World Authors 1995–2000

EDITORS
Clifford Thompson
Mari Rich

ASSOCIATE EDITOR
Olivia Jane Smith

ASSISTANT EDITOR
Martha A. Hostetter

EDITORIAL ASSISTANT
Carolyn Ellis

PRODUCTION STAFF
Gray Young (Manager)
Jeremy K. Brown
Tia Brown
Jennifer K. Peloso
Richard Joseph Stein

STAFF CONTRIBUTORS
Dimitri Cavalli
Andrew Cavin
Kathleen D'Angelo
Terence J. Fitzgerald
Peter G. Herman
Josha Hill
Virginia Kay
Christopher Luna
Christopher Mari
Edward Moran
Selma Yampolsky

The H.W. Wilson Company
New York ◆ Dublin
2003

Copyright © 2003 by The H. W. Wilson Company.

All rights reserved. No part of this work may be reproduced or copied in any form or by any means, including but not restricted to graphic, electronic, and mechanical—for example, photocopying, recording, taping, or information and retrieval systems—without the express written permission of the publisher, except that a reviewer may quote and a magazine, newspaper, or electronic information service may print brief passages as part of a review written specifically for inclusion in that magazine, newspaper, or electronic information service.

Library of Congress Cataloging-in-Publication Data

World authors, 1995–2000 / editors, Mari Rich, Olivia Jane Smith, Clifford Thompson ;
    assistant editor, Martha Hostetter.
    p. cm.
  ISBN 0-8242-1032-8
  1. Authors—20th century—Biography—Dictionaries. I. Rich, Mari. II. Smith, Olivia J.
III. Thompson, Clifford.

PN451.W676 2003
809'.049—dc21
[B]

2003045062

PRINTED IN THE UNITED STATES OF AMERICA

TABLE OF CONTENTS

Preface v

List of Authors vii

Biographical Sketches 1

Preface

Not taking into account the four-volume *World Authors 1900–1950*, published in 1997, *World Authors 1995–2000* is the 15th installment of the Wilson Author series, begun in 1942. This volume comprises biographical articles on more than 300 novelists, poets, dramatists, essayists, social scientists, biographers, and other authors who have published significant work within the period indicated.

Each article in *World Authors 1995–2000* provides a starting point for understanding the writer's unique contribution to the world of books, and, taken together, they reveal the wide variety of experiences, influences, opinions, and approaches to the creative process that shape contemporary literature.

Many of the authors profiled here have contributed autobiographical essays, solely for use in this book. A number of the essays detail a lifelong love of writing. Majgull Axelsson, for example, writes, "Myself, I knew by the age of eight that what I wanted to be was a writer," a fact that she attributes, in part, to a "conviction that since reading books was wonderful, writing them must be even more so." Fred Leebron quips, "As the youngest of five children, I was drawn to writing as the best chance to get all the words out before anyone interrupted."

Some authors lovingly pay tribute to a parent or professor who inspired them. Tom Wolfe writes of his father, the editor of an agricultural journal: "[He] was a man who sat at his desk writing with a pencil on a yellow legal pad. Two weeks later his not terribly legible handwriting would reappear as smartly turned out regiments of black type on graphically beautiful pages for thousands of people to read. To me that was magic. . . ."

Others thoughtfully examine their roles and obligations as authors. Rilla Askew writes, "In some ways I see myself not as a teller of stories but a re-teller, a balladeer, telling again the story of how we came to be here and what we've wrought." Aryeh Lev Stollman notes, "In my writing, I am continually trying to understand what might constitute one's place in this world. And even if I do not have the answers it is in this ongoing attempt that I feel most at home."

In these essays, writing is described variously as a passion, a compulsion, an honor, or a duty. Howard Bahr sees it as a gift. He explains, "That God has made me steward of such a talent, however humble, is proof that He looks after His wayward children. With it, I can explore the universals of the human heart in the context of the past. With it, I can hear the steam engines again, and the throb of an Indian motorcycle, and breathe air that is rich with the smell of burning leaves in autumn, of lantana [plants] and fried chicken in summer. Where I go in my writing, it still rains on summer afternoons, and a 'bad boy' is one who smokes cigarettes behind the gym and steals the lunches of little wimps like myself. For this, and for all things, I am grateful."

This volume has been a pleasure to edit, and I am grateful to the following people for their assistance in doing so: H. W. Wilson's staff of in-house writers and editors, listed on the title page; Gray Young and his entire production staff; the sharp-eyed Cullen Thomas; and Michael Schulze, H. W. Wilson's vice president for Editorial Services. My sincere thanks also go to Cliff Thompson and Miriam Helbok, who have provided me with immeasurable support and guidance.

—Mari Rich
April 2003

List of Biographical Sketches

André Aciman	1
Jonis Agee	3
Henry Alford	5
Tariq Ali	8
Hilton Als	13
Benjamin Anastas	15
Maya Angelou	17
Donald Antrim	23
Neal Ascherson	26
Rilla Askew	28
James Atlas	30
David Auburn	33
Ken Auletta	35
Majgull Axelsson	40
Howard Bahr	42
Murray Bail	44
Peter Balakian	47
Shauna Singh Baldwin	50
Paul Beatty	53
Elizabeth Benedict	55
Charles Bernstein	59
Michael R. Beschloss	62
Carol Birch	67
Herbert P. Bix	69
Edwin Black	70
Amy Bloom	74
Carol Bly	77
Dennis Bock	80
Robert Boswell	83
Carmen Boullosa	86
Clare Boylan	90
Alison Brackenbury	94
Rick Bragg	96
H. W. Brands	99
Mark Brazaitis	102

Connie Briscoe	104
Darryl Brock	106
Paul Brodeur	108
Michael Brodsky	113
Sylvia Brownrigg	115
Max Byrd	117
Ethan Canin	121
Kevin Canty	123
Lorene Cary	126
Louis Cha	128
Chang Ta-chun	131
Denise Chávez	133
Benjamin Cheever	135
Susan Cheever	138
Maxine Chernoff	141
Tracy Chevalier	143
Maxine Clair	145
Wanda Coleman	148
Billy Collins	151
Martha Collins	154
Gillian Conoley	156
Clark Coolidge	159
Rand Richards Cooper	161
Bernard Cornwell	163
Harold W. Coyle	167
Ann Crittenden	169
John Crowley	172
Victor Hernandez Cruz	174
Clive Cussler	176
Alice Elliott Dark	179
Peter Ho Davies	181
Kathryn Davis	184
Nicholas Dawidoff	186
Tom De Haven	189
Don DeLillo	191
Carl Dennis	197
Tory Dent	200
Hernando de Soto	201

Eric Jerome Dickey	204
Margaret Diehl	207
Slavenka Drakulic	209
Tom Drury	213
John Dufresne	215
Helen Dunmore	219
Stephen Dunn	222
Dorothy Dunnett	226
Paul Durcan	230
David Anthony Durham	232
Kelly Dwyer	234
Geoff Dyer	235
Cornelius Eady	239
Tony Earley	243
Louis Edwards	245
Jennifer Egan	247
Dave Eggers	249
Alistair Elliot	253
Joseph J. Ellis	255
Ben Elton	258
Carol Emshwiller	261
Anne Enright	263
B. H. Fairchild	265
Bruce Feiler	267
Alain Finkielkraut	269
William Patrick Finnegan	272
Daniela Fischerová	275
Richard Flanagan	276
Tim Fridtjof Flannery	279
Thomas Fleming	282
Maria Irene Fornes	288
Karen Joy Fowler	291
Lynn Freed	293
Darcy Frey	295
Alan Furst	297
Peter Gadol	299
Dorothy Gallagher	302
Forrest Gander	304

Gao Xingjian	306
Jane Gardam	309
Simon Garfield	313
Deborah Garrison	315
Barbara Garson	316
Timothy Garton Ash	320
Elizabeth George	322
Nelson George	325
Molly Gloss	329
Terry Goodkind	332
Anthony Grafton	334
Elizabeth Graver	338
Linda Gregg	341
Peter Guralnick	342
David Hajdu	345
Donald Hall	347
Erik Fosnes Hansen	352
Joy Harjo	354
William Harrison	357
Elizabeth Hay	360
Mo Hayder	362
Gar Anthony Haywood	363
Steven Heighton	365
Robin Marantz Henig	369
Patricia Henley	373
Michelle Herman	376
Jack Higgins	378
Raul Hilberg	382
Peter Hoffmann	387
Craig Holden	389
Sheri Holman	391
John Horgan	394
Nick Hornby	397
Helen Humphreys	399
Aislinn Hunter	401
Roland Huntford	403
Michael Ignatieff	405
Naomi Iizuka	410

John Irving	411
Dan Jenkins	415
Kaylie Jones	417
Thom Jones	419
Roger Kahn	420
Ken Kalfus	423
Alice Kaplan	426
Karen Karbo	428
Jonathan Keates	430
Faye Kellerman	433
Aileen Kelly	436
Brigit Pegeen Kelly	439
Elmer Kelton	441
Etgar Keret	444
Marian Keyes	447
Thomas King	450
László Krasznahorkai	453
Allen Kurzweil	455
Paul LaFarge	457
Jhumpa Lahiri	459
Anne Lamott	461
John Lanchester	463
J. D. Landis	465
Ann Lauterbach	468
Fred G. Leebron	470
Nancy Lemann	473
Nicholas Lemann	475
Mark Leyner	477
Sam Lipsyte	480
Robert Littell	482
Luljeta Lleshanaku	486
Sandra Tsing Loh	488
Rosetta Loy	490
Thomas Lynch	492
David Macfarlane	494
Eduardo Machado	496
Adewale Maja-Pearce	499
Kanan Makiya	502

Michael Malone	506
Ben Marcus	510
J. S. Marcus	512
Donald Margulies	513
Monika Maron	517
Jamie McKendrick	520
James McManus	522
James M. McPherson	524
Marion Meade	528
David Means	530
Perry Meisel	531
Louis Menand	535
Claire Messud	537
Anne Michaels	539
Andrew Miller	541
James Miller	544
Ron Milner	547
Anchee Min	550
Pankaj Mishra	554
Susan Mitchell	556
Herbert Mitgang	558
Deborah Moggach	561
John Mole	565
Mayra Montero	567
Mary McGarry Morris	570
Bradford Morrow	572
Katherine Mosby	577
Stanley D. Moss	579
Ferdinand Mount	581
Marcia Muller	584
Yxta Maya Murray	586
Gary Paul Nabhan	588
David Nasaw	591
Sena Jeter Naslund	594
Alexander Nehamas	597
Rob Nixon	598
Lewis Nordan	600
Howard Norman	602

Adam Nossiter	606
Josip Novakovich	609
Elizabeth Nunez	611
Sigrid Nunez	614
Sean O'Brien	617
Dennis O'Driscoll	618
Nuala O'Faolain	620
William L. O'Neill	623
Han Ong	627
Georg M. Oswald	630
Chuck Palahniuk	631
John Allen Paulos	633
Cathie Pelletier	636
Thomas Perry	638
Neil Powell	641
Thomas Powers	642
Wyatt Prunty	645
Jedediah Purdy	646
Michael Pye	649
Paul Quarrington	652
Joe Queenan	656
Ronald Radosh	658
Richard Rayner	664
Matt Ridley	667
José Rivera	670
Katie Roiphe	673
Roger Rosenblatt	675
Israel Rosenfield	679
Philip Roth	680
Ann Rule	686
Douglas Rushkoff	689
Richard Russo	692
Gene Santoro	694
George Saunders	696
Elaine Scarry	699
Bart Schneider	701
Helen Schulman	703
John Burnham Schwartz	705

Winfried Georg Sebald	706
Will Self	710
Vijay Seshadri	715
Alex Shakar	717
Alan Shapiro	719
Paula Sharp	722
Sam Shepard	725
Frances Sherwood	731
Jane Shore	733
Anita Shreve	735
Joan Silber	739
Tom Sleigh	742
Zadie Smith	744
Lemony Snicket	746
Andrew Solomon	749
Brent Staples	750
Robert B. Stepto	752
Jane Stevenson	755
Susan Stewart	758
Aryeh Lev Stollman	760
Ruth Stone	762
Tom Stoppard	765
Susan Straight	771
George Szirtes	773
Peter Tasker	776
Marcel Theroux	778
Jean Thompson	780
Rupert Thomson	783
Melanie Rae Thon	786
Adam Thorpe	790
Colin Thubron	792
Sue Townsend	796
David Trinidad	799
William R. Trotter	801
Omar Tyree	803
Jack Vance	805
Svetlana Vasilenko	807
Alfredo Véa	809

Kurt Vonnegut	811
Alice Walker	816
Ted Walker	822
Alan Warner	825
Sarah Waters	827
George Weigel	830
Mac Wellman	836
Geoffrey Wheatcroft	839
Kate Wheeler	840
Colson Whitehead	842
Ralph Wiley	844
Elizabeth Willis	846
Mark Winegardner	847
Tom Wolfe	849
Daniel Woodrell	857
C. D. Wright	859
Jay Wright	861
Akira Yoshimura	864
Simone Zelitch	866
Carl Zimmer	868
Paul Zimmer	870

World Authors 1995–2000

Sigrid Estrada/Courtesy of Farrar, Straus and Giroux

Aciman, André

1951– Memoirist; essayist

In *Out of Egypt* (1995) André Aciman, a professor of languages and literature, writes movingly of his Jewish family's experiences in Alexandria during the first half of the 20th century, from their initial prosperity to their eventual decline and exile due to Egypt's growing anti-Semitism. Though many of the events in this memoir took place before the author's birth, he describes family members, stories, and even moods in a richly lyrical prose, as if he had been a fly on the wall during those times. Since 1995 he has continued to write about his experiences as an exile, first as an editor of and contributor to *Letters of Transit: Reflections on Exile and Memory* (1999), and as the author of a new collection of essays, *False Papers* (2000).

André Aciman was born in Alexandria, Egypt, in 1951, the only child of a Sephardic Jewish father and an Arab Jewish mother. His family's roots in the city were planted in 1905 when his great-uncle Isaac moved there from Constantinople. At the University of Turin, in Italy, Isaac had become good friends with Fouad, the future king of Egypt, and subsequently Issac persuaded his family to move to his friend's country in the hope that the connection would help them to prosper. Isaac became the first—but not the last—of Aciman's family to enjoy success in Egypt; four generations called Alexandria home, living the good life in that city as traders, businessmen, bankers, and members of the bourgeoisie.

During World War II the family fully expected to wind up in a Nazi concentration camp after the German commander Rommel's forces pushed into Egypt. However, the British forces in El Alamein held off the German advances and the family remained in Egypt. After the war, nationalism swept across the country, hastening the departures of the last of the British and French nationals, as well as Egypt's Jews. The new Arab government began openly to practice anti-Semitism. Aciman's father watched as his textile factory was nationalized and the family began to lose money, without any means of making more. Aciman was taught anti-Semitic songs in school; once, after forgetting the words during a recitation, he was caned. In 1965, after a period in which they had received several threatening, anonymous phone calls each night, the family left Egypt, long after most of their friends and relations had already gone. In *Out of Egypt*, as quoted in a review by Michiko Kakutani in the *New York Times* (December 27, 1994), Aciman described his feelings as he sat near the ocean the night before leaving: "I wanted to come back tomorrow night, and the night after, and the one after that as well, sensing that what made leaving so fiercely painful was the knowledge that there would never be another night like this, that I would never eat soggy cakes along the coast road in the evening, not this year or any other year . . . I had caught myself longing for a city I never knew I loved."

The family traveled to Italy, where they had connections and, in some cases, citizenship, and later to France, before emigrating to the United States in the late 1960s. Aciman enrolled at Lehman College, in New York City, where he earned his bachelor's degree. Beginning in the early 1970s, he studied at Harvard University, in Cambridge, Massachusetts, earning both a master's degree and a doctorate there. Since that time he has taught French literature at Harvard, the New School for Social Research, Princeton University, and most recently, Bard College, in Annandale-on-Hudson, New York. He has also contributed essays and reviews to such publications as the *New Yorker, New York Times Magazine, New Republic, New York Review of Books,* and *Commentary.* In 1989 he published a translation of *Odyssey of the Bear: the Making of the Film by Jean-Jacques Annaud,* by Josée Bensabent-Loiseau.

Aciman's first book, *Out of Egypt* (1995), is a memoir of his family's time in Alexandria, beginning with his great-uncle's arrival there in 1905 and ending with their eventual emigration in 1965. In it Aciman describes the family's moneyed lifestyle: trips to the tailor for custom-made suits, daily outings to the beach, tennis lessons, and tutors for the children. He tells of his roguish great-uncle Vili who, during World War I, left the German army to fight with the Italians on the Allied side; during World War II he became an admirer of Mussolini and even gave lectures for the Hitler Youth in Germany while working as a British spy. Aciman also writes of his two grandmothers, one called "the Saint," who liked to play the victim, and the other known as "the Princess," who snobbishly manipulated people's emotions. He describes his parents' courtship, his father's obsession with his business and his extramarital affairs, and his mother's deafness and her fierce protection of her only son. Aciman wrote of his mother, as quoted by Kakutani, that there was "this truth about her ears, that she would always be deaf, never hear music, never hear laughter, never hear my voice." This made him realize, he continued, "what it meant to be alone in the world, and I would run to find her in this large house that became so quiet, so empty, and so very dark at night."

Out of Egypt was widely reviewed and received glowing notices. Evaluating the book for the *Chicago Tribune* (March 19, 1995), Mark Krupnick remarked: "Modest in manner, *Out of Egypt* gives much pleasure." Richard Eder, a senior book critic for *New York Newsday* (January 15, 1995), noted that the book "is beautifully remembered and even more beautifully written. Aciman writes of a dazzling time and place populated by lavish and theatrical characters." Michiko Kakutani, a longtime critic for the *New York Times* (December 27, 1994), proclaimed: "Andre Aciman . . . has written a remarkable memoir about Alexandria that's every bit as magical and resonant in its own way as [Lawrence] Durrell's quartet of novels, a memoir that leaves the reader with a mesmerizing portrait of a now vanished world." The book brought its author a 1995 Whiting Writers' Award, worth $30,000.

In 1999 Aciman edited a collection of essays entitled *Letters of Transit: Reflections on Exile and Memory.* The essays were written by men and women who came to America from countries around the world: Aciman himself; Eva Hoffman, a Polish exile who came to the United States via Canada; Edward Said, a Palestinian who moved to Egypt and subsequently to America; Bharati Mukherjee, a Bengali living in Berkeley; and Charles Simic, who left Yugoslavia in 1945. Each believes that his or her writing was heavily influenced by being in exile and the resulting feelings of duality—of being both an exile and an American.

Aciman has also written *False Papers* (2000), a new collection of his previously published essays about nostalgia, exile, and dislocation. Its title alludes in part to the slightly fictionalized nature of the memories depicted as Aciman reflects on his past in Alexandria, Rome, Paris, and New York. Aciman told David Holzel for *CNN.com* (August 8, 2000), "The 'me' in these stories is totally faithful. 'Me' is what I write about. The question is, are the furnishings around me real or not? The events are real, but I've reconfigured things." Aciman added that he views his work as neither fiction nor essay. "I don't feel comfortable in either style," he told Holzel, "and so I feel false to both." Included in the book are Aciman's accounts of glimpsing the sea during a train ride he took from Rome to Paris as a youth; fetching water for his grandmother in the Square Lamartine in Paris; and exploring a deserted, out-of-use subway station in New York. Holzel wrote that, read sequentially, the essays "form an eerily interlocking whole." Like *Out of Egypt,* this book received critical praise. A critic for *Kirkus Reviews* (June 2000)wrote, as excerpted on *Amazon.com,* "Although Aciman occasionally drifts into journalistic travelogue, more often he offers thoughtful, highly original aperçus through which run several themes: the meaning of the Passover seder and its remembrance of flight, the pleasures of city life and of discovering a city's forgotten past, and the difficulty of maintaining connections and memories across time and oceans."

André Aciman lives in New York City with his wife and children.

—C. M.

SUGGESTED READING: *Chicago Tribune* p3 Mar. 19, 1995; *Commentary* p48+ Jan. 1999, p40+ May 2000; *Kirkus Reviews* June 2000; *London Review of Books* p25 Nov. 2, 1995; *New York Newsday* p29+ Jan. 15, 1995; *New York Times* C p21 Dec. 27, 1994, C p15 Oct. 30, 1995; *New York Times Book Review* p7+ Feb. 5, 1995; *New York Times Magazine* July 11, 1999; *Washington Post* D p2 Feb. 15, 1995

SELECTED BOOKS: nonfiction—*Out of Egypt,* 1995; *False Papers,* 2000; as editor—*Letters of Transit: Reflections on Exile and Memory,* 1999; as translator—*Odyssey of the Bear: the Making of the Film by Jean-Jacques Annaud*

Courtesy of Jonis Agee

Agee, Jonis

May 31, 1943– Novelist; short-story writer; poet

Jonis Agee has a family history that includes Meriwether Lewis (of the explorers Lewis and Clark) and the outlaw Jesse James. With a heritage so colorfully tied to the American West, perhaps it's no wonder that Agee has forged a writing career documenting the life of small-town western Americans. "When I choose to write about small towns or remote areas," Agee said in one of a collection of interviews posted on the *Nebraska Center for Writers* (NCW) Web site, "it's because it is easier to explore human behavior in that setting. Small towns have all the internecine workings of large families." Beginning with her first volume of poetry, *Houses* (1976), and including several short-story collections, such as *Bend This Heart* (1989), and novels (*Sweet Eyes*, 1991 and *Strange Angels*, 1994), most of Agee's work has dealt with humble people of small-town America, whom she does not romanticize, but rather depicts with honesty and an attention to detail that bring her characters and settings to life realistically.

Jonis Agee was born in Omaha, Nebraska, on May 31, 1943, the daughter of Eugene and Lauranel Agee. From the time she was quite young, she knew she wanted to write. A restless child, Agee often woke up in the early morning, before anyone else had risen, to play outside. She later incorporated her habit of rising early into her writing routine, as she has with her love of exploring; Agee often points her car in a random direction and allows her own curiosities to guide her progress. "I forget about time as much as possible on the road and simply enter the place like wading into a river or lake," Agee said in an interview on the *NCW* Web site. "I might get twenty or thirty miles in a day, but I'll know what's at the bottom. I often write while actually in motion, in fact, taking down impressions, the things that poke out of the world at me: signs, people, structures, animals, weather, plants, rocks, etc."

Agee attended the University of Iowa, in Iowa City, where she received her bachelor's degree in 1966. She moved to the East Coast to pursue a master's degree, which she received in 1969, at the State University of New York at Binghamton. In 1976 Agee received her Ph.D. from the same university and began teaching creative writing at the College of St. Catherine, in St. Paul, Minnesota. She also released her first published work, a book of poetry called *Houses*. The volume explores Agee's family history; both Meriwether Lewis and Jesse James are represented, as well as other late relatives William Tecumseh Sherman Agee—a prosecuting attorney in Missouri—and Reverend Wilson, a female clergy member who was seriously injured while trying to cross a river to reach one of her parishioners. *Houses* also contemplated the interplay between the land and its inhabitants, thus setting the stage for her later works.

A year after *Houses*, Agee won a Minnesota State Arts Board Award in Fiction. On the heels of this award came another, a National Endowment of the Arts grant in fiction, in 1978. However, it wasn't until 1989, long after the publication of her second poetry collection, *Mercury* (1981), that Agee's first prose was published. That work, *Pretend We've Never Met*, found Agee working in the short story medium. Set in the fictional town of Divinity, Iowa, the book uses short sketches of various residents to assemble a picture of the setting as a whole. In an interview with Peter Catapano for the *New York Times Book Review* (March 31, 1991), Agee spoke about her use of setting: "I was always struck by authors who could create a universe. It's a way to express a moral geography without everyone getting mad at you." What many found striking about the collection was its compressed style, which would become an Agee trademark in her later short-short-story collections. The short sketches that comprise the stories of *Pretend We've Never Met* forced Agee to leave much to suggestion, including elements of plot. This technique later led Stewart Kellerman to write in the *New York Times Book Review* (October 17, 1999) "Much of the power in Agee's short fiction lies in what's left unsaid."

Agee published another collection of short stories in 1991, *Bend This Heart*, which abandoned the use of a cohesive landscape or setting. Instead, the stories in the collection were unified by the theme of love and relationships. Once again, Agee kept most of the stories very short, a difficult technique that reviewers found appealing and which helped the collection become a *New York Times* Notable Book of the Year. Nonetheless, some critics had reservations. Amy Hempel opined in her review for the *New York Times* (July 10, 1989) that "the parts are sometimes more interesting than the whole; they do not always add up, or add up to enough." However, she concluded on a positive note, stating "mostly these odd, original stories, keenly alive with language, make the heart *and* mind work."

In Agee's first novel, *Sweet Eyes* (1991), she returned to the town of Divinity, reintroducing many characters from *Pretend We've Never Met*, including the narrator, Honey Parish, a woman haunted by her dead lover and trying unsuccessfully to put his memory to rest by having new affairs. One of her lovers, Jasper, is the area's only black farmer. One day, to Honey's dismay, several of the locals nearly beat Jasper to death. Divinity, it turns out, is in many respects a violent and depressing place. Many of the characters are heavy drinkers, including Honey. She and Jasper share a dingy trailer and yell and pound tables rather than converse. Even Honey's own family members treat her poorly. Her father scars her head with a hammer, and her brother, Sonny Boy, shoots out her windows and wrecks her car. Sonny Boy is also part of a dark and violent secret that drives the book forward with suspense, as Honey gradually comes to terms with her past.

Reviewers of *Sweet Eyes* found promise in Agee's first novel. Andy Solomon, in his review in *Chicago Tribune Books* (February 17, 1991), found that the novel was a "meaty tale that captures American small-town life," and stated that Agee, "clearly shows herself to be a significant new novelist." Michael Malone was more critical, writing in the *New York Times Book Review* (March 31, 1991), "Her narrative line at times unravels; at other times, it clumps into a tangled ball as she is tempted to tell us too much, too often." However, Malone added, "Ms. Agee gives us an urgent sense of the primitive force of life, of the oppression of heredity and the fundamentals of human nature: the animal core at its heart of fear, sex, and violence." At the end of the year, the *New York Times* named the book a Notable Book of the Year.

For the setting of her next novel, *Strange Angels* (1993), Agee chose her home state of Nebraska—specifically, the barren dunes of the Sandhills. In preparation for the novel, Agee traveled to the Sandhills nearly every month for two years, to help her capture the mood of the place properly. In the novel, an old patriarch by the name of Bennett divides his ranch among his three children (two of whom are illegitimate), setting the stage for a series of conflicts. The younger son, Cody Kidwell, is a wild young man who kindles a love affair with an older widow named Latta Jaboy. The two are later estranged from one another when lies are spread about them in town. Then, after Latta's prize stallion is stolen, Cody (secretly knowing that his half-sister, Kya, is the culprit) sets out for Wyoming to retrieve it. In the process, Cody is shot twice by Kya's boyfriend. After lying unconscious for three weeks, Cody refuses to tell the police who shot him, nor will he reveal to Latta who stole her horse.

Despite his praise for the novel's authentic portrayal of Nebraska and ranch living, William Hauptman, a Nebraska native, found the clear lines of conflict in *Strange Angels* too outdated, writing in the *New York Times Book Review* (October, 17, 1993), "In this day and age, the conflicts are not this clear, and histrionics are a luxury. The collision between the modern world and the traditional is what makes life on the Great Plains interesting. . . . To make this life into a Greek tragedy is just too easy. . . . Ms. Agee is talented enough to do better." However, Donna Seaman, writing in *Booklist*, (August 1993) stated, "Agee has achieved a rare balance here between grit horse thievery, knockdown fistfights, rodeos, and blizzards—and breathtaking lyricism, sensuality, and catharsis." For the novel, Agee received her third *New York Times* Notable Book of the Year mention.

In 1995 Agee published another volume of short stories titled *A .38 Special and a Broken Heart*. Like her earlier volumes, many of the more than two-dozen stories were very short, creating brief impressions of the trials and tribulations of people, particularly women, in small-town America. Mary Caroll wrote in *Booklist* (May 1, 1995), "Agee's fans—and readers who appreciate the immediacy of good short-shorts—will find much to relish here." A reviewer for the *Hungry Mind Review*, as quoted on the *NCW* Web site, wrote, "While a few of these short-stories fail to get started or devolve into what feels like writerly warm-up exercises," the reviewer noted, "this collection as a whole has a thrilling freshness and immediacy."

The title of Agee's next work, *South of Resurrection* (1997), had a double meaning: In the novel, Moline Bedwell returns to her hometown of Resurrection, Missouri to resurrect her past after a long, deliberate absence. When Moline was 16, she witnessed a car crash that killed a local girl. Her boyfriend, Dayrell Bell, was wrongly implicated, yet Moline kept her silence rather than defend him. Back in Resurrection, Moline resumes her old love affair with Dayrell, while also dealing with the attempted takeover of her aunt and uncle's family farm by the Heart Hog Corporation. Despite the fact that Moline had found a settled life for herself in Minnesota, she gradually realizes that she had never completely left Resurrection behind. Coming to understand the good and bad aspects of the town becomes a process of self-discovery for Moline. Critical reaction to the novel was mixed. "Agee's obvious empathy for her vividly rendered characters underscores the mesmerizing resonance of the fluid narrative," noted Margaret Flanagan in *Booklist* (October 1, 1997), concluding that it was "a gripping contemporary fable." However, Dwight Garner, writing for the *New York Times Book Review* (November 23, 1997), found the novel too cute. "*South of Resurrection*, like its title is too sweet and strains for effect," wrote Garner. "There's something slightly off about it, like listening to Lucinda Williams try to pick through a batch of Debby Boone cover songs."

As with *Strange Angels*, the setting of Agee's next novel, *The Weight of Dreams* (1999), was the Nebraska Sandhills. It tells the story of Ty Bronte, whose family is devastated by the death of his little brother. His father is an abusive drunk, his mother is cold and unloving, and Ty gets in trouble with the law and has to flee Nebraska for Kansas. There, Ty becomes a horse trader, and Agee depicts the tough, physical life of that job. Stewart Kellerman noted in the *New York Times Book Review* (October 17, 1999), "Agee's descriptions of the backbreaking life of a Plains rancher—rounding up the cattle after a blizzard, pulling a trapped horse out of the mud, tearing a bawling cow away from her dead calf—are so real they make your muscles ache." Ty later becomes entwined with a woman named Dakota, who pushes herself upon him. The two of them return to Nebraska, where Ty's father is gravely ill and his mother refuses to lift the barriers she's always placed between herself and her family. In addition, Ty must face up to the crime that sent him fleeing from Nebraska in the first place. In an interview excerpted on the *NCW* Web site, Agee said, "I believe in forgiveness—that's kind of a mainstay—and mostly because it's the hardest thing in the world to do. I figure if it's that hard, it must be the right thing to try."

Some critics found the plot of *The Weight of Dreams* too amorphous and the narrative too long. "In tying up the plot," a reviewer for *Publishers Weekly* (May 31, 1999) wrote, "her direction scatters and each ambitious subplot grows broad and thin, diminishing the central struggle." However, the force of the character portrayals was undeniable, according to Carolyn See, who wrote in the *Washington Post* (August 13, 1999), "There are all kinds of reasons to disapprove of *The Weight of Dreams*, but in the end they don't really count, because Ty and Dakota and these godawful parents of his are so real, and so alive. You have to care about them."

For her most recent publication, a short-story collection called *Taking the Wall* (1999), Agee covers a subject near and dear to her heart: car racing. In an interview posted on the *NCW* Web site, Agee explained that she loves car racing because of the built-in drama and the ever-present element of chance. "Watching a race," Agee said, "is like watching a play written by Shakespeare, directed by Thomas Hardy with dialogue and extra scenes thrown in by Virginia Woolf and Andy Warhol, who have been resurrected as a couple for the occasion." The title of the novel refers to the act of crashing into the wall of the racetrack, and in this collection, Agee's characters flirt with crisis while displaying the noble human urge to survive and prevail. In "The Pop-Off Valve," Bobby is in danger of losing his wife because he is so obsessed with racing that he talks about the Indy 500 even while they're making love. The maimed ex-driver in "Over the Point of Cohesion" cannot keep himself from reliving his final crash every day, while in "The Trouble with Truth" two friends meet in a bar and discover that they are married to the same mechanic. Agee's latest collection garnered much acclaim. Critics enjoyed her economic prose and the fast-paced unfolding of her stories. Mary Park commented for *Amazon.com* (on-line), "The prose careens forward at a truly vertiginous speed, as Agee's characters learn that sometimes domestic life is the most spectacular car crash of all." Calling the stories "spare and muscular," Kellerman wrote in *New York Times Book Review* (October 17, 1999), "By writing just enough and nothing more, Agee forces us to imagine the rest."

In addition to writing prose and poetry, Agee has edited two fiction collections related to the Midwest, *Border Crossings: A "Minnesota Voices Project" Reader* (1984), and *Stiller's Pond: New Fiction from the Upper Midwest* (1991). She currently lives in Ann Arbor and teaches creative writing at the University of Michigan. Her book *Acts of Love on Indigo Road: New and Selected Stories* is scheduled for publication in 2003.

— P.G.H.

SUGGESTED READING: *MPLS. St. Paul* p135 Aug. 1993, with photo; *New York Times Book Review* p22 July 16 1989, p12+ Mar. 3, 1991, p26 Oct. 17, 1993, p15 Nov. 23, 1997, p18 Oct. 17, 1999; *Publishers Weekly* p67+ Aug. 18, 1997; *Washington Post* p4 Aug. 13, 1999

SELECTED BOOKS: novels—*Sweet Eyes*, 1991; *Strange Angels*, 1993; *South of Resurrection*, 1997; *The Weight of Dreams*, 1999; poetry—*Houses*, 1976; *Mercury*, 1981; short-story collections—*Pretend We've Never Met*, 1989; *Bend This Heart*, 1989; *A .38 Special and a Broken Heart*, 1995; *Taking the Wall*, 1999; as editor—*Border Crossings: A "Minnesota Voices Project" Reader*, 1984; *Stiller's Pond: New Fiction from the Upper Midwest*, 1991

Alford, Henry

Feb. 13, 1962– Humor writer

Henry Alford has been praised for turning journalism into performance art. Alford dreams up oddball situations in which he can play at least a supporting role, stages them, and then records the results, often to devastatingly comic effect. He has, for example, hired nude house cleaners to do his windows, met with a professional "humor consultant" who told him to listen to laugh tracks and "find the elf in yourself," and tried to sell the leftover pulp from his juicer machine to ceramics and particle-board manufacturers. Through a crisp style and sophisticated wit, Alford transforms the prose essay into an act of performance, prompting comparisons to Oscar Wilde, who also combined writing with theater, and Fran Lebowitz, who like Alford revels in the idiosyncracies of the Manhattan mind-set.

Henry Alford
Courtesy of Henry Alford

For *World Authors, 1995-2000*, Henry Alford writes: "I was born on February 13, 1962 in New Haven, Connecticut, the youngest of four kids. When an interviewer from the Foote School came to my family's house in New Haven to talk to me about attending kindergarten, I spent much of the interview under the living room coffee table, pretending to be a dog. We moved to Worcester, Massachusetts when I was six; I would live there until I was 13, whence I was sent off to the all-boy's boarding school Eaglebrook (my parents had divorced, I was living with my mother and sister, and it was felt that I would profit from having more male influences in my life). My childhood interests were theater, film and my Collie, Lucy, who I named after Lucille Ball. My first brush with humor came in 5th grade when, tears of laughter rolling down my cheeks, I read portions of Jean Kerr's *Please Don't Eat the Daisies* aloud to my deskmates at the Bancroft School. I studied film at New York University, thinking I wanted to write or direct films. I graduated in 1984. In my senior year I got an internship (and then was hired by) casting director Joy Todd, who cast feature films. I worked for her for three and a half years, and while wholly engrossed by the work, was increasingly drawn to comedy. At first I tried stand-up (disastrous), then I wrote a cabaret (mildly awful), and then published a single issue of a 'zine' (vaguely interesting). Increasingly, I found that my comedic impulses were best served by prose. I started writing short, humorous, unsolicited items and sending them to magazines, receiving bucketfuls of rejections until, finally, I found success with a new satirical magazine called *Spy*, which bought a list-based humor piece called "What If the Pope Were a Dog?" I followed up with more "What Ifs," and once *Spy* had published nine of them (and a few other short, unsolicited items), I asked them for a job. I worked as a staff writer at *Spy* for two years (1988–1990), receiving much help and guidance from editor Susan Morrison, who gave me a lot of assignments, including several of the first-person, Plimptonesque, participatory pieces (register for gifts at bridal registries even though I am not getting married; take a series of offbeat vocational tests; stay at Manhattan bed and breakfasts of questionable charm) that would appear in my first collection, *Municipal Bondage* (Random House, 1994) along with the "What Ifs.' (I got this book deal when Random House editor Jonathon Karp saw me give a reading with some other *Spy* writers).

"I seem to specialize in two kinds of work—the participatory journalism pieces, that sometimes involve an odd element or prank (these are sometimes referred to by my publisher as 'investigative humor,' I suppose to allude to the fact that some of the 'journalism' is conducted undercover); and 'found humor' pieces, in which, florist-like, I arrange stray information (e.g., misspelled items on menus in Manhattan delis and restaurants, phrases from phrase books for travelers, strange names of seashells) in an attractive manner. I tend to laugh at things that are based in reality, or that have some connection with fact; I respond to writing that is elegant and has a lot of voice. When entering a bookstore or library in search of something to read, I find that I am almost always safe if the author in question is dead and British.

"In 2000 I published *Big Kiss: One Actor's Desparate Attempt to Claw His Way to the Top*, an account of my misadventures as an aspiring actor. (Why acting? I wasn't getting enough rejections as a writer). The book gave way to a successful Off-Broadway show (*Big Kiss: New York's Funniest Unknown Actors Tell their Most Humiliating, Real-Life Audition Stories*) which I hosted and, with my editor Jonathon Karp, co-produced. I would love to write a comic novel, but am lazy and unskilled. I have gotten very used to having magazine editors hold a gun to my head. (Over the years, I have been a regular contributor to the *New York Times Magazine* and *Vanity Fair*; I have also written for the *New Yorker*, *Harper's Bazaar*, *Vogue*, *Travel and Leisure*, and the *Village Voice*.) I started out wanting to emulate essayists like James Thurber and Fran Lebowitz, but increasingly am drawn to novelists—P.G. Wodehouse, Jane Austen, Tom Wolfe. I've had the same boyfriend, Jess Taylor, for 9 years. A former literary agent (Curtis Brown, Endeavor), he now works as a freelance editor. We live in New York and Salisbury, Connecticut."

In his collection of essays about modern life in New York City, *Municipal Bondage* (1994), Alford reports on his encounters with nude house cleaners, who washed his apartment's street-level windows and carried splintery logs, and the staff at an upscale auction house, where Alford tried to have his "heirlooms" appraised—including two pieces of chalk, a pebble, pencil shavings, and a garlic husk. He describes his attempt to pass a dog-grooming certification exam with a borrowed cocker spaniel, which Alford douses with cologne and smears with rouge and lipstick. "I like a dog with a face," Alford recorded in his defense, as quoted in an interview with the journalist Mark Valenta on his Web site. In addition to such investigative pieces, Alford offers a series of lists describing telling moments in what he terms "What If" situations. "What if unemployed actors worked in banks instead of restaurants?" Alford asks, as quoted by Robert Plunket in the New York Times Book Review (March 20, 1994, on-line). "11:07 A.M. Teller gives customer 10 singles, vocalizing 'Ten! Tin! Tan! Tawn! Toe! Too!'" A critic for Kirkus Reviews (January 1, 1994) found these last "one-liner sideshows" an acquired taste, but wrote that, at his best, "Alford offers genuinely rueful takes on comic aspects of the urban experience."

While conducting his investigations, Alford plays the naïf, feigning credulity and artlessness in the service of comedy. "Alford's own face provides clues [to] how he gets away with so much," Valenta wrote. "He has earnest, little-lost-boy eyes and a jaw that's straight, like his demeanor. He could be the boy next door." Though his humor is always generous and self-effacing, Alford admits to sometimes suffering pangs of a guilty conscience for engaging in duplicity in order to get his stories. "I sometimes feel like a dirtball," Alford admitted to Valenta. "I assuage my guilt by not identifying people, by making myself look stupider, nuttier and by trying to be as charitable as possible."

When it comes to writing, however, Alford is anything but artless. In Booklist, as quoted on Amazon.com, Donna Seaman praised Alford's "dry-martini humor" and "deadpan wit," and Robert Plunket, in the New York Times Book Review, appreciated Alford's cosmopolitan sensibility. "With so much of today's humor bogged down in relationship jokes and tedious 'did you ever notice?' observations about daily life, it's a relief to find someone whose beat is a little more sophisticated," Plunket wrote. "Mr. Alford's world is one of restaurants, department stores, and Merchant and Ivory movies. His is a sensibility that reeks of Manhattan." Alford's humor is based in his precise handling of language. In an article for the New York Times Magazine (August 21, 1994) called "Al Dente," Alford puzzled out the strange behavior of celebrity biters whose ranks include, according to Alford, Mike Tyson, Sylvia Plath, and Sam Donaldson. "Biting other people is a habit that is, at best, unattractive. It lacks subtlety and nuance," Alford observed. "In many instances, biters opt for this peculiar form of self-expression because it conveys a pure, unmodulated message. The message is no." Alford's type of humor is, as Plunket wrote, meant "to be savored on the printed page . . . his sentences just so, with every syllable in place." Alford's affection for words is apparent in what he terms his "found humor" pieces such as a New Yorker article (August 10, 1998) in which a lover writes a letter composed around odd names of shells—including the "Unstable Limpet," the "Depressed Vitrinella," and the "Lurid Dwarf Triton."

Alford's second book, Big Kiss: One Actor's Desparate Attempt to Claw His Way to the Top (2000), is part memoir and part parable for would-be actors and starlets. "If you live in Blaine, Missouri, for example, and thrill each time you hear somebody sing 'New York, New York,'" wrote Jack Nichols for the Gay Today Web site, "then this is the book for you." In it, Alford once again launches into "participatory journalism," only this time he has an ostensible goal—to find celebrity and success as an actor. He starts by trying to talk Manhattan deli owners into posting his glossy head shot next to photographs of Telly Savalas, offering to write "Big Kiss" on it along with his autograph. He attends London's Royal Academy of Dramatic Art, a Wisconsin improvisational camp (along with his 69-year-old mother) and a ballroom dance class where he is asked to find a partner and "triple chasé sparkle sparkle" across the room. "The theater is full of Henry Alfords," remarked Jack Helbig in Booklist (February 15, 2000, on-line). "Funny, smart, earnestly devoted to their art but unsure of where they fit in, they spend their lives preparing for big breaks that never come." But Alford seems to enjoy himself along the way. In the Washington Post (March 9, 2000, on-line), Jonathan Yardley praised Alford's "manic ever-willingness to go do something, even if—especially if—the task requires ritual self-humiliation." In a series of character exercises, Alford tries playing a perfume salesman, phone-sex operator, and playing an extra in a crowd scene in the remake of Godzilla. When one of the movie crew tries to take away his prop camera, Alford first protests—"I based my character interpretation on that!" as cited by Scott Dickensheets in the Las Vegas Weekly (June 15, 2000, on-line)—then immediately concedes: "My work was getting proppy." As Fiona Maazel pointed out in the Village Voice Literary Supplement (May 17–23, 2000, on-line), there is a method to his madness, an element of satire that serves to "lance the pretensions native to show business." Although Maazel felt the book's many stories didn't cohere into a greater whole, she appreciated Alford's peculiar talents: "Taken on their own, these pieces are breezy and arch, funny and rife with the command of someone who has found his niche as commentator, voyeur, and in truth, showman," she wrote. Echoing many reviewers, Dickensheets characterized Alford as an accomplished purveyor of style: "It's a style that can be summed up in one perfectly apt word: sparkle. . . . He's got more sparkle than a diamond store. But, like a diamond, he's got some edge; the teasing sophistication and gentle ornateness of his writing don't turn it fey."

Alford tackled a new medium in his 2001 e-book, *Out There: One Man's Search to Find the Funniest Person on the Internet*, in which he explores a vast array of unique Internet personalities in search of the "funniest." Alford's zany subjects include everyone from the movie reviewer known as Filthy Critic to the on-line stock trader Tokyo Joe, who conducts most of his business in the nude. The book was also made available in a paperback edition.

—M. A. H.

SUGGESTED READING: *Booklist* (on-line) Feb. 15, 2000; *Las Vegas Weekly* (on-line) June 15, 2000; *New York Times Book Review* (on-line) Mar. 20, 1994; *Village Voice Literary Supplement* (on-line) May 17–23, 2000

SELECTED BOOKS: *Municipal Bondage*, 1994; *Big Kiss*, 2000; *Out There: One Man's Search to Find the Funniest Person on the Internet*, 2001

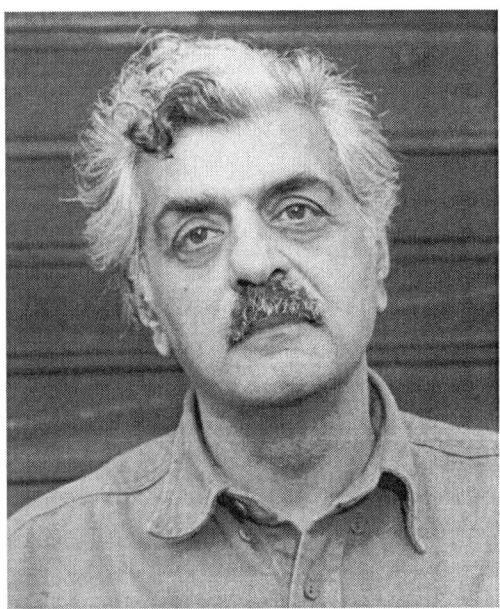

Courtesy of Verso Books

Ali, Tariq

Oct. 21, 1943– Journalist; novelist; playwright

Tariq Ali, the Pakistani-born writer and socialist leader, has been a very visible presence in Great Britain as an anti-war spokesperson, demonstration leader, satirical playwright, historian, and novelist. He has also produced television shows, including *Big Women* (1998) and *Black Athena* (1993), and made films, including *Wittgenstein* (1993), a biographical piece based on the philosopher Ludwig Wittgenstein. His first book, *Pakistan: Military Rule or People's Power?* (1970), was followed by other histories, biographies, and analyses related to the Indian subcontinent and numerous articles in such magazines as the *Guardian* and the *Nation*. Famous as the principal founder of the Vietnam Solidarity Campaign, Ali wrote several histories of the events of 1968, beginning with *1968 and After: Inside the Revolution* (1978). He has also written other works of political analysis, including *Introducing Trotsky and Marxism* (2000) with Phil Evans, and *The Clash of Fundamentalisms: Crusades, Jihads and Modernity* (2002). Ali's career as a novelist began in 1990 with *Redemption*, a satire about the Trotskyist movement and its leaders. That work was followed by four other historical novels, the latest of which is *The Stone Woman* (2000), which depicts the end of the Ottoman Empire through the lives of a Turkish family in 1899. Ali has also collaborated with Howard Brenton and others on several satirical plays about contemporary politics. One of these, *Ugly Rumours* (1998), depicts Margaret Thatcher extracting the socialism from everyone she encounters with a vacuum cleaner-like device.

Tariq Ali was born in Lahore in what is now Pakistan but was then British-ruled India, on October 21, 1943. His parents, despite being from the wealthy land-owning class, were dedicated leftists. His father, Mazhar Ali Khan, was an editor of the *Pakistan Times* and, later, of *Viewpoint*, a progressive magazine. His mother, Tahira Mazhar Ali, founded the Democratic Women's League and professed loyalty to the Communist Party and its principles.

Young Tariq was educated at St. Anthony's School and, later, Government College, both in Lahore. He was involved in radical politics from an early age, which soon got him into trouble. "My uncle, Brigadier Azmat Hayat, was head of military intelligence; he'd seen all my files," Ali told *Zameen* (December 1998), an on-line magazine. "He told my mother, 'If you want to keep this boy out of trouble you'd better send him abroad, here he'll just be locked up.'" In 1963 Ali left Pakistan for Exeter College at the University of Oxford, in England. He continued his political activities there, becoming the first Pakistani president of the Oxford Student Union in 1965 and one of the founders of the alternative paper *Black Dwarf*. Only one thing displeased him, he admitted: "It was nice, relaxed and liberating. But the thing I missed most . . . was Pakistani food. The food here was absolutely appalling."

During his time at Oxford, Ali made his first contact with Bertrand Russell, who congratulated the young student on a letter he had written to a newspaper, and from this encounter blossomed an enduring friendship. When the Vietnam War escalated in the late 1960s, Ali became one of its fiercest opponents, leading militant demonstrations in England and supporting the war's opponents with polemical writings. In 1966 he organized a teach-in at Oxford, which prompted a visit to the school by Henry Cabot Lodge, the former American ambassador in South Vietnam. When Lodge arrived, a union leader approached him and called him a mass murderer. "I had warned Henry Cabot Lodge that convincing this audience would not be as easy as organizing a coup in Saigon," Ali wrote in *Street Fighting Years: An Autobiography of the Sixties* (1987).

Ali visited Cambodia and North Vietnam in 1967 and reported on what he saw there to the International Crimes Tribunal organized by Bertrand Russell to publicize alleged American atrocities in Vietnam. He described how his party was unable to keep a scheduled visit to a hospital in the province of Thanh Hoa to interview victims of air raids because the hospital was being bombed. "At 4:00 P. M. we visited the hospital. . . . This was the hospital where we should have been at 2:30. At 3:00 it had been bombed and some of the patients killed. While they were being removed from the hospital and taken to the first-aid station, there was another attack and the first-aid station had been completely destroyed. Incendiary bombs had been used and some houses were still burning. When we visited Thanh Hoa, it was on fire. There were embers and flames everywhere. We saw a large crater caused by an American rocket. Anti-personnel weapons had been used." Ali termed that "the most traumatic experience" he had in Vietnam.

After editing the book *New Revolutionaries* (1969), Ali authored *Pakistan: Military Rule or People's Power?* (1970), which examined conditions in his homeland. Tracing Pakistan's history, from the nation's 1947 creation to the military overthrow of Ayub Khan's regime which ushered in martial law in 1969, Ali called his book "an unabashed and straightforward polemic against the feudal and capitalist class of Pakistan which has ruled the country since 1947 in varying guises." A reviewer for the *Library Journal* (October 15, 1970) noted that many would "consider it a plea long overdue," despite its reliance on Marxist doctrine. Other reviewers reacted adversely to *Pakistan*. A reviewer for the *Economist* (September 26, 1970) observed that, having "made his name as a student revolutionary in Britain, Tariq Ali has obviously approached the history of his own country with preconception." Alun Chalfont, writing in the *New Statesman* (September 25, 1970), agreed, taking exception to Ali's use of the word "bourgeois": "He scatters the word around like a demented sapper laying a minefield in the grip of some exotic fever." Chalfont termed the volume "an extended political pamphlet."

Ali continued to write books about the history and politics of his time, producing *The Coming British Revolution* (1972), *1968 and After: Inside the Revolution* (1978), *Trotsky for Beginners* (1980), *Can Pakistan Survive?* (1983), and *What Is Stalinism?* (1984). As a prominent and vocal "Trotskyist" until the 1970s, Ali was a member of the socialist organization Fourth International, one of whose foremost leaders was Ernest Mandel. Although the Fourth International characterized itself as an "open, critical approach to Marxist theory," and Ernest Mandel was widely recognized as an important political philosopher, it was actually a doctrinaire and sectarian organization.

Ali examined the history of Pakistan's neighbor and frequent rival in his 1985 work *An Indian Dynasty: The Story of the Nehru-Gandhi Family*. William Borders, in the *New York Times Book Review* (April 21, 1985), termed the book "a straightforward account of recent Indian history, told in terms of the country's greatest family." Borders, however, judged the volume a kind of potboiler, with writing that was "often flat and banal even when Mr. Ali tries to move from the political to the human plane." He concluded that the book contained "tiresome old anecdotes" and "no crackle, no fire and few people, except for politicians."

Ali's *Street Fighting Years: An Autobiography of the Sixties* (1987) dealt mainly with the impact of the Vietnam War on the consciousness of his generation. In this book he included an account of his childhood in Pakistan, which Nigel Fountain, writing in the *New Statesman* (November 6, 1987), termed "fascinating." He added that Ali "can be an informative, funny, and illuminating writer" with a "breadth of vision and a sympathy with struggle across the globe singularly lacking from most other British socialists." Sunil Khilnani, a reviewer for the *Times Literary Supplement* (November 27, 1987), thought that the "openness to, and presence of, other voices and opinions is one of the more engaging qualities of this chronicle." He found Ali's political analysis, however, less than "acute or theoretically imposing." Approving of Ali's style, he found that the "book's staccato prose does succeed in conveying a sense of the excitement of the period."

In the late 1980s Ali continued to produce articles for journals, such as the *New Left Review*, the *Nation*, and *Monthly Review*. He also published the 1988 book *Revolution from Above: Where is the Soviet Union Going?* Turning for the first time to literary methods of self-expression, Ali revealed his more splenetic side in the political satire that appears in his plays and novels. *Iranian Nights*, a play he wrote in 1989 with Howard Brenton, satirizes the Iranian reception of *The Satanic Verses*, the controversial novel by his friend Salman Rushdie. It was followed by another satire co-written with Howard Brenton called *Moscow Gold* (1990), about Mikhail Gorbachev's struggle for power in the Soviet Union.

Ali's first novel, *Redemption* (1990), is a roman à clef in which a world congress convenes an emergency session in Paris to deal with the implications of the collapse of the Berlin Wall. The congress is led by Ezra Einstein, who was described by L. Proyect for *Culture* (on-line) as combining "some of the qualities of an Old Testament prophet with the defects of a New Testament apostle, whose task was to interpret the words of the saviours in changing conditions." He is a thinly disguised Ernest Mandel, and Ali has him ultimately propose that the world's leftists infiltrate the major religions or create their own "Crislamasonism." The English Trotskyist Gerry Healy appears as the character Frank Hood, the volatile leader of the Hoodlums whose tirades frequently punctuate gatherings of the Hoodlum Politbureau. Also represented in *Redemption* is the Socialist Workers Party of the United States, which is called the Proletarian International Socialist Party of American Workers (PISPAW), led by Jim Noble, based on former SWP leader Jack Barnes. Also attending the fictional conference are representatives from other English Trotskyist sects, who Proyect called a "gallery of clowns. . . . Each one has a plan to maximize his own sect's personal interest out of the affair." Proyect continued, "The important political point that Ali is making about the shortcomings of all of these sect leaders is that none of them has a clue how to react to the collapse of the bureaucracy, except to say 'Now it is our time.' They . . . lack the self-awareness to understand the reason for their own collapse." Proyect found that while Ali "is unstinting in his bitter satire of this misbegotten movement, there is another element of the novel that demonstrates the serious concerns of Ali and his political milieu during 1990," which is that "Ali's book . . . provides the definitive satirical deathblow to a movement that has become ossified and irrelevant." Alamgir Hashmi, a reviewer for *SPAN: Journal of the South Pacific Association for the Commonwealth Literature and Language Studies* (1992, on-line), noted that "the possibility of redemption . . . is always considered tongue-in-cheek and the gloom caused by the collapse of the Alternative System is beaten out with wit and banter." He concluded that "solace and even blessedness . . . are found in the formation of positive personal relations and private worlds." As one comrade in Ali's novel says, "Something will be reborn . . . but how and when and in what shape it is impossible to predict. The whole world has to be remade," as quoted by Hashmi.

For the backdrop of his next novel, *Shadows of the Pomegranate Tree* (1992), Ali turned to 15th-century Spain. The first in a quartet depicting the conflicts between Muslims and Christians from a Muslim point of view, the work deals with the final destruction of the Islamic world in Spain and the expulsion of Muslims in 1492. Here, a noble family is forced to choose between conversion from Islam to Christianity and death. Amit Chaudhuri, writing for the *London Review of Books* (July 9, 1992), noted that the "emotions, conflicts and shifts in this novel are no more complex and layered than those to be found in the exhilarating lyrics of an Arab song about love or heroism, but it is a strangely refreshing work in that it gives us a warm and indulgent picture of a certain section of Islamic life. . . . Some of the characters are extremely talkative, even boring, but one forgives them because one knows they are to be silenced forever."

In *Fear of Mirrors* (1998), Ali returned to the present to explore contemporary socialist confusion. The novel spans the history of the 20th century, from the dissolution of the Austrian empire to the fall of Communism in Eastern Europe. Set in the former East Germany, it is the story of Vladimir Meyer, an old-fashioned socialist and father of Karl, an adherent of the new Social Democratic Party after German reunification. Karl's mother, Gertrude, is a Soviet agent and sympathizer whose lover, Ludwik, is the agent who recruited Kim Philby, the British spy. Vladimir, desiring reconciliation with his son, writes him a letter about the family history: "What I want . . . is to rescue the people in this story from the grip of those whose only interest in the past is to justify their version of the present."

Ali based his novel on the life of the real Ludwik, whose actual name remains unknown. Ali interviewed Ludwik's son Roman Bernaut in 1989, an experience he later related in an article in the *Guardian* (February 20, 1999). After "the carnage of the first world war, which had swept away human lives like rotting leaves," Ali wrote, "Ludwik and his friends refused to be mere spectators. The fall of the Kaiser and the Tsar filled them with hope. Rosa Luxemburg and V. I. Lenin appealed to their intellects. They saw themselves as bearers of a new idea. In their minds and hearts, they carried the vision of a world without oppressors and oppressed." Ali, in the article, described how he was inspired by one sentence in Peter Wright's book *Spycatcher*, in which Wright told how he had taunted Anthony Blunt, another British spy involved in Ludwik's ring, mocking his involvement in a "sordid enterprise." Blunt's reply, "Our generation was won over by the finest minds in Europe," spurred Ali to write *Fear of Mirrors* in order to portray the intellectual idealism of early supporters of the Soviet Union.

Fear of Mirrors "is a look over the wall at the somewhat taboo love for an ideology that first betrays and then is torn away," David Cline observed in *Booklist* (November 15, 1998), describing the work as "a densely packed novel" that "reveals a keen mind and strong political insight." A reviewer for *Publishers Weekly* (October 12, 1998) agreed that "the tight, cultlike atmosphere of Communist Party life, peopled by idealists who find their lives encumbered by betrayals, power grabs and corruption" makes for "a valuable book, especially for those interested in the current thinking of the European left." In London, Julian Ferraro of the *Times Literary Supplement* (July 3, 1998) found *Fear of Mirrors* "at its best in its examination of the painful and morally doubtful consequences of the compromises forced on those who live their lives in the service of political ideals, charting as it does the movement from utopian world revolution to Stalinist terror to the unsatisfactory realities of post-Communist Europe." He deemed it a "reasonably gripping" tale but objected that "the trite conclusion . . . seriously undermines the bleak complexities of the book."

The Book of Saladin (1998) is the second of Ali's novels depicting the confrontation between Muslims and Christians, this time during the reign of Saladin, the 12th-century sultan of Egypt and Syria who drove the Crusaders from Jerusalem after 77 years of occupation. Narrated from the point of view of the fictional Jewish chronicler Ibn Yakub and Saladin's servant Shadhi, this novel purports to be the complete biography of the only leader who was able to unite the Arabs, if only temporarily, against their common enemy. Ali intertwines Saladin's role as ruler with his personal life, including his relations with members of his harem. Rather than portraying him as the gallant knight of European legend, Ali presents Saladin as "charismatic yet not a hero of romance, a rather hesitant limping figure, a sultan whose preferred diet is soup and beans," wrote Jane Jakeman in the *New Statesman* (January 8, 1999). Jakeman went on to point out that even the women in the harem are "strong and intelligent . . . characters in a convincing story with a reality beyond that of historical cliché." In the novel, as quoted by Jakeman, Ali writes, "The sultan often asks himself if this bad dream will ever end or is it our fate as the inhabitants of an area which gave birth to Moses, Jesus and Mohammed to be always at war," a rumination which Jakeman said demonstrates in the author "the sadness of a radical who has seen the failure of ideals in his own lifetime. If this novel offers little comfort for the Crusader side of the story, its dense and multi-faceted explorations are also a plea against all religious bigotry." Jason Cons, reviewing the novel for *Bookpress* (November 1998), agreed that Ali had succeeded in presenting a critique of "Western religious imperialism," but he considered the novel more complex than a political discourse: "*The Book of Saladin* accepts the Middle East as a stage on which characters who are greater than their immediate selves rise to represent the whole. But while this stage does enclose the action of the novel, disparate elements from other lands wander on and off the stage to challenge fixed notions of religion, both Islamic and other." In the *Times Literary Supplement* (December 4, 1998), Ranti Williams praised *The Book of Saladin* as an attempt "to add to the conventional view of this humane, generous leader a sense of indecision and loneliness by presenting the contradictions at the heart of the great man." Williams concluded, however, that although "*The Book of Saladin* manages the grand historical sweep with a fair amount of colour and incident," the characters lack complete roundedness.

Also in 1998, Ali published, with Susan Watkins, *1968: Marching in the Streets*. The volume is a month-by-month review of the events of 1968, including the Prague Spring movement in Czechoslovakia, which was crushed by the Soviet Union; the student uprising in France; and the American pursuit of the war in Vietnam, which led to massive protest demonstrations in both the United States and England. Christopher Hitchens, in the *London Review of Books*, observed that the volume had "a kaleidoscopic feel. . . . Turn the pages in a hurry and you go from the Tet offensive in Vietnam to the strikes in Poland to the murder of Dr. King[,] . . . the invasion of Czechoslovakia, the drama in the streets at the Chicago Democratic Convention, the butchery at the Mexico Olympics." Hitchens concluded that these "imperishable vignettes" would be "better recollected in tranquillity." Karl Helicher, in *Library Journal* (June 1, 1998), called *1968* "an idealistic . . . survey" but criticized Ali for not identifying "overarching themes or root causes of the rebellions."

With his longtime dramatic collaborator Howard Brenton, Ali turned once again to the theater to write *Ugly Rumours* in 1998. A satire on New Labour, *Ugly Rumours* portrays Margaret Thatcher as a madwoman in the cellar of No. 10 Downing Street, who has sucked the socialism out of Tony Blair, the new prime minister. "Howard Brenton and Tariq Ali have done wisely to include Thatcher in their satire of new Labour," Kate Kellaway wrote in the *New Statesman* (November 13, 1998). In Kellaway's opinion, however, Blair as a character does not lend himself as well to "biting comedy," and "there is an obvious difficulty about satirising blandness that Ali and Brenton never quite overcome."

Ali and Brenton next joined with Andy de la Tour for *Snogging Ken*, their 2000 satire on the London mayoral election, which was won by Ken Livingstone in an upset. The three called themselves Stigma and banded together to create "disposable theatre," according to Nina Raine in the *New Statesman* (April 24, 2000). They issued the "Stigma Manifesto," which included the statement that "Stigma will challenge the insolence, the stupidity, the cliches and cadences of contemporary politics. It will lampoon the courtiers and sycophants of the New World Order. It will target those who send the message, but also shoot the messenger. Both are guilty. . . . Stigma will not aim to please. If more than a few critics ever like our work, we will be duty-bound to ask ourselves where we went wrong." One critic who liked their work was Lyn Gardner. In her review of a "Snogging Ken" production for the *Guardian* (April 20, 2000) she wrote, "It is terrific fun, plays cleverly on the idea that even the most rabid fantasies might have a grain of truth . . . and uses mockery to attack the smugness of New Labour. Not subtle, but subtly dissident."

In 2000, Ali returned to his novelizations of the history of Muslim-Christian relations with *The Stone Woman*, set in the final days of the Ottoman Empire in 1899. Iskander Pasha's family is gathered at its summer palace near Istanbul. Iskander's daughter, Nilofer, is the principal narrator, while the remainder of the narrative consists of the confessions of various characters before the "stone woman," a sculpture of a pagan goddess. "The plot coheres neatly as the stories interconnect," a reviewer for *Publishers Weekly* (June 26, 2000) wrote. "Ali's epic combines the luxuriant pacing of the old-fashioned novel of ideas with the 20th-century relish for sexual detail to conjure up an almost Chekhovian milieu." James Hopkin, in the *New Statesman* (September 11, 2000), concurred, noting that by drawing "on a rich tradition of myth-making and storytelling, Ali creates an enchanting, sometimes harrowing, fable of a family whose stability and harmony, like the empire to which they belong, is largely predicated on undisclosed information and recycled myths." He concluded that the "intertwining of political, religious and national posturing with simple tales of family life and love (suicide, madness, defiance) . . . makes *The Stone Woman* so captivating."

Ali returned to non-fiction with *The Clash of Fundamentalisms: Crusades, Jihads and Modernity* (2002), in which he explores several political and religious elements of Western and Muslim civilizations that have resulted in the current tensions afflicting international relations. He wrote the book in the aftermath of the terrorist attacks of September 11, 2001, after the U.S. had commenced its "war on terrorism" to deal with fundamentalist, terrorist groups around the world. Yet, throughout the book Ali explores "fundamentalism" as a characteristic of both the West and the East. He undertakes a brief history of Islam to identify the concepts driving fundamentalist movements within that religion, but also presents U.S. foreign policy as what he describes as "the mother of all fundamentalisms: American imperialism," as quoted by Mick Hume for the *New Statesman* (May 13, 2002). At the heart of his thesis, Ali suggests that the modern world is mired in "the clash between [an Islamic] religious fundamentalism . . . and an [American] imperial fundamentalism determined to 'discipline the world.'" Critical response to *The Clash of Fundamentalisms* was mixed. While some reviewers credited Ali with opening a worthwhile discussion, others felt that his interpretations of American history often lacked documentation. As James R. Holmes noted for *Library Journal*, as quoted on *Amazon.com*, "The book has no bibliography and only a handful of footnotes, largely from secondary sources. . . . In short, this isn't a serious work." In addition, some critics found the work lacking a clear focus, in what Hume called "this messy book's own identity crisis, caught as it is between Ali's original plan for a history of Islam and his post-11 September attempt to tack on a theory of everything." Nevertheless, writing for *The Nation* (July 8, 2002), Anthony Arnove praised numerous aspects of Ali's discourse, as well as his ability to explore history in a manner that is lyrical, passionate, and humane. While acknowledging some faults within the text, Arnove concluded: "None of this takes away from the importance of his argument that we are not living in a radically new epoch in history, but in a period with all too much continuity to the one before September 11." /TXT=Ali has arguably shown himself to be one of the few 20th-century writers who can maintain an irreverent attitude mingled with a total commitment to understanding and improving the world. He told Ardeshir Mehrdad in an interview for *Rahekargar* (on-line) that the "end of the Cold War, following the collapse of the Soviet Union was supposed to herald a 'New World Order' and the 'end of history.' A world that would be conflict-free and run in the interests of the global capitalist economy. In reality the world has become more dangerous, less stable and prone to nationalist, religious and ethnic conflicts of the most virulent sort." Although pessimistic, Ali has continued to raise a voice against oppression, through both his artistic endeavors, such as his novels, plays, and films, and through the expression of his political views in his nonfiction writings.

Tariq Ali is an editor of the *New Left Review* and resides in London.

— *S.Y.*

SUGGESTED READING: *Booklist* p564 Nov. 15, 1998; *Bookpress* (on-line) Nov. 1998; *Economist* p61 Sep. 26, 1970; *Guardian* p15, Oct. 28, 1996; T p34+ Feb. 20, 1999; *Library Journal* p3477 Oct. 15, 1970; *London Review of Books* p18 July 9, 1992; p14 June 4, 1998; *New Statesman* p82 Sep. 25, 1970; p28 Nov. 6, 1987; p55 Jan. 8, 1999, p43 Apr. 24, 2000; p56 Sep. 11, 2000; *New York Times Book Review* p25 Apr. 21, 1985; *Publishers Weekly* p47 June 26, 2000; *Rehecargar* (on-line); *SPAN: Journal of the South Pacific Association for the Commonwealth Literature and Language Studies* (on-line) 1992; *Times Literary Supplement* p20 July 3, 1998

SELECTED WORKS: nonfiction—*Pakistan: Military Rule or People's Power*, 1970; *The Coming British Revolution*, 1972; *1968 and After: Inside the Revolution*, 1978; *Trotsky for Beginners*, 1980; *Can Pakistan Survive?*, 1983; *What Is Stalinism?*, 1984; *An Indian Dynasty: The Story of the Nehru-Gandhi Family*, 1985; *1968: Street Fighting Years*, 1987; *Revolution from Above: Where is the Soviet Union Going?*, 1988; *1968: Marching in the Streets* (with S. Watkins), 1998; *Introducing Trotsky and Marxism* (with P. Evans), 2000; *The Clash of Fundamentalisms: Crusades, Jihads and Modernity*, 2002; fiction—*Redemption*, 1990; *Shadows of the Pomegranate Tree*, 1992; *Fear of Mirrors*, 1998; *The Book of Saladin*, 1998; *The Stone Woman*, 2000; plays—*Iranian Nights* (with H. Brenton), 1989; *Moscow Gold* (with H. Brenton), 1990; *Ugly Rumours* (with H. Brenton), 1998; *Snagging Ken* (with H. Brenton and A. de la Tour), 2000

Courtesy of the *New Yorker*

Als, Hilton

(ALZ)

1961– Journalist; memoirist

As a regular contributor to such publications as the *New Yorker* and *Grand Street*, Hilton Als has won acclaim for his insightful reviews on art and culture and thought-provoking articles in which he, as a gay African-American, explores his sexual and racial identity. Reviewers hailed Als's first book, *The Women* (1996), as an honest, well-written account of three interesting figures: his mother; the dramatist and poet Owen Dodson, who was Als's mentor and lover; and Dorothy Dean, an African-American woman who was a fixture in New York City's gay life during the 1960s and 1970s. In each profile Als also reveals important autobiographical details about himself and describes his emerging sexual identity during his adolescence. He has also explored gay themes in two films he co-wrote, *Looking for Langston* (1988) and *Swoon* (1992). Growing up in a modest brownstone home in the New York City borough of Brooklyn with his mother and five siblings, Als never expected that he would make a living as a writer. "It's so strange to be part of something you've always admired," he told Adam Kelly for the *Advocate* (December 12, 1996). "I just can't believe I made it to Emerald City."

Hilton Als was born in 1961. His parents had emigrated separately to the United States from Barbados and settled in Brooklyn. They met and enjoyed a 30-year relationship that produced four children. (Hilton's mother, Marie Als, never married his father, Cyprian Williams.) Raised in the Flatbush section of Brooklyn, Hilton had one brother, two sisters, and two half-sisters. Marie supported her family by working as a housekeeper, hairdresser, and teacher's assistant. (Als immortalized the beauty salon where Marie straightened hair during the 1960s in an April 6, 1997 *New York Times Magazine* article.)

In a piece published in the *New Yorker* (November 18, 1996), Als recalled that, as a child, he was completely fascinated by his mother. At age seven he began to experience a homosexual awakening. His fascination with his mother led him, as he wrote, "to a dark crawl space behind her closet, where I put on her hosiery one leg at a time, my heart racing, and, over the hose, my jeans and sneakers, so that I could have her, what I so admired and coveted, near me, always." A short time later he began living the life of what he called an "auntie man," a term for homosexual commonly used by Barbadians. Als wrote, "My mother responded to the Negress inside me with pride and anger: pride because I identified with women like herself; anger because I identified with women at all."

Als's father lived in the nearby Crown Heights section of Brooklyn and also influenced him. Cyprian Williams admired the Jews he encountered in New York City. As Als explained in his article for *Transition* (Spring 1997), "He was in love with the Jewish tradition of intellectual inquiry. My father wanted my brother and I to model ourselves after the smart Jews he knew; I was an anxious Yeshiva student to his brownskinned, well-dressed, mustachioed rebbe." Als came to believe that "Jews, unlike Negroes, had made something out of their suffering— something distinct, rich, and literary, to which I wanted to belong. For a long time I knew more about the suffering of the Jews than I did about being a Negro gentleman."

Hilton decided that he wanted to be a writer when he was eight years old. As he observed in *The Women* (1996), "Writing things down was the only way I understood how to be heard, there being so many women in my mother's house at various times, talking." After learning about his ambition to be a writer, his mother bought him writing tablets for Christmas and frequently gave him books, usually novels and collections of poems, which she bought from a local book store. A sympathetic neighbor gave him a typewriter.

When Als was 13 he became acquainted with Owen Dodson, an African-American dramatist and poet, and the two became lovers a few years later. In *Grand Street* (Winter 1995, on-line), Als wrote, "By the time I met him, he had, in effect, stopped writing. He drank, received pupils, former pupils, someone else's pupils, because the reflection and isolation required to produce writing, good, bad or indifferent, had never been as important to him as being liked." Dodson's health declined steadily, and he died in 1983, about two years after his relationship with Als ended.

Als enrolled in Columbia University, in New York City, to study art history. After dropping out of college, he got a job as a secretary with the *Village Voice*, a popular alternative newspaper. He began writing frequently for *Essence* magazine, most often covering the fashion scene, and later he started writing regularly for the *Village Voice*, contributing many reviews on books, films, television shows, theater productions, and art exhibitions.

In 1988 Als co-wrote the screenplay for the 42-minute film *Looking for Langston* with Isaac Julien, a director from the United Kingdom. An exploration of black gay sexuality, the movie suggested that the African-American poet Langston Hughes was homosexual. *Looking for Langston* was often screened during gay and lesbian film festivals in the United States and was broadcast on BBC television in Britain. In a review for the *Los Angeles Times* (January 26, 1990), Kevin Thomas wrote, "[The filmmakers treat] Hughes as an icon, as a point of departure to consider the oppressed state of black gays through the decades, of their exploitation by white gays, and of the specter of AIDS and of the bitter aftermath of the Harlem Renaissance [during the 1920s] when black artists and writers 'went out of style' with white sophisticates and intellectuals. The film . . . is exceptionally poignant and imaginative." The picture attracted controversy when the estate of Langston Hughes objected to its depiction of him as homosexual. Several scholars have said that there is no conclusive evidence that Hughes was gay, and the threat of legal action by the estate forced Julien to delete footage showing Hughes reciting one of his poems.

In 1992 Als co-wrote the screenplay for *Swoon* with Tom Kalin, who also directed the film. *Swoon* retells the story of the 1924 murder of 13-year-old Bobby Franks by Richard Loeb and Nathan Leopold, in Chicago. At that time, the murder and the subsequent trial of Loeb and Leopold caused a media sensation. The noted attorney and civil libertarian Clarence Darrow saved the pair from execution. Unlike previous films based on the case, such as *Rope* (1948) and *Compulsion* (1959), Als and Kalin focused on the killers' homosexuality, arguing that it was not a factor in the murder, as several other accounts suggested. Edward Guthmann, a reviewer for the *San Francisco Chronicle* (September 25, 1992), wrote that Kalin "builds his story coolly, elegantly, using a variety of narrative and visual techniques. He integrates old newsreel footage to enhance the '20s period, borrows from actual court transcripts and psychoanalytic sessions . . . and creates a series of voice-over journal entries read by both actors [portraying Loeb and Leopold], that trace the psychological roots of the crime." Guthmann criticized the film, however, for devoting little attention to the German philosopher Friedrich Nietzsche's concept of the "Superman" ("Ubermensch"), which is often used to explain Loeb's and Leopold's motivations for the murder. Both men were known to be impressed by Nietzsche's ideas, especially his proposition that the Superman achieves intellectual superiority by overcoming the boundaries—often in the form of morals and ethics—imposed on him by society.

Als joined the *New Yorker* as a staff writer in late 1994, thanks in part to a piece he had written for another publication about the *New Yorker* writer Ian Frazier. He regularly contributed profiles of notable individuals, reviews, and autobiographical pieces to the magazine. In 1996 Als published expanded versions of three of his articles—two from the *New Yorker* and one from *Grand Street*, in his first book, *The Women*. In the book Als discusses his relationship with his mother and Owen Dodson, and examines the life of Dorothy Dean, who used to describe herself as a white homosexual "trapped in a black woman's body." In each essay, Als reveals details and insights about his own sexual and racial identity and his background. Andrea Lee wrote for the *New York Times* (January 5, 1997, on-line), "A haunting sense of melancholy pervades the descriptions of all three: although the characters are very different, the reader is immediately aware that each is a tragic figure, yearning after an impossible dream and trapped by fear or laziness within the limits of a self-imposed identity." Lee praised the book, observing that its "almost magical cohesiveness is due to the peculiar talents of the author, who combines a quirky brilliance at analytical thought with a gift for visual and psychological description worthy of a novelist. The result has the hidden but compelling logic of a poem and, like the best poetry, suggests much more than it says." In a review for the *Library Journal* (September 1, 1996), Janice E. Braun wrote, "The predominant motif of this autobiographical tract is what Als calls the Negress. As a gay African-American, an 'auntie man'. . . Als both identifies and competes with his mother, sister and other representations of matriarchal society." Braun concluded that *The Women* is "deeply felt and beautifully written."

In 1997 Als edited *Our Town: Images and Stories from the Museum of the City of New York*. The book was published to commemorate the museum's 75th anniversary and included reprints of paintings, etchings, and photographs, along with essays on New York City's cultural life, by Louis Auchincloss and Arthur Gelb, among others.

In 2000 Als contributed an essay to *Without Sanctuary: Lynching Photography in America*, which was edited by James Allen. The book, which also served as a catalogue for the exhibit *Witness* at the New York Historical Society, is a collection of photographs that show lynchings of African Americans (and some whites) in the United States. The graphic and disturbing images in *Without Sanctuary* illustrate how common lynching and racism were in the United States at one time. Lynchings often attracted enthusiastic spectators, many of whom would often bring their children to see what was considered a form of entertainment, as well as a brutal and horrifying instrument of oppression. In his essay Als questions the purpose of such a collection of photographs and wonders if the people who view the images will identify with the victims or the oppressors. "Of course, one big difference between the people documented in these pictures and me is that I am not dead, have not been lynched or scalded or burned or whipped or stoned," Als wrote, as quoted on *nybooks.com*. "But I have been looked at, watched, and it's the experience of being watched, and seeing the harm in people's eyes—that is the prelude to becoming . . . like those seen here. . ." In an article for the *Los Angeles Times Book Review* (February 13, 2000), Benjamin Schwarz, while praising the book, wrote that "Als' short piece—in which he complains of the 'metaphorical lynching' he has experienced when his white editors and white fellow guests at parties 'watch' him—is self-aggrandizing and trivializes the subject." In the *Village Voice* (March 28, 2000), C. Carr described *Without Sanctuary* as a "powerful document of repressed history" and praised Als for having the courage in his essay to ask "the hard questions, the ones that make white people uncomfortable."

In addition to the *New Yorker*, Hilton Als often writes for *Grand Street*, *Artforum*, *Interview*, and *Vibe*, where he also serves as editor-at-large. Als's book, "The Group," which is tentatively scheduled for publication in 2004, will discuss the relationship between the African-American author James Baldwin and the intellectual Jewish authors who helped launch his career, including Saul Levitas, Elliott Cohen, Robert Warshow, and Philip Rahv. A reviewer for *Amazon.com* wrote that the book will analyse the "complicated, often volatile relationship between the intellectual and moral worlds of both the African-American and Jewish communities." Als wrote and directed the film, "Fine and Mellow," which tells the story of the love affair between the white actor Orson Welles and the popular black jazz singer Billie Holiday during the 1940s. The film has not yet been released.

Hilton Als lives in New York City.

—D.C.

SUGGESTED READING: *Advocate* p74 Dec. 12, 1996, with photo; *Grand Street* (on-line) Winter 1995; *Library Journal* p198 Sep. 1, 1996; *Los Angeles Times* p10 Jan. 26, 1990; *Los Angeles Times Book Review* p1 Feb. 13, 2000, with photos; *New York Times* (on-line) p7 Jan. 5, 1997; *New Yorker* p72+ Nov. 18, 1996, with photos; *San Francisco Chronicle* C p3 Sep. 25, 1992; *Transition* (on- line) Spring 1997; *Village Voice* p63 March 28, 2000, with photo

SELECTED WORKS: nonfiction—*The Women*, 1996; as editor—*Our Town: Images and Stories from the Museum of the City of New York*, 1997; as contributor—*Without Sanctuary: Lynching Photography in America*, 2000; films—as screenwriter—*Looking for Langston*, 1988; *Swoon*, 1992; as screenwriter and director—*Fine and Mellow*, 2001

Minna Proctor/Courtesy of Farrar, Straus and Giroux

Anastas, Benjamin

1969– Novelist

Benjamin Anastas is the author of two well-received novels, *The Underachiever's Diary* (1998) and *The Faithful Narrative of a Pastor's Disappearance* (2001). The former is a short novel written from the perspective of a young man named William, who has lived, since birth, in the shadow of his twin brother, Clive. Whereas Clive is a child prodigy who excels in all things, William obstinately devotes himself to a life of mediocrity. "I am proud to be a disappointment to almost everybody," William records in his "diary," as quoted by Celia Wren for the *Village Voice* (April 7, 1998). As William recounts the series of flukes and misadventures that punctuated his childhood and early adulthood, Anastas uses the opportunity to lampoon the liberal bourgeois culture of 1960s and 1970s Cambridge, Massachusetts. "There is real resonance in William, determined to make the least of his considerable gifts," Judith Kicinski wrote for *Library Journal* (February 1, 1998). Anastas's second novel, *The Faithful Narrative of a Pastor's Disappearance*, focuses on the gnawing discontent of a married suburban woman who had been having an affair with the local pastor until he mysteriously vanished. Jeff Zaleski for *Publishers Weekly* (April 23, 2001) called the novel an "unsparing take on the emptiness and desperation of a materialist society."

Little has been written about Benjamin Anastas's life. He was born in 1969 (although some sources list 1971), in Cambridge, Massachusetts. The son of a social worker, Anastas was born a fraternal twin; his sister's name is Rhea. He attended the University of Iowa Writers' Workshop, in Iowa

City. "The reason I went to an MFA program in the first place is that I wanted to be around writers," Anastas recalled in an on-line chat for the Barnes & Noble Web site. "I was very young, 22, when I went to Iowa—perhaps too young—and I found it a difficult but great experience. . . . When I was in college, writing was something that I had done in secret, and to all of a sudden meet 50 other people who had the same secret was liberating." While in Iowa Anastas worked as a fiction editor of the *Iowa Review*, for which he also wrote book reviews. His first short story was published in *Story* magazine, in 1992.

In *The Underachiever's Diary* William, who narrates the novel, was born seven minutes before his identical twin brother, Clive. After that brief triumph, things go downhill for him. While Clive delights his parents from the start—he is "a Green Beret in diapers," Anastas writes, as quoted by Christina Paterson for the Manchester *Guardian Weekly* (March 28, 1999)—William takes a perverse pleasure in his own shortcomings. The twins grow up in Cambridge, Massachusetts, in the 1960s, raised by middle-class liberals who encourage nudity and dinner-table discussions of masturbation. William has a hard time taking his parents' values seriously—they once toured Mexico "in search of armed insurrectionists and returned with the perfect dining-room set," Anastas writes, as quoted by Kicinski. He develops an incorrigible contrarian attitude that compels him to reject the prevailing ethos of success, conformity, and commercialism he sees around him. Accordingly, while Clive goes off to Harvard, William wiles away his time at an unimpressive college, courts an alcoholic girlfriend who can't remember his name, and makes his way through a string of dead-end jobs.

Anastas drew material for the book from his own upbringing in Cambridge. "I wanted to capture the particular mixture of class and progressive politics so prevalent there," he remarked in the on-line chat for the Barnes & Noble Web site. Anastas added, however, that he sees the characters of Clive and William's parents as "essentially good people." As a twin, Anastas is frequently asked how much of the novel is autobiographical. In the on-line chat for the Barnes and Noble Web site, he commented, "William is an entirely fictional construct, but I have filtered some autobiography through him. . . . I had always wanted to write about twins but didn't feel comfortable doing so until I was certain that I was writing fiction." The sharp contrast between the twins was inspired by a line from Fyodor Dostoevsky's 1863 novel *Notes from the Underground*. Anastas explained, "Toward the end of the book, Underground Man, the narrator, asks 'Which is better, cheap happiness or sublime suffering?' The question seemed unfairly weighted to me. So I thought a way to strike a balance might be to have one twin brother, Clive, represent cheap happiness, although since he is a fully rounded character, his happiness isn't all that cheap, and the other twin, William, represent sublime suffering, not that his suffering is always sublime. I guess the fact that I chose William to narrate the story shows that I am more sympathetic to the suffering side of the equation."

Reviews of the novel were predominately positive, although some critics expressed minor reservations. "Unfortunately, many witty sections of this deftly designed novel are marred by a self-conscious cleverness," Celia Wren remarked. "At its best, Anastas's writing unites a shrewd awareness of contemporary absurdities with metaphysical speculation. He has a knack for ringing, jazzy turns of phrase . . . and his adaptable style—now taut and poetic, now colloquial and relaxed—helps the narrative digress effortlessly from William's disastrous resume to musings on St. Augustine, the epic of Gilgamesh, single-sex schools, and the attractions of San Francisco. Anyone who has ever cringed at a sibling's or classmate's success will relish William's ambitious pursuit of defeat." An anonymous critic for *Kirkus Reviews* (January 1, 1998) described the novel as "a wearyingly discursive if often very funny fictional autobiography. . . . A skimpy chronological narrative that's nevertheless buoyed by Anastas's gift for offbeat comic phrasing." Christina Patterson praised Anastas for writing a "sparkling first novel. . . . It's all extremely funny, bursting with one-liners."

Anastas's second novel, *The Faithful Narrative of a Pastor's Disappearance*, pursues a similarly satirical vein—along with a more serious one—in it's thoughtful probing of suburban malaise in a small Massachusetts town. Thomas Mosher is the new pastor of the Pilgrims' Congregational Church. Although well-liked and respected, the half-black Mosher is something of an anomaly to the mostly white, upper-middle-class members of his congregation. The novel begins with Mosher's unexplained disappearance, and the confusion and anxiety it sparks among his parishioners. One woman is particularly stunned—35-year-old Bethany Caruso, a lonely and unfulfilled wife who, it quickly becomes clear, had been having an affair with the pastor. Bethany's life is perfect on the surface; she has a career, a husband, two kids, a nice home in a prosperous community—yet something is lacking. Her husband, a sex-obsessed man she doesn't love, has tried in vain to rejuvenate the marriage—by building a "fornicatorium," replete with dirty magazines and water bed, in a room above the garage. Her two children, meanwhile, are withdrawn and generally obnoxious. Although Bethany has recently tapered her daily dose of the antidepressant Zoloft, she continues to medicate herself with cheap wine and an occasional joint of marijuana. It was in hopes of finding some bit of solace that she turned to the Pilgrims' Congregational Church, where she ended up in the arms of the charming, but enigmatic Mosher.

Anastas's narrative moves back and forth in time and touches upon a host of minor characters—including the busybody Margaret Howard, a real-estate agent who discovers a note revealing Bethany's affair. When she publicly exposes Bethany and tries to turn the congregation against her, the plan backfires. Anastas has said that this plot line was influenced by Kenneth W. Starr's *Report of the Independent Counsel to the United States House of Representatives*, regarding the sex scandal involving former U. S. President Bill Clinton. Another important source for Anastas, referenced in the book's title, was *A Faithful Narrative of the Surprising Work of God*, a 1737 account of religious awakening in Massachusetts, by Jonathan Edwards, a Puritan. "The challenge I set for myself in writing the novel was to try to use secular language, which is rational, to talk about religious experience, which, at bottom, is quite irrational," Anastas told Philip Connors for *Newsday* (June 10, 2001). "Faith is something that's very private and very hard to explain. I'm not Christian, I don't practice any kind of religion, but I admire writers, like St. Augustine, who have a deep commitment to language as a way of attempting to explain the almost unexplainable."

As with *The Underachiever's Diary*, reviews of the novel were good, although occasionally tempered with criticism. Tom Beer for *Newsday* (May 31, 2001) described the novel as "odd and charming," adding that the "secondary characters . . . are the minor miracles of Anastas' book." Although Beer noted that the novel was "less successful . . . in its attempt to engage the broader existential questions that hover over Anastas' story," he confided that "one feels churlish complaining too loudly." He concluded, "If *The Faithful Narrative of a Pastor's Disappearance* falls shy of its loftiest ambitions, it's still a mighty good read. The characters and their social milieu are wonderfully drawn, and the writing is sardonic and memorable." "Suburban send-ups aren't normally this funny, or this serious. And they certainly aren't usually as good," Mark Luce wrote for the *Washington Post* (June 10, 2001). "Anastas exuberantly lampoons what passes for Christianity in today's upper-middle classes, but underneath the wit and farce of *The Faithful Narrative of a Pastor's Disappearance* breathes a quiet faith. And it's the best kind of faith, one that's loving, inclusive and abundantly aware of shared human foibles."

Anastas is a winner of the *Gentlemen's Quarterly* Frederick Exley Fiction Prize as well as *Story* magazine's college fiction competition. He received the James Michener/Paul Engle fellowship after graduating from the University of Iowa. He often contributes freelance book reviews to such periodicals as the *New York Times*, the *Washington Post*, *Salon*, and the New York *Observer*. His review of the Dave Eggers's book *A Heartbreaking Work of Staggering Genius* for the last publication drew immediate fire for its supposed vitriol, but Anastas told Phillip Connors for New York *Newsday* (June 10, 2001), "[My editors at the *Observer*] gave it a really obnoxious headline. They made what I thought was a quite respectful, if mixed, review seem like a hatchet job." Anastas is an editor of *Grand Street*, a quarterly magazine featuring art, poetry, short stories, and nonfiction. He lives in the New York City borough of Brooklyn.

—A. I. C.

SUGGESTED READING: *Kirkus Reviews* Jan. 1, 1998; *Library Journal* p109 Feb.1, 1998; (New York) *Newsday* B p2 May 31, 2001, B p11 June 10, 2001; *Publishers Weekly* p48 Apr. 23, 2001; *Village Voice* p8 Apr. 7, 1998; *Washington Post* T p10 June 10, 2001

SELECTED BOOKS: *The Underachiever's Diary*, 1998; *The Faithful Narrative of a Pastor's Disappearance*, 2001

Courtesy of Lordly & Dame, Inc.

Angelou, Maya

(AN-jel-oh, MIE-yuh)

Apr. 4, 1928– Memoirist; poet; educator; actress; activist

Maya Angelou, who is widely considered one of the most important voices in contemporary African-American literature, may be best known for her six-volume series of autobiographical memoirs, which commenced with the critically acclaimed *I Know Why the Caged Bird Sings* (1970). As one of the nation's most popular and accessible poets, Angelou made history on January 20, 1993, when she participated in President Bill Clinton's first inauguration, reciting her original poem "On the Pulse of the Morning." In addition to her celebrated work as a poet and autobiographer, Angelou has written plays, screenplays, and television scripts; recorded calypso songs and poetry; thrived in the theater as a singer, dancer, actress, producer, and director; taught and lectured at universities; and organized civil rights activists. Her writings often attest to her gift for survival in the face of hardship and injustice. "What I would really like said about me is that I dared to love," she told an interviewer for USA Today (March 5, 1985). "By love I mean that condition in the human spirit so profound it encourages us to develop courage and build bridges and then to trust those bridges and cross the bridges in attempts to reach other human beings." She has professed her desire to speak to and for people of all races and nationalities. "In all my work, what I try to say is that as human beings we are more alike than we are unalike," she told Catherine S. Manegold for the New York Times (January 20, 1993). "It may be that Mr. Clinton asked me to write the inaugural poem because he understood that I am the kind of person who really does bring people together."

Born Marguerite Annie Johnson on April 4, 1928 in St. Louis, Missouri, Angelou, who was called Rita in public, was given the nickname Maya by her older brother, Bailey Jr., who had been calling her "My" or "Mine." Her father, Bailey Johnson, was a doorman and naval dietician, and her mother, Vivian Baxter Johnson, worked variously as a card dealer, boardinghouse proprietor, and registered nurse. Shortly after their daughter's birth, the Johnsons moved with their two children to Long Beach, California. Three years later, in the wake of the dissolution of their parents' marriage, Maya and Bailey Jr. were sent to live with their paternal grandmother, Annie Henderson, who owned and managed a general store in the small town of Stamps, Arkansas.

In the mid-1930s, when Maya was seven, she and her brother left Stamps to live in St. Louis with their mother, who had returned there not long after her divorce. A few months after their arrival, Maya was raped by her mother's boyfriend. The crime was soon discovered, and when the offender was brought to trial, Maya was forced to testify. Several days later her assailant was found beaten to death in an alley, the victim, apparently, of the wrath of some of Maya's uncles. Shocked by the seeming connection between her words at the trial and the death of a man, Maya resolved to stop talking in public. "I thought he was killed because I spoke his name," she told Manegold. "That was the only logic I was able to employ. So I thought if I spoke, anybody might die." (In another source, Angelou said that she had stopped speaking because of the guilt she felt after lying in her testimony about a previous sexual assault by the same man, who had threatened to kill her brother if she revealed the molestation.) Several months after the trial, she and her brother were sent back to Annie Henderson, in Stamps.

For the next five years, Angelou maintained her silence while immersing herself in books and imbibing the power of language as it is written, spoken, and sung. A local woman, Bertha Flowers, whom Angelou later described as "the aristocrat of black Stamps," took a special interest in the girl's literary preoccupations and encouraged her to read. Along with an early fondness for the Bible and for the works of such black poets as Paul Lawrence Dunbar, James Weldon Johnson, and Langston Hughes, Angelou developed a great affection for the writings of William Shakespeare, Edgar Allan Poe, Matthew Arnold, and Charles Dickens. By the time she graduated from the eighth grade, in 1940, she had begun to speak again and had become known throughout the black community as a precocious and eloquent child. She later attributed to her self-imposed muteness her extraordinary ability to listen intently, remembering every inflection and every nuance of the words she heard.

Angelou and her brother moved to San Francisco in 1940 to be with their mother, who had remarried and was running a boardinghouse. While she was attending George Washington High School, in San Francisco, Angelou obtained a two-year scholarship to study dance and drama at the California Labor School. In addition to going to school day and night, she earned her own spending money. At the age of 16, she became the first black—and the first female—streetcar conductor in San Francisco. She graduated from high school in August 1945, just a few months before giving birth to her son, Clyde ("Guy") Johnson, an experience she later described as "the best thing that ever happened to me." Over the next five years, Angelou held a succession of jobs, including that of a cook in a Creole restaurant in San Francisco and a nightclub waitress in San Diego. During the time she lived in San Diego, she also worked as a madam, managing two prostitutes, until her guilty conscience compelled her to quit and move back to Stamps. Unable to tolerate the overt racism there, she soon returned to San Francisco. Hoping to obtain vocational training, she tried to enlist in the United States Army, but she was turned down after a security check of her background revealed that the California Labor School was listed as a subversive breeding ground by the House Un-American Activities Committee.

Following a three-year marriage to Tosh Angelos, a former sailor who was of Greek descent, in the early 1950s, Angelou bluffed her way into a job as a dancer and singer. A quick study whose winning appeal with the audience overcame any deficiencies in skill, she performed in the popular West Indian calypso style of dance at the Purple Onion, a cabaret in San Francisco. It was there that she adopted the stage name Maya Angelou (Angelou being a variation on her ex-husband's surname), which she soon began using in all of her endeavors. Her stage credits during this period included a stint as a featured dancer in a State Department–sponsored production of George Gershwin's opera Porgy and Bess, with which she toured 22 nations in Europe and Africa.

Upon her return to the United States, in 1955, Angelou settled in California. From her home base there, she took her cabaret act to Hawaii and to cities along the West Coast. Moving to New York City in the late 1950s, she became involved in a wide range of artistic activities. In 1957 she appeared in an Off-Broadway play, *Calypso Heatwave,* and recorded an album for Liberty Records entitled *Miss Calypso.* Spurred by her exposure to the works of Lorraine Hansberry, James Baldwin, and John O. Killens, who were dispelling myths about black Americans in their writings, Angelou began attending the weekly meetings of the Harlem Writers Guild, where she learned, among other things, that the difference between a talented writer and a published author lay in hard work and the ability to take constructive criticism. She supported herself during those lean years by singing at such legendary venues as the Apollo Theater in Harlem.

Angelou's theatrical flair dovetailed with her developing political awareness when, after hearing the Reverend Martin Luther King Jr. speak in a Harlem church, she decided to produce a play to raise money for King's Southern Christian Leadership Conference (SCLC). To that end, in 1960 she and her friend Godfrey Cambridge produced, directed, and starred in *Cabaret for Freedom,* a revue that she had written, at the Village Gate in New York City. A few months after the show closed, Bayard Rustin, the northern coordinator for the SCLC, told her that he had been impressed by her organizational abilities. At Rustin's suggestion, she succeeded him in 1961 as the SCLC's northern coordinator, a position she held for about a year. Her sensitivity to the politics of racism was heightened when she appeared, in May 1961, in an all-black, Obie Award–winning production of Jean Genet's *The Blacks,* a controversial play in which blacks overthrow their white oppressors only to become evil themselves under the corrupting influence of power.

Later in 1961 Angelou moved to Cairo, Egypt, with Vusumzi Make, a South African dissident lawyer whom she had married. Pressured by poor financial circumstances, Angelou took a job as an associate editor of the *Arab Observer,* an English-language paper published in Cairo. In 1963, after her marriage to Make had ended, she moved to Accra, in the newly independent African country of Ghana, to be with her son, who was attending the University of Ghana. There, she worked as an assistant administrator and teacher at the university's School of Music and Drama and also served as the feature editor of the *African Review* and as a writer for the *Ghanaian Times.* In 1966 Angelou returned to California, where, at the Theatre of Being, in Hollywood, she performed in a production of Jean Anouilh's modern recasting of Euripides's tragedy *Medea.* Angelou's own two-act drama, *The Least of These,* was also produced that year in Los Angeles. In addition, she wrote *Black, Blues, Black,* a 10-part television series about the prominent role of African culture in American life that was produced and broadcast in 1968 by National Educational Television.

Meanwhile, James Baldwin and the playwright and cartoonist Jules Feiffer had been encouraging Angelou to write the story of her life and to do so in a style that utilized the same rhythmical cadences with which she mesmerized her listeners at social gatherings. Angelou undertook just this task in *I Know Why the Caged Bird Sings*, which covers her childhood and adolescence until the birth of her son, when she was 17; the book was published in 1970 to overwhelming critical acclaim, including a nomination for the National Book Award. James Baldwin wrote, as quoted in Nancy Shuker's biography *Maya Angelou* (1990), "Not since the days of my childhood, when the people in books were more real than the people one saw every day, have I found myself so moved. . . . Her portrait is a biblical study of life in the midst of death." In an essay that appeared in the *Southern Humanities Review* (Fall 1973), Sidonie Ann Smith singled out for special praise Angelou's inspired use of language: "Her genius as a writer is her ability to recapture the texture of the way of life in the texture of its idioms, its idiosyncratic vocabulary, and especially in its process of image-making. . . . Here we witness a return to and final acceptance of the past in the return to and full acceptance of its language." Angelou told George Plimpton in an interview for *Writers at Work: Ninth Series* (1992) that in composing her autobiography, she had come to realize that she was "following a tradition established by Frederick Douglass—the slave narrative—speaking in the first-person singular talking about the first-person plural, always saying 'I' meaning 'we.'"

In the wake of *Caged Bird*'s popular and critical success, Angelou devoted herself to writing. She continued narrating her life story in *Gather Together in My Name* (1974), in which she describes her life through age 20, as well as the black community's bitter disillusionment over the entrenched economic disparity between its members and white Americans. Throughout the story, Angelou moves through this wasteland of disappointment, struggling to provide for her infant son. In the process she takes a variety of jobs, including stints as a Creole cook, a cocktail waitress, and even the amateur and absentee madam for two lesbian prostitutes. Annie Gottlieb, writing for the *New York Times* (June 16, 1974), called this book "engrossing and vital, rich and funny and wise," and particularly praised "the palpability, the precision and the rhythm of this writing. The reader is rocked into pleasure, stung into awareness. And the migrant, irresolute quality of the story—a faithful reflection of her late adolescence in the forties—resolves into a revelation. The restless, frustrated trying-on of roles turns out to have been an instinctive self-education, and the book ends with Maya Angelou finally gaining her adulthood by regaining her innocence."

Singin' and Swingin' and Gettin' Merry Like Christmas (1976) carries Angelou's life story into the 1950s. She writes of her short-lived marriage to

Angelos, her endless efforts to support her family, and the genesis of her theatrical career, studying dance with such legends as Martha Graham, Pearl Primus, and Anna Halprin, and drama with Frank Silvera and Gene Frankel. In a review of *Singin' and Swingin'* R. E. Almeida wrote, "Most Angelouphiles will find this a pleasant sequel in the ongoing autobiography of this fascinating woman. Her offbeat titles always intrigue, and she doesn't disappoint us." Almeida continued, "It is her perceptions of herself as a black, a woman, and a mother as well as her impressions of those she meets which distinguish this account. Her religious strength, personal courage, and her talent prevail."

In the fourth volume of her autobiography, *The Heart of a Woman* (1981), Angelou writes of her life through the late 1950s and early 1960s—the era of civil rights marches and the emergence of such African-American leaders as Dr. Martin Luther King Jr. and Malcolm X. During this period Angelou worked for the SCLC, organized *Cabaret for Freedom*, performed in *The Blacks*, and later moved to Egypt, where she married Vusumzi Make. The book chronicles her relationship with the African freedom fighter and also explores her struggles raising her teenage son. As Sheree Crute described for *Ms.* (July 1981), "Angelou makes the most of her wonderfully unaffected storytelling skills. . . . This memoir evokes a woman of strength who thrives on challenge and gives to her writing the energy and drive she gives to life." A reviewer for *Choice* (January 1982) observed, "Her first autobiography remains her best, . . . but every book since has been very much worth the reading and pondering."

In *All God's Children Need Traveling Shoes* (1986), Angelou describes the years she spent in the West African nation of Ghana during the 1960s. After her son, Guy, who was then in Ghana attending the university, nearly dies in an automobile accident, Angelou remains in Africa to be near him and becomes deeply involved in the community of black American immigrants who have moved there in search of a home. In the early 1960s, the young West African nation had recently earned its independence from Britain, and its progressive president, Kwame Nkrumah, was encouraging the integration of "American Negroes." Yet, as Angelou searches for her historical and spiritual "home," she confronts the cultural barriers that exist between native Africans and African Americans. As Barbara T. Christian wrote for the *Chicago Tribune* (March 23, 1986), "Angelou's journey into Africa is a journey into herself, into that part of every Afro-American's soul that is still wedded to Africa, that still yearns for a home—even as we create a new, yet African-derived culture in this new world." The book also features Angelou's experiences hosting Malcolm X when he visits the country, as well as her friendship with the black writer Julian Mayfield—two important leaders to whom she dedicates this volume. Critics again applauded Angelou's insight and candor in relating her life's experiences, with Jackie Gropman for *School Library Journal* (August 1986) declaring, "As in her previous memoirs, the poet's prose sings."

Angelou concluded her autobiographical series in 2002—more than 30 years after the original publication of *I Know Why the Caged Bird Sings*—with her sixth and final volume, *A Song Flung Up to Heaven*. In this work Angelou recounts her participation in the civil rights movement of the mid-1960s. The book opens with her return to the U.S. from Ghana, in 1964, to work with Malcolm X in establishing the Organization of African-American Unity; within days of her arrival, the activist is assassinated. "[Malcolm X's death] almost sent me over the edge," she told Sherryl Connelly in an interview for the *Daily News* (April 10, 2002). "After that, I couldn't imagine what I was going to be, what I was going to hook into." As Angelou finds her place in the black-power movement, she witnesses the historic 1965 riots that erupt in the South Central Los Angeles neighborhood of Watts. Later, she moves to New York City to work for Martin Luther King Jr. and again faces a devastating loss when the civil rights leader is assassinated. "I didn't know how to write it," she told Connelly, explaining why she took so long to conclude her memoirs. "I didn't see how the assassination of Malcolm, the Watts riot, the breakup of a love affair [with a man she will reveal only as 'The African'], then Martin King, how I could get all that loose with something uplifting in it." Critics found Angelou's exercise largely successful, although lacking the emotional impact of her previous autobiographical volumes. As Amy Strong explained for *Library Journal* (March 14, 2002), "Perhaps because this phase of Angelou's life is defined more by loss and withdrawal than conflict and struggle, this volume feels less profound, less intense than her earlier memoirs." James Hall, writing for the *Chicago Tribune* (April 7, 2002), observed, "More than any other of her volumes of autobiography, this one is motivated by some documentary urgency. . . . The historical sensibility that orders this book sometimes feels, if not shallow, extremely measured." Despite the mixed reviews, critics welcomed Angelou's perspective on this important era in African-American history.

Taken together, Angelou's volumes of autobiography have established her as a formidable presence on the American literary scene. In general, critics have applauded her for constructing a moving record of a modern African-American woman's life. In an essay that appeared in the *Washington Post* (October 4, 1981), David Levering Lewis examined the universal appeal and significance of Angelou's work: "Angelou has rearranged, edited, and pointed up her coming-of-age and going abroad in the world with such just-rightness of timing and inner truthfulness that each of her books is a continuing autobiography of much of Afro-America." Similarly, the National Public Radio correspondent Juan Williams told Connelly, "I think Maya Angelou occupies a singular space in

American cultural history. Her life story is a story of her people. And that's why so many people get emotional and caught up in Maya Angelou."

In addition to her memoirs, Angelou has published several volumes of verse: *Just Give Me a Cool Drink of Water 'Fore I Diiie* (1971), for which she was nominated for a Pulitzer Prize; *Oh Pray My Wings Are Gonna Fit Me Well* (1975); *And Still I Rise* (1978); *Shaker, Why Don't You Sing?* (1983); *Now Sheba Sings the Song* (1987); and *I Shall Not Be Moved* (1990). Grounded in the themes of love, friendship, community, African-American history, racial tensions in the United States, and her pride as a black woman, Angelou's poetry has become so popular that, according to Jacqueline Trescott of the *Washington Post* (January 16, 1993), audiences at her readings regularly "hoot out for her to recite 'Phenomenal Woman,' 'Still I Rise,' 'Weekend Glory,' and 'Seven Women Blessed Assurance,'" among other perennial favorites. A reviewer for *Publishers Weekly* (July 31, 1978) commended *And Still I Rise* and Angelou's earlier books of poetry for their "human warmth, honesty, strength, and deep-rooted sense of personal pride." However, other critics were less enthusiastic. Assessing the same volume for *Parnassus: Poetry in Review* (Fall–Winter 1979), R. B. Stepto described Angelou's verse as "slight" and "thin" and argued that she often relied too heavily on what Stepto viewed as more accomplished works by Langston Hughes and Gwendolyn Brooks, among others. In a lengthy review of Angelou's earlier work, *Oh Pray My Wings Are Gonna Fit Me Well*, Sandra M. Gilbert remarked, "I can't help feeling that Maya Angelou's career has suffered from the interest her publishers have in mythologizing her. [This] is such a painfully untalented collection of poems that I can't think of any reason, other than the Maya Myth, for it to be in print." Writing in the *Washington Post* (January 21, 1993), David Streitfeld commented on the unfavorable reviews that have often met Angelou's collections of poetry: "She's a people's poet rather than a poet's poet, which means she has a much bigger audience [than most poets] but doesn't win awards."

Despite critics' reservations about the artistic merits of her verse, Angelou made history in January 1993, when she read "On the Pulse of the Morning" at Bill Clinton's inauguration. She was only the second American poet to recite an original poem at a presidential inauguration; the first such poet was Robert Frost, who spoke at the 1961 inauguration of President John F. Kennedy. In words that seemed to address her listeners both as individuals and as members of one nation, Angelou placed special emphasis on the need for renewal: "Lift up your eyes upon / This day breaking for you. / Give birth again / To the dream." This work, which celebrated the diversity of American society, prompted a range of responses from her fellow artists. The novelist Louise Erdich spoke for many in praising both the poem and Angelou's forceful presentation of it: "I felt that this women could have read the side of a cereal box," she told David Streitfeld. "Her presence was so powerful and momentous, she made a statement that I was personally longing to see and hear." The poet David Lehman was less impressed. "She read the poem very well . . . ," Lehman conceded. "But if you ask me as a poet to be as ruthless on this poem as I would be on any other, I would have to say it's not very memorable." Again, despite the mixed reviews, Angelou's dramatic delivery of the poem helped renew readers' interest in her work. She included "On the Pulse of the Morning" in her 1994 book, *The Complete Collected Poems of Maya Angelou*; Angelou's recording of the poem earned her a 1994 Grammy Award for best spoken word or nonmusical album. That year she also published *Phenomenal Woman: Four Poems Celebrating Women*, a short volume that included four of her most memorable verses. In 1995, she composed another poem, "A Brave and Startling Truth," to celebrate the 50th anniversary of the signing of the United Nation's charter.

Angelou has also contributed to the genre of children's literature, publishing such celebrated works as *Life Doesn't Frighten Me* (1993), an illustrated poem, and *Soul Looks Back in Wonder* (1993), a children's anthology that she edited containing the writings of 13 African-American poets. The collection won the 1994 Coretta Scott King Award for illustration. In *My Painted House, My Friendly Chicken, and Me* (1994), Angelou presents Thandi, a Ndebele girl in South Africa, who takes readers on a tour of her village. *Kofi and His Magic* (1996) is a picture book about a young Ashanti boy and life in his West African village. Both works are illustrated with photographs by Margaret Courtney-Clarke.

Since the early 1970s, Angelou has also found time for a mind-boggling array of other projects. With the release of the film *Georgia, Georgia* (1972), about two black women who travel to Switzerland, she became the first black woman to have a screenplay produced. In 1974 she was involved in an adaptation of Sophocles's *Ajax*, at the Mark Taper Forum in Los Angeles, and she wrote and directed the film *All Day Long*. The following year, her performance in the Broadway production *Look Away* earned her a Tony Award nomination; she appeared as the dressmaker and confidante of Mary Todd Lincoln, the recently widowed former first lady, who was played by Geraldine Page. In 1977 she was nominated for an Emmy Award for her portrayal of Kunta Kinte's grandmother in the hugely popular television miniseries *Roots*, based on the book by Alex Haley. Rounding off an unusually productive decade, a film version of *I Know Why the Caged Bird Sings* was broadcast on national television in 1979, with the script and musical score provided by Angelou herself.

In 1982 Angelou's teleplay *Sister, Sister*, a dramatic rendering of the lives of the members of a middle-class black family, was aired by NBC. Six years later, in London, she directed Errol John's play *Moon on a Rainbow Shawl*, about the inhabitants of a tenement in Trinidad. In 1989 the editor Jeffrey M. Elliot compiled and published a collection of interviews with Angelou from the 1970s and 1980s in *Conversations with Maya Angelou*. In the fall of 1992 and again in January 1993, a play entitled *And Still I Rise*, based on Angelou's poetry, was staged in Winston-Salem, North Carolina. She wrote the poetry for John Singleton's film *Poetic Justice* (1993), in which she also appeared briefly in the role of Aunt June. In 1993 Angelou also published two collections of short essays, *Lessons in Life* and *Wouldn't Take Nothing for My Journey Now*. In an assessment of the latter volume for *Publishers Weekly* (September 27, 1993), a reviewer wrote, "These quietly inspirational pieces convey her sense of life as an ongoing adventure." In 1994 she read her poem "And Still I Rise" for an upbeat, new advertising campaign on behalf of the United Negro College Fund, in honor of the organization's 50th anniversary. In 1997 Angelou published another book of essays, entitled *Even The Stars Look Lonesome*, a collection that Donna Seaman for *Booklist* (August 1997) called a "potent sister volume" to *Wouldn't Take Nothing for My Journey Now*. Describing this work for *Publishers Weekly* (August 4, 1997), a reviewer opined, "Like a modern-day Kahlil Gibran, Angelou offers insights on a wide range of topics—Africa, aging, self-reflection, independence, and the importance of understanding both the historical truth of the African American experience and that art that truth inspired."

Angelou made her feature directorial debut with *Down in the Delta* (2000), an African-American family drama starring Alfre Woodard and Wesley Snipes. In 2002 she took part in the television specials *Roots: Celebrating 25 Years* and *Inside TV Land: African Americans in Television*. She also signed a contract with Hallmark to provide poems for a line of greeting cards, pillows, and other collectible items. While many of her fellow poets balked at Angelou's decision to commercialize her work, she remained committed to delivering her poetry to as many readers as possible. She explained her decision to Lynda Richardson for the *New York Times* (February 1, 2002): "I was once told that I shouldn't do it because the person said, 'You are the people's poet, the most popular poet in the United States, and you shouldn't trivialize your work.' So when I hung up the phone and thought about it, I said, 'If I'm the people's poet, then my work should be in the people's hands. There are many people who will never buy a book, but who would buy a card.' So I thought no, no. I'm going to do it." Angelou is reportedly writing a cookbook, which will include a collection of recipes and stories celebrating food.

Widely recognized for her achievements, Angelou has received numerous honors over the years, including a Yale University Fellowship (1970), a scholarship from the Rockefeller Foundation (1975), a presidential appointment to the American Revolution Bicentennial Council (1975), the North Carolina Award in Literature (1987), the Horatio Alger Award (1992), and approximately 50 honorary degrees. In the mid-1970s she served as writer-in-residence at the University of Kansas at Lawrence. She has also been a visiting professor at Wake Forest University, in Winston-Salem, North Carolina; Wichita State University, in Kansas; and California State University, in Sacramento. Since 1981, when she accepted a lifetime chair as the Reynolds Professor of American Studies at Wake Forest University, Angelou has taught one semester a year at Wake Forest and served as a visiting professor at other universities around the United States. She has memberships in the American Federation of Television and Radio Artists, the American Film Institute—for which she has served on the board of trustees since 1975—the Directors Guild, Equity, the Harlem Writers Guild, and the Women's Prison Association, among other organizations.

Angelou lectures to packed houses about 80 times per year and regularly receives about 500 letters each week. Over the years she has encountered fans in the most unlikely places, including a 1988 anti-apartheid rally in Berkeley, California, that she attended with the novelist Alice Walker. "We were arrested by a black policewoman," Angelou recalled to Nina Burleigh for the *Chicago Tribune* (May 28, 1989). "The policewoman was standing nearby, and we heard her say, 'Oh, my two favorite writers, and I get to arrest them.' When she fingerprinted me, her hands were shaking, and she asked me for my autograph."

Married several times since her divorce from Tosh Angelos, Angelou has generally declined to discuss her private life. She lives alone in a comfortable brick house in Winston-Salem that is decorated with the art that she avidly collects. Preferring to do her writing away from the distractions of her intimate surroundings, she habitually rises at five o'clock in the morning to go to a nearby motel room, where she reclines on the fully made bed—with a Bible, a dictionary, a thesaurus, and a bottle of sherry close at hand—and writes on yellow legal pads. While Angelou told Lynda Richardson that she is slowly succumbing to the trappings of age, as yet she has no plans to retire. "I'm a writer and I can do other things; I'm grateful for that," she said. "The way I describe myself to myself and to God is, 'Lord, you do remember me, Maya Angelou, the writer?'"

Angelou is fluent in French, Spanish, Italian, Arabic, and Fanti. She has one son and one grandson.

—K. D.

SUGGESTED READING: *Chicago Tribune* C p35 Mar. 23, 1986, C p1 Apr. 7, 2002; *New York Times* VII p16 June 16, 1974, C p1+ Jan. 20, 1993, B p2 Feb. 1, 2002; *Publishers Weekly* p54 Aug. 4, 1997; *Washington Post* G p1+ Jan. 16, 1993; *Washington Post Book World* p11 May 11, 1986

SELECTED WORKS: memoirs—*I Know Why the Caged Bird Sings*, 1970; *Gather Together in My Name*, 1974; *Singin' and Swingin' and Gettin' Merry Like Christmas*, 1976; *The Heart of a Woman*, 1981; *All God's Children Need Traveling Shoes*, 1986; *A Song Flung Up to Heaven*, 2002; poetry—*Just Give Me a Cool Drink of Water 'Fore I Diiie*, 1971; *Oh Pray My Wings Are Gonna Fit Me Well*, 1975; *And Still I Rise*, 1978; *Shaker, Why Don't You Sing?*, 1983; *Poems: Maya Angelou*, 1986; *Now Sheba Sings the Song*, 1987; *I Shall Not Be Moved*, 1990; *The Complete Collected Poems of Maya Angelou*, 1994; *Phenomenal Woman: Four Poems Celebrating Women*, 1994; children's literature—*Life Doesn't Frighten Me*, 1993; *My Painted House, My Friendly Chicken, and Me*, 1994; *Kofi and His Magic*, 1996; nonfiction—*Lessons in Living*, 1993; *Wouldn't Take Nothing for My Journey Now*, 1993; *Even the Stars Look Lonesome*, 1997; as editor—*Soul Looks Back in Wonder*, 1994; plays—*Cabaret for Freedom*, 1960 (with Godfrey Cambridge); *The Least of These*, 1966; *The Clawing Within*, 1966; *Adjoa Amissah*, 1967; *Encounters*, 1973; *And Still I Rise*, 1976

Ulrike Schmoni/Courtesy of Vintage Anchor Publicity

Antrim, Donald

1959(?)– Novelist; short-story writer

In his trilogy of novels, *Elect Mr. Robinson for a Better World* (1993), *The Hundred Brothers* (1997), and *The Verificationist* (2000), the American novelist and short-story writer Donald Antrim offers absurdist views of American life. *Elect Mr. Robinson* is set in a suburban community so dysfunctional that its members, while affable and polite, make war on one another. *The Hundred Brothers*, narrated by one brother, focuses on a gathering of 99 disparate siblings. *The Verificationist* spoofs a group of psychoanalysts whose own identities are strikingly fragile. All of Antrim's narrators are seemingly ordinary, yet mentally unhinged, and although his stories unfold in strikingly unreal situations, the author "somehow string[s] his readers along without letting us doubt what is taking place," Eric Wittmershaus wrote for *Flak Magazine* (April 1, 2000, on-line). Sven Birkerts, in a piece for *Esquire* (February 2000), echoed the reactions of many critics to Antrim's works: "For all the madness on the daily-life side of the spectrum, we have so little countering madness on the side of art. . . . It was only when I tumbled, perplexed, into Antrim's anxious fever dream that I realized how starved I had been for the other stuff, the literature that seeps into my dreaming centers and slowly turns me around."

Donald Antrim has chosen to let his writings speak for him and, consequently, has made few biographical details available. He was probably born in about 1959. In his interview with Eric Wittmershaus, he said, "I came from Southern Protestant families on my mother's side and on my father's side." He was educated at Brown University, in Providence, Rhode Island, where he majored in English and American literature and earned a bachelor's degree, in 1981. "I didn't do any writing at Brown . . . ," Antrim told an interviewer for the *Brown Daily Herald* (April 7, 1998, on-line). "I did a lot of theater instead. I lived off campus, I had some girlfriends. . . . I tried to have a good time and not be too depressed. I read a lot. Most of my reading was outside the syllabus with a few exceptions for classes that were quite challenging." He also said, "While I was at Brown I was trying to become someone, which is . . . one of the things college is for: becoming who you're going to keep being." After leaving Brown Antrim joined a professional theater company. "I didn't really like it so I left, . . . then I worked in publishing for a while," he told the *Herald*. "Then I started writing. At first what I wrote was depressing for me and for the reader: autobiographical short stories. When I began writing in earnest I realized that it's a long path to acquire real discipline and I am working on that."

Antrim's dark, satirical first novel, *Elect Mr. Robinson for a Better World*, was published in 1993. Pete Robinson, the narrator, is a third-grade teacher running for mayor of a seaside town whose previous mayor has been drawn and quartered by four motorists. Robinson is deranged, and he participates in the torture and murder of a little girl in his basement. He and his neighbors conceal large traps in their yards; shootings are common, and the town park is mined. In one scene Pete joins a group of men whose mission is to locate and deactivate the mines. Possessing no advanced technology, they hurl heavy reference books, taken from the library, in the direction of the suspected locations. Although Pete had qualms about using books in this way, he has put his reservations aside. Observing what he labels his "passivity," he muses on his participation in the operation:

> Was it a weakness, my facile desire to go along with the guys at the expense of the books? Or was it more complex, a sincere inclination to favor present human company, fellowship and community over the obscure pleasures of printed narratives? Certainly the air was cool at this time of evening. a wail of bird-song ascended from the gray-green trees. The men's voices were deep, the world seemed good, there were plenty of unimpaired books left in Tom's backpack. And in the end, what did it matter which books? The essence of a culture is found in all its artifacts.

When Degen Pener, who interviewed Antrim for the *New York Times* (October 10, 1993), asked him, "Was there a reason you were thinking about issues like a breakdown in civility in middle-class America?" the author—whom Pener described as an "intensely earnest 35-year-old"—responded, "The ideas and the issues raised in the book are probably related to things I think about, but they are also just in the air." Asked how people might view his producing so "dark" a novel, Antrim answered that while he had some concerns about readers' reactions, "that's the book I wrote. It's a work of fiction. . . . But it is also liberating to write a character who is not necessarily redeemed. That's a great freedom." The author of *The Virgin Suicides*, Jeffrey Eugenides, a classmate of Antrim's at Brown and a neighbor of his in the Park Slope neighborhood of Brooklyn, wrote for the *New Yorker* (July 1, 1996) that during the writing of *Elect Mr. Robinson*, Antrim "pasted all one hundred and seventy-eight manuscript pages to the walls of his apartment, so that he could literally live inside his book." The author "wandered the dim rooms for weeks, making small corrections," Eugenides reported. "Brushing his teeth, he'd change 'palm-covered' to 'palm-shrouded.' In the morning, he'd change it back. Such maniacal, punctilious traits bring to mind Mr. Antrim's own narrators, whom he exaggerates into such hilarious existence."

Elect Mr. Robinson impressed reviewers as a promising first novel. Calling Antrim "a writer of undeniable power and sensuality," Ed Weiner noted for the *New York Times Book Review* (November 7, 1993) that its characters "are either prehistoric or postapocalyptic, and experiencing a wingding of a breakdown: nervous, moral, societal." Weiner also expressed the view that Antrim had not succeeded completely in maintaining the narrative drive. Another critic, writing for *Kirkus Reviews* (June 15, 1993), felt that Robinson was well drawn: "Pete, though mad as a hatter, comments on the grisly goings-on (including his ritual burial of the ex-Mayor's body parts) with a cool, ironic intelligence; this dissonance is the novel's most striking feature—and effective up to a point. But Antrim's failure to orchestrate his flashy set-pieces leaves the impression of a first draft, albeit from a promising new talent with a wonderfully keen ear." Several years after the publication of *Elect Mr. Robinson*, Richard Eder described the novel in the *Los Angeles Times* (February 12, 1997) as an "absurdist comedy with menace underneath." "With a story of a whole suburban community going violently mad, the comedy was vigorous, unbelted, and had room to breathe and astonish—even though the dark lesson was fairly obvious," Eder wrote.

In his second novel, *The Hundred Brothers*, Antrim offered another satirical deconstruction of modern life. Ninety-nine of the 100 sons of a man whose ashes have been lost meet in their father's crumbling mansion, ostensibly to look for the urn that contains his remains but actually to engage in crazy family games. Alex Ivanovitch, who reviewed *The Hundred Brothers* for the *Times Literary Supplement* (May 30, 1997), called the siblings "a huge male mass that is subject to various subdivisions"—for example, chess players, young fathers, and football players. "All the brothers," Ivanovitch continued, "seem damaged in some way by their early family life, and almost all are slovenly and ageing ungracefully." What transpires—mostly in their father's private library—is viewed through the eyes of one mad brother, Doug. Addressing another brother's dog, Doug declares pompously, "Modern men had lost touch with ancient rhythms of death and regeneration, but . . . it was possible—if you took intoxicants and wore the right mask and costume—to regain connection with the primeval aspects of the Self."

"*The Hundred Brothers* is high-test literary absurdity," according to Paul Maliszewski, writing for the *Review of Contemporary Fiction* (Summer 1998). "It is fitting . . . that Antrim sets his novel about Western culture's collection of critical tools in the library. . . . The stacks meanwhile are in a maze, the shelving system's gone to pot, and books are piled on the floor. Antrim's library is both a physical place and a collection of conceptual signposts." A *Publishers Weekly* (January 6, 1997) reviewer enjoyed the surreal atmosphere Antrim created: "Like a Beckett play interlaced with elements of a medieval heroic chronicle and the comic anarchy of a Marx Brothers routine, the novel follows Doug . . . as he wanders about the library wreaking havoc, discoursing on bloodlines and inheritance and observing his brothers' bullying, grousing, and violent skirmishes." The *Publishers Weekly* critic concluded, however, "Drunk with language and surreal humor, Antrim's allegory never really coheres." Richard Eder, in his 1997 piece for the *Los Angeles Times*, agreed: "It is . . . as if the late S. J.

Perelman—lunacy without tears—were parodying the late Donald Barthelme—lunacy with not only tears, but droplets of Armageddon. After a while, though, the lunacy in *The Hundred Brothers* sticks in place; and the Armageddon—the dismaying message beneath the absurdity—turns out familiar and perfunctory." In a mixed but mostly favorable assessment, Ivanovich wrote that Antrim's "talent lies in creating these dark, floating worlds that retain uncertain and mobile links with our own." He felt that when events became "subject to a crude farcical entropy," the comedy sometimes veered toward slapstick, whereas when Antrim was at his best, "the comedy and image-making have a kind of skewed straight-facedness about them that makes the writing memorable." *The Hundred Brothers* was among five nominees for a PEN/Faulkner Award for Fiction in 1998. As one of the finalists, Antrim was awarded $5,000.

The Verificationist, the third novel in Antrim's trilogy, came out in 2000. The story is an account of a dinner meeting of psychoanalysts employed at a third-rate institution that is touted as the home of "Self/Other Friction Therapy." Slyly introducing a somewhat disorienting locale, Antrim has Tom, the narrator, describe their meeting place as the "modest, open-all-night Pancake House & Bar on Eureka Drive, way out past the book factory, down the perilously steep hill leading to our famous covered bridge and, beyond the bridge, the overgrown, abandoned airfield." Tom is so troubled that deciding what to order is a big struggle for him; while trying to select something, he ruminates about an empty room in his house, which he suspects his wife wants to use as a nursery, though she is not pregnant. Neither of them has been able to choose a color to paint the room:

> The wife in question (Jane) insists any color is fine with her. Her (Jane's) husband (I) secretly suspect(s) this is not the case. He (I) think(s) she (Jane) wants a sturdy, masculine blue, because he (I) feel(s) that she (Jane) is secretly hoping for a baby (ours) to live in this room, and he (I) suspect(s), judging from other things known about her (the wife) things better not explored in depth at this moment that she (my beloved) would, without a doubt, favor a boy.

Like the characters in Nigel Dennis's satiric novel *Cards of Identity*, about a convention of psychoanalysts, not only is Tom conflicted about having a baby, he is not even sure who he is. After one of his colleagues gives him a bear hug, he has an out-of-body experience, floating up to the ceiling and thus ratcheting up the action to surreal heights. "Antrim's art is to render the uncanny as if it were the canny," Sven Birkerts remarked in *Esquire* (February 2000). "The confessional matter-of-factness of Tom's voice plays beautifully against the preposterous scenario. . . . Slowly there emerges a portrait of the classic American boyman, the needy fellow full of sorrows and lyric longings. Tom is the therapist who cannot himself connect, the husband who can't make up his mind to fix the room at the head of the stairs because he keeps working through the emotional syllogism, 'If the room is a baby's room, then it is a baby's room missing a baby, and this of course is another way of saying that the room contains loss.'"

The first novel in Antrim's trilogy dealt with a man's place in society. The second addressed the individual's place in the family. *The Verificationist* "challenges the very notion of the individual," according to the *Publishers Weekly* (January 17, 2000) reviewer. "Antrim is a manic prose stylist, capable of balancing lush pastoral descriptions with outrageous turbocharged riffs on sex and marriage and psychoanalysis, and the novel hurtles toward its resolution at . . . breakneck speed. . . . Antrim has provided a striking meditation on the nature of self-identity and a fierce affirmation of the power of imagination," the *Publishers Weekly* critic declared. Discussing his narrators with Eric Wittmershaus, Antrim said, "I suppose these men have in common a certain grandiosity and sensitivity, or kind of an attempt at sensitivity and an attempt to, on their parts, articulate their experiences. . . . It was logical for one of them to be a psychoanalyst because they've all got a kind of analytic style."

Antrim's novels have neither chapters nor other breaks in the text. "These books require a fair amount of acceptance on the part of the reader," Antrim explained to Wittmershaus. "There's a suspension of disbelief that has to happen. Not that [the books] are fantastic, but because they're strung together with a certain amount of high tension wire. I was afraid [while writing] that if you got out of the narrative with a chapter break, it's a door out. . . . Even if you got out for a minute, you would see how flawed and unlikely the thing was."

Antrim's Park Slope neighborhood is home to many writers. "I feel that writing has made my life better and it's hard for me to imagine not doing it," he told the *Brown Daily Herald*. In its June 21, 1999 summer-fiction issue, the *New Yorker* included him among "20 Writers for the 21st Century." Antrim has been compared to such innovative novelists as Donald Barthelme and Thomas Pynchon, the latter of whom wrote a blurb that appears on the jacket of *The Verificationist*. While acknowledging that such recognition is "exciting," Antrim said to Wittmershaus, "I don't carry around praise or approbation for very long before I forget it all and feel lost and doomed as usual."

— S.Y.

SUGGESTED READING: *Esquire* p66+ Feb. 2000; *Kirkus Reviews* June 15, 1993; *Los Angeles Times* E p5 Feb. 12, 1997; *New York Times* IX p4 Oct. 10, 1993; *New York Times Book Review* p20 Nov. 7, 1993; *New Yorker* p96+ July 1, 1996, with photo; *Publishers Weekly* p64 Jan. 6, 1997, p43+ Jan. 17, 2000; *Review of Contemporary Fiction* p250+ Summer 1998; *Times Literary Supplement* p22 May 30, 1997

SELECTED BOOKS: *Elect Mr. Robinson for a Better World*, 1993; *The Hundred Brothers*, 1997; *The Verificationist*, 2000

Courtesy of Granta Books

Ascherson, Neal

Oct. 5, 1932– Journalist; nonfiction writer; essayist

The well-respected British journalist Neal Ascherson specializes in the study of small nations in Eastern Europe, Asia, and Africa. His writing displays a deep understanding of history and how it pertains to modern political and social problems. His first book was *The King Incorporated* (1963), an account of the life of King Leopold II of Belgium. He produced two books on Poland, *The Polish August: The Self-Limiting Revolution* (1982), about the emergence of the Polish Solidarity movement, and *The Struggles for Poland* (1987), a more complete history of that country. He has also published a collection of his political columns, *Games with Shadows* (1988), and *Black Sea* (1995), a history of the peoples and societies of that region. He has also written the introduction for a photography book on Berlin, *Berlin: A Century of Change/Die Gesichter Des Jahrhunderts* (2000).

Charles Neal Ascherson was born in Edinburgh, Scotland, on October 5, 1932, the son of a sailor, Stephen Romer Ascherson, and the former Evelyn Mabel Gilbertson. After serving in the Royal Marines from 1950 to 1952, he studied at Eton College, a preparatory school in Windsor, and then at King's College at Cambridge University, where in 1955 he received a master's degree, with first honors, in history. From 1955 to 1956 he served as a researcher at the East African Institute of Social Research, in Kampala, East Africa.

In 1956 Ascherson joined the Manchester *Guardian* (which is now published in London) as a cub reporter; three years later he became the British Commonwealth correspondent for the *Scotsman*. In 1960, not long after joining the staff of the Edinburgh *Scotsman*, he accepted an offer to become a foreign correspondent for the London *Observer*, for which he covered the Cold War events that were shaping Central Europe and East and West Germany. His work as a foreign correspondent enabled him to observe the forces that were shaping postwar Europe, as well as to understand the historical movements— colonialism, communism, fascism—that helped to shape Europe at the end of the millennium. He used this knowledge to great effect in his first book, *The King Incorporated*, a biography of King Leopold II of Belgium and his disastrous influence on the Congo Free State. As the monarch, Leopold sought to expand his country's influence by establishing a colonial empire. After organizing an association to explore the Congo, a European conference deeded the African country to his personal rule, thereby allowing him to make a fortune through the exploitation of its natural resources by means of forced labor. After significant scandals surfaced about his regime's brutal treatment of native workers, he was forced to turn over control of the country to the Belgian government in 1908, a year before he died.

The King Incorporated received great acclaim. "Mr. Ascherson's book is a brilliant composition," noted A. J. P. Taylor in the *New Statesman* (October 25, 1963). "It is lively, clear, good both as biography and as history." J. H. Plumb, writing for the *New York Review of Books* (April 30, 1964) proclaimed: "There is no rhetoric in [*The King Incorporated*], no special pleading, no weighted evidence, but a scholarly exposition of Leopold and all that he did." A reviewer for the (London) *Times Literary Supplement* (December 5, 1963) came to a similar conclusion, writing: "Mr Ascherson has written an admirable summary . . . compressing a lot of detail into a readable narrative. His book makes no pretense to originality but it will certainly stimulate the reader's curiosity about a remarkable product of the nineteenth century."

After three years with the *Observer*, in 1963 Ascherson was given the Central European beat, a position he held until 1968, when he became that paper's Eastern European correspondent. He left the *Observer*, in 1975, to rejoin the *Scotsman* as a political correspondent, holding that position until 1979. He then rejoined the *Observer* to serve as a foreign writer and columnist. (From 1985 to 1989 he was an associate editor of the publication.) While working in Central and Eastern Europe, he delved into the political and social unrest in Poland that led to the founding of the Solidarity movement. He wrote about this revolution in his widely reviewed book *The Polish August*. R. M. Watt in the *New York Times Book Review* (April

25, 1982) proclaimed: "All in all, [this] is a major work by an author who is at once a political scientist, a historian and a very good writer, indeed." In the *New Statesman* (January 8, 1982), Gustaw Moszez agreed, remarking that Ascherson "has surely written what will long remain the standard work on the antecedent risings which gave Solidarity its firm basis for the 1980 struggles." However, not everyone was so impressed with the work; as Leszek Kolakowski wrote in the *New Republic* (April 14, 1982): "I realize that the author makes no claim to provide . . . a scholarly analysis. This is a journalistic account . . . and it should be assessed accordingly. Nonetheless, this need not prevent the reader from noticing both the missing parts of the story and its ideological biases." In 1987 Ascherson published *The Struggles for Poland*, a wider-ranging history of that country, written in tandem with the BBC television series of the same name.

In 1984 Ascherson collaborated with Magnus Linklater and Isabel Hilton on *The Fourth Reich: Klaus Barbie and the Neo-Fascist Connection*, which was published in the United States as *The Nazi Legacy: Klaus Barbie and the International Fascist Connection*, in 1985. Primarily a biography of the infamous Nazi, the book also demonstrates how Barbie's 50 years as an international criminal involved connections with neo-Nazis in Germany, Italy, and Bolivia, as well as with the United States Army's Counter Intelligence Corps. Writing for the *New York Review of Books* (June 27, 1985), Francine du Plessix Gray noted that this book "is the first complete account of Barbie's fifty-year career in international crime. It is also a brilliant case study of how the Nazi ideology and techniques were exported throughout Latin American after the war and how this activity was abetted by the Western democratic powers, particularly the United States." James B. Street, in his review for *Library Journal* (January 1985), suggested that the volume "is especially valuable for its detailed presentation of Barbie's multifaceted services as advisor and operator for right-wing Latin American regimes and his connections with organized crime and right-wing terrorism in the 1960s and 1970s."

From 1985 to 1989 Ascherson wrote a political column for the *Observer* and collected many of these columns in *Games with Shadows*. He did a stint as an assistant editor at the London *Independent on Sunday*, from 1990 to 1998. His next book, *Black Sea*, published in 1995, was a series of reflections on the very historic region around that body of water, particularly noting the evolution of its peoples and ecology. Using his own explorations of the area and his knowledge of its past, he examines the history of the Black Sea region from ancient times until the end of the 20th century. The book received generally favorable reviews. Nader Mousavizadeh, in the *New Republic* (December 18, 1995), wrote: "It is by no means an exhaustive history of that vast and complex region, nor does it purport to be. Quietly, unambitiously, Ascherson tells a set of Black Sea stories, which together form a unique narrative of 'the interplay of circumstances,' of the hybrids of culture and ethnicity, of the irrepressible link between ages and people." In the *New Statesman and Society* (July 7, 1995), Stephen Brook approved of the work for the most part, though he did have some reservations about praising it whole-heartedly: "Ascherson has travelled exhaustively, read deeply, pondered hard. As a consequence *Black Sea* is stimulating and eye-opening. But the book requires a bit of a struggle. Shorn of narrative structure, it reads like a series of parentheses and excursions." He concluded, "The book comes to life most readily when we meet obsessive Cossacks, . . . the ministers of the new but impoverished Abkhazi state, and the Russian and Ukranian archaeologists and oceanographers struggling to continue their researches after their budgets and salaries evaporated overnight."

In 2000 Ascherson contributed the introduction for *Berlin: A Century of Change/Die Gesichter Des Jahrhunderts*, a photographic project documenting the city's history over the last century, from its glory before the world wars, its rise and fall during the Third Reich, and the post-war experience of Berliners.

For his journalistic achievements, Ascherson has received numerous awards, including two Granada Awards— Reporter of the Year (1982) and Journalist of the Year (1987); the James Cameron Award (1989); the David Watt Memorial Prize (1991); the Golden Insignia Order of Merit (1992), from Poland; the George Orwell Award (1993); and the Saltire Award for Literature (1995).

Neal Ascherson has been married twice. His first marriage, to Corrina Adam, in 1958, ended in divorce, in 1982. In 1984 he married Isabel Hilton. He has two daughters from his first marriage and a son and a daughter from his second. Since 1998 Ascherson, who has several honorary degrees, has been an assistant lecturer at the Institute of Archaeology at University College London. In 1999 he ran for a seat in the Scottish Parliament.

—C. M.

SUGGESTED READING: *Library Journal* p110 Jan. 1985; *London Review of Books* (on-line) Feb. 17, 2000; *Nation* p235 Sep. 11, 1982; *New Republic* p186 Apr. 14, 1982, p42 Dec. 18, 1995; *New York Review of Books* p6 Apr. 30, 1964, p32 June 27, 1985; *New York Times* C p21 Dec. 6, 1995; *New York Times Book Review* p11 Apr. 25, 1982, p17 Nov. 26, 1995; (London) *Times Literary Supplement* p1009 Dec. 5, 1963; *International Authors and Writers Who's Who*, 1997–98; *Who's Who*, 2001

SELECTED BOOKS: *The King Incorporated*, 1963; *The Polish August: The Self-Limiting Revolution*, 1982; *The Fourth Reich: Klaus Barbie and the Neo-Fascist Connection*, 1984 (published in the U. S. as *The Nazi Legacy: Klaus Barbie and the International Fascist Connection* in 1985); *The Struggles for Poland*,

1987; *Games with Shadows*, 1988; *Black Sea*, 1995

Marion Ettlinger/Viking Publishing

Askew, Rilla

1951– Novelist; short-story writer

The building blocks of Rilla Askew's fiction can be found in her experiences as a lifelong Oklahoman, as well as in the lives of the pioneer women from whom she's descended. *Strange Business* (1993), her collection of short stories, describes the lives of a group of characters in a small town in 20th-century Oklahoma. Her first novel, *The Mercy Seat* (1993), chronicles the experiences of a family who moves to the territory during the frontier days. Her most recent novel, *Fire in Beulah* (2001), explores relationships between black and white characters both before and during the Tulsa Race Riot of 1921.

In an autobiographical statement written in 2002 for *World Authors*, Askew discusses her life, work, and inspirations: "My family has lived in the mountains of southeastern Oklahoma for five generations. My maternal and paternal great-great-grandparents migrated from Mississippi and Kentucky into the Choctaw Nation in the late 1800's, settling in the valleys of the Sans Bois in a time when the forty-sixth state was still Indian Territory. I was born here—in Poteau, in 1951—and it's the place to which I perpetually return, in my life and in my fiction. It's a harsh, beautiful landscape, gorgeous to look at, filled with living things that can hurt you: cottonmouths in the streams, poison ivy in the timber, ticks, chiggers, rattlesnakes, stinging scorpions, copperheads, long black centipedes, brambles and briars and thorn trees; even the ponds have their snapping turtles lurking and dozing, ready to take your finger off with a quick snap. The harshness of the land has shaped the people I come from, given voice and form, a kind of simultaneous ruthlessness and cry for mercy, to my work. Folks here left the South a hundred years ago, but they're still Southerners, a hard working people, reckless users of the land but inextricably tied to it, lawless and law-abiding, independent, violent. They are also deeply religious—Southern Baptist, mostly—with a worldview inseparable from God's judgment and mercy. Their language is rich in idiom, steeped in the King James version of the Bible. They're all storytellers. From this land and these people my work takes its biblical themes.

"I grew up in an oil company town, the little city of Bartlesville located at the edge of the rolling tall-grass country in northeastern Oklahoma, where the earth is dominated by sky and wind—a gentler landscape than the mountains we moved from when I was three. Bartlesville had, in the years I grew up there, good schools, clean streets, a Frank Lloyd Wright building, one of the highest per capita incomes in the nation. It also had, secreted in certain discrete sections of the city, a shabby race-and-class-determined poverty far uglier and more hopeless than the rural poverty of southeastern Oklahoma. The town's stratified class structure, unrivaled west of the UK, was ordained, it seemed to me, by the powerful petroleum company that had its headquarters there. In Bartlesville I received my education in the magic of books; the hidden, inviolate borders of race; the unassailable forces of money, power, societal opinion. Growing up in a company town accounts for the sociological scope in my fiction, my interest in race, the timbre of social conscience that sounds through the work.

"In my twenties I lived on the banks of the Illinois River near Tahlequah, the capital of the Cherokee Nation. Tahlequah is in the Cookson Hills of eastern Oklahoma, a woody, clotted, tick-ridden land of clear waters and flinty hills thick with blackgum, dogwood, redbud—beautiful, mysterious, spirit-filled. As a child I was always told we were part Cherokee on my father's side, part Choctaw on my mother's (or "Black Dutch," as some would have it)—bloodlines never traced, so far as I know—but it was my years in Tahlequah that gave me my first deep connection to Native people, a force and source integrated throughout my fiction.

"These are the landscapes and people that determine the themes and characters, the stories, the power of place in my writing—far more so, I think, than the dynamics of family or my personal history. I'm a child of my generation, of course, and in the summer of 1969, not long after graduating high school, I ran away from home to try to go to the Woodstock Music Festival. I never made it outside the city limits of Bartlesville that summer, but twenty-one years later my husband and I bought a home a few miles from the festival site at Max Yasgur's farm—a sort of narrative book-ending which makes for a neat life symmetry but doesn't seem to have much to do with my work. The theatre informed me for many years, and still does, in the sense that the rising arc of drama so integral to plays, the imperatives of action, dialogue, gesture still come to mind when I'm making stories. I studied theatre in school, graduated from the University of Tulsa with a BFA in performance, moved to Manhattan in 1980 to pursue an acting career. Within a week I met the man who was to become my husband, Paul Austin, an actor, director, playwright, acting teacher, and with his encouragement I began to write seriously. I first tried my hand at plays, but very quickly turned to fiction, starting with a short story based in my childhood, which blossomed into a novella, which ballooned into a novel, which ultimately went into a drawer. But I was learning to write.

"We moved from Midtown to Brooklyn, and in 1987 I entered the MFA program at Brooklyn College, where I began the cycle of Oklahoma stories that would become my first book, *Strange Business*. Brooklyn College was where I first taught, and my students were almost all young people of color. In Brooklyn my godson Travis and his family came into my life, and I became more tightly bound to people of color through ties of love. It was in Brooklyn that I first learned—in 1989, while reading a biography of Richard Wright—about the Tulsa Race Riot of 1921. The deadliest race riot in the nation's history was at that time still a secret in Oklahoma, one I'd never heard whispered in all my growing-up years, The moment I read about it, I knew the riot would be the subject of my first novel—which turned out not to be the case; *The Mercy Seat* was written first—but I did begin researching the riot immediately, and so began a journey of making novels set in the historical past. Eventually my husband and I moved to the Catskills (to that little house near Yasgur's Farm), and I settled into a rhythm of long, closed-in winters, writing in the New York mountains, intercut with too-short, too-hot summers in Oklahoma, doing research, visiting family, refreshing my sources in the landscape and among the people who give voice and vision to my fiction.

"Oklahoma has always been the subject. The state's brief, violent history is, as I see it, a microcosm of all that's taken place on the North American continent for the past five hundred years—turned inside out, foreshortened, intensified. From the tragedy of the Trail of Tears to the frenzy of the white land runs to the hope in the all-black towns that sprang up here when Oklahoma was still the free "Injun Territory" toward which Jim and Huck Finn lit out, the drama of the three races has dominated Oklahoma's story. When I tried to find my way into the novel about the Tulsa riot—researching, talking to elders, reading—I kept going farther back in our history. I wanted to understand how racial attitudes that led to such a conflagration could have been carried into the state. I kept returning to old stories handed down in my family, how two brothers named Askew loaded up their families in wagons and left Kentucky in the middle of the night, headed for Indian Territory. In re-imagining my own family's story, I drew closer not only to painful attitudes about race but to the very sources of violence within us, to questions of guilt and repentance, which I continue to wrestle with in my work. That novel, *The Mercy Seat*, was titled after the holy of holies in the ark of the covenant, where the Hebrew priests went to commune with Yahweh, and where the Lord commanded them to sprinkle the sacrificial blood. I had to explore the elemental sources of violence—brother against brother, kin against kin—before I could comprehend the forces at work in the Tulsa riot.

"*Fire in Beulah* is the story not only of the 1921 riot, but also of oil wealth and greed, theft of oil rights from Native people, a painful, impossible friendship across color lines. It, too, receives its title from the Old Testament: *beulah* is synonymous with the Promised Land, which Oklahoma was for so many, black and white; it's also a Hebrew word meaning *married*—as the races are in this country. That's part of my vision. The triad of white, black, and red continues to weave through my work.

"In some ways I see myself not as a teller of stories but a re-teller, a balladeer, telling again the story of how we came to be here and what we've wrought. As a novelist, though, I'm most interested in demythologizing, deromanticizing America's master narrative—the comfort stories we tell ourselves. At this writing I'm at work on a novel set during the Great Depression, another mythic era in Oklahoma's past; it's a story that has its seeds in specific historical event—not among the well-known Dust Bowl refugees who fled to California. It's about what happened to the Okies who stayed home."

Askew published her first book, *Strange Business*, in 1992. It consists of 10 interlocking stories set in and around the town of Cedar, Oklahoma; each story is labeled with a year instead of an actual title. One of the central characters in the collection is teenaged Lyla Mae Muncy, to whom the reader is introduced in "1967." Lyla Mae, like many of the characters, is attempting to free herself of the ties that are holding her back—in her case, the old-fashioned values of small-town America. *Strange Business* received generally favorable reviews. In an article for the *New York Times Book Review* (August 6, 1992), Mark Childress compared Askew to Louise Erdrich and Ellen Gilchrist and wrote: "Although some of the stories reach moments of epiphany that seem either vague or a bit predictable . . . Ms. Askew is a writer with a very clear voice. She wastes few words, and her characters are memorable. You probably won't forget the man who likes to shock people by revealing the live rattlesnake he carries under his hat. And I'd be happy to read a whole novel about Lyla Mae."

In 1998 Askew published her first novel, *The Mercy Seat*, in which an 11-year-old girl named Mattie Lodi tells the story of her family's ruin. She begins in 1888, when her lawless uncle forces the family to leave their native Kentucky for Oklahoma, then part of the unsettled West. By the time they reach Oklahoma a series of tragedies has ripped the family apart—Mattie's mother and sister die, and her brother becomes brain-damaged. Finally a feud between her father and his brother threatens to destroy the clan entirely. The novel received very favorable reviews, including one from James Polk in the *New York Times Book Review* (October 12, 1997), who noted that "biblical echoes sound throughout Rilla Askew's powerful first novel as she artfully lays bare the sins and promises of a pioneer society." Emily Melton for *Booklist* (August 1997) concurred, remarking that Askew's "first novel is powerful, original, and beautifully written . . . It explores human nature and the nature of evil, and like biblical stories, Greek tragedies, or the plays of Shakespeare, it shows how seemingly small decisions can reshape the course of events, turning normal circumstances into tragedy." One of the few criticisms of the novel came from Editha Ann Wilberton who noted for *Library Journal* (July 1997): "The novel's weakness is the inconstancy in narration; Mattie's voice is so strong and true that other narrators pale in comparison, which causes confusion."

Askew's second novel, *Fire in Beulah* (2001), is a fictionalized study of one of the most infamous race riots in American history, the Tulsa Race Riot of 1921. The riot began on a warm day in June when a young black man named Dick Rowland stumbled and grabbed the arm of a white woman named Sarah Page for support. The police arrested him; local newspapers represented the incident as a sexual assault. Within hours white citizens of Tulsa had descended on the prosperous black section of town called Greenwood and begun lynching, burning, and shooting blacks. The blacks fought back but were unable to hold out against the white majority. In the end, more than 300 people died and Greenwood was all but destroyed. "I care deeply about race in this country, especially as it's manifest in the legacy of our original sins, slavery and genocide. I'm also passionate about the land and culture I come from, Oklahoma," Askew explained on her official Web site. "The Tulsa Race Riot . . . was the deadliest incident of racial violence in this nation, and it took place in my home state, and its history was hidden for seventy years. The subject was, for me, a natural."

Askew places her characters in the heart of this horrific scene, using multiple narrators, as in her previous novel, to tell the story, which centers on the relationship between Althea Dedmeyer, a rich white woman, and Graceful Whiteside, her young black housemaid. Reviews for the book were mixed. Peter Perl for the *Washington Post Book World* (February 4, 2001) remarked: "Askew . . . is a gifted storyteller who keeps the narrative moving. But some readers may be distracted by the author's use of multiple narrators, whose voices are signaled by several different typefaces. . . . But such narrative departures do not subtract too much from the power of Askew's novel. Her final hundred pages are a cinematic, apocalyptic denouement, as all the characters are swept up in the terrible racial tidal wave." In the *New York Times Book Review* (November 11, 2001), Adam Nossiter made a similarly mixed pronouncement: "The best parts of Askew's book come near the end, where she gives us a mob member's internal monologue, effectively getting inside the mind of the beat. Elsewhere, she is not well served by prose that can be overwrought, and by a tendency to spell out internal states that the reader should merely sense."

Rilla Askew has taught fiction writing at a number of universities, including Brooklyn College, Syracuse University, and the University of Central Oklahoma. She has received a number of awards for her fiction, including the Oklahoma Book Award for *Strange Business* in 1993 and *The Mercy Street* in 1998. In 1998 she also received the Western Heritage Award and was nominated for the PEN/Faulkner Award. She and her husband, the actor Paul Austin, live in the Catskill Mountains of upstate New York and in the Sans Bois hills of Oklahoma.

—C. M.

SUGGESTED READING: *Booklist* p1874 Aug. 1997; *Library Journal* p122 July 1997, p124 Feb. 1, 2001; *New York Times Book Review* p6 Aug. 9, 1992, p21 Oct. 12, 1997, p33 Nov. 11, 2001; Rilla Askew's Official Web site; *Washington Post* C p2 Mar. 12, 1998; *Washington Post Book World* p6 Feb. 4, 2001

SELECTED BOOKS: *Strange Business*, 1992; *The Mercy Seat*, 1997; *Fire in Beulah*, 2001

Atlas, James

Mar. 22, 1949– Biographer, critic, novelist

As a novelist, critic, and biographer, James Atlas has taken on hot-button subjects—from Jewishness in America and the "culture wars" at universities, to the literary lion Saul Bellow, about whom Atlas published a mammoth biography in 2000. Atlas has had a long career as a literary journalist, writing for the *New Yorker*, the *New York Review of Books*, the *Atlantic*, and *Partisan Review*, and serving as an editor for *Time*, *Vanity Fair*, and the *New York Times Magazine*, among others. His first book, a biography of the poet Delmore Schwartz, was nominated for a National Book Award, and since then his books have been widely reviewed. None, however, attracted as much notice as *Bellow: A Biography* (2000), the publication of which, because of its ambitions and its subject's prominence, was a major event in the literary world.

Courtesy of Viking Penguin
James Atlas

James Atlas was born in Chicago, Illinois, in 1949, the son of Donald and Nora (Glassenberg) Atlas. He attended Harvard University, in Cambridge, Massachusetts, receiving a B.A. degree, magna cum laude, in 1971, and was a Rhodes Scholar at New College, Oxford University, from 1971 to 1973.

Atlas developed a youthful love for poetry, and he served as editor of *Ten American Poets* (1973), the anthology. He then wrote *Delmore Schwartz: The Life of an American Poet* (1977); the book was published while Atlas was a book reviewer and staff writer for *Time*, a job he held from 1977 to 1978. Schwartz was born in Brooklyn, in 1913, and composed lyrical poems and short stories that are known for their expressions of cultural alienation. (Mentally unstable and an alcoholic, he was fictionalized by Saul Bellow in a 1975 novel, *Humboldt's Gift*, in which a Schwartz-like character oscillates between charismatic brilliance and disjointed ranting.) Most critics appreciated Atlas's portrait of the complex Schwartz, and several mentioned the thoroughness of his research. In a comment echoed by other reviewers, Leonard Michaels, writing for the *New York Review of Books* (March 23, 1978), applauded Atlas's "clear, precise, graceful" writing style, which, "makes the book read with the pleasure of a good novel." In *The Nation* (December 24, 1977), Erik Wensberg maintained that Atlas has "beyond doubt inquired everywhere and thought long, and has written a book as fair, full, and sympathetic as its subject may have had any right to hope for." However, in the *New Republic* (December 24-31 1977), Calvin Bedient found fault with the biography's "efficient bustle": "The young biographer . . . fails to bring passion of any sort to his task—love for the man or pity for his fate or scorn of his weakness or intelligent reverence for his work . . ." In a criticism that foreshadowed criticisms of *Bellow* as unduly influenced by Freud, Seamus Cooney disputed the notion of Atlas as a "fair" biographer. Cooney wrote for *Library Journal* (November 15, 1977) that Atlas's "main effort goes to elucidating the psychodynamics of Schwartz's self-destructiveness, thus undercutting the subtitle's claim to representative status." A year after the publication of *Delmore Schwartz*, Atlas edited and wrote the introduction for a reprint of Schwartz's 1938 short-story collection, *In Dreams Begin Responsibilities*.

Atlas published *The Great Pretender* (1986), an autobiographical coming-of-age tale, when he was 37 years old. Both Atlas and his fictional counterpart, Ben Janis, were born in Chicago to secular Jewish families; both attended Harvard and Oxford, developed an interest in poetry, and took practical jobs as journalists at *Time* magazine. "A lot of the things in [*The Great Pretender*] did happen," Atlas told John Blades for the *Chicago Tribune Book World*, as quoted in *Contemporary Authors* (2000), "but I hope that it has the feel of an invented world, that the issue of what's true and what isn't true, while necessarily interesting, is somehow secondary. . . . My own story is far more untidy, it lacks a dramatic unity and thematic motifs. It's just a life."

Atlas gave his character the name "Janis," a homophone of Janus, the two-faced Roman god who symbolizes duplicity. It's an apt name for Ben's character, who is torn between highbrow and lowbrow pursuits, between his parents' literary world (his father gives him Rene Wellek's *History of Modern Criticism* as a present) and his desire to stay home and watch *Leave it to Beaver* on television. Ben remains divided through the turbulent 1960s of his youth, attending antiwar protests and civil rights demonstrations, but not fully participating in them, and feeling torn between his desire for erotic adventure and his distaste for the company of women.

Leslie Fiedler noted for the *New York Times Book Review* (May 18, 1986, on-line) that Ben's father has taught him to admire the "New Chosen People"—a group of prominent gentile intellectuals, including Mary McCarthy, Robert Lowell, and Dwight Macdonald—and to read the "secular scriptures," which include *Partisan Review*, *Commentary*, and *New Yorker*. Fiedler focused on what he described as the "problematical" Jewishness of *The Great Pretender*; he felt that the story had less in common with the comic Jewish novels of an earlier age (Philip Roth's 1969 book *Portnoy's Complaint*, for example) than with the "covert self-pity and self-adulation reminiscent of James Joyce's *Portrait of the Artist as a Young Man*." Moreover, Fiedler felt that Atlas had failed to explore the experience of his Jewish character both in his all-Jewish suburban enclave and among the elite at Harvard or Oxford. Ben, Fiedler asserted, "remains, like his remote ancestors, ghettoized; though to be sure his is a cushy, book-lined ghetto with invisible walls. This constitutes, in any case, the last and best joke in a book which it would be churlish not to admit kept me laughing throughout. But I laughed, as my grandmother would have said, mit yashikes, with worms; since I was never quite sure who the joke was on—and to tell the truth, I was afraid to find out."

Other reviewers found that the central character, and thus the novel itself, are essentially static. "[Ben Janis] is so completely a precipitate of literary predecessors (eight-tenths Bellow, one-tenth each of Philip Roth and Henry Miller) that there is nothing left over that might have come out of life. . . . This is the ultimate cul-de-sac of self-consciousness," Sven Birkets asserted for the *New Republic* (May 12, 1986). In the *New York Times Book Review* (May 19, 1986), Christopher Lehmann-Haupt felt that, though the story was amusing, Ben's character failed to develop. "The more we nod knowingly at Ben's pretensions and confusions, the less patient we become with his inability to see beyond them. And a little too long before *The Great Pretender* ends, our patience runs out." In *Newsweek* (June 16, 1998), Laura Shapiro described Ben's experiences as a repetitive narrative: "women, poetry, identity crisis . . . women, poetry, identity crisis." "The one real pleasure in reading *The Great Pretender* comes from the portrayal of Ben's parents," Shapiro wrote, "who love him and worry about him and take care of him so openheartedly that Ben is genuinely moved by them. And so are we."

Atlas made bestseller lists with *The Book Wars* (1990), which examined the heated debate about the teaching of literature at American universities, involving clashes over values, inclusiveness, tradition, and pedagogy, among other things. In *The Book Wars*' succinct 90 pages, Atlas outlines the basic divide in academia between the traditionalists, who defend the value of the literary canon, and the deconstructionists, who call for a reassessment of so-called "universal" literary values.

The impetus for the book, Atlas writes, was his own shock at seeing how much the curriculum had changed at Harvard, his alma mater. He mounts a conservative but measured argument from the perspective of a literary critic outside academia. His central premise is that because the "Great Books" are no longer taught, the American university system is "producing a generation that has no stake in our society," as quoted in *Contemporary Authors* (2000). In *Commentary* (June 1993), Carol Iannone described the book as "an eloquent and heartfelt defense of the idea of literature," citing Atlas's claim that the movement toward political correctness causes the "fragmentation, politicization, and trivialization of education." Iannone felt that Atlas weakens his argument, however, by failing to defend absolutes values, making him "unable to fight the PC [politically correct] radicals effectively."

A contributor for the *Los Angeles Times Book Review* (July 20, 1990), as quoted in *Contemporary Authors* (2000), compared Atlas to Allan Bloom, the late educator and author of *The Closing of the American Mind* (1987), a controversial book in which Bloom described the impoverishment of American higher education and, as a result, of American democracy. "Don't believe James Atlas when he professes neutrality," the critic wrote, contending that Atlas's book is "little more than Bloom simplified." *The Book Wars* was reprinted in 1992 as *Battle of the Books: The Curriculum Debate in America*.

In 2000 Atlas published his much-anticipated *Bellow: A Biography*; in terms of heft (nearly 700 pages) and years in preparation (ten), Atlas's work joins a canon of substantial biographies, including Richard Ellmann's *James Joyce* (17 years in the making), or Edmund Morris's memoir of Ronald Reagan, *Dutch* (12 years). There are many connections between Atlas and his subject: Atlas was born in Bellow's fabled Chicago and wrote a Bellovian novel describing his life there; he later wrote a biography about a man (Delmore Schwartz) whom Bellow had recently fictionalized in a novel; and his *Book Wars* followed the line of argument set out by Bellow's good friend and like-thinker Allan Bloom. *Bellow* was widely and prominently reviewed, and nearly all of its critics prefaced their remarks by commenting on the difficulty of the task Atlas had undertaken. At the time the book was published, Saul Bellow was 85 years old, on his fifth marriage, and he had just fathered his first daughter. Considered a one-man literary tour-de-force, he is also known as a prickly and often controversial character. His novels, including *The Dangling Man* (1944), *The Adventures of Augie March* (1953), *Henderson the Rain King* (1959), *Herzog* (1964), and *Humboldt's Gift* (1975), present what the critic Robert Winder, in the *New Statesman* (October 23, 2000), termed "a bewitching brew of reckless soul-searching and damn-it-all worldliness," and have garnered for Bellow a Pulitzer Prize, three National Book Awards, and the 1976 Nobel Prize in Literature. After a string of critics pronounced his career finished, Bellow published the much-acclaimed *Ravelstein* in the spring of 2000. Bellow, who is candid about his novels being "bulletins" from his own life, didn't assist Atlas with his research, though he did give him permission to quote from his unpublished works.

John Leonard, in the *New York Times* (October 15, 2000, on-line), quotes Bellow's "Dangling Man" character—"If I had as many mouths as Siva has arms and kept them going all the time, I still could not do myself justice"—by way of saying that Bellow's life and character are enormously challenging subjects. But, Leonard writes, Atlas is an assiduous biographer: "If you know Bellow and aren't dead, Atlas will have talked to you. If you had an opinion but bought the farm, he's read your diaries, your F.B.I. dossier, and maybe your genome." Leonard appreciated how Atlas examined his subject from the perspective of a literary critic, a cultural historian, and even a psychotherapist, concluding that "we get the best of several worlds—colored by a wary disapproval." Leonard observed that Atlas's distaste for Bellow is palpable and speculated that the project was, for him, a "journey into knowing too much." Bellow's life is strewn with legendary literary squabbles, nasty divorces, and, instances of pettiness and ugliness. His early flirtations with Trotskyism gave way, in later years, to a pronounced social conservatism, tinged—some have said—with sexism, racism, and homophobia. Bellow once said of feminists, "All you're going to have to show for your movement 10 years from now are sagging breasts!" as quoted by Leonard. On another occasion he asked, rhetorically, "Who is the Tolstoy of the Zulus? The Proust of the Papuans? I'd be glad to read him," as cited by James Shapiro in his own *New York Times* article (October 16, 2000, on-line).

For Shapiro, Atlas's key insight about his subject is his assertion that Bellow tended "to tear up his life and feed it to his art," "as if he needed some obstacle, some impediment, to define himself against." Shapiro continued, "At the heart of this book is an unanswered question: Do the many unsettling facts Mr. Atlas unearths about Mr. Bellow's personal life devalue the novels, which he sees as emerging directly from Mr. Bellow's experiences? Or, alternatively, does Mr. Bellow's art somehow transcend the life, in which case why bother writing (or reading) literary biography?" Atlas's failure to answer this provoking question is, Shapiro wrote, the "only serious flaw in a biography unlikely to be surpassed for some time."

Christopher Hitchens's observations for the *National Review* (November 6, 2000, on-line) echo Leonard's and Shapiro's, but he draws harsher conclusions from them. "Atlas . . . seems to have developed a slight disdain for his chosen subject, without quite refining this disdain into a critique." Hitchens also argued that Atlas failed to invoke "the atmosphere of combat and urgency and excitement" surrounding Bellow's 1930s youth—the Depression, Fascism and Stalinism, the New Deal, and the approach of World War II—and spent too many pages on Bellow's personal life. "If you want to know about the novelist's wives, mistresses, indiscretions, alimony grudges, and alleged shortcomings in the sack . . . then Atlas is your man." While acknowledging the importance of such details, Hitchens argued that "they aren't always justified . . . by any real bearing on the life or the work."

Robert Winder, in the *New Statesman* (October 23, 2000, on-line), mounted a similar critique. "Like nearly all biographers," Winder wrote, "[Atlas] succumbs—too willingly for my taste—to the basic Freudian join-the-dots story by which any man's life is an extended conversation with his parents. . . . We spend a lot of time peering through the bedroom door, but hardly ever go into the study, where the real work was going on." And yet, like most critics, Winder found the biography immensely worthwhile and entertaining. (Bellow's witticisms, quoted throughout, are, Winder wrote, "like having a film scored by Mozart.") In the end, Winder concluded, "[Atlas's] book remains, at heart, a tribute, a respectful account of a warm tussle with greatness."

Atlas is the founding editor of the Lipper/Viking Penguin Lives Series. For the series, writers are matched with subjects and asked to produce brief biographies (around 150 pages). For example, the historian and cultural critic Garry Willis wrote about Saint Augustine for the series, and Larry McMurty, known for books set in the American west, examined the life of Crazy Horse. (The novelist Edmund White produced—miraculously—a short book on Marcel Proust.)

In 1975 Atlas married Anna O'Conor Sloane Fels; they have one son and one daughter.

—M. A. H.

SUGGESTED READING: *Commentary* p44 June 1993; *National Review* (on-line) Nov. 6, 2000; *New Statesman* (on-line) Oct. 23, 2000; *New York Times* (on-line) May 18, 1986, Oct. 15, 2000, Oct. 16, 2000; *Salon.com* Jan. 20, 2000

SELECTED BOOKS: *Delmore Schwarz: The Life of an American Poet*, 1977; *The Great Pretender*, 1986; *Book Wars*, 1990; *Bellow: A Biography*, 2000; as editor—*Attila Jozsef: Selected Poems and Texts*, 1973; *Ten American Poets: An Anthology of Poems*, 1973; *In Dreams Begin Responsibilities and Other Stories*, 1978

Auburn, David

1970 (?)– Playwright

David Auburn has achieved something rare for a young playwright—he has written a straight play that has been both critically celebrated and commercially viable. Since debuting Off-Broadway, in May 2000, and then moving to Broadway, *Proof* has played to sold-out crowds and cheering critics. It has won a multitude of awards, including 2001 Tony Awards for best play, best actress, and best director. Auburn himself has received many honors, most notably the 2001 Pulitzer Prize for Drama—the first time in eight years that a non-musical Broadway drama has won that award. (The last play to do so, in 1993, was Tony Kushner's *Angels in America*.) Despite the many accolades, Auburn says that his life hasn't changed much, and he remains humble about his achievements. "What is different— and very nice—is having professional opportunities that I wouldn't have had without *Proof*, and being able to write the next play with the assumption that it will be performed, rather than merely the hope," he told Wendy Aron for *Stage and Screen* (on-line). "Though that may or may not be an accurate assumption."

Courtesy of Writers and Artists Agency

David Auburn

Little has been published about David Auburn's early life, but it is known that he was born in about 1970 in Chicago, Illinois, and raised in Columbus, Ohio, and in Arkansas. In high school he developed an interest in the theater. When he returned to Chicago for college, he performed and wrote for an improvisational and sketch-comedy group. He soon realized how much he enjoyed writing sketch-comedy scenes, as he told Christian Parker for the *Dramatist Magazine* (on-line): "Gradually, the scenes got longer, and I wrote a one-act play, which I put on at college with friends. Eventually, I thought I'd try my hand at a full-length play, which I wrote the last year I was at college. I didn't know what to do with it, but I'd seen a poster advertising a writing fellowship with Amblin Entertainment at Universal Studios, where Steven Spielberg brought ten writers to L.A. each year. I sent the play to them and forgot about it, because I didn't think anything would come of it, but I got into the program."

Though shocked that he had won the fellowship, especially since he hadn't really considered a writing career up until that point, Auburn decided to take the opportunity before him and travel to Los Angeles to learn how to write screenplays. When the fellowship ended, however, he was out of money. At that point he had an epiphany. As he told Wendy Aron, "I decided pretty fast that if I were going to go broke trying to be a writer I'd rather do it trying to be a playwright in New York than a screenwriter in L.A."

Once in New York, Auburn supported himself with various day jobs—including a stint writing documentaries for the music channel VH1—while trying to write plays at night. He established a theater company with friends and had a few of his plays put on in small venues. He also spent two years in the playwriting program at the Juilliard School, in New York, which was then in its second year and supervised by the notable playwrights Christopher Durang and Marsha Norman. His time in the program proved invaluable to his writing. He told Parker: "Having people with [Durang and Norman's] level of experience talk about what you're doing is validating. Having actors as good as those at Juilliard do your work forces you to think seriously about how professional actors will approach the material you wrote. That was one of the best things about the program: learning what kinds of questions actors ask when they approach a new script and being able to think through those problems before you get it into rehearsal."

Nineteen ninety-seven was a turning point for Auburn. A short play, *What Do You Believe About the Future?*, was published in the *New England Review* and later reprinted in *Harper's*. More important, his first full-length play, *Skyscraper*, debuted Off-Broadway that year, albeit to poor reviews. The play takes place in a soon-to-be-demolished office building in Chicago, where chance meetings between six characters on the roof of the building lead to philosophical discussions on a number of subjects, including the passage of time. In the *New York Times* (October 3, 1997), Peter Marks wrote: "*Skyscraper* . . . fairly teems with intriguing notions. But none of them, ultimately, amount to much. Mr. Auburn has expended all of his energy on the structure of *Skyscraper* without paying enough attention to the people who inhabit it. As a result, the play . . . is as rigorous—and emotionally arid—as a master's thesis."

After *Skyscraper*'s short run Auburn quit his job and moved to London, England, to live with his girlfriend, who was then working there. Over the course of that summer, he worked on his next play, *Proof*. He had received encouragement from representatives of the Manhattan Theatre Club who, after seeing *Skyscraper*, asked Auburn to submit his next play to them. He received additional encouragement from the *New England Review*, which published his *Three Monologues* (Spring 1998) and a one-act play, *Fifth Planet* (Spring 1999).

When asked by Christian Parker how the idea for *Proof* originated, Auburn explained: "I felt that I wanted to write a more naturalistic play than my first play, which was a more conceptual, absurd comedy. I wanted to write something more realistic and grounded in character." Specifically, Auburn imagined two sisters, fighting over something left behind by their father after his death. He envisioned that one of the sisters would be concerned about inheriting the mental illness that had plagued their father. These ideas seemed, to Auburn, to be dramatic, and yet he still needed to decide what the sisters were fighting over. Eventually, he realized that the object of the argument could be a mathematical document, an idea that appealed to him for several reasons. "I thought the authorship of a mathematical proof could be called into question in some interesting ways that, say, a painting or a book manuscript couldn't be," he recalled to Parker. "Another [reason] was the historical fact that a number of well-known mathematicians have suffered from mental illness, which gave me a bridge between my two ideas. Once I had that, I wrote the play quickly."

Proof centers around Catherine, a guarded young woman who left college to take care of her father, a mathematical genius who, in his 20s, became famous for solving complicated mathematical proofs, but who suffered from dementia later in life. After her father dies, Catherine, who inherited his mathematical gifts, begins to worry that she may also suffer from his debilitating illness. When Catherine's sister Claire visits, to settle their father's estate, the sisters' relationship is tested, as is Catherine's sanity. Even more troubling for Catherine is the discovery by Hal, a former student of her father's, of an old notebook containing a profound mathematical proof with questionable authorship.

Proof debuted at the Manhattan Theatre Club, on May 2, 2000, to generally favorable reviews. David Kaufman, in the *New York Daily News* (May 24, 2000, on-line), proclaimed: "This play by David Auburn combines elements of mystery and surprise with old-fashioned storytelling to provide a compelling evening of theater. From its astonishing opening scene to its shocking Act I curtain line, the moral of *Proof* is that things often are not what they appear to be. This may be an ancient adage, but it acquires fresh vitality as Auburn's dialogue keeps spinning off in unexpected directions." In *New York* (June 5, 2000), John Simon cheered: "David Auburn's *Proof* is . . . a play about scientists whose science matters less than their humanity. Here, those of us who want their dramatic characters to be real people need not feel excluded . . . All four [main characters]—whether loving, hating, encouraging, or impeding one another—are intensely alive, complex, funny, human." But not all of the reviews were as favorable. A *New Republic* (November 13, 2000) critic believed that *Proof* suffered from a thin plot. "[Auburn] runs out of material so quickly that, by the middle of the second act, the play jerks to a halt and starts running in place. *Proof* sometimes looks like a rather austere stage version of *Good Will Hunting*, insofar as it features a whiz kid central character who is also an idiot savant."

Despite some negative reviews, *Proof*'s run at the Manhattan Theatre Club proved so successful that it moved to Broadway, where it again played to sold-out crowds. It also earned a host of awards for best play, including awards from the Drama League, the New York Drama Critics, and the Outer Critics Circle, as well as a 2001 Lucille Lortel Award, a 2001 Drama Desk Award, and the 2001 Tony. Mary-Louise Parker, who played Catherine in both the Off-Broadway and Broadway productions, earned widespread praise for her performance, and the 2001 Tony Award for best actress.

The director, Daniel Sullivan, also won many awards, including a Tony for best director. Auburn received the Hull-Warriner Award from the Dramatist's Guild, the John Gassner Playwriting Award, and the 2001 Pulitzer Prize for Drama. When asked if he thinks his next play will top the success of *Proof*, Auburn told Robert Hofler and Jonathan Bing of *Variety* (April 23–29, 2001): 'I don't think you try to. Every play is different. I'm glad this one has attracted an audience, and I hope the next one will too."

—C. M.

SUGGESTED READING: *Dramatist Magazine* (on-line); Harper's p30+ Aug. 1997; *New Criterion* p39+ Feb. 2001; *New England Review* p63+ Spring 1998, p21+ Spring 1999; *New Leader* p53+ Sep./Oct. 2000; *New Republic* p28+ Nov. 13, 2000; *New York* p106+ June 5, 2000; *New York Daily News* (on-line) May 24, 2000; *New York Times* E p3 Oct. 3, 1997; Official Web Site for *Proof*; *Stage and Screen* (on-line); *Variety* p27+ Apr. 23–29, 2001; *Vogue* p314+ Oct. 2000

SELECTED PLAYS: *Skyscraper*, 1997; *Proof*, 2000

Auletta, Ken

Apr. 23, 1942– Journalist, nonfiction writer

Ken Auletta has enjoyed a long and distinguished career as a business and media journalist. Over the last few decades he has written for such prestigious newspapers and magazines as *New York*, the *Village Voice*, the *Daily News* and the *New Yorker*. One of Auletta's strengths as a reporter is his ability to win the trust of important sources, who provide him with extraordinary access and information. He has published books on New York City's fiscal crisis during the 1970s (*The Streets Were Paved With Gold*, 1979); politics and reporting (*Hard Feelings: Reporting on the Pols, the Press, People and the City*, 1980); poverty (*The Underclass*, 1982); big business (*The Art of Corporate Success: The Story of Schlumberger*, 1984); corporate power struggles (*Greed and Glory on Wall Street: The Fall of the House of Lehman*, 1986); the television industry (*Three Blind Mice: How the TV Networks Lost Their Way*, 1991); the media (*The Highwaymen: The Warriors of the Information Superhighway*, 1997); and the antitrust case against the Microsoft Corporation (*World War 3.0: Microsoft and its Enemies*, 2001). "I go out and I meet interesting people and I wrestle with interesting subjects that are complicated and it's fun to try and master that," Auletta told Brian Lamb, the host of C-SPAN's *Booknotes* (October 6, 1991), as archived on their Web site. "Then at the end, I sit down, and I'm thinking about how I tell the story in the most truthful and interesting way that I can for the reader."

Ken Auletta
Lawrence Lucier/Getty Images

Ken Auletta submitted the following third-person statement for *World Authors 1995–2000:* "Ken Auletta is a journalist and an author. He has written the 'Annals of Communications' column for the *New Yorker* magazine since 1992. He is the author of eight books, including four national best-sellers: *Three Blind Mice: How the TV Networks Lost Their Way, Greed and Glory On Wall Street: The Fall of The House of Lehman.* His *The Highwaymen: Warriors of the Information Super Highway,* and his 2001 book, *World War 3.0: Microsoft and Its Enemies,* were national business best-sellers. Each was published by Random House.

"He was born on Coney Island [in the borough of Brooklyn, in New York City] on April 23, 1942, the second of three children sired by Nettie Tenenbaum and Pat Auletta (brother Richard was first, sister Bonnie was third). In the melting pot of Brooklyn's most southern precinct, inter-marriage among Italian and Jew was common. Two of Nettie's sisters married Italian-Americans, and one of Pat's brothers married a Jewish woman. Some neighborhood churches taught, 'The Jews killed Christ!' but an Italian who shared a stoop with a Jew was not likely to believe this.

"Auletta attended public schools. While his older brother, Richard, skipped two grades and was admitted to Brooklyn College at age 15, the first member of the Auletta or Tenenbaum tribe to enter college, Ken was stupidly unimpressed. His peers prided themselves on being tough guys. Study was for sissies. When he wasn't working at his dad's small sporting goods store on Stillwell Avenue, he spent hours on the baseball diamond and football field. In his junior year at Abraham Lincoln High School, he swiped a book of passes from a desk and handed it out to friends so they could all leave the building at will and hang out at the sweet shop across the street. Nabbed by the Dean, Ken was thrown out of school. Just some more free periods, he thought. His parents were distraught, and pleaded for a second chance. Ken wanted to rebel, but Pat Auletta kept a long black shaving strap, which he once applied to Ken's rear. The menacing strap caught his attention.

"The wily school principal, Abraham Lass, also captured his attention. 'Do you like school?' asked Lass.

'Not particularly,' said the teenager.

'Tell me, Kenneth, what you like about school?' asked Lass.

'Baseball and football,' responded the teenager.

'Well tell me, Kenneth, how you expect to play baseball and football for Abraham Lincoln if you no longer attend Abraham Lincoln?'

"The logic was impeccable, and so unassailable that it hit Ken as hard as his dad's strap once did. Lass now imposed the terms of the boy's surrender: he must sacrifice every free period and spend it in the principal's office; he must not leave the building during school hours; he must study harder and raise his grades. Do all that and he could stay in school and play ball. He obeyed, and forged a life-long friendship with Lass, who introduced him to the joys of reading. Still, Auletta's grade average was a miserable 64 percent, and the only college that showed an interest was the State University at Oswego, with a helpful nudge from their baseball coach.

"Over the next four years, Auletta met his first cow, and gradually became more studious. He was active in student government, and the International Relations Club, and organizing civil rights demonstrations, and writing thumping, righteous columns for the *Oswegonian.* He founded an off-campus underground paper, named it *Pravda,* which in Russian means truth. He graduated with a B.S. in history and a teaching degree. With an interest in government, politics and international politics, Auletta attended the Maxwell School of Citizenship and Public Affairs at Syracuse University. He entered a doctoral program in political science. He wrote a weekly column for the school newspaper, and edited the underground literary/humor magazine, *The Sword of Damocles.* He taught and trained Peace Corps volunteers. He imagined working in government.

"He got bored with school. Leaving after his second year, Ken went to work in late 1965 for Howard J. Samuels, a businessman who planned to seek the Democratic nomination for Governor. He would carry Samuels' coat, and write his speeches. Samuels lost. Auletta then became the first full time employee of the New York State Democratic party to work on advancing Senator Robert F. Kennedy's goal of getting the party more involved in community service activities. That dream lasted less than a year, hijacked by practical politics (youngsters were useful only if they joined the party). Auletta next served in the Army, then as Special Assistant to the U.S. Under Secretary of Commerce. Opposed to the war in Vietnam, he quit the Johnson administration and went to work in Senator Robert F. Kennedy's 1968 campaign for the Presidency. After Kennedy's assassination, he became Executive Editor of the weekly *Manhattan Tribune*. He was state Campaign Manager for Howard J. Samuels, helping him lose two races for Governor of New York. Under Samuels's Chairmanship, he was appointed the first Executive Director of the New York City Off Track Betting Corporation.

"He returned to journalism in 1974, becoming the chief political correspondent for the *New York Post*. He would become a staff writer and weekly political columnist for the *Village Voice* and a Contributing Editor of *New York* magazine. When Rupert Murdoch launched a hostile takeover of these publications, Auletta and more than 40 writers and editors quit in protest. Contacted by Editor William Shawn, he started writing for the *New Yorker* in 1977. Between 1977 and 1993, he also wrote a weekly political column for the New York *Daily News*. He also hosted numerous public television programs, and served as a political commentator for both WNBC-TV and WCBS-TV. He has written for numerous publications, including the *New York Times* and the *New York Review of Books*, written and narrated a 90-minute biography of Rupert Murdoch for PBS's *Frontline*, and has appeared regularly on *Nightline*, the *News Hour* with Jim Lehrer, and the *Charlie Rose Show*.

"The focus of his early writing was on New York and politics and urban affairs, subjects very much related to his schooling and work experience. He covered New York City's fiscal crisis in the mid seventies, and out of this experience grew his first book, *The Streets Were Paved With Gold*. He spent the better part of Edward Koch's first year as Mayor (1978) and Mario Cuomo's first year as Governor (1983) as a fly-on-the-wall, writing two-part *New Yorker* profiles of each. These pieces were included in his second book, *Hard Feelings*, a collection of his writing. He suggested to Mr. Shawn that he wanted to take a fresh look at poverty. This grew into a three-part series, 'The Underclass,' which was expanded into a book. Long before the notion was in the air, Auletta inserted this phrase, the underclass, into our national language, triggering praise from the left and right. 'Personal, vivid and irrefutable,' wrote Michael Harrington in the *New Republic*. James Q. Wilson in *New York* magazine wrote, 'Sympathetic and yet dispassionate . . . splendid . . .a call for intellectual honesty and political courage.'

"At a time when others were writing about the death of American business and what went wrong and why the U.S. was losing out to Japan, Auletta set out to explore why a company succeeds. This resulted in a two-part profile of Schlumberger and its ex-socialist CEO, Jean Riboud, which became a book, *The Art of Corporate Success*. Before insider trading scandals burst into our consciousness, Auletta wrote a two-part piece for the *New York Times Magazine* about the fall of Lehman Brothers, the oldest investment banking partnership on Wall Street. This tale captured the ethos of Wall Street in the mid eighties, and grew into a book, *Greed And Glory On Wall Street*, which attracted a chorus of praise and was a national bestseller. The *New York Times* wrote, 'A riveting chronicle of the lust for money, power and reputation. Invaluable.' The *Wall Street Journal* called it, 'A towering reportorial achievement.'

"Interested in how an industry did or did not adjust to change and to new technologies, he turned his attention to the broadcast industry. Nearly from the day the three broadcast networks (CBS, NBC and ABC) were acquired by new owners starting in 1985, Auletta for the next six years had a front row seat for his next bestseller, *Three Blind Mice: How The TV Networks Lost Their Way*. Frank Stanton, who was President of CBS from 1946 to 1973, hailed it as 'the best book ever written on network television.'

"Soon after that book was published, The *New Yorker* invited him in 1992 to cover the media and entertainment. He saw that technology was blurring the lines between once disparate industries such as broadcasting, cable, movie studios, computers, publishing, entertainment, software. Under the rubric of 'The Annals of Communication,' Auletta forged a new beat. He was among the first to popularize the so-called information superhighway with his February 1993 profile of Barry Diller and how he used his Mac laptop PowerBook to help search for something *new*. He profiled the leading figures and companies of the Information Age, including Bill Gates, Rupert Murdoch, AOL Time Warner, Viacom, John Malone, Ted Turner, and the *New York Times*. He dissected media meteors that fell to earth like 'push' technology and inter-active TV and Inside.com. He probed media violence, the PAC giving of communication giants, the fat lecture fees earned by journalist/pundits, and explored what 'synergy' may mean to journalism. Some of these pieces were included in his seventh book, *The Highwaymen: Warriors of the Information Superhighway*, which became a business bestseller. Appearing before the Financial Writers Association of America in 1997, *Wall Street Journal* Managing Editor Paul Steiger turned to him and declared, 'I really think that the kind of stuff you do for the *New Yorker* is terrific. I'd love to see more of that kind of stuff on the front page of the *Wall Street Journal*. . . . I think you set a standard.' In ranking him as America's premier media critic, the *Columbia Journalism Review* concluded, 'no other reporter has covered the new communications revolution as thoroughly as has Auletta.'

"He covered the Microsoft antitrust trial for the magazine. This would lead to his eighth book—*World War 3.0: Microsoft And Its Enemies*—about Microsoft and its historic antitrust trial, about Bill Gates and the battle for supremacy in the Information Age. *World War 3.0* prompted a media storm because of the more than ten hours of interviews Auletta conducted with the Microsoft trial judge, Thomas Penfield Jackson, and the unusual access he had to participants and to previously private documents. In a review, the book was hailed by renowned attorney Floyd Abrams this way: 'I cannot recall a book written about a complex civil trial that describes it as completely and compellingly . . . a journalistic tour de force.'

"Auletta has won numerous journalism honors. He has been chosen a Literary Lion by the New York Public Library, and one of the 20th Century's top 100 business journalists by a distinguished national panel of peers. He has been awarded the Chancellor's Medal from Syracuse University, and in addition to an M. A. in political science from the Maxwell School at Syracuse, the State University of New York awarded him a Doctor of Letters in 1990. He is the guest editor of the 2001 edition of *The Best Business Stories of the Year*, which is published by Random House. He has served as a Pulitzer Prize juror; is a judge of the annual Livingston national journalism awards; a Trustee (and member of the Executive Committee) of the Public Theatre/New York Shakespeare Festival; he was a Trustee of the Nightingale-Bamford School, and was twice a Trustee of PEN, the international writers organization. He is a member of the Author's Guild and of PEN.

"He is married to Amanda (Binky) Urban, co-head of the Literary Department at International Creative Management. They reside in New York City, and have a daughter, Kate."

In his first book, *The Streets Were Paved With Gold* (1979), Auletta analyzed the origins of the fiscal crisis that plagued New York City during the mid-1970s. By the end of the decade, the federal government had to bail out the city to keep it from going bankrupt. Auletta argued that the city's political leaders, and specifically Mayors Robert Wagner (1954–1966) and John V. Lindsay (1966–1974), were primarily responsible for the crisis. They borrowed huge amounts of money and increased spending to incredible levels to satisfy the demands of residents who wanted more government services and special interest groups. City politicians were particularly beholden to municipal unions, which could disrupt life in the city by going on strike if their members weren't awarded the pay increases they demanded. Auletta asserted that the political leadership lacked the courage to face up to economic realities and to simply say no to the demands for more services or pay increases. When city taxes were raised, he reported, the revenues went toward special interest groups instead of toward budget deficit reduction. He also blamed the crisis on the city's bankers, who supported the spending increases because their own institutions would profit, and the press, which failed to notice what was going on and sound the alarm. In his review for *Newsweek* (April 2, 1979) Tony Schwartz wrote that Auletta "builds his case by marshaling a mountain of statistical evidence: budget figures, labor costs (and demands), Federal-aid figures." Although Schwartz faulted the book's poor editing, he argued that this did not diminish the power of the book.

In 1980 Auletta published a collection of the political pieces he had written from 1976–1980 in his second book, *Hard Feelings: Reporting on Pols, the Press, People, and the City*. "Some of the pieces in this anthology are fascinating," Ken Nash wrote in his review for the *Library Journal* (June 15, 1980). "Auletta is best at catching nuances of personality and style. Issues take a back seat as he explores the kind of selling politicians do and the kind of buying reporters do."

Auletta turned his attention to poverty in his third book, *The Underclass* (1982). In expanding on a series of articles he had written for the *New Yorker*, Auletta explored the question of whether the chronic welfare recipients, street criminals, school dropouts, drug addicts, and drifters who populate America's inner cities have any hope of escaping poverty and becoming productive members of society. In addition to discussing the academic literature on the subject, Auletta reports on the seven months he spent attending classes with the Manpower Demonstration Research Corporation (MDRC), a federal program that works to encourage productive work habits and discourage self-destructive habits. Auletta warns that the underclass could grow, unleashing a wave of violent crime and threatening the quality of public schools. "As an introduction and overview to the contemporary debate over American poverty—its roots and proposed solutions—Auletta's book is invaluable," Juan Williams wrote in the *Washington Post Book World* (July 11, 1982). While acknowledging that the book is both "fascinating and well-written," Williams questioned what Auletta was trying to accomplish in reviewing expert opinions, interviewing members of the underclass, and then failing to offer any conclusions. He also criticized the book for failing to distinguish between the "poor," many of whom are able to escape their plight, and the "underclass," many of whom remain in their circumstances. "This leads to the question, unanswered by Auletta, of whether the nation should spend its social-welfare dollars on the poor or on the underclass, considering the differences in the cost of helping the two groups and the differences with the results," Williams added. In the *New Republic* (June 9, 1982), Michael Harrington asserted that "Auletta did something which no statistician in his right mind would ever do: he went out and talked to his subject matter. His reportorial portrait of the members of the underclass in a New York jobs program is personal, vivid, and irrefutable, as computer print-outs are not."

In his next book, *The Art of Corporate Success: The Story of Schlumberger* (1984), Ken Auletta profiled one of the nation's most profitable, but least known, companies. Schlumberger Limited provides technical information to companies that drill for oil. When the book was published, the company had 75,000 employees, 43 subsidiaries, and operated in 92 countries. (Schlumberger is still operating today.) "It began in France in 1927, when two Schlumberger brothers developed a technique for electrically analyzing the layers beneath the earth's surface to determine whether or not the terrain is right to sink a well," Anne Chamberlin explained in her review for the *Washington Post Book World* (May 13, 1984). "The Schlumberger brothers grew and prospered by perfecting their equipment and advancing their technology, always putting science and excellence ahead of personal profit." Another important factor in Schlumberger Limited's success was Jean Riboud, who had headed the company for more than 20 years when the book was published. Hired by the Schlumbergers in 1950, Riboud was a member of the French Resistance during World War II, was captured by the Nazis, and survived the Buchenwald concentration camp in Germany. Chamberlin noted that she was "ready to be swept off my feet by Auletta's Schlumberger saga. But somewhere along the line the chemistry gets lost." Although Auletta presented many impressive facts, Chamberlin asserted that the author's "dread *New Yorker* reporting style"—his piling on of details and lack of analysis—rendered the book dull. In contrast, Gary D. Barber praised the book in the *Library Journal* (April 15, 1984), writing that this "balanced account of a $20 billion corporation should be in all business collections."

Auletta chronicled the corporate struggle that led to the collapse of Lehman Brothers, one of the oldest and most respected investment banking firms in the U.S., in his fifth book, *Greed and Glory on Wall Street: The Fall of the House of Lehman* (1986). Peter G. Peterson, the former secretary of commerce in the Nixon Administration, became chairman of Lehman Brothers in 1973, helping to reverse the firm's misfortunes. According to Auletta, Peterson relied on Lewis L. Glucksman, a veteran trader and executive with Lehman, to administer the firm's internal operations, while he focused on long-term strategy. Although Glucksman was eventually promoted to co-chief executive officer, he personally disliked Peterson and wanted to run Lehman himself. On July 11, 1983 Glucksman met with Peterson for five hours and demanded the top position. Peterson stepped down nine days later without a fight. "Glucksman quickly moved loyalists into key jobs and proposed a radical shift of ownership shares and bonus money from the banking partners to the traders," Anthony Bianco related in his review for *Business Week* (January 27, 1986). "The latter generated two-thirds of the firm's income but held only one-third of the stock. Glucksman was able to buy off some influential partners with more power or bigger bonuses. But festering resentment turned to panic as key partners left, and a market slump and trading losses shriveled revenues." In 1984 Shearson/American Express Inc. acquired Lehman Brothers, saving it from liquidation. Although the name Lehman Brothers survived, the firm that once dominated Wall Street was gone. Bianco praised *Greed and Glory on Wall Street* as "a devastatingly authoritative account that leaves no doubt about what undid Lehman: greed, specifically the inability of its ruling partners to subordinate their self-interest to the interests of the partnership."

Auletta spent six years gathering research for his next book, which discussed television. He conducted many interviews with television executives and was permitted to attend corporate meetings at the networks anytime he wished. Published in 1991, *Three Blind Mice: How the TV Networks Lost Their Way* received substantial media attention. Three television networks—CBS, NBC and ABC—once dominated the airwaves, capturing as many as 90 percent of all viewers. By the end of the 1980s the number of viewers watching one of the networks had declined to about 60 percent. Auletta argued that the acquisition of each network by vast corporate conglomerates during the mid-1980s played the most significant role in their decline. The Loews Corporation, headed by Laurence A. Tisch, took over CBS; General Electric (GE) purchased NBC; and Capital Cities Communications bought ABC. In response to falling profits, the new corporate owners slashed budgets at each network. Additionally, Auletta observed that the networks weren't as powerful as originally thought. Networks served primarily as middlemen: they recruited advertisers and lured audiences for shows that were mostly made in Hollywood studios. The networks had prospered for so long due to little competition. According to Auletta, the end result of these corporate changes left CBS, NBC, and ABC at the mercy of increased competition from cable television, VCRs, independent local stations, and emerging new networks, like Fox. "Auletta's method—the numbing, *New Yorker*-style compilation of facts, irrespective of their larger significance—robs the narrative of any compelling focus," George Russell wrote in his review for *Commentary* (January 1992). "Sometimes Auletta scores a hit, as with his detailed story of the ouster of CBS Chairman Tom Wyman by Tisch and the network's late founder, William Paley. Other times he misses, as with his lengthy reconstruction of producer Aaron Spelling's dud series, *Nightingales*. In general, too much is unmemorable, and remains unmemorable." In the *Wall Street Journal* (September 20, 1991), Peter R. Kann concluded that the "book's fascination and fun lie in the detail—Mr. Auletta's extraordinary access to the principal players, his eye for color, ear for anecdote and reporter's instinct for conflict. The largely on-the-record recounting of a series of CBS board meetings in which a hapless Chairman Tom Wyman and his board allies are outmaneuvered by a sly (and rich) Larry Tisch ranks among the best of inside-the-board-room reporting."

In the early 1990s Auletta became the *New Yorker*'s media columnist. In 1997 he published a collection of his *New Yorker* profiles of prominent individuals in the media and entertainment industries, including Michael Eisner, Gerald Levin, John Malone, Rupert Murdoch, Michael Ovitz, and Sumner Redstone. The book, *The Highwaymen: Warriors of the Information Superhighway*, received mixed reviews. "Each of these executives has been profiled many times," Eric Nee noted in *Upside* (September 1997). "But author Ken Auletta digs deep enough—and was given enough access—to reveal the full personalities of these moguls in new and often captivating ways." Nee, however, criticized Auletta for republishing dated pieces and devoting little attention to the Internet— despite the book's title. "More effort should have been made to update the original pieces and add a few more profiles, such as one on [Bill] Gates," Nee wrote. "That would have turned a good book into a great book." In the *Los Angeles Times Book Review* (June 1, 1997), Eric Alterman observed that Auletta "is to media titans what Bob Woodward is to politicians: a human vacuum cleaner. An energetic reporter with unparalleled access to the high-powered world of billion-dollar deal-making, Auletta writes as if he were a fly on the wall of corporate boardrooms." However, Alterman expressed the opinion that there was a danger to this type of "access journalism." Noting that most of the profiles in the book were favorable treatments of their subjects, Alterman asserted that when "a reporter is tied to a given beat, a beat in which the sources are more powerful than he is, he will be tempted to write his stories in a manner that will flatter the vanity of the people who are spinning him. If he insults their own ideas of themselves, they will be unlikely to make themselves available to him the next time around. Access reporters almost inevitably end up writing for their sources rather than for their readers."

In his next book, *World War 3.0: Microsoft and its Enemies* (2001), Auletta discussed the U.S. Department of Justice's antitrust lawsuit against the software juggernaut headed by Bill Gates. Auletta enjoyed access to the most important players in the drama, including the federal judge Thomas Penfield Jackson, who presided over the trial and issued the judgment calling for the division of Microsoft into two separate companies. Jackson shared the handwritten notes he had taken during the trial and some of his personal opinions with Auletta—even going so far as to describe Microsoft's executives as liars. In the *New York Times Book Review* (February 4, 2001), Adam Liptak wrote that Auletta "has talked to everyone, has read everything and has set it all down, but he leaves it to the reader to make sense of a mountain of jumbled facts and impressions." *World War 3.0* became the subject of controversy. Microsoft appealed the court judgment and cited Judge Jackson's comments to Auletta and other reporters while the trial was still pending. As Adam Cohen, a writer for *Time* (March 12, 2001), explained, "Microsoft insists that Jackson's public comments showed judicial bias, and thus are grounds for reversing his liability ruling against the company." On June 30, 2001 the U. S. Court of Appeals voted unanimously to overturn Jackson's ruling. The Court sharply reprimanded Jackson for talking to the press during the trial and ordered him removed from the case.

Since 2001 Auletta has served as the co-editor of the anthology *The Best Business Stories of the Year*, which is published annually. Auletta told *World Authors* that he selects topics for his books carefully, explaining, "I generally like to take a little time between books to assure that I don't impulsively choose a topic that I am forced to live with or divorce."

—D. C.

SUGGESTED READING: *Business Week* p16 Jan. 27, 1986; *Commentary* p63+ Jan. 1992; Ken Auletta Web site; *Library Journal* p1374 June 15, 1980, p807 Apr. 15, 1984; *Los Angeles Times Book Review* p8+ June 1, 1997, with photos; *New Republic* p26+ June 9, 1982; *New York Times Book Review* p11 June 17, 1982, p7+ Feb. 4, 2001; *Newsweek* p84 Apr. 2, 1979; *Time* p60 May 12, 2001; *Upside* p158+ Sep. 1997; *Wall Street Journal* A p10 Sep. 20, 1991; *Washington Post* A p2 Jan. 7, 1977, A p3 July 1, 2001; *Washington Post Book World* p10 May 13, 1984

SELECTED BOOKS: *The Streets Were Paved with Gold*, 1979; *Hard Feelings: Reporting on the Pols, the Press, the People and the City*, 1980; *The Underclass*, 1982; *The Art of Corporate Success: The Story of Schlumberger*, 1984; *Greed and Glory on Wall Street: The Fall of the House of Lehman*, 1986; *Three Blind Mice: How the TV Networks Lost Their Way*, 1991; *The Highwaymen: Warriors of the Information Superhighway*, 1997; *World War 3.0: Microsoft and its Enemies*, 2001

Axelsson, Majgull

Feb. 14, 1947– Novelist; journalist; playwright

The Swedish novelist, journalist, and playwright Majgull Axelsson has built a solid reputation in her homeland for her powerful works of both nonfiction and fiction. She has earned a following in the U.S., as well, with the translation of two of her books into English: *Rosario Is Dead* (1997) and *April Witch* (2002). Her work often explores themes of modern-day Sweden and her native country's place in history.

Ulla Montan/Courtesy of Villard Books/Random House/Trade

Majgull Axelsson

Majgull Axelsson wrote the following autobiographical statement for *World Authors 1995–2000*: "They say Sweden is a country that has stepped aside from history and certainly, to an outsider, it may appear to be so. Here we are: a little nation on the periphery of the world, a country that has not been at war for nearly two centuries, in spite of being so close to all the battlefields of Europe, a country free from revolt and revolution, free from work camps and pogroms. A cool, dispassionate little country. Even a tad bit dull.

"But Sweden is also a nation of paradoxes: a socialist monarchy, more Americanized than any other country in Europe. An extremely secularized country in which, nevertheless, the public debate circles endlessly around ethics and morals (although, admittedly, we express more horror over gluttony than lechery). A nation which, for four decades, carried out a political experiment that, briefly, made us the wealthiest country in the world, and that gave us both the welfare state and a touching faith in human reason.

"I was born in this country on February 14th 1947. My father was a railway engineer, my mother sometimes a housewife, sometimes a factory worker, sometimes a waitress (notably at the Nobel Prize banquets). Myself, I knew by the age of eight that what I wanted to be was a writer. This may have been at least as much attributable to the fact that I was an unusually skillful liar as to my conviction that since reading books was wonderful, writing them must be even more so.

"Yes, I was a liar. An inveterate liar. I just couldn't help myself. When I started to tell my friends about something, reality was just not good enough. I began to fantasize, my stories took on a life of their own, and I was so deeply moved by the things I heard myself saying that I found it impossible to resist further embellishment. Wild birds landed on my shoulder! I was hunted by wolves! A young man I had never set eyes on before was head over heels in love with me!

"Of course I got caught. Of course I was punished—by my parents, my friends, and by my own superego. The superego was worst. In bed at night, I prosecuted myself. What had I prevaricated about that day? Would I stick to the truth tomorrow? Wouldn't I?

"In adolescence, I also began to doubt my own abilities. Suddenly I felt the dream of becoming an author to be asking too much of life, becoming a journalist would be quite good enough. What did a young woman like me have to write about? What did I—a high school drop-out, as it turned out—know about life and the world? So I shelved my dreams of authorship and decided to try to become a reporter, a superb calling for a person whose superego was unprepared to put up with lies but who refused to even consider the more conventional and secure jobs that my parents tried to suggest.

"I was 19 years old when I got my first job as a training reporter in a small town newspaper. During a couple of years I moved from town to town, from newspaper to newspaper, until I finally considered myself properly trained. At 27 I was made editor in chief of a small labor market magazine and accepted, although I was more interested in social issues than in labor market issues.

"One day in the 1980s, after more than 20 years of journalism, I found myself in the Philippines, where I stumbled into the story of Rosario Baluyot, an 11-year-old street child from Olongapo City. She had died six months earlier, because someone had shoved a massage bar so hard up her vagina that it was wedged irretrievably into her musculature. She went around with it inside her for several months and then died of peritonitis.

"When I sat down to write Rosario's story, I realized the language of the journalist would not suffice. This time it was not just a matter of checking on the facts and describing the superficial truth, this time I was face to face with a story that took a lot of questions to the extreme, questions not only about social, legal and economic conditions, but about what it means to be a human being on our earth, about what a human life is actually worth. And suddenly a new way of writing sprang up from inside me, a literary language that was creative and empathetic rather than descriptive and reporting. *Rosario Is Dead* turned into a documentary novel rather than journalism, and while I was writing it the idea took shape in my mind that I would resign from my position as editor-in-chief of a journal. From that moment on, I wanted to be in full control of what I would write and how I would write it.

"Since then, I have written three novels, two books of investigative journalism and a play. Perhaps the novel *April Witch* (1997) is the most significant of these works. It is the story of three women my own age and their extremely disabled sister. It is also a kind of coming to terms with contemporary Swedish history, with the hubris that afflicted us during the good years, and with the belief that we were living in a thoroughly rational and humane society. As I was writing it, it became clear to me that Sweden has never stepped aside from history at all, and that our belief is one we share with many people and many nations in the industrialized world.

"It should be added that, initially, I found writing fiction extremely difficult. My childhood superego perked right up, took to prosecuting me at night again. What was the point of sitting at my desk all day writing stories that weren't true? This time, however, I refused to give in to that stern judge inside me. Today I know that the core of truth we find in fiction and in art is far deeper than the superficial truth cultivated in journalism and science."

Majgull Axelsson's *Rosario Is Dead* (1991) was published in English in 1997. Lela E. Madijiah noted in the *Jakarta Post* (September 22, 1996), "Rosario's painful story . . . shocked the world when it became public . . . not only because of the grief it evoked in those who read it, but also because it accused the whole world of ignoring the spreading problem of sexual exploitation of children." Axelsson's 1997 novel, *Aprilhäxan*, was translated by Linda Schenck as *April Witch* in 2002. Axelsson took her title from a story by Ray Bradbury about a woman with strange and wonderful abilities. Her protagonist, Desirée, was born with cerebral palsy and is troubled in middle age by almost constantly recurring seizures. She has been institutionalized for life, as her body is completely useless; she is unable to walk or speak, except through computers. Nevertheless, her mind is so powerful that she can enter other people's lives, leaving her on the backs of crows and gulls to soar over the world. Eleanor J. Bader, who reviewed *April Witch* for *Library Journal* (February 1, 2002), called it "moving, suspenseful, and intense." Michelle Vellucci, in *People* (May 13, 2002), referred to a "haunting confrontation between a soaring mind and a body shackled by disease, family and society." *April Witch* won the August Prize.

—S.Y.

SUGGESTED READING: *Jakarta Post* p3 Sep. 22, 1996; *Library Journal* p129 Feb. 1, 2002; *Star-Telegram* L&A p1 Apr. 29, 2002; *Times-Picayune* L p1 Apr. 17, 2002

SELECTED WORKS IN ENGLISH TRANSLATION: *Rosario Is Dead*, 1997; *April Witch*, 2002

Bahr, Howard

1946– Novelist

Howard Bahr has described himself as out-of-step with his own time and bewitched by the past, so it seems fitting that he served for eleven years as curator of the Rowan Oak Museum, the antebellum estate where William Faulkner lived and worked for more than 30 years. Bahr told Alden Mudge in an interview for *BookPage* (April 1998, on-line) that when he was in his 20s he was "so deeply moved by the writing of Mr. William Faulkner that I wanted to be where he had written about." The Rowan Oak Estate, which Faulkner rescued from decay and named after a Scottish legend that claims that wood of the rowan tree, when nailed to a house's front door, will keep away ghosts, is close to the University of Mississippi, in Oxford, where Bahr taught in the English department for many years. He now teaches at Motlow State Community College in Tullahoma, Tennessee.

Bahr's first novel, *Black Flower: A Novel of the Civil War*, was first issued by a small publisher in Baltimore in 1997. Despite being nominated for four major awards, it escaped the attention of most reviewers and readers. In 1998, it was re-published in paperback by a larger publisher, and went on to win the Harold D. Vursell Award from the American Academy of Arts and Letters. It also became a *New York Times Book Review* Notable Book and garnered a wide readership. Bahr's second novel, *The Year of Jubilo* (2000), also subtitled *A Novel of the Civil War*, is a kind of sequel to the first; together, they describe the brutal inhumanity of war and the damage it inflicts upon individuals and communities, during the actual fighting and in its aftermath.

For *World Authors 1995–2000*, Howard Bahr wrote: "Folks often ask me why I always write about the past, and why I have so much to say about Time in my writing. Time has always been of interest to me, for the reason that I have never been comfortable in it. One of my chief joys in writing is to live, spend time with, even vicariously, people who are at home in their own period.

"I was born in Meridian, Mississippi in 1946, and lived in my grandparents' home—which is to say I lived among relics of the past, amid art, music, radio, the whistles of steam engines, the sound of people passing on the brick sidewalk at night. When I was nine, my mother remarried, and I was whisked from the black-and-white world of my grandparents to the absurd rotogravure of the Suburban American Dream. I have not recovered, and do not expect to.

"In 1964, I enlisted in the Navy and served on old, gallant ships that were the last of their kind, in a war that was the last of *its* kind. In 1968, I went

Howard Bahr

to work on the railroad in the twilight years of that wondrous profession, and saw the last of that way of life. I went to the University of Mississippi just in time to learn under professors of the Old School: Southern men who smoked pipes and had been in war and walked behind mules, and who revered literature as a thing of grace and beauty, and who are all gone now, replaced by Harvard graduates who ride bicycles and speak in 'isms.' I was at Faulkner's home, Rowan Oak, in the days of Dr. James Webb, when we kept a bottle of whiskey in the desk drawer, and a .22 rifle in the closet, and cut a Christmas tree every year, and invited pretty co-eds to play the piano in the parlor. Now it is a museum without a heart. So it goes.

"So it goes, indeed. Time has outrun me all my days, and I thank God for the gift of writing. That God has made me steward of such a talent, however humble, is proof that He looks after His wayward children. With it, I can explore the universals of the human heart in the context of the past. With it, I can hear the steam engines again, and the throb of an Indian motorcycle, and breathe air that is rich with the smell of burning leaves in autumn, of lantana and fried chicken in summer. Where I go in my writing, it still rains on summer afternoons, and a 'bad boy' is one who smokes cigarettes behind the gym and steals the lunches of little wimps like myself. For this, and for all things, I am grateful."

While *Black Flower* has been scrupulously researched, several critics note that in its formal and psychological complexities, Bahr's novel transcends the historical fiction genre, or any other category. David Rushing wrote in the *Daily Mississippian* (April 30, 1997), "His work is no maudlin Southern romance, clichéd military adventure, or regurgitated history. In fact, except for the period about which it is written, putting the book in a category is difficult." Writing for the *New York Times Book Review* (August 2, 1998, on-line), Robert Wilson agreed, arguing that *Black Flower* distinguishes itself from familiar Civil War narratives, such as *The Red Badge of Courage* and the film *Glory*. "Bahr's novel is too eccentric and too uneven to support such comparisons," Wilson asserted. "And at moments it's almost too good to support them."

Several critics commented on the gritty realism of the battle scenes. Rushing noted that the details of the violence, while never gratuitous, are vivid and precise. "One can almost hear bloody Ares' chuckling amongst the carnage to mingle with the groans of the wounded," Rushing wrote. Reviewing the novel for *BookBrowser* (March 23, 1998, on-line), Harriet Klausner identified Bahr's graphic depictions of violence as a sign of his late-20th-century sensibility. Robert Wilson concurred, praising the story's "post-Vietnam ferocity," but adding the caveat that the characters' cynicism feels "anachronistic," as if "the remnants of the Army of Tennessee were wreathed in marijuana smoke at firebases in the Central Highlands [of Vietnam]." In spite of this minor reservation, Wilson argued that Bahr's insistence on revealing the ugly realities of war—rather than dressing them up in the trappings of "glory" and "honor"—makes *Black Flower* "a deeply moral book." "You might expect blood and guts in a Civil War novel, but here are the actual gray, ropy entrails, the smell of corpses lying in a field," Wilson wrote. "You might expect a disquisition on the chaos and futility of battle, but Bahr insists on its grotesque malignity." Bahr has said that he mined his own experiences in Vietnam to portray the surreal aspect of battle. "There is a mystical quality to the experience because it is so awful," he said in his interview with Mudge. "When Bushrod gets into battle, his 'other' takes over. Although I was never in really bad combat, whenever we'd get in ticklish situations, I found that to be true. It was like I was watching somebody else doing it. Only later did I realize, or remember, that it was me."

Perhaps appropriately, then, the battle is narrated from a distance—from the vantage point of a group of women and children, who watches from a nearby farm that has been requisitioned by Confederate officers as a makeshift field hospital. After Bushrod is wounded, he is brought there and tended by Anna Hereford, who then helps him find and bury his two best friends. On the smoky battlefield, scavengers strip the corpses of valuables, and a crazed man prays to the heavens that God will forgive the South. Though his emotions have been blunted by three years of war, Bushrod feels stirrings of attraction to Anna, and she begins to warily return his interest. A critic for *Kirkus Reviews* (February 1, 1997), as quoted on *Amazon.com*, called the novel a "bleakly effective and economical account of men and women caught up in a bestial conflict."

Bahr's second novel, *The Year of Jubilo* (2000), takes up in the time period in which *Black Flower* leaves off. Set in the summer of 1865, the "jubilant" year that was supposed to end the hostilities between North and South, the novel follows Gawain Harper as he arrives in his hometown of Cumberland, Mississippi, and experiences what reviewer Robert Morgan, in the *New York Times Book Review* (June 18, 2000, on-line), termed the "scary, sickening emptiness" of peace. Before the war, Harper was a schoolteacher. He reluctantly joined the Confederate cause at the insistence of his fiancée's father, Judge Rhea, who demanded that Harper help the South win the war or give up any thought of marrying his daughter, Morgan. When Harper arrives in Cumberland, Northern troops are everywhere, and the violence and hostilities of the war have become local. The Union commander in charge is too traumatized to maintain order, and real power lies in the hands of a white supremacist named "King" Solomon Gault, who hopes to provoke a new rebellion that will sweep through the South and drive out the Northern occupiers. Judge Rhea gives Harper a final task before he can marry Morgan: to seek vigilante justice by murdering King Solomon. Harper must deal with questions of honor, revenge, and responsibility as he strives to achieve love and redemption.

The Year of Jubilo is longer and more complicated than Bahr's first novel. While David Rushing described *Black Flower* as "episodic," Robert Morgan termed *The Year of Jubilo* "cinematic," and claimed that the story reads "more like collage than drama." In a review for *Booklist* (April 1, 2000), Margaret Flanagan argued that the form of the book reflects its content. "Surrealistic, almost dreamlike, sequences serve to underscore the madness inherent in a world spinning out of control and the ambivalence of a man desperately seeking a moral compass in the midst of anarchy and despair," she wrote. Identifying a unifying theme, Robert Morgan wrote that "Descriptions of weather in this story function as a kind of choral commentary, setting the tone for sections and scenes. Through the continuing drama of the weather Bahr creates a sense of the timeless beyond the devastation."

Critics have noted that the narrative's several strands are enlivened by a vivid cast of minor characters. Robert Morgan cited Bahr's gift for "creating mentally damaged and physically repellent characters who come alive in disturbing and finally endearing ways." By way of example, he described "Old Hundred-and-Eleven," a canny grave digger in the tradition of Shakespearean fools, named after the "three streaks of tobacco juice that perpetually run from the corners of his mouth and the middle of his lower lip to form three ones." A reviewer for *Kirkus Reviews*, as quoted on *Amazon.com*, admired Bahr's creations of Harry Stribling, "self-proclaimed 'philosopher' and ironical observer of the South's stubborn vision of its own 'chivalry,'" and the "imperious, passionate Morgan and Gawain's flinty Aunt Vassar—two of the strongest female characters in the whole range of historical fiction."

While nearly all its critics remarked on *The Year of Jubilo*'s depiction of sorrow, anarchy, and defeat, some also found in it a note of hope. Robert Morgan located this hope in Bahr's evocation of place and time, writing that Bahr's "affection for the greening countryside and town of Cumberland, the loving detail of forest and river, soil and graveyard, are the true moral and poetry of this war story, showing that the life of a place transcends any one ruin or atrocity."

Bahr told Jonathan Baggs for the *Decatur Daily* (May 7, 2000, on-line) that *The Year of Jubilo* may be his last Civil War novel. He is working on a story set in 1939 in New Orleans, Louisiana, and his hometown of Meridian, Mississippi. "At last I can have characters talk on the telephone and smoke cigarettes and listen to the radio," Bahr said.

—M. A. H.

SUGGESTED READING: *Booklist* p1441 Apr. 1, 2000; *BookBrowser* (on-line) Mar. 23, 1998; *BookPage* (on-line) Apr. 1998; *Daily Mississippian* (on-line) Apr. 30, 1997; *Decatur Daily* (on-line) May 7, 2000; *New York Times Book Review* (on-line) Aug. 2, 1998, June 18, 2000

SELECTED BOOKS: *Black Flower: A Novel of the Civil War*, 1997; *The Year of Jubilo: A Novel of the Civil War*, 2000

Bail, Murray

Sep. 22, 1941– Novelist; short-story writer

Since publishing his first short-story collection in the mid-1970s, Murray Bail has been an innovator of the Australian literary tradition. According to Bruce King for *World Literature Today* (Autumn 1988), "Bail is part of the movement of the early 1970s . . . that transformed Australian fiction from dreary local realism to hip metafiction and brief, understated vignettes of contemporary urban life." More recently John Sutherland for the *New York Times* (November 14, 1999, on-line) called him one of three "indisputably world-class Australian novelists currently practicing." Often compared to the experimental Australian writers Peter Carey and Frank Moorhouse, Bail is known for his distinctive style, which emphasizes imaginative language and form over character and plot development. With the publication of *Contemporary Portraits and Other Stories*, in 1975, Bail began breaking new ground in the realm of the modern short story, a task that culminated when he edited *The Faber Book of Contemporary Short Stories* (1988). In this collection he showcased work from Australia's

Anthony Browell/Courtesy of Farrar, Straus and Giroux
Murray Bail

most original writers and, in the process, updated the country's short-fiction canon. In addition to short-story collections, Bail has published novels that have been praised for their virtuosity and self-consciously Australian themes, including *Homesickness* (1980), *Holden's Performance* (1987), and *Eucalyptus* (1998). In 1999 Bail was honored with the Miles Franklin Award for Australian literature and the Commonwealth Writers Prize. Bail, who is also an art critic, is the author of a 1981 biography of the abstract painter Ian Fairweather and editor of a 1994 collection of the painter's essays, entitled *Fairweather*.

Born on September 22, 1941 in the city of Adelaide, located in the territory of South Australia, Murray Bail later remembered his hometown in the short story "Healing," published in the *New Yorker* (April 16, 1979). Through the story's first-person narrative, Bail described childhood life in the town: "In Adelaide, a flat city, 'the city of churches,' we all went around on bikes." He later told Constance Casey for the *Washington Post* (October 2, 1981) that Adelaide was a dull place to grow up: "Nothing dangerous ever came out of Adelaide except my mother." In 1968, at age 27, Bail left Australia for India, where he lived for two years. From 1970 to 1974, he traveled and lived throughout Great Britain and Europe. During this time, Bail developed his interests in writing and art. "I have a taste for Latin American, Italian and French writers," he told Casey. "Anglo-Saxon ways of thinking are what I'm against at the moment." Soon after returning to Australia, Bail began publishing his fiction. In 1976 he became a trustee for the Australian National Gallery in the capital city of Canberra, a position he retained until 1981.

In his first publication, *Contemporary Portraits and Other Stories* (1976), Bail established himself as a writer eager to find new ways of depicting reality. (*Contemporary Portraits and Other Stories* was re-published in 1986 under the title *The Drover's Wife and Other Stories*. In 2002 it was published in the U.S. for the first time as *Camouflage: Stories*.) As Randall Stevenson noted for the *Times Literary Supplement* (June 19, 1987), "Several of the . . . stories contrast or examine pictorial, linguistic, or other forms of portraiture, questioning how 'Words. These marks on paper and so on' can 'attempt an imitation' of living being and reality." For example, in the opening story, "Heubler," a photographer considers ways to document the existence of every living person. In "The Drover's Wife," a jilted husband examines a well-known painting depicting the stolid country wife of a sheep driver, or "drover," by the Australian artist Russell Drysdale, and calmly asserts that its subject is his own runaway wife. In these and other stories, Bail demonstrates his interest in the different means of representing reality.

In the *Times Literary Supplement* (April 9, 1976) John Sutherland, who called Bail's stories "elegant" and "cool and clever," noted that, although Bail has spent part of his writing life abroad, "A couple of pieces in *Contemporary Portraits* may, however, be seen as peculiarly Australian." Such stories include "Camouflage," in which a docile piano tuner is drafted into the Australian Army in 1943 and finds a sense of creating "art" in the fulfillment of his duties. In "The Silence," a reclusive rabbit catcher—affected by the profound silence of the country's outback—avoids conversation with the truck driver who regularly picks up his catch. Finally, in "Life of the Party," a suburbanite hides in a tree house in his backyard, watching the interactions of his neighbors, who have arrived expecting a barbecue. Randall Stevenson credited Bail's collection for showing "a lively inventiveness in finding new forms," adding, "When Bail does seem to fall back into the old [Australian] fascination with wilderness and loneliness, it is with a new emphasis."

In 1980 Bail published his first novel, *Homesickness*, which Blake Morrison for the London *Observer* (August 24, 1980) called a "bizarre, playful and at times hilarious send-up of globetrotting, a postmodernist version of the Grand Tour." In this offbeat satire, Bail follows 13 Australians on a "trip-of-a-lifetime" to Africa, London, Ecuador, New York, and Moscow, poking fun at the popularity of modern "package" tours and the state of late-20th-century tourism, and exploring questions of cultural difference and national identity. The group visits a series of outrageous tour sites, such as a Museum of Legs in Ecuador and an Institution of Marriage in New York (featuring married sex shows and a preserved slice of Queen Victoria's wedding cake); at Moscow's Lenin Mausoleum, the travelers are locked inside the tomb and asked to verify the authenticity of the corpse. Peter Lewis for the *Times Literary Supplement* (September 19, 1980) noted: "The journey, like the novel, is long, bizarre, and Pynchonesque [a reference to the American novelist Thomas Pynchon]. The opening is realistic enough but the illusion of realism soon proves to be deceptive. Wherever the party go—and they are always going to museums—nothing is quite as they, or the reader, expect."

Homesickness was widely praised as a refreshing example of new Australian fiction, with Lewis comparing it to James Joyce's *Ulysses* "in its use of half-concealed motifs, submerged patterns, displays of erudition, and verbal high-jinks." However, while Lewis applauded the book's inventiveness, he also noted "a serious drawback too, in that the situations become more important than the thirteen main characters. Where they are and what they encounter take precedence over what they are themselves." John Sutherland, writing for the *New York Times* (November 14, 1999, on-line), placed Bail's novel in the context of the Australian oral storytelling tradition—which favors momentum and inventiveness—and concluded that Bail's "indifference to plot or character . . . concentrates the reader's attention on the novel's style." Although Sutherland credited Bail's writing for offering "numerous pleasures to be picked up by the connoisseur of smart writing," he called it "an acquired taste" for many readers. *Homesickness* earned Bail the 1980 National Book Council Award for Australian literature and *The Age* Book of the Year Award, which he shared with the novelist David Ireland for *Woman of the Future*.

Bail published his second novel, *Holden's Performance*, in 1987. Here, Bail continued his exploration of his home country; as Valentine Cunningham wrote for the London *Observer* (October 18, 1987), in the novel he tried to "arm-wrestle the bulk of modern Australia into pattern and significance." The epic story follows four stages of Holden Shadbolt's life, from his birth in Adelaide in the early 1930s, through his career as a bouncer and later a government bodyguard, to his eventual departure from Australia for the U.S. in the mid-1960s. Holden encounters larger-than-life characters, a group that Sophie Ratcliffe for the London *Times* (January 6, 2001) called "a cast of perverts and political shysters." Yet, despite the litany of colorful characters, according to Ratcliffe, "the satirical plays on geography and identity really steal the show." Bail used visual snapshots and catalogued experience to document the history of Australian popular culture and the Americanization of the country. Of this technique, Cunningham concluded: "Bail's prose scarcely leaves off pumping stylistic iron for a moment's breather. But still the clotted magnificence of this chortling midden of ratbags, pervs and wastrels does keep you reading." For *Holden's Performance*, Bail won the 1988 Victorian Premier's Vance Palmer Prize for fiction from the Australian state of Victoria.

Following the success of these novels, Bail tackled several different projects. He edited *The Faber Book of Contemporary Short Stories* and published *Longhand: A Writer's Notebook* (1989), in which he offered insights into his writing process and guidance to aspiring authors.

In 1998 Bail published his greatest critical success to date, *Eucalyptus*, a novel that a reviewer for the *Economist* (May 13, 2000) called "part fairy-tale, part catalogue, part love story, wholly original." Named for Australia's representative tree, the eucalyptus, or gum tree, Bail's novel delivers stories within stories, evocative of folklore; layered within these tales, he inserts scientific descriptions of hundreds of varieties of eucalyptus trees. The book's overarching plot reads like myth: A man named Holland moves with his young daughter, Ellen, to a remote property in the Australian territory of New South Wales. There, he blankets his lands with gum trees, planting every variety he can find and developing an extensive collection of obscure species. Through the years Holland's hobby becomes an obsession—so much so that when his daughter, a famed beauty, approaches an age to marry, he decides that he will only give her hand to a suitor who can identify every eucalyptus species on his property. After many men try and fail, a eucalyptus specialist, Mr. Cave, appears and effortlessly passes the test. Meanwhile, Ellen discovers a second man lying in one of her father's fields and becomes enchanted with his storytelling gifts.

Eucalyptus earned widespread critical acclaim. Michael Hulse for the *Spectator* (August 1, 1998) declared it a "masterpiece" and Erica Wagner for the London *Times* (June 25, 1998) called it "a strange, beautiful, compelling novel." Wagner continued: "Bail's language, charming, inventive, direct, marks his book out as a true original. His artfulness always avoids slipping into the arch, always saved by a dry humour that somehow echoes the tree-spiked, lonely landscape." Some critics lamented that the novel lacked such traditional elements of fiction as character development and a linear plot. Most reviewers, however, found that Blair's inventiveness carried the work. As Jack Sullivan wrote for the *Washington Post* (November 22, 1998), "Part of [the book's] charm is its style, the quirky sentences that rarely go where we expect, the sinister Arthur Machenesque [a reference to the British fantasy writer Arthur Machen] beauty of the landscape descriptions, the meandering stories that fail to deliver their expected allegories, that never really end but instead begin others." The novel earned Bail numerous literary prizes in 1999, including the Vance Palmer Prize for fiction, the Association for Studies of Australian Literature Gold Medal for literature, the Miles Franklin Literary Award, and the Commonwealth Writers Prize. In the announcement of the last award, as quoted in the *Dominion* (May 1, 1999), Professor Vincent O'Sullivan of Melbourne's Victoria University called *Eucalyptus* "a work of deeply imaginative originality that takes the reader into the domain of fable, yarn-spinning, and myth-making with wisdom, good humour, and impressive technical deftness. It is a story about the human need to keep hearing stories; about the difference between mere naming and true knowing. This is a highly entertaining and sophisticated piece of contemporary fiction."

Bail married Margaret Wordsworth in 1965; the couple later divorced. A later marriage to the Australian novelist Helen Garner ended in the late 1990s. Bail currently resides in Sydney.

—K. D.

SUGGESTED READING: *Economist* p14 May 13, 2000, Dec. 1, 2001; *Heat* IX p75 1998; London *Observer* p26 Aug. 24, 1980, p27 Oct. 18, 1987; (London) *Times* p43 June 25, 1998; *New York Times* (on-line) Nov. 14, 1999; *Times Literary Supplement* p445 Apr. 9, 1976, p1044 Sep. 19, 1980, p668 June 19, 1987, p19 July 3, 1998; *Washington Post Book World* p5 Nov. 22, 1998; *World Literature Today* p724 Autumn 1988, p233 Winter 2000

SELECTED BOOKS: short-story collections— *Contemporary Portraits and Other Stories*, 1975 (re-published as *The Drover's Wife and Other Stories*, 1985, and *Camouflage: Stories*, 2002); novels—*Homesickness*, 1980; *Holden's Performance*, 1987, *Eucalyptus*, 1998; nonfiction—*Ian Fairweather*, 1981, *Longhand: A Writer's Notebook*, 1989, *Fairweather*, 1994; as editor—*The Faber Book of Contemporary Short Stories*, 1988

John Hubbard/HarperCollins Publishers

Balakian, Peter

June 13, 1951– Poet; memoirist; critic

The American writer Peter Balakian, learning at the age of 23 about the Armenian genocide of 1915, realized that his happy childhood had been set within the cloud of his family's memory of that ghastly event. In his volumes of poetry, *Father Fisheye* (1979), *Sad Days of Light* (1983), *Reply from Wilderness Island* (1988), *Dyer's Thistle* (1996), and *June-Tree: New and Selected Poems, 1974-2000* (2001), he has evoked the era of the Turkish slaughter of the Armenians. His memoir *Black Dog of Fate* (1997) is a prize-winning hybrid of historical documents and reminiscences, particularly of how the strange tales told by his elders permeated his otherwise normal American childhood and aroused his curiosity about "the old country." A literary critic, Balakian also published *Theodore Roethke's Far Fields: The Evolution of His Poetry*, in 1989.

Peter Balakian was born on June 13, 1951 in Teaneck, New Jersey, to Arax Aroosian and Gerard Balakian. His father was a physician; his mother stayed at home to raise her four children. The family lived in prosperous circumstances, surrounded by relatives. "Every Sunday it's the same. Our extended Armenian family sitting around the dining room table in winter or out on the patio in summer for a full afternoon and more, and my grandmother quietly watching," Balakian wrote in *Black Dog of Fate*. At one point when Balakian was a child, his mother explained to him that his grandmother's pipe smoking stemmed from a custom of "the old country," leading Balakian to wonder where this "old country" was: "Since there was no picture of the old country in our house and since I didn't have one etched in my mind, the old country came to mean my grandmother," he wrote. "Whatever it was, she was. Whatever she was, it was." In spite of his family's connection to another place, on the surface Balakian's world was, as he wrote in the *Chronicle of Higher Education* (June 12, 1998), an "all-American" one. "My father, the physician, in his Brooks Brothers suits, leaving the house with his medical bag each morning. My mother, with her B.A. in chemistry, staying home—like a good mom of the '50s—to hover over her four children and whisk them to their Cub Scout, Brownie, and Little League events in her '57 lavender- and-white Chevy station wagon. My growing up was defined by rock 'n' roll, the New York Yankees and Knicks, friends and girlfriends, teenage pranks, and above all, high-school sports (I was captain of three varsity teams)."

Balakian was educated at Bucknell University, in Lewisburg, Pennsylvania, where he received his B.A. in 1973; New York University in New York City, where he was awarded an M.A. in 1975; and

Brown University in Providence, Rhode Island, where he earned a Ph.D. in 1980. Originally intending to become a painter, he had studied art history before deciding to become a writer; he went on to specialize in history, earning his doctorate in American civilization. He taught at the Dwight-Englewood School from 1974 to 1976. Meanwhile, from 1973 to 1979, he taught at Bucknell, in the writing department of the Pennsylvania Governors School for the Arts—a department he eventually chaired. He went to teach at Colgate University, in Hamilton, New York, in 1980 and became Donald M. and Constance H. Rebar Professor of the Humanities in the English department.

Balakian published his first poetry collection, *Father Fisheye*, in 1980. In collaboration with John Wheatcroft, he came out with *Declaring Generations*, another book of poetry, in 1982. In *Sad Days of Light*, his 1983 collection, Balakian—who had begun to come to terms with the Armenian genocide of 1915 only in his 20s—dealt with that tragic episode, which was the source of his family's secret sorrow. His grandmother, of whom he was so fond, had endured the murder of her first husband and had been driven out of Turkey with her two small daughters to perish in the Syrian desert. While the three of them survived, Balakian's grandmother lost her parents and all of her other relatives.

Robert Peters, reviewing *Sad Days of Light* for *Library Journal* (March 15, 1983), remarked that the best poems in the book were "collages commemorating the travels of Armenian relatives from Turkey to the U.S. . . . [H]e has something to say and celebrate." The *Christian Science Monitor* (August 12, 1983) reviewer, Steven Ratiner, called Balakian a poet "with an empowering vision that elevates personal experience to something equally vital to the distant reader." He noted that Balakian "portrays the history of the Armenian genocide of 1915 and the subsequent scattering of an entire people. His grandmother, a survivor of the diaspora, is a central figure in these poems. . . . If this book were political diatribe, it would never have the power to move us as it does."

About *Reply from Wilderness Island*, Balakian's 1988 poetry collection, Ben Howard noted in *Poetry* (September 1989) that Balakian's poems are dominated by images of loss. Balakian frequently writes about the loss of his father, "whose ghost frequents the poems. . . . A second, more general loss is that of Balakian's Armenian heritage, which survives in memory, or in the stories of uncles and aunts, or in images." Howard concluded that the biggest loss may be that of "a sense of oneness with the natural world." While he thought that Balakian had produced a "poetry of considerable pathos," he found that there were some "banal descriptions" in the volume. Nevertheless, "at its strongest," Balakian's poetry expressed his sense of loss "not in figures of speech but in densities of style."

Theodore Roethke's Far Fields: The Evolution of His Poetry is a work of criticism. The book is intended as a general introduction to Roethke's poetry rather than as a promulgation of a theory about the work of the American poet. B. Galvin, the *Choice* (November 1989) reviewer, praised Balakian's "relying on intelligent readings of the poems themselves rather than on previous interpretations or extraneous schematics." Galvin found *Far Fields* to be "a clear, refreshingly readable" book and thought Balakian "particularly good in his uncovering of William Carlos Williams's influence on Roethke and in his readings of the difficult 'Lost Son' poems." For Ronald A. Sharp, the critic for *American Literature* (June 1990), however, Balakian "sometimes errs . . . , settling for a mode of commentary that occasionally seems too miscellaneous." He concluded that precisely "because so many of his observations about both particular poems and larger patterns are so compelling, one finds the rather modest conceptual frame of the book, and the extraordinary brevity of many of his discussions of particular poems, a bit disappointing."

In *Dyer's Thistle*, Balakian's 1996 volume of poetry, he shows himself more deeply enmeshed in contemplation of the tragic Armenian genocide. "*Dyer's Thistle* deftly establishes connections between the self constituted by American pop culture and the war in Vietnam, on the one hand," John Naughton observed in *World Literature Today* (Winter 1997), "and the self which is the bearer of a 3,000-year-old Near Eastern culture that has been largely exterminated on the other. The familial memories of massacre and death permeate the poet's perception of the world and engender a genuine compassion as well as the uneasy awareness that 'there is no reign that executes / justice and judgment' anywhere in the world."

Rehabilitation and reconciliation were two of the goals Balakian set for himself in *Black Dog of Fate*, his 1997 memoir. The rehabilitation aspect involved bringing back to public consciousness the history of the Armenian genocide of 1915; the reconciliation entailed integrating the story of Balakian's happy American youth with the stories of his older relatives, who were survivors of that massacre and whose collective past hung like a cloud over his family. In *Black Dog of Fate*, termed "richly imagined and carefully documented" by Joyce Carol Oates in the *New Yorker* (March 23, 1998), Balakian not only told his family's story but supplemented it with documents from his grandmother's lawsuit against the Turkish government, filed after she had reached a safe haven in the United States. He also included references to such sources as *Ambassador Morgenthau's Story*, a 1918 memoir by an American ambassador to Turkey, Henry Morganthau, who detailed the Turkish killing of over one million Armenians. "I needed to tell a family story that came to haunt me as an adult," Balakian explained to Dinitia Smith during an interview for the *New York Times* (August 19, 1997), "to chart the affirmative, powerful and beautiful parts of my growing up and . . . this enormous, major moral event of the 20th century."

Balakian elaborated on that explanation in an article he wrote for the *Chronicle of Higher Education* (June 12, 1998), in which he noted that the "aromas of my mother's marvelous Armenian cooking" and the "Oriental carpets, fine porcelain, strange Near Eastern artifacts" and other accouterments of Armenian culture that lurked behind the bland American façade of their suburban home only masked the family's secret. "I came to understand that historical trauma is transmitted complexly across generations," he wrote. "The genocide had shaped our family, as it did every Armenian family of the 20th century, and no matter how hard my grandmother, aunts, and parents tried to repress this dark past, they couldn't. The trauma and its aftermath leaked through the sunny light of suburbia, expressing itself in an encoded way. In writing *Black Dog of Fate*, I finally began to decode those messages that I had received as a boy." He told Smith that the "Armenian holocaust deserves to take its rightful moral place in history. . . . For a generation for whom there could be no justice, the pain is compounded by the evil of denial."

The *Publishers Weekly* (April 7, 1997) reviewer found Balakian successful: by "spending Friday afternoons as a boy with his oddly magical grandmother, helping her bake . . . he felt he had 'access to some other world . . . something ancient, something connected to earth and words and blood and sky.' This connection, particularly to words, is a notion that Balakian pursues as only a word-loving poet can. The mystical tales and dreams of his grandmother transform over time into body counts, government documents, eyewitness reports quoted at length and family narratives at last given to the curious Balakian. In the book's crowning structural feat, they become the property of Balakian himself. At last the horrid story is in the words of the poet, and, in this quarter, the genocide becomes real and permanent."

The reviewer for *Choice* (December 1997) agreed, as did many other reviewers, that in *Black Dog of Fate* "Balakian deftly weaves personal accounts, brief excerpts of history and studies of survivor trauma. . . . This rare book is both lyrically evocative and informative in alternating passages that are seamlessly connected." *Black Dog of Fate* was included in the best books of the year lists of the *New York Times* and the *Los Angeles Times*. Balakian was given the PEN/Martha Albrand Award for the Art of the Memoir in 1998.

June-Tree: New and Selected Poems 1974-2000, an omnibus of Balakian's poetry was published in 2001. Balakian not only added new poems to his previous work but revised some of the older ones as well. "I'm a compulsive reviser," Balakian told Laura T. Ryan in an interview in the *Post- Standard* (April 5, 2001). "If I can look at a poem, and there's a little bit more that can be done there, I'll continue to tinker with it. I won't, if it alters its essential meaning or its core."

The Armenian tragedy is frequently present in Balakian's poetic consciousness. In "Ellis Island," Balakian writes, "Here is everything you'll ever need: / hemp-cords, curry-combs, jade and musk, / a porcelain cup blown into the desert / stockings that walked to Syria in 1915. /. . . . The weed and algae are floating like a bed, / and the bloodless gulls / whose breaths would stink to all of us / if we could kiss them on the beaks / are gnawing on the dead." The *Publishers Weekly* (February 19, 2001) reviewer noted that Balakian had been dealing with the Armenian genocide for a long time and that some "of his best poems on the subject ('The History of Armenia'; 'The Claim') appeared early on in his poetic career, and their reappearance after *Black Dog* should win them new readers." Susan Shapiro observed in the *New York Times Book Review* (April 15, 2001) that "*June-Tree* is political yet idiosyncratic" as well as "intense and soulful." She singled out "The Claim," the "longest and most moving poem," an application for reparations, as an example of how Balakian "manages to avoid generalities and abstract rage." The poem ends, "The deportation and the fiendish steps taken / against the Armenians in general being well / known by the civilized world, I do not mention / other evidences concerning this matter / Only / I assert that . . . / I am human herewith affidavit."

Balakian has continued to fight for the rightful place in history of the Turkish massacre of Armenians. He told Laura T. Ryan, "I think my exploration of the Armenian genocide, the transmission of trauma across generations . . . the American Revolutionary War, the Holocaust, World War II, Vietnam, Korea—all of these events get into my work in different angles, shapes and forms. . . . The muse of history is a notion I believe in." In 2003 Balakian edited a new edition of *Ambassador Morgenthau's Story*.

—S.Y.

SUGGESTED READING: *American Book Review* p15 Aug. 1989; *American Literature* p353 June 1990; *Choice* p482 Nov. 1989, p632 Dec. 1997; *Christian Science Monitor* B p7 Aug.12, 1983; *Chronicle of Higher Education* B p6+ June 12, 1998; *Library Journal* p587 Mar. 15, 1983, p80 Feb. 1, 1996; *New York Times* C p9 Aug. 19, 1997; *New York Times Book Review* p22 Apr. 15, 2001; *New Yorker* p94+ Mar. 23, 1998; *Poetry* p349 Sep. 1989; *Post-Standard* D p1 Apr. 5, 2001; *Publishers Weekly* p80 Apr. 7, 1997; *World Literature Today* p164+ Winter 1997

SELECTED BOOKS: poetry—*Father Fisheye*, 1979; *Declaring Generations* (with J. Wheatcroft), 1982; *Sad Days of Light*, 1983; *Reply from Wilderness Island*, 1988; *Dyer's Thistle*, 1996; *June-Tree: New and Selected Poems, 1974-2000*, 2001; nonfiction—*Theodore Roethke's Far Fields: The Evolution of His Poetry*, 1989; memoir: *Black Dog of Fate*, 1997; as translator—*Bloody News From My Friend: Poems By Siamanto* (with N. Yaghlian), 1996

Jerry Bauer/Courtesy of Random House of Canada

Baldwin, Shauna Singh

1963(?)– Short-story writer; novelist; essayist

A Canadian-born Sikh who was raised in India and now lives in Milwaukee with her Irish-American husband, Shauna Singh Baldwin has declared that she writes for a "hybrid, global audience—in short, for all of us who can read," as quoted from an essay she wrote for *Boldtype*, an on-line literary magazine published by Random House on its Web site. Baldwin, who is also an Internet e-commerce consultant and for a time produced public-radio programs, published stories in American, Canadian, and Indian small magazines before co-writing (with Marilyn Levine) her first book, *A Foreign Visitor's Survival Guide to America* (1992). Her collection of short fiction, *English Lessons and Other Stories* (1996), includes the story "Satya," which won a literary prize and was expanded by the author into a novel, *What the Body Remembers* (1999), about the cultural and social changes that accompanied the partitioning of India and Pakistan in 1947, as seen primarily through the eyes of two Sikh women.

Shauna Singh Baldwin was born into a Sikh family in Montreal, Canada, where she grew up speaking French and English; at the age of seven, she moved with her parents to India. On the occasion of her birth, her parents reportedly received congratulatory telegrams expressing the hope that their next child would be a boy. "So my mother named me Shanaaz," Baldwin told Suzanne Methot for *Quill and Quire*, as reprinted on the *Indigo.ca* Web site, "a Muslim name that means 'That of which emperors are proud.' It was her way of saying, 'Damn you all.'" It was when Shanaaz—later known as Shauna—was eleven years old that she harbored her first thoughts of being a writer. In Baldwin's keynote speech delivered to the Great Lake Writers' Conference in June 1998, and published on the *Sawnet* (South Asian Women's Network) Web site, she recalled that she had kept a writer's journal "sporadically through my teens converting personal angst, pain, and fun times to text," and that she had written poetry—"who doesn't?"—through her years at school and in college. But, she added, "as I grew older, the cacophony of the world grew ever louder and soon it seemed all the things that needed to be said were being said by others . . . I now know from other writers that even my experience in this is not unique. But at the time, I fell silent like a child who stops singing because the singers on the radio are so much better. The challenge of the adult writer is to recover that child who was so confident, ask it what it still needs to say, and find out what shape to give its thoughts that will hold a reader's attention." At the age of 18, after attending local schools in India, Baldwin returned to North America to enroll in an MBA program at the University of Wisconsin in Milwaukee. Even before her first books were published, her short stories appeared in a variety of small magazines, including *Fireweed* and *McGill St.* in Canada, *Manushi* in India, and *Calyx*, *Rosebud*, and *India Currents* in the United States. She worked as an independent public-radio producer from 1991 to 1994 and produced a show entitled "Sunno! The East Indian American Radio Show where you don't have to be East-Indian to listen." She later became a consultant to Internet companies, specializing in the area of e-commerce.

Baldwin's first book, *A Foreign Visitor's Survival Guide to America* (1992), co-authored with Marilyn Levine, was published by John Muir Press. This resource book for immigrants demystified American folkways and explained the practical difficulties involved in such transactions as renting an apartment or buying a car. Discussing the evolution of the book in her speech at the Great Lakes conference, Baldwin said that she and her co-author began "from an artless confidence that we had something to say, that there was a gap in the universe where this book should be, and that we were the ones who had both the lived experience and the research capability to do it." The book, she has said, was written with no specific immigrant community in mind, with the assumption that "economic necessity, more than national origin, shapes people's experience of the global community," in the words of Christopher Wiebe, in an article for *Edmonton Journal.com* (October 24, 1999).

Four years later, Singh's first story collection, *English Lessons and Other Stories* (1996), was published by Goose Lane Editions in Fredericton, New Brunswick, Canada. The book went into a third printing in September 1999, after having sold between five and six thousand copies, which Goose Lane's editorial director Laurel Boone described as "wonderfully well for a first book of stories by an unknown writer," as reported by Gordon Morash for *Edmonton Journal.com* (October 24, 1999). *English Lessons and Other Stories* presented narratives of Indian women trying to establish visibility and identity in, variously, India, Canada, and the U.S. Among the themes explored in the collection are mother-daughter relationships, as in "Simran" and "Toronto 1984"; the loneliness of immigrants dying in a foreign land, as in "Jassie"; and the conflicting demands of modern and traditional culture on young women, in such stories as "Devika" and "Montreal 1962." The longest story in the collection, and one of the most critically acclaimed, is "Family Ties," a tale narrated by a ten-year-old girl who learns some 20 years afterwards of the traumatic 1947 partitioning of India and Pakistan and her father's experiences during that period. Reviewing the collection for *India West* (August 15, 1996), as republished on the *Sawnet* Web site, Susan Chacko wrote that "Baldwin has a real gift for descriptive writing, and the stories often dwell sensuously on sensations, smells, and sounds. A simple description of washing becomes a metaphor for cultural strength:

> I placed each turban in turn on the bubbly surface and watched them grow dark and heavy, sinking slowly, softly into the warmth. When there were no more left beside me, I leaned close and reached in, working each one in a rhythm bone-deep, as my mother and hers must have done before me, that their men might face the world proud. I drained the tub and new colors swelled—deep red, dark black mud, rust, orange, soft purple, and jade green."

In her review of *English Lessons and Other Stories* for the literary magazine *India-Star* (on-line), Monika Fludernik, who teaches post-colonialist literature at the University of Freiburg, Germany, lauded this "wonderful new collection of stories about Indian women trying to come to grips with their situation of cultural displacement in North America. The stories are written in subtle prose, employing a variety of narrative strategies, some of them quite unusual. The tone is that of brisk unsentimental survival, sometimes bordering on (though not quite descending into) tragedy. Much of the writing is witty."

In 1998 Baldwin won considerable attention for another of her short stories. "Satya" won the prestigious Canadian Literary Award for 1998, which is sponsored by the magazine *Saturday Night*, the Canada Council, and the Canadian Broadcasting Corporation and carries with it $10,000 in prize money. Although "Satya" was not included in *English Lessons and Other Stories*, as the winner of the award, it was published in *Saturday Night* (June 1998). Goose Lane later anthologized "Satya" in *Emergent Voices: CBC Literary Award Stories 1979–1999* (1999), a collection edited by Robert Weaver.

Several years after the publication of *English Lessons*, Baldwin was quoted in the on-line version of the *Hindu* newspaper (March 7, 1999) as saying: "I'm very minimalistic in my writing. . . . Short stories to me are like windows, the reader has to work much harder whereas in a novel everything is spelt [sic] out." And yet her next writing project was *What the Body Remembers*, a novel that had its origins in the "Satya" story and was published by Alfred A. Knopf in 1999. Writing a novel proved to be a challenging enterprise for Baldwin, who was further quoted in *Hindu* (on-line): "I'm a very physical person and all of a sudden to sit in your room is too much. Some short stories might take a week or three weeks to finish but with a novel it's different. It's like a baby and you're sitting there to feed it [in] the morning and clean up at night. But it's a lovely process." Singh, who has continued to work as an e-commerce consultant in addition to writing, credits the Internet for facilitating the research and development of her novel. As she wrote in her essay on the book's origins for *Boldtype*, "To write a book with Sikh characters, you can't just go down to your corner library and check out books. Interlibrary loan brought me books from all over the world. It would have taken me about ten to twelve years to write this novel without the Internet. Not only are library catalogs and research sources on-line, there are listservs where I made friends and interviewed people. When I traveled to Pakistan to research the setting of *What the Body Remembers*, cyberfriends smoothed the way." In the on-line catalogue included on the Random House Web site, her publisher described *What the Body Remembers* as "deeply imbued with the languages, customs, and layered history of colonial India," and as a book that "tells the story of the Partition [the 1947 division of British India into the nations of India and Pakistan] for the first time from the Sikh women's point of view." In her manuscript, Baldwin purposefully neglected to include a glossary or even italics for the Punjabi words her characters sometimes used because she felt "these break the spell of the story," as she wrote for *Boldtype*.

The epic novel begins and ends with the birth of a child who is angry that she has once again been reincarnated as a girl. The story opens in Rawalpindi, in India's Punjab state, in 1937, during the final years of British colonial rule. Because his wife, Satya, has not produced any children for him, Sardarj, a wealthy Sikh, takes for his second wife a sixteen-year-old girl, Roop, whose mother died in childbirth and whose father is heavily in debt, and thus is elated by the prospect of her marriage. Baldwin creates complex characters and renders them with impartiality. "Indian men treat women harshly in this novel, but women at times do no better," Patricia O'Connell wrote in her review for the *San Diego Union-Tribune* (October 31, 1999, on-line), noting that Baldwin equitably credited British colonialism for its occasional progressive reforms, such as raising the legal marriage age. Christopher

Wiebe wrote, "While researching for the novel [Baldwin] realized she needed to 'set aside' [in her words] the assumptions of Western feminism, which recognized only the injustice of male privilege, and not the socioeconomic conditions that held it in place." He quoted Baldwin as saying, "Before, I didn't understand the economic reasons for polygamy. But now I see that it was a better alternative to divorce, which would have meant abandonment and destitution for Satya. . . . Sons become the only way for women to assert their status and provide for their old age." "*What the Body Remembers* is a very feminist book if you define feminism as the radical notion that a woman is a person," Baldwin wrote in her essay for *Boldtype*, adding, "It comments on woman to woman power relations, surrogate motherhood, and the two strains of feminism, strident and persuasive, that we have in operation today. Nevertheless, the men in this novel are also trapped in their gender, religions, times, and cultures too—as we all are in every time and culture; there is nothing new in the universe."

Reviews for *What the Body Remembers* were favorable. The author Amit Chaudhuri, writing in Canada's *National Post* (September 25, 1999, on-line), called Baldwin's novel an "impressive debut" and remarked, "The last chapters about the actual upheaval of India's partition are admirably controlled and manage to avoid the luridness of Hollywood—probably because Baldwin . . . is unobtrusively but deeply conscious of the fact that the trajectories of lives, with or without such upheavals, are always cruel, unexpected, and shocking. This is a novel whose many themes and characters have been orchestrated, for the most part, with great confidence and without sacrificing complexity." Elizabeth Buchan wrote in the London *Times* (September 25, 1999) that in the novel, "The individual stories and complex religious and philosophical divisions are woven into the larger picture with supreme confidence and a poetic intensity. The characters shimmer with life, their predicaments grab the reader by the throat, their fate has the reader on the edge of the seat, their individual psychological journeys are instantly recognizable." She concluded, "This book is an enthralling read." In Ron Carlson's appraisal for the *New York Times Book Review* (November 21, 1999), he wrote, "Three major themes converge in the book: the division of India, the sorrows of patriarchy, and a woman's role in the emerging nation-state. Along the way we are offered a sumptuous tour of that rich and poor and calm and chaotic country, including the manifold rituals of dressing, marital customs, manners, mores, foods of all sorts and other exotica of the sectarian Indian culture." While he criticized the way in which, in certain parts, characters were too close to their "representative type, serving the [book's] theme a little too neatly," he also added that "with her sharp focus on women in such turmoil, Baldwin offers us a moving and engaging look at 20th-century India's most troubled years."

In the keynote speech she delivered to the Great Lakes Writers' Conference in June 1998, responding to her own question, "For whom do you write?," Baldwin said: "I'm a hybrid of three cultures, Indian, Canadian, and American and I write from the perspective of all three. Today my answer is: I write for the people I love . . . for people interested in the process of becoming human, the ways in which we live, the influence of history, philosophy, culture, tradition, and memory on our sense of self." During their interview, she told Suzanne Methot, "I hate purity with a passion. I refuse purity. I'm pure blood, but my religion is a hybrid—it takes from the Hindu and the Muslim faiths. I love the hybrid world. I take what I like and I chuck the rest. Use what I can use. I'm reinventing myself every day."

Baldwin and Bisakha Sen, an economist on the faculty of the University of Central Florida, have issued a list of 22 "good resolutions" for the "South-Asian woman," published on the *Sawnet* Web site, beginning with "I resolve not to apologize for existing" and "I resolve not to apologize to men (unless I have really done something wrong)." Other resolutions urged women to assert their autonomy by declaring that they have a value independent of their husbands or children. In her 1998 speech at the Great Lakes Writers' Conference Baldwin said, "I'm still developing as a writer, letting the process teach me empathy as I venture deeper into the minds and hearts of selves I might have been if I wasn't me. I'm no longer quite as concerned about who will read my work, or even if anyone will. When it's published, my novel will sit on an overloaded bookshelf and invite some seeking soul to read it, and I hope he or she will find my characters good company. For myself, I hope I will have moved on by then to another book."

— E. M.

SUGGESTED READING: *Boldtype* (on-line); *Books@Random Online Catalog*; *Edmonton Journal* (on-line) October 24, 1999; *Hindu* (on-line), with photo; *India Currents* (on-line) Nov. 1999; *Indigo* (on-line) Aug. 30, 1999; *IndiaStar* (on-line); *India West* (on-line) Aug. 15, 1996; *National Post* Sep. 25, 1999; *New York Times Book Review* p70 Nov. 21, 1999; *San Diego Union-Tribune Books* p5 Oct. 31, 1999; *Saturday Night* June 1998; (London) *Times* (on-line) Sep. 25, 1999

SELECTED BOOKS: nonfiction—*A Foreign Visitor's Survival Guide to America*, 1992; novels—*What the Body Remembers*, 1999; short-story collections—*English Lessons and Other Stories*, 1996

Benoit/Courtesy of Random House

Beatty, Paul

1962– Poet; novelist

After publishing two books of verse, *Big Bank Take Little Bank* (1991) and *Joker, Joker, Deuce* (1994), Paul Beatty applied his gift for poetic language to the writing of his novels. *The White Boy Shuffle* (1996), set in Los Angeles, and *Tuff* (2000), set in New York's East Harlem, have solidified his reputation as an important chronicler and satirist of America's racial woes and of contemporary African-American life. Damon Smith, in the *Boston Globe* (May 28, 2000), called "this talented poet and novelist" one of the "preeminent voices in recent American fiction." Ken Foster in the *New York Times Book Review* (May 7, 2000) praised Beatty's "ability to write sentences that percolate not only with rhythm and attitude but also with a kind of transcendent observational truth," and further noted, "Beatty has a rare ability to fashion something more than just occasional sharp phrasing; word by word, sentence by sentence, paragraph by paragraph, the writing . . . is seamless and teeming with momentum."

Paul Beatty was born in 1962 in Los Angeles, California, and grew up in West Los Angeles, living with his mother and sisters. He told Oscar C. Villalon in an interview for the *San Francisco Chronicle* (May 29, 2000) that he and his mother often attended kung-fu movies in downtown Los Angeles in the 1970s, his passion for those films lasting into his adulthood. He admitted to Brian Alcorn for the *Los Angeles Times* (July 10, 1996) that his neighborhood was rough, adding, "It wasn't easy, but we just had a good time."

Beatty was a graduate student at Boston University, where he earned an M.A. degree in psychology, when one day "out of nowhere," as he was "walking down the street with a friend"—he decided that he would write poetry. As he explained to Beth Farnstrom for the *Brown Daily Herald* (April 6, 2001), "I was just like, 'you know what? I think that's what I'm going to try and do. . . .'" He went to New York to study writing at Brooklyn College, where he earned an M.F.A. degree. One of his teachers, Allen Ginsberg, championed his poetry.

In 1990 Beatty won the first poetry slam at the Nuyorican Poets Café, where those events originated. His first poetry collection, *Big Bank Take Little Bank*, was published in 1991. One of its signature poems, "Darryl Strawberry Asleep in the Field of Dreams," took on the popular baseball movie *Field of Dreams* as a way of commenting on the racial divisions that existed historically in the sport and in the rest of American life. Beatty wrote in lowercase, no-punctuation style, "and in film school heaven is / where white doctors who played / only an inning and a half in the show / can pray for a tinker everlastin chance to groove the 0-2 sinker / white boys steady leanin in / truly believin this is the best movie they've ever seen / but none of em asked josh gibson to slo-dance / across the color line that / falls in an iowa ball field / broken but unhealed." Reviewers, such as Thom Tammaro for *Library Journal* (January 1991), found that Beatty's poems were written "as though Beatty had found a way to plug in his be-bop mind to the outlet of language and instead of stream of consciousness there pours out a flood of consciousness of a young man growing up in late-20th-century America who sings the culture electric."

Scott Bryant-Poulson, the reviewer for the *Voice Literary Supplement* (March 1991), took a more measured view. Although he noted that Beatty's poems were a mixture of "hiphop anger, the beautiful cultural vulgarity of TV reruns, and the signifying, no-holds-barred imagination of a young black poet on a fin-de-siecle race-man mission," he also noted that what "keeps the work on track and away from the simple, funky race-conscious dramatics of many young black artists is his smooth but wired sensitivity to the levels and nuances of the black community." Joel Lewis, writing in *American Book Review* (January 1992), found in Beatty's poems the "detritus of our culture . . . diced up and spliced together in ways that are both startling and hilarious."

Although he became known as a performance artist, Beatty did not deliver his poems in the manner of a rapper but read in "a near mumble," according to Evelyn McDonnell, writing in *Rolling Stone* (August 5, 1993). He told McDonnell that while he valued his experiences in the café scene, he considered reading in coffee houses to be more of a means to an end than an end in itself. "It's very important for me as a black person to establish that the word is a written presentation. . . . If you really want to break new ground, then it definitely has to be done in writing," he declared. Beatty was later to tell Farnstrom that he hated performing and had become increasingly uncomfortable with it over time, particularly as poetry slams gained in popularity and intensity. Jeannine Amber in *Essence* (September 1994) referred to Beatty's "deadpan a capella delivery," and for Eric Murphy Selinger, writing in *Parnassus: Poetry in Review* (1998), every "gesture on the page of Beatty's poetry tells you to read it aloud with . . . jazzy 'Afrocentric' stylings. . . . Beatty himself, though, reads it in a deadpan monotone."

Like *Big Bank Take Little Bank*, Beatty's second poetry collection, *Joker, Joker, Deuce* (1994), struck reviewers as being informed by hip-hop imagery—despite Beatty's disdain for such comparisons: "Anything having to do with urban blacks and anything new they call hip hop," the *Times Union* (December 28, 1996) reported him as having said in the *Source*. "Someone has to work on an actual hip-hop aesthetic and start using the word in a way that means something other than a label." Jabari Asim noted in the *Washington Post Book World* (June 13, 1999) that in "both collections, Beatty displays a voracious appetite for popular culture. . . ." His takes on the world around him, however, according to Asim, are "filtered through a sensibility that is decidedly postmodern," with lines "that are equally indebted to the Beats and to the big guns of the Black Arts Movement." Asim found that unlike "the latter, Beatty is committed to sending up black American culture as much as he celebrates it. He's an intrepid parodist willing to sling literary spitballs at the sacred totems of black mythology."

The White Boy Shuffle, Beatty's first novel, was published in 1996. By then, Beatty, having achieved fame as a poet, was living in Germany on a writer's fellowship from that country. He had also been earning money by "working with the mentally ill," as he told Nicholas Wroe for the *Guardian* (November 20, 1996), and by performing on MTV.

Gunnar Kaufman, the main character in *The White Boy Shuffle* and "the only cool black guy at Mestizo Mulatto Mongrel Elementary, Santa Monica's all-white multicultural school," begins his narration: "Unlike the typical bluesy earthy folksy denim-overalls noble-in-the-face-of-cracker-racism aw shucks Pulitzer-Prize-winning protagonist mojo magic black man, I am not the seventh son of a seventh son. I wish I were, but fate shorted me by six brothers and three uncles." In the white enclave of Santa Monica, Gunnar and his sisters grow to regard other black children as "different," leading their horrified mother to move the family to "the hood," that is, a minority community. There, as a complete outsider ("In a world where body and spoken language were currency, I was broke as hell") who endures frequent beatings from his schoolmates, Gunnar "walked the dark streets of Hillside with my head down, looking for loose change and signs that would place me on the path to right-on soul brother righteousness." He survives by excelling at basketball and by learning to compose verse praising the local gang leaders: "My duties were similar to those of a Li Po or Lu Chaolin in the employ of a Tang dynasty warlord: immortalize the rulers and say enough scholarly bull . . . to keep from getting my head chopped off." After playing basketball at Boston University, Gunnar becomes a published poet and self-described "spokesperson" for the black community.

Critical responses to *The White Boy Shuffle* were uniformly enthusiastic. "Full of poetry skillfully metamorphosed into prose, Beatty's book is a clout upside your head delivered by the deacon nearest to the pew that you have been playing in," Nick Charles wrote in the *Nation* (July 8, 1996). "Laugh-out-loud funny and weep-in-silence sad . . . the book takes great risks when skewering what all too many hold to be self-evident, but for which there is little evidence. The . . . language is always vibrant and alluring." Terming the novel often "raucous, frequently profane and consistently funny," Jabari Asim observed in the *Washington Post Book World* (December 3, 2000) that *The White Boy Shuffle* "is ultimately about the universal human struggle to fit in. . . . His hero's travels allow Beatty to take on various stereotypes—including self-imposed ones—that often constrict black behavior. Slang, basketball, self-obsessed black 'spokespersons' and gangsta rap are just a few of the targets laid low by Beatty's caustic wit." Beatty told Wroe, "I couldn't have written the book without having written the poetry before. A lot of writers start out with poetry because you use skeletal bits of language and you can manageably explore whether a piece will be cognitive or linear or whatever. That process has really helped me."

Tuff, Beatty's 2000 novel, might be said to be more of a cognitive work than a linear one. Again, Beatty used an urban black male—Winston Forshay, known as Tuff—as the central character in a satire, this one concerning the mores of New York's East Harlem. A 22-year-old father and enforcer for a gang of drug dealers, Tuff decides to turn his life around after a brush with death. Other characters include Yolanda, the mother of Tuff's son and a believer in self-improvement; Inez Nomura, a radical Socialist who spent her early years in an internment camp for the Japanese during World War II and who helped to raise Tuff; Spencer Throckmorton, a black rabbi and urban sociologist from Big Brothers of America who wants to gain "insight into the lives of the working poor"; and Tuff's father, a former Black Panther who begins readings of his terrible poetry by firing a gun at the ceiling.

"*Tuff* is a richly textured and unforgettable work," Damon Smith wrote in the *Boston Globe* (May 28, 2000). "Beatty's inner-city Bildungsroman offers a fictional rumination on the politics of disenfranchisement that artfully yokes the Harlem Renaissance, sumo philosophy, classic cinema, and the humor of comics like Redd Foxx and Richard Pryor." Other reviewers agreed. Richard

Bernstein in the *New York Times* (July 11, 2000) wrote that "*Tuff* is a funny book, and Mr. Beatty's blunt, impious, streetwise eloquence has a kind of transfixing power.... The main ingredient of *Tuff* is portraiture, word-rich, profanity- and caricature-drenched tableaus of Winston and the off-kilter world in which he dwells." Bernstein praised the skill with which Beatty avoided "political-science language" in depicting "the subtle power of the inner city trap, with Winston and his friends hemmed in by stiff-necked victim-culture ideologies in one corner, self-defeating in-group machismo in another and an indifferent economic system in the third." Oscar C. Villalon, the *San Francisco Chronicle* (May 21, 2000) reviewer, found that "Beatty, who is also a poet, writes sentences as if he's throwing punches in the ring. He makes them tight and great to look at." He did find fault, as did others, with the novel's being "fueled by pop culture" to the point that "[i]ronically, Beatty's unique writing is . . . *Tuff*'s . . . weakness.

Though he dismantles stereotypes by pitting them against knowing caricature, the jokiness sometimes overflows."

Paul Beatty lives in New York City.

—S.Y.

SUGGESTED READING: *Boston Brown Daily Herald* (on-line) Apr. 6, 2001; *Essence* p58 Sep. 1994; *Guardian* TT p14 Nov. 20, 1996; *Library Journal* p107 Jan. 1991; *Los Angeles Times* p1 July 10, 1996; *Nation* P30+ July 8, 1996; *New York Times* E p6 July 11, 2000; *New York Times Book Review* p25 May 7, 2000; *Publishers Weekly* p247 Feb. 21, 1994; *Rolling Stone* p20 Aug. 5, 1993; *San Francisco Chronicle* R p3 May 21, 2000, E p1 May 29, 2000; *Voice Literary Supplement* p5 Mar. 1991; *Washington Post Book World* p12 June 13, 1999

SELECTED BOOKS: poetry—*Big Bank Take Little Bank*, 1991; *Joker, Joker Deuce*, 1994; fiction—*The White Boy Shuffle*, 1996; *Tuff*, 2000

Emma Dodge Hanson/Courtesy of Houghton Mifflin Company

Benedict, Elizabeth

Dec. 20, 1954– Novelist; nonfiction writer

Elizabeth Benedict is the author of four novels, *Slow Dancing* (1985), *The Beginner's Book of Dreams* (1988), *Safe Conduct* (1993), and *Almost* (2001), as well as a nonfiction writing manual. Many reviewers have praised Benedict for creating memorable characters, some of whom are partly based on herself, and thoughtfully exploring the nature of relationships between friends, married couples, parents and children, and lovers. "I'm interested in the subtle ways people change over a lifetime—much like the kind of changes that take place in the course of therapy or marriage, or just growing up," Benedict told an interviewer for *Contemporary Authors: New Revision Series, Volume 90* (2000). "Of course, the changes are fascinating to watch in kids, which is one of the reasons I write about them. . . . I suppose I'm interested in souls in flux—of all ages. So far, I've taken an optimistic outlook on the matter of change. I want my characters to change for the better—to become deeper, braver, more complete people."

Elizabeth Benedict writes for *World Authors: 1995–2000*: "I do not come from a literary family. My mother went to the Hartford Art School after high school and was a gifted painter and sculptor, though she spent much of her worklife as a secretary. My father, who studied to be an electrician at the Wentworth Institute in Boston, became a salesman, first of tangible objects, then intangible: insurance, pension plans. They were first generation Jews who believed in college education because it was a good way to meet a better class of people so that their daughters could marry up. But they also encouraged my sister and me to pursue our interests without prejudice. They never uttered the odious phrase: You can't do this because you're a girl. They aspired mightily to be part of the upper-middle class, and when I was eight, we moved to Manhattan, from Hartford, Connecticut; Columbus, Ohio; and Hartsdale, New York.

"We arrived in New York in 1962. My father was an ambitious businessman and alcoholic, although we didn't understand that at the time. My parents bequeathed to me the privilege of growing up in Manhattan and a sense of drama that came from their own friend-swept lives and the chaos and torment of their private lives. There were often friends of my parents—from the building and from out of town—in and out of our apartments in a way that more resembles a TV sit-com than any lives I have encountered since. And although there was much warmth and good will, several of our favorite visitors were troubled alcoholics whose lives were, at first, glamorous and grand, and later, desperate and ruined. The most dramatic of the visitors, a theatrical and strikingly beautiful woman, became the inspiration for the mother, Georgia, in my second novel, *The Beginner's Book Of Dreams*.

"My life took a literary turn at 12 or 13 when I became best friends with a girl at the local junior high school who was from a family of intellectuals, filmmakers and critics. My first boyfriend was a musical prodigy. Because of him, I became an odd New York City teenager in the late 1960s and early 70s, who, instead of protesting the war and yearning to go to the Haight and drop acid, hung out at the Museum of Modern Art and often went gallery hopping on 57th Street. At 15, I was directed to Dada, Surrealism, some version of the Avant Garde—anything but hippies and 'the counterculture.'

"When I began college at Barnard in 1972, I wanted to be an art historian. As a sophomore, a literature course in the Modern English Novel changed my life again. A prescient professor read my term paper—ostensibly about Samuel Butler's *The Way Of All Flesh* but really about my parents' recent divorce—and told me I was a good writer and that I 'obviously' wanted to write a novel. That was not obvious to me, and I would never have had the nerve to imagine it for myself. In high school, I'd written stories and poems and edited the literary magazine, but this professor's insight was electrifying. I decided that night that I was 'going to be a writer,' and I began obsessively keeping a journal, which I had done on and off all my life, and which I understood that night—somehow instinctively, not because anyone told me—would lead to my writing fiction.

"I was at Barnard during the height of the Women's Movement, when Virginia Woolf was being embraced by feminists and Joan Didion was beginning to write fiction and her early essays had just been collected in *Slouching Toward Bethlehem*. Favorite books at the time: *The Golden Notebook*, *New Grub Street*, *Clarissa*; I loved the feverish energy and obsession of it. I had a senior creative writing tutorial with Elizabeth Hardwick, and her languid encouragement kept me going for many years. The last week of my senior year, I won the Barnard poetry prize and second place in the prose prize—and learned I had flunked my science requirement, which I had taken pass/fail. That juxtaposition of events describes my appetites: I excel at what I love and don't much care about the rest.

"My first novel, *Slow Dancing*, came from a short story I wrote in my mid-20s. The professor who'd encouraged me to write in college read the story and said that it should be a novel. That gave me the courage to begin. I started taking haphazard notes in a small looseleaf notebook, because I was too intimidated to do more. I turned to it full-time about a year later, after I'd been laid off from a job as a publicist for a major civil rights organization, and finished it in a year. Since *Slow Dancing*, which appeared in 1985, I've written three more novels and *The Joy Of Writing Sex: A Guide For Fiction Writers*, as well as a raft of book reviews, personal essays, and journalism (some of the essays can be found at www.elizabethbenedict.com).

"Twenty years ago, I wrote a poem, never published, about my longing to be from a literary family instead of the family I am from. Part of what I longed for were books and ideas; and part was a young person's simple wish to have come from a happier, more stable home. But from this great distance, I see that my parents' literary lessons were many and profound:

"1. When I was 17, my alcoholic father left my mother. We became impoverished. We had upper middle class tastes and expectations but no money. I put myself through college and have taken care of myself since then. My mother's life became one of constant hardship and anxiety. Lesson: Work like a maniac; no one else will do it for you. It is not unusual for me to do 30 drafts of a piece of fiction.

"2. People change. Worlds previously unknown open up and offer beauty, joy, salvation. Lesson: Art matters.

"3. Life is full of sudden reversals. Lessons: Fiction is about transformation. Transformation is possible.

"4. My parents' many exuberant friends made the surface of our troubled family a lively place to be. Lesson: Make the surface of the writing lively, fun, funny, even if the characters are in excruciating pain, which they often are.

"Thus, two comments about my fiction make me especially happy: Anne Tyler wrote about *The Beginner's Book Of Dreams*: 'The world it spreads before us so convincingly is complex, fascinating, bewildering, sometimes morbidly funny, always underlaid with pain. The marvel is that such a sad book could be such a joy to read.' Reviewer Lisa Parsons wrote that my novel *Almost* 'moves like a Camry on a newly paved coastal highway. Slopes, curves, changing scenery; motion reliable, smooth, and sprightly. After a rest stop it merges back into action, 0 to 60 in 5 seconds, no road noise, no vibration.' (www.hippopress.com.)

"My fiction is autobiographical but not autobiography. Because I admit to this, readers figure the proportions must be: 85 percent true, 15 percent invented, but it is more accurately the other way around. I like these lines by Seamus Heaney:'How does the real get into the made-up. / Ask me an easier one.' ('Known World' in *Electric Light*.)

"I work on a laptop computer and rewrite constantly. I work chapter by chapter, print out what I've done at the end of every day and read it with a pencil that night. The next day when I make changes on the computer, I continue, printing out every day, reading the chapter every night from the beginning, so that by the time a chapter is done, it's been rewritten dozens of times, at least. But if the next chapter doesn't work—which I might find out a month into it—I might start rewriting the book from the beginning. I might do this five times in the course of writing a novel, keep returning to rewrite from the beginning, to propel and set up what happens much later.

"Several years ago at Office Max, I found a pad of giant Post-It Notes, 2 feet by 3 feet, made for easel presentations. I stick them up all over the walls, wherever there's room. When I don't know what to do, I stand at them with a marking pen and start writing—ideas, dialogue, anything. I don't censor myself. The size of the paper is liberating, and being able to write big is too; and so is seeing the notes on the wall when I look up from the desk. They're good reminders. I feel a little like Jackson Pollock throwing paint, but for me it's a way to loosen up so I can imagine things on a large scale, before I shrink everything down to the page and then obsess over every word."

Elizabeth Benedict is a pen name. The writer, who chooses not to reveal her given name, was born on December 20, 1954, in Hartford, Connecticut. In the mid-1970s she adopted the name Elizabeth Benedict. In an interview with Elizabeth Kastor for the *Washington Post* (April 26, 1988), Benedict explained that her new name "was easier to remember and spell than my other name." She continued, "I lived in San Francisco at the time, and I was sort of cut off from my family and my roots, as it were. And it was San Francisco, which is kind of a crazy place, so it didn't seem strange. It wasn't the most bizarre thing there." Benedict's father, Lester, worked as an insurance salesman, and her mother, Sara, was an artist. "They weren't happily married," Benedict wrote for the *Chicago Tribune* (September 25, 1988). "They are not married any longer, they split up when I was a senior in high school."

Benedict began writing poetry at age 13 and short stories while in high school. As a student at Barnard College, in New York City, she won the school's poetry prize in her senior year. At first, Benedict did not intend to become a professional writer and considered pursuing a career in art history or psychiatry. However, for one of her sophomore classes, she wrote a paper about her father. Benedict's professor was so impressed with the paper that he told her that she was a good writer and predicted that she would probably publish a novel one day. "That night, I went back to my little dormitory room, and I sat there with my typewriter and I said, okay, I am going to be a writer," Benedict recalled for her *Chicago Tribune* article. "I decided that what I had to do to be a writer was write every day. I don't know how I knew this, but I knew it. I said to myself, I have to write every day in a diary and one day, it's going to turn into fiction. That was how I decided what to do."

Benedict graduated cum laude from Barnard, in 1976. She then got a job as a computer typesetter. In her interview with *Contemporary Authors*, Benedict said that "two years out of college I finally was so sick of typing newspaper ads for department stores that I knew I could have written, and doing office temporary work, that I broke down and got a real job." In 1978 the Mexican American Legal Defense and Educational Fund (MALDEF), in San Francisco, hired Benedict on the strength of her typing and typesetting skills. A short time later, she relocated to Washington, D.C., to work for MALDEF as a lobbyist and public-relations assistant. Benedict lobbied for voting rights, immigration, and civil-rights legislation, and she frequently gave interviews to the press. Although she found the work rewarding, she was determined to become a writer. During the early 1980s, she began publishing her poetry and short stories. Her story "Feasting" was included in the O. Henry Prize collection in 1983. A year later, the American Society of Magazine Editors presented Benedict with their National Magazine Award for fiction for her story "An 80-Percent Chance."

Benedict left MALDEF in 1982 to write her first book, *Slow Dancing*, which was published in 1985. (The book was written in the kitchen of her unheated basement apartment; Benedict kept the oven ajar for warmth.) The novel tells the story of a friendship between two women: Lexi, an immigration lawyer who lives in Los Angeles, and Nell, a freelance writer living in New York City. The pair had been roommates at Barnard College a decade earlier, and although they are now separated by distance, Lexi and Nell keep in daily contact, talking about their lives and romantic relationships. In fact, the pair are so close that they are often suspected of being lovers. Both women, however, have had a number of unsatisfying relationships with men over the years and have grown tired and disillusioned by their failure to find the right man. The chemistry between Lexi and Nell is altered when Lexi meets David, a divorced reporter and the father of a 14-year-old girl.

"Benedict is a very sharp, funny writer who has produced a bright, bi-coastal love story that is great fun to read," Alix Madrigal wrote for the *San Francisco Chronicle* (March 10, 1985). "Her women are not bored, unfulfilled housewives . . . and her men are not selfish, loutish villains. They all find themselves grappling with the conflicts of romance and career, freedom and domesticity, and their confusions are recounted with sympathy." Although Madrigal wrote that "the problem with *Slow Dancing* is that Benedict is so good we expect more from her," the reviewer conceded, "with all the delights this novel offers, it seems ungenerous to complain that it isn't quite enough." Andrea Barnet, in a critique for the *New York Times Book Review* (March 3, 1985), opined that the scenes in the book between Lexi and David "are written in a clear bare-bones prose filled with tension and feeling." Despite asserting that the book was not "wildly imaginative," Barnet wrote that "the novel's strength is in its sympathetic portraits of three well-meaning people more comfortable in their public roles than in their private lives. Miss Benedict has written an unsentimental homage to a generation still struggling to grow up." *Slow Dancing* was a finalist for the American Book Award for first fiction and won the *Los Angeles Times* Book Prize for fiction, both in 1985.

Benedict's second novel, *The Beginner's Book of Dreams* (1988), has as its protagonist Esme, an unhappy girl with an unsupportive family. The novel chronicles a decade of Esme's life, starting when she is eight years old. Her alcoholic mother, a failed actress, has married several times, and Esme's biological father remains distant. As Esme gets older and more experienced, she learns that she has the power to escape her fate. In a review for the *Washington Post* (April 15, 1988), the novelist Alice McDermott praised the book. "Benedict knows her characters throughly, and each one of her details, from the description of Esme's first sexual experience to the account of her father as an aging hippie in a Rolls-Royce, rings absolutely true," McDermott observed. "She can pin down a character with a word, evoke a scene, a room or a city with a few perfect lines." In his review for the *Los Angeles Times* (April 24, 1988), Richard Eder expressed mixed feelings about the novel. "At times, it runs clear and distinct, with the verve that this talented writer brings to . . . her characters' feelings," Eder wrote. "Other times, it subsides into undifferentiated emotions that seem uncomfortably close to popular romance." Although he asserted that Benedict "has a genuine vision of Esme's painful journey" and "is quite brilliant at suggesting a complicated mixture of feelings," Eder observed that the author "flags here and there, as if losing concentration." The reviewer concluded that where "Benedict's heart is in Esme's struggles, her book is dry and moving in its restraint. Where the author's attention seems to stray, it goes soft and even sentimental."

Benedict published her third novel, *Safe Conduct*, in 1993. The book examines the marriage between Kate Lurie, a documentary filmmaker who narrates the story, and Mac, a former official of the State Department. Back in 1974, Mac was stationed in Leningrad (renamed St. Petersburg after the fall of the Soviet Union), where he had a short but passionate affair with a woman named Lida. Mac left the Soviet Union and Lida eventually settled in Paris, where she married and had a child. Nearly two decades later, Lida tracks Mac down in the United States and learns that he and Kate will be stopping in Brussels on their way to Turkey, where Kate will be filming a documentary. Lida travels to Brussels and meets the couple. Benedict used her personal experiences as material for the novel. As a diplomat living in Leningrad in 1974, Benedict's husband, Richard Harrington, had an affair with a Russian woman named Olga, who looked him up many years later. "We all arranged to meet in Brussels," Benedict told Joseph Olshan for *People* (June 21, 1993). "Of course I was a little nervous. I knew their affair had been passionate. But my husband was very assuring about his commitment to me. When I met Olga—who was very beautiful, brassy, emotional—I realized I would write their story. And so I kept my eyes peeled, for the novel but also for myself as a woman. Because I felt her sizing Richard up." (Benedict and Harrington later divorced.) For the *New York Times Book Review* (July 11, 1993) Jonathan Dee wrote that Benedict "explores the most complex emotional states with rare facility; unfortunately, at certain moments the strictures of the story she has chosen, with its cold war flourishes, force her into the language of the romance novel—a language in which her own considerably subtler talents can't always find suitable expression."

In 1996 Benedict published a nonfiction book, *The Joy of Writing Sex: A Guide for Fiction Writers*, which offers advice on how to write realistic sex scenes. Benedict presented the opinions of several writers whom she had interviewed, including John Updike, Dorothy Allison, and Joseph Olshan, and she discussed how such prominent authors as Joyce Carol Oates, David Lodge, Edmund White, and Alice Walker depict sex. Touching on marital sex, "safe" sex, and adultery, among other topics, she advises aspiring writers on how they can overcome their inhibitions (and the possible disapproval of their families) to construct believable sex scenes. "Benedict teaches both by precept and by example," Richard Dyer observed for the *Boston Globe* (August 30, 1996). "The precepts derive from sound, creative-writing principles, long standard because they make sense: Good writing about sex should meet the same requirements as good writing about anything."

In 2001 Benedict returned to fiction with *Almost*. In this novel, Sophy Chase, an alcoholic novelist, leaves her husband and her home on Swansea Island, off the coast of Massachusetts. Moving to New York City, she finds love with Daniel, an Englishman. When she receives news that her soon-to-be ex-husband, Will, has died, Sophy returns to the island. There, she confronts her painful past and tries to come to terms with her emotions. In his review for *Newsweek* (August 27, 2001), Jeff Giles wrote that *Almost* is "about grief and love, about figuring out who your friends really are and what, if anything, you owe everybody else." Giles called Sophy "an intriguing creation: smart, loving, combative, self-loathing." Although he criticized *Almost* for having a "harried plot," Giles concluded that "the book is funny, harrowing and just a little messy" and called it "the most engrossing novel I've come across in a long time." Reviewing the novel for *New York Newsday* (August 19, 2001), Claire Dedrer observed that "Benedict sometimes seems more concerned with pinning down the particulars of Sophy's mental journey than with making nice sentences or fashioning a shapely plot. But she so delicately pulls apart fragile moments that we get caught up in the drama all the same." Dedrer noted that Sophy often makes jokes, many of which fall flat, to deal with her pain. "Benedict seems to understand humor's real function: not to be funny, necessarily, but to get us through the day," the reviewer wrote. "She shows us that you can't write an honest novel about the life of the mind and leave out the jokes."

Benedict has taught at numerous institutions throughout her career, including George Mason University, in Fairfax, Virginia. She has served as a visiting writer at Swarthmore College and Haverford College, both in Pennsylvania. She was also a visiting professor at Haverford in 1991; Davidson College, in North Carolina, in 1992; and the University of Iowa at Iowa City, in 1993. From 1994 to 1998 Benedict lectured at Princeton University, in New Jersey, and in 1997 she also lectured at the New School for Social Research, in New York City. In 1997 and 1998 she taught at the New York State Summer Writers' Institute at Skidmore College, in Saratoga Springs.

Elizabeth Benedict has written for *Harper's Bazaar*, *Writer's Digest*, and *American Prospect*, as well as the *New York Times Book Review*, *Los Angeles Times*, *Washington Post*, *Boston Globe*, and the Japanese edition of *Playboy*. The author currently makes her home in New York City.

—D. C.

SUGGESTED READING: *Boston Globe* F p8 Aug. 30, 1996; *Chicago Tribune* VI p3 Sep. 25, 1988, with photo; Elizabeth Benedict Web site; *Los Angeles Times* p3 Apr. 24, 1988; *New York Times Book Review* p9 Mar. 3, 1985, p11 July 11, 1993; *New York Newsday* B p12 Aug. 19, 2001; *Newsweek* p58 Aug. 27, 2001; *People* p24+ June 21, 1993, with photo; *San Francisco Chronicle* p5 Mar. 10, 1985; *Washington Post* B p8 Apr. 15, 1988, B p1 Apr. 26, 1988 with photo; *Women's Review of Books* p30 July 1996

SELECTED BOOKS: novels—*Slow Dancing*, 1985; *The Beginner's Book of Dreams*, 1988; *Safe Conduct*, 1993; *Almost*, 2001; nonfiction—*The Joy of Writing Sex: A Guide for Writers*, 1996

Bernstein, Charles

Apr. 4, 1950– Poet; critic

The American poet and literary critic Charles Bernstein, in his collections of poetry and in his critical works, *Content's Dream: Essays 1975–1984* (1986), *A Poetics* (1992), and *My Way: Speeches and Poems* (1999), has interpreted modern life through the medium of Language poetry, of which he is one of the seminal creators. Developed in the late 1970s, Language poetry seeks to pay attention to words themselves as well as to what those words describe. Hank Lazer, another Language poet, observed in the *American Poetry Review* (October 1995) that the contribution of Charles Bernstein and the Language poetry movement to American poetry "may, oddly enough, not be principally based in formal innovation per se, but in altered professional conceptions of the poet and in re-directed and re-imagined relationships between reader and writer and in re-thinking earlier modernisms." Through his participation in conferences, his fostering of other poets' work, and his own prodigious output, Bernstein has been a major presence in the world of poetry for over two decades.

The youngest of three siblings, Charles Bernstein was born on April 4, 1950 in New York City. His father, Herman, worked in the garment business. Bernstein attended the Bronx High School of Science, a school for gifted students, then received a bachelor's degree in 1972 from Harvard University, where he majored in philosophy. His senior thesis, "Three Compositions on Philosophy and Literature," in part viewed Gertrude Stein's *Making of Americans* through the prism of Ludwig Wittgen-

Jill Kramer/Courtesy of Charles Berstein

stein's *Philosophical Investigations*; portions of the thesis were included in *Gertrude Stein Advanced*, Richard Kostelanetz's 1990 anthology.

Although Bernstein organized speakers' forums at Bronx Science and in college edited the literary magazines *Harvard Yard Journal* and *Writing*, there was little to suggest that he would become one of the most controversial spokespersons for a new poetic movement. The revolutionary nature of his approach to poetics can be understood, however, from a description by Marjorie Perloff in the *Virginia Quarterly Review* (Spring 1998) of a "historic" symposium, "What Is a Poet?," organized by Hank Lazer at the University of Alabama in 1984. There, sitting in for John Ashbery, who could not attend, Bernstein polarized many of the major voices in American poetry—among them Perloff, Louis Simpson, David Ignatow, Denise Levertov, Gerald Stern, Helen Vendler, Charles Altieri, Kenneth Burke, and Gregory Jay—by "set[ting] off the most vociferous debate on poetry I have ever witnessed at a public forum," as Perloff wrote. "Simpson, Levertov, Stern, and Vendler, as well as the then resident poets in Tuscaloosa, attacked Bernstein's work at every available opportunity; indeed Levertov told him in so many words that his poetry was a failure because it didn't 'move' anyone, a remark which led me to ask her how one would verify the state of being moved."

Bernstein, in fact, started his poetic career in obscurity. His first two books, *Asylums* (1975) and *Parsing* (1976), were published by Asylum's Press, run by Bernstein and his wife, the artist Susan Bee. Bernstein made his living by coordinating a free health-care clinic in Santa Barbara, California, from 1973 to 1975, then serving as a writer and editor for medical and health-care publications, including *Modern Medicine of Canada* and *Merck Minutes*, a tabloid journal for pharmacists. Bernstein viewed his career in health-care journalism with equanimity. He observed in an interview in *American Literary History* (Spring 1998) of his work on *Merck Minutes* that he "enjoyed" writing for this audience because the work was "clearly defined . . . without ambiguity of intent or style." When he proposed "a review essay on Michel Foucault's *Birth of a Clinic: An Archaeology of Medical Perception*," for example, he "was immediately ruled out of order. . . . Of course," he added, "if I had submitted my poems, or a review essay of Foucault's *Power/ Knowledge: Selected Interviews and Other Writings, 1972–1977*, to a national literary magazine at the time, I also would have been ruled out of order." For Bernstein, commercial strictures were easier to accept than their equivalent in the academy.

Although he held appointments as a visiting lecturer at the University of California, San Diego, Queens College of the City University of New York, and the New School for Social Research in New York, starting in 1987, Bernstein did not give up his career in medical journalism until 1989, when he was appointed David Gray Professor of Poetry and Letters at the State University of New York at Buffalo. Bernstein's independence from academic constrictions and the need to struggle for tenure had enabled him to write as he pleased and to conclude that "establishment" politics controlled poetry and the academy as well as the larger society. Deploring the dismantling of the National Endowment for the Arts (NEA) and the National Endowment for the Humanities (NEH), he called for a commitment on the part of artists and intellectuals to "make their work and the work they support available in public spaces . . . in forms that challenge, confront, exhilarate, provoke, disturb, question, flail and even fail." Only the university, he felt, remains a forum for such art, "although it is falling prey," as Bernstein put it, "to the same forces that have destroyed the NEA and diluted public broadcasting." He characterized those forces as "the mediocracy."

Bernstein went on to become not only a prolific poet, producing more than 20 books of verse, but also a prominent spokesperson for the Language poetry movement. In 1978 he and Bruce Andrews founded $L=A=N=G=U=A=G=E$, the movement's journal, which ran until 1981; the two also edited *The $L=A=N=G=U=A=G=E$ Book*, composed of selections from the magazine and published in 1984.

In Bernstein's 1983 collection, *Islets/Irritations*, appeared his most famous poem, "The Klupzy Girl." That long work sets forth Bernstein's poetic credo in its opening lines: "Poetry is like a swoon, with this difference:/ it brings you to your senses." Bernstein's *Content's Dream: Essays, 1975–1984* (1986) explored the boundaries of experiment in prosody. The book's publisher, Sun & Moon Press, maintained that the essays "help readers understand not only the aesthetic of $L=A=N=G=U=A=G=E$ poetry but also the importance of language itself." In *Content's Dream*, Bernstein discussed the work of his poetic cohorts, including William Carlos Williams, Louis Zukofsky, Charles Olson, Robert Creeley, Clark Coolidge, and Jackson Mac Low. The publisher cited the book as a document that is "central to the poetic theory of our day" and comparable in that regard to Ezra Pound's *Gaudier-Bzeska*, William Carlos Williams's *Collected Essays*, and Gertrude Stein's *How to Write*.

The Sophist, published in 1987, sets forth in poetic form Bernstein's core values concerning language's relation to truth and the political responsibilities of the poet in society. *The Sophist* contains 36 poems, some of them short, lyrical pieces, others "collage-like serial poems," according to the publisher, who termed it a work both "comic and intellectually challenging." One of the major poems in *The Sophist* is "Dysraphism," a coinage of Bernstein's that grew out of his knowledge of medical terms. A *raph* is a "seam," either an anatomical juncture or a created one. For Bernstein, as he wrote in a note to the poem, "dysraphism is misseaming—a prosodic device! But," he added, "it has the punch of being the same root as rhapsody (raph)—or in Skeat's—'one who strings (lit. stitches) songs together, a reciter of epic poetry.'" Bernstein has in all his poetic oeuvre attempted to create a disjuncture between the prosody of the past and modern methods of creation, while also employing "adjacency," which is both a recognition and a creation of similarity by juxtaposition. "I felt the abridgement of imperatives, the wave of detours, the sabre-rattling of inversion. All lit up and no place to go. Blinded by avenue and filled with adjacency. Arch or arched at," reads an often quoted passage from "Dysraphism."

The critic Marjorie Perloff, in *The Dance of the Intellect: Studies in the Poetry of the Pound Tradition*, wrote of Bernstein's exploitation in "Dysraphism" of "such rhetorical figures as pun, anaphora, epiphora, metathesis, epigram, anagram, and neologism" for the purpose of creating "a seamless web of reconstituted words," which become "an elaborate 'dysfunctional fusion of embryonic parts' and a 'disturbance of stress, pitch, and rhythm of speech' in the interest of a new kind of urban 'rhapsody.'"

Bernstein's *Rough Trades*, published in 1991, continues what he termed in *American Literary History* the invocation of "the necessity of the small-scale act, the complex gesture, the incontrovertible insinuation, the refractory insouciance of the intractable." He observed, referring to his own work, that "poetry is (or can be) about measure but it counts differently." *Rough Trades* is divided into three sections: "The Riddle of the Fat-Faced Man," "Rough Trades," and "The Persistence of Persistence." In the first poem in the volume, "The Kiwi Bird in the Kiwi Tree," Bernstein evoked the maker's craft:

> . . . The tailor tells of other tolls, the seam that binds, the trim, the waste. & having spelled these names, moves on to toys or talcums, skates & scores. Only the imaginary is real—not trumps beclouding the mind's acrobatic vers-ions. The first fact is the social body, one from another, nor needs no other.

The "lines of language, of thinking, intersect, dissect, converge, and emerge again as new ideas and emotions, hit and bounce and point and disappear over the horizon, only to reappear from the periphery," according to the publisher.

A Poetics appeared in 1992. A collection of 10 essays and an interview, from the years 1985 to 1990, *A Poetics* contains Bernstein's musings on the business of poetry, the effects that the immigration of large numbers of non–English-speaking people to the U.S. has had on the language available for poetry, and the uses of "absorptive" and "anti-absorptive" techniques in composing poetry. It includes "Pounding Fascism," an analysis of the centrality of fascist ideas not only to Ezra Pound's politics but to his poetry. In an article Bernstein later wrote for the *Yale Review* and also posted on his Poetics ListServe Web site, he maintained that "Pound's work . . . not only allows for but provokes an ideological reading; it insists that it be read, form and content, for its politics and its ideas. And it is precisely this that is one of the enduring values of his work. . . . The significance of 'the Pound tradition' requires that we interrogate it for what it excludes as much as what it makes possible: interrogate the assumptions of poetic lineages not just to acknowledge their effects but also to counteract their effects." Bernstein felt that "there is often a tendency among Americans to exoticize fascism; Pound did his best to bring it home" and, for that reason, Pound's ideas must be closely examined. Bernstein, as well, continued to dedicate himself to poetry as polemic and to an analysis of the politics brought forth by poetics.

Alan Golding, reviewing *A Poetics* for *American Literature* (March 1993), declared that Bernstein's "most interesting and significant work here challenges and expands the boundaries of that genre. His purpose is partly literary and cultural commentary, but equally it is to propose a poetics—his own poetics, personal and thus partial, implied in style, structure, and critical perspective as much as in explicitly articulated principles. . . . Books on poetics are rarely funny; this one often is, but seriously so."

Dark City, Bernstein's 1994 collection, was termed by his publisher "an at times comic, at times bleak, excursion into everyday life in the late 20th century," and, quoting from the *Village Voice* review, "a tireless attempt to regain our attention and bring us from inertia into discourse again." The on-line reviewer for *Taproot 7/8*, calling *Dark City* "a humorous, witty, informed collection of linguistic artifacts," found "form and rhyme and even reason here, an obsessive sense of the materiality of language." Again, Bernstein returned to the business of poetry, as in "The Lives of the Toll Takers," where, according to Hank Lazer, writing in the *American Poetry Review* (October 1995), he used "the rhetoric of investment calculation and market penetration . . . to investigate an issue in poetry of considerable seriousness":

> Our new service orientation meant not only changing the way we wrote poems but also diversifying into new poetry services. Poetic opportunities however, do not fall into your lap, at least not very often. You've got to seek them out, and when you find them you've got to have the knowhow to take advantage of them. . . . Poetry services provide cost savings to readers, such as avoiding hospitalizations (you're less likely to get in an accident if you're home reading poems), minimizing wasted time (condensare), and reducing adverse idea interactions. . . . Poets deserve compensation for such services. For readers unwilling to pay the price we need to refuse to provide such service as alliteration, internal rhymes, exogamic structure, and unusual vocabulary.

Although Bernstein's expression of the poet's dilemma is humorous, Lazer emphasized Bernstein's awareness of the question of "how to commodify poetry (for publication inevitably constitutes commodification) without destroying poetry's oppositional potential and the poet's position as a player in the enterprise of cultural criticism."

Raphael Rubenstein, in an article entitled "Gathered, Not Made: A Brief History of Appropriative Writing" in the *American Poetry Review* (April 1999), included Bernstein's "Emotions of Normal People" from *Dark City* in the ranks of important poetry created with "borrowed texts." "His unit is not the 'musical' phrase . . . but the discursive category," Rubenstein wrote. "Constructed out of the various types of language which constitute contemporary identity, . . . 'Emotions of Normal People' appear[s] to question the use of the self as an organizing principle, not only for poems but for the entire realm of human history." Bernstein, having consistently castigated the political and educational establishments, in *American Literary History* offered a more modest appraisal of his place in history: "I am a product of the US and an example of it; this is a source of considerable discomfort to me but this discomfort is perhaps the basis of my work. . . . [M]y themes, to call them that, have pretty consistently been awkwardness, loss, and misrecognition."

In a critical article in the *Times Literary Supplement* (April 30, 1999) entitled "Rattling the Chains of Free Verse: The Surprising Survival of Language Poetry and Poetics," Paul Quinn acknowledged, reviewing *My Way: Speeches and Poems*, that although the title of Bernstein's book was ironic and that "only in the most alternative of universes could Bernstein be imagined as . . . leader of his own literary Rat Pack," Bernstein had nevertheless entered a phase of acceptance both within and outside the academy (previous reviews of Bernstein and Language poetry in the *Times Literary Supplement* had been dismissive). Quinn noted "the book's caustic and cautionary comments on identity politics—the dominant preoccupation in American literary practice and theory." He termed *My Way* "a *bricolage* of poems in essay form, essays in verse, interviews, polemics, provocations . . . puns and jokes." Quinn praised the variety and inclusiveness of Bernstein's thought: "Bernstein's own poetry practice has been tireless in striving to find a language fit to reflect and affect the times. If his essays are an ambitious and exciting attempt at a formally various methodology, his poems are collages of extraordinary range and texture; no American poet since Ashbery has woven such multifarious material into his poems. This is allied to a full-blown and mordantly funny critique of the roles we are made to adopt, of socialization's masquerade."

Quinn pointed out that Bernstein's anti-authoritarian stance dated from his earliest works and was inherent in his verse, as in the poem "Asylum," collected in *Islets/Irritations* (1983). "The language of definition with all its damaging shorthand is again to the fore," Quinn wrote, "but proceeding in syntactically severed sentences, so that each line plunges us *in medias res*, encouraging the reader to construct a fuller sense, rather than take the word of authority on trust." As Bernstein wrote in the preface to *The Politics of Poetic Form: Poetry and Public Policy*, a book he edited in 1990, he and the other authors "are concerned with the ways that the formal dynamics of a poem shape its ideology; more specifically, how radically innovative styles have political meanings."

Bernstein has continued to attempt both poetic innovation and the effecting of changes in readers' perceptions of the world. In "Log Rhythms" (1998), a poem on which Bernstein collaborated with Susan Bee, he drew on the Manhattan Yellow Pages and other cultural artifacts and detritus. Quinn judged him successful in producing "bourgeois culture's thousand twangling instruments, humming about our ears." "Nursery rhymes," Quinn suggested, "have a special significance in Bernstein's verse: they offer both a reminder that ideology coos at us over the crib and a potential liberation from conventional sense, a dawning awareness that the world is still to be made." Quinn concluded that works "as stimulating, calculatedly cantankerous, and irrepressibly entertaining as *My Way* . . . suggest it will be worth following Language poetry and poetics for some time yet."

Bernstein's most recent book of poems, *With Strings*, was released in 2001.

— S.Y.

SUGGESTED READING: *American Literary History* p6+ Spring 1998; *American Literature* p173 Mar. 1993; *American Poetry Review* p35+ Oct. 1995, p31+ Apr. 1999; *Times Literary Supplement* p32+ Apr. 30, 1999; *Virginia Quarterly Review* p380+ Spring 1998

SELECTED BOOKS: poetry—*Asylums*, 1975; *Parsing*, 1976; *Shade*, 1978; *Poetic Justice*, 1979; *Senses of Responsibility*, 1979; *Controlling Interests*, 1980; *Disfrutes*, 1981; *The Occurrence of Tune*, 1981; *Stigma*, 1981; *Islets/Irritations*, 1983; *Resistance*, 1983; *Veil*, 1987; *The Sophist*, 1987; *Four Poems*, 1988; *The Nude Formalism*, 1989; *The Absent Father in Dumbo*, 1990; *Fool's Gold*, 1991; *Rough Trades*, 1991; *Dark City*, 1994; *The Subject*, 1995; *Little Orphan Anagram*, 1997; *Log Rhythms*, 1998; *Republics of Reality: Poems 1975–1995*, 2000; *With Strings*, 2001; essays—*Content's Dream: Essays 1975–1984*, 1986; *A Poetics*, 1992; *My Way: Speeches and Poems*, 1999

Beschloss, Michael R.

(BESH-loss)

Nov. 30, 1955– Nonfiction writer; historian

Michael R. Beschloss is one of the best-known presidential historians in the United States. Through his frequent appearances as a guest commentator and panelist on political news programs such as *NewsHour with Jim Lehrer*, *Nightline*, and *Meet the Press*, he has become a familiar face to millions of television viewers, with whom he shares his knowledge of history and thoughts on current political events. Beschloss earned his reputation as an expert historian with the books he has authored on important events that took place during the presidencies of Franklin Roosevelt, Dwight Eisenhower, John F. Kennedy, Lyndon Johnson, and George Bush, which have received critical acclaim from fellow historians, reviewers, and jour-

Michael R. Beschloss
Courtesy of Public Affairs Books

nalists. Furthermore, with several of these books Beschloss has achieved what few authors do: sparking major reinterpretations of history. Although they are considered works of serious scholarship, solidly documented with material he uncovers in various government archives, Beschloss's books have also proved accessible—and appealing—to the general public. Commenting on Beschloss's cross-over success in a profile published in the Washington Post (December 16, 1997), Howard Kurtz observed, "Through a mixture of sheer talent, prodigious research, movie star looks and dinner party prowess, Beschloss has charmed his way into the bosom of the media elite, making his mark as both writer of serious books and silky-smooth dispenser of television wisdom."

Michael R. Beschloss submitted the following statement to World Authors 1995-2000: "I was born in Chicago on November 30, 1955, attending public schools in Flossmoor, Illinois, until the age of 12, and then went to Eaglebrook School, Andover, Williams College and Harvard University.

"From the age of 10, I hoped to write history—particularly the history of American Presidents. Since I was more interested in writing than teaching history, I hoped to divide my professional life between writing history and not-for-profit foundation management, and hence took a degree in management at Harvard, but before I could go on to complete a doctorate in history, I was hired as a staff historian by the Smithsonian Institution in Washington, D.C.

"My first book, Kennedy and Roosevelt: The Uneasy Alliance (Norton, 1980), on the relationship between Joseph Kennedy and Franklin Roosevelt, originated as my undergraduate thesis at Williams under the supervision of the great political scientist James MacGregor Burns, who wrote the foreword. Having written biographies of FDR and two Kennedys, Burns had suggested the subject, saying that the relationship was richer than people realized. He also helped me to achieve access to Joseph Kennedy's then-closed private papers and diaries.

"I chose to write my next book, Mayday: Eisenhower, Khrushchev and the U-2 Affair (Harper, 1986) for a variety of reasons. At the time, Ike's second term was the most recent moment for which once-secret Presidential papers were being declassified. Eisenhower's reputation was undergoing energetic revision. We were beginning to learn more than ever before about the CIA's influence on postwar world affairs. The result was a book that showed that, contrary to previous historiography, the U-2 episode had a serious impact on the course of the Cold War, destroying the chance that both Khrushchev and Eisenhower wanted to relieve the harshness of the American-Soviet competition and paving the way for the confrontations of the early 1960s over Berlin and Cuba.

"The Crisis Years: Kennedy and Khrushchev, 1960-1963 (HarperCollins, 1991) continued the story, using newly-opened Kennedy White House documents as well as Soviet sources freshly opened under Mikhail Gorbachev's program of glasnost. It differed with previous works by Kennedy aides like Theodore Sorensen's Kennedy and Arthur Schlesinger, Jr.'s A Thousand Days, which suggested that, with the exception of the Bay of Pigs fiasco, Kennedy's foreign policy leadership was almost consistently masterful. My book concluded that while indeed JFK managed to take the West through the Berlin and Cuban Missile Crises without flare-up into nuclear war, he made grave mistakes that unnecessarily exacerbated the dangers of the Cold War.

"I collaborated with Strobe Talbott, then Time's Editor-at-Large, later Bill Clinton's Deputy Secretary of State, on At the Highest Levels: The Inside Story of the End of the Cold War (Little, Brown, 1993). At the start of 1989, Talbott suggested to me that the next three years were likely to be an historic period and ripe for collaboration between a journalist and historian. We repeatedly interviewed key figures on both the American and Soviet sides and gained privileged access to some documents to tell what turned out to be the story of George Bush and Mikhail Gorbachev as they presided over the last three years of the Cold War, culminating with an interview we had with Gorbachev in the Kremlin twelve days before he resigned as President of the Soviet Union.

"My trilogy on President Lyndon Johnson's tapes of private conversations began with a dinner I had with Harry Middleton, Director of the Johnson Library, in June 1994. Middleton told me that the Library had decided to open the nearly thousand hours of recordings and described them to me. I replied that if the tapes were as revealing as he said, they would provide a window on LBJ in private that could cause a lot of history to be rewritten. I went to Texas to listen to some of the tapes and decided to create three volumes of edited and annotated transcripts that would constitute a kind of biography of LBJ in the White House. The first volume, *Taking Charge: The Johnson White House Tapes* (Simon & Schuster, 1997), has, I hope, helped to fuel a serious reconsideration of Johnson's Presidency.

"*Reaching for Glory* takes LBJ's story up to the fall of 1965, covering the 1964 campaign, the height of the Great Society and the plunge into large-scale involvement in Vietnam. The greatest surprises for me in the tapes from this period were Johnson's private pessimism about winning the war in Vietnam and his severe private forebodings, as early as the summer of 1965, that a Vietnam catastrophe was in danger of destroying his Presidency and damaging the country.

"I began *The Conquerors* 11 years before it was finally published in 2002, having waited for years in the meantime for the opening of new World War II-era American, British and Soviet documents, which I ultimately used in the book. In it, I was critical of Franklin Roosevelt for what I considered to be his lassitude in taking direct efforts to save European Jews and in considering direct means to stop the Holocaust, but I warmly applauded both FDR and Harry Truman for their foresight in shaping World War II strategy in a way that has helped postwar Germany to ultimately become peaceful and democratic.

"While at work on the final [volume] of the Johnson trilogy, I am also writing a history of Abraham Lincoln's last days and his assassination, which will be published by Simon & Schuster. I have been fascinated by the subject since visiting the Lincoln monuments at New Salem and Springfield at the age of seven. As the father of two boys, six and four as of this writing, I hope that this demonstrates the importance of encouraging children to be interested in American history by taking them to historic sites."

According to Howard Kurtz, the name Beschloss is Austrian, and Beschloss's family is supposedly descended from a Polish king. Beschloss, whose father was part-owner of a company that manufactured industrial robots, showed an interest in presidential history at an early age. According to Howard Kurtz, Beschloss read Arthur Schlesinger Jr.'s biography of President John F. Kennedy, *A Thousand Days* (1965), as a schoolboy and can recite the book from memory. After Kennedy was assassinated in November 1963, Beschloss wrote to President Lyndon Baines Johnson, urging him to honor Kennedy by having his face carved on the Mount Rushmore Memorial in South Dakota. On a visit to the Johnson Library and Museum in Austin, Texas, in 1977, Beschloss asked an archivist to look for the letter, and it was found within minutes. As a high school student, Beschloss worked as an intern for United States Senator Adlai Stevenson III, the Illinois Democrat and the son of Adlai Stevenson Jr., the late governor of Illinois, three-time unsuccessful presidential candidate and United States ambassador to the United Nations. The same year he found his childhood letter at the Johnson Library, Beschloss graduated from Williams College in Williamstown, Massachusetts, with highest honors. He enrolled at Harvard University in Cambridge, Massachusetts to pursue an MBA degree. Beschloss explained to *World Authors* that he structured his studies in such a way that it would allow him to eventually complete a doctorate in history, if he desired. However, the Smithsonian Institution in Washington, D.C. hired him as a staff historian a short time after he received his M.B.A. in 1980. Beschloss advised the Smithsonian Institution on several projects such as an exhibit that commemorated the centennial of President Harry S. Truman's birth.

Beschloss published his first book, *Kennedy and Roosevelt: The Uneasy Alliance*, in 1980. An expansion of his undergraduate honors thesis, it discussed the relationship between businessman Joseph Kennedy and President Franklin Roosevelt, detailing the backgrounds and the political philosophies of both men. Kennedy supported Roosevelt's candidacy in 1932 and later served the president in several posts, including ambassador to the United Kingdom from 1938 to 1940. In that role, Kennedy openly disagreed with Roosevelt's foreign policy by opposing any intervention by the United States in World War II, which broke out in 1939. This disagreement lead to Kennedy's resignation in 1940. In the *New York Times Book Review* (June 22, 1980), Daniel Yergin wrote that the book "is a thoroughly professional account of a fascinating relationship told with balance, literary skill and authority. Mr. Beschloss had access to previously unseen papers and interviewed many of the other actors in the tale. He has used the material well." In the *New Republic* (April 19, 1980), historian Robert Dallek described *Kennedy and Roosevelt* as "a lively, often amusing account" that added "some fresh detail to our knowledge of Kennedy's public life and is particularly good on his ambassadorial career." Dallek, however, criticized the book for offering "a somewhat distorted picture of Kennedy," finding that it "ascribes a degree of importance to Kennedy he does not deserve."

In his second book, *Mayday: Eisenhower, Khrushchev and the U-2 Affair* (1986), Beschloss analyzed the implications of one of the most famous incidents of the Cold War: the downing of an American U-2 spy plane over the Soviet Union on May 1, 1960. The United States had formerly denied allegations that the U-2 flights took place. The Soviets publicly revealed that they had recovered parts of the plane and captured the pilot, Francis Gary Powers, alive. The timing of the U-2 incident couldn't have been much worse; President Dwight Eisenhower, Soviet Premier Nikita Khrushchev, British Prime Minister Harold Macmillan, and

French President Charles de Gaulle were scheduled to meet several weeks later at a summit conference in Paris in the hope of reducing tensions between the two blocs and thus the chances for a violent conflict that could lead to nuclear war. When Eisenhower refused Khrushchev's demand that the United States apologize for spying on the Soviet Union, Khrushchev canceled the summit. In the *New York Times* (May 4, 1986) Alexander Dallin wrote of Bescholoss's account, "Perhaps the most instructive part of *Mayday* is the reconstruction of the logic that drove both the American President and the Soviet [Premier] . . . to take a series of steps that inexorably undermined the Paris summit and brought Soviet-American relations to a new low." Dallin added, "Michael Beschloss skillfully integrates a lot of material from a lot of sources on a lot of subjects into a very readable and thoroughly documented account, which is part thriller and part political history."

In 1990 Beschloss published *Eisenhower: A Centennial Life*, which was illustrated with numerous photographs of the general and president. In an interview with *World Authors*, Beschloss described the book as a "90,000 word interpretive essay on Eisenhower's life." Beschloss added that he sought to correct what he considered the "overrevisionist view" advanced by Princeton University Professor Fred I. Greenstein, the author of *The Hidden Hand Presidency: Eisenhower as Leader* (1982), which presents Eisenhower as "almost obsessively manipulative, devious and in control of his administration."

Beschloss received substantial acclaim for his book *The Crisis Years: Kennedy and Khrushchev, 1960-1963*, published in 1991. Drawing from primary sources made available from both the American and Soviet archives, the author chronicled the most dangerous years of the Cold War, when tensions between the United States and the Soviet Union nearly escalated into nuclear war. Hostility between the two countries was fueled by such events as the failed American-sponsored Bay of Pigs invasion of Cuba in March 1961; the ongoing dispute between the United States and the Soviet Union over Western access to West Berlin; the nasty summit meeting in Vienna between President John F. Kennedy and Soviet Premier Nikita Khrushchev in June 1961; covert attempts by the CIA to assassinate Cuban dictator Fidel Castro (who was firmly in the Soviet camp); the fiery rhetoric on both sides; the construction of the Berlin Wall in 1961; and the Cuban Missile Crisis in 1962. Beschloss argues that both Kennedy and Khrushchev often misinterpreted each other's actions and made miscalculations that increased tensions unnecessarily. For example, Beschloss contends that after the Bay of Pigs fiasco, Khrushchev concluded that Kennedy was indecisive and could be intimidated. This perception deluded Khrushchev into thinking that Kennedy would never use military force to oppose the installation of Soviet nuclear missiles in Cuba.

In his review for *Time* (June 17, 1991), Bruce Van Voorst wrote, "Numbering more than 800 pages (including 62 pages of footnotes), *The Crisis Years* is a compelling piece of historical research. . . . Its attraction as a scholarly work, however, should not detract from its appeal to the casual reader, who can easily become immersed in this captivating description of how the U.S. and the Soviet Union almost blundered into World War III." In the *New Yorker* (August 26, 1991), Naomi Bliven also praised the book, writing that Beschloss's "solid construction solves every problem of narration and exposition, and he handles encyclopedic detail and constant shifts of time and scene without apparent effort. He has a mass of new material from the Russian side, as a result of *glasnost*, and even more from this country, where the passage of time has opened many archives. The new information does more than add trimmings to history; some of it changes our fundamental readings of events and our assessments of the actors." For example, as President Richard Nixon did after him, Kennedy often tape-recorded meetings with his advisors. Bliven noted that transcripts of these recordings, which had been kept secret, "reveal the inaccuracy of memoirists who we thought had given us factual firsthand reports."

For his next book, *At the Highest Levels: The Inside Story of the End of the Cold War* (1993), Beschloss collaborated with Strobe Talbott, an editor at *Time* magazine and later deputy secretary of state in President Bill Clinton's administration. The book focuses on the relationship between President George Bush and Soviet Premier Mikhail Gorbachev and their diplomatic efforts to negotiate an end to the Cold War. Beschloss, as a historian, was at a major disadvantage because important documents and other archival materials from the period would not be released for decades. However, Beschloss and Talbott were granted access to some classified documents and also interviewed the key players on both sides, including U.S. Secretary of State James Baker and Soviet Foreign Minister Eduard Shevardnadze. The authors, who decided to write the book in January 1989, were also confronted by rapidly changing events that dramatically affected the substance of their narrative, such as the fall of the Berlin Wall in late 1989, the reunification of Germany in 1990, and the final disintegration of the Soviet Union in 1991.

In his review for the *Chicago Tribune* (January 31, 1993), Timothy J. McNulty commented, "Students of diplomacy and foreign affairs will cherish this book, for it conveys in detail the quiet, mano-a-mano drama of international negotiations . . . and the thrill of being there as great events unfold." McNulty observed that there was a downside to the authors reliance on interviews with important officials in both nations, because "the recollections of such officials can be extremely self-serving." For instance, McNulty noted that in the book "all of Baker's accomplishments are notable while his missteps seem minor, especially to him." In the *Wall*

Street Journal (March 8, 1993), Gerald Seib, while acknowledging that *At the Highest Levels* presented a "stunningly detailed account of the tangled relationship between Mr. Bush and Mr. Gorbachev," criticized Beschloss and Talbott for providing "little analysis of whether the world was well-served by the way these two leaders handled the awesome events that unfolded before them. It's hard to tell whether Messrs. Beschloss and Talbott think the two did a good, bad or middling job." Beschloss explained to *World Authors* that he and Talbott sought to write a "straight narration with limited analysis" of those events, because a real history of the period could not be written without the benefit of archival documents.

The subject of Beschloss's next book was President Lyndon Johnson. In a departure from his previous works, Beschloss decided to let the late president speak for himself. When Johnson became president following John F. Kennedy's assassination in 1963, he installed a taping system in the Oval Office in order to have exact records of what his political colleagues promised him. Unlike President Nixon, who recorded his conversations for only a portion of his presidency, from 1971 to 1973, Johnson made such recordings from the beginning to the end of his presidency. In around 1994 Beschloss became one of the first to make use of the tapes after the Lyndon Baines Johnson Library and Museum decided to make public nearly 10,000 of Johnson's recorded conversations. Beschloss spent nearly three years listening to and transcribing the tapes, in part to hear for himself the nuances of the conversations, Johnson's tone of voice, and the words he emphasized. At first, Beschloss wondered if Johnson was simply performing for the microphone, thinking that the president would stage conversations that would make him look good to future historians. Although Beschloss found some evidence of this, his concerns were quickly alleviated after he listened to Johnson discuss damaging information about himself and others. For example, the president is heard authorizing the leaking to the press of confidential FBI information about his political opponents.

Beschloss decided to publish three volumes with selected, annotated transcripts of Johnson's recordings. The first book, *Taking Charge: The Johnson White House Tapes, 1963-1964*, appeared in 1997. Most reviewers enthusiastically praised the book, saying it offered valuable insights into President Johnson's character, personality, leadership style, political skills, views, and policies. In her review for the *New York Times* (October 10, 1997, on-line), Michiko Kakutani wrote, "In these pages, we hear Johnson slyly strong-arming his longtime friend Richard Russell into serving on the Warren Commission alongside Chief Justice Earl Warren. We hear Johnson gently trying to comfort the mother of the slain civil rights worker Michael Schwerner. . . . And we hear him muttering darkly to his aides about his distrust of Robert F. Kennedy." Kakutani added that the conversations show Johnson's efforts to get civil rights legislation and his Great Society anti-poverty programs approved by Congress. On the United States' growing involvement in Vietnam, Johnson expresses reservations about getting the nation embroiled in an unpopular and perhaps unwinnable war. However, at the same time, he does not want to be accused of being soft on communism. Kakutani also wrote that Beschloss "not only situates Johnson's conversations in a historical context but also provides illuminating footnotes that flesh out Johnson's thinking." Writing in the *New Leader* (December 29, 1997), Henry F. Graff observed, "Michael R. Beschloss . . . has superbly edited the tapes covering the first year of LBJ's Administration. Whatever follows in succeeding volumes, the complex Texan is fully revealed in these pages. Constantly on the phone, he is by turns choleric, charming, funny, cunning, affectionate, troubled, overbearing, and insecure."

The second volume of the transcripts, *Reaching for Glory: Lyndon Johnson's Secret White House Tapes, 1964-65*, was published in 2001. Beschloss revealed contradictions in Johnson's character. In one conversation with Nicholas Katzenbach, the attorney general, the president is heard expressing his moral objections to wiretapping. However, Johnson supports the FBI's continued wiretapping of Reverend Martin Luther King, the civil rights leader, in order to obtain damaging and embarrassing information about his private life. Although Johnson repeatedly expresses doubts about achieving victory in Vietnam, he is convinced that if the United States withdraws from the conflict, communism would eventually spread to Cambodia, Burma, Thailand, Indonesia, India, and the Philippines. Reviewing the book for the *Washington Monthly* (March 2002), David J. Garrow wrote, "Though phenomenally rich and valuable as historical documents, only dedicated political junkies will wish to plow through all of these dense—though often fascinating—conversations. Scholars of America's involvement in Vietnam will draw the greatest benefit from *Reaching for Glory*, though many other subjects, from [the president's military intervention in] the Dominican Republic to Johnson's own tormented psyche, are substantially illuminated."

In his next book, *The Conquerors: Roosevelt, Truman, and the Destruction of Hitler's Germany, 1941-1945* (2002), Beschloss wrote about the different policies the United States considered pursuing with regard to Germany after it was defeated in World War II. At Roosevelt's request in late 1944, the U. S. Secretary of the Treasury Henry Morgenthau drew up a plan to destroy Germany's industrial capacity and ensure that it would never rise again to threaten Europe. Germany's extermination of the Jews outraged Morgenthau, who was the only Jew in Roosevelt's Cabinet. Morgenthau, who considered Roosevelt a close friend, tried unsuccessfully to get the president to do more to help the Jews. Both Cordell Hull, the secretary of state, and

Henry Stimson, the secretary of war, objected to the "Morgenthau Plan" and leaked details of it to the press. The plan encountered substantial criticism, which forced Roosevelt to abandon it. After Roosevelt's death on April 12, 1945, his successor, Harry Truman, agreed to rebuild Germany's economy and turn it into a vibrant democracy that would help the West resist Soviet communism. "[Beschloss's] account includes new information unearthed from previously classified documents and private sources," Willie Drye wrote in his review for *American History* (April 2003). "Beschloss offers a detailed, highly readable interpretation of how Allied leaders, despite their flaws and squabbling, made certain the world would not confront another Hitler."

As he told *World Authors*, Beschloss estimates that about five percent of his time is taken up by his work as a commentator and analyst for PBS and his job as the ABC News historical consultant. He has also done freelance writing for *Vanity Fair* and the now-defunct political magazine *George*. In coming years, as the relevant documents and papers are made public, Beschloss hopes to write books about other recent presidents. He is also writing a book about Abraham Lincoln, who, as Beschloss told Adam Clymer for the *New York Times* (July 25, 1991), "is the greatest of our Presidents in my view." At the time of that interview, Beschloss had a portrait of Lincoln on the wall of his home office, where he did most of his writing. His interest in diplomatic history, Beschloss said to Clymer, arose in part from his desire "to try to find in history, lessons that can help to guide leaders of our own times." Howard Kurtz described Beschloss as "courtly" and "self-effacing," qualities that Kurtz believes have contributed to Beschloss's success.

Beschloss is married to Afsaneh Mashayekhi, who was born in Iran and is the director of investments for the World Bank. The couple resides in Washington, D.C., with their two sons, Alexander and Cyrus.

—D.C.

SUGGESTED READING: *American History* p62+ Apr. 2003; *Chicago Tribune* 14 p3 Jan. 31, 1993; *New Leader* p8 Dec. 29, 1997; *New Republic* p32 Apr. 19, 1980; *New York Times* A p12 July 25, 1991; *New York Times* (on-line) Oct. 10, 1997; *New York Times Book Review* p15 June 15, 1980, p7 May 4, 1986; *New Yorker* p77+ Aug. 26, 1991; *Time* p77 June 17, 1991; *Wall Street Journal* p10 Mar. 8, 1993; *Washington Monthly* p48+ Mar. 2002; *Washington Post* B p1 Dec. 16, 1997

SELECTED BOOKS: nonfiction—*Kennedy and Roosevelt: The Uneasy Alliance*, 1980; *Mayday: Eisenhower, Khrushchev and the U-2 Affair*, 1986; *Eisenhower: A Centennial Life*, 1990; *The Crisis Years: Kennedy and Khrushchev, 1960–1963*, 1991; *Sudden Victory: Bush, Gorbachev and the End of the Cold War* (with Strobe Talbott), 1992; *At the Highest Levels: The Inside Story of the End of the Cold War* (with Strobe Talbott), 1993; *Presidents, Television and Foreign Crises*, 1993; *The Digital Libraries in Our Future: Perils and Promise*, 1996; *Taking Charge: the Johnson White House Tapes, 1963–1964*, 1997; *Reaching for Glory: Lyndon Johnson's Secret White House Tapes*, 2001; *The Conquerors: Roosevelt, Truman and the Destruction of Hitler's Germany, 1941–1945*, 2002; as editor— *American Heritage Illustrated History of the Presidents*, 2000

Courtesy of Virago Press

Birch, Carol

Jan. 3, 1951– Novelist; storyteller

Carol Birch is the author of several novels, most of which detail the adventurous and sometimes self-destructive lifestyles of certain young people in the 1960s and '70s, and contrast them with the more settled lives of those same people as adults. D. J. Taylor, in the London *Guardian* (July 24, 1999), praised Birch's work and noted some of the distinguishing traits of her characters. "The people in her books," Taylor observed, "tend to be what the novelists of a couple of generations back would infallibly mark down as 'women of a certain age'—forty-something survivors looking wistfully, if sometimes thankfully, back on a crowded early life in which sensation came balanced by emotional turmoil, usually courtesy of the weak, directionless men to whom Birch females incline with the avidity of a compass point hitting North." Birch is also a well-respected storyteller who has performed her tales in many countries, including Australia, Canada, Germany, and Singapore. She has been heard on ABC's *Nightline*, CBS's *This Morning*, and on National Public Radio. In 1998 she received the National Storytelling Network's Circle of Excellence Award.

Carol Birch was born in Manchester, England, on January 3, 1951, the daughter of Frederick Fidler, a metallurgist, and Nancy (Rowe) Fidler. She received a B.A. from Keele University, in Keele, England, in 1972. After graduation she took a variety of jobs, including stints as an assistant at the English Folk Dance and Song Society, a library clerk, and a helper for people with learning difficulties. In 1987 she took a part-time position as a special-education teacher at South Thames College, in London, and as an outreach worker at the National Elfrida Rathbone Society, an organization that aids people with learning difficulties.

During the early 1980s Birch lived in a council estate, or government housing project. She told *Contemporary Authors* (1989) that the experience inspired her first novel, *Life in the Palace*, which was published in 1988. "*Life in the Palace* grew out of six years spent on a council estate described variously in the London press of the time as 'one of the worst slums in London,' a 'hell-hole,' and a 'playground for violence,'" Birch recalled. Many of the situations depicted in the novel were taken from real events that she witnessed at the council estate; the book was written "out of a sense of anger and injustice," she explained, "and a desire to set the record straight. Too many people who had not known the place and the people too easily dismissed and stereotyped them from a complacent distance."

Life in the Palace is a wandering narrative that depicts the lives of those living in a low-income London tenement. Among them are Judy Grey, an ex-teacher with a history of bad luck with men, Jimmy Raffo, a good-hearted but self-destructive roamer, and Loretta Booth, an overweight, chronic thief tormented by her repeated miscarriages. Birch's idiosyncratic characters are desperate and often unhappy, but they live on the fringes of society by choice. D. J. Taylor, in the *New Statesman* (March 6, 1996), applauded *Life in the Palace* and noted that it could serve as a sort of template for her succeeding novels. Judy Grey, Taylor wrote, typifies Birch's "cool-eyed and battle-scarred women on the cusp of middle age looking back at their lives with a wary mixture of nostalgia and unalloyed relief." Jimmy Raffo exemplifies the "charming, unreliable man, perennially enticing but with 'Must To Avoid' inked all over his shirt-front." Taylor called Birch an author of "extraordinary talents" and found the book involving despite Birch's "emphasis on ground-down interior brooding" rather than action. In the *Times Literary Supplement* (March 8, 1988), Julia Hamilton, as quoted in *Contemporary Authors* (1989), marveled at the "seething diversity reflected in the itinerant lives of the inhabitants, survivors of grim economic shipwreck, most of whom are clinging on to life by their fingertips." *Life in the Palace* won the 1988 David Higham Award for best first novel.

In 1989 Birch published *The Fog Line*, and in 1992 she published *Unmaking*. Her next novel, *Songs of the West* (1994), centers on a small village in County Cork, Ireland, where long-time villagers mix with "blow-ins," the recent transplants to the area, many of whom have artistic aspirations. The book's heroine, Marie, is a married local woman who falls in love with Bob, a blow-in writer. Ruth Pavey, in the *New Statesman & Society* (January 6, 1995), called *Songs of the West* a "rich, often funny novel."

In 1996 Birch edited *Who Says?: Essays on Pivotal Issues in Contemporary Storytelling*, a collection of essays by storytellers and folklorists. In 1998 she published the novel *Little Sister*, which is about Cathy Wren, a 37-year-old woman who supports herself by waiting on tables and giving piano lessons. One day an unexpected occurrence sends her on a search for the little sister she hasn't seen for 10 years.

In 1999 Birch published *Come Back, Paddy Riley*, the story of Anita, a well-off middle-aged mother of two, who works part-time in a bookstore and daydreams about her more exciting past. During the 1960s Anita's mother had worked as part of a traveling carnival show and was involved in a relationship with the show's "barker," Paddy Reilly. Anita herself, while on the cusp of adolescence, developed an infatuation with the roguish carnival worker. Years later she meets a man who reminds her of Paddy, and they begin a furtive affair.

Critics generally found *Come Back, Paddy Riley* to be a powerful, evocative novel. "Drifting through great swathes of lost English time, by turns sorrowful and matter-of-fact, *Come Back, Paddy Riley* is a riveting dispatch from a fictional world that ought to be better known," D. J. Taylor wrote in the London *Guardian* (July 24, 1999). "It's a delight to be back in the Birchforest." In the London *Times* (July 31, 1999) Christina Koning wrote, "This is a novel not so much about love as about the damage that people do to one another in the name of love—and is entirely convincing."

In 2000 Birch published *The Whole Story Handbook: Using Imagery to Complete the Story Experience*, a guide for adapting stories from text to spoken word. "[Birch] exhibits both wit and common sense; anecdotes, suggestions, and cautions are forthrightly communicated," Janice M. Del Negro wrote in the *Bulletin of the Center for Children's Books* (April 2001). "The author has the gift of specificity, expertly incorporating theory within concrete examples from specific tales."

Birch was a contributor to *Joining In: An Anthology of Audience Participation Stories and How to Tell Them* (1988). She has recorded audiocassettes of her own stories, in addition to producing and directing numerous audiocassettes for other storytellers. She is a frequent participant in the National Storytelling Festival, held annually in Jonesborough, Tennessee. Birch is a member of the Society of Authors.

—P. G. H.

SUGGESTED READING: *Bulletin of the Center for Children's Books* p323 Apr. 2001; (London) *Guardian* p8+ July 24, 1999; *New Statesman* p58 Mar. 6, 1996; *New Statesman & Society* p38 Jan. 6, 1995; (London) *Times* p22 July 31, 1999; *Times Literary Supplement* p21+ July 16, 1999

SELECTED BOOKS: *Life in the Palace*, 1988; *The Fog Line*, 1989; *Unmaking*, 1992; *Songs of the West*, 1994; *Little Sister*, 1998; *Come Back, Paddy Riley*, 1999; as editor—*Who Says?: Essays on Pivotal Issues in Contemporary Storytelling*, 1996; as contributor—*Joining In: An Anthology of Audience Participation Stories and How to Tell Them*, 1988

Courtesy of HarperCollins Publishers

Bix, Herbert P.

1938– Professor; historian; nonfiction writer

After winning the Pulitzer Prize in 2001 for his best-selling biography *Hirohito and the Making of Modern Japan*, Herbert P. Bix went from relative obscurity to being considered one of the foremost authorities on the Japanese emperor and postwar Japan. His thoroughly researched book dismantles the myth that Hirohito was a peace-loving figurehead who had no control of the Japanese military, and shows how both before and during World War II, he was, as Steven Butler described him in *U.S. News and World Report* (August 28, 2000), "in name and fact the supreme commander of Japanese military force—well briefed on all military activities from the bombing of Pearl Harbor to the atrocities committed by Japanese troops in Nanjing, and willing and able to intervene and issue orders." In addition to *Hirohito*, Bix wrote *Peasant Protest in Japan, 1590–1884* (1986) and is a frequent contributor to scholarly journals of Japanese and Asian studies.

Herbert P. Bix was born in Boston, Massachusetts, in 1938, and raised in nearby Winthrop. For his undergraduate studies he attended the University of Massachusetts at Amherst. After college he joined the U.S. Naval Reserve and did his tour of duty on ships stationed in Japan. Upon leaving the navy he began his graduate studies at Harvard University, in Cambridge, Massachusetts, where he earned a doctorate in history and Far Eastern languages. During his time at Harvard he helped to establish and contributed to a new journal on Asian studies: the *Bulletin of Concerned Asian Scholars*.

In Bix's first book, *Peasant Protests in Japan, 1590–1884*, published in 1986 and reprinted in 1992, he describes the development of feudalism in Japan and the causes of peasant uprisings during that period. He focuses on three fiefdoms on Honshu, Japan's central island, and notes that the causes of the protests there were the landowners' excessive demands on the peasants, who were subjected to inhumanly long working days and unreasonable production quotas. Bix also looks at the Japanese underclass in urban areas and describes how class structures were rocked by such uprisings.

Though Jeffery Broadbent complained in *Contemporary Sociology* (May 1987) about what he saw as Bix's disregard for modern sociological theories, he went on to remark: "[His] work remains one of the clearest, most insightful and sustained substantive expositions of the historical political-economic approach to social movements in the literature, for any country or time period." In *Choice* (December 1986), W. J. Donahue suggested that Bix has overstated the importance of these peasant uprisings, but maintained that "this is an excellent book that depicts the harshness of that era. It is well researched, documented, and written in a readable style."

In 2000 Bix published *Hirohito and the Making of Modern Japan*, a monumental biography of the longest reigning emperor in the history of Japan. Although Hirohito had long been considered a figurehead by Japanese and American scholars, Bix dismantles that myth with newly released documents that suggest the emperor fully encouraged and oversaw the planning of Japanese wars in Asia, in the 1930s; the bombing of the American base at Pearl Harbor, on December 7, 1941; and the final decision to surrender, in 1945. As Steven Butler noted: "[Hirohito] personally delayed the inevitable surrender for months essentially to protect his own skin and his divine imperial rule, while hundreds of thousands of Japanese citizens and soldiers died. Afterward, he lied about his role and sacrificed his chief lieutenants to the hangman. And, Bix writes, he did so with the full knowledge and encouragement of [U.S. General Douglas] MacArthur, who used Hirohito to smooth the progress of the occupation and to shore up Japan as an ally in the Cold War that provided key military bases in the western Pacific."

Hirohito and the Making of Modern Japan, the first complete English-language biography of the Japanese emperor, was lauded by critics and awarded the 2001 Pulitzer Prize in General Non-Fiction. Calling it an "important and provocative" book, Ronald Spector wrote in the *New York Times Book Review* (November 19, 2000): "Bix's Hirohito is neither a Hitler nor a pacifist but a deeply flawed statesman. Above all, he was no passive symbolic monarch but a behind-the-scenes wheeler-dealer whose words could make or break cabinets." "Meticulously researched, relying mostly on Japanese materials—diaries, letters, memoirs and apologias of Hirohito's military and civilian advisers and contemporaries—*Hirohito and the Making of Modern Japan* is an incisive work of scholarship," cheered Leonard W. Boasberg in the *Philadelphia Inquirer* (January 14, 2001). "It should put an end to the myth, contrived by Americans as well as Japanese, that Hirohito had been a peace-loving, passive puppet of the military."

Herbert P. Bix has taught Japanese history at a number of Japanese and American universities, including Harvard and the Graduate School of Social Sciences in Tokyo, Japan. He lived in Japan for 15 years before returning to the United States, in 2001, to teach history and sociology at Binghamton University, part of the State University of New York (SUNY). In addition to his books, Bix has written extensively for sociological and historical academic journals, both in the United States and in Japan.

—C. M.

SUGGESTED READING: *Asiaweek.com* (on-line); Binghamton University Web site; *Choice* p672 Dec. 1986; *Contemporary Sociology* p309 May 1987; *Economist* p77+ Sep. 2, 2000; *Foreign Correspondent/Australian Broadcasting Corporation* (on-line); *New York Times Book Review* p14 Nov. 19, 2000; *Philadelphia Inquirer* (on-line) Jan. 14, 2001; *U.S. News and World Report* p51 Aug. 28, 2000

SELECTED BOOKS: *Peasant Protest in Japan, 1590–1884*, 1986; *Hirohito and the Making of Modern Japan*, 2000

Black, Edwin

Feb. 27, 1950– Journalist; nonfiction writer; historian; novelist

Edwin Black has enjoyed a long and successful career in journalism. Writing for many different publications, Black has investigated noteworthy stories involving political corruption, insurance scams, and neo-Nazi skinheads. Black employed his skills as an investigative reporter for two nonfiction books, *The Transfer Agreement: The Dramatic Story of the Pact Between the Third Reich and Jewish Palestine* (1984) and *IBM and the Holocaust: The Strategic Alliance Between Nazi Germany and America's Most Powerful Corporation* (2001). *The Transfer Agreement* provides the first detailed account of a secret agreement between Zionist leaders and Nazi Germany that resulted in the emigration of 50,000 Jews to Palestine. *IBM and the Holocaust* reveals that the company placed profits over morality by providing Nazi Germany with punch-card machines that helped make the mass murder of Jews easier. Black has also published a novel, *Format C:* (1999), that tells the story of a wealthy computer magnate's attempts to take over the world.

Edwin Black's publisher submitted the following statement to *World Authors 1995–2000*: "Edwin Black's best-selling book, *The Transfer Agreement: The Dramatic Story of the Pact Between the Third Reich and Jewish Palestine*, won the Carl Sandburg Award for the best non-fiction of 1984 and was nominated by Macmillan Books for a Pulitzer Prize. In conjunction with the book, Black ap-

Anthony Marill/Courtesy of Crown Publicity/Random House

peared on some 200 TV and radio shows, including *CBS Morning News* and on an NBC affiliate documentary on the book, and enjoyed major feature coverage in the *Washington Post Sunday Magazine* and *Chicago Tribune Sunday Magazine*, as well as front page or spread coverage in publications across the country. In April 1998, the author was honored by Spertus Institute at a special ceremony in Chicago for donating the 35,000 archival documents gathered in the original research. Dialog Press has published an updated edition of *The Transfer Agreement*, with new material added by Abraham H. Foxman, national director of the Anti-Defamation League and Edward T. Chase, former editor-in-chief of *New York Times* Books. Carroll & Graf Books has published the latest edition, a trade paperback, with a new introduction by the author.

"Black is best known for his controversial, internationally best-selling book, *IBM and the Holocaust* (Crown Books, 2001). The massive international investigation details IBM's conscious involvement in Hitler's destruction of six million Jews. Simultaneously released in forty countries in nine languages on February 12, 2001, the book has already been the subject of massive media attention and almost universal acclaim by historians and experts of the period. Black subjected his book to the advance review of some 35 historians and other experts prior to publication and they unanimously endorsed the book. The book has already been the subject of front page and lead coverage in dozens of newspapers and magazines such as *New York Times, Washington Post, Los Angeles Times, London Times, L'Express, Der Spiegel, Le Monde,* most of whom verified the book in the months before publication and purchased reprint rights from the publisher. The *Los Angeles Times* syndicated excerpts to the top 100 foreign newspapers and magazines. Dozens of TV networks also advance verified the book and created news specials which aired in the first week of the book's publication.

"Black also wrote a novel. He wove images from the Holocaust and the true story of his parents' survival into his first novel, *Format C:* (Dialog Press 1999), an apocalyptic Y2K techno-thriller. *Format C:* has been met with critical acclaim. In May and June 1999, the author embarked upon a 15-city national tour of launch parties, receptions, speaking engagements and autograph signings.

"From 1986 until 1988, Black's weekly syndicated column, *The Cutting Edge* was published by newspapers in 50 cities across the United States and Canada. During 1987–88, the column originated from Jerusalem where Black was based as a foreign correspondent. From 1986 to 1988, the column received three nominations for the Pulitzer Prize. The enterprise and investigative column was noted for breaking stories on the Skinheads, the Aryan Brotherhood, the Black Hebrews, and Israeli religious strife. During his time in Israel, Black scored exclusive interviews with Prime Minister Yitzhak Shamir and Egyptian Ambassador Mohammad Bassiouny. He was the only non-Israeli print journalist to accompany Shimon Peres on his surprise February 1987 summit in Cairo. For the column, Black also accompanied the South Lebanese Army on patrol in Lebanon, Anti-Defamation League leaders during their Pollard crisis mission to Jerusalem, and the Jerusalem Bomb Squad during an outbreak of terror bombings.

"Black's writings have appeared in such diverse publications as *Der Spiegel, Playboy, Redbook, Mademoiselle, London Sunday Times, Washington Post, Chicago Tribune, Chicago Sun-Times, Business Week, Sports Illustrated, Downbeat, Medical Economics,* and *Journal of the American Bar Association.* His work is mainly (but not entirely) built on enterprise and investigative journalism. Topics and special achievements include exclusive interviews with Louis Farrakhan and Bishop Desmond Tutu, exclusive revelations and interviews on the notorious Gary Dotson-Cathy Webb rape recantation case, probes of maternal infanticide and child suicide, undercover investigations of the assassination of JFK, the enslavement of the Cocos Islanders, the lead investigation of Sen. David Durenberger's ethics violations that lead to his indictment, an undercover investigation of homeless conditions in Washington that led to the establishment of two federally funded health clinics, and in 1988 Black was the first to reveal the sudden emergence of the neo-Nazi bent of Skinheads in the U.S. Black has been featured on many broadcasts in conjunction with his writing, including *CBS Morning News, The Oprah Winfrey Show* (Skinheads investigation), *Dateline,* and many others.

"Black's major investigation of a network of corrupt malpractice insurance companies toppled the infamous Bramson global network of insurance companies, resulting in numerous indictments and imprisonments. The series led to Black's writing a cover story in the *Journal of the American Bar Association* in 1993, a cover story in *Medical Economics,* and, in 1994, he co-authored an article in *Business Week.* For his investigation Black was the focus of the 1993 season's premiere of *America's Most Wanted* on Fox-TV.

"Black is an avid reviewer and commentator on music, especially movie music. His frequent essays and reviews on film scoring have appeared in *Chicago Tribune, Chicago Reader, Film Music Magazine, Film Score Monthly, Music for the Movies, Spectrum Magazine,* and *Times Mirror's Hollywood Online,* and he moderates the movie music forum on Fox's Bix. In England, his work regularly appears in *Movie Music UK* and *Movie Wave.* In France, his work regularly appears in *Traxzone,* both in English and French. For his film music work, Black has interviewed such notables as Hans Zimmer and Jerry Goldsmith. Black's non-soundtrack essays and reviews—on a spectrum of schools from jazz to the classics—have appeared in *Chicago Tribune, Downbeat, International Musician, Country Music Magazine,* and *Earth Magazine*; for these, he has interviewed such diverse composers and performers as Dimitri Shostokovich, Aaron Copland, Sir Georg Solti, Ramsey Lewis, Minnie Ripperton, Cannonball Adderly, and Miles Davis."

Black himself submitted to *World Authors* this first-person account of his research for the book *IBM and the Holocaust: The Strategic Alliance Between Nazi Germany and America's Most Powerful*

Corporation: "What made me demand answers to the unasked questions about IBM and the Holocaust? I confronted the reality of IBM's involvement one day in 1993 in Washington at the United States Holocaust Museum. There, in the very first exhibit, an IBM Hollerith D-11 card sorting machine—riddled with circuits, slots, and wires—was prominently displayed. Clearly affixed to the machine's front panel glistened an IBM nameplate. It has since been replaced with a smaller IBM machine because so many people congregated around it, creating a bottleneck. The exhibit explained little more than that IBM was responsible for organizing the census of 1933 that first identified the Jews. IBM had been tight-lipped about its involvement with Nazi Germany. So although 15 million people, including most major Holocaust experts, have seen the display, and in spite of the best efforts of leading museum historians, little more was understood about this provocative display other than the brief curator's description at the exhibit and a few pages of supportive research. I still remember the moment, staring at the machine for an hour. I turned to my mother and father who accompanied me to the museum that day and promised I would discover more. My parents are Holocaust survivors, uprooted from their homes in Poland. My mother escaped from a boxcar en route to Treblinka, was shot, and then buried in a shallow mass grave. My father had already run away from a guarded line of Jews and discovered her leg protruding from the snow. By moonlight and by courage, these two escapees survived against the cold, the hunger, and the Reich. Standing next to me five decades later, their image within the reflection of the exhibit glass, shrapnel and bullet fragments permanently embedded in their bodies, my parents could only express confusion. But I had other questions. The Nazis had my parents' names. How? What was the connection of this gleaming black, beige and silver machine, squatting silently in this dimly lit museum, to the millions of Jews and other Europeans who were murdered—and murdered not just in a chaotic split-second as a casualty of war, but in a grotesque and protracted twelve-year campaign of highly organized humiliation, dehumanization, and then ultimately extermination.

"For years after that chance discovery, I was shadowed by the realization that IBM was somehow involved in the Holocaust in technologic ways that had not yet been pieced together. Dots were everywhere. The dots needed to be connected. Knowing that International Business Machines has always billed itself as a 'solutions' company, I understood that IBM does not merely wait for governmental customers to call. IBM has amassed its fortune and reputation precisely because it generally anticipates governmental and corporate needs even before they develop, and then offers, designs, and delivers customized solutions—even if it must execute those technologic solutions with its own staff and equipment. IBM has done so for countless government agencies, corporate giants, and industrial associations. For years I promised myself I would one day answer the question: how many solutions did IBM provide to Nazi Germany? I knew about the initial solution: the census. Just how far did the solutions go?

"In 1998, I began an obsessive quest for answers. Proceeding without any foundation funds, organizational grants, or publisher dollars behind me, I began recruiting a team of researchers, interns, translators and assistants, all on my own dime. Soon a network developed throughout the United States, as well as in Germany, Israel, England, Holland, Poland, and France. This network continued to grow as time went on. Holocaust survivors, children of survivors, retirees, and students with no connection to the Holocaust—as well as professional researchers, distinguished archivists and historians, and even former Nuremberg Trial investigators—all began a search for documentation. Ultimately, more than 100 people participated, some for months at a time, some for just a few hours searching obscure Polish documents for key phrases. Not knowing the story, they searched for key words: census, statistics, lists, registrations, railroads, punch cards, and a roster of other topics. When they found them, the material was copied and sent. For many weeks, documents were flowing in at the rate of 100 per day. Most of my team was volunteers. All of them were sworn to secrecy. Each was shocked and saddened by the implications of the project and intensely motivated. A few said they could not sleep well for days after learning of the connection. I was often sustained by their words of encouragement.

"Ultimately, I assembled more than 20,000 pages of documentation from 50 archives, library manuscript collections, museum files, and other repositories. In the process, I accessed thousands of formerly classified State Department, OSS, or other previously restricted government papers. Other obscure documents from European holdings had never been translated or connected to such an inquiry. All these were organized in my own central archive mirroring the original archival source files. We also scanned and translated more than 50 general books and memoirs, as well as contemporary technical and scientific journals covering punch cards and statistics, Nazi publications, and newspapers of the era. All of this material—primary documents, journal articles, news clips, and book extracts—was cross-indexed by month. We created one manila folder for every month from 1933 to 1950. If a document referred to numerous dates, it was cross-filed in the numerous monthly folders. Then all contents of monthly folders were further cross-indexed into narrow topic threads, such as Warsaw Ghetto, German Census, Bulgarian Railroads, Watson in Germany, Auschwitz, and so on.

"Stacks of documents organized into topics were arrayed across my basement floor. As many as six people at a time busily shuttled copies of documents from one topic stack to another from morning until midnight. One document might be copied into five or six topic stacks. A high-speed copier with a 20-bin sorter was installed. Just moving from place to place in the basement involved hopscotching around document piles. None of the 20,000 documents were flash cards. It was much more complex. Examined singly, none revealed their story. Indeed, most of them were profoundly misleading as stand-alone papers. They only assumed their true meaning when juxtaposed with numerous other related documents, often from totally unrelated sources. In other words, the documents were all puzzle pieces—the picture could not be constructed until all the fragments were put together."

The son of Holocaust survivors from Poland, Edwin Black was born on February 27, 1950 in Chicago, Illinois. He enjoyed writing from an early age. "Writing just took me," he explained to *World Authors*. Black began his career as a reporter, writing "hard news" for the *Chicago Tribune*, *Chicago Sun-Times*, *Chicago Daily News*, and *Chicago Today*. At the age of 18, he was the youngest writer admitted to the Author's Guild. Since the 1970s Black has worked for numerous publications as a foreign correspondent, columnist, music critic, reporter, and investigative journalist. Over the course of his career he has earned many prestigious awards. In 1978 he won the Chicago Award for securing an exclusive interview with the Jewish attorney who represented members of the American Nazi Party in their fight to march through Skokie, Illinois, where many Holocaust survivors lived. Black has also been honored with the Eagle Award (1978) for excellence in editing, the Smolar Award (1987) for excellence in public affairs journalism, the Rockower Award (1988) for excellence in Jewish commentary, two Folio Awards for excellence in magazine publishing, and an award from the Computer Press Association. Black has also been nominated for the Pulitzer Prize five times, the SDX Service Awards twice, and the IRE Award once.

In 1984 Edwin Black published his first book, *The Transfer Agreement: The Dramatic Story of the Pact Between the Third Reich and Jewish Palestine*. In August 1933 a group of Zionists concluded an agreement with Nazi Germany that enabled about 50,000 German Jews to emigrate to Palestine, where the State of Israel was created in 1947, and to take about $200 million of their assets with them. In exchange for these concessions, the Zionists agreed not to support the boycott of Germany that was organized by Jews in the United States and other countries. Under the terms of the agreement, the German Jews were allowed to access their frozen bank accounts back in Germany in order to purchase German goods that would then be exported to Palestine. After the goods reached Palestine, they were exchanged for cash. Black asserted that the transfer agreement strengthened the German economy and undermined the boycott of Germany—an action that required the support of Zionist leaders to be effective. In his review for *Commentary* (September 1984), Richard S. Levy wrote, "Black covers [this story] in mountainous and excessive detail. . . . Working from printed documents, unpublished letters, and private papers, Black is soundest in describing the complicated negotiations of various Zionist representatives and private individuals with the organs of the German government." Levy, however, faulted Black for ignoring secondary source literature and suggested that he relied "too heavily and uncritically on contemporary sources, newspaper accounts, and diplomatic reports." Writing in *Choice* (October 1984), C. Fink praised *The Transfer Agreement*. "Black is the first to investigate the origins of the August 1933 agreement, the international political and economic context in which it was drawn up, the leading persons involved, the repercussions within Jewish and Zionist organizations, and the long-term results," Fink wrote. The reviewer lauded Black for writing a "detailed, dramatic study" of the subject. *The Transfer Agreement* won the Carl Sandburg Award for best nonfiction book, in 1984, and was also nominated for a Pulitzer Prize. In 1999 and 2001 Black published updated versions of the book with new material.

In 1999 Black published his first novel, *Format C:*, a "techno-thriller" that tapped fears about the Y2K bug and incorporated elements of kabbalah (Jewish mysticism). In her review for the *Library Journal* (May 1, 1999), Debra Mitts wrote, "The richest man on earth, owner of the world's biggest computer company, uses Y2K to make a play for global domination. What results instead is a battle between good and evil, fought in the Holy Land as the millennium turns." Mitts described the novel as an "entertaining and provocative examination of our dependency on computers and the amount of information we reveal about ourselves each time we log on." In *Wired* (August 1999, on-line), Craig Engler had mixed feelings about *Format C:* Although he was intrigued by the battle between good and evil in the novel, Engler wrote that its characters "seem to live in cardboard reality, and [Black's] forays into Judaica and the Holocaust are unconvincing."

In 2001 Edwin Black received substantial publicity for his controversial book, *IBM and the Holocaust: The Strategic Alliance Between Nazi Germany and America's Most Powerful Corporation*. Drawing on numerous primary and secondary sources, Black detailed how IBM, under the leadership of Chairman Thomas Watson Sr., provided the Nazis with the Hollerith punch-card machines that were used to compile lists of Jews. Using these lists, the Nazis were able to exterminate Jews with greater speed. In an interview with Michael Dobbs, a reporter for the *Washington Post* (February 11, 2001), Black said, "The Holocaust would have occurred with or without IBM—but the Holocaust that we know of, the Holocaust of the fantastic numbers, this is the Holocaust of IBM technology. It enabled the Nazis to achieve scale, velocity, efficiency." In the book, Black noted that Germany was IBM's biggest customer in Europe. In fact, the Nazis honored Watson in 1937 with a medal, which he returned in 1940. According to Black, Watson directly oversaw the operations of Dehomag, IBM's German subsidiary. Black stressed that Watson was not motivated by anti-Semitism, but by a desire to increase profits. *IBM and the Holocaust* received mostly favorable reviews. "Black's study . . . contains a wealth of unknown or little-known details," the noted Holocaust historian Saul Friedlander wrote in the *Los Angeles Times* (May 20, 2001). "The author convincingly shows the relentless efforts made by IBM to maximize profit by selling its machines and its punch cards to a country whose criminal record would soon be widely recognized. Indeed, Black demonstrates with great precision that the godlike owner of the corporation, Thomas Watson, was impervious to the moral dimension of his dealings with Hitler's Germany and for years even had a soft spot for the Nazi regime." In his review for the *Washington Post* (March 18, 2001), Christopher Simpson asserted that "Black establishes beyond dispute that IBM Hollerith machines significantly advanced Nazi efforts to exterminate Jewry." In such places as the Greater Reich and Holland, Simpson wrote, the Nazis used IBM's punch-card machines to conduct "racial censuses that identified Jews for confiscation of their property and deportation to slave labor camps and death camps." Although he did not always agree with Black's arguments, Simpson concluded that "*IBM and the Holocaust* is a valuable contribution to our understanding of the Holocaust." The book became an immediate bestseller.

Black's next book, "The War Against the Weak: America's Crusade to Create a Super Race," about the history of eugenics and genetic engineering, is scheduled to be published in September 2003. The author resides in suburban Washington, D.C.

—D. C.

SUGGESTED READING: *Choice* p327 Oct. 1984; *Commentary* p68+ Sep. 1984; *Jerusalem Post* B p13 Mar. 10, 2000; *Library Journal* p108 May 1, 1999; *Los Angeles Times Book Review* p1+ May 20, 2001, with photo; *Washington Post* A p22 Feb. 11, 2001; *Washington Post Book World* p7 Mar. 18, 2001; *Wired* (on-line) Aug. 1999

SELECTED BOOKS: nonfiction—*The Transfer Agreement: The Dramatic Story of the Pact Between the Third Reich and Jewish Palestine*, 1984; *IBM and the Holocaust: The Strategic Alliance Between Nazi Germany and America's Most Powerful Corporation*, 2001; fiction—*Format C:*, 1999

Bloom, Amy

June 18, 1953– Novelist; short-story writer

In her fiction, Amy Bloom, a practicing psychotherapist, writes of the strivings of the human heart and the strange places to which love leads people. Her first short-story collection, *Come to Me* (1993), was a finalist for a National Book Award. For the stories, she drew on aspects of her own life and often narrated in a voice that might have belonged to her younger self. She broadened the range of her narrative concerns in her novel, *Love Invents Us* (1997). Although the novel's principal character came from a short story in *Come to Me*, Bloom also included a wide range of characters of different ages, races, and backgrounds. Some of Bloom's other characters reappeared in her next short-story collection, *A Blind Man Can See I Love You* (2000), in which transsexualism, cancer, birth deformities, old age, and illicit sexual relationships color the ways in which characters see each other. "Amy Bloom cuts deep. . . . Bloom ties and unties knots in the hearts of her readers," Susan Salter Reynolds wrote in the *Los Angeles Times* (September 24, 2000). "Rich in forgiveness," Bloom's writings "make you realize how badly you needed to be watered."

Amy Bloom was born in New York City on June 18, 1953 to Sydelle and Murray Bloom. Her mother was a writer, teacher, and psychotherapist, and her

Robert Birnbaum

father was a journalist and author. She grew up in Great Neck, on Long Island, New York, but on her Web page she notes that she has "never quite gotten Brooklyn out of my nature"; she explained in a note to *World Authors 1995–2000* that her claim on Brooklyn is purely ancestral, it being the early home of her parents and grandparents. She graduated from Great Neck North Senior High School and took a year off before attending Boston University for one year and Wesleyan University, in Middletown, Connecticut, for two, receiving her B.A. degree magna cum laude in 1975. Bloom intended to have a career in the theater and concentrated her undergraduate work in both theater and government. She earned her Master of Social Work degree at Smith College, in Northhampton, Massachusetts, in 1978.

Bloom had what might be called a typical writer's apprenticeship: "I've picked peanuts, scooped felafel, waitressed up and down the East Coast, tended bar, [and] written catalogue copy," she wrote on her Web page. She started her professional career not as a writer, however, but in the practice of psychotherapy "for both the worried well and the very ill," as quoted from her Web page. Journalist Beth Brophy remarked in an article on Bloom for *U.S. News & World Report* (January 27, 1997), "Psychotherapy and writing draw on common skills: listening, noticing small details that illuminate larger truths, distinguishing 'what's going on as opposed to what people tell me is going on,' Bloom says. Both spring from the impulse to [in Bloom's words] 'put your hands on people's lives, to be intimate.'"

In many of the stories in Bloom's first book, *Come to Me* (1993), psychotherapy and mental illness play a part; in "Silver Water," for instance, a woman describes her sister's descent into madness and her family's inability to help their mentally ill daughter. Bloom, however, wrote her stories from a human perspective rather than that of a practicing therapist or sociologist. A *Publishers Weekly* (May 3, 1993) reviewer remarked particularly on a story "in which Bloom achieves a soaring complexity in characters whose strange behavior eludes any simple psychological explanation." In *Library Journal* (May 1, 1993), Stephanie Furtsch praised Bloom's "psychological insights. Deviant human behavior is portrayed compassionately and honestly," she concluded.

Other types of human experience, beyond those of emotional distress and therapist-patient relationships, abound in Bloom's stories. A number of stories involve the recurring characters of the Silverstein and DiMartino families, and their "unharmonious entangling alliances," as Dan Cryer phrased it in *New York Newsday* (July 12, 1993). Cryer praised as "extraordinary" Bloom's ability "to light up more subtle transactions with enormous clarity," and her alchemy in "transmuting the messy dross of everyday life into the gold of artfully shaped fiction." For Anne Whitehouse, writing in the *New York Times Book Review* (July 18, 1993), there was an added dimension to the book in that several of the stories in *Come to Me* are related: "Several offer glimpses of the same people, who are related by blood or desire, thus suggesting a complex web of relationships and concerns and how they have changed over time." Whitehouse concluded that Bloom's stories are "about passion—shameful, blissful and perverse—about grief and guilt, about breakdowns, mental illness and death. Her voice is sure and brisk, her language often beautiful."

In contrast, Daniel McGuiness, writing in *Studies in Short Fiction* (Fall 1994), found it problematic that out of the 12 stories in *Come to Me*, five "concern a specific pair of suburban American couples: their infidelities, children, horror, coping strategies, and moments of eerie transcendence." Why, he asked, "would one not spin such stories out into a fully fashioned novel? . . . Reading contemporary short stories such as these can produce a feeling of something having been abandoned stillborn, something not worked through for some reason." He also noted that most of Bloom's stories were written "in the first person . . . , from the female (and exclusively youthful) point of view . . . and in the past tense."

Bloom's next book was the novel *Love Invents Us*, published in 1997. The protagonist, Elizabeth, is an only child from a middle-class suburb similar to the one in which Bloom grew up. Elizabeth wants to be loved, but her parents are remote—as she says of her mother, "Guilt and love were as foreign to her as butter and sugar"—and her classmates inimical to her bookish vocabulary and her "round trusting face and geeky glasses." Elizabeth bears a passing resemblance to Bloom, who described herself in an interview with Barbara Kaplan Lane in the *New York Times* (June 20, 1993) as having spent "a lot of time as a misfit. I remember . . . while in fourth grade, someone said, 'You might have friends if you didn't sound like you swallowed a dictionary.'" She told Mervyn Rothstein in another *New York Times* (August 21, 2000) interview, "I was definitely one of nature's observers. I loved to read a lot of 19th-century literature, which probably didn't do a lot for my playground skills. From the time I was a little kid I was waiting to grow up. At 9, for my birthday, I was asked what I wanted, and I said, 'my own apartment.'"

Love Invents Us begins with Elizabeth's first-person narration, repeated almost word for word from the story "Light Breaks Where No Sun Shines" in *Come to Me*. As a fat, ungainly, prepubescent girl, she visits the shop of a furrier who likes to look at her "beautiful skin" against his sables. When the furrier draws back from the brink of an illicit involvement with Elizabeth, she turns for companionship to her piano teacher, and then to a friendship with an elderly, almost blind, black woman whom the pastor of a nearby church has asked her to help, and who becomes almost a surrogate mother to her. She is also involved with Max Stone, her teacher and a married father who, unlike the furrier, allows her to obsess him. As Elizabeth gets older, she falls in love with a black high-school basketball star named Huddie. His father separates them after she has an abortion and he is absent from Elizabeth's life for a number of years, although he does enter the novel again. The last part of the novel, written in the third person, carries Elizabeth to a rueful middle age as an unmarried mother. Having lost Max, Mrs. Hill, and her strong emotional connection to Huddie, she describes herself as "happy every morning and . . . sad only late at night." She concludes, as quoted by Sarah Ferguson in the *New York Times Book Review* (January 19, 1997), "I've been alone my whole life. It may really be too hard and too late, not even desirable, after such long, familiar cold, to be known, and heard, and seen."

Reviewers' responses to *Love Invents Us* were for the most part laudatory. Novelist and short-story writer Gary Krist noted in the *Washington Post Book World* (February 27, 1997) that a "lesser writer might have chosen to end Elizabeth's long and harrowing trip to maturity in a swell of good feeling, with Elizabeth finally discovering the strength to be herself without the validation from others that she has always craved. Fortunately, however, Bloom is a true novelist rather than a propagandist; she allows her heroine no such easy triumph. Although her book is not flawless . . . its intelligence and passion never flag." The *Boston Globe* (January 12, 1997) reviewer Gail Caldwell found *Love Invents Us* "a lovely, harsh, reality-bound novel" containing "the truth about what really happens in a life lived somewhere in the vast middle between melodrama and nothingness," and in which "one is conscious of just how clear the authorial voice mostly is here, singing alone without any accompaniment to mask the false notes."

Wendy Brandmark, writing in the *Times Literary Supplement* (April 18, 1997), found that Bloom had failed to "fully exploit the Romeo and Juliet theme, the great racial divide." She judged *Love Invents Us* to be an obvious first novel, similar to a volume of short stories, in which Bloom "has not yet made the connections, discovered the patterns, which make a novel more than just a collection of brilliant moments." Jan Garden Castro, a reviewer for the *St. Louis Post-Dispatch* (February 9, 1997), wrote that in Bloom's depiction of the "interracial love story" of Elizabeth and Huddie, she had failed to "explore the correspondences and differences between their personalities and their respective Jewish and African-American backgrounds." Lynn Darling, the *Harper's Bazaar* (January 1997) reviewer, observed that "Bloom's subject is love, and she . . . is fascinated by its warty, messy, maddening ability to create chaos." Nevertheless, in *Love Invents Us*, according to Darling, though "the writing flashes fire throughout, the first half reads like a train of interconnected short stories; it is not until the abrupt switch in the second half from first to third person that the narrative takes wing."

Bloom returned to the short-story form in *A Blind Man Can See How Much I Love You* (2000), in which "eight stories shed insight on the healing properties of love, experienced through unexpected epiphanies, ardent sacrifices and impulsive acts of forgiveness," according to a review in *Publishers Weekly* (June 5, 2000). Characters from *Come to Me*, such as Julia and Lionel from the story "Sleepwalking," reappear in this collection. Lionel is a young black man, and Julia is his white stepmother, whom he calls "Ma" and refers to as "my mother." In "Sleepwalking," as Lionel and Julia experience grief over the death of Lionel's father and Julia's husband, their lives become irretrievably and illicitly linked when they fall into each other's arms. Margo Jefferson, in the *New York Times Book Review* (August 16, 1993), praised that story because "it makes race the backdrop, not the centerpiece." Jefferson observed that the stories in *Come to Me* are filled with people of different races, "in fact, people who live on the borders between races, religions and social or psychic certainties."

In "Night Vision," a story from *A Blind Man Can See How Much I Love You*, Lionel describes how he is persuaded by his brother to visit "Ma" after 15 years. He brings his French girlfriend and her young daughter along, but by the end of the story the reader understands that although Julia tells Lionel, "You do it, honey. You find someone smart and funny and kindhearted and get married so I can make a fuss over the grand babies," and he has told her "to think about marrying again," she lives alone and he is unable to make commitments because, as one says to the other, "I love you past speech." As they are entwined in each other's arms at that moment, it is not clear who is speaking. In "Light into Dark," another story involving Lionel and Julia, it is six years later, and Lionel has been married twice and has a stepson. "At the pace of a leisurely family Thanksgiving," Christine Wald-Hopkins wrote in the *Denver Post* (July 30, 2000), "[the story] becomes an examination of stepfamilies ('workable,' Lionel comments, 'only with people whose commitment and loyalty are much greater than the average'), the existence of Lionel's and his stepmother's one night having seared and soldered their lives."

Other stories in the book depict a mother who, upon learning that her daughter wants to become her son, sees her through her sex-change operation; a woman with cancer whose husband and lesbian best friend arrive at an understanding, although she wants only her husband's "absence"; and a woman who, while mourning the loss of her baby, forms a relationship in the hospital with an armless and resentful child and adopts him. "With fierceness and lyricism, Bloom catalogs the peregrinations of the human heart in these eerie, bittersweet stories that explore the joys and dangers of love in settings that test the limits of her characters—in cancer wards, hospital beds, sex-change clinics, and tension-ridden homes," Mark Luce observed in the *Atlanta Journal-Constitution* (July 30, 2000). Dottie Enrico, writing in *USA Today* (September 7, 2000), compared Bloom to Jill McCorkle and Lorrie Moore, noting that, like them, "Bloom uses humor and a wicked sense of the absurd to draw us into the complicated psyches of women and men unable to connect with one another." Enrico felt that Bloom had summarized her own life and artistic skills when, in a tale in the collection entitled "The Story," she wrote, "I have made the best and happiest ending that I can in this world, made it out of the flax and netting and leftover trim of someone else's life, I know, but made it to keep the innocent safe and the guilty punished, and I have made it as the world should be and not as I have found it."

Bloom's latest book, *Normal: Transsexual CEOs, Crossdressing Cops, and Hermaphrodites with Attitude*, was published on October 8, 2002. A collection of three essays examining the lives of people uncomfortable with their given gender, the book received mixed reviews. "The aspects of sexuality she writes about, Bloom says, may be unusual but they are not abnormal," wrote Erica Goode in a review for the *New York Times* (December 15, 2002). "Like the platypus and the blue potato, they represent nature's infinite variety, not its mistakes. If readers have not already reached similar conclusions, they are unlikely to be persuaded by the author's abruptly heavy hand."

Bloom has continued her dual careers as a private psychotherapist and author, although she has concentrated increasingly on the authorial side. She has also been a columnist, giving monthly advice on life to young women in *New Woman*. In her April 1998 column, entitled "What Are You Fit For?," she described finding herself doing some power walking with a young woman while staying at a resort. When they got back from one of their early walks, "a handsome young man" came up to them and asked the young woman, whom he addressed as "Honey," to stroll through an arboretum with him. Bloom expected the young woman to turn into "a puddle of affection, ready to meander and glow through the gardens." Instead, she told "Mr. Honey" that she preferred to go to a yoga class. Although modern standards of fitness upheld by women have proved "a joy, a solace, and an important part of the life we wish to build for ourselves and with others," Bloom wrote, "the gym, the trails and the climbing wall are all safer than relationships—and fundamentally less challenging than the larger world." "If we don't want to find ourselves at the end of the road, looking back on a life in which we've gotten a very high score but may have missed the point," Bloom added, "we need to greet emotional challenges with the same energy we bring to the physical ones."

Critics have praised Bloom's rich language and diction. In the story "Silver Water," she opened with a description of a voice, "like mountain water in a silver pitcher; the clear blue beauty of it cools you and lifts you up beyond your heat, beyond your body." Bloom is divorced and has three adult children, including one stepson and two daughters.

— S.Y.

SUGGESTED READING: *Atlanta Journal-Constitution* L p5 July 30, 2000; *Boston Globe* N p15 Jan. 12, 1997, with photo; *Denver Post* H p5 July 30, 2000; *Harper's Bazaar* p54 Jan. 1997; *Library Journal* p119 May 1, 1993; *New Woman* p44 Apr. 1998; *New York Newsday* p44 July 12, 1993; *New York Times* E p1 Aug. 21, 2000; *New York Times Book Review* p16 July 18, 1993; *Publishers Weekly* p293 May 3, 1993, p69 June 5, 2000; *St. Louis Post-Dispatch* C p5 Feb. 9, 1997; *San Francisco Review* p7 Apr. 1997; *Studies in Short Fiction* p694 Fall 1994; *Times Literary Supplement* p19 Apr. 18, 1997; *USA Today* D p9 Sep. 7, 2000; *Washington Post Book World* p3 Feb. 23, 1997

SELECTED BOOKS: novels—*Love Invents Us*, 1997; short-story collections—*Come to Me*, 1993; *A Blind Man Can See That I Love You*, 2000; essays—*Normal: Transsexual CEOs, Crossdressing Cops, and Hermaphrodites with Attitude*, 2002

Micah Bly/Courtesy of Carol Bly

Bly, Carol

Apr. 16, 1930– Short-story writer; essayist

The American short-story writer and ethical philosopher Carol Bly has created a body of work, including short fiction, essays, and poems, which reflects her passionate conviction that Americans, particularly those in small towns, can wrest their ethical and esthetic inner lives from the constricting hold of community life and its many demands. She has tried in her short-story collections *Backbone* (1985), *The Tomcat's Wife and Other Stories*

(1991), and *My Lord Bag of Rice* (2000) to show how some people transcend the almost deafening noise of the mundane to attain a kind of spiritual glory and to illuminate the path to fulfillment. Her essay collections *Letters from the Country* (1981), *Soil and Survival: Land Stewardship and the Future of American Agriculture*, co-written with Joe and Nancy Paddock (1986), and the autobiographical *An Adolescent's Christmas, 1944* (2000) also express her hope that Americans "live with passion, . . . have a sense of greatness in their lives," as Noel Perrin put it in the *New York Times Book Review* (May 24, 1981).

Bly was born April 16, 1930 in Duluth, Minnesota, to Mildred Washburn and C. Russell McLean. She was largely raised by an aunt in North Carolina and received her education at Abbott Academy, in Andover, Massachusetts, and Wellesley College, also in Massachusetts, where she received a B.A. in 1951. After college, Bly moved to New York City, where she "starved to death trying to write a novel," she told an interviewer for the *Long Prairie Leader* (March 30, 1994). "I wrote three novels, all horrible." She returned to Minnesota for graduate courses at the University of Minnesota, in Minneapolis, in 1954 and 1955. In 1955 she married the poet and leader of a men's renewal movement Robert Bly. They moved to Bly's hometown, Madison, Minnesota, and had four children before divorcing in 1979.

Bly began her career managing the poetry magazines published by her husband. These were called *Fifties*, in the 1950s, *Sixties*, in the 1960s, and so on. She remained as managing editor until 1971, the same year in which she co-founded the Prairie Arts Center in Madison. She then went into the crossword puzzle business and later became a humanities consultant and theme developer for the American Farm Project, a joint operation of the National Endowment for the Humanities and the National Farmers Union. She did similar work for the Land Stewardship Project, which she joined in 1982. She taught creative writing workshops at the University of Minnesota, where she also served as an instructor of ethics and literature beginning in 1989, while lecturing frequently at other colleges as well.

Bly's first book, a collection of essays titled *Letters from the Country* (1981), demonstrated how, for Bly, the country is not a place of idyllic virtue, but one of repression, narrowness, and over-involvement in community life, with a concomitant neglect of the individual's soul. According to Noel Perrin, however, Bly is not a passive complainer about small-town stultification. Perrin called *Letters from the Country* "a clarion call, fine silver notes meant to resound along a thousand Main Streets: These are letters to small towns. . . . Bly wants the farmers and small-town merchants of America to live with passion, to have a sense of greatness in their lives, to take themselves as seriously as a Beethoven or a Thoreau. . . . She is not the first to hold this grand Jeffersonian idea. But she is one of the first . . . who knows what to do with it." One of her recommendations, which she implemented herself, is that every town have what Bly calls a "mail-order servant." The mail-order servant, in the years before the Internet, acquired copies of such books as the *Whole Earth Catalog* or *Books in Print* and enabled the townsfolk to expand their minds through their use.

Rosellen Brown, in a review of *Letters from the Country* for the *New Republic* (June 20, 1981), praised Bly for her "concrete, even moving . . . instructions on how to talk with children if we want them to grow up to be thinking, rather than vacantly reverent people." Brown had somewhat less patience with Bly's proposal for holding an "Enemy Evening, at which all the discernible parties to a disagreement quarrel . . . openly, not behind shielding hands," finding Bly to have "too much faith in the magic of colloquy." Peter S. Prescott, a critic for *Newsweek* (June 15, 1981), judged Bly "not only a smart woman, but a wise one as well." Lauding the "graceful phrasing and deft wit" with which she set forth the book's numerous aphorisms, he agreed with many of them, such as, "Probably ethics are fun because they are a genuine inner form of campsite improvement."

After the publication of *Letters from the Country*, Bly co-wrote *Soil and Survival* (1986) with Joe and Nancy Paddock, fellow members of the Land Stewardship Project. A reviewer for the *Library Journal* (February 15, 1987) termed the book "poetic," describing it as "a call for agricultural reform—indeed, for ecological survival." The volume is not a scientific survey; it draws instead on religious and literary texts, including Native American sources, to call for land preservation and conservation. A reviewer for *Science Books & Films* (October 1987) faulted the volume for insufficient "scientific evidence" and for suggesting that the agricultural workforce in America should grow to 40 percent of the total workforce by 2000 (it accounted for four percent of the total in 1972), with "surprisingly little discussion of the reorganization of American society implied by such a massive realignment of the economy."

Bly's first short story was "Gunnar's Sword," about an 82-year-old woman's perilous journey from an old folks' home to visit her family farm, which has been sold by her son. Bly, according to the aforementioned interview in the *Long Prairie Leader*, sent "Gunnar's Sword" to the *New Yorker*, whose editor rejected it as too "long, earnest and tiresome." When it was published elsewhere, the same editor wrote her, this time "loving" the story and asking for more of her work. Bly displayed the two letters on her wall as a reminder to "never trust the establishment." "Gunnar's Sword" has been praised for its portrayal of the sense of loss that often accompanies the aging process and has been anthologized in *Full Measure: Modern Short Stories on Aging* (Graywolf, 1988).

In her first short-story collection, *Backbone* (1985), Bly continued to illuminate small town life. Tess Gallagher, in her review of the book for the *New York Times Book Review* (January 27, 1985), declared Bly the voice, not of the alienated and isolated, but of "active individuals who have remained socially conscious." Gallagher often used the term "individuals" when speaking of Bly's characters, possibly because Bly deals with people submerged in community life who must distinguish themselves by hewing to a sense of being "inner-directed." She often begins her stories with a description of minor characters, a delaying tactic which Gallagher said "works as part of a strategy that suggests no one character is simply incidental to the main character's situation. Indeed, the pettiness or kindness of such minor characters, intentional or not, is often illustrative of the weight under which the main character has to bear up." Gallagher observed that "imagination and the use to which we put it can serve as a constructive moral force," as demonstrated in Bly's story "Talk of Heroes," where a woman takes the microphone from a drunken speaker at a Norwegian-American cultural event to reveal to the audience the man's heroic resistance to Nazi torture during World War II. The audience members' imaginations can allow them to choose "whether to remember this man as the drunkard they see before them or as the heroic repository of those vanished acts." This woman, said Gallagher, has enabled heroism itself to move "from an individual to a communal plane." Three stories from *Backbone* were made into the film *Rachel River* (1987), directed by Sandy Smolan, with a screenplay by Judith Guest.

In 1990 Bly published *The Passionate, Accurate Story: Making Your Heart's Truth into Literature*. A return to her didactic approach, the volume is geared toward helping writers achieve emotional depth in their writing by concentrating, particularly in rough drafts, on feelings and intuition rather than logic and rules. This is easier said than done, however, as Bly noted in an on-line interview with Kelly Sagert for *Writersclub.com*. "Almost nobody has access to his or her own feelings," she told Sagert, "except for those who have, at some point, been in psychotherapy and those who once read literature as a child—and these numbers are certainly diminishing." In *The Passionate, Accurate Story* Bly, according to Sagert, recommends that writers clarify their own belief systems by listing two values that they think enrich life, two values that devalue life, two values missing from their lives, and two injustices that require their constant vigilance. She also recommends autobiographical writing, but not about childhood, because it is too easy to attach emotion to childhood events. "What writers need to know," writes Bly, as quoted by Sagert, "is that feeling attaches to adulthood."

Bly's 1991 collection, *The Tomcat's Wife and Other Stories*, marks yet another departure, this time into a dark world of violence and hypocrisy. Louis B. Jones, writing in the *New York Times Book Review* (March 31, 1991), commented that the characters in these stories are not "simply grotesques. . . . The defects in their flesh are not superficial; they are evidence of bone structure, genetic inheritance, injury, habits of soul, the local justice of teachers and cops. . . . Bly is entitled to her anger against these piety-stunted people because she had hoped to lift them up." In *The Tomcat's Wife* the lives of wife-beating husbands and their wives, who wait in bitterness for their husbands to die, are inextricably linked, as are the lives of firebugs, suicides, and even murderers, according to Jones, who observed, "Bly knows that a story is about its network of personal secrets and about the tug that every word, every detail, exerts to make the web tremble." The skill with which Bly portrayed these disturbing connections earned *The Tomcat's Wife* the Friends of American Writers Award.

By this time, Bly's former husband Robert had been receiving a great deal of attention as the ostensible leader of a new movement to liberate men's essential nature, an endeavor which, as quoted by *Washington Post* writer Phil McCombs (Feb. 3, 1991), Carol Bly found "frightening. The goal of invoking 'exhilaration' through regressive behavior isn't what's needed." She had more to say on this subject in an essay entitled "Male Initiation: An Ancient, Stupid Practice," published in *Beyond Borders: An Anthology of New Writing from Manitoba, Minnesota, Saskatchewan, and the Dakotas* (1992). In it, she discussed group psychology, as it is practiced particularly in the military. Once "someone is convinced that he is nothing, or at least, less, you give him a psychological tidbit to feed on," she writes. That tidbit is membership in a group: "Your squad is good. You yourself have no value, but the squad has." Group leaders, she says, will inculcate their members with the notion that "[t]he ideas we give you (such as anything *other* is wrong—it is all right to hurt *them* . . .) are not civilized ideas but at least you can have them *in your group*, all together, and that's comforting isn't it? Being together in a group?" She concludes, "Drill Instructors never talk about lemmings."

In *Changing the Bully Who Rules the World: Reading and Thinking About Ethics*, Bly's 1996 compilation of poems, essays, and stories, she casts herself as a modern-day ethicist. This was not a new stance for her, for in *Letters from the Country* she had maintained that every American has "an ethical and an esthetic nature." Bly's mission through the years was to help the folks of America's heartland in a quest for their inner lives. In *Changing the Bully*, she collects writings by Wendell Berry, Katha Pollitt, Jim Harrison, Charles Baxter, Will Weaver, Mark Helprin, and Arturo Vivante, along with her own essays, addressing such matters as the dangers of herd mentality, nostalgia for simpler times, and dead-end thinking, while arguing that empathy can be learned. Abigail Davis, in an interview in *PioneerPlanet* (October 20, 1996, on-line), called the volume "an outstanding anthology. Bly's arguments are well-advanced, challenging and passionate; the literature is first-rate."

In the 1990s Bly helped to found the Collaborative of Teachers and School Social Workers, established to counteract the "jeering and sneering" so prevalent in the nation's schools, she told an interviewer for the *Long Prairie Leader*. She admires social workers for their ability to teach non-aggressive styles of communication. "Social workers," she explained in the interview, "know so many specific conversational skills that change people. I have seen people change in 45 minutes." She also described a community development project which would encourage "community members of conflicting opinions, ideas, values or attitudes" to "learn how to have a conversation with someone they disagree with."

In Bly's short story "Chuck's Money," published in *TriQuarterly* (Winter 1999), she elaborated her characteristic themes through the story of a young couple who each go head-to-head with a small town's richest—and most evil—citizen, Chuck Mincesky. Leona, a bookkeeper, finds Mincesky's son Chucky's body in a motel where she is conducting an audit, the young man having shot himself to death. The story then spirals back to Leona's marriage to Allen, a misfit who is perennially underpaid, thereby prompting Leona to resign herself to being the family's chief breadwinner. As the story progresses, we learn that both Leona and Allen have highly developed ethical systems of which they are only half-conscious but which are tested by a series of crises, culminating in Allen's sentence to 90 days in prison for attacking Mincesky in a moment of righteous anger. As he is being led away, Allen smiles in a way that reminds Leona of the smile she had once received from a foreign diplomat when she worked in Washington: "He smiled at each one of them and he spoke perfect, friendly, American English. But she remembered thinking, even back then, that a person like that can talk to you gently and perfectly, but you can tell that they also know some very different language, a language that people speak in some country you may never get to in your lifetime." Although Allen is a complete failure by conventional measures, the "foreign language" that he possesses is his highly evolved ethical sense. Bly, it seems, would like the rest of us to try to understand that "language," as Leona does.

In 1992 Bly received an honorary degree from Northland College, in Ashland, Wisconsin. At the University of Minnesota, in St. Paul, she has also been the Visiting Hurst Professor in the Department of English and an Ethics professor. She lectures frequently, is a humanities consultant to the Land Stewardship Project, and serves on the Board of Directors of the Loft, a literary center in Minneapolis, Minnesota. Bly has continued to produce essays, poems, and stories in which she has mined small-town life in Minnesota for ethical lessons. In 2000 she issued the short-story collection *My Lord Bag of Rice*, the title story of which appeared first in *The Tomcat's Wife*. Her autobiographical volume *An Adolescent's Christmas, 1944*, about growing up in Duluth, also appeared in 2000. In 2001, her next book, *Beyond the Writers' Workshop: New Ways to Write Creative Nonfiction*, was released.
— S.Y.

SUGGESTED READING: *Library Journal* p155 Feb. 15, 1987; *Long Prairie Leader* (on-line) Mar. 30, 1994; *New York Times Book Review* p4 May 24, 1981, p19 Jan. 27, 1985, p14 Mar. 31, 1991; *Newsweek* p94 June 15, 1981; *PioneerPlanet* (on-line) Oct. 20, 1996; *Science Books & Films* p10 Oct. 1987; *TriQuarterly* p141+ Winter 1999; *Washington Post* F p1 Feb. 3, 1991

SELECTED BOOKS: fiction—*Backbone*, 1985; *The Tomcat's Wife and Other Stories*, 1991; *My Lord Bag of Rice*, 2000; nonfiction—*Letters from the Country*, 1981; *Soil and Survival: Land Stewardship and the Future of American Agriculture*, 1986; *Bad Government and Silly Literature*, 1986; *The Passionate, Accurate Story: Making Your Heart's Truth into Literature*, 1990; *An Adolescent's Christmas, 1944*, 2000; as compiler— *Changing the Bully Who Rules the World: Reading and Thinking About Ethics*, 1996

Bock, Dennis

1964(?)– Fiction writer

The Canadian writer Dennis Bock has earned notice for *The Ash Garden* (2001), a novel about the aftereffects of the bombing of Hiroshima, Japan, that brought an end to World War II. In an elliptical style, Bock tells the overlapping stories of three characters who experienced the war from different vantage points: a Japanese survivor; a German physicist who helped to develop the atomic bomb; and a Jewish woman who escaped Austria for Canada. The book, which contrasts the justifications for using the bomb with the intractable suffering it left behind, was lauded by many critics for providing a sensitive exploration of moral uncertainty. "Bock's achievement here is in creating characters with believably ambiguous edges, vulnerable people whose understanding of themselves and others is incomplete," Janice P. Nimura wrote for the *Washington Post* (September 9, 2001). "*The Ash Garden* quietly considers a few individuals in the context of terrifying forces that are and are not within their control. It pits human will against fate, and does not try to declare a winner." For Bock, withholding judgement is a fundamental part of artistic creation. "For me a novel doesn't try to solve riddles, but instead simply lay them out, expose, or state those riddles in new, arresting, and entirely crucial ways," Bock explained in an interview posted on the Alfred A. Knopf Web site. "In raising those questions—by positioning your characters, building your setting and your drama—you ap-

Dennis Bock
Andrea Bock/Courtesy of Dennis Bock

proach the heart of what it is to be human." Bock has also published a collection of short stories, *Olympia* (1998).

Dennis Bock was born in about 1964 in Belleville, Canada, a small town on the northern shore of Lake Ontario. When he was six, his family, which included four older siblings, moved to Oakville, west of Toronto. He knew from an early age that he wanted to be a writer. He began writing poetry and then tried fiction, inspired by Jonathan Swift's 18th-century satire, *Gulliver's Travels*. "That was the first book I read with the realization that it was an artifact, that it was created by an imagination," he told Mel Gussow for the *New York Times* (November 7, 2001).

Bock's family history provided material for his work. His parents had emigrated from Germany to Canada in the 1950s. "They were both kids during the war," he told Sandra Martin in an interview for *Globebooks.com* (August 25, 2001), "and I grew up hearing their stories and listening to what they saw and felt. It captured my imagination." His father, who had lived on a farm in Bavaria, was largely removed from the war. His mother was from an industrial town in Silesia, now part of Poland. "She ate cabbages and lived in bomb shelters in basements for months at a time," Bock explained. His mother's struggle to understand her relation to the war profoundly affected Bock. His grandparents "were not connected to the Nazi party, but still they lived in that context, kind of tainting," he told Gayle Feldman for *Publishers Weekly* (July 2, 2001). "I learned about German collective guilt when I was hauled over in the schoolyard as a kid."

Bock attended the University of Western Ontario, in London, Canada. After his junior year, he left school to write. He and a girlfriend moved to Spain and settled in Salamanca, northwest of Madrid. "It was a cold and austere town," Bock told Martin. With few distractions, he devoted himself to writing. Though he wasn't satisfied with the work he produced, he told Martin that he "proved [he] could hack it mentally."

After a year Bock returned to Western Ontario, graduating in 1989 with an Honors B.A. in English and philosophy. He then moved to Madrid, Spain, where he earned money by teaching English and studied the works of writers he admired. "I'd go to the one or two English bookstores in Madrid and they would have three Canadian writers—[Margaret] Atwood and [Mavis] Gallant and [Alice] Munro—and I would pick them up. . . . I read Alice Munro five times straight," he told Martin. "So much of writing is accident, but you also have to have the craft, and she is obviously one of the greatest craftsmen going."

Bock spent five years in Madrid, writing much of *Olympia*. In 1994 he returned to Toronto; by this time he had published a few short stories in literary journals, and on the strength of his work he was accepted into a writing program at the Banff Centre for the Arts, in Alberta, Canada. He also had residencies at Yaddo, an artist's colony in Saratoga Springs, New York, and the Fundacion Valparaiso, in Spain.

Bock's short-story collection, *Olympia*, revolves around three generations of a family of German immigrants in suburban Ontario. Peter, from the youngest generation, narrates a family history about Olympic ambitions and achievements that have been tainted by difficult memories of World War II. Peter's grandparents met while competing at the 1936 Olympics in Berlin (his grandmother was a champion diver; his grandfather, a sailor). After the war they moved to Canada. Peter's father, a yachtsman in the 1960 Olympics in Rome, now builds "unsinkable" boats. His younger sister, Ruby, is an aspiring gymnast. "We were Olympians," Bock writes in the voice of Peter, as quoted by Robert Lalasz for the *Washington Post* (August 9, 1999). "No miracle seemed misplaced on us. . . . I knew that normal people did not fly, could not breathe underwater. But we did. I believed we were evolving." The Olympic stature of the family's past serves as the backdrop for their present deterioration. In the opening story, "The Wedding," Peter's grandparents are renewing their vows on a boat in the middle of a lake when his grandmother is knocked overboard and drowns. In another story Peter's father diverts himself from his failing marriage by becoming a tornado chaser. Trying to raise money for cancer research, Peter attempts to break the record for the dead man's float by lying face down in a pool; when a sudden storm floods the town, he is swept into a river.

Reviews of the book were mixed. "The central problem with *Olympia*," Lalasz wrote, "is that while Bock is a fine writer of small metaphors . . . his big ones run away with the book. The relentless permutations of wetness soon become gimmicks that suffocate his characters." In a review for *Publishers Weekly* (April 26, 1999), Sybil S. Steinberg noted that "a strong sense of family bonds and an unspoken sadness pervade this work," in which Bock "looks lyrically at the past." She added that "the thematic use of water and air and a mystical tone finally become ponderous, but taken individually, these stories are subtle, gracefully constructed and rich in thoughts and images." *Olympia* received the Jubilee Award for short fiction from the Canadian Authors Association and the Danuta Gleed Award for best first collection of short stories from the Canadian Writers' Union, as well as the Betty Trask Prize for a first novel by a writer under 35 from England's Society of Authors. It was also a Toronto *Globe and Mail* 1998 Notable Book of the Year.

The Ash Garden takes on the psychic fallout from the bombing of Hiroshima at the end of World War II. "I have an obsession with history," Bock told Feldman about the genesis of this novel. "The past is never past. The relationship the individual has with large historical events—how the personal is interwoven with the political—I felt that as a kid." Bock introduces three characters whose lives intersect beneath the pall of suffering left by the war. Emiko is a Japanese survivor of the atomic blast. "One morning toward the end of the summer they burned away my face," she begins, as quoted by Richard Lourie for the *New York Times Book Review* (September 23, 2001). "My little brother and I were playing on the bank of the river that flowed past the eastern edge of our old neighborhood, on the grassy flood plain that had been my people's home and misery for centuries." Although Emiko is left horribly disfigured by the explosion, she becomes one of a lucky few who is sent to the United States to receive plastic surgery.

Many years later, Emiko encounters Anton Boll, a German physicist who came to America to assist in the development of the atomic bomb. Emiko also meets Boll's wife, Sophie, who is dying of lupus. Sophie is a half-Jewish refugee who lost her family to the war. She escaped from Europe on a ship that was then forced to sail the Atlantic for weeks until it found a hospitable port; she landed in a Canadian refugee camp, where she met and seduced Anton. A bond of resignation, rather than love, joins the couple: "That was one thing they agreed on, deep in the bones," Bock writes about this pairing, as quoted by Michiko Kakutani for the *New York Times* (September 21, 2001). "That happiness, pleasure, fulfillment were goals suitable only for the naive and foolish or extremely lucky. They were none of these." Boll was part of a team of scientists that went to Hiroshima to document the damage caused by the bomb. Since this harrowing experience he has struggled with guilt over his role in the creation of the bomb, and has become estranged from Sophie. Left alone with her suffering, Sophie has withdrawn into the small world of her topiary garden. Now near death, Sophie recalls the missed opportunities of her life. Bock's narrative segues between the characters as they struggle to understand their pasts.

Reviews of the novel have been largely positive. "From these three overlapping lives," Kakutani wrote, "Mr. Bock constructs an elegant, unnerving novel that illuminates the personal consequences of the war, transforming characters who might easily have been mere symbols or representative types into keenly observed individuals: people indelibly shaped, in anomalous ways, by their losses and their grief." Amanda Craig, in an assessment for the London *Times* (October 6, 2001), offered more tempered praise. "Novels addressing subjects of such magnitude often borrow a literary seriousness that they have not fully earned," she wrote. "*The Ash Garden* is remarkable for its ambition and for what it achieves as a narrative, but it also reads as the work of a young writer who is straining with too much effort after sorrows that it needs a lifetime to do justice to." Abby Frucht, writing for the *Far Eastern Economic Review* (December 20, 2001), concluded, "The novel's understated and paradoxically gentle evocation of violence is both edgy and surreal, while Bock's steady hand and absolute refusal to sensationalize gives his story added resonance and power."

In writing *The Ash Garden* Bock relied heavily on his imagination. In his interview with Mel Gussow, Bock said that he took the adage "write about what you know," and "threw it out the window." "I wanted to stick my neck out," Bock explained, "as far as it went—to test myself, to see if I could write about something I had absolutely no first-hand knowledge about." Bock confined his research to libraries, telling Gussow that he spent his time "trolling through the aisles between the stacks, pulling down books and stumbling across striking details." One such detail grabbed his attention: the scientists at Alamogordo who witnessed the first test explosion of the bomb wore suntan lotion, believing it would help protect them from the radiation. "You find a detail like that and you know it's going in the book," Bock remarked in his interview for the Alfred A. Knopf Web site. "And not just as an aside. . . . It becomes a crucial metaphor for the innocence of those times, of just how new this science was—even for the brilliant minds behind its creation."

Bock is married to Andrea Kellner, an editor and writer. With the money obtained from the advance on *The Ash Garden*, the couple recently bought a house in Guelph, Ontario.

—A. I. C.

SUGGESTED READING: *Christian Science Monitor* p20 Sep. 27, 2001; *Far Eastern Economic Review* p62+ Dec. 20, 2001; Globebooks.com Aug. 25, 2001; *New York Times* E p35 Sep. 21, 2001, E p3 Nov. 7, 2001; *New*

York Times Book Review p8 Sep. 23, 2001; Publishers Weekly p57 Apr. 26, 1999, p48 July 2, 2001; (London) Times p17 Oct. 6, 2001; Washington Post C p4 Aug. 9, 1999, p13 Sep. 9, 2001

SELECTED BOOKS: *Olympia*, 1998; *The Ash Garden*, 2001

Courtesy of Knopf Publicity

Boswell, Robert

Dec. 8, 1953– Novelist and short-story writer

Robert Boswell was one of the worst students in the creative-writing program at the University of Arizona, in Tucson. After concluding that he wasn't showing any improvement as a poet, one of Boswell's instructors persuaded him to try fiction. At first, Boswell's fiction was just as bad as his poetry. However, he never gave up and got better as he kept writing—often as long as 18 hours a day. In addition to earning his MFA in creative writing, Boswell's thesis, a collection of his short stories, received the 1985 Iowa School of Letters Award for Short Fiction. A year later he published his thesis as the book *Dancing in the Movies* and began his career as a novelist and short-story writer. Many of Boswell's characters are flawed, but decent, people who are forced to cope with extraordinary circumstances and life's difficulties. The dysfunctional family in his first novel, *Crooked Hearts* (1987), responds to the failure of its members by throwing a lavish party. In *Mystery Ride* (1993) a divorced couple works together to help their wild and troubled teenage daughter. In one of his most acclaimed novels to date, *Century's Son* (2002), a man tries to protect a co-worker who is being sought by the police. In an interview with William Clark for *Publishers Weekly* (January 25, 1993), Boswell said that "the writer's job is to embrace the next impossible task." He explained that he is "just trying to be honest and decent, to be true to the people I love and the things I hold dear, which includes literature—*the story*. Because I believe that storytelling is crucial to humans for existence, that in very complex ways, it helps us to see our own lives with more clarity."

Robert Boswell was born on December 8, 1953 in Sikeston, Missouri. For about 10 years of his childhood he lived on a tobacco farm in Wickliffe, Kentucky, near the point where the Mississippi and Ohio Rivers meet. Boswell recalled to Clark that this was "where Huck and Jim missed their turn" as they made their way down the Mississippi River in Mark Twain's classic tale *The Adventures of Huckleberry Finn* (1884). The novel greatly influenced Boswell and inspired him to be a writer.

Boswell's father was an elementary-school principal, and his mother worked as a realtor. During Robert's childhood Kentucky's schools became racially integrated. "I still remember the first black kid who came to school and how my father, that first recess, strolled around, keeping his distance, but really keeping an eye on the little black boy," Boswell told Dahleen Glanton for the *Chicago Tribune* (May 19, 1997). "He was afraid there would be a fight." When he was in sixth grade, Boswell and his family, which included two brothers and a sister, moved to Yuma, Arizona.

In high school Boswell played basketball and served in the student government. Coming of age during the late 1960s, he began experimenting with illegal drugs. "If you go the long way," he told Don Lee for *Ploughshares* (Winter 1996–1997, online), "Yuma is fifteen miles from the [Mexican] border, and there were a lot of drugs available cheap, a lot of people running across the border, and I found that an interesting pastime." In Yuma, Boswell made extra money by working in fields, picking wheat, cotton, and cantaloupes.

Boswell enrolled at the University of Arizona, in Tucson. Unfortunately, his addiction to drugs made it difficult for him to focus on his studies. "I finally made a conscious decision to quit doing drugs," he told Lee. "I thought I'd never get through college otherwise, and I knew I wanted to accomplish something. But it took me years, really, to quit." After briefly considering a career as a lawyer, Boswell abandoned studying government and switched his major several times. In 1977 Boswell finally graduated with a double major in English and psychology.

Boswell remained at the University of Arizona, obtaining a master's degree in rehabilitation counseling. "I was looking for a way to have a life that wasn't an obscenity, and this seemed like a possibility, doing important work," he told Lee. In 1979 Boswell found a job as a counselor in San Diego, California, helping the disenfranchised—

immigrants, the poor, and schizophrenics—to find job-training programs. In 1981 he quit his job to return to the University of Arizona as a student in the MFA program in creative writing. "My friends thought I was crazy to give up that job and my house on the beach in San Diego," he recalled to Clark. Among Boswell's classmates were David Foster Wallace and Richard Russo, future famous writers. At first, Boswell tried writing poetry, but quickly discovered that his work wasn't very good. A talk with Steve Orlen, one of his teachers, however, helped send him on a different creative path. Boswell recalled to Lee that Orlen had told him, "It seems to me you're always trying to tell a story. It seems to me that there's not much music in your poetry." Boswell explained that Orlen's observations were "a euphemistic way of telling me that I was writing one clunker after another, and the light bulb came on over my head that I should be writing fiction."

Boswell then threw himself into writing fiction, often working between 16 and 18 hours a day. Afterward, he would unwind at the Country Club Lounge until it closed. Although he concluded that his early fiction was poor, Boswell found that the quality of his work improved as he kept writing. His professional break came when the novelist Larry McMurtry visited the University of Arizona campus. McMurtry was impressed with one of Boswell's short stories, "The Right Thing," and introduced the young writer to his agent, Dorothea Oppenheimer. In 1983 the *Antioch Review* published "The Right Thing." Boswell received his MFA in 1984 and, one year later, his thesis, which was a collection of his short stories, including "The Right Thing," earned the Iowa School of Letters Award for Short Fiction.

In 1982 Boswell began working as a teaching assistant at the University of Arizona. Four years later, Northwestern University, in Evanston, Illinois, hired him as a teacher of creative writing. In 1989 Boswell joined the faculty of New Mexico State University, in Las Cruces, as a writing instructor and has taught there ever since.

In 1986 the University of Iowa Press published Boswell's thesis, with only slight modifications, as the book *Dancing in the Movies*. In "The Right Thing" Boswell writes about a veteran suffering from post-traumatic stress disorder. "Little Bear" is set during the Korean War and follows Joey Malone, a soldier who gets his feet blown off in battle. The title story of the collection explores an interracial relationship between Freddie, a white college student, and Dee, an African-American drug addict. An African-American police officer leaves New York City for Tennessee in "The Darkness of Love," to escape growing suspicions that he is being paid to arrest fellow African-Americans. "Boswell's stories . . . start from human lives in blood, bone, and flesh," Michael Kreyling observed in his review for *Studies in Short Fiction* (Fall 1986). "We are not permitted to forget that. These embodied creatures have memories—traumatic memories of delivering live babies from the wombs of their dead Vietnamese mothers; beautiful memories of constellations and love; puzzled memories with delayed meaning. . . . The stories say that memory lives as tenaciously as the flesh—perhaps more tenaciously, for Boswell's characters might lose limbs or prospects or illusions, but they never lose the memories that make them real."

In 1987 Boswell published his first novel, *Crooked Hearts*, which follows the dysfunctional Warren family. Edward and Jill Warren have four children: Charley, Tom, Ask, and Cassie. A former high-school history teacher, Edward was demoted to teaching driver's education after having a romantic relationship with a student. After getting divorced, Charley, the oldest sibling, gets Tom's girlfriend pregnant. In an effort to ease their collective pain, the Warrens respond to their failures by throwing lavish parties. (For example, when Tom comes home after dropping out of college, his family greets him with a party.) *Crooked Hearts* received mostly favorable reviews. "Mr. Boswell . . . uses the party motif to organize a prodigious quantity of material as the novel expands and contracts with family members' movements out into the larger world and back to one another," Sharon Sheehe Stark wrote for the *New York Times Book Review* (June 5, 1987). "Extras abound: friends, lovers, clients, classmates, each with a sad, sometimes horrific story worked expertly into the whole. The result is rich and vivid, an intriguingly busy view of the human adventure, the impossible family of man." Despite criticizing the book for over-using the party device, Stark concluded, "*Crooked Hearts* is an insightful, nicely turned, amazingly agile piece of work." In his review for the *Chicago Tribune* (May 31, 1987), Joseph Coates observed that too many novelists explore the theme of dysfunctional families and thus add little to what has already been written. Coates noted, however, "the measure of Robert Boswell's talent is that his first novel makes [the theme] absolutely new, with a richness of texture, solidity of characterization and technical finesse that most recognized third- or fourth-novelists would envy." The reviewer was impressed that Boswell's characters alternate narrating chapters, arguing that this device "refreshes the story with different voices, showing unsuspected motives or complications behind events." Coates wrote that "Boswell again and again deftly demonstrates the eternal presentness of the past in the lives of characters we come to care about deeply. His brilliant debut as a novelist will be a hard act to follow." In 1991 *Crooked Hearts* was adapted into a film starring Peter Coyote, Vincent D'Onofrio, and Jennifer Jason Leigh, but the movie attracted little attention.

In Boswell's second novel, *The Geography of Desire* (October 1, 1989), Leon Green, an American expatriate, operates a rundown hotel in La Boca, a town in an unnamed Latin American country. The twice-divorced Green is having affairs with two women: Pilar, a communist who is hiding from the repressive government, and Lourdes, who is passionately in love with him. Green's best friend and sidekick, Ramon Matamoros, seeks to provide his son Benjamin with a university education. In turn, Benjamin finds himself obsessed with Lourdes and often spies on her. Pilar shatters the refuge and peace that Green sought in La Boca when she shelters a dying political leader, who is being hunted by the army, in the hotel. In the *Washington Post* (October 5, 1989), Alberto Manguel faulted the book. "Central to this novel, as the title implies, is the idea that desire occurs within discernable limits, that it occupies certain spaces that it also creates," Manguel wrote. "But the geography of La Boca has not been created by Leon; we are told that it all was there before his arrival. His desire mapped out nothing. The supposedly marvelous place—even if its marvels were convincing, which they are not—seems unimportant even to Leon." As the story reaches its climax, the reviewer added, "It is difficult to understand why the reader should care, other than to mourn a hero who has lost his version of Club Med." By contrast, Paul Senazy was impressed with the novel in his review for the *Chicago Tribune* (October 1, 1989). He wrote, "Boswell this time turns his sensuous prose loose on a story of exile and self-discovery that mixes elements of the thriller and romantic adventure with Latin American storytelling traditions. The result is a sometimes too clever but often stunning blend of eroticism and intrigue, tall tales and seedy politics." Although critical of the book's "melodramatic kind of language" and female characters who seemed "stenciled from sentimental fiction," Senazy asserted that Boswell's "evocative prose and immense lyrical talents create a quietly self-conscious kind of narrative. He hasn't entirely mapped out the geography of desire that he seems to promise, but he has left us with provocative clues about the hazards of our search for any such state of grace."

Boswell's next novel, *Mystery Ride* (1993), begins during the early 1970s when newlyweds Stephen and Angela Landis move to a farm in Hathaway, Iowa. Although Stephen and Angela eventually have a daughter they name Dulcie, the marriage crumbles. Stephen stays on the farm and lives with a woman named Leah and her teenage daughter, Roxanne. Angela marries a theatrical agent and moves to southern California with Dulcie. The couple is reunited for the first time since their divorce when Angela brings Dulcie to the farm for the summer. Angela hopes the experience will help straighten out Dulcie, who has turned into an emotionally troubled and uncontrollable teenager. Gail Caldwell wrote for the *Boston Globe* (January 24, 1993), "[The] novel is rich and satisfying, with a wonderfully old-fashioned grasp of the way people actually feel." In his review for *Library Journal* (January 1993), David W. Henderson also praised the novel. "Life, indeed, can be a mystery ride," Henderson observed. "Who can explain the bonds that hold us together when the odds so often seem stacked against us? The answer lies best in works by novelists like Boswell . . . whose latest effort focuses on an American family separated by time, distance, and generation. . . . Combining wisdom, humor, and poignancy in equal measure, this well-told tale inexorably draws in the reader." *Mystery Ride* has been optioned for film.

In 1994 Boswell returned with *Living to Be 100*, a short-story collection. In the title story, a married couple, with doubts about the meaning of their lives, attempts to stitch together a carpet using scavenged rug remnants. "Glissando" explores the relationship between a bad, but well-meaning, father and his teenage son. The protagonist of "The Good Man" is an alcoholic trying to win back his estranged wife. "Boswell is so keen an observer of human nature and so adept at choosing apt details that every one of them is utterly believable," Claire Rothman wrote for the Montreal *Gazette* (June 4, 1994). She concluded that *Living to Be 100* "caught me by surprise, gave me great pleasure, enriched me; it is a book to be cherished." In 2002 "Glissando" was adapted into a film of the same name, but generated little interest among critics and audiences.

The title of Boswell's fourth novel, *American Owned Love* (1997), derives from the xenophobic practice of some business owners, particularly in the American West, who advertise that their establishments are "American owned" in an attempt to win customers. In the book Boswell writes about various characters who live in the fictional towns of Persimmon and Apuro, which lie on opposite sides of the Rio Grande, in New Mexico. The residents of Persimmon despise Apuro, which is nothing more than a squatters' camp without electricity, running water, or sewer lines. In his review for the *Los Angeles Times* (May 19, 1997), Michael Harris asserted that *American Owned Love* was "tightly plotted—no detail goes to waste—but it also flows as loosely and unpredictably as life. Boswell's prose never strains, but it's capable of delicate and powerful effects. His people are so real that we're reminded of what readers usually manage to ignore—that the characters in most novels are just bundles of stock attributes, snapped together like pieces of a Lego set."

Boswell's latest book, *Century's Son* (2002), received widespread critical acclaim. Set in a small town in Illinois, the novel examines the life of Zhenya Kamenev, the daughter of Russian immigrants and a political scientist and activist. When she was younger, Zhenya fell in love with and eventually married Morgan, a garbageman who helped organize his co-workers into a union. The couple is still haunted by the death of their teenage son, Philip, who hanged himself six years earlier. Their teenage daughter, Emma, has given birth to a child and will not name the father. Zhenya and Morgan clash over his efforts to protect Danny, a fellow garbageman who is wanted for murder. "Boswell's style, plain-spoken without being minimal, is a perfect fit for his approach to character, which, while without much in the way of adornment (Morgan doesn't even have a first name), is never simple," Jonathan Dee wrote in the *New York Times Book Review* (April 21, 2002). "In the end, the members of the accidental family cobbled together in the Forrest Avenue house have only the imperfect help of those who know them best, who share their private history of loss, to rely upon. Against an increasingly interconnected world, Boswell sets his vision of one family's painful, incomplete, unorthodox but still stirring return to life as an irremediably private matter." In her review for the *Chicago Tribune* (April 28, 2002), Sandra Scofield also hailed *Century's Son*. "Boswell writes a capacious, complex novel," she wrote. "There's so much going on you can't miss a line, but you wouldn't want to. He freely moves about in the consciousness of various characters, and within each he finds much worthy of comment, always sounding like the character and not an author. He proves that people of modest station can lead not only complicated lives, but intellectual ones as well."

Under the pseudonym Shale Aaron, Boswell also wrote the science-fiction novel *Virtual Death* (1995), which was named one of the year's best books in that genre by *SF Chronicle* and was shortlisted for a Philip K. Dick Award from the Philadelphia Science Fiction Society. Boswell also wrote a play, *Tongues*, which won the 1994 John Gassner Playwriting Award and was produced by the American Southwest Theater Company. Boswell has received a Guggenheim Fellowship; two National Endowment for the Arts fellowships; the 1995 PEN West Award for Fiction; and the 1996 Evil Companions Award, which celebrates authors who live in or write about the American West. (Boswell, however, does not care for the label of regional writer.) Boswell's short stories have been published in the *New Yorker*, *TriQuarterly*, the *Harvard Review*, and the *Colorado Review*, among other periodicals. His work has been widely anthologized, as well.

Robert Boswell, who is known to friends as Boz, supports a number of liberal causes, including the American Civil Liberties Union and the Southern Poverty Law Center. He is married to Antonya Nelson, a fellow novelist, short-story writer, and professor. (The couple met as graduate students at the University of Arizona and married soon after.) They have two children, Jade and Noah, and divide their time between Las Cruces, New Mexico, and a summer home in Telluride, Colorado.

—D. C.

SUGGESTED READING: *Boston Globe* Books p41 Jan. 24, 1993; *Chicago Tribune* Books p6 May 31, 1987, Books p6 Oct. 1, 1989, Tempo p1+ May 19, 1997, with photo, Books p1+ Apr. 28, 2002; (Montreal) *Gazette* Books p11+ Jun. 4, 1994; *Library Journal* p163 Jan. 1993, with photo; *New York Times Book Review* p12 Jul. 5, 1987, p10 Apr. 21, 2002; *Ploughshares* (on-line) Winter 1996–1997; *Publishers Weekly* p65+ Jan. 25, 1993, with photo; Robert Boswell Home Page; *Studies in Short Fiction* p461+ Fall 1986; *Washington Post Book World* p3 Oct. 3, 1989

SELECTED BOOKS: novels—*Crooked Hearts*, 1987; *The Geography of Desire*, 1989; *Mystery Ride*, 1993; *Virtual Death*, 1995 (as Shale Aaron); *American Owned Love*, 1997; *Century's Son*, 2002; short-story collections—*Dancing at the Movies*, 1986; *Living to Be 100*, 1994

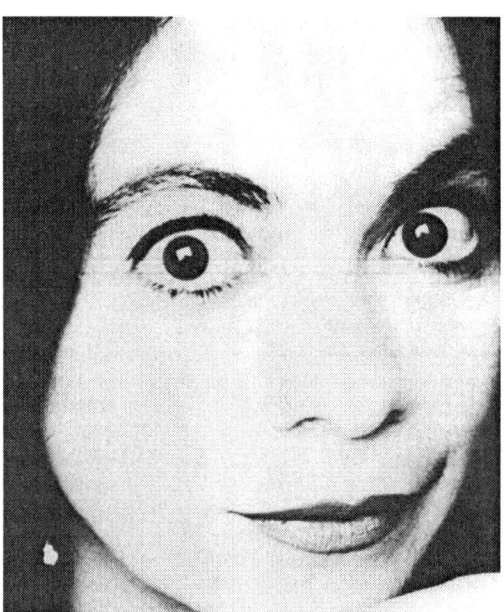

Raul Gonzalez/Courtesy of Grove/Atlantic

Boullosa, Carmen

(Boo-YO-sa)

Sep. 4, 1954– Novelist; poet; playwright

Carmen Boullosa has had a successful career in Mexico as a novelist, poet, and playwright for more than 20 years. Recent translations of her novels into English have introduced her to a wider audience. Her novels, which are filled with strange and supernatural events, explore Mexican identity and expose racism, sexism, political oppression, and injustice. In Boullosa's first book in English translation, *The Miracle Worker* (1993), a young girl has the power to heal the sick amid the poverty and political corruption in Mexico. For *They're Cows, We're Pigs* (1997), Boullosa turned to historical fiction, creating a colorful narrative about a band of 17th-century pirates who pillage and terrorize ships on the Caribbean Sea. In her latest novel, *Leaving Tabasco* (2001), a woman looks back 30 years to her unhappy childhood, spent in a village where unusual things—stones turning into water; people levitating above their beds—were commonplace. "I like placing myself in the shoes of strangers, foreigners, and all those who exist outside the world," Boullosa explained to Rubén Gallo for *Bomb Magazine* (Winter 2001), "perhaps that is why I write novels."

Carmen Boullosa writes for *World Authors 1995-2000*: "I am a woman, a Mexican and a writer, though it is for me the other way round: before anything else, I am a writer. Before being Mexican, or woman, or even Carmen Boullosa. I am a writer because I could build, construct, literally make myself with my vocation. I am a writer because through my profession I could track and find my own person.

"To write is not for me to transgress upon reality, nor to break the glass of Divine Order, nor to question intellectually the mysteries of life. It is not the tool to discover my identity and the masks that I need as a writer. It is not a game and a pleasure. It is not a way to understand and interpret, to read the things of life.

"But all these listed here have been a gift given to me by my profession. I have received many other gifts, like publishing my books and having readers.

"I was born in Mexico City [on September 4,] 1954, the second of a family of 6 children and 3 miscarriages. My parents were Catholic and had an intense and passionate relationship with religion. When I was seven years old, we spent a year as a missionary family in an Indian town, Huejutla. I remember walking in the market. The goods were displayed on the floor and nobody spoke Spanish. The priest said Mass in Otomi. Indians lived in extremely miserable conditions. We did not. My father was successful and he gave us a life surrounded by comforts, to which we returned after that one year experience. Except for 1962, and some months in Quebec in 1967, in a Catholic exchange program, I lived all my childhood in Mexico City.

"When I was 15, my boat sank. Writing was the wreck I could cling to in the disaster, my lifesaver. My mother died. I lost my family (without her the family crumbled), and I lost my city: Mexico City exploded, stopped being the peaceful place of my childhood. Since I was born, the number of people living in Mexico City has grown from 3 to more than 20 million, and it was in my teens that the demographic explosion sculpted the disfigurement of the beautiful city of my childhood.

"I had lost also my body, my child's body, the one I was used to having. I developed late, and it was when my mother died that I became conscious of the changes that were happening to my body.

"Without my familiar body, without my known city, without home (my father threw me out soon after he remarried, a year later), what could I do? Everything had turned not only unreachable, but each thing carried its own denial. Reality had betrayed me. Everything had turned its back to me, but even its back knew how to make me fall in love with it: I started wandering in the streets of the city, exploring the subway and its people, walking around corners I had never seen before. I had been a girl with a chauffeur at the door. I came and went from Las Lomas and Polanco (then the fanciest quarters of Mexico) to Santa Maria la Ribera (old, traditional, classy), where my grandmother lived. Now I was a pedestrian filled with appetite for the world. Feet weren't enough to walk as far as I wanted, nor were my skirts long enough to cover my legs, and that was the reason why going from one place to the other was a very risky adventure. I had to avoid hostile enemies. But the harassments did not stop me from discovering an extraordinary city, the new, the fractured, the chaotic, the magnificent Mexico City. And I felt I could have it under control, I could face it without any fear because I—or so I thought—I was going to write about it.

"And where was 'the most transparent region of the air,' as Alfonso Reyes described the Valley of Mexico? It was there, it had been born again in my eyes, not only because I learned to belong to the city by writing, but also because I started exploring the city by reading. Mexico City was there, perennial in literature. That way I learned that literature was invention as much as it was memory.

"I became a writer to survive, to make myself a new spine, a pair of eyes. But it is only by chance that I am Mexican. And it was because of this fate that I stumbled into a certain literary tradition. Instead of the chaotic metropolis, I found a city in splendid shape, a city that included the barren islet where the Aztecs erected their first temple, the colonial city of Palaces, the city that witnessed the Revolution, and the one with fountains and flowered boulevards of my childhood.

"I had joined a splendid literary tradition, that lived side by side with others—European, Asian, American and Hispanic—but also, without expecting it, I had arrived at the radical sense of literature. I had started to write only because of selfishness, but if I had needed to write for my survival and to make me be me, it was also true that reality needed the power of the Fable as much as I did. My personal trip was a parody of a collective need. Without the compass of the imaginary and the literary invention, the life of man loses its orientation.

"I started writing poems. In 1978 I published my first two collections, *La memoria vacia*, and *El hilo olvida*. None of my poems are at all descriptive. I wanted to touch the space of silence with them. After years of exercising in notebooks, I finally could fly, articulate and make comprehensible my obsessions: the body, the power of love, the fragility of life.

"In high school I tried to write plays for the first time, trying to make partners in crime. In 1980, answering an invitation of some of these former friends, I wrote for the stage professionally, *Vacio*. The play was a successful scandal. I was lucky. The people I worked with were very talented (Julio Castillo, now dead, and Jesusa, with whom I have done several other plays). Theater had bitten me, I felt its delicious poison, and I wanted to write more. I learned then that a dialogue is always present in literature, in one way or other. Writing plays made me grow as a writer. If I hadn't, I wouldn't have been able to write novels.

"Also in 1980 I dared write a novel. Dare is the wrong word: a novel trapped Carmen Boullosa, *Mejor desaparece*, fragmentary narrative. I can't describe the characters because they are all blurry. *Mejor desaparece* is not a novel of characters, but of atmospheres. All the characters had only one personality, they all had to share a very small amount of oxygen. The story is irrational and violent. A father picks up something in the street and brings *it* home. That '*it*' possesses the household, destroying all happiness and beauty. The language in which the story is told is impregnated by the so-called *it*. The novel is not beautifully but violently written. There's a phrase of Plotinus that has followed me through all my literary expeditions: 'to any vision must be brought an eye adapted to what is to be seen.' The novel was dirty and strange because the theme was bizarre and nasty: hate and violence between children.

"I kept the novel in a drawer six years, thinking I was not a novelist, but when I had almost finished my second novel, *Antes* (1989), which won the Prize Xavier Villaurrutia, the most prestigious in Mexico, I gave my first to the publisher. It appeared in 1987. In the meantime, I had a baby, Maria (b.1982), and owned a theater-bar. I had written a dozen plays, some of them staged in our own theater-bar. The father of Maria and Juan—born 1985, the year of the earthquake—is Alejandro Aura, an actor, and I wrote some of these pieces for him. We had a lot of fun, and sometimes even earned good money. That was the case with *X. E. Bululu*, (1983) a comic monologue, and of *Los Totoles* (1985), an adaptation of an Indian short story.

"The characters of *Antes* are more defined. They are also children. My second is less inclined to imagination than my first, has more realistic ingredients, but remains a novel of fantasy, with which I took (as I had done with the first) a sweet vengeance against reality. Reality had been harsh with me, this was my retaliation: I did not respect reality's order. My characters could go the way they wanted, against logic and normality, that was fair game. I had to betray reality. But I needed more space, another frame to go on working, and I chose (if writers really choose) Moctezuma, the king who had ruled the Aztec empire when Cortés arrived to Tenochtitlan, for my next novel, *Llanto: Novelas imposibles* (1992). Moctezuma comes back to life in Mexico City in 1989 with a particularly horrible headache, as you can imagine. The first thing he does, still in slumber, is remember some flashes of his life. Three women of my age find him where he has appeared, in a park, carry him to their car and show him around. He can't understand this is his city, Tenochtitlan. Nothing is familiar to him.

"After *Llanto*, I wrote *Son vacas, somos puercos*, (1992) a novel of pirates on the Caribbean Sea in the 17th century. I used a historical frame to talk again about violence and construction of the body. Why pirates? They had been with me all my life, as was the case with Moctezuma, and they had many meanings for me. But in that precise moment, I was obsessed by one feeling, that I could kind of touch with this verse by Eugenio Montejo: 'Soy el esclavo que perdio su cuerpo.' ('I am the slave who has lost his body.')

"By pure coincidence, I found a book by Esquemelin describing his piracy experience. I started to write my own version of his life. My novel is the story of a utopia, the first attempt to make a socialist society in the Isla Tortuga, where everybody is equal. And where women are forbidden. That interested me too.

"The historical frame gave me an enormous range of motion and freedom to imagine. My two children were small, my domestic life intense and peaceful (believe me, the combination exists), and there I was as a fish in the sea, among pirates.

"After that novel, I wrote seven others, some with historical frames, others not, some more realistic than others. I let my obsessions work in all of them: *La Milagrosa* (1993, *The Miracle Worker*); *Duerme*, (1994), which received the LiBeraturpreis in Frankfurt for its German version, and a year later, the Academy of the Arts of Berlin gave me the Anna Seghers Preis for all my work; *Cielos de la Tierra* (1997); *Treinta anos* (1999, *Leaving Tabasco*); among others.

"And now I have just finished a novel that is told by the very well-known Cleopatra. In none of my novels have I forgotten Plotinus' words, or my original training: form and content must come together. I want the phrases filled up with the substance, charged with the atmosphere of the story. *Duerme* is like a fairy tale of the 16th century, *Son vacas, somos puercos* like a picaresque novel of the 17th, *Treinta anos* is placed in the sixties, and revisits the novel that was so trendy then, magical realism. I say 'like,' meaning that I play my game between parody and homage. I have continued writing poems. A good number of them reinterpret Eden.

"In recent years, I have delivered lectures at several universities (Princeton, Irvine, Brown, Trinity College, Oxford, among others) and cities around the world. I have taught at Georgetown University (1998) and earlier have been a distinguished visitor at San Diego State University (1990). Last spring I held the Alfonso Reyes Chair at La Sorbonne, in Paris. Now I am a fellow at the Center for Scholars and Writers of the New York Public Library. I was a Guggenheim Fellow in 1991, and a member of the Sistema Nacional de Creadores of Mexico for 6 years. I live in Brooklyn, at Carroll Gardens, with Maria and Juan Aura, my daughter and my son."

After establishing herself as a literary talent in her native Mexico, Boullosa began, in the early 1990s, to receive critical notice abroad. In *Llanto: Novelas imposibles* (1992) the last Aztec ruler, Moctezuma, is brought to modern-day Mexico City—on the site of the ancient Aztec city of Tenochtitlan— and is shocked to find the civilization he knew and the empire he ruled gone. To dramatize Moctezuma's predicament, Boullosa drew on the work of Tzvetan Todorov, who, in a classic study, *The Conquest of America: The Question of the Other* (1982), described the confrontation between the Aztec and Spanish cultures in the New World. Reviewing *Llanto* for *World Literature Today* (Autumn 1993), Cynthia Tompkins noted that Boullosa has her narrator question the whole premise of the story, pointing out that the Aztec culture was based on an oral—rather than a written—tradition, and therefore "the attempt to recreate Moctezuma as a literary character is inherently self-defeating." Tompkins concluded that the "exploration of questions of national identity and writing in *Llanto* proves [Boullosa] to be one of the most intellectually stimulating and compelling voices in contemporary Mexican literature."

In 1993 Boullosa published another novel, *La Milagrosa* (*The Miracle Worker*). The title character is a young girl who has the power to heal the sick. Her story is told through her diary, tape-recorded conversations, and some papers found on a dead man. Although the book is partially a detective story, Boullosa revisits the question of Mexican identity and highlights many of the country's problems, including poverty and political corruption. "More thoughtful readers will find the correspondence between its characters and Mexican realities—or unrealities—alluring," Kay Pritchett observed in *World Literature Today* (Autumn 1994). "Readers seeking simple diversion will be entertained by its intrigue, for essentially it is a kind of whodunit. . . . Untypical of its genre, however, Boullosa's novel clarifies neither who did it nor exactly what was done. Readers will enjoy coming up with their own answers." In the London *Independent* (March 13, 1994) Tony Gould reviewed the English translation, *The Miracle Worker* (1994). He described the first half of the book, in which the girl performs her miracles, as "rewardingly specific. Through stories of deprivation, misery, petty viciousness— some no more than a paragraph long— Boullosa presents a powerful indictment of the Mexican predicament, if not the human condition." Gould faulted the second half, however, noting that "things fall apart as the windy tendencies of the Spanish language run riot. The Milagrosa worries that 'the I-syllable will dissolve into the banality of we.'"

Boullosa's next novel, *Duerme* (1994), is an adventure story set during the 16th century, when Spain colonized much of the New World and oppressed the indigenous Indian populations. The main character is Claire, a former prostitute, who disguises herself as a man and assumes the identity of Monsieur Fleurcy, a French pirate and smuggler. When she is captured by the forces of Conde Enrique de Urquiza, a subject of the Spanish king who is scheduled to be hanged for various crimes, she is forced to trade places with him on the gallows. She escapes and flees, assuming other identities including that of a mestiza, a person of mixed Indian and Spanish blood. In another incarnation, Claire leads a revolution against the Spanish. Boullosa told Gallo that she "became a compulsive reader of the laws passed during the early years of the Spanish colony. I read volume after volume of royal decrees, and their bans and prohibitions allowed me a glimpse into colonial life." Boullosa also consulted 16th-century maps of Mexico and historical commentaries from the 18th and 19th centuries. Writing for *World Literature Today* (Summer 1995), Rafael H. Mojica cited a scene in which Claire is wounded in her left breast. Her blood drains out and is replaced with water taken from the lakes surrounding Mexico City. "The exchange of French blood for Mexican water is perhaps the single most important narrative device . . . . It is an all-unifying device," Mojica wrote. "Indeed, in order for the story to proceed, the enabling flow of this water is necessary, since it is in its miraculous powers that Claire finds what she needs to withstand death on the gallows." Mojica praised *Duerme*, lauding the writer's "subtle blending of adventure narrative with the more complex textual components of the novel."

The English-language publication of *They're Cows, We're Pigs*, in 1997, brought Boullosa widespread attention in the United States. A translation of *Son vacas, somos puercos* (1991), the novel is an adventure story set in the 17th century among pirates on the Caribbean Sea. An old man named Jean Smeeks recalls being kidnapped from his native Flanders and sold into slavery. He eventually learns the healing arts and joins a band of murderous pirates as their ship's medical officer. The pirates call themselves "pigs" to show that they are unburdened by religion, nationalism, or women. The "pigs" contrast their lives with those of the "cows," land dwellers who are bound by traditional values. "The narrative is fractured into many different voices and stories, but this format appropriately reflects the restless, roaming pirate life, and all the strands knit together in a well-crafted closure," Sybil S. Steinberg wrote for *Publishers Weekly* (April 7, 1997). "Regarded as one of the most dazzling of Latin America's new generation, Boullosa justifies her laurels in this rich work." In his *New York Times Book Review* (July 13, 1997) Allen Lincoln wrote that "Boullosa's vivid and visceral descriptions provide hallucinatory images of the pirates' raping and pillaging, their battles in the jungle and at sea, and their post-looting orgies."

In *Leaving Tabasco* (2001), a translation of *Treinta anos* (2000), Delmira Ulloa, a writer living in Germany, recalls her childhood in Agustini, a village in the Mexican territory of Tabasco. In Agustini, birds fall from the sky and cooked lizards come back to life; it is, in the words of Sandra Tsing Loh in the *New York Times Book Review* (May 13, 2001), "a kind of Latin American magic realist Urtown." With a cold mother and absent father, the young Delmira finds solace in her grandmother's stories about their ancestors, Mexico's history, and the oddities of village life. After becoming involved in local politics, Delmira is forced to leave the village, and later is unsure if the strange events there actually took place. Boullosa told Gallo that the character of Delmira was a tribute both to her own grandmother and to "Delmira Augustini, the Uruguayan poet who wrote exquisite erotic texts. Both Delmira, the poet, and Delmira, my character, share an obsession: the elaboration of a body, the creation of their own bodies against the grain, the defense of their own eroticism against a hostile environment." Reviewing *Leaving Tabasco* for the *Boston Globe* (May 14, 2001), Monica L. Williams wrote, "By interspersing issues of sexual assault, sexism, and ethnic prejudice throughout the narrative, [Boullosa] adds enough realism to make the novel one of substance. . . . Boullosa's story thread appears frayed until the novel's midpoint. But each chapter is an adventure, and readers who stay the course will be rewarded as the strands eventually knit into a brilliant closure." In the *Washington Post* (March 18, 2001), Erica Da Costa described the novel as "a lovely, aromatic mix of small-town portraiture and coming-of-age story, heavily seasoned with magical realism." Although she asserts that "Delmira is too angelic to be entirely convincing," Da Costa also wrote that "her circumstances in Agustini are so rich that we happily share with her the myriad components of her life."

—D. C.

SUGGESTED READING: *Bomb Magazine* (online) Winter 2001; *Boston Globe* B p8 May 14, 2001; (London) *Independent* p32 Mar. 13, 1994; *New York Times Book Review* p18 July 13, 1997; *Publishers Weekly* p71 Apr. 7, 1997; *Washington Post Book World* p13 Mar. 18, 2001; *World Literature Today* p780 Autumn 1993, p788 Autumn 1994, p556 Summer 1995

SELECTED BOOKS IN ENGLISH TRANSLATION: *The Miracle-Worker*, 1994; *They're Cows, We're Pigs*, 1997; *Leaving Tabasco*, 2001

Boylan, Clare

Apr. 24, 1948– Novelist; short-story writer

The Irish novelist and short-story writer Clare Boylan is known for her wry wit and her probing, sometimes dark, depictions of Irish families. She has a gift for the fresh, surprising metaphor and for capturing the quirky rhythms of her characters' speech. Though she displays wistfulness for childhood and compassion for women who feel trapped by their duties to husband and family, her characters—both male and female—are never sentimentalized. "She toys with her characters before she sets them down," Lynne Truss wrote in the London *Times* (July 16, 1995), "rolling them hand to hand like marbles. . . . Being the protagonist of a Boylan story does not win you any instant sympathy." Published both in Great Britain and the U.S., Boylan is the author of more than a dozen short-story collections and novels, the most recent of which is the novel *Beloved Stranger* (2001).

Clare Boylan writes for *World Authors 1995–2000*: "I grew up in a red-brick suburb of Dublin. George Bernard Shaw, who spent his unhappy early years in a similar Dublin house, said that families stay together in order to protect the skeletons in their cupboard. A suffocating respectability combined with a feeling of being center stage (for God and the neighbours saw all things) meant we lived in a constant state of fear and stasis. Behind lace curtains, eccentricities, failures, petty scandals, loomed like monsters. Family secrets, and the poignant and comic efforts of people to conceal them, have remained a strong force in my fiction.

"The biggest influence of my childhood was my mother, an early feminist who wrote a very powerful little novel about a witch girl called Edith who

Mike Bunn/Courtesy of Clare Boylan and Little, Brown

used her spells to make bullies look absurd. From the start, my mother decided that I would be the writer of the family. I obliged, but intense mother-daughter relationships became a dominant theme in my work.

"My sisters and I led a dismally quiet life but like an inept trio of Brontës, wrought a ferment of creativity in our dark, suburban house. Mother painted one kitchen wall black and left a large box of chalks beside it so that we could draw to life size. We all wrote stories—entertaining one another far into the night with cliff-hanging serials.

"I went into journalism, writing (in the style of the Victorian Henry Mayhew) about the rich individuality of the marginalized. A series of articles on derelict women won me a Journalist of the Year award. I moved to fiction because it seemed much truer than factual narrative and because I loved to play with language. The late Sean O'Faolain (an Irish short-story writer) said he loved the short story for its mystery and its poetry. The mystery, he said, was the revelation of character. The poetry was the language. I've been criticized for a self-indulgent use of language, and I'm trying to cut back but I love the rich music of words and their infinite capacity to be misunderstood.

"I have always loved the short story, perfectly defined by the late Mary Lavin (an Irish-American short-story writer) as 'an arrow in flight.' My first novel *Holy Pictures* (written as a means of getting my stories published) was, like several other works, about the efforts of children to find a clear path to adulthood amidst the bumbling of deluded adults and as with its prequel *Home Rule*, was based on family myth and history. More recent family history featured in *Room for a Single Lady* and *Beloved Stranger*. The first was based on my own childhood in the 1950s. The latter was inspired by an incident in my family, when my father, at the age of seventy-five, lost his mind. After this painful and intensely personal work I find a change of direction and am now working on a novel set in Victorian London—the completion of an 18-page fragment written by Charlotte Brontë before her death.

"Now on my seventh novel, I feel I have become a more natural novelist and take almost equal pleasure in the very different forms of long and short fiction. My short stories frequently deal with self-revelation through relationships between men and women. All of my novels have had a domestic setting and in spite of widely differing plots, a common theme of intelligent women powerless to command their own destinies. My work has often been described as black comedy but I prefer Carol Shields' definition of it as 'serious comedy.'

"The craft of fiction writing has obsessed me as long as I have been writing and this led me to edit the anthology *The Agony and the Ego* in which eminent writers talk of the process of their creativity. *The Literary Companion to Cats*, my second anthology, was compiled with a view to revealing how in an era of emotional inarticulacy, we conduit our deepest feelings through our pets."

Clare Boylan was born in Dublin, Ireland, on April 24, 1948 (on April 21, according to some sources), the youngest of the three daughters of Patrick and Evelyn (Selby) Boylan. Evelyn Boylan was a writer who published several novels and many short stories, and she encouraged her youngest daughter to write as well. "From the time I was nine or 10," Boylan recalled in the London *Guardian* (April 3, 2000, on-line), "she focused her ambition on me. If I expressed an opinion, she'd say, 'Write it down.'" Boylan's mother was disappointed that her daughter never became a commercially successful author, along the lines of Jackie Collins, but Boylan asserts that "the kind of writer I became is all her own work. In the end, the relationship [between her and her mother], which dominated much of my life, became the substance and motivation of my fiction. All of my books, in one way or another, concern mothers and daughters."

Boylan was educated in Dublin and began her writing career in 1966, as a reporter for the Dublin *Evening Press*. In 1968 she accepted a position as an editor for *Young Woman* magazine, where she worked for two years before marrying Alan Wilkes, a journalist, on September 18, 1970. She became a feature writer for the *Evening Press* in 1972, and the following year she won Ireland's Journalist of the Year award. From 1981 to 1984 she worked as an editor for *Image* magazine. Boylan has also done radio and television broadcasting in Ireland.

In 1983 Boylan published her first novel, *Holy Pictures*. It depicts two sisters, Nan and Mary Cantwell, growing up in the 1920s in Ireland. While Nan, the 14-year-old elder sister, undergoes the traumas of adolescence and sexual awakening, young Mary's interests extend mainly to the welfare of the family cat and the adoration of her father, Cecil, who owns a corset factory. The sisters' lives are complicated when their father starts acting peculiarly. After traveling to India, he changes the family name to Webster and, not long after that, the mysterious Mrs. Mumtaz arrives from India and moves in with them. Their mother then leaves on an extended trip to Paris, and it is not until after her return that the girls finally begin to understand the tragedy that has befallen the family. "[Boylan's prose] tries too hard to be tinged with poetry; only Dylan Thomas could evoke a Celtic childhood in this manner," Roger Lewis wrote of *Holy Pictures* in the *New Statesman* (February 25, 1983). "Set in Dublin in the Twenties, it parades the usual tribulations of puberty: frumpy kisses, the menstrual sulks, a dreamed of trip to the glamorous movies. Perhaps the book would be better entitled Wholly Pictures for the effect is like a series of vignettes: magic lantern slides of a time gone by." In all, however, Boylan's first novel was fairly well received. "Clare Boylan's highly individual prose," wrote Abigail McCarthy in the *New York Times* (November 20, 1983, on-line), "is dense with rich visual images; it is suited to the sensibility shaped by film and television. It is not that her writing has not been influenced by Irish literature's oral tradition and exuberance of language. It has. But her apprehension of the meaning underlying the macabre and grotesque reminds me of our Southern writers. Like them, she juxtaposes the good and the sound with the perverse, the unacceptable and the shockingly haphazard." *Holy Pictures* was a *New York Times* Notable Book of the Year for 1983.

Also in 1983, Boylan published her first short-story collection, *Nail on the Head*. Many of the stories hinge on surprising reversals or unnerving revelations. "Often," Marguerite Quintelli-Neary wrote of the collection in the *Dictionary of Irish Literature* (1996), "Boylan's characters are chagrined to discover unexpected tendencies in spouses, lovers, and acquaintances, such as homosexuality in 'Black Ice,' a psychopathic murder history in 'Some Retired Ladies on Tour,' and geriatric sexual prowess in 'Bad-Natured Dog.'" Patricia Craig, in the *Times Literary Supplement* (March 11, 1983), as quoted in *Contemporary Authors* (1992), praised the "incontestable energy and skill" of the collection and noted that "one or two [of the stories] are very funny."

Boylan's next novel, *Last Resorts*, was published in 1986. It revolves around Harriet Bell, a middle-aged painter with three teenage children, who has been abandoned by her husband and whose only solace is an annual vacation to a pristine Greek island. Harriet, whose life has in many respects been a simple pursuit of love, is plagued instead by unremitting bad luck. She feels as if "she had been placed by fate under a leak in the world," Boylan writes, as quoted by Janet Madden-Simpson in the *San Francisco Chronicle* (March 2, 1986); why else, she asks herself, would "the slow drip of adversity have found her soft skull so unerringly?" Harriet lures her lover, a married man named Joe, to her Greek island retreat, but he leaves early after realizing that his tan will reveal that he has not been—as he had told his wife—on a business trip to Brighton, England. Meanwhile, with Joe gone, Harriet is besieged by her sulky, demanding teenagers and by real-estate developers looking to change "her" island. It remains for her to dig herself out of her mire of mishap and self-pity. Reviewers of the novel generally praised Boylan's wit and, as Madden-Simpson termed it, "linguistic virtuosity." However, some felt that Harriet's relentless misery cast a tedious pall over the book. "Boylan has set her in a whirlpool and means to extricate her," Richard Eder wrote in the *Los Angeles Times* (January 12, 1986). "But the book is mostly the whirlpool, and this creates problems. For one thing, we get no steady or reliable view of Joe and the three children, or of various neighbors who come and go. They are all seen from Harriet's own lurching perspective, and they go in and out of focus. From such a queasy vantage point, they are unable to provide much independent life to the book. It is all Harriet, and it is too much."

In her next novel, *Black Baby* (1989), Boylan explored the odd relationship between a depressive, white spinster and a young, energetic, black woman. When the 67-year-old Alice Boyle answers the door of her Dublin home, she finds "Dinah" (her real name is Cora), who has come—equipped with a wrench—to rob the old lady. Alice feebly attempts to grapple with the would-be robber, and Dinah, taking pity on her, finds she cannot go through with her plan. Instead, she embraces Alice, quotes bible scripture, and asks for money for a religious society. It soon becomes hard to determine what is real and what is the product of Alice's confused imagination: Alice comes to believe that Dinah was the African baby that, as a schoolgirl, she had donated money to "adopt," and that the adult Dinah has traveled from Africa to visit her. Dinah doesn't challenge this impression and she accepts Alice's invitation to move into her home. Once there, she immediately lifts Alice's somber mood, bringing friends over to redecorate, reviving the neglected garden, and even inviting a man—the first since the death of Alice's beloved father—into the house.

Reviewers of the novel commended its inventiveness, humor, and originality, although some found it self-consciously stylish and contrived. "The theme of an old and frozen character being thawed and rejuvenated by a stranger is not original," Richard Eder wrote in the *Los Angeles Times* (November 12, 1989), "but Boylan's blurring of the line between what happens and what is imagined gives it some freshness. Amid the adornment, there is writing that genuinely shines. But there is lethargy to the book that seems proportional to the quickness and reflexiveness of its author's fancy."

Boylan published another collection of short stories, *Concerning Virgins*, in 1989. As the title suggests, many of the stories depict characters dealing with situations with which they have had no previous experience. In 1992 Boylan published the novel *11 Edward Street* (titled *Home Rule* in the United Kingdom), which was offered as a prequel to *Holy Pictures*. Set in Dublin at the turn of the 19th and early 20th centuries, the novel follows the life of Daisy Devlin, the eighth of nine children in a family tainted by incest. Daisy's mother cares more for her three sons than her daughters, promptly pulling each girl from school when they reach the age of 13 so that they can take over the housekeeping duties. After Daisy's father dies, leaving the family destitute, Daisy is sent to a convent, from which she escapes through marriage to a handsome, young soldier. Daisy's happiness soon dissipates, however, as she falls into patterns with her new husband that reiterate the difficult family life she had hoped to escape. In the *Library Journal* (May 15, 1992) Ellen Kaye Stoppel asserted that the novel "attempts to cover too much material and too many years. The narrative is superficial, the characters little more than stick figures, and outside events so casually handled that even World War I makes little impact. Flashes of good writing demonstrate the reason for Boylan's previous successes, . . . but her fans may be disappointed this time." Deborah Singmaster, reviewing the book for the *Times Literary Supplement* (June 12, 1992), declared that *11 Edward Street*'s dark subject matter did not keep it from being enjoyable. "Buried deep underneath the surface fun," she wrote, "runs a wry lament for the unhappy lot of Irish wives, shackled to rotten men and dogged by the threat of perpetual pregnancy. . . . The plot of [the novel] moves at a cracking pace. Child abuse, death, attempted suicide, rape swirl past the reader in single paragraphs, leaving no time for pathos to settle. It is all a delightful, escapist romp."

Boylan next edited *The Agony and the Ego: The Art and Strategy of Fiction Writing Explored*, which was published in 1993. In 1995 she published a short-story collection, *That Bad Woman*, the title of which came from the section of Milton's *Paradise Lost* in which Adam berates Eve for tasting the forbidden fruit and thereby condemning him to unhappiness. In the London *Guardian* (July 11, 1995, on-line) Boylan offered her definition of "bad women": "[They] are neither young nor old," she wrote. "They are not looking for love or babies. After a lifetime of serving other people, what they are seeking is themselves. . . . The bad women of my stories are not out for revenge, but for revelation, and their first discovery is that (repressive societies aside) there are no conscious villains." The 15 stories in *That Bad Woman* chart the lives of Irish women as they negotiate their frustrated and frequently disappointing lives. "I found that a day after I had finished *That Bad Woman*, I could close my eyes and recall every single one of the 15 stories, like literary Pelmanism [memory training]," Helen Stevenson wrote of the collection in the London *Times* (August 19, 1995). "For this, Clare Boylan deserves lavish thanks and praise. . . . Similes and aperçus pop out with freshness, and the various narrative voices have the innocence and unselfconsciousness of those who are just learning to put words to feelings."

In 1997 Boylan published both a short-story collection, titled *Another Family Christmas*, and a novel, *Room for a Single Lady*. "When I set out to write my novel, *Room for a Single Lady*," Boylan explained in the *Guardian* (September 15, 1997), "it was as a tribute to a lost era of imaginative richness. I wanted to press out in its pages the magical episodes of my own growing up. Play was safe in the 1950s. With no television or telephones, we grew up in a fantasy world, childhood a series of hilarious dress rehearsals for the great drama of growing up." The novel, narrated by young Rose Rafferty, chronicles the ups and downs of the Rafferty family, who live in Dublin during the 1950s and supplement their meager income by taking on a succession of zany boarders. Among them are a woman whom the Raffertys dub "The Werewolf," due both to her hairiness and foul temper; Miss Taylor, an older woman who regales Rose and her two older sisters with Irish folk tales; and Minnie, a homely, middle-aged Jewish woman who is also clever, vivacious, and a great baker. Minnie is married to a mentally retarded man who is 20 years her junior, completely devoted, and a helper in her bakery. This odd couple offers Rose and her sisters their first glimpse of true love. "This is lovely, playful and quietly inventive writing," Katy Emck wrote of the collection in the *New Statesman* (December 19, 1997). "Boylan has a gift for capturing the poetry of life without belabouring it, and a lovely ear for the quirks and rhythms of individual speech. . . . Boylan is a funny, compassionate novelist who is unfailingly eloquent but never mannered or pretentious. *Room for a Single Lady* paints a vivid sketch of life's losers and victims and then shows them coming out on top—while remaining as weird as ever."

Boylan's previous short-story collections were compiled into *Collected Stories* in 2000. In 2001 she published the novel *Beloved Stranger*, in which she looks at a family on the edge of dissolution. Dick and Lily Butler have been married and living in the same Dublin neighborhood for 50 years. Lily has always tolerated her husband's surliness and temper tantrums, including the time, shortly after their wedding, when he systematically smashed her china until she agreed not to go back to work. Just when Lily begins to think that Dick has mellowed, his behavior becomes increasingly erratic. Previously a penny-pincher, he starts signing large checks written out to "cash." He rants to strangers at the local pub and insists on keeping the windows and doors open in the dead of winter, claiming that he feels claustrophobic. One night Lily finds him hiding under their bed, waving a shotgun at an imaginary intruder. Ruth, the couple's unmarried, middle-aged daughter, has always been exasperated by her mother's passivity. She calls in a psychiatrist, who diagnoses her father as having a bipolar disorder. For Ruth, the process of comforting her mother dredges up old memories and softens her attitude toward both of her parents. A romance with the sympathetic psychiatrist complicates her feelings. The novel received mixed reviews; too bleak for some critics, it was deemed refreshingly authentic by others. In the *Washington Post* (April 13, 2001) Carolyn See wrote of *Beloved Stranger*, "It's not that the novel isn't realistic. God knows, it is. But why on earth would anyone want to read it unless he or she were paid to? Lily Butler's life has been hell, and her 'enlightened' daughter . . . can't think of anything better to do than repeat it. Dick Butler is one of God's mean little jokes, impervious and reptilian. That's how it is over there in Ireland, according to chipper Ms. Boylan." In the *New York Times* (April 11, 2001) Richard Eder argued that "The truest and most evocative fictional characters take shape from the pinpoints of who they are—and from the undermining, even contrary flow of who they might otherwise be or possibly become." He maintained that Boylan's characters in *Beloved Stranger* had met these criteria and were governed by "their own free and unpredictable spirits. They do not prevail over what happens to them but neither they, nor we, are swamped. We read from the vantage of the little boats, not that of the dismal waves they sail against."

Boylan lives and works in Ireland. Her stories have been anthologized in various books, including *Territories of the Voice: Contemporary Stories by Irish Women Writers* (1989). The film *Making Waves*, based on her short story "Some Ladies on

Tour," was nominated for an Oscar in the Best Short Film category in 1988.

—P. G. H.

SUGGESTED READING: *Guardian* (on-line) Sep. 15, 1997, Apr. 3, 2000; *Los Angeles Times* p3 Jan. 12, 1986, p3 Nov. 12, 1989; *New Statesman* p28 Feb. 25, 1983, p82 Dec. 19, 1997; *New York Times* (on-line) Nov. 20, 1983, Apr. 11, 2001; *San Francisco Chronicle* p9 Mar. 2, 1986; London *Times* p1 Aug. 19, 1995; *Times Literary Supplement* p20 June 12, 1992; *Washington Post Book World* C p6 Apr. 13, 2001; Hogan, Robert ed. *Dictionary of Irish Literature*, 1996

SELECTED BOOKS: *Holy Pictures*, 1983; *Nail on the Head*, 1983; *Last Resorts*, 1986; *Black Baby*, 1989; *Concerning Virgins*, 1989; *11 Edward Street*, 1992; *That Bad Woman*, 1995; *Another Family Christmas*, 1997; *Room for a Single Lady*, 1997; *Beloved Stranger*, 2001

Courtesy of Carcanet Press

Brackenbury, Alison

May 20, 1953– Poet

"Summer Fruit," a short, early poem by the British poet Alison Brackenbury that was published in the pamphlet *Two Poems* (1979), displays the poet's style and technique:

> The stone is broken from its bed,
> The soft skin curls. I hesitate.
> Hot waves of Summer's scent
> It holds: a glowing world, where day is
> In orchards with the juice-stained pickers'
> Sweating, longing for Winter's tang;
> While perfect, undesired, the peaches hang.

Like much of Brackenbury's work, the poem is narrative and rhythmic, and carefully balances imagery and meaning. As Robyn L. Marsack wrote in the *Dictionary of Literary Biography* (1984–1987), in this remarkably sensual poem Brackenbury "is able to provide a luscious description of peaches, and to combine that with an intimation of how much more than fruit is being considered." Brackenbury treats a variety of subjects, some historical or imagined, and some that are personal, gleaned from her experiences living in the English countryside. In *The Oxford Companion to Twentieth Century Poetry* (1994), Peter Forbes described Brackenbury as a "countrywoman": "She writes of provincial lives—people who work in shops, watch a once-desired house grow derelict, drive home on wet Friday nights and find a frog in the road, balance the books at home—and these neglected byways become luminous in her poetry." Brackenbury has written five collections of poetry and received the Eric Gregory Award, in 1982. Her work has been published widely in literary periodicals and broadcast over the radio in Britain.

For *World Authors 1995–2000*, Alison Brackenbury wrote: "I was born in 1953 in Lincolnshire, a farming county in the English East Midlands. My mother taught at the village school and my father was a farm lorry driver. I went to the village school (Willoughton) and the local grammar school (Brigg). At eighteen I went to St. Hugh's College, Oxford, where I obtained a degree in English.

"I married in 1975, trained as a librarian and worked in a further education college in Cheltenham, Gloucestershire, until 1983, when my daughter was born. Since 1990 I have worked in the family metal finishing business.

"Poetry: The poetry which matters to me is memorable, not least through rhyme and rhythm. It is touched by the life of its subjects. It removes and recalls its readers. I have tried to write like this. I can see that my work has shifted from an early lushness to bare ballads. I can see that it has certain territories, including love, the past (as it lights the present), travel, and the strangeness of everyday life.

"Because I grew up in the country, my unchosen subjects also include brambles, mud, and buzzards. 'Nature' is too grand and abstract a word for this. I would like instead to borrow Thoreau's word: 'Wildness'. This may not be fashionable, but it should be.

'Wildness' is under threat, from many sides, and so are we.

"In short? I have my own life, and the poems have theirs. I can only commend them to strangers."

Several critics remarked on the original voice and remarkable skill evident in Brackenbury's first collection, *Dreams of Power and other poems* (1981), which was recommended by the Poetry Book Society. The collection includes both short and long poems, poems about English country life and family, and poems that address more oblique historical subjects. Looking back on this first collection in an article for the *Glasgow Herald* (August 3, 1991), James Aitchison observed that not only did the range of poems display "the creative intelligence one expects in a young poet," but they also showed proof of Brackenbury's "assured technical control over an equally wide range of modes."

During an interview with Brackenbury for *PN Review* (March/April 2000), Vicki Bertram quoted the words of the poet Grevel Lindop: "Speaking to the dead is one of [poetry's] great tasks; and how else, really, can we do that in any public setting?" Bertram observed that, in such historical poems as "Dreams of Power" and "Breaking Ground," Brackenbury does the opposite—she lends a poetic voice to the departed. The title poem of Brackenbury's first collection, "Dreams of Power," animates the historical figure Arbella Stuart, granddaughter to Elizabeth Hardwick, who was a long-time guardian of the dethroned and imprisoned Mary Stuart. While normally an obscure footnote to 16th-century English history, Arbella in Brackenbury's hands becomes a fascinating figure, raised in the company of women who came into and out of power and were unwillingly caught up in the ambitions and intrigues surrounding the English court. The poem is a long, dramatic monologue that spans years in Arbella's life, tracking changes in her position and attitude toward power through subtle modulations in her speech and diction. Robyn L. Marsack described the poem as "a dream in black and white . . . Held together less by chronology than by recurrent imagery, particularly that of the river and of winter light, and by the words *dream* and *power* in their varying appropriate contexts and combinations." Critics found "Dreams of Power" a daring and fascinating experiment; Aitchison claimed that it outgrew "the genre of monologue to become a first-person narrative that combines elements of drama and fiction, of political and amorous intrigue, in a tersely convincing verse novella," and Marsack likewise deemed Brackenbury's poem a success. "The danger Brackenbury courts, of mere costume drama, she evades by her ability to create a real, prickly, highhanded, vulnerable woman, caught in the dreams of others," she wrote.

The title poem in Brackenbury's second collection, *Breaking Ground* (1984), is another long poem about history, drawn in part from her family's own past. In it Brackenbury touches on the life of her great-grandmother, whose husband died of pneumonia after being forced to sleep in damp straw at an agricultural show while tending his employers' sheep. Widowed and with a family to support, Brackenbury's great-grandmother appealed to her Parish Board for help. The Board granted the widow's children relief, but denied her any financial support for herself. As Brackenbury told Bertram, a member of the Board countered her great-grandmother's plaint—"But how am I to live?"—by saying: "You're young and strong enough to work. Woman, where's your pride?" After a few years of hard work, the widow died and her children were left to fend for themselves.

This tale of one woman's tragedy is a kind of footnote to the poem's central narrative, which centers on another sad figure—a male poet who was a rough contemporary of Brackenbury's great-grandmother. This part of the poem takes the form of an imaginary dialogue: an unnamed female speaker, acting as a stand-in for Brackenbury, asks questions of the male speaker, who shares enough of his observations, loves, and disappointments that an attentive reader will discover that his character is based on John Clare. Clare was an 18th-century peasant from Lincolnshire who found modest success with a collection of poems inspired by nature, and then fell from favor and landed in an insane asylum, in Essex. In the poem, Clare recalls "the limping miles from Essex," as quoted by Marsack; in real life Clare escaped from the Essex asylum and walked the 90 miles home to his wife, Patty, whom he confused with his first love, Mary.

In the *Countryman* (1991), Kim Taplin interpreted "Breaking Ground" as a poem that says much about contemporary ecological concerns, underscoring what she called "the inescapable connection between the spiritual and the political which our attitudes to our shared land make plain." Taplin also noted "the wide and complex ironies" behind the poem's statement that Clare's popularity declined because 'nature fell from vogue.'" Robyn L. Marsack viewed "Breaking Ground" as more of a personal statement by the poet. She found that, in interrogating Clare about his loves and losses, Brackenbury seemed to arrive at a validation of her own life and work: "I once drank down / like you, the white and choking of despair, / from cramp and dazzle rescued, did not drown, / unlike you had an after." Marsack argued that, in "treating her breakdown in company with Clare, [Brackenbury] is invoking what could be crudely labeled the English tradition of 'mad nature poets.'" Ultimately, as the poem points out, Brackenbury seems to have found redemption in life and in writing, whereas Clare found only madness.

Brackenbury has often been called a lyric poet, a description that points to her evocation of intense, often personal emotions, and her use of rhythmic meter, which is suggestive of music, or song. In reviewing a third collection, *Christmas Roses* (1989), for the *Listener* (March 9, 1989), Peter Forbes noted that Brackenbury's work has "an insistent, insidious music that once learnt becomes addictive," and described her lyricism as being further apparent in the "supple, fluid line that taps the flux of life somewhere below quotidian consciousness" and "often dips into dream." Aitchison echoed these remarks, observing that "the best of the poems in *Christmas Roses* are prompted by a lyric impulse that takes the poet to the limits of experience and imagination." During her interview with Bertram, Brackenbury spoke of the lyrical facets of her work. "I think that poetry has far more in common with music than with any of the visual arts," she said, citing Tennyson, Keats, and the Georgians (a group of early 20th-century English lyric poets that included Robert Graves and Walter de la Mare) as having helped to tune her ear. Brackenbury also characterized her idiosyncratic use of punctuation and frequent line-breaks as ways of recording what she described to Bertram as "the skids and clutter of consciousness."

Another collection of poems, titled *1829*, was published in 1995. In 2000, Brackenbury's fifth collection of new poetry, *After Beethoven*, was published. According to Sue Wade in the *Poetry Review* (Autumn 2000), Brackenbury has said that the title of the collection comes from "a chance hearing on the radio of the story of a mysterious lady who turned up to Beethoven's funeral." In the title poem, Brackenbury muses about the identity of this "veiled lady," as quoted by Wade. Many of the poems in this collection engage with faraway times or places, and in his review of *After Beethoven* in *Orbis* (Spring/Summer 2000), William Oxley wrote that such "historical recreations . . . show Brackenbury at her best." He expressed some reservations, however, about the appeal of the nature poems also included in the collection. Asserting that "the rural has become a subject-cliché in itself," Oxley found that "[t]here are a number of competent but unexciting nature poems in this volume—a little editorial winnowing would have improved the collection." In spite of these reservations, he detected in Brackenbury the "special sense of joy" of the true lyric poet, and called the poem "Webs," "a true lyric poem."

— M.A.H.

SUGGESTED READING: *Glasgow Herald* Aug. 3, 1991; *Listener* Mar. 9, 1989, with photo; *Orbis* p87+ Spring/Summer 2000; *Poetry Review* p18+ Autumn 2000; *PN Review* p31+ March / April 2000; *Dictionary of Literary Biography*, 1984–1987

SELECTED BOOKS: *Dreams of Power and other poems*, 1981; *Breaking Ground*, 1984; *Christmas Roses*, 1989; *1829*, 1995; *After Beethoven*, 2000

Bragg, Rick

July 26, 1959– Journalist; memoirist

The journalist and memoirist Rick Bragg has been hailed for his sympathetic portrayals of the lives of the poor and working class in the American South. Many of his fellow southerners have discovered in his books echoes of their own childhood struggles and an occasion to indulge in nostalgia for a way of life that has found few exponents in American letters. Readers elsewhere have been enchanted by his heartfelt stories, written in a style that Diane Roberts, in the *Atlanta Journal-Constitution* (September 14, 2001), called "unabashedly lyrical." As a national correspondent for the *New York Times*, Bragg was awarded the Pulitzer Prize, in 1996, for feature writing. His first book, *All Over but the Shoutin'* (1997), describes his penurious childhood in northeastern Alabama, the deep love he felt for his supportive, caring mother, and his steady rise as a journalist. The book became a bestseller and was named a *New York Times* Notable Book of the Year. With *Ava's Man* (2001), Bragg reached farther back in time, to tell the story of Charlie Bundrum, his maternal grandfather, a rough-and-tumble southerner who made his own moonshine and grabbed whatever work he could to support his large family in the Depression-era Deep South. Some have compared *Ava's Man* to *Let Us Now Praise Famous Men*, the journalist James Agee's account of three tenant families during the Depression. "But where Agee approached their lives from the outside, Bragg writes from inside the culture," Robert Morgan wrote for the *New York Times Book Review* (September 2, 2001).

Courtesy of the *New York Times*

"The family he tells us about is his own. Often he lets the people speak for themselves, and the authenticity of the voices and the setting grab you from the first sentence."

Ricky Edward Bragg was born on July 26, 1959 in Piedmont, Alabama. The second of three sons (a fourth died in infancy), he grew up in Possum Trot, a rural area of Alabama in the foothills of the Appalachian Mountains. Bragg and his brothers, Sam and Mark, were raised primarily by their mother, Margaret Marie Bragg. Their father was an alcoholic Korean War veteran; on the rare occasions when he was around, he often beat Margaret and neglected the children. The family had very little money, surviving on $50 a month from Social Security checks and the pittance Margaret earned from picking cotton and cleaning houses. After high school Bragg attended Jacksonville State University, in Alabama, where he wrote for the campus newspaper. Months before his freshman year ended, he had to drop out, because he ran out of money.

Soon afterward Bragg got a job with the *Anniston Star*, an Alabama newspaper, and began covering sports. In 1985 he became a reporter for the *Birmingham News*, also in Alabama, and in 1989 joined the *St. Petersburg Times*, a Florida daily. At the latter, he covered such events as the 1989 riots in Miami; Hurricane Andrew, in 1992; and the political unrest in Haiti. In 1992 he studied journalism for a year at Harvard University, in Cambridge, Massachusetts, on a prestigious Neiman Fellowship. Two years later Bragg was hired by the *New York Times*.

During the next few years, Bragg reported for the *New York Times* on such events as the 1994 landing in Haiti of U.S. troops, whose mission was to restore the ousted president Jean-Bertrand Aristide to power; the trial in South Carolina of Susan Smith, who was convicted in 1994 of drowning her two sons; the shootings by a 13-year-old boy and his 11-year-old cousin at a Jonesboro, Arkansas, middle school in 1994, which resulted in the deaths of four students and a teacher; and the bombing in 1995 of the Alfred P. Murrah Federal Building in Oklahoma City, Oklahoma, by Timothy J. McVeigh, which left 168 people dead. "The Oklahoma City bombing story was easy to write because I had no time," Bragg told Chip Scanlon in an interview for the Web site of the American Society of Newspaper Editors. "I went on automatic. . . . You don't have any time to think about it. You just try not to get in the way of it. I was so full of the emotion of what I had seen and from talking to people, that not only was it clear how awful it was through the quotes and some of the images and details, but you could almost see the horror of it between the lines."

Among many other subjects he covered for the *New York Times*, Bragg also wrote about a Mississippi laundress named Oseola McCarty, who saved from her meager earnings the astonishing sum of $150,000 and, in 1995, when she was 87, donated it to the University of Southern Mississippi to establish a scholarship fund for African-Americans. Another of his stories focused on elderly prisoners in an Alabama penitentiary. Talking about that article, titled "Where Alabama Inmates Fade into Old Age," Bragg told Chip Scanlon, "I'm not really smart enough to write a story where I have to rely on telling people what I see. I have to use images and details to show them. An old editor at the Birmingham (Ala.) News, Clarke Stallworth, told me once, 'Show me, don't tell me.' That's really all I tried to do in this story, and others, to give some scenery, almost a backdrop, for the characters. Another good lesson came years ago from an editor who said, 'You don't have to be ashamed to make the stories personal.' He didn't mean that my feelings necessarily had to show, but that it was all right to make it as though the reader were wading through the story, to give images and details and, I hate to say, color—to care about it one way or the other. . . . I do like it when people come up later and say, 'I felt like I was there.'"

In 1996 Bragg was awarded the Pulitzer Prize for "his elegantly written stories about contemporary America," as stated on the Pulitzer Prize Web site. Bragg brought his mother to the awards ceremony, and for the occasion she bought herself a new dress—her first in 18 years. Bragg later told Susan Larson for the New Orleans, Louisiana, *Times-Picayune* (August 21, 2001) that one of his happiest moments was "having my mama go with me to [receive] the Pulitzer, and walking off the dais and handing it to my mama. It was just a natural thing to do. It's not in [my] house. It hangs in her living room, and when you walk in the house, it's the first thing you see."

Bragg's first book, *All Over but the Shoutin'*, was largely a tribute to his mother's selflessness. In it he recorded an early childhood memory, of how Margaret used to drag him along rows of cotton on a burlap sack while she worked long days in the fields. "It would have been easy for me," he wrote, as quoted by Richard H. Weiss in the *St. Louis Post-Dispatch* (October 20, 1998), "to just accept the facade of blind sacrifice that has always cloaked her, to believe my momma never minded the backbreaking work and the physical pain as she dragged me up and down a thousand miles of clay. . . . I would like to believe she didn't even notice how her own life was running through her hands like water. But the truth is she did know, and she did think about it in the nighttime when her children were put to bed and there was no one left to keep her company except her blind faith in God and her own regret." Diane Roberts noted, "When Bragg writes about his mother, worn down from poverty and pain, self-sacrificing and self-effacing, he will flat make you cry."

The book also reveals Bragg's bristling anger—toward his father for abusing Margaret and forsaking his children, toward those who looked down on his family because they were poor, and toward editors who discounted him for his lack of a college degree. Roberts wrote, "Bragg attacks the American class system like one of those little banty roosters who'll try to fight an elephant. It is rare—and welcome—to find a writer who knows that America's national boast of classlessness is a crippling lie." A critic for *Kirkus Reviews* (July 1, 1997) wrote that Bragg "has a strong voice and a sweeping style that, like his approach to newspaper writing, is rich, empathetic, and compelling. His memoir is a model of humility combined with pride in one's accomplishments." Francine Prose, in *People* (September 15, 1997), felt that "occasionally, Bragg's folksy tone ('The people who know about books call it a memoir, but that is much too fancy a word for me . . .') seems like an affectation," but nevertheless viewed the book as "a testament to a mother's grace and determination, to Bragg's courage and resilience, and to the kindness of the neighbors, relatives and strangers who helped a poor family survive and a determined young man succeed."

In conjunction with the appearance of the book, his publisher, Pantheon, sent Bragg on a national reading and book-signing tour. The large audiences he attracted were impressed by his sincerity and distinctive southern drawl, an accent he described to Alix Madrigal for the *San Francisco Chronicle* (September 9, 2001) as "more pool hall than syrupy Southern." "We knew our best weapon [in selling the book] would be to use Rick Bragg himself," Janice Goldklang, Pantheon's vice president and publishing director, told Steven M. Zeitchik for *Publishers Weekly* (February 2, 1998). "When we first met him we were just bowled over. He immediately started telling us stories." Bragg enjoyed the tour; as he recalled to Zeitchik, "It was as though every book signing became a front-porch taletelling session."

Sixty-five of Bragg's press pieces are gathered in his book *Somebody Told Me: The Newspaper Stories of Rick Bragg* (2000). Most were culled from the *New York Times*; five are from the *St. Petersburg Times* and one from the *Birmingham News*. The title of the volume reportedly derives from the answer Bragg has given when people ask him how he comes up with his remarkable tales. Telling Susan Larson that he regarded the collection as a good representation of his work, he compared it to the rooftops that his maternal grandfather built: "We'll go out around town, riding in the car, mama in the jump seat, and she'll say, 'Your granddaddy roofed that house.' And some of those old shingles are still on there. Even when some of those old barns are falling apart, you still see nails that he drove. He built houses that are still standing. And with *Somebody Told Me*, now, if I ever have a kid, I can show you: I never built a house, but I did this. That's what I did over a 10-year period of my life. I'm proud of it. I'm really proud of it."

The subject of Bragg's next book, *Ava's Man*, is his mother's father, Charlie Bundrum. Charlie was a roofer, a carpenter, a whiskey-maker, and a fisherman—a rough but tender patriarch who labored during the Depression years to provide for his wife and seven children. (An eighth died in infancy.) Even at times when the family had scarcely enough to eat, he shared what little they had with anyone who came to their door. He was also a drinker and a fighter who had his share of run-ins with the law. Charlie distilled moonshine; "He never sold a sip—not one sip—that he did not test with his own liver," Bragg wrote, as quoted by Jonelle Bonta in the *Atlanta Journal-Constitution* (August 29, 2001). Unlike many others, Charlie did not become violent after drinking heavily; rather, he liked to sing and play the banjo. But when angered he could be brutal; he once beat a man nearly to death for throwing a snake at one of his sons. He was almost universally loved and admired, and at his funeral cars from all over the county lined the blacktop for more than a mile.

Since Bragg never knew his grandfather—he died the year before Bragg was born—he gathered information for *Ava's Man* from talks with his mother and other relatives, who still so missed Charlie that their stories were often interrupted by tears. For Bragg, researching the lives of family members was more difficult than inquiring about those of strangers. "While you try to be conscientious with everybody, with your family you're walking on gilded splinters all the time," he explained to Alix Madrigal. "You don't want to hurt them, and you're not going to put the book out if it makes them unhappy. So there's always that fear, because you could not streamline or homogenize the man [his grandfather]. If you didn't use his foibles, his flaws and his sometimes out-and-out destructive nature, it wouldn't have rung true." Bragg also felt an obligation to his grandfather not to sugarcoat his story. "The one thing I am dead sure of," Bragg wrote in the book, as quoted by Bonta, "is that his ghost, conjured in a hundred stories, would have haunted me forever if I had whitewashed him. . . . A man like that, surely, would want a legacy with pepper on it."

Ava's Man quickly climbed the best-seller lists. Robert Morgan described the book as "a kind of sublime testimonial." "Bragg gets the combination of sentiment and independence and fear in this culture just right," he declared. Michael Kenney, in the *Boston Globe* (October 2, 2001), wrote, "It is a book that works on many levels—as an anecdotal social history of rural poverty, as the highly personalized sociology of a family, as an engaging compilation of regional folklore, and perhaps above all as just grand storytelling." A reviewer for *Publishers Weekly* (August 6, 2001) judged the work to be "a soulful, poignant portrait of working-class Southern life. . . . Bragg delivers, with deep affection, fierce familial pride, and keen, vivid prose that's as sharp and bone-bright as a butcher knife. In this pungent paean to his grandfather, Bragg also chronicles a vanished South that—like the once-wild Coosa River Charlie liked to ply in homemade boats—is becoming too tamed to accommodate those who would carve out a proud if hardscrabble living on its margins."

Bragg, who lives in New Orleans, has twice received the American Society of Newspaper Editors Distinguished Writing Award and has also earned more than 50 other writing honors. He has taught writing at Harvard University; the Poynter Institute for Media Studies, in St. Petersburg, Florida; Boston University, in Massachusetts; and the University of South Florida. In May 2003 Bragg resigned from the New York Times, amidst allegations that he had relied too heavily on the interviewing and reporting services of a freelance journalist while preparing an article on Florida oystermen. He defended the practice as being common among veteran newsmen, but felt that it was best to step down from his position in the wake of the controversy.

Bragg—who wrote in All Over but the Shoutin', "I love writing the way some men love women"—divorced after a few years of marriage in the 1980s. In 1996 he bought a house for his mother. When Chris Rose for the Times-Picayune (September 18, 2001) asked him what his greatest extravagance had been after his first book landed on best-seller lists, Bragg replied, "Truthfully, all the money from the books goes to my mom, my family, but I did buy a jacket—I call it my author's jacket, which I wear to book signings—for $67." Bragg has reportedly signed a $1 million contract with a large publishing house for two more books.

—A.I.C.

SUGGESTED READING: Atlanta Journal-Constitution L p10 Sep. 14, 1997, C p2 Aug. 29, 2001; Boston Globe F p2 Oct. 2, 2001; Kirkus Reviews p995 July 1, 1997; (New Orleans, Louisiana) Times-Picayune F p1 Aug. 21, 2001; New York Times VII p9 Sep. 2, 2001; People p42 Sep. 15, 1997, with photo; Publishers Weekly p34 Feb. 2, 1998, p74 Aug. 6, 2001; San Francisco Chronicle Sep. 9, 2001, with photo; St. Louis Post-Dispatch D p1 Oct. 20, 1998, with photo; Tallahassee Democrat D p4 Oct. 4, 2002

SELECTED BOOKS: All Over but the Shoutin', 1997; Somebody Told Me: The Newspaper Stories of Rick Bragg, 2000; Ava's Man, 2001

Courtesy of H. W. Brands

Brands, H. W.

1953 (?)– Historian; nonfiction writer

H. W. Brands is the author of, among other volumes, two well-regarded biographies: *T. R.: The Last Romantic* (1997), about former U. S. President Theodore Roosevelt, and *The First American: The Life and Times of Benjamin Franklin* (2000), which was a *New York Times* best-seller and a finalist for both the Pulitzer Prize and the *Los Angeles Times* Book Award for biography. Prolific in his output, he has written 17 books since 1988. His better-known works include *The Devil We Knew: Americans and the Cold War* (1993), *The Wages of Globalism: Lyndon Johnson and the Limits of American Power* (1995), *The Reckless Decade: America in the 1890s* (1995), *What America Owes the World: The Struggle for the Soul of Foreign Policy* (1998), and *The Age of Gold: The California Gold Rush and the New American Dream* (2002). Far from being dry or didactic, Brands's work has proven popular with the general public. "Most academics seem to be either unwilling or unable to reach ordinary readers. They're writing for each other," Jim Hornfischer, Brands's agent, told Sharyn Wizda Vane for the *American Statesman* (August 18, 2002). "[Brands] sees it as a calling. He's gifted with a novelist's skill—he knows how to sustain tension, how to build a scene." Brands has also edited or co-edited four volumes: *The Foreign Policies of Lyndon Johnson: Beyond Vietnam* (1999), *Critical Reflections on the Cold War: Linking Rhetoric and History* (2000), *The Use of Force After the Cold War* (2000), and *The Selected Letters of Theodore Roosevelt* (2001). His articles have appeared in numerous newspapers and journals, including the *New York Times*, *Wall Street Journal*, *Washington Post*, *International Herald Tribune*, *Boston Globe*, *National Interest*, *American Historical Review*, *Journal of American History*, *Political Science Quarterly*, and *American History*.

Brands is a distinguished professor of history and the holder of the Melbern G. Glasscock Chair in American history at Texas A & M University, in College Station. Of his teaching style, he told Vane, "I'll be the first to admit that when I'm giving a lecture, it's like giving a sermon. I know that I have to hook these students. Everybody at Texas A & M has to take two semesters of American history. I don't kid myself; most of them are there because they have to be. But I've got 'em for three hours a week. And if I can hook 'em, if I can make 'em think that this is interesting, then I can get 'em for the rest of their lives."

BRANDS

H. William Brands, known to friends and colleagues as Bill, was born in about 1953 in Portland, Oregon. He studied at Stanford University, in California, and in 1975 he received his B.A. in history. He worked as a traveling salesman for one year, in his family's cutlery business. After acknowledging that he lacked sales skills, he became a teacher at Jesuit High School, in Portland, where he taught history and math for five years. Meanwhile, he continued his education, receiving his M.A. in liberal studies from Reed College, in Portland, in 1978, and his M.S. in mathematics from Portland State University, in 1981. At that juncture, he was forced to decide whether to pursue doctoral studies in math or history. Wanting to contribute to the public debate and perhaps even influence public policy, he chose the latter. He received his Ph.D. in history from the University of Texas, in Austin, in 1985. He spent a year as an oral historian at the University of Texas Law School, then worked briefly in Nashville, Tennessee, as a visiting assistant professor of history at Vanderbilt University. In 1987 he joined the history department of Texas A & M University. The following year he published his first book, *Cold Warriors: Eisenhower's Generation and American Foreign Policy*. This was followed by several other well-received works on history and politics, including *Inside the Cold War: Loy Henderson and the Rise of the American Empire, 1918–1961* (1991) and *Bound to Empire: The United States and the Philippines* (1992). (Loy Henderson was a high-ranking official of the U. S. Department of State; his career spanned from 1922 to 1960.)

In *The Devil We Knew: Americans and the Cold War* (1993), Brands argues that the United States bears a larger measure of blame in perpetuating the Cold War than has been traditionally assigned to it. Writing in the wake of the Soviet Union's fall, in 1991, Brand criticizes American hard-liners for exaggerating Soviet military power and failing to perceive basic weaknesses in Soviet society. The Cold War could have been defused as early as the death of Joseph Stalin in 1953, Brands claims, and subsequent opportunities went equally unheeded. Tracing the history of the global conflict from the creation of the Central Intelligence Agency under president Harry Truman through the era of Ronald Reagan, Brands shows how the American preoccupation with fighting communism led the U.S. to involve itself in such questionable activities as helping to overthrow democratically elected governments in Iran and Guatemala, among other countries, supporting oppressive dictatorships abroad, and sacrificing human lives to fighting in Korea and Vietnam.

"*The Devil We Knew* should firmly establish [Brands's] reputation—at least among his professional peers—as one of the best and certainly one of the most prolific young historians of the postwar period," Kai Bird wrote for the *Washington Post* (September 26, 1993). "His work shows evidence of many hours spent in the archives. And yet his histories are eminently readable. He peppers his argument with wry observations about such well-known men as Harry Truman, J. Edgar Hoover, Dean Acheson, [and] Paul Nitze." "[This is] a sophisticated interpretation . . . that appears calculated to draw fire from the left as well as right," a critic noted for *Kirkus Reviews*, as quoted on the Amazon Bookseller's Web site. "In his mildly contrarian reckoning of the Red menace's socioeconomic and geopolitical implications, moreover, Brands displays an impressive flair for vivid phrasing." The reviewer concluded that *The Devil We Knew* was "a provocative audit of an adversarial world order whose passing, in retrospect at least, seems to have been long overdue."

T. R.: The Last Romantic (1997) charts the life of Theodore Roosevelt, the popular U.S. president who held office from 1901 to 1909. In the book Brands discusses Roosevelt's "romantic" perspective, which enabled him to see life as a clear-cut battle between good and evil—a moral standpoint that gave him the confidence, energy, and enthusiasm to drastically reshape the American presidency and maintain the adoration of the American people. "Theodore Roosevelt emerges as considerably more than his toothy Rough Rider legend in this extensively researched, psychologically penetrating biography of our 26th president," a critic for *Kirkus Reviews* noted, as quoted on the Amazon Bookseller's Web site. A reviewer for the *Christian Science Monitor* (February 5, 1998) called the book "engaging" and an ample examination of the former president's merits and talents.

In 1999 Brands published *Masters of Enterprise: Giants of American Business from John Jacob Astor and J. P. Morgan to Bill Gates and Oprah Winfrey*. The book examines the lives of 25 entrepreneurs to determine if they shared any common traits. He concludes, perhaps not surprisingly, that all had abundant health and energy, creative vision, and hunger for success. The book was generally well received and was called by various critics "invigorating" and a "treasure trove" of information.

When Brands was writing his acclaimed biography *The First American: The Life and Times of Benjamin Franklin* (2000), he had access to *The Papers of Benjamin Franklin*, a wealth of documents, some previously unpublished, gathered into 35 volumes by the American Philosophical Society and Yale University. At 759 pages, Brands's biography is the largest and most detailed biography of Franklin published in the last 60 years. The focus of the book is on Franklin's role as the leading figure in the movement to gain American independence from Britain, with special attention devoted to how Franklin's attitude towards Britain changed between 1763 and 1774, as he went from being a supporter of King George III to a staunch advocate for the American cause. Brands's thorough treatment also covers Franklin's achievements in each of his many areas of expertise—as scientist, businessman, philosopher, printer, journalist, author, inventor, and diplomat.

"Brands, a master storyteller . . . [has created] an absorbing portrait," Robert C. Jones opined in *Library Journal* (September 15, 2000). "Brands's eminently readable narrative is a worthy successor to Carl Van Doren's classic Pulitzer Prize–winning *Benjamin Franklin* [1938]." Max Hall noted in the *Boston Globe* (February 25, 2001), "[This is] a comprehensive, lively biography. Brands does not appear to have gleaned a lot of facts or insights that will be new to Franklin scholars. But I suspect that this was not his primary aim. He is a skilled narrator who believes in making good history accessible to the non-specializing book lover, and the general reader can read this book with sustained enjoyment."

Brands has said that he wrote the book to counter a decline in interest in Franklin over the last few decades. "To some degree I think it's sort of overexposure," Brands explained in an interview for the *Philadelphia Inquirer* (October 4, 2000). "Up until I was in high school, everybody read Franklin's autobiography in high school. By the 1950s and 1960s, dead white guys were falling out of fashion, and people were looking in other directions. . . . If my book does anything, I hope it restores Franklin as a real, vibrant, dynamic character." Brands added, "I consider him to be maybe the great American genius. He was talented in just about all facets of human activity. . . . To some degree, I suppose, one of the reasons that people lost interest in him is that he was just too good to be true. And, actually, he almost is."

In Brands's next book, *The Strange Death of American Liberalism* (2001), he argues that liberalism, which he defines as a willingness to trust the federal government to improve the lives of the American people, is not the norm in American history, but rather an anomaly. Brands claims that Americans have traditionally been skeptical of big government, and that it is only during wartime that expansive government policies are tolerated by the public. During the Cold War, Brands writes, America experienced a surge in domestic reformism—highway construction, education funding, civil rights legislation, for example—which the public viewed as an extension of foreign policy. However, liberal programs suffered a decline in popularity due to the erosion of confidence following the Vietnam War and the Watergate scandal—and were finally put to rest, Brands argues, after the collapse of the Soviet Union, in 1991.

Reviews of the book were not entirely laudatory. Amanda Heller, writing for the *Boston Globe* (December 23, 2001), found that Brands's thesis is "tidy if overgeneralized." In a critique for the *New York Times* (December 9, 2001), Joshua Micah Marshall wrote, "The book's real weakness . . . is its one-dimensional rendering of liberalism itself. For Brands, liberalism is all about bigness and power and centralized control. Equality, solidarity and rights-consciousness tag along like bit players in the drama." Many reviewers commented on the irony of the book's being completed shortly before the World Trade Center attacks of September 11, 2001 and noted that Brands's theories would be put to practical test in the wake of that catastrophic event.

Brands's most recent book is *The Age of Gold: The California Gold Rush and the New American Dream* (2002). Relying heavily on first-hand accounts—letters, memoirs, newspapers, and unpublished manuscripts—Brands shows how the 1848 discovery of gold by James Marshall in Coloma, California, became "a seminal event in history, one of those rare moments that divide human existence into before and after," as he writes. The gold rush, Brands argues, radically transformed the American character, as the East Coast puritan ethic of slowly and steadily building one's fortune over years of hard work was replaced almost overnight by the new dream of acquiring instant wealth, "won in a twinkling by audacity and good luck," as Brands writes. Through the stories of such famous figures as John Fremont, Leland Stanford, George Hearst, and Levi Strauss, and a host of lesser-known settlers, immigrants, and slaves, Brands examines the difficulties of the harrowing journey west; the creation of California society; the heated debate over whether California would be a slave state; and the xenophobia and racial tensions that characterized the time.

Janet Maslin praised the book in the *New York Times* (August 19, 2002) as "an engrossing, multifaceted history . . . [that] explores history, politics, geology, adventure and industry with omnibus enthusiasm. . . . [The] book unfolds in an evenhanded, instructive tone, without excess animation. But this is a serious, comprehensive study, filled with memorable visions and interesting observations. Its author, like the miners of the gold rush themselves, leaves no stone unturned." A reviewer for *Publishers Weekly*, as quoted on the Amazon Bookseller's Web site, wrote, "Noted biographer Brands . . . makes good use of a sparkling cast of characters. With solid research and a sprightly narrative, Brands's portrait of the gold rush is an enlightening analysis of a transformative period for California and America." David Kipen, writing for the *San Francisco Chronicle* (August 18, 2002, on-line), praised Brands's "witty, athletic prose," and deemed the book "a barn burner."

H. W. Brands lives in Austin with his wife, Ginger, and their five children. He is a frequent guest on radio and television talk shows. His books have been translated into Chinese, Japanese, and Korean. When working on a book, Brands usually spends from four to six hours writing daily. He prefers to type standing up, using a keyboard placed at about waist level. He is reportedly at work on a book about the Texas Revolution of 1835–36, while his comprehensive account of Woodrow Wilson's presidency, "Woodrow Wilson 1913–1921," co-authored with Arthur Schlesinger Jr., is set for release in June 2003.

—A. I. C.

SUGGESTED READING: *Boston Globe* C p2 Feb. 25, 2001; *Library Journal* Sep. 15, 2000; *New York Times* E p8 Oct. 10, 2000, VII p34, Dec. 9, 2001, E p7 Aug. 19, 2002; *Washington Post* X p1 Sep. 26, 1993

SELECTED BOOKS: *The Devil We Knew: Americans and the Cold War*, 1993; *The Wages of Globalism: Lyndon Johnson and the Limits of American Power*, 1995; *The Reckless Decade: America in the 1890s*, 1995; *T. R.: The Last Romantic*, 1997; *What America Owes the World: The Struggle for the Soul of Foreign Policy*, 1998; *Masters of Enterprise: Giants of American Business from John Jacob Astor and J. P. Morgan to Bill Gates and Oprah Winfrey*, 1999; *The First American: The Life and Times of Benjamin Franklin*, 2000; *The Strange Death of American Liberalism*, 2001; *The Age of Gold: The California Gold Rush and the New American Dream*, 2002; as editor or co-editor—*The Foreign Policies of Lyndon Johnson: Beyond Vietnam*, 1999; *Critical Reflections on the Cold War: Linking Rhetoric and History*, 2000; *The Use of Force After the Cold War*, 2000; and *The Selected Letters of Theodore Roosevelt*, 2001

Courtesy of Eberly College of Arts and Sciences

Brazaitis, Mark

July 23, 1966– Novelist; short-story writer; journalist

Mark Brazaitis is a novelist, short-story writer, poet, and journalist whose work has appeared in such publications as the *Journal of Sport Literature*, *Beloit Fiction Journal*, *Sun*, *Atlanta Review*, the *Washington Post*, and the *Detroit Free-Press*. Much of his fiction is set in Guatemala, where he spent time as a Peace Corps volunteer in the 1990s. His first short-story collection, *River of Lost Voices: Stories from Guatemala* (1998), won the Iowa Short Fiction Award. In it Brazaitis employs a deceptively simple style that borrows a certain lyricism from folktale forms, and uses short passages of dialogue to bring his characters to life. Brazaitis's first novel, *Steal My Heart*, was published in 2000.

For *World Authors 1995–2000*, Mark Brazaitis writes: "I was born in East Cleveland, Ohio, in 1966. I think I wanted to be a writer as soon as I understood what my father, a journalist, was doing. He used to type stories on a manual typewriter in the den. My sister and I were warned not to disturb him when he was writing; therefore, the act of writing took on, for me, an air of vital importance. Writing was a serious undertaking. It also sounded good—I loved the music of my father's fingers working the keys.

"My first 'success' as a writer occurred when I was in fourth grade. I wrote a story called 'Tommy the Talking Tomato,' and my teacher read it aloud to the class. It was a thrill to have an audience.

"I thought I would follow my father and become a journalist. For a while, I did. In college, I was the sports editor of the *Harvard Crimson*. I had summer internships at the *Richmond Times-Dispatch* and the *Detroit Free Press*. After college, I worked briefly as a stringer for the *Washington Post*. What I discovered was that what I most liked about working for newspapers wasn't finding the story—going to events, interviewing sources—but writing it. So I turned to fiction writing.

"I've always been a big reader. In junior high and high school, I read widely and deeply—Tolstoy, Turgenev, Hemingway, Steinbeck, Bowles. So I had a sense of what good writing was. This, however, didn't mean I could imitate it. The year after I graduated from college, I wrote a novel. It is, thankfully, buried deep in a trunk somewhere in my basement.

"I joined the Peace Corps in 1990 and served for three years in Guatemala. I worked with farmers to help improve their corn and bean seed and post-harvest storage methods; I also taught English in the junior high school in the small town where I lived. Stepping outside of my country and culture, I saw myself—and the world—as I'd never seen them before. I also had to operate in a new language (Spanish and, occasionally, Pokomchi, the local Maya language), and this helped me appreciate the importance of precise words. Saying 'thing' all the time wasn't going to help me get toilet paper at the local store.

"In Guatemala, I saw the world as I never had, and naturally I wanted to write about it. Toward the end of my time as a Peace Corps volunteer, I began to write the stories that would eventually appear in my first book, *The River of Lost Voices: Stories from Guatemala*. I was worried that once I left Guatemala, I wouldn't be able to recreate the world I was living in. But I found that when I returned to the States, I could close my eyes and be back on my doorstep in Santa Cruz Verapaz.

"*The River of Lost Voices* was inspired by people I met and stories I heard in Guatemala. All the stories are fictional, but each of them contains a kernel of truth. For example, 'José del Río,' the opening story, begins, 'I was born dead and I've never been allowed to forget it.' Down the street from my house lived a family with a son who was, so his sisters proclaimed, born dead. I was fascinated by the implications of this, and so I explored it in fiction.

"My novel, *Steal My Heart*, is also set in Guatemala. Ramiro Caal, who appeared in 'A Detective's Story' in my short story collection, returns to solve a series of cat burglaries and other small crimes. Unlike in *The River of Lost Voices*, several of the protagonists (and the chief antagonist) of *Steal My Heart* are North Americans.

"Guatemala continues to inspire my fiction, as well as my poetry and non-fiction. I've written several more stories set in Guatemala, and I have several more in mind."

In *Glamour* (June 1998) Brazaitis wrote about his eye-opening experience playing basketball with an amateur team in Guatemala. Guatemalans, who are exposed to American movies, sports stars, and scientific and technological achievements, but receive little other exposure to U.S. culture, often have lofty and unrealistic expectations of Americans, according to Brazaitis. Though he was a decent basketball player, his teammates expected him to be a superstar and insisted that he keep shooting the ball. They changed their opinions of Brazaitis only after the team started losing repeatedly. "I wasn't invited back on the team the following year," he wrote in the article. "Still, in a single season, I'd performed a valuable role. We North Americans enjoy too much acclaim in certain parts of the world. Preceded by the feats of our action heroes and sports stars, we are expected to perform miracles merely by virtue of where we were born. Playing basketball, I proved that we are capable of mediocrity. It wasn't a lesson I'd intended to teach, but there it was. And if I wasn't exactly consoled by the thought, at least I could retire from the team knowing I wouldn't be forgotten."

In 1993 Brazaitis returned to Ohio and taught creative writing at Bowling Green Junior High School. He also taught English at Bowling Green State University, where he was working toward a master of fine arts degree in creative writing. In 1995, after earning his degree, he again ventured abroad, this time to Mexico to participate in an agricultural aid program. Later that year he returned to Guatemala to work as a technical trainer for the World Learning Center program. After returning to the States in 1996, he became an adjunct English professor at the Helene Fuld College of Nursing in New York City. In 1998 he became an adjunct professor of English at Fordham University, in the New York City borough of the Bronx.

In 1998 Brazaitis published *River of Lost Voices: Stories from Guatemala*. As the title suggests, the collection drew heavily from Brazaitis's travels. The experience of living in Guatemala was so profound for Brazaitis that it necessitated a reevaluation of his entire life. In the on-line publication *Peace Corps Writers* (September 1999), Brazaitis is quoted as saying that in Guatemala he had to "learn a new language with which to describe my life, find new words to describe things, and fit the words to what it was that I saw. . . . In Guatemala, I was forced to wake up." Many of the stories in *River of Lost Voices* reflect the violence of the Guatemalan civil war as well as the everyday lives of villagers. In "Bathwater" a boy falls in love with Maria, the woman for whom he works as a housekeeper. Maria is the mistress of the wealthy and fierce Señor Prado, and their young housekeeper is forced to watch helplessly when they meet a violent end. In "The Liar" young Carlos's father pronounces him a liar when he returns from a hunting trip claiming to have seen a deer. In "Gemelas" a young woman is torn between happiness and jealousy when her twin marries a wealthy landowner, yet ultimately the two sisters suffer similar fates.

River of Lost Voices met with favorable reviews from critics and won the Iowa Short Fiction Award in 1998. In the *New York Times Book Review* (December 27, 1998) Maggie Garb wrote, "Mark Brazaitis's first collection of stories provides a harrowing account of life in a remote Guatemalan village where love is fleeting, poverty is commonplace, and violence erupts with casual regularity." Sybil S. Steinberg, in *Publisher's Weekly* (July 27, 1998), commented, "Adopting the conventions of folktales in sophisticated ways, Brazaitis controls his narrative with sparse dialogue and omniscient or calmly retrospective narrators. His admirable restraint anchors the stories and connects them by a tight chain of motifs, while his lucid prose directs attention away from itself and toward the characters who provide their color and drama."

In 2000 Brazaitis published his first novel, *Steal My Heart*. The story concerns the American expatriate Carlton James, and his maid, Rosario. Carlton is a small-time thief who steals from U.S. tourists and then offers them emergency loans that are paid back with interest, which goes to his "charity" organization. One night, after Rosario catches him red-handed, Carlton decides to let her in on his scam, and during their collaborations the two eventually fall in love. Because he is an American, Carlton had escaped the suspicions of the Guatemalan police; however, after Rosario joins him, their scheme attracts the notice of the authorities. With the help of a Peace Corps volunteer, the local policeman Ramiro Caal catches the duo and puts them in jail. Only afterwards, when a jailbreak ends tragically, do Ramiro and the volunteer feel remorse for apprehending the lovers. "The intense finale," Sybil S. Steinberg wrote for *Publishers Weekly* (September 18, 2000), "showcases Brazaitis's keen prose style and ends this Guatemalan love adventure on a luminous, dramatic note."

Brazaitis was awarded a National Endowment of the Arts creative writing fellowship in prose in 2000. On June 27, 1998 he married Juliet Penn, a marketer.

— P. G. H.

SUGGESTED READING: *Glamour* p98 June 1998; *New York Times Book Review* p15 Dec. 27, 1998; *Peace Corps Writers* (on-line) Sep. 1999; *Publishers Weekly* p53+ July 27, 1998, p86 Sep. 18, 2000; *U.S. Catholic* p30+ June 1999

SELECTED BOOKS: novels—*Steal My Heart*, 2000; short-story collections—*River of Lost Voices: Stories from Guatemala*, 1998

Courtesy of Random House

Briscoe, Connie

Dec. 31, 1952– Novelist

Like Terry McMillan, Connie Briscoe is an African-American writer whose best-selling novels—beginning with her first, *Sisters and Lovers* (1994)—deal with the romantic ups and downs of black women. Briscoe's work has also taken on such themes as political action and personal responsibility, in *Big Girls Don't Cry* (1996), and slavery, in *A Long Way from Home* (1999). In an article for *Essence* (July 1999)discussing her third novel, she wrote: "Our ancestors used their wits and intelligence to carve out a tolerable existence. . . . If they could do so much back then, I have no excuse on Earth for not getting ahead now. This is the message we ought to be handing down to our children." Briscoe returned to comic satire in *P.G. County* (2002), in which she explores the relationships between five African-American women in Maryland's affluent Prince George's County.

The older of two daughters, Connie Briscoe was born on December 31, 1952 in Washington, D.C. "I had a happy, normal childhood in every way," Briscoe wrote for the Author Biographies section of the Public Library of Charlotte & Mecklenburg County (PLCMC) Web site. "Although shy and quiet in my early years, I began to get a little rebellious in my teens—but nothing far out of the ordinary." She graduated from Hampton University, in Virginia, then enrolled in a graduate program in urban affairs at American University, in Washington. "The only thing unusual about my life," Briscoe wrote, is the hearing loss that runs in her father's family. By her late 20s, she had gone from a 20 percent hearing loss to an 80 percent loss. "First, you can't hear things on the phone. Then you can't hear it ring," Briscoe explained to Felicia R. Lee in an interview for the *New York Times* (September 2, 1999, on-line). "You make excuses for what's happening. Then you get to the point you can't ignore it anymore. I went through the period of the doctors, the emotional adjustment, but I'm lucky I have a supportive family."

After college and graduate studies, Briscoe did research for a time at a computer firm, then got an editorial job at the Joint Center for Political Studies in Washington, where she did not advance as quickly as she would have liked. "My career wasn't progressing the way I wanted it to because I couldn't use the telephone," she told *Essence* (July 1994) in an interview. She later joined the editorial staff at Gallaudet University, in Washington, the nation's only university for the deaf, eventually becoming managing editor of the Gallaudet publication *American Annals of the Deaf*. As she told an interviewer for the *Quarterly Black Review* (on-line), her career as an editor is tied to her fiction writing: "I can remember thinking about wanting to be a writer way back when I was a young girl, but back then during the 60s and 70s it was something I thought black people did not aspire to do. . . . So I pursued other things career-wise." But she finally entered the world of publishing, "because the need to work with the written word was so strong. In some ways I believe I was preparing myself slowly, making the transition. I can see how I was inching towards that novel. Working as an editor was part of that process, and it worked to make me a better writer." She told *Essence* that during "the period between losing my hearing and learning to cope with it," she started writing a mystery novel, which she never completed.

Briscoe married at the age of 28; the union ended after a few years. "Maybe I lowered my standards too far," she explained to David Streitfeld in an interview for the *Washington Post* (July 23, 1994). "Now I'd rather wait until I find the almost-perfect person." It was her ongoing search for the "almost-perfect person," and the difficulties faced by other African-American women engaged in that process, that inspired her first published novel, *Sisters and Lovers* (1994). The story of three sisters, Beverly, Evelyn, and Charmaine, and the men in their lives, it became a best-seller and enabled Briscoe to pursue a full-time career as a writer.

The character most closely identified with Briscoe herself is the unmarried Beverly, who endures many terrible dates in her search for a mate—an experience similar to the author's, according to Streitfeld. Beverly's sisters are married but have problems at home. Charmaine's husband is unfaithful, and Evelyn, a psychologist who has married a successful lawyer, fears the consequences—including the effect on her expensive lifestyle—if her husband quits his job and starts his own firm. Beverly's travails include clashes with her family over her choice to date a white man when she is unable to find a suitable black mate. Beverly is "almost 30, with not a thing to show for it except a halfway decent paycheck. No man, no kids, no house. Nothing that really mattered," Briscoe wrote.

Sisters and Lovers was for Stephanie B. Goldberg, the reviewer for the *Chicago Tribune* (July 31, 1984), "the perfect commentary on postmodern romance." Goldberg noted that in today's world, "the object isn't to be rescued by a handsome prince but merely to meet one's equal." A number of other reviewers echoed Goldberg's favorable assessment. Angela Washington-Blair, writing for the *Library Journal* (April 1, 1994), termed the novel "at once humorous, poignant, realistic, and romantic," with "witty but realistic dialog" that refreshingly portrays "black women in a positive light." Comparing Briscoe with Terry McMillan, Roz Spafford, who reviewed the novel for the *Washington Post Book World* (May 1, 1994), found that in contrast to McMillan, "Briscoe trusts plot and dialogue to carry her meaning." Although she wished for "more complexity in her characters' evolution as well as in the structure of the book itself," she deemed "Briscoe's message . . . a warm one and the novel . . . entirely readable."

A dissenting voice came from Karen Ray, who, writing for the *New York Times Book Review* (September 18, 1994), found the male characters "thinly portrayed" and called the novel "commercial fiction at its most commercial—a little preachy, a lot contrived." Reacting to such charges, Briscoe told Streitfeld, who called her "unabashedly a commercial writer," that reviewers were misguided when they compared her with "more literary women," such as Alice Walker or Toni Morrison. "I shouldn't be compared to them any more than you would compare, say, Judith Krantz to Edith Wharton," she declared.

That comment notwithstanding, Briscoe's second novel, *Big Girls Don't Cry* (1996), deals with themes more weighty than those addressed in most commercial fare—namely, political issues facing the African-American community. The main character, Naomi Jefferson, growing up in Washington in the 1960s, has to confront racism. Her father advocates patience, but her older brother is a radical. When her brother dies in an accident on the way to a civil rights demonstration, she picks up the torch of action, organizing a demonstration in response to her college statistics teacher's statement that African-American women are incapable of excelling at mathematics. "The prejudice against women and minorities in technological fields is one of Briscoe's main themes," Emily Listfield observed in the *Washington Post Book World* (April 28, 1996). "Briscoe, a talented writer, is not afraid to take on serious concerns: racism, the glass ceiling, the importance of personal responsibility." Naomi's first moves toward taking on responsibility are unsuccessful; the demonstration achieves nothing. Her disappointment is compounded when she discovers that her boyfriend is cheating on her, and she descends into drugs and promiscuity before recovering her bearings and going on to a successful career in a high-tech company. "The obstacles that Naomi faces are genuine, but they are drawn here with a sketchiness that undermines their impact," Listfield wrote. "Riddled with stock characters and pat answers, *Big Girls Don't Cry* never truly engages us the way Briscoe's wonderful first novel, *Sisters and Lovers*, did. Instead, it reads more like an inspirational allegory than a compelling tale."

After the publication of *Big Girls Don't Cry*, Briscoe entered a period of intensive historical research into her own family origins that was to culminate in her third novel, *A Long Way from Home* (1999), a story of founding father James Madison's slaves. Susan, who was Briscoe's great-great-grandmother, and Ellen are sisters born on the plantation owned by Madison; the identity of their father is unclear. In the novel Susan marries a former slave, Oliver, who has been able to buy his freedom. "While researching my slave ancestors . . . ," Briscoe wrote in a piece for *Essence* (July 1999), "I came across the usual grim tales of whippings, sales, and miscegenation. But I also uncovered stories of love and hope. One of the most heartwarming was the story my Grandma Corine told me about how my great-great-grandparents met in a park in Richmond, Virginia. Oliver would walk through the park on his way to the store, and Susan would take her master's children there to play. Oliver could write and had bought his freedom, and Susan was a slave. I don't know if Susan was literate, but she was clever enough to snag a smart, industrious brother like Oliver. I love that story. It shows, despite the bleakness of slavery, moments of tenderness and triumph."

In the novel, Oliver's plea for Susan's freedom is preempted by the fall of Richmond in the Civil War. As Susan flees, the master to whom she has been sold tries to give her a bag of coins to help her on her way. "But just like back then, he wasn't prepared to give her what he'd denied her all these years, what she wanted most. An identity. A real family. So she wanted nothing else from him," Briscoe explained, as quoted by Felicia R. Lee. Although her family lore places Briscoe in the Madison family, no real proof exists, as she told Lee. "It's a side of slavery and that era we don't talk about, but it's an open secret. There are a lot of us walking around who don't know who our great-grandfather was or hear stories about white ancestors."

Kim McLarin, who reviewed *A Long Way from Home* for *Emerge* (August 1997), praised the novel as being "lively, enjoyable, and original. . . . Briscoe effectively illuminates the dehumanizing and demeaning effects of slavery, even under 'good' masters." She concluded, however, that a defect in the novel was Briscoe's failure to make the history come alive. "Briscoe seems constrained by the history behind the narrative. There's not enough room for fictionalization to invigorate the book's more predictable elements. . . . By the book's end, the characters' stories don't haunt you the way the corrupt institution that inspired them continues to haunt our national imagination."

In 2002 Briscoe returned to comic satire with *P.G. County*, a novel exploring the lives of five African-American women in Prince George's County, Maryland. Briscoe weaves a complex plot connecting the protagonists, in the process revealing an intriguing story of love, secrets, and personal discovery. While most critics found the book more commercial than Briscoe's earlier works—what Mary Frances Wilkens for *Booklist* called, as quoted on *Amazon.com*, "fluffy stuff, to be sure, with more than a few hints of soap opera"—they nonetheless praised the author's knack for delivering authentic characters and an engrossing story.

According to Felicia R. Lee, Briscoe, who is "thin and sandy-haired," communicates by reading lips and employing a sign-language interpreter; she can speak, "although her diction is somewhat muffled." Lee wrote that Briscoe "spends no time feeling sorry for herself or other black people and says that awareness of the wrenching abuses that black people historically endured can put steel in the spine of African-Americans today." Briscoe told Lee that by "not looking into our history and our past in a realistic way, we are depriving our young people. We are too accepting of the history of ourselves that has been handed down and written about." As she wrote in *Essence*, "One of the things that kept me going is best expressed by the Ghanaian word *sankofa*, which means 'in order to move forward we must understand the past.'"

—S.Y.

SUGGESTED READING: *Chicago Tribune* XIV p5 July 31, 1994; *Emerge* p80 Aug. 1997; *Essence* p32 July 1994, p95+ July 1999, with photo; *Library Journal* p130 Apr. 1, 1994; *New York Times* (on-line) Sep. 2, 1999; *New York Times Book Review* p20 Sep. 18, 1994; *Washington Post* C p1 July 23, 1994; *Washington Post Book World* p11 May 1, 1994

SELECTED BOOKS: *Sisters and Lovers*, 1994; *Big Girls Don't Cry*, 1996; *A Long Way from Home*, 1999; *P.G. County*, 2002

Brock, Darryl

May 2, 1940– Novelist

In 1984 the novelist Darryl Brock proved himself to be a risk-taker, abandoning a successful career as a high school teacher to pursue writing. Brock tapped his passions for baseball and history to write three baseball novels set in the past, *If I Never Get Back* (1990), *Havana Heat* (1999), and *Two in the Field* (2002). Reviewers have praised Brock's descriptive writing for successfully bringing bygone worlds back to life within the pages of his books. In *Publishers Weekly* (May 6, 2000), Sybil S. Steinberg called Brock "one of the finest baseball fiction writers around, lucidly rendering the passions, disappointments, and excitement of the sport while capturing the defining details of the era he depicts."

Very little about Darryl Brock's background is publicly known, and he refused several requests for an interview from *World Authors*. He was born on May 2, 1940. In a message posted on *Amazon.com* (April 27, 2000), Brock wrote that he has been a resident of the San Francisco Bay Area, in California, for the last 30 years, and has previously lived in Oregon and Spain. Before becoming a writer, Brock taught history and English at a high school in Berkeley, California. In an interview with Patricia Holt, a writer for the *San Francisco Chronicle* (March 2, 1990), Brock recalled: "I had tried writing a young adult book but got jerked around for three years by publishers, so I finally stuffed it in my closet. But I wanted to try it again, so I retired from teaching after 20 years to live on my savings, married my sweetie a day after our seventh anniversary as a couple, bought a word processor and told everybody I was going to write. It's the way some people quit smoking: Burn your bridges and you have to do it."

Brock spent several years gathering research for his novel, which takes place in 1869, the year the Cincinnati Red Stockings came to San Francisco to play baseball, traveling across the country on the first transcontinental railroad. As Brock said to Holt, "I started in 1985 with my dog and drove 10,000 miles around the country, following the team's tour routes mostly, checking local libraries and history rooms, reading microfilm and studying regional language. It was great fun to photocopy 1869 maps and ask for directions at a local gas station. You get a wonderful reaction. People appreciated the fact that there was almost nothing physically left in most cities from that period."

Brock made use of his research for a nonfiction piece for *Sports Illustrated* (June 23, 1986) that described the Red Stockings' tour. In it, he wrote that the Red Stockings were baseball's first professional team. They were so skilled at the sport that they won 44 straight games in 1869. Baseball proved to be popular, and several cities in the United States soon had professional teams. In 1871, Brock wrote, "came the formation of the first association of pro clubs, and five years after that the National League was established."

Brock's first novel, *If I Never Get Back* (1990), tells the story of Sam Fowler, a present-day journalist plagued by a series of misfortunes. His wife leaves him, and his father dies. Fowler is also an alcoholic. After he collapses in an Ohio train station, Fowler wakes up in the year 1869 and becomes a member of the Cincinnati Red Stockings as they make their way west. In his review for the *Washington Post Book World* (February 6, 1990), Curtis B. Gans wrote that Brock's novel "creates in Fowler a hero who in one game dramatically uses trickery to save a victory from the jaws of defeat, who uses modern pugilistic techniques to defeat the opposing team's bully and who uses modern marketing techniques to create the first hot dog, hamburger, and beer concessions." Gans praised the novel's "exciting and fast-paced narrative and its rich detail," and was also impressed by Brock's vivid descriptions of such cities as New York, Cincinnati, and San Francisco and the honest way he portrayed the poor state of race relations in the post-Civil War United States. However he criticized the novel's use of "literary devices" that he felt typified time-travel stories, such as the presence of Mark Twain, who serves as a guide for Fowler, and the legendary outlaws Frank and Jesse James, who save Fowler's life. "Too much can at times be as unsatisfying and annoying as not enough," Gans declared. In a review for the *Los Angeles Times* (March 15, 1990), Keith Tuber lauded Brock for offering "an engaging view of baseball in its infancy and the colorful characters who took the game's first steps." Tuber noted that Brock "makes the cities come alive in a way that displays his considerable research without making it sound like a course lecture," and that his inclusion of actual members of the Red Stockings added "authenticity" to the novel. Although he criticized Brock for failing to explain "exactly how the time travel transpires," Tuber concluded that *If I Never Get Back* was "the wildest and most satisfying yarn since W. P. Kinsella's *Shoeless Joe*, which was made into a motion picture and renamed *Field of Dreams*."

After his success with *If I Never Get Back*, Brock had difficulty publishing his second novel. As he explained to Anneli Rufus for *East Bay Express* (May 2000, on-line), "My editor was fired. His replacement didn't like my second book and pulled the plug on it." The novel, "a Lincoln-era thriller" according to Brock's description, was never published. Throughout the 1990s, Brock wrote several articles on baseball for the *San Francisco Chronicle*.

In 1999 TotalSports published Brock's next novel, entitled *Havana Heat*. *Havana Heat* is a fictionalized account of Luther "Dummy" Taylor, a deaf-mute pitcher who played with the New York Giants from 1900 to 1908. The novel takes place in 1911. With his career in decline, Taylor is pitching in the minor leagues. He wants to make a comeback, so he approaches his former manager, John McGraw, for a tryout. McGraw agrees and Taylor joins the Giants in Cuba for a series of exhibition games. "I always knew [Taylor] would make a great hero," Brock said to Rufus. "In no way was he a victim. He was once thrown out of a game for cussing out the umpire in sign language." Rufus noted that Brock traveled to Cuba to do research for the novel.

In a review for the *Sporting News* (March 27, 2000), Steve Gietschier enthusiastically praised *Havana Heat*, commenting, "Brock has written a warm and compelling story, grounded in thorough research, that is so good it hurts to come to its end." In the *Milwaukee Journal Sentinel* (May 21, 2000, on-line), Kevin Baxter dismissed the novel as "a slow-paced story about an arm-weary baseball junkie" that "quickly dissolves into strange subplots that weave in santeria, Cuban race relations, U.S. imperialism, and Taylor's own insecurities." Baxter also criticized Brock's use of such real-life players as Christy Mathewson and Jose Mendez, arguing that this device makes it "difficult for the casual fan to know where history ends and the fable begins."

Brock released a sequel to *If I Never Get Back*, titled *Two in the Field*, in September 2002. The novel finds Sam Fowler returning to 1869 to reunite with his love interest from the first book. "With [an] uneven plot," wrote Jeff Zaleski for *Publisher's Weekly* (September 2, 2002), "Brock's competent but somewhat diluted sequel can't match its inspired forerunner."

Darryl Brock is married to Lura Dolas, an actress and teacher, and they reside in Berkeley.

—D. C.

SUGGESTED READING: *East Bay Express* (on-line) May 2000; *Los Angeles Times* E p13 Mar. 15, 1990; *Milwaukee Journal Sentinel* (on-line) May 21, 2000; *Publishers Weekly* p84 Mar. 6 2000; *San Francisco Chronicle* E p12 Mar. 2, 1990; *Sports Illustrated* p6+ June 23, 1986; *Sporting News* p69 Mar. 27, 2000; *Washington Post Book World* C p2 Feb. 6, 1990

SELECTED BOOKS: *If I Never Get Back*, 1990; *Havana Heat*, 1999; *Two in the Field*, 2002

Brodeur, Paul

May 16, 1931– Novelist; short-story writer; journalist

Paul Brodeur became famous as a staff writer for the *New Yorker* when he wrote a series of articles on "The Magic Mineral," asbestos, which works some very bad wizardry in human bodies. Brodeur had produced three well-received novels and a short-story collection when he began reporting on the scientific sleight of hand performed by officials covering up the workplace and residential health hazards associated with asbestos, microwaves, and power lines. Titles like *The Zapping of America: Microwaves, Their Deadly Risk and the Cover-Up* (1977), *The Asbestos Hazard* (1980), and *Currents of Death: Power Lines, Computer Terminals, and the Attempt to Cover Up Their Threat to Your Health* (1990) speak for themselves and aroused enormous controversy, polarizing Brodeur's opponents and supporters.

Paul Adrian Brodeur Jr. was born to Sarah M. (Smith) and Paul Brodeur, who was both an orthodontist and a sculptor, in Boston, Massachusetts, on May 16, 1931. He grew up in Boston and attended high school at Phillips Academy in Andover, Massachusetts, followed by Harvard University in Cambridge, Massachusetts, receiving his B.A. in 1953. While majoring in English, Brodeur studied writing with Kenneth Kempton and Albert Gerard and wrote his senior thesis on Ring Lardner. During his senior year at Harvard, Brodeur discovered, through a chance conversation, that he had an older brother with almost the same name. His father had tried to conceal his previous marriage and the existence of his oldest son from Paul, and Paul's brother and sister, until just before his death. After his discovery Paul hid his knowledge of his father's secret.

From 1953 to 1956 Brodeur served in the Army Counterintelligence Corps, where he was trained to hunt for communist spies during the McCarthy era. In Germany he was briefly stationed at the site of underground chambers for nuclear warheads. "Beneath a vault of trees, the subterranean igloos wrinkled the forest floor into elongated mounds of turf and needles, sprouting ventilators that looked like giant fungi," Brodeur wrote in his 1997 autobiography *Secrets: A Writer in the Cold War*. "The whole place seemed eerie and unreal, because it was the citadel of a future too close at hand to be comfortably imagined." He wondered whether future historians would be able to explain the remains, "Or would the excavators be forced, as with Stonehenge, to speculate on unknown treasures, obscure gods?"

Brodeur also described how, while briefly living in near isolation in the Palatinate, a district in Southwest Germany, he would meet at a restaurant the local Burgermeister, the school principal, and the area's doctor. The men kept volunteering their assurance that there had been no Jews in their area and that Nazi repression had been very light. After he visited the German archives in Heidelberg, however, he told them that he had "discovered that on *Krystallnacht*—November 9, 1938—Jewish families throughout Germany including some in nearby towns had been taken forcibly from their homes." He insisted that the local people must have known that the Jews would not be returning because those homes were "thoroughly looted." The men then rose from the table, said "*Guten abend* (good evening)" to each other and to the proprietor, and, with Brodeur, left the restaurant "for the very last time."

While living in France, Brodeur embarked on his professional writing career by writing about his experiences in Germany. When he returned to the United States, his short story "The Sick Fox"—"a commentary on the paranoia that informs intelligence work, as well as on the inclination of Germans to mistrust and harass strangers," Brodeur wrote in *Secrets*—was accepted by the *New Yorker*, where he joined the staff as a writer for the "Talk of the Town" section and wrote pieces on Charles de Gaulle's death and Robert F. Kennedy's funeral. Brodeur remained at the *New Yorker* until the 1990s. He began to specialize in scientific pieces because he had done a profile of Werner Heisenberg, the physicist, which William Shawn, the editor of the *New Yorker*, felt had succeeded in making Heisenberg's work accessible to the magazine's readers.

Brodeur expanded "The Sick Fox" into a novel, which was published in 1963. Although the plot does not echo his own experiences, the chief character, Harry Brace, is, as Brodeur was, an American intelligence agent assigned to guard a nuclear storage facility in a remote German town. Brace sees a fox with rabies, but he does not kill it. The townspeople, fearing the disease, become violently nationalistic, and Brace's failure to kill the fox earns him their enmity. They persecute a shepherd who has become Brace's friend, and he loses the man's companionship. Joseph P. Bauke asked in the *Saturday Review* (May 18, 1963) whether "The Sick Fox" could be called a "modern myth," an "Aesopian fable with a new twist," or a "philosophical whodunit." He praised Brodeur's "lucid, unaffected, and utterly civilized" language. Other reviewers also noted Brodeur's talent, with Whitney Balliett, the *New Yorker* (June 15, 1963) critic, calling it a "solemn, brooding, highly compressed book" with "the substance, and even the manner, of a large Jamesian novel." He did feel, however, that Brodeur concentrated too much on his main character, whom Balliett called "impulsive, illogical, seedy-minded," and wished Brodeur had not "rushed himself" so much.

Brodeur's second novel, *The Stunt Man*, was published in 1970. He described the experience of composing that novel in *Secrets*, explaining that he had been working on a story based on an episode of violence that had happened to him when he was a 19-year-old hitchhiker. While he was writing the novel, however, he and his first wife, Malabar

Schleiter, lost an infant boy to a choking accident. His obsessive anger at the doctor who had refused to help when they called him and grief at the loss of his child gave him writer's block. Then, he wrote in *Secrets*, in 1967 he was inspired to make the hitchhiker "a newly inducted army recruit, who is sent for help when a bus taking him from an induction center to a training camp unexpectedly breaks down. Seizing the opportunity, he deserts. While in flight, he crosses a desolate bridge, walks unwittingly into the middle of a movie stunt, and, believing that he is acting in self-defense, kills a stunt man who is making a film. Afterward, the fugitive is tricked by the mad, omniscient director of the film into replacing the dead stunt man in a movie about a man who is fleeing from the army." The AWOL soldier becomes enmeshed in the film, which mirrors his own life, and is required to perform more and more dangerous stunts. If he continues to follow the script, his last stunt will end in his death.

Brodeur admitted that he based the mad director, Gottschalk, partly on what he knew about Orson Welles and partly on Federico Fellini, whom he had once, at the urging of William Shawn, taken for a walk in a sleazy neighborhood, where Fellini's magnetism attracted the young prostitutes he hoped to film. Reviewers, such as Lawrence J. Davis of *Book World* (March 29, 1970), found a cinematic quality in *The Stunt Man*. "Using a format borrowed from the traditional chase move," Davis observed, "Brodeur has fashioned an existential novel . . . both intellectually powerful and artistically strong. . . . Brodeur displays a remarkable virtuosity in manipulating levels of meaning. It is rare to see symbols used so intelligently or action described so well." A reviewer in the *Library Journal* (March 15, 1970) thought that the "tug of war between film and reality develops into a surrealistic drama of spectator versus participant and the differentiation of which is which." This "stunning and important novel" was deemed a work "to captivate film buffs." Robert Scholes of the *Saturday Review* (April 18, 1970) found echoes of Pirandello in *The Stunt Man*, noting Brodeur's concern with "appearance and reality, the interpenetration of art and life," and his skillful use of myth and archetype. Laurence Lafore, writing in the *New York Times Book Review* (June 14, 1970) termed *The Stunt Man* "an allegory of immense intricacy, a study of art, illusion, and identity, of the relation between reality and man's confused awareness of it." "What was important," Brodeur wrote of his novel in *Secrets*, "was that it enabled me to put some degree of closure to the death of my child." He had done so "by stating in dramatic terms the basic conviction that I held about life at that time—that we were all stunt men in one of God's bad movies."

The Stunt Man became a motion picture directed by Richard Rush in 1980, with Peter O'Toole playing the character of the director. The film was highly praised by such masters as the French director François Truffaut. Missy Daniel, in an interview with Brodeur in *Publishers Weekly* (August 30, 1993), termed it "a cult film about Vietnam," but Brodeur told her, "It's an okay film that turned a serious allegory about running away from the war into a black comedy. . . . [T]he book was better."

Brodeur's third work of fiction was the 1972 short-story collection *Downstream*. A reviewer in the *Library Journal* (April 1, 1972) cited the "nostalgic charm" of the "evocations of childhood" in "A War Story" and "The Turtle," along with the "chromium cynicism" in "The Spoiler," a story of a man who drives people whom he considers "undesirable" away from his ski lodge. A critic for *Book World* (April 23, 1972) expressed admiration for "an author who knows how to resolve pain without bitterness yet still has a jeweler's eye for life's tricky facets and buried fissures" while projecting "a gentle tender wisdom." Although a critic in the *Saturday Review* (April 1, 1972) had some cavils about the stories' sentimentality, "Brodeur's clear, crisp prose" and "sheer narrative skill" won praise.

A piece about asbestos that Brodeur had published in the *New Yorker* in 1968 entitled "The Magic Mineral" was to set the direction for his next several books. Brodeur had interviewed Dr. Irving Selikoff, who was investigating the effects of asbestos exposure on people who had inhaled its particles. Selikoff's observations prompted the scientific community to investigate further, and Brodeur's article alerted the American public to the hazards of asbestos. His book *Expendable Americans* (1974) was based on that work and a five-part series of articles, "Annals of Industry: Casualties of the Workplace." Brodeur described *Expendable Americans* as exposing "working conditions in asbestos factories and other industrial facilities across the nation." He wrote that he also "uncovered the existence of a medical-industrial complex consisting of company physicians, industry consultants, and key occupational health officials . . . who were trying to prevent workers from finding out about the disease hazards to which they were being exposed and to discourage government health agencies such as NIOSH [National Institute for Occupational Safety and Health] from doing anything to remedy them."

Although Brodeur had been praised for his writing style in his fiction, some found that in *Expendable Americans* he was "agonizingly plodding, repetitive, and needlessly complex," quoting "sources directly and at great length, in precise but stilted language that sounds too edited to be accurately conversational," as Ed Magnuson put it in *Time* (October 7, 1974). Nevertheless Magnuson termed Brodeur an old-fashioned crusader who "should stimulate public concern over a largely unrecognized menace to hundreds of thousands of men and women." Peggy Champlin agreed in *Library Journal* (October 1, 1974) that in light of the fact that "an estimated 100,000 deaths result yearly from occupationally caused disease," Brodeur might "have used a more dramatic, old-fashioned, muckraking style," instead of giving "detailed information on investigations, inspections, hearings, and conferences."

Without departing entirely from his continued investigations of the hazards of asbestos, in his 1977 book Brodeur dealt with another hitherto unsuspected danger—*The Zapping of America: Microwaves, Their Deadly Risk and the Cover-Up*. In this exposé, Brodeur detailed the suppression of evidence that microwaves, then a relatively new technology, had negative effects on the human body. He disparaged the ability of scientists to be objective when their funds came from the producers of microwave appliances and others with vested interests in the outcome of experiments and studies. While nonscientific reviewers lauded Brodeur for his ability to amass evidence to prove his arguments, the scientific community was not sure he was qualified to present that evidence objectively.

Elting Morison, writing in the *New York Times Book Review* (November 13, 1977), saw *The Zapping of America* as having the quality of a morality play and described the people as "personifications of varied vices, virtues, motives, and appetites." He saw Brodeur's motive as "the fervor to establish, amid the swirl of self-seeking, venery, greed, sloth, deception, and sheer ignorance, a more edifying and redeeming proposition for the conduct of human affairs." On the other hand, Robert Claiborne, writing for the *Saturday Review* (January 7, 1978), took the position that Brodeur's arguments were vitiated because "the author's presentation of evidence falls well below his evaluation of it," and he claimed the reader could drown in a morass of detail and "trivia." The reviewer for *Science* (May 12, 1978) noted that Brodeur had cited "a mountain of reports . . . detailing telling aspects of government decision-making." But, W. A. Herman found "disconcerting . . . Brodeur's willingness to impute motives. He frequently proffers dramatic speculation, undocumented allegation, and even innuendo." Herman felt that Brodeur might have contributed to the "folklore" that had grown up around the "biological effects of microwaves and shortwaves."

Now deeply into his career as an investigative reporter, in 1985 Brodeur produced *Restitution: The Land Claims of the Mashpee, Passamaquoddy, and Penobscot Indians of New England*, based on his articles in the *New Yorker* about two lawsuits brought by Native Americans attempting to claim their rights to tribal lands. The tribes' claims were based on the Indian Nonintercourse Acts of 1789 and 1790. Those acts gave jurisdiction to the Federal Government over tribal lands, but the states of Massachusetts and Maine had seized those lands. Thomas Tureen, a lawyer, and his colleagues filed suit on behalf of the Native Americans in 1972, but the tribes settled before going to trial. "Can you imagine how a jury made up of 12 white landowners would judge the merits of our claim?" a tribal administrator asked, as quoted by Francis Jennings in the *New York Times Book Review* (September 22, 1985, on-line). The administrator elaborated on the reasons they feared a trial. "It was as if we had touched a raw nerve that extended back into the innermost recesses of the true personality of the white people around here and unleashed all their deep hatred for Indians, together with their guilt for what they had done to the Indians over all the years." Tureen, who wrote an afterward to *Restitution*, noted, as quoted by Jennings, "The United States will permit Indians a measure of recompense through the law—indeed it has done so to an extent far greater than any other nation in a comparable situation—but it ultimately makes the rules and arbitrates the game."

A reviewer for *Choice* (December 1985) called *Restitution* a "good, sympathetic, and very well written introduction to the consistently strong commitment of . . . tribes to their sociocultural identity and their pursuit of social justice." In the *New England Quarterly* (March 1986) Francis Paul Prucha deemed the book "valuable material for historians still to come," while Jennings found that Brodeur's brisk movement from one event to another, "even as he gracefully points up the significance of each step," made *Restitution* "the right book for anyone who would like to understand why the claims were made in the first place."

After *Restitution* Brodeur continued to expose what he had learned about asbestos while writing his 1980 work *The Asbestos Hazard*. In 1985 he produced *Outrageous Misconduct: The Asbestos Industry on Trial*, the story of litigation against asbestos companies, chiefly Manville, formerly Johns-Manville, which declared bankruptcy when faced with paying enormous damages to victims of asbestos-related diseases. Brodeur maintained that the company filed for bankruptcy to avoid paying those damages. Reviewers, even those like Eric Eckholm for the *New York Times Book Review* (November 24, 1985), who felt that Brodeur had produced "a legal brief, documenting an industry's dark history of callousness," never letting "us forget the pain of asbestos' real victims," found the book bombastic and "marred by the repetition of facts that should have been eliminated." Murray Kempton, writing in the *New York Review of Books* (January 30, 1986), also found *Outrageous Misconduct* ponderous reading. "His narrative flow is choked with weeds and snags," Kempton wrote. Others, such as Peter Huber of the *New Republic* (February 3, 1986), maintained that there was less to "the grand cover-up theory" than "meets Brodeur's eye." Huber admitted, however, that "for decades the asbestos companies and insulation contractors made no attempt to publicize the asbestosis [a disease of the lungs caused by the inhalation of asbestos particles] hazard. But this hazard was hardly a secret; it had been widely recognized since the 1930s. The cancer threat was not uncovered until much later, and it too was quickly publicized by Selikoff."

Brodeur did not cease to castigate those who would attempt to keep secret the potential harm to the public caused by substances or processes of which the people were unaware. He turned to electromagnetic fields at the end of the 1980s, first producing *Currents of Death: Power Lines, Computer Terminals, and the Attempt to Cover Up Their Threat to Your Health* in 1989. In that volume, Brodeur cited examples of workers, particularly telephone cable splicers, who had abnormally high rates of cancer, as well as examples of scientists paid by electric utility companies who declared that there was no danger from exposure to large amounts of electromagnetic fields of extremely low frequency (ELF), such as those generated by power lines, computer terminals, and electric blankets. Responses to *Currents of Death* were mixed. Stuart L. Shalat, in the *Bulletin of the Atomic Scientists* (April 1990), praised Brodeur's "wonderful prose style," terming his "ability to weave a good yarn . . . unquestionable," while denigrating the importance of a number of facts presented. Shalat then claimed that Brodeur "falls into the trap of accepting all studies at face value, failing to distinguish credible results from highly speculative ones." Shalat did admit, nonetheless, that the "sheer quantity of information in this book raises nagging questions."

The *Library Journal* (October 1, 1989) reviewer, Judith Eannarino, on the other hand, complained that "Brodeur is not master of the narrative flow," but she thought he had provided enough evidence to make readers suspect that the research into ELF from power lines, electric blankets, electrically heated waterbeds, and computers "has been ignored or covered up by the scientific community." M. Granger Morgan, writing for *Scientific American* (April 1990), took a middle ground. Calling *Currents of Death* "a dramatic and riveting story," he nevertheless thought Brodeur "deliberately oversimplifies and misrepresents the complexity of the scientific process and the evidence it has produced," citing the evidence "in a highly selective fashion" that "mixes and confuses adversarial legal and regulatory proceedings with honest scientific debate." He thought the weakness of Brodeur's arguments lay not in errors of fact but in "problems of interpretation."

Brodeur continued to hammer away at the power companies in his 1993 book *The Great Power-Line Cover-Up: How the Utilities and the Government Are Trying to Hide the Cancer Hazard Posed by Electromagnetic Fields*. In this work he singled out "clusters" of cancer found especially on one street in Guilford, Connecticut, and in an elementary school in Fresno, California, where exposure to electromagnetic fields (EMF) was especially high due to the presence of nearby power grids and lines. Brodeur maintained that government health agencies and scientists conspired with large corporations and power companies to cover up two things: one, that exposure to EMF causes cancer, especially in children; and two, that there were any cancer clusters at all.

An early reviewer of *The Great Power-Line Cover-Up* in *Publishers Weekly* (July 12, 1993) observed that Brodeur "lashes electric utilities, public health officials, and the Environmental Protection Agency for downplaying or denying what he sees as a major health crisis." The reviewer concluded that this "urgent book should be on Al Gore's desk as he tackles environmental health problems, and on Hillary Rodham Clinton's bookshelf as she reorders national health priorities." Later reviewers, however, took a more cautious position with regard to Brodeur's accusations. A *People Weekly* (February 7, 1994) contributor called the volume "a dangerous book, combining readability with troubling allegations." In the *Los Angeles Times* (September 28, 1993) Bettyann Kevles noted, "Brodeur is understandably outraged at the authorities' cavalier behavior. However, his dismissals of scientific literature are even more cavalier as he builds a case against the power companies by fixating on a single part of a complicated technological situation—the magnetic fields that are part of every alternating electric current." And yet she admitted that America needs "to spend whatever is necessary to investigate with greater imagination and rigor the ramifications of living in an electrically powered world."

The idea of spending whatever it costs to protect people from power lines by insulation and relocation encountered great resistance, and there was considerable backlash against Brodeur's book. A television report on *Frontline* in 1995 effectively debunked, in the opinion of many, Brodeur's conclusions and insisted that the American public was being deluged by scare tactics. For example, the libertarian journal *Reason* (January 1995), whose motto is "Free Minds and Free Markets," published a piece by Michael Fumento castigating Brodeur's Stephen King-like approach to writing about cancer. He quoted from the *Journal of Clinical Epidemiology* concerning the array of diseases Brodeur linked to EMF exposure, saying, "Surely it would be difficult to find a scientific basis for linking EMF exposure to this menagerie of ailments." Fumento cited criticisms of *Currents of Death* lodged by scientists, such as David Savitz of the University of North Carolina, who claimed there "is little evident attempt to separate legitimate criticism of the scientific evidence suggesting health harm from irrational resistance based on the implications of that evidence." More backlash came from Seymour Hersh, another investigative journalist. He had written a promotional blurb for *The Great Power-Line Cover-Up*, saying it should be required reading for every parent in America. When in 1997 the National Academy of Science published its findings that there was no evidence linking low-level radiation to any health hazards, Hersh renounced his blurb and called Brodeur a "crank," according to James Ledbetter, writing in the *Village Voice* (February 17, 1998). Brodeur responded bitterly, writing to various well-known journalists and editors.

Brodeur had spent so much of his life with secrets—first learning that he had a brother and keeping that knowledge a secret, then guarding American nuclear secrets in Germany, then exposing corporate and government cover-ups and lies with regard to asbestos, microwaves, ozone depletion, and power-line radiation—that when he published his autobiography in 1997, he entitled it *Secrets: A Writer in the Cold War*. Brodeur is oddly silent about whether he ever actually encountered his long-lost brother, but, encouraged by William Shawn, the *New Yorker* editor devoted to crusading journalism, he spent his career at the magazine "exposing secrets and the harm that secrecy engenders." He often linked his investigations to an inspiring person. He trumpeted the dangers of asbestos when the man who discovered them, Dr. Irving Selikoff, got little attention. At the end of the book he evokes "the lengths to which our FBI guardians went to protect us from Jean Seberg" (an actress who committed suicide after her private life was investigated and distorted by the FBI) and declares that "before I close out my interest in the shallow deceptions practiced by warriors for whom the Cold War became a game, and in the foulness that floated in their wake, I recall again the gratuitous cruelty of what they did to her, and the cowardice that lay behind it, not to mention their contempt for women."

The reviewer for *Publishers Weekly* (February 10, 1997) commented that, although Brodeur "combined polemic and memoir" in *Secrets*, it was his polemics that were "superb," as the author succeeded in "patiently assembling incontrovertible facts, then recording the evasions and hostilities of the industries he indicts—most notably the asbestos business and more latterly the electric companies. . . . It is in fact his revisiting of those massive controversies, and the way he places them in the context of an embattled America whose capitalist excesses were seen for nearly 40 years as the only bulwark against the menace of world communism, that is the most valuable part of the book."

As at least one critic has observed, Brodeur structured *Secrets* so that one event seems to have nothing to do with the next, but when the underlying theme is considered, the book's coherence and method become quite clear. "At first," *Washington Post Book World* (July 6, 1997) reviewer David Corn wrote, "you wonder what one reminiscence has to do with another. But slowly, as the road passes beneath, you start to see the links—explicit and otherwise—between the tales, and you become entranced."

Secrets was lauded by the *Harvard International Review* (Fall 1997), in which a reviewer described the volume as Brodeur's recounting of "a life spent in pursuit of truth." The reviewer observed that "Brodeur warns in his opening chapter, 'Now that the Cold War is over . . . people are falling over themselves to give their take on what it all meant—a rush to assessment.'" The *Review*, however, praised Brodeur's own "rush," noting that he "owes the richness of his tale to its rawness, its very lack of distillation through the sieve of time. His reader emerges with a sense of having lived through, rather than studied, the period he recalls."

Brodeur describes his retirement from the *New Yorker* as a very happy one. He is no longer involved in "the public health wars I waged in its pages." His children grown, he and his second wife, a bookstore owner in California, spend their time between Cape Cod and southern California. Intending to devote his retirement to resuming the writing of fiction, Paul Brodeur has nevertheless characterized himself for all time as "a kind of literary entomologist, one who overturns rocks in the dank garden of the private enterprise system as it presently exists and describes what he sees crawling out from underneath."

—*C. M.*

SUGGESTED READING: *Book World* p7 Mar. 29, 1970, p15 Apr. 23, 1972; *Bulletin of the Atomic Scientists* p47 Apr. 1990; *Choice* p658 Dec. 1985; *Harvard International Review* p72 Fall 1997; *Library Journal* p1046 Mar. 15, 1970, p1344 Apr. 1, 1972, p2463 Oct. 1, 1974, p112 Oct. 1, 1989; *Los Angeles Times* p6 Sep. 28, 1993; *New Republic* p39+ Feb. 3, 1986; *New York Review of Books* p31+ Jan. 30, 1986; *New York Times Book Review* p24 June 14, 1970, p25 Sep. 22, 1985, p22 Nov. 24, 1985, p10 Nov. 13, 1977; *New Yorker* p118 June 15, 1963; *People Weekly* p31 Feb. 7, 1994; *Publishers Weekly* p61 July 12, 1993, p70+ Aug. 30, 1993, with photo, p73 Feb. 10, 1997; *Reason* p22+ Jan. 1995; *Saturday Review* p30+ May 18, 1963, p30 Apr. 18, 1970, p76 Apr. 1, 1972, p35 Jan. 7, 1978; *Scientific American* p118 Apr. 1990; *Time* p113 Oct. 7, 1974; *Village Voice* p26 Feb. 17, 1998; *Washington Post Book World* p9 July 6, 1997

SELECTED BOOKS: fiction—*The Sick Fox*, 1963; *The Stunt Man*, 1970; *Downstream*, 1972; nonfiction—*Asbestos and Enzymes*, 1972; *Expendable Americans*, 1974; *The Zapping of America: Microwaves, Their Deadly Risk and the Cover-Up*, 1977; *The Asbestos Hazard*, 1980; *Outrageous Misconduct: The Asbestos Industry on Trial*, 1985; *Restitution: The Land Claims of the Mashpee, Passamaquoddy, and Penobscot Indians of New England*, 1985; *Currents of Death: Power Lines, Computer Terminals, and the Attempt to Cover Up Their Threat to Your Health*, 1990; *The Great Power-Line Cover-Up: How the Utilities and the Government Are Trying to Hide the Cancer Hazards Posed by Electromagnetic Fields*, 1993; *Secrets: A Writer in the Cold War*, 1997

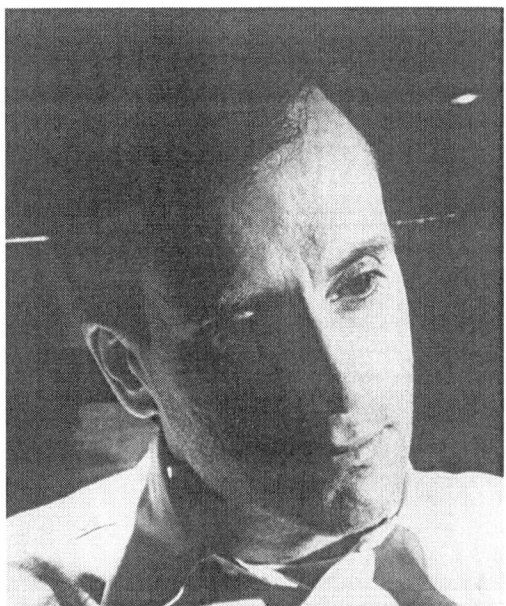
Arne Svenson/Courtesy of Four Walls Eight Windows

Brodsky, Michael

Aug. 2, 1948– Novelist; short-story writer; playwright

Novelist and playwright Michael Brodsky has gained notoriety among critics for his abandonment of old literary forms in favor of a boldly experimental use of language—a technique he believes pushes the boundaries of thought. "The true artist," Brodsky told *Contemporary Authors* (1994), "must continue to take his quantum leap, no matter how excruciating, out of the common plane, making himself or herself available to collision with the events that strain thought to the breaking point." Brodsky has often been compared to Samuel Becket for his learnedness and experimentalism, and his pioneering spirit has won him praise from many critics. However, his penchant for long, elliptical sentences injected with multiple tangents and obscure allusions makes his work challenging, and his determination to eschew plot and characterization has drawn harsh criticism and alienated many readers. Brodsky, nonetheless, remains steadfast in defending his sensibilities, maintaining that critics routinely misunderstand his work. "The reviews of my work so far have nothing incisive about them," he told *Contemporary Authors* (1981). "They merely underline the appalling stupidity of reviewers who, in order to earn their bread, pour out their dubious insights merely to cover a few pages."

Michael Brodsky was born on August 2, 1948 in New York, New York, the son of Martin Brodsky, a businessman, and Marian Brodsky, a clerk. In 1969 he received his B.A. from Columbia College, in New York City, and worked as a math and science teacher for a year before attending Case Western Reserve University, in Cleveland, Ohio, for two years. After leaving Case Western, from which he did not get a degree, Brodsky taught French and English in Cleveland from 1972 to 1975. Returning to New York City in 1976, he got a job editing an arthritis newsletter for the Institute for Research on Rheumatic Diseases and married Laurence Lacoste, with whom he would later have two children, Joseph Matthew and Matthew Daniel.

In 1977 Brodsky's first novel, *Detour*, was published. It is told in the first person by a narrator who somewhat resembles Brodsky: the son of middle-class Jewish parents, an avid movie-goer, and a chronic malcontent. Holding to no clear plot, the novel instead follows the peregrinations of the narrator's mind through long sentences that branch with ever-growing asides and amendments. "The more discriminating will conclude that this brilliant but grotesque first effort reveals a very real talent and a very real commitment to experimental writing," asserted a reviewer for the *Virginia Quarterly Review* (Spring 1979), as quoted in *Contemporary Literary Criticism* (1981). Robert Towers was equally impressed by the verbal virtuosity of Brodsky's sentences, writing in the *New York Review of Books* (June 15, 1978), as quoted in *Contemporary Literary Criticism* (1981), "The sentences . . . are stylistically impressive, demonstrating masterly control of diction and rhythm, an often startling metaphoric gift, and a range of effects extending from Swiftian bluntness to Proustian elaboration." However, Towers tempered his praise with serious reservations about Brodsky's multiple use of allusion. "The pleasures of recognition pall," he wrote, "and what had once been welcomed as an enlivening device becomes ultimately tiresome, a mere tic or fashionable reflex. Brodsky too often seems less a novelist than the brightest graduate student in the room." Daphne Merkin found further obstacles to reading *Detour*: namely, what she termed Brodsky's "precocity," writing in *Partisan Review* (no. 3, 1979), as quoted in *Contemporary Literary Criticism* (1981), "It is uneasily ahead of itself, racked by an off-putting discrepancy between intellectual savviness and emotional naivete. Too often Brodsky's precocity fails to rise to the occasion it sets for itself and totters into mere showing off. . . . One pays attention at such moments the way one would to a feverish, brainy child—wearily indulgent of its assumption that *every* permutation of thought, *every* vacillation of emotion is of supreme concern." Despite these reservations by some critics, Brodsky won a PEN Earnest Hemingway award for *Detour*.

Over the next couple of years, Brodsky pursued artistic endeavors outside of writing novels. His four-act play, *Terrible Sunlight*, played in New York City's South Street Theater in 1980. Two years later, Brodsky teamed up with illustrator Michael Hafftka to produce a short-story collection titled *Project and Other Short Pieces*. In 1985 he left his job as editor of the arthritis newsletter and became an editor for the scientific publisher

Springer-Verlag. That same year, he published his second novel, *Circuits*, and another short-story collection, *Wedding Feast*. Once again foregoing conventional plot development, *Circuits* is on one level the story of a man who flees authorities and then submits to imprisonment. The book's main emphasis, however, is on philosophical questions about the nature of knowledge and identity. In a dual review of *Circuits* and *Wedding Feast*, Lois Gordon wrote in the *New York Times* (September 14, 1986), "For someone willing to make the effort, these are unique meditations on being and reality."

Brodsky's next novel, *Xman* (1987), is a portrait of a man struggling against anonymity, and losing. In the story, the character known as Xman comes to New York looking to make a name for himself in the city. He observes the upper classes through the windows of their high-rise apartments and the lower classes in the street but never participates in city life himself. After struggling through a series of disheartening job interviews, he is hit by a truck and hospitalized. In the hospital he meets a terrorist, gets involved in the man's scheme, and, ultimately, kills himself and his fellow terrorists. Critics found the work puzzling and tended toward ambivalence in their appraisals. "The verbal pyrotechnics of this novel sometimes seem, as the narrator says in another context, 'too much the work of a seasoned performer running the gamut . . . purely as an exercise,'" Harry Marten noted in the *New York Times* (November 15, 1987). Marten added, however, that "at its best, *Xman* brings the reader to reflect anew on ways of knowing and truths of being in an uncertain world."

Brodsky next charted the adventures—or, in many cases, non-adventures—of different "X's" in the short-story collection *X in Paris* (1988). In the various stories, Brodsky's characters attempt to live meaningful lives but find themselves at odds with the world, forced to either accept mere survival without true fulfillment or be destroyed. One example of this conflict is provided by a character in "Picked Up On the Highroad (Out)," who is plagued by the paradox of recognizing his own depressed condition but not wishing to admit it for fear of making things worse. Reviewers were critical. Alan Gelb wrote in the *New York Times* (February 12, 1989), "Brodsky's sharp satire and invigorating rage degenerate into an overlong, one-note tune about the spiritual destruction of the artist thrown into a crass workaday world."

Brodsky followed his short-story collection with a novel, *Dyad* (1989), in which he once again ponders the nature and knowledge of being. The loose plot, which weaves its way through Manhattan and Long Island, tells the story of a man who meets the wealthy Mr. Jamms at a coffee shop in New York City. Dying of cancer, Mr. Jamms enlists him to try to convince his bohemian son, Jim, to visit him once more before he dies. The novel enjoyed greater success with critics than had many of Brodsky's earlier works. W. B. Warde, in *Choice* (July/August 1990), wrote that despite the sometimes meandering prose, "the novel demands thoughtful consideration." In *Library Journal* (November 15, 1989) Paul Hutchison wrote, "This extraordinary novel by the author of *Xman* continues Brodsky's evolution as one of the most important writers working today, and demands our attention."

In 1990 two of Brodsky's plays were staged in New York City. The first, *Dose Center*, appeared at the Theater for the New City, while *Night of the Chair* was performed at Theater Club Funambules through 1991. In that year, Brodsky's fourth novel, *Three Goat Songs*, was published, its title coming from the literal translation of "tragedy" from the Greek, meaning "goat song." In the work, the narrator entwines three tales that take place while he meditates along a rocky coast, watching a herd of goats. The narrator's wife and kids also come into the story, but the focus remains concentrated on the man's musings as Brodsky purposely deconstructs the traditional devices of plot and setting normally associated with the novelistic form. Once more, Brodsky's work aroused both scorn and admiration from critics. A reviewer for *Library Journal*, as quoted on Barnes&Noble.com, noted, "[Brodsky's] latest deconstructionist experiment fails miserably, consisting almost entirely of the pathetic projects, obsessions, rationalizations, and delusions of a character we are not given the slightest reason to care about." However, a reviewer for *Publishers Weekly*, as quoted on Barnes&Noble.com, found that "[The novel's] molten flow consumes all types of language—colloquialisms, legalese, and some eminently obscure vocabulary. The result is a vigorous, eccentric style that enables Brodsky . . . to bring a Swiftian gusto to the novel of ideas and write a challenging, at times dazzling book."

Having dispensed with just about every other novelistic convention in his previous works, Brodsky took the next step in 1994 by getting rid of the title as well. He simply dubbed his new novel ***. When asked by Sarah Lyall for he *New York Times* (November 3, 1993) how one should pronounce the title, Brodsky replied, "Ideally, you shouldn't say anything, but just visualize the asterisks. But I guess that saying 'Three Asterisks' is O.K." The plot centers around Stu Pott, a naive young man who works at a factory. When his boss, Dov Grey, is murdered, Stu decides to get to the bottom of the crime, only to discover that he is the main suspect. Brodsky intersperses plot-oriented chapters with chapters that offer commentary and other versions of the story. "From its title of three asterisks," a reviewer for *Kirkus Reviews* (April 1, 1994) wrote, "one can tell that the master of the oblique is out to make life miserable for those who dare to try to make sense of his purposefully impenetrable novel."

Brodsky next compiled a novella and seven stories into *Southernmost and Other Stories* (1996). Though the characters in the title story have names such as I, Z, and X, the poets Wallace Stevens and Hart Crane also figure into the mix, meeting each other in Key West, Florida. In "The Son, He Must Not Know," Brodsky examines father-and-son relationships. In "Bagatelle," "The $50,000 a Year Man," and "Partridges, and Nothing But," Brodsky critiques workaday life and echoes the odd stylings of Kafka. A reviewer for *Amazon.com* concluded, "Readers who enjoy wrestling with their books will find plenty to challenge them in *Southernmost*." However, Charles Salzberg, writing in the *New York Times* (March 9, 1997), preferred not to wrestle with the collection. "It would be nice," he wrote, "if the hapless reader didn't have to reach for the nearest bottle of Excedrin or take a nap between pages or could actually connect with a character or two in any of these frustratingly opaque stories. Language, which Michael Brodsky obviously has an affinity for, is supposed to communicate, not alienate; enlighten, not confuse."

Brodsky's most recent novel, *We Can Report Them* (1999), is about an advertiser named Bert who makes a TV commercial featuring a serial killer, played by an actor named Gift. Bert is regularly lambasted by Gift, as well as by his boss, B. Austin Samuels. He loses more clout when he is left off a Best Dressed list produced by the influential Floyd Flowers, and, to make matters worse, Bert must tend to his ailing parents. He responds to his tribulations with a string of monologues in which he ponders his plight and seeks to understand the philosophies of the serial killer whose life he is trying to depict. Jim Dwyer, decrying Brodsky's prose, wrote in *Library Journal* (November 1, 1999) that the book is, "Recommended only for the largest collections and for dilettantes wishing to impress people at cocktail parties by pretending they have slogged all the way through this depressing miasma." However, while Kristin Eliasberg, writing in the *New York Times* (October 10, 1999), found the novel frustrating, she also begrudgingly admitted, "Academic readers may get a charge out of Brodsky's unrelenting wordiness, and perseverance will yield the occasional insight."

In addition to writing fiction and drama, Brodsky contributes to periodicals such as the *Partisan Review*, the *Journal of Existential Psychology and Psychiatry*, and the *Santa Monica Review*. He also translated a Samuel Beckett play, *Eleutheria*, from the French in 1995, an effort which received favorable reviews. Despite the sometimes harsh criticism his work has received, Brodsky has stayed true to his vision of using rigorous experimentation with language in his bold attempts at literary revolution. As Brodsky told *Contemporary Authors* (1997), "I want it to be known for the record that I have devoted myself totally and absolutely to literature. . . . Not just literature, but film, philosophy, psychology, art history, philosophy of science and math—anything that can enrich my writing. I am always trying to break new ground NOT to be different for the sake of being different but because my vision of the world demands such a path, often without signposts."

— P.G.H.

SUGGESTED READING: *Library Journal* p105 Nov. 15, 1989, (on-line) Nov. 1, 1999; *New York Review of Books* p29+ June 15, 1978; *New York Times* (on-line) Sep. 14, 1986, Nov. 15, 1987, Feb. 12, 1989, Dec. 24, 1989, Jan. 26, 1992, Nov. 3, 1993, Mar. 9, 1997, Oct. 10, 1999; *Village Voice* p69+ June 20, 1995; *Contemporary Authors* vol. 41, vol. 102

SELECTED BOOKS: novels—*Detour*, 1977; *Circuits*, 1985; *Xman*, 1987; *Dyad*, 1989; *Three Goat Songs*, 1991; *[Three Asterisks]*, 1994; *We Can Report Them*, 1999; short-story collections—*Project and Other Short Pieces*, 1982; *Wedding Feast*, 1985; *X in Paris*, 1988; *Southernmost and Other Stories*, 1996

Jerry Bauer/Courtesy of Picador USA

Brownrigg, Sylvia

1964(?)– Novelist; short-story writer

Sylvia Brownrigg has been recognized as one of the most innovative young writers to emerge in recent years. She has produced three works—the short-story collection *Ten Women Who Shook the World* (1997), and the novels *The Metaphysical Touch* (1998) and *Pages For You* (2001)—characterized by their defiance of traditional storytelling techniques. Rather than emphasizing plot, Brownrigg, who has a background in philosophy, is known for relying upon social or philosophical themes to propel her stories.

Sylvia Brownrigg was born in about 1964 in Mountain View, California, and she was raised in both northern California and in England. She attended a high school in Oxford, England, which she described in an article for the *Guardian* (May 7, 2001) as a "cloistered place." Referring to coming out as a gay woman, she added, "It was not until I was at university in the U.S. that the door—not just to the closet, but to my imagination—swung wide open."

Brownrigg attended Yale University, in New Haven, Connecticut, where she studied philosophy. After graduating with a bachelor's degree in 1986, she considered pursuing an advanced degree in philosophy, but discovered that writing was her true passion. "At one time, I kept wondering if I would go back and do graduate work in philosophy, pursue the academic career," Brownrigg told Ron Hogan for the *Beatrice Interview* (1999, on-line). "It was an option I kept open for a long time, and in fact after I got my M.A. in writing, I did a year of graduate work in philosophy. But at that point I realized that my writing was too much of my life for me to be able to do it alongside philosophy."

Throughout much of the 1990s Brownrigg made her home in London, England, which she described to Hogan as "a good place for me to pull my resources together as a writer." She worked as a freelance writer, contributing numerous book reviews and articles to such publications as the *New York Times*, the *Guardian*, and the *Times Literary Supplement*.

In 1997 Brownrigg published her first book, *Ten Women Who Shook the World*, a collection of short stories, in England. (A U.S. edition was published in 2000.) Each of the book's ten stories presents a first-person narrative by a different quirky or unconventional woman. John Mark Eberhart observed for the *Chicago Tribune* (August 25, 2000), "Brownrigg's stories present a surreal but poignant view of the nature of femaleness and the roles women play—or are not allowed to play—in society." In the opening story, "Amazon," a mythical builder recalls how she and her female assistant constructed such impressive historical creations as the Egyptian pyramids, the Great Wall of China, and the Taj Mahal. When the assistant breaks out on her own, she focuses on tearing down existing factories and offices in order to reconstruct the rainforests. In other stories, such as "Hussy from the West" and "Lady in the Desert," Brownrigg explores familiar female themes from a fresh perspective, looking at, for example, patriarchal notions of promiscuity or women's obsession with dieting. The titles of other stories—"Broad from Abroad," "The Bird Chick," and "Mistress of Many Moons"—suggest the playfulness with which Brownrigg approaches her various subjects.

Some critics found Brownrigg's experimental style to be distracting. A reviewer for *Publishers Weekly* (May 22, 2000) wrote, "While the collection benefits from Brownrigg's intriguing iconoclasm, the author's tendency to over intellectualize deprives her work of real substance; without sympathetic characters or emotionally compelling plots, these stories fail to live up to their title's earthshaking promise." Nevertheless, others found much to hail. Writing for the *Times Literary Supplement* (June 13, 1997), Charlotte Mendelson admired the author's "linguistic playfulness," noting that her greatest gift is "her ability to confuse, muddling the familiar and the strange until all is equally odd, and equally reasonable." For *Library Journal* (July 2000), Mary G. Szczesiul opined, "There is something fragile yet life-affirming about Brownrigg's contemporary stories, which engage the reader and never let go." Dan Cryer for *New York Newsday* (June 27, 2000) concluded, "All in all, Brownrigg is blessed with one of the most exuberantly agile minds among younger American writers."

In 1998 Brownrigg published *The Metaphysical Touch*, an epistolary novel that explores several philosophical questions. Brownrigg examines the human impulse of letter writing as a means for making personal connections; the book's characters employ the modern communication medium of e-mail. Along the way, she uses the ambiguities of the Internet to pursue a more complex issue. "The novel's story is more abstract—it's about a person projecting a different self," she told Ron Hogan, "or perhaps recapturing an aspect of the self that was lost. There are a lot of different kinds of philosophical ideas in this novel, though, and actually more about metaphysics than there is about self and identity." The tale centers around two major characters: Emily Piper (nicknamed Pi), a philosophy graduate student who has lost all of her possessions in the 1991 Berkeley/Oakland fires, including her nearly completed dissertation on the German philosopher Immanuel Kant; and J.D., a depressed young man who has posted his "diery" on-line, documenting his plans to commit suicide. Overwhelmed by the loss of all her possessions, Pi quits school and moves into a summer house; without her books and her documents, she no longer considers herself a philosopher. (This attitude contradicts Kant's own notion of "idealism," in which he stated that the metaphysical side of the human mind—the world of ideas—represents the essence of existence, rather than material objects.) When a friend sends Pi a modem, she begins probing the Internet and encounters J.D. in an on-line chat room. The two commence a regular correspondence, which grows into a deepening friendship as each helps the other to re-enter life.

The critical response to *The Metaphysical Touch* was generally favorable. While some critics found the unstructured narrative style and meandering plot to be difficult reading, others celebrated the book as a "novel of ideas," in the words of Geoff Nicholson for the *New York Times* (July 11, 1999). Calling the story "a serious and intelligently wrought piece of fiction," he added, "We become involved with questions about ontology and epistemology, about absence and presence and where the physical and metaphysical worlds connect." Richard Hauer Costa, writing for the *Houston Chronicle* (August 22, 1999), affirmed, "The plot ought not to be taken too seriously, for the seriousness lies in the book's bounty of ideas about life and death, body and spirit, sexuality and engagement." Martyn Bedford wrote for the *New Statesman* (November 13, 1998), "One of several fine achievements in this novel is the balance struck between storytelling and ideas. This is a refreshingly intelligent work by an author unafraid to be serious, but saved from dryness by her humanity, the freshness of her prose and the passion of her characters." Other reviewers praised the believability of Brownrigg's characters. "One of the pleasures of this book is the thickness of its human reality: Each character, however tangential, is granted a full complement of emotions and intentions, a distinct personality and past," A.O. Scott opined for *New York Newsday* (June 6, 1999). "[Brownrigg] invents people so real that we can imagine their live continuing and ramifying beyond the confines of the book."

In her most recent book, *Pages for You* (2001), Brownrigg undertakes the theme of first love. "I had always wanted to set something at the time of the first year of college," she told Sara Scribner for the *Hartford Courant* (January 24, 2001), "and I was wondering if I could capture that feeling. This story just struck me, and I had to write it immediately and intensely. I just devoted myself to that. I wrote it in a way that was quite different from the other book. *Metaphysical Touch* had many layers, and I built it over a couple of years—I did a lot of forethinking. This story told itself in many ways." The novel is narrated by Flannery, a 17-year-old Californian in her first year at an East Coast university. There, she begins a romantic affair with Anne, the teaching assistant (TA) in her "Introduction to Criticism" class, who happens to be 11 years her senior. Flannery tells her story through several loosely linked short chapters, each reflecting on moments that the women shared and exploring the subtle reasons for the relationship's demise. Maria Russo wrote for the *New York Times* (April 22, 2001), "The novel is bathed in a joyful, cloistered mood of sensual celebration. Whether their love will be long-lasting or transient is determined by all the ordinary factors: the mysterious way any two personalities play off each other and how any two people discover the limits, or limitlessness, of their connection."

While many critics acknowledged the book's relatively simplistic plot, they praised Brownrigg's delicacy and authenticity in presenting the passion of an intense first love. Writing for *Women's Review of Books* (July 2001), Carole Maso observed, "The plot in fact is so prescribed, so familiar that it becomes virtually invisible. Hypothetically this might free the narrative to follow less tangible emotional drifts—better chronicle the small fleeting intimate shapes of a passionate affair, allowing for all sorts of odd and lovely and sorrowful and mysterious moments to arise." A reviewer for *Publishers Weekly* (February 19, 2001) wrote, "A lesser writer would be swamped in sentimentality, but Brownrigg handles her material with great good humor and vitality. . . . This exquisitely written, bittersweet Valentine of a novel is for any reader who has ever been in a romantic relationship and wants to remember and revel in all the foolish things we do for love." Some criticism focused on Brownrigg's matter-of-fact presentation of a same-sex affair. While some reviewers credited this decision, praising the universal nature of Brownrigg's story, others questioned her failure to explore the homosexual themes more deeply. Carol Guess wrote in the *Lamdba Book Report* (March 2001), "Since this is a realist novel (and a powerful one) Brownrigg might've spent more time tackling the inevitable difficulties such a relationship—taboo on most campuses for good reason—would generate. As blithe as the women are about the fact that Anne is TA for Flannery's class, they are even more blithe about their same-sex desires." Despite such reservations, Guess called the book "a seductive novel, brave in its attempts to outline 'the shape of what she kept unsaid.'" In 2002 *Pages for You* won the Lammy Award for romance fiction from the Lambda Literary Foundation, a group dedicated to the recognition and promotion of gay fiction.

Sylvia Brownrigg continues to divide her time between England and California. She is working on a new novel, which is set in England and devoted to the topic of celebrity.

—K. D.

SUGGESTED READING: *Beatrice Interview* (online) 1999; *Gay & Lesbian Review Worldwide* p43 July 2001; *Houston Chronicle* Z p23 Aug. 22, 1999; *Lambda Book Report* p23 Mar. 2001; *New York Times* VII p17 July 11, 1999, VII p15 Apr. 22, 2001; *New York Newsday* B p10 June 6, 1999, B p11 July 4, 1999, B p2 June 27, 2000; *Times Literary Supplement* p24 June 13, 1997; *Women's Review of Books* p32 July 2001

SELECTED BOOKS: short-story collections—*Ten Women Who Shook the World*, 1997; novels—*The Metaphysical Touch*, 1998; *Pages For You*, 2001

Byrd, Max

1942– Nonfiction writer; mystery writer; historical novelist

Max Byrd has found success in three different literary genres. He explored 18th-century English literature in *Visits to Bedlam: Madness and Literature in the Eighteenth Century*, *London Transformed: Images of the City in the Eighteenth Century*, and *Tristram Shandy*. Following in the footsteps of such mystery writers as Raymond Chandler, Dashiell Hammett, and Mickey Spillane, Byrd created a hard-boiled private detective, Mike Haller, who investigated cases in three novels: *California Thriller*, *Fly Away, Jill*, and *Finders Weepers*. Many

Karen Froyland/Courtesy of Bantam Books
Max Byrd

reviewers have applauded Byrd's three historical novels, *Jefferson*, *Jackson*, and *Grant*, which bring the past to life with impressive detail and accuracy. In an article published in the *Writer* (October 1993), Byrd noted, "Whether you're writing a detective novel, a comic novel, a historical novel, or a warm, sensitive contemporary novel about gun-running vampires in suburbia, the elements of plot are always the same: suspense (not surprise), a dominating image that works like a refrain . . . reversals, obstacles, active characters driven by obsessions."

Max Byrd writes for *World Authors 1995–2000*: "I grew up in rural Georgia, attended public schools there (Dublin, Georgia, near Macon), and then went to Harvard on a scholarship. At Harvard I studied American History and Literature, which was an official field of concentration. The most influential professors I had were Perry Miller, Bernard Bailyn, and especially the late W. J. Bate, the great Johnson scholar. I was on the *Harvard Crimson*. I graduated magna cum laude in 1964 and went to King's College, Cambridge for a year on a scholarship from Harvard. I then returned to Harvard for a Ph.D. in English (thereby avoiding the Vietnam War; had there been no war, I have often thought that I would have gone to work for a newspaper and become a journalist).

"In 1970 I joined the English Department at Yale as an Assistant Professor, specializing in 18th-century English literature; I published some scholarly books and articles and was promoted to Associate Professor, not a tenured position at Yale. In 1976 my wife, daughter and I moved to Davis, where I have taught ever since.

"At Yale I had begun to collaborate on a novel with my old Harvard friend Michael Crichton, but we never finished it; at some point I began trying to write a thriller on my own, and in 1979 or '80 my first novel, *California Thriller* was published as a paperback original by Bantam Books. I have continued to do some scholarly work, but most of my energy has been spent on writing fiction. I wrote a number of detective novels, then at the suggestion of Bantam tried my hand at an historical novel. The result was *Jefferson: A Novel*, about the years Thomas Jefferson spent in Paris. This has been followed by two more, *Jackson* and *Grant*. I hope to write several more historical novels, though not necessarily about American presidents.

"There are a number of things I find attractive about the historical novel—I like the research, which puts me in touch with interesting people and carries me back to my undergraduate interests; I like the forced objectivity of historical novels—it is hard to be too self-absorbed when you are writing about actual other people. And I like very much the feeling that I have been building a kind of version of American history with these books, my own very limited version, to be sure, but one that is based on a good deal of factual evidence. The kind of historical novel I try to write is not a costume drama, but a truthful evocation and recreation of a particular period or character. I believe, for instance, that Gore Vidal's *Lincoln* is a great novel, and I can only think of it with admiration and envy. The writers I know who have been important to me, besides Crichton, of course, who remains a good friend and inspiration, are Oakley Hall, Diane Johnson, Richard Ford, and most of the other regular members of the Squaw Valley Community of Writers, where I teach every summer.

"I will add that I have earned my money by teaching in the UC Davis English Department, not from my books. I regret now very much having entered academia (and stayed in it). I find most people in English Departments are not especially interested in literature; and in recent years, as political correctness has taken over the American university, I find much academic scholarship in English just plain goofy.

"Finally, if you were to ask what books are on my bedside table right now, I would report the newest collection of stories by my literary hero John Updike; a novel by Simenon; a collection of short stories by Balzac (both of these in French); and a novel by Alice Ellis."

Born in 1942, Max Byrd published his first book, *Visits to Bedlam: Madness and Literature in the Eighteenth Century*, in 1974. In it he explores how such authors as Jonathan Swift, Samuel Johnson, Alexander Pope, William Cowper, and William Blake presented insanity in their books. In his review for the *Times Literary Supplement* (March 28, 1975), Matthew Hodgart described the book as polished and skillful literary criticism that made an important contribution to the subject. Hodgart was impressed by Byrd's discussion of insanity as a theme in Pope's *Duciad*, cautious handling of Johnson's "vile melancholy" in *Rasselas*, and the introduction of "the rich topic of the English Malady," in which the "English believed themselves to be unusually splenetic, hypochondriac and given to suicide . . ." Reviewing *Visits to Bedlam* for *Library Journal* (October 1, 1974), H. G. Hahn lauded the book, writing that Byrd "never fails to notice the cultural and medical soil in which [insanity is] rooted: thus, this lucid study is as valuable to the historian of ideas as to the belletrist."

In his book *London Transformed: Images of the City in the Eighteenth Century* (1978), Byrd discusses such 18th-century authors as Daniel Defoe and Alexander Pope and their portrayals of the city of London. "Reading sensitively, Professor Byrd . . . finds Defoe and others softening this urban jungle by comparing it metaphorically with the human body," R. A. Sokolov observed in the *New York Times Book Review* (March 19, 1978). "Freshness is the chief virtue of this intelligent study, which, at first glance, may seem arbitrary in conception. Professor Byrd redeems his thesis over and over by leading us to well-known places by a new route."

In 1981 Byrd turned to fiction, with the publication of *California Thriller*, a mystery involving right-wing politics and mind-control drugs. In the book Byrd introduces Max Haller, a Boston-born private detective based in San Francisco. In an interview with Stuart Wavell for the Manchester *Guardian* (July 13, 1985), Byrd said that he "was frankly trying to imitate and update what [Raymond] Chandler had done." In her review for the *New Republic* (August 22, 1981), Robin W. Winks asserted that the first two-thirds of the novel were "as good a California thriller as one will find." However, she continued, "The last third resorts to so much violence to resolve the convolutions of its intricate plot that one feels the author has set out to prove that he can be nastier than the rest." Despite Winks' mixed assessment, the Private Eye Writers of America honored *California Thriller* with their Shamus Award, in 1982.

In the first sequel, *Fly Away, Jill* (1982), Haller travels to England to search for the missing daughter-in-law of a Mafia boss. In the *New Republic* (March 3, 1982), Robin W. Winks wrote: "Byrd is now on top of his plotting as well as his prose, and this tight, fast inquiry . . . is full of convincing characters, nasty types, wayward youths, and sound Englishmen."

In his third adventure, *Finders Weepers* (1983), Haller is hired to find a missing prostitute who stands to inherit $800,000. A reviewer for the *Times Literary Supplement* (December 27, 1985) described the novel as "Standard West Coast detective material, rescued from, run-of-the-millness by a fresh narrative voice and Haller's engaging eccentricities." By contrast, Newgate Callendar in the *New York Times Book Review* (October 30, 1983) wrote that everything in the novel "is predictable from the very first page to the last." Observing that the name Mike Haller is similar to Mike Hammer, the famous private detective who appeared in many books and several films and television shows, Callendar asked if "Mr. Byrd is trying to capitalize on the reputation of Mickey Spillane's old roughneck?" In his interview with Wavell, Byrd said that he had been unfamiliar with Spillane's thrillers and had actually named his protagonist after William Haller, an English scholar.

In 1985 Byrd returned to nonfiction with *Tristram Shandy*, a study of Laurence Sterne's book *The Life and Opinions of Tristram Shandy, Gentleman*, a bawdy treatise often referred to as the first modern novel. "Byrd addresses himself to the issue of Sterne's innuendoes, and is particularly good on the book's style, an area where so many others have been repetitious or dull," David Profumo wrote in his review for the *Times Literary Supplement* (November 29, 1985). "In his volume-by-volume reading of selected episodes, he assesses the strategies in which the novel's disorderly effects are organized. Byrd touches on many facets of this mosaic work—association, insanity, comedy—and has suitable respect for the protean nature of his subject."

In an article published in the *Writer* (October 1989), Byrd recalled that he wanted to write a fourth "Mike Haller" thriller, but his editor rejected the manuscript. "She wanted me to break out of the detective genre and try to write a bigger, more ambitious book," he wrote. "And, unlike my earlier novels, she wanted this one to be written in the third person." In the 1989 *Writer* article, Byrd discussed the advantages of writing a novel in the third person. First, it allows geographic expansion of the plot. "With a cinematic flick of the eye, while Mike Haller was still slowly boarding a plane, third person could change cities or even continents," he explained. Third person, he added, provides the novel with a greater cast of characters and increases the flexibility of the subplot.

Keeping the title of the previous manuscript, *Target of Opportunity*, Byrd wrote the novel his publisher had requested, which was published in 1988. Byrd's new hero, Gilman, follows his sister to Boston, where she seeks revenge on the man who murdered her husband. Reviewing *Target of Opportunity* for the London *Sunday Times* (November 19, 1989, on- line), Austin MacCurtain wrote, "The plot is tied up very neatly, if a touch implausibly. Byrd's narrative has an infectious speed which almost runs away with him at times, but overall this is a good thriller."

Another thriller, *Fuse Time*, appeared in 1991. In the book, David Renner, a former member of an English bomb squad, probes a series of bombings in Los Angeles. Jeff Black wrote in the *Jerusalem Post* (September 27, 1991, on-line) that the novel suffered from "a shaky plot, cardboard characters and dull dialog." By contrast, Peter Robertson, a reviewer for *Booklist* (March 1, 1991), praised the book, asserting that "Byrd's foreign characters are right on the money: their accents check out, and their reactions to being strangers in a strange land give the tale its richness."

Max Byrd turned to historical fiction with the publication of *Jefferson*, in 1993. Byrd offers an account of Thomas Jefferson, the third president of the United States, during the time he was United States Ambassador to France (from 1784 to 1789). The action is seen through the eyes of Jefferson's personal secretary, William Short, a character based on a real-life figure. In the *New York Times Book Review* (November 23, 1993), Michiko Kakutani wrote that Byrd "has focused on another contradiction in Jefferson's life—his inability to reconcile the promptings of his head and his heart—and has used this contradiction as a springboard for a wonderfully vivid novel that brings the sage of Monticello (or a version of him anyway) to life." Kakutani commended Byrd for skillfully describing Jefferson's day-to-day life and the atmosphere of pre-Revolutionary France, observing that "*Jefferson* has the organic intimacy of a novel that has sprung full-blown from the imagination of its creator." In her review for the *Washington Post Book World* (May 15, 1994), Alison Baker wrote, "We meet ribald Benjamin Franklin, strait-laced John and Abigail Adams, the slaves Sally Hemings and her brother, James. And we see Jefferson using the inventions and collecting the thousand-and-one curiosities and works of art that, 200 years later, are still on display at Monticello." Baker noted that by the end of the novel the reader is left with " a clearer sense of those supporting characters than of Jefferson. . . . Byrd leaves the mind of Jefferson a mystery to William Short, and so to us. But perhaps thus mixing of facts with mystery is as close as we can get to truth."

For the subject of his next book, Byrd chose Andrew Jackson, the general who served as president from 1829 to 1837. The book, *Jackson* (1997), is set during the presidential election in 1828. Jackson is seeking to unseat the incumbent, John Quincy Adams, who had defeated him four years earlier in a disputed election. (After all of the presidential candidates failed to receive the sufficient majority of votes in the Electoral College, the House of Representatives, following the protocol set forth in the U.S. Constitution, selected Adams.) The novel's protagonist is David Chase, a writer hired by Jackson's enemies to dig up damaging information about him and publish it a short time before the election. "But in the course of his year of research, Chase unearths something more significant," Keith Henderson wrote in his review for the *Christian Science Monitor* (April 4, 1997). "He begins to understand why countless thousands of his countrymen would willingly follow the unlettered, yet eloquent Jackson into the mouths of cannons." Chase becomes torn between publishing the truth and attacking Jackson as he was hired to do. "Like his creation, Chase, Byrd has mastered the spadework of writing," Henderson observed. "He musters vivid detail. . . . Byrd's rat-tat-tat narrative will propel readers with even a slight interest in American history on to the last page."

In 2000 Byrd returned with *Grant*. The book's structure was similar to the author's two previous historical novels; it details the adventures of Nicholas Trist, a one-armed writer and Civil War veteran, who is sent by a French magazine to cover President Ulysses S. Grant's efforts to win a third term. In her review for *Publishers Weekly* (July 10, 2000), Sybil S. Steinberg observed that "Byrd's research and literary knowledge are impressive, but while his re-creation of period detail, including product placement (Ivory Soap, E.C. Booze whiskey and Heinz pickles) is excellent, there are a few anachronisms. Even so, this is a fascinating read for any serious student of [the] period when modern politics and society were being mapped out of the smoky shadows of a devastating war." In the *New York Times Book Review* (August 20, 2000), Dante Ramos wrote that "Byrd adroitly deploys a small ensemble of Washington socialites, journalists and politicians to provide the sins and petty cruelties that push *Grant* along." The reviewer concluded that *Grant* is an "appealing tale about love and death in late 19th-century America."

In the October 1993 issue of *Writer*, Byrd explained how historical fiction should be written: "If a writer chooses a story that describes famous events or characters, the plot must be bounded and limited by the historical facts," he wrote. "Lincoln dies, Troy falls; unless it is historical *fantasy*, the South loses the Civil War." Although readers know that a novel about Abraham Lincoln will end in his assassination, Byrd asserted that it "only sets the heart beating faster as the carriage begins to roll toward Ford's theater."

Max Byrd edited the book, *Daniel Defoe: A Collection of Critical Essays* (1976), and he often contributes articles to the *New York Times Book Review*. Byrd and his family live in Davis, California.
—*D. C.*

SUGGESTED READING: *Booklist* p1320 Mar. 1, 1991; *Christian Science Monitor* p15 Apr. 4, 1997; Manchester *Guardian* (on-line) July 13, 1985; *Jerusalem Post* (on-line) Sept. 27, 1991; *Library Journal* p2278 Oct. 1, 1974; *New Republic* p39 Aug. 22, 1981, p38+ Mar. 3, 1982; *New York Times* C p20 Nov. 23, 1993; *New York Times Book Review* p16 Mar. 19, p31 Oct. 30, 1983, p7+ Aug. 20, 2000; *Publishers Weekly* p43 July 10, 2000; London *Sunday Times* Issue Sec. p1+ Nov. 19, 1989; *Times Literary Supplement* p328 Mar. 28, 1975, p689 June 23, 1978, p1352 Nov. 29, 1985, p1478 Dec. 27, 1985; *Writer* p12+ Oct. 1989, p12+ Oct. 1993

SELECTED BOOKS: nonfiction—*Visits to Bedlam: Madness and Literature in the Eighteenth Century*, 1974; *London Transformed: Images of the City in the Eighteenth Century*, 1978; *Tristram Shandy*, 1985; fiction—*California Thriller*, 1981; *Fly Away, Jill*, 1982; *Finders*

Weepers, 1983; *Target of Opportunity*, 1988; *Fuse Time*, 1991; *Jefferson*, 1993; *Jackson*, 1997; *Grant*, 2000

Courtesy of Picador USA

Canin, Ethan

July 19, 1960– Novelist; short-story writer

Ethan Canin is perhaps best known for *Emperor of the Air* (1988), a collection of nine short stories that reminded many critics and readers of the fiction of John Cheever. Observers noted the maturity of Canin's voice as he wrote about characters ranging from the adolescent son of a grocer to a biology and astronomy teacher in his late 60s. The volume, Canin's first, became a surprise best-seller, unusual enough for a writer's first book but even more rare for a collection of stories; it also earned him the prestigious Houghton Mifflin literary fellowship, which is given periodically to beginning writers of exceptional promise. (Previous recipients include such literary heavyweights as Robert Penn Warren, Elizabeth Bishop, Philip Roth, and Edward Hoagland.) In a review of *Emperor of the Air* for the *Washington Post* (January 20, 1988), Jonathan Yardley wrote, "The phrase 'auspicious debut' has for so long been used so casually and frequently by reviewers that it no longer means anything; this is a pity, for Canin's debut is indeed auspicious." Christopher Lehmann-Haupt also offered critical praise for the book, writing in the *New York Times* (January 25, 1988), "The way these stories transcend the ordinariness of human voices is . . . startling."

At the time of the book's publication, Canin was a 27-year-old, fourth-year medical student at Harvard University. For the next few years, he juggled his medical and literary careers before turning to writing full-time. In addition to *Emperor of the Air*, Canin is the author of *Blue River* (1991), *The Palace Thief* (1994), *For Kings and Planets* (1998), and *Carry Me Across the Water* (2001).

Of Jewish descent, Ethan Canin was born on July 19, 1960 in Ann Arbor, Michigan. His father, Stuart, was a violinist, and his mother, Virginia, a painter. The family moved several times during Canin's youth, following his father's musical pursuits first to Oberlin, Ohio, and then to Philadelphia before settling down in San Francisco, where Canin spent most of his childhood. His writing talents were first noticed while he attended the San Francisco University High School; one of his teachers, Danielle Steel, who would go on to win fame as a romance novelist, wrote the following appraisal of Canin's abilities, as quoted by *Publishers Weekly* (December 18, 1987): "Ethan has an extraordinary gift for writing. His work is nothing short of marvelous, crystal clear, perfect in nuance, adept in delivery." Canin received an "A" from Steel for his assignments, a "B+" for effort, and an "A+" for his final project. "I was so flattered," Canin told William Goldstein for the *Publishers Weekly* article, going on to explain his perplexity over Steel's approval of his work. "The stuff is terrible," Canin admitted. "I don't know what the other kids could have been doing to make me get an A."

Upon graduation from high school, Canin dismissed his teacher's suggestion that he follow a career in writing. Instead, he enrolled at Stanford University, in Stanford, California, to pursue a degree in engineering. In an interview for the *Writer* (May 2000), Canin told Lewis Burke Frumkes that his continuing to write was an accident. "I wandered into an English class one day," he recalled, "simply because it was listed on the next page in the course catalogue after engineering. I was looking for another class and ended up taking a creative writing course. . . . I began reading the stories of John Cheever, and that changed my life. Suddenly, I just wanted to be a writer." Like Steel, Canin's Stanford professors enjoyed his writing—enough to send two of his stories, on his behalf, to magazines, where both were accepted. One, called "Abe, Between Rounds," appeared in *Redbook* in August 1981.

After receiving his bachelor's degree, Canin entered the University of Iowa's esteemed Writers' Workshop, an M.F.A. (master of fine arts) program. The workshop was not what he had expected. In an interview with Jane Rosenzweig for the *Atlantic Online* (November 25, 1998), Canin recalled his unhappiness as well as his disillusionment during this two-year period. "I wrote almost nothing when I was in the workshop," Canin told Rosenzweig, "and I learned nothing. I was paralyzed—utterly paralyzed." Some of his memories of the Iowa

Writers' Workshop, however, were positive. "At the same time," he continued, "I know I wouldn't have been a writer if I hadn't come to the Iowa workshop. . . . Iowa is sometimes overwhelming, but when you leave you look back on your days here with nostalgia. You have two years to wander around this little Midwestern town with a hundred other impractical romantics, worrying about your next paragraph. Where else are you going to find that life?"

By the time he received his M.F.A. degree, Canin had all but given up on his career as a writer. He began taking undergraduate classes in order to fulfill his requirements for medical school, crediting the novelist John Irving with influencing his decision. He told Frumkes, "John Irving came to give a class. He read one of my stories and didn't like it at all. . . . I wondered, 'What have I done here?' I had a scientific background. I liked people, basically. And in a colossal failure of imagination, I went to medical school." In an interview with Nicholas A. Basbanes for *LitKit* (1998, on-line), Canin explained, "Writing had always been my first love, and the only reason I went into medicine in the first place was because I feared I could never support myself as a writer."

In 1984 Canin entered medical school at Harvard University, in Cambridge, Massachusetts. While there, far from abandoning his writing, he not only continued to produce short stories but had them published in such high-profile magazines as the *Atlantic*, *Esquire*, and *Ploughshares*. His work was also anthologized in the 1985 and 1986 editions of *Best American Short Stories*. During this time the publishing company Houghton Mifflin approached Canin with the idea of bringing out a collection of his work. Canin told Rosenzweig that he wrote most of *Emperor of the Air* during his first year at Harvard, "because I wasn't supposed to be writing. Miraculous trick. The idea of invention when you're in medical school is just beyond the pale." In his review of *Emperor of the Air* for the *New York Times*, Christopher Lehmann-Haupt wrote, "One can't help noting gratefully how much these remarkable stories are preoccupied with matters of ultimate concern—of life and death, of youth and aging, of wealth and poverty and of the heart not only as the seat of human emotions but also as the organ that pumps lifeblood through the system." Jonathan Yardley agreed, writing in the *Washington Post*, "Canin produces . . . evidence of unusual maturity." For *Emperor of the Air*, Canin won the Heinfield Transatlantic Review Award in 1989, the same year that he was given a National Endowment for the Arts grant.

Following the overwhelmingly positive reception of *Emperor of the Air*, Canin took a year's leave from medical school in order to concentrate on his next writing project. He traveled to Quito, Ecuador, and spent the better part of 1988 producing his first novel, which would be published three years later as *Blue River*. This book focuses on Edward and Lawrence Sellers, two very different brothers who are reunited after 15 years. *Blue River* received decidedly mixed reviews. Many critics, while judging the book to be good for a first novel, expressed their preference for his earlier work. In the *New York Times* (October 10, 1991), Christopher Lehmann-Haupt described *Blue River* as "promising but flawed" and added, "You have a wonderful future as a writer, Ethan Canin, but in *Blue River* you slipped." Jonathan Yardley, in the *Washington Post* (October 23, 1991), reached a similar conclusion: "[*Blue River*] is a narrative long on psychologizing but short on vivid character and incident—by no means a bad book, but well short of what its author is capable."

Canin continued to pursue a career in medicine. He graduated from Harvard Medical School in 1992 and immediately moved back to San Francisco, undertaking a residency at the University of California San Francisco Medical Center. Writing, though, remained very much a part of his life. Over the next three years, he would divide his time among pursuing a medical career, teaching writing at the University of Michigan, the University of Iowa, and San Francisco State University, and completing his third literary offering, *The Palace Thief* (1994), a collection of four novellas and the winner of the 1994 Commonwealth Club Gold Medal for Literature. Most critics agreed that *The Palace Thief* represented Canin's return to form and at least a partial fulfillment of the promise he had shown with *Emperor of the Air*. Dan Cryer wrote for *New York Newsday* (February 21, 1994), "Ethan Canin's achievement is one of both artistry and humanity." Abby Frucht in the *New York Times* (February 20, 1994) also praised *The Palace Thief*, writing, "Mr. Canin watches over his characters in much the same way that if you believe in God, you might imagine Him hovering over humankind—biting His mischievous tongue, stepping aside as we make our most touching, our most devastating mistakes."

As with his earlier works, publicists for this book took advantage of a selling point that went beyond the quality of the writing: the fact that Canin was a young, handsome doctor. He embarked on an extensive promotional tour. Joanne Kaufman, in the *Wall Street Journal* (March 22, 1994), explained why Canin's readings often attracted "many bookish young women," writing, "Mr. Canin is 33 years old and a hunk." While he was uncomfortable with all the attention, Canin found that the experience increased his confidence as a writer. In 1995 he left his post at the hospital and took on writing full-time. "I got halfway through my medical residency," he told John Kenyon for *IowaAlive.com*, "but I realized that if I became a practicing doctor, I wouldn't ever write again." The decision, though, was not an easy one to make. Indeed, the prospect of leaving the medical profession behind "terrified him," Robin Pogrebin reported in the *New York Times* (November 10, 1998). Canin explained to her, "I was leaving the most secure job in the world for the least secure, leaving a job I knew I could do for a job I still to this day have no idea whether I can do."

An opportunity that arose the next year, 1996, helped to calm Canin's fears: he was offered a tenured teaching position at the Iowa Writers' Workshop, from which he had graduated 12 years earlier. In addition to the financial security it provided, the position allowed Canin to maintain the flexible schedule he needed to finish his second novel, *For Kings and Planets* (1998). The story revolves around the characters Orno Tarcher and Marshall Emerson, freshmen at Columbia University in 1974. Orno is a wide-eyed midwesterner who is dazzled by his new friend Marshall, the son of two Columbia professors with connections to the Kennedy family. The book is a study in the attraction of opposites, one that Greg Johnson, in a review for the *Washington Post* (September 12, 1998), called "skillfully evoke[d]." Even more than *Blue River*, however, *For Kings and Planets* inspired a full spectrum of responses from critics. Lehmann-Haupt, writing for the *New York Times* (September 10, 1998), called the new book "shimmering" and concluded, *"For Kings and Planets* leaves you wounded and healed." Three days later, though, Rand Richards Cooper proclaimed in the *New York Times Book Review* (September 13, 1998) that the book was "a greedy monster of a novel that swallows up its creator's virtues and leaves only his weaknesses on display. . . . [Canin] should file *For Kings and Planets* under Lessons Learned and move on."

Canin's most recent book is *Carry Me Across the Water* (2001), a short but complex novel whose main character, August Kleinman, is a 78-year-old widower trying to make sense of his life. A number of critics agreed that the novel was less successful than some of Canin's earlier work. Michiko Kakutani of the *New York Times* (May 4, 2001) wrote, "This novel suffers from a certain lack of passion. It's a highly professional, highly polished performance, but in the end it remains just that: a performance that's conscientious and carefully fashioned, but somehow not deeply heartfelt." Kakutani concluded that the life of the story's hero was "devoid of any real interest." Other reviewers, however, were more generous. Carmela Ciuraru, in the *Wall Street Journal* (May 11, 2001), conceding that Canin had not "entirely sorted out Kleinman's jumble of memories," nonetheless called the book "compelling for its sensitive, elegiac portrayal of aging and grief."

A film version of the title story from *The Palace Thief*, entitled *The Emperor's Club* and starring Kevin Kline, was released by Universal Studios in late 2002. Canin had a cameo role in the movie. He currently resides in Iowa City, Iowa, with his wife, Barbara, and their two children.

—*J. H.*

SUGGESTED READING: *Los Angeles Times* E p1 May 22, 2001; *New York Times* E p9 Sep. 10, 1998, with photo, VII p12 Sep. 13, 2001; *Publishers Weekly* p19+ Dec. 18, 1987, with photo; *Washington Post* C p2 Jan. 20, 1988; *Writer* p19+ May 2000; *Contemporary Authors* vol. 135, 1992

SELECTED BOOKS: *Emperor of the Air*, 1988; *Blue River*, 1991; *The Palace Thief*, 1994; *For Kings and Planets*, 1998; *Carry Me Across the Water*, 2001

Courtesy of Vintage Books

Canty, Kevin

Jan. 1953– Short-story writer; novelist

Kevin Canty published his first short story at the age of 40. His first book, *A Stranger in This World: Stories*, was hailed by most reviewers as evidence of a fresh new talent. Critics have also applauded Canty's two novels, *Into the Great Wide Open* (1996) and *Nine Below Zero* (1999), which place ordinary people with difficulties in unusual circumstances and relationships. In 2001 Canty published a second anthology, *Honeymoon: And Other Stories*, which enhanced his reputation as one of the most talented short-story writers today. "So: apparently I've been interested in love, desire, appetite," he wrote in an essay posted on the Random House Web site. "Apparently I've been interested in food and sex, not necessarily in that order. . . . And what happens next? [I] hope that somewhere I can find two words to stick together, two sentences, the start of something that will, when it is done, surprise me. That's all I ask. But it's a lot to hope for."

For *World Authors 1995–2000*, Kevin Canty writes, "Born January, 1953 in the waning days of the Truman Administration, I think. Raised in the

Catholic faith--till I was 13, anyway—as the oldest of seven children.

"Until I was ten, we lived in California in a large, extended Irish family (my father's side) that had been established in the Bay Area for many years. My grandmother, for instance, survived the Earthquake, pushing her youngest brother and the day's baking away from the advancing fire in a baby carriage. My mother was from Montana, which seemed mysterious to me at the time. There were several pictures of her in high school and she was holding a cigarette and a bottle of beer in each of them.

"Our family moved East when I was ten, first to New Jersey and then to Washington, D.C., where I went to high school. This move from the large tribal Irish Catholic family to the isolated nuclear family was painful, though in the sense that it parallels the experience of a lot of this century it has been useful.

"Never quite finished high school. Instead I worked as the only white kid on an all-black construction crew in suburban D.C., from which I learned plenty. I continued my odd-job career in Montana, working as a carpenter, a gandy-dancer (railroad labor) and most memorably as a gopher-poisoner. In between I started at the University of Montana, where eventually I would study with the poet Richard Hugo and the essayist and short- fiction writer William Kittredge, among many others. In 1976, in the Liberal Arts Building at U.M. where my office is today, I met Lucy Capehart, to whom I am now married (though it would take us another 11 years to formalize ourselves with a wedding).

"Never quite finished college, either. I had (and have still) a low threshold of boredom which unsuited me for the rigors of General Education. And I did not have the discipline to get my writing done. Also by this time I was playing guitar in a series of bands and more and more involved with music. These were garden-variety bar bands playing around Montana, and no great shakes musically, but it was fun while it lasted.

"Lucy and I moved to Portland, Oregon next and spent nearly a decade there, Lucy working on her photography and me working in the sound reinforcement business. Somewhere in here I turned thirty, and then thirty-one, and it eventually occurred to me that if I wanted to be a writer it would be a good idea to get moving. I took an extension class from the Oregon Writers Workshop with Joyce Thompson, then started a writer's group that lasted a couple of years, then eventually ended up going to graduate school at the University of Florida and then at the University of Arizona, working with Padgett Powell, Harry Crews, Joy Williams and several other writers who had an influence on me. In the last year of the graduate school experience, I published my first story ('The Victim') in the summer fiction issue of *Esquire* magazine.

"My first book, a collection of short stories called *A Stranger In This World*, came out in 1994. We had come back to Montana with two small children and were living in a ten-sided log cabin (modeled on a Navaho hogan) as the book was being written. Shortly afterward we decamped yet again for a two-year stint at the University of North Carolina at Wilmington, where I taught fiction writing. At the end of this time I was offered a job teaching at the University of Montana, which I gratefully accepted. We bought a house on our arrival and threw the moving boxes away.

"Since moving back to Missoula I have published three more books: *Into the Great Wide Open* (a novel), *Nine Below Zero* (a novel), and *Honeymoon* (a short-story collection). My work—stories, articles and essays—has appeared in *GQ*, the *New Yorker*, the *New York Times Magazine*'s "Sophisticated Traveler," the *Oxford American*, *Vogue*, *Glimmer Train*, *Details* and many other places. Some of the books have been translated into French, Dutch, German, Spanish and English (the truck replaced with lorries, I guess, and the elevators with lifts) and the first two books were named as *New York Times Book Review* 'Notable Books.'

"We continue to live in Montana, for complicated reasons. It's a difficult and in some ways impractical place to live, with a long, cold winter and a first-class set of political crazies. But it's also very beautiful, and a decent place for our children—Turner, now age 12, and Nora, 8—and I do like teaching at the University, where the MFA program attracts some of the best students imaginable. Also, there's the fishing."

Kevin Canty recalled that reading was a "social thing" when he attended high school. "We would sit around and talk about books that I wouldn't be exceptionally proud of right now . . . but it really mattered," he told an interviewer for Oregon Live's *Book Spy* (March 17, 1998, on-line). "I think there's an aspect of reading that's like that, it really is, although it's solitary, reading really is a kind of social behavior. Out of that, I always thought, this is pretty interesting and what would happen if you could write [books]?" After dropping out of high school Canty earned his G.E.D. and eventually enrolled at the University of Montana, in Missoula. He graduated, in 1988, with a B.A. in creative writing. He then enrolled at the University of Florida, in Gainesville, receiving his M.A. in fiction, in 1990. Canty also received an MFA in fiction from the University of Arizona, in Tucson, in 1993. That same year he began publishing short stories.

A Stranger in this World, a collection of his short stories, was published in 1994. "Despite its range of subjects and forms, this collection has a distinctive and consistent voice—a voice that reminds one at times of Denis Johnson, Padgett Powell, even Flannery O'Connor," Michael Griffith wrote in the *Southern Review* (Spring 1995). "What Canty's stories share with Johnson's, besides their characteristic milieu—the ragged edge of disaster—is that they take place in a world of deadpan evil, a world where surprise is an unaffordable luxury." Griffith noted that the stories "Junk," about a man struggling with a drug problem and a failed marriage; "Blue Boy," about a young lifeguard's encounter with an older woman whom he had been ogling all summer; and "Pretty Judy," in which a 15-year-old boy becomes sexually involved with a mentally retarded girl, were the book's strongest. Griffith faulted the story "The Victim" for relying on "empty, slightly self-satisfied details" and borrowing too much from director Quentin Tarantino's film, *Pulp Fiction* (1994). In his review for *Booklist* (August 1994), David Cline wrote that "Canty's polished prose is spare: what he doesn't say carries as much weight as what he unflinchingly describes." Calling Canty a "powerful new talent," Cline observed that he "has the treasured ability of making his dark material palatable, shocking, and exhilarating at the same time."

Canty's first novel, *Into the Great Wide Open* (1996), received critical acclaim. Set in suburban Washington, D.C., the novel focuses on 17-year-old Kenny Kolodny, the son of an abusive father and a mother who resides in a mental institution. Although he is bright and shows potential as a writer, Kenny neglects his school work and smokes marijuana. His life changes when he meets the enigmatic Junie Williamson, a fellow student who also has family troubles. Several characters from stories in *A Stranger in this World* reappear in the novel. In her review for the *Los Angeles Times Book Review* (October 6, 1996), Erika Taylor observed that "Kenny has a presence, a kind of linguistic charisma that makes *Into the Great Wide Open* rank up there with some of the best coming-of-age novels." Taylor added that "Canty's writing lives in a slippery, teenage place where intense emotions—anger, sadness, ecstasy—lie between every word. He has near-perfect pitch." Writing in *USA Today* (October 3, 1996), Deirdre R. Schwiesow described the novel as "a beautiful book—both enchanting and painful to read." Favorably comparing the novel to J. D. Salinger's *Catcher in the Rye* and Scott Spencer's *Endless Love*, Schwiesow concluded that *Into the Great Wide Open* "chronicles the progression of the kind of overwhelming first love that never really dies, resonating with a poignant sense of doom on every page."

Canty published his second novel, *Nine Below Zero*, in 1999. During a winter in Montana, a Native American construction worker named Marvin Deernose, a former drug addict and alcoholic, rescues Senator Henry Neihart from a car wreck. Neihart convalesces from his injuries and an illness at Deernose's ranch, and his married granddaughter, Justine, arrives at the ranch to help take care of him. Marvin and Justine begin a secret love affair, and the situation becomes increasingly complicated with the arrival of Justine's husband and a major blizzard. "Effective in some places, the lyricism sometimes segues into excess," Kit Reed wrote in the *New York Times Book Review* (March 7, 1999). "Soberly and compassionately drawn, Justine and Marvin are too helpless to be appealing. It's hard to engage with characters who have so clearly lost the capacity for joy." In her review for the *Library Journal* (February 1, 1999), Nancy McNicol noted that each character in the novel "experiences a claustrophobic narrowing of psychological possibilities brought on by events past and present. Coupling such themes with an economy of language that propels the reader through the story, Canty inevitably draws comparison to Raymond Carver and Hemingway."

In 2001 Canty published another collection, *Honeymoon: And Other Stories*. "Kevin Canty's stories are short, spare and both beautiful and painful to read," Elizabeth Roca wrote in her review for the *Washington Post* (April 8, 2001), "beautiful in the poetic economy and intensity of their language, painful in their subject matter, which encompasses loneliness, loss and death." Roca was impressed by "Flipper," an encounter between an escapee from a weight-loss camp and a pregnant teenager, and "Carolina Beach," a love story between a divorced man and a terminally ill woman. Lauding *Honeymoon: And Other Stories* as a "very beautiful book" in the *New York Times Book Review* (April 22, 2001), Stacey D'Erasmo noted that Canty's "characters yearn unabashedly; they grieve; they are hilarious but rarely ironic." D'Erasmo noted that "Canty's dark humor finds its neatest expression in 'Little Debbie,' a folie à deux about a marriage between a woman who once couldn't stop eating . . . and a man who has no intention of not drinking a lot."

In 1999 Kevin Canty published *Rounders: A Novel*, an adaptation of the screenplay for the film *Rounders* (1999), written by David Levien and Brian Koppelman.

—D. C.

SUGGESTED READING: *Booklist* p2020 Aug. 1994; *Library Journal* p118+ Feb. 1, 1999; *Los Angeles Times Book Review* p14 Oct. 6, 1996; *New York Times Book Review* p7 Apr. 22, 2001; *Southern Review* p365+ Spring 1995; *USA Today* D p4 Oct. 3, 1996; *Washington Post* p13+ Apr. 8, 2001; Oregon Live Web site

SELECTED BOOKS: *A Stranger in the World: Stories*, 1994; *Into the Great Wide Open*, 1996; *Nine Below Zero*, 1999; *Rounders: A Novel*, 1999; *Honeymoon: And Other Stories*, 2001

Anne Ford Doyle/Courtesy of Knopf Publishers

Cary, Lorene

Nov. 29, 1956– Novelist; memoirist

When the novelist and memoirist Lorene Cary was a little girl, her grandfather told her a folktale about a woman who shed her skin every evening. The woman flew freely around her village without her skin, until the night her husband salted her skin, causing it to burn her when she put it back on. As a teenager Cary felt the sting of changing identities firsthand, as a student at St. Paul's, a prestigious prep school in New Hampshire. Cary, who is African-American and whose family was of relatively modest means, was uncomfortable in her new environment, as were some of her African-American friends. "What we were afraid of was that we would change in some way that would betray our people. We were afraid we would turn into [Uncle] Toms. It was hard to know ways to allow yourself to change," Cary explained to Jacqueline Trescott for the *Washington Post* (April 25, 1991). Cary later wrote about her St. Paul's experience in the acclaimed memoir *Black Ice* (1991), in which she noted her youthful mistake in adhering to an overly narrow definition of what it means to be African-American. The memoir was followed by her two novels, *Price of a Child* (1995) and *Pride* (1998), which take the question of African-American identity as themes, the former from a pre–Civil War perspective and the latter through the eyes of four African-American women going through midlife identity crises.

Lorene Cary was born on November 29, 1956 in Philadelphia, Pennsylvania, to John and Carole (Hamilton) Cary, and was raised in a primarily African-American suburb of the city. Carole Cary began grooming her daughter for the academic life when Lorene was young. She personally appealed to the principal of a prestigious public grade school outside their neighborhood to accept Lorene as a student, and literally dragged the girl to the site of the I.Q. test that subsequently placed her among the top pupils of her first-grade class.

At age 15, while attending public school and flipping burgers at a Woolworth's variety store in her free time, Cary heard that St. Paul's had recently begun an integration program and had set aside scholarship funds for black female applicants. Cary jumped at the opportunity, despite the fact that she had serious reservations about the school and what it meant for a black woman to join the ranks of its historically privileged white student body. "I was there in spite, despite, TO spite it," Cary told Trescott. "I was there because of sit-ins and marches and riots. I was there—and this I felt with extraordinary and bitter certainty—as a sort of liberal-minded experiment. And hey, I did not intend to fail." At St. Paul's, Cary was elected class vice president and won the Rector's Award for community service. After graduating from the school's two-year program, in 1974, she attended the University of Pennsylvania, in Philadelphia, where she earned a joint bachelor's and master's degree in English, in 1978. Afterward, she enrolled at the University of Sussex, in England, to study religious faith and doubt during the Victorian era; she completed the master's program in 1980.

That same year, back in the United States, she apprenticed as a writer for *Time* and then joined *TV Guide* as an associate editor. In 1982 she left *TV Guide* to work at St. Paul's as a teacher, coach, and dormitory master. In 1984 she became an adjunct professor at the University of the Arts, in Philadelphia, where she stayed until 1988. During this time Cary freelanced for such periodicals as *Essence*, *American Visions*, and the *Philadelphia Inquirer Sunday Magazine*.

In 1988 Cary wrote a short article for *American Visions* about her experience at St. Paul's, which gave her the idea to write a book of reportage about life at the school. She interviewed many St. Paul's alumni, mostly black men who had attended when it was still an all-male school, but she ran into a problem with her subjects. "People talked to me for hours," she explained to Rosemary L. Bray for the *New York Times Book Review* (March 31, 1991). "They told me all these things—their concerns about adolescence, about race and class—but they didn't want to see them between the pages of a book. The truth was I found I couldn't get down and dirty with anybody else's story but my own."

Cary's intention in writing *Black Ice*, as she told Trescott, was to explore African-American identity somewhat the way the abolitionist Frederick Douglass and the journalist and civil rights leader Ida B. Wells had in their works. "I did write it to be a part of a tradition that starts with the slave narratives," she said. "Who am I as a black American in America? There's that question." At the same time, she was aware that some might question the legitimacy of a comparison of her experience with racism at St. Paul's with those of slaves and ex-slaves who had led overwhelmingly difficult lives. "Sometimes I feel people are saying 'if it is not overt, then it is not bad,'" she told Trescott. "It is not true. That's very important for our generation. Slowly, slowly you can lose belief in yourself until you are paralyzed and you can't do it." Cary had performed well at St. Paul's, but she had also experienced a crisis of identity. In her memoir she described the pain of failing calculus, feeling perpetually out of place, and, most harrowing, being the victim of date rape. Although for a while she had even stolen from dorm rooms, she had never let down her guard around others and had never stopped playing the role of defiant overachiever. "I have been busy doing this little job, getting these little grades," she recalled to Trescott, "trying to be politically correct. But I have been so afraid. I have been holding myself, jacked up against the wall."

The title of her memoir may be a reference to Cary's veneer of aloofness, according to Phillip Lopate, who, in the *New York Times Book Review* (March 31, 1991), wrote that *Black Ice* is like "the icy self-control demanded by the situation of being a token or model minority student, and the anger it generated underneath. A price was exacted, the author seems to be saying . . . for the cool poise she needed to armor herself with as a teen-ager to get through the heaven of St. Paul's." While Lopate opined that the scope of the book "might be too slight to justify all the ambition [Cary] was bringing to bear on it," he also wrote, "*Black Ice* is an extraordinarily honest, lively and appealing book. The author expresses her desire to enter 'that unruly conversation' of black narratives that inspired her, and this she certainly has accomplished, weighing in with a wry, reflective, unpreachy voice all her own." Marcus Mabry, an African-American critic who attended a primarily white prep school, felt that Cary had failed to illuminate her experience of the racial dynamics at St. Paul's. In an assessment of *Black Ice* for *Newsweek* (June 24, 1991), he wrote, "She fails to develop her racial-identity crisis, her fear of becoming an Oreo (black on the outside, white on the inside)," and concluded, "What could be an extremely compelling memoir about the burden of race on adolescence stops short, leaving racial-identity issues boiling just below the surface." In *Journal of Reading* (March 1993), Susan Murphy and Joyce Graham came to the opposite conclusion about *Black Ice*: "This book is well written and full of honest anger and forthright accounts of what it means to be adolescent, to be Black in a predominantly White school environment, and to live within limited economic means in an affluent society," they wrote.

In 1992 Cary was awarded an honorary doctoral degree from Colby College, in Waterville, Maine. From 1993 to 1994 she worked as a contributing editor for *Newsweek*. Her first book-length work of fiction, *The Price of a Child*, an historical novel that takes place mainly in 1850s Philadelphia, was published in 1995. Its main character is Ginnie Pryor, a Virginia plantation slave whose master, Jackson Pryor, is the father of two of her three children. After Jackson is appointed ambassador to Nicaragua, he decides he must take Ginnie with him but that her youngest child, Bennie, must stay behind. When the two adults and the other two children stop in Philadelphia, where a ferry is to take them to New York, a group of men from the Vigilance Committee of Philadelphia help Ginnie and the children escape. (Before leaving Virginia she had sent a message to the Underground Railroad.) A well-connected African-American family, the Quicks, keep Ginnie and her children safe as Ginnie tries to adjust to her newfound "freedom." Although she is plagued by thoughts of the child she left behind and the trials associated with hiding from the law, Ginnie elects to put herself at further risk by speaking out at antislavery meetings throughout the North. This activity eventually leads to a greater danger that significantly affects her life.

"Even though the methods of memoir draw ever closer to those of the novel," Jonathan Yardley wrote in his review of *The Price of a Child* for the *Washington Post Book World* (May 31, 1995), "there is still a considerable distance between them—an imaginative leap, if you will—and Cary has not entirely crossed it." But Yardley agreed with other critics that Cary had nevertheless created a stirring portrait of a strong black woman from an era in which great strength was required. "She has created a believable heroine . . . and placed her in a time and place that have the feeling of reality; she faces great issues on an intimate level and deals with them in a convincing fashion." Fernanda Eberstadt's praise for the novel was less qualified. "She is a powerful storyteller," Eberstadt wrote for the *New York Times Book Review* (June 18, 1995), "frankly sensual, mortally funny, gifted with an ear for the pounce and ragged inconsequentiality of real speech and an eye for the shifts and subterfuges by which ordinary people get by. With *The Price of a Child*, Lorene Cary has produced a generous, sardonic, full-blooded work of fiction."

In 1995 Cary became a lecturer in the Department of English at the University of Pennsylvania and was awarded a Pew Fellowship in the Arts. In 1996 she won the Shirley Chisholm Award in the Humanities from the Philadelphia Congress of the National Congress of Black Women and was awarded an honorary doctor of letters degree by Keene State College, in Keene, New Hampshire. She founded the Art Sanctuary Community Lecture and Performance Series in Philadelphia in 1998, the same year in which her next book, *Pride*, was published. That novel is told from the points of view of four middle-aged black women, each of whom narrates her own story. Roz is married to a philandering politician, Hiram, and is recovering from breast cancer. Rather than join a support group, she vents her frustrations at a shooting range. Tam is a beautiful academic who has recently failed to gain tenure at her university. Arneatha is a widowed Episcopal priest who has never recovered from her husband's death. Audrey is a recovering alcoholic. *Pride* churns with plots and subplots, including the revelation of an affair between Tam and Hiram and an incident involving Roz's gun after she leaves it in Audrey's brother's car. Michael Rosner, reviewing *Pride* for the *New York Times Book Review* (March 22, 1998), called it "an up-to-the-moment morality tale about the dangers of compromising to get what you want," but felt that the numerous plot twists undermined the story and "begin to feel mass-produced." In *Emerge* (March 1998) Kierno Mayo applauded Cary's rendering of the relationships between her characters. "Cary makes their bond stronger and more substantive than many authors have done in contemporary Black women's literature," Mayo wrote. Nancy Pearl, in *Library Journal* (February 1, 1998), by contrast, wrote, "Calling a book 'commercial' doesn't mean it needs to have flat characters, hackneyed writing, and an uninteresting plot. Cary's novel, which exhibits all these traits, is simply bad commercial fiction and is not recommended."

Cary and her husband R. C. Smith, a former magazine editor, have been married since 1983. The couple, who lives in Philadelphia, have two daughters, Laura and Zoë. In 1999 Cary received the American Red Cross Spectrum Rising Star Award for community service. She has lectured throughout the U.S., at such schools as Rutgers University, Harvard University, Bryn Mawr College, and Case Western Reserve. Cary serves on the usage panel of the *American Heritage Dictionary* and the board of the Union Benevolent Association. She is a member of PEN and the Authors Guild and continues to teach English at the University of Pennsylvania.

—P. G. H.

SUGGESTED READING: *Emerge* p60 Mar. 1998; *Journal of Reading* p504+ Mar. 1993; *Library Journal* p110 Feb. 1, 1998; *New York Times Book Review* p7 Mar. 31, 1991, with photo, p12 June 18, 1995, p19 Mar. 22, 1998; *Newsweek* p65 June 24, 1991, with photo; *Washington Post* C p1 Apr. 25, 1991, with photos; *Washington Post Book World* B p2 May 31, 1995

SELECTED BOOKS: memoir—*Black Ice*, 1991; novels—*Price of a Child*, 1995; *Pride*, 1998

Cha, Louis

Feb. 6, 1924– Novelist; publisher

Louis Cha, a novelist and retired Hong Kong newspaper publisher, is better known to millions of Chinese readers by his pen name, Jin Yong. From 1955 to 1972 Cha wrote martial-arts novels, which were first published in serial form in newspapers. He created heroes and heroines who use their skills to battle corrupt rulers and defend their countrymen against enemy invaders. Although martial-arts fiction has not been given serious attention in Western countries, many critics trace the genre back thousands of years to the "knight errant" tradition in Chinese literature. In 1972 Cha stopped writing novels to devote more time to his newspaper, the *Ming Pao Daily News*, which began as a voice of opposition to China's government and has since evolved into a powerful publishing conglomerate. Cha's work enjoyed a revival during the 1980s, thanks to the lifting of bans on the publication of his novels in Taiwan and mainland China. Millions of readers became avid fans, and film and television adaptations of his stories increased his popularity. In the last several years, Cha has been introduced to English-speaking audiences with the translations of *Fox Volant of the Snowy Mountain* and *The Deer and the Cauldron* trilogy.

The descendant of scholars and the son of a wealthy banker, Louis Cha was born on February 6, 1924 in the town of Haining, in the Chinese province of Zhejiang. "We had a huge library in our

Reuters NewMedia Inc./Corbis

home and from a very young age I was in the habit of reading," Cha recalled to Kate Whitehead, a writer for the Hong Kong *South China Morning Post* (March 3, 2001). "My mother and father began teaching me simple Chinese characters when I was three, and at eight I was able to read by myself. I used to love reading novels, the Chinese classics and translations of foreign books."

In the 1930s Japan invaded China, occupying much of the country until 1945. "They were hard times," Cha recalled to Whitehead. "We didn't have enough food or clothing. Every day in class we could hear bombs going off in the distance. The cannons roared from morning to evening. Shelters were dug in the side of the mountain where we hid. The Japanese eventually occupied our town and took over our school." Many of Cha's classmates enlisted in the Chinese army to fight the Japanese. Believing that he was too physically weak to fight, Cha decided to enroll in a university to study diplomacy. In their article for the *South China Morning Post* (November 22, 1997), Winnie Chung and Elisabeth Tacey wrote that, against his parents wishes, Cha hitchhiked 3,200 kilometers to attend a university in Chunking, in 1941. He first studied at the Faculty of Foreign Languages of Chunking Central University. "I wasn't a very obedient student," he told Chung and Tacey, adding that he was expelled at least three times in eight years.

After the end of World War II, Cha enrolled in the Faculty of Law of Dongwu University, majoring in international law. After graduation he pursued other interests, telling Whitehead, "I was enthusiastic about literature, so I became a journalist and novelist." He found work as a translator and copy editor for the *Ta Kung Pao*, a pro-communist newspaper in China. Like many Chinese youth of his generation, Cha was sympathetic to the goals of Chinese Communists. In 1948 the newspaper sent him to Hong Kong, then a British colony, to open an office there. After the Communist forces of Mao Tse-Tung took control of China, in 1949, Cha remained in Hong Kong.

In addition to news, the *Ta Kung Pao* published adventure and martial-arts serials that were popular with readers. After the newspaper's regular serialist quit, in 1955, the editor asked Cha to fill in. Cha agreed, publishing the first chapter of what eventually became his first novel, translated as *Book and Sword* (1955). It was a hit with readers, and Cha began to write serials for the newspaper on a full-time basis. His next few novels were also successful with both readers and critics. By 1959 Cha had earned enough royalties to co-found, with Shen Baoxin, the Chinese-language daily newspaper, *Ming Pao Daily News*, in Hong Kong. Cha's sympathies for the Communist government had been eroded by its ongoing persecution of intellectuals. "I was disillusioned with the Communists distorting the truth," he explained to John Pomfret for the *Associated Press* (July 6, 1989). "So I quit and started my own newspaper."

Cha began to write serials under a pseudonym, Jin Yong, for his own newspaper. According to Sheila Melvin, a writer for the *Wall Street Journal* (March 9, 2000), between 1955 and 1972 Cha wrote 14 serial novels, each numbering hundreds of pages. "My novels are full of stories and very exciting developments," Cha explained to Simon Elegant for the *Far Eastern Economic Review* (September 5, 1996). "People like adventures, they like to read adventure stories."

In his article for *Sinorama* (December 12, 1998, on-line), Teng Sue-Feng noted that Chinese martial-arts literature dates back more than 2,000 years. "In ancient Chinese documents, the terms *xia* (knight) and *youxia* (wandering knight or knight errant) are seen very often," Teng wrote. "*Xia* first appeared in the Warring States' era [circa 420–200 B.C.]" He continued, "In his *Historical Records* [circa 1st century B.C.], the Western Han dynasty historian Sima Qian included a chapter in which he gave descriptions of Chinese knights errant and assassins: 'While the lives they lead may be immoral, they are true to their word, steadfast in their goals, and faithful to their promises. They are willing to put their lives on the line and will brave danger to save others.'"

Martial-arts literature in China nearly vanished, in 1911, with the overthrow of the Qing dynasty by revolutionary forces led by Sun Yat-Sen, who desired a democratic government and the modernization of the country. China's intellectuals found fault with traditional Chinese literature. "So they knocked down everything. They thought a modern and strong China should copy the Western countries," Cha explained to Elegant. "So they copied everything, even the style of literature." According to Teng, when the Communists took over China, in 1949, they immediately banned all martial-arts stories as "spiritual pollution." Many contemporary literary critics credit Cha with resurrecting the knight errant tradition and generally revivifying the martial-arts genre. Critics note in particular his inventive use of language. A writer for the Singapore *Straits Times* (November 23, 1997) observed that Cha "combined the writing techniques and expressions of Western literature with the traditional Chinese storytelling style. . . . Phrases from classical poetry added flavour to the text."

All of Cha's novels are set in China's distant past and follow a similar narrative: A hero, skilled in the traditional Chinese martial art known as kung fu, battles corrupt rulers and foreign invaders. Cha's fourth novel, translated as *The Condor Heroes*, follows the adventures of Guo Jing, a slow-witted swordsman who—à la Forrest Gump—is guided by honesty and generosity to fight for his country. "The author portrays a swordplay world in which the good and the bad are sharply contrasted," Zhu Hong wrote in the Singapore *Straits Times* (February 6, 1996). "As such, readers either love or hate a character. In the novel, the good are rewarded, the bad are punished and the lovers are united in marriage." Zhu described Guo as "honest and kind," observing that, while lacking ambition, "he is willing to assume the responsibility of upholding justice and defending his country any time." Zhu was also impressed with the "pretty and vivacious" heroine, Huang Rong, who "serves as a foil to Guo." He concluded that the "two perfect protagonists, complemented by an exciting plot and a number of distinctive characters, make up this enchanting novel."

In her article for the *New York Times* (January 3, 1989), Sheryl WuDunn argued that Cha "uses the martial arts as a literary device to express deeper ramifications of power and corruption. His heroic riders may somersault off horses, their spears may pierce an evil monk or the neck of a flying wild goose. But more important, they are entwined in relationships of love, friendship and familial piety, and their tales do not always end happily." Cha's later novels have a political edge, often attacking the Communist leadership of mainland China. A writer for the *Economist* (January 30, 1999) mentioned Cha's caricature of China's longtime Communist dictator, Mao Tse-Tung, in *Xiao Ao Jiang Hu* (*The Smiling and Proud Wanderer*). In this novel, Mao becomes a "deranged effeminate kung fu master," his slogans coming "straight from the mouths of grotesque characters hungry only for power and blood."

Cha's last novel, translated as *The Deer and the Cauldron* (1972), was another thinly veiled attack on Mao. In portraying an emperor who wants to rule all of China and whose power is facilitated by a cult of personality and fanatical devotion, Cha told WuDunn that he wanted to attack what he described as the "worship of the individual."

In 1972 Cha stopped writing martial-arts novels, but subsequent events brought his novels to millions of new readers. In 1979, in Taiwan—where the democratic opposition to the military government was gaining momentum—the ban on Cha's work was lifted. In 1981 the serialized novels were published for the first time in book form, and in 1984 the changing political climate in China allowed the publication of Cha's work there. (As many as 40 million illegal copies of his novels had been circulating underground in the country for many years.) Speaking to Simon Elegant, Cha noted that the Chinese government "accused me of being responsible for the lack of paper to print textbooks on." The novels have been adapted into movies and television shows in China and, in 2001, Chinese artists created the first kung fu–style Peking opera. Cha has inspired a devoted following, especially among Chinese youth, and he frequently receives requests to publish more martial-arts novels.

While writing novels, Cha was cultivating a loyal readership and international respect for the *Ming Pao Daily News*. Under Cha's leadership, the newspaper published strong editorials condemning Communist China and Mao Tse-Tung. In the late 1960s, the newspaper's attacks against the regime intensified during Mao's Cultural Revolution, in which intellectuals were persecuted and millions of Chinese citizens died. According to John Pomfret, Cha frequently received death threats from communist organizations in Hong Kong. Several bombs were sent to the newspaper, but they never exploded. Cha was placed under police protection. "During the Cultural Revolution the leftists wanted to burn me alive," he recalled to Stephen Vines, a writer for the Manchester *Guardian* (January 28, 1989, on-line).

The *Ming Pao Daily News* toned down its attacks on the Chinese government in 1978, when Deng Xiaoping took control. Deng reduced Mao's power, tacitly acknowledging that Mao had made mistakes, and initiated a program of reforms, which Cha enthusiastically endorsed. In 1981 Cha returned to China for the first time in several decades and met with Deng, a fan of his novels. Cha became an adviser to the Chinese government. Despite Cha's support for Deng, his newspaper continued to give sympathetic attention to Chinese dissidents. Cha resigned his position as an adviser, in May 1989, after Deng declared martial law to suppress the pro-democracy students in Beijing. One month later, on Hong Kong television, Cha tearfully condemned the government's massacre of the students in Beijing's Tiananmen Square. "Who could have expected that the magnificent ideals would vanish into thin air in less than one month," he wrote in the *Ming Pao Daily News*, as quoted by Pomfret. "Is it that the encouragement we had and the belief we held in the past ten or more years are nothing but an illusion, nothing but a fond dream?" In 1996 Cha agreed to serve on a government-appointed committee that supervised the transfer of control of Hong Kong, from Britain to China, in 1997.

Over the decades, the *Ming Pao Daily News* evolved into one of Hong Kong's most successful newspapers. The wealth it generated allowed Cha to set up Ming Pao Enterprise, a publicly traded conglomerate that controls a gossip magazine, a monthly magazine, a publishing company, a travel agency, a printing company, a Singaporean newspaper, and other businesses. In 1992 Cha stepped down as chairman of Ming Pao Enterprise and began selling off his shares. In late 1995 he sold the company to Tiong Hiew King, a timber and publishing magnate. Tiong has made the company profitable and steered the *Ming Pao Daily News* toward supporting the Chinese government.

Cha's fiction was introduced to English-speaking audiences, in 1996, with the publication of *Fox Volant of the Snowy Mountain* by Hong Kong's Chinese University Press. (Jin Yong was credited as the author.) Set in 1781, the story follows three separate bands of warriors as they search for a metal casket containing a precious dagger. A monk summons the three groups to a secluded mountain estate, where they compete for ownership of the dagger. Reviewing the book for the Canadian Asian Studies Association Web site, Adrian Hsia acknowledged Jin's talent as a novelist, but noted the difficulty in translating such works into English. "The translator requires a high sense of balance in retaining original flavour without alienating or boring Western readers," he noted. "Although I find the dialogues and monological thoughts tend to be stilted or wooden in the translation, the fighting scenes are usually well rendered."

In 1997 Oxford University Press published the first volume of *The Deer and the Cauldron*; the second and third volumes were published in 2000 and 2001. This trilogy, the last of Cha's martial-arts writings, is widely considered to be his masterpiece. It took John Minford, who teaches at Hong Kong Polytechnic University, eight years to translate the work. "There were a lot of considerations on how to best translate the martial arts moves," Cha explained to Chung and Tacey. "It is more difficult to express it in English. In Chinese *wushu* [martial-arts], when you fight it is very elaborate and complicated. In the English version, I think they had to simplify it because it would not appeal to a Western audience."

The novel centers on a comic figure named Trinket (Wei Xiaobao), who serves under Emperor Kang XI as a eunuch. Trinket is an unusual figure in Cha's fiction: witty, irreverent, and unskilled in martial arts, he is more of an antihero than a hero. "I wanted to write something different," Cha recalled to Chung and Tacey. "All the other books were about heroes and heroines who were very good in kung fu. Wei does not know kung fu at all and survives by his wit." Trinket takes part in the resistance to the occupation of China by the Manchus, a group of Tartar invaders. The three volumes span 20 years, move from desert islands to frozen tundras, and are rich in historical incident and characters—including fighting monks, song girls, Cossacks, dissidents, and a one-armed Princess with lethal kung fu prowess. Although the publication of *The Deer and the Cauldron* trilogy was mostly ignored by reviewers, there are plans to translate more of Cha's novels into English.

Over the years several of Louis Cha's admirers have lobbied to have him named the first Chinese recipient of the Nobel Prize in literature. (In 2000 this honor went to the writer Gao Xingjian, who was born in China but has since become a French citizen and now writes primarily in French.) In 1994 Cha was named an honorary professor at Beijing University. He is also an honorary fellow at St. Antony's College and the Wynflete Fellow at Magdalen College, both part of Oxford University. Cha currently writes nonfiction books on Chinese history and Buddhism.

Louis Cha has been married three times. He has two grown daughters and divides his time between homes in Hong Kong and mainland China.

—D. C.

SUGGESTED READING: *Associated Press* (on-line) July 6, 1989; Canadian Asian Studies Association Web site; *Economist* (on-line) Jan. 30, 1999; *Far Eastern Economic Review* p64+ Sept. 7, 1995, p38+ Sept. 5, 1996, with photos, p36+ Dec. 2, 1999, with photos; *Manchester Guardian* (on-line) Jan. 28, 1989; *New York Times* C p13 Jan. 3, 1989, with photo; *Sinorama* (on-line) Dec. 12, 1998; *South China Morning Post* p2+ Mar. 24, 1996, p9+ Nov. 22, 1997, Mar. 3, 2001; Singapore *Straits Times* p6 Feb. 6, 1996, p2 Nov. 23, 1997, p4 Feb. 21, 2000; *Wall Street Journal* A p24 Mar. 9, 2000

SELECTED BOOKS IN ENGLISH TRANSLATION: *Fox Volant of The Snowy Mountain*, 1996; *The Deer and the Cauldron*, 1997; *The Deer and the Cauldron: The Second Book*, 2000; *The Deer and the Cauldron: The Third Book*, 2001

Chang, Ta-chun

1957– Novelist and short-story writer

Chang Ta-chun is one of Taiwan's most popular literary figures. Although he is not well known outside of his native country, Chang has published many short stories and novels in the last 25 years. In 2000 his work gained attention with the English translation of two short novels, *My Kid Sister* and *Wild Child*, compiled in the book, *Wild Kids: Two Novels about Growing Up*. Both novels borrow from pop culture and traditional Chinese literature and paint a grim portrait of life for young people in contemporary Taiwan. Many reviewers lauded *Wild Kids* and expressed the hope that more of Chang's fiction will be translated into English.

Chang Ta-chun was born in 1957 in Taiwan. He attended Fu Jen Catholic University, in Taipei, receiving undergraduate and graduate degrees in Chinese literature. In his introduction to *Wild Kids: Two Novels About Growing Up* (2000), Chang's translator, Michael Berry, noted that Chang has been influenced by the Nobel prize-winning Colombian writer Gabriel García Márquez and the popular Italian writer Umberto Eco. In 1976 Chang received critical acclaim for his first published short story, *Xuandang* (*Suspended*). After completing two years of compulsory service in Taiwan's military, he became a reporter and editor for the *China Times*, one of Taiwan's leading newspapers. He later became a lecturer at Fu Jen Catholic University.

Chang's writing career took off during the 1980s. He published his first book, the short-story collection *Birds of a Feather*, in 1980. He proved to be a versatile writer; over the next two decades he produced short stories, historical essays, and political novels, as well as science-fiction tales and a martial-arts novel. His second short-story collection, *Gongyu daoyou* (1986, *Apartment Building Tour Guide*), established his reputation for inventiveness and dexterity. Berry described the title story as "an intricately woven portrait of how a group of seemingly alienated and disconnected urbanites living in an apartment complex in contemporary Taipei unknowingly affect one another's lives."

Chang Ta-chun
Courtesy of Columbia University Press

According to the literary critic and writer Yang Chao, as quoted by Berry, with this collection, "Chang Ta-chun ceased to cover up his impatience with traditional narrative conventions," and, in so doing, set off on a fruitful linguistic and literary journey.

Many critics were impressed with Chang's short-story collection, *Sixi yougo* (1988, *Lucky Worries About His Country*.) One of the stories, *Jiangjun bei* (*The General's Monument*), about a time-traveling general, was published right before China's lifting of the decades-old martial law in Taiwan. Berry wrote that the story "not only struck a sensitive chord in readers but also foreshadowed Chang's later politically and current event–inspired literary experiments."

One of Chang's most experimental works, *Da shouhuang jia* (*The Grand Liar*), grew out of Chang's reporting for the *China Times*. Beginning in 1988, Chang incorporated each morning's news into the novel he was writing; in turn, that segment of the novel was then published in the evening edition of the newspaper. Berry described the resulting work as "part hard-boiled detective fiction, part political satire, part fact, part fiction," and noted that this unusual format "served to challenge and deconstruct traditional narrative and literary structures."

In 1992 Chang began publishing novels under the pseudonym Datou Chun ("Big Head Spring"). In *Shaonian Datou Chun de shenghuo zhouji* (*The Weekly Journal of Young Big Head Spring*), Big Head Spring is a middle-school student who records the events of his life in a journal in a straightforward, sometimes startling style. Berry cites the literary critic Pang-yuan Chi marveling at Chang's new direction: "[His] speed in inventing new writing tactics can be compared with America's current speed at which it produces high-tech products." *The Weekly Journal of Young Big Head Spring* became immensely popular in Taiwan, remaining on best-seller lists for nearly a year, and prompted two more Big Head Spring novels, *My Kid Sister* (1993) and *Wild Child* (1996).

In 1996, the year of the first free presidential elections in Taiwan, Chang published a satirical novel, *Sahuang de xintu* (*Disciples of the Liar*), which was marketed as the Taiwanese version of Salman Rushdie's highly controversial *The Satanic Verses* (1988). Like Rushdie, Chang based his fiction on actual political events; the novel is a journey into the mind of Li Zhengnan, clearly based on Lee Teng-hui, then the president of Taiwan.

Michael Berry deserves credit for bringing Chang to international attention. A doctoral student of Chinese literature at Columbia University, in New York City, Berry discovered Chang's work while studying in Taiwan, in 1996. In 2000 Columbia University Press published Berry's translations of *My Kid Sister* and *Wild Child* as *Wild Kids: Two Novels About Growing Up*. In *My Kid Sister*, Big Head Spring, now in his late twenties, recalls his 1980s childhood, from the birth of his younger sister to her abortion, at the age of 19. What emerges from his disjointed narrative is a sense of a deep connection between brother and sister, forged against the backdrop of his parents' troubled, violent marriage. *Wild Child* follows Big Head Spring during his teenage years, as he drops out of school, explores Taipei's underworld, and becomes involved with gangsters. In a review for *World Literature Today* (Winter 2001), Sylvia Li-Chun Lin described *My Kid Sister* as a "haunting chronicle of a broken family and its offspring." Arguing that, "on a symbolic level, the narrator and his kid sister are two sides of the same person," Lin noted that "the maladies affecting the characters in the novel are both regional and universal: the specific social and historical conditions of Taiwan, and the universal themes of family and youth." About *Wild Child*, Lin wrote that "what makes the novel so enjoyable and engaging are the witty, sarcastic, and sometimes innocent narrator, whose observations on life are refreshing, and the author's ability to create memorable characters with fantastic backgrounds." In the *New York Times Book Review* (September 17, 2000), Maureen McLane observed that the "occasionally wisecracking tone [of *My Kid Sister*] does not diminish the delicacy of [the brother and sister] relationship, and story's end is stunningly, perfectly abrupt." McLane praised *Wild Child* as "brutal, pointedly anesthetizing, jaggedly written and willfully disorienting" and noted that it is "heavily and knowingly indebted to gangster movies and pop culture."

In recent years, Chang Ta-chun has become a cultural icon in Taiwan. He hosted and produced two television shows during the 1990s. In 1999 *My Kid Sister* was adapted into a stage production in

Taipei, and *Wild Child* was made into a movie for Taiwanese television.

Many of Chang's stories have been translated into English for journals and anthologies of Chinese literature, including "Birds of a Feather" (1983),"Speaker of the Aside" (1986), "The Wall" (1987), "The General's Monument" (1991), "Lucky Worries About His Country" (1991), "Alley 116, Liaoning Street (1992)", and "Ximi in the Metropolis (1999)".

Chang Ta-chun is married to Yeh Mei-yau, an editor at China Times Publishing. The couple has two children and resides in Taipei, Taiwan.

—D. C.

SUGGESTED READING: *Chronicle of Higher Education* A p22+ Sep. 8, 2000; *New York Times Book Review* p7 Sep. 17, 2000; *World Literature Today* p101 Winter 2001

SELECTED WORKS IN ENGLISH TRANSLATION: novels—*Wild Kids: Two Novels About Growing Up*, 2000; as contributor—"Birds of a Feather" in *Unbroken Chain: An Anthology of Taiwan Fiction Since 1926*, 1983; "The General's Monument" in *Worlds of Modern Chinese Fiction*, 1991; "Lucky Worries About Growing Up" in *Columbia Anthology of Modern Chinese Literature*, 1995; "Ximi in the Metropolis" in *A Place of One's Own: Stories of Self in China, Taiwan, Hong Kong, and Singapore*, 1999

Marion Ettlinger/Courtesy of Farrar, Straus and Giroux

Chávez, Denise

Aug. 15, 1948– Novelist; playwright; short-story writer

During her literary career Denise Chávez has written plays, novels, short stories, and essays. The publication of her short-story collection, *The Last of the Menu Girls* (1986), and two novels, *Face of an Angel* (1994) and *Loving Pedro Infante* (2001), brought her critical acclaim and established her as a definitive voice on the Chicana literary scene. Chávez draws from many sources, including her Mexican-American heritage, her three decades of experience as a waitress, her family's storytelling tradition, and her interest in acting and performance. "Writing for me is a healing, therapeutic, invigorating, sensuous manifestation of the energy that comes to you from the world, from everything that's alive," she explained to William Clark for *Publishers Weekly* (August 15, 1994). "Everything has a voice and you just have to listen as closely as you can. That's what so exciting—a character comes to you and you can't write fast enough because the character is speaking through you. It's a divine moment."

Denise Chávez was born on August 15, 1948 in Las Cruces, New Mexico. Her father, Ernesto, was a lawyer who struggled to overcome alcoholism; her mother, Delfina, helped support the family by teaching. During her childhood Chávez and her parents spent summers with their extended family in Redford, a small town in western Texas. She picked up the art of storytelling from these gatherings. "The untold stories were always the ones that, as kids, we found the most interesting," Chávez told Julio Moran for the *Los Angeles Times* (November 9, 1994). "Like the one about why one of my uncles had only half an ear. The story was that he'd been in a terrible accident, but we knew there was more to it. Back then people seemed to live life more deeply."

Recalling her childhood, Chávez told Moran that she "had no expectations of life. My dream was to work at the Dairy Queen." She loved reading and, at age eight, received a diary for a Christmas present. The diary became an important refuge for Chávez two years later when her parents divorced. "I began recording everything—how I felt hurt and unloved," she told William Porter for the *Phoenix Gazette* (September 6, 1994). "It was a private space. It became very sacred, a sacrament." Chávez also began writing poetry and short stories.

Chávez enrolled in New Mexico State University, in Las Cruces. She began writing plays and her first effort, *The Wait*, won the university's best play award, in 1970. She graduated in 1971 with a drama degree and then earned a master of fine arts degree from Trinity College, in San Antonio, Texas, in 1974. In 1982 she received a master's degree in creative writing from the University of New Mexico, in Albuquerque.

After a brief career as an actress, Chávez began teaching English and theater at the Northern New Mexico Community College, in Espanola, in 1975. She later taught at the American School of Paris (1975–1977), New Mexico State University (1988–1991), the University of Houston, in Texas (1988–1991), and briefly at the College of Sante Fe.

Since the early 1970s Chávez has written over 20 plays, many of which were produced in New Mexico, including *The Flying Tortilla Man* (1975), *The Adobe Rabbit* (1979), *How Junior Got Throwed in the Joint* (1981), and *Francis!* (1983). Her drama *Plaza* (1984) was staged in Edinburgh, Scotland, and at the Public Theater's Festival Latino, in New York City. Chávez also acted and toured nationally in her one-act play, *Women in the State of Grace* (1989), which features nine Latina characters, ranging in age from seven to 78.

In 1977 Chávez's work was published in two collections, *An Anthology of Southwestern Literature* and *An Anthology: The Indian Rio Grande*. In 1980 she edited her first book, *Life Is a Two-Way Street*, a poetry anthology.

Chávez received critical acclaim for her first short-story collection, *The Last of the Menu Girls* (1986). All of the stories revolve around the path to womanhood of 17-year-old Rocío Esquibel. In the title story, Rocío delivers menus to hospital patients, including an illegal alien injured during a barroom fight, a dietician, and a beautiful, embittered woman. In another story Rocío decides to become a writer, with her environment and experiences providing ample source material. "The stories are of two types: lyrical meditations on everyday objects and montages of dialogue that swiftly reveal character," Beverly Lyon Clark observed in the *New York Times Book Review* (October 12, 1986). "The former strain too hard for lyricism. The latter, though, show Ms. Chávez's strengths in dialogue and in juxtaposing evocative scenes." Clark concluded that Chávez showed considerable promise as a writer. Chávez told Porter that rereading *The Last of the Menu Girls* was like "looking at an old pair of jeans. You love them. The knees pooch out the way you want, the butt is loose, the waist is nice. But you move on." The title story won New Mexico State University's Steele Jones Fiction Award, and the book won the Puerto del Sol Fiction Award, both in 1986. In 1990 Chávez adapted the title story into a play.

In 1994 Chávez published her first novel, *Face of an Angel*, an epic saga about a Mexican-American family that she had been developing for years. "For the first four years I was really moving around in the book," Chávez explained to Porter. "I didn't start chronologically. I saw it as a series of interconnecting stories." When she finished, the manuscript was 1,200 pages. Working with her editor, Chávez spent the next few years honing the story into its final shape—456 pages. Borrowing from her experiences as a waitress, Chávez created the character of Soveida Dosamantes. At 15, Soveida takes a summer job at a restaurant in Agua Oscura, New Mexico, and stays for the next 30 years, gradually rising from bus girl to head waitress. The novel includes excerpts from Soveida's diary, which she wrote at age 12, and a manual she put together for the restaurant's other waitresses on etiquette and philosophy, *The Book of Service*. Through Soveida's eyes, Chávez offers sketches of the Dosamantes family, their dedicated maid, and the patrons and workers at the restaurant. "What unifies these fragments is the vision that even uneducated people can fulfill themselves through loyalty, sacrifice and love," Eileen Pollack observed in the *Washington Post* (December 26, 1994). "Even as Soveida comes to recognize the forces that have kept Chicana women powerless and poor, even as she urges them to break their thrall to their no-account men, she pleads with them not to think their lives worthless or abandon the values they've been taught by the church." Pollack had mixed feelings about *Face of an Angel*, writing that it "is a slow read because it lacks plot. Things happen, but without much cause or suspense. People die, but we don't know them well enough to care." She noted an exceptional scene—the passing of Oralia, the Dosamantes's maid. "[It] is described with such tenderness that the scene becomes uplifting; the people whom she has served all her life are now serving her, massaging her cold feet and stick-thin legs with warm oil, brewing tea from her garden," she writes. Chávez explained to William Clark that "character has always been more important to me than plot," adding that her "characters just come out, and they're composites of pieces of my own life, others' lives and inventions." Reviewing *Face of an Angel* for the *Los Angeles Times* (November 24, 1994), Emily Drabanski wrote that "Chávez pays tribute to everyday people—those who spend their lives serving others—the cooks, janitors, waitresses and maids. While they might live from paycheck to paycheck, Chávez recognizes that they live passionate, multidimensional lives as well, full of big drama, tragedy and joy." *Face of an Angel* won the Premio Axtlan Award and the American Book Award in 1995. That year, Chávez was honored with the Mesilla Valley Writer of the Year Award and the New Mexico Governor's Award in literature.

In Chávez's next novel, *Loving Pedro Infante* (2001), two female friends, Tere and Irma, spend their weekends looking for love at the La Tempestad Lounge, in Cabritoville, New Mexico. Both women are in their 30s and idolize Pedro Infante, the Mexican film actor who died in a plane crash in 1957; Tere is the secretary of the Pedro Infante Fan Club. For the two lovelorn women, Pedro Infante represents the ideal man—handsome, charming, adventurous, heroic—his films even providing practical advice for living. "I loved [Infante] when I was growing up," Chávez recalled to Bill Vourvoulias, a reporter for *Newsday* (May 27, 2001).

"He was so handsome. My mom and aunt would take me to see his movies at El Colon theater in El Paso [Texas]. . . . The hopes and the dreams of our culture were up on that screen." "There are few writers with as warm and generous a heart as Denise Chávez," Carolyn See wrote in the *Washington Post Book World* (April 6, 2001). "All of the characters in *Loving Pedro Infante*—even small-minded superstitious old bats—are treated with affection and respect. . . . All this manufactured heartbreak is treated as a comedy but in the gentlest possible way, without a trace of mean-spiritedness." In the *New York Times Book Review* (May 13, 2001), Maggie Galehouse wrote that in "hyperspecific and tireless detail, Chávez records the food, the hang-ups, the turn-ons and worldview of a thriving border culture." Galehouse, however, observed that this "zoom-lens approach can have its drawbacks: when the protagonist who makes sense of all the details falters, the narrative stumbles too. Tere begins to unravel about two-thirds of the way into the story when Lucio [her lover] makes moves to leave her. A series of subplots follows; as Tere wanders aimlessly through them, the reader has no choice but to follow." Despite these criticisms, she concluded that the "novel does come together with an ending that resists high drama and remains true to its protagonist's willful and slow-to-change nature."

Chávez has also published *The Woman Who Knew the Language of Animals* (1992), a children's book, and contributed essays to *Writing Down the River: Into the Heart of the Grand Canyon* (1998). Her next novel will be about a border guard.

Chávez is married to Daniel Zolinsky, a photographer and sculptor. They live in her hometown of Las Cruces, New Mexico, 40 miles from the Mexican border.

—D. C.

SUGGESTED READING: *Boston Globe* p61 Sep. 30, 1994, with photos; *Houston Chronicle* p16 May 6, 2001, with photos; *Los Angeles Times* E p1 Nov. 9, 1994, with photos, p6 Nov. 24, 1994; *Newsday* B p11 May 27, 2001; *New York Times Book Review* p28 Oct. 12, 1986, p17 May 13, 2001; *Phoenix Gazette* D p1 Sep. 6, 1994, with photo; *Publishers Weekly* p77+ Aug. 15, 1994, with photo; *Washington Post Book World* B p2 Dec. 24, 1994, C p6 Apr. 6, 2001

SELECTED BOOKS: novels—*Face of an Angel*, 1994; *Loving Pedro Infante*, 2001; short-story collections—*The Last of the Menu Girls*, 1986; juvenile literature—*The Woman Who Knew the Language of Animals*; as editor—*Life is a Two-Way Street*, 1980

SELECTED PLAYS: *The Wait*, 1970; *Elevators*, 1972; *The Flying Tortilla Man*, 1975; *The Mask of November*, 1977; *The Adobe Rabbit*, 1979; *Nacimiento*, 1979; *Sante Fe Charm*, 1980; *Si, hay posada*, 1980; *El santero de Cordova*, 1981; *How Junior Got Throwed in the Joint*, 1981; *The Green Madonna*, 1982; *El mas pequeno de mis hijos*, 1983; *Francis!*, 1983; *La morenita*, 1983; *Plaza*, 1984; *Plague-Time*, 1985; *Novena narrativas*, 1986; *Language of Vision*, 1987; *The Step*, 1987; *Women in the State of Grace*, 1989; *The Last of the Menu Girls*, 1990

Cheever, Benjamin

May 4, 1948– Novelist

For Benjamin Cheever, success as a writer came gradually. After spending two decades as a reporter and editor, Cheever received critical acclaim for his humorous novels, which borrowed from many of his personal experiences. His three novels, *The Plagiarist* (1992), *The Partisan* (1994), and *Famous After Death* (1999), explore father-and-son relationships, individualism, the world of publishing, romance, and society's obsession with celebrity. His most recent work, the non-fiction *Selling Ben Cheever: Back to Square One in a Service Economy, A Personal Odyssey* (2001), examines the sales world through his own experiences as a car salesman, bookstore clerk, and coffee-house worker, among others. "It's easy to write badly," Cheever explained in an interview with *World Authors* on June 3, 2000. "I want to write well. I think this is often a struggle. I'm like many writers: writing is what I hate most in the world; it's also the thing I value most highly in myself."

Benjamin Cheever submitted the following statement to World Authors 1995–2000: "My father was a successful writer. He was also a charming man. I wanted to be a writer too. There was no evidence that I could succeed. I was a good boy, but apparently a dumb one. I flunked the Second Grade. Plus, I was an outcast. I combined the social graces of a nerd with the intellect of a football star.

"I did love books. My parents read me Milne. My father used to hold his nose in order to dramatize Eeyore's melancholy voice: 'And if Eeyore's back snapped suddenly, then we could all laugh. Ha, ha! Amusing in a quiet way,' said Eeyore, 'but not really helpful.' I read Dostoyevsky, Thoreau and Albee to myself. Reading books I was not an outcast, or rather I was an outcast among outcasts. I imagined that writing might be like flying, like hearing an urgent message from the dead. Like smelling the body of God. But how to get off the ground? It didn't seem like carpentry. It didn't seem to be something you could learn. You had to be chosen first.

Benjamin Cheever
Courtesy of Bloomsbury USA

"I went to Antioch college in the late 1960s, when the culture was spinning apart. I was lonely. I read books to assuage my solitude. This was a good idea. I also got married, which wasn't a good idea. When I graduated from college, I went to work for the *Rockland Journal-News* in Nyack, New York. I wasn't a talented reporter, but I enjoyed the job.

"I spent a certain amount of time every couple of days hunkered over a blank piece of paper. I kept a journal. I was always buying new pens, new typewriters. I figured that if I could just locate the correct instrument, all those beautiful words would come flowing out of me, and I'd be that precious thing: I'd be a writer.

"I tried everything. I'd meditate before writing. I even bought a tape recorder. I got myself drunk once and tried to tell a story to the tape recorder. The story went like this: 'I'm sitting alone at the kitchen table. I've got this tape recorder. I'm going to tell this tape recorder a story. The story of my life. The sad, sad story of my life. But first I think I'll have another drink.' I woke up the next day with a headache. And nothing else of value.

"One of my favorite poems was *To A Friend Whose Work Has Come To Nothing*. Yeats wrote it. 'And like a laughing string / Whereon mad fingers play / Amid a place of stone / Be secret and exult / Because of all things known / That is most difficult.'

"I left the newspaper in 1976 and went to work for the *Reader's Digest*.

"Weekends, and evenings, when I wasn't cutting the lawn, I was starting a short story. I liked the way they began. I hated the way they ended. When they ended. Most of the stories just ran out of steam. The ones I did finish, I sent out. I had them turned down by some excellent magazines. I figured this was because I had no talent. Besides which, I was still waiting to be tapped. I used to imagine the writers' bus coming up the street I lived on, the driver knocking at our door: 'Calling all writers! Any writers in there?'

"When my father died, I edited a book of his letters and was shocked to discover that he'd had some horrid times too. His first novel was soundly rejected. 'I am like a prisoner who is trying to escape from jail by the wrong route,' he wrote in his journal. 'For all one knows the door may stand open although I continue to dig a tunnel with a teaspoon.'

"That was when I stopped waiting for talent. Instead of thinking about writing a lot, and writing very little, I started to write a lot and think about it less.

"I quit the *Reader's Digest* in 1988. I published the book of letters and three novels. I cracked a lot of those magazines that used to turn me down. It hasn't been easy. But you work at it, like anything else. It turns out I had a decent idea of what writing would feel like. It's like hearing an urgent message from the dead, like smelling the body of God. It feels like flying."

Benjamin Cheever was born on May 4, 1948 in New York City. He is the son of John Cheever, the celebrated short-story writer and novelist. Cheever grew up in Scarborough and later in Ossining in New York. He attended Antioch College in Yellow Springs, Ohio, majoring in English. Like many college students during the late 1960s, he protested against the Vietnam War. "I went to my share of anti-war demonstrations and spent three days in jail in Cincinnati, Ohio. We blocked an induction center," he recalled to *World Authors*.

In 1988 Cheever edited a collection of his late father's voluminous correspondence that was published by Simon & Schuster that year as *The Letters of John Cheever*. In his editorial introduction to the book, Benjamin Cheever wrote, "This will not be a collection of letters in the conventional sense, but rather, I hope, a picture of the man as revealed through his correspondence. No significant episode in my father's life passed without being recounted in letters. He wrote between ten and thirty a week, and he wrote them under all sorts of circumstances." Benjamin continued, "My father was a man of massive and fundamental contradictions. He was an adulterer who wrote eloquently in praise of monogamy. He was a bisexual who detested any sign of sexual ambiguity." By including such controversial material, Benjamin wanted to give readers a true sense of his father's life. In an interview with T. M. Pasca, a writer for the *Wilson Library Bulletin* (March 1993), Benjamin said, "Despite his troubles, and he had many troubles, and despite his failings, and we all have failings, my father lived his own life. He had a brilliant, individual life." *The Letters of John Cheever* received favorable reviews. "This breezy, fast-paced correspondence will delight [John] Cheever's fans," Michael Edmonds wrote in the *Library Journal* (December 1988). "Though occasionally savage toward other writers, the Cheever revealed here is generally light-hearted, warm, and confident." Reviewers also praised Benjamin Cheever's editorial introduction. In the November 28, 1998 edition of the *New York Times*, John Gross declared that "Benjamin's reflections and reminiscences are, in fact, often more interesting than the letters themselves."

In 1992 Benjamin Cheever's first novel, *The Plagiarist*, was published to critical acclaim. The novel's protagonist, Arthur Prentice, is the son of Icarus South Prentice, a famous writer and alcoholic. Arthur toils away as an editor at the *American Reader* magazine, which, like *Reader's Digest*, reprints articles from other publications. Arthur seeks to escape his father's immense shadow and live his own life despite overwhelming pressures from society and his own family to conform . As Cheever said to Pasca, "I don't know if you can grow up without being an individual, but there is no doubt in my mind that in America today you are not supposed to be an individual. . . . What you are supposed to be is predictable." Both readers and reviewers noticed the similarities between Arthur's life and Cheever's background. In *Newsweek* (June 1, 1992) D. Gates wrote, "What keeps you reading *The Plagiarist* isn't gossip value but entertainment value: witty dialogue, memorable characters, mini-zingers ending each episode." He added, "Like the novel itself, this parody of an Olympian father by a world-wise son is an affectionately bemused, sometimes snarky, always engaging declaration of independence." In the *New York Times Book Review* (April 30, 1992), Christopher Lehmann-Haupt declared that "Cheever shapes a story that is both touchingly sad and makes you laugh out loud every dozen pages. . . . The author has caught his mischievously witty father precisely." Lehmann-Haupt also said that Cheever's first novel "leaves the reader with a glowing promise of future writing."

Cheever's second novel, *The Partisan* (1994), explored the relationship between Nelson Ballard, who works for a free newspaper, and his stepfather, Jonas Collingwood, a successful writer. As Brooke Allen explained in the *New Criterion* (June 1994), "The themes of the novel are paternity and responsibility . . . the story once again is that of a young man cripplingly tethered to the talent of an older one, of a father who will neither acknowledge and love his son nor set him free." Allen wrote that the novel is "diffuse, foggy with tolerance: Jonas and his family even veer dangerously close to cuteness; in its meandering first half the story threatens to be a wacky tale of lovable eccentrics. Thankfully, it is much more than that, but Cheever erodes his narrative's power by softening its focus." However, in her review in the *Times* of London (August 18, 1994), Erica Wagner enthusiastically praised *The Partisan*: "This is an intriguing, subtle novel which confirms Benjamin Cheever as a skilled novelist in his own right, if such proof were needed. He has an eye for the tiny details that make up the real truth of life, the things we remember as both funny and poignant and absolutely right."

According to Linell Smith, a writer for the *Chicago Sun-Times* (February 13, 1994), Cheever said that writing "is an attempt to make sense out of things. . . . I think writing novels can be a wonderfully useful thing to do for yourself. The father figure who is godlike in my first book, for instance, is human in my second book—and probably won't exist in my third." Cheever also elaborated his writing philosophy to Wendy Smith, a writer for *Publishers Weekly* (March 29, 1999), stating that it is "traditional for people to write two vaguely autobiographical novels and then move on. That material's used up. When you write a book, it changes you. Whatever bothers you the most causes you to write the book, then it bothers you less, and whatever else is bothering you prompts the next one."

Cheever's third novel, *Famous After Death* (1999), explores society's obsession with fame. The novel's main character, Noel Hammersmith, edits diet books for Acropolis Press, which advertises itself as "the best little publishing house in America." Noel is frustrated because fame and women elude him, and he can't lose any weight. He sees an unusual opportunity to fulfill his desires when he is arrested as the suspect responsible for a series of terrorist bombings. Noel becomes a celebrity overnight, reaping substantial media attention and romantic interest from women. In his review for the *Washington Post Book World* (July 4, 1999), Mike Musgrove recognized that there are "a few good laughs tucked away in this trifle of a novel," but Noel "is nothing but a placeholder drawn forth from the void in order to serve as a patsy for a reasonably clever plot hook in an otherwise empty book." Musgrove concluded by saying that *Famous After Death* "reads more like the pitch [for a novel] than the finished product." In the *New York Times* (May 2, 1999), reviewer David Finkle identified the novel's strengths: "The sly author also makes many literate and playful jokes, frequently at the expense of the publishing business. . . . As a matter of nonfact, about one in five gags is laugh-out-loud funny, and only one in ten misses the mark. Not a bad ratio." Finkle also praised the novel's "numerous elements" that eventually come together "in a burst of grace, humor, and mad revelation."

Cheever's latest book, *Selling Ben Cheever: Back to Square One in a Service Economy, A Personal Odyssey*, was released in October 2001. The novel is a humorous look at Cheever's experiences working in a number of low-level jobs. "Selling Ben Cheever, to use what the publishing industry calls a 'selling quote,' is a smart, brave and unusual book that should be read by anyone interested in the shape of the modern workplace—that is, of modern life," D.T. Max wrote in the *Los Angeles Times* (March 17, 2002).

Cheever

Benjamin Cheever's first marriage, to Linda Boyd, ended in divorce in 1980. He is now married to Janet Maslin, the former film critic and current book reviewer for the *New York Times*. They reside in Pleasantville, New York. Cheever frequently contributes essays to both the *New York Times* and the *New York Times Magazine*. "I'd like to do fiction and nonfiction," Cheever said to Wendy Smith. "I think it's good to go out in the world and have something happen to you; being a naturally fearful person, if I don't force myself out, my big adventure will be getting a package in the mail, and that doesn't make for lively writing."

— D.C.

SUGGESTED READING: *Chicago Sun-Times* p14 Feb. 13, 1994; *New Criterion* p58 June 1994; *New York Times* C p21 Nov. 29, 1988, (on-line) Apr. 30, 1992; *New York Times Book Review* p18 May 2, 1999; *Publishers Weekly* p72 Mar. 29, 1999; (London) *Times* p34 Aug. 18, 1994; *Washington Post Book World* p8 July 4, 1999; *Wilson Library Bulletin* p59 Mar. 1993

SELECTED BOOKS: novels—*The Plagiarist*, 1992; *The Partisan*, 1994; *Famous After Death*, 1999; memoir—*Selling Ben Cheever: Back to Square One in a Service Economy, A Personal Odyssey*, 2001; as editor—*The Letters of John Cheever*, 1988

Sigrid Estrada/Courtesy of Simon & Schuster

Cheever, Susan

July 31, 1943– Novelist; memoirist

"The easiest road to the human heart is just to sit down and tell your story straight," author Susan Cheever explained to Lisa Meyer, a writer for the *Los Angeles Times* (March 1, 1999). In a writing career that has spanned 20 years, Cheever has told fascinating stories about her famous family, herself, and female characters who are struggling to find personal fulfillment in modern society in such works as *Looking for Work*, *Home Before Dark*, *Treetops: A Family Memoir*, and *Note Found in Bottle: My Life as a Drinker*. For many years, however, she deliberately avoided any attempt to write a book. In an interview with Christopher Kenneally in the *Los Angeles Times* (November 24, 1985), Cheever said, "I didn't start to write until I was ready to do it. It's the stability, it's learning how to write, it's knowing who you are . . . you need all those things."

Susan Cheever was born on July 31, 1943 in New York City and grew up in Scarborough and later Ossining in New York. Cheever comes from a writing family. Her father, John Cheever, received the Pulitzer Prize in 1979 for *The Stories of John Cheever* and won esteem from both readers and reviewers with his short stories and novels. Her brother, Benjamin, has also written several critically acclaimed novels. Susan attended Brown University in Providence, Rhode Island, graduating in 1965. After working as a teacher in Colorado, she returned to New York in 1971 and got a job as a reporter for the *Tarrytown Daily News*. Cheever profited from her experience as a reporter. As she told Kenneally, "A novelist, like any artist, ought to be trained in every aspect of writing. I learned to write [by working] on newspapers. I think that makes me like the painter who can also draw." Cheever joined *Newsweek* in 1974 as the religion editor and later served as the lifestyles editor.

Cheever's first book, a novel entitled *Looking for Work*, was published in 1980. Its main character, Salley Gardens, wants to be a writer. Unfortunately, her dreams are repeatedly frustrated because she follows her husband, whose own successful career as an editor takes them around the world. After five years of sacrificing her ambitions to meet his needs, Salley finds herself disillusioned and has an affair with a charming sculptor. After her marriage collapses, she sets out on her own and eventually finds work at a major magazine. (In a touch reminiscent of her father's kind of humor, Susan Cheever has John Cheever appear briefly in her novel as a minor character who attends Salley's wedding.) *Looking for Work* received mixed reviews. "Susan Cheever enlivens this well-trodden literary topography with some good descriptive writing," Susan Kennedy wrote in her review for the *Times Literary Supplement* (February 22, 1980). "Indeed, it is her unobtrusive technical assurance, her respect for the just use of words, that keeps the novel together." In her review in *News-*

week (January 14, 1980), however, Jean Strouse suggested that Cheever "has created something less than a novel"; she "scatters proper nouns to evoke a trendy New York world . . . but, lacking much narrative context, the names lie dead on the page."

In Cheever's second novel, *A Handsome Man* (1981), she tells the story of Hannah Bart, who goes on vacation in Ireland with her younger brother, Jake, her lover, Sam, and his estranged son, Travis. In the *Washington Post* (May 18, 1981), Michele Slung found that Cheever's "prose, when it is good . . . is seductive and tightly phrased," but added that "it is not always strong enough to fight off the scene-stealing proclivities of things Irish." Slung also praised the main character, Hannah, as "a real woman come alive on these pages. Both her doubts and wisecracks ring true."

A third novel, *The Cage*, followed in 1982. Cheever details the gradual disintegration of a marriage between Julia and Billy Bristol. Julia frequently contrasts her happy childhood growing up at Northwood, her father's estate, with her unsatisfying life with Billy. During a summer vacation on the estate, Julia "gets a predictable revenge [on Billy]," Sheila Ballantyne wrote for the *New York Times Book Review* (October 3, 1982), "and things eventually come to a surreal and melodramatic conclusion." Ballantyne also criticized *The Cage* for being "embroidered with glittery and often repetitive detail. . . . For a reader to care about either member of this doomed couple, something deeper in them has to be struck, and this Miss Cheever has failed to do."

Susan Cheever's journey into nonfiction began by accident. In an interview for *Contemporary Authors*, dated March 13, 1987, Cheever recalled that she began keeping a journal as a way to cope with the pain of seeing her father suffer from a terminal illness. John Cheever died in June 1982. "By this time I had more than two hundred [pages]," she added. "So I sat down with what I had already written and began to shape a little memoir." Cheever's memoir of her father, *Home Before Dark*, was published in 1984. In the *Washington Post Book World* (October 7, 1984), Brigitte Weeks described the work as "one of the most moving and intimate books I have read in years." Cheever discussed highly personal and controversial matters, such as her parents' turbulent marriage, John Cheever's battle with alcoholism, her occasionally difficult relationship with him, and his homosexual affairs, which were previously unknown to the public. "But *Home Before Dark* is no 'Daddy Dearest,' a child's settling of scores," Weeks noted. "The wonder of this book is the astonishing combination of dispassion and compassion with which Susan Cheever portrays her father. . . . Assembling her portrait, Susan uncovers the personality of her father layer by layer." *Home Before Dark* received a nomination from the National Book Critics Circle Award in 1984.

Susan discovered that her father had several homosexual relationships as she was looking through his personal journals following his death. She told Craig Little, a freelance writer for *Publisher's Weekly* (November 2, 1984), that at one point she "considered abandoning the book, in order not to be the person who revealed he was a homosexual." However, she continued, "I realized that if I didn't mention it in my book, then it would be only a matter of time before someone else did. I decided the best thing to do would be to present it in the way he would have wanted to, in a way that was very sympathetic, in a way that didn't have the force of revelation and in the context of his life."

Cheever returned to fiction in 1987 with the publication of *Doctors and Women*. As in her previous novels, Cheever focused on a woman's unhappy marriage. "In addressing her father's death and her mother's recently diagnosed cancer, Kate Weiss is thrown into an emotional maelstrom," Linsey Abrams wrote in the *Los Angeles Times* (May 17, 1987). "She realizes that she has lived automatically alongside her husband, David, a prominent lawyer, for the years of their marriage, and so begins an affair with Macklin Riley, her mother's doctor." Abrams highlighted several criticisms: "This title is indicative of one of the novel's basic assumptions: that men are defined by their work and women by their gender. Thus, over the course of the book, we follow Kate's obsession with Riley, Riley's impossible life as a cancer doctor. That we are robbed of Kate's sense of her life beyond men and Riley's sense of his life beyond work is, unfortunately, a serious flaw in these characterizations." Abrams also criticized the novel's "class-consciousness."

Another novel, *Elizabeth Cole*, appeared in 1989. In her review in the *San Francisco Chronicle* (December 1, 1989), Joan Dahlgren wrote, "Some authors have only one story to tell and Cheever . . . seems to be one of them. That's not necessarily a flaw, but in Cheever's case, it is dangerously close to writing by number. *Elizabeth Cole* presents the same basic situation as did Cheever's previous four novels: A woman from a socially and artistically prominent East Coast background struggles to shake off the yoke of Daddy and Daddy/husband." Dahlgren also criticized Cheever's characters whose "lives are veneered with a thick coat of money, polish, good taste, social and artistic pedigrees. . . . As they struggle to find themselves and their true loves, the reader keeps thinking, so what?"

In 1991 Cheever profiled her mother, Mary Cheever, in *Treetops: A Family Memoir*. In the *Los Angeles Times* (March 25, 1991), Carolyn See expressed enthusiastic praise for *Treetops*, which "may well be Susan Cheever's masterpiece." In the memoir, Cheever repeated themes discussed in her novels. Like her characters, the female members of Cheever's family often sacrificed personal happiness in order to meet the needs of the men in their lives. As See wrote, "This book is about in-laws and 'outlaws,' about haves and have-nots. Susan's great-grandfather, grandfather and father all had marvelous careers . . . but these men were generals in a familial army. The mothers, aunts, daughters were cannon fodder in the fight for their men's fame. The women paid dearly, in early death, insanity, depression, sad lives." See also praised Cheever for gaining in this book "a wonderful mastery over material that has eluded her time after time."

Cheever's book *A Woman's Life: The Story of an Ordinary American and Her Extraordinary Generation* (1994) was a biography of an "average woman" she met through a friend. Cheever protected the real woman's identity by changing her name in the book to "Linda Green." As Cheever explained to Joseph P. Kahn, a reporter for the *Boston Globe* (August 2, 1994), "At first I tried to convince her to use her real name, but as the story became more intimate I decided against it. The sexual stuff [i.e. extra-marital affairs], the pot smoking, the pot smuggling—you can see where a suburban mother living in a small town wouldn't want these things revealed. . . . My goal was for her not to get fired or divorced."

How did Cheever define "average"? According to Kelly Cherry, a reviewer for *America* (November 26, 1994), Cheever wrote in the book that she defined the "average American woman" as someone who was "unrecognized, unknown, and often unappreciated, trying to hold it all together—family, job, health, attractiveness, sanity." Cherry agreed that Linda Green was "a marvelous subject" because she had "an engagingly truthful and questing intelligence that has made her life interestingly complex." Linda was born in the borough of Brooklyn in New York City in the late 1940s and grew up in Passaic, New Jersey. Cherry noted that she changed from "cheerleader to commune hippie to suburban mother." After an unhappy first marriage, Linda's second marriage, to a lawyer, produced two children. Linda also became a Spanish teacher. "One of Cheever's important points is that women, who may have gone to work because a shifting economy obliged them to contribute to the family income, have achieved a new sense of themselves through work," Cherry wrote. "Certainly this is true for Linda, who discovered that teaching allowed her to effect real and useful changes in her students." Cherry concluded by describing *A Woman's Life* as an "absorbing and informative" book, and suggested that Cheever should write a second book about Linda Green in "10 or 15 years," to see how her life turned out.

In 1999 Susan Cheever published her third memoir, *Note Found in a Bottle: My Life as a Drinker*. Cheever chronicled her battle with alcoholism, which contributed to her three failed marriages. "Alcohol divorced cause and effect for me," Cheever explained to Lisa Meyer. "I thought I could not pay bills and somehow not get in trouble. I thought I could hurt other people and somehow they'd like me anyway." Writing in the *Library Journal* (November 15, 1998), reviewer Nancy Patterson Shires said, "This anecdotal memoir sometimes seems disjointed and incomplete—we never find out how Cheever finally gave up alcohol, for example—but her style is candid and moving."

The publication of *Note Found in a Bottle* also brought Cheever sharp criticism from noted *Washington Post* critic Jonathan Yardley. Reviewing the book for the *Chicago Sun-Times* (January 24, 1999), Yardley wrote, "Susan Cheever has now published nine books, fiction and nonfiction, all in one fashion or another about herself. . . . The central fact of Cheever's existence, as readers of her work know all too well, is that she is John Cheever's daughter." Yardley also accused Susan Cheever of having "exploited her paternal and familial connections to purposes that, in a less cynical age, would look more self-serving and opportunistic than revelatory and or even therapeutic. People who work in the literary subculture talk often about 'professional widows'; Susan Cheever is a professional daughter." Despite his severe criticisms, Yardley acknowledged that Cheever "is capable of writing smoothly professional prose," and that readers "who like the literature of confession will like this book."

Cheever published her fourth memoir, titled *As Good as I Could Be: A Memoir of Raising Wonderful Children in Difficult Times*, in 2001. In a series of essays, Cheever examines the difficulties of parenting, which are compounded by her battle with alcohol. The book received mixed reviews. "Although we learn a great deal about the inner workings of Cheever's family," wrote Diana McKeon Charkalis in *USA Today* (June 14, 2001), "there are no new insights. Instead, she treads familiar territory as if it were something new. It must have been a major aha! moment for Cheever when she realized that to be a good parent, you can't remain a child yourself. It's a point she makes at least eight times in the book."

Susan Cheever lives in New York City. She frequently contributes articles to such well-known publications as the *New York Times Book Review*, *Cosmopolitan*, *Harper's Bazaar*, the *New Yorker*, and *Architectural Digest*. She is the mother of two children, and her three marriages, all of which were to men who were previously married, have made her the mother of seven stepchildren. "Whenever I've failed, it always turned out for the best because it kept me going," she said to Christopher Kenneally. "My failure to be a writer when I was young was the best thing that ever happened to me."

— D.C.

SUGGESTED READING: *America* p22 Nov. 26, 1994; *Boston Globe* Living p57 Aug. 2, 1994; *Chicago Sun-Times* SHO p14 Jan. 24, 1999; *Los Angeles Times* VI p26 Nov. 24, 1985, E p6 Mar. 25, 1991, E p3 Mar. 1, 1999; *New York Times* VII p9 Oct. 3, 1982; *New York Times Magazine* p46 May 12, 1996; *Publishers Weekly* p79+ Nov. 2, 1984; *San Francisco Chronicle* E p13 Dec. 1,

1989; *Times Literary Supplement* p210 Feb. 22, 1980; *Washington Post* C p8 May 18, 1981; *Washington Post Book World* p1 Oct. 7, 1984; *Contemporary Authors* vol. 27, 1988

SELECTED BOOKS: memoirs—*Home Before Dark*, 1984; *Treetops: A Family Memoir*, 1991; *Note Found in a Bottle: My Life as a Drinker*, 1999; *As Good as I Could Be: A Memoir of Raising Wonderful Children in Difficult Times*, 2001; nonfiction—*A Woman's Life: The Story of an Ordinary American and Her Extraordinary Generation*, 1994; novels—*Looking for Work*, 1980; *A Handsome Man*, 1981; *The Cage*, 1982; *Doctors and Women*, 1987; *Elizabeth Cole*, 1989

Paul Hoover/Courtesy of Coffee House Press

Chernoff, Maxine

Feb. 24, 1952– Poet; novelist; short-story writer

The poet, novelist, and short-story writer Maxine Chernoff has been publishing her work in a variety of genres for nearly 30 years. While she initially focused solely on poetry, Chernoff has branched into fiction with both short stories and novels, producing the critically-admired collections *Bop* (1987) and *Signs of Devotion* (1993), and the novels *American Heaven* (1996) and *Boy in Winter* (1999). With her husband, poet Paul Hoover, Chernoff edits the literary journal *New American Writing*, which appears annually in early June and is recognized as one of the nation's best sources for innovative contemporary poetry. She currently serves as chairperson of the creative writing program at San Francisco State University.

Chernoff wrote the following autobiographical statement for *World Authors 1995-2000*: "I was born February 24,1952 in Chicago, Illinois, the second of two daughters to Idell Hahn and Philip B. Hahn, a housewife and a CPA. I was raised in Chicago in a bi-lingual household, which also contained my maternal grandmother, Rebecca Lubove, who had gone deaf as a child in Bialystok, Russia, and therefore only spoke Yiddish. A poet herself, some of her poems had been published in the *Jewish Daily Forward*.

"I led a normal childhood except for the fact that my mother was plagued by clinical depression and needed to be hospitalized and given shock treatments several times during my grade-school years. These were difficult times for me and made my bond with my older sister, Marsha, especially important to me. Since Marsha was nine years my senior, she left home when I was nine to attend college and then married immediately thereafter. I remember feeling very lonely the year she left, which happened to be the same year that my fourth grade teacher, a kindly woman named Mrs. Wahlberg, died suddenly of cancer. These two losses and a long hospitalization of my mother the same year caused a lot of anxiety in me.

"My mother's absences, which were prior to the time that mental illness was discussed in families, were largely treated with silence at home. I became a very mature and independent child quickly, an excellent student and an avid reader. I would often come home from school and read whatever books were available to me. I read everything from politics to spy novels to popular condensations of novels that my parents ordered from *Readers Digest*. Reading was a comfort and an escape, and I was a serious reader years before I became a writer.

"Graduating early from Bowen High School, I enrolled at the University of Illinois, Chicago, at the age of 16 and entered as a political science major. Never taking a political science class, I quickly became an English major after taking introductory literature classes in fiction and drama and finding myself in love with modern literature, from the wildly imaginative works of Ionesco, Pirandello, and Beckett to the amazing novels and short stories of James Joyce and Virginia Woolf.

"It was in my junior year of college in an American Literature class taught by Professor Fred Stern that I discovered contemporary poetry— [William Carlos] Williams, [Kenneth] Rexroth, and [Denise] Levertov, in particular, and decided that I wanted to write poetry. I showed my early works to Professor Stern, who was very kind and patient and encouraging. I wrote constantly and fervently. I would even pull over in my car to write a poem in my first few years of writing poetry.

"Around the same time, I quickly married and five months later left my college boyfriend, Arnold Chernoff. We were divorced the same year. Shortly after leaving him, I met my current husband, Paul Hoover, who had just finished the Program for Writers at the University of Illinois, Chicago. He was six years my senior and already a mature and talented poet. During our courtship in 1972, I began my graduate studies at the same university. More importantly, Paul introduced me to many major poets whose writing I still read and love: James Schuyler, Frank O'Hara, Kenneth Koch, Ron Padgett, Tom Clark, John Ashbery, Kenward Elmslie, Cesar Vallejo, Emily Dickinson, and Elizabeth Bishop were added to my list of favorite poets of that time.

"In 1974, I completed my MA degree in English. Paul and I married the same year (October 5, 1974), and I became an assistant editor of *Oink!*, a literary magazine he had founded with several other graduate students while in the MA Program at UIC. Eventually, the other editors dropped out, and Paul and I edited issues 9–19 together. In 1986, we changed the title of *Oink!* to *New American Writing*. The circulation increased to a high of 6,000 copies an issue, and we began to publish not only poetry and fiction but also special supplements including a censorship issue, an Australian issue, a British issue, a Brazilian issue, and a Russian absurdist issue.

"In the early seventies, I also started reading prose poems, first French writers such as [Henri] Michaux and [Francis] Ponge and Latin-American writers such as [Julio] Cortazar and [Clarice] Lispector. I also began noticing some American poets—[Russell] Edson, [James] Tate, [Robert] Bly, for instance, working in that form, and turned my attention to it. It seemed to capture both the eye and the ear of my writing. My first two published chapbooks, *The Last Aurochs* (Now Press, Iowa City, Iowa) and *A Vegetable Emergency* (Beyond Baroque Foundation, Venice, CA), were collections of prose poems. The *Paris Review* published several of my prose poems in 1974 when Michael Benedikt was the editor, and these early publications confirmed my sense of myself as a writer.

"From the early 1970s to the early 1980s, I wrote and published only poems. Around 1980, my interest in the prose poem led me to explore character further in some early brief pieces that seemed to be more story than prose poem. By the mid-1980s I had published a good number of these stories in various journals and was ready to put together a collection of them. Coffee House Press accepted a collection of my stories, *Bop*, for publication in 1985. When it was published in 1986, Francine Prose reviewed it favorably in the *New York Times*. It was subsequently picked up for reprint by the Vintage Contemporary Fiction Series in 1987.

"By then Paul Hoover and I had had three children, Koren, born in 1976, and twins Julian and Philip, born in 1985. Although I was writing fiction, I had never completely left poetry. More poetry book publications followed in 1979 (*Utopia TV Store*) and 1985 (*New Faces of 1952*, which won the Carl Sandburg Award). In 1988, I traveled to Australia on a writer's exchange with New South Wales, and I published my most experimental book of poems, *Japan* (Avenue B Press), which was an alphabet work consisting of 26 thin, sinewy poems connected by sound rather than image.

"The whole time I lived in Chicago, I taught English composition, English as a Second Language, and creative writing at a number of institutions including the University of Illinois, the City Colleges, the School of the Art Institute, and Columbia College, where Paul Hoover has been Poet-in-Residence since 1974.

"In 1991 my first novel, *Plain Grief*, was published by Summit, a division of Simon and Schuster. It concerns a mother's search for her runaway daughter. In that same year, Another Chicago Press brought out *Leap Year Day: New and Selected Poems*.

"In 1993 a second collection of stories, *Signs of Devotion*, was published by Simon and Schuster. It became a *New York Times* Notable Book of the Year and won the *Chicago Sun-Times* Fiction Award.

"In 1994, offered an Associate Professor position in Creative Writing at San Francisco State University, my family and I moved to Mill Valley, California. Paul Hoover arranged with Columbia College to stay on the faculty and teach only in the fall semester, which made our relocation to California possible.

"Since then, I have become Professor and Chair of the Creative Writing Program at SFSU. I have finished and published four more books: *American Heaven* (Coffee House Press), a novel set in Chicago in 1996. It deals with four residents of a Chicago high-rise—a gangster, a jazz musician, a Polish immigrant, and a young woman from Upstate New York—and the interconnections in their lives. It was runner-up for the Bay Area Book Reviewers Award in 1997. In 1999 I published *A Boy in Winter* (Crown Publishing), a novel about a child who accidentally kills his friend. In 2000 HarperCollins brought the book out in Australia, and in 2001 it was optioned by Showtime for a made-for-television film.

"In 2001, a new collection of poems, *World*, was published by Salt Editions (Cambridge, England), and in 2002, *Some of Her Friends That Year: New and Selected Stories*, appeared from Coffee House Press.

"During these years, Paul Hoover and I have read and discussed our work in many national and international forums including Glasgow, Scotland; Liege, Belgium; Cambridge, England; Sao Paulo, Brazil; and St. Petersburg, Russia. In addition, I was part of a group of Bay Area writers who were guests of Berlin's Literatur Werkstatt in fall of 1996.

"Early interests in the possibilities of language, sound, and image still characterize my work. To that I've joined an interest in the psychology of character, hoping to capture the complexities of consciousness. As one critic said of my work, 'Chernoff writes in a sleek, controlled vernacular about love, death, divorce, motherhood, alienation, and friendship. . . . She knows what she wants to write about, and writes about it deftly' (*Chicago Magazine*)." —S. Y.

SUGGESTED READING: *New York Times Book Review* p11 Sep. 21, 1986, p14 June 9, 1996; *Publishers Weekly* p237 Sep. 14, 1990, p56 July 5, 1991, p53 Mar. 4, 1996, p70 July 12, 1999; *Voice Literary Supplement* p6 Nov. 1991; *Windhover* (online)

SELECTED BOOKS: poetry—*Utopia TV Store: Prose Poems*, 1979; *New Faces of 1952*, 1985; *Leap Year Day: New and Selected Poems*, 1990; *World: Poems 1990-2001*, 2001; short-story collections—*Bop*, 1987; *Signs of Devotion*, 1993; *Some of Her Friends That Year: New & Selected Stories*, 2002; novels—*Plain Grief*, 1991; *American Heaven*, 1996; *Boy in Winter*, 1999

Jerry Bauer/Dutton Publicity

Chevalier, Tracy

October 1962– Novelist

The novelist Tracy Chevalier is the author of *Girl With a Pearl Earring* (2000), a fictional account of the origins of the painting of the same name by the 17th-century Dutch master Johannes Vermeer. The story centers on Griet, a young Dutch girl who becomes Vermeer's housekeeper and is drawn to the man and his enigmatic works of art. The book became a publishing sensation; after an initial printing of only 17,500 copies, it grew by word of mouth into a national best-seller with more than one million copies in print. Chevalier's next novel, *Falling Angels* (2001), is set in London, England, during the transformative period between the deaths of Queen Victoria, in 1901, and King Edward, in 1910. She has also published the novel *Virgin Blue* (1997).

Tracy Chevalier was born in October 1962 in Washington, D.C. She attended Oberlin College, in Ohio, earning a B.A. in English in 1984. Following graduation she moved to London, England, intending to stay only six months, but eventually marrying an Englishman and making it her home. She also began to write. "As a kid I'd often said I wanted to be a writer because I loved books and wanted to be associated with them," she recalled in an autobiographical essay posted on her personal Web site. "I wrote the odd story in high school, but it was only in my twenties that I started writing 'real' stories, at night and on weekends. Sometimes I wrote a story in a couple evenings; other times it took me a whole year to complete one." She took a night class in creative writing, and one of her stories was published in *Fiction*, a London-based magazine that folded shortly thereafter.

Chevalier worked for 12 years as a reference-book editor in London, where she edited several works, including *Twentieth-Century Children's Writers* (1989), *Contemporary Poets* (1991), and *Contemporary World Writers* (1993). "I wasn't having much fun in my job," she recalled in an interview posted on *Oprah.com* (November 2001). "But I hung on—I still loved editing books and thought things would eventually improve." This changed when she saw an advertisement for a reputed M.A. program in creative writing, one of only a few such programs in England, at the University of East Anglia. "I always thought any big changes I made in my life would be carefully thought out—every option analyzed, every angle considered, the pros and cons weighed up before I reached a rational decision," Chevalier explained during the interview. "I made the decision that changed my career in a split second, without any conscious thought at all." Chevalier enrolled at the University of East Anglia, in Norfolk, England, earning an M.A. in 1994. Among her instructors were the English novelists Malcolm Bradbury and Rose Tremain. "For the first time in my life I was expected to write every day, and I found I liked it," she recalled on her Web site.

During her year at East Anglia Chevalier conceived the idea for *The Virgin Blue*. The story centers on an American woman, Ella Turner, who moves to southwestern France with her husband to advance his career. She is not warmly received by her neighbors and begins having unsettling dreams. With time on her hands, she begins doing research on her French ancestors at a local library, where she is aided by a haughty but attractive librarian, Jean-Paul. She learns about a 16th-century Huguenot family that had converted from Catholicism to Protestantism, and a woman named Isabelle du Moulin, known as La Rousse because of her red hair. La Rousse, whose story is intertwined with Ella's, was forced to flee from religious persecution and met with a mysterious fate. As Ella unravels the forgotten tragedy she comes to understand what is happening in her own life. The novel is "very much about the outsider experience of being in a small town in a different culture," Chevalier told Gavin J. Grant for *Booksense.com* (March 2001). "I think outsiderness is one of those things I seem to do without even realizing I'm doing it."

Chevalier also explored the theme of the outsider in her highly acclaimed second novel, *Girl with a Pearl Earring*. Griet, an illiterate 16-year-old girl from a poor Protestant family, is forced to find work when her father, a tile painter, is blinded in a kiln explosion. Circumstances lead her to the Delft home of the painter Johannes Vermeer, who is gaining recognition for his luminous works. The Catholic Vermeer family takes her on as a housemaid, but tensions develop between Griet and the other members of the household, which includes Vermeer's five children; his pregnant and cavilling wife, Catharina; his watchful mother-in-law; and an older maid. Unlike the other women of the house, Griet is allowed into Vermeer's studio, where she is charged with the task of cleaning without moving anything—a skill that was as important when cleaning the home of her blind father as it is in the intensely visual world of a painter. In the artist's proximity she begins to acquire an appreciation for art and evinces an intuitive understanding of composition and form. Vermeer recognizes her talents and makes her his assistant, an arrangement that must be kept secret from his resentful and jealous wife. Eventually Vermeer's wealthy, lecherous patron insists that the girl be the subject for his next commissioned work. The resultant painting—with Griet reluctantly donning Catharina's pearl earrings at Vermeer's urging—provokes a scandal that will decide Griet's fate.

"Chevalier's story shares some of the striking qualities of Vermeer's paintings," Ron Charles wrote for *Christian Science Monitor* (December 30, 1999). "Her subject is a single woman caught in a private moment. Like the Dutch master, she's fascinated by the play of light, the suggestive power of small details, and the subtle thoughts beneath placid expressions." Michiko Kakutani for the *New York Times* (November 2, 2001) called *Girl* "a marvel of elliptical storytelling. . . . Though Ms. Chevalier's story of a young woman who goes to work as a maid in the painter's house was, at heart, a bildungsroman, the novel also illuminated Vermeer's alchemical art while coyly opening a window on 17th-century Delft." Richard Eder for the *New York Times* (January 24, 2000) wrote that the ideas of the novel "range among the dynamics and moralities of art and the artist, their claims upon life, life's claims upon them and the struggle of women to find their own values and place in a male hierarchy, specifically in a 17th-century painter's world. There is strong feeling, but it rises unforcedly from the book's tactile evocation of the social, material, and emotional detail of life in Delft of the time, and increasingly from the stormy clarity achieved by Griet as narrator and protagonist."

In an interview posted on the Penguin Putnam Web site, Chevalier described the book's conception. "A poster of [Girl With a Pearl Earring] has hung on the wall of my bedroom since I was nineteen," she explained. "I often lie in bed and look at it and wonder about it. It's such an open painting. I'm never sure what the girl is thinking or what her expression is. Sometimes she seems sad, other times seductive. So, one morning a couple of years ago I was lying in bed worrying about what I was going to write next, and I looked up at the painting and wondered what Vermeer did or said to the model to get her to look like that. And right then I made up the story." Chevalier began the novel in February 1998; working full time, she finished it in October 1998, two weeks before she gave birth to her son. "There's nothing like a fixed biological deadline to focus the mind!" she joked in the autobiographical essay on her Web site. "I don't think I'll ever write anything so quickly again. Since then I have juggled motherhood and writing, and feel lucky that I have a job with so much flexibility."

Her next novel, *Falling Angels*, is set in London during the opening decade of the 20th century. In January 1901, just after the death of Queen Victoria, two middle-class families, the Colemans and the Waterhouses, meet while visiting a cemetery where they have neighboring plots. The daughters of the two families—five-year-old Maude Coleman and Lavinia Waterhouse—become friends and begin meeting at the cemetery, wondering at the graves and ostentatious monuments while playing with the gravedigger's son, Simon Field. Whereas Lavinia is a somewhat spoiled, affected, and melodramatic girl—her fascination with the cemetery leads her to write a pamphlet titled "The Complete Guide to Mourning Etiquette"—Maude is coolheaded and rational, taking a scientific interest in what happens to the body after death. Together the two girls embody the conflicted ethos of the times, divided between Victorian and modern ways. Maude is neglected by her mother, Kitty Coleman, a beautiful woman who feels frustrated and oppressed. With the Queen's death Kitty coddles the hope that "England would miraculously slough off her shabby black coat to reveal something glittering and new," as quoted by Janice P. Nimura for the *New York Times* (November 4, 2001). She cannot understand how Gertrude, Lavinia's mother, has accepted the matronly role prescribed to her. Restless and headstrong, she begins an affair with the superintendent at the cemetery and later throws herself into the women's suffrage movement with equal abandon.

Chevalier did research for the book at Highgate Cemetery, the resting place of many famous Victorians in the north of London. (She still volunteers her time there, gardening and giving tours.) "I wanted to explore the change from Victorian to modern values, gauged through the changing attitudes to death and mourning," she explained in an interview with Jennifer Abbots for Bookreporter.com (October 19, 2001). "I think the way societies treat their dead says a lot about their social values. It thus made sense to set the book primarily in the cemetery. The thing about cemeteries, though, is that they are more about the living than about the dead. A lot of life goes on there, including sex!"

Reviews of the novel, while mixed, tended to be positive. "Chevalier is a master of voices," Janice P. Nimura observed. "In brief first-person narrations, she skips from parents to children to servants, touching on the details of life upstairs and down with grace and clarity, and delivering a considerable amount of social history without breaking stride. She paints the age with a palette of women." In the Christian Science Monitor (October 18, 2001) Ron Charles concluded that this narrative technique was ultimately unsuccessful. "The effect is elliptical," he wrote, "like watching the neighbors through a broad-board fence. We catch only glimpses of them, often glimpses that are called upon to convey enormous amounts of information, feeling, or dramatic irony." Charles also found Chevalier's depiction of the women's suffrage movement to be overly dismissive. In People (October 22, 2001), R. G. Sheinkin concluded that "the mix of personal and historical drama is not as convincing as in Chevalier's beloved novel about Vermeer. Still, Chevalier offers a thoughtful exploration of the ways people misread each other by being trapped in their own perspectives." Yvette W. Olson for Library Journal (October 15, 2001) wrote, "The novel is infused with enriching details. . . . Like an E. M. Forster novel filtered through a modern sensibility, Falling Angels takes us back to the early 20th century and keeps us there, waiting to see what Kitty and her crowd will do next."

Chevalier and her husband live in London with their son. Chevalier is reportedly working on a novel centered around the Lady and the Unicorn tapestries, which are believed to have been made in northern France or Flanders at the end of the 15th century.

—A. I. C.

SUGGESTED READING: Booksense.com Mar. 2001; Christian Science Monitor p21 Dec. 30, 1999, p21 Oct. 18, 2001; Library Journal p106 Oct. 15, 2001; New York Times p20 Jan. 23, 2000, E p12 Jan. 24, 2000, E p44 Nov. 2, 2001, p26 Nov. 4, 2001; Oprah.com Nov. 2001; People p53 Oct. 22, 2001

SELECTED BOOKS: The Virgin Blue, 1997; Girl With a Pearl Earring, 2000; Falling Angels, 2001

Clair, Maxine

1939(?)– Novelist; short-story writer; poet

For Maxine Clair, the path to a writer's life was far from direct. A medical technician for nearly 20 years, Clair decided at around age 40 that she wanted to pursue another goal and focused instead on becoming a fiction writer. With the 1994 publication of her short-story collection, Rattlebone, Clair, currently an assistant professor of English at George Washington University, in Washington, D.C., quickly distinguished herself as what Lee Martin for the Washington Post (October 7, 2001) called "a generous and marvelous writer." Both Rattlebone and her subsequent novel, October Suite (2001), have been widely praised for their strong literary merit. Clair, who is black, told Patrik Henry Bass for Essence (October 2001), "For me, writing is an act of faith and a spiritual exercise. I'm open to divine ideas, and I really do love language. I love how our people can speak it. I love what we do with it. I want to hear all of it in my work. I want to see myself, our people, in my work. Through our work we say, 'This is who we are.'"

Maxine Clair was born in Kansas City, Kansas, in 1939, the second of nine children, to Robert and Lucy Smith. Most of her childhood occurred in the years before Brown vs. Board of Education—the monumental 1954 Supreme Court case that helped end racial segregation. Clair recalled the experience to Connie Lauerman for the Chicago Tribune

Carol Clayton Photography/Courtesy of Random House

(July 6, 1994). "It was a kinder place and time," she said. "In my childhood during the 1950s in African-American communities, especially in the Midwest, there was a sort of tribal consciousness that was pervasive. It was because we were segregated. We lived together much more tightly, and that was disrupted in some ways with the civil rights movement. The civil rights movement was a wonderful thing to happen, but there was some sacrificing, I think. It changed the way we understood our lives." Neither of Clair's parents had completed high school, so reading was an activity rarely practiced in their home. Instead, as the oldest daughter, Clair spent a great deal of time helping her mother care for the younger children. Clair's mother, a talented singer and pianist, often played gospel, jazz, and swing music, leading sing-alongs with her children. As Clair explained to Mary Jane Dunlap for a University of Kansas (UK) press release (April 10, 2001) archived on the school's Web site, this early exposure to "mesmerizing rhythm and musicality" helped inspire her impulse to write. Through music, she said, she discovered the melodies of language, as well as the voices of many black poets who were building narratives around rhythms and beats.

Beyond developing a musical ear, Clair spent much of her early years under the positive influence of strong-minded teachers. "They had pushed us to be the best," she told Dunlap for the UK publication *OREAD* (February 16, 2001, on-line). "They always encouraged us to do more. They told us we needed to be twice as bright [as white children] and they told us 'you can be someone.' I felt a debt of gratitude for the foundation they had given me." One such high-school English teacher, Rebecca Bloodworth, introduced Clair to literature, especially women writers. "I read every word of [Elizabeth Barrett Browning's] sonnets, you know," Clair told Lauerman. "I remember coming alive to some of that, but it was something I related to in an intellectual way. It was beautiful, but I didn't see much of myself in it." In eleventh grade, Clair decided that she would attend college, despite the hurdles she knew she would face as a young black woman. "I wanted to become a legitimate person," she told Lauerman. "That's really what going to college was about for me. I just wanted to be something, anything, anything I thought I could do." With a vague interest in science, Clair enrolled as a science major at UK, telling Lauerman, "The thought of being a doctor died pretty fast, and then I decided on medical technology. I knew a medical technologist. I rode the bus with her. I was in awe of her, dressed all in white with patches on her coat and working in a lab."

In 1962 Clair graduated with a B.S. degree and embarked upon a successful career in medical technology. In 1967 she and her husband moved to Washington, D.C., where he attended Howard University Law School. (The couple divorced in 1975.) Throughout these years, a writing career remained far from Clair's mind, as she focused on raising her family—which eventually included four children—and advancing her career. By 1980 she was chief technologist at the Children's Hospital National Medical Center, in Washington, D.C., and a single mother, working to support her young children, who then ranged in age from nine to 16.

Despite achieving significant professional success, at around age 40, Clair began to experience a lack of fulfillment and realized that she wanted to make profound changes in her life. That year she decided to use her tax refund—about $1,200—to pay for a spiritual retreat to the Caribbean. "I went away for 18 days," she told Lauerman, "and every day I did my meditation and made the picture [in my mind] of what I might want. I visualized, although they didn't call it that then. I was reading some way-out books that I won't even *mention*. Essentially, I was programming myself to understand I could do something else, and I could have a different life." She continued, "When I came back, it was very clear: I was going to be a writer."

While Clair had no professional experience as a writer, she had kept a journal for many years. She compiled fragments from several journal entries that she considered to be poetic and sent these samples to the Pulitzer Prize–winning novelist Toni Morrison, who was then reading manuscripts for Random House. At the time Morrison was the only black woman that Clair had heard of working in publishing. Morrison explained that she was only reading fiction for the publishing company, not poetry, but she encouraged Clair to read more widely and continue writing. As Clair later told David Streitfeld for the *Washington Post* (July 6, 1994), "[My samples] weren't poems, and [Morrison] knew it and wanted me to find out what a poem was."

Soon after contacting Morrison, Clair came across a flyer announcing a free creative writing class at George Washington University and submitted her complete portfolio, which at the time consisted of a handful of poems. She was accepted into the workshop, and from there, she told Lauerman, "the whole world opened up."

Upon the recommendation of a writing teacher, Clair applied for admission to a master of fine arts program in creative writing at American University, also in Washington, D.C. She obtained a place for the fall of 1982—and a teaching assistantship to help defray the cost of tuition. Clair continued working, however, as a medical technician to support her children, often logging 16-hour days on the weekends. "I was working like a fool," she told Lauerman. "But my life depended on it. I don't always talk about how we didn't have the water and gas turned on and it was October already and the kids were really scared and when I was going to second-hand shops for their school clothes. That was part of making another life." Luckily she won a $10,000 fellowship that paid for her second year of tuition, and in 1984 Clair graduated with an MFA degree. She continued teaching at American University and the Writer's Center, in Washington, D.C., among other schools. Ultimately, she was offered a full-time professorship at George Washington University.

Throughout these years, seeing her work published was not her main objective; rather, she told Streitfeld, she measured success through "making these things happen on the page." She explained, "It was just amazing that you could sit there for three hours and then, before you knew it, you had six lines of something that made sense." Nevertheless, Clair did achieve publication in 1988 with a volume of poetry entitled *Coping With Gravity*.

Two years later, Clair turned to writing fiction, specifically short stories, and in 1992, published a short chapbook entitled *October Brown*. The work earned Clair the Baltimore Artscape Prize for Maryland Writers in short fiction and prompted an invitation for her to read the story at a local literary festival. After the reading, a woman approached Clair asking if she had more stories. She recommended that Claire contact a top literary agent in New York named Molly Friedrich. Clair wrote the name down, but did not use it at first, instead filing it in a box of notebooks. It was not until several months later, after a colleague at the university also urged her to find an agent, that she retrieved the scrap of paper and submitted her manuscript. What happened next was in Clair's own words, as quoted by Lauerman, "highly unusual." Friedrich, an eminent literary agent representing such best-selling authors as Terry McMillan and Jane Smiley, was so impressed with Clair's manuscript that she contacted her immediately, despite that fact that Clair's book was in the format of a short-story collection rather than a novel (which is often easier to sell to publishers). Shortly after, Friedrich called Clair again with astounding news: She had sent the manuscript to four large publishing houses, and three had responded with offers. As Clair recalled to Lauerman, "I can't even articulate how strange and wonderful that call was." By Friedrich's own account, the book became the first short-story collection she ever sold.

Rattlebone, published in 1994, told the story of a young girl, Irene Wilson, through a series of 11 related (and chronologically structured) stories revolving around her life in the fictional town of Rattlebone, on the outskirts of Kansas City, during the mid-1950s. Drawing comparisons to Sherwood Anderson's *Winesburg, Ohio* (1919) and Jean Toomer's *Cane* (1923)—two previous short-story collections that employed the linked-story form—*Rattlebone* was recognized as a work defying traditional categorization. Veronica Chambers for the *New York Times* (January 8, 1995) explained: "Although *Rattlebone* is a collection of stories with the same cast of characters and not a straight-ahead novel, it has the feel of a complete work of fiction. Rather than having the effect of breaking up the narrative, each story weaves a tighter web around the lives of Irene and her people." The reader first encounters Irene at age eight describing her teacher, October Brown, a woman with a troubled past and a white smudge, which the children call "a Devil's kiss," caused by the skin disease vitiligo upon her cheek. The story shifts when Irene observes her father talking with this teacher and soon after, he moves out of the Wilson home. In the subsequent stories, Clair introduces many characters within the town, often narrating the observations through Irene's eyes. Charles R. Larson noted for the *Chicago Tribune* (June 26, 1994), "The vignettes are rarely plotted stories; like ripples in a pond, they slip seamlessly into one another, the original source of agitation only hinted at." Michael Parker for the *Washington Post* (June 26, 1994) added that they "are told in a style that is memorable for its ability to shift tone and to capture, in rich and controlled language, new levels of consciousness." As a complete work, the stories within *Rattlebone* illustrate Irene's path from childhood to adulthood and her acceptance of certain tensions within her home. Many reviewers also noted the stories' success in conveying the landscape of Irene's African-American community, one that Veronica Chambers described as "less concerned with the racism of the world beyond its boundaries than it is concerned with the people who are neighbors, family, and friends." As Dinitia Smith described for *New York Newsday* (June 19, 1994), "*Rattlebone* is a celebration of the pleasures that make life possible here—jazz at the local club, Chez de Maurice's (Shady Maurice's), the music of Nat (King) Cole and Sara Vaughan, feasts of wild black morels and truffles, a glass of cold water on a hot afternoon."

Rattlebone became an immediate critical success, with one reviewer for *Publishers Weekly* (April 18, 1994) calling it "an utterly addictive collection by a writer to watch." Smith credited Clair with "a wonderful ear for language," while Chambers affirmed, "There is magic dust sprinkled over each and every page." The work earned Clair the *Chicago Tribune*'s Heartland Prize for fiction (1994), the American Library Association's Black Caucus Award (1995), and the Friends of American Literature Award (1995).

Following the success of *Rattlebone*, Clair began working on what she hoped would become a novel, telling Streitfeld in 1994, "I'm really asking the universe for a new book." In 1995 she won a Guggenheim Fellowship, which provided her with the financial resources to finish the project. In the resulting book, *October Suite* (2001), Clair resurrected the character of October Brown and developed a more sympathetic telling of her story, following the young schoolteacher through her adult life. The novel opens in an African-American teachers' rooming house, where October Brown is living in 1950. Here, October meets James Wilson, who as readers of *Rattlebone* will know is the father of one of Brown's students, and almost immediately falls in love with the married man. When October unexpectedly becomes pregnant and her lover just as quickly disappears, she is forced to move in with her sister, Vergie, and their aunts in Chillicothe, Ohio. October bears the child alone and agrees to allow Vergie and her husband to raise the baby as their own. Soon after, October realizes the depth of her mistake and must gradually come to terms with her choices. Meanwhile, she also confronts painful wounds from her past: The reader learns that when

October was five years old, her father brutally murdered her mother, leaving the young child and her sister to be raised by their aunts, who had forbidden any mention of the crime.

As Clair told Ali Ryan Scott for *Heart & Soul* (October 2001), she wanted to use the novel to explore themes of grace and forgiveness. She explained, "I have always wanted to say something about the fact that things can work out if you give them enough time; that no one is perfect, that we all have a good and a bad life. More than anything, I wanted to talk about the process of becoming who we are. It's the human thing, we all make mistakes. Usually our motivation is good, but things go wrong, and we have to live with our decisions. Drama unfolds in all of our lives and in every situation. That's what life is, and we become greater because of the mistakes that we learn from."

Critics largely applauded *October Suite* as, in the words of Lee Martin, "a novel that is notable not only for its compassionate, clear-eyed study of human nature, but also for the stylistic risks it takes and the enormous generosity of its vision." Rosemarie Robotham for *Black Issues Book Review* (November–December 2001) called the book "gorgeously written," affirming that "Clair has crafted an exquisite story of family with all its tender and violent devotions." In addition, Bart Schneider for the *New York Times* (November 11, 2001) noted that the novel offers "a rare view of African-American culture at midcentury, grounded as it is in black neighborhoods and schools and in country honky-tonks like Chez de Maurice." Nevertheless, Schneider acknowledged some problems with various plot devices—such as October's reunion with her father—that Clair uses to carry her story. He concluded, "Despite its sensual evocation of period and the promising conflict at its heart, *October Suite* is a novel in search of a credible emotional arc."

In 2001 Clair became the University of Kansas's Langston Hughes Visiting Professor of Literature. Currently, she resides in Landover, Maryland, and continues to teach creative writing at George Washington University. Of her life, she told Connie Lauerman: "I wrote a poem once about why I love winter. About the slick bark of cherry trees, about the smell of nutmeg and cabbage. Because winter holds things down, you have to push against it. It's not easy. You have to make soup from a stone and your lover doesn't come around, that sort of thing." She continued, "I was really accustomed to pushing against adversity. There was something attractive about that. And suddenly the adversity is not there and it's so strange. But it's great. I am no longer waiting for my life."

—K. D.

SUGGESTED READING: *Black Issues Book Review* p55 Nov.–Dec. 2001; *Chicago Tribune* XIV p1+ June 26, 1994, V p1+ July 6, 1994, with photo; *Heart & Soul* p35 Oct. 2001; *New York Newsday* p39 June 19, 1994, with photo; *New York Times* p23 Jan. 8, 1995; *New York Times* (on-line) Nov. 11, 2001; *Washington Post Book World* p5 June 26, 1994, p6 Oct. 7, 2001

SELECTED BOOKS: *Coping With Gravity*, 1988; *October Brown*, 1992; *Rattlebone*, 1994; *October Suite*, 2001

Coleman, Wanda

Nov. 13, 1946– Poet

The poet Wanda Coleman, born and raised in Los Angeles, captures in her writing the quintessential American experiences she has had: radicalization and emergence into black revolutionary consciousness during the Watts riots of 1965; success as a performance artist in the underground arena of poetry "slams"; self-education and the attainment of a shaman-like status. "Wanda Coleman, while staying firmly on her subject—a black girl's Bildungsroman, a black woman's transformations by and through passion and rage—displays a verbal virtuosity and stylistic range that explodes/expands the merely linear, the simply narrative, the straightforwardly lyric, into a verbal mandala whose colors and textures spin off the page," Marilyn Hacker wrote in the *Nation* (December 6, 1999), upon Coleman's receipt of the Lenore Marshall Poetry Prize. "Demotic, idiosyncratic, at once celebratory and embittered, Coleman's poems are not always easy or reassuring reading. But the generosity of their larger-than-life extravagance, their careful tempering of selfmockery, their elastic balance of overstatement and control, make them a continual, renewable reward."

In an autobiographical statement for *World Authors 1995–2000*, Wanda Coleman writes: "Restricted housing for Blacks in post World War II Los Angeles resulted in my mother and father renting a little house that had no visible address, but was then located at 1313 92nd Street, in Watts. I was delivered in that little ramshackle back house, off a long, broken, and muddy driveway, which was more a shed with its unfinished walls revealing tarpaper and chicken wire, by a doctor who made house calls. I was born with a caul over my face on Wednesday, November 13, 1946.

"Among my earliest memories is my mother's constant chase after the mailman, to be sure he delivered our mail. Those earliest of days, between cradle and aged three were the happiest days of my life, and the only period in which I felt consistently loved and accepted. By all accounts, I was a beautiful child, if frighteningly bright for my age.

Susan Carpendale/Courtesy of Wanda Coleman

Wanda Coleman

"My memories of those days are quite vivid. [Memories of] my favorite rose-colored velvet baby quilt; of seeing the faces of loved ones from my crib, of learning to identify my mother and father as distinct from other adults. I still have what remains of one of the lamp tables I used for balance, to pull myself up on in order to walk. I still maintain memories of being carried on my father's shoulder, watching him drink clabber milk, brushing his teeth, meeting 'cronies,' my mother called them, who came to the door. I remember the red-and-white gingham tablecloth. I remember playing with the neighbor kids, learning to run, frustrated by my efforts to keep up with the bigger kids. These are foremost among my early recollections, which make living in today's hate-filled world tolerable.

"I also remember when this joyful period came to an end with the death of my godmother, Virginia Clark. We called her Gin-Gin. She was a lovely woman, built like the proverbial brick (curves accented by one barrel-striped dress she favored), who had become my mother's best friend, and lived in the larger front house. Her husband pushed the refrigerator over on her during a late night fight, after he came home drunk. He served seven years in prison. The void Gin-Gin's death left in my life has never been filled. I still remember the exact moment I was told. All my attempts to fictionalize her story, or put it into verse, have failed. Something won't let me. We moved away shortly thereafter. Our new home was roughly three miles north, in the Florence-Graham district area of South Central Los Angeles. But I would begin school outside the neighborhood, at Trinity Street School, living part time with my great aunt Ora Douglas and her husband Harry, the family baby-sitters, until the age of five. The rest of my school years would be spent in South Central, a walk or bus ride away from home. My home life would be culturally rich as my parents provided lessons in all the fine arts. Prior to making a commitment to writing, I had studied to be a concert violinist. It remains my favorite instrument, although I also became adequate on piano—gifts that have atrophied.

"My years in the racist Los Angeles school system of the 50s were those of one prolonged nightmare that did not end until my graduation from Fremont High School in the summer of 1964. By the end of that summer, I was engaged to be married to my first husband, a White civil rights worker who had come to Los Angeles with Jesse Jackson, Vernon Jordan and Stokely Carmichael to raise funds for the Student Non-Violent Coordinating Committee (SNCC). This marginally educated young Georgia Cracker' began to teach me history and politics and together we joined what there was of L.A.'s emerging counterculture; however, my childhood ambition to become a poet & writer was fueled by the things he taught me, and by our experiences. In the aftermath of the Watts Riots of August 1965, we joined several arts and cultural organizations. And at that point, I began to outgrow our marriage. By the time we separated in 1969, I had two children, Anthony and Luanda, and manuscripts of fledgling poems, plays, short stories, and the outline for a yet unwritten novel.

"The coming 30 years would bring a mixed bag of false starts and dubious successes, as I became the major African-American poet in Los Angeles, a scriptwriter and journalist whenever I could get the work, marginally supporting myself with clerical jobs and the like. My second marriage in 1976 would produce my third child, Ian Wayne. I am presently married a third time, 19 years, to poet and visual artist Austin Straus. I have resided in Los Angeles, close to children, relatives, and friends. My father George Evans, an artist and advertising man, former sparring partner for Archie Moore (light-heavyweight champion 1952–1960), died in 1991. My mother Lewana Evans McDaniel, survived him to be recently widowed for a second time. I have three siblings: George, Marvin and Sharon. My daughter Luanda has made me a grandmother times three.

"Starting out as a 19-year-old college dropout, I am, as of this writing, the most prolific African-American poet in the history of modern Western verse. Among my early mentors were poets John Thomas (Venice West) and Henri Coulette. John Martin's Black Sparrow Press offered me shelter when others rebuffed me. Among my literary influences, I often credit the writings of Edgar [Allan] Poe and Lewis Carroll; Anne Petry's novel *The Street*, and Melville's *Moby Dick*. I have dwelled outside the American literary mainstream, not by choice, in the world of small presses and magazines, which proved nourishing ground. This happenstance has been fraught with its own frustrations, and I have not overcome them all. My literary success has come at a terrible emotional toll. I hope, someday, to have the quality time to tell my myriad stories in full. But the lack of that won't stop me though the lack of decent sleep may."

"Until the Watts Riots of August 1965," as Coleman wrote in *Native in a Strange Land: Trials and Tremors*, "there was no one other than my parents and a few inspired English teachers, outside of my grudgingly stubborn self, to imbue my life with value." Coleman's life as a poet started when, after the 1965 Watts riots—which saw the release of pent-up frustrations among the area's poor, predominantly black residents—creative arts programs were instituted in her community. After a poetry workshop, Coleman "emerged as a poet," according to Carol Schwalberg, who wrote about Coleman for *Poets & Writers Magazine* (October 1998). "Completing my off-and-on college education was not an option," Coleman explained in the introduction to *Native in a Strange Land*. "I was too proud to accept charity and terrified of credit. There was no local Ralph Ellison, James Baldwin or Gwendolyn Brooks to mentor me. There were no hotbeds of fledgling Black intellectuals, or intellectuals of any kind, within my reach, to thrive among. . . . Nevertheless, I did find my guides in unexpected places; an arts studio in post-riot Watts where I was introduced to, and developed a student-mentor relationship with, Bliss Carnochan, then professor in the Department of English at Stanford University." Another of her mentors was Lois Peyser, a scriptwriter. "Other guides, nameless and diverse, would eventually school me in the smarts mandatory for survival between the margins defined by poverty and race, presuming no escape," she wrote in her evocative style, using words such as "guides," for example, to bring in a dimension of African spirituality.

Her first book was a small chapbook of poetry published by Black Sparrow Press. Her second poetry collection, *Mad Dog Black Lady*, came out in 1979. All through the 1970s, Coleman, while not garnering much financial success, reaped other kinds of rewards from her poetry through choreographed and dramatically charged presentations—which became famous for eliciting emotional responses from audiences. Coleman worked as a scriptwriter as well as a poet, becoming the first African-American woman to win an Emmy Award, in 1976, for best writing for a daytime drama series, *Days of Our Lives*. Despite the Emmy, her career as a scriptwriter did not flourish, and Coleman, supporting herself and her family by a variety of what she termed "pink-collar jobs," continued to turn out a large body of poetry and stories. She also worked as an editor at men's magazines. Meanwhile, *Mad Dog Black Lady* and *Imagoes*, published in 1983, won her a National Endowment for the Arts (NEA) grant for 1981–82 and a Guggenheim poetry fellowship in 1984.

Coleman's 1987 volume, *Heavy Daughter Blues: Poems & Stories 1968–1986*, includes the poem "Josephine Your Big Mouth," in which Coleman ostensibly wrote about the entertainer Josephine Baker but clearly used Baker as a surrogate for herself:

. . . . they say it was your mouth was your
own worst enemy its caustic sooths and I
heard way back in the 60s how after all those
years you were still MUCH TOO LOUD

The cheer of a vital spirit often breaks through the bitterness that Coleman can sometimes convey. In "They'll Starve You," she wrote:

the future is a grave you won't get over sniffin clover it's your rump you've got to save. . . .

In the poem "Heavy Daughter Blues," Coleman revealed explicitly how she remains standing, despite a world that seems designed to drag her down:

I throw the symbols. I make reverberations
myth/my girlchild and me cackle joyfully in
the kitchen as we make cookies for the party
of the world

Coleman's first book consisting only of prose pieces, *A War of Eyes and Other Stories*, was published in 1988. Most of the stories deal with the harsher side of life in Los Angeles, as it is experienced by people of color. *A War of Eyes* was included in *500 Great Books by Women*, compiled by Erica Bauermeister, Jesse Larsen, and Holly Smith. Larsen, in her annotation of Coleman's book, termed it "Twenty-five Watts, Los Angeles, stories that whisper, scream, moan, and sing about people who smile and act nice to you but they ain't your friends," and about "women who sell their bodies—but not their anger—to feed their kids." Larsen concluded that through "deft use of dialogue, dream, description, and shimmering language, Wanda Coleman writes stories that feel and sound rough, gorgeous, strong, half-dead, brave, and terrified."

In a critical article in *Parnassus: Poetry in Review* (1998), Eric Murphy Selinger considered Coleman's 1990 volume *African Sleeping Sickness: Stories & Poems*; her 1993 poetry collection, *Hand Dance*; and *Native in a Strange Land*, a collection of short prose pieces, published in 1996. He discussed her response, in *The Best American Poetry 1996*, to a critic who "dismissed" her early work as "jazz poetry." She "decided to take that phrase and toot it as loud and long as possible," as she wrote. "Dipping into clashing dictions," Selinger observed, "her ears pricked as much by stammer, stumble, and cacophony as by the pleasures of swing, Coleman finds that the jazz poet's burden is to mock, meditate, imitate, and transform, using any and every literary trick and device—even cliches—at will. . . . When she carries it off, Coleman's 'fusionist' aesthetic gives her poetry a memorable, hectoring density."

A writer for *Book News, Inc.* (February 1, 1994) judged *Hand Dance* to be "hard brilliant strokes shot through with street music." The pieces in *Native in a Strange Land: Trials and Tremors*, mainly culled and revised from her *Los Angeles Times Magazine* biweekly column, cover much of the same ground as her poetry—and, like them, emerge organically from her life. Sandra K. Stanley, who critiqued the book for the *African American Review* (Summer 1999), found in it a window on "the lives of the disenfranchised and the dispossessed," pervaded by themes of "sexism, racism, dehumanization, and marginalization" that "relate Coleman's struggle in her own cultural war against poverty, racism, and hopelessness." The *Library Journal* (February 1, 1997) reviewer termed *Native in a Strange Land* "a nonlinear memoir" that expresses emotions "with integrity and subtlety."

Coleman's 1998 collection, *Bathwater Wine*, represents her mature period. In these poems, she considers herself a survivor: "and I who arrived late/and caught the last notes/am surprised by my laughter," she wrote in "The Sacred History of the Gone." The *Publishers Weekly* (June 29, 1998) reviewer called *Bathwater Wine* a "large, somewhat sprawling" book and "an encyclopedic, moment-by-moment accounting of left coast rage, witness and transcendence," in which the poems "move agilely from a tragic (yet comedic) resignation to verbal riffs and hijinks, to direct, in-your-face declarations of resistance and anger."

Mambo Hips and Make Believe, Coleman's first published novel, appeared in 1999. Many of the same themes and concerns that overlie her poetry and essays appear in fictional form in *Mambo Hips*. The story takes place in the context of a friendship between two women, Erlene and Tamala, with ambitions to be writers. Each of the 37 chapters is preceded by a transliteration from Japanese Zen wisdom, followed by a short homily that comments in Zen style on the action. Each chapter concludes with a letter or postcard from one of the women to the other. The *Publishers Weekly* (November 22, 1999) reviewer deemed the story of Tamala, a woman born with improperly developed sexual organs, "poignant" but "buried under the weight of excessive family history and awkward plot devices," while judging that Erlene "rarely emerges as an autonomous character." The reviewer concluded that "Coleman exhibits a colorful imagination" but that "the characters and events evolve in a dizzying blur."

In 1999 Coleman was awarded the Lenore Marshall Poetry Prize by the Academy of American Poets and *The Nation*, winning over other contenders who included Marie Ponsot, Arthur Sze, Alicia Ostriker, and Rachel Hadas. That award confirmed her rise in status from poet of potential to major American literary voice. Coleman's most recent book of poems, *Mercurochrome* (2001), was nominated for the 2001 National Book Award for poetry.
— S.Y.

SUGGESTED READING: *African American Review* p371+ Summer 1999; *Book News, Inc.* Feb. 1, 1994; *Denver Post* C p1 June 2, 1999; *Library Journal* p97 Feb. 1, 1997; *Parnassus: Poetry in Review* p356+ 1998; *Poets & Writers Magazine* p46+ Oct. 1998, with photo; *Publishers Weekly* p54 June 29, 1998, p44 Nov. 22, 1999

SELECTED BOOKS: fiction—*A War of Eyes and Other Stories*, 1988; *Mambo Hips and Make Believe*, 1999; poetry—*Mad Dog Black Lady*, 1979; *Imagoes*, 1983; *Hand Dance*, 1993; *Bathwater Wine*, 1998; *Mercurochrome: New Poems*, 2001; nonfiction—*Native in a Strange Land: Trials and Tremors*, 1996

Juliet van Otteren/Courtesy of Random House

Collins, Billy

Mar. 22, 1941– Poet

The American poet Billy Collins has established a reputation as one of the nation's most prolific troubadours of the 1990s, one for whom poetry can be at once entertaining, artful, and profound. "Billy Collins writes funny poems," Cynthia Magriel Wetzler wrote for the *New York Times* (November 30, 1997), "poems in which a dog barks out a solo with the oboes in a Beethoven symphony or in which the writer spends the morning shoveling snow with Buddha." Shunning the academic obscurity in which much of contemporary verse is cloaked, his trademark works frequently begin with humorous and inviting images that unfold into penetrating revelations. Due largely to his engaging and accessible style, Collins has attracted a wide readership and is credited with reintroducing poetry to the general public. He has been described by Bruce Weber in the *New York Times* (December 19, 1999) as "the most popular poet in America," and his collections have sold more than 100,000 copies to date—an astonishing number for books of modern poetry. Despite his blithe and popular approach to verse, Collins's work is taken seriously as literature: he has received fellowships from the National Endowment for the Arts and the Guggenheim Foundation, was named a "Literary Lion" by the New York Public Library, and has been singled out for numerous honors by *Poetry* magazine. He is currently serving his second consecutive one-year term as U.S. Poet Laureate, which expires in 2003.

Billy Collins was born in New York City on March 22, 1941. His father, William, was an electrician; his mother, Katherine, was a nurse. Having attended parochial schools throughout his youth, Collins earned a bachelor of arts degree from the College of the Holy Cross, in 1963, and a Ph.D. from the University of California at Riverside, in 1971. In the early 1970s Collins joined the English faculty at the Herbert H. Lehman College of the City University of New York, in the Bronx. While pursuing a career in academe, he wrote verse in his spare time.

After several years of publishing his poems in obscure literary and academic journals, Collins assembled his first full-length collection, which was published under the title *The Apple That Astonished Paris* by the University of Arkansas Press in 1988. Two years later his second manuscript, *Questions about Angels*, was selected by Edward Hirsch as a winner of the National Poetry Series competition. As part of his prize, the competition sponsored the collection's publication, in 1991, by William Morrow & Co. Based on the literary merit of his first two volumes, the University of Pittsburgh Press contacted Collins with an offer to publish future collections. His first with Pittsburgh was *The Art of Drowning* (1995), which was selected jointly by the *Nation* and the Academy of American Poets as a finalist for their 1996 Lenore Marshall Prize. "Collins is erudite and allusive without being pretentious, funny without being stupid," poet and critic Reagan Upshaw wrote about *The Art of Drowning* for the *Bloomsbury Review* (September/October 1996), as reprinted on the Web site *bigsnap.com*. "I picture him as a performer in one of his favorite imagined settings, the intimate jazz nightclub at 3:00 A.M. His slow saxophone solo evokes Bach, Mozart, and Brahms, while remaining jazz. It seduces listeners and warbles close to drunken sentiment at times, but never quite falls in. It's a music well worth hearing."

Collins continued to gain notice from all quarters of the literary establishment. In 1992 the New York Public Library selected him as one of its "Literary Lions," and *Poetry* honored him with its Poet of the Year Award for 1994. His work also appeared in *The Best American Poetry* anthology in 1992, 1993, and 1997. However, his work did not grab the attention of a readership beyond the traditionally insular world of American poetry until 1997, when the University of Pittsburgh Press published his volume *Picnic, Lightning*.

In tone and content a number of the poems in *Picnic, Lightning*, which is comprised of 43 poems divided into four sections, suggest a dialogue between Collins and his literary forebears: his "Lines Composed over Three Thousand Miles from Tintern Abbey," for instance, evokes William Wordsworth's "Lines Written a Few Miles above Tintern Abbey," and "Musée des Beaux Arts Revisited" was clearly inspired by W. H. Auden's "Musée des Beaux Arts." Such poems, however, appear not as parodies or burlesques, but as Collins's own commentary on Wordsworth and Auden. Taken as a whole, the poems in *Picnic, Lightning* possess Collins's conversational voice, which invites the reader to contemplate routine activities familiar to any late-20th-century American: shoveling snow, paging through a lingerie catalogue, or weathering a power outage at home. His art lies in juxtaposing such mundane occurrences with the jolt of an unexpected insight, creating offbeat scenarios that expose the extraordinary within the ordinary.

Collins's speaker in "Passengers," for example, contemplates mortality while waiting in an airport lounge:

> At the gate, I sit in a row of blue seats
> with the possible company of my death,
> this sprawling miscellany of people—
> carry-on bags and paperbacks—that
> could be gathered in a flash into a band
> of pilgrims on the last open road.

The speaker feels the need to eulogize himself and his fellow passengers but realizes, to comic effect, that airport security is a consideration:

> well, I just think it would be good if one
> of us maybe stood up and said a few
> words, or, so as not to involve the police, at least quietly wrote something
> down.

In reviewing *Picnic, Lightning* for *Virginia Quarterly Review* (Autumn 1998), an unnamed critic declared that "Collins has found his voice and hit his stride" in a collection that "impresses one with his light touch and his generally humorous take on things. His poems are conversational commentaries on his daily adventures, both real and imaginary. He writes easily about any number of topics: the various marginal comments he has encountered in borrowed books, the facial expressions people wear while listening to jazz, or the implied intimacies of looking at a Victoria's Secret catalogue." A brief review, also unsigned, in the *New Yorker* (July 6, 1998) was equally favorable: "Accessible and wry, the poems in this book belie a complicated sadness. What Collins does best is turn an apparently simple phrase into a numinous moment, as with a dream 'like a fantastic city in pencil,' which, come morning, 'erased itself.' Collins brings to mind the elegant wit of the sorely missed William Matthews, another poet of plenitude, irony, and Augustan grace."

Shortly after the publication of *Picnic, Lightning*, Garrison Keillor featured some of Collins's poems on the National Public Radio (NPR) program "Writer's Almanac." Collins then appeared as a guest on Keillor's immensely popular NPR show, "A Prairie Home Companion," which in turn caused the sales of his volumes to rise considerably. Since then, Collins has enjoyed prominence as both a critical darling and a best-seller, a unique status among most contemporary poets. His collections routinely sell in the tens of thousands and have remained on publishers' lists long after his contemporaries' collections have gone out of print.

Responding to his growing reputation and marketability, publishing giant Random House offered Collins, in 1999, a six-figure advance toward his next three collections of poetry. His first volume with Random House, *Sailing Alone around the Room*, a selection of new and previously published poems, was due to hit bookstores in February 2000, but was delayed due to a copyright dispute between Random House and Collins's former publisher, the University of Pittsburgh Press. The latter felt that their own back-list sales of Collins's work would suffer as a result of the Random House collection, and refused to grant permission to reprint many of Collins's poems. The two publishing houses eventually resolved their differences and *Sailing Alone around the Room* was released in 2001; within three months of its release, the book had 65,000 copies in print. Featuring poems from all of his previous books as well as 20 new poems, the volume was quickly deemed a commercial and critical success. As Dwight Garner noted for the *New York Times Book Review* (September 23, 2001), "There are brainy, observant, spit-shined moments on almost every page." Tim Gavin for *Library Journal* (September 1, 2001) added, "The surface structure of these poems appears simplistic, but subtle changes in tone or gesture move the reader from the mundane to the sublime. . . . The results are accessible but not trite, comical but not laughable, and well crafted but not overly flamboyant. Collins relies heavily on imagery, which becomes the cornerstone of the entire volume, and his range of diction brings such a polish to these poems that the reader is left feeling that this book 'once opened, can never be closed.'"

For Collins, keeping the reader in mind is a vital element in producing the kind of lively verse that he espouses, and he discounts claims from some quarters that American poetry is losing relevance among modern readers. "I think a lot of readers are frustrated with the obscurity and self-indulgence of most poetry," he opined to Gautam Naik for the journal *Magma* (Spring 1999, on-line). "I try very assiduously to court the reader and engage him. I am interested more in a public following than a critical one." "I just sense someone in the room with me. Poetry has a small but intense audience, like jazz," Collins elaborated to Cynthia Magriel Wetzler. "This lament for the diminished audience is a soap opera. . . . The facts are that good poetry is exorbitantly rewarded with grants, travel, fame, and positions in universities that were unthinkable 20 years ago. It's a wild time to be a poet." Explaining his own fascination with poetry, Collins told Magriel Wetzler, "When words are put together in fresh ways there is a pleasure-giving quality in language, which brings a release of endorphins." "Poetry is my cheap means of transportation," he added. "By the end of the poem the reader should be in a different place from where he started. I would like him to be slightly disoriented at the end, like I drove him outside of town at night and dropped him off in a cornfield."

In addition to the monies he has received from the NEA and Guggenheim Foundation, Collins has been granted a fellowship by the New York Foundation for the Arts, and has been awarded the Bess Hokin, Frederick Bock, Oscar Blumenthal, and Levinson Prizes, all by *Poetry*. In 2001 Collins was appointed the Library of Congress's Poet Laureate Consultant in Poetry, further securing his place of prominence in modern poetry. Of the honor, he explained to Stephen Whited for *Book* (September–October 2001), "Most gratifying to me . . . is hearing that people have been brought back to poetry by reading my work. I think there are many people who are ready to return to poetry. They had poetry in school, and either their love for it was beaten out of them by bad teachers, or they just marginalized poetry the way many people do. But I think there is a very basic need to get back to it." To assist in this process, Collins launched the "Poetry 180" program, designed to bring modern poetry into high schools. He accumulated an anthology of 180 poems—one for each of the roughly 180 days in a school year—which participating schools can use to expose students to a different type of poetry than what they may currently be studying. "The catchphrase for Poetry 180," he explained to Catherine Barnett for *Arts Education Policy Review* (March–April 2002), "has been to make poetry a part of your everyday life in addition to a subject to be taught." His aim is to provide "a more updated view of what's happening in poetry today" and "to seduce high school students to an affinity for poetry." While Collins hoped the poems would be read daily over the loudspeaker or some other system of public address, thus fostering the feel of a community reading, he did not want the poems to be "taught" in any traditional sense. Rather, the students should be given the opportunity to connect with the poems on their own terms. "You can't really get people to listen," he said. "It's up to the poems." Collins was reappointed Poet Laureate in 2002.

Described by Bruce Weber as "an unprepossessing but droll man, a lover of jazz and good whiskey in the manner of a 1950's-style hip intellectual," Collins has conducted summer poetry workshops for several years at University College Galway, Ireland, and has been poet-in-residence at Burren College of Art, also in Ireland. In 1999 he accepted a faculty appointment at Sarah Lawrence College,

in Bronxville, New York. In the spring of 2001 he was promoted to Distinguished Professor of English at Lehman College, where he has taught for more than 30 years. His most recent book of poems, *Nine Horses*, was published in 2002. Collins and his wife, Diane, who is an architect, live in Somers, a town in northern Westchester County, New York.
— E.M.

SUGGESTED READING: *New York Times* XIV (Westchester Section) p19 Nov. 30, 1997, with photo, I p1+ Dec. 19, 1999, with photo; *New Yorker* p73 July 6, 1998

SELECTED BOOKS: *The Apple That Astonished Paris*, 1988; *Questions About Angels*, 1991; *The Art of Drowning*, 1995; *Picnic, Lightning*, 1998; *Sailing Alone around the Room: New and Selected Poems*, 2001; *Nine Horses*, 2002

Doug Macomber

Collins, Martha

Nov. 25, 1940– Poet

The American poet, teacher, and translator Martha Collins is influenced by everything from mathematical theory to painting, sculpture, and political events. One of her critics compared her to a juggler, sending words and images flying and transforming them in the act of writing. The co-director of the creative writing program at Oberlin College, Collins has been published in a number of journals, has written four collections of poetry, and is at work on a fifth. In *Ms.*(March/April 1994), June Jordan describes Collins as part of a new feminist tradition, women who are writing twenty years after feminism's revolutionary heyday, but nonetheless "very hot, ingenious, and brilliantly willful sisters." Another critic reaches even farther back in history to locate Collins in a tradition of women's poetry. Reviewing Collins's work for the *Boston Book Review*, as quoted on the University Press of New England web-site, Pamela Alexander wrote: "The idiosyncratic territory of Martha Collins's work lies south of Emily Dickinson, west of H. D., a little to the left of Louise Bogan, and within easy commuting distance of Gertrude Stein."

For *World Authors 1995–2000*, Martha Collins writes: "Born in Nebraska and raised in Iowa, I was a late and only child who spent a great deal of time by myself. We were financially middle class until my father quit his job with a pharmaceutical company when I was ten. Later he opened his own pharmacy, where he struggled to make a living and all three of us worked. But we continued to enjoy middle class culture: I took piano and violin lessons, and it was expected that I would go to college. My father wanted me to be a doctor. My mother, who had been a fairly serious pianist, was less ambitious for me; but the musical background she gave me continues to be an important influence on my poetry: I usually hear the music of a poem before I begin to understand it."

"I wrote poems in grade school and high school, but didn't turn to poetry in a serious way for some years. Determined not to become a doctor, I slipped into an English major, where I discovered poetry. I abandoned plans for law school and began graduate study in English, but found it perversely unrelated to what I loved about literature. I dropped out briefly and managed a book store; a few years later I stumbled into a job at the University of Massachusetts-Boston. When I took a year off to finish my Ph.D and read Henry James for my dissertation, it finally became clear that I didn't want to write about writers—I wanted to be one."

"My first published collection of poems began with the discovery of the then-popular mathematical theory known as catastrophe theory; the rainbow was an example of how it worked, a situation 'where gradually changing forces or motivations lead to abrupt changes in behavior.' Painting was becoming an influence on my work at this time, and mathematical theory led, via the rainbow, to an exploration of color theory. *The Catastrophe of Rainbows* is filled with color; the sequential title poem moves through the spectrum, beginning with black and ending with white. Like many first books, *Catastrophe* has stories to tell, fictional and non-fictional; but a distrust of narrative as well as the influence of painting counter the linear impulse. I was reading Freud when I began the book, and was (as I continue to be) deeply interested in the often-unconscious motivations that constitute the undersides of our stories."

"Distrust of narrative becomes more pronounced in my second book, *The Arrangement of Space*, which is comprised of three long sequences. The second and longest, 'A Book of Days,' was written at the Bunting Institute, where the luxury of a year to write led me to use the single day as a structuring principle. These poems are even less linear than the earlier ones, and mark the beginning of a deliberate use of fragmentation. Shortly after I began them, I found a model in the sculptures of David Smith, so beautifully constructed of apparently disparate pieces."

"My third book, *A History of Small Life on a Windy Planet*, was the first that was influenced primarily by voice rather than visual art. I had always cared about the music of poems; my first book contained a number of experiments with loosened form. But reading John Ashbery helped me listen to a more vernacular language, and led me to open my poems to multiple voices."

"Meanwhile, my subject matter was becoming more expansive. Teaching at a working-class commuter school had led me to political involvements in the 60s and 70s, and I had participated in the anti-war movement; some of my first poems were attempts at protest. But it wasn't until the third book that these concerns really made their way into my work. The first poem was written during the Iran-Contra hearings, the last during the Anita Hill-Clarence Thomas hearings; war is a subject, as are various domestic issues. But the poems are not simply "about" these subjects. Ultimately, I had another visual metaphor: many of the poems are collages."

"After I finished this book, I began to work with the William Joiner Center at U. Mass.-Boston, which since the late 80s has held a summer workshop featuring Vietnam veterans as well as Vietnamese writers. Teaching a translation workshop there, I met Nguyen Quang Thieu, a Vietnamese poet born in 1957. The involvement with Thieu led me back to the time of the Vietnam War, when I had begun writing poems, and eventually to the publication of *The Women Carry River Water*, a co-translated collection of his work. In 1999, I began working on translations of poems by a contemporary Vietnamese woman, Lam Thi My Da."

"My fourth collection, *Some Things Words Can Do*, is concerned with ways of thinking and speaking that divide us; the longest poem, 'Pinks,' deals with race, and a sequence of unrhymed sonnets explores gender and racial differences, beginning with 'Points' and ending with 'Sides' (another mathematical echo). Collage continues to be an important technique, one that I think has allowed me to deal with personal experience and social concerns in a more integrated way; but the collection is also centrally aware of 'things words can do' (and things they can't) to bring together our fragmented selves and our splintered visions of society and the world."

"In 1997, I began teaching at Oberlin College, although I continue to live in the East half the year. At Oberlin, I began my fifth collection, *Working through the Night*. Influenced in part by the words of my aging mother, the collection carries the fragmentation of my earlier work a step further; but the poems also continue to be influenced by visual art and social issues, and the 'night' of the title is simultaneously the unconscious which helps to shape us, the evil amidst which we continue to struggle and fight wars, and the darkness into which, like my mother, we ultimately age and disappear."

Collins's second collection of poetry, *The Arrangement of Space* (1991), consists of three poetic sequences—the fragmentary narrative "Women in American Literature"; a sequence of thirty lyrics "A Book of Days"; and six poems, each of which has six parts, called "Six Suites." Reviewing the collection for *Small Press* (Spring 1992), Laurel Blossom praised the poet's technique. "The poems are free form, but that does mean they are uncrafted, or undercrafted," Blossom writes. "It means that their craft serves another end than the craft that aims at producing a shining jewel. These poems are more like rivers, ongoing, uncontainable, and moving. Openness is their central theme, womanhood their subject. . . ." Gardner McFall, in *American Book Review* (April/May 1992), also comments on the poem's dynamic movement. "One does not follow exactly the turns of a given sequence so much as ride them out with an ear to the underlying sense," she writes. Although McFall appreciated the expressions of "praise, despair, acceptance, outrage", the critic also felt there were poems that remain opaque. ". . . despite the poet's effort to create meaning through tone, her subject eludes us." Kathleen Norris, writing for *Library Journal* (August 1991), concurs. "This is extremely elliptical work, but too many words are missing; the connecting tissue that would flesh out the poems for the reader isn't there, and one often feels lost." And yet, Norris finds music in the lyrics, citing the poem "Wind Chill's" final stanza: "Open, as if the sun were a hole / in the gray sky, waiting for something to hold / in itself, the wind unlike the world / as a thing could be, the cold, the swell / of the organ, the chords, the rush / of snow blowing like God across the road."

Critics remarked on the intensity and control apparent in *A History of Small Life on a Windy Planet* (1993). In presenting the collection with the Alice Fay Di Castagnola Award, David Ignatow describe the poems as having a "unique ability to fix each passing phase of a swiftly moving, rootless society in triumphant style," as quoted by Judith Kitchen in the *Georgia Review* (Spring 1994). Kitchen also admires the book's "surrealistic" effects, achieved, she says, by "rapid shifts in perspective." "They challenge the reader to change gear as the poem turns sharply," Kitchen writes. ". . . twists back on itself as if on a hairpin curve, then rushes forward borne on its accumulated momentum."

The "history" of the collection's title refers to the connections that Collins explores between the individual self and the larger world. A reviewer for *Publishers Weekly* (June 7, 1993) finds in the poems a balance between the "horrific and the playful," citing one poem's invocation of a "friendly caboose" that, passing through pleasant farmland, evolves into cattle cars carrying Jews to their deaths. "With a few deft strokes," the reviewer maintains, "Collins endows the merely topical (the Gulf War, the news story about a murdered woman whose intestines were torn out) with universal dimensions." While Pat Monaghan, writing for *Booklist* (June 1-15, 1993), found that Collins captured the "ambiguities and urgencies of this life," Kitchen, in *The Georgia Review*, found that the poems are occasionally overdetermined, too concerned with "right thoughts." ". . . they can be felt to be written to a prescription. There's a little too much 'focus' in their final objective," she writes.

Collins's most recent book of poetry is *Some Things Words Can Do* (1998). In her review of the collection, Pamela Alexander echoed other critics by focusing on Collins's tonal balance: "While her poems deal with war and oppression, contemporary relationships, civil rights and censorship and homelessness, she is fluid, musical, full of wit and wordplay and suggestiveness."

Collins has received fellowships from the Ingram Merrill Foundation and the Bunting Institute, in addition to three Pushcart Prizes and a Witten Brynner Grant for translation. In 1990, she won a grant from the National Endowment for the Arts, at a time when that organization was under fire from some legislators who objected to the government support of exhibitions of works by the photographers Robert Mapplethorpe and Andres Serrano. Collins and other artists were asked to sign a letter promising to comply with the standards dictated by the Endowment. Specifically, artists were asked to refrain from producing artworks that include "depictions of sadomasochism, homoeroticism, the sexual exploitation of children or individuals engaged in sex acts and which, when taken as a whole, do not have serious literary, artistic, political, or scientific merit," as quoted by a reporter in the *New York Times* (March 10, 1990, online). In that article, Collins described her ambivalence about signing the agreement. "I signed because I can live with it, but I'm concerned by the tone—concerned that things could get worse instead of better," she told the reporter. ". . . It's ironic that we've spent all these years reading about restrictions on artists in Eastern Europe and just when they're gaining freedom we're beginning to feel restricted."

In a poem called "Day with Her," published in the *Gettysburg Review* (Winter 1999, online), Collins describes an encounter between an aging mother and her visiting daughter. In the final stanza, mother and daughter play out the scene of the child's coming into language: "First I taught you the vowels. O, I said, and you said O? / You were my first teacher. / And then the ah and ee, the other vowels, that are harder to say. / My first poetry teacher. / And then I taught you words. Pretty, I said one day, we were looking at a rose, I think. / Very pretty. / Pwitty, you said. And then I said Very Pretty. / Vewy pwitty. / But you said Vewy pwitty, and I said Very pretty again, to get the r. And then the accents too, not ver-y pret-ty, all the same, but vér-y prét-ty. / Vér-y prét-ty. / And that rose, you know, that rose was the most beautiful rose I'd ever seen, a perfect rose, I can see it now. / My poetry teacher, Mama. / Is that true? / You know, it is."

— M.A.H.

Arrangement of Space, 1991; *History of Small Life on a Windy Planet*, 1993; *Some Things Words Can Do*, 1998.

American Book Review p28 Apr./May 1992; *Booklist* p1773 June 1-15,1993; *Georgia Review* p162+ Spr. 1994; *Library Journal* p105 Aug. 1991; *Ms.* p70+ Mar./Apr. 1994; *New York Times* (on-line) Mar. 10, 1990; *Publishers Weekly* p65 June 7, 1993; *Small Press* p85 Spr.1992.

Courtesy of Nancy Lee Russell

Conoley, Gillian

1955– Poet

Over the last two decades, Gillian Conoley has been a lyrical spectator of small-town America, coloring the details of ordinary life with playful, vibrant, and emotionally complex works. Conoley has published five volumes of poetry, including *Some Gangster Pain* (1987), *Tall Stranger* (1991), which was nominated for the National Book Critics Circle Award, *Beckon* (1996), and *Lovers in the Used World* (2001). Following the lead of such women writers as Gertrude Stein and Jorie Graham, Conoley has developed a poetic style of contrasts, as Gail Wronksy described in *The Antioch Review* (Winter 1997), in which readers may find "the peculiarly American matter-of-factness of the small-town exotic coming face-to-face with the intellectual high-brow energy of language poetry."

For *World Authors, 1995–2000*, Gillian Conoley writes: "I was born in 1955 in Austin, Texas, though I did not grow up there. I grew up in Taylor, Texas, a small town of 10,000 people 36 miles northeast of Austin, culturally a world apart. My father grew up in the same town, and his father before him. Taylor is an old railroad town, and at one time was the biggest cotton producing community in the nation. There were many families of German, Mexican, and Czechoslovakian descent, and so it was not unusual, even in the 1950s and 1960s, to hear several different languages while walking down the street.

"Families tend to stay in Taylor for generations on end. My father lived there until his death in 2000; he had the same group of friends when he was 80 that he had when he was five. He had an identical twin brother. Both of them were adopted when they were six months old, by a devout Christian family that had adopted four other children already. The only time my father left this community for an extended period of time was during World War II, when he was a Marine, a recipient of both a Purple Heart and a Silver Star for heroism in Guam. Upon his release, he married my mother (who he had been engaged to for four years during the war) in La Jolla, California, and after a short trip to Niagara Falls, returned to Taylor, Texas.

"He started a grocery store with his twin brother, but this business eventually dissolved. My father started a new business on his own, the local radio station, KTAE radio, dial 1260, 'a little something for everyone.' Programming included Mexican polka, country and western, soul, and local and national news. National news came off the Associated Press wire. Local news was paraphrased from the town newspaper and for anything more immediate depended greatly on phone calls from town citizens, who would often call to report cows loose from fields, dogs running wild, school lunch menus. The radio station provided a real and necessary community function. My father hated music, but he loved community, and this was his impetus in starting the radio station to begin with.

"The rest of his family, however, did not hate music. My sister, my mother, and I listened to the radio all day long. I loved the plaintive notes and long, meandering rhythms of traditional country western music, but it was second to my love of soul. Second-rate soul performers would come through the town to perform. I remember a particularly riveting performance of 'Skinny Legs and All' by Joe Tex. Elvis Presley, before he was Elvis, came to the radio station once. He was on a car tour through central Texas hand-delivering 45's. My father, his accountant, and the radio announcer said that Elvis was a hoodlum. They wouldn't play his record.

"My mother is a sixth-generation Texan, with some more recent relatives residing in Louisiana and Georgia. Almost all of her relatives were farmers. She was a Psychology major at Sophie Newcomb in New Orleans, and was raised by a single parent, since her father died of tuberculosis when she was four. She spent most of her adolescence traveling from Texas city to city while her mother held different jobs as an English teacher in the schools or in the insurance industry. They moved almost constantly, particularly during the war years. She finished her degree in Psychology by attending three universities: Sophie Newcomb, the University of Texas, and Southwestern University, where she met my father. She helped him start the radio station, and raised two daughters. Throughout her life, she has had more than an abiding interest in the antique, in its link to the past. Over the course of 37 years, she gathered up much of her family's furniture, and imbued the furniture with the lore of her family. To this day, she has a keen eye for character.

"I grew up in a house that was previously owned by two brothers who had lived in it all their lives. They had been privately tutored in the house, and when they died, there was no one to leave the house to, and so a friend of their family sold it to my parents, fully furnished, and with floor-to-ceiling bookcases across the second floor landing. I remember in particular there were many volumes of Twain, Whitman, Thurber, Faulkner, Flannery O'Connor, Carson McCullers, Dorothy Parker, the Brontë sisters, as well as sort of 'book-of-the-month club' selections of the 1930s and 1940s of a lesser rank. The house burned down to the ground in 1998, taking with it almost all the family antiques, but I still have some of the books I retrieved from the house before the fire.

"Now I live about as far as one could from Taylor, Texas, both culturally and atmospherically; I live in California. My little block in Corte Madera, California, in the San Francisco Bay Area, 12 miles from the Golden Gate Bridge, feels like a sleepy little town though, on its best summer days. I have a white picket fence with wisteria that drapes over it, fully, almost choking it, every spring. I love the sense of endless possibility in California, what the Ohlone tribe called 'dancing on the edge of the world.' I love the 'there' in what Gertrude Stein called the 'no there, there.' I love the sun and the light.

"I have been married to Domenic Stansberry, a novelist and crime writer, for 16 years, and we have a daughter, Gillis Stansberry, who is nine. Gillis was named after my father. I teach at Sonoma State University, a small liberal arts college, and at Vermont College, a low-residency MFA program. I edit a literary magazine called *Volt*, which is committed to innovative poetry. I suppose editing *Volt* is an act of community, as my father's radio station was an act of community.

"I've been asked, in this biographical portrait, to discuss my motivations to write. I enjoy being in an imaginative state over long periods of time. All those years in a small town with not much cultural stimulation might have drawn me into the imagination more fully, and certainly for extended periods, since there was so much dead time to fill. I grew up loving language and its unpredictability and its fierceness and frailty. Poetry is an act of discovery. I think I write to see if there is anything I can know, if only momentarily. I don't think people 'know' anything, but I do think we have brief glances. It's the wily properties of language that draw me back to the page, the infinitudes of language, its relationship to human perception and consciousness."

In 1973 Conoley moved to Dallas, Texas, to attend Southern Methodist University, graduating in 1977 with a BFA degree. After college, she worked as a journalist for the *Irving Daily News* and the *Dallas Morning News*, but yearned to explore language in greater depth. Conoley soon became interested in poetry and its opportunities to test the boundaries of language, and enrolled in an MFA program at the University of Massachusetts at Amherst, earning her degree in 1983. There, she studied with such poets as James Tate and Madeline DeFrees. After graduating she taught at a number of universities across the country, including the University of New Orleans, Tulane University, Eastern Washington University in Spokane, California State University at Hayward, and San Francisco State.

In 1984, while teaching at the University of New Orleans, Conoley published her first book of poems, a chapbook entitled *Woman Speaking Inside Film Noir*. The book contains poems depicting Conoley's rural Texas, as well as others developing themes of urban life. In the title poem, Conoley speaks as a woman literally trapped inside the genre of noir. Dorothy Barresi for The *American Book Review* (July–August 1988) described, "Though [this poem's] world is an undeniably sensuous one, it is also characterized by the woman's inability to set herself free of unfulfilled longing." Barresi quoted from the poem: "What I want happens / not when the man leaning / on a lamppost / stares up to my room and / I meet his gaze / through the blinds, / but in the moment after, / in the neon's pulse, /when his cigarette / glows in the rain like a siren / and he looks away." Of the overall collection, Jared Carter for *Georgia Review* (Summer 1986) observed, "[The] sense of absence and loss, of things slipping away irretrievably, is characteristic of Conoley's poetic universe."

In 1987 Conoley published her second book, *Some Gangster Pain*, and began receiving wider critical attention. This book is divided into three sections, which Barresi described as "moving from Texas and the poet's own childhood, to the chronicling of real and imaginary women's lives, to a slightly less focused final section that takes on issues of mortality and time's passing." Critics applauded the book's range of topics, as well as Conoley's playful language, inventive imagery, and concentrated details. "These are poems," Barresi noted, "born of Flannery O'Connor's short stories, with their oddball grace, their undeniable redemption. It is Patsy Cline meets Susan Hayward. . . . It is Scarlett O'Hara, magically reincarnated into the 1980s." She concluded, "It is this odd hopefulness, this recourse to imagination which transforms the landscape of ordinary lives and longing into something rare, mysterious, and dangerous that are Conoley's special talent." A reviewer for *Choice* (November 1987) called the writing in part three the "strongest and surest," noting, "What begins as descriptions of the everyday—a bowl of fruit or rush hour—become meditations on the nature of the self and the world. Here, the rhythms are more lively and the syntax richer. The poems are tight, the images compressed and powerful. This is the work of a new poet worth watching."

In *Tall Stranger* (1991), Conoley again used the background of the small-town, rural South to explore emotional experiences relating to family, relationships, and place. In a review for *Small Press* (Summer 1991), Gary Soto described, "This is a tidy collection of twenty-five poems, all finely honed and rich with the slowness of a dead afternoon." Soto also emphasized the elegance of Conoley's depictions: "There is a deliberate attention to the odd graces of her characters. . . . Her people wear jeans and aprons, and when they dance, dust is kicked up from floorboards and there is a delightfully honest *twang* in Conoley's poetry." Donald Revell for *Denver Quarterly* (Winter 1992) observed, "[Conoley] finds in music a way to temporalize language and meaning, a way to make her poems happen in time." Overall, the book received critical praise; however, in a review for *Poetry* (August 1992), Sandra M. Gilbert expressed some reservations: "Conoley's book is uneven: sometimes the poems go on too long, sometimes the sardonic tone doesn't quite evolve into the mode of bittersweet poignancy toward which she tends to push it. But when she creates and celebrates the majestic eccentrics who haunt the American landscape, . . . she convinces me that she is indeed one of 'these new homegirls' upon whose singing her own 'American Muse' would look with favor." *Tall Stranger* was nominated for the National Book Critics Circle Award.

Through the poems collected in *Beckon* (1996), Conoley sought to look beyond the disordered realities of everyday life. Describing the book for *Poets & Writers* (January–February 2001), Kevin Larimer observed, "Conoley departs from the familiar Texas of her childhood, but retains a sense of its wide-open plains, and incorporates it into her poems in the form of white space. . . . She elevates the word above the media blitz and technological blur in order to explore the uncertainties of the modern world." For her, language is a way to explore truth, as the following excerpt from the title poem suggests: "Saddles left out to dry, / Vowels left up in the air as if something is better / left unsaid as if I could have. / And truth is music's mute half, / a sentence broken into." A reviewer for *Virginia Quarterly Review* (Autumn 1996) observed, "Whether describing an ordinary detail, such as that 'bootsoles leave little hexes / on the sidewalk' or tackling the complex emotional tangles of death, adultery, childbirth, or socio-economic turmoil, Conoley's writing is reliably crisp and fresh—often startlingly so." The reviewer also acknowledged Conoley's flare for language, noting, "Among Conoley's linguistic strengths are a keen ear for both staccato and lingering rhythms, and a knack for compressing entire relationships or experiences into a very few words." Writing for *The Gettysburg Review* (Spring 1997), Dorothy Barresi affirmed, "Embracing the world for Conoley means embracing lyric language. She is a first-rate maker of frayed-nerve music in these poems; she lays down quirky rhythms in language that is doubt-laden but also ready to dance."

In her most recent poetry collection, *Lovers in the Used World* (2001), Conoley lures readers back into her familiar playground of daily life, investigating celebrities, gas stations, and urban milieus. Along the way she dissects a "used" language, saturated with layers of meanings and associations. As Conoley told Larimer, "So much comes to us already used, already represented so many times, so copied, that the effort of seeing something in its original state is so difficult. . . . I want to write to a place where language breaks down." Throughout these poems, Conoley told Larimer, she tried to capture the emotion of silence. "I find myself very attracted to poetry that has a lot of white space lately," she explained. "I find that sort of work restful. Not to have a page covered with words is somehow more inviting. I want to go into that world."

As Eric Lorberer described for *Rain Taxi* (Spring 2001), "The discourse in *Lovers in the Used World* ranges from surreally down home . . . to the philosophically introspective. . . . Containing all these registers of a voice is a roving self, one brave enough to write a gorgeous love poem ('How Do I') and to leave us with a brighter notion of 'The World' than when we entered." A reviewer for *Publishers Weekly* (April 16, 2001) characterized the book as "best read as respectful homage" to the poet Jorie Graham, who also extracts religious and philosophical truths from the imagery of daily life. Of Graham's mannerisms, this reviewer noted that "though suited to Conoley's big topics—[they] overwhelm what Conoley has to say." *Lovers in the Used World* was nominated for the 2001 Bay Area Book Reviewers Association Award for poetry.

Since 1994 Gillian Conoley has been poet in residence and associate professor of English at Sonoma State University; she is also the founding editor of *Volt*, an annual magazine featuring experimental writing alongside more traditional forms. Conoley was the recipient of the 1995 Pushcart Prize and the 1999 Jerome J. Shestack Poetry Prize from *American Poetry Review*.

—K. D.

SUGGESTED READING: *American Book Review* July–Aug. 1988; *Antioch Review* p192+ Spring 1997; *Denver Quarterly* Summer 1988, Winter 1992;*Gettysburg Review* p157+ Spring 1997; *Poetry* p284 Aug. 1992; *Poets & Writers* p26+ Jan.–Feb. 2001, with photo; *Publishers Weekly* p60 Apr. 16, 2001; *Small Press* p65 Summer 1991;*Virginia Quarterly Review* p137 Autumn 1996

SELECTED BOOKS: *Woman Speaking Inside Film Noir*, 1984; *Some Gangster Pain*, 1987; *Tall Stranger*, 1991; *Beckon*, 1996; *Lovers in the Used World*, 2001

Christopher Felver/Corbis

Coolidge, Clark

Feb. 26, 1939– Poet

In an article for the *American Poetry Review* (March–April 1999), Raphael Rubenstein described the experimental poetry of Clark Coolidge in the following way: "For Coolidge, who speaks of his work as 'arrangements,' the poet seems to be a kind of sublime interceptor, tuning into all forms of communication and snatching at passing language fragments as they suit his purposes. It's important to note that Coolidge's mosaic poems cannot be elucidated by discovering the poet's sources. Like the great be-bop musicians, he takes a found phrase and draws out of it endless, wildly inventive variations."

Clarke Coolidge was born in Providence, Rhode Island, on February 26, 1939 to Arlan Ralph Coolidge and the former Sylvia Clark. Arlan Coolidge was a professor of music at Brown University, where his son studied geology from 1956 to 1958. Clark developed a passion for music as a teenager, learned how to play the drums, and joined a few local bands. In 1958 he became a disc jockey for WPFM-FM in Providence, but left that position in the summer to travel to Los Angeles, California. From there he wrote letters to friends back home, describing the beatnik scene on the West Coast.

In the fall of 1958 Coolidge moved to New York City. The bohemian scene in New York was even more inspiring to him than the one in California had been; in New York he found jazz clubs, art shows, and poetry readings in abundance. He took long walks around the city, soaking in the sights and the people, and soon began writing. He was greatly inspired by reading the works of Jack Kerouac, the poet, novelist, and advocate of a spontaneous, unrestrained form of writing, and the man who gave the Beat movement its name.

In 1960 Coolidge returned to his hometown of Providence, where he worked as a searcher in the order department of the Rockefeller Library, at Brown University. Within two years he had married. In 1964 he and a friend, Michael Palmer, founded and edited a literary magazine called *Joglars*, which folded two years later, after publishing only three issues. Coolidge's marriage ended in divorce, in 1966. He returned to New York and became acquainted with a number of poets now often described as the "New York School." New York School writers, including the poets Frank O'Hara and John Ashbery, came of age in the 1950s, rebelled against the formal, modernist poetry of the previous generation, and advocated open verse forms and rhythms, links to jazz and spontaneous improvisation, and the spoken word. Since the late 1960s, Coolidge has been associated with the New York School.

Although riddled with personal problems, 1966 proved to be a good year for Coolidge as well. He published his first book of poetry that year, *Flag Flutter and U.S. Electric*, a 22-page, stapled and mimeographed edition produced by Lines Books. He also met his second wife, Susan Hopkins, whom he married in December 1967. His first collection was quickly followed by two more: *Clark Coolidge*, published in 1967 by Lines Books, and *Ing*, published in 1968 by Angel Hair Books. With the exception of his next collection, *Space* (1970), published by Harper & Row, all of Coolidge's work has been published by small presses and literary magazines.

In the late 1960s, Coolidge still had more interest in becoming a drummer than in being a poet. In April 1967 he went to San Francisco, California, to join David Meltzer's Serpent Power band, which recorded an album that May for Vanguard Records. The highly experimental group, with influences from jazz, rock, and country music, fell apart quickly. In an interview with Tom Orange for *Jacket* (April 2001, on-line), Coolidge described the dissolution of the band: "People had an interest in supporting their families and staying alive, and I think there was always a tendency or a pull on any band to become more of a commercial or a dance band. We had arguments about that finally. Also I had just met Susan and was getting involved personally away from it. So the band came to an inevitable split-up, and I just started writing more."

Coolidge told Orange that one of the benefits of writing was that it was not a collaborative effort, that "you can always go home with a pencil and paper." After two more years in California, Coolidge and his wife moved to the Berkshires, in Western Massachusetts, his home for the next 27 years. He told Orange: "We never really intended to stay there that long, it's just inertia I guess. It was a good place to write; it was in the woods and quiet." He published more than 30 volumes in those 27 years. One of his works, *Solution Passage: Poems 1978–1981* (1986), is equivalent in size to the collected works of many better-known poets.

Coolidge's work can be described in three phases, the first of which stresses words, regardless of syntax. In an article for the *Dictionary of Literary Biography* (1998), Bruce Campbell noted that, in this phase, "Coolidge's work is not *about* something; it *is* something. This fact necessitates the reader's paying close attention to the words of Coolidge rather than to the ideas." This early work did not garner Coolidge much critical acclaim; many critics were baffled by the abstract arrangement of words without apparent order. In a review of *Space* for *Library Journal* (June 1, 1971), Jerome Cushman wrote that the poems "do present sound in image, but in a communicative shorthand that makes the strictest poetic condensation seem verbose. I spent too much time trying to put the syntax back to know what was going on." David Lehman, in a review of the same collection for *Poetry* (January 1972), remarked: "The abstract music, the nonsense verse, may delight fans of 'concrete poetry,' from whose company I generally exclude myself." Though critics were skeptical of Coolidge's talents, the editors of *An Anthology of New York Poets* (1970) included some of his poetry in their compilation. Other poetry collections in Coolidge's first phase include *The So: Poems 1966* (1971) and *Suite V* (1973).

Coolidge's second phase began in 1974, with the publication of *The Maintains*, an epic poem. *The Maintains* displays the influence of a group of poets known as the Language Writers; Coolidge used the sounds of words—rather than their meanings—to create a structure for this poem. In *Quartz Hearts* (1978) he uses the first-person voice for the first time, creating a greater sense of intimacy with his readers. Other volumes in this period include *A Geology* (1981), *American Ones: (Noise & Presentiments)* (1981), and *Research* (1982).

Coolidge's third and most extensive phase began in 1982, with the publication of *Mine*, and included such notable works as *The Crystal Text* (1986), *Solution Passage: Poems 1978–1981* (1986), and *Sound As Thought: Poems 1982–1984* (1990). During this period Coolidge received the critical praise that had long eluded him, in part because his work had become more accessible. In a review of *Solution Passage* for *Choice* (September 1986), J. M. Ditsky wrote that this was "one of the most unusual and remarkable volumes of verse to come along in years. Reminiscent, somewhat, of the linguistic experiments of Gertrude Stein, the economy of expression of Hart Crane, the creative syntax of E. E. Cummings, and the orality of the coffeehouse recital poetry of the Beats, Clark Coolidge's poetry is ultimately like nothing but itself." Robert Hudzik, writing for *Library Journal* (June 1, 1986), suggested that Coolidge's "approach can turn inward on itself and thus risks the patience and attention of its readers. But Coolidge is a serious and energetic poet whose work deserves a wider readership."

Coolidge's more recent work includes the *Rova Improvisations* (1994), poems that were inspired by the Rova Saxophone Quartet; *For Kurt Cobain* (1995), an ode to the late lead singer of the rock band Nirvana; *The Book of Stirs* (1998); *Now It's Jazz* (1999), a collection of essays on Jack Kerouac and jazz; *Bomb* (2000), which features photographic collages by Keith Waldrop; and *Far Out West: Adventures in Poetry* (2002), which was inspired by his childhood.

Since late 1997 Clark Coolidge has lived in Petaluma, California, with his wife, Susan. They have a grown daughter, Celia Elizabeth.

—C. M.

SUGGESTED READING: *American Poetry Review* p43+ Jan.–Feb. 1995, p31+ Mar.–Apr. 1999; *Choice* p118 Sep. 1986; *Jacket* (on-line) Apr. 2001; *Library Journal* p1985+ June 1, 1971, p126 June 1, 1986; *Poetry* p223 Jan. 1972; Sun and Moon Press Web site; *Dictionary of Literary Biography*, 1998

SELECTED WORKS: *Flag Flutter and U.S. Electric*, 1966; *Ing*, 1968; *Space*, 1970; *Polaroid*, 1975; *Quartz Hearts*, 1978; *Own Face*, 1978; *The Crystal Text*, 1986; *Solution Passage: Poems 1978–1981*, 1986; *Sound as Thought: Poems 1982–1984*, 1990; *The Rova Improvisations*, 1994; *Now It's Jazz*, 1999; *Bomb*, 2000; *Far Out West: Adventures in Poetry*, 2002

Cooper, Rand Richards

(?)– Fiction writer; essayist; travel writer

Fiction writer, essayist, and travel writer Rand Richards Cooper is the author of two short-story collections about men and family life: *The Last to Go: A Family Chronicle* (1988) and *Big As Life: Stories About Men* (1995). Cooper grew up in Connecticut and spent several years living in Africa in the early 1980s and in Germany a decade later. He began writing stories at Amherst and decided to become a full-time writer during his time in Africa. Cooper has also contributed fiction and essays to national periodicals as diverse as *Bon Appétit*, *Commonweal*, *Glamour*, *Harper's*, and the *New York Times Book Review*.

Rand Richards Cooper grew up in New London, Connecticut, and attended Amherst College in Amherst, Massachusetts. For his senior thesis, as he told Deborah Stead for the *New York Times Book Review* (November 13, 1988), he wrote a yet-unpublished novel "about jogging, God, and the nightly news." He had enrolled there as a premedical student but changed his major to English after taking a writing class with the novelist Robert Stone. At Amherst he also studied with Mary Gordon and William Pritchard, and interrupted his formal studies to spend time with an uncle in Kenya, where Cooper taught literature.

After graduating from college in 1981, Cooper returned to Africa thanks to a travel fellowship from the Watson Foundation. He spent a year in Kenya, then backpacked his way across Africa in 1982. These peregrinations informed several articles he wrote years later, including "A Zairian Journey," published in *Commonweal* (May 9, 1997), which reprised his three-month visit to Zaire, that "vast, varied, lovely land," as Cooper described the country. His time there, however, was marred by his confrontations with venal police officers and the "bribeocracy" in Kinshasa, Zaire's capital. He discovered that, as he recounted in *Commonweal*, "In Zaire, it turned out, all the rules were being broken," public services were in shambles, and the country's infrastructure was collapsing. "A man in Kinshasa told me that for 1000Z (about $60 at the time) you could get your enemy publicly beaten, or his girlfriend raped, or his car burned. There was nothing in Zaire you couldn't get by paying for it, and precious little you *could* get *without* paying for it." Cooper made a conscious decision to "rough" it by staying in a flophouse for three weeks and hanging out with locals in the town square, eating his share of "fiery stew and *kwanga*, the boiled cassava that had the consistency of playdough," as he wrote in his article. "I had been reading Henry Miller," he wrote, "and his wry twist on Emerson's dictum—that if it were true that a man was the sum of all he thought about during the course of a day, then he, Miller, was food—had been my touchstone for months; I was trying to pare my ambitions down to the shape of basic daily needs and means." During his months in Zaire, Cooper also read V. S. Naipaul's novel *A*

Bend in the River (1980), which depicts the anarchy and destruction that overtake an African town in the post-colonial period of the 1960s. The novel, which Cooper described in *Commonweal* as "bleakly nihilistic," seemed to him a mirror image of his day-to-day experiences. "Having trained my gaze through Naipaul's gloomy lens," he wrote, "I was looking for trouble in Mobutu's Zaire, and finding plenty of it."

Cooper lived in Mainz, Germany, in the early 1990s, where he witnessed firsthand the ferment and restructuring that immediately followed the fall of the Berlin Wall and the subsequent reunification of Germany. He recorded his observations on contemporary German politics and culture in an essay he wrote for *Commonweal* (May 7, 1993), entitled "It's Not Weimar All Over Again: The Strengths of German Democracy." (Weimar is a reference to the ill-fated and ineffectual republican government of Germany during the 1920s, immediately following the debacle of World War I and preceding the rise of Hitler.) In the article, Cooper expressed serious doubt that a right-wing or neo-Nazi group would take power in Germany again. "The foundations of democracy in today's Germany are rock-solid," he wrote, "the constitution of 1949 commanding public avowals of respect across the spectrum of political parties." Despite reports of xenophobic attacks against immigrants in Germany, Cooper pointed out that "the campaign against *Auslanderfeindlichkeit* (literally, 'foreigner-hostility') is an effort of humane propaganda spectacular in its breadth," with tee-shirts, billboards, sermons, and celebrity endorsements of a "Citizens Against Xenophobia" crusade. He also quoted the British historian A. J. P. Taylor, who argued that America's high-minded and self-righteous commitment to human rights issues should be viewed in context of its own "dark past" of slavery and hostility toward Native Americans.

Cooper's two story collections, *The Last to Go: A Family Chronicle* (1988) and *Big As Life: Stories About Men* (1995), solidified his reputation as an astute and sympathetic observer of the foibles of middle class (and aspiring working-class) families, with special emphasis on the male of the species. He began writing some of the stories in *The Last to Go* during his time at Amherst and on his travels to Africa, when his parents were in the midst of a divorce. In her profile of Cooper for the *New York Times Book Review*, Deborah Stead reported that "as he was floating down the Congo River on a barge, he found himself writing stories close to home—stories about 'what went wrong' [in his words] with his family." Despite their personal nature, Cooper did not think that the stories in *The Last to Go* would upset his parents. "Clearly, there have been things in [the book] that are difficult to deal with," he told Stead. However, even though the book was based on the story of his parents' initial romance, happy family life, and eventual breakup, Cooper asserted that "most of the events didn't happen in life. In some ways, my family sees it more as fiction, than, say, the neighbors will." Cooper acknowledged to Stead his parents' active participation in the creative process; they read and discussed his drafts and "we would have long talks afterward—literary, personal, and familial."

The Last to Go consists of a series of 16 interconnected stories spanning 30 years in the wedded life of Dan and Mary Ellen Slattery, who had met on a blind date in the 1950s just before Dan entered medical school. The stories follow them to Arizona, then back East, where Dan becomes a successful surgeon and the couple raises a family that is "truly contented, as happy as any family can hope to be," in the words of Robb Forman Dew, who reviewed the book for the *New York Times Book Review* (November 13, 1998). Of course there are shadows, including Dan's sexual wanderings, and their children's rebellion. The jacket copy for the book, published by Harcourt Brace Jovanovich, concludes, "Told variously in the first and third person, each tale is complete in itself. Taken together, they tell an eloquent story of happiness and disillusionment, dreams of success and invitations to failure, the terror at the heart of domestic life." At least one reviewer found this narrative approach confusing: Kimbery G. Allen wrote in *Library Journal* (November 15, 1988) that "the marital break-up that results is described from a number of different vantage points, beginning with a straightforward narrative and then switching from son to each daughter to neighbor. Although it offers a diversity of perspectives, this approach is not wholly successful: Transitions are sometimes confusing, and the reader is left wondering who is speaking and, in some cases, why." "The Last to Go," the title story and the final one in the collection, is narrated in the first person by Dan and Mary Ellen's son, the character who most closely resembles Cooper himself. In one passage the character relates his sense of having lost his moorings in the wake of his parents divorce:

> It didn't happen that way. Life at college did not proceed according to plan. First, my parents suddenly split up and then quickly sank into their misery, like stones in a pond. The silence from home was overpowering. . . . The stories my parents had always told me, stories about how the world worked and thus how my life in it should proceed, had fled from me like soldiers in a vast, hopeless retreat, leaving me standing alone on my little island of ego.

Whereas Cooper traveled to Africa, the protagonist of "The Last to Go" embarks on a three-year journey across "the real America, the limitless domain of laconic farmers, screaming evangelists, and soda jerks," as quoted from the story, finally concluding that the myth of everyone finding his or her one-and-only soul-mate is a chimera.

In his review Robb Forman Dew called the book "an enticing and, finally, a haunting work" that was reminiscent of a novel in the way that it spanned 30 years of change within a single family.

"There are only a few instances in this book that betray Mr. Cooper as a first-time and young writer," Dew added, finding fault with Cooper's minor but occasional lapses into "distracting and syrupy anthropomorphic images." Still, Dew concluded, "Mr. Cooper is impressively faithful to the elegance of his sensibilities; he is blessed with a generous and compassionate imagination and an unusual wisdom." *The Last to Go* was adapted by William Hanley for a made-for-television movie that aired on ABC in 1991, produced and directed by John Erman and starring Tyne Daly as Mary Ellen Slattery.

Cooper's second book, *Big As Life: Stories About Men,* was published in 1995 by Dial Press. This collection of 17 stories focuses on the emotional maturing of men of all ages: a ten-year-old coming to terms with racism, a high-schooler experiencing his sexual awakening, a man in his late twenties dating a girl ten years his junior, and middle-aged men experiencing the constricting of their ambitions, to name a few examples. In Michael S. Kimmel's review in the *San Francisco Chronicle* (June 25, 1995), he observed, "Each story is like a single slide in the slide carousel of seemingly isolated moments that together compose a man's life. The writer pauses at each frame, indicating how it turned out to be more important than it appeared at the time." Chris Goodrich, writing in the *Los Angeles Times* (August 17, 1995), called Cooper's men "attractive, sympathetic characters, often because they are willing to recognize their mistakes, to see that revelation is frequently predicated on error"; the story entitled, 'The Hoax,' Goodrich continued, is "one of a handful of memorable stories in this collection, and starkly outlines the adolescence that seems to run through the American man, a trait that can be both irresistible and hazardous, endearing and shameful."

In addition to essays and short stories, travel writing is yet another genre favored by the well-traveled Cooper. For *Bon Appétit,* he has written a gastronome's tour of old Lisbon (March 1997) and of Key West (February 1998). In the latter piece, he brings his literary consciousness to bear, as in the opening paragraph: "It sounds ghoulish, but the best place to start a Key West visit is in the graveyard. Check into your hotel, rent a bicycle—the sine qua non for exploring the island's palm-shaded square mile of Old Town—then head for Solares Hill and the cemetery where elevated tombs, poet James Merrill wrote, shine in the sun like 'whitewashed hope chests.'" He also reviewed a plethora of travel books for a special section in the *New York Times Book Review* (June 1, 1997).

Cooper has also delved into the war between the sexes, as in the article "Why Men Can't Resist Scaring Women," which appeared in *Glamour* (December 1996). An article Cooper wrote on euthanasia, which he opposes, in *Commonweal* (October 25, 1996) combines memories of his days in Africa with more recent images of visiting his aged grandmother in a nursing home: in the essay, he writes that "we experience a profound aspect of our humanity precisely in our intimate and awful knowledge of each other's physical neediness; and further . . . what we draw from this knowledge constitutes not only a spiritual good but a social good." While visiting his grandmother during the last months of her life, Cooper wrote, "She unexpectedly squeezed my hand, as if sending a last, bodily message from some strange place between being and not-being—all of that forms part of the story of my grandmother that I carry with me; and I feel I am the richer for all of it, endowed with a more expansive vocabulary of body and spirit, and also a more intimate acquaintance with death, it all its mystery and terribleness."

—E. M.

SUGGESTED READING: (Albany) *Times-Union* C p2 July 11, 1995; *Bon Appétit* p120+ Mar. 1997, p96+ Feb. 1998; *Commonweal* p11+ May 7, 1993, p24+ Oct. 6, 1995, p12 Oct. 25, 1996, p9+ May 9, 1997, p10+ Mar. 27, 1998, p11+ May 7, 1999; *Glamour* p286 Apr. 1996; *Hudson Review* p484+ Autumn 1989, p135+ Spring 1996; *Library Journal* p132 May 1, 1995; *Los Angeles Times* p6+ Aug. 17, 1995; *New York Times Book Review* p74 Aug. 26, 1988, p14 Nov. 13, 1988, with photo, p15 June 6, 1993, p3 June 5, 1994, p41 June 11, 1995, p22 July 4, 1999; *New Yorker* p114+ Mar. 27, 1989; *Publishers Weekly* p74 Aug. 26, 1988, p45 Apr. 3, 1995; *San Francisco Chronicle* p5+ June 25, 1995

SELECTED BOOKS: *The Last to Go: A Family Chronicle,* 1989; *Big As Life: Stories About Men,* 1995

Cornwell, Bernard

Feb. 23, 1944– Novelist

Since 1980, the historical novelist Bernard Cornwell has written scores of novels on the subjects of prehistoric and medieval societies, the Napoleonic and American Civil wars, and the French and American revolutions. His large body of collected works testifies both to his wide-ranging interests and his abundant story-telling gifts. A favorite of thousands of devoted fans, Cornwell is often besieged with requests for more stories in a particular series, or questions about the "lives" of his characters. Cornwell once described his work as "lazy man's writing" to a reporter for the *Economist* (September 28, 2000, on-line), noting that his novels usually consist of "a battle in the beginning, a battle in the middle and a battle at the end. Boom. Boom. Boom." But critics have been effusive in their praise, noting that Cornwell's meticulous research and ability to mix a swashbuckling narrative style with complex, multi-dimensional characters have helped him create some of the most original historical fiction of the past decades.

Courtesy of HarperCollins Publishers
Bernard Cornwell

Bernard Cornwell was born on February 23, 1944, the child of a Canadian airman and a married British woman who already had children and was awaiting her husband's return from World War II. As a result of the woman's circumstances, Cornwell was sent to an orphanage, and then became the fifth adopted child of a couple who belonged to an evangelical sect called the "Peculiar People," in reference to the biblical idea of being special, or chosen. "They were very peculiar indeed," Cornwell told Charles Laurence in the *Daily Telegraph* (April 14, 2000, on-line). "It was a very oppressive childhood of being force-fed religion, no point in saying otherwise. The idea was to cut us off from the modern world, which was sinful. We read the Bible a great deal, and there was no other entertainment. There was no sparing the rod." As a teenager in the 1960s, Cornwell rebelled, growing his hair, listening to what his parents termed "devil's music," and experimenting with drugs. He attended Monkton Combe, an evangelical boarding school that, nonetheless, as he told Laurence, "gave me [rugby] and cricket, which I love, and enough knowledge to conclude that my parents' religion was garbage. I knew what I had to do." After failing to get into the army because of his poor eyesight, Cornwell entered London University, graduating in 1967 with a degree in theology, a subject chosen as a form of rebellion against his strict religious upbringing. As Cornwell explained to Laurence, "I was looking for ammo. I wanted to come out a battleship with all guns blazing, and I did. And then I discovered there was no enemy." He then joined BBC television—"because, I suppose, television was forbidden," he told Laurence"—working as a producer in the current affairs department. In the late 1970s, he became head of current affairs in the war zone of Belfast, in Northern Ireland, and he married and had a daughter. That marriage soon ended, and he later married an American woman, Judy Acker. Cornwell agreed to move to America with his new wife, who did not want to live in England. He had been nursing an idea for a novel for years, and when he had difficulty obtaining a work permit in the U.S., he decided to become a writer, finding some of this themes in the nature of his upbringing. The first character he created, Richard Sharpe, was an orphan who overcomes adversity in his youth to become a hero. "With hindsight, I do have things to be grateful to my parents for," Cornwell told Laurence. "I learnt from them that childhood is a trap and that growing up is learning how to get out of it. And," he added, "a 17th-century mentality has proved useful to a historical novelist."

Cornwell is best known for his "Sharpe" series of novels, picaresque adventure stories set during the Napoleonic Wars (1792–1815) and named for their protagonist, the character Richard Sharpe. Cornwell became fascinated by the Wars as a youth, and decided to write about them after discovering that there were very few books that detailed Britain's military victories, though many recounted the country's defeats. According to the *FortuneCity* Web site, a HarperCollins editor read the manuscript of Cornwell's first novel, *Sharpe's Eagle*, and immediately offered Cornwell a contract for a ten-book series—an almost unheard of event in the history of publishing. Since 1980, Cornwell has written 20 novels in the Sharpe series, which together have sold more than 4 million copies and have been translated into nine languages.

Cornwell has described his Sharpe series as "shamelessly modeled on C. S. Forester's 'Hornblower' series," as quoted by a contributor to *Contemporary Authors* (1982). Forester's series of 12 novels, written during the first half of the 20th century, followed the progress of the British naval officer Horatio Hornblower, who rises from midshipman to admiral as a result of his naval victories against Napoleon. Cornwell set out to create a land-based counterpart to the Hornblower series by focusing on the Peninsular War of 1801–1814, in which English troops under the command of the Duke of Wellington fought Napoleon on the Iberian peninsula, in Spain and Portugal. Cornwell's series follows the life of Richard Sharpe, a fictional character named after one of England's great rugby players. Born in a London brothel, Sharpe is an orphan and petty thief who joins the army to escape being hanged. Each novel focuses on a different battle in which Sharpe distinguishes himself by an act of heroism, for example saving the Duke of Wellington's life or stealing the French standard, all the while conducting a series of romances on the fly. Through his skill and daring on the battlefield, Sharpe is promoted from a foot soldier to a rifleman and up through the ranks of the army, finally becoming a full colonel.

Cornwell's novels have been praised for including evocative, and accurate, historical details. "Whereas many other writers have been interested in little other than blood, romance, and costume drama, there is no doubt that the Sharpe novels are founded on a domination of the English-language sources that is probably all but unequaled," Charles Esdaile wrote in *Historian* (Winter 1999). In *Twentieth-Century Romance and Historical Writers*, as quoted in *Contemporary Authors* (2000), Geoffrey Sadler noted that "Cornwell's painstaking research, his sure grasp of authentic period detail, enable him to bring home to the reader the scent and feeling of those vanished times, forcing him to witness afresh the savage butchery of the battles, the squalor and corruption that marks life in the early-19th century."

In the early 1990s, British Central Television began filming versions of the Sharpe novels, and their subsequent broadcast increased the series' already healthy following. "I thought I was finished with Sharpe after Waterloo, but so many people wrote wanting more stories that he had to put on his green jacket and march again," Cornwell said, as quoted on the *Sharpe Appreciation Society* Web site. In 2000 Cornwell published *Sharpe's Trafalgar*, in which the author takes his hero out to sea to fight in the Battle of Trafalgar in 1805. The most recent books in the series include *Sharpe's Skirmish* (2002) and *Sharpe's Havoc* (2003).

In the 1990s, Cornwell embarked on a new series that takes place during the American Civil War. In order to capture the divisiveness of a war between countrymen, Cornwell created Nate Starbuck, a Northern-born son of abolitionist parents who finds himself in Virginia as the tensions between North and South escalate into full-scale war. In the first book of the Starbuck series, *Rebel* (1993), Starbuck joins the Confederate Army out of hunger for adventure—and to rebel against his father—rather than from any deep-seated belief in States' rights. Over the course of the next three books in the Starbuck series—*Copperhead* (1994), *Battle Flag* (1995), and *The Bloody Ground* (1996)—grim Civil War battles are recounted through Starbuck's eyes. *Booklist* reviewer Denise Perry Donavin, as quoted on *Amazon.com*, called Starbuck a "beguiling hero," and a reviewer for *Kirkus*, as quoted in *Contemporary Authors* (2000), concurred, commenting, "Starbuck is a worthy hero, smart enough to be interesting, callow enough to be real." The *Kirkus* reviewer went on to say that "Virginia is a great stage, teeming with Confederate and military politics, and the battle scenes, when they come, are presented with real mastery. They hurt."

More critically acclaimed than the Sharpe and Starbuck series and just as popular has been Cornwell's *The Warlord Chronicles*, a trilogy of novels based on the legend of King Arthur and Camelot, with an eye toward rediscovering the actual history behind the myths. In *Books*, as quoted in *Contemporary Authors* (2000), Cornwell stated that he decided to write about King Arthur because he "wanted to take him out of that romantic mystical land of fable and place him in the very real world where he is most likely to have lived." Rather than portray him as a wise king or a great lover, as other novelists have done, Cornwell wanted to depict Arthur as a soldier. "To survive at this time and obtain great power, Arthur must have been a brilliant military commander," Cornwell said in *Books*. Cornwell followed in the tradition of the historical novelist Mary Stewart who, in her 1960s *Merlin Trilogy*, transplanted the Arthurian legends from the traditional late Medieval setting (as in T. H. White's *The Once and Future King*, 1958) to the latter part of the fifth century. Cornwell's Arthur isn't a chivalrous knight, but a Celtic warlord in an area of England known as Dumnonia; rather than wearing a shining suit of armor, he is depicted in animal furs and fighting bloody, barbaric battles.

All of *The Warlord Chronicles* are told retrospectively, from the point of view of the character Derfel, who had been a trusted warrior under Arthur and has since become a Christian monk. For the benefit of Igraine, a British queen, Derfel narrates the story of Arthur, who is now dead. At one point, Igraine complains to Derfel that his story is too mundane, and lacks romance, magic, and grandeur. "To hear the tales told at night-time hearth, you would think we had made a whole new country in Britain, named it Camelot and peopled it with shining heroes," Derfel counters, as quoted by Robert K. J. Killheffer in *Fantasy and Science Fiction* (October/November 1997), "but the truth is that we simply ruled Dumnonia as best we could, we ruled it justly and we never called it Camelot. I did not even hear that name till two years ago." Killheffer noted that Derfel's debunking of the Arthurian legend "has a wistfulness about it that actually accentuates the tragedy of the tale."

The first book in the series, *The Winter King* (1996), focuses on the internal struggles for control of Britain. After the withdrawal of the Romans, Britain in the fifth century came under siege by opportunistic raiders—Angles, Saxons, and Jutes—who would eventually overrun the island and give it the name "Angleland," or England. *The Winter King* takes place in a period of relative peace before the unrest, when a courageous military leader, traditionally called Arthur, temporarily held off the attacks. In *World and I* (August 1996), Alan Lupack cited *The Winter King*'s opening sentence—"Once upon a time, in a land called Britain, these things happened"—as an indication of Cornwell's liberal blending of both the historic chronicle and romantic traditions. "This simultaneous evocation of the worlds of fairy tale and fact suggests that Cornwell wants to give himself the latitude to include elements of romance in the construction of what is predominantly a historical novel," Lupack observed.

The Winter King shows Arthur intent on trying to defang the tribal rivalries that he believes are tearing Britain apart. After agreeing to marry the daughter of another leader in order to forge peace, Arthur then falls in love with Guinevere and breaks off his former engagement, thus plunging the country back into civil strife. This act returns to haunt Arthur in the second book of the trilogy, *Enemy of God* (1997), in which the story of Tristan and Iseult appears. In Cornwall's version, Tristan, a friend of Arthur's, falls in love with the young and beautiful Iseult, who is supposed to marry Tristan's aging father, King Mark. The young lovers run off together, taking refuge in Arthur's territory. When King Mark threatens war, Arthur must choose between loyalty to his friend or a pragmatic acquiescence to King Mark. His choice is complicated by his own awareness of the fact that he, like his friend, once chose love over peace. Killheffer noted that, in instances such as this, Cornwell focuses on the moral struggles at the core of the Arthurian saga. "Cornwell strips the myths of their romance," he said, "but in so doing he recaptures their true potency." The battle scenes, Killheffer added, are unromanticized but nonetheless effective. Far from "Errol Flynn fencing duels," he wrote, the battles are "muddy, bloody, even boring pushing contests between opposing shield walls."

In *Excalibur* (1998), the trilogy's finale, Arthur's dream of a unified Celtic kingdom proves doomed, and Christianity displaces the pagan religions. Killheffer and Walsh both noted that because its outcome has been preordained by historical events, a sense of bittersweet tragedy pervades the trilogy. "What's great about Arthur," Killheffer noted, "is that we know, as he does, that in the long run his cause is doomed, and the best he can do is delay the inevitable."

Cornwell continued to take inspiration from the Celts in his next novel, *Stonehenge* (2000), which was nonetheless something of a departure for the author. In comparison to the Napoleonic Wars, for example, very little is known about Stonehenge, or the people who made it. Cornwell told Richard Lee, in an interview for the *Historical Novel Society* Web site, that "*Stonehenge* is by far the most difficult book I've ever written," and he is quoted as saying on the *HarperCollins* Web site that "all there was was a pile of rocks so everything had to be invented." In order to learn more about the structure, Cornwell did some archeological research, and even built a scale model of the monument to test one theory of its construction. However, his novel is not so much the story of the "pile of rocks" as it is an account of the society and culture that might have created it.

Stonehenge depicts three brothers, all vying for leadership of their Neolithic tribe. One brother is warlike, another pushes for peace, but the third, religiously minded brother succeeds in capturing the imagination of his people by proposing to build a glorious temple honoring the sun god. The story follows the transfer of the temple's stones, the capture of slaves to do the building work, and the conception of the ceremonial and religious import of the temple. Lee described the novel as "a remarkable feat of sustained imagination," recalling that "the overwhelming images . . . are wide skies, animal skins and bones, human squalor, and temples—not Stonehenge, that doesn't arrive till the end of the book, and even then it is not as we see it—but sordid, animal-smelling, superstitious, fear-inspiring temples." Writing in *Library Journal* (May 1, 2000), Laurel Bliss agreed that the work was rich in detail, although she felt that it was "slow paced and light on plot, while its characters seem one-dimensional."

Most recently, Cornwell published *Harlequin* (2000), the first in what promises to be a series of novels depicting the Hundred Years War, a conflict between England and France that lasted from 1337 to 1453. (In its U.S. release, *Harlequin* was retitled *The Archer's Tale*.) The novel begins on Easter morning in 1342 and depicts one of the opening rounds of the epic conflict. The treasure of Hookton, the sacred lance that Saint George is believed to have used to slay the dragon, is stolen from a village church on England's south coast by a band of Norman mercenaries. The raiders are led by a mysterious warrior named Harlequin, from the old French word "hellequin," which means a troop of the devil's horsemen. A group of Englishmen chase the sacred treasure and the Normans back to France, initiating a series of conflicts culminating in the battles of Caen and the famous battle of Crécy. A reviewer for the *Economist* commented that the narrative fabric of *Harlequin*, "with its rich mix of bloody conflict amid political and religious turmoil, marks a new maturity in Mr. Cornwell's writing." The reviewer speculated that future installments in the series will describe the Black Death, the papal schism, and other events that capture the "fear, faith, economic ravagement, and the imposition of political power" that riddled Europe in the tumultuous 14th and 15th centuries. The second book in the series, *Vagabond* (2002), continues the story of Thomas of Hookton as he returns to England to investigate his father's mysterious legacy. After surviving the Scottish invasion of 1347, he begins pursuing the Holy Grail, only to discover that a group of powerful men in France have embarked upon the same quest.

In the U.K. Cornwell has also published a series of contemporary thrillers, each of which features the background of sailing. These titles include *Wildtrack* (1988), *Sea Lord* (1989), *Crackdown* (1990), *Stormchild* (1991), and *Scoundrel* (1992). As Cornwell noted on his official Web site (www.bernardcornwell.net), "I enjoyed writing the thrillers, but suspect I am happier writing historical novels. I'm always delighted when people want more of the sailing books, but I'm not planning on writing any more, at least not now." His additional books include *Redcoat* (1987), an account of the Valley Forge winter during the American Revolution, and the recent *Gallow's Thief* (2001), a detective story set in 1820s London, featuring an ex-soldier-turned-investigator who works to save an innocent prisoner from being killed in the gallows.

Since 1980, Cornwell has lived in Cape Cod, Massachusetts, with his wife, who has three children from a previous marriage. "I'm married to this vegetarian pacifist," Cornwell told Richard Lee. "And I heard her talking in the kitchen one day, and a friend was asking, 'Do you actually read Bernard's books?' and my wife said, 'Yes, but I skip the battles.' So I shouted out, 'Bloody quick read isn't it?'" He spends 10 months of every year writing in a cabin behind their home or promoting his books, and the other two months sailing on his 24-foot Cornish Crabber sailboat. In order to win a bottle of whiskey in a bet among friends, he has published three novels under an assumed name, Susannah Kells. —M. A. H.

SUGGESTED READING: *Economist* (on-line) Sep. 28, 2000; *Fantasy and Science Fiction* p44+ Oct./Nov. 1997; *Historian* p9+ Winter 1999, with photos; *World & I* p244+ Aug. 1996, with photos

SELECTED BOOKS: novels—*Sharpe's Eagle*, 1981; *Rebel*, 1993; *Copperhead*, 1994; *Battle Flag*, 1995; *The Bloody Ground*, 1996; *The Winter King*, 1996; *Enemy of God*, 1997; *Excalibur*, 1998; *Sharpe's Trafalgar*, 2000; *Stonehenge*, 2000; *Harlequin*, 2000; *Gallow's Thief*, 2001; *Vagabond*, 2002; as Susannah Kells—*Crowning Mercy*, 1983; *Fallen Angels*, 1984; *Aristocrats*, 1986

Coyle, Harold W.

1952– Novelist

A former U.S. military officer, novelist Harold Coyle brings inside knowledge to his often best-selling war novels that allows him to create detailed, authentic portrayals of battle. A critic for *Kirkus Reviews*, as quoted on *Amazon.com*, called him "the modern master of life—under combat." Fueled by Cold War tensions, his novels written in the 1980s depicted hypothetical conflicts between the Soviet Union and the United States. In the early 1990s, Coyle took his cast of recurring characters into pitched battles in Mexico, Germany, and Colombia. In *Look Away* (1995), *Until the End* (1996), and *Savage Wilderness* (1997), Coyle marched back in time to the Civil War and the French and Indian War and proved his ability as a historical novelist. Coyle used turbulence in Eastern Europe as a jumping-off point in *God's Children* (2000), which is set in Slovakia. He has since featured a Russian nuclear crisis in the political thriller *Dead Hand* (2001), and a domestic terrorist attack by a disgruntled Gulf War veteran in *Against All Enemies* (2002).

Born in 1952, Harold Coyle graduated from the Virginia Military Institute, in Lexington, and spent 14 years on active duty with the U.S. Army, serving in capacities ranging from tank platoon leader to operations officer in Korea. He began his writing career with *Team Yankee: A Novel of World War III* (1987). In the book, Captain Sean Bannion, the leader of a tank battalion called Team Yankee, leads his troops into war against Soviet forces in West Germany, precipitating World War III. The novel became a best-seller and established Coyle as a strong newcomer in the genre of military fiction. He followed in 1988 with *Sword Point*, which was also about a war between the U.S. and the Soviet Union. In this case the conflict begins when the Soviets invade Iran in order to cut off U.S. oil supplies, and U.S. Army Lieutenant Illvanish leads a counterattack. Caught between the two military superpowers, Iran unleashes its secret nuclear arsenal, thus changing the scope and allegiances of the war. Once again, Coyle's novel became a best-seller. In his review for the *New York Times* (November 27, 1988), John Glenn criticized the novel for what he found to be weak and stereotypical characterizations, yet gave it a favorable review overall. "Mr. Coyle knows soldiers," he noted, "and he understands the brotherhood-of-arms mystique that transcends national boundaries."

Coyle's next novel was *Bright Star* (1990), in which Libyan terrorists attempt an assassination in Egypt, sparking a military build-up that gradually pulls the Soviet Union and the U.S. into battle. Though it, too, was a best-seller, the novel was generally considered inferior to Coyle's previous efforts. "The only thing that *Bright Star* has in its favor," Newgate Callendar wrote in the *New York Times Book Review* (June 17, 1990), "is authenticity when it comes to battle planning and warfare."

Critics were far more impressed by Coyle's next novel, *Trial by Fire* (1992). A group of revolutionaries intent on reform seize control of the Mexican government and take measures to stamp out corruption. Certain powerful drug dealers who are unhappy with the reforms use terrorist tactics to dupe the U.S. into a border war and thus bring their own new government under fire. A TV reporter, Jan Fields, attempts to uncover the drug lords' plot, while her lover, Lieutenant Colonel Scott Dixon, is forced into a misguided battle with Mexico. One of his troops is Lieutenant Nancy Kozak, the Army's first female combat officer. "This time," a critic for *Kirkus Reviews* (February 15, 1992) noted, "[Coyle] has sacrificed a little military detail for the sake of general readability. It's a sensible and worthwhile compromise."

Lieutenant Colonel Scott Dixon and Nancy Kozak, who has now been promoted to captain, returned in Coyle's next novel, *The Ten Thousand* (1993). This time, they lock horns with the German military. German Chancellor Johann Ruff is an old Nazi loyalist who, at age eight, was disfigured by a grenade after he threatened American troops with a knife. His chance for revenge arises when the U.S. president, a woman, seizes Ukranian nuclear weapons and has them brought into Germany. Ruff captures the weapons and orders American troops out of Germany, but General "Big Al" Malin refuses to surrender and fighting erupts. Reviewer Robert Denny's perception that the novel's action was too often interrupted by long technical passages and unwieldy sentences led him to ask in the *Washington Post Book World* (July 4, 1993), "Where are today's editors?" However, Harry Levins, in the *St. Louis Post-Dispatch* (June 27, 1993), wrote, "You can read it as a tactical primer for mechanized warfare in a European setting, and Coyle's Army background gives him a close-up and basically pessimistic view of combat."

Coyle's cast of Scott Dixon, who is now a General; his journalist wife, Jan Fields; and Captain Nancy Kozak find themselves in another dangerous situation in *Code of Honor* (1994). Dispatched on a peace-keeping mission, U.S. troops find themselves embroiled in guerilla warfare in the jungles of Colombia. Furthermore, they are endangered by Major General G. B. Lane, whose career ambitions often cloud his better judgment. A reviewer for *Kirkus Reviews* (February 1, 1994) pronounced *Code of Honor* "another winner for Coyle and his ongoing cast of heroines as well as heroes," noting that it also provided "credible portrayals of women at arms."

Shifting his focus from his previous preoccupation with high-tech warfare, Coyle looked backwards in history for his Civil War novel *Look Away* (1995). Two brothers, James and Kevin Bannon, are separated by their unscrupulous father, who places one in a military academy in the North, and the other in a similar institution in the South, in order to insure that he will have ties to the victor of the Civil War, whatever the outcome. Both brothers find love and happiness in their new locales, but their newfound allegiances come into conflict with their familial bond when they meet in combat at the Battle of Gettysburg. Coyle tells the brothers' respective tales through alternating chapters and includes historical information to offset his own fictional version of events. Jackie Gropman, in *School Library Journal* (May 1996), called the book "poignant" and lauded its "suspenseful, heart-wrenching climax."

Until the End, the sequel to *Look Away*, was published in 1996. Picking up from the Battle of Gettysburg, the novel follows the harrowing paths of the Bannon brothers as they confront the loss of their ideals, and ends with the final Union victory at Richmond, Virginia, the capital of the Confederacy. Reviews were mixed, with some critics opining that the sequel had lost some of the energy of its predecessor. A reviewer for *Publishers Weekly* (July 15, 1996) wrote, "Coyle renders the Civil War battlefields in stark and gripping detail. Gone, however, are the subplots that added spice and intrigue to the earlier book. The story line here is simpler, leading the two brothers down a predictable path to forgiveness and redemption."

Delving further into the past, Coyle's next novel, *Savage Wilderness* (1997), is set during the French and Indian War of the 1750s, when France and Great Britain battled for control of eastern North America. The main characters include Ian McPherson, a Scottish exile who lives in the British colonies and is forced to fight for Britain; Thomas Shields, a British army captain whose ambition outweighs his military skill; and Anton de Chevalier, a French artillery officer with a superior understanding of war and a love of the land for which he fights. Coyle's compelling descriptions of the New World led critics to esteem *Savage Wilderness* one of his finest works. A reviewer for *Publishers Weekly* (July 7, 1997) wrote, "Coyle's message is as clear as his storytelling is strong: great empires are won or lost by the blood, determination, and ingenuity of a few individuals, grappling on the dark fringes of civilization." A *Kirkus Reviews* (June 15, 1997) critic hailed the "vivid accounts of bloody engagements" and "resonant depictions of the men" and called the novel a "splendid period piece."

In 2000 Coyle published *God's Children*, in which he returned to the high-tech wars of the near-future depicted in his earlier novels. The plot concerns two young U.S. officers who join a NATO peace-keeping mission in Slovakia. Lieutenant Nathan Dixon is the son of Scott Dixon, the hero of some of Coyle's previous novels, while Lieutenant Gerald Reider is a recent graduate from West Point Military Academy. Coyle uses the two officers to illustrate different leadership styles, and when war flares up in Slovakia, the two officers clash. While critics accustomed to Coyle's fast-paced writing found his expositions on military mores intrusive, *God's Children* was nevertheless fueled by suspense, leading Budd Arthur, writing in *Booklist* (January 1, 2000), to state, "When it comes to military techno-thrillers, Coyle is as good as it gets."

In his 2001 political thriller *Dead Hand*, Coyle presents an ultra-nationalist Russian general who attempts to manipulate a national emergency for his own anti-Western agenda. When an asteroid hits Siberia, creating shockwaves similar to those from a nuclear explosion, the force is strong enough to activate Russia's retaliatory nuclear system, known as Dead Hand. With his finger now on the button, General Igor Likatchev decides to exploit the situation to stage a coup. Sensing Likatchev's madness, Moscow appeals to the U.S., NATO, and the French Foreign Legion to invade its own borders and destroy the nuclear missiles before the general can reach them. Although several critics acknowledged the story's political resonance, most found the book a disappointment, particularly because of Coyle's tendency to interrupt the plot with pedantic digressions. As one critic noted for *Publishers Weekly*, as quoted on Amazon.com, "[Coyle] shows a deep understanding of power politics and fighting techniques, but his exposition-heavy plot spends far too much time describing commandos readying themselves for battle, explaining military procedures and examining the specific qualities of the soldier mindset. When the action finally begins about two-thirds of the way through the book its course is predictable."

Coyle's next work, *Against All Enemies* (2002), features the familiar characters of General Scott Dixon; his journalist wife, Jan; his son, Nathan, an army lieutenant and recent graduate from the Virginia Military Institute; and Lieutenant Colonel Nancy Kozak. The story begins when a disgruntled Gulf War veteran launches a domestic terrorist attack by demolishing a federal building. The act inspires a group of Idaho militiamen, who call themselves "Patriots," to initiate their own attacks against the U.S. government. Ultimately, a bloody standoff ensues between the FBI and the Patriots when Idaho's right-wing governor and his attorney general refuse to arrest the militiamen after they are ordered to stand trial in Seattle. The governor goes so far as to use the Idaho National Guard to expel federal agents and Justice Department employees from his state. When Nathan's army unit is called in to "neutralize" the situation, and Kozak is given the task of keeping the state's ammunition away from both militiamen and the state's National Guard, tension mounts. The novel climaxes with an attack on the capital building in Boise, Idaho. *Against All Enemies* received mixed reviews. Again, critics bemoaned Coyle's tendency to pontificate on the political and military issues raised throughout the book. Nevertheless, most reviews praised the plot as being well-crafted, suspenseful, and action-packed.

Coyle's most recent book, *More Than Courage*, is set for release in April 2003.

— P.G.H.

SUGGESTED READING: *Booklist* p873 Jan. 1, 2000; *Kirkus Reviews* p889 June 15, 1997; *New York Times* VII p23 Nov. 27, 1988; *New York Times Book Review* p19 June 17, 1990; *Publishers Weekly* p54 July 15, 1996, p52 July 7, 1997; *School Library Journal* p148 May 1996; *St. Louis Post-Dispatch* C p5 June 27, 1993; *Washington Post Book World* p6 July 4, 1993

SELECTED BOOKS: *Team Yankee: A Novel of World War III*, 1987; *Sword Point*, 1988; *Bright Star*, 1990; *Trial by Fire*, 1992; *The Ten Thousand*, 1993; *Code of Honor*, 1994; *Look Away*, 1995; *Until the End*, 1996; *Savage Wilderness*, 1997; *God's Children*, 2000; *Dead Hand*, 2001; *Against All Enemies*, 2002

Crittenden, Ann

(?)– Nonfiction writer

Ann Crittenden, an award-winning journalist, is the author of *The Price of Motherhood: Why the Most Important Job in the World is Still the Least Valued* (2001). In this provocative and original book, Crittenden argues that mothers—in spite of their contribution to the "human capital" of the economy through raising the next generation of productive workers—are systematically disadvantaged in American society. They lose income and status when their careers are interrupted by pregnancy and child-rearing, and they face the risk of significant economic hardship in the event of divorce. Crittenden was a reporter on economic issues for the *New York Times* from 1975 to 1983, where her work brought her a nomination for the Pulitzer Prize. She was also a reporter for *Fortune*, a financial writer and foreign correspondent for *Newsweek*, and an economics commentator for CBS News. Her articles have appeared in numerous publications, including *The Nation*, *Foreign Affairs*, and *Working Woman*. She has been a visiting lecturer at the Massachusetts Institute of Technology, in Cambridge, and at Yale University, in New Haven, Connecticut. She is the author of two other books: *Sanctuary: American Conscience and the Law in Collision* (1988), which was a *New York Times* Notable Book of the Year, in 1988; and *Killing the Sacred Cows: Bold Ideas for a New Economy* (1993).

Courtesy of Henry Holt and Company

In an autobiographical statement submitted to *World Authors 1995–2000*, Crittenden writes: "I was born and raised in Dallas, Texas, where I attended college. There is still a great deal of Texas in me, such as a willingness to take risks, a love of opinionated, entrepreneurial people, and a strong dose of irreverence. Like many people who become writers, I was also a voracious reader from an early age, and a typical 'observer' of life, not much given to joining things and always skeptical toward authority. The one thing I wasn't skeptical about was the imagined glamour of far-away places, and when I did leave Texas to go to graduate school at Columbia University in New York City, I thought I had died and gone to Heaven.

"I eventually became a journalist, the perfect profession for the outsider temperament. I could read, travel, ask questions, and cast doubt on all the answers. The only problem was that at that time (the late Sixties) the best publications did not believe that women could be writers. At Time Inc., where I held my first job, a woman could be a researcher, but a female writer was a thing foreign. The world we covered agreed. I'll never forget having lunch with a source at a Wall Street club, and having a screen placed around our table so the other diners would not be offended by the sight of a woman. This sort of thing did not wear well, and in 1970 120 women sued Time Inc. for sex discrimination.

"We won our case, but I quickly moved over to *Newsweek*, which had just settled its own women's lawsuit. I became one of the first women writers hired since World War II. After a couple of months, I realized that I was grossly underpaid, so I asked for and received a raise. 'We are so happy,' an editor explained, 'that this experiment (hiring a woman writer) has worked.' Another editor paid me the supreme compliment: 'You write like a man.'

"I left the magazine to spend a year traveling in Southeast Asia, doing articles for various magazines, and *Newsweek* hired me back as a foreign correspondent. I was based in South America, where I covered the 1973 coup against Salvador Allende. From there I went to the *New York Times* as an economics reporter. All this time I had been entirely focused on my career. Once, when a new boyfriend asked me about myself, I essentially recited a job history. 'It sounds so impersonal,' he commented.

"Only when I hit my forties did I realize that the traditional male life, which I had been leading, was as narrow as the traditional female life, which I had escaped. I was hit with a sudden baby hunger; a deep desire to have a child. Fortunately, I did subsequently remarry and we had one son, James, who was born in 1982.

"It is impossible to exaggerate the impact that motherhood had on me. The experience was both transformative and radicalizing. It released feelings that I had suppressed all my life—the 'soft,' feminine side that both women and men have had to repress in order to be taken seriously in the world. I felt I had finally become a whole person; a feeling as well as a dispassionate, rational person. But I also discovered that while women had won respect for their ability to do a 'man's work,' they had still not won respect for their work at home, as caregivers and nurturers.

"I left the *New York Times* after my maternity leave, for in the early 1980s a new parent was expected to return to work as 'one of the boys,' as if she had had a brief operation. I became an independent writer. A few years later, at a cocktail party, a man came over to me and pleasantly asked, 'Didn't you used to be Ann Crittenden?'

"At that point I knew I had to write a book about all this. It became *The Price of Motherhood*."

During the 1980s, after quitting her job at the *New York Times*, Crittenden worked as a freelance writer, served as executive director of the Fund for Investigative Reporting, and was a project director for the Washington arm of the Aspen Institute. She soon published her first book, *Sanctuary: American Conscience and the Law in Collision*. Crittenden described the book to Ann Geracimos in *Publishers Weekly* (March 26, 2001) as "a nonfiction narrative about do-gooders." The book provides a history of the Sanctuary movement, which originated in 1981 when the Reverend John Fife and James Corbett, among others, began smuggling Central American refugees from southern Mexico across the U.S. border and into Tucson. Once in Tucson, the refugees, who had fled death squads and civil wars in Guatemala and El Salvador, received shelter from area churches. In 1985 11 of those involved in the movement were brought to trial, and eight of the 11 were convicted of "alien-smuggling." Crittenden used extensive interviews to produce a work of "good solid reportage," according to Richard Elman in a review for the *Los Angeles Times* (October 9, 1988). In the *New York Times Book Review* (September 25, 1988), Edwin Guthman noted that Crittenden does not "say categorically that the sanctuary workers were right in openly defying the United States Immigration and Naturalization Service. . . . But [she] sets forth a convincing case that in processing the Salvadorans and Guatemalans fleeing to this country, the Reagan Administration repeatedly violated the Refugee Act of 1980 and singled out the sanctuary workers for political reasons." *The Nation* (November 7, 1988) contributor Tom Miller concluded that "[Crittenden's] account of the inner workings of the Justice Department . . . is excellent."

Crittenden's next book, *Killing the Sacred Cows: Bold Ideas for a New Economy*, was a compilation of essays offering solutions to such pressing issues as welfare, public education, the budget deficit, and health care. She began the book in 1992, when it appeared to her that the United States was emerging from years spent in an ideological slumber. She writes in the introduction that, "like Sleeping Beauty, people were waking up and asking, 'Where am I? What happened? Where's my health insurance? Where's my pension? Where's my bank? Where's my job? How is my kid going to go to college?'" In proposing solutions to the economic troubles that faced the United States in the early 1990s, Crittenden drew upon the research of think tanks and policy institutes, the editorial sections of major publications, and interviews with scholars, businessmen, financiers, politicians, activists, and ordinary citizens. She found that the best ideas were those that did not fit neatly within either of the traditional liberal or conservative approaches, claiming in her introduction that "the either-or categories of 'private enterprise' and 'public sector' are passé; the economic reality is totally mixed." "Crittenden has masterfully used her position as a financial writer for the New York Times, Fortune, and other periodicals to assemble ideas concerning economic reform that she characterizes as the best and boldest that have been postulated," Gene R. Laczniak wrote in Library Journal (January 1993). "Unfortunately, her chapter on health-care reform is rather uninspired. . . . Nevertheless, all serious readers interested in economic policy should give this book their careful attention."

In The Price of Motherhood: Why the Most Important Job in the World is Still the Least Valued, Crittenden argued that women are penalized economically, legally, professionally, and personally for having children. The book, her most popular to date, received widespread media attention. Paul Starr praised the book in the New York Times (February 11, 2001): "Written with a fine passion and at times a biting wit, [The Price of Motherhood] challenges the received ideas of economists, feminists and conservatives alike and ought to be read by all of them. . . . [The book is] as informative and engaging in its details as it is compelling in its overall argument." In her review for the Washington Post (April 29, 2001), Shirley Burggraf described the book as "a modern mother's lament," and concluded that it "makes a significant contribution to understanding the supply side of our labor market: specifically, the years of hard, patient parental work required to develop a young person with the imagination, self-confidence and self-discipline to work, plan and save in a modern capitalist society." Crittenden spent five years researching her subject, conducting interviews in the United States and in Europe, and drawing upon current work in the fields of sociology, history, economics, child development, and law. "I've never written anything that took so much time, but I found I wasn't bored for one second," she told Geracimos. "I just loved it because, for one thing, there are so many disparate pieces. When I felt I was just running out of steam on one piece, I would wake up the next morning and say, 'I'm going to do this other one.' It was as though I was writing four or five stories at once. When I felt excited about one, that was the one I would work on that day."

Women who decide to have children suffer from a "mommy tax," Crittenden claims, which can add up to $1 million in lost wages, savings, Social Security, and pensions for college-educated mothers. Even mothers who return to work after a short leave of absence find themselves subject to a loss of respect and status, making professional advancement more difficult. Employers often view the special requirements of raising a family—leaving work early to pick up children, the difficulty in scheduling travel time—as a lack of commitment to the job. Crittenden points out that the wage difference between mothers and childless women under age 35 is larger than that between young women and men. It is this "mommy gap," even more than the glass ceiling, that Crittenden sees as preventing women from achieving equal pay and status.

The unfair treatment of mothers is largely due to a cultural bias that views motherhood as a voluntary decision. Crittenden cites a female lawyer who does not find fault with the fact that women's opportunities for advancement are limited if they choose to raise children. The lawyer equates motherhood with the decision of a male colleague to devote extra time to training for marathons; he is perhaps more likely to be passed over for a promotion, but that is a reasonable result of his choice of lifestyle. The problem with this argument, Crittenden asserts, is that choosing to be a mother is not the same as choosing to devote time to a sport or personal hobby. "The consequences of those decisions are private, of no concern to the rest of us," she writes, as quoted by Ruth Conniff in the Progressive (June 2001). Mothers, on the other hand, are nurturing and educating the next generation of workers. In an article for Women's eNews (February 21, 2001, on-line), Crittenden elaborated: "I knew that economists now agree that two-thirds of all wealth is created by human beings—through [the] skills, creativity and enterprise that is called 'human capital.' I also knew as a parent that these capabilities are nurtured, or stunted, in a child's earliest years. That makes mothers, and other early caregivers, the nation's principal wealth producers."

Crittenden contrasts the situation in the United States with Sweden, where employers grant mothers a year's paid leave of absence. In addition, the government gives mothers the right to a six-hour workday until the child is eight, tie the amount of child support to inflation, and provide a stipend for child care.

Women's organizations in the United States have traditionally been reluctant to take up issues related to motherhood, emphasizing instead the need for equality in business. Crittenden notes that, in the past, when mothers have united on such issues as drunk driving or gun control, they have wielded a remarkable amount of political influence. In an article for the Los Angeles Times (June 17, 2001), she wrote, "Mothers are the sleeping giant of American politics, and there is no telling what that giant can accomplish if she wakes up and gets her act together."

Crittenden resides in Washington, D.C. with her husband and son. She is the recipient of the World Hunger Media Award for her New York Times series, "A World to Feed."

—A. I. C.

SUGGESTED READING: *Christian Century* p18 May 23, 2001; *Christian Science Monitor* p17 Feb. 21, 2001; *Los Angeles Times* p6 Oct. 9, 1988, M p1 June 17, 2001; *Money* p19+ May/June 2001; *New York Times* p7 Feb. 11, 2001; *Progressive* p42+ June 2001; *Publishers Weekly* p57+ Mar. 26, 2001; *Washington Post* p4 Aug. 21, 1988, p9 Apr. 29, 2001; *Women's eNews* (on-line) Feb. 21, 2001

SELECTED BOOKS: *Sanctuary: American Conscience and the Law in Collision*, 1988; *Killing the Sacred Cows: Bold Ideas for a New Economy*, 1993; *The Price of Motherhood: Why the Most Important Job in the World is Still the Least Valued*, 2001

Courtesy of HarperCollins Publishers

Crowley, John

Dec. 1, 1941– Novelist; short-story writer; screenwriter

Since his first novel, *The Deep*, was published in 1975, John Crowley has received little serious critical attention because of his use of science-fiction and fantasy elements—despite the fact that his work contains broader themes and deeper characterizations than typically found in those genres. Writers like Crowley, who employ such genre devices in their work, have always been hard to classify, and have often had trouble finding readers because of this indistinct classification. Crowley, however, has generated a sizable, devoted readership over the years. (Despite this audience, his early books are often out of print.) Observers have theorized that his latest effort, *The Translator* (2002), has the potential to move Crowley from the rank of underappreciated cult writer into that of recognized literary great.

John Crowley was born in Presque Isle, Maine, on December 1, 1941, the son of Doctor Joseph B. Crowley and the former Patience Lyon. (Various sources list his birthplace as Vermont and his date of birth as 1942.) During his childhood, Crowley's family moved to Kentucky, before settling in Indiana when he was a teenager. In 1964 he received a bachelor of arts degree from Indiana University, where he majored in English and minored in film and photography. In the years after his graduation, Crowley worked as a photographer and commercial artist, but he nurtured dreams of becoming a filmmaker. In 1966 he began working as a screenwriter for various television shows, including documentaries and educational programs. In the early 1970s he grew fascinated by science fiction, particularly the work of such critically acclaimed and popular authors as Ursula K. LeGuin, Thomas M. Disch, and Brian W. Aldiss, and decided to try his hand at it.

Despite these exceptions to the rule, science-fiction authors then received little attention from critics or support from their own publishers—a fact that still holds true to some extent today. When Doubleday published Crowley's first novel, *The Deep*, in 1975, another book with the same title by Peter Benchley was being published by the company at the same time. "It's a sign of how highly regarded science fiction was at the time," Crowley noted in an interview with Robert K. J. Killheffer for *Publishers Weekly* (August 29, 1994), "that they didn't even know they were publishing two books with the same title. The right hand of bestsellerdom didn't know what the left hand of the genre was doing." In the *New York Times Book Review* (November 21, 1976), however, Gerald Jonas wrote about the book, "Paraphrase is useless to convey the intensity of Crowley's prose; anyone interested in the risk-taking side of modern science fiction will want to experience it firsthand."

With the publication of his next two novels, *Beasts* (1976) and *Engine Summer* (1979), Crowley was well on his way to becoming a cult writer, with a small but devoted following of fans. As he told Killheffer: "It was wonderful, just wonderful, to discover this subculture in which my work could be loved, admired, understood and taken seriously. It's hard to describe how important that is for a young writer."

In 1981 Crowley published his fourth novel, *Little, Big*, an intriguing mix of realism and fantasy that is considered by many to be one of his finest works. The two main characters, who meet and fall in love, are Alice Dale Drinkwater (who is nicknamed "Daily Alice") and Smoky Barnable. Alice's grandfather John had built a strange structure that he called the "folly house," employing disparate styles of architecture. The mysterious house also appears to be a portal to another place. The narrative intertwines Barnable's history with that of the town and reveals the Drinkwater family's association with the elves and sprites that live in the woods that border their ancestral home. Edmund Fuller, reviewing the novel for the *Wall Street Journal* (September 28, 1981), cheered: "*Little, Big*, with its overlapping realms of being . . . offers a refreshing, provocative adventure, with a gifted writer as our guide, entered not through a wardrobe or a looking glass, but through a 'folly house' of many styles." Fuller admitted though, "Much as I admire [the book] and responsive as I am to its odd genre, its intricacies began to exhaust me some three-quarters of the way through."

Bantam, Crowley's publisher at the time, tried to give *Little, Big* more exposure and thereby more access to the mainstream market. The book failed, however, to sell in large quantities. "Though I went through a succession of editors there, everybody was behind the book," he recalled to Killheffer. "I can't diagnose the problem, and I've never found anybody at Bantam who could diagnose it either." The mass-market paperback edition was ultimately issued on the company's science-fiction and fantasy list.

Bantam gave Crowley's next novel, *Ægypt* (1987), a huge push as well. *Ægypt* was the first novel in a planned series of four books, in which Pierce Moffett, an unemployed professor, begins to research a forgotten history of the world. Moffett's search brings him in contact with Rose Rasmussen, a mysterious woman who may hold the key to unlocking the secrets of a country once known as Ægypt. Though extremely complex, the novel generally received great praise. "[In a sense], *Ægypt* is a dense, slow, difficult book," John Peake wrote for the *Times Literary Supplement* (November 20-26, 1987). "But its own vivid reality is an absorbing one, and it leaves the reader impatient for the second volume." Colin Greenland, writing for the *New Statesman* (November 20, 1987), agreed: "This volume took five years to write. I hope the others materialize more rapidly. I want them now."

Greenland had to wait a number of years for the next installment, just as Crowley had to wait for another shot at the bestseller list; *Ægypt*, despite the push, sold no better than any of his previous novels. Crowley next published two collections of short stories, *Novelty* (1989) and *Antiquities: Seven Stories* (1993), and a highly regarded novella, *Great Work of Time* (1991); none of the volumes made great ripples commercially or critically, although Crowley's fans praised them. *Love and Sleep* (1994), the sequel to *Ægypt*, then became the next great test for the author. As the second book in the series, the novel advances the understanding of Pierce Moffett's character, while elaborating on the alternate history of the world he is researching. The book begins with a chronicle of Moffett's childhood in the 1950s, as he and his mother move from New York City to Kentucky, and follows him into adulthood, when he uncovers an unfinished novel about Renaissance magic and seeks to sell his own idea for an alternate history of the Earth to his literary agent.

Critics were divided over the merits of this novel. Phoebe-Lou Adams, writing for the *Atlantic Monthly* (September 1994), bemoaned: "This tale wanders plotlessly from the approximate present to Elizabethan England, encumbered by metaphysical and religious baggage, arcane references, and the philosophers' stone. There are ghosts, visions, and werewolves, but not even werewolves can locate any blood in these characters." Gregory Feeley offered a more positive assessment for *New York Newsday* (August 18, 1994): "With [a] half-realistic, half-magical touch, Crowley knits together the two halves of his novel and ends it with a note of satisfying resolution, while yet managing to keep matters up in the air. It is a bravura technical feat, and a superb ending for a strikingly original and affecting novel."

In 2000 Crowley published *Dæmonomania*, the third novel in the *Ægypt* series. The title refers to Samantha Mucho, a young girl who is believed to be possessed by a demon. This case of demonic possession draws the attention of Pierce Moffett and his friends in Faraway Hills, New York, who believe that the Mucho case foreshadows other shifts in reality. Like its predecessor, this novel received mixed reviews. Rachel Singer, in *Library Journal* (August 2000), wrote, "Crowley is at his best when illuminating the enchantment present in day-to-day life, yet in places he tends to allow his own cleverness to interfere with the stories of his characters." Writing for the *New York Times Book Review* (September 2000), Jeff Waggoner was also critical: "Crowley . . . interleaves Sam's story with those of the ancient black arts of alchemy and the more modern story of the struggle between faith and reason." He continued, "*Dæmonomania* is the work of a talented writer who, in this case, seems to work a kind of reverse alchemy—turning potential narrative gold into lesser materials."

In 2002 Crowley published *The Translator*, his first self-contained full-length novel since *Little, Big* more than 20 years earlier. The story takes place shortly before the Cuban Missile Crisis of 1962, at a Midwestern university where the reader meets Innokenti Falin, an exiled Russian poet and teacher, and his apprentice, Kit Malone. They are embarking on a huge endeavor—the translation of Falin's lyric poetry into English. Because relations between the United States and the Soviet Union are breaking down, many believe that the poet is a spy or worse. Within this framework, Crowley sprinkles magical elements: a group of "lesser angels" mentioned in one of Falin's poems, for example, is decidedly real. *The Translator* received mixed reviews. For *January Magazine* (April 2002, on-line), David Dalgleish wrote, "The novel hovers between realism and fantasy, but gains little from the ambiguity. The symbolic aspects of Falin's life and death lack the weight and texture of the novel's more mundane elements, which are superbly rendered. It is thus somewhat hard to credit the notion that poetry can save the world, but easy to believe that it can give Kit back her life." Although he bemoaned the book's reliance on "stock literary types," in a review for the Atlanta *Journal-Constitution* (August 11, 2002) Jerry Cullum wrote, "Crowley [uses] his characteristic blend of wit and intellectual magic, suggesting alternative interpretations for events and expanding our definitions of truth in the process."

In 1984 John Crowley married Laurie Block; they have twin daughters. The author lives in Massachusetts and is a visiting professor of creative writing at Yale University, in New Haven, Connecticut. In addition to his books, he has written more than 30 documentary films, some of them in collaboration with his wife. Crowley has been the recipient of numerous Hugo and Nebula Award nominations, and he has won a World Fantasy Award and an American Academy of Arts and Letters Award, among other honors.

—C. M.

SUGGESTED READING: *Atlantic Monthly* p112 Sep. 1994; *Library Journal* p168 Aug. 2000; *New Statesman* p31 Nov. 20, 1987; *New York Times Book Review* p9 May 3, 1987, p25 Sep. 17, 2000; *Publishers Weekly* p53 Aug. 29, 1994; *Village Voice* p60 Apr. 16, 2000; *Wall Street Journal* p26 Sep. 28, 1981

SELECTED BOOKS: *The Deep*, 1975; *Beasts*, 1976; *Engine Summer*, 1979; *Little, Big*, 1981; *Ægypt*, 1987; *Novelty*, 1989; *Antiquities: Seven Stories*, 1993; *Great Work of Time*, 1991; *Love and Sleep*, 1994; *Dæmonomania*, 2000; *The Translator*, 2002

Christopher Felver/Courtesy of Coffee House Press

Cruz, Victor Hernandez

Feb. 6, 1949– Poet

Though not much older than 50, Victor Hernandez Cruz has been publishing poetry in the U.S. and his native Puerto Rico for about 35 years. He is one of the vanguard of "Nuyorican" poets, émigré writers who merge their Puerto-Rican roots with their experiences in New York City to create a new poetic form. Cruz's poetry is characterized by a rhythmic quality, a nostalgic longing for home, and clever wordplay that melds English and Spanish. "My work is on the border of a new language, because I create out of a consciousness steeped in two of the important world languages, Spanish and English," Cruz is quoted as saying in *Contemporary Authors* (1999). "I write from the center of a culture which is not on its native soil, a culture in flight, living half the time on memories, becoming something totally new and unique, while at the same time it helps to shape and inform the new environment. I write about the city with an agonizing memory of a lush tropical silence. This contrast between landscape and language creates an intensity in my work." Carmelo Esterrich reflected in *MELUS* (Fall 1998), the journal of the Society for the Study of the Multi-Ethnic Literature of the U.S.: "'Nuyorican' writing has always been caught in the critical cross-fire between two national spaces—Puerto Rico and the U.S.— and between their literary and linguistic borders. Because of this conflict, Nuyorican writers have created an apparent instability in their own writing as one of their literary concerns, trying either to carve out a space for their writing or to create a new space." Cruz's 1995 poem, "The Lower East Side of Manhattan," which was published in *The Massachusetts Review* (Winter 1995/1996), reflects his concerns with history and place:

> By the East River Of Manhattan Island Where once the Iroquois Canoed in style A clear liquid Caressing another name For rock, Now the jumping Stretch of Avenue D Housing projects Where Ricans and Afros Johnny Pacheco/Wilson Pickett The portable radio night

Cruz was featured on the PBS poetry series, *Language of Life*, hosted by Bill Moyers, and has received major literary honors, including a fellowship from the National Endowment for the Arts, in 1980; a New York Poetry Foundation Award, in 1989; and a Guggenheim Award for artists from Latin America and the Caribbean, in 1991.

The son of Severo and Rosa (Hernandez) Cruz, Victor Hernandez Cruz was born on February 6, 1949 in Aguas Buenas, Puerto Rico. His grandfather was a cigar maker and also a poet respected for his powerful oratory. Cruz and his family immigrated, in 1954, to New York City's Lower East Side. Cruz eventually dropped out of high school, and, in 1966, while still a teenager, he self-published his first chapbook of poetry, *Papo Got His Gun!* Cruz moved to California's Bay Area, in 1968, and a year later his second poetry volume, *Snaps*, was published by Random House. The following year he co-edited, with Herbert Kohl, *Stuff: A Collection of Poems, Visions & Imaginative Happenings From Young Writers in Schools—Opened & Closed*.

Cruz was a guest lecturer at the University of California, at Berkeley, in 1971. That year he also returned to Puerto Rico, and, in 1973, he published *Mainland*, another poetry collection. In 1976 he published *Tropicalization*, which begins with a series of short poems about New York City and ends with several longer poems and short prose passages. "His poetry is a stunning batter of 'Spinglish' [often called Spanglish, a mixture of Spanish and English]," a reviewer wrote in *Choice* (February 1977), "with its ultimate stylistic roots in the far-out surrealism of Garcia Lorca—especially Lorca's *The Poet in New York*. This is very vital, energetic, fresh, innovative poetry, and it treats English just the way it should be treated—as its own kind of amalgam capable of easily incorporating into itself huge quantities of new words-syntaxes. Cruz is a poet to watch."

Cruz continued to explore language in *By Lingual Wholes* (1982), the title of which makes explicit his desire to synthesize a new language from two that had previously been separate. "Cruz allows the staccato crackle of English half-learned . . . to enrich the poems through its touching dictional inadequacy," Nancy Sullivan wrote in *Poetry*, as quoted in *Contemporary Authors* (1999). "If poetry is arching toward the condition of silence as [the composer and poet] John Cage and [the writer] Susan Sontag suggest, perhaps this mode of inarticulateness is a bend on the curve. . . . I think that Cruz is writing necessary poems in a period when many poems seem unnecessary."

Cruz published *Rhythm, Content, and Flavor*, in 1988, followed, in 1991, by *Red Beans*, which contains both poetry and essays. In an interview with Elizabeth Alexander for the *Voice Literary Supplement* (November 1991), Cruz described his new experience of writing essays. "If I bring a question up I feel I have to answer it in prose, whereas poetry is more suggestion. . . . The prose is like a map. I want to take [the readers] to a specific place and have them see a specific opinion I have." The subject material of *Red Beans* ranges from Columbus's arrival in the Americas, to Cruz's experience in poetry competitions, to bolero dancing. "Cruz is knowledgeable," Alexander wrote, "about the history and culture of the creolized Caribbean and its pre-diaspora roots; he claims African, Indian, and Iberian kin by weaving music and legends throughout the poems." In the *American Book Review* (February/March 1992) Anne C. Bromley wrote, "Hernandez Cruz has found a poetry that keeps alive lyrics and rhythms that used to emanate from coastal Caribbean beaches and towns, traditions that extended into the mists of Spain and Africa. [He] brings poetry back in many ways to its earlier public functions. His are poems that remember, poems that declaim, poems that celebrate language as a pathway into and out of dreams." Alexander declared, "What would be treacle in the hands of lesser souls is quirky and utterly lovely in *Red Beans* and in Victor Cruz. His nostalgia is a way of remembering as well as an avenue of response to the present."

In 1993 Cruz was a visiting professor at the University of California, in San Diego, and he returned to the same position, in 1995. In 1994 he was a visiting professor at the University of Michigan, in Ann Arbor. Cruz co-edited, with Leroy V. Quintana and Virgil Suarez, an anthology of poetry titled *Paper Dance: 55 Latino Poets* (1995), which included works by Julia Alvarez, Judith Ortiz Cofer, Juan Felipe Herrera, Pat Mora, Alberto Alvaro Rios, Luis J. Rodriguez, and Tino Villeanueva, among others. "This vibrant anthology . . . is a celebration of social, cultural, and private interfaces," Donna Seaman wrote in *Booklist* (March 1, 1995). "Their poems examine the complex and ever-evolving relationships between tradition and change, Spanish and English, rural and urban, private and public, female and male, young and old, past and present, native and immigrant, dream and reality, love and despair, joy and anger, art and life. . . . A poetry collection would usually be described as a chorus of voices, but the editors were right to choose dance for their title. These poems do dance in a dazzling array of tempos and moods. Some are elegant and graceful; others are clownish and mocking, frenzied, sultry, or threatening, but all are charged with the electricity of emotion, the current of thought and observation, and the rhythms of the body."

Cruz next published *Panoramas* (1997), a collection of poems and essays in which he seeks to illuminate his own art. In one essay, for instance, he writes, as quoted by Jabari Asim in the *Washington Post Book World* (January 25, 1998), "The encounter between rural and urban landscape, a debate released through migration, a discussion of spatial tempos, city versus tropical, these are steeped in my consciousness and echo through my poetic creations." Asim called Cruz an "exemplary poet, teacher and essayist" and described *Panoramas* as a "charming and easily digested blend of prose remembrances, new poems (in both Spanish and English), and insightful essays about Latin-American literature."

In 2001 Cruz published *Maraca: New and Selected Poems, 1965–2000*, which includes many of his unpublished poems from the previous four decades. "The poems as a whole evince a wryly matter-of-fact, documentarian approach to urban life that feels utterly contemporary," Michael Scharf wrote in *Publishers Weekly* (September 3, 2001). "And while bilingual work that jumpcuts across codes is now commonplace, Cruz's idioms hit highs and lows effortlessly, singularly and with political bite."

Cruz divides his time between the San Francisco Bay Area and Puerto Rico.

—P. G. H.

SUGGESTED READING: *American Book Review* p26 Feb./Mar. 1992; *Booklist* p1175 Mar. 1, 1995; *Choice* p1594 Feb. 1977; *MELUS* p43+ Fall 1998; *Publishers Weekly* p83 Sept. 3, 2001; *San Francisco Chronicle* p6 Apr. 2, 1989; *Voice Literary Supplement* p36 Nov. 1991; *Washington Post Book World* p9+ Jan. 25, 1998

SELECTED BOOKS: poetry—*Snaps*, 1969; *Mainland*, 1973; *Tropicalization*, 1976; *By Lingual Wholes*, 1982; *Rhythm, Content, and Flavor*, 1988; *Red Beans*, 1991; *Panoramas*, 1997, *Maraca: New and Selected Poems, 1965–2000*, 2001; as editor—*Stuff: A Collection of Poems, Visions & Imaginative Happenings From Young Writers in Schools—Opened & Closed* (with Herbert Kohl), 1970; *Paper Dance: 55 Latino Poets*, 1995

Courtesy of Putnam Publishing Group

Cussler, Clive

July 15, 1931– Writer; founder and chairman of the National Underwater and Marine Agency

While it is a truism that works of fiction reflect their writers' experiences, the channels through which life passes into fiction often remain a mystery, even to the authors themselves. For the most part, that is not the case for the action-adventure writer Clive Cussler, 20 of whose books have spent time on the *New York Times* best-seller list. Cussler bears a striking resemblance to his fictional alter ego, Dirk Pitt, who has been featured in more than a dozen of his creator's numerous books, among them *Raise the Titanic, Pacific Vortex, Deep Six, Treasure, Sahara Gold, Inca Gold, Flood Tide, Atlantis Found,* and *Valhalla Rising*. Like Pitt, Cussler is an avid underwater explorer: working with others connected with the National Underwater Marine Agency (NUMA), which he founded (and which employs Pitt), he has located the remains of more than 60 "historically significant wreck sites," as he reported on the NUMA Web site. Thanks to creative license, Pitt has certain advantages over Cussler: in 25 years, for example, Pitt has barely aged. Moreover, Pitt is dazzlingly charming, and his capacity for hairbreadth escape often beggars belief. But such discrepancies between life and fiction merely underscore the fact that Pitt is an idealized self-portrait; as Cussler declared to Harry Thomas for the *San Antonio Express-News* (October 5, 1997, on-line), "Pitt is me, of course."

Before launching his career as a novelist, Cussler worked for 18 years in the field of advertising. In a 1987 interview with Jean W. Ross for *Contemporary Authors*, he said that having to write "short, snappy ad copy" for so long prepared him "to write easy, understandable prose, and also to look at writing and publishing from a marketing angle. So I predetermined what I wanted to write—in fact, I spent months researching it—before I actually sat down and punched out the first chapter." Since the publication of *Raise the Titanic*, in 1976, Cussler has produced a Dirk Pitt novel every two to three years, on average. By and large the books offer the author's proven mix of derring-do, carefully researched historical detail, and exuberantly convoluted plotting. In total, the "Dirk Pitt" novels have sold more than 100 million copies worldwide; they have been translated into some 40 languages, and many have been published in large-print editions. "The old man of adventure," as Cussler has been called, has also commenced a new series, co-authored with Paul Kemprecos, which includes *Serpent* (1999), *Blue Gold* (2000), and *Fire Ice* (2002); each subtitled "A Novel from the NUMA Files," these books feature the NUMA field operatives Kurt Austin and Joe Zavala. (*Blue Gold* became Cussler's 17th best-seller shortly after its release.) A fourth book in that series, "White Death," is set for release in June 2003. Cussler's books of nonfiction include *The Sea Hunters* (1996) and *The Sea Hunters II* (2002), in which he and his co-author, Craig Dirgo, describe some of the shipwrecks Cussler has researched. For his first nonfiction work, which also became a best seller, Cussler was awarded a doctor of letters degree in May 1997 from the Board of Governors of the Maritime College, State University of New York. He has also produced *Dirk Pitt Revealed* (1998), written with Dirgo and Arnold Stern, which presents Cussler's account of the evolution of Pitt, synopses of all of the Pitt novels' plots, and a concordance that contains, among other things, the names of every major character and car model mentioned in the books.

The only child of a homemaker and an accountant, Clive Cussler was born in Aurora, Illinois, on July 15, 1931. He spent much of his youth in Alhambra, California, outside Los Angeles. In interviews he has recalled avidly reading adventure stories as a boy. Partly because of his fascination with such tales, he was never much of a student; as he told Walt Jayroe for *Publishers Weekly* (July 11, 1994), "I detested school. I was always the kid who was staring out the window. While the teacher was lecturing on algebra, I was on the deck of a pirate ship or in an airplane shooting down the Red Baron." After attending Pasadena City College, in California, for a short time, Cussler turned his back on formal schooling. In 1950, at the outbreak of the Korean War, he enlisted in the air force, motivated to some extent by a desire for adventure. During four years of service as a mechanic, he flew supply missions for the Military Air Transport Service throughout the Pacific but never saw combat. One of his fellow mechanics, Al Giordino, later materialized in Cussler's novels as the loyal sidekick of Dirk Pitt. Cussler has traced his longtime interest in sunken ships to his military experiences: while stationed in Hawaii he learned to scuba dive and explored underwater wrecks in his free time.

After his discharge from the air force, Cussler returned to California. He operated a gas station with a friend for a time and then landed a job as an advertising copywriter. From 1961 to 1965 he co-owned Bestgen & Cussler Advertising. During the next three years he worked as creative director at the D'Arcy Advertising Co., in Los Angeles (now part of D'Arcy Masius Benton & Bowles). His D'Arcy credits include the memorable slogan for Ajax detergent, "It's stronger than dirt," which he thought up with the help of friends. During his tenure at D'Arcy, he garnered several Clio Awards, an industry honor that recognizes creative excellence and has been called the Oscar of advertising. From 1967 to 1969 he was the advertising director at Aquatic Marine Corp., in Newport Beach, California. His last stint in the field (1970–75) was with Mefford Advertising, in Denver, Colorado, where he held the titles of vice president and creative director.

In spite of his successes at work, Cussler became restless, and by the late 1960s he had resolved to try his hand at writing. "When I decided to write, my wife was working nights at the local police department," he recalled to Lewis Frumkes for the *Writer* (September 1996). "I'd put the kids to bed and have nothing to do. What was I going to write? I didn't have the 'Great American Novel' burning inside me. So, I decided on a series. I was working in advertising then, and I looked at writing from a marketing angle. I went out and researched all the series' heroes, beginning with Edgar Allen Poe's Inspector Dupont, who was really the first one. Then, of course, Doyle's Sherlock Holmes, Ian Fleming's James Bond, and [Mickey Spillane's] Mike Hammer."

The first book that Cussler wrote, *Pacific Vortex*, features a diabolical hero-villain, a kind of combination of Fu Manchu and Aquaman whom Cussler described to Lewis Frumkes as an "old, evil guy with yellow eyes who lived under water with a gill system." Cussler told Frumkes that he had originally planned to reintroduce this amphibious scoundrel in his second novel, *The Mediterranean Caper*, but Dirk Pitt, who had been scripted for a minor role, "just took the book over." His two manuscripts interested neither literary agents nor publishers. As Cussler recalled to Pam Lambert for *People* (September 21, 1992), "People in publishing would say, 'Don't waste your time. Nobody buys adventure.'" Eager to prove them wrong, Cussler resorted to a desperate measure: using his father's Laguna Hills, California, address, he ordered business stationery bearing the letterhead of a fictitious writers' agency. Posing as "Charles Winthrop," he wrote to the literary agent Peter Lampack. Cussler recalled the text of the letter for Walt Jayroe: "Dear Peter, As you know, I primarily handle motion pictures, television and screenplays. I ran across a couple of book-length manuscripts that have a great deal of potential. I'd like to pursue them, but as I mentioned, I'm retiring." Lampack replied promptly: "Dear Charlie, I didn't like the first one [*Vortex*], but the second [*Mediterranean Caper*] is pretty good. Where can I sign Clive Cussler?" Four years later, in 1973, Lampack found a publisher (Pyramid Publications) for *Mediterranean Caper*, which sold fairly well.

Cussler's next book, *Iceberg* (1975), was published by Dodd. His breakthrough came in 1976, with the publication (this time by Viking) of *Raise the Titanic*. In *Titanic*, the tangled plot structure with which Cussler had experimented in *Iceberg*—and which he himself, speaking with Pam Lambert, called "horribly convoluted"—reached an even greater level of complexity. Indeed, dizzyingly baroque plots are a hallmark of the mature Cusslerian style. As *Titanic* opens, U.S. government scientists, covertly funded by a lame-duck president, have concocted a top-secret plan to erect an impregnable missile defense system, which would incorporate a device that concentrates sound waves. The scientists lack one crucial ingredient: byzanium, a rare (fictional) radioactive element. The only known specimen of byzanium, discovered on an island in Russia in Czarist times, sank with the *Titanic*, in 1912, along with the reckless band of Colorado miners who had stolen the entire stockpile of the precious substance. The task of recovering the byzanium has been delegated to Dirk Pitt, who, outfitted with an inflatable apparatus, must raise the sunken luxury liner from its frigid grave. But the Russians, in what was then the Soviet Union, learn of Pitt's plan, and will stop at nothing to retrieve the byzanium for themselves. Additional complications include a wayward hurricane, mysterious sabotage, a cadre of Soviet marines, a madman's dying words, a puzzling murder aboard a submarine, and an insane physicist unhappily married to an oversexed marine archaeologist.

Improbable as the plot may seem, *Raise the Titanic* sold more than 150,000 copies and remained on the *New York Times* best-seller list for 26 weeks. The critical response to *Raise the Titanic* was less enthusiastic. Evan Connell, for example, writing for *Harper's Magazine* (as quoted in the *New York Post* on January 15, 1977), declared that "if good books were rewarded with flowers and bad books with skunks, on a scale of one to five, *Raise the Titanic* would deserve four skunks." Opinions on whether the book succeeded on its own terms, as an action thriller, were divided. In the *National Observer* (October 16, 1976), Lee Ewing wrote, "Every story must meet some minimum standard of credibility, and the language, while it need not be elegant, at least should not hinder the telling of the tale. Judged by these less-than-lofty criteria, *Raise the Titanic* . . . scrapes over the shoal of credibility only to run aground on a reef of dead language." While Ewing conceded that Cussler's plot had engaged his curiosity in spite of its "preposterous" aspects, he found that he had been "distracted by the lack of craftsmanship in the writing, by awkward exposition, by abundant clichés and contrived dialog." He cited as an example a remark about a salvaged cornet; the instrument had been so well preserved, one character said, that "it shined up like a newborn baby's ass."

By contrast, Edmund Fuller, in the *Wall Street Journal* (November 8, 1976), mentioned the cornet, which Pitt and his investigators find before locating the wreck, as evidence of the "persuasive detail" that Cussler had used to flesh out the narrative. According to Fuller, the novelist had "spun skillfully a plot for the nuclear age." "Cussler resorts to dramatic overkill before he has finished, [but] he also fires, and thoroughly satisfies, our imaginations," Fuller wrote. While Fuller noted the novel's stylistic flaws—he described Pitt, for example, as a man "whose technical skills and daring are superior to his grammar"—he found that such blemishes did not significantly detract from the book, which he judged to be "a boldly conceived, well executed thriller."

Titanic's mixed reviews are fairly representative of critical opinion regarding Cussler's other novels. Positive assessments tend to emphasize the entertainment value of the books; they generally advise readers, in the words of Joe Collins, who reviewed *Inca Gold* (1994) for *Booklist* (April 1, 1994), to take Cussler's "breathless approach with a grain of salt and just relax and enjoy the adventures of Pitt and company." Many negative assessments contain the argument that the clichés and tangles of Cussler's prose interfere with the story. In a typical instance, the pseudonymous Newgate Callendar, critiquing *Inca Gold* for the *New York Times Book Review* (May 22, 1994), complained, "There is the germ of a story here. . . . But the writing! Mr. Cussler has revived the cliché and batters his reader with choice specimens: 'the cold touch of fear'; 'a set look of determination in the deep green eyes'; 'before death swept over him'; 'narrow brush with death.' In the Cussler style, virtually every noun has to have a modifier: 'morbid waters'; 'piercing eyes'; 'furtive dark eyes'; 'you thieving scum.' There are also unhissable hisses: 'We have no radio,' he hissed.'" Cussler himself admitted to Pam Lambert, "There's no literary merit in my books," and he told her that he is happy if his readers "reach the end and feel they got their money's worth." If sales are an accurate gauge of reader satisfaction, Cussler has ample reason to be happy. His books sell well abroad as well as in the United States; according to Walt Jayroe, "at least 40 percent of his sales are international and, like clockwork, he always hits No. 1 in Japan." Cussler's latest installments in the Pitt series include *Atlantis Found* (1999) and *Valhalla Rising* (2001), both of which soared to the top of best-seller lists.

Cussler's financial success has provided him with the means to indulge two passions that he shares with Dirk Pitt: restoring vintage automobiles and exploring undersea shipwrecks. His automobile collection includes more than 80 vehicles, including a 1930 L-29 Cord, the same model that Pitt drives. Since 1979, when he founded the National Underwater and Marine Agency, NUMA engineers and scientists have conducted dozens of underwater archaeological expeditions; among the wrecks they have either located or surveyed are the Confederate submarine *Hunley*, the German submarine *U-20* (which sank the British luxury liner *Lusitania* on May 17, 1915, an event often said to have precipitated the United States' entrance into World War I), and the Allied troop transport *Leopoldville* (which sank off the coast of Cherbourg, France, in 1944, during World War II). "We're dedicated to preserving our maritime heritage, and we do this by locating the lost ships of historical significance," Cussler, who chairs NUMA, told Jean W. Ross. "When we are lucky enough, after research and time and diving, to find and identify them, we turn over all the information to the state or federal government, or to museums, libraries, universities, and in some cases the navy, in the hope that someday the finds will attract the necessary funding and technology from either individuals, corporations, or the government to salvage and conserve the artifacts for public display, or perhaps raise the old shipwrecks themselves." Many NUMA expeditions have furnished material for Pitt's fictional exploits.

Cussler and his wife, the former Barbara Knight, married in 1955. They divide their time between Colorado and Paradise Valley, Arizona, an affluent suburb of Phoenix, where they own a winter home. The couple have three children—Teri, Dirk, and Dana—and two grandchildren. In December 2002, the 71-year-old Cussler announced plans to retire his pen for good. As he explained to a reporter for the *Los Angeles Times* (December 14, 2002), "The imagination is still working, but the drive is just gone. I can't explain it. I guess [after] 35 years of this stuff . . . I'm tired of it."

—P. K.

SUGGESTED READING: *National Observer* p19 Oct. 16, 1976 ; *People* p93+ Sept. 21, 1992; *Publishers Weekly* p58+ July 11, 1994; *Writer* p15+ Sep. 1996; *Contemporary Authors* New Revision Series Vol. 21, 1987; Cussler, Clive, Craig Dirgo, and Arnold Stern. *Dirk Pitt Revealed*, 1998

SELECTED BOOKS: *The Mediterranean Caper*, 1973; *Iceberg*, 1975; *Raise the Titanic*, 1976; *Cyclops*, 1986; *Vixen 03*, 1978; *Pacific Vortex!*, 1983; *Deep Six*, 1984; *Cyclops*, 1986; *Treasure*, 1988; *Dragon*, 1990; *Night Probe!*, 1992; *Sahara*, 1992; *Inca Gold*, 1994; *Shock Wave*, 1996; *The Sea Hunters: True Adventures with Famous Shipwrecks*, 1996; *Flood Tide*, 1997; *Serpent: A Novel from the NUMA Files*, 1999; *Atlantis Found*, 1999; *Blue Gold: A Novel from the NUMA Files*, 2000; *Valhalla Rising*, 2001; *Fire Ice: A Novel from the NUMA Files*, 2002; *The Sea Hunters II*, 2002

Sigrid Estrada/Courtesy of Simon & Schuster

Dark, Alice Elliott

1960 (?)– Short-story writer

Though most of Alice Elliott Dark's stories portray educated, upper-middle-class white characters, she tries not to be an exclusive author, nor does she hold herself above her readers. "I gave up the idea of trying to show how smart I am," she told Brenda Shaughnessy for *Publishers Weekly* (January 31, 2000). Instead, as she told Shaughnessy, she "believe[s] in popular culture, in what touches people." Her prose is carefully crafted to draw attention away from the author and create the most immediate connection between the reader and the text. "So much is a matter of getting out of your own way, your own ego," she told Shaughnessy. "When you see people through your own ego, as in daily life, you judge them, and it's separating. In my fiction I'm less judgmental and it's connecting.

I feel empathy for all my characters no matter how flawed they are." Dark's restrained prose is nevertheless able to generate powerful emotion, as in her short story about a mother and her dying son, "In the Gloaming," which was made into an HBO movie and included in *Best American Short Stories* (1994) and *Best American Short Stories of the Century* (1999). In addition to her two collections of short fiction, Dark recently published her first novel, *Think of England* (2002).

Alice Elliott Dark was born in about 1960. (Carlin Romano, a writer for the *Boston Globe*, noted in a November 9, 1991 book review that Dark was then 31.) Dark grew up in Bryn Mawr, Pennsylvania, an upscale suburb of Philadelphia. She began writing at a very early age. "I started with [Michael Bond's] *Paddington* [series]," she recalled to Jami Edwards in a *Bookreporter.com* interview (March 31, 2000). "That was probably my first huge influence. I read that book and immediately wrote my own bear book." As a teenager Dark took an interest in the romantic poetry of Shelley, Byron, Keats, and Rimbaud—"the really sensitive, nutty guys," as she called them in the *Bookreporter.com* interview. "It was my version of teeny-bopperness. The Beatles and Percy Shelley . . . the same thing a century earlier."

Dark graduated from an all-girls high school in Bryn Mawr and received her B.A. from the University of Pennsylvania, in Philadelphia, in 1976. She majored in Chinese, partly because after reading English literature voraciously on her own, she wanted to study something she could not easily learn independently. After graduating Dark went to London to pursue graduate studies in writing, during which time she was seduced by the rich possibilities of language and became enamored of ornate word usages. She began to write fiction, applying her poetic sensibilities to the form. "You can make things sound good that make no sense at all," she told Shaughnessy, recalling her early fiction experiments. "Some of the first fiction I wrote was very poetic but really made no sense." Dark soon rejected her fascination with language for language's sake. "Now I want the language to be transparent," she told Shaughnessy, "for people to totally forget they're even reading a book."

To achieve that effect Dark diligently crafts her prose. Though she had been writing assiduously for some time, her first book of fiction, *Naked to the Waist*, was not published until 1991. The book, which was published the day her son, Ascher, was born, contains two novellas and four short stories. The stories cover a broad range of characters and settings, though Carlin Romano found that they shared an "existentialist mix of freedom and danger." "Dark," Romano continued, "seems well acquainted with the precarious courage that results when an upper-middle-class sensibility stares risk in the face."

In the title novella a 30-year-old woman named Lucy Langworthy comes to realize that many of her past mates have embodied qualities that she wanted to cultivate; she was attracted to boys who wrote poetry, for example, when she herself wanted to be a poet. Similarly, in "The Comfortable Apartment," Janie, who is married to an abusive epidemiologist, lives vicariously through her more adventurous older sister. "Jean-Paul Sartre, call your trademark attorney," Romano quipped. "At the tender age of 31, Alice Elliott Dark has invented a new school of fiction called Main Line Existentialism. She writes like the unholy love child of Katharine Hepburn and Jack Kerouac." "Who can resist saying the obvious," Romano concluded, "Alice Dark's future is bright."

Many critics agreed with Romano, but Dark's next effort, a novel, was rejected by her publisher, and she was crushed. "I holed up, I went underground," she told Shaughnessy. "I didn't send anything out for a while." When she did resume sending out manuscripts a few years later, she met with success. Her story "In the Gloaming" was published in the *New Yorker*, in 1993. It was then selected for *Best American Short Stories* (1994) and *Best American Short Stories of the Century* (1999), the latter edited by John Updike. It was also made into two movies: one, directed by Christopher Reeve, was made for HBO, in 1997, and featured Glenn Close and Whoopi Goldberg; the other was produced by Trinity Playhouse, a small film company in Manhattan. The tragic story is about a young man, Laird, who returns to his parents' house after he discovers that he is dying of a debilitating disease. His impending death thaws the frosty relationship between him and his mother and forces his parents to reexamine their marriage. Dark was somewhat upset by HBO's loose interpretation of her story, partly because Laird's name was changed to Danny. This, Dark observed, removed the connotation of Laird as a "lord" or Christ figure. Dark explained to Jami Edwards, "He was 33 and it was the end of his life. I didn't write it to be the story of Jesus' last days, but I did feel there was an element of interpretation in saying that Jesus died for our sins, to redeem us, and here the parents coming together over his death is an example of that."

Dark's second short-story collection, *In the Gloaming*, was published in 2000. Many of the ten stories in the collection (including the aforementioned title story) take place in the fictional town of Wynnemoor, an upper-class suburban village whose residents are characterized by outward emotional restraint. As Michiko Kakutani pointed out in the *New York Times* (January 25, 2000, on-line), this restraint is often challenged as "Dark catches her well-bred, well-mannered characters in moments of extremis, when their guard is down and they are forced, by illness or mortality, divorce or disillusion, to re-evaluate their lives." In "Home" an elderly woman named Lil discovers that her handicapped husband, who has recently been admitted to a nursing home, has sold their house and checked her into a nursing home too. In "Maniacs" two sisters, Margaret and Diana, bump into an old acquaintance, Jerome. Diana used to date Jerome, while the more practical Margaret has long hidden her secret love for him, choosing to marry a wealthy, but dull man instead. After digging up some old diaries filled with adoring words for Jerome, Margaret is forced to admit her dissatisfaction with her life. Also trapped in a loveless marriage is Frannie, the central character in "Dreadful Language." Frannie, who had opted for a safe, passionless marriage after the love of her life died in an accident, finds that she has been deceiving herself. In "Watch the Animals" a fanatical animal-lover, who has lived on the periphery of Wynnemoor's society her whole life, reaches out to her neighbors, when, dying of lung cancer, she must find homes for her many cats and dogs. Though the other women of Wynnemoor resent her history of aloofness, they ultimately display their nobler tendencies when asked for help.

Critics applauded the collection, though some pointed out that not all of the stories were as poignant as the title piece. "The weaker stories in this volume," Kakutani wrote of Dark's collection, "tend to rely too insistently on sudden ironic plot twists to expose her characters' illusions, twists and turns that underscore Ms. Dark's authorial role as an O. Henryesque puppeteer." Katherine Dieckmann, who reviewed the collection for the *New York Times* (January 2, 2000, on-line), called the work a "microcosm of lily-white privilege, one that's tended and guarded with an implied disdain for the larger, messy world," though she conceded that Dark is able to "lay bare the most personal of troubles in controlled but devastating prose." In the *New York Review* (June 29, 2000) Joyce Carol Oates wrote, "*In the Gloaming* is a collection of beautifully composed, quietly narrated short stories . . . of love and loss. Each story exudes the gravitas of a radically distilled novel; though, in well-crafted short story fashion, we begin near the story's climax, we are brought through flashbacks into the protagonists' lives, and come to assess them in ways they aren't able to assess themselves."

In 2002 Dark published her first novel, *Think of England*, which traces the life of Jane MacLeod through three separate periods, as she confronts a painful childhood tragedy. The title refers to advice that Jane's grandmother often gave in times of crisis to "think of England," a phrase that comforts Jane. The first section is set in mid-1960s Pennsylvania, and depicts Jane at nine years old writing a book about the idyllic childhood she wishes she had. In reality, her parents have a strained marriage: her father, Emlin, is a heart surgeon who is rarely at home; her mother, Via, unhappy and resentful, often turns to drink. The young Jane assumes responsibility for her parents' marital woes. As the family gathers one evening in 1964 to watch the Beatles perform on *The Ed Sullivan Show*, a fight emerges when Emlin discovers the phone off the hook and assumes that Via has tried to block his emergency calls. (Via, in turn, accuses Jane.) Emlin leaves angrily for the hospital and is killed in a car accident. The next section picks up 15 years later, when Jane is living in London. Her relationships with a group of bohemian friends, as well as an affair with an American writer, help her confront the guilt she has long harbored over her father's death. In the final section, a middle-aged Jane—now a single mother with a daughter of her own—returns home for another family gathering, where she is finally able to resolve the tragedy of her past. Overall, Dark's first foray into full-length fiction was well received. In his review for *Publishers Weekly* (April 8, 2002), Jeff Zaleski called the book an "emotionally honest debut novel," concluding, "Although Jane's final revelation is no surprise, the author's languid yet affecting style and true-to-life dialogue make this a satisfying read for the baby-boomer set." Nevertheless, many critics found the story's pace to be somewhat slow. While one reviewer for *Kirkus Reviews* (March 1, 2002) found the book "smoothly written," and initially quite engaging, he determined that it was "at best, a qualified success," adding, "Dark's most accomplished work thus far remains her short fiction."

Dark teaches a writing workshop in New York City. She lives in Montclair, New Jersey, with her son and husband, Larry Dark, a production editor at *Businessweek*. Larry Dark also edits the O. Henry Award series, an annual collection of particularly noteworthy short stories chosen by him and a panel of jurors. Dark herself has won an O. Henry Award and has had a story included in the anthology.

—P. G. H.

SUGGESTED READING: *Boston Globe* p23 Nov. 9, 1991; *Harper's Magazine* p91+ Sep. 1999; *New York Review* p40+ June 29, 2000; *New York Times* (on-line) Jan. 2, 2000, Jan. 25, 2000; *Publishers Weekly* p74+ Jan. 31, 2000

SELECTED BOOKS: *Naked to the Waist*, 1991; *In the Gloaming*, 2000; *Think of England: A Novel*, 2002

Pat de Groot/Courtesy of Houghton Mifflin Publishing

Davies, Peter Ho

1966– Short-story writer

The British-born short-story writer Peter Ho Davies's two collections of short fiction, *The Ugliest House in the World* (1997) and *Equal Love* (2000), have been praised by critics for the way he "wields words with precision and delicacy, crafting stories admirable for their spare style, taut prose and arresting images," as a reviewer for *Publishers Weekly* (August 11, 1997) wrote. In the *New York Times Book Review* (March 19, 2000), Jacqueline Carey welcomed Davies's departure from the emphasis on "me" found in modern literature. "Virtually none of [Davies's] stories are dominated by a single, overweening voice," she wrote. "He emphasizes the most basic bonds between people rather than their individual opinions, their quirks of personality."

Peter Ho Davies, the son of a Chinese mother and a Welsh father, grew up in England. His parents were happily married, which is why, Davies told Liane Hansen for National Public Radio's *Weekend Edition Sunday* (April 2, 2000), he has often written about divorce. "I often write stories that deal with things that I either fear or I anticipate in some ways in the future. And so I think as a child of a happy marriage, I . . . grew up fearing divorce. I think I come from a generation of kids where we always had a sense that that was a possibility for our parents." Significant moments in his life pushed Davies toward becoming a writer. "When I was 18," he told Hansen, "my grandmother went into a geriatric home suffering from senile dementia and writing about that experience, painful family visits to her there, was one of the first moments that I realized the emotional potential of writing."

Davies attended Manchester University, in England, where he specialized in physics and the analysis of science and technology, receiving a B.S. in 1987. In 1989 he was awarded a B.A. in English by Cambridge University, also in England. After returning to the United States, he attended Boston University, in Massachusetts, earning a master's degree in creative writing in 1994. In 1997 he began teaching at the University of Oregon at Eugene, where he stayed until 1999.

Davies's first short-story collection, *The Ugliest House in the World*, appeared in 1997. Many of its stories deal with issues of pride and responsibility, and critics noted Davies's haunting plot twists and variety of settings and characters. The longest piece, "A Union," concerns a quarry town during a strike in 1899 and one couple who become "the eye of the storm" that is gathering about the town. "With the couple as his focus," Jay A. Fernandez wrote for the *Washington Post Book World* (January 4, 1998), "Davies explores the dangers idleness poses to a worker's pride; the moral ambiguities of a good man torn between loyalty to his fellow workers and obligation to his pregnant wife; and how easily Time can cause deep fissures in human relationships with less force than it takes a man to split a piece of slate." For Alex Chisholm, writing in the *Boston Book Review* (on-line), "A Union" is "a parable of complex characters, memorable action and an unforgettable sour humor" that manifests itself as the couple await their unwanted child, the end of the unsuccessful strike, and the need to sell the last of their furniture, an "elegant but 'mutilated' grandfather clock, functional, but tinged with shame," like themselves.

The title story of *The Ugliest House in the World* is a tale of parents and children, loss and reconciliation, both comic and tragic, and is told in a series of short bursts, each with its own title, a style adopted frequently by Davies. It concerns a young doctor who is not proud of his Welsh heritage. He is visiting his ailing father, who has bought a cottage near his boyhood home in the Welsh countryside. The relationship between the father and the son is often a rueful one:

> Every time I visit my father, I offer to whitewash the whole house. He always says, "I'll get to it. What's the rush? I'm a retired gentleman now." Since I found out he was living off sausages and baked beans I always bring a couple of bags of groceries when I come to visit him, but once I set four tins of paint on the kitchen table. He got angry and said, "I'll do it. I don't need your bloody help. Your heart's not in it, anyway." He means that I don't approve of him moving here. He's right.

Although the narrator has journeyed to where his father lives, over the course of the story, Davies makes it clear that he is going to Wales not just to visit his father but to attend a funeral. The reader does not learn whose funeral it is until well into the story, and the fact that a six-year-old boy is being buried comes as a shock. It is later revealed that the dead child's mother, the narrator's sometime lover, is the person he has really come to see. The situation becomes more complicated when the narrator's father, who had befriended the child, is held responsible for his death.

As Fernandez put it, the story is "a flawless rendering of the unexpectedly far-reaching arms of guilt—ethnic, familial and personal. . . . Davies writes with the graceful minimalism of Raymond Carver, uncovering with powerful understatement the complex emotions provoked by questions of home and family." For Chisholm, Davies drove home the point that the "ugliest house in the world, after all, is your own home when you are not welcome in it." He concluded that in "The Ugliest House" and in the "excellent" stories "Buoyancy" and "Coventry," Davies writes "with the poignancy and power of a perpetual outsider, someone who knows that one often feels most out of place in the very spot one calls home."

The *Publishers Weekly* (August 11, 1997) reviewer characterized Davies's stories as starting "benignly, often comically." But then, "inevitably there comes a moment when, with the briefest of phrases Davies startles the reader with a sudden turn down some melancholy and sometimes treacherous path." Describing "The Ugliest House in the World," the reviewer observed that "as in other tales, Davies delivers the full import of events with haunting realism," and concluded that in other stories in the volume, settings "that range from England to Patagonia, Africa and Asia are home to an appealing variety of characters whose voices are as distinctive as their accents."

In 1999 Davies left Oregon to teach at the University of Michigan at Ann Arbor. His second collection of short stories, *Equal Love*, was published in 2000. He took the title from a passage in E. M. Forster's *Where Angels Fear to Tread*: "For a wonderful physical tie binds the parents to the children; and—by some sad, strange irony—it does not bind us children to our parents. For if it did, if we could answer their love not with gratitude but with equal love, life would lose much of its pathos and much of its squalor, and we might be wonderfully happy." As Davies told several interviewers, including one from *OregonLive* (on-line), and Liane Hansen of National Public Radio (April 2, 2000), many of the stories in *Equal Love* touch on questions of parent-child relationships, particularly the predicament of that sandwich generation caught between aging parents and their own young children. "In fact," Davies told Hansen, "I think of the collection as sort of woven together so there are threads that run horizontally and threads that run sort of vertically. And the horizontal threads . . . that run through nearly all of the stories are the earlier sort of parental-child relationships. . . . Sometimes . . . young children, sometimes the way that older children relate to their aging parents. And if that's sort of the vertical thread, then the horizontal one . . . is the idea of equal love explored in various other ways between couples in a mixed race relationship. There's a story about a gay relationship, and . . . even stories that touch on class a little bit."

The first story in *Equal Love*, "The Hull Case," is about an alien abduction; it is based on the real-life case of Betty and Barney Hill, whom Davies calls Bessie and Bernie Hull. Bernie is a black veteran of Korea; Bessie is the white nurse who took care of him after he was wounded. As the story opens, they are describing their alien abduction to a colonel who has been sent to interview them. Davies's story was singled out by many critics: Susan Salter Reynolds, writing in the *Los Angeles Times Book Review* (February 6, 2000), observed that as the Hulls "report the incident to an army colonel, subtle questions of trust and credibility bubble up between the colonel, the black husband and the white wife. She is convinced that if she reveals everything about the abduction, she will be believed. He feels it is hopeless to expect that anyone will believe them; he isn't sure he believes it himself. How it feels to be doubted and denied trust is described with the same dignified precision Davies uses to describe the inner architecture of all his characters." "For . . . Hull . . . who's already 'had to work hard to be believed most of his life,' the project of reporting the alien encounter to an air force colonel becomes symbolic of the complex anxieties he, as a black man, suffers in his marriage to a white woman," the *Publishers Weekly* (November 22, 1999) reviewer wrote. Greg Changnon, assessing the book for the *Atlanta Journal-Constitution* (March 5, 2000), asked, "Who could ever find a metaphor for racism in alien abduction? Peter Ho Davies does, brilliantly, and with a straight face. 'The Hull Case' turns out to be heartbreaking."

Another story in the collection, "The Next Life," which is set in San Francisco, centers on the funeral of an old man who had been "the proprietor of the longest established Chinese newspaper on the West Coast." His son, Lim, plans an expensive, traditional funeral. He wants to make up for the fact that "even as a grown man . . . he had been afraid of his father." From Pang, a skilled artisan, he buys expensive paper furnishings to burn at the funeral, and he hires Pang and others to serve as mourners. The night before the burial, Lim, keeping vigil with the hired mourners, plays poker with them. He loses steadily until he goes to the table on which his father's glasses, a glass of brandy, and a cigarette have been laid out, for the "ghost." He puts on the glasses, drinks the brandy, and lights another cigarette. After that, he wins. In fact, with the collaboration of Pang, he recoups the funeral expenses. When his mother, upon learning what he has spent, says, "All this. . . . I never knew you loved him so much," Lim realizes that the ritual symbols represent a kind of love.

Davies explained to Hansen that "in the context of the story, I'm very interested in the way that the son, whose father has died, wants to find a way of very publicly expressing grief, a grief that he may not himself genuinely feel." Davies also said, "What really drew me to this story is that I knew in Britain particularly a number of Chinese students . . . from communities in Malaysia, in Singapore and Hong Kong, and . . . a lot of the sons of those families . . . would be going back after studying to inherit family businesses. I think one of the issues for them was that since they would go back they'd still even into their late 20s and 30s be almost boys within their families and still be very dutiful sons, not have the kind of freedom and independence that I think Western children sort of anticipate. And I was very interested in what it would be like for one of these men children to deal with the death . . . and . . . legacy of a parent like that." Jacqueline Carey, who critiqued *Equal Love* for the *New York Times Book Review* (March 19, 2000), felt that all "the stories in this collection are artfully constructed, but 'The Next Life' is written so exactly that each sentence seems to contain a hundred more within it. . . . 'The Next Life' may speak quietly, but it haunts."

When Hansen asked Davies why he liked to write short stories, he replied, "It really fits with the idea of equal love. I think one of the things in the Forster quote is that idea that equal love is not quite attainable. If only we could, we would be wonderfully happy. It feels as though it's a goal. It's impossible, and yet we have to . . . strive for it. [It's] sort of human and noble and brave to continue to strive for it. And oddly that parallels in some ways the way I feel about short stories when I'm trying to write them. I always begin with that notion . . . that it's possible . . . to write a perfect short story. I've . . . never attained that, by any means, but . . . always feel they're just out of reach. You . . . can stretch out your hand and brush it with your fingertips." When Hansen asked how he would know if a story were perfect, he had no answer, except that he would keep reaching. Davies won an O. Henry Award, a MacMillan Silver PEN Award, and a John Llewellen Rhys Prize for *The Ugliest House in the World*. The title story from that book was included in *The Best American Short Stories, 1995*, and another tale, "The Silver Screen," was included in the next year's compilation in *The Best American Short Stories* series.

Peter Ho Davies is currently the director of the MFA program at the University of Michigan. In 2003 he was named one of the 20 best young British writers of the decade by *Granta* magazine. (The list attempts to predict which authors will have the most impact on British fiction in the coming years, and it has been compiled once a decade since 1983.)

—S. Y.

SUGGESTED READING: *Atlanta Journal-Constitution* L p10 Mar. 5, 2000; *Library Journal* p190 Dec. 1999; *Los Angeles Times Book Review* p11 Feb. 6, 2000; *New York Times Book Review* Mar. 19, 2000; *Oregon Live* (on-line); *Publishers Weekly* p384 Aug. 11, 1997, p41 Nov. 22, 1999; *Washington Post Book World* p8 Jan. 4, 1998

SELECTED BOOKS: *The Ugliest House in the World*, 1997; *Equal Love*, 2000

Nancy Crampton/Courtesy of Houghton Mifflin Publishing

Davis, Kathryn

1946– Novelist; short-story writer

In the course of authoring five novels in little more than a decade, Kathryn Davis has become known for writing intellectually demanding, stylistically innovative books in which she often experiments with the novelistic form. Yet according to Davis herself, her essential approach to writing hasn't changed since she was a child. "Now, as then," Davis told Houghton Mifflin, her publisher, in an interview included in the author's press kit, "I'm interested in the plight of a character embarked on a journey through an utterly unfamiliar (and frequently fantastic) landscape, generally in order to track down something or someone of ambiguous importance. The quest itself has never interested me as much as the chance to describe that other world and its inhabitants, and to use the encounter as a way of analyzing the rules that govern the so-called real world." Indeed, all of Davis's novels—*Labrador* (1988), *The Girl Who Trod on a Loaf* (1993), *Hell* (1998), *The Walking Tour* (1999), and *Versailles* (2002)—portray characters whose lives are guided as much by their sometimes bizarre imaginations as by the realities of the outside world. Davis frequently blurs the distinctions between the two.

Kathryn Davis was born in Philadelphia, Pennsylvania, in 1946. She studied painting at the Pennsylvania Academy of Fine Arts, in Philadelphia, before attending Barnard College, in New York City, and received a B.A. from Goddard College, in Plainfield, Vermont. Her short stories and poems have appeared in *Esquire*, *Antaeus*, *Ploughshares*, the *Atlantic*, and the *Antioch Review*, among other publications.

In *Labrador* (1988), Davis depicts the world of two children, the sisters Kitty and Willie Mowbrey. The Mowbreys, who live in New Hampshire, are in many ways a typical middle-class family. Yet Mrs. Mowbrey is cowed by her angry, alcoholic husband, and Willie, the older sister, is beautiful and graceful, but also troubled. Her parents frequently send her to different specialists for psychological treatment. Most of the story is narrated by the younger daughter, Kitty, who retreats from family life into her imagination. Sometimes Kitty pretends that her parents are dead and that she and her sister are a pair of birds named Finch and Grackle. She also has an imaginary friend, a fallen angel named Rogni, who whispers strange tales in her ear. In one such tale, an old crone has a child with the King of Bears, and their little girl goes in search of a nonexistent sister before falling prey to evil strangers. Willie later leaves New Hampshire to become a ballet dancer, and Kitty journeys to Labrador, in the northern reaches of Canada, to visit her grandfather. It turns out, however, that although this land provides an escape from home, it is no paradise for Kitty.

Critics of *Labrador* were impressed by Davis's ability to use language to reveal the intensity of familial relationships. E. J. Graff, for example, commented in *Women's Review of Books* (January 1989), "*Labrador* narrates its relatively ordinary incidents in a poetically charged language that exposes emotional cruelty and gives family capriciousness mythic stature.... Nowhere else have I seen rendered such a powerful sister bond." Michiko Kakutani, conversely, saw Davis's tendency toward aggrandizement as affectation. In the *New York Times* (July 9, 1988), Kakutani wrote, "Ms. Davis's prose has a way of growing vague and purple.... As a result, the reader starts to feel estranged from the sisters while at the same time growing irritated with the author's pretensions." Davis's promising debut earned her the Janet Heidinger Kafka prize.

Davis's next novel, *The Girl Who Trod on a Loaf* (1993), was published five years later, and in it she delved into the world of opera. Helle Ten Brix, an older Danish woman and opera composer, retires to a small town in upstate New York where she meets Frances Thorn. The daughter of wealthy parents, Frances, despite her Julliard training, is now working as a waitress to support her two children. Like those of many operas, the novel's plot is circuitous, and its presentation of the story grandiose. Helle falls in love with Frances and becomes jealous of her lover, a professor of philosophy named Sam. Helle, realizing that she is dying, hosts a farewell costume party for herself during which she shoots and kills Sam. She is arrested but is later released, and spends her last days in Frances's care.

Before she dies, Helle bequeaths her opera-in-progress to Frances and asks her to finish it. The opera, entitled "The Girl Who Trod on a Loaf," is based on a tale by Hans Christian Andersen about a girl who is horribly punished for spurning domestic duties. Frances is left to piece together Helle's colorful past as a young lesbian cross-dresser living in Copenhagen.

In addition to its operatic qualities, *The Girl Who Trod on a Loaf* has a philosophical bent, as does much of Davis's writing: it is partly a meditation on feminist theory, and the way in which artistic pursuits can clash with the domestic responsibilities traditionally accorded to women. Critic Dinitia Smith, writing in *Newsday* (June 20, 1993), found the novel overly abstract. "*The Girl Who Trod on a Loaf*, although inspired by music, is a curiously muffled work," Smith opined. In the *New York Times Book Review* (October 10, 1993), Maggie Paley wrote that she occasionally found the novel self-consciously clever, although she praised it for this cleverness nonetheless. "Perhaps the most remarkable aspect of this complex, brilliant and occasionally irritating novel," Paley remarked, "is the richness of its texture. . . . It seems to approximate music—soaring, swirling, stating themes, returning to expand on them, hitting high notes, striking chords, moving, by indirection, unceasingly forward."

Davis's next book was *Hell* (1998), a complex narrative that both delighted and baffled critics. In the novel, Davis allows readers to peer into several different worlds, a technique of multiple perspective she had employed as a painter. As she said in her interview with Houghton Mifflin, "When I was in art school, I always set up my easel as far away from the model as possible, so I could include the heads of other students, as well as windows, doors leading down hallways, and other elements in my paintings. I liked the wider perspective afforded by looking at a subject from a distance." *Hell* focuses on four separate microcosms: a family living in Philadelphia in 1955, whose daughter, Dorothy D., narrates much of the book; a dollhouse in Dorothy's home, where the dolls are as alive as Dorothy's family; the residence of Edwina Moss, a "household management" expert living in the 19th century; and the kitchen of Antonin Careme, Napoleon's personal chef.

There is no central narrative uniting these four storylines, though there are several points of overlap. Events among the family of dolls living in the dollhouse, for example, sometimes echo scenarios from Dorothy's life, and Dorothy's maid shows up inexplicably in Edwina Moss's home. Considered experimental by virtue of its disregard for conventional narrative techniques, *Hell* provoked an array of reactions from critics. In the *Washington Post* (February 15, 1998), Melvin Jules Bukiet wrote, "*Hell* is one of the most gorgeously written books of our time." Tom LeClair, in the *Nation* (March 2, 1998), found the novel tiresome and categorized it as "postmodern," a literary genre he went on to disparage in his review. "No more fun-houses or dollhouses or hothouses," LeClair lamented. "For me, it's *Hell* and farewell to postmodernism."

In her next novel, *The Walking Tour* (1999), Davis returned to more traditional narrative forms; some reviewers described the book as a mystery novel of sorts. Around the year 2000, the characters Mr. Snow and Mr. Rose invent a strange device, the SnowWrite & RoseRead, that allows people to insert their own words into a preexisting text—in other words, to electronically rewrite the works of others. When Mr. Snow and Mr. Rose embark, along with their wives, on a walking tour of Wales, two of the four die, including the painter Carole Rose. Years later, in the mid-21st century, the Roses' daughter, Susan, tries to unravel the mystery surrounding their deaths from across time and space. Residing in her parents' decaying home in Maine, she uses court records, diaries, and the help of a vagrant who has camped on her lawn. The world in which Susan lives—hinted at rather than explicitly depicted in the novel—is in ruins. Society has been undermined, and propertyless nomads roam the land abiding by no laws. Civilization's unhappy fate seems linked to the SnowWrite & RoseRead, which has in effect eradicated intellectual property and thus taken away personal responsibility for ideas. In her interview with Houghton Mifflin, Davis explained her decision to place the book's narrator in the future, saying, "I knew I had things I wanted to say about the way we live now, but . . . the idea of speaking from the present seemed cramped and limited. . . . Clearly my best choice was to speak about the present from the future, except that then, God help me, I'd be writing science fiction, and the last thing in the world I wanted to hear coming out of my narrator's mouth was anything even remotely like, 'and then I climbed into my hovercraft . . .'"

The Walking Tour eschewed spaceships, laser guns, and other familiar trappings of science fiction, and it received much praise. In *Elle* (November 1999), Lisa Shea wrote, "Davis has written a fetching intellectual yarn, whose digressions and elaborations fascinate and delight." A. O. Scott, in *Newsday* (October 31, 1999), remarked, "Davis's approach to novel-writing is so original, and the results so magical, that trying to review her fiction in a thousand words on a tight deadline feels as doomed and inept as trying to review . . . one of your own dreams."

Davis shifted genres again in her most recent work, *Versailles* (2002), an historical novel chronicling the life of the doomed French queen Marie Antoinette. Told in a series of sketches, mostly from Antoinette's perspective, the novel begins with the 14-year-old girl leaving her home in Austria to join her fiancé, the eventual King Louis XVI, in France. In Davis's interpretation Antoinette never feels truly at home in France, though she does settle into the palace of Versailles, finding solace in the lavishly decorated rooms that separate her from the world outside. As the novel moves through Antoinette's life—and through the palace itself, describing rooms, gardens, and fountains—Davis presents the queen as naive and often eager to indulge in her own pleasures; yet, she is also clever, courageous, and devoted to her family. The novel follows the birth of Antoinette's four children, her widowhood, imprisonment, and eventual beheading. Critical response to the book was generally positive. While most reviewers acknowledged the creative liberties that the author took with history, they found the book's light, humorous, and often meditative tone appropriate for this unique presentation of Antoinette's story. Writing for *Library Journal* (August 15, 2002), David W. Henderson called the work "a refreshing change of pace from the typical historical novel." Nevertheless, some critics questioned the novel's focus, citing tonal discrepancies that frequently made the piece sound like a historical roster. As one critic observed for *Kirkus Reviews* (July 1, 2002), "It's unclear whether Davis's subject is Versailles itself and the famously rich profligacy of the Bourbons, or whether it's the queen herself, the real person, Marie Antoinette. . . . The tour-like information is always interesting, but it lacks any capacity for bringing the story's characters to life—not least its central figure and most frequent speaker, the queen." Ultimately, that reviewer found the novel "thoroughly researched, carefully composed—yet psychologically inert and unalive."

Davis received the 1999 Morton Dauwen Zabel Award from the American Academy of Arts and Letters. She has also twice received grants from the Vermont Council of the Arts and the National Endowment for the Arts. She is currently a professor in the English Department at Skidmore College, in Saratoga Springs, New York, and lives with her husband and daughter in East Calais, Vermont.
— P.G.H.

SUGGESTED READING: *The Nation* p30+ Mar. 2, 1998; *Newsday* p6 Aug. 8, 1988; *New York Times Book Review* p17 Feb. 8, 1998, p12 Nov. 28, 1999; *Village Voice* p71 Nov. 2, 1993

SELECTED BOOKS: *Labrador*, 1988; *The Girl Who Trod on a Loaf*, 1993; *Hell*, 1998; *The Walking Tour*, 1999; *Versailles*, 2002

Dawidoff, Nicholas

1963(?)– Nonfiction writer; journalist

Nicholas Dawidoff is perhaps best known for his writings on baseball; he began his career covering the game for *Sports Illustrated*, and his first book, *The Catcher Was a Spy: The Mysterious Life of Moe Berg* (1994), is a critically acclaimed volume about the eccentric baseball player who was recruited by the Office of Strategic Services during World War II. His more recent books—*In the Country of Country: People and Places in American Music* (1997) and *The Fly Swatter: How My Grandfather Made His Way in the World* (2002)—have been praised as thoroughly researched and comprehensive.

Nicholas Dawidoff was born in about 1963 and raised in New Haven, Connecticut. His parents divorced when he was very young, and because his father suffered from severe mental illness, Dawidoff and his sister were raised by their mother, Heidi, a high-school English teacher. He reminisced about his childhood in an essay for *Time* (September 8, 1997): "In most ways, I grew up like other kids in the late '60s and '70s. I had pets, played Little League, owned library and baseball cards, listened to *American Pie*, and every few months I was treated to a Whopper with fries and a movie like *Blazing Saddles* or *Animal House*." Nevertheless, his mother never allowed her children to watch television and refused to have a set in the house. According to Dawidoff's *Time* essay, his mother later told him, "I didn't want you growing up with something that would interfere with your imagination. . . . I thought it was better for us to find more creative ways to deal with the diffi-

Rebecca W. Carman/Courtesy of Vintage Anchor Publicity

cult hours—like at the end of the day, when we were tired from work or school—than by plopping you in front of a television set." Although some of his peers found the situation strange, Dawidoff grew accustomed to life without a TV. To fill the time, he became an avid reader. "I read before dinner, after dinner, even during dinner if my sister and I were feuding," he explained. "When I was especially tired or restless, I reread, with the result that I can still recite passages of *Johnny Tremain* and *The Willie Mays Story* from memory." He began writing for school newspapers as early as the first grade and went on to become editor of his high-school newspaper, as well as editor of two newspapers in college. "I learned to tell stories as a teller of true stories," he told Robert Birnbaum for *Identity Theory Interview* (on-line, 2002).

In addition to his passion for reading and writing, Dawidoff developed a love of baseball, largely because of his grandfather, Alexander Gerschenkron. Gerschenkron had emigrated to the U.S. in 1939 after being twice displaced—first from his native Russia and then from his adopted home in Vienna when Hitler came to power. Once in the U.S., he was recruited by Harvard University, in Cambridge, Massachusetts, where he became a well-known economic historian and somewhat of a legendary scholar. For Dawidoff, Gerschenkron served as a father figure, exposing the boy to Russian literature and baseball. "He introduced me to the Red Sox and Tolstoy when I was nine," Dawidoff told Donald J. Barr for *Sports Illustrated* (May 9, 1988). "We'd sit in his study and listen to games on the radio. He'd explain the subtleties that made Tony Conigliaro a better outfielder than his brother Billy and *War and Peace* a superior novel to *Resurrection*." As an immigrant Gerschenkron had embraced baseball largely because "it really made him feel American," Dawidoff explained to Lynn Neary for National Public Radio's *Weekend Edition Sunday* (March 31, 2002). "He felt that it was really emblematic of democracy, where, after the first half of the seventh inning, everybody stands up and stretches together."

Dawidoff attended Harvard, where he played as an infielder on the school's baseball team. In 1985 he graduated magna cum laude with a bachelor's degree in history and literature. Shortly after graduation he joined the staff of *Sports Illustrated* as a baseball reporter. After three-and-a-half years at the magazine, he was named a Henry Luce Foundation Scholar. (The foundation provides grants and internships for young Americans to live and work in Asia for a year, in hopes of fostering international understanding.) Dawidoff spent his year in Bangkok, Thailand, where he worked as a visiting professor of communication arts at Chulalongkorn University. Before leaving for this position, he told Barr for *Sports Illustrated* (June 12, 1989), "Two of the things I like best are American creations—baseball and jazz—and I look forward to helping people understand and appreciate both." Upon returning from Thailand, he resumed his work at *Sports Illustrated*, but stayed at the magazine only briefly. "I wanted to write books," he explained to Robert Birnbaum. "That's what I wanted to do with my life and I thought if I stay at *Sports Illustrated* I'm only going to be able to write sports books. . . . I thought I would have to go to work for the *New York Times* or a publication like that before I would be allowed to write books about just anything. And then I got offered a two-book contract."

Dawidoff spent the next several years working on his first book, *The Catcher Was a Spy: The Mysterious Life of Moe Berg* (1994), a biography of the former baseball player and government spy. As a third-string catcher for the Boston Red Sox, Berg was notable not for his athletic skills, but rather for his eccentricities: the child of Ukranian Jewish immigrants, he began playing baseball while studying at Princeton University, in New Jersey, and joined the Brooklyn Robins in 1923, soon after graduation. (The Robins would later become the Brooklyn Dodgers.) Early in his career, he juggled baseball and academics, earning a law degree at Columbia University, in New York City, during the offseasons; he enjoyed intellectual pursuits and was fluent in several languages—most sources estimate about a dozen. He was known to read up to 10 newspapers a day. Although Berg was generally considered a mediocre ball player, with a lifetime batting average of only .243, he remained in the major leagues for 19 years. One of his teammates is remembered for the quip, after being informed that Berg spoke several languages, "Yeah, I know, and he can't hit in any of them," as quoted by Dick Teresi for the *New York Times* (July 14, 1994). Dawidoff attributes Berg's longevity to his intellect and sophistication, which charmed sportswriters and critics. After leaving baseball, he worked for a time as a spy for the Office of Strategic Services, the precursor to today's Central Intelligence Agency, and was involved in investigating Germany's atomic-bomb capabilities. For his efforts during the war he was awarded the Medal of Freedom, which he refused on the grounds that he was uncomfortable with the honor. For the last 25 years of his life, Berg lived as a self-described "vagabond," with no job, no assets, no possessions, and no permanent address.

Dawidoff's portrait of Berg was widely celebrated for being thoroughly researched and elegantly written. Richard F. Shepard observed for the *New Leader* (August 15, 1994), "The biographer tirelessly tracked down every trace of Berg as remembered by his surviving friends and acquaintances. In addition, Dawidoff plowed through mountains of copy produced over decades by sportswriters marveling at an intellectual who pitched Sanskrit and caught fastballs for the Brooklyn Dodgers, the Chicago White Sox, the Washington Senators, and the Boston Red Sox." Writing for the *Jewish Advocate* (September 29, 1994), Jonathan Wasserman called the book "the most exhaustive piece of research on Berg ever written." Dick Teresi affirmed it as a "a wild ride through history," and opined, "*The Catcher Was a Spy* is relentlessly entertaining, and Mr. Dawidoff's style is so unobtrusive that you forget he's there. One story almost justifies the cover price by itself. It involves Babe Ruth, a geisha house, and Moe Berg's knowledge of katakana, the Japanese phonetic alphabet." The book was named a notable biography by both the *New York Times* and the *Washington Post*, and was later optioned for film by Miramax.

In his next book, *In the Country of Country: People and Places in American Music* (1997), Dawidoff explores American country music. He explained to Robert Birnbaum, "In one way or another country music never really got its due. Blues and jazz are taken so seriously as great forms of American music while country music is seen as something kitschy or tacky. I thought the great country musicians were making music that was just as profound." To research the book, Dawidoff traveled throughout the South, visiting with, as he asserts in his book, "some of the finest living American country musicians to learn about their lives in music," according to Terry Teachout for the *New York Times* (June 29, 1997). His historical account begins with country singer Jimmy Rogers, who is often called "the father of country" and who died in 1936, and continues with sketches of many legendary musicians, including the Carter Family, Bill Monroe, Earl Scruggs, Chet Atkins, Patsy Cline, Doc Watson, Johnny Cash, George Jones, Sister Rose Maddox, Kitty Wells, and Merle Haggard, and such younger country artists as Emmylou Harris, Iris DeMent, and Jimmy Dale Gilmore. Part of Dawidoff's intent was to distinguish country's greatest musicians from the pop artists that have monopolized recent country-music charts. "To call today's mainstream country music country at all is a misnomer," Dawidoff writes, as quoted by Alan Barre for the *Dallas Morning News* (June 8, 1997). "Hot country is really pop rock music for a prospering, mostly conservative white middle class . . . a lot like Disneyland . . . a safe adventure in a smoke-free environment."

In the Country of Country was a strong critical success. D. Gordon observed for *Choice* (September 1997), "The author manages to combine simple, well-told stories about many legendary country musicians . . . with complex revelations about the places and times that shaped them. This is a fine combination of clear writing, passion for subject, and solid scholarship." Other critics praised Dawidoff's interviewing skills and his ability, as an outsider, to present a balanced perspective on country music. "He is a shrewd and sensitive reporter and more," Richard Eder noted for the *Los Angeles Times* (March 30, 1997). "He can evoke as well as describe." While Teachout faulted Dawidoff's tendency to "romanticize his subjects," he nonetheless concluded: "Old hands will smile at the zest with which Dawidoff tells his thrice-told tales, but his book was not written to edify old hands; it is aimed at literate, uninformed readers who are curious about what country was like before the Grand Ole Opry became a theme park. For such folk, Dawidoff's enthusiasms will serve as an effective appetizer; his taste is sound, his prose style evocative, and he knows a good quote when he hears one."

Baseball: A Literary Anthology (2002), which Dawidoff edited, is a collection of more than 70 pieces of writing about the game. It features sports reporting from such writers as Roger Angell, Roger Kahn, Robert Kramer, and W. C. Heinz; essays from such authors as John Updike, Jonathan Schwarz, Gay Talese, Annie Dillard, Stephen King, and Thomas Wolfe; and fiction from Don DeLillo, Bernard Malamud, Ring Lardner, James Thurber, and Eric Rolfe Greenberg, among others. Dawidoff includes writings from Satchel Paige—the Negro League legend—as well as pieces from the baseball players Sam Crawford, Moe Berg, and Keith Hernandez. When asked why baseball has been mythologized by so many writers throughout the years, Dawidoff told Lynn Neary, "It's a game that's full of pauses, it's a game that's full of time . . . and the pauses sort of lend themselves to the imagination." In a representative appraisal, a critic for *Kirkus Review* (February 1, 2002) wrote, "This collection resurrects scintillating fragments of youthful summers and ultimately convinces readers that reflecting on baseball helps us understand our complicated national identity."

The Fly Swatter: How My Grandfather Made His Way in the World (2002) is a biographical memoir of Dawidoff's grandfather. In it he provides a complete picture of Alexander Gerschenkron, who had been a vivid, accomplished, and complicated character. Though his grandfather was not widely famous, Dawidoff found him an intriguing subject. "I was curious [about] who he was and everybody I knew who knew him was curious too," Dawidoff told Birnbaum "It was a recurrent theme in meeting people after he died. We'd start to talk and it would quickly evolve into lots of questions." To ascertain the answers, Dawidoff interviewed more than 300 surviving family members, Harvard colleagues, and former students. Beginning with Gerschenkron's difficult early years—including his political exile from Russia to Vienna, and later from Vienna to the U.S.—the book traces his life and professional successes as a scholar and economist. Famous for discovering in 1947 the "Gerschenkron Effect," which helped dispel the myth that the Soviet Union was economically superior, Gerschenkron was also an accomplished essayist; an avid reader of ancient Greek philosophy, Russian literature, classic novels, and poetry; and a speaker of some 24 languages. In an interview posted on the Pantheon Books Web site, Dawidoff recalled, "When I was a boy, what made him special for me was that he was the kind of man who could make ordinary experiences exciting. That was his real gift, he was a man who thought there was no such thing as a typical day and proved it with the way he comported himself. Everything was an adventure with him. . . . His drinking of a morning glass of juice was a dramatic ceremony."

The Fly Swatter was received warmly by critics, who noted the well-researched and objective nature of Dawidoff's portait. In a review for *Library Journal* (May 1, 2002), Amy Strong wrote, "Dawidoff offers an energetic and balanced study of his grandfather, and his book serves as a wonderful paean to scholarship, teaching, and the life of the mind." Writing for *Publishers Weekly* (June 24,

2002), another reviewer asserted, "Indeed, given that those supposedly close to Gerschenkron—[the English social historian and philosopher] Isaiah Berlin, physicist Philipp Frank, even Gerschenkron's sister—insist that they hardly knew him, it's to Dawidoff's credit that this finely wrought book is not just a collection of amusing Gerschenkron sketches, but movingly conveys something of the man's inner life."

Nicholas Dawidoff is a regular contributor to such publications as the New Yorker and the New York Times Magazine. He has been a Guggenheim Fellow and a resident at the artists colonies Yaddo and MacDowell. In 2002 he became a Berlin Prize Fellow at the American Academy in Berlin.

—K. D.

SUGGESTED READING: *Atlantic Monthly* p108+ May 2002; *Houston Chronicle* Z p24 Aug. 17, 1997; *Los Angeles Times* Books p13 Oct. 16, 1994, Book Review p2 Mar. 30, 1997; *New Leader* p17 Aug. 15, 1994, p29+ May–June 2002; *New York Times* VII p1 July 14, 1994, VII p34 June 29, 1997, VII p9 June 16, 2002; *Time* p16 Sep. 8, 1997; *Washington Post* T p13 June 23, 2002

SELECTED BOOKS: *The Catcher Was a Spy: The Mysterious Life of Moe Berg*, 1994; *In the Country of Country: People and Places in American Music*, 1997; *The Fly Swatter: How My Grandfather Made His Way in the World*, 2002; as editor—*Baseball: A Literary Anthology*, 2002

Courtesy of Santa De Haven

De Haven, Tom

May 1, 1949– Fiction writer; graphic novelist

Tom De Haven has had a varied and unique career, penning fantasy and young-adult fiction as well as conventional and graphic novels (books published in comic-strip form). Most notably, he has brought his love of comic strips to a trilogy of novels, *Funny Papers* (1985), *Derby Dugan's Depression Funnies* (1996), and *Dugan Under Ground* (2001), which follows the "life" of a comic-strip character as he evolves in the hands of different artists and through changing times.

Born on May 1, 1949 in Bayonne, New Jersey, Tom De Haven is the son of Clarence Richard De Haven and the former Margaret Elizabeth O'Hare. As a child De Haven wanted to be a syndicated comic-strip artist, but as he grew older he realized that his drawing skills were limited. By the time he had begun his undergraduate work at Rutgers, the State University of New Jersey, where he earned a bachelor's degree in 1971, he had given up hope of becoming a cartoonist. He then turned his attention to fiction and completed an MFA in creative writing at Bowling Green University, in Bowling Green, Ohio, in 1973.

De Haven began his career in 1973 as a managing editor for Magazine Associates, in New York City. In 1977 he became a freelance magazine editor. Around this time he began work on *Freaks' Amour* (1979), an offbeat novel about the mutant survivors of a nuclear explosion in New Jersey in 1988. He followed this with *Jersey Luck* (1980), which involves two black-market gangsters who find their livelihood threatened when one of them falls in love with the wife of an abusive husband. In 1981 De Haven began teaching creative writing at Hofstra University, in Hempstead, New York.

Funny Papers (1985), De Haven's third novel, is one of his best-known works. It is set in New York City during the 1890s, when the advent of comic-strips in newspapers launched a national craze. The novel follows the rise and fall of Georgie Wreckage, a newspaper illustrator who develops a comic strip based on an actual person, a young street urchin named Pinfold. "Pinfold and Fuzzy," the story of a streetwise young boy and his talking dog, becomes a runaway hit and is syndicated across the country. Though his strip earns him considerable wealth and fame, Wreckage starts drinking too much and has to employ an assistant, an ambitious teen named Walter Geebus, who develops a similar strip for a rival newspaper. Meanwhile the real-life Pinfold tries to exploit his sudden fame. The novel received mixed reviews. "*Funny Papers* has an odd, half-there feel that stems from its neglect of characterization," Dan Cryer remarked in a review for *Newsday* (March 6, 1985). "De Haven . . . seems so intent on writing a rollicking good tale that his characters are finally not much more substantial than the line drawings of the Sunday supplements." "Tom De Haven's *Funny Papers* is a nice idea and has a nostalgic, enchanted feel to it in many places," Robin Hemley wrote for the *Chicago Tribune* (May 5, 1985). Hemley concluded, however, that the story "gets bogged down in its wackiness. There's very little realistic grounding here, even though De Haven has done an admirable amount of research. Despite the turn-of-the-century feel, most of the characters have a cardboard flatness to them and just run around like giddy young kids who've been left untended by their parents too long."

In 1988 De Haven published two very different works: *Sunburn Lake*, a collection of three novellas, and *Joe Gosh*, a young-adult novel illustrated by Ralph Reese. *Sunburn Lake* is comprised of *Clap Hands!*, *Here Comes Charley*, *He's All Mine*, and *Where We'll Never Grow Old*, each a first-person narrative told by a different washed-up singer. In a review for the *Washington Post Book World* (August 7, 1988), as excerpted in *Contemporary Authors* (1991), John Calvin Batchelor cheered: "De Haven displays all his talents as in a burlesque review." The young-adult novel *Joe Gosh* introduces a has-been muscleman who is in love with a gangster's daughter. After he notices that junk mail is inexplicably appearing on top of his television set, he is launched into a series of fantastic adventures involving robots and zombies.

In 1989 De Haven made his first foray into the world of graphic novels with an adaptation, illustrated by Bruce Jensen, of William Gibson's 1984 science-fiction novel, *Neuromancer*. In 1990 he published *Walker of Worlds*, the first volume in his *Chronicles of the King's Tramp* fantasy trilogy, which was completed with *The End-of-Everything Man* (1991) and *The Last Human* (1992). In 1995 he published another graphic novel, *Green Candles*, featuring the art of Robin Smith and the lettering of Sean Knot. The next year he published his second young-adult novel, *The Orphan's Tent*, with illustrations by Christopher H. Bing.

In 1996 De Haven published a sequel to *Funny Papers*, *Derby Dugan's Depression Funnies*, which chronicles the misadventures of a Depression-era pulp writer named Al Bready. Bready has been hired by Walter Geebus—the ambitious, young comic-strip artist from *Funny Papers*, now older and worn-out—to help him revitalize his comic strips, including one called Derby Dugan. As the Depression has worn on, the Derby Dugan strip has grown grim and cheerless along with the times. Bready manages to breathe life back into it, but in the process he gets caught up in Geebus's mental and physical breakdown. "De Haven's sequel has a frill-free bittersweet quality equal to the era's best screwball comedies," Richard Gehr noted in the on-line magazine *Salon*. "Full of acid wisecracks and boozy faux pas, *Derby Dugan* deals in the little sins, mainly of omission, that comprise daily life. 'I've lived my life strictly work-for-hire,' [Bready] admits in the novel's haunting coda, having avoided the risks that might have brought him authentic happiness." In an assessment for the *Review of Contemporary Fiction* (Summer 1997), Joseph Witek noted: "De Haven's novel will be a romp for cognoscenti who can pick out the bits of historical and biographical fact that make up the novel's fictional bricolage, as fragments of comic-strip creators such as Rube Goldberg and Harold Gray emerge at different points, while 'Joe Palooka' artist Ham Fisher appears in proper persona. . . . Fans of comics history will need to read this book; other readers will simply want to." *Derby Dugan's Depression Funnies* won the 1997 American Book Award for outstanding literary achievement from the Before Columbus Foundation.

De Haven published another Derby Dugan novel, *Dugan Under Ground*, in 2001. The Dugan character falls on hard times in the 1960s, when his misadventures as a vagabond fail to find an audience among the era's hipsters. Over the years the Dugan comic strip has been passed from artist to artist; Candy Biggs, its latest interpreter, watches as Dugan becomes increasingly irrelevant and eventually disappears from syndication. Finding himself out of job, Biggs teaches Roy Looby, a talented young artist, about the comic-strip trade. Looby then reinvents Dugan as the Imp Eugene, a marijuana-smoking playboy who is embraced by the 1960s underground comic-book culture. The novel received mixed reviews. David Kamp, in the *New York Times Book Review* (October 21, 2001), opined that "De Haven's penchant for grotesquerie, which served him well in the gouty, pustulant Old New York realms of his earlier novels, merely seems curdled and gratuitous here. . . . *Dugan Under Ground* is, alas, the weakest entry in the Derby Dugan series, but collectively, the Derby books, with their multiple viewpoints, carefully interwoven plot lines and potted social-history lessons are a mighty accomplishment: John Dos Passos' *U.S.A.* trilogy as rendered for comic geeks." A critic for *Publisher's Weekly* (September 3, 2001) praised *Dugan Under Ground* as a "nostalgic romp through the funny-book business, as well as a compelling look at the people who struggle to make art out of four-color panels."

From 1987 to 1990 Tom De Haven taught American studies at Rutgers University. Since 1990 he has been a professor of American studies and creative writing at Virginia Commonwealth University, in Richmond. He is the recipient of two National Endowment for the Arts fellowships, and he contributes books reviews to *Entertainment Weekly* and the *New York Times Book Review*.

De Haven has been married to the artist Santa Sergio since June 1971; they have two daughters, Jessie Ann and Kate Marie.

—C. M.

SUGGESTED READING: *Chicago Tribune* XIV p34 May 5, 1985; *Newsday* II p31 Mar. 6, 1985; *New York Times Book Review* p9 May 31, 1998, p8 Oct. 21, 2001; *Publishers Weekly* p58 Sep. 3, 2001; *Review of Contemporary Fiction* p277+ Summer 1997; *Salon* (on-line)

SELECTED BOOKS: novels—*Freaks' Amour*, 1979; *Jersey Luck*, 1980; *Funny Papers*, 1985; *Walker of Worlds*, 1990; *The End-of-Everything Man*, 1991; *The Last Human*, 1992; *Derby Dugan's Depression Funnies*, 1996; *Dugan Under Ground*, 2001; graphic novels—*William Gibson's Neuromancer* (with art by Bruce Jensen), 1989; *Green Candles* (with art by Robin Smith and lettering by Sean Knot), 1995; young-adult fiction—*Joe Gosh* (with art by Ralph Reese), 1988; *The Orphan's Tent*, (with art by Christopher H. Bing), 1996; novella collections—*Sunburn Lake*, 1988

Joyce Ravid

DeLillo, Don

Nov. 20, 1936– Novelist; short-story writer; playwright

For three decades, in his disturbing but often witty novels, Don DeLillo has been anatomizing the games we play in the face of death and cultural disintegration. Often relying on ideas, metaphors, and patterns of association to shape his best work—*Ratner's Star* (1976), *White Noise* (1985), *Libra* (1988), *Mao II* (1991), and *Underworld* (1997)—DeLillo writes in a precise, musical language that has been celebrated by critics and readers alike. Writing for the London *Times* (September 5, 1991), Adrian Dannatt called him "a smart, cruel and somewhat sinister chronicler of contemporary culture, post-modernist in everything but the traditional storytelling values of his prose." Though many of DeLillo's earlier books remained in relative obscurity outside of academic circles—a circumstance which may be attributed to the fact that his work is sometimes seen as abstract and depressing—he has enjoyed a growing audience in recent years. *Underworld*, perhaps his biggest popular success to date, became a best-seller in several countries. DeLillo, who is often compared to such arcane writers as William Gaddis and Thomas Pynchon, has been honored over the years with the National Book Award for *White Noise*, the Aer Lingus International Fiction Prize for *Libra*, the PEN/Faulkner Award for *Mao II*, as well as the Jerusalem Prize, the William Dean Howells Medal, and the Riccardo Bacchelli International Award for *Underworld*. He received the Award in Literature from the American Academy and Institute of Arts and Letters in 1984, and the Lila Wallace–Reader's Digest Award for fiction in 1995. Linda Simon wrote for *World & I* (October 2001), "Concerned as [his] books are with politics, paranoia, and icons of popular culture; with terrorism, consumerism, and deathly ecological events, DeLillo considers transcendent questions (about time, knowledge, meaning, reality) and observes—lovingly, longingly, and with piercing acuity—the textures of everyday life."

Don DeLillo was born in New York City on November 20, 1936 and grew up in the borough of the Bronx. Little biographical information about his background is available, although he did tell Thomas LeClair in an interview for *Contemporary Literature* (Winter 1982) that "being raised a Catholic was interesting because the ritual had elements of art to it and it prompted feelings that art sometimes draws out of us. . . . Sometimes it was awesome, sometimes it was funny. High funeral masses were a little of both and they're among my warmest childhood memories." He has also informed several interviewers that he disliked college when he attended Fordham University from 1954 to 1958 and studied history, philosophy, and theology. He contends that the Jesuits taught him to be a "failed ascetic," as he told Robert R. Harris in an interview for the *New York Times* (October 10, 1982), and describes himself as having tried to emulate Stephen Dedalus—the protagonist in James Joyce's autobiographical novel *Portrait of the Artist as a Young Man*—although "the setting [at Fordham] wasn't quite right." The allusions to Joyce are perhaps significant, since most of DeLillo's books seem to be written with Joycean rigor and detachment, a quality that has led some critics to characterize his narrative voice as one from "another planet."

In addition to Joyce, DeLillo was also drawn to what he called the "comic anarchy" of Ezra Pound, Gertrude Stein, and other modernists. "Although I didn't necessarily want to write like them," he told Harris, "to someone who's twenty years old that kind of work suggests freedom and possibility. It can make you see not only writing but the world itself in a completely different way." He also became interested in avant-garde film, especially the movies of Jean-Luc Godard, Federico Fellini, and Howard Hawks, which had a greater impact on his early work than anything he read.

After graduating from Fordham, in 1958, DeLillo eventually landed a job at Ogilvy and Mather, a leading New York advertising agency. He worked there from 1961 until 1964, and in 1966 he began his first novel, *Americana*, setting out, like most ambitious first novelists, to capture "huge blocks of experience." Living on only $2,000 a year in an unheated Manhattan apartment, he often had to interrupt work on *Americana* to take temporary jobs, with the result that the novel took four years to complete. In spite of his privations and frustrations, however, he looks back upon that period of apprenticeship with nostalgia, perhaps because, when halfway through work on the novel, he began to view himself as a serious and committed writer. His only published work up to that time had been a story that appeared in the periodical *Epoch*.

Americana (1971) is a picaresque novel about a young television executive who quits his job and travels around the United States in an attempt to impose a pattern on his chaotic life by recording everything with a movie camera. Distinctive for its cinematic descriptions of barren landscapes and empty lives as well as for its flashy, self-reflexive language, the novel encountered a generally favorable reception when it was published. In his review for the *New York Times* (May 6, 1971), Christopher Lehmann-Haupt called the plot overfamiliar but found that the writing "soars and dips." Although Thomas Edwards, reviewing the novel in the *New York Times Book Review* (May 30, 1971), thought the book too obviously ambitious, he admired its "savagely funny portrait of middle-class anomie." One of the most encouraging pronouncements came from the acclaimed author Joyce Carol Oates, who called *Americana* "one of the most compelling and sophisticated first novels that I have ever read."

In discussing the writing of his next novel, *End Zone* (1972), DeLillo told LeClair, "I felt I was doing something easier and looser. I was working closer to my instincts." More compact and original than *Americana*, *End Zone* is narrated by Gary Harkness, a football star who comes to Logos College in western Texas after having been kicked out of four major football schools. As the team of misfits struggles through its scrimmages and games, the language of football comes to parody the jargon of nuclear war—Gary's other obsession, which, like football, is seen as a way to control experience. His obsession with control leads to setbacks on and off the field, and at the end of the novel Gary withdraws to a hospital with a mysterious brain fever. Yet *End Zone* is far from grim. What Thomas Edwards had written about *Americana* also applies to DeLillo's second novel: "To see a . . . serious imagination discover and possess a potent metaphor . . . is finally exciting and life-serving." *End Zone* also confirmed Edwards's earlier impression that "this richly inventive new talent looks like a major one."

Great Jones Street (1973) takes up where *End Zone* leaves off. Bucky Wunderlick, a rock star whose lyrics have degenerated from politics and self-exploration to mere babbling, has withdrawn to a tacky apartment in lower Manhattan. In establishing Bucky's almost catatonic point of view, DeLillo satirizes the American counterculture, the media, and corporate greed. For all its technical skill, inventiveness, evocative description, and flashes of humor, however, critics found that this "game at the far edge" lacked the charm of *End Zone*. Whereas most critics conceded that it extended DeLillo's range, they also considered it an "in-between book," or an obviously transitional novel.

Having explored the metaphors of advertising, sports, and rock music, DeLillo next addressed the field of science. In *Ratner's Star* (1976), which he has said he intended as a work of "naked structure," he combined mathematical theory with elements of children's literature. The book is divided into two sections to correspond with Lewis Carroll's *Alice's Adventures in Wonderland* and *Through the Looking Glass and What Alice Found There* to create a science-fiction novel that is also what LeClair called "a conceptual monster, a totalizing work like . . . Pynchon's *Gravity's Rainbow* or Barth's *Letters*."

In reviewing *Ratner's Star* in the *Atlantic* (August 1976), Amanda Heller admitted that there was "no way to describe . . . [this] cheerfully apocalyptic novel" about a fourteen-year-old genius and Nobel laureate, Billy Twillig, who is summoned to a space research center to decode a message from a distant planet. There, he encounters a collection of zany characters whose bizarre speech and behavior create a funny, if unnerving, picture of science run amok. Amanda Heller asked her *Atlantic* readers to imagine "*Alice in Wonderland* set at the Princeton Institute for Advanced Study." The abstraction, density, and recondite language of *Ratner's Star* frustrated some critics. In his *Newsweek* (June 7, 1976) review, Peter Prescott complained that it was an overlong imitation of Thomas Pynchon, and reviewers for *Time* and the *New Yorker* disliked DeLillo's cartoon characters. Among the critics who nevertheless found the novel to be elegant and funny were J. D. O'Hara of the *Washington Post Book World* (June 13, 1976), who praised DeLillo for combining serious mathematical ideas with wacky humor, and George Stade, who, in the *New York Times Book Review* (June 20, 1976), called it an example of Menippean satire—a form in which characters are reduced to the ideas for which they stand. Stade placed DeLillo in the tradition of Swift and Melville.

According to the literary critic Michael Oriard, *Ratner's Star* concluded a quartet of novels about a quest for an ultimate meaning that remains elusive. Although many of DeLillo's earlier themes of paranoia and anomie recur in his fifth novel, *Players* (1977), that search for meaning has been reduced to the characters' quest for excitement. Lyle and Pammy Wynant are quintessential married yuppies, bored with their jobs and each other. To escape their ennui, Pammy goes off to Maine with a homosexual couple—one of whom becomes her lover and commits suicide—while Lyle, a stockbroker, becomes involved with terrorists and urban guerrillas. In his enthusiastic review of *Players* in the *New York Times* (August 11, 1977), John Leonard celebrated its "wit, intelligence, and [incantatory] language." Other critics admired the brilliantly rendered, banal dialogue so listlessly exchanged between Pammy and Lyle and the novel's prologue, in which the characters, not yet introduced, watch and applaud a movie about hippie terrorists. In praising *Players* in the *New York Times Book Review* (September 4, 1977), the novelist and critic Diane Johnson noted DeLillo's lack of commercial success, attributing it to his habit of saying "deeply shocking things about America that people would rather not face," as quoted by Robert R. Harris.

DeLillo's next two books, *Running Dog* (1978) and the pseudonymous *Amazons* (1980), represent his partial retreat from what Johnson has characterized as high, if shocking, moral satire. *Running Dog*, a parody of a thriller, involves a race to obtain a supposedly pornographic film of Adolf Hitler's last orgy at the end of the war, which turns out to consist of scenes of Hitler doing Charlie Chaplin imitations for the amusement of the children of Joseph Paul Goebbels. *Amazons*, published under the pseudonym Cleo Birdwell, is a fictitious sports memoir about Ms. Birdwell's career as the first female hockey player in the National Hockey League. While both books are obviously less ambitious than DeLillo's earlier novels, reviewers saw them as fast-paced, if sordid, and extremely funny.

Funded in part by a 1979 Guggenheim Fellowship, DeLillo spent three years in Greece, the Middle East, and India. He described the experience to Harris, emphasizing how his travels influenced his writing in *The Names* (1982), his next novel. "What I found," he said, "was that all this traveling taught me how to see and hear all over again. Whatever ideas about language might be in *The Names*, I think the most important thing is what I felt in hearing people and watching them gesture—in listening to the sound of Greek and Arabic and Hindi and Urdu. The simple fact that I was confronting new landscapes and fresh languages made me feel almost duty bound to get it right. I would see and hear more clearly than I could in more familiar places." James Axton, the protagonist of *The Names*, works in Athens as a risk analyst for a firm that insures corporations against terrorism. Estranged from his wife and son, Axton feels cut off from himself and, in his self-alienation, becomes obsessed with a cult dedicated to murdering people in an almost random pattern based on their initials. His obsession gradually leads to the discovery that he has unwittingly been working for the CIA—which functions here, as in other DeLillo novels, as a sort of supercult.

Writing in the *New York Times Book Review* (October 10, 1982), Michael Wood felt that the digressive structure of *The Names* blurred DeLillo's insights; nevertheless he was impressed by the novel's intelligence, agility, and evocative atmosphere. Appraising it for the *New York Review of Books* (December 16, 1982), Josh Rubins saw DeLillo as having given up his fantastical satire and "flyaway characters" for a solid, almost Jamesian, narrator-hero and a direct approach to the problem of the contemporary corruption of American culture.

Since, on returning to the United States, DeLillo moved to the quiet suburb of Bronxville, New York, it is not surprising that his next novel, *White Noise* (1985), is permeated with the ambiance of suburbia. Its narrator is Jack Gladney, a professor of "Hitler studies" at a small college, who is happily married to Babette, a teacher of posture classes to the elderly and a reader of tabloids to the blind. Their several children from past marriages comment like a Greek chorus on the toxic gas leak that is the book's pivotal event. Terrified of outliving Jack, Babette has an affair with a researcher in order to obtain experimental pills that allegedly suppress the fear of death.

For all the book's almost surreal stylization, DeLillo's description of the Gladney family is lovingly rendered. Because of that departure, perhaps, *White Noise* received considerable attention from the media. In his *Washington Post Book World* (January 13, 1985) review, Jonathan Yardley dismissed it as a collection of tired political ideas, writing, "Until [DeLillo] has something to say that comes from the heart rather than the evening news, his novels will fall far short of his talents." Nevertheless, other critics were enthusiastic. In spite of his reservations—namely, that DeLillo was having too much fun writing the novel for readers to take the Gladneys' fear of death seriously—Thomas Disch admired *White Noise* in his *Nation* (February 2, 1985) review for its wit and dialogue. In his assessment for the *Village Voice* (April 30, 1985), Albert Mobilio seemed to be answering Yardley's objections when he wrote, "Critics who have argued his work is . . . overly intellectual should take notice: DeLillo's dark vision . . . strikes at both head and heart." In her evaluation for the *New York Times Book Review* (January 13, 1985), Jayne Anne Phillips wrote, "The voice guiding us through *White Noise* is one of the most ironic, intelligent, grimly funny voices yet to comment on life in present-day America." *White Noise* won the 1985 American Book Award for fiction.

After writing an article on the assassination of John F. Kennedy for *Rolling Stone* magazine in 1983, DeLillo bought a used copy of the 26-volume Warren Commission Report and spent three years reconstructing the events that led up to Kennedy's death. Since he felt particularly drawn to Lee Harvey Oswald—DeLillo discovered they had briefly lived in the same Bronx neighborhood in the mid-1950s—Oswald's sad, painful story makes up most of his tenth novel, *Libra* (1988). *Libra* is also shaped by various real and imaginary conspiracies: the United States government wants to invade Cuba; CIA agents want their revenge against Kennedy for his failure to give full support to the Bay of Pigs invasion; and Cubans want to thwart Kennedy's plans to achieve détente with Castro. In addition, DeLillo creates a CIA officer, Nicholas Branch, who is writing the CIA's secret history of the assassination. Branch's efforts to understand what happened link him to the author and afford DeLillo the opportunity to explore the nature of history and our changing perception of it. Of his impulse to revisit the Kennedy assassination in *Libra*, DeLillo told Jim Naughton for the *Washington Post* (August 24, 1988) he considered himself still "haunted" by the events that had taken place 25 years earlier. "I think that what's been missing since the assassination is a sense of coherent reality," he explained. "We seem to have entered a world of randomness, confusion, even chaos. We're not agreed on the number of gunmen, the number of shots, the time span between shots, the number of wounds on the president's body, the size and shape of the wounds. And, beyond this, I think we have developed a sense of the secret manipulation of history: documents lost or destroyed, official records sealed for 50 or 75 years, a number of extremely suggestive murders and suicides."

Because of its subject matter and DeLillo's growing reputation, *Libra* was widely reviewed. In *Time* magazine (August 1, 1988), Paul Gray criticized the book for advancing yet another dubious conspiracy theory (that the CIA planned to shoot at Kennedy and miss in order to galvanize public sentiment against Cuba): "There is a simpler possibility that *Libra* . . . skirts: a frustrated, angry man looked out a window, watched the President ride by, and shot him dead." And stepping up his earlier attacks on DeLillo's fiction, Jonathan Yardley of the *Washington Post Book World* (July 3, 1988) called *Libra* "fanciful journalism" and argued that DeLillo's doctrinaire left-wing politics kept his characters from coming to life. In his most acerbic comment, Yardley found DeLillo's technique of putting thoughts into the minds of living people to be "beneath contempt."

Yet, few critics agreed with those acidulous judgments. In an epilogue DeLillo makes clear that *Libra* is a work of imagination, not an historical document, and, as Terrence Rafferty pointed out in a review for the *New Yorker* (July 3, 1988), *Libra* is not so much *for* "conspiracy buffs" as *about* them. In fact, much of the novel's power is generated by the tension between aesthetically pleasing explanations and the brute facts of Lee Harvey Oswald's world and the assassination. DeLillo "might have written this novel to exorcise his own tendency toward paranoid mysticism," Rafferty observed, going on to note that *Libra* ends with Oswald's mother standing by her son's grave "howling with animal confusion, an intimation of the more terrifying world" outside the world of conspiracies. Thus, Rafferty maintained that *Libra* is DeLillo's best novel not only "because it goes right to the source—to Dallas in November, 1963, the primal scene of American paranoia," but also because DeLillo's portrayal of Oswald's life, in language that is as "weirdly eroticized as prisoners' poetry," transcends that paranoia.

Other reviewers were equally impressed. Christopher Lehmann-Haupt, writing for the *New York Times* (July 18, 1988), attributed the power of *Libra* to the seamlessness with which DeLillo bound the facts together with "every rumor, shadowy figure and crackpot theory." The novelist Anne Tyler, writing in the *New York Times Book Review* (July 24, 1988), admired the way DeLillo makes the reader less interested in "the . . . events of the assassination than in the pitiable and stumbling spirit underlying them." And John Leonard, who reviewed *Libra* in the *Nation* (September 19, 1988), linked DeLillo to Joseph Conrad, Franz Kafka, and T. S. Eliot. *Libra* was nominated for the National Book Award and the National Book Critics Circle Award, and in September 1989 it received the first annual Aer Lingus International Fiction Prize.

In his next work, *Mao II* (1991), DeLillo tells the story of Bill Gray, a reclusive author—suggestive of J.D. Salinger, Thomas Pynchon, or even DeLillo himself—trapped in his own self-induced seclusion. With only two books to his name, each of which have achieved cult status in part because of the author's elusive reputation, Gray spends his time working on his latest novel, rewriting the same sentences day after day. In his first step out of isolation, Gray allows Brita Nilsson, a photographer of both novelists and terrorists, into his home for a photo shoot. As he considers whether to publish his new book—his assistant, Scott, insists that his reputation will be better preserved by abandoning the project—Gray learns that an Arab terrorist group has kidnaped a young Swiss author. The fledgling publishing group that wants to produce Gray's novel convinces him to appear at an international press conference to appeal for the Swiss writer's safe return. The publicity, they figure, will be to all parties' benefit. As the novel progresses, it examines the power of writers and terrorists alike in post-modern culture. At one point Gray muses, as quoted by Sven Birkerts for the *Washington Post* (May 26, 1991), "What terrorists gain, novelists lose. The degree to which they influence mass consciousness is the extent of our decline as shapers of sensibility and thought. The danger they represent equals our own failure to be dangerous."

Critics largely commended the novel, with Birkerts calling it "one of [DeLillo's] best," and adding, "*Mao II* is also DeLillo's strongest statement yet about the crisis of crises. Namely: that we are living in the last violet twilight of the individual, and that 'the future belongs to the crowds.'" Likewise, Michiko Kakutani for the *New York Times* (May 28, 1991) affirmed, "Disturbing, provocative and darkly comic, *Mao II* reads, at once, as a sociological meditation on the perils of contemporary society, and as a kind of new-wave thriller. . . .

The writing, as usual, is dazzling; the book's images, so radioactive that they glow afterward in our minds." Despite the overwhelming praise, critics did note some flaws. According to Birkerts—who noted, "Indeed, if there is a problem with this novel, it's formal"—the novel's nonlinear structure diminished its climax, rendering the final pages "unfocused." Writing for the *New York Review of Books* (June 27, 1991), Robert Towers observed that "for all the brilliance of its parts, *Mao II* is not entirely satisfying as a whole." Nevertheless, he concluded: "[This] is the work of a major novelist writing almost, though not quite, at the top of his powers." For *Mao II* DeLillo won the 1992 PEN/Faulkner Award for fiction.

In *Underworld* (1997), DeLillo's next novel and perhaps most ambitious yet, he again tackles weighty themes of history, politics, and paranoia, presenting a detailed portrait of the ways in which the Cold War and the image-driven media have dominated late-20th-century American culture. The novel begins on October 3, 1951 at the historic New York Giants/Brooklyn Dodgers National League playoff game in New York, where outfielder Bobby Thomson won the pennant for the Giants with his home run, known as the "shot heard round the world." In the stands DeLillo places the real-life figure J. Edgar Hoover—then director of the FBI—who, in the novel, receives notice during the game that the Soviet Union has just tested a nuclear device. DeLillo then weaves his story through five decades of American history, focusing on a number of real and fictional characters and events. The main storyline, however, follows the life of the fictional Nick Shay, an analyst at a waste-management company, who is trying to distance himself from his delinquent past. The plot is anything but linear—and therefore difficult to summarize—bouncing back and forth through history, with many sections exhibiting no obvious connection to those that precede or follow them. Throughout the more-than-800 pages, DeLillo depicts a panoramic, post-modern epic of American life.

The response to *Underworld*—from critics, scholars, and readers—was overwhelming. Donna Seaman opined for *Booklist* (August 1997), "As DeLillo zooms in on each sphere of action, and each psyche, he achieves an unsurpassed intensity of sensory and psychological detail, which is rendered with exquisite tenderness. . . . *Underworld* is a ravishingly beautiful symphony of a novel." Writing for *Newsweek* (September 22, 1997), Malcolm Jones affirmed, "There's pleasure on every page of this pitch-perfect evocation of a sour, anxious half century. The pleasure comes from incident and insight, but more than anything else it comes from language."

While several critics lamented DeLillo's conspicuous underdevelopment of characters, claiming that many members of his cast sound alike, Vince Passaro, in his laudatory review for *Harper's* (November 1997), responded, "The point such critics miss is that DeLillo's books are purposely suffused with the language of the culture, the jargons and lingos of the public discourse of our time, snatches caught in supermarket aisles and on talk shows, the overpowering declamatory voice of the marketplace, of television, of business memos and the financial pages. His characters live in these worlds, and he shapes his own sentences to blend into their environments. He aims for an immersion in the clatter of almost sensible English, people talking over and through one another, lone souls on a rant." In other criticism, some reviewers found that *Underworld* failed to move beyond its political message. For example, James Wood declared in *New Republic* (November 10, 1997), "*Underworld* proves, once and for all, or so I must hope, the incompatibility of paranoid history with great fiction." Nevertheless, a majority of reviews emphasized the impact of DeLillo's vast exploration of the "underworld" of American life. Passaro observed, "That's the final and all-important meaning of the title *Underworld*. DeLillo wants us to see the things beneath our eyes, right on the surface but below the fantasies we insist on looking at, ordinary life as it has expressed itself among the people of a nation involved in a prolonged technological fantasy war, a fifty-year piece of theater at the end of the twentieth century, played out in the masks of strategic nuclear weapons and machines of despoilment." *Underworld* garnered DeLillo the 1999 Jerusalem Prize, the 2000 William Dean Howells Medal, and the 2000 Riccardo Bacchelli International Award.

DeLillo made a significant departure from the epic scope of *Underworld* in his next work, *The Body Artist* (2001). After calling the author's previous novel "a vast behemoth of a book," one reviewer for the *Economist* (February 17, 2001) noted, "*The Body Artist* could scarcely be more different. Though billed as a novel, it is really just a short story, as slight as a blade of grass." In it DeLillo introduces a young married couple, Lauren and Rey, a performance artist and a filmmaker who live in a large, remote home. Rey leaves one morning and commits suicide—the reader learns retrospectively that he has driven to the home of his ex-wife and shot himself. Lauren, while grieving, soon finds a small, possibly autistic man living in one of the empty bedrooms; she names him Mr. Tuttle. While the novel never explains Mr. Tuttle's identity or origin, it chronicles Lauren's increasing obsession with the little man, who demonstrates strange gifts of mimicry and memory. He is, for example, able to repeat exact conversations that Lauren once had with Rey.

Critics responded to *The Body Artist* with much curiosity, noting DeLillo's thematic deviation from his previous works in focusing here on one individual's emotional life rather than greater social or philosophical concerns. Writing for the *Los Angeles Times* (March 11, 2001), Nicole Krauss observed, "Possibly the most radical risk DeLillo takes with *The Body Artist* is his departure from so many things he is, well, good at. Incidental things to begin with, like the exhilarating collection of information, facts and evidence, which is the industry of suspicion and the foundation of any skilled opposition." She continued, "Only 124 pages, *The Body Artist* is spare, emptied of all that is not self-referential. But rather than serving as liberation, this stripping-down makes the writing feel drained and airless." While some critics recognized DeLillo's stylized gift for language, others found his writing inhibited by the material. In a *New York Times* (January 19, 2001) review, Michiko Kakutani noted, "His writing seems strangely attenuated in these pages, stripped of its usual pop and fizz, its tactile sense of detail." Stephen Amidon concluded in the *New Statesman* (February 5, 2001), "DeLillo has abandoned the provocative sizzle and black humor that sugared his nihilism in previous novels, creating instead a small, gloomy and forgettable book. The hope is that this is an aberration from his remarkable body of work, rather than a sombre, dead-end culmination of it."

DeLillo's most recent novel is *Cosmopolis* (2003). In this work he returns to the grander social themes of his earlier novels, depicting one day in the life of an accomplished "New Economy" billionaire. As the 28-year-old Eric Packer drives through Manhattan in his stretch limo, he encounters the chaos surrounding a presidential visit to the city, a violent anti-globalization protest, a rapper's funeral, and a film crew working in the streets. Throughout the day, Packer stages meetings in the limo, meets his new bride for lunch, and engages in two extra-marital encounters—all while a stalker plots his assassination. Meanwhile, he faces something of a financial crisis: Obsessed with the Japanese yen, he has taken up the dangerous habit of betting on the currency's value fluctuations. Despite losing millions, Packer increases his bet, thriving on his power to push the monetary system into chaos. Early reviews of the book have been mixed. While several critics praised DeLillo's masterful use of language—with Donna Seaman for *Booklist* (December 1, 2002) calling his descriptions "by turns breathtakingly poetic and devastatingly witty"—others found his characterization one-dimensional. As a critic noted for *Kirkus Reviews* (January 2003), "The crystalline metaphysician-ironist is only sporadically present in this distorted, frustratingly opaque world."

DeLillo has written several plays, including *The Day Room* (1989), which takes place in a hospital; *Valparaiso* (1999), the story of a business traveler who encounters a small measure of fame when he accidentally flies to Valparaiso, Chile; and *The Mystery at the Middle of Ordinary Life* (2000), a one-act play about a marriage. Two additional plays—*The Engineer of Moonlight*, published in the *Cornell Review* in 1979, and *The Rapture of the Athlete Assumed into Heaven*, published in *Quarterly* in 1990—have never been produced. Discussing the process of playwriting, DeLillo told Mark Feeney for the *Boston Globe* (January 24, 1999), "It's exciting. I think it's precisely because a novelist lives in a world of fragile autonomy that I welcome the chance to work with other people. It's certainly not something I would want to do exclusively, and for me there is an element in which each form is the antidote to the other." He continued, "It's very interesting to rediscover your play through the work of the actors. You can see levels of perception and motivation in a particular character based on the way an actor reads a certain line. This is one of the most exciting things about doing a play for me. In effect, the play isn't really written until performances begin." For the most part, DeLillo's plays have been well reviewed, particularly regarding the quality of the author's writing. Discussing a production of *The Day Room* at Los Angeles's Doolittle Theatre, Dan Sullivan for the *Los Angeles Times* (October 10, 1986) called DeLillo's work "a cunning and brainy play, and obviously a metaphor for larger societal issues." He added, "The writing is very clever." DeLillo has published a number of essays and short stories in such publications as *Harper's*, the *New Yorker*, the *New York Times*, *Sports Illustrated*, *Rolling Stone*, *Epoch*, the *Kenyon Review*, *Esquire*, *Atlantic*, and *Granta*.

Though Don DeLillo remains a reclusive figure, he generally agrees to interviews in conjunction with the publication of his novels, many of which have revealed him to be an articulate and gracious man of high seriousness, who is more comfortable talking about his work than about himself. While avoiding most of the literary world and its promotional circuit, DeLillo remains friends with other innovative writers, among them William Gass and William Gaddis. Of his approach to writing, he once wrote to a cybergroup discussing his work, as quoted by David Streitfeld for the *Washington Post* (November 11, 1997), "Fiction, at least as I write it and think of it, is a kind of religious meditation in which language is the final enlightenment, and it is language, in its beauty, its ambiguity and its shifting textures, that drives my work."

DeLillo continues to live in Bronxville with his wife, Barbara, a landscape designer.

—K. D.

SUGGESTED READING: *Boston Globe* H p1 Jan. 24, 1999; *Chicago Tribune* Books p1 Sep. 21, 1997; *Harper's* p72 Nov. 1997; *Los Angeles Times* Books p3 June 9, 1991, Books p2 Sep. 28, 1997; *New York Review of Books* p17 June 17, 1991; *New York Times* C p14 May 28, 1991, E p50 Jan. 19, 2001; *Newsweek* p64 Sep. 29, 1997; *Publishers Weekly* p55+ July 1, 1988; *Washington Post* C p1 Aug. 24, 1988, D p1 Nov. 11, 1997

SELECTED WORKS: novels—*Americana*, 1971; *End Zone*, 1972; *Great Jones Street*, 1973; *Ratner's Star*, 1976; *Players*, 1977; *Running Dog*, 1978; *Amazons*, 1980 (under pseudonym Cleo Birdwell); *The Names*, 1982; *White Noise*, 1985; *Libra*, 1988; *Mao II*, 1991; *Underworld*, 1997; *The Body Artist: A Novel*, 2001; plays—*The Day Room*, 1989; *Valparaiso*, 1999; *The Mystery at the Middle of Ordinary Life*, 2000

Courtesy of Carl Dennis

Dennis, Carl

Sep. 17, 1939– Poet

Joseph Parisi, the editor of *Poetry* magazine, once called Carl Dennis "a poet who has valuable things to say—about faith (or its absence) in the modern world, fear, loneliness, life's regrets—the great what-ifs and roads not taken—in ways that are personal and universal at the same time," as quoted in a State University of New York at Buffalo press release (April 12, 2000). Dennis's style is that of a poetic storyteller, rather than a lyricist; his poems are often soulful, free-verse meditations narrated in a conversational voice. Throughout his eight volumes of poetry—including the much-admired works, *The Near World* (1985), *The Outskirts of Troy* (1988), *Meetings with Time* (1992), and *Ranking the Wishes* (1997)—Dennis has emerged as an important poet, whose work contemplates the meaning of modern life in a tone at times as wry and ironic as it is eloquent and wise. He demonstrated his academic appreciation for poetry in his first critical work, *Poetry as Persuasion, an Essay for Writers* (2001), in which he reflects on the genre's influence. In 2000 he was recognized with the Ruth Lilly Poetry Prize—widely considered one of the most significant literary prizes in the English language—which carries a cash award of $100,000. In 2002 Dennis was honored again, this time joining the company of such celebrated poets as Robert Frost, Carl Sandburg, and Elizabeth Bishop, when his eighth book, *Practical Gods* (2001), won the Pulitzer Prize for poetry.

Of his approach to poetry, Dennis told Elizabeth Farnsworth in an interview for the PBS program *NewsHour with Jim Lehrer* (April 10, 2002), as quoted on the official transcript of the show, "I want to create an individual voice that the listener will find it worthwhile to engage with. . . . I think that's what the situation of poetry is. I've been very moved by something that [Ralph Waldo] Emerson wrote in his journals. He said he tried to write always for the unknown friend. I like 'friend,' of course, because you want a reader who's sympathetic and discriminating. But 'friend' in the singular, not the plural, because you don't want a corporate entity, you want to be talking to an individual; and unknown, because . . . you can't pitch your poem toward any easy appeal in terms of class or race or nationality. You have to try to reach something more fundamental than that."

For *World Authors 1995–2000*, Dennis writes: "Because my life has been somewhat bookish and uneventful, at least outwardly, I've made an effort to include as much of the world in my work as I can, though it's taken me some time to find ways to do this. I don't dislike autobiographical poetry, but I think one has to be very lucky to make it work, engaged almost despite oneself in an important political struggle, like [William Butler] Yeats, or born to a family like [Robert] Lowell's in which much of a region's history is deeply embedded. The danger of too personal a focus is the presumption that an event is important merely because it happened to the writer. On the other hand, all good poets must see their personal experience as representative, though they also must be willing as required to reconfigure it according to the demands of the imagination. Emerson was right when he wrote, 'To believe your own thought, to believe that what is true for you in your private heart is true for all men—that is genius.'

"The most important early influence on my work was Yeats. The book I wrote in my twenties, but was fortunately unable to publish, was full of Yeatsian imitations. From him I learned what a poem is and does, and was prompted to imagine how the practice of poetry might be a noble calling. And I was impressed by the way he was able to transform autobiography into something larger. Later, reading his doctrine of the mask, I came to realize how theatrically he conceived of the poetic voice. I was impressed by his distinction between the ordinary, everyday self that eats breakfast and the voice that he cultivates in the poems.

"The voice I've wanted in my own poems is in part a construction, stronger and less self-effacing than my natural voice, though familiar enough to let me explore my concerns. I would like my speaker to be capable of many moods, from estrangement to intimacy, now resisting what I think deserves to be resisted, now willing to attempt reconciliation and celebration. I think that poetry tries to make life more bearable, but that sometimes this service is performed simply by letting readers know that others too have endured regret and grief and loneliness, have tried to accommodate themselves to their lives and found the task hard going. Always for me there is a tension between the desire to accept the actual world and the desire to resist it, to make do with what is given and to keep alive certain wishes that may never be fulfilled but are part of the definition of what it means to be human.

"My stress on voice, on the need, if a poem is to be convincing, of establishing the presence of someone standing behind the lines, common I think to most traditional notions of poetry, would be criticized by contemporary skeptical theory as based on a faith in the unity and freedom of the self that we now know, or should know, to be fiction. I have tried to answer this critique in the introduction to my book on the rhetoric of poetry, *Poetry as Persuasion*, in which I point out that a unified speaker need not be monolithic, that the definition of self needs to be large enough to accommodate many voices. As far as freedom is concerned, a speaker need not be free of all historical influence to be free enough to hold up his beliefs to critical scrutiny. Even if this scrutiny is limited, it leads to discovery that a passive acceptance of fashion makes impossible. We can abandon the notion of a poet as the inspired announcer of timeless truth without embracing the notion that the poet is merely the unconscious transmitter of cultural convention. All poets inherit a dominant discourse, but the poets we admire seem to be able to transform it into personal speech, reshaping the conventions to create distinctive speakers that still move and challenge us.

"The very real threat to convincing personal speech that we must confront today is finally an argument not for abandoning the demand for such speech but for asserting the primacy of the speaker even more emphatically. In a time when the notion of 'self' is under attack, when the demand for the speaker's presence seems a relic from the files of an outmoded Romanticism, it is important to re-assert the peculiar value of poetry in making such a presence genuinely convincing. In this way poetry keeps us from falling asleep, by providing us with voices with whom we are eager to engage in continuous dialogue."

Carl Dennis was born on September 17, 1939 in St. Louis, Missouri, to Israel and Fay Dennis. Growing up in the Midwest, he told Stephen Watson for the *Buffalo News* (April 9, 2002), Dennis began writing "fitfully" as a teenager, though he did not consider becoming a poet for several more years. In 1957 Dennis attended Oberlin College, in Ohio, for one year before transferring to the University of Chicago; he switched schools again in 1959, this time relocating to the University of Minnesota and graduating in 1961 with a B.A. degree. Dennis pursued postgraduate work at the University of California at Berkeley, earning his Ph.D. in 1966. That same year he became an English professor at the State University of New York at Buffalo. As the institution was then a recent addition to the state university system—it had been acquired in 1962—New York Governor Nelson A. Rockefeller had been providing generous funding to establish a preeminent English department and to recruit distinguished faculty. "I came into a world where there was a poetry reading every night," Dennis recalled to Watson. Among Dennis's colleagues were such respected poets as Robert Creeley, Leslie Fiedler, and Irving Feldman—who remain at Buffalo today. With their encouragement he began pursuing his own interests in poetry. "I think I was about 28," he told Elizabeth Farnsworth of his decision to become a poet, "and I was already here teaching at Buffalo. And I found that writing poetry—which I didn't have a lot of time for then, because I was a new teacher—was the thing that gave me the most pleasure, the thing that I felt most alive when I was doing. So . . . I wanted to do as much of it as I could."

In *A House of My Own* (1974), Dennis commenced his practice of exploring everyday life, testing what Michael Madigan for *Library Journal* (November 14, 1974) called, "the limits of ambition, experience, and thinking." Helen Vendler for the *New York Times* (April 6, 1975) described the book as "a good natured, personal, social volume," adding that "Dennis's disarming advice is eminently readable, and even his bad moments have an open possibility for remedy hiding ready to blossom." Critics found some flaws in Dennis's first achievement, largely in his inability—at this stage in his artistry—to capture life's more complicated tones. Madigan observed, "Some of the character sketches are only cruel parody. . . . Loneliness and isolation are handled obscurely or glibly, while love is treated romantically or abstractly." He acknowledged, however, "[Dennis's] best poetry flows imaginatively and already has a remarkable scope and evocative power."

Most reviews of Dennis's second volume, *Climbing Down* (1976), focused on the poet's narrative voice—a tool that Rowe Portis for *Library Journal* (June 1, 1976) described as "relaxed, prosey diction which understates the quirky fantasies firing his imagination." A writer for *Choice* (October 1976) called it "that understated, deceptively informal, almost off-hand attitude toward eminently human situations." Here, Dennis again drew inspiration from common domestic settings, achieving his best epiphanies, according to Paul Kameen for *Best Sellers* (July 1976) "when he finds that spot at which the ordinary becomes compelling, at which matter and dream coincide to produce insight."

On the cover jacket of his next book, *Signs and Wonders* (1979), Dennis writes, "The poetry I most admire tries to relate society to solitude, common life to privileged life, and hope to memory," as quoted by Robert Pinsky in *Poetry* (November 1980). Dennis undertook a similar challenge, again using understatement to explore the wonders in his environment. "[The poems] engage in personal speech rather than self-display," Pinksy described, "and the personal speech itself is quiet: an odd, piping, intelligent utterance, shy and amiably comic, melancholy without despair or disillusion." Some critics, however, faulted Dennis's restrained poetic voice, with Rob Fure for *Library Journal* (May 1, 1980) calling it "frequently monotonous and timid, such that one soon must decide if one wants to listen after all." Nevertheless, Pinsky concluded, "Though it is perhaps not a style of enormous emotional range, it has a crisp quality of inquiring comedy and penetration."

In his next two works, *The Near World* (1985) and *The Outskirts of Troy* (1988), Dennis added literary, historical, and political allusion to his explorations of commonplace experience. Discussing *The Near World*, Vernon Shetley for *Poetry* (February 1986) challenged Dennis's reliance on narrative and mundane subject matter—despite the poet's references to Shakespeare and Greek myth. Shetley noted: "Dennis has certainly reached the limit of what can be done in the mode he practices; the aesthetic yield of any further advances in the poetics of insubstantiality is likely to be slender indeed." Tom Sleigh for the *New York Times* (July 21, 1985) opined, "[Dennis's] low-key poetical means are almost unbearably claustrophobic. And yet this claustrophobia entirely suits the diminished world he chronicles so fearlessly and artfully." Bruce Bennett for the *New York Times* (September 18, 1988), suggested Dennis's "dominant theme [in 1988's *The Outskirts of Troy*] is a search for perspective, a secure vantage point 'true to the way things stand / In the durable light of appearances.'" In this volume, Dennis used allusion to the past in order to better explore his modern backdrop. Bennett observed, "Almost every poem employs the technique of entering others' minds and lives, including the lives of fictional characters and animals. Yet the poet's voice remains consistent and distinctive, a peculiar, and peculiarly effective, blending of compassion, longing and regret." Bennett used as an example the poem "At Becky's Piano Recital," in which Dennis imagines a young piano student as she ages: "Even old age won't cramp her / if she loses herself on her evening walk / In piano music drifting from a house / And imagines the upright in the parlor / And the girl working up the same hard passages."

In *Meetings with Time* (1992), Dennis addresses themes of guilt, forgiveness, conflict, prejudice, and philosophical notions of time. Again, he presents a variety of characters, ranging from commonplace types, such as an immigrant woman or a neighbor, to such mythical and historical figures as Moses, Horace, Oedipus, and Sigmund Freud. Yet, within these shifting narratives, Dennis evokes the landscape of Middle America—setting his meetings at an ice-cream stand, a middle school, or a small-town appliance store. As Stephen Dobyns for the *New York Times* (December 13, 1992) observed, "Each poem gives the sense that [Dennis] has been struck by an exciting idea or emotion or metaphor and he is eager to share it. And he doesn't simply tell it. Instead, he creates an elaborate structure that convinces by its very authority, intelligence, deep feeling and humor." David Yezzi for *Parnassus: Poetry in Review* (1993) affirmed, "Dennis confidently questions, discusses, commands, conjectures, and turns directly to the audience, breaking the fourth wall and gathering us into his wanderings and musings with a candor so engaging we can't but follow."

Dennis's next collection, *Ranking the Wishes* (1997), contains a series of meditative poems linked by their theme of yearning. R. D. Pohl, writing for the *Buffalo News* (May 4, 1997), praised Dennis's book as "a subtle and disarming mixture of artful daydreaming and moral speculation." Pohl added, "His poems have the contemporaneous quality of imaginative thought with all of its twists and turns, its constantly shifting perspective, its self-questioning digressions and narrative irony." A critic for *Virginia Quarterly Reviewer* (Winter 1998) lauded the volume and hailed Dennis as "a poet who is both accessible and worthy of study."

In his most recent work, *Practical Gods* (2001), Dennis examines the concept of deities and the way they appear—or more often do not appear—in the ordinary miracles of everyday life. As Elizabeth Lund explained for *Christian Science Monitor* (April 25, 2002), "Dennis's gods and prophets are by turn Greek and Christian; sometimes they are historical figures or artists whom the poet has elevated to a new plane. At times, these gods inhabit vast realms, yet often they stand mute and aloof while the speaker struggles to absorb both large and small revelations." After naming his gods "practical"—an ironic technique, many reviewers concluded—Dennis tackles larger questions, such as, "Why aren't the gods more responsive, more helpful, more accountable?" according to Donna Seaman for *Booklist*, as quoted on the Amazon Books Web site. In addition, he uses the imagery of his deities to explore deeper issues of human values. In one of the book's most celebrated poems, "View of Delft," Dennis concludes (as quoted by Elizabeth Lund): "Don't be surprised if the painting lingers awhile in memory / And the trees set back on a lawn you're passing / Seem to say that to master their language of gestures / Is to learn all you need to know to enter your life / And embrace it tightly, with a species of joy / You've yet to imagine. But this joy, disguised, / The painting declares, is yours already. / You've been longing again for what you have."

Dennis explained to Farnsworth, "I'm not interested in theology or mythology for their own sake. I'm only interested in . . . how I can use, really, this perspective to help clarify my own more secular stances toward things. I mean, I want to enter into dialogue that I . . . can make use of in my own life." For *Practical Gods*, Dennis garnered the 2002 Pulitzer Prize for poetry. He said of the award to Stephen Watson, "I'm very pleased. For me it means that my publisher loves me, because now he'll be able to sell twice as many of my books. Which means he'll take my next book, which is all I care about."

Dennis's work has been featured in numerous literary journals, including *Atlantic Monthly*, *American Poetry Review*, *Ironwood*, *Kenyon Review*, *New Republic*, *Paris Review*, the *New Yorker*, *Poetry*, and *Salmagundi*; it has also appeared in such prestigious volumes as the *Pushcart Anthology*, *The Best American Poetry*, and *The Bread Loaf Anthology of Poetry*. In addition to the Ruth Lilly Poetry Prize and the Pulitzer Prize, Dennis has been honored with the Oscar Blumenthal Prize (1989), the Bess Hokin Prize (1995), and the J. Howard and Barbara M. J. Wood Prize (1997). He is the recipient of fellowships from the Guggenheim Foundation and the National Endowment for the Arts, as well as an artistic residency at the Rockefeller Study Center, in Bellagio, Italy.

Carl Dennis currently resides in Buffalo, New York, where he teaches courses at the State University of New York in American poetry, creative writing, and Greek and Roman literature in translation, among other topics. He also serves on the faculty for the nonresident master's program in creative writing at Warren Wilson College, in North Carolina.

—K. D.

SUGGESTED READING: *Buffalo News* E p8 May 4, 1997, A p1 Apr. 9, 2002, F p1 Apr. 28, 2002; *Christian Science Monitor* p15 Apr. 25, 2002; *New York Times Book Review* p24 July 21, 1985, p42 Sep. 18, 1988, p12 Dec. 13, 1992; *Parnassus: Poetry in Review* p460 1993; *Poetry* p159 Dec. 1992, p14 July 1998

SELECTED BOOKS: poetry collections—*A House of My Own*, 1974; *Climbing Down*, 1976; *Signs and Wonders*, 1979; *The Near World*, 1985; *The Outskirts of Troy*, 1988; *Meetings with Time*, 1992; *Ranking the Wishes*, 1997; *Practical Gods*, 2001; criticism—*Poetry as Persuasion, an Essay for Writers*, 2001

Courtesy of Sheep Meadow Press

Dent, Tory

1958(?)– Poet

Tory Dent was a graduate student in English, attending a writer's colony, when she received by telephone the devastating news that she was HIV-positive, in 1988. She went on to produce two remarkable books of poetry, *What Silence Equals* (1993) and *HIV, Mon Amour* (1999), that testify in brutal, yet beautiful, language to the experience of living directly under the specter of AIDS. Jusef Komunyakaa, in the citation he wrote acknowledging *HIV Mon Amour*'s receipt of the 1999 James Laughlin Award, termed it "a map where imagination and experiences collide, and what rises out of the landscape underneath is a poetry painful and truthful, beautiful and terrifying, lyrical and narrative, always engaging the intellect and body politic."

Tory Dent was born in around 1958. She obtained a master's degree at New York University, in New York City, and was pursuing a doctorate when she found out about her illness. In addition to her poetry, she has written art criticism that has appeared in such publications as *Arts*, *Flash Art*, and *Parachute*, and she has also contributed essays for various exhibition catalogs.

In an interview for *POZ* (September 1995, online) that was reprinted on the Web site *The Body: An AIDS and HIV Information Resource*, Dent recounted to writer Donna Minkowitz that the news that she was HIV-positive came as a complete shock. Furthermore, while during the 1990s new treatments made it possible for people with HIV to live in good health indefinitely, in 1988, as Dent told Minkowitz, "If you tested positive, you were going to die." In addition to the grief and anger that such news would likely engender in anyone, as a heterosexual woman, Dent also experienced a deep sense of isolation. "I didn't know any straight people who were living long enough to create a supportive community," she told Minkowitz. She continued, "It seemed all I had left was my writing. I don't know how I would have gotten through that first winter without writing these poems," speaking of the writing that made up *What Silence Equals*. "It was the essential initial component of my surviving HIV."

Dent's first poetry collection, *What Silence Equals* (1993), was published five years after she had been diagnosed. In her foreword to the volume, the poet Sharon Olds called it "a prayer for the creation of meaning, for an emergency of art equal to the emergency of life." Calvin Bedient, a critic for *Parnassus: Poetry in Review* (No. 1/2, 1995), referred to "Tory Dent's love-emptied, black-bottomed first book," terming it "a truth-telling that shows its teeth." He opined that Dent's is "a style that loves to hate itself," and that "hatred is Dent's spectacular, witchy muse." Bedient concluded, "There has never been a poetry quite like this before, so passionately and understandably barbaric in its deployment of uselessly learned words. And, withal, stormily beautiful at the border where beauty tolerates the sublime."

Other reviewers, such as Ellen Kaufman, writing in *Library Journal* (January 1994), were equally strong in their praise of the collection. Kaufman called the poems in *What Silence Equals* "intelligent and alive, emanating not from what the author terms the 'negative state of my positiveness' but from the vertiginous cavern's edge: they are not poems about a disease but weather reports from an existential state." In the *Women's Review of Books* (April 1995), Adrian Oktenberg concurred: "In searing poem after searing poem, without lessening the tension or giving any kind of relief, Dent describes exactly and precisely what is it like to be in her skin, in her head. . . . It is daily hell, fiercely described." Oktenberg found *What Silence Equals* "remarkable . . . a cry full of unappeasable longing . . . it is immediately one of the great, necessary books to come out of the AIDS crisis, flinging its challenge in the face of death."

In a poem entitled "Everybody Loves a Winner," published in *Ploughshares* (Spring 1996), Dent wrote: "It's hard to believe that you ever thought it beautiful / hasn't reality always been by virtue of the realistic aspect always / horrible / like the real rope that ties your ankles and wrists together / prepared like the modern-day equivalent of a virgin for slaughter." Despite her initial impression that her diagnosis was tantamount to a swift death sentence, Dent survived to publish a second volume of poetry, *HIV, Mon Amour*, in 1999. In addition to winning the 1999 James Laughlin Award, the volume was a finalist for the National Book Critics Circle Award for Poetry. In his citation of Dent's book for the former award, the poet Jusef Komunyakaa described Dent's use of long lines of text in her poems, unusual in contemporary poetry, as a "lifeline tethered to in-depth meaning and breathless pursuit." He quoted from a poem in the collection in which she described herself as "Egged on by an elaborate need to / mother like a goddess the ugly / within me." Komunyakaa observed that "these poems read like a breathy elegy for Dionysian happenstance; however, there are also passages . . . filled with hope and temporal grace, a language that craves a wholeness through acknowledgment and synthesis."

In *Library Journal* (April 15, 2000), Barbara Hoffert agreed with Komunyakaa, finding *HIV, Mon Amour* an "astonishing cri de coeur . . . in detail as harsh, exacting and whitely lit as the hospital corridors [Dent] frequents. . . . The lines pour out of her recklessly, as if she can barely contain herself and the knowledge that this may be her last chance." A reviewer for *Publishers Weekly* (October 25, 1999) wrote, "The title sequence contains the most annihilatingly subdued work in the book: 'Nothing, not the winter trees reduced to underbrush at this distance nor their moulin-like branches, so baleful, have conspired against you.' . . . Dent's second book records, unflinchingly, the mind's desperate clingings to life."

In Dent's poem "What Calendars Have Become," published in the *American Poetry Review* (February 2000), she recapitulated, in characteristic long-line hexameters, some of her major themes:

> Some fail quickly while some fail incrementally with time to absorb all the infinitesimal disappointments, the details, gory and beautiful, reflected in the shocked face continually reframed by the realization of its death forthcoming. Its features document the difference between a fatal accident and wasting away . . . the excruciatingly slow entry into the self-dug abyss like Eskimo elders excommunicated from the community—their footprints filling up immediately with fresh snow—evidence that the heavens are in agreement, acknowledged now and then in empty-canteen silence.

By documenting her coping with sickness and the prospect of early death, Dent has produced a body of poetry considered an important testament. She has reportedly begun work on an autobiography.

— S.Y.

SUGGESTED READING: *American Poetry Review* p32+ Feb. 2000; *The Body: an AIDS and HIV Information Resource* (on-line); *Library Journal* p119 Jan. 1994, p94 Apr. 15, 2000; *Parnassus: Poetry in Review* p197+ No. 1/2 1995; *Ploughshares* p41+ Spring 1996; *Publishers Weekly* p76+ Oct. 25, 1999; *Women's Review of Books* p10 Apr. 1995

SELECTED BOOKS: *What Silence Equals*, 1993; *HIV, Mon Amour*, 1999

de Soto, Hernando

1941– Economist

In 1981 Hernando de Soto was walking through the dingy shantytown that had cropped up outside of Lima, Peru—similar to the shantytowns that, over the past three decades, have cropped up outside many Third-World cities—and was struck by the black-market industry buzzing all around him. He began talking to the poor merchants living in makeshift dwellings and discovered that, even though the government frowned upon it, the black market—or the informal market, as de Soto calls it, to

Hernando de Soto
Alejandro Balaguer/Corbis SYGMA

distinguish it from the criminal market—made up a substantial portion of Peru's economy, accounting for anywhere from 29 to 40 percent of the gross national product (GNP). In 1982 (some sources say 1983) de Soto founded the Institute for Liberty and Democracy (ILD) to study Peru's "real" economy and to push for legal reforms. Since that time, de Soto and the ILD have tried to win property rights for the informal sector so that it can join the formal economy and begin developing in earnest. The ILD is "focused totally on creating modern legal frameworks that help the poor of the developing and ex-communist world access property rights and turn their assets into leverageable capital," according to the organization's Web site. Deemed the second-most important think tank in the world by the *Economist*, the ILD was responsible for creating 400 new laws and regulations under the former Peruvian president, Alberto Fujimori. De Soto has written two books that explore the potential of the informal sector to transform world economies, *The Other Path: The Invisible Revolution in the Third World* (1989) and *The Mystery of Capital: Why Capitalism Triumphs in the West and Fails Everywhere Else* (2000). *The Other Path* was the top-seller in every Spanish-speaking country in Latin America; *The Mystery of Capital* was Peru's best-selling book ever and has been widely praised abroad. De Soto's work has been endorsed by politicians from both sides of the political spectrum, including the former senator and left-leaning presidential candidate, Bill Bradley, and the more conservative Margaret Thatcher, Richard Nixon, Ronald Reagan, and George Bush, Sr. Bush said, as quoted in the *Washington Post* (January 27, 1991), that de Soto's "prescription offers a clear and promising alternative to economic stagnation." De Soto has advised Mexico's President Vincente Fox, Haiti's President Jean-Bertrand Aristide, Egypt's President Hosni Mubarak, and the Philippine's President Gloria Macapagal Arroyo.

Hernando de Soto was born in Arequipa, in southern Peru, in 1941. De Soto's father served as secretary to the president and, later, as an ambassador to various European countries; de Soto left Peru at age seven and was raised abroad. He returned to Peru to attend college and was struck by the country's overwhelming poverty. Why was there such a gulf between Europe and his homeland, Matthew Miller quoted him in the *New York Times* (July 1, 2001, on-line) as thinking, when "the quality of the people was the same?" In the 1970s he earned his master's degree, in international economics and law, from the Graduate Institute of International Studies, in Geneva, Switzerland. After graduation he worked briefly for the General Agreement on Tariffs and Trade (GATT) and ran a Paris-based organization of copper-exporting nations. At age 30 he became the managing director of the Universal Engineering Corporation, which was controlled by the Swiss Bank Corporation Consultant Group and was one of the largest such firms in Europe. In 1979 he returned to Peru to direct a gold-mining operation and soon learned that there were far more obstacles to running a business there than in Europe. Determined to explore the social and economic conditions that created such obstacles, de Soto made an unusual move—he invited 20 street vendors to a symposium, called "Democracy and the Market Economy," which was also attended by local and European intellectuals, including the Noble Prize–winning economist, Friedrich A. von Hayek.

Determined to understand how business worked in Peru, de Soto hired two young lawyers to count the number of laws and regulations enacted in Peru since World War II. They discovered that about 28,000 laws and regulations had been created per year to regulate how citizens produced and distributed wealth—about 100 laws for each working day. Seeking to understand this legal maze, de Soto set up a tiny garment factory in Lima (equipped with two sewing machines) and tried to get it licensed. It took five university students 289 days—working several hours per day—to obtain a legal license. (A similar licensing effort conducted in New York City several years later took only four hours.) The students were approached for bribes on 24 occasions and at least once were compelled to cooperate. The total cost of the licensing effort was 31 times the minimum monthly income for a Peruvian worker.

Sometime in 1982 or 1983, de Soto formalized his activities by founding the ILD. He and his research associates began walking through Lima's shantytowns and talking to the people that worked there. After tabulating their research, they discovered that substantial proportions of the country's economy were operating outside legal boundaries—including 90 percent of small industries, 60 percent of the fishing fleet, and 60 percent of grocery distribution, according to the ILD's Web site. These findings were big news in Peru; a 14-page cover story ran in a major news magazine and an hour-long television documentary aired. De Soto was approached by the Peruvian president, Fernando Belaúnde Terry, who offered to place the organization in an advisory position to the government. Soon the ILD was regularly drafting laws aimed at streamlining the country's economic system.

In 1986 de Soto published *The Other Path* (*El Otro Sendero*). Following its enormous success in Latin America, it was published in English, in 1989. The book's title is meant to suggest an alternative to the Shining Path, a revolutionary guerrilla group that had begun as an offshoot of the Peruvian Communist Party, and, in 1980, turned to violence and terrorism. (After publication of *The Other Path*, the Shining Path bombed the ILD's offices and machine-gunned de Soto's car.) Focusing primarily on Peru, but also discussing other Latin American countries and Africa, de Soto extols the power of the informal sector of the economy to reinvigorate poor countries. In Peru, de Soto found, the informal sector employs a majority of the population and produces a substantial percentage of the gross national product (GNP). Because many laws favor a few special interests and effectively shut out the rest, de Soto argues that Peru and other countries are not practicing free-market capitalism but rather a form of mercantilism, an economic system that privileges the merchant class. Elucidating de Soto's argument, Jeremy Main, in *Fortune* (January 16, 1989), compared the Peruvian economy to the New York City taxi system. "To own a cab in New York," he wrote, "you need a license from the city, known as a medallion. No new ones have been issued in the past 51 years, so newcomers have to buy one of the 11,787 existing medallions that trade for around $140,000 each. As a result, the city doesn't have enough cabs. An informal fleet of some 40,000 limousines and so-called gypsy cabs—often inadequately insured and unsafe—has sprung up. Now imagine that the entire U.S. economy works like New York's cab system. That's the economy of Peru and most of the Third World."

In the *Washington Post* (January 27, 1991), Peter F. Schaefer praised the novel economic approach put forth in *The Other Path*. He argued that both liberals and conservatives in the U.S. have erred in their third-world relief efforts. Liberals, he contended, tend to provide resources to the needy without doing much to alleviate the causes of poverty. Conservatives seek growth and development, but end up reinforcing the existing power structures and perpetuating more violence and unrest. "De Soto's ideas on reform," Schaefer wrote, "offer a way to bridge the gap between traditional liberal and conservative views about appropriate economic development—while contradicting both in important respects." Richard Gott, in *New Statesman & Society* (June 30, 1989), acknowledged the worth of de Soto's theories but felt that he had overstated his case. "De Soto's thesis is stimulating and intriguing. . . . The research is fine. The exact workings of the black economy—who benefits and why—makes a fascinating study. De Soto is also splendid when he details the limitations of Latin America's legal institutions and seeks to reform them. But the ideological superstructure that this research is obliged to bear is extremely dubious. . . . As a new recipe for emancipation for the deprived peoples of the third world, it leaves much to be desired."

In 1990 Peru's newly inducted president, Alberto Fujimori, asked de Soto and the ILD to help him devise an anti-drug policy that would seal a foreign-aid package from the U.S. One of de Soto's ideas was to offer incentives for the growers of coca, the plant used to make cocaine, to switch to other crops. "The major reason [farmers] make coca paste," de Soto explained to Dario Fernandez-Morera for *Reason* (February 1994), "is that these entrepreneurs have no security with respect to their property, because it is informal property and therefore not 'legal.' They have no incentive to plant, for example, oil palms, which in five years will give them an economic benefit six times greater than planting coca. To produce palm oil, you have to be able to wait five years, while coca grows like weeds, without any need for care and time. And if you don't have clear property rights, you can't get the credit necessary to grow crops that require more investment capital than coca." De Soto became one of Fujimori's main advisers. The formalization program he instituted brought titles to 1.6 million extralegal buildings, and 280,000 licenses to small businesses, according to Matthew Miller. Then, in early 1992, shortly before Fujimori suspended the constitution and dissolved the congress, de Soto resigned his post to demonstrate his disapproval of Fujimori's increasingly authoritarian rule. "It isn't that you have a villain in Fujimori," de Soto said, as quoted by Dudley Althaus in the *Houston Chronicle* (April 12, 1992). "You simply have another Third World leader who is trying to cope. . . . The whole system [in Latin America] has collapsed and Peru is right at the front. It's [like] France of the 18th century."

In *The Mystery of Capital* (2000) de Soto expands on the themes laid out in *The Other Path*. He argues that world poverty could be greatly alleviated by granting property rights to those who own informal businesses and homes. This would give poor people working capital to develop their properties and businesses and would stimulate the world economy. Entrepreneurs would be able to take out loans against their legally registered property and reinvest the money in business. Unlike agrarian reform, in which rural land deeds are created and parceled out, de Soto advocates recognizing the property lines already set up informally throughout the world—just as the U.S. did for the squatters and gold prospectors in the 1800s. "If you take a walk through the countryside," de Soto explained to Fernandez-Morera, "from Indonesia to Peru, and you walk by field after field—in each field a different dog is going to bark at you. Even dogs know what private property is all about. The only one who does not know it is the government. The issue is that there exists a 'common law' and an 'informal law' which the Latin American formal legal system does not know how to recognize."

Robert Skidelsky, in the *New York Times Book Review* (December 24, 2000), questioned the validity of de Soto's claims. Skidelsky maintained that poverty in rural areas was due more to low agricultural productivity than lack of property rights, and he noted that it is quite possible to generate significant capital in the informal economic sector—in some cases easier than in the legal sector. "And [de Soto] hardly considers the greatest obstacle of all: the land on which the poor squat and work is usually owned by someone else—whether government or private landlords. By what mechanisms of divestment or dispossession," he asked, "is this land to become the legal property of its occupiers?" He concluded that de Soto's book "needs a broader analytical framework and a deeper knowledge of history." Peter Coy agreed that *The Mystery of Capital* suffered somewhat from a lack of analytical scope, but in *Businessweek Online* (November 13, 2000) he called it a "provocative and elegantly written book." "Although de Soto oversimplifies the solution to poverty," Coy wrote, "he performs a valuable service by highlighting a problem that's often underestimated: the failure of the legal system to acknowledge and respect the property of the poor."

In the 1999 issue of *Time*, "Leaders for the New Millennium," the magazine's editors named Hernando de Soto as one of the five most important innovators of the century in Latin America. De Soto's 1989 book *The Other Path: The Invisible Revolution in the Third World* was recently re-released as *The Other Path: The Economic Answer to Terrorism* (2002).

—P. G. H.

SUGGESTED READING: *Fortune* p101+ Jan. 16, 1989; London *Guardian* (on-line) Sep. 11, 2000; *Houston Chronicle* p1 Apr. 12, 1992; *New Statesman & Society* p33+ June 30, 1989; *New York Times* A p17 Feb. 17, 1992, A p34 Oct. 26, 2000; *New York Times Book Review* p8+ Dec. 24, 2000; *Reason* p28+ Feb. 1994; *Wall Street Journal* p1+ Mar. 17, 1987; *Washington Post* C p5 Jan. 27, 1991

SELECTED BOOKS: *The Other Path: The Invisible Revolution in the Third World*, 1989; *The Mystery of Capital: Why Capitalism Triumphs in the West and Fails Everywhere Else*, 2000

Dickey, Eric Jerome

1961– Novelist

The African-American novelist Eric Jerome Dickey has written a group of novels, *Sister, Sister* (1996), *Friends and Lovers* (1997), *Milk in My Coffee* (1998), *Cheaters* (1999), *Liar's Game* (2000), *Between Lovers* (2001), and *Thieves' Paradise* (2002), in which young, African-American, urban professionals play the game of love. Sometimes they play amateurishly, sometimes almost professionally, and thanks to Dickey, they always seem to find themselves on a board with a lot of twists and turns. Dickey has been praised by critics for accurately reflecting, through his use of language and choice of situations, the mores of the African-Americans he portrays. He has been lauded also for his depictions of women, making him something of a rarity among male writers. As Dickey said during an on-line question and answer session for *USA Today* (June 22, 2000), "My primary concern is writing a story that . . . appears seamless and effortless even though it's a lot of hard work [to write it]. In the end, it holds together as a good story, and you don't see all the magic."

Eric Jerome Dickey was born in Memphis, Tennessee, in 1961. He "grew up on the south side," and attended Riverview Elementary and Junior High, and Carver High School, as he noted on his Web page. He graduated from Memphis State University (now the University of Memphis) with a B.S. in computer systems technology and went to work for the Rockwell company (now Boeing).

In 1983 Dickey moved to Los Angeles, where he worked by day as a software developer in the aerospace industry. During his off-hours, he also pursued a career as a comedian, writing his own stand-up act, and as an actor. When he lost his day job as a result of downsizing, he decided to become a writer. He joined International Black Writers and Artists (IBWA). The group offered development workshops and a scholarship for creative writing classes at the University of California, Los Angeles.

Dickey told an interviewer for *Chance22* (on-line) that, although during the nine years that he worked in the aerospace industry, he read mostly computer manuals and did technical writing, he "always had another, creative side. A silly side that didn't match my former occupation." He had written some short stories in high school and remembered "how much fun it was to make something out of nothing and get ALL of the credit for it," he told the interviewer. "I hadn't read a novel in umpteen years before I started writing, and had associated reading with school and work, never pleasure."

Eric Jerome Dickey

Dickey's first novel, *Sister, Sister*, came out in 1996. The book, which some might find oddly titled for a novel written by a man, deals with the lives of women in contemporary Los Angeles. The point of view shifts among Valerie, a married woman whose husband has lost interest in her; her sister Inda, whose boyfriend is also seeing Chiquita, and has a third "fiancée"; and Chiquita, who becomes close friends with Inda. Although Dickey's novels have been described as "urban," most of the characters are representative of the black middle class, people who earn salaries or have businesses and who are, to a certain degree, similar to Dickey himself, whether they're male or female. In an interview with Thomas J. Brady in the *St. Louis Post-Dispatch* (August 13, 1999), Dickey was careful to distinguish himself from his characters. He and a given character "may have been born in the same place and have gone to the same high school, but then we separate," he said. "I try to build individuals. . . . At some point, they go left, I go right. You let them do stuff you wouldn't do."

"The idea of an African-American 'sister' novel written by a man will strike many as suspicious," Lillian Lewis wrote in *Booklist* (September 15, 1996), "but Dickey accurately details the tangled relationships between both his female and male characters. . . . Valerie, Chiquita, and Inda share their thoughts and feelings about their interlocking relationship with one another, with men, with family members, and with the past. Remarkably, Dickey is able both to create believable female characters and to explore the 'sister-sister' relationship with genuine insight." A reviewer for *Publishers Weekly* (August 5, 1996) agreed that "Dickey's novel brims with humor, outrageousness, and an understanding of the generosity of affection." Nevertheless, the reviewer found fault with Dickey's use of multiple points of view, and also cited "an unevenness of characterization" in the novel.

Having formed very good work habits as a writer, Dickey published another novel, *Friends and Lovers*, in 1997. Although it appeared after *Sister, Sister*, Dickey told an interviewer for Amazon.com that *Friends and Lovers* was actually written first. Again, an intertwined group of characters—hip, single, and with good jobs—tell their stories of rejection, romance, and the tie that really binds, friendship. In the novel, Tyrel and Leonard are best friends, "ace-coon since elementary," as Tyrel puts it, who work together as software developers. Debra, a nurse, and Shelby, a stewardess, meet Leonard and Tyrel and pair off. Leonard, who also works as a comedian, and Debra get married. Shelby and Tyrel's romance takes a stormier course, but when a tragic event occurs in the lives of the married couple, Shelby and Tyrel learn something about the value of continuity in relationships. Lillian Lewis, writing in *Booklist* (September 1, 1997), called *Friends and Lovers* another "African-American novel for the bestseller list." She found Dickey "not only perceptive but also witty and moving in his portrayal of relationships." *Publishers Weekly* (September 1, 1997) applauded Dickey's "engagingly trendy dialogue."

With Jordan Greene, the protagonist of *Milk in My Coffee* (1998), Dickey created a Tennessee native relocated to New York. He hates the crowds and the cold: "A bad-tempered breeze from the direction of the East River kicked in, making everybody in Times Square bend, walk like hunchbacks, curse, and shudder, but nobody slowed down. Since I've been in New York, I've never seen anybody slow down. Even the dead keep moving. And no matter when, no matter where, there are so many damn people," Jordan declares at the beginning of the novel, as quoted from an excerpt published on Penguin Putnam's Web site. Jordan is complaining because he has walked a long way to Times Square, frozen his hands, can't feel his feet, and can't get a cab. "Paranoid punks never stop for a black man because they're afraid we might make them do something unreasonable, like drop us off in a black neighborhood. This is bull. I'm twenty-nine, work a nine-to-five, and have a wallet full of legitimate cash, and I still can't get a damn cab." His inability to make a driver stop for him turns out to be a stroke of luck: Kimberly, an artist, takes pity on him and lets him share her cab and, eventually, her life. A woman with a half-black father, Kimberly, who looks white, is in the novel's parlance the "milk in Jordan's coffee." Both Jordan and Kimberly have family problems, skeletons in their closets, and other troubles, and Jordan also experiences racism at work and loses his job. Jordan's best (or maybe not so good) friend Solomon, and his ex-girlfriend J'nette further complicate the picture. Jordan's Southern family has strong objections to his involvement with a nominally white woman, and a critic for *Kirkus Reviews* (September 1, 1998) noted that the "most chilling aspect of this romantic relationship" is the fact that virtually "without exception, Jordan's friends, relatives, and acquaintances are unwilling to accept Kimberly—and their hostility is convincing."

As a reviewer for *Publishers Weekly* (July 6, 1998) wrote, "Dickey has demonstrated once again his easy mastery of dialogue and voice (both romantic leads share narrator's honors with an omniscient third-person) and his cheerful, wittily acerbic eye for the troubles that plague lovers in the 1990s." Terming "Dickey's third novel of African-American romance and friendship" a story that is "definitely more developed than his two previous novels," *Booklist* (July 1998) reviewer Lillian Lewis praised *Milk in My Coffee* as "a good novel" with "a very satisfying conclusion." Tamala Edwards, in *Essence* (September 1998), opined that the novel wound up with "revelations worthy of daytime TV." However, she noted, "with all the flash, he scores with characters who come to feel like old friends; Dickey gets a big-up for writing in a female voice that is smart and believable." The *USA Today* (August 27, 1998) reviewer, Tamara Henry, objected to "the hip-hop lines," which she deemed "glib in the context of an interracial relationship." Nevertheless, Henry found that *Milk in My Coffee* "subtly teaches an appreciation for the complexities of life in America."

For *Cheaters* (1999), Dickey again used his convention of writing in the varied voices of a group of African-American singles in Los Angeles. The three narrators, Stephan, Chante, and Darnell, are rounded out by the other main characters, Tammy, Jake, and Karen. The tale begins with Stephan's flashback to when he was in the third grade. His father asks him, "How many womens you got now, boy?" Wanting to be a credit to his father, he answers calculatingly, "Got me three womens now." It proves the right answer. "We mens," his daddy declares. The male characters in *Cheaters* differ from the "monogamous, good-looking, charming, dreamy," types in Dickey's earlier novels, according to Rashod D. Ollison in the (Albany) *Times Union* (September 5, 1999). "In *Cheaters* . . . Dickey introduces readers to . . . men . . . who are slick and deceitful." Dickey told Ollison that the "guys in this book are more like the men a lot of women are dating. This book is about the good bad guys and the bad bad guys." As Ollison put it, "some cheaters gloss over their love games with romance, while others just flat-out use people."

The adult Stephan pursues women as his father did, but remains emotionally unsatisfied. His main girlfriend, Chante, decides she's been "dogged" enough, and now she's going to dog Stephan. Darnell, a lawyer, yearns to be a writer, but his wife, Dawn, can't understand why. He turns to an affair with Tammy, an actress. Stephan's friend Jake is appalled by thoughts of the aborted children that promiscuous Stephan leaves in his wake. Chante's friend Karen, single and determined to remain so, hurls bitter comments at the others, disparaging their love lives.

The *Washington Post Book World* (August 15, 1999) reviewer, Yolanda Joe, noted that although the title *Cheaters* might make readers "guess that the novel is about infidelity," unfaithfulness is only part of the story. "*Cheaters* is not simply about switching horses on the merry-go-round of romance. It is also about how we cheat ourselves through expectations, demands, desires, and emotion," she observed. Joe enjoyed the novel, noting that the "pacing is smooth and crisp, and the dialogue has enough wit that the reader can take time to savor the flip comebacks and the thought-provoking debates over what men and women want from each other—and what they actually get." Other reviewers agreed that Dickey had milked the definitions of cheating to the maximum in his novel. "As the title suggests," Michelle Williams wrote in the *Los Angeles Times* (August 4, 1999), "this is a book about dawgs. Not dogs, but d-a-w-g-s. Cheatin', lyin', no good, no-'count, dirty lowdown mendawgs and womendawgs. These dawgs don't just cheat on their spouses and lovers. Dickey explores the art of cheating: how we cheat on our friends, our family, ourselves. How we cheat ourselves into and out of relationships, good and bad. How we do this cheating all for the sake of stuff that . . . just ain't worth it." *Cheaters*, Emily Jones agreed in *Library Journal* (May 15, 1999), "not only makes readers examine their own behavior but keeps them laughing while doing so. Dickey improves his craft with each book."

With *Liar's Game* (2000), Dickey injected political commentary into the story of African-American singles in Los Angeles trying to escape from their messy pasts. Vincent's divorce has left him unable to see his young daughter, and his ex-wife reenters the scene disturbingly. Dana has left a bad relationship in New York to try her hand at the real estate business in L.A., and her former relationship also resurfaces during the course of the novel. The story's subplots involve Dana's friend Gerri, a stripper whose husband is involved with a female member of a rap group he manages, and Vincent's friend Womack, who cannot rely on his wife's faithfulness.

A *Publishers Weekly* (May 22, 2000) reviewer referred to Dickey's "standard themes of love, betrayal, and commitment-phobia," but observed that this book has the positive addition of "quips on political and cultural issues such as police brutality and justice, custody issues, and cultural conflicts between Africans and African-Americans." Tamara Henry, writing in *USA Today* (June 26, 2000), noted that the "magic" in the meeting of Vince and Dana did not prevent them from concealing their pasts from each other. The fact that the "plot is strong" and filled with entanglements "allows Dickey to pack in contemporary issues, steamy romance, betrayal, and redemption," Henry observed.

In Dickey's next novel, *Between Lovers* (2001), he presents a complex love triangle, characterizing his unnamed narrator with several autobiographical traits. The narrator, a Los Angeles–based African-American writer, encounters his ex-girlfriend, Nicole, at a book-signing event in Oakland. Seven years prior, Nicole had abruptly left him at the altar due to confusion about her sexuality and moved in with Ayanna, an intense attorney. Their meeting at the book signing reignites old feelings, and the two begin seeing each other regularly. Although the narrator is determined to win Nicole back, she remains committed to Ayanna. When Nicole insists that she wants a shared arrangement with both lovers, tension mounts between the characters and ultimately explodes in tragedy. Meanwhile, the narrator confronts expectations placed on him by his father and others to write black fiction of substance, rather than frivolity. *Between Lovers* was well received by fans and critics alike. As a reviewer noted for *Publishers Weekly*, as quoted on *Amazon.com*, "This is another spicy slice of African-American dramatic fiction from an author who seems only to get better."

In *Thieves' Paradise* (2002), Dickey delivers a love story that is also part coming-of-age tale, in which he explores the dark underworld of Los Angeles. When the 25-year-old Dante is laid off from his computer job, he is left with few prospects and is forced to turn to a life of crime. Dante and his best friend, Jackson, become involved with a master con artist, Scamz, who brings them into a set of high-level, life-threatening schemes. Meanwhile, Dante begins courting Pam, a thirty-something waitress and aspiring actress with financial problems of her own. When Dante convinces Pam to join the con game, the two begin an electrifying relationship. Yet, Dante's life soon spirals out of control. Like many of Dickey's earlier works, *Thieves' Paradise* became an instant hit among readers. As Jennifer Baker observed for *Library Journal*, as quoted on *Amazon.com*, "Dickey's talent for involving the reader in real-world problems while eliciting rueful smiles and creating characters who struggle to do the right thing ensure his latest novel's success."

Dickey lives in Los Angeles, and keeps himself fit by running. He mentors two children for Project Reach, and, as he has told interviewers, he keeps his personal life private. *Sister, Sister*, *Friends and Lovers*, *Milk in my Coffee*, and *Cheaters* all achieved the top ranking on the *Essence* Blackboard bestseller list, and *Cheaters*, *Liar's Game*, *Between Lovers*, and *Thieves' Paradise* were all national best-sellers. Dickey's latest book, "The Other Woman," in which he explores the hardships of the modern marriage, is set for release in May 2003. Some reviewers have referred to Dickey as the "male Terry McMillan," while others, such as Michelle Williams, have declared him better. In an interview with Alden Mudge for *Booksamillion.com*, Dickey objected to being "pigeonholed" as an African-American novelist. He told Mudge that although some "non-African-American editors . . . don't understand the culture or the style," he uses "that edge that you get when you're being honest" to appeal to all kinds of readers. "No one ever cries 'victim' in my books," Dickey told Don O'Briant in an interview in the *Atlanta Journal-Constitution* (July 15, 1999), and that forthright spirit has made his books appealing to a broad range of readers.

— S. Y.

SUGGESTED READING: *Atlanta Journal-Constitution* D p2 July 15, 1999; *Booklist* p220 Sep. 15, 1996, p56 Sep. 1, 1997, p1855 July 1998; *Essence* p84 Sep. 1998; *Kirkus Reviews* (on-line) Sep. 1, 1998; *Library Journal* p124 May 15, 1999; *Los Angeles Times* p4 Aug. 4, 1999; *Publishers Weekly* p428 Aug. 15, 1996, p92 Sep. 1, 1997, p47 July 6, 1998, p70 May 22, 2000; (Albany) *Times Union* J p4 Sep. 5, 1999; *USA Today* D p6 Aug. 27, 1998, D p8 June 26, 2000; *Washington Post Book World* p4 Aug. 15, 1999

SELECTED BOOKS: novels—*Sister, Sister*, 1996; *Friends and Lovers*, 1997; *Milk in My Coffee*, 1998; *Cheaters*, 1999; *Liar's Game*, 2000; *Between Lovers*, 2001; *Thieves' Paradise*, 2002

Diehl, Margaret

1955– Novelist; memoirist

In her memoir, *The Boy on the Green Bicycle* (1999), Margaret Diehl described a 30-year period in her life: "I grew, trading in sweets for marijuana, LSD, Southern Comfort, had visions, had sex, went to college, wrote poetry, got married to an older man with four children, drank far too much red wine, stayed up all night talking to the dead, published two novels." The two sparks that sent Diehl on this path were the death of her brother Jimmy and the suicide of her father, both in 1965. Like many artists, Diehl borrowed from painful experiences for her two novels, *Men* (1988) and *Me and You* (1990), and a family memoir, *The Boy on the Green Bicycle* (1999). In *Elle* (October 1988), Amy Boaz described Diehl's writing style as "lyrically ebullient, charged with moments of magic and myth that betray influences as diverse as Colette and García Márquez."

Margaret Diehl was born in 1955. As she wrote in *The Boy on the Green Bicycle*, her parents left the South and settled in New Jersey in 1962. "We were a family of six," Diehl recalled. "My father worked in publishing in New York, my mother took care of us." The Diehls lived in a large house and enjoyed a comfortable life. As a child, Margaret read fairy tales and played with her two brothers, Jimmy and Johnny, and sister, Charlotte.

The Diehl family's happy existence was shattered in February 1965 when Jimmy was killed in a traffic accident. As Diehl wrote in her memoir, Jimmy was her mother's favorite and was also popular with his three siblings because he was "clearly the best, smarter, older than Johnny, nicer than Charlotte, braver than me. He had a calm temperament, poise, deft hands and a good eye, a wide-ranging curiosity." Several months later, Margaret's father, who was overcome with grief over Jimmy's death, killed himself. The following year, Margaret's mother moved the family to New York City.

Diehl experienced a revelation during Jimmy's funeral. The minister concluded the service by reading from a poem that Diehl's mother had selected. "I read the poem at home, after the service, read it several times. Gradually I understood. Immortality belonged to poets," Diehl wrote in her memoir. "Jimmy and I had parallel destinies. His death was the necessary tragedy to make me a great poet, and my poetry would redeem his death. He was the one the invisible world chose to keep close at hand, while I, the dreamier, more passive child, was their agent on earth." According to Boaz, Diehl loves "reading poetry and novels because that's where you can find magic." She added that writing allows her "to bring something into being."

Diehl received publicity and substantial critical acclaim when she published her first novel, *Men*, in 1988. Its main character, 21-year-old Stella James, cruises the streets of New York seeking sexual partners. Stella is very successful and engages in a series of one-night stands with men who are virtually strangers to her. Stella eventually adopts monogamy, settling down with Frank, a San Francisco photographer. "From my own reading, I noticed that there wasn't very much about sex from a woman's point of view," Diehl explained to Marni Jackson, a reviewer for the *Toronto Star* (July 1, 1989). "Sex isn't all the same. To me it reveals so much about who the character is—and that's what a novel is about, revealing character." Diehl told Jackson that it is possible for a woman to love more than one man at a time, adding that infidelity is possible within a good marriage. "I'm not saying fidelity is better, or worse," she explained. "It's just a different kind of love, that's all."

In the *New York Times Book Review* (September 25, 1988), Howard Coale wrote that the best parts of the book are those in which "Ms. Diehl ranges back into Stella's memory." He described the passage in which Stella remembered losing her virginity at age 15 in a cold backyard in New Hampshire as "particularly wonderful," and said that in it Diehl achieved "a higher plane of vision." Coale concluded his favorable review of the novel by declaring, "Margaret Diehl is a novelist of subtle gifts. She writes about sex without a trace of self-consciousness. She suggests that through sex one can win oneself back, not by the body's ability to satisfy, but by its capacity to cleanse the mind."

In the *Wall Street Journal* (August 26, 1988), Cynthia Crossen, while acknowledging Stella's "poetic, convincing voice," observed an unrealistic quality in *Men*: "Words like AIDS and hepatitis are conspicuously absent, and Stella firmly dismisses the danger of getting slashed by a lunatic. Contraception is mentioned only once—when a lover conveniently says he has had a vasectomy. But for the nostalgic, these omissions are a treat. Sex without reality can be a beautiful thing." Diehl addressed these concerns in her interview with Boaz, explaining that *Men* is set before the onslaught of AIDS. "I don't see my novel as a prescription for people's lives," Diehl said. "Stella would be different in 1988; she'd carry a condom now, I'm sure." *Men* was adapted into a film starring Sean Young that was released in 1997.

As an adult, Diehl battled alcoholism before joining Alcoholics Anonymous. Her next novel, *Me and You* (1989), explored a recovering alcoholic's attempts to find love. After completing a recovery program, Gwen has an affair with Jack Price, an older man. Jack is married and also happens recently to have become the father-in-law of Gwen's sister Lucy. In a review in the London *Times* (March 4, 1990), Dorothy Wade praised Diehl's writing as "fluid and inspired, reflecting the three stages of Gwen's odyssey from alcoholism through lonely recovery to fulfilment." Wade noted that Diehl's writing "becomes a heady mix of hallucination and reality, past and present," as the affair between Gwen and Jack blossoms.

In the *San Francisco Chronicle* (April 22, 1990), reviewer Sherri Hallgren observed, "Diehl, however, doesn't provide a moral to this story or an easy psychological diagnosis. Although all involved are to one degree or another conscious of the patterns being acted out, Diehl's intention seems not to judge this setup but merely to examine it, thoroughly." Hallgren went on to identify the novel's main strength: "And here again, there is remarkable writing about the most impossibly dense and murky aspects of the psyche—parents and children, sex and intimacy. In rich, lyric prose and a narrative voice that is boldly honest, Diehl conveys what it is like to be inside alcoholic desire, alienation, withdrawal, fear."

Diehl waited nine years before publishing her next book and first nonfiction work, *The Boy on the Green Bicycle* (1999). In it she recalls her grief over the death of her brother Jimmy, whom she idolized, and the suicide of her father. "Jimmy was an American boy the way they used to make them in the early 1960s," Diehl wrote in the memoir. "He played football, he had a dozen friends, he was a cartoonist specializing in gangsters and tough women smoking cigarettes." After Jimmy's death, Margaret retreats into her imagination, which is filled with magic, fairy tales, and books, such as C. S. Lewis's classic series *The Chronicles of Narnia*, a particular favorite of hers.

In the *New York Times Book Review* (June 13, 1999), Stacey D'Erasmo wrote, "Diehl's descriptions of both the terrible events in her family and the golden stuff of her own interiority are so entrancing that one realizes too late—just as she does—that fairyland can be a gravityless hell."

D'Erasmo added that the memoir "scared me, and I mean that as a compliment. Instead of simply valorizing or sentimentalizing the imagination, Diehl gives it its due as a ferocious, drug-like force."

Reviewing the book for *New York Newsday* (August 1, 1999), Melanie Rehak wrote, "Although death obviously figures prominently in *The Boy on the Green Bicycle*, the book turns out to be less about the decimation of a family than about the stunning consciousness of a child. Diehl's descriptions of her mental wandering as a young girl verge on the poetic, the language bearing up seemingly effortlessly under the weight of the ruptures it describes." Rehak also praised the memoir as a "mesmerizing, even incantatory offering."

Margaret Diehl is married and lives in New York City. She is the stepmother of four grown children. Diehl also writes for the *New York Times Book Review*.

— D.C.

SUGGESTED READING: *Elle* p48 Oct. 1988, with photo; *New York Times Book Review* p38 Sep. 25, 1988; *New York Times Book Review* (on-line) June 13, 1999; *New York Newsday* Aug. 1, 1999; *San Francisco Chronicle* p9 Apr. 22, 1990; (London) *Times* June 22, 2000; *Toronto Star* M p24 July 1, 1989, with photo; *Wall Street Journal* Aug. 26, 1988

SELECTED BOOKS: novels—*Men*, 1988; *Me and You*, 1990; memoir—*The Boy on the Green Bicycle*, 1999

David Harrison/Courtesy of Viking Penguin Group

Drakulic, Slavenka

July 4, 1949– Novelist; essayist

The cosmopolitan writer Slavenka Drakulic, born and raised in Croatia, a now-independent region of Yugoslavia, has addressed in both nonfiction and fiction the subjects of communism, its decline, and the devastating wars in the Balkans. At least three of her books, the nonfiction *How We Survived Communism and Even Laughed* (1992), *The Balkan Express: Fragments from the Other Side of the War* (1993), and *Café Europa: Life After Communism* (1996), in which she surveyed how people, especially women, responded to the fall of communism and war in Eastern Europe, were written in English; they have not been published in her native Serbo-Croatian because in her homeland she is considered a traitor to the nationalist cause. She is the author of the novels *Holograms of Fear*, translated by Ellen Elias-Bursac in 1992; *Marble Skin*, translated by Greg Mosse from the French version in 1994; *The Taste of a Man*, translated in 1998 by Christina Pribichevich-Zorich; and *S: A Novel of the Balkans*, translated by Marko Ivic in 1999.

In an interview in the *Washington Post* (June 23, 1993), Drakulic described to Christine Spolar the methods she uses for writing both fiction and nonfiction: "The only way to do it is to talk about how you personally experience it and to take your guts out—to turn them out—and show them to everybody."

Slavenka Drakulic was born on July 4, 1949 in Rijeka, Croatia, a part of Yugoslavia, then under the rule of Josip Broz Tito; Croatia later broke away from the Yugoslav federation and became an independent nation. Her father was a decorated military officer, a member of the high echelons of the Communist Party, called the "nomenklatura." Her mother also worked for the Yugoslavian government.

Drakulic grew up in the most liberal Communist regime in Eastern Europe. The nation of Yugoslavia, consisting of various old Balkan principalities, nationalities, and religious groups, was united under Tito. Nevertheless, life there took place under conditions that, although relatively comfortable compared with those in other Communist countries, would have been viewed as intolerably repressive in more democratic societies. In the first book Drakulic published in English, *How We Survived Communism and Even Laughed*, she described going to the post office, where "it was perfectly normal not only to have to wait in line pressed tightly together, but to peer at each other's documents, accounts, letters and bills quite shamelessly. . . . Asking for the right to privacy meant you had something to hide. And hiding something meant it was forbidden. If it was forbidden, it must have been against the state. Finally, if it was against the state, you must have been an enemy." Drakulic earned a bachelor's degree in world literature in 1976. Three years later she became one of the founders of the first Yugoslavian feminist group. In 1987 she enrolled in the Writers' Workshop at the University of Iowa. She married Slobodan Drakulic, with whom she had a daughter; after that marriage ended, she was married twice more.

How We Survived Communism is a collection of essays that grew out of an assignment for *Ms.* magazine, for which Drakulic wrote about the lives of women in Hungary, Poland, Czechoslovakia, Bulgaria, and East Germany in 1990. She wrote the book as communism was collapsing and as civil war was about to erupt in Yugoslavia, bringing with it "ethnic cleansing," innumerable atrocities, and the complete "Balkanization" of Yugoslavia, now occupied by breakaway warring factions and nationalities. Cathy Young in the *New York Times Book Review* (April 19, 1992) described "The Day When They Say That War Will Begin," an essay from the book, as capturing "the numbing fear of waiting for catastrophe, even as life with all its trivialities goes on."

Young termed *How We Survived Communism* a "thoughtful, beautifully written collection of essays" and singled out Drakulic's "vivid picture of the compulsive recycling and collecting typical of Eastern European households, dictated not by environmental consciousness but by poverty and fear of shortages. 'While leaders were accumulating words about a bright future, people were accumulating flour and sugar, jars, cups, pantyhose, old bread, corks, rope, nails, plastic bags,' she writes. This desperate hoarding is, to her, the ultimate symbol of the failure of Communism."

Other reviewers, such as Erika Munk, the *Women's Review of Books* (May 1992) critic, found the book to be an important feminist document, "essential reading in every women's studies program." Munk praised "the beauty and precision of Drakulic's writing," noting that "we can feel these lives, walk into their rooms, smell their soup." An anonymous critic for the *Economist* (January 11, 1992), by contrast, praised Drakulic's writing style but found "a cloudy and romantic view of democracy" in *How We Survived Communism*. "Her idea of living standards in the West is still hugely inflated. She appears to believe that only under communism do women recycle things out of economic necessity. 'A nice, strong shoe box can have several purposes,' she informs the reader, as though no woman in the West would realise that." The *Economist* critic also faulted Drakulic for clinging to "the piety of the old order" and noted that she appeared to believe that "communism offered her native Yugoslavia (and other countries) some sort of cohesion, and a brutal guarantee against tribal warfare."

The next book by Drakulic to appear in English was the 1992 *Holograms of Fear*, translated from the Serbo-Croatian by Ellen Elias-Bursac. Originally published in 1988 in Yugoslavia, the novel is based on Drakulic's personal experience of having been treated by kidney dialysis for six years (she had a kidney transplant in 1986). The protagonist is a woman from Zagreb who is admitted to a Boston hospital, where she receives a new kidney. The novel draws parallels between the experience of being "in this limited world of the hospital," where "I'll never be wrong or responsible for anything," as the narrator puts it, and the experience of life under communism, where the same is true—where everything is taken care of by the state and individuals have no responsibility. The novel won high praise from such feminists as Barbara Ehrenreich and Alice Walker. Many journalists, however, Jenny Turner of the *London Review of Books* (April 23, 1992) among them, deemed the book "one of those . . . solipsistic, well-written memory-rambles about which there is nothing much to say." For Barbara Finkelstein, writing in the *New York Times Book Review*, the novel represented "a missed opportunity" to explore "a political system that has all but prepared her narrator for a life in which a properly functioning kidney is a bourgeois extravagance, like 'Christmas trees, nail varnish . . . salt, sugar, longing for love, longing for water, pleasure.' The connection between hereditary kidney disease and foundering Communism may be strained, but the author herself makes it, and then retreats." On the other hand, for Lindsey Hughes, the reviewer for the *Times Literary Supplement* (January 31, 1992), *Holograms of Fear* succeeded in creating powerful images of "death and decay." "This is assured writing, even in translation, which works on many levels, not least that of political metaphor: the security of the hospital that no one can leave."

The Balkan Express: Fragments from the Other Side of the War, published in 1993, chronicles the devastating civil war in Yugoslavia; the essays in the book were written between April 1991 and May 1992. "War," Drakulic wrote, "came upon us like some sort of natural calamity, like the plague or a flood, inevitable, our destiny." She told Jim Hoagland for the *Washington Post* (April 28, 1993) that the "myth of Europe, of our belonging to the European family and culture, even as poor relations, is gone. We have been left alone with our newly won independence, our new states, new symbols, new autocratic leaders, but with no democracy at all. We are left standing on a soil slippery with blood, engulfed in a war that will go on for God knows how long."

Drakulic attempted to make the world aware of what was going on in Yugoslavia and to try to articulate—and change—what she believed was the West's position: "You are Balkans, mythological, wild, dangerous Balkans. Kill yourselves, if that is your pleasure. We don't understand what is going on there, nor do we have clear political interests to protect."

"The essays that make up . . . *The Balkan Express* read like notes on learning how to survive in a land at war and how to absorb the successive shocks of violent change and disruption," Francine Prose wrote in the *New York Times Book Review* (May 23, 1993). In the book's first essay, Drakulic describes herself in Cambridge, Massachusetts, explaining her country's divisions to American friends. She then presents her return to Zagreb, in what became the nation of Croatia, her subsequent escape from the bombings to Slovenia, her return to Zagreb while the fighting continues, and her experience of living with the chaos of a war. For Anthony Borden, who reviewed *The Balkan Express* for the *Nation* (May 17, 1993), Drakulic captured essential elements of living in a war-torn land: "This is firsthand war reporting without body counts or strategic analyses; in-depth political commentary without the statements of presidents or the opinions of self-appointed experts. Drakulic focuses on individual lives . . . using the perversions that war forces onto everyday life to reveal the true complexity of the crisis and the enormity of the task of reconciliation." Amanda Mitchison in *New Statesman & Society* (January 29, 1993) agreed, praising the "verisimilitude" of the book. "Some of the most moving essays are Drakulic's attempts to explain astonishing acts of treachery. . . . Inevitably, war . . . undermines our trust in the power of language, and the writer trying to convey . . . heightened internal reality must call on enormous powers both of expression and of restraint. That Drakulic accomplishes this balance . . . is probably the greatest achievement in this wise, profound and original book."

Marble Skin, a novel, was published in an English translation by Greg Mosse in 1994; it originally appeared in Serbo-Croatian as *Mramorna Koza* in 1987. Telling a complicated story of mother-daughter relations, it has as its nameless narrator a sculptor who creates a marble statue that she calls "My Mother's Body." Her mother, after seeing a newspaper photograph of the sculpture, makes her second suicide attempt. The daughter goes to her mother's bedside, where during a two-day vigil she relives memories of her own and her mother's past and of the stepfather who had a negative effect on both their lives. "Deftly alternating recurring images involving hands, moisture, whiteness and dust between contexts of sexuality and sculpturing, the author brings to life the inner lives of mother and daughter with clarity and power," Nicholas Christopher wrote in the *New York Times Book Review* (March 13, 1994). "Drakulic deals unflinchingly, and without jargon, pop psychologizing or editorial comment, with child abuse, incest and rape, making them the more horrible for the nearly suffocated voice in which her heroine speaks of them. In dealing with issues of deadly seriousness to men as well as to women—both politically and emotionally—she speaks, like her heroine, as powerfully with her silences as with her words," Christopher concluded.

In a review in the *Los Angeles Times* (March 5, 1995) of two books, *Slaughterhouse: Bosnia and the Failure of the West* by David Rieff, and *Sarajevo Daily: A City and Its Newspaper Under Siege* by Tom Gjelten, Drakulic expressed again her feeling that no one could truly epitomize the war in her country: "I have to admit that in the four years since the war in the Balkans began, I have slowly developed an aversion to reading books on the topic. Perhaps I just got tired of them, of words in general—mine as a skeptical Croatian writer as well as someone else's. At a certain point you feel saturated by words, you feel that nothing more could be written on—or read about—the war." Despite these sentiments, in an article published in the *Guardian* (May 7, 1995), Drakulic described how, a few days before the article came out, bombing by Serbs had resumed in the city of Zagreb, which had been "the only untouched oasis of normality in a country of no peace and no war," but where the people had been living in "blind hope" and a "need to negate reality." Drakulic wrote, "Last week Zagreb was forced to learn a tough lesson: in this war there are no guarantees, no protected zones and no privileges. It is simple, there is no peace. . . . This war is going to be long, and one has to live with this truth. But to live with it means to accept uncertainty. This is the most difficult thing to accept. The idea that we are exposed, vulnerable, endangered all the time, is quite unbearable. But in a war and in a big city, we are." Her voice continued to be raised in the *Guardian*, as on November 26, 1995, after the bombing: "Anger is the strongest feeling I have at this moment. Not joy, not happiness, not even satisfaction—but an overwhelming rage. . . . I guess that, while the war went on, nobody had time to ask: Why? The question sinks in now, at the chance of peace. Why all the immense suffering, why Sarajevo, why Mostar, why the horrors of Srebrenica? To have ethnically cleansed territories and then to applaud each other? . . . The worst fear I have, though, is that all of this will soon be forgotten. For this not to happen, to remember what this war was all about, someone should hang first."

In *Café Europa: Life After Communism*, published in England in 1996, Drakulic continued her English-language examination of the motivations underlying the conditions of Balkan life. The people in Eastern Europe had seen themselves as victims of discrimination and marginalization on the part of Western Europe, but had still dreamt of becoming a part of that Europe. "For Ms. Drakulic, however," Michiko Kakutani wrote in the *New York Times* (February 21, 1997), "the failure of Western Europe to prevent or intervene in the Bosnian war has demonstrated that the dream of Europe is just that: a dream." Although she had married a Swedish journalist and begun living mainly in Vienna—and also in Zagreb—Drakulic wanted to tell "readers what's going on in her part of the world by describing the color of her life," according to Jennifer Gould, who reviewed *Café Europa* for the *Village Voice* (March 11, 1997). For

Drakulic, the "first person plural" is something to be avoided, since "'We' means fear, resignation, submissiveness, a warm crowd and somebody else deciding your destiny." She observed that the "war in the Balkans is the product of that 'us'; of that huge, 20 million-bodied mass swinging back and forth in waves, then following their leaders into mass hysteria." Combating totalitarianism, she wrote, begins with saying "I." For Gould, "Drakulic is a voice of sanity and compassion who has much to say about a part of the world that is too often ignored."

Terming *Café Europa* an "important book from a very talented writer," Mary Hemmings noted in *Library Journal* (March 15, 1997) that Drakulic "knows how to explain to the urbane reader the passions and desires of a marginalized Eastern culture. . . . Rather than using the language of traditional economic and political analysis, Drakulic offers the language of everyday life to describe a momentous cultural evolution."

Drakulic continued to wear two hats as a writer: also in 1996, her novel *The Taste of a Man* was published in an English version by Christina Pribichevich-Zorich. The book is told from the point of view of Tereza, a Polish poet and graduate student who is studying at New York University. There, she meets Jose, a Brazilian anthropologist who has a wife and children in Brazil; he is examining a group of Uruguayan rugby players who resorted to cannibalism to survive a plane crash in the Andes. Tereza's passion for Jose leads her to find an unusual path to permanent union with him: she kills him, dismembers the body, and eats parts of him. "As a professional academic," Starr E. Smith wrote in *Library Journal* (June 1, 1997), "Tereza is skilled at defending theses: she presents her motivation and reasoning in logical, even dry, locutions." The book "offers some wry commentary on modern mores and the degrees of separation inhibiting male-female communication," Smith concluded.

"Drakulic is a very interesting writer and worth following," Susan Salter Reynolds observed in her review of *The Taste of a Man* in the *Los Angeles Times* (September 19,1997). "She does fascinating things with sensuality that are never skin-deep. . . . There is a fine tradition in literature of experimentation with the dark voice of the soul . . . and it is almost always a voice that spills onto the page with alarming ease. As Drakulic says at the novel's end: 'In time the pain will evaporate, just like the smell.'" For Kate Bingham, the *New Statesman* (April 11, 1997) reviewer, the real tension of the story lies in Tereza's exploration of "the intricate memory-triggers and thought processes leading to her final decision. . . . In the controlled, dispassionate voice of a true obsessive intent on rationalising her behaviour, Tereza . . . introduces the story with a chapter devoted almost entirely to house-cleaning."

The horrors of the Balkan war dominate *S: A Novel About the Balkans*, published in Great Britain as *As If I Am Not There*, in a 1999 translation by Marko Ivic. S, a victim of the rapes inflicted on Muslim women in a camp where they have been herded by Bosnian soldiers, gives birth in a Swedish hospital but refuses to nurse her baby. Although she wants to forget what has happened, the immediate past—the other women and the suffering in the camp—remain alive for her. "All she has succeeded in obliterating is her previous life, in which she was a teacher, with parents and a sister who once lived in Sarajevo," the *Publishers Weekly* (November 29, 1999) reviewer wrote. "She has vanished . . . into the depersonalized world of the raped, the refugee, the woman without a country. This novel . . . is a terrifying, graphic story of a country's lost identity, told through the suffering of the nameless inmates of the camp and their attempts to rebuild their lives after liberation."

Drakulic has published numerous essays in the *New Republic*, the *New York Review of Books*, the *New York Times*, the *Nation*, and other journals and periodicals. In 1999, in an article entitled "Intellectuals as Bad Guys" in *East European Politics and Societies* (Spring 1999), she wrote that although "words are not bullets," intellectuals, journalists, poets, and other writers "were very efficient in preparing the war" in Yugoslavia that started in 1991. "In order for a war to start, a psychological preparation of people is needed, and this is where poets, journalists, historians, and writers come in handy, either as hired guns or as real zealots. I saw it happening in Yugoslavia where I saw that a war does not start by shooting, throwing bombs, and burning houses. It starts slowly and gradually by first creating an enemy, or digging out an old one, presenting him as a threat." Drakulic has attempted to counteract such dishonesty, both in fiction and journalism. As she told Christine Spolar in an interview for the *Washington Post* (June 23, 1993), "The rule of my writing in fiction and nonfiction is to go where it hurts."

—S. Y.

SUGGESTED READING: *East European Politics and Societies* p271+ Spring 1999; *Economist* p83 Jan. 11, 1992; *Guardian* O p17 May 7, 1995, O p21 Nov. 26, 1995; *Library Journal* p76 Mar. 15, 1997, p146 June 1, 1997; *London Review of Books* p17 Apr. 23, 1992; *Los Angeles Times* p1 Mar. 5, 1995, p10 Sep. 19, 1997; *Nation* p112 May 17, 1993; *New Statesman* p49 Apr. 11, 1997; *New Statesman & Society* p47 Jan. 29, 1993; *New York Times* C p34 Feb. 21, 1997; *New York Times Book Review* Apr. 19, 1992, July 5, 1992; *Publishers Weekly* p53 Nov. 29, 1999; *Times Literary Supplement* p23 Jan. 31, 1992, p20 July 30, 1993; *Village Voice* p55 Mar. 11, 1997; *Washington Post* p19 Apr. 28, 1993, with photos, C p1 June 23, 1993, with photos; *Women's Review of Books* p1 May 1992

SELECTED BOOKS: fiction—*Holograms of Fear*, 1992; *Marble Skin*, 1994; *The Taste of a Man*, 1998; *S: A Novel of the Balkans*, 1999; nonfiction—*How We Survived Communism and*

Even Laughed, 1992; *The Balkan Express: Fragments from the Other Side of the War*, 1993; *Café Europa: Life After Communism*, 1996

Nancy Crampton/Courtesy of Houghton Mifflin Company

Drury, Tom

Sep. 22, 1956– Novelist; short-story writer

Tom Drury has written three novels, *The End of Vandalism* (1994), *The Black Brook* (1998), and *Hunts in Dreams* (2000), that have been praised for their minute detailing of the lives of characters who thrive on vagueness and misdirection. "Drury is tender toward his characters," Richard Eder wrote for the *New York Times* (May 18, 2000). "Meaning well, they occasionally manage to do well." Drury has been called the "Brontë of the 1990s," and in *The Black Brook*, he intentionally drew "three slender threads" from the Brontë sisters, in his use of ghosts, his inclusion of French words, and his choice of setting. Drury has also published short stories, in *Harper's Magazine*, the *New Yorker*, and the *Mississippi Review*. Like his novels, many of his stories display a deadpan wit and feature characters who, in dealing with everyday concerns, undergo transformations.

Tom Drury was born on September 22, 1956 in Mason City, Iowa, where he grew up and attended Rockwell-Swaledale High School. He graduated from the University of Iowa at Ames, in 1980, and then enrolled at Brown University, in Providence, Rhode Island, where he earned an M.A. degree in English and creative writing in 1987. He remained in New England to work as a reporter, first for the *Providence Journal*, in Rhode Island; then for the *News-Times*, in Danbury, Connecticut; and then for the *Litchfield County Times*, also in Connecticut.

Segments of Tom Drury's first novel, *The End of Vandalism*, appeared in the *New Yorker* before the entire book was published, in 1994. Set in imaginary Grouse County, Iowa, the novel touches on the lives of many people but focuses on three, among them Sheriff Dan Norman. Drury told Alix Boyle in an interview for the *New York Times* (June 9, 1996) that covering the police beat as a reporter proved to be helpful to him in developing Norman's character. As a journalist, he said, "you learn a lot about what a difficult job it is. People can be corrupt and some soldier through." In his novel, Dan catches Tiny Darling, a plumber and a thief, in the act of vandalizing an anti-vandalism display at the local high school. He tells Tiny's wife, Louise, what has happened; soon afterward she leaves Tiny and becomes involved with Dan, eventually marrying him. A laid-back sheriff, Dan is unused to domestic life, and after Louise becomes pregnant with his son, he seeks psychiatric care. At one point Dan is interviewed on a television news show. Questioning him about a foundling and a stolen bolt of cloth, the interviewer asks, "When do you expect results?" His reply illustrates Drury's matter-of-fact humor and underlying seriousness: "I don't know if you've ever watched a spider making a web," said Dan. "But I have, Shannon, and it takes a long time. . . . And even when this web is done somebody might come along and destroy it just by their hat brushing against it. Know what I mean?" Louise picked up the phone and dialed Dan's number. She did not expect him to be home, and the phone rang in that neutral way it does when no one is going to answer. But he did.

"A spider?" she said. "What the hell is that all about?"

"It's a metaphor," said Dan.

Wendy Smith, the reviewer for the *Washington Post Book World* (April 17, 1994), found that Drury's "gently musing narrative voice suits his low-key tale. Although there are "plenty of events—the stillbirth of Dan and Louise's child, the near-death in a snowstorm of a Taiwanese exchange student, a hotly contested election for county sheriff," she didn't see "much forward motion in the text, which often seems as aimless as its protagonists." Nevertheless, she wrote, "Drury's delightfully quirky secondary characters and deadpan, dry-as-prairie-dust humor" will engage readers who don't "demand a lot of narrative energy in a novel."

Eric Kraft, writing about *The End of Vandalism* for the *New York Times Book Review* (March 20, 1994), drew attention to Drury's "precise and carefully worked, accumulating declarative sentences that echo the monotony of the characters' lives and the landscape." He also noted that with the occurrence of "something significant, poignant, personal and painful" about two-thirds of the way through the book, the "whole tone" of the story changes. At this point, he wrote, "*The End of Vandalism* becomes much more than just another denigration of working-class culture in the amusing Midwest. Faced with his characters' suffering, Mr. Drury seems to discover his affection for them. . . . The protective shell of irony cracks, and his compassion shows." By depicting a loss, "then carrying his characters through it," Kraft wrote, Drury seemed to have "discovered the kind of informed sympathy for the living that the visitor to hell feels upon returning to the light, even to the gray light of Grouse County."

In 1996 Drury, a resident of Litchfield, Connecticut, was named among the New England regional winners of the Granta Award for the best new writers under 40. (The judges included Henry Louis Gates Jr., Tobias Wolff, and Anne Tyler.) In his interview with Alix Boyle, Drury declared himself delighted to receive the award, and, as a teacher of fiction at Wesleyan University, in Storrs, Connecticut, he offered some advice to young writers: try, he said, "to glean emotion, mystery and humor from everyday life." His essay "Living Dangerously," published in the *New York Times Magazine* (September 22, 1996), demonstrates that approach. Although content with their house in Providence, Drury wrote in his essay, he and his wife, who were new parents, moved several times after reading about the dangers of living near electrical transformers. They wound up in a house in Litchfield, where they discovered, among other lurking dangers, that their "tap water [was] laced with radon." "Since our homes in many cases existed before us and will remain after we die," Drury noted in his essay, "it is probably not unusual to suppose that they in fact wish us dead. . . . Think of the walls, blank and sinister. Think of the crawl space. Think of the nail points hanging like stalactites from the attic roof. Think of lead. Think of asbestos. Trouble is everywhere and always has been. In Colonial days, beverages served in pewter mugs formed toxic substances, and the big roaring fireplaces did in so many children that frying pans had Fear Hell engraved on the handles."

Drury's second novel, *The Black Brook* (1998), is about an accountant, Paul, who has laundered money for mobsters. His wife, Mary, a painter, creates skillful imitations of famous artworks. The couple have to enter the Federal Witness Protection Program after Paul testifies against the Mob. Meanwhile, Mary inherits a hotel in Brussels, Belgium, and she and Paul become innkeepers. Paul insists on returning to the U.S., however, and takes on a job at a New England newspaper. His former college housemates, a married couple, live in the same town, and Paul starts an affair with the wife. He also enters into a relationship with the ghost of a woman who has drowned and seeks out her daughter in Scotland.

Reviewers were divided on the merits of *The Black Brook*. Luc Sante wrote in the *New York Times Book Review* (July 26, 1998), "Drury has taken a genre plot—standard-issue but fairly somber—and used it as a frame on which to hang a novel of deadpan whimsy." He concluded, however, that the book left him "with a residual impression of enormous sadness" and that the "humor, invention and whimsy can seem . . . like whistling past the graveyard." Donna Seaman, writing for *Booklist* (July 1998), called Drury a "unique voice," and observed that he displayed "the same flair for crazy yet significant detail that shaped his first novel." She also noted his "gift for dazzlingly hilarious dialogue and startling juxtapositions of the mundane with the extraordinary."

In his third novel, *Hunts in Dreams* (2000), Drury returned to Grouse County and Charles "Tiny" Darling. Darling has remarried, and Drury described his new, blended family:

Charles Darling lived with his wife, Joan, their son, Micah, and Joan's daughter, Lyris, on two acres south of the town of Boris. The house had been built a hundred years ago and added on to forty years ago, and the two pieces did not much match. The older part was a dormered cottage, the newer part a boot room. All in all, the place was too small, especially since the arrival of Lyris, the daughter whom Joan had placed for adoption sixteen years before.

Joan, an executive in the animal-rescue movement, goes to a convention, where she begins an affair with a doctor. The doctor recites lines from Tennyson's "Locksley Hall" (from which the book gets its title), using the poem as a way of pointing out the unsatisfactoriness of Joan's marriage: "Like a dog, he hunts in dreams, and thou art staring at the wall." Joan, following her inchoate longings, leaves her husband. Meanwhile, Charles has been trying to retrieve his stepfather's shotgun from the minister's widow who has gained possession of it. Lyris is stalked, captured, and rescued. Micah, seven years old, struggles to learn to ride a bicycle. Minutely detailing these events, Drury enlarges the tapestry he is weaving of life in Grouse County.

For the most part, the critical response to *Hunts in Dreams* was highly favorable. "In *The End of Vandalism*," D. T. Max wrote for the *New York Times Book Review* (May 14, 2000), "Drury showed a flexible new voice. . . . One left the book with a sense of humanity and the idiosyncrasies of love. *Hunts in Dreams* is a more limited effort. Its canvas is smaller. It is often obvious: When Joan is adrift, she swims in a pool. When Charles is worried, he shores up his barn's foundations. The narrative scheme undercuts any hope of redemption the characters have. . . . Don't dismiss *Hunts in Dreams*, though. . . . When linked with the stronger *End of Vandalism*, the book has more charm. It gives off a sense of passing time, of that particular pleasure of a multipart novel, the roman-fleuve."

Richard Eder, who reviewed *Hunts in Dreams* for the *New York Times* (May 18, 2000), was especially taken with a scene in which Micah, unable to sleep, goes outside in the middle of the night and wanders through the town's empty streets. "It is one of a number of lovely passages," Eder wrote, "stretched between lyrical and cockeyed that give a Puck-like air to Drury's midsummer night's dream-hunt (even to its subliminal 'what fools these mortals be')." The critic for *Library Journal* (April 15, 2000), Brian Kenney, characterized Drury as "an absolutely delightful writer who has carved out a world of his own in American fiction, one that is odd, revealing, and yet filled with love." In *Hunts in Dreams*, Kenney reported, "things fall apart, but at the same time and in a nearly magical way, they begin to come together." The *Publishers Weekly* (February 28, 2000) reviewer lauded Drury's ability to depict a family on the verge of a major transition, "smalltowners who must compromise their unruly desires and confront their failures and weaknesses. . . . Those who do manage to break out of their daily existence, like Joan, face the horrifying prospect of a life beyond the accepted pattern, where one finds not freedom but an abyss of confusion. Drury portrays this potential unmooring with persuasive clarity. His gift for dead-on realism and unfussy dialogue reveals the humorous, edgy pathos of his characters and invests his story with the ambiguity of real life and the poignancy of unrealized dreams."

In a story entitled "Chemistry," published in the *New Yorker* (May 1, 2000), Drury encapsulated many of his themes. The main characters are Keith, who works as a cook in a small town café, the Road House, and Stella, who sings and plays the piano in the Road House. On tentative dates in the past, Keith and Stella have failed to mesh. They are brought together while searching in the woods for an old, retired chemist who has failed to meet his daughter after a movie and has disappeared. They come upon a deserted orchard and a mysterious shack that contains a "life-size wooden likeness of a man with an apple for a head." They discuss life and death. Later, without their help, the old man is found at the café. Keith wonders where the man has been:

> "Did you go to an orchard, Mr. Geer?" asked Keith. "Are you a ranger?" "No, I'm a chef." "'Along the solitary plain we walked / Like one who seeks the road that he has lost, / And, till he finds it, seems to walk in vain,'" Mr. Geer said. "You're not answering me." "Not really." "Then it's a mystery," Keith said as he tied his apron behind his back.

Drury currently lives with his wife and daughter in Litchfield, and he remains on the faculty of Wesleyan University. When he was asked, "What does being a writer do for you?" Drury responded, as quoted by *Oregon Live* (on-line), "It gets me closer to understanding who the hell I am."

—S. Y.

SUGGESTED READING: *Booklist* p1180 Mar. 1, 1994, p1434 Apr. 1, 2000; *Library Journal* p122 Apr. 15, 2000; *New York Times* CN p10 June 9, 1996, E p9 May 18, 2000; *New York Times Book Review* p11+ May 14, 2000; *New York Times Magazine* p116 Sep. 22, 1996; *New Yorker* p202+ May 1, 2000; *Publishers Weekly* p56 Feb. 28, 2000; *Washington Post Book World* p7 Apr. 17, 1994

SELECTED BOOKS: *The End of Vandalism*, 1994; *The Black Brook*, 1998; *Hunts in Dreams*, 2000

J. Tomas Lopez/Courtesy of W. W. Norton & Company

Dufresne, John

(du-FRAYNE)

Jan. 30, 1948– Novelist; short-story writer

The author of four critically acclaimed works, John Dufresne is often hailed as one of the most promising fiction writers to emerge in recent years. His books—which include the short-story collection *The Way That Water Enters Stone* (1991) and the novels *Louisiana Power & Light* (1994), *Love Warps the Mind a Little* (1997), and *Deep in the Shade of Paradise* (2002)—are typically brimming with eccentric characters, humorous plot twists, and metafictional narrative techniques; yet, they are also deceptively relevant, exploring such serious themes as death, loss, religion, and love. Betsy Burton, a bookstore owner, told Brandon Griggs for the *Salt Lake Tribune* (March 28, 1999), "It's his oddness that sets him apart from other writers. It's not just his quirky characters but the way he views things. He has a distinctive take on the human condition." Dufresne is also known as a writer of regional fiction: Hailing from the small northeastern town of Worcester, Massachusetts, he attended graduate school and later taught in the American South; nearly all of his published works are set in one of these two regions. When asked about his reputation as a "Southern" writer, Dufresne told Robert Birnbaum for *IdentityTheory* (2002, online), "I think all writing is regional. And often the term 'Southern writing' or any regional term is used pejoratively. It's meant to limit you to some kind of place. Which I think is ridiculous because all writing has to take place somewhere. In America there is a great tradition of Southern literature. It was the literature I loved when I was growing up. It's not why I moved to the South, but it's why I felt at home there, in a way. My imagination had been there. . . . I felt at home and intrigued by the storytelling tradition of the South. So I started writing about it. I write about the North, too."

For *World Authors 1995–2000*, John Dufresne writes: "I was born on January 30, 1948, in Worcester, Massachusetts. We lived at 16 Security Road. Security Road was a dusty, gravel street in the Lincolnwood Public Housing Project, a temporary development on the edge of town, constructed out of converted navy barracks. My father stoked coal at Worcester County Electric, and my mother worked nights on a folding machine at U.S. Envelope.

"We followed most of our Lincolnwood neighbors and moved to the Curtis Apartments. On June 9, 1953, we were eating dessert when my father looked toward the window and bolted out of his seat. I turned and saw the small maple tree out front, the one to which our television antenna was incongruously attached, bend in a wind and then fly away down the street. The windows in the house exploded. In less than a minute, the tornado had passed.

"We moved to Grafton Hill when I was seven, back to the neighborhood where my parents had grown up. I was an altar boy throughout my childhood, found great solace in the mysteries of the Latin Mass, the dark and empty church, the winedark light of the stain glass windows. Every Sunday my grandmother cooked brown potatoes and pot roast and boiled the life out of some string beans. And when the meal was over, someone perked a pot of coffee, and then we sat around and talked about the family and the neighbors. These were stories my grandfather, Pepere, told about smuggling alcohol from Montreal to Worcester during Prohibition. Stories my memere told about Pepere's latest drinking bout, how he shot up the radio, emptied the icebox, and hid the food under his bed. Stories about people we'd just seen that morning at Mass and the no-good they were up to. Gossip. Turns out that's the fiction writer's job: Listen to the gossip and spread it as far as you can.

"I started writing earnestly in high school. First I wrote poems because poems were my first literary love. Then when I read *Catcher in the Rye*, I heard a voice that I recognized, if not as my own, at least as familiar and compelling. I loved being in Holden's world. I didn't want to come back to mine. I was so transported, was so clear of my miserable high school life, that I wanted to be able to perform that same magic, that enchantment, on someone else. I would cast a spell with words.

"At Worcester State College I was an editor of the paper, President of the Student Government, acted in the theatrical productions. I worked as a draft counselor, as a tutor at the Quaker meeting. I wrote innumerable political leaflets, worked for SDS and the Progressive Labor Party in the Vietnam Summer Project. I married Marilyn Virbasius in 1972. I was still more politically than literarily engaged. I wanted to change the world one person at a time. For the next seven years I worked at various not-for-profit social service organizations, mostly working with troubled kids. All the while I was writing stories, trying to teach myself the craft. They reflected, I think, the literary Zeitgeist. Metafiction, jazzing around.

"And then things fell apart, all at once, as I approached the end of my twenties. The marriage ended. And then the government decided to spend money on drug treatment rather than prevention. So I was out of a job. I applied for admission into a creative writing program. In order to become a writer I knew I needed to leave town, family, friends, expectations, commitments, and the pressure to remain the same. I got in at the University of Arkansas.

"After my first class, William Harrison, my professor, told me I knew how to write but had no idea what a story was. He explained plot and detail. I went off to George's Majestic Lounge, sat down with a beer, and started a story called "Addie" which would make it to the *Intro 14*, a journal of the best of the AWP programs. It won the Henfield Foundation/*Transatlantic Review* award for fiction as well. I wrote "Surveyors" for workshop. It won a PEN Syndicated Fiction award.

"Cindy Chinelly waited around while I finished up and got my degree, and then we both got jobs in Monroe, Louisiana, at Northeast Louisiana University. We married. Tristan was born. We stayed for three years, and that's where I learned to write. Just sitting at the kitchen table late at night and writing story after story. We were on non-tenured lines at NLU. It was five years and out. We spent a year in Binghamton, New York, at SUNY where we'd both gotten into the Ph.D. creative writing program.

"I sent three stories off to Dick McDonough and said if you like them, I've got more. He became my agent. I was teaching an intro class in creative writing. Cindy was taking classes, teaching and cleaning houses. Someone was stealing the electricity in our apartment, finagling with our meter. My fellow students in workshop didn't know what a peckerwood was or a shotgun house. All the grad students were into deconstruction. We needed to leave before we lapsed into despair. I landed a job in Augusta, Georgia. I ran the Sandhills Writers Conference, taught creative writing. Dick McDonough called one day to tell me that Norton had taken the story collection. We left Augusta after a year because I got the job I thought would only come after many years and several books—a job teaching in an MFA program at Florida International University.

"When we arrived in South Florida, I thought we wouldn't stay. We moved here in the wake of race riots in Miami. I didn't like the congestion, the traffic, the development. But I sure liked the beach down the road. And I liked teaching at FIU. We actually bought a house after eleven years in rental apartments. I don't have to write in the kitchen anymore. I've got a converted sun porch which looks out over a mangrove swamp. I can see herons, storks, ibises, egrets, and iguanas out my windows."

Dufresne published his first book, *The Way That Water Enters Stone*, in 1991. In this collection of short stories, he presents a number of eclectic characters, whom Sybil Steinberg described for *Publishers Weekly* (January 11, 1991) as "desperately seek[ing] a salvation that they suspect will never come." She continued, "And yet, in just muddling through, [Dufresne's] drifters, fast-food clerks, farmers, innkeepers, movie addicts, loners and losers achieve a certain dignity." In one of the book's most memorable stories, "The Freezer Jesus," a brother and sister in Louisiana believe they see "the very face of Jesus," as quoted by Steinberg, in a smudge on their yellow Amana freezer; after word gets out, people from around the country begin making religious pilgrimages to their farm. (Dufresne later adapted this story for film, winning a screenwriting contest at Grand Valley State University, in Allendale, Michigan, that allowed students to produce the piece.) In another story, "Must I Be Carried to the Sky on Flowered Beds of Ease?" a man dying of AIDS returns to the home of his estranged father. Dufresne's two award-winning stories—the aforementioned "Addie" and "Surveyors," about a man dismantling his beloved tomato garden—are also featured, as well as stories set in Massachusetts, Louisiana, and Florida. The collection was widely praised by critics, who often compared Dufresne to such classic short-story writers as Andre Dubus and Flannery O'Connor. The book was named a *New York Times* Summer Reading Choice.

One story from Dufresne's debut collection, entitled "The Fontana Gene," became the basis for his first novel, *Louisiana Power & Light* (1994). That story and the expanded novel feature the Fontana family of Louisiana's Ouachita Parish, a lineage often afflicted with tragedy, which Dufresne attributes to "bad water in the gene pool," as quoted by David Mehegan for the *Boston Globe* (March 28, 2002). While the novel reports on the family's long-cursed past—recounting how many of the town's problems, historically, can be attributed to various members of the Fontana clan—much of the plot focuses on the last living descendants, Billy Wayne Fontana, and his successive wives, Earlene and Tami Lynne. As the novel opens, nuns are raising the orphaned Billy Wayne and training him for the priesthood, in the hopes that his celibacy will ultimately end the troubled family line. Yet, the plan goes awry when the 19-year old Billy Wayne is sent to conduct acts of mercy at the local hospital and meets Earlene, a young woman being treated for "female problems." He is quickly overtaken by her charm and the two elope. After enduring a tumultuous marriage, Billy Wayne and Earlene separate when he takes a job at the electric company, Louisiana Power & Light. He weds his second wife, Tami Lynne, and the two become parents to Duane Pargoud and Boone Kyle (nicknamed Moon Pie), who is born with flippers instead of legs and is considered a genius. Ultimately, the novel encompasses the Fontana's family saga and much more, with Dufresne frequently interjecting tales about Louisiana politics and the eccentric Southern community. Jill McCorkle described for the *New York Times* (July 31, 1994), "Mr. Dufresne's storytelling methods reflect those of his townspeople. He offers a plot line as complex as the network of backwoods roads these people and their ancestors have committed to memory. The miraculous beauty of his tale-telling is that dead ends simply do not exist." Of Dufresne's frequently meandering sub-plots and colorful vignettes—delivered in "perfectly pitched Southern vernacular," according to McCorkle—the reviewer noted, "There isn't a single one that isn't well worth the time."

Writing for *Booklist* (July 1994), Bill Orr opined, "Dufresne's novel is a beguiling mix of [William] Faulkner and Barry Gifford. He takes this nearly surrealistic story of southern-style squalor well beyond parody, making us care about his white-trash cast even though we know our caring will lead to pain." In a review for the *Boston Globe* (July 31, 1994), Louise Kennedy praised the novel's depth, noting, "At its heart . . . is a profound and soulful seriousness. Not for nothing does the title evoke, besides a down-home utility company, thoughts of a more divine currency; the images of God's power and light are frequent and unmistakable. Over and over, Dufresne gets you laughing out loud, only to remind you, with a sudden phrase of deep and shuddering beauty, that what he is really writing is a very, very funny book about Life Itself—and about every other big issue from memory to religion, from the persistence of the past to the immortality of the soul." Peter Landry called the book "a spiritual farce" in the *Chicago Tribune* (August 10, 1994), and added, "Both raucous and wise, it lures us into introspection with humor, and amid guffaws brings home truths about faith and heritage, chance and genealogy." *Louisiana Power & Light* was selected as a 1994 *New York Times* Notable Book of the Year. Dufresne is currently completing a screenplay of the novel for Miramax, which has announced plans to produce the film, starring the actor-director Billy Bob Thornton.

In 1996 Dufresne collaborated with a group of 13 other Miami writers on the mystery novel, *Naked Came the Manatee*. (The title parodies another collaborative book, the controversial sex novel *Naked Came the Stranger*, which was written by a group of 25 journalists in 1969.) Along with such notable writers as Dave Barry, Carl Hiaasen, and Elmore Leonard, Dufresne contributed one chapter to the outlandish story. Of the experience he told Griggs, "It wasn't great literature. How could it be? But it was a hoot."

In his second novel, *Love Warps the Mind a Little* (1997), Dufresne sets the story in Massachusetts, this time presenting the first-person narrative of Lafayette Proulx (nicknamed Laf), a 36-year-old aspiring writer. Disenchanted with life, Laf quits his job as a high-school teacher, leaves his wife of 14 years (who kicks him out when she learns of his infidelity), and moves in with his girlfriend, Judi, a psychotherapist from a highly dysfunctional family. Laf spends much of his time writing stories at Judi's kitchen table and accumulating a mound of rejection letters from various fictional journals, including *Timber Wolf Review*, *Pond Apple*, and *Incomplete Flower*. He engages in another affair, with a clerk in a health-food store, and becomes suspicious that Judi has cheated on him as well. The novel builds towards its climax when Judi is diagnosed with ovarian cancer and Laf becomes her full-time caregiver. Dufresne explained his motivation for the plot shift to John Barron for the *Chicago Sun–Times* (March 2, 1997). "I thought the story would be about how this guy gets thrown out of his home and then works his way back to his wife," he said. "It would be about what he would learn about himself and his writing and how he learns that his marriage is important to him." Yet, when the vibrant character of Judi entered the novel, Dufresne found her too captivating to abandon. "She was just too good to leave," he told Barron. Ultimately, the novel explores the relationship between Laf and Judi, as it develops into genuine love. At one point Laf muses, "I used to believe that love and happiness were synonymous," as quoted by Karen Karbo for the *New York Times* (February 16, 1997). "I was a fool. . . . Judi and I had much love, I think, but little pleasure. And that's O.K. Pleasure is, after all, a luxury. It's love that's essential."

The critical response to *Love Warps the Mind a Little* was generally positive, though some critics lamented Dufresne's tendency to include too many extraneous characters and sub-plots, such as Judi's schizophrenic father or Laf's story-within-a-story about a couple named Theresa and Dale. Nevertheless, others applauded the humor and candor with which Dufresne presents the book's weightier material. As Richard Bernstein noted for the *New York Times* (February 7, 1997), "[The novel] could, given the dying girlfriend, become a maudlin melodrama, a kind of *Love Story* for the 1990s. But Mr. Dufresne . . . is an abundantly talented storyteller with a habit for droll, self-referential parody. He has fashioned a funny, tenderhearted, melancholy book marinated in a keen sense of the absurdities of everyday life." Dennis Drabelle, writing for the *Washington Post* (February 9, 1997), affirmed, "*Love Warps the Mind a Little* seems to have been not so much written as taken down while it was happening, with the real-life counterparts of its febrile characters gathered around, waving their hands, agitating for attention, clearing their throats to dictate their life stories." Several reviews acknowledged Dufresne's skill in presenting a novel that transcended what Karbo called "your usual comic romp," and Richard Bernstein opined, "The jokes are what make the deeper message bearable; it is about looking at the world the way it is and, as Laf says at the end, knowing not to turn away." Dufresne's second novel was named a *New York Times* Notable Book of the Year.

In *Deep in the Shade of Paradise* (2002), his third novel, Dufresne resurrects the Fontana clan, providing a sequel to the chaotic family tale he began in *Louisiana Power & Light*. He explained his impulse to Mehegan: "I wanted to know what was going on with Earlene, who was pregnant at the end of the story. To find out what she was up to and who this kid [Boudou] would be, I started writing. The only way to find out is to write. So I found out that he has this incredible memory. I was attracted to his innocence and his memory. I wanted him to remain innocent and see how that would affect other people, so I needed another central character, and I found this guy Adlai Birdsong." When the novel begins, 11-year-old Boudou—who was conceived on the day his father, Billy Wayne Fontana, died in 1988—is attending a wedding with his extended family at the brood's ancestral home, a plantation named Paradise in the Louisiana town of Shiver-de-Freeze. There Grisham Loudermilk (Earlene's cousin) is set to wed Ariane Thevenot, who works as a chicken-sexer at a poultry plant. Conflict arises when Grisham engages in a last lusty fling with an ex-girlfriend, and Boudou's cousin Adlai falls in love with the bride. In the meantime, a number of Dufresne's characteristically eccentric characters infiltrate the narrative with their own capricious subplots, each contributing to the chaotic nature of the story. Despite its exaggerated humor, the book examines such larger themes as loss and love. Many reviewers compared Dufresne's meandering narrative style to that of William Faulkner; and in a review for the *Los Angeles Times* (March 12, 2002), Bernadette Murphy likened the novel to Shakespeare's *A Midsummer Night's Dream*, told "in pungent Cajun-Creole fashion."

The critical response to *Deep in the Shade of Paradise* was decidedly mixed. Most reviews focused on Dufresne's excessive reliance on the grotesque, his tendency toward narrative experimentation, and his general evasion of a traditional, linear plot. While some critics found these qualities refreshing and imaginative, others lamented that they made for difficult reading. Jeff Zaleski noted for *Publishers Weekly* (November 19, 2001), "The all-out quirkiness of Dufresne's sparkling . . . novel may put some readers off, but others will surely think this talented writer's time has come." Erica Noonan described for the *Boston Globe* (February 22, 2002), "There are so many characters, vivid details, and story threads here; readers will have no choice but to flip back and forth to a set of family trees in the front of the book. But as the author himself asserts midway through, 'plots are for graveyards.' This novel is meant to read like a three-ring circus, helped along by an occasional narrator who cuts through the din, offering folksy advice and opinions." Nevertheless, she added, "There are a handful of moments where the story gets too outrageous for its own good." In a review for the *Washington Post* (April 14, 2002), Curtis Sittenfeld affirmed, "Though some readers will no doubt delight in Dufresne's colorful, exuberant language, the language is not enough to carry the book. Most scenes, no matter how consequential, are brief, and the dialogue is often unrealistic. . . . Ostensibly, Dufresne is celebrating wacky Southern culture. However, because it is so difficult to identify with or care about any of the characters, it's as if Dufresne is winking at the reader over the characters' heads." Bernadette Murphy, however, lavishly praised the book and called it "perfect for losing yourself in, for drifting off and forgetting about all the paperwork you need to gather for tax-filing day, the chores around the house calling for your attention and the grass you're supposed to be mowing. This is one to sweep you away to a gloriously off-center notion of paradise."

Dufresne has recently completed an instructive book on the writing process entitled "The Lie That Tells the Truth," which is set for release late in 2003. In addition, he is working on his second short-story collection and his fourth novel.

Dufresne has been honored with a *Yankee Magazine* Fiction Award (1988), a Florida State Arts Council grant (1992), and an honorary doctorate of literature from Worcester State College (1999). He holds memberships in the National Writers Union, the Authors Guild, the National Council of Teachers of English, and the Popular Culture Association in the South.

John Dufresne currently resides in Dania Beach, Florida, with his wife and son. Of his approach to writing fiction, he told Eve Richardson for *Poets & Writers* (March–April 2002, on-line), "The most important question a fiction writer can ask is 'Why?' I write to try to figure out the things in life I don't understand. I confront the human condition. What makes us human, what we have in common, is trouble." He added, "I'm dead serious in my books. I don't think tragedy is ever trivial. Illness and death are so serious, in fact, that we cannot bear them without relief."

—K. D.

SUGGESTED READING: *Boston Globe* B p27 July 31, 1994, D p4 Feb. 22, 2002, D p1 Mar. 28, 2002; *Chicago Sun–Times* p4 Mar. 2, 1997; *Chicago Tribune* p5 Aug. 10, 1994; *IdentityTheory* (on-line) 2002; *National Public Radio Morning Edition* Sep. 8, 1994; *New York Times* VII p9 July 31, 1994, C p33 Feb. 7, 1997, VII p11 Feb. 16, 1997, VII p24 June 9, 2002; *Poets & Writers* (on-line) Mar.–Apr. 2002; *Publishers Weekly* p46 Nov. 19, 2001, p47 Mar. 11, 2002; *Salt Lake Tribune* D p5 Mar. 28, 1999; *Telegram & Gazette* C p1 Mar. 1, 2002; *Washington Post* X p6 Feb. 9, 1997, T p6 Apr. 14, 2002; *World & I* p230+ July 2002

SELECTED BOOKS: short-story collections—*The Way That Water Enters Stone*, 1991; novels—*Louisiana Power & Light*, 1994; *Love Warps the Mind a Little*, 1997; *Deep in the Shade of Paradise*, 2002

Jerry Bauer/Courtesy of Grove/Atlantic

Dunmore, Helen

1952– Novelist; short-story writer; poet

In her early work, the English poet, short-story writer and novelist Helen Dunmore explored the lives of women through a feminist lens. Though feminist themes continue to surface in her writing, other themes appear in her later works, such as childhood innocence, the invasion of past into present, and the human propensity for evil. In *Literary Review* (September 1999), Barbara Trapido wrote, "In Dunmore's novels, the battered corpse, the drowned man, the homeless woman lying drunk in a doorway—any one of these could be you. There is the open-eyed stare at the seamier aspects of contemporary life, which she balances against the lovely, tender glimpses of childhood that linger to give the reader shreds of hope." These "tender glimpses of childhood" also appear in her many books for children. For Dunmore, childhood seems to offer the only real relief from the bleakness of adult life. "How can you call people good, knowing the capacity for evil that we all have, given the opportunity?" Dunmore asked interviewer Suzie Mackenzie in the *Guardian* (August 26, 1999). "Isn't that the story of our century, the lesson we have to learn? That only vigilance can prevent evil. That it's very easy to destroy structures and very hard to make them strong." Although, Dunmore's award-winning writing is at times stark, it also exhibits compassion, a keen sensuality, and a sharp eye for detail.

Dunmore was born in Yorkshire, England, in 1952, the second of four children. Her father, the manager of an industrial firm, was frequently forced to relocate. Dunmore told Mackenzie of her family's moves, "It made me an observer. I was always coming into situations from the outside." Dunmore was taught the typical skills that girls were expected to learn growing up in the 1950s, a tradition which Dunmore would later question in her writing. "I belonged to perhaps the last generation of little girls who learned to hand-stitch blouses in primary school," Dunmore wrote in the *Guardian* (January 6, 2000). "We cut out from cheap, vomit-colored cotton print, provided by our teacher." When she was 18, her parents moved to the United States, but Dunmore chose not to go. She attended York University and received a B.A. in English in 1973.

Her mother was a great storyteller, and as an adult Dunmore grew interested in telling stories herself. Her first book was a volume of poetry entitled *The Apple Fall* (1983). One theme addressed in the collection is the way male poets have often categorized women without giving real credence to women's voices. The volume also includes poems about the writers Zelda Fitzgerald and Virginia Woolf, as well as poems in which Dunmore rewrites familiar stories, such as that of the Virgin Mary. Dunmore's second collection of poetry, *The Sea Skater*, was published in 1986 and won the Poetry Society's Alice Hunt Bartlett Award. Many of the poems focus on the uncertain footing that women have in the world, as domestic relationships become strained and ecological disaster clouds the future. In another volume of poetry, *The Raw Garden* (1988), Dunmore contemplated the relationship between humans and nature, including the bond formed with nature through gardening. An avid gardener herself, Dunmore wrote in the *Guardian* (April 17, 2000), "A garden is a secret place, no matter how open it may appear. Only the gardener knows where the sun falls at each season of the year, where the frost pockets are, where extra drainage is needed, where red-hot pokers will blaze against a sunny wall, where valerian will self-seed in stony ground." *The Raw Garden* was awarded the Poetry Book Society Choice.

Dunmore's first novel, *Zennor in Darkness*, was published in 1993 and won the McKitterick Prize. It takes place during World War I and tells the story of a young painter named Clare Coyne and her awakening following her acquaintance with the writer D. H. Lawrence, who has moved with his wife to Clare's town. Like Lawrence, Clare is the product of a marriage of mixed classes. Her mother is the daughter of a tradesman, and her father is an Oxford scholar and amateur botanist. Clare confronts death when her lover and cousin, John William, returns from the war on leave and commits suicide. In the wake of this event, and partly with the guidance of Lawrence, who becomes her mentor, Clare wrestles to form her identity, which manifests itself through her art and her newly rekindled sexuality. Wendy Brandmark wrote in *New Statesman & Society* (February 1993) that Dunmore's characterizations were not always convincing, but that she "writes with the careful hand of the poet. Her touch is subtle, delicate: like any good poet she lets her images speak for her."

In 1994 Dunmore published *Recovering a Body*, a collection of poetry that Bill Greenwell, in *New Statesman & Society* (May 13, 1994), praised as "surefooted, observant, a lovely blend of surreal outings and glimpses of barefaced reality." Dunmore's second novel, *Burning Bright*, also came out that year. It tells the story of a young, rather naive woman, Nadine, who moves in with her lover, Kai, and his business partner, Tony. Also in the apartment complex is Enid, an elderly lady with whom Nadine forms a powerful friendship.

For her next novel, *Spell of Winter* (1995), Dunmore was awarded the 1996 Orange Prize for English Language Fiction, winning out over such authors as Amy Tan and Anne Tyler. The prize itself, first established in 1996, stirred up controversy in England because of its $46,000 purse, the largest in England at that time, and the fact that only women were eligible for the award. A. S. Byatt and Anita Brookner, two successful female authors, spoke out against the prize, criticizing it for encouraging the use of different critical criteria for male and female writers. The prize, intended in part to draw attention to the achievements of female writers, did stimulate sales of Dunmore's book. *Spell of Winter* tells the story of two siblings abandoned by their parents. Their father is committed to an asylum; their mother runs away. The children are left to raise themselves, and, later, to deal with the crushing bonds that tie them together. Dunmore's grandfather was abandoned by his mother, and the theme of abandonment is one that recurs in her writing. Her great-grandmother brought two of her children with her when she immigrated to Canada, but left two behind in England, including Dunmore's grandfather, because of economic necessities.

Talking to the Dead (1996) was Dunmore's first novel published in the United States. Nina, a London-based photographer, goes out to the country to visit her older sister, a beautiful, neurotic, housewife named Isabel. Having recently given birth to her first child, Isabel is obsessed with him to the exclusion of everyone else in her circle, including her husband, Richard, with whom Nina starts an affair. While ruminating over her sister's inattentiveness, Nina dredges up old memories, in particular, those of their baby brother, Colin, who had died 25 years ago, apparently of crib death. The novel takes on elements of a thriller as Nina questions whether Colin's death was indeed a natural one, and Isabel descends into madness. Critics praised Dunmore for weaving a compelling plot without losing the complexity of style and sophistication of theme often absent in plot-intensive genre fiction. "Helen Dunmore . . . takes a tale that could drive a thriller and weaves her linguistic spell around it," Carolyn Banks wrote in the *Washington Post* (August 10, 1997). "The result is brilliant and terrifying, an unbeatable combination." A reviewer for *People Weekly* (September 29, 1997) wrote, "The prose is limpid—the descriptions of food are voluptuous, the sex scenes urgent and raw—and Dunmore's plotting is masterful."

In 1997 Dunmore published a volume of poetry in the United States called *Bestiary* which includes poems with titles such as "Basketball player on Pentecost Monday" and "The Wasp." In *Library Journal* (January 1998) Louis McKee wrote, "Her menagerie includes tigers, toads, and tortoises, as well as muggers and murderers. Her keen sense of story and lyrical voice will reward many readers. . . . there's something for everybody here." Also in 1997, Dunmore published a collection of short stories entitled *Love of Fat Men*. The title story is about Ulli, who loves to sleep on the pillowy chests and shoulders of fat men. Many of the stories explore the multi-layered nature of relationships. In "North Sea Crossing" a father and son are forced into self-awareness by the crisis that ensues after an accident at sea. In "Short Days, Long Nights" a woman wakes up to find a strange man in her bed and isn't sure whether he's alive or dead.

Dunmore's novel *Your Blue-eyed Boy* (1998) is the story of a 38-year-old English district judge named Simone. When Simone receives a strange letter from Michael, an ex-lover who had taken nude pictures of her 20 years earlier, she suspects black-mail. Married, with two young children, working a job she dislikes, and facing financial difficulties, Simone is less than content with her life. When Michael shows up in her village she struggles to protect herself and her family from this intruder, but aspects of her past inevitably creep up and shed light on her present life. *Your Blue-eyed Boy* did not quite elicit the enthusiastic critical response that had met *Talking to the Dead*. In *Library Journal* (May 15, 1998), Caroline M. Hallsworth wrote, "Simone never emerges as a truly sympathetic character, and the novel lacks the spark to captivate readers totally." Similarly, Mark Lindquist wrote in the *New York Times Book Review* (September 6, 1998) that Dunmore "overloads her story with peripheral detail. By the end, the reader may be skimming pages, but not necessarily to find out what happens next." A reviewer for *Kirkus Reviews* (April 15, 1998) found more to like. "Dunmore confidently mines a number of subtle themes: the emotional perils of rendering judgment, the lure of vulnerability, the surprising power of memory, in spare, graceful prose. A haunting and psychologically dense exploration, then, that reads as effortlessly as a standard-issue thriller."

Once more, in *With Your Crooked Heart* (1999), Dunmore combined aspects of the thriller novel with a psychologically complex depiction of life. Louise is a sad, overweight woman who has lost custody of her child to her ex-husband, Paul, due to her alcoholism. Paul is a successful and ruthless businessman, who is trying to save his younger brother, Johnnie, from a life of crime. He doesn't realize that his daughter, Anna, is really Johnnie's, the product of Johnnie's affair with Louise years ago. When Johnnie gets into trouble with some vengeful crooks and looks to Louise for help, the two of them flee together. Meanwhile, the neglected, 10-year-old Anna and her friend have decided to run away with some of Louise's money, and Paul goes in pursuit.

With Your Crooked Heart is an unsentimental depiction of the downward spiral of a woman's life. Dunmore, in a article in the *Guardian* (November 11, 1999), wrote about her portrayal of Louise: "I wanted to trace the route she takes exactly, without cliché or sensationalism." The result is a stark novel, which led Dana Kennedy to write in the *New York Times* (March 12, 2000), "There's no real light in this twisting, sensually written tale." The children add to the novel a sense of relief and innocence, and Dunmore's skill in rendering Louise drew praise from critics. Katy Emck wrote in the *Guardian* (September 4, 1999), "What makes this desolate train of events into a compelling read is Dunmore's way of drawing you into the very fabric and grain of Louise's life and thoughts."

Dunmore's second collection of short stories, *Ice Cream*, was published in 2000. Ulli, who appeared in *Love of Fat Men*, makes her return in several stories. As a French exchange student, Ulli is lonely, unhappy, and pregnant. In another story, she goes home with a strange man whose various facial parts bear resemblance to exotic vegetables and who hordes religious icons in his apartment. In "My Polish Teacher's Tie," a school cafeteria worker is ashamed to admit she isn't a teacher when her Polish pen-pal makes a surprise visit to her at work. Dunmore experiments with science-fiction in "Leonardo, Michael, Superstork," in which women wear devices to screen out genetically inferior sperm and natural conception is widely replaced by cloned-embryo implantation. Though reviewer Harriet Lane felt the quality of the stories in *Ice Cream* was somewhat uneven, she wrote in the *Guardian* (April 9, 2000), "Dunmore's talent guarantees that the flavour lasts long after you've put the spoon down."

Most recently, Dunmore published *The Siege* (2001), a novel set in Leningrad, circa 1941, as the German army is rapidly advancing. When the Germans do invade during that winter, laying siege to the city and burning its only food reserves, the 22-

year-old Anna Levin, an artist and school teacher, battles desperation and starvation to keep her family alive. Enduring freezing conditions with food rations of only two slices of bread per day, Anna cares for her five-year-old brother, her invalid father, and her father's former mistress. In the harshest days of winter, she meets and falls in love with a doctor, Andre, in whom she finds a strong sense of hope for the future. *The Siege* was highly acclaimed by critics, who often praised Dunmore's authentic depiction of time and place. Writing for *Booklist* (December 1, 2001), Elsa Gaztambide described the book, "Heart-wrenching to read, but impossible to put down, this is quite an inspirational book." Meanwhile, Jeff Zaleski for *Publishers Weekly* (October 22, 2001) opined, "Dunmore has built a sizable audience [in the U.S.] with her seven previous novels, but this book should lift her to another level of literary prominence." *The Siege* was nominated for Britain's 2002 Orange Prize for fiction.

In 2001 Dunmore published a comprehensive collection of her poetry over the last 25 years, in *Out of the Blue: Poems, 1975–2001*. She has also written a number of children's books, which have been published primarily in England and include *Brother Brother, Sister Sister* (2000), *Zillah & Me* (2000), *Allie's Rabbit* (1999), *Allie's Apples* (1997), and *Amina's Blanket* (1996). Dunmore lives in Bristol, England and also works as a nursery school teacher. She is married and has several children of her own. As she continues to write, for both adults and children, she maintains that raising a family is not a restriction on her writing. In the *Guardian* (January 6, 2000) she wrote, "Women writers who have children are often asked about them as if they are nothing but an impediment, or even a shackle that prevents the writer soaring off into boundless creativity. But I think it's much more complex and fruitful than this."

—P. G. H.

SUGGESTED READING: *Guardian* (on-line) Aug. 26, 1999, Jan. 6, 2000; *Literary Review* (on-line) Sep. 1999; *New Statesman & Society* p38 Feb. 19, 1993; *New York Times Book Review* p12 June 1, 1997, p16 Sep. 6, 1998; *Washington Post Book World* p8 Aug. 10, 1997

SELECTED BOOKS: novels—*Zennor in Darkness*, 1993; *Burning Bright*, 1994; *Spell of Winter*, 1995; *Talking to the Dead*, 1996; *Your Blue-Eyed Boy*, 1998; *With Your Crooked Heart*, 1999; *The Siege*, 2001; poetry—*Apple Fall*, 1983; *Sea Skater*, 1986; *Raw Garden*, 1988; *Recovering a Body*, 1994; *Bestiary*, 1997; *Out of the Blue: Poems, 1975–2001*, 2001; short-story collections—*Love of Fat Men*, 1997; *Ice Cream*, 2000; juvenile—*Going to Egypt*, 1994; *In the Money*, 1995; *Amina's Blanket*, 1996; *Allie's Apples*, 1997; *Clyde's Leopard*, 1998; *Allie's Rabbit*, 1999; *Brother Brother, Sister Sister*, 2000; *Zillah & Me*, 2000

Courtesy of Matt Valentine

Dunn, Stephen

June 24, 1939– Poet

Over the course of a prolific career, the American poet Stephen Dunn has produced 12 collections of poetry, a collection of essays and memoirs, and a book of prose-poem meditations. Dunn's poetry has been described by critics as "wise," "witty," "gentle," "plain-spoken," and "passionate," and contrasted against the style and tone predominant in the poetry of his peers. Dunn's poems are often anecdotal or narrative; the poet and critic Jonathan Holden has described them as having the quality of a man "overhearing" himself, as quoted by Stan Sanvel Rubin in the *Literary Review* (Summer 1987). The poet and critic Stephen Dobyns, writing in the *New York Times Book Review* (January 28, 1990, on-line), described the poet's language as that of "a man remarking on the world around him, a sort of idealized speech." Dunn's unembroidered style and ironic humor have prompted comparisons both to the American poet William Carlos Williams and the film writer and director Woody Allen. In 1995 he received an Academy Award in Literature from the American Academy of Arts and Letters, and he has also earned fellowships from the National Endowment for the Arts and the Guggenheim Foundation. In addition, he garnered the 2001 Pulitzer Prize for poetry for his recent volume, *Different Hours* (2000). Since winning the New York City Poetry Discovery Award in 1971, Dunn has given hundreds of public readings at colleges, universities, and other venues.

In an autobiographical statement for *World Authors 1995–2000*, submitted in 2000, Dunn writes, "I was born in Forest Hills, New York, in 1939, and grew up there in a predominantly Jewish neighborhood. My parents, brother, and I lived in my maternal grandparents' house, a fact that I never questioned at the time, but which has seemed increasingly odd as I've grown older. My mother and father never moved out. My grandfather, Montefiore Fleischman, was a Jew who'd married Isabel MacKenzie, a Scotch Protestant. Their only child, my mother, married my father, a salesman who was Irish Catholic, and she converted to Catholicism eleven years after promising to do so. I was raised Catholic, a much-loved child in a family that for many years was harmonious. But that harmony broke down in my early teens (several of my early poems deal with this), causing a consciousness that not only made me turn inward, but with new empathy outward as well. My book of memoirs and essays, *Walking Light*, details this family drama.

"I was an athlete who eventually would go to Hofstra University [in Hempstead, New York] on a basketball scholarship and major in history. But more significantly, given what I've become, I was a Catholic with a somewhat Jewish sensibility. What that means exactly, I'm not sure. I suspect it has something to do with seeing the world as a place fraught with dangers, thus the need to circle the wagons, be suspicious and smart, trust that knowledge might save you. I suppose the unorthodox Catholic side of me made it easier for me to be relatively casual about such consciousness. I always told lies in Confession, which were no doubt among my earliest fictions. Though I went through First Communion and later was Confirmed, for some reason I never believed in Heaven or Hell. Even as a boy I suspected that one's rewards and punishments would occur here on earth.

"In retrospect, Jewish angst and Christian forgiveness, maybe with a tad of Irish élan, combined to form in me a certain awkward carriage, a way of being a stranger to myself and others. But athletics permitted me to get by with being such a stranger. I was my performance; little more was expected of me. It took years for me to realize that I was *all* of my personalities, and that multiple identities were not a form of insanity. Some of my early poems were for me clarifications and understandings of those truths.

"All my friends, except one, were Jewish. I never dated a non-Jewish girl until I was around twenty-one. We literally had no books in our house, but in his later years my Jewish grandfather every day would borrow a book from the lending library (at the local pharmacy), read it, and return it the next morning. I suspect he was the reason that I became a serious reader. He also was a very good storyteller. My father, whom I've come to think of as more heroic than tragic (as I originally thought), remained charming even when his luck turned bad. He may have instructed me in a certain stoicism and endurance. My mother believed in me even when it seemed she shouldn't have.

"In college I wrote a little fiction, no poetry. I had some facility with language, yet had few models for how to take myself seriously as a writer. One, Sam Toperoff, a friend, helped me considerably when I finally began to move in his direction. The others, though I didn't know they were so serving me, were the writers themselves—Dostoyevski, Hemingway, Frost, Stevens. At the time, they seemed too large to be emulated.

"After college I wrote brochures for a corporation in New York City and was alarmingly successful. In the evenings I would attempt to write stories. Perhaps the major turning point in my 'writing life' occurred after I met my wife (now of 35 years) Lois, an international flight attendant. She supported me when I wanted to quit that well-paying corporate job, and happily went with me to Spain where we lived for almost a year on $2200. I went to write a novel and ended up writing the poetry that would encourage me to believe I might have a chance of becoming a poet. I was twenty-seven.

"In graduate school at Syracuse University [in Syracuse, New York] in 1969, I was lucky enough to study with Philip Booth, George P. Elliott, Donald Justice, and W. D. Snodgrass. I knew very little about contemporary poetry when I arrived, or what it meant to be a poet. By the time I left, I had a rather keen sense of each. I had not only found a group of very good writers and teachers, but people who demonstrated, by example, a high-minded sense of the enterprise. It was exactly what I needed.

"I'd like to think I've been engaged in an ongoing process, a process that in great retrospect could look like a quest to write a poetry of intense clarities in service of the complexity and mystery of our daily lives. *Our*, I emphasize, not just mine. But, in practice, of course, I just wrote the poems that came to me. And since I was forty-five or so when I started to believe I knew something about that process and practice, I've been writing essays on poetics. My eleventh book of poems, *Different Hours*, will be published by Norton in October of 2000. And a new and expanded edition of my 1993 book, *Walking Light: Essays & Memoirs*, will be issued by BOA Editions Ltd. in the spring of 2001.

"I've taught poetry and fiction writing at Richard Stockton College of New Jersey [in Pomona] since 1974, where I'm presently Trustee Fellow in the Arts. I've taught at Columbia University and the University of Washington and will be visiting professor at the University of Michigan in the spring semester of 2001."

Dunn's first poetry collection is entitled *Five Impersonations* (1971). After the publication of Dunn's second collection of poetry, *Looking for Holes in the Ceiling* (1974), critics began to notice a voice remarkably different from the prevalent spirit of the age. In *New Letters*, Robert Wilson praised the collection, as quoted by *Contemporary Authors* (1998), as "poems which strike a blow for life" in the midst of the dark and suicidal themes in the poetry of Sylvia Plath and Anne Sexton, to name two prominent examples. Reviewing *Local*

Time (1986), a later collection of poems, for the *New York Times Book Review* (July 6, 1986), Andy Brumer alluded to Dunn's humanism. "Mr. Dunn is everybody's friendly neighbor. . . . He is good, and his obsession with moral and ethical propriety both distinguishes his poetry and slightly alienates those of us who cannot quite resolve our own problems with gentleness and understanding." Brumer goes on to describe another side to Dunn's poems in which there is "frustration and sadness, and a downright kinkiness," elements that, he suggests, counterbalance Dunn's obsession with propriety. In 1990 Stephen Dobyns echoed the observations of these earlier critics, describing Dunn as a poet agreeably out-of-step with his time. "In a period when obscurity and intellectual chill are increasingly celebrated in contemporary American poetry," Dobyns wrote, "it is a pleasure to look at poems in which clarity is a virtue and strongly felt emotion is a reason for being."

In spite of its title, the poems in Dunn's collection *Between Angels* (1989) are grounded in prosaic experience. Dobyns wrote that the poems are "modest without being small. . . . Not only does one come to care deeply about them, but they are a pleasure to read." When asked in his interview with Rubin for the *Literary Review* to describe his "realist lyric," Dunn made a distinction between lived reality and "reconstructed" experience. "I try to resist everything my conventional mind can say about experience, which I assume is not very interesting until it's made interesting," he told Rubin. Others have commented on the precise language with which Dunn chips away at observation and experience. Reviewing *Between Angels*, Dobyns calls Dunn a "master of the short phrase," and a poet who possesses the "same passionate attentiveness to the American cadence [William Carlos] Williams did." Dobyns in particular voiced appreciation for Dunn's control of phrasing, noting that his lines are often broken in mid-thought, so that closely related words fall on different lines. The effect of this device in Dunn's poetry, according to Dobyns, is to create "tension and build rhythm," and to achieve "a mixture of stillness and strong feeling."

New and Selected Poems, 1974–1994 (1994) offered readers a retrospective look at Dunn's career. Reviewing the collection for the *New York Times Book Review* (January 15, 1995, on-line), Anthony Libby identified some "inevitable risks" in Dunn's "plain-style celebrations." Dunn's language, Libby argued, is occasionally "colloquial to the point of triteness," making the sentiments seem threadbare. And yet, Libby expressed appreciation for Dunn's sustained efforts to develop an affirmative voice in the face of what Libby called "the cynical reader's resistance." The reviewer Jeff Parker Knight, writing for the *Virginia Quarterly Review* (Summer 1996), noticed that in nearly all of his poems, Dunn works in miniature, creating "finely observed moments, small triumphs and surrenders, microscopic epiphanies." "Is that enough?" Knight asked, and then concluded that it is, when, as in Dunn's case, the poet still manages to surprise us by finding "the miraculous lurking within the ordinary." As an example, Knight referred to Dunn's poem "The Sudden Light and the Trees," in which a narrator describes what it is like to have a violent neighbor, whose dog is taken away by the Humane Society, and whose abused wife remains. When a sparrow gets caught in their shared basement and the neighbor wants to shoot it, the narrator protests:

> I said I'd catch it, wait, give me
> a few minutes and, clear-eyed, brilliantly
> afraid, I trapped it
> with a pillow. I remember how it felt
> when I got it in my hand, and how it burst
> that hand open
> when I took it outside, a strength that must
> have come out of hopelessness
> and the sudden light
> and the trees. And I remember
> the way he slapped the gun against
> his open palm,
> kept slapping it, and wouldn't speak.

Knight remarked on the poem's seeming transparency. "Paying no heed to style, we read on to see what happens, until the peculiar syntax of 'burst / that hand open'"—a phrase that, Knight said, interrupts the narrative flow, and "increases the tension at the moment the suspense ought to end. . . . when the bird flies free the plot seems to be resolved. But the tension actually builds, now stemming from what is not said."

In the *Southern Review* (Autumn 1995), Sydney Lea used the occasion of the publication of *New and Selected Poems* to contrast Dunn's "mature vision" against that of his earlier poems. Lea noted in particular the sense of irony that Dunn finds in the "middleness" of middle-age. In one of the poems in this collection, "The Snowmass Cycle," Dunn writes "that piety will keep us small, imprisoned, / that it's all right to be ridiculous / and sway first to the left, then to the right, / in order to find our balance." Lea remarked that Dunn "remains open to the contradictions, fantasy coming to check a dull 'realism' just as realism mutes mere fantasy, humor blocks a lust for philosophical conclusion, and, commendably, a candid awareness of his comfort deflects Dunn from self-indulgent 'political' advocacy."

In *Loosestrife* (1996), a finalist for the National Book Critics Circle Award for poetry, Dunn reflects on contemporary events, including the Oklahoma City bombing that occurred in 1995, and the existence of street gangs and Satanists; he also observes the fragile beauty of the marshland along the New Jersey coast. Reviewing the collection for *Booklist* (September 1, 1996), Donna Seaman noted a new tone in Dunn's voice, "a deepening of his recognition of life's perversities." David Baker, writing in *Poetry* (August 1997), agreed. "[Dunn] brings important news, and warning, from the nearly paralyzed districts of American suburbia and middle-age. . . . *Loosestrife* seems to me a darker book than his others."

In *Riffs and Reciprocities* (1998), Dunn experimented with form. Following the principles of variation and improvisation at work in jazz, Dunn composed prose-poems by meditating on pairs of linked ideas. In his preface Dunn describes the genesis of the work: "I became intrigued with working in tangentially related pairs, each a discrete paragraph. . . . And each riff 'found' its reciprocity; I rarely began a paragraph knowing what the next paragraph would be." Each paragraph is a meditation on a single idea, which is then linked with another paragraph on a related theme. Some couplings are nearly complements, such as "Music/Noise," while others are more complex; their associations, while perhaps not obvious to readers at first, are embedded in the text. "Natives" is narrated by a man whose neighbor takes him on a walk and teaches him the names of trees and flowers; its counterpart, "Lovers," also involves the notion of naming, this time in a different setting. A couple comes to a strange city, where the "signs are in a language they've failed to learn. . . . Waiters bring them appetizers in seven different languages." This particular pair juxtaposes themes of country and city, love of nature and erotic love, foreignness and belonging.

In 1999 Dunn participated in the American Poetry and Literacy Project, which placed copies of a poetry anthology, *Songs for the Open Road*, on the driver's seat of every new Volkswagen sold in the U.S., as reported in the *New York Times* (April 9, 1999). In addition to Robert Frost's "The Road Not Taken" and "Ulysses" by Alfred Lord Tennyson, Dunn's poem "The Sacred" was included in the anthology. In this poem, Dunn recalls a theme familiar to many teenagers—the special kind of sanctuary afforded by a car: "the bright altar of the dashboard and how far away / a car could take him from the need / to speak, or to answer, the key in having a key / and putting it in, and going."

Dunn's next collection of poems, *Different Hours* (2000), further secured his prominence in American poetry, earning a 2001 Pulitzer Prize. In this volume, Dunn reflects on the "different hours" of his life, focusing largely on his present-day experience in latter-middle age, as well as the state of the world at this juncture in history. He explained the book's significance to Elizabeth Farnsworth for the *NewsHour with Jim Lehrer* (April 26, 2001), as quoted in an on-line transcript, "The book was composed in the years . . . the three or four years before I reached 60, and I guess I was sometimes consciously, probably more unconsciously aware that I was nearing the age that nobody in my family . . . no male in my family had ever reached. And I think that notion, that consciousness, colored a lot of the poems." In the tradition of Dunn's earlier work, *Different Hours* features a conversational, even simplistic, tone that invites the reader to join Dunn's deeper explorations of every-day experience. Yet, as Emily Nussbaum suggested in her review for the *New York Times* (August 19, 2001), readers should not "mistake that ease [of language] for lack of staying power." Rather, she described Dunn's poetry as "strangely easy to like: philosophical but not arid, lyrical but rarely glib, his storytelling balanced effortlessly between the casual and the vivid," adding that it "has an out-of-time quality, like a conversation with your smartest friend during a long-distance road trip."

The opening poem, "Before the Sky Darkens," exemplifies many of Dunn's larger themes throughout the book—a consciousness struggling to extract meaning and beauty from the world. In his reading of this poem to Farnsworth, Dunn opened, "Sunset's incipient storms, the tableaus of melancholy—maybe these are the Saturday night events to take your best girl to. At least then there might be moments of vanishing beauty before the sky darkens, and the expectation of happiness would hardly exist and therefore might be possible." As the poet considers "the ever-hidden God retreating even farther" from the world, he finds eventual solace in the most simplistic of gifts: "Then out of the daily wreckage comes an invitation with your name on it, or more likely that best girl of yours offers you once again a small local kindness." Other poems throughout the collection take on subjects of marriage, illness, human relations, life in the new millennium, today's news events, and ultimately, mortality. As Dunn's friend and fellow poet Gregory Djanikian explained to Robert Strauss for the *New York Times* (May 27, 2001), "[Dunn's] poems really quietly talk about our ordinary lives in extraordinary ways. They really show us washing the dishes, mowing the lawn or doing some daily task, the mysteriousness of all that. For poets as well, it is quite fine to discover one's life as full of realities which are special, where there are crevasses of unimagined beauty and feeling." *Different Hours* was widely acclaimed as a complex, powerful, and accessible collection of meditations on modern life.

Dunn's most recent work, *Local Visitations: Poems*, was released in February 2003. This book, divided into three sections, again features the poet's exploration of emotional landscapes and place. In the first, a modern-day, middle-aged Sisyphus searches for meaning in the mundane tasks of life. In the second, more personal, section Dunn explores themes of love. Finally, in what one reviewer for *Publishers Weekly*, as quoted on *Amazon.com*, called the "most ambitious sequence," Dunn envisions a roster of "Great Nineteenth-Century Writers" in his own present-day New Jersey. Of the book's merit, the reviewer noted, "Here as in his previous work, [Dunn] offers a plain and sometimes plaintive introspection, a panoply of lightly sketched driveways, shopping malls and seashores, a real attempt to represent his region as well as a nation's careful cocooning."

— M.A.H.

SUGGESTED READING: *Booklist* p57 Sep. 1996; *Literary Review* p559+ Summer 1987; *New York Review of Books* p47 Oct. 23, 1986; *New York Times Book Review* p23 July 6, 1986; *New York Times Book Review* (on-line) Jan. 28, 1990, Jan. 15, 1995; *New Yorker* p62 Apr. 10, 2000; *Poetry* p288 Aug. 1997; *Southern Review* p957+ Autumn 1995; *Virginia Quarterly Review* p558+ Summer 1996; *Contemporary Authors* vol. 53, 1998

SELECTED BOOKS: poetry—*Looking for Holes in the Ceiling*, 1974; *Local Time*, 1986; *Between Angels*, 1989; *New and Selected Poems, 1974–1994*, 1994; *Loosestrife*, 1996; *Riffs and Reciprocities: Prose Pairs*, 1998; *Different Hours*, 2000; *Local Visitations*, 2003; essays—*Walking Light: Essays and Memoirs*, 1993

Alison Dunnett/Courtesy of Vintage Anchor Publicity

Dunnett, Dorothy

(Aug. 25, 1923–Nov. 9, 2001) Historical novelist; mystery writer

The work of the Scottish historical novelist and mystery writer Dorothy Dunnett enjoys a loyal following around the world. Over the last few decades, Dunnett thrilled readers with two sets of historical novels. The six novels in the *Lymond Chronicles* series follow the adventures of Francis Crawford, a swashbuckling, Scottish-born rogue. The seven novels in the *House of Niccolo* series center around Nicholas, who is introduced to readers as a lowly apprentice in *Niccolo Rising* (1986); by the last novel, *Gemini* (2000), he is one of Europe's most wealthy and well-known bankers and merchants. Nicholas's exploits bring him in conflict with villains throughout the continent. Many reviewers and readers express admiration for the carefully researched historical details that Dunnett packed into every novel, as well as the action, intrigue, and romance. Dunnett also won acclaim for her *Johnson Johnson* mystery novels, which feature an American spy. About a year after announcing her retirement from writing, Dorothy Dunnett died in Edinburgh on November 9, 2001, leaving her devoted fans around the world saddened.

Shortly before her death in 2001, Dorothy Dunnett wrote for *World Authors 1995–2000*, "It was easier to become published forty years ago. It was made even easier for me because I had two good jobs (one in the Government, and one as a professional portrait painter), a lot of different interests (sailing, music, traveling, party-going) and, for half a century, a newspaper editor for a husband who assumed I could write and publish anything I wanted, so long as he never had to see or discuss it until it had been published (by somebody else). So I wrote twenty-two novels and sold every one that I wrote. Since Alastair thought this was normal, I thought it was normal. And it may well have been, for that time.

"It was a long time ago. I was born in Scotland on August 25, 1923, only child of a Scots engineer father and an English mother, who had met when my future father was wounded in France during the First World War and hospitalised in England. His was an army family: my grandfather had been a regimental sergeant major with the Cameron Highlanders (i.e. bossy). He and my grandmother married on the regiment's strength in Gibraltar, and my father was born when they were stationed in Valetta, Malta in 1895.

"My mother was a good letter-writer (they burned a thousand love letters the night before they got married in 1921, since there wasn't room to store them and, as they unsentimentally put it, they now had each other). It stayed that kind of marriage, which was pretty good. I went to the same Edinburgh school as Muriel Spark (we overlapped but didn't meet) and was taught by the same English and Latin teachers and found out I could paint and sing. I left during the war, aged sixteen and joined a Government department in Edinburgh to earn a living while I studied painting part-time, and had private singing lessons. (I did learn to sing opera, but never professionally.) I was going to be an artist. My sensible parents said that was fine, so long as I waited until I could earn a living that way.

"When I met Alastair and married in 1946, my home moved to Glasgow for ten years and I worked for the Board of Trade, still in the Government, and still studied painting and singing. By 1950 I was painting professional portraits—lawyers, actors, a captain's secretary in the navy—on canvases as big as five or six feet in height. I began to show regularly in the Royal Scottish Academy under my maiden name, Dorothy Halliday and that career has never stopped—my last commission was to paint one of the Queen's chaplains in his robes. But writing? Writing fiction? Never crossed my mind.

"Then my father died, and in the subsequent misery, I ran out of escapist reading—and Alastair suggested I write a historical novel of my own. As an afterthought he said, 'Make it a series. They're popular at the moment.' So (always co-operative) I did.

"*Game of Kings* was published in New York by Putnam's in 1961, a few years after we had moved home back to Edinburgh, where Alastair was to be editor and managing director of the *Scotsman*, and just after the birth of the first of our two sons in 1959. The novel had been turned down by five British publishers who liked it, wanted to publish it but said (rightly) that it was too long.

"I was busy on other exciting things. I didn't want to waste time on a non-starter, so did nothing about it. Then again on Alastair's advice ('they like long books in America'), I shoved it over to Lois Cole, who was a close friend of Margaret Mitchell (they both came from Atlanta) and had published *Gone with the Wind*. She said, it's too long, I love it, you will have to cut it, but here is a contract. And an option to take the rest.

"So 22 books followed. One was a non-fiction on Scotland done in collaboration with Alastair and a photographer, and seven are modern mysteries. All the novels have been published on both sides of the Atlantic, and the historical novels have been especially welcomed in translation in Italy, since their period is the early and late Renaissance. Researching them, I've enjoyed using what I know about painting and music techniques for the cultural background; my experience of sailing for the sea battles and voyages of exploration; my limited track record with horses (I generally fall off) to help avoid too many horsey mistakes. I suppose even my period with the Board of Trade has helped with understanding the commodity wars and early banking successes of the time. I've traveled a lot, so I don't mind going off on my own to Russia or Turkey or Iceland or Africa or the middle of the Sinai desert for that matter. I like adventures. And for each series (there are two, six about Francis Crawford of Lymond in the 16th century; eight about Nicholas vander Poele in the 15th), I have read or consulted up to 700 books, which is a lot of reading. Then in between, I wrote the single novel I'm proudest of, *King Hereafter*, a study of the great king who was the real King Macbeth, which took five years to research. And for light relief, seven modern mysteries about a guy called Johnson Johnson who is a portrait painter, working as an undercover agent from his yacht called the Dolly, which takes him to the more glamorous spots of the world. I enjoy researching those, too. In fact, the research sometimes makes a funnier story than the resulting novel; but don't . . . go into all that.

"There is a serious side. I've been fortunate: I was awarded an OBE by the Queen in 1992 for services to literature, and received another delightful literary award in 1993 from the Scottish Presbyterian College, Laurinburg, North Carolina. Alastair was knighted in 1995, with the main result that nobody knew what our names were. I've had an interesting life in other directions—13 years as a non-executive director of Scottish Television, 35 years a Trustee of the National War Memorial at Edinburgh Castle; many years on the Board of the Edinburgh Book Festival. I've served on film committees with John Grierson and acted as judge for all kinds of literary and other awards. I've been a Trustee, since 1986, of the National Library of Scotland, and for services to business, I was appointed in 1986 a Fellow of the Royal Society of Arts (the one connected with Captain Bligh and *Mutiny on the Bounty*).

"But chiefly I had discovered a deepening pleasure in my historical work. Novels are novels, and the leading character in each of mine is as charismatic as I can make him—to some effect. There have been world correspondence magazines about these books since 1984, and last year there were two international gatherings in Edinburgh and Philadelphia as well as a host of smaller ones, and nearly a dozen discussions groups on the Internet. Puzzle-minded people also quite like to follow the deliberate red herrings that run through all the books, making each series into a single many-volumed story whose greatest surprises are reserved for the end. (The two series are linked).

"They like, too, visiting the places in the books and following up the real history, with the help of Elspeth Morrison's *Dorothy Dunnett Companion*, being republished this summer by Vintage, with a second volume emerging next spring. By this time, anyway, I feel I know half my readers and they know me, even to their children who weren't born when I started to write and who are now indoctrinating their children into the world of Lymond and Nicholas."

In 1961 Dunnett published *The Game of Kings*, the first entry in her popular and acclaimed *Lymond Chronicles* series, which is set during the Anglo-Scottish War, in 1547. In an interview with Jean Richardson for *Publishers Weekly* (May 11, 1998), Dunnett recalled that she read many books about the period at the National Library in Edinburgh, Scotland, to familiarize herself with the era. "But these were the days before photocopying, so I had to spend long days in the library, and I've still got dozens of notebooks full of painstakingly copied material dating back from my early research," she told Richardson. *The Game of the Kings* follows the adventures of Francis Crawford of Lymond, a scholar and soldier of fortune, who is embroiled in a bitter feud with his older brother and considered a traitor in his native Scotland. In an interview with Delia O'Hara for the *Chicago Sun-Times* (December 10, 2000), Dunnett said that she intended Francis "to be the hero to end all heroes." A critic for *Kirkus* (August 15, 1961) praised The

Game of Kings, writing that Dunnett "has been extremely generous with plot, sub-plots and a whole array of colorful subsidiary characters." Describing the book as "a passionate, panoramic, suavely engineered tale," the critic added that the "confrontation between the two brothers towards the close of the book, and [Crawford's] treason trial, are gripping and psychologically rewarding." By contrast, Robert Payne criticized the novel in the *Saturday Review* (November 4, 1961). "Unhappily, most of the novel is written in the form of prolonged conversations," he wrote. "Throughout those interminable conversations we hear the authentic accents of modern speech with the archaisms dropped in at contrived intervals."

The commercial success of *Game of Kings* led Dunnett to continue Francis Crawford's adventures in five sequels. Crawford's adventures took him to France to protect the seven-year-old Mary, Queen of Scots, in *Queen's Play* (1964); to Malta to help fight a Turkish invasion, in *Disorderly Knights* (1966); into the Ottoman Empire to rescue his son, in *Pawn in Frankincense* (1969); to Russia, where he serves as an adviser and general to Ivan the Terrible, in *The Ringed Castle* (1971); and to France once again to lead an army against the English, in *Checkmate* (1975). The last book in the series received the Scottish Arts Council Award, in 1976. In discussing the series for the *New York Times Book Review* (December 24, 2000), Anne Malcolm described Francis Crawford as "impossibly charming, elegant and accomplished; a brilliant swordsman; an inspired leader of men. He is also highhanded, cynical and dangerous, with a 'cavalier way with opposition' that runs to knocking a girl unconscious or putting his dagger through the shoulder of an obstinate old man." Dunnett had told M. Melissa Pressley for the *Christian Science Monitor* (December 19, 1988) that "present-day people impose their own morality on the past and say, 'How awful.' It wasn't awful at all. This is the difficult thing about writing historical fiction, because you have to write about what to the modern reader are impossible horrors sometimes."

Malcolm wrote that "the six novels of *The Lymond Chronicles*—vivid, engaging, densely plotted—are almost certainly destined to be counted among the classics of popular fiction." Describing Dunnett as a "master of suspense and misdirection," Malcolm concluded that the author "will be remembered for having created the perfect romantic hero" in Francis Crawford of Lymond.

In 1968 Dunnett began a second series of books with the publication of the thriller *Dolly and the Singing Bird*. The author introduced Johnson Johnson, a wealthy American painter and undercover spy who sails a yacht named "Dolly." The *Johnson Johnson* books all follow the same structure, in which Johnson comes to the rescue of a woman, or "bird," who narrates the book in the first person. Johnson aids an opera star in *Dolly and the Singing Bird* (1968); a chef in *Dolly and the Cookie Bird* (1970); a doctor in *Dolly and the Doctor Bird* (1971); an astronomer in *Dolly and the Starry Bird* (1973); a nanny in *Dolly and the Nanny Bird* (1976); a make-up artist in *Dolly and the Bird of Paradise* (1983); and a secretary to a corporate executive in the last entry in the series, *Moroccan Traffic* (1991). In the United Kingdom Dunnett published the first four *Johnson Johnson* books under her maiden name, Dorothy Halliday. In the United States they were all published under her married name, and several books in the series were published with different titles. In his review for *Harper's Magazine* (October 1971), John Thompson wrote that *Dolly and the Doctor Bird* "is well ordered and has an arch and pleasant kind of elegance." Thompson concluded that the novel's "perils are suitably ingenious, and the whole charade is amiably maintained to its extravagant end."

In his review for the *Washington Post Book World* (March 18, 1984), Lawrence Block had mixed feelings about *Dolly and the Bird of Paradise*. He described the first half of the novel as "sluggish" and also faulted the book's narrator for committing a few "linguistic atrocities." However, Block praised the book's good qualities: "We get a good look at Madeira, at Martinique, and St. Lucia. The plot, once we're launched into it, has enough twists and turns to disorient almost everyone. The ending didn't seem to me abundant sense, but by the time it's reached Dunnett has sorted out so many complications that it would be arrant kvetchery to carp about the plausibility or the lack thereof."

In 1982 Dunnett returned to historical fiction with *King Hereafter*. The book offers a favorable image of the 11th-century Scottish king, Macbeth, and his wife—contrary to the villainous portrait of them presented in William Shakespeare's play. In the novel Dunnett calls Macbeth by his "Old Norse" name, Thorfinn. He later adopts Macbeth, which is his baptismal name. (According to Dunnett, Lady Macbeth's Old Norse name is Ingebord, and her baptismal name is Grua.) In his review for the *Washington Post Book World* (August 8, 1982), Thomas Flanagan, although expressing doubt as to the veracity of some of Dunnett's historical claims, wrote, "[She] has done a splendid work of restoring [Macbeth's/Thornfinn's] world, its colors, textures, sounds, the look of its seacoasts and mountains, the ways in which men measured their wills and strengths and their booty, one against another."

In 1986 Dunnett began her second set of historical novels with the publication of *Niccolo Rising*. The novel begins in 1459 and takes place in the vicinity of the Mediterranean Sea. The Renaissance has just begun in Italy, and the Turks have seized the city of Constantinople (later renamed Istanbul). England is torn by civil strife. Political intrigue and rivalry mark the relations among the Scots, the French, and the Italian city-states. Dunnett's new hero is Claes (who later adopts the name Niccolo), a 19-year-old apprentice employed by Marian Charetty, the widow of a wealthy merchant. As the action unfolds, Claes becomes the Widow Charetty's chief negotiator and strategist, visiting major banking centers in Europe, the courts of the Medici and Sforza families, and various heads-of-state, in order to benefit the Widow Charetty's business interests. In her review for the *Washington Post Book World* (September 21, 1986), the historical novelist Joan Aiken stated that Dunnett's novel left her "awestruck at the sheer volume of knowledge deployed in its construction, and at the energy and power of organization required to create and manipulate such a complicated plot, which is basically concerned with the trade and commercial dealings of 15th-century Europe."

In the first sequel, *The Spring of the Ram* (1988), Niccolo (formerly Claes) negotiates with the Medicis to obtain a loan and a ship, so he can bring a small army to Trebizond in the Byzantine Empire and offer it to the emperor to help defend his territory from Turkish aggression. Once he gets there, Niccolo also plans to purchase Persian silk, which he will resell in Europe. Niccolo's plans, however, are threatened by unforseen obstacles that include trouble from Pagano Doria, a rival merchant. "Mrs. Dunnett's gift lies in her ability to take history's bare bones and invest them with life," M. Melissa Pressley asserted in the *Christian Science Monitor* (December 19, 1988). "She does this by creating a central character and a circle of friends with whom one forms deep bonds, characters whose humor and pathos reach across the centuries." Pressley concluded that *Spring of the Ram* "is not just a book to read, but a book to revel in."

Dunnett often includes small "puzzles" in the books that, if solved correctly, reveal how the story develops. In an article for the Glasgow *Herald* (June 18, 1996), Jane Scott wrote, "It's a great game they play, Dunnett and the readers. She gives them immaculately researched, brick-length volumes of intrigue recounting the fortunes of her antihero.... The readers, for their part, correspond frantically across the world's continents, mulling over the detail and trying to second-guess the direction the story will take." Scott related that one of Dunnett's puzzles, a "text, half in Latin, half in French, found in some obscure book of medieval history in Paris was actually identified by an American reader (invariably more erudite than her European ones), thus giving away three or four years' worth of narrative in the *House of Niccolo* series."

In *Race of Scorpions* (1989), Niccolo (who becomes known in the novel as Nicholas Van der Poele) turns his attention to the island of Cyprus. Queen Carlotta and her brother, James, are fighting for control of the island, which is strategically important and boasts lucrative sugar crops. Both seek the support of Nicholas, who has become known throughout Europe. "Treachery and double-dealing are everywhere, especially as enormous sums of money are involved," Philippa Toomey wrote in her review for the London *Times* (November 25, 1989). "The excitement of Mrs. Dunnett's storytelling runs hand-in-hand with the erudition of her research though a high adventure."

In the fourth novel in the series, *Scales of Gold* (1992), Nicholas travels to Africa to search for gold. As in the three previous novels, he is besieged by enemies and circumstances that threaten his life and financial interests. In the next book, *The Unicorn Hunt* (1994), Nicholas searches for his new wife, who has disappeared and may be pregnant with his child. Reviewing the novel for the *Washington Post Book World* (September 4, 1994), Brian Jacob observed that Dunnett "has a knack for attaching her historical background to a strong story line, unlike those writers who hurl masses of blandly stated historical facts and try to impose a plot almost as an afterthought."

The sixth entry of the series, *To Lie With Lions* (1996), brings Nicholas to Iceland. His enemy this time is Gelis, his estranged wife and the mother of his son, Jordan. Gelis returns in *Caprice and Rondo* (1998). In this adventure Nicholas battles the Turks, making his way to Crimea, Russia, and Persia. Dunnett reveals a number of details about Nicholas's childhood in the course of the tale. To research this novel, Dunnett traveled to Poland and the Ukraine. She explained to Ann Donald, for the Glasgow *Herald* (October 31, 1997), that it "can be quite frightening and frustrating when you're traveling alone which I do all the time," but that she finds the experience very rewarding when she reaches "a place and get[s] hold of foreign books and find[s] a nugget buried beneath all those dates and places."

In 2000 Dunnett concluded the *House of Niccolo* series with *Gemini*, in which Nicholas returns to Scotland. "Anyone reading this novel, even as an introduction to Dunnett's work, will, I suspect join [her] admirers," John Sutherland observed in his review for the London *Sunday Times* (August 6, 2000). Dunnett also delighted her fans by establishing *Gemini* as a prequel to the *Lymond Chronicles* series. Cheslea Quinn Yarbro in the *Washington Post Book World* (August 7, 2000) lauded the book and noted that "[throughout] the series, Dunnett has maintained her consistency of vision, presenting the Renaissance in a multilayered collage, depicting in detail a world that in many ways set the stage for the onset of modernity in Europe. Readers are accustomed to seeing this degree of world-building in science fiction and fantasy. It is refreshing to find it in a work so grounded in actual events."

After the publication of *Gemini*, Dunnett announced that she would no longer publish historical novels—an announcement avidly discussed in the numerous Internet chat rooms and the two quarterly magazines exclusively devoted to her work. (These are *Marzipan and Kisses*, in the United States, and *Whispering Gallery*, in the United Kingdom.) In 1992 Queen Elizabeth II officially recognized Dorothy Dunnett's literary contributions by awarding her the Order of the British Empire (OBE).

Dorothy Dunnett's husband, Sir Alastair Dunnett, died in 1998. Dunnett died, at age 78, in Edinburgh on November 9, 2001. A short time before her death, Dunnett was collaborating with Elspeth Morrison on a second companion volume explaining the cultural and scientific details contained in her fiction. (The first had been published in July 2001.) She is survived by her two children, Ninian and Mongo, and two grandchildren.

—D. C.

SUGGESTED READING: *Baltimore Sun* D p1 Nov. 10, 1997; *Chicago Sun-Times* Show p16 Dec. 10, 2000; *Christian Science Monitor* p16 Dec. 19, 1988, p17+ Dec. 19, 1988; *Harper's Magazine* p120 Oct. 1971; (Glasgow) *Herald* p23 June 18, 1996, p17 Oct. 31, 1997; *Kirkus* p746 Aug. 15, 1961; *Los Angeles Times* p13 Nov. 16, 2001; *New York Times Book Review* p31 Aug. 2, 1964, p11 Dec. 24, 2000; *Newsday* B p2 May 14, 1998; *Publishers Weekly* p46+ May 11, 1998; *Saturday Review* p41 Nov. 4, 1961; (London) *Times* (on-line) Nov. 25, 1989; *Times Literary Supplement* p1225 Oct. 23, 1969, p511 Apr. 30, 1971, p959 Aug. 17, 1973; *Washington Post Book World* p3+ Aug. 8, 1982, p5 Mar. 18, 1984, p1 Sept. 21, 1986, p9 Sept. 4, 1994; Morrison, Elspeth *The Dorothy Dunnett Companion*, 1994

SELECTED BOOKS: fiction—*The Lymond Chronicles Series*: *The Game of the Kings*, 1961; *Queens' Play*, 1964; *The Disorderly Knights*, 1966; *Pawn in Frankincense*, 1969; *The Ringed Castle*, 1971; *Checkmate*, 1975; *Johnson Johnson Series*—(as Dorothy Halliday) *Dolly and the Singing Bird*, 1968 (published as *The Photogenic Soprano* in the United States, 1968); *Dolly and the Cookie Bird*, 1970 (published as *Murder in the Round* in the United States, 1970); *Dolly and the Doctor Bird*, 1971 (published as *Match for a Murderer* in the United States, 1971); *Dolly and the Starry Bird*, 1973 (published as *Murder in Focus* in the United States, 1973)—(as Dorothy Gallagher) *Dolly and the Nanny Bird*, 1976 (published in the United States in 1982); *Dolly and the Bird of Paradise*, 1983; *Moroccan Traffic*, 1991 (published in the United States as *Send a Fax to the Kasbah*, 1992); *House of Niccolo Series*: *Niccolo Rising*, 1986; *The Spring of the Ram*, 1987; *Race of Scorpions*, 1990; *Scales of Gold*, 1991; *The Unicorn Hunt*, 1993; *To Lie With Lions*, 1996; *Caprice and Rondo*, 1998; *Gemini*, 2000; other fiction—*King Hereafter*, 1982; nonfiction—(with Alastair M. Dunnett) *The Scottish Highlands*, 1988

Durcan, Paul

Oct. 16, 1944– Poet

Termed the "unofficial Poet Laureate of Ireland" by more than one critic, Paul Durcan has written 17 collections of poetry in a career spanning three decades. Indeed, with the exception of Nobel laureate Seamus Heaney, no other living poet is more widely identified with Ireland than Durcan. He has long been praised for his linguistic playfulness, humor, and creative use of metaphor; however, the views espoused in his poems, which tend to be critical of established religious and political institutions, have occasioned passionately divergent responses among critics. His 1990 collection, *Daddy, Daddy*, inspired by the death of his father, won the prestigious Whitbread Poetry Prize. His other books include: *O Westport in the Light of Asia Minor* (1975), *Teresa's Bar* (1976), *Jumping the Train Tracks with Angela* (1983), *The Berlin Wall Café* (1985), *A Snail in My Prime* (1993), *Give Me Your Hand* (1994), *Greetings to Our Friends in Brazil* (1999), and *Cries of an Irish Caveman* (2002).

The son of John and Sheila (MacBride) Durcan, both attorneys, Paul Durcan was born on October 16, 1944 in Dublin, Ireland. His youth was spent shuttling between his parents' home in Dublin and County Mayo, where his aunt owned a pub in the town of Turlough and his grandmother lived in Westport. "I was fostered, for want of a better word, to my aunt and my grandmother and my earliest memories are actually of those places, though Dart-

Courtesy of Random House Group

mouth Square [in Dublin] was officially my home. So in a funny way I'm neither one thing nor the other, Dublin nor Mayo," Durcan told Arminta Wallace for the *Irish Times* (February 18, 1999). "My parents—my father, in particular—never became Dubliners, really. Now I live most of my life in Dublin."

Between the ages of 19 and 27, Durcan spent the majority of his time working in London. Despite the infamous centuries-long friction between the English and Irish, Durcan formed an affection for the city. "I get angry when people start slagging England because, looking back, living in Ireland in those days was like being behind a sort of Iron Curtain—the pressure, the claustrophobia, the rigid conformity. The only way out was to get on the boat to England—and the other important thing was, that it was the only place you could get work," the poet explained to Wallace. "And in general—yes, I know there were signs saying no blacks or Irish—but in general, English people were the friendliest in the world. That was where I got married and where my children were born. So when I go to London it's a bit like going home, too—though, mind you, I'm always glad I'm coming back [to Ireland]."

In his 20s Durcan began publishing poems in small literary journals such as the *Holy Door*, whose editor, Brian Lynch, would later collaborate with Durcan on his first collection, *Endsville* (1967). In 1970 he returned to Ireland and lived in Cork with his now ex-wife, Nessa O'Neill, a teacher, and their two daughters, Sarah and Siabhra. He received a B.A. in archaeology and medieval history at the University College Cork, earning first-class honors. He was bestowed the Patrick Kavanagh Poetry Award in 1974, which encouraged him to publish, in 1975, his first solo poetry collection, *O Westport in the Light of Asia Minor*. Durcan went on to publish three more solid volumes of poetry in the 1970s, followed by the long poem *Ark of the North* (1982).

It was the 1982 publication of *The Selected Paul Durcan*, with an introduction by Edna Longley, however, that furthered Durcan's reputation in Ireland and abroad. This volume included 103 selections from his first five collections: one from *Endsville*, 30 from *O Westport in the Light of Asia Minor: Poems*, 22 from *Teresa's Bar* (1976), 35 from *Sam's Cross: Poems* (1978), and 15 from *Jesus, Break His Fall* (1980). Some of the poems, such as "Tribute to a Reporter in Belfast, 1974" and "In Memory of Those Murdered in the Dublin Massacre, May 1974," are poignant reminders of the sectarian violence that racked Ireland in the 1970s. Longley opened her introduction to the selection by noting that "the titles of Paul Durcan's four full collections . . . cover both the visionary and the Irish aspects of his poetry. They also imply a likely friction between the two; since Sam's Cross was the birthplace of the murdered Michael Collins, while *Teresa's Bar* represents an antidote to all the hurts and constraints of society."

As expected from such a large and varied volume, *The Selected Paul Durcan* touches on the major themes of human experience, such as faith and heritage. Both themes find a common ground in the poem "They Say the Butterfly is the Hardest Stroke," originally from *O Westport in the Light of Asia Minor*, in which the speaker equates his writerly heritage with a kind of religious faith, saying, "I have not 'met' God, I have not 'read' David Gascoyne, James Joyce, or Patrick Kavanagh: I believe in them."

However, organized religion, both its leaders and practitioners, often fares poorly in Durcan's hands. Edna Longley wrote in her introduction to the selected works, "Durcan's naturally religious cast of mind recoils from the Catholic Church's ingenious hostility to life and love. Many poems subvert puritanism, while 'Bishop of Cork Murders his Wife' hammers the accepted superiority of violence to sex, and maleness to femaleness." This poem, which originally appeared in the collection *Sam's Cross*, opens with the withering lines: "Such is the loyalty of his flock / That on hearing that their bishop had murdered his wife / Their immediate response was not of sympathy for the deceased / But of regret that the bishop had ever got married."

The 1980s proved to be a particularly fertile period for Durcan, resulting in six collections: *Jumping the Train Tracks with Angela*; *The Berlin Wall Café*; *Going Home to Russia* (1987); *In the Land of Punt* (1988), on which he collaborated with Gene Lambert; *Jesus and Angela: Poems* (1988), which collected the poems from *Jesus, Break His Fall* and *Jumping the Train Tracks with Angela*; and *Daddy, Daddy* (1990). Although the Whitbread went to *Daddy, Daddy*, many critics still consider *The Berlin Wall Café*, the second half of which Durcan drew from the breakup of his marriage to Nessa, his best volume yet.

The critical success of *Daddy, Daddy* and Durcan's place as one of Ireland's most important contemporary authors were supported by the 1993 publication of *A Snail in My Prime*, which presents new works with a selection of poems from his 10 previous collections. James Simmons, in his review for the *Spectator* (May 1, 1993), called this collection "a very substantial body of work, varied, original, funny, and profound." Simmons drew comparisons between Durcan's work and the later poems of Patrick Kavanagh while comparing the poet's satirical monologues to the scripts of the provocative American comedian Lenny Bruce. The following year Durcan published *Give Me Your Hand*, a collection inspired by the plastic arts. In was introduced by art critic Bryan Robertson, who observed, "In using painting as a point of departure for so many of his poems—and often traveling without a ticket, from the viewpoint of a sober art historian—Paul Durcan forges a strong personal link with a fascinating sequence of encounters between poets and painters." In her generally sympathetic review in the *New Statesman & Society* (April 8, 1994), Michèle Roberts stated how "a great many of these poems are monologues, confidently done. The poet inhabits any role or gender he likes." However, she found his female voices contrived, commenting that they "seem drawn from some conventional soap-opera sex war."

When his next collection, *Christmas Day*, was published by Harvill/HarperCollins in 1996, a reviewer for *Publishers Weekly* (November 25, 1996) paid tribute to Durcan's popularity in his country, noting that the poet "maintains a reputation as Ireland's most popular and entertaining poet . . . and yet is taken seriously by the Irish literary community as a poet extending the Celtic bardic tradition of the public balladeer." *Christmas Day* is a book-length poem that presents a Christmas celebrated by two Irish bachelors. The two men share a meal, drinks, and reminiscences that are almost Chaucerian in their bawdiness, all of which strike a particularly Irish tone. As the *Publishers Weekly* reviewer speculated, "It's a peculiar Irishness, perhaps, that permeates Durcan's poems, and may be the secret to his popularity."

Most contemporary poetry collections, which usually contain fewer than 50 poems, resemble pamphlets in thickness and heft. Durcan has run counter to the trend by providing readers with several beefy volumes of verse that exceed 200 pages. In *Greetings to Our Friends in Brazil* (1999), a collection of 100 poems covering more than 250 pages, Durcan has continued this practice. The volume stands in part as Durcan's poetic rendering of the years of Mary Robinson's presidency of Ireland (1990–1997), during which Irish society and politics stepped from beneath the shadow of Catholicism and emerged economically as a country to be reckoned with on the world stage. Throughout the collection he maintained his conversational voice, long-winded and challenging yet intimate and often cheeky. "There is a mateyness in Durcan's work that is never presumptuous," David Kirby wrote of the collection in the *New York Times Book Review* (November 7, 1999); "his speakers come across as gentle and intelligent, from a garbage collector describing pridefully his own body ('my nipples could jump over a government minister') to a musician meditating on his strangely happy isolation as he drives home at night, 'my audience all couples canoodling behind in the village.'" Durcan's most recent collection of poems, *Cries of an Irish Caveman*, was released in 2002.

Although his reputation as a poet continues to grow internationally, Paul Durcan is perhaps best known in the United States as a former lyricist and vocalist for Belfast rocker Van Morrison. In 1995 he was awarded the Heinemann Bequest by the Royal Society for Literature, and he is a member of Aosdána, an affiliation of 200 artists that, according to the organization's Web site, "was established by the [Irish] Arts Council in 1983 to honour those artists whose work has made an outstanding contribution to the arts in Ireland." He resides in the Ringsend section of Dublin.

— E. M.

SUGGESTED READING: *Irish Times* p15 Feb. 18, 1999; *New York Times* I p11 Jan. 1, 1994; *Poetry* p94+ Oct. 1995, p109+ May 1996; *Contemporary Authors* vol. 134, 1992; *Contemporary Literary Criticism* vol.43, 1987, vol. 70, 1992

SELECTED BOOKS: *Endsville* (with Brian Lynch), 1967; *O Westport in the Light of Asia Minor: Poems*, 1975; *Teresa's Bar*, 1976; *Sam's Cross: Poems*, 1978; *Jesus, Break His Fall*, 1980; *Ark of the North*, 1982; *The Selected Paul Durcan*, 1982; *Jumping the Train Tracks with Angela*, 1983; *The Berlin Wall Café*, 1985; *Going Home to Russia*, 1987; *Daddy, Daddy*, 1990; *A Snail in My Prime*, 1993; *Give Me Your Hand*, 1994; *Christmas Day*, 1996; *Greetings to Our Friends in Brazil*, 1999; *Cries of an Irish Caveman*, 2002

Courtesy of Random House

Durham, David Anthony

Mar. 23, 1969– Novelist

David Anthony Durham has emerged in recent years as a powerful voice in African-American historical fiction. His debut novel, *Gabriel's Story* (2001), presents a wholly original view of the American West, taking up the story of an emancipated slave who settles out west. The novel was praised by critics for its attention to a subject often ignored in historical fiction. In his most recent work, *Walk Through Darkness* (2002), Durham again explores the African-American experience in the 19th century. This novel, set in the years before the Civil War, presents the parallel struggles of a fugitive slave and the white man who has been sent to track him.

David Anthony Durham wrote the following autobiographical statement for *World Authors 1995-2000*: "I was born in New York City on March 23, 1969. Both my parents are of Caribbean ancestry, and I spent a couple of my early years in Trinidad.

When my parents separated my mother and I resettled in the D.C. Metropolitan area. I attended the University of Maryland, earning a BA in English in 1992 and an MFA in Creative Writing in 1996. While an undergraduate, I received a Creative Arts Scholarship from the University of Maryland Baltimore County, as well as their Braly Prize for fiction. In 1992, I was the first place winner of the Zora Neale Hurston/Richard Wright Fiction Award. My winning story, 'The Boy-Fish,' was published in *Catalyst*.

"After college I held a variety of jobs to support my writing habit. I worked as an Outward Bound Instructor in Maryland, Maine, and North Carolina and for whitewater rafting/kayaking companies in the Southeast, California, and Scotland. I also did my time in the shifting world of transient jobs: making sushi in Baltimore, shoveling manure in Eugene, Oregon, telephone sales in Portland, bartending in Edinburgh, Scotland. I've traveled in Central America, the Caribbean, and Europe, and in 1996 I moved to Great Britain, where I've published two stories, in *Staple* and *QWF*. During my first year in the United Kingdom, I met and became engaged to my wife, Gudrun Johnston.

"During Gudrun's first pregnancy I finished my first published novel, *Gabriel's Story*. I wrote the book primarily while living in Albertville, France. I stayed home writing while my wife went to work to support us. This was my last clean chance at making it as a writer. If it didn't happen with this book, I would've had to quit writing full time. We lived in a cheap studio apartment with cramped ceilings and walls that sweated constantly. To economize, I didn't turn the heat on during the day. Instead, I sat wrapped in a winter jacket, tucked into a sleeping bag, typing away with cold fingers. Some days I could see the mist of my breath. I knew the time I had on this novel was short and precious.

"*Gabriel's Story* sprang from a fusion of old and new ideas in my writing. On the older side, I'd written two novels before ever getting to *Gabriel's Story*. The first, 'Cicada,' is about a boy growing up within a dysfunctional family. It's a good book, and I hold out the hope that it may someday see publication. The second novel, 'August Fury,' is about a boy being raised by a single mother, dealing with his father's death, and coming to grips with the violence that he finds pervasive in the world around him. This book has many strong parts, but didn't quite have the narrative drive publishers were looking for.

"On the new side, the setting for the story developed while I was reading Cormac McCarthy's Border Trilogy. I wanted to write a Western similar to McCarthy's, except that I wanted to focus on the black and minority characters as much as the white ones. I quickly merged the Western setting with the story line I had developed in 'August Fury.' The novel became the story of a boy dealing with similar adolescent issues, seeking the answers not in his local (modern) community, but in the landscape of the American West. This is what Gabriel does, and in so doing he gets caught in a whirlwind of violence on a trek through the West and Southwest of the 1870s.

"Two months after Maya's birth I received a two-book publication offer from Doubleday and Anchor. It came at a wonderful time and provided us the financial boost so that I could quit my job of the moment—pushing Brit-pop as a sales consultant at Virgin Megastore in Perth, Scotland. Our son, Sage Anthony Durham, was born in March of 2001, right in the midst of the promotional push for *Gabriel's Story*. The novel went on to be a *New York Times* Notable Book, a *Los Angeles Times* Best of 2001 pick, a Booklist Editors' choice and an Alex Award winner from the American Library Association. It also won the First Novel Award from the Black Caucus of the American Library Association.

"My second published novel is called *Walk Through Darkness*. It's also historically set and follows two men on a trek through the Mid-Atlantic region in the 1850s. The first, William, is a runaway slave searching for his pregnant wife. The second is a Scottish immigrant named Andrew Morrison, who joins the hunt for William.

"Both *Gabriel's Story* and *Walk Through Darkness* illustrate my desire to engage with aspects of American history, to challenge and expand the myths central to our identity. By 'myths' I mean the organic melding of history, fantasy and storytelling that define us as a people, illustrating our world view, ideals, hero models and aspirations. The Old West is one such myth, recognizable both at home and abroad as central to the American identity. *Gabriel's Story* uses many of the traditional trappings of this genre but looks at the subject anew by focusing on African-American protagonists. *Walk Through Darkness* seeks to look beyond the traditional preconceptions about the lives of Antebellum slaves. William's story is a tale of enduring love and an Odyssey-like adventure set within our own landscape, in a time of bubbling turmoil. I hope that the story and characterization are credible on the surface, while being symbolically potent under closer scrutiny.

"My third novel is set in the Ancient Mediterranean. It's a fictional account of the Second Punic War and will be published by Doubleday and Anchor in the U.S. and by Doubleday U.K. and Bantam in Britain in 2004. Also, an excerpt from an earlier, unpublished novel, 'Cicada,' will appear in *Gumbo: Stories by Black Writers* in the fall of 2002."

The publication of David Anthony Durham's novel *Gabriel's Story* in 2001 brought him, almost overnight, a reputation as a major new black American literary voice. The 15-year-old Gabriel treks with his mother and younger brother from post–Civil War Baltimore to Kansas to join his stepfather, a farmer. Life on the Great Plains proves to be almost unbearably hard, leading Gabriel and his friend James to join what seems to be a benevolent band of cowboys but is actually a gang of horse thieves, rapists, and murderers. Hogg, their leader, appeals to Gabriel's consciousness of slavery in the recent past: "You got an anger in you just like all your race. Rightly so. All it takes is enough anger. Put the right person through the right ordeal, and they'll kill faster than they can think." Hogg, "like . . . Milton's Satan in *Paradise Lost*, is the novel's villain and existential hero," Brad Vice noted in the *San Francisco Chronicle Book Review* (January 26, 2001). When Gabriel escapes the gang and goes back to his family, evil—personified by Hogg—follows him.

In the *New York Times Book Review* (February 25, 2001), Maria Russo characterized *Gabriel's Story* as a "bold and richly imagined . . . novel." In addition to its literary qualities, Russo judged that the book filled in a "historical lacuna. From the Underground Railroad to the Great Migration, the journey north is so important to African-American history and culture that it's easy to overlook the many black people who headed west instead." She added that in "sonorous yet disciplined language," Durham "constantly juxtaposes the twin realities of Western life, the itinerant cowboy and the industrious homesteader, mutually exclusive yet interdependent. . . . The moral weight of the novel rests on the virtues of farming and creating a stable home. Solomon, a former slave who lives in daily gratitude for the chance to build a life for his family, is a figure of quietly heroic proportions. . . . *Gabriel's Story* is both artistically impressive and emotionally satisfying, a serious work that heads off in exhilarating directions." The *Publishers Weekly* (December 4, 2000) reviewer concurred: "Durham is a born storyteller: each step of Gabriel's descent into hell proceeds from the natural logic of the narrative itself, . . . inevitable even as it's totally surprising. Equally impressive is Durham's gift for describing the awful beauty of the American West: 'The April sky was not a thing of air and gas. . . . Rather it lay like a solid ceiling of slate, pressing the living down into the prairie.'"

Walk Through Darkness, Durham's 2002 novel, is set in an earlier period—before the Civil War. In it, William, a slave with a cruel master and a pregnant wife, escapes when his wife is taken to Philadelphia. After being recaptured twice, he finally reaches Philadelphia, with no idea of how to find his wife. By this time his story has been joined with that of Morrison, a Scottish immigrant who is trying to track William. Chapters that deal with Morrison alternate with William's narrative, until the climax, when the guilty secret in Morrison's past is revealed to involve William. "The abominable treatment of slaves is always in the foreground," the *Publishers Weekly* (April 1, 2002) reviewer wrote about the novel, "but Durham never succumbs to sentimentality. . . . In the thrilling climax, Morrison reveals an unexpected tie that binds him to William and makes a gesture that he hopes will redeem his sins. Durham's writing is forceful and full of startling imagery as he testifies to the courage (and sometimes the ambivalence) of people who, in one way or another, rebelled against the great injustice in American history."

—*S. Y.*

SUGGESTED READING: *Christian Science Monitor* p18 Jan. 25, 2001; *January Magazine* (on-line) 2001; *New York Times* E p9 May 16, 2002; *New York Times Book Review* p7 Feb. 25, 2001, p33 June 9, 2002; *Publishers Weekly* p54 Dec. 4, 2000, p50 Apr. 1, 2002; *San Francisco Chronicle Book Review* (on-line) Jan. 28, 2001

SELECTED BOOKS: *Gabriel's Story*, 2001; *Walk Through Darkness*, 2002

Dwyer, Kelly

Feb. 28, 1964– Novelist

Kelly Dwyer is the young author of two novels, *The Tracks of Angels* (1994) and *Self-Portrait with Ghosts* (1998). Her characters struggle to make sense of loss and death and to unsnarl the emotional entanglements of familial relationships. Belying its title, *The Tracks of Angels* drew the applause of critics partly for its down-to-earth sensibility. *Self-Portrait with Ghosts* was praised for its convincingly intricate picture of depression and the way it hinders its victims' will to confront the daunting realities of everyday life. Dwyer is the recipient of a James Michener/Paul Engle Fellowship, a Wisconsin Arts Board grant, and an award from the Wisconsin Library Association.

Born on February 28, 1964 in Torrence, California, Kelly Dwyer is the daughter of Richard Stanley Dwyer and Sharon Arlene (Speigler) Dwyer. In 1984 she worked as a field manager for the Voting Power Action Committee in Berkeley, California. She earned a B.A. from Oberlin College, in Oberlin, Ohio, in 1987, and her MFA in creative writing from the University of Iowa, in Iowa City, in 1990. From 1994 to 1996 she was a visiting assistant professor at Oberlin College.

The Tracks of Angels, as Dwyer noted to Greg Shapiro for *Outlines* (January 20, 1999, on-line), was unintentionally published at a time when angels were the latest fad, and the book may have profited from this, despite the fact that its taciturn angel is decidedly unstylish. The book is narrated by 18-year-old Laura Neuman, who has recently lost her mother to cancer and her father to suicide. (Laura is part-Jewish and part-Catholic, the same as Dwyer herself.) She flees California and ends up in Boston, where she finds a job as a waitress and gets romantically involved with a young man. Her new relationship helps her heal from her parents' untimely deaths, as do imagined visits from her irritable, dingy guardian angel, who refuses to give her any insight into the nature of God.

"Ms. Dwyer's narrative can be a bit too delicate at times, and it suffers occasionally from weak story and character development," Mindi Dickstein wrote in the New York Times Book Review (March 13, 1994). "But there are enough flights of lyricism in *The Tracks of Angels* to make it a moving inquiry into the nature of loss." Noting Laura's observation that God and love are like cats because neither comes when called, Susan Dooley wrote in the *Washington Post Book World* (January 23, 1994), "Laura learns that even if you can't whistle love in with the wind, you can come to understand it. In this beautifully written book, Dwyer and her grubby angel help the reader to do the same."

Self-Portrait with Ghosts is the story of an estranged family reunited by tragedy, (although it was mistakenly listed as a horror novel by the online bookseller Amazon.com, because of its title). Kate Flannigan is a sculptor and the divorced mother of 13-year-old Audrey. Ten years ago Kate left her husband, Sam, after she found out that he was having an affair with her beautiful sister, Colleen. Since then Kate has broken ties with Sam and Colleen and concentrated on sculpting mythic figures, often modeled after her family members. Just as she has begun a statue of herself as Zeus giving birth to Audrey from her head (as Zeus did to Athena), her older brother, Luke, commits suicide. Through flashbacks the reader learns how Luke helped his mother raise his two younger sisters after the death of their father in a car accident. Always a caring brother, he was nevertheless plagued by depression, which at times paralyzed him. Dwyer explained to Shapiro why she chose depression as a topic: "I think it's because it's just so ubiquitous. I've read some statistics that seemed kind of horrifying to me, and one of them is that one in five adults suffer from depression at any given time. Others say one in ten, but still that seems really high." Luke's deadly bout with the disease has a positive aspect in that it helps to reconcile Kate, Sam, and Colleen, and enables Audrey to meet the father she hardly knows.

Wendy Brandmark, writing in the *Times Literary Supplement* (March 19, 1999), felt that the novel was too pat and marred by "sentimentality or coy cuteness." "Maybe she is too close to her characters," Brandmark offered, "too determined to resolve their conflicts and round off her book, rather than leave her readers with some nagging questions." Other critics were not bothered by the story's optimistic resolution. "Dwyer is a master at depicting the ghosts haunting modern life—loss, alienation, guilt—without being maudlin," Reba Melinda Leiding wrote in *Library Journal* (November 15, 1998). In *Publishers Weekly* (October 26, 1998) Sybil S. Steinberg—though she complained that "at times the dialogue is stagy, the symbolism is obvious and the characters naively portrayed"—concluded that these were "minor defects. Dwyer moves gracefully from character to character and from past to present. She gets the intergenerational dialogue just right, often with a flash of humor, and the distinctive voices ring true. Even jaded readers will be moved by this novel of quiet metamorphosis."

Dwyer married Louis A. Wenzlow on January 5, 1991; they live outside of Chicago, where she is working on a third novel.

—P. G. H.

SUGGESTED READING: *Library Journal* p90 Nov. 15, 1998; *Los Angeles Times* p6 Mar. 6, 1994; *New York Times Book Review* p18 Mar. 13, 1994; *Outlines* (on-line) Jan. 20, 1999; *Publishers Weekly* p41 Oct. 26, 1998; *Times Literary Supplement* p24 Mar. 19, 1999; *Washington Post Book World* p6 Jan. 23, 1994

SELECTED BOOKS: *The Tracks of Angels*, 1994; *Self-Portrait with Ghosts*, 1998

Valerie Guglielmi/Courtesy of Farrar, Straus and Giroux

Dyer, Geoff

June 5, 1958– Nonfiction writer; journalist; novelist

Geoff Dyer's work consistently refuses to fit into any one genre. *But Beautiful: A Book About Jazz* (1992) is ostensibly a sweeping biography of some of jazz's greats, but Dyer infuses their stories with his own sharply imagined fictive details. *Out of Sheer Rage: Wrestling with D. H. Lawrence* (1998) at first appears to be a scholarly work on Lawrence, but it soon turns into an examination of writer's block and a general commentary on modern life. Even Dyer's novels—*The Colour of Memory*, 1989; *The Search*, 1993; and *Paris Trance*, 1998— downplay narrative structure in favor of atmospheric evocation and philosophical investigation. *The Search*, for instance, borrows from Mickey Spillane crime novels and Arthurian legends, using the mystery and quest forms to investigate the nature of truth, motivation, and character. Such eclecticism has exposed Dyer to criticism from some quarters that he lacks focus and discipline. Yet his work consistently attracts widespread interest, and he remains one of the most talked-about young authors in England. Dyer has also written for such journals as the *New Statesman*, *Listener*, *City Limits*, and *New Society*.

Geoff Dyer writes for *World Authors 1995–2000*: "I was born in Cheltenham, Gloucestershire (our little English version of the mid-west) in 1958. For many people Cheltenham is synonymous with 'upper-middle-class' but ours was a working-class family (my dad was a sheet metal worker and my mum worked as a 'dinner lady' at the local school). I had no brothers and sisters and, if I remember rightly (I probably don't), I was often bored and lonely. I passed the 11-plus and went to the local grammar school—the first steps along the well-trodden route of the scholarship boy. When I was about 15 or 16 I fell under the influence of my English teacher, Bob Beale, started doing well at school and began to read a lot. D. H. Lawrence, obviously, was a huge presence, but, like many people of my generation, I was drawn to American rather than British fiction and, to this day, my two favourite novels are *On the Road* and *Tender is the Night*. I got three grade 'A' A-Levels (which, sadly, is still my greatest achievement) and then went to Oxford to read English. I was—and still am—the only person in my family to go to university but I wouldn't want to exaggerate the 'pulled myself up by my own bootstraps' aspect of this: I just rode an educational escalator that had been functioning efficiently—if selectively—for many years before I stepped aboard.

"Unlike many people I knew exactly what I wanted to do when I graduated: sign on the dole. Oxford had given me a taste for idleness which the heyday of Thatcher-induced unemployment provided ample opportunity to indulge. It was a great time to be unemployed because the previous regime's provisions for social security were still in place. Also, since so many other people were out of work (especially in Brixton, south London, where I was living), there were plenty of people to hang out and smoke pot with in the afternoons. I still regard this period of state-funded leisure—from about 1980 to 1984—as the time of my greatest intellectual development. This was when I read Adorno, Foucault, Barthes, Calvino, Raymond Williams and, crucially, John Berger. My immersion in American fiction was kind of counterbalanced by European 'theory' (though Barthes and Foucault for me are great *writers* rather than theorists). At university I thought that you were either a writer (which meant you wrote novels) or a critic (which meant you wrote about other people's novels); now I became aware of another way of being a creative writer without having to think up stories or plots. I still find myself kicking against the widespread, unthinking assumption that the novel is the loftiest perch of imaginative creation in prose. There is more imaginative daring in a page of Rebecca West's *Black Lamb, Grey Falcon* or Berger's *Success and Failure of Picasso* than there is in many conventional literary novels. At the risk of sounding immodest I think that three of my books *But Beautiful*, *The Missing of the Somme* and *Out of Sheer Rage*—inhabit this unclassifiable, highly original region between different genres.

"In the early 80s I started writing book reviews for magazines and gradually got more freedom to write other, more imaginative pieces. My first book was a dull critical study of John Berger who has been the most important influence on my writing life. From him I got the confidence to write about whatever interested me, rather than pursuing any kind of specialism. I tend to write about something to find out about it and I lose interest in it once I've finished writing about it. As a result I think I've found it hard to build up a consistent readership: jazz lovers know the jazz book, people who are into Lawrence know the Lawrence book etc. Maybe this is why the book that means most to me is *Anglo-English Attitudes*, a collection of bits and pieces published in magazines and papers over the last fifteen years: the unruly range of my interests all held together in a single volume.

"My first novel, *The Colour of Memory* is a kind of elegy for that idyllic period of hanging out, unemployed, in Brixton. Originally it was going to be a non-fiction type account of my life. At that time I often found myself wishing I had a sister and I suddenly had a great insight into the liberating potential of fiction. You want a sister? Easy: invent one! Even better, invent one you'd like to sleep with. At this time I was starting to fall in love with jazz and despite the fact that I knew almost nothing about it, in 1989, a few months after *The Colour of Memory* came out, I went to New York to write a book about jazz. This gave me a taste for living abroad. I next went to live in New Orleans to write *The Search*. Then I went to live in Paris to try to write a novel that was, I hoped, going to be a contemporary version of *Tender is the Night*, but I failed to make any progress and actually wrote two other books—*The Missing of the Somme* (occasioned by a visit to the First World War cemeteries in northern France) and *Out of Sheer Rage*—before doing so. I eventually wrote the *Tender* book in Paris and Rome in the late 90s. I was going to call it *The Awakening of Stones* (a line from Rilke's poem 'Memory') but my English publisher wanted something with the word 'Paris' in the title. I settled on *Paris Dream-time* even though that didn't feel quite right. Then, at the last moment, just before the cover was printed, at a party in North Carolina, I thought of *Paris Trance* which was perfect, even better than the Rilke.

"My life has fallen into a recognisable pattern since I first lived outside of England in 1989: travel, living in different countries, interludes in England, idleness and boredom leading to a descent into despondency that is hopefully arrested by some new, all-consuming enthusiasm. The theme running through all my work is, I think, a sense of purposelessness briefly evaded. When asked 'Why do you climb?' a French mountaineer answered, 'To conquer the uselessness.' I suppose I feel the same about writing.

"At this point, however, rather than defining myself in terms of my individual literary comings and goings, I prefer to locate myself within the context of a larger movement. In 1999 I went to Burning Man in the Black Rock Desert, Nevada, [an annual gathering of artists and others that terms itself an experimental community] and have been back each year since. I don't consider myself a British or European writer. Ultimately, in fact, I don't even consider myself a writer. It's enough—more than enough, it's everything I could ever have dreamed of—to be a citizen of Black Rock City."

Born on June 5, 1958, Dyer had an early fascination with American comic books, which exposed him to a fantasy world and gave him his first conception of large American cities, where many comic books are set. Comics, as Dyer explained in an autobiographical essay in *Harper's Magazine* (February 1999), also set the stage for his adult literary preferences. "Superhero comics not only had what [D. H.] Lawrence called 'a profound influence on my childish consciousness'; they also formed my tastes as a reader and, to a degree, my style as a writer. The very pervasiveness of their influence in this regard makes it difficult to pin down precisely."

Dyer earned a B.A. with honors from Corpus Christi College, Oxford University, in 1980. Among his favorite writers as a student were the novelist D. H. Lawrence, the playwright John Osborne, and the art critic John Berger, about whom he wrote his first book, a critical biography called *Ways of Telling: The Work of John Berger*, published in Great Britain in 1986. In a later book, *Anglo-English Attitudes* (1999), Dyer, as quoted by a critic for the *Complete Review* (on-line), described *Ways of Telling* as "my dull little book about [John Berger]." (The title refers to Berger's seminal 1972 work, *Ways of Seeing*, which discusses the intersections of art and capitalism.) The *Complete Review* critic was more sympathetic, calling it a "useful, though now dated (i.e. not up-dated), survey of John Berger's life and work. It still has value as such. The great value of this book, however, is in what it reveals about Geoff Dyer. Dyer is one of the more interesting writers of this age. Stylistically superior to Berger (and most other writers), though still lacking a certain critical acumen, Dyer practices as Berger preaches."

In 1989 Dyer published his first novel, *The Colour of Memory*. Thin on plot and substantial in its philosophical and literary concerns, the book contains allusions to Friedrich Nietzsche, Italo Calvino, Roland Barthes, and others. It follows a group of young people living "on the dole," or public assistance, in the southern London neighborhood of Brixton. In the*New Statesman & Society* (May 19, 1989) Paul Oldfield called it a "cross-section of south London life in the eighties that shows us all the right cultural signifiers in pin-sharp prose: warehouse parties, jazz revival, Baudrillard." In his withering review for the *Spectator* (September 2, 1989), Nicholas Lezard described the novel as being "self-obsessed and deluded at the same time." He pointed to the novel's meandering narrative and many literary and pop cultural allusions as evidence of its essential weakness.

Dyer next wrote *But Beautiful: A Book About Jazz* (published in the U.K. in 1991, and in the U.S. in 1992), a loose biography of the jazz greats Lester Young, Thelonious Monk, Bud Powell, Charles Mingus, Ben Webster, Chet Baker, Art Pepper, Duke Ellington, and Harry Carney. Dyer, as he warns in the introduction, takes liberties in relating the incidents of their lives; he elaborates from the core facts and invents dialogue and details. Most of all, he attempts to capture in words the improvisational flights of music that characterized each man's unique genius. Of the bassist Charles Mingus, Dyer writes, as quoted by Richard Bernstein for the *New York Times* (March 20, 1996), "Some people played the bass like sculptors, carving notes out of an unwieldy piece of stone; Mingus played it like he was wrestling, getting in close, working inside, grabbing at the neck, and plucking strings like guts. . . . Then he'd touch the strings softly as a bee landing on the pink petals of an African flower growing some place no one had ever been. When he bowed it he made the bass sound like the humming of a thousand-strong congregation in church."

Critical response to the book was overwhelmingly positive; it was considered by many to be one of the best recent books about jazz. Bernstein wrote, "*But Beautiful* is . . . beautiful, an ingenious and brilliantly written book. Even readers not fascinated by jazz above other kinds of music are likely to find Mr. Dyer too good a literary craftsman to put the book down." In the *Library Journal* (November 15, 1995) Dan Bogey wrote, "Dyer evokes the rhythm and feeling of the music as his words echo the forlorn, aching sound of a midnight solo."

In 1992 Dyer won the Somerset Maugham Prize for *But Beautiful*. With the prize money, he moved to New Orleans, Louisiana, where he worked on his next novel, *The Search* (1993), which is set in fictional American towns. The novel begins like a conventional detective novel. At a party, Walker, a "tracker," or finder of missing persons, meets an alluring woman who asks him to search for her missing husband, Malory. The trail is weak: there is only a fuzzy photograph of Malory and the name of a town, some distance away, where he recently rented a car. Not long after Walker begins his search, he realizes he is being followed by a man named Carver, who is also looking for Malory. Walker continues to cross paths with Carver as he travels across a surreal landscape, through a town called "Avlona," which is completely deserted, and another town in which everyone is frozen in mid-gesture. Dyer tells his story in the stark tone of film noir, yet *The Search* also bears comparison to a medieval, Arthurian quest. Malory, for example, refers to Sir Thomas Malory, author of *Morte d'Arthur*, and Walker is explicitly linked to Sir Lancelot.

Reviews of *The Search* were mixed. In the *New Statesman & Society* (November 26, 1993) Peter Jukes noted that Dyer "has a poet's gift with metaphor as well as an ability to grasp ideas, hold them up to the light, pass them on." But he concluded that "it's both the greatest strength and salient weakness of *The Search* that none of its fictional characters is as vocal, powerful or interesting as their author." Nicholas Royle wrote in the London *Guardian* (November 30, 1993), "A short, brilliant novel, *The Search* offers more in 150 pages than most books twice that length."

In 1994 Dyer published *The Missing of the Somme*, an extended essay about World War I. The title refers to the Battle of the Somme, in which English and French troops launched an offensive against the Germans in northern France, near the Somme River, and where more than a million men perished. Dyer, whose grandfather fought in the war, injects the essay with both personal and philosophical observations about this incredible loss of life. Jason Cowley, writing in the London *Guardian* (October 18, 1994), called Dyer an "unusually interesting writer," yet was ultimately dissatisfied with the fluid structure of *The Missing of the Somme*. "It meanders and drifts, taking in film, poetry, sculpture and painting; ideas flicker and dazzle, lighting up the pages like flares, before incandescently fading. Yet, paradoxically, the book's formlessness—its inclusiveness, indiscipline and intellectual promiscuousness—works in the end against Dyer. He has so much to say, yet allows himself so little space in which to say it." A radio adaptation of *The Missing of the Somme*, entitled "A Shadow into the Future," was broadcast on BBC on the eve of the 80th anniversary of the Battle of the Somme.

In 1995 Dyer set out to write a scholarly study of one of his literary heroes, D. H. Lawrence, but he was continually distracted from his task, especially by ideas for a new novel. The result of his quandary was *Out of Sheer Rage: Wrestling With D. H. Lawrence* (1998), a book as much about the process of writing as about Lawrence. Dyer, along with his girlfriend, Laura, follows Lawrence's trail through Paris, Rome, Greece, and Oxford, and finally ends up in Taos, New Mexico, where Lawrence died. Along the way Dyer writes about everything from his own genius for procrastination to the decline, as he sees it, of the novel; he also considers the absurdities of modern life, and to a lesser extent, the works of Lawrence. Critics generally applauded Dyer's genre-bending book. In the *Washington Post Book World* (September 6, 1998) Kelly Murphy Mason wrote, "*Out of Sheer Rage* is smart and furious enough to justify its many detours." Christopher Lehmann-Haupt, in the *New York Times* (April 20, 1998), wrote, "Mr. Dyer's plight might seem tedious, even depressing, but for the fact that the book he can't write—or rather the book about the books he can't write—keeps unwinding before your eyes in sinuous, comic prose. . . . [It] keeps circling its subject in widening loops and then darting at it when you least expect it to."

Dyer's third novel, *Paris Trance*, was published in the U.S., in 1998. It is the story of four expatriates living in Paris. Luke and Alex are young English wanderers who meet in Paris and soon find themselves in romantic relationships with, respectively, Nicole, a Yugoslav immigrant, and Sahra, an American. A latter-day incarnation of the 1920s "Lost Generation," as chronicled by Ernest Hemingway, F. Scott Fitzgerald, and others, the young expatriates move aimlessly through Paris, looking for amusement and distraction. An encounter with a trapped stag bleeding in a snowy field provides a thematic center to the novel, whose characters seem similarly trapped.

Critical responses to the novel were mixed. Some critics, such as Richard Eder, writing in the *New York Times* (June 2, 1999), thought that Dyer failed to bring substance to his material. "Mr. Dyer, depicting a culture that is divorced from consequences and suffers the consequences of the divorce, voices his theme too abstractly," Eder wrote. "He locates but does not quite deliver the 'lost' of his contemporary lost generation." Others saw *Paris Trance* as a definitive portrait of the "new" lost generation. "There are books, such as *The Great Gatsby*, whose callowness is itself profound, whose charm is persistingly, enduringly transient," Candia McWilliam wrote in the *New Statesman* (April 17, 1998). "Geoff Dyer has written such a book." McWilliam concluded, "It takes a writer as clear as this to show us what we are up to and as charming as this to make us able to sit still and face the mischief we make."

In 1999 Dyer published a collection of his essays and journalistic writings, *Anglo-English Attitudes: Essays, Reviews, Misadventures 1984–99*. The book covers many topics, which, as John Berger listed them in the London *Guardian* (November 13, 1999), include "photos, prizefighters, Bosnia, Roland Barthes, kids' comics, Cartier-Bresson, jazz, Graham Greene, techno, being in love, model aircraft, Coltrane playing 'My Favorite Things,' Def Leppard, General Franco, flying MiG jets." Critics found the essays consistently illuminating and praised both Dyer's breadth of knowledge and the clarity and originality of presentation. Paul Bonaventura, in *Modern Painters* (Spring 2000), wrote,

"Anglo-English Attitudes is one of the most rewarding books to emerge from Britain in the past twelve months, 'fiction' and 'non-fiction' alike." In the London Times (November 27, 1999) Jason Cowley lauded, "Dyer's has long been a name to look out for amid the gossip, prurient interviews and celebrity trash of modern newspapers. That he exists at all, in such ruthlessly materialistic times—unattached to any newspaper, always on the move—is a celebration in itself. This book, a tribute to his persistence and originality, deserves to have a long afterlife."

In 2000 Dyer co-edited, with Margaret Sartor, What Was True: The Photographs and Notebooks of William Gedney, the 20th-century American photographer. The following year he edited Selected Essays: John Berger (2001). Dyer's most recent book, Yoga For People Who Can't Be Bothered to Do It (2003), a collection of 11 personal essays about his travels around the world, was deemed another critical success.

—P. G. H.

SUGGESTED READING: Guardian Oct. 18, 1994; Harper's Magazine p29+ Feb. 1999; Library Journal p76 Nov. 15, 1995; Modern Painters p135 Spring 2000; New Statesman p49 Apr. 17, 1998; New Statesman & Society p25+ May 19, 1989, p46+ Nov. 26, 1993, p13 Jan. 1994; New York Times C p20 Mar. 20, 1996, E p8 Apr. 20, 1998, E p8 June 2, 1999; Spectator p31 Sept. 2, 1989; London Times p21 Nov. 27, 1999

SELECTED BOOKS: novels—The Colour of Memory, 1989; The Search, 1993; Paris Trance, 1998; nonfiction—Ways of Telling: The Work of John Berger, 1986; But Beautiful: A Book About Jazz, 1992; The Missing of the Somme, 1994; Out of Sheer Rage: Wrestling With D. H. Lawrence, 1998; Anglo-English Attitudes: Essays, Reviews, Misadventures 1984–99, 1999; Yoga For People Who Can't Be Bothered to Do It, 2003; as editor—What Was True: The Photographs and Notebooks of William Gedney, 2000 (with Margaret Sartor); Selected Essays: John Berger, 2001

Eady, Cornelius

1954– Poet

"[Cornelius] Eady . . . is quickly emerging as one of the most skilled and sensitive African American writers," Rochelle Ratner observed in a critique for Library Journal (March 1, 1995). Indeed, since publishing his first collection of verse, Kartunes, in 1980, Eady has released six additional critically admired volumes that reflect his experiences as an African-American male. His poems often invoke music—both in their subject matter and their lyrical nature—and echo the poet's passion for the cadences of language. Eady has adapted two of his books for the stage, collaborating with the composer Diedre L. Murray in the Off-Broadway musical productions of You Don't Miss Your Water (1997) and Brutal Imagination (2002); he also wrote the text for Murray's award-winning jazz opera Running Man (1999).

Cornelius Eady was born in 1954 in Rochester, New York, and spent his entire childhood there. Since the early 20th century, Rochester had been a popular destination for blacks seeking union-protected jobs and the opportunity to buy property. Eady's parents had migrated from Florida for these reasons, and by the time their son was born, they were living comfortably in a conservative community that seemed ideal for raising a family. Despite these pleasant surroundings, Eady's home life was far from idyllic; his parents endured a tumultuous relationship and never legally married. His backyard was situated close to the Pennsylvania Railroad, and he spent much of his childhood roaming the area and imagining what lay beyond his hometown. When this hunger for knowledge

Courtesy of Chelsea Forum

could not be satisfied through simple youthful exploration, he turned to the public library, voraciously reading everything he could find. He was particularly drawn to poetry and began reading a diverse collection of verse by such poets as William Carlos Williams, Amiri Baraka, Pablo Neruda, and Allen Ginsberg. Eady often sampled the library's eclectic music collection, as well, sitting for hours and listening to classical music, jazz, blues, and rock.

Eady's fascination for the sounds of music and language soon merged, and he began writing poems of his own. While his father regarded the hobby as impractical because it provided little means to make a living, Eady received encouragement from his teachers, who noticed his skills in using rhyme and lyrical language. One of his earliest poems dealt with the assassination of Martin Luther King Jr. and, as he recalled to Natasha Trethewey for *Ploughshares* (Spring 2002, on-line), it garnered much attention from his peers and teachers. "People were coming up to me, telling me how they had been thinking exactly what I'd articulated for them in the poem," he said. "I realized then poetry's larger implications." For his junior and senior years of high school, Eady attended Rochester Educational Alternative, a school known for its liberal curriculum. There, he told Trethewey, he spent most days absorbed in "marathon writing sessions" that allowed him to further develop his poetic craft. For college he remained in Rochester and enrolled at Empire State University, majoring in English with a concentration in creative writing. He began seeking out collections of verse by African-American poets. On discovering the work of Yusef Komunyakaa, Eady recalled to Trethewey, "I was thrilled because it was that moment when you actually find yourself in the books you're reading." He later attended the prestigious MFA program at Warren Wilson College, in Asheville, North Carolina.

In 1980 Eady released his first book of poems, *Kartunes*, which received little critical attention. However, his next book, *Victims of the Latest Dance Craze* (1985), helped distinguish him as an important emerging poet: this volume won the 1985 Lamont Poetry Prize from the Academy of American Poets, an honor that recognizes a poet's second work. In this collection Eady presents conversational poems that explore various forms of dance and, to a lesser degree, the musical energy behind them. Referencing styles from ballet to the twist, Eady examines dance's varied influence on his subjects, who range from ordinary speakers to such classical figures as Shakespeare's Ophelia. Critics praised the work as vibrant and original. H. Fox wrote for *Choice* (September 1986), "The book is full of uplift. It is written with a helium pen." The reviewer continued, "Never really simply descriptive, Eady is always evocative, splicing the everyday with undreamed-of, off-the-wall image partners. If he can keep up the energy, extend and amplify it, if he can 'last' on the writing track over the years, what we have here could be a future Whitman." Thomas Swiss, writing for the *New York Times* (November 30, 1986), noted that there was "much to admire in Mr. Eady's work." Swiss concluded, "Individual poems, especially long ones, can veer off wildly, changing the subject or multiplying images until there is too much action on stage. . . . But this is a poet of great energy and resourcefulness. If he digresses more than we would like him to, we nevertheless admire his particular vision."

Eady's next book, *Boom Boom Boom* (1988), received few reviews, but the critical success of his fourth collection, *The Gathering of My Name* (1991), secured his reputation as an innovative lyrical poet; the volume was nominated for the 1991 Pulitzer Prize for poetry. In it Eady returns to musical themes, even addressing several poems to such jazz and rock legends as John Coltrane, Elvis Presley, Thelonious Monk, and Hank Mobley. In the poem "Thelonious Monk," he employs a fragmented narrative style that recreates the tone of Monk's own jazz music. As Eady explained to Daniel Kane in an interview for *Teachers & Writers* (April 22, 1999, on-line), the poem was intended to pay homage to Monk, while invoking the musician's distinct style. "That was the idea—finding a way of duplicating the playfulness in Monk's music," he said. "It's a playfulness that's also very deliberate in Monk. It took people years to find out that what they thought was Monk hitting bad notes or off notes was actually a strategy, reimagining what musical sound could be about. So I was trying to find a way within language to duplicate that—that's why you get those odd line breaks, that odd meter."

The volume also includes several verses with messages about racism and urban life. Leslie Ullman observed for the *Kenyon Review* (Summer 1992), "Most impressive about this collection is Eady's ability to use language to translate, through evocation, what can't be translated directly without tremendous loss of resonance. He does this brilliantly enough in his poems that evoke dynamics of music, but he does it at an even more effective level in several poems that translate the experience of being Black in America. It's no easy thing, at this time, for an African-American poet to find language that breaks through sociological and political configurations to sting us directly and afresh with a taste of his of her experience." In "Song," for example, he tells of having racial slurs "spat" at him in Lynchburg, Virginia. "Sherbet," which deals with being denied service by a waitress while sitting with his white wife, as quoted by Ullman, includes the lines:

. . . What poetry
Could describe the
perfect angle of

This woman's back as
She walks, just so,
Mapping the room off

Like the end of a
Border dispute, which
Metaphor could turn

The room more perfectly
Into a group of
Islands? And when

The manager finally
Arrives, what language
Do I use

To translate the nervous
Eye motions, the yawning
Afternoon silence, the

Prayer beneath
His simple inquiries,
The sherbet which

He then brings to the table personally,
Just to be certain
The doubt

Stays on our side
Of the fence?

After *The Gathering of My Name*, Eady published *You Don't Miss Your Water* (1995), a collection of poems dealing with his father's death from cancer. Despite the thematic departure, he again relied heavily on musical motifs. The book's title, for example, alludes to a song lyric that reads, "But when you left me, / O how I cried. / You don't miss your water / till the well runs dry," as quoted by Robert Hass for the *Washington Post* (June 21, 1998). Eady explained to Orlando Ramirez for the California *Press–Enterprise* (February 16, 1997) that each poem within the collection takes its title from a song lyric. "[The titles] serve as a subtext to anchor the central metaphor of [the] poem and give you a sense of the emotional location of the poem," he said. "Sometimes we remember songs incorrectly and the way we remember our parents aren't always reliable memories. I use that as a way to get clarity or understanding about the relationship." The poems in this collection often resemble short prose monologues more than traditional verse. "This is a big story I wanted to tell," Eady told Ramirez, "but I had to tell it in pieces. It is not a memoir, but I wanted to approach it at the level of a poem. It took me a while to realize this was the mode that worked best."

The 21 poems in *You Don't Miss Your Water* describe painful aspects of Eady's relationship with his father, as well as the difficult circumstances that characterized the elder man's demise. In "A Little Bit of Soap," for example, Eady recalls his father's distaste for dark skin, which the poet describes as "skin that seemed born to give up." The elder Eady often told his son, who was of a darker complexion, "Maybe you ought to wash more," as quoted by Hass. In another poem, Eady describes how his mother refuses to legally commit to the man on his deathbed, even though she will be denied ownership of her home and access to his pension after his death. "In a voice that could damn a saint," Eady writes, as quoted by Anthony Tommasini for the *New York Times* (June 28, 1997), "she is telling us she'd rather starve on her anger than feed off his slow regret." Later in the book, the poet discusses his sister's anger over discovering a "secret" half-sister whom his father had concealed. The critical response to this collection was overwhelmingly favorable. A reviewer for *Publishers Weekly* (February 27, 1995) declared, "This is a small book of tremendous power and grace. . . . Like a high-wire walker moving steadily along an almost invisible tension, Eady writes with simplicity and apparent ease." In June 1997 the book was adapted for the stage in an Off-Broadway musical production at New York's Vineyard Theater. Featuring music by the jazz cellist and composer Diedre L. Murray, *You Don't Miss Your Water* received generally positive theatrical reviews. While some theater critics found Murray's musical score somewhat muted, Tommasini observed, "The words are so strong, it's understandable that in providing music for them Ms. Murray mostly stays out of the way. . . . There is elegance and honesty in Mr. Eady's words, and these characters will stay with you."

The Autobiography of a Jukebox (1997), Eady's next book, is divided into four sections; it includes a group of poems about his family, another documenting his reaction to the Rodney King beating, and a group of poems labeled "Small Moments." Many critics considered the strongest verses to be those in a fourth group, which deals with jazz. For example, in the poem "Why Was I Born? A Conversation Between John Coltrane and Kenny Burrell," Eady invents a dialogue between these two legendary musicians. Writing for the *Buffalo News* (April 2, 2000), R. D. Pohl observed, "No contemporary poet has explored the complementary relationship between the lyric voice and popular music or jazz more productively than Eady."

In 1999 Eady teamed again with Murray to write the text for a jazz opera she composed entitled *Running Man*, about a black child prodigy whose life runs a disastrous course. Murray developed the story as a fictionalized account of her brother, who died of a heroin overdose at age 49. The play begins with the title character's sister, Miss Look, standing at a slave cemetery, where she encounters an oracle named Seven who guides her toward understanding her brother's road to self-destruction. Murray's musical score combined elements of jazz, opera, gospel, and soul, and generally defied traditional musical categorization. Of his role in the project, Eady wrote in the program notes, as quoted by Pheralyn Dove for the *Philadelphia Tribune* (November 9, 1999), "When Diedre asked me to provide the text for this piece—a cycle of poems which was then 'imploded' by her into dialogue and songs—her concept was to compose an elegy to all the lost 'runners' out there." The production, which opened in New York City and was later revived in Philadelphia, received critical acclaim, garnering two 1999 Obie Awards (for best musical score and lead actor in a musical) and nominations for the New York Drama Critics Circle Award for best musical and the Pulitzer Prize for drama. Pamela Renner, writing for the *Village Voice* (March 16,

1999), characterized Eady's contribution: "[His] text, elliptical and suggestive, gives *Running Man*'s voyage a poetic compass to chart its course."

Eady published the text for *Running Man* in his seventh volume of poems, *Brutal Imagination* (2001), which also featured a series of poems about a fictional black criminal, known as Mr. Zero. Here, Eady invents Mr. Zero as the persona of the black male who was accused of abducting Susan Smith's children in South Carolina, in 1994. (The Susan Smith case made national news headlines when Smith alleged that she had been car-jacked by an African-American male, who, she claimed, then drove off with her children. After a nine-day search, during which several witnesses came forward contending to have seen the culprit, Smith admitted that she had made up the story and had in fact rolled her Mazda into a lake, drowning her two sons in the backseat.) Eady's book explores the genesis of this mythical figure and examines his relationship with both Smith and greater society. He places Mr. Zero within a long legacy of invented black characters, including Aunt Jemima, Uncle Tom, Steppin' Fetchit, and Buckwheat—many of whom deliver monologues in the collection. In a review for the *Village Voice* (January 22, 2002), Alisa Solomon noted, "Eady's ingenious idea in *Brutal Imagination* is to bring this phantasmagoric, threatening everyman to life, and to let us hear what it's like to be, as he puts it, 'a stray thought, a solution,' and 'the scariest face you could think of.'" The book received widespread critical acclaim and earned a nomination for the 2001 National Book Award for poetry. *Brutal Imagination* was adapted for the stage in 2002, opening Off-Broadway in New York's Vineyard Theater and again teaming Eady with Murray and the director Diane Paulus (who had directed *Running Man*). While most theater critics acknowledged Eady's bold political message, they found the piece less effective as theater than as a book of poetry. In a review for the *New York Times* (January 10, 2002), Ben Brantley wrote, "It's the kind of concept that grabs you instantly and ferociously, and a corresponding excitement glitters through the opening moments." He continued, "The excitement, however, is intellectual, which in theater in enough to arouse interest but not to sustain it." Gordon Cox wrote for *New York Newsday* (January 10, 2002), "While the intellectual ripples stirred by Mr. Zero are well-examined, the visceral push-and-pull between Smith and Mr. Zero never quite comes to theatrical focus."

Eady has published his work in numerous literary journals, including *Callaloo, American Scholar, Kenyon Review, Prairie Schooner,* and *Ploughshares.* His poems have been anthologized in *Every Shut Eye Ain't Asleep: An Anthology of Poetry by African Americans Since 1945* (1994) and *The Vintage Book of African American Poetry* (2000).

In 1996 Eady collaborated with the poet Toi Derricotte in founding Cave Canem, a nonprofit organization dedicated to providing a strong, nurturing community for African-American poets. "It began as a series of conversations with various black writers and scholars," he told Trethewey, "loose talk that often ended when the question of money arose. Then Sarah, my wife, suggested we just pay for it ourselves. For the first two years, we did." Since then the organization has sponsored summer retreats at the Mount St. Alphonsus Retreat Center on the Hudson River, where approximately 52 fellows are invited each year to craft poems and discuss their work with mentors and peers. Cave Canem has also established an annual book prize for young poets and is widely recognized for helping expand and celebrate the canon of African-American literature.

Throughout his prolific career, Eady has received many prestigious fellowships and awards, including a National Endowment for the Arts fellowship in literature (1985); a John Simon Guggenheim fellowship in poetry (1993); a Lila Wallace–*Readers Digest* Traveling Scholarship to Tougaloo College, in Mississippi (1992–1993); a Rockefeller Foundation fellowship in Bellagio, Italy (1993); and the Prairie Schooner Strousse Award (1994).

Eady has taught at many institutions across the country, including the State University of New York at Stony Brook, where he directed the school's Poetry Center; Sarah Lawrence College, in Bronxville, New York; New York University; New York City's 92d Street Y; George Washington University, in Washington, D.C.; and the College of William and Mary, in Williamsburg, Virginia. With his wife of 23 years, Sarah Micklem, he resides in New York City, where he is the Distinguished Writer-in-Residence at the City College of New York.

—*K. D.*

SUGGESTED READING: Academy of American Poets Web site; *American Visions* p30 Oct. 1, 1999; *Associated Press* Jan. 16, 2002; *Boston Globe* F p5 Aug. 30, 2000; *Kenyon Review* p174+ Summer 1992; *New York Times* VII p17 Nov. 30, 1986, I p15 June 18, 1997, E p5 Jan. 10, 2002; *Ploughshares* (on-line) Spring 2002; *Teachers & Writers* (on-line) Apr. 1999; *Weekend All Things Considered* Feb. 11, 2001

SELECTED WORKS: poetry—*Kartunes*, 1980; *Victims of the Latest Dance Craze*, 1985; *Boom Boom Boom*, 1988; *The Gathering of My Name*, 1991; *You Don't Miss Your Water*, 1995; *The Autobiography of a Jukebox*, 1997; *Brutal Imagination*, 2001; plays—*You Don't Miss Your Water*, 1995; *Running Man*, 1999; *Brutal Imagination*, 2002

Jim Herrington/Courtesy of Algonquin Books

Earley, Tony

June 15, 1961– Novelist; short-story writer; essayist

The American writer Tony Earley has preserved his family's Southern heritage in the short-story collection, *Here We Are in Paradise* (1994), and a novel, *Jim the Boy* (2000), as well as in his numerous essays. Earley first created the character Jim Glass, of the fictional town of Aliceville, North Carolina, for several stories in *Here We Are in Paradise*. Earley then placed the character back in his Depression-era childhood in *Jim the Boy*, creating a "radiant, knowing, pitch-perfect parable of childhood," in the words of Janet Maslin in the *New York Times* (June 8, 2000). Earley's most recent work, *Somehow Form a Family: Stories That Are Mostly True* (2001), is a collection of personal essays chronicling his childhood in a small Southern town, his entrance into adulthood, and his search for a spiritual life.

Tony Earley was born on June 15, 1961 in San Antonio, Texas, where his father was stationed while serving in the U.S. Air Force. As soon as they were able to relocate, his parents moved back to the North Carolina mountains, where they both were raised, to bring up their son in Rutherfordton, near Asheville. Earley's father became a welding supervisor in a factory that made office furniture. Earley found his calling at a young age. "My second-grade teacher made us write a story every Monday about what we did on the weekend," he told Beverly Keel in an interview for the *Nashville Scene* (October 4, 1999). "And one Monday morning she read mine and said, 'This is very good. You should be a writer.' I thought, 'OK, I'll be a writer,' and I never really got over that."

Earley was educated at Warren Wilson College, in Swannonoa, North Carolina. During his first year there, his only sibling, a younger sister, was killed in an automobile accident, and his father left his mother. "I was really a sweet kid until my sister got killed, then the rest of my college career I was pretty acerbic and nasty," he told Keel. He managed to finish college, despite his grief and depression. "I would start to sabotage things—I wouldn't go to class, I made bad grades, and later there were periods when I drank too much—then this miraculous thing would appear in front of me which I knew I didn't deserve, so I would make another mess and another thing would appear," he said to Keel. "I think God and I have a deal: I'll keep writing and he won't make me do something stupid."

After receiving a bachelor's degree in 1983, Earley worked as a features writer, sports reporter, and editor for a couple of newspapers in Columbus and Forest City, North Carolina. Although he learned much about writing sentences while working on newspapers, he realized life as a journalist was not his cup of tea. In 1988 he received a fellowship to study creative writing at the University of Alabama, in Tuscaloosa.

During his time at the University of Alabama, he crafted the stories "Charlotte" and "The Prophet from Jupiter." Although other students in the workshop gave negative criticism to his writing, he sent the stories to *Harper's* magazine, and they were published. *Harper's* won a National Magazine Award for fiction in 1993, and "The Prophet from Jupiter" was cited as one of the reasons. Both stories were anthologized in *New Stories from the South* and *Best American Short Stories*. The following year marked the publication of Earley's first book, *Here We Are in Paradise*, a collection of short stories. Earley was living in Pittsburgh at the time because his wife, Sarah Bell, was working on a degree there, at Trinity Episcopal School of Ministry.

In the collection's title story, a woman fighting a losing battle with breast cancer summons the courage to tell her husband that he has never understood her, and then realizes that it doesn't matter. She decides that "it had been a good enough way to live." The story "Charlotte" is set in Charlotte, North Carolina. A young bartender is obsessed with professional wrestling, and embittered because a wrestler "gathered up all the good and evil in our city and sold it four hours south"—in other words, Charlotte's pro-wrestling league has relocated and been replaced by an NBA team. The bartender is also despondent because he wants his girlfriend to admit that she is in love with him. In the final pro wrestling bout in Charlotte, Lord Poetry goes up against Noxious Bob in a "Final Battle for Love," and the narrator laments, "Gone is Lord Poetry, and all that he stood for." The character Jim Glass appears in the stories "Aliceville," "Story of Pictures," and "My Father's Heart." In the later of the three, the narrator says, "We live in stories, and our stories go on. Do not worry, our stories go on." Ellen Currie wrote in the *New York Times Book Re-*

view (March 27, 1994), "That is true, and one wishes only for more of them from Tony Earley."

In Currie's laudatory review of *Here We Are in Paradise*, she observed that Earley's "sense of place is beautifully specific and profound, yet these stories are not 'regional' in any limiting sense. Their territory is bolder and broader than that; it is the whole unruly campus of the heart. Mr. Earley's tough subject is love in all its guises . . . love and the failure of love and its even more alarming triumphs." A *Publishers Weekly* critic (November 15, 1993) wrote, "In each of these stories, Earley deftly weaves together several thematic strands to create complex, richly rewarding fiction. His tales connect with the heart."

When *Here We Are in Paradise* appeared, Earley had begun work on a novel. In 1996 the British literary magazine *Granta* included him on their list of the most promising young fiction writers in the United States. Earley told Bob Summer in a *Publishers Weekly* (June 12, 2000) interview that, although he was deeply depressed when the *Granta* list came out, the opportunity it represented was not lost on him. "I was making a minimal living . . . as a freelance writer. . . . So when the *Granta* list came out I was smart enough to realize that if I was ever going to get a date for the prom, it was that year," he said to Summer. Earley got a semester appointment as writer-in-residence at the University of the South, in Sewanee, Tennessee, and went on to become a writing teacher at Vanderbilt University, in Nashville. "I love teaching creative writing," he told Summer.

For his novel *Jim the Boy*, published in 2000, Earley revisited Jim Glass of Aliceville, the character and town he had used in *Here We Are in Paradise*, this time returning him to his childhood in the 1930s. Although the novel has autobiographical elements, Jim's family configuration is very different from Earley's. Jim's father died before he was born, and he is an only child, living with his mother and her three bachelor brothers. Jim "has my heart and feels the way I feel," Earley told Keel. "He has my heart, but I made him the biggest kid in the class and the best athlete, a leader. I never was that."

The book tells the story of Jim's 10th year, including learning from his uncles, winning a greased-pole climb, and watching his mother being courted. The anecdotes lead to a kind of epiphany at the end, as Jim begins to understand who he is. "Part of the challenge I've set myself with this book is to use the simplest possible lines to tell a complex story, to have the story say things without saying them," Earley told *Brightleaf Review* (January 1998), an on-line publication. "*Jim the Boy* is essentially the tale of how a moral person develops in the care of loving adults," Ron Charles wrote in the *Christian Science Monitor* (June 1, 2000), terming the novel "a reminder of the wonder of life before one's hopes and fears are clearly demarcated and cataloged, when everything is raw and dazzling." The following passage is excerpted from the novel.

During the night something like a miracle happened: Jim's age grew an extra digit. He was nine years old when he went to sleep, but ten years old when he woke up. The extra number had weight, like a muscle, and Jim hefted it like a prize. The uncles' ages each contained two numbers, and now Jim's age contained two numbers as well. He smiled and stretched and sniffed the morning. Wood smoke; biscuits baking; the cool, rivery smell of dew. Something not quite daylight looked in his window, and something not quite darkness stared back out.

Reviewers generally found that Earley had succeeded in making his simple style illuminate Jim's life. Laudatory blurbs came from such writers as Allice McDermott, who praised the "marvelous language, honest emotion and authentic characters," and Andrea Barrett, who declared that Earley rendered "luminous one boy, one family, one very small town—and by delicate implication, the wide world just beyond that charmed circle." In *Newsweek* (June 5, 2000) Malcolm Jones wrote, "In the finest scene in this dazzling first novel about boyhood, the Depression-era town of Aliceville, N.C., gets electricity. . . . The little miracle in this scene is how . . . Earley balances the genuine wonder at electrification with the slow realization that while something has been won, so something is lost. . . . The bigger miracle is that there are a dozen such scenes" in the novel. "By the end of the book, the life of this boy and his family blaze at you like a whole town of lights."

Jonathan Miles, writing in the on-line magazine *Salon* (June 13, 2000), held out a dissenting opinion from the chorus of praise for *Jim the Boy*. Terming it "a polite, sincere, and ineffusive novel bearing a kind of balmy ministerial charm that will endear it to mamas everywhere," Miles found that *Jim the Boy* "drifts about like cheap air freshener—cloyingly sweet . . . and smelling like no mountain meadow anywhere in the whole gosh-darn big world."

In his essays, Earley shows a propensity for combining family history and reminiscences with an almost scholarly appreciation of language and the past. In "The Quare Gene," published in the *New Yorker* (September 21, 1998), Earley discusses the Appalachian dialect employed by his family, which he described as having been lost with his generation. "Words and blood are the double helix that connect us to our past," he wrote. "As a member of a transitional generation, I am losing those words and the connection they make. I am losing the small comfort of shared history. I compensate, in the stories I write, by sending people up mountains to look . . . for the answers to their questions, to look down from a high place and see what they can see. My characters, at least, can still say the words that bind them to the past without sounding queer, strange, eccentric, odd, unusual, unconventional, or suspicious. 'Stories,' says the writer Tim O'Brien, 'can save us.' I have put my faith in the idea that words, even new ones, possess that kind of redemptive power."

In another *New Yorker* (July 3, 2000) article, Earley expressed different reasons for preserving family heritage by telling stories. He described a trip his grandmother had made to look for her errant teenage son, explaining how in retelling the story many years later, "In an alchemy of will, she had taken a bus, a bridge, and a failed journey and had transformed them into the culmination of a life. It wasn't lying, exactly, but, rather, burnishing memory until it looked like hope."

Many of these essays were collected in Earley's most recent work, the widely acclaimed *Somehow Form a Family: Stories That Are Mainly True* (2001). The volume features glimpses of his childhood in North Carolina, observations on family relationships, his grief over his sister's death, his efforts to attain a spiritual life, and many later journalistic adventures. Critics praised the book's elegant, unsentimental language and accessibility. Cliff Glaviano observed for *Library Journal* (April 1, 2002), "These stories will stick with the listener for quite some time." In her review for *Booklist*, as quoted on *Amazon.com*, Candace Smith affirmed, "Earley draws the reader in with his deceptively simple prose and a sharp eye for the telling detail. A willingness to share painful memories, including his struggles with depression and a sometimes dysfunctional family life, makes these memoirs especially effective."

Tony Earley lives in Tennessee.

—S. Y.

SUGGESTED READING: *Brightleaf Review* (on-line) Jan. 1998; *Christian Science Monitor* II p17 June 1, 2000; *Nashville Scene* (on-line) Oct. 4, 1999; *New York Times* (on-line) June 8, 2000; *New York Times Book Review* p8 Mar. 27, 1994; *New Yorker* p80+ Sep. 21, 1998, p33+ July 3, 2000; *Newsweek* p74 June 5, 2000; *Publishers Weekly* p69 Nov. 15, 1993, p49 Apr. 17, 2000, p48+ June 12, 2000, with photo; *Salon* (on-line) June 13, 2000

SELECTED BOOKS: *Here We Are in Paradise*, 1994; *Jim the Boy*, 2000; *Somehow Form a Family: Stories That Are Mostly True*, 2001

Edwards, Louis

1962– Novelist; short-story writer

Like many Southerners before him, the African-American fiction writer Louis Edwards has been inspired by the rich cultural landscape of Louisiana—from New Orleans to its surrounding rural towns—and has featured it throughout much of his published work. As Susan Larson, the book editor for the *Times-Picayune*, told Debbie Elliott for *Morning Edition*, according to a transcript of the August 9, 2001 show posted on the Nation Public Radio Web site, "Louis put a gloss on [New Orleans] that no one ever has." While Edwards admitted to Elliott that he resists being classified solely as an African-American or Southern writer, he also acknowledges the importance of his heritage and his awareness of the South's longstanding literary tradition, to which many critics now consider Edwards a welcome addition.

Louis Edwards was born in 1962 in the rural town of Lake Charles in southwest Louisiana. With French-speaking Creole grandparents, Edwards grew up with a unique understanding of his African-American ancestry. As a young man, he became interested in journalism, history, and the South's own historical narrative. One of the first stories that Edwards composed in high school was a parody of *The Glass Menagerie*, a play by the Southern writer Tennessee Williams. In 1985 Edwards moved to New Orleans, where he fell in love with the city's character, studying it in an intense manner that has since allowed him to capture its essence through his writing.

Photo by Girard Mouton III/Courtesy of Greywolf Press

Edwards published his first novel, *Ten Seconds*, in 1991. In it, he tells the story of Eddie, a former high-school track star, who is now a 26-year-old refinery worker, husband, and father of two young children. As Eddie watches a 100-yard dash event at the high-school track in his small Louisiana town, he reflects upon his life. Through Edwards's carefully constructed narrative, the book moves in a nonlinear fashion through Eddie's past, present, and future, traveling back to his loss of virginity at age 17 and ahead to his disillusionment at age 35. Using this disjointed chronology, Edwards juxtaposes images of who Eddie once was with who he is to become. As Mason Buck wrote for the *New York Times* (August 11, 1991), the book's structure "allows the events of the future to illuminate those of the past." For example, in one scene Edwards depicts the young Eddie pledging to honor his new bride; yet through his placement of that scene—after a chronologically later one in which Eddie's wife threatens to leave him if he does not curb his drug use and womanizing—Edwards infuses his narrative with additional layers of meaning. Ultimately, the book's 10 chapters correspond with the 10 seconds it takes for the runners Eddie is watching to complete their 100-yard dash. Michael Erik Ross for the *San Francisco Review of Books* (Fall 1991) observed, "With marathon Faulknerian passages [alluding to another Southern writer, William Faulkner], Edwards touches all the bases: the joys and agonies of friendship and marriage, of raising children and accepting the changes of modern life. . . . The chronology is haphazard . . . but the payoff is real as the disappointments and victories of the human condition are seen through a black man's eyes."

Critics praised the book for its authenticity in depicting the young protagonist's life. Albert E. Wilhelm for *Library Journal* (May 1, 1991) acknowledged the novel's "considerable skill in characterization and elegance in style," while Mason Buck asserted that "the writing always rings true," particularly in passages depicting Eddie's relationships with his wife and his best friend. E. S. Nelson for *Choice* (December 1991) added, "Without retreating into sentimentality or sociology, [Edwards] has managed to create in his work an immensely recognizable image of black manhood. His use of an elaborate athletic metaphor to shape the narrative structure succeeds marvelously, even as it helps intensify the novel's thematic resonances." *Ten Seconds* earned Edwards the PEN Oakland/Josephine Miles Award for excellence in literature in 1991 and was named one of *Publishers Weekly*'s best books of that year.

In 1996 Edwards published his short story, "The Insiders," in the anthology *Street Lights: Illuminating Tales of the Urban Black Experience*, a book featuring 49 stories by African-American writers with each work set against the backdrop of an urban environment. While many of the stories take place in New York City, Edwards brought his characters to New Orleans, where he captured the experience of two high-school graduates bidding farewell to various city landmarks. Of the story, Susan Larson wrote for the *Times-Picayune* (September 1, 1996), "It's a wonderful idea, and Edwards evokes the place—and the emotions of farewell—in his gentle, insightful and unforgettable way."

On the heels of overwhelming critical acclaim for his first book, Edwards received a prestigious Guggenheim Fellowship, in 1993, that allowed him to work toward completing his second novel, *N: A Romantic Mystery*, which was published in 1997. According to Edwards, the "N" of the title stands for many things, but most importantly for New Orleans and "noir." In an interview with Larson for the *Times-Picayune* (May 18, 1997), Edwards explained, "I was just obsessed with [noir]. It's such a beautiful word, there's poetry in just the sound of the word, and that's even before we get to defining it in its literal meaning and its idiomatic meanings. It turns into something even more wonderful once we do that. . . . It means black in French and it also defines a style." The noir style of fiction is an American literary tradition that dates back to the 1930s and 1940s. Within the broader genre of crime fiction, the noir novel features a "hard-boiled" antihero who ultimately succeeds in finding dignity and spiritual triumph in his bleak environment. Many popular noir films, including *The Maltese Falcon* (1941) and *The Postman Always Rings Twice* (1946), began as books (in these examples by noir architects Dashiell Hammett and James Cain, respectively).

Edwards explained to Susan Larson: "New Orleans is such a noir city. And here we come back to the meaning of the word in all its fullness. New Orleans is a very black city, and you can put that word in quotation marks, but it is. There are a lot of black folks here, and it's said that the white folks here are pretty black. It's so true. I think there's an integration of spirit, maybe, if not a physical integration." He also told Larson his reasons for examining the sadness that underlies New Orleans' modern character. "I just could not see another television news program," he said, "about some black kid killing some other black kid for God knows what—we don't know what—and not do something. . . . I just thought I should take up some artistic challenge of trying to find out something about it, to document it, to somehow explore this real, real tragedy." Although Edwards's book carries the subtitle "A Romantic Mystery," he insists that his novel is more a literary work. Using a term most often heard in relation to jazz, he explained to Larson, "I'm riffing on romance and mystery."

This novel tells the story of Aimee DuBois, who is described by one character as somewhere between Blanche DuBois from the Tennessee Williams play *A Streetcar Named Desire*, and the 20th-century black intellectual W. E. B. DuBois, as she embarks upon a quest to determine her identity. A well-educated Creole woman who has inherited a black weekly newspaper, DuBois sets out to find the truth behind a local black man's murder. Like Edwards, she lives in the French Quarter of New Orleans, but through her investigation she is forced to explore a harsher side of the city, the mostly African-American neighborhood of Central City. There she encounters a small-time drug dealer, with whom she falls in love, and several other dangerous characters, who ultimately help her piece together the life of the murdered man. Along the way DuBois struggles with her own crisis of race, sex, and identity. Using a narrative device similar to the one he used in *Ten Seconds*, Edwards constructs the novel through a series of flashbacks, a technique that critics found largely successful. Dulcy Brainard for *Publishers Weekly* (March 3, 1997) wrote, "With constant shifts in tense, point of view and typeface, [Edwards] reaches into the postmodern armory of fragmentation techniques, but his prose is fluid and a story does emerge from beneath all the stylistic wrinkles." Rex E. Klett for *Library Journal* (April 1, 1997) praised Edwards's "attention-getting mixed narrative viewpoints and rhythmic, ultimately entrancing prose." Critics largely applauded the book; one writer for *Kirkus Reviews* (April 1, 1997) opined that "Edwards brilliantly deconstructs the language of race in America, a country and culture he celebrates for its invigorating mix, much like this smart and genre-bending book."

Edwards published his third novel, *Oscar Wilde Discovers America*, in early 2003 to mixed reviews. The story fictionalizes the U.S. travels of the Irish writer Oscar Wilde, as told through the narrative of his black valet. Of his decision to explore new geography within his writing, Edwards told Debbie Elliott, "[It] is not uncommon for my generation of Southerners at all [to] mov[e] from being strictly regional to being national. And maybe it's part of the evolution of America and not necessarily that we're giving up on the region, but there's a greater geography to be explored, and why not explore it?"

In addition to his other honors, Edwards won the Whiting Writers' Award in 1994. He currently resides in New Orleans' historic Lower Quarter, the residential side of the city's famous French Quarter. When he is not writing, Edwards serves as associate producer for Festival Productions, the company that stages the New Orleans Jazz & Heritage Festival and the Essence Festival.

—K. D.

SUGGESTED READING: *Choice* p591 Dec. 1991; *Kirkus Reviews* Apr. 1, 1997; Nation Public Radio (NPR) Web site; *Publishers Weekly* p67 Mar. 3, 1997 *Times-Picayune* E p1+ May 18, 1997

SELECTED BOOKS: *Ten Seconds*, 1991; *N: A Romantic Mystery*, 1997; *Oscar Wilde Discovers America*, 2003

Egan, Jennifer

Sep. 7, 1962– Novelist; journalist; short-story writer

Jennifer Egan has intrigued critics and audiences alike with the clarity of her prose, the relevance of her themes, and her honest depictions of young heroines struggling to understand themselves and their worlds. Her first novel, *The Invisible Circus* (1995), is about a teenage girl who is trying to come to terms with her older sister's death. In 1996 Egan published a collection of her short fiction, *Emerald City and Other Stories*, which includes such tales as "Why China?" and "Sacred Heart." Her most recent book, the novel *Look at Me* (2001), is an ambitious examination of the troubled lives of individuals adrift in the contemporary, media-saturated culture of the United States; that widely discussed work earned a nomination for the 2001 National Book Award. Egan has published short fiction in prominent periodicals that include the *New Yorker*, *Harper's*, and *Ploughshares*. Her journalism has appeared in the *New York Times Magazine*, where she has written about modeling, self-mutilation, and gay teenagers' use of the Internet, among other issues.

The daughter of Donald Egan, a lawyer, and Kay Kimpton, an art dealer, Jennifer Egan was born in Chicago, Illinois, on September 7, 1962. She was raised in San Francisco, California. Eager to travel before attending college, she worked as a model for six months after her high-school graduation with the aim of saving for her trip. As she later told Michael Kenney for the *Boston Globe* (February 28,

Courtesy of Brennan Photography

1996), despite having the right height—five feet, nine inches—and "the basic bone structure," she was ill-suited for modeling. "I felt a desire to vanish and to speak—the two things you can't ever do as a model," she explained to Kenney. When she had saved enough money, she purchased a backpack and caught a flight to London, England. From there she traveled widely in Europe, her perambulations providing material that she would later develop in *The Invisible Circus*. Upon her return to the United States, she enrolled at the University of Pennsylvania, in Philadelphia, where she majored in English and began writing seriously. She graduated from the university with a B.A. in English in 1985. Following graduate study at St. John's College, in Cambridge, England, where she earned an M.A. degree in English literature in 1987, Egan embarked on a series of travels to China and other regions of Central Asia. "Why China?" a short story published in the *New Yorker* on April 24, 1995 and later included in *Emerald City and Other Stories*, grew out of her experiences during that period.

Egan's debut novel, *The Invisible Circus*, is a coming-of-age story about a young girl who treks across Europe, hoping to gain insight into her elder sister's life and mysterious, untimely death. It opens in 1978 in San Francisco, where 18-year-old Phoebe is living with her widowed mother. It has been eight years since her sister, Faith, fell to her death from a cliff along the coast of Italy. Faith had been a 1960s flower child—reckless, adventurous, and carefree. Following the death of their father, Faith had run off to Europe with a boyfriend, sending postcards from the places she visited. One day the postcards stopped coming, and the family learned that she had died. Phoebe, who grew up in the shadow of these events, is convinced that life has already passed her by. After her high-school graduation and some troubling incidents at home, Phoebe makes an impromptu decision to go to Europe. Once there she follows the trail indicated by her sister's postcards, and in the process pieces together the events leading to Faith's death. Along the way she encounters the remnants of the once-lively 1960s scene and has some psychedelic experiences of her own; she also uncovers disturbing truths about her sister's past.

The Invisible Circus was well received by critics. Jesse Lee Kercheval, writing for *Ploughshares* (Spring 1995), called it a "marvelous first novel" and declared, "Only rarely does Egan's deft touch at integrating history into her characters' lives fail. . . . But for every occasional weak spot, there are a dozen luminous evocations of the period. To read *The Invisible Circus* is to see the sixties again in all its glimmering and illusive promise." Erica Abeel, in a review for *New York Newsday* (January 1, 1995), noted that Egan displayed "a sure command of narrative tension impressive in a first novelist." In 2001 the novel was made into a little-noticed movie starring Jordana Brewster as Phoebe, Cameron Diaz as Faith, Blythe Danner as the girls' mother, and Christopher Eccleston as Faith's boyfriend, Wolf.

The characters in Egan's next work, the collection *Emerald City and Other Stories*, are reminiscent of Dorothy, the heroine of L. Frank Baum's *The Wonderful Wizard of Oz*: in various ways they are struggling to cope with the trauma of disillusionment. In the story "Sacred Heart," a young Catholic-school girl named Sarah nurses an obsession with a mysterious new classmate, Amanda, who, in Egan's words, "wore silver bracelets embedded with chunks of turquoise" and "would cross her legs and stare into space in a way that suggested she lived a dark and troubled life," as quoted by Ginia Bellafante in *Time* (January 15, 1996). Sarah soon discovers that, in reality, Amanda is less mysterious than she seems. In the tale "Why China?"—which Susan Wood, in the *Houston Chronicle* (March 31, 1996), considered to be "perhaps the collection's most remarkable story"—a businessman takes his family on an outing to China, hoping to find release from his work and an escape from recent allegations of fraud. In Kunming he encounters a man who once conned him out of $25,000, and decides to accompany the swindler on a trip to some Buddhist caves. "Emerald City" focuses on Stacey, an aspiring model who has moved to New York City from Cincinnati, Ohio, to pursue her dream. She suffers a blow when a photographer tells her that her classic good looks are no longer in style. "Beauty today is ugly beauty," he tells her, as quoted by Linda Simon in *New York Newsday* (February 25, 1996). "Look at those girls, they're monsters—gorgeous, mythical monsters." Rory, a photographer's assistant, is in love with Stacey; he comes to the realization that New York City is "a place that glittered from a distance even when you reached it," as quoted by Jodee Stanley in *Ploughshares* (Spring 1996). As the story ends, Stacey and Rory are setting their sights in search of new horizons. In a review of *Emerald City and Other Stories* for *People* (February 26, 1996), Louisa Ermelino wrote that Egan "displays a gift for cool, clean, wrenching prose. [She] has modern life down pat, and in this smartly crafted collection, she hands it over." Linda Simon wrote that despite the despair evoked in some of the tales, Egan "sees a glimmer of happiness, even of deliverance, for her bewildered characters. She tempers cynicism with compassion; she believes in hope."

Look at Me, Egan's second novel, has generated a lot of interest, both critically and commercially. The book alternates between two narratives, each about a protagonist named Charlotte. Charlotte Swenson, a fashion model living in New York City, is recovering from a car crash in which she suffered multiple fractures of her facial bones. Charlotte Hauser, a teenager growing up in Rockford, Illinois, is leading a double life. An ordinary student by day, the young Charlotte begins an affair with her enigmatic math teacher. She is also being tutored by her uncle, Moose Metcalf, a mentally troubled cultural-studies professor with an obsessive interest in the Industrial Revolution. (Moose had been a rising academic star before he nearly blew up part of the Yale University campus while carrying out an experiment.) While taking walks with Charlotte in Rockford, Moose discourses on the unsettling effects of the Industrial Age, with the hope that his niece will be taken with the vision that has come to dominate his life. Charlotte increasingly retreats into the worlds of the two older men, thereby isolating herself from her friends and family. Charlotte Swenson, meanwhile, gets involved in a reality-based Web site that turns people's real lives into a form of entertainment.

In an interview posted on the Web site of the publisher Nan A. Talese (a division of Random House), Egan admitted that she had intentionally made the connection between the two Charlottes obscure. "After writing *The Invisible Circus*," she said, "in which the action of the novel is rather fully explained psychologically, I wanted to write a book whose connections were felt rather than understood, a book that was more deeply mysterious." She also said, in commenting on the shifting boundaries between reality and fantasy in contemporary American life, "I think that our culture's image saturation has resulted in a kind of media hangover—a longing for experience that is unmediated, or 'authentic.' . . . [Reality] has been fetishized into a style: a simulacrum of authenticity that appears to satisfy the viewer's genuine longing for it, but, in fact, leaves him empty. And the media respond to that emptiness with ever greater contortions of simulated reality, which is what I wanted to explore in *Look at Me*." Reviews of the book have tended to be mixed but appreciative. For example, in his assessment for the *Washington Post* (November 4, 2001), David Mulcahey wrote, "Ambitious as Egan is, she lets her narrative bloat. Subplot after subplot comes along . . . leaving the reader to wonder whether they add to the whole." "Nonetheless," he concluded, "Egan has created some compelling characters and written provocative meditations on our times." Katherine Dieckmann offered a similar assessment in the *New York Times Book Review* (September 23, 2001): "Just as Charlotte [Swenson]'s new face is held together with 80 titanium screws, a set of fragile pieces forever threatening to become dismantled, Egan's book is a tenuous assembly that manages to compel despite its occasionally confounding construction."

Egan has received fellowships from the National Endowment for the Arts and the Guggenheim Foundation. In 1992 she won the *Cosmopolitan*/Perrier Short Story Award for "Sacred Heart." She lives in the New York City borough of Brooklyn with her husband, David Herskovits, a theater director, and their son.

— A.I.C.

SUGGESTED READING: *Boston Globe* p73 Feb. 28, 1996; *Los Angeles Times* p2 Mar. 5, 1995; *Nation* p42+ Nov. 26, 2001; *New York Newsday* p33 Jan. 1, 1995, Feb. 25, 1996; *New York Times Book Review* p22 Sep. 23, 2001; *People* p32 Feb. 26, 1996; *Ploughshares* p193+ Spring 1995, p205+ Spring 1996; *Time* p72 Jan. 15, 1996; *Washington Post* T p6 Nov. 4, 2001

SELECTED BOOKS: *The Invisible Circus*, 1995; *Emerald City and Other Stories*, 1996; *Look at Me*, 2001

Eduardo de la Manzana/Courtesy of Simon & Schuster

Eggers, Dave

1970– Editor of McSweeney's; writer; graphic artist.

A reader encountering a book called *A Heartbreaking Work of Staggering Genius* might assume that the author either suffers from an inflated ego or is painfully self-aware. In the case of Dave Eggers, whose first, autobiographical book bears that very title, the latter is true. "Like most titles, it was a place-marker for a long time, and it kind of became too late to change it," Eggers told Sarah Lyall for the *New York Times* (February 10, 2000). "And it made me laugh." A partly fictionalized account of how Eggers dealt with the loss of his parents to cancer and accepted the responsibility for raising his younger brother, Toph (short for Christopher), the book has succeeded critically and commercially and inspired pronouncements that its 30-ish author is the voice of his generation. Publishing rights to the book have been purchased around the globe, and there have been rumors that several film studios are interested in the story. The book's boastful, attention-grabbing title notwithstanding, Eggers seemed unprepared for the reception it received upon its publication, in early 2000. "I didn't write the thing to have it read by a lot of people. That's not the sort of audience I've ever sought," he told Nadine Ekrek for the *Washington Post* (February 11, 2000). "It's nice when people say they enjoyed it. But I had no idea when I finished it that anyone would like it at all. It seemed to me like a very strange and ugly book. But either I was very wrong, or strange and ugly books are now very popular."

With such modest protestations Eggers has risked sounding disingenuous, mainly because he spent the latter half of the 1990s as a rising star in the publishing world. Beginning with *Might*, the doomed but celebrated satire magazine he founded in San Francisco in 1994, and continuing with his cheeky and influential literary journal *McSweeney's*, Eggers has made a career of criticizing—from the sidelines—the mainstream media's affinity for hype. The success of *A Heartbreaking Work of Staggering Genius*, however, has launched him from the periphery of the media into their midst.

At the root of all the attention—and the best evidence that Eggers is sincere in his response to it—is his particular vision. Like *Might* before it, *McSweeney's* is defiantly uncommercial and reflects its founder's tastes and sensibilities. *A Heartbreaking Work of Staggering Genius*, by turns funny, tender, sad, and maddeningly self-aware, is no less a product of Eggers's artistry, insecurity, and integrity. His book, Michiko Kakutani wrote for the *New York Times* (April 22, 2000), "uses all the latest postmodern hardware: his account of his parents' deaths and his rearing of his eight-year-old brother is prefaced with a coy discussion of the major themes of the book, 'Rules and Suggestions for Enjoyment of This Book,' and an emotional flow chart; it demonstrates, however, that such devices can enhance, rather than undermine, the emotional power of his story."

The third of four siblings, David Eggers was born in Boston in 1970 and raised in Lake Forest, Illinois, a tony suburb of Chicago most famous for being the setting for the 1980 film *Ordinary People*. His father practiced law, and his mother taught in an elementary school. Eggers led a seemingly unremarkable childhood. "I never rebelled. Not in any conventional way. I wanted to please my parents," he told Amy Benfer for *Salon* (February 22, 2000, on-line). "When I liked an album, I wanted them to like it too. I was desperate to make connections with them, and I really liked doing that. So I don't ever identify with the idea that you try to upset your parents in some deliberate way." Despite his father's chronic drinking problem, which he described in *A Heartbreaking Work of Staggering Genius*, Eggers has characterized his mother and father as good parents, both loving and supportive. In particular, he has praised his mother's ability to interact with children. "She was a parenting genius. I'm not the only one who would say that," he told Benfer. "She taught for many years and had hundreds of kids and I think almost all of them would say that."

The relative quiet of his early life ended during his third year at the University of Illinois at Urbana-Champaign, where Eggers was studying painting and journalism. That year his mother endured drastic surgery for stomach cancer, and shortly thereafter doctors found tumors in his father's brain and lung. In 1991, about six months after his father's diagnosis, Eggers's parents died, within 32 days of each other. "On the one hand you are so completely bewildered that something so surreal and incomprehensible could happen," Eggers told Sarah Lyall, describing his reaction to his parents' deaths. "At the same time, suddenly the limitations or hesitations that you might have imposed on yourself fall away. There's a weird, optimistic recklessness that could easily be construed as nihilism but is really the opposite. You see that there is a beginning and an end and that you have only a certain amount of time to act. And you want to get started."

In the wake of the family's tragedy, Eggers dropped out of college, assumed the lion's share of responsibility of raising Toph, and moved with his younger brother to the San Francisco Bay area to be closer to his sister, Beth, who was pursuing a law degree at the University of California at Berkeley. "People said, 'That's so nice of you to do that,'" Eggers told Lyall about raising his younger brother. "But I would rather have had Toph as a roommate than anybody else, and the alternative was much worse. What were we going to do, break up the family and send Toph to a salt mine?"

The unconventional situation and Eggers's age led some to question his ability to care for an adolescent. In his book Eggers wrote at length about acquaintances and neighbors who would never have questioned the judgment of a 40-year-old mother yet didn't think twice about challenging his own parental decisions. "I think a lot of parents assumed that our house was a young bachelor pad, chaotic sort of thing," he recalled for Amy Benfer. Contrary to the expectations of such people, Eggers filled the parental void for Toph, mingling a brotherly playfulness with the protectiveness of a more conservative parenting philosophy. "I think there is a strange American Puritanism, of course, that's always there, right below the surface, that favors incredible simplicity and austerity for the raising of a child. And I did too in a way," he said to Benfer. "I really believe strongly that kids should be spared the runoff of their parents' lives and problems."

As for the effects of becoming a guardian so unexpectedly at a time when most young adults are looking to ease into responsibility and pursue an active social life, Eggers has said that living with a youngster did not really hinder his lifestyle. "I never went out a whole lot. Never more than once a week, usually. I always attributed that fact to the conviction I had that something horrible would happen to my brother if I left, obviously, and that I would pay for it the rest of my life," Eggers explained to Benfer. "But a lot of it had to do with work. I like working. I like staying home and working on things and pretending to work on things. And half the time I prefer hanging out with Toph at home to just going to a bar. We had real fun. We had pingpong."

As he and Toph got used to the new familial roles and responsibilities thrust upon them, Eggers took a job as a graphic designer with *SF Weekly*, an alternative news and arts paper, and reunited with his high-school friend David Moodie, who was also living in the area. Media junkies both, Moodie and Eggers decided to take over *Cups*, an arts publication that was circulated free of charge and served as an accoutrement to San Francisco's pervasive café culture. They published the periodical in their spare time. "At first we thought it would be fun to have a place where we could run our own stuff," Eggers told Joel Selvin for the *San Francisco Chronicle* (January 27, 1994). "But soon it was, like, when we were done with all our other work, we'd go and spend a week without sleep." Having decided that running *Cups* was no longer worth the effort and having failed to secure a buyer, they gave the publication away. The duo then began working on a concept for a new publication, this time with another high-school friend, Marny Requa, who had moved to California. The result, *Might*, was launched in January 1994.

Might's title, taken from a literary journal the three had worked on at Lake Forest High School, was intended to evoke the word's two primary but separate connotations: ambiguity and power. Its first issue was a fairly straightforward celebration of 20-something achievement, far different from the bitingly satiric bimonthly into which it quickly evolved. "After the second issue we stopped preaching," Eggers told Laurie Sandell for *Shift* (January/February 2000, on-line). "It's sort of that the people we attracted were, like, a little too earnest for us." With a puny budget that rarely allowed the editors to pay contributors, *Might* lacked the polish of typical newsstand glossies but offered funny and often trenchant commentary on rampant consumerism and the ways of the media. One oft-cited example was a cover story reporting the alleged murder of former child actor Adam Rich, who portrayed Nicholas on the TV show *Eight Is Enough*. The hoax, perpetrated with the actor's knowledge and cooperation, lampooned the media's willingness to capitalize on the misfortunes of even minor celebrities and ultimately proved its point: it prompted the *National Enquirer* and television's *Hard Copy* to contact *Might* for follow-up stories they were planning.

Although several of the publication's essays—a selection of which was published by the editors in the anthology *Shiny Adidas Tracksuits and the Death of Camp* (1998)—are considered contemporary classics of the genre, the magazine was best known for its asides and marginalia. Fake footnotes and retractions would pop up on random pages; one example read: "On page 111, in our 'Religious News Round-up,' we reported that Jesus Christ was a deranged, filthy protohippy. In fact, Jesus Christ was the son of God. We regret the error." Another favorite was the magazine's bogus contents page, which promised nonexistent articles with outrageous and sardonic titles. In typical David-versus-Goliath fashion, *Might* often used this page to take on such media giants as the *New York Times*. For instance, one issue's contents page announced the piece "Harrummph harrummph harrummph," by conservative *Times* editorial columnist and word maven William Safire, and another by *Times* theater critic cum political commentator Frank Rich, called "Politics! Entertainment! Can't Tell the Difference!"

Such editorial fearlessness won *Might* and its editors a rabid cult following and frequent requests for their services. Microsoft tapped the editors for freelance submissions for its Generation X magazine *Mint*, and *New York* asked them to contribute an article to its Academy Awards coverage. But with circulation figures that never broke the 30,000 mark, the publication was bound for failure. In an effort to prolong the magazine's life, and maybe even earn a living from it, Eggers, Moodie, and Requa approached several publishers for financial backing. (They later mocked their own actions, by reprinting a rejection letter from Hearst Magazines.) "We didn't do anything that we were supposed to do to appeal to the people that give money to magazines," Eggers acknowledged to Nadine Ekrek. "We probably could have shaped it in such a way as to be solvent, but, you know, I just didn't give a [expletive] about any of that." Their best prospect for solvency came from the magazine *Wired*, but when that deal fell through, *Might*'s editors closed shop, in 1997, after their 16th issue.

Throughout the life of *Might*, Eggers had supplemented his income with freelance design work from the graphics studio he and Moodie had started. For a time he also edited the "Media Circus" section of the on-line magazine *Salon*. After *Might* folded, *GQ* and *Esquire* each approached Eggers about a plum staff position; he accepted *Esquire*'s and moved with Toph to New York. At first, being an editor at large for a magazine that he had revered for years seemed to him a great opportunity. Eggers quickly grew disdainful, however, of the mainstream tone *Esquire* was increasingly adopting to compete in a men's-magazine market dominated by such titles as *Maxim* and *Details*, which feature scantily clad models and puerile humor alongside service journalism. "It was a learning experience, the first real job I'd ever had," Eggers told Laurie Sandell. "I learned that I could never have a regular job. It's good to know that early on." Eggers often voiced his distaste for *Esquire*'s new direction. "After a few months, no one listened to me. I was always complaining about misogyny and stupidity," he said to Michael Colton. "I was a lunatic screaming from the woods." Before leaving the magazine, in 1998, Eggers used his numerous contacts to solicit contributions for a literary and humor publication he planned to launch, titled *Timothy McSweeney's Quarterly Concern*.

Indicative of Eggers's imagination and sense of humor, *McSweeney's* (as the quarterly and its accompanying Web site, *Timothy McSweeney's Internet Tendency*, are commonly called) is named after a mentally ill man who once claimed to be a relative of Eggers's. An idiosyncratic hodgepodge of literary fiction and nonfiction, Eggers's own artwork and designs, and overtly silly, made-up tales about the lives of buttoned-down public figures, particularly the political pundit David Gergen, *McSweeney's* allows its contributors to pursue virtually any topic, however eccentric, they choose. "*McSweeney's* is an effort to experiment with form," he explained to Sarah Lyall. "It's an effort to tell the same story, in a different way, without taking it too seriously."

As with *Might*, what sets *McSweeney's* apart from other publications are its digressions and marginalia: fine-printed footnotes dot the perimeter and simultaneously add to and divert attention from the main text. The journal's structure changes from issue to issue (one recent issue was sent to subscribers in the form of 14 slender, individually bound volumes wrapped in a custom-made carton); but its basic design concept gives it the look and feel of a 19th-century periodical. "We'll keep upping the ante," Eggers declared to Mark Horowitz for *New York* (January 31, 2000). "Whether doing them in hardcover, or putting in every bell and whistle we can: die cuts, vellum, different paper stocks. That stuff interests me as much as—sometimes even more than—the words on the page." Also unique to *McSweeney's* is its quixotic, self-conscious tone, often described as postmodern.

Although contributors are not paid for their submissions, Eggers has attracted notable contemporary writers, including David Foster Wallace and Rick Moody, thus acquiring cultural cachet for his journal. In addition to longtime Eggers fans and admirers of postmodern writing, the journal has become a "must read" among book and magazine editors looking for fresh new voices. Within its first four issues, the press runs of *McSweeney's* have jumped from about 2,000 to 12,000.

Further boosting the journal's appeal was the launch, in February 2000, of Eggers's much-anticipated book, *A Heartbreaking Work of Staggering Genius*. *A.H.W.O.S.G.*, which is said to be Eggers's preferred acronym for the book, chronicles Eggers's life from the onset of his parents' illnesses to his and Toph's move from California. The bulk of the memoir (a word Eggers prefers not to use to describe the book, because he changed some names, conflated some incidents, and fabricated most of the book's dialogue) recalls Eggers and Toph's years in California. Interspersing the core story with contrived conversations and interviews, which act almost as Socratic dialogues that expose his internal conflicts, Eggers painted a vivid picture of the turmoil that for a time marked his and Toph's lives.

In spite of the sobering events Eggers wrote about in the book, he incorporated many of the same peripheral elements familiar to readers of *Might* and *McSweeney's*. On the copyright page, normally reserved for legal disclaimers, Library of Congress information, and the like, the reader learns, among other things, that the author is five feet 11 inches tall, weighs 170 pounds, and rates a three "on the sexual-orientation scale, with one being perfectly straight, and 10 being perfectly gay." There are 32 pages of prefatory notes and acknowledgments that comment on the major themes of the book and anticipate reader reaction: "[The author] would also like to acknowledge that no, he is not the only person to ever lose his parents, and that he is also not the only person ever to lose his parents and inherit a youngster. But he would like to point out that he is currently the only such person with a book contract. . . . And that he too is well aware of all the book's flaws and shortcomings, whatever you consider them to be, and that he tips his hat to you for noticing them." The acknowledgments section also gave Eggers the opportunity to indulge his affinity for marginalia, including charts further inventorying the book's themes and metaphors, a breakdown of how he has spent the $100,000 advance he received from his publisher, Simon & Schuster, and a drawing of a stapler.

Predictably, the physical form the book would eventually take proved to be an important element of the writing process for Eggers, who wrote his memoir late at night on a computer program that allowed him to see the text as it would appear on a page. "I had to see it right in front of me. I had to see how the paragraph breaks looked, with the margins a certain way," Eggers told Fred Kaplan. "I'm really reluctant to write for something where I don't control the design." He insisted on being involved in the book's final design, choosing the artwork for its dust jacket and urging that the word "memoir" be stricken from the title. "I bullied my way," he joked to Anne Fulenwider for *Vanity Fair* (March 2000). "I'm a pain in the ass."

A.H.W.O.S.G. spent nine weeks on *Publishers Weekly*'s best-seller list and earned Eggers a largely laudatory critical response. "To call this book brazen is like calling a blizzard white—it's true, but it leaves out most of the story," the *Boston Globe* (February 27, 2000) chief book critic, Gail Caldwell, wrote in her review. "Dave Eggers's memoir-maybe is a defiantly Not Tragic soliloquy; it's also hip, funny, wildly intelligent, and as flushed with narrative energy as anything I've read in some time." She concluded, "It's a carnival ride of insights from a writer who can be breathtakingly articulate, and who (it must be said) comes off sounding like a really cool guy." Sara Mosle, in her appraisal of *A.H.W.O.S.G.* for the *New York Times Book Review* (February 20, 2000), found "Eggers's book, which goes a surprisingly long way toward delivering on its self-satirizing, hyperbolic title," to be "a profoundly moving, occasionally angry, and often hilarious account of those odd and silly things, usually done in the name of Toph." Above all, in Mosle's estimation, "Eggers's real achievement is to provide a counterweight to what Ian Frazier once called 'the encroaching Hefty bag of death,' and to write about it, in our age of irony, with genuine, unsentimental poignancy."

In light of his recent celebrity, Eggers does not allow journalists to interview Toph, now in his teens, and has conceded only that his brother has read the book and liked it. Despite *A.H.W.O.S.G.*'s popularity, Eggers has claimed that he has not read it since it was written and doesn't even own a copy of it. He told Fred Kaplan, "There are five or six parts of the book—the rough ones to write, the raw, more emotional parts—I don't know what's on those pages." Eggers, who has said that he will not write another memoir, admitted that he is working on his first novel and on an art book with the Russian artists Vitaly Komar and Aleksandr Melamid, who provided the dust-jacket artwork for Eggers's first book.

In late 2002 Eggers published his first novel, *You Shall Know Our Velocity*. Chronicling the misadventures of two friends traveling around the world, the book received mixed reviews.
—*T. J. F.*

SUGGESTED READING: *Boston Globe* F p1 Feb. 22, 2000, with photo; *Brill's Content* (on-line) Mar. 1999; *Salon* (on-line) Feb. 22, 2000; *Shift* (on-line) Jan./Feb. 2000; *New York* p31+ Jan. 31, 2000, with photo; *New York Times* E p1 Feb. 10, 2000; *Newsweek* p71 June 19, 1995, with photo; *Washington Post* C p1 Feb. 11, 2000

SELECTED WORKS: nonfiction—*A Heartbreaking Work of Staggering Genius*, 2000; fiction—*You Shall Know Our Velocity*, 2002; as editor—*Might*, 1994–97; *Shiny Adidas Tracksuits and the Death of Camp*, 1998; *Timothy McSweeney's Quarterly Concern*, 1998–

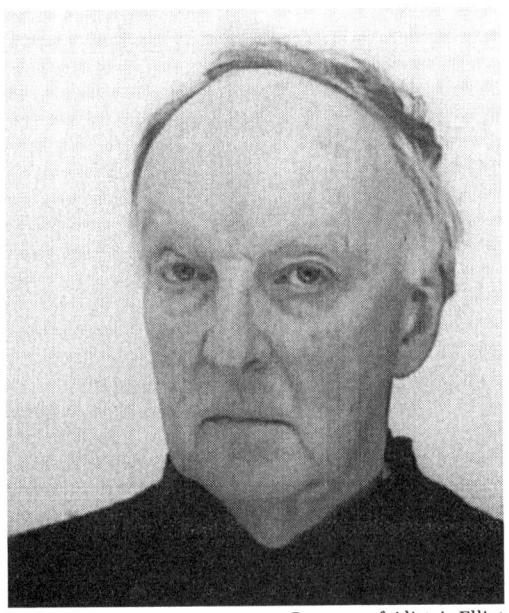

Courtesy of Alistair Elliot

Elliot, Alistair

Oct. 13, 1932– Poet; translator

The British poet Alistair Elliot has quietly made a name for himself as one of the premier translators into English of verse from French, German, Italian, and classical Greek authors. His translation of *Medea*, published in the U. S. in 1993, was performed in London and New York City to great acclaim. Critics have been equally enthusiastic about his original collections of poetry: *Contentions* (1977), *Kisses* (1978), *Talking Back* (1982), *On the Appian Way* (1984), *My Country: Collected Poems* (1989), *Turning the Stones* (1993), and *Facing Things* (1997). Mick Imlah, writing for the *New Statesman & Society* (December 13, 1991), explained that he had chosen Elliot's poem "At Appleby Horse Fair" as the best poem to have appeared in the magazine that year because of "its unobtrusive technical skill" and "its cool delineation of its subject." Indeed, Elliot has been widely praised as a versifier who "has developed and refined a rhythmic and verbal self-consciousness."

Alistair Elliot composed the following autobiographical statement for *World Authors 1995–2000*: "I was an eldest child, born in Liverpool but never lived there. My first years were spent in Wigan, where my two sisters were born, and in Hoylake, beyond Liverpool to the west. Summer holidays were nearly always spent with our father's family in the far north of Scotland, but I do remember one holiday in Hanslope, Buckinghamshire, where our Sassenach (English) mother grew up: it ended when my very young sister Anne used in front of her grandparents a bad word learned obviously from me and both our mouths were washed out with soap. Language!

"In November 1940 (I was just eight) my mother took the three of us across the Atlantic—I remember ships in the convoy being sunk—and left us with our generous but previously unknown Anglophile hosts just before Christmas. We stayed there, wintering in Palm Beach and summering in Southampton, Long Island (our host was the businessman Charles E. Merrill, father of the poet James Merrill) for the next four and a half years, becoming, I suppose, American children, though remaining foreigners. When we came back to England in 1945 we found our parents had produced a new brother for us.

"Almost immediately I was sent away again for five years at a boarding-school in Edinburgh, still therefore a foreigner, though my American accent gradually changed to a Scottish one, and then I went up to Christ Church (Oxford University) to study 'Greats' (classics, plus ancient history and philosophy). That meant joining yet another tribe, the living citizens of the ancient world, and that may well be my deepest nationality; I get on with classicists and Americans as if we were old friends. I do however pronounce the dead languages with some uncertainty, for Latin and Greek were spoken differently by every new teacher in those days.

"Graduating in 1955, I got married (to another half-Scot) and began a confused period of jobs of all sorts, including supply teaching and acting, but the poet's practical problem of earning a living was solved for me when I saw a notice outside Kensington Public Library asking for library assistants. I spent the next 25 years working in libraries, mainly of universities in Britain, but with an interesting two years in Shiraz, Iran, in the 1960s, and a final 15 in Newcastle where I was in charge of manuscripts and other special collections. Then I took early retirement and concentrated on writing poems and translating other people's poems or plays. Recently I have even written poems on commission—an 'Epithalamion' was in the *Times Literary Supplement*.

"I started writing verse when one of my teachers in Edinburgh made us write a poem for 'prep' (homework), and have been writing it ever since. The 'subjects' of these poems are so various they don't seem to me to form a category; I think what is recognisably mine about my work (the voice) is in the rhythms and perhaps the 'angle,' not the 'subjects' themselves; in fact, I believe the 'subject' of a poem is largely irrelevant to the quality of the work. This is a serious credo, but at the same time I cannot altogether think it true, for when I find some other poet has used an image I had been keeping on my own shelf, high and perhaps never to be reached, I feel slightly upset, as if slightly robbed, materially. Also, I did in 1982 apply for a grant to re-cross the Atlantic in the hope of writing a book of poems that would in some sense be 'about' America; it seemed to me at the time (and not just as a person thinking up an excuse for a grant) that there was some sort of 'copy' (a promising shadow of work) in the situation of returning after 38 years, with a kind of museum of 1940's America inside me. (Poems did result, and I collected them in my book called *My Country*, alluding to the American patriotic song which goes to the British national anthem.)

"What happens when people ask me pointblank what I write about, is that I step back and say first that I nearly always use metre and rhyme or half-rhyme (the unspoken question being whether I am 'modern') and then I say the poems are 'about' Iran, submarines, sailing, Scotland, America drifting away from Europe, slugs, walking in the country, a tree nearly falling on me as I drove by, radios (why do they go strange when you put your head near them?), snipers, fossils, anabiosis, coincidences that brought me towards meeting Sylvia Plath, learning Spanish, a blanket, travelling from Rome to Brindisi, finding a copy of *Le Roman de la Rose* on sale at an airport, until one of these 'subjects' gets us onto a less personal line of conversation than where I pick up my seeds.

"Some of my poems have won prizes, but the success that has pleased me most is that one was published by the British Medical Journal as my father's obituary—he was a g[eneral] p[ractitioner] (family doctor). I can say that my book of Verlaine translations (obscene and never shown to my parents) is a good piece of workmanship, and so is my version of Euripides' *Medea* that did well on the stage, thanks to Diana Rigg's marvellous performance and Jonathan Kent's direction. But otherwise, if my work is mentioned, I go shy and . . . British."

Alistair Elliot was born on October 13, 1932 in Liverpool, England. He received an undergraduate degree in 1955 from Christ Church College, Oxford University, England and also earned an M.A. there in 1958. He became a librarian in 1959, serving in British public and university libraries until 1965. He then went to Pahlavi University in Shiraz, Iran, remaining there as an acquisitions librarian for two years. When he returned to England in 1967, he was hired as the special collections librarian at the University of Newcastle upon Tyne, where he remained until 1982; since then, he has devoted himself to writing and translating full-time.

Elliot has displayed amazing range as a translator. He has rendered into English the verse of Heinrich Heine from German and Paul Verlaine from French, as well as works by the classical Greek playwright Euripides and the Latin epic poet Virgil. Elliott has also published English versions of several modern Arabic poems, in collaboration with Matthew Sorenson, and produced a collection of translations of Italian landscape poetry. Marilyn Gaddis Rose, writing in *Library Journal* (December 15, 1983), thought Elliot's bilingual edition of Paul Verlaine's French erotic poetry, *Femmes, Hombres/Women, Men* (1979), to be possibly the "definitive" edition of its kind. She commented that Elliot "has successfully rendered 19th-century French slang into contemporary English slang." John Mole, a reviewer for *Encounter* (April 1983), applauded Elliot's "dexterous, juicy versions" of Verlaine's poetry, which he said created "a catalogue of mutual delights without what Burns (and Elliot) calls the 'consequential sorrows.'"

For his original work, Elliot has mined his trips to North America for poetic ore. "I am a very lucky traveller and meet the most interesting people wherever I go," he wrote in a letter to *World Authors*. *My Country: Collected Poems* contains many poems that "entertain the historical and social forms inscribed . . . in the modern United States," as Michael Walters wrote in his review for the *Times Literary Supplement* (March 23, 1990). "In this context, claims of language to arrest and pin down the poet's experience are teased for their duplicity. A hotel-room's decor is sleepily mistaken for a prairie-vista: 'and the crossed fingers of teepees / Against the light swear that today is clear.' If such poems speak with a forked tongue, it is to a forked and uncertain condition that they address themselves. . . . Elliot is . . . a poet for whom the visible world exists."

Elliot's collection *Facing Things*, published in 1997, seemed to Stephen Knight, who reviewed it for the *Times Literary Supplement* (August 22, 1997), to resemble "a well-stocked Egyptian burial chamber . . . packed with objects of affection—radios, birds, a wristwatch and shaving-brush that belonged to the poet's late father, boats, a tomato knife, books—along with a range of subjects from the area between the shoulder-blades and rheumatism to bentonite and the Big Bang." Knight found that the poet's more recent verse "has accreted to *My Country: Collected Poems* rather than pushed forward to develop new techniques or fresh concerns, so that work published since that volume can sometimes feel like addenda." Nevertheless, Knight called *Facing Things* a "thoughtfully structured collection," which marks "Elliot out as a memorialist, his poems as a stay against time or even an attempt to strip away the years." Knight concluded that Elliot is "patiently building an impressive body of work that is amused and amusing, elegiac, humane, and—in its self-effacing autobiography—quintessentially English."

Indicative of the volume's tone is "Sylvia and Me." The poem notes slight parallels between the lives of the speaker and a woman named Sylvia. Beginning with the description, "We both get born in ports, only a fortnight apart, but the Atlantic / separates our doubtless identical cots," the poem catalogs the coincidences that simultaneously mark their separate lives. By the time the reader reaches the point in the poem when the speaker and Sylvia do meet, he or she will have recognized "Sylvia" to be the American poet Sylvia Plath, who would gain fame for her intense confessional poetry and tragic suicide. The coincidences culminate in a brief, uneventful meeting at a party. Then, years later, the speaker discovers one final connection with Sylvia.

Alistair Elliot has received awards and fellowships from the Arts Council of Great Britain, in 1979; the Ingram Merrill Foundation, in 1983; the Djerassi Foundation, in 1983; and the Prudence Farmer Award from the *New Statesman & Society*, in 1983 and 1991. He and his wife, Barbara Demaine, married in 1956; they have two sons, William and Matthew.

—S. Y.

SUGGESTED READING: *Encounter* p69 Apr. 1983; *Library Journal* p2335 Dec. 15, 1983; *New Statesman & Society* p40 Dec. 13, 1991; *Times Literary Supplement* p327 Mar. 23, 1990, p25 July 9, 1999

SELECTED BOOKS: poetry—*Contentions*, 1977; *Kisses*, 1978; *Talking Back*, 1982; *On the Appian Way*, 1984; *My Country: Collected Poems*, 1989; *Turning the Stones*, 1993; *Facing Things*, 1997; as translator—*Alcestis*, 1965; *Femmes, Hombres/Women, Men*, 1979; *Lazarus Poems*, 1979; *French Love Poems*, 1991; *Italian Landscape Poems*, 1993; *Medea*, 1993; *Le Jeune Parque*, 1997

Ellis, Joseph J.

July 18, 1943– Historian

Joseph J. Ellis is the rare historian whose writing is both learned enough for academics and colorful and accessible enough for casual readers. Most of Ellis's six books are straightforward works of intellectual or cultural history that demonstrate an interest less in complex theory than in clearly illuminating the past and revealing the way people once lived and thought. Ellis received a 1997 National Book Award in nonfiction for *American Sphinx: The Character of Thomas Jefferson* and a Pulitzer Prize in history for *Founding Brothers: The Revolutionary Generation* (2000). A self-professed "throwback," as he told Mark Feeney for the *Boston Globe* (November 1, 2000), he pens most of his work in an elegant, longhand script. Ellis is known for his lively and witty prose and has written for such publications as *American Heritage*, the *Boston Globe*, the *Washington Post*, the *New York Times*, the *Chicago Tribune*, the *New Republic*, and *Civilization*.

Joseph John Ellis was born to Joseph and Jeanette (Sigafoose) Ellis in Washington, D.C., on July 18, 1943, and grew up in Virginia. Ellis earned a B.A., in 1965, from the College of William and Mary (Thomas Jefferson's alma mater), in Williamsburg, Virginia, where he was a member of the Reserve Officers Training Corps (ROTC). Ellis then attended Yale University in New Haven, Connecticut, where he earned an M.A., in 1967, and his Ph.D., in 1969. (Ellis previously claimed to have served a tour of duty in Vietnam, but after he won the Pulitzer Prize for *Founding Brothers*, an investigative reporter for the *Boston Globe* obtained public records indicating that those claims were false. Also proven to be false were claims that Ellis made about his involvement in the antiwar and civil rights movements during the 1960s.)

In 1968 Ellis became an instructor in the American Studies Program at Yale. Then, in 1969, he became an assistant professor at the U.S. Military Academy at West Point, New York, in order to fulfill his ROTC obligations. "I'd go back to New Haven to visit," Ellis recalled to Feeney, "and graduate school friends of mine would say, 'Oh, it must

Jim Gipe/Courtesy of Vintage Anchor Publicity
Joseph J. Ellis

be so awful to be up there with these Neanderthals.' I'd say, 'It's not awful at all, and a lot of these guys are a lot smarter than you.'"

In 1972 Ellis made the dramatic transition from West Point to Mount Holyoke College, in South Hadley, Massachusetts, where he became an assistant professor of history. (The nation's oldest women's liberal-arts college, Mount Holyoke was established in 1837.) Ellis, at first, was viewed with suspicion by some students, and was even followed around during his first year there by a "truth squad," a group organized to place people or events under public scrutiny. Soon, however, he became an admired member of the faculty at Mount Holyoke College, respected for his individual outlook on history and teaching. Ellis "has his own take on things and delivers it compellingly," one of his associates at Yale told Feeney. "It's not what's in fashion. It's not about gender or ethnicity. Political and intellectual history are not in fashion in the academy, and that's what he does." Unlike some historians, who prefer to teach at research-oriented universities and work with graduate students, Ellis is committed to teaching at the undergraduate level. "I much prefer to teach undergraduates than graduate students," he told Feeney. "To me, the kind of questions that are posed at the liberal arts college level, by undergraduates, are more interesting. I have no desire to produce PhDs in history who will then be unemployed." In 1975 Ellis was promoted to associate professor with tenure; he became a full professor at Mount Holyoke in 1979. (When the news broke, in 2001, that Ellis had falsified his background, he was suspended from the college for one year without pay and asked to step down from his endowed chair.)

In 1973 Ellis published his first book, *New England Mind in Transition: Samuel Johnson of Connecticut, 1696–1772*, in which he looks at the life of Johnson—a clergyman and educator, not to be confused with the English poet—as indicative of a transition in the religious and intellectual climate in Puritan New England, from strict doctrinairism toward increased tolerance and liberalism. "At times," a reviewer wrote of the book for *Choice* (February 1974), "the author's explanations tend to become tedious. . . . But there is independence of judgement, a refreshing candor, and reliable accuracy throughout his chapters; they can serve undergraduates as well as specialists in cultural history, philosophy, and religious thought."

Ellis coauthored his next book, *School for Soldiers: West Point and the Profession of Arms* (1974), with another ex-teacher at West Point, Robert Moore. In the book, Ellis and Moore evaluate the academy in terms of its academic quality by referring to their own experiences and by interviewing cadets, faculty, and administrators. In *America* (November 30, 1974), Donald Smythe wrote of *School for Soldiers*, "[The authors] respect the Academy and are concerned about it, but they are certainly not blind to its faults. . . . Enough evidence exists, and is clearly laid out in this well-documented book, that not everything is right concerning the curriculum, the honor code and the basic educational approach. . . . In presenting this, the authors have done a real service to the academy. The book is highly recommended, both for those who love West Point and those who do not."

In 1979 Ellis published *After the Revolution: Profiles of Early American Culture*, in which he looks back at American culture between the time of the revolution for independence from England and the 1830s and the problematic role of the artist during those decades. Ellis examines the life and work of Charles Wilson Peale, Hugh Henry Brackenridge, William Dunlap, and Noah Webster. "Ellis demonstrates that the writers and artists were reduced to a kind of artistic paralysis by their divided loyalties," D. M. Hunter wrote in the *Journal of American History* (September 1980). "Their desire to be 'virtuous citizens' was at odds with their need to succeed by entrepreneurial skills in the market place; their aesthetic and intellectual judgements often warred with their regard for the public's preferences." In *Choice* (April 1980) a reviewer of the book wrote, "[Ellis's] ideas are not innovative in terms of theory, but his feel for his subjects and the warmth and skill of his narrative make this book very readable. . . . [It] will be of great value to students of history and literature."

One of Ellis's favorite historical figures is America's second president, John Adams. As he told Feeney, "I am of the opinion that John Adams is the most underappreciated great man in American history. . . . He deserves our respect and our interest as much as, or more than, any of the other figures [who are prominent in the nation's early history]." Ellis attempted to set the record straight in *Pas-*

sionate Sage: The Character and Legacy of John Adams (1993). He devotes only one chapter to Adams's life during the Revolutionary War and during his presidency, concentrating instead on Adams's later years, when the somewhat embittered ex-president was attempting to vindicate himself in the eyes of Americans. Unlike Thomas Jefferson, who is known for his liberal idealism and his unflagging faith in the American populace, the Adams that Ellis presents was somewhat suspicious of human nature and favored a more restrained form of democracy. An individualistic, even eccentric man, Adams was not skilled at making political allies and often felt that his own adherence to moral principles precluded his enjoying great popularity. "Adams' perspective," Ruth Helm wrote in the *Historian* (Winter 1995), "illuminates his own time and, Ellis asserts, may even reverberate in ours. Adams' call for restraint and accountability to the community while the new nation plunged into an era of unlimited opportunity and individual freedom, gives his political legacy a curious immediacy. . . . Adams believed it was his fate to be misunderstood, but this book does much to prove him wrong." In the *Journal of American History* (September 1994), John Howe praised Ellis's colorful portrait of Adams, asserting that "no other study of John Adams captures so persuasively the robust personality of this remarkable member of the revolutionary generation." However, he added that "Ellis's presentation raises troubling questions of interpretation. Though the book offers an extended psychological portrait of Adams, it reveals little about the psychological premises on which that portrait is grounded."

Following his work on Adams, Ellis turned his attention to a man who, at least for a time, was one of Adams's most fervent political opponents, Thomas Jefferson. In *American Sphinx: The Character of Thomas Jefferson* (1997), Ellis points out several lamentable incidents in Jefferson's career, such as his assertion that people of African descent are mentally inferior to white people, his employment of character assassins against political opponents, and his attempts to revise his old correspondence to downplay his support of the French Revolution. Ellis portrays Jefferson as an idealist capable of resorting to morally questionable behavior for the sake of his ideals, and as the title suggests, also capable of changing guises to suit his assorted purposes. Jefferson, according to Ellis, was a man who could be dishonest with himself—as indicated, for instance, in his holding slaves after earlier speaking out against slavery. Jefferson had "the internal agility to generate multiple versions of the truth, the deep deviousness only possible in a dedicated idealist," Ellis wrote, as quoted by Michiko Kakutani for the *New York Times* (February 11, 1997, on-line).

American Sphinx was roundly applauded by critics as an insightful and balanced, though critical, assessment of Jefferson, and in 1997 it won the National Book Award in the nonfiction category. In the *New York Times* (March 23, 1997, on-line) Brent Staples wrote, "Mr. Ellis. . . is a remarkably clear writer, mercifully free of both the groveling and the spirit of attack that have dominated the subject [of Jefferson] in the past." Kakutani wrote of *American Sphinx*, "[Ellis situates] Jefferson's philosophy and actions within a social context, providing the lay reader with a remarkably vivid feel for the period's mood, conventions and concerns. . . . Though the reader may not agree with all Mr. Ellis's assessments, he writes so intelligently and knowledgeably that it's impossible to read this book and not reconsider Jefferson's role as a thinker, writer and politician."

In *American Sphinx* Ellis maintained that Jefferson had probably not had sexual relations with his slave Sally Hemings, a matter that had long been under debate. However, after DNA tests of one of Hemings's descendants strongly suggested that Jefferson had fathered a child with her, Ellis publicly reversed his view and supported the scientific findings. "I found that because I had not supported that conclusion in the pre-DNA days, I had some kind of professional, if not moral, responsibility to take an upfront position on it right away. So I did," he told Feeney. "[Some] people said, 'How can you change your mind so fast and do a 180?' I said, 'Look, if you ask me if Lee Harvey Oswald acted alone in killing John F. Kennedy, I'll say that's my conclusion. But if tomorrow some dying Mafia don confesses and gives us evidence about the complicity of the Mafia and the CIA and maybe Cuba, I'm open to that."

In 2000 Ellis published *Founding Brothers: The Revolutionary Generation*, in which he makes the point that it might be more productive to view America's founding fathers as brothers, or relative equals, in order to better understand America's early history. "I'm on a bit of a crusade to do something so old-fashioned some people might regard it as fresh and novel," he told Feeney. "*Founding Brothers* represents an attempt to say these figures who are larger than life and demigods need to be made not larger than life, not demigods, [but] into human beings with foibles. At the same time, they need to be rescued from the people who regard them as the deadest, whitest males in American history." Ellis, in the book, examines George Washington, Benjamin Franklin, Thomas Jefferson, John Adams, Alexander Hamilton, James Madison, and Aaron Burr by focusing on six significant occurrences that greatly affected all of them and America as well. These include the famous duel between Burr and Hamilton; a dinner held by Jefferson in which he convinced Hamilton and Madison to have the federal government assume the states' debts in exchange for moving the nation's capital to what is now Washington, D.C.; Congress's failed attempt to deal with the slavery issue in 1790; Washington's farewell address; the shifting alliances between all of the "founding brothers"; and the stormy relations between Jefferson and Adams that ended in a final reconciliation. The backdrop for nearly all of these events is the enduring disputes between the Federalists, who advocated a strong, centralized government, and the Republicans, who supported state rights and more checks and balances on the federal government.

"In lesser hands the fractious disputes and hysterical rhetoric of these contentious nation-builders might come across as hyperbolic pettiness," Joyce Appleby wrote of *Founding Brothers* in the *Washington Post Book Review* (November 26, 2000). "Ellis knows better, and he unpacks the real issues for his readers, revealing the driving assumptions and riveting fears that animated America's first encounter with the organized ideologies and interests we call parties." Ellis's book elicited enthusiastic reviews from many critics, including David M. Shribman, who wrote in the *Boston Globe* (November 12, 2000), "In this volume are friendship and betrayal, loyalty and philosophy, conspiracy and collaboration, high ideals and petty rivalries—in short, the entire human condition. It is the miracle of the founding brothers that they took these raw materials of human character and molded them into something bigger than themselves—into an idea that endures in a time that couldn't be more different from the founding period. It is the enduring achievement of Joseph J. Ellis that he was able to portray that process, all the more remarkable for its improbability, in a vivid and unforgettable fashion." In 2001 the book won a Pulitzer Prize.

Ellis is the editor of *What Did the Declaration Declare?* (1999) and *Thomas Jefferson: Genius of Liberty* (2000). He is married, has three children, and lives in Amherst, Massachusetts. His awards and honors include the Frederick Carr Award (for outstanding graduates of the College of William and Mary), in 1965; a distinguished Teacher Award from West Point Academy, in 1972; a National Endowment for the Humanities Senior Research Fellowship, from 1975 to 1976; a John Simon Guggenheim Memorial Foundation Fellowship, from 1988 to 1989; and an Alumni Medallion Award from the College of William and Mary, in 1998.

—P. G. H.

SUGGESTED READING: *Boston Globe* C p1 Nov. 1, 2000, A p16 Apr. 17, 2001; *Boston Globe* (on-line) June 18, 2001; *Choice* p1843 Feb. 1974; *Historian* p380+ Winter 1995; *Journal of American History* p398 Sep. 1980, p659 Sep. 1994; *New York Times* (on-line) Feb. 11, 1997; *U.S. News & World Report* p67+ Nov. 9, 1998; *Virginia Quarterly Review* p541+ Summer 1997; *Washington Post* B p3 Feb. 7, 1999; *Washington Post Book Review* p3 Nov. 26, 2000

SELECTED BOOKS: *New England Mind in Transition: Samuel Johnson of Connecticut, 1696–1772*, 1973; *School for Soldiers: West Point and the Profession of Arms*, 1974; *After the Revolution: Profiles of Early American Culture*, 1979; *Passionate Sage: The Character and Legacy of John Adams*, 1993; *American Sphinx: The Character of Thomas Jefferson*, 1997; *Founding Brothers: The Revolutionary Generation*, 2000; as editor—*What Did the Declaration Declare?*, 1999; *Thomas Jefferson: Genius of Liberty*, 2000

Elton, Ben

May 3, 1959– Television writer; playwright; novelist

A prominent member of the new wave of British comedy writers that emerged during the 1980s, Ben Elton has been a contributing writer for several acclaimed television sitcoms and variety shows, including such hits as *The Young Ones*, *The Man From Auntie*, and the *Blackadder* series. Known for his satirical attacks on Margaret Thatcher in the 1980s, Elton has also written several plays and novels, the latter of which include *Popcorn* (1996), a satire on American serial killers and Hollywood violence; *A Blast from the Past* (1998), about a romance between a U.S. military man and a leftist social worker; and *Infertility* (1999), an offbeat look at the psychological perils of trying to conceive a child. His most recent novel is *Dead Famous* (2001), a send-up of the "reality" television program craze. In 1999 Elton collaborated with Andrew Lloyd Webber on *The Beautiful Game*, a musical about the intersection of soccer, romance, and terrorism in Northern Ireland.

The youngest of four children, Ben Elton was born with the given name Benjie Ehrenberg on May 3, 1959 in South Catford, London. He grew up in a family steeped in education. His grandfather, Victor Ehrenberg, was a professor who had fled Czechoslovakia in the 1930s to escape Nazi domination. Elton's mother, Mary, was a teacher, and his father, Lewis Ehrenberg, worked as a nuclear physicist and later became a professor of higher education at Surrey University. Elton studied at Godalming Grammar School and joined a number of amateur theater groups as a teenager. He wrote his first play when he was 15 years old, and by the time he received his bachelor's degree in drama from Manchester University in 1980, he had written 20 more plays.

After he graduated Elton began writing humorous sketches for the Leicester Square Comedy Store, which had just been formed. According to a profile of Elton in the *Guardian* (March 30, 1998), "He did a turn at the Comedy Store in 1981 because he was short of money, and the rest, as they say, is hysteria." Within two years he was a contributing writer for *Alfresco*, a television variety show that

Shannon Morris/Getty Images

Ben Elton

aired on Granada TV. Shortly afterward his college friend Rik Mayall asked him to develop material for a new comedy series called *The Young Ones*. The series, which Elton co-wrote with Mayall and Lise Meyer, ran in 1982 and 1984, with Elton appearing in cameo roles in a couple of episodes. "For a generation brought up on the sometimes tired formulas of the conventional 'Terry and June'-style sitcom, there was something glorious about the show's celebration of the emetic," a writer for the *London Observer* (March 25, 1990) opined.

Over the next 15 years, Elton wrote, co-wrote, or produced dozens of scripts for situation comedies, including *Happy Families* (1985) and *Filthy Rich and Catflap* (1986), a short-lived sequel to *The Young Ones* that lasted only six episodes after critics gave it a thumbs-down. With Richard Curtis, Elton took over writing duties for the *Blackadder* series and penned *Blackadder II* (1987), *Blackadder the Third* (1988), and *Blackadder Goes Forth* (1989); the series featured the comic actor Rowan Atkinson as Edmund Blackadder, a character who appears in various historical epochs. In a 1996 interview that appears on the British Comedy Library Web site, Elton told Lowe that *Blackadder* was "much more conventional. It didn't chop and change as much as *The Young Ones*. I think it was extremely original, but it was a different kind of originality—not the *Young Ones* kind where someone suddenly flies up to space or we go into a kind of sub-Beckett dialogue in the cellar. With *Blackadder*, Richard Curtis and I discarded enormous amounts of material, and that was where I started learning the lessons about not being too precious and editing yourself."

Gradually, Elton started appearing in front of audiences as a performer and a stand-up comic. In addition to undertaking several comedy tours, he hosted the television comedy shows *Saturday Live* (in 1987) and *Friday Live* (in 1987–88). He also wrote and starred in the popular series *The Man From Auntie* (1990), the title of which spoofed the 1960s spy series *The Man From U.N.C.L.E.* Four years later he wrote another season of *The Man From Auntie* (1994), which became a hit on British television. Other popular television shows he worked for include *Mr. Bean*—which he co-wrote with Rowan Atkinson, Robin Driscoll, and Richard Curtis—and *The Thin Blue Line*, a mid-1990s comedy series about policemen that Elton wrote and produced. In 1998 he appeared in *The Ben Elton Show*, which featured his own stand-up routines as well as those of guest comedians.

During the period when he was establishing himself as a comedy writer and performer, Elton also wrote a number of plays, some of which were performed in London and elsewhere. The more prominent of these include *Gasping* (1990), *Silly Cow* (1991), and *Blast from the Past* (1998), which also became a novel.

Elton's early novels are black comedies about the environmental destruction caused by capitalism. "I don't see myself as a political comedian," he told *Jam! Showbiz* (July 27, 1997, on-line), "but I'm very, very committed to environmental causes. I've been with Greenpeace for a long time." His first novel, *Stark* (1989), is set in the barren outback of Western Australia, where a conspiracy with planetary consequences evolves. *Gridlock* (1991) is a savage comment on how a petroleum-based economy is destroying urban life. *This Other Eden* (1993) also imagines an end-of-the-world scenario involving ecological disaster.

The publication of Elton's novel *Popcorn* (1996) brought him to the attention of American readers. A critique of the violence in Hollywood films, *Popcorn* focuses on hip director Bruce Delamitri, whose blood-drenched film *Ordinary Americans* wins an Oscar. Though the film has reportedly inspired a spate of copycat killings by Wayne and his girlfriend Scout (known in the media as the Mall Murderers), Delamitri denies any responsibility for their behavior. After the Oscar ceremonies, the murderous pair turn up at Delamitri's Hollywood mansion. In a positive review Joanne Wilkinson wrote in *Booklist* (November 1, 1997) that "Elton sends up film directors like Quentin Tarantino and Oliver Stone while making cogent points about taking responsibility for our society's fascination with violence." In a more negative review, Jess Bravin noted in the *Washington Post Book World* (January 18, 1998) that "*Popcorn* was well-received in Britain, where perhaps it provided some comfort to a nation whose own film industry long ago became a costumed subsidiary of Hollywood. But to anyone who has actually been to Hollywood—or, for that matter, the Eastern Seaboard, *Popcorn* rings false. Start with its surfeit of British-isms: American breakfasts aren't famed for their crumpets and scones, and the organization called the Girl Guides in Britain is known over here as the Girl Scouts." After pointing out other factual errors that "might be quibbles in an otherwise worthwhile novel," Bravin concluded that "Elton offers a take on American society that is pedestrian when not patronizing or simply ignorant. . . . *Popcorn*, then, has little to show us about America or the things we do in Hollywood. Except, perhaps, that the lure of Tinseltown can infect even the most supercilious British writer; the jacket copy proudly proclaims that Warner Bros. has 'optioned the book for director Joel Schumacher.'" *Popcorn* was performed as a play in England and won a Laurence Olivier Award in 1998.

Elton's novel *Blast from the Past* (1998) was described by Bob Lunn in the *Library Journal* (August 1999) as "a black-humor take on the stalker-thriller genre." The novel focuses on General Jack Kent and social worker Polly Slade, who had an affair in the 1980s, when he was a young American soldier and she was a peace activist and quasi-pantheist who called herself "Sacred Cycle of the Womb and Moon." Still in love with Slade 16 years after their fling, Kent revisits her just as she realizes she is being stalked by one of her former clients. Lunn wrote that "those expecting social commentary from Elton . . . will not be disappointed; the 16-year gap allows him to skewer some of the less savory political elements of the Eighties, including Reagan and Thatcher. Those looking for a John Sandford thriller, however, might find that the author's wit dilutes the frightfulness of the stalkings." *Blast from the Past* originated as a play and enjoyed a run of several weeks at the Yorkshire Playhouse before its publication as a novel. This fact, Alex Clark argued in the *Guardian* (September 5, 1998), gave the novel a dramatic feel: "In fact," he wrote, "*Blast from the Past* reads like nothing more than a script or a screenplay, its action set more or less in one room, during a few hours of one night, with past history simply being inserted through flashbacks and reminiscences. What this means is that the action is tight and well-plotted, the dialogue is punchy, and the whole thing rolls along so nicely that you never have to feel that you're reading a book at all." In a less glowing review, Emily Hall wrote in the *New York Times* (September 12, 1999) that Elton's "one-dimensional characters drone on and on about politics; there is little chemistry between them; had they at least jumped into bed together it would have relieved the tedium."

In 1998 Elton reportedly signed a two-book deal for more than a million and a half pounds, an amount that made him one of the highest paid authors in England. He also wrote and performed the initial ad for Divine chocolate, a "socially conscious" brand that seeks to return greater profits to growers in West Africa. The following year he began a collaboration with Andrew Lloyd Webber to create a musical, *The Beautiful Game*, about soccer, romance, and terrorism in Northern Ireland. Patrick O'Connor, writing in the *Guardian* (May 5, 1999), commented on the unlikely partnership between Webber and Elton: "Lloyd Webber, who supports several football teams, and Ben Elton, who has often sneered at the sport, may be just the oil-and-vinegar necessary. The greatest musical collaborators have often been like chalk and cheese."

Published by Bantam in 1999, *Inconceivable*, describes how Sam and Lucy Bell's various attempts to conceive a child wreak psychological havoc on the pair. Frank Egerton, who reviewed the novel for the *Spectator* (October 2, 1999), expressed annoyance with the "variety show" tone of the novel's first half ("Sensitive writing still has to compete with farce, motor-mouth comedy, and slapstick humour," Egerton wrote), but praised the book's eventual outcome. Midway through the novel, Egerton noted, "the 'knob gags' and endless feeble euphemisms for masturbation disappear and [Elton] is writing a tender, beautifully balanced romantic comedy."

In 2001 Elton published *Dead Famous*, a satire of the modern trend in "reality" television, in which a group of strangers is forced to live together for a number of weeks while the cameras record the action. About four weeks into the program, one of the contestants is murdered, though none of the cameras positioned throughout the house reveal the identity of the murderer, and a grizzled detective is forced to sift through hours of footage hoping to find a clue to the killer's identity.

Elton married Sophie Gare in 1994. In his spare moments he does not spend a lot of time investigating other comics. He told Andy Lowe, "I know next to nothing about today's comedy. And it's not just me being poncey. I just don't use comedy as a recreation; I spend so much time trying to create it. Obviously, I love good comedy. I've just seen the latest Woody Allen, I'm enjoying the Ab Fab repeats . . . but I generally don't seek it out. I'm not a comedy junkie in the slightest."

—E. M.

SUGGESTED READING: *Guardian* p46 Jan. 22, 1994, with photo, p18 Jan. 26, 1994, with photo, p7 Apr. 14, 1998, p25 Sep. 30, 1998, pT016 May 5, 1999; (London) *Observer* p17 Mar. 25, 1990

SELECTED WORKS: drama—*Gasping*, 1990; *Silly Cow*, 1991; *Blast from the Past*, 1998; novels—*Stark*, 1989; *Gridlock*, 1991; *This Other Eden*, 1993; *Popcorn*, 1996; *Blast from the Past*, 1998; *Inconceivable*, 1999; *Dead Famous*, 2001; television—*The Young Ones* (with Rik Mayall and Lise Meyer), 1982, 1984; *Happy Families*, 1985; *Filthy Rich and Catflap*, 1986; *Blackadder II* (with Richard Curtis), 1987; *Saturday Live*, 1987; *Friday Live*, 1987–88; *Blackadder the Third* (with Richard Curtis), 1988; *Blackadder Goes Forth* (with Richard Curtis), 1989; *The Man From Auntie*, 1990, 1994; *The Thin Blue Line*, 1995–96; *The Ben Elton Show*, 1998

Courtesy of Small Beer Press

Emshwiller, Carol

Apr. 12, 1921– Novelist; short-story writer

The fiction of novelist and short-story writer Carol Emshwiller defies easy categorization. Although her overlying theme has been the emotional predicaments of women, especially in the domestic sphere, she also uses elements of fantasy and science fiction in portraying her often-troubled female characters. Though Emshwiller's stories can be outrageous, they are always delivered with understatement and reserve. For example, in a short story entitled "Mrs. Jones" that appeared in *Omni* (August 1993), Emshwiller tells of an aging spinster who captures a strange, winged creature in her backyard, names him Mr. Jones after her deceased dog, and forces him to marry her. "She tells him she loves him several times," Emshwiller writes in the story, "kisses him on the cheeks and then on the neck, just below the choke collar." Emshwiller's eccentric imagination, wit, and stylistic techniques, including subtle irony, economical prose, and restrained use of metaphor, render her work unique. In *Twentieth-Century Science-Fiction Writers* (1986), Douglas Barbour observed, "Emshwiller's fictions force us to look again at the supposedly ordinary domestic world and see it as truly weird and, yes, unknown. How she does this is through prose so precise it cuts away conventional perceptual fat like a surgeon's scalpel." Though now in her 80s, Emshwiller continues to be productive; her most recent publications include *Reports to the Men's Club* (2001), a collection of stories, and *Mount* (2002), a novel.

Carol Emshwiller was born in Ann Arbor, Michigan, on April 12, 1921, the daughter of Charles Carpenter, a professor, and Agnes Fries. In 1945 she received a B.A. in music from the University of Michigan, in Ann Arbor, and went on to get a second bachelor's degree, in design, from the same school, in 1949. That same year she married Edmund Emshwiller, a filmmaker and science-fiction illustrator. She was a Fulbright Fellow at the Ecole Supérieure des Beaux-Arts, in Paris, from 1949 to 1950. Her writing began appearing in science-fiction publications in the mid-1950s, including *Dangerous Visions*, *Orbit*, and *2076: The American Tricentennial*. Although Emshwiller's early writings were not typical of the science fiction genre, her work was lumped into that category from the beginning, in part because of her association with her husband. Some of her early stories include "This Thing Called Love" (1955), "The Piece Thing" (1956), "Murray is for Murder" (1957), "Two-step for Six Legs" (1957), and "Puritan Planet" (1960).

As she grew more confident, Emshwiller's style grew more experimental. For *Science-Fiction Writers,* she told Douglas Barbour, "Formal/structural concerns have always interested me the most, so once I had learned to plot and had published numerous science-fiction stories (and a few mystery stories), I decided to learn how *not* to plot. My concerns were for the various ways of forming a story and keeping forward movement without plotting." In 1974 some of Emshwiller's many stories were collected in her first book, *Joy in Our Cause*. The stories included are all experimental in nature. Although she did not publish a second short-story collection for 15 years, she continued to publish stories in journals. Some of her works from this period include "Escape is No Accident" (1977), "Abominable" (1980), "The Start of the End of the World" (1981), "Queen Kong" (1982), and "Verging on the Pertinent" (1984). In 1973 she received a MacDowell Fellowship, and in 1975 she received a Creative Artists Public Service grant.

Meanwhile, Emshwiller began to teach writing at universities and writers workshops. From 1972 to 1973 she taught at the Clarion Science Fiction Workshop in Lansing, Michigan. In 1974 she began teaching writing as a member of the continuing education faculty at New York University, in New York City, a post she would hold for many years. In 1975 and 1976 she organized writing workshops at New York City's Science Fiction Bookstore, and she became a guest faculty member at Sarah Lawrence College, in Bronxville, New York, in 1982.

In 1989 Emshwiller's second collection of short stories, *Verging on the Pertinent*, was published. Many of its 17 stories focus on the sexual imagination of women. In "Yukon," a neglected housewife treks into the mountains and moves in with a bear. After a tawdry love affair, the bear starts wandering in at three in the morning and ignoring her, just like her husband had. In another story, a woman who lives inside a statue in New York City's Washington Square Park outrages a male guard by hanging her underwear between the statue's knees. In "Queen Kong," a giantess scales a tall building holding a plump male executive in her fist. Gregory Feeley wrote in his review of the collection for the *Washington Post* (April 9, 1990), "Emshwiller's stories are lithe, sharply observed, humane, and unfailingly funny, besides having the most inviting titles of any writer anywhere: 'Biography of an Uncircumcised Man (Including Interview),' 'Slowly Bumbling in the Void,' 'There Is No God but Bog.'" While Deborah Stead in the *New York Times* (March 8, 1990) found some of the stories "too cerebral, too cooly ironic," she also wrote, "When the aliens land, I hope Carol Emshwiller is around to explain what's up with Earth women these days. She certainly knows how to take the Martian view of ordinary domestic life—how to get at the truth of things by rendering them strange."

Emshwiller's first novel, *Carmen Dog*, was published in England in 1988 and came out in the U.S. in 1990. A feminist fable about the domination of women by men, the heroine of the novel is a dog named Pooch, who, after a series of adventures, transforms into an opera-singing young woman. Scores of women in the novel go through the reverse process, changing from humans to animals. Some women sprout webbed feet, while others grow wings. When Pooch's master turns into a snapping turtle and bites her own baby, Pooch takes the child and flees. Pooch's life out in the world is anything but easy. Among other adventures, she narrowly escapes a dog-catcher and endures a doctor's experiments before joining up with the animal-women's movement and making her triumphant singing debut in the opera "Carmen." Writing in the *New York Times* (April 29, 1990), Charlotte Innes found the novel, "Warm, compassionate and refreshingly jargon-free . . . a gentle exposition of human folly that nevertheless makes some tough points about the inequalities between the sexes—especially the ways in which women learn how to be the willing victims of men." In general, critics applauded the novel for its stylistic accomplishments, which inspired comparisons to the writing of James Thurber. Some critics, however, felt the book's feminist sentiment was oversimplified and lacked subtlety. "The underlying message kills this book," Marianna Hofer wrote in *Small Press* (June 1990), "and, what's worse, it's applied with a trowel."

Emshwiller's third short-story collection, *The Start of the End of It All*, was published in 1991. Thematically, it shared common ground with her previous collection, in that she used satire and fantasy to critique the plight of women from a feminist perspective. In the title story, aliens visit Earth to advise a group of divorced, middle-aged women on how to change the world. Their sage advice is to kill all cats. In "Glory, Glory," a woman on vacation with her husband takes pleasure in being identified as a goddess by the natives. Her husband, however, reminds her not to get too uppity, because she hasn't finished college. Eventually, she parts ways with her spouse and remains where she is truly appreciated. "Emshwiller's fabulisms court a sense of the sacred but cleverly undercut that sense with tongue-in-cheek playfulness," a critic noted in *Kirkus Reviews* (April 15, 1991). "The ensuing deft balance between mystery and skepticism is touching—and often aesthetically triumphant."

In 1992 Emshwiller's novella, *Venus Rising*, was published, though it attracted little attention. *Ledoyt*, a Western of sorts set in post-World War I California, was published in 1995. In the novel, Oriana Cochran, an only child of proper New England parents, flees to the West to raise her illegitimate daughter, the progeny of a rape. Plagued by self-loathing, Oriana meets a man, Bill Ledoyt, who is completely different from her in every way, except for their shared self-contempt. The two marry, have a son of their own, and also raise Oriana's daughter, Lotti. Lotti grows into an angry, strong-willed young woman, whose wildness threatens to tear Oriana and Bill apart. Critics complimented Emshwiller's strong characterizations and her feel for the rugged terrain of the West. In the *Library Journal* (October 1, 1995), Janet Ingraham wrote, "Emshwiller knows well the marvelous inexplicability of love, jealousy, and heroism." Fellow science-fiction writer Ursula K. Le Guin, writing in *Women's Review of Books* (January 1997), called *Ledoyt* "an unsentimental love story, an unidealized picture of the American past, a tough, sweet, painful, truthful novel." Walter Satterthwait commended the novel in the *New York Times* (October 29, 1995), despite finding Lotti an unsympathetic character. "[Emshwiller] creates, in only a few words, people whose bravery and pride and tortured honesty are almost palpable," Satterthwait observed. "There are moments in this book that are remarkably moving; there are scenes of great power. I just didn't like that kid."

Leaping Man Hill (1999) was Emshwiller's next novel, a sequel to *Ledoyt* also set in California. It begins with Lotti, now known as Charlotte, who is grown up and just barely keeping a ranch afloat with the help of her younger brother, Fay, while also raising her little boy, Abel. She brings in a young woman, Mary Catherine, to teach Abel at home, though he would rather climb trees than speak, much less learn to write. Mary Catherine, young and innocent herself, soon falls in love with a half-crazed World War I veteran named Henry, whose favorite activity is starting fights and losing them on purpose. When Fay runs away from home and Charlotte dies in pursuit, Mary Catherine is left alone. In the meantime, she has given her love to Henry with full abandon and is left to raise his child after he disappears. In a review for the *San Francisco Chronicle* (October 10, 1999), Gerald Haslam praised the book, noting, "*Leaping Man Hill* is a satisfying novel, with complexities not susceptible to easy summary, as well as those quirky characters and some playful language. Finally, though, it is dominated by Emshwiller's sure development of Mary Catherine. Readers who grow with that young woman may remember this book a long time."

Though now over 80 years old, Emshwiller is still remarkably productive. In recent years she has published *Reports to the Men's Club* (2001), a collection of stories, and *Mount* (2002), a well-received novel. In *Science-Fiction Writers*, she recounted her strategy as an author: namely, to attempt to chart the inner landscape of the mind. "I tried to do away with character, and substituted what I called 'selves,' which, in my mind, were more real than 'characters' (though perhaps just different). I used the first person and tried for a kind of internal, psychological realism." In 1980 she received a National Endowment for the Arts grant; she has also won a Pushcart Prize. Her son, Peter Emshwiller, is a writer of science fiction. Emshwiller also has two daughters, Eve and Susan, and lives in New York City.

— P.G.H.

SUGGESTED READING: *New York Times* (on-line) Mar. 18, 1990, Oct. 29, 1995; *Newsday* p17 Mar. 18, 1990; *San Francisco Chronicle* (on-line) Oct. 10, 1999; *Washington Post* C p3 Apr. 9, 1990; Smith, Curtis, ed. *Twentieth-Century Science-Fiction Writers*, 1986

SELECTED BOOKS: novels—*Carmen Dog*, 1990; *Venus Rising*, 1992; *Ledoyt*, 1995; *Leaping Man Hill*, 1999; *Mount*, 2002; short-story collections—*Joy in Our Cause*, 1974; *Verging on the Pertinent*, 1989; *The Start of the End of It All*, 1991; *Reports to the Men's Club*, 2001

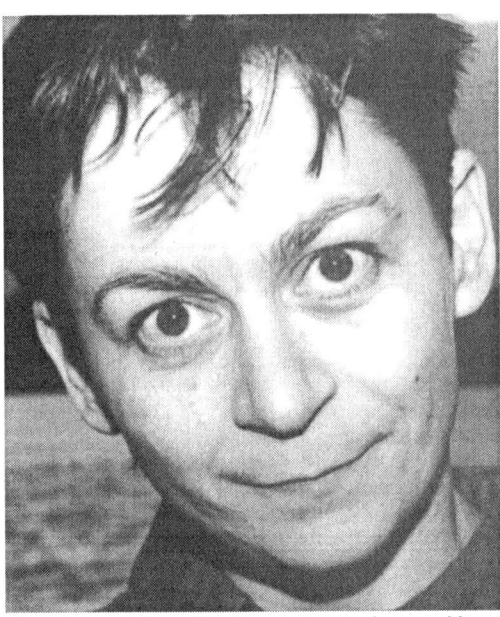

Courtesy of Grove/Atlantic Publicity

Enright, Anne

1962– Novelist; short-story writer

Among the ranks of modern Irish writers, Anne Enright is "an important emerging talent," as Robert MacFarlane wrote for the *Times Literary Supplement* (March 3, 2000). Additionally, Amy Halloran observed for *Rain Taxi* (Winter 2001, on-line), "Her writing is pithier and more intelligent than much of what is billed as contemporary literature." A television producer turned writer, Enright has published several critically admired works: a collection of short stories, *The Portable Virgin* (1991), and three novels, *The Wig My Father Wore* (1995), *What Are You Like?* (2000), and *The Pleasure of Eliza Lynch* (2003). Known for her sharp language and biting humor, Enright told an interviewer for the *Independent* (March 2000, on-line), "The irony I use is not literary. It's my mother's. A lived, inherited irony—not from books."

Anne Enright was born in Dublin, Ireland, in 1962. She spent her childhood in Ireland; then at age 16, she began attending school in Canada. She returned to Dublin to enroll at Trinity College. She later matriculated at the University of East Anglia, in Norwich, England, where she studied creative writing with the noted British writers Angela Carter and Malcolm Bradbury. After completing her university education, Enright worked as an actress and later as a television director and producer, most notably producing the popular show *Nighthawks*, which was set in a fictional bar and often featured improvisational dialogue. Speaking of the experience, Enright told the *Independent* reporter, "It was like packing to go on holiday every day. I'd wait for the script, have the actors standing by, the props, but you never knew what you were going to need. . . . It was anarchic."

Despite the heavy scheduling demands of producing a regular television series, Enright found time to write fiction, as she recalled in her *Independent* interview: "I'd come home on Friday, go to the pictures, then write all weekend." In 1991 she published her first book, a short-story collection entitled *The Portable Virgin*, which depicts several unconventional female characters. In "(She Owns) Everything," for example, Enright presents Cathy, a handbag saleswoman who becomes obsessed with matching her customers with the perfect bags, which may "take them one step beyond who they thought they might be," as quoted by Penelope Fitzgerald in the *London Review of Books* (March 2, 2000). One day, when Cathy is unable to arrange the perfect union between customer and bag, her ordered life begins to fall into disarray. In another story, "Luck Be a Lady," Enright introduces a 55-year-old bingo champion, Mrs. Hanratty, who falls for the only man at her bingo games. Enright writes, as quoted by Fitzgerald, "She wanted him. It was as simple as that. A woman of 55, a woman with 5 children and 1 husband, who had had sexual intercourse 1332 times in her life and was in possession of 14 coal-scuttles." "Several of these stories are concerned with the crucial moment when human nature cannot stand any more," Fitzgerald explained, adding, "Enright has a tender heart, with great pity for women, who seem set on their course of hard daily work and uncomfortable dreams." A reviewer for the London *Observer* (January 5, 1992) wrote of Enright, "She writes with a kind of controlled battiness, sometimes with egregious whimsicality, but always with originality. Amazingly assured debut from a new Irish writer, bursting with talent, and obliquely moving." *The Portable Virgin* won the 1991 Rooney Prize for Irish literature and was a candidate for the 1991 *Irish Times*/Aer Lingus Irish Literature Prize.

In 1995 Enright published her first novel, *The Wig My Father Wore*, a book that John Tague, writing for the *Times Literary Supplement* (March 31, 1995), called "an intellectually inventive fable, polished with a comic light touch." The book begins when Grace, a Dublin television producer who works for a flamboyant dating show called *The Love Quiz*, is visited by an angel named Stephen. Stephen committed suicide in 1934 and has been assigned to return to earth to help a mortal. He moves into Grace's home to help her overcome her personal confusion about love, motherhood, Roman Catholicism, sex, and redemption. As Grace falls in love with this comical angel, she deals with her ailing father, who has been rendered inarticulate by two strokes. During the scenes in which Grace dutifully visits her parents' home, Enright indulges in humorous anthropomorphism, animating the father's wig: "I was very fond of it as a child," she has Grace say, as quoted by Tom Gilling in the *New York Times* (November 18, 2001, on-line). "I thought it liked me back." According to Kate Kellaway in the London *Observer* (March 12, 1995), the wig "is perhaps the most frisky character in the book." Describing the hairpiece during a cycle in the washing machine, Kellaway quoted Enright as writing, "I like to think of it as spinning around with [my mother's] knickers and bras like a rat on holiday."

Most critics applauded *The Wig My Father Wore* for its inventive wit and tone; Kellaway praised Enright as "someone who knows how to wisecrack her way into and out of trouble, who is quick to answer back, slow to question and too busy talking to allow pain—of which there is a great deal here—any air time." Gilling called Enright's distinct prose "often beautiful but demanding to read" and wrote, "Enright writes exhilarating sentences, strewn with surprising conjunctions of words that capture the ambiguities and contradictions inherent in love and religion and family life." While John Tague judged the novel to be "intellectually ambitious," he complained that it resembled "an overgrown short story" rather than a novel. "The narrative continually, and claustrophobically, folds inward into Grace's own mind," Tague explained, "and so the pacing of the story is severely limited to one rhythm."

In 1997 Enright participated in writing a group novel with six other authors representing Dublin's literary elite. Along with Dermot Bolger, the Irish novelist who conceived the idea (and edited the final manuscript), Enright collaborated with Roddy Doyle, Hugo Hamilton, Jennifer Johnston, Joseph O'Connor, and Colm Tóibín. Each wrote one chapter, all without attribution. The result, *Finbar's Hotel*, is a multilayered narrative told through seven linked stories, each set in a Dublin hotel scheduled for demolition. The novel features a colorful cast of characters, beginning with a husband who acts upon his long-held wish to spend one night alone in a hotel before he dies. As the man ventures from his room in search of a mini-bar, he encounters several other guests, including an electrician who has stolen his ex-girlfriend's cat, two feuding sisters, an ill woman who is skipping her cancer treatment, and an art thief. Wroe declared the book to be "an intriguing literary puzzle," while Katherine Weber in the *New York Times* (May 2, 1999) wrote, "This unusual novel is far more than a curiosity, although no one—its own authors included—would presume to call it an important work of literature."

In her 2000 novel, *What Are You Like?*, Enright presents a complicated story of twin sisters separated at birth, beginning it with what a reviewer for *Publishers Weekly* (July 17, 2000) called "a flawlessly rendered first chapter." Martha K. Baker, writing for the *St. Louis Post–Dispatch* (November 5, 2000), noted the book's gripping first line, which introduces a baby whose mother has died in childbirth: "She was a small monster, with the slightly hurt look that monsters have and babies share, the same need to understand." Raised by her father and his new wife, this child, Maria, grows into a conflicted and despairing young woman, who at one point ventures to New York but later returns to Dublin, where she becomes a changing-room clerk in a boutique. Meanwhile, the reader learns of the existence of a twin who has been given up for adoption; this girl, Rose, grows up in England, becomes a social worker, and eventually chooses to seek out her biological family. The two girls share a parallel sense of isolation and a lack of self-esteem, always feeling that something of themselves is missing—though neither one knows of the other's existence. Enright's narrative shifts back and forth abruptly between the girls' lives. As the *Publishers Weekly* reviewer put it, the book is "fractured like the family it illuminates." Yet, Baker observed, "You're willing to forget what, on the surface, is confusing or tedious after you realize that [Enright] had to do it this way. . . . Otherwise, writing wouldn't be so much fun."

Critics found much to praise in *What Are You Like?*, with Halloran calling the book "gruelingly beautiful," and Ruth Scurr, in the *New Statesman* (April 10, 2000) opining, "Enright turns this raw, unwieldy material into a delightful novel." Scurr wrote of Enright's style, "She is an intense and frenetic writer, jumping from one perception to the next, always on the accelerator or the brakes, sometimes dashing, sometimes silly, but never boring." Robert MacFarlane observed, "Enright is a meticulous writer in the very best sense of that adjective, paying attention to rhythm, and to the individual image, without ever seeming over-intricate." Nevertheless, MacFarlane noted that "the ambitious architecture of the book seems to prevent Enright from creating any emotional impetus." He concluded, "In the end, reading [Enright's novel] feels like putting on a suit of armour. You admire the workmanship and gleam of the individual segments, but find the whole outfit rather unwieldy and disjointed." Despite the mixed criticism, *What Are You Like?* won the British-based Encore Award for best second novel and was short-listed for the prestigious Whitbread Novel Award.

Enright has published short stories in such periodicals as the *New Yorker*, *Harper's Magazine*, and the *Paris Review*; she also writes regular columns for the *London Review of Books* and the *Irish Times*. She is a frequent commentator for BBC Radio 4, which broadcasts news throughout Great Britain, and RTE, Ireland's national broadcasting company. She resides in Dublin with her husband, the Irish actor Martin Murphy. Her most recent book is *The Pleasure of Eliza Lynch*, which was published in 2003. Based on an Irishwoman who became widely known as the "Eva Peron" of Paraguay in the 1850s, the novel was generally well received.

—K. D.

SUGGESTED READING: *Independent* (on-line) Mar. 2000; *London Review of Books* p8 Mar. 2, 2000; *New Statesman* p61 Apr. 10, 2000; *New York Review* p90 Sep. 21, 2000; *New York Times* (on-line) Nov. 18, 2001; *New York Times Book Review* p19 May 2, 1999; *Times Literary Supplement* p22 Mar. 31, 1995, p23 Sep. 26, 1997, p21 Mar. 3, 2000

SELECTED BOOKS: short-story collections—*The Portable Virgin*, 1991; novels—*The Wig My Father Wore*, 1995; *What Are You Like?*, 2000; *The Pleasure of Eliza Lynch*, 2003.

Fairchild, B. H.

Oct. 17, 1942– Poet

"It's common for people to think that the place from which they come has no poetry in it," B. H. Fairchild explained in an interview for the *Dartmouth Contemporary* (Summer 2000, on-line). "I thought that the last thing that could be a subject for poetry could be the small, wind-blown, dusty, working-class town that I came from. . . . But then I learned of and read poets such as William Stafford, James Wright and Richard Hugo, all of whom came from the same kind of place and the same social environment as I do and, lo and behold, I realized, 'Well you can write poems about it. You can get poetry out of it.'" Fairchild's poetry collections include *The Arrival of the Future* (1985) and *The Art of the Lathe* (1998), which take as their subjects the dreary existence and frustrated desires of working-class laborers in the small lonely towns of the Midwest. He has contributed poetry and articles to numerous publications, including *Poetry*, *Southern Review*, *Hudson Review*, *TriQuarterly*, *Sewanee Review*, *Salmagundi*, and the *Threepenny Review*, and has been described by Robert Phillips for the *Houston Chronicle* (October 18, 1998, online) as a poet "who should be better known." His most recent poetry collection is *Early Occult Memory Systems of the Lower Midwest* (2002).

Bertram H. Fairchild Jr. was born on October 17, 1942 in Houston, Texas, the son of Bertram, a machinist, and Locie. He grew up in small towns in west Texas, Oklahoma, and Kansas. He received a B.A., in 1964, and an M.A., in 1968, from the University of Kansas, in Lawrence. In 1975 he received a Ph.D. from the University of Tulsa, a private in-

Joanna E. Morrissey/Courtesy of W. W. Norton & Company

stitution affiliated with the Presbyterian Church, in Oklahoma. Fairchild discovered poetry in college. As he recalled for the *Dartmouth Contemporary* interviewer, "Life seemed so superficial and unreal and phoney—in the Holden Caulfield way—and I wanted something that could carry me down to the very bone of existence, whatever that was. I got to college and began reading poetry, and after a couple of classes and a lot of reading, something dawned on me: what I had wanted was what poetry is." It was a propitious discovery for Fairchild, who spent his summers working at C & W Machine Works, his father's machine shop in Liberal, Kansas. "At college, it would all be life of the mind, an intellectual world," Fairchild told the interviewer. "Back home I would do only physical work; I could feel my IQ dropping. Later on in college I realized that poetry was the one thing that brought the physical and the intellectual worlds together."

Fairchild's first published book was a critical study titled *Such Holy Song: Music as Idea, Form, and Image in the Poetry of William Blake* (1980); it examined the influence of music on the Romantic poet, focusing on two of his well-known works, *Songs of Innocence and of Experience* and *The Four Zoas*. The volume was generally well received. A reviewer for *Choice* wrote, as quoted by *Contemporary Authors* (1999), that Fairfield treated his subject "clearly and effectively," and praised the work as "the first direct attempt to render as accurately as possible the musicality" of Blake's poetry.

Fairchild has published some small-press collections of poetry, including *Flight* and *The System of Which the Body Is One Part*. His first major collection, *The Arrival of the Future*, was published in 1985 and included illustrations by Ross Zirkle. (*The Arrival of the Future* was re-issued in 2000 by Alice James Books.)

The Art of the Lathe, Fairchild's next published collection of poetry, is a unified series of poems that portray the lives and frustrations of working-class Midwesterners: machinists, welders, farmers. The first poem, "Beauty," is narrated by a man who grew up in the machine shops of Kansas and Oklahoma. As the poem begins the narrator is in Italy with his wife (as posted on the Alice James Books Web site):

> We are at the Bargello in Florence, and she says / what are you thinking? And I say, beauty, thinking / of how very far we are now from the machine shop / and the dry fields of Kansas, the treeless horizons / of slate skies and the muted passions of roughnecks / and scrabble farmers drunk and romantic enough/ to weep more or less silently at the darkened end / of the bar out of, what else, loneliness, meaning / the ache of thwarted desire, of, in a word, *beauty,* / or rather its absence, and it occurs to me again / that no male member of my family ever has used / this word in my hearing or anyone else's except / in reference, perhaps, to a new pickup or dead deer.

Another poem, "Body and Soul," examines a group of off-duty miners and oil-field workers who have gathered for a game of baseball. One man short, they allow a 15-year-old boy that is hanging around the field to join the game. The boy, as it happens, is the young Mickey Mantle (the legendary baseball player), and he humiliates the older men by hitting five home runs with ease. The narrator asks (as posted on the Billie Dee's Electronic Poetry Anthology Web site):

> Why in hell didn't they just throw around the kid, walk him, / after he hit the third homer? Anybody would have, / especially nine men with disappointed wives and dirty socks / and diminishing expectations for whom winning at anything / meant everything. . . .

The poet then gives the answer:

> And they did not because they were men, and this was a boy. / after smoking their Chesterfields in the cool silence and / listening to the big bands on the radio that sounded so glamorous, / so distant, they glanced over at their wives and noticed the lines / growing heavier around the eyes and mouth, felt what their wives / felt: that Les Brown and Glenn Miller and all those dancing couples / and in fact all possibility of human gaiety and lightheartedness / were as far away and unreachable as Times Square or the Avalon / ballroom. They did not because of the gray linoleum lying there / in the half-dark, the free calendar from the local mortuary / that said one day was pretty much like another, the work gloves / looped over the doorknob like dead squirrels. And they did not / because they had gone through a depression and a war that had left / them with the idea that being a man in the eyes of their fathers / and everyone else had cost them just too goddamn much to lay it / at the feet of a fifteen year-old-boy.

The Art of the Lathe earned high praise from critics. Robert Phillips called the work a "triumph," declaring that "Fairchild's poems combine the worlds of labor and physical danger with those of high art and history." "Fairchild's ability not only to choose a story but to pace it and to reveal its meaning through the unfolding of the narrative is probably unmatched in contemporary American poetry," Kate Daniels wrote for the *Southern Review* (Autumn 1998). "The incisive psychology, the vividly descriptive diction, the large repertoire of vocabulary, the weightiness of his settings and plots: all these contribute to the delightful sensation that one is reading, simultaneously, the best poetry and the best prose. I cannot think of another living poet capable of delivering such pleasure." *The Art of the Lathe* has received numerous awards, including the 1999 William Carlos Williams Award, the 1999 PEN Center USA West Poetry Award, the 1999 Kingsley Tufts Award, and the 1999 California Book Award.

Fairchild's most recent collection of poetry, *Early Occult Memories of the Lower Midwest* (2002), reflects on his youth in Kansas in the 1950s. In a representative review for *Booklist*, as quoted on *Amazon.com*, Ray Olson observed, "If strong emotion courses through Fairchild's work, it never makes it lachrymose, thanks to concrete vocabulary and images, direct syntax, and propulsive rhythms. Poetry book of the year?"

Fairchild is an English professor at California State University, in San Bernardino, where he teaches classes on modern and contemporary poetry and creative writing. In addition he has received Guggenheim, Rockefeller, and National Endowment for the Arts fellowships, a California Arts grant, and a National Writers' Union first prize. He is married, has two children, and lives in Claremont, California. —A. I. C.

SUGGESTED READING: *Dartmouth Contemporary* (on-line) Summer 2000; *Houston Chronicle* p23+ Oct. 18, 1998; *Poetry* p276+ Jan. 2001; *Southern Review* p736+ Autumn 1998

SELECTED BOOKS: criticism—*Such Holy Song: Music as Idea, Form, and Image in the Poetry of William Blake*, 1980; poetry collections—*The Arrival of the Future*, 1985; *The Art of the Lathe*, 1998; *Early Occult Memory Systems of the Lower Midwest* (2002).

Andrew Feiler/Courtesy of HarperCollins Publishers

Feiler, Bruce

Oct. 25, 1964– Nonfiction writer

Bruce Feiler is a highly respected travel writer, known for his ability to submerge himself in other people's cultures and lives. His first book, *Learning to Bow* (1991), chronicled the year he spent teaching in a small Japanese town. *Looking for Class* (1993) covered his time as a graduate student at Cambridge University and was notable in that it dismissed the popular belief that the English educational system is one of the best in the world. To write *Under the Big Top* (1995), Feiler lived out a childhood fantasy and joined the circus, and for *Dreaming Out Loud* (1998) he shadowed three of country music's biggest stars in order to better understand the evolution of country music, as well as his native South. In *Walking the Bible* (2001), Feiler traveled 10,000 miles across the Middle East to visit places mentioned in the Bible and explore his own faith.

Bruce S. Feiler was born in Savannah, Georgia, on October 25, 1964. His father, Edwin J. Feiler, Jr., was a developer; his mother, the former Jane Abeshouse, was a small-business owner. Growing up in a Jewish family in the traditionally Christian South, Feiler realized, as he remarked to Wendy Smith in *Publishers Weekly* (April 30, 2001), that he was "at the nexus of two great storytelling traditions, the Jewish and the Southern. Now I realize that there is this deeper, older storytelling tradition of the Bible that they both come from."

In 1983 Feiler left the South to study at Yale University, in New Haven, Connecticut. He found himself out of sorts with his Northern classmates who, after noting he was from Georgia, asked him sarcastic questions like "Do you have running water?" or "Where do you keep your slaves?" as he recalled in an interview for *Contemporary Authors, vol. 145* (1995). Such stereotyped remarks drove Feiler to study Southern history in order to better understand a place he had known all his life. "Little did I know, but this process of being an outsider inside a strange place, in this case a Southerner in the North, would become a driving force behind my work," Feiler told the *Contemporary Authors* interviewer.

In 1987 Feiler received a bachelor of arts degree from Yale and then joined the Japan Exchange and Teaching Program, sponsored by the Japanese Ministry of Education. For the next year he served as a teacher in a junior-high school in Sano, a rural town north of Tokyo, where the population has had little exposure to foreigners. He wrote letters back home about his experiences, and— encouraged by his friends and family—decided that he might turn the letters into a book. Feiler's mother happened to meet someone who had published a book, and secured the name of a literary agent for her son. Within a few months, Feiler had an agent and a book contract. As he related to Wendy Smith: "I was 24 years old! It doesn't happen that way, but it happened to me because you couldn't pick up a newspaper at that time without reading an article about Japan or education, and this was a book about Japanese education."

Learning to Bow was published by Ticknor and Fields, in 1991, to much critical acclaim. Reviewers praised Feiler's analysis of how the Japanese emphasis on teamwork in school prepares them for the workplace. In particular, Feiler drew attention to the social etiquette of bowing, which is the cornerstone of formal Japanese business practices. Japanese students practice bowing up to an hour each day. Shirley L. Hopkinson, in *Library Journal* (August 1991), called *Learning to Bow* "a lighthearted yet extremely perceptive analysis of [the Japanese] educational system." In *School Library Journal* (March 1992), Judy McAloon pointed out: "Readers cannot help comparing the Japanese society to ours, sometimes finding ours, theirs, or both wanting. American students (and teachers) will be particularly interested to learn how Japanese schools instill in students a sense of responsibility to the group and the state, using activities that would set up a howl if suggested here."

After his experience as a teacher in Japan, Feiler returned to school, at Cambridge University's Clare College, in England. He studied international relations and received his M.Phil. (akin to an American master's degree), in 1991. His experiences at one of the world's oldest and most prestigious institutions of higher learning served as the impetus for his next book, *Looking for Class*, published in 1993. Feiler describes the social mores and traditions of the university, including tea breaks, rowing, and student drinking binges and, as in his first book, includes personal anecdotes about his difficulties in adapting to a foreign culture. *Looking for Class* is harsher in tone than *Learning to Bow*, and pointedly critical of the British educational system. It received mixed reviews. In *Library Journal* (September 1, 1993), Scott Johnson remarked: "Feiler's wit and humor shine through as he relates his encounters with academic protocols, bedders, porters, rowing, alcohol consumption, social gatherings, tutorials, debates, adjustments to the Queen's English (almost a foreign tongue, he claims), sharking and interpersonal relationships as a 'colonist.'" Simon Sebag Montefiore's review for the *New York Times Book Review* (October 31, 1993) was much more negative: "Mr. Feiler serves up a feast of clichés that underestimates both the complexity of British society and the sophistication of American readers."

After Cambridge, Feiler returned to the States and pursued a childhood dream—he ran away to join the circus. In high school he had juggled and had been a mime; before going to Yale he had even considered going to clown school. In order to research his next book, *Under the Big Top* (1995), he spent the 1993 season as a clown in the Clyde Beatty-Cole Brothers Circus, which claims to be the world's biggest tented circus. His account of circus life dismantles the conventional view of the circus as being a real-life cartoon, and instead presents real people with real problems. *Under the Big Top* received high praise in the press, including a glowing review from Jean Hanff in the *New York Times* (July 23, 1995): "Bruce Feiler has written an engaging account. . . . [He] is a keen and thoughtful observer, at his best when describing the love of circus people for their difficult, dangerous and financially torturous way of life." In the *Christian Science Monitor* (August 3, 1995), Keith Henderson wrote that Feiler's book "should make anyone yearn to go out and see the circus's spectacle because, considering what goes on all around the canvas cathedral, it's an even bigger show than it's billed to be."

After completing his tour with the circus, Feiler turned his attention to more familiar territory. "I wanted to write a book about the death of the South and the Southificiation of America; it was going to be about stock car racing and country music and barbecue, all these things in one huge, undoable book," he told Smith in *Publishers Weekly*. "I went to Nashville on a scouting trip, and everyone was so welcoming. . . . I just got up and moved there." His early research formed the basis for "Gone Country," an extensive article published in the *New Republic* (February 5, 1996), in which Feiler analyzes the mainstream appeal of country music. As he began writing the book, he realized that—instead of the overview of modern Southern society that he had planned—he should focus on country music as a mirror for larger cultural changes in the South. Feiler shadowed three country music stars—Garth Brooks, Wynonna Judd, and Wade Hayes—for three years in the mid-1990s. The result, *Dreaming Out Loud*, was published in 1998 to generally favorable reviews. In *Library Journal* (April 15, 1998), Kathleen Sparkman cheered, "One hopes that [Feiler's] first book on country music is not his last, for he is a savvy author and journalist who can sort through misconceptions about country music and analyze the historical background with a clarity that other writers sometimes lack." Mike Tribby, writing for *Booklist* (April 1, 1998), remarked, "Feiler's assessment of the country music environment comes at a time when country has attained the pinnacle of pop cultural accomplishment. His take on whether it will now descend into vapidity makes good reading for those who care."

In 2001 Feiler published *Walking the Bible*, an account of his 10,000-mile pilgrimage around the Holy Land in search of famous biblical sites. On his journey, Feiler—who had not been a particularly devout Jew—discovered that his faith was strengthened by visiting the places where Abraham nearly sacrificed Isaac, for example, and where Moses parted the Red Sea. The book received mixed reviews. In *Newsweek* (April 2, 2001), David Gates wrote that—while he was happy that Feiler rediscovered his faith—"after finishing *Walking the Bible*, a 451-page slog from one Biblical said-to-be-the-place-where to the next—with epiphanies lurking behind every crumbling stone and earnest conversations at every pit stop—I was even happier to part company." In a review for *Amazon.com*, however, Michael Joseph

Gross found that Feiler's "attentiveness, intelligence, and adventurousness enliven every page of this book. And the lessons he learned about the relationship between place and the spirit will be useful for readers of every religious tradition that finds its origins in the Bible."

Abraham: A Journey to the Heart of Three Faiths, an examination of Abraham's role in Judaism, Christianity, and Islam, was published on September 17, 2002. "Feiler has a keen sense of what is at stake when these three religions claim Abraham as their father," observed a writer for *Publisher's Weekly* (July 22, 2002). "This is a joy to read."

In addition to writing travelogues, Bruce Feiler is a on-air contributor to National Public Radio and a writer for *Gourmet* magazine. Of his journalism, he remarked to Smith: "It's nice to have an outlet for an idea that's not 110,000 words. My books can be meat and potatoes; journalism can be dessert. I feel like I've got the balance right, financially and emotionally."

—C. M.

SUGGESTED READING: *Booklist* p1291 Apr. 1, 1998; *Christian Science Monitor* p15 Nov. 15, 1993, p13 Aug. 3, 1995; *Entertainment Weekly* p86+ Apr. 3, 1998; *Library Journal* p114 Aug. 1991, p82 Apr. 15, 1998; *Life* p114+ Apr. 1999; *New Republic* p19+ Feb. 5, 1996; *Newsweek* p60 Apr. 2, 2001; *New York Times Book Review* p20 Oct. 31, 1993, p14 July 23, 1995; *Publishers Weekly* p48+ Apr. 30, 2001; *School Library Journal* p268 Mar. 1992, p200 Sept. 1, 1993

SELECTED BOOKS: *Learning to Bow*, 1991; *Looking for Class*, 1993; *Under the Big Top*, 1995; *Dreaming Out Loud*, 1998; *Walking the Bible*, 2001; *Abraham: A Journey to the Heart of Three Faiths*, 2002

Courtesy of Editions Gallimard

Finkielkraut, Alain

1949– Philosopher; nonfiction author

Alain Finkielkraut is one of France's most prominent intellectuals and philosophers. A frequent presence on French television and radio, Finkielkraut has written many books about such topics as post-Holocaust Jewish identity and humanism. Finkielkraut shuns identification with both the political left and right in France, but he is well known as an opponent of totalitarianism and Marxism. A committed secularist and a partisan of Enlightenment values, he has published blistering attacks on multiculturalism and faulted moral relativism. During the 1990s Finkielkraut began to receive notice and acclaim outside of Europe, when several of his books were translated into English. These include: *Remembering in Vain: The Klaus Barbie Trial and Crimes Against Humanity* (1992), *The Imaginary Jew* (1994), *The Defeat of the Mind* (1995), *The Wisdom of Love* (1997), and most recently, *In the Name of Humanity: Reflections on the Twentieth Century* (2000). "The idea of passing on a legacy is based on the fact that the present does not have all the answers," Finkielkraut told Anne Rapin for the *Business Recorder* (April 28, 2000, on-line). "We have to know how to distance ourselves from ourselves, and the works of the past can help us here." He continued, "I would say that we have to bequeath an obligation to pass down [our legacy] and one primary value, which is the passion to understand."

The only child of Polish Jewish immigrants, Alain Finkielkraut was born in June 1949 in Paris, France. His father had left Warsaw for Paris during the early 1930s. His mother had also left Poland with her family, and they settled in Germany before the Nazis took power in 1933. During World War II Finkielkraut's father was deported to the Auschwitz death camp, but he managed to survive. His mother eluded the Nazis, in both Germany and occupied Belgium, using false identity papers. Finkielkraut's parents met in Paris in 1948 and married soon after. Finkielkraut's father worked in the leather business, and his mother remained at home, showering Alain with love and attention. "Deeply scarred by the war, Finkielkraut's parents responded like many other survivors and chose not to pass down Jewish traditions to their son, either religious or secular," Judith Friedlander wrote in her book, *Vilna on the Seine: Jewish Intellectuals in France Since 1968* (1990). "For them, Yiddish culture had disappeared in Poland, together with their families and friends. Their Alain would be culturally French, free of every trace of his Polish Jewish origin."

Growing up, Finkielkraut enjoyed a comfortable, middle-class upbringing, and he was educated in some of the best schools in Paris. He attended a two-year program at the Lycée Henri IV school in Paris in order to prepare himself for an entrance exam for the Écoles Normales Supérieures de Saint-Cloud, a prestigious university.

Finkielkraut, however, interrupted his studies at the Lycée Henri IV to participate in the student revolts that rocked France in 1968. "The place history had accorded us, the posterity of the baby boom, was the ludicrous agony of growing up during the 'phony peace,'" he recalled in *The Imaginary Jew*. "Our favorite pastime in an era so devoid of significance was transforming it into war or insurrection. Nothing was going on, so we fashioned the nothingness that befell us into the gaudy garb of revolution." Finkielkraut identified himself as a Maoist and frequently argued with his parents over politics and the current events of the day. He eventually resumed his education and was admitted to the École Normales, where he majored in French literature.

Finkielkraut gradually became disillusioned with radicalism. After studying the works of such philosophers as Hannah Arendt and Emmanuel Levinas, Finkielkraut became a militant opponent of totalitarianism and Marxism and a champion of such Enlightenment values as reason, tolerance, and individualism. According to Richard Bernstein, writing for the *New York Times* (April 2, 1987), Finkielkraut was once arrested in the Soviet Union and then expelled for campaigning on behalf of Soviet Jews, who were being persecuted by the Communist government.

After completing his education, Finkielkraut embarked on a teaching and literary career, cowriting two books with Pascal Bruckner, who later gained international recognition as a novelist: *Nouveau désordre amoureux* (1977) and *Au coin de la rue, l'aventure* (1979). During the 1980s Finkielkraut took his place among France's prominent intellectuals with such notable books as *Le juif imaginaire* (1980), an autobiographical study of Jewish identity after the Holocaust; *Avenir d'une négation: réflexion sur la question du génocide* (1982), which examined Holocaust denial; *Réprobation d'Israël* (1983), a discussion of Israel's invasion of Lebanon in 1982; *Défaite de la pensée: essai* (1987), a best-selling critique of multiculturalism; and *Mémoire vaine: du crime contre l'humanité* (1989), a look at the trial of the Nazi war criminal Klaus Barbie. In 1984 Finkielkraut was awarded the Prix Europeen de l'Essai "Charles Veillon."

Mémoire vaine was translated into English as *Remembering in Vain: The Klaus Barbie Trial and Crimes Against Humanity* (1992). During World War II, Barbie, the Gestapo chief in Lyon, France, ordered the deportation of tens of thousands of Jews to the concentration camps and the torture and murder of other civilians and members of the French Resistance. After the war Barbie escaped to Bolivia. In 1983 Barbie was handed over to France to stand trial. Finkielkraut attended the trial, which began in May 1987. Although Barbie was found guilty and sentenced to life in prison, Finkielkraut, in the book, expresses disappointment with the trial itself. Finkielkraut observed that instead of educating a new generation about the Holocaust, the media coverage turned the proceedings into entertainment. The main strategy of Jacques Vergès, Barbie's radical defense attorney, was to indict the Western world for its racism and colonialism. Vergès claimed that France had no moral right to try Barbie because of its own past crimes, especially in Algeria, a former French colony, which, in his opinion, were equivalent in severity to the Holocaust. Many journalists and commentators allowed themselves to be influenced by Vergès's arguments, which shifted attention away from the charges against Barbie. Finkielkraut also raises legal questions about the trial; he writes, for example, that it was inappropriate for a French court to try Barbie for the murder of members of the French Resistance, because the statute of limitations for these crimes had expired. Finkielkraut argues that Barbie should have been tried instead by an international tribunal, which would have been based on a higher legal standard than the laws of any individual state and would have successfully represented the human race as a whole at the trial. In his review for the *Times Literary Supplement* (April 2, 1993), David Cesarani wrote that *Remembering in Vain* was packed "with insight and irony," concluding, "Finkielkraut may bemoan the degradation of memory into sentimentality, and remembrance into instant consumption, but his book is evidence that when it comes to the past, they do things differently, and better, in France."

The publication of *The Imaginary Jew*, a translation of *Le juif imaginare*, brought Finkielkraut substantial attention in the United States. In it he discusses Jewish identity after the Holocaust, recalling how he struggled with his own Jewish heritage. Although his parents decided against passing Judaism's traditions and practices down to him, Finkielkraut, as a young man, learned to take pride in being Jewish because it allowed him to be different than his compatriots, most of whom were Gentiles. In the book he elaborates: "The Judaism I had received was the most beautiful present a postgenocidal child could imagine. I inherited a suffering to which I had not been subjected, for without having to endure oppression, the identity of the victim was mine. I could savor an exceptional destiny while remaining completely at ease. Without exposure to real danger, I had heroic stature: to be Jewish was enough to escape the anonymity of an identity indistinguishable from others and the dullness of an uneventful life." He eventually realized that adopting such an identity—without personal risk—for opportunistic reasons made him an "imaginary Jew." For Finkielkraut, the Holocaust destroyed the secular Jewish culture that represented identity for many Jews in pre-war Europe. Finkielkraut maintains that those Jews who were alive before the war and who survived the Holocaust have a connection to that culture through memory. Jews who were born after the war, he opines, have no memory of that culture and are forced to seek new means to affirm their Jewish identities. "Finkielkraut's book is an insightful and compelling study of the sense of *déracinement* felt by those who live in the aftermath of the death camp," Alan L. Berger wrote for the *Journal of Religion* (July 1996). "His sense of exclusion is exacerbated by the realization that what was lost can never be recovered. The search for *enracinement* carries with it the recognition that, as [the novelist and critic] Maurice Blanchot contends, 'the disaster ruins everything.' Beneath the masks of cultural identity lies the void of the Holocaust. The arguments of *The Imaginary Jew* have lost none of their force in the years since they first appeared." In his review for the *New Leader* (December 19, 1994), David Singer criticized Finkielkraut's arguments. "Finkielkraut is a man who has painted himself into a corner," Singer explained. "What he values in Jewish life no longer exists, and what exists he does not value. One would have expected that a careful thinker intent on forging a meaningful Jewish identity for himself would adopt an incrementalist approach, carefully sifting through the various possibilities and keeping all his options open. The radical either/or stance he assumes instead quickly narrows the range of acceptable Jewish experience to virtual zero."

In 1995 Finkielkraut's best-selling 1987 book, *Défaite de la pensée: essai*, was translated into English as *The Defeat of the Mind*. In it Finkielkraut traces the intellectual origins of contemporary multiculturalism back to the German thinker Johann Gottfried Herder (1744–1804), who argued that different cultures produce different types of human beings. Herder's ideas clashed with the Enlightenment values articulated by many French philosophers, who asserted that human nature transcended racial and ethnic barriers and championed the rights of the individual. Finkielkraut noted that during the 1960s, elements of nationalism and Marxism were combined to form an ideology of liberation in many Third World countries against the colonialism, racism, and exploitation of Western Europe. He concludes that multiculturalism, with its exclusive emphasis on racial identity, threatened freedom, justice, and individuality, which were the foundation of many developed countries. "The life of the mind has been quietly moved out of the way, making room for the terrible and pathetic encounter of the fanatic and the zombie," he warned in the book. In his review for *Commentary* (November 1995), Thomas Pavel observed that Finkielkraut echoed many of the themes of such American authors as Allan Bloom and Christopher Lasch, writing, "With *The Defeat of the Mind* Finkielkraut joins their ranks, offering a vibrant, persuasive plea for individualism and reason which should fortify critics of the multiculturalist orthodoxy on today's campuses—and enlighten anyone who thinks that multiculturalism is a strictly American affair." In the *New Yorker* (September 4, 1995), Paul Berman wrote, "Finkielkraut has reverted to an earlier, superior mode of French writing. It is a style of lucidity and logical reasoning, which . . . comes to us slightly chipped and dented, owing to the unavoidable hardships of translation (plus some avoidable hardships in the form of straight-out errors)." Berman added that the author "sometimes comes off as a scold, airily instructing us on which arts should be held in high esteem (literature, Duke Ellington) and which in low (movies, rock). . . . Finkielkraut has the kind of talent for generalization which allows his subject to be vast and his book to be short and the reader to be satisfied even so."

In *The Wisdom of Love*, a 1997 translation of *Sagesse de l'amour: essai* (1984), Finkielkraut examines the ideas of the prominent Lithuanian-born Jewish philosopher Emmanuel Levinas (1906–95). "Finkielkraut does not present a discussion of Levinas' thought in any systematic or exegetical manner," Robert Gibbs wrote in his review for *Shofar* (April 30, 2000). "He takes Levinas' central concept . . . and then explores how it relates to other aspects of our culture: to love, to antisemitism, to revolutionary politics, and so on." Gibbs observed that the "excitement of Finkielkraut's book, then, is to parse that infinite responsibility through a series of important cultural contexts, showing how responsibility and the wisdom born of it can help us discern the ethical dimension of culture. . . . Without focusing on issues in Levinas scholarship, this book offers the intellectual world a chance to see what Levinas' difficult and demanding ethics might mean in the world of politics, hatred, and ideas."

Finkielkraut examines the roots of Holocaust denial in his book *The Future of a Negation: Reflections on the Question of Genocide* (1998), a translation of one his early works, *Avenir d'une négation: réflexion sur la question du génocide*. While it is widely known that neo-Nazis and anti-Semites frequently insist that the Holocaust never happened in an attempt to rehabilitate the reputation of Adolf Hitler and Nazism, Finkielkraut points out that elements of the radical left in France also deny the Holocaust. As Rafael Medoff explained in his review for *Judaism* (Spring 2000, on-line), "In their mental universe, Western capitalism is the chief enemy of mankind and Western accusations about Nazi atrocities are seen as an attempt to distract the proletariat from its real foe." Medoff wrote that Finkielkraut "concentrates on the philosophical implications of Holocaust-denial, the deniers' motives, and French society's response to their activity. It makes for compelling reading."

During the early 1990s Finkielkraut turned his attention to the turmoil in Yugoslavia. In June 1991 Croatia and Slovenia declared their independence from Yugoslavia, whose government was dominated by Serbs. Slobodan Milosevic, Yugoslavia's president, attempted to keep Yugoslavia together with military force, attacking both Croatia and Slovenia and supporting Serb minorities in both countries who were violently resisting the independence campaigns with guerilla warfare. Several Western nations, including the United States, France, Germany, and Great Britain, attempted to resolve the crisis without success. Although the fighting stopped in Slovenia, the war between Yugoslavia and Croatia dragged on for the next several years and, in 1992, the violence spread to Bosnia-Herzegovina, which was also seeking independence from Yugoslavia. Finkielkraut published many op-ed pieces on the Balkan conflict for the Paris daily newspaper Le Monde and other periodicals. Finkielkraut passionately championed Croatia's bid for independence and criticized the Western response to the conflict, especially by the French President Franqois Mitterrand. In 1992 a collection of Finkielkraut's pieces were published in the book Comment peut-on être Croate?, which subsequently appeared in English as Dispatches From the Balkan War and Other Writings (1999). "Finkielkraut is nothing if not passionate and opinionated," a reviewer for Publishers Weekly (November 29, 1999) wrote. "He offers no pretense of impartiality and no in-depth knowledge of the region. While cleverly laying bare some of the inadequacies of the world's response to the Balkan crises, he seriously confuses the motivations at play in the region. In defending Croatia, he believes he is defending an authentic idea of humanity and democracy. Readers aware of Croatia's record on human rights may disagree with his views."

Finkielkraut offers a critique of humanism in his book In the Name of Humanity: Reflections on the Twentieth Century (2000), a translation of Humanité perdue: essai sur le XX siécle (1996). The author questions how and why humanism, which asserts that all human beings regardless of their race, ethnicity, and culture are equal and should respect one another's rights, failed in the last century—as evidenced by the Holocaust, as well as the murder of as many as 100 million people under Communist regimes. In discussing the historical development of humanism, Finkielkraut asserts that the skepticism of the Enlightenment—which unleashed the forces of democratic egalitarianism—also undermined society's "sacred" foundations, which provide a higher standard of morality than the laws of any individual state. Divorced from these foundations, Finkielkraut theorizes, humanism was unable to provide a sufficient challenge to both Nazism and Communism. Finkielkraut argues that present-day humanism is insufficient to provide a foundation for political morality. In his review for First Things (January 2001), Brian C. Anderson found Finkielkraut's assessment of globalization and the Internet to be too bleak, but concluded that In the Name of Humanity "is a significant book. Finkielkraut is right to see the weakness of an ungrounded humanism. . . . Solving the deeper problem that Finkielkraut leaves unaddressed—how such a restoration might happen—is the challenge we face today."

Alain Finkielkraut teaches literature and philosophy at the École Polytechnique, one of France's most elite institutions of higher learning, in Paris. He hosts a weekly radio show on the arts, frequently contributes op-ed articles to Le Monde and other French newspapers, and edits the journal Le Messager Européen, which he founded.

—D. C.

SUGGESTED READING: Business Recorder (on-line) Apr. 28, 2000; Commentary p134+ Nov. 1995; First Things p41+ Jan. 2001; Hudson Review p152+ Spring 1996; Journal of Religion p509+ July 1996; Judaism (on-line) Spring 2000; New Leader p31+ Dec. 19, 1994, with photograph; New Statesman & Society p62+ Dec. 18, 1992, with photographs; New York Times A p4+ Apr. 2, 1987, with photos; New Yorker p93 Sep. 4, 1995; Publishers Weekly p62 Nov. 29, 1999; Romanic Review p131+ Jan. 1990; Shofar p171+ Apr. 30, 2000; Times Literary Supplement p26+ Apr. 2, 1993, with photo; Friedlander, Judith. Vilna on the Seine: Jewish Intellectuals in France Since 1968, 1990

SELECTED BOOKS IN ENGLISH TRANSLATION: Remembering in Vain: The Klaus Barbie Trial and Crimes Against Humanity, 1992; The Imaginary Jew, 1994; The Defeat of the Mind, 1995; The Wisdom of Love, 1997; The Future of a Negation: Reflections on the Question of Genocide, 1998; Dispatches from the Balkan War and Other Writings, 1999; In the Name of Humanity: Reflections on the Twentieth Century, 2000

Finnegan, William Patrick

Nov. 17, 1952– Journalist

William Finnegan is recognized for his ability to take confusing and disturbing situations and, with characteristic balance and vividness, make them real to readers. In three celebrated works of literary journalism set in Africa—Crossing the Line: A Year in the Land of Apartheid (1986), Dateline Soweto: Travels with Black South African Reporters (1988), and Complicated War: The Harrowing of Mozambique (1992)—Finnegan entered as a relatively uninformed observer into potentially dangerous circumstances. The resultant books, with their clear and unique perspectives, impressed even experts. Finnegan, who has been a staff writer for the New Yorker since 1987, turned from apartheid to a dif-

Courtesy of the *New Yorker*
William Patrick Finnegan

ferent sort of stratification: that between the American upper and lower classes. In *Cold New World: Growing Up in a Harder Country* (1998) he makes an extended visit to a bleak world of teens and young adults who feel untouched by American prosperity and trapped by an absence of opportunity. "The most remarkable of William Finnegan's many literary gifts is his compassion," Robert Christgau wrote in a review of *Cold New World* for the *Village Voice* (May 12, 1998). "Not the fact of it, which we have a right to expect from any personal reporting about the oppressed, but its coolness, its clarity, its ductile strength."

William Patrick Finnegan was born on November 17, 1952 in New York City. His parents, William R. Finnegan and Patricia (Quinn) Finnegan, were both film producers. After earning his B.A. from the University of California at Santa Cruz, in 1974, Finnegan received his MFA from the University of Montana, in Missoula, in 1978.

Finnegan first found his way to South Africa toward the end of an extended surfing excursion that had begun in Asia. In 1980 he began teaching at Grassy Park High School, near Cape Town. Grassy Park was a school for "coloureds," the mixed-race population, who shared the language and religion of the Afrikaner ruling class, but were segregated because of their non-white ancestry. *Crossing the Line: A Year in the Land of Apartheid* gets its title from Finnegan's daily crossing from the segregated white sector into the coloured sector to get to work. Finnegan describes the experience of gradually winning over a student body that was at first skeptical about the young American surfer. Departing from the curriculum—which he saw as skewed toward a white perspective—he provides alternative education and tries to cultivate a thirst for knowledge among his students. When the students boycott the school, demanding equal treatment regardless of race, Finnegan provides instruction at informal tutoring sessions initiated by the students. (Nearly 100 schools joined Grassy Park in the boycott before it ended, later in 1980.)

In the course of describing his own experience, Finnegan sheds much light on the twisted bureaucracy that was the South African government. "This may be the best book to give to an American trying for the first time to understand the agony of South Africa," Norman Rush wrote in the *New York Times Book Review* (September 21, 1986). "Even those familiar with the structure and history of apartheid will encounter much that is new and important to think about in this detailed story of life in the Cape Flats." Some reviewers faulted *Crossing the Line* for not offering solutions to the bleak realities of apartheid. A reviewer for the *Economist* (November 22, 1986), for example, wrote, "Mr. Finnegan describes lucidly, analyses cleverly, predicts darkly, but fails to prescribe." *Crossing the Line* was named one of the ten best nonfiction books of the year by the *New York Times*.

Finnegan's next adventure in South Africa took place in 1986, when he traveled around with several black reporters from the *Johannesburg Star*. *Dateline Soweto* is an account of how these reporters consistently risked themselves to cover the atrocities being perpetrated by the South African government. Though it was published at a time when there were many other writings about South Africa, Finnegan's book stood out from the rest, several reviewers agreed. In *Quill & Quire* (January 1989) Paul Stuewe wrote, "Amid the many titles dealing with contemporary South Africa, *Dateline Soweto* impresses as an unusually knowledgeable contribution. . . . The book is also a compelling personal document, alert to the complicated dynamics that make interracial relationships in South Africa a minefield of explosive possibilities, and extremely well written to boot." Jill Nelson, writing in the *Washington Post* (December 22, 1988), called Finnegan's vision of South Africa "one of the clearest I have read. In *Dateline Soweto*, Finnegan displays the attributes of a great reporter: an open mind, a sensitivity to nuance and a constant battle with his own subjectivity. Perhaps best of all, Finnegan has the ability to see through the white privilege—and government-appointed black leaders—that are the bulwark of apartheid." In 1988 Finnegan spent several months in the ravaged African country of Mozambique, where for some 15 years civil war had raged between the socialist government, known as the Front for the Liberation of Mozambique, or Frelimo, and a rebel guerilla group known as the National Resistance of Mozambique, or Renamo. (The civil war ended, in 1992, and in 1994 the country had its first democratic elections.) War, combined with severe drought in the early 1980s, had devastated the population and left millions starving and homeless. In *A Complicated War: The Harrowing of Mozambique*—much of which appeared as a series of articles in the *New Yorker*—Finnegan interviews peasants, displaced persons, and Frelimo officials, though he was unable to make significant contact with any member of the Renamo. Finnegan learns that many of Mozambique's people do not know the name of their president, nor the difference between the Frelimo and the Renamo; they know only the intense hardships they must endure every day. Among the many horrors he describes, Finnegan also tells of a man, accused by the Renamo of being a spy, whose lips, nose, ear and hand were hacked off. *A Complicated War*'s formidable task is to try to make sense of the extreme violence of a civil war that is senseless even to many of Mozambique's inhabitants.

Rand Richards Cooper acknowledged in *Commonweal* (December 18, 1992) that "readers interested in third-world politics will appreciate [*A Complicated War*] for the resourceful work of political journalism that it is." However, he had two major misgivings about the book—first, that Finnegan is able to describe the violence but not explain its source, and second, that his account of the civil war is slanted toward the Frelimo party, which "makes him seem like a rearguard PR man for Frelimo and for third-world Marxism generally." Mario Azevedo, a scholar born and raised in Mozambique, was at first wary that Finnegan might not have enough background to write about Mozambique and that his information might be unreliable because it was authorized, and to a degree assisted, by the Frelimo. Yet Azevedo concluded in the *Black Scholar* (Summer 1995), "Finnegan's volume deserves to be placed among the best works, if not the best, in the literature on contemporary Mozambique not only for its critical and accurate analysis of post-1975 Mozambique society but, most importantly, for its non-partisan approach to the war in Mozambique. It is a solid work of scholarship, undergirded by sound and enriched social science methodology."

For his next book Finnegan turned from Africa to his own country, where unexpectedly depressed conditions defied his expectations. In the introduction to *Cold New World: Growing Up in a Harder Country* Finnegan recalls, "I started out with a set of relatively neat, received ideas about what I would find in this country under headings like race, class, poverty, and the drug trade. My tidy ideas were upended, in any case, at every turn. American real life is rowdier, more disturbing, more charming than anything dreamt of in your or my philosophy. This country was (and is) in a strange, even an unprecedented, condition. While the national economy has been growing, the economic prospects of most Americans have been dimming." For his book Finnegan interviewed and hung around with youths from Washington State to Connecticut, noting the setbacks and hardships that many low- and middle-class kids contend with even in an era of supposed economic opportunity. "We are a country with a 50 percent divorce rate and sky-high rates of child neglect and juvenile crime," Finnegan wrote in the *New York Times* (June 12, 1998), touching on a theme similar to that expanded on in *Cold New World*, "and our behavior toward our young people—not our expressed concerns, but our behavior—suggests that we are actually more interested in their shopping patterns (and, should they break the law, in locking them up) than in their well-being."

In *Cold New World* Finnegan assembles in-depth profiles of various troubled young people—Terry, a fifteen-year-old drug dealer in New Haven, Connecticut; Mindy, a neo-Nazi in a suburb of Los Angeles; Juan, a drifter in Washington state; and a group of youths who endure the fallout after crack cocaine is introduced to their little town, in East Texas. "Finnegan convincingly connects the wayward events in these people's lives," Jack Hitt wrote in the *New York Times Book Review* (June 14, 1998), "to the messages and forces they detect around them—whether from a fractured home, a school tracking system that subtly winnows out the losers from the gifted or just plain despair inherent in what Finnegan calls our national religion of 'liberal consumerism.'" Hitt added, "Finnegan's hanging-around technique yields riches among the kind of people that most reporters would strenuously avoid. His stories do not concern a trial of the century, a perfect storm or the ascent of a tall mountain. Instead, they are about powerless people left battered and grounded by an economy that may be richly rewarding the educated, but is cruelly punishing many others." Hitt's compliments were echoed by reviewers all over the country. "Finnegan catches perfectly the way ordinary America today may pass through some moral looking glass," Lance Morrow wrote in *Time* (May 25, 1998), "into a devouring universal consumers' bazaar wherein the remotest locales sell the fanciest drugs and perversions, and the minds of the young, ungrounded by their absent parents' experience or protection, become unrecognizably weird." Morrow concluded, "Finnegan's book, a status report on the American Dream, gets its power the way a good novel does: from sheer story—the unpredictable, rich specifics of people's lives. Alas, every syllable of the book rings true." *Cold New World* was a *New York Times* Notable Book of the Year, a *Los Angeles Times* Best Nonfiction of 1998 selection, and among the *Voice Literary Supplement*'s 25 favorite books of 1998.

William Finnegan lives in New York City and continues to write for the *New Yorker*.

—*P. G. H.*

SUGGESTED READING: *Africa Today* p94+ Jan./Mar. 1997; *Black Scholar* p49+ Summer 1995; *Commonweal* p18+ Dec. 18, 1992; *Economist* p97 Nov. 22, 1986; *Los Angeles Times* p1 Aug. 17, 1986; *New York Times* A p21 June 12, 1998; *New York Times Book Review* p7 Sep. 21, 1986, p9 June 14, 1998; *Quill & Quire* p31

Jan. 1989; *Time* p80 May 25, 1998; *Washington Post* C p3 Dec. 22, 1988

SELECTED BOOKS: *Crossing the Line: A Year in the Land of Apartheid*, 1986; *Dateline Soweto: Travels with Black South African Reporters*, 1988; *Complicated War: The Harrowing of Mozambique*, 1992; *Cold New World: Growing Up in a Harder Country*, 1998

Courtesy of CatBird Press

Fischerová, Daniela

Feb. 13, 1948– Short-story writer; children's book writer; playwright; librettist

Daniela Fischerová is a prominent member of the generation of Czech writers that followed Ivan Klima and Milan Kundera. She has written children's stories, plays, librettos, song lyrics, and short fiction, and two of her works have been published in English. Her *Dog and Wolf*, translated by A. G. Brain, a play about the murder trial of François Villon, is included in Barbara Day's *Czech Plays* (1994). In the style of magical realism, the drama uses ahistorical characters and modern artifacts, such as the tape recorder. A collection of Fischerová's short stories, *Fingers Pointing Somewhere Else* (2000), translated by Neil Bermel, was "highly recommended" by Eleanor J. Bader in the *Library Journal* (January 2000).

Daniela Fischerová was born on February 13, 1948 in Prague, in what was then Czechoslovakia and is now the Czech Republic. Her father was Jan Fischer, a well-known composer who was also a writer. Jan Fischer wrote the lyrics for 10 of his own operas as well as words to many of his songs, and he later set some of his daughter's writings to music.

Fischerová graduated from the FAMU, the film division of the Academy for Performing Arts in Prague, and obtained employment as a scriptwriter for film, television, and radio. During her third year at the Academy, the country was occupied by Soviet troops. The possibilities for artistic self-expression were severely limited from then until the "Velvet Revolution" of 1989, when the Communist government was replaced by a more democratic one under president Vaclav Havel. Fischerová also worked as an editor at a publishing house and a writer of children's stories.

Fischerová's first play was *Hodina mexi psem a vlkem*, translated into English by A. G. Brain and given the title *Dog and Wolf* (the Czech title refers to a time of day between "the hour of the dog and the hour of the wolf"). The play was given three performances in Prague in 1979, but then government authorities ordered that it be closed, and, as Fischerová expressed it in 1998 to a gathering of foreign writers invited to Limoges, France, she was forbidden from staging her work for the next eight years and was forced to return to writing children's stories.

Dog and Wolf, about the life of François Villon, concerns "the universal struggle of free people to resist arbitrary authority," as Fischerová said in Limoges, in 1998. Although it takes place during Villon's trial for murder in the 15th century, modern journalists—and modern technology, such as spotlights and tape recorders—intrude on the action as well. A surreal, almost dadaist spirit pervades the opening scene, as a character, The Father, calls out the names of the participants in the trial from his "register." One of them, Monsieur Régnier de Montigny, subsequently known as The Wolf, is leader of the criminal gang to which the accused belonged. After most of those whose names are called exit the scene, a character called Angèle, whose name has not been announced, remains on stage with The Father and The Wolf. "And what about me, then?" she asks, as quoted from the play. When at first Angèle says she is Villon's bride, Régnier dismisses her as "a phantom. A romantic fiction of Villon's biographers." It is then that Angèle identifies herself as Villon's guardian angel. According to Lauren McConnell, in the abstract of her paper "Czech Women Playwrights of the Transition: Exploring New Directions," published on-line, *Dog and Wolf* "explores issues of artistic freedom in a repressive society."

In 1998 Fischerová published *The Lights Are Playing a Game*, a short play that she described as a "cosmic drama," on Czech photographer Michal Macku's Web site. The "aim" of the play, according to its stage directions, "is to recover the human face from nothingness." The characters in the play are the Sun, the Moon, and the planets, also called the "lights," as Fischerová refers to them. Each speaks of the characteristics with which it endows human faces: Venus, for example, "with an endlessly stirring, out of breath hoarseness of an aging bar singer," gives "the face everything that makes it lovely. A smile. Rosy cheeks, pupils spilling like drops of Indian ink on blotting paper." Venus concludes, "I am the mirror which will never tell her: 'Snow White.' I am the mirror which will always tell her: 'You.'" At the end of the play, as quoted from the stage directions, "the Sun begins to create endless variations of human faces with its eruptions. . . . Nobody reacts to the creative flow of the Sun, which is bringing into being face after face. Mercury momentarily fastens his gaze on the creation and makes a grimace with one corner of his mouth. Only Venus eagerly looks at the faces and, fascinated, whispers to them: 'You!'"

Fischerová's play *Princess T.* (1984) was mounted in English in 1999 as a joint production of the University of Toronto's graduate program in drama and its Centre for Russian and Eastern European Studies, to mark the 10th anniversary of the Velvet Revolution. The play itself was written before the Velvet Revolution, and was one of three plays by Fischerová allowed to be produced under the Communist regime, another being *Legend* (1988). The "T." in the play's title stands for Turandot, and the story is based on a Chinese fairy tale of that name. Turandot is a princess who refuses to marry unless her suitor is able to solve three riddles, and anyone who answers incorrectly gets his head chopped off. The play begins after the 10th suitor has been decapitated and China is in an uproar. A new potential groom arrives on the scene, "a captivating, charming, intelligent stranger who breaks down all [the Princess's] defenses and wins her heart," according to Keith Fernandes for *UTPulse Magazine* (on-line). Fernandes criticized the production, however, describing it as jumping "from Commedia dell'Arte to melodrama to 20th century realism."

In Fischerová's collection of short stories, *Fingers Pointing Somewhere Else*, which was published in an English translation by Neil Bermel in 2000, the author returned to China, or a place like it, in the story "The Thirty-Sixth Chicken of Master Wu." In this tale an emperor's aging chef and his nephew, a subversive poet who is hiding out in his uncle's kitchen, combine forces to create a new chicken dish, as the chef is required to do for each of the emperor's birthdays. The poet's work and the cook's make a masterful blend of flavors.

"A Letter for President Eisenhower" is narrated by a 10-year-old Czech girl, who has already written a prize-winning essay and is assigned by her principal to write a letter to President Eisenhower that may prevent "the West," which is "secretly preparing for war" as quoted from the story, from attacking. The girl describes herself and her life as follows: "Fourth grade took something out of me. Just last year I swam through life like a fish through water. Now I'm a dry cork on the surface. I tread water and try to get down inside it. Life's every-day certainties are gone." During the course of the story, she loses her best friend and falls in love with an older girl, the 13-year-old Sasha, with whom she spends the summer playing an erotic game in which she is Mount Everest and Sasha is Mount Kilimanjaro. In the fall, when she returns to start fifth grade, she discovers that the letter to President Eisenhower was only a game as well. "There was no hope it would reach its addressee; it was just pretend. It too was a gesture that missed its mark—a finger that might point somewhere, but somewhere it will never touch." According to Kathleen Hayes, writing in *Central Europe Review* (August 1999), "Letter for President Eisenhower" is "an amusing and ironical piece about a fatuous young girl's first sexual and artistic experiences." For the *Library Journal* (January 2000) reviewer, the story is one in which "Cold War angst meets burgeoning adolescent sexuality. Like a voyeur, readers will experience the ribald fantasies of a young girl and cheer her as she eludes the despair that has deadened the adults around her." Although the reviewer described Fischerová's language as "unusual" and her images as "odd," she noted that "the overall impact of this anthology is unmistakable"; it asks "profound existential questions in a rambling, stream-of-consciousness style" that is "deeply moving."

Fischerová was described in *Publishers Weekly* (January 3, 2000) as a writer who, although best known for her plays, has demonstrated a "mastery of the genre" of the short story. The reviewer also praised the adroitness of Neil Bermel's translation, and wrote that *Fingers Pointing Somewhere Else* "is an excellent introduction to one of the most influential Czech writers in the literary generation following that of Milan Kundera, Ivan Klima, and Josef Skvorecky."

—S. Y.

SUGGESTED READING: *Central Europe Review* (on-line) Aug. 1999; *Library Journal* p164+ Jan. 2000; *Limousin-culture* (on-line); *Michal-Macku* (on-line); *Publishers Weekly* p58 Jan. 3, 2000

SELECTED WORKS IN ENGLISH TRANSLATION: short-story collections—*Fingers Pointing Somewhere Else*, 2000; plays—*Dog and Wolf* (included in *Czech Plays*, B. Day, ed.), 1994

Flanagan, Richard

1961– Novelist; nonfiction writer

Richard Flanagan's three novels, *Death of a River Guide* (1994), *The Sound of One Hand Clapping* (1997), and *Gould's Book of Fish* (2001), have won him critical acclaim. His fiction is characterized by a rich, poetic prose (although some have called it purple) and contains strains of magical realism, with its intermingling of the fantastic and mundane. A native of the Australian territory of Tasmania, Flanagan draws on the island's exotic landscape and its tragic history in his novels. His his-

The *Mercury*/Courtesy of Grove/Atlantic
Richard Flanagan

torical bent, however, doesn't interfere with the deeply personal nature of his writing. "The great freedom—but the great difficulty—of being a writer," Flanagan told Giles Hugo for the *Write Stuff* (March 31, 1995, on-line), "is that you allow yourself access to parts of your soul that most people in everyday life, for a very good reason, leave closed off. . . . I think to really write something of worth you've got to go back within yourself, dredge your soul, and that's a profoundly disturbing thing to do because it goes beyond simply feeling sad or happy—it takes you to that aspect of yourself that you may or may not like or wish to describe."

Richard Flanagan was born on the island of Tasmania, off the coast of Australia, in 1961, the fifth child of an Irish Catholic family. Their ancestors had been among the prisoners transported to the island in the late 1840s, when it was a prisoner's exile called Van Dieman's Land. As a boy, Flanagan was fascinated by stories told to him by members of his family, and in his novels, he has tried to recapture their storytelling methods. "When people tell stories here," Flanagan told Murray Waldren for *Literary Liaison* (1997, on-line), "they digress endlessly but always return where they began, with no real ending. Yet the tales stay with you, and grow in richness. They don't impose explanations or analysis, and that's part of their joy." Despite his interest in stories, Flanagan found the subject of language arts challenging. "I had trouble at school because I don't think grammatically," he explained to Hugo. At age 16 Flanagan dropped out with the intention of becoming a carpenter. Unable to find a job in that field, he worked as a surveyor's chain man in the Australian bush for a year before the company went bankrupt. Then, in a dramatic reversal, he returned to school and became an exceptional student, winning the prestigious Rhodes Scholarship to attend Oxford University, in England. He later received a Master of Letters from Oxford.

After finishing school, Flanagan decided he wanted to write. While working in a succession of jobs, including river guide, doorman, and general laborer, he spent his free time writing, a pattern he continues to this day. "In a typical year," Flanagan told Hugo, "I'll do laboring, river guiding, and writing in various forms, film work, television work. . . . I work with an architect sometimes, coming up with ideas. It's a very difficult balancing act. You must be focused on what you want to be as a writer. But at the same time some of those jobs are actually good for you, because they take you beyond your immediate concerns, reopen your eyes once more."

Though Flanagan wanted to write novels, his first books were works of nonfiction, because he felt that in that genre he stood a better chance of getting his writing published. In 1991 he co-authored *Codename Iago: The Story of John Friedrich* with John Friedrich. That same year saw the publication of Flanagan's *Parish-fed Bastards: A History of the Unemployed in Britain, 1884–1939*. Here, he focuses on the political activism of the unemployed, starting with the formation of the National Unemployment Workers Movement (NUWM) in 1884 and ending with the dissolution of the group in 1939. Other themes he touches on include the relationship between unemployment and industrialism, the resolution of class conflicts, and the power of individuals to exert influence through activism. Though Richard Lewis, reviewing the book in the *American Journal of Sociology* (November 1992), felt that it did little to prove that the NUWM was an effective organization, he concluded, "The book is particularly useful, however, in two specific respects. First, it helped to kill the once widely held but erroneous idea that the NUWM was simply a front for the Communist Party of Great Britain. Second, it has a valuable chapter on the role of state-supported voluntary social service for the unemployed." J. H. Wiener was less enthusiastic. In *Choice* (June 1992) he wrote, "Unfortunately, [Flanagan's] efforts at scholarship are drowned in a sea of anticapitalist rhetoric. Most of his conclusions are unreliable and there are many factual errors."

After the Literature Board of the Australia Council refused Flanagan a grant to work on his first novel, Arts Tasmania gave him $14,000. In 1994 Flanagan published *Death of a River Guide*. The central event of the novel is the drowning of Aljaz Cosini, the river guide of the title. His last visions follow his own life from birth through his failed marriage, and expand beyond his personal history into images of his ancestors' often sordid pasts, including their persecution of the Aborigines and their participation in the destruction of the environment through the timber, mining, and hydroelectric industries. Flanagan was intent on telling the truth about Tasmania in the novel, by not glossing over its gruesome history or ignoring its positive qualities. "There are a series of responses to Tasmania," Flanagan told Hugo. "One is to present it as a Gothic horror land, and the other is to present it as this Utopia. But nobody wants to look at truths that might be more complex. . . . The great problem with a lot of Australian writing, I think, is that it's constantly in flight from the truths of this place rather than engaging with it."

Flanagan weaves strange, magical tales into his narrative, such as the story of an eagle that carries a child off to its nest and raises it to adulthood, and a banquet attended by tigers, lobsters, and stray cats and dogs who share barbecued delicacies around long tables. Ultimately, *Death of a River Guide* is a story of redemption, as Cosini, in his dying moments, comes to terms with his past crimes and the crimes of his ancestors. The novel was well-reviewed and lauded as a landmark in Australian literature. Vivian Smith, in the *Times Literary Supplement* (October 3, 1997), wrote, "There are marvelous descriptions of rain forests and clouds, of eel-catching and gum trees flowering and yellow-tailed black cockatoos; and topographical views of the Franklin gorges that have an almost surreal power. . . . [Flanagan's] novel marks one of the most auspicious debuts in Australian writing since the advent of David Foster, a writer with whom Flanagan has a deal in common." In *World Literature Today* (Spring 1998), John Scheckter wrote, "*Death of a River Guide* powerfully extends the tradition of Australian representations of character in the animate, transcendent landscape of the spirit." The novel won the 1995 Victorian Premier's Award for First Fiction, the Adelaide's National Fiction Literary Award, and the 1996 Australian Fiction Award.

While working on *Death of a River Guide* in 1991, Flanagan also began writing a screenplay. Upon its completion, he tried to generate interest among film producers, without success. He decided, instead, to turn the script into a novel, and in 1997 *The Sound of One Hand Clapping* was published. It tells the story of a Slovenian family that immigrates to Tasmania after being displaced by World War II. The central character is Sonja Buloh, the daughter of Bojan Buloh and his wife, Maria. Bojan works on one of Tasmania's hydroelectric dams, and he and his family live as second-class Australian citizens in ramshackle huts. One day when Sonja is three years old, her mother, no longer able to tolerate the mean conditions of their existence, walks off into a snow storm and never comes back. Sonja is left in the care of foster parents until her father decides to reclaim her. Bojan drinks to assuage his despair and beats Sonja whenever he falls into a drunken stupor. Eventually Sonja escapes and the subsequent portion of her life, as a clerk in Sydney, Australia, is dedicated to forgetting her former existence. After a time she finds, however, that she cannot run away from her grief, and she returns to Tasmania and her father to confront her past.

A central theme in the novel is the way in which history and individual lives are intertwined: history affects even those who are ignorant of it, yet each person also has an inner life that is independent of the collective past. Some reviewers found the novel's dark tone overbearing and its style awkward. In the *New York Times Book Review* (April 2, 2000, on-line), Nina Sonenberg wrote, "One snowy night in Tasmania, a young Yugoslav refugee abandons her three-year-old daughter and walks into a blizzard, never to return. Why? Perhaps to escape the maudlin despair and overwrought prose to follow in Richard Flanagan's overly long second novel." Most reviews, however, were positive. In the *San Francisco Chronicle* (May 21, 2000, on-line), Bella Stander called it a "beautiful if crushing novel." Peter Green, in the *Los Angeles Times* (March 12, 2000), wrote, "This novel is a rare and remarkable achievement. Given its subject matter it could have been as grittily depressing as anything by Zola or Orwell, yet somehow, amid all the relentless squalor, what Orwell called the 'crystal spirit' shines indomitably through. Flanagan blends a strong yet delicate psychological sensibility with the kind of sharp, vivid, original prose more common in good poets. His outcasts really got past my emotional guard." *The Sound of One Hand Clapping* won the Australian Booksellers Book of the Year Award and the Vance Palmer Prize for Fiction.

Shortly after Flanagan submitted the completed manuscript of *The Sound of One Hand Clapping* to his publisher, he finally got a reply from a film producer interested in his script. Flanagan ended up writing and directing the film version of the story, and it proved to be a challenging experience for him. "Directors are an odd combination of the guardian of the soul of the film and a sort of security guard for the project to stop people busting in and wrecking it," he told Greg King for *Beat* (April 22, 1998). "You have to be a bit of a street fighter—one part artist, one part politician, really. I wasn't prepared for that aspect of the business." The film, which was released in 1998 and starred Kristof Kaczmarek and Kerry Fox, won a prize at the 25th Flanders International Film Festival.

Flanagan's third novel, *Gould's Book of Fish*, was published in 2001. In it he returns to the 19th century to tell the story of William Buelow Gould, who is sent to a penal colony in Van Diemen's Land, now Tasmania, where a prison doctor uses Gould's artistic talents to help him complete a book on the native wildlife of the penal colony. Many critics agreed with Brendan Dowling, who wrote in *Booklist* (as quoted on *Amazon.com*): "Taken from historical accounts of the real-life Gould, Flanagan's novel vividly re-creates the penal colony's conditions and its eccentric cast of characters. Gould's story is framed by the tale of the present-day writer (somewhat of a raconteur himself), who discovers Gould's collection in an antique store and soon becomes obsessed with the multifaceted text. Readers will be similarly entranced with this richly detailed work that calls attention to a major new talent."

Flanagan lives in Tasmania with his wife, Majda Smolej, who, like his heroine in *The Sound of One Hand Clapping*, is originally from Slovenia. They have three daughters. As he told Hugo, "I've had enough hard times with writing to know that the next one could be a total dud and then nobody would be interested again. And that doesn't mean the book's not as good. And so I'll continue to write without hope and without despair."

— P.G.H.

SUGGESTED READING: *Beat* Apr. 22, 1998; *Literary Liaison* (on-line) 1997; *Los Angeles Times* p8 Mar. 12, 2000; *New York Times* (on-line) Apr. 2, 2000; *San Francisco Chronicle* (on-line) p7 May 21, 2000; *Times Literary Suppplement* p21 Oct. 3, 1997; *World Literature Today* p453+ Spring 1998; *Write Stuff* (on-line) Mar. 31, 1995

SELECTED BOOKS: nonfiction—*Codename Iago: The Story of John Friedrich* (with John Friedrich), 1991; *Parish-fed Bastards: A History of the Politics of the Unemployed in Britain, 1884–1939*, 1991; novels—*Death of a River Guide*, 1994; *Sound of One Hand Clapping*, 1997; *Gould's Book of Fish* (2001)

Andrea Raynor/Courtesy of Atlantic Monthly Press

Flannery, Tim Fridtjof

Jan. 28, 1956– Science writer; mammalogist; paleontologist

The scientist and writer Tim Fridtjof Flannery, who was named for the Norwegian polar explorer Fridtjof Nansen, is an explorer in his own right. During the years of research he conducted in order to write *Mammals of New Guinea* (1990), Flannery braved numerous hazards, battled life-threatening diseases, and befriended many of the island's sheltered, mountain-dwelling inhabitants. He chronicled those adventures in the popular *Throwim Way Leg* (1998), and he has edited several books of material written by early explorers, including the sailor John Nicol. Flannery is also an explorer in a different sense: he has done pioneering work in paleontology and mammalogy, discovering new species and locating important new fossil sites. In the best-selling *Future Eaters* (1994), he advanced the controversial notion that the modern trend toward unlimited consumption originated among the highly advanced humans that dwelled on the Australian continent thousands of years ago. An outspoken and unique voice among conservationists, he published *The Eternal Frontier* (2001), in which he maintains that humans hunted the megafauna—giant mammalian animals, such as mammoths—to extinction and have continued to stamp out other forms of life at an unprecedented rate.

Tim Fridtjof Flannery was born in Melbourne, Australia, on January 28, 1956 and grew up in the Melbourne suburb of Sandringham. As a child he was very interested in Australian wildlife. He kept live lizards and often visited the Victorian Museum to see the natural-history exhibits. He even collected kangaroo carcasses so he could boil them down and inspect their skeletons. In 1977 Flannery received a B.A. in English from La Trobe University, in the Australian state of Victoria. (Though immersed in the sciences, Flannery has remained interested in literature, specifically the literature of the English Restoration and medieval periods.) After graduating he found a job at the Museum of Victoria in the vertebrate paleontology department. This rekindled his interest in the earth sciences and led him back to school. In 1981 he earned an M.S. in earth science from Monash University, in Victoria, and in 1985 he received his doctorate in zoology from the University of New South Wales, in Sydney.

While at Monash University, in 1980, Flannery discovered several dinosaur fossil sites along the southern coast of Victoria, the first to be unearthed in that region in some 80 years. In 1983 he began studying the known megafauna species of New Guinea from the Pleistocene Epoch, lasting from about 1.6 million to 10,000 years ago. In 1985, after becoming the principal research scientist for the Australian Museum, in Sydney, he joined a group of Australian scientists that found mammalian fossils from the Cretaceous Era, about 144 million to 66 million years ago. These fossils were 80 million years older than any existing Australian mammalian fossil record, and the findings were published on the cover of *Nature.*

In 1985 Flannery, along with Michael Archer and Gordon C. Grigg, published *Kangaroo,* based on Flannery's doctoral work, in the course of which he described 29 new species of kangaroo. In 1990 he published two books, *Australia's Vanishing Mammals: Endangered and Extinct Native Species* (with Paula Kendall and Karen Wynn-Moylan) and *The Mammals of New Guinea.* The latter book is still the only comprehensive text on New Guinea's mammalian species.

In 1994 Flannery published the book that brought him to international prominence, *Future Eaters: An Ecological History of the Australasian Lands and People.* The book details Australia's history dating back to early fossil records. Neanderthals, Flannery argues, first came to Australia from Southeast Asia about 60,000 years ago. They found a bountiful environment full of prey, including megafauna, which had not co-evolved with humanoid life and therefore had few defenses against human hunters. Within approximately 20,000 years, 95 percent of Australia's large mammals were wiped out, and the Aborigines, who had ample food and some leisure, evolved new technologies faster than the humans on the Afro-Eurasian homeland. "They were the world's first future eaters," Flannery explained to Claire Hutchings for *Geographical Magazine* (January 1997), "eating into the capital resource base, exhausting it rather than using it sustainably, and eating away their own future. Today, almost everyone alive is a future eater. My guess is that it was this move to Australia, and to a new ecology, that allowed people to develop without the restraints of the co-evolved ecosystem and the limits put on human activity by prey." Soon the Australian Aborigines ventured out to other parts of the world, including Europe, where more primitive Neanderthals lived, and spread their influence. "Changes in technology and thought undergone by the Aborigines changed the course of evolution for humans everywhere," Flannery told Hutchings.

Future Eaters was a best-seller for more than a year and won numerous awards; it was named book of the year by the Melbourne magazine, *The Age,* in 1995, and also won the South Australian Premier's Literary Award, in 1996. David Attenborough named it his book of the year in the London *Sunday Times.* In *New Scientist* (October 29, 1994) Ian Lowe wrote, "The intellectual scope of [*Future Eaters*] is awesome. . . . It should be compulsory reading for politicians who mumble vaguely about sustainable development without the biological knowledge to distinguish a bacterium from a bandicoot." Matt Ridley, in the *Times Literary Supplement* (March 17, 1995), wrote, "[Flannery] . . . tells his beautiful story in plain language, science-popularizing at its antipodean best. Moreover, Flannery is a true ecologist, in the rather old-fashioned meaning of that term. He is fascinated by how the jigsaw of species fits together to make an ecosystem; he is not pious or sentimental about the role of mankind."

In 1995 Flannery, as a companion piece to *The Mammals of New Guinea,* wrote another comprehensive description of the mammalian species of an area, this time the *Mammals of the South-West Pacific and Moluccan Islands.* Gary J. Wiles, who reviewed the book for the *Journal of Mammalogy* (August 1997), complained of oversights, some misinformation, and the "absence of any discussion of conservation." "The book falls short of being a definitive guide to the mammal fauna of these islands," Wiles wrote, "but does serve as a starting point for anyone wanting to learn more about the species of the region."

In 1996 Flannery edited *1788: Comprising a Narrative of the Expedition to Botany Bay,* a compilation of historical accounts of the British colonization of Australia that became Flannery's second best-seller. The following year he edited *The Life and Adventures of John Nicol, Mariner.* Nicol was a Scottish sailor who, shortly before his death, in 1825, documented his sea-faring adventures with smugglers, whalers, and Australia-bound convicts. Flannery also wrote an introduction to Nicol's tale. Sara Wheeler, writing in the *Spectator* (April 1, 2000), admired the book's "prose of beguiling simplicity" and called it an "enchanting tale of gunpowder, hammocks and a whole world gone."

Flannery charted his own adventures in *Throwim Way Leg: Tree-Kangaroos, Possums, and Penis Gourds—On the Track of Unknown Mammals in Wildest New Guinea* (1998). The main title comes from a New Guinean pidgin expression for the first step of a new journey. Flannery's New Guinea is a land of rich rain forests and high mountain ranges, inhabited by exotic animals and thousands of unique mountain tribes, whose traditional ways of life are jeopardized by the modernization creeping onto the island. In the course of searching for the island's mammals, Flannery befriends many of the natives. "Readers will share his respect for their intelligence," D. J. R. Bruckner wrote in the *New York Times Book Review* (March 7, 1999), "and his delight in their cutting sense of humor, especially about sex, and in their practical jokes, childish but shrewd tests of the wit of their targets." Flannery discovers three-foot-long rats, fruit bats thought to have been extinct for 12 millennia, giant anteaters, and many other mammals; he also undergoes his share of hardships, including dangling over a thousand-foot chasm, contracting a near-fatal bout of typhus, and suffering from tropical ulcers and flesh-eating boils. His many escapades culminate in the discovery of a new species of tree kangaroo, capable of jumping 60 feet in one bound. He introduces the kangaroo to the scientific world as the dingiso, the name the Aborigines use for it.

Most critics found *Throwim Way Leg* extremely absorbing. Laurence A. Marschall, in *Sciences* (July/August 1999), compared the experience of reading it to "the way the ancient Athenians must have felt on hearing travelers tell of giant one-eyed natives and mountains made of gold." In *Sierra* (May/June 1999) Rebecca Shotwell wrote, "Whether literally going out on a limb to capture an 'extinct' bat, nearly getting killed when a hostile group identifies him as a member of the hated 'wildlife' clan, or solving the mystery of a tree kangaroo with a white man's face, Flannery combines diligent science, heart-pounding adventure, and a respect for ancient cultures to create a compelling tale. Initially titillated by the exotic, the reader is soon swept up on a tour that might rattle Indiana Jones himself."

In 1998 Flannery edited an anthology of adventure stories, *Explorers: Stories of Discovery and Adventure from the Australian Frontier*. These 67 accounts form a history of the island's exploration—from 1606, the date of the earliest recorded visit by a European, to 1977, when a physician drove into the desert during an extreme drought to rescue an elderly Aboriginal couple. Joseph L. Carlson wrote in *Library Journal* (September 1, 2000) that the stories "often read like science fiction and sizzle with suspense. Flannery's . . . thoughtful introduction and his comprehensive bibliography are alone almost worth the price of the book." In 2000 Flannery edited *The Birth of Sydney*, a compilation of writings by early residents of the Australian city.

When, in 1997, Flannery first traveled to North America, to Boston, Massachusetts, he was "stunned," as he told Brian Bethune for *Maclean's* (July 9, 2001). "It was mid-September," Flannery recalled, "100 per cent humidity, a vast biomass of plants and insects, dazzling green colours. Six weeks later, it was all gone. That doesn't happen in Australia, or anywhere else." North America's extreme climatic fluctuations are caused by north-south air currents that are funneled and intensified by the Rockies, Appalachians, and other mountain ranges, which also run north-south. These extreme changes, Flannery notes, have made North America "the eternal frontier."

The Eternal Frontier: An Ecological History of North America and Its Peoples (2001) surveys the continent's natural history, beginning 65 million years ago, when it is believed that a huge asteroid crashed near the Yucatan Peninsula, in present-day Mexico. The ensuing molten rock and tidal waves wiped out most North American life forms, including dinosaurs, and triggered a new direction in evolution that gave rise to megafauna—mammoths, ground sloths, bison with six-foot horns, saber-toothed tigers, giant armadillos, and bears twice the size of today's grizzly bears. By about 13,000 years ago these megafauna had mostly disappeared. Competing theories attempt to explain the causes of this disappearance, citing disease, climatic change, and as Flannery posits, over-hunting by humans. He offers abundant evidence for this controversial theory, including the fact that extreme temperature reductions in other parts of the world did not harm megafauna, and that the megafauna disappeared too gradually to have been caused by catastrophic climatic changes. The megafauna's extinction, Flannery argues, marked the beginning of a trend in North America in which humans indiscriminately consume available resources without concern for other species or their own future.

Patricia Nelson Limerick, writing in the *Washington Post* (June 24, 2001), disputed the book's premise. She wrote that "Flannery's brisk, superficial commentaries do this important topic a big disservice," and wondered why Flannery had failed "to think searchingly about the biological components and consequences of human behavior." Conversely, Richard Ellis wrote in the London *Times* (June 6, 2001), "*The Eternal Frontier* is history (and evolution, anthropology, palaeontology, and extinction theory) written intelligently, gracefully and thoughtfully, chock-full of useful, sometimes astonishing information, and yet all worked almost seamlessly into a larger story."

Flannery's latest book, *A Gap in Nature: Discovering the World's Extinct Animals* (2001), was published in conjunction with an exhibit at the South Australian Museum, in Adelaide, where Flannery serves as museum director. The book features the artwork of the wildlife artist Peter Schouten and catalogs 104 creatures that have become extinct since 1492 due to European expansion. Flannery describes how each animal lived and how it became extinct.

Flannery's awards and honors include the Edgeworth David Medal from the Royal Society of New South Wales (1990), the South Australian Arts Festival Award (1996), the Rudi Lemberg Travelling Fellowship from the Australian Academy of Science (1996), and the Eureka Pol Prize for environmental research (1996).

—P. G. H.

SUGGESTED READING: *Geographical Magazine* p26+ Jan. 1997; *Houston Chronicle* p12 July 26, 1994; *Journal of Mammalogy* p984+ Aug. 1997; *Library Journal* p238 Sept. 1, 2000; *Maclean's* p49 July 9, 2001; *New York Times Book Review* p7+ Mar. 7, 1999; *New Scientist* p64 Oct. 29, 1994; *Sciences* p45 July/Aug. 1999; *Sierra* p75+ May/June 1999; *Spectator* p49 Apr. 1, 2000; London *Times* II p10 June 6, 2001; *Times Literary Supplement* p7 Mar. 17, 1995; *Washington Post* p12 June 24, 2001

SELECTED BOOKS: *Kangaroo*, 1985; *Australia's Vanishing Mammals: Endangered and Extinct Native Species* (with Paula Kendall and Karen Wynn-Moylan), 1990; *The Mammals of New Guinea*, 1990; *Future Eaters: An Ecological History of the Australasian Lands and People*, 1994; *Mammals of the South-West Pacific and Moluccan Islands*, 1995; *Throwim Way Leg:*

Tree-Kangaroos, Possums, and Penis Gourds—On the Track of Unknown Mammals in Wildest New Guinea, 1998; *The Eternal Frontier: An Ecological History of North America and Its Peoples*, 2001; *A Gap in Nature: Discovering the World's Extinct Animals*, 2001; as editor—*1788: Comprising a Narrative of the Expedition to Botany Bay*, 1996; *The Life and Adventures of John Nicol, Mariner* 1997; *Explorers: Stories of Discovery and Adventure from the Australian Frontier*, 1998; *The Birth of Sydney*, 2000

Jerry Bauer/Courtesy of Wiley & Son Publishers, Inc.

Fleming, Thomas

Jul. 5, 1927– Nonfiction writer; novelist; historian

Thomas Fleming has produced more than 40 books in a career spanning five decades. He has won acclaim as the writer of both nonfiction books, mainly centered around the American Revolution, and historical novels. The novels explore city politics (*All Good Men*, 1960, *King of the Hill*, 1966, and *Rulers of the City*, 1977), his Roman Catholic faith (*Romans, Countrymen, Lovers*, 1969, *The Sandbox Tree*, 1970, and *The Good Shepherd*, 1975), different periods in American history through the eyes of the wealthy Stapleton family (*Promises to Keep*, 1978, *Dreams of Glory*, 1983, *Spoils of War*, 1985, *Remember the Morning*, 1997, *The Wages of Fame*, 1998, and *When This Cruel War is Over*, 2001), and two world wars, *Time and Tide* (1987) and *Over There* (1992). In his nonfiction work, Fleming has written biographies of such figures as George Washington, Thomas Jefferson, and Benjamin Franklin; has published a much-heralded history of the U. S. Military Academy at West Point; and has analyzed such key events in American history as the Battle of Bunker Hill, the duel between Alexander Hamilton and Aaron Burr, and President Franklin Roosevelt's policies during World War II.

In a statement for *World Authors 1995-2000*, Thomas Fleming writes: "'Shake hands like a man,' my father told me from the age of three. 'Aim High!' my mother wrote in my 8th grade autograph book. My mother, Katherine Dolan Fleming, was a beautiful darkhaired romantic, the daughter of a prosperous carpenter. My father, Thomas J. 'Teddy' Fleming, was born poor, the son of an illiterate laborer. On both sides, my grandparents were born in Ireland.

"In World War I Teddy Fleming was commissioned in the field during the battle of the Argonne. Frank Hague, leader of the Irish-American political organization that dominated Jersey City and the state of New Jersey for over thirty years, decided my father's battlefield exploits gave him voter appeal. My mother fell in love with the war hero, who soon became leader of Jersey City's gritty working class Sixth Ward, where he had been born.

"At election night parties, I absorbed the ethos of the Hague Organization. It was 'us—the Irish-Catholics—against 'them'—the Anglo-Saxon Protestants who ran the rest of New Jersey. In parochial school nuns and priests taught us always to tell the truth, to obey the law, to trust God and love mankind, ideals my mother earnestly seconded. In the streets of the Sixth Ward, nerve was what counted—the readiness to silence opposition with a nightstick if necessary and pile up the votes with a nice combination of threats and rewards, including cold cash on election day. The goal was power and jobs for the Democratic Party's faithful.

"This clash between my mother's soaring ideals and my father's tough realities stirred not a little anxiety in my young soul—and soon played a major role in my literary imagination. Years later, when I read Edmund Wilson's *The Wound And the Bow*, I realized I was walking talking proof of this theory of how writers are born.

"In 1946, when I was 19, just out of the U.S. Navy, I discovered Irish literature and was enthralled. Joyce, Yeats, Synge were my idols for a while. But I soon decided they were writing about a foreign country. I turned to American writers, especially Herman Melville, William Faulkner and Robert Penn Warren. Their stories were rich in history, a subject that became more and more relevant to me as I struggled to emerge from my Irish-Catholic ghetto into the full dimensions of the American experience. History helped me to understand my father's generation who were scarred by the anti-Catholic and anti-Irish-American prejudice that was rampant in New Jersey—and many other states—for over 100 years.

"Soon after I graduated from Fordham College, I became assistant to Fulton Oursler, a gifted writer and editor whose early novels were compared favorably to Sinclair Lewis. He impressed on me the importance of narrative in both fiction and nonfiction. He also urged on me a middle style, simple and sturdy, with a minimum of 'fine writing.' Thanks to him I was able to support myself as a journalist while getting started as an historian and novelist. I was a frequent contributor to the *New York Times Magazine, American Heritage, Reader's Digest* and other magazines.

"My first books alternated between nonfiction on the American Revolution and a series of novels (*All Good Men, The God of Love, King of the Hill* and *Rulers of the City*) about the collapse of an Irish-American political machine (the Hague organization fell apart in 1949) and its impact on the lives of the leaders, the followers and their families. Critic and novelist Roger Dooley called this cycle, set in the imagined city of Hamilton, 'a powerful fictional experience that relegates other novels on big city politics to the whimsical realm.' Dean of American historians Allan Nevins said my second history book, *Beat the Last Drum*, the story of Yorktown, was 'assuredly one of the outstanding historical works of the year.'

"This praise led to an invitation to write a history of the U.S. Military Academy. In the course of three research years at the school, I got to know many officers and their wives. I found in the military experience a clash between ideals and reality similar to the one that permeated my boyhood in Jersey City. In the West Pointers' case, the ideals were sharply articulated as duty, honor, country. In the real world of the Army, they had to figure out how to fit these noble words into a business that often involved throat-cutting careerism and the possibility that the bottom line was death.

"Army wives, who were both participants and observers, saw this conflict more vividly than their husbands. In the decade after I finished my history of West Point, I wrote *The Officers' Wives*, a novel that dealt with three very different women who married graduates of the class of 1950 and followed them through the disillusions and heartbreaks of Korea and Vietnam. The book was an international best seller.

"Meanwhile, I had begun writing a series of novels about a powerful American family called the Stapletons. Modeled loosely on the Stocktons and the Stevenses, two notable New Jersey families, the Stapletons carry with them a large freight of American history as they progress from colonial merchants (*Remember the Morning*) to Gilded Age industrialists (*The Spoils of War*) and from Federalist politicians (*Dreams of Glory*) to Washington, D.C. power brokers (*The Wages of Fame*). In the best American tradition, Stapleton sons repudiate fathers, marry women with ideas of their own about the pursuit of happiness, bleed in America's wars and barely survive the nation's financial panics and depressions.

"Ultimately my Stapletons intersect with the Irish-Americans of my political cycle. In *Promises To Keep*, Jim Kilpatrick is hired to write the biography of Paul Stapleton, the war hero scion of the 20th Century branch of the family. Disillusioned by the death of a son in Vietnam, Kilpatrick declines to write a panegyric. He digs into the gritty underside of Stapleton's career. Eventually he discovers that in the 1930s, this supposed WASP paragon paid a huge bribe to the Democratic politicians who ruled New Jersey to enable him to move the family's textile mills to North Carolina without ruinous legal and financial complications.

"When Kilpatrick confronts Stapleton with the evidence, he admits everything—and informs him that he gave the money to Kilpatrick's father, who was the chief justice of New Jersey's supreme court at the time. 'We're all in this together, Jim,' Paul Stapleton says.

"He meant (and I meant) we were all—WASPS, Irish-Americans, Jewish-Americans, Italian-Americans, Polish-Americans, African-Americans—in the American experience together, with its confusing mix of ruthless competition and dreams of brotherhood, of repression and liberation, of wrenching loss and inexplicable spiritual gain.

"While ranging across U.S. history with the Stapletons, I retained a strong interest in the American Revolution. I wrote a well received novel, *Liberty Tavern*, set in New Jersey, which portrayed the conflict as a civil war. I also wrote biographies of Thomas Jefferson (*The Man From Monticello*) and Benjamin Franklin (*The Man Who Dared Lightning*) to enlarge my grasp of the Revolution's ideas and ideals. I decided my youthful view of the conflict was too narrowly military and wrote *1776: Year of Illusions*. The book demonstrates that both the Americans and the British were in the grip of delusions of moral and military grandeur which evaporated in the harsh realities of this pivotal year.

"In the next two decades I broadened and deepened my exploration of the clash between America's realities and its ideals. *Time And Tide* is a novel about the USS Jefferson City, a morally stained cruiser that sails symbolically through the Pacific War. The captain is an anti-Ahab figure who refuses to abandon the American dream of brotherhood in spite of multiple betrayals. *Over There* portrays a cynical American general astonished to find himself in love with a redheaded feminist ambulance driver in the cauldron of World War I's Western Front. *Loyalties* is about an American intelligence officer who loves a woman involved in the German Resistance to Hitler. In this book I became convinced that to confront radical evil, idealism needs religious faith—even if it is only a spark in the prevailing darkness.

"In 1997, I summed up my thinking on my favorite historical era in *Liberty! The American Revolution*, the companion volume to the award-winning PBS series. It was a main selection of the Book of the Month Club. Their editors told me I was the only writer in their 70 year history to have won this kudo in both fiction (*The Officers' Wives*) and nonfiction.

"*Liberty!* moves beyond the semi-debunking tone of *1776: Year of Illusions* to a perception of Revolutionary America as a multi-ethnic society, with over 40 percent of the population Irish, German, Dutch and African American. Liberty, was the force, the idea, that galvanized and sustained this new people.

"In 1999, *Hours of Gladness*, portrayed heirs of New Jersey's Irish-American chieftains, out of power and tragically out of sympathy with two IRA men who attempt to smuggle weapons from Cuba for the civil war in Northern Ireland. I have also continued my time-travels with the Stapletons. In March [2001], Forge Books published *When This Cruel War Is Over*, a novel about Major Paul Stapleton, a West Pointer who struggles against disillusion in the last summer of the Civil War.

"I am also widening my nonfiction reach. In 2001 Basic Books published *The New Dealers' War: Franklin D. Roosevelt and the War Within World War II*. The book explores the problems and failures of flawed idealism during the war that shaped the second half of our century.

"In January 2003 I published a novel on which I have been working for a decade, *Conquerors of the Sky*, about an aircraft company in California. It explores the often savage clashes between idealism and realism in this quintessentially American business over the course of more than 50 years. In the late spring 2003 I will publish *The Illusion of Victory: America in World War I*. Here the theme is how idealism, in the person of Woodrow Wilson, can lead to tragedy for a man and a nation. In the fall 2003 I will publish *The Louisiana Purchase*, a volume in the Turning Points series being published by John Wiley. I have also become senior scholar at the new National Center for the American Revolution at Valley Forge.

"If I were asked to sum up my subject matter as a writer, I would say it all in one word: America. I will never tire of exploring in the past and present the tension between its ideals and its realities and the impact of this great dichotomy on individual men and women, on the conduct of America's wars and its politics and ultimately on the soul of this vanguard nation, to whom the world looks for leadership."

The descendant of Irish immigrants, Thomas James Fleming was born on July 5, 1927 in Jersey City, New Jersey. After attending Catholic elementary and high schools, and after having turned 18, Fleming enlisted in the U.S. Navy, in July 1945. World War II, however, ended one month later, and Fleming left the Navy after one year.

With the benefit of the G. I. Bill, which gave veterans the opportunity to attend college, Fleming enrolled at Fordham University, in the New York City borough of the Bronx. He majored in English and received his A.B. degree in 1950. After pursuing postgraduate studies at Fordham's School of Social Work, he took a job as a reporter for the *Herald Statesman* newspaper in Yonkers, New York, in 1951. Fleming left that job the same year to become an assistant to Fulton Oursler, a novelist and mystery writer, and also began writing freelance articles for several magazines. After Oursler died in 1952, Fleming became the executor of his estate. In 1954 Fleming joined *Cosmopolitan* magazine, working as an associate editor and later executive editor. He left the magazine in 1961 to write books on a permanent basis.

In his first book, *Now We Are Enemies: The Story of Bunker Hill* (1960), Fleming discusses one of the most important battles of the American Revolutionary War from the point of view of both the colonial and British troops. On June 17, 1775 colonial forces defended a strategic point outside Boston called Breed's Hill, which later became known as Bunker Hill, from British attack. Although they were eventually forced to retreat, the colonists inflicted heavy losses on British troops despite being greatly outnumbered. The battle resulted in the substantial weakening of the British military position in Massachusetts, setting the stage for future American victories, and also boosted the morale of the colonists, many of whom were ready to give up their quest for independence. In his review for the *Chicago Sunday Tribune* (September 18, 1960), Vincent Starrett wrote, "Fleming has written an important and fascinating book about a great day that may be in danger of being forgotten. It should be read by everybody who believes in and cares about the greatness of America."

For his first novel, *All Good Men* (1961), Fleming borrowed from his relationship with his father and his recollections of the Democratic Party political machine that dominated Jersey City for several decades. The novel's protagonist is Jake O'Connor, a recent law-school graduate and the son of Ben O'Connor, a prominent local politician. Although Jake has negative feelings toward his father, and hates politics, he agrees to take his father's place when he becomes ill. "Mr. Fleming's novel benefits from a rich fund of precinct lore and a headlong pace that keeps the reader on edge until the last vote is bought," Martin Levin wrote in the *New York Times Book Review* (October 1, 1961). By contrast, in his review for *Library Journal* (October 1, 1961), Earl Tannenbaum faulted *All Good Men's* "turgid writing, stock characters and overt moralizing," which, he argued, detracted from the book's strengths. Jake O'Connor returned in two sequels, *King of the Hill* (1966) and *Rulers of the City* (1977).

In 1963 Fleming published *Beat the Last Drum: The Siege of Yorktown*, an account of the battle in Virginia that resulted in the surrender of British troops under the command of General Charles Cornwallis in 1781, bringing an end to the Revolutionary War and ensuring the independence of the United States. In his review for *America* (November 9, 1963), William D. Hoyt Jr. praised *Beat the Last Drum* as "the best book on the subject," one that makes "military history interesting and even exciting reading." Hoyt wrote that Fleming "describes the movements of troops and vessels, and the details of their clashes, in such a manner that the reader feels much like an eyewitness."

In his novel *King of the Hill* (1966), Fleming explored big-city politics once again. This time, he focused on the role played by Irish Americans in politics. This was also the first of Fleming's novels to examine the impact of the Roman Catholic Church on its flock. Reviewing the book for *Commonweal* (April 1, 1966), Roger B. Dooley wrote that the world Fleming revealed was "one of total, brutal corruption, Machiavellian double-dealing and power struggles literally to the death—to several deaths, in fact, two cold-blooded murders, another threatened and a dubious accident." Dooley found that Fleming's attacks on the Catholic Church detracted from the novel's strengths. "It seems a violation of the writer's objectivity when his tone becomes shrill with the sound of grinding axes," he wrote. Despite this criticism, he concluded that *King of the Hill* was written in "generally powerful prose" and "is a compulsively readable novel, full of harsh, undeniably true observations on how our cities are run."

The Catholic Church plays a central role in three more Fleming novels: *Romans, Countrymen, Lovers* (1969), *The Sandbox Tree* (1970), and *The Good Shepherd* (1974). In writing the stories Fleming aired his own frustrations with his strict Catholic childhood and education. In an interview with Jean Ross, a contributor to *Contemporary Authors* (1982), he recalled that "in the course of going through sixteen years of Catholic schools, I had become thoroughly sick of being lectured at and told how lucky I was to be educated by these wonderful Jesuits, etc. It was the old Catholic church of pre-Vatican II, of course, and very authoritarian, which naturally set my Irish-American teeth on edge."

Fleming completed the first draft of *The Sandbox Tree* in 1952, but was unable to get the novel published because, as he told Ross, many publishers at the time were leery of publishing works that attacked the Church. The novel follows the plight of an unhappy Irish Catholic girl, a senior at college in 1948, who gradually loses her faith. After Fleming revised the draft eight times, the novel was finally published, in 1970.

In general, Fleming's novels about the Church received mixed reviews. Writing for *Library Journal* (July 1974), D. E. Weston praised *The Good Shepherd* (1975), about a liberal cardinal named Matthew Mahan who opposes the Church's teachings on contraception and divorce. "Fleming gives a superb characterization of Mahan's inner conflicts and his harassments by both friend and foe, radical and reactionary," Weston wrote. "A provocative, well-researched portrayal of today's Church." In the *National Review* (February 28, 1975), Priscilla L. Buckley described the novel as a "compelling book with a number of flaws: some characters are overdrawn, others stereotyped, the women are one dimensional. Some incidents are inherently impossible, others downright impossible." *The Good Shepherd* won the Catholic Press Association's Religious Book Award in 1974. In spite of his criticisms, Fleming has never left the Catholic Church, telling Ross, "I think the post-Vatican II Church has definitely lessened the gap between the religious experience of American Catholics and that of the country as a whole." In a telephone interview with *World Authors*, Fleming said that he continues his efforts to reconcile his Catholic faith with his belief in American historical traditions.

In 1969 Fleming published a nonfiction book, *West Point: The Men and Times of the U. S. Military Academy*. Using personal papers, correspondence, archival records, and information gathered from interviews, Fleming constructed a history of the military academy that produced many of the country's greatest military leaders, including Ulysses S. Grant, William T. Sherman, George McClellan, Thomas "Stonewall" Jackson, James "Jeb" Stuart, Robert E. Lee, Philip Sheridan, George Custer, John J. Pershing, George Patton, Douglas MacArthur, Omar Bradley, Dwight Eisenhower, and Norman Schwarzkopf. In the *New York Times Book Review* (May 4, 1969), as excerpted in *Contemporary Literary Criticism* (1986), Charles Bracelen Flood described it as "the best book written about the United States Military Academy at West Point" and "also one of the best books ever written about any American educational institution." Flood added that, in "describing the decades from the Civil War to the onset of World War I," Fleming makes "his most original contribution."

Fleming's biography, *The Man from Monticello: An Intimate Life of Thomas Jefferson* (1969), received mixed reviews. For example, despite faulting Fleming for making "some serious factual errors" and accepting interpretations that most historians have abandoned, a *Choice* (October 1969) reviewer concluded that the biography, which is targeted to a general audience, "has an enchanting engrossing style." In 1970 the book won an award from the Christophers, a religious organization. It was also named one of the outstanding books of the year by the *New York Times*, in 1970.

Another biography, *The Man Who Dared the Lightning: A New Look at Benjamin Franklin*, appeared in 1971. "It is impossible not to be impressed all over again by a man of such extraordinary parts as Ben Franklin. The author fondly presents them all," a *Time* (May 31, 1971) reviewer noted. "What is unexpected and particularly touching in the book is Fleming's account of Franklin's stormy relationship with his son."

Fleming continued to write about the American Revolution. In his book *1776: The Year of Illusions* (1975), he argued that both the Americans and the British misunderstood and underestimated one another, eventually producing a series of disasters for both sides that prolonged the conflict. As Henry Wilkinson Bragdon wrote in his review for the *Christian Science Monitor* (November 12, 1975), as quoted in *Contemporary Literary Criticism*, "Both sides shared the expectation that the war would be short. The British overestimated the numbers of men still loyal to the crown and so despised the rebels that they underestimated their will to fight. The Americans were rendered over-optimistic by a series of dazzling early successes." Bragdon enthusiastically recommended the book, writing that "it shows how, amid disaster and disillusion, Washington grew in confidence, in decisiveness, and in ability to lead men." *1776* was named one of the outstanding books of the year by the American Library Association, in 1975, and received the Annual Book Award from the American Revolution Round Table, in 1976.

In his novel *The Officers' Wives* (1981), Fleming portrays military life from the point of view of several women who marry graduates from the West Point class of 1950. "What energizes this novel . . . is the war between the sexes," Peter Davison observed in the *Atlantic* (April 1981). "The officers' wives spend their lives watching their men die, or advance in rank, or grow disillusioned or hard or corrupt. . . . Sometimes cumbersome, but often passionate or reflective, Fleming's fictional account of the alterations in our attitude toward military service recapitulates the entire course of recent American history."

In 1978 Fleming published *Promises to Keep*, the first of a series of novels that follows the lives of a wealthy American family, the Stapletons, during different periods of American history. In the first novel, set in the present, Jim Kilpatrick, the lead character from *Romans, Lovers, Countrymen* (1969), is hired to write the Stapleton's family history. While conducting his research, he uncovers a number of embarrassing secrets about the family. The second novel, *Dreams of Glory* (1983), portrays the Stapletons during the American Revolution and centers around a British plot to kidnap George Washington. "Fleming's historical background is accurate and evocative," Loralee MacPike wrote in the *West Coast Review of Books* (September–October, 1983), as quoted in *Contemporary Literary Criticism*. "The richness of incident and character which makes the book seem so true to our ideals of Revolutionary America, however, also makes it very difficult to keep the characters straight and to follow the overly complex action." Fleming wrote four other novels about the Stapletons: *Spoils of War* (1985), *Remember the Morning* (1997), *The Wages of Fame* (1998), and *When This Cruel War Is Over* (2001). In the *New York Times Book Review* (April 21, 1985), Jack Sullivan dismissed *The Spoils of War*, arguing that the characters are underdeveloped and concluding that "Fleming is far more convincing as a historian than as a novelist." However, in her review for the *Library Journal* (August 1997), Barbara Conaty praised the characterizations in *Remember the Morning*, which also takes place during the American Revolution, citing in particular Fleming's "stereotype-smashing insights into the psychology of ambitious, conflicted young people."

Conaty called the book "a marvelously fresh reinterpretation of an era."

In an article published in the *Writer* (February 1995), Fleming discussed the vital role of research in creating historical novels. "The first and most important reason is the commitment every writer, both in fiction and nonfiction, has to the truth," he wrote, adding that research can also "deepen an imaginary character, transform a key scene, and even alter a novel's plot." While planning his novel, *Over There*, Fleming discovered 40 memoirs written by American women who went to France during World War I, on a dusty library shelf at Yale University, in New Haven, Connecticut. After reading the women's recollections, Fleming totally reworked his novel's plot. Instead of the story of an eccentric general and his division that he had been planning, Fleming was inspired to create the character of Polly Warden, a feminist who goes to the front lines in France to prove that women, too, could be heroic in war.

In his nonfiction book, *Duel: Alexander Hamilton, Aaron Burr and the Future of America* (1999), Fleming analyzed the events that led Vice President Aaron Burr to shoot his archnemesis, Alexander Hamilton, on July 11, 1804 in Weehauken, New Jersey. Hamilton died the next day from his wounds. Fleming writes that by 1804, the political careers of both men, who once held one another in high regard, were in serious decline. The Federalist Party, which Hamilton headed, lost the presidency in 1800 to Thomas Jefferson, a member of the Democratic-Republican Party, which eventually became today's Democratic Party. Burr became Jefferson's Vice President, but eventually came to earn his distrust and suspicion. In 1804, after Jefferson dropped him as his running mate in his re-election bid, Burr ran for governor of New York State, in an effort to save his political career. He lost by a landslide, however, thanks to opposition by both Jefferson and Hamilton. During the campaign, the New York press vilified Burr, publishing many of Hamilton's statements attacking him. Burr blamed his defeat on these statements, which he considered inflammatory and libelous. Hoping to salvage his honor and resurrect his political career, Burr challenged Hamilton to a duel. After killing Hamilton, he fled New Jersey to avoid being arrested for murder. He was later placed on trial for treason after he conspired to separate the Western Territories from the United States and then rule the newly created nation. Although a jury acquitted him of treason, Burr's political career was finished. In his review for the *Boston Globe* (October 19, 1999), Robert Taylor praised *Duel* as a "carefully researched narrative history" that "probes behind the scenes to show the temperaments of the adversaries within the context of their minds."

In *The New Dealers' War: Franklin D. Roosevelt and the War Within World War II* (2001), Fleming examined the prewar and wartime policies of the president who was elected four times and served from 1933 until his death in 1945. Fleming dissents from the view held by many historians that Roosevelt was a visionary and a great wartime leader. According to Fleming, Roosevelt frequently deceived the public, which was overwhelmingly isolationist and opposed to intervention in the European war, and tried to lure Japan into attacking the United States as a pretext to enter World War II on the side of the Allies. The author faults the president's leadership, objecting to Roosevelt's commitment to the policy of unconditional surrender, which lengthened the duration of the war and cost more lives, and to his attempts to influence Josef Stalin, the Communist dictator of the Soviet Union who ordered the deaths of millions of people and went on to dominate Eastern Europe after the war. "Fleming obviously knows his stuff," Richard Pearson wrote for the *Washington Post* (July 1, 2001). "He paints a devastating portrait of a Roosevelt whose health and powers were in steep and terminal decline after 1940. The evidence he assembles seems authoritative, irrefutable and has seldom been gathered in one volume." Pearson, however, asserted that a major flaw of the book "is that in portraying the wartime FDR—no doubt accurately—as a broken and fumbling man, Fleming has given us only part of the truth. The book begs for a portrait that includes the Roosevelt of the first two terms, the vibrant, unforgettable voice that moved and mobilized a nation in the depths of despair."

In late 1998 Thomas Fleming was the subject of several stories in the press. In 1968 he had traveled to France to explore the Argonne forest, where his father, Teddy, served during World War I. While climbing an embankment, Fleming lost a ring his father had given him in 1957. Frank Hague, a former mayor of Jersey City who had encouraged his father's entrance into politics, had presented his father with the ring to honor his election as sheriff. The ring was inscribed: "From Mayor Frank Hague to Sheriff Teddy Fleming 1945," as quoted by David Gonzalez, a reporter for the *New York Times* (December 5, 1998). The younger Fleming desperately looked for the ring, but never found it.

In 1998 Fleming received a telephone call from Gene Scanlon, a friend who worked for Bret Schundler, then mayor of Jersey City. Scanlon reported that a French photographer named Gil Malmasson found the ring in 1985, when he was using a metal detector to hunt for shells, rifles, bayonets, and other war souvenirs in the Argonne. At the time, he contacted American diplomatic and military offices in Europe to see if they could help him locate the ring's owner, but they couldn't provide any assistance. In 1998, Malmasson performed an Internet search and discovered that Frank Hague had served as mayor of Jersey City. He then contacted the mayor's office in Jersey City, and learned that Teddy Fleming had worked for Hague. Scanlon put Malmasson in touch with Fleming, who immediately flew to France to recover the ring on the exact spot where he lost it 30 years earlier. "I was deeply moved," he told Gonzalez. "I had this indelible rush of emotion that my father was in some sense in my life again in this mystical way I didn't understand. The more I thought about it, the more I thought there has to be some meaning to it."

In addition to writing history books and novels, Thomas Fleming contributes frequently to the *New York Times Book Review* and other publications. He has also written several nonfiction books intended for children. He served as the president of the American chapter of PEN from 1971 to 1973 and is a fellow of the New Jersey Historical Society and the Society of American Historians. The author is married to the former Alice Mulcahey. They live in New York City and have four children. In 2001 the Flemings celebrated their 50th wedding anniversary. In 2003 Fleming published another novel, *Conquerors of the Sky*.

—D. C.

SUGGESTED READING: *America* p583+ Nov. 9, 1963, p296 Oct. 17, 1970; *Atlantic* p122 Apr. 1981; *Boston Globe* D p5 Oct. 19, 1999; *Chicago Sunday Tribune* p1+ Sep. 18, 1960; *Choice* p1100 Oct. 1969; *Christian Sciene Monitor* p23 Nov. 12, 1975; *Commonweal* p59+ Apr. 1, 1966; *Library Journal* p3300 Oct. 1, 1961, p1847 Jul. 1974, p126 Aug. 1997; *National Review* p236 Feb. 28, 1975; *New York Times* B p1 Dec. 5, 1998, with photos; *New York Times Book Review* p38 Oct. 1, 1961, p10+ May 4, 1969; *Publishers Weekly* p12+ Jul. 4, 1977, with photo, p51 Jan. 20, 2003, with photo; Thomas Fleming Writer Web site; *Time* p89 May 31, 1971; *Washington Post Book World* p10 Jul. 1, 2001; *West Coast Review of Books* p53+ Sep.–Oct. 1983; *Writer* p9+ Feb. 1995; *Contemporary Literary Criticism*, Volume 37, 1986; *Who's Who in America*, 2001

SELECTED BOOKS: nonfiction—*Now We Are Enemies: The Battle of Bunker Hill*, 1960; *Beat the Last Drum: The Siege of Yorktown*, 1963; *One Small Candle: The Pilgrims First Year in America*, 1964; *The Man from Monticello: An Intimate Life of Thomas Jefferson*, 1969; *West Point: The Men and Times of the United States Military Academy*, 1969; *The Man Who Dared the Lightning: A New Look at Benjamin Franklin*, 1971; *The Forgotten Victory: The Battle for New Jersey*, 1973; *1776: Year of Illusions*, 1975; *New Jersey: A History*, 1977; *Downright Fighting: The Story of Cowpens*, 1988; *Liberty! The American Revolution*, 1997; *Duel: Alexander Hamilton, Aaron Burr and the Future of America*, 1999; *The New Dealers' War: Franklin D. Roosevelt and the War Within World War II*, 2001; as editor—*Affectionately Yours, George Washington: A Self-Portrait in Letters of Friendship*, 1967; *Benjamin Franklin: A Life in His Own Words*, 1972; *The Living Land of Lincoln*, 1980; fiction—*All Good Men*, 1961; *The God of Love*, 1963; *King of the Hill*, 1966; *A Cry of Whiteness*, 1967; *Romans, Countrymen, Lovers*, 1969; *Sandbox Tree*, 1970; *The Good Shepherd*, 1974; *Liberty Tavern*, 1976; *Rulers of* the City, 1977; Promises to Keep, 1978; A Passionate Girl, 1979; The Officers' Wives, 1981; Dreams of Glory, 1983; Spoils of War, 1985; Over There, 1992; Loyalties: A Novel of World War II, 1994; Remember the Morning, 1997; Lights Along the Way, 1998; The Wages of Fame, 1998; Hours of Gladness, 1999; When This Cruel War Is Over, 2001; Conquerors of the Sky, 2003; juvenile literature—First in Their Hearts: a Biography of George Washington, 1968; Battle of Yorktown, 1969; Golden Door: The Story of American Immigrants, 1970; Give Me Liberty: Black Valor in the Revolutionary War, 1971; Thomas Jefferson, 1972; Behind the Headlines: the Story of American Newspapers, 1990; Harry S. Truman: President, 1995

Courtesy of Bill Giduz/Davidson College

Fornes, Maria Irene

May 14, 1930– Playwright

Maria Irene Fornes, the Cuban-American playwright, has been writing innovative and experimental plays for Off-Broadway and Off-Off-Broadway theater since the early 1960s. During that time she has amassed a remarkable nine Obie Awards, the highest form of recognition for non-Broadway productions. Despite her many critical successes, she has not achieved popularity with mainstream audiences, but instead has become a favorite of theater aficionados, who admire her originality and longevity. While most of her contemporaries from the 1960s avant-garde theater community have either disappeared from view or gone on to do work in film or on Broadway, Fornes is one of the few who has succeeded in forging a career in Off-Broadway theater. Her work has influenced playwrights as diverse as Tony Kushner, Paula Vogel, and Eduardo Machado. Bonnie Marranca, in *American Playwrights: A Critical Survey*, as quoted in *Contemporary Literary Criticism* (Vol. 61), described Fornes's plays as "whimsical, gentle and bittersweet, and informed with her individualistic intelligence. Virtually all of them have a characteristic delicacy, lightness of spirit, and economy of style. Fornes has always been interested in the emotional lives of her characters, so human relationships play a significant part in the plays. . . . She apparently likes her characters, and often depicts them as innocent, pure spirits afloat in a corrupt world which is almost always absurd rather than realistic. . . . Political consciousness is present in a refined way." Although Fornes's work has been linked to various groups, including feminists, lesbians, Hispanics, and Cuban-Americans, Fornes herself resists attempts to fit her plays into any one category. She acknowledges their political relevance, but emphasizes that she creates without any conscious intentions. "I never feel that I want to write something," she explained during an interview with Alisa Solomon for the *Village Voice* (September 15–21, 1999, online). "Something is there and I respond to it. Creativity can't have any restriction or instruction. It's like dreams. If you say you want to dream about this or that, it won't come out." Her work has a broad range, from the surrealism in her early works to the elements of dramatic realism of her more recent dramas. Her nearly 40 plays include *Promenade* (1965), *The Successful Life of 3: A Skit for Vaudeville* (1965), *Fefu and Her Friends* (1977), *Eyes on the Harem* (1979), *The Danube* (1982), *Mud* (1983), *Sarita* (1984), *The Conduct of Life* (1985), *Abingdon Square* (1987), and *Letters from Cuba* (2000). They have been published in three collections—*Promenade and Other Plays* (1971), *Maria Irene Fornes: Plays* (1986), and *Lovers and Keepers* (1987). Fornes frequently directs her own productions.

Maria Irene Fornes was born in Havana, Cuba, on May 14, 1930 to Carlos Luis, a public servant, and Carmen Hismenia (Collado) Fornes. The youngest of six children, Fornes grew up in a poor family and attended school regularly only until the sixth grade. After her father's death, in 1945, she immigrated to New York City with her mother. She initially pursued a career in painting and drawing. In the 1950s she traveled to Paris, where she lived for three years and for a time studied under the painter Hans Hofmann. While in Paris she attended Roger Blin's 1954 production of Samuel Beckett's *Waiting for Godot*, which was written in French. "I didn't know a word of French. I had not read the play in English," Fornes recalled in an interview with Scott Cummings for *Theater* (Winter 1985), as quoted on a geocities Web site devoted to Broadway. "But what was happening in front of me had a profound impact without even understanding a word. Imagine a writer whose theatricality is so amazing and so important that you could see a play of his, not understand one word, and be shook up."

Fornes returned to New York, in 1957, and became part of the emerging Off-Broadway theater movement, joining the experimental Judson Poet's Theater and the Open Theater during the 1960s. She described the avant-garde scene in New York to Matthew Barber in an interview for the *San Francisco Independent* (November 15, 1990), as quoted on the Brava Theater Web site: "When I started writing plays, there were really very few people who were involved in non-traditional, non-commercial theatre. We were not aspiring to create commercial theatre. It was right at the very beginning of the Off-Broadway movement, and there were perhaps only a dozen writers in the whole country, at most, who were involved in writing theatre that was experimental. And there were only four places in New York where this kind of theatre was done—two cafés and two churches."

One of Fornes's earliest plays was *Tango Palace* (1963), a dark face-off between two male characters—alternately behaving as lovers, father and son, and teacher and student— that shows the clear influence of *Waiting for Godot*. She achieved her first major critical success, in 1965, when she received an Obie Award for *Promenade* and *The Successful Life of 3: A Skit for Vaudeville*. *Promenade*, a musical, follows two working-class prisoners, known only as 105 and 106, who escape from their jail cell and embark on an unusual quest to discover evil. In a *Dictionary of Literary Biography* essay, as quoted in *Contemporary Authors* (Vol. 28), Phyllis Mael remarked on the disjunction between *Promenade*'s comic action and its despairing lyrics, which comment on "unrequited love, the abuse of power, the injustice of those who are supposed to uphold the law, and the illogical and random nature of life." Bonnie Marranca noted that "*Promenade* has the *joie de vivre*, the disregard for external logic and spatial convention, the crazy-quilt characters that one associates with the plays of Gertrude Stein. . . . The satire seems almost effortless because the playwright's touch is so playful and laid back. Yet Fornes makes her point, and there's no confusion as to whose side she is on in this comedy of manners."

The Successful Life of 3 parodies conventional romantic comedy by creating a love triangle involving He, She, and 3. In 10 short scenes that span years, Fornes presents her characters trying on a variety of roles, forever re-imagining their lives and their relationships with each other. Marranca argued that the play "represents Fornes at her comic best. This beautifully orchestrated piece, with its crisp, precise dialogue, peculiar internal logic, and short, cinematic takes is a wonderful display of comic anarchy. Forget about conventional observations of time and place; they don't exist for these successful three. The pacing is at times rigid, at other times rapid, but the overall rhythm of this tightly structured piece is as smooth as the story is unbelievable."

One of Fornes's best-known works is *Fefu and Her Friends* (1977). The play is set in 1935 in a country home, where eight women have gathered for the weekend to plan a fund-raising event. This domestic setting and conventional premise marked a step toward realism for Fornes, and yet the play is no straightforward domestic drama. It is most noted for its innovative dramatic structure. The play is comprised of six scenes; the first and last are set in a living room, with the entire audience watching. The middle four scenes take place in different areas of the house and are performed simultaneously in different locations around the theater. The audience, which is divided into four groups, physically moves from scene to scene, so that each group watches the four scenes in a different order. "Fornes, you see, is literally asking her audience to 'track down' her characters," David Richards noted in the *Washington Post* (July 1983), as quoted in *Contemporary Authors* (Vol. 28). "Theater-goers are being transformed into sleuths." Joan Larkin, in a review of the play for *Ms.*, as quoted in *Contemporary Literary Criticism* (Vol. 61), recalled the experience: "In the kitchen we sit—witnesses rather than remote spectators—watching two women deal with their finished love affair. In the backyard, during a game of croquet, we overhear Fefu's bravado and her pain. In the bedroom we sit, literally surrounding Julia's bed, and share her haunted visions of women's visceral loathsomeness." Richards concluded that "the strength of this production is that it has you thinking, 'If only I could look into one more room, catch one more exchange, come back a minute later.' In short, it lures you into a labyrinth of the mind." Not all of the reviewers appreciated the experience. Edith Oliver, in her review for the *New Yorker*, as quoted in *Contemporary Literary Criticism* (Vol. 61), noted that "Miss Fornés is a subtle, stylish writer, but she can also be a distressingly whimsical one. As for the evening as a whole, I must say with regret that I ran out of steam before she ran out of play."

The Conduct of Life (1985) is a political drama set in an unidentified Latin American country. Fornes introduces an army captain whose job it is to torture prisoners for an oppressive military regime. Rather than dramatize his acts of torture, Fornes shows how his brutality spills over into his home life, where he is abusive of his wife and a female servant. The drama garnered much praise for its subtlety and visceral impact. A reviewer for the *Village Voice*, quoted in *Contemporary Literary Criticism* (Vol. 39), noted that "Fornes's freedom from psychological, naturalistic, and didactic conventions lets her explore what happens to this man, his wife, his young mistress, his childhood pal, and his servant without exploiting subject or audience. The events are as direct and mysterious as life, and as surprisingly funny. There's nothing goody-goody or hectoring about this most ethical play, and despite its surface simplicity I am still . . . finding new possibilities in the web of class, sex, and character she has woven."

In 1998 Fornes's *The Summer in Gossensass* was presented by New York City's Women's Project as the concluding attraction of its 20th-anniversary season. The title refers to a spa town in the Austrian Alps, where an aging Henrik Ibsen fell in love with a much younger woman, who then became the prototype for the title character of his 1890 drama, *Hedda Gabler*. Fornes's play is a meditation on the initial reception of, and enduring fascination with, this classic work. She introduces two young actresses, actual historical figures who mounted the first English-language production of the play, in London, in 1891. Lawrence Van Gelder, writing for the *New York Times* (April 23, 1998), described *The Summer in Gossensass* as "something of a comic valentine to the antediluvian [e.g. 19th-century] avant-garde, a consideration of the evolution of acting styles and a trip back through time to a period when ideas about the psychological underpinnings of characters and those who play them constituted a thrilling novelty." Michael Feingold, reviewing the play for the *Village Voice* (April 14, 1998), noted that "a Fornes play may be a mess—and *The Summer in Gossensass* is as elliptical and digressive a mess as she ever concocted—but it springs from a core of feeling, a sense of emotional awareness coupled with intellectual curiosity, that sends out provocative tendrils in every direction."

The Signature Theatre Company of New York City devoted its 1999–2000 season to Fornes—a significant honor, considering that in previous years the theater had devoted seasons to such mainstream playwrights as Sam Shepard, Arthur Miller, and John Guare. Alisa Solomon, in an article previewing the season for the *Village Voice* (September 15–21, 1999, on-line), quoted the Signature Theatre artistic director, James Houghton, who described Fornes's work as "funny, tough, relentlessly truthful, and full of surprises." Solomon also quoted the Tony Award–winning playwright Tony Kushner, who has acknowledged Fornes as an influence upon his career: "[Fornes's] work is both intensely private, closed, elusive, and at the same time incredibly political."

Mud, one of Fornes's Obie-winning plays, which was first produced under her direction in 1983, was revived for the Signature Theatre season. Seventeen short scenes are played out in an impoverished, rural household headed by a young woman named Mae. Mae, who is learning to read, becomes enmeshed in a battle of wills between Lloyd, a dim-witted figure who helps around the farm, and Henry, a newcomer who seems to offer hope for a better life. Fornes built the play around some wooden chairs, a hoe, and an ironing board that she bought at a flea market; all the scenes are set in the kitchen, and feature Mae cleaning, ironing, preparing food, and, occasionally, trying on lipstick or learning new vocabulary words. Alisa Solomon noted that "*Mud* is one of several beautiful and painful plays Fornes wrote in the 1980s in which a woman's inchoate desire for fulfillment disturbs her world, and thus destroys her." Les Gutman, reviewing the Signature Theatre production of *Mud* for *CurtainUp* (September 27, 1999, on-line), noted, "As the assault of rapid-fire scenes Fornes unleashes on us start to sink in, and the raw power of their base, violent, unpleasant, indeed repulsive, vulgarity recedes, it is the stunning, expressive portrait of Mae that seems most durable. It is drawn with words that shift repeatedly from the most visceral to the incredibly poetic." Peter Marks, in a mixed review of the same production for the *New York Times* (September 27, 1999), concluded that "Ms. Fornes's inventive voice, with its embrace of the surreal, will remain a marginal one. Still, it's worth a listen, if one is willing to listen patiently. Her plays have the meticulous composition of still lifes, which means at times they are strikingly balanced and at others opaque, impassive. . . . She is perhaps best when writing in short strokes, which reveal her clever employment of dramatic structures without lapsing into turgidity."

Many critics have interpreted Fornes's plays, including *Mud*, as feminist parables. In a conversation with Kathleen Betsko and Rachel Koenig for *Interviews with Contemporary Women Playwrights*, as quoted in *Contemporary Literary Criticism* (Vol. 61), Fornes argued that, in *Mud*, having a female protagonist "is a more important step toward redeeming women's position in the world than whether or not *Mud* has a feminist theme, which it does not. The theme is just a mind that wants to exist and has difficulties. The difficulties have nothing to do with gender, but the fact that this mind is in a woman's body makes an important feminist point."

Fornes has taught playwriting at several institutions, including the Yale School of Drama, in New Haven, Connecticut; New York University, in New York City; and the International Arts Relations (INTAR) Hispanic American Arts Center, also in New York City. She was the 2001 McGee Professor at Davidson College, in North Carolina. In addition to her nine Obies, she has received a New York State Governor's Arts Award, a Distinguished Artists Award from the National Endowment for the Arts, a Lila Wallace-Reader's Digest Literary Award, an award from the American Academy and Institute of Arts and Letters, and grants from the Rockefeller Foundation and the Guggenheim Memorial Foundation.

—A. I. C.

SUGGESTED READING: *New York Times* E p5 Apr. 23, 1998, II p7 Sep. 19, 1999, E p5 Sept. 27, 1999; *Village Voice* p129 Apr. 14, 1998, p51 Sep. 21, 1999, with photo; *Contemporary Literary Criticism* Vol. 39, 1985, Vol. 61, 1990

SELECTED BOOKS: *Promenade and Other Plays*, 1971; *Maria Irene Fornes: Plays*, 1986; *Lovers and Keepers*, 1987

Courtesy of Karen Joy Fowler

Fowler, Karen Joy

Feb. 7, 1950– Novelist; short-story writer; science-fiction writer

At the age of 30, Karen Joy Fowler, a college-educated homemaker in California, became a writer. Starting in the mid-1980s, she began publishing science-fiction–themed short stories on a regular basis for many different publications. Her science fiction has earned her several Nebula Award nominations, from the Science Fiction and Fantasy Writers of America, and the 1987 Hugo Award, from the World Science Fiction Society, for best new science-fiction writer. Fowler has also won acclaim for her novels, *Sarah Canary* (1991), *The Sweetheart Season* (1996), and *Sister Noon* (2001), which explore life for women in different historical eras. Reviewers have singled out Fowler's well-drawn characters and her narrative style.

Karen Joy Fowler was born Karen Joy Burke on February 7, 1950 in Bloomington, Indiana. Her father, Cletus, worked as a psychologist at Indiana University, in Bloomington, and her mother, Joy, taught school. "Along with basketball, my family loved books," Fowler recalled in a statement posted on her official Web site. "The day I got my first library card there was a special dinner to celebrate. And before I could read myself, I remember my father reading the *Iliad* to me, although really he was reading it to my older brother, I just got to be there. A shocking book!"

In 1961 Fowler's father got a job with the *Encyclopedia Britannica*, and the family relocated to Palo Alto, California. Her parents, who were raised in California, were happy to return there. By contrast, Karen was sad that she had to leave Bloomington, the only home she knew. "Palo Alto was much more sophisticated than Bloomington," Fowler wrote for her Web site. "At recess in Bloomington we played baseball, skipped rope, played jacks or marbles depending on the season. In Palo Alto girls my age were already setting their hair, listening to the radio, talking about boys. I considered it a sad trade." Fowler remained a voracious reader and was particularly fond of *The Hobbit*, by J.R.R. Tolkien.

After graduating from Palo Alto High School, in 1968, Fowler enrolled at the University of California at Berkeley. At the time, students on college campuses across the country were demonstrating for civil rights and against the war in Vietnam. On many occasions, the protests turned into violent clashes with the police. The Berkeley campus was one of the major centers of the student protest movement in the United States. Fowler, who majored in political science, actively participated in the anti-war movement. "I was in Berkeley during People's Park, when the city was occupied and there were tanks on the street corners, and I was there during the Jackson State/Kent State killings," she wrote for her Web site.

Fowler graduated from Berkeley, in 1972, with a B.A. The same year she married a fellow student, Hugh Fowler. She continued her education, receiving a master's degree in political science from the University of California at Davis, in 1974. Shortly before she completed graduate school, Fowler gave birth to her first child. A second child followed two years later. Still unsure of her career goals, Fowler settled down as a mother and homemaker with her family in Davis, California.

In an interview with the journalist Elisabeth Sherwin, as posted on the University of California at Davis Web site, Fowler recalled that in 1980 she and her two children drove to Berkeley University to pick up her undergraduate diploma. At Sproul Hall on campus, they discovered a long line. Fowler began telling the children a story. "My idea was to pre-empt any bad behavior by telling these cautionary tales about two children named Cheryl and Ralph," she said. "The people in line were enormously impressed and supportive of my story and I felt strangely entitled to this. I got a round of applause when I reached the window. One woman said I should be a writer." Fowler decided to try writing. She began publishing science-fiction stories in such publications as *Asimov's Science Fiction*, the *California Quarterly*, *Fantasy and Science Fiction*, and *Helicon 9*.

In 1986 Fowler published her first book, *Artificial Things*, an anthology of five of her stories. Although the book was ignored by most reviewers, it won the prestigious Hugo Award for best new science-fiction writer, in 1987. A second anthology of her work, *Peripheral Vision*, appeared in 1990. In his review for the *Washington Post Book World* (April 29, 1990), Gregory Feeley wrote that Fowler's stories "are quieter, self-questioning rather than self-assertive, and very funny. Fowler's stories tend to be contemporary tales, which often tilt toward fantasy but without shifting their centers of gravity." Although Feeley observed that none of Fowler's stories "has achieved a perfect fusion of language, structure and theme," he concluded that she was a "writer of clarity and humor, and this brief volume . . . suggests she is still growing." In an interview with *Locus* magazine (July 1999, online), Fowler said, "Particularly in a commercial field like ours, the escapist aspect is something to think about. It's seldom admired, and yet it seems to me often that if people's lives are hard and a book takes you out of it for a few hours, what's wrong with that? Why isn't that an admirable thing for a writer to have done?"

In 1991 Fowler published her first novel, *Sarah Canary*, which takes place in the Pacific Northwest in 1873. The title character appears one day at a Chinese railway camp and attracts the attention of Chin An Kin, one of the workers. Since the woman cannot speak or even communicate, Chin has no idea who she is or where she came from. He calls her "Sarah Canary" because the only sounds she can make are chirping noises. Chin brings Sarah to an insane asylum in the Washington Territory from which he thinks she must have escaped. Their journey turns into an adventure as they encounter bigotry and post-Civil War lawlessness and meet several interesting characters. Most reviewers praised *Sarah Canary*. In the *American Book Review* (April/May 1992), Brooks Landon wrote that the novel "is so firmly grounded in the marvelous historical marginalia of 1873 that its every action draws from and reflects upon that history. . . . No personal story can match the cultural story that Fowler unfolds in a book ever concerned with injustice but ever playful." In his review for the *San Francisco Chronicle* (November 17, 1991), Jeffrey Pepper Rodgers observed that Fowler's "narrative brims over with invention." Rodgers added, "By the end of the novel, the question remains: Who is Sarah Canary? A ghost, a madwoman, an emblem of female power, a symbol of dream and desire for the outcasts of America? Clear answers are not forthcoming, and maybe that's just as well. Readers may feel a bit like [Fowler's characters] here—as if we have been led on a memorable trip to strange locales we can't easily describe for some purpose we can't pinpoint. But given another chance, we'd probably go again." *Sarah Canary* won the Commonwealth Club Medal, in 1991.

In her second novel, *The Sweetheart Season* (1996), Fowler explores the life of Irini Doyle, a 19-year-old girl who lives in the small, Midwestern town of Margit, in 1947. Irini works in the scientific research division of a company that manufactures breakfast cereal. The novel's narrator is Irini's daughter, who tells the audience about her mother's life after World War II. During the late-1940s, women were expected to find a husband and settle down, but unfortunately Margit has practically no marital prospects for Irini or the other young women, because after the war ended, most of the men decided not to return to their hometown. As a solution, Henry Collins, the 92-year-old who owns the cereal company, organizes a women's baseball team. Collins hopes that by traveling to other towns to play baseball, the women will meet suitable husbands. In the *Los Angeles Times* (September 29, 1996), Richard Eder criticized the novel for "a certain lack of conviction, an anticlimactic quality. It organizes a plot and plots are not the author's best talent." However, Eder wrote that the characters in the book, especially Irini, "make an alluring crew for [Fowler's] time-travel venture into the mysterious universe that lies half a century behind us." In the *New York Times Book Review* (October 13, 1996), Deirdre McNamer praised the novel, writing that Fowler's "shadowy humor and the elegant unruliness of her language, all elevate her story from the picaresque to the grand."

Fowler published her third anthology of short stories, *Black Glass: Short Fictions*, in 1998. Like her two previous anthologies, it contained her best science-fiction stories. In her review for the *Boston Globe* (March 8, 1998), Amanda Heller cited "Black Glass," "The Faithful Companion at Forty," and "The Elizabeth Complex" as the best stories in the book. "Encounters with the uncanny, played sometimes for humor and sometimes for chills, Fowler's fictions are a heady brew of sensibilities from feminism to sci-fi," Heller wrote. "Each piece puts us on notice in its own way that an intriguing intelligence is at work." In the *New York Times Book Review* (March 8, 1999), Jenny McPhee observed that there "is much that is fantastical about Fowler's fiction, but also much that is rooted in a solid emotional reality; in fine-edged and discerning prose, she manages to re-create both life's extraordinary and its ordinary magic."

In 2001 Fowler published her third novel, *Sister Noon*. Like her two previous novels, *Sister Noon* takes place in the distant past. The protagonist, Lizzie Hayes, serves as the treasurer of the Ladies' Relief and Protection Society Home in San Francisco during the 1890s. One day, Mary Ellen Pleasant, a mysterious older woman who is the subject of much local gossip, brings a young girl to stay at the home. "Every character's tale is complicated, unpredictable and often engrossing," Jeff Zaleski wrote in his review for *Publishers Weekly* (April 9, 2001). "Mrs. Pleasant, for instance, is a former slave (or is she?), wealthy as a railroad baron, charitable, a witch and a legendary cook. Still beautiful at 70, she is a purported dealer in underground markets where sex, opium and even murder are for sale." Zaleski lauded Fowler for moving her characters "through time and space seamlessly and gracefully, and exquisitely render[ing] San Francisco as it grows from outpost to city. The temporal shifts and the unreliability of some characters' histories may be temporarily disorienting, but readers who bear with Fowler will be handsomely rewarded." Writing in *USA Today* (May 31, 2001), Jocelyn McClurg asserted that "*Sister Noon* never lives up to its early promise." The reviewer also observed that "Fowler's prose, while often pretty, has an ethereal vagueness that makes Gilded Age San Francisco seem ghostly, rather than inhabited by the living dead, which is what we want from historical fiction."

Karen Joy Fowler is one of the founders of the James Tiptree Jr. Memorial Award, an annual prize that celebrates the contributions of women to the field of science fiction. She won a 1988 grant from the National Endowment for the Arts, and she has taught a workshop every summer at Cleveland State University, in Ohio, since 1990. In 2003 Fowler edited the fiction anthology *Mota 2003: Courage*. She and her husband, Hugh, continue to live in Davis, California. They have two grown children.

—D. C.

SUGGESTED READING: *American Book Review* p10 April/May 1992; *Boston Globe* E3 Mar. 8, 1998; *Locus* (on-line) July 1999; *Los Angeles Times* p2 Sep. 29, 1996; *New York Times* (on-line) Oct. 13, 1996; *Publishers Weekly* p48+ Apr. 9, 2001; *San Francisco Chronicle* p3 Nov. 17, 1991; *USA Today* D p9 May 31, 2001, with photo; *Washington Post Book World* p3 Apr. 29, 1990

SELECTED BOOKS: short-story collections—*Artificial Things*, 1986; *Peripheral Vision*, 1990; *Black Glass: Short Fictions*, 1998; novels—*Sarah Canary*, 1991; *The Sweetheart Season*, 1996; *Sister Noon*, 2001

Mary S. Pitts/Courtesy of www.lynnfreed.com

Freed, Lynn

July 18, 1945– Novelist

Lynn Freed's books, which include *Home Ground* (1986) and *The Bungalow* (1993), reflect her experiences as a white person of Jewish descent growing up in South Africa during apartheid. Speaking of the task of recording the harsh realities of institutionalized racism in her native country, Freed told Sarah Anne Johnson for the *Writer's Chronicle* (October/November 1999, on-line), "This is the writer's job: to write what there is." She continued, "What I'm saying, I suppose, is that you write as if everyone [you are writing about] is dead. Then you face the music. I don't know any other way to keep the teeth sharp and the spirit alive."

Lynn Freed was born in Durban, South Africa, on July 18, 1945 to Harold Derrick Freed, an actor, and Anne (Moshal) Freed, a theater director. She began writing at an early age. "I can't ever remember ever wanting to write. I just wrote," she told Johnson. "At first, as a child, and for a number of years into adolescence, I seemed to write partly to show off. I'd write a story or play—I wrote a lot of plays, mostly awful—and I'd run downstairs to read it to my mother. She was a completely honest critic: harsh and fair. If she came forth with praise, I knew that what I had written wasn't fake."

After receiving a bachelor's degree from the University of Witwatersrand, in Johannesburg, Freed moved to the United States to study English literature at Columbia University, in New York City. "I had spent my childhood in South Africa both loving the place and, concomitantly, dreaming of getting out," she told Johnson of her decision to come to the United States. "These are not as mutually exclusive as one might imagine. South Africa is an outpost. When I was growing up it was a quasi-colonial outpost. Anyone who grows up in such a place understands the need to get out—at least temporarily—to go north to the source, to what is fondly known as 'the real world.'" In 1969 Freed received her master's degree. She considered studying law and took the standard Law School Admission Test, but quickly decided against that path. As she told Johnson, "I chose to write, and, more or less, to struggle." She continued studying at Columbia, and in 1972 she earned a doctoral degree in English literature.

Freed moved to San Francisco, California, in the early 1980s and there began her first novel, *Heart Change* (1982), which was reprinted in 2000 as *Friends of the Family*. The novel, about a doctor who breaks out of her stagnant life after meeting her daughter's music teacher, featured an a primarily American cast and was far removed from Freed's experiences in South Africa. The book made few ripples, either commercially or critically—in part, Freed believes, because she based so little of it on her own life. She explained to Johnson how she realized her error: "My first novel was in galleys when, one evening, I was having dinner with [the writer] Gail Godwin. I was telling her about my family, my background. Then she asked whether I had written about them, and when I said no, she said, 'Well, for God's sake!' So home I went and began *Home Ground*. One finds permission to write when one is ready to receive it, I suppose."

Home Ground was published in 1986. The novel explores the relationships among a large cast of characters living in South Africa—Jews, Indians, whites, and blacks. The book examines their ties to the country, where whites live in protected enclaves, while blacks are forcibly segregated; Indians long for ancestral homes in England; and the main character, Ruth Frank, who is Jewish, is so out of place that she considers South Africa home only after she has left it. *Home Ground* caused a stir in South Africa when it first appeared, and there were rumors that the book would be officially banned. (It was not.) Despite that, Freed did not see her tale as overly political. She told Ari L. Goldman in an interview for the *New York Times Book Review* (August 17, 1986), "I feel terribly helpless about South Africa. It is a beautiful place, it is home. I'm not a revolutionary, I'm a subversive—not a subversive in the political sense but as a writer. Any writer to be effective, has to have this quality."

Janette Turner Hospital, in a critique of *Home Ground* for the *New York Times Book Review* (August 17, 1986), wrote, "What is extraordinary about this book is its perspective . . . Lynn Freed's guileless child-narrator takes us *inside* the neurosis of South Africa. We experience it in a way that is qualitatively different from watching the most graphic of news clips. Ms. Freed may not have quite the literary reach of [the South African writer] Nadine Gordimer, but her vantage point of privileged outcaste gives, I think, a more disturbing inner view of that awful, intricate symbiosis between black and white, of the patronizing glibness of those who take black servitude for granted." *Home Ground* was named a *New York Times* Notable Book of the Year.

Freed's next novel, *The Bungalow* (1992), is a sequel to *Home Ground*. In it, Ruth, now older, returns to South Africa after escaping a loveless marriage in New York. At home an affair reignites between her and Hugh Stillington, an ex-lover who lives in a bungalow overlooking the Indian Ocean. Ruth's affair with Stillington, a white liberal who is 20 years her senior, gives her a sense of peace that she has never felt before; her family, however, insists that she return to America and reunite with her husband. Carolyn See wrote for *New York Newsday* (December 29, 1992), "Lynn Freed creates a racist South Africa where everyone is both subservient to and lording it over someone else. . . . We begin to see apartheid in different, familial terms." Glenda Adams agreed, writing for the *New York Times Book Review* (March 21, 1993): "We see in Lynn Freed's fiction what we might fail to recognize from passing news stories about political change." *The Bungalow*, too, was named a *New York Times* Notable Book of the Year.

In 1997 Freed published her fourth novel, *The Mirror*, which tells the story of an English-born housekeeper, Agnes La Grange, who makes her fortune in South Africa. Beginning with an old Jewish man by whom she becomes pregnant, Agnes uses men to gain financial security, while resolving never to fall in love with any of them. A critic for *Kirkus Reviews* (July 1, 1997) wrote, "Candor, passion, and love of life put Agnes on a par with the Wife of Bath, while Freed adds the treats of succulent place and period flavor, even 20 black-and-white photographs of the very places where Agnes walked, slept, loved, and lived. A pleasure." Margot Mifflin, writing for *Entertainment Weekly* (September 12, 1997), noted, "Agnes is Moll Flanders without excuses—an enchanting and infuriating heroine, both admirable and wrongheaded in her commitment to honesty and her pursuit of adventure."

Freed's most recent novel, *House of Women*, was published in 2002. Its protagonist, a teenage girl named Thea, is taken from her mother's South African home by her estranged father, who has promised her in marriage to a wealthy Syrian cousin. Thea's mother, Nalia, has taught her to fear men, in part because of her own experiences in concentration camps during World War II. Despite these fears, Thea marries the cousin and moves with him to an island where she gives birth to twin daughters, who are then ripped from her by her husband's half-sister to be raised. Polly Shulman noted for *New York Newsday* (February 17, 2002) "This odd, hypnotic little book turns its view . . . inward, beyond domestic interiors to the hidden places of the psyche. The world it inhabits follows Freud's floor plans, with all the plumbing and major appliances—like the child's desire for the mother or the parent's wish to reabsorb the child—just where psychoanalysts placed them." In her review for the *Fort Worth Star–Telegram* (February 28, 2002), Catherine Newton wrote, "In this upside-down fairy tale, the world is, for the most part, an ugly place despite its physical beauty. The primary male characters are powerful but misogynistic. The female characters are unhappy victims. But those who stick with *House of Women* will find, in the end, its redeeming message, hidden deep in the psychological scarring and angst that make this fantasy so unsettlingly real."

Lynn Freed has taught at the City College of San Francisco; St. Mary's College, in Moraga, California; the University of California at Berkeley; the University of Montana at Missoula; the University of Oregon at Eugene; and the University of Texas at Austin. She has had visiting professorships at numerous other institutions and is a frequent participant in such prestigious gatherings as the Bread Loaf Writers' Conference and the Bennington Writing Workshop. She is currently a professor of English at the University of California at Davis, and a member of the faculty for the MFA program at Bennington College, in Vermont.

Freed's articles, short stories, and reviews have been featured in several periodicals, including *Harper's*, *Mirabella*, *Travel and Leisure*, *Washington Post Book World*, and the *New York Times*. Her work is included in the anthologies *Shaking Eve's Tree: Short Stories of Jewish Women* (1990), *The Confidence Women: 26 Women Writers at Work* (1991), and *Best Short Stories of 1992* (1992), among others.

Freed has won fellowships from the Guggenheim Foundation, the Rockefeller Foundation, the National Endowment for the Arts, and Yaddo. She has one daughter, Jessica Peta.   —C. M.

SUGGESTED READING: *Atlantic Monthly* p38+ Nov. 1, 1998; *Chicago Tribune* p6 Apr. 15, 2001; *Entertainment Weekly* p 132+ Sep. 12, 1997; *Fort Worth Star–Telegram* Feb. 28, 2002; *Harper's Magazine* p71+ May 1, 1999; *Kirkus Reviews* p970 July 1, 1997; Library of Congress Web site; Lynn Freed's Official Web site; (New York) *Newsday* p36+ Dec. 29, 1992, with photo, D p24 Feb. 17, 2002; *New York Times Book Review* p 7 Aug. 17, 1986, p17 Mar. 21, 1993

SELECTED BOOKS: *Heart Change*, 1982 (republished as *Friends of the Family*, 2000); *Home Ground*, 1986; *The Bungalow*, 1993; *The Mirror*, 1997; *House of Women*, 2002

Frey, Darcy

1960(?)– Nonfiction writer; journalist

"In today's jargon, we call Darcy Frey a literary journalist," Andrea Cooper wrote in a profile of Frey for *Writer's Digest* (November 1998). "In another time, we might have used the word storyteller, before that description became inexorably linked with fiction." A regular contributor to such publications as the *New York Times Magazine*, *Rolling Stone*, and *Sports Illustrated*, Frey conveys stories through snatches of dialogue and scene descriptions, appealing not only to a reader's intellect, but also to his or her emotions. In 1994 Frey published his first book, *The Last Shot: City Streets, Basketball Dreams*, which developed out of an award-winning essay he wrote for *Harper's Magazine* about four black teenagers trying to obtain college-basketball scholarships to escape the ghetto. Frey documented the teens' encounters with wily basketball recruiters, the Scholastic Aptitude Tests (SATs), and the neighborhood drug scene. The resulting work—what Evan Thomas for *Newsweek* (November 21, 1994) called "an achingly good book"—received widespread praise and was named a *New York Times* Notable Book of the Year. Frey's memoir about his father's deadly battle with emphysema, *The Words Between Us*, was published in 1999 (some sources say 2000).

After graduating from Oberlin College, in Oberlin, Ohio, Darcy Frey accepted a job writing for *American Lawyer*, an investigative magazine focusing on the legal profession. He then worked for *New England Monthly*, a now-defunct magazine that featured a narrative style of journalism. These professional experiences helped Frey develop strong reporting and storytelling skills. Frey worked for one year as an editor at *Harper's Magazine* and then embarked on a freelance writing career.

Frey wrote several pieces on inner-city life and wanted to focus a book on that topic. "I thought maybe I should write about one floor of a housing project or one playground or one city block," he explained to Cooper. "I decided that if I wrote about a high school basketball team, I'd have a nice narrative structure—with a school year or school season, games and practices to hang the story on." After scouting for the right location, Frey settled on Coney Island's Abraham Lincoln High School, in the New York City borough of Brooklyn. Lincoln High had turned out such alumni as the novelist Joseph Heller, the playwright Arthur Miller, and three Nobel laureates in physics, but the school that Frey encountered in 1991 was characterized by insufficient budgets; a poor, African-American, student body; and a powerful basketball team. As Brent Staples wrote for the *New York Times* (November 13, 1994): "Lincoln has become a virtual annex of Coney Island's basketball courts." The neighborhood of Coney Island, once synonymous with its famous amusement parks, had become the victim of misguided urban renewal plans that razed row houses and built high-rise housing projects, which became occupied by some of the city's poorest blacks. Within this congested slum, Frey found two separate and distinct circles of young men—one dominated by drug culture and the other by basketball.

Frey befriended four of Lincoln's star basketball players—Russell Thomas, Tchaka Shipp, Corey Johnson, and Stephon Marbury—and planned to follow them from June of their junior year through graduation. He followed the boys to summer basketball camps, sat in on numerous interviews with college recruiters, and spent most nights with them at a neighborhood basketball court known as "the Garden," in homage to New York City's Madison Square Garden, the home court of the New York Knicks. However, midway through the 1991–1992 school year, Frey ran into obstacles to his plan: one boy's mother became suspicious of Frey's relationship with her son, while another parent demanded money for his son's involvement in the book. Finally, the National Collegiate Athletic Association (NCAA) ruled that Frey could not accompany the boys to college campuses while they were being recruited. Unable to complete his full year of observations, Frey abandoned the project as a book, instead developing it into a 15,000-word essay for *Harper's Magazine*. "But," he told Cooper, "I still had half a story—I didn't know how to give it a beginning, middle and end." An editor convinced Frey to incorporate the obstacles he had encountered into his story, and the resulting essay, "The Last Shot," earned Frey the 1994 National Magazine Award for feature writing and was later collected in the 1994 volume of *The Best American Essays*.

Frey revisited his material and began to shape it into a book, albeit a different one than he originally envisioned. "For *The Last Shot*, I'd imagined an upbeat story about kids using basketball to further their education and playing their way out of the ghetto," he recalled to Cooper. "The more I got into it, the more I realized I'd stumbled on a much deeper, darker story about the exploitation of high school athletes. It was, in fact, about all the obstacles that are thrown up in the way of these kids and how incredibly difficult it is to land a scholarship and make good on that promise." Frey showed that coaches, colleges, and sneaker companies all manipulate would-be basketball stars for their own financial gain. While success in basketball is sold as a version of the American Dream, less than one percent of high-school basketball players obtain scholarships to Division One colleges, and only one percent of those who play in college go on to play professionally. Frey concluded, as quoted by Donna Britt for the *Washington Post* (March 21, 1995), "Hard work alone—although preached . . . as the one sure route to success—does not suffice in these circumstances. . . . If the NCAA is so concerned about education . . . [why not] allow . . . scholarships to players who don't pass the SATs as long as they stay off the team until the school brings them up to speed . . . or eliminate freshman eligibility across the board so that every player's first year would be devoted to schoolwork?"

The Last Shot, published in November 1994, was an immediate critical success. Brent Staples called the book "compellingly written, with elegance, economy and just the right amount of outrage," while George F. Will for the *Washington Post* (November 24, 1994) described it as "an elegantly told sad story of young black men playing with literally life-and-death desperation." Alex Kotlowitz for the *Washington Post* (December 11, 1994) added, "[Frey's] honest coming-to-terms with the tragic world around him is as dramatic and exhilarating as the unfolding lives of the four young basketball stars." Of Frey's success in documenting this environment, Staples wrote, "Mr. Frey shows us levity and light in Coney Island's grimmest corners. His portraits of its young men and boys are warmly, even lovingly written. He cares for them and lets it show. He also reminds us that the basketball players are vulnerable, breakable—and still children, despite the fact that they appear to us as giants." Frey's book was often compared to *Hoop Dreams*, a 1994 documentary about high-school basketball players in Chicago.

In 1999 Frey published *The Words Between Us*, a memoir about coming to terms with his father's death from emphysema. "While the events I wrote about were taking place," he explained to Cooper, "I was keeping a journal and taking notes. Still, it's very much a work of memory. Memory is a fallible thing. I tried to be as rigorous with myself as possible. But I'm sure I got some details wrong."

Frey continues to write freelance articles. He has written memorable pieces about a young couple struggling to save their four-months-premature baby, a homeless woman murdered in a racially divided New England town, and a scientist studying a colony of Arctic seabirds who uncovers clues about global warming. One of Frey's stories, for the March 24, 1996 issue of the *New York Times Magazine*, explored the high-pressure environment of air-traffic control at New York City's Terminal Radar Approach Control Center, which monitors America's most congested airspace. Frey documented the enormous stresses placed on air-traffic controllers by an ailing trafficking system. "Something's Got to Give" became the basis for a movie on the same subject, *Pushing Tin* (1999), featuring the actors John Cusack and Billy Bob Thornton.

"You have to be in love with the process [of writing]," Frey told Cooper, "as much as you are with the topic you've chosen. You have to be drawn to lengthy projects. For a long time, you'll be in a tunnel, not seeing any light. I think patience is the key, and faith that if you hang around long enough, interesting things will happen. With this kind of reporting, you can't parachute into a situation, gather up the information that you need, and get airlifted out. You have to dig in for the long haul." Darcy Frey currently resides in Boston.

—K. D.

SUGGESTED READING: *Chicago Tribune* XIV p5 Nov. 27, 1994; *New York Times* C p18 Nov. 7, 1994, with photo, 7 p1+ Nov. 13, 1994; *Newsweek* p101 Nov. 21, 1994, with photo; *Washington Post Book World* p2 Dec. 11, 1994; *Writer's Digest* p32+ Nov. 1998

SELECTED BOOKS: *The Last Shot: City Streets, Basketball Dreams*, 1994; *The Words Between Us*, 1999

Robert Birnbaum

Furst, Alan

Feb. 20, 1941– Novelist

The American author Alan Furst gained fame as a writer of thrillers set in 1930s and 1940s Europe, mainly France—the years before and during World War II. *Shadow Trade* (1983), *Night Soldiers* (1988), *Dark Star* (1991), *The Polish Officer* (1995), *The World at Night* (1996), *Red Gold* (1999), and *Kingdom of Shadows* (2001) gained critical approbation and a wide readership. Robert Chatain wrote in the *Chicago Tribune* (February 26, 1995), "Alan Furst's ongoing novel series, beginning with the superb *Night Soldiers*, . . . portrays ordinary men and women caught out on the sharp edge of military intelligence operations in wartime: the partisans, saboteurs, resistance fighters and idealistic volunteers risking their lives in causes that seem lost. Dozens of major and minor characters are vividly drawn; the books are rich with incident and detail. . . ." The *Library Journal* (December 2000) reviewer observed that Furst's "noir heroes navigate a world of betrayed promises and lost friends, seeking to derail Nazi lackeys and only half believing in their own chance of success or survival."

Alan Furst was born February 20, 1941 in New York City. He was educated at Oberlin College, in Oberlin, Ohio, receiving his B.A. in 1962, and at Pennsylvania State University in University Park, where he was awarded his M.A. in 1967. After completing a Fulbright Fellowship in 1969, Furst started his career as a writer. His first book, *Your Day in the Barrel*, published in 1976, was nominated for an Edgar Award, an honor given by the Mystery Writers of America. His second novel, *The Paris Drop*, followed in 1980, and his third, *The Caribbean Account*, in 1981. It was with *Shadow Trade*, published in 1983, that Furst made his mark as an authority on the events behind World War II, as seen from the vantage points of intelligence operatives of the Soviet Union, Germany, France, and Great Britain.

In 1983 Furst visited Moscow, as part of an assignment to write about Eastern Europe for *Esquire*. He arrived on the day Soviet planes shot down a Korean Airlines jet. Furst told Genie Chipps Henderson during a *Publishers Weekly* (February 5, 2001) interview that the fear among the people of Moscow was palpable; they constantly looked to the sky, expecting American missiles to rain down on them at any time. "I'd never experienced a totalitarian culture before," Furst said. "It was a huge shock. The police were everywhere."

The country that captured Furst's heart, however, was France, for the remnants of World War II history that linger there. As a Fulbright fellow, he lived in France for a year in the late 1960s. Furst explained to *George Jr.* (September 1996, on- line) why he has made his literary niche the years before and during World War II in Europe, particularly France—and why he continues to be absorbed by that time and place: "In French hearts and minds," he observed, "the war never ends. It defines heroism and honor and sacrifice and nationality—it was really the worst of times but it brought out the best in some people. There was real evil, and breath-taking goodness, people torn between opportunism and self-sacrifice. None of the peoples in this war can forget it or leave it behind—the Russians, the French, the Japanese, the British and the Americans—we're still living out the destinies forged in that time."

In the 1980s Furst and his wife, Karen, an ornamental horticulturist, moved from rural Bainbridge Island, Washington, to Paris, where Furst could write and do research full time. The product of his work during that period was *Night Soldiers* (1988). For that book, Furst chose as his hero a man from the ranks of the NKVD, the Soviet secret police network that was the precursor of the KGB. As a very young man, Khristo Stoianov, a Bulgarian, sees his brother murdered for mocking the fascists who have taken over his country. He is recruited by the NKVD and sent to Moscow for training. His first assignment is in Spain, where the Soviet government has liquidated the revolutionary groups who were trying to save Spain from the coming fascist takeover; Moscow wanted the anarchists, who predominated in Republican Spain, eliminated. Khristo is not enthusiastic about his job and escapes from the NKVD to Paris. After a spell in prison, engineered by spiteful Britons and evil Bulgarians, Khristo joins the French Resistance (known as the Maquis) against the German occupation in 1943. In his new job, sabotaging trains, he is led by an American sent by the OSS, the predecessor of the CIA. At the close of the war, Khristo goes back to the mouth of the Danube to rescue an old comrade from Soviet clutches.

"The book springs alive in the scenes of Khristo's training by the NKVD and his employment of the skills of subversion across Europe. His exploits with the Maquis make first-rate spy stuff," Walter Goodman observed in the *New York Times* (January 30, 1988). "Khristo's derring-do doesn't blow too big a hole in credibility; he is always constrained by circumstances and is not often triumphant. . . . Though Khristo remains in shadow, his simple decency is highlighted. His politics consist of opposition to the brutes, be they Fascist or Communist."

"Everything about this book seems right," the historian Geoffrey C. Ward wrote in his review for *USA Today* (January 14, 1988). Although, he remarked, the politics of Eastern Europe and "the sometimes deadly conflicts among rival antifascist organizations before and during the war" are "opaque" to many people, "in *Night Soldiers*, it is all somehow made to seem perfectly clear. . . . All the settings are vividly rendered, too, from the muddy Bulgarian village where the story begins with a vicious killing, to the Manhattan waterfront where it finally ends."

Furst's 1991 novel, *Dark Star*, also deals with Eastern Europe during the early days of World War II. A journalist, Andre Szara, a Polish Jew, is drawn into working for the NKVD full-time when he discovers proof that Stalin had worked for the czar's secret police before the Revolution. Some factions of the secret police want to use the information against Stalin; others support him. Szara is thus dragged out of what Furst described in the novel as "a kind of dream world, a mythical country where idealistic, intellectual Jews actually ran things, quite literally a country of the mind." Meanwhile, World War II is approaching, and the need to defeat Hitler will take precedence over intranational conflicts. Josephine Woll, the *Washington Post* (June 4, 1991) reviewer, wrote, "Furst has created a stimulating and satisfying novel out of the stuff of history: dates, names and places certainly, but the no less significant realities of human fears and courage." Herbert Mitgang, in the *New York Times* (June 12, 1991, on-line), agreed: "Furst . . . has surpassed himself in *Dark Star*. . . . Szara is a secret agent with soul. . . . The historical background and intelligence information are woven into the novel seamlessly. . . . Furst is particularly effective on the subject of intelligence, salting his narrative with references to tradecraft that add flavor to his story. . . . *Dark Star* casts a strong new light on the old world of espionage."

In 1994 Furst returned to World War II–era Poland with *The Polish Officer*. Captain Alexander de Milja of the Polish military intelligence, the eponymous hero, smuggles the Polish gold reserves out of the country so that they will not fall into the hands of the Germans. The year is 1939, and his rail trip is fraught with danger. He goes on to join the French underground, posing as a Russian émigreé poet in Paris; later, he becomes first a coal merchant with a plan to ambush Luftwaffe pilots, then a train saboteur working out of a Ukrainian forest. "De Milja is a thoroughly fleshed-out character: a cartographer conscripted into service by the political remnants of a defeated nation; a husband whose wife has lost touch with reality; a gentle lover; an individual driven by intense love of his country and a burning passion for freedom," Charles P. Thobae commented in the *Houston Chronicle* (April 2, 1995). He added that Furst's "greatest talent lies in getting into the heads of his characters and making their moral choices fit. . . . *The Polish Officer* is a classic spy story replete with the moral ambiguities found in a world at war." Thobae commended the novel's "profound sense of history, its suspense and the quiet heroism of its characters."

The World at Night, Furst's 1996 novel, is another story of World War II espionage, this time set mainly in occupied Paris. The hero, Jean Casson, is a movie producer whose series of documentary films about the French army comes to an end with the army's defeat by the Germans. Escaping back to Paris from the field, he returns to work under the aegis of a German film executive. On a trip to Spain, however, while ostensibly scouting locations, he engages in a failed mission for British intelligence. Again in Paris, he pursues the movie star Citrine, an old flame. (The character Citrine is generally believed to be a portrait of Arletty, the great French actress who starred in *Children of Paradise*, a film made during the German occupation.) Recruited by German intelligence to become a double agent—"condemned to heroism," as Richard Eder wrote in the *Los Angeles Times* (June 2, 1996)—Casson turns triple agent.

In his interview for *George Jr.*, Furst admitted that Casson and Citrine were "based on real people" and that "at least two film producers I know of were involved in spying for resistance movements." He added that reading about French film had inspired him: "The occupation was certainly one of its greatest periods." Furst also explained that in *The World at Night* he had tried to capture the French character. "The French believe in making love, in drinking wine, in staying up all night and talking about life. Certainly the hero of *The World at Night* believes in little else. But he—like a few hundred French men and women—tries to resist, to fight back against the Germans. He does it wrong, at least at the beginning, but at least he tries. Why does he fight? For the right to remain French."

"Furst," Eder observed, "has a splendid feeling for moods, gestures, landscapes and the sweet and acrid aspects of France. The moral desolation of occupied Paris is tangible: the vile graffiti of German uniforms against that great wall of history, the Seine embankment; the fury of a French waiter serving ersatz coffee."

Casson returns in *Red Gold*, Furst's 1999 novel. In it, Furst writes of Casson: "June 1941, off the Normandy coast, just at the moment of escape, as the fishing boat turned toward England, he had jumped into the sea and swum for the shore, British special operatives waving their Stens and calling him names. . . . He'd had a thousand francs, faked papers, and love in his heart." Casson has come back for Citrine, but she has vanished. "He survived it—maybe he survived it. Wandered north for a time, to Bourges, to Orléans, to Nantes. Where he'd been a stranger. Always a bad thing in France, and now a dangerous thing just waking up in these places felt wrong. . . . So he came home to Paris to die." Although at the beginning of *Red Gold* Casson nearly dies of starvation, he survives to join his old captain in an underground group that seeks to work together with the Communist-led resistance.

"This sequel to *The World at Night* just may be better than its superb predecessor," Bill Ott remarked of *Red Gold* in *Booklist* (February 1, 1999). "What makes Casson so appealing, and this novel so entertaining, is the way Furst refuses to let his hero off the hook; here's a resistance fighter whose cynical antiheroism doesn't evaporate in the last reel. Casson fights out of weary pragmatism, and he dreams mainly of a good meal and a decent glass of wine."

Nicholas Morath, the hero of Furst's 2001 book, *Kingdom of Shadows*, is Hungarian. Traveling to Paris in the late 1930s to try to rescue Eastern Europeans forced into exile by Hitler, Morath acquires faked passports, military documents, and cash, which he transports to the East. "Morath time and again returns in thankless triumph to the glittering salons of Paris," the *Publishers Weekly* (November 6, 2000) reviewer wrote. "Furst expertly weaves Morath's apparently unconnected assignments into the web of a crucial 11th-hour international conspiracy to topple Hitler before all-out war engulfs Europe again, counterbalancing scenes of fascist-inspired chaos with the sounds, smells and anxieties of a world dancing on the edge of apocalypse. The novel is more than just a cloak-and-dagger thrill ride; it is a time machine, transporting readers directly into the dread period just before Europe plunged into its great Wagnerian gotterdammerung."

Furst's latest novel, *Blood of Victory*, arrived in bookstores in August 2002. In the *New York Times* (August 22, 2002), Janet Maslin noted that the author "glides gracefully into an urbane pre-World War II Europe and describes that milieu with superb precision. The wry, sexy melancholy of his observations would be seductive in its own right—he is the Leonard Cohen of the spy genre—even without the sharp political acuity that accompanies it."

Among the magazines to which Furst has contributed is *Esquire*. There, his article "The Golden Age of Goo" appeared in 1984; it was later turned into the book *One Smart Cookie*, Debbi Field's story of how she started her cookie business. In 1988 *Esquire* published Furst's "Secrets of a Paris Café," which told readers how to deal with the "unwritten rules of life" in which Paris abounds. Furst returned to the United States from France in the early 1990s. He made his home in the town of Sag Harbor, on the South Fork of Long Island, while becoming a participant in the café life of New York City's "seedy boites and frowsy rooms," as Ruth La Ferla put it in the *New York Times* (October 14, 2001). Furst led La Ferla on a tour of some of the clubs on the Lower East Side soon after the destruction of the World Trade Center by terrorists. He told her that he could "find none of the gloom that used to hang like a fog over those war-torn European refugees" whom he encountered in his days of prowling the area at night. "But he did pick up a whiff of anxiety," La Ferla wrote. "The last few weeks have been hard on everyone," he said. "People are asking, 'How are you? No, really how are you?' In other words, did you lose anybody? Are you afraid?" He compared the atmosphere to that in London during World War II. "In nervous times," he found, "the spirit rises."

—S. Y.

SUGGESTED READING: *Atlantic* p108 Apr. 1991; *Booklist* p964 Feb. 1, 1999; *Chicago Tribune* XIV p5 Feb. 2, 1995; *Detroit News* D p28 May 27, 1995; *Economist* R p3+ June 19, 1999; *George Jr.* (on-line) Sep. 1996; (London)*Guardian* II p12 Feb. 27, 1997, p8 Aug. 5, 2000; *Library Journal* p187 Dec. 2000; *Los Angeles Times* p2 Apr. 28, 1991, p2 June 2, 1996; *New York Times* I p16 Jan. 30, 1988, C p17 June 12, 1991; *New York Times Book Review* p10 Apr. 11, 1999; *Publishers Weekly* p67 Nov. 6, 2000, p62+ Feb. 5, 2001, with photos; *Spectator* p30 Feb. 22, 1997; *USA Today* D p6 Jan. 14,1988; *Washington Post* C p12 Jan. 18, 1988, B p3 June 4, 1991

SELECTED BOOKS: fiction—*Your Day in the Barrel*, 1976; *The Paris Drop*, 1980; *Shadow Trade*, 1983; *Night Soldiers*, 1988, *Dark Star*, 1991; *The Polish Officer*, 1995; *The World at Night*,1996; *Red Gold*, 1999; *Kingdom of Shadows*, 2001; *Blood of Victory*, 2002; nonfiction—*One Smart Cookie: How a Housewife's Chocolate Chip Recipe Turned into a Multimillion-Dollar Business: The Story of Mrs. Field's Cookies* (with D. Fields), 1987

Gadol, Peter

Apr. 15, 1964– Novelist

Peter Gadol has created a body of work in which characters' relationships shift and change, and reality is not always as it seems. Readers of his novels *Coyote* (1990), *The Mystery Roast* (1993), *Closer to the Sun* (1996), *The Long Rain* (1997), and *Light at Dusk* (2000) meet inside their pages despairing men, who often make choices with which readers might find it hard to sympathize. "Gadol deals in dreams and terrors that are shaped by the landscape but float a little above it, like mist. It's a trib-

Art Gray/AMG Photography/Courtesy of Picador USA
Peter Gadol

ute to his skill as a writer that he nails most of them down," Michael Harris wrote in the Los Angeles Times (February 12, 1996).

Peter Gadol was born on April 15, 1964 to Sybil (Rickless) and Norman Gadol, a business executive. Gadol grew up in Westfield, New Jersey, a suburb of New York City, and was educated at Harvard University, in Cambridge, Massachusetts, graduating in 1986. There he studied under the Nobel Prize-winning poet Seamus Heaney, and wrote an undergraduate thesis on the work of Wallace Stevens, under the guidance of the noted critic Helen Vendler. Gadol served as an editor of the Harvard Advocate and, while he was still in college, was an intern at the Atlantic Monthly.

Gadol published his first novel, Coyote, to great acclaim when he was 26 years old. The story is set in a desert landscape of hills that resemble animals and lonely cacti, which "had to remain apart" because if "the cacti bunched up too much they would strangle one another," as quoted from an excerpt of the novel published on Gadol's Internet home page. The protagonist is Coyote Gato, a young man who grew up in the desert and goes to a mysterious ashram looking for a giant meteorite that was stolen from his mentor, the unconventional physicist and astronomer Frog Reading. Coyote becomes involved with Madeleine, an investigative journalist trying to find out more about Guru B, who runs the ashram, and his mysterious cult. Coyote also helps Amy, an archeologist trying to unearth an Indian city, and falls in love with her brother Matthew, a sculptor. Patty O'Connell, in the Washington Post (January 29, 1993), described Coyote as a "visionary" novel that showcases the American Southwest, and "ultimately . . . a love story involving secrets and dreams, anxieties about fulfillment and intimacy."

The title of Gadol's 1993 novel, The Mystery Roast, refers to the secret blend of coffee served in a New York City café of that name, in Manhattan's West Village. The story revolves around Eric, who, after having recently left his wife, moves into the building in which the café is located. Accompanying him is a statue, the 4500-year-old Goddess of Desire, which he has stolen from a major art museum. Eric's old friend Timothy lives in the building, as does Inca, a woman who designs gadgets. Inca persuades Eric and Timothy to reproduce the statue. They do, unleashing Desire into the world in the form of mass-produced figurines, T-shirts, and buttons. The characters become romantically entangled with one another: Timothy with Andre, the cafe proprietor, and Eric with Inca. Eric's mother, Lydia, who knows Timothy from childhood, is smitten with the museum official who is investigating the theft of the statue. Lydia's ex-husband, Jason Maldemer, the author of the novel Esidarap Found, serves as a kind of deus ex machina.

Gadol employs a kind of magical realism in describing the strange happenings in The Mystery Roast. At the beginning of the novel, "midway through a winter of mystifying warmth, a polar bear escaped from the zoo. She was spotted charging north across the vast lawn of the park, an amorphous, vanilla beast making one mad, hopeless break for freedom. The zookeepers . . . had to fire five tranquilizer darts into her rump to capture her. Around three o'clock, a helicopter weighted with an arctic pendant flew low across the western sky as it carried the doped truant back to her exile. . . . And yet no one in New York City that afternoon noticed the airborne bear," as quoted from an excerpt from the novel published on Gadol's Internet home page. Also quoted on that page, writer Nick Davis described Gadol as "that rare writer who can create a universe as disturbing as our own, but softer somehow, gentler." A critic for Publisher's Weekly, in a starred review also quoted on Gadol's home page, wrote, "This novel is too modern and raw to be called fabulist or fantastic, and too full of comic turns and virtuoso storytelling to be labeled realistic. . . . Mystery Roast is a brew of exotic strains whose strengths and nuances connoisseurs will enjoy tasting for themselves." Gadol, Patty O'Connell noted in the Washington Post (January 29, 1993), "writes convincingly about both gay and heterosexual relationships, about the concerns of young people starting out and older folk looking back. The dialogue is often funny, sometimes touching and always illuminating. . . . This novel is an accomplished mystery and a savory spoof of trends."

The protagonist of Gadol's next novel, Closer to the Sun (1996), asks his grandfather what it was like to lose his first love. The grandfather describes how he went off to war, returned, married another woman, and started a family after the early death of his first wife: "I fell into the sweep of time," he said, as quoted from an excerpt of the novel printed on Gadol's home page. The narrator remembers his grandfather's words when he comes to inhabit his own "province of grief," after falling in love with a man and believing "that I would spend the rest of my life with him," as quoted from the novel. After seven years, his lover has died, and the narrator has "wandered and . . . drifted," landing in California, where he spies on and then joins forces with a couple who is building a house. They have experienced their own tragedy, having lost their child in the fire that destroyed their previous home. Fires, a recurring image in the novel, are essential to the action.

Los Angeles almost figures as a character in the novel. "Southern California has rarely seemed more symbolic," Michael Harris wrote in the *Los Angeles Times* (February 12, 1996). "The symbols aren't exactly new, but Gadol's prose burnishes them to a shimmering luster." Although Harris found Gadol's style at the beginning of the novel somewhat "mannered, overpure," he found the book's middle more satisfying. "The otherworldly atmosphere of the canyon where these three flawed but likable people rise and sink, help and hurt one another is nicely balanced by the complexity of their relationship and the details of carpentry, plumbing, wiring, and painting—details so evocative of basic human needs that the barest description is meaningful, and Gadol's descriptions are rich." Maggie Garb, writing in the *New York Times Book Review* (January 21, 1996), also enjoyed Gadol's "exuberant descriptions of the process of building a home." In *Closer to the Sun*, she wrote, the "steady rhythm of hammering shingles, of lifting and placing roof joists, offers momentary transcendence from a chilling portrait of his characters' . . . grief."

In *The Long Rain* (1997) Gadol again used California as his setting, in this case the Northern California wine country near San Francisco. The book's narrator, Jason Dark, has left his law practice after becoming separated from his wife and young son. He returns to his family's vineyard, "drawn to the process of cultivating and nurturing plants," as Scott Martelle phrased it in the *Los Angeles Times* (September 28, 1997). Dark "finds in his vines the success in rearing he didn't achieve with his son and his marriage," Martelle wrote, and is gradually able to start a new law practice and reunite with his wife and son, who come to live with him at the vineyard. However, he continues his habit of soothing himself by driving back roads in the mountains. He muses, "I would head up into the foothills, where the air was bluer and cooler and the tall trees were not oak, but all pine, where I could lose myself in the wend of the mountain road as it traced the sheer granite cliffs and slouched back into the verdant run of the forest, a road that would, if I was lucky, carry me into the singed dust settling over a new valley," as quoted from an excerpt of the novel on Gadol's home page. One night, driving on a rain-slicked road, he accidentally kills a teenage boy. He decides to keep his role in the accident a secret, but a drifter and car thief is arrested and charged in the boy's death and even believes he may be guilty. Jason, as a lawyer, is morally obliged to defend someone charged with a crime he himself has committed.

The suspense in *The Long Rain*, according to Clea Simon, the reviewer for the *Boston Globe* (September 22, 1997), lies in "whether we can empathize with Jason Dark as he lies about his crime (and by extension destroys several lives) to protect his pleasant life." While Simon noted that the novel sets its readers up to experience sympathy for Dark by virtue of his recent return to happiness after difficult times, she deemed the novel unsuccessful in making Dark a character with whom readers can identify. "Gadol rationalizes and explains and ultimately sets himself a tad too far from his main character for empathy. This distance—the slip between author and first-person narrator—is just enough so that emotions are explained, rather than described, scenes described rather than felt." A *Publishers Weekly* (July 28, 1997) reviewer, however, disagreed, writing that "Gadol keeps the solutions to his hero's moral dilemmas surprisingly complex."

Although Gadol used Paris as a backdrop in *Light at Dusk* (2000), the novel's main characters are Americans. The City of Light is in this book a place where right-wing terrorists menace immigrants, kidnapping their children and setting off bombs. In one scene, Pedro Douglas is followed by a group of skinheads who confront him threateningly before, he runs away in a panic. "Maybe I should have declared myself an American; that very well might have ended the encounter. But what difference would it really make? My complexion was still brown, a darker nut in shadow, and that was enough," Pedro thinks, as quoted from a passage from the novel printed on Gadol's home page. Pedro, an architecture student, is joined by his former lover Will Law, who has left his post in Mexico, in the U.S. Foreign Service, for reasons that turn out to have tragic resonance. Will and Pedro become embroiled in the search for Nico, the four-year-old child of Jorie, another American, who is involved in a relationship with a Lebanese man.

In a starred review, a critic for *Publishers Weekly* (February 28, 2000) declared *Light at Dusk* "a spellbinding narrative," and a "novel of perception and misperception, of light refracting reality." The reviewer concluded that "Gadol blends ruminative philosophical passages within the framework of a crisp, action-packed story. The intricate plot remains lucid with finely wrought crystalline writing." The *Library Journal* (March 15, 2000) reviewer found it "an interesting story with well-constructed characters."

Peter Gadol lives in Los Angeles and teaches creative writing in the MFA program at the California Institute of Arts.

— S.Y.

SUGGESTED READING: Boston Globe C p9 Sep. 22, 1997; Library Journal p126 Mar. 15, 2000; Los Angeles Times p3 Feb. 12, 1996, p13 Sep. 28, 1997; New York Times Book Review p21 Jan. 21, 1996; Peter Gadol Home Page (on-line); Publishers Weekly p51 July 28, 1997; Washington Post C p2 Jan. 29, 1993

SELECTED BOOKS: Coyote, 1990; The Mystery Roast, 1993; Closer to the Sun, 1996; The Long Rain, 1997; Light at Dusk, 2000

Sylvia Plachley/Courtesy of Vintage Anchor Publicity

Gallagher, Dorothy

Apr. 28, 1935– Memoirist; biographer; journalist

Dorothy Gallagher, the author of the critically acclaimed memoir *How I Came Into My Inheritance: And Other True Stories* (2001), started her book-writing career with two biographies. The first, *Hannah's Daughters: Six Generations of an American Family* (1976), is an oral history of a clan of farmers from rural Washington. The second, *All the Right Enemies: The Life and Murder of Carlo Tresca* (1988), chronicles the fascinating life of an Italian-American anarchist. Gallagher told Mel Gussow for the *New York Times* (June 5, 2001) that in her memoir she tried to retain "the kind of detachment that I brought to biography." This is apparent in the memoir's lack of sentimentality. Though *How I Came Into My Inheritance* relates sometimes heartbreaking events in the author's life, it is also characterized by a pervasive wry humor. Nevertheless, Gallagher's love and affection for the friends and family who inhabit the book shines through, adding warmth to the wit—a combination that many critics applauded. Speaking of her parents, Gallagher told Gussow, "They were my gods when I was growing up. They were brave, they were quarrelsome, they were part of a spectacular generation. I hope the book is saying that I love them because I did."

Dorothy Gallagher was born in New York City on April 28, 1935, the only child of Eastern European Jewish immigrants. Upon coming to America, her father, Isadore Rosen, worked odd jobs, including selling bananas, before opening a mechanic shop. Gallagher's mother, Bella, helped out at the garage, despite the fact that she knew nothing about cars, because her husband could not afford to pay an assistant.

During the 1940s Gallagher and her parents lived in the Manhattan neighborhood of Washington Heights. Her parents and some of her relatives expressed deep admiration for communism, which had a great effect on Gallagher's early life. The "D" in her first name was meant to honor Georgi Dimitrov, a Bulgarian communist, and her first crush was on the boy who delivered the *Daily Worker*, a communist-associated publication. For years Gallagher thought that a portrait of the Soviet leader Vladimir Ilich Lenin that hung in their attic was actually a picture of her grandfather. In an essay for *Raritan* (Summer 1997) that later became one of the chapters of her memoir, Gallagher recalled her early perceptions of her family's political ideas: "I listen when adults talk. I pick up words and phrases and sentences. I hear 'Bolshevik,' and 'Stalin,' and 'The Party,' and 'class struggle,' pronounced with reverence. I hear 'Trotskyite,' 'objectively an agent of Fascism,' and 'reactionary,' and 'class enemies' spoken contemptuously." In her teens Gallagher attended Camp Wochica (Workers' Children's Camp), where she was exposed to more communist ideas. Eventually she joined the Labor Youth League, previously called the Young Communist League. However, as she grew older she became estranged from her parents' political ideals and the conformity these ideals seemed to demand.

In the early 1950s Gallagher attended Hunter College, in New York City, and dropped out before graduating. She began her writing career working for a series of gossip magazines, where along with such other budding writers as Mario Puzo and Bruce Jay Friedman, she fabricated stories about celebrities. Gallagher worked at the magazines from 1960 to 1964. She was reportedly fired for failing to notice that a photo of an actress used to illustrate a story had an obscene line of graffiti plainly visible on the wall behind her. In 1966 Gallagher took the position of associate editor at *Redbook*. In 1970 she turned to freelance writing, eventually publishing her work in such periodicals as the *New York Times Magazine*, *Harper's Magazine*, *Playboy*, and the *Village Voice*.

Gallagher's first published book was *Hannah's Daughters: Six Generations of an American Family* (1976), an oral history of Hannah Lambertson Nesbitt and her female descendants, all of whom lived in remote areas of the state of Washington. The majority of the book consists of the women relating their experiences in their own words, with Gallagher authoring brief prologues before each woman's story. The book also features many photographs of Hannah's family. In *Commonweal* (September 30, 1977), S. B. Warner wrote, "Hannah and her daughters and their families are representatives of the fringes of the westward migration of the American poor. . . . Theirs is the culture of poor American farmers—independent, hard-working, isolated. The suffering and heroism in their lives rests in the conflict between the ways of the old rural society and the skills and disciplines of the new urban and industrial world. I don't recall ever having read a more convincing account of the human costs which that enormous social transformation exacted."

In 1988 Gallagher published *All the Right Enemies: The Life and Murder of Carlo Tresca*. Tresca, an anarchist agitator and publicist, had come, in 1904, to America from Italy, in flight from a political trial. He began editing an Italian-language paper called *Il Proletario* and became deeply involved in the American pro-labor movement. Among those whom Tresca publicly criticized was the Italian mafia. By the 1920s Tresca had become an outspoken opponent of fascism and communism, both of which he lambasted in his paper *Il Martello* (The Hammer). Then, on January 11, 1943, he was shot to death. The mobster Carmine Galante was arrested for the crime. It remains unclear, however, who hired Galante, and Gallagher, in addition to offering a sociopolitical history of the period, turns her narrative into a detective story of sorts, as she unravels the evidence for and against the possible culprits. Was the mafia responsible, or could the communists have been behind Tresca's death?

Gallagher's intended publisher for *All the Right Enemies* rejected the book, calling it unpublishable, but she succeeded in selling the book to another house, which released it to mostly favorable reviews. Maurice Isserman, who reviewed the book for the *Nation* (October 10, 1988), thought that Gallagher's attempts to preserve suspense kept her from writing a fully developed work of history, but he concluded that "on the whole it is a fine, lively biography of an important and neglected figure in the history of American Radicalism." In *Commentary* (November 1988) Stephen Schwartz wrote, "The drawbacks of *All the Right Enemies* consist of a number of gaps and errors," but he acknowledged that Gallagher "has effectively recreated the atmosphere and attitudes of the Italian radical labor movement in America during the first half of this century, and she has extensively researched certain accessible but neglected subjects."

When Gallagher was caring for her parents during their final days, she took some notes about her feelings and observations. Only years later did she feel able to look over the notes, along with some old letters and photographs that had belonged to her parents. Initially she had intended to write a brief, single story about her parents, "to make order out of the total chaos of the last five years of their lives," as she told Gussow. Then, her third and current husband, the writer and editor Ben Sonnenberg, encouraged her to keep writing. "By the time I had done three [pieces]," she told Gussow, "I knew I could do a book."

How I Came Into My Inheritance: And Other True Stories (2001), which consists of a series of self-contained essays, begins with an account of her parents near the ends of their lives, when they are living in a dilapidated cottage built by her father. Her father's mind is failing him, allowing him to fall prey to a money-grubbing con man. Her mother, unable even to walk, has retreated into a fantasy world. As Laura Shaine Cunningham noted in the *New York Times* (March 4, 2001, on-line), Gallagher begins to imagine headlines: "STARVING OLD COUPLE EATEN BY RATS: MILLION DOLLARS FOUND IN MATTRESS." Eventually Gallagher is forced to move her parents to a nursing home. Many of the stories in the memoir tell of childhood memories, and other members of Gallagher's family people the book: Aunt Lily scrapes out a living by selling silk lingerie to prostitutes; Cousin Meyer, who lost most of his family during the Nazi invasion of Russia, commits suicide at 87. Gallagher also recalls her growth into adulthood, her career moves, and her book-writing experiences, eventually returning to the topic of her parents' deaths. Her grief over their passing hits her in stages, sometimes unexpectedly. "Grief took me by surprise," Gallagher writes, as quoted in the New Orleans *Times-Picayune* (March 3, 2001). "Would you believe, for instance, that while standing on line in the supermarket I'd be engulfed by a memory so overwhelming that I'd hear myself moaning aloud? When something like that happens in a public place, it's best to be nicely dressed." The memoir ends with a chapter called "Night Falls on Transylvania," in which Gallagher returns to her parents' homeland. In her typical wry fashion, she writes, as quoted by Cunningham, "And now in this odd and wracked corner of the world, on this hill . . . grief slipped away. I felt as happy as the day is long. Maybe it was the schnapps."

How I Came Into My Inheritance was a critical success and received positive reviews from such literary notables as Alice Munro, Susan Minot, and James Salter. A reviewer for the *Times-Picayune* wrote that it was "filled with hard won truths about history and love and writing, and of course, grief." Cunningham wrote of the memoir, "Gallagher's uncompromising presentation of both the beautiful and the abhorrent aspects of [her relatives'] lives has a cumulative effect. Readers who relish the truth—served straight up, 120 proof—will be intoxicated by her book and will accept her inheritance as their own."

Dorothy Gallagher and her husband live in New York. —P. G. H.

SUGGESTED READING: *Commentary* p 66+ Nov. 1988; *Commonweal* p628 Sep. 30, 1977; *The Nation* p322+ Oct. 10, 1988; *New York Times* (on-line) Mar. 4, 2001; *Raritan* p59+ Summer 1997; *Time* p157+ Mar. 19, 2001; New Orleans *Times-Picayune* E p1 Mar. 3, 2001

SELECTED BOOKS: *Hannah's Daughters: Six Generations of an American Family*, 1976; *All the Right Enemies: The Life and Murder of Carlo Tresca*, 1988; *How I Came Into My Inheritance: And Other True Stories*, 2001

Courtesy of Forrest Gander

Gander, Forrest

Jan. 21, 1956– Poet

Forrest Gander is regarded as one of the most important experimental poets writing today. His books are characterized by their unique subject matter, form, and rhythm, which vary from poem to poem. While many of his poems reflect his academic background in geology, Gander does not limit his topics to science or nature. He often tackles larger philosophical questions, such as reflections on the self, the complexities of relationships, or even the purposes of language itself. His most recent books include *Science and Steepleflower* (1998) and *Torn Awake* (2001). In addition, Gander translates Mexican poetry and has edited the bilingual anthology *Mouth to Mouth: 12 Contemporary Mexican Women Poets* (1993).

In 2002 Forrest Gander wrote the following autobiographical statement for *World Authors 1995-2000*: "Born in the Mojave Desert in 1956, I grew up mainly in Virginia. My physiological father ran a bar on Bleecker Street in Greenwich Village through the sixties and early seventies. It morphed from a college-crowd peanut bar to a gay bar to The Showboat to The Mod Scene as the times changed, but it was consistently a failure. My mother was a hugely loved elementary school teacher in Fairfax County, an avid birder, and a willing harborer of my extensive childhood bestiaries. My two younger sisters and I spent part of each summer with our father, but it was our mother who raised us until she remarried, when I was in tenth grade. We were glad to take on our new father's name, Gander, and to pick up two brothers, one my age and one the age of my oldest sister. It wasn't an easy joining, exactly, but we grew into each other like tree bark and barbed wire, and we became the same stuff.

"My grandfather was a Swede, and during my childhood, in the absence of my father, he had a profound influence on me. He loved birding and fishing, and we spent weekend afternoons on the C & O Canal, beside the Potomac, catching bluegills and snapping turtles, frogs and catfish. He used to declaim 19th-century poems with charismatic ebullience, and he taught me a rhymed prayer in Swedish that my sisters and I have recited before every Christmas dinner that I can remember. He and my mother, who would often read aloud poems by Edgar Allan Poe and Carl Sandburg, her favorites, introduced me to poetry.

"At The College of William and Mary, I majored in Geology and English, and I studied poetry with Peter Klappert, whose seriousness and rigor also impacted me. In Washington D.C., after graduation, I worked in sundry jobs before I was diagnosed with third stage melanoma. I had already lost my spleen, appendix, and tonsils, and had a hernia repaired. After the cancer operation, and the loss of some lymph nodes a year later, a fevered seriousness visited upon me. I looked like a veteran of some awful conflict and I was ready to change my life.

"I returned to the state of my birth and studied Creative Writing in San Francisco where the Language Poets were holding forth at 80 Langdon Street and all my poetic assumptions were called to question. At San Francisco State University I met C. D. Wright in the poetry room where I was reading my way through the notable library. On our first date, I prepared sushi and served raw octopus. We chewed through that milky, rubbery octopus, which is never supposed to be eaten uncooked, and we plotted a journey together.

"In 1981 we headed down to Mexico. I spoke some Spanish, but neither of us had been out of the country. We lived in Dolores Hidalgo for six months before my depressed immune system gave out to amoebic dysentery, colitis, and God knows what else. Before we returned to the U.S., though, I amassed a collection of poetry books by women who were writing the most interesting work that I was seeing, and who were also often founding presses to publish books that the more traditional and patriarchal venues would not. This body of poetry, translated and edited, became *Mouth to Mouth: Poems by Twelve Contemporary Mexican Women*. Since that anthology, I have published two more books of translations, *No Shelter: Selected Poems of Pura López-Colomé* and (with Kent Johnson) *Immanent Visitor: Selected Poems of Jaime Saenz*.

"Although I love the city, my grandfather's devotion to what we used to call Nature, our evening trips to the woods' edge where we tapped the ground to call out nightcrawlers, his knowledge of animal tracks and bird songs may underlie my passion for geology and some of my subsequent interest in Merleau-Ponty's phenomenology. My most recent books of poems, *Torn Awake* and *Science & Steepleflower*, explore, among other things, the complex collaboration between subjectivity and world, and they reveal my sense of selfhood as a construction of reciprocally reflective relations. The ceaseless shifting, within the poems, from particularity to abstraction, from lyric to meditation, and from figure to ground and back, enacts my own felt experience. In many poems, a linguistic materiality comes to the forefront and then recedes. In a corollary rhythmical movement within the larger rhythmical contraction and expansion of syntax and line, we see through the words; then syntax and lexicon thicken and we see the words themselves; and then we see through the words again to their meanings. Such orchestration provokes, I hope, a deeper physical engagement with the poem and a fuller emotional resonance.

"Now, in 2002, I am working on a new book of poems, a more supple, propulsive line. I am translating, and I am also developing a poem called 'Circle of Blades' as a dance performance. With C. D. Wright, I raise, so to speak, a brilliant and bullheaded teenage boy, Brecht. In the last five years, my professional position has peregrinated from Providence College to Harvard University to Brown University, where I am currently Professor of English Literature and Director of the Graduate Creative Writing Program."

For Christina Zawadiwsky, reviewing *Rush to the Lake* for *Small Press* (June 1989), Gander has been successful in uniting "image and idea. . . . Certainly idea and image marry and remarry in these poems, as symbolized in these lines from 'anti-image': 'No matter how good you are, something / happens and you live in the shadow of that event . . . the lonesome / cage burst out and something changed in me as I was falling." The images in the poems, with their juxtapositions of opposites, were what captured the admiration of Jessica Grim of *Library Journal* (August 1988). "The poems pose interesting polarities," Grim wrote, "between East and West, sexuality and asceticism, the pushes and pulls of life and language: '. . . The black bar in the gold circle / of the goat's eye / shifts.' It is a similar shift—a movement just a bit surprising . . . that produces the slight skew of images and language that makes these poems so interesting."

During the years 1991 to 1994, Gander produced three poetic works: *Eggplants and Lotus Root* in 1991, *Lynchburg* in 1993, and *Deeds of Utmost Kindness* in 1994. As an editor, Gander has taken seriously a mission to deliver to the English-speaking public the work of Mexican women poets. Reviewing *Mouth to Mouth: Poems by Twelve Contemporary Mexican Women* (1993), S. A. Cavallo noted in *Choice* (October 1993), "Gander, the editor and translator of some texts, is a poet, as are all of the translators. This explains their deftness at rendering rhythm, tone, and diction of originals."

Gander's 1998 collection, *Science and Steepleflower*, contains *Eggplants and Lotus Root*, first published as a chapbook in 1991. *Eggplants and Lotus Root* has a structure like that of a musical fugue, entwining recurring themes of sex, violence, and sensuous appreciation. Each of its five sections, "tea scripture," "monitory," "a macula of light," "close to water," and "moon in the afternoon," is divided into movements: "geometric losses," "violence's narrative continues," and "meditative." Tod Marshall, reviewing *Science and Steepleflower* in the *Boston Review* (March 1999), found the "paratactic energy, associative web, and unusual imagery" of *Eggplants and Lotus Root* "representative of Gander's methods."

In *Torn Awake*, his 2001 collection, Gander wrote about spirituality that is entirely apart from the strictures of organized religion: "I have lost the consolation of faith / though not the ambition to worship." David Kirby, in the *New York Times Book Review* (January 20, 2002), observed that it "isn't long before the ethereal quality of these poems begins to remind you of similar effects in the work of T. S. Eliot and the 17th-century Anglo-Welsh mystic Henry Vaughan, both of whom are cited as influences by Gander in his notes to this collection."

Gander has received many honors. He has twice been a recipient of the Gertrude Stein Award for Innovative North American Writing. He has also won an NEA Fellowship in Poetry and a Whiting Award. His most recent translations include *No Shelter: The Selected Poems of Pura López-Colomé* (2002) and *Immanent Visitor: Selected Poems of Jaime Saenz* (2002)

—S. Y.

SUGGESTED READING: *American Poetry Review* p29+ Oct. 2001; *Boston Review* (on-line) Mar. 1999; *Choice* p296 Oct. 1993; *Library Journal* p161 Aug. 1988; *The Nation* p29+ July 13, 1998; *Ploughshares* p58+ Winter 2002; *Publishers Weekly* p58+ Jan. 10, 1994; *Small Press* p48 June 1989; *Southern Review* p84+ Win. 1995; *Washington Post* X p12 May 2, 1999

SELECTED BOOKS: poetry—*Rush to the Lake*, 1988; *Eggplants and Lotus Root*, 1991; *Lynchburg*, 1993; *Deeds of Utmost Kindness*, 1994; *Science and Steepleflower*, 1998; *Torn Awake*, 2001; as editor and translator (with Zoe Anglesey)—*Mouth to Mouth: Poems by Twelve Contemporary Mexican Women*, 1993; *No Shelter: The Selected Poems of Pura López-Colomé*, 2002; *Immanent Visitor: Selected Poems of Jaime Saenz*, 2002

Courtesy of Homa & Sekey Books

Gao Xingjian

Jan. 4, 1940– Novelist; dramatist; Nobel laureate

In October 2000 the novelist, dramatist, and painter Gao Xingjian became the first Chinese writer ever to win the Nobel Prize for Literature. The Chinese government perceived the award as a slight, because Gao's work is banned by the Chinese Communist Party (CCP) and he has lived in France since 1987. Gao's plays first appeared in China during the 1980s and exerted a great influence by combining experimental Western dramatic forms with Chinese themes and traditional Chinese performance arts. Several of these avant-garde plays were denounced or banned by the CCP. The Swedish Academy, which selects the winners of the Nobel Prize, particularly cited Gao's epic novel *Soul Mountain* as a great work. It recounts a physical and spiritual journey through rural China using an unusual form characterized by frequent shifts in narrative voice. Gao is also an accomplished painter and has supported himself mainly through the sale of these works since he moved to France. His art work has been exhibited in many countries, and his ink paintings adorn the covers of his books.

The dissident exiled Chinese writer Gao Xingjian has won the Nobel Prize for Literature for the year 2000. Although he is one of the least political of Chinese dissidents, his victory instantly became a political issue as the prize was immediately denounced by the Beijing government. Even though Gao is an exile practically unknown to readers in contemporary China, and a French citizen since 1998, in the West he is likely to be turned into a representative of China. prize.

The writer and artist Gao Xingjian was born on January 4, 1940 in Ganzhou, China, located in the eastern province of Jiangxi. His father was a bank official, and his mother was an amateur actress who was a member of a YMCA theater troupe prior to the Communist Revolution. She also had a serious interest in Western literature. "Thanks to her," Gao told Alan Riding for the *New York Times* (November 21, 2000, on-line), "we had lots of books everywhere, translations of classics, Balzac, Zola, Steinbeck. That's why I began to read at a very early age." Gao was also a highly creative child. He told Riding, "I always had a dream of being a writer or actor or playwright. My mother and I would do little theater pieces at home. Sometimes my father was the only audience. I wrote my first novel when I was 10. It was an adventure story. At the same time, I painted. Early on, I was doing oils, water colors, calligraphy—all sorts of things." Educated in China's public school system, he earned a degree in French in 1962 from the Department of Foreign Languages in Beijing. His second language afforded him further exposure to Western literature, in particular experimental dramas by such writers as Eugene Ionesco, Samuel Beckett, Jean Genet, and the writings of theater theorist Antonin Artaud, all of whom he claims as key influences. As part of his studies, Gao translated the works of French surrealist poets, and he later translated French dramas into Chinese as well, including Ionesco's *The Bald Soprano*.

In the early 1960s, as part of the economic initiative known as the Great Leap Forward, Gao, like many others, was sent to a re-education camp where he labored for six years as an agricultural worker. His mother drowned in an accident at one such camp. Gao wrote extensively during this period, although, due in part to warnings from friends, he did not attempt to publish his work. In 1966 Mao Zedong, the chairman of the Chinese Communist Party (CCP), launched the Cultural Revolution, his attempt to bring the Party back under his control and to eliminate elitist and capitalist elements from society. During this tumultuous episode in Chinese history, Gao's own wife denounced him as a traitor to the Party, and Gao felt it necessary to burn a suitcase full of stories, plays, and essays that he thought might incriminate him. "In China, I could not trust anyone, not even my family," Gao is quoted as saying in the *Detroit News* (October 13, 2000).

In 1979, after the Cultural Revolution had ended, Gao began to publish short stories, essays, and dramas in Chinese literary magazines and he was able to travel abroad, to France and Italy. In 1981 he published a collection of essays, which has been published in English as *Contemporary Technique and National Character in Fiction*, and which sparked a debate in China about modernism versus realism. In 1985 he published a narrative work, which can be translated as "A Pigeon Called Red Beak", and a collection of plays. Another book of nonfiction, which can be translated as "In Search of a Modern Form of Dramatic Representation," was published in 1987.

Several of Gao's plays were performed in China in the 1980s while he was a writer and director with the People's Art Theater in Beijing. There, according to Anthony Kuhn for the *Los Angeles Times* (October 16, 2000), "Gao was part of a group of directors who used bold visual imagery, lighting, sound, and acting techniques to introduce Chinese audiences to postmodern Western drama." Gao's plays were among the first to take inspiration from Western dramatic forms in order to create a new genre of contemporary Chinese theater. Horace Engdahl, the permanent secretary of the Swedish Academy, stated at a press conference in Stockholm that "Gao has been one of the most important writers in creating what didn't exist before: a spoken drama in China as distinct from music drama, dance, and the old traditions," as quoted in the *Los Angeles Times* (October 13, 2000). An October 12, 2000 press release published on the Nobel e-Museum Web site notes that Gao's plays are also influenced by such traditional and popular Chinese performance arts as masked drama, shadow plays, drumming, and opera. Through his plays and his involvement with the People's Art Theater, Gao was part of a burgeoning avant-garde arts movement in China that has continued following his departure and, due in part to a loosening of governmental restraints on art, flourished.

In 1982 Gao made his debut as a playwright with *Warning Signal*, the "first experimental play staged in Beijing in years," according to John-Thor Dahlburg for the *Los Angeles Times* (October 13, 2000). Deemed a success within the avant-garde community, the play provoked a polemic from the government but was not banned. In 1983 Gao further established his reputation with a production of *Bus Stop*, perhaps his best-known play, which he'd written in 1981 but was considered too experimental to be performed at that time. Bearing similarities to Samuel Beckett's *Waiting for Godot*, *Bus Stop* implies that life itself is a form of waiting. The play begins with eight people waiting in line for a bus at a bus stop. Though their hopes that the bus will come are often aroused, they are repeatedly disappointed. One day they realize with shock that they have been waiting for the bus for years. Simultaneously, they discover that they are now only seven; a silent man left the group long ago, they now remember. A spotlight suddenly illuminates the man, behind the audience on a raised platform, and the people at the bus stop are filled with remorse. They, too, should have walked. As the play closes, each of the actors addresses a different section of the audience at once, ruminating over the time they have wasted. In a critical essay in *Modern Drama* (Fall 1998) comparing *Bus Stop* and *Waiting for Godot*, Harry H. Kuoshu noted that Beckett's play seems to view waiting as inherent to the human condition, while Gao's seems to ascribe it to the inhibiting presence of a repressive political climate. "*Bus Stop*, after all, is not as nihilist as *Waiting for Godot*," Kuoshu wrote. "It attributes existential absurdity more to the political result of totalitarian control than to an epistemological crisis." According to Dahlburg, a Chinese official denounced *Bus Stop* as "spiritual pollution," a term used to refer to undesirable Western influences, and called it "the most pernicious text written since the creation of the People's Republic [of China]." Rather than deliver a public self-criticism as was ordered by the Party, Gao embarked on a 10-month walking tour, tracing the course of the Yangzi River in southwestern China from its source all the way to the coast. This trip figured largely in *Soul Mountain*, which he had begun writing in 1982. "I said to myself, 'I have already subjected myself to self-censorship, and still I was attacked,'" Gao told Alan Riding. "So I started writing a novel just for myself without thinking of having it published."

In 1985 a production of a new play by Gao, *Wild Man*, was mounted at the People's Art Theater and provoked derision from the CCP. Around that time, according to Riding, the political climate had again shifted and Gao could no longer publish his work. In 1986 Gao's play *The Other Shore* was banned by the party, and none of his plays have been produced in China since. Following the reception given *The Other Shore*, Gao was blacklisted as a writer, but he was allowed out of the country as a painter. In 1987 he left China and about a year later established residence in Paris as a political refugee. After hundreds of pro-democracy demonstrators were killed in Beijing's Tiananmen Square in 1989, Gao formally withdrew from the CCP. Following the publication of his play *Fugitives*, which uses the Tiananmen Square incident as its backdrop, he was declared persona non grata in China, and all of his writings were banned by the government.

A number of Gao's works have been translated into English, including *Wild Man*, published in 1990, and *Fugitives*, published in 1993. In 1999 the Chinese University Press, in Hong Kong, published a collection of five of Gao's plays translated by Gilbert C. F. Fong, under the title *The Other Shore: Plays by Gao Xingjian*. Included in the volume are *The Other Shore, Between Life and Death, Dialogue and Rebuttal, Nocturnal Wanderer*, and *Weekend Quartet*. The description of the collection posted on the Chinese University Press Web site reads, "One finds poetry, comedy, as well as tragedy in the plays, which are graced by beautiful language and original imagery. Combining Zen philosophy and a modern world view, they serve to illuminate the gritty realities of life, death, sex, loneliness, and exile, all essential concerns in Gao's understanding of the existence of modern man."

Soul Mountain was first published in Taiwan in 1990. An English translation, by Mabel Lee, was published in 1999 in Australia, where it became a best-seller. The novel recounts a spiritual journey through remote regions of China and is told from a variety of perspectives. The narrator speaks in the first-, second-, and third-person, which is also characteristic of the characters in Gao's dramas. "The book is a tapestry of narratives with several protagonists who reflect each other and may represent aspects of one and the same ego," according to the Swedish Academy press release. "With his unrestrained use of personal pronouns Gao creates lightning shifts of perspective and compels the reader to question all confidences. This approach derives from his dramas, which often require actors to assume a role and at the same time describe it from the outside. I, you, and he/she become names of fluctuating inner distances." During the course of the journey, the narrator encounters many strange people and phenomena. Shamanistic beliefs and customs still hold sway in these regions of China, and in the novel old myths seem to come to life. At one point, the head of a village encourages the narrator to visit a magical hunter named Grandpa Stone, who once wove enchantments but has been dead for many years and supposedly still lies in his hut impervious to decomposition. His magical rifle, which never misses its target, is said to be still hanging in the hut as well. The narrator's journey in *Soul Mountain* is also an escape from the confines of intellectualism and the literary life. The narrator, who like Gao is a writer, feels that his concepts of life have often kept him from experiencing life more directly. "In those contaminated surroundings I was taught that life was the source of literature," says the narrator, "that literature had to be faithful to life, faithful to real life. My mistake was that I had alienated myself from life and ended up turning my back on real life. However, real life is not the same as manifestations of life." The Swedish Academy cited *Soul Mountain* as "one of those singular literary creations that seem impossible to compare to anything but themselves."

When Gao received the phone call informing him that he'd won the Nobel Prize, "They announced it to me very simply and told me I had to prepare a 45-minute speech. I said that's very long," Gao told Reuters Television in French after receiving the award, as reported by Dahlburg. In China, the Academy's choice was roundly criticized. Some Chinese intellectuals argued that there were plenty of Chinese authors still living in the country and sanctioned by its government who were of greater stature than Gao. China's Foreign Ministry, according to Anthony Kuhn, said the decision "shows again the Nobel literature prize has been used for ulterior political motives, and it is not worth commenting on." Shu Yi, the head of China's National Museum of Modern Chinese Literature, in Beijing, had a more moderate reaction. "We should congratulate [Gao] for his award," Kuhn quoted Shu as saying. Shu continued, however, "The award is stimulating and provocative for China. It makes us feel awkward—we don't know whether to laugh or cry."

On December 7, 2000 Gao gave his Nobel lecture, focusing on the importance of keeping literature free from the constraints of politics, commercialism, and reductive literary theories. "What I want to say here is that literature can only be the voice of the individual and this has always been so," Gao said, as translated from the Chinese on the Nobel e-museum Web site. "Once literature is contrived as the hymn of the nation, the flag of the race, the mouthpiece of a political party or the voice of a class or group, it can be employed as a mighty and all-engulfing tool of propaganda. However, such literature loses what is inherent in literature, ceases to be literature, and becomes a substitute for power and profit." The most valuable aspect of literature, said Gao, is that it is a "spiritual communication" between the reader and an author. "During the years when Mao Zedong implemented total dictatorship . . . to write even in secret was to risk one's life. . . . It was only during this period when it was utterly impossible for literature that I came to comprehend why it was so essential: literature allows a person to preserve a human consciousness."

Soul Mountain was published to great acclaim in the United States in 2000. Gao's second novel, *One Man's Bible*, was published in English in 2001 or 2002. The latter is an autobiographical fiction based on Gao's experiences during the Cultural Revolution. Gao continues to live and work in the Paris suburb of Bagnolet. He was awarded the Chevalier de l'Ordre des Arts et des Lettres, the French government's equivalent of knighthood, in 1992.

—D. C.

SUGGESTED READING: *Denver Post* Oct. 13, 2000; *Detroit News* Oct. 13, 2000; *Los Angeles Times* Oct. 13, 2000, Oct. 16, 2000; *Modern Drama* Fall 1998; *New York Times* (on-line) Nov. 21, 2000, Dec. 8, 2000; Nobel e-Museum Web site

SELECTED WORKS IN ENGLISH TRANSLATION: drama—*Fugitives* (in *Chinese Writing and Exile*), 1993; *The Other Shore: Plays by Gao Xingjian*, 1999; fiction—*Soul Mountain*, 1999; *One's Man's Bible*, 2002; nonfiction—*Contemporary Technique and National Character in Fiction*, 1981.

Gardam, Jane

July 11, 1928– Novelist, short-story writer; children's writer

"I've never stopped writing stories, ever since I was a child," Jane Gardam explained to Kathy O'Shaugnessy for the London *Daily Telegraph* (April 13, 1996). "I think it's a sort of Yorkshire-Cumbrian thing," she added, referring to growing up in Yorkshire, England, and holidaying in Cumbria—a popular spot in the northwest of England—where her grandfather had a farm. "We were always saying, Mrs. So-and-so came by this morning; you've never seen anything like it!—and off we'd go. Things shaped themselves into anecdotes." Despite her love of storytelling and writing, Gardam didn't start publishing books until she was more than 40 years old. She first became known for her children's stories and soon began publishing adult fiction as well, including such notable novels as *Black Faces, White Faces, God on the Rocks, Crusoe's Daughter, The Queen of the Tambourine, Faith Fox,* and *The Flight of the Maidens.* With her distinctively English style, she routinely inspires comparisons to such writers as Jane Austen and Barbara Pym. For someone as laden with awards as Gardam—she has won the David Higham Prize, the Katherine Mansfield Prize, the Winifred Holtby Prize, and two Whitbread Awards—she is surprisingly little known, perhaps owing to her earlier reputation as a children's writer; enthusiastic critics have thus hailed her as the "invisible novelist" and the "unsung heroine" of English fiction.

In an autobiographical statement submitted to the *Fifth Book of Junior Authors and Illustrators* (1983), Gardam writes: "I was born in Yorkshire, England, by the cold North Sea, but I spent three months of every year on my grandparents' farm in the English Lake District—Arthur Ransome, Beatrix Potter country. When I was seventeen I went to college in London, did research there afterwards, became a journalist, got married, and had three children. I have lived in London now for thirty years—but I go 'home' as much as possible—and we have a little house at the head of one of the English dales. When I go back I begin to speak with a Northern accent. Everybody knows me and remembers my family and is interested in my children as though they were country children. They even like my London lawyer husband who is what they call a foreigner. All my children's books have been about the North, but not because I yearn for the past or for my childhood. Probably because the people up there seem to talk more, and better, and have more dramatic lives than in towns or in the South. And the weather's exciting.

"I wrote about girls first—a five-year-old, then a twelve-year-old, then a sixteen-year-old, then a younger teenager who ends up middle-aged. Lucy, Jessica, Athene, Marigold. I like Jessica (*A Long Way from Verona*) best, but I'm glad she's not my daughter. Too exhausting. I'd have got no books written. Then I wrote two First Readers, *Bridget and William* (1981) and *Horse* (1982), because so many late readers have said to me, 'Why should all reading books be so young?' Then I got tired of girls and wrote *The Hollow Land*, which is mainly about a town boy and a country boy who are friends all their lives. They go on being friends until 1999, when the book ends. I enjoyed putting a toe into the future. The illustrations in this book are all of our house in the country and the places and people round about, even our kitchen furniture.

"I never write about people I know, but I never write about people I don't know—i.e., have not experienced in some way. My characters have bits of many people in them, but, if they work, all the bits have to be swirled up together like in an electric mixer and come out transformed: like the oil and eggs in mayonnaise.

"I didn't try to publish anything until I was nearly forty. I am glad. What I wrote earlier was very heavy and labored and earnest and boring. I didn't work at all for very long after I was married. I meant to. I left my desk at the newspaper to have my first son and intended to be back in three weeks. But it was fifteen years before I took the typewriter out of its case again. I had three children who were always getting ill or doing something sensational at the wrong moment. My husband became a Queen's Counsel and being his wife became almost a job in itself. We have traveled to and worked in Hong Kong, Singapore, the West Indies, Indonesia, and Bangladesh as well as in Europe. I didn't try to write until the third child was at school all day—not on principle (I think they'd have quite liked me out of the way), but because I couldn't concentrate. My son Timothy is now a producer at BBC Television; my daughter, Kit, is doing research in Mediaeval History and spends her time crawling about cathedral floors with a measuring tape; my son Tom, when not climbing 500-foot rock faces on the end of a rope, is still at school. For four years he went to an American school in London—he was a late reader and we were told that Americans took dyslexia seriously. You do—he was reading in a month. So we have a lot to thank America for. My American publisher, Susan Hirschman of Greenwillow, invited me to America in 1979 and we went to California and the East Coast and to Madison [Wisconsin] in the middle. Meeting readers from far away is one of [life's] great amazements. One of the big prizes. Just seeing America itself, and this year as a guest of the Adelaide Arts Festival, Australia, are the most unexpected and wonderful prizes of all.

"I don't write for children only but for everyone. It makes me sad that those who read my 'children's books' have never heard of my 'adult books'—and vice versa. My favorite author is Dickens—with a dozen others thundering at his heels.

"There is no book, however, I would not put down to go to the theatre. When I am old I want to live in a rabbit-hole house under London's Waterloo Bridge and then I can totter out each night to a play not five minutes from home. Of course I'll pick the book up again as soon as I get back. I hope I may even be writing it."

Jane (Pearson) Gardam was born on July 11, 1928 in Coatham, Yorkshire, England, where her father, William, taught math and physics at Sir William Turner's School, a boys' institution. She started writing shortly after entering school at age five, but lost her earliest stories when they caught fire in her bedroom fireplace. "I remember not minding much. Thinking—oh well, I'll write it again," she said, as quoted in *Major Authors and Illustrators for Children and Young Adults* (1992). "How easy it is to write, before the age of ten."

Gardam received a scholarship to study English at Bedford College, in London. "It was probably the nicest time of my life," she told Candida Crewe for the London *Times* (May 10, 1997). "I had so longed for more theatre, more books—there was only a very small library in Coatham—and to see some paintings. And in London, there it all was. I didn't want to go home for the holidays." After receiving her B.A., with honors, in 1949, she stayed on to do graduate work in 18th-century literature, but had to return home when her grant ran out. She found a job proofreading for *Weldons Ladie's Journal*, but was let go when she didn't take seriously the content of the publication, which dealt heavily with the aesthetics of flower arrangement and other domestic topics. She met David Gardam, a young naval officer turned lawyer, and married him in 1952. She started working as an assistant editor at the literary weekly *Time and Tide*, a position she enjoyed as it enabled her to work with such writers as T. S. Eliot. She left *Time and Tide* in 1955 to give birth to her first son. She had two more children, and raising them kept her too busy to write. However, "as soon as the last of them was at school," she told Anne Chisholm for the *Sunday Telegraph* (January 19, 1992), "I began writing at once: the very day the last one was deposited at the school gate I exploded and have not stopped writing since."

In 1971 Gardam published her first two books of children's fiction: *A Few Fair Days* was a collection of nine short stories about a girl's life in pre-war England; *A Long Way from Verona* is a novel narrated by a young girl named Jessica Vye, a preacher's daughter living in Britain during World War II. The latter work was highly praised both in England and in the United States. Suzanne Curley, in *New York Newsday* (October 9, 1988), called it "beautifully written. . . . [Jessica's] passage through her early teens amidst air raids, food rationing and first encounters with the opposite sex is told with wit and grace." *A Long Way from Verona* was named a Notable Book by the American Library Association in 1972.

After writing another children's book, *The Summer after the Funeral* (1973), Gardam published her first work of adult fiction, *Black Faces, White Faces* (1975). A collection of linked short stories set in Jamaica, it won Britain's David Higham Prize for fiction and the Royal Society of Literature's Winifred Holtby Award. "Gardam has proved to be especially good at observing the receding tide of British imperialism and the aftermath, poignant and comic, of lost power on ex-governors and their former subjects," Anne Chisholm wrote of the book. In 1976 the volume was published in the United States as *Pineapple Bay Hotel*. Gardam's next children's novel, *Bilgewater* (1976), is about a young girl growing up in a boys' school where her father, Bill, is schoolmaster. Bilgewater, a distortion of "Bill's daughter," is her nickname. Gardam subsequently wrote *God on the Rocks* (1979), which was a runner-up for the Booker Prize and made into a television movie, and *The Sidmouth Letters* (1980), a collection of short stories. *The Hollow Land* (1981), her next effort, is a collection of interlinked stories set in England's Cumberland Fells, where a London family is vacationing and getting to know their farmer neighbors. That work won Gardam her first Whitbread Award.

The Pangs of Love (1983) is a work of adult fiction containing 11 short stories; the title notwithstanding, they are not about traditional romance. The title story's heroine is the younger sister of the mermaid who died for love in one of Hans Christian Anderson's fairy tales. Gardam's mermaid is a new breed of woman—she decries the subordination of women and the lack of self-respect that longing for romance can lead to. She demands a test of her would-be prince, but the sacrifice she requires (his legs, his tongue, and other important anatomical features) proves beyond his capacity. "This story is the most gutsy of the collection," Nigella Lawson wrote for the London *Financial Times* (February 26, 1983). "Witty, innovative, ironic, its style—if it is at all possible to imagine—is a mixture of Damon Runyon and Jane Austen." *The Pangs of Love* won the 1984 Katherine Mansfield Award.

Gardam's next two children's books were *Kit* (1984) and *Kit in Boots* (1986). Gillian Cross, in a London *Daily Telegraph* (November 14, 1998) review of a 1988 reissue that combined the two tales into one volume, *The Kit Stories*, wrote, "Kit does nothing more frantic than deal with an escaped bull and visit London to be an artist's bridesmaid, but she does them in a real world, full of solid characters. Jane Gardam writes with the calm authority of someone who does not need to bludgeon or astound her audience. She simply tells the stories. That is the rarest skill of all."

Crusoe's Daughter, Gardam's 1986 adult book, tells the story of a girl named Polly Flint. After her mother's death, her father, a sea captain, leaves Polly in the care of her aunts, who live in an isolated salt marsh in northeast England. Her father then dies at sea. A precocious child, the orphaned Polly reads extensively, learning about the world from such books as George Eliot's *Middlemarch* and Daniel Defoe's *Robinson Crusoe*. The hero of the latter book proves to be an important source of strength and inspiration for her: "He didn't go mad," she says, as quoted by a reviewer for *People* (April 1, 1986). "He was brave. He was wonderful. He was like women have to be almost always, on an island. Stuck. Imprisoned. The only way to survive it is to say it's God's will." Enduring difficulty and hardship is a recurring theme in the novel, which follows Polly through several reversals, from the death of a childhood friend to her abandonment by Theo, the son of a German-Jewish family, whom she loves.

Linda Barrett Osborne, writing for the *Washington Post* (April 21, 1986), praised *Crusoe's Daughter* as the "story of an indomitable woman who survives disappointment and solitude with her lively spirit intact." Osborne wrote that the novel "unfolds with the assurance of writing that creates a completely imagined world. . . . It is beautifully detailed and self-contained, rendered with clarity and humor." The *People* reviewer described *Crusoe's Daughter* as "deeply plotted, wonderfully old-fashioned," and wrote, "This post-Victorian charmer is an engrossing delight."

Gardam's next work, *The Queen of the Tambourine* (1991), chronicles the descent into madness of Eliza Peabody, a middle-aged woman living in a prosperous neighborhood in south London. The book is composed of a series of letters that Eliza, a gossip and a busybody, writes to a neighbor named Joan. In the first letters Eliza smugly patronizes Joan for making too much of a hurt leg, explaining that her work with "the Dying" at an AIDS hospice has taught her that life is "a wonderful thing." After Joan suddenly departs—abandoning her husband and children to go off and see the world—Eliza's letters (some not sent) lengthen and gradually become more delusional and preposterous; Joan never writes back. As the novel progresses Gardam's clever social comedy becomes a study of Eliza's emotional breakdown.

Michael Upchurch, writing for the *Seattle Times* (August 11, 1996), called *The Queen of the Tambourine* "hilarious yet poignant," and asserted, "[In] this jigsaw puzzle of a novel, [Gardam] keeps up the suspense to the end, writing like a sorceress in the meantime." A writer for *Kirkus Reviews* (June 1, 1995) called the book "a loony, funny tale," and deemed Gardam "an author with a refreshing take on the familiar." Gardam received the Whitbread Book of the Year Award for *The Queen of the Tambourine*.

Although Gardam does not usually cater to contemporary literary fashion, she explained to Anne Chisholm, "I did want *Queen of the Tambourine* to reflect the times we live in. . . . The disintegration of the woman mirrors the disintegration of the nation." She told Amanda Craig for the London *Independent* (January 11, 1992), "I'm very interested in the theory of madness. . . . However, it would be more true to say that what I really write about is sanity: the idea that often you can cure yourself if, like Eliza, you're brave enough to look. My characters become sane."

The characters in *Going Into a Dark House* (1994), a collection of short stories, are largely middle-aged women and their mothers, or elderly mothers and their sons. They are sometimes haunted by ghosts, but are more threatened by the specters that appear in old-age—death, senility, and loneliness. "Flawlessly written," Victoria Glendinning wrote in a review for the London *Daily Telegraph* (October 1, 1994), "with dialogue so angular and sparky, and descriptions—of landscapes and food—so lovely and hard-edged, that they are a revelation of the extraordinary effects ordinary language can achieve." "In these carefully crafted stories," Fiona Patterson wrote for the London *Times* (September 29, 1994), "Gardam shows us the ageing with the kind of perceptiveness and humour usually found in Barbara Pym. . . . She can capture loneliness, and everyday pain with a rare gentleness that has come to be expected of her." Gardam received the Macmillan Silver Pen Award for *Going Into a Dark House*.

Faith Fox (1996) revolves around a baby named Faith, born to Holly and Andrew Fox, in Surrey, in the south of England. When Holly dies in childbirth, Faith is left in the hands of her overworked and seemingly indifferent father. After initially placing her in the care of an upper-crust friend, Andrew decides to send the baby north for a while. There she is looked after by the Fox's lower-class relatives: the quirky uncle Jack and his wife Jocasta (who live in a religious community in the Northumberland moors), and the quarrelsome grandparents, Toots and Dolly. "As north and south become entangled over the fate of baby Faith, the novel becomes a cluttered farce of distrusting relations, minor betrayals and encounters between the conventional and the eccentric," Sylvia Brownrigg wrote for the *Guardian* (May 3, 1996). Although Brownrigg noted that Gardam "has a wonderful ear for the absurd, and an eye for the mad colours of local costume and ritual," she added that the book's conclusion "offers less satisfaction than the comic pleasures of the jumbled, vivid sightseeing along the way." Boyd Tonkin wrote for the London *Independent* (March 8, 1997), "There has always been a blackly comic streak buried in Jane Gardam's novels and here it finds full and exuberant expression. On one level, Gardam's tale is a simple story of the great North/South divide—the geographical split that shuts off one end of Britain from the other, but it is also a story about love and redemption, sex and death recounted in dazzling style."

Gardam's darker comedic impulses come to the fore in the collection of short stories *Missing the Midnight: Hauntings and Grotesques* (1997). In the title piece, a distraught college girl has failed her exams, lost her lover, and become ill with appendicitis; she is traveling home to visit her family on Christmas Eve and sorely dreading the encounter. "With economy and a fine ear, Gardam plays out the dull rhythms of the London-bound train and the narrator's own earthbound, imprisoned spirit to their inevitable conclusion," Fiona Maddocks wrote for the *Manchester Guardian Weekly* (January 4, 1998). The title story is one of five labeled "carols" in the volume, all of which are variously related to the Christmas season. Each of next five tales, called "grotesques," features a character who exhibits some type of physical oddity—a man who works at a chemical plant and has an unexplained diamond embedded in his neck and a magazine editor whose ears begin to sprout long golden hair, for example. "These skillful, modern-day fairy stories touch the darkest recess of the imagination, producing strangely magical tales of the night," Claire Allfree and Daniel Britten wrote for the London *Daily Telegraph* (January 2, 1999). "These delicious horrors delight the soul while sending shivers down the spine."

The coming-of-age story Gardam presents in her most recent novel, *The Flight of the Maidens* (2001), takes place during the summer of 1946. Three girls living in a Yorkshire seaside town have won prestigious university scholarships, and the book follows them in the few weeks before they depart for school. Hetty Fallows is trying to wrest her independence from her overbearing and highly possessive mother, Kitty. Hetty seeks escape in reading, perhaps inspired by her father; an intellectual who suffered emotional damage in the trenches of World War I, he is now a gravedigger with a philosophical bent. Hetty's best friend, Una Vane—whose father committed suicide some time ago—feels responsible for her eccentric, widowed mother. Una is involved with a young leftist, who teaches her about politics as well as love. Lieselotte Klein is a German-Jewish refugee living with a Quaker family; she arrived in England in 1939 on the Kindertransport, in which trains filled with Jewish children escaped Nazi Germany; her parents' fate is not known. The shadows of the war loom large in Gardam's novel; the memories of antiaircraft fire, food rationing, and kisses stolen by parading soldiers are still fresh in the girls' minds, forming the backdrop for their sometimes painful struggles into adulthood.

"Gardam's characters are acutely and compassionately observed," Juliet Barker wrote for the *Atlantic Monthly* (July 1, 2001), in a review of *The Flight of the Maidens*. "[The] lean, fast-paced prose is at turns hugely funny and deeply moving. We care about her characters and want to know what happens to them." Charles Taylor wrote for *New York Newsday* (August 5, 2001), "The *Flight of the Maidens* offers the pleasures of a straightforward narrative, well-drawn characters and that particular province of the English novel, the accumulation of detail that defines social status and thus outlook, prospects, character." He continued, "Gardam does it all with a nice balance of compassion and dry wit that keeps the emotional passages from descending into gush." A critic for *Kirkus Reviews* (June 1, 2001) described the story as "essentially familiar," but found the book "redeemed by invigorating detail (especially the piecemeal portrayal of how wartime hardships were patiently endured)

and an elegiac affection for the excesses and absurdities of youth on the puzzling, intimidating threshold of maturity."

Gardam lives in a large historic house in Sandwich, Kent, in England, but still spends her summers in Yorkshire, where she has a farmhouse. Many reporters have commented that her appearance is that of an average middle-aged, middle-class Englishwoman. "Jane Gardam looks like the archetypical lady who writes fiction as a supplement to needlepoint," Amanda Craig wrote. Anne Chisholm commented on "her neat full skirts and jumpers, smart but sensible low-heeled shoes, pretty rounded face and slightly shaggy silvery hair." Chisholm added, "Gardam's reassuring appearance and manner serve, perhaps deliberately, as a cover for an unnerving preoccupation with suffering and a taste for subversive comedy; and her impeccable sense of structure and limpid prose are weapons deployed to expose the strategies whereby middle-class England has always attempted to hide from awkwardness and avoid emotional extremes." Gardam has insisted, "There's no point in writing anything if it doesn't disturb you in some way," as quoted by Kathy O'Shaughnessy. "A novel must be about what everyone is thinking, but nobody dares say. And then reading it, people say, 'Oh yes, God, we don't usually admit this.' That's why it's never boring to write, because you go deep down. You talk about what people are really thinking."

—*A. I. C.*

SUGGESTED READING: *Atlantic Monthly* p161 July 1, 2001; (London) *Daily Telegraph* p7 Oct. 1, 1994, p4 Apr. 13, 1996, p4 Nov. 14, 1998, p4 Jan. 2, 1999; (London) *Financial Times* I p14 Feb. 26, 1983; *Guardian* T p17 May 3, 1996; (London) *Independent* p27 Jan. 11, 1992, p8 Mar. 8, 1997; *Kirkus Reviews* June 1, 1995, June 1, 2001; *Manchester Guardian Weekly* p22 Jan. 4, 1998; *New York Newsday* p19 Oct. 9, 1988; *People* p18 Apr. 1, 1986; *Seattle Times* M p3 Aug. 11, 1996; (London) *Times* Sep. 29, 1994, May 10, 1997; *Washington Post* B p3 Apr. 21, 1986; *Major Authors and Illustrators for Children and Young Adults*, 1992

SELECTED BOOKS: *A Long Way from Verona*, 1971; *Black Faces, White Faces*, 1975; *Bilgewater*, 1976; *God on the Rocks*, 1979; *The Pangs of Love*, 1983; *Crusoe's Daughter*, 1986; *The Queen of the Tambourine*, 1991; *Going into a Dark House*, 1994; *Faith Fox*, 1996; *Missing the Midnight*, 1997; *The Flight of the Maidens*, 2001

Diane Samuels/Courtesy of W. W. Norton & Co., Inc.

Garfield, Simon

(?)– Nonfiction writer

Simon Garfield, the popular British journalist, has made a name for himself by writing unique and insightful histories. His books are best described as pieces of extended journalism; they are thoroughly researched and draw on extensive interviews. Most of his works have been explorations into various subcultures of contemporary British society. His most recent book, *Mauve: How One Man Invented a Colour That Changed the World* (2001), stretches farther back in time, to mid-19th-century Britain, when the first artificial dye was created, and expands to shed light on scientific progress, industry, and medicine. He has written two books about the music business, *Money for Nothing: Greed and Exploitation in the Music Industry* (1986) and *Expensive Habits: The Dark Side of the Music Industry* (1986), and three micro-histories, or works that examine a place and time through a particular lens: *The End of Innocence: Britain in the Time of AIDS* (1994), winner of the Somerset Maugham Award; *The Wrestling* (1996), about the popularity of that sport, in Britain, in the 1960s and 1970s; and *The Nation's Favourite: The True Adventures of Radio 1* (1998), about the battles over who would define popular culture.

The End of Innocence: Britain in the Time of AIDS was the first of Simon Garfield's books to garner widespread media attention. It is a stark portrayal of what is widely regarded as a failure on the part of the British government to respond adequately to the problem of AIDS. Relying on interviews with doctors, scientists, activists, politicians, and people who have tested positive for HIV, including the film director Derek Jarman and the singer Holly Johnson, the book documents events in the history of AIDS from the early 1980s until its publication, in 1994. The rapid escalation of the epidemic during this time was formidable: In March of 1983, there were six reported cases of AIDS in Britain; by June of 1994, 6,388 people had died of the disease. Garfield traces the attempts of individuals and organizations to raise awareness and initiate appropriate public policy in the face of enormous reluctance and often outright hostility from a government that was woefully ignorant about the realities of this epidemic.

Featured prominently in Garfield's account is Norman Fowler, Britain's secretary of state for social services during the mid-1980s, who reportedly remarked to a colleague at a meeting, "Oral sex? I had no idea you get [AIDS] from talking dirty," as quoted by Stuart Jeffries in the (London) *Guardian* (November 25, 1994). Yet compared to his colleagues, Fowler emerges as one of the more soberminded members of his government. He resisted the efforts of groups like the Conservative Family Campaign, whose proffered solution to the AIDS epidemic was to isolate all the infected and recriminalize homosexuality. An admirable figure to emerge from Garfield's reporting is Sir Donald Acheson, England's chief medical officer for most of the 1980s, who managed to convince the Cabinet of the importance of dealing with the AIDS crisis. Acheson encountered a great deal of resistance; according to Garfield, Margaret Thatcher, then prime minister, believed that AIDS was a small problem, confined to the homosexual community, and accordingly one that the gay community should handle by themselves.

The End of Innocence was widely reviewed. Nicholas Royle, writing for the (London) *Guardian* (November 19, 1995), described it as a "levelheaded, exhaustively researched and utterly reliable report on the history and current state of AIDS [in the UK]. . . . Not only are the facts assembled with great clarity and authority, but the human stories told here by Garfield's interviewees, in a variety of voices and reflecting a range of experiences, instantly acquaint the reader with the grim reality of the disease. By choosing selectively to dramatise the subject without either sensationalising it or relying on the accumulation of information, Garfield delivers a gripping read." While critics were mostly appreciative of Garfield's efforts, some felt that the book would have benefitted from a more pronounced critical dimension. Virginia Berridge, in a review for the *British Medical Journal* (December 10, 1994), argued that "the journalistic format defeats the author's intentions. Garfield reduces the social and structural to the personal. Delay by the government and the Medical Research Council, homophobia, and the 'degaying' of AIDS may be valid explanations for some issues, but the evidence needs to be assessed and contextualised. . . . The book has no concluding analysis." Garfield's book was adapted into a television special for BBC2, by Nigel Evans. Lynne Truss, writing in the (London)

Times (December 6, 1995), judged *Fine Cut: The End of Innocence*, which aired in 1995, to be "powerful, cool and intelligent. . . the best programme yet made about AIDS in this country."

Following his sobering research into the AIDS epidemic, Garfield next turned his attention to the popularity of wrestling in the Britain of the 1960s and 1970s. His book on the subject, *The Wrestling* (1996), is an oral history compiled through interviews with famous wrestlers and other men and women associated with the sport. Although Garfield includes commentary from such cultural critics as Roland Barthes and Peter Blake, he mostly lets the wrestlers speak for themselves. One such figure is wrestling legend Mick McManus, who related the following anecdote to Garfield, as quoted by Robert Crampton in a review of the book for the (London) *Times* (December 7, 1996): "At the ringside, the ladies would be running up. I used to make sure that I didn't get too near the ropes, otherwise someone came up and banged you on the head with a shoe or a bag. If you get banged on the head with a high-heel shoe, especially with the heel, it can give you a nasty lump." Crampton gave *The Wrestling* a favorable review, noting that "this entertaining, poignant and occasionally extremely funny tribute to the grapple game reads very easily indeed." Crampton also praised Garfield's handling of composition and tone: "Garfield allows his subjects to describe the rise and fall of their sport with humour, intelligence and affection. He could mock them, and he does not. Extended journalism of this sort is a subtle art. Striking the correct balance between the general and the particular, between gentle irony and due respect, is not easy, but Garfield does just that. An honourable achievement."

Garfield's next book, *The Nation's Favourite: The True Adventures of Radio 1* (1998), was a behind-the-scenes look at a tumultuous time in the history of Radio 1, when the top executives Matthew Bannister and Chris Evans went head-to-head in a series of spats that were well publicized in the British tabloids. For years the only national pop radio station in Britain, Radio 1 began losing listeners in the 1990s, with the arrival of competing stations. Bannister was brought in as controller, in 1993, to retool the station's image. When Evans later joined the station, he had his own ideas for bringing Radio 1 in line with popular culture. A bitter dispute ensued, and Evans eventually left Radio 1 for Virgin Radio. Garfield spent a year covering the clash and documented it in *The Nation's Favourite*. Patrick Humphries, in a review for the (London) *Times* (October 17, 1998), wrote that, "although largely made up of Garfield's interviews with DJs and executives, this is nonetheless a compelling account of the end of the old and the arrival of the new. Having eavesdropped on the crucial playlist meetings, and at press conferences where the disastrous ratings were announced, Garfield also offers some irresistible tales of media spin doctoring." *The Wrestling* and *The Nation's Favourite* were adapted into plays by Alex Lowe and produced at the Jermyn Street Theatre, in London, as a double bill, in early 2000. Hettie Judah, writing in the (London) *Times* (January 11, 2000) commented on Lowe's decision to transfer such unconventional material into dramatic form: "These are not storybooks, but well presented histories of corporate takeover, management power struggles and audience statistics. They have no dramatic structure, precious few surprises and no love interest whatsoever. What they do have in their favour, and what presumably attracted Lowe to them in the first place, is the most accurate characterisation and on-the-dime speech-writing possible, largely because it was all harvested from the characters themselves, most of whom are still alive."

In 2001 Garfield published *Mauve: How One Man Invented a Colour That Changed the World*, his most popular book to date. Garfield tells the story of William Henry Perkin, the man who accidently invented the color mauve, in 1856, and thereby ushered the field of industrial chemistry into being. Perkin was only 18 at the time, experimenting with coal tar as a way to produce artificial quinine to fight against malaria, which was rapidly killing off British troops in India. Although unsuccessful in achieving this goal, Perkin found that the dark, oily sludge that he had created dyed his shirt a lustrous purple. He stained a silk cloth with the substance and found that it didn't fade with washing or exposure to light, unlike other dyes of the period. Realizing that there could be profit in his discovery, he took out a patent for the manufacture of the dye. Although today Perkin's name is hardly remembered, during the 19th century he enjoyed widespread fame and retired wealthy at the age of 36. He was knighted shortly before his death, in 1906.

In *Mauve*, Garfield outlines how the invention of the purple dye led to the creation of the synthetic-dye industry, which in a short time revolutionized standards of dress. Until Perkin's discovery, dyes were primarily derived from such natural sources as shellfish, insects, vegetables, and plant matter; he had discovered a superior dye that could be made artificially, from an industrial waste. The hue became the hallmark of fashion in England and France in the 1860s. Empress Eugenie, the wife of Napoleon III, decided mauve matched her eyes and began wearing it on public occasions; and Queen Victoria wore mauve to her daughter's wedding, in 1858, and later wore it in mourning for her husband. Although the mauve mania died out, around 1869, numerous artificial dyes took its place.

Garfield describes how Perkin's discovery affected science and industry. In the field of medicine, for example, artificial dyes came to be used in the study of chromosomes and in preliminary research on diseases. Experimentation with coal tar led to the production of such pharmaceuticals as aspirin, which is derived from a dye product. In industry, Perkin's example proved that profits could be made through the commercial application of chemical discoveries. Coal-tar derivatives came to be used in photography, the manufacture of perfumes, the preservation of canned foods, and the creation of saccharin. Garfield punctuates his account of the Victorian era with flash-forwards to the concerns of modern chemistry, and includes in his discussion the health hazards and environmental dangers that followed developments in industry.

Reviews of *Mauve* have been favorable. Anthony S. Travis, in an appraisal for *American Scientist* (July/August 2001), wrote that, "*Mauve* is an inviting cocktail of Perkin biography, account of the dye industry and where it led, and social and cultural history of the color mauve up to the present. It is a very successful and instructive mix, certainly for the intended popular audience; it succeeds in providing sufficient background to retain the nonscientist's attention and to convey the excitement and sense of achievement at the various pioneering enterprises." Marcia Bartusiak, writing in the *New York Times Book Review* (April 15, 2001), called *Mauve* an "engaging and airy history. . . . Garfield has inspired me to wear a bit of mauve this spring to honor this inventive man."

Garfield lives in London, where he is a journalist for the *Independent*.

—A. I. C.

SUGGESTED READING: *American Scientist* p364+ July/Aug. 2001; *British Medical Journal* p1591 Dec. 10, 1994; (London) *Guardian* Nov. 20, 1994, Nov. 25, 1994, Nov. 29, 1994, p23 Jan. 8, 2000, p7 Sep. 21, 2000; (London) *Times* p1 Dec. 6, 1995, p1 Dec. 7, 1996, p22 Oct. 17, 1998, p36 Jan. 11, 2000; *Melody Maker* p13 Oct. 24, 1998; *New York Times Book Review* p17 Apr. 15, 2001; *Wilson Quarterly* p8+ Summer 2001

SELECTED BOOKS: *Money for Nothing: Greed and Exploitation in the Music Industry*, 1986; *Expensive Habits: The Dark Side of the Music Industry*, 1986; *The End of Innocence: Britain in the Time of AIDS*, 1994; *The Wrestling*, 1996; *The Nation's Favourite: The True Adventures of Radio 1*, 1999; *Mauve: How One Man Invented a Colour That Changed the World*, 2001

Garrison, Deborah

Feb. 12, 1965– Poet; editor

Poetry collections usually attract few buyers, and of those that have sold well, few have earned critical acclaim in respected periodicals. Among the small number of volumes that fall into the latter category is Deborah Garrison's book, *A Working Girl Can't Win: And Other Poems* (1998), a highly accessible collection that deals with the everyday struggles of a young working woman trying to make sense of her hectic life. Sales figures for the hardcover edition of *A Working Girl Can't Win* have reached more than 20,000—making it a bestseller among books of poetry, which usually sell around 1,000 copies—and a paperback edition is now available. Garrison wrote the poems in *A Working Girl Can't Win* over a period of 10 years, often after hours at the *New Yorker* magazine, where she worked from 1986 until 2000. Currently, she is the poetry editor at the publishing house Alfred A. Knopf as well as a senior editor at Pantheon Books, a division of Knopf, where she edits fiction and nonfiction.

The second of Joel and Naomi Gottlieb's three daughters, Garrison was born Deborah Gottlieb on February 12, 1965 in Ann Arbor, Michigan. Her father, an anesthesiologist, died of heart failure when she was 14 years old. Her mother, an accountant specializing in nonprofit institutions, was 40 when she was widowed. "She had these three girls to take care of, and her whole life ahead of her, and she went ahead and did it," Garrison told Dana Jennings for the *New York Times* (April 23, 2000). Around the time of her father's death, Deborah began to develop an interest in poetry, and during her teens she began writing poems. She attended Brown University, in Providence, Rhode Island, where she earned a B.A. degree with honors, in 1986, and was elected to Phi Beta Kappa. She later received a master's degree in English from New York University. In her interview with Jennings, she said that she began to get serious about her poetry only after joining the staff of the *New Yorker*, in 1986; she began there as a word processor and worked her way up to editor. "I was inspired to write by the talent at the *New Yorker*. There was a desire to please a literary parent." During her early years at the magazine, she would remain after her workday ended, to type and retype her poems on an electric typewriter. After returning to her apartment, in the East Village section of New York City, she would revise them in her head during her frequent bouts of insomnia. "You feel very free to let your mind go in any direction, and you know you have the night," she recalled to Jeanne Tift for the Random House publication *At Random* (February 1998, on-line). "That's really when I've had most of my ideas. I find that distracted, nighttime thinking brings me much closer to the writing self."

At the *New Yorker* Garrison edited the work of such esteemed writers as Martin Amis, Simon Schama, John Irving, and Joan Acocella, an experience that aided her in developing a critical eye and also enabled her to accept criticism about her own work. Her work as an editor did not, however, help her to think of herself as a writer. As she told Tift, "So much of being an editor involves judgment, and when you write, basically you want to let go of all your inhibitions and find some other part of yourself that isn't so controlled. It's hard to do that sometimes after a long day examining other people's sentences. I wish I knew how to press the button and say, 'Okay, now I'm in poetry mode.'" Thus influenced by her editorial mindset, she worked on her poetry only intermittently until 1995, when an editor at Random House suggested that she put together a collection.

Though many of Garrison's poems appeared in *Elle*, the *New York Times*, *Slate*, and even the *New Yorker*, she did not collect them until 1998, the year that Random House published *A Working Girl Can't Win: And Other Poems*. The collection focuses on a young working woman who seeks to balance her professional and private lives, who is devoted to her husband but fantasizes about flirting with other men, and who has a strong sense of herself as a woman but still wonders what her late father would think of her now. In an assessment for *Newsweek* (February 23, 1998), Jeff Giles called *A Working Girl Can't Win* "a wonderful collection, full of candor, bereft of b.s. It will speak both to women and to those hunting for clues to same. . . . Garrison's poems are full of ambivalence—how could any honest poems about love and work not be?—but they don't seem soaked in self-pity. That's partly because the language is so user-friendly, partly because it's full of such unexpected rhymes and sly humor." (One example of such rhymes and humor can be found in the title poem: "Is she Jewish, / self-hating? Past her sell-by date, / or still ovulating?"Another example can be found in "An Idle Thought": "I'm never going to sleep / with Martin Amis / or anyone famous.") Walter Kirn, writing for *Time* (March 30, 1998), reacted similarly, calling Garrison's collection "an airy, appealing first book," and adding, "As Garrison's book proves, not all good poems are hard poems, and sometimes the lines you can hum are also the lines you can't forget." Garrison's positive reviews are best represented by Nicholas Christopher's concluding paragraph in the *New York Times Book Review* (March 8, 1998): "*A Working Girl Can't Win* is an intense, intelligent and wonderfully sly book of poems that should appeal as much to the general reader as to the poetry devotee, a book in which working women and men—overwhelmed, overstimulated, and often overcome by love—ought to find Garrison clearly and generously speaking their language. However emphatically this particular working girl tells us she can't win, she certainly can write."

Other reviewers have not praised the book. Some, like Judy Clarence in *Library Journal* (February 15, 1998), felt that the poems showed that Garrison could turn a phrase but were thin on subject matter. "One only wishes that Garrison would use her vivid skills with the language ('the sun's fuzzy mouth sucking the day back') to explore issues and scenery that more deeply touch the reader's soul . . . ," Clarence wrote. "Garrison entertains but shallowly." In a harsh appraisal for *Parnassus: Poetry in Review* (Volume 24, No. 1, 1999), David Catron speculated that the acclaim lavished by some critics on the book could be attributed to Garrison's acquaintance with people in the literary world. "Like the verdict in the State of California vs. Orenthal James Simpson, [the acclaim] stands as proof that it is sometimes possible to get away with murder if one has the right connections. . . . [This book] is a study in mediocrity. Very few of its 28 poems rise above the level of workshop doggerel. Indeed, many are so poorly conceived and sloppily executed that they fail to reach even that modest altitude." By her own account, Garrison has ignored such criticism, for the most part, and has continued to write poems.

As the poetry editor at Alfred A. Knopf since February 2000, Garrison is concerned that people will assume that the poems she herself has written reflect her poetic taste. "My own poetry is irrelevant to my role as an editor," she told Dana Jennings. "My book would have never been on the Knopf list." She hopes to increase sales of Knopf's poetry books by paying attention to marketing details, ranging from the title of each book to the way the volume is presented to Knopf's sales force. But her most important function at Knopf is editing. "My job is to ask [each writer], 'What are you really trying to say here?'" she told Jennings of the occasional trouble spots in her authors' poetry. "People only respect you for you saying what you think. . . . And poetry has more burden to be clear than any other form."

Deborah Garrison and Matthew C. Garrison, an attorney, have been married since 1986. The couple have two daughters, Daisy and Georgia, and live in Montclair, New Jersey.

—C. M.

SUGGESTED READING: *At Random* (on-line), Feb. 1998; *Cybergrrl* (on-line); *New York Times* I p19 Sep. 4, 1995, E p9 Feb. 26, 1998, I p31 Aug. 15, 1999, XIV p1 Apr. 23, 2000, with photos; *New York Times Book Review* p15 Mar. 8, 1998; *Newsweek* p68 Feb. 23, 1998; *Parnassus: Poetry in Review* p306+ Vol. 24 No. 1 1999; *Time* p68 Mar. 30, 1998, with photo; *Contemporary Authors* vol. 169, 1999

SELECTED BOOKS: *A Working Girl Can't Win and Other Poems*, 1998

Garson, Barbara

1941– Playwright; nonfiction writer

Barbara Garson is perhaps best known for her controversial 1966 play, *MacBird!*, which satirizes many of the leading figures in American politics of the era, including President Lyndon B. Johnson, the former attorney general and senator Robert F. Kennedy of New York, and the chief justice of the U.S. Supreme Court Earl Warren. Garson has also written three books on labor, *All the Livelong Day: The Meaning and Demeaning of Routine Work*

Barbara Garson
Bernard Gottfried/Courtesy of Penguin Putnam, Inc.

For *MacBird!*, Garson parodied William Shakespeare's style. "I kept a copy of Shakespeare open in front of me continuously [while writing,]" she told Coleman. "I would try to think of what there was in Shakespeare that would correspond to the political situation. I was unhappy when I couldn't find a corresponding scene—then I had to write the scene myself."

President Lyndon B. Johnson is the title character of the play—an ambitious politician, much like Shakespeare's Macbeth—who becomes president after the assassination of John Ken O'Dunc, with the late President John F. Kennedy in the King Duncan role. Lady Bird Johnson is skewered in a parody of Shakespeare's Lady Macbeth. John Ken O'Dunc has two brothers: Robert Ken O'Dunc (Robert F. Kennedy, the former attorney general who was elected to the U.S. Senate in 1964, in the MacDuff role) and Ted Ken O'Dunc (Senator Ted Kennedy from Massachusetts). Garson included such other characters as Lord McNamara (Secretary of Defense Robert McNamara, one of the chief architects of the Vietnam War); the Egg of Head (Adlai Stevenson, the former governor of Illinois and an unsuccessful Democratic candidate for president in 1952 and 1956, who was frequently ridiculed by political opponents as an intellectual "egghead"); the Wayne of Morse (Senator Wayne Morse of Oregon, an early opponent of the war); and the Earl of Warren (Earl Warren, the Supreme Court chief justice who headed a presidential commission that concluded that Lee Harvey Oswald acted alone in assassinating President Kennedy in 1963).

The play borrowed from the public's growing suspicions that Kennedy may have been the victim of a conspiracy, despite the Warren Commission's conclusions to the contrary. In one scene, MacBird summons the Earl of Warren, asking him to conduct an investigation into John Ken O'Dunc's assassination and put a grieving and suspicious nation's mind at ease. The Earl agrees, intoning, "Oh, curs'ed spite / That ever I was born to set things right." MacBird immediately corrects him, saying: "I don't believe you understand the job. / I wouldn't say you're asked to set things *right*. / I think you get the point." The Earl replies, "Oh, whine and pout, / That ever I was born to bury doubt." A pleased MacBird then says, "You get the picture now." *MacBird!* proved to be slightly prophetic. At the end of the play, Robert Ken O'Dunc comes to depose MacBird. In real life, after a poor showing by Johnson in the 1968 New Hampshire Democratic primary, Robert F. Kennedy announced that he would challenge him for the Democratic Party nomination for president. (Johnson then dropped out of the race, but Kennedy, after winning several primaries, was shot by an Arab extremist on June 5, 1968, the night of the California primary in Los Angeles, and died the next day.)

MacBird! was first published in 1966 by the Independent Socialist Club of Berkeley and excerpted in the local magazine *Despite Everything*. The first printing, about 2,000 copies, sold out in six

(1975), *The Electronic Sweatshop: How Computers Are Turning the Office of the Future into the Factory of the Past* (1988), and *Money Makes the World Go Round: One Investor Tracks Her Cash Through the Global Economy, from Brooklyn to Bangkok and Back* (2001). "Work is what most people do most of their waking lives," Garson explained to Claudia Dreifus for the *Progressive* (January 1990). "Writing about it shouldn't be such an unusual thing. But work is a kind of dirty word in our culture; it's the only secret thing that people don't talk about."

Barbara Garson was born in 1941 in the New York City borough of Brooklyn. During the early 1960s, she enrolled at the University of California at Berkeley (UC Berkeley) and became involved with the Free Speech Movement (FSM), a group of left-wing student activists and protesters who clashed with the university administration over the use of school facilities for political purposes and the censorship of student leaflets. While at UC Berkeley, she edited the FSM newsletter and married Marvin Garson, a fellow FSM activist. She graduated with a B.A. in history.

The genesis of Garson's satirical play, *MacBird!*, came in August 1965, when she was speaking during a student protest against the Vietnam War. "I made a slip of the tongue," Garson told Kate Coleman for *Newsweek* (February 27, 1967). "I called Lady Bird Johnson [the wife of President Lyndon B. Johnson] Lady MacBird Johnson. Later I thought about the slip and thought it would make a good skit." Garson originally planned *MacBird!* as a 15-minute skit to be performed at a major antiwar demonstration, the "International Days of Protest," in October 1965. She ended up, however, writing a full-length play.

weeks. Major publishers shunned the play, however, because of its controversial nature. Garson and her husband then set up Grassy Knoll Press to publish and sell *MacBird!*. (The "grassy knoll" refers to the spot in Dallas from which many conspiracy buffs believe another assassin fired shots at President Kennedy's motorcade.) After the play proved impressive sales, Grove Press, which had previously rejected it, began publishing *MacBird!*; it eventually sold more than 500,000 copies. "*MacBird!* became a major cultural event because 'we'—the politically concerned counterculture—had our own audience that we had organized ourselves," Garson told Dreifus.

In early 1967 *MacBird!* was performed at the Village Gate, a nightclub in New York City. Several literary figures, including George Plimpton, the author and editor of the *Paris Review*; Victor Navasky, the editor of *Monocle* magazine and the future editor of *The Nation*; Paul Krassner, the editor of *Realist* magazine; and the poet Robert Lowell, helped finance the production. Although *MacBird!* was a hit with audiences, the play sharply divided reviewers. In the *New York Times* (February 23, 1967), Walter Kerr wrote, "Barbara Garson, the author of *MacBird!*, is like someone who has suddenly thought of something funny to say at a party, who has blurted out the beginning of the joke only to realize that it is hurtling toward embarrassing consequences, and who has then plunged on anyway—hurriedly, boldly, wistfully, boorishly hoping against hope that something, *anything*, would turn up to save the day." By contrast, Jack Kroll, writing for *Newsweek* (March 6, 1967), observed that "*MacBird!* turns out to be better seen than read, that in its mixture of bile, laughter and concern it qualifies as genuine satire, and that it succeeds in being an authentic theatrical event—making a real and lasting impact on its audience." *MacBird!* helped launch the careers of several mainstream actors and actresses, including Stacy Keach and Rue McLanahan.

After the success of *MacBird!*, the eventual dissolution of the FSM, and the birth of her daughter, Garson retreated from the public spotlight. She went to work at the Shelter Half, an antiwar coffeehouse in Tacoma, Washington, near the Fort Lewis Army Base. Garson told Dreifus that she "worked with soldiers being made to fight the war in Vietnam, and I felt I was trying to raise ordinary people's sense of confidence—to make them feel good about themselves. We listened to the GI's stories and made them feel significant."

In 1975 Garson published her first nonfiction book, *All the Livelong Day: The Meaning and Demeaning of Routine Work*, which discusses how employees cope with the effects of such mundane and repetitious jobs as packing Ping Pong paddles in boxes or processing tuna fish at canneries. Garson spent two years interviewing workers in different parts of the country and took several jobs herself to personally observe working conditions. She is critical of managers and unions, arguing that they ignore the workers' best interests. *All the Livelong Day* received mixed reviews. "This is a loving book," J. D. Moorhead wrote for the *Christian Science Monitor* (October 1, 1975). "It celebrates man's vitality and ingenuity under intense pressures designed to turn him into a machine. The gritty realities of life on America's assembly lines come through loud and deadening." Although Moorhead observed that Garson offers few solutions, the reviewer concluded that "as a look at what the days of millions of American workers are probably like, the book is fascinating." In his review for *Newsweek* (September 29, 1975), Peter S. Prescott faulted the book. "I'm not unwilling to be taken in by socialist optimism, but [Garson] hasn't made her case: she'll let women ramble on . . . , but with no more than a contemptuous smirk she cuts managers off at their knees," he wrote. "Garson is a playwright; she knows what dialogue is, and how to shape a scene, but she has no sense at all of how to shape an argument that persuades." In 1994 Garson published an updated version of *All the Livelong Day*.

In her next book, *The Electronic Sweatshop: How Computers Are Transforming the Office of the Future into the Factory of the Past* (1988), Garson argued that the increased presence of computers in the workplace has been detrimental to many workers. "Jobs that once required a lot of discretion have become routinized, standardized, packaged—so that creative people do monotonous, repetitious, and highly controlled work," she told Dreifus. "One would have thought that the introduction of computers into the workplace would free people, but instead systems have been designed that make employees work at breakneck speeds that kill their ingenuity, and that monitor their every action." Garson's research revealed that at McDonald's, the popular fast-food chain, computers tightly regulate the production of a meal and can even detect if a worker places too many bits of minced onion on a hamburger. Computers have also allowed managers and supervisors at many places to closely monitor their employees's every move. In fact, Garson experienced electronic monitoring when she was working at a data-entry job as part of her research for an article for *Mother Jones* magazine. "I was working in an office where hundreds of women sat keying in data with three fingers of one hand and turning little slips of paper over with the other," she recalled to Dreifus. "It amazed me: Nobody was talking. This was in a sub-basement, there was no supervisor there, and still it was absolutely silent." She continued, "After I had been there a few days, I was called into another department, shown my print-out, and told my keystroke count had fallen to 9,000 an hour after lunch two days in a row. I was supposed to do 15,000 keystrokes an hour. So the supervisor was *inside* the machine all along!" *The Electronic Sweatshop* received mostly favorable reviews. In his review for the *Los Angeles Times* (April 24, 1988), Alex Raskin wrote that "through dozens of interviews with 'professional clerks'—from airline reservation agents whose 'talk time' and 'conversation rate' are monitored second-by-second to 'automated social workers'—Garson convincingly argues that our current definition of productivity is inadequate: 'Any system that spends so much money on limiting instead of using human creativity,' she writes, 'has got to be inefficient.'" While disagreeing with her claim that corporations have deliberately dehumanized some jobs, Raskin concluded that Garson provides a "compelling warning that in the computer age, big-business could become like Big Brother." Writing for Long Island *Newsday* (July 27, 1988), Christopher Hitchens was also impressed by *The Electronic Sweatshop*. "In this vivid and humane book Barbara Garson has confirmed the suspicions of many lay critics about the use of computerization," Hitchens observed. "It may still be that microtechnology will turn out to be liberating, but Barbara Garson has shown that the technique is not neutral and that in the hands of the short-sighted and the over-specialized it has become another reinforcement for the Organization Man."

Garson's third book, *Money Makes the World Go Round: One Investor Tracks Her Cash Through the Global Economy, from Brooklyn to Bangkok and Back*, appeared in 2001. Garson deposited part of the advance she received for this book into the Bank of Millbrook, in New York, and the Mutual Series funds, which were managed by the noted investor Michael Price. She then traced her deposits through several different financial institutions, which used it for purchases, interest payments, loans, and issuing letters of credit. Although it was impossible to find out exactly where her money went, Garson managed to narrow down the possibilities by using bank records and interviewing bank officials. After depositing her money in the Bank of Millbrook, Garson learned that the bank sent $1 million to its "correspondent" bank, the Chase Manhattan Corp. (now J. P. Morgan Chase), to satisfy a Federal Reserve funds requirement. In turn, Chase made loans to a firm in Brooklyn that imported frozen shrimp from Malaysia and to Caltex, an oil concern that was building refineries in Singapore and Thailand. For research Garson traveled to all three countries, observing the companies' impact on local communities and the effect of globalization. She interviewed numerous workers, managers, street vendors, and shrimp fishermen. In Bangkok Garson met a woman whom she nicknamed "Squirrel," who left the rice paddies to find factory work in the city. Squirrel worked as a seamstress in a sweatshop and as a street vendor outside an oil refinery, but then mysteriously disappeared after fighting with another vendor. In an interview with Jane Slaughter for *The Witness* (November 2001, on-line), Garson recalled that Squirrel preferred working all day in front of a sewing machine to "standing in the paddy fields with leeches on her legs." While globalization and the spread of capital gave impoverished individuals such as Squirrel opportunities to improve their economic status, such opportunities vanished during the Asian economic crisis of 1997–1998. Speaking with Slaughter, Garson blamed the crisis on U.S. banks and the International Monetary Fund (IMF), which made substantial loans to Asian governments and banks, with such tight controls that devaluation of their currencies and economic hardship resulted.

Garson's investment with Mutual Series allowed her to follow the plight of the Sunbeam Corp., which manufactured outdoor furniture and household appliances. At the time of Garson's investment, Mutual owned 20 percent of Sunbeam, which had been experiencing financial difficulties. In an effort to turn the struggling company around, Michael Price pressured Sunbeam's board of directors to hire Albert Dunlap as the chief executive officer (CEO). A tough and ruthless executive, Dunlap, who became nationally known as "Chainsaw Al," had established a successful track record in turning floundering companies around by cutting costs and laying off thousands of workers. Garson visited Sunbeam plants targeted for closure by Dunlap to see how workers there responded to the layoffs. She found that the closing of a plant in Portland, Tennessee, devastated many of the town's families, especially those without health insurance. Unionized employees in a Biddeford, Maine, plant fared somewhat better; they were able to buy the facility, which made electric blankets, from Sunbeam and keep it running. (Although the new company eventually declared bankruptcy, it was purchased in 2002 by the Taiwanese conglomerate Microlife Corp. and is still in business today as Biddeford Blankets.)

Money Makes the World Go Round divided reviewers. "For the most part, the points that Garson is making are hard to find," Trudy Lieberman wrote in her review for the *American Prospect* (August 13, 2001). "Too much dialogue at times obscures the larger picture. And there are too many digressions. Concerning the Asian oil refinery operations, for example, we learn about a Japanese overseer of the international labor force and are told about his Sunday golf game. It's hard to see the point." Lieberman added that "Garson's conclusions are not very far reaching. Noting that what she saw in her travels 'awakened all the old international optimism,' she maintains that capital should be controlled more democratically and that the idea of regulating capital flows and humanizing the economy will come back into vogue. But how and when? She doesn't go there." In contrast, Marilyn Harris praised the book in a review for *Business Week* (March 5, 2001). "Garson's sketch of [Albert] Dunlap is memorable," Harris wrote. "With gusto, she exposes what she sees as his hypocrisy and the line of baloney he fed investors and analysts." Harris concluded that by interviewing people around the world, "Garson manages to extract universal lessons about the unceasing pressure of capital and the nature of the global economy."

Garson, who attended the Yale School of Drama in addition to UC Berkeley, has written other plays, although they did not bring her the same critical attention she received for *MacBird! Dinosaur Door*, a children's production, did earn a special citation from the Obie Awards in 1977. Garson is the recipient of grants from the Louis M. Rabinowitz Foundation and the New York State Council on the Arts. She has won fellowships from the National Endowment for the Arts and the Guggenheim Foundation. Garson has written for such publications as the *Progressive*, the *New York Times*, the *Boston Globe*, the *Los Angeles Times*, *Newsweek*, *Harper's*, *Mother Jones*, and *The Nation*. She was the vice presidential candidate for the Socialist Party in 1992.

Barbara Garson makes her home in New York City. Her daughter, Juliet, is also a playwright.
—D. C.

SUGGESTED READING: *American Prospect* p46 Aug. 13, 2001; *Business Week* p22 Mar. 5, 2001; *Christian Science Monitor* p18 Oct. 1, 1975; *Los Angeles Times* Book Review p4 Apr. 24, 1988; *New York Times* p38 Feb. 23, 1967, with photo; (Long Island) *Newsday* II p13 Jul. 27, 1988; *Newsweek* p99 Feb. 27, 1967, with photo, p79 Mar. 6, 1967, with photo, p90 Sep. 29, 1975; *Progressive* p30 Jan. 1990, with photo, p2 Jan. 1997; *The Witness* (on-line) Nov. 2001; Kaye, Phyllis J. ed. *National Playwrights Directory*, 1981

SELECTED BOOKS: plays—*MacBird!*, 1966; nonfiction—*All the Livelong Day: The Meaning and Demeaning of Routine Work*, 1975; *The Electronic Sweatshop: How Computers Are Transforming the Office of the Future into the Factory of the Past*, 1988; *Money Makes the World Go Round: One Investor Tracks Her Cash Through the Global Economy, from Brooklyn to Bangkok and Back*, 2001

Garton Ash, Timothy

July 12, 1955– Journalist; historian

Timothy Garton Ash's uncommon approach to reporting—a blend of personal observation, careful research, lucid analysis, and elegant prose—has made him one of the most well-respected writers on European affairs. Equal parts journalist and scholar, Garton Ash studied modern history and then focused his knowledge on contemporary affairs, becoming what one of his admirers termed a "historian of the present." He has covered the Polish Solidarity movement of the 1980s, the division and reunification of Germany, the revolutions in Eastern Europe in 1989, the fall of the Soviet Union, and the rise of ethnic wars in Eastern Europe in the post–Cold War world. He has written for the London-based *Times*, *Spectator*, and *Independent*, as well as the *New York Review of Books* and other publications. His essays have been collected in *The Polish Revolution: Solidarity* (1983), *The Uses of Adversity* (1989), *We the People* (1990), and *In Europe's Name* (1993). His most recent works are *The File* (1998), about the information gathered on him by East German secret police, and *History of the Present* (1999), essays about Europe in the 1990s.

Timothy Garton Ash was born on July 12, 1955 in London, England. He studied modern history at Exeter College, Oxford University, and then did graduate work at Oxford's St. Antony's College. In order to write his doctoral dissertation about Berlin under Hitler's rule, he traveled to the divided capital to do research. He studied at the Free University, in West Berlin, and in 1980 enrolled for a semester at Humboldt University, in East Berlin, becoming the first British student to study in Com-

Courtesy of Hoover Institution/Stanford University

munist East Germany. As a student of the Third Reich, Garton Ash wanted to understand how people behave under a dictatorship—why some collaborate and others resist, as he explained to Harry Kreisler in a April 4, 1996 interview archived on Berkeley University's "Conversations with History" Web site. "That was quite difficult to find out from the archives, many of which were still closed," he told Kreisler. "But people were *living* those dilemmas in East Germany at that time, so I started writing about [C]ommunist East Germany and thence about Eastern Europe."

Garton Ash's first book, written and published in Germany in 1981, was *"Und willst Du nicht mein Bruder sein. . ." Die DDR heute*, about the German Democratic Republic and Erich Honecker. A lifelong political activist, Honecker had resisted Hitler, helped found the Socialist Unity Party, and led East Germany for nearly two decades.

After completing his studies, Garton Ash traveled around East Germany and other Eastern Bloc countries, becoming an eyewitness to the various uprisings occurring against Communist rule. "I talked to everyone I met," he told Kreisler of this period, "I went home and made notes on these conversations, read voraciously, went to the theater. . . . But at the same time, unlike a classic newspaperman . . . I was very consciously looking for the larger historical significance of what I was writing about." When Polish workers occupied the Lenin Shipyard, in Gdansk, in August 1980, he was there as a reporter, but he soon began to see the larger context of history at work: the worker's strike grew into the Solidarity movement, which effectively dismantled the totalitarian Soviet regime from within. For more than a year, Solidarity's peaceful demonstrations brought about reforms, including the creation of independent trade unions; then, on December 1981, the military shut the movement down. Garton Ash chronicled these events in *The Polish Revolution: Solidarity* (1983), which received favorable reviews from critics. Gary Mead, in a review for *New Statesman* (November 11, 1983), cheered: "Garton Ash has written one of the finest books currently available on Solidarity, its history and wider significance." In *Choice* (September 1984), L. K. D. Kristof wrote that, while the book offers "nothing really new for the specialist," it is a lively and important introduction to the subject: "If someone can afford to read only one book about Poland 1980–81, this is it," Kristof concluded. Abraham Brumberg, in a review for the *New Republic* (September 10, 1984), judged: "Of all the works on recent Polish history, none matches Garton Ash's lucid account of the nature and history of the Solidarity movement." *The Polish Revolution: Solidarity* won the 1984 Somerset Maugham Award from the British Society of Authors.

During the 1980s Garton Ash covered European affairs for the British newspapers the *Spectator*, *Independent*, and the *Times*, and also contributed articles to the *New York Review of Books*. He collected his writings on Central and Eastern Europe into *The Uses of Adversity* (1989), which includes essays on the division of Germany, repression in Prague, the Holocaust and its effect on European history, and life under the oppressive regime in East Germany. Like its predecessor, this essay collection received glowing reviews. In the *New Leader* (October 2–16, 1989), Michael J. Kaufman remarked, "One of [this book's] greatest strengths is that the essays are not written within the dispassionate and disinterested conventions of journalism or relativistic history. They never imply that truth lies midway between adversarial poles, nor do they shun passion as bias. . . . The author truly knows the countries he writes about . . . . Timothy Garton Ash's book is stimulating and probably indispensable." In the *New York Review of Books* (March 1, 1990), George F. Kennan praised how Garton Ash "writes primarily as a witness to the events he is treating, and not just as an outside witness. . . . Yet the sense of the historic dimensions of the events in question is never lost. And the quality of the writing places it clearly in the category of good literature. . . . This is a kind of writing—it could be called the history of the present— for which it is not easy to find examples in earlier literature." *The Uses of Adversity* won the 1989 Prix Europeen de l'Essai from the Charles Veillon Foundation.

Throughout 1989 Garton Ash bore witness to the remarkable revolutions throughout Eastern Europe, in which the people of East Germany, Poland, Hungary, and Czechoslovakia rose up against their Soviet occupiers. The year culminated in the destruction of the Berlin Wall, which had divided the German capital for nearly 30 years. His 1990 book *We the People* (published as *The Magic Lantern* in the United States) brought together four essays detailing the events that occurred in Berlin, Warsaw, Budapest, and Prague, as well as two essays on the causes and effects of Eastern Europe's rejection of communism. As Robert Marquand wrote in the *Christian Science Monitor* (July 19, 1990), "No one is better qualified to tell this story than Ash. . . . The book has more weight and content than its 156 pages would indicate." Writing for the *New York Times Book Review* (July 22, 1990), Jan T. Gross noted: "Mr. Garton Ash . . . offers in his essays a wonderful combination of first-class reporting, brilliant political analysis and reflection."

In 1993 Garton Ash published *In Europe's Name*, a painstakingly researched account of East-West relations in the divided Germany after World War II. The main subject is the concept of *Ostpolitik*, the name for the West German effort to stabilize relations with East Germany, the Soviet Union, and the rest of the Warsaw Pact countries— Albania, Bulgaria, Czechoslovakia, Hungary, Poland, and Romania—which had signed a security treaty in 1955. He looks at the policies of détente and brinkmanship between the United States and the Soviet Union and how this had an impact on West German policy with the East. *In Europe's Name* received generally favorable reviews. In the *Historian* (Spring 1995), Marion F. Deshmukh proclaimed "this volume is essential reading for its deftness of analysis, for its many astute observations on continuities in West German foreign policy, and for its broad vision of Germany's role within the larger European community." In a review for the *Washington Post Book World* (December 12, 1993), Marc Fisher noted that *In Europe's Name* differs from Garton Ash's earlier works. "Like the people and country it studies, this book immerses itself in the rational," Fisher wrote. "The author even apologizes for doing what he does so well elsewhere—exploring, through the prism of his own experience and ideas, the social forces that drive politics. Here, examining the path toward revolutions powered from below, he restricts his survey to policy ordained from above. The result is a superb work of research, one that will define the Who Was Right debate. But it is not the Garton Ash who captured the spirit and striving of the Poles and the Czechs, even as he explained why and how their leaders acted as they did."

Though he spent only a single semester in East Germany as a graduate student, Garton Ash became the subject of a surveillance file put together by the East German State Security Service, most often known as the Stasi; the file contained more than 300 pages of information about his activities while inside the country. When Germany reunited, in 1990, the new government made the Stasi files available to their subjects. After reviewing his file—and realizing that ordinary people had spied on him at the behest of the East German government—Garton Ash hit on a idea: why not contact the people who had spied on him to find out why they had become informants? In the course of his research, Garton Ash discovered that the British Security Service had compiled a file based on his conversations with fellow British citizens in East Berlin; as a student, he had a visa to travel throughout East Germany while journalists and diplomats were generally restricted to the city, and he was thus an important source of information—and an unwitting spy. The result of Garton Ash's research into this period in his life was The File (1998), part memoir and part philosophical exploration into the ethics of spying. Reviewing the book for the New York Times (September 17, 1997), Richard Bernstein remarked: "Via these case histories Mr. Garton Ash tries to understand something about the system itself, as well as about human nature. The result is a thoughtful, utterly absorbing exploration of the very purpose, meaning and character of control and collaboration in an insecure dictatorial society." In a review for the Washington Post Book World (August 24, 1997), Dusko Doder summarized the questions Garton Ash raises about the proper restraints placed on the intelligence community in a free society. "Who is to determine what is too far or too reckless?" Doder asked. "The author provides no clear answer. But his book is a valuable contribution to the debate in the West focusing on finding a new and different place for intelligence services in the new post–Cold War era."

Garton Ash's most recent book, History of the Present (1999), collects his essays about Europe in the 1990s. (The title came from George Kennan's New York Review of Books discussion of The Uses of Adversity.) This volume received mixed reviews. As Michael D. Mosettig wrote in Europe (April 2001), "As a vehicle to present Garton Ash's valuable insights to a wider public . . . this book is a success. As a literary device, the verdict is more mixed. It is often odd to be reading predictions written in the early nineties when you already know the outcome. This work is clearly an assemblage and bears the drawbacks of that genre. That said, for any serious student of Europe—Western or Eastern—this is an essential book." However, Steve Kettmann, reviewing the book for the Washington Monthly (November 2000), praised Garton Ash for "writing with both empathy and hard-won understanding, knowing the people and what they are really talking about, not just during television interviews. He's careful with facts, and maybe even more careful with ideas. He is, in short, someone whose approach and sensibility are completely at odds with all current trends in American journalism."

Timothy Garton Ash is the Kurt A. Körber Senior Research Fellow in contemporary European history at St. Antony's College, Oxford, and is also a senior fellow at the Hoover Institution, a think tank based on the campus of Stanford University, in Stanford, California. In addition to prizes for specific books, he has won the 1989 David Watt Memorial Prize for the essay "Mourning Becomes Europa." In 1990 he was named Commentator of the Year by Granada Television. He has also been honored with the Order of Merit from both Poland and Germany.

—C. M.

SUGGESTED READING: Berkeley University's "Conversations with History" Web site; Choice p188 Sep. 1984; Christian Science Monitor p13 Oct. 20, 1989, p14 July 19, 1990; Europe p48 Apr. 2001; Historian p629+ Spring 1995; New Leader p14 Oct. 2–16, 1989; New Republic p35 Sep. 10, 1984; New Statesman p28 Nov. 11, 1983; New York Review of Books p3 Mar. 1, 1990; New York Times p8 Sep. 17, 1997; New York Times Book Review p29 July 22, 1990; Newsweek p95 Nov. 13, 1989; Washington Monthly p53 Nov. 2000; Washington Post Book World p5 Dec. 12, 1993, p1 Aug. 24, 1997

SELECTED BOOKS: The Polish Revolution: Solidarity, 1983; The Uses of Adversity, 1989; We the People, 1990; In Europe's Name, 1993; The File, 1998; History of the Present, 1999

George, Elizabeth

Feb. 26, 1949– Mystery writer

"It's important for a writer to write about what she loves and is interested in," Elizabeth George told Anita Manning for USA Today (December 2, 1999, on-line). "For me, that means writing about British culture, with British characters and stories set in England." George is the author of several mystery novels and a collection of short stories, all of which offer detailed accounts of British life, highly atmospheric descriptions of British locales, and dialogue peppered with British slang. They present

Figge Photography/Courtesy of Elizabeth George/Bantam Books

Elizabeth George

those details with such accuracy that many of her readers have mistakenly assumed that she is a native of Great Britain. But the American-born George, who has spent most of her life in California, is simply a passionate Anglophile. "England really works for me artistically," she told Lynn Carey for the *Contra Costa Times* (August 7, 1997, on-line). "The topography is emotionally charged for me and suggests elements of plot." In the *Writer* (January 1994), George reported that her books "are sometimes called literary mysteries, sometimes novels of psychological suspense, sometimes detective stories, sometimes police procedurals, sometimes British novels." But, she added, they "are always—at least to my way of thinking—'real novels' from start to finish."

George's mysteries feature Detective Inspector Thomas Lynley of New Scotland Yard, his sidekick, Sergeant Barbara Havers, and his best friend, the forensic specialist Simon St. James, and the stories describe not only the criminal investigations that occupy this trio but their emotional ups and downs as well. "To write a mystery-suspense [story] that is a 'real novel' is to write largely about character," George observed in the *Writer*. "In these novels, the characters and the circumstances engendered by those characters drive the story forward, and not vice versa. . . . Mystery-suspense novels that are 'real novels' end where they begin: with an examination of the human heart—in conflict, in despair, in peace, in anguish, in love, in happiness, in fear. When a writer decides to create a novel of character within this genre of mystery-suspense, she challenges herself to move beyond the simple mechanics of plotting, to drive from her mind the temptation to adhere to a formula, and to take a risk. She decides to begin with character and to use character as the foundation for the hundreds of pages and thousands of words that will follow that character's creation. This is what I have attempted to do with my novels." George's last three books—*In the Presence of the Enemy, Deception on His Mind*, and *In Pursuit of the Proper Sinner*—have all been best-sellers.

The writer was born Susan Elizabeth George on February 26, 1949 in Warren, Ohio. Her father, Robert Edwin George, was a salesman for a conveyor company; her mother, the former Anne Rivelle, was a nurse. "We weren't a family that had a lot of money," George told Marjorie Rosen for *People* (August 23, 1993). "We turned to the world of imagination." When Elizabeth's older brother, Rob, suffered an eye injury at age six and had to have his eyes bandaged, her parents "spent hours reading to him, and I listened," George recalled to Rosen. When Elizabeth was seven her mother gave her a used, 1930s manual typewriter, and throughout her elementary-school years, she composed short stories. Her favorite books included the Nancy Drew mystery series.

George continued to write for pleasure while attending Holy Cross High School in Mountain View, California. As a junior or senior, she visited England for the first time. "I was very interested in English history, English literature, England's contribution to the creative arts as well," she told Anita Manning. After her graduation from high school, she enrolled at Foothill Community College, in Los Altos Hills, California, where she earned an A.A. degree, in 1969. She then transferred to the University of California at Riverside, from which she received a B.A. degree, in 1970. The following year she married Ira J. Toibin, a business manager and, later, school superintendent. During the 1974–75 academic year, George taught English at Mater Dei High School, a Catholic school in Santa Ana, California. She was fired from that position for "union agitation," as she put it in an interview with Lisa See for *Publishers Weekly* (March 11, 1996). She spent the following dozen years teaching English at El Toro High School, in Orange County. "I called my remedial students scholars," she told Rosen. "At first they thought I was making fun of them, but it was a rare student who didn't rise to my expectations." In 1981 the Orange County Department of Education named her teacher of the year. Two years earlier she had gotten an M.S. degree in counseling and psychology from California State University.

All the while, George told See, "I knew I wanted to write, but I didn't have a lot of confidence." When, in 1983, her husband bought a computer, she said to herself, "This is put up or shut up time," as she recalled to See. That semester she was teaching a course that focused on mystery novels, and she decided to produce one herself. Almost immediately after she started to write it—on June 28, 1983—she felt moved to set her story in England. "The English tradition offers the great tapestry novel," she explained to See, "where you have the emotional aspect of a detective's personal life, the circumstances of the crime and, most important, the atmosphere of the English countryside that functions as another character." Completed within three months, George's first novel was a basic drawing-room mystery written in a style associated with Agatha Christie. It marked the debut—though not in public, since it was never published—of George's regular stable of characters: Inspector Thomas Lynley of New Scotland Yard, who is also the wealthy eighth earl of Asherton; Lynley's partner, the unattractive, aggressively plebeian Detective Sergeant Barbara Havers, who simmers with resentment against the aristocracy; Lynley's best friend, the independent forensic scientist Simon St. James; St. James's wife, Deborah, a one-time love interest of Lynley's; and Lady Helen Clyde, the inspector's most-recent flame. "The characters are strictly from my imagination, though each possesses a quality that I have," George told Linda Carey. "I am intellectual as St. James is; I am sort of ironic, casual, and slob-oriented like Barbara Havers. I am hesitant and melancholy the way Deborah is. I think I have Lynley's tendency to hot passion; he's the kind of person who's going to say something and then regret it." When she created Havers, George told Anita Manning, she tried to make her Lynley's "antithesis, because [Lynley] was a character who might be somewhat unbelievable—a detective inspector with a title in the family for 250 years, a belted earl, handsome, rich. He sounded pretty unreal. When you create a character who is unrealistic or has too much going for him, the tendency is for the reader to not like him." To nip the reader's antipathy in the bud, George had Havers describe Lynley in highly unfavorable terms before the inspector made his first appearance, so that, as George explained to Manning, "when we meet Lynley, we see he's really not so bad."

Of the various publishers to whom George sent a sample chapter of her book, only one responded—Scribner, whose representative, Suzanne Kirk, rejected it, on the ground that novels written in the "drawing-room style" were no longer commercially viable. But Kirk encouraged George to continue writing. Having decided to seek, in her words, a "buffer against rejection" from publishers, George obtained a list of agents from the organization Mystery Writers of America and sent samples of her work to 10 agents at a time; eventually, she secured the services of Kathe Trelingator. Meanwhile, during her vacations, she traveled in England and worked on two new novels, *A Great Deliverance* and *A Suitable Vengeance*. A series of rejections greeted them, and Trelingator severed her ties with George.

In September 1986 George acquired a new agent, Deborah Schneider, who sent George's two novels to Kate Miciak at Bantam Books. Bantam turned down *A Suitable Vengeance* but bought *A Great Deliverance* and agreed to take George's next novel.

Published in 1988, *A Great Deliverance* follows George's sleuths as they investigate the decapitation of a rich man and his daughter's questionable confession to the murder. Enthusiastically praised by most critics, *A Great Deliverance* won an Anthony Award (named for Anthony Boucher, the pseudonym of a well-known writer, critic, and fan of the mystery genre) and an Agatha Award (named for Agatha Christie). In addition, it was nominated for a Macavity Award (named for the mystery cat from T. S. Eliot's *Old Possum's Book of Practical Cats*) and an Edgar (named for Edgar Allan Poe, who has been called the father of the modern detective story), the most prestigious prize bestowed by the Mystery Writers of America. In France, *A Great Deliverance* won Le Grande Prix de Littérature Policière.

Payment in Blood (1989), George's second published work, is about the gory murder of a controversial playwright. Most reviewers found fault with the book but also much to admire. Rex E. Klett, for example, who critiqued it for *Library Journal* (July 1989), complained that it was "a bit mechanical in places, and slow-moving in others, but steadily absorbing and masterful overall"; he also described it as "literate, vastly detailed, and intricately characterized." In the *New York Times* (November 12, 1989), Josh Rubins, put off by what he called the novel's "foolishness and excess," rated it "unequal" to its predecessor; nevertheless, he wrote, "the crisp, literate narration firmly draws us in," and he noted that the book's "page-by-page satisfactions—dry humor, juicy dialogue, smartly paced shifts from one viewpoint to another—are considerable."

In the next five years, Bantam published five other books by George, including *A Suitable Vengeance*, in 1991. The others were *Well Schooled Murder* (1990), *For the Sake of Elena* (1992), *Missing Joseph* (1993), and *Playing for the Ashes* (1994). George's eighth Lynley mystery, *In the Presence of the Enemy* (1996), earned decidedly mixed reviews, with James Hynes, in the *Washington Post* (February 29, 1996), dismissing it as "the longest, slowest, dullest book I have ever read," while Mark Harris, in *Entertainment Weekly* (March 15, 1996), considered it "superb." Despite such negative assessments, *In the Presence of the Enemy* became the first of George's books to reach the best-seller list, where it remained for eight weeks. Inspired by the kidnapping and murder of 12-year-old Californian Polly Klass, in 1993, the novel chronicled the abduction of the illegitimate daughter of a member of Parliament. "It was the easiest one to write," George told Carey. "I only had two bad days on it. That's not to say I didn't groan and moan, but I never had that sense of, 'Oh, this is too big for me, I must be out of my mind.' I felt the story was solid, but I never thought it would take off the way it did."

In her ninth book, *Deception on His Mind* (1997), George dispensed with Lynley and St. James, and focused solely on Barbara Havers. The story is about Havers's investigation of the murder of a Pakistani immigrant. The idea for the plot came to George after she met Kay, a young Anglo-Pakistani woman, during the writer's research into Muslim culture. The product of a dysfunctional family, Kay had been victimized by an abusive husband. "Kay is 90 per cent of the reason the book exists, though it's not her life story," George told Syrie Johnson for *london.com* (on-line). "The first time we met we talked for four hours in which she did nothing but tell the story of her life and of the arranged marriage which she had agreed to and from which she then fled." "George doesn't disappoint with her latest mystery, which offers more than 600 pages in which fans may luxuriate," a reviewer for *Booklist* (May 15, 1997) declared. *Deception on His Mind* became George's second best-seller.

In *New York Newsday* (October 24, 1999, on-line), Matthew Flamm reported that a postcard George found discarded on a London street, offering the services of a "hot stunning Thai girl," triggered the idea for her 10th mystery, *In Pursuit of the Proper Sinner* (1999). In devising the plot, the writer, who is childless, also had in mind the saying "A thankless child is sharper than a serpent's tooth." Like its predecessors, the novel offers an intricately woven plot, this time centering on a brutal double murder that has taken place at the site of an ancient circle of stones known as a henge. Complicating the investigation is the identity of one of the victims—she was the daughter of a former Scotland Yard colleague and mentor of Lynley's—and Lynley's increasingly troubled relationship with Sergeant Havers, who has been demoted for behavior that the inspector belatedly discovers was justifiable. "Lynley makes mistakes," George told Matthew Flamm. "He has such difficulty seeing the shades of gray in life. I never wanted to have the detective as Godhead. That's obnoxious to me." She also said, "Self-doubt is the great leveler. If I can reveal a character's self-doubt and weakness, then I'm immediately creating a bond between the reader and the character." In a review of *In Pursuit of the Proper Sinner* for *BookBrowser.com* (July 13, 1999, on-line), Harriet Klausner wrote, "Once again . . . Elizabeth George creates a fantastic police procedural that will satisfy her legions of fans. . . . The who-done-it is superbly set up and well executed by linking two separate incidents that appear to have nothing in common. . . . The strained relationship between Barbara and Thomas provides insight into both characters as well as an understanding about police partnering." *In Pursuit of the Proper Sinner* debuted at number seven on the September 19 *New York Times* best-seller list and remained on the list for several weeks.

In 2001 George published the 11th Lynley and Havers mystery, *Traitor to Memory*, in which the detective duo are sent to Hampstead to puzzle over the vehicular death of a wealthy woman. A year later she published *I, Richard* (2002), her first-ever collection of short stories.

George has traveled extensively in the United States on book tours. The British writer, critic, and American-studies specialist Malcolm Bradbury has been commissioned to write scripts for *A Great Deliverance* and *A Suitable Vengeance* for BBC television.

George told Matthew Flamm that she considers three weeks of research sufficient preparation for each of her novels. In planning each book, she first chooses a killer, a victim, and the motive, and she decides how the story will end. She writes an outline and then a first draft. Next, she composes a second outline, adding new ideas, if any have occurred to her. She starts writing each day at 9:00 a.m. and sets a quota for herself of at least five pages a day. Since her divorce, in 1995, she told See, "I've built a family amongst my friends. Divorce has allowed me to enrich my friendships by becoming vulnerable and allowing my friends to give me support." George lives most of the year in Huntington Beach, California; within the past few years she has acquired a residence in England as well. "When the plane comes down in England," she told Valerie Takahama for the *Albany Times Union* (April 9, 1996, on-line), "I feel as if I'm coming home."

— J.K.B.

SUGGESTED READING: *Contra Costa Times* (on-line) Aug. 7, 1997; *Entertainment Weekly* p56+ Mar. 15, 1996, with photo; *New York Times* E p1+ Dec. 14, 1999, with photo; *People* p59+ Aug. 23, 1993, with photos; *Publishers Weekly* p38+ Mar. 11, 1996, with photos; *USA Today* (on-line), Dec. 2, 1999

SELECTED BOOKS: *A Great Deliverance*, 1988; *Payment in Blood*, 1989; *Well-Schooled in Murder*, 1990; *A Suitable Vengeance*, 1991; *For the Sake of Elena*, 1992; *Missing Joseph*, 1993; *Playing for the Ashes*, 1994; *In the Presence of the Enemy*, 1996; *Deception on His Mind*, 1997; *In Pursuit of the Proper Sinner*, 1999; *Traitor to Memory*, 2001; *I, Richard*, 2002

George, Nelson

Sep. 1, 1957– Novelist; screenwriter; critic

The African-American social critic, novelist, and film writer Nelson George got an early start chronicling the rise of hip-hop culture and its influence on—and reflection of—the larger American scene. In 1978, as a 21-year-old neophyte music critic, he covered a rap concert for the *Amsterdam News*, and his writing career has continued to flourish. He wrote a biography of the pop superstar Michael Jackson when he was 27 years old and went on to pen *Where Did Our Love Go?: The Rise and Fall of the Motown Sound* (1986) and *The Death of Rhythm & Blues* (1988), books that detailed changing tastes and mores in the world of black music

Daniela Federici/Courtesy of Simon & Schuster
Nelson George

Nelson George was born on September 1, 1957 in Brooklyn, New York, the son of Arizona Bacchus, a teacher, and Nelson E. George. His parents separated when he was young, and he was raised mainly by his mother. In a dialogue with Nathan McCall published in *Essence* (November 1995), George revealed that he had learned to respect women by watching the affectionate interaction between his mother and "a guy she went out with for about seven years." "So much of that respect comes from seeing how your father, or an adult male, deals with women on an individual basis," he said.

Prior to his graduation from St. John's University in Queens, New York, George had become a part-time staffer at the *Amsterdam News*, an African-American newspaper. He then embarked on a career as a critic of black music, on which he became an authority. He served as black music editor first for *Record World*, from 1981 to 1982, and then for *Billboard*.

George became a book author early in his career, publishing *Top of the Charts: The Most Complete Listing Ever* in 1983, when he was only 26 years old. The following year brought *The Michael Jackson Story*, termed one of George's two "classics of pop music journalism" by Al Young in the *New York Times Book Review* (December 11, 1988), and in 1985 he was a principal author of *Fresh, Hip Hop Don't Stop*. It was with *Where Did Our Love Go?: The Rise and Fall of the Motown Sound* (the other "classic") in 1986 that George solidified his reputation as a chronicler of the various forms of black music in America. *Where Did Our Love Go?* explores the creation of the Motown record label, which propelled the hit records of the Supremes, the Temptations, and Marvin Gaye, among others, by its legendary founder, Berry Gordy. Catherine Foster, writing in the *Christian Science Monitor* (February 26, 1986), termed the book "a clear-eyed, sometimes affectionate look at a remarkable man and his company that so fit the times. *Where Did Our Love Go?* is much more than a record industry book. It shows Motown to be an anthem of black pride and the sound of an era." George De Stefano, the reviewer for a more left-leaning publication, the *Nation* (August 23, 1986), however, deplored George's acceptance of "the black capitalist myth." He questioned whether such enterprises as Motown could "do anything but enrich a few entrepreneurs while increasing numbers of blacks fall into an impoverished underclass," noting that George evaded such questions.

George's *The Death of Rhythm & Blues* (1988) was written while he was black music editor of *Billboard*, the magazine where the term "rhythm & blues" was coined. The book is an elegy for the music that was once recorded on so-called "race" labels, music created, played, and disseminated by and for African-Americans. George discussed the effects of trying to sell that music to nonblacks, a process that caused some vitiation of the heritage of the blues- and gospel-based sound. He placed

and that were based largely on the expertise he had gained as a critic of black music for *Billboard* and as a columnist for the *Village Voice*. *Elevating the Game: Black Men and Basketball* (1992) and *Buppies, B-Boys, Baps & Bohos: Notes on Post-Soul Black Culture* (1992) delved further into the shaping influence of African-Americans on modern American mores. Films that George co-wrote, *Strictly Business* (1991) and *CB4* (1993), provided some of the background material for *Blackface: Reflections on African-Americans and the Movies* (1994), his examination of how blacks are depicted in American films and treated by the film industry—and of how the genre of "blaxploitation" films arose. *Hip Hop America* (1998) is a complete history of the rap-music industry and its various commercial offshoots, taking full account of the ironies inherent in the fact that the music and style of the underclass is appropriated by the mainstream. More recently he was the co-author of *Life and Def: Sex, Drugs, Money and God* (2001) with Russell Simmons.

George's novels, *Urban Romance: A Novel of New York in the 80s* (1993) and *Seduced: The Life and Times of a One-Hit Wonder* (1996) are fictional explorations of the relationship of young black men to their "roots." The protagonist of *Urban Romance* is a "buppie" who needs the help of a mailroom clerk to romance the woman he desires. In *Seduced*, the hero, after being seduced by the music business, returns to the core values of his upbringing. His more recent novels include *One Woman Short* (2000) and *Show and Tell* (2001), as well as the upcoming "Night Work," due to be published in June 2003.

the assimilation of black music into white culture in its historical context. Al Young, critiquing the volume in the *New York Times Book Review* (December 11, 1988), responded favorably to its "dispiriting conclusions." "Like many a 'race,' 'sepia,' 'ebony,' 'rhythm and blues' or 'soul' lyric, Nelson George's book is a many-leveled work. Its challenge to 'black artists, producers, radio programmers and entrepreneurs of every description to recapture their racial identity, and . . . the right to exist on their own terms' is mountain high and river deep, expressed with loving urgency," Young concluded. D'Evelyn Thomas, the reviewer for the *Christian Science Monitor* (July 27, 1988), agreed, calling George "a brilliant journalist—a historian prophet" and observing that *The Death of Rhythm & Blues* "is about hope as well as despair. . . . must reading."

George edited the 1990 volume *Stop the Violence: Overcoming Self-Destruction* for the National Urban League and wrote *In Living Color: The Authorized Companion to the Fox TV Series*, which was published in the following year. A film that he co-wrote, *Strictly Business*, was released in 1991. That comedy focuses on a young black real-estate salesman who has a decidedly middle-class fiancée but falls in love with a much hipper young woman—then seeks a mailroom employee's help in becoming hip enough to succeed with his new love. *Strictly Business* was not a critical success. Vincent Canby, who reviewed it for the *New York Times* (November 8, 1991), dubbed it "a junk bond of a movie" that has "the satiric edge of a damp croissant."

George, now writing a column for the *Village Voice* entitled "Native Son," had a bumper year in 1992. First came *Elevating the Game: Black Men and Basketball*, a consideration of the contributions made by black players to the game of basketball, from its origins in 1891 to the contemporary predominance of African-Americans in the sport. Robert Lipsyte, a sportswriter for the *New York Times* (February 7, 1992), termed George "a shrewd and sensitive observer of the connections among basketball, drugs, music and the streets" who looks at basketball "through the prism of the black esthetic." He deemed *Elevating the Game* a "smart, lively, funky required book." Michael E. Ross in the *New York Times Book Review* (March 29, 1992) praised "this folksy yet scholarly study," particularly for the way George "likens basketball to jazz and to the nervous, insistent rhythms of rap," making for "a rich, welcome addition" to the literature.

With *Buppies, B-Boys, Baps & Bohos: Notes on Post-Soul Black Culture*, also published in 1992, George continued his analysis of issues that concern African-Americans. Culled largely from his *Village Voice* columns, the pieces in this volume deal with politics, economics, racism, sexism, music, film, sports, literature, drugs, violence, and crime, among other topics. Through portraits of Spike Lee, Toni Morrison, and Al Sharpton, among others, George observed the beginning, in 1971, of four ways of characterizing American blacks that appeared in the media—as "buppies," or black yuppies; B-boys, streetwise products of hip-hop culture; baps, who resembled in their attitudes so-called Jewish-American princesses and princes; and bohos, a category made up largely of artists, who behaved in a nonconformist or nonstereotypical manner. George observed that these labels did not fit neatly and that most African-Americans fall into "some combustible compound" of the types. Margaret Flanagan in *Booklist* (February 1, 1993) called the book's assertions "[i]nsightful urban sociology." For Matthew Rees, who reviewed *Buppies, B-Boys, Baps & Bohos* for the *Washington Post Book World* (May 9, 1993), the volume provided "an entertaining trip through many aspects of post-soul black culture, ranging from a testimonial to *Ebony* magazine publisher John H. Johnson to a provocative work on what it means to be a black man." George displayed animosity toward those who, he felt, failed to acknowledge themselves as part of the black community. For example, he noted Colin Powell's and Bryant Gumbel's "crisp, polished" analyses of the U.S. invasion of Panama, opining that the two men's "affable explanations of imperialist aggression demonstrated that my race's quest for a piece of the pie has produced the best-paid house niggers in history." Rees called George's approach a "slash-and-burn style" that "makes his book eminently readable." He referred to George as "one of America's leading cultural critics."

George was honored with a Grammy Award in 1992 for his contribution to the liner notes for James Brown's album *Startime*. The film *CB4*, co-written by George and its star, the comedian Chris Rock, and co-produced by George, appeared in 1993. The movie's zany plot has a group of middle-class rappers pretending to be street thugs. Hal Hinson, reviewing *CB4* for the *Washington Post* (March 12, 1993), found it "primarily a collection of sight gags that lovingly poke fun at the whole rap scene, blaxploitation pictures and most of black culture." The movie looks at rap "with affectionate and tolerant nostalgia," Hinson added.

George's first novel, *Urban Romance: A Novel of New York in the 80s*, came out in 1993. The main plot of the novel concerns Dwayne, a critic writing about the rise of rap music, and Danielle, who leaves a publishing job to go to the Columbia University School of Journalism. Their romance is thwarted when Danielle gets pregnant. In a subplot, Danielle's roommate, Jacksina, a law clerk, is having an affair with an older judge. She too becomes pregnant; although the judge is married, he and Jacksina want to have the child. "The result: one failed romance, one happy couple—one yawning audience," the *Kirkus Reviews* (November 1, 1993) critic wrote. Most reviewers agreed with George Packer of the *Washington Post Book World* (March 6, 1994), who called George "a better sociologist and satirist than novelist." Critics also found the surrounding cast of characters more interesting than the main protagonists. "The novel is tiresome on love and relationships but offers a sharp insider's guide to the loose urban American subculture that includes Bronx rappers and Manhattan lawyers bound by race and divided by class," Packer wrote. Patricia O'Connell, in the *New York Times Book Review* (February 13, 1994), dubbed George "an excellent chronicler of the political climate, styles, club scene and rap music culture of New York," but she objected to the "many consumer brands, record titles and restaurant names" that "seem to crowd out the characters."

"More a memoir than a critique," according to George himself, *Blackface: Reflections on African-Americans and the Movies* (1994) deals with the image of African-Americans in film; Melvin Van Peebles, who pioneered the blaxploitation genre; Spike Lee, in whose first successful film, *She's Gotta Have It*, George invested some of the profits from his biography of Michael Jackson; the films of Sidney Poitier and Richard Pryor; and the making of *CB4*. The *Booklist* (October 15, 1994) reviewer, Benjamin Segedin, found the book to be "filled with keen observations and sharp analyses of the development of black cinema." He thought too much emphasis was placed on *CB4*, however, which was a box-office disappointment. The novelist Charles Johnson, who reviewed *Blackface* for the *Washington Post Book World* (October 23, 1994), deemed the subject of the book "the perennial artistic struggle of storytellers to create a cinema for black audiences in an industry where the figure for African-American directors and writers hovers at about 2 percent, and where everyone sooner or later comes to realize, 'you can't be a real rebel in the Black nationalist's sense, or be completely oppositional within the Hollywood system of compromise.'" Johnson gave George a vote of thanks for a contribution that "will have a place in the history of Hollywood's nerds and B-boys."

Seduced: The Life and Times of a One-Hit Wonder, George's second novel, came out in 1996. Narrated in the first person, it purports to be the story of Derek Harper, "a tunesmith, a hack, an artist, and a thief depending on the year, the place, and the speaker," as he describes himself. He begins his story in the 1960s in Queens, where he grows up as the son of an undertaker—at whose table conversation about the assassination of Martin Luther King "centered on the autopsy, the embalming, which Atlanta funeral home would land the contract, and how this prestigious job surely secured their future." Derek progresses through the music business, "seduced" by women, glitter, and instant success; he becomes a commercial jingle writer and a "one-hit wonder" before coming back to Queens, by way of Hollywood and Philadelphia, dedicated to serving his community with an arts center. The novel was widely praised for George's expert chronicling of the music business and his depiction of "the shark tank of the early 80s music biz," with its "rising rappers, wannabe stars and predatory record producers," as the *Washington Post Book World* (February 16, 1997) reviewer put it.

Hip Hop America (1998), the story of rap music from its origins in the South Bronx to its permeation of the wider society, was termed by Laura Jamison in the *New York Times Book Review* (November 15, 1998) a "rich cultural history." The "multi-billion dollar industry" spawned by hip-hop culture encompasses fashion and food and beverages, as well. "So powerful has been hip-hop's presence in American culture that nearly every black public intellectual has been compelled to either validate or scorn its presence," Mark Anthony Neal wrote in the *Washington Post Book World* (January 10, 1999). "Everyone from tenured Ivy League professors to the CEOs of multinational conglomerates have benefited from hip-hop's rise, whether or not their sympathies lie with the black urban underclass," he added, calling the book "a solid examination of black youth culture's continued influence on American society." Other mainstream publications, such as *Booklist* (September 15, 1998), also praised *Hip Hop America*. Michiko Kakutani, the reviewer for the *New York Times* (December 4, 1998), conceded George's argument that "the social conditions that forged hip-hop—poverty, drugs, deteriorating schools—continue to be problems, and that hip-hop continues to reflect and internalize 'our society's woes.'" She quoted George's premise that the reason hip-hop "has managed to remain vital, abrasive and edgy for two decades" is that it can "communicate dreams and emotions that make outsiders uncomfortable." Although some readers expressed disappointment with *Hip Hop America's* focus on "the MTV-approved face of rap, not the true story," George has obviously succeeded in putting forth the music he loves for America to understand and appreciate.

Most recently, George has co-authored *Life and Def: Sex, Drugs, Money and God*, with Russell Simmons, which tells of the music entrepreneur's rise in the hip-hop world. He has also authored the novels *One Woman Short* (2000) and *Show and Tell* (2001), both of which focus on the young urban black scene. A new novel, "Night Work," is expected in June 2003.

—S. Y.

SUGGESTED READING: *Booklist* p959 Feb. 1, 1993, p390 Oct. 15, 1994, Sep. 15, 1998; *Christian Science Monitor* p17 July 27, 1988; *Essence* p96+ Nov. 1995; *Kirkus Reviews* Nov. 1, 1993; *Newsweek* p66 Feb. 24, 1992; *New York Times* C p13 Nov. 8, 1991, B p11 Feb. 7, 1992, C p22+ Feb. 27, 1992, II p11 Mar. 1, 1992, E p45 Dec. 4, 1998; *New York Times Book Review* p16 Dec. 11, 1988, p16 Mar. 29, 1992, p18 Feb. 13, 1994; *Washington Post* D p7 Mar. 12, 1993; *Washington Post Book World* p6 May 9, 1993, p9 Mar. 6, 1994, p12 Apr. 17, 1994, p4 Oct. 23, 1994, p12 Feb. 16, 1997, p1 Jan. 10, 1999

SELECTED WORKS: novels—*Urban Romance: A Novel of New York in the 80s*, 1993; *Seduced: The Life and Times of a One-Hit Wonder*, 1996; *One Woman Short*, 2000; *Show and Tell*, 2001; nonfiction—*Top of the Charts: The Most Complete Listing Ever*, 1983; *Fresh, Hip Hop Don't Stop*, 1985; *Cool It Now: The Authorized Biography of New Edition*, 1986; *Where Did Our Love Go? The Rise & Fall of the Motown Sound*, 1987; *The Death of Rhythm & Blues*, 1988; *Buppies, B-Boys, Baps & Bohos*, 1992; *Elevating the Game: Black Men and Basketball*, 1992; *Blackface: Reflections on African Americans and the Movies*, 1994; *Hip Hop America*, 1998; *Life and Def: Sex, Drugs, Money and God*, 2001; screenplays—*Strictly Business*, 1991; *CB4*, 1993

Barbara Gundle/Courtesy of Houghton Mifflin Company

Gloss, Molly

Nov. 20, 1944– Novelist; short-story writer

In an interview for *Oregon Live* (1999, on-line), novelist and short-story writer Molly Gloss said, with characteristic modesty, "I am, foremost a reader. But when I can't find the book I want to read, then I shamelessly sit down and write the thing myself." She began her first novel, *Outside the Gates* (1986), when she wanted something good to read to her son as a Christmas present. It became a critically acclaimed young-adult fantasy book. Partly because she felt that Westerns, of which she had read many as a child, generally lacked strong female characters, she decided to write a story of a woman pioneer alone in the great West. The result, *The Jump-off Creek* (1989) featuring the steely character Lydia Sanderson, was a fi-

nalist for the PEN/Faulkner award. Her most recent novel, *Wild Life* (2000), also presents a female protagonist meeting the challenges of the West with moxie and a fierce independence. If Gloss's writing has been a response to a perceived lack in literature, it hasn't been without unifying themes. "One of the questions I always seem to be holding in my hand," Gloss told Heather Vogel Frederick for *Publishers Weekly* (July 10, 2000), "is the question of the human response to wilderness." Wilderness figures heavily in the works so far mentioned, as it does in her third novel, *Dazzle of Day* (1997), in which a group of Quakers pilots a spaceship in search of a new planet to settle. Like her other works, it was noted by critics for its originality and thoughtful composition.

In an autobiographical statement submitted to *World Authors 1995-2000*, Molly Gloss writes, "I'm frequently asked if I've always wanted to be a writer. I like to answer that I've always liked to write but no one ever told me I could grow up to be a writer. In the time and place I grew up, smart girls—girls who wanted to go to college—were encouraged and expected to grow up to be teachers or nurses while they waited to marry and have children, after which time they were expected to be housewives and mothers. Which is what I did, to a point. I taught only long enough to realize and admit I hated it, and then I took a clerk's job at a freight company—a job for women who hadn't gone to college—where I worked only until I had a child. Then I planned to devote myself to mothering. During all this time, I was writing, yes, but I never had finished anything, never had shown my writing to anyone, probably never had written anything very interesting. And no, I never had imagined that I would or could actually become a writer.

"The heroic myth of the Artist is almost always of a man writing in terrible but splendid isolation, sacrificing family for his art, and women, most women, have been excluded from this myth by their motherhood. Still, and yet, my life as a writer began with motherhood.

"Motherhood isn't trivial; its activities may be trivial, but they put you in touch, deeply and immediately and daily, with the great issues of Life: heavy duty things like Love and Loss, Growth and Tolerance and Dignity, Control and Conflict and Power—which are the issues, incidentally, that make great novels. I might have become a writer eventually without having first become a mother, but it's hard for me to imagine it.

"Of course, at the time, I thought I was writing to escape the trivialities and redundancies of mothering. I was finding a coherent space for Molly, now that I was always and only Mother and Wife. To give birth and bring up a child is to be about as awash in Life as you can be, and I was swimming hard, looking for a log to hang onto. I took to writing while my baby was sleeping, and later when he was in nursery school two mornings a week. I wrote a rather desperate journal, at first, and as I became a little less desperate I wrote short fictional anecdotes, bits and pieces of things, beginnings, middles or ends of imitative novels and stories.

"In August the year my son was six and registered for Fall kindergarten, I read about a competition for a Western novel by an unpublished writer. I was certainly unpublished. And I'd been a Western reader since I was 12, had begun with Ernest Haycox and Luke Short and worked my way up through the genre to H. L. Davis and Willa Cather and A. B. Guthrie, Jr. So I undertook to write a novel for this competition. The deadline was March 31st. For five months, I wrote about four hours a day—two in the early morning while my son slept, two in the afternoon while he was at school. In the last month, March, I rented an electric typewriter and began to spend 6 or 8 hours every day madly typing the thing up, rewriting as I went. And I mailed the novel on the afternoon of March 31st.

"It was a perfectly awful book. But everything (almost everything) I know about writing, I learned from writing that novel. The best way to become a writer, I discovered, is to practice writing a lot. And after that winter of steady writing, I always considered myself a writer. When strangers asked me what I did, I sometimes even had the nerve to answer that I was a Writer, even though their inevitable next question was 'Are you published?' and when I had to answer 'No' I could see them relegating me to a certain category of drowning mother, the sort who scribble anecdotes about her children and send them off to the Reader's Digest like desperate notes in bottles.

"But I knew by then, just by the act of daily writing, and the accomplishment of finishing a whole, a true novel (and even though it wasn't very good, there were good things in it: fine paragraphs, beautiful pages, lovely scenes) that I had, in fact, grown up to be a writer. For a while, it was difficult to take any pride in that—no money was being paid to me. We all know, in our culture, how little respect is attached to work that is unpaid. But my husband was unbegrudging, willing to keep on supporting me while I went on writing—which for a mother and a writer and a wife is the most fundamental and valuable kind of affirmation. So I kept at it, and in another year or so I sold a story for $35, and half a year later another one for $100, and after that I sold regularly, as they say in the business world, 'in the low three figures.' And by the time *The Jump-Off Creek* brought in heady sums—'low five figures'—my friends and relatives had begun to believe that I was a writer, and to describe me so to others. They even began to avoid calling me during my 'work hours,' for which I am deeply grateful—though they persist, to this day, in asking me 'Are you still writing?' as if it might be a mere phase I'll one day be finished with, or a temporary job I've taken until I decide to get on with my Real Life."

Molly Gloss was born in Portland, Oregon, on November 20, 1944. Her father, Charles David, was a railroad switchman, and her mother, Eleanor Marie (Bettey), worked as a housekeeper for a hospital. Gloss's family did not have a lot of money to spend on books, but every week they walked to the local library, where Gloss's father would take out a traditional Western novel and Gloss would raid the children's book shelves. Eventually Gloss outgrew juvenilia and acquired her father's literary tastes. She loved to ride horses and pretend that she was a cowboy herself. Because her father was originally from Texas, the family traveled there every summer to visit relatives, a custom that Gloss refers to as her "covered-wagon experience," as she told Frederick. "There were five of us and two big dogs and a huge umbrella tent, and driving across that glorious Western landscape that I read about in those adventure stories, sitting in front of a campfire every night—those books were perfect for me at that time of my life," she said.

Gloss received her B.A. in social science and English from Oregon's Portland State University in 1966; she then got her secondary teaching certificate. In June 1966 she married a truck driver by the name of Edward G. Gloss and started teaching in a junior high school in Portland. She disliked teaching, however, because she could not get the children to mind her, so she left the profession in 1967 to become a correspondence clerk for a local shipping company. "I might have gone on to be vice president of Consolidated Freightways," Gloss said during the *Oregon Live* interview. "I was on track for that, when I quit to have a baby."

Gloss left Consolidated Freightways in 1970. She later enrolled in a writing workshop taught by the novelist Ursula K. LeGuin at Portland State University. The positive feedback she got from LeGuin gave Gloss new confidence in her abilities as a writer. In 1981 she sold her first story, "Doe," to *Calyx: A Journal of Art and Literature by Women*. In 1984 "Joining" and "Seaborne" were published in the *Magazine of Fantasy and Science Fiction*, in the June and December issues respectively. That year Gloss's "Interlocking Pieces" was anthologized in *Universe 14*, edited by Terry Carr. "Field Trial" and "Wenonah's Gift" were published respectively in the February and July 1986 issues of *Isaac Asimov's Science Fiction Magazine*.

Gloss published her first novel, *Outside the Gates*, in 1986. In the story a young boy named Vren is banished from his city when he is discovered to have the ability to talk to animals. In the wilderness, he meets an older man, Rusche, who can manipulate the weather. Soon Vren meets many others who have an assortment of strange abilities. One day Rusche vanishes and Vren goes in search of him, only to discover that Rusche and others with powers like theirs have been captured by an evil spellbinder. Holly Sanhuber wrote about the book for *School Library Journal* (March 1987), "The conflict is cerebral and symbolic, and because the characters are ciphers, this mental conflict is bland and will not hold the interest of most readers." More typical of the novel's critical reception was Roger Sutton's review in the *Bulletin of the Center for Children's Books* (October 1986), in which he called *Outside the Gates* a "quiet, evocative fantasy." "The pacing is deliberate but never slow, and the drama unfolds carefully and subtly," he continued. "The depiction of the outcasts is powerful: scorned as children, living in separate solitude in the great forest, afraid to trust others like themselves."

Gloss set her next novel, *The Jump-Off Creek* (1989), close to home, but in an era long before Portland became a big city. The novel's protagonist, Lydia Sanderson, sells everything she owns after her husband's death and moves from Pennsylvania to the rainy wilderness of Oregon. The story takes place in 1895, a time when lone women are rare on the frontier. Lydia embraces a life of complete self-reliance and rejects most of her neighbors' offers of help. She encounters hardship and loneliness, yet she refuses to think of loneliness as anything other than a fact of life. Ursula Hegi, reviewing the novel in *New York Newsday* (August 20, 1989), felt that it was overly bleak and not revelatory of Lydia's deepest feelings. "[Gloss] documents Lydia's external journey with many convincing details," wrote Hegi, "but fails to explore her inner journey." Judith Freeman had the opposite reaction to Gloss's minimalist approach. "In fewer than 200 pages, Molly Gloss, in her first novel, has created a classic of its kind," Freeman wrote in her assessment of the book for the *Los Angeles Times Book Review* (November 5, 1989). "It's a case where what's been left out contributes as much to the success of a story as what's been put in. You tend to read between the lines of *The Jump-Off Creek*, and what you find in those undescribed spaces separating witheringly cruel events is enough valor to make an ordinary life seem heroic." In another, later review in the *Los Angeles Times Book Review* (September 26, 1999), Susan Salter Reynolds appreciated Gloss's unique portrait of loneliness, in which "the white space and the black letters seem to gleefully record the distance between us." *The Jump-Off Creek* was a finalist for the PEN/Faulkner Award and won the Oregon Book Award and the Pacific Northwest Booksellers Association Award.

Because it took critics and the literary establishment about a year to recognize Gloss's achievement in *The Jump-Off Creek*, she was initially convinced the book was a failure. Consequently, she decided to go back to what she knew best: science fiction. *The Dazzle of Day* was published in 1997 and tells the story of a group of Quakers who travel through space in search of a new planet after Earth becomes uninhabitable. The Quakers, who speak Esperanto and are predominantly of Latin American origin, travel aboard their ship, the Dusty Miller, for more than a hundred years. When they finally reach the planet on which they intend to settle, they discover a cold, relatively unfertile world. Some want to continue searching for a better planet, while others wish to make do with the one they've found. A general malaise settles over the group. One man commits suicide by slashing his spacesuit while on an exploratory mission. A virus, perhaps spread by several people who have explored the surface of the new planet, begins to spread through the ship. However, they refuse to surrender their ideal of living a virtuous life, and they must resolve the conflicts through discussion and unanimous agreement.

Gloss had some difficulty getting *The Dazzle of Day* published, partly, she said, because it did not fit into the categories of either conventional science fiction or mainstream fiction. "The literary houses," Gloss explained to Frederick, "would read it and say, gee, this is beautiful, it's lyrical and poetic, but there's a spaceship in it, and the science fiction houses would say, gee, this is beautiful, it's lyrical and poetic, but there are no robots or laser guns." A critic for *Kirkus Reviews* (April 15, 1997) echoed the sentiment of the publishing houses, describing *The Dazzle of Day* as "either a meticulous, utopian study of character and society whose natural mainstream audience won't relish the sf [science fiction] setting, or an sf adventure unsatisfyingly deficient in incident and up-front problem-solving." Sybil S. Steinberg, writing for *Publishers Weekly* (May 26, 1997), seemed not to mind the novel's lack of "incident": "This is a novel of ideas, in the utopian tradition, but every idea finds its way to the reader through one or more characters. Intelligent and entertaining, it demonstrates why Gloss was a recent winner of a Whitman Writer's Award." Indeed, *The Dazzle of Day* earned a Whitman Award, as well as an Oregon Book Award and mention as a *New York Times* Notable Book.

Gloss returned to the West for the setting of her next novel, which also features a female heroine living in Oregon—this time in the early 1900s. In *Wild Life* (2000) Charlotte Bridger Drummond, a mother of five who supports her family by writing pulp adventure novels, sets out on an adventure of her own, joining a search party for her housekeeper's daughter, who has disappeared near a logging camp in the wilderness. A stubborn individualist, Charlotte smokes cigars and dresses in men's clothing to shock her neighbors. Through Charlotte's narration, excerpts from her diary, and her other writings, the reader follows her over hills and through valleys, into caves and dense forests. Although most of her novels are set in the wilderness, she has never experienced it firsthand. Therefore she is unprepared to face the rigors of the wild when she becomes separated from the rest of the search party after fleeing a sexual assault. She is rescued by a clan of giant, hairy bigfoots, which resemble creatures she has written about in her own stories. They are peaceable, and though they don't speak, they communicate through gestures. Free from the constraints of language and society, Charlotte reexamines her life and realizes that she is not satisfied with writing pulp fiction and living in a

GOODKIND

fantasy world. "Unfortunately, the heavily stylized Victorian prose of Charlotte's adventure stories is often self-consciously campy, and her lengthy feminist tracts prove didactic and repetitive," wrote Norah Labiner for *Minneapolis-Star Tribune* (July 30, 2000). Ultimately, Labiner concluded, "Gloss's *Wild Life*, though uneven, is a bold and inventive novel about how the stories we consume come to define us." Many critics agreed that *Wild Life* was bold and inventive, and few disliked the voice of Gloss's narrator. In the *Denver Post* (June 18, 2000, on-line) Kristen Iversen wrote, "In stunningly lyrical prose and a tone that exercises just the right degree of restraint, *Wild Life* is sure to mark a solid place for its author in the ranks of contemporary women who challenge the way the West has been written." In the *Detroit Free Press* (June 18, 2000, on-line), Susan Hall-Balduf gave the novel four out of four stars, stating "I have been asked why I write book reviews as if the people in a novel were real. The answer is simple: Authors like Molly Gloss make them real."

Gloss was recently widowed and lives in Portland. After finishing *Wild Life*, Gloss's next course of action was to "shovel out the house, and work my way down to the bottom of the unanswered mail," as she told *Oregon Live*. She then began another novel, tentatively set in Washington in 1910 and narrated by a female ornithologist. However, her writing was interrupted when her husband died. "With all the changes that have taken place in my life," Gloss said to Frederick, "I'll just have to look at it and see, when I get back to it, whether it still interests me."

—P. G. H.

SUGGESTED READING: *Bulletin of the Center for Children's Books* p26 Oct. 1986; *Detroit Free Press* (on-line) June 18, 2000; *Los Angeles Times Book Review* p21 Nov. 5, 1989; *Minneapolis-Star Tribune* F p14 July 30, 2000; *Newsday* p13 Aug. 20, 1989; *New York Times Book Review* p24 June 22, 1997; *Oregon Live* (on-line) 1999; *Publishers Weekly* p71 May 26, 1997, p36+ July 10, 2000; *Washington Post* D p2 Mar. 9, 1990

SELECTED BOOKS: *Outside the Gates*, 1986; *The Jump-off Creek*, 1989; *Dazzle of Day*, 1997; *Wild Life*, 2000

Goodkind, Terry

1948– Fantasy novelist

Terry Goodkind is the author of the best-selling *Sword of Truth* series. His fresh take on the fantasy genre has earned him many fans and a place on best-seller lists worldwide. Though he did not begin writing professionally until his 40s, Goodkind feels that writing had always been his calling. As he told James Frenkel in an interview posted on *Prophets, Inc.*, his official Web site: "When I'm not writing, I generally feel I'm wasting time." He continued, "It's the thing I absolutely love to do more than anything I've ever done in my life. Writing is magic for me. Maybe that's why I feel such a deep connection to fantasy, to magic." Despite that, Goodkind feels that his books transcend the genre for most of his readers. "I have yet to receive a letter from a fan telling me they love the books because of the magic," he told Frenkel. "They all say they love the books because they can empathize with the characters and are enthralled with the tale."

Terry Goodkind was born in 1948 in Omaha, Nebraska. He was dyslexic and found reading difficult. "From the beginning, teachers dealt with this learning disorder by ridiculing and humiliating me," he recalled to Frenkel. "What they actually taught me was to hate reading. Reading became a form of punishment. . . . I felt like I was being told by the adults that I wasn't good enough to read, that I wasn't trying hard enough." Despite his academic difficulties, he had an active imagination and constantly created characters and adventures in his head. He never tried getting his tales on paper,

Courtesy of Jeri Goodkind

however. "Because of my dyslexia, I'm a lousy speller," he told Frenkel. "So everything I wrote down was simply more fuel for ridicule. I wasn't about to add more fuel to that fire." Although Goodkind hated his teachers' assigned readings, which he found boring and irrelevant, he did read at home, sometimes hiding in his closet to peruse books he had snuck out of the local library. Mark

Twain and Edgar Rice Burroughs were particular favorites, and he devoured nonfiction books on astronomy and rocket science.

In Goodkind's senior year in high school, he finally connected with one of his English teachers. Though she pointed out his grammatical and spelling errors, unlike other teachers she also made him understand that there was something in writing just as important as the mechanics—the story. She enjoyed his compositions and read them to his classmates, and he soon began staying after school, talking with her about his assignments and stories he had written outside of class. "She let me touch something noble," Goodkind told Frenkel. "This changed my world."

Goodkind, who had always shown a talent for painting and drawing, attended art school after high school. He then embarked upon a career as a respected wildlife artist, as well as a cabinet maker, a violin maker, and a restorer of rare artifacts—all the while continuing to imagine stories in his head. In his 40s, while building a house in the woods for himself and his wife, Jeri, vivid scenes began occurring to him, and characters started to develop. He told Frenkel, "I guess you could say that it [was] a little like seeing a movie." When he completed the house, he began to write the story down. His art background helped. "In order to paint, you have to see what is really there," he explained on his Web site. "When I [imagine] these things in my head, and it comes time to write them down, that artistic ability helps me to describe in an accurate way what I'm seeing, what is really there. I think it helps me bring texture and life to my writing." Within 13 months he had finished his first novel, *Wizard's First Rule*, which was sold at auction in 1994. After earning more than six times the record price for a first fantasy novel, *Wizard's First Rule* quickly became a worldwide best-seller upon its publication later that year.

The novel, set in a fantastic world populated with wizards, warriors, and dragons, is the first part of Goodkind's *Sword of Truth* series, and in it the reader is introduced to the two main characters, Richard Cypher, a forest guide and future wizard, and Kahlan Amnell, a mysterious woman who becomes his great love. War is about to break out, and Richard, as the only one who knows the secrets kept in the "Book of Counted Shadows," is presented with the Sword of Truth, thus becoming a "Seeker of Truth." He rescues Kahlan from assassins, and they join forces with a wizard named Zedd to prevent Darken Rahl, an evil despot, from enslaving humanity and destroying the world. In an essay posted on *Prophets, Inc.*, Goodkind described Richard as "someone who I admire, someone who has qualities I look up to—qualities of honor, integrity, and honesty—but who at the same time makes mistakes just like the rest of us." Jackie Cassada, writing for *Library Journal* (September 15, 1994), remarked that the novel "offers an intriguing variant on the standard fantasy quest."

In the second novel in the series, *Stone of Tears* (1995), Goodkind reveals that Richard has discovered that Darken Rahl, whom he had banished to another world in *Wizard's First Rule*, is actually his father and that Zedd is in fact his grandfather. Still reeling from these revelations, Richard must do battle with the Keeper of the Underworld. Meanwhile, Kahlan pits her young army against Rahl's conflict-tested warriors in what a *Publishers Weekly* (September 25, 1995) reviewer called "one of the most vigorous battle sequences written for a heroine in modern fantasy."

The adventures of Richard and Kahlan continued with *Blood of the Fold* (1996), in which Kahlan goes into hiding to avoid being executed by her own people. Richard, accepting his lineage as a wizard, must unify the Midlands in a battle against a diabolic emperor. In the fourth book, *Temple of the Winds* (1997), the duo go on a quest in search of a mythical temple that had vanished 3,000 years earlier. In the series' fifth episode, *Soul of the Fire* (1999), Richard and Kahlan seek a way to summon the three Chimes—powerful, magical creatures. They must also contend with Emperor Jagang, who is making war in D'Hara. The war against Jagang and his evil forces continues in *Faith of the Fallen* (2000), in which Kahlan is badly wounded and Richard is enslaved. A reviewer for *Publishers Weekly* (July 24, 2000) described the plot's political subtext: "Goodkind's fans—and they are legion—will revel in vicarious berserker battle scenes and agonize deliciously as Richard . . . toils to establish a bastion of Capitalism in the cold gray heart of the Stalinesque Old World." In an interview posted on his Web site, Goodkind, who described his books as "a cry of defiance into the descending storm of tyranny," touches on his political leanings, writing, "We live in one of the most politically repressive times in our nation's history. The McCarthy era was small potatoes compared to the thought-police in this dark age of political correctness."

In 2001 Goodkind wrote *Debt of Bones*, a prequel to the *Sword of Truth* series that details the adventures of a younger Zedd, who is asked by a poor peasant woman named Abby to rescue her town. Jackie Cassada, reviewing the book for *Library Journal* (December 1, 2001), had much praise for it: "This revised version of a novella that first appeared in the fantasy anthology *Legends* illuminates the period in history before the events of Goodkind's *Sword of Truth* series. The conflict between love and duty forms a central theme in this brief and touching tale of people caught up in events they cannot fully control."

When Goodkind returned to the series with *Pillars of Creation* (2002), he focused on Darken Rahl's illegitimate daughter (and thus Richard's sister) and her struggles to find the truth about her ancestry. Jeremy Pugh, a reviewer for *Amazon.com*, remarked, "Loyal readers . . . may find this book tedious as they wonder when Lord Richard Rahl and Mother Confessor Kahlan are going to swoop in and save the day. But Goodkind appears to be challenging readers, and perhaps himself, to see the benevolent administration of Richard Rahl from its underside and from an opposition perspective. The change in perspective works up to a point. Goodkind has created a fast-paced adventure story that might be appreciated by diehard fans if they can leave their longing for the status quo at the door." A new novel featuring Richard and Kahlan, "Naked Empire," is expected to be published in July 2003.

Goodkind, for his part, returns the devotion of his die-hard fans. "I have always considered it an honor that readers would give me that most precious of commodities: time," he wrote for his Web site. "I feel duty bound to give them value in return for their investment. I endeavor not to waste their time—to make it worth their while from the first sentence."

—C. M.

SUGGESTED READING: Booklist p28 Sep. 1, 1994, p254 Oct. 1, 1995, p576 Nov. 15, 1996; Kirkus Reviews p1147 Aug. 15, 1995, p 1434 Oct. 1, 1996; Library Journal p94 Sep. 15, 1995, p91 Oct. 15, 1995, p131 May 15, 1999, p181 Dec. 1, 2001; Prophets, Inc.—The Official Terry Goodkind Web site; Publishers Weekly p65 Aug. 29, 1994, p48 Sep. 1995, p66 Oct. 7, 1996, p73 July 24, 2000, p52 Nov. 19, 2001

SELECTED BOOKS: *Wizard's First Rule*, 1994; *Stone of Tears*, 1995; *Blood of the Fold*, 1996; *Temple of the Winds*, 1997; *Soul of the Fire*, 1999; *Faith of the Fallen*, 2000; *Debt of Bones*, 2001; *Pillars of Creation*, 2002

Denise Applewhite/Courtesy of University Press

Grafton, Anthony

May 21, 1950– Historian

The historian Anthony Grafton has written several books about intellectual life during the Renaissance. Grafton's work has brought the period to life for both academics and the general reader with detail and scholarly analysis that are solidly documented with primary sources. Among Grafton's best-known books are the two-volume *Joseph Scaliger: A Study in the History of Classical Scholarship* (1983 and 1993), *Forgers and Critics: Creativity and Duplicity in Western Scholarship* (1990), *Defenders of the Text: The Traditions of Scholarship in an Age of Science, 1450–1800* (1991), *The Footnote: A Curious History* (1997), *Cardano's Cosmos: The Worlds and Works of a Renaissance Astrologer* (1999), *Leon Battista Alberti: Master Builder of the Italian Renaissance* (2000), and *Bring Out Your Dead: The Past as Revelation* (2002). Discussing his research with Scott McLemee for the *Chronicle of Higher Education* (July 5, 2002), Grafton said, "There's a sensibility from this era that I grow more impressed with over time. It's the understanding that tradition, a sophisticated tradition anyway, like that of the classics, always knows more than you do."

The son of a journalist, Anthony Grafton was born on May 21, 1950 in New Haven, Connecticut. He recalled the spirited discussions that took place over the family dinner table to McLemee: "It was the serious talk of serious people about serious things; it made a compelling way to encounter some of the complexities of the world and history for the first time." After high school Grafton enrolled at the University of Chicago in Illinois. There he took a course on Renaissance humanism and discovered the body of scholarship and literature that had been published between the periods of the Middle Ages and the Enlightenment. This study of "neo-Latin" texts, as they were called by scholars, appealed to him because most of those in academia had given little attention to the works, studying instead ancient Greek and Roman texts. "I could read Latin and Greek, and I really liked this later writing, with its dense thicket of allusions," he explained to McLemee. In 1970 Grafton received his bachelor's degree in classics. He continued his education at the University of Chicago, earning his master's degree in 1972 and his Ph.D. in 1975. After receiving his doctorate, Grafton became an assistant professor of history at Princeton University in New Jersey. He was promoted to associate professor in 1976 and full professor in 1985. Grafton has been Princeton's Andrew Mellon Professor of History (1988–93) and its Dodge Professor of History (1993–2000). He was also named Behrman Senior Fellow in the Humanities (1994–95). Since 2000 he has served as the Henry Putnam University Professor at Princeton.

In 1983 Grafton published the first book of a two-volume biography of Joseph Scaliger, a 16th-century humanist scholar. Thomas D'Evelyn reviewed *Joseph Scaliger: A Study in the History of Classical Scholarship, Volume 1: Textual Criticism and Exegesis* for the *Christian Science Monitor* (April 4, 1984), writing, "Scaliger translated the texts from the ancients and balanced the technical discussion—fascinating as a record of a fusion of rational and rhetorical method—with absorbing discussions of the disputes, characteristic of national awakening, between scholars from opposing parts of Europe." The reviewer continued, "Joseph Scaliger is one of the great scholars and, as Grafton's readable and exact book shows, an exceedingly interesting man. Scaliger was an original. With full faith in his ability to establish accurate texts for ancient authors, he managed to leave his stamp on many of the classics to this day. Grafton clearly cares about his subject and about making him available to intelligent general readers as well as scholars." In the *Times Literary Supplement* (August 18, 1983), E. G. Kennedy wrote, "Grafton's analyses of [his] works bring out sharply [Scalinger's] strengths and weaknesses as a scholar. . . . Grafton occasionally gives him the benefit of the doubt when he does not really deserve it." Despite this mild criticism, Kennedy concluded that the first volume was a "fine characterization of a supremely gifted scholar and thoroughly mixed-up-man." The second book, *Joseph Scaliger: A Study in the History of Classical Scholarship, Volume 2: Historical Chronology*, appeared in 1993. "The new volume is huge and complex, covering a wide variety of mostly unfamiliar materials, often highly technical and at the time deeply controversial," Timothy J. Reiss wrote in his review for the *Renaissance Quarterly* (Autumn 1996). "It is packed with detail."

In 1986 Grafton and Lisa Jardine published *From Humanism to the Humanities: Education and the Liberal Arts in Fifteenth- and Sixteenth-Century Europe*. "In so far as it sets out to demythologize humanistic education," J. B. Trapp wrote for the *Times Literary Supplement* (July 24, 1987), "this book will seem harshly reductive to some and gaff-blowing to others, according to their sympathies. The disinterested reader will raise an eyebrow at some of its generalizations. None of this should obscure the solid merits or the importance of Grafton and Jardine's investigation. Its great value lies in its close scrutiny of the modern historiography of Renaissance education and its insistence that historians should give practice as much attention as theory. Above all, it is welcome for the mass of new information that is revealed by its determined realism. Not the whole story, but a necessary part of it, is here told with great learning and skill."

In *Forgers and Critics: Creativity and Duplicity in Western Scholarship* (1990), Grafton explores the history of literary forgery, writing about such figures as James MacPherson (1736–96), Thomas Chatterton (1752–70), Carlo Sigonio (1524–84), Giovanni Nanni (1487–1546), and Desiderius Erasmus (1466–1536). Grafton discusses such scholars as Porphyry (232–305), Isaac Casaubon (1599–1671), and Richard Reitzenstein (1861–1931), who studied and exposed numerous forgeries. "Porphyry, Casaubon, and Reitzenstein, united by the Hermetic forgeries which drew out their critical skills, are heroes of Grafton's book," the British historian Hugh Trevor-Roper wrote for the *New York Review of Books* (December 6, 1990). "Together they illustrate the thesis which periodically emerges and then sinks again in the rich and, alas, necessarily compressed detail around it, viz: that forgery and criticism are interdependent; that their basic techniques, though sophisticated, haven't changed since Hellenistic times, and that forgery, by provoking critical antibodies, ends by fortifying scholarship itself."

In 1990 Grafton and Ann Blair co-edited *The Transmission of Culture in Early Modern Europe*, a collection of eight academic papers that had been delivered at the Shelby Cullom Davis Center for Historical Studies at Princeton. "The results appear more as a series of interesting studies, than as a structured attempt at shared discourse, and this is on the whole to be accounted a virtue," Felicity Heal wrote in her review for *History Today* (June 1991). "The themes of papers range from fairly traditional ideas history—Alan Charles Kors on 'Theology and Atheism in Early Modern France'—through Anthony Grafton's entertaining study of the forgeries of Annius of Viterbo, an exercise in the reconstruction of Renaissance mentalities—to Inga Clennidinnen's ambitious examination of non-communication between cultures, 'Cortes, Signs and the Conquest of Mexico.'" Heal concluded that the collection was "rather a mixed bag, but one which should contain something of interest for most scholars of the early modern period."

In his next book, *Defenders of the Text: The Traditions of Scholarship in an Age of Science, 1450–1800* (1991), a collection of nine essays, Grafton asserts that the humanistic tradition remained vibrant and influential several centuries after the Renaissance. Grafton's essays cover such topics as the German scientist Johannes Kepler; Isaac Casaubon's exposure of the *Corpus Hermeticum*, central texts of the Gnostic tradition; Joseph Scaliger's work on chronology; and the controversy between two 15th-century teachers of rhetoric, Cristoforo Landino of Florence and Giovanni Pietro of Lucca. In the *English Historical Review* (April 1992), Peter Burke wrote, "Grafton's essays show him at his best. All nine pieces are learned, lucid, witty and incisive and all have something important to say." Burke continued, "Grafton has a gift for synthesizing the work of others, while adding ideas of his own. It is difficult to fault the specific arguments of any of these essays, or indeed to find errors." In the *Times Literary Supplement* (August 16, 1991), Oswin Murray also praised *Defenders of the Text*, describing it as a "sheer delight—a real feast of intellectual scholarship and a hilarious account of the mannerist fantasia that was the European intellectual scene in the sixteenth and seventeenth centuries."

In 1992, with April Shelford and Nancy Siraisi, Grafton published *New Worlds, Ancient Texts: The Power of Tradition and the Shock of Discovery*, a catalogue that accompanied an exhibition mounted by the New York Public Library. The catalogue examines how the discovery of the New World affected the intellectual life of Europe during the Renaissance. Many scholars of the period, deeply influenced by ancient texts, were forced to revise their views of the world to accommodate the discovery, and intense disagreements ensued. "By carefully selecting from the New York Public Library's vast collection, Anthony Grafton and his colleagues April Shelford (who curated the exhibition) and Nancy Siraisi capture the vitality of European intellectual history during a period of momentous change," Carla Rahn Phillips wrote for the *Journal of American History* (June 1994). "They demonstrate how sophisticated thinkers gradually assimilated new knowledge about the world and interpreted it for their contemporaries. Handled with imagination, the texts define a world in flux, struggling to make sense of itself. Europe's intellectual dilemma had important moral and ethical dimensions. It responded to the encounter with unfamiliar peoples and situations, but it was timeless in a concern for justice, honor, religion, ethics, and other human issues." *New Worlds, Ancient Texts* was honored with the 1993 *Los Angeles Times* Book Prize.

Grafton edited *Rome Reborn: The Vatican Library and Renaissance Culture* (1993), for an exhibition of the Library of Congress in Washington, D.C. The essays in the catalogue discuss the history of the *Biblioteca Apostolica Vaticana*, the Vatican Library, which has one of the most extensive collections in the world. Pope Nicholas V, who had a personal collection of about 1,200 volumes, conceived the idea of a Vatican library a short time before his death in 1455. His successor, Sixtus IV, organized the library and appointed its first custodian in 1475. Since then, the Vatican Library has amassed an extensive collection containing millions of books, manuscripts, archival materials, works of art, prints, drawings, maps, and artifacts, making it an important source for scholars around the world.

In their book *The Foundations of Early Modern Europe, 1460–1559* (1994), Grafton and Eugene F. Rice analyze the economic, cultural, political, intellectual, historical, and religious forces that contributed to the development of Europe. In his review for the *Sixteenth Century Journal* (Fall 1995), D. Darek Jarmola expressed mixed feelings about the work. "The early parts of the book, primarily chapters 1 and 2 (on technological inventions and economic expansion), tend to leave the reader with an unfinished story, the text having produced more questions [than] answers," Jarmola wrote. "The authors are at their best, however, when dealing with intellectual and political history (chapters 3 and 4). Their accounts of the rediscovery of the Greek classics and their impact on the European's new understanding of history, education, art, philosophy, and human dignity are presented with outstanding clarity." Although the reviewer faulted Grafton and Rice for excluding large sections of Europe from the book's focus, Jarmola concluded that the "authors' ability to explain various aspects of history in a concise and clear manner makes this volume an excellent textbook for courses in European history since 1500."

Grafton's next book was *The Footnote: A Curious History* (1997). Grafton found several extremely early examples of footnoting: Krateros of Macedon, who visited the archives in Athens in the fourth century B. C., used a method of citation in his work, and Manetho, an Egyptian priest, and Berosus, a Chaldean, produced footnoted histories of their peoples for Alexander the Great in the third century B. C. According to Grafton, European humanists such as the French writer Jacques-Auguste de Thou popularized the use of the footnote among scholars, as part of improved standards of research and proof. "Grafton's essay itself is an example of the best erudition and reasoned argument," Patricia H. Smith wrote for the *Journal of American History* (December 1999). "[Grafton's] fondness for the republic of letters, present and past, as well as his passion for the messy, equivocal craft of history come through clearly in this elegant work."

Grafton next published *Cardano's Cosmos: The Worlds and Works of a Renaissance Astrologer* (1999), a biography of the accomplished Italian scholar, who lived from 1501 to 1576. Although he was a proficient mathematician and physician, Cardano is most remembered as an astrologer who drew up horoscopes for the wealthy and the powerful. During the Inquisition, the Church condemned Cardano, who was sentenced to house arrest. "The combination of telling detail and intellectual sweep in *Cardano's Cosmos* is irresistible, and it shapes Grafton's book as Cardano once shaped his disparate empirical data into system," Ingrid D. Rowland wrote for the *New York Review of Books* (February 22, 2001). "We do not accept the system now, but Cardano himself, as [Grafton] makes movingly clear, still 'deserves to be heard.'" Writing for the *Wilson Quarterly* (Spring 2000), Laura Ackerman Smoller was also impressed by the book. "Grafton's methodology, a combination of old-fashioned intellectual history and the newer discipline of the history of books and readers (what he calls the perspective of 'the parachutist and the truffle-hunter'), makes this book more than just an examination of Cardano," Smoller noted. "Through wonderfully vivid prose, the reader enters Cardano's cosmos—a place no more unreasonable or contradictory, the author points out, than a world in which scholars 'use computers to write and fax machines to submit the conference papers in which they unmask all of modern science as a social product.'"

In 2000 Grafton published another biography, *Leon Battista Alberti: Master Builder of the Italian Renaissance*. Alberti (1406–1472) mastered philosophy, music, literature, mathematics, and architecture and was one of the most important figures of the Renaissance. He wrote several notable treatises on architecture and designed the Santa Maria Novella, a church in Florence, as well as the San Andrea and San Sebastiano churches in Mantua. Alberti's designs influenced architecture for the next several centuries. "This fully documented volume seeks to understand the man and his entire body of work," Ellen Bates wrote in her review for the *Library Journal* (November 1, 2000). "This wholly absorbing account of a man who became a bridge between the literary and engineering worlds and elevated the arts to a status above craft will appeal to serious general readers as well as specialists." In the *New York Review of Books* (September 20, 2001), Joseph Connors concluded that the book "is a powerful attempt to see a unified personality behind the practitioner of so many different professions. [Grafton] is superb on historiography and his range of reference is extraordinarily wide."

In *Bring Out Your Dead: The Past as Revelation* (2002), Grafton writes in a series of essays about the intellectual life of several Renaissance scholars. "Many of the scholars who between the 15th century and the 19th recovered the ancient world and created the disciplines of modern learning were weird," D. J. R. Bruckner wrote for the *New York Times Book Review* (June 23, 2002). "And no one captures their grit, brawling and glory like Anthony Grafton. Or with such humor; I can't think of another intellectual historian of his stature who would give a book a title that invokes, among other jokes, a classic Monty Python scene [from the 1975 film *Monty Python and the Holy Grail*]." Bruckner observed that Grafton's "passion is for understanding and, as he confronts its pioneers, who are themselves responding sharply to ancient and contemporary writers, the polyphonic conversation becomes a discourse about how we have become who we are. Like the contentious people in his book, he wants to leave behind students who are in love with discovery."

Grafton has been the co-editor of such scholarly works as *Secrets of Nature: Astrology and Alchemy in Early Modern Europe* (2001), with William R. Newman; *Historians and Ideologues: Essays in Honor of Donald R. Kelly* (2001), with J. H. M. Salmon; and *Conversion: Old Worlds and New* (2003) and *Conversion in Late Antiquity and the Middle Ages: Seeing and Believing* (2003), both with Kenneth Mills.

Anthony Grafton's work has been translated into numerous languages. He is the recipient of an honorary Woodrow Wilson fellowship, a Danforth fellowship, a Fulbright-Hays fellowship, a Guggenheim fellowship, and grants from the National Endowment for the Humanities, among other honors. His awards include the Sixteenth Century Studies Conference's 1998 Bainton Prize for Literature and the American Historical Association's 2000 Marron Prize.

Anthony Grafton is married and is the father of two children. He and his family live in Princeton, New Jersey.

—D. C.

SUGGESTED READING: *Christian Science Monitor* p22 Apr. 4, 1984; *Chronicle of Higher Education* p12+ July 5, 2002; *English Historical Review* p397 Apr. 1992; *History Today* p61 June 1991; *Journal of American History* p233 June 1994, p1312+ Dec. 1999; *Library Journal* p78 Nov. 1, 2000; *New York Review of Books* p26 Dec. 6, 1990, p29+ Feb. 22, 2001, p73+ Sep. 20, 2001; *New York Times Book Review* p7+ June 23, 2002; *Renaissance Quarterly* p669 Autumn 1996; *Sixteenth Century Journal* p765+ Fall 1995; *Times Literary Supplement* p871 Aug. 19, 1983, p787 July 24, 1987, p5 Aug. 16, 1991; *Wilson Quarterly* p131 Spring 2000

SELECTED BOOKS: *Joseph Scaliger: A Study in the History of Classical Scholarship, Volume 1: Textual Criticism and Exegesis*, 1983; *From Humanism to the Humanities: Education and the Liberal Arts in Fifteenth- and Sixteenth-Century Europe* (with Lisa Jardine), 1986; *Forgers and Critics: Creativity and Duplicity in Western Scholarship*, 1990; *Defenders of the Text: The Traditions of Scholarship in an Age of Science, 1450–1800*, 1991; *New Worlds, Ancient Texts: The Power of Tradition and the Shock of Discovery* (with April Shelford and Nancy Siraisi), 1992; *Joseph Scaliger: A Study in the History of Classical Scholarship, Volume 2: Historical Chronology*, 1993; *The Foundations of Early Modern Europe, 1460–1559* (with Eugene F. Rice), 1994; *The Footnote: A Curious History*, 1997; *Commerce with the Classics: Ancient Books and Renaissance Readers*, 1997; *Cardano's Cosmos: The Worlds and Works of a Renaissance Astrologer*, 1999; *Leon Battista Alberti: Master Builder of the Italian Renaissance*, 2000; *Bring Out Your Dead: The Past as Revelation*, 2002; as editor—*Secrets of Nature: Astrology and Alchemy in Early Modern Europe* (with William R. Newman) 2001; *Historians and Ideologues: Essays in Honor of Donald R. Kelly* (with J. H. M. Salmon), 2001; *Conversion: Old Worlds and New* (with Kenneth Mills), 2003; *Conversion in Late Antiquity and the Middle Ages: Seeing and Believing* (with Kenneth Mills), 2003

Debi Milligan/Courtesy of Elizabeth Graver/Hyperion

Graver, Elizabeth

July 2, 1964– Novelist; short-story writer

The American novelist and short-story writer Elizabeth Graver has used varied approaches in dealing with a common theme—the relationship between parents and children and the ways in which young people are fostered and brought to maturity. Her first novel, *Unravelling* (1997), is set in 19th-century New England, but its story of a young woman's growth to a mature understanding of the world and an ability to come to terms with its harshness—as well as that of her own mother—has universal implications. Her second novel, *The Honey Thief* (1999), which also deals with a young girl's growing understanding and a mother's dilemmas, has a contemporary flavor. In a laudatory review in the *Atlanta Journal-Constitution* (August 17, 1997), Carolyn Nizzi Warmbold observed of *Unravelling* that the "voice, the plot, the characters all weave a beautiful fabric of fiction that is rare in these days to behold." *The Honey Thief* received an equally warm critical reception. With her volume of short stories, *Have You Seen Me?* (1991), Graver won the Drue Heinz Literature Prize.

Elizabeth Graver sent the following autobiographical statement to *World Authors 1995-2000*: "I was born in Los Angeles, California, in 1964, but my family moved to a small town in Western Massachusetts when I was two weeks old, and it is there that I grew up—in a town nestled in the Green Mountains and filled with woods and ravines, fields, brooks, and old stone walls. My parents are both English professors, so my childhood was filled with books; in my memory, I am always either reading, drawing, writing, or playing 'pretend games.' I was, as a young reader, both voracious and undiscerning. I read pretty much anything I could get my hands on: serials like Nancy Drew, classics like *The Secret Garden* or *Charlotte's Web*. When I was around nine, I wrote my first long rhymed poem and remember the feeling of delight, almost awe, that the links, echoes, and symmetry those end-rhythms could make me feel. I also wrote story after story as a child—many of them 'genre' pieces in one way or another: mystery or romance, fable or fairy tale. I would illustrate them, bind them with yarn, and present them proudly to my parents, who saved them all in a big drawer amidst my sister's and my own report cards, our birth bracelets, even (or am I inventing?) a baby tooth or two.

"When I look back at my childhood, it seems to have taken place in two spheres: the 'real,' where I played with my sister, chatted with my parents, went to school; and the 'pretend.' The 'pretend' (which sometimes felt more real) took place partly in my deep plunges into reading and writing stories, but it was most powerfully present in the long, intricate, ongoing fantasy game I played with my best friend Nancy, who lived down the road. In this game, Nancy and I were the proprietors of a large farm and lived in a vaguely distant past. We each had a precocious daughter (in the form of two unremarkable, foot-high plastic dolls, hers with freckles, mine without), but we also 'spoke' the voices of a large cast of characters: farmers and neighborhood children, princes and doctors, horse trainers and thieves. This game of ours went on for over six years. We wrote out baby books for our 'children.' We read Dr. Spock and books on horseback riding with titles like *Heads Up, Heels Down*. We played for hour upon hour in the woods and fields between our houses. We never planned what would happen; we never said 'you do this voice, I'll do that.' Our games were often filled with melodrama, even violence: a doll we found was possessed and we had to punch her eyes out and drown her in the brook. Our children were ill; we had to put leeches (slugs?) on them, to drain their blood. Coming back into the real world after a day of playing with Nancy was like swimming up out of a dream.

"Then I turned 13. At 13, it became an impossible embarrassment to play with dolls. I remember recognizing this fact with a grim sense of inevitability and grief. For awhile, Nancy and I snuck around, played dolls deep in the woods where no one would see us. Don't change, we pleaded with each other. Promise me you'll never change. But our bodies ran away with us. Breasts appeared, signaling to me, at first, nothing but loss. I tried to push them back inside my chest.

"Looking back, I can see that the only way I managed not to lose hold of this childhood world of deep play and full imagination was through writing. I wrote more and more as an adolescent, in equal measure to 'playing' less and less. When I write, I drop myself down into a world where things unfold almost of their own accord. I take on voices, riff and improvise. I play. The world of a novel or a story when I am far inside it is a place that is at once full of surprises and deeply connected to my most central concerns. When I am not writing—too busy teaching or dealing with life's daily demands—I feel less alive. It was not until I had finished my first novel, *Unravelling*, that it occurred to me how connected its story was to the childhood game I played with Nancy. A 19th-century woman lives on a farm, spins yarn, peers into a bog. . . . She bears two children, loses them, befriends a mute and wounded girl. I might have been 10 years old, inventing. Through writing, I have been able to keep the most vital strand of my childhood alive, and I am forever grateful that what I do for grown-up work is really childhood play.

"Writing has thus always been, for me, a process of discovery, where I begin with a glimmer—a voice, an image, a hint of a situation, sometimes even the hazy residue of a dream—and then move forward, each word leading to the next until I arrive in a new place, one I couldn't have begun to imagine until the language led me there. As a result of the intuitive, almost groping nature of my writing process, my sense of my own work's themes and concerns is formed largely through a series of backward glances. Although I only rarely set out, in any conscious way, to 'experiment,' I can see, in looking back, how the pieces of fiction, non-fiction, and poetry I have written constitute a series of experiments in subject matter, language, structure, tone, and voice.

"The stories in *Have You Seen Me?* are, it seems to me, largely efforts to explore the interior worlds of people who find themselves marginalized—a woman with a nerve injury, a girl stuck between countries, a lonely child whose mother awaits the end of the world. Like much of my other work, they examine how the self is paradoxically both essentially isolated and essentially social. I try, here, to chart the complicated relationship between the psyche and the outside world, finding myself drawn to characters whose imaginative landscapes are vivid, almost all-consuming places, 'worlds' unto themselves. Many of these stories portray people on some sort of cusp—a boy on the brink of adolescence, a woman dying, another about to give birth. Like the borders between the self and the outside world, or between one body and another, these 'cusp' moments strike me as rich with possibility and fraught with danger. Identity becomes unstable here, the old world about to be lost, the new one still unknown.

"In many of the stories I've written since the publication of *Have You Seen Me?*, I have attempted to move beyond the fevered inner state of one self to explore the self in community, or the intersections of several selves. 'Between' is about, among other things, the ways in which notions of family and community in late 20th century America can be interrogated and stretched. In 'Vines and Other Climbing Plants,' I look at how the world of virtual reality provides an imaginative community for a man otherwise unable to venture forth. My essays 'Two Baths' and 'Three Mothers' experiment with the effects of juxtaposition, playing with the odd energy that gets created when several narratives sit next to one another, linked, but in only fairly oblique ways. 'Two Baths' also explores the theme of memory—both historical and personal—and looks at how (as John Berger puts it in the quote I use as the essay's epigraph) 'sometimes first impressions gather up some of the residue of centuries.'

"My novel *Unravelling* is my most extended experiment in venturing into a world far from the one I inhabit. Set in 19th-century New England and narrated in the voice of a woman named Aimee Slater, it is a fictional autobiography, an exploration of a woman's attempt to create a life for herself in a culture that allows her little room to explore her own passions and desires. Writing this novel allowed me to make use of my long-standing interests in women's studies and 19th-century American prose. My research included learning about the Lowell textile mills and reading numerous frontier and factory narratives. In imagining, from a late 20th-century perspective, the life of a fictional 19th-century woman, I hoped to give voice to much that was left unspoken or repressed in 19th-century texts. Aimee's relationship to her body and sexuality are writ large here, rather than being submerged or circled around. The novel is also literally in dialogue with earlier texts, since I borrowed fragments—letters, mill descriptions—from 19th-century writings, collaging them into the story. In this way, I see *Unravelling* as situating itself, more than most of my other writing, in an overtly historical context.

"My second novel, *The Honey Thief*, takes place at the tail end of the 20th century and explores (among other things) themes of memory and repression, safety and danger, narrative and truth-telling. The setting is a rural town in upstate New York; a woman, Miriam, and her eleven-year-old daughter, Eva, have just moved there from the city because Miriam thinks the country is a safe place to raise a child. One strand of the book involves Eva's growing friendship with a male beekeeper down the road. With a mite epidemic wreaking havoc on the bee population (and thus threatening pollination, and so crop production), what appears at first to be a rural life of milk and honey turns out to be much more layered and complex. The book has a parallel movement back in time, in which Eva slowly gains more access to the story of her father's death, which took place when she was six. Here, too, I am interested in juxtaposing worlds—past and present; country and city; the intricate, tiny world of the beehive and the human world—and in playing with the possibilities opened up by the gaps in perspective between various points of view.

"There are many writers whose work sustains and nourishes me: Alice Munro, for the layered intricacy of her stories, as well as for their precise and lovely language; Howard Norman; Flannery

O'Connor; Charlotte Bronte; George Eliot; Toni Morrison; Marilynne Robinson; John Berger, Virginia Woolf, Anita Desai. . . Younger writers whose work I have read recently and admired include Jhumpa Lahiri, Lorrie Moore, Lauren Slater (who is also my closest writing friend). When I read, I look for writers who create a world—a place with its own thick sense of being, what Alice Munro calls 'a sturdy sense of itself, of being built of its own necessity, not just to shelter or beguile you' (Munro, Introduction to *Selected Stories*). So, too, do I strive for this worldness in everything I write."

Elizabeth Graver was born on July 2, 1964. Her parents, Suzanne Levy Graver and Lawrence Graver, were both English professors. She was educated at Wesleyan University, where she received her B.A. degree in 1986, and at Washington University, in St. Louis, where she earned her M.F.A. degree in 1990. She also pursued doctoral studies at Cornell University, in Ithaca, New York, for a time. She was a fellow of the Bread Loaf Writers' Conference, in Middlebury, Vermont, in 1986 and studied in Neuilly-sur-Seine, France, on a Fulbright grant in 1987–88. Graver has worked as a freelance journalist and has taught creative writing at Washington University and at Cornell University. She became known as a "Boston writer" when she began teaching at Boston College and settled in the area.

The stories in Graver's first book, *Have You Seen Me?*, "deal tellingly with themes of nurture," according to Benjamin DeMott, writing in the *New York Times Book Review* (August 17, 1997), and were widely praised. Graver's stories have been honored by inclusion in the *O. Henry* and *Best American Short Stories* anthologies. Her story "Islands Without Names" won the American Fiction Prize in 1994.

Graver's short stories tend to have autobiographical elements and to focus on life's small crossroads. A girl of 12 leaves a very small town to live in a city for a year in "What Kind of Boy," published in *Southwest Review* (Summer 1995); in "Scavenger Bird," which appeared in *Ploughshares* (Spring 1995), a young woman begins to understand that her Jewish heritage may be an obstacle in her relationship with her boyfriend.

Graver told *Amazon.com* in an on-line interview that her novel *Unravelling* was inspired by a dream—"the only historical dream I have ever had," she explained—"in which I was a 19th-century mill girl walking barefoot through the snow looking for my mother." Aimee Slater, whose story is told in the novel, is born in New Hampshire in 1829 and, attracted by the glamour of living independently and by dreams of personal growth, becomes a mill worker in Lowell, Massachusetts, starting at the age of 15. She quickly becomes disillusioned; impregnated by a mechanic at the mill, she gives birth to twins and is forced by her mother to give them up for adoption. Now an outcast, she goes to live in a shack at the edge of her father's land and takes the "town cripple" as a lover. Her redemption comes in the form of her ability to help an orphan. She becomes self-sufficient and proud enough, after 25 years, to tell her story. The novel "is partly about provisioning, survival, pride in self-sufficiency," observed Benjamin DeMott, who saw in the novel layers of regret on the part of the protagonist: "At its core, Aimee's story is about the slow cumulative registering, over years, of the weight and meaning of one's own misjudgments. The heroine winces at her recollected credulity—her shock at the unconcern of the factory mechanic who impregnated her, her beamish enthusiasm for the mill that employed her. . . . She's also abashed at a larger misjudgment: her fierce condemnation of her elders." At the end, as her mother is dying, Aimee is able to achieve a kind of reconciliation with her. Most reviewers concurred that *Unravelling* was a "strong and affecting first novel," as the *Publishers Weekly* (June 23, 1997) reviewer put it. That critic wrote that the book's "depiction of the dissonance between what Aimee's heart tells her and what her world expects of her is genuinely haunting."

Graver's second novel was so deeply concerned with issues of nurturing that many reviewers called it a novel about parenting. In *The Honey Thief* (1999), 11-year-old Eva is taken by her widowed mother from New York City's East Village to the cleaner, safer environs of Ithaca, New York. Eva has been caught shoplifting, and her mother, Miriam, although she doesn't understand why Eva steals small things, fears that the habit may become ingrained. Her deeper worry is that Eva has inherited mental illness from her father, who committed suicide when Eva was six. Eva's reason for stealing is that possessing a new object temporarily calms her fears of losing everything she has—in other words, her mother.

"Though it is neither torpid nor uneventful, the action in *The Honey Thief* builds quietly, deployed in a network of scenes in which convincing characters make small, revelatory gestures and choices," Katharine Weber wrote in her *New York Times Book Review* (September 5, 1999) notice. The *Publishers Weekly* (June 7, 1999) reviewer concluded that Graver's "touch is both subtle and honest, grounded in reality but acknowledging the essence of human striving for companionship and happiness." The reviewer further found "nuanced, fallible characters who doggedly strive to go on with imperfect lives," which adds "emotional resonance."

In addition to the Drue Heinz Literature Prize, Elizabeth Graver has won fellowships from the National Endowment for the Arts, in 1992; the MacDowell Artists' Colony, in 1994 and 1998; and the Blue Mountain Center Artists' Colony, in 1996. She is director of the creative writing program, of which she was one of the designers, at Boston College.

— S.Y.

SUGGESTED READING: *Atlanta Journal-Constitution* L p13 Aug. 17, 1997; *Boston Globe* D p2 Aug. 1, 1999; *Library Journal* p173 Aug. 1999; *New York Times Book Review* p7 Aug. 17, 1997, p7+ Sep. 5, 1999; *Ploughshares* p94+ Spring 1995, p215+ Winter 1998; *Publishers Weekly* p69 June 23, 1997; *Review of Contemporary Fiction* p247+ Fall 1997; *Southwest Review* p260+ Summer 1995

SELECTED BOOKS: short-story collections—*Have You Seen Me?*, 1991; novels—*Unravelling*, 1997; *The Honey Thief*, 1999

Courtesy of Greywolf Press

Gregg, Linda

Sep. 9, 1942– Poet

Linda Gregg's poetry has a spare, direct style that critics have described as moving and brutally honest, likening her work to classical Greek poetry. A widely published contemporary American poet, her work has appeared in such notable publications as the *New Yorker*, the *Paris Review*, the *Atlantic Monthly*, and the *American Poetry Review*, among others. Her most notable collections include *Too Bright to See* (1981), *Alma* (1985), *The Sacraments of Desire* (1991), and most recently, *Things and Flesh* (1999).

Linda Alouise Gregg was born in Suffern, New York, on September 9, 1942. Her parents, Harold Gregg and the former Frances Rumnal, migrated across the country and raised their daughter in Marin County, California. Gregg was educated at San Francisco State College (now University), where she received a bachelor's degree in 1967. In that same year she taught at Humboldt State College (now University) in Arcata, California. She received a master's degree from San Francisco State in 1972.

Gregg's writing career truly began in 1975 after her poems were published in such magazines as the *Paris Review*, the *Nation*, and the *Kenyon Review*. That same year her poetry was selected for inclusion in *The American Poetry Anthology*. In her first collection of poetry, *Too Bright to See* (1981), the poems were grouped into three sections, "Alma," "The Marriage and After," and "After That." In each, she writes about "the pain of being female," according to Stephen Yenser in the *Yale Review* (Autumn 1981). *Too Bright to See* received mixed reviews. William Logan, writing for *Library Journal* (July 1981), praised the collection, commenting that "[Gregg's] terrifying acquaintance with fear and psychological pain drives this book from the commonplaces of marriage toward an individual accounting of the self: the result is not confession but exposure. The reader will forgive local weaknesses in order to have lines like 'The body goes into such raptures of obedience' and these fine dark poems." An anonymous reviewer for *Choice* (January 1982) wrote that "One feels a thoughtful, sensitive, and serious craftsman at work. . . . But none of this makes one like these poems or want to read them often. It is not the fact that they are filled with loss, uncertainty, and pain, but that they are coupled with a strange pride in having experienced suffering."

Gregg published a second volume of poetry, *Eight Poems*, in 1982. Though that collection met with little fanfare, the same cannot be said for *Alma*, published in 1985. Much of *Alma* focuses on "harsh landscapes which Gregg explores until she can discover her connection to them," as described by Rosaly DeMaios Roffman in a review for the *Library Journal* (February 15, 1985). Roffman continued, "[The author] speaks with authority in confronting the ghosts of the past. . . . The poetry is confessional, sturdy, and occasionally veers toward prose pronouncement. . . . A spareness of language also serves the poet well." "Much of *Alma* is set in Greece's elemental landscape, and Miss Gregg is very much a poet of essentials—motives bared and emotions clarified," J. D. McClatchy noted in the *New York Times Book Review* (March 16, 1986). "Sometimes it is true, she has whittled poems down to a monotonous simplicity. And her range is narrow. But within these limitations, her poems shimmer in the cool mysterious light her passion and intelligence cast on them."

For several years Gregg did not publish a new collection of poetry, although she continued to publish works in such periodicals as the *American Poetry Review*, the *New Yorker*, *Poetry East*, *Antaeus*, *Ironwood*, *Columbia*, and the *Iowa Review*. In 1991 she published *The Sacrament of Desire*. This collection is organized into four suites, each of which refers to an episode in Gregg's life: the author's travels in Greece; the end of her marriage and the strange sensation of freedom that came afterwards; a trip to Central America during which she was confronted with true poverty; and her affair with a married man. Like *Alma*, this collection received mostly favorable reviews. M. P. White, in *Choice* (April 1992), remarked: "This book confirms what was evident from the first: the scope of her work is large, her intention is weighty, and her passion deeply felt." A reviewer for the *New Yorker* (March 8, 1993) described the collection as "devotional poetry celebrating the mysteries of eroticism: poetry 'of stars and stone and the ordinary'. . . . The landscape is at once contemporary and of antiquity, and Gregg's typical language is silvery and agile, her tone level and concentrated." Steven Cramer, in his review for *Poetry* (January 1992), wrote that the book "unites lyric grace with shapely precision," and noted that "Despite [a] pervasive attention to self's story, Gregg at her best doesn't come across as narcissistic. . . . After [the] finely understated 'airings' in Parts I and II, [the book] begins to falter. Part III, set mainly in Mexico, contains lovely moments . . . but it also features poems of social comment that, despite admirable intentions, strike me as self-aggrandizing."

Gregg published another collection, *Chosen by the Lions*, in 1994. In her most recently published work, *Things and Flesh* (1999), the poems are spare and, as David Orr noted in *Poetry* (August 2000), are often "built around words like 'heart,' 'body,' 'love,' and 'spirit.' The book's animating principle is sacrifice: by forgoing lushness and intricacy, Gregg hopes to attain the sort of authenticity that leaves a ringing stillness in the air." He continued, "When Gregg's poems succeed, they have the elegance of Greek statuary and the good-humored poise of haiku. . . . Of course, the problem with writing this way is that, when it doesn't work, the reader has an awfully hard time breathing. Just as we find ourselves pleased on an almost intuitive level when Gregg gets it right, we wince with particular discomfort when she gets it wrong. Her simplicity leaves her vulnerable to two enemies, sentimentality and smugness." Similarly, William Logan, in his review for the *New Criterion* (June 2000), remarked, "The sour intensity of Gregg's poems is an acquired taste, and her failings make it tempting to dismiss her. The poems are repetitive in mood and manner (grindingly so), the poet preening in her discontents, the gloomy tone so unrelieved you think the author is beyond, not simple pleasures, but simple enjoyment of pleasure. Boiling everything away to banalities, the poems give the trivial unbearable significance. Gregg has been flayed toward sacredness (she doesn't ask to be liked, and that makes you like her). After the weary irony of so much contemporary poetry, written by victims who aren't victims, it's a relief to read poems whose mysteries are deep in what they must say."

In addition to teaching at a number of writers workshops and conferences, Linda Gregg has taught at the University of Tucson; Louisiana State University; the College of Marin and Napa State College, both in Northen California; Lafayette College, in Easton, Pennsylvania; Hampshire College, in Amherst, Massachusetts; the University of Iowa; and the University of Houston. She has won a Guggenheim fellowship, a National Endowment for the Arts grant, a Whiting Writer's Award, and six Pushcart Prizes. Her poetry has been published in a number of anthologies, including the *Ardis Anthology of New American Poetry* (1977), the *Poet's Choice* (1980), *Random Review* (1982), *Women Poets of the World* (1983), and *Nineteen New American Poets of the Golden Gate* (1984).

—C. M.

SUGGESTED READING: *American Poetry Review* p5 Sep./Oct. 1999; *Choice* p626 Jan. 1982, p1224 Apr. 1992; *Library Journal* p1427 July 1981, p183 Feb. 15, 1986; *New Criterion* p63 June 2000; *New York Times Book Review* p12 Mar. 16, 1986; *New Yorker* p111 Mar. 8, 1993; *Poetry* p223 Jan. 1992, p294+ Aug. 2000; *Contemporary Authors*, vol. 113, 1985

SELECTED BOOKS: *Too Bright to See*, 1981; *Eight Poems*, 1982; *Alma*, 1985; *The Sacrament of Desire*, 1991; *Chosen by the Lion*, 1994; *Things and Flesh*, 1999

Guralnick, Peter

1943(?)– Biographer; music journalist; novelist

A prolific chronicler of blues, soul, and early rock music, Peter Guralnick has earned the admiration of critics for his profiles and interviews of hundreds of musicians in those genres. "I aspire to be a good interviewer," he told Wendy Smith for *Publishers Weekly* (October 3, 1994). "I hope that at least I'm open to hearing people. You have to recognize the legitimacy of people's experience, that whatever formulations you have made about a subject and however much the person you're talking to may be contradicting those formulations, they have a very personal, vivid memory that is valid for them. Then the problem is trying to bring all these different versions together." His latest publication, a two-volume biography of Elvis Presley, earned high praise from reviewers, many of whom were impressed by the extent of his research into the life of the rock legend. In the *New York Times Book Review* (October 30, 1994), Stephen Wright wrote of the first volume of the set, "Mr. Guralnick's narrative is rendered with an intimate, restrained intensity eerily reminiscent of the plaintive tone of Presley's ballads, that tremulous yearning of America itself, the promise the country makes to each of its children and keeps for all too few."

The son of a dental surgeon, Peter Guralnick was born in about 1943 in Brookline, Massachusetts, a suburb of Boston. Since his early childhood, he harbored dreams of being a novelist but doubted

Courtesy of Little, Brown and Company
Peter Guralnick

that his experiences were the stuff of which fiction was made. "It seemed like everybody else—Hemingway, Faulkner—had this wonderful world that they came out of, and I didn't. I said to myself, 'Who could ever write anything about Brookline?'" he told Wendy Smith. "It may have been a stupid perspective, but it led me to seek out other people's worlds." Described by Smith as a "quiet rebel" during his high school years, the teenage Guralnick developed a keen interest in the world of blues and folk music. After graduating high school Guralnick attended Columbia University, in New York City, before dropping out and moving to England with his future wife, Alexandra. After returning to the United States, Guralnick finished his bachelor's degree in 1967 at Boston University, where he stayed on as a classics instructor.

In the meantime, Guralnick wrote a novel that was never published and began crafting profiles of musicians for magazines, an activity he began at the behest of friends who worked in journalism and were familiar with his clean prose style and love of music. In 1971 he compiled a series of such profiles—Muddy Waters, Charlie Rich, and Jerry Lee Lewis among them—into his first book, *Feel Like Going Home: Portraits in Blues and Rock 'n' Roll* (1971), which a reviewer for *Publisher's Weekly* (September 17, 1971) called a "graceful and moving survey." Two years after the publication of the book, Guralnick experienced what he has called an epiphany. His tenure at Boston University had ended, and he had begun searching for another job. After one promising interview for a teaching post at a local college prep school, he went on assignment to a nearby blues club to cover Bobby "Blue" Bland, who was performing there.

On his way home early the next morning, Guralnick realized that he preferred writing about music to teaching.

Abandoning teaching, Guralnick pursued writing full-time. Although he still hoped to develop his fiction, music journalism provided his income. In 1979 he published an anthology of articles profiling country-western artists under the title *Lost Highway: Journeys and Arrivals of American Musicians*. In his review for *Rolling Stone* (April 17, 1980), Greil Marcus described *Lost Highway* as a "companion volume" to *Feel Like Going Home* and wrote that Guralnick's "technique is the interview, woven seamlessly into biography, reporting, musicology." Among the articles highlighted by Marcus are Guralnick's "major analysis of the career of Elvis Presley," a "shattering account of Charlie Rich," and "a historic conversation with Sam Phillips, founder of Sun Records." The Before Columbus Foundation, a non-profit organization that promotes multicultural literature, honored *Lost Highway* with their American Book Award in 1983.

In 1980 Guralnick published his first novel, *Nighthawk Blues*, an account of the life and career of a washed-up blues singer, the fictional character Screamin' Nighthawk. "It was my seventh or eighth novel," he told Wendy Smith, "and I felt that it and *One Way Out*, the [unpublished] novel that preceded it, were the first times I achieved enough distance so that they were entirely independent of my experience." Although he criticized the novel for having a slow pace and a distracting romantic subplot, Harry Sumrall, writing for the *Washington Post* (August 11, 1980), praised *Nighthawk Blues* as "an engrossing and evocative portrayal of the character and commitment of rural blues musicians." Sumrall also lauded Guralnick for being "consistently convincing in a musicological as well as a personal sense" and added that the book "is most moving in his depiction of [Screamin' Nighthawk] himself."

Guralnick returned to nonfiction in 1986 with the publication of *Sweet Soul Music: Rhythm and Blues and the Southern Dream of Freedom*, which has chapters on such music legends as Sam Cooke, Ray Charles, Otis Redding, Jerry Butler, and Solomon Burke. Guralnick spent five years researching the book and accumulated over 100 interviews. In the *Chicago Tribune* (August 6, 1986), Daniel Brogan called *Sweet Soul Music* "the definitive history of soul's rise and fall," writing that it contained "remarkable portraits" and hailing it as both a "scholarly work," and a "whole lotta fun." Brogan was especially fascinated by Guralnick's "startling argument about the racial nature of soul. The story of black music is all-too-often a tale of white hustlers exploiting black artists. But in the case of Southern soul, for a brief, marvelously creative period, blacks and whites collaborated in almost blissful harmony."

In 1989 Guralnick published *Searching for Robert Johnson*, a reprint of a magazine essay he had written about the legendary blues artist from Mississippi with the addition of rare photos. Guralnick's task in writing the article had been complicated because Johnson was murdered in 1938, and very little information about him existed. The author was able to construct a brief portrait of Johnson by interviewing several musicians who had played with him. According to Guralnick, Johnson often traveled alone, had vanished for an extended period of time, was both extremely shy and popular with women, and often performed under different names. "Guralnick recounts the facts and legends around Johnson's life, tries to sift the influences on Johnson's art, quotes Johnson's friends, and sketches the history of researchers of Johnson's life," John Litweiler wrote for the *Chicago Tribune* (January 5, 1990). Litweiler went on to criticize the book for being "padded with reveries and romantic speculation, much of it murky or silly or both," and took issue with Guralnick's description of Robert Johnson's life as "shadowy." Litweiler said that this term was inappropriate because Johnson and "millions of Americans, black and white . . . lived amid similar circumstances." However, Litweiler concluded by saying that *Searching for Robert Johnson* was "a rewarding appetizer" for Johnson's fans until they could read Mack McCormick's anticipated, more extensive portrait, *Biography of a Phantom*, which had not yet been published.

In 1988, Guralnick embarked on his most ambitious project to date, a biography of Elvis Presley. "I didn't set out to explode any particular myths, but to see Elvis as a person who lived a life of very real ambitions, as an omnivorous taster of music of all kinds," Guralnick told Bill Eichenberger, the book critic for the *Columbus Dispatch* in Ohio (January 10, 1999, on-line). "I was interested in describing life as it was lived. If I confirmed that some myths were in fact true, that was fine with me, too." Guralnick soon expanded the biography to two volumes, a move that caused him to lose his initial publisher. As Guralnick explained to Eichenberger, the first 600 pages he wrote ended with the death of Presley's mother in 1958. Guralnick saw this event as the best way to divide the biography. In an interview with D. C. Denison for the *Boston Globe Magazine* (February 5, 1995), Guralnick said, "The main thing is that when his mother died, which happened while he was in the Army, something went out of his life that never came back. . . . I realized there was such a division after his mother's death, it was almost as if a curtain had come down. He never really recovered from that sense of spiritual desolation. That's when I decided to break the biography into two volumes."

The first volume, *Last Train to Memphis: The Rise of Elvis Presley*, was published in 1994. In the *Los Angeles Times Book Review* (October 2, 1994), Frank Rose expressed mixed views about the book. "What we have here is a biography that is at once magisterial and quirky," Rose wrote. "Guralnick has produced the definitive chronicle of Elvis' early years. But in his zeal to 'rescue' Elvis from the mass adulation he inspired he is strangely singleminded. He refuses to delve into messy questions of motivation and psyche. He declines to acknowledge exactly what it is he's rescuing Elvis from." Rose also criticized Guralnick for failing to explain why Presley allowed himself to be exploited in "situations that mocked his talents and diminished his possibilities," such as his appearance on the *Steve Allen Show* in July 1956 when he sang "Hound Dog" to a basset hound. However, other opinions were far more positive, and *Time* named *Last Train to Memphis* one of the best books of 1994.

The second volume of the Presley biography, *Careless Love: The Unmaking of Elvis Presley*, was published in 1998. In the book, Guralnick documented Presley's life from his time in the Army in 1958 until his death in 1977. In his review for the *Washington Post Book World* (January 24, 1999), Richard Harrington wrote, "Like its predecessor, *Careless Love* is assiduously researched, meticulously assembled and beautifully written, equal parts Shakespearean tragedy and psychological mystery. The book delineates the decline and fall of an American icon with musical, social and psychological details that will appeal to both Presley die-hards and doubters." Harrington lauded Guralnick for using "a depth and wealth of material that illuminate the complexity of [Presley's] story," and noted that Guralnick had won the trust of Presley's manager, the legendary "Colonel" Tom Parker, who provided valuable insights and unprecedented access to many of Presley's former associates.

In 1999 Guralnick and Ernst Jorgensen, the author of *Elvis Presley: A Life in Music* (1998), collaborated on the book, *Elvis Day by Day*, a chronology of Presley's life and career that begins with the birth of his mother on April 25, 1912 and ends on October 3, 1977 (almost two months after his death) with the broadcast of his last concert on the CBS television network. "Rich in photos and reproductions of documents such as letters, telegrams, and even Presley's 6th-grade report card, *Elvis Day by Day* is certain to be a prime Elvis reference work for the forseeable future," Tom Popson wrote in his review for the *Chicago Tribune* (December 12, 1999).

In 2000, Guralnick wrote and produced a documentary about Sam Philipps, the recording industry executive and founder of Sun Records. The documentary, *Sam Philipps: The Man Who Invented Rock 'n' Roll*, aired on the cable television channel A&E. Performers such as Johnny Cash, Roy Orbison, Jerry Lee Lewis, Charlie Rich, and Elvis Presley made their first recordings in Philipps' Memphis, Tennessee studio. Philipps, who is white, also recorded such African-American blues artists as B. B. King, Howlin' Wolf, and Roscoe Gordon at a time when the South was still racially segregated. According to Wald, Philipps was extremely pleased with the documentary. "I think that Peter really probably understands me, for better or worse, as much as anybody," Philipps explained to

Elijah Wald for the *Boston Globe* (June 11, 2000). "With his mind, and having been exposed to me the way he was, without underarm deodorant, he probably does feel somewhat a little twitch of my soul. And I wouldn't want it to be in better hands."

Peter Guralnick and his wife, Alexandra, live in West Newbury, Massachusetts. They have two grown children. Wendy Smith wrote of him, "It's easy to see how he wins the trust of his interviewees. . . . [Guralnick] seems genuinely nice, [and] reluctant to speak badly of anyone." In addition to his books and articles, Guralnick has also written liner notes for various records. In 1985 he won a Grammy Award for "Best Album Notes" for *Sam Cooke Live at the Harlem Square Club, 1963*. "You write a 10,000-word essay, nobody makes any changes and you're selling something you believe in," Guralnick told Smith, discussing his love for the liner-note format. In coming years, Guralnick hopes to publish more fiction. He is currently working on a novel entitled, "Democracy."

—D. C.

SUGGESTED READING: Boston Globe D p1+ Jan. 5, 1999, with photo, L p2 June 11, 2000; *Boston Globe Magazine* p12 Feb. 5, 1995; *Chicago Tribune* V p3 Aug. 6, 1986, V p3 Jan. 5, 1990, Books p2 Dec. 12, 1999; *Columbus Dispatch* (on-line) Jan. 10, 1999; *Los Angeles Times Book World* p1 Oct. 2, 1994; *New York Times Book Review* (on-line) Oct. 30, 1994; *Publishers Weekly* p47 Sep. 20, 1971, p47 Oct. 3, 1994, with photo; *Rolling Stone* p29 Apr. 17, 1980; *Washington Post* C p9 Aug. 11, 1980, G p1 Jan. 24, 1999

SELECTED BOOKS: novels—*Nighthawk Blues*, 1980; nonfiction—*Feel Like Going Home: Portraits in Blues and Rock 'n' Roll*, 1971; *Lost Highway: Journeys and Arrivals of American Musicians*, 1979; *Sweet Soul Music: Rhythm and Blues and the Southern Dream of Freedom*, 1986; *Searching for Robert Johnson*, 1989; *Last Train to Memphis: The Rise of Elvis Presley*, 1994; *Careless Love: The Unmaking of Elvis Presley*, 1998; (with Ernst Jorgensen) *Elvis Day by Day*, 1999

Hajdu, David

Mar. 8, 1955– Nonfiction writer

"All I've ever done was write," David Hajdu remarked in an interview with Wendy Smith in *Publishers Weekly* (June 11, 2001). "It was the second job I ever wanted—the first was to be a garbage man, when I was four! I had some early breaks, and by the time I was a senior in high school, I was writing for the local paper, the *Easton Express*." Hajdu has taken advantage of those early breaks and has since made a name for himself by profiling influential musicians, starting with his 1991 guide *Discovering Great Singers of Classic Pop*, co-authored by Roy Hemming. In 1996 he published the highly regarded *Lush Life: A Biography of Billy Strayhorn*. This study of jazz musician Duke Ellington's little-known collaborator went on to win numerous awards and was optioned for treatment as a feature film. His most recent book, *Positively Fourth Street* (2001), has been praised for its intimate rendering of the early-1960s New York folk scene, as seen through the relationships between Bob Dylan, Joan and Mimi Baez, and Richard Fariña.

Of Hungarian descent, David Hajdu was born on March 8, 1955 to Charles and Angelina Hajdu in Phillipsburg, New Jersey. He attended New York University, where he learned dramatic writing under the guidance of the playwright Tad Mosel. As Hajdu recalled to Wendy Smith, "[Mosel] taught me how to demonstrate, not state, and how to express feelings and ideas through behavior and scenes. Even in nonfiction, I prefer to leave things suggestive so readers can come to their own conclusions." As an undergraduate, Hajdu submitted

Courtesy of Farrar, Straus and Giroux

articles to the *Village Voice*, the *New York Times*, and *New York*. Though most were rejected, he had a few music articles published in the *Village Voice* before earning his B.A., in 1977. In 1978 and 1979 he wrote about music for *Rolling Stone*.

After getting married and having children in the early 1980s, Hajdu decided to put his career on firm financial footing by joining the *New York Times Magazine* as an editor. He told Smith that editing "was good solid work, and I could make a living in publishing without having to write about things I didn't want to." After a few years at the Times, he spent 10 years as an editor for Entertainment Weekly. While there, he edited Video Review's Best on Home Video (1985), an early guide to home videos.

In 1991 Hajdu co-authored Discovering Great Singers of Classic Pop with Roy Hemming, a guidebook covering the lives and careers of over 50 masters of American pop music. Divided into two sections covering the best artists of the pre- and postwar eras, it received solid reviews. A reviewer for Publishers Weekly (June 21, 1991) noted, as quoted in Contemporary Authors (1999): "The analyses of the singers' styles are perceptive," adding that the book was "entertaining, and refreshingly free of biographical trivia." In Booklist (February 1, 1992), also quoted in Contemporary Authors, a reviewer noted, "The authors' affection for this genre is evident in these enjoyable profiles."

Hajdu's first solo performance came with his celebrated 1996 work, Lush Life: A Biography of Billy Strayhorn, the first major study of Duke Ellington's longtime collaborator, songwriter, and arranger. Throughout their collaboration (from 1938 until Strayhorn's death, in 1967), Strayhorn remained in Ellington's shadow—on purpose. As an openly gay man at a time when most gays were closeted, Strayhorn's behind-the-scenes role as Ellington's right-hand man allowed him to live the life he wanted to live, while at the same time enabling him to have his music played by one of the greatest bands of the era. Unfortunately, in shunning the limelight, Strayhorn hasn't been properly credited for his contributions to the Ellington band, including the composition of its signature tune "Take the 'A' Train." Critics applauded Hajdu's work for its insights and contribution to jazz history. In the Washington Post Book World (June 23, 1996), a reviewer cheered: "David Hajdu's biography of Billy Strayhorn comes as a surprise and a most welcome one. It is the work of a journalist . . . but it meets standards of research and analysis that any scholar would respect and many would envy. Its prose is straightforward, and so is its structure; it tells us as much as we need to know about its subject without indulging in biographical excess; and, most important of all, it gives its subject his due." After calling the work "one of the finest of jazz biographies" in the New York Times (July 14, 1996, on-line), Will Friedwald proclaimed, "The detail that Mr. Hajdu has uncovered, particularly concerning the early Pittsburgh years and including the copious testimony of nearly 200 of Strayhorn's and Ellington's associates, is staggering, especially in light of how little has been previously published on Strayhorn."

Lush Life received many awards, including the Deems Taylor Award for music writing from the American Society of Composers, Authors, and Publishers, the New Visions Award for best nonfiction work, and a nomination for the National Book Critics Circle Award in biography. Film rights to the book have been optioned by the noted screenwriter Jack Cocks (The Age of Innocence and Titanic).

Hajdu's next book, Positively Fourth Street (2001), explores the artistic and personal relationships between Bob Dylan; his fellow musician and girlfriend, Joan Baez; Joan's younger sister, Mimi (also a singer and songwriter); and Mimi's husband, the novelist and songwriter Richard Fariña. The two couples worked together, influenced one another, and competed to make their marks in the folk-music scene of New York's Greenwich Village in the early 1960s. Positively Fourth Street received favorable reviews. In the Nation (June 11, 2001), Gene Santoro remarked: "Hajdu has written an engrossing page-turner. . . . At its best, his fluent style floats information with deceptive lightness, but he's not lightweight. . . . He uses his narrative's inherent elasticity to open perspective and depth of field naturally, then skillfully dollies around and pans in and out of larger contexts as illuminating backdrop for his two odd couples." In her review for the New York Times (May 17, 2001), Janet Maslin was similarly impressed with Hajdu's book: "With this lovely madeleine of a book, a hauntingly evocative blend of biography, musicology and pop cultural history, it is as if David Hajdu has struck a tuning fork and summoned the spirit of the folk singing 1960's all over again. It is also as if Mr. Hajdu has discovered that within every movement, however pure, there is a healthy whiff of soap opera to be found."

David Hajdu is divorced from the mother of his children, Jacob and Victoria, and is now married to the actress Karen Oberlin.

—C. M.

SUGGESTED READING: Entertainment Weekly p6 Aug. 23, 1996; Los Angeles Magazine p99+ June 2001; The Nation p18+ June 11, 2001; New Republic p42+ Sept. 30, 1996; New York Review of Books p9+ July 19, 2001; New York Times (on-line) July 14, 1996, May 17, 2001; Publishers Weekly p52 June 11, 2001; Time p68 Aug. 5, 1996; Washington Post Book World p3 June 23, 1996; Wilson Quarterly p102 Winter 1997

SELECTED BOOKS: Discovering Great Singers of Classic Pop (with Roy Hemming), 1991; Lush Life: A Biography of Billy Strayhorn, 1996; Positively Fourth Street, 2001; as editor—Video Review's Best on Home Video, 1985

Courtesy of Beacon Press

Hall, Donald

Sep. 20, 1928– Poet; essayist; critic; editor; children's writer

Over the course of almost five decades, Donald Hall has established a sterling reputation as a poet, prose stylist, children's writer, literary critic, and editor. Critics have savored his musicality, humor, and lyricism, and his colleagues have admired the versatility of his technique, which has ranged widely over the years from classical meters to syllabics, free verse, and surrealism. Although Hall is not by strict definition a "New England poet" like Robert Frost, much of his work has dealt with his experiences in that region. Since 1975, when he gave up his tenured position as an English professor at the University of Michigan, he has lived on his family's homestead in New Hampshire, the source for much of his inspiration. As the poet Richard Tillinghast noted in the *New York Times* (February 24, 1991), "About 15 years ago Mr. Hall found his true place and his true subject. Readers of American poetry have reason to be grateful." Over the last several years, Hall has begun to explore aging, mourning, and death in his poetry. His most recent collections—*The Old Life* (1996), *Without* (1998), and *The Painted Bed* (2002)—chronicle his experiences with recurrent cancer and the death of his second wife, the poet Jane Kenyon, from leukemia. In addition to writing and to giving hundreds of poetry readings, Hall has been associated with several BBC radio shows (from 1959 to 1980); has served as host, from 1974–75, of a series of television interviews called *Poets Talking*; and has recorded albums of poetry by Longfellow and Whittier, among others. He has published several collections of prose essays, produced books for children, and served as editor for a number of poetry anthologies. Hall has received numerous prestigious awards, including the National Book Critics Circle Award, the Robert Frost Silver Medal, the New England Booksellers Association Award, and the Ruth Lilly Prize; he also served as New Hampshire's Poet Laureate from 1984–89 and again from 1995–99.

Donald Andrew Hall Jr. was born to Donald Andrew and Lucy (Wells) Hall in New Haven, Connecticut, on September 20, 1928. He grew up in the nearby town of Hamden, where his father was the treasurer for the family dairy business. Surrounded by books as a child, he quickly became engrossed in them, with the encouragement of both his parents. His mother often read poetry to him, including his childhood favorite, "The Moon's the North Wind's Cooky," by Vachel Lindsay. An only child, Hall turned to books for companionship and entertainment. At first he read such staples of juvenile fiction as the *Hardy Boys* and *Bobbsey Twins* series, but he soon discovered the works of Edgar Allan Poe, who became his literary idol. He recalled in an autobiographical article for the *New York Times Book Review* (January 16, 1983): "I wanted to grow up and be like Poe; I wanted to be mad, addicted, obsessed, haunted and cursed; I wanted to have eyes that burned like coals, profoundly melancholy, profoundly *attractive.*" Not surprisingly, his early short stories and poems, which he began to write when he was twelve, were rather morbid and in the Gothic tradition. The subject of his first poem, which he wrote to impress a baby-sitter, was death, for example, and his later juvenilia bore such chilling titles as "Blood" and "Night-Walker."

From the time he was six, Hall spent at least part of every summer vacation at Eagle Pond, his maternal grandparents' farm in New Hampshire. During the mornings he read or wrote, and later in the day, he helped his grandfather Wesley Wells with the haying or other chores. He preferred the farm to his lonely life in Hamden and especially enjoyed listening to his grandfather talk about his ancestors or recite such poems as "Casey at the Bat" or "What the Deacon Said" from his seemingly inexhaustible repertoire. "I sat in the tie-up on a three-legged stool," Hall reminisced in his *New York Times Book Review* article, "watching him milk his Holsteins as his dear voice kept time with his hands and he crooned wonderful bad poems with the elocutionary zeal of another century."

Although he continued to write fiction until he was twenty, Hall increasingly began to concentrate on writing poetry—and gradually T. S. Eliot and Hilda Doolittle dethroned Poe as his idols. During his two years at Hamden High School, he began submitting his poems to major magazines, including the *New Yorker*, the *Nation*, and the *Atlantic*, but with no success. However, "Wind-in-Storm," his imagistic poem patterned on the work of H. D. (as Doolittle was known), was published in the high school's annual literary magazine, the *Cupola*, which awarded it a first prize for poetry. Several obscure magazines published some of his other poems in 1944. That fall Hall transferred to Phillips Exeter Academy, in New Hampshire, and the next summer his parents sent him at his request to the Bread Loaf Writers' Conference, sponsored by Middlebury College, in Vermont.

In 1947, after illness forced him to miss a total of about a half-year's schooling, which he had to make up, Hall graduated from Exeter. That fall he entered Harvard. As a staff member of the *Harvard Advocate*, the university's prestigious literary magazine, he was associated with undergraduates who would later become some of the country's most renowned poets. In 1950, as a tribute to the magazine on its 85th anniversary, Hall edited *The Harvard Advocate Anthology*, an anthology of poetry and fiction that had been previously printed in the *Advocate*. Among the famous Harvard graduates whose work appeared in the anthology was Arthur M. Schlesinger Jr., the poets Wallace Stevens and T. S. Eliot, and Theodore and Franklin D. Roosevelt. The poet and translator Dudley Fitts, himself a Harvard alumnus, observed in the *New York Times Book Review* (April 8, 1951) that "no more fitting commemoration could be imagined than Mr. Hall's admirably chosen anthology."

During his years at Harvard, Hall was influenced by his friendships with Robert Bly, John Ashbery, and Adrienne Rich, among others. Their discussions of poetry did more, perhaps, to shape his work and convince him that he was a writer than did his association with Robert Frost, Archibald MacLeish, Richard Eberhart, and other distinguished "elders," as he has called them. "My early poetry concentrated on form entirely," Hall explained in *World Authors, 1950–1970*. "I was concerned that poetry should be only technique, and perfectly finite." His honors thesis, entitled "Yeats's Stylistic Development as Seen Through a Consideration of His Published Revisions of 'The Rose,'" reflected that interest. Moreover, the Lloyd McKim Garrison Prize that he received for his poetry collection *A Single Look* (for which he used the pseudonym of Rhadamanthus Gall), reflected his growing mastery of his craft. In 1951 Hall also received Harvard's John Osborne Sergeant Prize for Latin translation.

After graduating from Harvard with a B.A. degree in 1951, Hall was given a fellowship to attend Oxford University. He studied "theoretical prosody, typical of [his] interests at that time," as he recalled in *World Authors*. He was also secretary, and later, president, of the Oxford Poetry Society. In 1952, for his long poem "Exiles" he won the Newdigate Prize for narrative poetry, an honor rarely accorded an American. After obtaining his bachelor of letters degree from Oxford in 1953, he returned to the United States and studied for a year at Stanford University, in California, as a creative-writing fellow under the eminent poet and critic Yvor Winters.

For the next three years, as a Junior Fellow in the Society of Fellows at Harvard, Hall enjoyed what he has called a "long episode of freedom," during which he "did nothing but read and write." In 1955 he published *Exiles and Marriages*, which included his Newdigate Prize–winning poem and was a Lamont Poetry Selection of the American Academy of Poets. The poems in the collection concerned some of his early experiences and his marriage but were primarily about his grandfather Wesley Wells. According to Hall, they were "keens over the dead, glorifying him as a saint of a destroyed civilization." *Exiles and Marriages* won praise from many reviewers for its wit, lyricism, and technique. According to a critic for *Time* (December 5, 1955), it was distinctive for "its own true tone composed in almost equal parts of intelligence and imagination."

In 1957 Hall joined the faculty of the University of Michigan at Ann Arbor as an assistant professor of English. A year after he moved to Michigan, he published *The Dark Houses* (1958), which consisted of two sections, "Houses on Residential Streets" and "Men Alone." Hall described it as "the book of [his] father's death, [which] largely examined the outward details of the life of the American suburbs" but also explored "an alternative to that life." Critical reaction was mixed. Although several reviewers expressed disappointment in what they considered to be his witty, but shallow, treatment of his subject, they once again singled out his technique for special praise. "Perhaps the principal achievement of the book," concluded the poet Thom Gunn in the *Yale Review* (December 1958), "is in Hall's use of syllabics and a kind of syllabic blank verse, two techniques by which he produces an effect where the deliberate flatness of a certain type of free verse is combined with the emotional control of regular meter."

Hall's next book of poetry, *A Roof of Tiger Lilies* (1964), evinced a marked change in his style and thematic emphasis. He recalled in *World Authors* that as early as 1954 he "had begun to distrust the vanity of technique" and gradually envisioned "poetry as exploration of the inward continent of the spirit." Consequently, the verse in this collection, much of which had been published previously in periodicals, often had a surrealistic, dreamlike quality. "Many of these poems," the writer of the dust jacket explained, "seem to consist wholly of direct actions and sensuous images; they often deal with magical transfiguration or metamorphosis, with the experience of *breaking out*." The critics generally welcomed Hall's shift of direction. In *Encounter* (March 1965) Martin Dodsworth called *A Roof of Tiger Lilies* an excellent, if at times perplexing, book, and though Robert Mazzocco complained in the *New York Review of Books* (April 8, 1965) that "psychologically, these poems do not fulfill themselves," he concluded that "aesthetically, [they are] Hall's most impressive achievement." Hall's next book, *The Alligator Bride* (1969), consisted mainly of revisions of poems from earlier collections. A critic for the *Virginia Quarterly Review* (Spring 1970) discerned in them evidence of Hall's "continually deepening poetic awareness."

Hall continued his spiritual exploration in his next three poetry collections: *The Yellow Room* (1971), *The Town of Hill* (1975), and *A Blue Wing Tilts at the Edge of the Sea* (1975). Of the three, *The Yellow Room*, a recounting of a failed love affair, was accorded the warmest critical reception. In her review for *Poetry* (January 1972), Phoebe Pettingell extolled Hall's use of imagery to "create a sensual picture conveying an emotion" and applauded his use of surrealism. She concluded, "Keeping his vision personal, without straining for generalities about love and loss, he writes honestly. . . . [This] is a commendable attainment."

Hall's teaching position at the University of Michigan had not made overwhelming demands on his time, and money he earned from giving poetry readings enabled him to take frequent leaves of absence. Nevertheless, in 1975 he "jettisoned tenure to live the improvised day," as he has said, and moved with Jane Kenyon to Eagle Pond Farm, which he had bought after the death of his grandmother Kate Wells. His return to the farm that his family had owned for over a century allowed him to concentrate full-time on his writing, but perhaps more important, it gave him a sense of his familial past. The poems in *Kicking the Leaves* (1978), all of which focus on death, grew out of his reflections on his ancestors and on his own place in the "continuum [of] the decades." The book, which was generously praised by many critics, is generally considered Hall's breakthrough work. The noted poet Hayden Carruth, writing in *Harper's* (November 1978), found the collection "both excellent and deeply moving."

In his next book, *The Happy Man* (1986), Hall reflected on aging and mortality. In the opening poem, "Great Day in the Cows' House," which celebrates the cycles of life on the farm, he establishes what Robert Pinsky for the *Nation* (October 31, 1987) called "[the book's] characteristic, penetrating emotion: the feeling that happiness is relative and must inhere in daily life along with the pain and labor, or else nowhere." Throughout the next three sections, Hall presents varying narratives that address the idea of finding a "home," both in nature and in the domestic sphere. As Joseph Garrison described for *Library Journal* (August 1986), "After building, burning, or rebuilding various figurative houses, Hall's happy man finally discovers 'a mortal house' where he can smell the 'double scent of heaven and cut hay.' His affirmation is hard earned." David Shapiro observed in *Poetry* (April 1987), "[This] is a very powerful volume, and it makes a rare combination of phantasmal and shattering narratives with natural description of a high precision." Widely acclaimed, *The Happy Man* earned Hall the 1986 Lenore Marshall Poetry Prize.

Hall next published *The One Day: A Poem in Three Parts* (1988), which he had begun writing in 1971. It took more than 15 years for him to structure the piece into three distinct sections. In the first, an aging man proclaims his fate as "unfit / to work or love," as quoted by Thom Gunn for the *Los Angeles Times* (November 5, 1989); a female voice then joins him in his lamentations. In part two the narratives are disrupted by "Four Classic Texts," each of which presents satirical remarks on rage, history, destruction, and love. In part three the original speakers return fully restored and capable of experiencing joy. Many reviewers interpreted the progression of the three sections as an evocation of a maturing mind—accepting the pleasures of life, as well as the inevitability of death. Critics praised *The One Day* for its subtle depiction of complex themes; Liam Rector wrote for the *Los Angeles Times* (February 5, 1989), "I suspect those of us who come to poetry for an ultimate spareness of expression—and for even another reason: wisdom—will be pulling this book from our shelves for some time." Hall told David McDonald for the *American Poetry Review* (January–February 2002) that he considers this book "probably the best thing I've done." *The One Day* won the 1988 National Book Critics Circle Award for poetry, the 1990 *Los Angeles Times* Book Prize in poetry, and a nomination for the Pulitzer Prize.

In 1990 Hall published *Old and New Poems*, a collection that includes poems from his other books as well as 22 new poems written over the previous four years. In *The Museum of Clear Ideas* (1993), his next major work, he presented "Another Elegy," a seven-page elegy to a fictitious poet, William Trout. Yet, as Hall explained to Noah Adams in an interview for National Public Radio's *All Things Considered* (November 26, 1993), as archived on an official transcript, the poem was in fact based on many writers Hall had known. "[It] started as an elegy for one poet, my dear friend James Wright," Hall explained. "And for many years, I tried to write it as an elegy for him. And there is Jim Wright in this William Trout figure, but not only him. There's also Ray[mond] Carver. . . . And there was John Logan, there was Dick [Richard] Hugo. Then there are also the living in there. I mean, there's a bit of Galway Kinnell, who's a dear friend in there. There's Robert Bly and Louie [Louis] Simpson. . . . And there's certainly me in that as well, finally." Following "Another Elegy," Hall presents two long poems that comprise the remainder of the book: The first, "Baseball," consists of nine, nine-line stanzas and explores the topic of baseball as art; in the second, "The Museum of Clear Ideas," which Daniel Guillory for *Library Journal* (February 1, 1993) called a "witty little masterpiece," Hall presents classical odes reminiscent of the odes of Horace, a Roman lyrical poet born around 65 B.C. who celebrated love, friendship, and the beauty of life. In the *Yale Review* (October 1993) Vernon Shetley wrote that the volume was "as shrewd, sharp-tongued, and genuinely funny a group of poems as American poetry has produced in many years."

In 1996 Hall published *The Old Life*, in which he again presents poems about Eagle Pond Farm ("The Night of the Day") and baseball ("The Thirteenth Inning")—though the majority of the book consists of the 97-page title poem, an exploration of his life. Writing for *Booklist* (May 1, 1996), Ray Olson called this lengthy poem "an involving, entertaining, poignant life testament that surpasses such similar contemporary efforts as Charles Bukowski's rants and even Andrew Hudgins' fine *Glass Hammer*." In the *Library Journal* (June 1, 1996) Tim Gavin called it a poem "without any weaknesses" and characterized the overall work as one that "solidifies [Hall's] reputation as a major poet."

The final poem of *The Old Life* became the title poem for Hall's next book, *Without* (1998), a series of poems about Jane Kenyon's death from leukemia, in April 1995. The work chronicles her deterioration as well as Hall's grief throughout the year following her death. He explained to David McDonald that the book "was constructed out of wild loss and screaming" and took part of its inspiration from Thomas Hardy's elegies for his deceased wife. "I have loved Hardy since I was about thirty," he said, "and the poems I have loved the most are the grief poems out of the death of his first wife. . . . But it never occurred to me to try to follow his example until four years ago—writing in improvised and repeated stanza forms, sometimes with a Hardy-like awkwardness." Though Ray Olson for *Booklist* (May 1998) considered the book "less brilliant" than Hall's two previous works, most critics considered the book deeply compelling. In a review for *New York Newsday* (August 9, 1998), Heller McAlpin wrote, "Donald Hall's heartbreaking account of his wife's battle with leukemia is everything you could ask for in poetry: accessible, riveting and extraordinarily moving." Leslie Ullman for *Poetry* (February 1999) concluded, "His grief, so keenly and elegantly sustained, provides a map for others to follow if they risk, as he has, loving what they may well lose."

Hall continued to explore Kenyon's death, and his own life since then, in *The Painted Bed* (2002). J. T. Barbarese observed for the *New York Times* (April 14, 2002), "Perhaps only a poet of Hall's stature and powers could pull of a book like this—filled with raw sexual disclosures, rowdy anger and a self-blasting mockery. . . . Hall's grief matures into something like a rugged, outraged, Job-like comedy that is nearly a comment on the poet's own emotional state—he's inconclusive, a noble wreck, but still talking and writing poems." As an example of what he thought was uneven quality, Barbarese quoted lines from a poem titled "Kill the Day": "Without prospect or purpose, who dares to love meat / that will putrefy?"

Although Hall has several volumes of poetry to his credit, he has not limited his writing to verse. He has written numerous prose essays, including five collections of essays about poetry: *The Pleasures of Poetry* (1971), *Goatfoot Milktongue Twinbird: Interviews, Essays, and Notes on Poetry, 1970–76* (1978), *The Weather for Poetry: Essays, Reviews, and Notes on Poetry, 1977–81* (1982), and *Poetry and Ambition* (1988). From 1953 to 1962 Hall was the poetry editor of the *Paris Review*, and he has edited several highly regarded poetry anthologies, including *The New Poets of England and America* (1957) with fellow poets Louis Simpson and Robert Pack, *Contemporary American Poetry* (1963), *A Choice of Whitman's Verse* (1968), and *The Best American Poetry* (1989). One of Hall's most critically acclaimed prose works, *Remembering Poets: Reminiscences and Opinions* (1978), examines the last years of four great 20th-century poets: Ezra Pound, Dylan Thomas, T. S. Eliot, and Robert Frost, all of whom he knew personally. (The book was revised and republished as *Their Ancient Glittering Eyes* in 1992.) Hall modestly termed his work "literary gossip," but according to Seamus Cooney in a review for *Library Journal* (February 15, 1978), "His book blends well-honed anecdotes with amateur psychologizing and intelligent criticism in an agreeably readable fashion. . . . Interpretation, whether plausible or strained, is properly subordinated to the vivid sense of the living presence of the four poets."

Hall's additional prose projects include two plays—*An Evening's Frost*, a tribute to Robert Frost, and *Bread and Roses*—and two biographies *Henry Moore: The Life and Work of a Great Sculptor* (1966) and *Dock Ellis in the Country of Baseball* (1976), which were highly regarded by reviewers. His critical study *Marianne Moore: The Cage and the Animal* (1970) was also warmly received. In his more recent essay collections, *Fathers Playing Catch with Sons: Essays on Sport (Mostly Baseball)* (1985) and *Principal Products of Portugal: Prose Pieces* (1995), Hall examines sports, reflecting largely on his passion for baseball. In 1987 he published a collection of short stories, *The Ideal Bakery*. Perhaps his best-known—and certainly his best-selling—work is the textbook *Writing Well* (1973), which was published in its eighth edition in 1994.

Hall has documented his love for New England in several collections of autobiographical essays, beginning with *String Too Short to be Saved* (1961), in which he re-creates days of haying and blueberry picking and pays tribute to the way of life that died with his grandparents. More recently, he has recorded life on Eagle Pond in his books *Seasons at Eagle Pond* (1987) and its companion, *Here at Eagle Pond* (1990). In both collections Hall describes his quiet, reflective life on the farm and reminisces about the rural culture of New England in the past and present. In his 1993 memoir, *Life Work*, Hall again celebrates life in New Hampshire, this time focusing on the pleasures of being absorbed in one's work. Inspired by his grandparents' dedication to the endless chores they endured in caring for the farm, Hall discusses his life's work as a full-time writer. In the second half the memoir concentrates on Hall's diagnosis with liver cancer. Critics praised *Life Work* for its captivating prose and its exploration of the minute details of a quiet life. In one such laudatory review, Barbara Hoffert for *Library Journal* (October 15, 1993) concluded, "Hall writes cleanly, crisply, and with a gentle conviction that will push readers out of their easy chairs and set them to working, too. He inspires such absorbedness that the task of reading is done in an instant."

Over the last four decades, Hall has also built a reputation as an accomplished author of children's books, including *Andrew the Lion Farmer* (1959), *Riddle Rat* (1977), *Ox-Cart Man* (1979), *The Man Who Lived Alone* (1984), *Summer of 1944* (1994), *I Am the Dog, I Am the Cat* (1994), *Lucy's Christmas* (1994), *Lucy's Summer* (1995), *When Willard Met Babe Ruth* (1996), *Old Home Day* (1996), and *The Milkman's Boy* (1997). In a *Horn Book* review (February 1980) of *Ox-Cart Man*—which earned the 1980 Caldecott Medal from the American Library Association—M. M. Burns called the book "a pastoral symphony translated into picture book format [in which] the stunning combination of text and illustrations re-creates the mood of nineteenth-century rural New England. . . . Quiet but not static, the book celebrates the peacefulness of a time now past but one which is still, nevertheless, an irrefutable part of the American consciousness." Hall explained to David McDonald this impulse to record the past: "One of the major goals of my writing—look at the children's books like *Ox-Cart Man*, *Lucy's Christmas*, and *The Milkman's Boy*—has been to preserve the past and pass it on. Yes, I want to hand on a sense of old times, not only in my writing, but to my children and grandchildren." In addition to writing children's books, he has edited *The Oxford Book of Children's Verse in America* (1985)—for which he was included on the 1986 *Horn Book* honor list—and *The Oxford Illustrated Book of American Children's Poems* (1999).

Hall has contributed numerous stories and articles to such publications as the *New Yorker*, *Esquire*, *Playboy*, *Transatlantic Review*, and *American Scholar*. Among the many honors he has received are the Edna St. Vincent Millay Award of the Poetry Society of America (1955), the Longview Foundation Award (1960), two Guggenheim fellowships (1963–64 and 1972–73), the Robert Frost Silver Medal from the Poetry Society of America (1991), the New England Booksellers Association Award (1993), the Ruth Lilly Prize from the American Council of the Arts (1994), and honorary doctorates from ten distinguished colleges and universities. He enjoys giving public readings of his work and has appeared at more than 1,500 poetry readings at colleges, libraries, schools, and community centers around the world. In September 2003, his next book of essays, "Breakfast Served Any Time All Day: Essays on Poems New and Selected," is scheduled for release.

Donald Hall continues to reside at his farmhouse on Eagle Pond, where he rises every morning around 5 a.m. and spends his days engaged in a range of writing projects. By his marriage to Kirby Thompson, which ended in divorce in 1969, he has two grown children, Andrew and Philippa. Hall has said his current focus is writing verse "in which the sound itself keeps the listeners intent." He explained, "The listener doesn't have to understand this poem intellectually, but to enjoy it as a sensual object, to take it into the ears and be moved by it." In his *New York Times Book Review* article, he summed up his dedication to the craft of writing: "If you continue to write, you go past the place where praise, publication or admiration sustains you," he said. "The more praise the better—but it does not sustain you. You arrive at a point where only the possibilities of poetry provide food for your desires, possibilities glimpsed in great poems that you love. What began perhaps as [the poem "The Moon's] the North Wind's Cooky"—what continued variously as affectation and self-love; what zaps crazily up and down in public recognition—finds repose only in love of the art, and in desire, if not precisely the hope, that you may make something fit to endure with the old ones."

—K. D.

SUGGESTED READING: *American Poetry Review* p17+ Jan.–Feb. 2002; *Atlantic* (on-line) Oct. 1996; *Commonweal* p21+ Sep. 24, 1993; *Esquire* p68+ Jan. 1984; *Los Angeles Times Book Review* p10 Nov. 5, 1989; *The Nation* p496 Oct. 31, 1987; *New Republic* p41+ Feb. 14, 1994; *New York Times* C p1 Apr. 1 1981, VII p18 Feb. 24, 1991; *New York Times Book Review* p7+ Jan. 16 1983; *Ploughshares* p270 Fall 2001

SELECTED WORKS: poetry—*Exiles and Marriages*, 1955; *The Dark Houses*, 1958; *A Roof of Tiger Lilies*, 1964; *The Alligator Bride: Poems, New and Selected*, 1969; *The Yellow Room: Love Poems*, 1971; *The Town of Hill*, 1975; *A Blue Wing Tilts at the Edge of the Sea: Selected Poems, 1964–1975*, 1975; *Kicking the Leaves*, 1978; *The Toy Bone*, 1979; *The Happy Man*, 1986; *The One Day*, 1988; *Old and New Poems*, 1990; *The Museum of Clear Ideas*, 1993; *The Old Life*, 1996; *Without*, 1998; *The Painted Bed*, 2002; essays—*String Too Short to be Saved: Recollections of Summers on a New England Farm*, 1961; *The Pleasures of Poetry*, 1971; *Writing Well*, 1974; *Goatfoot Milktongue Twinbird: Interviews, Essays, and Notes on Poetry*, 1978; *Remembering Poets: Reminiscences and Opinions—Dylan Thomas, Robert Frost, T.S. Eliot, Ezra Pound*, 1978 (republished as *Their Ancient Glittering Eyes*, 1992); *To Keep Moving: Essays, 1959–1969*, 1980; *The Weather for Poetry: Essays, Reviews, and Notes on Poetry, 1977–81*, 1982; *Fathers Playing Catch with Sons: Essays on Sport (Mostly Baseball)*, 1985; *Winter*, 1986; *Seasons at Eagle Pond*, 1987; *Poetry and Ambition*, 1988; *Here at Eagle Pond*, 1990; *Life*

Work, 1993; *Death to the Death of Poetry: Essays, Reviews, Notes, Interviews*, 1994; *Principal Products of Portugal: Prose Pieces*, 1995; children's books—*Andrew and the Lion Farmer*, 1959; *Riddle Rat*, 1977; *Ox-Cart Man*, 1979; *The Man Who Lived Alone*, 1984; *Summer of 1944*, 1994; *I Am the Dog, I Am the Cat*, 1994; *Lucy's Christmas*, 1994; *Lucy's Summer*, 1995; *When Willard Met Babe Ruth*, 1996; *Old Home Day*, 1996; *The Milkman's Boy*, 1997; as editor—*The Harvard Advocate Anthology*, 1950; *The New Poets of England and America*, 1957; *Contemporary American Poetry*, 1963; *The Faber Book of Modern Verse*, 1965; *A Choice of Whitman's Verse*, 1968; *The Modern Stylists: Writers on the Art of Writing*, 1968; *American Poetry: An Introductory Anthology*, 1969; *The Pleasures of Poetry*, 1971; *Galway Kinnell, Walking Down the Stairs*, 1978; *William Stafford, Writing the Australian Crawl*, 1978; *The Oxford Book of American Literary Anecdotes*, 1981; *To Read Literature: Fiction, Poetry, Drama*, 1981; *Claims for Poetry*, 1982; *To Read Poetry*, 1982; *The Contemporary Essay*, 1984; *The Oxford Book of Children's Verse in America*, 1985; *To Read Fiction*, 1987; *The Best American Poetry*, 1989; *The Oxford Illustrated Book of American Children's Poems*, 1999

Annica Thomsson/Courtesy of Farrar, Straus and Giroux

Hansen, Erik Fosnes

June 6, 1965– Novelist

Erik Fosnes Hansen is one of Norway's best-known novelists. He found literary success early, publishing his first novel in 1985, at the age of 20. Hansen has written four books—three novels and one biography. His work has been translated into many languages, including English. In *Psalm at Journey's End* (1996), the first of his novels translated into English, Hansen writes about the backgrounds and experiences of the musicians who played aboard the *Titanic*, which sank after hitting an iceberg during its maiden voyage, in 1912. Hansen's *Tales of Protection* (2002), which was published to critical acclaim in the United States, explores the phenomenon of coincidence; it is comprised of several stories that take place in different times and places, but are nonetheless linked narratively. "Having written so extensively on disaster, I thought it would be interesting to write about disasters that didn't happen. Those saved-by-the-bell and by-the-skin-of-your-teeth experiences," Hansen told Carol J. Williams for the *Los Angeles Times* (May 31, 2000) of his decision to tackle the unusual topic.

Erik Fosnes Hansen was born on June 6, 1965 in New York City. A short time after his birth, Hansen and his family moved to Oslo, Norway, where he grew up. For two years, Hansen studied in Stuttgart, Germany, where he became fluent in the German language.

In 1985 Hansen made his literary debut with the publication of his novel *Falketårnet* ("The Falcon Tower"). The book did well with both literary critics and the public and was eventually translated into several languages.

Hansen's second novel, *Salme ved reisens slutt* (1990), earned the Riksmålprisen, one of Norway's most prestigious literary prizes. It sold 100,000 copies, a remarkable feat given that the population of Norway is just slightly more than four million. In 1996 the book was translated into English as *Psalm at Journey's End*. The novel focuses on a diverse group of musicians who are hired to play as the orchestra aboard the doomed ocean liner *Titanic*. Much of the novel presents the musicians' individual stories, which provide a look at the moral and cultural values in the years leading up to World War I. The son of an English doctor, Jason enjoyed a happy childhood—until his parents died tragically during a medical mission in India. Shattered by the loss, Jason becomes self-destructive and emotionally indifferent. After getting expelled from medical school, the young man finds himself living on the streets of London. Jason later finds redemption and begins to heal after he saves the life of a young prostitute half-buried in the snow. In turn, she encourages him to begin playing a violin that his mother had given him. Jason turns his life around, eventually becoming the *Titanic*'s orchestra leader.

Leo, a German pianist who is nicknamed "Spot," wanted to become a composer. His father, however, insisted that he continue playing the piano, thinking a musician would make more money than a composer. Alex, the first violinist and a former thief, had fled Russia, leaving behind a younger brother who needed him. David, the second violinist and a young member of a wealthy Jewish family in Vienna, had his heart broken by a girl who left him for an older man, a famous actor. At the novel's climax, as the *Titanic* sinks, the musicians attempt to calm the passengers on the deck by performing. As the ocean liner's lights go out, they finally go their separate ways one by one. In his review for the *Los Angeles Times* (August 18, 1996), Richard Eder had mixed feelings about the novel. "The *Titanic* scenes are told delicately, with restrained though absorbing detail, and at a poetic, almost offhand distance," Eder wrote. "Trying as the individual stories can sometimes be, they do succeed, cumulatively, in giving us the sense of an engorged, decadent and ailing world. It is a heavy cargo to take on board, but without it, the author's airy, quicksilver account of the ship's days and destruction would work a less startling transmutation." The reviewer concluded that for "much of the time Hansen is callow and self-indulgent. His mystical vision summons all kinds of spirits from the deep, and many simply refuse to come. A few do, though, and his novel, with its undependable allure, floats in the imagination for quite a while after it sticks in judgment." By contrast, in the *Chicago Tribune* (September 29, 1996), Philip Graham observed that many of the musicians's "stories are nearly novellas in themselves, smaller books within the larger narrative of this structurally audacious novel. Though the setting for this novel is the Titanic's journey, Hansen is primarily concerned with the psalms of inner experience, and he brilliantly connects his characters' exploration of the past—their secret wounds—with the varied cultural histories of Europe at the turn of the century." Although he criticized the novel for ignoring some of the musicians or giving them "less-developed stories," Graham concluded that "what lingers in the reader's mind, what most commands admiration in this ambitious and often dazzling novel—fluidly translated from Norwegian by Joan Tate—is Hansen's balance of compelling narratives, his accomplished portrayal of a wide range of European cultures, and above all his masterly invention of the inner landscapes of his characters, all bound together by the ever-present music of his poetic prose." The popularity of James Cameron's film, *Titanic* (1997), which grossed more than $1 billion at the box office, helped generate interest in Hansen's novel.

In 1998 Hansen published his third book, *Beretninger om beskyttelse*, which received the Booksellers' Prize. In 2002 the novel was translated into English as *Tales of Protection*. In it Hansen offers three long stories and several shorter ones that are loosely connected despite taking place in different countries and times. The first story, set in present-day Norway, opens with Wilhelm Bolt, a wealthy mine engineer, lying in his coffin. Bolt has left his entire fortune to his grandniece, Lea, a runaway who had dropped by for a visit, but ended up staying at his home for two years. The narrative traces back through Bolt's life, and the reader learns that after nearly dying in a mine years before, Bolt had become fascinated with the ideas of the Austrian biologist Paul Kammerer (1880–1926), who attempted to develop a scientific theorem that explained synchronicity—coincidences that appeared to be unrelated. In fact, Bolt had compiled many examples of coincidence by subscribing to a newspaper clipping service and paying informants in an effort to build on Kammerer's ideas and prove that seeming coincidences are the result of unseen forces in the world. The second tale follows Enberg, who works at a lighthouse on a Swedish island, in 1898. An accident had cut short Enberg's promising career as a singer and left him nearly mute. Although Enberg is devoted to his job and to his co-workers, he once failed to pick up a ship's distress signal, allowing it to run aground. Several sailors died in the accident, and Kalle Jacobbson, the lighthouse keeper, is troubled by the deaths. Jacobbson's epileptic daughter, Josefa, whose life was saved by Enberg on the day she was born, occasionally sees and hears the ghosts of the dead sailors. In the third story, which takes place in 1497 Italy, during the Renaissance, a young merchant named Lorenzo del Vetro suffers from a painful and disfiguring skin disease. The medical treatments that were available at the time do not work, but Lorenzo is miraculously cured after seeing a painting of the Virgin Mary in a rundown church. Determined to learn the history of the painting, which he initially considered ugly, Lorenzo dispatches his servant, Fiorello, to Padua to track down an old blind man who was the artist's apprentice. "Hansen favors the Russian doll approach to stories, in which one story is nested inside another," Jeff Zaleski wrote in his review for *Publishers Weekly* (June 3, 2002). "His 'serialism' is romantic in the deepest sense—allegories and narratives contain the deep structure of the world, while math and science are merely the mutable surface. The craft of 19th-century fiction and the complexity of 20th-century thought make this a gloriously rewarding novel." In *Newsday* (July 28, 2002), John Freeman favorably compared Hansen to the Danish novelist Isak Dinesen (1885–1962). "Like Dinesen, Hansen seems more comfortable in a century not his own," Freeman observed. "*Tales of Protection* bulges with all the wonderfully strange, arcane, information of centuries ago—how to read nautical charts, interpret rock formations, create aquamarine paint or gild a detail on a fresco. Hansen paints these details so thickly onto his canvas that, in order to read this book, one must enjoy the process of learning about bygone ways." The reviewer added, "Hansen ends each tale with an unfinished sentence that begins in the following tale. Following his prose from one tale to the next, a reader is made to feel like a bird, migrating backward and forward in time with an ease that congratulates the power of storytelling."

In 2001 Hansen published his first nonfiction book, *Underveis: et portrett ab Princess Märtha Louise*, a biography of Norway's Princess Martha Louise that was officially commissioned by Norway's royal family. Hansen also serves as the literary critic for the *Aftenposten*, one of Norway's major newspapers. Hansen and his family live in Oslo.

—D. C.

SUGGESTED READING: Cappelen Publishers Web site; *Chicago Tribune* Books p6 Sep. 29, 1996; *Los Angeles Times* Book Review p2 Aug. 18, 1996; *Newsday* D p26 July 28, 2002; *Nordic Business Report* (on-line) Nov. 15, 2000; *Publishers Weekly* p59 June 3, 2002

SELECTED BOOKS IN ENGLISH TRANSLATION: *Psalm at Journey's End*, 1996; *Tales of Protection*, 2002

Hulleah Tsinhnahjinnie/Courtesy of Mekko Productions, Inc.

Harjo, Joy

May 9, 1951– Poet; screenwriter; musician; educator

The work of the award-winning poet Joy Harjo reflects her strong feelings of connectedness to her Native American heritage and to the landscape of the American Southwest. Often autobiographical, Harjo's poems are rooted in memory as well as in myth, history, and the environment. "I feel strongly that I have a responsibility to all the sources that I am: to all past and future ancestors, to my home country, to all places that I touch down on and that are myself, to all voices, all women, all of my tribe, all people, all earth, and beyond that to all beginnings and endings," the poet told *Contemporary Authors* (2000). "In a strange kind of sense [writing] frees me to believe in myself, to be able to speak, to have voice, because I have to; it is my survival." Harjo has written several volumes of poetry; the first, *The Last Song*, was published in 1975, and the most recent, *How We Became Human*, was published in 2002. *A Map to the Next World: Poems and Tales*, came out in 2000. Her most highly celebrated book is *In Mad Love and War* (1990), which won the William Carlos Williams Award of the Poetry Society of America, among other honors. Harjo has taught creative writing and poetry at a half-dozen universities. She also plays alto saxophone; her readings of her poems to the accompaniment of the band Joy Harjo and Poetic Justice have been recorded on three CDs.

"I don't believe I would be alive today if it hadn't been for writing," Harjo told Laura Coltelli for *Winged Words: American Indian Writers Speak* (1990), as excerpted in *Contemporary Literary Criticism* (1994). "There were times when I was conscious of holding onto a pen and letting the words flow, painful and from the gut, to keep from letting go of it all. Now, this was when I was much younger, and full of self-hatred. Writing helped me give voice to turn around a terrible silence that was killing me. And on a larger level, if we, as Indian people, Indian women, keep silent, then we will disappear, at least in this level of reality. As Audre Lorde says [in her 1996 book, *Sister Outsider: Essays and Speeches*] . . . , 'Your silence will not protect you,' which has been a quietly unanimous decision it seems, this last century with Indian people."

A registered member of the Muscogee Nation (also known as the Creek or Muskoke tribe), Joy Harjo was born on May 9, 1951 in Tulsa, Oklahoma. Her father, Allen W. Foster, was Muscogee; her mother, Wynema (Baker) Foster, was part French and part Cherokee. Native Americans of mixed heritage as well as white families lived in the neighborhood where Harjo was raised, on the north side of Tulsa. Harjo's Muscogee grandmother, Naomi Harjo, and great-aunt Lois Harjo Ball were both painters who earned bachelor of fine arts degrees in the early 1900s; her great-aunt became young Joy's mentor. "From the time I was very small you could always find me drawing, whether it was in the dirt or on paper. That was the one thing that made me happy," Harjo told Marilyn Kallett for the *Kenyon Review* (Summer 1993). As a teenager Harjo studied painting and theater at the Institute of American Indian Arts, an innovative program in Santa Fe, New Mexico. After she graduated, in 1967, she joined a Native American dance troupe and took a number of odd jobs.

Harjo spent one semester as a pre-med student at the University of New Mexico before switching her major to painting. She also took courses in the language of the Navajo Nation. After attending readings by Galway Kinnell, Simon Ortiz, Leslie Marman Silko, and other poets, she gave up painting and began writing poetry. "I found that language, through poetry, was taking on more magical qualities than my painting," Harjo explained to Laura Coltelli. "I could say more when I wrote. Soon it wasn't a choice. Poetry-speaking 'called me' in a sense. And I couldn't say no." Ortiz's performance in particular showed her that "the voice of a poet can be a natural speaking voice, and poetry can include the experience of a person of the Southwest like me," as she explained for the *Heath Anthology of American Literature Newsletter* (Fall 1991, on-line). In 1976 she earned a B.A. degree from the University of New Mexico.

Harjo then entered the prestigious Iowa Writers' Workshop, at the University of Iowa, where she took classes with Leslie Silko. At that time Harjo was a single mother raising two children (a son, Phil, and a daughter, Rainy Dawn). When she first arrived at the university, she told Marilyn Kallett, she felt as if she had "walked into a strange land in which I had to learn another language. This comes from being of native background, from the West, but it also comes from being a woman in that institution. I heard the Director say once to a group of possible funders—I was one of the people they chose to perform for them in the workshop—he told them that the place was actually geared for male writers, which is honest; it was true, but I was shocked. I remember [the novelist] Jayne Anne Phillips and I looking at each other, like 'Can you believe this? Then why are we sitting here?'" Harjo received a master's degree in fine arts from the university in 1978. She told Kallett that although she "learned a lot about technique" at the Iowa Writers' Workshop, she was disappointed to find "the art of poetry had broken down into sterile exercises. And yet, I know I admire some of the work of those people who taught me. But the system had separated itself from the community, from myth, from humanhood."

Earlier, in 1978, Harjo had begun teaching at the Institute of American Indian Arts, where she remained until 1979. Her first full-length volume of poetry, *What Moon Drove Me to This?*, was released the following year; included in the text were nine connected poems originally published in 1975 as a 15-page chapbook entitled *The Last Song*. From 1980 to 1983 Harjo served as a writer and consultant for two private organizations—the Native American Public Broadcasting Consortium and the National Indian Youth Council—and a federal agency, the National Endowment for the Arts (NEA). Harjo's experience with the NEA was at times both "comical" and "bizarre," as she explained to Laura Coltelli. "When I was on the National Endowment for the Arts literature panel I was often the spokesperson-representative for Indian people, black people, all minority people, including women's, lesbian, and gay groups. It was rather ridiculous and angering at the same time, for we were all considered outside the mainstream of American literature. And it's not true, for often we are closer to the center."

Repetition of phrases marked some of the poems in Harjo's second book, *She Had Some Horses* (1983). For example, in a poem about the rape of a child, the line "She thought she woke up" serves as a refrain. Some of Harjo's early poems, such as "Kansas City" and "Heartbeat," feature Noni Daylight, a character Harjo created as a means of telling the stories of women. Noni Daylight began "as a name I gave a real-life woman I couldn't name in a poem," Harjo explained to Laura Coltelli. "Then she evolved into her own person, took on her own life. And then she left my poems and went into a poem by Barney Bush, a Shawnee poet, and I never saw her again. She never came back!" The image of the moon also recurred in Harjo's early work, as a symbol both of the past and of female energy. Often labeled a feminist writer, Harjo has not hesitated to acknowledge that her poetry is "woman-identified," as she described it to Coltelli. "One of the funniest questions I have been asked as a visitor to an Indian-culture class in a university is, by a male student, 'Where are the men in your poems?' He was offended because he didn't see himself, not in the form that he looked for. I truly feel there is a new language coming about—look at the work of Meridel Le Sueur, Sharon Doubiago, Linda Hogan, Alice Walker—it's coming from the women."

As Harjo explained to Laura Coltelli, her poems "begin with the seed of an emotion, a place, and then move from there." She told Coltelli that she has come to view each poem as the culmination of "an often long journey that can begin years earlier, say with the blur of the memory of the sun on someone's cheek, a certain smell, an ache." The resulting poem is "sifted through a point, a lake in my heart through which language must come." Harjo's work is informed by her belief that art emerges from a place "beyond us . . . from that source of utter creation, the Creator, or God," as she told *Contemporary Authors*. "We are technicians here on Earth, but also co-creators. . . . Ultimately humans have a small hand in it. We serve it. We have to put ourselves in the way of it, and get out of the way ourselves." Harjo's approach does not involve "taking established forms and developing them," as she explained to *Contemporary Authors*. "I admire a finely constructed sonnet but I do not wish to work in that Euro-classical form. I honor that direction, but I am working to find my own place. . . . I am influenced by Muscogean forms, European and African forms, as well as others that have influenced me [such as] Navajo. . . . [The Navajo language] influenced me deeply because intimate to the language were the shapes of the landscape, the history. I became aware of layers of meaning marked by sandhills, by the gestures of the earth." Harjo was also inspired by the civil rights movement and the activities of the American Indian Movement, an organization responsible for sparking "an intertribal awareness in [the U.S.]," as she told Paul Seesequasis for the magazine *Aboriginal Voices* (1995, on-line). "I started writing out of that need for that river of concern. Up to that point a lot of us felt shame for what we were. That movement helped galvanize us and open us up like nothing else."

Harjo collaborated with the astronomer and photographer Stephen Strom on *Secrets from the Corner of the World* (1989), a book of 60 prose poems set in the Southwest, each of which was accompanied by one of Strom's photographs. From 1985 until 1988 she was an assistant professor at the University of Colorado at Boulder, during which time she began playing the saxophone. She spent the following two years as an associate professor at the University of Arizona at Tucson before becoming a tenured professor at the University of New Mexico at Albuquerque, where she taught from 1991 to 1997. She took a leave of absence from academia to concentrate on her work with Poetic Justice.

Poetic Justice evolved out of a collaboration between Harjo and the drummer Susan M. Williams in 1992. In addition to Williams and Harjo, who provides vocals and plays the saxophone, for a while the band featured the guitarist William Bluehouse Johnson, the bassist John L. Williams, the guitarist Richard Carbajal, and Frank Poocha, a percussionist who also performs tribal songs. The band has made three recordings: *Furious Light* (1986), *The Woman Who Fell from the Sky* (1994), and *Letter from the End of the Twentieth Century* (1997); a fourth, tentatively titled "Crossing the Border," is in the works. Following the release of *Letter from the End of the Twentieth Century*, Poetic Justice received an award for Outstanding Musical Achievement from First Americans in the Arts (1998); the recording was also nominated for awards in eight categories at the 1998 National Native Music Awards. The band's music incorporates elements of rock, jazz, reggae, and tribal music. Recently Harjo has been traveling with a rotating group of musicians known as Joy Harjo and Her Poetic Justice Band.

African-American music in particular has "been critical to my development as a writer and musician," Harjo told *Contemporary Authors*. "There is history and a relationship between Africans and Muscogean peoples begun in the southeastern U.S. We've influenced each other, yet this influence is rarely talked about. I can hear the African influence in our stomp dance music, and can hear Muscogean influence in jazz, the blues, and rock. . . . The first poetry I heard and recognized as pure poetry was the improvised line of a trumpet player on a jazz tune on the radio when I was four years old. . . . I've been trying to get it right ever since."

The year 1990 marked the appearance of Harjo's fourth volume of poetry, *In Mad Love and War*, a very personal take on such subjects as politics, heritage, and the healing power of poetry. It contains pieces dedicated to the Native American activists Jacqueline Peters and Anna Mae Pictou Aquash, the jazz saxophonist Charlie Parker, and the pop singer Nat King Cole. *In Mad Love and War* received several awards in 1991, among them the Josephine Miles Award for excellence in literature, the William Carlos Williams Award, and the American Book Award, as well as prizes from the Poetry Society of America and the Before Columbus Foundation. Later, in 1995, the book also received the Delmore Schwartz Memorial Award and the Mountains and Plains Booksellers' Award. In a review for *Prairie Schooner* (Summer 1992), Kathleen West wrote, "*In Mad Love and War* has the power and beauty of prophecy and all the hope of love poised at its passionate beginning. It allows us to enter the place 'we haven't imagined' and allows us to imagine what we will do when we are there."

The title of Harjo's next volume of poetry, *The Woman Who Fell from the Sky* (1994), refers to an Iroquois creation myth. The book, which contains a number of prose poems, was sold along with a cassette featuring Harjo's poetry and the music of Poetic Justice; it received an Oklahoma Book Arts Award in 1994. In 1997 Harjo and Gloria Bird coedited *Reinventing the Enemy's Language: North American Native Women's Writing*, a social and political call to arms that includes work by approximately 80 women, among them the writers Louise Erdrich and Mary Brave Bird and various activists, including Wilma Mankiller, Beatrice Medicine, and Winona LaDuke. The year 2000 saw the release of Harjo's fifth full-length collection of poetry, *A Map to the Next World: Poems and Tales*, as well as a children's book, *The Good Luck Cat*, about a girl's friendship with her pet cat, Woogie.

In 2002 Harjo published *How We Became Human*, a collection of 13 new poems as well as selected poems from her earlier collections and chapbooks. As quoted on *Amazon.com*, a reviewer for *Publishers Weekly* observed, "Harjo . . . contends that poetry is not only a way to save the sanity of those who have been oppressed to the point of madness, but that it is a tool to rebuild communities and, ultimately, change the world: 'All acts of kindness are lights in the war for justice.' Alive with compassion, pain and love, this book is unquestionably an act of kindness."

In 1982 Harjo completed a nondegree program at the Anthropology Film Center in Santa Fe, New Mexico. She has since written a number of screenplays, including "When We Used to Be Humans" (which has never been published) and *Origin of Apache Crown Dance* (1985). From 1987 to 1990 Harjo was a member of the board of directors of the Native American Public Broadcasting Consortium. She also completed a songwriting workshop at the Berklee College of Music, in Boston, Massachusetts, in 1998. Harjo provided narration for a series on Native Americans that aired on Turner Network Television and the Emmy Award–winning 1995 *National Geographic Explorer* segment on the Navajo "code-talkers" who, using the Navajo language during World War II, helped to encode military messages that eluded Japanese cryptographers.

Harjo, who currently lives in Honolulu, Hawaii, is a member of the advisory boards of the New Mexico and the national chapters of the writers' organization PEN, and she has served on the editorial boards of such publications as *Contact II*, *Tyuonyi*, and the *High Plains Literary Review*. Her many honors include the Academy of American Poetry Award (1976); a Lifetime Achievement Award from the Native Writers' Circle of the Americas (1995); the New Mexico Governor's Award for Excellence in the Arts (1997); the Lila Wallace–Reader's Digest Award (1998); and a Distinguished Achievement Award from the Western Literature Association (2000). She has received poetry fellowships from the National Endowment for the Arts (1978) and the Wittner Byner Poetry Foundation (1994). In 1998 she received an honorary doctorate from St. Mary-in-the-Woods College, Indiana, and was appointed to the National Council on the Arts by then–president Bill Clinton.

"Today, just about everything inspires me to continue writing," Harjo told an interviewer in connection with the 1998 edition of the *Heath Anthology of American Literature* (one of the many anthologies that include her poetry), as cited on the Georgetown University Web site. "My granddaughter inspires me to think about the future. I have intense dreams and visions that inspire me. And I have an amazement for survival that keeps me writing."

—C. L.

SUGGESTED READING: *American Indian Quarterly* p13+ Summer/Fall 1999; *MELUS* [The Society for the Study of the Multi-Ethnic Literature of the United States] p5+ Spring 1989/1990; *New York Times* C p11 Apr. 21, 1997, with photos; *Progressive* p22+ Mar. 1992; *Contemporary Authors* new rev. ser. vol. 91, 2000; *Contemporary Literary Criticism* vol. 83, 1994; Pearlman, Mickey. *Listen to Their Voices: Twenty Interviews with Women Who Write*, 1993

SELECTED BOOKS: *The Last Song*, 1975; *What Moon Drove Me to This?*, 1980; *She Had Some Horses*, 1983; *Secrets from the Center of the World*, 1989; *In Mad Love and War*, 1990; *The Woman Who Fell from the Sky*, 1994; *The Good Luck Cat*, 2000; *A Map to the Next World: Poems and Tales*, 2000; *How We Became Human*, 2002

SELECTED RECORDINGS: with Poetic Justice—*Furious Light*, 1986; *The Woman Who Fell from the Sky*, 1994; *Letter from the End of the Twentieth Century*, 1997

Harrison, William

Oct. 29, 1933– Novelist; short-story writer; screenwriter

The publication of his latest book, *The Blood Latitudes* (2000), marked the fifth decade of William Harrison's career as a novelist. Like many of his previous novels, *The Blood Latitudes* is set in Africa. Harrison's novels and stories typically present characters who find themselves in unfamiliar and even threatening surroundings. "Harrison's world is an aggressive place, and his characters are scammers, grifters, guys and gals on the make," Erin McGraw observed in the *Georgia Review* (Summer 1999). "In Harrison's fiction only the shrewd survive."

Harrison submitted the following third-person statement to *World Authors 1995–2000*: "William Harrison was born in Texas on October 29, 1933 and attended Texas Christian University where he was the editor of the student newspaper. He later attended Vanderbilt University and the University of Iowa. At Vanderbilt he studied at the theological school with the intention of teaching comparative religion, but began to write his earliest fiction as well as poetry and drama. At Iowa's writing workshop he sold his first novel and the first of several stories published in *Esquire* magazine during the 1960s and 1970s.

"His second novel gained him wider attention. John Leonard of the *New York Times* wrote about the author when *In a Wild Sanctuary* was published in 1969 that 'he is a young writer who writes equally well about action and ideas.' During this same period one of the author's *Esquire* stories, 'Rollerball,' became the futuristic film by that name: a story about a player in a death sport during a time when giant corporations have replaced nations.

"Since 1958 he has been married to Merlee Portman Harrison, and they have three children: Laurie, Sean, and Quentin. Although the author has been a university teacher for most of those years the Harrisons have also been world travelers, living for lengths of time in London, on the Spanish coast, and in Malibu, California.

"In 1976 the author made the first of many extended trips to Africa and began to write about Americans and Europeans on that continent. He subsequently published five novels with African settings: *Africana* (1977), *Savannah Blue* (1979), *Burton and Speke* (1982), *Three Hunters* (1990) and *The Blood Latitudes* (2000). He also co-wrote the script to *Mountains of the Moon* directed by Bob Rafelson in 1990 and based on the novel *Burton and Speke*.

"His short stories and essays have appeared in the *Paris Review, Esquire, Playboy,* the *Saturday Evening Post, Cosmopolitan, Anataeus, Redbook* and other magazines, and have been collected in two volumes: *Rollerball Murder and Other Stories* (1973) and *The Buddha in Malibu* (1998).

"He began his teaching career in North Carolina, then taught briefly in Texas before coming to the University of Arkansas in 1964. There with James Whitehead he became co-founder of the Program in Creative Writing. His students have included Barry Hannah, Ellen Gilchrist, Lee K. Abbott, Lewis Nordan, Jim Crumley, Steve Yarbrough, and others. He retired in 1998 as University Professor.

"He has been awarded a Guggenheim Memorial Fellowship in fiction, the Christopher Award for television (*A Shining Season,* CBS, 1979), and the Columbia School of Journalism Prize in association with *Esquire* magazine.

"He says of his work, 'I've always written about outsiders and my African novels, especially, are designed to place my characters in an exotic and hostile environment. In this regard I suppose I've been influenced by Graham Greene, but especially by Joseph Conrad. I also think I'm close in spirit to all those writers—one of my favorite contemporary writers, Paul Theroux, comes to mind—who use foreign settings to reveal character.

"Americans, after all, are very wealthy nomads roaming the world nowadays, not just products of their own small backyards back home. Most of us aren't just Southerners or New Yorkers or locals. We're everywhere—and involved in the political and social lives of many others very different from ourselves. We're also a people with an abiding arrogance that we can change things for the better wherever we go. Between such lofty expectations and the hard realities there's always a drama happening.

"In this regard I've been very like a reporter as a writer, never autobiographical, and always looking for other people's stories—people far more interesting than my own rather conventional life has been. At times I've felt like a thief of good anecdotes or particularly interesting characters, but all writers have that sort of larceny in them. It was great impertinence, for instance, to write about Richard Burton and John Hanning Speke. They belong to British history and to that daring time in the 19th century when men searched in Africa for the source of the Nile. But Speke's homosexuality and his dyslexia stood in sharp contrast to Burton's womanizing and his extraordinary gift for languages, so I became bold enough to take them on. Mine was a revisionist view of their relationship and their accomplishment, then, and, after all, any historical work should be revisionist in spirit—or shouldn't be written in the first place.

"There's yet another reason why I went to Africa to find my material. That's language, the art of language in literature. I've never been a hip American. In many ways I'm a Victorian, but aside from that I looked for a world that required a measure of poetry. After all, storytelling is a matter of creating a series of surprises: the unexpected surprises of plot, of characterization, of point of view, of closely observed detail, and of language itself.'"

Harrison tapped his background in religious studies for his first novel, *The Theologian* (1965). At a theological seminary in Tennessee, Randle Fast pursues a doctorate despite having little interest in religion. According to Eleanor Smith's review in the *Library Journal* (September 1, 1965), he "becomes involved in an affair with the wife of an influential professor and simultaneously slips from orthodox theology toward the occult." Randle later marries Dora, the daughter of a wealthy man, and takes a teaching job in Texas. Feeling trapped by his unhappy life, Randle eventually turns to murder. "This is a well-written first novel but a depressing one since it is developed entirely from the point of view of the protagonist, who is psychotic from the start," Smith wrote. She also observed however that few of the novel's characters are well-developed. Writing in the *New York Times Book Review* (October 24, 1965), Martin Levin observed that Randle's relationship with Dora in the novel "has a synthetic, literary flavor when added to the solidly realized foundation of character and atmosphere that the author has earlier established."

In Harrison's next novel, *In a Wild Sanctuary* (1969), four troubled college students form a suicide pact. As a review in the *Times Literary Supplement* (December 12, 1970) explained, "Each has some cause for suicide, each has—to some degree—the inclination: Adler is neurotically introverted, Stoker's sexual failures have become almost debilitating, Pless is depressive; most complex of all, though, is Clive, whose manic, near-uncontrollable energy provides a focal-point for the others. He, it appears, generates the nervous tension which keeps the idea of the pact alive." In the *New York Times Book Review* (November 30, 1969), Martin Levin wrote, "Mr. Harrison has saved his book from drowning in a muddy sea of interior monologue by shoring it up with a suspenseful plot. . . . As [Clive's] activities gain momentum, so does the novel, overcoming the tide of introspection to reach a shattering denouement."

In 1971 Harrison published *Lessons in Paradise,* a love story between Baskin, a mathematical genius, and Kate, an older, divorced woman. A reviewer for *Publishers Weekly* (January 11, 1971) wrote, "The breakdown of genius into man is always fun and Mr. Harrison has a sure touch and knows his subject. The love story is very simple and there is both humor and compassion for Baskin and Kate."

In 1974 Harrison published his first collection of short stories, *Rollerball Murder and Other Stories*. Harrison adapted the title story into a screenplay for the film *Rollerball* (1975), which starred James Caan and John Houseman. The film was a hit with audiences. In 2002 a remake of *Rollerball* was released, but it received mostly negative reviews and failed at the box office.

In 1977 Harrison wrote the first of his novels set in Africa. *Africana* is an adventure story centered around three characters: Leo, a solider of fortune; Val, a British correspondent; and Harry, a Vietnam veteran. United Nations Secretary-General Dag Hammarskjöld, a real-life figure who died in a plane crash in the Congo in 1961, also appears in the novel. Writing in the *Times Literary Supplement* (December 2, 1977), Robert Brian described the conflict between the novel's opposing forces: "Violence is set against tameness, the wild against the domestic, war against peace, the individual against the group, man against women." As Brian noted, different characters in the novel represent these different forces; Leo, for example, embodies violence and wild nature, while Hammarskjöld represents peace, culture, and order. Brian had a generally favorable view of *Africana*: "The adventure is neatly told; the fable has simple, fairy-tale cadences; and the philosophy is poetic." However, Brian criticized Harrison's dialogue as "undistinguished," observing that while "Leo is Welsh, Harry is Texan, and Val a Londoner, they all speak American." In the *Atlantic Monthly* (June 1977), E. S. Duvall also praised *Africana* as an "ambitious novel [that] is an exploration of the savagery that lies at the heart of modern civilization."

In Harrison's next novel, *Savannah Blue* (1981), an Englishman named Quentin Clare tries to protect African culture from foreign influences by poisoning American businessmen. In the *Chicago Tribune Book World* (May 10, 1981), Eric Zorn wrote, "The core idea of Harrison's book is excellent: A man obsessed with the collision of cultures in the modern world goes on a one-man spree of savage disobedience." However, Zorn added that the novel "ends up with sort of an unseasoned jambalaya of a story: There's not enough suspense to make this book thrilling; not enough social commentary to make it 'meaningful'; not enough carnage to make it Hitchcockian; and not enough sex to make it titillating." Under the title, "Crimes Against Fiction," Anatole Broyard in the *New York Times* (February 7, 1981) dismissed *Savannah Blue* as "poorly written" with no believable characters.

Harrison turned to historical fiction in 1982 with the publication of *Burton and Speke*. The novel chronicles the exploits of British explorers Richard Francis Burton and John Hanning Speke, who in 1857 sought to find the source of the Nile River. In his review in the *Washington Post* (November 23, 1982), Dennis Drabelle discussed the novel's plot: During the expedition, Burton is disabled by illness, and Speke continues alone, eventually finding a large lake in East Africa that he believes is the source of the Nile. Although Speke has promised Burton that he will keep his findings secret until Burton recovers, Speke announces his discovery to the Royal Geographical Society in London, and even denounces Burton. After Burton publicly disputes Speke's claims, Speke, as Drabelle wrote, "feels compelled to answer Burton at one of those grand public debates the Victorians love so well, and the stage is set for the tragic climax." Drabelle described *Burton and Speke* as a "sure-handed historical novel" that is flawed only by "its pedestrian style." Drabelle added, "Harrison's version of the Burton-Speke relationship also has an ironic intensity rarely found in contemporary fiction. As in classical tragedy, the reader is both disheartened by the characters' self-defeating actions and delivered from chaos by the fateful pattern they form." Harrison adapted *Burton and Speke* into a screenplay for the critically acclaimed film *Mountains of the Moon* (1990).

Harrison waited seven years before publishing his next novel. In *Three Hunters* (1989), a father and his two sons come together to hunt a ferocious leopard that has been devouring the residents of a refugee camp. The trio were legendary game hunters who were forced into retirement when the sport was outlawed. In the *Los Angeles Times* (July 2, 1989), reviewer Sonja Bolle wrote, "This is a novel of restless men and the bonds between them, a terrific adventure story as well as a profound meditation on the intoxication of risk-taking." A film based on the novel is expected to be released in 2004.

In 1998 Harrison's second collection of short stories, *The Buddha in Malibu*, was published. In the *Georgia Review* (Summer 1999), Erin McGraw remarked on both the strengths and weaknesses of the collection. For example, she criticized Harrison's stories for being "stocked with caricatures—wealthy paranoids, vulgar social climbers, [and] agile swindlers," and relying on plot twists instead of "character development." However, McGraw also noted that Harrison's stories "do generate some real narrative power," because he gives his characters "interesting work to do." Among the best stories in the collection, according to McGraw, are: "The Rocky Hills of Trancas," which details the conflict between a teenager and his father, who is a screenwriter and an adulterer; "Magic of Soweto," which concerns a thief; "The Arsons of Desire," which discusses firefighters; and "The Good Ship Erasmus," which has a cigarette smuggler taking a smoke-free cruise. McGraw concluded by writing, "Illusions in this book are powerful, but the people who hold them are not; they live in hells they themselves constructed. It's a bleak vision, but at their best the stories in *The Buddha in Malibu* give it credible heft and dimension by grounding Harrison's perspective in a world of interesting, intricate, sometimes brutal work."

In Harrison's most recent novel, *The Blood Latitudes* (2000), Will Hobbs, a retired journalist, goes to war-torn Rwanda to search for his missing son, Buck, who is also a journalist. In the *Seattle Times* (May 7, 2000, on-line), Ginny Merdes wrote, "Harrison writes best when his characters are in country. He has us watching the African jungle turn roads into muddy trails. He launches chapters with beast sounds. And like a journalist who can't turn away from a good story, no matter how gruesome, Harrison describes the torture of young children." While Merdes concluded that *"Blood Latitudes* is no *Heart of Darkness*, the heroic standard against which all books of its ilk must be measured," she praises Harrison for offering "some powerful scenes in the jungle dealing with the big questions: man against man."

In 1990 Harrison donated his private papers to the University of Arkansas in Fayetteville.
—D. C.

SUGGESTED READING: *Atlantic Monthly* June 1977; *Chicago Tribune Bookworld* p7 May 10, 1981; *Georgia Review* Summer 1999; *Library Journal* p3475 Sep. 1, 1965; *Los Angeles Times Book Review* p6 July 2, 1989; *New York Times Book Review* p52 Oct. 24, 1965; *Publishers Weekly* p69 Jan. 11, 1971; *Seattle Times* (on-line) May 7, 2000; *Times Literary Supplement* p1437 Dec. 12, 1970, p1397 Dec. 2, 1977; *Washington Post* D p4 Nov. 23, 1982

SELECTED BOOKS: novels—*The Theologian*, 1965; *In a Wild Sanctuary*, 1969; *Lessons in Paradise*, 1971; *Africana*, 1977; *Savannah Blue*, 1981; *Burton and Speke*, 1982; *Three Hunters*, 1989; *The Blood Latitudes*, 2000; short-story collections—*Rollerball Murder and Other Stories*, 1974; *The Buddha in Malibu*, 1998; screenplays—*Rollerball*, 1975; *Mountains of the Moon*, 1990

Don Denton/Courtesy of Elizabeth Hay

Hay, Elizabeth

Oct. 22, 1951– Novelist; poet; essayist; memoirist

In three memoirs, *Crossing the Snow Line*, *The Only Snow in Havana*, and *Captivity Tales: Canadians in New York*, Elizabeth Hay has delved deeply into her Canadian heritage and written about her love of her native region as well as her travels to other places. Her book of stories, *Small Change*, and her novel, *A Student of Weather*, deal with life lived under the burdens of harsh climes and economic hardship.

Elizabeth Hay provided the following statement for inclusion in *World Authors 1995–2000*: "Until the age of 15 I was convinced that I couldn't write at all.

"My first five years were spent in Owen Sound, Ontario, a small city on Georgian Bay at the base of the Bruce Peninsula, where I was born on October 22, 1951. The next five years were passed in Wiarton, a tourist and fishing town of 2,000 people, located farther up the peninsula.

"Those were happy years. I had a close friend, I learned how to read and I read a great deal, I wandered freely around town and the town was interesting, as towns beside water always are. Wiarton's geography was simple and beautiful, formed by water, limestone cliffs, hills, trees and rock. It was a place, too, that was full of characters. The rich brick and stone houses of the doctors and lawyers were located on the long hill that led down into town, and the poor houses, smaller, ramshackle, home to boys whose hands were covered with warts and to girls who swore, were set farther back on the hill, as was our house.

"My father was the high school principal, and my mother a full-time mother with four children. Now and then she found time to do the painting that later, after her kids left home, would occupy her completely. We were comfortably off, but lived in some ways as if we were poor. This, because of my mother's stubborn frugality. We owned very few books, using the public library instead. We had no television until I was nine, at which time we inherited my grandmother's TV and were allowed to watch it for two hours a week. It stopped working a few years later, and wasn't replaced.

"When I was nearly 10, we left Wiarton and moved inland and farther south to a small town in the heart of agricultural Ontario. It was flat, neat, very conservative. We lived in a rented bungalow on the highway for almost five quite unhappy years. Once, my father looked down at me seated in a chair with my book and said, 'You read so much. Have you ever thought about writing?' It was a kind thought, but hopeless. The only writing I knew were the panic-filled essays and exams at school. It wasn't until we moved again that I found a way to write.

"My father had got it into his head that we would go to London, England, for a year, where he would finish his master's degree in education. It was 1966. The change from small town Ontario to the city of London was stunning. The world opened wide, and with it another door. One day, at the Camden High School for Girls, my English teacher asked us to read a D. H. Lawrence poem, then turn over our books and write down whatever came into our heads. I wrote rapidly, astonished that there was something in my head and that it had a way of coming out. From that moment I was hooked on this private source of pleasure. Over the years the difficulty of finding a form— stories that were deemed stories by anyone else, for instance— eroded my pleasure in writing, and I felt enormous frustration. I realized only a few years ago that I hadn't really learned my lesson from that moment in the classroom when I was 15. What made it possible to write then was the poem I had just been reading. It distracted me from myself, allowing other thoughts and images to well up. To write more freely I needed to forget myself.

"After attending the University of Toronto, I moved west to British Columbia and then north, finding work with the Canadian Broadcasting Corporation in Yellowknife. For some years I continued to work for CBC Radio both in Canada and as a freelancer in Latin America. My first three books, *Crossing the Snow Line*, *The Only Snow in Havana*, and *Captivity Tales: Canadians in New York*, were all written while I was living outside the country, in Mexico and New York; all three are poetic chronicles that weave together early Canadian history with my own life and travels. In 1992, driven by homesickness, I returned to Canada, determined to expand my range as a writer by cracking what I called the fiction nut. Living in Ottawa, I wrote a series of fictional stories about friendships gone wrong that became the book *Small Change*, and then the novel *A Student of Weather*, using as my starting point the Great Depression, which affected my mother's life so deeply.

"Since I've worked largely in isolation, by choice and temperament, the few writers I've known have meant a lot to me. For years I corresponded with the Vancouver writer Daphne Marlatt, always heartened by her endless generosity. Others I've relied on include Stan Dragland and Bob Sherrin.

"When I lose my way in my work, I turn to books to regain my balance, picking up Elizabeth Bishop, for instance, or Chekhov. In the last several years the nominations I've received for literary awards have given me a taste of confidence, but my reason for writing remains the same: to keep myself company, and to feel more alive.

"I have been married twice. My second husband and I have two children, and we live in Ottawa."

Elizabeth Hay's *The Only Snow in Havana* (1992) details her travels with Alec, an American with whom Hay was in love, from Mexico to Havana to Salem, Massachusetts, and New York. Alec desired the warmth of Mexico; when Hay became pregnant, she brought Alec with her back to her beloved North, a move that highlighted differences in their priorities. The book recounts the discovery of those differences, the effort to reconcile them, and Hay's examination of her own personality, which she places in the context of her nationality. Misao Dean, writing in the *Canadian Forum* (April 1992), found *The Only Snow in Havana* to be "at once poetic and political, offering strongly felt images of northern and southern sensuality, flowers, snowflakes, candles, to explore the reality of nationality, gender, motherhood, exploitation, love." For Jerry Horton, the reviewer for *Quill & Quire* (November 1992), *The Only Snow in Havana* "weaves quiet, powerful prose poems from the most banal of Canadian raw materials. Snow, rock, fur, 'lives of the Esquimaux' and explorers: these are her tropes. . . . Hay's strategy of reading the personal present through the historical past succeeds in re-animating the dusty stuff of Canadian history and culture, while lending an almost mythological depth to the events and situations she culls from her own life."

The result of Hay's six-year sojourn in New York City, recorded in her 1993 volume, *Captivity Tales: Canadians in New York*, melds her reflections on her experiences with tidbits about the lives of other Canadians, such as Glenn Gould, Marshall McLuhan, Emily Carr, Paul-Emile Borduas, Teresa Stratas, Joyce Wieland, and Michael Snow, who also spent time in New York. Pat Smart noted in the *Canadian Forum* (May 1994) that "Hay's narrative (of marriage and motherhood, her walks around New York, her meetings with other Canadians and her constant quest for the meaning of home) is bound up in a soft, shimmering web of sensations, images that float up from memory and facts gleaned from her readings that make the reader aware of the impossibility of separating the personal from its political or cultural dimensions (and vice versa)." In the *Voice Literary Supplement* (April 1994), Katherine Dieckmann remarked that Hay had taken into account the fact that Canada "remains forever neutral, even undifferentiated, to most U.S. minds. . . . Canada's mythology is the mythology of not having one, of being inarticulate about our past. Like a deep blush, this can be eloquent in itself."

In *A Student of Weather* (2000), Hay's first novel, the eponymous student arrives in 1938 at an isolated Saskatchewan farm to disrupt the lives of two sisters, one eight and one 17, who both fall in love with him. The novel traces the lives of these three characters over 30 years, moving from the farm to Ottawa to New York City. The beautiful, placid older sister, Lucinda, makes sacrifices for the good of her motherless family; the younger, Norma Joyce, strange in both behavior and appearance, is in a sense the victor in the contest between the sisters, as she gets Maurice—the "student"—to be the father of her child, if not her husband.

The *Time* (February 12, 2001) reviewer Paul Gray praised the "added luster" given to what might have been an ordinary story by Hay's "deft variations on and additions to familiar themes" and her "fine descriptive flourishes." For the *New York Times Book Review* (February 11, 2001) critic Liza Featherstone, however, *A Student of Weather* was much more than an enjoyable variation on an old theme. Terming the novel "spare and elegiac," Featherstone particularly lauded Hay's character development: "Hay is keenly attuned to how circumstance forms character in paradoxically opposite ways. Both sisters have endured scarcity, but while Lucinda hates waste, allowing herself just one careful drop of hand lotion a night, Norma Joyce is all reckless, voluptuous desire, stealing the fruitcake Lucinda bakes and hoarding it in her room to eat before breakfast. They treat Maurice the same way: Lucinda is aloof, even seeming stingy with her affections; Norma Joyce never hesitates to boldly stake her claim. . . . Hay deftly renders her characters' disconcerting moral ambiguities. . . . *A Student of Weather,* . . . like its maddening characters, is nearly impossible not to like. Even as a child, Norma Joyce 'has to make everybody uncomfortable.' Hay seems to share that impulse—and in this disquieting novel she succeeds." *A Student of Weather* was shortlisted for the Giller Prize, a Canadian literary award.

In an essay, "In the Garden of a Scientist," published in *Canadian Geographic* (August 2000), Hay described the life of one Bill Dore, a botanist of Ottawa, who died in 1996, when Hay "had the great good fortune to move into his house and inherit his garden." She noted that Dore had published *Grasses of Ontario* and grown in his garden "wild rice . . . and patches of big bluestem and sweet grass and pampas grass; wood anemones; a spindle tree; hops; Jerusalem artichokes that he dug up in October and tried to palm off on his neighbours; many varieties of allium; hundreds of bulbs; and ivy that he brought from his grandfather's grave in England." Hay deemed Dore "a brilliant, unconventional civil servant whose writings, collections and garden are reminders of the sort of person Ottawa has nourished and been nourished by." Hay consulted Dore's work for *A Student of Weather*, and she has continued his legacy as an artist "Ottawa has nourished and been nourished by."

—S. Y.

SUGGESTED READING: *Canadian Forum* p43 Apr. 1993, p42 May 1994; *Canadian Geographic* p82+ Aug. 2000; *New York Times Book Review* Feb. 11, 2001; *Publishers Weekly* p63 Dec.11, 2000; *Quill & Quire* p27 Nov. 1992; *Time* p86 Feb. 12, 2001; *Voice Literary Supplement* p32 Apr. 1994

SELECTED BOOKS: fiction—*Small Change*, 1997; *A Student of Weather*, 2000; nonfiction—*The Only Snow in Havana*, 1992; *Captivity Tales: Canadians in New York*, 1993

Hayder, Mo

Jan. 2, 1962– Novelist

Since the publication of her best-selling crime novels *Birdman* (1999) and *The Treatment* (2001), the British crime writer Mo Hayder has built a solid reputation as one of the most promising authors within the genre. Her psychological and forensic thrillers have been compared to those of Patricia Cornwell and Lynda La Plante. While her books often tackle raw and gruesome material, Hayder has been widely praised for her powerful sense of storytelling and suspense.

Hayder wrote the following autobiographical statement for *World Authors 1995-2000*: "My poor parents—they realised early that I had a morbid curiosity. It was the way I'd beg them to drive slowly past traffic accidents, the way, aged ten, I rejected Enid Blyton [a popular British children's author] in favour of Kafka's *Metamorphosis* (forget the dark psychology—just get a load of that *beetle*!). They had to teach me that this sort of fascination wasn't quite 'nice,' and fairly soon I learned to keep it quiet that I was at least as fascinated by death as I was by life itself. But, of course, these things don't stay hidden long.

"In my 20s I was something of a traveller. Somehow I'd wound up in Japan, and was working as a hostess in a Tokyo nightclub when one of the other hostesses was attacked and raped. At the time I was working 70 hour weeks, had very few friends and was reading far too much of the batty Japanese novelist Mishima, so I was probably vulnerable to shock and the old interest in the dark side of life resurfaced; I found myself obsessing about what the rapist had been thinking, *why* had he done it, *what* was in it for him. Three years previously an acquaintance in London had been tortured and ritualistically murdered, and although I hadn't been deeply affected by it at the time, in Tokyo it came back to haunt me. I became obsessed with this display of violence and the meaning behind it and why some people feel compelled to inflict brutality on others.

"I went back to England determined to write some of this down. Like an exorcism I wanted it out of my system—so I started playing around with plot lines. Fairly soon I woke up to the fact that what I was writing was a crime novel. This surprised me—I hadn't been a great fan of the genre, and hadn't read a lot of classic crime fiction, but I

Andre Heeger
Mo Hayder

did know what gripped me was meticulously researched fiction (Patricia Cornwell for example) so I went to the specialist unit in London's Metropolitan Police Force that deals with violent serial attacks, AMIT, and asked them to tell me about their investigative techniques. They were wary of me at first; they didn't know how to discuss details of brutal sexual attacks in front of a woman, and a civilian at that, but slowly they relaxed. In fact they relaxed to the point where they began teasing me. In the first meeting I attended everyone spoke like B movie cops: 'Don't worry guv, he'll soon be singing like a canary' or: 'He's got a rap sheet as long as your arm'. The chief shouted across the incident room to a junior officer: 'Show the young lady the head they brought in last night, will you? You know, the one in the filing cabinet.' I, rather touchingly, fell for it all and for quite some time believed sincerely that the police kept body parts amongst their paper work. But when I wised up I began to learn a lot. Much of what I saw the police dealing with was so gruesome it couldn't be fictionalised, but I got direct inspiration for my first novel, *Birdman*, from one case in particular: Colin Ireland was a serial murderer in London—killing 5 men in a very short burst of activity at the beginning of the '90s. In one instance he also killed the victim's cat and decorated the victim with the corpse. Involving an animal in this ritualistic way gave me the central idea in *Birdman*: a sexual psychopathic killer operating in Greenwich, London, and using a bird in his macabre decoration of his victims.

"I was astonished at the success of *Birdman*, for a first time novel it did enormously well, being sold in a bidding war, published in 13 countries (making the bestseller lists in many of those) and due to be made into a feature film. . . . Detective Inspector Jack Caffery, the central character, is a young police officer—a deeply flawed obsessive who struggles to maintain a veneer of normality in his relationships. He is consumed by the hunt for his brother Ewan, who has been missing since their childhood. Caffery is convinced that Ewan was the victim of a paedophile, and in my second novel, *The Treatment*, he becomes involved in a hunt for another predatory paedophile in a case with uncanny parallels to his own past. *The Treatment* became my second UK bestseller.

"Since becoming a full time novelist I've completed an MA in creative writing, had my first child, a little girl, Lotte Genevieve, and moved away from one of my primary inspirations: London. I'm based in the English countryside now, and living outside the city I find that my scope for backdrops in my novels has widened. I'm currently working on a novel set in Tokyo: a psychological thriller, it draws together two strands of Japanese life—the Japanese mafia (the 'yakuza') and the country's involvement in the second world war, particularly its part in one of the worst massacres of last century, the Nanking massacre in China. Last year I visited Nanking to research and this year I'll be returning to Tokyo to try to get a job again in one of the hostess bars I worked in during the 80s. I'm pushing forty now—will I still get a job? And if I do will I still get the occasional thousand dollar tip as I did in the wealthy 80s? I doubt it, but either way I know the timbre of the book will be as dark as *Birdman* and *The Treatment* because it's difficult for me to write 'feelgood' books. The act of writing, for me, is all about excavating and examining the worst in the human condition. I believe, now as much as I did as the ambulance chaser child, that the morbid is as worthy of our interest and scrutiny as any other part of life."

—S. Y.

SUGGESTED READING: *Economist* p3 July 15, 2000; *Guardian* p10 Dec. 18, 1999, II p6 June 4, 2001; *Library Journal* p132 Nov. 1, 2001; *New Statesman* p57 Feb. 7, 2000; *New York Times Book Review* p14 Dec. 29, 1999, p28 Feb. 2, 2002; *Publishers Weekly* p34+ Oct. 29, 2001; *Tangled Web* (on-line) Jan. 14, 2000

SELECTED BOOKS: *Birdman*, 1999; *The Treatment*, 2001

Haywood, Gar Anthony

1954– Novelist

The African-American crime novelist Gar Anthony Haywood has developed two successful detective series. The novels *Fear of the Dark* (1988), *Not Long for This World* (1990), *You Can Die Trying* (1993), *It's Not a Pretty Sight* (1996), *When Last Seen Alive* (1998), and *All the Lucky Ones Are*

Dead (1999) feature Aaron Gunner, a private investigator who dredges the mean streets of Los Angeles. The humorous dialogue and occasional comic situations in those books belie the seriousness of the underlying themes. Not nearly so gritty are the tongue-in-cheek books *Going Nowhere Fast* (1994) and *Bad News Travels Fast* (1995), narrated by Dottie Loudermilk, who with her husband, Joe, lives in a trailer and travels the country—mainly to escape their adult children, who embroil them in trouble no matter how far they roam. "There was a threshold beyond which an investigation became more about his own hunger for the truth than his client's, and somewhere over the last 48 hours, Gunner had stepped over it," Haywood wrote in *All the Lucky Ones Are Dead*, and "Gunner . . . not only steps over that threshold, he carries the reader with him like an eager bride," the *Publishers Weekly* (December 6, 1999) reviewer added. Kate Mungor, writing in the *Washington Post Book World* (January 30, 2000), concluded that "there is . . . always an underlying intelligence in Haywood's work that shines through."

Born in 1954, Gar Anthony Haywood grew up to become a field engineer for Bell Atlantic, but from the age of seven he dreamed of writing detective fiction. His ambition was fueled by the "books with lurid covers" the science fiction, mystery, and detective novels he found in his father's room, according to Denise Hamilton, who interviewed Haywood for the *Los Angeles Times* (January 20, 1999). Reading those books as a child, Haywood wondered why they contained no black characters; as an adult he decided that the world of detective fiction "could use some people of color," as he told Hamilton.

Haywood moved to Los Angeles, the home of his detective, and burst upon the crime-fiction scene to great acclaim with his first Aaron Gunner novel, *Fear of the Dark*. In 1988 the book was awarded the prize for Best First Private Eye Novel of the Year by the Private Eye Writers of America. Aaron Gunner was to remain an enduring and endearing figure in crime fiction. While he is unusual in detective fiction in that he is African-American, he is in other ways a quintessential specimen of the genre. Haywood, the *Publishers Weekly* (July 8, 1988) reviewer declared, possessed "a good ear for the sour voice of the true private eye and the sense of tired hopelessness of the underclass they have always served." In *Fear of the Dark*, Gunner is led back into the detective's career he had abandoned when a black-power activist is murdered, along with the bartender whose customer he had been. The activist's sister persuades Gunner to hunt down her brother's killer.

While most reviewers were greatly impressed by Haywood's debut, Kathleen Maio, writing in *Wilson Library Bulletin* (February 1989), "would have found Gunner more interesting if he hadn't been so consistently abusive. . . . His attitude toward women was particularly troubling." As an example, Maio pointed out that after talking to one female, Gunner 'left her before the impulse to slap his third woman in six days grew too strong to overcome.'"

Haywood produced two more Aaron Gunner novels, *Not Long for This World* and *You Can Die Trying*, before coming out with *Going Nowhere Fast* in 1994. That novel introduced Joe and Dottie Loudermilk, a retired couple who buy a trailer, name it Lucille, and travel around the country, finding trouble both inside and outside their family of five grown (but not mature) children. When their son Theodore nicknamed Bad Dog—shows up at the trailer, a corpse appears simultaneously. Soon the Loudermilks are being chased by the mob, the police, and assorted other odd and dangerous characters. "Haywood uses the Airstream life style to sidesplitting advantage," Sparkle Hayter declared in the *New York Times Book Review* (November 13, 1994). She praised, in addition, Haywood's creation of the narrator, Dorothy, declaring it "impressive . . . how the versatile author, a father of two, so convincingly speaks in the voice of a mother of five. Wry, wise, tough and, when the occasion demands it, credibly sentimental, Dottie is one of the most lovable fictional mothers around." In an interview with Carolyn Tillery for *American Visions* (May 1997), Haywood explained that Dottie "was the driving force, and she told the story." He had originally planned to have Dottie and her husband alternate as narrators, but Dottie's voice proved too powerful for him to let another voice take over.

Dottie and Joe returned in 1995 in *Bad News Travels Fast*. This time, their son Eddie, a political radical, is arrested for murder in Washington, D.C. In the course of trying to clear their son, Dottie and Joe get mixed up in another murder investigation and in a plot involving a senator. Dick Richmond, who reviewed the audiotape version of the book for the *St. Louis Post-Dispatch* (December 29, 1996), found the second Loudermilk book not as funny as the first but "entertaining nonetheless." The reviewer for the *Houston Chronicle* (October 1, 1995), Amy Rabinovitz, disagreed, declaring *Bad News Travels Fast* "brisk, witty and believable . . . one of the most enjoyable books to hit the shelves for a long time."

Aaron Gunner returned in 1996 in *It's Not a Pretty Sight*, a novel about the detective's former girlfriend Nina, a recently murdered resident of a home for abused women. In that same year Haywood won both an Anthony Award and a Shamus Award for "And Pray Nobody Sees You," a short story featuring Gunner.

In Haywood's 1998 Aaron Gunner novel, *When Last Seen Alive*, the main action concerns Gunner's search for Elroy Covington, last seen alive at the Million Man March. Covington's sister hires Gunner to search for him because she has traced her brother to Los Angeles, where Gunner lives. Hearing her version of events is "like listening to a stereo with one speaker missin'," Gunner says. "You could tell you weren't always hearin' all the notes to the song." Covington is a pseudonym, it turns out, for a disgraced Chicago journalist who has fabricated an award-winning story. Covington's friends and associates, to whom Gunner turns for a glimpse into his past, are an exceedingly sinister bunch.

"L A. gets it good in this one—the pols are every bit as scummy as they were in Chandler's day," Richard Lipez wrote in his *Washington Post* (January 18, 1998) review. "But Haywood saves most of his venom, some of it quite funny, for the American book publishing industry, which comes off here as greedy as the Baetican olive oil plotters [a gang from another mystery], and a lot dumber." The reviewer for the *Atlanta Journal-Constitution* (January 29, 1998) felt that the worst crime connected with *When Last Seen Alive* was "that more people haven't embraced the Los Angeles-based gumshoe. . . . Haywood does a masterful job cutting between the unrelated cases, treating us along the way to Gunner's trademark tongue-in-cheek observations about life in the city of tarnished angels." Dick Lochte, writing in the *Los Angeles Times Sunday Brunch Bookshelf* (December 21, 1997), agreed: "Haywood is particularly adept at sliding social commentary into his carefully plotted tales. And his descriptions of Southern California are sometimes worthy of Raymond Chandler: 'Silver Lake was the Los Angeles capital of schizophrenia. It was Caucasian and Hispanic, gay and straight, young and old. It was picturesque, and it was garish; quaint and charming here, plastic and phony there. . . . [Silver Lake] offered a little something for everybody. Including the dumb and dumber.'"

In *All the Lucky Ones Are Dead*, published in 1999, Gunner is drawn—or dragged—into both investigating the death of a rap star after the case has been declared a suicide and checking into death threats against ultraconservative talk-show host Sparkle Johnson. The Defenders of the Bloodline, a radical black nationalist group that figured in the plot of *When Last Seen Alive*, reappear. Reviewers praised Haywood's depiction of South Central Los Angeles and his ability to skewer pretensiousness. Bill Ott wrote in *Booklist* (December 15, 1999) that Gunner "relishes exposing poseurs, politics be damned." He added that Haywood's view of South Central "reveal[s] a community of ordinary people struggling with the dailiness of living. His canvas is wonderfully detailed, with vivid supporting characters—including the regulars at Lily's Acey Deuce Bar—and careful evocation of the neighborhood's sights and sounds. Haywood never shies away from a tough issue, either." The *Publishers Weekly* (December 6, 1999) writer was equally enthusiastic about *All the Lucky Ones Are Dead*: "Haywood juices his compelling mystery with sharp dialogue, and Gunner's savvy intelligence makes it a pleasure to follow the PI through a maze of betrayals and greed. As Gunner navigates the meaner, deadlier streets of L.A., Haywood infuses the hard-boiled genre with renewed vigor."

—S.Y.

SUGGESTED READING: *Atlanta Journal-Constitution* E p5 Jan. 29, 1998; *American Visions* p18 May 1997; *Booklist* p759 Dec. 15, 1999; *Houston Chronicle* p23 Oct. 1, 1995; *Los Angeles Times* B p9 Nov. 14, 1997, p9 Apr. 16, 1998; p1 Jan. 20, 1999; *Los Angeles Times Sunday Brunch Bookshelf* p2 Dec. 21, 1997; *New York Times Book Review* p19 Nov. 13, 1994; *Publishers Weekly* p43 July 8, 1988, p56 Dec. 6, 1999; *Washington Post Book World* p8 Jan. 18, 1998, p13 Jan 30, 2000; *Wilson Library Bulletin* p89 Feb. 1989

SELECTED BOOKS: *Fear of the Dark*, 1988; *Not Long For This World*, 1990; *You Can Die Trying*, 1993; *Going Nowhere Fast*, 1994; *Bad News Travels Fast*, 1995; *It's Not a Pretty Sight*, 1996; *When Last Seen Alive*, 1998; *All the Lucky Ones Are Dead*, 1999

Bernard Clark/Courtesy of Houghton Mifflin

Heighton, Steven

Aug. 14, 1961– Writer

The Canadian poet and novelist Steven Heighton is widely recognized one of Canada's most promising contemporary writers. For his first collection of verse, *Stalin's Carnival* (1989), he earned the Gerald Lampert Award for best first book of poetry and the 1989 Canadian Authors Association's Air Canada Award. His later books of poetry, *Foreign Ghosts* (1989) and *The Ecstasy of Skeptics* (1994), have also received wide acclaim. Heighton's poetic sensibilities were apparent when he began writing fiction. His first efforts include the short-story collections *Flight Paths of the Emperor* (1992), based on his travels in Japan, and *On Earth As It Is* (1995). He has also composed a book of essays on the devaluation of literature in a postmodern world, entitled *The Admen Move on Lhasa: Writing and Culture in a Virtual World* (1997). Most recently, Heighton completed his first novel, *The Shadow Boxer* (2000), a semi-autobiographical tale about a young Canadian man who is determined to become a novelist.

For *World Authors 1995-2000*, Steven Heighton writes, "I was born in Toronto, Canada, to an English father and a Greek mother, and raised in Balmertown—a gold-mining town in northern Ontario—and then in a generic middle-class Toronto subdivision. It's probably too neat, too plausible to suggest that restlessness with those tidy surroundings made me the kind of writer I am—a chronicler of things foreign as opposed to a detailer of dailiness, or curator of domestic phenomena. Most writers, I think, generally hew to home or tend to ramble. Among the homebodies are Alice Munro, William Faulkner, Charles Dickens, Flannery O'Connor, John Cheever; among the exotics, Joseph Conrad, Malcolm Lowry, William Shakespeare, Herman Melville, D.H. Lawrence, Mavis Gallant. I love all these writers, but my own writing seems by instinct to seek admission to the camp of the nomads, the exotics. Why blame that on the bland innocuous suburb I grew up in? One thing you discover on becoming a parent is that children launch into the world with a personality that is remarkably distinct and consistent. Maybe travellers are as much born as they are formed.

"After high school graduation I backpacked through Australia and Europe, funding my way largely by busking with a guitar and neck-brace harmonica. I was writing songs that owed too much—yet at the same time not nearly enough—to Bob Dylan, Neil Young, Bruce Springsteen, Mark Knopfler et al. I returned to Canada and attended university where, under the influence of the EngLit curriculum, my derivative lyrics mutated into derivative lyric poems, and by my third year of studies morphed again into poems that now definitely had something original in them—though weighing that originality now, I'm reminded of Dr Johnson's famed note of rejection to a poetaster: 'Sir, your work is both original and good; unfortunately the part that is good is not original, and the part that is original is not good.' Still, I was learning at that apprentice pace that's only maintainable once in a writer's life, and I was beginning to land poems with the literary magazines. Soon I was publishing stories there too. Over the course of my MA year I actually wrote and revised most of my first full book of poetry *during the seminars*—a productive truancy that convinced me I no longer belonged in the ivied halls.

"After graduating and having that first book, *Stalin's Carnival*, accepted for publication, I travelled to Asia on the stingily preserved vestige of a scholarship. My girlfriend Mary Huggard and I backpacked through parts of China just recently opened to foreigners and through a barely-opened Tibet, and then through Nepal, Thailand, Malaysia, Indonesia, and Singapore. During this seven-month journey I drafted a second book roughly in the *utaniki* or 'song-diary' form (essentially a travelogue in poetry and prose) made famous by Matsuo Basho-in his *Oku no hosomichi*, or *Narrow Road to the Deep North*. This one I called *Foreign Ghosts*—a slightly inaccurate but telling translation of the Mandarin epithet for foreigners.

"And being a foreigner, an outsider, was something I savoured, above all in Japan, the booming country we headed for when our money ran out. Like thousands of expatriates before and since, we soon landed jobs teaching English (and teaching myself Japanese became my night-light sideline, a labour of love). I was fortunate to get hired by a new school that still had only a few students, so that in the gaps between classes I could do some writing. I began to shape stories about expatriates in Japan, part of a postmodern Lost Generation—or perhaps Scattered Generation. Their linked stories would eventually combine into my first book of fiction, *Flight Paths of the Emperor*, published in 1992.

"Returning to Canada in '88, we settled in Kingston, Ontario, a picturesque but volatile city, its population a densely contiguous mix of professionals, prisoners, parolees, college students, bikers, artists, soldiers, and army officers, on the eastern end of Lake Ontario (the lower intestine of the Great Lakes). My first books were published close together—first the one I'd written in my graduate seminars, then *Foreign Ghosts*—and I was asked to edit the literary magazine *Quarry*. So that suddenly I felt 'established' in a small way, both personally and professionally. For a while it was a good feeling; for a while it stifled those intimations of imposture that had been heckling away at me since I first began swamping the magazines with my work. Naturally in time the feeling came back. It's with me still, often enough. And perhaps the self-doubt the painful self-scrutiny can and should be seen as aspects of a functioning esthetic immune system, the enemy of self-indulgence and other occupational vices. Or simply as the price of improvement. You need—I tell myself—to harbour a high degree of bafflement about life and art in order to create with the requisite intensity. Can there be any real passion where there's certainty? Maybe there can for religious writers of a certain kind, but not for me. Not only will the conscientious writer never 'arrive' but should not even wish to.

"I published (in '94) a third book of poetry, *The Ecstasy of Skeptics*, then (in '95) a second collection of stories, *On Earth as It Is*, and then (in '97) a book of essays, which I now largely dislike; intent on avoiding any whiff of scholarly decorum or dullness, I aimed in some chapters at the sort of vexed and hectoring tone you find in Ezra Pound's polemics on verse, or in D. H. Lawrence's cocky screeds in his *Essays on Classic American Literature*. But this cranked-up tone was a poor fit for my temperament. In trying to shun one kind of ponderousness I achieved another.

"In the novel I was then drafting, *The Shadow Boxer*, I was likewise using a voice ratcheted above the vernacular—lyrically torqued and elevated in a Thomas Wolfian vein—but which was still somehow my own. In this course I was incited partly by fury at a critic's complaint about the short story writer Katherine Mansfield; the critic regretted how, because of Mansfield's early death, 'Time had not been able 'to temper a too-ardent sensibility.' But (I shouted back) isn't that just the proper mood of youth and of youthful creation? Austere Austen, austere Auden—of course they're both glorious in their ways but where would we stand without their antimatter, the Lawrences and Lowrys and Hopkinses of the world? Especially now, amid a discourse so dominated by shallow and mechanical irony. I decided to write about an anachronistic young man—a postmodern Innocent Abroad—and to write about him in a prose meant to re-enact the vision of one described by a British reviewer as embodying 'the romantic soul adrift in the cynical postmodern world.'

"*To re-enact the vision*, I wrote. I could as easily have written, *to translate the vision*. These days I seem to be doing more and more translation, and not just metaphorically but actually. Usually I work from French, although at times I experiment with texts in languages I have no knowledge of whatsoever (I have decided to view this as a technicality). Translation, of course, entails another intimate encounter with 'otherness,' foreignness, the Uncrackable Code in its various local and linguistic manifestations. It allows me to collaborate with, and thus to learn from, dead writers I revere: the process of translation as a virtual Master Class. Currently I'm working on a version of Rimbaud's hundred-line surrealist masterpiece *Le Bateau ivre*, while at the same time trying to continue editing the work of students and friends, because that too feeds my hunger for border-crossings—entering the country of another mind and helping to smuggle meanings out across verbal and personal frontiers."

Steven Heighton was born on August 14, 1961. As he told Jeffrey Canton in an interview for *Eye* (May 25, 2000), he "came to consciousness in northern Ontario. . . .—the basic, essential geography" to which he compares everything else. Heighton has expressed a desire to interviewers to reveal little about his private life or upbringing, except that he lives in Kingston, Ontario, with his wife and daughter.

Heighton published *Foreign Ghosts*, a poetry collection, in 1989, winning in that year the Air Canada Award for poems and stories published in literary magazines. *Stalin's Carnival*, another book of verse was also released in 1989 and won the 1990 Gerald Lampert Award for best first book of poetry. His poetry collection *The Ecstasy of Skeptics*, which was published in 1994, was a finalist for the Governor General's award in 1995.

Heighton explained to Canton that he had always written both poetry and prose and made little distinction between the genres, except for the amount of revision necessary for each: "I wrote fiction and poetry right from the beginning. I didn't matriculate from one form to the next. . . . I'm just as attentive to the rhythms of a prose sentence as I am to a line of poetry." He added, "Sometimes mistakes become embedded in a book and you can't get them out. That doesn't happen with a poem. With a poem, you throw it out and start over. But you're not likely to throw out a novel you've been working on for four years."

Heighton first collected his stories in *Flight Paths of the Emperor*, published in 1992. The volume, for which he drew upon his stay in Japan, was a finalist for the 1993 Trillium Award. "Each story is a little snapshot of everyday life, schools, offices, restaurants, and love hotels. And each story, through its simplicity, captures the complexities of Japanese society," a reviewer wrote for *TG Magazine* (1997).

On Earth As It Is, Heighton's 1995 story collection, contains stories that range from Nepal to Greece to Canada to the Arctic, and includes the novella *Translations of April*. In many of the stories, Heighton subjects his characters to moments of epiphany, often just before they die. "The blurb on the back of . . . Heighton's collection . . . promises an 'exploration' of 'the interlocking worlds of the erotic and religious,'" Tamas Dobozy wrote for *Canadian Literature* (Summer 1998). "The book delivers. Both the ending of the story 'Downing's Fast' and *Translations of April* offer a recovery of love through death, a death often paired with the ocean and drowning, common symbols of spiritual rebirth and fertility." He concluded, however, that "Heighton plays it safe, offering spiritual rapture followed by a swift descent back to Earth; the fifth section of *Translations of April*, entitled 'The Flower in the Face of God,' follows the same pattern as the ending of 'Downing's Fast': a sailor experiences an illumination which releases him from all physical needs except to tell at least one person of his experience before dying."

Sarah Hurst, in a review of *On Earth As It Is* for *Granta Books Literary Review* (on-line), was also struck by Heighton's references to death: "Those few characters who emerge unscathed from the labyrinth of deathtraps designed for them by . . . Heighton can count themselves lucky. The author is a man with a message, transmitted from Hades into the mind of a fictitious research assistant: 'Everything is vanishing. Do not waste your life.'" Hurst commented that the fact that Heighton is a poet "is evident in his reflective style. . . . He imbues ordinary objects with a magical beauty." But despite the varied types with which Heighton fills his stories, "the leading character is fate. . . . We are entirely at the mercy of chance and the elements."

In the story "Sounds of the Water," published in the *Arkansas Review: A Journal of Delta Studies* (Volume 26, Issue 4), a man looks back on the Christmas holiday when he was 10 years old, recalling how his foreign correspondent father, briefly home between assignments, left the family for the last time. Young Jason pretends to be an animal, "a frog, or some scaly exotic amphibian—the member of a scarce and endangered species." During the course of the story, Jason, unable to bear the pain of his parents' breakup and his father's unfaithfulness, inserts earplugs and wears a blindfold in a vain effort to escape. He also stops eating, and, although the story is told in flashback, the reader fears for him. Nevertheless, at the story's close, after Jason, his mother, and his sister Pandora (called Dora), see his father off at the airport, "Our mother is perfectly composed. She is herself again, patient and predictable, vulnerable, necessary. Smiling her kind conspiratorial smile, she reaches down and pulls the remaining plug from my ear." The family has returned to Earth as it is.

The Admen Move on Lhasa: Writing and Culture in a Virtual World, Heighton's 1997 book is, according to John Walker for the *University of Toronto Quarterly* (Winter 1999), a collection of "casual essays which function as a critique of Western society in the stages of late capitalism." The book's title comes from an observation that even in Tibet, advertising men have begun to appear. "I'm nostalgic and no doubt a bit poetic and naive when it comes to Lhasa and places like it, not only because I see and feel how far our own cities and our own art fall short of the visionary standards set by doomed worlds like Lhasa, or Nepal, or precolonial Tahiti," Heighton wrote. Lawrence Mathews, in *Essays on Canadian Writing* (Spring 1998), expressed the view that Lhasa, "a living and visionary place which until recently showed how a city could be a lasting work of art," in Heighton's words, became "a metaphor for the product of the artist's labours. But as the literal Lhasa of 1997 is not what it used to be, so literary art is under siege by the ubiquitous 'admen': '. . . Lhasa of only a decade back: an open book, a richly illuminated, multitudinous conclave of poems, not a Chamber of Commerce brochure, not a catalogue.'" For Heighton, the difference between art and advertising is similar to that between a beautiful city with many attractions and a theme park. "The importance of literary art and the need to struggle against the forces that would deform or destroy it are the almost constant focus for Heighton's meditation," Matthews concluded. He had the cavil about Heighton's book, however, that Heighton placed too much emphasis on art in the century of fascism, communism, the Holocaust, and the threat of thermonuclear annihilation. His advice to Heighton: "Lighten up, kid. Get a grip."

Although Heighton continues to believe in the power of art to heal society, he expresses doubts, according to Walker, about "the phenomenon of postmodernism, which, supposedly revolutionary, has turned out instead to be a kind of cultural Trojan Horse which elevates the cool, ironic detachment of the computer geek. . . . Revising Spengler, Heighton recasts the postmodern age, the 'Age of Clowns,'" a time when "pain without purpose has made the world retreat behind a leering mask and set the word 'love' in quotation marks. . . . When 'virtual' realities crowd out visceral and the passionate context of nature and the body. When it becomes impossible to stay earnest and reverent about anything without looking like a dupe or a dangerous fanatic." Walker concluded that the basis of Heighton's philosophy lies in that of Henry Miller. "Heighton sees 'literature' returning to its ancient rhetorical function: art as 'an invitation to change what can be changed—one's self, first and finally—and to cherish what is receding, vanishing, as all things are.'"

The Shadow Boxer, published in 2000, is Heighton's first novel. Many critics considered it a semiautobiographical story and described it as a "Kunstlerroman," from the German word for "artist novel." The novel centers around the young Canadian Sevigne Torrins, who after abandoning his ambitions to become a boxing champion, discovers that he wants to be a novelist. After his father, a drunken sailor and former boxer with whom he has a troubled relationship, dies, Torrins leaves for Egypt, where his mother has lived for years with her second husband. His travels take him back to Toronto and later to a remote island, where the rigors of a Canadian winter nearly kill him. Nevertheless he finishes his novel "The Islands in the Nile," sections of which are presented in Heighton's book. Over the course of his odyssey, Torrins has passionate relationships with two women, first Una and later Mikaela, with whom he eventually has a daughter.

"The technical challenge that I set for myself in this book was to create a character who would win the reader over in the first section," Heighton told Lachlan Mackintosh for *FFWD Weekly* (June 29, 2000), "fall from grace with the reader in the second section, and in the third section win the reader's sympathy back." Most reviewers deemed him successful. Jennifer Andrews noted in *Canadian Literature* (Spring 2001) that "instead of dying in isolation, Sevigne survives, and goes from the remote island back to the civilized world where he discovers that he can change the patterns of his parents' past through his own relationship to his daughter and his writing career."

In his review of *The Shadow Boxer* for *Essays on Canadian Writing* (Winter 2000), Stephen Ross found Heighton to be a practicing literary modernist. According to Ross, the novel shows the influence of T. S. Eliot, James Joyce, and Virginia Woolf and "acknowledges, plays with, and lays to rest 'the anxiety of influence' attendant on all literarily conscious first novels." Ross found *The Shadow Boxer* quintessentially Canadian, suggesting that "if Canada is going to persist as a nation, then it will have to do so as an 'imagined community.'

The promise of continuity for that imagined community appears in the closing vignette: standing on the shore of Lake Erie, Sevigne's daughter claims to be able to see Rye Island in the distance. Sevigne himself sees nothing, but he promises to take her there 'some day,' at once echoing his father's perpetually deferred (though not devalued) promises and establishing a new narrative trajectory. Leaving the shore of the lake, they strike out west across Canada with the promise of a usable past as their best hope for the future."

—S. Y.

SUGGESTED READING: *Arkansas Review: A Journal of Delta Studies* p143+ Vol. 26, Iss. 4; *Canadian Literature* p176+ Summer1998, p160+ Spring 2001; *Essays on Canadian Writing* p167+ Spring 1998, p118+ Winter 2000; *Eye* (on-line) May 25, 2000; *FFWD Weekly* (on-line) June 29, 2000; *Granta Books Literary Review* (on-line); *TG Magazine* (on-line) 1997; *University of Toronto Quarterly* p405+ Winter 1999

SELECTED BOOKS: poetry—*Foreign Ghosts*, 1989; *Stalin's Carnival*, 1989; *The Ecstasy of Skeptics: Poems*, 1994; fiction—*Flight Paths of the Emperor*, 1992; *On Earth As It Is*, 1995, *The Shadow Boxer: A Novel*, 2000; nonfiction—*Admen Move on Lhasa: Writing and Culture in a Virtual World*, 1997

Courtesy of Robin Marantz Henig

Henig, Robin Marantz

Oct. 3, 1953– Science writer

Robin Marantz Henig is an award-winning science writer. Working as a freelance journalist since 1980, she has become well known through her substantial output of magazine and newspaper articles, in which she discusses various topics in science and medicine. Henig's early books include *Your Premature Baby: The Complete Guide to Premie Care During that Crucial First Year* (1983), with Dr. Anne B. Fletcher; *How a Woman Ages: Growing Older—What to Expect and What You Can Do About It* (1985), with the editors of *Esquire* magazine; and *Being Adopted: The Lifelong Search for the Self* (1993), with David Brodzinsky. Many reviewers have praised her books for making difficult scientific topics accessible to the average reader. Henig refuted popular stereotypes about memory loss and aging in *The Myth of Senility: Misconceptions about the Brain and Aging* (1981); explained how previously unknown diseases, such as AIDS, suddenly appeared in *A Dancing Matrix: How Science Confronts Emerging Viruses* (1993); and chronicled the history of public health in the United States in *The People's Health: A Memoir of Public Health and Its Evolution at Harvard* (1997). Henig's *A Monk in the Garden: The Lost and Found Genius of Gregor Mendel* was published in 2000; the account of the 18th-century monk widely considered the father of genetics was a finalist for the National Book Critics Circle Award, one of several prestigious awards Henig has received over the course of her career.

Robin Marantz Henig writes for *World Authors 1995–2000*: "I always knew I wanted to write, way back when I wrote my first little article for a classroom newspaper in sixth grade. By the time I entered graduate school at Northwestern University's journalism school in 1973—a spanking new English degree from Cornell marking me as essentially unemployable without an advanced degree—I burned with some of the same change-the-world fervor that sent a lot of my classmates on the path of Woodward and Bernstein. I basically wanted to bust stereotypes, to provide information that would dash conventional wisdom about how the world works. My earliest writings—about teaching sign language instead of lip reading to deaf children; breaking the taboo of talking about dying; recognizing that aging and senility do not always go hand in hand—did indeed defy conventional wisdom. But what they also did, it turned out, was focus on issues in medicine, health, psychology, and science policy—subjects that have been drawing me ever since.

"I think of science writing as having two types: explanatory and narrative. For most of my writing career I have focused on the explanatory, using as many writing tools as possible to make complex topics comprehensible to an informed and interested lay readership.

"Like my colleagues, I have often turned to metaphor and analogy to make an important point—though I've recently come to believe that metaphor can be a trap for the science writer, often serving to obfuscate the truth rather than clarify it. Those of us who write about science, as well as our readers, are at times left in the absurd position of believing we understand the analogy, and yet having no clue about how the thing actually works in the real world. In the popular imagery used to explain DNA, for instance, we science writers often describe its structure as being 'like' a spiral staircase, its chemicals 'like' letters, with genes that are 'like' words and chromosomes that are 'like' sentences. But of course there's no staircase inside us, no letters, nothing really to read at all. And the analogy brings us no closer than we were before to understanding what goes on in our cells, or what precisely DNA does.

"I've struggled against this trap in all my explanatory writing, which has been the bulk of my work to date. In my 1993 book, *A Dancing Matrix: How Science Confronts Emerging Viruses*, for instance, I explained the basics of virology—based on broad readings in the subject and lengthy interviews with such eminent virologists as Bernard Field and Stephen Morse—by self-consciously avoiding the anthropomorphizing so common in this kind of popular science writing. Viruses, I took care to point out, are not 'wily,' are not our 'enemies,' do not set out to 'trick' our cells. Instead of metaphors, I turned to facts and, as often as I could, to case studies that brought to light the many ways in which new viruses emerge.

"Now I have shifted gears, moving into the second type of science writing, the narrative. In *The Monk in the Garden: The Lost and Found Genius of Gregor Mendel*, I used many of the tools of the novelist—plot, character development, scene setting, attention to detail and an appeal to all five senses— to tell the story of the early days of genetics. Writing the book in this new style, including reading my final draft into a tape recorder and then listening to the tape I'd made, led me to a greater awareness of what goes in to crafting a work of science writing, both narrative and explanatory.

"I loved the 'creative nonfiction' aspect of writing *The Monk in the Garden*; it was one of the most rewarding experiences of my professional life. And, happily, the book I so loved writing has also won its share of awards: it was a finalist for the National Book Critics Circle Award, and was named one of the year's '25 Books to Remember' by the New York Public Library. It appeared three times on the *Washington Post*'s alternate bestseller list, based on sales at the metropolitan area's independent bookstores. And in England, where it was published by Weidenfeld & Nicolson under the baffling title, *A Monk and Two Peas*, it made the list of the year's Top 10 bestselling science books.

"In between writing my books I did what most freelancers have to do: I sold my stuff to whomever was interested in it. I've had articles published by just about every woman's magazine in the supermarket, but my favorites have been for the general interest magazines that usually pay less but allow me the elbow room to really get into subjects of some significance: *Civilization, Discover, Ms.*, the *Washingtonian*, and the *New York Times Magazine*. The *Times Magazine* in particular has let me explore nice juicy subjects— gene therapy, breastfeeding, fetal surgery, privately funded cancer research—in a way that did not talk down to readers. My 1983 article in the *Times Magazine* on AIDS was one of the first such articles in a national publication (and, a colleague trolling the Internet told me recently, the first to state explicitly, in those more decorous days, that the disease could be transmitted through anal intercourse). And three of my articles—on senility, neonatology, and adoption—turned out to be so rich that I ended up writing books about them after the articles appeared in the *Times*.

"I'm not too interested in going back to writing for women's magazines; I'll consider myself lucky if I can make a living mostly writing books from now on. It's the interesting stuff I want to sink my teeth in to, the stuff where I go beyond metaphor and analogy to a true demonstration of how the natural world works. And I hope to be able to stick with the narrative approach to my science writing. My next book will be another exercise in storytelling, about the very early days of 'test tube baby' research in the 1970s. Before Louise Brown, the world's first test tube baby, was born in 1978, people truly believed that in vitro fertilization would lead to genetic monstrosities, and yet, within a very few years, IVF had become absolutely mundane and almost entirely accepted. Is this the likely outcome of the genetic manipulations, such as human cloning or the engineering of sex cells, that today we consider ethically untenable? That is one of the questions I hope to answer in my book.

"After more than 20 straight years working as a freelance writer—with the exception of four months in 1987 when I took a temporary full-time job as staff writer at the *Washington Post's* Health section—I must admit that the freedom it offers is a mixed blessing. While it's a great job for a woman trying to raise a family (my husband Jeff, a professor of political science at George Washington University, and I have two daughters), it's a strain to be so isolated. I've been active in several writers groups, both to cure the freelancer's occupational hazard of loneliness, and to give back something to a profession that I care a great deal about. I am on the board of directors of the National Association of Science Writers, and have been active in the D.C. Science Writers Association and the American Society of Journalists and Authors. In addition, I meet regularly with a group of other nonfiction book writers from Washington and Baltimore that calls itself, with its tongue in its cheek, the 'Midlist Club.' We're a rag-tag group of journalists with only one rule: any member who makes it to the bestseller list has to buy dinner for everybody else."

Robin Marantz Henig was born Robin Marantz on October 3, 1953 in the New York City borough of Brooklyn. Her father, Sidney, was a business executive, and her mother, Clare, worked as a secretary in a high school. In 1973 she graduated from Cornell University, in Ithaca, New York, with a B.A. In 1974 she received her MSJ degree from Northwestern University, in Evanston, Illinois. After completing her education, Henig went to work as an associate editor for *Comprehensive Therapy* magazine, in Chicago, Illinois. In 1975 she became an assistant editor for *New Physician*, in Schaumburg, Illinois. Two years later she joined *The Blue Sheet*, serving as an assistant managing editor and reporter. In 1978 she became the features and news editor for *BioScience* magazine and the Washington, D.C. correspondent for *Human Behavior* magazine. In 1980 Henig left both positions to begin her career as a freelance writer.

In 1981 Henig published her first book, *The Myth of Senility: Misconceptions about the Brain and Aging*. Citing the medical studies available at the time, Henig explains why memory loss increases with advancing age and argues that environmental and psychological factors play an important role in the aging process. In his review for the *Library Journal* (October 1, 1981), O. A. Gillespie described the book as a "timely and well-written book on the psychology and physiology of aging." The reviewer added that Henig's excellent "analyses of the normal functional changes accompanying aging (which have little to do with day-to-day functioning and enjoyment) are contrasted clearly with the effects of disease processes, particularly those occurring in Alzheimer's disease." In *Science Books & Films* (March/April 1982), C. H. Owen criticized the book for being "too long and irritatingly repetitious." However, Owen acknowledged that *The Myth of Senility* was "readily understandable and, if condensed, would make an excellent book for general readers." In 1982 the book won a first prize for excellence from the American Medical Writers Association.

In 1983 Henig and Dr. Anne B. Fletcher, the chief of neonatology at the Children's Hospital of the National Medical Center, in Washington, D.C., co-wrote the book, *Your Premature Baby: The Complete Guide to Premie Care During that Crucial First Year*. The authors offered parents a wide range of helpful guidelines from how to communicate effectively with hospital staff, family, and friends, to the best ways for parents to bond with their premature infants. The book also examined the plethora of medical equipment, procedures, and testing used on premature infants. In his review for *Science Books & Films* (November/December 1983), Gerald Golden lauded *Your Premature Baby* as a "superb guide." Although he faulted the book for its length and undue optimism in parts, Golden wrote that the "material is presented directly, and potentially upsetting issues are not glossed over. There is, however, a skillful mixture of case histories and constant attention to the thoughts and feelings of the parents, which makes the book highly readable."

Henig's third book, *How a Woman Ages: Growing Older—What to Expect and What You Can Do About It* (1985), written with the editors of *Esquire* magazine, also offered practical advice to readers. "Robin Henig, one of the clearest expository writers to tackle medical and scientific topics for the layman (she's written books about premature infants and senility), seeks to demythologize aging, specifically female aging, by detailing the facts of its process, then explaining how to cope," a writer for the *Washington Post Book World* (May 26, 1985) observed. "Her message, loud and clear, is two-fold: clean living makes aging easier, and a positive attitude is essential to well-being."

In their book, *Being Adopted: The Lifelong Search for Self* (1992), Henig and David M. Brodzinsky explored how people can cope with the psychological effects of adoption and lead an emotionally healthy life. A reviewer observed for *Child Welfare* (March 1994), "*Being Adopted* is different from so many of the publications on adoption that deal with how-to or parenting. This book illustrates a model of normal adjustment to being adopted as that adjustment takes place throughout the life span."

Henig's next book, *A Dancing Matrix: How Science Confronts Emerging Viruses* (1993), addressed the phenomenon of how viruses that were never known to have existed, such as AIDS and "mad cow disease," suddenly appeared. The author argues that millions of seemingly "new" viruses have always existed in nature, but caused no harm because they occupied areas of the world—such as the African and South American rain forests—that were mostly isolated from major population centers. In recent decades, however, global warming, population shifts, the destruction of rain forests, and the decline of sexual morality have unleashed deadly viruses from their habitats. As an example, Henig theorizes that Haitian professionals unknowingly brought the AIDS virus from Zaire, Africa, into Haiti. In turn, people vacationing in the Caribbean introduced the virus to North America and Europe, spreading it through sexual contact and intravenous drug use. In her review for the *Washington Post Book World* (March 1, 1993), Jean Hanff Korelitz wrote that Henig "provides a very technical primer illuminating the ways and means of viral survival, travel, and reproduction." The reviewer concluded that although the book was "hardly a gripping read, *A Dancing Matrix* does offer a wealth of information, and, for those who never quite recovered from [Michael Crichton's] *The Andromeda Strain*, even the occasional thrill." In the *Wall Street Journal* (March 11, 1993) Michael Waldholz wrote "that some viral encounters are indeed hazardous to humans, Ms. Henig argues, is often 'simply because people have put themselves in some dangerous virus's way.' Her book is a wonderfully well-written, simply stated and often dramatic explanation of this single fact and what it means to future public health, the environment and the future of the planet."

In 1997 Henig published her sixth book, *The People's Health: A Memoir of Public Health and Its Evolution at Harvard*. Henig provides an overview of issues that affect public health, such as infectious diseases, air and water pollution, pesticides, poverty, and violence. She also commemorates the 75th anniversary of the Harvard School for Public Health in Cambridge, Massachusetts. The book received mixed reviews. "Unfortunately, in trying to achieve its secondary purpose of celebrating Harvard's role, the book is at odds with its primary goal of educating the general public," Thomas J. Van Gilder, Arthur P. Liang, and Andrew L. Dannenberg wrote in their review for the *Journal of the American Medical Association* (June 25, 1997). "The author's choice of topics seems driven more by the academic interests of the alumni and faculty interviewed than by the public health importance of the topic. Most of the second half of the book dwells on research findings with little attention given to accomplishments in policy or prevention." However, they described Henig's writing style as "entertaining and engaging," noting that she weaves "the tales of public health triumphs and failures, its challenges and responses, into a coherent story." The reviewers were also impressed by her extensive research and interviews, adding that "her bibliography would make a remarkable public health library."

In 2000 Henig turned to biography for her next book, *The Monk in the Garden: The Lost and Found Genius of Gregor Mendel*, which received substantial acclaim from most reviewers. Gregor Mendel, who is widely considered to be "the father of genetics," lived in a monastery during the 19th century, in the city of Brno, in what is today the Czech Republic. Mendel disproved the theory of the time that if plants or animals with different heights, colors, and shapes were crossed, the offspring would have the combined traits of both parents. For example, it was believed that if a tall plant were crossed with a short one, the result would be a plant of medium height. From 1857 to 1863, Mendel conducted numerous breeding experiments, observing more than 28,000 pea plants to see how individual traits were passed along. He discovered that the offspring inherited separate and distinct traits from each parent. The child of a father with blue eyes and a mother with green eyes, therefore, would have either blue or green eyes, not some color combination of the two. Mendel also concluded that traits were passed along at random and would reappear in successive generations. Mendel wrote two papers summarizing his findings for the proceedings of a local academic society. His conclusions, however, received no attention, and he died in 1884. In 1900 three scientists, who had reached similar conclusions separately, discovered Mendel's published papers and brought public recognition to his scientific contributions. Mendel helped give birth to a new branch of science, genetics, and his work led to the eventual discovery of chromosomes, genes, and DNA. "Henig's account of Mendel and the conflicting currents of his time is rich, clear, and filled with wonderful evocations of Mendel's world," Richard Saltus wrote in the *Boston Globe* (July 2, 2000). "In her research, she gleaned so many details of place, weather, sounds, and sights that the book has an unexpectedly sensual texture making it pleasurable to read as a superbly written travelogue." In a review for *Science News* (July 1, 2000), Cait Goldberg praised the book. "Henig draws a provocative portrait of the modest man commonly recognized as the father of genetics," Goldberg observed. "Henig eloquently reveals the idiosyncratic genius of a man ahead of his time."

Robin Marantz Henig has won the American Academy of Pediatrics's Journalism Award, in 1982; the American Heart Association's Howard Blakeslee Award in science writing, in 1984; the American Psychological Association's National Media Award, in 1987; and the American Society of Journalists and Authors's June Roth Memorial Award for medical writing, in 1993 and 1994. The American Society of Journalists and Authors named her author of the year, in 1994. Henig has also won a science writers fellowship from the Marine Biological Laboratory, in 1990; a grant from the Alfred P. Sloan Foundation, for 1998–1999; a fellowship from the Knight Foundation for Science Writing at the Massachusetts Institute of Technology (MIT), in December 1999; and a journalism research fellowship from the Alica Patterson Foundation, in 2001. Henig's next book, tentatively entitled, "Pandora's Baby," will discuss the early days of in vitro fertilization research. She lives with her husband in Takoma Park, Maryland, which she describes on her Web site as "a funky little suburb of Washington, D.C., that for some reason is a haven for book writers."

—D. C.

SUGGESTED READING: *Boston Globe* E p1 July 2, 2000; *Child Welfare* p187 Mar. 1994; *Journal of the American Medical Association* p1979 June 27, 1997; *Library Journal* p1937 Oct. 1, 1981; Robin Marantz Henig Web site; *Science Books and Films* p205 Mar./Apr. 1982, p93 Nov./Dec. 1983; *Science News* p2 July 1, 2000; *Wall Street Journal* A p12 Mar. 11, 1993; *Washington Post Book World* p12 May 26, 1985, p3 Mar. 1, 1993

SELECTED BOOKS: *The Myth of Senility: Misconceptions About the Brain and Aging*, 1981; (with Anne B. Fletcher) *Your Premature Baby: The Complete Guide to Premie Care During That Crucial First Year*, 1984; (with the editors of *Esquire*) *How a Woman Ages: Growing Older—What to Expect and What You Can Do About It*, 1985; (with David M. Brodzinsky) *Being Adopted: The Lifelong Search for Self*, 1992; *A Dancing Matrix: How Science Confronts Emerging Virsues*, 1993; *The People's Health: A*

Memoir of Public Health and Its Evolution at Harvard, 1997; *The Monk in the Garden: The Lost and Found Genius of Gregor Mendel*, 2000

Mary Ruth Cowgill/Courtesy of Random House

Henley, Patricia

1947– Novelist; short-story writer

The author Patricia Henley's fiction is firmly grounded in a sense of place, whether it be the jungles of Guatemala or the back roads of the American West. In her short story "Same Old Big Magic," published in *Ploughshares* (Winter 1990–1991), a woman reminisces about a former lover while sifting through a box of maps. The maps landmark the high and low points of their love affair, which took place as they wandered across the country from Arizona to Oregon. Here and in other stories Henley uses place as backdrop to record collisions of character and circumstance, allowing emotions and discoveries to take center stage. Henley has published three collections of short stories and two novels, and her work has been anthologized in *Best American Short Stories* and *The Pushcart Prize Anthology*.

In 2000 Patricia Henley wrote for *World Authors 1995–2000*: "I was born in Terre Haute, Indiana, in 1947, the oldest of eight children in a working-class family. My parents had both served in WW II, my mother at Wright-Patterson Air Force Base and my father in the South Pacific. I was given to understand that they, like many, came home from the war desirous of family life and stability; thus they married and I was born eleven months later, but my mother was deeply troubled and had her first psychological breakdown when I was six months old. The loss of my mother during her hospitalizations is the primary wound of my childhood and I'm certain I write with that as an undercurrent. She was a complicated woman, given to bursts of singing and angry diatribes. For the most part, she did not work outside the home. My father worked away, as a telecommunications equipment installer. Their families did not approve of their marriage; one was Catholic, one was Protestant; one was Democrat, one Republican. My mother converted to Roman Catholicism when I was ten years old. We lived in several homes while I was growing up, moving to accommodate more babies. The one I remember best is a humble cement block house on a narrow blacktop road not far from the Illinois state line. It was surrounded by hardwood trees and cornfields, and the ecstasy of tromping through the sycamore leaves and wandering among the May apples, of observing the seasons, has been a feeling that has stayed with me and made town living always seem like a temporary necessity. When I am able to set aside my parents arguments and my mother's illnesses, I remember the countryside, the air, the snowy fields in winter, and becoming a voracious reader while we lived there.

"My paternal grandmother, Anna Swiezy Cowgill, came to the United States from Bohemia when she was ten years old. She never went to school again, but worked in factories and as a census-taker. Her high, black Royal typewriter had a place of honor on her desk and I wanted to type stories before I could read. When I was nearly five years old my grandmother took me to Sarah Scott Junior High School where there was a public library in the basement. She borrowed children's books for me and with her help I learned to read before kindergarten. My childhood was spent reading and figuring out how to garner more time for reading. It sounds so dull to admit it, but I was the sort of antisocial child who would read on the playground at recess. We did not have many books in our home—my father's detective novels and a few volumes of condensed novels—but I brought home stack after stack of library books and read late into the night. I read *The Secret Garden* and *A Tree Grows in Brooklyn* several times over the course of years. With their heroines who heal and grow, they are perhaps the most influential books of my childhood.

"Still, I thought I needed a profession more reliable than writing, and I set out to become a high school English teacher. The nuns who had educated me were the only intellectuals who inhabited my world, and I could envision modeling after them as a teacher, although at puberty I fled from the common Catholic girlhood notion of becoming a nun. I felt the deep conviction that I had to write and would when I read Anne Sexton's poems—*All My Pretty Ones*—when I was nineteen years old. I was standing outside my professor's office door in a slant of late afternoon light, waiting for a conference. The cover of the book was black and purple and I still have my rain-damaged copy. I just knew.

I began writing poetry and was a declared poet while in the master's program at The Johns Hopkins University.

"Stories were my first love, however, and as soon as I matured enough to sit still, I began writing stories. My first stories arose as a result of moving to Washington State in 1975 to live in an anarchist back-to-the-land community. Living that way—without running water (in winter) and indoor plumbing, growing some of the food I ate, caring for a dairy cow, spending much of the day outdoors in a paradisiacal, remote canyon—renewed that childhood ecstasy, and I felt boundaries dissolve between me and what the philosopher David Abram calls the more-than-human world. That feeling, in conjunction with the westerners I met, gave rise to the stories that are collected most recently into a volume titled *Worship of the Common Heart*.

"I thought I would always be satisfied with writing short stories, but in 1989 I traveled to Guatemala with a woman friend. I had always been interested in Latin America and we wanted to see for ourselves what had happened in Guatemala during the 1980s when the government suppressed the human rights movement. The first glimmers of *Hummingbird House* were evident within two weeks of arriving in Antigua, where most of the novel is set. Writing *Hummingbird House* allowed me to bring together so much of what concerns me at this stage of my life: mysticism, sexual healing, human rights, the abuse of power.

"I teach in an MFA program at Purdue University. Interviewers often ask me if my teaching feeds my writing and I have to say, No, I don't believe it does. But I have been grateful to be a writer taken under the wing of a university and I teach to give back what I can to my community. I live with my husband and two cats on a country road not far from campus, with long green views of the Indiana fields."

The publication of her first book of short stories, *Friday Night at Silver Star* (1986), brought Henley recognition as a strong, new voice. The collection was featured as an Editor's Choice in both the *New York Times Book Review* and *Publishers Weekly*, and won the Montana Arts Council First Book Award for 1985. In *Esquire*, a reviewer described Henley as an "up-and-coming" author, as quoted by Charlotte M. Wright in *Studies in Short Fiction* (Spring 1994). Set in the 1980s against the conservatism and booming-economy of the Reagan era, the collection's stories feature characters in their middle years who feel out of place and time; in the words of Wright, they "came of age in the 60s and early 70s [and are] trying to bring the past and present into perspective." These aging members of the counterculture have names such as Little Egypt, Obadiah, Rein, and Sunbow and live in renovated school buses and tepees scattered across Montana and the Northwest. They live on cheap food and wine, occasionally picking apples for cash and pairing off with other members of their tribe. In the *New York Times Book Review* (July 6, 1986, on-line), W. D. Wetherell admired the "skill and sensitivity" with which Henley sketches the people that populate her stories, but noted that she sometimes fails to transcend her material, succumbing instead to the same "blahs" as her characters. "We can see that Ms. Henley knows everything her characters know; we need to see she knows more," Wetherell wrote. Wetherell also praised the collection, stating that a writer at the beginning of a career needs to seek "a patch of land and, through skill, sweat, and determination," make it their own. In this respect, he argued, Henley's first book—in treading a "fairly narrow path"—stakes "a claim on our imaginations in a readable and convincing style." Wright applauded Henley's technique but, like Wetherell, found that she wanted more than the book delivered. "What bothers me is the sameness of those characters, who seem recycled from story to story. Nearly all are wanderers, with '60s attitudes towards drugs, sex, and health foods. I am of the right age to appreciate such attributes, but I found that after a few stories, I wanted to see the author's lively, polished, and accessible style applied to different types of characters."

Henley's second collection of stories, *The Secret of Cartwheels* (1992), is also set in the American West. This time the characters are not so much lost as unsettled, their lives in turmoil from divorce, death, or abandonment. "Lessons in Joy" introduces a 40-year-old woman who becomes unhinged after the deaths of her parents. Fearful that her own time is running out, she seeks out young lovers and tries to identify with her teenage son. At the story's end, "in a wild leap of mind that made her feel almost as though she'd left her body," as quoted by David Wong Louie in the *New York Times Book Review* (January 31, 1993, on-line), she finds love with a white-haired, 55-year-old man. In the much-praised title story, an adolescent narrator named Roxie wants to adopt her mother's confirmation name, Joan—"a name to carry into battle," as quoted by Wong Louie. She hopes the name will lend her the emotional armor she needs to deal with her alcoholic mother, whose despair hangs over the house like a curse and who burdens her daughter with secrets and troubles too weighty for Roxie to bear. When her mother is committed to a mental institution, for a moment Roxie thinks she has been released from her troubles, only to find herself drawn unwillingly into the past.

The stories turn on moments of sudden understanding, leaps of faith, or acts of sheer desperation. In the orphanage in which she ends up, Roxie is offered some advice on taking such leaps: "The secret of cartwheels . . . [is to] catch yourself before you kill yourself," as quoted by Wright. "In this and other stories," Wong Louie observed, "Ms. Henley . . . displays a command of her subject, the complex emotions that motivate and chill people."

About the collection as a whole, Wong Louie remarked, "Ms. Henley's narrative strengths tend toward the descriptive. Stories turn on the strength of her elegant, homespun prose, rich with stunning images and quick wisdom, rather than on an unfolding of events. Conflict is present, but its role is minimized."

In her next work Henley tackled a time and place defined in the popular imagination by conflict—the war-torn Central America of the 1980s. *Hummingbird House* (1999), Henley's first novel, received widespread critical attention and was a finalist for both the National Book Award and the New Yorker Best Fiction Book Award. During the 1980s, Henley made several trips to the Chiapas state of southern Mexico and to Guatemala and Nicaragua, during which she gathered first-hand accounts of the violence and oppression in those countries from refugees, activists, and Indian women. For Henley, writing about these difficult subjects is part of her political activism; she also donates a portion of the book's royalties to human rights causes worldwide. "I wanted other people to come to know the story of Central America and understand what is happening there," she told Amy Lotierzo during an interview for the *Butler Collegian* (October 28, 1999, on-line). Over nearly a decade of writing, Henley's research material evolved into a novel due to the richness and complexity of the subject matter, as she told Lotierzo. "Writing a short story is like a trip to the Bahamas and writing a novel is like a sickness," Henley said.

In *Hummingbird House*, Kate Banner, an American nurse and midwife, has come to Mexico for what she thought would be a three-week visit; eight years later, she is still south of the border, fighting social injustice with a group of mostly North American activists. Kate takes a job at a women's health clinic in Nicaragua, and the novel opens with the scene of her delivering a baby in a half-sunken boat in the aftermath of a hurricane. While the baby survives, the mother dies soon after giving birth, and the incident becomes a catalyzing event for Kate. Exhausted after eight years of hard work, beaten down by the grinding poverty and unending violence, Kate decides she wants to go home. However this means leaving Deaver, her long-time lover and a gun-runner for the Sandinistas (a socialist group that governed Nicaragua throughout the 1980s while fighting the Contras, or counter-revolutionary forces). Although Deaver is drawn as a fanatical, selfish, and unlikable character, who once called Kate a "lightweight" and a "spoiled North American woman," as quoted by Jeannie Pyun in the *New York Times Book Review* (November 7, 1999, on-line), Kate mourns the loss of their relationship.

These events, which are told mostly through memory and flashback, form the backdrop to the book's central plot. On her way back to the U.S., Kate stops off at a friend's home in Antigua, where she meets Father Dixie Ryan, an activist and priest who, like Kate, is experiencing doubts about his vocation. Kate and Ryan become involved in helping Vidalz, a Mayan woman whose husband has been detained, and Marta, a traumatized girl from the streets who doesn't speak. Meanwhile, they begin to fall in love, and make plans to move to a farm and start a peasant cooperative—Hummingbird House. Just as the book seems to be moving toward a happy ending the facts surrounding Guatemala, circa 1989, reassert themselves: army death squads are operating, and as a worker for the resistance, Ryan is in danger. Even after the group of characters leaves Antigua for the countryside, they face further violence and tragedy.

The plot's liberal interweaving of history, politics, and romance generated sharply divided critical opinions. Writing for *City Pages* (June 30, 1999, on-line), Amy Weivoda observed that Henley is "able to pen such lush descriptions of the tropical landscape and glue-sniffing children, but is pretty thin when it comes to the what's-actually-going-down complexities." Weivoda wrote that Henley's "vision is more in focus when she's gazing into small domestic battles and victories, and that's where the tale, amid so many dead, comes to life." Jeannie Pyun expressed appreciation for Henley's point "that personal connection is the wellspring of political involvement," but wished that Henley had supplied the novel with "more geopolitical context." A writer for *Kirkus Reviews*, as quoted on *Amazon.com*, found the story "overwrought. . . . a not-so-subtle homily," and lamented that "Kate and her good deeds don't shine as brightly as they should in this schematic take on the suffering of the innocents."

Writing for the *National Catholic Reporter* (May 7, 1999, on-line), Teresa Malcolm dissented from the aforementioned reviews, finding the personal and political elements of the story in perfect balance. "Author Patricia Henley convincingly blends the ordinary—the smell of tortillas, the sound of jazz, children playing, [a character's] fear of rainstorms—with the brutality of Guatemala in the late 1980s," Malcolm wrote. "The mundane startles the reader with the realization that life carries on with some semblance of normality, even with violence and fear around every corner."

In *Cross Currents* (Fall 1999), Kenneth Arnold conveyed yet another impression of the novel, describing it as "about vocation, who we are at the center of our being." Both Kate and Ryan must grapple with how to live, work, and love in the face of incredible misery and injustice. In the book, Henley quotes the Guatemalan poet Otto Rene Castillo: "What were you doing while the poor were suffering, their humanity and their lives consumed by flame?" as cited by Pam Johnston in the *Missouri Review* (on-line). Even while pointing out the novel's weaknesses, most reviewers appreciated Henley's willingness to address such persistently troubling questions.

Henley's third collection, *Worship of the Common Heart: New and Selected Stories*, was published in September 2000. The 19 stories included are mostly anthologized from her previous two collections, and the new characters are familiar Henley types—rootless searchers strung across the country, looking for comfort and meaning apart from mainstream society. Roxie from "The Secret of Cartwheels" reappears as an adult and is once again startled into a recognition of her pain, this time by news of her mother's impending death. A reviewer for *Publishers Weekly* (August 14, 2000) praised the book enthusiastically, citing Henley's talent for capturing defining moments in otherwise ordinary lives. "These stories, by a marvelous writer who speaks from both the heart and the head, are as comfortable as well-worn denim."

Henley's second novel, "In the River Sweet," (2002), is a family saga set in the author's home state of Indiana. Generally well reviewed, the book touches on themes of homosexuality, marriage, and war, among other topics.

—M. A. H.

SUGGESTED READING: *Butler Collegian* (on-line) Oct. 28, 1999; *Cross Currents* p403+ Fall 1999; *Missouri Review* (on-line); *New York Times Book Review* (on-line) July 6, 1986; *Ploughshares* p193+ Winter 1990–91

SELECTED BOOKS: novels—*Hummingbird House*, 1999; *In the River Sweet*, 2002; short-story collections—*Friday Night at Silver Star*, 1986; *The Secret of Cartwheels*, 1992; *Worship of the Common Heart*, 2000

Courtesy of Michelle Herman

Herman, Michelle

Mar. 9, 1955– Novelist

Since the publication of her first book, *Missing*, in 1990, Michelle Herman has been recognized as a strong talent, particularly in the genre of Jewish-American fiction. The winner of numerous awards and fellowships, she has been hailed for her colorful and compelling characters, whom a reviewer for *Publishers Weekly* (June 1, 1998) called "intellectually rich but emotionally uncertain."

Michelle Herman was born in the New York City borough of Brooklyn to Morton and Sheila (Weiss) Herman on March 9, 1955. She attended Brooklyn College of the City University of New York, earning her B.S. degree in 1976. After completing college she worked as an editor and reporter for the Associated Press and later enrolled in the prestigious Iowa Writers' Workshop at the University of Iowa, where she received a teaching/writing fellowship in 1985; she earned her MFA degree the following year.

In her first novel, *Missing* (1990), Herman presents an 89-year-old Jewish widow, Rivke Vasilevsky, who is literally and symbolically taking inventory of her life as she prepares for her death. The mother of five children and numerous grandchildren, Rivke spends much of her time alone, save for regular visits and phone calls from her favorite granddaughter, Rachel. As Rivke packs her belongings in her Brooklyn apartment in preparation for a move—to a nursing home, hospital, or perhaps a funeral home, depending on the state of her health—she decides to make Rachel a necklace out of a special set of beads she has been saving for years, but she cannot find them. While Rivke confronts the loss of the beads, even composing a list of suspects whom she believes may have stolen them, she reflects on other things she has lost throughout the years: her husband, Sol, who died two years earlier; her five children, whose spouses she does not like; and—as her body deteriorated with age—her own hope, independence, and mobility. As Rivke, Herman narrates the story with the sharp tongue of a brittle, unhappy old woman. In a review for the *Voice Literary Supplement* (October 1990)—transcribed on Michelle Herman's Ohio State University Web site—Ralph Sassone observed, "Herman wisely avoids turning Rivke into a martyr.'" Instead, Herman portrayed a complex character who is achieving what Sassone called "gradual recognitions" about her life. He added, "Herman has an impressive command of Rivke's syntax ('Sol used to buy the *Forward* [a Yiddish newspaper] every day, and from cover to cover he would read it.') as well as the mental rearrangements the woman must perform to keep herself sane. And Herman's a brave writer: she refuses to enliven her narrative with outside events." An exploration of Rivke's interior life, the novel records the claustrophobic musings of memory and the subtle dramas that occur within the walls of her dusty apartment. Susan Spano Wells, writing for the *Bloomsbury Review* (April–May 1991), as transcribed on Herman's Web site, called it "an impressive, gutsy debut." Wells continued, "Judging by her photo, Herman is young enough to be Rivke's granddaughter. Still, in *Missing*, she creates the silent, hazardous world of the elderly with strikingly sure and clear strokes."

Some reviewers criticized Herman's mundane depictions of her protagonist's existence. For example, in the *New York Times Book Review* (February 17, 1991), Frances A. Koestler wrote, "What's really missing in *Missing* is an editorial blue pencil to correct awkward diction and bad grammar and do away with the plethora of needless Yiddishisms. What are all too present are repetitious, self-pitying memories and the tedious details of Rivke's daily life." Overall, however, the novel received more praise than criticism. Ralph Sassone drew favorable comparisons between Herman and the acclaimed Jewish-American writer Cynthia Ozick and concluded, "The novel's achievement is that [Rivke's] sad life is handled with such seriousness and sympathy that it's nearly impossible to remain unmoved." *Missing* won the 1991 Harold U. Ribalow Award for best Jewish fiction and was named one of the *Voice Literary Supplement*'s 25 Best Books of the Year.

Nearly a decade passed before the publication of Herman's next book, a collection of three novellas entitled *A New and Glorious Life* (1998). The first novella, "Auslander," is about an accomplished literary translator (known only by her last name, which is the novella's title), who begins translating the work of a Romanian poet. After the poet's husband contacts Auslander to request her services—without his wife's consent—the reclusive translator reluctantly becomes involved in the poet's life and work and soon discovers that the situation is not as it first appeared. The story ends with a terrifying tragedy, one that a reviewer for *Publishers Weekly* (June 1, 1998) called "both inescapable and completely earned." This novella first appeared in the 1986 anthology *Twenty Under Thirty: Best Stories by America's New Young Writers*. In a review of this collection for the *New York Times* (March 23, 1986), Phillip Lopate called "Auslander" "the best story in the book—certainly the most commanding." In "A New and Glorious Life," the second and longest novella in the volume that bears its name, Herman presents an unhappily married composer, Gad, who, while on a six-week retreat at an artist's colony, meets Hannah, a poet from New York City. The story explores the development of the couple's relationship as they fall in love and decide to begin "their real lives . . . Their real life, together. A new and glorious life," as quoted by Kevin Clay in *American Literary Review* (Fall 1999) and transcribed on Herman's Web site. In "Hope Among Men," the third novella, Hope, an art conservator, suffers through two dysfunctional relationships with men known only as "Misery" and "Heartache," each of whom leaves her in turn.

In the *Columbus Dispatch* (May 2, 1998), Margaret Quamme wrote that the three novellas are much less focused on "material objects than in a meticulous analysis of [the characters'] emotional lives, so Herman relies more on internal and external dialogue than on physical description. Not much happens in these stories, but Herman wrings suspense out of the characters' slow decision-making." She added, "On the surface, the dilemmas involve simple sets of relationships. . . . Underneath the surface, the dilemmas are moral rather than emotional. The stories scrutinize the ways our minds work to justify our desires." *A New and Glorious Life* received a great deal of acclaim, with a reviewer for the Cleveland, Ohio, *Plain Dealer* (May 10, 1998) noting, "It's clearly the work of a resourceful and sophisticated writer." The same reviewer concluded, "In Michelle Herman we find a distinctive stylist who also possesses a spirited intelligence and a wonderfully screwy sense of humor. That combination makes for some rare and unbeatable reading." Writing for *Our Town* (September 1998), as transcribed on Herman's Web site, Carol Parikh affirmed, "Herman is a generous writer, and her prose is so clean that you can only appreciate its artfulness later . . . when you find yourself wondering for the umpteenth time about Auslander's terrifying final deed and how Gad and Hannah are getting on these days."

Herman has published stories, novellas, and essays in numerous literary journals, including *Story Quarterly*, *Nebraska Review*, *Brooklyn Literary Review*, *Iowa Journal of Literary Studies*, the *Village Advocate*, *Three Plum Review*, *Northwest Review*, and *North American Review*. In addition, her work has been anthologized in such collections as *Ariadne's Thread, An Anthology of Contemporary Women's Journals* (1984), and *Jewish-American Fiction: A Century of Stories* (1998). She has been recognized with a National Endowment for the Arts Fellowship (1986), a James Michener Fellowship (1987), two Individual Artist's Fellowships from the Ohio Arts Council (1989 and 1998), a Lilly Foundation Fellowship (1990), and two research awards from Ohio State University (1990 and 1991). In 1986 she earned a Syndicated Fiction Award from PEN for her short story "All I Want to Know."

Michelle Herman currently serves as the director for the MFA program in creative writing at Ohio State University, where she is also an associate professor of English. In 1999 she was recognized with the institution's highest teaching honor, the University Alumni Distinguished Teaching Award. Along with the poet Kathy Fagan, she co-edits the *Journal*, the university's nationally distributed literary magazine. Herman resides in Columbus, Ohio, with her husband, Glen Holland, an artist, and their daughter, Grace; she is currently at work on a novella and a novel. —K. D.

SUGGESTED READING: (Cleveland, Ohio) *Plain Dealer* I p11 May 10, 1998; *Columbus Dispatch* H p4 May 2, 1998; *New York Times* VII p12 Mar. 23, 1986; *New York Times* (on-line) Dec. 20, 1998; *Publishers Weekly* p52 June 1, 1998

SELECTED BOOKS: *Missing*, 1990; *A New and Glorious Life*, 1998

Courtesy of Putnam Publicity

Higgins, Jack

July 27, 1929– Novelist

Harry Patterson, better known by the pen name Jack Higgins, overcame poverty and sectarian violence in Northern Ireland during his childhood to become one of the most prolific and popular writers of espionage and action novels in the world. He began writing thrillers in 1959 to make extra money for his family; because he was paid so little for each book, he wrote as many as possible in his spare time, publishing one or two novels a year, under his real name, Harry Patterson, and the pseudonyms, Martin Fallon, Hugh Marlowe, James Graham, and Jack Higgins. Despite his prodigious output, the writer remained relatively obscure until the mid-1970s. His big break came in 1975 with the publication of *The Eagle Has Landed*, which features a team of German paratroopers who attempt to kidnap the British Prime Minister Winston Churchill during World War II. Millions of readers were enthralled by the character of Liam Devlin, a well-read and personable guerilla with the Irish Republican Army (IRA), who collaborates with the Germans. Higgins's novel became a worldwide best-seller, and in 1977 it was adapted into a film of the same name. The success of both the book and the film made Jack Higgins an international celebrity and brought him greater wealth and fame than he had ever imagined. Since then, Higgins has published about one thriller a year.

In *Eye of the Storm* (1992), Higgins introduced another popular protagonist, Sean Dillon, a former IRA gunman, who has since appeared in several best-selling sequels. In the London *Evening Standard* (April 2, 2001), John Kercher estimated that Jack Higgins's books have sold more than 250 million copies worldwide. His popularity rivals that of other best-selling thriller authors such as Alistair MacLean and Robert Ludlum. Higgins concedes that his novels are primarily entertainment and do not qualify as literature. "I think the type of book I'm writing, and the type that Robert Ludlum writes, is also a kind of social history of our times," Higgins explained to Edwin McDowell for the *New York Times* (July 28, 1982). "People who read them a few years from now will actually get some idea of what was happening politically in our time."

The son of an Irish mother and a Scottish father, Jack Higgins was born Harry Patterson on July 27, 1929 in Newcastle-on-Tyne, in the United Kingdom. When Higgins was two years old, his mother took him to live with relatives in the city of Belfast, in Northern Ireland, leaving his father behind. During the 1930s tensions between Catholics and Protestants divided Belfast, and acts of violence by political extremists on both sides were common. ("The Troubles," as the situation in Northern Ireland has been frequently described, continued through the next six decades.) Although he was baptized in the Presbyterian faith, Higgins had several Catholic relatives. "My aunt used to take me to the Catholic church," Higgins told Linda Das for the London *Mail on Sunday* (March 19, 2000), "and I recall the priest saying goodbye to all the congregation and, as I left, him patting me on the head and saying: 'This boy's black Orange soul is going straight to Hell.'" (The color orange is associated symbolically with Protestant loyalists.) One time, when Higgins was on a trip to the local movie theater to see *King Kong*, an IRA terrorist threw a bomb into the crowd. As a schoolboy, he was often accosted on the street by both Catholic and Protestant hoodlums. "I soon learned to second-guess whether a potential attacker was a Catholic or Protestant and act accordingly," he recalled to Das. "If I guessed that they were Catholic, I'd [make the sign of the cross] in the vain attempt of warding them off, but I invariably got it wrong and would end up being beaten and having my money stolen. It was a very violent upbringing yet, strangely, I don't recall ever feeling particularly scared." Another time, when Higgins was older, his mother shielded him from IRA gunfire during a ride aboard a tram. During the Battle of Britain in World War II, Higgins often took refuge in the cellar as German aircraft bombed the nation.

When he was nine years old, Higgins and his mother moved back to England, living in the city of Leeds. Since her ex-husband was not obligated to provide her with child support under the laws at the time, Higgins's mother supported him by working as a waitress. For a time, he lived with his grandmother in Belfast. When he was 13 years old, Higgins returned to Leeds to live with his mother, who had remarried. "My stepfather never liked me," Higgins told Das. "He was incredibly jealous of the relationship I had with my mum. When he was [disqualified from the Royal Air Force] after an accident, he felt very much like a failure in life and seemed to take it out on me. My time at school from then on wasn't very happy either. I was once given nine strokes on the backside for throwing snowballs at the school clock." Higgins was told by both his stepfather and the headmaster at the school that he would never amount to anything.

Higgins dropped out of school at age 15, which outraged his stepfather. He forced Higgins to take a school correspondence course, which gave him some academic qualifications. (Higgins has said that in the end he realized that his stepfather had done him a favor by insisting on the correspondence course.) The young man also worked as a clerk and messenger with the Leeds cleansing department, a government agency. In 1947 Higgins fulfilled his compulsory national service by joining the British Army's Royal Horse Guards (also called the Household Calvary). A test given at the time revealed that Higgins had an I.Q. of 147, and learning those results gave him greater confidence than he had ever had. "The army gave me a sense of what I was capable of," he told Grania McFadden for the *Belfast Telegraph* (July 20, 2000), "and I thoroughly enjoyed serving on the East German border during the Cold War." After leaving the army in 1947, Higgins worked at several different jobs, including stints as a clerk, circus-tent hand, tram conductor, driver, and cigarette salesman.

In about 1955 Higgins decided to change professions. "I bumped into a friend of mine in the park, and he said he was going to be a teacher," he told Kercher. "That made me think that maybe I could be one too. I hadn't realised that you could retrain at 26." Higgins received a small grant, which allowed him to enroll at the Leeds Training College. He paid for his tuition by working in the post office at night. In 1958 Higgins earned a certificate in education. The same year, he married Amy Margaret Hewitt, a student at the college, and began teaching history at the Allerton Grange Comprehensive School, in Leeds. In 1962 Higgins earned a degree in social psychology and sociology from the University of London. Two years later he became a lecturer in liberal studies at the Leeds College of Commerce. In 1968 Higgins joined the faculty of James Graham College, in New Farnley, Yorkshire. From 1971 to 1973 he served as a tutor at Leeds University.

Higgins had dreamed of being a writer since childhood. During his teenage and young-adult years, he often wrote stories. "I once entered a [writing] competition in the *Yorkshire Post*," he recalled to Das. "I didn't win, but one of the judges—the Yorkshire novelist Leo Walmsley—wrote to me saying: 'I was very impressed with your work, and I want you to know one thing—you are a writer.' That certainly gave me confidence, and I think it must have been the first time someone told me that I could do something well."

To support his family, which eventually included four children, Higgins began writing stories in his spare time. In 1959, under his given name, Harry Patterson, he published his first novel, *Sad Wind from the Sea*, an adventure set in communist China. Among the novels Higgins published as Harry Patterson were *Cry of the Hunter* (1960), *The Thousand Faces of Night* (1961), *Hell Is Too Crowded* (1962), *Thunder at Noon* (1964), and *Wrath of the Lion* (1964). The main character of *Cry of the Hunter* is an IRA assassin named Martin Fallon. In 1962 Higgins began using that name as a pseudonym. As Martin Fallon, Higgins introduced Paul Chavasse, a British intelligence agent, in the thriller *The Testament of Caspar Shultz* (1962). Chavasse returned in five sequels, *Year of the Tiger* (1964), *The Keys of Hell* (1965), *Midnight Never Comes* (1966), *Dark Side of the Street* (1967), and *A Fine Night for Dying* (1969). "While I was a struggling schoolmaster I was trying very much to make some kind of living by writing, but I couldn't because the return on each book was so small," Higgins told Edwin McDowell for the *New York Times Book Review* (July 20, 1980). "That meant I had to publish books one after another, so I used several names."

As Hugh Marlowe, Higgins published *Seven Pillars to Hell* (1963), *Passage by Night* (1964), and *A Candle for the Dead* (1966), the last of which details a plot to break an IRA terrorist out of prison. In 1968 *A Candle for the Dead* was adapted into the film *The Violent Enemy*, which was banned in Britain because of its political content. Borrowing the name of the college where he taught, Higgins, as James Graham, wrote *A Game for Heroes* (1970), *The Wrath of God* (1971), *The Khufra Run* (1972), and *The Run to Morning* (1974). In 1972 *The Wrath of God*, an adventure set in Mexico during the 1920s, was released as a film; it co-starred Robert Mitchum, Frank Langella, and Rita Hayworth in one of her last performances.

In 1968 Harry Patterson began writing under the name of Jack Higgins. "I used to visit my great uncle Jack Higgins [in Belfast] every Sunday," Higgins recalled to McFadden. "He was a notorious Orange gunman, and I remember that before he went out of the house, he would open a secret drawer under the stairs, where he kept an array of handguns, and select one to take with him." The first Jack Higgins novel was *East of Desolation* (1968), a thriller set in the forbidding climes of Greenland. In Higgins's *Night Judgment at Sinos*

(1970), a Greek shipping tycoon hires Jack Savage, a deep-sea diver and former British commando, to free a man being held at a prison on the Greek island of Sinos. "Higgins has a good ear for dialogue, handles his love scenes without mawkishness, and is well up on Mediterranean politics," Newgate Callendar observed of the book for the *New York Times Book Review* (April 4, 1971). "This one you won't put down."

Although the character of Martin Fallon died in the novel *Cry of the Hunter* (1960), Higgins resurrected him for *A Prayer for the Dying* (1973). In that novel, Fallon, a career IRA assassin, accidentally kills children aboard a school bus during a botched terrorist attack. With both the police and the IRA after him, Fallon decides to flee the country and approaches a local gangster for help. The gangster agrees to provide Fallon with a forged passport on the condition that he commit one last murder. Fallon agrees, but then confesses the crime to a priest, who is bound by the seal of the confessional and cannot report him to the police. Higgins told McFadden that writing *A Prayer for the Dying* "took a hell of a lot out of me, and made me question God, religion, and my feelings towards everything." In 1987 *A Prayer for the Dying* was adapted into a film with Mickey Rourke as Fallon and Bob Hoskins as the priest. The film failed at the box office and received many negative reviews.

By his own account Higgins's writing improved after he read F. Scott Fitzgerald's unfinished novel *The Last Tycoon*, which was published with the author's notes in 1941, a year after Fitzgerald's death. Higgins was impressed by Fitzgerald's observation that character is action. "It was quite a revelation," Higgins said to McDowell for the *New York Times* (July 28, 1982). "I think in my early works I fell into the trap of thinking of a plot and making the characters act it out. Now I start with a concept, then create the characters, and let the characters make it happen, like in real life."

Jack Higgins had his first international best-seller with the historical novel *The Eagle Has Landed* (1975), which eventually sold more than 30 million copies. The book takes place in late 1943, as the Allies continue to push back Nazi Germany. The German dictator Adolf Hitler hatches a desperate scheme, ordering a team of elite paratroopers to abduct or kill the British Prime Minister Winston Churchill during his brief sojourn on the Norfolk coast in England. Higgins introduced one of his most popular characters, a charming IRA guerilla named Liam Devlin, who aids the paratroopers. "There are elements of heroism, duplicity, and heavy irony, plus considerable bloodshed, in this action-oriented yarn," F. H. Guidry wrote in his review for the *Christian Science Monitor* (June 25, 1975). "Mr. Higgins's book features a lot of movie-like cross-cutting between German and English locales, dialogue that is mostly routine, and a sufficiently fantastic plot to keep readers wondering not whether Churchill will be spared but precisely how those overreaching Germans will muff the intricate kidnaping assignment." In 1977 the film version of the novel, with Donald Sutherland, Michael Caine, and Robert Duvall, was a box office hit and helped establish Higgins's reputation as a master storyteller. The success of both the novel and the film led the author to adopt the pseudonym Jack Higgins on a permanent basis, and many of the earlier novels he published as Harry Patterson, Martin Fallon, Hugh Marlowe, and James Graham have been republished in paperback under the Higgins name. However, as Harry Patterson, Higgins wrote two more novels that take place during World War II, *The Valhalla Exchange* (1976), a best-seller, and *To Catch a King* (1979), which was adapted into a 1984 television movie. Under that name he also revised *Thunder at Noon* (1964), a fictionalized account of the Depression-era criminal, John Dillinger, as *Dillinger* (1983).

Higgins set *Day of Judgment* (1979) right before President John F. Kennedy's visit to West Berlin in June 1963. In the book, the East German communists kidnap Sean Conlin, a Catholic priest who helps smuggle refugees to West Germany, and try to brainwash him into confessing that he is a CIA agent during a public trial that they hope will embarrass Kennedy and undermine the impact of his visit. The United States, however, dispatches a group of agents to rescue the priest before he breaks. "Higgins has brought together a rich mixture of ingredients, and a plot which is implausible—particularly when one considers what was actually happening in East Germany in the Early '60s," Joseph McLellan wrote in his review for the *Washington Post* (March 31, 1979). "He is a master at involving his readers in the fate of his characters and in the storyteller's most basic art—keeping alive the eagerness to see what happens next. He manages to put the Catholic Church into a suspense novel with more expertise than anyone else who has tried in recent memory except Morris West, and if [Higgins] makes an occasional slip in small details . . . this is not likely to bother most of his readers."

Higgins brought Liam Devlin back for *Touch the Devil* (1982), which is set during the early 1980s. Semi-retired from his days as an IRA operative and teaching English literature at Trinity University, in Dublin, Ireland, Devlin is kidnaped by Group 4, the elite anti-terrorist unit of the British security services. Charles Ferguson, the head of Group 4, forces Devlin to rescue Martin Brosnan, a Vietnam veteran and IRA terrorist, from a French island prison. Once freed, Brosnan and Devlin must track down an elusive terrorist who attempted to assassinate the British foreign minister and supplies arms and money to different left-wing terrorist groups across Europe. In Higgins's *Confessional* (1985) Devlin hunts a KGB-trained rogue agent who is planning to assassinate Pope John Paul II during his visit to England. In the London *Financial Times* (August 3, 1985) Brian Ager described *Confessional*, which was made into a television miniseries in 1989, as one of Higgins's "most intricate tales."

Higgins returned to World War II with *Night of the Fox* (1987). In it, an army colonel who has extensive knowledge of the Allies' plans to invade Nazi-occupied Europe on D-Day is captured by the Nazis on the Channel Island of Jersey, the only British territory that was occupied by Germany during the war (and where Higgins currently makes his home). The Allies send Harry Martineau, a secret agent, to rescue the colonel or keep him from revealing crucial information. In her review for the *Christian Science Monitor* (February 6, 1987), Jane Stewart Spitzer observed, "Higgins knows how to tell a good story, and he writes in a fast-moving, hard-to-put-down style that works to his advantage. If the novel is read too slowly, the improbable plot points and weak characterizations stand out too clearly for comfort. *Fox* also lacks the sympathetic heroes in [*The Eagle Has Landed*] and the tension created by the reader's desire to root for the bad guys. Still, *Night of the Fox* is fun to read." The novel was made into a television film in 1990.

In 1990 Higgins published *The Eagle Has Flown*, which picks up where *The Eagle Has Landed* left off. In the sequel, Liam Devlin accepts an offer from Heinrich Himmler, the head of the Nazi SS, to rescue Kurt Steiner, one of the paratroopers sent to kidnap Churchill in the previous novel, who is being held prisoner in the Tower of London. In his review for the *Atlanta Journal and Constitution* (March 10, 1991), Don O'Briant wrote that although it wasn't as good as the previous novel, *The Eagle Has Flown* was superior to many "technothrillers that glorify hardware more than humans." O'Briant added that by "skillfully blending historical facts with imagination, the author creates a plausible world in which men find themselves fighting for a rotten cause. Devlin, the Irish poet with a cynical view of life, is an especially sympathetic anti-hero. He and Steiner always try to do the right thing even when they are on the wrong side."

In 1992 Higgins began a new series of novels with *Eye of the Storm*, which marked the first appearance of Sean Dillon, a former IRA terrorist who works as a hired gun. Higgins was inspired to create Dillon after a failed IRA mortar attack on No. 10 Downing Street, the residence of the British prime minister in London, on February 7, 1991. A master of disguise and a convincing actor, the champagne-sipping Dillon is irresistible to many women. Higgins explained to McFadden that Sean Dillon is the Liam Devlin of the 1990s. In the novel, Dillon is hired by the Iraqis during the 1991 Persian Gulf War to assassinate the former British Prime Minister Margaret Thatcher during a visit to France. After that attack fails, Dillon targets her successor, John Major, and his entire Cabinet. The British send Martin Brosnan, one of the heroes of *Touch the Devil*, to stop Dillon. (Liam Devlin also briefly appears in the novel.) In the *Washington Times* (July 13, 1992), Elizabeth M. Cosin faulted *Eye of the Storm*, writing, "This story of the exploits of superhuman terrorist Sean Dillon, who can transform himself into almost any character with or without makeup, is simply contrived and shallow." By contrast, in the *Calgary Herald* (October 10, 1992), Bob Stallworthy wrote that "Higgins spins a credible tale" and succeeded "in weaving together terrorists, a love interest, disenchanted KGB officials, an old IRA character, the British and French intelligence communities, which are just smart enough, and the underworld." Despite the varying critical reviews, *Eye of the Storm* was a best-seller.

In Dillon's second adventure, *Thunder Point* (1993), the British security services have taken him into custody and are about to execute him secretly. Dillon, however, is saved by Charles Ferguson, the head of Group 4, who was first seen in *Touch the Devil*. Dillon accepts Ferguson's offer of a full pardon in exchange for his services. For his first job as a "good guy," Dillon must destroy a sunken German U-boat that contains documents that reveal that many important individuals in Britain sympathized with the Nazis. Dillon goes on a similar mission in *On Dangerous Ground* (1994), in which he must locate an important document before it falls into the wrong hands.

Sean Dillon battles such enemies as anarchists, Arab terrorists, and mobsters in several more books: *Angel of Death* (1995), *Drink With the Devil* (1996), *The President's Daughter* (1997), *The White House Connection* (1999), *Day of Reckoning* (2000), *Edge of Danger* (2001), and *Midnight Runner* (2002). The books were all commercially successful, although some received more favorable critical notice than others. In the *Library Journal* (March 1, 1995), Elsa Pendleton dismissed *Angel of Death* as a "rather predictable shoot-'em-up," adding that "it is disappointing to find the characters barely sketched and the plot clunking from one episode to the next." Reviewing *The White House Connection* for *Booklist* (April 15, 1999), Budd Arthur hailed the novel as an "entertaining read." A critic for *Publishers Weekly* (February 28, 2000) was impressed with *Day of Reckoning*, concluding, "The action is sleek and intensely absorbing, but the supreme pleasure is in those Higgins celebrates—tarnished warriors who value honor over life and who get the job done no matter what the cost."

The actor Rob Lowe portrayed Sean Dillon in two films, *Eye of the Storm* (1995), which went directly to video, and *On Dangerous Ground* (1996), which was made for cable television. Kyle MacLachlan also played Dillon twice, in the cable-television films *The Windsor Protocol* (1996), a loose adaptation of the novel *On Dangerous Ground*, and *Thunder Point* (1998).

Before writing a novel, Higgins conducts extensive research. "There are two kinds of research," Higgins told Tim Murray for the Bergen, New Jersey *Record* (January 23, 1987). "One is fresh research in which I go around and talk to people and find out the right sources and read up on technical things. The other is what I can draw upon from several years of reading and listening. For instance, I've read and seen everything there is on [General and President Dwight] Eisenhower. When I say in a book that he took tea and not coffee for breakfast, I can quote you chapter and verse from memoirs of other generals that bear that out."

Jack Higgins's marriage to Amy Margaret Hewitt, with whom he had four children, ended in 1984. Speaking to Lynda Lee-Potter for the London *Daily Mail* (June 5, 1993), Higgins blamed his success as an author for the break-up. "I'd no idea then I was going to become a world famous bestselling author and it was not something that sat well with Amy," he explained. "One of the problems with great success is it's like setting out to sea on a big ship. It's all right for you, but your family aren't given a choice. In the end Amy wanted something that was hers, she wanted a life of her own." Higgins's second marriage, to Denise Palmer, an Oxford-educated ex-model, also ended recently.

To escape England's high taxes, Jack Higgins lives on Jersey, one of the Channel Islands. The author has both British and Irish citizenship. He uses a pen and paper to write his books. "Writing in longhand is a personal thing, like painting," Higgins observed to McFadden. His next thriller, "Bad Company," is scheduled for publication in June 2003.

—D. C.

SUGGESTED READING: *Atlanta Journal and Constitution* Arts & Entertainment p10 Mar. 10, 1991; *Belfast Telegraph* (on-line) July 20, 2000; (Bergen County, New Jersey) *Record* D p1 Jan. 23, 1987; *Booklist* p16 Apr. 15, 1999; *Christian Science Monitor* p23 June 25, 1975, p6 Feb. 6, 1987; *Library Journal* p102 Mar. 1, 1995; (London) *Daily Mail* p14 June 5, 1993, with photo; (London) *Evening Standard* p27 Apr. 2, 2001; (London) *Mail on Sunday* p23 Mar. 19, 2000, with photo; *New York Times* C p22 July 28, 1982, with photo; *New York Times Book Review* p51 Apr. 4, 1971, p22 July 20, 1980; *Publishers Weekly* p61 Feb. 28, 2000; Unofficial Jack Higgins Home Page; *Washington Post Book World* p2 Mar. 31, 1979; *Washington Times* D p5 July 13, 1992

SELECTED NOVELS: as Harry Patterson—*Sad Wind from the Sea*, 1959; *Cry of the Hunter*, 1960; *The Thousand Faces of Night*, 1961; *Comes the Dark Stranger*, 1962; *Hell Is Too Crowded*, 1962; *Pay the Devil*, 1963; *The Dark Side of the Island*, 1963; *A Phoenix in Blood*, 1964; *Thunder at Noon*, 1964 (revised and republished as *Dillinger* in 1983); *Wrath of the Lion*, 1964; *The Graveyard Shift*, 1965; *The Iron Tiger*, 1966; *Brought in Dead*, 1967; *Hell Is Always Today*, 1968; *Toll for the Brave*, 1971; *The Valhalla Exchange*, 1976; *To Catch a King*, 1979; as Martin Fallon—*The Testament of Caspar Shultz*, 1962; *Year of the Tiger*, 1964; *The Keys of Hell*, 1965; *Midnight Never Comes*, 1966; *Dark Side of the Street*, 1967; *A Fine Night for Dying*, 1969; as Hugh Marlowe—*Seven Pillars to Hell*, 1963 (republished as *Sheba* in 1994); *Passage By Night*, 1964; *A Candle for the Dead*, 1966; as James Graham—*A Game for Heroes*, 1970; *The Wrath of God*, 1971; *The Khufra Run*, 1973; *The Run to Morning*; 1974 (published in England as *Bloody Passage*); as Jack Higgins—*East of Desolation*, 1968; *In the Hour Before Midnight*, 1969 (published in the United States as *The Sicilian Heritage* in 1970); *Night Judgment at Sinos*, 1970; *The Last Place God Made*, 1971; *The Savage Day*, 1972; *A Prayer for the Dying*, 1973; *The Eagle Has Landed*, 1975; *Storm Warning*, 1976; *Day of Judgment*, 1978; *Solo*, 1980 (also published as *The Cretan Lover*); *Luciano's Luck*, 1981; *Touch the Devil*, 1982; *Exocet*, 1983; *Confessional*, 1985; *Night of the Fox*, 1986; *A Season in Hell*, 1989; *Memoirs of a Dance Hall Romeo*, 1989; *Cold Harbour*, 1990; *The Eagle Has Flown*, 1991; *Eye of the Storm*, 1992; *Thunder Point*, 1993; *On Dangerous Ground*, 1994; *Angel of Death*, 1995; *Drink with the Devil*, 1996; *The President's Daughter*, 1997; *Flight of Eagles*, 1998; *The White House Connection*, 1999; *Day of Reckoning*, 2000; *Edge of Danger*, 2001; *Midnight Runner*, 2002

Hilberg, Raul

June 2, 1926– Holocaust historian, memoirist

Although many books and articles have been written about the Holocaust in the last few decades, there were few works published about it in the 15 years following World War II. Apart from the public trials of the Nazi war criminals in Nuremberg, there was little public discussion of the Holocaust, including among Jews themselves. The situation began to change in 1961 with three developments. David Ben-Gurion, then prime minister of Israel, announced the capture of Adolf Eichmann, often characterized as the chief architect of the Holocaust. Eichmann's subsequent trial in Jerusalem was broadcast around the world, bringing the Holocaust to the attention of millions of people, many of whom knew little about it. Despite his claim that he was following orders, and therefore not culpable, Eichmann was convicted of crimes against humanity and later executed. The release of the Stanley Kramer film, *Judgment at Nuremberg* (1961), with Maximillian Schell, Spencer Tracy, Burt Lancaster, and Marlene Dietrich, also brought public attention to Nazi atrocities during the war. The publication of the historian Raul Hilberg's massive book, *The Destruction of the European Jews* (1961), provided one of the first major scholarly analyses of the Holocaust. Using material from German archives and published sources, Hilberg documented the extermination of the Jews in nearly every nation that had been under Nazi Germany's control. Although many readers objected to his assertion that the Jews' failure to offer resis-

Courtesy of Ivan R. Dee, Publisher
Raul Hilberg

tance to Nazi Germany made them accomplices in their own deaths, Hilberg's book received substantial attention from the media and favorable reviews from prominent historians in major publications. Hilberg is widely credited with helping to create Holocaust studies, setting the stage for future Holocaust historians, including Sir Martin Gilbert, David Wyman, Saul Friedländer, and Christopher Browning. In 1985 Hilberg expanded *The Destruction of the European Jews* into three volumes, ensuring its reputation as one of the definitive works about the Holocaust. He has also explored the Holocaust in several other books: *Documents of Destruction: Germany and Jewry, 1933–1945* (1971); *The Warsaw Diary of Adam Czerniakow: Prelude to Doom* (1979); *Perpetrators, Victims, Bystanders: The Jewish Catastrophe, 1933–1945* (1992); *The Politics of Memory: The Journey of a Holocaust Historian* (1996); and *Sources of Holocaust Research: An Analysis* (2001). Discussing his research into the Holocaust with Colin Campbell, a writer for the *New York Times Book Review* (August 11, 1985), Hilberg said, "A lifetime is not sufficient to do justice to it."

Raul Hilberg was born on June 2, 1926 in Vienna, Austria. In his memoir, *The Politics of Memory: Journey of a Holocaust Historian* (1996), Hilberg recalled that his father, Michael, worked as a "middleman," which "consisted of buying household goods for people who needed credit and who paid him in installments."

Raul's interest in politics and history began at age 10, when he received an atlas, which was required reading at his school. "A masterpiece of cartography, it was made for the eye, with maps so finely shaded that they highlighted the distinctions between major and minor rivers, deeper and more shallow waters, higher and lower mountains," he wrote in the memoir. "Railroad tracks were always sketched in red, and cities were shown with circles and lettering denoting their size." Although he never pursued geography due to his shortcomings in mathematics, the atlas led him to discover "the topographical features to the international frontiers. . . . something new: the political world, the world of power." This—together with the outbreak of war in Europe—led to his interest in history.

In March 1938 the Nazis marched unopposed into Austria, unifying the two German-speaking nations in the *Anschluss*, or annexation. In his memoir Hilberg recalled that his father was arrested during a major round-up of Viennese Jews, in November 1938—right after *Kristallnacht*, an outbreak of government-sanctioned violence against the Jews in Germany. Hilberg and his mother, Gisela, were expelled from their apartment at gunpoint, the assailant screaming at them that the Jews had always exploited the German people. "At this moment my mother replied calmly that my father had always worked honestly and that he had never broken the law," Hilberg recalled in his memoir. While in custody Hilberg's father noticed his name on a list with the letter "D" marked next to it. This led him to conclude that he would be sent to Dachau, one of Germany's first concentration camps. He managed to win his release by telling two Gestapo officers about his World War I service, convincing them he wasn't lying by recalling the precise names of his stations, which happened to be in the same area where one of the Gestapo officers had served. Apparently thinking that a war veteran should not be dispatched to a concentration camp, the two officers released him.

The growing anti-Jewish climate in Austria destroyed Michael Hilberg's business. Those who owed him money either could not afford to or refused to pay him. The Hilbergs fled Austria, arriving first in Cuba, and then winning asylum in the United States because Gisela had relatives there. On September 1, 1939, the day World War II broke out, the family entered the United States, settling in the New York City borough of Brooklyn a short time later. Hilberg's parents went to work in a factory in the city.

Hilberg attended Abraham Lincoln High School, in Brooklyn. In his memoir, he described the school's atmosphere as "totalitarian," with students patrolling the hallways and abusive teachers. After his graduation he enrolled in Brooklyn College and also worked part time in a factory. His father urged him to major in chemistry, thinking it guaranteed a viable career. Although he heeded his father's advice, Hilberg preferred literature and history.

Hilberg's studies were interrupted when he turned 18. As he quipped, the U.S. Army "liberated me from chemistry," by drafting him for service in World War II. "I was not wounded and received no medals," he recalled in the memoir. "Unlike so many American soldiers, I was not shelled at Anzio, did not cross the Rapido River, and did not wade ashore under withering fire on Omaha Beach. For years and decades I was told that I could not imagine what it was like."

In April 1945, just before the war in Europe ended, Hilberg's unit arrived in Bavaria, in southern Germany. One night a group of German soldiers attempted to overrun the unit, but were stopped by machine-gun fire. "All over the field the bodies of the Germans lay motionless, rifles stuck in the ground to mark their location," Hilberg recalled. "One corpse was on its back, its eye sockets filled with blood. What, I asked myself, could have compelled these men at this late stage of the war to run into almost certain death?" After marching into Munich Hilberg's unit was housed in the Nazi Party's former headquarters there. While exploring the building, Hilberg discovered crates containing books from Adolf Hitler's personal library.

After his discharge from the army, Hilberg returned to Brooklyn College. He abandoned chemistry, majoring instead in history and political science. He graduated in 1948 and then began graduate studies at the Department of Public Law and Government at Columbia University, in New York City. He became increasingly interested in the Holocaust—in trying to comprehend the series of steps taken by Nazi Germany that eventually led to the extermination of six-million Jews. During his first year of graduate school, Hilberg approached the renowned scholar and Jewish refugee, Franz Neumann, to ask for help on a research paper entitled, *The Role of the German Civil Service in the Destruction of the Jews*. Neumann accepted the proposal and referred Hilberg to Columbia's Butler Library, which housed mimeographed copies of Nuremberg War Crimes Trial documents. These were the first primary sources about the Holocaust that Hilberg examined; over the next few years he would examine thousands of such documents. "The evidence, the facts that came out of the documents . . . were so overwhelming that I said to myself, 'This is what I want to study, and not to study it, not to write about it would be an evasion,'" he said to Marilyn Henry, a writer for the *Jerusalem Post* (March 27, 1997). Hilberg concluded that his original topic was too large for a term paper and, with Neumann's approval, turned the results of his research into a master's thesis. After reading the first draft, which numbered about 200 pages, Neumann asked Hilberg to delete a passage in the conclusion. "It was my statement that administratively the Germans had relied on the Jews to follow directives, that the Jews had cooperated in their destruction," he explained in the memoir. "Neumann did not say that this finding was contradicted by any facts; he did not say that it was underresearched. He said, 'This is too much to take—cut it out.' I deleted the passage, silently determined to restore it to my larger work." Hilberg received his M.A. in 1950.

He remained at Columbia to pursue a doctorate, with Neumann as his dissertation advisor. He wanted to write about the civil, military, industrial, and political aspects of the Holocaust, thereby drawing a comprehensive picture of the Jew's persecution as a massive, highly orchestrated effort. He recalled that Neumann "knew that at this moment I was separating myself from the mainstream of academic research to tread in territory that had been avoided by the academic world and the public alike. What he said to me in three words was, 'It's your funeral.'"

Hilberg went forward with the project, spending the next few years performing substantial research and writing his dissertation. (Neuman's tragic death in a car accident delayed Hilberg's work, forcing him to find another dissertation advisor.) After completing his dissertation, which he titled *The Destruction of European Jews*, Hilberg received his doctorate, in 1955. Columbia University honored Hilberg with the prestigious Clark F. Ansley Award, which recognized excellence in doctoral work in the social sciences. Hilberg was pleased with the award because it included a contract with Columbia University Press to have the dissertation published as a book.

In 1954, while he was still a doctoral student, Hilberg began teaching four courses in American government at Hunter College, in New York City. He supplemented his income by helping the War Documentation Project catalogue new materials that were gradually being released from the German archives. He copied much of the new material by hand, so that he could use it for his own research. In 1956 he accepted an offer from the University of Vermont, in Burlington, to teach in the political science department, where he later received tenure.

Hilberg expanded his dissertation, incorporating more research and adding many more details. The final manuscript numbered 789 pages. Columbia University Press and other publishing houses rejected the manuscript for publication, claiming it was too unwieldy. In April 1958 Hilberg mailed it to Yad Vashem, the newly established Holocaust memorial and research center in Jerusalem, Israel. On August 24, 1958 he received a letter of rejection signed by Dr. J. Melkman, Yad Vashem's general manager. Melkman wrote that although Yad Vashem's editorial board concluded that the manuscript "possessed numerous merits, it also had certain deficiencies," as quoted by Hilberg in his memoir. Yad Vashem's editors asserted that Hilberg relied too heavily on German sources to the exclusion of primary sources in European languages, Hebrew, or Yiddish. The editors also objected to his conclusions about Jewish cooperation with the Nazis, echoing Neumann's criticism years earlier. "Here was the first negative reaction to my manuscript, and these bullets were fired at me from Jerusalem," Hilberg wrote in the memoir. "For ten years I had imagined that the Jews, and particularly the Jews, would be the readers of my work. It was for them I labored. And now this."

Quadrangle Books, a small publisher in Chicago, Illinois, finally accepted Hilberg's manuscript, publishing *The Destruction of the European Jews* in 1961. The book tracks the Nazi's repressive measures against German Jews, including stripping them of their citizenship, forbidding them from marrying non-Jews, or "Aryans," and expelling them from various professions. Sometime in 1941, after the expulsion of Jews from Europe proved impractical (one scheme had called for Jewish resettlement on the African island of Madagascar), the Nazis decided on a "final solution" to the Jewish question: complete extermination. According to Hilberg, this presented the Nazis with a bureaucratic problem; they first had to define what constituted Jewishness, then identify individual Jews, establish the means to round them up, and finally send them to places where they would be worked—often to death—or exterminated. This plan required the coordination and cooperation of many different agencies, including the Nazi Party's political machine, the German Foreign Ministry, the Gestapo, the SS, and the military. Concentration camps had to be built, and the most efficient means of transporting the Jews to the camps also had to be set up. Hilberg's narrative details the administrative handling of the persecution of Jews in each of the occupied and satellite nations. He also repeats the highly controversial argument that most Jews failed to show resistance, and that some cooperated with the Nazis in their own destruction. *The Destruction of the European Jews* received substantial media attention. The British historian H. R. Trevor-Roper devoted 8,000 words to a review for *Commentary* (April 1962), the journal of the American Jewish Committee. "This is not merely a compilation or a recapitulation of the now documented facts," Trevor-Roper wrote. "It is not yet another chronicle of horrors. It is a careful, analytic, three-dimensional study of a social and political experience unique in history: an experience which no one could believe possible till it had happened and whose real significance still bewilders us." A substantial part of the review cited many examples from the book that show how the Jews, who were organized into administrative groups called *Jüdenrate*, or Jewish Councils, often led by rabbis and other community leaders, offered little resistance and even helped to expedite German orders. Although he agreed with Hilberg's thesis, Trevor-Roper predicted—correctly—that many people would reject it. In the months after his review, angry readers flooded *Commentary* with letters and protests. Oscar Handlin, a professor at Harvard University, in Cambridge Massachusetts, published an article in *Commentary* (November 1962) that challenged Hilberg's conclusions, arguing that Jewish resistance to the Nazis had taken place more often than he had claimed. As Hilberg relates in his memoir, Handlin accused him of an "impiety" that was "defaming the dead." Other reviewers, while recognizing the book as a major achievement and a contribution to scholarship, took issue with Hilberg's approach. "The story is told in great detail and is based on painstaking research in all available primary sources of German origin and in some of the writings on the epoch," Jacob Robinson wrote in the *Political Science Quarterly* (March 1962). "The hundreds of footnotes, the dozens of tables, the geographical maps—all bear evidence to the author's conscientious effort." However, like the editorial board at Yad Vashem, Robinson criticized Hilberg for relying too heavily on "German official documents without comparing them with official sources of at least Germany's satellites." Despite—or perhaps because of—its controversial nature, *The Destruction of the European Jews* helped give birth to Holocaust studies. Many more books on the Holocaust, Nazism, and related issues were published over the next few decades.

Raul Hilberg waited 10 years to publish his next book, *Documents of Destruction: Germany and Jewry, 1933–1945* (1971). He edited a collection of reports, taken from German archives, letters, and eyewitness accounts of the Holocaust. "Together with the introductions, this collection serves as a valuable documentary introduction for the layman and a sometimes valuable sampler for the specialist (the source of each document is labeled)," a reviewer for *Choice* (June 1972) wrote. "It supplements a growing literature on the topic with fresh material, evenly balanced, well introduced, and rationally arranged." By contrast, S. M. Batzdorff in the *Library Journal* (August 1972) asserted that the book "will interest students of the Nazi persecutions, but the editor has added little introductory or connecting text. The documents are the book: they contribute no new knowledge, but serve to reinforce what the world already knows through following the Eichmann trial and reading the earlier historical studies."

In 1968 Josef Kermisz, an archivist at Yad Vashem, informed Hilberg that he had the diary of Adam Czerniakow, the chairman of the Jewish Council of the Warsaw ghetto, where hundreds of thousands of Jews were confined in miserable conditions during World War II. The Nazis had established Jewish Councils to help implement their orders and appointed Czerniakow to the position of chairman in the Warsaw ghetto. He recorded his entries in code, so his diary would not be discovered by the Nazis and destroyed. Czerniakow began writing on September 6, 1939, five days after Germany invaded Poland, and stopped on July 23, 1942, the day when he was supposed to have assisted the Nazis in deporting Jews from the ghetto to the death camps. He described the human suffering in the ghetto, and his futile attempts to improve conditions by appealing to the Germans. On the day of his last entry, Czerniakow committed suicide by swallowing a potassium cyanide pill, thinking it was the only noble choice left for him. In his memoir, Hilberg wrote that a Jewish woman named Rosa Braun, who had escaped the Nazis by hiding outside the Warsaw ghetto, had sold the diary for $10,000 to the state of Israel. How she had obtained the diary was unclear. Hilberg concluded that the diary was genuine, explaining in his memoir that "a reading of even half a page convinced me that no one could have possibly made up such a manuscript with its wealth of references to specific occurrences and people." Hilberg believed the diary should be translated into English because it provided a valuable account of life in the Warsaw ghetto. Stanislaw Staron and Josef Kermisz deciphered the diary and translated it into English. *The Warsaw Diary of Adam Czerniakow: Prelude to Doom* was published in 1979 with Hilberg, Staron, and Kermisz serving jointly as editors. Reviewing the diary for the *Washington Post Book World* (April 22, 1979), Peter Osnos wrote that Czerniakow had no choice in obeying the Nazis' orders "to have people turn in their personal possessions or submit to forced labor and other pointless indignities as though there were some governmental, administrative reason for them. Hence the lunacy of Czerniakow's account, a nightmare Alice-in-Wonderland." Osnos described the diary as "remarkable" and "a mirror of that time," adding that the "newsreel effect and the absence of commentary (expect for the elaborate, essential introduction and useful footnotes) makes the message all the more stark." He concluded that as "a chronicle of the ghetto and the personal memoir of a fundamentally decent man in Hades, the diary of Adam Czerniakow makes a deep, deep impression."

In 1985 Hilberg republished *The Destruction of the European Jews*, expanding it to three volumes. He corrected mistakes he had made in the earlier edition and included material from archival sources that had become available. Despite the earlier criticism, Hilberg also stood by his claim that the Jews cooperated with their extermination. "The book marshals a vast array of sources, including archives in Germany, Israel and the United States," the Holocaust historian David S. Wyman observed in the *New York Times Book Review* (August 11, 1985). "It is superbly organized. The scholarship is thorough and careful. All information in it is clearly footnoted. The writing is clear, readable, often graceful." In his review for the *Times Literary Supplement* (March 8, 1995), Michael R. Marrus also lauded *The Destruction of the European Jews*, writing that no "single book has contributed more, even to its critics, to an understanding of Nazi genocide. In its originality, scope and seriousness of theme, this is one of the greatest historical works of our time."

In his next book, *Perpetrators, Victims, Bystanders: The Jewish Catastrophe* (1992), Hilberg explored the roles of many of the parties involved in the Holocaust: the Nazis and their collaborators; the Jews and the Allies; neutral nations; churches; and others. In his review for *Commentary* (February 1993), Edward Alexander asserted, "Readers will find in Hilberg a reliable and shrewd guide to the main topics of Holocaust research, and one still capable of the cold contempt for the killers and their protectors that has always characterized his work." In *Newsday* (September 15, 1992) Jonathan Rosen faulted the book, arguing that Hilberg "has abandoned the approach that made his earlier history so successful: the slow, methodical accretion of crushing fact. Here his chapters are emblematic rather than comprehensive, and his mechanical prose simply cannot meet the challenge of distilling so vast and terrible a subject into such an ambitiously small space."

In 1996 Raul Hilberg published his memoirs, *The Politics of Memory: The Journey of a Holocaust Historian*, in which he recalls growing up in Vienna, attending American high school, writing *The Destruction of the European Jews*, and defending his thesis from attacks. The memoir received mixed reviews. In *Library Journal* (August 1996) Frederic Krome recommended the book for graduate students, noting that Hilberg "gives important insights on research, writing, publishing, and job hunting." Writing in the *Times Literary Supplement* (March 7, 1997), Michael André Bernstein dismissed the book as a spiteful settling of old scores, arguing that "Hilberg seems to remember every slight, every negative review, theoretical dispute, or contrary perspective he has confronted over the years, and his thoroughness of recall is matched by an inability to drop any quarrel in which he was ever embroiled."

In his next book, *Sources of Holocaust Research: An Analysis* (2001), Hilberg argued that the source materials used by historians and scholars to write about the Holocaust should be studied closely to determine their adequacy and reliability. "Indeed, the entire work seems like an exercise in paleography; what saves it from sterility are the anecdotes that bring the people and the tragedy to life," Mark Rotella, Charlotte Abbott, and Sarah F. Gold wrote in their review for *Publishers Weekly* (June 25, 2001). "The result is a dry, academic treatise that resembles a how-to-research-the-Holocaust essay."

Raul Hilberg retired from teaching at the University of Vermont, in 1991. He is married to the former Christine Hemenway, a fellow teacher. The Hilbergs have two grown children, David and Deborah, and live in Burlington, Vermont.

—D. C.

SUGGESTED READING: *Choice* p565 June 1972; *Commentary* p 351+ Apr. 1962, p159+ Aug. 1962, p398+ Nov. 1962, p32+ Feb. 1993; *Jerusalem Post* p5+ Mar. 27, 1997, with photo; *Library Journal* p2496 Aug. 24, 1972, p75 Sept. 15, 1992; *New York Times* C p19 May 30, 1985, with photo; *New York Times Book Review* p3+ Aug. 11, 1985, with photos; *Newsday* p42+ Sept. 15, 1992, with photo; *Political Science Quarterly* p125 Mar. 1962; *Publishers Weekly* p58+ June 25, 2001; *Times Literary Supplement* p3 Mar. 7, 1997, p247+ Mar. 8, 1985; *Washington Post Book World* p5 Apr. 22, 1979; Pacy, James S. and Alan P. Wertheimer, Eds. *Perspectives on the Holocaust: Essays in Honor of Raul Hilberg*, 1995

SELECTED BOOKS: *The Destruction of the European Jews*, 1961; *The Destruction of the European Jews*, rev. ed. 1985; *Perpetrators, Victims, Bystanders: The Jewish Catastrophe, 1933–1945*, 1992; *The Politics of Memory: The Journey of a Holocaust Historian*, 1996; *Sources of Holocaust Research: An Analysis*, 2001; as editor—*Documents of Destruction: Germany and Jewry, 1933–1945*, 1971; *The Warsaw Diary of Adam Czerniakow: Prelude to Doom*, (with Stanislaw Staron and Josef Kermisz), 1979

Hoffmann, Peter

Aug. 13, 1930– Historian

The German-born historian Peter Hoffmann is widely considered to be the preeminent authority on the various groups that loosely made up the German Resistance during Adolf Hitler's dictatorship. Hoffmann's books have been published in several languages and have impressed many reviewers with their detail and extensive use of primary sources. Four of Hoffmann's books are available in English: *The History of the German Resistance, 1933–1945* (1977), *Hitler's Personal Security* (1979), *German Resistance to Hitler* (1988), and perhaps his most acclaimed work, *Stauffenberg: A Family History, 1905–1944* (1995). Despite the many plots and conspiracies that were hatched—including some by disgruntled military officers—the Resistance ultimately failed in its efforts to overthrow or kill Adolf Hitler; it remains, however, a subject of interest among many historians today. "On the one hand, [the Resistance] is proof that there were brave and just people in Germany," Hoffmann explained to Daniel McCabe for the *McGill Reporter* (March 7, 1996, on-line). "On the other hand, there clearly weren't enough of them. It forces people of that era to realize that there were Germans who fought the Nazis and that they were not among them. Certainly, the resistance achieved some things. They managed to save the lives of some individuals but on the whole, it was too small. It was completely ineffectual."

Peter Conrad Werner Hoffmann was born on August 13, 1930 in Dresden, Germany. In January 1933 the Nazi Party, led by Adolf Hitler, took power and established a brutal dictatorship that ruled Germany until its 1945 defeat in World War II. During the war Allied bombing destroyed most of Hoffmann's native city. Many years later, as a doctoral student, Hoffmann learned that his father, Wilhelm, a librarian, had been active in the German Resistance. Wilhelm had played a small role in a conspiracy by army officers to assassinate Hitler by smuggling a bomb into his bunker on July 20, 1944. "One of the men who was hung for his involvement in the assassination attempt could have named my father," Hoffmann told McCabe. "If he had, my father would have been executed."

Hoffmann studied at the University of Stuttgart and the University of Tübingen, both in what was then West Germany. He also spent a year at the University of Zurich, in Switzerland, and briefly attended Northwestern University, in Illinois. After completing his undergraduate education, he enrolled at the University of Munich as a doctoral student. After receiving his doctorate, in 1961, Hoffmann embarked on an academic career. He was a lecturer at the University of Maryland's satellite campus in Heidelberg, West Germany, from 1961 to 1965. Hoffmann also spent a year (1964–1965) lecturing at the German campus of Schiller College, an American institution with campuses around the world. In 1965 he came to the United States, joining the history department of the University of Northern Iowa, in Cedar Falls. In 1970 McGill University, in Montreal, hired Hoffmann as a history professor. In 1988 he was named the William Kingsford Professor at McGill.

In 1963 Hoffmann published his doctoral dissertation as the book *Die diplomatischen Beziehungen zwischen Württemberg und Bayern im Krimkrieg und bis zum Beginn der Italienischen Krise, 1853–1858* ("The Diplomatic Relations Between Württemberg and Bavaria During the Crimean War and to the Beginning of the Italian Crisis, 1853–1858"). Hoffmann had become interested in the German Resistance after learning about his father's involvement in it. "Friends of my father, who were also involved in the resistance, asked me if I would be interested in writing about their experiences," Hoffmann explained to McCabe. "I had nothing else planned, and they offered me access to documents that no other historian had ever seen. To be the first scholar to examine important records. That's almost impossible to resist." In 1977 Hoffmann's book *Widerstand, Staatsstreich, Attentat: Der Kampf der Opposition gegen Hitler* (1969), was translated into English as *The History of the German Resistance, 1933–1945*. In it Hoffmann writes about the opposition to Hitler by senior officials in the military and other German groups, as well as several botched attempts to oust or kill him. A reviewer for the *Economist* (May 28, 1977) wrote, "This admirable book goes right to the heart of the conspiracy to kill Hitler that misfired on July 20, 1944, to the last fascinating detail: the senior officers who could not make up their minds, the junior officers who missed their chances, the sergeant major who interrupted the hero who was actually to place the bomb-in-a-briefcase—Claus von Stauffenberg—so that there was no time to fit enough explosive into the briefcase to kill everybody present when it went off, and the appalling reprisals that Hitler exacted afterwards." The reviewer noted that Hoffmann "combines industry, integrity, sympathy and objectivity to an unusual degree. This is a powerful study of lasting interest, as well as a piece of first-rate scholarly detection." In a more mixed assessment for the *New York Times Book Review* (April 3, 1977), Walter Laqueur wrote, "Hoffmann's study is a valuable contribution toward the understanding of the age of fascism, even though the American publishers have done him a disservice by giving the translation of this painstaking work a title that is overambitious and thus quite misleading, instead of the original German version ('Resistance, Coup d'état, Assassination Plots')." Despite praising the book as the "most detailed and reliable [account] available," Laqueur concluded that "on the personalties involved [in the German Resistance], their motives, their thoughts, it has little to say." Hoffman has published updated editions of *The History of the German Resistance* several times, the most recent in 1996.

Hitler's Personal Security (1979) is a translation of Hoffmann's 1975 volume, *Die Sicherheit des Diktators: Hitlers Leibwachen, Schutzmassnahmen, Residenzen, Hauptquartiere*. "Hoffmann concludes that despite Hitler's supposed unconcern for his safety, he in fact took a keen and even irrational interest in his own protection," a reviewer for *Choice* (April 1980) wrote. "Most of the attempts on his life failed only after security had already been defeated by the would-be assassins." The reviewer concluded, "Although the book has no bibliography, the footnotes are an extensive and useful guide to Hoffmann's sources, and the study includes illustrations, and an index." A critic for the *Economist* (May 5, 1979) wrote, "[Hoffmann] has examined the administrative archives of the various SS bodies responsible for Hitler's safety—so many of them that they often counteracted each other—and counts nearly 50 unsuccessful attempts to kill him. He provides a mass of scholarly detail to support every statement, has some admirable photographs, and concludes of Hitler that 'almost everything he did proved self-defeating in the end.'"

Hoffmann's next English-language book, *German Resistance to Hitler*, was published by Harvard University Press in 1988. In it he provides a brief and general discussion of his previous findings. "After a rather dull introduction on Hitler's rise to power, Hoffmann's story becomes more lively," Peter Alter observed in his review for *History* (February 1990), "as he describes the various groups and personalities in the Resistance from 1933 onwards, the diversity of their thinking and planning for a Germany after Hitler's fall, and their contacts abroad." Reviewing the book for *Choice* (October 1988), D. H. Norton asserted that some of the book's documentation was inadequate, but concluded that it was as "good an account as readers are likely to get for some time."

In *Stauffenberg: A Family History, 1905–1944* (1996), a translation of *Claus Schenk Graf von Stauffenberg und seine Brüder* (1992), Hoffman profiled the German family that is most closely identified with the Resistance. The Stauffenbergs, an old Catholic aristocratic family, initially backed the Nazi regime. They gradually became disillusioned with Hitler, however, because of his reckless invasion of several countries and his efforts to exterminate the Jews. The most famous member of the family was Claus von Stauffenberg, who served in the army as a lieutenant colonel. (Both of Claus's brothers, Alexander and Berthold, were also active in the Resistance.) Assigned to North Africa in 1943, Claus was seriously wounded, losing an eye, part of his right arm, and two fingers on his left hand. After he recovered he joined the army staff in Berlin and hatched an ambitious scheme to kill Hitler. On July 20, 1944 Claus attempted to assassinate the dictator by smuggling a briefcase bomb into his bunker outside of Berlin. After placing the bomb in the room where Hitler was meeting with his aides, he left the bunker. The bomb exploded, but Hitler escaped with only minor injuries. After the failure of the July 20 attempt, Claus and Berthold von Stauffenberg, along with others who were involved in the plot, were arrested and immediately executed. Writing for the *New York Review of Books* (June 6, 1996), Noel Annan praised Hoffmann for describing Claus von Stauffenberg's career in such great detail and "exploring the mind of an energetic, attractive, and outstandingly efficient officer who step by step is driven by his upbringing both to honor and to break the code of the German General Staff." In a critique for the *American Historical Review* (June 1997), Robert W. Whalen also recommended *Stauffenberg: A Family History*, hailing it as a "model of dispassionate historical investigation and exposition" that, like Hoffmann's previous books, made extensive use of primary sources. The reviewer observed that controversy "will undoubtedly continue to swirl around the conspirators of July 20, but it will, one hopes, be informed by Hoffmann's exhaustive scholarship. This book is a both a major contribution to a specific historical discussion and a model of immense erudition, exhaustive research, and intense moral concern."

In 2001 Hoffmann was presented with the Officer's Cross of the Order of Merit of the Federal Republic of Germany. He often writes articles for various scholarly journals and is a frequent contributor to the *New York Times Book Review*. Since 1959 Hoffmann has been married to the former Helga Luise Hobelsberger. They have two children, Peter and Susan. Hoffmann currently lives in Montreal.

—D. C.

SUGGESTED READING: *American Historical Review* p843+ June 1997; *Choice* p276 Apr. 1980; *Economist* p140 May 28, 1977, p133 May 5, 1979; *History* p172 Feb. 1990; *McGill Reporter* (on-line) Mar. 7, 1996; *New York Review of Books* p20 June 6, 1996; *New York Times Book Review* p13 Apr. 3, 1977; Nicosia, Francis R. and Lawrence, D. Stokes. *Germans Against Nazism: Nonconformity, Opposition and Resistance in the Third Reich: Essays in Honour of Peter Hoffmann*, 1990

SELECTED BOOKS IN ENGLISH TRANSLATION: *The History of the German Resistance 1933–1945*, 1977; *Hitler's Personal*

Security, 1979; *German Resistance to Hitler*, 1988; *Stauffenberg: A Family History, 1905-1944*, 1995

Marion Ettlinger/Courtesy of Simon & Schuster

Holden, Craig

1960(?)– Novelist; crime writer

"I flinch a little whenever anyone introduces [me as] 'the mystery writer,'" Craig Holden remarked in a speech delivered in 1999, as archived on his Web site. "It's not that I don't enjoy genre mysteries or thrillers or suspense novels," he elaborated. "It's just that I've never seen myself in that light, and I don't like to think that my future works will follow some set of conventions that will allow them to be fit into a category. But crime offers a fascinating, I would even say unequaled, view into character, into personality." While Holden's books *The River Sorrow* (1994), *The Last Sanctuary* (1995), *Four Corners of Night* (1998), and *The Jazz Bird* (2002)— prominently feature intrigue and mystery and tend to be labeled crime novels or thrillers, readers have often noted his ability to play with conventions and transcend those genres.

Craig Holden was born in about 1960 in Toledo, Ohio, to parents who were both schoolteachers. He attended the University of Toledo, in Ohio, and in 1983 he received his B.A., with honors, in a combined major of psychology, biology, and philosophy. Having planned to pursue a medical career, during his senior year he worked at a medical center drawing blood. He eventually began working there full-time and remained at the job for three years. "I just worked at night, drank too much, and wrote during the days," Holden recalled in an autobiographical statement posted on his Web site. He also worked intermittently as a substitute highschool teacher.

After abandoning his ideas of medical school, Holden decided to seek an MFA degree in creative writing. He applied to three programs and gained acceptance to one, at the University of Montana in Missoula. He moved there in 1984, "firmly believing that writing could not be taught," he wrote, as posted on his Web site. "I went to grad school because I wanted to not have to work full time anymore, and to have more time to write. But to my surprise, Bill Kittredge [a well-known Montana writer] and Earl Ganz [now a professor emeritus] taught me plenty. My real education as a writer began, and during my two and a half years there, I began to write stories that people noticed and responded to." While in Missoula Holden also worked in a lumber mill, taught classes, and edited fiction for *Cutbank*, a literary magazine.

Holden enjoyed editing, and after earning his MFA he took a publishing course given at Radcliffe College, in Cambridge, Massachusetts. (The publishing course has since been moved to the Columbia University School of Journalism, in New York City; Radcliffe has joined forces with Harvard University and is now called the Radcliffe Institute for Advanced Study.) Holden subsequently moved to New York City to look for an editing job, but he was unable to find work. When he ran out of money, he was forced to move back to Ohio, where he taught at a junior college for a year and got engaged to Lisa Dilworth, a legal assistant. In the summer of 1988, he returned to New York City once again; this time he landed a job with a literary agent. (His biggest coup at the agency was selling the movie rights to the Richard Russo novel *Nobody's Fool*.)

In 1989 Holden, by then married, was in need of some quick money. "So I had the brilliant inspiration to write a bad novel, quickly," he told an interviewer for the *Book Report*, as posted on his Web site. "I saw these being sold all the time. Good genre story, mediocre writing. I figured I too could write a bad novel." With the idea that he could draw upon what he had learned during his days as a lab assistant, he decided to write a detective story with a doctor as the protagonist. The project did not proceed as planned, however. "I couldn't write this schlocky book," he told the *Book Report* interviewer. "Instead, I got interested in the characters, and slipped back into the voice I had developed in grad school, and spent four years writing that book." "I realized fairly quickly that if I was going to write books at all, they needed to be good books," Holden told Yuri Kageyama for the Associated Press (January 13, 1995). "I don't ever want to write a book that's not a very compelling story."

Holden's efforts resulted in *The River Sorrow*. The story follows Adrian Lancaster, an emergencyroom doctor in a small-town hospital in southern Michigan. Lancaster, a former heroin junkie, is troubled when familiar faces from his drug-using days start turning up, dead or near dead, around town. Some appeared to have been murdered, and linking the deaths is a strong synthetic heroin, known on the street as Fang, which Lancaster's former girlfriend had a role in designing. When federal agents take the case, Lancaster—who had lost his previous job as a doctor in Detroit when his drug habit was discovered—immediately comes under suspicion. Convinced that he is being framed somehow, he delves into his past and into the underground world of drugs to piece together the answers to the mystery. He receives help from a seductive and mysterious woman named Storm—an addict friend of one of the murdered victims—and Frank Brandon, a police detective who believes in his innocence.

"Holden throws everything but the kitchen sink into *The River Sorrow*, from corrupt politicians, lawless federal agents and figures in mysterious disguises to snowmobile drug deals, high-speed shootouts and tape-recordings from the dead," Chris Goodrich wrote for the *Los Angeles Times* (October 10, 1994). "The potboiler origins of *The River Sorrow* are unmistakable," Goodrich added, "but Holden has transcended the genre with aplomb." In the *Washington Post* (November 13, 1994), Dwight Garner praised the novel as "both intelligent and stripped down, built for speed," and concluded, "*The River Sorrow* is a joy to read for its plot alone; there's a well-delivered surprise around every corner."

In Holden's next novel, *The Last Sanctuary*, a Persian Gulf veteran named Joe Curtis is driving from Detroit to Seattle to come to the aid of his substance-abusing brother when his car breaks down in the middle of North Dakota. He hitches a ride with a young couple, Rick and Kari, followers of an obscure religious cult known as Amonism, who are also on their way to Seattle. In Idaho, however, things go awry, as Joe gets snared into helping Rick hold up a country store—a crime that results in the murder of three men. Joe must run from a host of law-enforcement agencies that includes the local police, the FBI, the Canadian Mounties, and U.S. military intelligence. Also on his trail is Leanne Red Feather, an agent with the Bureau of Alcohol, Tobacco and Firearms (ATF); one of the murdered men was a suspected arms dealer under surveillance by her agency.

"Crowded with lots of near misses and narrow escapes, *The Last Sanctuary* presents deftly realized characters as they are sucked into a shady nether world of cults and militias," James Polk wrote for the *New York Times Book Review* (March 31, 1996). "Holden's balanced view of the cult members conveys understanding without condescension or approval; these folds may be deluded, but they aren't simply evil. Instead, they are seeking real answers to real questions." "*The Last Sanctuary* is a fine thriller, but it goes beyond that as a quick treatise on what's going on in parts of America's heartland," M. R. Aig opined for the Associated Press (June 21, 1996). "Holden has crafted a novel that will keep the reader going and going and going almost breathlessly until the end, when Joe's desperate nightmare becomes an absurd dream of a lifetime." An anonymous critic for *Kirkus Reviews* (December 1, 1995) praised the work as "an artfully crafted and often thought-provoking entertainment that barrels along at a spirited pace."

Speaking of his inspiration for the story, Holden told Margaret Carlin for the *Denver Rocky Mountain News* (May 5, 1996), "I wanted to write a novel set in the Northwest, especially Alaska. I used to hitchhike and camp all through that country, including Canada and Alaska. It always seemed the last frontier to me, a place where people can still hide out, try to live free." One of Holden's sources of information for *The Last Sanctuary* was a friend and former ATF agent, from whom he learned some of the unpublicized details of the standoff between federal agents and the Branch Davidians at Waco, Texas. (The Davidians were a doomsday cult led by David Koresh. On April 19, 1993, following a two-month siege by the FBI, which believed that Koresh was stockpiling illegal weapons, a firefight took place, igniting the Davidian compound and killing most of those inside, including more than 20 children.) "I found out how much I didn't know about modern weapons, about what goes into making a bomb—delayed reaction and that kind of stuff," Holden told Carlin. "Terminology can be tricky too—details about cops, the way they talk and work, law and the courts, the inner workings of the Bureau of Alcohol, Tobacco and Firearms."

Four Corners of Night, Holden's third work of fiction, is a crime story that focuses on the relationship between two cops, Mack Steiner and Bank Arbaugh. Lifelong friends, the two are also partners on the police force. When a 12-year-old girl is kidnapped in their unnamed Ohio town, it is revealed that seven years earlier, Arbaugh's own daughter mysteriously disappeared one day, on her way to a softball game. The mystery has never been solved, but parallels between the two cases start to emerge as the investigation continues. Steiner narrates the story, alternating between the present and flashbacks to the past. He slowly pieces together the clues, and in the process examines the history of his relationship with Bank.

Reviews of *Four Corners of Night* were positive, although some critics voiced minor reservations. Christopher Lehmann-Haupt, in the *New York Times* (January 14, 1999), commented, "The switches back and forth in time are sometimes confusing. The plot grows so complicated that some of its details feel implausible. And here and there, the narrative piles up a few too many words to sustain its threatening mood. Yet everything becomes more or less justified by the surprising turn the plot eventually takes, a twist that makes you reread the first half of the book in wonder at how the story has fooled you." A reviewer for *Publishers Weekly* (October 26, 1998) wrote, "Aside from the astonishing ending, what makes Holden's latest work noteworthy is the depth of the characterizations and the assuredness with which he handles chronological leaps to develop parallel plots and subplots. Holden is an accomplished storyteller who delves deeper beneath the surface with each successive book." Susan Gene Clifford, writing for *Library Journal* (November 15, 1998), called the novel "a compelling and gut-wrenching thriller that will further solidify Holden's reputation as an emerging master of the genre."

Holden received the Great Lakes Book Award, sponsored by the Great Lakes Booksellers Association, for *Four Corners of Night*. In his acceptance speech at the 1999 awards ceremony, as posted on his Web site, he said: "My first two books . . . while being, I think, novels of character as well as of plot, relied fairly heavily on some of the conventions of the Thriller or the Mystery. And that was fine. They taught me an awful lot about writing novels. But when I came to begin what would become *Four Corners of Night*, I felt both emboldened by the two earlier books, and yet also restricted by them." Holden explained that he had difficulty writing the novel and had subjected it to constant revisions, until he realized he had been trying to force it into a mold that no longer applied. "*Four Corners of Night* marked a change for me, a move away from what I saw as the conventions of genre thrillers, and into a realm more of my own imagining."

The Jazz Bird, Holden's fourth novel, was based on a true story—the 1927 murder of Imogene Ring, the beautiful daughter of a prominent Cincinnati lawyer. The assailant was her own husband, George Remus, a notorious bootlegger. After gunning her down in the street, he calmly drove to the police station and turned himself in. Holden's story focuses on the high-profile trial that followed the murder, when Remus entered the then-uncommon plea of temporary insanity and elected to defend himself. When asked how closely he had adhered to the known facts of the case, Holden said in an interview posted on his Web site, "As far as the major characters other than Imogene are concerned, things happen more or less as they happened in real life. The trial is somewhat simplified in the book, because it was Byzantine in its detail, but the basic outline of it and all the major turning points are true to life."

Holden's narrative moves between the drama of the courtroom and the relationship between Remus and Imogene—a flamboyant couple whose wealth and extravagant parties were a hallmark of the Jazz Age. "I like to say that this is a love story in which the man shoots the woman on the first page," Holden wrote, as quoted on his Web site. "It's fascinating to me how you can love someone and at the same moment kill them. That was what was driving the story. But it all came together with the social and political backdrop of the big money, the whiskey, the betrayal, the general loosening of society, the jazz scene, and the overriding ambition that brought Remus down."

The novel was well received. "[Holden] has created a striking, meticulously evoked Jazz Age saga that holds its own with the prose of F. Scott Fitzgerald and John O'Hara," Dick Lochte wrote for the *Los Angeles Times* (January 16, 2002). (There has been speculation that Fitzgerald based the character Jay Gatsby on Remus.) Jeff Zaleski, in *Publishers Weekly* (October 29, 2001), praised *The Jazz Bird* as "deftly written" and added, "The poignancy of the story lies in Holden's uncanny ability to make his creations believable, flaws and all, and in his evocation of the charged and sultry 1920s." "Holden has marvelously blended history, romance, and legal thriller," Susan Clifford Braun noted for *Library Journal* (October 15, 2001). "Reminiscent of E. L. Doctorow's *Ragtime*, this is an exceptional period piece that portrays the roller-coaster life of the Prohibition era with color, verve, and consistency."

Holden lives just outside of Ann Arbor, Michigan, with his wife and their four children. His office is located in an old refurbished factory nearby. He has taught creative writing as a visiting professor at his alma mater, the University of Toledo.

—A. I. C.

SUGGESTED READING: Associated Press Jan. 13, 1995, June 21, 1996; *Kirkus Reviews* Dec. 1, 1995; *Library Journal* p91 Nov. 15, 1998, Oct. 15, 2001; *Los Angeles Times* E p3 Oct. 10, 1994; *New York Times* p9 Jan. 14, 1999; *New York Times Book Review* p18 Mar. 31, 1996; *Publishers Weekly* Oct. 26, 1998, p32 Oct. 29, 2001

SELECTED BOOKS: *The River Sorrow*, 1994; *The Last Sanctuary*, 1995; *Four Corners of Night*, 1998; *The Jazz Bird*, 2001

Holman, Sheri

June 1, 1966– Novelist

In her novels *A Stolen Tongue* (1997) and *The Dress Lodger* (1999), Sheri Holman has succeeded in creating magical bridges that transport her readers back to the wonders and horrors of the past. *A Stolen Tongue* is a kind of mystery set in the 15th century, involving the disappearance of the enshrined pieces of St. Katherine of Alexandria's body. *The Dress Lodger* takes place in early 19th-century England, as the industrial revolution and a cholera epidemic dominate the life of the heroine Gustine, a 15-year-old prostitute, and the novel's other characters, including a surgeon who has engaged in body-snatching in the name of promoting science. Hitting on the elements of the macabre in Holman's writing, Annette Kobak wrote in the *New York Times Book Review* (February 13, 2000, online), "Bodies are at the heart of both novels, bodies dead and alive. But it's the dismembered ones that seem especially freighted with symbolism, with

Jerry Bauer/Courtesy of Random House
Sheri Holman

our age-old anxieties about life, desecration, and the afterlife." Her most recent book, *Sondok, Princess of the Moon and Stars* (2002), is a children's novel that explores the life of a girl who became queen of ancient Silla (part of modern South Korea) at a young age. Holman's next novel, *The Mammoth Cheese*, is expected in mid-2003.

Sheri Holman was born on June 1, 1966 in Hanover County, Virginia. She grew up in a rural area, "the woods," as she described it in an interview with George Dawes Green in *Contents* (April 1997, on-line), "far away from malls and movie theaters and video arcades." In that same interview, Holman described her parents as "not big readers." She chose for herself an eclectic mix of Robert Louis Stevenson and Nancy Drew mysteries. Holman told Green, "My mother encouraged me to tell her stories that she would transcribe, so I grew up with a false idea that an audience existed for my work." Holman majored in theater at the College of William and Mary, in Williamsburg, Virginia.

A Stolen Tongue was published in 1997, after Holman had tried a career as an actor and then gotten a job at a literary agency in New York City. Friar Felix Fabri, the novel's protagonist and a real-life historical figure recreated and fictionalized by Holman, is possessed by an almost superhuman devotion to the long-dead St. Katherine of Alexandria, whom he considers his spiritual bride. In 1483 Felix embarks on a group pilgrimage to Mount Sinai to visit St. Katherine's relics, which rest in various shrines along the group's route, and *A Stolen Tongue* is a kind of travel diary written by Felix along his journey. As the pilgrimage progresses, the travelers discover that the Saint's relics—actual pieces of her body that have been preserved—have been disappearing from the holy sites that housed them. One element of the plot concerns a young woman, Arsinoë, who, possibly suffering from madness, converses with the saint and is called the Tongue of St. Katherine. Felix, meanwhile, is in possession of St. Katherine's actual tongue, his personal relic. During their interview, Green asked Holman whether she identified with the "more plodding and ethical" Felix, or "his nemesis Arsinoë," represented in the novel as "pure passion," according to Green. Holman replied, "Arsinoë is the side of me at 25, when I had my nervous breakdown. I had just moved to New York and suffered a complete loss of self. Like Arsinoë, I existed for, and fed off the idea that I could 'reflect.' I could be anything any man wanted me to be. What that leaves, however, is a completely hollow center. You don't know who you are, and so often, as with Arsinoë—as with many young women that turns into a death wish. I was lucky and snapped out of it. Now, I would identify more strongly with Felix."

In the course of her research for the novel, Holman made her own journey to the monastery of St. Katherine, at the foot of Mount Sinai. The monastery is the oldest in continuous use in Christendom, and because of its isolation in the Sinai desert, it possesses religious icons that escaped destruction at the hands of the iconoclasts. Holman described her arrival at the monastery in an essay that appeared in *Bold Type* (February 1998), a literary magazine published on the Random House Web site. She recounted an encounter with an orthodox nun who had been denied a visa to stay in Jerusalem and, by the end of Holman's visit, was denied the right to stay in a hut on the grounds of the monastery because of her gender. "She has been rejected from Israel," Holman wrote, "and she may be rejected here, but most of God's saints were rejected, she says, and there is holiness in that state."

When Holman was received by the Archbishop of Sinai, Father Paolo, he allowed her a glimpse of the relics of St. Katherine:

I am led into the darkened sacristy behind the altar, where Father Paolo reaches into a box and takes out a small silver ring. Then he moves slowly to a square silver and jeweled box, unlocks it, and holds it out to me. Inside, lying on a bed of silk is a narrow skeletal hand, dark brown and oily looking. Each finger is circled up to the knuckle with diamond rings, even the thumb. This is it, I realize. This is what Friar Felix Fabri traveled months to see, what he, like many pilgrims before him, risked attack, disease, loss of life to venerate. This bit of bone and skin, like other bits of bone and skin in churches the world over, has the power to summon us across seas and over deserts, can command mass migration of men. . . . I lean down to kiss the relic and breathe in the sweetest scent, something like sandalwood and jasmine; faint but unmistakable. I asked Father Angelos [the translator] what it is, but he merely smiles and says, "The grace of God." Holman goes on to describe how Father Paolo touched the small silver ring to this and the monastery's other relics of St. Katherine, which include the top of her head. He then blessed the ring, and put it on Holman's finger. "I feel myself part of that great historical tide, that is for me, faith; seeing clearly my infinitesimal place in it as it rushes past to include all those who will come after—and for that brief instant I *understand*. Then it is gone, and I am left staring at a silver ring I know I will never take off," Holman wrote in the essay.

Holman's empathy for the religious devotions of the past were evident in her novel. As Sybil S. Steinberg noted in *Publishers Weekly* (November 4, 1996), although modern readers might find Felix Fabri's devotion to a dead saint odd, "such eroticized spirituality was not uncommon at the time." The review lauded Holman for pulling "her readers along with odd riddles and careful suspense," and concluded that as "absorbing as . . . her portrayal of the premodern world is, her feel for timeless ironies is also sure: Felix decries the strange, unholy ways of the 'Saracens' while he searches for his dead 'wife,' whose dried-out tongue he keeps in a pouch around his neck." Steinberg called *A Stolen Tongue* "an often enthralling yarn that draws the reader right in among the pilgrims on their harrowing trek." The *Library Journal* (December 1996) reviewer, Rex E. Klett, praised the vividness with which Holman evoked the life and times of Felix Fabri. "Fifteenth-century culture springs to life through the voice of this educated, religious, witty, and well-spoken observer," he remarked. *Mystery Guide* (July 6, 1999), an on-line magazine, termed *A Stolen Tongue* "a superb evocation of mediaeval pilgrimage conditions and a psychological thriller in the truest sense."

Although Holman's second novel, *The Dress Lodger* (2000), is also a historical one, it is set in an entirely different era from that of *A Stolen Tongue*. Its title refers to the protagonist, 15-year-old Gustine, a prostitute who does not own, but merely "lodges" in the expensive dress lent to her by her pimp in order to attract a better class of customer. Gustine lives in the English town of Sunderland in the 1830s, just as the industrial revolution is transforming the lives of the English masses, mainly for the worse, and not long after the Napoleonic Wars have ended. At the same time, fervor for industrial works has swept over England, and Sunderland in particular is the site of a bridge that is one of the wonders of the newly emerging world. In an excerpt from the novel published on its own Internet Web page, Holman describes how "every child in Sunderland, including Gustine, can recite the famous pledge buried inside the foundation stone: 'At that time when the mad fury of the French citizens, dictating acts of extreme depravity, disturbed the peace of Europe with an iron war; we the people of Sunderland, aiming at worthier purposes, hath resolved to join the steep and craggy shores of the River Wear, with an iron bridge.'"

Gustine works by day for a potter, and in her nighttime occupation, as a street walker, she comes across corpses—mainly the victims of a cholera epidemic—and informs a surgeon interested in anatomy of their whereabouts. This doctor, Henry Chiver, has recently come to Sunderland to escape from his former association with the notorious Burke and Hare, Edinburgh criminals who dug up graves and murdered beggars to acquire corpses to sell to medical researchers. Gustine has a baby who was born with an external heart, a rare defect that fascinates and increasingly preoccupies Henry, and the survival of this infant is her most dire concern. Gustine is followed constantly by a malevolent old woman with one eye, called the Eye, who is employed by Gustine's pimp, Whilky, to ensure she doesn't steal the valuable dress. Although the cholera epidemic is the worst since the bubonic plague, the corpses it provides are not enough to satisfy Henry's scientific curiosity, and, according to a description of the book published on the Web site *Bestsellers@Any-Book.com*, Gustine "must turn to her mortal enemy, the Eye, in her battle for the life and afterlife of her only child."

Annette Kobak wrote in her review, "If [Holman] flirts with melodrama, it is only in the way that *Wuthering Heights* does, or the novels of Dickens: that is, it is merely the exuberance of an outstandingly generous and fertile imagination. *The Dress Lodger* is an even better book than Holman's first, with prose that's more limber and vivid—and with, appropriately enough, more heart." Advance reviews, such as the starred one that appeared in *Publishers Weekly* (November 15, 1999), which called the novel a "dazzlingly researched epic," were equally enthusiastic. "Holman . . . delivers a wealth of morbid, authentic detail. . . . The major characters are buttressed by a vivacious cast of minors: Whilky's cowed daughter, Pink; a troupe of traveling thespians; pawnbrokers; rat catchers; and sailors. Holman's style is risky and direct, treating scenes . . . with unflinching emotional precision." Grace Fill, a reviewer for *Booklist* (November 1, 1999), concluded that "Holman's vivid writing, rife with historical social commentary, renders Sunderland's residents and their sometimes macabre interactions disturbingly real."

In her children's novel, *Sondok, Princess of the Moon and Stars* (2002), Holman again reflects on the significance of religious devotion. The book centers on the real-life young Sondok, who in 632 A.D. became the first queen of Silla. Little is known about her reign, except that under her authority Buddhism flourished and that she built the oldest still-standing astronomical observatory in Asia. Holman's Sondok is torn between the powerful influence of Confucianism in neighboring China, the ancient teachings of shamanism, and the modern ideas of Buddhism. In a review for *School Library Journal*, as quoted on *Amazon.com*, Be Astengo called the book "a well-written story that will inspire young readers to learn more about other wise women from Asia."

Holman wrote in *Bold Type* that she continues to wear St. Katherine's ring, and tries never to take it off. "It is my tenuous connection to that moment when I realized that there are people in this world who can see what I, back in New York, have become too sinful to see." Her new novel, "The Mammoth Cheese," will be published in mid-2003.

—S. Y.

SUGGESTED READING: *Bold Type* (on-line) Feb. 1998; *Booklist* p508 Nov. 1, 1999; *Contents* (on-line) Apr. 1997; *Dress Lodger* (on-line); *Library Journal* p150 Dec. 1996, p106 Oct. 15, 1999; *Mystery Guide* (on-line) July 6, 1999; *New York Times Book Review* (on-line) Feb. 13, 2000; *Publishers Weekly* p62 Nov. 4, 1996, p56 Nov. 15, 1999

SELECTED BOOKS: *A Stolen Tongue*, 1997; *The Dress Lodger*, 1999; *Sondok, Princess of the Moon and Stars*, 2002

Jack Slomovitz/Courtesy of Houghton Mifflin Company

Horgan, John

June 23, 1953– Science writer

In his first two books—*The End of Science: Facing the Limits of Science in the Twilight of the Scientific Age* (1996) and *The Undiscovered Mind: How the Brain Defies Replication, Medication and Explanation* (1999)—the science writer John Horgan interviews well-known scientists and philosophers and advances the sweeping, controversial claim that all the great scientific discoveries have already been made. Horgan believes that the best contemporary scientists can hope to achieve is to fill in some of the details of the great scientific paradigms—evolution, general relativity, and quantum mechanics, for example—that have already been discovered. He also asserts that the big questions on the origins of life and the nature of consciousness will never be answered because the human ability to understand these matters is limited. Most reviewers have praised the liveliness of his interviews, the clarity of his style, and the vividness of his portraits of contemporary scientists, but many have denied the validity of his general thesis. His most recent book, *Rational Mysticism: Dispatches from the Border Between Science and Spirituality* (2003), explores the similarities and differences between spirituality and hard science, with an eye towards neither converting agnostics nor dismissing the importance of either religion or scientific advancement.

In an autobiographical note for *World Authors 1995–2000*, Horgan writes: "In retrospect, it seems inevitable that I would become an author of books about the limits of knowledge, but it took me a while to get there. I was born in New York City on June 23, 1953, and spent most of my upbringing in New Canaan, Connecticut. I graduated from New Canaan High School in 1971 with vague fantasies about becoming a novelist. I drifted around the U.S. for several years, doing odd jobs in places like Key West, Nantucket Island, and Tucson, before settling down in Denver in 1975 and starting a house-painting business.

"During this period I wrote dozens of short stories, but none was ever published. In the late 1970s I started taking classes at a small state college in Denver, and in 1980 I moved to New York City after being accepted at Columbia University's School of General Studies. I graduated with a degree in English in 1982, and a year later I received my master's degree from Columbia's School of Journalism. By that time, I had decided that what I really wanted to write about was science, which had fascinated me ever since I was a kid.

"From 1983 to 1986 I worked at IEEE [Institute of Electrical and Electronics Engineers] *Spectrum*, a magazine for electrical and electronics engineers, where I wrote articles about biotechnology, arms-control, intelligence and other national-security issues. Then in 1986 *Scientific American* hired me as a staff writer. I continued covering technology and natural security issues, as I had at *Spectrum*. I also wrote about virtually every major field of science—including astronomy, particle physics, behavioral genetics—as well as mathematics and the philosophy of science. [He wrote about 400 articles for *Scientific American*. In 1987–88 he also taught journalism at Polytechnic University, in New York City.]

"In the late 1980s I became fascinated less with the prospects for progress in science—which is the focus of most science journalism—and more in the limits of scientific knowledge. The initial goad to my thinking was that physicists like Steven Weinberg and Stephen Hawking were proposing that physics might soon achieve a 'final theory' of physics, one that would solve all the major problems of the field. Intrigued by this possibility, I began to question prominent scientists and philosophers of science about what limits, if any, would constrain science in the future.

"My research culminated in my first book, *The End of Science: Facing the Limits of Science in the Twilight of the Scientific Age*, which was published in 1996. In that book, I argued that the glory days of science might be over; scientists are unlikely to discover anything rivaling Darwin's theory of evolution, quantum mechanics, the big bang theory or DNA-based genetics.

"*The End of Science* provoked debate worldwide. One common critique was that research into the human mind will surely yield discoveries as profound as any we have already witnessed. In June 1997, I left *Scientific American* to write a book addressing this point. Published in 1999, *The Undiscovered Mind: How the Brain Defies Replication, Medication and Explanation* examines the many different fields of science that purport to explain the human mind, treat its disorders and replicate it in computers. I argue that, given the poor record of mind-related science thus far, the mind may be in certain respects scientifically irreducible.

"Each of my first two books concludes with a brief consideration of whether mystical experience might yield insights into reality that science alone cannot give us. This possibility will be the topic of my next book, which is tentatively titled 'The Wonder of It All: Searching for the Meaning of Mysticism.' My model (obviously wildly ambitious) is William James's *The Varieties of Religious Experience*, although my style will be more journalistic. What I admired most about James's book was that he managed to be empirical and 'scientific' without succumbing to reductionism.

"'The Wonder of It All' will present the views of people who can talk about mystical experience from the inside and the outside, objectively and subjectively—and who have struggled to reconcile their mystical worldview with modern science. I also want to explore whether mystical knowledge can help answer what for me is the most important of all theological questions: If the universe is unfolding according to some divine plan, why must the plan involve so much suffering for so many innocent creatures?

"I have been married since 1989 to Suzie Gilbert, a children's book author. We have two children, MacNeil and Skye, born in 1993 and 1995, respectively. We live in Garrison, New York, a hamlet just across the Hudson River from West Point."

Horgan became interested in science while studying literary criticism in college. As he wrote in *The End of Science*, he grew frustrated with the lack of certainty in the discipline: "After too many cups of coffee, too many hours spent slogging through yet another interpretation of James Joyce's *Ulysses*, I had a crisis of faith. Very smart people had been arguing for decades over the meaning of *Ulysses*. But one of the messages of modern criticism, and of modern literature, was that all texts are 'ironic': they have multiple meanings, none of them definitive. . . . Arguments over meaning can never be resolved, since the only true meaning of a text is the text itself." Horgan was drawn to science because he thought that clear, concrete answers were more forthcoming in that discipline.

As he studied science in greater depth, however, Horgan realized that science often resembled literature. Like fiction writers suffering from "anxiety of influence" (a term coined by Harold Bloom to describe the difficulty of creating original literature in the shadow of literary giants), scientists struggle to make discoveries on par with those of Isaac Newton, Charles Darwin, and Albert Einstein. More often than not, according to Horgan, scientists are reduced to the practice of "ironic science": "Ironic science resembles literary criticism in that it offers points of view, opinions, which are, at best, interesting, which provoke further comment," he wrote in *The End of Science*. "But it does not converge on the truth. It cannot achieve empirically verifiable surprises that force scientists to make substantial revisions in their basic descriptions of reality." One of Horgan's favorite examples of the limitations of science is superstring theory, which claims to be a theory that accounts for all forces in the universe—in essence, a theory of everything. The theory posits that the most basic element of the universe are multidimensional strings that are much smaller than the smallest particle currently visible with the aid of the most up-to-date scientific instruments. To observe such strings, Horgan points out, would require a supercollider a thousand light years around. (The circumference of the solar system is only one light day around.) Thus, arguing about the validity of superstring theory may be as futile as arguing about how many angels can dance on a pinhead.

For *The End of Science*, Horgan interviewed prominent philosophers and scientists about the limits of their fields. Among the many scientists and thinkers he talked to were physicists Sheldon Glashow and David Bohm; artificial intelligence researcher Marvin Minsky; philosophers Karl Popper and Paul Feyerabend; evolutionary biologist Stephen Jay Gould; Lynn Margulis, proponent of the Gaia hypothesis; molecular biologist Francis Crick, one of the discoverers of the double helix; the linguist Noam Chomsky; and scientists of the mind Gerald Edelman and Roger Penrose.

One of many "end of" books published near the end of the second millennium, *The End of Science* became a best-seller and was translated into 10 languages. In the *New York Times Book Review* (June 30, 1996), Natalie Angier wrote that *The End of Science* is an "intellectually bracing, sweepingly reported, often brilliant and sometimes bullying book." Many critics found the irreverent portraits of individual scientists to be particularly vivid. John Eggebrecht, the reviewer for *Educational Leadership* (November 1996), noted, "Delightful anecdotes reveal the humanity, and often arrogance, of many of those who are interviewed." Tom Wilkie wrote in his review for the *New Statesman* (May 23, 1997) that "Horgan has a novelist's eye for character-revealing detail, and we can almost see, as well as hear these scientists engaging in their passionate arguments. . . . Horgan has both sympathy and understanding." Reviewers disagreed, however, over the substantive claims of *The End of Science*. In the *Smithsonian* (May 1997), Paul Trachtman claimed that Horgan ignored evidence of scientific advances: "As Horgan buries biology, for example, that discipline is just beginning to explore the uncharted terrain of messenger molecules, replacing our concepts of the nervous, immune and endocrine systems with an as yet undeciphered language of peptides." Tom Wilkie had another viewpoint on why scientific research may not be as vibrant as in the past: "Though Horgan's conclusions are wrong, his intuition may be right. Science as we have known it since the second world war is coming to an end, but this is the result of social and economic changes, not the intellectual nihilism that Horgan portrays. Governments, so impressed by the fruits of science during the war, would at one time just give scientists money to go off and do what they wanted, in the expectation that useful technology would surely follow. Now governments want science to pay its way. Simultaneously commercial companies are moving into pure research—and are capturing it as their private intellectual property. The old values of science—knowledge for its own sake, financial disinterestedness, serving the public good—are coming to an end, or at least being transformed."

Horgan again provoked a storm of controversy by publishing an op-ed piece in the *New York Times* (March 21, 1999) in which he chided humans for believing that cures for mental disturbance and even mortality would be found. Entitled "Placebo Nation," the article agreed with the claims of Jerome Frank, a psychiatrist who had written a book warning that the placebo effect might account for most of the therapeutic effect of psychiatric remedies. Horgan concluded that the "latest research supports Dr. Frank's finding: psychiatrists, psychologists and other 'scientific' healers are really exploiting the power of human belief, just as shamans and witch doctors do." Many psychiatric patients and psychiatrists wrote letters in protest, arguing that the latest antidepressants had enabled them to return to normal lives from the depths of depression.

In *The Undiscovered Mind: How the Human Brain Defies Replication, Medication, and Explanation*, Horgan focused on current attempts to understand the human brain. Noting that Congress had declared the 1990s "The Decade of the Brain," Horgan set out to deflate that optimistic projection by interviewing prominent scientists in a variety of brain sciences, including Freudian psychology; psychiatric pharmacology; genetics; evolutionary psychology (which attempts to explain personality and cognition by examining evolutionary history); and artificial intelligence. Despite notable advances in brain scanning technology (positron-emission tomography and magnetic-resonance imaging) and the ongoing discoveries of new aspects of brain chemistry, Horgan asserted that scientists do not have a clue as to how all the disparate elements of the brain form consciousness and selfhood. Horgan has called this problem the "Humpty Dumpty Dilemma." In a *Washington Post* (October 17, 1999) article adapted from *The Undiscovered Mind*, he argued that it is foolish to "hope that neuroscience will be delivered from its current impasse by a genius who discerns patterns and solutions that have eluded his or her predecessors." Still, Horgan doesn't believe that neuroscientists should stop trying or that Congress should stop funding projects to understand the brain. "Neuroscience's potential is so vast that it cannot be abandoned now, or ever," he wrote in the *Washington Post*. "As long as we remain mysteries to ourselves, as long as we suffer, as long as we have not descended into a utopian torpor, we will continue to ponder and probe ourselves with the instruments of science. How can we not? Inner space may be science's final—and eternal—frontier."

Jim Holt, reviewing *The Undiscovered Mind* for the *Wall Street Journal* (September 15, 1999), termed the book "engaging and informative" and "full of fascinating vignettes in which noted brain-researchers are often caught thinking out loud." Yet for Holt, "Horgan disappoints as a philosopher of science" by not having proven his central thesis. In the *New York Times* (October 31, 1999), Paul Churchland suggested that trying to predict what science can't do in the future is as impossible as trying to prove what science can do. "For any puzzling phenomenon, there is an infinity of possible conceptualizations and explanations," Churchland wrote. "Each major success opens a new domain of unseen experimental techniques and new puzzles to go with them in turn. Running out of addressable problems and candidate theories to explain them is the last thing science needs to worry about."

In 2003 Horgan published *Rational Mysticism: Dispatches from the Border Between Science and Spirituality*. In it, he asks how such mystical manifestations as visions, prayer, and trances work scientifically. He also examines how "mystical technologies," including mind-altering drugs like LSD, allow users to feel as if they have experienced spiritual enlightenment. Horgan interviewed many prominent experts for the book, including the scientist Andrew Newberg, the chemist Alexander Shulgin, and the theologian Huston Smith, among others. In a review for *Publishers Weekly*, reprinted on *Amazon.com*, a reviewer noted, "Here and there, the book drops tantalizing hints of a gnostic universe created by a neurotic God terrified of being alone, but it never fully loses the rationalist framework Horgan uses to avoid succumbing to spirituality's alluring excesses. The result is a title with crossover appeal: believers can point to Horgan's willingness to grapple seriously with their tenets, while skeptics can find ample support for the argument that it's all in our heads."

Horgan won the Society of National Association Publications Award for Investigative Reporting, in 1985; the American Association for the Advancement of Science Journalism Award, in 1992 and 1994; the National Association of Science Writers Science-in-Society Award, in 1993; and the American Psychiatric Association Certificate of Commendation for Outstanding Reporting on Psychiatric Issues, in 1997. —S. Y.

SUGGESTED READING: *Bulletin of the Atomic Scientists* p60+ Nov./Dec. 1996; *Educational Leadership* p89 Nov. 1996; *New Statesman* p45+ May 23, 1997; *New York Times* IV p15 Mar. 21, 1999; *New York Times Book Review* p30 Oct. 31, 1999; *New York Times Book Review* (on-line) June 30, 1996 (on-line); *Smithsonian* p128+ May 1997; *Wall Street Journal* A p30 Sep. 15, 1999; *Washington Post* B p1 Oct. 17, 1999

SELECTED BOOKS: *The End of Science: Facing the Limits of Science in the Twilight of the Scientific Age*, 1996; *The Undiscovered Mind: How the Human Brain Defies Replication, Medication, and Explanation*, 1999; *Rational Mysticism: Dispatches from the Border Between Science and Spirituality*, 2003

Tessa Hallman/Courtesy of Penguin Putnam Inc.

Hornby, Nick

Apr. 17, 1957– Novelist; memoirist

Nick Hornby has been called the most successful British author of his generation, an assertion based mostly on the widespread opinion of critics and readers, which holds that his work is accessible and fun to read while remaining true to life and emotionally astute. Hornby's writing focuses on the lives of average young men in contemporary society, who seem to be more committed to their interests in pop culture or sports than to any relationship. As Merritt Moseley commented in the *Dictionary of Literary Biography* (1999), "What Hornby offers to many readers is honesty about emotion and an awareness of the deficiencies of modern men, an awareness that is charming rather than defensive or apologetic." Hornby spent most of his 20s teaching and writing occasional reviews for small literary magazines while attempting to write plays. His scripts were never performed and he soon found himself looking to his interests for inspiration, one of which—his obsession with soccer (known outside the U.S. as football)—became the basis for his highly successful memoir *Fever Pitch* (1992). He then turned to fiction, producing the cult novel *High Fidelity* (1995), about a commitment-phobic record store owner who obsesses about pop culture. Three years later Hornby published a second, equally successful novel, *About A Boy* (1998), which looks at the life of professional slacker and cool guy Will Lightman and his unlikely relationship with Marcus, a 12-year-old boy who gets picked on in school because he does not fit in. His most recent novel is *How To Be Good* (2001), about a liberal young doctor who is about to divorce her slacker husband, only to discover that he has remarkably transformed himself into a decent and upright man.

Nick Hornby was born on April 17, 1957 and spent his early years in the Home Counties, outside of London, England. Though his father, Sir Derek Hornby, is an international businessman, Hornby's upbringing was middle-class. After his parents' divorce, he went to live with his mother and his younger sister, Gill. He spent weekend afternoons with his father, who, in search of a way to entertain and connect with his son, took him to football matches. Father and son began attending the matches of the Arsenal Football Club regularly, and over time Hornby's football obsession grew.

Hornby was educated at Jesus College, in Cambridge, where he received his degree in English. He then worked for a year as a gas station attendant before attending two years of teacher's training at Kingston Polytechnic. He taught English at a comprehensive school in Cambridge, an experience which he claimed helped both his writing and reading, though not necessarily his understanding of people. When asked by Eve Claxton of *Time Out New York* (May 14–21, 1998, on-line) if teaching high school gave him new insight into human nature, Hornby responded, "Well, no, not human nature—only kids' nature, maybe. There's a lot that I was left with as a result of teaching. One of the things was knowing what kind of books I wanted to write. As part of the quest of looking for stuff for kids all the time, I found lots of writers who wrote very simply, and I felt that was the kind of writing I enjoyed."

After deciding to devote his energies to becoming a writer, Hornby moved to London and supported himself by teaching English as a second language. He then took a job teaching English to Korean employees of the Samsung electronics company. In interviews he has claimed that he didn't get serious about his writing until his late 20s, and indeed, at age 35 he still hadn't developed much of a literary career. Though he was a freelance contributor to London's *Sunday Times*, the *Times Literary Supplement*, and the *Literary Review*, by his own admission he seemed to have more success at expanding his ever growing record collection than he did at writing. His first book-length publication came in 1992 with *Contemporary American Fiction*, a collection of essays on American writers of the "dirty realist" school, as it had been defined by *Granta*, a prominent British literary journal. Writers discussed in the collection included Richard Ford, Raymond Carver, Ann Beattie, and Tobias Wolff. Hornby hoped to give British readers the cultural context necessary to appreciate American writers, as well as to convey what makes each of the selected authors worth reading. While this book received some respectable reviews, it was not a breakthrough success.

That same year Hornby published *Fever Pitch*, his memoir about growing up as a fan of British football and his obsession with the Arsenal club. In it, the author delves into the male passion for sports, using his own experiences to illustrate his points. He makes it clear that he does not continue to follow Arsenal because it is an enjoyable experience. In the chapter describing the first match he attended with his father, he writes, as quoted by Merritt Moseley, "What impressed me most was just how much most of the men around me hated, really hated, being there. As far as I could tell nobody seemed to enjoy, in the way that I understood the word, anything that happened during the entire afternoon." Rather, Hornby explains, he watches because he has a pathological connection with every victory and defeat, every brilliant play and foolish move. The book was lauded by critics in both the United Kingdom and the United States, where the book was published in 1994. Matthew Engel, reviewing the book for the *Guardian* (November 28, 1992), wrote, "This one has everything to do with Arsenal, and nothing at all. It is a book passingly about sport, more profoundly about sport's role in our relationships and lives. That has to be said but it probably does Hornby a terrible disservice by making *Fever Pitch* sound boring." In the *New York Times Book Review* (June 19, 1994), Christopher Clarey remarked that "this book is as much about obsession and a sensitive young man's search for direction and community as it is about goals and penalty kicks. It is also wry and relatively accessible, except for the occasional passage that leaves you longing for a British-American dictionary."

In 1995 Hornby published *High Fidelity*, his first novel. As many critics have noted, this book, like *Fever Pitch*, is also concerned with addictions, in this case to making lists and collecting rock albums. The main character, Rob, is a 35-year-old record store owner and world-class failure: his store is going out of business and he has just broken up with his girlfriend, Laura. Unable to commit to anything serious, particularly relationships, Rob and his two store assistants, Barry and Dick, spend their time compiling top-five lists—top five *Cheers* episodes, the top five Elvis Costello songs, and the top five bands who will have to be shot come the next musical revolution, to name a few. Instead of having real emotional reactions to things, Rob fills his life with popular culture, so much so that it becomes the very thing that guides him as he ruminates about his life, especially his relationships with women. Eventually, in an attempt to reunite with Laura, Rob is willing to do what she asks of him, namely, to lose his central philosophy: "That what really matters is what you like, not what you are like." *High Fidelity* was praised on both sides of the Atlantic. "Mr. Hornby captures the loneliness and childishness of adult life with such precision and wit that you'll find yourself nodding and smiling. To his credit, he knows better than to use popular culture as a form of character padding," Mark Jolly noted in the *New York Times Book Review* (September 3, 1995). Jolly concludes, "*High Fidelity* fills you with the same sensation you get from hearing a debut record album that has more charm and verve and depth than anything you can recall." Kathy O'Shaughnessy, in her review for the *Financial Times* (March 25, 1995), called the novel "true to life, very funny, and moving. Hornby writes about relationships, the good things and the petty things. He maps out feelings with rigour, searching out the awkward little emotions we shove aside."

Will Lightman, the main character in Hornby's second novel, *About a Boy* (1998), is a consummate slacker. Because his father wrote a ridiculously popular Christmas song in the 1930s, Will remains very comfortably unemployed. He passes his days smoking pot, watching television, and questioning why his married friends are so obsessed with their children, wondering, even, why anyone would want children at all. However, in an effort to meet women, he starts attending a single-parent support group, which leads to his meeting Marcus, a 12-

year-old boy whose suicidal single mother, Fiona, has taken Marcus away from his pot-smoking father in the hopes of giving him a better life. Marcus is bullied at school, in part because he has not been exposed to popular culture; for instance, he thinks that Kurt Cobain, the late lead singer for the hugely popular band Nirvana, played football for Manchester United. Though Will has spent his whole life avoiding emotional situations, he feels compelled to help Marcus overcome his cluelessness, and he also wants to make sure that Fiona does not go off the deep end. Rob Spillman noted in his review for *Details* (May 1998), "Hornby's naturalistic, slyly comic writing is as effortless and playful as always."

In 2001 Hornby published his third novel, *How To Be Good*. The novel focuses on the disintegrating marriage of Katie and David Carr. Katie, a general practitioner, believes herself to be a good woman, wife, and mother, in part because she tolerates her cranky, frequently unemployed husband, who writes a local newspaper column titled "The Angriest Man in Holloway." After having an affair with another man, Katie decides to divorce her husband, only to discover that David, upon hearing of the affair, has decided to stop being angry instead. He's become religious and struggles to emulate the goodness he reads about in the Gospels. In a review for *Booklist*, as reprinted on *Amazon.com*, James Klise wrote, "Breezy without being shallow, truth seeking (and, egad, spiritual) without being sentimental, Hornby's novel explores the theme of goodness with tremendous fun. The novel's final message seems to be the potentially deadly 'There's no place like home,' but Hornby succeeds, in large part because he's got the heart, the brain, and the courage to prove it quite convincingly."

Hornby is the editor of *My Favourite Year: A Collection of New Football Writing* (1993) and, with Nick Coleman, *The Picador Book of Sportswriting* (1996). He also served as the editor for *Speaking With the Angel* (2001), an anthology of first-person stories by noted writers Dave Eggers, Zadie Smith, Irving Welsh, Roddy Doyle, Helen Fielding, and Melissa Bank, among others. Part of the proceeds for the book were given to autism charities worldwide. In late 2002 Hornby published *Songbook*, a collection of short, personal essays about 31 of his favorite songs and songwriters. The book is packaged with a CD featuring 11 songs, and proceeds were once again given to charity.

Hornby wrote the screenplay for *Fever Pitch*, which was adapted into a film starring the British actor Colin Firth in 1995. A film version of *High Fidelity*, starring John Cusack, debuted in 2000, and the film version of *About A Boy*, starring Hugh Grant, debuted in 2002. Hornby and his wife, Virginia, from whom he separated in 1998, have a son, Danny. Danny, who is autistic, lives with his mother.

—C. M.

SUGGESTED READING: *Salon* (on-line) Mar. 31, 2000; *Details* p84 May 1998; *Entertainment Weekly* p19+ June 12, 1998; *Financial Times* 2 pVIII Mar. 25, 1995; *Guardian* p16 Nov. 28, 1992; *Harper's Bazaar* p128+ May 1998; *Interview* p64 May 1998; *New York Times Book Review* p14+ June 19, 1994, p6 Sep. 3, 1995; *Observer* p16 Mar. 17, 1996; *Time Out New York* (on-line) May 14–21, 1998; *Weekend Guardian* p4+ Sep. 5–6, 1992; *Contemporary Authors* Vol. 151, 1996; *Dictionary of Literary Biography* vol. 207, 1999

SELECTED BOOKS: memoir—*Fever Pitch*, 1992; novels—*High Fidelity*, 1995; *About a Boy*, 1998; *How To Be Good*, 2001; as editor—*Contemporary American Fiction*, 1992; *My Favourite Year: A Collection of New Football Writing*, 1993; *Speaking with the Angel*, 2001

Jerry Bauer/Courtesy of Picador USA

Humphreys, Helen

Mar. 29, 1961– Poet; novelist

Helen Humphreys became a published poet in her native Canada while she was in her mid-20s. Her poetry collections, *Gods and Other Mortals* (1986); *Nuns Looking Anxious, Listening to Radios* (1990); *The Perils of Geography* (1995); and *Anthem* (1999), have won several Canadian awards. Her first published work of fiction, the novella *Ethel on Fire* (1991), was followed by the novels *Leaving Earth* (1998), the story of a 25-hour flight by two women, and *Afterimage* (2000), a fictional portrait of a 19th-century English photographer, told from the point of view of her maid. Reviewing *Leaving*

Earth, Robert Taylor, writing in the Boston Globe (December 16, 1998), referred to it as a "poet's novel, with limpid evocations of space, landscape, and sky." Her latest novel is The Lost Garden (2002), which explores the life of an English woman during World War II.

Helen Humphreys was born in England on March 29, 1961 to Anthony and Frances Brett Humphreys. When she was three years old, the family moved to Canada. Humphreys grew up in Kingston, Ontario; she taught for a time in the continuing-education division of Ontario's George Brown City College. Beginning in 1989, she pursued an editorial and research career at Resources for Feminist Research, a scholarly journal published by the Centre for Women's Studies in Education at the University of Toronto.

Humphreys starting her writing career by publishing several volumes of poetry. The first, Gods and Other Mortals, dealt with subjects ranging from her own life to retellings of Greek myths; the volume was praised for Humphreys's use of words as "flares sent up in desperation," as the reviewer for the Toronto Star put it. The collection Nuns Looking Anxious, Listening to Radios appeared in 1990. Humphreys published her first work of fiction, the novella Ethel on Fire, in 1991. It was brought out under the aegis of a small press and did not receive major attention.

In The Perils of Geography, Humphreys's 1995 volume of poetry, she focused on metaphors involving space: "Distance is narcotic, ride it to / the brink of stupor. Grit in your teeth, / cramp in your throttle hand. Pebble shot / of bees and rough rasp wind. Take / the straight line through the corners," she wrote in "Motorcycle Lesson." Lee Anne Phillips, writing in Women's Books Online (July 11, 1996), termed The Perils of Geography "very lean and physical poetry" filled with "crystaline poems," in which "Humphreys examines closely the maps that chart the ways people lose each other, themselves, half-starved and alone in the wide presence of the world. . . . Sometimes distance looks like freedom, the road beckons like a lover, like the rush of speed or drugs, . . . but all too often it looks up close like the empty maps that fail to span wide oceans, like the far journey we have yet alone to go. . . ."

Anthem, Humphreys's 1999 collection, was nominated for the Pat Lowther Award for best book of poetry published by a woman and won the 2000 Canadian Authors Association Award for Poetry. Reviewer Anne Simpson wrote in the Antigonish Review (January 5, 2000) that Humphreys "takes poetry back to its in lines like these: 'Wanting is a word that fills / and empties, a word that, like the sea, remembers / itself each time differently.'"

Leaving Earth, Humphreys's first full-length work of fiction, was widely celebrated for capturing the era of the Great Depression, in which people, despairing of finding joy on Earth, looked to the skies to provide them with wonders and to such heroic figures as airplane pilots to supply the glamour that could not entirely be captured by movies. In Leaving Earth, a famous aviator, Grace O'Gorman, tries to beat her husband's record for continuous flying by staying aloft, in a plane called Adventure Girl, over the Toronto lakefront for 25 days. When her chosen co-pilot is unable to accompany her, she is forced to choose an inexperienced young woman as her companion. The novel also follows the 12-year-old, hero-worshiping Maddy, who wants Grace for her "real mother."

The fliers in the novel may exhaust themselves, but, as Carolyn See wrote in the Washington Post (October 2, 1998), "within fatigue lies the possibility of transcendence. On Earth, nobody cares. Only Maddy really yearns for them; only Maddy keeps track. Every other character here is caught in the pressing exigencies of the real world." See termed the book "beautifully written, extremely controlled" and noted that it is partially about "the limits and extensions of language." The critic found, as well, that "the earthbound sections are far more vivid" than those about flight, comprising "a condensed, controlled encyclopedia of flimsy diversions in a menacing world. Great Depression pastimes of the poor—boxing, flying, dancing, marching, flagpole-sitting, rowing, racing, going to fairs, watching fireworks displays—all show a great and dizzy courage."

David Willis McCullough, writing in the New York Times Book Review (October 25, 1998), also found that the book provides a good sense of the time in which it is set: "The Great Depression is not quite over. Camps for workers have been set up near the city. Hitler is becoming a disturbingly familiar name. A gang of pro-Nazi blueshirts roams the amusement park midway." McCullough praised in addition Humphreys's "spare uncluttered prose," her "great knack for evoking unspoken love," and her talent for "finding stark beauty in matters as diverse as the sight of a burning ship at night or the creation of a silent language." Humphreys won the 1998 Toronto Book Award for Leaving Earth.

Afterimage, Humphreys's 2000 novel, takes place in England in the mid-1860s. Its central character, Isabelle Dashell, who is loosely based on Julia Margaret Cameron, a pioneering photographer, avoids grieving for her stillborn children by immersing herself in taking photographs for which her household servants and the local village people are models in tableaus that she creates. Her husband, Eldon, is a would-be explorer and mapmaker who never leaves home. Into their household comes a new maid, Annie Phelan, who uses reading as an escape from her own deprived past: her parents died in the Irish potato famine, and she was raised in a workhouse. Annie harbors hopes that her new post will make her life comparable to that of Jane Eyre, the eponymous heroine of Charlotte Brontë's novel. Instead, she is fated to become Isabelle's principal model.

"Eldon's character is often obscured by his sadness," Andrea Barrett wrote in the New York Times Book Review (April 15, 2001), "while Isabelle, more sharply drawn, exists almost entirely in the intensity of her longing to make photographs: 'Art is like a light,' she says to Annie. 'Isn't it? Always burning with the same brightness, no matter how long we've been gone from the room.' But Annie . . . is fully imagined and gloriously herself. . . . Immensely touching . . . Annie is altogether admirable, sometimes perhaps too much so. When her own fumbling first efforts with the camera give Isabelle the key to a new photographic technique, or when a casual comment reshapes Isabelle's thinking about proper representations of women, Annie can seem both too good to be true and anachronistic, her character shaped by class and gender issues that belong to our time and not hers."

The reviewer for the Washington Post Book World (April 1, 2001), John Freeman, saw the character Annie from another viewpoint. "While Humphreys deftly depicts the couple's desire to transform their servant, she's less skilled at fleshing out Annie's interior life. Nevertheless," he concluded, "*Afterimage* builds elegantly toward its crescendo, in which Annie is forced to choose whether to continue her modeling for Isabelle or to look into the terra incognita of her own past." Humphreys won the Rogers Writers' Trust Fiction Prize for *Afterimage*. Ruth Gledhill, writing in the London Times (August 12, 2000, on-line), praised the book thus: "In *Afterimage*, every phrase is succinct, every sentence perfectly balanced. So beautifully written, it leaves its own lasting poetic image on the mind." Others have seen the same poetic elements in all of Humphreys's writing.

In 2002 Humphreys published a new novel, *The Lost Garden*, which explores an English woman's search for her place in a world ravaged by World War II. Gwen Davis is a horticulturist who leaves London to manage a team of women growing vegetables on a country estate as part of the war effort. Struggling to manage her young charges—who are more interested in the Canadian soldiers stationed nearby than in growing crops—she finds herself involved in a love affair, with alcoholic Captain Raley. In a review for *Publishers Weekly*, as quoted on Amazon.com, a critic observed: "Humphreys renders convincingly [Gwen's] first, fleeting experience of deep friendship and love. Unfortunately, the story is sometimes marred by overwrought or cloying prose, though Humphreys's language also has its moments of elegance (during the blitz, "houses become holes. Solids become spaces. Anything can disappear overnight"). Humphreys doesn't quite have the narrative energy of Pat Barker and Jane Gardam, but fans of those authors may enjoy this exploration of the impact of WWII on English life."

—S. Y.

SUGGESTED READING: *Antigonish Review* (on-line) Jan. 5, 2000; *Boston Globe* E p4 Dec. 16, 1998; *Economist* (on-line) May 3, 2001; *New York Times* p14 Aug. 12, 2000; *New York Times Book Review* p25 Oct. 25, 1998; *Washington Post* D p2 Oct. 2, 1998; *Washington Post Book World* p15 Apr. 1, 2001; *Women's Books Online* July 11, 1996

SELECTED BOOKS: poetry—*Gods and Other Mortals*, 1986; *Nuns Looking Anxious, Listening to Radios*, 1990; *The Perils of Geography*, 1995; *Anthem*, 1999; fiction—*Ethel on Fire*, 1991; *Leaving Earth*, 1998; *Afterimage*, 2000; *The Lost Garden*, 2002

Glenn Hunter/Courtesy of Aislinn Hunter

Hunter, Aislinn

1969– Short-story writer; poet; novelist

In 2001 Aislinn Hunter established herself as a promising young Canadian writer with the publication of two books, *What's Left Us*, a collection of her short stories, and *Into the Early Hours*, a poetry collection. *What's Left Us*, which explores religious themes and portrays affecting characters in difficult situations, won wide critical acclaim. *Into the Early Hours* was a finalist for the 2002 Dorothy Livesay Poetry Prize (named for a well-loved Canadian poet and bestowed by the British Columbia Teachers' Federation) and won the 2002 Gerald Lampert Award (presented by the League of Canadian Poets). In 2002 Hunter's first novel, *Stay*, was published to critical acclaim in Canada.

Aislinn Hunter writes for *World Authors: 1995–2000*: "I was born in Belleville, Ontario in the autumn of 1969. Growing up my family moved every year or two to a new, developing Ontario town, following my father who was a Xerox salesman. In

1973 I was the only kid I knew who had a photocopier in my house. My love of books started with that monstrosity of a photocopier and the hours I spent photocopying the best parts of my bedtime story books. I started writing in grade two, the first thing being a poem for my mom, a bad poem, but one that said something important to me, a poem that talked about how much I loved her. My parents didn't particularly encourage me to write, we weren't a literary family in the least, and for a large part of my childhood I was naive in terms of world literature. When I reached the age of twelve a huge void opened up in terms of what kinds of books I could get my hands on. In the end I read anything I could find—my sister's high school English books (Timothy Findlay's *The Wars*) or the romances on my mother's bookshelf. A year later I told my mother I wanted to read a book called *Ivanhoe*. She promptly took me to the University of Windsor bookstore and bought me a copy. That was when my love affair with reading began. And it wasn't just Scott's epic romance, it was being in that grown-up bookstore and realizing just how many books there were to read, how many worlds those books contained.

"I started writing seriously in University. Patrick Lane, the poet, walked into my first year creative writing class at the University of Victoria and he read us a Gwendolyn MacEwan poem, 'Gahzala's Foal.' My world shifted off its axis and I remember looking around to see if anyone else felt what I felt. Jack Hodgins was another mentor at UVic. My first two books are really the result of all my experiences until then—living in Ireland in particular—and the rush I got from working with such great writers.

"In terms of inspiration I'd say I'm inspired by a mix of my own ideology and by people and places. I write about a way of seeing the world that is ultimately, I hope, optimistic, meliorist. I write about Ireland and history and love. I'm afraid of being sentimental in my work which is, I hope, an optimist's way of censoring their work. My work has been influenced by a number of Irish and Canadian writers, mostly poet-novelists like Dermot Healy, Michael Ondaatje, Seamus Deane and Anne Michaels. Though early on I was reading all these great women like Lorrie Moore, Jeanette Winterson, Anne Enright and Janice Galloway, Elizabeth Smart, very strong, feminine voices. It was exciting back then to realize I didn't have to write like Alice Munro or Flannery O'Conner, two amazing writers who didn't really excite me much as a reader. I love them now, but at the start I wanted more passion, less control.

"One of my central preoccupations, and something that shows up in my story collection *What's Left Us* and in my poetry collection *Into the Early Hours*, is the question of place and heritage and home. Having moved a lot as a child I think it's in me to be unsettled, but I also think that I'm looking for a sense of history that we, in Canada, don't really have. Ireland is 'home' in the sense that a part of me is more attuned, more comfortable there, and that's why I think the writing comes back to Ireland again and again. And the Irish writers have a way with language, a cadence, a general air that seems to go beyond what I've found anywhere else. There have been times in my life, especially recently, when I've queried how a writer can be good, and I mean really good, at more than one genre. There is a mentality in the literary world that demands that a writer stake his or her claim in either the world of poetry or fiction. I have always felt an equal affinity to both. But there came a time in 2000 when I was writing in both genres and working as a backfill producer/broadcaster on an arts show at CBC Radio. That's when I realized that a person can't be good at everything, that it's impossible to split yourself up into different people and wow everyone. For a while I started thinking I should throw my hat into one ring or the other, master the craft of one genre. I dropped the radio work. My first two books came out. Things were going okay. Then the nominations came. Two for *What's Left Us* and two for *Into the Early Hours*. I am not a believer in awards in so much as I am totally aware of their subjective nature. A different day of the week, a different experience in the juror's morning might mean someone else ends up on the short list. But to be nominated twice for each book was incredible. It was the boost I needed.

"[My first novel] *Stay* was published in October 2002. The story is set on the west coast of Ireland and follows Abbey, a young Canadian, her 55-year-old lover, Dermot, and the local villagers of Spiddal. It centres around the excavation of a local bog body, the filming of an Irish soap opera and the tourism boom in Ireland. This is a book about our relationship with history, how we can become mired in it even when the world is carrying on.

"Right now I'm looking to the next project and I'm teaching which is a privilege and a good deal of fun. I'm eying the East Coast and a cottage in Sligo and consulting my husband on some kind of five year plan. Mostly I'm thinking about the craft—or crafts—because fiction and poetry are each their own set of equations. But in the end, I think, the answer is the same. We write and we read to know ourselves and our world better. To be outside of ourselves, sure, but ultimately to place ourselves on a larger map, to step back and say 'of course' as if we always knew we were there, right there, exactly, but moving in new and demanding directions."

Aislinn Hunter graduated from the University of Victoria, in British Columbia, with a BFA degree. She then received her MFA from the University of British Columbia, in Vancouver. For several years Hunter lived in Dublin, Ireland. After returning to Canada, she began teaching creative writing at the University of Victoria.

The first half of *What's Left Us* is composed of six short stories, including "Hagiography," about a young Catholic girl who tests her faith by going to work at a theater in Dublin that shows pornographic films; "We Live in This World," about a woman in Vancouver trying to hail a taxicab during a rainstorm; and "The Last of It," in which a Canadian writer visits her boyfriend in Dublin. The stories are followed by the title novella, which follows Emma, a single woman who is eight months pregnant, as she traces her baby's family roots in Ireland. Reviewing the book for the *Vancouver Sun* (May 19, 2001), Annabel Lyon wrote, "Reading [the first six stories] straight through is rather like watching a jeweler try the same stone in a series of different settings, each finely worked, each striking slightly different lights off the facets of a single theme." Lyon observed that Hunter "is concerned with love—love of God, of husbands, of sisters and brothers and boyfriends and guys in argyle socks at the bus stop—and the way characters lose something in themselves when they love others." Citing Hunter's "wry wit and intelligence," Lyon concluded that *What's Left Us* "is alive and kicking, a strong healthy debut that's cute and fierce and wails like a banshee." In a review for the *Hamilton Spectator* (July 21, 2001), Judy Pollard Smith found Hunter's work "an interesting blend of both Canadian and Irish culture." She opined, "Hunter writes in a witty, clear style with vivid metaphors to enhance the reader's perceptions." As an example Smith quotes lines from "We Live in This World," in which the heroine describes her mother as a "secretary in a secretarial pool . . . which evokes an image of [the swimmer and actress] Esther Williams. Sometimes I've imagined her and her co-workers sitting at their desks in rubber swim caps, wearing nose-clips. I imagine for sport they practice synco-typing, flipping their feet around under the desks as if they're in a wading pool."

Into the Early Hours, Hunter's volume of poetry, also received critical attention. In his review for the *Vancouver Sun* (February 16, 2002), George Fetherling wrote, "Hunter's stance is engaged and participatory as well as withdrawn and analytical. Her discourse is calm, measured—and often startling." As one example of the poems' sometimes startling nature, Fetherling quotes the lines "The slim-wristed dead are with you again, / in their ruffled blouses and long white skirts." He noted that Hunter's imagery occasionally references such other poets as Stephanie Bolster and Gwendolyn MacEwen. "But such acts of homage proceed from self-assurance," he observed. "How rare it is to find a genuine ambidexter, equally gifted in fiction and poetry." Writing for *Eye* (January 17, 2002, on-line), Kevin Connolly was less impressed by the collection: "The noted Vancouver short-fiction writer has the smooth, writing-school currency down cold," Connely wrote. "Even the titles ('What We Have,' 'Burning Ground') shiver with borrowed import, while individual pieces labour with an affected poeticism suggesting learned rather than discovered craft. At times, Hunter is so brazenly derivative she leaves you speechless." In 2002 *Into the Early Hours* was nominated for the prestigious Dorothy Livesay Poetry Prize and won the Gerald Lampert Award.

In Hunter's first novel, *Stay* (2002), a young Canadian woman named Abbey visits Spiddal, a small town on the Irish coast. Abbey meets and eventually falls in love with Dermot, a 55-year-old former university professor who was fired for having an affair with a student. Both characters are forced to address their painful pasts and watch as Spiddal's status as a tourist spot gradually changes the town. In her review for the Toronto *Globe and Mail* (October 12, 2002), Michelle Berry wrote that Hunter "tackles the theme of time and all its implications—ever-changing and moving, elastic and stiff. She plunges us through history to the present and back again with ease." Berry concluded that for "all the complexity in Hunter's rich book—the compounding of character, narrative, history and an arching, multi-layered plot—there is also a certain quietness and simplicity to the prose, a minute attention to detail and an elegance in the natural dialogue. Hunter heaps ideas on you, ideas you want to stop and think about, in such a subtle, tender way that you never feel assaulted, but rather protected."

Aislinn Hunter has contributed to two anthologies, *Write Turns, New Directions in Canadian Fiction* (2001) and *Constellations: 20 Years of Stellar Poetry from Polestar* (2001). Hunter and her husband make their home in Vancouver.

—D. C.

SUGGESTED READING: *Eye* (on-line) Jan. 17, 2002; Toronto *Globe and Mail* D p15 Oct. 12, 2002; *Hamilton Spectator* M p11 Jul. 21, 2001; Raincoast Books Web site; *Vancouver Sun* E p18 May 19, 2001, D p18+ Feb. 16, 2002; Writer's Union Web site

SELECTED BOOKS: poetry—*Into the Early Hours*, 2001; short fiction—*What's Left Us*, 2001; novels—*Stay*, 2002

Huntford, Roland

1927– Nonfiction writer; biographer; journalist

Trained as a reporter, Roland Huntford has produced some of the most thoroughly researched biographies available. He has frequently written about explorers, including several that hail from Scandinavian countries. His first such effort, *Scott and Amundsen* (1979), a dual portrait of explorers on competing quests to reach the South Pole, was adapted as a seven-part PBS documentary called *The Last Place on Earth*. In addition to two other important biographies, *Shackleton* (1985) and *Nansen: The Explorer as Hero* (1997), he has written a critique of the socialist government in Sweden and a historical novel.

Little has been written about Roland Huntford's early life. He was born in 1927 in England, and he served as a foreign correspondent for the London *Observer* in Stockholm, Sweden. His interest in Scandinavia was not confined to his journalistic output; he eventually began writing full-length books about the region, its history, and notable figures of Scandinavian descent. The first of these books is *The New Totalitarians* (1972), a treatise condemning the Swedish government as an oppressive bureaucracy that sought to stifle any signs of individuality among its citizens. In the *New York Times Book Review* (February 27, 1972), P. B. Austin wrote: "There is no doubt that [Huntford's] critique, if at times heavily loaded with pejorative epithets, not to say slanted facts . . . is extraordinarily acute. It is a major study by an unsympathetic observer of Swedish social democracy in all its aspects." A reviewer for *Choice* (June 1972) called the book a "polemic" and wrote, "Many native Swedish critics have analyzed the conformity, group-mindedness, personal timidity, and cultural sterility of their countrymen, and Huntford performs a service by raising these issues in an English language forum. His presentation is weakened, however, by his serious misinterpretation of Swedish history."

For his next book Huntford turned to historical fiction. *Sea of Darkness* (1975), which was not widely reviewed upon publication, follows a young Christopher Columbus, who travels aboard a Norwegian ship to the Americas—some 20 years before his famed 1492 expedition. With *Scott and Amundsen*—republished in 1985 as *The Last Place on Earth* in connection with the PBS documentary—Huntford details the extraordinary competition between Robert Falcon Scott, an Englishman, and Roald Amundsen, two early-20th-century explorers who raced each other to be the first man at the South Pole. Amundsen beat Scott to the Pole by a month, arriving on December 14, 1911. When Scott arrived, on January 18, 1912, he and his party were depleted by the 81-day trip and sorely disappointed in their failure to be first at the site. The weather was particularly bad during their return trip, and Scott and his four companions perished 11 miles from their base. Still, Scott was considered a national hero, and his widow was given a knighthood in honor of his bravery and patriotism.

Huntford challenges this picture of the English explorer. He portrays Scott instead as a reckless and unprepared leader who sacrificed his crew because of his pride and lack of foresight. By contrast, Huntford depicts Amundsen, who is frequently overlooked by historians, as a paragon of resourceful determination. The dual biography was widely lauded in the press. Gwyn Jones, in the *New York Review of Books* (July 17, 1980), wrote, "Roland Huntford has written a book which is at once exciting and sobering. . . . It is not just a retelling, however knowledgeable and purposeful, of an old story. It is a thoughtful and thought-provoking study." A reviewer for the *New Yorker* (June 2, 1980) praised the work with similar zeal, writing, "It is a skillful and probing study of the contrasts in character between the Norwegian and the Englishman, out of which comes a new appraisal of Captain Scott. . . . Mr. Huntford has done a vast amount of research for this book, and he relates his iconoclastic story without relish."

In 1985 Huntford published *Shackleton*, a comprehensive biography of the English explorer Sir Ernest Henry Shackleton, who attempted three expeditions to the South Pole during the early 20th century, each ending in failure. M. C. Mangusso wrote for *Choice* (May 1986), "Students of Edwardian England will learn why the British of that era approached Antarctica with horses and grim determination but without dogs, skis, or Scandinavian-style common sense." J. F. Husband, in *Library Journal* (January 1986), wrote: "Huntford . . . has written the definitive life of Shackleton. Some readers may be shocked by the negative portrayal of Scott, Shackleton's rival, and the revelations of British ineptitude in polar exploration, and others may be overwhelmed by the profuse detail, but this book belongs in all exploration collections." Peter S. Prescott, in *Newsweek* (January 13, 1986), agreed: "To read so exhaustively detailed a book leaves a reader feeling as if he had stumped over the glaciers himself. Shackleton's personality is, in the end, of only limited interest, and he dealt exclusively with men less interesting than he. We are left with what he did, and its staggering physical and psychological cost. . . . [Huntford's] is a story of masochism on a heroic scale, and he has told it very well."

Huntford's next work, *Nansen: The Explorer as Hero*, is a thoroughly researched biography of the Norwegian explorer and humanitarian Fridtjof Nansen, who won the Nobel Prize for Peace in 1922. Known for his early exploration of Greenland, later in life Nansen became a diplomat; he assisted in the separation of Norway from Sweden in 1905, repatriated prisoners of war from Germany and Austria-Hungary after World War I, found homes for the 1.5 million refugees from the Russian Revolution of 1917, and rallied a relief effort for starving Soviets in 1921. Reviewers had little but praise for Huntford's biography. In the *Atlantic Monthly* (August 1999), Phoebe-Lou Adams wrote: "Mr. Huntford, with much material to quote from and a lively period in both exploration and politics to cover, has produced a splendid biography of a splendidly versatile man." Annette Kobak, in the *New York Times Book Review* (May 16, 1999), was equally enthusiastic: "A great virtue of Huntford's extraordinarily well-researched book is that it allows one to ponder the cost of the ideas Nansen so energetically lived up to. . . . Huntford is masterly at weaving Nansen's life into his times."

Roland Huntford is also the editor of two books, *The Amundsen Photographs* (1987) and *The Sayings of Henrik Ibsen* (1996).

—*C. M.*

SUGGESTED READING: *Atlantic Monthly* p94 Aug. 1999; *Choice* p596 June 1972; *Library Journal* p79 Jan. 1986; *New York Review of Books* p33 July 17, 1980; *New York Times Book Review* p6 Feb. 27, 1972, p16 May 16, 1999; *New Yorker* p139 June 2, 1980; *Newsweek* p66 Jan. 13, 1986

SELECTED BOOKS: fiction—*Sea of Darkness*, 1975; nonfiction—*The New Totalitarians*, 1971; *Scott and Amundsen*, 1979 (republished as *The Last Place on Earth*, 1985); *Shackleton*, 1985; *Nansen: The Explorer as Hero*, 1997; as editor—*The Amundsen Photographs*, 1987; *The Sayings of Henrik Ibsen*, 1996

Courtesy of Princeton University Press

Ignatieff, Michael

May 12, 1947– Novelist; historian; biographer; memoirist

The Canadian-born writer Michael Ignatieff has made his mark as a novelist, memoirist, historian, biographer, and talk-show host and producer and writer of documentaries for British television. His two novels are *Asya* (1991), which traces the life of a woman born into the Russian nobility in 1900, and *Scar Tissue* (1993), about the narrator's loss of his parents and the breakup of his marriage. His book *The Russian Album* (1987), a family memoir, won Canada's Governor General Award and the Heinemann Prize of Britain's Royal Society of Literature in 1988. His highly praised *Isaiah Berlin: A Life* (1998), about the life and work of the distinguished philosopher, diplomat, writer, and college president, is "a masterpiece of contemporary biography," according to John Gray in the *New Statesman* (November 20, 1998). In *Blood and Belonging: Journeys Into the New Nationalism* (1994), *The Warrior's Honor: Ethnic War and the Modern Conscience* (1988), and *Virtual War: Kosovo and Beyond* (2000), Ignatieff provided eyewitness accounts of armed conflict in a half-dozen of the world's hot spots, along with insightful discussions of the nature and implications of contemporary nationalistic fervor and ethnic pride. In his review of *Blood and Belonging* for *New York Newsday* (April 7, 1994), Richard Eder wrote, "Ignatieff has admirably used a cosmopolitan sensibility to find what is recognizable and human in what, to him and to many of us, seems most strange." Ignatieff's most recent book is *Human Rights as Politics and Idolatry* (2001), a collection of essays by him and a number of other authors. For more than 15 years, Ignatieff has contributed articles to the *New York Review of Books*, a journal of ideas as well as reviews. His byline has also appeared in the *New York Times Magazine*, the *New Yorker*, the *New Republic*, the *Wilson Quarterly*, and the *World Press Review*, among other periodicals.

Michael Ignatieff was born on May 12, 1947 in Toronto, Ontario, Canada, to George Ignatieff and the former Alison Grant. His mother was an artist; his father, a diplomat. In 1958 and 1959, when George Ignatieff was serving in the Canadian embassy in Yugoslavia, the family lived in Belgrade. Ignatieff attended the University of Toronto, where he received a B.A. degree in 1969. As an undergraduate, from 1966 to 1967, he worked as a reporter for the Toronto *Globe and Mail*. In 1971 he became a teaching fellow at Harvard University, in Cambridge, Massachusetts. He earned a Ph.D. in history from Harvard in 1975 and a master's degree from Cambridge University, in England, three years later.

Meanwhile, from 1976 to 1978 Ignatieff taught history at the University of British Columbia, in Canada. Next, from 1978 to 1984, he held the title of senior research fellow at King's College, a division of Cambridge University. In 1985 he was a visiting fellow at the École des Hautes Études in Paris, France. By that time Ignatieff had become a member of the "brain trust," a group of public intellectuals in Great Britain, thanks largely to his work as the host of Britain's Channel 4 television series *Voices*, an interview program on which such distinguished writers as Czeslaw Milosz and Susan Sontag appeared. From 1989 to 1992 he hosted the BBC's *Late Show*, where, after a time, as he told Norman Oder for *Publishers Weekly* (November 30, 1998), he began to feel like "a kind of well-mannered butler at other people's intellectual conversation." From 1990 to 1993 he was an editorial columnist for the London *Observer*.

Religion and International Affairs (1968), which he edited with Jeffrey Rose, was Ignatieff's first book. It is a compilation of articles prepared for the "International Teach-in" held in Toronto in 1967. His next book, *A Just Measure of Pain: The Peni-*

tentiary in the Industrial Revolution, 1750–1850 (1978), is a study of conditions in English prisons during the Industrial Revolution. In *A Just Measure of Pain*, Ignatieff analyzed the concept of prison as punishment and also considered the development of the penal-reform movement. Earlier, Ignatieff had worked as a volunteer in a Massachusetts prison. "I learn from books, but I learn most from raw, painful experience," he told Oder.

With Istvan Hont, Ignatieff edited *Wealth and Virtue: The Shaping of Political Economy in the Scottish Enlightenment* (1983), which examines the ideas of the economist Adam Smith and other great thinkers of 18th-century Scotland. That book was followed by *The Needs of Strangers* (1984), which brought Ignatieff to the attention of a wider public. In four essays that form that volume, he explored human needs other than the material, focusing on "fraternity, love, belonging, dignity, and respect." The first and fourth essays—in the latter of which he presented an imagined dialogue between Adam Smith and the philosopher Jean-Jacques Rousseau—deal with community and the need for membership. The second and third concentrate on spiritual needs, discussing the nature of "tragedy, . . . Christian sin, . . . [and] human passion."

For the most part, reviewers of *The Needs of Strangers* admired the lucidity, beauty, and power of Ignatieff's prose but questioned his merging of the political and the spiritual. Although Ignatieff maintained that modern society has created "a new possibility for fraternity among strangers in public places," according to Alan Tonelson in the *New York Times Book Review* (May 5, 1985), "nothing in his description of the urban community suggests that its members acknowledge any obligations to those materially, psychologically or spiritually incapable of experiencing 'the joy of modern life, its fleeting and transient solidarity.' Members of these communities seem supremely content to let the 'arteries of the state' discharge their responsibilities to the needy—and to accept the consequent neglect of nonmaterial needs." Tonelson noted that in the United States today, "the gap between human needs and society's willingness to meet them seems even wider than the author's emphasis on nonmaterial needs indicates." The *Commonweal* (June 21, 1985) reviewer, Wilson Carey McWilliams, wrote, "Despite Ignatieff's graceful prose and his fine sympathies, his argument has its own tragic flaw. Ignatieff maintains that 'human nature is historical.' . . . [But] at crucial points, Ignatieff speaks ahistorically, referring to the human condition as such rather than the condition of human beings in this or that time and place." Michael Walzer, whose review appeared in the *New Republic* (May 13, 1985), praised Ignatieff's "skill and penetration" and declared the essays to be "very good." He had a serious compliant, though: "Ignatieff writes well so long as he has a subject to write about . . . ," he wrote, adding, "Political theory has to be about something, and the human need for earth, God, and love is not something it can plausibly be about."

In his 1987 memoir, *The Russian Album*, the cosmopolitan and politically liberal Ignatieff paid tribute to his aristocratic and monarchist paternal grandparents, Paul Ignatieff, the last Russian czar's minister of education, and his wife, Princess Natasha Mestchersky. Drawing on family photographs, diaries, and other sources, Ignatieff evoked the personal lives of the Russian aristocracy as well as the events and environment surrounding them. One of Ignatieff's ancestors helped Czar Nicholas I destroy the Decembrist movement in 1825 and was appointed minister of the interior. Another of his forebears helped to create the state of Bulgaria. His grandparents barely escaped becoming victims of the Bolshevik Revolution of 1917; leaving behind their estates, Doughino and Kroupodernitsa, they fled to England and ultimately settled in Canada.

"The family's glorious past was like a treasure too heavy to be borne very far into the 20th century," Walter Goodman noted in his review of *The Russian Album* for the *New York Times* (August 1, 1987). "The future shadows their chronicle. Noting that the peasants at the estate of Doughino . . . are largely absent from the memoirs and from the photographs, Mr. Ignatieff muses, 'In just 20 years these peasants were to burn Doughino to the ground and make the owner. . . sweep out the latrines in the prison yard at Sichevka.'" Referring to Ignatieff's discovery of a trunk in which his grandmother had placed histories written by an ancestor, a silver basin, and the jeweled necklace that she sold piece by piece, Goodman noted that the trunk proved to be empty, "but the past has been recaptured."

Most reviewers reacted favorably to *The Russian Album*. In *Quill & Quire* (July 1987), John Sewell wrote that he had found only one "discordant note"—"a hodgepodge of half-digested ideas [in the first chapter] entitled 'The Broken Path.' In it, Ignatieff recounts the struggle he experienced in writing the book. . . . Thankfully, the author has let the characters speak for themselves in the rest of the book. The result makes *The Russian Album* an engaging, powerful, and satisfying work." Anne Denoon, by contrast, in an assessment for *Books in Canada* (October 1987), declared, "The opening and closing chapters telling of his own ambivalence toward the claims of illustrious ancestry and his dealing with his father and uncles—the last surviving generation to have lived through the Revolution—are in many ways more compelling than the respectful, seamless narrative he has created from the drama and chaos of his ancestors' lives."

Ignatieff published his first novel, *Asya*, in 1991. The eponymous heroine, a Russian aristocrat, becomes pregnant as the result of an affair with a military officer. After the outbreak of the Russian Revolution, she settles in Paris, where she lives among other Russian émigrés. Her lover, Sergei, turns up and marries her, but he repeatedly disappears and then vanishes forever. With the approach of World

War II, Asya relocates to London, where she becomes involved with another man. Nevertheless, she remains in love with Sergei, even though she cannot decide whether he is a war hero or a traitor. Years later, when she visits Moscow for the last time, she learns the truth about him.

"This big, old-fashioned novel, with Dr. Zhivago-like settings and dialogue, displays a traditional Russian sensibility and grandeur that are to the minimalist short story what blini and caviar are to a Triscuit," the *Publishers Weekly* (August 9, 1991) critic wrote, terming *Asya* "a rich feast of plot, character and history." To Muriel Spanier, the *New York Times Book Review* (December 1, 1991) critic, the book had an "historic sweep," and "Ignatieff's superb multilayered rendering of Asya makes her an utterly memorable heroine." Daniel Jones, in *Quill & Quire* (July 1991), joined the chorus of praise, deeming *Asya* "a narrative that explores not only the way history affects the lives of individuals and is altered by those lives, but also the ways that the past survives and continues to inform the present." He found Ignatieff to be "truly as fine a novelist as he is a historian—categories that here merge in a compelling vision of the world as a whole." The London *Observer* (February 24, 1991) critic Valentine Cunningham noted that Ignatieff's "magically realist way with the potency of objects" gave the book moments "powerful enough to make one forgive much, even the historical awkwardness, the nervy links, the novel's creaky start and its early flat adjectives." In a dissenting opinion, Anthony Quinn, who reviewed *Asya* for *New Statesman & Society* (March 1, 1991), complained that "Ignatieff hasn't drawn one remotely believable character" apart from Asya herself. "His pages are crowded with people who laugh and drink and sulk around Asya, but Ignatieff doesn't seem to notice that none of them is alive," he wrote. Catherine Bennett, in the London *Guardian* (February 28, 1991), was even more negative. "Ignatieff has . . . succeeded in convincing *himself* that he is an all-purpose intellectual, for whom writing fiction is a simple career choice," she wrote. "Anyone trying to write an ambitious first novel might have written *Asya*, but only a fool would have published it."

In *Scar Tissue*, Ignatieff's second novel, the unnamed narrator witnesses his mother's decline as she suffers the ravages of Alzheimer's disease. He leaves his wife and child and devotedly takes care of his mother until her death. His brother, a neurologist, remains mostly on the sidelines; during the course of the story, his father suddenly dies. The book starts with a painful memory:

> I do not want to remember her last hour. I do not want to be eternally condemned to think of her as she was in those final moments, when we held her hands, my brother and I, and she fought for life and lost, her mouth stretched open, gasping for breath, her eyes staring sightlessly up into the lights. . . . I still have days when everything she ever was, everything she ever meant to me is entirely erased by the memory of those great agonising breaths, that frail body wracked with spasms, those lips wet with blood.

"The narrator exhibits a fixed and angry love . . . ," Jane Vandenburgh wrote in an review of *Scar Tissue* for the *Washington Post Book World* (September 25, 1994). "This character has become so enthralled by his own incapacity that he seems finally to exist solely in relationship to someone who cannot remember him. 'Memory,' he says, 'is the only afterlife I have ever believed in. But the forgetting inside us cannot be stopped. We are doomed to betray.'. . . On page after page of this dark story there are starbursts of insight when Michael Ignatieff's deep knowledge of his subject lights up, irradiated by his brilliant command of language." The *New Statesman & Society* (April 16, 1993) reviewer termed *Scar Tissue* "a graceful, meticulous examination of our various responses to family illness and death. . . . The last pages are a gorgeous cascade of theories, memories and finally settled positions: of death as a 'pure and heartless reality' that can barely be imagined, but whose light will now illuminate the narrator's life. No recent . . . novel has traversed the worlds of reason and emotion, the human presence and its annihilation, so effectively and directly." *Scar Tissue* was shortlisted for the Booker Prize, Great Britain's most prestigious literary award.

With his 1994 volume, *Blood and Belonging: Journeys into the New Nationalism*, Ignatieff produced a partly first-hand account of late-20th-century internecine conflicts. On a BBC assignment, he had traveled in Germany, the Ukraine, Quebec, Kurdistan, Northern Ireland, and the former Yugoslavia, where conflicts suppressed for decades had once again ignited. Both the resulting television series, also called *Blood and Belonging*, and the book encapsulate the lessons Ignatieff learned about the destructive forces unleashed by nationalism and tribalism.

"In a compelling mix of interviews, history, vivid impressions and sharp reportage," the *Publishers Weekly* (February 21, 1994) reviewer wrote, Ignatieff "argues that nationalism can be a constructive, welding force, but that, in its extreme, authoritarian form, it serves as collective escape from reality, whose adherents, inhabiting a delusional realm of noble causes and tragic sacrifice, straitjacket themselves and other groups in the fiction of an irreducible ethnic identity." According to Gary Gerstle, writing for *Tikkun* (December 1994), Ignatieff viewed the "ethnic rage" that too often accompanies such identifications "as part of an epochal development in world history, a turn away from what he calls 'civic' nationalism and toward 'ethnic' nationalism." Gerstle explained that Ignatieff "grew up thinking that ethnicity was on the wane and that nations committed to the principle of ethnic purity had been swept into the dustbin of history. These feelings intensified as he gravitated, in his youth, to a Left politics that characteristically underestimated the power of tribal appeals. . . . Hence the nightmare of his present: Montreal . . . , choking from the grip of Quebecois nationalism; Britain, the land he now calls home, unable to stop the terror in Northern Ireland; Sarajevo, the exotic cosmopolitan city he visited as a boy, lying in ruins. . . . He never tries to hide his distaste for ethnic nationalism, or his anger, nausea, and incomprehension at some of what he observes. But he rarely allows his feelings and views to interfere with his explorations or cloud his search for understanding." The *Washington Post Book World* (April 10, 1994) reviewer, David Fromkin, found Ignatieff "at his best when suggestive. . . . He does try gamely to find a common theme in his six areas of conflict, but it eludes him, very possibly because it isn't there. In his title and subtitle, at least, Ignatieff seems to be saying that in all six cases nationalism—the primitive call of blood and belonging—is the troublemaker; but it isn't so. In Northern Ireland, the overriding conflict isn't national but religious: Protestant versus Roman Catholic. The tragedy of Kurdistan is that it has never had enough nationalism to overcome its paralyzing tribalism. East and West Germans resent one another despite, not because of, nationalism. Quebec separatism seems to be at least as much a question of language, culture and social status as of nationality." Although Fromkin concluded that while Ignatieff had not answered the central question—why nationalism, which once unified, now divides—there was much of value in *Blood and Belonging*. "Vivid and readable, it provides unforgettable impressions of societies that are going in the wrong direction on the highway to brotherhood and unity." *Blood and Belonging* won the Lionel Gelber Award for the best writing on foreign affairs, and the Overseas Press Club honored it with the Cornelius Ryan Award.

In *The Warrior's Honor: Ethnic War and the Modern Conscience* (1998), Ignatieff again dealt with ethnic conflict, this time concentrating on nations and individuals that had attempted to intervene in such wars. "What impulses led us to supervise elections in Cambodia, try to protect the Kurds from Saddam, send UN troops to Bosnia, restore democracy to Haiti, bring the warriors to the table in Angola?" Ignatieff asked. He theorized that "human rights have little or no purchase on this world of war. Far better to appeal to these fighters as warriors than as human beings, for warriors have codes of honor; human beings—qua human beings—have none."

Reviewers differed in their responses to Ignatieff's "alternative narrative of moral commitment," as David Rieff phrased it in the *New Republic* (March 16, 1998). Rieff found Ignatieff's positing of a "shared human rights culture" a "worthy", but inadequate enterprise. "Ignatieff has written a book about the Western conscience and the Western response to certain types of contemporary disaster; but he thinks that he has written about something universal," Reiff wrote; the danger is that "universalism easily declines into sentimentalism, into a tortured but useless distance from the particulars of human affairs. Ignatieff's universalism is too sweeping, and his moralizing rhetoric is too stipulative." Jean Bethke Elshtain, reviewing *The Warrior's Honor* for *Commonweal* (October 9, 1998), felt that Ignatieff "doesn't really get beyond the themes of *Blood and Belonging*, here repeating his argument about the ways in which, given a particular concatenation of circumstances, even minor differences get magnified into incommensurabilities that blind human beings to the suffering of others and justify wounding those same others." She concluded that Ignatieff's asking "that we should call up and call upon whatever is in our cultural and political armamentarium to interdict killing . . . is surely right. . . . *The Warrior's Honor* is vivid in description, thin in prescription. But we are all in Ignatieff's debt for his insistent plumbing of the heart of contemporary darkness."

Ignatieff was a friend and interlocutor of Isaiah Berlin during the last 10 years of Berlin's life, and he was chosen as the older man's official biographer. His book *Isaiah Berlin: A Life* (1999) summarizes, in fewer than 500 pages, the life and ideas of Sir Isaiah, who died in 1997 at the age of 88. Among most other philosophers and scholars, Berlin had long been regarded as a lightweight, a man with a brilliant surface and not much depth or productivity. Since his death, scholarly opinion has come to hold Berlin in higher esteem and to recognize the value of his contributions as a liberal thinker. A Russian Jew born in Riga, Latvia, Berlin was brought to England as a young boy. He was elected to a fellowship at All Souls College, a division of Oxford University. In 1940 he spent time in the United States as part of the British effort to persuade the U.S. to join the war effort on the Allied side and to keep Prime Minister Winston Churchill informed about what was going on in Washington. After his retirement from All Souls, Berlin raised money for and founded Wolfson College at Oxford University, becoming its first president. A quintessential liberal, he believed in progress, the solubility of human problems, and the power of reason to effect change.

Reviewers of Ignatieff's biography lauded the work while often giving more space to evaluating Berlin than they did to *Berlin*. Although "Berlin was a lifelong, steadfast champion of the values of the Enlightenment," John Gray observed in the *New Statesman*, "such Enlightenment hopes were not at the heart of his defence of liberal freedoms. He chose instead to ground the value of freedom in the necessity of choice among values that will always be at odds. The result is an intensely original contribution to political philosophy and this country's truest account of liberal values." Ian Buruma, in the *New Republic* (November 16, 1998), called *Isaiah Berlin* "a fine biography . . . light in the best sense: entertaining without ever lacking in seriousness. Ignatieff's subject was not a tortured genius, and so he has written the life of a man who was honored and loved, and who took grateful pleasure in his good fortune." Ignatieff also presented his subject's darker side. According to Buruma, "The inner life of Berlin was never as tranquil as his college and clubland surroundings. In the 1960s, Ignatieff tells us, Berlin felt like 'a man beset: disliked by the left, held in suspicion by the right; too sceptical to be trusted by the committed; too committed to be at home among defenders of the status quo. He managed these conflicts with a gay, sardonic public surface; but underneath, he was often troubled with a sense, if not of tragedy, then certainly of the inevitability of losing someone or something dear whenever he made a commitment.' . . . Ignatieff has taken Berlin's resolution of these dilemmas as the main theme of his book."

Ignatieff returned to the subject of the former Yugoslavia in his collection of essays *Virtual War: Kosovo and Beyond*, published in 2000. In it he expressed his fears about the ability of nations and organizations to conduct war from a distance and with no danger to one side, as NATO forces did in Kosovo in 1999. While he believed that that war was waged unethically, he deemed the "humanitarian" rationale for NATO's actions in Kosovo morally correct. But he warned that democratic countries "may remain peace-loving only so long as the risks of war remain real to their citizens."

John Simpson, who reviewed *Virtual War* for the *New Statesman* (April 3, 2000), covered the 1990s war in the Balkans himself until he was expelled from the region for "speaking 'disrespectfully' on BBC radio about Slobodan Milosevic," the Serb leader. "Michael Ignatieff, who has written with such clarity about the events of the past decade in the Balkans (and unlike most other writers on the subject, has actually risked his neck by going to these places and seeing for himself what he calls 'Balkan Physics'), would probably have called me an appeaser . . . ," he wrote. "But by the end of this excellent, thought-provoking essay, which forms a natural completion to his two other books on the Balkan crisis of the 1990s, Ignatieff seems to feel about the war rather as I do: 'We see ourselves as noble warriors and our enemies as despicable tyrants. We see war as a surgical scalpel and not as a bloodstained sword. In doing so we misdescribe ourselves as we misdescribe the instruments of death. We need to stay away from such fables of self-righteous invulnerability.' . . . *Virtual War* is not a comfortable book. I admire Ignatieff all the more for facing up to the uncomfortable, and allowing it to alter his views accordingly." In an appraisal for the *New York Times Book Review* (June 11, 2000), Fouad Ajami wrote that in *Virtual War*, Ignatieff "straddles a moral fence of sorts. . . . He can't give himself over to the morality of the new interventionists; he can't sanction the indifference of the realists. Back and forth he goes between these two sensibilities, and the tension can be felt in the book." Ajami concluded that he understood "Ignatieff's point about the 'virtuality' of the war and the discrepancy between NATO firepower and Serbian capabilities." But, he maintained, "Ignatieff exaggerates the novelty of this." Michael Mosettig, the reviewer for the journal *Europe* (July 2000), praised *Virtual War*, which he described as a "treatise on modern war and its military and political consequences." The book, he wrote, "raises a key question of whether Western nations are now more likely to embark on military campaigns if they appear so risk free. . . . And there is the ultimate question: if Western nations are so concerned about maintaining standards of human rights in the Balkans or elsewhere, to what degree are they ready to risk the lives of soldiers on the ground to match their oratory?"

In 2001 Ignatieff published *Human Rights as Politics and Idolatry*, a collection of essays written by himself and by scholars such as K. Anthony Appiah. The book opens with two long essays by Ignatieff on the politics of human rights and is followed by four essays from scholars commenting on his ideas. A reviewer for *Publishers Weekly*, as quoted on the Amazon.com Web site, noted, "The strength in this sensible, dense collection of essays about the burgeoning human rights movement lies not in the answers it gives but in the questions it raises. . . . Those looking for specific policy proposals for addressing these difficult issues may be unsatisfied. But Ignatieff illuminates complexities likely to make headlines as the call for intervention regarding worldwide human rights continues to grow. This book will undoubtedly provoke controversy within the human rights community."

Ignatieff is the director of Harvard University's Carr Center of Human Rights Policy.

—S. Y.

SUGGESTED READING: *Books in Canada* p26 Oct. 1987; *Commonweal* p378 June 21, 1985, p25+ Oct. 9, 1998; *Europe* p48 July 2000; *Index* (on-line) No 397; (London) *Guardian* p24 Feb. 28, 1991; (London) *Observer* p62 Feb. 24, 1991; *New Republic* p36+ May 13, 1985, p27+ Mar. 16, 1998, p32+ Nov. 16, 1998; *New Statesman* p48+ Nov. 20, 1998, p53+ Apr. 3, 2000; *New Statesman & Society* p36 Mar. 1, 1991, p40 Apr. 16, 1993; *New York Newsday* B p10 Apr. 7, 1994; *New York Times* I p19 Aug. 1, 1987; *New York Times Book Review* p20 May 5, 1985, p70 Dec. 1, 1991; *New York Times Magazine* (on-line) Apr. 1, 2001; *Publishers Weekly* p46 Aug. 9, 1991, p242 Feb. 21, 1994, p46+ Nov. 30, 1998; *Quill & Quire* p68 July 1987; *Tikkun* p68+ Dec. 1994; *Washington Post Book World* p5 Apr. 10, 1994, p5 Sep. 25, 1994

SELECTED WORKS: nonfiction—*A Just Measure of Pain: Penitentiaries in the Industrial Revolution 1750–1850*,1978; *The Needs of Strangers*, 1984; *The Russian Album*, 1987; *Blood and Belonging: Journeys Into the New Nationalism*, 1994; *The Warrior's Honor: Ethnic War and the Modern Conscience*, 1988; *Virtual War: Kosovo and Beyond*, 2000; *The Rights Revolution*, 2001; *Human Rights as Politics and Idolatry*, 2001; as editor—*Religion and*

International Affairs (with J. Rose), 1968; *Wealth and Virtue: The Shaping of Classical Political Economy in the Scottish Enlightenment* (with I. Hont), 1983; fiction—*Asya*, 1991; *Scar Tissue*, 1993; screenplays—*Eugene Onegin*, 1998

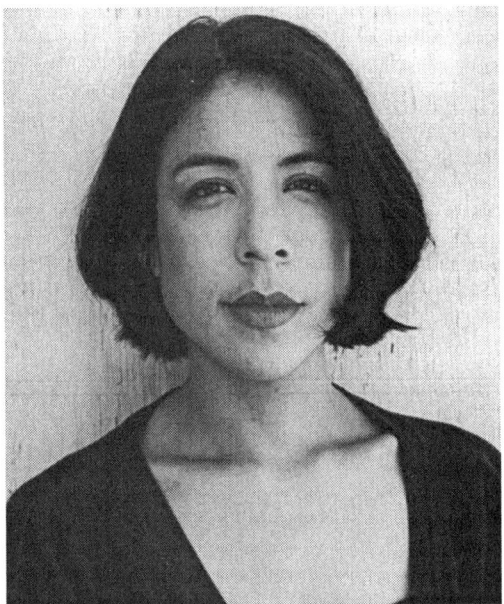

Sioban Dixon/Courtesy of Dramatists Play Service, Inc.

Iizuka, Naomi

1965– Playwright

"The theatre artists who are working in the most exciting ways are creating new fusions or hybrids from old material," the playwright Naomi Iizuka wrote in her essay "What Myths May Come" in *American Theatre* (September 1999). "They sing old songs in their own strange, wild, utterly singular voices. . . . They spin out new yarns with old thread. I can think of few skills more useful in the times in which we live." Iizuka has become known for her modern renditions of classic myths and stories. Her play *Polaroid Stories*, for instance, uses homeless teenagers to retell the Greek myth of Orpheus and Euridyce. In another play, *Skin*, she introduced a modern-day version of Georg Büchner's drama *Woyzeck*. "I like theatre that startles me, and that makes me reappraise my relationship to the real," she told Misha Berson for *American Theatre* (September 1998). "I think that's probably more readily accessed by going towards myth . . . something that's not, strictly speaking, realistic."

Iizuka was born in Japan in 1965 to a Spanish-American mother and a Japanese father who worked as a banker. Raised partly in the Netherlands, she also lived in Chevy Chase, Maryland, where she attended the National Cathedral School, a private Catholic school that served mostly children of diplomats. She majored in classics at Yale University, in New Haven, Connecticut, then attended Yale Law School. Bored with her legal studies, she dropped out and entered the University of California at San Diego (UCSD) to study playwriting. One of the teachers who influenced her the most was Adele Edling Shank. "Her work is hyperrealism, and I think what I took from that is a sense of creating an event that happens in real time, a theatre event that sort of washes over and hits the audience as it struggles for a certain kind of honesty."

After Iizuka received her MFA in 1992, she worked at UCSD with Anne Bogart and Robert Woodruff. One of her early plays, *Carthage*, transports the doomed romance of Dido and Aeneas to contemporary Los Angeles. *Tattoo Girl* focuses on a trumpet-player named Perpetua, who embarks on a magical quest. Iizuka's play *Marlowe's Eyes* was performed in New York, in 1996. The play's protagonists include the 16th-century English dramatist Christopher Marlowe; the 20th-century Italian poet and filmmaker Pier Paolo Pasolini; Queen Elizabeth I of England; and Ruth Riddle, a member of the Branch Davidians, whose compound at Waco, Texas, was stormed by federal agents, in 1993. The play is "about how visionaries can be crushed by assassins of the state," according to Brian Parks who reviewed it for the *Village Voice* (April 2, 1996). Parks added that Iizuka demonstrated "how strong spirits, especially gays, are doomed to be smothered by repressive orders . . . Iizuka tries to show how those who most embrace life are fated to die young, while those who want death are destined to escape it."

The 1997 Humana Festival, in Louisville, Kentucky, presented Iizuka's plays *Polaroid Stories* and *Songs from a Girl with No Tongue*. For *Polaroid Stories*, Iizuka drew on Ovid's *Metamorphoses* and other Greco-Roman myths to portray the lives of homeless teenagers who gather at a pier. The play was originally commissioned by a New York theater company as a site-specific work. Iizuka based much of her material on her 18-month stay in Minneapolis, Minnesota, which was sponsored by a Jerome Foundation fellowship and a McKnight advancement grant. "In Minneapolis I lived near an area where a lot of street kids congregated, kids who hopped freight trains and traveled a lot . . . ," Iizuka told Berson. "I found them to be very smart—a lot of them write and draw and lead rich, creative inner lives. It would be a mistake just to call them victims." M. S. Mason, writing in the *Christian Science Monitor* (April 23, 1997), described *Polaroid Stories* as "experimental and riveting." The "play is full of unique rhythms, poetic flights, and raw street language," Mason concluded. In a review of a San Francisco production of the play, Bob Graham wrote for the *San Francisco Chronicle* (July 20, 1998) that the "play is about finding love and losing it." One of the organizers of the Humana Festival told Misha Berson in an interview for *American Theatre* (September 1998) that he thought Iizuka "had the zapline to the Greeks through a kind of passion and obsession and desire that also applies to today's fringe culture of outcasts, runaways, and drug addicts. . . . Their sense of need and fear seemed a perfect match for the emotions of the Greek myths, but the contemporary settings and characters gave you a new understanding of those myths that was emotional and visceral, not academic." *Polaroid Stories* received an award from the PEN Center USA West, in 1998.

Describing her views on myth, Iizuka wrote in "What Myths May Come" that "we are sleeping beauties, all of us. We live in a culture saturated by myth—myths about what's normal and what's freakish, what's appropriate and what's obscene. The myths we know by heart are the most dangerous." Nevertheless she believes that mythology is "the homeland of the muses, the inspirers of art, the inspirers of poetry." For Iizuka myth "is a crash course in metaphor" and the mine in which she searches for dramatic gold. She declared that "myth is memory" and concluded that "making theatre is the act of remembering, remembering again and again. . . . This is how we make sense. . . . This is how we conjure anew."

Skin, staged in 1998 in Los Angeles, is Iizuka's reworking of *Woyzeck*, an unfinished 19th-century play by Georg Büchner about a poor man who kills his girlfriend in a jealous rage. In Iizuka's play the principal character, Jones, is a factory worker, abused by his boss, harassed by the police, and betrayed by his girlfriend. Laurie Winer wrote in the *Los Angeles Times* (June 19, 1998) that "Jones is a trapped Everyman, a powerless philosopher, who is so attuned to death that he can imagine how things would sound from underneath the ground. His father once threw him in the ocean, it seems. At times, *Skin* seems as if it is underwater too, lugubrious but with moments of unreal beauty."

In 1999 the Humana Festival featured another Iizuka work, *Aloha, Say the Pretty Girls*. In a review for the *Cincinnati Enquirer* (March 12, 1999, on-line), Jackie Demaline called the play "high energy and desperately wacky" and added that "*Aloha* isn't sitcom, it's 'threatcom.' It leaves you feeling brow-beaten into having fun. If you're not having fun, well, there must be something wrong with you." Celia Wren, in a review for *American Theatre* (July/August 1999), believed that the play represents "Iizuka's vision of discontinuity and rootlessness in the global village. . . . After kicking off with the image of a komodo dragon piñata, the play proceeds to twine around a python, tattoos, a holdup in a pet store, a florist in Alaska, surfboards in Hawaii, the seer Tiresias, and a man who turns into a lizard. The looping paths of the characters (including an airline steward, a hula dancer, and Demi Moore's personal assistant) cross and recross so many times that a bird's eye view would look like a Jackson Pollock painting." Wren added, "Detractors will blame *Aloha* for self-indulgence but the play's zany shapelessness does have a purpose:

to express the fragmentation and confusion of modern life. 'I don't believe in fate,' one character aptly remarks. 'I think everything is kind of random.' Fate once meant social coherence and a sense of place. These days, we have airports."

Iizuka recently wrote *War of the Worlds*, a play about the life of Orson Welles. The play, directed by Anne Bogart, was performed at the Humana Festival in 2000. Iizuka was also selected by the Sundance Institute to participate in the organization's 2000 Theatre Lab. The three-week workshop allowed her to work on *36 Views* (2003), a series of 36 scenes and moments centered around an art dealer and an art historian's discovery of an ancient Japanese pillow book. As the characters attempt to confirm the book's authenticity, the play examines authenticity in love and art. A critic for the *Village Voice*, in a review quoted on *Amazon.com*, called the play "chock full of charm, intelligence, and compassion."

—S. Y.

SUGGESTED READING: *American Theatre* p56+ Sep. 1998, with photo, p49 Aug. 1999; *Christian Science Monitor* XV p1 Apr. 23, 1997, with photo; *Cincinnati Enquirer* (on-line) Mar. 12, 1999; *San Francisco Chronicle* E p1 July 20, 1998; *Village Voice* p76 Apr. 2, 1996

SELECTED PLAYS: *Carthage*, 1993; *Marlowe's Eyes*, 1996; *Polaroid Stories*, 1997; *Songs from a Girl with No Tongue*, 1997; *Skin*, 1998; *Aloha, Say the Pretty Girls*, 1999; *War of the Worlds*, 2000; *36 Views*, 2003

Irving, John

Mar. 2, 1942– Novelist; short-story writer; essayist; screenwriter

John Irving is that too rare kind of writer, both critically considered and wildly popular. His books—jam-packed with colorful characters and an assortment of plot twists and revelations—have been best-sellers since the 1978 publication of *The World According To Garp*, which became an international sensation. Irving's richly detailed style has earned him comparison to some of the world's greatest 19th-century authors, including Charles Dickens, but it has also earned him scorn from some critics, who deride his plots as convoluted and his language as inelegant. Like Dickens, Irving does not shy away from controversial social issues in his writing; his topics have included abortion (*The Cider House Rules*), religion (*A Prayer for Owen Meany*), and unusual relationships—sexual and otherwise. Critics have accused him of writing pulp fiction for the masses; Irving says he is just trying to write good stories that people will want to read, believing that novelists have a responsibility to entertain. He once told an interviewer, "I want to move you—that's the important

John Irving
Courtesy of Random House

thing. . . . It's only bad art that's given soap opera a bad name. I'm an artist, but I want to jerk tears." A novelist, according to Irving, is also obliged to write as clearly and accessibly as he can: "It's no triumph to be difficult to read or understand, in fact I think it's a triumph to be readable," he told the interviewer. "I don't find that an aspect of commercialism, but part of a writer's responsibility."

John Winslow Irving was born John Wallace Blunt Jr. on March 2, 1942 and raised in Exeter, New Hampshire. His father was John Wallace Blunt Sr., an air force pilot during World War II whose plane had been shot down over occupied Burma. (Blunt and his crew walked to China and were found after being reported missing for 40 days.) His mother, Frances Winslow Irving, had divorced John Wallace Blunt Sr. before Irving was born. She remarried when her son was six years old; her new husband, Colin F. N. Irving, adopted him and changed his name. John's stepfather was a teacher of Russian history and the treasurer at Phillips Exeter Academy, a prestigious New Hampshire prep school. The author attended Exeter, where he excelled in English and history and was a champion wrestler. Upon graduation from prep school, he chose to go to the University of Pittsburgh because of its strong wrestling program. Wrestling has been an important part of Irving's real life and his creative life. His characters are frequently wrestlers, and he often uses the terms of the sport as metaphors for larger ideas; he likens the concentration necessary for writing, for example, to that required for winning at wrestling.

Outside of New England, Irving found himself outclassed as a wrestler, and his year in Pittsburgh was not successful. He returned home to attend the state university at Durham. He realized there that he wanted to be a writer, and after two semesters he went off to study at the University of Vienna. Chosen because it sounded more exotic than the other possibilities, Vienna proved to be a fertile ground for him; the city has appeared repeatedly in his work.

Irving had met Shyla Leary in 1963 and corresponded with her while he was in Europe. On August 24, 1964 they were married, and Irving returned to the University of New Hampshire, receiving his degree *cum laude* in 1965. From there he went on to the Writers' Workshop at the University of Iowa, where he tended bar and sold pennants and souvenirs at college football games to support his family (a son, Colin, had been born by then). Irving was awarded a master of fine arts degree in 1967, and the family moved back East, to a converted barn in Putney, Vermont. Irving taught English at a small local college and wrote his first novel, *Setting Free the Bears* (1969). A picaresque tale of two university dropouts who hatch a plot to release the animals from a Vienna zoo, the novel exhibits what were to become some of Irving's hallmarks: Vienna, bears, what the novelist Anne Tyler once called "manic high spirits" and "jaunty heroics," and an imaginative, complex plot.

Irving spent the next several years in Vienna and Putney, working on the screenplay of *Setting Free the Bears* and on his next novel. The Irvings' younger son, Brendan, was born in 1970. In 1972 Irving returned to the University of Iowa as a writer-in-residence, a position he would hold for three years. That year *The Water-Method Man*, a dark comedy for which Irving had received a Rockefeller Foundation grant, was published. The protagonist, Bogus Trumper, is a graduate student at the University of Iowa, working on his dissertation and trying to cope with his failing marriage while an underground documentary is being made of his life. Abundant sex—with and without love—and bathroom humor (the title refers to the treatment prescribed for Trumper's urinary infection) were featured prominently throughout the book. A reviewer for the *New Yorker* (July 22, 1972) wrote, "The novel flips back and forth through Bogus's life as if it were telling three or four stories at once, and it's often three or four times as funny as most novels." Paul Majkut, writing for *Best Seller* (July 1, 1972), however, complained, "[This book] is not exceptionally funny, though it is typical of what has come to pass as funny these days in the American comic novel. That is, it is light, well-trained, even risqué, and it avoids every real human issue present throughout the land."

Irving's third novel, *The 158-Pound Marriage* was published in 1974. One of its four protagonists is the wrestling coach at a small New England college. The story tells of the complicated relationships among two married couples. A *Washington Post* critic, as quoted on the Amazon Bookseller's Web site, opined, "Irving looks cunningly beyond the eye-catching gyrations of the mating dance to the morning-after implications."

Irving was 36 years old when the publication of his fourth novel, *The World According to Garp* (originally titled "Lunacy and Sorrow"), catapulted him to prominence. *Garp* made him a celebrity and provided enough financial comfort that he was able to retire from Mount Holyoke College, where he had taught since 1975. T. S. Garp, the protagonist of the 1978 book, is an engaging, utterly human writer of great talent; an adoring, anxious father; and a loving—though occasionally unfaithful—husband, whose vision of the world appears, from all evidence, to be close to Irving's own. The novel shot to the top of the best-seller lists, and was nominated for a National Book Award. The paperback version, which was published the following year, was awarded an American Book Award as the best paperback novel of 1979. In 1982 the book was made into a film starring Robin Williams as Garp. Irving later remarked that this was the first novel in which he had created characters he genuinely admired and cared for.

While reviewers praised the warmth, humanity, and readability of the book, most noted that the rape, mutilation, dismemberment, and violent death so integral to the plot exceeded anything Irving had written previously. Walter Clemons wrote for *Newsweek* (April 17, 1978), "The middle section of this novel is vividly disturbing. . . . Irving here deals out Grand Guignol shocks leading to a hushed, heart-stopping revelation of irreparable grief." In a review for *Time* (April 24, 1978), R. Z. Sheppard, called the book "extraordinary" and concluded, "At 36, [Irving] moves into the front rank of America's young novelists."

Garp's widespread popularity led some critics to question whether a book so successful commercially could be considered art. Joseph Epstein, the author of several volumes of critical scholarship, has noted the emphasis on the physical in Irving's work, the academic "game-playing" of Irving's intricate plot constructions, Irving's failure to investigate moral questions, and his "strained effort to be, simultaneously, adorable and gruesome." Epstein has concluded that the basis of Irving's appeal to such large audiences is his ability to "make his readers feel advanced in their views yet fundamentally sound in their emotions."

Irving had ample opportunity to answer his detractors; his success made him news beyond the confines of the literary pages, and he was the frequent subject of interviews. To the charges of excessive violence, he repeatedly replied that the news in any newspaper on a given day is of equal or surpassing violence, and that he used violence for artistic reasons only. He defended his black humor on the grounds that was intended to make more bearable the events he describes. He often pointed out that art and entertainment are not contradictions, and he deplored the obscurity of writing that requires the intervention of critics and academics for interpretation.

Conceived as a modern fairy tale, Irving's fifth novel, *The Hotel New Hampshire* (1981), recounts the vicissitudes of Wyn and Mary Berry and their children: Frank, Fanny, John, Lilly, and Egg. Sustained by strong family bonds and tenacious courage, they encounter violence, rape, homosexuality, deformity, sudden death, and incest. The title refers to the three hotels inhabited by the family: the first is a converted girl's school in New Hampshire; the second is a Viennese fleabag—by day the workplace of a team of revolutionary terrorists, by night of a team of aging prostitutes; the third, in Maine, doubles as a rape crisis center.

Benjamin DeMott, writing for the *Atlantic* (October 1981), praised the "surprising narrative rhythms and a sharply distinctive tone," but questioned the rationale behind Irving's pairing of "the nightmare and sunshine." A reviewer for *The Nation* (September 26, 1981) found the novel "Not only confusing . . . but boring."

In 1985 Irving published what many readers considered one of his finest books, *The Cider House Rules*. In this novel of New England, set in the 1940s, Homer Wells grows up at St. Cloud's Orphanage, having never been adopted. He is reared by Dr. Larch, St. Cloud's administrator, who educates his young charge about abortion procedures. (Many of the couples who come to St. Cloud's are there not to adopt but to receive illegal abortions from Dr. Larch.) As Homer grows into his teens, he learns everything about being a doctor from his surrogate father, but he is unwilling to perform abortions. He's not quite sure he even wants to be a doctor. He eventually leaves St. Cloud's to find his own place in the world. Upon its publication the novel received mixed reviews. In the *New York Times Book Review* (May 26, 1985) Benjamin DeMott cheered: "By turns witty, tenderhearted, fervent and scarifying, *The Cider House Rules* is, for me, John Irving's first truly valuable book." Anthony Burgess, however, denounced the book in the *Atlantic* (July 1985): "If I do not like this book, it is because it seems to me to lack art. An artist would have thought of compression, not the wind-filled prolongation that makes for the best seller. . . . It also lacks the qualities that I think desirable in fiction—wit, irony, even good, honest, knockabout humor." In 2000 Irving received an Academy Award for Best Adapted Screenplay for his work on the film version of *The Cider House Rules*, which starred Michael Caine and Tobey Maguire.

Four years later Irving completed *A Prayer for Owen Meany* (1989), an ambitious novel that vented moral outrage at everything from dubious religious faith to the Vietnam War. The story of Owen Meany is told by his childhood friend John Wheelright; Owen, cursed with a diminutive stature and a gravelly voice, may or may not be a spiritual reincarnation of Jesus Christ. But Owen is unlike any representation of Christ readers have ever seen before: he drinks and smokes, he belittles and orders his parents around, he speaks bluntly to everyone.

When he accidentally kills John's mother with an errant baseball, he begins to consider himself an instrument of God. In the *Globe and Mail* (April 1, 1989), Jay Scott called the book "Irving's finest fictional hour so far. Commentators who find the plot of this yuppie Dickensian novel too far-fetched, and who deem too cynical Irving's emphasis on the distressing tendency of fate to wreak vengeance on the innocent, are probably commentators who get all the news they need on the weather report; they certainly have not bothered to read the Bible." The novelist Stephen King, in a review for the *Washington Post Book World* (March 5, 1989), cheered: "John Irving, who writes novels in the unglamourous but effective way Babe Ruth used to hit home runs, deserves a medal for not only writing this book but for the way he has written it. He does not dance, duck, dodge or beat around the burning bush; he simply walks up to the subject of divinity and briskly smites it, hip and thigh. He does not come away unbruised, but he does come away a clear winner. *A Prayer for Owen Meany* is a rare creation in the somehow exhausted world of late 20th century fiction—it is an amazingly *brave* piece of work."

In *A Son of the Circus* (1994), Irving tells the story of Dr. Farrokh Daruwalla, a surgeon born in Bombay and living in Toronto. Though the doctor returns to Bombay every year to aid disabled children and conduct research on dwarves (all while stimulating his imagination for his secret work as a screenwriter for a highly successful series of Indian films), he feels very much a stranger wherever he is, especially in his native land. A number of transvestites, prostitutes, and transsexuals spur the plot along, as well as a pair of identical twins separated at birth and an Iowa-born hippie who is married to an Indian homicide detective. A reviewer for *Entertainment Weekly* (September 9, 1994) bemoaned: "Every novel is an act of audacity, but if any book has ever deserved the catchphrase 'monstrous presumption,' it would be [this one]. Monstrous, that is, both in its immense, stultifying length (633 pages) and in its author's preoccupation with physical deformities and sexual curiosities pretty much for their own sake." In the *Globe and Mail* (September 3, 1994), Suanne Kelman noted, "some of the early reviews of *A Son of the Circus* made it sound completely turgid, which is untrue. Parts of it are compulsively readable, intelligent and moving. . . . but other sections are unforgivably slack. Irving's introduction mentions that he did have an editor, who pruned the novel down from an initial 1,094 pages. Yet *A Son* still suffers from repetition and inexplicable padding."

In *A Widow For One Year* (1998), Irving returned to the world of writing that he had last depicted in *Garp*. Several of the book's character's are writers: Ruth Cole, the main character, is a critically acclaimed and highly popular novelist; her womanizing father is a successful children's writer and illustrator; and her mother's former lover is a writer, though a considerably less successful one.

The novel commences in 1958 when Ruth is four, and details how her mother, Marion, spends her days staring at walls filled with photos of her two dead sons before beginning a summer-long affair with her husband's 16-year-old assistant. At the end of the summer Marion simply disappears, leaving both her daughter and her lover lost without her. Many critics believed this novel to be a return to form for Irving. "*Widow* stands as one of Irving's best novels and a worthy thematic sequel to his most famous creation," Tom De Haven wrote for *Entertainment Weekly* (May 15, 1998). "A combination of vaudeville, romance, and sentimentality, *A Widow for One Year* is never entirely convincing, but like a warm bath, it's a great pleasure to immerse yourself in."

Irving's most recent novel is *The Fourth Hand* (2001), which depicts how Patrick Wallingford, a tabloid televison reporter, loses his hand to a lion while covering a story. The scene is witnessed on live televison, forever altering people's perceptions of Patrick. He is forever known as "the lion guy," and he meets this newfound fame with some ambivalence. Among the people who have seen Patrick's accident on television are a noted hand surgeon named Nicholas Zarjac and Doris Clausen, a housewife, who manages to convince her husband, Otto, to give Patrick his hand in the event of his death. When Otto dies shortly thereafter, Doris has the appendage shipped to Patrick—with instructions that she is to have visiting rights to the hand. The novel received mainly mixed reviews. Donna Seaman, in a *Booklist* critique quoted on the Amazon Bookseller's Web site, complained of Irving's "pedestrian social commentary," but called the novel "compulsively readable" and a "crazy but sweet little love story."

In addition to writing novels, John Irving is the author of *Trying to Save Piggy Sneed* (1996), a well-regarded collection of his short fiction and essays, and *My Movie Business* (1999), which details his struggle to bring *The Cider House Rules* to the screen. Irving divorced Shyla Leary in 1981 and was remarried, in 1987, to Janet Turnbull, a former editor who is now his literary agent. John Irving has three sons—two from his first marriage and one from his second.

—*C. M.*

SUGGESTED READING: *Atlantic* p256 July 1985; *Entertainment Weekly* p75 Sep. 9, 1994, p92 May 15, 1994; *Globe and Mail* C p6 Apr. 1, 1989, C p10 Sep. 3, 1994; *Maclean's* p63 Apr. 3, 1989; *New York Times* (on-line) Apr. 28, 1998, July 8, 2001, *Newsweek* p64 Apr. 10, 1989; *Washington Post* (on-line) July 2, 2001; *Washington Post Book World* p1 Mar. 5, 1989; Miller, G. *John Irving*, 1982

SELECTED BOOKS: *Setting Free the Bears*, 1969; *The Water-Method Man*, 1972; *The 158-Pound Marriage*, 1974; *The World According to Garp*, 1978; *The Hotel New Hampshire*, 1981; *The Cider House Rules*, 1985; *A Prayer for Owen*

Meany, 1989; *A Son of the Circus*, 1994; *Trying to Save Piggy Sneed*, 1996; *A Widow for One Year*, 1998; *The Fourth Hand*, 2001

(c) 2002 AP Wide World Photos

Jenkins, Dan

1929– Novelist; sportswriter

Though well known for many years as a sportswriter for various newspapers and magazines, most notably *Sports Illustrated*, Dan Jenkins came to even greater fame with his 1972 novel *Semi-Tough*, a rough-and-tumble look at professional football and one of the first books to depict sports heroes in a truly unvarnished manner. *Semi-Tough*, which spawned two sequels, became a national bestseller and established its author as arguably one of the wildest and funniest novelists of the era. Jenkins' fiction rails against everything from sportswriters and professional golf to gold-digging women and political correctness. He is sometimes criticized for his blunt language, but such criticism has never deterred him from speaking his mind. "I always thought it takes tremendous ego to be a writer," he told Stephanie Mansfield for the *Washington Post* (November 10, 1984). "To sit down and put your name on it and presume to tell people. But I enjoy it. Because I goddam well *do* know more about it than they do and I want to inform them."

Dan Jenkins was born in Fort Worth, Texas, in 1929. His father, a salesman, deserted the family when Jenkins was a young boy. He has described his mother, who was in the antiques business, as "half-crazy." Jenkins was raised by his grandmother and aunt and has stated in interviews that, having received an abundance of love and humor from them, he remembers his childhood fondly despite its tribulations.

Jenkins' love of sports began early; as a boy he would buy the *Fort Worth Star-Telegram* every day just to read the sports pages. He soon knew he wanted to be a reporter. "I think Clarke Gable did it," he told Mansfield. "Seeing him in an old movie at the age of 10, a guy with the press card in his hat who got to go through life [not taking any nonsense is] what made me want to be a journalist." His grandmother bought him a typewriter, which he used to type out the sports stories he saw in the newspaper. Then, as he told Mansfield, "One day I started trying to improve on [a story]. I thought, 'This guy's an idiot. I can do better than this.' It hasn't stopped since."

As a senior at R. L. Paschal High School, Jenkins was noticed by Blackie Sherrod of the *Fort Worth Press*, who was impressed by an article he had written for the high-school paper. When Jenkins went on to attend Texas Christian University (TCU) and captain the school's golf team, Sherrod arranged a part-time job for him writing for the paper. Upon graduation he began working as a sportswriter for the *Fort Worth Star-Telegram*, a position he held for 10 years. He then moved to the *Dallas Times-Herald* for two years before taking a position at *Sports Illustrated*, sometimes known informally as *SI*. The job at *SI* required Jenkins to move to New York City. He immediately felt at home. "He got to New York and in two weeks every maitre d' in town knew his name," Gary Cartwright, a fellow sportswriter, told Jason Cohen for *Texas Monthly* (November 1998). Jenkins soon became well known in the city's most exclusive establishments for both his wit and his capacity for drink.

"The sixties were *SI*'s golden years," Jason Cohen noted, "and as the country's leading college football expert as well as a preeminent golf writer, Jenkins was untouchable. . . . His combination of clout and creativity was so potent that he was able to cover the Masters [one of the country's preeminent golf tournaments], an event he has now documented for 47 straight years, seemingly without ever leaving the clubhouse. Instead the story would come to him between alternating doses of J&B [scotch] and coffee. . . . His work at *SI* ultimately earned him a place in the pantheon of American's greatest sportswriters." In 1970 Jenkins published *The Dogged Victims of Inexorable Fate*, a collection of his best *SI* golf stories from the 1960s.

When Jenkins began writing his first novel in the early 1970s, he had no agent or publisher ready to receive it. Despite that, *Semi-Tough* became a hit as the first novel to depict the rough language, racial banter, and sexism that pervaded pro football at the time. The narrator of the novel is Billy Clyde Puckett, a fullback for the New York Giants who is recording his memoirs (for a nice profit) a week before his team plays the New York Jets in the Super Bowl. With the help of his good buddy, "Shake" Tiller, he relates his impressions of marijuana smokers, oil barons, Arabs, and orgies, among other topics. "Jenkins . . . has written a book that is about sports, but not about sports, and it is a very funny book," David Halberstam wrote for the *New York Times Book Review* (September 17, 1972). "Jenkins' writing and his ear recall—there is no higher compliment—Ring Lardner, though in different times and different Americas. . . . In Lardner, we were looking at the bush [minor-league] ballplayer. In Jenkins, the ballplayer is no longer so bush, and he is looking at us." Larry L. King, writing in *Life* (September 29, 1972), proclaimed: "If you have the stomach for belly laughs, semi-tough language and spoofing just about everything in modern-day America, then this book should be your stick of tea."

Jenkins quickly followed *Semi-Tough* with a variation on the same theme—the 1974 novel *Dead Solid Perfect*, in which golf pro Kenny Lee Puckett is struggling to get into contention for the U.S. Open. The novel received mixed reviews when it was published (although in recent years it has been looked at more favorably). Eric Moon, in *Library Journal* (October 1, 1974), complained, "Jenkins is reaching too hard, missing too many fairways and too many putts to make par this time." Barry Hannah, in the *New York Times Book Review* (November 3, 1974), had similar complaints: "It may be the intent of the author to elevate self-conscious banality into an art form, but I thought the whole affair came off as tacky." On the other hand, Pete Axthelm in *Newsweek* (November 11, 1974) praised the book, writing, "This is vintage Jenkins—profane, outrageous and sharp-eyed in its parody of the overblown world of big-time golf. It is also distinguished by Beverly, the first really believable female Jenkins has created, and by a climatic golf match that may be the funniest scene he's ever written. But for aficionados, the real joy is still in the one-liners."

Jenkins published two more novels, *Limo* (1976) and *Baja Oklahoma* (1981), which sold well. In 1984 he completed a sequel to *Semi-Tough* titled *Life Its Ownself*, which picks up more than a decade after the events of the first novel. Billy Clyde Puckett has returned, although because of an injury his career may be over, and his marriage is troubled. "Shake" Tiller has retired from the Giants and is writing a book about biased referees. The novel received mixed reviews. In a representative appraisal Michael Dorman wrote for *Newsday* (October 31, 1984): "[Jenkins] tosses off some semi-funny one-liners. And he still has an ear for the idiom of the pro-football locker room or the Fort Worth honky-tonk. But, when you get down to it, the cliche holds in this case: The sequel never lives up to the original."

Jenkins shifted gears for *Fast Copy* (1988), a period novel about Texas in the 1930s. The plot revolves around Betsy Throckmorton and her husband, Ted Winton, who are convinced by Betsy's wealthy father to move back to Claybelle, Texas. The couple, who work for *Time* magazine, agree only after Betsy's father promises to give her control of his newspaper and Ted control of the local radio station. Back in Texas, Betsy and Ted try to make the newspaper and radio station more sophisticated by introducing news from Europe and swing music, but the denizens of Claybelle prefer listening to the radio for the local football game and the latest installment of *The Shadow*. Christopher Lehmann-Haupt called *Fast Copy* a "lively new novel" in his review for the *New York Times* (October 27, 1988) and praised its leisurely pace, which allows time for detailed period descriptions and interesting asides. "It's a delicate trick that Mr. Jenkins tries to pull off, like a bicyclist on a tightrope moving so slowly he nearly topples over," he wrote. "What saves the act is the performer's awareness that if he stops he is bound to fall. Fortunately for the reader, Mr. Jenkins keeps his balance."

When Jenkins returned to the realm of fiction in 1991 with *You Gotta Play Hurt*, he drew on his own experience as a well-known national sportswriter. Jim Tom Pinch, the protagonist of the novel, is sick of dealing with the problems associated with magazine journalism, in particular, editors who hack his stories to pieces. Pinch works for *The Sports Magazine,* or *SM*, a rival of *Sports Illustrated*. He is concerned that a talented researcher named Neil Woodruff might be passed over for promotion to managing editor in favor of the nephew of the magazine's new publisher. Problems at the office are compounded by problems at home when he is forced to choose between his girlfriend, Nell, and Jeanne, a columnist for the *Los Angeles Times*. Christopher Lehmann-Haupt noted for the *New York Times* (December 9, 1991), "What makes this novel special is the author's vitriolic view of the sportswriter's venue and the smooth yet pungent prose in which he vents his outrage."

The second sequel to *Semi-Tough*, *Rude Behavior*, was published in 1998. In it the reader is reintroduced to Billy Clyde Puckett, who finds himself in trouble as a former pro-football star turned team owner when he and his wealthy father-in-law win the rights to the West Texas Tornadoes, an NFL expansion team. The novel received mostly favorable reviews. "A Jenkins novel is like a Robin William appearance on The David Letterman Show: a frenetic, often-hilarious interlude that leaves one breathless from both laughter and the breakneck speed with which the jokes are being delivered," Wes Lukowsky noted for *Booklist* (September 1, 1998). "The novel won't linger in your mind for long, but don't be surprised to hear yourself mumbling 'damn gubmint' at inappropriate moments." Marylaine Block, in *Library Journal* (September 15, 1998), had similar praise: "Anyone who has read *Semi-Tough* will not be surprised that this book . . . is sexist, racist, redneck, antigay, politically incorrect, and guaranteed to offend virtually every category of human being. It is also rolling-on-the floor funny."

In 2001 Jenkins returned to the world of professional golf tours with *The Money-Whipped Steer-Job Three-Jack Give-Up Artist*. Bobby Joe Grooves is a touring pro golfer who has been around the golf circuit long enough to collect two ex-wives; he needs to be around a little longer to keep them supplied with alimony. He also has to deal with a hack sportswriter who wants to ghostwrite his memoirs, media junkets with dot.com millionaires, and the commercialization of his sport—a trend he decries. The book received mostly favorable notices. In *Publishers Weekly* (July 9, 2001) a reviewer called the book "a blasphemous roasting of the PGA [Professional Golfers Association]" and wrote, "this goofy encyclopedia of golf shines with rays of simple truth." On the other hand, Tobin Harshaw was somewhat more critical in the *New York Times Book Review* (August 12, 2001), noting: "It's not that Jenkins hasn't written another laugh-out-loud funny—and unabashedly politically incorrect—insider's look at the tour. But if the new book compares unfavorably with [*Dead Solid Perfect*], it's because his characters have suffered a bit from the game's corporate transformation."

In 1959 Jenkins married his third wife, June Burrage. They have three children, Marty, Danny, and Sally, who is also a sportswriter. Jenkins has been a contributor to *Golf Digest* and *Playboy*, and his articles have been collected in *You Call It Sports, But I Say It's a Jungle Out There* (1989) and *Fairways and Greens* (1995). He has also published *Bubba Talks of Love, Sex, Whiskey, Politics, Foreigners, Teenagers, Movies, Food, Football, and Other Matters That Occasionally Concern Human Beings* (1993), in which he examines the archetype of the Southern "good old boy" in a collection of short humourous pieces.

—C. M.

SUGGESTED READING: *Booklist* p118 Sep. 15, 1993, p1758 June 1–15, 1994, p6 Sep. 1, 1998; *Business Week* p12 Sep. 16, 1972; *Chicago Tribune* I p12 Oct. 28, 1981; *Library Journal* p2176 June 1, 1970, p112 Sep. 15, 1998; *Life* p24 Sep. 29, 1972; *New Republic* p31 Sep. 16, 1972, p30 Dec. 28, 1974; *New York* p52+ Sep. 9, 1974; *New York Times* C p25 Oct. 27, 1988, C p18 Dec. 9, 1991; *New York Times Book Review* p2 Sep. 17, 1972, p69 Nov. 3, 1974, p44 Oct. 24, 1976, p67 Nov. 14, 1993, p5 Aug. 12, 2001; *Newsday* II p31 Oct. 31, 1984; *Newsweek* p112 Nov. 11, 1974; *Publishers Weekly* p43 July 9, 2001; *Saturday Review* p35 Oct. 2, 1976; *Texas Monthly* p56+ Nov. 1998; *Washington Post* D p1+ Nov. 10, 1984

SELECTED BOOKS: nonfiction—*Dogged Victims of Inexorable Fate*, 1970, *You Call It Sports, But I Say It's a Jungle Out There*, 1989, *Fairways and Greens*, 1994; fiction—*Semi-Tough*, 1972; *Dead Solid Perfect*, 1974; *Limo*, 1976; *Baja Oklahoma*, 1981; *Life Its Ownself*, 1984; *Fast Copy*, 1988; *You Gotta Play Hurt*, 1991; *Rude Behavior*, 1998; *The Money-Whipped Steer-Job Three-Jack Give-Up Artist*, 2001

Jones, Kaylie

Aug. 5, 1960– Novelist

Although the American novelist Kaylie Jones has written extensively about her famous father—the novelist James Jones—particularly in her autobiographical novels *As Soon as It Rains* (1986) and *A Soldier's Daughter Never Cries* (1990), she has not adopted the themes or style of James Jones's brutal anti-war realism. Rather, she writes, as a *Publishers Weekly* (February 21, 2000) reviewer put it, of "tangled loves and shattered dreams." She drew on her experiences as a student in Moscow for her novel *Quite the Other Way* (1989) and wrote in *Celeste Ascending* (2000) of the way in which a young woman's childhood experiences helped drive her toward an abusive relationship and alcoholism.

Kaylie Jones was born in Paris, France, on August 5, 1960 to James and Gloria Jones. Her early years were spent in Paris, where her father was the center of a group of writers and artists. In the Jones's home, James Baldwin would often mount a replica of an 18th-century wooden pulpit, an item that the family used as a bar. "Baldwin . . . often preached late at night," Jones wrote in an essay in the *New York Times* (September 17, 1998). "My father had a rule that anyone with a point to make could take the pulpit and speak uninterrupted for up to 10 minutes. Baldwin, who came from a long line of Baptist preachers, loved to expound on racism, maintaining that all white Americans were racist, which enraged my father, who believed he had thrown off the shackles of his puritan upbringing." Jones was permitted as a small child to drag her blanket to the living room and observe her parents' get-togethers, despite their friends' comments that the goings-on might not be suitable for a child.

The family later moved to Sagaponack, Long Island, partly because of James Jones's ill health. Jones received her B.A. degree from Wesleyan University, in Middletown, Connecticut, in 1981. She went on to attend Columbia University, where she was awarded a master of fine arts degree in creative writing in 1983 and then stayed on to study Russian language and literature. She has also studied at the Pushkin Institute, in Moscow, and taught creative writing at Southampton College of Long Island University.

Jones's first novel, *As Soon as It Rains*, published in 1986, was begun as her master's thesis in writing. It is an autobiographical story of a young woman, Chloe, overwhelmed by the death of her father, a famous writer. (Jones made the father character a playwright rather than a novelist.) Chloe goes to college in Connecticut, as did Jones,

Frederic Reglain/Courtesy of Kaylie Jones
Kaylie Jones

and returns to Paris, where her family had lived on the Ile St. Louis, for a year abroad— finally accepting her loss and reconciling herself to her family back on Long Island. "My book is about that terrible feeling of being alone," Jones told James R. Genovese in an interview in the *New York Times* (March 16, 1986).

John House, writing in the *New York Times Book Review* (March 9, 1986), termed "[a]cademic indecision, a difficult love, a semester abroad," subjects he found in Jones's novel, to be "familiar clippings from a college diary." He observed that to be the "stuff of a novel," those subjects require "a reader's complicity; they depend for effect on having been shared." Jones, he felt, "comes shy of the conviction needed to confront the questions she asks" and "treats her heroine's grief in an oblique, tentative way." In spite of those failings, however, "the absence of irony and affectation in the book is as rare as Chloe's unmannered innocence, and as welcome," he concluded.

With her second novel, *Quite the Other Way*, Jones was deemed by David Finkle in the *New York Times Book Review* (August 27, 1989) a worthy successor to her father and fit company for Martin Amis and Susan Cheever, both children of famous writers who are successful in their own right. Jones drew on her experiences in and study of Russia for the novel, in which Clinton Gray, the daughter of a prominent American journalist, spends a semester in Moscow studying Russian culture and seeking information about her father's stay there during World War II. Despite what he saw as too much day-to-day minutia in the book, Finkle concluded that Jones's "account of Clinton's quest for fragments of her father's past and her coming to terms with life and love in today's Soviet Union is touching, disturbing, funny, frustrating and as charming in its way as . . . earlier adventures of Americans-abroad Emily Kimbrough and Cornelia Otis Skinner."

It was with her 1990 novel, *A Soldier's Daughter Never Cries*, that Jones achieved fame. The autobiographical story of a girl's life in Paris and return to America with her parents, the book details the coming-of-age of the protagonist, Channe. The novel is divided into three parts, the first dealing with the integration of Billy, a French boy, into the household, and Channe's initial rejection and ultimate acceptance of him. The second part involves Channe's relationship with a flamboyant schoolmate—who feels rejected when the teenage Channe becomes interested in boys. In the last section, Channe must come to grips with her beloved father's mortality, as he is slowly claimed by illness. *A Soldier's Daughter Never Cries* was well-received and was made into a film in 1998.

Jones's 2000 novel, *Celeste Ascending*, although it is a coming-of-age story, is not obviously based on the story of Jones's own life. Celeste, the main character, is a New Yorker—a teacher, writer, and student at Columbia University. She encounters Alex, an investment banker, who is able to provide her with the luxuries that teaching in Harlem cannot. What Alex is unable to do is drive away the lingering pain from Celeste's past, which tinges her new relationship and leads her to consume ever greater amounts of alcohol. The *Publishers Weekly* (February 21, 2000) reviewer praised "Jones's affinity for her vividly executed characters." The *Library Journal* (March 1, 2000) reviewer, Caroline M. Hallsworth, agreed, citing Jones's "decisively . . . clear prose that cuts directly to Celeste's soul." She saw the novel as one that would cause readers to think about "partner abuse and alcohol dependency," since Celeste is aware of Alex's "manipulative force but . . . is unwilling or unable to recognize Alex's lethal aspect." The novel's strength lies, according to Hallsworth, in Jones's "exploring and understanding this paradox."

In an on-line interview with *Teachers & Writers*, Jones, in describing her techniques as a teacher of creative writing, expressed her own approach to the art: "I take the approach that no story is boring or unimportant, that characterization and motivation are crucial to a story. . . . 'Does this move you?' is my primary question."

—S. Y.

SUGGESTED READING: *Denver Post* E p14 Apr. 2, 1999; *Library Journal* p124 Mar. 1, 2000; *New York Times* XI p19 Mar. 16, 1986; *New York Times Book Review* p24 Mar. 9, 1986, p16 Aug. 27, 1989; *Pitch Weekly* (on-line) Jan.20, 1999; *Publishers Weekly* p65+ Feb. 21, 2000; *Teachers and Writers* (on-line); *Washington Post* B p5 Sep. 25, 1998

SELECTED BOOKS: *As Soon as It Rains*, 1986; *Quite the Other Way*, 1989; *A Soldier's Daughter*, 1990; *Celeste Ascending*, 2000

Jones, Thom

1945– Short-story writer

The American fiction writer Thom Jones had an apprenticeship that included service in the marines, boxing, and advertising as well as janitorial work. Similarly, his writing is characterized by a wide variety of subjects and locales; his three collections of short stories, *The Pugilist at Rest* (1993), *Cold Snap* (1995), and *Sonny Liston was a Friend of Mine* (1999), range in setting from the American heartland, to Vietnam, to Africa and India. His characters, as Joyce Carol Oates described them in the *New York Times Book Review* (June 4, 1995), are "a gallery of the walking wounded," including soldiers, doctors, and boxers. Oates observed that "though they are all in dire states, the last thing they demand is pity. Bleakly and outrageously comic, the inhabitants of Mr. Jones's fictional landscape are never less than articulate about their fates. . . . The vision . . . is bleak and intransigent. Yet, over all, Thom Jones's stories . . . quiver with their own manic life. The thrilling urgency of his voice transcends his subject."

Thom Jones was born in 1945. His first book, *The Pugilist at Rest*, was not published until 1993, when he was in his late 40s. Its title story appeared in the *New Yorker*, thus attracting the attention of literary agents and publishers; Jones thereafter had little trouble getting his stories published. The *Nation* (September 6, 1993) critic Ted Solotaroff found "several interactive furies in the writing persona of Thom Jones," making *The Pugilist at Rest* "seem like a three-car collision on the Indy 500. Lots of power and lots of wreckage pile up as each situation races along its violent or otherwise 'wired' premise to its baleful destination." The characters in *The Pugilist at Rest* vary from amphetamine-addicted veterans of the Vietnam War to a janitor to a dying woman. "The themes dominating [the book] are violence, adultery, alcoholism, epilepsy, and madness," according to Mark Annichiarico, the reviewer for *Library Journal* (April 15, 1993). Some of the characters suffer from the same physical problems that have plagued Jones himself. Jones's writing is notable, and has won him acclaim, in part because of its comic riffs. "Theogones was the greatest of gladiators," one of Jones's narrators says, in discussing the Roman statue *The Pugilist at Rest*. "It was the approximate time of Homer, the greatest poet who ever lived. Then, as now, violence, suffering, and the cheapness of life were the rule." The contrasting of the classical statue and the poet of the *Iliad* with an evocation of Hollywood noir is representative of Jones's ability to draw upon disparate elements in a short space.

"Giving voice to the deepest instincts of man is what Thom Jones is after," the novelist Robert O'Connor wrote in his *Washington Post* (June 29, 1993) review of *The Pugilist at Rest*. "His characters, having bought into the Hemingwayesque code of violence, excitement, misogyny, and danger, are hard up against it and are looking for some new answers to the old questions. . . . These stories show, unapologetically, the gritty side of life as a man, not only in our time but throughout time. By courageously confronting not only the how but the why of life and war and love, Thom Jones offers not redemption, but understanding."

Because *The Pugilist at Rest* won such praise—as well as a place for its title story in *The Best American Short Stories 1992* and a nomination for the National Book Award in 1993—Jones's next book was awaited with great eagerness. For most reviewers *Cold Snap* did not disappoint. Another collection of "gritty yarns," according to Bill Marx, commenting in the *Boston Globe* (February 4, 1999), *Cold Snap* drew raves for "Jones's depictions of macho mayhem among the permanently deranged." In *Cold Snap* Jones added to his gallery of desperate women and men struggling to maintain their way of life in contemporary America. "Jones writes best about the partially deranged, semi-sensible ideas that dash through men's minds when they're by themselves (or should be)," Scott Bradfield noted in the *Times Literary Supplement* (May 17, 1996). His "characters don't so much speak as assault one another with ideas about donor-weariness, Rumpelstiltskin, or the best way to pack sardines. Their recurring obsessions and Jones's as well, it seems, are Jaguars, dogs, drugs (both over and under the counter), rock and roll, existentialism, and boxing. As soon as the opening bell sounds, Jones's characters come out, prepared to beat one another into the ropes with anything available, even words." Jones, too, according to Bradfield, "delivers his punches with a steady, even accuracy." He concluded that "as a writer of vision, integrity, and conscience, [Jones] keeps coming at you, and never holds back any of his best stuff." In an on-line interview with Amy Firis for *Citybeat* (1996), Jones spoke of his surprise that his audiences at readings are mainly female. Yet Jones has clearly reserved much of his deepest sympathy for the women in his stories, who are as battered by life as the men but are usually less able to give "payback."

Although readers and critics were looking forward to a hinted-at novel, Jones's next book was *Sonny Liston Was a Friend of Mine*, another collection of stories. Again the volume is filled with tales of losers who manage to pull a kind of victory of bare moral survival out of the jaws of defeat. In the title story, Kid Dynamite, a high-school boxer, draws as his opponent in a tournament the best boxer in the league. The Kid's hand already contains a number of losing cards: an indifferent mother, a stepfather—called Cancer Frank—who has no faith in him, and little chance for the college education that awaits his girlfriend. Kid Dynamite manages to win the bout, but afterward he comes to a realization:

> Suddenly, definitely, boxing was over. For years, it had protected him in ways he never entirely understood—a buffer, a cushion, a

thing he had to do. By turning his back on it he knew that he was losing something that had given his life a magical sense of meaning and simplicity. The real world had seemed far away; now it was upon him.

The acceptance of a world that has little to offer them is a choice many of Jones's characters must make as an alternative to death, and there is usually a kind of joy in the acceptance.

Most reviewers continued to laud Jones, but some had cavils about *Sonny Liston Was a Friend of Mine*. Matt Barnard, the *New Statesman* (February 26, 1999) reviewer, found "a rough poetry" in Jones's language and praised his "powerful and original imagination," maintaining that "Jones belongs to the American tradition in which the writer and the writing are inseparable." Nevertheless, Barnard found Jones to be "straining" against the bounds of the short story, "wanting to escape into the freedom of the novel." Kasia Boddy, the *Guardian* (March 6, 1999) reviewer, disagreed. She observed that although hints about an impending Jones novel continued to be dropped, "Jones's talent seems very much suited to the short story form. With great skill he exploits . . . the scope of an individual piece while retaining its separate identity . . . without needing to resort to the type of progressive development associated with the novel. Each story informs and modifies the others. Within each collection patterns of juxtaposition and comparison build up, and over the three collections these become increasingly complex." Boddy found that Jones had found a new way of dealing with masculine reality: "Whereas Hemingway hoped to carry over the codes of ritualised male life into a wider context and so achieve some kind of redemption, for Jones the two worlds are fundamentally incommensurable. . . . There is nonetheless a more optimistic view of human intimacy here."

Among Jones's experiences have been mystical ones. "The ecstasy was almost unendurable," he told Susannah Hunnewell in an interview in the *New York Times Book Review* (June 13, 1993). "I had to read philosophy to figure out what I had experienced. There was such a certainty that God exists. Even though people are suffering and the world is a sorry place, it's all necessary. . . . When I write, I am searching for that kind of rapture. Art is the closest way to get at it if you're not crazy."

—S. Y.

SUGGESTED READING: *Boston Globe* E p2 Feb. 4, 1999; *Guardian* p10 Mar. 6, 1999; *Nation* p254+ Sep. 6, 1993; *New Statesman* p57 Feb. 26, 1999; *New York Times Book Review* p7 June 13, 1993, p8 June 4, 1995, p38 Mar. 14, 1999, p2 Apr. 4, 1999; *Studies in Short Fiction* p122+ Winter 1997; *Time* p60 June 19, 1995; *Times Literary Supplement* (on-line) May 17, 1996; *Washington Post* D p4 June 29, 1993

SELECTED BOOKS: *The Pugilist at Rest*, 1993; *Cold Snap*, 1995; *Sonny Liston Was a Friend of Mine*, 1999

Courtesy of Harcourt Publicity

Kahn, Roger

Oct. 31, 1927– Novelist; short-story writer; journalist

The baseball writer, novelist, journalist, and historian Roger Kahn is known principally for his 1972 book, *The Boys of Summer*. That work combines the story of Kahn's youth in Brooklyn and the saga of the Brooklyn Dodgers, the legendary baseball team that he covered during their years of glory. In all, Kahn has written more than 15 books, and while his fame rests on his coverage of baseball, he has explored a variety of subjects, in such volumes as *The Passionate People: What It Means to Be a Jew in America* (1968), *The Battle for Morningside Heights: Why Students Rebel* (1970), *Joe and Marilyn: A Memory of Love* (1986), and *A Flame of Pure Fire: Jack Dempsey and the Roaring '20s* (1999). His most recent book is *October Men* (2003), the story of the 1978 World Champion New York Yankees.

Roger Kahn was born in Brooklyn, New York, on October 31, 1927, the son of Olga Rockow Kahn and Gordon Jacques Kahn, both of whom taught at Thomas Jefferson High School. An editor and historian, Gordon Kahn was to become one of the originators of the radio quiz show *Information Please*; he was also passionately interested in baseball and claimed to have played for City College of New York. Olga Kahn much preferred literature to baseball and for a time led the family in weekly readings from James Joyce's novel *Ulysses*.

Perhaps the defining event of Kahn's life was his birth in Brooklyn in the late 1920s; his formative years coincided with the heyday of the Dodgers, the fabled team known affectionately as "dem bums." Part of the Dodgers' mystique was the love they inspired among fans, despite the fact that they seldom won a World Series. Throughout Kahn's youth he followed the team closely, witnessing such historic events as the integration of major-league baseball, when the gifted African-American player Jackie Robinson joined the Dodgers' lineup, in 1947.

In the same year, after having attended New York University on and off, Kahn followed his interest in both writing and sports to a job with the *New York Herald Tribune*. Five years later, when he was 24, the *Tribune* made him its Dodgers reporter. By 1955 Kahn was the highest-paid sportswriter specializing in baseball in New York City; he was also the co-author of a baseball almanac. Although he was taken off the Dodgers beat in 1953, after he referred to the team's stadium—Ebbets Field—in print as a "sarcophagus" (which means "coffin"), he maintained contact with Jackie Robinson. He collaborated with the athlete, who became his close friend, on a series of articles for *Our Sports*, a magazine intended for an African-American audience. Black star players were still a new phenomenon in baseball when Kahn, now assigned to cover the New York Giants, began writing about Willie Mays—whom he would call the "most exciting player" he had ever seen. In 1956 Kahn went to work for *Newsweek* as sports editor. He also published pieces in other magazines, such as *Sports Illustrated*, the *Saturday Evening Post*, and *Esquire*. While he lived and wrote mainly in a world of sports and the hard-bitten reporters who covered them, Kahn was interested in modern poetry and symphonic music as well (although he did not write about them). In 1962 he published *Inside Big League Baseball*; intended for young people, the book was widely praised as good reading for baseball fans of all ages.

Kahn's first major book to deal with a topic other than baseball was *The Passionate People: What It Means to Be a Jew in America*, a mixture of character sketches and history. While the *Library Journal* (May 1, 1968) reviewer found the book to be "a fascinating combination of flavor and fact, entertainment and information," other critics were not so kind. Marshall Sklare, the *Commentary* (October 1968) reviewer, declared that *The Passionate People* was "replete with technical errors" and that, in its attempt to beguile readers, it offered "vulgarity and distortion." For *Christian Science Monitor* (June 27, 1968) writer Michael J. Bandler, the book "overemphasizes the vulgar and ignores many important issues."

Like his fascination with the Dodgers, Kahn's 1970 book, *The Battle for Morningside Heights: Why Students Rebel*, came about partly as a result of geography: he lived near the Morningside Heights campus of New York's Columbia University, and during the 1968 student rebellion—which constituted a protest against the Vietnam War and racial injustice as well as a demand for "participatory democracy" on campus—he was able to interview many of the participants, including students, professors, police, and neighbors, to create an overview of the events. Critics were divided over the merits of the book. A. L. Fessler, in *Library Journal* (March 15, 1970), praised Kahn's indictment of "both racism and Big Education as the *agents provocateurs* of much of the violence on our campuses," and thought that his "account of the police bust, the finest writing in the book, resonates with the vulgarity, clangor, and terror of that night." The *New York Times Book Review* (November 8, 1970) critic, Samuel McCracken, found "Kahn's weakness for the wildly irrelevant . . . obtrusive" and "his analysis . . . little more than uncritical recitation of S. D .S. [Students for a Democratic Society] verities." In the opinion of the *Time* (March 23, 1970) reviewer, Kahn demonstrated "a fine eye for the humor and irony in the midst of turmoil."

Kahn's national reputation was achieved with his 1972 work, *The Boys of Summer*, an account of his youth as a baseball fan and of the lives of those who played for the Brooklyn Dodgers in the early 1950s. Joe Black, Roy Campanella, Billy Cox, Carl Erskine, Carl Furillo, Gil Hodges, Clem Labine, Andy Pafko, Pee Wee Reese, Jackie Robinson, Preacher Roe, Duke Snider, and other members of the Dodgers captured the imaginations of Americans, and Kahn chronicled their last seasons playing in Brooklyn; their 1955 World Series win; the team's 1958 move to Los Angeles; and the players' lives after baseball. The book, which takes its title from a poem by Dylan Thomas, was widely acclaimed and has been reprinted in several editions.

In an article entitled "Dem Bums Become the Boys of Summer: From Comic Caricatures to Sacred Icons of the National Pastime," which appeared in *American Jewish History* (March 1995), Frederic M. Roberts examined what lay behind the durability of *The Boys of Summer*. "Almost all of the critics describe *The Boys of Summer* as nostalgic," he wrote. "In fact, a major reason *The Boys of Summer* is a classic is that Kahn excelled at what could be termed mature nostalgia—a fine balancing of a fond and reassuring view of the past with a realistic appraisal of its faults. . . . Mature nostalgia allows the reader to never feel that he has forgotten one of the most important and painful lessons learned during the '60s and early '70s—avoid illusions and naiveté: at almost any cost. . . . That lesson . . . is inherently reinforced by the Brooklyn Dodger 'story.' For the story's unhappy ending—Walter O'Malley's removal of the team to Los Angeles . . . is remembered by many as one of their earliest and most traumatic introductions to the facts of the 'real world.' They discovered that in America when the values of loyalty and community clash with power and greed, the latter forces almost inevitably prevail." Peter Prescott, a contemporary reviewer of *The Boys of Summer* for *Newsweek* (March 13, 1972), caught the tone of the book itself when he wrote: "Kahn's book is knowledgeable, leisurely, and anecdotal. . . . But it is more: Kahn never forgets that he is writing about men in relation to a certain discipline, a certain level of achievement, a certain process of decline, and as such his book acquires a cumulative power. It is not just another book about baseball or a boy growing up to like baseball, but a book about pain and defeat and endurance, about how men, anywhere, must live."

Kahn's next volume was a collection of articles, *How the Weather Was* (1973). *A Season in the Sun*, another nonfiction book about baseball, followed four years later. The year 1979 saw the publication of Kahn's first novel, *But Not to Keep*, a story of divorce and a custody battle over a 14-year-old boy. The protagonist of the novel is, like Kahn, a journalist who enjoys great art. A *Kirkus Reviews* (March 15, 1979) writer found fault with the book: "Kahn, embarrassingly, interrupts his narrative early to announce: 'Aside from genius and politics, talent and venality, you always rooted for the artist over the reviewer, provided only that the artist did his honest best. Bardic best. Symphonic best. Bad best. Best, any best, deserved decency. It was frightening to stand naked out there, naked and vulnerable and stained by hope.' Kahn stuffs the novel with this kind of anxious, self-dramatizing filler." Michael J. Bandler, in the *Christian Science Monitor* (July 18, 1979), took the opposite viewpoint, finding *But Not to Keep* to be a "sensitive, occasionally frustrating, yet honest and credible first novel." Bandler pointed out that in addition to condemning divorce as practiced by Americans, Kahn "confronts other beleaguered institutions, such as religion and race, and vents himself on the hypocrisy and bigotry that incessantly pollute the rarefied air of 'Society.'" Kahn returned to baseball for the subject of his 1982 novel, *The Seventh Game*. A sentimental story of an over-the-hill pitcher reminiscing about his past, the book was reviewed in such a way as to make it Kahn's last foray into the novel form to date.

Good Enough to Dream (1985) was Kahn's nonfiction account of how he became the president and part-owner of a minor-league baseball team, the Utica (New York) Blue Sox. The team, Paul Stuewe wrote in *Quill & Quire* (March 1986), was "characterized by marginal players, an explosive manager, and a patchwork playing field. How these volatile elements coalesced into a rollercoaster ride of horsehide high jinks is the engaging subject of this immensely enjoyable book."

Joe and Marilyn: A Memory of Love, Kahn's 1986 book about the romance, marriage, and lives of baseball legend Joe DiMaggio and screen icon Marilyn Monroe, was received warmly by some reviewers as a collection of fascinating anecdotes if not a penetrating analysis of its subjects' personalities. Also in 1986, Kahn received an assignment to ghost-write the autobiography of Pete Rose, the star hitter for the Cincinnati Reds, whose career was later derailed by accusations of illegal gambling. Before the book was completed, tragedy entered Kahn's life: his son Roger committed suicide, in 1987. Kahn included mention of his son's addiction to drugs and death at the age of 22 in *Pete Rose: My Story*, his 1989 book. Although written with—and about—Rose, the book is told chiefly in Kahn's voice. Elliott J. Gorn, the reviewer for the *Nation* (January 22, 1990), called *Pete Rose* "a disappointing work, nowhere near what Kahn achieved in his lyrical *The Boys of Summer*. Kahn is too taken with Rose to explain him." Nevertheless, Gorn found that just "reading about Willie Mays, Hank Aaron, and Sandy Koufax, about the Big Red Machine, the 1975 World Series and Charlie Hustle's quest for hit number 4,192 revives old passions. What is missing from *My Story*, however, is a sense of the complexity of the game." In an interview for *Publishers Weekly* (October 4, 1993), Kahn told Craig Little that he "wouldn't collaborate" with a sports figure again. "There are people who are better at that than I am," he said.

Baseball was the subject of Kahn's next two books, *Games We Used to Play: A Lover's Quarrel with the World of Sport* (1992), his second collection of articles, and *The Era: 1947–1957, When the Yankees, the New York Giants, and the Brooklyn Dodgers Ruled the World*, published in 1993. With *The Era*, Kahn, who had already created a baseball classic in *The Boys of Summer*, returned to the time before the Dodgers left Brooklyn to cover 11 seasons of New York baseball, beginning with the arrival of Jackie Robinson. Bill Ott, reviewing the volume for *Booklist* (September 1, 1993), remarked that Kahn "brings to the familiar story of the Giants, Yankees, and Dodgers not only an eyewitness perspective . . . but also a willingness to dig beneath the surface, look beyond the legends. . . . The best stories always bear retelling, and Kahn is the right man to retell the story of baseball's greatest decade." Kahn continued to mine the golden era of baseball in *Memories of Summer: When Baseball Was an Art and Writing About It a Game*, published in 1997.

Many years earlier, in 1969, Kahn's friend Jack Dempsey—the former heavyweight boxing champion of the world—had asked him to get his "story straight." Kahn did so, 16 years after Dempsey's death, with *A Flame of Pure Fire: Jack Dempsey and the Roaring '20s*, published in 1999. While the book offered detailed descriptions of Dempsey's legend-making fights with Jess Willard, Luis Firpo, and Gene Tunney, many reviewers felt that the best part of the book was Kahn's description of Dempsey's impoverished childhood, early struggle for survival, and emergence as a boxer in mining camps before he was 20. Michiko Kakutani of the *New York Times* (December 14, 1999) judged that Dempsey did not live up to Kahn's portrait of him as an iconic figure of the "roaring '20s," and that "Kahn's determination to open out Dempsey's story into something larger causes him to lard the boxer's tale with dozens of panoramic asides. . . . These asides—about everything from Sacco and Vanzetti to Warren G. Harding, from women's suffrage to Prohibition—have little to do with Dempsey, and they end up feeling irrelevant and pretentious." Kakutani added that Kahn "is at his best in this volume describing Dempsey's actual fights, capturing the thrashing, deadly violence of the boxer in the ring."

The Head Game: Baseball Seen from the Pitcher's Mound (2000) is about pitching. Kahn described how the underhand toss of baseball's early days evolved into pitching, and he covered the careers of such great pitchers as Warren Spahn and Don Drysdale. Alan Schwarz, in an assessment for the *New York Times Book Review* (September 10, 2000), found fault with *The Head Game*: "Kahn spends so much time swooning" at what the pitchers did, he complained, "that he veers away form the promise of his book, which is to explore and explain the beauty of how they did it." Schwarz also felt that Kahn focused too much on pitchers from the 1960s and before, missing such greats as Pedro Martinez and "a chance to offer a comprehensive depiction of pitching today and where it is headed."

In his most recent work, *October Men* (2003), Kahn recalls the remarkable championship season of the 1978 New York Yankees, when the team came back from 14 games behind first place to win the World Series. The team also faced internal struggles, both on the field and off, including heated battles between the Yankees owner, George Steinbrenner, manager, Billy Martin, and marquee players like Reggie Jackson, who helped to lead the team to victory after Martin's departure in mid-season.

Roger Kahn married Katharine C. Johnson, his third wife, in 1989. He has two surviving children from previous marriages. —S. Y.

SUGGESTED READING: *American Heritage* p87+ Oct. 1999, with photo; *American Jewish History* p51+ Mar. 1995; *Commentary* p82 Oct. 1968; *Nation* p93 Jan. 22, 1990; *New York Review of Books* p60+ Nov. 4, 1993; *New York Times Book Review* p45 Nov. 8, 1970, p32 May 5, 1972, p5+ July 3, 1977, p12 Apr. 6, 1997, p43 Sep. 10, 2000; *Newsweek* p94 Mar. 13, 1972, p82 Nov. 10, 1986; *Publishers Weekly* p49+ Oct. 4, 1993, with photo; *Quill & Quire* p78 Mar. 1986

SELECTED BOOKS: *Inside Big League Baseball*, 1962; *The Passionate People: What It Means to Be a Jew in America*, 1968; *The Battle for Morningside Heights: Why Students Rebel*, 1970; *The Boys of Summer*, 1972; *How the Weather Was*, 1973; *A Season in the Sun*, 1977; *But Not to Keep*, 1979; *The Seventh Game*, 1982; *Good Enough to Dream*, 1985; *Joe and Marilyn: A Memory of Love*, 1986; *Pete Rose: My Story*, 1989; *Games We Used to Play: A Lover's Quarrel With the World of Sport*, 1992; *The Era: 1947–1957, When the Yankees, the New York Giants, and the Brooklyn Dodgers Ruled the World*, 1993; *Memories of Summer: When Baseball Was an Art and Writing About It a Game*, 1997; *A Flame of Pure Fire: Jack Dempsey and the Roaring '20s*, 1999; *The Head Game: Baseball Seen from the Pitcher's Mound*, 2000; *October Men*, 2003

Kalfus, Ken

1954– Short-story writer; journalist

Ken Kalfus has been widely recognized as "one of the United States' most inventive and important contemporary fiction writers," according to Frank Caso for the *Moscow Times* (November 13, 1999). With the critical success of his two short-story collections, *Thirst* (1998) and *Pu-239 and Other Russian Fantasies* (1999)—which was a 2000 PEN/Faulkner nominee—Kalfus has been compared to such influential authors as Ernest Hemingway, John Updike, and Jorge Luis Borges. Kalfus lived abroad for much of the last decade, in such countries as Ireland, France, Yugoslavia, and Russia, and the influence of these travels are visible in nearly every piece of his fiction. As Caso observed, "For Kalfus, geography seems to be the primary starting point and the bridge between his own life and his fiction: [his] is a deep identification with place." In 2003 Kalfus published his first novel, *The Commissariat of Enlightenment*.

Ken Kalfus was born in the New York City borough of the Bronx in 1954; he grew up in Plainview, Long Island, where his parents moved soon after his birth. As early as seventh grade, Kalfus began studying Russian, inspired by dreams of becoming an astronaut. "I was interested in science and astronomy," he told Thomas J. Brady for the *Philadelphia Inquirer* (December 23, 1999), "and I figured Russian would be an advantage." Kalfus had another connection with Russian; his maternal grandparents had emigrated to the U.S. from the Ukraine. His fascination with Russian continued through high school—Kalfus visited the Soviet Union for the first time with his high school Russian class in 1971—and college, when he attended Sarah Lawrence College and later New York University. (He dropped out before obtaining a degree from either institution.) Rather than pursuing a career in space exploration, however, he became interested in writing and ultimately decided on a career in journalism. His first such experience occurred while he was still a student at Plainview-Old Bethpage High School in the early 1970s, when he edited a comic newspaper called *The Daily Raunch*.

After leaving college Kalfus held a series of odd jobs, including a stint as a driver for a livery business in New York City. He soon settled into more regular work as a freelance writer, providing articles for various publications, including numerous

Ken Yanoviak/Courtesy of HarperCollins Publishers
Ken Kalfus

book reviews for the *New York Times*. In 1990 he edited a series of essays by the writer Christopher Morley for *Christopher Morley's Philadelphia*. In perhaps his most traditional position as a journalist, Kalfus spent two years working as a writer and editor for a Philadelphia-based science publication. Of his success as a reporter, he told Dwight Garner for the on-line magazine *Salon* (July 23, 1998), "I don't think of myself as a journalist, but I do try my hand at it occasionally. I see myself as a bit of a journalist manqué. I have never been great at it. I discovered after a while that the key thing about a journalist's craft is calling up people you don't know and asking them questions. And I found I didn't like it so much. I much preferred calling people—I discovered this when I was working for a science newspaper—and telling them my opinions. That's really absurd, because they were scientists and I wasn't." Throughout this time Kalfus was also writing fiction, and in 1981 he began publishing short stories in magazines. "I've been writing fiction since I was a little kid," he told Garner. "At one point I thought that being a journalist was a way of getting into fiction. But I actually think now that to do good journalism is harder."

After Kalfus married Inga Saffron, a fellow journalist, the couple began traveling the world, often in connection with one or both of their jobs. In the 1990s Kalfus and Saffron spent two years in Dublin, Ireland—where he worked for a current affairs magazine—a year in Paris, France, and another year in Yugoslavia. One of their longest stints abroad took place from 1994 to 1998, when they lived in Moscow, Russia, while Saffron served as the Moscow bureau chief for the *Philadelphia Inquirer*. Kalfus later described the extent to which his travels influenced his fiction: "When you live abroad, even your ordinary life is very stimulating," he told Garner. "I have a Yugoslav friend who says that when you're abroad, nothing's provincial. Just the idea of going out to get your milk and coffee is an adventure. You see everything fresh. It gives you a chance as an adult to see things in a more childlike way. . . . If you're trying to be an artist, it helps to see things in the fresh light of living abroad."

In 1998 Kalfus published *Thirst*, his first collection of short stories. Many of the stories had been written over the previous 10 years, and several had already been published in magazines. Nevertheless, the book's publication marked a significant achievement for the struggling author. "Many times I swore if nothing's coming up by the time I'm [aged] 35," Kalfus told Dan Cryer for *New York Newsday* (October 17, 1999), "I'm going to give this up and make a real career. Here I am at 45 and still trying to hold on as a writer." The wait for validation was at times frustrating, he admitted to Garner, adding, "We live in a society that celebrates success at an early age; the 25-year-olds have the field. Writers get discouraged these days if they're not famous by 25, which is absurd. It's this culture of success we're living in. I feel lucky to have had the chance to learn some skills."

Nevertheless, Kalfus's patience paid off; with the publication of *Thirst*, he was soon receiving wide critical acclaim for his work. *Thirst*, which contains a series of 14 short stories exhibiting widely varying themes and settings, was a somewhat unusual debut for a short-fiction collection, which typically contain stories linked by theme, backdrop, or emotion. Instead, these stories take place in varying times and places, including Venice in 1849, modern Paris, Southeast Asia, Bulgaria, New Hampshire, and Long Island. While the first two stories, "Bouquet" and "Thirst," involve the same character—a young Irish au pair who confronts aspects of her sexuality—the collection quickly shifts gears to explore vastly different territories. In "The Republic of St. Mark, 1849" Kalfus tells a story that resembles both fable and historical document, in which Austrian soldiers try to infiltrate the besieged Italian city of Venice. In contrast, "The Joy and Melancholy Baseball Trivia Quiz" provides a comical narrative of questions and answers about fictional baseball statistics. In "Among the Bulgarians," a high-school student who has just returned from a summer in Bulgaria to his Long Island hometown, comes to terms with the friends who have moved on without him and is overwhelmed by "the fundamental strangeness of being home," as quoted by Ron Carlson for the *New York Times* (July 26, 1998).

Garner wrote for the *Village Voice* (June 2, 1998), "Kalfus is one of those rare writers whose travels haven't colored his prose with cosmopolitan cynicism. He's absorbed emotional truths, not showy surface details. His supple, unfussy stories have something in common with Hemingway's best work; he's willing to let moments speak for themselves." Garner called the book "easily the most potent debut book I've read this year." Writing for *Salon* (July 23, 1998, on-line), Laura Miller affirmed, "It's exhilarating to discover a young writer with so much range and so little self-consciousness about exploring it. The publication of *Thirst* marks the debut of a major talent." *Thirst* was named a *New York Times* Notable Book of the Year, one of *Salon*'s best books of 1998, and one of the *Village Voice*'s top 20.

Kalfus followed up his successful debut with another critically admired collection of short stories, *Pu-239 and Other Russian Fantasies* (1999). This time Kalfus set the book's six stories and one novella in Russia, though at varying times and places in that nation's history. All of his characters are genuinely Russian, as he told Albert Mobilio for the *Voice Literary Supplement* (April 13, 1999). It is a book in which "not a single American expatriate appears," he explained. "In Russia, human life and history are so much on the surface, you can't help getting big ideas." The title story, "Pu-239," which takes its name from the chemical symbol for weapons-grade plutonium, finds Timofey, an engineer at a nuclear-weapons plant, recently made ill by radiation. In making preparations for his family's security after his impending death, he steals a canister of plutonium and attempts to sell it on the black market in modern-day Moscow. Laura Miller for *Salon* (October 25, 1999, on-line) noted the story's "pitch-black humor," which Kalfus managed to extract from such grim circumstances. The story later earned Kalfus a Pushcart Prize, awarded to the best literature from small or independent publishing companies.

Other stories in the collection examine life through various periods of Soviet history. "Birobidzhan," which Donovan Hohn for *Civilization* (October–November 1999) called "one of the most remarkable stories in the collection," takes its title from the name of the town thousands of miles east of European Russia to which more than 40,000 Russian Jews relocated in the late 1920s in an attempt to establish a homeland. (Today only approximately 3,000 Jews remain in the area.) In it Kalfus describes the plight of Jewish pilgrims fleeing the anti-Semitism that characterized the Soviet Union in the years following the revolution; when they arrive at the harsh, unpopulated lands near the Chinese border, they find conditions nearly uninhabitable. Kalfus explained to Thomas J. Brady for the *Philadelphia Inquirer* (December 23, 1999) that the story was in part inspired by the experiences of his grandparents in the 1920s. "I thought, what if, instead of coming here [to the U.S.], they had gone to Birobidzhan instead?" In "Anzhelika, 13," he tells the story of a 13-year-old girl's coming-of-age, when she gets her first period on the same day of the Soviet leader Joseph Stalin's death. In the collection's novella, "Peredelkino," set in 1968, Kalfus describes a Soviet novelist who faces a moral dilemma when he is instructed what to write in order to save his politically troubled career.

Critics celebrated Kalfus's achievement in evoking a genuine Russian narrative style. As Albert Mobilio described, "Kalfus channels the emotional plentitude of Chekhov as well as Gogol's wry comedy—in short, he gets a good portion of the Russian heart on paper." When Thomas J. Brady asked Kalfus if he intentionally tried to conjure a Russian voice, the author explained, "I didn't want to pretend to be a Russian writer, but I wanted people to be able to read the book without being reminded that I was American." Kalfus had traveled throughout Russia interviewing as many people as he encountered in his bid for authenticity. These efforts succeeded: As Paul Richardson noted for *Russian Life* (January–February 2000), "It is exceptionally difficult for a foreigner to write about Russia and get it right. Ken Kalfus gets it right. Again and again." *Pu-239 and Other Russian Fantasies* was named a *New York Times* Notable Book of the Year and was a finalist for the 2000 PEN/Faulkner Award.

In 2003 Kalfus published his first novel, *The Commissariat of Enlightenment*, which tracks the two turbulent decades in Russia between Leo Tolstoy's death in 1910 and the rise of Josef Stalin through the eyes of a young cinematographer who has come to believe that film has a power to shape political ideals. As Russia moves through the revolution of 1917 towards Communism, the cinematographer comes in contact with the Soviet Commissariat of Enlightenment, who is charged with reforging Russian principles and institutions into the new Soviet order. As quoted on the *Amazon.com* Web site, a reviewer for *Publishers Weekly* wrote, "Told in supple, witty and gritty prose, the story exhibits all the vigorous intelligence and vision readers have come to expect from Kalfus."

Ken Kalfus resides in Philadelphia, Pennsylvania, with his wife and daughter, Sky.

—K. D.

SUGGESTED READING: *Moscow Times* Nov. 13, 1999; *New York Times* VII p9 July 26, 1998; *New York Newsday* B p2 Aug. 20, 1998, B p11 Oct. 17, 1999; *Philadelphia Inquirer* Dec. 23, 1999; *Salon* (on-line) July 23, 1998, Oct. 25, 1999

SELECTED BOOKS: *Thirst*, 1998; *Pu-239 and Other Russian Fantasies*, 1999; *The Commissariat of Enlightenment*, 2003

Courtesy of University of Chicago Press

Kaplan, Alice

June 22, 1954– Historian; essayist; memoirist; translator

Alice Kaplan, the American cultural critic and memoirist, has devoted her life and writing to teaching the French language and examining French culture. She has specialized in the literature of fascism as it appeared in France, in the works of such writers and intellectuals as Louis-Fernand Céline, Maurice Bardèche, and Robert Brasillach. Her *Reproductions of Banality: Fascism, Literature, and French Intellectual Life* (1986) is a study of fascist literature in 1930s and 1940s France. She continued her study of that period with *The Collaborator: The Trial and Execution of Robert Brasillach* (2000), in which she "employs the skills of a biographer and literary critic to flesh out the life of Robert Brasillach," according to a reviewer for *Publishers Weekly* (February 28, 2000). Kaplan's most popular book to date is *French Lessons: A Memoir* (1993), "in which a young Jewish woman from Minneapolis questions, affirms, and complicates the various facets of her identity and culture and experiences the privilege of 'living in translation,'" as Stephen Lehmann phrased it in *MultiCultural Review* (March 1994).

Alice Yaeger Kaplan was born in Minneapolis, Minnesota, on June 22, 1954, the youngest of three children. Her mother, Leonore Yaeger Kaplan, was a social worker, and her father, Sidney J. Kaplan, was a lawyer who had been a prosecutor at the Nuremberg war crimes trials of German Nazis following World War II. He died when Alice was eight and, not long after, she found stacks of photographs of concentration camp victims in his old desk. She brought them to school with her. "I believed that my friends had no right to live without knowing about these pictures," she later wrote in *French Lessons*. "I explained to them about the camps, Hitler, how many Jews had died. To shock them. They had to know! I had to tell them. Or was it just that I missed my father. I was trying to do what he would do, be like him." Kaplan continued to follow those threads throughout her life, informing others about Nazi crimes and, in a sense, carrying on her father's work.

From kindergarten through ninth grade, Kaplan attended Northrup Collegiate, a private girls' school. At age 15 she was sent to boarding school in Switzerland, where she first became enchanted with the French language, the eventual conquest of which became a source of great pleasure and pride. Kaplan was admitted to Vassar College, in Poughkeepsie, New York, but left there after her freshman year to attend the University of California at Berkeley. After spending her junior year abroad, at the University of Bordeaux in France, she received her B.A. from Berkeley in 1975. She then went on to pursue graduate work at Yale University, in New Haven, Connecticut, where she embarked on her life-long study of French fascism. At Yale, one of her professors was Paul de Man, the chief American proponent of the deconstruction movement in literary criticism. Kaplan was to write of him in *French Lessons* that, although many thought de Man was out to destroy literature, no "one had ever paid more attention to literature than de Man did. We responded to him because of his ability to trim away anything that wasn't literature—he was the only literary critic we had ever encountered who seemed to know exactly what he was studying." In her memoir, Kaplan also discusses the scandal created when it was revealed, after his death, that de Man had written anti-Semitic and pro-Nazi articles for a collaborationist Belgian publication during World War II.

After receiving her Ph.D. in 1981, Kaplan embarked on an academic career, teaching at a "state school," as she described it, and at Columbia University, in New York City. In 1986 she landed her "dream job," at Duke University, in Durham, North Carolina, as professor of Romance studies and literature, and director of undergraduate studies for the program in literature. In 2000 she was named director of Duke's newly established Institute for French and Francophone Studies.

Kaplan's principal interest lies in history and memory in post-World War II France. Her first book, which was published in 1986, is titled *Reproductions of Banality: Fascism, Literature, and French Intellectual Life*. She described in *French Lessons* her personal connection to the topic of fascism: "In his last year of life my father had read Hannah Arendt on the Eichmann trials. I tried to get into his head by reading it. I fixed on the phrase that Arendt had used to describe the horrors of the Nazi mentality, the phrase I wanted to ask him about: 'The Banality of Evil.' How could so many people—soldiers and bureaucrats but also intellectuals and poets—be blind to so much horror?"

As Russell Berman wrote in the foreword to *Reproductions of Banality*, "Fascism . . . reduces politics to necessity, that appears simultaneously as banality and discipline. 'Banality' is therefore not that which is shared by all of humanity, but the substance of the individual who, relinquishing humanity, only submits to discipline and necessity and is consequently 'natural.'" Kaplan's study of the aesthetics of fascism centers on Robert Brasillach, a journalist and critic; Louis-Fernand Céline, a novelist; and Maurice Bardèche, a literary and film critic, as well as "the dean of antifascism and father of postwar letters," in her words.

Reproductions of Banality concludes with an interview with Maurice Bardèche. In addition to being a literary and film critic, Bardèche was the brother-in-law of Robert Brasillach, who was executed for collaboration with the Nazis in 1945. Kaplan interviewed Bardèche because Céline, Brasillach, and Drieu la Rochelle, "the most decadent of the [French fascists]," were dead. "Like many intellectuals, Bardèche did not see himself as 'political' in the 1930s but rather as 'attracted' to what he understood as a new fascist culture," she wrote in *Reproductions of Banality*.

In a series of events Kaplan recalled in *French Lessons*, Bardèche tried to charm her during her interview with him, attempting to come off as the avuncular professor. After Kaplan had returned to the U.S., he wrote her a letter revealing that he had been playing with her. "Bardèche was offering me, a Jew," she wrote, "the Holocaust without guilt. 'The Jews just died like flies,' he said." To her, his denial of the murder of Jews by the Nazis and their collaborators and his attribution of their deaths to disease bespoke "submammalian genetic weakness." After having buried his letter for five years and then retrieving it, she rewrote the chapter, "making him more evil, more monstrous, conforming to the portrait he paints of himself."

In 1988 Kaplan published *Sources et citations dans "Bagatelles pour un massacre."* In this volume, written in French, Kaplan examines the background of Louis-Fernand Céline's racist tract *Bagatelles pour un massacre* (1937), which in English might be translated as "Trifles for a Massacre." A novelist in the French tradition of Rabelais, but more black and bitter than comical, Céline's most famous work is *Voyage au bout de la nuit* (1932, *Journey to the End of the Night*, 1934). He was also a virulent anti-Semite and fascist. Kaplan spent three years researching the "cheap anti-Semitic leaflets Céline had scavenged to write *Bagatelles pour un massacre*," the first and longest of his polemics. Kaplan described in *French Lessons* how she told a colloquium that the cultural forces that shaped *Bagatelles* could be found "right in the pages of [his] book." Céline's technique was to refer constantly "to his immediate daily context . . . to texts the narrator claims to have read at that very instant, provoking him to write." Although Kaplan was able to discourse ably on the negative aspects of Céline's writings, she also admired the power of his novels: "I got hooked on Céline because he was the farthest from official French I could get in a book. . . . I love Céline for language and emotional directness I don't have. But in the end—I always want to put a 'but' at the beginning of every sentence I write about him—he was paranoid; his reactions distorted the harsh realities he sensed so acutely, but couldn't tolerate."

In *French Lessons: A Memoir* (1993), Kaplan tells the story of her discovery and gradual mastery of the French language, including the pleasure of conquering the pronunciation of the elusive French "r" and the equally difficult French "u," as in "tu." This process awakened Kaplan to the joys of intellectual discovery and led her down a path of teaching, writing, and research. In the memoir, Kaplan also analyzes her own fascination with French fascist thinkers and Jewish-American identity, recalling a newspaper photograph of her father, wearing headphones while listening intently to the proceedings of the Nuremberg trial. Kaplan eventually came to understand "how much I owed to his death, his absence a force field within which I had become an intellectual; his image, silent and distant with headphones over his ears, a founding image for my own work."

Calling *French Lessons* "beautifully, elegantly written," Hephzibah Roskelly in *College English* (October 1995) praised Kaplan's ability to recognize "the loss and the damage that occur when personal experience and intellectual inquiry get divorced." *French Lessons* "confesses, and tells truths, truths that are more powerful for having been learned in more than one language," Roskelly concluded. In his review of the book for *Canadian Literature* (Spring 1996), Norman Ravvin agreed that it was "an uncommonly good book," "wedding the ethnographer's keen eye to the novelists's appreciation for the movement of words and memory." Kaplan, he added, "chastises herself for perhaps having 'reproduced the dry analysis' and 'emotional deadpan' she recognizes in her teacher's [Paul de Man's] literary style. But there is nothing dry or deadpan about *French Lessons*." For Arthur Goldhammer, the reviewer for the *Washington Post Book World* (January 23, 1994), the value of *French Lessons* lay in "its plainspoken, homespun frankness. Told in a 'staccato Midwestern style,' her story of becoming French is arrestingly all-American."

Kaplan, in an essay entitled "The Trouble with Memoir" published in the *Chronicle of Higher Education* (December 5, 1997), recounted a few of the benefits she received from having written *French Lessons*: the book was nominated for a National Book Critics Circle Award, and she became famous and a part of the larger literary world. As she put it in the essay, "I had reached that elusive 'general audience' that we academic writers aren't supposed to have access to." She was invited to lunch in Paris with Edmund White, also a famed autobiographer. Nevertheless, Kaplan had "to fight the feeling that my life was over. There it was, between covers. What if nothing else good or interesting ever happened to me?" she wrote in the essay. The writing of her book had also unleashed a flood of confessions from acquaintances of her family who wanted to reveal dark secrets about themselves that Kaplan had not been privy to. She "had unwittingly opened a bureau des pleurs," Kaplan wrote. A "bureau des pleurs," literally, an "office of tears," is, in her words, "the person you weep and moan to." Then there were people like the English teacher who claimed that Kaplan had been her favorite student. "Reading my memoir made her forget what she actually knew about me: that I had done terrible work in her class. Then and there," Kaplan wrote, "I felt the treachery of memory and the bribe of memoir."

Notwithstanding the downsides Kaplan named, commentators have hailed the recent interest in the genre of scholarly memoir. In the *New York Times Book Review* (September 4, 1994), Ben Yagoda praised what he saw as these memoirs' "more accessible, belletristic writing," adding that Kaplan and a group of scholars like her "have . . . made a transition from sometimes impenetrable high theory to prose, often explicitly autobiographical in cast, that is suitable—and intended—for comparatively wide audiences."

Kaplan's most recent work, *The Collaborator: The Trial and Execution of Robert Brasillach* (2000), dealt with the case of a famous French intellectual who became an editor of fascist magazines such as the anti-Semitic, anti-Republican *Je Suis Partout* ("I Am Everywhere"). Although he was also a novelist and a poet, during the Nazi occupation of France he not only wrote Nazi propaganda but was the editor of a publication that identified Jews by name. Naming, or denouncing, Jews was a way of sending them to almost certain death in the German concentration camps. Nevertheless, although Kaplan believed Brasillach's conviction for treason was justified, she expressed doubts about his execution. Brasillach, who had signed no death warrants personally, was executed, while others who had signed such warrants got off much more lightly. By way of partial answer Kaplan wrote that at the time of Brasillach's trial, crimes against humanity and complicity in deportations were not yet fully understood and had not been granted a place in the French legal code. She further noted that Marcel Reboul, the prosecutor at Brasillach's trial, "played on the real fear and hatred of homosexuality that was alive in the culture," as quoted by Richard Bernstein in the *New York Times* (May 10, 2000, on-line).

"What [Kaplan's] own arguments suggest," Bernstein wrote, "though she does not make this point explicit, is that France in 1944 was readier to punish imputed homosexuality than the murder of Jews." Bernstein concluded that Kaplan's "fine book in this sense shows that the passage of time illuminates different understandings, and she leaves it to us to reflect on which understanding is better." Eugen Weber, the reviewer for the *Los Angeles Times* (May 21, 2000), lauded Kaplan's "fine job plumbing scarce and murky records." *The Collaborator* "provides rich portraits of Brasillach's defender and of his prosecutor," he added. David A. Bell, in the *New York Times Book Review* (April 30, 2000), went even further, observing that Kaplan brought to the somber subject "the same fluidity and grace and even something of the same light, seductive touch with which she earlier described her lifelong love affair with the French and their language." He deemed *The Collaborator* "one of the best-written, most absorbing pieces of literary history in years." The *Publishers Weekly* (February 28, 2000) reviewer proclaimed that "Kaplan . . . brilliantly demonstrates how a trial, and the lives of individuals, can serve as a metaphor for an entire nation."

In addition to doing her own writing, Kaplan has translated several books, including three by Roger Grenier (*Another November*, 1998; *Difficulty of Being a Dog*, 2000; and *Piano Music for Four Hands*, 2001) and one by Louis Guilloux (*Ok, Joe*, 2003).

— S.Y.

SUGGESTED READING: *Canadian Literature* p173+ Spring 1996; *Chronicle of Higher Education* B p4+ Dec. 5, 1997; *College English* p713+ Oct. 1995; *Los Angeles Times* p8 May 21, 2000; *New York Times* E p11 May 10, 2000; *New York Times Book Review* (on-line) Sep. 4, 1994, p10 Apr. 30, 2000; *Publishers Weekly* p70 Feb. 28, 2000; *Washington Post Book World* p9 Jan. 23, 1994

SELECTED BOOKS: nonfiction—*Reproductions of Banality: Fascism, Literature, and French Intellectual Life*, 1986; *French Lessons: A Memoir*, 1993; *The Collaborator: The Trial and Execution of Robert Brasillach*, 2000; as translator—*Another November*, 1998; *Difficulty of Being a Dog*, 2000; *Piano Music for Four Hands* (2001); *Ok, Joe* (2003)

Karbo, Karen

1956– Novelist

Karen Karbo, who originally set out to write screenplays with tragic themes, has instead made her reputation with novels that strike sharp blows at reviewers' funny bones. In *Trespassers Welcome Here* (1989), the story of a group of Russian expatriates in Los Angeles, she captured the foibles and accents of a community desperate to adapt to American mores. *The Diamond Lane* (1991) contrasts documentary filmmaking with Hollywood crassness, and *Motherhood Made a Man Out of Me* (2000) turns a jaundiced eye on the world of motherhood. Her most recent work is the nonfiction volume *Generation Ex: Tales from the Second Wives Club* (2001). In an interview for the *New York*

Karen Karbo Courtesy of Bloomsbury USA

women, each in her own way, pursue the American dream.

"Karbo is a very funny writer," Elin Schoen Brockman wrote for the *New York Times Book Review* (May 21, 1989), in an assessment of *Trespassers Welcome Here*. "And what is amazing about her humor is not merely its abundance but its range—from near slapstick to a wry wit, evident even in the wonderfully ironic title . . . and also its depth. For shining through the shenanigans of the various characters are poignant revelations not only about strangers in a strange land, but about their American friends, lovers and nemeses, and about Soviet-American relations at their most intimate and basic."

Like *Trespassers Welcome Here*, *The Diamond Lane* is set in Los Angeles. Karbo told Graeber for the *New York Times Book Review* interview that she conceived of *The Diamond Lane* as a twist on the book *You'll Never Eat Lunch in This Town Again*, a nonfiction Hollywood exposé by Julia Phillips. "I think of it as 'You'll Never Eat Lunch in This Town in the First Place,'" she said. "And the characters are people who would love to have lunch." The adventures of two sisters form the core of the book. One sister, Mouse, has been in Africa

Times Book Review (May 19, 1991), Karbo told Laurel Graeber that she "never tries consciously to be funny," invoking the comic actor Charlie Chaplin's maxim that humor must "come from how you look at life." Her own belief is that life is "hopelessly tragic and hilarious."

Karen Karbo was born in 1956 in Detroit, Michigan, to Joan and Richard Karbo. She was educated at the University of Southern California in Los Angeles, receiving a B.A. in 1977 and an M.A. in 1980. For a screenwriting class, as Laurel Graeber reported, Karbo wrote a script "about a crippled pianist who falls in love with a religious guitar player in the Paris Metro." She told Graeber, "I thought it was *Imitation of Life*," referring to the 1959 film melodrama. "But my instructor said, 'This is the funniest thing I've ever read.' It struck me then that maybe I wasn't aimed for high drama." While writing screenplays in Los Angeles, Karbo supported herself as a dog groomer and a Hollywood agent's assistant, among other jobs. But she found no buyers for her screenplays. "It's depressing . . . when you try to sell your soul and nobody wants it," she told Graeber. So she decided to try her hand at fiction.

Karbo's first book was *Trespassers Welcome Here*. In that novel Karbo explored the lives of four Russian women who have emigrated to Los Angeles and work in the Slavic languages department of a university. Bella Bogoga is obsessed with shopping; Valeria Chalisian teaches "Russian with an Emphasis in Sports Vocabulary," or "Russian for jocks," as it is known on campus; Tanya Zlopak, an actress, is desperate for a Hollywood film role; and Marina McIntyre, who works as a KGB agent, is married to an unsuspecting American. All four

with her boyfriend, making a documentary film about tribal marriage customs; the other, Mimi, who is divorced and works as an assistant to a Hollywood film producer, is romantically involved with a married man—who, like her, dreams of success as a screenwriter. "Karbo has done her job brilliantly," Robert Ward wrote of *The Diamond Lane* for the *New York Times Book Review* (May 19, 1991). "Not only is the plot ingenious, but the writing remains deft all the way through. . . . Karbo is smart enough and good enough to know when to slow down and reveal the little terrors that people feel in Tinseltown, but she is also clever and sophisticated enough to know that the Hollywood experience is essentially a comic one. And it remains so even as Mouse and Mimi and their boyfriends stagger toward an unforgettable (and darkly funny) wedding." "Part of what Karbo is satirizing in this novel, in an often very wicked fashion," Judith Freeman commented in the *Los Angeles Times* (June 21, 1991), "is the way the ordinary rituals and activities in life—love, work, marriage—get twisted into the most bizarre shapes when money and Hollywood values enter the picture." Karbo, Freeman continued, "understands the banalities and excesses, the contradictions and absurdities of living in a place where knowing not to put glitter in your stucco is construed as good taste. . . . Karbo sustains her tale by contrasting misery and humor, real filmmaking (real documentary) and the crass commercial product, poor humble Africa and fat, gluttonous America."

Karbo was a contributor to the 1995 volume *Home: American Writers Remember Rooms of Their Own*. Her piece evoked her mother, for whom "the dining room is a vortex of impeccable etiquette and laborious buffets," as Bernard Cooper noted in the *Los Angeles Times* (December 24, 1995). He found Karbo's second-person narrative "hilarious, but never at the expense of the conservative mother who values self-control above other virtues. That Karbo can sustain this tone without one note of condescension is no small feat, and it is a tone that becomes all the more chilling as a tumor slowly destroys her mother's capacity for self-control."

For the 1997 nonfiction book *Big Girl in the Middle*, Karbo served as co-writer with Gabrielle Reece, a tall former professional model who had abandoned that career to join Team Nike in the Bud Light Professional Beach Volleyball Tour in 1991. Reece's story centered on her team's unsuccessful 1996 season, one in which, as the *Publishers Weekly* (May 26, 1997) reviewer wrote, "Captain Reece maintained her perspective and her resolve to keep plugging away. This account should give a boost to the morale of female athletes."

In the 2000 novel *Motherhood Made a Man Out of Me*, Karbo took on the pitfalls of pregnancy and new motherhood. The protagonist, Brooke, has a baby daughter, Stella, whose arrival has effectively ended Brooke's career as a film producer. Brooke's husband, Lyle, is an aspiring artist who repairs photocopiers for a living, spends a great deal of time playing computer games, and generally proves to be less than ideal as a father. Brooke's best friend is the pregnant Mary Rose, who "functions largely as a straight woman for the narrator," David Kipen observed in the *San Francisco Chronicle* (July 5, 2000), "smiling along as Brooke confides yet more witty observations, e.g., 'She didn't see me. No one does of course. Being the mother of a beautiful baby is the next best thing to being in the Witness Relocation Program.' . . . Karbo plainly has a lot to say—much of it amusing—about both pregnancy and new motherhood. By synchronizing Mary Rose's pregnancy with Brooke's first nine months as a mom, Karbo covers both topics in half the time."

While Ann Hodgman, writing in the *New York Times Book Review* (June 18, 2000), found *Motherhood Made a Man Out of Me* to be "peevishly hilarious," she tempered her praise with mild criticism: "What [Brooke] might as well be saying is: 'I'm trying to tell a whole big story but the baby keeps getting in the way'. . . . Throughout the novel, characters are thrown at us and we're just expected to keep track of them somehow. . . . The city where this is all taking place is never mentioned by name. It must be Portland, Ore., because it's always rainy and people are always watching Trail Blazers games. . . . In the same way, segments of plot bob up without warning from under a thick layer of domestic detail. (The details are very funny; there are just so many of them!) . . . But that's because this book is really about having babies, and it's the plot that keeps getting in the way." Hodgman concluded, however, that "*Motherhood Made a Man Out of Me* should be clutched to the 'corn-silo-sized' breasts of every new mother."

Karbo's *Generation Ex: Tales from the Second Wives Club* was published in the spring of 2001. That nonfiction book examines, from the points of view of five women who meet to trade stories, the complications that result from having "exes" in one's life: an ex-husband, a husband's ex-wife, and the children of the various unions. A *Library Journal* (March 1, 2001) reviewer, who considered *Generation Ex* a self-help book, noted that Karbo had hit "all the major minefields." A *Publishers Weekly* (March 5, 2001) critic termed the ex-spousal encounter a "hilarious" mix of "screwball comedy, tragic drama, feel-good fantasy and stalker flicks." Laura Jamison, writing for the *New York Times Book Review* (April 8, 2001), also found *Generation Ex* "wildly funny," and she praised Karbo's use of "solid statistics."

Karen Karbo lives in Portland, Oregon, with her husband, a filmmaker. Her previous marriage ended in divorce. She is a contributing writer for *Sports for Women*, and her articles have appeared in other publications, including the *New York Times Book Review*.

—S. Y.

SUGGESTED READING: *Los Angeles Times* p5 June 21, 1991, p1 Dec. 24, 1995; *New York Times Book Review* p11 May 21, 1989, p9 May 19, 1991, p27 June 18, 2000; *New York Times Book Review* (on-line) Apr. 8, 2001; *New Yorker* p95+ Sep. 16, 1991; *Quill & Quire* p29 May 1991; *San Francisco Chronicle* D p1 July 5, 2000; *Virginia Quarterly Review* V p20 Winter 1998; *Voice Literary Supplement* p13 May 9, 1989

SELECTED BOOKS: fiction—*Trespassers Welcome Here*, 1989; *The Diamond Lane*, 1991; *Motherhood Made a Man Out of Me*, 2000; nonfiction—*Big Girl in the Middle* (with Gabrielle Reece), 1997; *Generation Ex: Tales from the Second Wives Club*, 2001

Keates, Jonathan

1946– Novelist; biographer; travel writer

Jonathan Keates is something of a throwback to an earlier era in literature. His prose is often ornate, his long sentences march behind bevies of commas, and he has a fondness for antiquated vocabulary. He is conversant in literature, Renaissance art and architecture, and classical music, and he frequently decorates his work with erudite references. Much of his fiction is set in the past, and his celebrated biographies—*Handel: The Man and His Music*, *Stendhal*, and *Purcell: A Biography*—concern figures whose popularity and renown have endured through the passing of many years. He has produced several travel volumes, writing most often of Italy. His book reviews appear widely in such publications as the *Times Literary Supplement* and the London *Guardian*.

Jonathan Keates was born in 1946, and he began teaching English literature at the City of London School in the 1980s. His earliest publications focus on travel, art, and architecture; these include *The Companion Guide to the Shakespeare Country* (1979), *Historic London* (1979, with Angelo Hornak), *Canterbury Cathedral* (1980, with Hornak), and *The Love of Italy* (1980).

His first work of fiction, *Allegro Postillions*—a collection of four related stories—was published in 1983 in Great Britain and in 1985 in the U.S. Each of the stories is set in 19th-century Italy and has an artist as a main character. In "Morn Advancing" Cattermole, an English landscape painter, travels on horseback through the Kingdom of Naples. When a violent local uprising interrupts his painting, he is more disturbed by the inconvenience to himself than by the loss of lives around him. In "Enthusiastic Fires" a young narrator visits an aging but respected composer, Hippolyte Jolliot, in Venice. At first blinded by his admiration of Jolliot, the narrator eventually sees him for the mean-spirited narcissist that he is. The artist in "The Distinguished Elephant" is Giovanni Andrea Pellegrini, a poet who has been exiled from Villafranca to Genoa because of his subversive poetry. In the more permissive Genoa, Pellegrini cannot find his muse and is forced to pass off his old writings as new material. In "A Slight Disorder" Flora, the young wife of an artist named Lionel (whose artistic interests bore her), considers having an affair with an Austrian officer in Venice.

Allegro Postillions won the 1983 James Tait Black Memorial Prize and the Hawthornden Prize. Jonathan Penner, in the *New York Times Book Review* (April 14, 1985), suggested that the "archaic language, rhetorically full-blown, seems appropriate to the period. Also appropriate from the standpoint of consistency, though sometimes distressing from that of art, is the author's reliance on 19th-century artifice: characters who stand for ideas, plots made to convey messages. Clearly, Jonathan Keates is not interested in verisimilitude." In the *Christian Science Monitor* (July 25, 1985) L. S. Klepp maintained that the stories in *Allegro Postillions* "are subtle, ironic meditations on art and illusion; they are also triumphs of a rich, finely shaded historical imagination. [This] is a remarkable literary debut, an exquisite and memorable book."

Keates's first biography was *Handel: The Man and His Music* (1985), which David Owens in the *Christian Science Monitor* (August 21, 1985) said might as easily have been called "The Man and His Music—and the Music, Poetry, and Politics of Everyone Else at the Time Besides." Owens relished Keates's thoroughness and called him a "most graceful stylist." Anthony Hicks, however, complained in the *Times Literary Supplement* (December 20, 1985) that the book's virtues "have to be filtered effortlessly out of an exuberant flood of information and opinion, much of it questionable in relevance, unreliable in detail or obscure in sense." Hicks added, "the most insidious errors are those arising from plausible-sounding but misguided attempts at original scholarship."

Keates published a novel, *The Strangers' Gallery*, in 1987, followed by a series of Italian travel books, *Tuscany* (1988), *Umbria* (1991), *Italian Journeys* (1991), and *Venice* (1994). Determinedly unorthodox in its tastes, *Italian Journeys* focuses on little-known artists and locales rather than those for which Italy is most famous. Keates states, for example, his preference for Umbria over the more popular province of Tuscany, and for Bologna over touristy Florence. He is also unafraid to voice generalities about Italians. He writes, for instance, as quoted by Rupert Scott in the *Spectator* (June 15, 1991), that "no one could write a novel [about Italians, because] their outwardness proclaims no inwardness." Scott suggested that one drawback of *Italian Journeys* is that "the author feels obliged to devote a good part of the . . . 17 chapters to proving his point, *ad*, if not *nauseam*, then *exhaustiam*," but he concluded, "for all its mild irritations this is unquestionably the finest book of its genre to appear in many years. Radiating intelligence and vivacity, it is a performance that anyone seriously interested in Italy would be unwise to miss."

Keates published *Stendhal*, the biography of the French writer (whose real name was Marie-Henri Beyle), in 1994. Stendhal (1783–1842) lived a short, but eventful life and left a literary legacy that consisted primarily of two novels, *The Red and the Black* (1830) and *The Charterhouse of Parma* (1839). Keates's biography treats Stendhal's life almost as a third work of art. He focuses on Stendhal's bold determination to live a happy life—which consisted primarily of indulging his senses—and on Stendhal's rejection of virtue for the Italian notion of "virtu," or sublime creative power. The biography drew mostly favorable reviews. "Having chosen the chronicler's pace," Dan Hofstadter wrote in the *Wall Street Journal* (March 25, 1997), "[Keates] offers a train of incident so even, so uniformly diced, as to seem at times almost inventorial, so that readers may be surprised to discover, somewhere around the middle of the book, that they feel they know Stendhal rather well. Suddenly he seems alive, entertaining, perhaps even lovable in his bearish way: One anticipates with regret the moment of leave-taking that looms ahead." In the *New York Times Book Review* (May 4, 1997) Frederick Brown wrote, "It is regrettable that Mr. Keates has not worked a closer examination of Stendhal's novels into his narrative. . . . But Mr. Keates tells the story of the life exceptionally well." Brown added, "His prose twirls through Stendhal's peripatetic career like a gentleman's stick, striking sparks when it taps a point home. In general, he proceeds with an air of easy omniscience, as if early-19th-century France were very much his province (the evocation of Grenoble [a city in southeastern France] is admirable) and the novelist a confidant who must every so often be flushed from behind some new self-invention."

Keates's *Purcell: A Biography* was published, in 1995, on the 300th anniversary of its subject's death. Henry Purcell's reputation as a preeminent English baroque composer—whose work includes the opera *Dido and Aeneas*, the cantata *Odes for St Cecilia's Day*, and the song "Orpheus Britannicus"—has continued to grow after his death, despite a dearth of information about him. Keates manages to paint a vivid portrait of the man and his work, as was noted by many critics. "He has made excellent use of his own enthusiasm for Purcell's music to kindle interest even in more out-of-the-way pieces," Genevieve Stuttaford wrote in *Publishers Weekly* (September 9, 1996); "his detailed treatment of much of the music is the best so far in a popular study. He is intelligent also on the complex religio-political history of the time, and casts a knowing eye on the French and Italian influences on Baroque music, influences that Purcell thoroughly absorbed into a distinctive English style that has inspired native composers ever since." In *Choice* (March 1997) W. Metcalfe called the book the "most appealing biography of Purcell to emerge from the tercentenary of his death. . . . [Keates's] descriptions of a huge amount of Purcell's music in all genres are persuasive, if occasionally over-enthusiastic, and readily accessible to nonspecialists. . . . His vocabulary is occasionally irritatingly English—'hugger mugger,' 'over-egged-pudding quality'—but always colorful and pointed."

In 1997 Keates published *Soon To Be A Major Motion Picture*, a collection of short stories. "Caliginous," like many of the stories in the volume, is peopled by the wealthy—in this case a young woman who complains about social climbers to a gay man who she hopes will change his sexual preferences for her. In "The Cherry Thief" two rich Italian cousins, Enrico and Giorgi, track down a maid who has stolen some cherries, only to be shamed when they find out the reasons for her theft. In "La Dolce Prospettiva" a gay American art professor visits a Venetian church to look at some paintings with a wealthy woman friend.

In his review of *Soon To Be A Major Motion Picture* for the *Guardian* (April 17, 1997) Steven Poole wrote, "Fewer titles could be more ironical. Cinema is a kinetic medium: character is illuminated primarily through gesture and action; in Keates's highly crafted stories, character is worried at by heavy paragraphs of exegetical prose, with a few tiny actions and modulations of feeling assuming mythical proportions." On a more positive note, Russell Celyn Jones wrote in the London *Times* (April 17, 1997), "In every one of these stories there is a glancing moment of great personal change, which Keates freeze-frames," but he asserted that the characters "feel more resurrected than invented and their membership [in] a hermetically sealed class means they cannot quite reach their feelings, as if all emotion were on a shelf too high." In the *Spectator* (May 31, 1997) Andrew Barrow cheered, "Once you have got the hang of Mr. Keates's wonderfully fancy style and subject matter, everything goes swimmingly."

In 2000 Keates published *Smile Please*, about the lives and relationships of a group of friends living in London. The story centers around Adam, a gay man in his early 30s, who is in love with a dancer named Frankie. Adam's roommate, Theo, is a gay black man engaged in a destructive relationship with a bigot. Also involved are the middle-aged housewives Alice and Serena. Plot twists involve a case of mistaken identity and the death of a goose. Offering his assessment of the book's essential ingredients, Tim Teeman wrote in the London *Times* (February 5, 2000), "Take an easy recipe. For one formulaic British gay-themed novel you will need: a protagonist whose fogeyish demeanor belies an obsession with sex; a group of straight friends composed of dissatisfied, archly camp women and ineffectual husbands called Jeremy; a sexy flatmate with whom the withdrawn protagonist is mildly obsessed; some dirty sex to show double life . . . [and] lots of references to art and literature to show the author is not just writing a gay version of an Aga bonkbuster [aristocratic romance novel]. Which pretty much sums up *Smile Please*." Katie Grant had more appreciation for Keates's wit and linguistic aptitude and offered some guarded praise. In the London *Spectator* (February 5, 2000) she wrote, "Readers will find in *Smile Please* a gentle camp comedy of modern manners that minces along in perfectly unobjectionable, even whimsical fashion, with tableaux of homoerotic sex in carefully chosen settings strategically placed to keep up the interest if you like that sort of thing."

Keates continues to write book reviews for the London *Spectator*, *Times Literary Supplement*, *Guardian*, and *New York Times*, among other periodicals.

—P. G. H.

SUGGESTED READING: *Choice* p1172 Mar. 1997; *Christian Science Monitor* p24 July 25, 1985, p22 Aug. 1985; (London) *Guardian* II p1 Apr. 17, 1997; *New York Times Book Review* p18 Apr. 14, 1985, p13 May 4, 1997; *Publishers Weekly* p73 Sep. 9, 1996; (London) *Spectator* p31 June 15, 1991, p42+ May 31, 1997, p34+ Feb. 5, 2000; (London) *Times* p41 Apr. 17, 1997, p18 Feb. 5, 2000; *Wall Street Journal* A p5 Mar. 25, 1997

SELECTED BOOKS: nonfiction—*The Companion Guide to the Shakespeare Country*, 1979; *Historic London* (with Angelo Hornak), 1979; *Canterbury Cathedral* (with Hornak), 1980; *The Love of Italy*, 1980; *Handel: The Man and His Music*, 1985; *Tuscany*, 1988; *Italian Journeys*, 1991; *Umbria*, 1991; *Stendhal*, 1994; *Venice*, 1994; *Purcell: A Biography*, 1995; fiction—*Allegro Postillions*, 1983; *The Strangers' Gallery*, 1987; *Soon To Be A Major Motion Picture*, 1997; *Smile Please*, 2000

Jonathan Exley/Courtesy of Warner Books

Kellerman, Faye

July 31, 1952– Mystery writer

Since her first novel, *The Ritual Bath*, appeared in 1986, mystery writer Faye Kellerman has published more than a dozen novels and numerous short stories, all with characters and settings drawn from her Orthodox Jewish background. She is best known as the creator of the series starring Rina Lazarus, a young Jewish widow and *mikvah* attendant, and Peter Decker, a Christian detective. Kellerman has also authored two books outside of the series: *Quality of Mercy* (1989), a historical novel about William Shakespeare and a Jewish girl, and *Moon Music* (1998), a detective novel set in Las Vegas. Her short stories have appeared in the *Sisters in Crime* series, *Ellery Queen's Magazine*, and several prominent anthologies, including *A Modern Treasury of Great Detective and Murder Mysteries*. She is the wife of Jonathan Kellerman, a clinical psychologist who has written several best-selling mystery novels.

Faye Marder Kellerman was born in St. Louis, Missouri, on July 31, 1952, the daughter of Oscar, a delicatessen owner, and Anne Steinberg Marder. The family moved to Sherman Oaks, California, when Faye was four years old, and she grew up in the San Fernando Valley, not far from Los Angeles. When she was 18 years old and just starting college classes, she met Jonathan Kellerman at a volleyball game sponsored by a Jewish community center in Los Angeles. She sometimes worked the cash register at her father's deli, so Jonathan took a job bagging groceries to be near her. They became engaged shortly thereafter and married in 1972.

Kellerman received her bachelor's degree in mathematics, in 1974, from the University of California at Los Angeles, and a doctorate in dentistry from the same university, in 1978, when she was seven months pregnant with her first child. She never did go into professional practice, though she did work as a dental internist at a hospital emergency room when she was in graduate school. One day she helped an elderly man who had suffered severe injuries in a mugging; the thieves took only a $20 Social Security check. "That was just so sad," Kellerman told Sean Mitchell for the *Los Angeles Magazine* (August 1995). "It affected me for a long time, and I thought, I'm going to get these guys. If I can't get 'em in real life, I'll get 'em in fiction."

Sometime around the birth of her first child, she began writing, turning out a large number of romance novels that never saw the light of publication. As she told Bettijane Levine, for the *Los Angeles Times* (April 21, 1996), "I was a poor English student more comfortable with symbols than with language, which is why I majored in math." Nonetheless, despite a brief stint as an apprentice luthier (a maker of stringed musical instruments), she stuck with the writing. She realized that the romance novels did not work, so she turned her attention to mysteries, a genre she enjoyed reading. After deciding not to write from the point of view of a dentist or a female detective, she asked herself (as she told Sean Mitchell), "What do I have about me that's unique? I am an Orthodox Jew. Why don't I write about my religion the way Tony Hillerman is writing about the Indians, the way Walter Mosley writes about blacks in the '50s? There's a lot in my culture that's rich and not very well explained in the world of literature." In 1986 her first mystery, *The Ritual Bath*, was published by Arbor House; it won that year's Macivity Award for best first novel.

The Ritual Bath is the first in a series of mystery novels built around the fictional characters of Rina Lazarus and Peter Decker. In the novel, Detective Decker is called on to investigate a brutal rape that took place outside a *mikvah* (a Jewish ritual bath) where Rina Lazarus, a young Orthodox Jewish widow with two small sons, is an attendant. Like Kellerman's later novels, *The Ritual Bath* combines traditional detective-work with richly drawn portraits of the people and practices of an ethnic/religious community whose daily rhythms are not often portrayed in popular fiction. As the series progresses, Decker and Lazarus deal with the growing tensions of cross-cultural relationships, until, in a later novel, Decker finally reclaims his Judaism—he had been born a Jew but raised as a Christian by his adoptive parents—in order to marry Lazarus, and the two remain partners in life and criminal investigation for the rest of the series. Kellerman has endeavored to ensure that Lazarus is not seen as a stereotypically insular Jewish woman; in a 1996 *People Online* conference, she explained that "Rina will continue to be both more worldly and orthodox. The two aren't incompatible, although sometimes it appears that way."

In an article entitled "Assimilated, Acculturated, or Affirming: The Jewish Detective in America," published in *Judaism* (Winter 1997), Lawrence W. Raphael commended Kellerman's interest in portraying Orthodox Jewish life. Raphael, a Reform rabbi, placed Kellerman in the category of novelists who "have merged their interest in solving a crime with their desire to illuminate some aspect of traditional Judaism and the Jewish community" and have created "affirmative Jewish protagonists." Raphael contrasted Kellerman with such writers as Linda Barnes, Michael Katz, and others, whose protagonists are "almost always highly assimilated and often intermarried."

Kellerman's first two books, *The Ritual Bath* and *Sacred and Profane* (1987), both published by Arbor House, established the Decker/Lazarus series and Kellerman's reputation as a mystery writer. Her next book, however, departed from the mystery genre and started a relationship with a new publisher, William Morrow, who has published all of Kellerman's books since that date. *The Quality of Mercy* (1989) is set in Elizabethan London. The protagonist—Rebecca Lopez, a Spanish Jew and the daughter of Queen Elizabeth's personal physician—joins a theatrical troupe while masquerading as a man; meanwhile, William Shakespeare smuggles Jews who are trying to escape persecution in Spain into London. A decade after its publication, *The Quality of Mercy* became the focus of controversy when Kellerman brought a lawsuit in federal court against Marc Norman and Tom Stoppard, the screenwriters of the 1999 Oscar-winning film *Shakespeare in Love*; she claimed that the pair had stolen the plot of the screenplay from *The Quality of Mercy*.

Kellerman resumed the Peter Decker/Rina Lazarus series with *Milk and Honey* (1990), the book in which Decker finally embraces Orthodox Judaism to marry Lazarus. Then followed *Days of Atonement* (1992); *False Prophet* (1992); *Grievous Sin* (1993); *Sanctuary* (1994); and *Justice* (1995), in which Decker and, to a lesser extent, Lazarus, investigate the death of a teenager whose murder is blamed on her prom date, an amateur cellist who is the adopted son of a mobster. *Prayers for the Dead* (1996) recounts the grisly murder of Dr. Azor Sparks, a heart-transplant surgeon and a religious fundamentalist who took pleasure in riding with a motorcycle gang; one of Sparks's sons is a Catholic priest named Abram, who is an acquaintance of Lazarus's. *Publishers Weekly* (November 4, 1996) listed *Prayers for the Dead* as one of the best books of 1996 and described the plot as "a complex and absorbing moral tangle." In an earlier issue of *Publishers Weekly* (July 8, 1996), a reviewer declared that the book was "powerful, assured, and absorbing" and concluded that "Kellerman succeeds brilliantly in making the search for understanding as compelling as the search for the murderer." In the next book, *Serpent's Tooth* (1997), Decker investigates a mass murder by a gunman who opened fire in a fashionable restaurant in Los Angeles.

For her 1998 novel, *Moon Music*, Kellerman once again abandoned her regular series and her usual setting in Los Angeles. *Moon Music* takes place in Las Vegas, where homicide detective Romulus Poe—who has a twin brother named Remus—tries to solve the murder of a prostitute whose past romantic entanglements include a brief fling with Poe's cop-buddy, Steve Jenkins. Poe travels from the glitzy world of Vegas casinos to the eerie Yucca Flats test site, where atomic bombs were routinely detonated during the 1950s (often before audiences of schoolchildren on field trips, as the detective's mother, Emma Poe, recalls). Oline H. Cogdill described the book in the *Chicago Tribune* (September 30, 1998) as "a far-reaching tale of mysticism, horror, science fiction, and mystery." Cogdill argued, however, that such a combination proved detrimental to the narrative, and added, "By mixing too many elements, Kellerman never achieves the cohesive story or intimate look at characters that have made her a best-selling author."

A year after her Las Vegas detour with Romulus Poe, Kellerman's next novel, *Jupiter's Bones* (1999), returned to Rina Lazarus and Peter Decker in a narrative that finds them searching southern California cults for clues about the death of Dr. Emil Ganz, an eccentric astrophysicist who had vanished for 10 years only to reappear as Brother Jupiter, the leader of a cult called the Order of the Rings of God. In her review of this novel for the *Houston Chronicle* (August 1, 1999), Amy Rabinovitz wrote: "Uppermost in Decker's mind is the fear that Jupiter's 200-plus followers will decide to follow the leader. Discovering that the great man had been receiving signals from an alternate universe for the past six months does little to ease his mind. . . . Murder, mystery, action, and drama make this another winner for the popular author who neatly wraps the plot in very human emotions, a trademark of the series."

In 2000 Kellerman took the Decker-Lazarus series in a new direction with *Stalker*, a mystery that focused primarily on Cynthia Decker, Peter's daughter. A rookie cop in Los Angeles, Cynthia is strong-willed, brash, and opinionated—and desired by most of the male police officers on the force. She must help solve a series of car jackings while at the same time defending herself against her own stalker. The book received mixed reviews. In a critique for *Amazon.com*, Jane Adams stated that the book did not gain momentum until Peter Decker arrives on the scene late in the novel. "Sadly," Decker wrote, "Cindy's not quite ready for prime time; perhaps she'll grow up in her next outing. Or better yet, Kellerman will bring us more adventures by Peter and Rina."

The next Decker-Lazarus novel, *The Forgotten*, was published in 2001. It deals with Rina's teenage son, Jacob, whose many problems include his association with Ernesto Golding, a classmate who recently defaced Rina's synagogue. When the boy and his therapists are murdered some months later, a tantalizing clue is revealed: Ernesto's grandfather might have been a Nazi who fled to South America by posing as a Jew. In a review for *Amazon.com*, Jane Adams cheered: "Kellerman skillfully keeps the dramatic tension going as she pulls all the pieces of her complex plot together. But what makes this novel her best yet is her acutely revealing portrait of Jacob, struggling with the existential angst of adolescence as he attempts to reconcile his devotion to Judaism with the temptations of contemporary life, from drugs to sex. She brilliantly limns his search for identity, intimacy, and independence even as he redefines his relationship to Peter and Rina, in a scenario that resounds with psychological truth. *The Forgotten* is a terrific addition to the Kellerman oeuvre."

Kellerman's most recent Decker-Lazarus mystery is *Stone Kiss* (2002), in which Decker hunts for his relative's murderer and the victim's teenage niece, who has disappeared after witnessing the murder. In order to find her, he must team up with a known psychotic—Chris Donatti, first introduced in *Justice* (1995)—who may hold the keys to the mystery. As quoted on the *Amazon.com* Web site, a *Publishers Weekly* reviewer observed, "Whether Kellerman is depicting the ultra-Orthodox Jewish community or a pornographer's studio, she is utterly convincing. Amid the wreckage of lives taken or thrown away, Kellerman's heroes find glimmers of hope and enough moral ambiguity to make even her most evil villain look less than totally black."

Describing her writing process to Sean Mitchell, Kellerman stated, "First I come up with an idea. *Sacred and Profane* was bodies found in the desert; *Milk and Honey* was a child found alive but in a neighborhood where she didn't belong. Then I investigate a theme I want to talk about. *Sacred and Profane* is, literally, how can you keep any sort of spirituality in a profane world? *Day of Atonement* talks about the expiation of guilt. *False Prophet* is all about jealousy." When she has settled on an idea and theme, Kellerman creates an outline: "Then I have notes that contradict my outline and I re-outline. Then I do a character outline. By the time you're sitting down to actually write, your characters have spoken to you and you've discovered how they're going to act. Now you're ready to get close to them. And when you get close to people, you discover secrets." During the *People Online* conference, Kellerman identified "passion" as the prominent motivator of her characters: "I like people who have burning drives and who are obsessive in their pursuit of justice." When the moderator asked Kellerman whether she, as a female writer, had any difficulties writing male characters, Kellerman replied, "I've grown up with brothers, and I've been married to Jonathan so I've had a lot of experience. I listen to what they have to tell you."

Kellerman's husband also writes mysteries, most notably the series featuring Alex Delaware. Bettijane Levine reported that, as of 1996, his 14 novels had sold 22 million copies, while Faye Kellerman's 10 books had sold 2 million. Comparing Faye Kellerman's work with that of her husband's, Sean Mitchell wrote, "She and her husband write in markedly different styles. Jonathan is known for leisurely pacing and painterly descriptions of the L.A. people and places encountered by his clinical-psychologist detective Alex Delaware. Faye's books are more terse, with greater emphasis on dialogue, a pattern she attributes to childhood reading difficulties that forced her to learn as much as possible by ear. 'He writes like a camera; I write like a tape recorder,' she says." The Kellermans work in separate offices in their Beverly Hills home and never collaborate, "because," as Faye Kellerman told Levine, "every other area of our lives is about collaboration." They do, however, read each other's work in all its stages and give editorial commentary. Jonathan told Levine, "What's important to Faye is what's important to me. Values, morality, right and wrong. I think that's why we write mysteries, because they deal with real and important issues." In a *People* (February 19, 1996) profile entitled "Home Sweet Homicide" and subtitled "Mysteriously, the thriller-writing Kellermans cohabit without bloodshed," Jonathan described Faye as "sexy, stable, and brilliant. I'm glad I was smart enough not to be threatened by someone smarter."

The Kellermans have four children—Jesse Oren, Rachel Diana, Ilana Judith, and Aliza Celeste—and maintain a kosher household. Bettijane Levine described Faye Kellerman as a "delicate-boned woman with curly hair, no need for makeup, and a gauzy ankle-length dress that enhances her air of fragility. Don't be deceived. Her husband calls her 'cut-to-the-chase Faye,' and 'the "Rawhide" of the family, who moves the herd on and gets 'em out.'" He also calls her "Betty Crocker with a 'tude," according to Salter Reynolds, who interviewed Faye Kellerman for *Publishers Weekly* (August 18, 1997). To balance home life with work, she told Reynolds, "A writer has to be able to focus, and men and women think differently in this regard. I can work in very short bursts when I need to, accomplishing a lot in 20 minutes. I think this is a part of being the family's primary caretaker . . . it forces you to sustain interruptions." Despite her success as an author, Kellerman believes that writing takes only second place in her life. "I may be a working girl," she told Reynolds, "but I don't consider it nearly as tough as being a mother, and certainly nowhere near as important."

—E. M.

SUGGESTED READING: *Atlanta Journal* A p1 Mar. 23, 1999; *Belles Lettres: A Review of Books by Women* p53 Winter 1993; *Chatelaine* p12 Dec. 1995; *Chicago Tribune* TEMPO p3 Sep. 30, 1998; *Houston Chronicle* p21 Aug. 1, 1999; *Judaism* p122+ Winter 1997; *Los Angeles Magazine* p167+ Aug. 1995, with photo; *Los Angeles Times* p1 Apr. 21, 1996, p14 Jan. 11, 1998, with photo; *New York Times* C p11 Oct. 16, 1996; *New York*

Times Book Review p17 Aug. 23, 1992, p28 Oct. 1, 1995; *People* p57+ Feb. 19, 1996, with photo; *Publishers Weekly* p64+ Aug. 18, 1997, with photo; *St. Louis Post-Dispatch* E p2 Sep. 2, 1998; *Virginia Quarterly Review* S p131 Autumn 1991

SELECTED BOOKS: *The Ritual Bath*, 1986; *Sacred and Profane*, 1987; *The Quality of Mercy*, 1989; *Milk and Honey*, 1990; *Day of Atonement*, 1992; *False Prophet*, 1992; *Grievous Sin*, 1993; *Sanctuary*, 1994; *Justice*, 1995; *Prayers for the Dead*, 1996; *Serpent's Tooth*, 1997; *Moon Music*, 1998; *Jupiter's Bones*, 1999; *Stalker*, 2000; *The Forgotten*, 2001; *Stone Kiss*, 2002

Kelly, Aileen

July 7, 1942– Historian

The British historian Aileen Kelly has set into motion a reexamination of what she sees as a rich and neglected Russian intellectual tradition. In *Toward Another Shore: Russian Thinkers Between Necessity and Chance* (1998) and a companion volume, *Views from the Other Shore: Essays on Herzen, Chekhov, and Bakhtin* (1999), Kelly has proved herself to be an agile thinker, moving easily from philosophy, to literature, to history; she is no less at home in the subjects of English, French, and German thought than in her own area of expertise—19th and 20th-century Russia. With reference to such Russian political figures as Alexander Herzen and such literary figures as Tolstoy, Chekhov, and Dostoevsky, Kelly charts what she views as the essential Russian debates—between faith and doubt and between idealism and nihilism. With a passion and moral vision not often found in contemporary academic writing, Kelly insists that the past and its ideas must be used to inform the future. Kelly is a lecturer in Russian Studies at Cambridge University, and a fellow at King's College, at Cambridge.

For *World Authors 1995–2000*, Aileen Kelly composed the following statement: "I was born in South Africa and have lived mainly in England since I was 14. A multicultural background (Irish emigrant parents, South Africa under apartheid, an English convent-school and university education, followed by two years in the Soviet Union) was a recipe for rootlessness, but I discovered that early exposure to a variety of cultural, ideological, and geographical perspectives is a great advantage for an intellectual historian. I acquired some more perspectives from my Czech-Scottish-Australian husband, a speaker of about a dozen languages.

"My interest in Russia began at my convent school, where Russia was presented as the home of atheism and therefore the origin of the worst evils threatening our time. There were no sources on Russia in my school library—we were expected to pray for Russia's conversion, not learn about its culture—but the effect of the propaganda made me want to do just that. I decided to start with the language and found a way of filling the compulsory hours in the school chapel by folding hand-copied lists of Russian vocabulary inside my prayerbook and studying them. In school vacations I borrowed books on Russian history from the public library. I had a parallel interest (inspired initially by the French Revolution) in French, which it was possible to indulge in school by more orthodox means.

"I studied both languages for a B.A. at Manchester University where I developed my interest in periods when dogmatic systems were being questioned by writers and thinkers. My undergraduate dissertation considered the transition from religious to secular notions of political power and the development of the notion of toleration in seventeenth-century France.

"I decided to specialise in Russian thought for my graduate studies because I was attracted by Russian writers' obsession with what Dostoevsky called the 'accursed questions' of the meaning of life, and their iconoclastic refusal to take on trust the solutions offered by western political and philosophical systems. At Oxford University where I completed my doctorate, by far the strongest influence on my work was that of Isaiah Berlin. Russian intellectual history was not (and is not) taken seriously in Britain, and even intellectual history itself is treated with some suspicion. It was therefore a great relief to find a thinker of such distinction who believed that what I had chosen to do was worth doing, shared my passion for the field and was happy to make time to discuss it at length though not being my supervisor.

"As I have said in one of my books, Berlin's 'moral vision has been the constant standard by which I have measured [Russian writers'] failings and their strengths.' The central idea associated with his work is a defense of value pluralism as the basis of liberty against monistic doctrines which hold that all desirable goods can be harmonised and integrated into a single system. My own experience had led me to the same position, and I became fascinated by the way in which the political and moral consequences of monistic and pluralistic views of the world were discussed and acted out by writers, revolutionaries, and conservatives in Russia. It became something of a mission in my books and in my writing for publications such as the *New York Review of Books*, to overturn the stereotypical view of Russian thinkers as fanatical extremists on the margins of Europe. I treat pre-Soviet Russian thought as an integral part of the European tradition, fertilized by all its groundbreaking thinkers, from Francis Bacon to Marx, Darwin, J. S. Mill, and Nietzsche, but distinctively Russian in its intoxication with the power of ideas and concern with their practical effects on political and moral life. I strongly believe that the history of Russian thought can be of great value in reminding intellectuals in the West of the still unexhausted destructive as well as creative potential of ideas that are now a familiar part of our cultural heritage.

With this aim I wrote my first book, on Bakunin (subtitled 'A Study in the Psychology and Politics of Utopianism'); I have since mainly focused on the countercurrent of anti-utopianism in Russian thought and literature, which predicted with astonishing prescience the horrors that would ensue when Russian (and European) dreams of a brave new world were implemented in practice and which drew on the latest discoveries in Western science to articulate a new humanism that anticipates much post-modern philosophy by grounding human freedom in the openness of time.

"The collisions of Russian utopians and anti-utopians are depicted in my book *Toward Another Shore*, while my latest book, *Views From the Other Shore*, is mainly concerned with the pioneering humanism of the brilliant writer Alexander Herzen, one of Russia's most original thinkers, whose insights I believe are highly relevant to current debates about how to ground morality after the collapse of ideological certainties.

"In general, while I judge individual thinkers on their merits, I am predisposed to those whose commitment to ideas is more intense than is common in Anglo-Saxon cultures. This distinctive flavour in the Russian character is well illustrated by the novelist Ivan Turgenev's account of a philosophical debate with the critic Belinsky. After some hours, Turgenev was feeling hungry and suggested that they stop to eat. No, Belinsky replied, 'First we will settle the existence of God, and only then will we have dinner.'"

Aileen Kelly was born in South Africa on July 7, 1942 and educated in England. As a student at Oxford University, she studied with the political theorist and intellectual historian Sir Isaiah Berlin, who is regarded as one of the leading liberal thinkers of the 20th century. Kelly is the co-editor of Berlin's seminal work *Russian Thinkers* (1978), in which he cited the ancient Greek proverb of "The Hedgehog and the Fox": "The fox knows many things, but the hedgehog knows one big thing." Kelly's work builds on Berlin's description of two strains of Russian intellectuals: hedgehogs, or monist thinkers, who are in the grip of a single, all-encompassing vision; and foxes, or pluralists, who are receptive to multiple points of view. Kelly has asserted that most intellectuals have gone through both "hedgehog" and "fox" stages in their thinking, engaging along the way in fierce debates with each other and themselves about faith and doubt, ideology and nihilism, and utopian and anti-utopian dreams.

Kelly's first book, *Mikhail Bakunin: A Study in the Psychology and Politics of Utopianism* (1982) is an intellectual biography of this prominent 19th-century propagator of anarchism. A Russian revolutionary who was influenced by Hegel and Marx, Bakunin rejected all forms of political control and centralization and agitated for revolutions against Europe's monarchies, insisting that "the passion for destruction is also a creative passion," as quoted in an article about him on *Britannica.com*. In an example of her storm-the-tower approach to scholarship, Kelly challenges the commonly held views of such major Bakunin scholars as E. H. Carr, who saw in Bakunin "one of the completest embodiments in history of the spirit of liberty," as quoted by James Joll in *History* (February 1984). Kelly views Bakunin as a figure whose own psychological needs drove his interest in politics, and argues that his life and thought demonstrated how an alienated individual might utilize a mass movement as a vehicle for the realization of personal wholeness, in the process creating an illogical and potentially dangerous political doctrine.

Toward Another Shore: Russian Thinkers Between Necessity and Chance (1998) is a collection of 17 of Kelly's essays, written over the course of 20 years. Taken as a whole, the essays serve as a reassessment of political thought during the 19th and early 20th centuries. Writing for the *New York Times Book Review* (August 9, 1998), Michael Scammell discussed Kelly's book in the context of contemporary debates about Russia's future. "Whither Russia? Who is to blame? What is to be done?" are some of the rhetorical questions that, Scammell wrote in his article, plagued Russians in the 19th century and, with the recent collapse of the Soviet Union, have returned with a vengeance. The importance of Kelly's work, Scammell suggested, is that clues to the future can often be found in the past.

Kelly's central argument, however, is that Russia's past has been misinterpreted by both the Soviets and the West. She questions the truism that hindsight is 20/20 by arguing that historians and others tend to distort the ideas of the radical intellectuals of 19th-century Russia by viewing them through the prism of the 20th-century revolution. The Soviets championed 19th-century populist thinkers as their own forebears, but in fact the populist ideas of mutual help and cooperation evolved from more widespread and homegrown traditions, of which the fanatical, revolutionary arm was only one aspect. By the same token, Western critics are wrong to condemn early Russian radicals as having sown the seeds of revolution that led to the excesses of Soviet Communism; in fact, Kelly argues, populist ideas could have led down many different paths. "While the Soviet Union was still a threat, to argue (as I do in this book) that we might be morally enlightened by the insights of the Russian radical humanists was to swim against the ideological stream in the West," Kelly asserts, as quoted by John Bayley in the *New York Review of Books* (November 19, 1998). "Liberal societies had never been more secure in their goals and values, and historians who identified with those values were not disposed to concede merit or insight to those whom they saw as having prepared the ground for the evils of Bolshevism." In light of the end of the Cold War and the moral certainties it created, Kelly argues for a more contextual approach to history, one in which thinkers are "re-appraised in the light of how they themselves viewed their goals and achievements," as quoted by a reviewer for the *British East-West Centre Journal.*

Specifically, Kelly proposes a more nuanced understanding of the range and diversity of reformist ideas among Russian writers and thinkers of 1840s to the 1870s. Groups of nihilists, socialists, and radical humanists debated several possible courses of action with the goal of implementing their reforms, Kelly asserts: the revolution of 1917 was by no means the only possible outcome of 19th-century Russian thought. In one essay, "Liberal Dilemmas and Populist Solutions," Kelly argues that a viable liberal tradition did not exist in Russia; even the liberalizing Czar Alexander II upheld repressive Government policies. Kelly maintains that the only alternative to autocracy was the "Russian humanitarian socialism" advanced by Alexander Herzen and the Populists. Their idea—that by developing a peasant commune system, Russia could avoid what they viewed as a pattern of large-scale industrialization and social alienation in the West—was "no more utopian than the hopes of [Western] liberal constitutionalists," Kelly wrote, as quoted by Michael Scammell.

In her appraisal of *Toward Another Shore* for the *Russian Review* (January 2000), Marina Kostalevsky voiced appreciation for Kelly's "commitment to a moral perspective." According to Kostalevsky, Kelly's work is comprised of more than just a "set of opinions" or "fashionable verbal games," and the critic compared it favorably to much of contemporary academic writing. And yet, Kostalevsky opined, there are instances in which Kelly's sympathy for the populist agenda leads her astray. "The book never mentions the vulgar utilitarianism of Dmitry Pisarev [a 19th-century nihilist], with his effort to demolish even Pushkin as socially pernicious," Kostalevsky observed, adding that Kelly's intellectual approach also scants discussion of Christianity's complex role in Russian society.

John Bayley described Kelly's work as a rare combination of conviction and accessibility. "*Toward Another Shore* is a masterpiece of its kind, so absorbing that one wants to read it all in one sitting despite its variety and its length. . . . At the same time, it argues a case—its own kind of case—illuminatingly and with great subtlety and distinction," he wrote. Michael Scammell emphasized the book's significance in terms of its potential to further understanding of post-Communist Russia. "[Kelly] has performed a signal service by inviting Russia's thinkers back into the mainstream of political discourse," he wrote. "I hope someone is already hard at work translating this essential book into Russian."

Views from the Other Shore: Essays on Herzen, Chekhov, and Bakhtin (1999) is a companion volume to *Toward Another Shore* in which Kelly examines in detail the humanist strand of Russian thought. "The Russian intellectual tradition that triumphed under Joseph Stalin fostered nationalism, xenophobia, collectivism, and messianic utopianism," Milton Ehre wrote in the *Washington Times* (September 19, 1999, on-line). "Aileen Kelly reminds us of another Russian tradition—'the other shore'—writers who were more modest in their aspirations and realistic in their assessments." Kelly presents as evidence of this counter-tradition the clear-eyed integrity of the playwright and short-story writer Anton Chekhov, the pluralism of Mikhail Bakhtin's literary theory, and especially the moral autonomy advocated by the political philosopher Alexander Herzen (1812–1870).

According to Kelly, Herzen has been vastly underappreciated in the West and ignored in Russia, largely because he was Lenin's favorite philosopher. Herzen and many of his contemporaries experienced an intellectual crisis and loss of faith, captured in Nietzsche's announcement of the "death" of God; some turned to cynicism and despair, while others sought out new ideologies, including communism. According to Kelly, Herzen was among the first of the 19th-century thinkers to challenge the assumptions underlying the Hegelian doctrine of historical development, or progress. Rejecting the notion of teleological history, Herzen decided that society's fate was instead ruled by chance and human will. He advocated moral autonomy, free from all formal principles and systems, including the notion of progress. Though an active writer and advocate of peasant communes, Herzen was also a skeptic and an ironist, someone whose example, Kelly writes, ought to speak to the situation in contemporary Russia, with its rampant corruption and demoralized populations. Kelly argues that, in the writings of Herzen and others, there is an indigenous and honorable set of ideas available with which Russians can remake their self-image and their nation.

In the *New York Times Book Review* (October 31, 1999), Barry Gewen called Kelly "one of the finest intellectual historians now writing," and praised *Views from the Other Shore* as even better than *Toward Another Shore.* "It may be narrower in scope," he wrote, "but it is more coherent, even more accessible, and it provides an excellent distillation of Kelly's own thought."

—M. A. H.

SUGGESTED READING: *History* p74 Feb. 1984; *New York Review of Books* p37+ Nov. 19, 1998; *New York Times Book Review* p12 Aug. 9, 1998, p34 Oct. 31, 1999; *Russian Review* p126+ Jan. 2000

SELECTED BOOKS: *Mikhail Bakunin: A Study in the Psychology and Politics of Utopianism*, 1982; *Toward Another Shore: Russian Thinkers Between Necessity and Chance*, 1998; *Views from the Other Shore: Essays on Herzen, Chekhov, and Bakhtin*, 1999

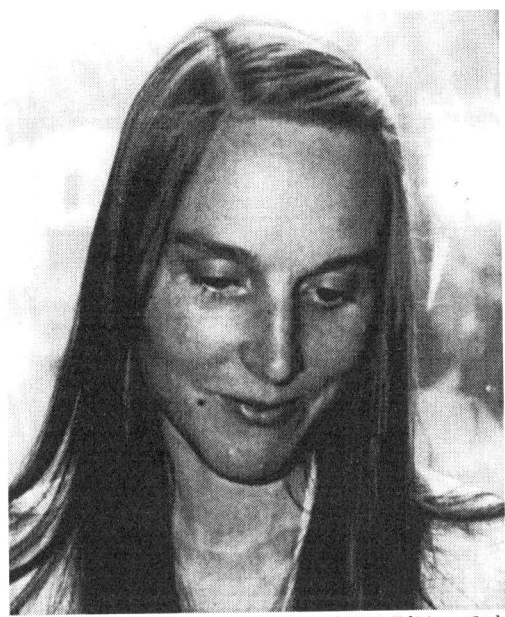
Courtesy of BOA Editions, Ltd.

Kelly, Brigit Pegeen

1951– Poet

With just two volumes to her credit, Brigit Pegeen Kelly has been honored with some of the most prestigious poetry prizes currently available, including the 1987 Yale Series of Younger Poets Award, the 1994 Lamont Poetry Award, and the 1996 Whiting Writers Award. Her collections, *To the Place of the Trumpets* (1988) and *Song* (1994), display a unique lyrical voice and often use simple imagery to explore deeper spiritual, mythical, and psychological themes. In making the Yale Series Selection, the poet James Merrill compared Kelly's work to folk art, saying that her imagination "breeds heresies as innocent and plentiful as mayflies," as quoted by Judith B. Newman for *Horizon* (November 1987), while her language "retains the wild transforming eye of childhood."

Brigit Pegeen Kelly submitted the prose poem "Windfall" to *World Authors 1995–2000*, noting that its content addresses her writing process:

Windfall

There is a wretched pond in the woods. It lies at the north end of a piece of land owned by a man who was taken to an institution years ago. He was a strange man. I only spoke to him once. You can still find statues of women and stone gods that he set up in dark corners of the woods, and sometimes you can find flowers that have survived the collapse of the hidden gardens he planted. Once I found a flower that looked like a human brain growing near a fence, and it took my breath away. And once I found among some weeds a lily, white as snow......No one tends the land now. The fences have fallen and the deer grown thick, and the pond lies black, the water slowly thickening, the banks tangled with weeds and grasses. But the pond was very old even when I first came upon it. Through the trees I saw the dark water steaming, and smelled something sweet rotting, and then as I got closer, I saw in the dark water shapes, and the shapes were golden, and I thought, without really thinking, that I was looking at the reflections of leaves or of fallen fruit, though there were no fruit trees near the pond and it was not the season for fruit. And then I saw that the shapes were moving, and I thought they moved because I was moving, but when I stood still, still they moved. And still I had trouble seeing. Though the shapes took on weight and muscle and definite form, it took my mind a long time to accept what I saw. The pond was full of ornamental carp, and they were large, larger than the carp I have seen in museum pools, large as small trumpets, and so gold they were almost yellow. In circles, wide and small, the plated fish moved, and there were so many of them they could not be counted, though for a long time I tried to count them. And I thought of the man who owned the land standing where I stood. I thought of how years ago in a fit of madness or high faith he must have planted the fish in the pond, and then forgotten them, or been taken from them, but still the fish had grown and still they thrived, until they were many, and their bodies were fast and bright as brass knuckles or cocks' combs. I tore pieces of my bread and threw them at the carp, and the carp leaped, as I have not seem carp do before, and they fought each other for the bread, and they were not like fish but like gulls or wolves, biting and leaping. Again and again, I threw the bread. Again and again, the fish leaped and wrestled. And below them, below the leaping fish, near the bottom of the pond, something slowly circled, a giant form that never rose to the bait and never came fully into view, but moved patiently in and out of the murky shadows, out and in. I watched that form, and after the bread was gone and after the golden fish had again grown quiet, my mind at last constructed a shape for it, and I saw for the space of one moment or two with perfect clarity, as if I held the heavy creature in my hands, the tarnished body of an ancient carp. A thing both fragrant and foul. A lily and a man's brain bound together in one body. And then the fish was gone. He turned and the shadows closed around him. The water grew blacker, and the steam rose from it, and the golden carp held still, still uncountable. And softly they burned, themselves like flowers, or like fruit blown down in an abandoned garden.

Brigit Pegeen Kelly was born in Palo Alto, California, in 1951. She grew up in Indiana, where her father was a professor of English at Indiana University. She recalled to Newman that her father liked to read aloud to his children and often required them to perform daily writing exercises. "How many people have heard all of *Bleak House* read out loud?" Kelly said. "It's how I fell in love with the sound of words, even when I didn't understand what the words meant." She described her home life as "permeated with rationalism—which may be why I love to tap into the irrational today." Kelly coupled her father's rationalism with strict discipline and self-denial, and she ultimately developed anorexia as a teenager. Though her parents were non-practicing Catholics, she sought out a strong religious framework in which to address the questions of doubt and faith that had plagued her since childhood. At age 18, she joined an order of silent nuns in New Mexico, where she spent nine months as a postulant. "I was a little too young to become a postulant," she later told Newman. "If I had entered a few years later, I'm sure I would still be there today. I loved that life, and in fact, I think in some ways my life here mimics my life there. Like being a nun, being a poet is isolated and contemplative in a society that doesn't value these qualities."

After Kelly left the convent, she spent some time in England working at a youth hostel. During the next decade, she moved in and out of school, trying on a variety of potential careers: She worked as a nurse in Indiana, as a printmaker in California, and as a therapist in Oregon. She had her first child, Huck, out of wedlock, and her second child, Maria, with another man, whom she later married. The marriage lasted only a short time, however, and despite her religious convictions, Kelly consented to divorce. (She later married the award-winning poet Michael Madonick). The difficult period of her divorce corresponded with her first attempts to see her poems in print; she was quickly rewarded with publication in several literary journals. Of her career as a writer, Kelly told Newman she considers it a combination of all her previous jobs; "It's drama, it's psychology, it's myth," she said.

Kelly published her first volume of poems, *To the Place of Trumpets*, in 1988, after winning the Yale Series of Younger Poets Award. (This distinction is one of the most prominent honors available for poets who have not yet published a book. As part of the prize, her book was published by Yale University Press.) Kelly's debut collection largely celebrates the common-place details of life, from the shops and church on a familiar Main Street (as in "The House on Main Street"), to the banality of chores on a Sunday afternoon (as in "Doing Laundry on Sunday"). Alfred Corn, writing for *Poetry* (January 1989), praised her "kinesthetic vision" and opined, "The nearest comparison I can think of is [Marc] Chagall's rural paintings, where cows, steeples, human figures, and stars are all swept up into new spatial and spiritual relationships." Many of the poems in the volume—including "Imagining Their Own Hymns," which deals with hypocrisy in the Catholic Church; "Above the Quarry," which explores salvation; and "To the Place of the Trumpets," which imagines heaven—reflect specifically spiritual themes. While her poems often examine the process of finding, losing, and rediscovering faith, she told Newman she is careful about being identified too narrowly as a "Catholic" poet. "Poetry has an independent life," she said. "The poetic spirit operates outside of doctrine." Fred Muratori, reviewing the book for *Library Journal* (May 15, 1988), concluded, "Kelly has a talent for coaxing out the world's ghosts and then fixing them in personal landscapes of fear and uncertainty. . . . Smoothed by nuances of sound and rhythm, her poems exude an ambiguous wisdom, an acceptance of the sad magic that returns us constantly to the lives we might have led."

Kelly's second volume, *Song*, appeared in 1994 to significant critical praise. The book's 27 poems delve into mythical, spiritual, and religious questions, while employing personal, everyday imagery. Mary Ann Samyn observed for *Cross Currents* (Fall 1995), "The title provides a key not only to the poems' thematic concerns but to their method as well. These haunting, lyrical poems often turn on narrative, employing the musical strategies of refrain and verses, melody and harmony, to explore the role of revision in the act of storytelling and the ways in which narrative is often not linear, just as memory is not simply a straightforward recall of events." The book's title poem—which was often praised as its most haunting and powerful—presents an almost fable-like tale of a young girl whose goat has been brutally murdered by a group of boys. "Listen: there was a goat's head hanging by ropes in a tree," the poem begins, as quoted on the Web site for the Academy of American Poets. "All night it hung there and sang. And those who heard it / Felt a hurt in their hearts and thought they were hearing / The song of a night bird." As the poem delivers weighty themes of sacrifice, cruelty, guilt, redemption, and grief, it moves toward a transcendent conclusion about death: "There / Would be a whistle, a hum, a high murmur, and, at last, a song, / The low song a lost boy sings remembering his mother's call. / Not a cruel song, no, no, not cruel at all. This song / Is sweet. It is sweet. The heart dies of this sweetness."

Many critics praised Kelly's original language and narrative style. Mary Ann Samyn, for example, concluded, "Kelly's combination of lyrical and narrative, of image-making and storytelling, works to create poems that are as memorable for their songs as for their singing, the whole collection echoing with their strange, enchanting music." Writing for *Booklist* (February 1, 1995), Patricia Monaghan affirmed, "In *Song* . . . Kelly is both lavish and demanding. Her images unfold intuitively, hypnotically. Her rhythms and repetitions drive the poems beyond mere logic into passion. . . . Kelly's poetry is symphonic, and each poem is best appreciated as a total composition rather than as a series of melodic lines." In an article for *Poetry* (April 1996), David Baker also praised the collection, writing, "There is not a weak poem . . . in *Song*, and not one sounds like anybody else's. [Kelly's] talent is great and her embrace is large, from the singular determinations of familial belonging to the most metaphysical explorations of history, faith, and language. She is not an ecstatic poet, but one for whom mystery and adventure are best approached in humble, if certain, song." *Song* was awarded the 1994 Lamont Poetry Award for the best second book by an American poet and was a finalist for the 1995 *Los Angeles Times* Book Prize.

Kelly's poems have been published in a number of literary journals, including the *Gettysburg Review*, *Kenyon Review*, and *Yale Review*. Her work was featured in both the 1993 and 1994 volumes of *The Best American Poetry*, *The Extraordinary Tide: New Poetry by American Women* (2001), and *Poets of the New Century* (2001). She has won fellowships from the National Endowment for the Arts, the Illinois State Council on the Arts, and the New Jersey Council on the Arts. In addition, she has received several other honors, including a "Discovery"/*The Nation* Award (1986), the Cecil Hemley Award from the Poetry Society of America, a Pushcart Prize, the Theodore Roethke Prize from *Poetry Northwest*, and a Whiting Writers Award (1996), which included a $30,000 cash prize.

Brigit Pegeen Kelly described her writing process to Judith B. Newman: "You always fail. As a poet you have to accustom yourself to the idea that you conceive beyond what you can execute." Kelly resides in Urbana, Illinois, where she and Madonick are professors of English at the University of Illinois.

—K. D.

SUGGESTED READING: *Cross Currents* p424+ Fall 1995; *Horizon* p39+ Nov. 1987, with photo; *Library Journal* p84 May 15, 1988, p107 Jan. 1995; *Poetry* p234+ January 1989, p41+ Apr. 1996; *Prairie Schooner* p179+ Apr. 1996; *Southern Review* p761+ Autumn 1996

SELECTED BOOKS: *To the Place of Trumpets*, 1988; *Song*, 1994

Kelton, Elmer

Apr. 29, 1926– Novelist

Perhaps the most honored of all Western writers, the native Texan Elmer Kelton has been writing about the American West for more than 50 years. For much of his writing life, he maintained dual careers as a journalist and novelist, penning more than 40 novels and several works of nonfiction. Kelton's books explore a variety of Western themes spanning many historical eras. His series of historical novels on the post–Civil War experiences of the Texas Rangers have been widely praised for their historical accuracy. Throughout his lengthy career, Kelton has been honored with seven Spur Awards and four Western Heritage Awards from the National Cowboy Hall of Fame; he was also voted the all-time best western author by the Western Writers of America. In addition, Kelton has written several books under the names Lee McElroy and Tom Early.

Kelton contributed the following autobiographical statement to *World Authors 1995–2000*: "People who write about me usually describe me as a Western writer. Some think they are being kind by describing me instead as a regional writer inasmuch as most of my writing has been about Texas, past or present. I happily accept the 'Western writer' description. Having grown up in the 1930s on a West Texas ranch, around people who had lived in open-range days or even remembered the Civil War, I was keenly aware from early boyhood of history and my personal Texas heritage. It has always been my favorite subject.

Jim Bean Professional Photography/Courtesy of Forge Books

"As a boy I loved Western stories and films, though I recognized that the cowboys of stories and screen were not always like the ones among whom I was growing up. Fictional cowboys spent a lot of time celebrating in town or rescuing ranchers' daughters and helpless schoolmarms from men of evil intent. The ones who worked with my father spent their time riding horses that were always looking for a chance to buck them off, or working cattle, digging postholes, repairing fences, and indulging in other forms of strenuous manual labor that seldom befell the make-believes. I resolved that when I grew up I would write stories about the real ones as in Ross Santee's *Cowboy*, or in the books Will James was writing and illustrating such as *Smoky*.

"An early convert to the folklore tales of J. Frank Dobie, I also reveled in the colorful adventure-filled Westerns of Zane Grey. I read the pulp stories of writers like Walt Coburn, W. C. Tuttle, and S. Omar Barker. Barker, known as the 'poet lariat' of New Mexico, later became a personal friend and something of a mentor. His humor-tinged Western stories always smacked of reality, and his cowboys sometimes actually worked cows.

"Though fiction writing was my primary ambition, it seemed reasonable that I needed to make a living while I learned the art and the craft of it. Partly through the influence of teacher Paul Patterson, I majored in journalism at the University of Texas. Newspaper work appeared to be a logical gateway. I did not seriously try for publication until my return from World War II military service in 1946. I lacked three semesters to finish at the university. In spare time after classes and homework I wrote short stories and sent them to Western pulp magazines. Sometimes it seemed as if they beat me home from the post office.

"In my final semester, however, I sold a story to Fanny Ellsworth, editor of *Ranch Romances*. Though she had rejected previous offerings, she would write encouraging letters pointing out my shortcomings and encouraging me to keep trying. Mrs. Ellsworth was the first of three lady editors who furthered my writing career. The second was Betty Ballantine, who in 1955 published my first novel, *Hot Iron*, for the company she and husband Ian Ballantine had just started. A third, years later, was Judy Alter of Texas Christian University Press, who reprinted many of my bigger novels originally published by Doubleday.

"Having sold my first story and feeling confident that riches and fame were just around the corner, I nevertheless expected that it might be a year or so before my dreams came to full fruition. After graduation I accepted a job as an agricultural reporter on the San Angelo *Standard-Times*, assuming it would be of limited duration. It lasted 15 years, followed by a five-year stint as editor of *Sheep and Goat Raiser Magazine* and 22 years as associate editor of *Livestock Weekly*.

"The economics of fiction writing made me keep two parallel careers for 42 years, but I enjoyed both. One often complemented the other. Situations and events observed in newspaper work became central to my fiction. A notable example was a seven-year drought, my daily running news story during the 1950s. It led to what many consider my signature work. I could never have written that book had it not been for my experience as a West Texas farm and ranch reporter.

"The work gave me an opportunity to travel widely and learn history on the ground where the events had occurred.

"Some have commented that I could have written many more books had I not had to spend so much time on the job. The fact is that I could not have written some of those books had it not been for knowledge gained as a reporter.

"In a strong sense newspaper work had a liberating influence on my fiction. It made a living for my family so I was not dependent upon the fiction for income. It freed me to write books I wanted to write instead of being forced to knock off something I might be ashamed of because I needed a quick check for the mortgage payment or to put food in the pantry.

"After 40 novels and more than 50 years as a professional writer, I can think of little I would want to change if given the opportunity to do it over. I am grateful for what both careers have given me."

Elmer Kelton was born on the Scharbauer Cattle Company's Five Wells Ranch, near Andrews, Texas, in 1926. His father, R. W. "Buck" Kelton, was a cowboy, and his mother, Bea, was a schoolteacher. He grew up in Crane, Texas, on the McElroy Ranch, where his father was the foreman. As a boy he learned the cattle business, but found that he liked reading about the life of cowboys just as much as he liked living it. He decided that he wanted to become a writer of Westerns and figured that to support himself he should study journalism. In an interview with Dale L. Walker for the on-line magazine *ReadWest.com*, Kelton recalled that his father accepted the news stoically, but fixed his son with a "look that could have killed Johnson grass," and said, "'That's the way with you kids nowadays. You all want to make a living without having to work for it!'"

Kelton entered the University of Texas at Austin in 1942. His schooling was interrupted by World War II, and he served two years in the United States Army, from 1944 to 1946, including a period of combat-infantry service in Europe. There he met and fell in love with Anna Lipp, an Austrian, who returned with him to America. The couple were married in 1947. The following year Kelton completed his degree in journalism and began his career as an agricultural reporter.

Despite the amount of work required in his various positions as reporter and editor, Kelton proved to be a prolific fiction writer. Since the publication of his first novel, *Hot Iron*, in 1955, Kelton has produced an average of a book a year. In 1956 he won his first Spur Award from the Western Writers of America, for best Western novel of the year, for his second novel, *Buffalo Wagons*. As his writing progressed, his novels tended to become longer, more complex, and more historically based. For example, *Massacre at Goliad* (1965), is based on the execution of 280 Texan prisoners in Goliad in 1836, by order of the Mexican president Antonio López de Santa Anna. This trend was even more pronounced in *The Day the Cowboys Quit* (1971), a groundbreaking novel based on a little-known 1883 cowboy strike on the Canadian River. Kelton also began to place more emphasis on character rather than plot, although character development was something that he had been working on since his early days at Ballantine Books, when Betty Ballantine was his editor. In the interview with Walker, Kelton explained, "[Betty] was always more interested in why a character fired a gun than in simply showing the character firing a gun. She always valued strong characterization over strong plotting and she exerted an important influence over my manner of writing, then and now."

Among readers of Western fiction, Kelton's ability to create memorable personalities has become a hallmark of his work. In *The Time It Never Rained* (1973) Kelton introduced one of his most well-known characters, Charlie Flagg, a proud, hard-headed cowboy who refuses to abandon his principles, at considerable cost to himself and his family. Other notable Kelton characters include Hugh Hitchcock in *The Day the Cowboys Quit*; Gideon Ledbetter, Gray Horse, and Hannah York in *The Wolf and the Buffalo* (1980); Frank Claymore in *Stand Proud* (1984); and Wes Hendrix in *The Man Who Rode Midnight* (1987).

Kelton's interest in strong characters extends to females as well, unusual in a genre that until recently has not been noted for including challenging representations of women. Kelton commented to Walker, "In the older Westerns, in the words of the late Stephen Payne, the woman's function was mainly 'to be chased, and chased, but to remain ever chaste.' She was put there for the hero to rescue, and not much else. But, in real life, women had a very important part in the settlement of the West, and it took a strong-minded one to survive. I think back to my two grandmothers and to the one great-grandmother I was privileged to know. . . . Survival was a struggle, but they all met life head-on, never wasting time waiting around for my grandfathers to rescue them from anything. They could take care of themselves, thank you, and did."

Kelton has also made important inroads in his genre through his inclusion of black and Hispanic characters. As he told Walker, "Hispanics and blacks were a factor in the history of the part of the country I write about—West Texas—and to ignore them would be to deny part of history." In *Massacre at Goliad*, for example, a Texas-born cowhand named Josh Buckalew falls in love with a Mexican woman named Teresa. The novel takes place shortly after the siege of the Alamo, in 1836, when tensions between white Texans and Mexicans are high, and Josh finds himself torn between two worlds. In *The Wolf and the Buffalo*, the Civil War has just ended and Gideon Ledbetter, a freed slave with no money and no job prospects, joins the U.S. Cavalry and heads west to make a life for himself. There, however, he is drawn into a conflict with a Comanche warrior, Gray Horse Running, who is fighting to defend his way of life. A poignant struggle ensues between the two men, who are revealed to be mere pawns in a tragic confrontation of much larger proportions.

An overriding theme of Kelton's fiction is the ways in which individuals face the challenge of changing times. As Kelton explained to Walker, "Nothing stands still for very long; no generation goes untouched by change, usually drastic change. Our history has been one of constant challenge to the status quo. And in using this universal theme, we don't have to create a white hat and a black hat to make a story. We can use two gray hats, one trying to bring about change and one trying to resist it."

The novels for which Kelton has received the Western Writers of America Spur Award are *Buffalo Wagons*, *The Day the Cowboys Quit*, *The Time It Never Rained*, *Eyes of the Hawk* (1981), *Slaughter* (1992), *The Far Canyon* (1994), and *The Way of the Coyote* (2001). His four books to win the Western Heritage Award from the National Cowboy Hall of Fame are *The Time It Never Rained*, *The Good Old Boys* (1978), *The Man Who Rode Midnight*, and *The Art of Howard Terpning* (1992). *The Good Old Boys* was made into a 1995 TV miniseries directed by and starring Tommy Lee Jones. Kelton's recent novels include *Honor at Daybreak* (1991), *The Pumpkin Rollers* (1996), *Cloudy in the West* (1997), *The Smiling Country* (1998), *The Buckskin Line* (1999), and *Badger Boy* (2001). Kelton has also written several works of nonfiction. He has explicated the works of Western artists in *The Art of Howard Terpning*, *The Art of Frank McCarthy* (1992), and *The Art of James Bama* (1993). *Texas Cattle Barons: Their Families, Land and Legacy*, a book of photographs by Kathleen Jo Ryan with text by Kelton, was published in 1999.

Kelton's 40th novel, *Ranger's Trail*, the fourth installment in his *Texas Ranger* series, was published in 2002. In a review of the book for *Publishers Weekly*, as quoted on *Amazon.com*, an anonymous critic wrote: "Kelton is a master storyteller who offers more than just blood and gunsmoke. The right blend of action, drama, romance, humor and suspense makes this a handsome addition to his ongoing saga of the Old West."

Kelton has received numerous other honors and awards for his work. In 1987 he received the Barbara McCombs/Lon Tinkle Award for "continuing excellence in Texas letters." In 1990 he received the Distinguished Achievement Award from the Western Literature Association. The Texas Legislature proclaimed Elmer Kelton Day in April 1997. In 1998 he received the first Lone Star Award for lifetime achievement from the Larry McMurtry Center for Arts and Humanities

Although the literary world in general continues to disregard Westerns as a serious form of fiction, Kelton hopes that will change. "Today we have many writers in the Western genre who take their history seriously and who weave a really valid human story into the Western locale," he told Walker. "But the critical establishment still ignores them in favor of works that are often poorly conceived and shoddily written but are considered 'important,' mainly because they are negative toward traditional American values. For many critics, a writer is important only when he savages his subject matter. If he writes with understanding and hope, with respect and love, he is considered trivial."

Kelton and his wife, Anna, live in San Angelo, Texas. They have two grown sons, a daughter, four grandchildren, and five great-grandchildren.
—A. I. C.

SUGGESTED READING: *Boston Globe* p91 Mar. 5, 1995; *Houston Chronicle* p6 Aug. 12, 1990, p12 July 23, 1990, p24 Mar. 3, 1991, p27 June 16, 1996, p6 Apr. 16, 2000; *Los Angeles Times Book Review* p4 Sep. 6, 1987; *Publishers Weekly* p65 Sep. 28, 1992, p56 June 27, 1994; ReadWest.com; *San Angelo Standard-Times* (on-line) Apr. 24, 2000, p80+ Dec. 1995, with photo; *Texas Monthly* p80+ Dec. 1995 with photo, p104 Mar. 1996, p22 June 2000; *Texas West* (on-line) June 24, 1990

SELECTED BOOKS: novels—*Hot Iron*, 1955; *Buffalo Wagons*, 1956; *Barbed Wire*, 1957; *Shadow of a Star*, 1959; *The Texas Rifles*, 1960; *Donovan*, 1961; *Bitter Trail*, 1962; *Horsehead Crossing*, 1963; *Massacre at Goliad*, 1965; *Llano River*, 1966; *After the Bugles*, 1967; *Captain's Rangers*, 1968; *Hanging Judge*, 1969; *Bowie's Mine*, 1971; *The Day the Cowboys Quit*, 1971; *Wagontongue*, 1972; *The Time It Never Rained*, 1973; *Manhunters*,1974; *The Good Old Boys*, 1978; *The Wolf and the Buffalo*, 1980; *Stand Proud*, 1984; *Dark Thicket*, 1985; *The Man Who Rode Midnight*, 1987; *Honor at Daybreak*, 1991; *Slaughter*, 1992; *The Far Canyon*, 1994; *The Pumpkin Rollers*, 1996; *Cloudy in the West*, 1997; *The Smiling Country*, 1998; *The Buckskin Line*, 1999; *Badger Boy*, 2001; *The Way of the Coyote*, 2001; *Ranger's Trail*, 2002; as Lee McElroy—*Joe Pepper*, 1975; *Long Way to Texas*, 1976; *Eyes of the Hawk*, 1981; as Tom Early—*Sons of Texas, Book 1*, 1989; *Sons of Texas, Book 2*, 1989; *Sons of Texas, Book 3*, 1990; as Alex Hawk—*Shotgun Settlement*, 1969; short-story collections—*The Big Brand*, 1986; *There's Always Another Chance*, 1986; nonfiction—*Looking Back West*, 1972; *Frank C. McCarthy: The Old West*, 1981; *The Art of Howard Terpning*, 1992; *The Art of Frank McCarthy*, 1992; *The Art of James Bama*, 1993; *My Kind of Heroes*, 1995; *Texas Cattle Barons: Their Families, Land and Legacy*, 1999

Keret, Etgar

1967– Novelist; short-story writer

Over the last decade the iconoclastic writer Etgar Keret has established a loyal following among young people in Israel. Keret has written short stories, sketches for television, comic books, screenplays, and a musical. While many have praised his deliberately offhand style and wit, his satirical talent has made him a controversial figure. Some Israelis, particularly members of an older generation of writers, have criticized Keret's work as lacking political or ideological significance. "I think my writing is ideological," Keret told Emily Gitter for the *Forward* (October 26, 2001, on-line). "But in Israel, when people talk about ideology or morals, they're always talking about politics. And I think there's a lot more to ideology and morals than politics."

Etgar Keret was born in 1967 in Ramat Gan, a suburb of Tel Aviv, Israel. In an interview with Moshe Temkin for the *Jerusalem Report* (March 29, 1999), Keret described his writing as reflecting his "suburban, middle-class upbringing." He elaborated, "I don't write about brokers who do coke." His mother experienced difficulties while she was pregnant with him, and a physician advised her to have an abortion. However, she dreamed about a tall, blond man playing the piano in a crowded auditorium and—imagining that her son would be a renowned musician—decided to have the baby.

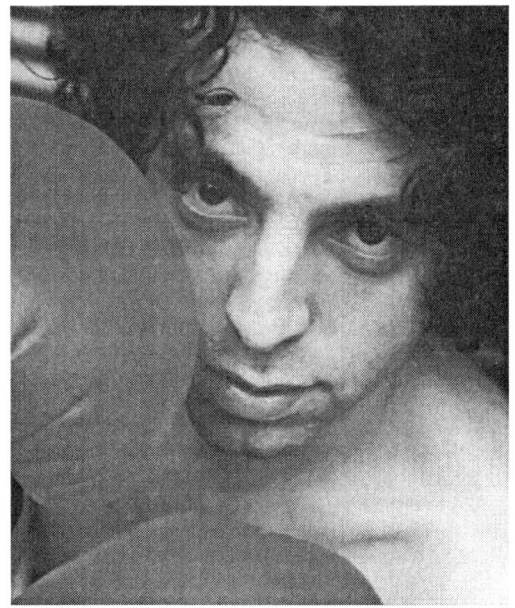

Eldad Rafaeli/Corbis

"When I was born, her first shock was that I wasn't blond," Keret told Allison Kaplan Sommer for the *Jerusalem Post* (July 28, 1995). "And after a while it became clear I wouldn't be tall either." The given name his mother chose for him means "challenge" in Hebrew.

Keret's father held a series of jobs, including running a plastic-container factory and a coffee shop, managing an oil-truck company, and working as an electrician. "My father changed his occupation every three years, claiming that staying in the same job made him bored and grumpy," Keret explained to Gitter. He added that his "parents taught me to be true to myself, and not be afraid to fight for my point of view."

As a child Keret had poor motor skills, which made writing difficult. In high school he focused on mathematics and science. After graduation he did his compulsory service in the Israeli Defense Force, serving as a computer programmer. Keret told Gitter that the strong sense of independence that his parents had inculcated in him got him into trouble in the army, and "was one of the main reasons why I was court-martialed more than 20 times." In spite of his unhappiness as a soldier, Keret experienced an intellectual and literary awakening during this time. He started writing and discovered the works of American authors, including John Cheever, Kurt Vonnegut, and Raymond Carver. "It was very difficult for me to identify with the characters in Israeli literature," he told Gitter. "They always seemed better than me—stronger and more charismatic." Keret found that he identified in particular with the characters in Vonnegut's *Slaughterhouse Five* (1969), telling Gitter that they "were less heroic and more ironic; they could recognize a problem, but they couldn't think of a way to solve it."

After leaving the military Keret enrolled at Bar-Ilan University, in Ramat Gan, graduating with a B.A. in philosophy and computer science. He then earned an M.A. from Hebrew University, in Jerusalem. He also studied at Tel Aviv University's Interdisciplinary Program for Fostering Excellence.

After school Keret worked briefly in Tel Aviv as a construction worker. "I became a writer when a manager in Jerusalem refused to hire me for his site and told me I was too short and frail for the job," he explained to Moshe Temkin for the *Jerusalem Report* (March 29, 1999). In 1991 he found work as a reporter and columnist for the *Kol Ha'ir* newspaper, which also published some of his short stories. In addition he wrote for the newspapers *Hadashot* and *Ma'ariv*, contributed a comic strip to the *Zman Tel Aviv* daily newspaper, and worked as a freelance copywriter for several advertising firms and as a researcher for *Fact* magazine.

In 1992 Keret published his first collection of short stories, *Tzinorot* (Pipelines), which sold about 8,000 copies in Israel. The next year Keret co-wrote the comic musical *Operation Entebbe* with Jonathan Bar Giora, who also composed the music. The musical is a satirical look at the events of 1976, when a team of Israeli commandos freed Jewish airline passengers who had been taken hostage by Palestinian terrorists at the airport in Entebbe, Uganda. The commando who led the raid, Lieu-tenant Colonel Jonathan "Yoni" Netanyahu, the brother of the future prime minister, Benjamin Netanyahu, was killed in the fighting and became a revered figure in Israel. According to Calev Ben-David for the *Jerusalem Report* (1994, on-line), the musical portrayed Yoni Netanyahu as "a trigger-happy glory-seeker." In spite of its irreverence, *Operation Entebbe* won first prize at the 1993 Acre Alternative Theater Festival, in Acre, Israel. After this success, Keret was asked to write sketches for *Cameri Quintet*, a comedy show on Israel's Channel 1. According to Allison Kaplan Sommer, the Israeli Broadcasting Authority censored some of Keret's sketches because they were deemed too controversial.

Most critics in Israel hailed the 1994 publication of Keret's second short-story anthology, *Ga'aguai Le-Kissinger* (published in English in 1993 as *Missing Kissinger*). The book was also a popular success, but some Israeli writers, including the novelist and playwright A. B. Yehoshua, dismissed Keret's stories as frivolous. For his part, Keret argued that it is a mistake to judge writers in terms of their public lives and political involvements rather than their literary talents. "Take two authors, Vaclav Havel and Charles Bukowski, for example," Keret explained to Temkin. "One became president of his country, the other wanted to booze. Who's to say which of them was the more important writer?"

Several of Keret's stories sparked controversy. In "Siren," for example, a boy runs away from a group of bullies as the memorial siren on Holocaust Remembrance Day goes off—a moment when Israelis are asked to stand at attention. Some schoolteachers refused to teach "Siren" when it was included in the school curriculum, fearing their own students would begin to ignore the siren. "I was criticized for that story," Keret told Temkin. "How can you make light of the Holocaust, someone wrote me. But I wasn't. That kid related to the siren in his own private way. It had special meaning for him. Most people stand still during the siren and think about what they have to do at the bank later. Isn't that making light of the Holocaust?" In "Rabin's Dead" two boys find a cat in the area where Prime Minister Yitzhak Rabin was assassinated in 1995 and name it after the slain leader. After the cat is run over by a car, one of the boys reflects on the meaning of Rabin's death. In another story a frustrated Israeli soldier—under orders not to fire his gun—trades places with a Palestinian militant who has been taunting him. The soldier puts on a mask, gives his rifle to the Palestinian, and begins to provoke him. The Palestinian then tries to shoot the soldier, but the rifle jams. "I received two angry letters about that story," Keret told Sommer. "One said I finally showed my true face, that I'm a left-wing goody-two-shoes after all. And the second letter said they were shocked to discover that I was such a fascist. I really don't believe I am either."

Keret's third book, *Hakaitana shel Kneller* (Kneller's Camp), which appeared in 1998, includes a novella and several stories. Writing for the *World Literature in Review* (Spring 1999), Yair Mazor noted that Keret's stories "continually conduct a reciprocal dialogue involving seemingly realistic plots consisting of daily petty occurrences and the most overwhelmingly absurd events, motivations, and verbal expressions." In "Wine Stinger from Hell," for example, Keret introduced a fictional place that has no remarkable features, except that the entrance to Hell is located there. During their once-in-a-century reprieve, damned souls emerge from Hell to visit the locals. Mazor observed that the language in the stories is "deliberately elementary, full of slang, and even grammatically incorrect," and he concluded that the "stories both possess and produce a unique appeal that simultaneously tantalizes and duns the reader while rewarding his or her intellectual curiosity." Reviewing the collection for the *Jerusalem Post* (January 22, 1999), Jeff Green observed that the characters in the stories "are mainly secular Tel Avivians in their 20s who don't see much point in settling into their middle-class destinies." Green was impressed with the novella, "Kneller's Camp," which describes the afterlife of people who have committed suicide. With gaping wounds, the walking dead go to bars, have romances, and otherwise behave like living human beings. "Obviously life doesn't mean much to these characters, since they've intentionally shuffled [off] the mortal coil," Green noted, "which raises the question of what life means to the rest of us, who are sticking it out."

In 2001 Keret's work was introduced to readers in the United States, with the publication of *The Bus Driver Who Wanted to Be God*, a translation of 21 of his short stories and the novella from his previous collection, here re-titled "Kneller's Happy Campers." "Neither trite nor heavy lifting, the extraordinary collection *The Bus Driver Who Wanted to Be God* has the kind of writing that could hook a lot of readers, including some who rarely open a book," Jules Verdone observed in the *Boston Globe* (November 19, 2001). "Keret's voice is hard to resist, with its distinctive mix of insight, humor, tenderness, indelicate language, and a hopeful kind of cynicism." Verdone singled out "Breaking the Pig," in which a child saves money in a piggy bank to buy a Bart Simpson doll, but then becomes too attached to the pig to smash it for the coins. Discussing "Kneller's Happy Campers," about the afterlife of suicides, Verdone noted that the story is "guileless and thoughtful," rather than morose. Verdone pointed to the narrator, whose impression of the afterlife is different than he had imagined. "I'd always imagine these beeping sounds, like a fuzz-buster, and people floating around in space and stuff," Verdone quoted him as saying. "But now that I'm here, I don't know, mostly it reminds me of Tel Aviv." In the *New York Times Book Review* (October 28, 2001), Benjamin Anastas expressed disappointment with the book. "There are 22 stories in all, more than enough to define an author's worldview or—even better—to embody a realized fictional world," Anastas wrote. "One of the disappointments here is Keret's apparent lack of interest in using narrative to explore his ideas (which are often provocative) in any depth: each story can be summed up in a sentence and, like a skit on *Saturday Night Live*, manages to deliver less, not more." Anastas concluded, "Keret's stories, if they speak for anything, seem to advocate the writer's freedom to provoke without consequence, entertain without investment and value above all things the pursuit of fleeting pleasures. Life in the midst of conflict? Maybe. Or it could just be that Keret, like his readership, would rather be watching TV."

Etgar Keret is the co-author of two comic books, *Lo Banu Lehenot* (Nobody Said It Was Going to Be Fun, 1996), with Rutu Modan; and *Simtaot Ha-Zaam* (Streets of Rage, 1997), with Assaf Hanuka and Zmora Bitan. Keret has also branched into filmmaking. His screenplay for the short film *Devek Metoraf* (Crazy Glue), which explores a divorce, won a "special mention" award at the Munich Film Festival in 1994. Two years later Keret directed and appeared in the short film *Malka Lev Adom* (Literally meaning Malka Red Heart, the title has been translated as Skin Deep), which won a prestigious Israeli award for best film as well as the first prize at the Vienna short film festival, in 1996. Keret has also written other short films, including *Ha-Chavera Shel Korbi* (Korby's Girlfriend, 1994) and *Mashehu Totali* (Total Love, 2000). Film students in Israel have produced more than 40 short films based on Keret's short stories.

Etgar Keret resides in Tel Aviv and lectures at the Tel Aviv University School of Film.

—D. C.

SUGGESTED READING: *Boston Globe* C p2 Nov. 19, 2001; *Forward* (on-line) Oct. 26, 2001; *Jerusalem Post* p13+ July 28, 1995; *Jerusalem Report* p24 Jan. 22, 1999, p46+ Mar. 29, 1999; *Jerusalem Report* (on-line) 1994; *New York Times Book Review* p7 Oct. 28, 2001; *World Literature in Review* p388 Spring 1999

SELECTED BOOKS: *Selected Stories*, 1997; *The Bus Driver Who Wanted to Be God*, 2001

Mark McCall/Courtesy of William Morrow/Avon Publicity/HarperCollins Publishers

Keyes, Marian

Sep. 10, 1963– Novelist

Over the last decade the Irish author Marian Keyes has emerged as one of the leading innovators in women's fiction. Often compared to the British writer Helen Fielding, whose novel *Bridget Jones's Diary* won international fame, Keyes has produced six books addressing the complex, and often humorous, challenges of modern women. Yvonne Nolan, writing for *Publishers Weekly* (June 17, 2002), described Keyes's novels as "brightly colored, chunky books featuring self-deprecating heroines with 'issues,' body dysmorphia and unreliable taste when it comes to men." She continued, "Whilst in the wake of the success of *Bridget Jones's Diary*, many writers and critics have sought to dismiss chick-lit as froth, Keyes's fiction is so genuinely funny, sharply observed and winning as to make such reservations seem stuffy and wrongheaded. Nor is she afraid to tackle darker, more serious themes. In fact, it is a hallmark of her work that she manages to combine her great comedy-writing skills with an ability to examine issues like addiction or abortion with clarity, empathy and delicacy."

Keyes's books, while not considered "literary novels," have proven immensely popular with readers around the globe. They have been published in 35 countries, as well as in several different languages, resulting in sales of more than six million copies worldwide; Keyes is one of Ireland's best-selling authors, surpassed only by the novelists Maeve Binchy and Roddy Doyle. Of the debate over the literary value of her fiction, Keyes told Alex O'Connell for the London *Times* (October 2, 1999), "There is a growing acknowledgement for what I write, but it's not going to win the Booker Prize, as people are fond of telling me. There is more than one set of criteria for judging a book. If you divert people, take them away from their own situation, that is valid."

Marian Keyes was born on September 10, 1963 in Limerick, Ireland, the eldest of five children (three girls and two boys) to Timothy and Mary Keyes. Over the next several years, the family moved to Cork, Galway, and Cavan. They settled in Dublin when Keyes was 11, because her father, a government worker, had taken a job there. As a child, Keyes enjoyed reading and was an obsessive fan of the British children's writer Enid Blyton. Her home was filled with storytelling, laughing, and entertainment—traditions that were emphasized by her mother and grandmother. Yet, Keyes never considered becoming a writer herself. "It didn't occur to me that ordinary people could be writers," she told Amanda Linnell for the Auckland *Sunday Star-Times* (February 11, 2001), "I thought they were special people who were born that way." Keyes excelled at her studies in school—while also demonstrating an adventurous streak. While attending secondary school at the Presentation Convent, in Dublin, she often defied the nuns by wearing make-up and short skirts. "I had a great thing about justice," she recalled to O'Connell, "not doing what people wanted me to."

Keyes worked as a clerk in Dublin for one year before enrolling at University College of Dublin. She earned a degree in 1986, intending to pursue a career in law. She soon realized, however, that she had no passion for such a career and instead moved to London to follow other interests. London, at the time, was mired in recession, and Keyes was forced to support herself by working as a waitress. She then took a job in the accounts department of an architectural college, a position she retained for the next eight years. While in her mid-20s she applied for a coveted position in a graduate journalism program in Dublin, but was denied. "I was very upset," she told Georgina Brennan for the *Irish Tribune* (August 7, 2001), "I had such low self esteem. I thought they didn't let me in because I was crap. So I continued to work and just got on with it."

By age 30 Keyes was suffering from serious alcoholism. She had begun drinking as a teenager "like everyone else," as she explained to Linnell. "There was nothing unusual about it and everyone was experimenting." Eventually, however, she found herself drinking larger quantities and drinking even when she was by herself. "It was a very lonely, dreadful, paranoid, isolated time for me," she told Linnell. "I knew I had a problem, but I didn't really. I wondered why my life was so dreadful and I was so terribly confused." After a suicide attempt in 1994, Keyes returned to Ireland to undergo three months of treatment at a rehabilitation facility in Dublin; since beginning her recovery she has reportedly not touched any alcohol.

Keyes next returned to London, where, with the support of her family and close friends, she seriously pursued writing fiction. In an interview posted on her official Web site, she recalled, "I began writing short stories four months before I finally stopped drinking, and after I came out of rehab I decided to send them off to a publisher. So that they'd take me seriously, I enclosed a letter saying I'd written part of a novel. Which I hadn't. I had no intention of so doing either—I was much more into the instant gratification of short stories. But they wrote back and said, send the novel, and for once in my self-destructive life I didn't shoot myself in the foot. I wrote four chapters of my first novel *Watermelon* in a week, and was offered a three-book contract on the strength of it." Keyes's debut novel was released in 1995. That same year she married Tony Baines, a computer analyst who has since become her freelance editor and public-relations agent.

In *Watermelon* Keyes tells the story of Claire Webster, a 29-year-old woman whose husband, James, has just left her for an older woman, mere hours after the birth of their first child. With few options available, Claire leaves London and takes her baby daughter to Dublin, where she can recuperate among her eccentric family. Her younger sisters, Anna and Helen, help her lose the pregnancy weight and set her up with a handsome local. When James arrives to win her back, Claire must decide between her new life and her old. *Watermelon* quickly became a best-seller, with reviewers generally praising the book for its outrageous humor and entertaining plot. A critic for *Kirkus Reviews*, as quoted on *Amazon.com*, opined, "A grand first novel by Irish writer Keyes is a hilarious treatise on love's roller coaster. . . . A candid, irresistibly funny debut and perfect summertime read." A reviewer for *Publishers Weekly* (April 13, 1998) wrote, "Much of the hilarity generated by Claire's funky family . . . wears thin, but readers will identify with Claire's flaws, applaud her irreverent wit and rejoice at her triumphant recovery. Like the fruit it's named for, this overlong novel is short on nutrition but long on refreshment."

In her second novel, *Lucy Sullivan Is Getting Married* (1996), Keyes presents Lucy, a 26-year-old Londoner who visits a fortune teller with a group of friends and is told she will soon be getting married. Though skeptical, Lucy begins believing the prophecy is destined to come true after several of her friends' unlikely fortunes are realized. A humorous account of Lucy's adventures in dating commences, as she searches for Mr. Right. Along the way, however, Keyes introduces more serious themes of clinical depression and alcoholism. Almost immediately *Lucy Sullivan Is Getting Married* became an instant best-seller; it was the top-selling book in Ireland for 10 weeks and reached the third spot on the U.K.'s best-seller list for a period. It met, however, with less critical success then her debut. Some reviewers found the character of Lucy to be self-pitying and tiresome, while others found the novel's neat resolution lacking credibility. On the other hand, many critics celebrated the book's surprising depth. As one reviewer noted for *Publishers Weekly* (June 21, 1999), "Throughout, the effervescent narrative is fueled by witty repartee; though its outcome may be predictable, its sentiments are heartfelt, and its progress is sprightly." *Lucy Sullivan Is Getting Married* was later adapted into a 16-part miniseries for British television.

A spirited Irishwoman named Rachel Walsh is the heroine of Keyes's third novel, *Rachel's Holiday* (1998), about a woman recovering from addiction. When Rachel (who is a member of the Walsh family from *Watermelon*) wakes up in a New York hospital after overdosing on cocaine, her friends and family encourage her to seek professional help for her addiction. Though Rachel denies that her cocaine habit is a problem, she checks into an Irish treatment center—anticipating daily massages and celebrity sightings. Rachel's experiences in recovery and her dawning realizations about her life and her decisions form the basis for the narrative. This book, which spent several months on Ireland's best-seller list, was also deemed a critical success. Though some critics found the novel too long and the ending too predictable—Keyes has a penchant for happy endings—most applauded the author's manner in approaching such weighty material. As Monica L. Williams observed for the *Boston Globe* (August 17, 2000), the novel "is her most serious, and yet her funniest." Williams continued, "[Keyes's] touch in *Rachel's Holiday* is sometimes heavier, and the narrative is a bit long, but what easily could have been a grim shelf-warmer turns out to be a delightful page turner, propelled by its unforgettable heroine and her supporting cast of eccentric sidekicks." Deloris Tarzan Ament for the *Seattle Times* (September 10, 2000) affirmed, "Keyes has a fine knack for capturing the awkwardness of self-conscious laughter, and sexual collisions in which both parties are too polite to call a halt to proceedings gone awry. Her character descriptions are dead-on devastating. . . . The book is a crash course in the faces of addiction and the forms it can take, the denials that are part of its pathology and a glimpse into some of its causes." She concluded, "*Rachel's Holiday* rings with authenticity."

Last Chance Saloon (1999) chronicles the lives of three friends in London. Katherine is a beautiful and aloof 31-year-old accountant, who shuns all advances from men. Tara, a computer analyst, struggles with her weight while remaining trapped in an emotionally destructive relationship; though her boyfriend, a bitter high-school geography teacher, treats her poorly, she is terrified of being alone. The girls' best friend is Fintan, a gay man who discovers that he has cancer. Of her decision to tackle the cancer storyline, Keyes told Brennan, "This book was about people in their thirties looking for love. Shortly into it, I wanted it to be something with a bit more depth, I wanted something more profound. I had explored alcoholism and abandonment before and I then thought that the idea of illness in a young person was worth exploring. I had a lot of research to do though." Keyes continued, "There is a myth that when you get very ill you suddenly find serenity. The people that I spoke to talked of frustration and resentment of others. So I wanted to write an honest account of the illness not hearts and flowers." Again, critics responded warmly to Keyes's inclusion of more serious themes, with Paul Davies for the London *Mirror* (October 15, 1999) calling *Last Chance Saloon* "a terrific book, probably Keyes' best." In a laudatory review for *New York Newsday* (August 26, 2001), Emily Gordon praised Keyes for having "a terrific ear for dialogue, a brisk pace and the knack of quick description." Gordon continued, "Keyes never falters in her fidelity to her creations, who are inconsistent, irrational and sometimes downright self-delusional—in short, true to life. She is also utterly realistic about tragedy; while people are suffering, as Keyes puts it, 'life [takes] the liberty of going on.' Even in its grimmest chapters, *Last Chance Saloon* is deeply hilarious . . . and unexpectedly deep."

In her fifth novel, *Sushi for Beginners* (2001), Keyes focuses on three co-workers at a women's magazine in Dublin. When Lisa, a London-based editor, is passed up for a promotion, she finds herself in Dublin, where she is assigned the task of overseeing a new magazine. Her assistant editor, the provincial and dowdy Ashling, has low self-esteem and a history of clinical depression. Their friend Clodagh, who on the surface appears to have the perfect husband, children, and home, is bored and unhappy in both her professional and personal lives. Lesley McDowell observed for the London *Independent* (November 12, 2000), "The novel is not so much about finding a partner in an increasingly time-starved world, or about the highly amusing observations of office life, or even about adapting to new environments, although all those elements are there. It is, of course, about the nature of relations between women, how they negotiate their friendships, share their joys, pass on their pain. Keyes has a real talent for making it all seem fresh and funny; easy to identify with but also new."

Other critical response to *Sushi for Beginners* was generally positive. In a London *Times* review (June 9, 2001), Wendy Holden called Keyes's greatest strength "her unerring eye for comic vulnerability." She continued, "Though perceptible and funny (in particular with her descriptions of . . . glossy magazine life), she is a sympathist, rather than a satirist. Gifted with a wonderful turn of phrase, she is the warm-hearted poet of everyday anguish." Bernice Harrison, writing for the *Irish Times* (June 16, 2001), affirmed, "What separates Keyes from all the other wannabes is her exuberant and extremely clever writing style. She has the ability to mix the fluffy handbag stuff with real issues such as depression, divorce and even homelessness without a drop of worthy earnestness dripping from her pen." She asserted, "Anyone who's inclined to thumb their noses snootily at this type of fiction should think again."

In her most recent book, *Angels* (2002), Keyes sets her story for the first time in the U.S., as she chronicles the adventures of Maggie, another Walsh sister. Maggie, a 33-year-old whose own family describes her as "room temperature vanilla yogurt"—as quoted by Carolyn See for the *Washington Post* (June 6, 2002)—discovers that her husband of nine years is having an affair. Unable to concentrate at work, she is fired. After moving in with her parents for a time, she accepts an invitation from Emily, a childhood friend who is now a struggling screenwriter in Los Angeles, to recuperate in sunny California. Once there, Maggie becomes caught up in the fast-paced, glamorous life of Hollywood studios, designer shopping, fashionable parties, and romance. The novel's darker themes include Emily's struggle to sell her script, Maggie's grief over her failed marriage and the two miscarriages she has suffered, and both women's search for happiness in a somewhat shallow world. Again, critics applauded the novel as entertaining and honest in its portrayal of more serious topics. While some reviewers found the plot twists silly or sordid, others celebrated Keyes's humor and refreshing observations about Los Angeles. Carolyn See noted, "Understand, this is nothing but froth, and presents itself as nothing but froth." Nevertheless, she continued, "Marian Keyes doesn't do any trashing. . . . She creates a balmy, welcoming emotional climate where sex is at once low-key and energetic, imaginative but not ridden with guilt." Writing for *New York Newsday* (July 21, 2002) Emily Gordon affirmed, "[Keyes] sketches her characters deftly, and her prose is bright and fast-moving, full of wordplay and impish jokes. She builds her story well, too, cutting flashback and background into the narrative; the effect is deceptively light and offhand." A reviewer for *Publishers Weekly* (June 3, 2002) concluded, "Keyes's observations may be familiar . . . , but her cleverly hilarious approach, especially as a foreigner, keep them fresh. Although this is unquestionably a fun read, Keyes refrains from turning it into fluff and delivers a well-rounded story."

In addition to her novels, Keyes has published a collection of articles gathered from a regular monthly column she writes for the *Irish Tatler*. In *Under the Duvet: Notes on High Heels, Movie Deals, Wagon Wheels, Shoes, Reviews, Having the Blues, Builders, Babies, Families, and Other Calamities* (2001), the author discloses many realities of her often unglamourous life as a writer. All proceeds from the book's Irish sales were contributed to the Simon Community, a charity dedicated to helping the homeless. In 2001 Keyes participated in the group novel *Yeats is Dead!*, with a number of Irish writers, including Roddy Doyle and Frank McCourt. She has also produced a short novel, *No Dress Rehearsal* (2000), aimed at adults just learning to read; again, Keyes donated all royalties to charity.

KING

Marian Keyes and her husband, Tony Baines, currently reside in the Dublin suburb of Dun Laoghaire. Of her approach to writing, Keyes told Yvonne Nolan, "I write the books I write to keep me positive and optimistic about the human condition because I'm too prone to melancholy. It makes me feel hopeful. I know I might get better reviews if I wrote downbeat endings, but I just couldn't. I write for myself."

—K. D.

SUGGESTED READING: *Boston Globe* E p2 Aug. 17, 2000; *Boston Herald* Books p59 Aug. 8, 1999; *Chicago Tribune* p3 Aug. 1, 2001; *Courier Mail* M p5 Feb. 3, 2001; *Europe* p45 Apr. 1998; (London) *Independent* p77 Nov. 12, 2000; Marian Keyes's Official Web site; *Mirror* p27 Oct. 15, 1999, p23 Oct. 27, 2000, p34 Sep. 7, 2002; *New York Newsday* B p14 Aug. 26, 2001, D p33 July 21, 2002; *Publishers Weekly* p48 Apr. 13, 1998, p53 June 21, 1999, p63 July 30, 2001, p62 June 3, 2002, p37 June 17, 2002; *Seattle Times* Books p8 Sep. 10, 2000; (Auckland) *Sunday Star-Times* p2 Feb. 11, 2001; *Washington Post* C p3 June 6, 2002

SELECTED BOOKS: *Watermelon*, 1995; *Lucy Sullivan Is Getting Married*, 1996; *Rachel's Holiday*, 1998; *Last Chance Saloon*, 1999; *Sushi for Beginners*, 2001; *Under the Duvet: Notes on High Heels, Movie Deals, Wagon Wheels, Shoes, Reviews, Having the Blues, Builders, Babies, Families, and Other Calamities*, 2001; *Angels*, 2002

Courtesy of HarperCollins Canada, Ltd.

King, Thomas

1943– Novelist; short-story writer

As a writer of Native American heritage who has never lived on a reservation or been closely affiliated with a particular tribe, Thomas King has a unique perspective on the clash between native and non-native cultures in North America. "I can't really write about the reservation experience," King told Jeffrey Canton for *Paragraph* (Summer 1994), "but I can write about the experience that contemporary Indians have in trying to manage living in the more contemporary world while maintaining a relationship with that more traditional world." In several novels and a collection of short stories, King has explored questions of Native American identity with an eye toward moving beyond stereotypical views. He told Canton, "I don't think that I need to stay away from some of the problems that Native communities face—alcoholism, drug abuse, child abuse—but I do have a responsibility *not* to make those such a part of my fiction that I give the impression to the reader that this is what drives Native communities. . . . It's my responsibility to make my readers understand what makes Native communities strong." King accomplishes this with a prose influenced by the Native American oral tradition and infused with his wicked sense of humor—Jace Weaver called him a "Native American Kurt Vonnegut" in *Publisher's Weekly* (March 8, 1993)—as well as by using fantasy grounded in careful and intimate depictions of his fictive Native American communities.

Born in Roseville, California, in 1943, Thomas King is of Native American, Greek, and German descent. His father, a Cherokee, abandoned the family when King was about five years old. Though he and his brother sometimes visited his Cherokee relatives in Oklahoma, they were primarily raised outside of Native American culture by his mother and grandmother in California. King has said that this outsider status gives him an advantage as a writer. "In some ways, I'm this Native American writer who's out there in the middle, not of nowhere, but I don't have strong tribal affiliations," King told Weaver. "My responsibilities are to the story and to the people from whom I get some of the stories. Other than that, I feel rather free to ask some of the really nasty questions that other writers may not want to ask or may not be in a position to ask. One of the questions that's important to ask is, 'Who is Indian? How do we get this idea of Indianness?'"

King received his B.A. and his M.A. in English from California State College at Chico in the early 1970s, after which he traveled to New Zealand and Australia, where he found work as a photojournalist. King later returned to the U.S. and entered a doctoral program in American Studies and English at the University of Utah, in Salt Lake City, where he did his dissertation on Native American oral tradition. This mode of storytelling later influenced his writing, as he explained to Canton. "What I learned from storytelling—from oral stories—was that those stories help to create a fantastic universe in which anything can happen. You're free to create that as you will."

While in New Zealand and Australia, King had experimented with writing fiction. However, he did not become serious about writing until he met his second wife, Helen Hoy, in 1980, at which time he was teaching Native American studies at the University of Lethbridge, in Alberta, Canada, where he lived with his son from his first marriage. "I dinked around with my own writing," King told Val Ross for the Toronto *Globe and Mail* (November 13, 1993), "but I got serious to impress Helen." To pass the time in tiny Lethbridge, King, in addition to teaching and writing, also joined an all–Native American basketball team (King is six feet, six inches tall), which gave him the opportunity to get to know a number of Blackfoot Indians. The experience provided him with material for some of the short stories that he later wove into his first novel, *Medicine River* (1990).

In 1986 King completed his Ph.D. at the University of Utah. The following year he edited, along with his wife and Cheryl Calver, a book of essays entitled *Native in Literature*. The volume was a modest success. In *Choice* (November 1988) Larry Evers wrote, "The volume is a step toward a more comprehensive, hemispheric consideration of the subject. . . . The quality of the essays spans the usual range: the embarrassingly uninformed and mundane to the illuminating and riveting, with a lot of competent work in between. . . . A necessary purchase for all colleges with undergraduate and/or graduate programs in 'American' literature."

In 1989 King was granted a month-long writer's residency at the Ucross Foundation in Wyoming, during which time he completed *Medicine River* and wrote a first draft of his second novel, *Green Grass, Running Water*. Around this time, the writer Margaret Atwood reviewed two of King's stories, "Joe the Painter and the Deer Island Massacre" and "One Good Story, That One" in *Canadian Literature* (Spring–Summer 1990). "They seem to me to be 'perfect' stories," Atwood wrote, "by which I mean that as narrations they are exquisitely timed, that everything in them appears to be there by right, and that there is nothing you would want to change or edit out. . . . They ambush the reader. They get the knife in, not by whacking you over the head with their own moral righteousness, but by being funny." King's use of humor is born of a conscious decision to leaven his outrage at the treatment of Native Americans so that his words won't fall on deaf ears. "I think of myself as a dead serious writer," King told Canton. "Comedy is simply my strategy. I don't want to whack somebody over the head, because I don't think that accomplishes much at all."

In 1990 *Medicine River* was published. Sewn together from a number of short stories and adapted into a novel by King, he actually prefers to call it a "cycle of stories," or a group of stories that stand on their own yet are interrelated, as he told Constance Rooke for *World Literature Written in English* (Autumn 1990). "It's . . . a form that's very prominent in Native oral literature and probably that had something to do with my choosing it," he said. The protagonist is Will Butler, a photographer who is half white and half Blackfoot. After his white lover is unfaithful to him, he leaves Toronto, Canada, and comes to Medicine River, a small town on the edge of a Blackfoot reservation in Alberta. Through Will's memory flashbacks, the reader learns that Will's mother, Rose Horse Capture, was a Blackfoot who fell in love with a white rodeo star, who left her not long after Will's birth. Both parents are dead by the time Will gets to Medicine River, and he is not allowed to live on the Blackfoot reservation itself, because he is not full Blackfoot. Will undergoes a sort of identity crisis; soon, however, the meddlesome Harlen Bigbear gets Will involved with the tribe when he asks him to play center for the all-Native basketball team that Harlen coaches. Harlen also gives Will a packet of letters written by his father to his mother and tries to spark a romance between Will and Louise Heavyman, the accountant who does the reservation's taxes. King interweaves Will's story with numerous subplots involving still more characters from the reservation, thus painting a vivid picture of reservation life.

Medicine River was well received by critics. Jack Butler, in the *New York Times Book Review* (September 23, 1990), called it "economical, precise, and elegant," and praised its subtlety. "But," he added, "the finest of all Mr. King's many subtleties involves Will—for in his uncertain parentage and lack of drive, he is formed as an image for the state of all the Blackfeet. Native North American but disconnected from their heritage, citizens but not at home in the ambitions of the world, they drift with their fates." In *Canadian Literature* (Winter 1991) M. A. Gillies wrote, "King does not use the novel as a platform from which he can lecture non-natives about native Canadians; he chooses the harder, and more effective, route of drawing the reader into the daily lives of Louise, Harlen, and Will. He succeeds where polemics would surely fail."

King won a PEN/Josephine Miles Award and was runner-up for the Commonwealth Writer's Prize for *Medicine River*. Following this success, King wrote the script for a made-for-television movie, starring Graham Greene and Tom Jackson, based on the novel. In 1990 King also edited a collection of fiction entitled *All My Relations: An Anthology of Contemporary Canadian Native Fiction*. In 1992, the 500-year anniversary of Christopher Columbus's arrival in America, King published a children's book, *A Coyote Columbus Story*, which retells the story of Columbus from a Native

American perspective. In the early 1990s King also became chair of the Native American studies department at the University of Minnesota at St. Paul.

In 1993 King published *Green Grass, Running Water*, a novel that got its name from the treaties between whites and Native Americans in the 18th and 19th centuries: in order to signify perpetuity, these treaties often contained the clause, "As long as the grass is green and the water runs." Much of *Green Grass, Running Water* takes place on a Blackfoot reservation in Alberta where the grass is no longer green—or capable of supporting much agriculture—and a nearby river is about to be dammed. Lionel Red Dog is a 40-year-old TV salesman who lives in the nearby town of Blossom and whose aunt is constantly pestering him to come back to the reservation because she is afraid he is turning into a white man. Lionel's sometime girlfriend is Alberta Frank, a college professor from Calgary, for whose attention Charlie Looking Bear is also competing. Charlie is a somewhat unscrupulous lawyer who represents the construction conglomerate that is building the dam. Another important character is Lionel's Uncle Eli: an ex-college professor who left his job to come back to the reservation, he owns a little cottage that is the only remaining obstacle to the completion of the dam, and he staunchly refuses to move. *Green Grass, Running Water* is full of subplots and secondary characters, so much so that King drew flowcharts to help him keep track of them while he was writing. In addition to the characters already mentioned, there are four old shamans who periodically escape from a mental institution to mend troubles in the world and who, on this particular outing, take on the identities of the Lone Ranger, Ishmael (from the novel *Moby-Dick*), Robinson Crusoe, and Hawkeye (from the novel *The Last of the Mohicans*). They are accompanied by Coyote, the trickster of many Native American myths.

King's busy and ambitious novel drew mixed reviews. "Mr. King's working premise is that the linear version of a story leaves out its most interesting aspects—that truth lies somewhere in the digressionary minutiae," James McManus wrote for the *New York Times Book Review* (July 25, 1993). He concluded, "Mr. King, however, carries this premise several stages too far, both by making it repetitively explicit and by spending similar numbers of words on characters much less intriguing than Lionel or his uncle. His novel thus verges on becoming a reductive parody instead of a telling example of its own central narrative principle." Conversely, in *Newsweek* (April 12, 1993), Malcolm Jones Jr. wrote that "At his best, [King] is as savagely and darkly funny as [Mark] Twain," and called *Green Grass, Running Water* a successful mix of "realism and myth, comedy and tragedy (and any writer who can bring off a talking coyote has to be called successful)." *Green Grass, Running Water* was runner-up for the Governor General's Award in 1993 and won the Canadian Author's Award for fiction.

In 1993 King also published his first collection of short stories, entitled *One Good Story, That One*. Like his novels, the stories use both realistic and fantastic elements—such as blue coyote space aliens, singing totem poles, and the presence of the biblical characters Adam and Eve—to highlight and examine tensions between Native Americans and their successors on the continent. In "Trap Lines" a teenager refuses his father's invitation to go fishing, opting to watch TV instead. In "Magpies" an old Native American woman nearing death insists that her body be wrapped and placed in the boughs of a cottonwood tree after she passes away, according to Native tradition. Her daughter, however, keeps urging her to follow the burial rites of the Catholic Church. In "A Seat in the Garden" King parodies the baseball movie *Field of Dreams*, while in the title story, he sends up the Garden of Eden myth. "Despite a tendency to stereotype non-Natives as uncomprehending and officious," Kenneth Radu wrote in *Books in Canada* (October 1993), "and despite a couple of narratives that are more sketchy than complete, *One Good Story, That One* is an engaging and worthwhile collection." Scott Anderson's praise, in *Quill & Quire* (September 1993), was less qualified. "Told with humor and humility, these tales resonate with the inescapably anguished history of North American Indians," he wrote. "Like the coyote—that sly prankster of Native folklore who lurks close to the heart of King's work—these tales at once trap you in their jaws, tickle with waggish tongue, and howl with ironic wit."

King's next novel, *Truth and Bright Water*, was published in Canada in 1999. The narrator is a 15-year-old boy named Tecumseh whose naive point of view serves as a comic device in the novel. The action commences one night when he and his cousin, Lum, see a woman dancing beside the Shield River. Suddenly, she jumps in and although she apparently does not reemerge, they cannot find her body. Instead, they dredge up a child's skull. Tecumseh and Lum subsequently embark on a quest for the truth, though from early on it is evident to readers that the truth will evade them. *Truth and Bright Water* is a highly allegorical novel, whose action takes place in a white settlement in the U.S. called Truth, and in Bright Water, a Native reservation across the Shield River from Truth, in Canada. The river, with its shimmering surface, symbolizes art as a reflection of reality. Most of the Natives in the novel are artists, including Munroe Swimmer, whose goal is to erase all signs of American colonization in Truth; at one point, he buys the town's missionary church and magically paints it out of existence.

Warren Cariou's reaction to the novel, in the *Canadian Forum* (December 1999), was mixed. He admitted that it is possible to "delight in the depth and cleverness of King's web of symbols, which gives off an almost inexhaustible supply of meanings," but concluded that "The problem here is that *Truth and Bright Water* is so weighed down by the groaning architecture of its symbolism that there is hardly any room for the characters to have an appearance of agency or depth." Irene D'Souza was not bothered by the novel's overarching symbolism. In *Prairie Fire Review of Books* (on-line) she wrote, "There is no doubt that King has a keen understanding of what is wrong with this world: race and economic deprivation come into the fray. His brooding exploration in *Truth and Bright Water* of that infinite quarrel of the what-ifs will continue to haunt the reader long after the book has been finished."

In mid-2001 King published *Coyote Sings to the Moon*, a children's book with illustrations by Johnny Wales, which tells the story of a singer named Coyote who is offended when the Old Woman refuses to allow him to serenade the Moon. In a review for *School Library Journal*, as quoted on *Amazon.com*, Linda M. Kenton remarked: "This story is far too long to be read aloud, and only determined independent readers will get through the stilted dialogue. The illustrations are beautifully rendered in smoky grays and browns that perfectly reflect the nighttime setting. Translucent brush strokes and lines give the images the distinctive look and feel of Japanese paintings. Coyote's sauciness and the moon's haughtiness are elegantly captured. The illustrations, however, cannot overcome the weaknesses of the plot."

Since 1995 King has been teaching Native American literature and creative writing at the University of Guelph, in Ontario, Canada. He hosts a radio show called the "Dead Dog Café Comedy Hour," which is recorded in Edmonton, and continues to do photography. One of his several major projects is a series of portraits of Indians throughout North America. He has three children, two with Helen Hoy and one from his previous marriage.

—P. G. H.

SUGGESTED READING: *Books in Canada* p36+ Oct. 1993; *Canadian Forum* p38+ Dec. 1999; *Canadian Literature* p212+ Winter 1991; *Chicago Tribune* 5 p1+ Apr. 21, 1993, with photo; *Christian Science Monitor* p13 Oct. 13, 1990; (Toronto) *Globe and Mail* C p3 Nov. 13, 1993; *Newsweek* p60 Apr. 12, 1993, with photo; *New York Times Book Review* p29 Sep. 23, 1990, p21 July 25, 1993; *Paragraph* p2+ Summer 1994; *Publishers Weekly* p56+ Mar. 8, 1993; *Quill & Quire* p61 Sep. 1993; *World Literature Today* p201 Winter 1995; *World Literature Written in English* p62+ Autumn 1990

SELECTED BOOKS: novels—*Medicine River*, 1990; *Green Grass, Running Water*, 1993; *Truth and Bright Water*, 1999; *Coyote Sings to the Moon*, 2001; short-story collections—*One Good Story, That One*, 1993; as editor—*Native in Literature*, 1987; *All My Relations: An Anthology of Contemporary Canadian Native Fiction*, 1990

Krasznahorkai, László

Jan. 5, 1954– Novelist, short-story writer

László Krasznahorkai is the author of five novels *Sátántangó* (1985, usually translated as "Devil's Tango"); *Az ellenállás melankóliája* (written in 1989, the book was published in English translation as *The Melancholy of Resistance*, in 2000), *Az urgai fogoly* (1992, "The Prisoner of Urga"); *Théseus-általános* (1993, the title is sometimes translated as "The General Theseus" or "Theseus Universal"); and *Háború és háború* (1999, "War and War"). He has also written a collection of short fiction, *Kegyelmi viszonyok* (1986, "Circumstances of Grace"). He has collaborated with the Hungarian director Béla Tarr on several screenplays adapted from his fiction. Those films—which include *Kárhozat* ("Damnation," 1988); an adaption of *Sátántangó* (1994); and *Werckmeister harmóniák* ("Werckmeister Harmonies," 2000, which was adapted from *Az ellenállás melankóliája*)—although not widely known, have received high praise from critics. "Among the 'second generation' writers of fiction bent on portraying the unspeakable horrors, utter hopelessness, and almost eerie apocalypse of the socialist reality of Eastern Europe," Clara Gyorgyey wrote for *World Literature Today* (Winter 1995), "Krasznahorkai marches in the vanguard."

László Krasznahorkai was born on January 5, 1954 in Gyula, Hungary, the son of Gyorgy Krasznahorkai, a lawyer, and the former Julia Palinkas, a government administrator. He studied at the József Attila University, in Szeged, receiving his law degree in 1977. He earned degrees in literature and philology from Eötvös Loránd University, in Budapest, in 1983. Before writing his first novel, Krasznahorkai moved from town to town across Hungary, taking odd jobs and working as an editor.

Krasznahorkai's first novel, *Sátántangó*, was published in 1985. George Gomori wrote in *World Literature Today* (Summer 1993), that the novel was "structurally tight" and marked "by a certain timelessness." Béla Tarr read *Sátántangó* while it was still an unpublished manuscript and began making plans with Krasznahorkai to turn it into a film. The project took several years to complete, but the final work, with the screenplay co-authored by Tarr and Krasznahorkai, was heralded as a landmark of modern cinema by such esteemed critics as Susan Sontag and Jonathan Rosenbaum. First screened at the 1994 Berlin Film Festival, *Sátántangó* offers a stark portrayal of the disintegration of Communism in Eastern Europe. In the *Chi-*

László Krasznahorkai — Horst Tappe/Courtesy of New Directions

cago Reader (May 10, 1996, on-line), Rosenbaum described the story as "brilliant, diabolical, sarcastic," as it "gradually unravels the dreams, machinations, and betrayals of a failed farm collective over a few rainy days, two of them rendered more than once, from the perspectives of different characters." Despite the high praise, the film's length (seven hours) and glacial pace have prevented its wide distribution.

Prior to *Sátántangó*'s release, Krasznahorkai and Tarr had jointly written the screenplay for *Kárhozat*. The critic Rob Tregenza, writing for the Cinema Parallel Web site, found that their "fruitful collaboration brought about a maturity, and a more profound philosophical and artistic depth to Tarr's work that was lacking in [his] earlier films." The minimalist plot concerns Karrer, a morose and lonely man who spends his days wandering the bleak, rain-swept streets of a Hungarian coal-mining town. In the evenings he frequents the Titanik, a local bar where his former lover is a lounge singer. Karrer is obsessed with her and determined to regain her affection.

Az ellenállás melankóliája, Krasznahorkai's second novel, is his only book to be translated into English thus far. Originally written in 1989, it was published as *The Melancholy of Resistance*, in 2000, in a translation by George Szirtes. The story takes place in a small town in the Hungarian countryside, where the lives of several inhabitants are disrupted by the arrival of a traveling circus show which brings with it a host of mysterious, unsavory characters. The show boasts that its main attraction is the carcass of the "World's Largest Giant Whale," but rumors circulate that something more sinister is at work, and a deformed character known as the Prince seems to be at the center of it. As menace grips the town, a young dreamer named Valuska is haplessly drawn in by the carnival's sensationalism, while his older friend, the musicologist Mr. Eszter, succumbs to a bitter nihilism. It falls upon Mr. Eszter's obstreperous, power-hungry wife, recently made the president of the women's committee, to free the town from the intruders.

"It's all too rare . . . we have the opportunity to encounter a voice as knowing, sympathetic, dark and beguiling as Krasznahorkai's," Chris Lehmann wrote for the *Washington Post Book World* (December 24, 2000), as quoted on Amazon.com. Krasznahorkai writes in a lugubrious style, with very long sentences and without paragraphs, creating what George Szirtes describes in his introduction as a "slow lava flow" of narrative and a "vast black river of type." "The writing (and translation) is so accomplished, though, that it does not suck you under," Carrie O'Grady wrote for the *Guardian* (August 28, 1999). "You're lifted along in lunar leaps and bounds." Maya Mirsky, in a review for the on-line journal *Critique*, noted that the "difficult, elastic style . . . takes some effort. Nevertheless, this unheroic saga of entropy makes for a strangely enthralling book." "For narrative sophistication and acute discernment of contemporary social unrest, Krasznahorkai's artistry merits serious notice," Michael Pinker wrote in the *Review of Contemporary Fiction* (Spring 2001). "Unraveling his long, rhapsodic sentences, which suggest a language of bad dreams, proves captivating entertainment. May further translations grant him the wider notice he deserves among English-speaking readers." It reportedly took Krasznahorkai six years to write the book and Szirtes four years to complete his English translation. Krasznahorkai collaborated with Tarr on a film adaptation of the novel, released internationally as *Werckmeister Harmonies* in 2000.

In *Az urgai fogoly*, Krasznahorkai's third novel, the narrator describes a long and gloomy train ride that takes him from Urga (the former name of Ulan Bator), the capital of Mongolia, through China. During the trip, the protagonist attends a performance of a Chinese opera, where a young actress's singing leaves him enchanted. "Although ingenious and modern in its structural solutions, [the novel] captures us with its sinuous, delicately balanced style and with the vulnerable subjectivity of the story itself," George Gomori wrote. "Whether fictitious or not, it feels real and authentic."

Théseus-általános, Krasznahorkai's 1993 novel, contains three lectures—as the book's subtitle, which translates to "Secret Academic Lectures" implies. The lectures are delivered by an anonymous male speaker, with no indication of the purpose of the lectures or the audience being addressed. The first lecture begins with an obscure academic discussion of sorrow, but concludes with a sobering recollection of the speaker's childhood in a provincial town, where he felt "indescribably deep sorrow at the sight of a giant whale carcass dragged all over the land," as quoted by Clara Gyorgyey. By the commencement of the second lecture, something ominous has taken place "outside." As his talk on rebellion progresses, the speaker subtly conveys that the lecture hall is now sealed and that he has been made a prisoner. It soon becomes clear that he is being held in the building by paramilitary police, confined to a cell, and that outside a revolution is in the making. During the third lecture, which was intended to be a discussion on property, the speaker delivers an elegy of sorts, lamenting the current meaninglessness of the term: as translated by Gyorgyey, one passage reads, "There was a world once in which it was possible to define property, and this could be defined by pointing out that the meaning of this property exists only and alone given that peace prevails in human and natural relations." Gyorgyey commented, "Krasznahorkai juxtaposes order (academia) and chaos (society at large), hope and hopelessness, with pathological precision." Although she opined "the often grotesquely abstract, sometimes mockingly 'naturalistic' text is a challenging read," and that "the author's new experiment with double endings frequently invalidates any effect already achieved," Gyorgyey found that "the long, often convoluted sentences and overtly methodical details, set amid lyric descriptions or humourous asides, are bold innovations in Hungarian prose."

The book won a 1994 award as best book of the year in Germany, where Krasznahorkai is very popular.

Two of Krasznahorkai's short stories were included in *Thy Kingdom Come* (1998), an anthology of short stories by Hungarian authors translated into English. Clara Gyorgyey, writing for *World Literature Today* (Spring 1999), found fault with the collection on the whole, but wrote that Krasznahorkai's contributions were works of "social criticism and political satire, delivered with a savage grin and spontaneous mockery."

Krasznahorkai lives in the hills of Szentlászló, Hungary. After a previous marriage to Aniko Pelyhe, which ended in divorce, in 1997 he wed Dora Kopcsani. He has three children—Kata, Agnes, and Panni. An English translation of his newest novel, *Háború és háború* (1999, War and War) is scheduled for publication by New Directions in 2003.

—A. I. C.

SUGGESTED READING: *Chicago Reader* (online) May 10, 1996; Cinema Parallel Web site; *Guardian* p11 Aug. 28, 1999; *Review of Contemporary Fiction* p188 Spring 2001; *World Literature Today* p643 Summer 1993, p192 Winter 1995

SELECTED BOOKS IN ENGLISH TRANSLATION: *The Melancholy of Resistance*, 2000

Kurzweil, Allen

1961(?)– Novelist

Allen Kurzweil, who in 1996 was named one of the best young American writers by *Granta* magazine, has combined his love of history, mechanics, and art to produce two highly imaginative novels of personal exploration and adventure. His first novel, *A Case of Curiosities* (1992), was the result of five years of research into the lives of 18th-century French clockmakers and inventors. His second novel, *The Grand Complication* (2001), explores the life of a New York librarian who aids an eccentric collector in finding a long-lost object.

Allen Kurzweil was born in about 1961 to Viennese Jews who had escaped to Italy during World War II. His father was a mechanical engineer and a designer of machine tools, and his mother was a professor of sociology. His early years were spent living in both the United States and Europe. Kurzweil studied history at Yale University, in New Haven, Connecticut, and initially planned on following his mother into academia. Though interested in history he was bored by the rote recitation of historical events, the endless procession of "famous men doing famous or infamous things," as he told John Blades in an interview for the *Chicago Tribune* (February 11, 1993). He won a Fulbright fellowship and used it to study in Italy, where he began writing for various Italian newspapers. He ultimately accepted freelance jobs all over the world.

Courtesy of Hyperion

While researching an article for the *Herald-Tribune*, in Australia, in 1985, Kurzweil met his future wife, Françise Dussart, a French anthropologist who was there studying Aboriginal sign language. Over dinner he told her about the frustrations of journalism, and she urged him to try his hand at a novel instead. The pair married and moved to Paris, and Kurzweil began to work on his first novel, the seeds of which had germinated after his discovery of a partitioned box filled with ordinary objects from a man's life. "I though that was an interesting conceit," he told Blades. "We all narrate our lives in the objects we gather around us."

Kurzweil spent the next five years researching and writing his novel. He made numerous forays to the French national library, traveled to Geneva to visit watch workshops, and went to the Isle of Man to interview the biographer of a well-known clockmaker. His home filled with the results of "all the unnecessary explorations," as he told Blades. "I had two binders of photocopies on the history of playing cards that have almost no relevance to the story. But I wanted to steep myself in the culture and understand the period." At one point Kurzweil, who has referred to himself as a "collector of facts," had 24,000 footnotes compiled for the book.

Four publishers vied for Kurzweil's work; *A Case of Curiosities* was ultimately published by Harcourt Brace Jovanovich, in 1992. The novel begins in an auction house in Paris in 1983, where the narrator has just bought a strange box filled with such ordinary objects as a button, a shell, and some dried plant material. An Italian art historian approaches the narrator, offering to pay him a great sum of money for the box, but is rebuffed. Despite his disappointment, the art historian explains to the narrator that the box is a "memento hominem," filled with objects that symbolize one man's life. After six years of research, the narrator discovers that the box belonged to Claude Page, an 18th-century French inventor. Possessed of an artistic nature and mechanical ability, Page as a young child is made the apprentice to the Count of Tournay, who—among other pursuits—fashions watches painted with pornographic scenes for decadent noblemen. As the Count's student, Page learns the intricacies of watchmaking. He then journeys to Paris where he attaches himself to a bookseller who specializes in obscene material. Page takes a mistress and becomes embroiled in the low life of the city. He remains obsessed, however, with becoming a great inventor and a true artist. He finds fame as the creator of a mechanical man, named the Talking Turk, who can be made to proclaim "*vive le roi*," (long live the king)—a particularly dangerous thing to say in a Paris about to burst into revolution.

The book received generally favorable reviews. Joseph Coates wrote for the *Chicago Tribune* (January 12, 1992), "Kurzweil's novel is anything but a cold clockwork confection. More like a joint effort by Henry Fielding and John Barth, it is clever, indeed, but also riotous, melodramatic and erotic, full of lore and lewdness and crackling with ideas and exhilarated imagination." (Many reviewers of *A Case of Curiosities* drew comparisons to the works of Fielding, Barth, and Umberto Eco, causing Kurzweil to quip to John Blades, "It's forced me to rush out and buy the books of writers who supposedly influenced me.") In a more mixed review, Dan Cryer for *New York Newsday* (January 27, 1992) noted: "For all his deft storytelling and adherence to historical authenticity, the author reveals his own apprenticeship in one significant aspect. Claude Page and his compatriots are certainly believable characters, but it's harder to find them involving. Since Kurzweil is so bent on avoiding sentimentality, he keeps his characters at an emotional distance, and so do we. On an intellectual level, however, *A Case of Curiosities* has no trouble holding our attention." The book was a finalist in the 1992 *Irish Times*–Aer Lingus International Fiction Prize.

In 2001 Kurzweil published his second novel, *The Grand Complication*, a sequel of sorts to *A Case of Curiosities*. The story begins with an overview of the life of a modern-day New York City librarian named Alexander Short. Short has sought to bring order to his disorderly life (his parents have died, he is impotent, and his neighborhood is filled with crime and drugs) by throwing himself into the rules and regulations of the Dewey Decimal System. He nurses a fascination with the secret compartments sometimes built into antique furniture—a fascination that is compounded by his encounter with Henry James Jesson III, a collector whom Kurzweil's readers will recognize as the unnamed narrator of his first novel. After submitting a call slip for a book titled *Secret Compartments in 18th-Century Furniture*, Jesson meets Short and the pair embark on a mission to find a missing object from the memento hominem that is the centerpiece of Jesson's collection.

The Grand Complication received varied reviews. Michael Dirda, writing for the *Washington Post Book World* (August 5, 2001), lamented: "Instead of a firecracker novel, Kurzweil . . . has published a real dud, a major disappointment. . . . *The Grand Complication* isn't so much complicated or grand as very, very slow, interminably, relentlessly slow: Nothing happens for the longest time, and when something finally does it's inconsequential." D. T. Max in the *New York Times Book Review* (August 19, 2001), however, praised the book, calling it "engaging" and noting that it "should be approached with a mood of casual curiosity. Puns, obscure words, a quick course in library science, a world of boxes in other boxes whiz by. Try to go with the book and not master it." Ron Charles, a reviewer for the *Christian Science Monitor* (August 9, 2001, on-line), concurred and called the book "a rollicking, witty suspense tale."

Kurzweil's new book *Leon and the Spitting Image* is scheduled to be published in October 2003. He currently lives in Connecticut with his wife and their son.

—C. M.

SUGGESTED READING: *Christian Science Monitor* (on-line) Aug. 9, 2001; *Chicago Tribune* XIV p7 Jan. 12, 1992; D p11 Feb. 11, 1993; *New*

York Newsday p44 Jan. 27, 1992; *New York Times* C p15 Oct. 6, 1992, E p5 Apr. 5, 1999; *New York Times Book Review* p1 Jan. 26, 1992, p7 Aug. 19, 2001; (London) *Observer* p62 Mar. 22, 1992; *People* p27 May 4, 1992; *Washington Post* T p12 June 17, 2001; *Washington Post Book World* p9 Jan. 12, 1992, p15 Aug. 5, 2001

SELECTED BOOKS: *A Case of Curiosities*, 1992; *The Grand Complication*, 2001

Carol Shadford/Courtesy of Farrar, Straus and Giroux

LaFarge, Paul

1970– Novelist; short-story writer; journalist

Paul LaFarge has emerged as a promising young writer in the last few years. His first novel, *The Artist of the Missing* (1999), about a man who paints portraits of missing persons, won the California Book Award, and his second, *Haussmann, or the Distinction* (2001), which is derived from the life of Georges-Eugène Haussmann, the 19th-century planner who built modern Paris, received some favorable critical attention. Writing allows LaFarge to gain a greater comprehension of his experiences and surroundings. "By telling stories, and by listening to stories," he observed in an article for the Commonwealth Book Club Web site, "we take all the materials (perceptions, feelings, memories, etc.) out of which we ordinarily make a world, and we put them together in a new way, and in doing so we learn something about what kind of materials we're working with, and what kind of world we inhabit."

Paul LaFarge was born in New York City in 1970. He studied comparative literature at Yale University, in New Haven, Connecticut, and at the University of Paris. LaFarge graduated summa cum laude from Yale in 1992. After briefly teaching French in a New York City high school, he enrolled at Stanford University, in California, to pursue a doctorate in comparative literature. While there he became interested in "automatic writing," a technique first practiced by mediums and psychics and later adopted by the Surrealists, in which departed spirits supposedly guided their pens.

LaFarge left Stanford after one year; in 1994 he settled in San Francisco, California, where he worked at a variety of jobs, including stints as a neurologist's assistant, legal secretary, curriculum director for a media activism center, and teacher of Web site design.

In 1998 LaFarge was named writer-in-residence at the Camargo Foundation, which sponsors projects in the humanities and social sciences related to French culture, in Cassis, France. The next year he earned the Dorothy and Granville Hicks Residency at Yaddo, a writers' retreat in Saratoga Springs, New York, as well as a residency at the MacDowell Colony, which allows writers to pursue their projects in a comfortable environment without distractions, in Petersborough, New Hampshire.

For his first attempt at writing a novel, LaFarge explored life in Paris during the student revolts of May 1968. However, in his article for the Commonwealth Club Web site, he explained that he became "so tangled in the plot of that book that I had to stop for a while and write something I had a hope of finishing." He explained the strategy that resulted in *The Artist of the Missing* in an article for the *Village Voice* (April 17, 2001): "I decided to write something easy, unplanned, and above all fast, something I could finish in, say, two weeks. I took a nap, woke up, and started typing. And strangely, 15 days later I had the first draft of a novel, which has since been published (albeit after two years of more or less painful revision)." *The Artist of the Missing* focuses on two lifelong friends, Frank and James, who leave their home on a farm for life in a big unnamed city, so that Frank can look for his parents, who disappeared mysteriously when he was five years old. In the city Frank falls in love with Prudence, a police photographer. A short time later Prudence also vanishes without a trace, and as Frank searches for her, he discovers that many other people in the city have also disappeared. Frank uses his drawing skills to sketch portraits of the missing based on the descriptions he receives from their acquaintances. He becomes widely known as "the artist of the missing," and is eventually jailed for his art.

The Artist of the Missing received mixed reviews. Writing for the *Los Angeles Times* (August 20, 1999), Michael Frank asserted that "LaFarge is probably at his best when he conveys the magically layered quality of the city's life and landscape: the cellars in iron buildings that fill each night with smoke and music; the railroad station where 'time itself seems to have been held up by an unexpected delay somewhere farther down the line.'" The reviewer, however, found fault with much of the novel. "Allegories are not easy to sustain over 241 pages, and at about midpoint LaFarge's novel begins to falter," Frank observed. "The elements in the story that at first beguiled—Frank's sad origins, his picaro-like adventures in this queer urban landscape, his tender romance with the elusive Prudence . . . begin to feel arbitrary, too episodic, and insufficiently rooted in emotional and psychological reality. It is hard, in the end, for a reader to stay fully with a character whose interior life remains so spare and unvaried." In the Boston Globe (July 25, 1999), Jodi Daynard wrote, "From the onset, LaFarge creates a strange, original landscape as full of mystery and wonder as it is anarchy and nascent danger." The reviewer criticized the novel, however, for sinking into "a political allegory of the artist in totalitarian society—a dusty trail already well traveled by Franz Kafka and others." Despite the fact that it did not receive universal acclaim from critics, in 1999 The Artist of the Missing won the California Book Award, a prize established in 1931 to acknowledge literary excellence among that state's writers.

In his second novel, Haussmann, or the Distinction (2001), LaFarge offers a fictionalized account of Georges-Eugène Haussmann (1809–91), the civic official who modernized Paris in the 19th century. Appointed by Emperor Napoleon III in 1853, Haussmann implemented plans that resulted in the installation of gas lighting in Paris and the construction of modern streets, more than 100,000 apartment buildings, and 320 miles of sewer lines. He also designed the Arc de Triomphe, one of the city's best-known landmarks, and the Bois de Boulogne, a public park with two artificial lakes and 320,000 trees. When work was finally completed, in 1870, very little of the old feudal city was left standing. LaFarge's novel purports to be an English translation of an obscure French biography that was written about Haussmann in 1922, which was recently discovered in the Bibliothèque Nationale, France's equivalent of the Library of Congress. To give his "translation" additional authenticity, LaFarge includes a "Notes to the English Edition" section.

The novel's protagonist is an abandoned girl named Madeleine, who is thrown into the river by her mother and rescued by a passing lamplighter who takes her to a convent to be raised. She is eventually adopted by de Fonce, who earns a living tearing down portions of the city and selling its treasures to collectors; he soon becomes her lover as well. Haussmann, who is a frequent guest at de Fonce's home, also falls in love with Madeleine and begins a secret affair with her. The result is a complicated love triangle that brings serious consequences, especially when Madeleine becomes pregnant. In the New York Times Book Review (October 21, 2001), Edmund White recommended Haussmann, or the Distinction for its imaginative approach and "compelling storytelling," but took issue with the author in several areas. "Most of the comparisons in the book (and there are three a page) sound pretty kooky," White wrote, using as an example the passage: "Like Napoleon in Russia, Madeleine grew breasts; unlike the emperor she grew taller as well." White also questioned the novel's treatment of the historical figure on which it's based: "The [great] enigma is why Haussmann, who is perhaps the most interesting French power broker of the 19th century after Napoleon Bonaparte, should have become the subject of a whimsical novel that fails to explore his character or deal with his achievement." In a review for Publishers Weekly (August 27, 2001), Jeff Zaleski praised the novel more enthusiastically. "LaFarge . . . neatly integrates geographical and cultural references into the tale, making this as much an enlightening history of Paris as it is a tragic, affecting love story," Zaleski wrote. "An astonishing amount of research, a believable tone, and a captivating story all come together to make this work a stunning success."

Paul LaFarge has written short fiction that has appeared in Story and McSweeney's, among other periodicals. His nonfiction pieces have been published in the Village Voice and the on-line magazine Salon. He serves as the director of the Paraffin Arts Project, a community arts group in San Francisco, where he currently resides. Paraffin publishes 6,500 Magazine, a literary journal, and hosts a monthly reading series featuring new and established writers. The group also sponsors the Paraffin Press, which produces small print runs of handmade books of poetry, fiction, and children's literature, using archival material. LaFarge's Paraffin Press fiction includes The Cell Game (1996), Demons (1997), The Sleepwriter (1998), and The Observers (1998), as well as the children's books The Bug (1996), The Yerblew (1997), The Pool Shark (1998), and Ratliffe (1999). LaFarge's next novel, which is tentatively titled "Luminous Airplanes," will be about the history of aviation, meteorology, and stand-up comedians, among other topics.

—D. C.

SUGGESTED READING: Boston Globe C p1 July 25, 1999; Commonwealth Book Club Web site; Los Angeles Times p4 Aug. 20, 1999; New York Times Book Review p20+ Oct. 21, 2001; Paraffin Arts Project Web site; Publishers Weekly p51 Aug. 27, 2001

SELECTED BOOKS: The Artist of the Missing, 1999; Haussmann, or the Distinction, 2001

Marion Ettlinger/Courtesy of Houghton Mifflin

Lahiri, Jhumpa

1967– Short-story writer

In 2000 Jhumpa Lahiri became both the youngest person and the first of Asian descent to win the Pulitzer Prize in fiction, which was awarded to her for her short-story collection, *Interpreter of Maladies* (1999). Though Lahiri, who is Indian American, usually features characters of Indian descent, her narrators represent both genders (four of the nine stories in *Interpreter of Maladies* are told from the male point of view), all ages, and several countries of residence. Lahiri's ability to convincingly capture these diverse voices is one of the reasons for her popularity with critics, but she does not write from these varying points of view to please reviewers. "I believe what first drove me to write fiction was to escape the pitfalls of being viewed as one thing or the other," she wrote in an essay for *Feed* (July 24, 2000, on-line). "As an author, I could embody any individual my imagination enabled me to, of any origin. This sense of freedom is one of the greatest thrills of writing fiction, and for a person like me, who has never been confident of what to call herself or of where to say she is from, it is a solace." As noted on the Houghton Mifflin Web site, the acclaimed author Amy Tan once said, "Lahiri is one of the finest short-story writers I've read." In addition to the Pulitzer, Lahiri has won the Hemingway/PEN award and the O. Henry Award. She was named among the 20 best writers under the age of 40 by the *New Yorker*, was included among 19 other prominent writers in that magazine's 1999 summer fiction issue, and has had short stories anthologized in the *Best American Short Stories* series.

Jhumpa Lahiri was born in 1967 in London, England, and grew up in South Kingston, Rhode Island. Her father worked as a librarian, and her mother, who earned an advanced degree in Bengali literature, was a teacher; both parents are originally from Calcutta, in the East Bengal province of India. Despite the fact that Lahiri grew up in the U.S., her mother always told her to identify herself as Indian, and consequently Lahiri was somewhat confused about her identity. "If I say I am from Rhode Island," Lahiri explained to Sumit Mitra and Arthur J. Pais for *India Today* (April 24, 2000), "nobody is satisfied. They want to know more, based on things such as my name and my appearance. If I say I am from India, a place where I was not born and never lived, this is also inaccurate." Growing up Lahiri often traveled with her sister and parents to Calcutta (where some of her stories are set). Rather than affirm her identity, the visits exposed her differences from the people of her parents' homeland. "People knew we weren't from India," she recalled to Daphne Uviller for *New York Newsday* (July 25, 1999). "My sister and I speak Bengali with an accent, and there's something about the way we carry ourselves that makes us easy to spot as foreigners. It was their curiosity with the smallest of details that made me realize I was very different from my Indian relatives." As she told Uviller, "being an outsider is the fundamental way I view myself."

Like her literary parents, Lahiri took an interest in reading, though rather than her mother's Bengali literature, she liked books "with tension between the real world and other worlds," as she told Uviller. The fantasy-oriented works of Lewis Carroll and C. S. Lewis appealed to her because she "always had access to another world." Having cultivated a love of reading, it seemed natural for her to write. "When I learned to read, I felt the need to copy," she told Vibhuti Patel for *Newsweek International* (September 20, 1999), "I started writing ten-page 'novels,' during recess, with my friends. Sitting around the sandbox, we'd say things out loud. At playtime, we'd be princesses in a castle in France. Writing allowed me to observe and make sense of things without having to participate. I didn't belong. I looked different and felt like an outsider."

Lahiri eventually discovered the works of Virginia Woolf, Katherine Mansfield, James Joyce, Vladimir Nabokov, and Franz Kafka, among others. The first stories she wrote as an adult were composed in India during visits to her extended family. "I had come to regard India as a place both in which and about which to write fiction," she wrote in *Feed*. "During visits there I was idle, unmoored, intensely curious about what I saw: an alternate life, which, had my parents chosen not to live their lives abroad, would have been mine." While critics in India have taken pride in Lahiri, some have complained that her portrayals of the country and its people lack authenticity and that, as she interpreted their qualms in *Feed*, she lacks "the cultural ambidexterity to write about Indian life in an authentic way." She continued, "I have been accused of setting stories in India as a device in order to woo Western audiences. . . . Even after I won the Pulitzer, *India Today*, a national news magazine, wrote that my setting stories in Calcutta was 'an unwise decision.'"

Lahiri earned a B.A. from Barnard College, in New York City, in 1989. Her applications to several English graduate programs were rejected, and she took a job at a nonprofit organization in Cambridge, Massachusetts. There she took advantage of her computer to work on stories before and after work. Having amassed a body of work, she applied and was accepted to the graduate creative-writing program at Boston University, in Massachusetts, earning her M.A. in 1993. Still unsure of a career path, she continued on at Boston University, earning another master's degree, in comparative studies in literature and the arts, in 1995, and a Ph.D. in Renaissance studies, in 1997. While in school she held an assortment of jobs, including stints as a waitress, a clothing-store clerk, and, in 1997, an intern for *Boston Magazine*.

Lahiri's writing career dramatically accelerated after she was accepted into the Fine Arts Work Center, in Provincetown, Massachusetts, where she was given a $550 monthly stipend, free lodging, and plenty of time to write. Within seven months her agent succeeded in getting one of Lahiri's stories published in the *New Yorker* (where she has since had two other stories published) and signing a book deal with Houghton Mifflin. *Interpreter of Maladies* was published in 1999. Most of the nine stories in the collection portray people of Indian heritage, living either in America or India. In "When Mr. Pirzada Came to Dine" a 10-year-old girl named Lilia begins to understand the hardship caused by political upheaval when a man, who was separated from his family during the Pakistani civil war of 1971, comes to her parents' house. In *Feed* Lahiri remembered the story as a "turning point" for her. "In this story," she wrote, "I felt I was, for the first time, conveying that intimate Bengali of my upbringing, both spoken and otherwise, into English. . . . What concerned me . . . was the precise explanation of certain gestures and details—the manner in which the family eats, for example, and their preoccupation, while living in a small New England town, with the Pakistani civil war. My focus in this story wasn't the unilateral translation of a place or a language. Instead it was a simultaneous translation in both directions, of characters who literally dwell in two separate worlds." In "Third and Final Continent," which was included in *Best American Short Stories 2000*, a 36-year-old Indian man tells the story of his travels from India to England, and finally, to the U.S., where he rents an apartment from a very old woman. When his wife, whom he barely knows, comes to the U.S., he finds that seeing her through his landlady's eyes helps him warm up to her. (The idea for the story came from Lahiri's father, who, as he was fond of recalling to Lahiri, had once rented an apartment from a 103-year-old woman in Cambridge.) In "A Temporary Matter" a married couple whose relationship has suffered after the stillbirth of their son is forced into intimacy during a series of electrical shutdowns. This intimacy, however, reveals how irreparably deteriorated their relationship has become. In the title story, which was included in the *Best American Short Stories 1999*, an Indian tour guide who is showing an American-born Indian couple through his country realizes that their marriage seems no better than his own, even though his was an arranged marriage.

When asked by Uviller why she seems to have a grim view of marriage, Lahiri answered, "Partly, it's just a way of pitting two characters against each other to get a story going. But part of it is that I started writing these stories at a time when a lot of my friends were getting married. I was intensely curious about marriage, and I started to imagine what could go wrong. I do dwell, often morbidly, on worst-case scenarios." Such predilections were not apparent in *Interpreter of Maladies*, at least in the opinion of Deirdre Donahue, who wrote in *USA Today* (August 12, 1999), "Often, authors display a pronounced tendency to either gloom or cheer. Thus, all their short stories end with a certain repetitive thump. Lahiri deftly plays all the cards in her deck, happy and sad." Reviews of *Interpreter of Maladies* were overwhelmingly positive. Michiko Kakutani, in the *New York Times* (August 6, 1999, on-line), wrote, "Ms. Lahiri chronicles her characters' lives with both objectivity and compassion while charting the emotional temperature of their lives with tactile precision. She is a writer of uncommon elegance and poise, and with *Interpreter of Maladies* she has made a precocious debut." In the *San Francisco Chronicle* (June 24, 1999) David Kipen praised Lahiri's "subtle characterization" and "meaningful but never portentous detail." "In places," Kipen continued, "she suggests one of those artists who can capture a likeness with two or three pencil strokes. But Lahiri keeps sketching until the face begins to breathe and change before our eyes."

Upon first hearing that she had won the Pulitzer Prize in fiction, Lahiri was stunned. (It is rare enough for a book of short stories, rather than a novel, to win the prize, but for a debut work to win is even more extraordinary.) "I just try to sort of keep it in its place," she told Vanessa E. Jones for the *Boston Globe* (November 9, 2000), "which is that it's an honor for this book that I've written, but . . . I'm moving on to other things. You know, prizes are wonderful, but they don't help you write the next book or your next story." In 2001 Lahiri married Alberto Vourvoulias, an editor for *Time*'s Latin American edition, in a traditional Bengali ceremony held in Calcutta. She lives in New York City and is working on a novel, a new form for her. "I've had to exercise new muscles in a way and push myself in ways that are a bit unfamiliar," she told Jones. "But I like sort of working in a territory where I don't feel completely at home and just seeing what comes of it."

Lahiri's next book, *The Namesake*, is scheduled to be be published in the fall of 2003.

—P. G. H.

SUGGESTED READING: *Boston Globe* E p1 Nov. 9, 2000; *Feed* (on-line) July 24, 2000; *India Today* p89 Apr. 24, 2000; *New York Newsday* B p11 July 25, 1999; *Newsweek International* (on-line) Sep. 20, 1999; *New York Times* (on-line) Aug. 6, 1999; *San Francisco Chronicle* E p1 June 24, 1999; *USA Today* D p7 Aug. 12, 1999; *Washington Post* C p8 Oct. 7, 1999

SELECTED BOOKS: *Interpreter of Maladies*, 1999; *The Namesake*, 2003

Scott Braley/Courtesy of Riverhead Books/Putnam Publishing

Lamott, Anne

Apr. 10, 1954– Novelist; nonfiction writer; memoirist

Though Anne Lamott had published four novels, including *Hard Laughter* (1980), *Rosie* (1983), *Joe Jones* (1985), and *All New People* (1989), it was not until she published her first nonfiction book that she received widespread critical and popular acclaim. Alternately humorous and poignant, *Operating Instructions: A Journal of My Son's First Year* (1993), is an insider's view of raising a child as a single parent. She followed this book with another nonfiction work, *Bird By Bird: Some Instructions on Writing and Life* (1994), which presented illuminating and funny stories about the creative process. In 1997 she returned to fiction with the long-awaited sequel to *Rosie—Crooked Little Heart*. She has also published a collection of essays on her conversion to Christianity entitled *Traveling Mercies: Some Thoughts on Faith* (1999); her most recent novel is *Blue Shoe* (2002).

Anne Lamott was born in San Francisco, California, on April 10, 1954, the daughter of Kenneth Lamott, a writer, and Dorothy Lamott, an attorney. Much of her childhood has been documented in her essays, in which she has noted that as a young girl she was very tense and suffered from low self-esteem, due in part to her parents' often difficult marriage. As a result of her insecurities, she became something of an overachiever, excelling in school and becoming a high-school tennis star who played on the California circuit. From her father she learned about the discipline and dedication necessary to being a writer, and after two years at Goucher College (1971 to 1973), she dropped out to become one herself. In order to support herself, she gave tennis lessons, cleaned houses, worked in a restaurant, and slowly began doing freelance work for magazines such as *Mademoiselle*. From 1974 to 1975 she was a staff writer at *Women Sports*, a magazine whose offices were located in San Mateo, California.

Though Lamott was making progress in her quest to become a writer, her personal life was more problematic. In college she had begun experimenting with drugs and alcohol, to which she quickly became addicted. She was bulimic. She was also having difficulty maintaining relationships with men, often because the ones with whom she chose to involve herself were married. At the same time, however, she was beginning to become aware of her own nascent spirituality. Though her parents objected to organized religion, she began to believe that God had been a presence in her life since early childhood. She recalled praying at her bedside as a little girl; in college, according to her book *Traveling Mercies*, she noted how "a puzzling thing inside me . . . had begun to tug on my sleeve from time to time, trying to get my attention." In interviews she has said that, at the time, she had not completely accepted her faith—and often tried to submerse the whole idea in a haze of drugs and alcohol—but she believes that it helped her get through the difficult next phase of her life.

In the late 1970s Lamott's father was diagnosed with terminal brain cancer. She began writing short pieces about the effects of the disease as well as the reactions of her family, and these became chapters of her first novel, *Hard Laughter*. She had been sending some of her writing to her father's literary agents in New York without success, but the novel quickly grabbed their attention. Lamott attempted to complete the book before her father died; he was able to read the entire rough draft except for the first and last chapters. She has since called the book "a present to someone I loved who was going to die," as quoted by Ruth Reichl in an interview with Lamott for the *New York Times* (December 1, 1994, on-line).

Hard Laughter opens with a northern California family discovering that their father has just been diagnosed with a terminal brain tumor. The family consists of a father and mother, and three grown children, all of whom use a great deal of humor to cope with the impending tragedy. Throughout the course of the novel they learn about their individual strengths and weaknesses while growing stronger as a family. The novelist Anne Tyler, writing for the *New York Times Book Review* (October 12, 1980), noted that "it's a moving and strangely joyful book, a kind of celebration, and it's written with an assurance far beyond the reach of most first novelists."

Lamott's next book, *Rosie*, focuses on the relationship between a mother and daughter. Rosie, the daughter, is four years old when her father is killed in a freak auto accident, leaving her mother, Elizabeth, to raise her alone. As the years go by Elizabeth, on the surface an educated and attractive perfectionist, turns more and more to alcohol, creating the need for Rosie to care for her mother. The pair are in many ways night and day: Rosie is an assertive and precocious troublemaker while Elizabeth, supported by a trust fund, barely has enough strength to look at the job advertisements or invest herself in a new relationship with a man. Diane Cole, writing for the *New York Times* (January 29, 1984, on-line), gave the book a decidedly mixed review: "In presenting Rosie's world from the quirky point of view of a preteen, [Lamott] succeeds where many other writers have failed. After a fine beginning, however, the novel beings to suffer from its lackluster plot, and one wonders whether it would not have made a more satisfying—and more powerful—novella or short story."

While writing her next novel, *Joe Jones*, Lamott's addictions to drugs and alcohol caused her to hit bottom. The book that resulted from this period is about a San Francisco Bay area restaurant named Jessie's Café that specializes in neo-hippie food. The main action centers around the intersecting lives of an eclectic group of characters at the restaurant: Jessie, the owner; her gay, pastry-chef grandson; Louise, the head cook; and Joe, the bartender of the title, with whom Louise is involved in a relationship. The book received scathing reviews, most of which complained about its lack of structure. In the *Chicago Tribune* (January 5, 1986), James Kaufmann wrote: "Lamott has a gift for the unusual image and simile, though sometimes she stretches too far, and the irrepressibly episodic structure of *Joe Jones* showcases that aspect of her talent all the more. The problem is that all the fine and funky metaphors accumulate into not much— the novel seems to lack purpose, though not drive, and it pushes its contemporaneity too hard." "When *Joe Jones* came out I really got trashed, I got 27 bad reviews," Lamott recalled in her interview with Ruth Reichl. "It was kind of exhilarating in its way. I was still drinking and I woke up every morning feeling so sick, I literally felt I was pinned to the bed by centrifugal force. I wouldn't have very many memories of what had happened the night before. I'd have to call around, and I could tell by people's reactions whether I'd pulled it off or not. I was really humiliating myself. It was bad."

Lamott quit drinking and taking drugs in 1986 with the help of an Episcopal priest who became a good friend. She soon found herself visiting a small church, St. Andrew Presbyterian in Marin City, California, initially because she liked standing in the doorway and listening to the songs. After a while she began to listen to the sermons as well and considered being baptized. After a year of being sober, she told the minister at the church that she felt she "wasn't good enough yet." His response, according to Patrick Henry in *Theology Today* (January 2000), was, "You're putting the cart before the horse. So—honey? Come on down."

Lamott's sobriety and her growing Christian faith enabled her to resume writing after having taken an extended break. The result was her fourth novel, *All New People*, which was published in 1989. In it, the main character, Nanny, has returned to the town where she grew up, leaving a failed marriage behind her. Throughout the book Nanny serves as the narrator, detailing the lives of her family over the course of two decades: her father, a writer, never makes enough money from his work; her mother is very religious but suffers from depression; her brother gets deeply involved in the drug scene in San Francisco in the late 1960s; her uncle has fathered a child during a separation from his wife. On the whole, the book received favorable reviews, such as one by Richard Bausch, writing for the *New York Times Book Review* (October 22, 1989): "*All New People* is about life being more powerful than death; its true subject, its deepest impulse, is love. A comedy in the best classical sense of the word, it faces the dark and still manages to give forth the sound of laughter." Other critics, including Dan Cryer in *New York Newsday* (November 20, 1989), weren't as kind: "[This novel] sets up a wealth of sympathy for some of its characters then fails to probe them. In the end, the reader remains extremely frustrated, tantalized but unsatisfied."

Around the time *All New People* was published, Lamott became pregnant. The baby's father wanted her to have an abortion, and when she decided that she wanted to give birth, he left. Lamott documented her pregnancy and her life as a single parent in her next book, *Operating Instructions: A Journal of My Son's First Year*, a nonfiction work published in 1993. She writes of her struggles following the baby's conception, from telling the father about her pregnancy, to learning how to deal with a baby all on her own, to coping with her good friend's death from cancer. The book received critical and popular acclaim and increased Lamott's stature in the literary world. "Throughout [the book], Lamott provides a sense of ordinary domesticity, interrupted and then rendered extraordinary by moments of peripatetic musings," a reviewer for *Kirkus Reviews* (March 15, 1993) noted. "One need not be a new parent to appreciate Lamott's glib and gritty good humor in the face of annihilating weariness. She'll nourish fans with her entries, and give birth to new ones as well."

In 1994 Lamott published *Bird By Bird: Some Instructions on Writing and Life*, which became a national best-seller. This how-to book on writing is full of autobiographical bits relating how she developed her craft, as well as exercises for getting started and getting over humps. She received high critical praise for her effort. In the *Christian Science Monitor* (October 2, 1995), David Conrads wrote, "Lamott is a skillful and witty writer, and a wonderful storyteller. If nothing else, this is one of the funniest books on writing ever published." Carol Muske Dukes, writing for the *New York Times Book Review* (March 4, 1995), called it a "hilarious, helpful, provocative book."

Lamott returned to fiction in 1997 with the publication of *Crooked Little Heart*, the sequel to her 1983 novel *Rosie*. Rosie is now a 13-year-old tennis phenomenon whose mother, Elizabeth, is now remarried to a man named James. Throughout the course of the novel Rosie faces challenges ranging from puberty to her mother's alcoholism. This coming-of-age novel received mixed reviews. A critic for *Publishers Weekly* (February 17, 1997) wrote, "[Lamott] writes with integrity and tenderness of the failure of parental love to protect children, and of the resilience that helps children step over that threshold to maturity." Benjamin Cheever, writing for the *New York Times* (August 17, 1997), completely disagreed with that appraisal, finding Lamott's fiction lacking when compared to her nonfiction: "What happened to the giggly, absurd character who wrote two popular nonfiction books? That mind set out for parts exotic and also highly, fiendishly familiar. . . . Why would an intelligence so lively in this world invent another universe in which so little happens?"

In 1999 Lamott published a collection of essays about her conversion to Christianity, entitled *Traveling Mercies: Some Thoughts on Faith*. Like her other nonfiction works, it was enthusiastically praised by reviewers. Donna Seaman, writing for *Booklist* (January 1, 1999), noted, "Squeezing every last drip of meaning out of even the smallest things, Lamott writes agilely about such watershed events as the deaths of her father and closest woman friend, and the birth of her son and life as a single mother, all the while tracing her slow crawl back to faith with wonder, gratitude, and an irrepressible love of a good story." In an editorial review for *Amazon.com*, Gail Hudson wrote: "Lamott keeps her spirituality firmly planted in solid scenes and believable metaphors. As a result, this is a richly satisfying armchair-travel experience, highlighting the tender mercies of Lamott's life that nudged her into Christian faith."

In 2002 Lamott published her sixth novel, *Blue Shoe*. In it, Mattie Ryder, a newly divorced mother of two, returns to her childhood home and is forced to reevaluate her life by dealing with her mother's senile dementia as well as her own children's emotional problems. In a review for *Amazon.com*, Regina Marler wrote: "Some of the action in this novel could have been compressed, and the major subplot involving Mattie's father fails to excite, but the strengths of *Blue Shoe*—humor, unflinching characterization, and keen observation—more than compensate for its weaknesses." TXT=Anne Lamott was the recipient of a Guggenheim Fellowship in 1985. From 1995 to 1999 she wrote a column for the on-line magazine *Salon*. The column has recently been reintroduced. She lives in the San Francisco area with her son, Sam.

—C. M.

SUGGESTED READING: *Booklist* Jan. 1, 1999; *Christian Century* p742+ Aug. 4, 1999; *Chicago Tribune* 14 p31 Jan. 5, 1986, 6 p3 July 18, 1993; *Christian Science Monitor* p14 Oct. 2, 1995; *Newsweek* p71 May 3, 1999; *New York Newsday* Part II p4 Nov. 20, 1989; *New York Times* (on-line) Jan. 29, 1984, Dec. 1, 1994, Aug. 17, 1997; *New York Times Book Review* p8 Oct. 22, 1989, p19 Mar. 4, 1995; *New York Times Magazine* (on-line) Feb. 20, 2000; *New Yorker* p187 Dec. 4, 1989; *Sojourners* p52+ May/June 1999; *Theology Today* p608+ Jan. 2000; *Contemporary Authors*, vol. 74, 1999

SELECTED BOOKS: fiction—*Hard Laughter*, 1980; *Rosie*, 1983; *Joe Jones*, 1985; *All New People*, 1989; *Crooked Little Heart*, 1997; *Blue Shoe*, 2002; nonfiction—*Operating Instructions: A Journal of My Son's First Year*, 1993; *Bird By Bird: Some Instructions on Writing and Life*, 1994; *Traveling Mercies: Some Thoughts on Faith*, 1999

Lanchester, John

1962– Novelist

Since the mid-1990s John Lanchester has gained a reputation for being one of the most versatile British novelists working today. His first book, *The Debt to Pleasure* (1996), is an unusual combination of journal, cookbook, and murder mystery. For his second novel, *Mr. Phillips* (2000), he completely changed directions; the book focuses on the everyday life of a man who has recently been fired after working for the same company for three decades. With his most recent novel, *Fragrant Harbor* (2002), Lanchester has written an epic story of Hong Kong, as told by three narrators. When asked about his versatility by Sybil Steinberg for *Publishers Weekly* (July 8, 2002), Lanchester noted, "The difference between [my] books is obviously very striking, because everyone has commented on it. It's less apparent to me because it's like listening to your voice on the Dictaphone—it always sounds like your voice."

Jason Bell/Courtesy of *London Review of Books*
John Lanchester

The only child of British subjects, John Lanchester was born in Hamburg, Germany, in 1962. His father, Bill Lanchester, worked for the Hong Kong Shanghai Bank, which necessitated frequent moves. When he was just six weeks of age, Lanchester moved with his family to Hong Kong, then a British colony, after several short stops in Burma, India, Malaysia, and Brunei. Exotic locales were not unknown to the Lanchester clan; Bill had been born in Cape Town, South Africa, in 1926, and Jack Lanchester, John's grandfather, had moved to Hong Kong in the 1930s with his wife, the former Dora Bosomworth, who was a nurse.

Lanchester frequently heard the story of Jack and Dora when he was growing up. Jack Lanchester had, after several years as a teacher, earned a degree in dentistry. At the time, he and his family were living in a small town in Rhodesia (now Zimbabwe), where there were few patients wealthy enough to afford quality dentistry. He decided to move the family to Hong Kong, correctly presuming that there would be more wealthy patients there. In a short time he became the official dentist for the British government in Hong Kong. When war broke out with Japan, in December 1941, Lanchester's grandparents were sent to the infamous Stanley Internment Camp and were not released until August 1945. Dora regaled her grandson with tales of savoring the blackened rice burnt onto the bottom of the pot, simply because it tasted different from the white rice that constituted most of their rations.

Lanchester remembers his childhood as pleasant; the family took frequent weekend trips by boat, and he could see Hong Kong's bustling harbor from his window. In 1972 Lanchester left Hong Kong for England to study. There he attended Gresham's Boarding School, in Norfork. He had no idea of what England would be like, other than "flat and green," as he told Tim Teeman for the London *Times* (June 26, 2002). He found the pervasive class snobbery in England unpleasant, and he dreaded his periodic 21-hour flights back to Hong Kong. (In the early 1970s, flying over Chinese or Vietnamese airspace was forbidden.) In 1979 Lanchester's parents returned to the United Kingdom, eliminating the need for the lengthy flights. Lanchester himself did not return to Hong Kong until a visit in 1997, and, he told Teeman, "The city I had grown up in wasn't there. The centre of the town had so many buildings it was unrecognizable." He continued, "Where once there were [rice] paddy fields, there were towns with half a million people."

Lanchester attended Oxford University, but in 1986 he left a graduate program there to become an editorial assistant at the *London Review of Books*. The job paid poorly, so he supplemented his income with sports and obituary writing. During this time he was also working on his first novel, *The Debt to Pleasure* (1996), which he had begun while sharing a house with five other men at Oxford. His mother had given him a detailed recipe for pasta "right down to how to turn on the gas taps," as he told Teeman. "She clearly assumed I had the capabilities of a not very bright amoeba." He discovered, however, that he loved to cook. He began buying numerous cookbooks; he was fascinated by the form, especially as written by such masters as M. F. K. Fisher and Elizabeth David. "I thought: what if you had a cookbook that was actually a story," he told Sybil Steinberg. "Then I thought: it has to be a murder story. The idea came to me in one go." Lanchester optimistically took a three-month leave of absence from his job at the *London Review of Books* to work on the project. The book was not fully completed for five years, however.

The Debt to Pleasure is narrated by Tarquin Winot, an English gourmet who has decided to tour France and write down his ideas about good food. Throughout his narrative, Tarquin makes references to a darker aspect of his life; we learn he sometimes wears disguises and that several of the people in his life have died violently. The novel received differing reviews. Gerald Howard praised it in *The Nation* (May 6, 1996), writing: "Cocksure, obtuse, increasingly sinister, Tarquin Winot is a brilliant creation—as compelling an unreliable narrator as we've had since Nabakov set the gold standard with Charles Kinbote in *Pale Fire*." He concluded, "It was inevitable that somebody was going to write a high-toned serial killer novel with a literary pedigree, and considering the potential awfulness of such a book, we must be grateful for Lanchester for bringing it off so beautifully. He has conjured up an immensely stylish literary dish and served it with a wit and knowingness that will delight foodies and bookies alike." Adam Mars-Jones, writing for the *Times Literary Supplement* (March

16, 1996), was less laudatory. He described the book's style as "pseudo-tedious" and argued that "this material isn't satisfactorily strung on the thread of a story. . . . [Winot] is an unrealized character, inflated by a steady stream of esoteric knowledge and provocative opinions, but leaking interest and plausibility from many vents."

In 2000 Lanchester published *Mr. Phillips*, his second novel. The title character has just been laid off from the catering-supply company at which he has worked for more than 30 years. The book chronicles a single day in which Phillips wanders through London contemplating his life and the effects of having so much taken from him so quickly. The novel received mostly favorable reviews. Veronica Scrol wrote for *Booklist* (February 15, 2000), "It takes real courage and talent to write a novel about an unexceptional man living an unremarkable life, but Lanchester pulls it off with grace and wit." Martin H. Levinson, writing for *Etc.* (Fall 2000), agreed: "In Mr. Phillips, [Lanchester] skillfully portrays a character who seems to be in many ways an Everyman for these downsizing times—a human being with fanciful dreams and fantasies who lives a life with many set obligations." In his review for the *New Statesman and Society* (January 31, 2000), Christopher Tayler wrote, "Overall, the novel does not quite cohere—which is, of course, partly the point (life being incoherent, after all)—but also brings its own set of frustrations. None the less, at its best the book vividly conveys a certain level of London reality rarely encountered in fiction."

The title of Lanchester's next book, *Fragrant Harbor* (2002), refers to the port of Hong Kong—in a somewhat ironic manner. "Hong Kong harbour has an incredibly distinctive smell, a kind of warm, oily, fishy aroma," Lanchester wrote for the London *Daily Telegraph* (June 8, 2002). "And because smell takes you straight back in time, [when I'm there] I feel an extraordinary psychic vertigo, as one part of my mind is saying, this is a place you don't recognize, it's got nothing to do with you, while another part is saying, this is where you grew up, this is your childhood, this is the exact spot you were standing on when you were five years old. If I had to boil the inspiration for the novel down to one moment or one sensation, it would be that."

The novel encompasses much of the 20th century—from the 1930s to the new millennium—and traces the evolution of Hong Kong from a British colony to the modern center of the global economy that it is today. The book has three narrators; the central one is Tom Stewart, a British expatriate. Stewart's story stretches from his arrival in Hong Kong in the 1930s to World War II, when he is imprisoned and tortured by the Japanese. Another narrator is Dawn Stone, a journalist in Hong Kong in the mid-1990s hoping to make her career by exposing the organized-crime roots of some of the city's wealthiest citizens. The final narrator is Matthew Ho, a wealthy business executive who bribes his way to the heights of power and influence.

Sophie Harrison, writing for the *New York Times* (June 30, 2002, on-line), opined, "*Fragrant Harbor* is not an enormous novel, but it feels like one—it is bursting with ideas. Lanchester takes on almost every major theme and succeeds with most of them: race, class, love, war, the fall of rulers and the rise of the ruled. The novel's sharpest insights are into the nature of success, its best passages careful dissections of how a disenfranchised community of poor refugees turned the colony into one of the richest societies in the world." She cautioned, however, "There are some costs to this broad scope. One is pacing. . . . In *Fragrant Harbor* the decades race by. The scope is that difficult thing called 'epic,' the setting a period of exceptional eventfulness. To achieve such a level of detail, Tom's narration has to cover both historical background and personal foreground, a feat of memory that has some cost for his credibility." Dan Cryer, writing for *New York Newsday* (July 11, 2002), agreed: "Despite its more than 300 pages, *Fragrant Harbor* is a story that feels crammed with too much history. It moves too fast for its own good. The Thirties, World War II, Cold War and end-of-millennium economic explosion whiz by in a blur." He concluded, "A few snapshots from selected periods rather than a camera kept rolling would have tightened the focus."

John Lanchester lives in Clapham Junction, outside London, with his wife, Miranda Carter, also a writer. She is perhaps best known for *Anthony Blunt: His Lives* (2001), a critically acclaimed biography of the Cambridge art historian turned Soviet spy. The couple have one son, Finn. As of July 2002 they were expecting a second child.

—C.M.

SUGGESTED READING: *New York Times* (on-line) June 30, 2002; (London) *Daily Telegraph* p1 June 8, 2002; *Etc.* p380 Fall 2000; *New York Newsday* C p30 Apr. 14, 1996, B p2, July 11, 2002; *New Statesman and Society* p33 Mar. 15, 1996, p129 Jan. 31, 2000; *Publishers Weekly* p24 July 8, 2002; (London) *Times* June 26, 2002

SELECTED BOOKS: *Debt to Pleasure*, 1996; *Mr. Phillips*, 2000; *Fragrant Harbor*, 2002

Landis, J. D.

June 30, 1942– Novelist; juvenile-fiction writer

The American novelist and writer of young-adult fiction J. D. Landis first learned the book trade as an editor and publisher. While working in the publishing business, he wrote the juvenile novels *The Sisters Impossible* (1979), *Daddy's Girl* (1984), *Love's Detective* (1984), *Joey and the Girls* (1987), *The Band Never Dances* (1989), and *Looks Aren't Everything* (1990). He went on to become an acclaimed writer of books for mature readers with *Lying in Bed* (1995), the story of an unusual marriage

Courtesy of Marion Ettlinger

J. D. Landis

in which conversation is as important as sex, and both dominate the couple's lives. In *Longing* (2000), which *Publishers Weekly* (July 10, 2000) termed "expansive and engrossing . . . historical fiction at its best, true to its subjects and steeped in the past," Landis told the story of the romance between composer Robert Schumann and his wife, Clara Wieck. The novel chronicles their relationship through Schumann's last years in an insane asylum, when Johannes Brahms served as a go-between for Clara and her husband, whom she was not allowed to visit.

James David Landis, known to readers as J. D. Landis, was born June 30, 1942 in Springfield, Massachusetts, to Eve Saltman, a painter and teacher, and Edward Landis, a lawyer. Landis was educated at Yale University in New Haven, Connecticut, where he received his B.A. in 1964.

Landis started his professional life as an editor. He first worked for the publisher Abelard-Schuman, in New York City, and then went on to Morrow, in 1967, where he later became publisher and editor-in-chief of various divisions. Landis edited the work of such noted writers as Robert Persig, author of *Zen and the Art of Motorcycle Maintenance*, and the poet Amiri Baraka. While working as an editor, Landis wrote and published novels under a pseudonym, though he now declines to identify their titles. In 1991 he retired from publishing to become a full-time writer, and he moved from New York City to Exeter, New Hampshire, in 1994.

During his first years as a writer, Landis produced a number of novels directed essentially at an audience of teen-age girls. After *The Sisters Impossible*, which came out in 1979, Landis went on to write *Daddy's Girl*. The novel is the story of Jennie, a 13-year-old New York teen who attends a "feminist day school." Jennie catches her father in an adulterous affair and attempts to deflect the incident so that her mother, a psychologist, will not get hurt. How Jennie does so forms the heart of the book's plot. Terming *Daddy's Girl* "a splendid entertainment," in the *New York Times Book Review* (September 30, 1984), Barbara Thompson observed that the "plot is wonderfully rich and inventive." She praised the diversity of the characters—Jennie's boyfriend, Howie Simonize; the head of the school Jennie attends, who has an "ovary-shaped office loaded with dolls of feminist heroines," in Thompson's words; and the richest girl in the school, who is also the biggest shoplifter. Thompson concluded that the book was filled with "warmth and understanding."

In Landis's novel *Joey and the Girls*, the title character—a good person, a great tennis player, and a bright guy—finds himself in over his head when too many girls choose him as the object of their affections. A reviewer for the *New York Times Book Review* (April 12, 1987) characterized the book as "a breezy, often funny novel about teenagers and sex." Landis's 1989 young-adult novel, *The Band Never Dances*, has as its central character 16-year-old Judy, who becomes a drummer for a touring rock band. Attempting to overcome her grief at her brother's suicide, she enters into complex relationships with the other musicians in the group.

Another 16-year-old, Rosie, is the heroine of *Looks Aren't Everything*, which was published in 1990. After dating numerous guys, Rosie falls in love with her best friend Jeannie's older brother, Handsome Harry. Jeannie falls for Spud, so-called because he always wears a potato suit, and Rosie's mother, who is divorced, also has a romantic involvement. Handsome Harry is not interested in Rosie, and she finds herself temporarily alone. "Despite occasional flashes of brilliance (the description of teen boys' kisses is hilariously, achingly perceptive), Landis's latest is not as engaging as *The Band Never Dances*," a *Publishers Weekly* (January 19, 1990) reviewer wrote.

Lying in Bed, Landis's first adult novel not published under a pseudonym, came out in 1995. The principal narrator, John Chambers, a wealthy, word-obsessed intellectual and Nietzsche fanatic, is awaiting the return of his wife, who calls herself Clara Bell. While he seldom leaves their loft, she spends time at her shop, where she sells antique quilts, but this time she has gone on a mysterious errand. "No topic for us is interdicted, though neither tells the other all we know. We share a healthy respect for the dangers of depletion and the potential vacuity of the future. Nothing must diminish the ardor with which we live with one another," John says, as quoted by Maggie Paley in the *New York Times Book Review* (June 11, 1995). Clara is the novel's other narrator by way of her diaries, which John reads. "Landis brilliantly catches the two very distinct voices of John and Clara—he's an egghead; she's impulsive, pragmatic, funny—and the reader quickly becomes enmeshed in the dreamily concupiscent atmosphere of their partnership, in which audacious sexuality is the norm," a *Publishers Weekly* (March 30, 1995) reviewer commented. "*Lying in Bed* . . . offers some genuine insights—discomforting, exultant, even comic—into the power of sex."

Tom De Haven, who reviewed *Lying in Bed* for *Entertainment Weekly* (June 23, 1995), found John Chambers so paranoid—"quite possibly a lunatic"— that readers might speculate as to whether Clara really exists or is merely a product of John's disordered imagination. "Is anything that Chambers tells us reliable information? This is a tricky book, but too coy, even smug for its own good," he concluded. Donna Seaman, on the other hand, writing in *Booklist* (June 1, 1995), agreed that "Landis has constructed a veritable hall of mirrors, all reflection and seduction," but she regarded it as a successful construction, "an annoying if captivating novel," which "we both like and resent." For James Polk, who reviewed the novel for the *Washington Post* (May 18, 1995), "the airless and self-contained world the two characters have constructed for themselves is not meant for outsiders to understand. . . . But while the existence they share is singular in its weirdness, the fearsome exaggerations of the novel provide an off-center insight into human behavior that a more conventional approach couldn't touch."

Landis's next novel, *Longing*, delves into romantic despair and passion, again with a heroine named Clara. Based on what is known about the marriage of Clara Wieck and 19th-century German composer and pianist Robert Schumann, *Longing*, according to Michael Spinella for *Booklist* (August 2000), is a "gripping real-life story full of love, music, madness, and intrigue." Schumann, who died insane at the age of 46, is considered one of the foremost romantic composers. Clara, also one of the great pianists of her time, was famously involved with Johannes Brahms, and she and Schumann were part of a circle of well-known European artists that included Franz Liszt, Felix Mendelssohn, Ivan Turgenev, Hans Christian Andersen, and Jenny Lind.

Landis described to David A. Walton in an interview for *Publishers Weekly* (July 10, 2000) how the idea for the novel developed in the mid-1970s, as he listened to Schumann's music. "I realized that theirs is the greatest of all true love stories because of the separations they suffered, and the obstacles put in the way by Clara's father, and the children that they had. These were two very great artists who married, which always causes tremendous conflict. Then to realize that when Robert went into the Endenrich Asylum in 1853, Clara didn't visit for two and a half years, until she came to see him die—that was when I saw a story. I wanted to know why a husband and wife would be separated for two and a half years. Especially since before that they were rarely apart."

Although Landis used a modern-day narrator, who speaks from the vantage point of the 20th century, and footnotes, which are unusual in fiction, "There are no made-up characters," he told Walton. "Everything is real, filtered through my imagination." The critic who reviewed the novel for *Publishers Weekly* (July 10, 2000) observed that rather than "strive for literary or stylistic effect, Landis relies on the truths of Schumann and Wieck's passion, writing with the earnestness, playfulness and fervor characteristic of the era he chronicles." Even the footnotes "paradoxically . . . enhance immediacy," the reviewer noted. Landis's own favorite footnote, he told Walton, "involves the duel between Lester Young and Coleman Hawkins at Nightsie Johnson's nightclub in Harlem. I couldn't put that into the text. So it's there in the context of musicians' duels. Musicians had confrontations where they would play against one another, and be judged as to who was the better pianist."

Longing was met with general critical acclaim. James Polk noted in the *New York Times Book Review* (September 17, 2000) that "Landis has seamlessly interwoven his text with ideas (about language and music, genius, imagination and the nature of human devotion) that are very much his own. The strikingly original narrative that he has constructed, while it may present the facts, is about much more than facts alone. Of course, music dominates. . . . Even conversations are constructed like musical compositions, infused with melodic elements. . . . It is almost as if Landis himself were conducting a score, with the two characters his human instruments."

Landis won the Morton Dauwen Zabel Award from the American Academy and Institute of Arts and Letters in 1996. The citation stated in part, "Landis is a gifted writer who has the courage and strength to take chances."

—S. Y.

SUGGESTED READING: *Booklist* p1729 June 1, 1995, p2113 Aug. 2000; *Entertainment Weekly* p46 June 23, 1995; *New York Times Book Review* (on-line) Sep. 30, 1984, Apr. 12, 1987, June 11, 1995, Sep. 17, 2000; *Publishers Weekly* p111 Jan. 19, 1990, p40 Mar. 20, 1995, p41 July 10, 2000, p42+ July 10, 2000; *Washington Post* C p2 May 18, 1995

SELECTED BOOKS: juvenile fiction—*The Sisters Impossible*, 1979; *Daddy's Girl*, 1984; *Love's Detective*, 1984; *Joey and the Girls*, 1987; *The Band Never Dances*, 1989; *Looks Aren't Everything*, 1990; novels—*Lying in Bed*, 1995; *Longing*, 2000

Lauterbach, Ann

Sep. 28, 1942– Poet; essayist

Ann Lauterbach first gained the attention of critics with her poetry collection *Many Times, But Then* (1979). Her subsequent books, including *Before Recollection* (1987), *Clamor* (1991), *And for Example* (1994), *On a Stair* (1997), and *If In Time: Selected Poems, 1975–2000* (2001), have made her a prominent voice in today's poetry world. "Ann Lauterbach's poetry is of ravishing presence pressured and fired by memory, desire, myth, and dream," James McCorkle wrote in the *Dictionary of Literary Biography: American Poets Since World War II* (1998). "To read Lauterbach's poetry is to immerse oneself in the rich textures of language as well as to participate in the re-visioning of the modernist lyric. Hers is not a didactic, discursive, or instructional poetry; rather it is a poetry moved by intuition, juxtaposed fragments, oblique narratives, and stunning images."

Ann Lauterbach was born on September 28, 1942 in New York City. She has described her parents, Richard Edward and Elisabeth Stuart Wardwell Lauterbach, as "active leftists," who attended Ivy League schools; they were married in Moscow while still undergraduates. In an interview with Molly Bendall for the *American Poetry Review* (May/June 1992), Lauterbach recalled that her parents "passionately believed that individual action could change the world, and that art could unite it." In an essay for the book *Conversant Essays: Contemporary Poets on Poetry* (1999), Lauterbach recalled that as a child she felt exceedingly vulnerable when her father's work as a foreign correspondent took him away from home for extended periods of time. She considered his typewriter a magical tool. "Words would eventually become the agent of my Oedipal attachment to him and to the world he represented," she wrote in the essay. "Touching the keys of the typewriter, I resemble and imitate him, and I almost touch him: an intimate mimicry."

Lauterbach attended a small, progressive school with leftist leanings; her music teacher there was the folk legend Pete Seeger. She then enrolled at the High School of Music and Art, in New York City, intending to become a painter. "When I was young I discovered what many children discover," she told Bendall, "that the act of painting is profoundly absorbing in an almost literal sense: you can disappear, so to speak, into the space or place you are making, and as you are doing it, temporality ceases; you escape your own narration, your own subjectivity." In high school, Lauterbach found herself fascinated with the work of the abstract expressionists for their combination of sensuousness and mystery, telling Bendall that "they seemed to answer something in me, to substantiate the encounter with the unknown. It seemed like pure encounter, pure response, and to elicit something both private and subject-free; you could bring your own investments to the place of the painting. A lot of my poems aim at a similar idea."

In 1964 Lauterbach graduated from the University of Wisconsin at Madison with a B.A. in English. Two years later she received a Woodrow Wilson graduate fellowship to study contemporary literature at Columbia University, in New York City. After what she has called "a disastrous year" at Columbia, Lauterbach embarked on a three-week visit to London, Paris, and Dublin. Her brief tour of Europe turned into a six-year stay. "I wrote to anyone vaguely interested in my fate that I had decided to become 'a poet in Dublin, not a career girl in New York," she told Bendall. Lauterbach fell in love with a man who worked for the British Broadcasting Corporation (BBC) and lived with him in his flat in London's Covent Garden. She was hired as an editor for the publisher Thames and Hudson and taught at the Saint Martin's School of Art. She eventually became co-editor of a monthly magazine on the history of modern art and later the director of publicity for the Institute of Contemporary Arts (ICA), where she introduced a poetry reading series. The culmination of the series was an appearance by the American poet John Ashbery, who had just completed his volume *Three Poems*. Hearing Ashbery read "changed my life," Lauterbach told Molly Bendall. "I realized that a poem could be at least as capacious as prose, that it need not be a tidy little bouquet of words tied in a ribbon."

In 1974 Lauterbach returned to New York City. She found an apartment on Spring Street in the downtown Manhattan neighborhood known as Soho and went to work at a local bar. One day, a tall man came in and introduced himself. In an article for the *New York Times* (May 12, 1996), Lauterbach wrote that the man was "Max Protech, who owned a gallery in Washington and who had just opened a second gallery on Spring Street on the fourth floor of the building directly across from my lone window. He had built himself a loft bed from which he could see directly into my life." Protech invited her to drive down to Washington, D.C., to see his first gallery. "Given the sense of reckless trust that pervaded downtown [New York], it seemed priggish not to accept," she wrote. "All the way down, we talked about art." Two weeks later, Protech offered her a job as the director of his new Spring Street gallery. "It seemed better than a proposal of marriage to me," she explained. In 1984 she became assistant director of the Washburn Gallery, also in New York City.

Lauterbach began her teaching career in 1985, working as an assistant professor in the master of fine arts program in writing at Brooklyn College. Over the next several years, she taught writing and poetry at Columbia University, Princeton University, and the University of Iowa. In 1992 she started teaching at the Graduate Center of the City University of New York (CUNY) and joined the university's English department two years later. In 1998 Lauterbach became the Ruth and David Schwab II Professor of Language and Literature at Bard College, in Annandale-on-Hudson, New York.

In 1971 the Seafront Press, in Dublin, published her first chapbook, *Vertical, Horizontal*. When she returned to the United States, she published a second chapbook of her work, *Book One* (1975). Her first extensive critical attention came, however, for her collection *Many Times, But Then*, which was published by Texas University Press in 1979. In his review for the *Times Literary Supplement* (January 18, 1980), John Fuller criticized the collection, writing that there was "a superfluity of mystery in Ann Lauterbach's poems, due I think to a heavy reliance on the ad lib." Fuller continued, "There is no reason why a controlled stream of consciousness should not make its effect, but when it doesn't make an effect there is not very much to say about it." A critic for *Choice* (March 1980), however, praised *Many Times, But Then*. "Fashionably urban and intellectual in the manner of John Ashbery, the poems are elaborate constructions in which the emotions are as muted as the chiaroscuro of 'anywhere where there is profuse / nothing, nothing but air in motion / and distances to boggle the imagination,'" the critic wrote. "Lauterbach's poetry is somewhat narrow in range, but it is accomplished according to the rules of the New York School. There are poems of promise here and a few fine achievements." (The New York School refers to a movement that came to prominence in the 1950s and '60s. Its participants included Ashbery, Kenneth Koch, and Frank O'Hara, who wrote poems that were urban in spirit and inspired by such modern painters as Willem de Kooning and Jackson Pollack.)

Lauterbach published several more chapbooks during the early 1980s. Her second collection, *Before Recollection*, appeared in 1987. Reviewing the book for *Choice* (December 1987), M. Gillan argued that most of Lauterbach's poems "are abstract to such a degree that they seem unconnected to human life. Often the point of the poems is unclear and the impact almost nonexistent." Although the critic acknowledged that several of the poems in the collection, including "Naming the House," "Like Moths to the Flame, " and "Here and There," achieved some success, Gillian concluded that the "poems are flawed because they lack specificity and clarity."

Lauterbach's next book, *Clamor*, received sharply contrasting reviews from critics. "*Clamor* is a book of noise punctuated by embarrassing howlers," Mark Jarman wrote for the *Hudson Review* (Spring 1992). "In 'Mountain Roads,' the poet says, 'It we say often, and it is always the same it.' The poems in this book are constantly proposing an *it*— that thing poets must try to define—and never telling us what the poet has in mind, expect to offer unforgettable, ingenuous hermetica, as in 'Forgetting the Lake': 'Everything I am thinking of rhymes with *spires*.' All one can say in response is 'Surely not everything.'" In her review for the *Washington Post* (February 16, 1992), Harriet Zinnes was more impressed with *Clamor*. She points out that although the work owes much to the movement called "Language Poetry," in which broken syntax and disassociation are common features, "[Lauterbach] can't help her talent for the memorable phrase. She can't help taking the reader down a sonorous path where intelligence is striking and verbal dexterity everywhere."

Lauterbach's fourth collection, *And For Example*, was published in 1994, and she followed it, in 1998, with *On a Stair*. In his review for *Poetry* (August 1998), David Yezzi faulted the latter book, noting its "dispiriting, academic cast." He explained, "One poem actually poaches extensively on the language of [Jacques] Derrida [the French deconstructionist]—it's poetry only a graduate student could love." Yezzi added that much "milage is gotten from the tensions between sensuality and intellectual unease, tensions often dissipating into bathos, as in 'the shopping cart's / cinematic rampage' or a sudden cry of 'Mom, what's for dinner?' Such feints promise humorous, Ashberyian relief from blanket tonal sobriety; it's a shame, therefore, that they are rarely really funny." By contrast, an anonymous critic for the *Virginia Quarterly Review* (Winter 1998) hailed *On a Stair*. "If this is postmodern poetry, then I am a convert to postmodernism." The critic continued, "Lauterbach has a calm assurance, almost a command, an authority, that one doesn't usually associate with experimental poetry."

In 2001 Ann Lauterbach published, *If in Time: Selected Poems 1975-2000*, which includes poems from her previous books, as well as 19 new pieces. "The most apt comparison for Lauterbach's career is to that of Jorie Graham [an American poet known for her abstract, intellectual verse]," Michael Scharf wrote in *Publishers Weekly* (February 12, 2001), "the two MacArthur fellows are near contemporaries [and] use free verse and open field composition to tackle the philosophical implications of travel, art and relationships from a postfeminist perspective." In her review for the *Village Voice* (May 15, 2001), Cathy Hong wrote that for "over two decades, Lauterbach's poetic trajectory has been unique, constellating the tattered fabric of self with language full of auguries, parenthetical asides, found slogans and glass-cut images." Hong asserted that the poems republished from *Clamor* and *And for Example* were the strongest in the book, praising them for their "lyric intensity" and "erudition." The reviewer, however, expressed disappointment with the new poems in the collection, arguing that "in them language becomes a tired and coy subject."

Ann Lauterbach has received many grants and awards during her career, including a Creative Arts Public Service Grant (1978), a Guggenheim Foundation Fellowship (1986), an Ingram Merrill Foundation Grant (1988), a New York State Council for the Arts Grant (1988), the Jerome J. Shestack Prize from the editors of the *American Poetry Review* (1990), and a 1993 John D. And Catherine T. MacArthur Fellowship. She been awarded several residencies by Yaddo, an artistic community in Saratoga Springs, New York, as well as by the Isabella Stewart Gardner Museum, in Boston, and the Atlantic Center for the Arts, in New Smyrna Beach, Florida. Maintaining her ties to the art world, Lauterbach has written four catalogues for museum exhibitions. Her next book, "The Night Sky," will be a collection of essays on poetry and art that she originally published in the *American Poetry Review* from 1996 to 1999.

—D. C.

SUGGESTED READING: *American Poetry Review* p19+ May/June 1992 with photo; *Choice* p75 Mar. 1980, p622 Dec. 1987; *New York Times* II p51 May 12, 1996; *Poetry* p292+ Aug. 1998; *Publishers Weekly* p203 Feb. 12, 2001; *Times Literary Supplement* p65 Jan. 18, 1980; *Village Voice* p101+ May 15, 2001; *Virginia Quarterly Review* p28 Winter 1998; *Washington Post Book World* p11 Feb. 16, 1992; McCorkle, James, ed. *Conversant Essays: Contemporary Poets on Poetry*, 1990; *Dictionary of Literary Biography, American Poets Since World War II*, 1998

SELECTED BOOKS: *Vertical, Horizontal*, 1971; *Book One*, 1975; *Many Times, But Then*, 1979; *Later That Evening*, 1981; *Closing Hours*, 1983; *Sacred Weather*, 1984; *Before Recollection*, 1987; *Clamor*, 1991; *And For Example*, 1994; *On a Stair*, 1997; *If In Time: Selected Poems, 1975–2000*, 2001

Tom Levy/Courtesy of Harcourt Publishing

Leebron, Fred G.

1961– Novelist; short-story writer

"I have a writer friend who once said that she hated writing about real people, because real people are messy, and she didn't want that mess on the page," Fred G. Leebron noted in an interview for the *Mountain Times* (July 25, 2001, on-line). "I want that mess, the awful mix of the passive and the active, the smart and the dumb, the mean and the kind, that I believe we're all made of." He continued, "Realism to me means embracing and exploring the contradictions that reside in people and in the situations in which they find themselves. For me it's the only reason to write."

Fred Leebron submitted the following autobiographical statement to *World Authors 1995–2000*: "I was born in Narberth, Pennsylvania, a suburb of Philadelphia, in 1961. As the youngest of five children, I was drawn to writing as the best chance to get all the words out before anyone interrupted. When my eighth grade teacher gave us an assignment to write a story, I handed in five. In eleventh grade, I switched to poetry, because I liked how much of it was unspoken and how much of it depended on sound. I was living in a small town in Denmark then, as a Rotary Exchange Student, and I read so many novels that I really didn't want to add to the mass of fiction out there. But like any writer, I came to writing through reading. I read all of Dostoevsky and Camus and Sartre and Turgenev and Kafka and Joyce and McCullers and Flannery O'Connor and Thomas Mann, among others, and I made myself read material that I wouldn't normally read, such as James Michener and John LeCarré. So, naturally, when I returned to school in the States, I returned to fiction. I liked the apparent excess of it, and my poetry was pretty terrible anyway.

"After a senior year at boarding school, I worked in the locked unit of the Philadelphia Psychiatric Center, took a fiction writing course at the University of Pennsylvania, and applied to college. Eventually, at Princeton, I majored in comparative urban affairs at the Woodrow Wilson School, and traveled to do research in Hong Kong and Chicago, among other places. In between Princeton and graduate school (at Iowa, Johns Hopkins, and Stanford), I lived in Copenhagen and Singapore. And after those four years of graduate study, my wife—who is a poet and memoirist—and I lived in San Francisco, where I worked in nonprofit housing and children's rights advocacy, and then Provincetown, Massachusetts, where I directed the Fine Arts Work Center, a residency program for artists and writers, and Charlotte, North Carolina, where I taught fiction writing . Despite the fact that for the past five years we have been living and working in Gettysburg, Pennsylvania, I think I have an urban imagination, one that is fueled by chance encounters, imagined and real dangers, and justified paranoia. And so I mention all these cities.

"*Out West*, the first novel I wrote after placing a dozen diverse stories at various literary magazines, reflected this sense of justified paranoia, culled from my own experiences in San Francisco's gritty Tenderloin neighborhood, where I had worked for four years. The novel was an attempt, in its early stages, to reimagine Nathaniel West's own years as a clerk at a low-income residential hotel in Los Angeles. To keep it loose—in other words, absolutely untied to and unconstrained by the truth—I set it in contemporary time and in San Francisco. Every morning I sat with a stenographer's notebook (smaller pages that would lead to less pressure to fill them) and wrote. I had about an hour each day. Usually I stole this hour on the commuter train (I had gotten the idea for this kind of routine from reading about how Scott Turow drafted his first legal thriller). And I learned to let the characters do whatever they wanted to do, regardless as to what I wanted them to do. I had no idea what would happen in it from day to day. I just followed the characters. Sometimes what they did repulsed me, sometimes it surprised me, sometimes it disappointed me. I wanted her to kill him. She never would. I wanted him to rise up and be more of a man. He couldn't. In a year they finished whatever they were going to do together, and I was finished as well. I had a mess on my hands. It took me three years to line-edit it. But it was a novel. It was a novel in the sense that it was new to me as I wrote it, that I had no idea what would happen until it did, and that I never dictated what would happen, I just followed it to find out.

"When I re-read the novel during the publication process, I was surprised by how gritty it was. It was almost offensive (perhaps it was actually offensive, but I am hard to offend). But I could not bring myself to change any of it, because I wanted it to be true to the characters, and I felt that it was. My own philosophy about grotesque material in fiction had been forged reading Dostoevsky and Kafka and Flannery O'Connor. As long as the content came from the characters, I thought that the content was justified. And, as a witness, I had made the choice to look at the various grotesque scenes, rather than look away.

"For *Six Figures*, I decided to try to create more mainstream characters who, I expected, would surprise me but be less graphic and more complex in their surprises. When they bored me or they got tired of hearing themselves think I followed other characters. I followed the point of view of a five-year-old and the point of view of a six-month-old and the points of view of two sixty-five-year-old women. I did not care what they said or thought or did as long as it was them saying or doing or thinking, and I didn't think of anybody reading it, I just thought of them doing it, and I had no idea what would happen when it did or how it would end. When the central act occurred I followed it and watched it and wrote it, and in those respects I might as well have been a journalist, covering the days of my characters, except that they offered me access to their interior worlds as well as whatever it was they felt like doing in public. When the ending came I still had doubt as to some essential truths but I didn't care because I doubted that there ever was just one essential truth ever for anybody. One editor had written me years before that "a little ambiguity never hurt anybody," and I had read Tim O'Brien's work and decided that in ambiguity actually there was an even more essential truth. The truth of many possible and potential truths. The thread to revelation wasn't singular, it was plural, and you could follow any of a number of these threads and they all took you to one understanding or another and there was not any single understanding that was a total or an all-encompassing understanding, and that, too, became a not knowing, because you could never tell on which particular path which particular understanding would be reached until you arrived at it.

"My most recent novel, *In the Middle of All This*, was also part of a conscious decision to try to find more universal issues. While *Six Figures* and *Out West* pivoted on literal crime, I wanted to write a novel that pivoted on something that I believe all of us are guilty of—psychological crime. And I wanted to set it in the most universal arena available—the arena of our mortality. When the central mystery emerged, I wanted to continue following all of the players for several reasons. First, I think, was because this was my most autobiographical novel, in that my sister was as ill as one of the main characters was, and I wanted to know as much as I could as what was happening to her. Second, I was worried that allowing this character to leave the book in such shrouded circumstances was too much of a surrender to the natural ambiguity of mortality. But I couldn't access this character without feeling that I was creating something less authentic than I had hoped. And so, again, the book ends in what I hope is a natural ambiguity that is also artful.

"As a writer, I tend to write from the personal into the imagined; I write from a dilemma I have been in and follow what happens to these characters who are confronted with the same problems that have confronted me. In new work, I'm getting further away from the personal, while still exploring the universal; thus, I'll have a stake in what I write, while at the same time being able to distance myself in a way that will allow me to be more ambitious with my writing."

Fred G. Leebron earned a B.A. from the Woodrow Wilson School of Public and International Affairs at New Jersey's Princeton University in 1983. He received a master's degree in writing from the Krieger School of Arts and Sciences at Baltimore's Johns Hopkins University and then attended the Iowa Writers' Workshop, earning an MFA. Leebron has lived for more than four years abroad and has visited Central America, Europe, Southeast Asia, and Peru, among other places. He worked as an apartment painter in Paris and as a baker in Copenhagen.

In 1996 Leebron published his first novel, *Out West*, the sordid tale of Ben, an intelligent and sympathetic ex-con, and Amber, a teacher with VISTA (Volunteers in Service To America). Ben is attempting to straighten out his life by working nights at a welfare hotel in San Francisco. (Leebron himself worked for a time at a nonprofit agency in the seedy Tenderloin district of San Francisco.) When the two meet, however, they end up embarking on a crime spree that will change their lives forever. The novel received mixed reviews overall, and Leebron frequently got shocked reactions when he performed live readings, due to the graphic nature of his narrative. Despite that, *Out West* was named a Barnes & Noble Discover Great New Writers selection, and Dick Alder, writing for the *Chicago Tribune* (November 3, 1996), called it "an impressive debut novel" and opined, "Leebron is so good at chronicling [his characters'] fears and aspirations that you'll be totally engrossed."

In his second novel, *Six Figures* (2000), Leebron explores the struggles of the shrinking number of middle-class Americans. The protagonists, Warner and Megan Lutz, have two young children and live in Charlotte, North Carolina. Walter is the head of a struggling nonprofit charity, and although the book takes place during one of the greatest economic booms in the history of the United States, the couple can't seem to make ends meet. While mansions rise around the area, families at the opposite end of the financial spectrum live across town in houses without running water. Danise Hoover wrote for *Booklist* (March 15, 2000): "This sharply written novel is populated by seriously flawed individuals, but the compelling immediacy of the story will carry readers regardless of the outcome." Rob Spillman wrote for the *New York Times Book Review* (May 14, 2000), "[*Six Figures*] is a morally challenged novel, an engrossing portrait of a husband and wife left in the wake of the booming economy and an examination of what each is willing to believe about the other in order to stay together. As a social critique, as a study in the evolving dynamics of a couple with young children and as a suspenseful story, *Six Figures* is right on the money."

In *The Middle of All This*, Leebron's third novel, was published in 2002. In it, Martin and Lauren Kreutzel, a pair of anthropology professors with two small children, must come to grips with the imminent death of Martin's sister, Elizabeth, from cancer. They are also contending with Richard, Elizabeth's feckless husband, who is able to act self-indulgently because Elizabeth says nothing about her suffering. Mary Rourke for the *Los Angeles Times* (August 9, 2002) cheered: "Leebron has a talent for revealing his characters, men and women, with the sure hand of a builder hammering nails." In a review for the *Washington Post* (August 20, 2002), Deborah Sussman Susser was more reserved in her judgement, writing: "This is an ambitious novel, and Leebron isn't afraid to tackle difficult themes. Unfortunately, it's tough to grasp what really drives his characters, beyond their current predicaments. We're told that Elizabeth blames her mother for her illness—she believes that the childhood spankings and humiliation she suffered led her to pick an abusive job and eventually develop cancer. But that's just it: We're told, rather than made to feel this information." Susser continued, "In much the same way, we're told that Martin and Lauren are anthropologists—a vocation ripe with possibility but there's little in their daily lives to convince us of this fact. They might as well be professors of English or philosophy or botany." She concluded, "These shortcomings are a shame, because there's so much here that's worthwhile."

Leebron's short fiction has been published in such periodicals as *Double Take*, the *North American Review*, *Grand Street*, and *TriQuarterly*. His work has earned him numerous awards and honors, including a Fulbright Scholarship, a James Michener Award, a Wallace Stegner Fellowship, and a Pushcart Prize. In addition to his work as a fiction writer, he has also served as an editor, with Andrew Levy, for *Creating Fiction: A Writer's Companion* (1995) and, with Paula Geyh and Andrew Levy, for *Postmodern American Fiction: A Norton Anthology* (1998).

Leebron has taught literature and writing at Johns Hopkins University, California's Stanford University, and the University of North Carolina in Charlotte. He has served as a director of the Fine Arts Workshop, a residency program for writers and artists, in Provincetown, Massachusetts. During the past decade he has helped to develop numerous literacy and writing programs in Baltimore and San Francisco. He is currently an assistant professor of English and creative writing at Gettysburg College, in Pennsylvania, where his wife, an author of nonfiction and poetry, also teaches creative writing. They have a daughter and a son.

—C. M.

SUGGESTED READING: *Mountain Times* (online) July 25, 2001; *Booklist* p1328 Mar. 15, 2000; *Chicago Tribune* C p9 Nov. 3, 1996; *Los Angeles Times* V p3 Aug. 9, 2002; *New York Times Book Review* p41 May 14, 2000; *Washington Post* C p3 Aug. 20, 2002

SELECTED BOOKS: fiction—*Out West*, 1996; *Six Figures*, 2000; *In the Middle of All This*, 2002; as co-editor—*Creating Fiction: A Writer's Companion*, 1995; *Postmodern American Fiction: A Norton Anthology*, 1998

Lemann, Nancy

Feb. 4, 1956– Novelist; nonfiction writer

When she came to New York in the early 1980s to pursue a publishing contract, Nancy Lemann was "just a hick from the South," as she described herself to Eric Pooley for *New York* (July 22, 1985). The New Orleans native has since published four novels—*Lives of the Saints* (1985), *Sportsman's Paradise* (1992), *The Fiery Pantheon* (1998), and *Malaise* (2002)—that feature characters who exhibit the Southern virtues that Lemann admires, such as kindness, a sense of duty, good manners, and often, eccentricity. "Literature should teach you how to act, and it should give you hope," she told Michael Schumacher for his book *Reasons to Believe: New Voices in American Fiction* (1988). "It's like religion or ethics. I wouldn't want to write about a bunch of depressed people who are living life wrong, and to some extent I'm actually out to provide a certain amount of lighthearted, escapist entertainment. My aim is to provide a world that you would want to dwell in while you're reading the book—a world you wish you could dwell in when you close the book. My aim is to give hope and consolation." Lemann is also the author of one nonfiction volume, *The Ritz of the Bayou* (1987), in which she examines the corruption trials of Edwin Edwards, the governor of her home state.

Nancy Lemann was born on February 4, 1956 in New Orleans, Louisiana. Her father, Thomas, was a lawyer. "I get my love of eccentrics from my father," she told Schumacher. "My father is an incredible eccentric, and that's what I was raised on." Lemann majored in English literature at Brown University, in Providence, Rhode Island, graduating in 1978. At the age of 20, she completed her first novel, *The Lives of the Saints*, but was unable to find a publisher. Lemann returned home to New Orleans and worked at several different jobs, including positions at a law firm, a publishing company, and the local housing preservation society. In 1982 Susan Minot, a classmate from college who also went on to enjoy success as a novelist, invited Lemann to move to New York City to increase her chances of finding a publisher for her work. Although Lemann was reluctant to leave the city she loved, she relocated and enrolled in Columbia University's creative writing program. "They can't teach you how to write," she told Schumacher. "No one can. What New York and writing school did for me was give me the chance to see who the editors and publishers were. I could see the different people and what they were like." In 1984 Lemann received her MFA from Columbia.

After completing her education, Lemann found a publisher (Knopf) for *Lives of the Saints*, which chronicles the gradual decline of the Colliers, an eccentric family of New Orleans aristocrats. The narrator of the book is a young woman named Louise Brown, who works for a law firm as a proofreader. Louise, a frequent guest at the Colliers home, falls in love with Claude Collier, a bright, but troubled Southern gentleman. Unsure of what to do with his life, Claude spends his time drinking and going to parties. After the tragic death of a five-year-old relative, Claude begins a downward spiral; he leaves New Orleans and indulges in drinking binges in other cities. Many reviewers enthusiastically praised Lemann's debut novel. In the *New York Times* (May 25, 1985), Michiko Kakutani hailed *Lives of the Saints* as "a lovely, grave elegy for lost innocence, for lost youth and a vanished world" and a "dense, musically patterned novel, in which repetitions of scenes, images and phrases—varied by mood and time—acquire a cumulative power: An exchange of non sequiturs at a party that seems silly, even pointless on first hearing, can reverberate with much darker tones when it surfaces again later." Kakutani added that "in the end, it is a resonant, loving portrait that Louise assembles; and in telling her story, Miss Lemann has succeeded in creating not only a finely etched picture of the South, but also a lyrical prose poem about a young woman's coming of age." In a review for the *New Republic* (June 24, 1985), Anne Tyler also praised the novel. "Think of *Lives of the Saints* as a long poem—a hysterically funny poem that is also beautifully written, if you can imagine such a thing," Tyler wrote. "It doesn't exactly tell a story. It violates all kinds of rules. (The narrator, for instance, is part of the events but never fully explains herself; she's both there and not there, and on at least two occasions describes scenes from which she was absent.) Even so, the book works—perhaps because of its sheer exuberance, its enthusiasm for its characters, its peculiarly Southern habit of telling us not so much what happened as to whom." Tyler concluded that *Lives of the Saints* "is an almost hypnotic portrait of unforgettable people in a strange and magnificent city."

Lemann turned to nonfiction for her second book, *The Ritz of the Bayou* (1987). She researched the book by attending the two corruption trials, in 1985 and 1986, of Edwin Edwards, the Democratic governor of Louisiana. A notorious womanizer and gambler, Edwards was widely considered a throwback to the siblings Huey Pierce Long (1893–1935) and Earl Kemp Long (1895–1960), two Louisiana politicians who managed to remain popular with many voters despite numerous scandals. Edwards' first trial ended with a hung jury. In the second trial, he and seven co-defendants were acquitted of racketeering and other charges. (In 2000, however, the 72-year-old Edwards, who had been elected governor four times, was finally convicted of extortion.) Despite writing about Edwards, Lemann had no real interest in government. "I actually pride myself on having written something that doesn't have one line about politics in it, although it took place in a political arena, with politicians," she explained to Schumacher. "Politics is not my beat," she continued. "I was looking at it as a tragedy, the downfall of a man by his own flaws. It's called the human condition. I saw the dark side, but also the atmosphere, the characters, the very South, sangfroid, grace in adversity and in defeat."

Richard Eder, writing for the *Los Angeles Times* (September 30, 1987), had harsh criticism for the book. "The first rule of journalism is: Get out of bed in the morning," he asserted. "Lemann, in her highly mannered account . . . brings her bed with her. She ventures out, is overwhelmed by the heat, the light, the color, the strangeness; and retreats back into bed. She pulls the sheets over her head and, surrounded by sensibility, refashions what she has seen." Although he praised Lemann as a "writer of skill, sensitivity and sophistication," Eder faulted the book's quirky language, which included repeated uses of the words "jolly," "jovial," and "joshing," and references to "smoldering" nightclubs and a "jazz-crazed assistant prosecutor." In contrast, Douglas Seibold wrote for the *Chicago Tribune* (September 21, 1987) that with *The Ritz on the Bayou*, Lemann had "created an idiosyncratic piece of journalism that seems to obey the dictates of her own sensibility as much as the actual progress of the case." The reviewer noted that "desperate gaiety is the chief distinguishing feature of Lemann's book; everyone seems to spend all of their nonworking hours going to bars and parties and carrying on wittily through every manner of emotional crisis." Seibold concluded that such episodes make for fine entertainment, and he applauded Lemann's ability to control the tone of the book. "Whenever the scene is about to deteriorate into complete silliness," he wrote, "Lemann is usually able to revive it with some pithy insight into the trial's workings or the nature of the South."

Lemann waited five years to publish her third book, *Sportsman's Paradise* (1992), a novel that revisits the Colliers. In this book, the New Orleans eccentrics are vacationing at an estate on Long Island, in New York. The book's narrator is Storey Collier, a young woman who works as an advice columnist for the *New York Examiner* newspaper. Her cousin Claude Collier, one of the main characters from *Lives of the Saints*, is undergoing alcohol rehabilitation back in New Orleans. In Long Island Storey is joined by a host of characters, including her former lover, Hobby Fox, who is the international editor at the *New York Examiner*; Stokes Underwood, their tough boss at the newspaper; Grace Fox, Hobby's aunt and the owner of the estate; Claude's three children; and an accident-prone woman named Margaret. Hobby is interested in rekindling his relationship with Storey, who frequently seeks the assistance of Al, Claude's 3-year-old son, when writing her advice column. In *New York Newsday* (May 18, 1992), Dan Cryer dismissed *Sportsman's Paradise* as "so unbelievable and so phony that a critic can only shake his head in amazement." Despite praising Lemann's "nice feel for lovely, lyrical language," Cryer argued that the author wasted her talents by writing a novel that lacked an engaging plot and characters. Sven Birkets, however, observed for the *New Republic* (May 18, 1992) that the novel's "real point—and triumph—is its registration of sensibility. Of emotional susceptibility. *Sportsman's Paradise* (the tag on Louisiana license plates) is, like *Lives of the Saints* before it, a vast exhalation of romantic yearning. Which is another way of saying that it is filled to spilling with old-fashioned—and culturally unfashionable—sentiments and stances." Birkets noted that "the point of writing is not to create anyone's idea of a right-thinking person, but to open up pockets in which we can dream our lives in other directions. This Nancy Lemann has done. Her wonderfully rhythmic, off-center prose installs the reader squarely inside the life of a foolish, obsessive, but emotionally forthright young woman. Storey's quaint devotions set her apart from her fictional peers. But like it or not, she is who she is, the queen of her scattershot dreams."

In Lemann's next fictional work, *The Fiery Pantheon* (1998), Grace Stewart is engaged to be married to Monroe Collier, whose family graced Lemann's two previous novels. For Grace, Monroe embodies the traditional Southern values she cherishes, including devotion to family. Monroe is frequently absent because he is visiting ailing relatives. During one such absence, Grace meets Walter Sullivan, a New Orleans native who relocated to New York City to work as a securities analyst on Wall Street. Grace and Walter soon discover a mutual attraction; he follows her and her extended family as their vacation takes them through New York City, Cairo, Istanbul, and Rome. "Which man will Grace love?" Elizabeth Graver asked in a review for the *Chicago Tribune* (March 8, 1998). "That is the question the novel half-pretends to ask, yet it quickly becomes clear that the love triangle is little more than a pretext for other questions Lemann wants to explore—questions about language, nostalgia, obsession, and the powerful, often-blind human attachment to place, history and home." Despite her criticism of the book's constant repetition of certain words and phrases—she gives as examples "debonair," "gaiety," and "decorum"—Graver wrote that where "the novel shines is in its precise renderings of the pitfalls and lures of tradition; in its vivid, painterly descriptions of place; and in the marvelous moments when it abandons realism completely and enters a stylized, skewed realm all its own." In a similarly mixed review for the *Boston Globe* (March 11, 1998), Robert Taylor observed that at her best, Lemann suggests "a New Orleans Jane Austen." Taylor enjoyed the first two-thirds of the book, which take place in Virginia and New York City, but wrote that the "final foreign episodes sag a bit; the characters in the last third of the story get shunted aside by the travelogue."

In 2002 Lemann published another novel, *Malaise*. The story revolves around Fleming Ford, a woman from Fort Defiance, Alabama, who has moved to Southern California with her husband and two children. Fleming's husband, Mac, is a geologist who spends a lot of time away from home drilling for water in the Mojave Desert. One day, Fleming meets Harry Lieberman, a British tycoon and a widower. Despite being attracted to Harry and visiting him in Los Angeles, she has moral reservations about cheating on her husband. "Lemann is not simply a quirky stylist steeped in the sometimes impenetrable ways of the South, not just a sharp observer of the less regional, if equally mystifying, ways of the human heart," Karen Karbo wrote for the *New York Times Book Review* (June 2, 2002). "She's also terrifically funny and can write a story that rocks." A native Southern Californian herself, Karbo praised Lemann's knack of making many of the typical complaints about California, such as the lack of intellectual rigor and the obsession with health and beauty, "sound new, accurate and hilarious." Of Fleming Ford, Karbo wrote, "Rarely has a heroine been so believable in her determination to do the right thing." In a critique for the *Library Journal* (May 1, 2002), Wilda Williams compared Lemann to the authors Walker Percy and James Wilcox and wrote, "You either love the [book's] eccentric, almost bizarre characters and quirky, playful style, or you are bored and irritated by the lack of plot and constant repetitions. For this reviewer, these mixed qualities add to the charm of Lemann's witty comedy of manners."

Nancy Lemann lives in San Diego.

—D. C.

SUGGESTED READING: *Boston Globe* C p3 Mar. 11, 1998; *Chicago Tribune* Tempo p3 Sep. 21, 1987, Books p3 Mar. 8, 1998; *Library Journal* p134 May 1, 2002; *Los Angeles Times* V p2 Sep. 30, 1987; *New Republic* p36 June 24, 1985, p48 May 18, 1992; *New York* p22 July 22, 1985, with photo; *New York Times* I p13 May, 25, 1985; *New York Times Book Review* p11 June 2, 2002; *New York Newsday* II p44 May 18, 1992; Schumacher, Michael. *Reasons to Believe: New Voices in American Fiction*, 1988

SELECTED BOOKS: novels—*Lives of the Saints*, 1985; *Sportsman's Paradise*, 1992; *The Fiery Pantheon*, 1998; *Malaise*, 2002; nonfiction—*The Ritz of the Bayou*, 1987

Lemann, Nicholas

Aug. 11, 1954– Journalist; nonfiction writer

Nicholas Lemann has made a name for himself as an author of books about recent American social history, and he has used his skills as a journalist to research aspects of his topics that have not previously been highlighted. His first book, *The Fast Track* (1981), a collection of essays profiling people who have struggled to succeed, asks readers to redefine their negative perceptions of ambition. *Out of the Forties* (1983) is a collection of photographs of American life during that crucial decade, to which Lemann contributed accompanying text that sheds light on the lives of the people depicted. He has also written *The Promised Land* (1991), a history of the migration of black Americans from the South to the urban North from the 1940s to the 1970s. Lemann's most recent book is *The Big Test* (1999), which is both a history of the Scholastic Aptitude Test (SAT) and its founders as well as a critical discussion of the test's importance in achieving success in the United States.

Nicholas Lemann was born in New Orleans, Louisiana, on August 11, 1954. He is the son of Thomas B. Lemann, a lawyer, and the former Barbara M. Landon, a psychologist. Lemann graduated from Harvard University, in Cambridge, Massachusetts, in 1976, and although he was expected to attend Harvard Law School and join the family firm, he decided instead to pursue a career in journalism. After earning his bachelor's degree in American history and literature he joined the staff of the *Washington Monthly*, in Washington, D.C., where he became managing and contributing editor. Two years later, in 1978, he joined the staff of the *Texas Monthly*, based in Austin, Texas, and he

Sigrid Estrada/Courtesy of Farrar, Straus and Giroux

went on to serve as that publication's contributing and executive editor from 1981 to 1983.

Beginning in 1979 Lemann served as a reporter for the *Washington Post* while also working at the *Texas Monthly*; he relinquished his position at the *Post* in 1983 to become a national correspondent for the *Atlantic Monthly*. At that magazine Lemann distinguished himself as a social historian of modern America, whose articles on education, television, politics, civil rights, affirmative action, and generational gaps formed the basis of many of his best-selling nonfiction books. In addition to writing feature articles, he also contributed to the magazine's travel section and book reviews. Lemann left the *Atlantic Monthly* in 1998 to become a staff writer at the *New Yorker.*

Lemann's first book was *The Fast Track: Texans and Other Strivers* (1981), a collection of eight previously published essays about people whose ambition brought them success in their respective fields, including medicine, real estate, and theater. The book received high praise. Anne Tyler, in a review for the *New Republic* (June 13, 1981), commented: "*The Fast Track* is . . . an absorbing collection—a crisply written, clear-eyed study of America's travels upward." In a review for *Library Journal* (August 1981) Jack Forman wrote that Lemann's "aim is to show . . . the many faces of ambition and to expose the unjustified bad press this human motivation had been given. . . . [It is] an involving and thought-provoking collection of journalistic features."

In Lemann's next book, *Out of the Forties* (1983), the author shows how life has changed in the United States since that decade through a collection of photographs originally commissioned in the late 1940s and early 1950s by Standard Oil as part of a public-relations initiative intended to boost the company's image. The pictures convey a great deal about the American experience of the time: schoolboys going to a concert, cowboys playing cards in a bunkhouse, teenagers watching their first television, a family resting on a service station porch, a father fixing his car as his young daughter looks on. Not content to let the images stand alone, Lemann tracked down many of the people in the pictures and interviewed them about how their lives had evolved since the photos were taken, in the hopes of not only documenting the inevitable changes in a 40-year period but also to question the meaning of nostalgia itself. While some critics agreed with Melvin L. Grotberg's assessment in *Library Journal* (June 15, 1983) that "the idea is good and the photos are excellent, but unfortunately the text is a rambling, disjointed narrative," most believed that Lemann's written contributions added greatly to the value of the book. "Mr. Lemann combines arresting photographs of the 1940s with his own inspired detective work of the 1980s. . . . The images assault, caress, beckon, haunt," Peter Davis noted in the *New York Times Book Review* (July 31, 1983). "This would be enough to make an excellent book, but Mr. Lemann only begins with the photographs. The heart of *Out of the Forties* is in the stories he collects about some of the people in the pictures."

In *The Promised Land: The Great Black Migration and How It Changed America* (1991), the 1940s also featured prominently, in that this was the decade in which blacks living in rural areas of the South moved to northern urban centers in the hope of securing better lives for themselves and their families. Blacks moved north for a variety of reasons, but mainly because the mechanized cotton picker had rendered their jobs as sharecroppers obsolete. More than four million men and women migrated north between 1940 and 1970, forever changing the makeup of such large American cities as New York, Boston, the District of Columbia, Philadelphia, and Chicago. Despite their efforts and the subsequent development of a black middle class, many found themselves fairing no better in northern cities. Poverty, inadequate education, and racism were among the factors that relegated large numbers of blacks to crumbling neighborhoods rampant with crime. Many descendants of these migrant families live in an abject state not unlike that from which their parents or grandparents escaped.

The Promised Land received rave reviews and made Lemann a best-selling author. In *Library Journal* (February 15, 1991), Thomas J. Davis "highly recommended [it] for all collections on contemporary America." Richard Lacayo, reviewing the book for *Time* (March 11, 1991), asserted that "*The Promised Land* is an important cornerstone in the effort to understand why so many travelers . . . never reached the land of milk and honey." Seymour Martin Lipset, in the *Times Literary Supplement* (May 31, 1991), wrote that "On very rare occasions, a book can turn a nation's social and political outlook around. This one is good enough to do it. Much of Lemann's account reads like a novel; or rather like a series of short stories, which enable the reader to understand the lives of the characters in them."

Lemann's most recent book, *The Big Test: The Secret History of the American Meritocracy* (1999), looks at the history of the SAT, examining how this test became a central part of the college application process and created a new "meritocracy" in the U.S. The SAT's story begins in the 1930s with James Bryant Conant and Henry Chauncey, president and dean, respectively, of Harvard University. Both men were intent on reforming the process by which students were admitted to America's top universities, whose student bodies had, up until that time, been limited to the sons and daughters of America's upper class. Conant and Chauncey wanted to seek out students of varying races and social and economic backgrounds from all over the United States to give "flux to the social order." In order to accomplish their goal, they turned to standardized testing, and in doing so, Lemann argues, unwittingly lead to the establishment of a new elite that, while different from the old, has not proven more equitable. In an interview for the *Atlantic Monthly* (October 6, 1999, on-line), Lemann outlined what he believed to be the inherent flaw in standardized testing: "The SAT is intended to do a very specific thing in regard to educational opportunity, which is to make great opportunities available to the very high scorers—the top one percent of the distribution. And it has done that. But it hasn't done that much to provide educational opportunity for the other 99 percent. People who are in the top one percent tend to think, *Well, it worked for me, so it must be working for everybody.* Serving the top one percent is not in itself the sign of a good system that provides opportunity for all." Lemann also describes the evolution of the Educational Testing Service, which administers the SAT, and the lives of a number of college students in the late 1960s and early 1970s whose paths were changed by the opportunities the SAT opened to them. He also discusses the development of the state-run University of California system, and the rise of affirmative action, which was designed in part, Lemann argues, to compensate for the SAT's deficiencies. He concludes by calling for a new system of college admissions in the U.S., one that would rest on a student's mastery of a nationally mandated high-school curriculum.

Many critics praised *The Big Test*, including Mary Carroll, who wrote in *Booklist* (August 19, 1999): "Lemann . . . infuses a potentially dry topic with life and energy by capturing the commitment of the crusaders who made testing an essential rite of passage and by clarifying their crusade's internal contradictions and the unintended consequences those contradictions produced." Erin Kelly, in *Fortune* (October 25, 1999), concurred, calling *The Big Test* a "fascinating and thoughtful new book." Kelly went on, however, to say that "Lemann's description of this transformation—the rise of the SAT and the fall of the WASP—in the first part of the book is eye-opening stuff. But he runs into trouble when he gets past the history and into the implications. The breadth of his reporting is wonderful, but he sometimes stretches too far when he tries to explain a vast swath of post-war U.S. social history—the development of the public university system in California, the debate over affirmative action in college admissions, and the rise of Ronald Reagan—through the SAT lens." Christopher Lehmann-Haupt was far more harsh in his assessment when he wrote in the *New York Times* (October 4, 1999, on-line), "If the SAT's, while being unfair, do accurately predict academic performance, as Mr. Lemann admits, how should colleges accommodate those who perform less well on them and are admitted through affirmative action? . . . Lemann doesn't explore such questions. He just assumes that readers will share his outrage at the present system."

Nicholas Lemann is married to the editor Judith Shulevitz. He has two sons, Alexander and Theodore, from his previous marriage to Dominique A. Browning, which ended in divorce. In addition to his work as an author, he has co-edited *Inside the System* (1979) with Charles Peters.

—C. M.

SUGGESTED READING: *Atlantic Monthly* (on-line) Oct. 7, 1999; *Booklist* (on-line) Aug. 19, 1999; *FEED* (on-line); *Fortune* p68+ Oct. 25, 1999; *Library Journal* p1560 Aug. 1981, p1256 June 15, 1983, p207 Feb. 15, 1991; *New Republic* p31 June 13, 1981, p35 May 27, 1991; *New York Times* (on-line) Oct. 4, 1999; *New York Times Book Review* p9 July 31, 1983; *People Weekly* p187+ Nov. 22, 1999; *Time* p72 Mar. 11, 1991; *Times Literary Supplement* p5 May 31, 1991; *U.S. News & World Report* p16 Oct. 25, 1999

SELECTED BOOKS: nonfiction—*The Fast Track: Texans and Other Strivers*, 1981; *Out of the Forties*, 1983; *The Promised Land: The Great Black Migration and How It Changed America*, 1991; *The Big Test: The Secret History of the American Meritocracy*, 1999; as co-editor—*Inside the System* (with Charles Peters), 1979

David Plakke

Leyner, Mark

Jan. 4, 1956– Novelist; short-story writer

When the novelist and short-story writer Mark Leyner submitted his first story for a college creative-writing class, the teacher, Alan Lelchuk, had some words of advice for him. As Leyner recalled in an interview with William Grimes for the *New York Times Magazine* (September 13, 1992), "He told me, 'This is a real tour de force, but you can't keep it up beyond one story.' I took that as some sort of challenge that I still feel." Lelchuk's reservations were understandable; Leyner's prose was bombastic and densely packed with references to popular culture. "The goal was to make every sentence seem like a tabloid headline, so to speak," he explained to Grimes, "to turn up the volume on every sentence, to deliver a constant surprise." Proving Lelchuk wrong, Leyner has, in fact, maintained the frenetic style of his writing throughout three novels, a short-story collection, and a volume of essays, and has become, according to Henry Alford for the *Village Voice* (October 14, 1997), "one of our preeminent comic postmodernists." Grimes aptly described Leyner's unique style: "The writing comes in short, disconnected takes, slices of contemporary experience that add up to a strange, unsolicited pizza-with-everything delivered at top speed. The language is rhetorical, mingling the public, pop-culture voices of hard-boiled detective fiction, television news, advertising, and public relations. The images, stitched together surrealistically, are cartoonish, violent, sexual, and scatological, with a rich store of arcane biological and medical information . . . Leyner is the poet laureate of information overload."

As several journalists have noted, Mark Leyner's life has been considerably tamer than his fiction. He was born on January 4, 1956 in Jersey City, New Jersey. His father, Joel Leyner, was a successful lawyer, and his mother, Muriel (Chasan) Leyner, worked as a real estate agent. As Joel Leyner's practice prospered, the family moved to the more affluent New Jersey suburbs of West Orange and Maplewood. With tongue in cheek, Leyner wrote for *Esquire* (November 1997), "[I began] hating my parents for not traumatizing me in any way that I could parlay into a big nonfiction best-seller. How they could have just blithely treated me with such abiding respect as a child I'll never understand. . . . No abuse, no beatings, no addictions, not even a teensy soupçon of incest—my God! What am I supposed to write about? Surely, a paradisiacal childhood is the cruelest hand an aspiring author can be dealt."

Leyner, always a voracious reader, avidly consumed books, newspapers, and magazines in search of interesting or amusing information, even as a child. In an interview with Eric Levin for *People* (April 24, 1995), Leyner said that he was then in the process of simultaneously reading a guide to hair coloring, a book on capital punishment, and a biography of the rock band Sonic Youth, as well as issues of *Corrections Today*, *Gastroenterology*, and *Packaging World*. "One thing people like about my work," Leyner explained, "is the surprise of it, that your expectations are confounded at every turn. To give the reader that experience, I have to have a similar experience writing. So I try not to get habituated to any one kind of reading. . . . One of the joys of life is being shocked and amazed. . . . "

In high school Leyner read everything from the Beat writers, such as William Burroughs and Jack Kerouac, to the romantic poets. Inspired by his favorite authors, he tried to cultivate the image of a rebellious outsider, but classmates have reported that he was actually quite popular. Leyner wrote a regular column in his high-school newspaper and, exhibiting a touch of the egomania later displayed by some of his fictional characters, insisted that his byline be printed larger than everything except the paper's masthead. In his junior year he ran for vice president of the student body, using sensational campaign tactics that nevertheless resulted in his losing by one vote. After the election Leyner convinced friends to fabricate an anonymous letter by a student who guiltily confessed that he had voted twice for the other candidate. The letter worked, and a re-vote was ordered. Ironically, Leyner lost again, this time by a wider margin. During his teens Leyner formed a rock band that practiced in his parents' basement, and his continued love of rock music has greatly influenced his writing. "There's an unmodulated volume and intensity to [rock] which is not supposed to be a part of writing," Leyner told Jonathan Bing for *Publisher's Weekly* (March 6, 1995). "I work endlessly on these sentences because I'm really after that unmodulated intensity." Leyner wrote several poems while still in high school and would eventually have one, which he dedicated to the singer Tina Turner, published in *Rolling Stone*.

After graduating from high school, Leyner spent nearly a year living on a kibbutz in Israel and traveling through Europe. He then enrolled at Brandeis University, in Waltham, Massachusetts, where he studied with Alan Lelchuk. At Brandeis Leyner turned his focus from poetry to prose, though he strove to maintain the lingual concentration of verse in his work. Graduating from Brandeis in 1977, he went on to the writing program at University of Colorado at Boulder and received an MFA in 1979.

After finishing graduate school, Leyner undertook a series of jobs. First, he waited tables in a restaurant, where he met his future wife, Arleen Portada. The two of them then started a cleaning business together, and Leyner would often compose pieces in his head while vacuuming. In Hoboken, New Jersey, Leyner served briefly as an editor of the *Hoboken Reporter*, a weekly newspaper. In 1981 he was hired by the Panasonic Company in New Jersey to write advertising copy and also taught part-time at both Brooklyn College and Jersey City State College. Later, he became a copywriter for a medical advertising agency, Falcone & Associates, a job that he often found amusing. "Watching a client's face light up," Leyner explained to Bing, "because you said 'the greatest balloon angioplasty catheter tips ever,' and they know that no one's ever put it that way—there's something sublimely ridiculous about it."

At the University of Colorado Leyner had become involved with the Fiction Collective, an alliance of experimental writers dedicated to publishing writing overlooked by the mainstream presses. The Fiction Collective published Leyner's first major work in 1983, a collection titled *I Smell Esther Williams*. The volume contained 26 pieces, including short stories, a five-scene play, and dialogue sketches. Although Leyner has expressed discomfort with this early effort, calling it "nakedly derivative," the book received good reviews and became an underground hit among college students, selling 3,000 copies. In *American Book Review* (March–April 1994), as reprinted in *Contemporary Literary Criticism* (1996), Charlotte M. Meyer wrote, "The stories are finally *about* language: they are full of unheard-of associations, mixed metaphors by the cascading streamful, fantastic transmogrifications of the familiar into the strange, lists of disparate items held together in newly-invented categories, distortions in space and time. . . . The book is very rich."

Leyner continued to work for Falcone & Associates, composing pieces in his head while driving to work and then rushing to his desk to type them out before he forgot them. Now that he was out of academia and working in advertising, Leyner grew impatient with what he saw as the elitist, anti-commercial stance of the writers of the Fiction Collective and parted company with the group. "It is the responsibility of writers to keep people in the fold," he told Grimes. "If you don't want people to abandon literature, then write books that will engage readers. It's not enough to complain about dumb kids who watch TV all the time." Leyner began to enjoy widespread recognition as a writer who could speak to the members of the "MTV generation," because of his familiarity with their language and nonlinear mode of thinking. "All our attention spans have been affected by the grammar of television," Leyner said to Trish Hall for the *New York Times* (June 10, 1990). "It's not something I bemoan. We live in an age of dense, fast information."

In 1988 Larry McCaffrey, an English professor at San Diego State University, included Leyner's "i was an infinitely hot and dense dot" in a special cyberpunk edition of the *Mississippi Review* that he was guest editing. McCaffrey told Hall that his students loved Leyner's writing. "It speaks to them, somehow, about this weird milieu they're swimming through," McCaffrey said. After appearing in the *Mississippi Review*, Leyner's story was excerpted in *Harper's Magazine*, and a contract with Harmony Books soon followed. Leyner's first novel, *My Cousin, My Gastroenterologist*, was published by the company in 1990. The novel was so offbeat that critics even debated whether it should rightly be called a novel. Certainly, it did not follow a traditional plot line. Jonathan Yardley wrote for the *Washington Post* (June 27, 1990), "What ties *My Cousin, My Gastroenterologist* together is neither character nor plot but the author's own wry, irreverent intelligence." Some of the characters who make appearances in the novel—and then exit like participants in a vaudeville act—include a kids' show host named Big Squirrel, an octogenarian woman with the body of a male Olympic swimmer, a swarm of lovesick mosquitos flying through Manhattan in search of human genitals, and a girl with a brain the size of the Houston Astrodome.

The novel was well reviewed, and critics found in Leyner's hyper-kinetic prose an analogy for the fast-paced chaos of contemporary life. "By putting an odd spin on the mundane," Yardley wrote, "by twisting the ordinary into the improbable, Leyner at once ridicules and illuminates the preposterous juxtapositions of modern life—which is to say that, at a certain level, Leyner makes a great deal of sense." *My Cousin, My Gastroenterologist* sold approximately 18,000 copies in its first two years, which was considered a lot for an "experimental" writer such as Leyner.

His success, coupled with his experience in advertising, provided the theme of his next novel, *Et Tu, Babe*, which was narrated by an egomaniac named, not coincidentally, Mark Leyner. "I wondered," Leyner told Grimes, "what happens when the narratives of our lives are refracted through the language of advertising and celebrity." The novel begins with Leyner, a full-fledged celebrity writer, living in a stucco mansion protected by mines. Beautiful women, such as Sonia Braga, Elle Macpherson, and Claudia Schiffer, rhapsodize about Leyner's muscular body. Reviewers gush, and one writes that after Leyner's (fictional) play, "Varicose Moon," "I think it will be unnecessary for playwrights to write any new plays for some time now: 'Varicose Moon' should suffice. In fact, I think it would be vulgar for playwrights to burden the public with their offerings given the creation of this coruscating master work." Leyner dolls show up in toy stores, and Leyner cartoons appear on TV. A crystal bottle of Team Leyner perfume sells for $3,500. Soon Leyner is swept away by his own celebrity. At the writing workshops he teaches, he employs a "phalanx of bionic elderly bodyguards" who attempt to assassinate any potential young rivals. By the end of the novel, Leyner has mysteriously vanished, but the public is invited to call 1-800-T-Leyner to hear "an exhortatory message from Mark Leyner to his fans recorded in the heroic hours before his disappearance!"

Michiko Kakutani, writing for the *New York Times* (October 13, 1992), lost patience with the book: "While *Et Tu, Babe* attests to Mr. Leyner's vitality as a writer—his inventiveness, irreverence, and shrewd ability to satirize the wretched excesses of a society obsessed with fame—a little bit goes a very long way," she wrote. In *New York Newsday* (September 27, 1992) Richard Gehr wrote, "As fractured as an evening spent foraging anxiously through 72 channels, *Et Tu, Babe* runs the risk of glossing everything and revealing nothing. The non-stop yucks are justified, however, by the author's awe-inspiring control and formidable comic timing."

Despite such mixed reviews the book enjoyed some popularity. After it was released, Leyner appeared on *Late Night with David Letterman* and was featured on the cover of the *New York Times Magazine*. He was now able to support himself entirely with his fiction writing, along with freelance articles he wrote for *Time*, the *New York Times*, the *New Yorker*, and *Esquire*. In 1995 he published a collection of writings, primarily satirical essays reprinted from these publications, called *Tooth Imprints on a Corn Dog*. In "The (Illustrated) Body Politic," senators exhibit their power and political connections with colorful tattoos. In "Oh, Brother" Leyner investigates a pair of twins who kill their parents after becoming convinced that their innocuous behavior could only be concealing an underlying and potentially threatening abnormality. In "Eat at Cosmo's" Leyner proposes inserting product endorsements into classic literature: Shakespeare's phrase "a gap in nature" would thus become "The Gap in nature."

Michiko Kakutani wrote for the *New York Times* (March 7, 1995), "While some of these pieces are laugh-out-loud funny, they tend to have the emotional afterlife of a mayfly. In fact, in sending up our appearance-mad society, Mr. Leyner has consciously or unconsciously created pieces that echo the very culture he intends to spoof: pieces that are clever and amusing and willfully superficial." Nancy Jo Sales, however, reviewing the book for *People* (April 24, 1995), commended Leyner's sharp satire. "How do you spoof a world that has become a parody of itself?" she wrote. "In *Corn Dog*, Leyner . . . confirms that he is the American writer best suited for this daunting task."

According to Henry Alford, writing for the *Village Voice* (October 14, 1997), Leyner's next book was promoted by his publisher as his "first 100 percent BONA FIDE NOVEL—story, characters, everything!" Indeed, *The Tetherballs of Bougainville* (1997) does follow a plot line of sorts. The protagonist, again named Mark Leyner, is a teenaged writer slated to win an award given to the author of the best screenplay by a student at Maplewood Junior High School, a prize worth $250,000 per year for life. The only catch is that he has not written the screenplay yet and must do so by the next day. Meanwhile, his father, a PCP addict accused of killing a mall security guard with a Cuisinart blender and a Teflon-coated ice-cream scoop, is scheduled to be executed, but is so accustomed to toxins that the lethal injection doesn't kill him. One of the officials present at the attempted execution is a beautiful female warden with whom Leyner strikes up a torrid relationship. The first portion of the book is the narrative of these situations, while a second portion takes the form of the screenplay, "The Vivisection of Mighty Mouse, Jr.," that he ultimately submits for the award. An extended review of an imaginary movie featuring Leyner and his father on an island in the Solomon Sea comprises the third section.

Unlike some reviewers, Alford discerned a theme beneath Leyner's bizarre story: "The novel," he wrote, "is studded with reminders that, in the present, we are wholly reactive and instinctual, like PCP-addled beings, and that it is only in reflection that we are able to bring order to our lives. . . ." While Alford noted that Leyner "creates dazzlingly unique situations and knows how to mine them for their comic ore," he also wrote, "that we ultimately don't care about or become emotionally involved with his characters is testament to the limitations of his disjunctive and highly digressive style." In a more consistently positive review, Joanne Wilkinson wrote for *Booklist* (October 15, 1997), "Combining vitriolic humor with a heightened sense of the absurd . . . Leyner turns in his funniest, most inventive novel yet." Mike Musgrove, however, concurred with Alford that Leyner's comic routine was wearing thin. He wrote for the *Washington Post* (Oct. 27, 1997), "It's a brilliant spectacle but, lacking any human emotion whatsoever, it's starting to feel a little empty."

Leyner currently lives in New Jersey with his second wife, Mercedes, and their daughter, Gabrielle, who was born in 1993. In 2000 he collaborated on a screenplay for the gritty ABC television show "Wonderland," which was set in the psychiatric ward of a New York City public hospital.

—*P. G. H.*

SUGGESTED READING: *Esquire* p60+ Nov. 1997; *New York Times* 1 p46 June 10, 1990, C p17 Oct. 13, 1992; *New York Times Book Review* p14 Sep. 27, 1992; *New York Times Magazine* p35+ Sep. 13, 1992, with photo; *People* p27+ Apr. 24, 1995; *Publishers Weekly* p44+ Mar. 6, 1995; *Village Voice* p7 May 8, 1990, p67 Oct. 14, 1997, with photo; *Washington Post* B p2 Jun. 27, 1990

SELECTED BOOKS: short-story collections—*I Smell Esther Williams*, 1983; novels—*My Cousin, My Gastroenterologist*, 1990; *Et Tu, Babe*, 1992; *Tooth Imprints on a Corndog*, 1995; *Tetherballs of Bougainville*, 1997

Lipsyte, Sam

1968– Novelist; short-story writer

Sam Lipsyte has made a name for himself by writing about unusual characters in bizarre situations. In his first book, a short-story collection entitled *Venus Drive* (2000), the author explores the seedier side of life—with a twist: a drug dealer saws off part of his thumb and gives it to his mother; an addict deals with his mother's death by mixing her ashes with his morphine; a peep-show customer assaults his comatose sister. Lipsyte's first novel, *The Subject Steve* (2001), is a black comedy that looks at the life of a man seemingly dying of complete boredom with modern life.

In an autobiographical statement for *World Authors 1995-2000*, Lipsyte writes: "I was born in 1968 in New York City. We moved to a town in New Jersey called Closter when I was two, and that's where I grew up. My father was (and is) a sports columnist for the *New York Times* who wrote several non-fiction books and a slew of novels for young adults. My mother had been a reporter at the *Times*, too. She later edited a feminist newspaper and published a novel. Our house was full of all kinds of books and I spent most of my childhood reading indiscriminately. I think I started to write because I saw my mother and father giving each other manuscripts to edit and I wanted in on the action. My parents never pressured me but they seemed pleased that I was interested. I guess it's somewhat akin to all of those ballplayers who are the children of ballplayers. You are around it, you are around people who understand it. The pleasure of language was cultivated in our house. We all talked too much.

"I was a fat and self-conscious kid. I was very dreamy. I wasn't quite what you'd call a geek. I lifted weights and was a shot-putter and could fend for myself, but I remember feeling pretty disconnected from things, even when I participated. I had a few great teachers but mostly I holed up in my room with rock records and novels. In my early teens I started reading Robert Stone and Thomas McGuane. Stone's intensity and McGuane's sentences were beacons for me. I read a lot of so-called classics in school but with the exception of *Moby Dick*, the nineteenth century novels tended to bore me. I'll chalk it up to callow youth.

"When I went to Brown University I already knew I wanted to be a writer. I had a very quaint idea of what this was, however, and I had a rude awakening at school. The author was apparently dead. The artist seemed like some kind of vestigial organ, or else looked upon as a discomfiting necessity. I know this is a foolish notion of literary theory, but I was certainly a fool. I read the deconstructionists and took some writing workshops but never felt we were getting to anything. I did read some great fiction—Kafka, Beckett, Bernhard, Elkin, DeLillo, Hannah. They formed me anew. This was brilliant, funny stuff. Scared the hell out of me. By the time I was graduated I'd become appropriately disenchanted with my juvenilia. I started a punk band with some equally disaffected classmates. We lived and played in Providence and New York for a few years. We toured the South a bit. We also did a lot of hard drugs, so that was the end of that.

"I'd been sending the occasional story to Gordon Lish at *The Quarterly*, mostly for his wonderful form rejection letters, which would often have something encouraging at the bottom: 'Keep going!' Finally he accepted a few stories and invited me to his class in New York. I'd heard all the horror stories about his seminar but I jumped at the chance. I was pretty hollowed out by things at that point and I guess I craved the rigor. I was working a crappy job and living at home with my mother. She'd been diagnosed with cancer and it was a very strange time, a very heightened time. I was discovering myself while watching my mother waste away.

"What Lish did, besides teach us how to make sentences, was to help us see ourselves as people who write, rather than people who want to be writers. The distinction was crucial. I'd felt stymied by years of expectations but now I realized that none of it mattered. I worked at an online magazine and wrote my first book at night. *Venus Drive*, a collection of stories, came out in 2000. It's a very autobiographical book, as I guess a lot of first books are, but my concerns were fairly formal when I wrote it. Somebody said to me, 'Well, you solved the problems raised by metafiction by just forgetting about them,' but I don't think that's quite true. I was painfully aware of what I was ignoring. I was after something else, something apart from both a self-reflexive literature of ideas and the typical American workshop story. Ideas, characters, plots, they may all be in evidence, but that's not why we read fiction, or at least it's not why I read it. I want to be enthralled by a lingual event.

"My first novel, *The Subject Steve*, came out in 2001. Its stance is perhaps more strictly absurdist than the stories, and it's certainly a far cry from autobiography, but I see similarities. There's death's governance again, and our futile attempts to connect with each other and our world in its shadow. I wrote both books with comedy in mind, though that's often lost on people. They tell me it's all so dark. I think that's a marketing term at this point. I don't know what dark means. I know I don't write to communicate, or express myself. I write from compulsion. It's like that man who built the Watts towers. [The towers to which Lipsyte refers are located in Los Angeles, California. A series of nine steel structures, the largest almost 100 feet in height, they are heavily decorated with found objects.] Why did he spend all those years with pieces of metal and glass shards and bottle caps? When they asked him he said, 'You gotta make something they don't got 'em in this world.'"

In *Venus Drive* Lipsyte presents stories of down-and-out men—addicts, drug dealers and peep-show afficionados—who may know the difference between right and wrong, but have grown too callous to care. The author gives the reader little reason to admire these characters, and critics have been divided over the merits of such tales. James Hannaham, reviewing the collection for the *Village Voice* (June 14–20, 2000, on-line), wrote: "It's something of a testament to Lipsyte's ability that in wry, stripped-down language, he captures brief flashes of [his characters'] complex, addled humanity, and smashes a window into their hopelessness for a punchy and cinematic, if bleak, read." Monica Drake, writing for the *Portland Mercury* (August 24–30, 2000, on-line), opined: "For the most part [*Venus Drive*] reads as show and posturing. It's hard to sell a first story collection, and hard to distinguish oneself from all the other clamoring new authors. Sam Lipsyte wants to be recognized as a bad ass. He's following in the wake of [John] Fante [and Charles] Bukowski . . . each one dropping the softer elements of the one before in an effort to break new ground." In December 2000 the editors of the *Village Voice Literary Supplement* named *Venus Drive* one of their 25 favorite books of the year.

The protagonist of Lipsyte's first novel, *The Subject Steve*, has an unknown illness with symptoms that correlate suspiciously with those of complete boredom. Although his doctors can't figure out exactly what's wrong with him, they name his condition Goldfarb-Blackstone Preparatory Extinction Syndrome (after themselves), and assure him that the disease will eventually kill him. When Steve discovers that his doctors are frauds, he decamps to a clinic in upstate New York run by an extorture expert known only as Heinrich of Newark. When Heinrich's treatments also prove fruitless, Steve heads west to join a cult. In a critique for *Publisher's Weekly* (August 13, 2001), a reviewer noted that the author "has come up with an intriguing experimental concept, but the absence of coherent, linear plot means the commentary must be particularly sharp and interesting, and much of what Lipsyte offers is rambling, self-absorbed and at times just plain annoying." Michael Schaffer, in a review for the *Washington Post* (September 23, 2001), wrote, "[Lipsyte] is a funny guy. His dialogue lands with a terse deadpan that makes up in zip what it shuns in realism. And while the wacky postmodern satire is pretty well-worn territory, Lipsyte still manages to land some zingers." He continued, "But despite the funnies—or maybe because of them—[the] novel quickly begins to grate. The acid he pours over contemporary culture doesn't just strip away pretension; it strips away any motivation to care about Steve's allegedly short life." Schaffer concluded, "Funny and mean, in this case, are just not enough: At novel's end, you're no more certain than the doctors about just what's eating Steve—or the world around him."

Sam Lipsyte lives in Astoria, in the New York City borough of Queens.

—C. M.

SUGGESTED READING: *Portland Mercury* (on-line) Aug.24–30, 2000; *Publishers Weekly* p284+ Aug. 13, 2001; *Salon* (on-line) July 13, 2000; *Village Voice* (on-line) June 14–20, 2000; *Washington Post Book World* p7 Sep. 24, 2001

SELECTED BOOKS: *Venus Drive*, 2000; *The Subject Steve*, 2001

Jean-Regis Roustan/Courtesy of The Overlook Press

Littell, Robert

Jan. 8, 1935– Suspense novelist

"If Robert Littell didn't invent the American spy novel, he should have," declared the best-selling author Tom Clancy in a statement quoted on the cover of Littell's most recent book, *The Company* (2002). An epic Cold War thriller, *The Company* mixes fact and fiction to deliver a sprawling history of the Central Intelligence Agency (CIA) from the 1950s to the 1990s. At almost 900 pages in length, it is perhaps the longest spy novel ever written, and is, according to Otto Penzler in a review posted on the Amazon Booksellers Web site, "destined to become the definitive novel about the CIA." The covert machinations of the American intelligence organization, as well as the KGB (its Soviet counterpart), provide the material for the bulk of Littell's more than a dozen novels, the first of which is *The Defection of A. J. Lewinter*, published in 1973 and now regarded as a classic of the genre. In such novels as *The October Circle* (1976), *Mother Russia* (1978), *The Amateur* (1981), and *The Sisters* (1986), Littell established himself as a master of black comedy and mischievously complicated plot lines that mirrored the "byzantine" workings of the spy rings he depicts. A *New York Times* critic labeled him "the American [John] le Carré," referring to the British author of *The Spy Who Came In From the Cold*—a comparison which Joseph Finder, writing for the *Washington Post* (August 11, 1997), found to be largely accurate: "They're both clever, literate and graceful writers—but le Carré's novels, whether they 'transcend' the genre or not, take the conventions seriously, while Littell is deftly playful with them. Everything about his stories, from plot to characterization, from the first line to the payoff, is infused with irony and mordant wit."

In an interview with Nancy Beth Jackson for the *New York Times* (February 2, 1986), Littell confessed that most of his knowledge regarding the inner workings of intelligence agencies came from reading—especially the memoirs of former CIA and KGB agents. His only personal experience was conversations with dissident writers in Moscow when he was working for *Newsweek* in the 1960s. The inspiration for his novels, he explained, came from newspaper headlines. "To get readership, you have to deal with what people are familiar with. East-West conflict is the gist of the front page, what consumes the world. A well-written novel in which the characters are well developed is exciting to read but also offers a supplement to the front pages." When reading his novels, it becomes clear what Littell means when he describes the East-West conflict of the Cold War as "an unwitting conspiracy" between the two intelligence communities against American and Soviet citizens. "I have an exaggerated view, I admit," he said to Jackson, "But it's not that far off."

Robert Littell, the grandson of Russian immigrants, was born in the New York City borough of Brooklyn, on January 8, 1935. He attended Alfred University in New York and received his B.A. in 1956. After graduating, he joined the U.S. Naval Reserve and eventually earned the rank of lieutenant junior grade. In the navy Littell learned about code-breaking, which would later figure heavily in his fiction writing. "No account of my education would be complete without mentioning my four years in the Navy," Littell remarked in an interview for the "Meet the Writers" feature of the Barnes & Noble Web site. "I served on board the USS John R. Pierce (DD753) where I was, variously, the ship's navigator, antisubmarine warfare officer, communications officer and deck watch officer. These years were extremely formative for me." Upon his release, however, Littell was dismayed to find that the experience had not prepared him for a career. "I used to say that the only thing I could do at the age of 24 was hunt submarines," Littell told Herbert R. Lottman for *Publishers Weekly* (April 29, 2002).

Littell landed his first job as a journalist for a newspaper in Long Branch, New Jersey, where he was made the bureau chief of a nearby town—"chief because I was the only one in the office," Littell remarked to Lottman. He later moved to the United Press, then *Newsday*, and finally to *Newsweek*, where he served as an Eastern European and Soviet-affairs editor. While at *Newsweek*, he took a leave of absence to drive from France through Eastern Europe to the Soviet Union, and in the process he learned a great deal about the region. In 1967 he worked on the magazine's cover story commemorating the 50th anniversary of Russia's October Revolution, in which the Bolshevik Party, aiming for a socialist system, had led workers and peasants under the slogan, "All Power to the Soviets."

Littell then edited a collection of reports and testimonies, published by the Czechoslovak Academy of Sciences, Institute of History, detailing the events of August 1968, when armed forces from the USSR and its satellite countries entered Czechoslovakia to enforce a return to a Soviet-style political system. Published later that year under the title *Sedm prazskych dunu* (Seven Days in Prague) and translated into English as *The Czech Black Book*, the volume contains speeches, leaflets, eyewitness reports, newspaper articles, transcripts of radio broadcasts, official announcements and documents, and notes from high-level clandestine meetings. A reviewer for *Choice* (May 1969) called *The Czech Black Book* "a remarkably detailed and extensively documented history . . . [that] can stand on its own as a unique tribute to the spirit of Czechoslovak democracy and socialist humanism."

In 1970 Littell left *Newsweek* to devote his time to writing fiction. He moved to France with his wife and two young sons, and in 1973 he completed his first novel, *The Defection of A. J. Lewinter*. "[My agent] fired me," Littell told Lottman of his experience in submitting the manuscript. "And then a cousin of mine in publishing read [it] and suggested I go back to my job at *Newsweek*." Undaunted, Littell procured a new agent, and Houghton Mifflin agreed to publish the book.

Reviews of the novel were strong. "[This] is an unromantic spy thriller, illuminated by flashes of wit and darkened by shadows of treachery," H. C. Velt wrote for *Library Journal* (January 1, 1973). "The game is deception and doublecross, embellished with stupefying inefficiency on both sides. Interesting and beautifully done." Lewinter is an American scientist who has labored for years in a relatively low-level position in the military-industrial complex. At an academic conference in Tokyo, Japan, Lewinter contacts the KGB and informs them that he has U.S. military secrets in his possession and wants to defect. The Russians, however, doubt his sincerity, and the Americans aren't sure exactly what Lewinter knows. Lewinter finds himself in the middle of a prickly contest of intelligence and counter-intelligence—a morass of treachery that blindly steamrolls over friendships and loyalties. "The whole point, beautifully made, is the futility of the intricate espionage game whose histrionics, however fascinating, are duplicated in kind on each side of the Iron Curtain," O. L. Bailey commented in the *Saturday Review of the Arts* (March 1973). "What [the author] tells us about the future, defections and freedoms here and there, is thought-provoking and unique." The book won the Crime Writers Association's Golden Dagger award and an Edgar Allan Poe Award for best first novel.

The October Circle (1976) is about a group of Bulgarians—a celebrated magician, a popular circus dwarf, a former anti-Nazi partisan, a famous poet, an opera singer, and a champion cyclist who owns the world's speed record in the sport. When the Soviets invade Czechoslovakia, in 1968, the group decides to protest, but the Bulgarian bureaucracy delivers a fierce response, first suppressing any record of their actions, then assassinating the members themselves. "Littell writes with wit and sympathy, and he has a feel for the telling detail," Dennis Pendleton opined for *Library Journal* (November 15, 1975). "The tone throughout is one of gentle irony, just on the edge of black humor. It's a good novel, even though one comes to feel that ultimately it's neither black enough nor comic enough." Peter D. Zimmerman, in a review for *Newsweek* (January 19, 1976), praised the novel's "exotic setting, constantly surprising imagery and clockwork plot," adding that "Littell writes crisp, inventive entertainments disguised as thrillers. . . . [He] lightens the proceedings with accomplished artifice, sketching in the brightly colored world of Sofia cabaret society, serving up brittle banter, pulling a charming story out of his hat at one moment, introducing a droll character the next."

Littell's next novel, *Mother Russia* (1978), is a black comedy about an inventive hustler trying to survive in Moscow during the 1970s. Robespierre Isayevich Pravdin is a social deviant who sells information to American journalists and spends his time spraying graffiti and dodging police. His eccentric neighbor, who is known as Mother Russia, and a disguised KGB agent enlist him to destroy the reputation of a Nobel Prize–winning Soviet author—a crusade that rapidly escalates beyond Pravdin's control. "Littell has tackled the absurdities of the police state in his previous novels, but never more effectively than in this zany satire on the frustrations of contemporary Soviet life," James N. Baker wrote for *Newsweek* (July 3, 1978). "Littell perceives a foreign society with the piercing irony of an insider."

Despite positive reviews, sales of the novel were poor. Littell attributes this to the failure of his publisher, Harcourt Brace Jovanovich, to sufficiently promote the book. In financial difficulty, Littell was nearly forced to abandon the writer's life in France, but his next novel, *The Debriefing*, brought him the commercial success he needed to carry on.

The plot of *The Debriefing* (1979) is set in motion when Kulakov, a Soviet courier with a briefcase of classified documents chained to his wrist, places himself in the hands of the United States Embassy in Athens, Greece. Agent Stone, the head of an elite American intelligence agency, is in charge of debriefing the defector. Concerned that he may be a Soviet "plant," Stone travels to Russia to dig up information about Kulakov's past, and along the way he meets such intriguing characters as an 80-year-old Joseph Stalin look-alike who used to stand in for the Russian dictator at public events and now lives in retirement with his transvestite lover. "Littell plays his cards with clarity and elegance," Walter Clemons wrote in *Newsweek* (July 23, 1979). "I count it a definite plus that I was able to grasp the multiple final betrayals without having to flip backward through the book to find out who was who. Littell excels at lucid complication." Henri C. Veit, writing for *Library Journal* (July 1, 1979), called it "a superior espionage thriller, as smooth as cream and full of gloom." He concluded that the book was "riveting in spite of a pervasive use of the present tense, and the cynical switch at the end is brilliant."

Charlie Heller, the protagonist of *The Amateur* (1981), is a cryptologist for the Company—as the CIA is known to insiders—and in his spare time he uses his computer to try and discover a cryptogram in the works of Shakespeare that will reveal the author's "true identity." When Heller's girlfriend is taken hostage and murdered by international terrorists in West Germany, the grieving man goes to his superiors, who refuse to get involved. In his rage, Heller decides to hunt the killers himself. In possession of top-secret information, he blackmails the agency into training him as a field agent and sending him to Czechoslovakia, where he goes about obtaining his revenge. Although the CIA has decided to exterminate him, Heller manages to elude his pursuers, find new love, and meet someone who may know the answer to the Shakespeare conundrum.

Making reference to two masters of the genre, Michael Malone wrote for the *New York Times* (May 10, 1981), "*The Amateur* has a taut, chilling plot and a protagonist as memorable as one of Len Deighton's heroes or le Carré's George Smiley." He continued, "Acid etchings of agents and officials fill *The Amateur* with characterizations as graphic and incisive as [Littell's] evocation of Communist Prague." Anatole Broyard, writing for the *New York Times* (May 13, 1981), found the book to be "even better" than *The Debriefing* and *The Defection of A. J. Lewinter*. "While good suspense novels are usually cool and ironical, this one is remarkably warm-hearted. It has another irresistible appeal: its hero is an amateur in a world of professionals, which means that the book really pits us against them, all the professional thems in government everywhere." Littell also helped write the screenplay for a movie version of *The Amateur*, which was directed in 1981 by Charles Jarrott.

In *The Sisters* (1986), two male CIA operatives, Francis and Carroll, devise "a perfect crime"—the assassination of a head of state on a ceremonial visit, which will then be blamed on the Russians. To implement their plot, the duo—known within the agency as "the sisters Death and Night" in reference to a Walt Whitman poem—circuitously employ a Russian "sleeper" agent stationed in the U.S., who mistakenly believes he is under orders from the KGB. "About a third of the way into [*The Sisters*] it dawns on the reader what the author is really up to this time," Christopher Lehmann-Haupt wrote for the *New York Times* (January 30, 1986). "And it seems all at once so clever, outrageous and cynical that first your breath is taken away and then, when you remember it's only a story, you giggle. The giggle is embarrassing to confess, but I blame it completely on empathy with the mad, fascinating characters who populate this book." "I don't know of anyone who seems to have more fun spinning out complicated spy stories than Robert Littell," Peter Andrews wrote for the *New York Times* (February 2, 1986). "Mr. Littell has a good and properly cynical eye for the more outlandish aspects of covert operations as they are currently being practiced in Washington and Moscow. . . . Once again [he] delivers the goods in fine style."

The Revolutionist (1988), a fast-paced and ambitious tale set in Russia, spans the period from the October Revolution of 1917 to the death of Stalin, in 1953. The novel's protagonist, Alexander (Zander) Til, is a young, idealistic Russian immigrant living in New York City, where he and his friend Atticus Tuohy are on the run from the FBI. Together they leave for Russia in 1917 to participate in the Bolshevik coup. There Zander falls in love with Lili, a woman who is also dedicated to the cause. Soon the revolution they longed for begins to sour; Zander is arrested and interrogated, and Lili is executed. Zander survives to experience the harsh reality of Soviet industrialization and collectivization, as well as the terror of Stalin's rule. Walter Berkov called Littell "a first-rate storyteller" in the *Washington Post* (April 25, 1988). "He also [incorporates] elements of many types of novels: proletarian, political, adventure, spy and historical romance. . . . [The book has] the virtues of a crackerjack commercial novel, and it's written with passion and a vast knowledge of and sympathy for Russian suffering."

As the Soviet Union dissolved during the 1990s, Littell adapted his fiction to suit the times. *An Agent In Place* (1991) is set in Russia during the era of Mikhail S. Gorbachev's leadership, where *perestroika* (restructuring) and *glasnost* (openness) are disdained by hard-line operatives who long for a return to the old methods of coercion. Linda Barrett Osborne, writing for the *Washington Post* (December 15, 1991), asserted that the book was "all a thriller should be—intricately plotted, suspenseful, and convincing in its details of protocol and intrigue." In *The Visiting Professor* (1994), a famous Russian theorist accepts a teaching position at the Institute for Advanced Interdisciplinary Chaos-Related Studies in upstate New York, where he expects to find that "the streets are paved with Sony Walkmans," as quoted by Chris Petrakos in the *Chicago Tribune* (March 20, 1994). Instead, as Petrakos notes, he finds "a 23-year-old hairdresser named Occasional Rain who introduces him to dope, wild sex and environmental activism." For *Walking Back the Cat* (1996) Littell "gathered into an ambitious plot some traditional antagonists with names like Parsifal and La Gioconda," as James F. Clarity noted in the *New York Times* (August 3, 1997), "then added two disillusioned American gulf war veterans, . . . a pizza-chomping mafioso and a clan of casino-owning Apaches and set them all down in the New Mexico desert."

The idea for Littell's most recent novel, *The Company*, came from Peter Mayer, the head of Overlook Press. Mayer was already a fan of Littell's work when the pair met, in 1997, and he suggested that Littell write a multigenerational saga of the CIA. Littell enthusiastically crafted a 25-page proposal, for which the publisher offered a large advance. The outlay was recouped when only months later Mayer sold translation rights in six countries for about $600,000. Littell spent a year doing research—traveling to Russia, Eastern Europe, and Pakistan—and two years writing.

The Company begins during the night of September 28, 1978, when the Pope is mysteriously assassinated at the Vatican. The scene is only four pages long, and the mystery is not resolved for almost 700 more pages. After the brief Vatican scene, the novel's action flashes back to Berlin at the end of World War II, where the division of Germany into sectors by the victorious Allies has laid the foundations for the ensuing Cold War and the rise of the CIA. Littell follows two generations of characters—both fictional and historical—through the major events of the period, including the 1956 Hungarian Revolution; the 1961 Bay of Pigs invasion in Cuba; CIA involvement in Afghanistan during the mid-1980s; and the right-wing Soviet coup, in 1991. The main protagonists of the story are two fictional agents—Harry Torriti, known as the Sorcerer, and Jack McAuliffe, a handsome Yale graduate—but at the heart of the novel is a mole hunt led by the paranoid and obsessed real-life counterespionage chief James Jesus Angleton. Other historical figures who enter into the plot include: William F. Buckley Jr, G. Gordon Liddy, William Casey, and the U.S. presidents John F. Kennedy and Ronald Reagan.

"Using historic figures amplified by artfully drawn figments of his abundant imagination, Littell also dramatizes the internal feuds and cutbacks that left the CIA, already vulnerable on the moral knife-edge of espionage, barely able to meet the challenges of a changing world," Barbara Conaty wrote for *Library Journal* (December 1, 2001). "Gathering its power slowly, the novel accelerates as events become more and more familiar and current. This is a work of fiction, yet its scholarship and analysis are outstanding. Littell avoids the didactic in favor of wit, irony, and ambiguity." Patrick Anderson remarked in the *Washington Post* (April 14, 2002), "Besides being hugely entertaining, *The Company* is a serious look at how our nation exercised power, for good and ill, in the second half of the 20th century." He concluded, "Although its story plays out on a worldwide stage, it is at bottom a Washington novel, one of the most important I have ever read. . . . This is popular fiction at its finest."

Robert Littell lives in the southwest of France with his wife, Victoria, a painter, in an old manor house on a hill overlooking the Dordogne River. In the winters, the Littells travel to Santa Fe, Venice, Sienna, Rome, and Ireland, among other places. The author has spent several recent winters in Jerusalem, where his upcoming novel is set. Littell's interest in Eastern Europe and Russia has been passed on to his children: one son now lives in Moscow, the other in Prague. An amateur mountain climber, once or twice a year Littell enjoys a trek into the French Alps. "It is probably the only place," he remarked in the Barnes & Noble interview, "where I forget the faults of the book I am working on at the moment."

—A. I. C.

SUGGESTED READING: *Chicago Tribune* C p7 Mar. 20, 1994; *Library Journal* Jan. 1, 1973, Nov. 15, 1975, July 1, 1979, p173 Dec. 1, 2001; *Newsweek* p74 Jan. 19, 1976, p79 July 3, 1978, p77 July 23, 1979; *New York Times* VII p15 May 10, 1981, C p33 May 13, 1981, C p19 Jan. 30, 1986, VII p9 Feb. 2, 1986, VII p16 Aug. 3, 1997; *Publishers Weekly* p36+ Apr. 29, 2002; *Washington Post Book World* p7 Dec. 15, 1991, p1 Apr. 14, 2002

SELECTED BOOKS: *The Defection of A. J. Lewinter*, 1973; *The October Circle*, 1976; *Mother Russia*, 1978; *The Debriefing*, 1979; *The Amateur*, 1981; *The Sisters*, 1986; *The Revolutionist*, 1988; *Walking Back the Cat*, 1996; *The Company*, 2002

Mark Alice Durant/Courtesy of New Directions

Lleshanaku, Luljeta

(lool-YET-tah leh-sha-NAH-koo)

1968– Poet

"Luljeta Lleshanaku is a pioneer of Albanian poetry," Peter Constantine declared in his introduction to *Fresco: Selected Poetry of Luljeta Lleshanaku* (2002). "She speaks with a completely original voice, her imagery and language always unexpected and innovative. . . . We have in Lleshanaku a completely original poet." As the child of anti-Communist dissidents, Lleshanaku spent much of her life under Albania's strict Stalinist rule. However, since the emergence of democracy in the early 1990s, she has become one of the youngest and most well-regarded poets of her generation. Lleshanaku has produced four volumes of poetry over the last decade, and the collected work *Fresco* was recently translated for U.S. publication.

Luljeta Lleshanaku was born in Elbasan, Albania, in 1968, at a time of escalating turmoil in her nation's history. The Communist prime minister, Enver Hoxha, had been governing the People's Socialist Republic of Albania as a Stalinist regime since 1946; yet by 1968, he had broken ties with the Soviet Union (after Soviet Premier Nikita Krushchev began denouncing Stalin in the late 1950s) and had allied himself instead with Communist China's Chairman Mao Zedong. When Mao commenced his oppressive Cultural Revolution in 1966, Hoxha followed suit, launching a strict campaign to purge all non-Marxist elements from Albanian culture, particularly literature. As Constantine described in *Fresco*, "Poetry and prose were no longer to be tainted by: abstract humanism, anarchism, bourgeois objectivism, bureaucratism, conservatism, decadentism, ethnologism, folklorism, formalism, imperialism, individualism, intellectualism, mysticism, nihilism, patriarchalism, revisionism, or sentimentalism, to name a few." In addition, Hoxha banned numerous religious books—including the Old Testament, the New Testament, the Koran, the Talmud, and all Buddhist texts—and in 1967 declared Albania the world's first officially atheist nation. In this climate writers were often persecuted for producing what Hoxha's censors considered to be subversive works. Many prose writers turned to poetry "since it proved easier to follow the strict guidelines of Socialist Realism in the more concise forms of verse," as Constantine explained. For this reason, Albanian poetry actually began to flourish throughout the late 1960s and early 1970s, with poets enjoying a wide readership among miners, laborers, and factory workers, as well as educated professionals. Throughout Lleshanaku's childhood, poetry was widely available in books, magazines, leaflets, and on the radio. Yet, in 1972 the restrictions on content were further tightened. After Mao welcomed U.S. President Richard Nixon to China, Hoxha became disillusioned with China's commitment to Communism. In response, he further isolated Albania from the rest of the world, enforcing a near total moratorium on the circulation of foreign books. The poets who managed to survive during this period almost exclusively produced political verses extolling the virtues of Stalinist Albania.

Albania's political circumstances greatly strained Lleshanaku's childhood—a situation that was exacerbated by her family's own political background. Her maternal great-uncle had fought against the Communists in the years following World War II. After the Stalinists ascended to office, his entire family was sent to prison camp for five years. Later, when one of Lleshanaku's uncles tried to escape, the family was tortured. Lleshanaku's mother was only five years old when she was given electric-shock punishments. On Lleshanaku's paternal side, her family carried a similar political stigma. Her paternal grandfather had organized armed rebellions against the Stalinists taking power after the war. He was arrested and, with his family, spent many years in internment camps; he eventually died in prison. Because of the family's history, Lleshanaku's parents were severely restricted by Hoxha's government. Her father was condemned to work as a bricklayer, while her mother labored in a factory, making woolen filters for tractors. No member of the family was allowed to pursue higher education, hold political office, or even obtain a professional job of any prestige. Lleshanaku and her sister grew up essentially under house arrest. They were treated as outcasts in school and were refused any academic honors. When Lleshanaku was forbidden to enter college, she began working at a carpet factory—the only job the state would allow her to perform. In 1989 she secretly married Lazer Stani, who was then a respected journalist for the newspaper *Zeri i rinise*. When the state discovered the couple's marriage, they instructed the newspaper to issue Stani a strict ultimatum: He must either leave his job or his wife. Stani stayed with Lleshanaku and was promptly fired from *Zeri i rinise*. To find work Stani moved his family to Klloja, Albania—a small town north of Tirana, the capital city. There, he became a schoolteacher. During this time many citizens petitioned for Stani's reinstatement at the paper; to counter such efforts, the government spread a rumor that Lleshanaku and Stani had been killed crossing Albania's borders for refuge in Yugoslavia.

The couple spent several years in Klloja, and soon benefitted from dramatic political changes taking place in Albania in the early 1990s. Since Hoxha's death, in 1985, another Stalinist dictator, Ramiz Alia, had taken control of the People's Socialist Republic of Albania, but after more than a decade of complete isolation from rest of the world, the nation was disintegrating. Alia's dictatorship ended in December 1990, when his party consented to allow the existence of opposition parties. With the country's infrastructure and government crumbling, free elections were held in March 1992, and the Democratic Party won by a landslide. Party officials quickly moved to break from Albania's oppressive past, promising complete freedom for all citizens and an improved national economy.

Although Lleshanaku had been writing poetry for many years, the Communist regimes under Hoxha and Alia had suppressed her work. As the national poet Dritëro Agolli later confirmed, publishers had been forbidden from printing Lleshanaku's poetry. (Agolli had access to such information because he had headed the government's notorious literary censor, the Albanian Writers Union, for 20 years.) In 1992, with Albania's new emphasis on freedom of expression, Lleshanaku published her first book, *Sytë e Somnambulës* (The Sleepwalker's Eyes). Agolli wrote the collection's introduction. In 1994 she published *Këmbanat e Së Dielës* (Sunday Bells) and followed it, in 1996, with *Ysmëkubizëm* (Half-Cubism), for which she won the Eurorilindja Award for Poetry. While many poets of Lleshanaku's generation were composing overtly political poems attacking the precepts of Socialist Realism, she took a different approach. Constantine observed in *Fresco*, "One of the elements that distinguishes Luljeta Lleshanaku's poetry is the absence of direct social and political commentary. Her poetry's remarkable variety of themes, which avoids simplistic reactions to a terrible past and an unstable present and future, is perhaps one of the elements that makes her poems contemporary classics of world literature. . . . She speaks individually to her readers, the mark of a true poet able to transcend time and culture." In 1999, Lleshanaku published her fourth collection, *Antipastorale* (Anti-Pastoral). Though each of these volumes met with significant critical acclaim in Albania, none is currently available in the U.S.

In 2002 the American poet Henry Israeli edited and translated a collection of Lleshanaku's poems for U.S. publication. (He also relied on the assistance of 10 co-translators, including Lleshanaku and her sister, Albana.) *Fresco: Selected Poetry of Luljeta Lleshanaku* includes 57 poems from previously published works, plus several new poems. As Israeli described in the afterword, he did not organize the poems chronologically or thematically but rather "intuitively, using the poem 'Memory,' a philosophical rumination on memory real and memory historic, as a point of departure." That poem, which opens the collection, reads:

There is no prophecy, only memory.
What happens tomorrow
has happened a thousand years ago
the same way, to the same end—
and does my ancient memory
say that your false memory
is the history of the featherhearted bird
transformed into a crow atop a marble mountaintop?

Among poetry scholars and critics, *Fresco* was considered an important collection for exposing U.S. readers to one of Albania's most prominent contemporary poets. On the book jacket, the American poet Eliot Weinberger characterized Lleshanaku as "a young poet who seems to have been writing for a hundred years in a language that's only been around for a hundred years; an erotic lyricist in the ruins of a state." He continued, "Luljeta Lleshanaku is the real thing, and as unexpected as an oasis behind a mountain on the moon." While a contributor to the *Complete Review* (on-line) questioned the accuracy of the translation—the critique nonetheless concluded, "Still, the collection affords a glimpse of a largely unknown European culture, with Lleshanaku giving some sense of life there and how difficult it was for the individual to endure in such an environment. [The collection] offers a decent introduction to a clearly talented poet, despite the fact that her work has perhaps not quite broken through the immense barrier that is translation."

English translations of Lleshanaku's work have appeared in *Grand Street*, *Quarterly West*, *Seneca Review*, *Fence*, *Tin House*, *Modern Poetry in Translation*, *Anthology of American Verse & Yearbook of American Poetry 1997*, and *Visions–International*, for which Lleshanaku was awarded the 1996 Translation Award. Her poems have also been translated into German and French.

Although Albania's Socialist Party was returned to power in 1997, Lleshanaku has been able to continue writing her poetry freely. She was also able to pursue the college education she had been denied under Stalinist rule. In 1999 she was invited to participate in the International Writers Program at the University of Iowa, where she delivered a talk on "Albania Before and After the War in Kosovo." That same year she was granted residency at the MacDowell Colony, in New Hampshire. In addition to writing poetry, Lleshanaku has worked for the Albanian cultural magazine *Drita* and is currently editor in chief of *Zeri i rinise*. She writes essays and reviews, many of which she is publishing in an upcoming collection, and is translating John Ashbery's poems into Albanian.

Luljeta Lleshanaku currently resides in Tirana, with her husband, Lazer Stani, and daughter. When asked about the future of Albanian poetry, she told Israeli, according to his afterword, "Albanians have no shortage of things to write about and they need never look far to find a rich cultural heritage. But first, they must search inward—not to larger cultures or overarching ideologies—to find their inner rivers."

—K. D.

SUGGESTED READING: *The Academy of American Poets* (on-line); *The Complete Review* (on-line); *Publishers Weekly* p58 Feb. 25, 2002

SELECTED WORKS IN ENGLISH TRANSLATION: *Fresco: Selected Poetry of Luljeta Lleshanaku*, 2002

Michael Boutefeu/Getty Images

Loh, Sandra Tsing

Feb. 11, 1962– Novelist; nonfiction writer; performer

Sandra Tsing Loh's comic riffs on Generation X slackers in Southern California, as well as her own hilarious stories of growing up as the half-German/half-Chinese daughter of immigrants, have garnered her high praise in the media and a growing fan base. She began her career as a performance artist and musician but found her true calling—according to many observers—while writing a column in *Buzz* magazine about the unsettled lives of people her own age. Her first book, *Depth Takes a Holiday: Essays from Lesser Los Angeles* (1996), was a collection of those columns. She has since published two other nonfiction works, *Aliens in America* (1997) and *A Year in Van Nuys* (2001), as well as a novel, *If You Lived Here, You'd be Home by Now* (1997). Loh is also a radio commentator on KCRW, in Santa Monica, California, and on National Public Radio (NPR). She remains an active composer, musician, and performer.

Sandra Tsing Loh was born in Los Angeles, California, on February 11, 1962, the third and youngest child of recent immigrants to the United States. Her German mother, Gisela, came to the U.S. after Germany's defeat in World War II; her Chinese father, Eugene, arrived in 1948, after having been orphaned at the age of 12 and having lived in poverty in Shanghai. They met in the late 1950s, at the swimming pool on the California Institute of Technology's (Cal Tech) Pasadena campus, where Eugene was studying aerospace engineering.

Despite their differences in background and temperament (Loh's mother was extremely outgoing and gregarious, while her father was introverted and reserved), Eugene and Gisela fell in love and married. (Eventually, their differences drew them apart, and they divorced when their children were adults.) Growing up, Loh and her siblings had piano and ballet lessons and were taught to study hard, particularly in the sciences. Sandra expressed a childhood interest in painting, and continued painting through her college years. She also began composing music for the piano. She studied at Cal Tech, earning a bachelor of science degree, in physics, in 1983. She vacillated between following in her father's footsteps and becoming an aerospace engineer, and leaving the sciences and exploring her artistic side. After graduation she went to work for the Hughes Aircraft Company, designing computer programs for use with an infrared camera. She found this work unappealing, however, and soon quit her job. She went back to school to pursue her creative interests. "It was a very big issue," Loh recalled in an interview with the journalist Douglas Eby, archived on members.aol.com/douglaseby/sloh.html. "In our family, with our values, it was kind of a failure not to go on to your Ph.D. in physics. . . . I was the youngest in my family, but the first to break out of that, and it was all very shocking to everyone, and it looked like I was at the beginning of a tragic tumble into living as a street person."

From 1983 to 1989 Loh attended graduate classes, in English, at the University of Southern California. While there she took classes in playwriting and began doing performance art. In her first high-profile event, Loh played her musical compositions on a piano on the roof of a parking garage, near the Harbor Freeway in Los Angeles. "They said I had one-third of the amplification at a U2 concert," she told Dinitia Smith in the *New York Times* (July 24, 1996). "Cars were stalled in front of me. It was Labor Day weekend between 4 and 6 P.M. Some people had the experience of wondering if a radio was on and looking around."

Loh's stunt garnered her press coverage in the *Wall Street Journal*, *People Weekly*, *Gentlemen's Quarterly*, and *Glamour*. Johnny Carson even mentioned her in his *Tonight Show* monologue. Buoyed by this interest, she did another performance, entitled *Self Promotion*, in March 1988. During the performance Loh's assistant threw 1,000 dollar bills—each one autographed by Loh—over her as she played piano. (This idea was inspired by Loh's unwillingness to hire a publicist; she told her friend who had suggested the idea, "Why don't I take the money and throw it out the window!," as quoted by Smith.) A year later 1,000 people attended a concert at which Loh and a symphony orchestra played a concerto for fish spawning on a Malibu beach at midnight. In 1991 she composed and recorded an album, *Pianovision*, a collection of jazz music for piano.

In 1992 Loh got a job as a columnist for *Buzz*, a magazine based in Los Angeles. Some of her columns were collected in *Depth Takes a Holiday* (1996), an assortment of essays on the confused lives of the overeducated and underemployed in Los Angeles. The disaffected youth she describes complain about never dating anyone interesting, but spend their nights watching bad television shows and surfing the Internet. The collection was widely praised in the press. An anonymous reviewer for *Publishers Weekly* (March 25, 1996) noted, as excerpted in *Contemporary Authors* (1999): "Loh succeeds in making Generation X angst far more appealing and sympathetic than usual." In *Entertainment Weekly* (April 19, 1996), also as quoted in *Contemporary Authors*, Erica K. Cardozo wrote that "all the pieces are terrific: intimate, acerbic, . . . subtle and perspicacious—and really, really funny."

In 1996 Loh took her talents to the stage at New York City's Second Stage Theater, where she premiered her one-woman show, *Aliens in America*. The performance had three sections: one about her father's search for a Chinese wife after her mother's death; another describing a horrendous family vacation to Ethiopia, in 1969; and a final section on returning home after her first year in college, only to discover that she hadn't completely escaped her parents' influence. In his review of the show for the *New York Times* (July 20, 1996), Ben Brantley noted that "in the wake of all too many performance pieces about dysfunctional families and ethnic identities, Ms. Loh has at least managed to stake out an individual territory and style. She may be stranded in terra incognita, but the shape she has given it is her own." *Aliens in America* was published as a book, in 1997.

Loh's first novel, *If You Lived Here You'd Be Home by Now*, was published the same year. Her protagonist, a 30-year-old graduate student named Bronwyn Peters, struggles to balance her bohemian ideals with her desire for middle-class comforts. Her friends have all embraced a materialistic lifestyle while she pursues women's studies and her boyfriend, Paul, struggles to sell his screenplay. Just as Bronwyn and Paul began to explore a different lifestyle, the Los Angeles riots begin. The novel received mixed reviews. In *Booklist* (August 1997), as quoted in *Contemporary Authors*, Kevin Grandfield remarked that the book "resonates with . . . wit and incisive observations," and noted that it was "a quick, humorous read, with a good moral at the end." A reviewer for *Publishers Weekly* (July 28, 1997), also quoted in *Contemporary Authors*, concluded that the novel "holds more promise than what's delivered" and judged that Loh "never does lob the firebombs she so accurately aimed in her previous books."

Listed as nonfiction but reading more like a fictionalized memoir, *A Year in Van Nuys* (2001) introduces a neurotic writer, Sandra, who is suffering from a mid-life crisis, which manifests itself in an obsession about her eye bags and a burning envy of other people's achievements. When a degree of success finally does come her way, her own egotism propels her back to the neurotic mess she had been before. Overall, the book received solid praise. In the *New York Times Book Review* (September 2, 2001), Mark Athitakis remarked: "Pop culture, eye bags, therapists, life in Southern California: Loh isn't charting new frontiers in comedy here. But her gift is her ability to approach those subjects in a way that goes beyond cheap, hey-what's-up-with-that riffing."

In 1998 Loh returned to the stage to perform another one-woman show at Second City, *Bad Sex with Bud Kemp*. *Sugar Plum Fairy*, a solo stage comedy about a young girl who dreams of playing Clara in the *Nutcracker* Christmas ballet, premiered at the Seattle Repertory Theatre in November 2002. Loh also remains active as a musician and composer. She composed the score for and also performed in Jessica Yu's Academy Award–winning documentary, *Breathing Lessons: The Life and Work of Mark O'Brien* (1997), and is again collaborating with Yu for an HBO documentary about the Living Museum. She received a Pushcart Prize, for fiction, in 1995, and a MacDowell fellowship, in 1996.

On September 2, 1995 Loh married Mike Miller, a guitarist.

—C. M.

SUGGESTED READING: *Booklist* p1879 Aug. 1997; *Entertainment Weekly* p72 Apr. 19, 1996; *Mother Jones* p64+ Sep./Oct. 1997; *New York Times* C p11 July 20, 1996, C p9 July 24, 1996, E p7 May 6, 1998, E p10 June 12, 1998, C p6 Dec. 19, 1998, II p 29 Sep. 26, 1999; *New York Times Book Review* p19 Sep. 2, 2001; *People Weekly* p28+ July 29, 1996; *Publishers Weekly* p76 Mar. 25, 1996, p52+ July 28, 1997

SELECTED BOOKS: fiction—*If You Lived Here, You'd Be Home By Now*, 1997; nonfiction—*Depth Takes a Holiday*, 1996; *Aliens in America*, 1997; *A Year in Van Nuys*, 2001

Valerio Giannetti/University of Nebraska Press

Loy, Rosetta

May 15, 1931– Novelist; memoirist

The Italian novelist and memoirist Rosetta Loy has been celebrated in Europe for her seven novels, which have won literary prizes. Only one has been published in English translation: *The Dust Roads of Monferrato* (1990), translated by William Weaver, "crisscrosses 19th-century Piedmont—elegantly and swiftly," according to Joan K. Peters, writing in the *New York Times Book Review* (July 21, 1991). Loy's memoir, *First Words* (2000), translated by Gregory Conti, is a description of her almost idyllic childhood in Fascist Italy.

Rosetta Loy was born Rosetta Provera on May 15, 1931, the daughter of Evelina Di Ginolamo and Angelo Provera. Her father was an engineer, and she and her two siblings grew up in privileged middle-class surroundings. She graduated from the Instituto dell'Assuntione in 1950. In 1955 she married Guiseppe Loy, and the couple had four children.

La bicicletta (The Bicycle), a novel for which Loy won the Viareggio prize opera primo (for first books), was published in 1974. *Le strade di polvere* (1988) won the Campiello prize and the Viareggio prize and was translated into English by William Weaver as *The Dust Roads of Monferrato* in 1990. A historical saga set in the Piedmont region in northwest Italy, *The Dust Roads of Monferrato* follows the fortunes of four generations of descendants of "the Great Masten," a landowner who acquired "so many acres that he had to hire extra hands," as quoted from the novel by Joan K. Peters. He builds the grand family home at the end of the 18th century and remains in the story as a ghost, appearing during a flood in 1839. His son, il Giai, also returns after death, as an apparition who plays the violin. "Others among the dreamily evoked figures include a neighbor who uses her granddaughter's powers of attraction to gain young lovers for herself; a bevy of impoverished but worldly sisters who offer their beauty as dowries; [and] an ingenue born of an illicit, much-regretted tryst," the *Publishers Weekly* (February 8, 1991) reviewer wrote. "Unlike other grand Italian sagas such as *The Leopard*, this novel presents subjects unbowed by the demands of historical change; rather their lives constitute a history in and of themselves."

For Joan K. Peters, the "novel's enchantment . . . is that of a medieval tapestry, one on which numerous tiny figures are woven into exquisitely detailed scenes of the hunt and the hearth, of men going off to battle. Half a dozen wars do, in fact, affect the four generations of the family . . . but this strife forms only part of a larger human landscape—just as, ultimately, the family does too." Peters describes how, later in the novel, il Giai's ghost plays his violin until all the descendants have left and "the whole house creaked like a vessel lying at anchor." For Loy's readers, Peters wrote, "il Giai's sweet, sad music lingers. It is the sound of the book's real protagonist—the Piedmont."

Peters praised William Weaver's translation, calling it a "lucid, often lyrical rendition." However for Tim Parks, writing in the *Times Literary Supplement* (November 9, 1990), "William Weaver never comes close to finding an English idiom to match the ease and fluency of the Italian." He hoped readers would, nevertheless, enjoy the novel "for the fine narrative that it is," detailing "misplaced affections, the dowries of embroidered bed linen, the hard work and dusty roads." The *Library Journal* (March 1, 1991) reviewer, Ulla Sweedler, also found Weaver's translation "stiff" and hoped readers could overcome it to enjoy the novel's "clear, evocative prose," depicting "passionate love affairs, beautiful people, and dramatic events such as wars, floods, epidemics, and a solar eclipse."

In 1995 Loy published *Cioccolata da Hanselmann* (*Hot Chocolate at Hanselmann's*), which was translated into English in 2003. The book's title refers to a café in St. Moritz, and the family depicted, like most of the others in Loy's novels, is an upper-middle-class Roman one. Two stepsisters are in love with Arturo, a young Jewish scientist who, unknown to them, has killed a relative of theirs, Eddy, after learning that Eddy was about to betray him to the Nazis during World War II. After the war, one of the women marries Arturo and goes with him to the United States. When he confesses to Eddy's murder, both women lose their love for him. In her review of the English translation for *World Literature Today* (Spring 1996), Rosetta Di Pace-Jordan summed up the novel's impact: "The aim of Loy's book . . . is not nostalgia but the revelation of a religiously motivated sacrifice, which is made to emerge through the shifting points of view of the key characters. . . . The chorality of this low-keyed elegy gets to the heart of the matter through the magic of the author's art." Di Pace-Jordan considered "the surplus of meaning and interest that Rosetta Loy can bring to her minimalist page-turners through perfect construction and economy of means" to be "truly amazing."

Loy's memoir, *La parola ebreo* (The Jewish Word), was published in English as *First Words* (2000), in a translation by Gregory Conti. Loy's childhood was a happy one, spent in Rome and at the seaside in Ostia, in a "world of velvet and lace, airy apartments, indulgent nannies and summers in the mountains," according to a description of the memoir on the Henry Holt Web site. She was born, however, in 1931, during the Fascist regime of Italian dictator Benito Mussolini. Although some of her neighbors, including a family named Levi, were Jewish, Loy wrote in her memoir that while she was enjoying her privileged childhood, she remained largely unaware of her country's increasing persecution of its Jewish citizens. Gradually forbidden from going to resorts, giving lectures, selling art, and entering public libraries, many of Italy's Jews were eventually sent to death camps after the Nazis occupied the country. Loy, detailing Fascist outrages, makes it clear that, despite her own blissful ignorance, her childhood was set in a scene of horror. "There is a black border around those guiltless days of ours," Loy wrote in the memoir, as quoted by Jonathan Yardley in the *Washington Post* (August 17, 2000, on-line). "If the Levis didn't defend themselves and were unable to imagine the inconceivable, surely it is not least because they considered themselves, like all other Romans, beneficiaries of certain guarantees. For too long they had shared with us happy days and sad, fears, cowardice, hopes. Going up and down the same stairs, drinking the same tea, stirring the spoon in the cup, they had spoken the same language, in the lexical sense but also in the emotional sense, for far too long to think of themselves as other."

When Pope Pius XI, who publicly decried nationalism and racism, died in 1939, his successor, Eugenio Pacelli, who became Pope Pius XII, was silent in the face of the atrocities committed by the Nazis. Although Loy wrote in the memoir that her father was "allergic to Fascism," as quoted in the *Savannah Morning News* (August 13, 2000, on-line), he stood by with helpless passivity while his Jewish neighbors disappeared. "Loy explains that, as a Roman Catholic, she carries an 'unbearable burden,'" according to a reviewer for *Publishers Weekly* (June 12, 2000). "Her scathing denunciation of the Vatican's support of Hitler and the willful passivity of Italy's intelligentsia forms a powerful act of atonement." Jonathan Yardley agreed. "To the little girl that Rosetta Loy was then, there was 'no impulse to scream, to do something for that boy with the cheerful face who used to ring their bell, his leather ball tucked tightly under his arm.' This book is her protest. It comes many years after the fact, but that in no way diminishes its passion or its quiet power."

The English translation of Loy's *The Water Door* is scheduled for publication in July 2003.

— S. Y.

SUGGESTED READING: *Booklist* p1996 July 2000; *Library Journal* p117 Mar. 1, 1991; *New York Times Book Review* p18 July 21, 1991; *Publishers Weekly* p47 Feb. 8, 1991, p59 June 12, 2000; *Washington Post* (on-line) C p2 Aug. 17, 2000; *World Literature Today* p378+ Spring 1996

SELECTED WORKS IN ENGLISH TRANSLATION: novels—*The Dust Roads of Monferrato*, 1990; *Hot Chocolate at Hanselmann's*, 2003; memoirs—*First Words*, 2000

Joe Vaughn/Courtesy of W. W. Norton & Company

Lynch, Thomas

1948– Poet; essayist

Although Thomas Lynch is known in literary circles as a poet and essayist, his fellow residents in Milford, Michigan, know him better as the town undertaker, a trade he learned from his father. While his three volumes of poetry, *Skating with Heather Grace* (1987), *Grimalkin and Other Poems* (1994), and *Still Life in Milford* (1998), and his two essay collections, *The Undertaking: Life Studies from the Dismal Trade* (1997) and *Bodies in Motion and at Rest* (2000), have won him critical acclaim and widespread recognition, he has no plans to give up his job at Lynch & Sons, the funeral home he has run for more than a quarter of a century. Death and mortality are frequent themes of Lynch's writing; for him those concerns are inextricably connected to poetry. "I remember the first poem I ever heard, the first dead human body I ever saw," he told Phil Nugent for the *Times–Picayune* (June 25, 2000). "Neither scarred my psyche but each changed my life. Each gave it meaning by holding forth a mystery." In *Bodies in Motion and at Rest*, he writes, "The arrangement of flowers and homages, casseroles and sympathies; the arrangement of images and idioms, words on a page—it is all the same."

Thomas Lynch composed the following autobiographical statement for *World Authors 1995–2000*: "I was born in Detroit in 1948, the second of nine children of Rosemary O'Hara and Edward Lynch, and named after my father's uncle—a priest who had died young some years before. I was schooled by nuns and Christian Brothers and spent a few years at university in the late 1960s.

"The poems of Yeats and fictions of Joyce were among the things I learned from studying with Michael Heffernan in 1968 at Oakland University in Rochester, Michigan. He was the first living poet I had ever met. These were times when to be a poet seemed more a function of lifestyle than language. This owed mostly to my ignorance: the mistaken sense that to be a poet one should be driving west in a fashionably down-market mini-bus, wearing distinctively off-brand footwear and more hair than I was ever going to have. Heffernan was, by contrast, a fellow Detroiter, on his first teaching assignment, worried about rent, driving a Buick, living, by all the evidence, an ordinary life and writing, at the same time, extraordinary poems. I began to think I could be a poet too. And my first efforts at same are coincidental with and correlated to my meeting of Michael Heffernan and his poems.

"I'd drawn a high number in the Nixon draft lotto so I didn't have to go to Vietnam. In February of 1970 I went to Ireland on a one-way ticket, intent on reading and writing and finding my way. I'd written to and been welcomed by my third-cousins, Tommy and Nora Lynch of Moveen West, Kilkee in Co. Clare. They were brother and sister, neither ever married, peasant farmers in their late 60s then. Their grandfather and my great-great-grandfather was Pat Lynch, our common man. It was out of their cottage in Moveen, between the Mouth of the Shannon and the North Atlantic, on Clare's westernmost peninsula, that my great-grandfather had come in 1890 to Jackson, Michigan. I was the first of my family, in three generations, to go back. It changed my life.

"Rural Ireland in 1970 was nearer to 18th century life than late 20th century suburban American life. The house that Nora and Tommy Lynch welcomed me to had no plumbing, no central heating, no telephone or toilet or television. It had two light sockets and a radio that got the BBC and one Irish Channel on which the Angelus was played at noon. They kept cows, saved hay, went to the creamery by ass and cart and to Mass on Sundays. I stayed that first winter until spring. The next couple of years I spent back and forth between Ireland, the Continent and Michigan.

"In 1972 I married. In 1973, I graduated from Wayne State University Department of Mortuary Science and moved to Milford in 1974 when our family bought the funeral home there. I was the only funeral director in town. I published my first poems in *Poetry* in 1980. The marriage ended in 1984. We had a daughter and three sons. I was 'awarded' custody of the children and spent the next seven years as a single parent dividing my duties between the funeral home and family obligations. I was much assisted in the latter by Mary Tata to whom I was married in 1991.

"My first book of poems was published by Gordon Lish at Alfred A. Knopf, Inc. in 1987. My second collection was published by Robin Robertson at Jonathan Cape in London who had heard me read in Dublin in 1988. It was Gordon Lish who first asked me to write an essay for *The Quarterly* which he edited in the late 1980s. It was later published in *The London Review of Books* by John Lanchester, and in *Harper's Magazine*. It became the title piece for the collection of essays called *The Undertaking* which was published in 1997. It won awards and was translated into six languages. My third collection of poems, *Still Life in Milford*, was published in 1998 by W. W. Norton and Jonathan Cape in London. A second collection of essays was published in London and New York in 2000, titled *Bodies in Motion and at Rest*.

"I continue to work as a funeral director in Milford and am given leave to write and travel by the labor of my brother and sisters and sons who work with me. Still, the trust and custom of my townspeople is a treasure to me and something that makes me, I believe, a better writer. I think being a writer makes me, likewise, a more able funeral director. Poems and funerals share the effort to shape some meaningful utterance in the face of what is thought to be otherwise, unspeakable.

"By great good fortune and the gift of Nora Lynch, I inherited the cottage in Moveen my people came out of and I first returned to years ago. I go there now whenever bookish duties take me there, usually two or three times a year. When I'm not there, I let it out to writerly friends and family for their own purposes.

"In my work I like to examine the dynamics between language and life, faith, death, desire, family, remembrance, hope, ritual and customs. What it means to be human and alive in our own times seems the proper concern of writers. To the extent that the language in all its incarnations is available, I've tried to address these concerns."

Thomas Lynch was born in Michigan. His father was a funeral director in the town of Birmingham. After working in the state asylum and in a home for alcoholic priests, Lynch enrolled in Oakland University in Rochester, Michigan, where he studied literature. He then went on to study mortuary science at Wayne State University and then bought a funeral home in Milford, in 1974, when marriage and a family made earning a steady income necessary. Lynch's first published poem, in a 1980 issue of *Poetry* magazine, was called "A Death" and concerned the death of a childhood friend from cancer. His first collection of poems, *Skating with Heather Grace*, was published in 1986. Rosaly DeMaios, writing in *Library Journal* (March 1, 1987), praised Lynch's "craft and careful language." Matthew Flamm in the *New York Times Book Review* (October 4, 1987) also professed admiration for Lynch. He wrote, "Mr. Lynch is a master of Irish-influenced invective, an echo of brogue recalling the days when a poet's curses meant something." According to Flamm, Lynch "never places too much emphasis on technique. His loose iambic lines give him just the support from tradition he needs, while the irregular rhymes show both a love for lyric and a crusty refusal to be tamed." Although many of the poems in the volume deal directly with death—such as "Damage," which is about a suicide—Wayne Koestenbaum, the reviewer for *Commonweal* (September 11, 1987), was disappointed to find few new insights into the topic. "What the book offers us, in lieu of the extraordinary, are facts of a regular life presented with such velocity that—as the expertly-scanned, jauntily-iambic lines speed past us—we almost feel that swiftness itself conveys a profundity. An illusion of wisdom comes with his distinctive line."

Lynch's next book of poetry, *Grimalkin and Other Poems* of 1994, dedicated to his second wife, Mary Tata, became widely known for its title poem, in which Lynch writes about his loathing for a cat belonging to his 12-year-old son, Mike, and fervently wishes for the animal's demise. He dreams of abandoning the cat in a desert town where she'll be taken in "by kindly tribespeople who eat her kind /on certain holy days as a form of penance." Lynch imagines a funeral at which he'll give the homily, "making some mention of cat-heaven where /cat-ashes to ashes, cat-dust to dust," and concludes with a sort of credo:

I'll turn Mike homeward from that wicked little grave and if he asks, we'll get another one because all boys need practice in the arts of love and all boys' ageing fathers in the arts of rage.

Grimalkin was followed in 1997 by a collection of essays, *The Undertaking: Life Studies from the Dismal Trade*, the idea for which grew out of a piece he wrote for a literary magazine called *The Quarterly*. In "Burying the Ungrateful Dead" Lynch tells of a pompous priest who requests only the simplest burial, wanting to be, as Lynch puts it, "an example of simplicity, of prudence, of piety and austerity." When Lynch somewhat caustically tells him that he needn't wait for death to set a good example, "that he could quit the country club and trade his luxury sedan for a used Chevette, that free of his Florsheims and cashmeres and prime ribs he could become the very incarnation of Saint Francis himself or Anthony of Padua," the priest is aghast. "What I was trying to tell the fellow was, of course, that being a dead saint is no more worthwhile than being a dead philodendron or a dead angelfish," Lynch concludes. "Living is the rub and always has been." In several of the essays Lynch defends the profession of undertaking against opponents such as Jessica Mitford, whose book *The American Way of Death* is particularly critical of the funeral industry.

Calling *The Undertaking* "one of the most life-affirming books I have read in a long time," the *Nation* (June 9, 1997) reviewer Tom Vanderbilt wrote that Lynch sees "every day [as a] matter of life and death, to be greeted with the tradesman's workaday pragmatism and the poet's capacity for transcendence." The poet Dennis O'Driscoll, who reviewed *The Undertaking* for the *Times Literary Supplement* (May 2, 1997), called the book "stunningly original" and observed that Lynch "reveals as much about our mores as our mourning."

Much of *Still Life in Milford*, Lynch's 1998 poetry collection, deals with the theme of death, perhaps most graphically in a poem titled "That Scream if you Ever Hear It," in which Lynch explicitly describes an accident that kills two small children and a motorcyclist. A portion of the book, however, is devoted to poems inspired by his Irish roots, including "The Moveen Notebooks," a 13-page tribute to his cousins in County Clare. Roger Gilbert wrote for the *Michigan Quarterly Review* (Winter 2000) that "death and its vicissitudes are Lynch's true subject, not his Catholic boyhood or Irish ancestry," but other reviewers were more tolerant of Lynch's fascination with his Celtic heritage. "Lynch has surely earned his portion of the family holdings by his tending of the flame," Thomas M. Disch wrote for the *Hudson Review* (Summer 1999), "and this may be taken as a metonymy for the task of poetry, remembering and rendering tribute to the works and days from which our civilization is compounded."

In *Bodies in Motion and at Rest*, an essay collection published in 2000, Lynch continued to write about the exigencies of the funeral business and parenthood. Susan Salter Reynolds, a reviewer for the *Los Angeles Times* (July 2, 2000), called Lynch "one of our most elegant cogitators," and concluded that "[he] writes most beautifully in these essays about passage and about echoes throughout generations. . . . It's clear that he's found some peace and quiet and that his god speaks through him." Richard Bernstein wrote for the *New York Times* (May 31, 2000, on-line), that the new book "is less thematically focused than *The Undertaking* and it is angrier in places, as if Mr. Lynch has now decided to relax his hold on avuncular bemusement and confide to us his private agony." He notes, however, that readers will still find "the pungent compassion, the unabashed lyricism, and the homespun repudiation of vanity and banality that bathed Mr. Lynch's earlier writings in their considerable glow."

Lynch, whom Bernstein praised as a cross between Garrison Keillor and William Butler Yeats, is a frequent contributor to *Harper's*, *Paris Review*, and the *London Review of Books*, among others. His distinctive appearance has occasioned much comment. Richard Bak wrote for the *Detroit News* (August 12, 1997), "He is perhaps the only literary figure in the Rust Belt states who can wear a Homburg and bowtie without coming across as a poseur. . . . Put a bible in one hand and a shovel in the other and he could be the frontier undertaker from an episode of 'Gunsmoke.'" Phil Nugent, commenting on Lynch's rather antiquated style of dress, wrote that "in his [book] jacket photos Lynch looks as if he'd just put on his Sunday best to tell a newsreel cameraman what he thinks of President Truman," and Joanne Kaufman, writing for the *Wall Street Journal* (September 15, 1997), described Lynch as "the fellow most likely to be cast as the stage manager in a community theater production of 'Our Town.'"

—S. Y.

SUGGESTED READING: *Booklist* p1954 Aug. 1998; *Harper's* p26+ Dec. 1995; *Hudson Review* p313+ Summer 1999; *Library Journal* p79 Mar. 1, 1987; *Los Angeles Times* p11 July 2, 2000; *Michigan Quarterly Review* p149+ Winter 2000; *Nation* p28+ June 9, 1997; *New York Times* (on-line) June 8, 2000; *New York Times Book Review* p24 Oct. 4, 1987; *Times Literary Supplement* p26 May 2, 1997; *Times-Picayune* D p7 June 25, 2000

SELECTED BOOKS: poetry collections—*Skating with Heather Grace*, 1986; *Grimalkin and Other Poems*, 1994; *Still Life in Milford*, 1998; essays—*The Undertaking: Life Studies from the Dismal Trade*, 1997; *Bodies in Motion and at Rest*, 2000

Macfarlane, David

Aug. 19, 1952– Memoirist; novelist; journalist

David Macfarlane is a veteran writer whose magazine and newspaper articles made him well known and highly respected throughout his native Canada before he ever published a book. His family memoir, *The Danger Tree: Remembrance and Loss in a Newfoundland Family* (1991), and novel, *Summer Gone* (1999), have earned him critical acclaim and attention abroad.

David Macfarlane was born on August 19, 1952 in Hamilton, in the Canadian province of Ontario. Macfarlane's father, Blake, an ophthalmologist, grew up in Ontario, while his mother, Betty, was a native of Grand Falls, Newfoundland. In an interview with his hometown newspaper, the *Hamilton Spectator* (October 11, 1999), Macfarlane recalled, "There were lots of books in my parents' home. As well, we were encouraged to make use of the public library. . . . And—as J. D. Salinger pointed out—in order to be a writer, you have to first be a reader."

Macfarlane received his B.A. from the University of Toronto in 1975. After graduation, he began working to finance a trip to Europe. By 1976 he had saved enough money, and he spent the next two years living in London, Paris, and the Tuscany region of Italy. Macfarlane also developed his writing skills by penning short stories, poetry, and reviews while living abroad.

After returning to Ontario, he got a job with *Weekend* magazine, where he worked in several different capacities during his tenure. Macfarlane found his experiences there invaluable. As he later told Ken McGoogan, a reporter for the *Calgary Herald* (October 3, 1999), "It was almost as if someone had designed a course for me. It was a fantastic introduction to the magazine business." After *Weekend* folded, Macfarlane joined *Saturday Night* magazine as a staff writer, in 1983. The same year, he began writing for *Macleans* as a freelance contributor. Throughout the 1980s, Macfarlane was a prolific journalist, publishing numerous reviews of books, films, and television programs. In 1987 he became an associate editor at *Saturday Night*. The next year, he left to become a senior writer for *Toronto Magazine*. In the *Hamilton Spectator* (September 4, 1999), Jeff Mahoney observed, "During all this time he developed an enviable reputation in the business as a consummately 'writerly' journalist. Not a just-the-facts-ma'am kind of stenographer of events, he would bring himself to his material with wit, colour, detail, powers of observation, and a sensibility one associates with fiction more than non-fiction." Macfarlane won Canada's National Magazine Award 10 times and was also honored with the Sovereign Award for Magazine Journalism in 1987.

In his late 30s Macfarlane became more conscious of his Newfoundland roots. As a child, his only contact with Newfoundland had been through visits from his maternal grandparents. As an adult, he began to realize that he was the product of two very different societies. Ontario, where Macfarlane grew up, is Canada's most affluent province. By contrast, the coastal province of Newfoundland, part of which lies on a large island of the same name and much of which is rich in natural resources, has nonetheless often been plagued with unemployment and poverty, due in part to its harsh climate and rugged terrain.

Macfarlane's first book, *The Danger Tree: Remembrance and Loss in a Newfoundland Family* (1991), explored his roots by profiling his mother's family, the Goodyears. (The book was published as *Come From Away: Memory, War and the Search for a Family's Past* in the United States and the United Kingdom.) For the memoir, Macfarlane conducted substantial research, consulting public records, old newspapers, and family letters and interviewing relatives, including his ailing grandmother. Macfarlane's grandfather, Joe Goodyear, made a good living working in the construction business, but never became rich. When World War I broke out in 1914, Joe and four of his brothers, Ken, Stanley, Raymond, and Hedley, quickly volunteered. At the time, Canada was still part of the British Empire. Stanley, Raymond, and Hedley were killed in France and were among the many Newfoundlanders who never returned home. Grief over those lost in the war added to the existing suffering in Newfoundland. "It was a different family after the war," Macfarlane wrote in the book, as quoted by Jonathan Yardley in the *Washington Post* (October 2, 1991). "Something was gone from the heart of it. Ray's innocence and enthusiasm would never temper Ken's guile and ambition; Stan's charm and level-headedness would never leaven my grandfather's stubbornness; Hedley's wisdom and learning would never sustain Roland's [another Goodyear brother] flights of fancy. Somehow the wrong combination survived. Fights erupted in their absence. A balance was never regained."

Most reviewers enthusiastically praised *The Danger Tree*. In the *Toronto Star* (April 27, 1991), Philip Marchand wrote, "In presenting [the Goodyears], Macfarlane rarely indulges in any facile or gratuitous fictionalizing. The reader has the strong impression that every scene or conversation from the past that is recreated on the page is based on solid, scrupulous research. What is imagined is rooted closely in fact. But the fact is also, in this book, transformed by a high degree of art." Marchand was impressed by Macfarlane's narrative style, which borrows from the storytelling techniques of his Newfoundland relatives. "He adopts their habit of starting tales, abandoning them, and then coming back to them," Marchand explained. "A story like the death of Hedley Goodyear is told in a series of separate episodes, interspersed in the larger narrative. Each incomplete episode gains in meaning from being juxtaposed with other, seemingly unrelated stories, and the irony and pity of his death, in the end, is magnified." In his review for the *San Francisco Chronicle* (September 15, 1991), Steve Jensen observed that the war passages in the book "are the only ones that don't succeed; perhaps it's a mistake to try to bring to life men who died so young and left so little behind. The passages evoking death in the trenches, alone among all the stories in the book, bear traces of self-conscious artiness." Despite these criticisms, Jensen concluded that Macfarlane's book is "consistently brilliant" and filled with many fascinating stories about his Goodyear relatives. *The Danger Tree* received a nomination for the Trillium Award, a major Canadian literary prize open to residents of Ontario, in 1992 and won the Canadian Author's Association Award for nonfiction in 1992. In 1998 Macfarlane adapted *The Danger Tree* into a documentary broadcast on Canadian television.

In 1997 Macfarlane assisted George Cohon, the senior chairman of McDonald's Restaurants of Canada, with writing his book, *To Russia With Fries*, in which Cohon recalled his efforts to bring McDonald's to the Soviet Union. In his review for Montreal's *Gazette* (November 1, 1997), Mark Abley ridiculed the book, expressing doubts that Cohon's "hamburger-packed life is worth relishing over 339 pages." Abley argued that the book was far beneath Macfarlane's considerable talents as a journalist and author, and asked what Macfarlane was doing "ghost-writing a book for a guy who genuinely seems to believe that the collective wisdom of the human race can be summed up by the credos of McDonald's?"

For his next book, Macfarlane decided to write a novel. "People would say to me, 'You're nonfiction is so fictional, why don't you try writing a novel,'" he said to Mahoney. "I took them at their word and thought maybe it would not be such a big leap. But it turned out to be quite a different fish." For Macfarlane, the experience of a writing a novel proved difficult. He explained to Mahoney that, in nonfiction, there is a set "template," as he put it, specifically real characters and real events from which the narrative flows. By contrast, he said that such templates do not exist in fiction, telling Mahoney, "If you find yourself at a spot where it's not working, you would think, maybe the narrator should be female or this should be happening 20 years earlier." The novel went through many drafts before Macfarlane settled on the final version.

Summer Gone, Macfarlane's first novel, was published in 1999. The plot concerns Bay Newling, a divorced magazine editor, who takes his estranged 12-year-old son on an ill-fated canoe trip. Macfarlane told McGoogan that the biblical story of God asking Abraham to sacrifice his son, Isaac, inspired the idea for the novel. Macfarlane had long been haunted by the story, and had been seeking a way to meditate on it. In a review for the *Calgary Herald* (August 14, 1999), Shane Rhodes praised the novel, writing, "Through the simple use of images and repeated scenes, Macfarlane combines what could have been 20 different stories into one impressive garment of a novel. The way he has written this story, its perambulations, its twist and turns, is almost as interesting as the plot itself. Macfarlane has discovered and mastered tricks that even more experienced writers are unwilling to attempt." In the *New York Times* (April 23, 2000), Katherine Wolff declared, "Gently, as with a fine ghost story, Bay's complicated past is lived and relived from different points on a shadowy time line. The pain of lost innocence ripples through this remarkable novel." Wolff added that the novel's language "evokes the freshwater lakes and rivers that the characters navigate." *Summer Gone* received a nomination for the Giller Prize, one of Canada's most prestigious literary awards.

David Macfarlane is married and has two children. He writes a weekly column for the *Globe and Mail* newspaper in Toronto, where he and his family live. In the early 1990s they rented a cottage on an island in northern Ontario with no electricity and running water, and they have spent their summers in that area ever since. As of 2000, Macfarlane had plans to publish three more nonfiction works: a collection of his magazine and newspaper articles entitled "A Living"; "Somebody Running," a collection of essays inspired by what he thinks about when he jogs in cities around the world; and a travel book about Tuscany's marble quarries, tentatively called "Reading the White Stone: Travels in the Italian Marble Quarries."

—D. C.

SUGGESTED READING: *Calgary Herald* G p9 Aug. 14, 1999, C p4 Oct. 3, 1999; (Montreal) *Gazette* K p3 Nov. 1, 1997; *Hamilton Spectator* W p1 Sep. 4, 1999, C p6 Oct. 11, 1999; *New York Times Book Review* p18 Apr. 23, 2000; *San Francisco Chronicle Sunday Review* p5 Sep. 15, 1991; *Toronto Star* J p11 Apr. 27, 1991; *Canadian Who's Who*, 1997

SELECTED BOOKS: fiction—*Summer Gone*, 1999; nonfiction—*The Danger Tree: Remembrance and Loss in a Newfoundland Family* (published in the United States and the United Kingdom as *Come From Away: Memory, War and the Search for a Family's Past*), 1991; *To Russia With Fries* (with George Cohon), 1997

Courtesy of Coconut Grove Playhouse

Machado, Eduardo

June 11, 1953– Playwright

The work of the Cuban American playwright Eduardo Machado exhibits an ongoing concern with what it means, politically and socially, to be Hispanic, but Machado is equally concerned with depicting universal human drama. "The minute you say 'we're doing Hispanic theater, we're doing Chicano theater' is the minute you feed stereotypes," he told Jan Breslauer for the *Los Angeles Times* (October 16, 1994). "I'm not doing any of that: I'm doing theater. If I was concerned with the struggle of people coming over the border, I'd better be over at the border doing something about it. I'm concerned about my art." In an opinion piece for *American Theatre* (May/June 1997) Machado elaborated. "Isn't it my duty to write about . . . the entire canvas that has been my life?" he asked. "But we divide ourselves in the theatre according to the color of our skin, birthplace, etc., etc., etc. Isn't idealism, either artistic or political, more binding than blood, color or gender? To show life here on Earth. Isn't that our job? Why waste time fighting about anything else? Truth in art is individualistic, not communal. The writer's truth. This is all a playwright owes to himself, her community, and the writers that came before." Machado is the author of more than 25 plays, including four plays about Cuban families that he combined into the epic, *Floating Island Plays*. His work has been produced at such theaters as the Long Wharf Theater, Mark Taper Forum, Actors Theater of Louisville, Ensemble Studio Theater, American Place Theater, Williamstown Theater Festival, Magic Theater, and Theater for the New City.

Eduardo Machado, the son of Othon Eduardo and Gilda (Hernandez) Machado, was born on June 11, 1953 in Havana, Cuba. In 1961, in the wake of Castro's revolution, Machado—like many other Cuban children—was sent to live with relatives in Miami. His parents emigrated a year later, and moved the family to Los Angeles, California. Some members of Machado's wealthy family were heavy drinkers, and Machado grew up in what he describes as an abusive environment. "My childhood was a combination of isolation and desperation," he wrote in a short essay for *American Theatre* (October 1994). "I wanted to believe that it was because, when I came to America from Havana when I was eight years old, I thought I was going to come here for the weekend. But in fact, I was full of isolation and desperation in Cuba. In fact, isolation and desperation were the only things I ever felt."

Machado discovered the world of the stage at age 14, when he sang a song from the musical *Mame* at his junior-high school. By the time he was 17 and attending Van Nuys High School, in California, he was devoted to becoming an actor. He found an agent and changed his name to Ben Machado. "I tried to get a tan so I could play hoods," he recalled in his essay, "and I grew a moustache. I started working with this wonderful acting teacher named David Alexander, who was a Russian Jew. He taught me everything I knew about theatre."

With help from President Carter's Comprehensive Employment and Training Act (CETA), a job creation program intended to prop up the flagging 1970s economy, Machado started his own theatre. In 1979 he attended the Padua Hills Playwrights Festival and Workshop, where he came into contact with such established playwrights as Sam Shepard, Maria Irene Fornes, and John Steppling, the latter of whom cast Machado in several of his plays during the '80s. But Machado soon grew disillusioned with acting. "When I was in John [Steppling's] plays, my job was to create this other person that had little to do with my instincts," he told Breslauer. "And because I wasn't playing Latins, I was expressing less and less of myself. There was this world that I wanted to express—being Latin and Cuban—and there was no literature for me to express [it]. Because of that I stopped acting." At the same time, he found himself enamored with the work of the Cuban American playwright Maria Irene Fornes, whom Machado referred to in his essay as "perhaps the most important person in my life." "I wrote my first play," Machado recalled, "because I walked into one of Irene's classes by mistake, and she made the tragic mistake of telling me what I wrote was good."

Machado began writing in earnest and received fellowships from the National Endowment for the Arts (NEA) in 1981, 1983, and 1986, and from the Rockefeller Foundation, in 1985. In 1983 his play, *The Modern Ladies of Guanabacoa* (the first of the four plays incorporated into the *Floating Island Plays*), was published by the Theatre Communications Group (TCG). The play was inspired by a photograph of his grandmother that had been labeled with the note, "The day we cut our hair." "It's . . . based on the fact that my grandmother cut her hair in 1929 and she thought it was a big rebellious act," Machado told Breslauer, "that my grandfather lost his bus company when Fidel nationalized . . . and that I lived in an extremely alcoholic family. But of course it's my re-imagination of all these things." *The Modern Ladies of Guanabacoa* takes place between 1928 and 1931 in Cuba and follows the Ripoll family: Maria Josefa is a traditional, somewhat downtrodden mother; Arturo is the stern, philandering patriarch; Manuela is the daughter, who wants to rebel and bob her hair; and Mario, the eldest son of three sons, who seeks to hide his homosexuality from his family. It is the Jazz Age, the world economy is blossoming, women are starting to smoke and wear their hair short, and these changing times impinge upon the family's traditional life. Arturo becomes involved with an ambitious cab driver who hopes to start a bus company, and in so doing brings the whole family along with him into the new era.

In the second play of the *Floating Island* series, *In the Eyes of the Hurricane*, three decades have passed, and Arturo's bus company has become a success. The Ripoll's wealth has not brought them real happiness, however, nor has it eased the friction caused by Mario's homosexuality. *Fabiola*, the third play in the series, depicts another family, the Marquezes, during the upheaval of Castro's ascension to power and the events leading up to the Bay of Pigs battle, in which U.S.–backed Cuban rebels attempted to overthrow the Castro regime. Paralleling the political crisis are eruptions within the Marquez family, in which two brothers are involved in an incestuous, homosexual relationship. The play opens with a family seance held to contact Fabiola, the dead wife of one of the brothers. "There's a reason why Fabiola is the play's title" Sylvie Drake wrote in her review for the *Los Angeles Times* (October 12, 1985) of an Ensemble Studio Theatre production, in Hollywood. "She's a symbol of cosmic reproach—the eye of the hurricane, the specter of sin, anguish, innocence, revolt, of the ailing, trampled Cuba itself. And she won't leave this family alone." Though Drake disparaged the production, she recognized that *Fabiola* is an "important work, not just because it is written well, but also because few plays, if any, have dealt with the immigrant experience of the mid-20th century and none—to my knowledge—with the culture shock of pampered, often arrogant upper-middle-class Latinos suddenly plunged into an American environment that sees them all as laborers and domestics."

The series concludes with *Broken Eggs*, set in the 1980s, in Southern California, where most of the Ripolls and Marquezes have settled. The families meet for the wedding of one of the daughters, who has become a thoroughly American "Valley Girl." In 1991, *Floating Island Plays* was published in book form. In 1993 Machado was awarded a TCG/Pew Charitable Trust grant of $100,000 to stage a production of the complete *Floating Island Plays* at the Mark Taper Forum, in Los Angeles. One evening, not long after receiving the grant, Machado proved he was willing to risk his life for his life's work. Walking from the Mark Taper Forum back to his hotel late one night, Machado was approached by a man with a gun. Machado surrendered his wallet and wristwatch, but—when the mugger asked for his computer disks—Machado balked. "He put the gun against my head," he recalled to Richard Stayton and Oliver Mayer for *American Theatre* (January 1995), "and he very slowly ran the gun down my back from the top of my head to my buttocks. He asked me what part of my body wanted the bullet." Noticing the mugger was Hispanic, Machado explained to him in Spanish that the disks contained the text of his four *Floating Island Plays*, plus notes for condensing them for an upcoming performance. Fifteen minutes passed, and neither of them would back down. Finally, the mugger walked away. "I will always remember the feeling of that gunmetal against my spine," Machado said.

Floating Islands premiered at the Mark Taper Forum, in 1994. The process of condensing and reworking the four plays for a single, six-hour viewing proved difficult for Machado—who trimmed hundreds of pages from the scripts—as well as for the play's director and cast. They were not fully prepared for the opening night performance. John Lahr, in the *New Yorker* (November 14, 1994), defended the plays and blamed the production's shortcomings on the director, Oskar Eustis, but most reviewers didn't try to decide whether the writing or the directing was responsible for the performance's perceived shortcomings. Dick Lochte wrote in *Los Angeles* (December 1994), "Six hours of drama severely tests even the most dedicated theatergoer. The material must be so extraordinarily engrossing that time loses its meaning. With its epic aspirations and ornate family histories, *Floating Islands* doesn't quite turn the trick."

The *Floating Islands* plays have enjoyed critical success when staged independently, as have many of Machado's other works. One such play was *A Burning Beach* (which premiered at the American Place Theatre, in New York City, in 1988), though Machado himself was far from happy with the staged productions. During a staged reading of *A Burning Beach* at a Los Angeles theater, Machado decided to play a joke on the audience and told the stage manager that, at the end of the play, a dresser should start bleeding and cover everything on stage in blood. To his chagrin, this flashy device was seen by many, including the director, as a highly effective example of magical realism, wherein fantastic events are treated as everyday occurrences. "I get this call from the American Place Theatre that they want to do the play," Machado told Breslauer. "I go in there and they [begin talking about] 'that amazing moment of magic realism when the dresser bleeds.' I say, 'Oh no, that's a joke.' And they say, 'No, you're wrong.'" At the Los Angeles Theatre Center, in 1989, the bleeding dresser scene was again left in, against Machado's wishes. "Every night I would have to see this dresser bleed and I would just die, I would be so embarrassed that this dresser was bleeding," he told Breslauer. "But I know that that play would not have gotten two productions if the dresser hadn't bled."

Set in Cuba, in 1895, *A Burning Beach* revolves around four female characters. Two sisters, who live on a plantation, have just lost their father and must run the estate by themselves. Their black maid and a beautiful American girl also figure in the story, as do their half-brother and Jose Martí, the leader of Cuba's movement for independence from Spain. In his review of a 1989 Los Angeles Theatre Center production for the *Los Angeles Times* (February 6, 1989), Dan Sullivan described *A Burning Beach* as an allegory, albeit a somewhat inchoate one. "The young American woman," he wrote, "stands for seductive American imperialism. The black maid . . . stands for voodoo and heat. The half-brother is Cuba . . . realizing that its mixed-blood is its strength. The two sisters? The frilly one . . . is the patrician class, beautiful but ineffectual. The angular one . . . is harder to read. She shows considerable spirit, up to a point, but ultimately accepts being defined as an onlooker rather than a maker of history. Maybe we need to know more of the actual history here, or maybe Machado hasn't made his statement clearly enough." Sullivan concluded, "To marry the allegorical and the personal is a tough trick. *A Burning Beach* doesn't quite give us characters in whom we can believe, yet doesn't quite give us a clear and compelling social parable either." Mel Gussow's *New York Times* (November 5, 1988) review of a different production, as quoted in *Contemporary Authors* (1991), was more positive. In particular, Gussow appreciated the play's "provocative intensity" and "air of intrigue."

Machado's two-act musical, *Stevie Wants to Play the Blues*, was produced by the Los Angeles Theatre Center, in 1990. Loosely based on the story of the jazz pianist Billy Tipton, the story centers on Stevie, a female jazz musician who dresses up as a man because she is convinced it is the only way to be taken seriously as a musician. Her plan works, and she is hired by a band, but, much to her surprise, Ruth Scott, a beautiful, heroin-addicted singer, falls for her. Stevie returns her affections, while still maintaining her secret, though inevitably her plan ends in disaster. Sylvie Drake, who reviewed the Los Angeles production for the *Los Angeles Times* (February 19, 1990), appreciated the music and production to some extent, but wrote, "The play's major hurdle is its lack of subtext. We can second-guess where it's headed pretty early on and nothing Machado inserts alters the destination. . . . If we are to derive more from the event than a story stylishly told in dramatic and musical riffs . . . it's hard to tell what it might be."

In 1998 Machado's *Broken Eggs* was performed in Havana, Cuba, by Repertorio Espanol, marking the first time Cuban Americans had been invited to perform in Cuba since 1961. In 1999 Machado directed his play *Crocodile Eyes* at the Theater for the New City, in New York City. It is based on Federico García Lorca's *The House of Bernarda Alba* (1941), in which the recently widowed Bernarda cloisters her five daughters in their house, forbidding them—quite against their wishes—to associate with a host of interested suitors and threatening to keep them in mourning for eight years. Lorca's play offered a metaphor for political oppression, and the Spanish dictator Francisco Franco had him executed after it was staged. In *Crocodile Eyes* Machado concentrates on the suitors who are forbidden to enter Alba's home. The play opens with a group of them boasting of their sexual conquests of the night before. Pepe el Romano, a Don Juan figure and ardent Franco supporter, has succeeded, despite Bernarda's wishes, in courting both the eldest daughter (who has the largest dowry) and the youngest (who is the prettiest). The gentle poet Joaquin tries unsuccessfully to change Pepe's political viewpoints. Pepe continues headlong down a path that results in tragedy. Reviews of *Crocodile Eyes* were mixed. Charles McNulty wrote in the *Village Voice* (May 11, 1999), "Like many works inspired by the classics, *Crocodile Eyes* has trouble striking a balance between the original story and the new one. Though narrative clarity is typically the playwright's strong suit, his vision here seems unusually blurry."

Machado's *When the Sea Drowns in Sand* was staged at the 2001 Humana Festival of New American Plays, a major theatrical event in Louisville, Kentucky, and was generally viewed as one of the finest offerings of the festival. Inspired by his own experience, Machado tells the story of Federico, a Cuban American who was sent to America as a child in the 1960s, and who, 40 years later, returns to Cuba to look for his old family home. His guide is Ernesto, who disapproves of Federico's nostalgic trip, and a clash of cultures ensues. Michael Phillips, writing in the *Los Angeles Times* (April 3, 2001) called *When the Sea Drowns in Sand* the highlight of the Humana Festival, a "lovely and rueful comedy" and a "tight, crafty and exceptionally eloquent play about identity politics, on every scale."

Machado is an associate professor of theater and the director of the graduate playwriting program at Columbia University, in New York City.

—P. G. H.

SUGGESTED READING: *American Theatre* p30+ Oct. 1994, p14+ Jan. 1995, p15+ May/June 1997; *Los Angeles* p173 Dec. 1994; *Los Angeles Times* p1 Oct. 12, 1985, p1 Feb. 6, 1989, p1 Feb. 19, 1990, p9 Oct. 16, 1994; *San Francisco Chronicle* E p3 Jan. 18, 1990; *Village Voice* p140 Mar. 24, 1998, p135 May 11, 1999

SELECTED PLAYS: *Rosario and the Gypsies* (with Rick Vartoreila), 1982; *The Modern Ladies of Guanabacoa*, 1983; *Broken Eggs*, 1984; *Fabiola*, 1985; *When It's Over* (with Geraldine Sherman), 1987; *Why to Refuse*, 1987; *A Burning Beach*, 1988; *Don Juan in New York*, 1988; *Once Removed*, 1988; *Wishing You Well*, 1988; *Cabaret Bambu*, 1989; *Stevie Wants to Play the Blues*, 1990; *Floating Islands*, 1994; *In the Eyes of the Hurricane*, 1994; *Crocodile Eyes*, 1999; *When the Sea Drowns in Sand*, 2001

Maja-Pearce, Adewale

June 3, 1953– Journalist; short-story writer

The British-Nigerian author and journalist Adewale Maja-Pearce has emerged as one of the leading champions of human rights and freedom of expression in Africa, especially Nigeria, where he lived as a child and where his father was born. Although Maja-Pearce has earned a reputation as a versatile writer, publishing books in several different genres, his work is mostly devoted to that continent. He has written a travel book, *In My Father's Country: A Nigerian Journey* (1987); a well-received reflection on his British-Nigerian heritage, *How Many Miles to Babylon? An Essay* (1990); a short-story anthology, *Loyalties* (1987); a bold collection of articles condemning political persecution in Africa, *Who's Afraid of Wole Soyinka? Essays on Censorship* (1991); and an acclaimed work of literary criticism, *A Mask Dancing: Nigerian Novelists of the Eighties* (1992). "Nigeria is such a big, bad, beautiful country," he said to Ginny Dougary for the London *Independent* (June 20, 1990). "All I had to do was turn up in a new place for an adventure to happen."

The son of a Nigerian father and British mother, Adewale Maja-Pearce was born in London, England, on June 3, 1953. According to Dougary, Adewale's father, who was a surgeon in Nigeria, encountered racism when he studied medicine in England, and often heard such comments as "Speak up, you're not in the jungle now; can't you talk proper English?" Adewale grew up in Ikoyi, an affluent section of the city of Lagos, Nigeria, populated by expatriates. The family was wealthy enough to afford servants and gardeners, and Adewale and his brother often swam in the nearby lagoon. His parents eventually divorced. "The same thing happened to parents of all my friends who were from similar backgrounds," Maja-Pearce told Dougary. "Mostly, it was Nigerian men and British women. The men had problems coming to terms with who they were. They had grown up in a colony and (post independence) were suddenly thrust into the position of being in charge." Maja-Pearce concluded, "Being married to white women worked both for and against them. There was no way these marriages could survive."

After his parents' divorce, Adewale went to live with his grandparents, in Streatham, England. He later returned to Nigeria to attend boarding school. When he turned 16, Maja-Pearce went back to London to live with his mother. "I'd spent five years willing myself back in Britain," he recalled to Dougary, "but as soon as I got there the first thing I wanted to do was return to Nigeria." The young man felt that he did not belong to either country. In England, his schoolmates often called him a "wog," which is a racial epithet. By contrast, he was called "paleface" in Nigeria.

Maja-Pearce graduated from the University College of Swansea, part of the University of Wales, in 1975, with a B.A. In 1986 he received a master's degree from the School of Oriental and African Studies, in London. His career as a writer began in 1986. He became a researcher for the *Index of Censorship*, a London-based magazine that champions the freedom of the press around the world and often features articles by writers who cannot publish in their own countries due to political oppression. Maja-Pearce later became the magazine's Africa editor. In 1986 he also began working as a consultant for Heinemann Education Books, a publisher in Oxford, England.

That year Maja-Pearce edited the book *Collected Poems*, an anthology of the late Nigerian poet Christopher Okigbo. In 1987 Maja-Pearce published two books. The first, a travel book entitled *In My Father's Country: A Nigerian Journey*, was mostly ignored by reviewers. In her article, Dougary wrote that the book "focuses on the too many languages, too many wives (polygamy is legal), too much family, too much squalor, too many [corrupt] aspects of Nigerian life." The second, *Loyalties and Other Stories*, is a collection of his short stories. The stories are all set in Nigeria, reflecting the country's repression and social and political problems. Reviewing the second edition of the book for *World Literature Today* (Winter 1992), Nadezda Obradovic observed that the "plots unfold in cities and villages alike, and almost all aspects of Nigerian life are covered." Among the stories that Obradovic found interesting were "An Easy Death," about a mother who cannot part with the body of her dead child; "Loyalties," in which "raised hopes for an independent Biafran state are dashed by wholesale death and suffering; "The Occupation," about the violent oppression of villagers by government troops; and "Lagos Brothel" and "Lovers," two pieces that "furnish insights into the seamier facets of Lagos life." The reviewer concluded that *Loyalties and Other Stories* "is a fine book. With its brief sentences and clear language, it reads very easily, and once it is finished, one regrets that there is not more."

In 1990 Maja-Pearce's book *How Many Miles to Babylon?: An Essay* received critical acclaim. In it the author offers a discussion of racial identity and explains what it was like for him, as a "mulatto," considered white in Nigeria and black in England. Reviewing the book for the London *Independent* (July 29, 1990), Mihir Bose asserted that the author "is best when narrating his own experiences in his mother's country. The beginning, describing his struggles to become a writer in the marginal society around Ladbroke Grove as he mingles with black West Indians and their white paramours, is a haunting echo of V. S. Naipaul's *Mimic Men*." Mihr added that "Maja-Pearce's journey through his 'mulatto' origins is very touching, and the section on the meaning of 'mulatto' is a minor classic." The reviewer, however, expressed disappointment that Maja-Pearce failed to devote more attention to his Scottish grandparents. Bose concluded that a "more autobiographical exploration of this fractured existence, which provides so many insights denied to others, would have been valuable." In the London *Sunday Times* (August 19, 1990), Paul Bailey wrote that "Maja-Pearce is as scathing about sentimental left-wing notions of working class nobility as he is towards an equally sentimental High Toryism, anxious to maintain a now-obsolete status quo." He concluded that the "short book is dense with ideas, and deserves to reach a wide audience, at every level of British society."

In 1991 Maja-Pearce published a collection of 13 essays, most of which had previously appeared in the *Index on Censorship*, in the book, *Who's Afraid of Wole Soyinka? Essays on Censorship*. (Wole Soyinka is the renowned Nigerian playwright, poet, and essayist who won the Nobel Prize for literature, in 1986. He has been an outspoken advocate for human rights and freedom of expression and an eloquent opponent of oppression in his native country.) In his review for the *International Journal of African Historical Studies* Vol. 2 (1993), Ketu H. Katrak observed that in "Maja-Pearce, one senses a deep sense of compassion and a relentless need to expose the brutality of repressive regimes that deny human beings their basic dignity." Katrak added that the book would appeal "to a broad audience that is concerned about the harsh realities under several military regimes in Africa today." In the *Los Angeles Times* (November 24, 1991), Charles Solomon hailed the book as "an impassioned plea for justice on that troubled continent," writing that although "he condemns the corrupting influence of Western wealth and colonial ideologies, he reserves his harshest criticism for the black Africans who oppress, torture and murder other black Africans."

Maja-Pearce turned to literary criticism in *A Mask Dancing: Nigerian Novelists of the Eighties* (1992). The author argued that many Nigerian writers, including the acclaimed Chinua Achebe, have failed to offer a moral vision that challenges the corruption and political oppression in their country. According to Maja-Pearce his subjects, who write in English, ignore the language's wider implications. He feels that for Nigeria, the English language should connote both the nation's colonial history and the wider world influenced by European culture. Many contemporary Nigerian writers have ignored these important connections and do not comprehend how colonialism and the European world have formed modern Nigeria. The end result, Maja-Pearce concludes, is poor literature that ignores the true state of contemporary Nigeria and placates the status quo. "*A Mask Dancing* is a radically different book of criticism written with . . . skill," Bruce King wrote in *World Literature Today* (Summer 1993). "It steps on many toes, and its claims need serious thought. The title comes from an Igbo proverb which speaks of the need for change, modernization, and relativism as necessary for the broader, wiser perspective required for success: 'The world is like a mask dancing; if you want to see it well you do not stand in one place.'" In his review for *College Literature* (February 1994), Derek Wright described *A Mask Dancing* as "a necessary book, one that had to be written. It is, moreover, refreshingly rugged and robust polemic, with a shrewd eye for the phoney and pretentious . . . and it is fired by a raw, exhilarating vigor that has not been surpassed in Nigerian critical thinking. It rises above its subject matter and is that rare phenomenon, a good book about bad ones." Wright, however, offered some minor criticisms of the book, observing that Maja-Pearce devotes too much space to summarizing plots and makes a few careless mistakes, such as alleging that a character in one novel commits suicide when he actually dies in a car accident. The reviewer also faulted the author for exempting Wole Soyinka, whom Maja-Pearce greatly admires, from criticism—despite the fact that his novel *Season of Anomy* (1973) reduces women to objects of male fantasies, a literary practice that *A Mask Dancing* strongly condemns in the work of other Nigerian novelists.

In 1994 Maja-Pearce edited the book, *Wole Soyinka: An Appraisal*, a collection of 12 essays that assessed Soyinka's work and celebrated him on the occasion of his 60th birthday. In his review for *Research in African Literatures* (Summer 1996), Richard K. Priebe wrote that the book is "an interesting collection of commentary that yields some sharp criticism of Soyinka's achievements while also recognizing his well-earned stature as both a writer and a public man." The book includes Soyinka's 1986 Noble Lecture dedicated to Nelson Mandela and an interview he gave to Maja-Pearce in 1993. Although Priebe had favorable reactions to the book, he noted that some of the pieces had already been published elsewhere and were somewhat dated. "Whatever faults one can find in this book, however, are minor in relation to the importance of the collection as a whole," Priebe observed. "No one who is seriously interested in Soyinka should fail to read it. . . . In fact, no other single work does so much to advance our understanding of the ways Soyinka is deeply committed both as artist and public individual." In *World Literature Today* (Spring 1995), Tanure Ojaide asserted that *Wole Soyinka: An Appraisal* "is a strong and balanced book that deserves to be read by any serious scholar of African and world literatures."

In 1995 an article that Maja-Pearce wrote for the *Index on Censorship*, with assistance from Dulue Mbachu, was republished as a pamphlet, *The Press in Nigeria*. Although it was only 32 pages long, the pamphlet caught the attention of the editors of the *Review of African Political Economy* (September 1995). A reviewer for that publication wrote that the pamphlet "tells a depressing and familiar story of successive regimes from the colonial period onwards engaged in harassing the press for embarrassing them, usually with true exposes of abuses or corruption, and provides many short case studies." The reviewer added that *The Press in Nigeria* is weakened "by crude political commentary in which the [I]slamic, ignorant and reactionary Northern elite use control or harassment of the press as one weapon against the [C]hristian, educated and progressive South. Thus while useful as a descriptive account of assaults on press freedom, it has little value as an analysis of why they occur." The same reviewer also discussed the book, *Who Rules the Airwaves? Broadcasting in Africa*, which was published in 1995. Although no author or editor is officially credited, the reviewer noted that Maja-Pearce contributed "five of the nine short country case studies that comprise the bulk of the book." Focusing on Malawi, Namibia, and Mozambique, the book's essays, the reviewer wrote, "are descriptive and have as their central theme the extent of official control of radio and TV, which are for most Africans the only source of news other than gossip and foreign broadcasts."

In 1997 Maja-Peace published a comprehensive guide to African newspapers and magazines in *The Directory of African Media*. The increase in the number of democratic states in Africa during the 1990s resulted in the dramatic growth of independent newspapers and magazines. More than just a list, *The Directory of African Media* included brief overviews that discussed the growth of the free press in many African nations, as well as examples of censorship and legislation relating to the press. In *Research in African Literatures* (Summer 1997), Nancy J. Schmidt described the book as "important in calling attention to this recent growth in journalistic activity and the need to become familiar with it." Schmidt hailed the publication of *The Directory of African Media* as "an important beginning" and expressed the hope that it would be updated on an annual or biennial basis.

Adewale Maja-Pearce edited *The Heinemann Book of African Poetry in English* (1990). He is a member of International P.E.N., a group devoted to promoting understanding and cooperation among writers. He resides in Hastings, England.

—D. C.

SUGGESTED READING: *College Literature* p188+ Feb. 1994; London *Independent* Living p18 June 20, 1990, Sunday Review p30 July 29, 1990; *Index on Censorship* (on-line); *International Journal of African Historical Studies* p462+ 1993 Vol. 2; *Los Angeles Times* Book Review p10 Nov. 24, 1991; *Research in African Literatures* p201+ Summer 1997; *Review of the African Political Economy* p374+ Sep. 1995; London *Sunday Times* (on-line) Aug. 19, 1990; *World Literature Today* p191+ Winter 1992, p659+ Summer 1993, p420 Spring 1995

SELECTED BOOKS: nonfiction—*In My Father's Country: A Nigerian Journey*, 1987; *How Many Miles to Babylon? An Essay*, 1990; *Who's Afraid of Wole Soyinka? Essays on Censorship*, 1991; *A Mask Dancing: Nigerian Novelists of the Eighties*, 1992; as editor—*Collected Poems* (of Christopher Okigbo), 1986; *The Heinemann Book of African Poetry in English*, 1990; *Wole Soyinka: An Appraisal*, 1994; *The Press in Nigeria*, (with Dulue Mbachu) 1995; *The Directory of African Media*, 1997; *From Khaki to Agbada: A Handbook for the February, 1999 Elections in Nigeria*, 1999; short-story collections—*Loyalties*, 1987 (republished as *Loyalties and Other Stories* in 1990)

Paula Hajar/Courtesy of Vintage Anchor Publicity

Makiya, Kanan

(kah-NAN mah-KEE-ah)

Aug. 13, 1949– Nonfiction writer; novelist

Kanan Makiya's first book, *Republic of Fear: The Politics of Modern Iraq*, was published under the pseudonym of Samir al-Khalil in 1989. It was a scathing indictment of the Iraqi dictator Saddam Hussein and his Baathist (also called Ba'th or Ba'ath) regime, and Makiya, an Iraqi expatriate then living in the West, dreaded the possible repercussions to himself and his family were he to reveal his identity. His position was further complicated by the fact that not only had his father, a prominent Iraqi architect, recently been in the employ of the Iraqi state, but Makiya had also worked for his father's firm for years. Makiya's book initially attracted little attention, but after the 1990 Iraqi invasion of Kuwait, it became a best-seller. Makiya revealed his identity in 1991, and shortly thereafter published *Cruelty and Silence: War, Tyranny, Uprising and the Arab World* (1993). This bold and incendiary book sharply criticized Arab intellectuals for what Makiya perceived as a failure to condemn the tyranny of Saddam Hussein. Makiya recently published *The Rock: A Seventh-Century Tale of Jerusalem* (2001), a work of historical fiction about Mount Moriah, a holy site that occupies a central place in the Jewish, Christian, and Islamic religions.

In an autobiographical statement submitted to the H.W. Wilson Company, Makiya writes: "I was born in Baghdad, Iraq, on August 13, 1949, of an Arab Muslim father and an English mother. The larger family which I knew growing up was that of my father in Iraq seeing as how my relations on my mother's side disapproved of the marriage and her intention to settle in Iraq. Nonetheless I grew up fluent in both Arabic and English, and, through the efforts of my mother (and the services of the British Council in Baghdad), was exposed at an early age to many of the great classics of English and European literature (Thomas Hardy, and Fyodor Dostoevsky were favorites).

"I attended Baghdad College, a high school run by American Jesuits with a strong science bias. Many of my teachers came from Boston College in Boston, Mass., and with the encouragement of my mathematics teacher, Reverend J. McDonell, S.J., I ended up applying to M.I.T. [Massachusetts Institute of Technology] and coming to the United States as a student in 1967. The six years I spent at M.I.T. (bachelor of science in Arts and Design followed by a stint as a site architect working on the island of Bahrain in the Persian Gulf before returning to M.I.T. where I completed a two-year master's in architecture) were, perhaps, the most glorious and eye-opening years of my life. Like most young Arabs of my generation, I was drawn to politics by the devastating defeat of the Arab armies in the June 1967 Arab-Israeli war. The then new and still untested Palestinian Resistance movement was the rising star to which our dreams and hopes were attached.

"But I was also very active in the civil rights and anti-Vietnam war movement that was sweeping American campuses. I recall with near total clarity what was perhaps a decisive turning point in my life: the assassination of Martin Luther King. With the rest of my American peers, I dropped everything I was doing and, in spite of having only the sketchiest of knowledge of the American civil rights movement, collaborated on a huge 'instant' memorial exhibition of King's life and work at M.I.T.

"But the politics of the Middle East is what ended up being the great passion of my life. Disillusionment with the Palestinian Movement, and the leftism of my twenties, set in as a result of three seminal events: the Lebanese civil war which broke out in 1975; the Iranian revolution of 1979; and the eight year long Iraq-Iran war which broke out in 1980. My whole world system collapsed in on itself with the onset of these events. Nothing in my previous ten years of political activism had prepared me for understanding why these great historic events were taking place, and what they meant. In the meantime terrible stories were being filtered to me through friends and relatives about what was going on in Iraq. Thus began a moral and intellectual journey away from ideological politics and grand schemas of 'Palestinian revolution,' 'Arab liberation,' and 'socialism' in the abstract, to a concrete understanding of what was going on in my native country Iraq.

"The result was my first book, *Republic of Fear: The Politics of Modern Iraq*, which I wrote under the pseudonym of Samir al-Khalil. The book owed a great deal to the writings of Hannah Arendt [a German-American political scientist of Jewish descent] which I discovered in the course of trying to make sense of what was going on in Iraq. It described the regime created by the Ba'th in 1968 as a classic totalitarian police state, whose closest analog was Stalinism in the Soviet Union and fascism in Nazi Germany. No Arab or Middle Eastern state had ever been described in such a way before.

"*Republic of Fear* took six years to write. Only a handful of friends knew I was writing it. It was finished in 1986. I spent three years trying to get it published. I have around 70 rejection letters from a whole variety of publishing houses in the United Kingdom and the USA. Finally, the University of California Press took a chance on publishing a book by an author whose identity was kept secret from his publishing house (this was a problem for the Board of Trustees of UC Press, but they took a vote and made an exception in my case). Two academics vouched for my existence. The book finally appeared in 1989, just one year before Saddam Husain [an alternative spelling of Hussein] invaded Kuwait in August 1990. But then the book would not sell. A few hundred copies at most sold in that first year (1989–1990), largely to Iraqi dissidents among whom word of the book spread fast. Otherwise no one was interested. Saddam Husain had after all been a strong ally of the West in the 1980s, which had in a whole variety of ways kept him from being defeated by Iran during the latter years of the Iraq-Iran war.

"Once Saddam entered Kuwait, the book became an overnight bestseller (several weeks on the *New York Times* best-seller list). I was sought after by the media and universities. But I kept my identity secret until the beginning of the uprising that followed the Gulf war. Then I went public in a major event organized by Professor Roy Mottahedeh at the Center of Middle East Studies at Harvard University. At that event I did the unthinkable for an Arab of my generation (formed on the 1967 Arab defeat in the six-day war): I called on the United States to finish the 1991 Gulf war, take out the tyrant, and march on Baghdad. Much of the rest of my life has been spent pursuing that argument in print and in politics.

"While waiting for *Republic of Fear* to find a publisher, I wrote about the degradation of culture in Saddam Husain's Iraq. That book, *The Monument: Art, Vulgarity and Responsibility in Iraq*, was also published by the University of California Press under my pseudonym in 1992. [Some sources list 1991 as the publication date.] It was followed in 1993 by *Cruelty and Silence: War, Tyranny, Uprising and the Arab World*. This was the first book to be published under my own name. It relies on the eyewitness reports of Iraqis and Kuwaitis who witnessed or survived terrible acts of cruelty. I tried to tell their stories in their own words. In the second half of the book, I launched a severe critique of Arab and pro-Arab intellectuals of my generation who were eloquent in their critiques of what they called "imperialism" and "Zionism" but who more often than not failed to make a priority of the terrible cruelties in their own backyard. This book was highly controversial, lauded in some circles and attacked in others. No one could remain neutral about it. It won the Lionel Gelber award for the best book on international relations in English for 1993.

"After 1993, I withdrew from the maelstrom of 'public' life. I began teaching at Brandeis University [a nonsectarian Jewish-sponsored institution], the first Arab I believe to do so. I remained active on human rights issues involving Iraq and the Middle East. I started the Iraq Research and Documentation Project at Harvard University which is attempting to put online approximately three million pages of classified Iraqi police and intelligence documents captured by the Kurds in the uprising that followed the Gulf war. I began writing my first novel, a work of historical fiction rooted in early Muslim, Jewish and Christian sources entitled *The Rock: A Tale of Seventh Century Jerusalem*. It tells the story of the building of the Dome of the Rock as a Muslim enterprise intended to celebrate a Jewish rock. Everything about Muslim-Jewish-Christian relations in the seventh century is a completely inverted version of what they are today. That is what attracted me to the idea. And I needed a break from the politics of the modern Middle East."

Kanan Makiya was born to Mohamed, a celebrated Iraqi architect trained in England, and Margaret, an Englishwoman who broke with her family to return with Mohamed to Baghdad. Makiya enjoyed a pleasant and largely peaceful childhood. He did well in his Jesuit-run high school, where he excelled in mathematics. Although as a youth he was largely oblivious of politics, he was very affected by the 1963 coup, when a military group and the Baathist political party wrested power from the reigning prime minister, Abdul Karim Kassem. (The Baathists came to power by espousing pan-Arabism and opposing the West.) Makiya later traced his political awakening to the violence of this coup, when the Baathists repeatedly displayed on television Kassem's dead body, with a man pointing out the bullet holes and spitting in the corpse's face. Another moment of revelation, which Makiya related to Lawrence Weschler for the New Yorker (January 6, 1992), occurred during the Six Day War of 1967 between Israel and the Arab states of Jordan, Egypt, and Syria. In the face of mounting evidence to the contrary, Arab news reported that victory was imminent, and that the Israelis were being defeated on battlefields and in the air. "I don't know why," Makiya told Weschler, "but I just remember immediately thinking, This is such bullshit, these are all such lies, we *deserve* to lose."

Eager to study abroad, Makiya applied to M.I.T., in Cambridge. He was accepted and began taking classes in 1967, shifting his focus from math to sculpture, and eventually to architecture. Meanwhile, he became increasingly politically active, participating in anti–Vietnam War activities and reading extensively on the politics of his native land. During this time Makiya met his future wife, Afsaneh Najmabadi, an Iranian graduate student of physics at Harvard University, in Cambridge. Makiya took a year off from school, which he spent as an apprentice in his father's architectural offices in Bahrain, an island nation off the coast of Saudi Arabia. He returned to M.I.T. and earned his master's degree in architecture, and then moved with Afsaneh to England, where he entered a year-long postgraduate program in urban and regional planning at the London School of Economics. He then went to work for his father's firm, Makiya Associates, which had relocated to London in 1974. (As a Shiite Muslim and an intellectual, Mohamed Makiya was out of favor with the Sunni Muslim–dominated Baathist regime, and his name appeared on a list of suspicious persons.)

Then, in 1980, the elder Makiya was invited by Saddam Hussein to direct a huge architectural project—the redevelopment of major sections of Baghdad. He was divided: although he recognized Hussein as an untrustworthy figure, he eventually accepted the assignment, judging that his architectural contribution would be for the future of his country, and not for the current regime, which he believed would be short-lived. Kanan Makiya disagreed, but out of loyalty to his father he continued to work for the firm. Father and son fought frequently, and the younger Makiya finally left the firm in 1983. He and his wife moved back to the U.S., where he began working on a book.

Republic of Fear, which Makiya completed around 1986, provides an in-depth look at the institutional violence in Baathist Iraq. Makiya argued that the state, including its network of police, surveillance networks, prisons, and torture chambers, maintains "security" by instilling in the population an overriding sense of fear and isolation. The intention of this system, he concluded, as quoted by Lawrence Weschler, is "the transformation of everybody into an informer." Makiya acknowledged that the Baathist Party had modernized parts of Iraq, but felt such gains were undermined by the regime's dehumanizing controls. Many Iraqis were literate, for example, but censorship placed severe restrictions on available texts. The status of women had nearly approached that of men, yet both men and women were routinely deprived of basic human rights. Makiya also described the centralization of power in the person of Saddam Hussein—whom he referred to as "the only genuinely free man in Iraq," as quoted by Weschler.

Makiya had a difficult time finding a publisher for the book; many editors felt that the subject was too peripheral and that the approach was too specialized. Meanwhile, Makiya worked on two other books. *Post-Islamic Classicism: A Visual Essay on the Architecture of Mohamed Makiya* (1990) was a tribute to his father's works, which Makiya published under his own name. *The Monument: Art, Vulgarity and Responsibility*, published under his pseudonym, criticized Iraqi artists for debasing themselves by catering to the tastes of Saddam Hussein. Makiya was particularly interested in Hussein's self-aggrandizing plans to construct a huge monument and military parade ground in Baghdad, to consist of a Victory Arch, commemorating Iraq's victory in the war with Iran (which at the time was still going on), and a pair of 60-foot-high bronze arms, molded from plaster casts of Hussein's own arms.

Eventually an editor at the University of California Press took an interest in *Republic of Fear*, and the book was published in 1989. It sold very few copies in the first year. Then Iraq invaded Kuwait on August 2, 1990, and almost overnight Makiya's book emerged as one of the few authoritative texts on Iraq and its leader. Lawrence Weschler cited a *New York Times Book Review* critic who called it "required reading for anyone with a serious interest in Iraq or in the political dynamics of dictatorship." *Republic of Fear* sold well in the U.S. and Britain and was translated into French, German, and Arabic. Now a sought-after authority on Iraq and Hussein, Makiya wrote editorials, under his assumed name, for the *New York Review of Books* and the *New York Times*, and began granting interviews during which his voice and appearance were disguised to preserve his anonymity. He also met with members of Congress to share his views.

As the Persian Gulf War drew to a close, Makiya decided to reveal his identity in order to air his belief that the U.S. should lend support to the Iraqi opposition. In March 1991, at a symposium put together by Harvard's Center for Middle Eastern Studies, Makiya stunned the crowd with the proposal that the U.S.—which had by this time won the war—should enter Baghdad and remove Hussein from power. While the idea found supporters among Iraqi expatriates, most Arab intellectuals were outraged. Edward Said, the prominent Palestinian intellectual and Columbia University professor, told an interviewer, as quoted by Lawrence Weschler, "[Makiya] is intelligent, fluent, but unable to attach himself to anything but an issue of the moment, with no realism in perspective. He's suddenly discovered he's got to do something, and what does he do? He appeals to the United States . . . to come and rescue him! It's astonishing." According to Michael Massing for the *New Yorker* (April 26, 1993), Said further accused Makiya of being a "careerist," who, "aside from hysterical and only occasionally informative polemics against Saddam," is "quite incapable of argument, scholarship, or rational exchange."

Makiya responded to the tide of scorn with *Cruelty and Silence: War, Tyranny, Uprising and the Arab World*. The first half of the book, titled "Cruelty," includes a series of firsthand accounts of the horrors experienced under Hussein's rule. One story depicts the regime's brutal treatment of the Kurdish ethnic minority through a boy named Taimour, who was 10 when Iraq led a 1988 campaign against the Kurds. While the men in Taimour's village were rounded up and never seen again, the women and children were taken in trucks to the Saudi border, where they were thrown into vast pits and machine-gunned. Taimour escaped by playing dead, huddling among the corpses that included his mother, his three sisters, and three of his aunts. Another account relates the atrocities committed against the Shiite Muslims, who had attempted to rebel after the Gulf War. Hussein's tanks entered the Shiite holy city of Najaf, destroying mosques, libraries, seminaries, and cultural monuments. Scores of Shiites were executed, and witnesses reported that children who refused to reveal the location of their parents were sprayed with gasoline and set on fire. Makiya gathered the material for this part of the book through a series of interviews he conducted in 1991, during a trip to northern Iraq. It was his first return to the country since 1968. "I found the cumulative effect of the stories unbearable," Makiya writes, as quoted by Michael Massing, "deadening to all rationality, a threat even to my own sanity."

The second part of the book, called "Silence," was a virulent attack against the Arab intellectual community, which, Makiya argued, had failed to speak out against Iraq's invasion of Kuwait and on behalf of the Kurds and Shiites who had stood up to Hussein after the war. Makiya acknowledged that many Kurds and Shiites had indulged in violent acts against their rulers, but he insisted that their opposition movements were important because they had broken through the stranglehold of fear that had long gripped the populace. "Not one of the intellectuals," Makiya wrote, as quoted by Massing, "who fulminated against the West for getting itself involved over Kuwait wrote or spoke up in defense of a people that had finally gathered the courage to rise against the regime that had napalmed, gassed, tortured, and terrorized them for twenty-three years." Makiya singled out Edward Said and his influential book, *Orientalism* (1979). In this book, Said accused the West of maintaining its dominance over the East, or the "Orient," by holding to an unrealistic and demeaning image of its people and society. Makiya contended that Said's argument—which had found a sympathetic audience among Arab intellectuals—obscured the real problems of the Middle East by deflecting blame from Arab leaders to the West. The writings of Said and other Arab thinkers, according to Makiya, covered up the crimes of Saddam Hussein with pro-Arab rhetoric. Makiya's conclusion, as quoted by Michael Massing, was that it is not the "tyrannies, monarchies, and autocracies that wield the guns," but "the intellectuals who generate the ideas" whom "young Arabs must hold accountable for the moral collapse of their world."

Geraldine Brooks, in an appraisal for the *Wall Street Journal* (April 7, 1993), called *Cruelty and Silence* "one of the most important books ever written on the state of the modern Middle East." Other reviewers praised Makiya's passion and conviction but expressed reservations about what they viewed as his one-sided arguments. Stanley Reed, writing for the *New York Times* (June 27, 1993), concluded that Makiya "overrates the influence of intellectuals. The rise of the modern state, not the cowardice of writers, is largely responsible for the emergence of leaders like Saddam Hussein." "Still," Reed added, "Mr. Makiya has a point in arguing that Arab political thinking is badly in need of a thorough shake-up." "In Makiya's marshalling of evidence, righteousness frequently wins out over rigor," Michael Massing wrote, asserting that Makiya's selective references failed to do justice to the scope of Said's writings. "And yet," Massing continued, "in a way, Makiya's zeal seems understandable: he is seeking to change the terms of debate in the Arab world." Indeed, in the *Washington Post* (June 6, 1993), Milton Viorst quoted Makiya in arguing for nothing less than a revolution in Arab thought, which must begin not with Arab nationalism or political Islam but "with an Arab groundswell of revulsion at cruelty in the Arab home and cruelty on the Arab street, a groundswell which views someone like Saddam Hussein as the principle of cruelty incarnate, not as the principle of Arab strength." In 1993, *Cruelty and Silence* was awarded The Lionel Gelber Prize for the best English-language book on international relations.

Makiya's next work took him into the distant past. *The Rock: A Seventh-Century Tale of Jerusalem*, Makiya's first novel, was published in 2001. The title refers to Mount Moriah, a site steeped in religious significance for the three major monotheistic religions of Judaism, Christianity, and Islam. It is believed to be the site where God appeared on Earth after the sixth day of Creation, where Adam landed after his expulsion from Paradise, where Abraham prepared to sacrifice Isaac, where Jesus preached, and where the prophet Muhammad ascended to Heaven. It is also the former site of Solomon's Temple, which is described in the Old Testament, and it is where the Dome of the Rock stands today as the oldest surviving Islamic building. The novel imagines the period leading up to the construction of the Dome, which took place after the Arab conquest of Jerusalem in the seventh century. Since historical sources about the building of the Dome are incomplete, Makiya drew from legends and myths. "We know too little," Makiya wrote in an appendix to the book, as quoted by Jonathan Kirsch in the *Los Angeles Times* (December 1, 2001). "So much has been irretrievably lost." To make up for it, Makiya explained, "Fiction has stepped into the breach."

The Rock is narrated by Ishaq, the son of Ka'b al-Ahbar, an actual historical figure. Born a Jew, Ka'b converted to Islam and became an advisor to the Islamic caliph, Umar, who had seized Jerusalem from the Christian Romans in the 630s. The Muslims allowed Jewish settlement in Jerusalem for the first time in five centuries. When the novel opens, Ka'b has died, and Ishaq, an architect, has been commissioned to carry out the construction of the Dome. In the course of his narration, Ishaq recalls the complicated relationships that had developed over the planning of the Islamic monument between his father, Umar, and Sophronius, the Christian patriarch who conceded Jerusalem to the Arabs. In Makiya's telling, Ka'b passes on aspects of Jewish theology through his discussions with Umar, thus demonstrating the possibility for harmony between the faiths. "The fact that the author never indicates which scripture he's quoting is part of his strategy to emphasize unities rather than divisions," Daniel Mendelsohn wrote for *New York* magazine (December 17, 2001). "Readers who haven't been to Sunday school in a while will have to search the 70 pages of dense notes at the back of the book to figure out whether they're getting the Koran, or the Old Testament, or the New."

Makiya "triumphs in this inspired and lyrical book," Jana Riess wrote for *Publishers Weekly* (October 15, 2001). "The novelization is pure magic, as Makiya brings history to life for contemporary readers." For the *Washington Post* (December 9, 2001), James Reston Jr. noted that "[Makiya's] vivid renderings are so well grounded in the sources that he succeeds in overcoming the normal complaints about historical fiction. The result is a solid, interesting, accessible and highly illuminating tome for our time." Jonathan Kirsch opined that "the same passion for human dignity and human diversity that Makiya brings to his work in politics shines through in his storytelling."

Makiya lives in Cambridge, Massachusetts, and teaches Middle East studies at Brandeis University, in Waltham, Massachusetts. He has written for the *New York Times*, the *New York Review of Books*, the *Times Literary Supplement* and the (London) *Times*. He also directs the Iraq Research and Documentation Project at Harvard University. Makiya and Afsaneh Najmabadi divorced in 1986. They have two children.

—A. I. C.

SUGGESTED READING: *Los Angeles Times* B p22 Dec. 1, 2001; *New York* p68 Dec. 17, 2001; *New York Times* p7 June 27, 1993; *New Yorker* p40+ Jan. 6, 1992, p114+ Apr. 26, 1993; *Publishers Weekly* p67 Oct. 15, 2001; *Wall Street Journal* A p12 Apr. 7, 1993; *Washington Post* p6 June 6, 1993, p4 Dec. 9, 2001

SELECTED BOOKS: nonfiction—*Republic of Fear: The Politics of Modern Iraq*, 1989; *Post-Islamic Classicism: A Visual Essay on the Architecture of Mohamed Makiya*, 1990; *Cruelty and Silence: War, Tyranny, Uprising and the Arab World*, 1993; fiction—*The Rock: A Seventh-Century Tale of Jerusalem*, 2001

Malone, Michael

Nov. 1942– Novelist; nonfiction writer; short-story writer

Michael Malone has developed a career by defying traditional genre categorization. Whether he's producing inventive picaresques, suspenseful mysteries, or absorbing television scenarios, Malone often colors his works with large casts of characters, sprawling plots, and what Jean M. White, writing for the *Washington Post* (November 20, 1983), called "a stylish gift for language." Malone, who has taught at Yale University, Swarthmore College, and the University of Pennsylvania, among other schools, is known for his liberal use of literary allusion. By his own account, his writing is indebted to the "friendship, nudges, winks, and wise teaching" of his favorite canonical authors, most notably Charles Dickens, Henry Fielding, and Miguel De Cervantes, whom he acknowledged in the prologue of his 1986 novel, *Handling Sin*. Likewise, many critics have drawn comparisons between Malone's style and those of his literary mentors. Frances Taliaferro wrote for the *Washington Post* (April 13, 1986), "What distinguishes all three masters [Dickens, Fielding, and Cervantes] is their energy—a

Michael Malone
Courtesy of Source Books

yeasty and irrepressible bubbling-up of life. Like Dickens, especially, Malone cannot resist peopling his narrative with quirky souls who add nothing to the plot and everything to the texture of the novel." Malone has crafted several critically admired novels, including *Dingley Falls* (1980) and *Foolscap* (1991). He has contributed to the mystery genre with *Uncivil Seasons* (1983), *Time's Witness* (1989), and *First Lady* (2001), three books set in the fictional southern town of Hillston, North Carolina, and featuring what Evan Hunter for the *New York Times* (November 13, 1983) called "two of the most memorable police detectives ever to appear in mystery fiction." In 1991 Malone took a five-year hiatus from writing novels to become head writer on the ABC soap opera *One Life to Live*; more recently, he has produced a collection of award-winning short stories, *Red Clay, Blue Cadillac* (2002). Malone is also the author of several plays, screenplays, nonfiction books, articles, and reviews. Of his adventurous approach to fiction, he told Judith Weinraub for the *Washington Post* (February 7, 1992), "I'm a real fictional democrat. I don't think any one form or genre is superior to any other."

Michael Malone was born in the Piedmont region of North Carolina in November 1942, the eldest of six children of Thomas Patrick Malone, a psychiatrist, and Faylene Malone, an English teacher. A natural storyteller from an early age, Malone often penned short plays as a child and forced his brothers and sisters to act in his productions. Recalling a particular childhood incident that illustrated his precocity, Malone told an interviewer for *Sourcebooks.com*, "[My mother] once defended me to my elementary school principal. I'd told the principle my mother had been unable to sign my report card because she'd come down with the blue bonnet plague. 'He's not a liar; he has a wonderful imagination,' [she said]. 'He's going to be a writer.'"

After a stint at Syracuse University, in New York, Malone obtained a B.A. degree from the University of North Carolina, where he also earned a master's degree. He then completed additional postgraduate study at Harvard University, in Cambridge, Massachusetts, where he worked toward completing his Ph.D. in the early 1970s; Malone's Harvard dissertation on the archetypes of innocence and eroticism in American film formed the basis of his later nonfiction book, *Heroes of Eros: Male Sexuality in the Movies* (1979). While at Harvard Malone met his future wife, Maureen Quilligan—whom he described to Michael Neill and David Hutchings for *People* (February 24, 1992) as "a real scholar"—while she was pursuing her Ph.D. in Renaissance literature. The couple married in 1975. (Quilligan has since developed an accomplished career in academia and is currently chair of the English Department and a professor of Renaissance studies at Duke University, in North Carolina.)

During his years at Harvard, Malone began working on his first novel, *Painting the Roses Red* (1975), written from the point of view of an indecisive Berkeley graduate student, Constance Mennagan, who is torn between her husband and another student. The novel explores the insulated environment of Berkeley, California, in the 1960s. The book received few reviews; however, one critic for *Publishers Weekly* (March 3, 1975) observed, "Innocence is what characterizes the novel and ultimately what goes wrong with it. . . . What's off the mark here is Mennagan's sensibility; the author simply isn't wise enough yet to understand the turmoil in her head."

In *The Delectable Mountain* (1977), Malone produced his first picaresque. (A picaresque is a type of fiction that presents a series of episodic adventures; the main character is often roguish.) This novel depicts a young protagonist who comes to an understanding about life through his experiences working with a theater company in Colorado. Writing for *Library Journal* (January 1, 1977), Larry Gray observed, "The characters of *The Delectable Mountain* are a catalog of stereotypes. . . . By every right this novel should be corny, but it isn't. Despite [the] clichés and the author's disconcerting habit of writing in fragmentary and sometimes awkward sentences, the book succeeds. . . . This is not just a funny novel. It is a comedy in the best sense of the word." That year, Malone also published his first nonfiction book, *Psychetypes: A New Way of Exploring Personality* (1977).

Dingley Falls (1980) became Malone's first widely reviewed literary novel and was again written in picaresque form. Here, Malone creates the fictional New England town of Dingley Falls, Connecticut, and "peoples it," according to Susan

Fromberg Schaeffer for the *Chicago Tribune* (June 15, 1980), "with the sort who would actually live in it—wealthy wives and their husbands, bored teen-agers, frustrated blue-collar workers, the elderly, the eccentrics." The novel chronicles the lives of some 50 characters within Dingley Falls as they confront a mysterious illness plaguing their town; throughout, Malone weaves numerous subplots into his narrative, creating what Alan Cheuse for the *New York Times* (May 11, 1980) called "an extremely busy novel." According to Cheuse, "[*Dingley Falls*] is full of matters—large ones, such as love, conscience, politics and health, and small ones, such as gossip, sexual habits and the trivia of contemporary American culture—that will hold the attention of readers both serious and casual." Malone's novel was largely a critical success, with Ross C. Murfin for *The Nation* (August 30–September 6, 1980) calling it, "effective social satire as well as dark human comedy." Murfin added that the novel "sometimes reads like the work of a New England Faulkner," but concluded, "*Dingley Falls* . . . ultimately owes more to Dickens than to any single American novelist." Schaeffer observed, "So beautiful is this novel rendered, scene by scene, character by character, sentence by sentence, that the end of the journey is much less important than the journey itself." She opined, "*Dingley Falls* is one of the best books I have read in a long time."

In 1983 Malone produced his first mystery novel, *Uncivil Seasons*, which according to White, "bears [Malone's] imprint—the vividly drawn ambience of a small Southern milltown with an old-family structure that dominates local society and politics." Amidst this backdrop, Malone introduces Justin Savile V, a police detective and a recovering alcoholic who still turns to the bottle during times of stress. When Cloris Dollard, the wife of Justin's uncle—a state senator—is murdered, Justin and his partner, police chief Cuddy Mangum, manage the investigation and discover several mysteries along the way about Justin's own family history.

Several critics praised Malone for his development of rich and interesting lead characters; Evan Hunter also observed, "Equally engaging are the colorful characters the detectives encounter in their search for the truth." While Hunter noted some flaws—such as an unconvincing romance between Justin and a female character—the reviewer said, "These are minor problems, and they are compensated for by the rich diversity of the cast, the compelling plot and the often poetically haunting beauty of Mr. Malone's prose." Hunter concluded, "Mr. Malone has written a rattling good mystery; he has also written an excellent novel. The two need not be incompatible." A reviewer for *Quill & Quire* (August 1989) concurred, calling *Uncivil Seasons* "a brilliant example of the mystery novel's literary potential."

After completing his first mystery, Malone returned to the genre of the episodic novel with *Handling Sin* (1986), a book chronicling what Thomas D'Evelyn for the *Christian Science Monitor* (March 26, 1986) described as "the madcap adventures of the hero, who strikes me as a combination of Odysseus, Don Quixote, and Tom Jones." The novel begins with the disappearance of Raleigh Hayes's father, a defrocked Episcopalian minister who escapes the hospital where he is being treated for a heart condition, leaving a taped message of instructions for his son. At his father's request Raleigh, at the start an uptight, middle-aged insurance salesman, embarks on a series of adventures across the South, picking up various people and objects of significance to his father before meeting the elder Hayes in New Orleans. Despite the sprawling narrative and continually shifting plot, Terrence Rafferty for *The Nation* (June 21, 1986) observed, "The novel's structure is tight as a fitted sheet: everything gathers perfectly at the end."

Handling Sin received widespread critical praise, with several reviewers comparing the novel to John Kennedy Toole's southern satire, *A Confederacy of Dunces* (1980). Writing for the *New York Times* (April 13, 1986), A. C. Greene elaborated, "The humor of *Handling Sin* is superior to that by now assumed classic. Mr. Malone's twists and turns and surprises are downright phenomenal, verging on genius. There are entire chapters in this book that are funny, sentence by sentence." While Thomas D'Evelyn suggested that Malone's novel lacked the satirical bite of Toole's work, he characterized *Handling Sin* as "romantic and sentimental, but in the highest sense." Some critics found flaws within Malone's meandering plot. For the *Times Literary Supplement* (January 9, 1987), Brian Morton wrote of the novel, "For all its mythic pretensions, [it] never manages to be more than the sum of its occasionally entertaining parts." Terrence Rafferty noted, "The problem with *Handling Sin* is, perhaps, the most forgivable one a novel can have: even this maximum capacity structure can't quite contain everything the author fits into it."

In 1989 Malone resurrected the characters of Lieutenant Justin Savile V and his partner, Cuddy Mangum, in his second mystery novel, *Time's Witness*. This time around, Mangum, who is fiercely opposed to capital punishment, narrates the multilayered story of two murder investigations. Valerie Sayers wrote for the *New York Times Book Review* (April 23, 1989), "[Malone's] narrative offers a complex and satisfying plot, a rich panorama of a class-stratified Southern town and dense portraits of even minor characters." Of Mangum and his staunch views, Sayers noted, "Creating a character with such strong beliefs is a risky business, of course, since the novelist . . . must never abandon the all-important story while veering off on a moral crusade. Mr. Malone never does."

Throughout the 1980s Malone produced several plays; in 1987 he wrote a screenplay adaption of his 1986 book *Handling Sin*. He returned to the picaresque genre with *Foolscap* (1991), a comedic romp satirizing the worlds of academia, theater, and publishing. The story chronicles the adventures of Theo Ryan, a reserved professor of the English Renaissance at the fictional Cavendish University. Ryan, who is the son of theater performers and himself a closet dramatist, has been authorized to write the biography of the legendary playwright—and flamboyant alcoholic—Ford Rexford. After Rexford helps Ryan revise his only play, *Foolscap*, which is written in the language of an Elizabethan drama, he takes the piece to London, leaving behind an unfinished play of his own. Soon after, Rexford dies in an car accident, prompting Ryan to complete the elder playwright's final work and bring it to the London stage in order restore Rexford's diminished reputation. While in England Ryan arranges to have his own play discovered as a "lost" work of the Renaissance figure Sir Walter Raleigh. As a reviewer for *Atlantic Monthly* (November 1991) described, "Mr. Malone's novel is basically the old tale of the fellow who starts out from dreary circumstances, encounters and, with the help of a supernatural mentor, survives outrageous adventures, and ultimately finds true love and a pot of gold. On this antique foundation the author has erected an amusing, satirical, marvelously convoluted modern structure inhibited by characters of Dickensian gaudiness." Meanwhile, Richard Bausch for the *New York Times* (December 8, 1991) called the book a "vibrant, unruly, playful and cannily plotted caper through our foolishness." Of his own intentions, Malone told Susannah Hunnewell for the *New York Times* (December 8, 1991), "I've spent my whole life with academic zanies and they fell together on a canvas. It's a fascinating, dramatic time in academia. I wanted to write about a university that was obsessed with political correctness and fame."

Critics applauded *Foolscap* for its humorous tone and entertaining characterizations. Richard Bausch opined, "Perhaps Michael Malone's greatest gift as a novelist—apart from his reckless, ingenious and always exhilarating way of spinning a tale—is his ability to make distinctive, substantive characters out of his comic creations." Writing for *Commonweal* (February 14, 1992), Paul Elie thought the novel faltered when Malone favored parody or plot device over deeper characterization, noting, "Malone's easy reliance on caricature keeps him from developing the themes on which his plot is founded." Elie concluded, "*Foolscap* stands or falls not on the verities of plot and character and theme but on the degree to which we find its authorial voice entertaining."

In the early 1990s Malone took a highly unprecedented step for a literary novelist and accepted a position as head writer for the ABC daytime soap opera *One Life to Live*. The opportunity arose after the producer Linda Gottlieb, whom Malone had met years earlier during negotiations over movie rights to one of his novels, was hired to revive the 23-year-old program. Gottlieb wanted a veteran writer who could coordinate multiple story lines while developing interesting characters and moments of drama, suspense, and humor. "She told the network she needed a novelist, someone who wrote huge-canvas novels," Malone recalled to Michael Neill and David Hutchings, "and that's when a mutual friend called my wife and told her." He continued, "[My wife] didn't even bother to tell me about it. She laughed and said I'd never be interested. A week later I got the call from Gottlieb, and I started watching the show." Malone quickly became interested in what he described as "an endless chance to tell stories," as well as the opportunity to write adventurous story lines, craft elaborate characters, and collaborate with a team of other writers. "I couldn't resist it," he told Susannah Hunnewell. "I think Dickens would have done it. I make up characters and there they are in the flesh. I have my own Shakespeare company." Less than one year after Malone took charge of the show's writing staff, *One Life to Live* had jumped from eleventh place in daytime television ratings to fourth. During his five years as head writer for *One Life to Live*, Malone received four nominations for the Daytime Emmy Award for outstanding drama series writing team; he brought home the award in 1994.

After five years of writing television drama, Malone returned to writing fiction. In 2001, a decade after the publication of his last book, Malone released *First Lady*, the third mystery built around the characters of Justin Savile V and Cuddy Mangum. This novel, narrated by Savile, depicts the detectives' investigation into an apparent serial murderer. John Orr for the *San Jose Mercury News* (October 23, 2001), applauded Malone's return to fiction, calling *First Lady*, "a terrific whodunit, with clever plotting and clue strewing that make it a real page-turner; it is beautifully written, with graceful turns of phrase and thoughtful looks into the hearts of well-conceived characters." The book features Malone's signature subplots, rich characterizations, and large amounts of local lore. Jesse Berrett for the *New York Times* (September 23, 2001, on-line), found the wealth of detail a distraction and noted that "the plot is repeatedly interrupted by rambles through local history and mores that sometimes feel luxuriantly digressive and sometimes merely wearying." Nevertheless, Berrett concluded, "Malone sets loose his collection of eccentrics and lets them do their worst, alternately horrified and amused by the varieties of mischief they get up to—in best Southern tradition, but with a self-consciously modern twist."

In 2002 Malone published a collection of 12 short stories entitled *Red Clay, Blue Cadillac*, which included "Stella: Red Clay," a story that had earlier won the Edgar Allan Poe Award from the Mystery Writers of America, and "Meredith: Fast Love," the winner of the 1982 O. Henry Award. Joanne Wilkinson wrote for *Booklist* (February 1, 2002), "The main focus of this collection is southern women, ranging from a smoldering, light-fingered femme fatale with an Elvis obsession to a phenomenally rich socialite whose fifth wedding is marred by murder." Another reviewer for *Publishers Weekly* (February 18, 2002) found the collection uneven, but called it "more than worthwhile, including some of the best stories to come out of the South in years."

Also in 2002, Malone published the novel *The Last Noel*, which follows an evolving interracial romance between Noelle "Noni" Tilden and John "Kaye" King. As quoted on the *Amazon.com* Web site, Joanne Wilkinson wrote for *Booklist*, "Malone walks a fine line here between the mawkish and the moving. The plotline can sometimes feel soap opera-like, with its detours into infidelity and illness, but Malone is such a fine writer that at every turn he provides insightful glimpses into an exceptionally appealing cast of characters."

Over the years Malone has contributed numerous articles and reviews to such publications as *Viva*, *The Nation*, *Human Behavior*, *Harper's Magazine*, *Playboy*, *Mademoiselle*, and the *New York Times Book Review*. He is currently working on his next novel, a romantic odyssey entitled "The Four Corners of the Sky." Of his urge to write novels, he told the reporter for *Sourcebooks.com*, "I believe that in the end, art we make—our books and plays, music and paintings, gives to our nation, to our world, one of the strongest weapons we have to defend our freedom and preserve our humanness. I think that these days more than ever we should read and talk and teach and sing and laugh together. When we do, the community we make becomes a shield of light. I keep thinking of Gandhi being asked, 'What do you think of western civilization?' and his replying, 'I think it would be a good idea.'"

Malone resides in Hillsborough, North Carolina. He and his wife, Maureen Quilligan, have one daughter.

—K. D.

SUGGESTED READING: *Chicago Tribune* VII p4 June 15, 1980; *Commonweal* p27 Feb. 14, 1992; *The Nation* p195+ Aug. 30–Sep. 6, 1980, p860 June 21, 1986; *New York Times* (on-line) Sep. 23, 2001; *New York Times Book Review* p14+ May 11, 1980, p14 Nov. 13, 1983, p11 Apr. 13, 1986, p12 Dec. 8, 1991, with photo; *People* p57+ Feb. 24, 1992, with photo; *San Jose Mercury News* Oct. 3, 2001; *Washington Post* B p1 Feb. 7, 1992, with photo; *Washington Post Book World* p10 Nov. 20, 1983, p3 Apr. 13, 1986, p5 Oct. 13, 1991

SELECTED BOOKS: novels—*Painting the Roses Red*, 1975; *The Delectable Mountain*, 1977; *Dingley Falls*, 1980; *Uncivil Seasons*, 1983; *Handling Sin*, 1986; *Time's Witness*, 1989; *Foolscap*, 1991; *First Lady*, 2001; *The Last Noel*, 2002; short-story collections—*Red Clay, Blue Cadillac*, 2002; nonfiction—*Psychetypes: A New Way of Exploring Personality*, 1977; *Heroes of Eros: Male Sexuality in the Movies*, 1979

Joyce Ravid/Courtesy of Vintage Anchor Publicity

Marcus, Ben

Oct. 11, 1967– Novelist; short-story writer

With the publication of *The Age of Wire and String: Stories* (1995), a collection of short ruminations about meaning, Ben Marcus emerged as an innovative writer whose quirky, succinct style and unconventional word usage earned his work comparisons with James Joyce's *Finnegan's Wake* and William Faulkner's *The Sound and the Fury*. "Using short, unsentimental orbs of prose, Marcus describes an odd North America in which plain people live as normally as they know how," Stacey Levine noted for the *Alt-X Online Publishing Network*. In her interview with him for that publication, Marcus said, "Maybe your real life is everything you don't know about, ideas and feelings you haven't confirmed or even imagined yet. The writing is instantly more powerful if there is an act of discovery on the writer's part. . . . The task, for me, is to build beyond what my daily life has evidenced, to discover the outer possibilities of my heart and mind and possibly, as a result, produce a new kind of animal." Marcus's subsequent publication, *Notable American Women* (2002), an unconventional, fragmented novel about a protagonist named Ben Marcus who undergoes a process of "emotion removal," has helped to foster a cult-like following for the inventive author.

Ben Marcus was born in Chicago on October 11, 1967. He received a bachelor's degree in philosophy from New York University, in New York City, in 1989, and a master's degree in fiction writing from Brown University, in Providence, Rhode Island, in 1991. Marcus's first book, *The Age of Wire and String: Stories* (1995), is a collection of 41 short prose pieces that forgo plot and character;

rather, Marcus acts as a creator, cataloguer, and taxonomist of what Blake de Pastino, who critiqued the book for *Weekly Wire* (on-line), described as "a ghostly, vaguely America-like world." "This is a place where 'difficulties with dog populations' are said to have 'generated the mass suffocation of Ohio.' Where the people of Montana use 'food costumes,' including something called a 'fudge girdle, a one-piece garment that spreads from waist to feet,'" de Pastino wrote. In a brief "Argument" in the collection, Marcus states:

> This book is a catalog of the life project as prosecuted in the Age of Wire and String and beyond, into the arrangements of states, sites, and cities and, further, within the small houses that have been granted erection or temporary placement on the perimeters of districts and river colonies. . . . There is no larger task than that of cataloging a culture, particularly when that culture has remained willfully hidden to the routine in-gazing practiced by professional disclosers, who, after systematically looting our country of its secrets, are now busy shading every example of so-called local color into their own banal hues.

The Age of Wire and String is divided into eight sections, titled "Sleep," "God," "Food," "The House," "Animal," "Weather," "Persons," and "The Society," each of which includes five brief essays and a glossary of terms, except for "The Society," which has a sixth essay. Throughout the book, Marcus uses the language of speculative academic discourse, arranging his ruminations in a style that combines the "high modernist's" search for meaning with the encyclopedist's passion for classification. "There is something cheerfully lipogrammatic in the book's architecture," Steven Poole wrote in his review for the *Times Literary Supplement* (November 14, 1997), adding that Marcus's "often comical pseudo-scholarship" suggests "the voice of a fusty library-haunter" and that *The Age of Wire and String*—"a treasury of interconnected fables of violence and hope," as he described it—"stands out as an exhilarating work of literature."

Marcus's penchant for subverting the familiar meanings attached to commonplace words is especially evident in the glossaries that accompany each section; the glossaries co-opt familiar names in the service of the author's utopian fantasies, in which inanimate objects take on an organic vitality. "Albert," for example, is defined in the "Sleep" glossary as "nightly killer of light, applied to systems or bodies which alter postures under various stages of darkness. Flattened versions exist only in the water or grass. They may not rise until light is poured upon them." Similarly, "Jennifer" is defined as "the inability to see. Partial blindness in regard to hands. To jennifer is to feign blindness. The diseases resulting from these acts are called jennies." The unconventional way Marcus uses language led the writer Robert Coover to declare, in a blurb for the jacket of *The Age of Wire and String*, that Marcus is a "unique new talent in American letters" and that the publication of the book was "the most audacious literary debut in decades—witty, startlingly inventive, funny but fundamentally disturbing, language itself held together here by whimsical bits of wire and string."

In 2002 Marcus published *Notable American Women*, his first novel. The dystopian tale is set in a futuristic Ohio, where the main character, a boy named Ben Marcus, is raised by his mother and a sect of radical women called the "Silentists." The Silentists, lead by the austere matriarch Jane Dark, believe that they can attain power by withholding speech and altering the conventional means of communication. To achieve silence and stillness they subject themselves to cult-like forms of behavior modification—a taxing regimen that includes swimming in a "learning pond," drinking "behavior water," and taking "language enemas"—which Ben not only witnesses but is subjected to by his mother, an enthusiastic Silentist. Ben once had a younger sister who died from the stress of an experiment in which her parents changed her name daily. Ben's father, who introduces the book with a bitter message for the reader, has been banished by the Silentists to an underground cell in the backyard. The Silentists also advocate a form of "emotion removal" and Ben has been taught to eschew personal expression; as a result the narrative he presents is an assortment of utilitarian instruction-manual prose, historical time lines, a manual of Silentist behavior, and disquisitions on such topics as female names. Yet throughout, the author conveys the protagonist's sense of distress and anxiety caused by his situation.

Critics who approved of Marcus's first book warmly welcomed *Notable American Women*. "Marcus combines an audacious yet assured style with fragmented structure to create a bitterly funny critique of 21st-century family dynamics," Michael Porter wrote in the *New York Times* (April 28, 2002). "The reader pieces this strange history together from bits of narrative, invented chronologies, health and dietary information and detailed instructions on how to read the book. What unites these elements—and keeps the novel from sinking into stale allegory—is Marcus's vigorous imagination and scathing humor." Ross Doll, in a review for *Amazon.com*, called the book "strange and fantastical. . . . Most accurately classified as science fiction, (though often darkly humorous), *Women* maintains an unsettling balance between absurdity and horror, shifting its subject from the academic to the domestic. . . . A heart can be found in the novel, however, that is well worth discovering: beyond its detached creepiness lies an allegory deeply concerned with the dangers of conformity and the maniacal pursuit of human advancement."

In his interview with Stacey Levine, which took place before the completion of *Notable American Women*, Marcus explained that in that book he was planning to "create a system [of language] that might read like an 'essay' or a religious text." He added: "My struggle is formal. When it comes down to it, my model for fiction is more of a religious than narrative one."

Marcus's most recent work is *The Father Costume* (2002), an art book joining Marcus's text with drawings by the artist Matthew Ritchie. The story takes place in a mythological world made mostly of water, where clothing changes people's behavior. According to the book description, as posted on *Amazon.com*, "Matthew Ritchie's striking images blend scientific diagramming with vivid, colorful renderings of the apocalypse, while writer Ben Marcus's cold prose plumbs the inner workings of two boys caught out at sea with a father whose costumes grow increasingly menacing."

In the early 1990s Marcus acted in several experimental videos and films that he directed and wrote or co-wrote. Notable among them is a 15-minute, 16mm black-and-white film entitled "Nine Feet Tall," which Marcus directed and co-wrote with Bob Mowen. "Nine Feet Tall" won a prize at the New York University film festival in 1991 and was shown in 1992 at film festivals in Arizona and Dallas.

Marcus is currently an assistant professor in the graduate writing program at Columbia University, in New York City. Before that he taught for three years at Brown University, where he was the editor and founder of the on-line journal *Impossible Object*. He has also served as an adjunct lecturer at the City College and Lehman College campuses of the City University of New York and as a visiting assistant professor at both the University of Texas at Austin and Old Dominion University, in Virginia. He is currently the fiction editor of *Fence* magazine. His short fiction and book reviews have appeared in a wide range of literary and other periodicals, including the *Iowa Review*, *Grand Street*, *Mississippi Review*, *Story Quarterly*, the *Village Voice*, and *Conjunctions*; he has also served as senior editor for the latter publication. Among other honors, Marcus is the recipient of a Whiting Writer's Award, in 1999, an NEA in fiction, and two Pushcart Prizes.

—E. M.

SUGGESTED READING: *Grand Street* p31+ Fall 1994; *St. Louis Post-Dispatch* D p13 Dec. 7, 1998; *New York Times* VII p21 Apr. 28, 2002; *Times Literary Supplement* p23 Nov. 14, 1997; *Village Voice* p90 Oct. 26, 1999

SELECTED BOOKS: short-story collections—*The Age of Wire and String: Stories*, 1995; novels—*Notable American Women*, 2002

Marcus, J. S.

(?)– Novelist; short-story writer; journalist

Between the time he published his first short-story collection, *The Art of Cartography*, in 1991, and his first novel, *The Captain's Fire*, in 1996, J. S. Marcus's writing style changed dramatically, from one of highly crafted and refined minimalism to one filled with references and digressions. However, despite the stylistic differences, the characters and themes Marcus wrote about remained similar. In both works he created young characters who are pursued unendingly by self-consciousness and their own pasts. Seemingly possessed of an innate detachment from life and other people, they exhibit aimless restlessness and loneliness. As Michael Miller remarked in the *Village Voice Literary Supplement* (March 5, 1996), their predicaments are aptly described by a character from the short story "Everywhere," in which a native New Yorker waiting tables on an exotic island echoes the words of Greek poet Constantine Cavafy: "You will find no new lands. . . . You will find no other seas. The city will follow you."

J. S. Marcus grew up in the suburbs of Milwaukee, Wisconsin. His short stories began appearing in such magazines as the *New Yorker* and *Harper's* in the mid-1980s. In 1991 he published a collection of some of his stories, entitled *The Art of Cartography*. In the collection, Marcus displayed little interest in complex plots, and most of the stories featured characters in their 20s engaging in ordinary activities. In one story a photographer who takes pictures of the shadows of wires visits a couple whose apartment is littered with unfinished woodworking projects. Another story is about a young American bank trainee in London. In another, a woman drops out of law school to move in with her ex-boyfriend, Everett. "How heavy we seemed," she reflects, "Everett and I, back where we began, but not exactly, as if all we could do in our lives was shift weight," as quoted in the *New York Times Book Review* (April 21, 1991). This theme of the ineffectuality of travel and of attempts to change one's circumstances—of the inability to escape one's origins—recurs in many of the stories in *The Art of Cartography*.

In a review of the collection for the *New York Times Book Review* (April 21, 1991), Elizabeth Gleick wrote that there was "some good writing here . . . along with some real intelligence. Just not enough." She lamented the sameness of Marcus's characters and his tendency to encapsulate themes. "Like cookie fortunes," Gleick wrote, "Mr. Marcus's stories are not necessarily untrue. Sometimes they're even apt. They're just not as deep as this clearly talented writer could make them." In the *Nation* (April 8, 1996), Scott McLemee found Marcus's writing indistinguishable from that of other young writers publishing work in the 1980s. Commenting on the writing of this group as a whole, McLemee observed, "The style was disjunctive, ironic, minimalist. The people were creatures of pure anomie: They did little, felt less and thought about almost nothing at all. Narrators were prone to sudden aphorisms, particularly toward the end of the story. . . . Hundreds, if not thousands, of writers began turning out work in this mode." However, Marcus won several awards for the collection, including a 1992 Whiting Writing Award, worth $30,000. He was also short-listed by the literary magazine *Granta* in 1993 for the publication's 20 Best Young American Novelists award.

In the early 1990s Marcus went to live in Germany and wrote several travel articles about that country for the *New York Times*. His first novel, *The Captains's Fire* (1996), was also an outgrowth of Marcus's experiences abroad. It is narrated by Joel LaVine, a bisexual, American Jew in his early 30s who leaves Milwaukee to take a job as an English teacher in Berlin, Germany. Much of the novel consists of his observations about the city as he travels from place to place. Joel laments Berliners' wishes to forget the Holocaust and turn the concentration camps into tourist attractions under the unified country's relatively new capitalist system. The narrative is punctuated with a rich store of references to German-speaking Jewish writers, including Franz Kafka, Walter Benjamin, Gershom Scholem, and Hannah Arendt. While Joel is preoccupied by self-reflection and his avid reading, his students trash him in evaluations, and his duties are gradually lessened. Finally, Joel is dismissed from his job. To make matters worse, he is served an eviction notice at his apartment and is forced to take a job selling videos at a flea market in order to make ends meet. Over the course of the novel, Joel finds himself in several romantic relationships that inevitably stall as he is unable to become emotionally intimate. Finally, he returns to America, determined to stay put. Toward the novel's end, an unidentified "I," either Joel or another, unknown narrator, ponders writing "the opposite of a travel article—an attempt to make people stay at home. . . . I want them to see where they are differently, as a new place," as quoted from the novel by McLemee.

As in *The Art of Cartography*, dreamed-of destinations always prove illusory in *The Captain's Fire*, and this pattern extends to Joel's relationships. "*The Captain's Fire* relentlessly substitutes Joel's origins for his destinations," Miller wrote. "His relationships are all botched departures—constant, futile yearnings to be elsewhere on the map of desire. After he sleeps with a woman he wants to sleep with a man and vice versa." Janet St. John, writing in *Booklist* (March 1, 1996), noted that "Marcus demonstrates the kind of curiosity, patience, and wisdom that cannot go unpraised." On the other hand, McLemee, while appreciating the book's complexity and viewing it as a major improvement on Marcus's short stories, felt that the novel suffered from being tied too closely to the narrator's perspective: "The problem with the book lies in its effort to hold as many levels of information and reflection as possible (and as nearly simultaneously as possible) within the frame of a single character's consciousness. . . . Other char-

acters are names, little more." In the *New York Times Book Review* (April 21, 1996), John David Morley wrote that "since [Marcus] is hindered by an ingrained cultural antipathy [against Germany], he is not prepared to offer much in the way of understanding." However, he also complimented Marcus on his "astute grasp of the historical and cultural issues of 20th-century Germany, particularly as they are reflected in the work of the Jewish writers he knows well."

Not long after Marcus returned to the U.S. from Germany, his mother died. In an article for the *New York Times Magazine* (May 11, 1997), he wrote about returning to Milwaukee to mourn her death and becoming caught in a cycle of sorrow that was broken only after he got in a car accident. He had taken to driving around Wisconsin, exploring little towns "with paper mills and bait-and-tackle shops and gas stations selling cheese curds at the register." One evening he was driving along an icy road and went into a slide just in front of a tractor trailer. Though Marcus's car landed upside-down in a ditch, he was unharmed. "For a while after that," Marcus wrote in the article, "I was, in some sense, elated—no longer mourning my mother but celebrating the fact of my survival." He was able to overcome his grief and return to New York City, where he currently lives.

—P. G. H.

SUGGESTED READING: *New York Times Book Review* p23 Apr. 21, 1991, p41 Apr. 21, 1996; *New York Times Magazine* p70 May 11, 1997; *Village Voice Literary Supplement* p16 Mar. 5, 1996, with photo

SELECTED BOOKS: novels—*The Captain's Fire*, 1996; short-story collections—*The Art of Cartography*, 1991

Margulies, Donald

1954– Playwright; screenwriter

After the playwright Donald Margulies won the 2000 Pulitzer Prize in drama for *Dinner with Friends*, he said that the award "meant a lot personally and professionally" and that it "creates new interest in my other works," as cited by Everett Evans in the *Houston Chronicle* (April 8, 2001). Even before the Pulitzer, however, Margulies had been a successful and popular playwright, known for his stylistically and thematically daring work, which is often grounded in relationships and the inevitable conflicts that bedevil them. An early play, *Found a Peanut* (1984), found much critical success, his succeeding work met with many awards, and his *Sight Unseen* (1992) and *Collected Stories* (1998) were both finalists for the Pulitzer Prize. Margulies has also written scripts for Tri-Star, Touchstone, Warner Brothers, and other film and television production companies, and his

Courtesy of Theatre Communication Group
Donald Margulies

credits include the television feature *Divorced Kids' Blues* (1987) and an episode of the television series *Once and Again* (1999). Many of Margulies's plays deal with the Jewish experience, but they also take on such universal themes as marriage, father-and-son relationships, and the costs of success. "Just about everything I've written is the result of some sort of a consistent troubling notion," Margulies told Kathy Janich for the *Atlanta Journal-Constitution* (October 1, 2000). "Whether it's something from my past or something I'm experiencing in the present—something that I am seeing around me with fresh eyes that moves me to want to make drama out of it. It's one of those mysteries of creativity. It seems to emanate from a certain place of churning deliberation."

Donald Margulies was born in the New York City borough of Brooklyn, in 1954, the son of Bob Margulies, a wallpaper salesman, and Charlene Margulies, a homemaker. When not occupied with his six-day-a-week job, Bob Margulies enjoyed listening to cast albums from Broadway musicals, watching old movies, and, occasionally, going to the theater. When Margulies was around nine, instead of spending vacation in the Berkshire Mountains or Pennsylvania Dutch Country, as the family had done in previous summers, Bob Margulies took his wife and sons to spend a week in Manhattan, going to Broadway shows. Young Margulies fell in love with the theater. "Herb Gardner's [A] *Thousand Clowns* was the first nonmusical play I ever saw," he recalled in an autobiographical essay for the *New York Times* (June 21, 1992), "and I remember how the muscles in my face hurt from grinning in pleasure for two hours. I felt privileged being in a grand Broadway theater packed with well-dressed adults and being let in on jokes they so obviously enjoyed; I was thrilled to add my small sound to all that laughter."

While Margulies's father passed on his love of movies and theater, he did not share his sons' love for books and learning. "As my brother and I grew more intellectually and creatively curious, he began to distance himself," Margulies wrote in the *New York Times*. "We were, no doubt, challenging sons for a stolid, unanalytical father; he responded by abdicating, by leaving our education entirely up to my mother. We were fortunate that she loved to read and instilled that love of books in her children." Later in life Margulies found that writing provided him with a way to comprehend his mainly absent father. "Not until I was an adult did I understand that, in his lonely abdication, my father sought refuge from his demons, from the terrible fear that, not having had a relationship with his own father, he wouldn't know how to be a father himself," Margulies wrote in his essay; "rather than try and fail, he simply retreated into silence. Years after I became a playwright, I realized that playwriting—the craft of dramatizing the unspoken—provided me with the tools I needed to get inside my father's head and figure out what he was thinking. Through the echoes of my father that occur in my plays, I have been able to give him a voice he only rarely used in life."

In addition to reading extensively—particularly the works of Arthur Miller, J. D. Salinger, Philip Roth, Harold Pinter, and William Faulkner—Margulies also liked to draw. Encouraged by his parents and teachers to pursue the visual arts as a career, he enrolled in the Pratt Institute, in Brooklyn, where he was offered a scholarship. A year and a half later, after having failed to find any mentors at Pratt, he transferred to the State University of New York (SUNY), in Purchase, where, while continuing to study the visual arts, he became increasingly interested in writing. "I was a disgruntled art major with literary aspirations when I walked into the office of Julius Novick, the theater critic, who taught dramatic literature at Purchase," Margulies recalled in his essay. "I boldly asked if he would be willing to sponsor me in a playwriting tutorial. He said yes and could not have imagined the impact that his decision was to have on my life: I was given permission to write."

Margulies worked as a graphic designer after he graduated from SUNY, and wrote plays in his free time. The Jewish Repertory Theatre, in New York City, commissioned him to write a one-act play inspired by the short story "In Dreams Begin Responsibilities," by Delmore Schwartz. That play, *Luna Park*, premiered in 1982 and was followed the next year by *Gifted Children*—his first, full-length professional production, also at the Jewish Repertory Theatre. Also in the early 1980s, Margulies met and befriended Joseph Papp, a theater director and producer who founded and ran New York City's Public Theater and cultivated many young writing talents. Margulies's *Found a Peanut* debuted at the

Public Theater, in 1984, and was published the same year. Set in 1962, the play introduces a group of children (played by adult actors) who gather in a backyard in Brooklyn; their interactions and the pecking order they establish cast light on the intersections between child and adult behavior. One of the children, Smolowitz, is a bookish Jewish boy who constantly gets picked on by his two friends. He is given the chance to assert himself when the children, in the course of digging a grave for a dead bird, find a buried envelope full of money. A series of quarrels ensue, and Smolowitz proves that he may be more worthy of respect than his peers had thought. According to Stephanie Coen, in *American Theatre* (July 1994), Joseph Papp described *Found a Peanut* as one of the most powerful plays about anti-Semitism he had read. Alan Kennedy, who reviewed a revival of the play by the RAKKATHAMM!!! Theatre Company of New York City for the *Village Voice* (December 17, 1991), described the play as "By turns funny, poignant, and horrifying," adding that it "resonates with the cruelty of early encounters with fairness, greed, loyalty, and injustice."

Another of Margulies's early plays, *The Model Apartment*, which was written in 1986 and premiered at the Los Angeles Theatre Center in 1988, depicts two Holocaust survivors, Max and Lola, who leave Brooklyn for a Florida retirement community, hoping to escape their disturbed, obese daughter, Debby. Because their home is not yet complete, they are put up in a model unit; they soon discover that—like their lives since the Holocaust—the apartment is superficially functional, but hollow: the television is fake, the refrigerator doesn't work, and the ashtrays and other bric-a-brac are glued down to the tables. Debby shows up with her homeless teen boyfriend, and terrifies her parents with her inappropriate behavior and disrespectful attitude toward the horror of their pasts. "[*The Model Apartment*] doesn't sentimentalize or coddle its audience," Margulies told Coen. "It's 90 uninterrupted minutes, and I didn't put an intermission in for good reason—I think people wouldn't come back. It's a very sad play, and very wrenching. But I like that."

For Laurie Winer, who reviewed a production at the La Jolla Playhouse, near San Diego, for the *Los Angeles Times* (July 29, 1997), the play was too wrenching. "There's something deeply unfunny," she wrote, "about watching a pair of elderly Holocaust survivors look on horrified as their daughter has sex with her homeless boyfriend who has just broken into their condominium where they have come for a little peace at the end of the day." Conversely, Robert Skloot wrote in the *Nation* (November 16, 1998): "That Margulies can make us laugh at human suffering while respecting the 'facts' of the Holocaust and the blighted victims who survived it is proof that, in the hands of a skilled and courageous playwright, the astonishing artistic possibilities of a post-Holocaust, 'Americanized' vision can move us mightily." *The Model Apartment* won the Obie Award for best new play in 1996.

Margulies's play, *The Loman Family Picnic*, debuted at the Manhattan Theatre Club, in 1989, and was published in 1994. It is inspired, in part, by Arthur Miller's *Death of a Salesman*, which chronicles the travails of a traveling salesman, Willy Loman, and his family as they pursue what they take to be the American dream. "I was 11 years old when I read *Death of a Salesman*," Margulies wrote in his *New York Times* essay, "and I remember the guilt and shame I felt for recognizing in the Lomans truths about my own family: that my mother shared Linda's chauvinism and, most frightening of all, that my father, then barely 40, might turn out to be a Willy himself. But the play's uncanny reflection of my life and worst fears also exhilarated me and made me feel less alone. I studied it with great fascination, as if it were a key to understanding what was happening to the people I loved, so that I might somehow alter my family's fate."

The Loman Family Picnic depicts a hardworking, Jewish family in the Brooklyn of the mid-1960s. Doris, the mother, delivers a monologue about how perfect her life is, but as she speaks, she tears up her wedding dress to make a "Bride of Frankenstein" Halloween costume. Herbie, the father, works long hours selling fixtures, yet still cannot provide enough money to satisfy his family. His older son, Stewie, is anticipating lavish gifts at his upcoming bar mitzvah, and the younger son, Mitchell, observes his unhappy family and wishes for better. Mitchell's escape fantasies evolve into an optimistic musical called "Willy!," which recasts his family as characters from *Death of a Salesman*; scenes from his fantasy musical are acted out toward the end of the play. Other odd moments punctuate the realistic domestic drama. Doris and Herbie imagine each others' deaths as if relating funny anecdotes, and Doris converses with her long-dead aunt, who crawls through their 10th-story window. Instead of providing a single resolution, the play actually has several, consecutive endings—ranging in tone from the sentimental, to melodramatic, to a final, bittersweet ending that implies that the family will continue to live as it always has. Stephanie Coen referred to *The Loman Family Picnic* as "perhaps Margulies's most audacious play," an assessment some other reviewers shared. However, Bill Marx, in the *Boston Globe* (April 23, 1998), asserted that Margulies's "new spin on a worn dreidel" sometimes "falls into overly familiar territory." *The Loman Family Picnic* was made a Burns Mantle selection for the "Best Play" series, and its second New York production, in 1993, was a Drama Desk Award nominee for best revival of a play.

Margulies achieved widespread acclaim for his next play, *Sight Unseen*, which was commissioned and produced by the South Coast Repertory theater, in Costa Mesa, California, in 1991, and published the next year. The play concerns a successful painter who travels to England to attend a retrospective of his work after the death of his father. As Margulies described it in his *New York Times* essay, "The father is offstage, a shadowy figure whose recent death jolts the protagonist, the painter Jonathan Waxman, into examining his loss of cultural identity and artistic purpose. His journey leads him to Patricia, the woman with whom he long ago had a relationship, which symbolized the themes of his life and which remains unresolved." Jonathan meets Patricia and her husband, a bland but intelligent archeologist, in their humble farmhouse. Patricia and Jonathan reminisce about their romantic past, and flashback scenes conjure up the early stages of their love affair, when Patricia was an inspiration for Jonathan's art. It emerges that Jonathan, who has grappled his way into a prominent position in the art world, is afraid that his talents are dwindling; scenes between him and a somewhat hostile German art critic demonstrate Jonathan's waning confidence.

Reviewing a production of *Sight Unseen* at the Alternative Repertory Theatre, in Santa Ana, California, T. H. McCulloh wrote in the *Los Angeles Times* (April 17, 1999), "Margulies' script is as taut as a violin string and reverberates with intensity. It is built as a piece of music, in movements: the present, the past and brief glimpses of a disturbing interview with a German art critic. . . . The result is a rewarding and intriguing evening in theater." In the *Wall Street Journal* (February 14, 1992) Melanie Kirkpatrick, reviewing a 1992 production of the play at the Manhattan Theatre Club, observed that Margulies successfully handles the subjects of "embittered love, artistic inspiration and the corruption that success can bring," and called *Sight Unseen* an "intellectually ambitious play also blessed with witty dialogue," despite the fact that she felt its "unconventional structure doesn't always work." *Sight Unseen* won a 1992 Obie Award for best new American play, a Burns Mantle "Best Play" citation, and a Dramatists Guild Hull-Warner Award. It was also a finalist for the Pulitzer Prize in drama.

Margulies's one-act play, *July 7, 1994*, commissioned and first produced at the Actors Theatre of Louisville, in 1995, follows a day in the life of Kate, a doctor who works in an inner-city health clinic. (Margulies's wife, Lynn Street, is a physician in a family-health clinic in New Haven, Connecticut.) Kate wakes early from a nightmare about her son and listens to her husband relate his dream about the Nicole Brown Simpson murder case. At work she is visited by an African-American patient, who has apparently been physically abused; the subject of the O. J. Simpson trial comes up, and the patient defends the football player, in spite of his purported history of domestic abuse. Kate's other patients include a Puerto Rican woman who fails to comprehend her diagnosis of clinical depression and a single mother of five with AIDS. Kate's encounters result in an outpouring of grief when she returns home to her husband that evening. "*July 7, 1994* goes to the heart,*"* Stephanie Coen wrote for *American Theatre* (July 1995), about a production at Kentucky's Actors Theatre of Louisville, "and though it offers no answers, the play's wrenching, generous spirit gives salve to the pain that envelops, to use a well-worn phrase, the way we live now."

In 1996 *Collected Stories* premiered at the South Coast Repertory Theatre, where it had been commissioned, and later well-received productions were mounted at the Manhattan Theatre Club and the Lucille Lortel Theatre, both in New York. It depicts two fiction writers—a young student named Lisa, and the 60-something Ruth, her mentor and an accomplished short-story writer. Ruth, who enjoyed her heyday in the Greenwich Village literary scene of the 1950s, is a concerned, but sometimes harsh, critic of Lisa's work. Over the course of six years, Lisa publishes a short-story collection, becomes a great success, and then, fishing for new material, decides to fictionalize Ruth's Greenwich Village experiences. Ruth is angered by this intrusion, and by the fact that Lisa has accentuated the sexual escapades and scandals to appeal to modern tastes. Their anger at one another is complicated when Ruth's health begins to fail.

Michael Feingold, who reviewed a production at the Lucille Lortel Theatre, appreciated the many complex questions raised by *Collected Stories*, as he listed them in the *Village Voice* (August 25, 1998): "What limitations, if any, are there on an artist's right to use the lives of others as material? What rights, if any, does identity have over creativity? Does the quality of the work, or of the time for which it's created, change the rules?" In a review of the published play for *Booklist* (September 15, 1998), Jack Helbig wrote, "Beautiful, heartfelt, tightly written, the play never resorts to easy cliches or cinematic notions of what it is to be a writer: there are no great scenes of agonized genius at work—or at play. Instead, Margulies shows us . . . the everyday moments that make up two lives, the small disappointments and smaller triumphs, the white lies and seemingly minor betrayals that mark a relationship. And it all makes fascinating reading. Once started, the 85-page play is hard to put down." *Collected Stories* was a finalist for the Pulitzer Prize in drama, and won the Los Angeles Drama Critics' Circle Award for outstanding new play and the Drama-Logue Award.

Describing the impetus for his next play, *Dinner with Friends*, (commissioned and first produced at the Actors Theatre of Louisville, in 1998), as cited by Everett Evans, Margulies said, "What I've learned from 40-odd years of living is that time is the co-player in one's life. You have no way of knowing what impact time will have on your relationship with another person. In midlife, some people feel the need to begin again. Sometimes one person changes and the partner does not. The play is about one of the gifts, and terrors, of growing older: that you attain wisdom at great cost." *Dinner with Friends* focuses on the lives of two middle-aged couples—Gabe and Karen, and Beth and Tom—who have been friends for many years and currently live relatively affluent lifestyles. One evening Gabe and Karen, who are both food writers, invite their friends over for a sumptuous meal; Beth arrives alone, claiming that Tom is away on business. Soon, however, she breaks into tears and admits that Tom has left her for another woman. Margulies switches back and forth in time, interspersing the couples' pasts with the present. With their sympathies for their friends pulled in different directions, Gabe and Karen also find that their friends' breakup forces them to question their own relationship.

Critics roundly applauded *Dinner with Friends*, praising its ability to examine relevant, familiar issues in novel ways. "In pondering issues of intimacy, passion and the pleasures and dolors of conjugal routine," William Tynan wrote of the play in *Time* (January 17, 2000), "Margulies writes about relationships with such intelligence and spiky humor that his comedydrama . . . becomes something quite wonderful." Benedict Nightingale wrote in the London *Times* (June 30, 2001), "I've usually found American plays about the shifting emotions of the Tristate yuppie class too small and insular; but the sensitivity, shrewdness, humour and sadness of *Dinner with Friends* lifts it to another level. It's a Rorschach blot for our times, a touching comedy that, unlike many before it, deserves the Pulitzer Prize it received last year."

When asked by Maureen Dezell for the *Boston Globe* (October 29, 2000) to respond to those who classify *Dinner with Friends* as a play about yuppies, Margulies, in addition to pointing out that the characters are neither young nor urban, replied, "'Yuppie' is a facile label, and I resist labels. The territory of this play is the aging boomer—the graying boomers who are now dealing with the quality of midlife in ways that are different from previous generations. The nature of their discourse, the expectations of husbands and wives are different now than they were in the past." In addition to the Pulitzer Prize, *Dinner with Friends* won the Lucille Lortel Award, the Outer Critics Circle Award, the Dramatists Guild/Hull-Warriner Award, and the American Theatre Critics Association New Play Award. Margulies wrote a screenplay version for a 2001 HBO movie of the same title, which starred Dennis Quaid, Andie McDowell, Greg Kinnear, and Toni Collette.

Margulies's other plays include *What's Wrong with this Picture?*, *Pitching to the Star*, and *God of Vengeance*, a loose reworking of a 1906 Yiddish play of the same title, by Sholom Asch, which had its world premiere at Seattle's A Contemporary Theatre, in 2000. He recently published *Luna Park: Short Plays and Monologues* (2002), a collection of writings drawn from his 20-year career. He is working on new plays, continues to write screenplays, and currently teaches playwriting at Yale University, in New Haven, Connecticut. He lives in New Haven with his wife and son, Miles.

—P. G. H.

SUGGESTED READING: *American Theatre* p46+ July 1994, p62 July 1995, p95+ Jan. 1996; *Atlanta Journal-Constitution* L p3 Oct. 1, 2000; *Boston Globe* N p1 Mar. 8, 1998, D p4 Apr. 23, 1998, N p2 Oct. 29, 2000; *Houston Chronicle* Z p11 Apr. 8, 2001; *Los Angeles Times* F p6+ July 29, 1997, p2 Apr. 17, 1999; *The Nation* p20+ Nov. 16, 1998; *New York Times* II p5 June 21, 1992; *Village Voice* p125+ Dec. 17, 1991, p141+ Aug. 25, 1998; *Wall Street Journal* A p9 Feb. 14, 1992

SELECTED PLAYS: *Found a Peanut*, 1984; *Model Apartment*, 1990; *What's Wrong with this Picture?*, 1991; *Sight Unseen*, 1992; *Pitching to the Star*, 1993; *The Loman Family Picnic*, 1994; *July 7, 1994*, 1997; *Collected Stories*, 1998; *God of Vengeance*, 1998; *Dinner With Friends*, 2000; *Luna Park: Short Plays and Monologues*, 2002

Courtesy of the University of Nebraska Press

Maron, Monika

1941(?)– Novelist

Monika Maron is one of the best-known writers to come out of the former German Democratic Republic (GDR), also known as East Germany. Maron is part of the postwar generation of German intellectuals that initially embraced socialism, which seemed to offer a break from Germany's Nazi past. For a period in her early adult life, Maron was a member of the Communist Party. She soon became disenchanted with the Communist state, however, and, in 1988 and at the age of 47, she defected to the West.

Monika Maron was born in Berlin in around 1941. After the official establishment of two separate German states in 1949, Maron's mother, Hella, became a Communist and remarried, to a high-ranking GDR official. Maron then moved with her family from West Berlin to East Berlin, where she studied drama and art history, and later worked for television and theater companies and as a journalist.

Maron's writing is a measure of her disenchantment with the Communist state. Her first three novels are set in East Germany and feature characters who struggle to achieve self-definition while living under repressive regimes. These early novels were banned in the GDR, though they were published and received favorable attention abroad. In all of her work, Maron shows a keen interest in history and politics, as well as in the processes of memory and character formation. Maron has written four novels, a volume of essays, and a family memoir, and her work has been published widely in the West and translated into many languages around the world. In 1992, she received the Kleist Prize, one of Germany's highest literary honors.

Maron's first novel, *Flugasche* (1981, *Flight of Ashes*, 1986), follows the story of Josefa Nadler, an ambitious, 30-year-old journalist who is sent by a Berlin magazine to B., an industrial city, to write monthly reports profiling a hardworking comrade at the local power plant. Instead of these reports, Josefa produces a muckraking account of the outdated, polluting plant that she discovers, including details about the horrific working conditions and contaminated local environment. Her friends and colleagues urge her not to pursue the story, but Josefa will not be dissuaded, even though there will be dire consequences in both her professional and private life.

The novel is written in a realistic, reportorial style. According to a listing in the *Bloomsbury Guide to Women's Literature*, it was the first artistic work in East Germany to deal with issues of pollution and the environment. R. A. Zipser wrote in *Choice*, as quoted on the *Barnes and Noble* Web site, that the novel "has much to say about the lives of workers, the position of women, and the press in the German Democratic Republic." Arthur Waldhorn, writing in *Library Journal* (October 15, 1986), noted that although the story of the idealistic young journalist struggling against an indifferent bureaucracy is of interest, much of the novel lacks vitality. "[Josefa's] loneliness as a divorced mother; her starchy colleagues, selfish lover, Orwellian antagonists—all are comfortably novelistic cliches," he wrote. A reviewer for *Publishers Weekly*, as quoted on the *Barnes and Noble* Web site, observed that the novel's publication in English was timely, coinciding with reports of the worst nuclear reactor disaster in history, which occurred in 1986 at the Chernobyl nuclear power plant in the former U.S.S.R.

In *Die Uberläuferin* (1986, *The Defector*, 1988), Maron introduces the character Rosalind Polkowski, a historian who finds herself living in a kind of limbo: for two days, she lies in bed or sits in chairs, feeling no desire to sleep, eat, or relieve herself. None of her friends or colleagues seems to miss her. As a reviewer for *Publishers Weekly* put it, as quoted on the *Barnes and Noble* Web site, Rosalind defects "not from a country, but from her life." With time spreading out before her, Rosalind decides to gather her memories to compose the history of her own life, starting with "the first catastrophe of my life . . . my birth," as quoted by the *Publishers Weekly* reviewer. In ruminating over childhood memories, failed relationships, and forgotten friendships, Rosalind seeks to be released from the pull of the past. This kind of "internal imprisonment," observed the *Publishers Weekly* reviewer, is a kind of analog to "the exterior yoke of Communism."

In Maron's next novel, *Stille Zeile sechs* (1991, *Silent Close No. 6*, 1993), the character of Rosalind reappears, and makes another gesture toward achieving personal freedom. Rosalind quits her job at a research institute, no longer willing to sell her intellect to a government she abhors, and instead plans to pursue her pet projects, which include learning to play the piano. Her scheme is interrupted when she meets Herbert Beerenbaum, an aging Communist Party functionary with a palsied hand and failing health. Before he dies, Beerenbaum wants to record his life experiences. Out of good will, and because she needs the money, Rosalind agrees to visit Beerenbaum at his home on Silent Close, a secluded Berlin street, and transcribe his memoirs. But it soon becomes clear that Beerenbaum is a representative of everything that Rosalind hates—an embodiment of the Communist Party, its jargon, its pieties, and its crimes, and a reincarnation of her dead father, who had also been a loyal party member. Furthermore, Rosalind learns that Beerenbaum was responsible for the imprisonment and torture of one of her friends 20 years earlier. Rosalind indulges in fantasies of Beerenbaum's death, which she allows herself to imagine hastening.

Maron sets Rosalind's recollections of her afternoons at Beerenbaum's home among scenes of his funeral in a Berlin cemetery, within sight of the Berlin Wall and its guarded towers. Critics identified Maron's use of the narrative technique of cross-cutting between the present and scenes from the past as a way of indicating Rosalind's preoccupation with her own history and how she came to be who she is. Writing in *World Literature Today* (Summer 1992), Ursula Love described the novel as a variant of the "father-novel" of the 1980s, in which German writers dealt with how the Nazi pasts of West German fathers affected their children. In *Silent Close No. 6*, Maron "attempts to show the crippling and silencing effect of socialist authority figures," according to Love. "[Rosalind] is no longer touched by the experience of socialism as hope for a better future," Love wrote, "but experiences it as a dangerous deformation of reality and of her own individual potential, even though she recognizes, admires, and even envies the antifascist resistance elements in the history of many party members." Rosalind blames the ideology of Communism for robbing her of an identity, and plans to make a new start after Beerenbaum and his ilk pass away. However, even though Rosalind refuses to look at the manuscript of Beerenbaum's autobiography that has been bequeathed to her, Maron suggests that Rosalind (and all East Germans) are necessarily formed by their fathers', and their fatherland's, pasts.

Rand Richards Cooper, in the *New York Times Book Review* (June 27, 1993), described the novel as a "bitter valedictory to the German Democratic Republic," which had ceased to exist the year before the book's publication, when, following political upheaval and the fall of the Berlin Wall in 1989, East and West Germany were officially reunified. He also called it an "early profession of doubt . . . about the new [Germany]." "The novel bubbles over with death, decay, and disgust," he observed, noting that such intrusions counter the "sterile, stale claims of socialist idealism" and, in his view, bespeak a gloomy future. Although Cooper and other critics admired the novel, they lamented the English translation, which they found inadequate. "It's a shame that American readers will have to encounter Monika Maron's challenging novel in the warped mirror of a faulty translation," Cooper wrote.

Although *Nach Massgabe meiner Begreifungskraft: Artikel und Essays* (1993) has not been translated into English, its title might be interpreted as "According to my Ability to Comprehend: Articles and Essays." In 20 articles, Maron writes about subjects ranging from the reunification of Germany, to art and literature, to the process of writing itself. Erlis Glass, a reviewer for *World Literature Today* (Autumn 1993), singled out for praise an essay on abortion rights, and an essay on the 19th-century German dramatist Heinrich von Kleist, written on the occasion of Maron's receipt of the Kleist Prize. "It is not only the excellent style of Maron's essays which highly recommends this collection," Glass wrote, "but also the honesty and passion with which she presents her thoughts."

Reunification left many Germans reeling from the sudden joining of two diametrically opposed political and economic systems, and became a central preoccupation in German literature of the 1990s. *Animal Triste* (1996, 2000), published under the same title in both German and English, is a love story set in post-reunification Berlin. Like *The Defector* and *Silent Close No. 6*, this story is told retrospectively, through the unreliable and fragmentary memories of an East German woman. Standing beneath the looming skeleton of a brachiosaurus at the National History Museum, the woman, a paleontologist, meets a West German scientist, and the two embark on a passionate and ultimately doomed love affair. Both are already married, with families at home. In a possibly tongue-in-cheek detail, Maron justifies the traditionally illicit affair with the novel excuse that the previous isolation of East Germany had made it nearly impossible for certain individuals to have met. The novel's narrator is now at least 90 years old by her own reckoning, lives holed up in a shabby apartment, and spends her days mentally reliving her past with her lover, whom she calls Franz because she has long ago forgotten his real name. All else, including her family, the new Berlin, and her failing health, she ignores. "Besides my lover and the brachiosaurus," Noah Isenberg quoted her as saying, in the *New York Times Book Review* (March 19, 2000, on-line), "there is not much else I like to think about."

Reviewers noted that the failed East-West love affair mirrors the incompatibility of the two halves of the reunited Germany. "For the couple, in particular the female narrator, the end of communism holds out the promise of redemption through love; and love promises initially to liberate from the burden of the past. However, love cannot surmount history and politics," Alison Lewis argued in the *German Quarterly* (Winter 1998). She concluded, "If the old saying holds that post coitum mankind is an animal triste, then the title of Maron's book suggests that in the wake of unification Germany, like the abandoned lover of the book, has much to mourn about."

Isenberg pointed out that the novel's interest extends beyond its historical significance. "There is also a deep mythical resonance," he wrote, "owing to Maron's deft appropriation of classical and modern sources." He mentioned in particular Maron's repeated use of the line "to win your heart or to die," from Kleist's *Penthesilea*, a drama that depicts the passionate and bloody encounter between the proud Greek Achilles and the Amazon Queen of the play's title. Like *Penthesilea*, Maron's tale is one of strangers who come together across different cultures, and whose meeting brings love, obsession, madness, and violence. (The narrator repeatedly imagines murdering her lover's wife, and her lover eventually meets an untimely death.) In *Booklist*, as quoted on the *Amazon.com* Web site, Bonnie Johnson described the love story as a demonstration of "the relationship between passion and our instinctive animal selves."

In *World Literature Today* (Winter 1997), Erlis Glass-Wickersham singled out the image of the brachiosaurus as a symbol both of endurance (the bones have survived) and transience (the dinosaurs did not). As such, Glass-Wickersham noted, it introduces the themes of time and memory into the love plot, so that the middle-aged lovers appear dinosaur-like, trying to forge new relationships even though their lives "are calcified into patterns that are difficult to disrupt." Like the lovers, he continued, the new Germany is in a state of limbo, formed by rules of the past and as yet unable to forge a new present.

While some critics found David N. Marinelli's translations of Maron's earlier novels unsatisfactory, Isenberg praised Maron's new translator. "Maron's exquisite language, highlighted at times by lyrical flourish, retains much of its splendor in English, thanks to the fine translation by Brigitte Goldstein," he commented.

Like her fictional character in *The Defector*, in her most recent work Maron sets out to examine her own past. *Pawels Briefe: Eine Familiengeschichte* (1999) has not yet been translated into English. The title refers to the letters of Pawel, Maron's maternal grandfather and the family's only Jewish member, who was deported and murdered by the Nazis. Maron quotes from the letters he wrote from the ghetto to his cancer-stricken wife and adult children. The subtitle might be translated as "family history," and the rest of the book is comprised of family stories, descriptions of how politics affected domestic life, and reflections on remembering and forgetting. Many passages describe the relationship between Maron and her mother, Hella, who was a committed Communist. The book also includes illustrations and photographs, which were arranged by Maron's son, Jonas.

In *World Literature Today* (Autumn 1999), Irmgard Elsner Hunt admitted that while he was drawn to the book's concept, he found Maron's storytelling unsuccessful. "The author tends to return hurriedly to the recording of this and that incident, delivering, in rather dry and brittle language, an often confusing report on the family," he wrote. Nevertheless, Hunt concluded, the letters and the images formed an emotional core to the book.

In 1992, Maron, along with fellow East German writers Heiner Müller and Christa Wolf, became embroiled in a debate about politics and artistic freedom when the files of the Stasi (the former East German secret police) were opened. As reported by Monica Munn in *German Life* (April/May 1996, on-line), it was revealed that Maron had met with Stasi agents on several occasions in the 1970s, although there is no evidence that Maron collaborated with the police in any way. Refusing to be drawn into what had become a kind of literary witch-hunt, Maron told reporters that "out of curiosity" she would probably still meet with Stasi agents today, as she did years ago, as quoted by Munn.

—M. A. H.

SUGGESTED READING: *German Quarterly* p30+ Winter 1998; *New York Times Book Review* p11 June 27, 2000; *New York Times Book Review* (on-line) Mar. 19, 2000; *World Literature Today* p505 Summer 1992, p822 Autumn 1993, p137 Winter 1997, p733 Autumn 1999

SELECTED BOOKS IN ENGLISH TRANSLATION: *Flight of Ashes*, 1986; *The Defector*, 1988; *Silent Close No.6*, 1993; *Animal Triste*, 2000

Norman McBeath/Courtesy of Jamie McKendrick

McKendrick, Jamie

1955– Poet

During the 1990s, Jamie McKendrick emerged as a leading poet of Britain's "New Generation" of writers. His five collections of poetry, *The Sirocco Room* (1991), *The Kiosk on the Brink* (1993), *The Marble Fly* (1997), *Sky Nails: Poems 1979–1999* (1999), and *Ink Stone* (2002), received favorable critical attention in England. Having taught in Italy and translated the work of Italian and Spanish poets, he is often described as being closer—in style and subject—to continental Europe than the British Isles. His poems convey raw emotion and danger, but he is also noted for his lightness of touch and wry humor.

Jamie McKendrick was born in 1955 in Liverpool, England. He began writing poetry around 1979, and taught English, at the University of Salerno, in Italy, from 1984 to1988. He has translated several poems by the 20th-century Italian poet Valerio Magrelli into English and has published poetry and book reviews in such periodicals as the *New Republic*, *Times Literary Supplement*, London *Independent*, London *Guardian*, and London *Observer*. He currently teaches creative writing at Hertford College, Oxford University, where he also serves as poet in residence.

In 1991 *The Sirocco Room*, McKendrick's first collection, was published by Oxford University Press as part of its Oxford poets' series. Tim Dooley, a contributor for the *Times Literary Supplement* (May 10, 1991), found that "McKendrick emerges as a poet with individuality of style and perspective." The collection's title refers to an interior room, once found in Sicilian mansions, that offered wealthy inhabitants shelter from the sirocco, a hot wind that carries sand northward from the Libyan deserts. Dooley noted that "the contexts of his poems, whether Hackney, Liverpool or the South of Italy . . . are tenderly and judiciously observed." He noted in particular a poem that moves from talking about the weather to imagining the wind of a nuclear winter, and another group of poems about "Lost Cities" in which the "citizens of Heaven" try to "trace some lost Before / Which if it ever was we can't recall.'"

McKendrick followed *The Sirocco Room* with *The Kiosk on the Brink*, in 1993. In his review for the Glasgow *Herald* (August 28, 1993), Alasdair Macrae explained that the kiosk of the title "refers to a flimsy sweet-shop perched on the crater of Vesuvius," the volcano in southern Italy that violently exploded in 79 A.D., and that has been intermittently active since then. McKendrick lived for four years in Salerno, in the shadow of Vesuvius, and many of these poems reflect the sense of impending violence—an ominous background of distant rumbling. Macrae observed that McKendrick "succeeds in devising poems which are tautly dramatic and not at all melodramatic. Although we have a strong awareness of an observing personality, the poems are not centred on any authorial anguish, they don't slide a hand into our emotional wallet." Dooley described the collection as "highly intelligent, beautifully crafted, endlessly surprising" and noted that the poet's "wry humour, usually at his own expense, defuses any histrionic gestures." In his review for the *Times Literary Supplement* (March 11, 1994), Mark Wormald noted that *The Kiosk on the Brink* builds on the fertile ground of McKendrick's first collection. "The atmosphere is still sultrily Mediterranean," Wormald noted, "but the sources of volcanic eruptions are now named. The poet becomes 'The Vulcanologist,' tracking one Athanasius Kircher as 'He visited Etna and Vesuvius, / and Vesuvius he entered.'" Both Dooley and Wormald appreciated McKendrick's adaptations of work by the Italian poet Eugenio Montale and the Spanish poets Antonio Machado and Francisco de Quevedo; McKendrick's inclusion of these works indicates that he is "a talent at ease with tradition," according to Wormald. "It is with an expression of the freedoms such encounters can afford that this fine collection ends," Wormald observed, "as Jamie McKendrick recalls a dead friend's voice: 'I still catch your accent, travelling / backwards, / knocking the usual patterns of speech awry / to open meanings in the hearts of words, / ironic and mobile in their sleeves of air.'"

In 1997 McKendrick published his most critically acclaimed book, *The Marble Fly*. In "Taken Awares," McKendrick displays his characteristically wry, self-deprecating humor:

> I fall into every trap
> they set for me
> mantrap, mousetrap, birdlime.
> Every time I take the bait
> the worm, the cheese, whatever.
> I pluck the wire
> that shifts the lever
> that springs the teeth.
> Then, in the calm before death,
> I flatter myself
> I'd seen it all a mile off.
> I even manage a small laugh.

In the *Times Literary Supplement* (August 1, 1997), Sean O'Brien noted McKendrick's use of familiar classical sources and observed that McKendrick's "talent is to make us re-examine what might seem to have become a riff: the world he presents is both conventional . . . and hauntingly inventive . . . and the leathery irony of a well-travelled scholar turns out to be a means of focusing on and then evoking powers not susceptible to reason." O'Brien concluded that "*The Marble Fly* is not an especially showy book, and the easy charm with which McKendrick writes serves the subject and the reader rather than poet-as-personality." In his review for the London *Times* (July 3, 1997), Michael Hofmann described *The Marble Fly* as "consistently excellent," noting the "appealingly dry and musical voice" that leads the reader through several anecdotal poems. "Where McKendrick scores is in his expert salvaging of beauty from squalor, wit from adversity, delicacy from grossness," Hofmann noted. "There is not a poem in the book that is not immediately attractive, well-turned and well-crafted." *The Marble Fly* won England's prestigious Forward Prize, in 1997.

In 1999 McKendrick published his fourth book, *Sky Nails: Poems 1979–1997*, which included poems from his three previous collections. In his review for *English Studies* (February 2001), Charles Bennett wrote that McKendrick's "graceful poems dart and twist in numerous directions, and yet are always rewarding" and quoted from the title poem, which described sky nails as having "unbreakable heads / That will nail anything / To nothing / And make it stay." Bennett praised his use of language and place, asserting that "the appeal of McKendrick's poetry lies in just this movement from the actual experience into something more profound and unexpected. This is exactly the transition that turns the lived experience into something more than an anecdote." In her review for the *New Statesman* (March 13, 2000), Lavinia Greenlaw characterized McKendrick's work as "a poetry of parts." "Every subject and scene is provisional, breakable, on the point of collapsing, erupting or being blown away," she explained. "Threat looms in the form of an ill wind, a rock fall, a split hair or spider's web." Like Bennett, Greenlaw detected a "European" quality in McKendrick's style and subjects, and concluded that "*Sky Nails* charts an impressive and strengthening body of work."

McKendrick's fifth collection of poems, *The Ink Stone*, appeared in 2002. In her review for the *Guardian* (February 15, 2003), Lavinia Greenlaw lauded the book. "Like many poets of the generation who grew up on ready-broken metre, McKendrick has become increasingly interested in form and here we have sonnets, haiku and terza rima,"

Greenlaw wrote. "In his hands, they are more like origami than architecture—we glimpse a living shape rather than stand before an edifice. His final lines resist the dramatic twist or any other kind of rhetorical boom-boom, and he leaves room for us to come and meet him, making his poetry a more than usually active pleasure to read. *Ink Stone* is a mature and compassionate work, always serious, never posturing."

Jamie McKendrick makes his home in Oxford, England.

—D. C.

SUGGESTED READING: *English Studies* p53+ Feb. 2001; Glasgow *Herald* p14 Aug. 28, 1993; *New Statesman* (on-line) Mar. 13, 2000; London *Times* p43 July 3, 1997; *Times Literary Supplement* p23 May 5, 1991, p27 Mar. 11, 1994, p26 Aug. 1, 1997

SELECTED BOOKS: *The Sirocco Room*, 1991; *The Kiosk on the Brink*, 1993; *The Marble Fly*, 1997; *Sky Nails: Poems 1979–1997*, 1999; *Ink Stone*, 2002

Jon Randolph/Courtesy of Farrar, Straus and Giroux

McManus, James

Mar. 22, 1951– Novelist; short-story writer; poet

Early in his career, because of such novels as *Out of the Blue* (1984) and *Chin Music* (1985), James McManus was known for his verbal deftness, stylistic boldness, and chaotic, disorienting narratives. In the *Los Angeles Times* (December 1, 1985) Dick Roraback called him "the most exuberant, indecipherable, imaginative, poetic (undisciplined?) writer since [James] Joyce." More recently, with the novel *Going to the Sun* (1996), McManus has disciplined his verbal dexterity to serve the interests of character development and storytelling, which by his own admission he had neglected in his earlier works. He has also written several short-story collections and a volume of poetry, *Great America* (1993). His work, both fiction and nonfiction, has appeared in such publications as the *New York Times*, *Atlantic Monthly*, *Paris Review*, *Harper's Magazine*, *New Directions*, *Harvard Magazine*, *Washington Post*, and *DoubleTake*.

James McManus was born in New York City on March 22, 1951, the son of Kevin McManus, a salesman, and Mary (Madden) McManus, a secretary. He earned his B.A. from the University of Illinois at Chicago, in 1974, the same year he married the sculptor and painter Susan Romanelli. In 1977 he received his M.A. from the Program for Writers, at the University of Illinois, and then began teaching at the school. McManus also taught at Kalamazoo College, in Michigan, and at Loyola University, in Chicago, before becoming a visiting assistant professor in liberal arts at the Art Institute of Chicago, in 1981.

McManus published a collection of poetry and prose pieces, *Antonio Salazar is Dead*, in 1979. His first novel, *Out of the Blue*, was published in 1984. In it five-year-old Elizabeth Exley is abducted from her suburban Chicago elementary school by kidnappers who have mistaken her for the daughter of Burke Rawls Jr., the wealthy CEO of North Central Industries. Realizing their mistake, the kidnappers nevertheless demand a ransom from Rawls, setting off a series of unusual interactions between Exley's parents, Rawls, and the FBI. Adam Gussow, who reviewed *Out of the Blue* for the *Wall Street Journal* (May 14, 1984), saw the book as a statement about the disorderly nature of existence. "What do you do if the truth you have to tell is that the world makes very little sense?" Gussow asked. McManus, in Gussow's interpretation, chose to tell the truth anyway, which produced mixed results for the reviewer. "Mr. McManus," Gussow wrote, "tells his story in a series of fragments. . . . He unsettles us by keeping us entirely outside his characters, by turning away from them unexpectedly to focus on some apparently meaningless detail of their physical environment. The result is a crime story that is precise yet withholding, gripping yet strangely impersonal."

In 1985 McManus published *Curtains: New and Selected Stories*, a collection of 16 short stories, many set in Chicago. That year he also published the novel *Chin Music*. Like *Out of the Blue*, *Chin Music* throws the reader into a world of chaos. As the U.S. enters into a nuclear war, Chicago awaits the impact of several nuclear bombs already headed its way. Ray Zajak, a pitcher for the Chicago White Sox, has been in the hospital for a head injury caused by an opposing pitcher's fastball. Still addled and suffering from amnesia, he leaves the hospital to discover that World War III has begun and that people are rioting and looting in the streets. Meanwhile, his wife is searching for him and their son, who is off on a quest of his own, hoping to locate his girlfriend amid the pandemonium.

Dick Roraback commended McManus's daring as a writer and called him "an author with a tenuous hold on control, caught in the dissonant rhythm of his creation. Trying, as is everyone in *Chin Music*, to get it in, all of it, before the holocaust. Impossible, of course. But he tries. Lord, does he try!" In the *Chicago Tribune* (September 22, 1985), as quoted in *Contemporary Authors* (1998), Jerome Klinkowitz wrote, "McManus is smart enough to know that if an atomic holocaust were to happen, it would not be a strange event at all, but rather something growing from the fabric of our most familiar lives. The same culture that creates the possibility of an Earth-ending bomb also crafts our daily lifestyles, and seeing how close these two are wedded makes [*Chin Music*] a devastatingly life-like book."

McManus's next novel, *Ghost Waves* (1988), focuses on Linda Krajacik, a 19-year-old student at the School of the Art Institute of Chicago whose father was killed in the Vietnam War before she was born and whose mother is going out with a rich stock-trader named Richard Baum, whom Linda hates. "Her hatred of Richard," Benedict Cosgrove explained in the *San Francisco Chronicle* (January 31, 1989), "her loyalty to a father she never knew and what she sees as her mother's betrayal of her father, serve as the framework for the story's often hallucinatory, unabashedly Freudian, frequently riveting tension." After her mother and Richard get married, Linda is asked to join them on their honeymoon to Paris, where the three characters are forced to confront one another. Cosgrove found some of the dialogue artificial, and the story in general somewhat slow, but concluded that, "with all its flaws and lapses, *Ghost Waves* convincingly portrays the anguish of a young woman growing up with few signposts and fewer friends to guide her. It contains more than a few memorable scenes, a heroine that the reader fears for and cares about, and an assured, celebratory acknowledgment of the English language's efficacy and power. A chilling document of much that is threatening and bewildering in America today, it succeeds as an illustration of the skewered logic of both dreams and contemporary urban realities."

McManus, who had divorced his first wife, married Jennifer Arra, in 1992. In 1993 he published a poetry collection entitled *Great America*. His poetry often has a humorous, conversational tone. For example, "Your what Hurts?," which appeared in *Salmagundi* (Spring/Summer 2001), begins, "Can it hurt, sir, as much as a speckled hyena can hurt / hunkered on your nipples, crushing the oxygen / from your lungs? As trapped inside your khaki shirt / a mamba, madam, can hurt you?" The poem is a litany of similarly bizarre and painful scenarios.

Great America's title piece is a long, rambling poem about the Gulf War. Throughout the volume McManus details, and ridicules, American pop culture, mentioning stars, musicians, video games, and Michael Jordan's jump shot, among other things. In the *Antioch Review* (Spring 1994) Daniel McGuiness observed that the poems "are fun to read: sonnets about exercise machines, scripts of post-feminist jokes, a long title poem that has epic ambitions, great ISO [In Search Of] ads, and Jimi Hendrix. But they dissolve in your mouth like lifesavers of Prozac. This book joins those already piled high and handsome on heaven's streetcorner: Olson, Pound, Ginsberg, Lindsay, the great griefstricken line of those with too much to say, for whom the page is not enough prison, with whom we suffer when we get home from work." Robert McDowell, who reviewed the volume for the *Hudson Review* (Spring 1994), as quoted in *Contemporary Authors* (1998), stated that, in reading the poems, "we find ourselves in the company of a novelist-on-a-spree. In fact, rather than poetry *Great America* is really a Day Book, the things one jots down when not writing a novel, when building towards a new one."

By the time McManus wrote his fourth novel, *Going to the Sun* (1996), his ideas about writing had changed. As he told John Blades for the *Chicago Tribune* (May 27, 1996), as quoted in *Contemporary Authors* (1998), "A lot of people whose opinion I trust say that my books were obscure, which to a great extent they were, and sexist, which I'm less certain about. But [James] Joyce was my hero for so long that I felt it was a badge of honor to really challenge the reader, image by image, sentence by sentence. I don't feel that way anymore." McManus also told Blades, "As a writer, I think I've been a very slow learner. . . . By the time I got to [*Going to the Sun*] I had learned some things about characters' emotions and storytelling that I just wasn't good at, or interested in, earlier."

The narrator of *Going to the Sun*, Penny Culligan, is a young diabetic woman whose boyfriend has died. Years later she is still distraught over his death and struggling with her dissertation on the novels of Samuel Beckett. As McManus told Ron Hogan in a 1996 interview for the on-line magazine, *Beatrice*, Penny's character is a composite of women he knows. "A colleague of mine had lost her fiancé in 1981, and she still hasn't fully recovered from that fifteen years later," he said. "My daughter has diabetes, and my sister has been in a graduate program for about seventeen years unable to finish her dissertation. Under those circumstances, it seemed inevitable that the protagonist of my novel would be female, and after that I considered it as a literary challenge, inspired by other men who had written from a female perspective, particularly Joyce's Molly Bloom and Norman Rush's novel *Mating*."

The novel begins as Penny and her boyfriend, David St. Germaine, are on a camping trip in Alaska. David is horribly mauled by a grizzly bear and rushed to the hospital. His eyes, nose, and much of his body are destroyed, and, when he tells Penny that he wishes to die, she gives him a lethal dose of her insulin. The novel then skips to seven years later, when Penny decides to bike more than 3,000 miles from Chicago to the scene of the catastrophe. Along the way she meets a flashy young African-American man, Ndele Rimes, and the unlikely pair become friends. The novel has a surprise conclusion and ends, as James Marcus expressed it in the *New York Times* (February 18, 1996, on-line), in an "existential cul-de-sac, from which [Penny] can envision only a single, rather shocking exit." Some thought that McManus had misfired with the ending, including Vincent Coppola, who reviewed the novel for the *Atlanta Journal-Constitution* (March 24, 1996) and declared that "McManus ran out of gas." Most reviewers, however, applauded the book in its entirety. "In a sense, *Going to the Sun* is a long, Americanized gloss on Beckett," Marcus wrote, "with last lines that echo the conclusion of *The Unnameable*. This is a bold—even a reckless—move, since few novels can hold a candle to such an exalted model. But in Penny's brilliant, funny and sometimes harrowing travelogue, Mr. McManus manages the comparison quite nicely. And that's about the highest compliment I can pay him."

In 2000 *Harper's Magazine* sent McManus to Las Vegas, Nevada, to cover the World Series of Poker, a $23-million-dollar championship event. McManus initially set out to report on the growing involvement of women in the sport as well as the murder of Ted Binion, the tournament's host, who was allegedly killed by a stripper and her boyfriend in a highly unusual manner. Then, believing that the only way to write about the poker game accurately was to experience it for himself, McManus risked his entire *Harper's* advance to join the competition. As McManus recalled in the article for *Harper's Magazine* (December 2000), he entered the event having learned the game mainly from playing computer poker and reading several books on poker strategy. Nevertheless, he managed to finish in fifth place, out of 512, and win $247,760. However, because he had come within one hand of possibly winning the tournament, he wrote, "What it feels like is fifth out of six." McManus turned his experience into a book—to be titled *Positively Fifth Street: Murderers, Cheetahs, and Binion's World Series of Poker*— scheduled for publication in May 2003 by Farrar, Straus and Giroux.

McManus's awards and honors include a Guggenheim fellowship in poetry, National Endowment for the Arts fellowships in poetry and prose, a Shifting Foundation grant, Carl Sandburg Prize, Society of Midland Authors Award, Bellagio Residency, and a Rockefeller Foundation grant. He lives near Chicago with his wife, Jennifer. The couple has two grown children, Bridget and James, and a young daughter, Beatrice. He continues to write and teach writing at the School of the Art Institute of Chicago.

—P. G. H.

SUGGESTED READING: *Antioch Review* p371 Spring 1994; *Atlanta Journal-Constitution* Mar. 24, 1996; *Beatrice* (on-line) 1996; *Harper's Magazine* p71+ Apr. 2000, p39+ Dec. 2000; *Los Angeles Times* p2 Dec. 1, 1985; *New York Times* (on-line) Feb. 18, 1996; *Salmagundi* p192 Spring/Summer 2001; *San Francisco Chronicle* E p4 Jan. 1989; *Wall Street Journal* p1 May 14, 1984

SELECTED BOOKS: fiction—*Out of the Blue*, 1984; *Chin Music*, 1985; *Curtains: New and Selected Stories*, 1985; *Ghost Waves*, 1988; *Going to the Sun*, 1996; poetry—*Antonio Salazar is Dead*, 1979; *Great America*, 1993

Patricia McPherson/Courtesy of Oxford University Press

McPherson, James M.

Oct. 11, 1936– Historian

James M. McPherson has become one of the nation's preeminent Civil War historians, despite the fact that he often writes for popular audiences—as in his Pulitzer Prize–winning *Battle Cry of Freedom: The Civil War Era*—as well as for academia. "There is a tendency to look down on popular history in academia," McPherson told William R. Ferris for *Humanities* (March/April 2000, on-line). "The word 'popularization' is a word that can be almost a kiss of death for young faculty members trying to get ahead, trying to gain tenure." However, McPherson continued, "There is a real hunger out there [in the general public] which is not always reached by academic historians. I think they ought to reach out more than they do, and that is what I try to do." McPherson has been publishing books about the abolitionist movement and the Civil War since the mid-1960s and has become known for his clear, concise, and evocative style, his exhaustive research, and his breadth of knowledge. He has been teaching history at Princeton University, in Princeton, New Jersey, since 1962. In 1991 he was named to the U.S. Senate Civil War Sites Advisory Commission, and in 2000 he was chosen to deliver the prestigious Jefferson lecture, sponsored by the National Endowment for the Humanities (NEH).

James Munro McPherson was born on October 11, 1936 in Valley City, North Dakota, the son of James Munro McPherson, a high-school teacher, and Miriam (Osborn) McPherson, an elementary-school teacher. He lived for six years in Valley City before moving with his family to Minnesota. He married Patricia (Rasche) McPherson on December 28, 1957, and in 1958 he received his B.A. from Gustavus Adolphus College, in Saint Peter, Minnesota. Being confined to cold northern climates sparked McPherson's interest in the distant and, to him, exotic South, and he decided to study history at John Hopkins University, in Baltimore, Maryland, where he studied under C. Vann Woodward, one of the leading historians of the post–Civil War South. "Living in Baltimore," McPherson recalled in an interview for *Something About the Author* (1979), "during my years of graduate study, and also during the early years of the civil rights movement (1958–1962), I became fascinated by the history of race relations in the South. Being a northerner, I became further interested in the role that northerners had played in trying to change southern race relations in the past."

While in Baltimore, a border city, McPherson participated in the Civil Rights movement. He received his Ph.D., in 1963, and, in 1964 published his dissertation as *The Struggle for Equality: Abolitionists and the Negro in the Civil War and Reconstruction*. Reviewing a new edition of the book in the *Black Scholar* (Summer 1995), Maize Woodford called it an "important and timely analysis of the abolitionist movement and the legal basis it provided for the civil rights movement of the 1960s." The book won the Anisfield Wolff Award from the Cleveland Foundation, for books that contribute to the understanding of racism.

Continuing to explore his interest in southern race relations, McPherson next wrote *The Negro's Civil War: How American Blacks Felt and Acted During the War for the Union* (1965), which he adapted for a younger audience, in 1967, under the title, *Marching Toward Freedom: The Negro in the Civil War, 1861–1865*. The books employed extensive quotations from slaves, freedmen, and politicians to document this crucial period for African-Americans. In *Book World* (May 5, 1968) P. M. Angle called *Marching Toward Freedom* a "well-documented account" and an "impressive study, reinforced with passages from the letters and diaries, song and oratory of its protagonists."

McPherson won a Guggenheim fellowship in 1967. In 1975 he published *The Abolitionist Legacy: From Reconstruction to the NAACP*, an examination of the lives of abolitionists during the period of approximately 1870 to 1910. He argues that, contrary to the opinions of some historians, white abolitionists continued to take passionate strides on behalf of African-Americans after the war, particularly in areas such as education and civil rights. Critics generally considered the book to be a thorough and thought-provoking work on the abolitionist movement. In the *New England Quarterly* (September 1976) R. E. Luker wrote that, despite some confusion over terminology and the somewhat narrow scope of the book, *The Abolitionist Legacy* "confirms James McPherson's reputation as the leading authority on the later history of abolitionism" and demonstrates an "admirable sensitivity to the complexity of the issues which it probes."

In 1977 McPherson was awarded a Huntington fellowship from the NEH. In 1982 he co-edited, with J. Morgan Kousser, *Region, Race, and Reconstruction: Essays in Honor of C. Vann Woodward*. He also published *Ordeal by Fire: The Civil War and Reconstruction*, which, starting in 1800, analyzes the roots of the war, explores the war and subsequent reconstruction, and ends at the dawn of the 20th century. J. C. Mohr wrote in the *Journal of American History* (December 1982), "Experts will recognize a great many points where interpretative inconsistencies lurk just beneath the surface. Some may even accuse McPherson of being on all sides of several historiographical disputes, as, in fact, he appears to be." Like most critics, Mohr nevertheless considered *Ordeal by Fire* to be an instant classic among comprehensive historical surveys about the Civil War era. "Professor McPherson has accomplished what one is tempted to describe as a miracle," P. L. Adams wrote in the *Atlantic* (March 1982). "[This] is an extraordinary feat of organization and condensation and definitely the book for any reader wishing to understand the Civil War in all its aspects and effects."

McPherson received a fellowship from the Huntington-Seaver Institute, in 1987. In 1988 he published his Pulitzer Prize–winning *Battle Cry of Freedom: The Civil War Era*. The book, which was part of the Oxford American History series, begins in 1845, with the start of the Mexican-American War, and ends in 1865, with the close of the Civil War. McPherson characterizes the secession of the southern states as a "pre-emptive counterrevolution." It was a response, he argues, to the challenge to slavery, but also to the challenge to the largely agrarian way of life that was still prevalent in most of the U.S. In this way, McPherson points out, the Old South was more a part of the U.S. mainstream than the handful of industrialized northern states. McPherson also reminds us that the Union victory was far from assured and was contingent on both political factors, such as the re-election of Abraham Lincoln, and military factors. "There were many times during the Civil War when the South came quite close to victory," McPherson told Walter W. Ross for *Contemporary Authors* (1990), "partly because what victory meant for the South was much different from what it was for the North. The South merely had to compel the North to give up its attempt to put down the insurrection, give up its attempt to invade, conquer, occupy, and suppress the war of independence by the Southerners, in the same way that the United States in 1776 had to persuade Britain merely to give up. But the North in 1861 did have to invade, conquer, occupy, and basically destroy the infrastructure that supported the Confederate war effort. That's a much larger undertaking, and that was why the South, even with a smaller population and far inferior industrial resources, had a good chance to win its independence a number of times between the beginning of the war and the fall of 1864."

Battle Cry of Freedom was nearly universally acclaimed. Thomas L. Connelly, writing in the *Washington Post* (March 13, 1988), was overawed by McPherson's ability to sift through such a vast amount of research and still avoid the pitfalls of oversimplification. He called the book an "absolutely brilliant narrative" and "the finest single volume on the war and its background." In the *New York Times Book Review* (February 14, 1988) Richard E. Beringer wrote, "[This] is the best one-volume treatment of its subject I have ever come across. It may actually be the best ever published. It is comprehensive yet succinct, scholarly without being pedantic, eloquent but unrhetorical. It is compellingly readable. I was swept away, feeling as if I had never heard the saga before. It is most welcome. . . . a deeply satisfying book." *Battle Cry of Freedom*, in addition to the Pulitzer, received a 1988 National Book Award nomination and a 1988 National Book Critics Circle nomination. It remained on the *New York Times* best-seller list for almost five months, and Ballantine Books bid more than $500,000 for the paperback rights.

In 1990 McPherson published a collection of seven essays titled *Abraham Lincoln and the Second American Revolution*, in which he examines the legacy of our 16th president and explores the effects of the Civil War. The war, he argues, had such a deep and overarching effect on the U.S. that it can be seen as a second revolution. McPherson, as summarized by William E. Gienapp in the *Washington Post* (February 3, 1991), shows how the Civil War "ended the South's national political dominance and altered permanently the relations between the two sections; how it destroyed southern wealth, stimulated northern industrialization, consolidated the power of industrial capitalists and furthered the process of modernization; and how it created a more expanded and open-ended concept of liberty that depended on the extensive use of government power." Gienapp called the collection a "succinct statement of both the importance of the Civil War in American History and Lincoln's central role in shaping that legacy." In the *New York Times Book Review* (January 20, 1991) Frederick Allen called it "crystal clear, well-reasoned, supremely informed."

McPherson reviewed thousands of letters and diaries of both Union and Confederate Civil War soldiers for *What They Fought For, 1861–1865* (1994). These led him to the conclusion that, unlike in some other wars, the Civil War combatants were passionately engaged in the ideological issues that caused the conflict. In the *Times Literary Supplement* (June 9, 1995) David Herbert Donald wrote, "McPherson plausibly argues that these thousands of letters and diaries give persuasive evidence that both Union and Confederate soldiers thought of themselves as 'custodians of the legacy of 1776,' who were fighting to defend republicanism and to sustain liberty."

In 1996 McPherson published a collection of 15 essays titled *Drawn with the Sword: Reflections on the American Civil War*. Revisiting and reinforcing some of the themes covered in *Battle Cry of Freedom*, McPherson argues that the causes of the Civil War were not only disputes over slavery but a clash between traditional and modern societies. He states that Union and Confederate troops were engaged in and deeply invested in an ideological war and that the North's victory was narrower than many assume. He also notes that Lincoln's at times ruthless leadership was essential to the North's unconditional victory, which permanently transformed the country. The book was well received by critics, including Steve Forbes, who wrote in *Forbes* (May 6, 1996), "The combination of an always fascinating subject, the American Civil War, and an author with an absorbing, lucid, succinct style of writing gives you a book that you won't be able to put down."

In 1997 McPherson and his wife, Patricia, edited *Lamson of the Gettysburg: The Civil War Letters of Lieutenant Roswell H. Lamson, U.S. Navy*. Lamson's letters relate most of the naval action along the South Atlantic coast during the Civil War, and the McPhersons help place the events he describes in an historical context. Also in 1997 McPherson published *For Cause and Comrades: Why Men Fought in the Civil War*, in which he expands upon the theme of *What They Fought For, 1861–1865* and sheds light on the motivations of Civil War soldiers. In an October 3, 1997 discussion of the book with David Gergen, posted on the PBS Web site, McPherson recalled that one of the initial impetuses for the book was a field trip of Princeton students to the site of the decisive Union victory at the Battle of Gettysburg, in Gettysburg, Pennsylvania. There, as he told his students, Confederate troops withstood heavy artillery fire over a mile-long stretch of open ground, and most did not survive the battle. "They asked me, what motivated these guys to do that?" McPherson recalled. "How could they walk into this wall of bullets? You could never get me to do that. And I thought about it, and I tried to give them an answer, but I wasn't satisfied with my own answer. And that planted the seed of an idea to write a book about the motivation of Civil War soldiers for facing that wall of bullets." McPherson's research entailed reading over 25,000 letters, 250 private diaries, and information from 22 different research libraries. Acknowledging that peer pressure and outright coercion from officers impelled some soldiers to fight, McPherson nevertheless maintains that most of the soldiers in the grisly war were motivated by political, patriotic, and religious ideals. *"For Cause and Comrades* presents a valuable broad portrait of Civil War soldiers and their experiences," Heather Cox Richardson wrote in the *Historian* (Winter 1999). "Aside from its use in filling in our picture of the war, McPherson's book is highly readable. Soldiers' voices carry the narrative, giving an extraordinary immediacy to the material. At the same time, McPherson's relentless enumeration of the deaths of his speakers connects the reader directly to the sheer carnage of the war. In *For Cause and Comrades*, McPherson has managed to combine his usual excellent scholarship with the intensity of a good novel." *For Cause and Comrades* won the 1998 Lincoln Prize from Gettysburg College, for the finest scholarly work in English about the Civil War.

In 1998 McPherson applied his knowledge of the Civil War to other regions and time periods in *Is Blood Thicker Than Water?: Crises of Nationalism in the Modern World*. He compares the regional nationalism of the American South around the time of the Civil War to the nationalism that threatens to separate Quebec from the rest of Canada. He also draws parallels to the ethnic nationalism that tore apart the former Soviet Union, Czechoslovakia, and Yugoslavia.

In 2000 McPherson was awarded $10,000 and the honor of delivering the NEH Jefferson speech at the Kennedy Center, in Washington, D.C. He spoke for an hour about Abraham Lincoln's definitions of liberty, which the president had elaborated upon in a speech delivered in 1864. Lincoln differentiated between the definitions of liberty used by the Union and the Confederacy, which McPherson respectively termed "positive liberty" and "negative liberty." Positive liberty, which Lincoln championed, is the government-protected freedom to do something, such as vote or receive wages for labor. "The concept of negative liberty," McPherson said in his speech, as quoted by John Pancake in the *Washington Post* (March 29, 2000), "is perhaps more familiar. It can be defined as the absence of restraint, a freedom from interference, by outside authority, with individual thought or behavior." These competing definitions of liberty are still significant in today's political climate, McPherson held. "The Democratic Party," he said, "once the bastion of negative liberty, states' rights and limited government, donned the mantle of positive liberty, while most Republicans invoked the mantra of negative liberty. How these matters will play out in the new millennium remains to be seen."

Crossroads of Freedom: Antietam (2002) is McPherson's recent contribution to the Oxford University Press's academic series, *Pivotal Moments in American History*. The book provides a pithy account of the events of September 17, 1862, when about 6,500 Union and Confederate soldiers died, and an additional 15,000 men were wounded, in the Civil War battle near Antietam Creek in Maryland. McPherson argues that by late summer of 1862, with the Union effort on shaky ground, a Confederate win at Antietam—dubbed "the Bloodiest Day in American History"—could have had a drastic effect on the future of the United States. "This deceptively slim volume emphasizes why fine history is always worth reading," Katharine Whittemore remarked in an article for *Salon.com* (September 17, 2002). "Don't fear an arid chronicle of charging regiments. *Crossroads of Freedom* is not specifically a work of military history. Rather, it meticulously, seemingly effortlessly, constructs a context through which the reader can clearly see the pivotal nature of the battle by witnessing its consequences. It delivers the 'what if' mode of historical writing, but always sticks to the facts."

McPherson continues to teach at Princeton University, where, in 1982, he became an Edwards Professor of American History. He lives with his wife in New Jersey. The couple have a daughter, Joanna.

—P. G. H.

SUGGESTED READING: *Atlantic* p88 Mar. 1982; *Black Scholar* p71 Summer 1995; *Book World* p30 May 5, 1968; *Forbes* p24 May 6, 1996; *Historian* p396+ Winter 1999; *Humanities* (online) Mar./Apr. 2000; *Journal of American History* p705 Dec. 1982; *New England Quarterly* p483 Sept. 1976; *New York Times Book Review* p9 Feb. 14, 1988, p13 Jan. 20, 1991; *Times Literary Supplement* p11 June 9, 1995; *Washington Post* p1 Mar. 13, 1988, p6 Feb. 3, 1991, C p8 July 18, 1993, C p1 Mar. 29, 2000; *Something About the Author*, 1979

SELECTED BOOKS: *The Struggle for Equality: Abolitionists and the Negro in the Civil War and Reconstruction*, 1964; *The Negro's Civil War: How American Blacks Felt and Acted During the War for the Union*, 1965; *Marching Toward Freedom: The Negro in the Civil War, 1861–1865*, 1967; *The Abolitionist Legacy: From Reconstruction to the NAACP*, 1975; *Ordeal by Fire: The Civil War and Reconstruction*, 1982; *Lincoln and the Strategy of Unconditional Surrender*, 1984; *How Lincoln Won the War with Metaphors*, 1985; *Battle Cry of Freedom: The Civil War Era*, 1988; *Abraham Lincoln and the Second American Revolution*, 1990; *What They Fought For, 1861–1865*, 1994; *Drawn with the Sword: Reflections on the American Civil War*, 1996; *For Cause and Comrades: Why Men Fought in the Civil War*, 1997; *American Journey* (with Joyce Appleby and Alan Brinkley), 1998; *Is Blood Thicker Than Water?: Crises of Nationalism in the Modern World*, 1998; *Civil War and Reconstruction*, 1999; *Crossroads of Freedom*, 2002; as editor—*Region, Race, and*

Reconstruction: Essays in Honor of C. Vann Woodward, 1982; *Battle Chronicles of the Civil War* (with Richard Gotlieb), 1989; *American Political Leaders* (with Steven O'Brien, et al.), 1991; *Why the Confederacy Lost* (with G. S. Boritt), 1992; *Atlas of the Civil War*, 1994; *"We Cannot Escape History": Lincoln and the Last Best Hope of Earth*, 1995; *Lamson of the Gettysburg: The Civil War Letters of Lieutenant Roswell H. Lamson, U. S. Navy* (with Patricia R. McPherson), 1997; *Writing the Civil War: The Quest to Understand* (with William J. Cooper), 1998; *Liberty, Equality, Power: A History of the American People* (with John M. Murrin), 1999; *Personal Memoirs of U.S. Grant*, 1999; *Encyclopedia of Civil War Biographies*, 2000; *"To the Best of My Ability": The American Presidents*, 2000

Meade, Marion

Jan. 7, 1934– Biographer; novelist

Although Marion Meade has written several novels and children's books, she is known primarily for her biographies of such diverse figures as Eleanor of Aquitaine, Helena Petrovna Blavatsky, Dorothy Parker, Buster Keaton, and Woody Allen. In an interview with Allene Symons, a writer for *Publishers Weekly* (March 11, 1983), Meade said that a biographer is "almost like an undertaker or detective." To obtain information on her subjects, Meade relies on countless interviews and substantial research using both primary and secondary sources.

Marion Meade was born on January 7, 1934 in Pittsburgh, Pennsylvania. She graduated from Northwestern University in Chicago, Illinois, in 1955. In 1956 she received her M.S. from Columbia University in New York City.

Meade's early books reflected her feminist beliefs. As she explained to Symons, "I want to write about women as survivors rather than as casualties—women who have survived men, children, wars, history, [who] have even survived victimization." Meade's first book, *Bitching* (1973) explored how, in Meade's view, most women live their lives; namely, according to rules set by society. Meade interviewed a number of women who voiced their opinions, complaints, and frustrations about marriage, sex, dating, and relationships, tape-recording each interview and then presenting them in the book. In a review in the *Library Journal* (April 1, 1973), Gloria Gehrman wrote, "Since the title is accurate, Meade's audience will be those dissatisfied with the status quo and not afraid to say so. Perhaps her approach is not the most objective, but it sure as hell is fun to read." In a radically dissenting view, the *Times Literary Supplement* (November 30, 1973) dismissed *Bitching* as "one of the most vulgar books anybody has ever written about anything."

In the mid-1970s Meade published four children's books, *Tennis* (1975), *Free Woman: The Life and Times of Victoria Woodhull* (1976), *Little Book of Big Riddles* (1976), and *Little Book of Big Bad Jokes* (1977). During this period Meade also published her first biography, *Eleanor of Aquitaine* (1977). Her sympathetic account of the 12th-century woman who became queen of France and then England received mixed reviews. "Meade quotes historical sources frequently, but does not hesitate to venture into the realm of speculation and conjecture. Scholars would certainly question many of her interpretations," F. X. J. Homer wrote in *Best Sellers* (August 1977). However, reviewer Irene Mahoney, writing in the *New York Times Book Review* (August 28, 1977), said, "Eleanor of Aquitaine has been well-served by her recent biographers. . . . Marion Meade's biography takes its place on the same shelf." Mahoney also praised Meade's writing and concluded that she handled the evidence about her subject "with skill and prudence."

Meade's first novel, *Stealing Heaven: The Love Story of Heloise and Abelard*, was published in 1979. In the *Los Angeles Times* (July 11, 1979), Diana Sherman described the book as "historical fiction of epic proportion, centering on one of the most famous love stories in European history." According to Sherman, Meade made use of Abelard's own autobiography, actual love letters exchanged between the doomed couple, and other 12th-century sources in writing a novel about this medieval tale. "I consider myself a biographer, and the novels I've done have been risky propositions for me," Meade told Symons. "When a man picks a historical theme, his fiction is taken seriously; when a woman picks a historical theme, for many people her fiction falls into the category of romances with heart-fluttering females." In 1989 a film version of *Stealing Heaven* was released to mixed reviews.

In 1980 Meade profiled Helene Petrovna Blavatsky, the 19th-century occultist who founded the theosophy movement and referred to herself as "H. P. B." In the *New York Times Book Review* (October 5, 1980), Paul Zweig described *Madame Blavatsky: The Woman Behind the Myth* as a "fascinating biography" that is both "full and rich." Zweig added "Miss Meade traces H. P. B's life from her childhood in provincial Russia, through her early travels to Egypt and Western Europe, to the founding of the Theosophical Society in New York, and her emergence as a somewhat disreputable but engrossing figure. Later Madame Blavatsky would make extravagant claims about her early life: She had visited the interior of Tibet; she was a virgin and never married; she had been wounded fighting with Garibaldi in Italy. These myths became cornerstones of Theosophical faith; but, as Miss Meade proves beyond all doubt, the reality was sadder, although adventurous enough." In the *Library Journal* (August 1980), J. H. Byer praised the book, saying, "Meade is painstakingly objective

... [The book] is also a highly intelligent and well-researched account, abounding with insightful analysis and historical and personal detail."

For her next book, Meade intended to write a biography about one of a number of female poets who lived during the Middle Ages. Unfortunately, as Meade explained to Symons, she was unable to find exact information about the lives of any of the 24 women from that era whose poetry survived to the present day. Instead of the biography, Meade wrote a novel, *Sybille*, which was published in 1983. Set in 13th-century France during the war between the Roman Catholics and the Albigensian heretics, the novel tells the story of Sybille d'Astarac, a poet and the daughter of a noble family, who struggles to survive in her bleak world. (Sybille is a composite character based on the medieval poets about whom Meade had read.) Marina Walker, writing in the *New York Times Book Review* (April 17, 1983), discussed the book's weaknesses: "The dialogue—veering from 'I want to thump you' to 'Shall I lie with you, lady?'—gives the novel the stiff, play-acting, costume feeling of a movie." Walker also suggested that Meade's depiction of 13th-century France resembles "a hippie commune struggling for self-realization in the Vermont woods."

Meade returned to biography for her next book, *Dorothy Parker: What Fresh Hell Is This?* (1988). Meade profiled the sharp-tongued 1920s-era writer who became famous as a member of the Algonquin Round Table, a group of wits whose members traded daily barbs and insults during lunch at the New York hotel for which the table is named. In the *Times Literary Supplement* (May 6, 1988), Shena Mackay applauded Meade for writing "a glossy, exhaustively researched, blow-by-blow account" of Parker's life. Mackay concluded by saying that "Meade's book, while perhaps underemphasizing [Parker's] talent (whatever and whoever else she may have abused, she did not abuse that), is a balanced and generally sympathetic study of an artist and her era, rich in detail and gossip." Mackay also noted that the book's subtitle was Parker's usual response to a ringing telephone or doorbell. Meade's book established her as an authority on Dorothy Parker. In an article she wrote for *Brill's Content* (March 2000), Meade recalled that fact-checkers from *Vanity Fair* and the *Reader's Digest* consulted her regarding articles they were publishing about Parker.

After spending two decades writing mostly about women, in 1995 Meade published a biography about Buster Keaton, the silent-film comedian. In *Buster Keaton: Cut to the Chase*, Meade explained that her aim was "to reveal a more detailed picture of the artist, which perhaps will further illuminate his art." In a review in *Choice* (February 1996), T. Lindvall enthusiastically praised the book: "Building on Buster Keaton's autobiography *My Wonderful World of Slapstick* (1960) and on hundreds of personal interviews, Meade constructs a solid literary monument to the stone-faced comedian. . . . The book provides the context of family and friends (including Charlie Chaplain and Fatty Arbuckle) behind Keaton's career, and in doing so adds flesh and humanity to the funny bones and gags that have entertained and marveled audiences for decades. A remarkably gentle and insightful story of a silent comic riddle."

According to Janny Scott, in an article for the *New York Times* (October 6, 1996), Meade considered writing another biography about a "dead person." When editors expressed reservations about her proposal, Meade suggested a living person, film director Woody Allen. Meade told Scott that in writing her book she did not seek Allen's cooperation because she wanted to remain objective. Meade did inform Allen that she was writing a book about him, but he never responded. The result, *The Unruly Life of Woody Allen: A Biography*, was published in 2000. "From a purely pragmatic point of view, you can't really blame Meade for what she has chosen to emphasize— approximately the final two-thirds of the 384 pages of *The Unruly Life of Woody Allen* are devoted to Allen's relationships with Mia Farrow and Soon-Yi Previn, and the preceding pages, as the prologue indicates, are essentially designed to lay the groundwork," Mim Udovitch stated in the *New York Times Book Review* (March 5, 2000). Udovitch acknowledged that the book "is accurate to its sources" and "follows what has become, unfortunately for him, the consensus of opinion on its subject, depicting him as self-involved, misogynist, egotistical, inconsiderate, isolated, and stagnant. And there certainly isn't much evidence out there that contradicts this portrait."

In his review for the *Montreal Gazette* (February 26, 2000), Victor Swoboda, while acknowledging the book's good points, argued that it was incomplete: "Meade, a veteran biographer, does not undertake a critical examination of Allen's work or assess his place in the context of American filmmakers. As a result, the biography seems a bit lightweight, focusing on Allen's personal and professional relationships, with more than half of the text devoted to his tribulations with Farrow. The book is more *Vanity Fair* than *Cahiers du Cinema*." Swoboda elaborated, "The facts are here, the quotes and anecdotes are amusing, the author's observations sometimes telling. But a mountain of research cannot fill in the inevitable hole left in a biography whose principal subjects refuse to speaks [sic] to the author. Until they do, this account of the life of Allan Konigsberg, aka Woody Allen, is probably as good as we'll get."

In *Brill's Content*, Meade complained that biographers are often plagiarized by "magazines and newspapers, cable networks and film companies" in order to "satisfy their ceaseless need for product—at no cost." As an example, Meade recalled her dispute with Fine Line Features, which released a film about Dorothy Parker's life in 1994, *Mrs. Parker and the Vicious Circle*, starring Jennifer Jason Leigh. Meade wrote that Fine Line Features had invited her to brief Leigh about Parker. Meade agreed on the condition that she could see the script. When Fine Line Features' representatives refused, she suspected that they "had something to hide." Meade's agent obtained a copy of the script, and Meade was shocked to discover that Fine Line Features had plagiarized her book by placing "my prose (my words, not Parker's!) verbatim into their dialogue and stage directions." *Brill's Content* showed Meade's article to Alan Rudolph, the director of *Mrs. Parker and the Vicious Circle*, however he declined to respond to her allegations. Meade considered taking legal action against Fine Line Features, but eventually decided against it. After *Mrs. Parker* was released, Meade told Valerie Takahama, a writer for the *Baltimore Sun* (December 30, 1994), that the film was an inaccurate portrayal of Parker's life. "I found it rather boring. It didn't seem to go anywhere," she said. Meade added that the film downplayed Parker's achievements and skill as a writer and literary critic.

Marion Meade is currently writing a book about the novelist F. Scott Fitzgerald. She lives in New York City and frequently contributes to such periodicals as *Ms., Commonweal, Cosmopolitan*, the *New York Times*, the *Village Voice*, and *McCall's*.
—D. C.

SUGGESTED READING: *Best Sellers* p148 Aug. 1977; *Brill's Content* (on-line) Mar. 2000; *Choice* p958 Feb. 1996; *Montreal Gazette* J p3 Feb. 26, 2000; *New York Times Book Review* p11 Oct. 5, 1980; *New York Times Book Review* (on-line) Mar. 5, 2000; *Publishers Weekly* p26 Mar. 11, 1983; *Times Literary Supplement* p1473 Nov. 30, 1973, p497 May 6, 1988

SELECTED BOOKS: nonfiction—*Bitching* (1973); *Eleanor of Aquitaine* (1977); *Madame Blavatsky: The Woman Behind the Myth* (1980); *Dorothy Parker: What Fresh Hell Is This?* (1988); *Buster Keaton: Cut to the Chase* (1995); *The Unruly Life of Woody Allen* (2000); fiction—*Stealing Heaven: The Love Story of Heloise and Abelard* (1979); *Sybille* (1983); juvenile fiction—*Tennis* (1976); *Free Woman: The Life and Times of Victoria Woodhull* (1976); *Little Book of Big Riddles* (1976); *Little Book of Big Bad Jokes* (1977)

Means, David

1961– Short-story writer

The short stories of David Means are nearly all characterized by a certain bleakness and despair, yet as Maria Russo wrote in the *New York Times* (September 10, 2000, on-line), "His bracing realism shouldn't be confused with pessimism. He has an uncompromising, humane vision that makes stringent, difficult stories almost unaccountably lovely." His short stories have appeared in several prestigious periodicals, as well as compiled into two collections, the latter of which won the 2001 *Los Angeles Times* Book Prize in the fiction category.

David Means was born in 1961. His first short-story collection, *A Quick Kiss of Redemption & Other Stories*, was published in 1991. The stories, many of which explore male sexuality, are generally somber in tone. In the title story a boy has his first sexual experience while kissing in church during the services. In "A Myth of Devotion" a couple vacationing in Costa Del Sol find their marriage in jeopardy. In "A Matter of Direction" and "Her Story With Mine" the narrator recalls his painful interactions with his mentally ill and drug-addled sister. In "Close Your Eyes" a neighbor finds two men, one white and the other African-American, kissing in the yard. Carolyn See, who reviewed the collection for the *Los Angeles Times* (July 22, 1991), found that the sadness of the pieces ultimately had a cathartic effect. "In two heartbreaking tales here," she wrote, "the material is so agonizing that the reader guesses the writer can hardly deal with it, something like jamming his fist into a Cuisinart and holding it there. . . . It takes consider-

Geneve Patterson/Courtesy of David Means

able artistry to rise above this kind of material; to take scenes of such flat desolation and make them alive and somehow un-sad enough that the reader won't throw down the book and burst into tears." Conversely, a reviewer for *Kirkus Reviews*, as quoted on Amazon.com, found that the stories failed to make a strong impact. "Means's stories all have their moments and, in most cases, an ease of voice—but without a strong sense of place or exceptional dialogue, they fail to leave a lasting impression."

Following the publication of *A Quick Kiss of Redemption & Other Stories*, Means's work appeared in a number of prominent magazines and literary journals, including *Harper's Magazine, Esquire*, the *Paris Review*, and the *Antioch Review*. In 2001 he published a second collection of stories, *Assorted Fire Events*. Many of the stories take place either in the northern Midwest or along the Hudson River north of New York City, not far from where Means currently lives, in Nyack, New York. Adrienne Miller wrote of the collection for *Esquire.com*: "Means's world is populated by beaten people, characters whose luck is so bad it's damn near Russian. . . . These are stories about loneliness, about the difficulty of human connections . . . and yet, wonder of wonders, they remain, above all else, generous, redemptive, and hopeful." In "Coitus" a man involved in an adulterous affair with a neighbor finds his mind drifting during the sexual act to his wife, his church, and the death of his brother. In "The Grip" a vagrant's all-night struggle to cling to a speeding freight train that is due to arrive in Santa Fe at dawn serves as a metaphor for the human ability to weather uncertainty and hardship. "The Gesture Hunter" presents a man in search of the authenticity behind false gestures. In the "Railroad Incident, August 1995" a man who is desperately upset due to a financial mishap and the death of his ex-wife, walks down a set of railroad tracks that parallel the Hudson River. After he encounters a group of hoodlums and then gets hit by the much-foreshadowed train, the narrative suddenly switches over to the point of view of the train's engineer.

Such narrative unconventionalities caused Jonathan Levi, who reviewed the collection for the *Los Angeles Times* (April 29, 2001), to imagine a reader "jumping up from the chair and shouting at the page: 'Wait a second, you can't do that!'" Levi added, however, that Means is good enough to "tweak the trust of his reader with every gesture (or lack thereof) and still push him back down onto his seat with a final narrative coup that leaves him gasping in wonder. . . . Means's ability and will to leap blind off high stories and grab the heart at the last minute . . . give *Assorted Fire Events* a place in my lineup of memorable fiction." Many other critics echoed Levi's enthusiasm. Maria Russo wrote, "To write fiction of such serious intent without coming off as moralizing takes both philosophical sophistication and stylistic audacity, and Means has these qualities to spare. There's not a cheap emotion or a predictable conclusion to be found in *Assorted Fire Events*." She continued, "[He] is constantly pulling back to correct an impression or to offer a plausible alternative, shifting the point of view slightly so that we don't fool ourselves into thinking we've got it all figured out. He never rests easy or settles comfortably into a simple explanation for human behavior, from adultery to pyromania."

Means is currently an adjunct assistant professor at Vassar College, in Poughkeepsie, New York.

—P. G. H.

SUGGESTED READING: *Antioch Review* p463+ Fall 1999; *Harper's* p79+ Sep. 2000; *Library Journal* p140 Nov. 1, 2000; *Los Angeles Times* E p2 July 22, 1991; *Los Angeles Times Book Review* p4 Apr. 29, 2001; *New York Times* (online) Sep. 10, 2000; *Publishers Weekly* p23 May 14, 2001; *Review of Contemporary Fiction* p200+ Spring 2001

SELECTED BOOKS: *Quick Kiss of Redemption & Other Stories*, 1991; *Assorted Fire Events: Stories*, 2001

Courtesy of Perry Meisel

Meisel, Perry

(MY-zell)

Jan. 26, 1949– Nonfiction writer

Perry Meisel has had a long career as a professor, author, and literary critic. His books on English literary modernism include *Thomas Hardy: The Return of the Repressed, A Study of the Major Fiction* (1972), *The Absent Father: Virginia Woolf and Walter Pater* (1980), and *The Myth of the Modern: A Study of British Literature and Criticism after 1850* (1987); they have provoked strong reactions from reviewers for several prestigious publications. In 1985 Meisel and Walter Kendrick published *Bloomsbury/Freud: The Letters of James and Alix Strachey, 1924–1925*, which provided valuable insights into the psychoanalyst and translator James Strachey and his wife. Meisel's most recent book, *The Cowboy and the Dandy: Crossing Over from Romanticism to Rock and Roll* (1998), theorized that there is a link between English Romanticism and modern rock music.

Perry Meisel submitted the following third-person account to *World Authors 1995–2000*: "[He] was born in Shreveport, Louisiana, [on January 26, 1949], the son of I. S. Meisel, businessman, and the former Rebecca Abramson. The family moved to Dobbs Ferry, New York, in 1955, where Meisel attended public schools; in 1963, he became a student at the Horace Mann School in Riverdale, New York, from which he graduated in 1966. Meisel entered Yale College in the fall of 1966, taking his B.A. in English and History in 1970, and receiving a number of undergraduate prizes, one of which, the Wrexham Prize, for his senior essay on Thomas Hardy, led to the publication of his first book by Yale University Press in 1972, *Thomas Hardy: The Return of the Repressed*. From 1970 to 1971, he was Carnegie Teaching Fellow in English at Yale; he remained at Yale for graduate study in English, and continued to teach. In 1974, he taught at Wesleyan University. After taking the M. Phil. in 1973, in 1975, he completed a doctoral dissertation on Virginia Woolf, still a canonically marginal figure, for which he received the Ph.D.

"A Zionist during his school years, Meisel spent the summer before Yale in Israel, touring the country and working on a kibbutz. In 1967, after the Six Day War, he returned to Israel at the end of a summer spent working in London. He found the country much changed. In the fall of 1967, he returned to Yale for his second year, and found the revolution of the late 1960s in full bloom. He became a cultural radical. Combining the ethos of literary modernism with that of late-1960s jazz, particularly John Coltrane, Meisel played saxophone in Jazz Praxis; studied literature, history, and psychoanalysis; and, in 1968, edited a special issue of the *Yale Literary Magazine* on the Beatles.

"In 1971, Meisel began his career as a rock and jazz critic, writing, while in graduate school at Yale, for *Rock*, the *Boston Phoenix*, *Fusion*, and *Crawdaddy*. He also played saxophone with a number of rock bands, including Tenderloin, Powerhouse, and Karen and the Pistons.

"Meanwhile, in the milieu of the Yale English Department, which assumed a continuity between high and 'low' culture, Meisel fell under the influence of the new European criticism—structuralism, semiotics, and deconstruction. His liberationist beliefs of the 1960s were challenged by thinkers such as Roland Barthes, Michel Foucault, Jacques Derrida, and Jacques Lacan, for whom the self is not, to use James Taylor's phrase, 'a churning urn of burning funk,' but an agency socially produced by language and culture. In both his literary and his rock criticism, Meisel began to make adjustments in his assumptions, particularly those of his study of Hardy, notably the belief that culture represses a gregarious nature. Music had already taught him the central importance of form in art, and had made him aware of the historical factors involved in its production. Ironically, Meisel's literary criticism had to catch up with his writing on music.

"In the fall of 1975, Meisel moved to Greenwich Village. He began teaching at New York University as an assistant professor of English, and, within months of his arrival, began writing rock and jazz criticism for the *Village Voice*. He chronicled the jazz-rock 'fusion' movement of the 1970s; his conversion to punk rock in the later 1970s; and the New Wave rock and roll that followed it in the 1980s. He also contributed articles to the *Voice* on books, television, and football; 'Everything You Always Wanted To Know About Structuralism But Were Afraid To Ask' (1976) attracted particular attention among his non-musical pieces.

"By now he was also writing articles on literature, criticism, and psychoanalysis for *Partisan Review*, the *Ontario Review*, the *Nation*, *October*, *Salmagundi*, and the *Atlantic*. From 1977 to 1981, he was also a fellow of the New York Institute for the Humanities. In 1984 he served as consulting editor for a special issue of *October* on psychoanalysis. In the same year, he also began contributing to the *New York Times Book Review*.

"Writing for the *Village Voice* incurred the wrath of the senior members of the New York University English Department, whose antipathy to avant-garde literary criticism added fuel to their dislike of 'popular' culture and journalism. The publication of two new books, *The Absent Father: Walter Pater and Virginia Woolf* (1980) and *Freud: A Collection of Critical Essays* (1981), did little to pacify them. Thanks to an alliance with a newly enlightened university administration, Meisel was made associate professor of English in 1981; in 1987, he was made full professor. In the 1980s he also taught at Columbia University as a visiting professor.

"*The Absent Father* and *Freud* were the initial yield of Meisel's absorption of new critical approaches to literature. *The Absent Father* combined psychobiographical criticism with 'intertextual' literary history to show Woolf's influences, particularly as an essayist. In *Freud*, Meisel assembled classical estimates of Freud's relation to literature, from Thomas Mann and W. H. Auden to Lionel Trilling and Jacques Derrida. In a long introductory essay entitled 'Freud as Literature,' he showed how the 'truth' of psychoanalysis depends, in large part, on Freud's skill as a writer. Psychoanalysis, he argued, is a consensual mythology engineered by the conflicting responses Freud's writing generates.

"In 1985 with his friend and collaborator, the late critic and journalist Walter Kendrick (who also served as professor at Fordham University and as an editor of the *Voice Literary Supplement*), Meisel brought out the selected letters of Freud's English translators, James Strachey and his wife, Alix, under the title *Bloomsbury/Freud*. 'The book not only illuminates the continued power and relevance of the Strachey translation of Freud's text,' wrote Harold Bloom, 'but also provides one of the authentic inside visions of the context in which Virginia Woolf and E. M. Forster found their aesthetic and spiritual home.' The letters also chronicle the background of Melanie Klein's emigration to London from Berlin, where she and Alix had become friends while both were in analysis with Freud's disciple Karl Abraham.

"In 1987 appeared *The Myth of the Modern*, the first revisionist study of the modern British literary canon since it was established by the thematic critics of the 1950s. Using the techniques of deconstruction, Meisel challenged customary beliefs about modernism, from Hardy and Pater to Joyce and Woolf. 'Much of the literature now honored as modernist purports to confront the alienating complexity and spiritual depletion of modern life,' said the *New York Times*. 'Perry Meisel's new book persuasively calls this popular assumption into question.' *The Myth of the Modern*, wrote Richard Poirier, editor of *Raritan Quarterly*, was a 'permanently valuable redirection of critical thinking about literary modernism.' Not a quest for the 'authentic,' modernism, Meisel argued, is a self-conscious adjustment to the burdens of history and precedent from which no one can be entirely free. Modernism and postmodernism are thereby also continuous.

"In 1999 Meisel published *The Cowboy and the Dandy: Crossing over from Romanticism to Rock and Roll*, a synthetic account of modern literary culture and rock music, tracing the latter to its roots in African-American music and culture. The rock sensibility, Meisel argued, comes from a combination of two Romantic myths—the gunslinging rangehand and the urbane fop—a crossing that provides Anglo-America a medium of exchange with Afro-America other than minstrelsy. Although some reviewers complained about the admixture of academic critical methods and 'pop' materials, the admixture was precisely the book's point. The cultural resistance Meisel had experienced as a young assistant professor writing for the *Village Voice* in the 1970s was still very much in evidence among 'high' culture apologists. Other critics, however, found the approach by now natural, and the book, as the *Chronicle of Higher Education* put it, 'elegantly written.'

"Meisel continues to live in Greenwich Village, teach at New York University, and contribute essays and reviews to a number of publications. In 2001, he was appointed contributing editor to the psychoanalytic journal, *American Imago*. Current work-in-progress includes a book on 'pop' culture that takes up rock, jazz, film, television, pornography, and 'pulp' fiction; the book also explores the history of the 'popular' and the problems involved in maintaining the distinction between 'high' and 'low' culture."

Perry Meisel published his first book, *Thomas Hardy: The Return of the Repressed, A Study of the Major Fiction*, in 1972, when he was still in graduate school. In it he explores how the fiction of the British modernist author Thomas Hardy (1840–1928) gradually changed. According to Meisel, in his early novels, Hardy showed how a society is changed for the worse by outsiders who bring different values to the community. In later novels Hardy presented the same conflict, but from a different perspective, focusing on the individual's efforts to resist society's powerful influence. "The book is largely a patchwork of quotations stitched together by commentary marked to a considerable degree by arid obfuscation," a reviewer for *Choice* (September 1972) observed. "Meisel's book offers a few interesting insights but on the whole it does not add much to our understanding of Hardy's fiction." By contrast, a reviewer for the *Times Literary Supplement* (June 16, 1972), praised the book, writing that "There is also much in Mr. Meisel's view that Hardy's human sympathies with these intruders develops until, from *The Woodlanders* on, he begins to reverse the process, stating the case for the self-alienated individual against the society." The reviewer concluded that "Mr. Meisel makes his points well, if in a somewhat academic style."

Meisel's second book, *The Absent Father: Virginia Woolf and Walter Pater*, appeared in 1980. In it the author discusses the literary relationship between Woolf (1882–1941) and Pater (1839–1894), a critic and essayist. Meisel argues that Woolf's language and vision were heavily influenced by Pater, whom she later rejected. Reviewers were split on Meisel's thesis. In the *Times Literary Supplement* (September 12, 1980), Eric Warner wrote that this "ingenious case rests on some questionable guesswork about her life and an extremely wilful handling of facts which will convince few impartial readers. The argument grows even more tendentious when Meisel states that Pater became 'the absent father,' a literary patriarch no less fearful whom Woolf spent the rest of her creative life trying to outwit and evade." In her review for the *Library Journal* (February 15, 1980) Mary McBride believed that Meisel proves his case, writing that he "demonstrates that Woolf's reading of Pater and her studying with his sister Clara from 1898 to 1905 had a profound effect on her theory of literature and novelistic practice. Just as Woolf rejected the patriarchal influence of her father Leslie Stephen, however, she also established her independence from Pater by neutralizing and sublimating his influence in her essays and novels."

In 1985 Meisel and Walter Kendrick co-edited *Bloomsbury/Freud: The Letters of James and Alix Strachey, 1924–1925*. James Strachey helped translate the works of Sigmund Freud, the Austrian pioneer in psychoanalysis, from German to English. The final result, which took 21 years to complete, was the 24 volumes of *The Standard Edition of the Complete Psychological Works of Sigmund Freud*; Strachey was credited as the general editor of the series. Strachey and his wife, Alix, both went to Freud to have themselves analyzed and to learn his methods, which they later used to psychoanalyze their own patients. For almost two years the couple were separated, with James in London and Alix in Berlin. They corresponded almost daily. Their letters reveal their love, give observations about the cultural life in Berlin and London, and relate insights into the process of psychoanalysis. "Mr. Meisel and Mr. Kendrick . . . have also written a substantial introductory essay and an epilogue that bring James and Alix into focus much more clearly than before," John Gross wrote in his review for the *New York Times* (November 15, 1985). "In the introduction, for instance, we learn exactly how James came to analysis, at a time when it had made very few inroads into English life, and how he found in it the sense of direction that had previously been lacking in his career." As for the Stracheys' letters, Gross observed that "they reflect a keen intellect and a lively curiosity; they are severe in their judgments, but witty and observant as well, and along with a racy account of Weimar Berlin in general, they offer an informal, uninhibited picture of the German psychoanalytic community at that time that—in English at least—is surely without parallel." Writing in the *Washington Post Book World* (December 29, 1985), Joseph Caruso noted that "during the period of these letters, they were truly neophytes. We see them struggling to understand, practice, and translate Freud's work. They had found in psychoanalysis a venture to shape their talents, as fledgling as that young movement."

Meisel discussed literary modernism, which sought to break with literary traditions of the past and find new techniques and styles to convey ideas, in his next book, *The Myth of the Modern: A Study in British Literature and Criticism After 1850*. Meisel contrasts the work of such authors as Matthew Arnold and T. S. Eliot, whom he labels "weak" modernists, with such "strong" modernist writers as Thomas Hardy, Walter Pater, Joseph Conrad, James Joyce, E. M. Forster, and Lytton Strachey. Meisel concludes that literary modernism was, in the end, unsuccessful. In his review for the *Journal of Modern Literature* (Fall 1998), Daniel T. O'Hara wrote that Meisel's "scholarship, although generally impeccable, is incomplete at points, especially with regard to earlier critics elaborating similar revisionary, arguments, with respect to Eliot and Pater; similarly, . . . some treatment of [the poet William Butler Yeats] would have made the book more comprehensive." Despite these reservations, however, O'Hara concluded that *The Myth of the Modern* "is a very valuable book" because "it is the first, nearly full-scale treatment, from this influential point of view, of most of the major and very different components of British Modernism in literature and criticism that cover the hundred-year period of its development and its demise." In the *Literary Review* (Spring 1990), Martin Green asserted that the book, although difficult to read at times, "is a tour-de-force reinterpretation of the modernist canon as a struggle over how to accommodate the anxiety of influence. The desire to make things new, the will to modernity, leads to a sense of belatedness that becomes a burden for those who fail to recognize its inevitability." Green argued that Meisel's assessments of Joyce, Woolf, Hardy, and Conrad were persuasive, but faulted him for his analysis of Strachey's *Elizabeth and Essex*, which stretches "beyond the limits of language (and logic)" and gives the work greater significance than it deserves.

In *The Cowboy and the Dandy: Crossing Over from Romanticism to Rock and Roll* (1998), Meisel argued that modern rock music is the product of both 19th-century English Romantic literature and African-American blues music. In her review for the *Library Journal* (December 1998), Susan Hamburger wrote that to support his thesis, "Meisel alternates literary and musical chapters while drawing parallels between them." The reviewer, however, criticized the book, writing that Meisel's "writing style—paragraph-length sentences full of words demanding a dictionary—is inaccessible and incomprehensible to all but the most persevering literary scholar and obfuscates an otherwise intriguing premise." In their review for *Notes* (December 2000), Peter Mercer-Taylor and Eunice Schroeder described *The Cowboy and the Dandy* as "an important book, well argued and highly inventive," adding that it "should be considered essential reading for scholars of rock and roll and of popular culture in general, and it forms an original contribution to late-romantic literary studies as well."

Perry Meisel has also edited the books *Freud: A Collection of Critical Essays* (1981) and the Henry James anthology, *The Turn of the Screw and Other Short Novels* (1995). Meisel contributes frequently to the *New York Times Book Review* and lives in New York City.

—D. C.

SUGGESTED READING: *Choice* p815 Sep. 1972; *Journal of Modern Literature* p232+ Fall 1988; *Library Journal* p55 Feb. 15, 1980, p110 Dec. 1998; *Literary Review* p403+ Spring 1990; *New York Times* C p31 Nov. 15, 1985; *Notes* p358+ Dec. 2000; *Times Literary Supplement* p687 June 16, 1972, p1006 Sep. 12, 1980 *Washington Post Book World* p8 Dec. 29, 1985

SELECTED BOOKS: *Thomas Hardy: The Return of the Repressed, A Study of the Major Literature*, 1972; *The Absent Father: Virginia Woolf and Walter Pater*, 1980; *The Myth of the Modern: A Study of British Literature and Criticism after 1850*, 1987; *The Cowboy and the Dandy: Crossing Over from Romanticism to Rock and Roll*, 1998; as editor— *Freud: A Collection of Critical Essays*, 1981; *Bloomsbury/Freud: The Letters of James and Alix Strachey, 1924–1925*, (with Walter Kendrick), 1985; *The Turn of the Screw and Other Short Novels* (by Henry James), 1995

Joe Tabacca/Courtesy of Farrar, Straus and Giroux

Menand, Louis

1952– Nonfiction writer

Louis Menand, the Pulitzer Prize–winning author, professor, and cultural critic, has been described by Carlin Romano in *The Nation* (June 11, 2001) as "the crossover star of his academic generation, a bi-Manhattan emissary between campus and media whose prose travels only first-class, the public intellectual whose pay per word every public intellectual envies." Romano continued, "In [New York City] the media capital of the last superpower, where thousands of professors undoubtably think they, too, with a little Manhattan networking, could be a contributing editor (and editor heir apparent) of the *New York Review of Books* or staff writer at the *New Yorker*, or contributor to the *New Republic*, Menand has actually pulled it off . . ." A distinguished professor of English at the Graduate Center of the City University of New York, Menand is, indeed, also a contributing editor to the *New York Review of Books*, a staff writer for the *New Yorker*, and a contributor to numerous other publications. For more than a decade, he has produced witty and informative essays on a variety of topics, including the Beatles, Stanley Kubrick, Saul Bellow, and Toni Morrison. He is the author of the highly acclaimed *The Metaphysical Club: A Story of Ideas in America* (2001), which recounts the rise of pragmatism, an influential 19th-century American philosophy and important precursor to modern liberalism. Menand has also edited several well-regarded anthologies on academic issues, most notably *The Future of Academic Freedom* (1996).

Louis Menand III, known to associates as Luke, was born in Syracuse, New York, in 1952, the son of a political-science professor. (Some sources list his specific birth date as January 21.) After graduating from a Massachusetts prep school, in 1969, Menand enrolled at Pomona College, in Claremont, California. He later transferred to the University of California at Berkeley, but he was dissatisfied and reentered Pomona. Upon graduating with a bachelor's degree in 1973, he returned to the East Coast, where he attended Harvard Law School, in Cambridge, Massachusetts. Again, however, he was not content, and after a year he took a leave of absence. He applied for two programs at Columbia University, in New York City—the School of Journalism and the doctoral program in English. "When I was admitted to both of them, I went to talk to the dean of the journalism school," Menand explained to Stephen Burt in an interview for *Publishers Weekly* (May 28, 2001). "I said, 'Should I go to your school or should I go to get a Ph.D. in English?' He said, 'What kind of writing do you want to do?' and I said, 'I want to write for the *New Yorker*.' And he said, 'You don't need journalism school for that.' So I went to graduate school for English instead."

Menand completed his doctorate in English and comparative literature at Columbia in 1980; his thesis concerned modernist critics' views of the Victorians. "Like many people who start Ph.D. programs and imagine themselves not teaching, I decided that actually I like to teach," he told Burt. After teaching for seven years at Princeton University, in New Jersey, he was turned down for tenure. "I was sitting in my office about a month after I was told I wasn't going to be promoted, and the phone rang and an editor at the *New Republic* called and said she was going to go on leave for a year." She wanted to know if Menand could replace her, he explained to Burt. "I said, 'Are you kidding? I'll do it in a second.' It was the luckiest thing that ever happened to me. Everything worked out."

At the *New Republic*, based in Washington, D.C., Menand edited book and film reviews as well as the magazine's political coverage. "I had a good time," he told Burt, but he and his wife missed New York. He applied successfully for a position at Queens College, a division of the City University of New York (CUNY), where he became one of the few professors who ably straddles the worlds of academia and journalism. While teaching English at CUNY, he wrote articles for the *New Yorker* and the *New York Review of Books*. He was also a literary editor at the *New Yorker* from 1993 to 1994 and has been a contributing editor to the *New York Review of Books* since 1994 (only the second person to hold that position in the magazine's history). In 2000 he became a staff writer for the *New Yorker*. He is also a frequent contributor to the *New York Times Magazine*. Menand has acknowledged that such a career would be difficult to maintain outside New York City. "It's helpful to have personal relations with people," he told Burt. "It's nice to go out to lunch with them and to know what's happening. I like to be involved with magazines more than just as a writer. I like to have a sense of what they're up to, that's part of the fun of it."

Menand is sometimes compared to such New York intellectuals of the 1940s and 1950s as Irving Howe, Lionel Trilling, and Alfred Kazin. Although he has admitted to reading their work and being influenced by their example, he has not identified himself as a descendant of that tradition. He has cited instead such *New Yorker* writers as Joan Didion, Janet Malcolm, and Pauline Kael. "Those are the people who really inspired me," he told Burt. "I don't think of myself as an academic who writes for a larger audience the way that Irving Howe did. I think of myself as a magazine writer. . . . I'm not interested in being a moral authority or a cultural authority or the conscience of a generation. I'm much more interested in writing stuff that seems to be able to be entertaining and interesting."

Menand's first book, published in 1987, was *Discovering Modernism: T.S. Eliot and His Context.* In it he examines the poet's early views on literature and his later reversal of those views. Menand theorizes that Eliot's changing attitude reflected the general changes that occurred during the early 20th century in our understanding of literature. "*Discovering Modernism* pleases initially with the high polish of its prose and with the audacity it shows," Margaret Moran wrote for *American Literature,* as quoted by *Contemporary Authors* (2002). "In the end, the book attains a rarer achievement by growing more admirable after being pondered." *Discovering Modernism,* which has been out of print, is scheduled to be reissued in paperback in January 2003.

Menand subsequently edited several collections of essays; *The Future of Academic Freedom* (1996) contains essays from such prominent academics as Richard Rorty, Edward Said, and Henry Louis Gates Jr. and offers discussions of multiculturalism and the imposition of campus speech codes, among other topics. "The essays are not only sharp, elegant and lucid, but extremely well-informed about the history of American battles over academic freedom," Alan Ryan wrote for the *Times Higher Education Supplement* (April 25, 1997). Menand's editorship of another volume, *Pragmatism: A Reader* (1997), riled some specialists in the field of American philosophy, who considered him an outsider. The book includes essays by Richard Rorty, George Herbert Mead, Hilary Putnam, Joyce Appleby, Lynn Hunt, and Richard J. Bernstein, among others.

Pragmatism is also the subject of Menand's most recent book, *The Metaphysical Club: A Story of Ideas in America* (2001), considered by many to be his most important work to date. . . .in it Menand traces the development of pragmatism from 1861 to 1919, through the lives of its four primary exemplars: Oliver Wendell Holmes Jr., William James, Charles Sanders Peirce, and John Dewey. The book took Menand 10 years to complete. "It was a challenge to avoid "skat[ing] over the difficult philosophical problems that these writers had to deal with or explain," he told Burt. Menand became interested in Holmes after reading an article in a law journal that led him to deepen his research into pragmatism. "I put off starting it for a long time because I was afraid it was too much to do. . . . There were all kinds of things I had to look up. One of them was the history of biology and evolutionary theory; the other which I knew nothing about was probability theory. It was a pleasure trying to condense the explanation of those into my narrative."

In January 1872 Holmes, James, and Peirce were the most prominent members of a small group of educated men, calling themselves the Metaphysical Club, that began holding a casual discussion group in Cambridge, Massachusetts. (Dewey was not affiliated with the club; only 13 years old at the time, he would later come under the influence of Peirce and James.) The club was in existence only for a short time and was scarcely mentioned in any of the members' writings, but it is there that Menand locates the first articulation of pragmatism's central tenet—that a belief is to be judged true not by virtue of its accurate representation of an objective reality, but by the degree of its utility and adaptability. As Lee Siegal explained for *Harper's Magazine* (October 2001), "Pragmatism is an American product with a simple heart. Its animating principle is that truth is social and constructed rather than transcendent and objective. It holds that ideas prove their worth in action, and that the results of an idea are the best criteria by which to judge its merit. And since what works for me might not work for you, pragmatism advocates a strenuous openness to all perspectives." Siegal concluded, "With its insistence on the fusion of being and doing, thought and action, pragmatism has one foot in academe and the other in everyday life."

Menand links the roots of his subjects' radical skepticism to various personal and social influences, but primarily to the effects of the Civil War and the 1859 publication of Charles Darwin's *On the Origin of Species.* "The Civil War swept away the slave civilization of the South, but it swept away almost the whole intellectual culture of the North along with it," Menand writes, as quoted by Janet Maslin in the *New York Times* (June 4, 2001). "It took nearly half a century for the United States to develop a culture to replace it, to find a set of ideas, and a way of thinking, that would help people cope with the conditions of modern life." *The Metaphysical Club* begins with a chapter on Holmes (a future U.S. Supreme Court justice), who fought in the Civil War and was wounded three times. The exposure to horrendous slaughter left him deeply disillusioned. "The lesson Holmes took from the war," Menand writes, as quoted by Maslin, "can be put in a sentence. It is that certitude leads to violence." In subsequent chapters Menand focuses on such topics as the Pullman strike of 1894; the creation of Johns Hopkins University, in Baltimore; the Confederate victory at

Ball's Bluff, in Virginia; the influential naturalist Louis Agassiz's field trip to Brazil; and the Harlem Renaissance.

The book received considerable accolades. "*The Metaphysical Club* casts a vast, brilliant light on the human subtleties of America's most influential philosophical achievement," Carlin Romano wrote for *The Nation*. "It's a feast of canny wisdom and sophisticated entertainment, and one hopes Menand's already privileged position in the intellectual elite, and the envy of the specialists, won't muffle the sounds of celebration." Janet Maslin, who complained that the narrative was somewhat disjointed, nevertheless found that "the larger philosophical constructs at work are exciting and radical enough to rivet attention in their own right." Overall, she judged the work to be "an immensely impressive and valuable achievement. . . . As both a landmark work of scholarship and a popular history of profound, sweeping change, it is of enormous worth." The editors of the *New York Times* (December 2, 2001), who named *The Metaphysical Club* one of the best books of 2001, noted, "The ground [Menand] has to cover is vast: legal theory with Holmes, psychology and religion with James, educational development with Dewey, mathematics and philosophy with Peirce. But the large personalities of his principal players let him explain ideas in a series of connected stories that help the reader digest the learning. This approach also gives his thesis a kind of theatrical excitement that no severe intellectual history could engender." "*The Metaphysical Club* is that rare thing, an intensely pleasurable intellectual history offering insights (even laughs) on almost every page," John T. McGreevy wrote for *Commonweal* (August 17, 2001). "[It is] exhilarating, as is Menand's conviction that a better understanding of these figures provides us with a better understanding of our own time." The book was a *New York Times* best-seller and won Menand the 2002 Pulitzer Prize for history.

Menand lives in Manhattan with his wife, Emily Abrahams, and their two sons. He works from an office across the street from the Empire State Building. He has received fellowships from the National Endowment for the Humanities and the John Simon Guggenheim Memorial Foundation. He was vice president of the PEN American Center from 1995 to 1996 and the program director of the New York Institute for the Humanities at New York University from 1992 to 1994. His most recent book, *American Studies*, appeared in late 2002. A wide-ranging cultural history, it covers such topics as William James's nervous breakdown, the anti-Semitism in T. S. Eliot's writing, and the connection between Larry Flynt's *Hustler* and Jerry Falwell's evangelism. "I don't think of there being any division between my academic career and my career in journalism," Menand told Stephen Burt. "To me, I'm just a writer. . . . And it happens that some of my interests are relatively scholarly and some are not."

—A. I. C.

SUGGESTED READING: *American Enterprise* p56 Jan./Feb. 2002; *Commonweal* p22+ Aug. 17, 2001; *Harper's Magazine* p84+ Oct. 2001; *National Review* p44+ July 9, 2001; *New York Times* E p9 June 4, 2001, VII p11 Dec. 2, 2001; *Publishers Weekly* p42+ May 28, 2001; *Times Higher Education Supplement* p28 Apr. 25, 1997

SELECTED BOOKS: *Discovering Modernism: T.S. Eliot and His Context*, 1987; *America in Theory*, 1988; *The Future of Academic Freedom*, 1996; *Pragmatism: A Reader*, 1997; *The Metaphysical Club: A Story of Ideas in America*, 2001; *American Studies*, 2002

Robin Farquhar-Thomson/Courtesy of Harcourt Publishing

Messud, Claire

1966– Novelist; short-story writer

The American novelist Claire Messud writes with great insight about other cultures: in her first book, *When the World Was Steady* (1995), two British sisters search for spiritual comfort in such diverse places as the Isle of Skye, in the United Kingdom, and the Indonesian island of Bali; in her second, *The Last Life* (1999), Messud writes of French colonials in North Africa who are exiled to their mother country after the Algerian war for independence. Both novels received critical acclaim and established Messud as a new light on the literary scene. Frequently praised for her lyrical prose, Messud is also highly regarded for her complex characterizations and insights into human psychology. *The Hunters* (2001), a collection of two novellas, was a finalist for the 2001 Pen/Faulkner Award.

Claire Messud was born in the United States to a French-Algerian father and Canadian mother. She was raised in Connecticut; Toronto, Canada; and Sydney, Australia; before studying at Yale University in New Haven, Connecticut, and Cambridge University, in England. She began writing shortly after completing her studies, publishing fiction in the journals *Zoetrope: All Story* and *Granta*. She also wrote book reviews and articles that were published in periodicals, such as the *Washington Post*, the *New York Times*, the *Times Literary Supplement*, and the London *Times*.

In 1995, at age 29, Messud published *When the World Was Steady*. The novel's action centers around two sisters, Emmy and Virginia, both born in London during World War II. Since childhood they have led remarkably different lives: Emmy quickly left England for Australia to marry the heir of a wealthy family; Virginia remained in their native country to care for their mother. After Emmy's husband leaves her for one of her friends, she travels to Bali to escape her feelings of humiliation and immerse herself in a completely foreign culture. Though she goes so far as to take part in a Balinese religious ritual, she realizes that she cannot run away from herself. Upon returning to Australia, she has come no closer to recovering from her loss or to self-discovery.

Meanwhile Virginia is having a crisis of her own. She has long since given her fate over to divine providence, believing that human destiny could not possibly lie in the hands of fallible people. She gains fortitude from her devout belief in God, but this does not stop her from snapping at her closest friend, or prevent her boss from assigning her mandatory sick-leave to overcome her nervous tension. Then, just as she is about to seek spiritual guidance from her reverend, she discovers him in the rectory having sex with another man. Virginia subsequently flees to the Isle of Skye to recover her spiritual strength but finds she has to deal with her cantankerous mother, Melody, who imagines that she will be dead before the end of the trip.

James Marcus, reviewing the book for the *New York Times Book Review* (September 24, 1995), called it an "assured and engaging debut," noting that "we may not admire this trio of sad sack searchers, but Ms. Messud makes us eager to see them get their rare shot at bliss." Reviewing the work for the *Chicago Tribune* (December 24, 1994), Joseph Olshan wrote, "*When the World Was Steady* is an extremely contemporary novel because it treats the world as a virtual microcosm in which we can bear witness to psychic hardships that are occurring thousands of miles apart. . . . But this is also a very traditional novel, for Messud writes beautiful cadenced prose, and proceeds, sentence by sentence, image by image, character by character, to create a fully realized, multi-layered world." *When the World Was Steady* was nominated for a PEN/Faulkner Award for Fiction in 1996.

The Last Life, Messud's second novel, was published in 1999. Its narrator, Sagesse LaBasse, is a teenage girl coming of age on the French Riviera as the daughter of an Algerian-Frenchman who returned to France only after being forced to leave Algeria during its war for independence. On the Riviera, Sagesse's grandfather establishes a hotel, which his son Alexandre, Sagesse's father, helps to run. There the family's members hope to reinvent themselves among the vacationing bourgeoisie, though they continue to pine for the colonial Algeria they called home. By the late 1980s Sagesse's father's life is full of troubles: his marriage to Sagesse's mother, an American, is failing; his only son, Etienne, is mentally retarded and confined to a wheelchair, and his business successes add up to nothing more than the opportunities his overbearing father has given him. He consoles himself with womanizing and staying out late. Observing her family's disintegration, Sagesse is forced to roll with the punches through a series of traumatic events in which her grandfather breaks down and shoots at one of her friends for swimming in the hotel pool late at night, her father commits suicide, and her mother escapes to Nice with a rich lover. Sagesse, realizing that her world will never be the same again, leaves for the United States and her own exile, not from a country, but from her family and their way of life.

The Last Life garnered Messud high praise. Margaret Flanagan, writing for *Booklist* (September 15, 1999), called it "A spellbinding and perceptive glimpse into a tortured adolescent soul from a tremendously gifted and empathetic writer." "*The Last Life*," Jay Parini wrote in the *Nation* (October 18, 1999), "is a complex instrument, a harp whose many strings are always in tune." In the *New Criterion* (November 1999), Brooke Allen noted that "where Messud outstrips the competition is in her tenacious grip on psychological realism; she plumbs the moral shallows of her characters with a brutal regard for honesty. The novel's social gatherings . . . are observed with cruel wit, and Sagesse functions perfectly as observer and chronicler."

The Hunters (2001) contains two thematically unrelated novellas. In "A Simple Tale," an elderly cleaning woman in Toronto, Canada, loses a client to a nursing home. She is led to reflect on her own life story: her experience as a teenager in the Ukraine during World War II, when she was transferred to the Nazi labor camps; her arrival in Canada after the war; her son's unfortunate marriage; and the death of her husband. "The Hunters" tells of an American academic living in London who has acquired an obsession with her two downstairs neighbors, a mother and daughter who raise rabbits. "Messud's two narratives share common themes of loneliness and isolation, but they're as different as night and day," Zofia Smardz wrote for the *Washington Post* (August 18, 2002). "While the first opens out into light to celebrate the miraculous in the mundane, the second is dark, foreboding—and hauntingly unresolved."

In January 2003 Messud received a Strauss Living Award, which offers a $250,000 prize paid out over five years. Previous winners of the award, which is sponsored by the American Academy of Arts and Letters, include Cynthia Ozick and Raymond Carver. Messud has also been the recipient of a Guggenheim Fellowship and the Addison Metcalf Award from the American Academy of Arts and Letters, a prize presented each year to "a young writer of great promise."

In addition to writing, Claire Messud has taught creative writing at Warren Wilson College, in North Carolina, and in the graduate writing program at Johns Hopkins University, in Baltimore, Maryland. She has served as writer-in-residence at the University of the South in Sewanee, Tennessee, and as a visiting writer at Amherst College, in Massachusetts. She lives in Washington, D.C., and will spend the 2003 spring semester as the visiting Thomas Professor of Creative Writing at Kenyon College, in Gambier, Ohio.

—C. M.

SUGGESTED READING: Amherst College Creative Writing Center Web site; *Booklist* Sep. 15, 1999; *Chicago Tribune* p4 Dec. 24, 1995; *Granta* p163+ Summer 1999; *Harborfront Reading Series* (on-line); *Nation* p25+ Oct. 18, 1999; *New Criterion* p60+ Nov. 1999; *New Statesman* p57 Sep.13, 1999; *New York Times* C p18 Mar. 21, 1996; *New York Times Book Review* p23 Sep. 24, 1995; *Pan Macmillan on-line*; *Salon* (on-line) Sep. 3, 1999

SELECTED BOOKS: *When the World Was Steady*, 1995; *The Last Life*, 1999

Courtesy of McClelland & Stewart Ltd.

Michaels, Anne

1958– Novelist; poet

It is not uncommon for contemporary poets to apply their exploration of language, imagery, and form to the task of writing fiction. Commenting on this growing list of poet-novelists, W. S. Di Piero noted for the *New York Times* (April 20, 1997, on-line), "Poets are just as capable of writing drab prose as anyone else, but a few poets—and the Canadian Anne Michaels is among them—are capable of producing the sort of sumptuous economies of language we expect from a superior novel." Since the mid-1980s the Toronto-born writer Anne Michaels has penned three critically admired collections of poetry, including *The Weight of Oranges*, *Miner's Pond*, and *Skin Divers*, gaining an international reputation as "one of the finest and most respected poets of her generation," according to Branko Gorjup for *World Literature Today* (Winter 2001). Often infusing her work with motifs of natural history, geology, meteorology, and biology, Michaels presents narrative poems, sometimes invoking historical and political personalities. In 1996 she published her first novel, *Fugitive Pieces*, the story of a young boy, Jakob Beers, who is rescued by a Greek geologist during the Holocaust. The book became an undisputed critical success, with Mark Abley for *Saturday Night* (June 1996) calling it, "a breathtaking work of art—a first novel that catapults Anne Michaels to the front rank of Canadian writers." *Fugitive Pieces* earned Michaels Ontario's Trillium Award, the Chapters/Books in Canada First Novel Award, The Beatrice and Martin Fischer Award (the main prize in the Jewish Book Awards), the American Lannan Literary Award, Italy's Giuseppe Acerbi Literary Award, and Britain's prestigious Orange Prize. Discussing the rewards of writing across genres, Michaels told Kathleen O'Neill for *WordsWorth Books* (April 25, 1997, on-line), "A novel allows you to be with the reader long enough to let time and thought enter the equation. . . . In poetry communication is instant and precise, although hopefully the effect lasts a long time. But the use of time is so different in poetry and the novel."

Anne Michaels was born in Toronto, Canada, in 1958, the youngest of four children—and the first daughter—born to Isaiah and Rosalind Michaels. Her father was a Polish Jew who had immigrated to the country in 1931 at the age of 13; her mother had been born in Canada. Michaels studied at the University of Toronto, graduating in 1980 with a B.A. in English.

In 1986 Michaels published her first book of poetry, *The Weight of Oranges*, which Louise Longo for *Books in Canada* (May 1986) called "an impressive debut." While many of its poems tackle themes of love and loss, or what Longo called "almost standard poetic fare," the reviewer concluded, "what [Michaels] makes of them certainly is not." For example, in the poem "Memoriam," Michaels displays her flair for striking imagery through such lines as, "The dead leave us starving with mouths full of love," and later, "Memory has a hand in the grave up to the wrist. / Earth crumbles from your fist under the sky's black sieve. / We are orphaned, one by one." In other poems Michaels explores themes of sexuality and creativity, and contemplates the demands of making art. "Words for the Body," for example, presents a conversation between a writer and a musician, as they consider the relationship between music, language, and memory: "In a voice that came from the highway / you described the blackness where music waits, / tormenting until you draw it out, / a redemption. / Then the fear of forgetting notes / disappears, the fingers have a memory / of their own." Paul Dutton for *Quill & Quire* (January 1987) praised the book as "the work of a poet whose intensely visual imagery is rife with painterly perceptions. The poems reveal a precise intellect and refined sensibilities, the language wielded with appropriate precision and refinement." He continued, "The writing is richly sensuous, sombre without being ponderous, compassionate without being sentimental—and at a few peak points—elegantly moving." *The Weight of Oranges* earned Michaels the 1986 Commonwealth Poetry Prize for first book.

With her second collection, *Miner's Pond* (1991), Michaels again elicited praise from reviewers. As Charlene Diehl-Jones noted for *Books in Canada* (October 1991), "An intelligent and inquisitive mind is at work here, wrestling with problems of language and memory, history and desire, and the body in art and in the world." Throughout many of these poems, Michaels applied her fascination with science and historical biography, often inserting artistic and political personalities into her narratives. She portrays, for example, the writers Marina Tsvetaeva, Osip Mandelstam, Anna Akhmatova, Alfred Doeblin, and Isak Dinesen; the painters Pierre Auguste Renoir, Paula Becker, and Lunia Czechowska; and the astronomer Johannes Kepler. According to Rhea Tregebov for *Quill & Quire* (June 1991), "Michaels's dramatic monologues are an intriguing test of the limits of the poetic imagination." In the title poem Michaels combines an autobiographical narrative of childhood with an elegy, introducing the characters of her young brothers and recalling their curiosity with science. Throughout the poem she presents powerful language, such as "A family is a study of plate-tectonics, flow-folding. / Something inside shifts; suddenly we're closer or apart," and later: "Overhead the geese are in a line, / a moving scar. Wavering / like a strand of pollen on the surface of a pond. / Like them, we carry each year in our bodies. / Our blood is time." Of the startling images in "Miner's Pond," Diehl-Jones concluded, "They take you over, press other readings into your eyes. Michaels's work is a celebration of lyric possibility, refreshingly free of nostalgia and narcissism." Tregebov affirmed, "Michaels is a writer willing to take risks, to flex her voice and her imaginative range. Her successes are reflective of this boldness." For *Miner's Pond* Michaels won the Canadian Authors' Association Award for poetry, the National Magazine Gold Award for poetry, and was short-listed for the Governor General's Award and the Trillium Award.

Shortly after the publication of *The Weight of Oranges*, in 1987, Michaels had begun working on her first novel, a story set during the Holocaust. "I had the beginning and the ending in my mind even as early as 1980," she told an interviewer for a student publication from the University of British Columbia, the *Ubyssey* (November 8, 1996, on-line), "but I didn't let myself begin writing until quite a few years later, 1986, after my first book came out. It's important that the facts have a chance to ferment, to be absorbed, in order to try and fathom whatever meaning is hidden among those facts. I did years of reading, years of research, followed all kinds of strange and stray paths and just let that material sink into me." Michaels wrote and polished her manuscript for more than nine years before publishing *Fugitive Pieces* in 1996. Of her interest in presenting a story of Holocaust survival, Michaels told Mark Abley, "For me, it's natural that when the first half of the century was dominated by war, the second half should try to come to some understanding of that."

On the first page of *Fugitive Pieces*, the reader learns that a fictional poet and translator, Jakob Beers, has been killed by a car in Greece and that shortly before his death he had begun writing his memoirs. In the first section of what follows, Michaels presents these memoirs, with Beers narrating the collection of layered images and scenes that have comprised his life; in the second section, Michaels writes from the perspective of Ben, a meteorologist who is a strong admirer of Beers's writing—and is himself the son of Holocaust survivors—as he travels to Greece in search of the poet's lost diaries. Jakob's recollections begin with a day in 1939 that changed his life: At age seven, when Nazi soldiers invade his home, killing his parents and abducting his 15-year-old sister, Jakob saves himself by hiding behind a wall. He escapes to a nearby forest, hiding for days in the mud, until he is rescued by a Greek geologist, Athos, who smuggles him to the island of Zakynthos to hide for the duration of the war. Throughout these years, Athos teaches Jakob poetry, botany, astronomy, shipbuilding, and geography, always encouraging the young boy to overcome his silence by writing. Later in the book, Jakob recalls, "I already knew the power of language to destroy, to omit, to obliterate," as quoted by Molly E. Rauch for *The Nation* (April 7, 1997). "But poetry, the power of language to restore: this is what . . . Athos [was] trying to teach me." After the war, Jakob and Athos settle in Toronto, where Jakob marries and eventually heals through memory, language, and love. In the second section, in which Ben nurses his own Holocaust wounds, Di Piero observed, "The discovery of Jakob's journals, with their subtle story of love's redemptions, frees Ben into new recognitions." For the *Times Literary Supplement* (February 7, 1997), Kasia Boddy discussed Michaels's themes: "The idea that we must recreate history, forever reliving other lives as well as our own, lies behind the novel's complex metaphorical texture. The metaphors . . . inform the novel's structure; its 'fugitive pieces,' like fossils or fragments of ancient civilization, are buried and excavated, their secrets need to be delicately prised away."

Critics celebrated *Fugitive Pieces* for its complexity and originality in depicting the emotional destruction suffered by Holocaust survivors. Paul Gray and John Skow noted for *Time* (March 3, 1997), "Michaels not only creates an imaginary poet, she also examines the ways in which a poetic imagination can arise out of horror." Of the book's authentic texture, Rauch added, "*Fugitive Pieces* is so compelling in part because it reads like philosophy, or history, or even a scholarly treatise on peat-bog preservation—anything other than the novel that it is. Jakob is fabricated, but Michaels has written him with an interior tenderness that makes one feel guilty for reading, as if one had stumbled on Jakob's journals and were reading the secrets of his life." While some critics lamented that many of the novel's characters appeared as mere sketches in Jakob's memoirs, they applauded Michaels's "wondrous evocation of place," as Nancy Wigston wrote for *Quill & Quire* (May 1996), adding, "She makes unfamiliar landscapes in Poland and Greece intimately real. . . . Toronto is approached as if it were an archeological dig. Ravines, the overflowing banks of the Humber River, layers of rock and layers of history." Rauch concluded, "It's not only Michaels's restorative language that merits celebration; it's also her rare and genuine hopefulness. That love can survive grief is indeed a miracle." According to Anne Michaels's Web site, rights to the novel have been sold in 19 countries.

In 1999 Michaels published her third book of poems, *Skin Divers*, a collection dedicated to exploring biological motifs and the interconnectedness of all living things. As Branko Gorjup observed, "The landscape in these poems assumes another dimension: it becomes overlaid with thick strata of biological memory. Though the poems are still concerned with burials and excavations . . . they also explore . . . the mystery of how these surviving fragments continue to live with new cell-life." Throughout the book, Michaels employs scientific language to explore the world's mysteries. Additionally, she again invokes historical narratives, giving voice to such characters as the French chemist Irene Curie, daughter of Marie, (in "The Second Search") and the sculptor Kathleen Scott (in "Ice House"). In this latter poem, which Gorjup named "probably one of the most moving," Michaels examines the emotional connection between Scott and her husband, Robert Falcon Scott, an Antarctic explorer who died while returning from the South Pole. Describing the merits of *Skin Divers*, Gorjup described the work as "infused with insight, technical sophistication, and a powerful vision of a world that is both near and far-off—near because it is in our skin and our bones, far-off because we cannot see it with our unaided eye." Two years later, Michaels published a complete collection of her three volumes of poetry in *Poems: The Weight of Oranges, Miner's Pond, Skin Divers* (2001). While Robert MacFarlane for the *Times Literary Supplement* (May 25, 2001) observed, "Every now and then her sincerity congeals into mawkishness and truism," he nevertheless affirmed the most memorable moments are "when Anne Michaels combines her potent sense of wonder with her gift for precise description."

Of harnessing the poetic effects of language, Michaels told Diane Turbide for *Maclean's* (December 22, 1997), "For me, writing is a question of supreme control and complete surrender. Both are essential, and you need to know when to do each." When she is not writing, Michaels teaches creative writing in Toronto and composes musical scores for the theater. A member of the League of Canadian Poets, she is currently working on her second novel.

—K. D.

SUGGESTED READING: *Books in Canada* p43 May 1986, p49 Oct. 1991; Books on Kensington Web site; *Maclean's* p61 July 1, 1996, p40+ Dec. 22, 1997; *The Nation* p35 Apr. 7, 1997; *New York Times* (on-line) Apr. 20, 1997; *Quill & Quire* p32 Jan. 1987, p39 June 1991; *Times Literary Supplement* p23 Feb. 7, 1997, p26 May 25, 2001; WordsWorth Books Web site; *World Literature Today* p120 Winter 2001

SELECTED WORKS: poetry—*The Weight of Oranges*, 1986; *Miner's Pond*, 1991; *Skin Divers*, 1999; *Poems*, 2001; novels—*Fugitive Pieces*, 1996

Miller, Andrew

Apr. 29, 1960– Novelist

"There are some writers who are particularly skilled in the art of description, of evoking images and characters, visual effect and connotation, of being able to suggest the full ambience of their craft," Hamilton Smith wrote in Australia's *Cranberry Times* (May 22, 1999). "[Andrew] Miller certainly belongs to this category. His power of narrative, precise forming of sentences and paragraphs is often quite exquisite, even mesmerizing in its ex-

Andrew Miller
Rui Xavier/Courtesy of Harcourt Publishing

ecution." With three novels to date—*Ingenious Pain* (1997), *Casanova in Love* (1998), and *Oxygen* (2001)—Miller has been widely celebrated for his authentic and inventive historical fiction, which is often set in 18th-century Britain. However, Miller's work is not limited to that setting. His most recent book, *Oxygen*, takes place in England's West Country in 1997, with forays into 1956 Hungary. Throughout the writing process, as Miller told Nadine O'Regan for the *Sunday Business Post* (as posted on his official Web site), research is only the first step toward recreating another time. "I don't research obsessively," he explained. "I try to be accurate, but this is like a dream. . . . This is a 21st century person dreaming of another time. There are things which are just hard for people to know—what it was like to wake up in 1760, how it smelled. I'm not trying to do a reconstruction as an archaeologist might from fragments. It's much freer than that."

Andrew Miller was born in Bristol, a city on Britain's southwestern coast, on April 29, 1960. He spent his early childhood in Flax Bourton, a small village in Somerset County, where his father was the local doctor. When Miller was four years old, his parents divorced, and he and his older brother moved to Bath to live with their mother. Never a good student, Miller failed his 11-plus exams—a standardized test that all British students then took at age 11—and was sent to Dauntsey's School, a private boarding school in Wiltshire. (The 11-plus test was discontinued in Britain in the 1970s but is still administered in Northern Ireland.) His grades continued to suffer; Miller excelled in only one subject—English. One day in 1978, as he told O'Regan, after reading D.H. Lawrence's acclaimed novel *The Rainbow*, he decided he would become a writer. "After that," he explained, "although I did many different jobs in different parts of the world, I was always an undercover writer."

Miller's first such job was at a chicken abattoir, where he spent his days pulling the legs off slaughtered chickens. He then worked for three years with British Social Services, assisting children with learning disabilities. At age 22, having gained some distance from his challenging years in secondary school, Miller applied to Middlesex Polytechnic—now Middlesex University—in North London to study English, history, and philosophy. He recalled to Peter Kingston for the London *Guardian* (May 25, 1999), "I had to write an essay to show I was capable of the course. It was about D.H. Lawrence and was wonderfully chaotic, but it got me in." In his third year he transferred to Crewe and Alsager College, part of the Manchester Metropolitan University, where he took his first creative writing course and graduated with high honors in 1985. (At Crewe and Alsager he also met his future wife, whom he married in 1985 and divorced in 1990.) After completing college Miller continued working a variety of odd jobs, including stints as a bookseller, an agency nurse, and a bartender.

In 1991 Miller returned to school to embark on the prestigious creative writing course at the University of East Anglia, where he worked with such notable British writers as Malcolm Bradbury, Lorna Sage, and Rose Tremain. Despite his regard for the program's faculty, Miller told Penny Fox for the Glasgow *Herald* (March 5, 1998) that he didn't much enjoy the experience. "It's no reflection on [the professors]," he explained. "Gaining a place on it gave me one of those 'little bits of success,' I felt I was being taken seriously. It makes you more professional and rigorous, you have to take responsibility for what you put down on paper. And there is a great deal of scrutiny. But nine months is probably long enough; it may not be a good thing for a writer to be exposed to too much scrutiny, too many people looking over your shoulder." Miller completed the course in 1992, earning an M.A. in creative and critical writing, and then spent time teaching English in Spain, in both Avila and Barcelona, and later in Tokyo, Japan. Soon after, he began a doctoral program at Lancaster University under the tutelage of Professor David Craig; there, he worked extensively on his first novel (which would become *Ingenious Pain*) and finished his Ph.D. in creative writing in 1995. Since 1996 Miller has been writing full time.

Ingenious Pain is set in 18th-century Britain and explores the life of James Dyer, a gifted surgeon who is unable to feel any physical or emotional pain. Conceived when his mother is raped on a frozen river, Dyer is mute, strange, unfeeling, and emotionally cold. The first part of the novel consists of Dyer's picaresque adventures as he encounters a series of roguish characters who exploit his peculiarity. He eventually rises to become one of

England's most brilliant brain surgeons. In the second portion of the book, he travels to Russia—another icy environment—to innoculate Catherine the Great against smallpox. En route he undergoes a mysterious rebirth that awakens all the pain he has experienced and suppressed throughout his life. The shock of this newfound affliction drives Dyer mad, and the novel closes with his admission to a mental hospital in London. Of his inspiration for the book, Miller told James Urquhart for the London *Independent* (September 1, 2001), "I started looking into the conditions of surgery in the 18th century and realised the kind of hell it was not just for patients, but for surgeons, too. Then I had the thought: what would it be like to live in the midst of a world like that but not actually to feel any pain or have any empathy with suffering—what kind of person would that be?"

Ingenious Pain received near-universal praise from critics, some of whom compared it to *The French Lieutenant's Woman* (1969), by John Fowles, or Graham Swift's *Waterland* (1984). Like Fowles and Swift, Miller presents 18th-century England in a way that is historically authentic and yet, as Patrick McGrath described for the *New York Times* (April 13, 1997), "entirely its own creature, a mature novel of ideas soaked in the sensory detail of its turbulent times." McGrath elaborated, "The 18th century had a strong appetite for the freaks and peculiarities of the natural world, and Andrew Miller has cleverly deployed his various specimens so as to draw out characteristic features of the period: the casual cruelty and sheer hard slog of life; the gullibility and superstition of the popular mind; but mostly the vigorous new spirit of scientific inquiry, particularly in the fields of medicine and anatomy, then sweeping away established patterns of thought." Writing for the *Times Literary Supplement* (February 28, 1997), Alison Woodhouse affirmed, "The novel's evocation of the period, down to the finest detail, is thoroughly confident; and many of its minor characters are memorably vivid. . . . *Ingenious Pain* achieves a difficult blend of sadness and loss, joy and laughter. Skillfully constructed, reaching imaginative heights and emotional depths, this fine first novel explores the question of what it means to be human." *Ingenious Pain* earned Miller the James Tait Black Memorial Prize for fiction; Italy's Grinzane Cavour Prize; and the IMPAC Dublin Literary Award, which carries a cash prize of approximately $135,300 (£100,000)—an impressive honor for a first-time novelist. The book has been published in more than 20 countries and is currently being adapted for film.

Miller again focused on the 18th century in his second novel, *Casanova in Love* (1998), a fictional account of the real-life Giacomo Casanova's experiences in London, circa 1763, and narrated by the aging legend himself. (Casanova was an Italian adventurer, known for his scandalous womanizing and his multi-volume memoirs entitled *History of My Life*.) The novel highlights Casanova's unrequited obsession with Marie Charpillon, a smart young woman who repeatedly deflects his affections. When Casanova arrives in London, thinly disguised as the "Chevalier de Seingalt," he encounters Charpillon—another real-life figure—and is immediately taken by her beauty. Because the girl's mother owes him a large sum of money, Casanova believes his seduction will prove successful; yet, the novel chronicles his defeat through a series of often-comical courtship frustrations. Along the way, Miller depicts a less-confident side of the serial lover. According to Christina Del Sesto for the *Washington Post* (November 8, 1998), "Miller gives us a unique portrayal of the Venetian seducer. Not only is he cruelly rebuffed, but he is lovesick and aging. Casanova, the symbol of virility, is vulnerable." She added, "Watching Casanova doubt and struggle with mortality . . . is thought-provoking. Miller finds the right balance between the infamous but predictable, swaggering Casanova and the bumbling, somewhat endearing, doubtful one."

Casanova was widely praised for its rich illustration of the 18th century and its complex depiction of its historical protagonist. Writing for New York *Newsday* (October 11, 1998), Sylvia Brownrigg observed, "Miller . . . is astonishingly assured in handling the novel's lush complexities of time and place, of nationality, and of the intricate workings of Casanova's troubled mind. Miller brings to vivid life the textures of 18th-Century London: nightboats along the Thames, sodden carriage rides, the drinking of chocolate by a drawing-room fire. Miller has a lovely way with sensuous details." John Elson for *Time* (October 19, 1998) opined, "Miller's limning of London in 1763 and 1764, with its acrid stenches and incessant rains, has the picturesque grunge of a [William] Hogarth sketch." Amid such applause, some critics found Miller's characterization of Charpillon lacking. Del Sesto noted, "Ultimately, Charpillon is uninteresting. She is a frustrating tease, and Casanova's obsession with her rejection raises the question of whether he was really ever in love with her. . . . Defining Charpillon's character and telling more about the courtesan world at the turn of the century would have added a welcome dimension to the book." Nevertheless, critics found much more to praise in *Casanova in Love* than to criticize. In a review for the Chicago *Sun-Times* (January 6, 1999), Kyrie O'Connor concluded, "If Andrew Miller's novel *Casanova in Love* is not entirely successful, it lingers in your head far longer than many novels that meet all their less-daring objectives." *Casanova in Love* was named a *Publishers Weekly* best book of the year for 1998.

In his next work, *Oxygen* (2001), Miller abandoned the 18th-century themes that had characterized his previous works and instead set his story in modern-day England. In the novel Alice Valentine, a 60-year-old widow, is dying of cancer in her West Country home and is dependent on an oxygen tank for immediate survival. Her younger son, Alec, a literary translator, has returned to visit her from London and has brought with him his most promising job to date—he has been hired to translate the Hungarian exile and playwright Laszlo Lazar's work, *Oxygene*. Struggling against his own insecurities and his mother's impending demise, Alec is on the brink of a nervous breakdown. His older brother, Larry, returns home with his own set of problems in tow: Larry was once a successful tennis-star-turned-soap-opera-actor in the U.S., who is now facing drug and alcohol addictions, a crumbling marriage, and a failing career. Amid this domestic chaos, Miller weaves a second storyline of Laszlo Lazar's own crisis, as he grapples with his own haunted memories of the 1956 Hungarian uprising in which he failed to save his lover's life. (An actual event, the uprising started in October of that year when members of the working class rebelled against their Soviet oppressors and briefly established their own government.) Miller described his intentions for *Oxygen* to James Urquhart: "One of the themes I was very interested in was how little we know even of people who are very close to us, and that lack often does make it very difficult for us to say or do the necessary things." He added, "The idea that love redeems everything is very strong in our culture, but maybe love isn't always enough. It's about the best we've got, but sometimes it doesn't give you the privileged insights into another person that can cement the relationship."

Oxygen received generally favorable reviews, though some critics opined that the novel failed to capture the merits of Miller's previous works. Writing for the *Seattle Times* (April 15, 2002), Scott Stolnack observed, "While certain scenes are rendered beautifully and lucidly, nothing here compares to the startling vividness of his two earlier novels." David Matthews for the *Australian* (October 13, 2001) called the book an exploration of the "masculine anxiety" of his male characters—a tradition pioneered by such modern writers as Ian McEwan and Graham Swift in the 1980s and 1990s. Matthews added, "It's not that this is not worth looking at again, just that for a writer who really had established his own place it's slightly disappointing to see him falling into line with some well-established preoccupations." Nevertheless, many other critics celebrated the work, particularly Miller's development of characters and his perspective. In his favorable review for the *Chicago Tribune* (March 31, 2002), Michael Upchurch noted, "Miller has researched his contemporary realities—Alice's illness, Larry's hedonistic California, Laszlo's Paris and Budapest—as diligently as he did the 18th Century backgrounds of his first two novels. And his care and precision with them bring alive every chapter of this meditation on the nature of exile and home, love and responsibility, discontent and happiness." *Oxygen* was short-listed for the 2001 Booker Prize and the 2002 Whitbread Novel Award.

Andrew Miller has lived for extended periods in Dublin, Paris, and London. He currently resides in Brighton, on the southern coast of Britain, and is reportedly working on his fourth novel.

—K. D.

SUGGESTED READING: *Australian* R p12 Oct. 13, 2001; *Chicago Tribune* C p7 July 27, 1997, C p2 Mar. 31, 2002; *Glasgow Herald* p14 Mar. 5, 1998; *Irish Times* p12 Jan. 22, 1998; (London) *Independent* p5 Sep. 22, 1998, p9 Sep. 1, 2001; *New Statesman* p51 Sep. 10, 2001; *New York Times* VII p10 Apr. 13, 1997; *New York Times* (on-line) Oct. 25, 1998, May 5, 2002; (New York) *Newsday* B p14 Oct. 11, 1998; *Washington Post* X p4 Nov. 8, 1998

SELECTED BOOKS: *Ingenious Pain*, 1997; *Casanova in Love*, 1998; *Oxygen*, 2001

Miller, James

Feb. 28, 1947– Philosopher; biographer; essayist; music critic

In the 1970s James Miller, once a member of Students for a Democratic Society (SDS), emerged as a popular-music critic and as editor of the *Rolling Stone Illustrated History of Rock and Roll* (1976). He then went on to a career as a professor of political philosophy. His books include *History and Human Existence: From Marx to Merleau-Ponty* (1979), a study of two phenomenologist philosophers; *Rousseau: Dreamer of Democracy* (1984), an examination of how Rousseau's life contributed to his theory of democracy, which in turn formed the basis for modern political theories; *"Democracy Is in the Streets": From Port Huron to the Siege of Chicago* (1987), an account of the rise and decline of the efforts of the New Left to create participatory democracy in the United States; *The Passion of Michel Foucault* (1993), a biographical study of the iconic 20th-century philosopher and post-structuralist who tried to live his philosophy; and *Flowers in the Dustbin: The Rise of Rock and Roll, 1947–1977* (1999), a history of the music genre that first excited and then disappointed the author, who feared that jazz and gospel would be vitiated by the newest trends in rock. Miller might have been speaking of his own life and work when he wrote in *Social Research* (Winter 1998), "When Socrates received an injunction from the oracle at Delphi, it was not to write books or to teach seminars in logic. It was rather, as he said, 'to live the life of the philosopher, to examine myself and others.'"

James Miller was born in Chicago, Illinois, on February 28, 1947 to Barbara Anderson and James E. Miller Jr., a professor of English and the author of *The American Quest for a Supreme Fiction: Whitman's Legacy in the Personal Epic* (1979). Miller received his B.A. degree from Pomona College, in Claremont, California, in 1969 and was awarded a Ph.D. by Brandeis University, in Waltham, Massachusetts, in 1975. During this period, Miller—who had been a journalist since the late 1960s, as a contributor to *Rolling Stone*, *New Times*, and *Real Paper*—started an academic career, becoming a professor of government and political science at the University of Texas in Austin in 1976. He remained there until 1980, when he left for New York. There, he put his teaching career on hold and at first gave the major portion of his time to writing and editing for *Newsweek*, where he reviewed books and music.

The Rolling Stone Illustrated History of Rock and Roll, edited by Miller, was largely well received. Mark C. Miller wrote in the *New York Review of Books* (February 3, 1977) that the "book tries to be groovy and monumental at the same time" and is "most successful when least authoritative." A revised edition, published in 1992, provided up-to-date coverage of the rock scene. While he was still teaching at the University of Texas, Miller produced the first book that was all his own: *History and Human Existence: From Marx to Merleau-Ponty*, published by the University of California Press, was considered an academic book and as such did not receive wide critical comment. In the book, Miller examined the relationship of two philosophers, Karl Marx and Maurice Merleau-Ponty, to materialism and phenomenology.

By contrast, *Rousseau: Dreamer of Democracy*, published when Miller was an editor at *Newsweek*, attracted critical notice. One of Miller's enduring interests has been the history of democratic reform and revolutionary movements; in *Rousseau*, Miller analyzed Rousseau's theory of democracy, as expressed in *Social Contract*. Rousseau, who was persecuted for his views, died in 1778, before the French Revolution. During that revolution, his theories were adopted, particularly by Robespierre, who used them largely as a pretext for violence. Miller argued that Rousseau's dream of democracy was "something of a mirage and a less than reliable paradigm for modern democracy," according to the *Choice* (December 1984) reviewer, C. A. Linden. "Miller does a fine job of drawing out the central democratic-populist thread in Rousseau's thought, which is so easily lost among the diverse interpretations, both past and present, that his well-known paradoxes invite. Miller combines a fair-minded and scholarly appreciation of Rousseau's place in the first ranks of political philosophers with a searching and telling criticism of the flaws he detects in his arguments," Linden concluded.

Miller continued his exploration of the meaning and practice of democracy with *"Democracy Is in the Streets": From Port Huron to the Siege of Chicago*, an account of the 1962 creation, at Port Huron, Michigan, of the SDS manifesto. The book goes on to trace the subsequent lives and careers of the organization's founders, up to and after the Democratic National Convention in Chicago in the summer of 1968 and the final SDS convention in 1969. The SDS manifesto called for "the establishment of a democracy of individual participation, governed by two central aims: that the individual share in those social decisions determining the quality and direction of his life; that society be organized to encourage independence in men and provide the media for their common participation." Miller used this idea of participatory democracy as the organizing principle of the narratives in the book, which include the story of Tom Hayden, an architect of the Port Huron manifesto, who became one of the Chicago Seven (defendants accused of inciting rioting) and later a more mainstream political figure in California. Miller himself had joined SDS and was present at its final convention. He wanted the ideals laid out by the founders of SDS to survive the subsequent descent of the organization into "a loonier incarnation of the same sectarian marginality it had set out, at Port Huron, to transcend," according to Hendrik Hertzberg, writing in the *New York Times Book Review* (June 21, 1987).

Miller wrote the book to correct myths and misunderstandings about the New Left, the movement of which SDS was a prominent part. He wanted to convey "the extraordinary intensity and seriousness" with which he and his associates tried to build a grassroots movement, as he told E. J. Dionne Jr. for an interview in the *New York Times Book Review* (June 21, 1987). Miller explained that "as a mood of smug tranquility began to settle over the political culture of the United States in the early Eighties, I found myself increasingly uncomfortable with both the neoconservative scorn and the facile nostalgia that have typified popular attitudes about the Sixties." Miller was careful to interview those he wrote about and to allow them to correct, if they so desired, what he had written. Nicholas Xenos, the reviewer for the *Nation* (July 25, 1987), judged Miller successful: "His approach works wonderfully, giving us the story from a number of perspectives, but with the question of participatory democracy at the center." Hendrik Hertzberg agreed with that assessment, deeming Miller "a fine guide—accurate, sympathetic, critical, learned."

In 1992 Miller resumed his academic career as a professor of political philosophy at the New School for Social Research, in New York City. With his 1993 offering, *The Passion of Michel Foucault*, he returned to a study of a philosopher's life and the interaction between that life and his work. "Trying to sum up a philosopher's life is always hazardous, particularly if one wishes . . . to explore the ethos of a philosophy—that is, the way in which a deliberately cultivated way of thinking shaped (or failed to shape) a life into a chosen form," Miller was to write in *Salmagundi* (Winter/Spring 1996). In his study of Foucault, Miller explored questions of guilt and responsibility, as Foucault inspired a great deal of controversy by his actions. Foucault was a philosopher who devoted himself to living out Nietzsche's injunction to "become what one is." He thus engaged in "transgressive sexuality" and many other forms of revolt against middle-class mores, believing that social institutions work to mold people into beings who contribute willingly and efficiently to their own exploitation in capitalist society. Above all, he underscored "the lyrical core" of life, which he believed was revealed by death; Foucault himself died of AIDS. He had consciously engaged in dangerous, even life-threatening activities in order to enter the void beyond language, "the occluded, Dionysian dimension of being human," as Miller phrased it. In "The Prophet and the Dandy: Philosophy as a Way of Life in Nietzsche and Foucault," published in *Social Research* (Winter 1998), Miller explained some of what had attracted him to writing about Foucault: "With Foucault . . . one of the things I most admire is a certain kind of heroic openness to the possibility of transforming, through philosophizing, his ethos, a noble trait perhaps most movingly displayed at the end of his life, when he faced death with what an eyewitness like Paul Veyne has described as a striking serenity. . . . It is as if the dandy, measuring up to one teaching of a prophet who he never ceased to admire, could, in the end, do one of the most important things that Nietzsche had enjoined: that is, affirm without irony or apparent regrets the life he had actually led, taking comfort perhaps from what he had become: a self-reliant philosopher of true courage and singular style."

"Miller gives enormous prominence to Foucault's sexual adventures, as well as to his death," P. N. Furbank noted in the *London Review of Books* (July 22, 1993). Observing that Foucault's own writings on sexuality were quite sober, Furbank went on to criticize Miller, arguing that "the plot—the gospel-story of Foucault as visionary and prophet—leads Miller to depreciate [Foucault's] *The Order of Things*, that endlessly rewarding text, as somehow inauthentic, even dull." The *Entertainment Weekly* (February 5, 1993) reviewer of *The Passion of Michel Foucault* had a different opinion, judging that Miller's book had "its intended effect of making you respect Foucault as you can't help respecting his greatest influence, Nietzsche, whether or not you agree with him." The reviewer concluded that "Miller does a breathtaking job of rescuing the philosopher from the dogmatic clutches of his academic acolytes." The reviewers for the *New York Review of Books* (April 8, 1993), Alan Ryan; the *New York Times Book Review* (January 10, 1993), Isabelle de Courtivron; and the *Times Literary Supplement* (March 26, 1993), Lilla Mark, also praised the book. For Ryan, it gave one "a good sense of the kind of personality that would find modern liberal societies peculiarly oppressive" and stood as a volume that would "enhance Foucault's reputation." The *New York Times* selected *The Passion of Michel Foucault* as one of the Notable Books of 1993. The volume was nominated for a National Book Critics Circle Award in 1994.

As a professor of political philosophy, Miller continued to be occupied with the lives and thoughts of major philosophers of the 20th century. One of those, Martin Heidegger, a German, who had been considered one of the greatest philosophers of his time, became a spokesman for the Nazi party when Hitler came to power in Germany. In 1933, having become famous for his book *Sein und Zeit* (*Being and Time*), Heidegger was installed as rector of Freiburg University. He had pledged his loyalty to Hitler and vowed to rid the university of Jews and Jewish influences. After World War II, Heidegger obfuscated—but never renounced—his Nazi past.

As Miller described it in his Winter/Spring 1996 *Salmagundi* essay, titled "Heidegger's Guilt," Heidegger—in a Nazi ceremony he had planned—spoke of how the future did not belong to "meek and spineless pedants"; rather, "confronted with a 'moribund pseudocivilization' morbidly reproducing enervating pseudovalues, the restoration to health of a 'truly spiritual world' . . . requires 'the placing of one's existence in the most acute danger in the midst of overpowering being.'" Miller summed up the contrast between the hermit ascetic that Heidegger later became and his earlier assumption of a powerful position: "Two images, one man: the philosopher at the pinnacle of his worldly power, the otherworldly thinker in retreat. Two emblems of a man of two minds torn between guilt and pride, contemplative isolation and pitched battle, the mystery of 'overpowering Being' and the Promethean hubris of a self-avowed hero of the philosophical life—tragically flawed, defiantly unrepentant." What Heidegger was guilty of in the end, according to Miller, was "allowing his theory of history to hinge on a 'moment of vision' that could not be submitted to any kind of reasoned analysis" and using "the synthetic power of imagination in order to manufacture new myths for his compatriots and for himself," thus creating "a fantasyland fascism populated by Promethean philosophers, militant students, and resolute German soldiers braving death with Hölderlin and Nietzsche in their knapsacks."

Miller's philosophical investigations extended into the field of music, specifically rock music, on which he is a recognized authority. In an interview with Marc Woodworth and Robert Boyers for *Salmagundi* (Summer 1998), he explored some of the misconceptions attached to the culture of rock, especially the music's association with "images of disorder and disruption." For example, discussing the philosopher Theodor Adorno, whose "aversion to popular music is coded as a cultural critique," Miller presented Adorno's dismissive attitude as both elitist and uninformed by any understanding of the music he dismissed. But he contrasted Adorno's attitude with the "pseudo-religious terminology" used by critics of popular music, who should have simply described some of what they were analyzing as "just fun or entertaining," in Miller's view. Miller also observed that pronouncements about the effects of rock music on society were exaggerated: "As a historian, I would say that the invention of the pill was probably far more important than Elvis Presley to the sexual revolution. . . . It's not obvious to me that rock and roll represents a revolutionary leap forward from the bobby-soxers who screamed for Frank Sinatra, or the flappers in the roaring 20's who participated in orgiastic dance contests during the wee hours of the morning." Miller did, however, "defend the contention that there are pieces of popular music which are sublime." Still, he added that "sublimity is a rather rare event not only in popular culture but in high culture as well. . . . The main difference between rock and literature is that the market for bad poetry isn't as large as the market for bad popular music."

Miller's survey of the sublime in rock music, *Flowers in the Dustbin: The Rise of Rock and Roll, 1947–1977*, was published in 1999. Although Miller wrote at the beginning of the book, "Inspired by the Beatles, a new generation of performers, from Bob Dylan to Jim Morrison and the Doors, helped choreograph a cultural revolution that turned rock and roll from a disparaged music for kids into a widely watched, frequently praised mode of serious cultural expression," the book also displayed Miller's more pessimistic view of popular music. Reflecting on the creativity of such artists as the Beatles, Bob Dylan, Marvin Gaye, Jimi Hendrix, and the Rolling Stones, Miller concluded that rock music went into something of a decline in the 1970s, with the advent of punk. "After 1967, Miller shows rock heading downhill fast," Jon Pareles wrote, reviewing the book for the *New York Times* (August 26, 1999). "Nihilism and mere obnoxiousness start to replace rock's sense of possibility," Pareles continued, going on to quote Miller: "Nobody, young or old, could any longer experience the core feelings—of wonder and surprise—that rock and roll had really excited, once upon a time." Although Pareles praised some of Miller's writing and his "loving precision about the details of the music," he felt that "as *Flowers in the Dustbin* marshals facts to back up its cynicism, it misses the sheer pleasure that rock can deliver, and the way that pleasure can still transform a receptive fan."

By contrast, Ken Tucker, who reviewed *Flowers in the Dustbin* for *Entertainment Weekly* (August 6, 1999), found the volume "insightful and energetic." Tucker was not put off by Miller's seeing a decline in rock and roll or his ending his account of rock's rise with the death of Elvis Presley. "*Flowers* blossoms in chapters devoted to Bob Dylan and the Beatles, whose combined efforts, claims Miller, turned rock & roll into 'a medium fit for communicating autobiographical intimacies, political discontents, spiritual elation'. . . . Yet Miller's own chilly disillusionment with the genre never freezes his thoughts."

James Miller, married to a psychiatrist, has three children. In 1992 he became a professor of political philosophy and director of liberal studies in the graduate faculty of the New School for Social Research. "To be a philosopher," he wrote in *Social Research* (Winter 1998), once "entailed striving for happiness, or peace of mind, aiming at one's goal by living one's life according to a thoughtfully examined set of precepts and beliefs, embodied in word and deed." Miller has examined in his books the lives of those who attempted or failed to live up to those Socratic ideals.

—S. Y.

SUGGESTED READING: *Choice* p619 Dec. 1984; *Entertainment Weekly* p48 Feb. 5, 1993, p56+ Aug. 6, 1999; *London Review of Books* p11+ July 23, 1993; *New Republic* p28 Aug. 17, 1987; *New York Review of Books* p12 Apr. 8, 1993; *New York Times* Aug. 26, 1999; *New York Times Book Review* p9 Sep. 16, 1984, p1+ June 21, 1987; *Salmagundi* p178+ Winter/Spring 1996, p 206+ Summer 1998; *Social Research* p871+ Winter 1998; *Times Literary Supplement* p365 Mar. 29, 1985, p3 Mar. 26, 1993; *Voice* p90+ May 4, 1993; *Washington Post Book World* p5 Jan. 3, 1993

SELECTED BOOKS: *History and Human Existence: From Marx to Merleau-Ponty*, 1979; *Rousseau: Dreamer of Democracy*, 1984; *"Democracy Is in the Streets": From Port Huron to the Siege of Chicago*, 1987; *The Passion of Michel Foucault*, 1993; *Flowers in the Dustbin: The Rise of Rock and Roll, 1947–1977*, 1999

Milner, Ron

May 29, 1938– Playwright

The African-American playwright, critic, and director Ron Milner has experimented with many different dramatic forms in order to portray contemporary African-American experiences. Several of his plays, including *Who's Got His Own* (1966), *The Warning: A Theme for Linda* (1969), and *What the Wine-Sellers Buy* (1974) are set in urban ghettos, depicting familial and generational conflicts and characters burdened by their pasts and facing uncertain futures. *What the Wine-Sellers Buy* and three other plays, *Jazz-Set* (1980), *Checkmates* (1990), and *Urban Transition* (1995), were published in 2001 in the collection *What the Wine-Sellers Buy Plus Three*, which included a forward by acclaimed poet/playwright Amiri Baraka (formerly LeRoi Jones) and an introduction by Woodie King, Jr. Milner has also written history plays, including *Roads of the Mountain Top* (1986), which dramatizes episodes from the last three years in the life of Martin Luther King, Jr., and *Defending the Light* (2000), in which a 19th-century victim of racial injustice is defended at trial by William Seward, who later became secretary of state under President Lincoln. Some of Milner's energies have gone into creating musical theater, as in

Jazz-Set, in which the characters are named for the instruments they play, and *Don't Get God Started* (1987), which includes gospel music.

Ronald Milner was born in Detroit, Michigan, on May 29, 1938. His parents separated, and Milner was raised "in a split home" with his sister, as he told Don Shirley in an interview in the *Los Angeles Times* (July 12, 1987). "I never felt poor," Milner said, "but I had to wait a while to get the things I wanted." Milner grew up on Hastings Street in a Detroit neighborhood called "The Valley," known as the home of both famous preachers and various kinds of criminals. The neighborhood was "pretty infamous and supposedly criminal," Milner told David Richards for the *Washington Star-News*, as quoted in *Contemporary Authors Online* (2000). He continued, "The more I read in high school, the more I realized that some tremendous, phenomenal things were happening around me. What happened in a Faulkner novel happened four times a day on Hastings Street. I thought why should these crazy people Faulkner writes about seem more important than my mother or my father or the dude down the street. Only because they had someone to write about them. So I became a writer." Remaining in his hometown, Milner attended Northeastern High School, Highland Park Junior College, and the Detroit Institute of Technology. He also studied at Columbia University, in New York City, for a time.

Milner married at age 21, and he and his wife had three children in a short time. He worked in sales and at a variety of odd jobs to earn a living, but he was confident that he would one day become a writer. In the early 1960s he was awarded several grants, including a John Hay Whitney fellowship and a Rockefeller grant. With this financial support he was able to work on a novel, which he has said will never be published. He soon turned to drama, thinking, as he told Shirley, that "a play was simply dialogue, that I could write one at lunchtime." After discovering that it took longer than a lunch hour to write a play, Milner joined a group of artists who staged productions at a Detroit coffee house called the Unstable. The first of his plays to be produced there was a one-act called *Life Agony*. Milner was inspired by his interactions with the custodians who swept the theater at Unstable. They watched rehearsals of his plays and booed or applauded his lines, thus setting him in a direction he was to follow for the rest of his career. "I realized," he told Shirley, "that if I'm going to write for them, I'd better write in the oral, participatory tradition rather than a strictly literary one."

Milner's first full-length play, *Who's Got His Own*, which was produced in New York in 1966, is a psychological drama about a family trying to work out their embattled relationships with one another, and with their racist society. After the death of a family's breadwinner, his widow and two children act out their problems, the son violent and distrustful, and the daughter trembling with emotion. "[Milner] would like to use the stage as though it were really a bear pit, with a point at the center where all angers must cross," Walter Kerr wrote in his review of the production for the *New York Times* (October 13, 1966). Kerr continued, "And he would like us to see his victims gored to death in full view, harried and helpless and beyond hope." While admiring the drama's explosiveness, Kerr felt that Milner failed to include the audience in the evening's upheavals. "The [characters] cry real tears now and again; but we are merely alert, strictly attentive, still detached from the felt heart of the matter."

In *The Warning: A Theme for Linda*, produced at the Brooklyn Academy of Music in 1969, Milner depicts a young black woman at a crossroads, unsure of what role she should play with respect to the men in her life. Her models are her grandmother and mother, who are both embittered by their experiences, one to the point of man-hating, the other to the point of alcoholism. The 17-year-old Linda daydreams and fantasizes of ideal men, but finally reconciles herself to reality and demands an equal relationship with her boyfriend.

Milner's *What the Wine-Sellers Buy* was first produced in 1973 at the New Federal Theatre in New York, and then, with the backing of the legendary producer Joseph Papp, became the first play written by a black playwright to be staged at the Vivian Beaumont Theatre at New York's Lincoln Center, opening on Valentine's Day in 1974. A condensed version of the play toured New York's parks the following summer, and the show then embarked on what became a hugely successful national tour. The drama is set in the Detroit of Milner's youth, and concerns a 17-year-old, Steve, who is pulled in different directions by his girlfriend, Mae, and Rico, a seductive street hustler and pimp. Steve's situation is further complicated when his mother becomes ill and needs expensive medicine, and Rico cajoles him to turn Mae into a prostitute. The play ends on an optimistic note, with Steve resisting Rico's influence and taking Mae in his arms, declaring "We ain't goin' his way, it costs too much," as quoted by Walter Kerr in the *New York Times* (February 24, 1974).

In his review of the production, Kerr saw Milner as having taken a step toward "an authority that no amount of righteous finger-wagging will ever equal"; namely, the authority of human emotions laid bare. He praised in particular a scene in which Mae, after being given a tongue-lashing by her mother, begs her mother to hit her instead. "When you stopped whipping, you just took your hands away," she cries, as quoted by Kerr. In the end, though, Kerr felt that Milner had not moved far enough from the atmosphere of a morality play, writing that he would "do well to let impulse interrupt him oftener, let people speak for themselves instead of steadily saluting the evening's cause."

Milner's forays into musical theater produced mixed reviews. In *Jazz-Set*, which premiered in Los Angeles in 1980, a group of six musicians are the main characters in a drama based on their own experiences. Named after the instruments they play, the characters tell their stories—about imprisonment, rape, sharecropping for white landowners, and other forms of oppression—in music and while talking between sets. Reviewing a revival of the play in the summer of 2000 for *Detroit News* (August 19, 2000), Michael H. Margolin heralded the production's "undeniable authenticity," but found the musical as a whole "off-key": Milner's "riffs are clumsily enacted and do not connect the history and the emotion," he wrote. He found "the plea for brotherhood and love . . . as cliched as some popular songs—glib but unsubstantial."

Another musical project of Milner's was *Don't Get God Started*, which was produced in Los Angeles in 1986. Milner conceived of the idea for the musical together with its producer, Barry Hankerson, wrote the book, and directed the production. Sylvie Drake, in a review for the *Los Angeles Times* (September 3, 1986), observed that "*Don't Get God Started* may have created its own genre: a musical sermon dramatically delivered in a gospel/revivalist tradition." She termed it "a pious lesson in morality for the already converted that might work as a new form of religious service"; as theater, however, she deemed it a "world-and-a-half away from Milner's memorable *Jazz-Set*."

Checkmates, which had its premiere in Los Angeles in 1987, is Milner's best-known play, and the first to treat the experiences of the African-American middle class. This comic drama introduces two married couples sharing a two-family home in Detroit. The Coopers are the older and somewhat cantankerous landlords, whose values have been shaped by the Depression, World War II, and a blue-collar sensibility. They find themselves hopelessly out-of-touch with their tenants, the Williamses, who are younger, professional, and upwardly mobile. The drama derives from the conflict between the generations; while the Coopers have been through marital ups and downs and have become a rock-solid couple, the Williamses don't know where their marriage is headed. "It's dangerous to identify with [the Williamses]," Milner told Don Shirley during an interview for the *Los Angeles Times*, "because you can't tell what they might say or do next. They aren't fixed. They can't say, 'These are the values I stand for.' The point of the older couple's lives was to build for the future. Now here is the future, and there are no rules left for the younger couple."

Dan Sullivan, writing in the *Los Angeles Times* (July 20, 1987), termed *Checkmates* a "funny, likeable play," that needed some rewriting in order to become "absolutely first-rate." He found Milner's evocation of contemporary society particularly acute. "*Checkmates* gives us a specific sense of today's corporate jungle and its particular risks for blacks, however hip, however educated. . . . 'Last hired, first fired' goes for middle-management, too."

A production of *Checkmates* that opened in New York in 1988 found little critical favor with Frank Rich. Writing in the *New York Times* (August 5, 1988), he castigated Milner for the play's "inexhaustible supply of clichés," "canned speeches," and "lack of dramatic propulsion." He complained that the "older couple's sequences . . . fail to move the play forward. . . . The Coopers, who have been married 45 years, not only recite family history as if they had just met each other, but they also re-enact that history in flashbacks drenched in purple lighting that precisely matches the tone of the prose."

Milner paid tribute to Martin Luther King, Jr. in *Roads of the Mountain Top*, which depicts the final three years of King's life, from his accepting of the Nobel Prize to his assassination in 1968. The play was first performed in 1986 at New Brunswick, New Jersey's Crossroads Theater, and then opened in Washington, D.C., in 1992 in a production Milner directed. As Milner told Neil Novelli in the (Syracuse) *Post-Standard* (March 5, 1999), the play evokes several different aspects of the legendary Dr. King. "He was a public icon, larger than life. But we also show his personal side, and that doesn't make him any less a hero." The play alternates between the private and the public, between scenes of King's personal life presented as realistic drama and public events presented in a Brechtian, epic style. Seven actors shift between portraying historical figures, including Dr. King, Reverend Ralph David Abernathy, and Coretta Scott King, and functioning as a chorus, commenting on the historical events. Novelli praised a 1999 Syracuse production of *Roads of the Mountain Top*: "Milner . . . manages to crystallize the crisis-filled feeling of those crucial years—riots, Vietnam, assassinations, but above all the steady drive toward civil rights and justice," he wrote. He added that Milner showed historical events "obliquely, from behind the scenes. The tactic gives a fresh, offhand feeling to what might have seemed merely a history lesson."

In his next history play, *Defending the Light*, which was staged in New York in 2000, Milner reaches back to the events of March 12, 1846, the night a black man knifed to death a white family—husband, wife, grandmother, and child—in Auburn, New York. The drama presents the historical figure of William Freeman, a young black man from Auburn who had been unjustly convicted of stealing a horse and imprisoned under extremely inhumane conditions. After he was released from prison, utterly changed from the promising, bright young man he had been, he became the prime suspect in the murder of the white family. Based on the novel *Seward for the Defense*, by Earl Conrad, which also depicts these real-life events, Milner's play is part courtroom drama and part morality tract. In the play, as in life, Freeman is defended at trial by William Seward, who later became Abraham Lincoln's secretary of state, and Seward enters a controversial plea for his client: not guilty by reason of insanity. According to Lawrence van Gelder, who reviewed the production for the *New York Times* (March 3, 2000), Milner's drama poses troubling questions: "Could not such treatment by such a society drive a man mad? Does not such treatment hold a mirror to the society that inflicts it?" Alluding to the play's title, van Gelder argued that ultimately, Milner's play puts on trial our nation, "on charges of extinguishing the bright lights among its young blacks, depriving them of education and hope of equality." In her review for the *Village Voice* (February 22, 2000), Alisa Solomon noted that, though historical, *Defending the Light* has contemporary relevance, given that "the criminal justice system hasn't changed much for African-Americans in the last 150 years." Nevertheless, she lamented that the playwright had made his points with a heavy hand, and the director allowed the cast to deliver "every line as a holy pronouncement," making the play "far simpler and far duller than it has any reason to be."

Milner has gone through two divorces. Mainly residing in or near New York City, he returns frequently to Detroit, where he has established several theater companies. He has also served as a mentor to young authors, and given workshops all over the country for black playwrights.

— S. Y.

SUGGESTED READING: *Detroit News* D p5 Nov. 7, 1996, p6 Aug. 19, 2000; *Los Angeles Times* p6 Sep. 3, 1986, p45 July 12, 1987, p1 July 20, 1987; *New York Times* p52 Oct. 13, 1966, II p1 Feb. 24, 1974, C p3 Aug. 5, 1988; (Syracuse) *Post-Standard* p25 Mar. 5, 1999; *St. Louis Post-Dispatch* D p3 May 26, 1996; *Village Voice* p85 Feb. 11, 1997, p70 Feb. 22, 2000; *Washington Post* D p2 Mar. 9, 1991

SELECTED PLAYS: *Who's Got His Own*, 1966; *The Warning: A Theme for Linda*, 1969; *What the Wine-Sellers Buy*, 1974; *Jazz-Set*, 1980; *Roads of the Mountain Top*, 1986; *Checkmates*, 1987; *Don't Get God Started*, 1987; *Defending the Light*, 2000

Min, Anchee

Jan. 14, 1957– Memoirist; novelist

The Chinese-born author Anchee Min first attracted widespread notice in 1994 with her striking memoir *Red Azalea*, which detailed her life growing up in China during the upheaval of Mao Zedong's Cultural Revolution. Min writes in English, despite having spoken barely a word of that language until the age of 27. In the opinion of many critics and readers, Min's recent familiarity with English brings a freshness and directness to her writing, though her handling of the language has also been disparaged by some. Min's negative experiences in China have made her an outspoken critic of Chinese communism and a great admirer of the freedoms granted to citizens of the United States. In her first novel, *Katherine* (1995), Min explored the collision of the two cultures through the story of a brazen American teacher who comes to China and greatly influences her students. In *Becoming Madame Mao* (2000), Min painted a fictionalized and somewhat sympathetic portrait of the much-maligned, real-life figure Jiang Qing, Mao Zedong's wife. Her most recent novel, *Wild Ginger* (2002), tells the story of two young friends who come of age during the Cultural Revolution.

Anchee Min was born on January 14, 1957 in Shanghai, China, the eldest of four children born to Naishi Min, an astronomy instructor and his wife, Dinyun Dai, also a teacher. As a young girl, Min became entangled in the Cultural Revolution, which was initiated by Chinese Communist Party (CCP) chairman Mao Zedong in 1966. The Cultural Revolution was Mao's attempt to bring the CCP back under his control and to eliminate capitalistic

Michele Dremmer/Courtesy of Houghton Mifflin Company

and elitist elements from society. Toward this end, he established the Red Guard, a mobilization of Chinese youth whom he encouraged to attack traditional values and criticize party officials. The Red Guard organized rallies and spread propaganda, attacking officials, teachers, and any whom they deemed unfriendly toward the new China. By 1967 the Guard had broken into factions and began to quarrel over which of them espoused Mao's true principles. Their numbers eventually grew to as many as 11 million, and it is estimated that several hundred thousand people were executed at their hands.

During the Cultural Revolution, Min's family lost its Shanghai apartment and was sent to live in the squalid conditions of a communal house. Min's father was dismissed from his job teaching astronomy because he had discussed sunspots in the classroom. "They told him the sun represents Chairman Mao," Min told A. O. Scott for the *New York Times Magazine* (June 18, 2000), "and that talking about sunspots is criticizing the chairman." Despite the fact that Min herself had suffered at the hands of the Party, she was a fervent supporter as a member of the Little Red Guard, a younger branch of the Red Guard. In *Red Azalea* Min described her behavior as a student: "I always began my compositions with this: 'The East wind is blowing, the fighting drum is beating. Who is afraid in the world today? It is not the people who are afraid of the American imperialists. It is the American imperialists who are afraid of the people.' These phrases won me prizes." Min admits that she denounced one of her teachers to prove her loyalty to the Party and that the teacher was beaten and humiliated in front of an assembly of two-thousand people and forced to admit to being an American spy.

The Red Guard eventually caused such major disruptions in China that they were encouraged to retire into the countryside. In 1974, at the age of 17, Min was separated from her family and sent to the Red Fire Farm, a labor camp of some 13,000 people located near the East China Sea. Though the soil there was too salty to support the intended cotton crop, the workers were forced to continue farming anyway. After months of backbreaking work, hunger, and repression, Min's faith in the Party began to wane, and she longed to escape from the harsh life at the camp. One day, in 1975, as she was working in the fields, a group of talent scouts for a Shanghai film studio spotted Min and thought she had the right look to star in a propaganda film titled *Red Azalea* about the life of Mao Zedong's wife, Jiang Qing. After intense competition, Min was finally selected to play the part. However, following Mao Zedong's death in 1976, Qing fell out of favor with the Party leaders and the movie was canceled. Min, because of her association with the film, was an outcast in the new political climate. For six years, from 1977 to 1984, she performed menial tasks at the studio, and it was a miserable time of her life. "I was treated like a machine," she wrote in an article for *Chicago Tribune Magazine* (November 6, 1994). "I had tuberculosis but was not allowed to take any leave. Completely exhausted, I could see no end to my misery. I collapsed and passed out on the set many times and coughed blood." Min even contemplated suicide, staring at the gas jets one night at the communal house where she lived.

Finally, a friend whom Min had met years before in the studio intervened on Min's behalf. Her name was Joan Chen, the actress who starred in the film *The Last Emperor*. She helped Min get into the School of the Art Institute of Chicago (SAIC), because it was the only school without an English proficiency requirement. One problem still remained for Min, however: She needed a visa from the U.S. consulate in order to leave China. Many young people were being turned down in those days, and Min and her family were worried that she, too, would be rejected. A friend prepared a self-introduction for Min in English, so that she could memorize it and appear fluent. On the day of the meeting with the consul she borrowed her mother's green skirt and white blouse for good luck. Upon her return home, her parents were so nervous about the outcome of the meeting that they could not bring themselves to ask Min whether her visa had been granted. Min simply pulled out her passport and showed them the visa stamp. "Letting out a huge breath, my father lost his strength," Min wrote in *Chicago Tribune Magazine*. "He almost fell on his knees. He struck my shoulders and said loudly: 'My monkey daughter, I can't believe this! Our ancestors are going to be proud of you. I am, because it's my character you inherited.'"

Though Min was happy to be enrolled in school and headed to the United States, plenty of challenges lay ahead when she arrived in 1984. She spoke no English and had few friends or acquaintances in the States. She forbid herself to speak Chinese, so that she would learn English faster. Her first English teachers, as she told Jeff Lyon for *Chicago Tribune Magazine* (June 18, 1995), were the characters of children's and daytime television. "To learn English, I'd turn TV on in the morning and watch Sesame Street and Oprah," said Min. "Her show played a big role in convincing me to get my story out, the way she encourages guests to reveal their past by telling them it's all right to speak out about what they consider shameful." Min also took English classes at Chicago's University of Illinois and learned English well enough to succeed at the SAIC, where she eventually received her B.F.A. and her M.F.A. and graduated in 1991.

Min supported herself with a variety of jobs, among them assisting a plumber, waiting tables, painting flowers on women's underwear, and baby sitting. At SAIC Min took a writing class with writer Jim McManus, who asked the class to compose an essay about their lives at age 12. That was when she began to cull the material that would eventually become *Red Azalea*. Though her English was still rough, she chose not to write in Chinese. "We didn't have any words for what happened to us," Min explained to Scott. "There was no way for me to describe those experiences or talk about those feelings in Chinese. The Chinese language for me was taken over by Mao [Zedong] and Jiang Qing." McManus praised Min's story but told her she was a poor writer. Undeterred, Min kept at it, and the material, at first, took several forms. Min first completed a short story called "White Chrysanthemum," which she submitted to the *Mississippi Valley Review*'s 20th anniversary competition. Min was so poor that she decided to save money by making her own envelope out of brown paper and Scotch tape. Despite the humble packaging, her story won first prize. Afterwards, Min had the story published in the respected literary magazine, *Granta*.

Min's painful and extraordinary youth continued to fuel her writing, and over the course of eight years, she honed her material into *Red Azalea*. As Min told Roxane Farmanfarmaian for *Publisher's Weekly* (June 5, 2000), the process of writing was difficult for her: it was, said Min, "like a long line of ants walking for blocks carrying one crooked cricket leg." Even more challenging was forcing herself to be honest about her own character. "Whenever it comes to self-examination," Min explained to Briggs, "you try to portray yourself, naturally, as a good person, a good guy. You don't intend to reveal your jealousy. I wrote [*Red Azalea*] that way, and I knew the parts I wasn't 100 percent honest."

Red Azalea was finally published in the United States in 1994. (In the United Kingdom it was published in 1993.) The process had been so traumatic that upon completion, as Min told Penelope Mesic for *Chicago* magazine (January 1994), "I was vomiting, my whole body was shaking after a year of living my past life and having to face myself." In spare, simple language consisting primarily of short, declarative sentences, *Red Azalea* recounts her story from her early childhood until her arrival in the United States. Though some critics found the language jarring, most thought it perfectly suited to her sorrowful story, and the book garnered mostly favorable reviews as well as a *New York Times* Notable Book of the Year Award of 1994. Scott wrote that Min's language "is marked by an emotional nakedness and a sexual intensity that overwhelms history, narrative, and even sometimes the English language," and compared Min to Emily Dickinson: "Her prose, crude and powerful, with some of the sharp lyric compression of an Emily Dickinson poem, is full of raw, unassuaged anguish." Many critics noted the sexual content of *Red Azalea*, which they considered remarkable coming from a writer who grew up in a country where premarital sex was punishable by death, and even interest in sex was considered unpatriotic. As Min explained in *Red Azalea*, as quoted in *Contemporary Literary Criticism* (1994), "A good female comrade was supposed to devote all her energy, her youth, to the Revolution; she was not permitted to even think about a man until her late 20s." In her memoir, Min recounts her affair with Yan, a female party secretary at Red Fire Farm. A friend of Min's at the camp, a woman named Little Green, is caught having an affair with a man. After he is executed for their crime, Little Green begins to go mad, and Yan, who had initiated the public discovery of the lovers, comes to regret her own actions and tries to comfort her. "They were like two lost boats drifting over the sea in a dense fog," Min writes as quoted by Judith Shapiro in the *New York Times Book Review* (February 27, 1994). Drawn to Yan by her show of compassion and her beautiful playing of the erh-hu (a Chinese classical instrument), Min befriends her. After helping Yan compose a love letter to her boyfriend, the two of them consummated their own affair, which becomes their only solace from the brutality and isolation of life at the camp. Shapiro wrote, "This memoir of sexual freedom is . . . a powerful political as well as literary statement." In *English Journal* (April 1997), Regina Wiegand commented that "*Red Azalea* journeys into a world as vivid, exotic, and distant as its title promises. Anchee Min's amazing courage [and] literary and artistic abilities took my breath away."

Red Azalea was banned in China. However, after it was a success, Min was invited to China to make some public appearances. "They allow me back because they think I brought the country honor and respect," Min told Mesic, and added with a laugh,"That's before they read the book." Indeed, there is little that is flattering to China in Min's book. Describing her purpose in writing *Red Azalea* to Achy Obejas for *Chicago Tribune* (February 11, 1994), Min said "I wrote this to lay out history, to do my best to make sure it doesn't happen again, that it doesn't happen to my daughter's generation."

Min had married Chinese painter Qigu Jiang in 1991 and later gave birth to a girl, Lauryan. In 1994, after divorcing Jiang, she and Lauryan moved to Los Angeles, where she worked on her first novel, *Katherine* (1995). The novel is about a beautiful, free-spirited American teacher, Katherine, who goes to China to teach English and unwittingly creates a revolution in the spirits of her students. The story is narrated by Zebra, a 29-year-old Shanghai factory worker and student. Katherine's influence on her students is profound. For example, after she offhandedly remarks that black clothing is a good solution when one doesn't know what to wear, her students come to school the next day all dressed in black. In her ignorance and innocence, Katherine continues to espouse freedom, laughter, and nonconformity, bringing herself and her students into inevitable conflicts. Min explained her aims in writing *Katherine* to Lisa See for *Bazaar* (May 1995). "I want readers to know how it feels to live in mental darkness," said Min, "then to breathe a little fresh air. I want readers to see the good and bad in Chinese people." The novel received mixed reviews. Sarah Smith, writing in *New Statesman & Society* (August 25, 1995), found the characterizations and themes too simple. "This is a guileless book," she wrote, "about a far from guileless time, and a difficult story, too simply told." The critic Sally Eckhoff was less put off by Min's undisguised directness in addressing her themes. In *Village Voice* (June 20, 1995), she wrote of the novel, "It's wrenching, melodramatic, and totally over the top, and yet real enough for both sparkling entertainment and deep, dark tragedy."

Min's next novel was titled *Becoming Madame Mao* (2000). Writing the novel was an arduous task for Min, and, indeed, it was rejected by her two previous publishers. When she showed it to her tough-minded agent, Sandy Dijkstra, Min was prepared for the worst. "I told Sandy, I don't want to know anything about it," Min related to Farmanfarmaian. "Don't tell me who's bidding, who's not. I am prepared fully to accept that this thing is not going to be published. I did it because I had to. I told her to put it in the trash can." *Becoming Madame Mao* is a fictionalized account of the life of Jiang Qing, Mao Zedong's wife, and one of the most vilified women in China's history. Qing was the architect of much of the propaganda that surrounded the Cultural Revolution. She also used her power to take revenge on those who had slighted her earlier in life, and her policies caused innumerable deaths. Min, in the novel, alternates between third-person omniscient narration and first-person narration told from Madame Mao's point of view. The story begins moments before Qing (or Ching, as Min renders her name) takes her own life while in prison. Then it sweeps back to Ching's early memories: how her feet were bound and how she refused to keep the bindings on when they became painful; how her parents abused her; and how they fought with each other. After Ching goes to live with her grandfather, he introduces her to traditional Chinese operas, which immediately capture her imagination. Eventually, she becomes an opera singer, marries an abusive husband, falls in love with a Communist, and is imprisoned for cheating on her husband. Ching first meets Zedong on a visit to a new Communist base in Yenan after attracting his attention by writing a critique of bourgeois art. Zedong falls in love with her and they marry. However, after he comes into power and is named chairman of China, he becomes estranged from her. Ching emerges as a tragic figure worthy of at least some measure of pity.

Reviews of the novel were mixed. In *Salon* (June 1, 2000, on-line), Gary Krist wrote, "The portrait of Jiang that emerges is satisfyingly complex—that of a consummate actress who spent her entire life looking for the role that would define her, all the while being tossed about on the conflicting tides of politics and her own ambition, insecurity, and romantic yearnings." Then he went on to say that Min's narrative technique "makes for a choppy and remote reading experience," that her use of language sounds like an "awkward and unidiomatic translation," and that "too much of the dialogue is just plain awful." Though Judy Lightfoot wrote in *Seattle Weekly* (June 1, 2000, on-line) that Min's "spirited, research-based narrative sweeps us right into modern China's political torrents and a woman's raging need for approval," she also lamented that "sometimes Min is so busy explaining Jiang's character she fails to create it." Sheryl WuDunn, writing in the *New York Times Book Review* (July 9, 2000) concluded that, for all its faults, *Becoming Madame Mao* is an important book. "Readers who remember the hundreds of thousands of people who died during the Cultural Revolution may wince at *Becoming Madame Mao*, seeing it as the moral equivalent of a sympathetic portrayal of Hitler," wrote WuDunn. "But then again, this is a novel, not a historical assessment. And what renders it compelling and penetrating is precisely its empathy for a woman normally thought of as inhumanly evil."

In *Wild Ginger* (2002) Min again draws on her own experiences to bring together world-historical events and the lives of ordinary individuals. The coming-of-age story begins in 1969 in Shanghai, where two teenage girls, Maple and Wild Ginger, ostracized by their peers, form a lasting friendship. As she grows up, Wild Ginger, who was always picked on and abused for her light-colored eyes (her father was part French), determines to overcome this "inadequacy" by devoting herself to the Maoist regime. Maple, the narrator of the story, also yearns to embrace Maoism, but is an independent thinker who cannot help but question the policies of the Communists. Wild Ginger rises quickly through the ranks, eventually joining the Red Guard and even attracting the attention of Mao himself. Her love for a young man named Evergreen, however, soon brings her into conflict with the Maoist prohibition on romantic love. When Maple herself falls for the same man, a tragic ending becomes unavoidable.

Although some critics complained that the novel lacked the complexity and depth of *Becoming Madame Mao*, most concluded that the shortcomings were outweighed by the novel's expressiveness and the vivid representations of life under Mao. "Her characters seldom step out of the preordained roles dictated by their allegorical names," Melvin Jules Bukiet noted in an assessment for the *Los Angeles Times* (April 14, 2002). Bukiet added, however, that "Min's lament for wasted years and wasted lives under tyranny is potent, and the image she creates of a world marching lock-step is as chilling as her casual mention of 'mind-brushing schools' for those out of step." "Min's language isn't elegant, and her storytelling is often plain and worn as the threadbare wardrobe of her youth," Lisa Schwarzbaum commented in *Entertainment Weekly* (April 19, 2002). "But the blunt intensity of the telling," she added, "and the way Min grimly returns to reexamine pain, communicates its own spare dignity."

In 1999 Min married an English teacher named Lloyd Lofthouse. They currently live outside Los Angeles with Min's daughter from her previous marriage. Her next novel, *The Last Empress*, about the life of Tsu Hsi, the final imperial ruler of China who died in 1907, is due to be published in fall 2003. Min still listens to the propaganda operas she grew up with during the Cultural Revolution and teaches Lauryan to dance the ballets that accompany the music. Earlier, Min wrote in the *Chicago Tribune Magazine* (November 6, 1994), "I plan to take Lauryan to China every year and teach her

Chinese. I think it is important that she is made to be aware of how different life could have been for her."

— P. G. H.

SUGGESTED READING: *Chicago* p55+ Jan. 1994; *Chicago Tribune* 5 p3 Feb. 11, 1994, with photo, 5 p1 July 14, 1995; *Chicago Tribune Magazine* p24 Nov. 6, 1994, with photo, p8 June 18, 1995; *English Journal* p87 Apr. 1997; *New Statesman & Society* p33 Aug. 25, 1995; *New York Times* (on-line) July 9, 2000; *New York Times Book Review* p11 Feb. 27, 1994, p31 Sep. 10, 1995; *New York Times Magazine* p45+ June 18, 2000, with photos; *Publishers Weekly* p66+ June 5, 2000; *Salon* (on-line) June 1, 2000; *USA Today* (on-line) Dec. 2, 1999; *Village Voice* p69+ June 20, 1995

SELECTED BOOKS: novels—*Katherine*, 1995; *Becoming Madame Mao*, 2000; *Wild Ginger*, 2002; nonfiction—*Red Azalea*, 1994

Mishra, Pankaj

(MISH-ra, PAN-kahj)

1969– Novelist; journalist

In articles for the *New York Review of Books*, *New Statesman*, and other periodicals as well as in his two books, the travelogue *Butter Chicken in Ludhiana* (1995) and his acclaimed novel *The Romantics* (2000), Pankaj Mishra explores how the interaction of Eastern and Western cultures has affected his native India, which was under British colonial rule for more than 150 years until it won independence in 1947. "The East-West encounter has defined this country more than anything else in the past 150 years," Mishra told Robert Marquand for the *Christian Science Monitor* (February 1, 2000). "You can't escape it—it's part of who we are. The problem is, we like to pretend it isn't true, which creates a split in us. As the world globalizes further, that split is becoming more pronounced."

Pankaj Mishra was born in India in 1969. In an article for the *New York Review of Books* (April 9, 1998, on-line), Mishra detailed his background: "I was upper-caste myself, without family wealth, and roughly in the same position as my father had been in freshly independent India when the land reform act of 1951—another of Nehru's attempts at social equality, it was meant to turn exploited tenants into landholders—reduced his once well-to-do Brahmin family to penury. My mother's family had suffered a similar setback. Like many others in my family who laboriously worked their way into the middle classes, I had to make my own way in the world." Mishra's father worked on railways, and Pankaj grew up in a series of small towns throughout India that he has described as "dead-end places." In an interview with Kate Chisholm for the *Evening Standard* (February 15, 2000), Mishra elaborated, "We (my friends and I) were destined for oblivion, and yet because of our English schooling we were given a sense of a larger world. It gave us a perpetual dissatisfaction with who we were, what we were."

In 1985 Mishra enrolled in Allahabad University in the city of the same name in northern India. Although it was once known as "the Oxford of the East," in his article for the *New Statesman* (February 7, 2000) Mishra noted that the university "had ceased to be a place for higher learning. Instead, it had become a battlefield for rival caste groups, a setting for the primordial struggles of food, shelter, and terror." At age 19, after speaking Hindi for his whole life, Mishra began instead speaking and thinking in English, a language that he has said offered "the possibility of social inquiry." He explained to Chisholm that his "whole experience of the world is [now] mediated through English; through what is a foreign language in India because so few people speak it." Mishra's eventual fluency in English led to an intellectual awakening during his years at Allahabad University. He became a voracious reader, studying English translations of Tolstoy, Dostoevsky, and Nietzsche on his own. "I read randomly, whatever I could find, and with the furious intensity of a small-town boy to whom books are the sole means of communicating with, and understanding, the larger world," Mishra wrote for the *New York Review of Books*.

Mishra's discovery of German philosopher Friedrich Nietzsche brought new insights. Although he did not understand Nietzsche at first, Mishra was fascinated by the subtitle of Nietzsche's last book, *Ecce Homo: How One Becomes What One Is*. "Only now have I managed to figure out [its] meaning," Mishra wrote in the *New Statesman*. "And this required not only becoming a writer, but also an acknowledgment of my diverse inheritance: the feudal Brahminical past and the half-learnt ways of another civilisation. It required the acquisition of a language, English, that offered the possibility of social inquiry; it required a recognition, implicit at first, of the many ways in which we had been shaped by the West in the past two centuries, the ways its civilisation had created, along with much random destruction, a new sense of human possibility wherever it had traveled."

Mishra graduated from Allahabad University with a B.A. in English literature and later received his master's degree in philosophy from Jawaharlal Nehru University in Delhi. While still at the university he began writing book reviews for *The Pioneer*, primarily of Indian fiction that had been written in English or Western fiction about India. He quickly received notice in India's literary circles for his keen insights and concise language, and many of his readers were surprised to learn that he was still a student in his early 20s.

In 1995 Penguin Publishing's Indian division published Mishra's first book, *Butter Chicken in Ludhiana*, a travelogue of several small towns in India. A reviewer for the *Complete Review* Web site (January 1, 2000) wrote, "Mishra is particularly interested in the people he encounters, and he has a great deal of contact with the locals, though almost as a mere passerby. Mishra describes the people and his interaction with them well, an interesting cross-section of Indian society." Although the reviewer was critical of the book's lack of focus and direction, the reviewer praised *Butter Chicken in Ludhiana* for giving "a good impression of a fast-changing society, offering many vantage points and vistas." The book sold well in India, although it was not readily available outside the country, and Mishra resumed writing reviews and literary criticism for various publications.

When Mishra was just 26 years old, he accepted a job as an editor for the Indian division of the large publishing company HarperCollins. In April 1996, during a train trip to Delhi, Mishra read a manuscript, *The God of Small Things*, by first-time author Arundhati Roy. He was impressed by Roy's honest examination of love and the caste system in rural India, which although written in English didn't pander to the Western taste for exotica or exaggeration. Mishra was so enthralled by the book, which he considered the most important Indian novel since Salman Rushdie's prize-winning *Midnight's Children* (1980), that he hopped off the train miles from Delhi to call Roy from a phone booth. He introduced her to a literary agent in the United Kingdom, who sold the world publishing rights to Random House. Mishra's actions resulted in his termination by HarperCollins. In her article for *The Week* Web site (November 2, 1997), Debashish Mukerji explained that many publishers in India prefer to obtain the exclusive right to sell a first-time author's book around the world. However, since they lack the resources to compete in American and British markets, Mukerji observed that most Indian publishers rarely "make an effort to sell these books outside of India." On account of these restrictive contracts, many Indian authors are forbidden from having other publishing houses market their books in other countries. Although he ensured that Roy would reach a far wider audience by having her published in the United States, Mishra's actions outraged his superiors at HarperCollins, who fired him for disloyalty. *The God of Small Things* was eventually published by Random House in 1997. It reportedly sold over three million copies worldwide and won the Booker Prize in the United Kingdom, thereby validating Mishra's enthusiasm for it.

For the next several years, Mishra was a frequent contributor to the *New York Review of Books* and *New Statesman*, among others. Some of his articles were autobiographical, while others discussed Indian literature or politics. In a lengthy piece published in the *New York Review of Books* (June 25, 1998), Mishra criticized India's obsession with developing a nuclear arsenal. "What is clear is that nuclear muscle-flexing will not go any way toward solving India's gigantic problems of poverty, illiteracy, malnutrition, and overpopulation," Mishra declared. He added that India's political system has neglected the basic needs of most Indians and "survives only through its ability to enrich people venal enough to be part of it."

Mishra discussed his views on literature in an article entitled, "Little Inkling," published in 1999 on the *Outlook India* Web site. "This is the truest function of a national literature: it holds up a mirror in whose unfamiliar reflections a nation slowly learns to recognize itself," he wrote. "The writer, exercising his talent and imagination, discovers new subjects, or deepens old discoveries; and he himself grows in the process." Mishra criticized contemporary Indian literature in English for failing to portray the current state of India, especially its widespread poverty, to the rest of the world, arguing that "writing has become yet another technical skill to be acquired from the West in the private pursuit of social and financial glory." English-language novels by Indian authors, Mishra added, tell their audiences "just about everything except who we are." In 2000 he conducted a well-publicized feud with Salman Rushdie, whom many consider to be the elder statesman of Indian literature. He had a particular distaste for magic realism—a style that Rushdie frequently employed in which magical occurrences or characters are presented in realistic settings. According to Chisholm, Mishra dismissed Rushdie's work as "witless buffoonery" and "essentially adolescent stuff." The veteran author responded by calling Mishra "a young punk and a straw in the wind," as quoted by Baldev Chauhan in the *Statesman* (February 21, 2000).

After the success of Arundhati Roy's *The God of Small Things*, many prestigious publishing houses in the United States and the United Kingdom sought out other Indian novelists who write in English. Mishra would soon be competing with Rushdie, not only in print, but on the bookshelves. Random House purchased the rights to Mishra's first novel, *The Romantics*, for $450,000, the second largest advance ever for an Indian author.

The novel, which was published in 2000, follows the maturation of Samar, a young Brahman student who befriends several wealthy expatriates from the West and develops a romantic relationship with one of them. Through these relationships, Mishra explores how the interaction of Western and traditional Indian cultures has shaped modern India. "*The Romantics* is a first novel of astonishing maturity," David Robson wrote in his review for the *Sunday Telegraph* (February 20, 2000). "I read it in a sitting, utterly absorbed in its characters, entranced by its lush prose, saddened, but never depressed, by its core of melancholy." Robson praised Mishra as "one of those magical writers who can capture the sights and smells of everyday life in aching detail. Every chapter boasts descriptive passages which you want to re-read and savor for their wonderful word-painting. This bright new star is the real thing." In the *Boston Globe* (March 10, 2000), Bill

Marx wrote that the novel "offers a surprisingly assured, provocatively balanced meditation on the familiar culture clash, focusing on a generation of Indian youth bewildered about the value of an ancient heritage others find indispensable." Marx observed that Mishra "skillfully covers the extremes of Indian poverty and piety with a detachment reminiscent of V. S. Naipaul." Other reviewers compared Mishra to E. M. Forster and Gustave Flaubert, whose own book, *Sentimental Education*, figures in the plot.

The Romantics was translated into eight languages and brought Pankaj Mishra international recognition and acclaim. A shy and private person, Mishra had even refused to provide a photograph for the book's cover, and he was extremely uncomfortable with his growing fame. "I'm slightly depressed actually," he confessed to Martin Spice, a reviewer for the *New Straight Times* (June 7, 2000) in Malaysia. "In the UK there are many authors who get this sort of money but in India there are very few. The attention here can be very oppressive. Everyone thinks they have the right to talk to you."

In 2002 Mishra edited the book *Writer and the World: Essays*, a collection of short pieces written by the famed Trinidad-born travel writer V. S. Naipaul, who won the Nobel Prize for Literature in 2001. Mishra and Michael Dibdin will co-edit another anthology of Naipaul's writings in August 2003, entitled *Literary Occasions: Essays*.

Pankaj Mishra lives in India, dividing his time between New Delhi and the town of Shimla (spelled Simla in some sources). Mishra told Chisholm that he would never leave India, saying "I can't write about it if I am living in London. Perhaps one could, but not in the way I want to write about it." Mishra is currently writing a novel about the Buddha.

—D. C.

SUGGESTED READING: *Boston Globe* D p12 Mar. 10, 2000; *Christian Science Monitor* (on-line) Feb. 1, 2000; *Complete Review* (on-line) Jan. 1, 2000; (London) *Evening Standard* (on-line) Feb. 15, 2000; *New Statesman* p58+ Feb. 7, 2000; *New York Review of Books* p25+ Apr. 9, 1998, with photos, p55+ June 25, 1998, with photos; *Outlook India* (on-line) 1999; (London) *Sunday Telegraph* p13 Feb. 20, 2000; *The Week* (on-line) Nov. 2, 1997

SELECTED BOOKS: nonfiction—*Butter Chicken in Ludhiana*, 1995; novels—*The Romantics*, 2000; as editor—*Writer and the World: Essays*, 2002

Mitchell, Susan

Jan. 20, 1944– Poet

Susan Mitchell has proved herself a poet's poet, with her collections *The Water Inside the Water* (1984); *Rapture* (1992), with which she garnered a National Book Award nomination, the first Kingsley Tufts Poetry Award, a Guggenheim fellowship, and a Lannan Literary Fellowship in Poetry; and *Erotikon* (2000). She composed the following autobiographical statement for *World Authors 1995–2000:* "I grew up in New York City, and I often think of myself in my early years as a dandified child, already sophisticated, with worldly tastes. Probably, this is just a fantasy. Closer to the truth, I was an only child surrounded by a large family of doting aunts, uncles, and grandparents, and I spent more time, certainly more pleasurable time, with adults than with other children. My father was an Assistant United States Attorney who later went into private practice. My mother, at least until I was born, was an editorial assistant at the *New York Times*. Dinner conversations were frequently about my father's clients, and it was always assured that my observations and suggestions for possible lines of defense were of value. My mother was passionate about the arts. Our apartment was sensuous and lush, filled with paintings, flowers, books, sculptures, and musical instruments, first a Baldwin spinet, later, when my piano playing improved, a Steinway baby grand. I began piano lessons at the age of seven, ballet lessons the following year, and the piano lessons continued through my first two years at college. From a very early age, I loved going to the ballet, the opera, the theater, and to concerts. How a poem sounds is very important to me (I say my poems aloud as I write them), and I love to create rich sonic textures, which is one reason that I weave into my poems snatches of other languages—Old English, Middle English, Provençal, and German.

"Education was very important to my parents, but so were the pleasures of living, and this love of living perhaps explains why they thought nothing of taking me out of school for two months every winter so that we could stay in Florida where my days were filled with ocean, beaches, shells, exotic animals, birds, and plants, and my nights with glimpses of a sophisticated, glamorous life. The split between my life in New York City, which stressed education and the arts (from seventh to 12th grade I went to an academically rigorous private school) and my life in Florida, which was sensuous, hedonistic, and utterly free, is one of several dichotomies that have had a strong impact on my poetry.

"When I look at my adult life, with its back and forth movement between America and Europe, scholarship and poetry, teaching and writing, it seems to imitate the pattern of my childhood with its movement between New York and Florida. After receiving my B.A. from Wellesley College, I lived for a while in Paris and Rome. This stay in Europe was followed by graduate study at Georgetown University where I was a teaching fellow. Once I received my M.A. in English Literature from Georgetown, I returned to Italy, then came back to New York City to continue my studies in English Literature in the doctoral program at Columbia University.

"My first book, The Water Inside The Water, draws on only a small portion of my life; but the poems in my second book, Rapture, bring together New York City and Florida, the artificial and the natural, the medieval and the modern, the intellectual and the sensuous, Europe and America. As a person, I am heterogeneous, rather than homogeneous; I am inclusive, rather than exclusive. And in my poems, I want to make worlds as hybrid as I am. One way I do this is by creating a language that is macaronic, rather than pure, a language made up of many languages, with shifting levels of diction. My third book, Erotikon (HarperCollins, 2000), continues my interest in creating complex narrators who are themselves concerned with what a self is: 'Who am I who speaks to you?' is the way one of these narrators states the problem. Perhaps the question that most preoccupies these narrators is: what is the meaning of life?

"Life for me is gorgeous and terrifying, thrilling and absurd, so there is something dark and disturbing in many of my poems. To quote another one of my surrogate selves, the narrator of "Venice" (Erotikon); 'There's a vertigo to history different/from the vertigo of sex/The children sold into slavery, into brothels./The sores. The futility of crying and the futility/of stories that gradually wash up/on other shores. To what purpose all this/telling, version by version/deteriorating like silk.' I write against and despite such feelings of futility. One is, after all, situated not only within a family but also within a world, and my childhood was situated between two wars. Of World War II, I remember blackouts, the absence of two uncles stationed overseas, butter rationing, and stories of concentration camps; of the Korean War, I remember air raid drills in school and the sudden increase in New York City of men missing legs and arms. More disturbing were horrific pictures in magazines which I could not bring myself to discuss with anyone and adult conversations overheard and only partially understood by me. In Rapture, 'Smoke' is concerned with World War II and 'Havana Birth' with the Cuban Revolution, but I rarely deal with the political so directly. Instead my poems are concerned with suffering's antidote, desire and appetite—and with the precariousness of joy and pleasure."

Susan Mitchell was born on January 20, 1944. Before attending graduate school at Georgetown University, where she earned an M.A. degree in English literature in 1970, she worked at Time in New York as a copy reader. She started her academic career at Northeastern Illinois University, where she was poet in residence from 1981 to 1985, and went on to teach in Vermont as a visiting assistant professor at Middlebury College (host of the Bread Loaf Writers' Conference) from 1983 to 1986 and in the Vermont College graduate program in creative writing from 1986 to 1993. She moved to Florida Atlantic University, where she became Mary Blossom Lee Professor of English, in 1987.

Mitchell's first book of poetry, The Water Inside the Water, was greeted with acclaim on its publication in 1984. The poet Stanley Kunitz lauded Mitchell's "heightened sense of reality" as well as her "fantastic eye," "depth, range, and brilliance," which produced what he called "a book of memory and nightmare, changes and epiphanies." Another poet, Richard Eberhart, observed that in Mitchell's poems, although they have a "hard reality," a "spirit of transformation tends to make everything become something else. This makes for an astonishment of mysteries enriching our consciousness."

The New York Times Book Review (March 11, 1984) chose poet Alfred Corn as its critic for The Water Inside the Water. Corn associated Mitchell's poems with "the dreamlike, portentous mode that was popular during the 70's, a poetry developed under the influence of Latin American surrealism. An effect of timelessness is sought, with places, people and objects reduced to nearly generic form—the road, the table, the grandmother. Recurrent preoccupations inhabit emblems such as knives, bread, milk, shadows, thorn trees, blood. . . . The sensibility is less visionary than phantasmagoric." Terming this kind of poetry "hospital Gothic," he admitted that Mitchell "has worked through her Gothic apprenticeship" and presented "waking reality" with vividness. When Mitchell, in "Once Driving West of Billings, Montana," described being struck by lightning, "branches shooting stars down the windshield, poor car shaking like a dazed cow," her sense of humor helped "bring down the sense of enormity to credible levels," Corn concluded. "Mitchell has the earmarks of a survivor," he wrote, "energy, boldness, perseverance."

Mitchell's energy and perseverance in writing poetry were apparent when with her second book, Rapture, issued in 1992, was nominated for a National Book Award. In 1993 Mitchell won the first Kingsley Tufts Poetry Award, a prize accompanied by $50,000, for the book. The previous year she had become a Lannan fellow and a Guggenheim fellow and had received the Denise and Mel Cohen Award for the Outstanding Poem in Ploughshares. Poems in Rapture have as a major theme the deepening and enriching of the self through the understanding of ordinary experience. The poet James Merrill found in Rapture "a kind of centripetal rhetorical field into which casual idiom and arcane allusion are irresistibly drawn," along with the reader.

Two of Mitchell's free-verse poems, "Golden Bough," which appeared in the New Republic (June 16, 1997), and "Golden Bough: The Feather

Palm," published in the *Atlantic Monthly* (August 1997), begin with the words "as if." The poet then observes, in both poems, the work of the bees in creating honey, writing in "Golden Bough" of "workers dipping whatever is thought into huge vats, gold-/plating, stirring the possible until/it hums, the buttery, the sorghum—/I would have preferred some salt, some brine/the brackish even, some unripe to/lick from the stream from the miele, mela, meglio, melisma/the way a bear takes it, stings and all/the unkempt gold like a wedding of finches:/who would dare break it off?" In "Golden Bough: The Feather Palm," Mitchell deals again with questions of taste—the rough and the smooth—in sensual and natural terms, wedding the visual and aural senses with touch and taste: "flies and wasps and bees smear their/mouths and eyes with spangled, with vulgar/with not at all good taste like those beaded/curtains hung up as room dividers/from a distance peroxide and honey up loud/a xanthous, a luteolous, a gilded, auric/screech, who said the past/was chaste."

Erotikon, Mitchell's 2000 collection of poetry, containing the "Golden Bough" poems, was described in the *New Yorker* (May 22, 2000) as a "roll in the hay with the dictionary." The reviewer found "less of the world here than there was in her last book, *Rapture*, and more of the heady fumes of language," but admitted that some of the poems "have the divine spark." The *New York Times Book Review* (April 16, 2000) critic, Melanie Rehak, also thought *Erotikon*—"crammed with wordplay and complicated, occasionally archaic diction"—produced at times "a mellifluous effect."

Mitchell lives in Boca Raton, where she holds the Mary Blossom Lee endowed chair in creative writing at Florida Atlantic University.

— S. Y.

SUGGESTED READING: *Atlantic Monthly* Aug. 1997; *New Republic* p44 June 16, 1997; *New York Times Book Review* p26 Mar. 11, 1984, p23 Apr. 16, 2000; *New Yorker* p95 May 22, 2000; *Paris Review* p96+ Fall 1998

SELECTED BOOKS: *The Water Inside the Water*, 1982; *Rapture: Poems*, 1992; *Erotikon*, 2000

Mitgang, Herbert

Jan. 20, 1920– Historian; critic; novelist

Herbert Mitgang is a prolific writer of nonfiction and literary and cultural criticism. In such historical works as *Lincoln as They Saw Him* (1956), *The Man Who Rode the Tiger: The Life and Times of Judge Samuel Seabury* (1963), *The Fiery Trial: A Life of Lincoln* (1974), *Dangerous Dossiers: Exposing the Secret War Against America's Greatest Authors* (1988), and *Once Upon a Time in New York: Franklin Roosevelt, Jimmy Walker and the Last Battle of the Jazz Age* (2000), Mitgang combines thorough research with the art of a good storyteller to bring past times to life. A longtime writer and critic for the *New York Times*, he has gathered his journalistic work into *America at Random, From the New York Times' Oldest Editorial Feature, "Topics of the Times," a Century of Comment on America and Americans* (1969), *Working for the Reader: A Chronicle of Culture, Literature, War and Politics in Books from the 1950s to the Present* (1970), and *Words Still Count With Me: A Chronicle of Literary Conversations* (1995). In addition to his 14 works of nonfiction and criticism, he has written four novels and a play.

The son of Benjamin and Florence (Altman) Mitgang, Herbert Mitgang was born on January 20, 1920 in East Harlem, in the New York City borough of Manhattan. From 1938 to 1939 he was a sports stringer for the *Brooklyn Eagle*. He earned a bachelor of law degree from St. John's University, in New York City, and was admitted to the New York State Bar in 1942. During World War II, from 1942 to 1943, Mitgang worked in counterintelligence in

© 2002 AP Wide World Photos

the U.S. Army Air Forces. For the next two years he was an army correspondent, and later managing editor, for the military newspaper *Stars and Stripes* in Oran, Algeria; Casablanca, Morocco; and Sicily, Italy. He became a sergeant and received six battle stars. (In his office he still keeps a photograph of himself and General Dwight Eisenhower on the beach of Normandy, France, where the June 6, 1944 D-Day invasion took place.)

After the war, in 1945, Mitgang found a staff position at Universal Pictures—working both in Hollywood, California, and New York City. That same year he embarked on a decades-long career at the *New York Times*, where he served on the editorial board, edited the drama section, and wrote book reviews and editorials. (He retired in the early 1990s.) For a year in the late 1940s he also taught English at City College (now City College of the City University of New York). Yet, as busy as Mitgang was with his journalism, he was most interested in writing a book. "To me, a book is still a book," he told Terry Golway in *Publishers Weekly* (January 24, 2000). "You can have a pile of your old newspaper clippings, but that's tomorrow's fish wrapping. Somehow, a book has a life."

In 1956 Mitgang edited his first book, *Lincoln as They Saw Him*, a compilation of Union, Confederate, and European newspaper articles, dating from 1832 to 1865, about Lincoln's congressional career, the Lincoln-Douglas debates, Lincoln's presidency, and his leadership during the Civil War. Mitgang arranged the articles and offered commentary, attempting to present Lincoln in the context of his own time. "I've always been a big believer, as an amateur historian, in going as much as possible to original sources," he told Golway. "When I pick up a book, I turn to the back, and ask, 'Is this author quoting other authors' books, or is he or she going back to the scene, going back to contemporary sources.'" Many critics appreciated Mitgang's thorough approach. Herbert Cahoon wrote in *Kirkus Reviews* (September 15, 1956) that "it is very evident that Mr. Mitgang has turned a great many yellowed folio pages, for his research has brought a number of interesting items to light." Cahoon noted in particular that Lincoln endured a great deal of criticism among his contemporaries—a potentially surprising fact for many modern readers. "Those who fear that such talk," K. E. Wilson wrote in the *San Francisco Chronicle* (November 18, 1956), "no matter how incongruous it sounds today, detracts somehow from the Lincoln hero-legend can rest at ease because out of it all Lincoln emerges more human than ever." The book was republished, in 1971, as *Abraham Lincoln: A Press Portrait*, and had two subsequent re-printings.

In 1959 Mitgang edited *Civilians Under Arms* (reprinted with the subtitle *The Stars and Stripes, Civil War to Korea*, in 1996). That year he also published his first novel, *The Return*, which is about Joseph Borken, an American veteran of World War II who returns to the battlefields of Sicily a decade after he had fought there. Now a geologist, Joseph works for a large oil company that is searching for a particular type of ore found in volcanic soil. In Sicily he reunites with his war-time lover, Franca Florio, who has been married and widowed and is now engaged to Eduardo. Joseph and Franca rekindle their relationship, adding another layer of conflict to the battle raging between peasants and landowners over the rights to the land being surveyed by Joseph's company. Some critics characterized Mitgang's literary style as lifeless, including J. A. Burns in the *Library Journal* (April 1, 1959), who wrote, "Instead of a hearty minestrone, the author serves up a rather thin broth." Reviewers differed in their assessments of the novel's intellectual and moral ambitions. In the *San Francisco Chronicle* (March 18, 1959) William Hogan called *The Return* a "daring novel of ideas and unfashionable but profound moral thinking," but Taliaferro Boatwright wrote in the *New York Herald Tribune Book Review* (April 12, 1959), "Like the 'proletarian' novels of the Thirties, [*The Return*] is more an effort to dramatize a set of convictions, or preach a sermon, than a story about real people in a believable situation."

Mitgang next wrote *The Man Who Rode the Tiger: The Life and Times of Judge Samuel Seabury*, a nonfiction account of the judge's attempts to squelch the corrupt practices of New York City's Democratic Party organization, known as Tammany Hall, for its meeting place. (The political cartoonist Thomas Nast used a fiercely aggressive tiger as an emblem of Tammany Hall in the 1870s; the "Tammany Hall Tiger" image became famous and outlasted Nash's cartoons.) "The Seabury investigations had an enormous impact on the politics and moral climate of New York," R. A. Low wrote in the *Saturday Review* (March 30, 1963), adding that Mitgang "has performed a real service in bringing to the public this immensely readable story of the man who rode the tiger."

In 1968 Mitgang edited the correspondence of a prominent Abraham Lincoln biographer in *The Letters of Carl Sandburg*. The following year he edited a collection of *New York Times* articles, *America at Random, From the New York Times' Oldest Editorial Feature, "Topics of the Times," a Century of Comment on America and Americans*. The collection, which included articles from the 19th century but focused mostly on more recent decades, celebrated the tradition of the journalistic essay, in which such writers as E. B. White, Marianne Moore, and Eugene McCarthy mused on a range of topics, including fashion, literature, and politics. "Side by side, without the separation of the sevenday week, the [columns] make . . . better reading than ever," S. W. Little wrote in the *Saturday Review* (July 12, 1969). "Taken together, [they] have an uncanny way of getting at what lies just below the surface of the mind and bringing it up for inspection in easy, informal prose." He noted E. B. White's essay on the "robot-written" numbers at the bottom of checks, and J. A. Morsell's probing of the distinctions between the terms "black," "Negro," and "Afro-American." "In sum, the essays make for about as good a collection of short, occasional essays as one could find," he concluded.

In 1970 Mitgang published *Working for the Reader: A Chronicle of Culture, Literature, War and Politics in Books from the 1950s to the Present*. In this collection of book reviews, many of which had been published in the *New York Times*, Mitgang attempts to demonstrate how historical and cultural events manifest themselves in books. The reviews "reveal and express an almost passionate effort to understand, distill and pass on the themes and concerns of this time," S. W. Little wrote in the *Saturday Review* (November 14, 1970). "[His] book is more valuable for its service as cultural history than mere literary summary." Not all critics perceived the book's benefits, however. "The lack of a unifying idea wouldn't matter if the writings were invigorating or contained any special insights," J. A. Avant opined in the *Library Journal* (December 1, 1970). "Mitgang's book reviews have no special distinction, and he comes across as a nice left-wing man who has read a lot."

Mitgang again turned to fiction with *Get These Men Out of the Hot Sun* (1972), a satirical novel about the Richard Nixon/Spiro Agnew administration that masquerades as a fictional account of the future. In the novel, which opens in 1976, President Nixon has become a cipher and his vice president, Spiro Agnew, conspires to control the nation's communications and media. "Before all else, let it be said that journalist Herbert Mitgang has nerve," Frank Trippett wrote in the *New York Times Book Review* (March 26, 1972). "Let it also be said that he has given us a good little yarn. . . . A spare but unsparing tale that is often funny even as it builds suspense and finally fills us with horror." In the *Saturday Review* (April 8, 1972) Arthur Cooper described Mitgang as a "writer with a quiverful of sharp satirical shafts" to aim at the Nixon administration. "What an angry book Mitgang has written! What a joy parts of it are. And what a pity he failed to sustain it all the way," Cooper wrote, noting that the novel's "verve and bite" eventually succumb to the needs of a suspenseful plot.

In *The Fiery Trial: A Life of Lincoln* (1974) Mitgang again takes on one of America's storied public figures. As he had done in earlier works, he attempts to see Lincoln as a product of the 19th century, rather than judge him through the clouded lens of history. Critics were divided in their opinions of the results. "Once in a while comes a gentle, humanizing point of view such as [this study]," Kelly Fitzpatrick wrote in *Best Sellers* (July 1, 1974). "Mitgang effectively presents Lincoln's concepts of slavery and white supremacy, stressing the need to look at the times and to study the full picture." J. G. Polacheck, writing in *Library Journal* (November 15, 1974), found Mitgang's approach untenable, calling the book "a confusing biography which follows no order either chronologically or topically." *New York Times Book Review* (June 30, 1974) contributor Frank Vandiver found the biography as a whole "brilliantly written" but noted that, in making "Lincoln's importance for our own time" his real theme, Mitgang is guilty (like those whom he criticizes) of mixing eras "like metaphors." In the late 1970s, Mitgang wrote a one-man play, *Mister Lincoln*, that became the first play about the president to be performed in the Ford's Theater, where Lincoln was shot. It appeared on Broadway, in 1980.

Dangerous Dossiers: Exposing the Secret War Against America's Greatest Authors (1988) was the result of Mitgang's digging into thick government agency files on writers and artists. His research was made possible by a 1974 amendment to the Freedom of Information Act (originally passed in 1967) that made surveillance files—including the jealously guarded files kept by the FBI under the former director, J. Edgar Hoover—subject to disclosure. According to the terms of the law, Mitgang was able to request his own file, and the file of anyone deceased; after he published his preliminary findings in the *New Yorker*, in the fall of 1987, such living writers as the economist J. K. Galbraith and the Beat poet Allen Ginsburg requested their own FBI files and shared them with Mitgang. *Dangerous Dossiers* excerpts from the many dossiers of writers and artists—including Pearl S. Buck, Georgia O' Keefe, Thomas Mann, E. B. White, Edmund Wilson, Ernest Hemingway, Thornton Wilder, and Pablo Picasso—who were under surveillance for their writings or their activities, or both. A *Boston Globe* (October 4, 1987) reviewer cited the example of Ernest Hemingway, who was spied upon as a "premature anti-fascist" for his support of the Spanish Republic against Franco, Hitler, and Mussolini. Mitgang supplements the dossier excerpts with historical contexts and analysis. Critics united in their praise for his laborious research, noting however that the files he obtained are heavily censored and thus incomplete. "Reading Herbert Mitgang's summaries of the F.B.I. files of some 35 American writers is like re-entering the 1950's," Elinor Langer wrote in the *New York Times Book Review* (April 10, 1988). "But the book is not so much an analysis of the relationship between the Federal Bureau of Investigation and the American literary community as a compilation of the crude materials out of which such studies will one day undoubtedly be written." In the *School Library Journal* (June/July 1988) Anne Paget noted the book's contemporary relevance: "*Dangerous Dossiers* analyzes the current situation for writers and the fact [that] they are often suspect because of their independent thoughts that appear in print."

Words Still Count With Me: A Chronicle of Literary Conversations (1995) is a collection of 64 interviews—many previously published—that Mitgang conducted with writers from 1962 to 1995, out of his desire to speak with "the authors I most respected in the world," as Elizabeth Hanson quoted him as saying in the *New York Times Book Review* (October 15, 1995). He introduced them with an essay, "The Art of Writing and the Craft of Interviewing." An *Economist* (March 23, 1996) reviewer described the interviews as "short, sharp and stylised" and Hanson concluded that "in the aggregate they show much about the craft of writing, the demands of the writer's life and the reclusive nature of many successful writers."

In *Once Upon a Time in New York: Franklin Roosevelt, Jimmy Walker and the Last Battle of the Jazz Age* (2000) Mitgang picks up on the story of

Judge Samuel Seabury (the subject of *The Man Who Rode the Tiger*). He describes the events of 1932, when Seabury's investigations into New York's political corruption led him to City Hall and toppled the popular, carousing "Night Mayor of New York," Jimmy Walker. Walker's fellow Democrat and New York's governor, Franklin Roosevelt, became personally involved in the proceedings. By the end of the year, Walker had fled to Europe—Broadway showgirl in tow—and Roosevelt was headed for the White House. Mitgang drew on contemporary newspaper accounts of the political battle and interviews that he had conducted over the years with Eleanor Roosevelt; the city planner, Robert Moses; and Thomas Dewey, a celebrated New York attorney. Mitgang uses the political and legal battle as a window onto Jazz Age–New York, which was—as David Walton put it in the *New York Times Book Review* (January 9, 2000)—"a city of 32,000 speakeasies and more than 200 plays in production every year" and in which "more than half of [taxable real estate] went to pay city jobholders, thousands of them appointed directly by the mayor and Tammany Hall." In *American History* (August 2000), Joseph Gustaitis praised the book as "history that goes back to the source and does it with style and authority." Many other critics echoed his praise, including Jeff Zaleski, who wrote in *Publishers Weekly* (November 15, 1999) that Mitgang "delivers some sharp social insight, but he never forgets that scandal makes good narrative."

In the mid-1960s Mitgang made a brief foray into television to produce the CBS documentary, *D-Day Plus Twenty Years*, which featured the reminiscences of General Eisenhower, the commanding officer of the battle. He also produced documentaries on Carl Sandburg, the sculptor Henry Moore, and others.

Upon his retirement from the *New York Times*, in 1992, Mitgang received the George Polk Award for his life's work in journalism. The award cited Mitgang's work on behalf of civil rights, court reform, gun control, and copyright reform, among other causes.

—P. G. H.; M. A. H.

SUGGESTED READING: *American History* p69+ Aug. 2000; *Best Sellers* p34 July 1, 1974; *Library Journal* Nov. 1, 1956, p94 Aug. 1969, p99 Nov. 15, 1974; *New York Herald Tribune* p9 Apr. 12, 1959; *New York Times Book Review* p40 Mar. 26, 1972, p14 June 30, 1974, p14 Apr. 10, 1988, Jan. 9, 2000; *Publishers Weekly* Nov. 15, 1999, p287+ Jan. 24, 2000; *San Francisco Chronicle* p24 Nov. 18, 1956, p35 Mar. 18, 1959; *Saturday Review* p52 July 12, 1959, Mar. 30, 1963, p53 Nov. 14, 1970, p55 Apr. 8, 1972

SELECTED BOOKS: nonfiction—*Lincoln as They Saw Him*, 1956; *The Man Who Rode the Tiger: The Life and Times of Judge Samuel Seabury*, 1963; *America at Random, From the New York Times' Oldest Editorial Feature, "Topics of the Times,"* a Century of Comment on America and Americans, 1969; *Working for the Reader: A Chronicle of Culture, Literature, War and Politics in Books from the 1950s to the Present*, 1970; *The Fiery Trial: A Life of Lincoln*, 1974; *Dangerous Dossiers: Exposing the Secret War Against America's Greatest Authors*, 1988; *Words Still Count With Me: A Chronicle of Literary Conversations*, 1995; *Once Upon a Time in New York: Franklin Roosevelt, Jimmy Walker and the Last Battle of the Jazz Age*, 2000; fiction—*The Return*, 1959; *Get These Men Out of the Hot Sun*, 1972

Moggach, Deborah

June 28, 1948– Novelist; short-story writer; screenwriter; television writer

After starting out as a journalist, Deborah Moggach moved into writing novels, short stories, and, later, television and movie scripts. What unifies her work is her concern with domestic life. She has built her prolific career on witty explorations of family and relationships, as well as suspenseful plots that keep her readers turning pages. Her ability to cut quickly yet smoothly from scene to scene in her fiction has prompted critics to compare her writing techniques to the skills of a movie editor. Moggach appears to move effortlessly between her novels and her writing for television and film. While critical reactions to her work have been mixed, books such as *To Have and To Hold* (1987) and her best-selling *Tulip Fever* (1999) have attracted an enthusiastic readership.

In an autobiographical statement submitted to *World Authors 1995–2000*, Deborah Moggach writes, "One of four sisters, I was born into a family of writers; my father, Richard Hough, wrote over 100 books which included naval history, children's stories and adult novels, while my mother, Charlotte Hough, wrote and illustrated children's books. Our house, a gothic cottage on the outskirts of London, was filled with the sound of tapping typewriters. This made fiction both ordinary and mysterious—ordinary because it was simply what my parents did, a job of work, and mysterious because I would find my own life—my pony, my exploits—appearing on the page. From an early age I read their manuscripts and was asked my opinions.

"It was a marvellous upbringing for a writer, though at the beginning I rebelled—I didn't want to do what my parents did, what child does? It was only in my mid-twenties, when I went to live in Pakistan, that I began writing seriously. Being in a distant place helped because it gave me the perspective to make sense of my past and shape it. I started my first novel there. *You Must Be Sisters* is deeply autobiographical, a coming-of-age novel about a rebellious girl at university. When I returned to England in the mid-seventies I wrote my second novel, *Close To Home*, which also drew largely from my own life. By that time I had two small children and worked in the mornings while they slept.

"After that I left my own life behind and launched into a purely fictional world. Eleven novels followed over the next twenty-five years. *Porky* was a tough, curdled novel narrated by a victim of incest; *The Ex-Wives* was a comic, modern-day fairy story; *Hot Water Man* was set in Pakistan and dealt with Islam, East-West relationships and a holy man. *The Stand-In* was a thriller set in the movie business, while *Driving in the Dark* was narrated by a coach driver who travelled over Britain trying to trace his lost son. I've tackled some difficult themes whilst, I hope, also writing an entertaining story; I feel that humour is present in even the most tragic situation and I'm also a believer in the pleasures of a strong plot. Having three sisters myself, sibling feelings emerge in many of my novels and several of them—*Seesaw*, *Stolen*, *To Have and To Hold*—deal in various ways with family relationships and the damage to children from divorce, kidnapping, parental abduction and the general implosion of the nuclear family. Life is changing so fast that I feel one has to run to keep up with it, and to reflect what's happening now. I offer a mirror to reflect people's own experiences; I hope they can recognize their own lives and feel companioned, as I do by the writers I love best.

"I've also written two volumes of short stories and a number of TV screenplays. I'm unusual in that I adapt many of my own novels as TV dramas, and sometimes create novels out of my own screenplays (*Close Relations* and *Seesaw* are two examples), and I've also adapted other writers' work. For adapting Anne Fine's *Goggle-Eyes* for the BBC I was awarded the Writers Guild Best Adapted TV Series prize, and I've just adapted two of Nancy Mitford's novels—*The Pursuit of Love* and *Love in a Cold Climate*—for the BBC.

"My latest novel, *Tulip Fever* has been bought by Steven Spielberg's DreamWorks. This novel is unusual for me, in that it's set in the past—17th century Amsterdam. I've never written anything remotely historical and found it exhilarating, as if I had walked into a Vermeer painting and found myself at home. It's a story about art, illusion, and doomed love and is set during the tulipomania craze of 1636. It tells the story of a painter who falls in love with a young married woman and who gambles everything, disastrously, on tulip bulbs. I illustrated it with reproductions of Dutch old masters—Vermeer, de Hooch—and so far it's been translated into twelve languages.

"I live in London, in a house overlooking Hampstead Heath, where I walk a great deal and swim in the ponds. If a novel is going well I move around like a sleepwalker; that secret life grows more substantial than my own."

Deborah Moggach was born on June 28, 1948 in London, England, to Richard Alexander Hough and Charlotte Woodyat Hough. "Because I come from a booky family, in some ways I've taken writing for granted," Moggach said in an interview for the *Bookseller* (April 2, 1993). "It's like coming from a family of butchers and going into the meat trade. I can't imagine life outside it. What I do worry about is that some day, somebody's going to find me out. Because, if it's going well, it's a wonderful way to live." In 1970 she graduated with honors in English from the University of Bristol in England, and began working as a librarian at Oxford University Press. In 1971 she married Anthony Austen Moggach, a publisher. The following year, they moved to Pakistan, where Moggach contributed to local newspapers and magazines as a freelance journalist. She and her husband moved back to England in 1974, and Moggach continued her freelance writing career, working as a journalist, book reviewer, and movie critic. In 1975 she won the Young Journalist Award from the Westminster Arts Council. Meanwhile, she began taking an interest in writing fiction. "A great turning point for me was the day I wrote my first sentence of fiction in my mid-twenties," Moggach told Lucy Miller for the *Daily Express* (February 7, 2000, on-line), "because I suddenly realized that you can plunge into another world and make it as real as you are able. I walk around as the characters I write about. Writing is more of an acting exercise than people think."

As she herself has stated, Moggach didn't have to stretch her acting ability too far in writing her first novel, *You Must Be Sisters* (1978). The novel chronicled the lives of three young, middle-class, English sisters—Claire, Laura, and Holly—focusing on the restless adolescence of Laura, who moves into a dilapidated apartment as a college freshman and has her first experiences with sex and drugs. The novel received favorable reviews and was seen as a promising first effort. Cyrisse Jaffe wrote in the *School Library Journal* (May 1979), "The writing style is refreshingly observant; characters, firmly developed; and the world of Claire, Laura, and Holly recreated with insight, sympathy, and humor." Valentine Cunningham, who reviewed the book for *New Statesman* (February 17, 1978), was less enthusiastic, though still complimentary. "For all the sense of deja vu that must grip the reader of yet another novel about undergraduate life," Cunningham wrote, "this one manages to be warm and witty and even from time to time actually to seem fresh. . . . Moggach may not have exploited all the possibilities her novel spots, but she can at least catch family life most achingly bared."

Moggach did most of the writing for her second novel at her kitchen table while her two young children, Tom and Lottie, were asleep. *Close to Home* (1979) examined new motherhood—and its effects on marriage—through the eyes of two neighboring families who gradually get to know each other over the course of a summer. As Moggach told Angela Neustatter for the *Observer* (January 7, 1990), "I have written around issues to do with children always, because they are the thing I care about most."

Moggach's next novel, *Quiet Drink* (1980), was more removed from her own direct experience than her previous novels had been, and she found the process of creating characters dissimilar to herself a kind of revelation. "For me this was a breakthrough," she told *Contemporary Authors* (1986). "All novelists realize that they must step out of their own limiting experience, otherwise after a couple of autobiographical books they get into a repeating pattern or else dry up altogether." The novel follows the separate lives of two characters. Claudia is a dynamic and willful woman whose husband has just left her for a more passive mate. Steve is a cosmetics salesman who is starting to lose interest in his pretty, rather dull young wife. Steve and Claudia wind up meeting over a quiet drink toward the end of the novel and find a deep connection.

Moggach drew on her experiences in Pakistan to write her next novel, *Hot Water Man* (1982). Duke Hanson, a middle-aged American business man, travels to Pakistan and has an affair with a young Pakistani woman that ends in disaster. Meanwhile, a young couple arrives in Karachi, Pakistan, where they seek to solidify their relationship in the unfamiliar setting of South Asia.

Moggach has said that she sometimes imagines her characters so vividly that she can picture them haunting the neighborhoods she frequents. Such was the case with Porky, the title character of Moggach's next novel, published in 1983. "The girl [Porky] lived in a subsiding smallholding near Heathrow Airport—which is actually where Penguin Books is," Moggach explained in her interview with the *Bookseller* (April 2, 1993). "When I go past, I wonder what has been happening to her in the intervening years, and that's very odd." In *Porky* a young woman who is the victim of incest by her father recalls her trauma years later. Over the course of a long, disturbing evening, she is able, for the first time, to revisit the memory that haunts her and makes her relationships with men so difficult.

"When I'm writing, everything in my normal life becomes useful for the book. I'm like a great vacuum cleaner hoovering up everything as I go along," Moggach told the *Bookseller* interviewer, "or like a catfish sucking up all the rubbish in an aquarium." For *To Have and To Hold* (1986), Moggach once again used an experience from her own life as a skeleton for her plot. The novel chronicles the lives of two sisters, Ann and Viv, who grow up in London and mature into very different people. Ann is plain-looking, lacks confidence, and likes to stay at home. Viv is beautiful, wilder than her sister, and seeks out adventures of all kinds. Both sisters marry, and while Viv gives birth to two children, Ann is unable to conceive. Viv agrees to conceive a child for Ann, and instead of using artificial means, she goes to a hotel with Ann's husband, Ken. Ken falls in love with Viv, and, toward the end of the novel, Viv must decide whether to keep the child or give him to Ann as planned. Moggach, years before writing the novel, had agreed to have a child for her infertile sister. Unlike what transpires in the novel, the sisters decided not to go through with the plan. In a rather unusual reversal, Moggach adapted *To Have and To Hold* into a novel based on a script she had previously written for a television mini-series. The series was praised by critics, as was the novel, to a lesser extent. "*To Have and To Hold* clips along at a brisk pace. The prose is clean, the characterizations are deft if one-dimensional, and the author cuts from scene to scene with the dexterity of a film editor," Ellen Feldman wrote in the *New York Times Book Review* (March 29, 1987). "But," Feldman continued, "the book is marred by a fuzzily sentimental view of parenthood and an inauthenticity of fact. All the women, from a boss's wife to a once-promising school dropout, begin to quiver at the mere thought of having a child."

In 1987 Moggach published a collection of short stories, *Smile*, many of which focus on domestic themes. In 1988 she published *Driving in the Dark*, a novel about a father who is thrown out of the house by his wife and goes in search of his son from a previous tryst. *Stolen* (1990), another novel, deals with the subject of child abduction. Moggach decided to write the story—which she also wrote as a television series that began airing the same day the book appeared in stores—after reading a newspaper article about a woman whose Algerian husband took their children back to his native country. In the novel, Marianne, a beautiful, audacious young woman, marries Salim, a Pakistani man. After their children, Yasmin and Bobby, are born, Salim becomes serious and remote, seemingly concerned only with his paternal duties. Weary of her situation, Marianne takes a lover, and when Salim discovers her infidelity, he smuggles the children to Pakistan. To better acquaint herself with the issues, Moggach met with members of Reunite, an abduction support group. However, Moggach avoided making her story simple or one-sided. "Some of the mothers may find it offensive because Marianne is portrayed as feckless and not a perfect mother," Moggach told Angela Neustatter, "and Salim, although motivated by anger and revenge, sincerely believes that his children will have a better upbringing in Pakistan."

In 1991 Moggach published *The Stand-in*, a thriller about a British actress who acts as a body double for an American actress and is gradually consumed by jealousy. *The Ex-Wives* (1993) also portrayed the life of an actor, in this case an aging stage performer and radio persona named Russell Buffery, also known as Buffy. After three unsuccessful marriages, Russell meets a young woman, Celeste, and falls in love once more. Russell believes his love is reciprocated, but unbeknownst to him, Celeste tracks down his ex-wives and children. Her motive is revealed only at the novel's end. Moggach's second short-story collection, *Changing Babies*, came out in 1995. The subjects of the stories range from life in a caravan park, to Belgian lovers, to a rock star attempting to write his memoirs. The collection was popular with readers, due in part to Moggach's infectious sense of humor. It met with less enthusiasm, however, from critics. For example, Charlotte Raven commented in the *Spectator* (August 12, 1995), "Deb Moggach's gal-pals at Cosmo are the sort who'd think it dazzlingly original to point out that when women speak, *men never listen*. If they have as little to say as this lady, all good feminists had better pray that it is so."

Moggach published two more novels in 1997. *Seesaw* is a thriller about a kidnaped girl who is put up for ransom. *Close Relations* tells the story of contractor Gordon Hammond, who has a heart attack while climbing a ladder and then falls in love with the nurse who nurtures him back to health. After he abandons his marriage of 40 years, his daughters are left to take care of their mother, and, in the process, they reach new conclusions about themselves and their relationships with each other. Kate Chrisholm, reviewing the book for the *Electronic Telegraph* (March 22, 1997, on-line), found the characters absorbing and the writing skillful, but was ultimately bothered by what she saw as a contradiction in the novel. "*Close Relations* is an involving study of the complex feelings that both bind and tear apart families, and Deborah Moggach creates powerful characters whom we, as readers, begin to care about," Chrisholm wrote. "But there is something intensely irritating about the way she controls and manipulates what happens to Gordon and his family, on the one hand trying to pretend that these are just ordinary people, and yet on the other investing their lives with far more excitement than can ever be the lot of Mr. and Mrs. Average Consumer."

Moggach made her first foray into historical fiction with *Tulip Fever* (1999), a novel that takes place in 17th-century Holland. The Dutch at that time had developed a passion for tulips that verged on mania, and a rare bulb might be valued as highly as a horse, a house, or an entire fortune. In the novel, Sophia, the young bride of an older gentleman named Cornelius Sandvoort, falls in love with Jan van Loos, a painter commissioned to do her portrait. Sophia is soon consumed by love and hatching plots to earn herself and Jan freedom from Cornelius. Her schemes—which involve lead coffins filled with sand, evil doctors and the bubonic plague, and the flowers of the book's title—gradually endanger her and Jan's lives, as well as those of others. Moggach vividly reproduces life in this period of Holland's history and intersperses descriptions of Dutch paintings into the narrative. "There is something of the first-rate thriller about *Tulip Fever*," Jane Gardam wrote in the *Spectator* (May 15, 1999), "but Moggach's feeling for paintings and love of Amsterdam—and what must have been some considerable research—makes it more than that. She takes us into 17th-century Holland as if she has walked its streets and fields." Catherine Osborne, in the *New York Times* (May 28, 2000, on-line), complimented Moggach's language as "rich and concentrated as oil pigments" and wrote that her "sumptuous prose creates an impression of serenity that belies the passions just beneath the surface of Amsterdam in the 1630s." *Tulip Fever* is being made into a movie by Steven Speilberg's DreamWorks studio and Miramax. Scheduled for release in 2003, it will be directed by John Madden, from a screenplay adapted by Tom Stoppard.

Final Demand (2001), Moggach's recent novel, is about a woman named Natalie, a 32-year-old office worker living in Leeds. Somewhat bored with her life and frustrated by financial setbacks, she concocts a scheme to bring in some extra income. At NuLine Telecommunications, where she works, customers occasionally submit checks made out to N.T. All she has to do, she reasons, is marry someone whose surname begins with a T, thereby making her initials N.T., and start depositing the checks into a separate checking account. After a few failed liaisons, she succeeds with a man named Stumpy Taylor, and all is going well until a computer miscalculation leads to unexpected consequences—some good, some tragic. Reviews of the novel were mixed. "This book may disappoint the many admirers of *Tulip Fever*," Patrick Gale wrote for the London *Daily Telegraph* (October 20, 2001). "There was an almost gleeful cruelty to the plot and telling of *Tulip Fever*, and a well-judged ambivalence to its characters, so that even as they were chewed up in traps of their own making, the reader discovered their hidden depths and humanity. Natalie is a charmless minx who barely develops until the final page." Gale added, however, that "The novel's human interest lies in the glimpses into the lives of Natalie's victims. A charming encounter with a retired schoolmistress who stumbles into love, and a clear-eyed portrait of a family crippled by poor communication and then destroyed by an act of random violence are teasing reminders of Moggach on top form." Frank Egerton, in a review for the London *Financial Times* (October 20, 2001), commented: "There are moments during the book's denouement, as at its very beginning, when the narrative comes perilously close to cliche . . . too many coincidences, too many characters behaving as types. But the tension between Moggach the popular fiction writer and her mature impulse to push her themes to the limit make for a highly exciting, stimulating and, at times, profoundly moving novel."

Moggach lives in London and continues to write novels, as well as television and film scripts. She is a fellow of the Royal Society of Literature and chairman of the Society of Authors. She divorced Anthony Austen Moggach in the 1980s and married a cartoonist named Mel Calman, who died in 1994. Her children are now both in their 20s, and

Moggach uses her free time to travel. She also continues to find her career rewarding. "I feel very lucky," she told Miller. "I feel like someone is going to find me out and tap me on the shoulder, saying, 'You've got away with it long enough, Deborah. Now you've got to be a proper grownup.'"
—P. G. H.

SUGGESTED READING: *Bookseller* p44+ Apr. 2, 1993; *Daily Express* (on-line) Feb. 7, 2000; (London) *Daily Telegraph* p5 Oct. 20, 2001; (London) *Financial Times* p4 Oct. 20, 2001; (London) *Observer* p33 Jan. 7, 1990; *New York Times* (on-line) May 28, 2000; *New York Times Book Review* p19 Mar. 29, 1987; *Spectator* p31 Aug. 12, 1995, p41 May 15, 1999

SELECTED BOOKS: novels—*You Must Be Sisters*, 1978; *Close to Home*, 1979; *Quiet Drink*, 1980; *Hot Water Man*, 1982; *Porky*, 1983; *To Have and To Hold*, 1986; *Driving in the Dark*, 1988; *Stolen*, 1990; *The Stand-in*, 1991; *The Ex-Wives*, 1993; *Seesaw*, 1997; *Close Relations*, 1997; *Tulip Fever*, 1999; *Final Demand*, 2001; short-story collections—*Smile*, 1987; *Changing Babies*, 1995

Mole, John

October 12, 1941– Poet; children's writer; teacher

John Mole is the rare poet who has written successfully for both children and adults, though he has often maintained that one ought not to discriminate too sharply between the these two types of audiences. As he told a writer for *Something About the Author* (1984), "If I were to choose one quotation to pin above my desk while writing poems for the young it would be this—from an essay on Walter de la Mare by W. H. Auden: 'There are no good poems which are only for children.'" Mole's aptitude for understanding and relating to children also informs his adult poetry; he is known for his clear and direct style, as well as the warmth and compassion exhibited in his lines. Mole's poetry frequently celebrates life, and yet it is also often suffused with an underlying melancholy. For example, his poem "To a Blackbird at First Sight," which appeared in the London *Spectator* (April 28, 2001), begins, "Clasp whatever branch you may land on / and, just for the joy of it, from a full throat / sing, before flight, of yet another season / coming into leaf." Later in the poem, Mole writes, "may your song / resist interpretation much as beauty does / the suffering it causes." In *Encounter* (September/October 1984), as quoted in *Contemporary Authors* (1994), a reviewer stated that Mole offers "proof, if any were needed, that poetry is as necessary in ordinary circumstances as in times and places of crisis. His poems are light in the best sense—lucid, sharp, economical."

Mole writes for *World Authors 1995–2000*: "I was born in 1941 in the Somerset village of Staplegrove which at the time seemed an independent community, though it has since become a residential satellite for the nearby town of Taunton. When I was six, our family moved three miles further into the countryside to Kingston St. Mary at the foot of the Quantock Hills. This area has also become more populated although it still preserves much of its natural beauty which appealed to Wordsworth and Coleridge—who lived there for a while. As a young man, the Quantocks became a formative landscape and environment for me, a world to explore on solitary walks and in which to absorb a sense of history and discover horizons which challenged my own. My father was a chartered accountant, my mother a full-time housewife (though she had briefly been a teacher before marriage) and our family, also including my younger sister, a good example of post-war, middle-class English life. This meant financial security, much to be grateful for, yet at the same time a degree of constraint bound in by good manners and the implicit imperatives of social convention.

"Looking back, it occurs to me that my future was determined by these circumstances. When, after a respectable but undistinguished career at school and University I moved to Hertfordshire and became a teacher, my parents were happy enough—though it had been hoped that I would follow my father into the accountancy firm set up by *his* father—but when I started to take myself seriously as a writer it seemed that the more I published the more my parents were determined to see this work as a sideline, a hobby. My books and articles never joined others on their shelves (i.e. the real books) but were kept in a drawer as if for safety, as if at some time I might ask for them back when it was all over. I recall this with gratitude for the love and patience I was always shown, and sympathy for the bewilderment I caused. In some ways, too, I have remained the dutiful child caught between two worlds. Yeats once observed that the poet makes poetry out of the quarrel with himself, and I suppose that my quarrel has always been between the safely domestic and the dangerous edge of things. It also occurs to me that this may be the reason why many of my poems, whether for adults or younger readers, take a child's eye view of the world, domesticity and danger being so intimately conjoined in a child's experience and imagination.

"From 1964 to 1998 I taught school in England, almost without a break although I came with my wife to Riverdale in New York on a year's exchange and took time off to be Poet in Residence at my old Cambridge college, Magdalene. The exchange came early in my career (1969–70) and it coincided with a period of intense political activity on campus. Many of the high school students I found myself teaching might soon find themselves fighting in Vietnam, and my own ambiguously privileged situation as a guest in a country whose foreign policy I opposed became as much a political education for me as an academic one for those I was somewhat presumptuously teaching. When, after returning to England, our first son was born, the experience of fatherhood came in the wake of the concern I still felt for the future of my students, and this, I think, affected the poetry I was writing. If one's overt subject matter is domestic it is always likely to be open to the charge of complacency but I hope that my work at that time—and indeed subsequently— can be seen to have a sub-text which challenges the comfortable response.

"While holding down my day job as teacher, I wrote and published poems, reviewed for many of the British literary journals and, between 1982 and 1988 was the regular poetry reviewer for *Encounter*. My pieces on a range [of] British and American [poets] were collected as a volume (*Passing Judgements*) in 1989. With a fellow poet and teacher, Peter Scupham, I helped to set up The Mandeville Press which for many years published small handset editions of poetry by emergent poets or those we felt to have been unjustly neglected.

"An important shift in my writing life occurred in 1987 when, along with several others, I was dropped by the publisher I had been with for over ten years. Invited back to Peterloo Poets, which had published my first book in 1973, I brought out *Boo to a Goose*, a collection of poems for children— illustrated by my wife—which was well received and won the Signal Award. Since then I have written for adults and children, often not deciding until the last minute whether to include a particular poem in an 'adult' or 'children's' book. I agree entirely with E. B. White who insisted that 'anybody who shifts gears when he writes for children is likely to wind up stripping his gears.' A good poem for children is simply a good poem, and a bad poem is a bad poem whomever it is for.

"My retirement from teaching to go freelance in 1998, has led to diversification and a more chancy way of life: more reviewing, lecturing, residencies and appearances as a jazz clarinetist. Jazz has always been an enthusiasm of mine, and a number of my poems have witnessed to this. The relationship between fixed form and improvisation has always preoccupied me as poet and musician. Indeed, one of the remarks most applicable to my writing and playing (and which, in a way, unites them) was made by the great pianist Earl Hines. However familiar the tune, he said, he always tried to find a fresh way of journeying through it, 'and when you see me smiling you know I'm lost.'"

Mole's first volume of poetry, *The Love Horse*, was published in 1973. In 1975 he published the poetry volumes *Landscapes* and *Partial Light*, and in 1977 he published *Mortal Room* and *Our Ship*. In *Thames Poetry* (1977), as quoted in *Contemporary Authors* (1986), a reviewer of *Our Ship* called Mole, "intelligent, witty, self-deprecating, a lively and delighted observer of the oddities of persons." A reviewer for *Sunday Telegraph* (May 8, 1977), also quoted in *Contemporary Authors* (1986), wrote, "*Our Ship* established Mole as an anti-romantic with a warm, human sympathy and the ability to embody these attributes in an almost primitive clarity."

In 1978 Mole was invited into several schools to read his work. For this purpose he decided to put together some verse riddles based on an old Anglo-Saxon model, some of which were collected in *Once There Were Dragons* (1979). The book was illustrated by his wife, Mary Norman, whom he'd married on August 22, 1968, and the illustrations provided hints to the answers of the riddles. Alan Brownjohn, in the *Times Literary Supplement* (July 18, 1980) wrote of the book, "It has a nice metaphysical touch; and it might jump an alert child straight into the tone of poems much more serious than playful riddles: children may learn by leaps as well as by painful steps. Many of John Mole's riddles will function as excellent poems in their own right."

From 1979 until the mid-1980s, Mole published mostly children's poetry, often culling from poems he had written for his own children, Simon and Benjamin. His publications during this time included *From the House Opposite* (1979) and *Feeding the Lake* (1981). In 1984 Mole published a poetry volume entitled *In and Out of the Apple*. Martin Dodsworth, who reviewed the book for the *Guardian* (October 11, 1984), found the poems diverting, but lacking in impact. "The poems seem to have to force their way into being against the poet's will," Dodsworth wrote, "which is why, perhaps, they are such slight, pale offspring—appealing, but very waif-like."

In 1987 Mole published one volume of poetry for adults, *Homing*, and one for children, *Boo to a Goose*, for which he won the 1988 Signal Award for outstanding contribution to poetry for children. *Homing* was widely considered to be one of his finest works. A critic for the *Poetry Review* (June 1987), as quoted in *Contemporary Authors* (1994), called Mole a "poet at the height of his powers, finding new strength with each volume and with a considerable body of work to his name. *Homing* will make it still more difficult to fail to see him as one of the most accomplished and salutary poets of the age."

In 1989 Mole published a collection of his critical writings entitled *Passing Judgements*. The following year saw another of Mole's poetry books for children, *Mad Parrot's Children*. In 1993 he published *Depending on the Light*, and two years later his poetry from previous works was collected into *Selected Poems*. Vernon Scannel, who reviewed the collection for the *Sunday Telegraph* (June 25, 1995), noted that "much of the work has a peculiarly English melancholy" and that Mole "can be very witty." Scannel concluded, "Virtually all of these poems are expertly and variously crafted and are sure to give pleasure to readers who respond to the tested traditional qualities of the best English poetry."

In 1999 a London-based group called Poet in the City appointed Mole as its poet in residence, making Mole essentially the first "official poet" of London and charging him with the responsibility of organizing poetry readings in the city's schools and businesses. In a speech posted on the Poet in the City Web site (www.poetrysoc.com), Mole said, "My hope is that throughout the rest of my term of 'office,' I shall be able to do more to build bridges . . . between the high-risers of the Square Mile [London's financial district] and all those kids from the less glittering high-rises who need every advantage they can possibly be given."

Mole's most recent poetry collection, *For the Moment*, was published in 2001. In it he explores several themes, including death, childhood, and the desire for freedom and spontaneity. In "The Waterfall," as quoted by Sarah Broom in the *Times Literary Supplement* (June 8, 2001), Mole dreams of "throwing caution to the winds / that still might offer me the gift of danger / in this only lifetime, leaping free." Broom felt that his attempts to throw caution to the wind were for the most part unconvincing, writing, "Mole's collection does not quite manage to gather up the new energy described in [some of the poems], instead feeling rather backward-looking and ponderous." She was impressed, however, by his ability to "capture the intricacy of emotion lying behind the simplicity of a child's voice." Broom concluded, "Most of this collection comprises poems which are sensitive, thought-provoking and technically impressive, including several accomplished jazz-inspired poems which achieve a smooth rhythmical momentum, catching effortlessly and successfully at the 'chancy modulation.'"

In addition to his writing, Mole has had a long career in academia. In 1964 he began teaching English at the Haberdashers' Aske's School, in Elstree, Hertfordshire. He left in 1973 to teach English and head the department at the Verulam School, in St. Albans. In 1981 he became the head of the English department at the St. Albans School, also in St. Albans; he remained there until 1998. During his years at St. Albans, Mole also taught numerous residential creative writing courses and, in 1996, he became the poet in residence at Magdalene College. In 1998 he was a visiting poet at the University of Hertfordshire. As of 2002, he was the City of London poet in residence.

Mole is also a literary critic and has been a regular reviewer for the *Times Literary Supplement*, *Times Educational Supplement*, *New Statesman*, *Listener*, and *Cambridge Review*. He has appeared on the BBC Radio programs *Poetry Now*, *Forget Tomorrow's Monday*, *Time for Verse*, *Pick of the Week*, and *Poetry Please*. His awards and honors include the Eric Gregory Award from the Society of Authors (1970) and the Cholmondeley Award for poetry from the Society of Authors (1994).

—P. G. H.

SUGGESTED READING: *Guardian* Oct. 11, 1984; *Sunday Telegraph* Books p10 June 25, 1995; *Times Literary Supplement* p810 July 18, 1980, p25 June 8, 2001; *Something About the Author*, 1984

SELECTED BOOKS: children's literature—*Once There Were Dragons*, 1979; *Boo to a Goose*, 1987; *Mad Parrot's Children*, 1990; *Copy Cat*, 1997; literary criticism—*Passing Judgements*, 1989; poetry—*The Love Horse*, 1973; *Landscapes*, 1975; *Partial Light*, 1975; *Mortal Room*, 1977; *Our Ship*, 1977; *From the House Opposite*, 1979; *Feeding the Lake*, 1981; *In and Out of the Apple*, 1984; *Homing*, 1987; *Depending on the Light*, 1993; *Selected Poems*, 1995; *For the Moment*, 2001

Courtesy of HarperCollins

Montero, Mayra

(MY-rah mon-TEHR-oh)

1952– Novelist; journalist

Mayra Montero, who was born in Cuba, worked for many years as a journalist in Puerto Rico before beginning her career as a novelist. As her popularity spread throughout Latin America and Spain, her prose, described by critics as "hypnotic" and "imaginative," raised comparisons to such acclaimed authors as her fellow Cuban novelist, Alejo Carpentier. Critics also praise her spare, precise writing—something she credits to years of journalism—and her attention to recent historical and scientific events. *In the Palm of Darkness* (1997), her fourth novel, was the first to be translated into English. The story, which follows an American herpetologist and his Haitian guide on an expedition into the mountains of Haiti in search of the potentially extinct blood frog, was widely praised by American critics. Janet Ingraham, in a review for *Library Journal* (April 1, 1997), called the book "a shocking, absorbing, beautifully written tale from a writer to watch." Other translations soon followed, including *The Messenger* (1999), a novel loosely based on the assassination attempt made on the life of the Italian tenor Enrico Caruso, and *The Last Night I Spent With You* (2000), an erotic tale about selfishness, power, and guilt. *The Red of His Shadow* (2001), Montero's most recent novel to receive an English translation, provides a window into the world of Haitian voodoo, set against the background of poverty and misery in the Dominican Republic sugar industry.

Mayra Montero was born in Havana, Cuba, in 1952. She was educated at a Catholic school. After the Cuban Revolution that culminated on January 1, 1959, when Fidel Castro wrested power from the dictator, General Fulgencio Batista, life became difficult for her family. Montero's father, a well-known television writer and actor, moved the family to Puerto Rico. "When I was 17, I was kicked out of the college preparatory school because we were leaving," Montero recalled during an interview with the Cuban writer José Manuel Prieto for *Bomb Magazine* (on-line). "My family's situation was terrible: my parents couldn't work, we lived out of the generosity of our extended family. I didn't travel around, I didn't have any privileges, I was never a Young Communist or even a Pioneer. In other words, I had a terrible time throughout my adolescence."

Montero studied journalism in Mexico and Puerto Rico, and by the age of 20 she was covering baseball games as a sportswriter for the *El Nuevo Día*, a newspaper in San Juan, Puerto Rico. She found work at other magazines and newspapers, doing interviews and writing feature stories. She later joined *El Mundo*, Puerto Rico's oldest newspaper, as a correspondent for Central America and the Carribean. She covered politics and popular uprisings in the region, including the 1979 Sandinista revolution in Nicaragua. Eventually she became an editorial writer for the paper. "That is where I became a real journalist and it's a vocation I never turned my back on," Montero told Prieto. "I think journalism is excellent training for anyone who wants to become a writer. It has given me flexibility, ease in front of the blank page and something more important: it has allowed me to approach literature from a journalistic point of view. When the time comes to research the subjects of my books, it is much easier because I have that journalistic training. When it comes time to write, I also feel that I maintain an economy of language which is the result of journalistic practice."

Montero's first novel, *La Trenza de la Hermosa* (The Braid of the Lovely Moon), was published in 1987 by Anagrama Publishing in Barcelona, Spain. She drew material for the book from stories she heard from her contacts in Haiti. The plot centers on the friendship between two men, a voodoo priest and a sailor, who meet after many years in Port-au-Prince during the last days of the Haitian dictator Jean-Claude "Baby Doc" Duvalier, who was overthrown in 1986. The novel, which has not been translated into English, was a finalist for the Premio Herralde award, sponsored by Anagrama Publishing.

In the Palm of Darkness (originally published in Spanish as *Tú, la Oscuridad*, in 1995), also explores the relationship between two men of different backgrounds on the island of Haiti. Joking to Prieto that she is "a frustrated biologist," Montero said the idea for the novel came from a *New York Times Magazine* article about the decline of amphibians and reptiles that had fascinated her. In the novel, Montero introduces Victor Grigg, an American herpetologist who is on a quest to locate a specimen of an amphibian on the verge of extinction. He hires a Haitian local, Thierry Adrien, to be his guide. The two men search for the frog in the dangerous mountains outside Port-au-Prince, a region plagued by the violence and mayhem created by the "Tonton Macoutes," gangs that protected Haiti's longtime dictators, Francois and Jean-Claude Duvalier, by torturing and murdering scores of their opponents. While Grigg struggles to hold on to his scientific reason, Thierry describes his life amid his country's mysteries and crushing violence. Interspersed between these two men's narratives are journalistic accounts of the ominous disappearance of frogs and other amphibians from many regions in the world. Sybil S. Steinberg, who described the book as a "literary pageturner" for *Publishers Weekly* (March 31, 1997), wrote that "As Thierry's unfolding story sheds light on the troubled soul of Haiti (where zombies and other otherworldly threats are made to seem as real as the worldly threats of corruption and poverty), Victor finds himself, despite his academic detachment and pragmatism, pulled ever further into the mysteries of the land and its alien logic. Montero accomplishes much here with an extraordinary blend of power and economy." Alisa Valdes, writing for the *Boston Globe* (August 22, 1997), called *In the Palm of Darkness* "a graceful novel that climbs gradually to a surprising and goose-bump-raising finale. . . . Montero manages in only 183 pages to make a heartbreaking link between the modern and enigmatic disappearance of the blood frog (grenouille du sang) from the hills of Haiti and the disappearance of kindness and humanity from Haiti, and by association, the Carribean."

Montero's next novel to be translated into English, *The Messenger* (*Como un Mensajero Tuyo*, 1998), is based on a famous incident that took place in Havana, Cuba. On June 13, 1920, the celebrated Italian tenor Enrico Caruso was performing in the opera *Aida* when a bomb exploded at the Teatro Nacional. Suspecting that the bomb had been planted by members of the Black Hand, a Sicilian crime gang that extorted money by threatening—and often going through with—assassination attempts, Caruso fled into the street, still costumed as the Egyptian soldier Radames, and disappeared for several days. Montero fills in those unaccounted-for hours by delivering Caruso into the arms of Aida Cheng, the daughter of a Cuban mother of African origins and a Chinese immigrant father. Aida's godfather is Jose de Calazan, a powerful priest of the Santería faith, which blends Catholic and Yoruba traditions. Jose has foreseen the explosion and Aida's ill-fated affair with Caruso, and determines to keep the two lovers apart. Aida, however, commits herself to Caruso and her fate. The story of star-crossed lovers parallels Verdi's tale in *Aida*, and each chapter bears a title taken from the opera's libretto. "In an adventurous plot of escapes, kidnappings, and trysts, [Montero] creates an imaginative yet believable saga," Lawrence Olszewski wrote for *Library Journal* (May 1, 1999). The narration—delivered partly by Aida and partly by her daughter born of the affair, Enriqueta, who 30 years later interviews witnesses to the explosion—creates "a haunting duet that mixes Afro-Cuban ritual, Chinese folklore, opera and documented history," Janice P. Nimura noted for the *New York Times Book Review* (June 20, 1999). For *Publishers Weekly* (March 22, 1999), Sybil S. Steinberg observed that "Montero's authorial dexterity avoids grandiose pageantry, keeping the action clear and the pace right. The result is a novel, rich in metaphor and allusion, that will leave most readers breathless as its final curtain drops."

The Last Night I Spent With You is an erotic tale about a middle-aged couple on a cruise in the Carribean. Fernando and Celia, after 25 years of marriage, are estranged from one another; on the rare occasions when they make love, it is a passionless, mechanical event—"As if we were packing suitcases," Montero writes, as quoted by James Polk for the *New York Times Book Review* (July 16, 2000). Fernando, who has had a few previous affairs, seduces Julieta, a 40-year-old white-haired woman who is also a passenger on the boat. Pretending not to notice her husband's infidelities, Celia recalls an unhappy affair she had years earlier, when she repeatedly had sex with a man who was nothing more than a stranger: "I barely recognized myself in that submissive, flushed woman who walked behind him, unbuttoning her skirt," Celia recalls, as quoted by Polk. She is further ashamed that the affair caused her to neglect her father, who was dying at the time. When her emotional anguish becomes overbearing, Celia tries to distract herself in a sexual liaison with a local boatman.

"Sex in middle age," Polk wrote in his review of the book, "becomes less a rediscovery of a lost sensuality for [these characters] than an endless struggle for power and control, a destructive series of betrayals, deceits and mutual degradations all played out to the erotic yet melancholic musical strains of haunting boleros, the peculiarly Latin songs of love and loss." Bonnie Johnston, in an assessment for *Booklist* (June 1/June 15, 2000) called *Last Night* an "intensely passionate and disturbing novel." The novel generated a stir in Puerto Rico and other Spanish-speaking countries when it was first published, in 1991, as *La Última Noche que Pasé Contigo*. It became a finalist for Spain's Sonrisa Prize for erotic literary fiction. In her interview with Prieto, Montero explained that she had not planned to write an erotic novel. "I think eroticism is a good hook—and a good alibi—which allows us, as writers, to develop the personality and psychology of our characters," she said. "Eroticism perturbs us, makes us face forgotten feelings, reveals a courage and series of sensations that we didn't even know were in us."

Montero's *The Red of His Shadow* (*Del Rojo de su Sombra*, 1992) explores an erotic relationship that has become dangerous. Zule Reve, the story's protagonist, is a young priest of the Voudon, or Haitian voodoo, tradition. She emigrates with her father from Haiti to the Dominican Republic. For the laborers working under the brutal conditions of the Dominican Republic's sugar industry, voodoo rituals offer their only solace. As Holy Week begins, Zule and a retinue of her followers embark on a pilgrimage across the region's sugar fields. The journey will be a perilous one for Zule; Simila Bolosse, a rival priest and Zule's former lover, has threatened her life. A few years earlier, Zule had found Bolosse near death; she nursed him back to health and a passionate romance ensued. Bolosse, however, is now a "bokor," a Voudon priest who works for good and evil. Having fled Haiti after the overthrow of dictator Jean-Claude Duvalier, Bolosse is also a drug trafficker with ties to the former secret police of the violent regime. Bolosse now wants Zule to join him in an "alliance." If she refuses, he has vowed to kill her.

"In this fierce tale, Montero mines the viscera of Voudon's secret society with the deftness of a journalist and arresting images reminiscent of Alejo Carpentier," Nelly Rosario wrote for the *Village Voice* (August 28, 2001). "Structured like a braid that weaves past and present toward a final showdown," she continued, "*The Red of His Shadow* puts a hypnotic amarre [or spell] on its reader." Jana Giles, writing for the *New York Times Book Review* (August 12, 2001), called the novel "transfixing," noting that it "offers potent insights into a highly complex world." She added that "the brevity of the novel allows us to focus on its tightly wound plot and its timeless archetypal confrontation." "At once a brutal, expressionistic voodoo fairy tale and an indictment of the plight of Haitian cane workers in the Dominican Republic," Jeff Zaleski wrote for *Publishers Weekly* (August 20, 2001), "this demanding novel proves that Montero is capable, like Zule, of 'looking at the sun for a long time, searching with staring eyes for the temporal cause of its fury.'"

"People often ask me if I practice these religions," Montero remarked to Prieto. "I tell them that I respect them profoundly and have a great aesthetic, even philosophic affinity, with these magicoreligious systems. That is why I have an altar in my house . . . on that altar, voodoo gods cohabit with gods from Santería and Madonnas. . . . This wonderful mixture is what we are, what gives us depth and spirituality as a people."

Montero lives in San Juan, Puerto Rico, where she is a columnist for the newspaper *El Nuevo Día*. She often writes for *El País* and ABC News in Spain, and for *Revista Rumbo*, a magazine in the Dominican Republic. Her other works include *Aguaceros Dispersos* (2000), a collection of journalistic essays, and *Púrpura Profundo* (2000), a novel that will be published in English in 2003 as "Deep Purple." —A. I. C.

SUGGESTED READING: *Bomb Magazine* (on-line); *Booklist* p1860 June 1/June 15, 2000; *Boston Globe* F p1 Aug. 22, 1997; *Library Journal* p128 Apr. 1, 1997, p111 May 1, 1999; *New York Times Book Review* p16 June 20, 1999, p18 July 16, 2000, p29 Aug. 12, 2001; *Publishers Weekly* p61 Mar. 31, 1997, p68 Mar. 22, 1999, p59 Aug. 20, 2001; *Village Voice* p68 Aug. 28, 2001

SELECTED BOOKS: *In the Palm of Darkness*, 1997; *The Messenger*, 1999; *The Last Night I Spent With You*, 2000; *The Red of His Shadow*, 2001

Jim Rogash/AP Photo

Morris, Mary McGarry

1943(?)– Novelist

After a lifetime of writing, conducted mostly in secrecy and in spare moments while raising five children, Mary McGarry Morris made what the *New York Times* (June 4, 1999, on-line) book reviewer Michiko Kakutani called "a startling and powerful debut," at age 45, with the publication of her novel *Vanished* (1988). For years, Morris had told only her family that she was working on a novel in the hope of avoiding the inevitable questions about how the book was going or when it might be published. For a long while, it seemed as though *Vanished* might never actually reach publication. Morris sent the book to almost 30 agents and publishers, all of whom rejected it. "With ignorance comes courage," she explained to Elizabeth Mehren for the *Los Angeles Times* (March 7, 1991), "I had no idea how many manuscripts were landing on top of mine." Finally her persistence paid off, and she was signed by the agent Jean V. Nagger, who quickly sold *Vanished* to Viking Publishers. "It seemed unreal," Morris told Mehren of the sale. "It seemed a very fragile thing. I would not have been a bit surprised if a phone call had come saying it was all a big mistake." Once recognition came, it did so steadily and from high-profile quarters: *Vanished* was nominated for both the PEN/Faulkner Prize and the National Book Award, Morris's second novel, *A Dangerous Woman* (1991), was made into a feature film, and the influential television talk-show host Oprah Winfrey endorsed her third novel, *Songs in Ordinary Time* (1995), launching Morris onto bestseller lists for weeks.

Mary McGarry Morris was born in the New York City borough of Brooklyn, and moved with her parents to Rutland, Vermont, when she was six. Her father, an "educated and witty" man who doted on his only daughter, as Morris told Roger Cohen for the *New York Times* (January 28, 1991, on-line), was also an alcoholic, and couldn't keep a job long enough to support Mary or her three younger brothers. Her parents separated when she was eight, and Morris's mother remarried a chef.

After graduating from a parochial high school, Morris enrolled at the University of Vermont but soon transferred to the University of Massachusetts at Amherst to be with her husband, Mike, now a lawyer, whom she had married during her sophomore year. She left school altogether at age 19 in order to raise a family, giving birth to four children in the space of six years. Although she worked briefly at a Massachusetts welfare office to earn money for the children's education, Morris concentrated on running her home and snatching spare moments between chores to write. "But I always felt guilty," Morris told Patti Dolen, for the *Boston Globe* (February 19, 1991). "Guilty that I wasn't spending time working in the community or volunteering at my children's schools. I always had an excuse. But no one knew the real excuse—

writing. If someone would arrive at my door unexpectedly, I'd jump up and run to the kitchen so they wouldn't catch me at my typewriter." Many journalists have commented about the apparent contradictions between Morris's own life—spent with her husband and children in the quiet Boston suburb of Andover, in a Victorian house full of family portraits and lace curtains—and the sordid, desperate lives of many of her characters. "Why does everyone find it so surprising that a woman from the suburbs can write what I write? Would they have the same questions if I were male?" Morris asked Dolen. "What I write about seems natural enough to me. These people, my characters, have the same basic human reactions as everyone else . . . they have the same longings and the same feelings of loss." All of Morris's novels are set in the kind of small New England town she knows best, where people tend to mind each others' business. "I'm fascinated by the raw circumstances of lives colliding, coming so close, veering apart," Morris told Weinraub.

In a letter to her editor, Morris explained the central character of her first novel. "There are countless Aubrey Wallaces in this world," Morris wrote, as quoted by Caryn James in the *New York Times* (June 20, 1988, on-line), "little people, pale lives, the briefest, simplest human creatures. They are the shadows in early morning doorways and the solitary late night climbing of wooden stairs. They wash dishes in restaurants and mop floors and pick up litter in the park, and they are always startled to be spoken to, because no one ever does." The character of Aubrey Wallace in *Vanished* is a gentle but dim-witted man, abandoned by his father, then bullied into an unhappy marriage with a wife who constantly reminds him of his stupidity and fecklessness. While working on a road crew one day, Aubrey encounters Dotty, a half-naked, wild-looking teenage girl who has just killed her sexually abusive father. The two join forces, and, when Dotty impulsively kidnaps a baby, they embark on a five-year odyssey of back roads, petty crime, and cheap motels. The trio gradually forms a kind of heartbreaking family, but their situation becomes increasingly surreal and desperate, culminating in further violence. "Though Ms. Morris's book creates a terrifying portrait of rootlessness in America," observed Michiko Kakutani, "it is not, at heart, another on-the-road study in affectlessness and alienation." Instead, Kakutani described the novel as belonging firmly to the tradition of the Southern gothic and notes its particular affinity with the stories and novels of Carson McCullers. "It aspires, like McCullers's works, to examine the perversities of passion: the illogical nature of love and the crippling effects of its absence," she wrote. Patti Down, in the *Boston Globe* (February 19, 1991), admired how Morris anchored the sensational plot with realistic characters. "[Aubrey and Dotty] are fully developed, albeit crippled, human beings. Dangerous innocents," she noted.

The eponymous character of *A Dangerous Woman* (1991) is someone "for whom the wind's a little too strong, the sun just a little too bright," in the diagnosis of a fellow townsman, as quoted by David Gates in *Newsweek* (April 8, 1991). Martha Horgan—"Marthorgan," an ogre's name to the children who torment her—is emotionally clumsy and compulsively honest. Her breed of "solitary oddball," Gates observed, is a literary archetype common in American literature. As Gates sees it, Martha, who as a teenager is assaulted by a gang of boys and then blamed for provoking the attack, is a kind of social barometer for the people in her small Vermont town. "Martha merely sets up the moral choices for those around her," Gates wrote. "They end up with a keener (if more painful) sense of who they are; she never has a clue." When Martha does attempt to take a job and form real bonds with others, the clashes that ensue seem inevitable, given the collision of character and circumstance. Reviewing the book for *New Statesman* (July 24, 1998), Amanda Craig called it "as compelling as Ruth Rendell, as haunting as Jane Hamilton," and concluded that "*A Dangerous Woman* is also tender and hilarious, a magnificent novel of rare quality."

Songs in Ordinary Time (1995) is set in a picture-postcard New England, complete with steepled churches, bandstand, and a drugstore with lunch counter. The novel takes place in 1960, before John F. Kennedy's assassination and the war in Vietnam. Unlike many writers, however, Morris does not depict this era as a more innocent time. Atkinson, Vermont, where the story takes place, is an ailing community: the doctor is a quack, the priest seduces young girls, dead bodies go undiscovered, and con men flourish. Because of its colorful characters and intricate plot, *Songs in Ordinary Time* prompted a critic for *Kirkus Reviews* to dub its author a "contemporary Dickens," and a reviewer for the *Boston Globe* to deem the book as "deep and thick as a long, hot summer, a fully realized world . . . wrought with fearless detail," both as quoted on the *Amazon.com* Web site. Some critics, however, found Morris's narrative unwieldy and emotionally unconvincing. Kakutani, who termed Morris's first two novels "narrative tours de force," wrote for the *New York Times* (August 4, 1995, on-line) that *Songs in Ordinary Time* is "a sprawling, episodic narrative filled with subsidiary characters and rambling asides—asides that undercut the urgency of the main story and that are tied together only by portentous remarks about 'the disaster that's coming' and the 'implacable cadence of doom.'" Lee K. Abbott, in the *Los Angeles Times Book Review* (August 13, 1995), found that, although the novel's scope allows for evocative descriptions and telling detail, ultimately the many narrative strands toppled the drama. "too many of these songs . . . sound the same notes," he wrote. Though reviewers of both *Vanished* and *A Dangerous Woman* praised Morris's ability to leaven sensational plots with realistic and recognizable emotion, many, including Kakutani, observed that, in

Songs in Ordinary Time, the narrative swerves toward melodrama. Jim Shepard wrote that the characters' unrelenting venality and misery seem overdone, and Kakutani wrote that "everyone in the town of Atkinson seems like a dysfunctional refugee from a talk show." In a dissenting opinion for *USA Today* (on-line), Susan Kelly described all the characters as sympathetically portrayed. "[Morris] opens the doors to these people's souls, showing all their fears and flaws without making them seem ridiculous or unworthy," she wrote.

In spite of mixed reviews, *Songs in Ordinary Time* achieved considerable success, thanks in great part to the efforts of Oprah Winfrey, a talk-show host who regularly devoted shows to discussing current books that she has enjoyed. Although some critics have denigrated Winfrey's taste, citing her preference for sentimental or formulaic novels, she has enormous influence on the American public, and a reported 11 percent of all U.S. book sales are of those she has recommended. In 1997, two years after the publication of *Songs in Ordinary Time*, Winfrey called Morris to inform her that she was going to feature the novel on her show. Fearful that she had been the victim of a prank, Morris immediately called her publisher, who confirmed that it had indeed been Winfrey on the phone. The book, which had sold only modestly before, went on to sell 1.5 million copies and Morris, who had been stung by the many negative reviews, felt vindicated. "If [Winfrey] hadn't come along I would never have felt right about *Songs*," Morris told Joanna Coles for the *London Times* (June 9, 2000). "It is a remarkable book and I worked very hard on it for a very long time."

Fiona Range (2000) introduces a small-town bad girl into Morris's cast of misfits and rebels. Fiona, while not economically disadvantaged like many of the others, has been abandoned by her unwed mother and taken in by a disapproving aunt and uncle. A college dropout and waitress at the local greasy spoon, Fiona has a reputation for getting attention and love any way that she can. But, after waking up to find herself in bed with her close friend's husband, Fiona tries to change her life—by reaching out to an unstable Vietnam veteran rumored to be her father, and by trying to repair relations with her adoptive family. True to Morris's pattern, a character's attempt to form emotional bonds is prey to both capricious fate and human treachery. Sherie Posesorski, writing for the *Toronto Star* (June 23, 2000), called the story "high-end soap opera—emotionally intelligent, entertaining, even the most minor characters portrayed with depth and intensity—but soap opera all the same." Posesorski wrote that the novel doesn't "raise all those unanswerable questions and sour truths that keep us awake and unconsoled at night as [Morris's] other novels so viscerally do." Monica L. Williams, in the *Boston Globe* (June 25, 2000, on-line), warned readers, however, not to mistake the story for a lightweight romance, insisting that it is both "full of mystery and suspense" and "a grim and complex tale of love."

Morris's life hasn't changed dramatically since she found an audience for her work. She still writes five hours a day, with a line by the French novelist Gustave Flaubert taped to her desk. "Be regular and orderly in your life," it reads, as quoted by Judith Weinraub in the *Washington Post*, "so that you may be violent and original in your work." She rarely attends parties, preferring to spend time with her family instead, and avoids both the New York and Boston literary scenes. "I am not part of any literary world," she told Roger Cohen. "And I have no desire to move into a literary world. I am wary of letting an aura take the place of the effort of writing." She concluded, "The core of my life is writing. Without that, I'd be very miserable."

— M. A. H.

SUGGESTED READING: *Boston Globe* p25 Feb. 19, 1991; *Boston Globe* (on-line) June 25, 2000; *Los Angeles Times Book Review* p2 Aug. 13, 1995; *New York Times* (on-line) June 4, 1988, July 3, 1988, Jan. 4, 1991, Aug. 4, 1995; *Newsweek* p61 Apr. 8, 1991; (London) *Times* June 9, 2000; *Toronto Star* June 25, 2000; *Washington Post* B p1 Mar. 26, 1991

SELECTED BOOKS: novels—*Vanished*, 1988; *A Dangerous Woman*, 1991; *Songs in Ordinary Time*, 1995; *Fiona Range*, 2000

Morrow, Bradford

Apr. 8, 1951– Novelist; poet; editor

"Bradford Morrow has been quietly solidifying his reputation as one of the United States' best young novelists," John G. Cawelti wrote for the *Lexington Herald-Leader* (April 16, 1997). In an issue of *Review of Contemporary Fiction* (Spring 2000) dedicated entirely to surveying Morrow's body of work, the novelist Jonathan Safran Foer observed, "Morrow is an American writer insofar as he is a writer of the Americas. His narratives careen from the American West, to Central America, to the Northeastern United States, connecting these blazing sites like a sign of the zodiac that had never before been noticed." With six volumes of poetry and five novels to his credit to date, Morrow has become known for employing complex narratives and timely themes. His work is often informed by the rich landscapes of his settings, as he explained to Wendy Smith for *Newsday* (April 23, 1995): "Place is very important to me. The first thing I buy when I get interested in a place is a map, because it gives a sense of what a person has done to understand that place on earth." As the editor of the avant-garde literary magazine *Conjunctions*, which he founded in 1981, Morrow has played a significant role in shaping contemporary literature. Whether publishing the work of innovative young poets and short-fiction writers or providing a forum for established literary figures, *Conjunctions* has been

Michael Eastman/Courtesy of Viking Penguin
Bradford Morrow

called "an international treasure, created and enjoyed literally around the globe," according to Foer.

Bradford Morrow was born on April 8, 1951 in Baltimore, Maryland, the son of Ernest Dean and Lois (Hoffman) Morrow. During Morrow's early childhood, the family moved west to Littleton, Colorado, a suburb of Denver, where he was largely raised. His father, a geologist, worked as a recruiter for the Martin Marietta Corp., gathering physicists, chemists, and mathematicians to conduct work in early aerospace projects, as well as weapons delivery systems. Throughout most of his childhood, Morrow spent much of his time exploring the outdoors; his youthful interests lay in music, nature, painting, and medicine—rather than literature. He "never read a book all the way through until I was 17," he told Michael Coffey for *Publishers Weekly* (June 14, 1991), adding, "We had a set of Dickens on the mantle, but no one was allowed to touch it. What did I know?"

Because of his interest in medicine, Morrow assumed he would become a doctor, and at age 16 he earned a grant to join the Amigos de las Americas—a group of approximately 20 pre-medical students traveling throughout South America. That year, 1967, he was sent to rural Honduras as a medical assistant, distributing smallpox inoculations and attending to soldiers wounded in border disputes with Nicaragua. Upon his return, Morrow found himself significantly changed. "No question," he told the novelist Patrick McGrath in an interview for *Review of Contemporary Fiction* (Spring 2000). "Honduras changed my life. I wanted to be a doctor, or so I thought. When I came back, even though still in high school, everything was politicized for me, immediately. There were the politics of my parents, the politics of Vietnam, the politics of ideas, the politics of a girlfriend, the politics of a car, the politics of trees. I was hyper-politicized by the experience of seeing and experiencing Honduras's abject poverty."

His father's work in the weapons industry became a source of conflict between them. "I didn't want to know what he did," Morrow told McGrath. "He didn't particularly want me to know what he was doing. We had a very iffy, although loving, I must say at the same time, relationship during the late sixties and into Nixon's presidency. What he embraced, I needed to consider as wrong." Morrow applied for and earned an American Field Service Scholarship, which allowed him to spend his final year of high school as an exchange student in Cuneo, Italy. While in Italy Morrow became severely ill with dysentery and a strain of hepatitis C he had caught in Central America. (This bout with illness would become the first of many for Morrow; he has since contended with such maladies as diverticulitis and peritonitis, which required him to undergo five surgeries in the mid-1990s.) During his months of recovery in Italy, he stayed in a home stocked with classics from English and American literature. There, Morrow developed his love for books, enjoying works by William Shakespeare, Dante Alighieri, and Henry James, among others.

In the late 1960s Morrow returned to the U.S. to attend the University of Colorado, where he studied politics and comparative religion. During this period, he married his first of two wives (both marriages eventually ended in divorce). He moved for a time to Paris, where he began writing short stories, which he never published. When he ran out of funds, he returned to the University of Colorado, graduating summa cum laude with a B.A., in 1973. Morrow then took on several unusual jobs: He worked as a studio musician (playing with such artists as blues musician Albert King and rock legend Leon Russell), taught classical guitar lessons, learned book restoration, and dabbled in painting. He earned a scholarship to pursue graduate study at Yale University, in New Haven, Connecticut, but remained there only a year. He told McGrath, "When I went to Yale in the mid-seventies, what they offered was not coincident with what interested me." Instead, he pursued his own course of study by reading the works of Ezra Pound and other canonized authors. "I read *The Cantos*," he told Coffey, "and *How to Read, Personnae*, Eliot's *Selected Essays of Pound*. I followed Pound's leads. If he said go read Cavalcanti, I would go read Cavalcanti. Through Pound I discovered Brancusi, Gaudier-Brzeska, the Troubadors. Pound was my first guide to culture." Morrow also became interested in the British painter and novelist Wyndham Lewis, and he spent some time at New York's Cornell University studying Lewis's papers. In 1978 he published the annotated volume *A Bibliography of the Writings of Wyndham Lewis*, with Bernard

Lafourcade. "I devoured Lewis," Morrow told Coffey. "His language was so bristling and alive. . . . It's where I learned that a prose that had a rhythm, the right kind of bite to it, could be as strong as poetry, with the added value of narrative."

While working on the Lewis bibliography, Morrow moved to Santa Barbara, California, where he opened a rare-book store. There, he met and befriended the American poet Kenneth Rexroth, who had been a mentor to the beat writers Jack Kerouac, Allen Ginsberg, and Gary Snyder, among others. He recalled to Coffey, "To be arguing with this polymathic, 70-year-old who had been everywhere and done everything was yet another education. Rexroth became both my dear friend and outrageous, idiosyncratic post-graduate-manque professor." With Rexroth's encouragement, Morrow began to write poetry. The duo launched the literary magazine *Conjunctions* in 1981. (Morrow sold his book store to finance the undertaking.) The project started out as a single Festschrift, dedicated to James Laughlin, the founder of the publishing house New Directions. (A Festschrift is a volume containing writings in tribute to an accomplished individual.) The enterprise grew, however, into the acclaimed and influential journal *Conjunctions* is known as today. In an editor's letter recently posted on the magazine's Web site, Morrow noted, "For over a decade and a half, *Conjunctions*' specific contribution to the literary community has been to provide a forum for the now over 800 writers and artists whose work challenges accepted forms and modes of expression, experiments with language and thought, and is fully realized art." George Plimpton, the editor of the *Paris Review*, called it "the most interesting and superbly edited literary journal founded in the last decade," according to Robert S. Boynton for *Newsday* (July 7, 1991).

In 1982, just before his death, Rexroth named Morrow as the literary executor of his papers. In this capacity, Morrow has since edited the following collections of the poet's works: *The Selected Poems of Kenneth Rexroth* (1984), *Kenneth Rexroth, Classics Revisited* (1986), *World Outside the Window: The Selected Essays of Kenneth Rexroth* (1987), *Kenneth Rexroth, More Classics Revisited* (1989), and *The Complete Poems of Kenneth Rexroth* (2002). Throughout the early 1980s, Morrow also published several volumes of his own poetry, including *Passing from the Provinces* (1981), *Posthumes: Selected Poems, 1977–1982* (1982), *Danae's Progress* (1982), *The Preferences* (1983), and *After a Charme* (1984). His well-known 1991 collection, *A Bestiary*, consists of 36 illustrated prose-poems about animals, including everything from plankton to elephants. In addition, he edited *Thirty-Six Poems of Tu Fu* (1987), a collection by the famed eighth-century Chinese writer, and co-edited the anthology *The New Gothic: A Collection of Contemporary Gothic Fiction* (1991) with Patrick McGrath.

In 1988 Morrow published his first novel, *Come Sunday*, an intricate story about a man in pursuit of the secret for prolonging life. Owen Berkeley, a wealthy man from upstate New York, hires Krieger, a crooked businessman who specializes in selling Central American treasures through the black market, to transport a tribal chief—who is reportedly 400 years old—from the border region of Nicaragua and Honduras. The situation becomes complicated when Krieger attempts to smuggle heroin in the process, and Berkeley's children take steps to halt the exchange. Richard Eder, writing for the *Los Angeles Times* (May 19, 1988), described the book as "an accomplished anthology of current literary themes and ways of delivering them. It touches on sickness, both the indigenous and the American variety, in Central America; on corruption and drugs in our cities; on the new rootlessness of our countryside; on the severed links among our generations; on the dissolution of our social and personal ties; on the blurring of lines between enterprise and criminal enterprise." *Come Sunday* received mixed reviews from critics. While Eder praised Morrow's writing as "complex but controlled," and noted the inventive situations he creates for his characters, the reviewer nonetheless concluded, "For all its expert elaboration, its interweaving of moral, emotional and political textures, and a trance-like atmosphere suggestive of large messages, there is nothing much left in *Come Sunday* once its puzzles are nudged at." In an assessment for *Library Journal* (April 1, 1988), Paul E. Hutchinson found the novel "tediously overwritten and burdened with plot lines that seem mere afterthoughts."

Morrow followed up his debut novel with *The Almanac Branch* in 1991. Narrated by Grace Brush, a 33-year-old woman, the book explores her unresolved traumas stemming from childhood incest and a lifetime of severe migraines. When at the age of seven Grace attests to seeing "Flare Man"—a hallucination brought on by a headache—her family moves from the New York City borough of Manhattan to a farm on New York's Shelter Island in order to better soothe the child's affliction. Yet, the idyllic environment of Shelter Island becomes the site for even greater family dysfunction: Grace engages in inappropriate sexual behavior with her brother Desmond, which her other brother, Berg, witnesses. When Desmond dies falling out of a tree in which he is perched to spy on his mother and her lover, Grace's parents separate. She becomes estranged from her mother and even more dependent on her emotionally distant father. Eventually, Berg begins making pornographic films as part of his father's sprawling business and tries to cast Grace in the lead roles. Writing for the *Washington Post* (August 11, 1991), Gregory Feeley described, "This gothic machinery sounds more lurid in summary than in its presentation, as the diaphanous scrims of Morrow's prose set both action and memory at a meditative remove. The novel retains its musing, impassive air despite a steady quickening of its plot, which eventually encompasses blackmail, a 30-year-old secret that threatens the family business with ruin, and the surviving brother's embezzlement of company funds to realize his dream of a definitive 'art film' of his family obsessions."

The Almanac Branch was generally praised by critics, who found it a complex psychological study of a troubled mind. Morrow himself told Coffey, "Originally I was interested in memory, how it functions as a part of imagination; specifically, how memory reorganizes the realities we live through." In her review for the *Voice Literary Supplement* (June 1991), Polly Shulman praised Morrow's careful treatment of Grace's condition, which she said keeps the book "from being manipulative or titillating, despite its melodramatic outline." She continued, "Avoiding exploiting Grace is a magical, impossible feat. . . . Modestly, delicately, and with unobtrusive, laudable self-doubt, Morrow has written a precise study of the sexual and artistic conscience." For the *New York Times* (July 14, 1991), Howard Coale opined, "Although this is a tangled novel, from time to time it shines with a mysterious and ingenious beauty." Gregory Feeley concluded, "[This is] a highly sophisticated novel, written in full appreciation of such postmodern themes and strategies as unreliability of memory, the deployment of tests within the narrative, and the deep ambiguities of metaphors. . . . Uneasy in its larger structure, Morrow's novel remains a pleasure in its prose and quirky intelligence." *The Almanac Branch* was a finalist for the 1992 PEN/Faulkner Prize for fiction.

In his third novel, *Trinity Fields* (1995), Morrow moved from the northeastern U.S. setting of his first two books to the more expansive environment of the American Southwest. He told Wendy Smith he had conceived of the novel while visiting a New Mexican church, El Santuario de Chimayo, in 1991. "Traveling across the desert, you go down into the lip of this valley that had been sacred for thousands of years before the Spanish built a little church there in the 19th Century," he said. "Suddenly I realized that 25 miles behind me was Los Alamos and I thought: My God, here you've got the most high-tech place in this country, and 25 miles away you have the magic and spiritual quality of Chimayo. That was the day the book got born." Named for the code name given to the site where scientists first tested the atom bomb in 1945, the novel explores the relationship between two lifelong friends whose fathers are both scientists at Los Alamos. The two boys—Brice McCarthy and Kip Calder—who were born on the same day in 1944, remain best friends throughout their youths, taking rebellious stances against what they consider their fathers' amoral work. The tumultuous 1960s bring about an ideological rift. Both characters fall in love with the same woman, Jessica Rankin, during college; Brice then joins a peace movement, and Kip goes off to serve in Vietnam. There he joins a covert military operation in Laos and remains in Vietnam for more than two decades after the war.

Now dying from exposure to Agent Orange, he has returned to New Mexico to make peace with Brice, who has been raising Ariel, Kip's biological daughter with Jessica, as his own. In addition to exploring the men's intricate friendship, Morrow told Dick Williamson for the *Denver Rocky Mountain News* (May 28, 1995) that he had a larger political mission throughout the novel. "Laos was the most secretive place during the Vietnam War, and Los Alamos was the most secretive place during World War II," he explained. "I wanted to see if there was a connection between Vietnam and World War II. There definitely was. My whole bias against the Vietnam War was born of that childhood sense that after the detonation near Alamogordo in 1945, the apocalypse was in our hands. Wars were never the same after that."

Trinity Fields was deemed a critical success, with many reviewers praising Morrow's original approach to historical events, such as the construction of the atomic bomb and the polarization in the U.S. over Vietnam. Bruce Powe for the Toronto *Financial Post* (September 9, 1995) said of the book, "I admire this strongly written, strong-minded, fictional chronicle of the generation following the Second World War. It is a novel about connections and purgations." While some critics found fault in various aspects of Morrow's storytelling technique, they generally concluded that the novel's message overcame its stylistic problems. Bruce Allen, for example, writing for the *New York Times* (July 9, 1995), observed, "There are problems, particularly when Kip's thoughts are filtered through Brice's analytical scrutiny, so we're not always sure whose words we're hearing. And yet, despite such confusions (and an unfortunate excess of flat pronouncements), Mr. Morrow's assiduous probing of the intricacies of moral choice hits us where we live—or ought to live. *Trinity Fields* is distinguished by the seriousness of its concerns and by the force of [Brice's] passion to understand and be forgiven, and to forgive." In her review for the *Review of Contemporary Fiction* (Fall 1995), Brooke Horvath affirmed, "A meditation on the conservation of wholeness and integrity, on the complementarity of what changes and what endures, on the inescapable personalness of history as something in which we must always find ourselves implicated if we ever hope at all to find either ourselves or our national identity, *Trinity Fields* is one of this year's notable books, and a book that we will still be reading when this year is itself history."

In *Giovanni's Gift* (1997), his fourth novel, Morrow adopted the genre of mystery fiction, narrating the story from the perspective of Grant Morgan, an American expatriate who has been teaching English in Rome. When Grant's aunt and uncle, Henry and Edme, are terrorized by a strange intruder, Grant returns to Ash Creek—their remote estate high up in Colorado's Rocky Mountains—to investigate the problem. Once there he discovers a probable link between the family's current circumstance and the mysterious murder of Henry's friend, Giovanni Trentas, some years before. Just prior to his death, Giovanni had given Henry a cigar box containing items that ultimately provide clues to unraveling the story. Along the way Grant falls in love with Giovanni's daughter, Helen, with whom he sets about to solve the crime.

The critical response to *Giovanni's Gift* was decidedly mixed. While some critics found the complex plot contrived and overwritten, others praised the book as an old-fashioned mystery. Most of the positive reviews focused on Morrow's skill in pacing the story to maximize the suspense and in successfully evoking the myth of Pandora's box, which the cigar box represents. Acknowledging in her critique for the *Miami Herald* (February 26, 1997) that "most readers will figure out the secret of Giovanni's cigar box long—way too long—before Grant does," Margaria Fichtner nonetheless concluded: "This is a brisk, extremely appealing tale about characters—likeable and often refreshingly unlikeable—whom we gladly grant our close attention if not our respect." John Gregory Brown, writing for the *Chicago Tribune* (March 9, 1997), called the novel "a beautifully written and well-plotted tale, a Gothic story of darkness and light, of love lost and, perchance, regained." "Truth be told," he added, "on certain dark and stormy nights, that's quite enough for the reader to handle." Other critics were not so favorably inclined. In the *New York Times* (March 9, 1997), Walter Kirn opined, "Everything that know-nothings and philistines accuse the literary novel of being—precious, hysterical, contrived, in love with its own nobility—Bradford Morrow's *Giovanni's Gift* resolutely and horrifyingly is. An unintentional campy blend of artistic ambition and commercial cynicism, it's a case study in the novel as gilded kitsch—a book that proposed to elevate its readers even as it takes calculated aim at their presumed stupidity." While Jeff Giles for *Newsweek* (March 10, 1997) found the first chapter "wonderfully stark and spooky," he noted that Morrow's characterization of Grant, whom he considered "prissy and dithering," did little to propel the story. "Grant himself is unlikable. Not in any interesting way, but in the old-fashioned way: you just don't like him," Giles wrote. A reviewer for *Publishers Weekly* (November 18, 1996) concluded, "Somehow, the human drama never lives up to the epic quality of Morrow's prose, and the book, for all its beauties and some passages of fine romantic ardor, never quite comes to life."

In *Ariel's Crossing* (2002), Morrow returned to the story he began in *Trinity Fields*, this time focusing on Kip's biological daughter, Ariel Rankin, who is now a grown woman working at a New York publishing house. Raised by Brice, Ariel discovers that he is not her real father only after Kip contacts her through a letter. While she is not moved to action initially, she eventually seeks out a connection with her biological father when she becomes pregnant. The novel chronicles Ariel's pursuit to find Kip before he dies of lymphoma. When the father and daughter reunite, Kip is living with a family in New Mexico, in a home haunted by the benevolent spirit of a descendent of the conquistadors. Later, Kip assists the family in recovering land that the U.S. government had taken for the purposes of nuclear testing. While some critics found Morrow's characterization of Ariel somewhat flat, the author himself described his protagonist as a symbolic figure—the resolution between Brice and Kip. "She represents the search for unity between these two extremes," he told Lynn Neary in an interview for *All Things Considered* (July 17, 2002), "the anti-war activist vs. the warrior; the runner vs. the stayer, the kind of extremes of how we think, what we can be, what we can do in life." A reviewer for *Publishers Weekly* (June 24, 2002) called the book "yet another outstanding, thought-provoking novel from one of America's major literary voices as he continues to explore the issues that made *Trinity Fields* so compelling and memorable."

Morrow has contributed stories, poems, and essays to such publications as the *Paris Review*, *Village Voice*, and *Washington Post*. His awards and honors include the Coordinating Council of Literary Magazines Editor's Award (1984 and 1988), the General Electric Foundation Award (1985), the General Electric Foundation Younger Writer's Awards for editing *Conjunctions* (1985 and 1988), a New York Foundation for the Arts grant in fiction (1989), and an Academy Award in Literature from the Academy of Arts and Letters (1998). He holds memberships with the PEN American Center—for which he served on the board of trustees from 1998–2002—and the New Writing Foundation, among other groups. Morrow has taught at several prestigious schools, including Princeton University, Columbia University, Brown University, and the Naropa Institute.

Bradford Morrow is currently a Bard Center Fellow and professor of literature at Bard College, in Annandale-on-Hudson, a town located in the Hudson River Valley of upstate New York.

—K. D.

SUGGESTED READING: *All Things Considered* July 17, 2002; *Chicago Tribune* Books p5 Mar. 26, 1995, Books p3 Mar. 9, 1997; *Denver Rocky Mountain News* A p79 May 28, 1995; *Los Angeles Times* V p18 May 19, 1988; New York Times VII p7 Mar. 9, 1997, VII p13 June 30, 2002; *Newsday* p34 July 7, 1991, p30 Apr. 23, 1995; *Publishers Weekly* p61 May 3, 1991, p41+ June 14, 1991, p60 Nov. 18, 1996, p41 June 24, 2002; *Review of Contemporary Fiction* Fall 1995, Spring 2000; *Washington Post* X p3 Aug. 11, 1991

SELECTED BOOKS: novels—*Come Sunday*, 1988; *The Almanac Branch*, 1991; *Trinity Fields*, 1995; *Giovanni's Gift*, 1997; *Ariel's Crossing*, 2002; poetry—*Passing from the Provinces*, 1981; *Posthumes: Selected Poems, 1977–1982*, 1982; *Danae's Progress*, 1982; *The Preferences*, 1983;

After a Charme, 1984; *A Bestiary*, 1991; as editor—*A Bibliography of the Writings of Wyndham Lewis*, 1978 (with Bernard Lafourcade); *A Bibliography of the Black Sparrow Press, 1966–1978* (with Seamus Cooney), 1981; *The Selected Poems of Kenneth Rexroth*, 1984; *Kenneth Rexroth, Classics Revisited*, 1986; *Thirty-Six Poems of Tu Fu*, 1987; *World Outside the Window: The Selected Essays of Kenneth Rexroth*, 1987; *Kenneth Rexroth, More Classics Revisited*, 1989; *The New Gothic: A Collection of Contemporary Gothic Fiction* (with Patrick McGrath), 1991; *The Complete Poems of Kenneth Rexroth*, 2002

Courtesy of HarperCollins

Mosby, Katherine

1957– Novelist; poet

"Katherine Mosby writes like no one working today," Heller McAlpin observed in a critique of the novelist and poet for *Newsday* (March 31, 2002). "Not for her the edgy anomie of modern urban bleakness, the laundry list of domestic catastrophes or the one-line bulletins from the psychic front." In contrast to the minimalism of many other contemporary writers, Mosby typically presents absorbing, epic tales that showcase her evocative, often poetic, prose. McAlpin described Mosby's two books to date—*Private Altars* (1995) and *The Season of Lillian Dawes* (2002)—as "lushly descriptive and deeply nostalgic, old-fashioned yet by no means quaint." Mosby's work has garnered much critical acclaim and has also proven commercially popular with readers; *Private Altars* was awarded the Book-of-the-Month Club's First Fiction Award. In addition to her novels, Mosby has published a collection of poems, *The Book of Uncommon Prayer* (1996).

Katherine Mosby was born in 1957 and raised in New York City. From an early age she had a passion for writing. She recalled in an interview posted on the HarperCollins Publishers Web site, "I had acclimated my family early on in my childhood to the notion of my becoming a writer. It had always been what I wanted to be when I grew up: not only did I like to make up stories and write poems, collect words and read books, but it was the only job I could think of where you got to work in your pajamas if you wanted." Mosby attended private schools in Manhattan before leaving the city for Concord Academy, a boarding school in Concord, Massachusetts. She later attended Princeton University, in New Jersey, where she earned a degree in medieval literature. After college Mosby used the money she had earned in a poetry competition to live for a year in Paris. She returned from her sojourn abroad to pursue advanced degrees at Columbia University and New York University (NYU), both in New York City. "Finally," she told John Habich in an interview for the Minneapolis *Star Tribune* (May 8, 2002), "my family said, 'It's time to get a job.' Otherwise I'd still be in school." She began teaching business writing at NYU and creative writing at New York City's 92nd Street Y; she also conducted poetry workshops in several of the city's public schools.

Although her poetry was featured with some regularity in various periodicals, Mosby did not publish any fiction until 1995, when her first novel, *Private Altars*, appeared. She recalled in the HarperCollins interview that she had been inspired initially to write about a young woman in mid-century New York, but she found the tale moving in a different direction. "As I came to know [the character] and her circumstances, I realized that her story was so deeply informed by her mother, Vienna's story that that story needed to be told first," she explained. Thus, Mosby's first novel takes up the story of the mother—Vienna Daniels—an educated, spirited Northerner who moves to Winsville, West Virginia, to marry Willard, a conservative Southerner. Vienna finds it difficult to adapt to the intolerance of the 1920s South, and her marriage becomes increasingly strained. Her defiance of social convention, coupled with her husband's excessive drinking, causes an explosive conflict. Soon after, Willard abandons his wife—with a small daughter, Willa, to care for and a second infant on the way. Left to raise Willa and the newborn, Elliot, alone, Vienna begins translating Latin poetry and spends 15 years working on a 12-volume epic poem. Throughout the saga, which follows her through World War II, Vienna remains a social misfit who raises her children to embrace independence and to live by their own standards.

For a debut novel from a relatively unknown author, *Private Altars* received significant critical attention, with many reviewers praising the poetic and lyrical qualities of Mosby's language. In his review for the *Los Angeles Mirror* (May 12, 1995), Frank Levering wrote, "This is a prose of high order, and Mosby can reach these heights consistently, creating a density of language that borders on being an extended prose poem." In a review for *Time* (February 27, 1995), Ginia Bellafante affirmed, "*Private Altars* is about more than the strife Vienna is forced to endure; it is about language. In sentence after lush sentence, Mosby is intent on showing the reader that she was primarily a poet before turning to fiction." Several critics compared the book to Sinclair Lewis's 1920 novel *Main Street*, which also provides a portrait of an intolerant small town, and Hayden Trenholm, writing for the *Calgary Herald* (September 16, 1995), called it "a beautiful addition to the genre often referred [to] as Southern Gothic." Despite such praise, the critical response was not entirely positive: Louisa Ermelino, reviewing *Private Altars* for *People* (March 27, 1995), found Mosby's story to be thin. "Mosby . . . writes with fluid grace but fails to give fresh life to the southern gothic form," Ermelino wrote. "Her images are magical, but her narrative has no momentum, and her central characters are too ethereal to have any real bite." John Stark Bellamy II, writing for the Cleveland *Plain Dealer* (February 26, 1995), called the novel "overwrought and overwritten" and observed that Mosby's lyrical skills were "not well served in prose by her inability to resist overblown metaphor and simile."

In 1996 Mosby published her first poetry volume, *The Book of Uncommon Prayer*. The collection presents a series of spiritual pieces that combine elements of poetry and prayer. In his review for *Library Journal* (January 1996), Henry Carrigan Jr. called the book "a strikingly beautiful tapestry of lyrical poems." He added, "Her imagistic poem-prayers integrate the sensuality of the physical world with the transcendence of the spiritual world. . . . Lovingly and hauntingly crafted, Mosby's spiritual lyrics evoke the power and mystery of divine love."

"[*The Season of Lillian Dawes*] is a sequel to *Private Altars*," Brooke Allen wrote of Mosby's 2002 novel, "but to describe the link between the two books would give away more of the plot than is fair to reader or author." Describing her decision to include some of the same characters in both of her novels, Mosby told the HarperCollins interviewer, "One of the ideas I was exploring was the notion that we are, as personalities, in a state of flux, permutating and evolving as time and circumstance shape us. I was reminded of the famous quotation from [the Greek philosopher] Heraclitus, 'You could not step twice into the same river; for other waters are ever flowing on to you.' I wanted to examine the difficulties that creates in 'knowing' someone. . . . I think that readers encountering a character at a different point in life, in a different place, under wildly different circumstances can assume that they will be seeing new aspects of that character and will need to get to know the character anew, just as in life, when we reconnect with someone as an adult whom we have not seen since childhood."

The Season of Lillian Dawes is narrated by Gabriel Gibbs, a mischievous 17-year-old orphan who has been expelled from his private boarding school for smoking cigars and sent to live with his older brother, Spencer, in Manhattan. Although his family expects him to pursue a career in law, Spencer is instead working on a collection of short stories. While Spencer writes, Gabriel explores New York City, observing the life of the social elite in Manhattan's most upscale neighborhoods. There, he first encounters Lillian Dawes, a mysterious young woman of immense talents: she is beautiful, sophisticated, charming, intellectual, fluent in French, and a superb painter, horsewoman, and dancer. Gabriel's adolescent crush becomes increasingly complicated when Lillian begins a relationship with Spencer. As she further infiltrates the brothers' lives, Lillian's secrets gradually unravel, revealing her tragic past. Joyce Johnson wrote of the title character for the *Washington Post* (June 30, 2002), "Who is this ragged waif we first see having tea with a soft drink tycoon at the Plaza? Or this behatted society beauty at the racetrack? Or this Central Park equestrienne perched in a tree? Or this auburn-haired dancer doing the tango in the kitchen of a Brazilian restaurant? Not to give too much away, let us just say that it is a character from *Private Altars*."

Critical response to Mosby's second novel was mixed. While many reviewers compared the book to those of such writers as Edith Wharton, F. Scott Fitzgerald, and Henry James—who often explored the conflict between "old" and "new" money in New York's elite social circles—others found Mosby's references pretentious. Most of the critical praise centered on Mosby's skill in evoking 1950s New York. Polly Paddock observed in her review for the *Charlotte Observer* (April 24, 2002), "The novel is at once a coming-of-age tale, a finely rendered portrait of a time and place, and a meditation on the often blurred line between appearance and reality, the true and the false." A reviewer for *Publishers Weekly* (January 14, 2002), however, called the story "long on atmosphere but short on credibility," and observed: "Mosby works too hard at making Lillian enchanting and multitalented and Gabriel presciently ubiquitous, and at portraying the rich as caricatures. . . . The melodramatic denouement, clumsily foreshadowed from the beginning, moves the book into the realm of overheated romantic fiction." A critic for *Kirkus Reviews* (January 15, 2002) noted, "[Mosby's] characters seem to have been borrowed from the movies . . . and in spite of all the period detail carefully layered in, the tale has an artificial, unlived quality." While Brooke Allen also considered Lillian "merely a stock character," she nevertheless concluded: "There is so much to enjoy in *The Season of Lillian Dawes* that it seems pointless to dwell on its faults. The period color, the depiction of a long-vanished

New York, is exquisite: date-nut-and-cream-cheese sandwiches at Chock Full o' Nuts, riding on the jump seat in Checker cabs, Schrafft's, the Oak Room back in the pre-Trump days. . . . Mosby recreates such scenes lovingly and with a meticulous attention to language that betrays her origins as a poet."

Katherine Mosby currently resides in New York City, where she is working on her third novel, which is said to have characters in common with the previous two.

—K. D.

SUGGESTED READING: *Charlotte Observer* Apr. 24, 2002; *Library Journal* p105 Jan. 1996, p141 Apr. 1, 2002; *Los Angeles Times* E p7 May 12, 1995; *Minneapolis Star Tribune* E p3 May 8, 2002; *New York Times* VII p8 June 9, 2002; *Newsday* D p27 Mar. 31, 2002; *Publishers Weekly* p36 Jan. 14, 2002; *Washington Post* T p7 June 30, 2002

SELECTED BOOKS: fiction—*Private Altars*, 1995; *The Season of Lillian Dawes*, 2002; poetry—*The Book of Uncommon Prayer*, 1996

Courtesy of Seven Stories Press

Moss, Stanley D.

June 21, 1925– Poet

Stanley Moss has been writing poetry for almost seven decades, publishing his work in a diverse group of journals, magazines, and newspapers. Many of his poems concern religious themes, such as God's existence and the Bible; others convey longing, anguish, and hope. Moss has collected his work in four volumes: *The Wrong Angel* (1966), *Skull of Adam* (1979), *The Intelligence of Clouds: Poems* (1989), and *Asleep in the Garden* (1997).

Stanley David Moss was born on June 21, 1925 in New York City and grew up on Long Island. His father, Samuel, taught history at Columbia University, in New York City. As a child he traveled with his father during sabbaticals from the university, to Greece, Spain, Italy, and Egypt, among other places. During a visit to Algiers at age nine, Stanley got lost in the city's "red light" district and was accidentally shot in the leg a few weeks later by Greek revolutionaries. "That was just part of the mythology of my childhood," he explained to Joe Ryan for the *Riverdale Press* (November 1, 2001).

During World War II Moss served in the navy, earning a Silver Star and a Purple Heart. After the war he enrolled at Trinity College, in Dublin, Ireland, where he received his bachelor's degree. Moss later obtained a master's degree from Yale University, in New Haven, Connecticut. After graduating from Yale Moss found employment with New Directions, a publisher of avant-garde writing, editing the works of such authors as Ezra Pound, Franz Kafka, and Dylan Thomas.

Moss began a career as an art dealer in 1951, at a gallery on 57th Street in New York City, with no formal art history education. "I have a very good eye," he told Ryan, "and I am able to see things in a dirty painting that others don't see." Five years later he established his own art dealership, Stanley Moss & Co. Moss eventually became well known and respected around the world as a major art dealer. His clients have included the National Gallery of Art, in Washington, D.C.; the Getty Museum, in Los Angeles, California; the Minnesota Institute of Arts; the National Gallery of Canada; and the National Gallery of Australia. Moss acquired a reputation for tracking down important art works for clients by investigating every lead. "If you told me your Aunt Molly had a Leonardo in her apartment in Jackson Heights [Queens], I'd go take a look," he quipped to Lee Rosenbaum for *ARTnews* (March 1979). In the late 1970s Moss discovered a painting by the Italian artist Bernardo Strozzi (1581–1644) that was being sold at a garage sale in New York State. "It was one of 20 paintings there," Moss explained to Rosenbaum. "Nobody knew it was a Strozzi. I identified it, and others agreed." He sold the painting to the De Young Museum, in San Francisco. In 1978 Moss received attention in the press for selling a painting by the 15th-century Italian artist Piero della Francesca to the Louvre museum, in Paris, for $2 million. Despite these high-powered transactions, Moss has said that art dealing bores him, and that he does it only for the money, which allows him to pursue his passion for poetry.

Moss began writing poetry at age seven. He published his first poem in the *Angry Penguin*, an Australian magazine, when he was 18. Since the late 1940s Moss's poetry has been published in

American Poetry Review, *New Republic*, the *New York Times Magazine*, the *New Yorker*, *Poetry*, the *Sewanee Review*, *Tikkun*, and the *Times Literary Supplement*, among other publications. Using the money he made from art dealing, Moss also founded his own publishing company, Sheep Meadow Press, in 1977. Moss explained to Joe Ryan that the purpose of Sheep Meadow Press was to help out friends, "who needed to be published." The company has published books by Stanley Kunitz, Yehuda Amichai, David Ignatow, and many others.

In 1966 *The Wrong Angel*, Moss's first collection, was published; it contains poems that he had written from 1949 until 1966. Reviewing the book for *Poetry* (December 1966), Arthur Freeman observed that the tone of the majority of poems "for the most part is somber and brooding, like self-exile." Freeman asserted that a "defect, however, turns up in a few aspects of technique: the meters of many of these poems . . . are haphazard and distended, the rhymes often oddly, and I think unsuccessfully, experimental . . . and there is almost always a war between Moss and punctuation which augurs ill for the understander." In his review for the *Library Journal* (July 1966), E. H. Walden was more impressed by *The Wrong Angel*. "[Moss's] terse style develops solidity and concreteness in his free verse form and one rereads to grasp obscure meanings," Walden wrote. "Original phrases and thoughts predominate." Moss published a slightly longer edition of *The Wrong Angel*, in 1969.

Moss's next collection, *The Skull of Adam* (1979), also explored religious themes. In the *New York Times Book Review* (September 2, 1979), Charles Molesworth wrote that despite "poems entitled 'Snot' and 'Vomit,' the shocks in the book seem willed, forced. For me a key line was 'If only I could coin nightmares,' where the slack metaphoric verb drained the energy from the longing to know fear." The reviewer asserted that many of the poems in the book "often conclude on a strained or flat note." As an example, Molesworth cited "The Debt," which opens with the line "I owe a debt to the night," and closes with, "It is the night itself that provides / a forgiveness." G. E. Murray praised the collection in his review for *The Nation* (May 19, 1979). "These poems are accessible, simple almost to the point of artlessness, but with surprising rewards," Murray wrote. "Often autobiographical or commemorative, Moss never lapses into confession or sentimentality." Murray concluded that Moss "does what other poets are supposed to do: he puts life into words and gives words a life of their own."

Most reviewers lauded Moss's third book, *The Intelligence of Clouds: Poems* (1989). "Moss intimates a dark view of the universe, seen as the 'greatest of all crap shoots, / . . . and darkness was the big winner,'" Barbara Hoffert observed in her review for the *Library Journal* (May 15, 1989). "But to find the poems themselves dark is mistaken; they are luminous if complex, not so much visually as verbally striking." Hoffert described Moss as "a poet of great perceptiveness; his intelligence and dignity set him far above the crowd." Reviewing the book for *Poetry* (August 1989), Robert B. Shaw asserted that "Stanley Moss's poetry is ambitious in its range of cultural allusion as well as simply in the geography it covers. His new poems move from New York to the near East, from Germany and Italy to Japan and China." Shaw added that in "many fine poems in this book, Moss manages to sustain [a] haunting simplicity of statement, bittersweet in image and tone."

In 1997 Moss published his fourth book, *Asleep in the Garden: New and Selected Poems*, which included poems from his previous three volumes. A critic for the *Virginia Quarterly Review* (Summer 1998) praised the collection, writing, "Moss gives the impression of having meditated for a long time over each poem, crafting them with an eye on readers as well as his own experience, which he conveys with a strength and power that is odd in a poetry so unconfessional." Based on his understanding of most of the poems, the reviewer concluded that Moss "is an unbeliever who finds the observation of the world and the writing about it a powerful religious experience. . . . Still, he identifies especially with religious artists and the symbols they used—the Virgin [Mary], the rainbow, the poor, mourning—as he writes about his creative process in a refreshingly unselfconscious way." Writing in *Booklist* (November 15, 1997), Donna Seaman asserted that "Moss' voice echoes the boom of the Old Testament, the fluty trill of Greek mythology, and the gongs of Chinese rituals as he writes about love, nature, war, oppression, and the miracle of language. He addresses the God of the Jews, of the Christians, and of the Muslims with awe and familiarity, and chants to lesser gods of his own invention, such as the 'God of paper and writing,' with jocosity and gratitude." Seaman concluded that in "every surprising poem, every song to life, beautiful life, Moss, by turns giddy and sorrowful, expresses a sacred sensuality and an earthy holiness."

Stanley Moss has edited César Vallejo's *Trilce* (1992), *Interviews and Encounters with Stanley Kunitz* (1993), *The Sheep Meadow Anthology* (1999), and *To Stanley Kunitz With Love* (2001). In 1967 he received a Rockefeller Foundation grant. In 2003 Moss is scheduled to publish "A history of Color: New and Gathered Poems."

Stanley Moss's first marriage ended in divorce, in 1960. He is now married to Jane Zech, a sociologist, and has two sons. Moss resides in the Riverdale section of the North Bronx, in a 150-year-old villa overlooking the Hudson River. He spends as many as 20 hours a day reading and writing poetry.
—D. C.

SUGGESTED READING: *ARTnews* p168+ Mar. 1979; *Booklist* p538 Nov. 15, 1997; *Library Journal* p3443 July 1966, p72 May 15, 1989; New York Times C p21 Mar. 17, 1978; *New York Times Book Review* p14 Sep. 2, 1979; *Poetry* p191 Dec. 1966, p285 Aug. 1989; *Riverdale Press A* p1+ Nov. 1, 2001, with photo; *Virginia Quarterly Review* p103 Summer 1998

SELECTED BOOKS: poetry—*The Wrong Angel*, 1966; *Skull of Adam*, 1979; *The Intelligence of Clouds: Poems*, 1989; *Asleep in the Garden: New and Selected Poems*, 1997; as editor—*Trilce* (by César Vallejo), 1992; *Interviews and Encounters with Stanley Kunitz*, 1993; *The Sheep Meadow Anthology*, 1999; *To Stanley Kunitz With Love*, 2001

Courtesy of the *Times Literary Supplement*

Mount, Ferdinand

July 2, 1939– Novelist; journalist

The British political commentator, policy maker, and novelist Ferdinand Mount began his writing career with the novel *Very Like a Whale* (1967). He went on to produce an examination of political life in Britain, *The Theatre of Politics* (1973), before embarking on two novel series: the elegiac *A Chronicle of Modern Twilight*, featuring the character Gus, whose life in some ways parallels that of Mount; and *Tales of History and Imagination*. Mount's other nonfiction books include The *Subversive Family: An Alternative History of Love and Marriage* (1982). In 1991 he became the editor of the *Times Literary Supplement*.

Ferdinand Mount sent the following statement to *World Authors 1995-2000*: "I was born in Hampstead, London, on July 2, 1939, but was immediately transported to a small village on Salisbury Plain, not far from Stonehenge, where I spent all my childhood and youth. My father was an amateur steeplechase jockey who had been invalided out of the Commandos. He was a man of sensitivity and charm, averse to work but not to drink. He was a great influence on me, and something of him is celebrated in my second novel *The Man Who Rode Ampersand*. I did not go to school until I was nearly nine years old. My mother—laconic, highly intelligent and somewhat recessive—taught me most things. She died of cancer when I was 17. After being educated on scholarships at Eton and Oxford, I scraped a living as a journalist, with some hazy view of a political career. This led nowhere much, except to becoming a political columnist on the *Spectator* and later on the *Times* and *Daily Telegraph*. My only active participation in public life was as head of Mrs. Thatcher's Policy Unit between 1982 and 1984. After this, a brief spell as literary editor of the *Spectator* was followed a few years later by a 10-year stint as editor of the *Times Literary Supplement* (1991–). I began to write novels in the late 1960s. They have gradually divided into two streams: an occasional series of novels of modern life covering the latter half of the 20th century and grouped under the title *A Chronicle of Modern Twilight*; these comprise so far *The Man Who Rode Ampersand* (1975); *The Selkirk Strip* (1987); *Of Love and Asthma* (1991), which won the 1992 Hawthornden Prize; *The Liquidator* (1995); and *Fairness* (2001). I have also written two *Tales of History and Imagination*: *Umbrella* (1994) and *Jem (and Sam)* (1998); and three works of nonfiction: *The Theatre of Politics* (1972), *The Subversive Family* (1982), and *The British Constitution Now* (1992).

"Any novel worth reading creates a sort of moral poetry, by which I mean that the questions of human choice and of how life is to be lived are intrinsic to it. Of course, a satisfying novel will include all sort of other things—vivid imagery, funny and touching and disgusting scenes, memorable characters— but without a moral liveliness running throughout the book it will be empty. Though a good novelist (and a bad one, too) will have his own signature—quirks of grammar or syntax, preferred flights of fancy, characteristic blind spots— the end product will be mere tinkling on a xylophone unless it exhibits some human connection. A novel is not like a painting or a piece of music; it's not even like a poem. The relation to life is different. Music's raw material is resonance and the intervals between notes; the novel's material is motivation and the intervals between people. Poetry can deal in single moments, the effect of light upon water or window sills; but novels must deal in consecutive moments and the effect of people upon one another. It is a social and hence, in some measure, a narrative art, because what people do or don't do to one another has consequences which must be followed through. However cunningly disguised, there has to be a story in there somewhere. To get rid of the consequences and let your text float freely, arbitrary and unconstrained by time, is to discard what is most interesting. I am with Dickens and Evelyn Waugh, against Sterne and William Burroughs."

The journalist and novelist was born William Robert Ferdinand Mount, the son of Lady Julia Pakenham Mount and Robert Francis Mount. His mother was the daughter of the Earl of Longford, and Mount himself inherited a baronetcy from his uncle. He has never used the title.

In the *National Interest* (No. 64, on-line) Mount wrote about his stint, in the winter of 1962–63, as "assistant courier and general dogsbody [helper] to Selwyn Lloyd." Lloyd had been chancellor of the Exchequer under Prime Minister Harold Macmillan but was relieved of his duties during an episode known as the Night of the Long Knives, a misguided attempt by Macmillan to regain his popularity. Lloyd was mollified by getting an assignment to find out what was ailing the Conservative Party. "We traveled the length and breadth of England and Wales," Mount wrote. "To a young man from the soft south of England who knew only the gentle undulations of Salisbury Plain and the antique serenity of Eton and Oxford, this odyssey was an education. In those narrow rain-swept valleys of Lancashire and Yorkshire, it seemed as though nothing much had happened since the first Industrial Revolution." Mount saw derelict factories and interviewed owners and managers of dying industries. He predicted the further decline of the old industrial base in England.

After the publication of his first novel, *Very Like a Whale* (1967), he turned to nonfiction with *The Theatre of Politics*, in 1973. Mount held that politics is "not a battle of interests, or a quest for truth, or a voyage of progress it was an aesthetic performance, to captivate an audience," according to the political philosopher Perry Anderson, writing in the *London Review of Books* (October 22, 1992). "But it was not high theatre. . . . It was more like commercial theatre, the drama of the boulevards that plays to our emotions or embarrassments—Rattigan rather than Racine." Mount continued his elegiac (rather than nostalgic) tone in his *Chronicle of Modern Twilight*. *The Man Who Rode Ampersand* (1975), the first novel in that series, is the story of an amateur jockey who rode Ampersand, a horse that won the Gold Cup. His decline is chronicled by his son, Aldous—known as Gus—a somewhat autobiographical character who reappears in Mount's fiction. As the father "falls further into his cups, his son, Aldous, watches on with amused, occasionally shocked, detachment," Isabel Montgomery wrote in the *Guardian* (March 24, 2001). "There is nothing attention-grabbing about Mount's style, but that is its dependable charm." The second novel in the series, *The Selkirk Strip*, was published in 1987.

After another novel, *The Clique* (1978), Mount produced *The Subversive Family: An Alternative History of Love and Marriage* in 1982. Mount contended that the nuclear family, contrary to received modern opinion, has always been the basis of human social organization, and that the mutual support provided by its members is not a modern innovation. The word "subversive" in the title refers to Mount's theory that the family works against, rather than in conjunction with, the institutions of church and state, in that it is self- directed and resistant to outside interference. The book produced a storm of controversy, particularly in the United States (where it appeared 10 years after its British publication), because its depiction of the nuclear family—father, mother, and children conceived out of love—as the most "natural" and oldest form of social organization went against the mores of contemporary life, in which single-parent families abound. Mount cited diary entries, letters, and court documents to support his belief that the family, rather than evolving from a primitive to a more "advanced" state, has been based on the enduring values of love and affection—rather than material gain—throughout history. The reviewer for the *Christian Century* (April 7, 1993) observed that when it was published in Britain, *The Subversive Family* "enraged the Marxists, irritated many Catholics, jolted those nostalgic about the 'traditional family' and upset those who hoped the book would jettison the very idea of the family. . . . Mount is a creative demythologizer, and in the end . . . a true supporter of the fallible marriage and family."

On the other hand, Mount did not take a sentimental view of the family. According to Ann Hulbert, writing in the *New Republic* (August 16, 1993), Mount "celebrates the 'selfish and materialistic, inward-looking' nature of the institution. Passion, pride, possessiveness, jealousy, narcissism, competition, acquisitiveness—the typical roster of anti-family values—are all encompassed by Mount's depiction of family life as an invigoratingly strenuous emotional endeavor that makes 'other experiences, both pleasant and unpleasant, seem a little tame and bloodless.'" Hulbert concluded that "Mount's . . . view . . . suggests that the alternative to piety about the nuclear family doesn't have to be earnest neutrality about all variations on it. . . . If much of family life is not fulfilling in the most elevated terms, plenty of it is satisfying in some of the most immediate and time-bound ways."

The third novel of Mount's *Chronicle of Modern Twilight* series was *Of Love and Asthma*, published in 1991. That book was followed by the nonfiction work *The British Constitution Now* (1992). The so-called constitution in England, Mount observed, is a patchwork of laws, customs, treaties, and historic accommodations to prevailing conditions. In Mount's lifetime there has been a groundswell of demand for a written constitution, such as the United States and many other nations of the world have. One reason given by Mount for this demand was that the majority party in Parliament, led by the prime minister, can "force through any measure . . . without fear of modification or delay," as Mount said in a lecture ("The Recovery of the Constitution," May 11, 1992). He decried the fact that "exactly the same procedure is gone through, regardless of whether the measure is some profound constitutional alteration or the Hairdressing (Scotland) Amendment Bill." He added, "Defenders of the status quo will argue that this system has served us well over the centuries, that our parliamentary traditions have combined stability and flexibility and that we should not cast away in a minute what has taken generations to build. . . . I am not insensible to this line of argument. But it has to be said that the status quo is not what it was." Mount called for reform, such as a separate legislative assembly for Scotland and a Supreme Court to decide on the appropriateness of laws.

"'Constitutional theorists who wish to hold our attention must charm as well as instruct; this is not so, I think, in other countries,' writes Ferdinand Mount," as Perry Anderson noted in the London Review of Books (October 22, 1992). "Who better to illustrate the claim. Few figures in the world of English letters possess such a combination of credentials. . . . Mount's account of the framework of the United Kingdom, and what repair it may call for, has already beguiled readers across the political spectrum." Anderson went on, however, to counter the book's premise, suggesting that Mount was being disingenuous in seeming to advocate more checks and balances in the government. Citing Mount's praise of certain practices in the higher circles of British power, Anderson noted, "At every point, the imperatives are centralised authority, efficacy, secrecy. These are the values Mount served then and upholds today." Anderson allowed, however, that whatever "one's attitude towards [those values], his report of their machinery is compelling."

The title of Mount's 1995 novel, *The Liquidator*, refers to two characters in the book. One liquidator is a priest of the Maronite rite in Lebanon at the beginning of the 20th century. His job involves faking a miracle, which makes it appear as though oil is running out of St. Mary Magdalene's tomb on her feast day. The second liquidator is the priest's descendant, who presides over the liquidation of bankrupt companies. To some, liquidation means that they are freed of past responsibilities and can begin again; to others it is a destructive end to the past and its traditions. The novel's complicated plot involves terrorists in Lebanon, the strange behavior of the son of the last man hanged in England, who attempts to exact vengeance on everyone who watched his father's execution, and the comical mores of musical producers and suburban tennis-club members. "The shadowy narrator attempts to supply motive, to find meaning and continuity, but the characters with whom he is obsessed re-make themselves with no feeling for the past," Sean French noted in the (London) *Times* (September 21, 1995). The characters "behave arbitrarily, revealing attributes of which we, and the narrator, were unaware. . . . Everything we might assume to give continuity to our existence—family names, property, relationships, institutions, memory—proves fallible and temporary. Mount gives a brief nod to *The Satanic Verses* and he uses the hallucinatory metamorphism of that book, but in a deliberately humdrum way. . . . There are considerable risks in writing a novel founded on arbitrariness and rootlessness, with a deliberately dour narrator. . . . [T]his novel itself is an almost reckless example of the temporariness that is its subject. . . . isn't it peculiar that the sequence's name, *A Chronicle of Modern Twilight*, is a wry, self-deprecating reference to another novel sequence, Henry Williamson's *Chronicle of Ancient Sunlight*, which is virtually forgotten and unobtainable? Mount's account of affectlessness is surprisingly effective, but is he making a further, ironic point by discouraging people from reading it?"

The first of Mount's *Tales of History and Imagination*, *Umbrella: A Pacific Tale*, appeared in 1994. The next, *Jem (and Sam): A Revenger's Tale*, was published in 1998. The eponymous Sam is Samuel Pepys, who occasionally mentioned in his famous diaries of the 17th century a drinking companion named Jeremiah Mount (known as Jem)—who may or may not have been an ancestor of the author. Jem becomes a man on the make in 17th-century London, competing with the successful political career of Pepys, sleeping with the duchess of Albemarle, and becoming chamberlain to General Monck. He decides to keep a diary "to tell the world the aspect of great matters from the underside"—unaware that Pepys is doing the same. The *Publishers Weekly* (June 14, 1999) reviewer called Jem "a sort of Salieri to Pepys's Mozart," who "manages to be always on the fringe of things, giving the reader a view, from the cheap seats, of historic events such as the Great Fire of London and the plague."

"It is a sign of Ferdinand Mount's extraordinary gifts that one is tempted to review the novel as if it were a genuine autobiography, " Michael Upchurch wrote in the *New York Times Book Review* (July 18, 1999). "Mount is careful to include salient passages from Pepys's diaries, where they apply, providing all the familiarity with the actual source that's needed to enjoy the novel. . . . The historical detail feels rich and accurate, seamlessly integrated into the text. . . . The prime attraction is Jem himself, ever on the move from one adventure to another. . . . In fact, Jem in emphasizing how failure opens our eyes to the real nature of the world, almost makes us feel we've had the better of Sam. The truth is we are most of us Jems—creatures of accident, poor judgment, muddled feeling. . . ."

In *Fairness*, published in 2001, Mount returned to his *Chronicle of Modern Twilight* and its central character and narrator, Gus. As a teenager in the 1960s, working as a tutor for the children of a rich American family in France, Gus meets Helen, a nanny for some Iranian children. He spends the next two decades pursuing Helen fruitlessly, while also becoming a civil servant who works in intelligence. "Those . . . 20 years are packed with surprises that touch one or both of them, love affairs, marriages, shady business deals, political strikes, sudden death, pedophilia and six suicide attempts (only two successful)," Michael Dirda wrote in the *Washington Post Book World* (July 29, 2001). Dirda termed the novel "subtle and amusing" and praised the minor characters, whom he found to be "as vivid as carnival grotesques, as memorable as Chaucer's Canterbury pilgrims." Michael Gorra, the *New York Times Book Review* (August 19, 2001) critic, also found in *Fairness* "more eccentric characters than you'll find in any two British sitcoms combined, and some wonderfully crack-brained schemes. . . . Best of all are the precisely observant throwaway lines that belie without quite undercutting Gus's rather colorless self-presentation." Nevertheless, Gorra had the complaint that "*Fairness* is a book of scenes and sketches that, while amusing, don't build to anything much."

Christopher Hitchens, in the *Atlantic Monthly* (August 2001), argued that Mount was one of the novelists who "have the ability to narrow the divide between youth and maturity and to make both states . . . real and immediate." Hitchens appreciated Mount's historic sense: "In a few sentences Mount can evoke the Britain of the 1960s and 1970s, the Thatcher years, and the onset of the present. . . . The Englishness of it all is extraordinary; even when Gus goes to America in Her Majesty's service, he encounters only grotesques and caricatures." He observed that "the word 'fair' is an ancient word for 'beautiful.' In our day it has acquired a second relationship, with the banal, as in 'fairly good,' 'fair enough.' The abyss between these meanings is the one that swallows up poor Aldous."

Although Mount has written novels in an elegiac tone, he has, through his own engaged life and through works that deal with major questions of late 20th century, given the lie to the sense of being a passive observer of the passage of time.

—S. Y.

SUGGESTED READING: *Atlantic Monthly* (on-line) Aug. 2001; *Christian Century* p379 Apr. 7, 1993; *Guardian* (on-line) Mar. 24, 2001; *National Interest*, No. 64 (on-line); *New Republic* p26+ Aug. 16, 1993; *New York Times Book Review* (on-line) July 18, 1999, Aug. 19 2001; *Publishers Weekly* p48 June 14, 1999; *Washington Post Book World* p15 July 29, 2001

SELECTED BOOKS: fiction—*Very Like a Whale*, 1967; *The Man Who Rode Ampersand*, 1975; *The Selkirk Strip*, 1987; *Of Love and Asthma*, 1991; *Umbrella*, 1994; *The Liquidator*, 1995; *Jem (and Sam)*, 1998; *Fairness*, 2001; nonfiction—*The Theatre of Politics*, 1972; *The Subversive Family*, 1982; *The British Constitution Now*, 1992; as editor—*The Inquiring Eye: The Writings of David Watt*, 1988

Courtesy of Tom Graves

Muller, Marcia

Sep. 28, 1944– Mystery writer

Marcia Muller's San Francisco private eye, Sharon McCone, is as appealing as a fictional female detective can get. Tough, beautiful, resourceful, and packing serious heat (she carries a .357 Magnum handgun), McCone has been on the case for more than two decades, beginning with *Edwin of the Iron Shoes* in 1977. Unlike other fictional private investigators—male and female—who have come before her, McCone ages, develops intricate relationships, and grows as a character. "Sharon is like a real person to me," Muller told Dulcy Brainard in a interview for *Publishers Weekly* (August 8, 1994). "I'm not tired of her because I keep making changes in her life and her circumstances."

Marcia Muller was born on September 28, 1944 in Detroit, Michigan, to Henry J. Muller, a marketing executive, and the former Kathryn Minke. In a statement submitted to *World Authors*, the author discusses her life and motivations as a crime novelist: "I grew up in a suburb of Detroit, Michigan, in a houseful of books, with a father who was a great storyteller. After graduating from the children's classics and popular series, I was given free run of my parents' library. My idea of a good time was an afternoon with a book, and my heroes were authors. In retrospect, I realize that much of my reading was for escape: my siblings were much older than I and, at home, I was the only child in a family of adults; at school, I was an introvert among extroverts. At age twelve I attempted to follow in my heroes' footsteps and wrote—on my Tom Thumb typewriter—a one hundred-page 'novel' about my dog, complete with very bad illustrations.

"My literary aspirations were derailed in my teens by the usual things—boys, clothes, and cars—until, in my junior year at the University of Michigan, I took a creative writing course. At its conclusion the instructor, a failed novelist, informed me that I would never be a writer because I had nothing to say. Of course I hadn't! I was a very sheltered and naive nineteen-year-old. But my instructor's pronouncement was sufficiently discouraging that I switched course and eventually earned a master's degree in journalism. It was not a good career move: rather than report the facts, I tended to embellish my stories; it seemed the things I could make up were much more compelling than reality. Unfortunately, a number of editors didn't see it that way, and I rapidly became unemployable.

"A move to California, the state which provides the setting for most of my work, proved an inspiration, and I again began experimenting with fiction, but I lacked focus until I happened upon the works of Raymond Chandler and Ross Macdonald, fell in love with the crime novel, and recognized it as a vehicle for the kinds of issues I wanted to explore. After several abortive starts, my first novel, *Edwin of the Iron Shoes*, emerged from an assignment in a writers' workshop, and sold to the first editor who looked at it. Although it was a moderate success, I was unable to sell another word for the next four years—possibly due to what my present agent calls my 'spectacularly passive approach' to the business aspects of my career.

"I continued to write, however, and produced two more manuscripts chronicling the life and times of the heroine of my first novel, San Francisco private investigator Sharon McCone. Eventually my future husband and collaborator, crime writer Bill Pronzini, asked to see my manuscripts and introduced me to several editors; one of them, at a house which had previously turned down my efforts, bought both, and my career was back on track.

"It wasn't until I'd been writing for a number of years that I realized what had drawn me to the crime novel: a series of violent events occurring during my teens and young adulthood. A teacher at my junior high school was fatally stabbed by her husband. My dentist shot and killed his wife and son. A next-door neighbor in my college dormitory took her own life. The war in Vietnam heated up, and friends died violently. For me, the crime novel is a way of working out these and subsequent issues, and although I've written in different forms—nonfiction, mainstream, and western—I inevitably come back to the exploration of why human beings commit such acts and what their effects are on others."

When Muller began writing about Sharon McCone, there weren't many female detectives in fiction for her to emulate. "There were a few perfectly horrible female private-eye novels written by men," Muller remarked to Dulcy Brainard. "But the women were just men in drag, either obnoxiously aggressive or too clinging for words." Muller has been quick to point out that although she is credited with being the first American woman to publish a novel featuring a strong, confident female detective, Sue Grafton and Sara Paretsky, fellow novelists, were right on her heels.

When Muller started working on the first Sharon McCone story, in 1972, she knew that she did not want McCone to be a clone of herself. As she noted in an article for the *Writer* (May 1997): "I therefore began building McCone's character by giving her a background as different from mine as I could make it. She is a native Californian; I am not. She comes from a large blue-collar family; I do not. She put herself through the University of California at Berkeley by working as a security guard; I was supported by my parents during my six years at the University of Michigan. And Sharon has exotic Native American features and long black hair, is enviably tall and slender, and can eat whatever she likes without gaining weight. Since I don't possess such qualities, I wanted to spend time with a character who did." (McCone's name came from a combination of the author's college roommate's name, Sharon, and that of John McCone, the former head of the CIA.)

Muller fleshed out the character by giving her parents and siblings, as well as political opinions and religious beliefs. She populated McCone's world with a variety of interesting secondary characters and allowed all the characters to age and develop throughout the years. "McCone," Muller noted in an interview with *St. James' Guide to Crime and Mystery Writers* (1996), "is a woman with day-to-day problems and a fully developed personal life, who must deal with the increasingly complex pressures and issues posed by modern society."

Muller's first McCone manuscript was never published. She has since noted in interviews that it is so bad she keeps it locked up and has left instructions to have it burned in the event of her death. However, each of her subsequent efforts has received great praise from fans and critics alike. In a review of the 2002 McCone novel *Dead Midnight* for the *Post and Courier* (August 18, 2002), Christine W. Randall proclaimed: "Muller began publishing the McCone series back in 1977 and has managed to keep her heroine fresh and entertaining in the more than 20 novels since then. Through the years, McCone has uncovered secrets in her own family tree, learned to fly a plane and started her own agency. This latest case brings her up to speed on computer and Internet technology without feeling forced or manipulative. And the subplots involving her family, friends and employees add depth to the stories. Let's hope Muller keeps her investigator on the trail for another 25 years."

In addition to the McCone mysteries, Muller has published three novels—*The Tree of Death* (1983); *The Legend of the Slain Soldiers* (1985); and, with Bill Pronzini, *Beyond the Grave* (1986)—featuring Elena Oliverez, a curator at the Museum of Mexican Arts, in California. Unlike Sharon McCone, Elena has no desire to do detective work; she does so only because she needs to prove that she is innocent of her boss's murder. Muller is also the author of the Johanna Stark mysteries: *The Cavalier in White* (1986), *There Hangs the Knife* (1988), and *Dark Star* (1989); the novels' protagonist is a partner in a security firm in San Francisco. She has written two non-series novels as well. The first, *The Lighthouse: A Novel of Terror* (1987), was co-authored by Bill Pronzini and concerns a murder in a small Oregon town. *Point Deception* (2001) features Rhoda Swift, a California deputy sheriff tormented by a mass murder committed in her town more than a decade before. "Muller's intricate plotting and strong narrative flow have won a dedicated fan base for her Sharon McCone series, and both qualities are on full display here," Jane Adams wrote in a review for the Amazon Bookseller's Web site. "A terrific read from a master of the genre, *Point Deception* is Muller at her best."

Widely anthologized herself, Muller has also edited or co-edited (with Bill Pronzini) numerous anthologies, including *The Web She Weaves: An Anthology of Mystery and Suspense Stories by Women* (1983), *Chapter and Hearse* (1985), and *Detective Duos* (1997). She has received a great number of honors and awards for her work, including the 1989 American Mystery Award for *The Shape of Dread*, the 1991 Shamus Award from the Private Eye Writers of America, the 1993 Private Eye Writers of America Life Achievement Award, and two Anthony Boucher Awards.

In 1966 Marcia Muller received a bachelor's degree in English from the University of Michigan, and in 1971 she earned a master's degree in journalism. Her first marriage lasted from 1966 to 1981; in 1992 she married Bill Pronzini.

—C. M.

SUGGESTED READING: *Kirkus Reviews* p838 June 1, 1997; *Post and Courier* E p3 Aug. 18, 2002; *Publishers Weekly* p361+ Aug. 8, 1994; *Writer* p7+ May 1997

SELECTED BOOKS: Sharon McCone mysteries—*Edwin of the Iron Shoes*, 1977; *Ask the Cards a Question*, 1982; *The Cheshire Cat's Eye*, 1983; *Games to Keep the Dark Away*, 1984; *Leave a Message for Willie*, 1984; *There's Nothing To Be Afraid Of*, 1985; *Eye of the Storm*, 1988; *There's Something in a Sunday*, 1989; *The Shape of Dread*, 1989; *Trophies and Dead Things*, 1990; *Where Echoes Live*, 1991; *Pennies on a Dead Woman's Eyes*, 1992; *Wolf in the Shadows*, 1993; *Till the Butchers Cut Him Down*, 1994; *A Wild and Lonely Place*, 1995; *The McCone Files*, 1995; *The Broken Promise Land*, 1996; *Both Ends of the Night*, 1997; *While Other People Sleep*, 1998; *McCone and Friends*, 1999; *A Walk Through Fire*, 1999; *Listen to the Silence*, 2000; *Dead Midnight*, 2002; Elena Oliverez mysteries—*The Tree of Death*, 1983; *The Legend of the Slain Soldiers*, 1985; *Beyond the Grave* (with Bill Pronzini), 1986; Joanna Stark mysteries—*The Cavalier in White*, 1986; *There Hangs the Knife*, 1988; *Dark Star*, 1989; non-series novels—*The Lighthouse: A Novel of Terror* (with Bill Pronzini), 1987; *Point Deception*, 2001

Murray, Yxta Maya

(EEK-sta)

1968(?)– Novelist; lawyer

By her late 20s Yxta Maya Murray had successfully navigated law school, become an associate professor of law, and published her first novel, *Locas*. About two Latina women who take divergent routes to find their own places as women in a gang society, *Locas* reveals Murray's preoccupation with Latino identity. "As a lawyer interested in Latino rights," she explained to David L. Ulin for the *Los Angeles Times* (November 13, 1997), "I spend a lot of time thinking about what it means to be Latino, female, legal." Her recent novel, *The Conquest* (2002), explores the concept of identity through an adroitly bifurcated narrative, moving between a present-day story about a rare book restorer in Los Angeles and a 16th-century Spanish manuscript about a young Aztec princess who was kidnaped by the explorer Hernán Cortés and taken to Italy. The *Los Angeles Times* named *The Conquest* among the best books of 2002. Murray has also contributed articles on Latino culture to periodicals as diverse as *Buzz*, *Glamour*, *North American Review*, and *ZYZZYVA*. She was a finalist for the 1996 National Magazine Award for fiction and received a Whiting Award for literature in 1999.

Yxta Maya Murray was born in Long Beach, California, in about 1968, the daughter of a Los Angeles schoolteacher. Living in an area where the blue-eyed blonde is the standard for beauty, Murray's Latino family made "no secret of their admiration for Anglo looks," as she wrote in an essay for *Glamour* (October 1996). She explained, "My eyes have always been the same color—brown with a few dots of green—but year by year my mother and grandmother claim my eyes are lightening. 'Ay, no, they're greener, *linda!*' is what I hear each Christmas, and as a teenager I would dream of the day when my eyes' true emerald beauty would emerge. I eventually grew out of this. My eyes can turn gold or hazel, but at bottom they are a rich, felicitous Mexican brown."

Murray graduated cum laude with a bachelor's degree from the University of California at Los Angeles. She then earned a doctorate in law with distinction from Stanford University. When she was a third-year student there, an article of hers on employee liability was published in the *Stanford Law Review* (January 1993). Entitled "Employer Liability After *Johnson Controls*: A No-Fault Situation," it offers an overview of legal opinion about Title VII of the Civil Rights Act of 1964 and how tort law might be applied to punish employees who subjected their pregnant female workers and their fetuses to dangerous levels of lead. Murray concluded that "employee liability is not the answer, but the need for fetal redress remains."

In 1995 she joined the faculty of Loyola Law School, in Los Angeles, where she teaches courses in the administration of criminal justice, feminist jurisprudence, sexual orientation and the law, and sentencing. A year later she recalled in her essay for *Glamour* the dichotomies Latinas face. "Most of the Latinas I know want to celebrate their own version of beauty, but they often feel a lingering ambivalence about whether it's better to assimilate. One reason they are tempted to blend in is that Latinas in the United States have been stereotyped in a variety of ways—as the timid housekeeper, the lazy welfare mother, the sexual spitfire—and their looks can unintentionally promote these prejudicial images." Murray, too, fell into this trap. When she began her own round of job interviews, she'd remind herself, "Blot your lipstick, girl. . . . Spitfires may get dates, but they don't get into law firms."

On top of her success in the worlds of law and academe, Murray nurtured an interest in literature and creative writing. She published short fiction in several magazines and contributed remarks to a symposium on L.A. literature organized by the *Los Angeles Times*. "Los Angeles is as haunted as Flannery O'Connor's South and Nathaniel Hawthorne's Salem," she was quoted as saying in the *Los Angeles Times* (April 25, 1999). "We have old, old ghosts here, as well as recent blood-guilts and burnings. . . . Los Angeles is a place of ancient themes—you can imagine dark Cleopatra planning intrigues here, if not draped in silk and shouting orders from inside the glittering walls of the Getty [Museum], then at least flashing her violet eyes and purring promises to Richard Burton in front of movie cameras and an expensive director." Murray went on to explain that her vision of L.A. literature is epitomized by "a brown-skinned woman at a Wilshire bus stop, which has a poster of [actresses Greta] Garbo or [Gwyneth] Paltrow beaming behind thick, graffiti-scarred plastic." This prototypical woman, she continued, is one who's "got that ageless anger, but she's also created out of the city you see outside your window right now, with its heat, noise, dread, and lunatic glamour." Murray selected four books to represent her "Los Angeles literature" list: Mona Simpson's *Anywhere But Here*, Michele Serros's *Chicana Falsa*, Hector Tobar's *The Tattooed Soldier*, and Robert Penn Warren's *All the King's Men*, the last for its "enchanting description" of her hometown, Long Beach.

In 1997 Grove Press published Murray's first novel, *Locas*, a quick-paced, slice-of-life portrayal of gang life in East Los Angeles as narrated in the first person, in alternating chapters, by Lucía and Cecilia. The novel traces their development over a 17-year period, from 1980 to 1997. Lucía is determined to smash gender stereotypes by wresting power from her boyfriend, Manny, the leader of the gang the Lobos, while Cecilia, Manny's adoring younger sister, hopes to find self respect as a *mamacita*, a single mother. While Lucía adopts an increasingly swaggering, menacing vernacular, Cecilia crafts a voice out of her own desperation. Murray told David L. Ulin that *Locas* was inspired in part by contemporary events. "I was watching a news report on the beating of undocumented immigrants in Riverside, and somehow I tripped up on this one voice." An anonymous reviewer for *Publishers Weekly* (March 3, 1997) opined that both narrators voices are "insistent, unvarnished, in-your-face tough." While most reviewers praised the book, Celeste Fremon, who has written about life in the *barrios* of East Los Angeles, wrote a mixed review for the *Los Angeles Times* (June 15, 1997). "With *Locas* . . . one ignores the cultural context into which the book arrives only at one's peril. Imagine publishing a novel that depicts Native Americans as pitiless savages during the Indian-hating 1850s. Such a book, no matter how skillfully crafted, could not help but be a part of the problem. As a coming-of-age fable, Murray's story is passionate, poetic, and, in so many ways, dazzling, but as a window into real life, it's a saddening misstep."

Grove Press published Murray's second novel, *What It Takes to Get to Vegas*, in 1999. Like *Locas*, this book draws on the Hispanic street culture of Los Angeles and centers on a young woman who wants more for herself. When Rita Zapata is branded a slut by her peers, she decides to do all she can to live up to the sobriquet. She eventually hitches her wagon to the rising star of a Mexican-born boxer named Billy Navarro, who wins money and fame in a title bout in Las Vegas. Rita's success is short-lived, however, for Billy leaves her for another woman and Rita's neighborhood is destroyed by rioting. Reviewing the novel for *Publishers Weekly* (June 28, 1999), Sybil S. Steinberg wrote: "The novel is populated by colorful, richly drawn characters who tell stories so fascinating that at times they detract from the narrative's focus, but nothing matches Rita's own fabrications. Everything she gains, she attains by deceit, and Murray never spells out a moral position, leaving it for the reader to decide whether Rita has taken responsibility for her actions and come to any true understanding of herself." Most critics, however, remained mixed in their assessments of the book, appreciating the fine writing but deploring the unimaginative plot. In her review for the *New York Times* (October 3,

1999), Barbara Sutton praised Murray's skill at characterization, writing that "despite the selfishness behind Rita's repeated missteps, we're touched by how ignorantly she desires the consumer goods that she associates with respectability—from custom-interior Cadillacs to the complimentary bottles of fancy shampoo you get in your room at Caesars Palace." But, Sutton continued, "After a while . . . Rita's upbeat though fated-for-deflation epiphanies become taxing, as does the incongruity of street language spiked with more 'literary' metaphors."

In *The Conquest* 32-year-old Sara Rosario Gonzales is a rare book restorer for the Getty Museum, in Los Angeles. Unable to commit to her long-term boyfriend, a Marine captain named Karl Sullivan, she risks losing him to another woman. While trying to win him back, she becomes captivated with a 16th-century manuscript that describes the life of an Aztec princess who was captured by Cortés and brought to Rome as a present for the Pope. Dubbed Helen by the Italians for her beauty, she performs as a juggler to gain favor with her captors. Soon she falls in with the painter Titian, for whom she serves as both model and lover, all the while concealing her true objective—to kill the Holy Roman Emperor Charles V and avenge the destruction of her people. Although scholars unanimously believe the manuscript, titled "The Conquest," to be the fanciful work of a Spanish monk, Sara becomes convinced that Helen is in fact the true author. The story of Helen's exploits alternates with Sara's attempts to establish the identity of the manuscript's author and her romantic maneuvering to regain Karl's affections.

Many critics praised *The Conquest* as a major step forward for Murray. As Salvador Carrasco noted in a review for the *Los Angeles Times* (October 27, 2002), *The Conquest* finds Murray "creating a hybrid garden of literary intricacies that might have amused even Jorge Luis Borges. . . . *The Conquest* tackles the excruciating question of how to redress loss, whether it be in the form of a 500-year-old conquest that has deprived the indigenous people of the universe as they knew it, the loss of a lover or the gradual erosion of one's cultural identity in the modern world." According to Ariel Swartly, writing for the *Los Angeles Magazine* (November 1, 2002), "*The Conquest* is a rarity among novels: philosophical and amorous, serious and deliciously entertaining. . . . For the first time Murray is writing fiction in a voice that's close to her own—educated, professional, analytical."

In her articles that have appeared in such publications as *Buzz*, *Glamour*, *North American Review*, and *ZYZZYVA*, Murray has written about Latino identity issues and pop culture, such as the Latina quest for a more Anglo appearance (achieved through the application of cosmetics). Murray has also tackled civil-rights issues. She contributed an article entitled "Merit-Teaching" to a symposium titled "The Meanings of Merit: Affirmative Action and the California Civil Rights Initiative."

Murray has a simple writing philosophy. "A person who really wants to write," she told David L. Ulin, "will just write for the joy of it and stop worrying about the other stuff. Although it's not great for writers to toil in obscurity, it can open a space for creativity and free up the imagination."
—E. M.

SUGGESTED READING: *Glamour* p90 Oct. 1996, with photo; *Hispanic* p94 Sep. 1997, with photo; *Los Angeles Magazine* p134 Nov. 1, 2002; *Los Angeles Times* E p3 Nov. 13, 1997, R p2 Oct. 27, 2002; *New York Times Book Review* p19 Aug. 24, 1997, p21 Oct. 3, 1999

SELECTED BOOKS: *Locas*, 1997; *What It Takes to Get to Vegas*, 1999; *The Conquest*, 2002

Mark Klatte/Courtesy of W. W. Norton & Company

Nabhan, Gary Paul

Mar. 17, 1952– Ethnobotanist; nature writer

In an interview with Susan Ives for *Land and People* (on-line), Gary Paul Nabhan bemoaned the lack of environmental knowledge of inner-city children like those from his hometown of Gary, Indiana: "Not only had these kids never been around horses, for example, but they didn't know how to plant the very foods in their daily diet. Urbanization had diminished their familiarity not only with domesticated plants and animals that form the basis of their diets, but with wild plants and animals as well." Once, Nabhan explained, "every person, not just biological experts, could rattle off between 500 and 3,000 names for plants and animals on their home ground. So it's not simply that we're losing the capacity to classify and inventory species in our immediate surroundings. We're also losing all the stories and symbols and ethical lessons these plants and animals once taught." In one Native American community, for instance, a local tree is not just an assemblage of roots, branches, and leaves. "That plant was a person once, just like you and me," Nabhan quoted an Indian elder as saying. "It was turned into a plant when the waters from a great flood touched its heels. But because it's a person, if you break off a branch or if you pull a seedling up out of the ground . . . winds will come and destroy our village. We can't hurt the tree without hurting ourselves."

Currently the director of the Center for Sustainable Environments at Northern Arizona University, in Flagstaff, Arizona, Nabhan has struggled to preserve those cultures and communities that treat the environment with respect. For Nabhan, who has won a MacArthur Fellowship for his innovative ecological investigations, a "sense of place" is one of the most important ingredients in establishing a harmonious relationship with nature. "Much of my activist work has been building cross-cultural coalitions to protect places that are part of the historical, cultural heritage of several different ethnic groups," he told Susan Ives. In such books as *The Desert Smells Like Rain: A Naturalist in Papago Indian Country* (1982), *Gathering the Desert* (1985), *The Forgotten Pollinators* (1996), and *Cultures of Habitat: On Nature, Culture, and Story* (1997), Nabhan demonstrates how a strong sense of place can contribute to environmental well-being. A former director of conservation and science at the Arizona-Sonora Desert Museum, he also helped establish the Sense of Place Project, one of the Desert Museum's outreach programs, and he was a co-founder of Native Seeds/SEARCH, a regional seed bank. In the *New York Times Book Review* (November 30, 1997), Mark Dowie described Nabhan as a writer "whose small but inspiring stories from the far outposts of humanity teach us about the tense and tenuous relationship between culture and biological diversity."

Of Lebanese descent, Gary Paul Nabhan was born on March 17, 1952 in Gary, Indiana, to Wanda Mary Goodwin and Theodore B. Nabhan. Steel mills dominated the landscape of his native city. "The playgrounds of my childhood were built from cast-offs of the local Gary, Indiana, steel mills," Nabhan told Susan Ives. "There were big steel-barred slides and swing sets, and pig-iron cinder was spread across the ground. I saw one wild animal on those playgrounds the whole time I was growing up, a butterfly that happened by. . . . It seems incredibly sad to me that we were literally in the midst of Indiana Dunes National Lakeshore and, with a few notable exceptions, science education took place almost entirely indoors." Nabhan spent as much time as he could walking in the wilds, picking flowers and observing squirrels. In junior high school, he often cut class to visit the local dunes and marshes. He dropped out of high school, but less than a year later, he attended college and took field biology courses "in which I could do what I had always had the most fun doing—turning over rocks and old logs looking for snakes and lizards," as he explained to Ives. He obtained a Ph.D. in botany and environmental sciences and became a professional ethnobotanist.

Nabhan's first book, *The Desert Smells Like Rain: A Naturalist in Papago Indian Country* (1982)—reprinted in 2002 as *The Desert Smells Like Rain: A Naturalist in O'Odham Country*)—stemmed from his fieldwork among the Papago people in southern Arizona and Sonora, Mexico. The volume describes how the Papago have adapted to life in the desert region, which receives an average of only 25 centimeters of rain a year. Without resorting to irrigation, the Papago can still get enough food from farming and foraging. Nabhan also investigates the Indian's legends and songs, which contain information about the weather and appropriate agricultural practices. In a review for *Science Books & Films* (February 1983), John Cole wrote that Nabhan "brings people and desert ecology to life. . . . Ritual, myth, history, technology, world view, and especially ecology are treated sympathetically and usefully although perhaps romantically."

Nabhan continued his investigation into desert ecology with *Gathering the Desert* (1985). Illustrated by Paul Mirocha, the volume contains essays on Sonoran desert plants, including amaranth, creosote bush, chile, devil's claw, mescal, organpipe cactus, palm, panicgrass, sandfood, tepary bean, and wild gourds. In a review for *Choice* (February 1986), R. Mellor remarked, "Each chapter . . . includes enlightening and entertaining anecdotal material that carries deeper messages about the use, misuse, and abuse of the earth." In his notice for *Natural History* (March 1986), Hugh H. Iltis was more critical, finding that in Nabhan's "lonely battle for an idiosyncratic cause (automatic respect for the nontechnical or primitive)," Nabhan sometimes displayed a "whiff of anti-intellectualism."

Another discussion of Native American farming methods came in Nabhan's *Enduring Seeds: Native American Agriculture and Wild Plant Conservation* (1989). The book focuses on survival in the desert, which requires attunement to weather patterns and soil conditions to make maximum use of plant foods. In a review for *Choice* (February 1990), D. A. Falk termed *Enduring Seeds* a "poetic work of the highest order" with elements of "narrative, biography, ethnobotany, and natural history." He added, "The book is as much about the cultural significance of biological diversity as it is about the seeds themselves. In addressing the deep accommodation of traditional agricultural systems to the local ecology, *Enduring Seeds* reveals the profound influence of place on human societies."

In 1990, after experiencing a bitter divorce in 1988, Nabhan traveled to Italy to walk the "Franciscan Way," the path in Tuscany and Umbria traversed by St. Francis of Assisi. Nabhan's reasons for embarking on the journey included a desire to experience the Mediterranean region. He was also a Third Order Franciscan, which had required a year of training; the position enjoined him to honor the legacy of St. Francis by preserving endangered species. Finally, Nabhan wanted to see whether "the folk knowledge of nature—and the example of St. Francis—that had accumulated over generations had served Italian farmers, foragers, and foresters well enough to have kept their land from losing all of its wildness," as he was quoted as saying by Peter Bernhardt for the *New York Times* (July 11, 1993). Nabhan described his journey, which he undertook with conservationist Ginger Harmon, in *Songbirds, Truffles, and Wolves: An American Naturalist in Italy* (1993). Bernhardt called Nabhan's book "his most personal book to date." In a review for *Booklist* (June 15, 1993), Eloise Kinney wrote, "The book is lush with descriptions of the land, its people, and the history of plant life. . . . Quotes from other essayists, as well as Nabhan's own well-crafted insights, make this an engaging exploration of the frailties and resilience of life on Earth."

In 1993 Nabhan edited *Counting Sheep: Twenty Ways of Seeing Desert Bighorn*, a compendium of essays in which naturalists describe sightings of rare bighorn sheep. "As the subtitle suggests," Jim Dwyer wrote for *Library Journal* (September 15, 1993), "this book is as much about how the bighorns roam the hearts and minds of the watchers as it is about the elusive sheep themselves. Most of the authors take a very personal approach to doing science, with Terry Tempest Williams, Ann Zwinger, and Charles Bowden offering particularly powerful narratives."

With entomologist Stephen L. Buchmann and illustrator Paul Mirocha, Nabhan published *The Forgotten Pollinators* in 1996. The book called attention to the disappearance of the plant pollinators that are crucial for the reproduction of common plants. According to one estimate, one in every three mouthfuls eaten by the average person comes from plants that need to be pollinated. "Imagine Thanksgiving without cranberries or Halloween without pumpkins," Cait Anthony wrote in a review for *Science News* (January 3, 1998). "While these scenarios may seem unlikely, Buchmann and Nabhan point to the survival crisis now facing pollinators of these and other fruits and vegetables—bees, butterflies, hummingbirds, moths, and bats." These pollinators are threatened by a variety of causes, including pesticides and habitat fragmentation and destruction. Launching the Forgotten Pollinators Campaign along with the book, Nabhan and Buchmann have put out a call for a national pollination policy. Some reviewers, however, have criticized the book's anecdotal style for not providing enough scientific proof of the growing ecological crisis.

In 1997 Nabhan published *Cultures of Habitat: On Nature, Culture, and Story*, a collection of 24 essays on the relationship between culture and ecology. In opposition to some biologists who believe that biodiversity is best enhanced by excluding humans from ecological preserves, Nabhan claims that biodiversity can be protected by maintaining cultural diversity. When human communities are rooted in a place for a long time, Nabhan argues, the inhabitants learn to interact with their environment, to the benefit of both humans and biodiversity. The knowledge is encoded in songs, myths, legends, and practices. Such knowledge is lost when humans either migrate, or when their community is destroyed by an imperialist power. Nabhan writes, "Whenever empires have spread to suppress other cultures' languages and landtenure traditions, the loss of biodiversity has been dramatic." The problem for conservationists, then, is to match the right human communities with the right ecological habitats. In a review for *Audubon* (February 1998), Verlyn Klinkenborg wrote, "[Nabhan's] elegant, heartfelt essays . . . remind the reader that the human presence in nature can actually increase the complexity of the natural world."

In *Coming Home to Eat: The Pleasures and Politics of Local Foods* (2002), Nabhan argues that a local biosystem, or foodshed, can provide its inhabitants with all the food they need—plants and animals, wild and domesticated—for a healthy and enjoyable diet. In preparation for writing the book Nabhan spent 15 months on a diet in which 90 percent of his food was grown or gathered within a 250-mile radius of his home in Flagstaff. In humorous anecdotes he relates his attempts at growing his own food, foraging in the desert, raising turkeys (and his inability to slaughter them), and discovering a community of "local eaters," many of them Native American. He stuck to his diet, even when traveling, by explaining to his hosts, "'While I'm with you, I have to eat what is locally produced,'" as quoted by Patricia West-Barker in the *Santa Fe New Mexican* (October 9, 2002). "It's not like it's chicken [I] can't eat," Nabhan added. "I can't eat globalized food." Nabhan argues passionately against the commercialization and dehumanization of the food industry, which he links to the deterioration of local food culture and the dilemmas facing modern farmers. Nevertheless, he finds hope in the perseverance of those who enjoy local foods. "There's a hidden economy all over America of people selling paw-paws and persimmons at swap meets in the Midwest, or making their own jam from berries that they find up in the mountains," he told West-Baker. "It's one of the things that people take the most pride in, connecting them to place in the deepest way. The globalized food system is so pervasive in its advertising that it seems like it has overwhelmed the American food system, where, inevitably, there are pockets of persistence in every area of the country."

"While many of the topics covered are fascinating and important, they are touched on only superficially," Karen Munro wrote in a review of the book for *Library Journal*, as quoted on *Amazon.com*. "Nabhan undoubtedly knows his material, but he too often depends on flowery writing in a book that as a whole feels disorganized." Other reviews were more positive. "Most Americans have no idea where their food comes from, how it's grown, handled, or shipped, but many are starting to wonder, as Nabhan does, what our society has sacrificed for the sake of convenience," Donna Seaman noted in *Booklist*, as quoted on *Amazon.com*. "Warmhearted, innovative, and respectful of life, Nabhan inspires readers to think twice about corporate domination of the food supply and the old adage You Are What You Eat."

In addition to writing, Nabhan has sought other ways of educating people about ecology. With the Sense of Place Project, Nabhan has sponsored workshops "to help identify the common values and symbols of place that unite us," as he explained to Susan Ives. "The premise is that if communities can identify and map places of great cultural and symbolic value, they will be better able to stave off threats to those places. Too many times, people rally behind protecting a place only after some plan has out to destroy it. We need to find new ways to honor the past and integrate it into our lives before such threats arise." The organization has also started handing out Keepers of the Desert Treasure awards, given to people who have accumulated a vast amount of ecological knowledge for their communities. The first recipients of the award were honored in October 1997.

Nabhan has been the recipient of many honors, including a Burroughs Medal in 1987, a MacArthur Fellowship in 1990, and a Lannan Literary Award in 1999. Nabhan is also a member of Al-Rawi, a professional association of Arab-American writers.

In a 1999 article in *Audubon* entitled "A Sense of Place—Land of Contradictions," Nabhan described one of his favorite spots on earth: an oasis called Quitobaquito, in the Sonoran Desert, where he baptized his first child. "It has refreshed and renewed my life in ways that I can't explain," he wrote. "Perhaps I am just one more of the anomalous aspects of the history of Quitobaquito and the gran desierto, a Lebanese-American who has adopted a desert home far from the country of his Arab forefathers. And yet, I am no more anomalous than the desert oasis itself, with its Mediterranean figs and pomegranates growing next to native capers and cacti. Quitobaquito's natural and cultural legacies are full of juxtapositions: wet and dry, sacred and profane, native and exotic. And that's why I like it—I see myself reflected in its waters."
— S. Y.

SUGGESTED READING: *Audubon* p95 Feb. 1998; *Audubon* (on-line) 1999; *Booklist* p1774 June 15, 1993, p440 Nov. 1, 1997; *Choice* p1448 June 1982, p888 Feb. 1986, p972 Feb. 1990; *Library Journal* p100 Sep. 15, 1993; *New York Times Book Review* p14 July 11, 1993, p33 Nov. 30, 1997; *Natural History* p74 Mar. 1986; *Santa Fe New Mexican* C p1 Oct. 9, 2002; *Science Books & Films* p121 Feb. 1983; *Times Literary Supplement* p515 May 9, 1986

SELECTED BOOKS: nonfiction—*The Desert Smells Like Rain: A Naturalist in Papago Indian Country*, 1982; *Gathering the Desert*, 1985; *Saguaro: A View of Saguaro National Monument and the Tucson Basin*, 1986; *Enduring Seeds: Native American Agriculture and Wild Plant Conservation*, 1989; *Songbirds, Truffles, and Wolves: An American Naturalist in Italy*, 1993; *The Geography of Childhood: Why Children Need Wild Places* (with S. Trimble), 1994; *Desert Legends: Re-Storying the Sonoran Borderlands* (with M. Klett), 1994; *Canyons of Color: Utah's Slickrock Wildlands* (with C. Wilson), 1995; *The Forgotten Pollinators* (with S. L. Buchmann), 1996; *Cultures of Habitat: On Nature, Culture, and Story*, 1997; *Coming Home to Eat: The Pleasures and Politics of Local Foods*, 2002; as editor—*Arizona Highways Presents Desert Wildflowers* (with J. Cole), 1988; *Counting Sheep: Twenty Ways of Seeing Desert Bighorn*, 1993

Courtesy of the Graduate Center/NYU

Nasaw, David

(NAY-saw)

July 18, 1945– Nonfiction writer; biographer; historian

David Nasaw is the prize-winning author of the biography *The Chief: The Life of William Randolph Hearst* (2000). Drawing on Hearst's personal correspondence and papers that were not previously available to authors and researchers, Nasaw produced what many reviewers called the best and most comprehensive account of the influential publisher, whose newspapers reached tens of millions of readers across the United States. *The Chief* won several prestigious literary prizes, and Nasaw has also earned critical attention in major newspapers and magazines for his other books, which explore sociological trends in American history; these include *Schooled to Order: A Social History of Public Schooling* (1979), *Children of the City: At Work and Play* (1985), and *Going Out: The Rise and Fall of Public Amusements* (1993).

David Nasaw submitted the following third-person statement to *World Authors 1995-2000*: "David Nasaw received his Ph.D. degree from Columbia University in 1972. His dissertation, sponsored by Professor Leonard Krieger, was entitled *Jean-Paul Sartre: Apprenticeship to History* and examined the generation of French intellectuals that disdained politics and commitment in the 1920s only to have their philosophies and world views turned upside down by the events that convulsed and transformed daily life in France in the late 1930s and 1940s.

"On graduating from Columbia, Nasaw was appointed as Assistant Professor at Staten Island Community College of the City University of New York where he taught in the 'Youth and Community Studies Program.' (In 1978, Staten Island Community College was merged with Richmond College to form the College of Staten Island.) While at Staten Island, he wrote his first book, *Schooled to Order: A Social History of Public Schooling*. In this book, published by Oxford University Press in 1979 and now in its tenth printing, Nasaw described how American public schooling was democratized in the 19th and 20th century, but imperfectly. As the nation's common schools in the 1830s and 1840s, then the high schools at the turn of the 20th century, and the nation's public colleges in the 1950s and 1960s opened their doors to those who had earlier been excluded, they directed these newcomers into a less demanding, more vocationally oriented 'tracked' curriculum.

"Nasaw's second book, *Children of the City: At Work and Play*, was published by Doubleday in 1985 and, in paperback, by Oxford University Press in 1985. It is a highly readable narrative history of the process by which the city's immigrant and working children acculturated and socialized themselves, not necessarily in the public schools, but on the streets of the city where they worked and in the new public amusement spaces (vaudeville houses, nickelodeons, amusement parks, etc.) where they played.

"Following the publication of *Children of the City*, Nasaw was awarded a Fulbright Lectureship at Hebrew University, where he taught in the American Studies department in the spring of 1987. On his return to the College of Staten Island, he was awarded a fellowship from the American Council of Learned Societies to continue work on what would become his third book, *Going Out: The Rise and Fall of Public Amusements*. Published by Basic Books in 1993 and subsequently released in paperback by Harvard University Press, *Going Out* looks at the ways in which the growth of public amusements transformed the daily life as well as the culture and politics of the city in the decades surrounding the turn of the twentieth century. While *Going Out*, like *Children of the City*, demonstrates how the new amusements brought together immigrants and native-born, rich and poor, male and female, it also examines in some detail the processes by which people of color were excluded or segregated in the audience, though over-represented in parodic form on the stage of the vaudeville hall, in the early cinema, in world's fair exhibits, and at the amusement park.

"In 1994, Professor Nasaw was appointed Executive Officer of the Ph.D. Program in History at the Graduate Center of the City University of New York. He served in that capacity until [being appointed] Director of the Center of the Humanities at the Graduate Center.

"*The Chief: The Life and Times of William Randolph Hearst* was published by Houghton Mifflin in 2000 to commercial and critical acclaim. The book was awarded the Bancroft Prize in History, the J. Anthony Lukas Book Prize for Non-Fiction, and the Ambassador Book Award for Biography and was a finalist for the National Book Critics Circle prize for biography. *The Chief* [will be] released in paperback by Houghton Mifflin in the fall of 2001 and is being translated into Japanese and Spanish.

"Nasaw has published several scholarly articles, is a regular participant in the annual conferences of the American Historical Association and the Organization of American Historians, and has written for a number of general-interest publications, including the *Nation* and the *New Yorker*. He is a regular contributor to *New York Times Book Review*, has been a consultant to a number of television documentaries, and has lectured extensively throughout the country. He lives in New York City with his wife, Dinitia Smith, a national cultural correspondent for the *New York Times*. His twin sons, Daniel and Peter, are entering their senior year in college, Daniel at the University of Chicago, Peter at Brandeis University."

David Nasaw was born on July 18, 1945 in Cortland, New York. His father, Joshua, was a lawyer, and his mother, Beatrice, worked as a teacher. Nasaw graduated from Bucknell University in Lewisburg, Pennsylvania, in 1967, receiving a B.A. in history. "Since graduating from college, I knew that I wanted to teach on the high school or college level and write scholarly works that would have some sort of appeal beyond the classroom," he explained to *World Authors*. In 1972, the year he received his Ph.D. from Columbia University, in New York City, Nasaw edited the book, *Starting Your Own High School*, which was published by Random House. The next year, he began teaching at the College of Staten Island of the City University of New York (CUNY).

In 1979 Nasaw published the book, *Schooled to Order: A Social History of Public Schooling in the United States*. The author discussed how public education expanded in the nation, starting in the 1830s. The gradual increase of public elementary schools, then high schools, and finally public colleges provided more educational opportunities to the poor and middle classes, minorities, and immigrants, all of whom had been previously excluded from getting a quality education. In his review for the *Washington Post* (May 13, 1979), Jonathan Kozol criticized the book, writing that Nasaw "fails to go beyond those whose pace-setting books he quotes repeatedly and, therefore, he adds little to the sense of leverage that we already possessed in 1970. He tells us in orderly fashion all that we knew before, or else could readily learn from any one of the major books, published in the previous 10 years, to which he constantly alludes." By contrast, a reviewer in *Choice* (September 1979) was not bothered by Nasaw's use of well-known sources and wrote that his "analyses and interpretations are based largely on works published over the past 40 years, and include many of the best scholars in the areas of general and educational history and sociology." The reviewer concluded that *Schooled to Order* is "a worthwhile contribution to the literature."

Nasaw's next book, *Children of the City: At Work and at Play* (1985), portrays the lives of children in urban areas at the turn of the 20th century, when boys sold newspapers, fruit, and various used items to make money, and girls worked in factories, offices, schools, and stores, before marrying. (Other girls worked at home, serving as unpaid babysitters, housekeepers, laundresses, and cooks.) Nasaw estimates that hundreds of thousands of boys who grew up in American cities during this time sold newspapers, and the "newsboy" holding up a paper, yelling "Extra! Extra! Read all about it!" was an image depicted in countless old films. In New York City, in 1899, the newsboys organized a strike to protest increases in the wholesale price of newspapers owned by William Randolph Hearst and Joseph Pulitzer. The strike crippled sales, and within two weeks, two of the most powerful newspaper owners in the country were forced to capitulate. In the *New York Times Book Review* (April 28, 1985), Avery Corman wrote that Nasaw "has assembled *Children of the City* from archives, early reports by journalists and settlement house workers, oral history collections and published reminiscences." Although he faulted the book for oversimplifying the economic problems of the time, Corman praised Nasaw for bringing to life "these color pieces from the remnants of our urban landscape." In his review for the *Journal of American History* (December 1985), LeRoy Ashby lauded the book for showing that the children "were not simply passive recipients of a culture. They were superbly creative and adaptive within the limits of the environment in which they found themselves." He continued, "Cities were dangerous and dirty, but for many children they were also places of promise and variety. The almost seventy photographs that Nasaw includes to dramatize that point are in themselves splendid parts of a thoughtful and pioneering book."

In *Going Out: The Rise and Fall of Public Amusements* (1993), Nasaw explored how Americans entertained themselves at the start of the 20th century, when technological advances and improvements in working conditions gave people more leisure time. Nasaw wrote that people spent their off-hours frequenting movie theaters, amusement parks, dance halls, vaudeville shows, and baseball games. These activities did more than provide Americans with inexpensive entertainment and relief from boredom; according to Nasaw, they broke down barriers among people of different economic classes and ethnic groups—such as the Irish and the Poles—and promoted a sense of community. However, as he observed, racism resulted in the exclusion of African-Americans from these pastimes, and blacks were sometimes victimized in the pursuit of amusement. For example, a popular game at Coney Island, in New York City, featured a caged African-American at whom players would toss balls. The age of television and the flight to suburban areas during the 1950s changed the nature of American leisure and brought an end to many public amusements. In her review for *Booklist* (November 15, 1993), Donna Seaman wrote, "Nasaw paints a vivid and animated picture of urban nightlife around the turn of the century, when 'going out' was all the rage for white-collar workers." The reviewer concluded that the book was a "fresh and intriguing assessment of American entertainment at its most spontaneous and uninhibited." Reviewing *Going Out* for the *Washington Post Book World* (November 21, 1993), Jonathan Yardley disagreed with Nasaw's claim that the white exploitation and ridicule of African-Americans in public amusements was a conscious and ideological tool of racial oppression. "That manifestations of racism in public amusements had an 'ideological' cast is ludicrous on its face," Yardley argued. "They occurred because white Americans took it as a matter of course that blacks were inferior, and they kept on occurring until, in the 1950s, blacks started to force America into confronting the lie it had permitted democracy to become."

In 2000 Nasaw published his first biography, *The Chief: The Life of William Randolph Hearst*, in which he profiles the influential newspaper baron, whose media empire survives today as the Hearst Corporation. "I didn't set out to write a biography originally but to do a monograph about culture, media, and politics," Nasaw explained to *World Authors*. "My intent was to use Hearst, a millionaire and media mogul, as a case study of the ways in which the media and politics have become intertwined in the 20th century. But once I began to look at the material on Hearst, I became fascinated by the man and all he did and was swept away into a new project—a biography." The son of a wealthy

U.S. senator, Hearst took over the *San Francisco Examiner* newspaper in 1890 and turned it into a profitable rival to the *San Francisco Chronicle*. He later purchased New York's *Journal* newspaper, bringing him into direct competition with Joseph Pulitzer's *World*. Hearst eventually acquired 28 newspapers around the nation and also opened a movie studio in Hollywood. Politically ambitious, he served two terms as a New York representative in the U.S. House and unsuccessfully sought the Democratic Party nomination for president, in 1904. During the 1930s, Hearst clashed with President Franklin Delano Roosevelt over his New Deal reforms and internationalist foreign policy. Hearst was also the unacknowledged inspiration for the director Orson Welles's classic film, *Citizen Kane* (1941), which is considered by many critics to be one of the greatest films of all time. In his review for *Time* (August 7, 2000), John F. Stacks wrote, "This is at least the fourth biography of Hearst and is far and away the best. Given access to Hearst's correspondence with his editors and family, Nasaw has used the raw material brilliantly to paint a richly textured picture of the man who for decades did so much to shape the political debate." In the *Los Angeles Times Book Review* (June 18, 2000), Kevin Starr hailed the book, writing that it "is part of a larger pattern of extraordinarily well-researched books of American history and biography, based on new sources, envisioned and executed in the grand spirit of the 20th century novel." Starr added that Nasaw "brings us to a new understanding of just how important Hearst was in the creation of Hollywood, in which he was no mere interloper but a silent and dominant partner, among other things, in the emergence of the studio system."

David Nasaw earned a fellowship from the National Endowment for the Humanities for college teaching for 1981–82. He is a member of the American Historical Association, the Organization of American Historians, and Educators for Social Responsibility. In 1987 Nasaw edited the two-volume book, *Course of United States History*. Nasaw told *World Authors* that his next book will probably be another biography.

—D. C.

SUGGESTED READING: *American Heritage* p27+ Dec. 2000/Jan. 2001; *Booklist* p596 Nov. 15, 1993; *Choice* p891 Sep. 1979; *Journal of American History* p709 Dec. 1985; *Los Angeles Times Book Review* p1 June 18, 2000, with photos; *New York Times Book Review* p15 Apr. 28, 1985; *Time* p86 Aug. 7, 2000; *Washington Post* K p7 May 13, 1979; *Washington Post Book World* X p3 Nov. 21, 1993

SELECTED BOOKS: *Schooled to Order: A Social History of Public Schooling in the United States*, 1979; *Children of the City: At Work and at Play*, 1985; *Going Out: The Rise and Fall of Public Amusements*, 1993; *The Chief: The Life of William Randolph Hearst*, 2000; as editor—*Starting Your Own High School*, 1972; *Course of United States History*, 1987

Naslund, Sena Jeter

1942(?)– Novelist; short-story writer

Imagine *Moby-Dick*, that great bastion of masculinity and literature, as told through the eyes of a woman. Sena Jeter Naslund did just that in her best-selling novel *Ahab's Wife: or, The Star-Gazer* (1999). In Naslund's version of the American classic, Ahab's story is sidelined while the onshore adventures of his young wife, Una Spenser, unfold. The novel put Naslund on the literary map and introduced her to a national readership. A longtime professor at the University of Louisville, where she once directed the writing program, Naslund has written two other novels: *The Animal Way to Love* (1993) and *Sherlock in Love* (1993), the latter a fictional recreation of Sherlock Holmes's final years. She has also authored two collections of short fiction—*Ice Skating at the North Pole* (1989) and *The Disappearance of Water* (1999)—and is an editor of the *Louisville Review*.

The only daughter of three children, Sena Jeter Naslund was born in about 1942 in Birmingham, Alabama. She grew up in West Virginia and Louisiana, where her father, a physician, worked; he died when Naslund was 15 years old. Naslund's mother, a music teacher, was a voracious reader, and Naslund shared her mother's literary appetite. When Naslund was a freshman in high school, the provenance of a book report she wrote on *Moby-Dick* was challenged by a teacher who could not believe the girl's precociousness and thought the essay was written by an art critic. Recalling this incident about 40 years later in "Origins of Writing Ahab's Wife: or, The Star Gazer," an essay put out by her publisher, Naslund wrote, "I was stunned not at the question of my honesty—which was quickly assured (and accepted)—but with the hint of information: there were art critics, and I wondered where one could read what they'd written, and did this mean that a novel was a form of *art*?"

Naslund's talent for writing fiction quickly became apparent when she was asked by her English teacher to write a scene that might have been edited out of Shakespeare's *Julius Caesar*. Foreshadowing her later interest in developing minor female characters from the male-dominated canon, Naslund imagined Portia, Brutus's wife, dying after having "swallowed fire," an incident that is merely alluded to in the play. Naslund later explained to Katy Yocum for the *Louisville Magazine* (September 1999, on-line), "I loved this assign-

Sigrid Estrada/Courtesy of HarperCollins
Sena Jeter Naslund

ment of taking an already established character, a character who seemed in some sense underdeveloped, and letting this bud open. So I wrote a 19-page playlet. And my teacher gave me an A-plus-plus-plus. It was like the trail of a comet, those pluses after my A."

During her formative years Naslund also nurtured an interest in music. A talented cellist, she played in the school orchestra and with the Alabama Pops Orchestra. When she graduated from Birmingham High School, she turned down a music scholarship from the University of Alabama and enrolled at Birmingham-Southern College, where she studied English and creative writing. At the urging of a professor who recognized her ample talents, Naslund participated in the Breadloaf Writers' Conference, in Vermont. After she received her bachelor's degree, she attended the Iowa Writers' Workshop, at the University of Iowa, and received her master's and Ph.D. degrees in creative writing.

In 1971 Naslund became a visiting professor in the master of fine arts program at the University of Montana, and in 1972 she joined the faculty of the University of Louisville, her present appointment. For a dozen years, beginning in the mid-1970s, she directed the university's creative-writing program, increasing enrollment from 20 students each semester to more than 250; in 1980 her achievements earned her the first Distinguished Teaching Award presented by that institution. Naslund's commitment to nurturing aspiring writers also extended outside of the classroom. She founded the literary journal *Louisville Review*, in 1976, and, 20 years later, the Fleur-de-Lis Press to help new writers get their works published. She remains ardently devoted to both ventures; in the early 1990s, when the periodical was threatened with extinction because the University of Louisville ended its subsidy, a determined Naslund vowed to keep it alive. She ran the magazine from her own office and inaugurated a writing competition that has attracted thousands of manuscripts from writers around the world, whose entry fees helped keep the journal afloat. In 1998 Spalding University began subsidizing the *Louisville Review*, and Naslund continues to serve as one of its editors. She is also on the creative-writing faculty of Vermont College.

Naslund first published her short fiction in such prestigious journals as *The Paris Review*, *The Georgia Review*, and *The Iowa Review*; a story published in the *Michigan Quarterly Review* won the Lawrence Prize in fiction. Her first book, a collection of short stories entitled *Ice Skating at the North Pole*, was published in 1989. In its title story, set in a remote wilderness, a mother slays a mountain lion that threatens her daughter's life when it enters their trailer.

Naslund's first two novels appeared in 1993. *The Animal Way of Love*, published by Ampersand, is a coming-of-age story. *Sherlock in Love* made a much bigger splash, becoming a Quality Paperback Book-of-the-Month Club selection. Intended as an explanation of Holmes's final, unsolved case, in which he is confronted by his nemesis Moriarty at the Reichenbach Falls, Naslund explained in a 1999 essay that her novel "had been written partly to insist that there were women who were the equivalent of any imaginatively convinced male figure." George Grella, writing for the *Washington Post Book World* (November 21, 1993), panned the book as "embarrassingly clumsy." But Tobin Harshaw, reviewing the novel for the *New York Times* (November 21, 1993), called it a "sentimental adventure," adding that Naslund was "largely faithful to Sir Arthur Conan Doyle's style, and her narrative entertains at breakneck speed."

Two more of Naslund's books made their debut six years later. The first of these, *The Disobedience of Water*, a collection of eight short stories and a novella, was published by Godine. The renewal of life is an important motif in the collection, which includes stories such as "Madame Charpentier and Her Children," about a woman starting afresh after a friend's suicide, and "The Shape You're In," about a 20-something artist from Atlanta who finds that a move to Montana cannot fully erase the ghosts of her past. Reviewing the collection for the *New York Times Book Review* (April 25, 1999), Maud Casey called it a "fiercely beautiful story collection" and concluded that Naslund "has an eye for odd, telling details and a gift for rendering (and respecting) this oddness in language so sharp and precise that it is sometimes pleasantly painful."

Several months after the publication of *The Disobedience of Water*, *Ahab's Wife: or, The Star-Gazer* was published by William Morrow, with antiquarian-style illustrations by Christopher Wormell. Described by Paul Bresnick, a Melville aficionado-cum-executive editor at Morrow, as "the most thrilling acquisition I've ever made," the manuscript reportedly was auctioned for more than half a million dollars, according to John F. Baker in his "Hot Deals" column in *Publishers Weekly* (December 21, 1998). The book became the most-talked-about literary property of the season, snagging a spot as a Book-of-the-Month Club main selection and rising to the top of best-seller lists soon after its publication. In the *New York Post* (September 26, 1999), Michael Glitz wrote: "Of course, the mere idea of going toe-to-toe with Melville's epic is shocking to some. Naslund admits that a few 'very well-known writers' said to her, 'How *dare* you?' And when she told her friend and fellow author Wendell Berry what she was working on, he said, 'You don't lack for boldness, do you?' Naslund now laughs. 'Well, no, I don't,' she says."

The 688-page novel is narrated by Una Spenser, wife of the captain of the Pequod in Herman Melville's classic novel *Moby-Dick*. While Melville only briefly referred to Ahab's wife in a handful of passages in *Moby-Dick*, Naslund lends a voice to the invisible woman and even permits her to reweave the elements of Melville's universe. Una's mother entrusts the girl to the care of relatives (lighthouse keepers in faraway New England) to insulate Una from her father, a religious zealot. She runs away to sea disguised as a boy and then survives a shipwreck and a first marriage before marrying Ahab, who fathers her first child. After losing Ahab, she remarries and gives birth to two more children, Justice and Felicity, and becomes involved in the abolition movement. She meets many famous historical figures and eventually lives out her days in a commune of freethinkers on Nantucket. With its provocative opening lines—"Captain Ahab was neither my first husband nor my last"—the novel depicts a 19th-century woman who tries to remake her identity on her own terms.

Although it took her six years to complete the novel, Naslund has recalled that the idea for *Ahab's Wife* came "in a flash" in 1993, while she was in Boston for the publication of *Sherlock in Love*. *Ahab's Wife*'s opening sentence leapt into her head, followed by the image of Una on her widow's walk, searching the starry night for a sign of Ahab. At about this time, Naslund and her daughter often took long drives while listening to abridged audiotape-versions of *Moby-Dick* and classic novels by Dickens and Twain. Although Naslund had, from childhood, been captivated by these novels, especially *Moby-Dick*, she and her daughter realized how few women appeared as characters. "I feel a certain mission to redeem the territory," she said, "not historical territory but imaginative territory—for women. To say, 'Hey, we were there; we lived and died too'—fictively." In "Origins of Writing Ahab's Wife," Naslund explained, "I've written *Ahab's Wife* somewhat as a child dreams, or almost dreams. When I *was* a child, I had severe insomnia. . . . So that I wouldn't toss and turn, betraying my restlessness, I imagined continued stories. . . . Though *Ahab's Wife* has been heavily (and very gratefully) revised, it came to me like those dreamy stories, as a friend, a ready companion, a world easily entered, fascinating and fulfilling. The rewriting has been like polishing a favorite piece of wood, my hand enchanted by the surface, in love with touching it again."

Naslund invested a lot of herself in this novel, and she has acknowledged a spiritual bond between herself and the character of Una Spenser. "You know, it's not me. It couldn't be me," she told Katy Yocum. "But I wanted a name I felt akin to." Karen Mann, Naslund's colleague on the *Louisville Review*, told Yocum that she recognized much of Naslund's personality in Una. "I don't mean it's autobiographical," Mann stated, "but the brilliance of Una is the brilliance of Sena. They share the desire to search out their individual meaning of life. And there's a vitality, a zest for life in both of them."

Reviewers and critics hailed the publication of *Ahab's Wife* as one of the most important novels of the season, though not without reservations. A *Kirkus Reviews* (August 15, 1999) critic called the novel an "extraordinary tale: a ravishingly detailed re-creation of the worlds of 19th-century antebellum America and of Melville's seminal *Moby-Dick*"; the reviewer gushed that it was a "genuine epic of America: an inspired homage to one of our greatest writers that brilliantly reinterprets, and in many ways rivals, his masterpiece." But Edward Rothstein, in his essay for the *New York Times* (October 16, 1999), opined that "while Ms. Naslund ostensibly preserves Melville's literary tools—the exclamations, the alliteration, the sharply contrasting chapters, the occasional archaic phrase—she also chases her subject in ardent 20th-century fashion, with self-conscious proclamations of political virtue" and that she is quite "intentional in her dismantling" of *Moby-Dick* as a mythic novel. To Rothstein, Naslund has rejected "the very premises of Melville's universe: Biblical beliefs are replaced by a good-natured agnosticism. Metaphysical broodings are supplanted by sentimental musings. Grim eroticism is turned into maudlin romance." In her front-page analysis for the *New York Times Book Review* (October 3, 1999), Stacey D'Erasmo suggested that *Ahab's Wife* "may well turn out to be Melville's worst nightmare: *Moby-Dick* rewritten by a woman as a conventionally constructed popular novel with an unflaggingly virtuous heroine and a happy ending." D'Erasmo concluded that "Una is an innate feminist, but she is inscribed into a landscape that rarely opposes or disappoints her for long. . . . On the roiling, dark terrain of Melville's wildness and disintegration, Naslund has erected a glistening pink utopia, every word of which argues by harmonious example, 'Now, isn't this better?' . . . The book insists on happiness, sometimes to the exclusion of even the most generous reading of history. But why not? Men have got rich from their big harpoons and mythic beasts and improbable heroics. Don't women deserve their own fantastic voyages?"

Naslund lives in Louisville, Kentucky, with her husband, John C. Morrison, an atomic physicist, and her daughter, Flora, who shares her mother's fascination with literature and Melville. Both Morrison and Naslund have been longtime faculty members at the University of Louisville, but the couple did not meet until 1994, when Morrison heard Naslund reading from *The Disobedience of Water* at a literary program. Captivated by her work, he introduced himself and learned that the novelist had begun delving into physics texts as part of her bedtime reading.

—E. M.

SUGGESTED READING: *Booklist* p257 Oct. 1, 1993, p263 Oct. 1, 1993, Aug. 1999; *Kirkus Reviews* Aug. 15, 1999; *Library Journal* p104 Oct. 15, 1989, p105 Sep. 15, 1993, p112 Mar. 15, 1999; *New England Review & Bread Loaf Quarterly* p98+ Autumn 1989; *New York Post* p46 Sep. 26, 1999, with photo; *New York Times Book Review* p24 Nov. 21, 1993, p20 Apr. 25, 1999, p1+ Oct. 3, 1999; *North American Review* p61+ June 1991; *Publishers Weekly* p58 Aug. 25, 1989, p98 Sep. 13, 1993, p17 Dec. 21, 1998, p48 Mar. 8, 1999, p340 Aug. 9, 1999; *Time Out* p75 Sep. 30–Oct. 7, 1999; *Variety* p6 Dec. 14–20, 1998; *Washington Post Book World* p5 Nov. 21, 1993

SELECTED BOOKS: novels—*The Animal Way to Love*, 1993; *Sherlock in Love*, 1993; *Ahab's Wife: or, the Star Gazer*, 1999; short-story collections—*Ice Skating at the North Pole*, 1989; *The Disobedience of Water*, 1999

Courtesy of Alexander Nehamas/the Council of the Humanities

Nehamas, Alexander

Mar. 22, 1946– Nonfiction writer; translator

An important voice in philosophy, Alexander Nehamas is noted for his argument that many of the greatest philosophers in history not only developed theories but were also able to put those theories into practice in their own lives. Nehamas expounded on this postulate in *Nietzsche: Life as Literature* (1986), his study of the great German philosopher's life and work, as well as in *Art of Living* (1998), in which Nehamas argues that such philosophers as Plato, Nietzsche, Montaigne, and Foucault are some of the best representatives of Socrates' belief that one must succeed in creating a unique identity in order to live a truly fulfilling life. Most recently he has published *The Virtues of Authenticity* (1999), a collection of essays about Plato and Socrates.

Born in Athens, Greece, on March 22, 1946, Alexander Nehamas is the son of Albert Nehamas and the former Christine Yannuli. At the age of 18 he immigrated to America where he attended Swarthmore College, in Swarthmore, Pennsylvania, and received his bachelor's degree in 1967. He continued his education at Princeton University, in Princeton, New Jersey, earning his Ph.D. in 1971. Upon leaving Princeton he taught philosophy at the University of Pittsburgh as an assistant professor; he received a promotion to associate professor in 1976 and was made a full professor in 1981. Five years later he joined the philosophy department at the University of Pennsylvania, in Philadelphia. In 1990 he became a professor of philosophy at Princeton, where he is also a professor of humanities and comparative literature. In addition to teaching courses on Greek philosophy, philosophy of art, European philosophy, and literary theory, Nehamas is the head of the Council of the Humanities.

Nehamas published his first book, *Nietzsche: Life as Literature*, in 1985. A study of the 19th-century German philosopher Friedrich Wilhelm Nietzsche, it discusses Nietzsche's ideas about truth, knowledge, science, morality, and the self while primarily addressing Nietzsche's ideas on aestheticism (i.e. viewing the world and people as a literary text and characters) and perspectivism (the belief that there are no absolute truths, only interpretations). R. L. Perkins, in *Choice* (February 1986), called Nehamas's work "an original and important interpretation of Nietzsche." Michael Tanner, writing in the *Times Literary Supplement* (May 16, 1986), believed it to be "the best and most important book on Nietzsche in English. . . . This book can be greeted with relief and gratitude: one hopes that the study of Nietzsche will never be the same again."

Nehamas's next book, *The Art of Living: Socratic Reflections from Plato to Foucault,* was published in 1998. In it the author uses such philosophers as Socrates, Nietzsche, the 16th-century French essayist Montaigne, and the 20th-century critical theorist Michel Foucault as examples of thinkers who have based their philosophies on lessons learned from real life. Philosophy, Nehamas argues, is the means through which one betters oneself and creates a successful life by forging a unique personality. This book received mostly favorable reviews. Terry C. Skeats, in *Library Journal* (November 1, 1998), called it "an intelligently written and closely argued book. . . . This original work should be part of all philosophy collections." J. Bussanich, in *Choice* (March 1999), agreed, writing: "In this elegant, stimulating book, Nehamas . . . identifies Socrates as the source and inspiration of two ways to do philosophy: 1) the systematic, universalist approach, developed by Plato, which sees philosophy as offering one ideal life for all, and 2) an individualist, self-creative path traveled by those he calls 'philosophers of the art of living,' exemplified by Montaigne, Nietzsche, and Foucault."

In late 1998 Nehamas published *Virtues of Authenticity,* a collection of what he considers to be his 16 most important essays on Plato and Socrates. Divided into four sections that discuss various aspects of Socratic and Platonic thought, the book is unified by Nehamas's central idea that Plato was most concerned with distinguishing what is real from what is not. Like Nehamas's other works, *Virtues of Authenticity* garnered solid reviews. In *Library Journal* (November 1, 1998), Terry C. Skeats wrote: "These essays are all well written and well argued; for those who are not familiar with Nehamas's work in Greek philosophy, this collection provides an excellent introduction."

In addition to his work as an author, Alexander Nehamas has also translated Plato's *Symposium* (1989) and *Phaedrus* (1995), and he co-edited *Aristotle's Rhetoric: Philosophical Essays* (1994). Over the years he has contributed to a number of journals including *History of Philosophy Quarterly, Ancient Philosophy, Journal of Modern Greek Studies,* and *Arion,* among others. He married Susan Glimcher on June 22, 1983, and they have one child, Nicholas Albert.

—C. M.

SUGGESTED READING: *Choice* p879 Feb. 1986, p1280 Mar. 1999; *Chronicle of Higher Education* Ap24 Sep. 18, 1998; *Library Journal* p112 Dec. 1985, p86 Nov. 1, 1998; *New Republic* p32+ Jan. 4–11, 1999; *New York Review of Books* p41+ May 6, 1999; *New York Times Book Review* p25+ Oct. 25, 1998; *Times Literary Supplement* p519 May 16, 1986; *Who's Who in America* 2000

SELECTED BOOKS: nonfiction—*Nietzsche: Life as Literature,* 1985; *The Art of Living: Socratic Reflections from Plato to Foucault,* 1998; *Virtues of Authenticity: Essays on Plato and Socrates,* 1998; as co-editor—*Aristotle's Rhetoric: Philosophical Essays,* 1994; as translator—*Plato's Symposium,* 1989; *Plato's Phaedrus,* 1995

Nixon, Rob

1954– Memoirist; nonfiction writer

Rob Nixon left his native South Africa during the apartheid era, in 1980, and has since enjoyed a distinguished career as an academic and journalist in the United States. His first book, *London Calling: V. S. Naipaul, Postcolonial Mandarin* (1992), focused on the novels and nonfiction works of this internationally known author. In 1997 Nixon explored life in post-apartheid South Africa and the ties between South Africa and the West in his book, *Homelands, Harlem, and Hollywood: South African Culture and the World Beyond.* He blended personal memoir, political commentary, and travel narrative with a history of the ostrich trade for his third and most unusual book, *Dreambirds: The Strange History of the Ostrich in Fashion, Food, and Fortune* (2000), which brought him international acclaim. In an article he published in the *Chronicle of Higher Education* (March 31, 2000), Nixon wrote, "I have found *Dreambirds* shelved in bookstores under memoir, biology, biography, history, and travel. If I were asked, I wouldn't know where to place it myself. Memory, to me, is all of the above."

Robert Nixon was born in Port Elizabeth, South Africa, in 1954. His grandparents had emigrated to the country from Scotland and Ireland in the early 20th century. His father published a weekly gardening column under the pseudonym "Babiana" for a local newspaper, the *Eastern Province Herald.* Nixon explained in *Dreambirds* that the babiana is a tiny ground orchid, hardly noticeable until the spring rains cause it to burst into deep-blue bouquets. "The name suited Dad," he wrote. "By nature, he hugged the ground, belonging where he was in a deep-rooted, unobtrusive way. In all his deepest sentiments, he was a local man."

Nixon's father often took his son to the Feather Market Hall, in Port Elizabeth, to see Gilbert and Sullivan musicals, cello recitals, and Christmas concerts. An amateur botanist, his father also took Nixon on field trips around the Karoo, the vast, scrub desert lying just beyond the city. While his father collected information on plants, Nixon became fascinated with birds, especially the ostriches that populated the desert. At age 11 he began keeping a diary, called "Flying Things," in which he recorded his observations. "Becoming a writer was an accidental spin-off of my fidelity to birds," Nixon wrote in *Dreambirds.* At age 15 he published an excerpt from his diary in *The Ostrich*, the official journal of the South African Ornithological Society. Nixon reported the sighting of a European Oystercatcher, a bird that had apparently been blown southward—far from its usual path of migration—by gale-force winds.

As a child Nixon enjoyed reading. However, he was continually disappointed when he failed to find the world around him described in books. Then, on his 11th birthday, his father gave him *Trader on the Veld*, by Albert Jackson. In 1888, at age 15, Jackson had left his native Poland (then called East Prussia) to seek his fortune in South Africa, in what was then a booming ostrich feather trade. Nixon was thrilled to finally read something that described the world he knew. "As I turned the pages, they all came tumbling out: ostriches, merino sheep, mimosa thorn trees, the Karoo, our town of Port Elizabeth and the Feather Market Hall," he recalled in *Dreambirds*.

Nixon, who is white, lived in South Africa during apartheid, the legal system that institutionalized racial segregation between the nonwhite majority and the white minority. In an article published in the *Atlantic Monthly* (July 1999), Nixon recalled that he and his family had to listen to Neil Armstrong's walk on the moon, in July 1969, on a radio. The apartheid-era government outlawed television, fearing it would undermine the foundations of a socially conservative, strictly segregated society. (In response to a public outcry, the government eventually allowed videotapes of the event to be broadcast at local planetariums. In 1977 South Africa permitted the introduction of one television channel, which the state firmly controlled.)

Nixon attended Rhodes University, in South Africa. He graduated, in 1977, receiving a B.A. in African languages. In 1980, at the age of 25, he left South Africa to avoid being drafted in the army. "I entered an exile of sorts, though I had always felt, from early childhood, that my destiny lay overseas, that emotionally I would have to leave," he wrote in *Dreambirds*. He emigrated to the United States. "South Africa still haunted me as a shadowland, but as a place composed purely of politics," he recalled. "For [the next] twelve years, the anti-apartheid cause became my passion, my revenge against an injustice and an illusion. This obsession stood at the heart of it all: my teaching, my journalism, my scholarship, my political and private life."

Nixon settled in Iowa City, where he attended graduate school at the University of Iowa. He also taught rhetoric and creative writing at the university. He received his master's degree in 1982, and then moved to New York City to pursue a doctorate, in literature, at Columbia University. Nixon earned his Ph.D. in 1989. A short time later, he joined Columbia's faculty as a professor of English and comparative literature. He also began writing articles and book reviews for such publications as *Critical Theory, Transition, London Review of Books, New York Times, South Atlantic Quarterly, Village Voice, Times Literary Supplement, New Yorker, Intermedia*, the *Guardian*, the (London) *Independent*, and the *Nation*.

In 1992 Rob Nixon published his first book, *London Calling: V. S. Naipaul, Postcolonial Mandarin*. Nixon examined the work and legacy of the novelist and travel writer V. S. Naipaul, a Trinidadian of Indian descent who emigrated to England, in 1950. Nixon challenged the popular description of Naipaul as a bridge between first- and third-world cultures. He maintained that Naipaul's ideas are, in fact, rooted in a Western tradition of thought. In his review for *World Literature Today* (August 1992), Reed Way Dasenbrock observed several contradictions in Nixon's book. "It will seem fairly obvious to most readers that Nixon is writing from precisely the 'metropolitan' intellectual position he criticizes Naipaul for attaining," Dasenbrock argued. "Writers as complex as Naipaul tend to escape pat formulations, whatever their nature; and although Nixon is remarkably adept at criticizing the pat formulations of those who have promoted Naipaul, his own critique creates a new set of pat formulations." Despite these criticisms, Dasenbrock concluded that *London Calling* "is a welcome addition to studies on Naipaul" because of its detail and formidable challenge to Naipaul's popular image. In *Choice* (October 1992), T. Ware wrote, "Nixon offers many insights into travel writing as a genre and many illuminating comparisons between Naipaul and other travel writers. This is the best of many books on Naipaul and a major contribution to postcolonial studies."

The apartheid regime in South Africa collapsed in the early 1990s, during the reign of President F. W. de Klerk. In 1993 Nixon returned to his homeland, for the first time, to attend his father's funeral. A short time later he returned again, this time to vote in the nation's first multiracial elections. His next book, *Homelands, Harlem, and Hollywood: South African Culture and the World Beyond* (1997), is a collection of nine essays relating to South Africa and the post-apartheid era. Nixon wrote about ethnic violence, the effects of the cultural and sports boycott on the apartheid regime (South African sports fans—for so long starved for international competition—have been particularly enthusiastic since the end of apartheid and the lifting of the boycott), the exile of the novelist Bessie Head, and the role of Nelson Mandela, among other topics. In her review for *Research in African Literatures* (Summer 1997), Rosemary Jolly described Nixon's arguments as "intelligent, soundly argued, and for the most part, fiercely original in their careful positioning of South Africa in relation to international debates." Although Jolly criticized Nixon for failing to give a complete picture of certain issues, she concluded that *Homelands, Harlem, and Hollywood* "is as prescient about the future as it is intelligent about the past, and can be both vastly informative . . . and tactfully moving: the chapter on Bessie Head is the best piece of writing I have seen on her life and work in a long while."

In 1999 Ron Nixon became the Rachel Carson Professor of English at the University of Wisconsin, in Madison. The same year, he published his most acclaimed book, *Dreambirds: The Strange History of the Ostrich in Fashion, Food, and Fortune*, in the United Kingdom. (The American edition was published in 2000.) Nixon incorporated his childhood memories of South Africa's ostrich country and his relationship with his father into a history of the nation's ostrich trade. According to Nixon, Jews fleeing persecution in Eastern Europe during the late 19th century settled in the South African town of Oudtshoorn. The immigrants discovered the ostriches that populated the nearby Karoo desert and began collecting and selling their feathers, which were used in European fashions. Within several decades, the feather merchants amassed vast personal fortunes and Oudtshoorn became known as the "Jerusalem of Africa." However, with the outbreak of World War I, the market for ostrich feathers vanished, and the feather merchants were financially ruined. Oudtshoorn decayed and never recovered. Recently, American entrepreneurs have begun to promote ostrich ranching among Southwestern ranchers; instead of feathers, the ostrich promoters hope to generate a market for ostrich-hide leather and ostrich-meat steaks. "The writing of *Dreambirds* took me on a journey that spanned two centuries and three continents," Nixon explained in the *Chronicle of Higher Education*. "I encountered an extraordinary cast of people, contemporary and historical, people whose lives had been turned upside down by ostriches. What emerged was a book about immigrant memory and hope: about the human capacity to dream up fantastic schemes." A reviewer for the *New Yorker* (May 8, 2000) praised *Dreambirds*, avowing that Nixon's "tale, like the feather palaces constructed by flush ostrich barons, is a 'promiscuous fantasmagoria' of history, ornithology, and episodes from his own coming of age under apartheid. Ultimately, the book does what the awkward bird Nixon clearly loves cannot: it soars." A reviewer for *Publishers Weekly* (February 7, 2000) noted that Nixon made an odd subject magical. "Nixon narrates these tales in their fascinating glory and tragedy, presenting a rich socioeconomic tale of the ostrich's rise and decline during the 20th century. Tugging at this alternatingly humorous and bizarre background is the author's honest and fresh attempt to revisit two ghosts from his past—his father . . . and South African apartheid. Who would have suspected that ostriches could provide the ballast for such a moving memoir?"

Rob Nixon is married. He and his family live in Madison, Wisconsin.

—D. C.

SUGGESTED READING: *Atlantic Monthly* p12+ July 1999, with photos; *Choice* p300 Oct. 1992; *Chronicle of Higher Education* B p4+ Mar. 31, 2000; *New Yorker* p120 May 8, 2000; *Publishers Weekly* p75 Feb. 7, 2000; *Research in African Literature* p190+ Summer 1997; *World Literature Today* p764 Aug. 1992

SELECTED BOOKS: *London Calling: V. S. Naipaul, Postcolonial Mandarin*, 1992; *Homelands, Harlem, and Hollywood: South African Culture and the World Beyond*, 1997; *Dreambirds: The Strange History of the Ostrich in Fashion, Food, and Fortune*, 1999

Nordan, Lewis

Aug. 23, 1939– Novelist; short-story writer

Lewis Nordan's short stories and novels are rooted in the literary tradition of the American South. His fiction has been compared to that of legendary southern writers William Faulkner and Eudora Welty, because, just as they did, he sets his stories in a fictionalized home town and uses recurrent characters. His unique fusion of comedy and tragedy, however, moves his work beyond such comparison. The author first gained notice in literary circles after the publication of his two short-story collections, *Welcome to the Arrow-Catcher Fair* and *The All-Girl Football Team*, and he received critical and popular acclaim with the publication of *Wolf Whistle*, his fictionalized account of the 1955 lynching of Emmett Till. He has published two celebrated novels, *The Sharpshooter Blues* and *Lightning Song*, and has completed a memoir, *Boy with Loaded Gun* (2000). Nordan's fiction, which depicts life's comic and tragic aspects side by side, defies categorization. "I became a comic writer," he said, as quoted on the *Mississippi Writers Page* (on-line), "but I always see writing from the same place, that is that deeply serious, melodramatic horror that's at the heart of my work."

Lewis Alonzo Nordan was born in Jackson, Mississippi, on August 23, 1939, the son of Lemuel Alonzo Nordan and the former Sara Hightower. Nordan's father died when he was 18 months old, leaving, as he wrote in his memoir, only one picture "in which he holds me." His mother, a schoolteacher, eventually remarried, and the family moved to Itta Bena, Mississippi, where he was raised. Frustrated by the limits of small-town life, he longed to escape Itta Bena. He ran away twice, first to Memphis, Tennessee, and later to New York City, yet each time he returned home. "I left Itta Bena to try to find a life in the larger world," he remarked in his memoir. "I was running from myself when I left home, not from the people who loved me." In 1958, at the age of 19, he joined the United States Navy and served for two years. When he returned from his tour he enrolled in Millsaps College in Jackson, Mississippi, graduating with a bachelor of arts degree in 1963. For the next two years he was a teacher in Titusville, Florida public schools. In 1965 he received his master's degree from Mississippi State University. A year later he moved to Auburn, Alabama, to become an English teacher at Auburn University; there he earned his doctorate in Shakespeare studies in 1973. From 1971 to 1974 he taught English at the University of Georgia, in Athens.

Nordan left teaching in 1975, primarily because of a shortage of teaching posts. Between 1975 and 1981 he supported himself alternately as an orderly, a clerk, and a night watchman and focused on writing fiction. He had some early success, winning the John Gould Fletcher Award from the University of Arkansas in 1977 for his short story "Rat Song"; he then received a grant from the National Endowment for the Arts in 1978, which allowed him to complete his first collection of stories *Welcome to the Arrow-Catcher Fair* (1983). In 1986 he released a second collection, *The All-Girl Football Team*, for which he won the 1987 Porter Fund Prize. Selected stories from both collections, which are populated by strange characters, were published again under the title *Sugar among the Freaks*, in 1996. Edward B. St. John, reviewing *Sugar among the Freaks* for *Library Journal* (April 1, 1996), praised the volume's "delightfully eccentric situations and colorful language" and recommended it for "all collections of Southern fiction."

Nordan's next published work, *Music of the Swamp* (1991), was difficult for many critics to categorize—some termed it a collection of short stories, others a novel. The book centers on the 11th year of Sugar Menkin, a recurrent character that appears in several of Nordan's short stories. Throughout the work many unusual things happen to Sugar: he and a friend find a man's body in the swamp, he hears a cow sing in a tenor voice, and he digs up a well-preserved woman buried in a glass coffin beneath his family's house. Sugar's home life is equally bizarre: his father accidentally gives his morphine-addicted druggist friend a lethal dose and lapses into alcoholism. "None of this black-humored drama is uncommon to southern fiction," a reviewer for *Kirkus Reviews* (July 1, 1991) remarked, "but Nordan brings wit, warmth, elegance, grace, and an original, persuasive love of his hidebound, inarticulate characters to territory previously covered by Faulkner, O'Connor, and especially . . . McCullers."

Wolf Whistle (1993), Nordan's first work to be universally accepted as a novel, is based on the case of Emmett Till. A 14-year-old black boy, Till was beaten to death in 1955 by a gang of white men for calling a white woman "baby." Two men were brought to trial for the murder but were later acquitted. Around the time of the lynching, Nordon was growing up in Itta Bena near Money, Mississippi, where Till was killed. In Nordan's fictionalized account, the brutality of the crime is offset by his breezy and comedic style. "By the book's end the reader will have been witness to an amazing display of technical virtuosity, particularly with regard to point of view," Leon Roake opined for the *Washington Post Book World* (October 3, 1993), "*Wolf Whistle*, to state matters clearly, contains a number of scenes that will astound and electrify. The novel as a whole is an illuminating, even uplifting achievement." Randall Kenan, reviewing the book for the *Nation* (November 15, 1993), concurred: "Lewis Nordan has written an outrageous, audacious book that should be applauded not only as a brave social act but as an extraordinary aesthetic achievement. Few today are writing with such verve, intelligence, and compassion." In a dissenting view, Jack Sullivan argued in the *New York Times Book Review* (January 2, 1994), that "Unfortunately, Mr. Nordan . . . gives us so many portents and flourishes that they eventually work against him, crowding out his novel's central tragedy rather than deepening its horror."

As did his previous fiction, Nordan's 1996 novel, *The Sharpshooter Blues*, takes place in the imaginary town of Arrow Catcher, Mississippi. It follows the exploits of Hydro, a simple-minded young man who does odd jobs around town: pumping gas, keeping store, and even selling moonshine at a grocery store outside of town. When a brother and sister attempt to rob the store, Hydro kills both of them, though no one believes he could possibly have done it. The incident affects the whole town; since no one thinks Hydro capable of such an act, Louis McNaughton, Hydro's friend and an eyewitness to the killings, blames it on Morgan, a young thug who happens to be having an affair with Louis's mother. Eventually all of Arrow Catcher is involved with the murders, though somehow their lives improve because of it, especially Hydro's. "Nordan expertly mines this vein of narrative gold, revealing the good will and humor, the versatility the tragedy brings out in his overwrought characters," John Albert Casey wrote for the *Voice Literary Supplement* (October 1995), echoing the virtually unanimous praise the book received. "This is not just a good book, this is a marvelous book." Karen Angel wrote for the *Washington Post Book World* (Feb. 4, 1996) that she believed that "minor inconsistencies and a tendency to mawkishness" had an effect on her reading of the work, but noted that they "vanish before Nordan's magical writing, which brings to life the ghostly otherworldliness of the swamp and the powerful emotions that lurk there."

One year after the appearance of *The Sharpshooter Blues* on bookshelves, Nordon published *Lightning Song* (1997), in which he introduced readers to Leroy Dearman, a 12-year-old boy confused by his developing sexuality. This bittersweet coming-of-age tale, which features Nordan's trademark comedic style and oddball scenarios, was a departure for the author in that it was his first to be set in a locale other than Arrow Catcher, Mississippi. Harold Augenbraum, writing for *Library Journal* (April 1, 1997), praised the novel for its "grace, charm, and humor" and noted that "its

'American-ness' may remind readers of the work of Wallace Stegner." A reviewer for *Publishers Weekly* (March 10, 1997) was more critical of *Lightning Song* but still found much to like about the novel: "Nordan's meandering plot is balanced by the rich cadences of his prose, however, and by the powerful moment in which Leroy's 'dark history was suddenly bathed in light' and he embodies his family's frustration and pain." "Given a choice between eerie and cutsey, Nordan will almost always choose cutesy, and that's a shame, because it's deeply disappointing when, at the end of this book, we lose track of Leroy's story," Maud Casey complained in her on-line review of the book for *Salon* (May 24, 1997). "Generic family love ultimately triumphs here, and in the end, the lightning of Nordan's prose comes to feel like a showy—but empty—display."

In February 2000 Nordan published a memoir, *Boy with Loaded Gun*. In it he looks back on his remarkable childhood on the Mississippi Delta and contrasts it with his more depressing adulthood, in which he cheats on his first wife, finds love with another woman only to cheat on her too, and loses two sons. In the *New York Times Book Review* (February 13, 2000), Roy Hoffman found the memoir enjoyable but opined that "Nordan writes of himself more effectively as a boy than as an adult, and it is in the latter sections of this memoir that the book, like Nordan himself, often loses its way."

Since 1983 Lewis Nordan has been a professor of English at the University of Pittsburgh, in Pennsylvania. In 1962 he married Mary Mitman; they divorced in 1983. In 1986 he married Alicia Blessing. His first marriage produced three sons: Russell Ammon, Lewis Eric, and John Robert. Some of Nordan's more recent awards include the Notable Book Award from the American Library Association, in 1992, and the Best Fiction Award from the Mississippi Institute of Arts and Letters, also in 1992.

—C. M.

SUGGESTED READING: *Mississippi Writer's Page* (on-line); *Salon* (on-line) May 25, 1997; *Harper's* p22+ Sep. 1995, p39+ Dec. 1999; *Kirkus Reviews* July 1, 1991; *Library Journal* p121 Apr. 1, 1996, p128 Apr. 1, 1997, p120 Mar. 15, 1998; *Nation* p592+ Nov. 15, 1993; *New York Times* p9 May 25, 1997; *New York Times Book Review* p14 Jan. 2, 1994, p34 Feb. 13, 2000; *Publishers Weekly* p47 Mar. 10, 1997, p28 Jan. 3, 2000; *Southern Literary Journal* p96+ Spring 1998; *Voice Literary Supplement* p14 Oct. 1995; *Washington Post Book World* p4 Oct. 3, 1993, p8 Feb. 4, 1996

SELECTED BOOKS: novels—*Music of the Swamp*, 1991; *Wolf Whistle*, 1993; *The Sharpshooter Blues*, 1996; *Lightning Song*, 1997; short-story collections—*Welcome to the Arrow-Catcher Fair*, 1983; *The All-Girl Football Team*, 1986; *Sugar among the Freaks*, 1996; memoir—*Boy with Loaded Gun*, 2000

Courtesy of Farrar, Straus and Giroux

Norman, Howard

Mar. 4, 1949– Novelist; translator; short-story writer; folklorist

One might assume that Howard Norman is Canadian: most of his fiction—including all four of his novels—has been set in Canada, often in the nation's remote, northern terrain. Nevertheless, Norman is a wholly American writer, born and raised in the Midwest. He explained his attraction to Canada to John DeMont for *Maclean's* (December 14, 1998): "It is where my imagination, for better or worse, comes alive." With a background in folklore and translation and a general fascination with Native American culture, Norman spent 16 years living for extended periods in Canada, Greenland, and Newfoundland, observing and recording tribal tradition. Fluent in three Algonquin and Eskimo dialects (and passable in another two), Norman has produced several translated volumes of Native American poems and folklore for adults and children, including *Northern Tales: Traditional Stories of Eskimo and Indian Peoples* (1990) and *The Girl Who Dreamed Only Geese, and Other Tales from the Far North* (1997). His translation work provided him with a type of literary apprenticeship that prompted him to begin writing his own fiction in the early 1980s. His first two novels, *The Northern Lights* (1987) and *The Bird Artist* (1994), were each nominated for the National Book Award, while his remaining works, *The Museum Guard* (1998) and *The Haunting of L.* (2002), have also garnered widespread critical praise. In addition to his novels, Norman has penned two volumes of short stories, *Kiss in the Hotel Joseph Conrad* (1989) and *The Chauffeur: Stories* (2002), as well as numerous articles and reviews, documentaries, plays, and commissioned screenplays. The recipient of grants and fellowships from the National Endowment for the Arts, the National Endowment for the Humanities, the Mrs. Giles Whiting Foundation, and the John Simon Guggenheim Memorial Foundation, Norman has been recognized, according to Drake Bennett for *Boston Review* (April–May 2002, on-line), as "a quiet writer . . . who knows how to get your attention."

Howard Norman was born in Toledo, Ohio, on March 4, 1949. He was one of four boys born to Jewish parents of Russian and Polish descent. After Norman's family settled in Grand Rapids, Michigan, where he attended school, the young boy experienced a tumultuous childhood. His father abandoned the family, and his mother was forced to work as a nanny to earn a living. Norman learned to cope by frequenting bookmobiles and libraries. "I went to four different elementary schools," he told Margaritte Huppért and Donald Lee for *Ploughshares* (Winter 1997–1998). "Libraries were the one continuity. And from early on, through books, I projected a life—I daydreamed north. This is makeshift psychologizing, but perhaps part of it was that such open, vast spaces, such a sense of mystery and severe, compelling landscapes, served to counteract the claustrophobia of an inwardly collapsing home life." During these years, Norman became extremely close to a schoolmate, Paul, and the boy's family; he was devastated when Paul abruptly died from a rare blood disease. To escape the trauma Norman eventually dropped out of school and moved to Canada, living with friends outside of Toronto. One summer, he worked on a brush fire crew and became intrigued by the culture and storytelling traditions of many of his co-workers, who were largely Cree Indians.

After earning his high school equivalency, Norman returned to Michigan to attend Western Michigan University, in Kalamazoo, where he studied English and zoology; he often spent his summers in Canada as a student of the country's native culture. Throughout college he also worked in Kalamazoo's Athena Book Store, where he developed a passion for the work of the naturalist and bird artist Edward Lear. Norman told Huppért and Lee, "Every extra dollar I earned went into a print by [Mark] Catesby [an English naturalist] or one of Edward Lear's parrots." Norman completed his B.A. degree and enrolled at the Folklore Institute of Indiana University, graduating in 1976 with a master's degree; shortly after, he was offered a three-year fellowship at the University of Michigan, which allowed him to concentrate on translations. Through his post-graduate work and his own personal contact with tribal peoples, Norman had developed linguistic skills in several Algonquin and Eskimo dialects. He focused on transcribing and translating Native American poems and folktales from oral tradition, which had rarely, if ever, been written down. As Norman told Huppért and Lee, "I listened to, recorded, kept notebooks on hundreds of stories. Sometimes under formal circumstances, most often not. And even if you are slow to grasp the true emotional and historical dimensions and generosities of these myths and folktales, still, a lot of it sinks in. The structures, the rhythms, the wild episodes, the sheer inventiveness and unpredictability of incident. Of course, as a Westerner—an outsider—one can't ever think in those languages. But you can work at it. I was dogged, if nothing else. One project, transcription and translation of just ten shaman stories from around Hudson's Bay, is just now getting completed almost to my satisfaction, after twenty years or so. That's pretty much how it has gone for me. Translation was a good education. Sitting at family tables in locales such as Churchill or Eskimo Point, filling notebooks, botching it, botching it, getting a little right."

In 1978 Norman assembled his first collection of translations, *The Wishing Bone Cycle: Narrative Poems of the Swampy Cree Indians*, for which he won the Harold Morton Landon Translation Award from the Academy of American Poets. Norman shared this prize with the poet and translator Galway Kinnell. (He reportedly shares his royalties and honoraria with the Cree Indians.) After publishing the book Norman continued traveling through Canada and various Arctic regions, often working as a freelance writer. His projects included field reports for several journals and museums, travel articles, radio plays, documentaries, and children's books; he also worked as an interpreter for such international organizations as the World Society for the Protection of Animals. He told Huppért and Lee, "Deep down, I think I still harbored some hope of constructing a life somewhat like my hero at the time, Edward Lear. He was a rather eccentric traveler, and of course a wonderful artist. . . . I had this notion of reporting back from remote places and including my sketches and drawings. An utterly autonomous life. The central failure in my thinking was that I simply could not draw."

In 1981 Norman was invited to spend Thanksgiving with the poet Philip Levine and his wife, Fran; there, he met another poet, Jane Shore, with whom he fell in love. (The couple married in 1984.) With Shore's encouragement Norman began working on his fiction and soon submitted several pages of a novel to an editor of the literary magazine *Ploughshares*. The piece was published, and the exposure helped Norman obtain an award from the Whiting Foundation, which allowed him to complete his book. Norman published *The Northern Lights* in 1987. At around that time, he also published three children's books of folklore, *The Owl Scatterer* (1986), *Who-Paddled-Backward-With-Trout; A Cree Indian Naming Story* (1987), and *How Glooskap Outwits the Ice Giants, and Other Tales of the Maritime Indians* (1989).

In *The Northern Lights* Norman presents the coming-of-age story of the young narrator, Noah Krainik, raised in an isolated village in northern Canada. Told through a series of flashbacks, the novel explores Noah's world, from his absentee father, a cartographer who travels 11 months out of the year, to his best friend, Pelly, a talented, half-Cree artist who dies in a tragic unicycle accident. The novel shifts when Noah's mother, whose secluded surroundings have pushed her to madness, moves to Toronto to re-open a rundown movie theater, the Northern Lights. "Norman paints [the novel's] landscape lovingly," W.D. Wetherell observed for the *Washington Post* (April 28, 1987), "with such detailed attention to character that every word seems to spring from and suggest a remarkable clarity of vision. . . . In his simplicity and artlessness, we are convinced of the authenticity of both his locale and his characters." Other critics responded warmly to *The Northern Lights* as well, with Ceil Cleveland for the *New York Times* (April 12, 1987) calling the work "a striking achievement," and Austin MacCurtain for the *Times Literary Supplement* (March 11–17, 1988) affirming it as "funny, tender, and written with simplicity and integrity: a modest book of great originality, utterly faithful to its subject." While some reviews noted that the novel's second half was not as powerful as the first—either visually or emotionally—they more often emphasized Norman's flare for narrative. Wetherell concluded, "Artlessness requires a tremendous amount of art, and it's no disparagement of Norman to say he hasn't quite refined it yet in this stage of his career. What he does have is natural story-telling talent that carries much before it." *The Northern Lights* was nominated for the 1987 National Book Award.

Norman followed his successful novel with a collection of seven short stories. The settings within *A Kiss in the Hotel Joseph Conrad and Other Stories* (1989) were often such secluded environments as Nova Scotia, Halifax, and Vermont. Richard Eder noted for the *Los Angeles Times* (September 3, 1989), "The stories strike odd notes of extremity. In some, the oddity seems contrived, a quirk. In the best of them, it is a rip in our insulation; the winter seeps in and we feel the anguish that has been discovered in us, not inflicted." The collection's most memorable stories deal with themes of survival and isolation. "Jenny Aloo," for example, is about an old Eskimo woman who believes her missing son is trapped inside a jukebox, and "Old Swimmers" depicts several elderly women at their annual meeting to commemorate their survival during a ferry sinking in World War II. While Eder acknowledged that the book's pieces "are not perfect—Norman is still a little unhandy at such scut-work of fiction as plots, transitions and the amount of heralding you need to make a point," he concluded, "their modal distances are unforgettable."

Norman's second novel, *The Bird Artist* (1994), became perhaps his most critically acclaimed to date; the work also commenced what Norman has called his "Canadian Trilogy." Narrated by a fictional bird artist, Fabian Vas, who grew up in Witless Bay, Newfoundland, at the beginning of the century, the novel opens with Fabian's confession that "I murdered the lighthouse keeper, Botho August, and that is an equal part of how I think of myself," as quoted by Eder for the *Los Angeles Times* (July 10, 1994). As the novel unfolds, Fabian explains the events leading up to this murder, including Botho's affair with Fabian's mother, the deflated relationship between his parents, Alaric and Orkney, and Fabian's own unconventional association with the animated and alcoholic village personality, Margaret Handle, who is four years his senior. Norman told Lynn Karpen for the *New York Times* (July 10, 1994) that he conceived the original idea for the novel in 1978 while conducting research for a documentary in Newfoundland. "I was put up in this village in an abandoned church," he explained. "It was rather monastic and the only decoration was a painting of an ibis, unsigned but dated 1911. A very elderly woman recalled that the artist had long ago been charged with murdering the local lighthouse keeper." Norman investigated this intriguing story until, as he told Huppért and Lee, "what I was finding out—facts—began to trespass on what I *imagined* might have taken place."

The Bird Artist earned Norman near-unanimous critical praise, with Eder calling it "light and magical . . . one of the most perfect and original novels that I have read in years." A reviewer for *Wilson Quarterly* (Spring 1995) celebrated the work as "a novel for the ear," elaborating, "Norman favors pared-down sentences and broken dialogue, most of which convey some odd, savory turn of phrase that salts—and hermetically seals—the story in its own packing of language. This language, at once simplified and oddly poetic . . . is the real subject of this novel." Commenting on Norman's success in depicting the unique inhabitants of Witless Bay, Robert Hellenga for the *Washington Post* (July 24, 1994) noted that the novel's strength lay in "the capacity of the villagers . . . to surprise us over and over again without becoming merely eccentric." *The Bird Artist* was named one of *Time* magazine's five best books of the year and earned Norman the New England Booksellers Association Prize in fiction, the Lannan Literary Award, and another nomination for the National Book Award.

In addition to his fiction, Norman continued to work on translations; he published *Northern Tales: Traditional Stories of Eskimo and Indian Peoples* in 1990; this collection presented 116 folktales that he had amassed from various cultures throughout Siberia, Greenland, northern Canada, and the Aleutian Islands. In 1997 he published *The Girl Who Dreamed Only Geese, and Other Tales of the Far North*, a collection of Inuit stories for young readers. Although the book is aimed at a preteen audience, Denise Anton Wright observed for *School Library Journal* (November 1997) that it contains "fascinating, magical, and funny stories that can be enjoyed by anyone." The collection was named one of the *New York Times Book Review*'s best illustrated books of the year, as well as a best book of the year by *School Library Journal* and a notable book for children by *Smithsonian* magazine. In 1999 Norman published another collection of Algonquin tales for children, entitled *Trickster and the Fainting Birds*.

Of *The Museum Guard* (1998), the second novel in his Canadian Trilogy, Norman explained to Huppért and Lee: "In the past, I'd pretty much tended to write about open spaces, how wilderness and isolation affected character, and so on. But in *The Museum Guard*, the attempt is something different. . . . This novel resides largely in interior spaces. Museums, hotel rooms, hotel lobbies. And the larger 'backdrop,' if you will, is Europe—across the ocean—and the war building up." As in *The Bird Artist*, the narrator of *The Museum Guard*, Defoe Russet, begins the novel with a confession: "The painting I stole for Imogen Linny, *Jewess on a Street in Amsterdam*, arrived to the Glace Museum, here in Halifax, on September 5, 1938." Through the ensuing story, Defoe explains his relationship with Imogen Linny, the caretaker of Halifax's Jewish cemetery, and Linny's growing obsession with the character in the painting. Defoe, who was orphaned at age eight when his parents died in a zeppelin crash and raised by his Uncle Edward, leads a quiet life sleeping in the Lord Nelson Hotel and working at the Glace Museum. Yet, his life becomes more complicated as Linny begins to believe that she is the Jewess in the painting and journeys to Amsterdam to locate the artist, Joop Heijman, whom she believes is her husband.

Critics praised Norman for his imaginative characters and settings. One reviewer for *Publishers Weekly* (May 18, 1998) wrote, "Norman again creates eccentric characters whose oddities seem quite natural." Fernanda Eberstadt observed for the *New York Times* (August 30, 1998, on-line), "[Norman] has mastered a narrative voice so dry, so laconic, so humbly self-denying that the most muted gestures can have the force of a scream." However, several critics found Norman's development of Imogen Linny lacking. For example, Phil Whitaker, writing for the *New Statesman* (March 5, 1999), called the scenes of Linny in Amsterdam "mired . . . in melodrama," adding, "The reader is left churning through page after page, wondering what on earth happened to the engaging novel they started out with." Eileen Pollack for the *Boston Globe* (August 16, 1998, on-line) noted a similar problem, but reasoned, "In its first 30 pages—and for most pages after that *The Museum Guard* provides more pleasure than many novels can provide in 10 times as much prose. If a character like Imogen Linny draws a reader in, then begins behaving in a way the reader finds infuriating, maybe that is a testament to the powers of her creator."

Norman completed his Canadian Trilogy with *The Haunting of L.* (2002), this time narrated by Peter Duvett, another orphaned young man who has come to Churchill (a town on the southern shore of the Hudson Bay) to work for a villainous photographer, Vienna Linn. The day Duvett arrives, he begins an affair with Linn's new bride. As the novel details Linn's evil scheme of manipulating accidents in order to be the first photographer on the scene, Peter must reconcile his own involvement in the crimes of adultery and ultimately murder. Throughout the novel, according to Drake Bennet, Norman reflects upon themes established in his previous works, such as "what is genuine in art, the extremes to which loss drives people, and what happens when those two issues get jumbled together." Writing for the *Toronto Star* (April 7, 2002), Elizabeth Johnston observed another similarity between *The Haunting of L.* and its predecessors, noting that Norman "once again explores the shallow depths of ordinary men who, swept up in extraordinary circumstances, remain steadfastly, even tragically, ordinary."

Critics offered varying reviews for the book. Bennett, who characterized the novel as a catalogue of motifs, observed, "After a while, the reader starts to crave something more than motifs and themes." Michael Dirda for the *Washington Post* (March 31, 2002, on-line), however, called the novel "classically artful" and concluded, "Howard Norman's darkly mesmerizing novel of people pushed to, and even beyond, their limits manages to transform contrivances into urgencies. That might almost be a definition of art."

In 2002 Norman also published his second collection of short stories, entitled *The Chauffeur*. He currently teaches one semester per year at the creative writing department of the University of Maryland. He resides for half of the year in Washington, D.C., and the remainder of the year at his 150-year-old farmhouse in Vermont. Norman and Jane Shore have one daughter.

—K. D.

SUGGESTED READING: *Boston Globe* (on-line) Aug. 16, 1998; *Boston Review* (on-line) Apr.–May 2002; *Los Angeles Times* V p1+ Mar. 18, 1987; *Maclean's* p80+ Dec. 14, 1998; *New Republic* p46 Mar. 25, 2002; *New Statesman* p55 Mar. 5, 1999; *New York Times* (on-line) Aug. 30, 1998, Apr. 10, 2002; *New York Times Book Review* p16 Oct. 8, 1989, p7 July 10, 1994; *Washington Post Book World* p3 July 24, 1994

SELECTED BOOKS: short-story collections—*A Kiss in the Hotel Joseph Conrad and Other Stories*, 1989; *The Chauffeur*, 2002; novels—*The Northern Lights*, 1987; *The Bird Artist*, 1994; *The Museum Guard*, 1998; *The Haunting of L.*, 2002; transcriptions and translations—*The Wishing Bone Cycle: Narrative Poems of the Swampy Cree Indians*, 1978; *The Woe Shirt: Caribbean Folk Tales*, 1980; *Where the Chill Came From: Cree Windigo Tales and Journeys*, 1982; *Northern Tales: Traditional Stories of Eskimo and Indian Peoples*, 1990; children's folklore—*The Owl Scatterer*, 1986; *Who-Paddled-Backward-with-Trout; A Cree Indian Naming Story*, 1987; *How Glooskap Outwits the Ice Giants and Other Tales of the Maritime Indians*, 1989; *The Girl Who Dreamed Only Geese, and

Other Tales from the Far North, 1997; *Trickster and the Fainting Birds*, 1999

David Rae Morris/Courtesy of Houghton Mifflin

Nossiter, Adam

June 4, 1960–Nonfiction writer

In two books that detail the human stories behind epoch-making events, the American writer Adam Nossiter has explored the way that the past influences—and exists in—the present, often in hidden ways. *Of Long Memory: Mississippi and the Murder of Medgar Evers* (1994) shows how the civil rights movement in the American South prevailed, as evidenced by the fact that the murderer of the civil rights leader Medgar Evers could be convicted after three decades; the climate of opinion had shifted from one of almost universal white sympathy for Evers's killer to a desire for justice on the part of the majority. In *The Algeria Hotel: France, Memory and the Second World War* (2001), Nossiter dealt with the hidden wounds left by World War II in people who refused to acknowledge the past. "If memory can be so easily distorted, history needs to take extra pains to ensure that the dialogue between past and present is free of self-serving cant and propaganda," Lawrence N. Powell wrote in the New Orleans *Times-Picayune* (July 22, 2001), judging that Nossiter's writing of history served the purpose of clearing away the cobwebs of self-serving distortions of that history.

Adam Nossiter's autobiographical statement for *World Authors 1995–2000* follows: "I was born in the United States, grew up mostly in Europe, and have spent most of my professional life as a journalist in the American South. These biographical elements have contributed to my main preoccupation, which I have explored in two books: the overhang of the past. In Europe, in the Paris of the mid-1960s and later in London in the 1970s (my father was a newspaper reporter in both places) the recent past of World War II was part of the landscape, inside the family house and out. In the South, the past of civil rights, civil war, and slavery was the constant subtext on reporting trips for the several newspapers I've worked for over the last two decades—the *St. Petersburg* (Fla.) *Times*, the *Atlanta Journal-Constitution*, and the *New York Times*. I am haunted by the idea that the past doesn't actually disappear, that it continues to exist in some form, and that elements of, for instance, traumatic historical events persist in present-day behavior. My task has been to find these elements, and to uncover their coherence. My first book dealt with the South—with the murder of the civil rights leader Medgar Evers in 1963, and how the American state of Mississippi tortuously came around, over three decades, to judging his killer. In my second book I sought to look even more closely at the persistence of the past by examining three places in France troubled by the memory of World War II and German Occupation. My objective was to get as close as possible to answering the question of what it means to live with old events.

"One of my own earliest childhood memories is of the house my family inhabited in Paris. It had once belonged to a famous French surgeon who shot himself on the second floor on the day the Germans marched into Paris in 1940. This story made a strong impression on me as a child, partly because it seemed to impress my parents a great deal. In addition, friends of my parents had survived concentration camps, been in the French Resistance, lived through the London Blitz. These things were brought up as a matter of course. So from early days I had a sense that what had happened in a distant time could in some way linger. This sense was reinforced by my study of French history at Harvard in the early 1980s. We were taught not only the facts of the past, but also the ongoing debate in France surrounding them. We were made very conscious of contemporary disputes between historians, and initiated into the sense that what is referred to as 'history' is actually rather fluid and changeable. So here too was further evidence of a living connection to old events.

"My work as a newspaper reporter fueled my preoccupation with these questions. As a reporter, I was strongly influenced by my father's approach to journalism; it was his passion to read as much as he possibly could about the areas he was covering. He was an unusually bookish journalist. Yet in newspaper reporting it is difficult to bring this knowledge to bear, to find space or time to look closely at the elements beneath what you are witnessing, or the commentary you are listening to. You feel nonetheless, whenever you are reporting a story, and almost instinctively, that there is a whole world beneath.

"Elements from the past, acknowledged or otherwise, make up this world, it seems to me. It was a desire to uncover it that led me to my two books. In Mississippi, for instance, where I roamed for a number of years as a reporter, how could you understand the hostility of whites to reviving the Medgar Evers case without knowing the larger history of institutional oppression? That hostility was itself the best discrediting of white claims that the murder of Evers was just 'history.' It was an event that continued to provoke and agitate long after its occurrence, and in that way to intrude into ordinary existence.

"I wanted to get as close as possible to the question of what it means to live with the past, and France seemed to me an ideal laboratory for doing so. My book about the memory of the wartime past in three French towns in no way sets out to be about whether or not the French feel guilty, or should feel guilty, about this past. Nor does it seek to be about whether or not the French collaborated. These are old questions, and I saw no point in revisiting them. Instead, I wanted to see the particular form agitation over old events takes in ordinary lives. I looked for signs of it not systematically—it seemed to me foolish to pursue a rigid, linear approach to such old memories—but in a multitude of interviews, some random and some not, in buildings, and wherever I could observe them, in habits of behavior. I looked for patterns in what people were telling me; I attempt to let people have their say (often it was ugly), and by juxtaposing their words, weaving them together, to arrive at a sense of the unease engendered by the past's intrusions. The book does not set out to be a morality tale about France during the war—that tale has already been told—but an attempt to uncover what it means to live simultaneously in both past and present."

Adam Nossiter was born in Washington, D.C., on June 4, 1960 and moved to Paris, where his father was a reporter for the *Washington Post*, in his early childhood. He followed in his father's profession, reporting on the American South for the *Atlanta Constitution* and on New Orleans for the *New York Times*. He has also written for the *Houston Chronicle*; the New Orleans *Times-Picayune*; the *San Francisco Chronicle*; the *Guardian*; and *The Nation*, among other publications.

Nossiter's method in his books and articles has been to concentrate on the story behind the story, often favoring interviews and personal testimony over so-called objective analysis. Nossiter covered the final trial of Byron de la Beckwith, who was indicted in 1990 and convicted in 1994 for the 1963 murder of Medgar Evers in Mississippi, after two trials in the 1960s had ended in hung juries. Nossiter's book *Of Long Memory* deals with the assassination and its aftermath and repercussions, leading to Beckwith's conviction, which exemplified the gradual change that had made equal participation in civil and political life possible for African-Americans in Mississippi and the other southern states.

Nossiter commented on the roles of Evers, and such others as Vernon Dahmer and William Waller, a prosecutor who tried to get Beckwith convicted in the 1960s, in obtaining civil rights. "They helped make integration a fact. They made an idea that had seemed extraordinary in Mississippi—the idea of whites sharing social and political institutions with blacks as coequals—ordinary," Nossiter wrote in the book. He also emphasized the contrasts in the family backgrounds of Evers and Beckwith, showing that Evers had received guidance from his upright parents, who were great believers in education, while Beckwith had an abusive, alcoholic father who died when he was five; his mother died six years later, leaving him in the care of male relatives who also abused him.

Evers was an outspoken proponent of civil rights and became famous for his vocal opposition to conditions under which African-Americans had to struggle in Mississippi. Beckwith, driven by an obsessive racism, became a hero to white people who would not have followed his path but who agreed with him in principle. Nevertheless, the first time Beckwith was tried for the murder, six members of the all-white jury voted for conviction, unusual in an area where no white man had ever been convicted of murdering a black man and acquittal had been expected; no verdict was reached. Beckwith's second trial also resulted in a hung jury. While he was never actually acquitted, neither was he convicted until his third trial, in 1994, after new evidence of previous jury tampering emerged. In an article in the *Houston Chronicle* (December 21, 1990), published just after Beckwith had been newly indicted, Nossiter explored the themes on which he would elaborate in the book: "Mississippi's official spokesmen, white and black, have hailed the reindictment of Beckwith . . . as evidence of the state's willingness to deal with the uglier aspects of its past. But for many, the revival of the case has been troubling. . . . For many whites, Beckwith is an uncomfortable reminder of a period when the state reaped national disgrace for its violent defense of segregation. For blacks, there is muted satisfaction at seeing Beckwith once more in the dock." Nossiter included in the book commentaries and stories from many observers, giving a sense of how the movement Evers personified finally led to Beckwith's conviction.

Critical response to *Of Long Memory* was generally favorable. Marilyn Chandler McEntyre, the reviewer for the *Washington Post Book World* (July 10, 1994), commended Nossiter's dispassionate approach: "Nossiter is a Jewish non-Southerner, hence a member of one of the white supremacists' target groups. But his treatment of individuals and of the culture of racism is even-handed, non-sensationalized and compassionate: He even imagines the lives and fears of those who appear as the villains in this historical drama. . . . He manages to avoid idealizing Evers and he endows the now aged Beckwith with real pathos even as he cites damning facts. It . . . vividly reminds readers of our past and provides hope that history has something to teach us." William Ferris, writing in the *New York Times Book Review* (July 24, 1994), concurred, citing Nossiter's observation that "Medgar Evers's death in 1963, the 'first of the decade's political assassinations,' was the first civil rights murder that drew national attention."

Nossiter later turned his investigative and analytic skills to an examination of the climate of opinion in France long after the German occupation of World War II. His *The Algeria Hotel: France, Memory and the Second World War*, published in 2001, takes its title from the hotel in Vichy that was used as the headquarters for the identification of Jews, the confiscation of their property, and their deportation to death camps. Nossiter began *The Algeria Hotel* with his own childhood memories of being in Paris during the years that Charles de Gaulle was the president of France; the confidence and air of prosperity that characterized that era formed a contrast with the somber tales of the past that the young Nossiter heard. De Gaulle, who "was God in those years," as Nossiter wrote, referring to the 1960s, was instrumental in creating the postwar image of France as having refused to accommodate the Germans. "The late war continued to exist in this optimistic world," Nossiter wrote of his childhood years, "but only as a kind of negative foil. The country was moving forward; de Gaulle, as everybody knew, had triumphed in those war years, incarnating the essence of France with his refusal to collaborate. His version of the war's aftermath—nothing of the country's murky collaborationist regime subsisted, and France had been reborn—was the accepted one." Although the nation's citizens knew that the received version of recent history was not necessarily the true one, they buried their memories. Nossiter set himself the task of revealing the effect of those buried memories. He covered mainly Bordeaux, where Maurice Papon was tried in 1997 for war crimes committed in the early 1940s; Vichy, chosen as the capital of the Nazi-accommodating French regime for its plethora of hotel rooms, used to house government officials; and Tulle, a small town where the Germans hanged 99 men and sent 101 others to concentration camps in revenge for Resistance activity in 1944, just after the Allied invasion of Normandy, which began Germany's defeat. *The Algeria Hotel* tells the story of three years Nossiter spent traveling around France, listening to people's stories and tracing the relationship of their pasts to their daily lives in the present. Richard Bernstein, writing in the *New York Times* (August 1, 2001) observed that "as . . . *Algeria Hotel* reveals, outsiders [such as Nossiter] still have something special to bring in the way of insight to the most troubling years of 20th-century French history and the way those years are remembered."

Bernstein described *The Algeria Hotel* as "intelligent, intimate and elegantly presented" and predicted that readers would "feel as if something essentially bitter, unflattering to the human species has been disclosed about the ways that men and women practice self-deceit." Eric Weinberger, the reviewer for the *Boston Globe* (August 12, 2001), agreed, observing that *The Algeria Hotel* is "a book without heroes, and testament to our own worst nature." The *New York Times Book Review* (July 15, 2001) critic, Christopher Caldwell, called *The Algeria Hotel* a "sensitive but oddly detached book," adding, "Nossiter writes from a standpoint of moral neutrality that is an asset for a reporter but a liability for an author. The absence of judgmentalism doesn't make his narrative more objective; it makes it more psychiatric. . . . For the French, the torment of Vichy lies in resolving whether they were the Nazis' sidekicks or their victims. This has proved impossible to do, as the answer is both. One can sympathize with the difficulty. But next to punishment for the perpetrators and remembrance for the lost, therapy for the witnesses is a matter of secondary importance."

The reviewer for the *St. Louis Post-Dispatch* (July 30, 2001), Suzanne Rhodenbaugh, found *The Algeria Hotel* to be "a very contemporary kind of project," an "exploration of how memory per se is qualified, provisional, changing and so on, especially in regard to a history whose proportions of evil make any connection to it—even in time, even in physical proximity—suggestive of guilt to one degree or another. . . . Because the implied judgment is of memory, not actions, and because guilt by association is also implicit, the author's stance tends to blur the lines between the patently guilty, the heroic, the victimized, the 'uninvolved' and the innocent. . . . The book does, however, raise significant questions, the most important of which Nossiter frames as 'the moral continuity of past and present.' He convinces us that such continuity does, and must, exist."

That is indeed Nossiter's goal, as shown in his first two books: to demonstrate "moral continuity." He pointed in *The Algeria Hotel* to a French lawyer who started his career by defending Nazi collaborators before going on to do work of more benefit to the public; that lawyer's life can be seen, Nossiter wrote, as a seamless whole, while that of Maurice Papon, who sent Jews to their deaths from Vichy and then became a government official in postwar France, was one of discontinuity, distortion, and deformity, the distortions themselves amounting to immorality. In Nossiter's view, it is possible for people to evolve gradually into their better selves, as they did in the American South depicted in *Of Long Memory*.

Adam Nossiter lives in New Orleans.

—S. Y.

SUGGESTED READING: *Boston Globe* D p4 Aug. 12, 2001; *Houston Chronicle* p8 Dec. 21, 1990; *New York Times* E p8 Aug. 1, 2001; *New York Times Book Review* p9 July 15, 2001; *St. Louis*

Post-Dispatch D p3 July 30, 2001; *Times-Picayune* D p6 July 22, 2001; *Washington Post Book World* p11 July 10, 1994

SELECTED BOOKS: *Of Long Memory: Mississippi and the Murder of Medgar Evers*, 1994; *The Algeria Hotel: France, Memory and the Second World War*, 2001

Courtesy of White Pine Press

Novakovich, Josip

Apr. 30, 1956– Short-story writer; nonfiction writer

The Croatian-born short-story and nonfiction writer Josip Novakovich has earned significant attention in the U.S. for his heartfelt depictions of life in the former Yugoslavia. Whether through his critically acclaimed essays—collected in *Apricots from Chernobyl* (1994)—or his innovative short stories—presented in *Yolk* (1995) and *Salvation and Other Disasters* (1998)—Novakovich often explores the complexities of life in his troubled native region. Novakovich, who has lived in the U.S. since the age of 20, writes exclusively in English and has composed two books of instruction on writing fiction. He has received the 1995 Richard J. Margolis Award, a Cohen/Ploughshares award, an Ingram Merrill award, and a fellowship from the National Endowment for the Arts.

Novakovich composed the following autobiographical statement for *World Authors 1995-2000*: "You are a writer in so far as you write and when you write. These days I am distracted with travel and moving to Pennsylvania, where I teach at Penn State University, so I don't write enough to talk about myself as a writer, but I can tell about how I came to write at all. In my boyhood, I read passionately partly because of frequently being ill and partly because in my small hometown, Daruvar, Croatia, not much went on. I wanted to play tennis, but there was no tennis club; I loved chess, but there was no real chess club. I loved music, and began to learn how to play the violin, but a retired military orchestra conductor was my only teacher, who liked to whack me over the fingers with his bow, which may not have thwarted my love of music as much as breaking my left arm in playing soccer did. I thought my primary talent lay in drawing; however, drawing did not excite me. I had many ambitions. I wanted to be a doctor and a psychiatrist and philosopher. I started studying medicine in Novi Sad, but got a chance to spend a couple of years in the States at Vassar as a liberal arts student, which I took. The American optimism influenced me to think that what I wanted could be done. I could write. I wrote in English as a second language, many essays, so writing in the language seemed natural to me when I remained in the States and grew disenchanted with philosophy and theology at Yale. Partly because of the rigid way in which books of philosophy were translated, I grew to detest reading philosophy, and found it a great pleasure to read fiction, with unrestrained playful sentences. So, almost by default I resorted to writing fiction, seeking pleasure in lively expression, in absurdities. Here I found something subversive, an arena of freedom. Still, I wanted to do nearly everything that I didn't do in the other arts and endeavors right there in fiction—to reach for the understanding of psychology, of human motivation, violence, of suffering, death. The story that influenced me most and drove me to the writing desk was 'The Death of Ivan Ilych' by Tolstoy. I had witnessed my father's death when I was 11, and I wanted to come to grips with his death and my fear of death in writing, and so I wrote a couple of stories in which death was the central theme. But, I didn't want writing to be a grim affair, so I joked as much as I could, and I read Beckett and Kafka, and imitated them. I learned to write mostly from reading, and the notion that you could go to a workshop to learn how to write did not appeal to me at all. However, when I did odd jobs in NYC, and wrote aimless narratives which nobody would publish, I decided to go to workshops, somewhere warm, and went to Austin, Texas. Not that I learned there much, but I had a lot of time, and I wrote many stories and drafts of two novels. I learned how to send them off to magazines and began to publish. David Bradley published my first story in *New Virginia Review*. He first accepted one of them, and wrote me a five page letter, detailing how I should revise it. His letter taught me more than some of my workshops did. It showed me how writers could be educated by other writers and editors, through feedback. Too bad that the art of editing has declined, so that these days it would be hard to imagine the kind of apprenticeship Babel underwent with Maxim Gorky. There were a few other editors who taught me the art of revision and compression. Anyhow, in the States culture could be recouped artificially. If people don't walk in their daily routine as part of culture, well, they could go to the gym or go on organized hikes; if they don't exchange ideas about writing in a salon, well, they could go to a university writing workshop and do something similar.

"I could tell the story of how I came to write in many ways, and they would all be true, to some extent, so it seems there are many roads that lead to Rome. One of them, letter writing, is perhaps the most direct. When I got to the States, I wrote long letters to my friends in Croatia. In return I got postcards. That was painful, but I realized I still enjoyed writing the letters, and instead of writing to them, I wrote to nobody, journals, essays, sketches, stories, but throughout, I kept that initial impulse of writing a letter as the paradigm.

"Writing started much before letter-writing, however. I tried to write when I was 13. I sprained my ankle in basketball, and while staying in bed, I wrote the beginning of a western, in which everybody shoots everybody, so pretty soon I ran out of antagonists. I would have managed to continue and to revive the antagonists if my leg hadn't got better and my chess partners hadn't visited me. At school, we had to write, for a grade, once a week, for two hours, various compositions. I enjoyed being silly, and a couple of times, my teachers were entertained so much that they took my compositions to other classes to read out loud. That gave me a notion that people liked what I did with words on the page. Since I was a bit of a stutterer, and had stage-fright for a long time, this was an unexpected overcoming of my inferiority in communication. I remembered that I could do that—whenever there was something to say, I wanted to write it.

"Later, I ran into many great conversationalists, whose jokes were better than mine, who could tell great anecdotes, and while I couldn't reciprocate in the tavern, I could attempt on the page to do something similar. The page became my tavern. I could bring in my favorite guests, seat them any way I liked, and order a round of muddiest wheat-beer.

"Maybe much is lost through my writing in English as a second language, although by now, it is chronologically my second language and pragmatically my first—I have written ten times more in English, and my words flow much less self-consciously, even naturally, than in my native language. I could say the language is my second nature now—but any language is, we aren't born with it. Nothing is lost in translation since I don't translate but write directly in English. However, when I set scenes in Croatia, and have people who would ordinarily speak in slang converse, then I am at a loss—I don't translate into an equivalent American slang . . . so there's a bit of distance that results from this handicap, and the conversations aren't realistic. That in a way drives me to write imaginatively, not to recreate the realities of the Balkans, but to transform them into an expressive picture with a touch of surrealism. On the other hand, the dreamy and sometimes nightmarish atmosphere in my fiction could at some level be a more direct and accurate portrait of the region's souls than a strict surface reproduction—at least I hope so. And at the same time, no matter whether I illuminate much, I play, and I hope that the playfulness in the stories can bring along a few readers to imagine the things I relate to them in words.

"Recently I have been a writing fellow at the New York Public Library. My term started on September 10, just a day before WTC vanished. I am working on a novel about Croatian and Slovenian immigrants in the States in the first two decades of the last century. We'll see how that works."

When Novakovich published his first book, *Apricots from Chernobyl* (1993), he was teaching creative writing in the English department of the University of Cincinnati, where he worked from 1993 to 2001. He left in that year for a position in the M.F.A. program at Pennsylvania State University in University Park. *Apricots from Chernobyl* is a collection of 17 essays in which Novakovich evoked life in the "old country" and described the experiences of a newcomer to American shores.

The 17 short stories in Novakovich's next book, the 1995 collection *Yolk*, "send the reader through the core of the former Yugoslavia in a way that broadcast media never will," Susan M. Olcott wrote in *Library Journal* (October 1, 1995). "More than the chest is bared here—we get to see the heart." Novakovich's 1998 book, *Salvation and Other Disasters: Short Stories*, was similarly well received. His most recent work, *Plum Brandy: Croatian Sojourns*, was published in February 2003.

The first of Novakovich's writers' manuals, *Fiction Writer's Workshop*, appeared in 1995. It was followed by *Writing Fiction Step By Step* in 1998. Novakovich's technique is to present exercises, such as dramatizing a conflict or presenting a lyrical description, which can form connecting links to larger pieces, such as complete short stories or novels.

—S. Y.

SUGGESTED READING: *Christian Science Monitor* p14 June 23, 1995; *Library Journal* p123 Oct. 1, 1995, p126 Apr. 1, 1998; *Magill Book Reviews* (on-line) Nov. 1, 1999; *MultiCultural Review* p68 Dec. 1995; *New York Times Book Review* p27 Dec. 10, 1995, p19 July 5, 1998; *World Literature Today* p526+ Summer 1999

SELECTED BOOKS: nonfiction—*Apricots from Chernobyl: Narratives*, 1994; *Fiction Writer's Workshop*, 1995; *Writing Fiction Step By Step*, 1998; fiction—*Yolk: Short Stories*, 1995; *Salvation and Other Disasters: Short Stories*, 1998; *Plum Brandy: Croatian Sojourns*, 2003

Akeem Photos/Courtesy of Ballantine Books

Nunez, Elizabeth

(NOON-yez)

1944(?)– Novelist

As a college professor and the founding director of the National Black Writers Conference (NBWC), Elizabeth Nunez frequently takes part in discussions on African-American literature; but more than simply debating and illuminating the topic, Nunez has helped expand black literary achievement through her own four novels, which together tackle the difficult themes of race, class, colonialism, gender, and culture.

In a statement sent to the H.W. Wilson Company, Elizabeth Nunez writes: "I was born in Trinidad, West Indies, the third child of 11 children of my parents, Waldo and Una Nunez. I suppose my passion for creative writing and teaching was evident from childhood. I was seven when I won a juvenile short-story competition in a local newspaper. By that age, I was also already rounding up my brothers and sisters to play school with me, I, of course, being the teacher.

"Education was highly prized in my family. For my parents, it was the only way for their children to break past the limits for native Trinidadians implicit under a colonial system administered by the English government. Both my paternal grandparents were teachers; before he became the warden officer for the northern district in Trinidad, my grandfather was a headmaster. My father also taught early in his career; later he was Commissioner of Labor for the colonial government, and then a director for the Shell Oil Company in Trinidad and the Lesser Antilles. Until his retirement two years ago, at the age of eighty-five, he was a consultant for both private industry and the government in labor disputes.

"My mother, an avid reader, was her children's first teacher. She made certain that each of us could read, write and do simple arithmetic before we began school. The success of my brothers and sisters is a credit to my mother's efforts as our teacher. Three of my five brothers are physicians; of the others, one is an actuary and the other a businessman. One of my five sisters is a midwife; two hold top managerial positions, one in banking and the other in insurance; one is a lawyer, who has published two definitive books on law in the Caribbean; and the youngest is an actuary, the only actuary on the island of St. Vincent where she lives.

"I won an exhibition scholarship to the prestigious high school, St. Joseph's Convent, Port of Spain. After secondary school, I was awarded a scholarship to Marian College, in Fond du Lac, Wisconsin, and graduated from there with a B.A. honors degree in English. I returned to Trinidad and taught at the Woodbrook Secondary School before migrating to New York in 1968. I began graduate school at New York University in the fall of 1968. In 1971, I graduated with a M.A. degree, and in 1977, a doctorate in English Literature, both from New York University. I joined the faculty of Medgar Evers College in 1972. In 1983, I was elected chairman of the Humanities Division; in 1987, I was promoted to full Professor; and in 2001, I was awarded the title of Distinguished Professor of the City University of New York. The year before, in 2000, my alma mater, Marian College, honored me with an honorary doctorate in Humane Letters for contributions to the arts and education.

"I have served as an evaluator for national and local programs in the arts and education and raised over $10 million dollars in grants for educational, social and cultural programs in the Ocean-Hill Brownsville district of Brooklyn, New York. My awards and honors include the Urban Strategies award for contributions to the Ocean-Hill Brownsville community, several community service awards from organizations in Long Island, the YWCA Woman of Distinction Award, the Sojourner Truth Award from the National Association of Black Business and Professional Women's Clubs, the Carter G. Woodson Outstanding Teacher of the Year Award, and fellowships at the Yaddo Artists Colony, the MacDowell colony and the Paden Institute. Since 1986, I have been the director of the National Black Writers Conference, which is sponsored by the National Endowment for the Humanities. Considered the premier conference of its type in the US, NBWC panelists have included notable black writers such as Gwendolyn Brooks, Alice Walker, Maya Angelou, Derek Walcott, John Edgar Wideman, Terry McMillan, Bebe Moore Campbell, Jill Nelson, Ishmael Reed, Amiri Baraka, Walter Mosley, Marita Golden, George Lamming, Ntozake Shange, John A. Williams, Margaret Walker Alexander, Paule Marshall, Mari Evans, Henry Louis Gates, Jr., Arnold Rampersad, Stanley Crouch, and

Maryse Condé, among others. Close to 2000 people attend these conferences which are open to the general public.

"Until 1983, when the writer John Oliver Killens came to Medgar Evers College as writer-in-residence, most of the writing I did was for scholarly journals or academic conferences. My articles have appeared in journals at the University of Arkansas, Purdue University, the University of Michigan, the University of Wisconsin, and Howard University, among others, and I have presented over two hundred papers at workshops and conferences. More recently, I co-edited the collection of essays *Defining Ourselves: Black Writers in the 90s*.

"But in 1983, I took a sabbatical and joined Killens's creative writing workshop on Saturdays. In that workshop were Terry McMillan, Arthur Flowers and Doris Jean Austin. None of us had written a novel. All of us were wannabes. However, within a few years, all four of us published novels that we had worked on in that workshop. Terry McMillan published *Mama*, Arthur Flowers published *De Mojo Blues*, Doris Jean Austin published *After the Garden*, and I published my first novel, *When Rocks Dance*.

"Killens had a great influence on my development as a writer. From him I learned that writers have an obligation to write responsibly. As a writer who happens to be black, I do feel responsible for rectifying the distorted images of black people that persist in the media even today, and for pointing out the lie in instances of racial stereotyping, but primarily I am concerned with telling the truth. I want to make my characters as multidimensional as I can. I want to portray them in all their human potential for good and for evil. For me, their ethnic or racial background has no bearing on their moral and ethical choices.

"I have written four novels: *Discretion* (Ballantine, 2002); *Bruised Hibiscus* (Seal Press, 2000); *Beyond the Limbo Silence* (Seal Press, 1998); and *When Rocks Dance* (Putnam, 1986 and Ballantine, 1992). Ballantine will publish my fifth novel, *Grace*. Much of my fiction has been the subject for academic papers, some for dissertations for the masters and doctoral degrees. I would define my life's work as a commitment to empowering my students so that they can maximize their potential as human beings and good citizens as well as their ability and means to enjoy the Good Life. I am as committed to developing my talents as a writer as I am to doing the same for others. To that end, I lecture widely and give creative writing workshops across the country. I am chairman of the board of the Center for Black Literature at Medgar Evers College and chair of the PEN American Open Book Program, a project which focuses on providing access for people of color to various aspects of the publishing industry."

Nunez's first novel, *When Rocks Dance*, published in 1986, is a mythical tale exploring the historical and cultural heritage of her native Trinidad. According to Bahadur Tejani in his critique for *World Literature Today* (Winter 1994), Nunez "gives definition to the passions of African, Indian, and Caribbean cultures in her land, submerged under waves of European invasions. The ideological and artistic design in her novel is to make the pre-Columbian cultures present a united front against the onslaught of Western cultures." The story, set in rural Trinidad, depicts one woman's struggle to achieve landownership amidst the cultural synthesis of African, Indian, and Caribbean traditions—three cultures that Tejani called "symbolic of the trinity in the Trinidad." At the start, Emilia, recently freed from bondage following the abolishment of slavery in Europe and the Americas, recognizes that she can only achieve true freedom through the acquisition of land. Her consort, a white European landowner named Hrothgar, promises her the title to a piece of land if she will produce an heir for his colonial kingdom; his own wife is sterile. After three sets of her twins die in childbirth despite the medical assistance of a Western doctor on the island, Emilia consults an African healer trained in the obeah tradition of her ancestors—a system of beliefs that relies upon herbal medicine, sacrifice, and magic ritual. On the advice of this elder, Emilia offers her fourth set of twins for the appeasement of the gods, who then reward her with the birth—and survival—of her ninth child, Marina, who possesses the spiritual strength of the eight children who preceded her. Emilia instills in Marina her own compelling drive for land acquisition. As the two women continue their quest for land, they encounter a number of characters representing the various historical perspectives on the island. According to Tejani, the deeply symbolic depictions of Nunez's characters, their struggles, and their ambitions have a wider application for modern readers: "The unique strength of *When Rocks Dance* resides in the fact that it provides Trinidadians with a cultural synthesis which is operative today and which includes elements of the traditions of the island's three major groups. . . . In the actions of ordinary people like Emilia and Marina, struggling to acquire genuine independence, there is a message for a broad range of readers, especially in the Caribbean."

Nunez again addresses the themes of colonialism and race in her second novel, *Bruised Hibiscus*. In the opening pages a fisherman discovers the body of a white woman floating in Freeman's Bay, an event based on an actual incident in 1954, in which a Trinidadian physician strangled his German wife, removed her intestines, and dumped her body in the Gulf of Paria. While the investigation of this murder is not central to the novel, the discovery of the body—and the news of a second violent killing on the island—serve as catalysts for the remaining plot, in which two women from different racial and social backgrounds begin rejecting their own oppressive marriages. Nunez told V. R. Peterson for *Essence* (November 1994), "The takeoff point for me in this novel was the historical story of an Indian doctor who murdered his White wife. But what really concerned me were questions about why a woman enters into an abusive relationship and why she would stay. And why, in the case of slaughter, society so often remains on the side of the man." The main characters—Zuela, who is white, and Rosa, who is Hispanic—are inseparable as children growing up on a plantation; but when the two young girls witness a rape from their hiding place behind a hibiscus bush, their friendship is changed forever. When the women accidentally meet 20 years later, Rosa is imprisoned in a sexually abusive marriage to a black school headmaster, and Zuela has had 10 children with an opium-addicted Chinese immigrant who is more than three times her age. After reconnecting, Rosa and Zuela seek each other's support as they confront their destructive marriages.

Critical responses to *Bruised Hibiscus* were largely favorable. Writing for the *Voice Literary Supplement* (April–May 2000, on-line), Luis H. Francia noted, "For one thing, the work accurately reflects how in a country like Trinidad the present is intimately linked to the injustices of the past. For another, while she sometimes exhibits a tendency to overwrite, Nunez uses these linkages to wrap her complex characterizations and nifty plot around, thereby creating a powerful, disturbing exposé of a society that has felt the heavy hand and heel . . . of the white man's oppressive longing." Jana Giles highlighted some of the novel's shortcomings in a book review for the *New York Times* (April 9, 2000): "Nunez's shrewd employment of native dialect enlivens the narrative, but without efficiently enhancing plot or character. She fails to handle suspense well. And she interrupts what could have been a fluid fictional dream with too much commentary and too many descriptive passages." Nevertheless, Giles wrote, "In its finest moments, the novel leaves us with difficult lessons about the postcolonial new world order we still struggle to negotiate." *Bruised Hibiscus*, which was originally published in 1994 and republished in 2000, was awarded the American Book Award in 2001.

In her third novel, *Beyond the Limbo Silence*, published in 1998, Nunez explores the racial and cultural differences of three Caribbean immigrants amidst the background of the 1960s American civil rights movement. The story focuses on the experiences of Sara Edgehill, a young Trinidadian immigrant of mixed racial ancestry who has come to the United States on a scholarship to the all-white College of the Sacred Heart, in Oshkosh, Wisconsin. There Sara befriends the only other black students on campus: Courtney, a scholarship student from St. Lucia and a strict follower of African and Caribbean rituals; Angela, a scholarship student from British Guiana who adapts easily to the all-white community; and Sam, a black law student from Milwaukee who becomes deeply embroiled in the struggle for civil rights. "Through the triangular friendship among Courtney, Angela, and Sara," Heather Hathaway wrote for *African American Review* (Fall 2000), "Nunez proves differing patterns of immigrant adjustment in what turns out to be the most alienating of environments. . . . Nunez uses the disparate reactions of each character to this circumstance to illustrate a range of possible responses to the pressures and opportunities posed by migration." Hathaway suggested that the character of Sam is a tool "to examine yet another dimension of intercultural interaction—that between native-born and foreign-born blacks." Sara begins an affair with Sam and in the process becomes educated about civil rights; she is ultimately inspired to declare the movement's political and social struggle her own. Her involvement intensifies when Sam becomes entangled in events in Mississippi, especially after the murders of the real-life civil rights martyrs Andrew Goodman, James Chaney, and Michael Schwerner. While Nunez weaves such historical details into her fictional plot, Kwame Dawes, writing for the *Washington Post* (December 31, 1998), concluded: "Sara and her story are totally distanced from the historical events described in the novel. . . . Sara's life remains completely removed from the experience of African Americans, and her recognition of a connectedness is rooted in the largely intellectual acceptance of the shared brutality of slavery. This is fascinating but not compellingly new, and not enough."

Dawes described Nunez's goal as "ambitious: to write a novel that is at once politically astute and almost polemic, and at the same time to tell a gripping, character-driven story." While he considered Nunez's success in this goal incomplete, another reviewer writing for *Americas* (May–June 1999) praised the novel as "a celebration of Afro-Caribbean traditions as well as a sad reminder of a difficult time in U.S. history," and Hathaway opined: "Nunez makes a significant contribution to the body of fictional literature addressing the Civil Rights Movement; her consideration of this exceptional moment in American history through regional and international lenses adds a new and important dimension to our understanding of the period."

Nunez's fourth novel, *Discretion*, published in 2002, explores a lover's triangle between an African foreign ambassador to the United States, his wife—the daughter of his country's president—and an American artist with whom he falls in love while in New York City. Nunez tells the story through the voice of Oufoula Sindede, a man torn between his responsibilities to Africa and his passion for the West. In a representative review Jeff Zalesky for *Publishers Weekly* (November 26, 2001) wrote, "This rich, multilayered narrative is powerful in its sweep and moving in its insight."

Most recently Nunez published *Grace* (2003), in which she explores the struggles of a modern-day marriage. Justin Peters is a Trinidadian-born, Harvard-educated professor of literature in Brooklyn, who strictly adheres to his department's "dead white men" canon of literature, while abandoning the Afro-centric line of study he pursued in college. His wife, Sally, is a primary-school teacher who has lost her dream of becoming a poet. Despite their comfortable life with their young daughter, Giselle, Sally has become dissatisfied—particularly when she compares her accomplishments to those of her father, a courageous doctor who was murdered in her youth by the Ku Klux Klan. When Sally abruptly moves out of the couple's house and in with her best friend, Justin suspects the two women are having an affair. His feelings of distress are increased when a colleague accuses him of being an "Uncle Tom." With the relationship threatened, both characters embark on a path of self-discovery. Early reviews of the book were mixed, though critics acknowledged Nunez's gift for narrative. In his review for *Publishers Weekly* (January 20, 2003), Jeff Zaleski said of the book, "As in most of life, there is no shattering epiphany here but, rather, a subtly shaded landscape, at once familiar and pitted with hidden challenges."

In 1986 Nunez founded the National Black Writers Conference, a four-day conference sponsored by Medgar Evers College and grants from the National Endowment for the Humanities in which black writers, scholars, and critics engage in discussions on the status of African-American literature and publishing; Nunez directed the conference in 1991, 1996, 1998, and 2000. Following a surge in the publication of African-American writers, the Fourth National Black Writers Conference in 1996 posed the question, "Black Literature in the 90s: A Renaissance to End All Renaissances?" Nunez later co-edited many of the papers presented throughout the conference for the 1999 book, *Defining Ourselves: Black Writers in the 90s*.

—K. D.

SUGGESTED READING: *African American Review* p552 Fall 2000; *Americas* p61+ May–June 1999; *New York Times* C p13 Mar. 21, 1996, with photo; *New York Times Book Review* p 35 Apr. 9, 2001; *Publishers Weekly* p36 Nov. 26, 2001; *Voice Literary Supplement* (on-line) Apr.–May 2000; *Washington Post* C p3 Dec. 31, 1998; *World Literature Today* p53+ Winter 1994

SELECTED BOOKS: *When Rocks Dance*, 1986; *Beyond the Limbo Silence*, 1998; *Bruised Hibiscus*, 2000; *Discretion*, 2002; *Grace*, 2003; as editor—*Defining Ourselves: Black Writers in the 90s* (with Brenda M. Greene), 1999

Nunez, Sigrid

1951– Novelist

Sigrid Nunez is known for writing books that often cross the boundary between fact and invention. Building upon the "hybrid" model established by such modern novelists as Elizabeth Hardwick and W. G. Sebald, Nunez has published four critically admired works, including her memoir-like first novel, *A Feather on the Breath of God* (1995), and her most recent, *For Rouenna* (2001). Throughout her career, as Megan O'Grady observed for *Vogue* (November 2001), Nunez has had "a taste for unusual perspectives," and "in exploring them spins tales that blur fiction and reality."

For *World Authors 1995–2000*, Nunez writes: "I was born on Staten Island, New York City, in 1951. Both my parents were immigrants. My mother was from Germany, and my father, who was half Chinese and half Panamanian, spent most of his early life in China. Neither of my parents spoke the other's native language, and both spoke English imperfectly. I never learned to speak either German or Chinese myself. We lived in a public housing project on the Island's north shore.

"As I remember it, I wanted to write from an early age. For a long time, I thought I would grow up to be a poet or a writer of children's books. I stopped even thinking about writing poetry before I was twenty years old, but I have always kept the hope of one day writing something for children.

Jerry Bauer/Courtesy of Farrar, Straus and Giroux

Like most writers, I was also a big reader as a child, and the library was always a favorite place and beloved haven. When I was in high school, I began to study dance and decided to abandon all literary ambitions and become a ballerina. This dream was short-lived, but I would draw on this period of my life and on my struggles as a young dancer when I came to write my first novel.

"At seventeen, I went away to Barnard College [in New York City] where I majored in English and studied with Elizabeth Hardwick, who taught the first writing class I had ever taken. She was also the first professional writer I had ever met. Hardwick would turn out to be an important and enduring influence on my work—much more by her writing, however, than by her teaching. I still hear echoes of her voice and catch something of her cadences in my own prose. In 1979, Hardwick would publish *Sleepless Nights*, an essay-novel that belonged to the kind of hybrid genre to which I myself would be irresistibly drawn one day.

"After I graduated from Barnard, I worked for a year as an editorial assistant at the *New York Review of Books* before returning to school for an MFA. In the writing program at Columbia University [in New York City], I took classes with, among others, Richard Yates, but in fact I have never found fiction workshops to be particularly inspiring or useful to me. As a teacher myself, I would always begin by telling my students that they would learn far more from reading other writers than they ever could from any writing class, and I still believe this is true.

"Soon after getting my MFA, I was back at the *New York Review*, where I met Susan Sontag, a regular contributor to the magazine at the time. She, too, would turn out to be an important influence. Sontag introduced me to the work of countless writers, as well as other artists, many of them European, and to a wealth of ideas about literature and art. Inevitably, in helping shape my intellectual development, Sontag also helped shape my writing, and although my fiction has not been influenced by Sontag's writing as it has been by Hardwick's, I surely would not have become the same writer had Sontag not been a mentor. Sontag's attitude of high seriousness towards literature and her exalted view of the writer's vocation struck deep chords in me and helped show me how the serious writer makes his or her way.

"Proust, Rilke, Milan Kundera, Peter Handke, Philip Roth, V. S. Naipaul, W. G. Sebald—these, along with Hardwick and Sontag themselves, were some writers who had written works in which the lines between genres were blurred or ignored. Composed of both fictional and nonfictional elements, these works might be part novel, part history, part journal, part travel book, part essay, part memoir—and they (their originality, their dazzling possibilities) enthralled me. In my first book, *A Feather on the Breath of God*, I used material from my immigrant parents' lives and from my own life along with material that was wholly invented. Although much of it is factually true, the book is a work of imagination and not at all the memoir it has sometimes been mistaken for. It seemed important to me, however, to try my hand also at a novel strictly in the traditional genre, and that is what I set out to do with my next book, *Naked Sleeper*.

"My third book, *Mitz: The Marmoset of Bloomsbury*, was conceived as a jeu d'esprit: a mock biography of Leonard and Virginia Woolf's pet monkey. Inspired by *Flush*, Virginia Woolf's biography of Elizabeth Barrett Browning's cocker spaniel, Mitz's story was drawn from the Bloomsbury archives, and, once again, though based solidly on historical fact, it is indisputably a work of imagination.

"*For Rouenna*, my most recently published novel, is another (if very different) kind of fictional biography. The subject of the biography is a former US Army nurse who served in the Vietnam war. But the novel is as much about the writer-narrator as it is about her subject, how and why she came to write the nurse's story, and what it means for a writer to imagine the life of another person.

"People have sometimes asked me how I would describe my major preoccupations as a writer, and my answer has been: language, memory, identity, class, the lives of women, and writing itself. None of this has been the result of any particular agenda; it is just what I have found myself writing about.

"In addition to my four books, I have written some short fiction that has been published in various literary journals, including the *Threepenny Review* and *Iowa Review*. Some of my work has been anthologized, in particular excerpts from my first book, which have appeared in several anthologies of Asian-American literature. I have been the recipient of two Pushcart prizes, a Whiting Writer's Award, and of two awards from the American Academy of Arts and Letters: the Richard and Hinda Rosenthal Foundation Award and the Rome Prize in Literature. I have taught at Amherst College, Smith College, and Columbia University."

Nunez's first novel, *A Feather on the Breath of God* (1995), is a fictionalized depiction of the author's own coming-of-age as a first-generation American, the daughter of a German-born mother and a Chinese-Panamanian father. Like Nunez, the book's narrator grows up in a New York City housing project, where she regularly confronts the complexities of cultural identity and the frustrations of the immigrant experience. The narrator's father, born in Panama to a traveling Chinese businessman and given the name Carlos Chang, sheds his Chinese surname—adopting that of his Hispanic mother—when he emigrates to New York City. While serving in World War II, Carlos meets a young German woman, Christa, whom he impregnates; the ill-suited couple marries and returns to New York City. Throughout the novel, the narrator, who is the couple's third child (and who, incidentally, never reveals her first name), examines the divisions that plague her parents, who can barely communicate in a common language, as well as the conditions they endure as isolated immigrants. The narrator struggles to make sense of her mixed heritage after her father's death. She had seen him as "the only Chinese thing" in the family home, "sitting like a Buddha himself among the Hummels and cuckoo clocks and pictures of Alpine landscapes," as quoted by Bharati Mukherjee for the *New York Times* (January 8, 1995). Christa, angry and bitter at having to endure a life of poverty, remains a harsh, overbearing figure, uncomfortable in both America and Germany.

As the narrator explores her cultural identity, she embraces a traditional "American" life and discovers liberation through her passion for ballet. Later, as an English instructor, she becomes romantically involved with a troubled Russian immigrant named Vadim. Thomas Deignan, writing for *World & I* (September 1995), called the ballet passages, "the novel's strongest because they embrace so much, cutting so close to the skin that separates the interior and the exterior, the intellectual and the emotional, the personal and the political." Overall, *A Feather on the Breath of God* was received well by critics. Mukherjee, for example, called it, "a forceful novel by a writer of uncommon talent." Lori Marie Carlson wrote for the *Washington Post* (January 29, 1995), "As for elegant language, Nunez nearly transforms literature into ballet." Deignan acknowledged that the book may be "too tight, or too cynical, and that aspects of the plot seem unnecessary or even melodramatic," but concluded: "Nunez navigates this dual immigrant experience and the accompanying emotions with compassion, and intelligence. She is a provocative chronicler of our 'strange culture,' circa the mid-late twentieth century, and a fine guide into the human heart."

In *Naked Sleeper* (1996), Nunez again displayed what a reviewer for *Publishers Weekly* (July 29, 1996) called "the range of her talent, especially her sensitivity to the wellsprings of character and behavior." Nunez's second novel explores a woman's quest to reconnect with her heritage. The narrator, Nona, is a 40-year-old English teacher working on a book about her father, a painter with whom she lost touch as young child and whose reputation has grown since his early death. Though married to a loving husband, Nona begins an affair with a loathsome, married man. Throughout the novel, as Nona learns more about her father—and herself—she comes to realize the effects of her self-destructive actions.

Naked Sleeper garnered mixed reviews: *Publishers Weekly* called the book "a haunting story, resonant with hard-won wisdom," crediting Nunez with exhibiting "impeccable control of her narrative." Christine Schwartz Hartley, writing for the *New York Times* (December 1, 1996, on-line) praised Nunez's "well-pitched prose and her eye for telling contemporary details." Hartley went on to observe, however, that "because Nona spends a considerable amount of time simply thinking, dreaming and remembering, the novel eventually takes on an analytical quality, which can be grating." She added that Nunez "sometimes lapses into frustratingly elliptical observations." Jacob Molyneux, writing for the *Village Voice* (December 4, 2001) acknowledged *Naked Sleeper* as "a beautifully reflective novel occasionally marred by unnecessary plot twists."

Nunez again wove fiction and fact for *Mitz: The Marmoset of Bloomsbury* (1998), in which she imagines the life of Leonard and Virginia Woolf's sickly pet monkey, Mitz, a gift from their friends the Rothschilds in 1934. While the book offers an image of life inside the Woolf household, it also, according to Frank Caso for *Booklist* (May 15, 1998), "reconstructs a fading Bloomsbury, whose surviving members are in physical decline and for whom the hint of tragedy is ever present." Real-life friends and colleagues of the Woolfs, including Vanessa Bell, T. S. Eliot, and Vita Sackville-West, often appear in the book, authenticating the details of Nunez's picture. A reviewer for *Publishers Weekly* (March 16, 1998) wrote, "Nunez observes the similarities between Virginia and Mitz, 'two nervous, delicate, wary females . . . relentlessly curious . . . both in love with Leonard.'" The slim book was hailed by Yvette Weller Olson for *Library Journal* (April 15, 1998) as "a charming novel." The *Publishers Weekly* reviewer affirmed it as "a moving commentary on the trajectory of [the Woolfs'] lives."

The narrator of *For Rouenna* (2001) is a middle-aged writer who has recently published her first novel; she begins correspondence with a fan—an overweight, uneducated clothing-store manager named Rouenna. An unlikely friendship develops between the two women, who hail from the same housing project in Staten Island: Rouenna, a former army nurse who served in Vietnam, asks the narrator to assist her in writing a book about her experiences. The narrator declines and, soon after, Rouenna takes her own life. Haunted by their brief friendship, the narrator (who is never named) takes up Rouenna's story, telling it through a varying mix of remembered conversations, investigation, and imagination. Thomas Curwen wrote for the *Los Angeles Times* (December 16, 2001), the resulting novel "is a story about the debt survivors owe to the dead."

For Rouenna was largely deemed a critical success. Although Curwen felt that Nunez had fallen somewhat short of her mission "to take the measure of another person's life," he characterized Rouenna as "brilliantly drawn." Jeff Zalenski, writing for *Publishers Weekly* (October 8, 2001), attributed the book's strength to "its assertion of the danger of looking backwards." Zalenski continued, "Nunez's insightful examination of the way collective cultural memory whitewashes the uncomfortable past is at once a memorialization of an era and a declaration of the insufficiency of memorials when the past remains very much a part of our present." Merle Rubin wrote for *Atlantic Monthly* (December 2001), "There is a conspicuous lack of pretension about her writing, a refreshing earnestness. Reading her, we feel that everything is out in the open."

Sigrid Nunez currently resides in New York City and is working on her fifth book, a novel that begins in the late 1960s and spans many years.

—K. D.

SUGGESTED READING: *Atlantic Monthly* p145 Dec. 2001; *Los Angeles Times* Dec. 16, 2001; *New York Times* VII p12 Jan. 8, 1995; *New York Times* (on-line) Dec. 1, 1996, Nov. 18, 2001; *Publishers Weekly* p69 July 29, 1996, p52 Mar. 16, 1998, p41 Oct. 8, 2001; *St. Louis Post–Dispatch* D p5 May 31, 1998; *Washington Post Book World* p8 Jan. 29, 1995; *World & I* p276 Sep. 1995

SELECTED BOOKS: *A Feather on the Breath of God*, 1995; *Naked Sleeper*, 1996; *Mitz: The Marmoset of Bloomsbury*, 1998; *For Rouenna*, 2001

O'Brien, Sean

Dec. 19, 1952– Poet; nonfiction writer

Sean O'Brien's poetry grows out of his love of commonplace things and events. He takes the stuff of his life—his father's socialist political leanings, his Irish heritage, his feelings about the policies of the former British prime minister Margaret Thatcher—and melds them. His poems, therefore, present detailed accounts of everyday living, as well as sweeping views of modern British life. Bruce Woodcock observed in *Critical Survey* (1998): "O'Brien's poems often use . . . simultaneously particular and imaginary places, the two blurring across each other as reality and imagination meet and inform each other in peculiar ways: real places become vehicles for exploration and are transformed as poems progress, until we are somewhere else entirely."

Sean O'Brien was born in London, England, on December 19, 1952 and grew up in the port city of Hull. His father, who was of Irish descent, had a great impact on his son's political views. As a self-educated socialist, the elder O'Brien took his young son to Hull Labour Party meetings and railed against the class system in England and the country's discrimination against its Irish citizens. O'Brien developed a sense of displacement and a feeling that he was, as an Irishman, essentially stateless and isolated from English society. He received his formal education at Selwyn College, part of Cambridge University, where he received his bachelor's degree, in English, in 1973. He completed his master's degree three years later at Birmingham University. Between 1976 and 1979 he took some classes at Hull University, but he received his post-graduate certificate from Leeds University, in 1981.

From 1981 to 1989 O'Brien served as a teacher at the Beacon School, in Crowborough, East Sussex and also worked on his poetry. During that period he completed two collections of realistic, socially conscious poems, *The Indoor Park* (1983) and *The Frighteners* (1987), both of which drew their inspiration from the city of Hull. As quoted by Woodcock, "The Police," a poem from *The Indoor Park*, is a veiled comment on police brutality: "The police, when they pot their begonias, / Press down with both thumbs, like that . . . " O'Brien told *Contemporary Authors* (2000), "I am particularly interested in history, politics, and place." He continued, "The conditions of the 1980s seem to me to have presented poets with a problem which has gone largely unaddressed, that of writing poetry which confronts moral and economic barbarism while remaining art." On the strength of these volumes, O'Brien won a creative-writing fellowship for the 1989–90 school year at the University of Dundee, in Scotland.

During the next decade O'Brien published *HMS Glasshouse* (1991) and *Ghost Train* (1995). Bruce Woodcock observed of the latter: "As its title suggests, *Ghost Train* as a whole is obsessed with the dead and with journeys which often go into the past, or more bizarrely, through which the past journeys into the present. The past comes back to haunt the present in strangely unsettling ways, as a familiar spirit almost co-existent with the present, and as an exiled land of lost or missed opportunities." Woodcock described the governing experience in *HMS Glasshouse* as "an imaginative wandering around Dundee, the city in which O'Brien had a writing fellowship, something he 'celebrates' in 'In Residence: A Worst Case View,' a manic nursery rhyme about being a writer-in-residence and an audaciously funny exercise in biting the hand that feeds you. In these poems city life is savage, an end-of- the-world vision of life in the 1990s with Dundee as an emblem of inner-city desolation, inhabited by urban dossers, boozers, headbangers, scroungers, deadheads and 'wasters.'"

In 1998 O'Brien published *The Deregulated Muse*, a collection of essays on modern British and Irish poetry. In an on-line article for the *British Council*, a reviewer noted that the books showed "O'Brien as a critic with definite views about poetry which he communicates with confidence: he has a fluent and thoughtful writing style and, as with all critics of note, the reader does not have to agree with his views to find them illuminating. . . . It is the most readable book of poetry criticism to appear for a while."

That same year, O'Brien edited *The Firebox*, a collection of post–World War II poems from Great Britain and Ireland. The volume was considered by many to be one of the most comprehensive of its type. A *British Council* (on-line) reviewer noted: "O'Brien's short prose introductions to the work of each poet are of special importance. Many of these are models of their kind: to the point, informative, keeping a balance between biographical and bibliographical information and, most important of all, providing incisive critical opinion."

O'DRISCOLL

Sean O'Brien is currently a poetry critic for the Sunday (London) *Times* and an editor of *The Printer's Devil*, a literary magazine he established with Stephen Plaice, in 1990. His recent books include *Downriver* (2001) and *Cousin Coat: Selected Poems, 1976–2001* (2002).

—C. M.

SUGGESTED READING: *The British Council* (online); *Critical Survey* p33+ 1998; *Southern Review* p897+ Autumn 1995

SELECTED BOOKS: poetry—*The Indoor Park*, 1983; *The Frighteners*, 1987; *HMS Glasshouse*, 1991; *Ghost Train*, 1995; *Cousin Coat: Selected Poems, 1976-2001*, 2002; nonfiction—*The Deregulated Muse: Essays on Contemporary British and Irish Poetry*, 1998; as editor—*The Firebox: Poetry in Britain and Ireland After 1945*, 1998

O'Driscoll, Dennis

Jan. 1, 1954– Poet

The basis of much of the writing of the Irish poet and critic Dennis O'Driscoll is the fact that he began working in the Irish civil service when he was 16 years old. Many of the poems in his collections *Kist* (1982), *Hidden Extras* (1987), *Long Story Short* (1993), *Quality Time* (1997), and *Weather Permitting* (1999) deal with the daily life of work and office politics. Robert Hass observed in the *Washington Post Book World* (September 21, 1997) that O'Driscoll "writes in a dry, ironic way—something of W. H. Auden and something of Philip Larkin in the style—about office life." Hass called him, in addition, "one of the best-known reviewers and commentators on Irish poetry."

Dennis O'Driscoll composed the following autobiographical note for *World Authors 1995–2000*: "Drunken cheers, car horns, train whistles and a sugar factory siren greeted my birth. Nothing personal—I just happened to be born in the first minutes of a new year. On January 2, 1954, the day after my birth in Thurles (a small town in County Tipperary), Pope Pius XII in Rome warned against the threat which television posed to family life. He was preaching to the converted in my family's case. Not only were we—like most Irish people—Roman Catholics, but we were never to own a television during my upbringing. Two forms of Sunday worship—one sporting, the other spiritual—offered alternative forms of mass spectacle: hurling games (to which I failed to respond with the requisite level of enthusiasm) and church ceremonies (by which I was moved and enthralled, especially when incense wafted and plainchant wavered).

"'I remember, I remember, / The house where I was born,' Thomas Hood's most famous poem begins. As a child, I repeatedly read an illustrated edition of this poem, embellished with olde-worlde depictions of rustic thatch and rose-budding gardens. Although the book is long mislaid, I remember, I remember the words of the poem—not least, the final lines (as stirring to me at the age of ten as they seem sentimental to me now) about having believed that the 'slender tops' of the fir trees 'were close against the sky': 'It was a childish ignorance, / But now 'tis little joy / To know I'm farther off from heav'n / Than when I was a boy.' The actual house in which I read Thomas Hood, by a coal-burning range, was roofed with slate instead of thatch and was home to six children (I was the second of the four boys) and our parents. Whatever about thatch, our pinkly perfect climbing roses and our tall, tapering fir trees were worthy of Thomas Hood's illustrator. Both of my parents were from farms and my father, who loved the soil, proved to have Martian-green fingers where gardening was concerned.

"All roads around Thurles lead to its central square and it was as a 'square', uncool schoolboy that I grew up about a mile from the town. Not only was my TV-viewing restricted to other people's sets and my cinema-going restricted to the few occasions when parental permission—akin to a censor's license—was forthcoming, but I had no record collection, never attended a dance or disco and never bedecked myself in denim (denim being the definitive sign of trendiness during what passed in Thurles for the Sixties). After I left Thurles, at the age of 16, for a civil service job in Dublin (working first in the Death Duties office, later in the Stamp Duties office and, more recently, in Customs), my TV-viewing skills remained rudimentary; worse still, I rarely achieved my cinema target of one film per annum. Poetry (from Elizabethan to modern East European) and painting (from Zurbarán to Rothko) have been constant passions—my lunch-breaks are spent in contemplation of gallery walls and bookshop stocks.

"When I attended University College, Dublin—on day release from my office cell—it was Law, not Literature, that I studied during my three years there. I resisted the temptation to contribute to college magazines, preferring to blush my way through a private rather than public apprenticeship; but I made the acquaintance of student writers like Aidan Mathews, Colm Tóibín and Ronan Sheehan through the English Literature Society. I began to publish poems and reviews only when (in 1977) two Australian poets independently engaged in forms of benign intervention on my behalf. Vincent Buckley, a regular visitor to his ancestral Ireland, recommended me as a reviewer to Nuala Mulcahy (literary editor of a lively Dublin-based weekly, *Hibernia*). Soon I was the magazine's poetry editor and its principal poetry reviewer. My resistance to publishing my 'poems' (I would have used the disparaging quotation marks even more vehemently at the time) was overcome by a postcard from a thirtysomething poet, living in Sydney, who was beginning to make an international name for himself. That name was Les Murray. I had met him at Seamus Heaney's house a short time before; and his elegantly hand-written message indicated that a poem of mine which I had shown him there had lodged in his mind. Could he publish it in *Poetry Australia*? It was a long way from Tipperary to New South Wales, a safe distance at which to put a short poem to the test, to exercise a degree of remote control. Yes, certainly he could publish the poem (and, as a concession to the happy event, I cagily detached the qualifying quotes from the word 'poem').

"I never planned a career in poetry; everything that happened simply occurred. I have avoided writers' workshops and artists' colonies. My poems and reviews are written after work or on weekends in a house beside a glossy County Kildare racecourse in which my wife, Julie O'Callaghan (a Chicagoan who has published poetry for children and adults), and I brood in our separate studies. Having saturated my imagination all week, a poem may burst its banks on a Saturday morning and spill out on to the page. Sometimes the poem will be one in which the everyday and the transient are momentarily transformed. Other poems will be cries of bewilderment at the complexity and perplexity of the world. I write occasionally about office life—my most sustained poem, 'The Bottom Line,' tries to wrench something permanent from the evanescent jargon of business and bureaucracy. I am embarrassed by the weaker poems in my first collection, *Kist* (1982); but dissatisfaction is as good a motive as any for writing and it has sustained me for four further collections to date: *Hidden Extras* (1987), *Long Story Short* (1993), *Quality Time* (1997), and *Weather Permitting* (1999), each of which is intended to provide a measure of compensation for the shortcomings of its predecessor. The unwritten collection of poems, the one which glows with potential in my imagination, is the book which excites me most. I live in hope."

The fact that Dennis O'Driscoll had an almost bucolic upbringing is secondary in his poetic work. He is a poet of modern life—of the urban, and especially of the office. He has, in a sense—although not necessarily stylistically—placed himself in the company of the American poet Wallace Stevens, an insurance executive, and Herman Melville, the author of *Moby-Dick*, who worked as a customs functionary. Although O'Driscoll has written poetry evoking the pastoral, such poems deal on a deeper level with eternal verities, such as death and loss. "Riches of hay were hoarded/away in the barn,/a cache/stuffed under a mattress," O'Driscoll wrote in "Hay," published in the *Yale Review* (October 1998), establishing an ironical contrast between hay and gold, the usual object of hoarding.

In an article for the *Washington Post Book World* (September 21, 1997), Robert Hass, a former poet laureate of the United States, characterized O'Driscoll's poetic examination of office life as "the antithesis of the intensely poetic subject matter Americans associate with Irish poetry." O'Driscoll took the title of his collection *Quality Time* from the line, "Quality time at weekends, domestic bliss," which he viewed in contrast to: "All of the mornings of all of the weekdays / I leave for work; my office bin fills / with the shredded waste of hours /A pattern regular as wallpaper or rugs / and no more permanent than their flowers."

A representative comment on O'Driscoll's work was made by John Taylor, who noted in his review of *Quality Time* in *Poetry* (July 1998), the "initial thrust of O'Driscoll's office-life poems is satiric, but what defines his approach more deeply is an ultimate pity for his targets; he seeks to express 'the hidden pain of offices,' and this is why his work surpasses the limitations of satire. . . . O'Driscoll . . . strips off professional mask after professional mask until the primal fears and aspirations inhabiting these at once ambitious and cowering men come to the surface, usually 'in the dark filling/of the night' when 'doubts gather with the rain/. . . spreading as predicted from the west.' At this point, the poet . . . lets us ponder the pathetic spectacle, which is also our own, of course."

O'Driscoll wrote in "Troubled Thoughts: Poetry Politics in Contemporary Ireland," an essay published in the *Southern Review* (Summer 1995), of "the stifling bell-jar of Irish literary life, where rivalries and resentments are experienced with a scalding edge and intimacy." Nevertheless, with gentle humor and intellectual panache, O'Driscoll has made himself an authority on Irish poetry. In addition, he has gleaned from the press the thoughts of poets on various topics, which he presents in a column, "Pickings and Choosings," published in *Poetry Ireland Review*. Michael Glover gathered what he considered the best of the columns into *As the Poet Said*, published in 1996. Some of the themes on which such poets as C. H. Sisson, Seamus Heaney, and the American John Ashbery have offered opinions are work, death, money, drink, sex, prayer, and spirituality. The *New Statesman* (January 2, 1998) reviewer observed that the book provided "a composite portrait of the modern poet and the world in which he struggles to make his mark."

As O'Driscoll noted in his autobiographical statement, he is, if not quite an optimist, one who has hope for the future. In his poem "Jet Age," published in the *New England Review* (Summer 1998), he envisioned a world in which airplanes no longer exist, "where swaying grass will replace windsocks, fuel trucks rust on apron cracks," but where there will nevertheless be "stories we will regale our grandchildren with" about that vanished jet age and its travelers: "So inured to mystery, we will say, they took for granted/sprayed glitter of night cities, towns riveted to the ground,/but stirred from newspaper or snooze to adjust their watches/and their headrests, choose a complimentary liqueur."

O'Driscoll frequently contemplates the future. In "Tomorrow," published in *Poetry* (July 1999), he wrote: "Tomorrow I will start to be happy. . . . I will put my shapeless days behind me, fencing off the past, as a golden rind of sand parts slipshod/sea from solid land. It is tomorrow I want to look back on, not today. Tomorrow I start to be happy;/today is almost yesterday." In 1999 O'Driscoll won the Lannan Award for poetry. He was included with Padraig J. Daly, John F. Deane, Richard Kell, and MacDara Woods in David Lampe and Dennis Maloney's collection, *Five Irish Poets*. In 2001, O'Driscoll published *Troubled Thoughts, Majestic Dreams: Selected Prose Writings*.

—S. Y.

SUGGESTED READING: *New England Review* p50 Summer 1998; *New Statesman* Jan. 2, 1998; *Poetry* p230+ July 1998; *Southern Review* p639+ Summer 1995; *Washington Post Book World* p2 Sep. 21, 1997; *Yale Review* p69+ Oct. 1998

SELECTED BOOKS: *Kist*, 1982; *Hidden Extras*, 1987; *Long Story Short*, 1993; *Quality Time*, 1997; *Weather Permitting*, 1999

Perry Ogden/Courtesy of Riverhead Books

O'Faolain, Nuala

(O-FWAY-lon, NOO-la)

1940– Memoirist; novelist; columnist

In 1996 Nuala O'Faolain was compiling a collection of her best columns from the *Irish Times*. As she sat down to write a 500-word introduction for the collection, which was being published by New Island Books, in Dublin, she recalled the pain and anguish of her childhood and her life. O'Faolain wrote, in detail, of her impoverished youth, her neglectful parents, her sexual awakening in Ireland's repressive culture, her several love affairs—including one with the journalist Nell McCafferty, who lived with her for almost 15 years—and her battle with alcoholism. When she finished, the "introduction" was about 190 pages long. New Island Books agreed to publish it as a memoir instead. Although O'Faolain thought the book, *Are You Somebody?: The Accidental Memoir of a Dublin Woman*, would sell only a few copies, she had struck a nerve with many Irish people, and it quickly became a best-seller. When it was published in the United States and the United Kingdom two years later, in 1998, it also sold well and received favorable reviews in those countries. O'Faolain's first novel, *My Dream of You*, which explores the effect of the Irish potato famine on present-day Ireland, was published, in 2001, to similar acclaim. In 2003 O'Faolain published her second memoir, *Almost There: The Onward Journey of a Dublin Woman*.

Nuala O'Faolain writes for *World Authors 1995–2000*: "I was born in Dublin, Ireland in 1940 the second child of a couple of brainy, handsome young Dubliners, the stars of their quiet, lower-middleclass families. They were madly in love. Ireland was a very poor country at the time, however, and they had no money and they had no skills with what money they had. My mother, therefore, lived outside Dublin where there were cheap homes to rent with us, who eventually ran to nine living children out of thirteen pregnancies. My father meantime was more and more in the city, and a small and then a bigger celebrity. As Dublin life became more sophisticated he became its chronicler in the daily social column he wrote for an evening newspaper called *Dubliner's Diary*. He was a dapper, clever, reticent, man, and he treated the family as if he had met them at a cocktail party. My mother began to drink too much, from loneliness. She developed into a total alcoholic. He pretended to ignore her condition. At some level and in ways we children didn't understand they were a real couple. But they were neglectful parents, and their children paid, then and now, for the times and the society they were born into and for having such parents. On the other hand, neglect also means autonomy, and we were not used or manipulated in any way. We also had the example if not the encouragement of parents who were exceptionally and genuinely as cultured as they could be in the Ireland of the 1940s and 1950s. Though few around us did, my father knew and loved recorded classical music, and my mother vas a voracious and demanding reader. They were also heartbreakingly charming.

"If my autobiographical sketch begins with them it is because they made me a writer. Writing about them was my bid for mental and even physical health, which I was not able to make until I was in my fifties. I was always confused until then, or drinking too much, or unsuccessfully in love, or something in the family was pulling me down.

"I was an intelligent but wild child. At fourteen, when I was lost in storms of puberty, I was expelled from the convent school in the small town we lived in then, because I went to the big working-class dances, to meet boys. This was a sin against the nuns' class pretensions. I was sent to an Irish-speaking convent boarding school far away, on the border with Northern Ireland. The nuns there gave us a splendid education and I was not allowed to leave till I had done the final state examination. From then on my life oscillated between the opportunities I got through education, and my desire to ruin myself with 'love' and drink. By the skin of my teeth, and with the help of this or that individual who turned up in my life, I got to college in Dublin: then got a scholarship to do postgraduate work in an English provincial university; then got a more difficult scholarship to the University Of Oxford, where I did a B. Phil degree, by thesis and examination. Then I returned to my old university—University College, Dublin, alma mater of James Joyce—as a lecturer in the Department of English.

"Since then I have had good, professional jobs, as a lecturer, then as a producer of educational television programmes for the BBC in London and elsewhere, then as a general television and radio producer, then as a journalist, and now as an opinion columnist with the 'Irish Times'—Ireland's newspaper of record. My personal life had many ups and downs. However, I did, after years in England return to Ireland, a country I have come to love passionately, and that was a saving move. My parents died in their sixties. Gradually, after that, and with the help of a good relationship with a strong woman, I began to find my feet.

"When I was 55, and once more alone, a modest Irish publisher—New Island Books—asked whether they could collect some of my old opinion columns. I accepted, though I knew only a handful of people would ever want to read old opinion columns of mine or anyone's. Secure in the knowledge that though I would have an audience it would be very small and on my side already, I wrote a long, personal introduction to the columns. I called it *Are You Somebody*? This was the place where I tried, through words, to see my parents and the shape of my life as clearly as I could. The introduction escaped from obscurity, took on a life of its own, and after a long and sensational career on the Irish best-seller list was bought by publishers in England and the USA, and was translated into several languages.

"Throughout this amazing change in my life, I went on working for the *Irish Times* and even moved to Belfast, to write from the conflict situation there. But fans in the USA kept asking me about my next book, and eventually I came to believe that I might be able to write a novel. I applied to Yaddo in upper New York State. They gave me a five-week residency. I had never been accepted as an artist before, or thought myself a possible artist, and I had never been in a place where I had nothing to do but my preferred work. I wrote a treatment for *My Dream of You* in Yaddo; it was contracted for, I moved to Manhattan, got a room and a cat out of a shelter, and wrote it. It was published in the USA, the UK, Ireland and various non-English-speaking countries in 2001, to some acclaim—it went on to the *New York Times* best-seller list in its first week.

"I am now trying to write a second novel. A leading theme of the last book was what women will do for passion. The present one explores the curve of life as it naturally moves away from passion, in late middle age. What then? How do you unlearn what have been the yearnings of a lifetime? I still work for the *Irish Times*. Some of my sisters and a brother and I have just gone on our first ever holiday together—all of us with grey hair, but better late than never. I move between Dublin and the west of Ireland and my ambition is to also spend winters in Manhattan. My companions are a cat and a dog."

In an interview with Janet Kinosian, a contributor to the *Los Angeles Times* (April 26, 1999), O'Faolain recalled, "A lot of us suffered in the Ireland of my day. We came out of a culture where woman were utterly powerless and children had no value. If you were hit at school, you were hit at home for being hit at school. It goes without saying there was no sex education. The only education a lot of us got was in neglect and being unloved."

Despite neglecting their children, the O'Faolain parents raised them in a relatively cultured environment. Nuala's mother read to them frequently, and her father taught them the words to German songs. Growing up, they also listened to such musical works as *Swan Lake* on the gramophone. Nuala found solace in reading. She obtained books from the local library and the larger one maintained by the United States Information Service, in Dublin. Among the authors she enjoyed were James Joyce, John Dos Passos, and Theodore Dreiser.

After working at University College as a lecturer, O'Faolain moved to London to work as a producer for BBC television. In an interview with Daphne Merkin, a contributor to the *New York Times Magazine* (February 18, 2001), O'Faolain described life in her 30s as "a wasteland of misery and loss and mourning and drinking." Like her mother, O'Faolain became an alcoholic, and after the death of her father, she was hospitalized for a time in a psychiatric institution. She managed to recover and eventually regained control of her life. In the late 1970s Radio Telefís Éireann (RTÉ) in Ireland hired her as a producer and announcer.

In 1990 Conor Brady, the editor of the *Irish Times*, offered O'Faolain the opportunity to write an opinion column for the newspaper, after hearing a radio interview with her. O'Faolain immediately became popular with readers. "She just took off," Brady explained to Merkin. "She'd get these amazing mailbags from people because she touched something very elemental in their lives." O'Faolain covered many different topics, such as politics and religion, along with issues that were considered taboo by many in Ireland, such as domestic violence and homosexuality.

O'Faolain explained to Kinosian that writing *Are You Somebody?: The Accidental Memoir of a Dublin Woman* was "more about my personal loneliness, the fact that I've no lover, no child in a country that only upholds that role for a woman and here I am near 60. I wanted to find the answer to the question: How did this happen?" She never expected the book to be a success. "I wanted a small print run because I was so ashamed about how many would be left over," she recalled to Emma Cook, a reporter for the London *Independent* (September 14, 1997). After O'Faolain made a promotional appearance for the book on Ireland's popular television program *The Gay Byrne Show*, *Are You Somebody?* became an overnight bestseller. Many Irish people, especially women, strongly identified with her tale. In an interview with Robin Dougherty, a reporter for the *Boston Globe* (May 27, 2001), O'Faolain recalled that she received 3,000 supportive letters within a short time after the book was published, and people often stopped her on the street to praise what she had written. (Not everyone, however, was pleased with the book; O'Faolain's surviving siblings were unhappy because the memoir disclosed personal and painful matters.) O'Faolain's publishers marketed her as a female Frank McCourt, the best-selling Irish author of *Angela's Ashes* (1997); McCourt has extolled O'Faolain's work, and the two authors have occasionally appeared together during promotional tours. Most reviewers praised *Are You Somebody?*, and in *Library Journal* (February 1, 1998), Denise S. Sticha invoked McCourt's name, writing, "In the best tradition of Irish storytelling, O'Faolain shares what it was like growing up as one of nine children . . . in an Ireland scarred by its past, dominated by the patriarchy of church and academe. . . . [The book] is a beautifully written, well-crafted memoir revealing the growth of a writer whose complexities mirror her times. Comparisons will be made to Frank McCourt's *Angela's Ashes*, but O'Faolain can stand on her own merit." In her review for the *Washington Post* (April 19, 1998), Alice McDermott observed that O'Faolain's excellent writing and honesty distinguished the memoir from others. McDermott concluded that the "final chapter of the book, a recounting of a Christmas Day O'Faolain spends alone, facing a middle age without a partner or child, wondering how it all happened, is a beautiful exploration of human loneliness and happiness, of contentment and longing."

After the critical and commercial success of *Are You Somebody?*, many publishers solicited O'Faolain to write a novel. O'Faolain found writing fiction more difficult than writing a memoir. Speaking to Noreen Taylor, a writer for London's *Times* (April 12, 2001), O'Faolain related that after several attempts she "wrote nothing. Ireland drained my confidence. So I moved to Manhattan, since everyone there seems to be writing. But some days I'd open the laptop and start crying because I thought: I can't do this, whatever led me to believe I could? Why am I sitting here, a grown woman, making up stories when I could be doing my columns?" O'Faolain kept trying, and within two years she had completed the manuscript. The novel, *My Dream of You*, was published in 2000. Its protagonist is Kathleen de Burca, a middle-aged travel writer. Kathleen, who is single and childless, returns to her native Ireland—which she had left behind decades before—to research the "Talbot Judgment," a mid-19th-century divorce decree between a wealthy Anglo-Irish landlord and his wife, who was having an affair with an Irishman. "The Talbot Judgment is a real document," O'Faolain told Heidi Benson for the *San Francisco Chronicle* (March 21, 2001). "The affair happened in 1849–1852, and I could not ignore the country it happened in." Kathleen's research leads her to the Great Potato Famine, which took place during the time of the Talbot Judgement and in which about one million people starved. "The famine is much more important than any us believe," O'Faolain told Liam Fay for London's *Sunday Times* (January 28, 2001). "It's very close in time. There are people alive whose parents lived through it. It's very contentious in rural Ireland because of land. We never faced it or talked about it. But this was the point when Ireland broke. It lost its whole history." *My Dream of You* became a best-seller and also earned O'Faolain substantial critical acclaim. Catherine Lockerbie observed in the *New York Times Book Review* (March 4, 2001), "The real virtues of *My Dream of You* are . . . entirely traditional: they lie in involving storytelling and in the depiction of a vivid and warm cast of characters, people about whom it is possible to care." In her review for the *Irish Times* (January 27, 2001), Kathy Cremin wrote that the novel "evokes the author's powerful political and social commentaries on Irish life." Cremin added that "O'Faolain gives readers a well-crafted, though not happy book: a work, in fact, of mourning which overtly locates a reservoir of anger and grief that women feel about women, in a way that is significantly unexplored in Irish fiction."

In 2003 O'Faolain published a second memoir, *Almost There: The Onward Journey of a Dublin Woman*. She revisited material that she had previously explored in *Are You Somebody?*, including her painful upbringing, and she wrote about the success and the overwhelming response to that book. O'Faolain wrote about her relationship with John, a twice-divorced Jewish lawyer from the borough of Brooklyn in New York City and the father of an eight-year-old daughter, whom she met through Match.com, an Internet dating service. In the *New York Times Book Review* (February 23, 2003), Deborah Mason had mixed feelings about the follow-up. "O'Faolain has a tangy, storytelling style, nurtured in a mordant Irish sense of irony and an Oxford-trained sleekness of thought," Mason wrote. "The most vivid of her ruminations—on 'the first man I ever adored,' on her 'muddy, ferny,' secret hideout as a child—have the rush of elegant daydreaming. Others go on too long or are annoyingly preachy. And with all due respect to what she describes as her sacred bond with readers, she has included too many of their letters to her." Mason wrote that the book was not for readers who expected loose ends to be tied up in neat bows, adding that O'Faolain's "unrepentant honesty—and her almost childlike determination to do better—that gives her book its strength."

O'Faolain currently writes a column for the *Irish Times* based on her personal experiences. Despite her successes, she told Daphne Merkin, "I can't wait to be an old lady. I'm dying to wither up so I can stop hurting." She concluded, "I'm going to live in a pub as soon as I get the old-age pension. Old ladies are always treated with great respect in pubs."

—D. C.

SUGGESTED READING: *Boston Globe* D p4 May 27, 2001; (London) *Independent* p6 Sep. 14, 1997; *Irish Times* p71 Jan. 27, 2001; *Los Angeles Times* E p3 Apr. 26, 1999; *New York Times Book Review* p7 Mar. 4, 2001, p30 Feb. 23, 2002; *New York Times Magazine* p6+ Feb. 18, 2001; *Publishers Weekly* p58+ Mar. 12, 2001; *San Francisco Chronicle* C p2 Mar. 21, 2001; (London) *Times* (on-line) Apr. 12, 2001

Selected Books: nonfiction—*Are You Somebody?: The Accidental Memoir of a Dublin Woman*, 1996 (Published in the United States and the United Kingdom in 1998); *Almost There: The Onward Journey of a Dublin Woman*, 2003; fiction—*My Dream of You*, 2001

Courtesy of William L. O'Neill

O'Neill, William L.

Apr. 18, 1935– Historian; biographer

William L. O'Neill is a historian and the author of many books on 20th-century American history. He examines changing attitudes toward divorce in *Divorce in the Progressive Era* (1967) and covers early 20th-century feminism in *Everyone Was Brave: The Rise and Fall of Feminism in America* (1969) and *The Woman Movement: Feminism in the United States and England* (1969). O'Neill attracted controversy with a favorable biography of Max Eastman, a leading American radical, in *The Last Romantic: A Life of Max Eastman* (1978) and a book detailing the American Left's dilemma over the Soviet dictator Josef Stalin in *A Better World: The Great Schism—Stalinism and the American Intellectuals* (1982). Both books opened old wounds among some leftists, who considered Eastman a traitor and believed that those on the left who supported Stalin did no visible harm to the United States. In *American High: The Years of Confidence, 1945–1960* (1986), O'Neill argues that the dramatic social change that defined the 1960s actually began during that 15-year period. He also explores how an ill-equipped United States managed to win World War II, despite numerous mistakes, in *A Democracy at War: America's Fight at Home and Abroad in World War II* (1993). His latest book, *The New Left: A History*, was published in 2001.

William L. O'Neill writes for *World Authors 1995–2000*: "I was born in Big Rapids, MI on April 18, 1935 to John P. and Helen E. O'Neill, becoming the eldest of three sons. I graduated from Big Rapids High School in 1953, and from the University of Michigan in Ann Arbor in 1957. I majored in history at Michigan and became a member of Phi Beta Kappa. I received my M.A. in history from the University of California, Berkeley in 1958 and my Ph.D. in 1963. My graduate career was interrupted by six months spent on active duty with the U.S. Army Reserve. I also married Elizabeth Carol Knollmueller in 1960, who later gave birth to two daughters, Cassandra in 1965 and Catherine in 1968. I took a one year appointment as an assistant professor in the history department of the University of Pittsburgh in 1963, and spent the next two years as a regular member of the history department at the University of Colorado, Boulder. From 1966 to 1971 I was a member of the history department of the University of Wisconsin, Madison, where I was promoted to associate professor in 1969. I spent the academic year 1969–70 as a visiting assistant professor at the University of Pennsylvania. In 1971 I joined the history department of Rutgers University as a full professor, where I have been ever since. These frequent moves were a function of the remarkable expansion of the college population during the 1960s, when enrollments doubled and the supply of Ph.D.s could not keep up with demand. Beginning in the 1970s colleges and universities began using part-timers and graduate students to do much of the teaching and faculty hiring and turnover has greatly declined as a result.

"My first publication in 1966 was an anthology of a socialist magazine. Quadrangle [my publisher] called the book, *Echoes of Revolt: The Masses 1911 to 1917*. As so many leading writers and artists were radicals during this period *The Masses* was beautifully written and illustrated, hence the continuing interest in it which led Ivan R. Dee, Inc. to bring out a paperback edition in 1989. In 1967 I published my dissertation, *Divorce in the Progressive Era*, a study of the efforts to bring down the rising divorce rate during the last historical period when there was a chance of doing so. In 1969 I published *Everyone Was Brave: The Rise and Fall of Feminism in America*. This was the book that made my academic reputation as it was the first professional history of the old feminist movement that came to an end with the enfranchisement of women. It was also the first book to point out that getting the vote proved to be a mixed blessing for feminists as once suffrage disappeared as an issue the movement lost its center and faded away. My career as an historian of women faded away also in the early 1970s since once it became a recognized field of specialization women's history was essentially closed to male scholars.

"*Coming Apart: An Informal History of America in the 1960s* (1971) was the only one of my books to write itself. At the suggestion of Ivan Dee, my editor at Quadrangle Books, I began writing it in 1969 and finished the following year. I had been on the margin of the civil-rights, student, and anti-war movements of the period and had been disillusioned by all of them, as also by the Johnson administration, so fueled by anger and disappointment the pages poured out of my typewriter. The book remained in print for 30 years so I obviously was not alone in feeling as I did.

"*The Last Romantic: A Life of Max Eastman* (1978) and especially *A Better World: The Great Schism: Stalinism and the American Intellectuals* (1982) did me more harm than good professionally as the Cold War was still on and academics considered it bad form to be anticommunist, the correct position being neutrality. I had met Max Eastman when I was editing *Echoes of Revolt* and became very fond of him personally. After his death I decided to write a biography of him as no full length work on him existed, although he had written a beautiful two-volume autobiography. I could not improve upon his own creation but I tried to put his life in historical context. Max had begun his career as a socialist, became a Communist after the October Revolution, then an anti-Stalinist after Trotsky's fall, and in the 1940s a conservative. The reasons for his evolution were fairly simple. Max had spent several years in the Soviet Union during the 1920s, learned Russian, married a woman whose brother was an important Soviet official, and made many friends among Russian political activists and artists. In the fight between Stalin and Trotsky Max took Trotsky's side and left the country after Trotsky's defeat. During the purges of the 1930s almost everyone Max knew or cared about in the Soviet Union was murdered by Stalin. That changed everything for Max. He tried to remain an anti-Stalinist radical, but eventually concluded that not just Stalin but Marxism itself was wrong and responsible for all the horrors in Russia. In working on Max's life I became an anti-Stalinist too, although I did not follow him into conservatism. This led inevitably to my writing *A Better World*, a history of the struggle between pro and anti-Stalinist intellectuals from the 1930s into the '70s. As I sided with the anti-Stalinists I became anathema to the many academicians who, while not Communists themselves, sided with the American Stalinists who were regarded chiefly as victims of McCarthyism. After the Cold War ended and many Soviet and American documents came to light proving that every accusation ever made by anti-Communists against both the USSR and the Communist Party USA were true, sentiment changed—too late to do me or my book any good. I have no regrets and consider the hostile reviews *A Better World* received to be merit badges.

"After writing *American High: The Years of Confidence, 1945–1960* (1986) I turned to a subject that had fascinated me since I was a child, the result being *A Democracy at War: America's Fight at Home and Abroad in World War II* (1993). As I was only ten when the war ended I do not remember much about it, but my hometown had its National Guard rifle company sent to New Guinea in 1943, where Company E was wiped out. At the end of the Buna-Gona campaign only six men were still on their feet, most having fallen prey to disease rather than enemy fire. It won a presidential unit citation for valor. The survivors were heroes to my town and to me growing up and I wrote the book in their honor. I also wrote it because no other history linked the home front to the fighting fronts. So far as I know all the many books on America during WWII deal either with military matters or domestic affairs, none except mine linking the two. The book received probably the best reviews I have ever gotten. I am now working on a book about the 1990s and the end of the American Century, which I expect will annoy many reviewers, my usual fate."

For his first book, *Echoes of Revolt: The Masses 1911 to 1917* (1967), O'Neill edited a collection of articles, editorials, poetry, short stories, drawings, and cartoons that had been previously published in the socialist magazine, *The Masses*, beginning three years before the outbreak of World War I. The collection offers insights into American radicalism of that time. Such prominent individuals as Pablo Picasso, Jack London, Stuart Davis, John Reed, and William English Walling contributed to the magazine. In the *New York Times Book Review* (December 11, 1966), Peter Lyon wrote that O'Neill "has modestly restrained the length of his notes and commentary, with the result that there is more space for the superb reports by John Reed and Inez Haynes Gillmore and Frank Bohn of strikes and industrial struggles. . . . *Echoes of Revolt* is a splendid achievement, and we are all the luckier to have this bonny reminder of the good old, golden days of American radicalism."

In his next book, *Divorce in the Progressive Era* (1968), O'Neill explores the increase in the number of divorces in the United States from 1890 to 1920. In the *American History Review* (June 16, 1968), B. M. Solomon had mixed feelings about the book. Although he described it as a "welcome addition to the small body of scholarly work in this field," Solomon criticized O'Neill for injecting "his own sympathetic view of divorce in a way that distracts from the historical focus of the book."

In 1969 O'Neill published two books about feminism, *Everyone Was Brave: The Rise and Fall of Feminism in America* and *The Woman Movement: Feminism in the United States and England*. In the first book, O'Neill discusses how the success of its mission undermined the early feminist movement. In 1920, through effective political activism, feminist organizations secured the right to vote. O'Neill argued that, with that battle won, feminists lost the need for political activism, and their influence declined. "What is particularly valuable in O'Neill's explication of events is that he faces the influence of political action on moral problems, and of moral imperatives . . . on political judgments," Elizabeth Janeway wrote in the *Saturday Review* (October 11, 1969). Janeway praised the book for providing vivid descriptions of various feminist leaders and such organizations as the Women's Trade Union League and the Consumers League. Janeway concluded that *Everyone Was Brave* is "a truly intelligent discussion of what the issues were." In the second book, O'Neill provides a detailed history of feminism in the United States and England. The book includes 22 pieces written by both feminists and critics of the movement. "O'Neill, in a masterful introductory essay based on extensive research and fine scholarship, takes a fresh and challenging approach," Gerda Lerner observed in her review for the *Journal of American History* (March 1970). "He deals with the subject of woman's emancipation as a whole, seeing feminism as merely one aspect of the problem. By comparing British and American feminism, he is able to view the issue from a new vantage point. . . . This small book is an important challenge to scholarship in the field."

In his book, *Coming Apart: An Informal History of America in the 1960s* (1971), O'Neill chronicles the turmoil of the decade, which saw widespread student unrest, growing opposition to the Vietnam War, the civil-rights movement, race riots in several major cities, and the assassinations of President John F. Kennedy, the civil-rights leader Dr. Martin Luther King, and Sen. Robert Kennedy, who was seeking the Democratic Party's nomination for president, in 1968. The book received mixed reviews. D. A. Bower lauded it in the *Library Journal* (July 1971), writing that "O'Neill brilliantly discriminates, synthesizes, and arranges the most significant events, writing in language so clear that no reader will be bored or fail to grasp the links between the politics and culture of the day." By contrast, in the *New York Times Book Review* (October 24, 1971), Benjamin DeMott faulted *Coming Apart* for its "intellectual thinness," concluding that although it was a good "quickie read, it doesn't light up the period."

In the biography, *The Last Romantic: A Life of Max Eastman* (1978), O'Neill profiled the prolific author, intellectual, and former radical. In 1917 Eastman militantly opposed the United States's entry into World War I. An avid communist, he lived in the Soviet Union from 1922 to 1923 and wrote one of the first major biographies of Leon Trotsky in English. Eastman's political outlook gradually changed over the next few decades. After he returned to the United States, Eastman turned against the Soviet dictator Josef Stalin, a move that brought condemnation from much of the American Left. By the late 1930s Eastman had abandoned Marxism and become a staunch opponent of the Soviet Union. During the 1950s he backed Senator Joseph McCarthy's witch-hunts against alleged communists in government and elsewhere, and he contributed articles to the conservative magazine, *National Review*. In his review for the *American Scholar* (Summer 1979), Sidney Hook, who had often clashed with Eastman throughout his life, identified several factual errors in the book, noting, "I come in for a number of mentions in Professor O'Neill's biography of Max Eastman, and I ought to say straightaway that my own recollection of the events he describes is often very different from his historical resuscitation of them." Hook admitted that the great virtue of O'Neill's book "is that he meticulously documents the stages in Eastman's intellectual odyssey from American syndicalism and pragmatism to Bolshevik Leninism and, after several ideological ports of call, the safe harbor of free enterprise to which he was piloted by Friedrich Hayek [an Austrian economist and author]." He concluded, however, "There is nothing so revelatory of O'Neill's intellectual limitations as his failure to grasp, or even to state accurately, the issues in this dispute, or indeed any of the theoretical disputes in which Eastman was engaged. He does not analyze any ideas or examine the arguments or evidence presented in their behalf. His statement of the issues is superficial and unilluminating." In the *New York Times Book Review* (December 19, 1978), Jerome Charyn was more impressed with *The Last Romantic*. Although Charyn strongly disagreed with O'Neill's claim that Eastman never acquired "adult traits" such as sexual fidelity, the reviewer concluded that O'Neill successfully "rescued" Eastman by establishing his intellectual importance. "Eastman did play out so many of the bumps and twists of the 20th century," Charyn wrote. "And he sang his own odd and often heroic song: 'I'm a black sheep that wandered away and fell into the chasm between literature and science.' Professor O'Neill exposes a large area of that chasm to us."

In *A Better World: The Great Schism—Stalinism and American Intellectuals* (1982), O'Neill details a major dispute in the old American Left. During the mid-1920s, many left-wing intellectuals and activists embraced Stalin, thinking that the nation he ruled offered hope for a world free of poverty, inequality, and injustice. Many intellectuals, however, turned against Stalin, after the purge trials of the late 1930s that killed millions of people, his alliance with Nazi Germany from 1939 to 1941, and his domination of Eastern Europe after World War II. O'Neill writes that these intellectuals began separating Stalin or "Stalinism" from Marxism and radicalism in order to preserve their credibility. By contrast, a number of left-wing intellectuals continued to back Stalin, dismissing the disclosure of his crimes as anti-communist propaganda or even justifying them as necessary evils. In his review for the *New York Times* (December 31, 1982), Walter Goodman agreed that the split between the Stalinists and anti-Stalinists "deserves periodic retelling for its political and moral relevance, and Mr. O'Neill tells it in straightforward if not particularly stylish fashion." Goodman noted that O'Neill's "main sources for progressive thought or avoidance of thought in the 1930s and '40s are such magazines as the *Nation* and the *New Republic*. The anti-Stalinists of the time are represented by the *New Leader*, *Partisan Review*, and Dwight MacDonald's iconoclastic *Politics*. Mr. O'Neill has mined these journals and the papers of some of the major players thoroughly enough to spare future researchers some exertion." In his review for the *New Republic* (March 14, 1983), Dennis Wrong hailed *A Better World*. "One feels immense gratitude to O'Neill for having faithfully reported a record that has been the subject of so much myth-making," Wrong asserted. "He sticks close to the immediate issues under debate at all times, avoiding excessive psychologizing or motive-mongering, and his verdicts are pithy, balanced, and expressed with wit and economy."

In 1986 O'Neill published his next book, *American High: The Years of Confidence, 1945–1960* (1986). In it he argues that those 15 years, in addition to being a time of great national self-confidence and optimism for many Americans, were a period of dramatic social and economic change. Citing several examples, O'Neill notes that median family income doubled during those years, and housing was affordable and plentiful. The civil-rights movement had begun in the mid-1950s, galvanized by *Brown v. Board of Education of Topeka, Kansas*, the 1954 Supreme Court decision that declared racial segregation unconstitutional, and the birth control pill was approved by the FDA, in 1960, helping to spark a sexual revolution later that decade. Contrary to the opinions of many historians, O'Neill concludes that President Dwight Eisenhower was a capable leader, who preserved both peace and prosperity. In his review for the *Washington Post Book World* (February 1, 1987), Ronald H. Spector hailed the book as "a lively and provocative new look at those years," writing that O'Neill's "judgments are invariably rendered with style and verve, and many, in my opinion are right on target." Spector, however, disagreed with O'Neill's favorable assessment of Eisenhower, arguing that a "detailed examination by historians of specific foreign policy issues and episodes in our relations with Asia, Latin America, and the Middle East during the Eisenhower period have uncovered few successes and numerous instances of misperception, lost opportunities, and good old-fashioned muddle." Reviewing the book for the *Atlantic* (February 1987), William E. Leuchtenburg concluded that O'Neill wrote "a book that is lively and stimulating," but offered a few criticisms. "Most of his argument is cursorily stated at the beginning or very end of the book in a series of one-liners," Leuchtenburg observed, "and the bulk of *American High* does not elaborate his theme but offers a history of public policy, war, and diplomacy in which topics too often seem to be chosen at random."

In 1993 O'Neill published another book on American history, *A Democracy at War: America's Fight at Home and Abroad in World War II*. In it he explores how the United States managed to achieve victory in World War II, when the war effort was plagued by military and political mistakes. (He reports, for example, that the mobilization effort, which involved the drafting and training of millions of soldiers, was slow and inefficient.) "The book is written in a style and manner intended to appeal to the general reader," George Q. Flynn wrote in the *American Historical Review* (February 1995). "Although O'Neill uses many fine secondary works, he eschews archival material and provides no bibliography. Citations are infrequent and too often point to *Life* magazine as the authoritative source on the American experience." Despite these criticisms, Flynn was impressed with O'Neill's discussion of the war effort at home, noting that his "chapter on 'everyday life' is a minor masterpiece in which he repeatedly captures a new trend in a pithy phrase."

O'Neill has also published several textbooks, including *Looking Backward: A Re-Introduction to American History* (1974), *The Progressive Years: America Comes of Age* (1975), and *World War II: A Student Companion* (1999). In 2001 O'Neill revisited American radicalism with the publication of *The New Left: A History*. In his review for the *History Teacher* (February 2002, on-line), Robert C. Cottrell wrote that O'Neill "delivers a blistering indictment of the largely young rebels and radicals who grabbed their nation's attention during the 1960s." Although he criticized the book for being weak in several areas, Cottrell agreed that "*The New Left* has much to offer students of the subject."

In 2002 O'Neill edited the *Oxford Essential Guide to World War II*. He is also the editor of the "Scribner Encyclopedia of American Lives," which is scheduled for release in 2004.

O'Neill and his wife live in Highland Park, New Jersey.

—D. C.

SUGGESTED READING: *American Historical Review* p1661 June 1968, p255 Feb. 1995; *American Scholar* p404+ Summer 1979; *Atlantic* p91+ Feb. 1987; *Booklist* July 1999; *History Teacher* (on-line) Feb. 2002; *Journal of American History* p935 Mar. 1970; *Library Journal* p2337 July 1971; *New Republic* p34 Mar. 14, 1983; *New York Times* C p20 Dec. 31, 1982; *New York Times Book Review* p1+ Dec. 11, 1966, p63 Oct. 24, 1971, p13 Dec. 10, 1978; *Saturday Review* p27 Oct. 11, 1969; *Washington Post Book World* p5 Feb. 1, 1987

SELECTED BOOKS: *Divorce in the Progressive Era*, 1967; *Everyone Was Brave: The Rise and Fall of Feminism in America*, 1969; *The Woman Movement: Feminism in the United States and England*, 1969; *Coming Apart: An Informal History of America in the 1960s*, 1971; *Looking Backward: A Re-Introduction to American History* (with Lloyd C. Garner), 1974; *The Progressive Years: America Comes of Age*, 1975; *The Last Romantic: A Life of Max Eastman*, 1978; *A Better World: The Great Schism—Stalinism and the American Intellectuals*, 1982; *American High: The Years of Confidence, 1945–1960*, 1986; *A Democracy at War: America's Fight at Home and Abroad in World War II*, 1993; *World War II: A Student Companion*, 1999; *The New Left: A History*, 2001; as editor—*Echoes of Revolt: "The Masses," 1911 to 1917*, 1966; *American Society Since 1945*, 1969; *The American Sexual Dilemma*, 1972; *Women at Work*, 1972; *Insights and Parallels, Problems and Issues in American Social History*, 1973

Ong, Han

1968(?)– Playwright; novelist

The playwright and novelist Han Ong's talent became evident in his teenage years, not long after he moved to the United States from the Philippines. Though English is not his native language, his plays exhibit verbal dexterity and elegant simplicity. In 1997, at the age of 29, he became the youngest playwright to receive a MacArthur "genius" fellowship. Generally considered an avant-garde playwright, he tends to subsume plot and characterization beneath a prominent conceptual framework. He has resisted being categorized as an Asian or homosexual playwright, but his work is often concerned with issues relevant to these groups. "I want theatre to do several contradictory things," he told John Lahr for the *New Yorker* (April 26, 1993). "I want it to be pop and profound at the same time. I think I want it to be a confluence of many illegitimate and bastard forms, such as music videos, anthropological lists, dry news reportage, comic books, fashion shows. Why? I have a problem with authority figures. I have always resented being told these things aren't theatre. I disagree, and I want to prove these people wrong." Ong is a prolific writer who has produced approximately three dozen plays and a novel, *Fixer Chao* (2001). His plays include *The L.A. Plays, Reasons to Live. Reason to Live. Half. No Reason., Bachelor Rat, Symposium in Manila, Airport Music*, and *Middle Finger*.

Courtesy of Farrar, Straus and Giroux

Han Ong was born in Manila, the Philippines, in about 1968, the second of the five children of Solomon Ong, an insurance executive, and Jane Ong, a homemaker. Ong's grandparents had emigrated from China to the Philippines to escape poverty and drought. In 1984 Ong and his family moved to Los Angeles, California, where they settled in the neighborhood known as Koreatown. Ong's parents were strict Catholics, but their authority was weakened once they moved to America. "They wanted to remain the sole arbiters of right and wrong for us," Ong wrote in *Natural History* (March 1998), "consequently drawing lines around our conduct that, in the harsh light of America and its emphasis on personal liberty, were revealed to be outdated, unfair, inhuman. Still, their hold on us would have remained firm had we not felt that they were in some sense weakening, their authority manifestly cracking, when required to confront white people and a country whose language and systems exposed them as mere virgins: so many tasks, like having to talk to the phone company people, say, to ask about a bill; or to the grocer to finesse the difference between one brand of rice and another—tasks for which we, the children, had to intercede on their behalf—turned us into the new adults of this new place and our parents into infants, their threats and injunctions growing day by day into watery things."

Because of overcrowding in the public schools in Koreatown, Ong was bussed to the predominantly white Grant High School in the San Fernando Valley. There he began writing plays, mostly because he could not find any published dramas that had roles to which he could relate. In general, he found America an inhospitable place for nonnatives. "It was horrible," he told Jan Breslauer for the *Los Angeles Times* (November 29, 1992), "as if adolescence wasn't bad enough. Nothing in the atmosphere of the city and, correlatively, in the country, made me feel as if this was my place." Though he had hated the Catholic school he attended in the Philippines, Ong soon realized that his education there was far better than the one he received at his American public high school, which he has described repeatedly as "terrible." In 1986, after his sophomore year, he dropped out and studied for his high-school equivalency exam, which he passed. He also moved out of his parents' home and began taking temporary clerical jobs. He worked briefly as an assistant at the Mark Taper Forum, a Los Angeles theater where he made friends who later helped him get some of his work produced. While living with a high-school friend and her family, Ong began exploring the street life of Los Angeles and "gravitated to the subculture of homosexual hookers," as he told Kevin Kelly for the *Boston Globe* (April 4, 1993). Through "this real world experience," he told Kelly, he discovered "freedom he had never known."

Ong became a member of the Los Angeles Theatre Center's Young Playwrights Lab and the Asian American Theatre Center. His experience with the underground gay culture of Los Angeles inspired two short plays, *In a Lonely Country* and *A Short List of Alternate Places*, which were then combined into *The L.A. Plays*, tied together through a central character named Greg, a homosexual Asian American street hustler. *The L.A. Plays*—which was the first of Ong's works to be produced—debuted at the Mark Taper Forum in 1990. In the first act Greg takes the stage alone and is confronted by an authoritarian offstage voice, which disparages his appearance and tells him to change it. Greg then has a series of encounters in an unglamourous cityscape of bus stops, street corners, and telephone booths. Though he wants to be an actor, he settles for being a part-time prostitute because it offers evidence of his desirability and provides a sense of belonging. Ong, in *The L.A. Plays*, presents a collage of scenes rather than a continuous narrative and traditional character development, a technique that he employed in subsequent plays and that elicited an array of responses from critics. *The L.A. Plays*, for the most part, was very successful; it appeared in theaters around the country and in Britain and attracted the attention of the prominent director Robert Brustein, who gave Ong the opportunity to showcase his work at the American Repertory Theater, in Boston. Some critics, however, found Ong's approach to playwriting unsatisfying. "There's breadth here but not a lot of depth," Sheridan Morley wrote of *The L.A. Plays* for the *Spectator* (November 20, 1993): "we never really get to know any of the characters for long enough to care about their displacement, and in the end Han Ong's play resembles nothing so much as one of those coach tours of movie stars' homes on which we are left with our noses pressed up against the glass of the bus, desperate to learn more of lives that are only flickeringly on public show."

The L.A. Plays offered a statement about the illusory quality of the American dream for those on the periphery of society, including many Asian Americans and gays. And yet, Ong himself has expressed an ambivalent attitude about being described as an "Asian" or a "gay" writer. "I think that when you present people under the banner of 'multiculturalism,' you're just finding another way of categorizing them," he told Dennis Harvey for the *San Francisco Chronicle* (April 5, 1992). "It's often assumed that ethnic people in the arts are only interested in creating kvetch festivals about their history of oppression, because our models have been the theater of social protest. So it's easy to sweep new work under the same carpet, as 'typically Asian American' or whatever." Ong has made a concerted effort to bring the range and complexity of minority experience to center stage, to move beyond merely portraying minorities as oppressed. "This humanist agenda is laudable," he told Breslauer, "but it is politically first-rung. We ought to have evolved further. The fact that we need to restate every year that black people are human too is a sorry state of affairs. Knowing the humanist agenda that the past generation of playwrights has accomplished and knowing the satiation point, I want to move on to the next level."

Following the success of *The L.A. Plays* Ong continued to write prolifically. In 1992 three of his plays—*Symposium in Manila*, *Bachelor Rat*, and *Reasons to Live. Reason to Live. Half. No Reason.*—were staged simultaneously in San Francisco.

Symposium in Manila, a monologue that Ong performed himself, is about an Asian American artist who feels his career is not taking off despite current trends in multicultural theater. Following the advice of his grandfather, the artist goes to the Philippines to try to find himself, but U.S. colonization has rendered the country an imitation of America. *Bachelor Rat* is a surrealistic portrait of a young man named Dada. "It's not really plot-driven," Ong told Harvey, "but more an accretion of scenes in the life of the lead character, who is a young, promiscuous gay man. It's almost a sort of faux anthropological documentary." *Reasons* depicts Rudy, an ex-con who has recently served 15 years for killing his nagging mother. "After his release, he basically tries to create a prison for himself again to seclude himself," Ong explained to Harvey. "When his girlfriend wants him to better himself, it echoes the ways that his mother had kept harping at him to do the same. You gradually see the history of constant mental and emotional oppression which led to his original outburst of violence." Steven Winn, writing in the *San Francisco Chronicle* (April 24, 1992), found fault with the characterizations in *Reasons*. "[It] is more promise than delivery, unfortunately," he wrote, "a fragmented journey that opens Rudy's experience to us only in brief and elusive flashes. A good deal of the action is built around prototypical encounters that generate synthetic dialogue, some of it written in tepid free verse."

In 1994 Ong collaborated with Jessica Hagedorn on *Airport Music*. As Luis H. Francia described it in the *Village Voice* (May 17, 1994), the play presents "fragments of stories about exile, the incongruous and awkward juxtaposition of cultures, with a clear emphasis on the personal." The material ranges from satirical speeches on American footwear to descriptions of the 1904 St. Louis World's Fair, where tribal Filipinos were displayed for mostly white crowds. Francia continued, "Not all the notes resonate. Some of the material is merely clever, some quite thin. But the work has an inquisitive intelligence and edges away from the preachiness that often mars drama on any diaspora. And it's brave enough to show its rough edges."

Ong has often spoken of his disenchantment with American theater. While continuing to write plays, he has also worked on several novels. He wrote three, in fact, before his first, *Fixer Chao*, was published, in 2001. In an article on PublishersWeekly.com Ong explained to an interviewer how he came up with the idea for *Fixer Chao* while attending a play. "There was an instance where I was bored and my mind drifted," he said. "Suddenly, instead of what I was watching on the stage, I saw a set filled with white furniture. I saw this character walking around, making suggestions about the furniture arrangement, and I realized he was a feng shui master. And I knew, for some reason, that he was telling lies." In the novel, a gay Filipino hustler named William Narciso Paulinha—upon the urging of his friend Shem C—makes a career move. He had been turning tricks in a New York City bus station bathroom, but now begins advising the city's elite in feng shui, the ancient Chinese spiritual practice of arranging one's domestic environment in a harmonious manner. William, who becomes known around town as Master Chao, excels as a con man. His clients follow his advice, even when it is purposefully spiteful. For instance, Master Chao tells one particularly detested client to put a mirror somewhere where she will see it first thing in the morning. "This furious—and occasionally infuriating—book is relentless in its exposure of the frauds that fuel the American Dream," Mark Rozzo wrote in the *Los Angeles Times* (April 29, 2001), "irate, and inchoate as it takes on race and origin and sexual orientation, self-consciously microcosmic in its exploration of class and, to the last, baffling, ambiguous and nearly euphoric in its anger." In the *New York Times* (April 5, 2001, on-line) Janet Maslin wrote, "Mr. Ong's gift for quick, acerbic caricatures and piercing observations about contemporary culture far outstrips his plotting. The book sprawls, although it doesn't entirely run out of steam. In the meantime there are enough tart observations to keep it vivid as a running commentary, which is perhaps its true purpose after all."

In September 2000 Ong's *Middle Finger*, an adaptation of the German playwright Frank Wedekind's *Spring Awakening* (1909), was presented by the Ma-Yi Theatre Company in New York City. It is a story of Filipino boys coming of age, told in a more naturalistic manner than many of Ong's other plays. "If I told this story in an avant-garde style," he told Lenora Inez Brown for *American Theatre* (February 2001), "there would be no rules, a sense that anything goes, and the boys would have nothing to chafe against. In naturalism, I not only had to reveal character through speech, I had to do it so that they would sound convincing within the characters' circumstances. I came to understand that I was avoiding naturalism because I considered it a bag of tricks used by generations before me, and that it wasn't young and hip. And then I realized I'm really not young and hip, and it's great to know that!"

Ong lives in New York City. His play, *The Suitcase Trilogy*, will be performed by the Ma-Yi Theatre Company in New York City in 2003.

—P. G. H.

SUGGESTED READING: *American Theatre* p29+ Feb. 2001; *Boston Globe* B p30 Apr. 4, 1993; *Guardian* Nov. 8, 1993; *Los Angeles Times* p5 Nov. 29, 1992; *Natural History* p50+ Mar. 1998; *New Yorker* p112+ Apr. 26, 1993; *New York Times* (on-line) Apr. 5, 2001; *San Francisco Chronicle* p44 Apr. 5, 1992, C p7 Apr. 24, 1992

SELECTED WORKS: novels—*Fixer Chao*, 2001; plays—*The L.A. Plays*, 1990; *Reasons to Live. Reason to Live. Half. No Reason.*, 1992; *Bachelor Rat*, 1992; *Symposium in Manila*, 1992; *Airport Music*, 1994; *Middle Finger*, 2000

Martin Fengel/Courtesy of Random House

Oswald, Georg M.

(GAY-org)

1963– Novelist

Georg M. Oswald is a successful author in his native Germany. He has written four novels, which explore violent crimes and other misdeeds committed by some of society's more affluent professionals. In 2001 Oswald's latest novel, which tells the story of a banker who becomes mixed up with drug dealers, was translated into English as *All That Counts*.

Georg M. Oswald was born in 1963 in Munich, in what was then West Germany. After completing his education, Oswald became a lawyer, but wrote in addition to practicing law. In 1995 he published his first novel, *Das Loch*. His second novel, *Lichtenberg's Fall* (1997), brought him some attention outside of Germany. "A sense that the best stories are from people on the fringes seems . . . to have inspired Georg Oswald," a writer for the *Economist* (October 18, 1997) observed. "*Lichtenberg's Fall* tells of a young, successful Munich yuppie whose life goes into a tailspin when he is accused of killing his mother-in-law. (In German ein Fall is both a fall or collapse and a law case.) Strikingly, the novel takes the form of an extended response to a police interrogation."

Oswald's third novel, *eine Karriere* (Party Boy), was published in 1998, and his fourth, *Alles, was zählt*, in 2000. That year *Alles, was zählt* earned the International Prize, which is awarded by several European publishing houses. In 2001 the book was translated into English as *All That Counts*, as well as into several other languages. (The "all" of the title refers to money.) The novel's main character is Thomas Schwarz, an arrogant deputy manager who works in a bank's foreclosing and liquidation department. Schwarz enjoys his work, saying, "It's like a sport—I squeeze the last drop of blood out of people, and when no one believes there's any left, I give him a good shake, and lo and behold, there's a couple of more drops," as quoted by Geoff Nicholson in the *New York Times Book Review* (October 7, 2001). Schwarz is fired when he fails to solve a two-decade-old bank case. When his wife leaves him in the wake of the firing, he becomes involved with two crooks, who use a furniture store to launder money from their illegal sales of steroids. Schwarz then hatches a scheme to double-cross his new associates and run off with their money. "This is a book full of small, cumulative pleasures," Nicholson wrote. "Schwarz starting an argument in the fish department of a supermarket, making a fool of himself at a party where he tells a lot of highly respectable rich people that he can help them set up anonymous Swiss bank accounts, accompanying a bailiff to an ill-fated store called the Gothic Place, which sells comics, horror videos and death metal CD's." Although he asserted that "it is impossible to tell Oswald's own moral viewpoint," Nicholson concluded that the "*All That Counts* delivers a taut climax," and that the novel "is a parable about the extent to which money is, or is not, destiny. This is a high ambition, one that Oswald tackles without pretension. That he manages to make it look easy is the real confirmation of his talents." By contrast, Jeff Zaleski faulted the book in his review for *Publishers Weekly* (August 6, 2001). "German novelist Oswald proves that it's a small world, after all, by writing a bitter sendup of consumerism and corporate culture that's every bit as shallow, ham-fisted and self-congratulatory as anything penned by his wannabe-hip American or British counterparts over the past decade," Zaleski wrote. "Oswald's all-out assault on the soullessness of big business and the pervasive numbness and lack of direction of today's young professionals is largely unsuccessful, full of uninspired sociological observations and peopled exclusively by militantly unpleasant characters, making for a short but onerous read."

Georg M. Oswald currently lives in Munich.

—D. C.

SUGGESTED READING: *Economist* p14+ Oct. 18, 1997; *New York Times Book Review* p7+ Oct. 7, 2001; *Publishers Weekly* p61 Aug. 6, 2001

SELECTED BOOKS IN ENGLISH TRANSLATION: *All That Counts*, 2001

Chris Saunders/Courtesy of the Doubleday Broadway Publishing Group

Palahniuk, Chuck

(PA-LUH-nik)

1962 (?)– Novelist

Chuck Palahniuk's novels have spawned a cult following among young readers, who see themselves rebelling against the same societal constraints that Palahniuk mocks in his work. In *Fight Club* (1996), men feel so powerless that they choose to beat one another up in order to feel a sense of vitality; in *Survivor* (1999), a survivor of a religious cult taps into the modern American obsession with money, marketing, and televangelists; in *Invisible Monsters* (1999), the American standards of beauty are dissected through the misadventures of a transsexual and a disfigured model; in *Choke* (2000), compulsive behavior, sex, and religion are put to task by way of a main character who may or may not be the second coming of Jesus Christ, and who earns a living by faking choking episodes in restaurants, and then exploiting those who save him. Palahniuk experimented with the horror genre in his fifth novel, *Lullaby* (2002). "What's really remarkable about Chuck," fellow Portland writer Tom Spanbauer remarked to Frank Bures in *Poets and Writers Magazine* (May–June 2001), "is his wit and how caustic it can be. He can turn that wit on just about anything and shred it."

Of Russian and French descent, Chuck Palahniuk was born in about 1962 in Burbank, Washington. His father, Fred, worked on the railroad and his mother, Carol, worked for a nuclear power plant; because his parents fought so often and eventually divorced, Palahniuk and his three siblings were raised on his grandfather's cattle ranch, in eastern Washington. "My grandfather had so many scams," Palahniuk recalled for Emily Jenkins in the *Village Voice* (October 13–19, 1999, on-line). "The scene in *Invisible Monsters* about feeding stale Hostess treats to the pigs [to fill their intestines with extra poundage before sale]—my sister and I always had to do that, open all those packages and throw them in."

In order to keep out of his parents' arguments, Palahniuk escaped into books and soon began imagining himself as a writer. After high school he took a messenger job at *The Oregonian*, a Portland newspaper where, he hoped, he would be able to get started in journalism. He then studied journalism at the University of Oregon, receiving his bachelor's degree, in 1986. He found no mentors among his professors: one wanted him to drop his fiction class; another told him that he would never have an original thought. He was original enough, however, to get out of scrapes by inventing "Nick," his alter ego. He recalled during an interview for *IGN for Men* (October 15, 1999, on-line): "All through college I had an alter-ego named 'Nick.' So whenever we went out drinking and semi-illegal carousing I would always be 'Nick.'. . . That way if somebody called the house asking for 'Nick' I would know that it was gonna be bad news."

After graduation Palahniuk took a job at a local paper, but quickly discovered the frustrations of being a reporter, including the poor wages ($5 an hour). He quit before long. "It was eighty percent money, twenty percent frustration," he told Frank Bures. "I was starting to see how my editor would send me out specifically to start conflict so I would have something to report on. I just felt very used by the whole process." He then decided to take a mechanics class, and found a job at the Freightliner truck-manufacturing plant. "I worked two years on the assembly line then I got this documentation specialist job, which everyone seems to interpret as diesel mechanic," he explained to Dawn Taylor in an interview for the *DVD Journal* (January 25, 2000, on-line). "But basically I did service procedures on trucks, and timed myself, then wrote about the repair times. So I did work on trucks, but I also wrote about it."

"I hated my job so much," Palahniuk told Bures, "that all of my free time was spent trying to forget what I did for a living." His life outside of work consisted of drinking and getting into bar fights, and going to open houses and raiding people's medicine cabinets for drugs. He was angry, frustrated, and resentful. His life changed dramatically in the early 1990s, when he moved to a small house outside of Portland. Since the house was located near a hill, he couldn't get any reception on his television at all. Though at first upset by this, Palahniuk eventually found that—without television—he could settle into a new, more reflective rhythm. He had more time to read, and scoured library shelves for books that interested him. He discovered the works of Junot Diaz, Amy Hempel, Jo Ann Beard, Denis Johnson, and Mark Richard—

young writers who use language in a concise, effective way, and whose stories often combine misery and humor. He also began to write more.

Palahniuk published two stories in the literary journal, *Modern Short Stories*, and then attempted to write a novel. The result was the manuscript "If You Lived Here You'd Be Home Already," which Palahniuk has described as 700-pages long, autobiographical, and awful. He then began *Invisible Monsters*, about a disfigured fashion model who takes to the road with an attractive, pre-operative transsexual. It was read and ultimately rejected by several editors, who deemed it to be too outrageous and bleak. Palahniuk was undaunted, as he remarked in his interview for *IGN for Men*: "I thought I could either write something that's less dark and upsetting or I could write something that's 10 times as dark and upsetting. So I wrote *Fight Club* to punish those people. . . . I'm not going to change my style for you. You figure out how to market dark and upsetting."

Three days after Palahniuk sent his *Fight Club* manuscript out, it was accepted by Norton, and published in 1996. The novel is told by a 30-year-old unnamed narrator, who relates the story of Tyler Durden, a projectionist and waiter, who organizes underground fight clubs for men. Through membership in these fight clubs, men vent their frustrations about their mundane lives by beating each other senseless. Since the men of Durden's generation have had no sacrifices by which to define themselves, their lives are so empty that they can only define themselves by what they own. As Tyler remarks in the novel [quoted by Stuart Jeffries in the *Guardian* (May 14, 2000) and posted on *The Age* Web site]: "Our generation has had no Great Depression, no Great War. Our war is spiritual. Our depression is our lives." The fight clubs help them reconnect with their manhood, test their endurance, and make them question the society that created them. Though the book was not widely reviewed, it quickly started selling by word of mouth to younger readers, who recognized in the novel a reflection of their own lives. It became a runaway underground success, and won an Oregon Book Award for best novel and a Pacific Northwest Booksellers Award. In 1999 *Fight Club* was made into a movie, starring Brad Pitt, Ed Norton, and Helena Bonham Carter.

After the success of *Fight Club*, Palahniuk published a short story about the survivor of a suicide cult who becomes a religious television star through the influence of the media. He expanded that idea into a novel and published it as *Survivor*, in 1999. In the novel, Tender Branson tells his life story to an airplane's flight-data recorder, just before the plane is about to crash in the Australian outback. He recalls his evolution from a member of the Creedish religion, an isolated Christian sect in Nebraska, where Branson worked for 17 years as a humble housekeeper, to his life as a made-over televangelist, constructed for and by the media. Branson is catapulted into this new life when the rest of his sect commits mass suicide, and news of his survival reaches book agents, talk-show hosts, and other would-be handlers. A scathing criticism of fame, modern religion, and the media, *Survivor* received mixed reviews. In the *Village Voice* (February 24–March 2, 1999, on-line), Lily Burana wrote: "Palahniuk is an original talent. It's just that, in contrast to his first novel, *Fight Club* . . . *Survivor* seems lazy. Funny, but lazy. One wonders why someone with such a unique mind would bother with such overstudied ideas." Frank Bures, in *The Oregonian* (March 10, 1999, on-line), found *Survivor* interesting, but ultimately disappointing. "The seeds of brilliance are present in *Survivor*. Its ideas are fresh, its voice is original and its wit is cutting. It is an entertaining story that reads smoothly. But in the end, each seed seems to have grown along its own course without circling back to a central motif. As a result, *Survivor* lacks cohesion."

Later in 1999 Palahniuk published a revised version of *Invisible Monsters*, as a Norton paperback original. Dashing back and forth with little regard for chronology, the narrative begins and ends with the disfigured model, Shannon McFarland, confronting her former friend Evie Cottrell, on the day of Evie's wedding. In between, Palahniuk chronicles Shannon's misadventures on the road with the beautiful transsexual, Brandy Alexander. The pair moves from town to town, pretending to be celebrity confidantes at open houses and stealing drugs from medicine cabinets. Along the way the characters' true motivations and personalities begin to emerge. The book received mostly favorable reviews. "There's no point in trying to make sense of it all," Anouk Hoedeman warned in the *Toronto Sun* (on-line), as posted on Canoe, Canada's Internet Network. "The bizarre characters, the drugs, the scams, the mutilation—it's a very strange, funny and hallucinogenic trip, best enjoyed if you don't overthink it. Just let its giddy waves sweep over you. You'll come out of it feeling exhilarated. And so glad your own anatomy is still more or less intact." In the *San Francisco Chronicle* (September 12, 1999, on-line), as posted on the *SF Gate* Web site, James Sullivan wrote: "It's Palahniuk's least successful effort to date, yet there are more than enough moments of insight to recommend *Invisible Monsters*."

In 2001 Palahniuk published his fourth novel, *Choke*, about the life of the scam artist Victor Mancini, who supports himself and his ailing mother by feigning choking in restaurants, having someone "save" his life, and then hitting up those saviors—now sentimentally attached to him—for money. Victor explains his scam in the novel, as quoted by John Foyston in *The Oregonian* (May 13, 2001, on-line) and posted on OregonLive.com: "By choking, you become a legend about themselves that they'll cherish and repeat until they die. They'll think they gave you life." Like most of his other books, *Choke* received mixed reviews. Foyston compared Palahniuk's strengths and weaknesses. "His most endearing trait—the thing that keeps me reading—is that marvelous quicksilver voice," he wrote, lamenting that Palahniuk did not create "a plot any deeper than what's needed to support all that glittering wordplay" or "characters any more warm and lovable than millipedes scuttling back under a rock." "For now," Foyston concluded, "the exuberance of his language makes it still worthwhile to brave these often chilly waters." In the *New York Times* (May 27, 2001, on-line), Jennifer Reese had a similar opinion: "Palahniuk is a gifted writer, and the novel is full of terrific lines. . . . But they can't hold the book together. . . . This book is dark, but it's not deep." Despite the mixed criticism, *Choke* became a surprise *New York Times* best-seller.

In his most recent novel, *Lullaby* (2002), Palahniuk took a different approach to his story, this time combining horror and humor to explore the absurdities of the modern world. "It's my attempt to reinvent the horror novel," he explained to Adam Dunn for *Publishers Weekly* (September 2, 2002). "I'm 40 years old this year, and I just can't be the angry young man for the rest of my life." *Lullaby* presents the story of a 40-something reporter, Carl Streator, who lost his young child and wife 20 years prior. Assigned to write a series of stories on sudden infant death syndrome, or SIDS, Streator discovers an ancient African lullaby that may be the cause. The "culling song," which he finds featured in a children's book of world poems, is lethal to anyone who hears it. Streator memorizes the lullaby and goes on somewhat of a killing spree before recognizing his crimes and the extent of the song's deadly potential. He collaborates with Helen Hoover Boyle, a witch who makes a lucrative living as a real estate agent, selling—and reselling—haunted houses to unsuspecting buyers. A romance develops as the two embark on a road trip to collect and destroy all copies of the lullaby. Throughout the often satirical story, Palahniuk probes a deeper contemporary issue: the notion that information has become a deadly weapon. *Lullaby* was generally well received, particularly for its comic elements. Yet, as one critic for *Publishers Weekly* noted, as quoted on *Amazon.com*, "The chief significance of this novel is Palahniuk's decision to commit himself to a genre, and this horror tale of both magic and mundane modernity plants him firmly in a category where previously he existed as a genre of one."

In addition to his novels, Palahniuk's writing has been featured in such magazines as *Playboy*, *Gear*, *Nest*, and *Black Book*. His next book, an autobiographical travel piece about his hometown, entitled "Fugitives and Refugees: A Walk in Portland, Oregon," is set for release in July 2003. He is also expected to release his sixth novel, tentatively titled "Diary," in 2003. Palahniuk lives with his wife in Portland.

—C. M.

SUGGESTED READING: *Book Browser* (on-line) Oct. 30, 1999; *Book Reporter* (on-line) Oct. 29, 1999; *DVD Journal* (on-line) Jan. 25, 2000; *Guardian* (on-line) May 14, 2000; *IGN for Men* (on-line) Oct. 15, 1999; *New York Times* E p14 Oct. 15, 1999; *New York Times* (on-line) May 24, 2001, May 27, 2001; *The Oregonian* (on-line) Mar. 10, 1999, May 13, 2001; *Poets and Writers* p24+ May–June 2001; *San Francisco Chronicle* (on-line) Sept. 12, 1999; *Toronto Sun* (on-line) Jan. 9, 2000; *Village Voice* (on-line) Feb. 24–Mar. 2, 1999, Oct. 13–19, 1999; *Washington Post Book World* p6 Dec. 1, 1996

SELECTED BOOKS: *Fight Club*, 1996; *Survivor*, 1999; *Invisible Monsters*, 1999; *Choke*, 2001; *Lullaby*, 2002

Courtesy of John Allen Paulos

Paulos, John Allen

July 4, 1945– Mathematician and nonfiction writer

The mathematician John Allen Paulos is on a crusade. Dismayed by the widespread ignorance of mathematics in the United States, Paulos is trying to encourage people to make sense of the statistics and figures that inform their lives. And, contrary to popular belief, he insists that mathematics is easy to learn and understand. Ignorance of basic mathematical concepts, Paulos argues, discourages critical thinking and results in costly mistakes and misguided decisions by both political leaders and ordinary people in their everyday lives. Three of his books, *Innumeracy: Mathematical Illiteracy and Its Consequences* (1989), *Beyond Numeracy:*

Ruminations of a Numbers Man (1991), and *How a Mathematician Reads the Newspaper* (1995), were best-sellers and well received by most critics. "I'm distressed by a society which depends so completely on mathematics and science and yet seems so indifferent to the innumeracy and scientific illiteracy of so many of its citizens, with a military that spends one quarter of a trillion dollars each year on ever smarter weapons for ever more poorly educated soldiers," he said to a writer for *Omni* (April 1993), "and with the media, who invariably become obsessed with this hostage on an airliner or that baby who has fallen into a well and seem insufficiently passionate when it comes to addressing problems such as urban crime, environmental deterioration, or poverty."

John Allen Paulos was born on July 4, 1945 in Denver, Colorado. After living in Chicago, Illinois, Paulos and his family moved to Milwaukee, Wisconsin, when he was five years old. He traces the roots of his fascination with mathematics to an incident in school, when he was 10. Paulos calculated that the Earned Run Average (ERA) of one of the Milwaukee Braves' less-talented pitchers was a poor 135. His teacher informed him that he must be wrong, claiming that the highest ERA a pitcher can have is 27. Paulos later consulted the *Milwaukee Journal Sentinel*'s sports pages and discovered that his figure of 135 was correct. "I remember thinking of mathematics as a kind of omnipotent protector," he explained to the *Omni* interviewer. "You could prove things to people, and they would have to believe you whether they liked you or not."

Paulos received his doctorate in mathematics from the University of Wisconsin, at Madison, in 1974. The same year, he became an associate professor of mathematics at Temple University, in Philadelphia, Pennsylvania. He specializes in symbolic logic, computer languages, and artificial intelligence.

In his first book, *Mathematics and Humor* (1980), Paulos argued that mathematical and logical concepts form the basic structure of humor—riddles, paradoxes, non sequiturs, and jokes. After reviewing the literature on humor, he analyzes a particular joke using a mathematical model. In the *New York Times Book Review* (January 18, 1981), Douglas Hofstadter elaborated the book's strengths and weaknesses. "Mr. Paulos does bring up a good number of excellent ideas from mathematics and philosophy, and attempts to apply them to some jokes with success," he noted. "He has brought all these ideas together so that non-technical readers can get an idea of the wealth of concepts that mathematicians and computer scientists can draw on in making metaphors to understand human behavior." And yet, he noted, Paulos presents such concepts "too haphazardly and shallowly." Reviewing the book for the *Times Literary Supplement* (December 19, 1980), Stuart Sutherland observed that Paulos's "examples of mathematical reasoning are often highly ingenious and are always lucidly presented." Sutherland concluded that "Paulos has certainly succeeded in looking at jokes in a new way, though whether the result is the discovery of new truth or the invention of a good joke must be left to the reader to decide." Paulos next wrote *I Think, Therefore I Laugh* (1985), which he described on his Temple University Home Page as "in part, an exemplification of a remark by [the philosopher and mathematician Ludwig] Wittgenstein that a good and serious work in philosophy could be written which consisted entirely of jokes."

He received substantial attention and critical acclaim for his third book, *Innumeracy: Mathematical Illiteracy and Its Consequences* (1989). According to Paulos, innumeracy, or the ignorance of mathematics and logic, is a widespread condition in the U.S. Weather forecasters, stock analysts, politicians, political activists, journalists, and others often cite misleading or incorrect figures to make judgments and support claims. In turn, many individuals accept the veracity of statistical data without question because they fail to adequately comprehend the meaning of numbers and mathematical concepts. As an example, Paulos recalled that he and his wife visited a doctor to learn about a minor medical procedure that she was scheduled to undergo. "Within 20 minutes, the doctor said there was only a million- to-one shot of something going wrong, that it was a 99 [percent] safe procedure, and then he said that it usually went quite well," Paulos told Kay Bartlett, a reporter for the *Los Angeles Times* (March 26, 1989). The doctor did not understand when Paulos observed that he just said three completely different things. "Even in their area of expertise, people just use numbers, not knowing what they mean," he said to Bartlett. Paulos claimed that, as a result of this "innumeracy," people make poor decisions in both their public and private lives. To remedy the problem, he called for better education. "You might expect a book about mathematics to be loaded with formulas and abstract reasoning," Langdon Wales wrote in the *Christian Science Monitor* (February 14, 1989). "Paulos avoids this, presenting his concepts entirely in words. Such hitherto abstruse topics as conditional probability, or permutations and combinations, are treated in a brief, entertaining, and comprehensible way without use of a single equation." In the *New York Times Book Review* (January 15, 1989), Morris Kline observed that Paulos's "aim is to inspire a mathematical way of looking at the world that does not depend on much actual mathematics—and sometimes depends on none at all." The reviewer noted that Paulos "provides a wealth of examples from the real world that demonstrate the variety of questions that can be treated with these simple tools." *Innumeracy* became a best-seller and was eventually translated into 11 languages. "Anyone can master the elements of mathematics," Paulos told Bartlett. "The unfortunate thing is that some of it is kind of ugly. It's like learning to parse a sentence. That's not fun, but it's necessary to get to the fun things like literature. Before you play with patterns and structures and have fun with math, you have to go through the ugly part too."

The commercial and critical success of *Innumeracy* led Paulos to publish a sequel, *Beyond Numeracy: Ruminations of a Numbers Man* (1991), a collection of 70 brief essays, arranged alphabetically, on mathematical topics from algebra and analytical geometry to vectors and voting systems. He even ventures into the relationships between mathematics, art, and music. In his review for the *Wall Street Journal* (May 22, 1991), Jim Holt compared *Beyond Innumeracy* to Voltaire's *Philosophical Dictionary* (1764); like Voltaire's dictionary, *Beyond Numeracy* "makes for an often-jolly little book." He continued, "Mr. Paulos does reasonably well in conveying the aesthetic appeal of mathematics. . . . If there is much to take issue with in *Beyond Numeracy*, there is also much to be amused and enlightened by." Curt Suplee, a contributor to the *Washington Post Book World* (April 21, 1991), was also impressed. "The book is at its best when explicating concepts that most readers might justly regard as unapproachably arcane, such as 'e' (the miraculous constant that is the basis of natural logarithms), 'i' (the square root of -1), or how 'matrix' and 'vector' math enables us to model economic and physical events. . . . Paulos painstakingly presents even the most recondite ideas in concrete, [visual] terms," Suplee noted, also complimenting Paulos's "wry and literate style, his slightly morbid sense of humor" and "his instinct for the killer example."

In *A Mathematician Reads the Newspaper* (1995) Paulos uses newspaper articles to explain mathematical concepts, for example citing a story on the economy to examine prediction, statistics, and game theory. In order to understand everyday events, Paulos suggests, journalists and readers alike should be well versed in mathematics. In his review for the *Christian Science Monitor* (May 31, 1995), Robert Schultz admired Paulos's "self-effacing sense of humor and awareness of the 'professional myopia' among mathematicians." As an example, Schultz cited a story in the book about three statisticians on a duck hunt: "The first fired, and his shot sailed six inches over the duck. Then the second fired, and his shot flew six inches below the duck. At this, the third statistician excitedly exclaimed, 'We got it!'" In the *New Scientist* (July 15, 1995), Robert Matthews found that "Paulos's attempts to link mathematics to newspaper issues are sometimes a little strained," adding that "he also tends to underestimate just how difficult some of the issues he raises really are." In spite of these reservations, Matthews concluded that "this book should be mandatory reading for every journalist—as well as the readers, viewers and former tutors they supposedly serve."

In *Once Upon A Number: The Hidden Mathematical Logic of Stories* (1998), Paulos looks at stories in which numbers play an important part; in so doing, he hopes to "limn the intricate connections between two fundamental ways of relating to our world—narratives and numbers," as he told Simon Singh in an interview for *Scientific American* (February 1999). Singh found that the narratives provided "an ideal environment for nonmathematicians to encounter mathematical ideas and examine them in comfort, without fear usually associated with the subject," adding that "one of Paulos's great strengths is his ability to invent new stories or at least add twists to old ones." "This book is packed with fresh ideas, unorthodox connections, and new interpretations," J. Mayer concurred, in *Choice* (April 1999), "but they are tossed together haphazardly and often are badly worded."

Paulos received national attention during the disputed 2000 presidential election between George W. Bush and Al Gore. In an article published on *ABCNEWS.com* (November 20, 2000), Paulos argued that "the margin of error in the vote count in Florida is more than an order of magnitude greater than the total number of votes now separating the candidates." He quipped that measuring "this very small difference with the gross Florida election apparatus is akin to measuring the width of a DNA molecule with a yardstick," and suggested that the election be decided by "flipping a specially-minted Gore-Bush coin in the Capitol Building in Tallahassee." On December 9, 2000 the Florida Supreme Court ordered a recount in several counties. In his dissent, Charles T. Wells, the Chief Justice of the Florida Supreme Court, wrote that "this case has reached the point where finality must take precedence over continued judicial process" and cited Paulos's article, according to the *St. Louis Post-Dispatch* (December 10, 2000). As a result, Paulos received e-mails and telephone calls from people around the country. In an interview with Melanie Burney, a reporter for the *Philadelphia Inquirer* (December 10, 2000), Paulos explained that "the comments I made are more consistent with a different conclusion. It's become clear since the election that more people intended to vote for Gore."

Paulos sits on the editorial board of the *Philadelphia Daily News* and writes a monthly column for *ABCNEWS.com*. He also contributes articles to such publications as *The Nation*, the *New York Times*, *Washington Post*, *Christian Science Monitor*, and *Philadelphia Inquirer*. His next book, "A Mathematician Plays the Stock Market," will be published in 2003.

John Allen Paulos and his wife, Sheila, a romance novelist, reside in Philadelphia, Pennsylvania. They have two children.

—D. C.

SUGGESTED READING: *ABCNEWS.com* Nov. 20, 2000; *Choice* p1495 Apr. 1999; *Christian Science Monitor* p13 Feb. 14, 1989, p14 May 31, 1995; John Allen Paulos Web site; *Los Angeles Times* p22 Mar. 26, 1989; *New Scientist* p46 July 15, 1995; *New York Times Book Review* p26 Jan. 18, 1981, p9 Jan. 15, 1989; *Omni* p34+ Apr. 1993; *Philadelphia Inquirer* A p25 Dec. 10, 2000; *Scientific American* p102 Feb. 1999; *St. Louis*

Post-Dispatch A p14 Dec. 10, 2000; *Times Literary Supplement* p1430 Dec. 1990; *Wall Street Journal* A p12 May 22, 1991; *Washington Post Book World* p3 Apr. 21, 1991

SELECTED BOOKS: *Mathematics and Humor*, 1980; *I Think, Therefore I Laugh*, 1985; *Innumeracy: Mathematical Illiteracy and Its Consequences*, 1989; *Beyond Numeracy: Ruminations of a Numbers Man*, 1991; *A Mathematician Reads the Newspaper*, 1995; *Once Upon A Number: The Hidden Mathematical Logic of Stories*, 1998

Pelletier, Cathie

1953– Novelist; poet; screenwriter

Cathie Pelletier has won literary approbation as a "Maine writer" with her novels *The Funeral Makers* (1986), *Once Upon a Time on the Banks* (1989), and *The Weight of Winter* (1991), all of which are set in the fictional town of Mattagash, and *The Bubble Reputation* (1993) and *A Marriage Made at Woodstock* (1994), which are set in other parts of Maine. With *Beaming Sonny Home* (1996), Pelletier returned to Mattagash. Pelletier has also written as K. C. McKinnon (a pseudonym based on Pelletier's grandmother's name). McKinnon made her first appearance in 1997, with *Dancing at the Harvest Moon*, a sentimental story about a woman seeking her first love. *Candles on Bay Street*, another McKinnon "heartwarmer," followed in 1999. Stephen McCauley, writing for the *New York Times Book Review* (August 7, 1994), described Pelletier as "an accomplished and extremely witty writer." He called her style "Southern Gothic with frostbite" and praised the "smart vitality" of her prose and her "keen observations."

The youngest of six children, Cathie Pelletier was born in 1953 in Allagash, Maine, and grew up in that village, which is in a rather desolate part of the state. Her father was in the lumber business. At the end of her freshman year at the University of Maine, she was expelled for breaking curfew and setting off a false fire alarm; after hitchhiking around the country for a while, she returned to school and finished her degree. She then moved to Nashville, Tennessee, where she rented an apartment from a family of undertakers. She became the companion of Jim Glaser, a country-music singer-songwriter, and moved with him to a wooded area near Nashville. Pelletier's first book was a collection of poetry, *Widow's Walk*, which came out in 1976. She published *The Funeral Makers*, her first novel, in 1986. A mordant comedy, *The Funeral Makers* takes place in a town called Mattagash, which closely resembles Allagash. Mattagash is divided into a Catholic side, represented by the Gifford family, and a Protestant side, represented by the McKinnons. The novel recounts the last days of Marge McKinnon, who is dying of beriberi, a result of limiting her diet to tea and rice. Marge's sisters Sicily and Pearl and their husbands and children gather to await the end and arrange "Mattagash's finest send-off." Pearl's husband, Marvin, and her son, Marvin Jr., are undertakers. "It really helps to have a head start like this," Pelletier explained in her story. "Most people don't know one of their loved ones has died until the very last minute." Susan Kenney, writing in the *New York Times Book Review* (June 1, 1986), found *The Funeral Makers* "at once hilariously irreverent, comic, tragic and lyrical." According to Kenney, Pelletier depicted "with impressive sympathy as well as irony the various ways her characters' lives and expectations are constrained, warped and in some cases ultimately destroyed by generations of living in a place so remote that indoor plumbing is still a novelty." Kenney enjoyed the spectacle that Pelletier created out of the situation and suggested that the author might be "at her best in these gruesomely and poetically rendered accounts of the last thoughts of people dying." In the *Atlantic* (July 1986), Phoebe-Lou Adams found fault with Pelletier's tendency to "bounc[e] back and forth between sentimental sympathy and grotesque comedy" and her failure to successfully integrate the two. She found some scenes effective, however, and declared, "Pelletier writes with an energy and inventiveness that promise well for her future work."

Once Upon a Time on the Banks, the next volume in Pelletier's Maine trilogy, was published in 1989. In this continuation of the Mattagash saga, Pelletier described the preparations for a wedding. Sicily's daughter Amy Joy is going to marry Jean Claude Cloutier, to whom Sicily objects because he is French and Catholic. All 456 Mattagash residents eagerly await the wedding, which is to take place during a cold, snowy, northern Maine spring. "What happens on the day of the wedding and who gets out of town alive?" Fannie Flagg wrote for the *New York Times Book Review* (October 22, 1989), noting that in the answer to that question "lies the hilarious and tragic tale." Pelletier, according to Flagg, "accomplishes what every great novelist should. She creates a place and . . . allows you to get to know the people." Once Pelletier "has you listening to the life that goes on along the banks of the river," Flagg continued, "she rushes you by the doors of the past, the present and the future. And she reminds you that some things are as inevitable as the flow of that same river." Dan Cryer, the *Newsday* (October 22, 1989) reviewer, characterized *Once Upon a Time on the Banks* as "a hilarious, high-spirited, it's-great-to-be-alive hoot of a novel" that is bolstered by a "quiet truth."

Pelletier returned to Mattagash in *The Weight of Winter* (1991). There is much more sorrow than comedy in this novel, the final volume of the Mattagash trilogy. Sicily has grown old, and Amy Joy wants to place her in a nursing home. Amy Joy is single and middle-aged, but town gossips suspect that she is pregnant. Commenting on the disproportionate number of suicides in Mattagash, one character says, "Little towns were like big families. Sometimes the child prospers in the family. Sometimes the child suffers. And it's the suffering child, the child who can hear and see things that other children, happy at play, can never see and never hear, it's this child, who holds the gun to his or her own head." Pelletier uses the image of snow as a leitmotif signifying the weight of the everyday world, which can be oppressive and suffocating but also beautiful.

Joseph Olshan, who reviewed *The Weight of Winter* for the *Washington Post* (November 5, 1991), labeled Pelletier "an ambitious, fearless novelist" and noted that one of her "most successful ventures" was having several chapters narrated by Mattagash's oldest resident, Matilda Fennelson, who is over 100 years old. Only Matilda's mind is still active. "Pelletier's sentences are as sharp and unique as snowflakes when Mathilda describes her life before World War I . . . ," Tim Sandlin wrote for the *New York Times Book Review* (November 24, 1991). "Even though Mathilda lives in her brain, without sensory perceptions, she has become an integral part of her surroundings." The *Publishers Weekly* (September 6, 1991) reviewer, too, found Mathilda's memories "poetically charged" and thought "the geography of Mattagash . . . as important as any character." *The Weight of Winter* earned for Pelletier the 1992 New England Book Award for fiction.

The Bubble Reputation, Pelletier's 1993 novel, also takes place in Maine. Although many of the characters are eccentric—among them Uncle Bishop, an immense gay man; Mother, who is completely insane; and Miriam, the strange sister who dresses only in green—they are not the backwoods types of the Mattagash trilogy. These people revolve around Rosemary, a teacher, who has lived with an artist named William for eight years. Now William has deserted her, by going to London to commit suicide. Rosemary's intense grief is interrupted by a bevy of crazy house guests, both family members and friends. Disgusted, she moves into a tent to get away from them. Later, she learns that her father, for whom she also grieves, had had a lover, a revelation that makes her understand his references to the "sugar" and "sweetness" of life. "'Levels of consciousness depend upon the light,' William had said," Susan Dooley wrote in a review of *The Bubble Reputation* for the *Washington Post* (May 21, 1993), "and the phrase haunts Rosemary and becomes the theme of Cathie Pelletier's sad and funny book. . . . *The Bubble Reputation* is a book in which Pelletier brilliantly shows how it is the persistence of the living that provides the final level of light."

The title of Pelletier's novel *A Marriage Made at Woodstock* (1994) conveys an ironic subtext. Chandra and Frederick met at Woodstock in 1968, got married, and lived together in Portland, Maine, for 20 years. Maintaining her 1960s attitude toward life, Chandra runs psychological seminars on such subjects as self-actualization by means of participation in demonstrations and name changes. (Born Lorraine, she herself took the name Chandra, which is Sanskrit for "moonlight.") Her husband, however, has morphed from an English major into an accountant who cares only for his computer. After Chandra leaves Frederick, he falls apart, staying in bed and drinking; then he has an affair with a married woman. "This is a book about major midlife transitions, not just a comedy about divorce," Mary Ellen Quinn noted in *Booklist* (May 1, 1994), deeming Pelletier successful in presenting the "deeper meaning" in "a very funny novel." Karl Ackerman, the *Washington Post* (July 18, 1994) reviewer, disagreed, observing that although "Pelletier has a gift for comedy and a loose, easygoing writing style . . . too much of the humor is at Freddy's expense, and he becomes a caricature." Jeanie MacFarlane of the Toronto *Globe and Mail* (July 23, 1994) observed of *A Marriage Made at Woodstock*, "Pelletier fritters away the Woodstock legacy. Where did it all go, and what is it like to wake up alone in this very big chill?" She concluded, "The joke goes that if you remember the sixties you weren't really there. If you wonder about them, don't steal this book." Pelletier collaborated with George Stevens Jr. to write the screenplay for *A Marriage Made at Woodstock*.

The Gifford family of Mattagash are the principal characters in Pelletier's novel *Beaming Sonny Home* (1996). They include Mattie Gifford, now 66 years old, whose mother committed suicide and whose husband was a skirt chaser, Mattie's three greedy daughters, with whom she does not get along, and her spoiled son, Sonny, whom she adores. Sonny sparks a crisis when he takes two women and a poodle hostage in his ex-wife's trailer. His sisters go to their mother's house to watch the news reports about their brother; smoking, eating pizzas, and quarreling, the daughters irritate Mattie. The *Booklist* (May 1, 1996) reviewer, Joanne Wilkinson, found Pelletier's depiction of Sonny's sisters fine, and she deemed "the sharp-tongued Mattie—addicted to picture puzzles, haunted by memories of her bad marriage, regretting the way she coddled Sonny . . . one of [Pelletier's] most sublime creations." Ruth Coughlin, in an assessment for the *New York Times Book Review* (August 18, 1996), wrote, "Despite some heavy-handed symbolism involving a jigsaw puzzle featuring Jesus, *Beaming Sonny Home* is often both funny and unexpectedly moving." The *Publishers Weekly* (February 19, 1996) reviewer, however, felt that the book was "marred by the depiction of the Gifford sisters" as "an unappealing bunch who verge on caricature and whose behavior in the family's darkest hour is more the stuff of sitcoms than real life." "While much of the narrative is entertaining and affecting," this reviewer concluded, "the ending is a major disappointment that nearly negates the homespun wisdom" that Pelletier had supplied earlier in the story.

Dancing at the Harvest Moon, for which Pelletier used her pseudonym, K. C. McKinnon, came out in 1997. The story focuses on Maggie, a college teacher of comparative literature. After her husband leaves her, Maggie returns to Harvest Moon, a summer resort where she worked and met her first love, Robert, years earlier. Kimberly B. Marlow, writing for the *New York Times Book Review* (November 9, 1997), compared *Dancing at the Harvest Moon* to Robert James Waller's sentimental best-seller *The Bridges of Madison County*. Finding "very little that seems remotely engaging in the wooden prose of K. C. McKinnon," Marlow rated Pelletier's other novels "vastly superior."

The next book to bear K. C. McKinnon's name was *Candles on Bay Street* (1999). Set in Fort Kent, Maine, where Pelletier taught at a branch of the University of Maine, it revolves around Dee Dee, who is dying of cancer. Her only wish—to live a little while longer, so as to take care of her son, Trooper—has been fulfilled. *Candles on Bay Street*, for which Pelletier received a $1 million advance, appeared in *Good Housekeeping* magazine in June 1999.

Pelletier then edited *A Country Music Christmas* (1996), a collection of stories and recipes from country-music performers, and, with the country musician Skeeter Davis, she wrote *The Christmas Note* (1997), a children's book. In 2000 she received an honorary doctorate of humane letters from the University of Maine at Orono, where she delivered the commencement address. "Through her dry and sometimes biting humor, her captivating story-telling and her fascinating cast of characters, Cathie Pelletier has established herself as another of Maine's literary treasures," Peter Hoff, the president of the university, declared on that occasion.

Pelletier has written songs that have been recorded by the Glaser Brothers, the Texas Tornadoes, David Byrne, and other artists. She and her husband, Tom Viorikic, have recently formed a film-production company, and she is currently engaged in writing screenplays.

—S. Y.

SUGGESTED READING: *Atlantic* p79 July 1986; *Booklist* p1584 May 1, 1994, p1489 May 1, 1996; *Chicago Tribune* XIV p6 June 6, 1993; *Good Housekeeping* p189+ June 1999; *New York Times Book Review* p7 June 1, 1986, p21 Oct. 22, 1989, p13 Nov. 24, 1991, p11 Aug 7, 1994, p20 Aug. 18, 1996, p22 Nov. 9, 1997; *Newsday* p23 Oct. 22, 1989; *People* p80 Nov. 3, 1988; *Publishers Weekly* p96 Sep. 6, 1991; (Toronto) *Globe and Mail* C p8 July 23, 1994; *Washington Post* B p3 Nov. 5, 1991, B p2 May 21, 1993, D p2 July 18, 1994, D p2 Oct. 24, 1997

SELECTED BOOKS: juvenile—*The Christmas Note* (with S. Davis), 1997; novels—*The Funeral Makers*, 1986; *Once Upon a Time on the Banks*, 1989; *The Weight of Winter*, 1991; *The Bubble Reputation*, 1993; *A Marriage Made at Woodstock*, 1994; *Beaming Sonny Home*, 1996; poetry—*Widow's Walk*, 1976; as K. C. McKinnon—*Dancing at the Harvest Moon*, 1997; *Candles on Bay Street*, 1999; as editor—*A Country Music Christmas*, 1996

Perry, Thomas

Aug. 7, 1947– Crime novelist

Since the publication of his first book in 1982, Thomas Perry has proven himself an inventive crime novelist who uses humor to leaven his portraits of killers and those who hunt them. Throughout his 13 books, Perry has created both series and stand-alone novels that have won the approval of readers and critics alike. His first, *The Butcher's Boy* (1982), about an adopted boy who grows up to become a hit man, earned him an Edgar Allan Poe Award (or "Edgar") from the Mystery Writers of America for best first novel. His later books include *Metzger's Dog* (1983), *Big Fish* (1985), *Island* (1987), and *Sleeping Dogs* (1992), another story of the "butcher's boy." In the mid-1990s he commenced the *Jane Whitefield* series, which includes *Vanishing Act* (1995), *Dance for the Dead* (1996), *Shadow Woman* (1997), *The Face Changers* (1998), and *Blood Money* (1999). These books focus on a woman with Seneca blood who uses ancient Native American woodcraft and modern computer skills to hide people from unsavory pursuers. Most recently, Perry has published the thrillers *Death Benefits* (2001), *Pursuit* (2001), and *Dead Aim* (2002). Having written both series and stand-alone novels, Perry told Suzanne Mantell for *Publishers Weekly* (October 23, 2000) about some of the differences in tackling these genres: While he enjoyed creating Jane Whitefield with "an absolutely unique set of philosophical and personal beliefs and rules for her behavior, " he said, he did not intend to explain them over and over. In contrast, with a stand-alone book, he added, the "good news is you can earn a living with a blank page and a pencil. The bad news is the same: All you have is a blank page and a pencil. You never know whether you will go anywhere or reach a dead end. It's more exciting but riskier to start fresh every time."

Thomas Perry submitted the following third-person statement to *World Authors 1995–2000*: "Thomas Perry was born in Tonawanda, New York on August 7, 1947, the youngest of three children. His parents, Richard and Elizabeth, were both public school teachers. He attended Tonawanda elementary and secondary schools, and graduated from Tonawanda Senior High School in 1965.

Thomas Perry
Jerry Bauer/Courtesy of Random House

"He enrolled in the College of Arts and Sciences at Cornell University in Ithaca, New York, and graduated cum laude in English in 1969 with an honors essay on the novelist John Barth. From 1969 through 1974 he studied English and American Literature at the University of Rochester on an N.D.E.A. Fellowship. He interrupted his graduate studies in 1970 for active duty in the Air Force, and resumed his studies after training. The subject of his doctoral dissertation was the works of William Faulkner, and he received his Ph.D. in English in 1974.

"He spent the 1974–75 academic year as a commercial fisherman on an abalone diving boat in Santa Barbara, California, then began work in May 1975 as Assistant to the Provost of the College of Creative Studies at the University of California at Santa Barbara, where he worked in the administration of undergraduate programs in art, biology, chemistry, literature, mathematics, music, and physics, and taught some courses in literature and in prose writing.

"In 1980, Perry married Jo Anne Lee, a lecturer at the college. A few months later they moved to Los Angeles, where they both found employment at the University of Southern California. During that year, Perry completed his first novel, *The Butcher's Boy*. It was accepted for publication by Charles Scribner's Sons, and was given the Edgar Allan Poe Award for best first novel by the Mystery Writers of America in 1982. Perry's second novel, *Metzger's Dog*, was a *New York Times* Notable Book for 1983.

"From 1984 through 1989, Thomas and Jo Perry worked as writers/producers on the staff of the prime time network television shows *Simon & Simon* (at Universal Studios), *Sidekicks* and the *Oldest Rookie* (at Disney Studios), and *Snoops* (at Viacom). Thomas Perry completed the novels *Big Fish* (1985) and *Island* (1987). At the end of 1989, when their first daughter was born, the Perrys left full-time television work so they would have more time with their child (and two years later, their second child). During the next few years they wrote scripts on a freelance basis for such television series as *Star Trek: The Next Generation* and *21 Jump Street*. In 1992, *Sleeping Dogs*, Perry's sequel to *The Butcher's Boy*, was published.

"In 1995, Perry published *Vanishing Act*, which was selected as one of the 100 favorite books of the 20th century by the Independent Mystery Booksellers' Association. In it and the novels which followed—*Dance for the Dead* (1996), *Shadow Woman* (1997), *The Face Changers* (1998), and *Blood Money* (1999)—Perry presents five years in the life of a half-Seneca woman named Jane Whitefield who saves likely murder victims by transporting them away from their enemies and teaching them to live elsewhere as new people.

"Perry's next novels, *Death Benefits* and *Pursuit* (both 2001), have concerned other characters and situations. He lives in Southern California with his wife and two daughters, and continues to work as a novelist."

Thomas Perry grew up in Tonawanda, New York, near Buffalo. His Ph.D. dissertation was entitled "Epistemology in the Novels of William Faulkner." "I was a typical English major," he told Patricia Ward Biederman in an interview for the *Los Angeles Times Book Review* (May 9, 1996). However, Perry discovered that in addition to epistemological investigations, he enjoyed reading mysteries and decided to try his hand at writing them.

After *The Butcher's Boy* (1982) won an Edgar from the Mystery Writers of America for best first novel, Perry's reputation as a writer of humor-laden—but nevertheless noir—crime novels was established. *The Butcher's Boy* tells the story of an unnamed hit man who was raised by a butcher. Because his facial knife scars make him easily identifiable, he becomes a target for both the U.S. Justice Department and the Mafia boss who had initially hired him. His principal opponent is Elizabeth Waring, an analyst for the Justice Department.

Metzger's Dog, Perry's 1983 novel, was another widely praised mystery story. In this work, a small gang, led by a man called Chinese Gordon, connives to steal cocaine from a university laboratory. While lifting the cocaine, they acquire a document that details American involvement in Central and South America. When they attempt to sell the top-secret document back to the CIA, the agency refuses to pay; instead the CIA assassinates the professor who conducted the research and hatches schemes costing $35 million (rather than the $5 million demanded by Chinese and his gang). In turn, the gang is forced to shut down the city of Los

Angeles. The eponymous Dr. Henry Metzger is Chinese's cat, and the dog is a ferocious junkyard mutt that becomes the cat's property. As Jim Barlow noted in the Houston Chronicle (May 19, 1985), "Perry specializes in unusual characters and events." Critics responded favorably to what Lawrence Block in the Washington Post Book World (September 18, 1983) termed a "riotously funny" book that is neither a comedy nor a spoof, but rather a taut thriller. "Perry has tucked imagination and ingenuity sufficient for 10 books into Metzger's Dog," Block concluded. "Thomas Perry's writing is clean and crisp and lively, his California sets vivid, his characters at once wacky and tough-minded, his plot a wondrous construction."

Following the success of Metzger's Dog, Perry received an offer to write for television. He told Biederman that he enjoyed "the collaborative craft of writing for TV," and added, "Writing for TV teaches you what a scene is. . . . It teaches you to think of where the camera is when visualizing a scene in a novel, and it teaches you to use, if not enjoy, criticism."

Perry followed up Metzger's Dog with Big Fish (1985), a novel featuring a husband-and-wife duo who engage in gun running and assist a Hollywood agent in resolving a mess involving drug dealing. The agent is then recruited into their business, along with a movie director. When a Japanese client comes into possession of nuclear weapons, a chaotic world chase ensues.

Another husband-wife team involved in illegal dealings turns up in Island, Perry's 1988 novel. "A tour de force is like jazz; you may not be able to define it but you recognize it when you meet it," Charles Champlin wrote for the Los Angeles Times (February 14, 1988). He pronounced Island "indisputably a tour de force, an antic, unconventional, unpredictable, witty and surprising tale" of con artists who create an artificial Caribbean island that becomes "a haven for tax dodgers, money launderers and other sly operatives from around the world," as well as for a few surviving Carib Indians.

The eponymous—but unnamed—butcher's boy reappears in Perry's 1992 novel, Sleeping Dogs. Here, under the name of Shaeffer, he is living in Bath, England and romancing the "Honorable Meg," an aristocratic beauty. When the two go to the races, however, corpses begin to appear. "In thriller fiction there are two sure-fire plots: the lone figure who, against all the odds, goes up against a vastly more powerful enemy, and the aging professional who is forced out of retirement to fight one last battle," Michael Dirda observed in the Washington Post Book World (April 20, 1992). "In Sleeping Dogs Perry combines them both as Shaeffer goes home to murder his way back to tranquility and a good night's sleep in the arms of the Honorable Meg." Dirda concluded that Sleeping Dogs is "a wish-fulfillment power fantasy" and "an exceptionally old-fashioned thriller, with aging dons running things from prison, capos vying for power, cocky punks out to make their bones or their reps, dumb body guards, officious bureaucrats and, not least, a killer who lives by the code of the spaghetti western." Dirda found Sleeping Dogs a somewhat nostalgic reflection on a time when there seemed to be honor among thieves. He concluded that Perry's vision was "of a male world of internecine violence, intense loyalty, very little sex and the passing of hunting skills from a warrior to his adopted son." While Dirda found The Butcher's Boy to be a richer, more complex novel, he cautioned against trying to wrestle Sleeping Dogs away from somebody half-way through. "No telling what might happen."

With his 1995 novel, Vanishing Act, Perry introduced the Jane Whitefield series, which was to comprise Dance for the Dead (1996), Shadow Woman (1997), The Face-Changers (1998), and Blood Money (1999). Jane Whitefield has a Seneca background and comes from the same region of upstate New York—though disguised with a fictional name—as Perry. She draws upon her Native American background for her work—helping those who are in trouble disappear. "I show people how to go from places where someone is trying to kill them to other places where nobody is," she says. Biederman described her as "a self-reliant modern woman and a woman with primal, ancient insights and instincts as well."

The character of Jane drew significant admiration from reviewers, with the sole cavil being that she is "humorless." In her review of Vanishing Act for the New York Times Book Review (February 5, 1995), Marilyn Stasio observed that Perry "lets Jane travel light and carry the heavy stuff in her head." In concluding, she noted that Perry "rarely recycles, but Jane deserves a longer life." Perry granted this very wish when he featured Jane in four additional novels. Dance for the Dead, Shadow Woman, and The Face Changers, the next books in the series, were widely praised for their spellbinding and thrilling plots. (With The Face Changers, Jo Ann Vicarel in Library Journal [May 15, 1998] pronounced Perry to have "hit his stride.") Perry concluded the series with Blood Money, though he chose not to terminate the character of Whitefield with his series, instead giving his readers hope for her future. The plot of Blood Money has Jane covering up for the faked suicide of an aged mob banker; she collaborates with a group trying to steal mob money and donate it to charity. "Even readers who find the setup farfetched," Ronnie H. Terpening noted in Library Journal (October 1, 1999), "will enjoy the fast pace of this entertaining thriller with its resourceful heroine, fascinating characters, convincing development of intrigue, and ever-present menace."

For his 2001 novel Death Benefits, Perry created the data analyst John Walker, "the kind of numbers cruncher who adds up the weight of people crowding onto an elevator with an eye on the posted limit," as one reviewer noted for People (February 5, 2001). Walker is counterbalanced by the older, more relaxed fraud investigator Max Stillman; the two uncover an insurance scam involving Walker's former lover, pursuing clues all across the U.S. Marilyn Stasio, in the *New York Times Book Review* (January 28, 2001), highly approved of the "applications of wit" Perry used to "energize the tutor-pupil dynamic between Walker and Max Stillman." Many reviewers agreed that Perry had successfully made the insurance business fascinating.

In *Pursuit* (2001), Perry's next novel, 13 bodies are found in a restaurant. Although the police think it is the work of a madman, forensic expert David Millikan believes a hired killer has done his work all too well. To catch the killer Millikan recruits Roy Prescott, a skilled manhunter who is not overly scrupulous about presumptions of innocence; he usually catches his man and brings him back dead. The man he hunts, James Varney, is his "most worthy opponent," according to Robin Vidimos for the *Denver Post* (January 13, 2002). While the reader knows who the murderer is, the suspense lies in the pursuit and the act of guessing who will survive. The novel is narrated in the first person by Millikan, Prescott, and Varney in alternating chapters, providing, as Vidimos wrote, "a structure that gives the reader inside information and increases the tension. Knowing each man's plan gives little clue as to how the plans will ultimately play out. . . . The result is a novel that is an expertly crafted mind game."

In *Dead Aim*, Perry's second book of 2002, the author sets his novel in a self-defense training camp that has a side purpose of producing mercenary assassins. The faculty there "includes a number of beautiful, angry, aggressive women—lethal versions of the strong, motivated women who often take charge in Perry's thrillers," Marilyn Stasio noted in the *New York Times Book Review* (December 29, 2002).

Perry has built a career of challenging his readers to engage in thrilling mind games. Writing for the *Boston Globe* (January 30, 2000), Robin Winks summed up Perry's talents as "an ability to make the reader feel 'right there,' on the street corner watching, in the back seat of the car listening; a powerful sense of plot; an ear for how many different people speak; an eye for the turn in the road, not this one but the next one."

—S. Y.

SUGGESTED READING: *Boston Globe* E p3 Jan. 30, 2000; *Denver Post* (on-line) Jan. 13, 2002; *Entertainment Weekly* p62 Apr. 12, 1996; *Houston Chronicle* p22 May 19, 1985; *Library Journal* p116 May 15, 1998, p136 Oct. 1, 1999; *Los Angeles Times Book Review* p1 May 9, 1996; *New York Times Book Review* p30 Feb. 5, 1995, p16 Jan. 28, 2001, (on-line) Dec. 29, 2002; *People Weekly* p39+ Feb. 5, 2001; *Publishers Weekly* p63 Apr. 21, 1997; *Washington Post Book World* p9 Sep. 18, 1983, p1 Apr. 20, 1992

SELECTED BOOKS: *The Butcher's Boy*, 1982; *Metzger's Dog*, 1983; *Big Fish*, 1985; *Island*, 1987; *Sleeping Dogs*, 1992; *Vanishing Act*, 1995; *Dance for the Dead*, 1986; *Shadow Woman*, 1997; *The Face Changers*, 1998; *Blood Money*, 1999; *Death Benefits*, 2001; *Pursuit*, 2001; *Dead Aim*, 2002

Powell, Neil

Feb. 11, 1948– Poet; critic; editor

The English author Neil Powell is a traditionalist, both in his poetry and criticism. An admirer of such orthodox postwar poets as Donald Davie, Philip Larkin, and Thom Gunn, he produces pieces that display the same devotion to traditional theme and structure that has characterized English poetry for centuries. He is the author of several volumes of poetry including, most recently, his *Selected Works* (1998), and he has also published books of nonfiction, including *Carpenters of Light* (1979), a volume of criticism, and *Roy Fuller: Writer and Society* (1995), a biography.

Neil Powell was born on February 11, 1948 in London and was raised in Surrey and Kent. His original passion was music, but, as he told *Contemporary Authors* (vol. 34, 1991), "I was too lazy to practice at it." He turned instead to writing. In high school he wrote stories, edited the school literary magazine, and attempted to write a novel, which he has described as "dreadful." After joining a poetry writing group at the invitation of one of his teachers, he fell in love with that form.

Powell studied English and American literature at the University of Warwick, in Coventry, England; he received a bachelor's degree, in 1969. As an undergraduate he edited the university's literary magazine and reviewed books. (The year of his graduation he won the Gregory Award from the Society of Authors.) He received his master's degree from Warwick, in 1975, and his master's thesis formed the basis of his critical study of modern English poets, *Carpenters of Light* (1979).

In *Carpenters of Light*, Powell focuses on the work of several poets, including Davie, Larkin, and Gunn, and argues that their work is firmly placed on "the main road" of traditional English poetry styles. The book received mixed reviews. A critic for *Choice* (May 1980) wrote: "Powell's book is lucid, careful, and judicious when dealing with specific poems, but frequently it turns caustic when dealing with those critics who do not agree that experimentation presupposes ignorance." In the *New Statesman* (December 7, 1979), Peter Levi was equally critical, observing: "Neil Powell has made a decent attempt to discern good from bad; the effect is perhaps inevitably more dogmatic than he intended, and the sharpness of his tone somehow reinforces the chilly atmosphere which exclusive criticisms always generate. It is one of the least attractive missions of the modern critic to tell poets what they should do to be saved. Gunn and Davie and Larkin are fine poets, but when you set them up in a row and talk about a tradition, something has got lost." He concludes, however, that "this is [still] a highly intelligent and fascinating book."

Powell began producing collections of poetry with the 1974 chapbook *At Little Gidding*; he followed it, in 1975, with another, *Suffolk Poems*. His first book-length collection of poetry, *At the Edge*, was released in 1977 and received solid reviews. Merrill Leffler, in *Library Journal* (May 1, 1978) remarked: "[*At the Edge*] demonstrates a technical mastery of traditional prosodic forms." Writing for the London *Times Literary Supplement* (July 1, 1977), Andrew Motion noted that "while the frequency of this emphasis on formality seems rather dogged, Neil Powell's preferences have in fact served him well; his book adroitly practices what it preaches, and represents a professional, serious and distinguished debut."

Powell's next collection of poems, *Season of Calm Weather*, was published in 1982, and in 1990 he edited *Fulke Greville: Selected Poems*. These were followed by two volumes of his own poetry, *True Colors* (1991) and *The Stones of Thorpness Beach* (1994). The latter features numerous poems about his childhood, his love of music, and fondly remembered landscapes. The title poem evokes the changing Suffolk seashore: "While on the beach in random rows/ The enigmatic stones compose/ A silent staveless variation/ The music of regeneration."

In 1995 Powell published *Roy Fuller: Writer and Society*. In this biography of the well-respected though underrated poet, Powell examines Fuller's life outside literature, initially as a law clerk and attorney, and later as a member of the BBC's board of governors and a chairman at Oxford University. Calling the book "a brilliant interleaving of life and works," Bernard F. Dick went on to note in his review for *World Literature Today* (Winter 1997): "Powell has succeeded magnificently in resurrecting the shade of a poet who only needed a sympathetic interpreter to make him accessible. It is now up to the academy to grant him more than just a few poems in the latest anthology of modern verse."

In November 1997 Carcanet Books published Powell's *The Language of Jazz*, a reference book of terms relating to the musical form. The volume includes commentary on the nicknames of selected jazz notables, such as "Duke" Ellington and Charlie "Bird" Parker and an examination of notable venues, such as the Cotton Club and Minton's. In the introduction Powell argues that the great jazz era lies between the early 1920s, when its formative elements started to coalesce, and the late 1970s, when it began to merge with other musical forms.

Powell's *Selected Poems*, a collection of his best work throughout the years, was published in 1998. In a review for the *New Statesman* (April 24, 1998), Michael Glover proclaimed Powell "an exceptional poet of place, and of the East Anglian coast in particular," and added that this collection "thoroughly defines the peculiar atmospheres of that bleak landscape and seascape: its rigorous beauty, its unostentatious appeal, its enduring, melancholy drag on our emotions."

In addition to his work as a writer, Powell taught English for many years at various schools, including the Kimbolton School, in Huntingdon, England, and the St. Christopher School, in Letchworth, England. In 1986 he left teaching to become a bookseller in Baldock, England. He is currently a freelance writer, editor, critic, and lecturer. He is a member of the Eastern Arts Association, the Poetry Society, and the Society of Authors. Apart from music, his other passionate interest is gardening.
—C. M.

SUGGESTED READING: *Choice* p17 May 1980; *Library Journal* p103 May 1, 1978; *New Statesman* p98 Dec. 7, 1979, p56 Apr. 24, 1998; (London) *Times Literary Supplement* p801 July 1, 1977; *World Literature Today* p166 Winter 1997

SELECTED WORKS: poetry—*At Little Gidding*, 1974; *Suffolk Poems*, 1975; *Season of Calm Weather*, 1982; *True Colors*, 1991; *The Stones on Thorpness Beach*, 1994; *Selected Poems*, 1998; nonfiction—*Carpenters of Light*, 1979; *Roy Fuller: Writer and Society*, 1995; as editor—*Fulke Greville: Selected Poems*, 1990; *Gay Love Poems*, 1997

Powers, Thomas

Dec. 12, 1940– Nonfiction writer; journalist; novelist

The journalist Thomas Powers is known for writing works of nonfiction that often challenge conventional wisdom about the recent events they depict. His first book, *Diana: The Making of a Terrorist* (1971), discusses the life of a young woman from an upper-middle-class background who became a left-wing radical. In his next book, *The War at Home* (1973), Powers argues that the anti-war movement in the United States directly aided in bringing the Vietnam War to a close. *The Man Who Kept the Secrets* (1979) is a biography of CIA director Richard Helms and a study of the agency under his leadership. Powers's fourth book, *Thinking About the Next War* (1983), is a collection of his essays about the threat of nuclear warfare. *Heisenberg's War: The Secret History of the German Bomb* (1993) is a biography of the German physicist Werner Heisenberg who, Powers claims, prevented the Nazis from building an atomic bomb. Most recently he has completed a spy novel entitled *The Confirmation* (2000), and a collection of essays exploring U.S. intelligence services since 1941 in *Intelligence Wars: American Secret History from Hitler to al-Qaeda* (2002).

Thomas Moore Powers was born on December 12, 1940 in New York City, to Joshua Bryant Powers and Susan Moore Powers. He received his bachelor of arts degree in 1964 from Yale University, in New Haven, Connecticut, and began his career as a reporter the next year at the *Rome Daily American* in Rome, Italy. He remained on the staff of that newspaper until 1967, when he returned to New York to become a reporter for United Press International (UPI).

In 1970 Powers left the UPI to become a freelance writer. That same year, he wrote a series of five articles with Lucinda Franks about Diana Oughton, a well-educated young woman from a wealthy family who had become a militant revolutionary and was subsequently killed in an explosion in a Greenwich Village townhouse where she and others had been manufacturing bombs. In their investigation, Powers and Franks went inside the Weathermen, a radical wing of the Students for a Democratic Society of which Oughton was a member and which ran the bomb-making operation. They also interviewed Oughton's friends and family. The articles were published by UPI and earned the pair a Pulitzer Prize for national reporting in 1971. Powers expanded the articles into his first full-length book, *Diana: The Making of a Terrorist* (1971). In it, he uses Diana's life to shed light on the trend toward political and social activism among young members of the upper and middle classes, in particular students, during that era. According to Powers, this activism was fueled in part by this group's awareness of their own privileged status. As Susan Brownmiller observed in her critique of the book for the *New York Times Book Review* (April 11, 1971), "Revolutionary ardor became a kind of absolution from class." Many of these activists, like Diana, became dissatisfied with the results of nonviolent protest and began to form groups that supported the violent overthrow of the establishment. According to Brownmiller, Powers's attempt to relate Diana's life and death to the larger picture "works, and brilliantly, for Diana's story *is* the evolution of Weatherman, and by placing her in a political, rather than a personal or psychological, context, her inexorable descent into the basement workshop of the townhouse becomes a history lesson of critical importance, a tragedy of alienated rage performed by some of America's most brilliant, sensitive, and privileged youth." G. A. White, in a review for *Commonweal* (October 22, 1971) was less enthusiastic, writing that "[Powers' account] seems strangely distant, forced, moralistic, although fascinating. . . . [The author's] colorless prose captures the broad outlines in tracing Diana's life."

Powers wrote his next book, *The War at Home: Vietnam and the American People 1964–1968* (1973), during the waning days of the Vietnam War. In it he postulates that the antiwar movement brought about President Lyndon Johnson's decision not to seek reelection and caused a radical shift in the average American's feelings about the conflict. The book received mixed reviews, some of which took issue with Powers's controversial argument. "When the American people began turning against the war, it was mostly because of its interminableness and hopelessness, not, in all probability, because they had in any way been 'reached' by the antiwar movement," Steven Kelman wrote in the *Saturday Review* (September 11, 1973). "[This] is a disappointingly pedestrian account, the main sources for which appear to be the *New York Times* and books on the subject." While arguing that the book "demonstrates the difficulty of writing interpretive history on the fly," John Kifner in the *New York Times Book Review* (October 14, 1973) also praised Powers's book, writing that it is "most valuable when he traces the roots of the antiwar movement back to the struggles of the Student Non-Violent Coordinating Committee, a piece of history so overrun by events as to have almost been forgotten."

In 1979 Powers published *The Man Who Kept the Secrets: Richard Helms and the CIA*, a study of the American intelligence organization and the man who headed it from 1966 to 1973. Powers questions the role of such an organization in a democratic society, and whether or not the CIA overstepped its authority in international situations such as the Bay of Pigs invasion and the revolution in Chile. The book received many favorable reviews, including one from the novelist John le Carré in the *New York Times Book Review* (October 14, 1979), in which he stated: "Mr. Powers has the wit to stand nowhere, and in consequence has given us a splendid spy story, the best I have read for a long time, and all the much better for being nonfiction. He tells us as much about the Presidency as he does about the C.I.A., and he leaves me scared stiff of both." Edwin Warner, in a review for *Time* (November 12, 1979) agreed: "With near clinical detachment, Powers has produced a remarkably realistic portrait of American intelligence beset by bureaucratic rivalries, personality clashes, and presidential caprice." David Wise, in the *New Republic,* disagreed with these assessments, claiming that "Powers became enamored of his subject, and the result is a book that is defensive, semi-adulatory (as its title suggests), and often querulous in tone."

Four years later Powers published *Thinking About the Next War* (1983), a collection of essays originally published in *Commonweal* between 1976 and 1982, all of which reflect on the possibility of nuclear conflict. Topics range from the military's assessment that there is very little likelihood of a nuclear war, to what the author feels he should tell his daughters about nuclear weapons. "Inconsistent here and there, guilty of a stream-of-consciousness fault on occasions, it is nevertheless a provocative and stimulating reflection on the continuing nuclear debate," Michael McDowell wrote in his review for the Toronto *Globe and Mail* (March 26, 1983). In a review for the *Nation* (January 29, 1983), David Corn concurred: "Powers's reflections may not add up to a pragmatic program for averting war, but they are valuable for the lucid manner in which they address the subject. We should all be such good thinkers on the issue, especially [President] Reagan and the rest of the gang."

In his next book, Powers examines the life of German physicist Werner Heisenberg, who won the Nobel Prize in 1932 for his "uncertainty principle" and was among the chief scientists involved in the Nazi effort to build an atomic bomb during World War II. In *Heisenberg's War: The Secret History of the German Bomb* (1993), Powers argues that Heisenberg, arguably Nazi Germany's greatest physicist, intentionally worked to slow down his government's campaign to build nuclear weapons by discouraging officials, telling them, for example, that it would be too costly and difficult successfully to build a bomb. Although Powers was not the first to make this argument, it is considered controversial among historians, many of whom attribute the Nazis' failure on this front to several other reasons. These include the Nazis' initial belief that they would win the war before their scientists would have time to build an atomic bomb, and the fact that by the time they realized the war would be protracted, resources needed to build the bomb had become difficult to obtain. In a second narrative that runs through the book, Powers documents the Allies' wartime efforts to assess the threat posed by Germany's nuclear program, a task which included keeping a close eye on Heisenberg. Writing for the *New York Times Book Review* (March 14, 1993) David A. Hollinger wrote that Powers's book "is the most carefully documented and sensitively developed version" of the argument that Heisenberg retarded the Nazis' atomic bomb program. However Hollinger concluded that in presenting his case, Powers "falls victim to the mystique of the individual scientist-hero on whose thoughts and deeds the world's destiny depends." G. Pascal Zachary, in a review for the *Wall Street Journal* (March 25, 1993), agreed, noting that "the case for Heisenberg's conscience and good intentions is unconvincing."

Powers changed direction with his next work, *The Confirmation* (2000), a spy novel whose plot concerns Frank Cabot, a CIA man in line for the agency's directorship. Since he already holds the post of acting director, both the U.S. president and the confirmation committee chairman want Cabot for the job. However, when they discover that an American soldier listed as missing in the Vietnam War has turned up in the Soviet Gulag, American officials begin to wonder if Cabot and his associates know more than they're letting on. The novel received generally negative reviews. Erik Tarloff, in the *New York Times Book Review* (July 16, 2000), wrote that "The prose . . . reads as if it had been put together by an engineer. . . . More troublesome, the book never quite comes alive, never transcends its author's meticulous calculations."

In 2002 Powers returned to nonfiction—and to his exploration of the U.S. intelligence community—with *Intelligence Wars: American Secret History from Hitler to al-Qaeda*. Timothy Naftali for the *New York Times* (February 23, 2003) observed, "The essays in *Intelligence Wars* provide a useful introduction to a missing dimension of American history, from Wild Bill Donovan and the Office of Strategic Services during World War II to Sept. 11 and beyond. There is as yet no single book that synthesizes all that we have learned in the past 10 years here and in Moscow about American intelligence since 1941. For the moment this collection fills the gap." Powers's analysis of such national events as the Bay of Pigs debacle, the Kennedy assassination, the Aldrich Ames scandal, and the terrorist attacks of September 11, 2001, helped illuminate the CIA's successes and failures over the last three-quarters of a century. Powers also addressed the issue of whether the CIA is equipped to face today's international challenges.

Thomas Powers married Candace Molloy on August 21, 1965, and they have three daughters, Amanda, Susan, and Cassandra. As of 1999, the family resided in Vermont. In addition to his books, Powers writes frequently for such publications as the *Atlantic Monthly*, the *New York Review of Books*, *Harper's*, the *Nation*, and the *New York Times Book Review*.

—C. M.

SUGGESTED READING: *Atlantic Monthly* (online); (Toronto) *Globe and Mail* E p8 Mar. 26, 1983; *Ms.* p23 Jan. 1983; *New Republic* p34 Nov. 3, 1979; *New York Newsday* II p46 Mar. 16, 1993; *New York Times Book Review* p4 Apr. 11, 1971, p32 Oct. 14, 1973, p1 Oct. 14, 1979, p3+ Mar. 14, 1993, p8 July 16, 2000; *Newsweek* p118 Oct. 22, 1979; *Time* p130 Nov. 2, 1979; *Saturday Review* p35 May 1, 1971, p37 Sep. 11, 1973; *Wall Street Journal* A p12 Mar. 25, 1993

SELECTED BOOKS: nonfiction—*Diana: The Making of a Terrorist*, 1971; *The War at Home: Vietnam and the American People, 1964–68*, 1973; *The Man Who Kept the Secrets: Richard Helms and the CIA*, 1979; *Thinking About the Next War*, 1982; *Heisenberg's War: The Secret History of the German Bomb*, 1993; *Intelligence Wars: American Secret History from Hitler to al-Qaeda*, 2002; novels—*The Confirmation*, 2000; as editor—*Total War: What It Is, How It Got That Way* (with Ruthven Tremain), 1988

Ms. Berkley/Courtesy of Sewanee Writers Conference

Prunty, Wyatt

May 15, 1947– Poet; nonfiction writer

Wyatt Prunty's evocative verse about everyday life, buoyed by its traditional meter and rhyme, has received high praise from critics of postwar American poetry. His carefully assembled structures betray a great attention to sound and detail. Prunty writes with a calm, almost detached tone; he creates uncommon poetry about common occurrences and finds meaning in the most mundane of life's tasks. He has published six collections of poetry, including his warmly received collection of new and selected poems, *Unarmed and Dangerous* (2000). He has also published a study of American poetry written since World War II, *Fallen from the Symboled World* (1990).

Eugene Wyatt Prunty was born in Humbolt, Tennessee, on May 15, 1947, the son of Merle Charles Prunty, a geographer, and the former Eugenia Wyatt. During his childhood his family lived in the college town of Athens, Georgia, where his father taught at the University of Georgia, and spent summers and holidays on a farm in Newbern, Tennessee. The duality of this life is reflected in Prunty's work. "The patterns found in the landscape of [Newbern] still inform some of his writing," noted a reviewer for *Poetry Net* (June 1998, on-line). "In addition, there was the double vision created by living in an academic community most of the year, but an agricultural one the rest of the time. New ideas were taken on vacation to the old predicaments of race and poverty, situations that were changing and aging but in the 1950's and 1960's still visible in the rural south. . . . During Prunty's early years when home was an overlay of both city and farm this double view seemed natural. Now it appears in poems that have their origins in puzzlements over the contrasts between a privileged city life and a raw agricultural existence."

Prunty was educated at Sewanee, The University of the South, in Sewanee, Tennessee, and graduated with honors, in 1969. Shortly after his graduation, with the Vietnam War on his mind, he joined the United States Navy. From 1969 to 1972 he served as a deck and gunnery officer, and eventually made lieutenant. After completing his tour of duty, he returned to the U.S. to continue his education, receiving a master of arts degree from Johns Hopkins University, in Baltimore, Maryland, in 1973, and a doctoral degree from Louisiana State University, in 1979.

While still an undergraduate Prunty published poetry in the *Sewanee Review*, The University of the South's literary journal, which had gained a national reputation in the 1940s under the editorship of the poet and critic Allen Tate. Tate was a champion of New Criticism, which held that the language and imagery of literary works should be considered independently, without consideration of the biographical or historical contexts. Many critics link Prunty's formal aesthetic to the New Critics, but also point out that Prunty does not maintain strict formality in all of his work. From early in his career, however, he has employed formal strategies, including rhyme and meter. Early poetry collections include *Times Between* (1982), *What Women Know, What Men Believe* (1986), and *Balance as Belief* (1989).

In 1990 Prunty published *Fallen from the Symboled World*, a treatise on postwar American poetry. He argued that such poetry is not so much defined by the battle between free and formal verse as it is by a rejection of symbol and allegory in favor of simile and simile-like structures, which reflect the era's doubts about language and tradition. In a review for *Choice* (November 1990), B. Wallenstein remarked: "This fairly recondite study of contemporary U.S. poetry owes as much to philosophical texts and linguistics as to the old formalists, the 'New Critics.' Most valuable about [Prunty's] steady, if somewhat dogmatic, analysis is the attention given to poets generally slighted in books about U.S. poetry since WW II." Wallenstein cited in particular the poets Howard Nemerov, Richard Wilbur, John Hollander, Elizabeth Bishop, and Robert Pinsky. Clive Wilmer's assessment, in the *Times Literary Supplement* (February 1, 1991), was more negative: "Metre, for Prunty, is the trilby hat which all good poets wear, while the essence of poetry is figurative language. But surely we have heard all this before? . . . One is mainly struck by the staleness of the argument, especially since it is so similar to that once used to justify the Modernists themselves."

Prunty published two poetry collections in the 1990s, *Run of the House* (1993) and *Since the Noon Mail Stopped* (1997). In the *Hudson Review* (Autumn 1999), Richard Tillinghast described the poems in *Since the Noon Mail Stopped* as the work of a poet "firmly planted in the middle of things. . . . His keen interest in other people shows that he might just as easily have turned his talent for observation to fiction rather than to poetry."

Prunty's most recent collection is *Unarmed and Dangerous* (2000), which brings together selections from his five previous collections with 10 new poems; it has been the most celebrated and widely reviewed work of his career. In *Poetry* (January 2001), Bruce F. Murphy expressed some reservations, but concluded that "Prunty shows that he has a real talent for verse." In the *Sewanee Review* (Winter 2000), George Core remarked: "The best of the new poems are as good or better than anything [Prunty] has previously published—a positive sign, especially for a selected volume." Melanie Rehak, writing for the *New York Times Book Review* (March 19, 2000), proclaimed: "Prunty was born and raised in the South, . . . and his poems often draw on the rich langour of his home territory. Life moves by at just the right pace for examination, and while many of the events chronicled in his work are entirely average, Prunty holds everyday experience up to the light in such a way that it seems anything but." Rehak singled out for praise one of the new poems, "A Child's Christmas in Georgia, 1953," in which Prunty recreates his boyhood confusions over death and loss:

His infant older brother who never
Came home, two cousins lost in war, an uncle
Who captained his ship over the flat world's edge,
And one fleece-lined pilot lost years now inside
The stilled weather of a relative's box camera.

Prunty began teaching literature at Louisiana State University, in 1978. Since that time he has taught at Washington and Lee University, in Lexington, Virginia; Virginia Tech, in Blacksburg, Virginia; the Bread Loaf School of English and the Bread Loaf Writers' Conference, both associated with Middlebury College, in Middlebury, Vermont; and Johns Hopkins University. He is currently the Carlton Professor of English at Sewanee, The University of the South, and the founder and director of the Sewanee Writers' Conference. He edited *Sewanee Writers on Writing* (2000), a series of lectures by playwrights, novelists, and poets about the process of writing.

—C. M.

SUGGESTED READING: *Choice* p488 Nov. 1990; *Hudson Review* p507+ Autumn 1991; *New Republic* p40 July 1, 1996, p40 Feb. 8, 1999; *New York Times Book Review* p14 Mar. 19, 2000; *Poetry* p279+ Jan. 2001; *Poetry Net* June 1998; *Sewanee Review* II Winter 2000; *Southern Review* p286+ Spring 1997, p479+ Summer 1999; *Times Literary Supplement* p19 Feb. 1, 1991

SELECTED BOOKS: poetry—*Times Between*, 1982; *What Women Know, What Men Believe*, 1986; *Balance as Belief*, 1989; *Run of the House*, 1993; *Since the Noon Mail Stopped*, 1997; *Unarmed and Dangerous: New and Selected Poems*, 2000; nonfiction—*Fallen from the Symboled World*, 1990; as editor—*Sewanee Writers on Writing*, 2000

Shoreline Studios/Courtesy of Knopf Publicity

Purdy, Jedediah

1974– Nonfiction writer

Hebrew scripture tells of Jeremiah, a sixth and seventh-century B.C.E. prophet who was pessimistic about his society and foresaw a calamitous future; because no one wanted to hear unpalatable truths, he was ignored, placed in stocks, and eventually jailed. At age 24 and bearing his own Old Testament–style name, Jedediah Purdy published *For Common Things: Irony, Trust, and Commitment in America Today* (1999), his attempt to speak to his society about its failings and to make prescriptions for change. The controversial book has placed him in what Wilfred M. McClay, in *Commentary* (November 1999), has called "the long American tradition of the jeremiad." In *For Common Things* Purdy identifies a corrosive irony that, in his opinion, permeates American culture, dampens our enthusiasms, and cripples our capacity for hope. To counter this irony, Purdy advocates sincerity and calls for a renewed engagement with the moral and political problems of our time. In part because of Purdy's young age and personal history, and in part because of his book's polemics, *For Common Things* has been alternately championed and ridiculed, evincing deep divisions within contemporary American culture. In his most recent book, *Being America: Liberty, Commerce, and Violence in an American World*, released in February 2003, Purdy takes the first step toward fulfilling his agenda from *For Common Things*, initiating an earnest dialogue in which he reflects on America's political and cultural role in the world.

Jedediah Purdy was born in 1974, and that same year his parents moved from Pennsylvania to the rural hamlet of Chloe, West Virginia, where they hoped to revive an agrarian ideal of self-sufficiency. His mother, Deirdre, later described the family's intentions to Marshall Sella for the *New York Times* (September 5, 1999). "We believed what Wendell Berry [the poet and agrarian philosopher] wrote about—living in a certain place and making what you can of the place," she said. The Purdy family built a home in the hills, raised and slaughtered their own cattle, and grew crops on fields that they plowed using a team of draft horses. Purdy and his younger sister were home-schooled. Apart from a few hours of math a week, they had no formal lessons and instead followed their interests, reading, working, and playing alongside their parents. At age 14 Purdy entered the local public high school, where he spent three years. He then wrote to an admissions officer from New Hampshire's prestigious Phillips Exeter Academy, a private preparatory school, and won a scholarship to attend his senior year there. After graduation Purdy spent time traveling and working at home as a carpenter and for the West Virginia Environmental Council. In the fall of 1993, he enrolled at Harvard University in Cambridge, Massachusetts, graduating in 1997 with a degree in social studies. In 1999 he began a course of graduate study in law and forestry at Yale University in New Haven, Connecticut; he later earned his law degree from Yale.

Purdy's encounters with the codes of behavior in public high school and in the largely privileged and sophisticated environs of prep school and Harvard influenced his thinking about American culture. At Harvard, for instance, there is a custom among incoming freshman to view the movie *Love Story* as a group. As Purdy described this ritual to Sella, the freshman are encouraged to mock the film's depressing story of young lovers who get together despite the odds, only to have one of them die from leukemia at the end. For example, when Ali McGraw, who plays one of the lovers in the film, steps into a cab, a student in the audience yells, "To the morgue—and step on it!" "Placing this at the beginning of the orientation seemed an induction of students into a cold, self-satisfied manner," Purdy told Sella.

After leaving Harvard, Purdy began expanding an article he had written in 1998 for *American Prospect*, a liberal journal based in Boston. As he worked, the article became a 200-page manuscript, which he then submitted to a literary agent. It was noticed by a young assistant editor at the publishing company Alfred A. Knopf, who saw in the book an opportunity to reach readers in their twenties. According to Sella, it was only later that the editor learned that Purdy was 24 and had been home-schooled. "It may sound like we chose him from Central Casting," the editor told Sella, "but that's not the way it worked. The kid from nowhere has valuable things to say."

Purdy has described the book as part poem and part essay, the product of six years of thinking about cultural and political trends. Its tone is unabashedly romantic, even rhapsodic, and its purpose defined in the preface as "one young man's letter of love for the world's possibilities," as quoted by Sella. It is the world's possibilities, Purdy believes, that are obscured by the cultural code of irony, which he defines as "a refusal to believe in the depths of relationships, the sincerity of motivation, or the truth of speech—especially earnest speech," as quoted by Katherine Marsh in the *Washington Post* (October 24, 1999). As many of the book's reviewers have pointed out, irony is difficult to define. Traditionally a rhetorical device used by such writers as Socrates, Shakespeare, and Cervantes, in common usage irony has come to refer to an easy form of sarcasm, or flippant wit. This seems to be what Purdy has in mind when he identifies the comedian Jerry Seinfeld as "irony incarnate" and writes that Seinfeld's television sitcom, one of the most popular series of the 1990s, "perfectly echoed the tone of the culture." "The ironic individual," Purdy writes, as quoted by Walter Kirn in *Time* (September 20, 1999), "is a bit like Seinfeld without a script; at ease in banter, versed in allusion, and almost debilitatingly self-aware." Although it was the book's attack on irony that garnered public attention, Purdy actually identifies two types of irony—positive and negative. If the negative kind is disabling, according to Purdy, positive irony "uncovers, in what is ordinarily imagined to be unimportant or banal, something that elicits surprise, delight, and reverence," as quoted by Christopher Lehmann-Haupt in the *New York Times* (September 9, 1999, on-line). "This irony is ecstatic, in the etymologically strict sense of drawing us out of our stasis. It is the irony of discovery. It moves us," Purdy writes.

Purdy expands his critique of irony, citing it as one of the causes of a general breakdown in civic life. Politics, he writes in the book, was once "Promethean"; that is, it aspired to "bring about basic changes in the human predicament," as quoted by Caleb Crain in *Salon* (September 7, 1999, on-line). In the wake of the Watergate scandal, Vietnam, and the Cold War, Purdy asserts, people have become disillusioned with politics on a grand scale, and instead seek escape, whether it be through New Age beliefs in guardian angels, or utopian dreams of cyberspace. The magazines *Wired* and *Fast Company*, he claims, promote greed and self-absorption by encouraging readers to strive toward a vision of a high-tech paradise. Purdy also cites the management guru Tom Peters, who teaches his disciples to market themselves as the "brand called You," as an example of the culture's wholesale endorsement of self-involvement. President Clinton practices "therapeutic politics" in Purdy's view, "apologizing" for slavery, for example, instead of working for real change. Meanwhile, Purdy points out, destructive practices, such as the strip-mining of the West Virginia hills, something close to his experience, continue with apparently no thought of future generations.

In the place of what he perceives as self-defeating fantasies and empty words that do little to affect change, Purdy proposes a return to reality—specifically, the often messy, frustrating, but, in his view, tangible realities of civic life. Drawing on his understanding of philosophy, including Henry David Thoreau's concept of self-sufficiency, Jean-Jacques Rousseau's theory of the social contract, and George Orwell's call to political engagement, Purdy argues the necessity and satisfactions of civic and political involvement. He articulates a plan for renewal of America's moral, social, and natural systems—the "common things" of the title—including a justice system that is more just, an economic system that reduces inequalities between classes, and a natural world that flourishes long beyond the current generation.

The response to Purdy's book has been drastically divided. A reviewer for *Publishers Weekly* (July 26, 1999) found the book "inspiring in its thoughtfulness, in its commitment to the idea that politics should be about more than divvying up the pie and in the care with which it is written. The ideas expressed aren't complicated, but Purdy grapples with them with a seriousness that puts more seasoned—and ironic—commentators to shame." Writing for *Commentary*, Wilfred McClay regretted that the book's themes, laudable in themselves, are not, in his opinion, applied with any degree of sophistication. McClay pointed out that Purdy fails to identify possible root causes of the deterioration of public life, and went on to point out several in his review. "Purdy might have considered, for instance . . . the 'culture wars' that have arisen . . . making it virtually impossible to agree on those things that compose our 'commons'; and the reign of politically-correct speech, which has done so much to sap the vitality and honesty of public discourse." Jonah Goldberg, writing for the *National Review* (October 25, 1999), described Purdy's longing for the civic-minded spirit of his parents' generation as that of a "typical liberal. Throughout much of the 1990s, liberalism has been awash in nostalgia."

In the media Purdy has often been portrayed as a kind of cultural relic, a Rip Van Winkle who "slept through" the disillusionment of the late 1970s and early 1980s because of his unusual upbringing. Indeed, many commentators have rankled at how neatly Purdy's personal history fits into a promotional package. McClay asserted, "If we did not know who Jedediah Purdy is—an improbable combination of Appalachian authenticity and Harvard-yard smarts—we would read his words very differently, if at all." Roger D. Hodge, in *Harper's* (September 1999), described Purdy as part of a fad in recent publishing that includes Dinesh D'Souza, Katie Roiphe, and Wendy Shalit, smart young writers whose books were heavily marketed toward readers in their 20s. Facetiously titling his review "Thus Spoke Jedediah," Hodge called Purdy's ideas trite and second-hand, stating that "Down-home piety is no substitute for a natural wit." In *Salon*, Caleb Crain was equally dismissive, describing Purdy as both "treacly" and "snide," and finding fault with the structure of his argument. "Purdy is not a disciplined thinker. Strip mining reminds him of integrity, which reminds him of Czeslaw Milosz's essays about Communist intellectuals."

In an article for *Time*, Walter Kirn depicted the hostile reactions to Purdy's book in terms of cultural warfare, in which the "chattering classes"—which Kirn identified as readers of *Harper's* and other "disaffected Eastern elite"—are pitted against Purdy and those who might agree with him. "Among New Yorkers whose daily bread is irony, heavily buttered with sarcasm and ridicule, Purdy's message of earnest civic-mindedness was as welcome as a vice cop at a bachelor party," Kirn opined. Purdy told Sella that negative reviews, such as Hodge's, were "disappointing" to him. "Wallace Stevens refers to the cynical realist who was still vital because 'under every No lay a passion for Yes that had never been broken'—but reading Hodge, it's No all the way down. [His review] is purely and woefully an exercise in contempt," he said.

Even those who dismiss Purdy's book acknowledge that many of his cultural observations are apt. As Crain wrote, "Irony, of course, has limits, and all the best ironists know it." By way of example, Crain cites the writing of both the 19th-century Danish philosopher Søren Kierkegaard and the contemporary writer David Foster Wallace. Sella also cites Wallace, who, in his 1997 essay collection *A Supposedly Fun Thing I'll Never Do Again*, described irony and ridicule as "agents of a great despair and stasis in U.S. culture." Sella also points out that Senator John McCain declared a "war on cynicism" during his 2000 presidential campaign. Although Christopher Lehmann-Haupt found Purdy's tone "self-righteous," he also wrote, "You always sense what he's getting at, and you have to admire him for taking on the disease of irony. . . . If many will not heed him, at least he has articulated a cure." Nearly all his critics focused on Purdy's youth as a primary consideration in any assessment of his book. Purdy's ambition and earnestness, perceived by some as weaknesses, might also be seen as the prerogatives of youth. Part of Purdy's intention in writing, as Lehmann-Haupt quoted from *For Common Things*, was "so that I will not forget what I hope for now."

In February 2003 Purdy published *Being America: Liberty, Commerce, and Violence in an American World*, a book that continued many of the themes from *For Common Things* yet extended the dialogue, this time examining America's political and cultural role in the world. Following the terrorist attacks of September 11, 2001, Purdy—then a recent law-school graduate—embarked on a trip through Egypt, India, Indonesia, Cambodia, and China. Speaking to a variety of groups around the world, he set out to glean a better understanding of how people perceive America abroad. He often found them divided, simultaneously expressing contempt for the U.S. while longing to emigrate there themselves. Throughout the book Purdy examines common perceptions of the U.S. and explores the underlying causes; in the process, he takes up such big issues as AIDS, globalization, environmentalism, nationalism, refugees, imperialism, and freedom. He even questions the merits of capitalism itself, assessing the value of political extremes on both the left and the right. Like *For Common Things*, Purdy's second book generated significant critical attention, though many reviewers were divided about the merits of the author's arguments. Nevertheless, most critics applauded Purdy's efforts to take on such difficult questions at this juncture in history. As one critic noted for *Publishers Weekly* (January 13, 2003), "For someone young, yet who thinks so hard about so many befuddling issues, he comes across as wonderfully sane: the writing is unadorned, lucid and without cynicism. . . . Purdy is already among the most inspiring political thinkers writing today, and his ideas resonate like the clear ring of a bell through a cacophony of better-known pundits."

Purdy has served as a fellow at the New American Foundation and currently clerks for a federal judge in New York City. He was named one of *Esquire* magazine's "Best and Brightest" for 2002.

—M. A. H.

SUGGESTED READING: *Commentary* p62+ Nov. 1999; *Harper's* p84+ Sep. 1999; *New York Times* (on-line) Sep. 9, 1999; *New York Times Magazine* p56+ Sep. 5, 1999, with photos; *National Review* p67+ Oct. 25, 1999; *Salon* (on-line) Sep. 7, 1999; *Time* p74+ Sep. 20, 1999, with photos; *Washington Post* F p1+ Oct. 24, 1999

SELECTED BOOKS: *For Common Things: Irony, Trust, and Commitment in America Today*, 1999; *Being America: Liberty, Commerce, and Violence in an American World*, 2003

Pye, Michael

Oct. 25, 1946– Nonfiction and fiction writer

Michael Pye has written extensively in a variety of genres, working as a newspaper and magazine journalist, historian, and novelist. As he said in a statement for *Contemporary Authors* (2000), most of his writing has been an attempt to elucidate frequently misunderstood ideas. "I've always thought that much of the problem with ideas that fascinate me is that they are almost willfully obscured by language—that giving access to those ideas is a democratic imperative," Pye said. "That means making thrillers out of real politics, trying to use tools like semiotics without self-consciousness in critical work, and explaining money and power in their curious and complex relations with industries and arts like the movies." He added that "it is . . . an approach which allows the making of connections—sometimes usefully, sometimes not—across the boundaries of apparently unrelated disciplines." Pye began his writing career with *The Movie Brats: How the Film Generation Took Over Hollywood* (1979). He then authored a well-received history in 1981, *The King Over the Water*, about the experiences of the Duke and Duchess of Windsor while in exile from England. His latest works have all been novels, *The Drowning Room* (1995), *Taking Lives* (1999), and *The Pieces from Berlin* (2003).

David Godlis/Courtesy of Knopf Publicity

Michael Pye was born in Manchester, England, on October 25, 1946, the son of Reginald William, a teacher, and Marjorie (Stoneley), a nurse. He received his B.A. with honors from St. John's College, in Oxford, and received his master's degree there in 1967. Upon graduation he took a position as a staff writer for the *Scotsman*, a newspaper published in Edinburgh, Scotland. He stayed with the *Scotsman* until 1971, when he became a staff writer for the (London) *Times*, a job he held until 1978. He was also a consultant for Coca-Cola Europe from 1968 to 1974. From 1976 to 1978 he was a program consultant for the Edinburgh Film Festival. In 1978 he began his career as a freelance writer, writing primarily arts and culture articles for such publications as the *Atlantic Monthly*, the *New York Times*, *Geo*, *New Society*, the London *Observer*, and *Plays and Players*. During this time he lived for an extended period in New York City.

Pye's first book was a collaboration with Lynda Myles entitled *The Movie Brats: How the Film Generation Took Over Hollywood* (1979), an analysis of the filmmakers Francis Ford Coppola, George Lucas, Brian De Palma, John Milius, Martin Scorsese, and Steven Spielberg. Using interviews and exposition, Pye and Myles argue that the deterioration of the American film industry in the 1950s and 1960s set the stage for this new breed of filmmaker, whose strengths and weaknesses they discuss. *The Movie Brats* was generally well received by critics. "The book allows American film and American society to illuminate one another," Marshall Deutelbaum wrote in *Library Journal* (May 15, 1979), "and helps us to see ourselves in our films." Even R. F. Moss, who complained in the *Saturday Review* (June 23, 1979) that in *Movie Brats* "a simple horror story like *Jaws* . . . is forced to disgorge not only human corpses but elaborate Freudian symbolism," also conceded that "in its own domain, it is well above average. Pye and Myles have turned in an informative, hard-working, fairly intelligent report."

Pye focused on the business aspects of the entertainment industry in his next book, *Moguls: Inside the Business of Show Business* (1980), profiling six prominent producers of television, theater, movies, and music: Jules Stein, William S. Paley, David Merrick, Peter Guber, Trevor Nunn, and Robert Stigwood. David Edgar summed up the main thesis of the book in the *Times Literary Supplement* (November 28, 1980). "The argument," he wrote, "is that the old-style, individual showman has been inevitably supplanted by a new breed of surrogate mogul, publicly still the lord of all he chooses to survey, but privately beholden to the multinationals who finance his operations." In *Library Journal* (June 1, 1980) J. M. Fuchs wrote that *Moguls* "serves as an unsettling reminder that much of popular culture is thrust upon the masses by a select few." Although Edgar was interested in Pye's subject, he felt that his approach was misguided. "Pye's chosen medium—the individual career profile—often seems to deflect, if not to contradict, his message," he wrote. "Indeed, it could be argued that Pye offers inadequate proof of the corporate takeover of Show Business."

Pye's next book was entitled *The King Over the Water* (1981), the story of Great Britain's duke of Windsor, the former King Edward VIII, who abdicated the throne in 1936 in order to marry a divorcée, Wallis Warfield Simpson of the United States. The book explores the period from 1940 to 1945, when the duke served as governor of the Bahamas, then a colony of the United Kingdom. Pye details the duke's political decline, concentrating on his failed attempts to launch an ambassadorial career through his tenure in the Bahamas. Barbara Goldsmith, in the *New York Times Book Review* (July 26, 1981), called it a "meticulously researched book" and celebrated the characterizations, which she said were "as colorful as in any pirate adventure story." While she opined that "the tale Michael Pye has to tell is far more interesting than the way he tells it," she added that "what he has to say is fresh and absorbing and profoundly sad. Both the Duke and Duchess emerge as people who are ultimately defeated by their fears, selfishness, pretensions and vanity."

In 1983 Pye published his first novel, *Eldorado*, which attracted little critical notice. In 1989 he wrote the commentary for the *Pirelli Calendar Album: The First Twenty-five Years*, and in 1991 he published *Maximum City: The Biography of New York*, in which he looked at New York's past in order to understand its present circumstances. Several years after its publication, Iain Finlayson, in the *Financial Times* (July 22, 1995), called *Maximum City* "a masterpiece of journalistic judgment. It compressed the history of the city as tightly as a concertina which he fingered and squeezed in a busking, impertinent, peripatetic performance from City Hall to Carnegie Hall."

In 1995 Pye wrote another book, *The Drowning Room*, that delves into the early history of New York City, or New Amsterdam as it was once known. *The Drowning Room* is a historical novel based on a real-life character, Gretje Reyniers. All that is known about Gretje from historical records is that she moved from Amsterdam to New Amsterdam in the early 1600s, appeared in court over debts and slander charges, and worked as a prostitute in the city before she was banished, eventually to return years later. From this information Pye weaves the tale of a woman who lives a singular life, full of virtue and vice. The novel begins just after the death of Gretje's second husband, Anthony the Turk, whose corpse lies in a coffin in Gretje's yard, waiting for the spring thaw to be buried. Gretje, in her sorrow, relates her life story to Tomas, an unfortunate mute, and Pieter, a mysterious stranger described as an "angel," "white, vague, made of unused skin and muscles, haloed with blond hair and smiling," as quoted by Richard Bernstein in the *New York Times* (January 3, 1996). The plot thickens when Anthony's corpse is first mutilated and then stolen. Pye interweaves the past and present, gradually revealing Pieter's secret purpose in coaxing Gretje to tell her life story. *The Drowning Room* was applauded by critics and named a *New York Times* Notable Book of the Year, in 1996. Richard Bernstein observed that "Gretje . . . is a very recognizable literary type, the innocent voyager cut loose from the usual bonds of social life and forced to make her way alone in an ungenerous world. That kind of story depends on two factors: the voyager has to have enough inner power to sustain interest, and the adventures that befall her have to be pungent and unexpected. Mr. Pye succeeds on both counts." In the *Washington Post* (January 3, 1996) Jonathan Yardley wrote, "Michael Pye captures in earthy detail the muck and mire of both the old and new Amsterdams, and the occasional flicker of gilt as well. He reminds us that at its best historical fiction is another way of telling history, and a wholly legitimate one."

The idea for Pye's next book, *Taking Lives* (1999), came to him from a real-life experience. He had been living in a small town in Portugal and through mutual acquaintances had met a Danish man who mysteriously disappeared one day. It was later revealed that he had killed at least one person, in a particularly violent manner. "I started thinking about what happens when a monster passes through ordinary lives," Pye said in an interview posted on the Random House Web site. "The very idea of such a sophisticated killer in such a remote, rural place was fascinating. And there was something else. I was close to a turning point in my life, thinking about leaving New York and all those Jasper Johns and Sharon Stone profiles and moving to this same forest town in Portugal. I was about to reinvent myself. And here was a man who knew just how to do that, so it seemed—but with a chainsaw." In *Taking Lives*, Martin Arkenhout, a Dutch foreign-exchange student, is traveling in Florida with another student, Seth Goodman, when their rental car breaks down, and they are forced to hitchhike. Seth is hit by a passing car, which fails to stop, and is left seriously mutilated, but still alive. Martin impulsively smashes Seth's head with a rock—justifying the murder as an act of mercy—and then exchanges his belongings with Seth's and assumes his dead companion's identity. Thus begins a string of murders in which Martin takes over the lives—and the bank accounts—of his victims. For nearly 10 years he follows this pattern, until he murders Christopher Hart, a British art scholar wanted for stealing valuable artworks from a London museum. John Costa, the curator of the museum, had been looking for Christopher, and eventually tracks Martin (now impersonating Christopher) to a small town in Portugal. There, the two men become involved with the same woman, a local lawyer, and the novel culminates in surprising revelations and reversals. Like *The Drowning Room*, *Taking Lives* is a meditation on the nature of identity, an aspect of the book many critics were quick to commend. As Michael Upchurch wrote in the *New York Times Book Review* (March 14, 1999), Pye's "urgent focus on the fragility of the self commands attention, as do Costa's thoughts on 'how reason hides reality.'" Upchurch, however, felt that Pye's narrative was plagued by inconsistencies and unbelievable coincidences, making the book feel "heavily stage-managed." Michiko Kakutani concurred with this assessment in the *New York Times* (March 23, 1999), but added, "What enables the reader to overlook these jerry-rigged developments—and even the novel's contrived ending—is Mr. Pye's ability to combine psychological insight with Hitchcockian suspense and vivid novelistic descriptions."

In the Random House interview Pye outlined his literary plans: "Another novel, another killer but a very different one: a moral monster. If Arkenhout is a twisted version of ambition and hope, this one is twisted virtue—a truly good murderer. It's the good things in life that kill you, always." Pye delivered on this goal in *The Pieces from Berlin*, released in February 2003, in which he takes on the moral question of whether survival is justified when it requires complicity with evil. Inspired by a real case from secret criminal files, the novel explores the life of the fictional Lucia Muller-Ross, who collected and sold valuable antiques entrusted to her by their German-Jewish owners during World War II. After smuggling many of these pieces into Switzerland, Lucia opens an antique shop in Zurich. Sixty years later, Lucia is now a proud, frail antiques dealer, who has told her son and granddaughter little of her mysterious past. When a former neighbor passes Lucia's store and identifies a valuable table that she had once owned, a process is begun to bring Lucia to justice. As the trial approaches, each of the characters struggles to face his or her own painful memories of the war. *The Pieces from Berlin* received largely favorable reviews, particularly for Pye's powerful psychological approach to the Holocaust.

—P. G. H.

SUGGESTED READING: *Financial Times* II p11 July 23, 1995; *Library Journal* p1156 May 15, 1979, p1303 June 1, 1980; *New York Times* C p15 Jan. 3, 1996; *New York Times Book Review* p11 July 26, 1981, p8 Mar. 14, 1999; *Saturday Review* p41 June 22, 1979; *Times Literary Supplement* p1356 Nov. 28, 1980; *Washington Post* B p2 Jan. 3, 1996

SELECTED BOOKS: *The Movie Brats: How the Film Generation Took Over Hollywood*, 1979; *Moguls: Inside the Business of Show Business*, 1980; *The King Over the Water*, 1981; *Eldorado*, 1983; *Pirelli Calendar Album: The First Twenty-five Years*, 1989; *Maximum City: The Biography of New York*, 1991; *The Drowning Room*, 1995; *Taking Lives*, 1999; *The Pieces from Berlin*, 2003

Courtesy of Douglas & McIntyre/Greystone Books

Quarrington, Paul

July 22, 1953– Novelist; playwright; humorist; sportswriter

The Canadian novelist, playwright, and humorist Paul Quarrington has specialized in the creation of quirky and eccentric characters inhabiting fringe, or twilight, worlds. Some are physical freaks, and others are based on such real figures as Brian Wilson of the Beach Boys and the magicians Siegfried and Roy. "Most of my characters try to exclude themselves from life and then get drawn back in," Quarrington told Val Ross in an interview for the Toronto *Globe and Mail* (September 3, 1994). His novels *The Service* (1978), *Home Game* (1983), *The Life of Hope* (1985), *King Leary* (1987), *Whale Music* (1989), *Logan in Overtime* (1990), *Civilization* (1994), and *The Spirit Cabinet* (1999), have varied backgrounds—sports in *Home Game*, *King Leary*, and *Logan in Overtime*, and various aspects of show business in *Whale Music*, *Civilization*, and *The Spirit Cabinet*, to name two prominent examples. Although many of his characters are alcoholics or in some other state of dissolution, Quarrington exhibits an almost religious concern with redemption. No withdrawal is permanent, and hope is always present.

Quarrington has written or co-written the scripts for many films, among them *Perfectly Normal* (1990), *Giant Steps* (1992), *Camilla* (1994), and *Whale Music* (1994), as well as a number of plays, including *The Invention of Poetry* (1989), *Checkout Time* (1997), *Dying Is Easy* (1997), and works for television. His nonfiction books, *Hometown Heroes: On the Road with Canada's National Hockey Team* (1988), *Fishing with My Old Guy* (1995), and *The Boy on the Back of the Turtle* (1997), share the concerns of his novels—the magic and absurdity of life and the need to feed the spirit. Quarrington has told several interviewers that, although "screenplays make more money," the novel is his preferred form.

Paul Quarrington was born in Toronto, Ontario, on July 22, 1953 to Mary Ormiston Lewis and Bruce Joseph Quarrington, both of whom were psychologists and amateur musicians. He grew up in Don Mills, a suburb of Toronto, with his two brothers, who are professional musicians. Quarrington, too, was musically inclined from childhood, playing guitar, clarinet, squeeze box, bass, harp, and piano. He always thought of himself as an imaginative writer as well; he has attributed that talent to the personality tests his mother would administer to him and his brothers as a sort of experiment connected with her work with disturbed children. "We became quite adept at achieving truly frightening results on these tests so as to please mama. I believe this helped me develop a novelistic imagination," he told R. W. Megens in an on-line interview for *quarrington.org* (on-line).

Quarrington launched his musical career at 15, as "a chubby white blues guitarist," in his words. From the late 1970s through the early 1980s, he was a singer/songwriter with a rock band called Joe Hall and the Continental Drift. "Baby and the Blues," a song that he wrote and performed with one of his band mates, Martin Worthy, became a hit single, reaching the top of the Canadian charts in 1980. The age at which Quarrington produced his first novel has been reported as nine by some sources and 12 by others; its plot, by his own account, involved a Sherlock Holmes–type detective and, perhaps, the Loch Ness monster. He told John Gault in an interview for *Maclean's* (May 29, 1989) that writing was a way of "indulging my fantasies"; describing himself as "a driven person," he said that he has never been able to stop writing.

Quarrington attended the University of Toronto from 1970 to 1972. His first published novel, *The Service*, came out in 1978. He told Megens that one reviewer declared it "not a very impressive book, but . . . quite an impressive debut." In *The Service*, the main character pays a huckster $50 to solve all his problems. Val Ross, who profiled Quarrington for the *Globe and Mail* (September 3, 1994), called the "series of odd encounters between eccentric freaks and a frustrated, average-guy drunk" a foreshadowing of the writer's future work. Justin Smallbridge noted in *Maclean's* (October 3, 1994) that Quarrington's ability to temper "a mordant wit with sympathy and affection" were "elements . . . apparent in his first novel."

With his second novel, *Home Game* (1983), Quarrington achieved a large measure of success in Canada; there, the book was nominated for a Stephen Leacock Award. Quarrington wrote *Home Game*, his longest work to date, during the last tour of Joe Hall and the Continental Drift—a difficult task, as he told Megens, because, in that pre-computer era, he had to produce fairly clean typed copy. The difficulty of the job enters the novel as its framing device; as part of the plot, a grandfather is forcing his grandson to type the book itself. The story involves a group of circus freaks and a bizarre bunch of religious sectarians, who compete in a baseball game to determine which group will have to leave town. The religious sectarians are led by Tekel Ambrose, a baseball great. Another baseball player, Nathanael Isbister, fallen on bad times, becomes the freaks' coach. According to the publisher, "During these all-important nine innings we learn that, despite all appearances, these eccentric characters cannot deny the humanity that makes them all members of a single team." The book enchanted a reviewer for the *Toronto Star* who, as quoted by *quarrington.org*, characterized the story as what might be produced "if the Brothers Grimm and the Brothers Marx had conspired to perform pratfalls while Freud was looking on, shaking his head." *Home Game* struck Andrew Bartlett, in an assessment for *Canadian Literature* (Summer 1998), as "cartoon like" and its humor as "juvenile, adolescent"; he also reported that "Quarrington's narrative energy pick[ed] up at the game itself."

The Life of Hope, Quarrington's 1985 novel, also takes place in a village whose residents include a dwarf, a monster, a man with a talking stomach, an Indian with an Oxford accent, and a giant oracular fish, Ol' Mossback. Paul, an alcoholic novelist, comes to the town to visit a professor friend, in the hope of ridding himself of the writer's block that has prevented him from completing his second novel. He becomes involved in the present-day life of the town and fascinated by its history as well. (The place was founded by a 19th-century religious leader who believed in nudism and communal sex.) Flashbacks tell of the Perfectionists, who engaged in strange rituals but had a practical streak that enabled them to make a lot of money from the sale of fishing aids of their own invention. The Toronto *Globe and Mail* (September 21, 1985) reviewer, William French, wrote that he was "not quite certain" about what Quarrington meant to satirize, but he speculated that the author's targets included "environmental issues, religion, the dangers of nuclear annihilation, sex, the bromide that there's nothing new under the sun, the difficulty of sorting out history from legend." French also declared, "*The Life of Hope* combines the historical and hysterical novel," in which any "attempt to trap . . . meaning is like trying to catch a firefly in a bottle: just as you sneak up on him, he turns off his taillight and zips off in another direction." Louise Longo, writing for *Quill & Quire* (September 1985), agreed that *The Life of Hope* is "skilled, funny, racy, whimsical and heavily ironic" and possesses "a subtle emotional subtext." Among other reviewers who joined in the chorus of praise, Ronald B. Hatch termed its defects a kind of strength, because Quarrington's aim was "to create not the perfection of form but the excitement and vigour of language as expressed in the passing moment," as he wrote for the *Canadian Forum* (April 1986).

Quarrington turned to hockey for the setting of *King Leary* (1987), in which the main character, Percival Leary, is partly based on Francis Michael Clancy, the hockey star who became vice president of the Toronto Maple Leafs. Leary, an old man who lives in a nursing home, makes his last trip to Toronto, where he is to appear in a television commercial for ginger ale. Unlike Quarrington's previous novels, in which a narrator enters the action in a postmodernist ploy that makes the existence of the author obvious, *King Leary* takes place entirely in the mind and memory of its protagonist, with the novelist manipulating his creations from behind the scenes. "Memory Lane was never like this," Ron Carlson commented in the *New York Times Book Review* (May 1, 1988). "The dead in this hall of fame don't stay in their display cases. Clay Clinton—Leary's oldest friend, a flamboyant entrepreneur and bootlegger, the owner of the Ottawa Patriots—appears with disturbing frequency, as do Leary's wife and son. But the central apparition is Manfred Armstrong Ozikean, Manny Oz, the man who could have been King. He's been dead 50 years, having suffered an acute alcoholic insult to the brain . . . in 1937. Or did he die of a broken heart? . . . So . . . Quarrington thickens the broth. What starts out to be the life story of the King of the Ice changes into something more like a mystery. . . . As the layers of memory peel away, Leary is wide-eyed at what he finds his life has been, and he moves toward atonement. The book has come to earth; the comedy serves the tragedy." *King Leary* won the 1987 Stephen Leacock Award for Humour. Nevertheless, Quarrington told Megens in his on-line interview, in "no way do I see myself as a humorist. When I was a young man . . . novels were humorous. Think of [the novelists Richard] Brautigan, [Kurt] Vonnegut, [Joseph] Heller, [Philip] Roth. I just thought being funny was a part of the job."

Quarrington followed *King Leary* with *Hometown Heroes: On the Road with Canada's National Hockey Team*, a work of nonfiction that appeared in 1988. In it, he recounted the exploits during a tour of Europe and North America of what the publisher described as "the most original cast of stickhandlers and puck-stoppers ever to lace up a skate." His next book, the novel *Whale Music* (1989), is based on the life of Brian Wilson of the Beach Boys. Quarrington told Smallbridge that he wanted to enter the mind of someone like Wilson, who became a recluse, because "everyone just assumes that the man's crazy. But I bet you I can construct a predicament for him where this kind of response—to hide yourself away—is really the most sane response." In *Whale Music*, the rock star Desmond Howell, acting like a beached whale, has holed up in his house by the sea. His brother Danny, with whom he made his hit records, is dead, and Des spends his time composing a rock symphony for whales. (Whales surrounded Danny after he crashed his car into the ocean.) Drugs, jelly doughnuts, and alcohol are Des's preferred companions. He muses, "We were all of us born too late, that's a sad fact. . . . This age is a strange new neighborhood, cheaply constructed and stuck out in the middle of nowhere. None of us belongs." His seclusion is imperfect, however, as intruders from the music world keep appearing. The unexpected arrival of Claire, an escapee from a Toronto mental asylum, lifts Des out of his funk. After they quarrel and Claire leaves, Des searches for her in Los Angeles. He finds her, and the novel ends on a note of redemption.

Jack MacLeod, the reviewer for *Books in Canada* (July 1989), deemed *Whale Music* "full of effective one-liners and aphorisms"; he reported that the novel demonstrated "that Quarrington can write a lean, spare prose" and displayed "comic capering and the rush of epiphany" expressed with "taut control, . . . an artistic restraint and even a suggestion of wisdom," all of which were quite unlike the "untamed . . . exuberance" of his earlier works. In the *Canadian Forum* (August 1990), Julie Mason called *Whale Music* "immensely likeable . . . funny and poignant and rich with eccentrics." American critics, such as Tom Schnabel, writing for the *Los Angeles Times Book Review* (April 15, 1990), tended to focus on Quarrington's biographical skills. Although Schnabel termed *Whale Music* "stylishly and inventively written," he would have preferred "either straight biography or a new set of characters not so transparently linked to real people, dead or alive." Margot Mifflin, the critic for the *New York Times Book Review* (February 25, 1990) and herself a rock musician, called the Brian Wilson story one "that would strain credulity even if it were printed as fiction." Although she felt that Quarrington's "ability to create rounded and colorful characters" almost compensated for "his novel's lack of originality," she declared that "truth, where the Beach Boys are concerned, is not only stranger than fiction, it's better." *Whale Music* won the Governor General's Literary Award for fiction. The film *Whale Music*, which Quarrington co-wrote, opened the Toronto International Film Festival in 1994.

Quarrington's play *The Invention of Poetry* premiered in Toronto in 1989 and appeared in book form in 1990. Its chief characters are two residents of a fleabag hotel, an alcoholic baseball player and an alcoholic poet, who one night decide to try to redeem their failed lives. "Tonight the plan is to stay sober and to create a poem of beauty and a joy forever. But writing poetry requires a muse . . . ," Quarrington wrote in his introduction. According to Val Ross, writing for the *Globe and Mail* (September 3, 1994), "Male bonding, slapstick and sports talk abound" in the play. Also published in 1990 was Quarrington's novel *Logan in Overtime*, the story of a has-been goaltender who makes a comeback in a game of hockey against the Hope Blazers.

Quarrington spent the next few years writing mainly for cinema and television. The Quarrington-scripted *Camilla* (1994) was the last film in which Jessica Tandy appeared. Desson Howe, who reviewed the movie for the *Washington Post* (March 24, 1995), described *Camilla* as "a minimally involving, female-bonding road movie . . . for fans of the late actress only." *Civilization (And Its Part in My Downfall)*, Quarrington's next major novel, was published in 1994. It is narrated from a prison cell by Thom, who became a cowboy hero and had an affair with Thespa Doone, a silent-screen siren. The events that led to his incarceration began when he realized that there will be no part for him in the forthcoming epic film *Civilization*, which a major director is making. Quarrington told Megens that his narrative strategy in *Civilization* was "halfway between" the technique of the authorial intervention he used in *The Service*, *Home Game*, and *The Life of Hope* and the more traditional narrative technique of *Whale Music*, "because we know someone is in the act of producing the artifact, the book. It's just that it's not me, it's Thom Mass, the hero." In a review of *Civilization* for the on-line Toronto publication *eye*, Richard Sutherland praised the atmosphere its author had created: "Woven together from scraps of the mythologies of baseball, the Wild West, and the silver screen, it's a world of prodigies and mysteries like tule rooters and the Order of Ancient and Lucid Druids" where all of the "outlandish folks" are "totally believable, finely and even sensitively drawn."

Fishing with My Old Guy: The Hilarious Quest for the Biggest Speckled Trout in the World (1995), is the true story of Quarrington's trip along the Broadback River in northern Quebec with his mentor Gordon Deval—his "Old Guy"—and two other men. Their outboard motor soon becomes waterlogged, but not "much happens while fishing and not much happens in this modest volume," Tom Hawthorn wrote for *Canadian Geographic* (February 1996). Nevertheless, Hawthorn did not fault Quarrington for the hubristic self-review of his subtitle: characterizing the author's writing style as "both smoother and more facile than his casting technique," he wrote, "Among the spirited and intoxicating volumes in the piscatorial library, Quarrington's contribution is proof that a fisherman's style can be wry, rather than rye." The *Publishers Weekly* (August 19, 1996) reviewer noted that despite the hostile terrain, the "unrelenting, freezing wind, lots of rain and at least one ice storm," this "humorous account" had resulted.

In *The Boy on the Back of the Turtle* (1997), Quarrington offered another chronicle of an expedition with an "old guy," in this case his father, and also one of his two daughters. Driven by the idea that "there must be a God, because how else can the wonderful interlocking complexities of nature be explained?," as John Bemrose put it in *Maclean's* (December 8, 1997), Quarrington set out to "introduce" his daughter to God by taking her and his father to the Galapagos Islands. Bemrose noted that when Quarrington's father reaches for the hands of his son and his granddaughter while they are watching dolphins, the "passage catches a moment of love between the generations, while simultaneously evoking the mystery of the natural world. When Quarrington finally concludes that God is not so much a maker present from the beginning of the world, as He is a state towards which humanity is struggling, it is such tender family scenarios that lend his argument weight." Nevertheless, Bemrose expressed skepticism about how seriously to take the book, because whenever "a hint of real spiritual angst leaks out, Quarrington quickly dilutes it with humor." Quarrington's humor especially impressed Barb Minett, who, in a quote posted on *quarrington.org*, praised his "very funny fascinating account" and his revelations of "many endearing power struggles with both his father and daughter." Quarrington's play *Checkout Time* (1997) also depicts power struggles, this time between a Hollywood director and a novelist working in a hotel room on an adaption of a novel into a screenplay. An ambitious chambermaid becomes their interlocutor. The play starred Quarrington's wife, the actress Dorothie Bennie, in its premiere at the Toronto Fringe Theatre Festival.

The eponymous artifact of *The Spirit Cabinet*, Quarrington's 1999 novel, supposedly belonged to the great magician Houdini. The cabinet represents the real magic that Jurgen, a member of a three-person Las Vegas magic act, longs to achieve. The magicians are said to be modeled on Siegfried and Roy, who have performed in Las Vegas for years. Jurgen's partner Rudolfo is the "tamer" of Samson, "an elderly albino leopard with a rich inner life who may alone be worth the read," in the words of Judith Kicinski, the reviewer for *Library Journal* (February 15, 2000). The other partner in their show is Miranda, whose huge, nearly naked body distracts the audience from the magicians' maneuvers. Jurgen and Rudolfo, the victims of miserable childhoods in Germany that are described in flashbacks, fall in love and live together in a mansion in the Nevada desert. After Jurgen acquires the Davenport Spirit Cabinet at an auction, he spends much of his time inside it. Strange things happen to him: he loses color, emits light, and enters a state of increasing weightlessness. "Jurgen slowly disappears into the realm of pure spirit," Jennifer Schuessler wrote for the *New York Times Book Review* (April 30, 2000), "but the novel seems preoccupied with the often disgusting business of having a body. . . . All the gross-out descriptions underscore Quarrington's somewhat hokey point that we're all freaks at heart." Schuessler nevertheless concluded on a favorable note: "Considering all the ham-fisted weirdness that has gone before, Quarrington pulls an ending of surprising delicacy and sweetness out of his hat. He comes close to making good on the characters' often trite disquisitions of the human need for wonder and magic. . . . Paul Quarrington knows some neat tricks." Jay Currie, in a review of *The Spirit Cabinet* for *January Magazine* (on-line), felt that "the glitz of Vegas" got in the way of "the mystery and fascination of magic," but for other reviewers, the magic outweighed the novel's defects. Kicinski called the book "Darkly comic, deeply sad, and always ironic" and maintained that Quarrington "shows us that the difference between true magic and everyday charlatanism depends on a willingness to suspend disbelief and open oneself to miracles." The *Publishers Weekly* (February 7, 2000) reviewer found "philosophical enlightenment in a novel to be treasured, even by those who don't believe in magic."

In 2001 Quarrington published *Fishing for Brookies, Browns and Bows: The Old Guy's Complete Guide to Catching Trout*, a humorous guide to trout fishing. He offers more insights on fish, middle age, and marriage in his 2003 book, *From the Far Side of the River: Chest-Deep in Little Fish and Big Ideas.*

—S. Y.

SUGGESTED READING: *Books in Canada* p25+ July 1989; *Canadian Forum* p39 Apr. 1986; *Canadian Geographic* p85 Feb. 1996; *Canadian Literature* p170+ Summer 1998; *Eye.net* (on-line); *Library Journal* p198 Feb. 15, 2000; *Los Angeles Times Book Review* p8 Apr. 15, 1990; *Maclean's* p61 May 29, 1989, p52 Oct. 3, 1994, p94 Dec. 8, 1997; *New York Times Book Review* p26 May 1, 1988, p12 Feb. 25, 1990, Apr. 30, 2000; *Publishers Weekly* p62 Feb. 7, 2000; *Quill & Quire* p78 Sep. 1985; (Toronto) *Globe and Mail* E p6 Sep. 21, 1985, C p7 Sep. 3, 1994; *Washington Post* N p43 Mar. 24, 1995

SELECTED WORKS: novels—*The Service*, 1978; *Home Game*, 1983; *The Life of Hope*, 1985; *King Leary*, 1987; *Whale Music*, 1989; *Logan in Overtime*, 1990; *Civilization*, 1994; *The Spirit Cabinet*, 1999; nonfiction—*Hometown Heroes: On the Road With Canada's National Hockey Team*, 1988; *Fishing With My Old Guy*, 1995; *The Boy on the Back of the Turtle*, 1997; *Fishing for Brookies, Browns and Bows: The Old Guy's Complete Guide to Catching Trout*, 2001; plays—*The Second*, 1981; *The Invention of Poetry*, 1989; *Checkout Time*, 1997; *Dying Is Easy*, 1997; films—*Perfectly Normal*, 1990; *Giant Steps*, 1992; *Camilla*, 1994; *Whale Music*, 1994; as editor—*Original Six True Stories from Hockey's Classic Era*, 1996

Courtesy of Running Press Book Publishers

Queenan, Joe

Nov. 3, 1950– Satirist; critic

"When Joe Queenan is good he is very, very good. But when he is bad, he's a lot better," John Anderson wrote for New York Newsday (January 26, 1994). Once described as a "cheerful nihilist," Queenan has a reputation for disliking much of contemporary pop culture. A short list of his peeves includes: virtually everyone associated with Hollywood, New Age philosophy, the proliferation of cable channels, sports stars as role models, and magazine writers who write about magazine writers. Celebrities tend to avoid him, prompting him to title his second book *If You're Talking to Me, Your Career Must Be In Trouble*. "My chronic nastiness and obdurate refusal to look on the bright side of things goes far beyond garden-variety misanthropy," he wrote in *My Goodness: A Cynic's Short-Lived Search for Sainthood* (2000). "In a very real sense, I am a complete and utter bastard." His vituperative criticism has appeared in many magazines and seven books. Blending performance art with his critical duties, he has also engaged in a variety of stunts that mock his designated objects of derision. Once he tried to make a movie for less than $7,000 to show that anybody could make a film; in another stunt, he paraded about as the Bad Movie Angel and offered moviegoers a refund after watching films he considered rancid. Although some readers have found his writing and antics funny, many of his fellow critics have wondered whether his wit needs to be wasted criticizing the likes of singer John Tesh, writer Joan Collins, and the Olive Garden chain of restaurants.

The son of Joseph and Agnes (McNulty) Queenan, Joe Queenan was born on November 3, 1950 in Philadelphia, Pennsylvania. Coming from a working-class, Catholic family helped shape his cynical attitude toward mass culture. "Blue collar people like me have zero tolerance level for the problems of celebrities," he told Janet Maslin for the *New York Times* (March 23, 1994). He studied English and French at St. Joseph's College. After he graduated, in 1972, he lived in France, then returned to the U.S. and worked at various odd jobs, such as loading trucks and selling tennis racquets.

Sick of the drudge work, he decided to become a journalist. His journalism career started in 1986, when he produced "an acrid but thought-provoking op-ed piece in the *Wall Street Journal* entitled 'Ten Things I Hate About Public Relations,'" as he explained in his book *My Goodness: a Cynic's Short-Lived Search for Sainthood*. He worked for *Barron's*, a financial publication, and was senior editor at *Forbes* from 1989 to 1990, after which he became a full-time freelance writer, contributing to several publications, including the *Wall Street Journal*, the *Los Angeles Times*, the *New York Times*, *Rolling Stone*, *Movieline*, and the *Washington Post*.

Queenan's first book, *Imperial Caddy: The Rise of Dan Quayle in America and the Decline and Fall of Practically Everything Else* (1992), offers a satirical look at President George Bush's vice president, Dan Quayle, as well as commentary on previous vice presidents and the nature of the news media. Joseph Sobran wrote in the *National Review* (August 31, 1992), "The question naturally arises: Do we need Quayle jokes at all? . . . It's risky to try to top a man who loses a battle of wits with a sixth-grader over the spelling of potato." Molly Ivins, who reviewed the book for the *New York Times Book Review* (October 11, 1992), found that Queenan was aware of "the absurdity of writing an entire book about a subject as slight as Mr. Quayle." She called Queenan "a funny writer," but she thought that "in long stretches he reads like a poor imitation of P. J. O'Rourke. The problem is that, like Mr. O'Rourke, Mr. Queenan has only one note. . . . Several times Mr Queenan starts to address the larger question: What does it say about us as a nation that Dan Quayle, at least at one time, appeared to be almost inevitable as the Republican nominee [for president] in 1996? Mr. Queenan's only answers are predictable cynical quips." She concluded, "There comes a time when one must drop the pose of being above the fray by virtue of one's superior cynicism. . . . Queenan has talent. He will write better books when he has the courage to risk standing for something."

In 1994 Queenan's essays about movies and movie personalities were collected in *If You're Talking to Me, Your Career Must Be in Trouble: Movies, Mayhem, and Malice*. Many of the essays make fun of what he considered overhyped Hollywood icons, including Barbra Streisand, Woody Allen, Oliver Stone, Mickey Rourke, and Martin

Scorsese, among others. A piece entitled "Don't Try This at Home" satirizes improbable movie plots, such as the murder scheme in Alfred Hitchcock's *Dial M for Murder*. Writing for the *New York Times Book Review* (February 27, 1994), Hal Goodman judged Queenan's attempt to skewer Hollywood "resolutely sarcastic. Too resolutely. . . . By sticking so gleefully to the sarcastic, Mr. Queenan does a disservice not to his victims, who in almost all cases deserve what they get, but to his readers and himself. One can't help wondering what insights Joe Queenan might bring us about something he liked." In a review for *Library Journal* (February 15, 1994), Judy Quinn agreed that "unmitigated gall gets a bit tiresome," but she found Queenan's "debunking of sacred cows like Barbra Streisand and Woody Allen . . . on the money" and the whole book "a fun and illuminating read."

Not content with merely writing about motion-picture icons, Queenan went on to make his own movie, *Twelve Steps to Death*, and to write about the experience in *The Unkindest Cut: How a Hatchet-Man Critic Made His Own $7,000 Movie and Put It All On His Credit Card* (1995). The book, which contains the script to the film, recounts Queenan's discovery that Robert Rodriguez had made *El Mariachi* for $7,000. Queenan thought that he could outdo Rodriguez by making a film for $6,998. Gilbert Taylor reported in *Booklist* (February 1, 1996) that Queenan "hired actors who would follow orders and work for nothing (family and neighbors), and controlled travel costs by filming entirely on location—his backyard and environs. Result: a pretty atrocious movie with pretty good publicity." Queenan later learned that it was impossible to make a film on such a paltry sum; the studio that purchased *El Mariachi* had actually spent another $107,000 on the film to tidy it up; similarly, the cost of Queenan's less-polished film ballooned an extra digit. Adam Mazmanian wrote for *Library Journal* (January 1996) that the script, a murder mystery involving a psychiatrist, "is hilarious, promising the kind of offbeat, indie film that studios are buying by the boatload these days." Mazmanian also wrote that the book "is a readable guide to making a movie; but this is more a cautionary tale than a how-to manual."

For his next stunt, Queenan decided to write a novel in three 12-hour stints. The act was in part inspired by pulp-fiction writer Georges Simenon, who wrote a novel in seven days in a glass cage in Paris in 1927. The result of Queenan's frantic scribbling was *Serb Heat*, an 18,000-word novel serialized on the *Mr. Showbiz* Web site from April 30 to May 2, 1996. With an improbable plot about Serbian killers who travel to the U.S. to wreak vengeance on a journalist who insulted them on the Internet, *Serb Heat* did not get too many positive reviews and was deemed unpublishable. "Perhaps to fill up space, Queenan uses the word *very* very much," Peter Kobel suggested in *Entertainment Weekly* (May 17, 1996).

In his next book, *Red Lobster, White Trash, and the Blue Lagoon: Joe Queenan's America* (1998), Queenan explored contemporary American pop culture. He concluded that almost all of it is pathetically bad, though he was surprised to find value in Barry Manilow, Jerry Lewis, Wayne Newton, and the Sizzler chain of restaurants; the unexpected revelations led him to coin a new term, *scheissenbedauren*, to describe the feeling of regret when something is not as horrid as one expected it to be. As Lance Gould observed in the *New York Times Book Review* (July 26, 1998), because "the vulgarity of American pop culture is fecund comedic ground and . . . Queenan . . . is a proven comic talent, the book's premise is promising. . . . However, Queenan relies on the subject matter to serve as its own punch line—as if the names Geraldo Rivera and Donald Trump alone incite laugh riots." London-based critic James Delingpole wrote for the *Spectator* (July 25, 1998) that Queenan's critique of American popular culture "may be like using a sledgehammer to crack a nut." Delingpole found that "cracking nuts with sledgehammers can be really good fun" but that "there are only so many times that you can use the 'x was so bad it makes y look like z' formula before it loses its impact."

Queenan's next book, *Confessions of a Cineplex Heckler: Celluloid Tirades and Escapades* (1999), is another collection of his essays about film. In the book he confessed that "I am one of those people who has never lost his childlike belief that the next motion picture he sees could be the worst film ever made." One piece details his founding of the Antonio Banderas Research Institute, to determine when, if ever, the actor was going to become a superstar. In another essay, "Don't Try This at Home, Part II," Queenan used himself as an experimental subject to disprove the viability of such movie premises as: a white man beating a black man in a game of basketball (*White Men Can't Jump*); hot candle wax being erotic instead of unbearably painful (*Body of Evidence*); or the deadliness of toppling bookcases (*Howard's End*).

For his next book, *My Goodness: A Cynic's Short Lived Search for Sainthood* (2000), Queenan investigated whether he could become less acerbic. He wrote that in 1998 "I began to succumb to the cumulative effects of a lifetime spent being clinically unpleasant. As I approached my fiftieth year and felt the footsteps of mortality just a few yards in my wake, I found myself questioning whether I wanted to spend the rest of my life as a human adder. . . . I was tired of people telling me that I was clever; I wanted people to start telling me that I was good." He decided to emulate such do-gooders as Tom Chappell, founder of Tom's of Maine; Susan Sarandon, the movie star; Anita Roddick, founder of the Body Shop; and many other famous people who "seemed incapable of scooping up a piece of litter or giving a blind dwarf a nickel without issuing a 12-page press release apprising the general public of their awesome munificence." Queenan found, however, that he could not resist the temptation to return to being mean when he saw, for example, that Robin Williams was still making movies.

When Susan Carpenter asked in an interview for the *Los Angeles Times* (February 2, 2000) how it felt to be back to his old cynical self, Queenan quipped, "Great, because it's so much more lucrative." Queenan has also said that his malice is "cheerful, life affirming . . . not the noxious, downbeat variety." "Just because you think things are absurdly stupid . . . it doesn't make you miserable," he told a writer for the *St. Louis Dispatch* (July 20, 1998).

In 2001 Queenan published *Balsamic Dreams: A Short but Selfish History of the Baby Boomer Generation*, an acerbic and witty analysis of his own generation. The book was generally well-received by critics. As one reviewer noted for *Library Journal*, as quoted on *Amazon.com*, "At least when he knocks baby boomers, Queenan has the decency to be funny."

Most recently, Queenan edited *The Malcontents: The Best Bitter, Cynical, and Satirical Writing in the World* (2002). His next book, "True Believers: The Tragic Inner Life of Sports Fans," is set for release in June 2003. Queenan resides in Tarrytown, New York.

—S. Y.

SUGGESTED READING: *Booklist* p910 Feb. 1, 1996; *Library Journal* p162 Feb. 15, 1994, p102 Jan. 1996, p114 Jan. 2000; *Los Angeles Times Magazine* p31 Nov. 7, 1999; *Los Angeles Times* E p2 Feb. 2, 2000; *Nation* p547+ Nov. 9, 1992; *National Review* p69 Aug. 31, 1992; *New York Times Book Review* p13 Oct. 11, 1992, p26 Feb. 27, 1994, p10 July 26, 1998, Mar. 5, 2000; *Publishers Weekly* p60 Dec. 6, 1999; *St. Louis Post-Dispatch* E p1 July 20, 1998; *Toronto Sun* (on-line) July 26, 1998; *Washington Post* C p2 Feb. 17, 2000

SELECTED BOOKS: *Imperial Caddy: The Rise of Dan Quayle in America and the Decline and Fall of Practically Everything Else*, 1992; *If You're Talking to Me, Your Career Must Be in Trouble: Movies, Mayhem, and Malice*, 1994; *The Unkindest Cut: How a Hatchet-Man Critic Made His Own $7,000 Movie and Put It All on His Credit Card*, 1995; *Red Lobster, White Trash, and the Blue Lagoon: Joe Queenan's America*, 1998; *Confessions of a Cineplex Heckler: Celluloid Tirades and Escapades*, 1999; *My Goodness: A Cynic's Short Lived Search for Sainthood*, 2000; *Balsamic Dreams: A Short but Selfish History of the Baby Boomer Generation*, 2001; as editor—*The Malcontents: The Best Bitter, Cynical, and Satirical Writing in the World*, 2002

Radosh, Ronald

Nov. 1, 1937– Historian

The historian Ronald Radosh has been described as "the Zelig of the American Left," meaning that he, like the title character in the Woody Allen film *Zelig* (1984), has been a participant in many key events and has known many noteworthy individuals. The child of Communist immigrants and trade union activists, Radosh grew up a leftist. As a college student, he was a co-founder of the New Left, which opposed the Vietnam War during the 1960s. After receiving his doctorate Radosh intended to serve the Left as an academic and historian. Many of Radosh's early books, including *American Labor and United States Foreign Policy* (1969) and *Prophets on the Right: Profiles of Conservative Critics of American Globalism* (1975), reflected his views. However, like such prominent leftists as Arthur Koestler, Stephen Spender, Richard Wright, Frank Meyer, and Whittaker Chambers, Radosh eventually turned against Communism. One major factor that severed Radosh's ties to many of his leftist colleagues was his study of Julius and Ethel Rosenberg, who were executed in 1953 for providing atomic secrets to the Soviet Union. Radosh had always believed the Rosenbergs were innocent and wanted to write a book that would finally exonerate them. However, after he studied the evidence, which included about 200,000 pages of newly re-

Courtesy of Encounter Books

leased FBI documents, Radosh was forced to conclude in his book, *The Rosenberg File: The Search for the Truth* (1983), that Julius Rosenberg was, in fact, guilty of espionage, and that his wife, Ethel, was probably an accomplice in his crimes. Although the book received many favorable reviews, it outraged many leftists, who had always insisted that the Rosenbergs were innocent. By the end of the 1980s, Radosh had abandoned the movement completely and moved to the right. He continued writing, publishing the books *Divided They Fell: The Demise of the Democratic Party, 1964–1996* (1996); *The Amerasia Spy Case: Prelude to McCarthyism* (1996), with Harvey Klehr; and his memoir, *Commies: A Journey Through the Old Left, the New Left, and the Leftover Left* (2001).

Ronald Radosh was born on November 1, 1937 in New York City. His father, Reuben, immigrated from Poland, where he manufactured women's hats. A short time after he arrived in the United States, Reuben Radosh was drafted by the U.S. Navy during World War I. After completing his military service, he went to work in a millinery factory in New York City. Radosh's mother, Ida Kreichman, had left Russia at an early age and settled in New York City's teeming Lower East Side. Ida found a job as a cutter in a garment factory. Reuben and Ida first met during a meeting of the International Ladies Garment Workers' Union. They fell in love and eventually married. The couple, who joined the Communist Party, shared a passion for radical activism and became members of the trade-union movement in New York City. In his memoir, *Commies: A Journey Through the Old Left, the New Left and the Leftover Left* (2001), Radosh wrote, "Politics notwithstanding, they were devoted and loving parents who continually sought my best interests, which sometimes meant shielding me from the [Communist] movement's dark side."

Radosh grew up as a "Red-diaper baby," and eventually adopted his parents' political views. "One of the photographs I have inherited shows me as a baby, one and a half years old," he wrote in *Commies*, "bundled in a stroller and about to be paraded down Fifth Avenue in the yearly Communist Party celebration [held on May 1 or "May Day"] that went through the garment center of the then radical needle trade unions, ending with a mass rally at Union Square—for decades the historic center of radical protest. That day, it seems to me, was my baptism into the world of Jewish radicalism, a world so small and insular that existed inside a political and social ghetto." Radosh's parents sent him to the Camp Woodland for Children, a summer camp in Phoenicia, New York. "It was created by Communists and fellow travelers so their children could be together in the protected atmosphere of Phoenicia, New York," Radosh recalled in the book, "enjoying a pleasant setting where the ideas, values and culture of the parents could be transmitted painlessly to their Red-diaper babies."

Radosh attended Elisabeth Irwin High School, a private school run by Communists in New York City, named after one of the leaders of the progressive-education movement. As a student during the early 1950s, Radosh handed out leaflets on behalf of Julius and Ethel Rosenberg, who were convicted and then sentenced to death for providing atomic secrets to the Soviet Union. Many leftists in the United States and the rest of the world alleged that the American government fabricated the charges against the Rosenbergs because they were Jews and Communists and demanded clemency and a new trial for the them. Radosh and other leftists tried to rally American Jews on behalf of the Rosenbergs. "My mother and father, after all, were also progressive activists steeped in the secular *Yiddishkayt* culture, people who cared for Russians, who favored civil rights for Negroes, and who had fought in or supported the valiant fight of the Abraham Lincoln Brigade against fascism in Spain," he explained in the memoir. "We convinced ourselves that unless the decision to execute the Rosenbergs was overturned, the same fate might await our own loved ones." (Radosh, however, pointed out the hypocrisy in that many Communists who asserted that the Rosenbergs were the victims of anti-Semitism denied that anti-Semitism played any role in the conviction and execution of 11 Jews in 1952 by the Communist government in what was then Czechoslovakia.) On the evening of June 19, 1953, when the Rosenbergs went to the electric chair at Sing Sing prison in Ossining, New York, Radosh joined over 10,000 activists who gathered near Union Square to protest the executions. "We stood with tears in our eyes, ignoring the thundering words of the speakers and continuing to weep at the Negro ballads sung by the Communist Party folk singers," he wrote in his memoir.

While many of his left-wing friends decided to attend City College, a branch of the City University of New York (CUNY), Radosh enrolled at the University of Wisconsin at Madison. In *Commies* he explained that the university appealed to him because it had no mathematics requirement and was the only campus in the United States that had a recognized chapter of the Labor Youth League (LYL), a branch of the Communist Party. Radosh added that he "came to Madison with the desire to study history—the queen of the sciences, according to [Karl] Marx—and to become a leader in the American Communist movement." As an undergraduate, Radosh broke with the Old Left, which had long supported the Soviet dictator Joseph Stalin, who died in 1953. Many Communists became disillusioned with Stalin after learning that his successor, Nikita Khrushchev, had secretly denounced him as a criminal in a speech delivered in 1956 to the 20th Party Congress in Moscow. After reading the work of the historian Isaac Deutscher, who had been expelled from the Communist Party in 1932 for publicly criticizing Stalin, Radosh concluded that he could remain a consistent leftist while opposing Stalinism.

During the late 1950s, Radosh and other students who shared his views founded a radical movement that became known as the New Left, which helped mobilize students on college campuses across the country against the Vietnam War during the next decade. In 1959 Radosh graduated from the University of Wisconsin with a B.A. in history. A year later, he received a master's degree in history from the University of Iowa, in Iowa City. He then returned to the University of Wisconsin, where in 1967 he earned a doctorate. (While there Radosh studied under the author and historian William Appleman Williams, a leftist who had shunned Communism.)

In 1964, while he was still a doctoral student, Radosh began teaching history at Queensborough Community College, a branch of CUNY. He also taught at the CUNY Graduate Center and various other CUNY campuses. Radosh supplemented his income by teaching courses at the Polytechnic Institute in New York, and Rutgers University, in Newark, New Jersey. Radosh taught at Queensborough and the Graduate Center until his retirement in 1992. He later received a fellowship from the John M. Olin Foundation to teach at Adelphi University, in Garden City, New York, from 1994–1996.

During the 1960s Radosh joined the Committee to Stop the War in Vietnam. Radosh recalled in Commies that the group "aligned itself with those who wanted unilateral withdrawal from Vietnam rather than negotiations. Our intention was never so much to end the war as to use antiwar sentiment to create a new revolutionary socialist movement at home."

In 1967 Radosh and Louis Menashe co-edited the book Teach-Ins: U.S.A. During the mid-1960s professors on many college campuses began organizing "teach-ins," informal protests outside of class. The teach-ins attracted numerous students and became effective vehicles for political protest and activism. The book includes articles from professors, students, journalists, activists, and government officials and provides a history and assessment of the impact of the teach-in movement.

In American Labor and United States Foreign Policy (1969) Radosh criticizes many of the nation's powerful labor leaders, including Samuel Gompers (1850–1924), John Spargo (1876–1966), George Meany (1894–1980), and Jay Lovestone (1898–1990), asserting that they consistently supported the foreign policy of the United States during World War I, World War II, and the Cold War without the input and consent of the members of their unions. "Much unpublished source material is cited that may have value for labor historians interested in writing a fair-minded history of the period covered by this book," Philomena Mullady wrote in her review for America (May 16, 1970). "The volume is unnecessarily long and frequently detailed about irrelevant material. This, combined with the author's lack of objectivity, makes for rather tedious reading." In the Journal of American History (September 1970), S. J. Scheinberg, who expressed mild criticisms of American Labor and United States Foreign Policy, still concluded that "Radosh has written a useful book . . . [which] will serve the needs of the specialist in this field."

In 1971 Radosh edited the book Debs, a volume devoted to the American Socialist Eugene V. Debs (1855–1926), who was variously a journalist, the president of the American Railway Union, and the Socialist Party's candidate for president in five elections. Debs strongly opposed the United States's entry into World War I, and his activism led to his conviction of violating the 1917 Espionage Act and a sentence of 10 years in prison, which was subsequently commuted, in 1921, by President Warren G. Harding. The book includes many of Debs's speeches and articles and statements about him from contemporaries, activists, and historians, including President Woodrow Wilson, President Theodore Roosevelt, Samuel Gompers, Emma Goldman, and Arthur Schlesinger Jr.

As a left-wing critic of American foreign policy, Radosh discovered that he shared several views with members of the staunchly isolationist Old Right, who were vocal opponents of globalism and armed intervention. In 1972 Radosh co-edited the book, A New History of Leviathan, with the libertarian economist Murray Rothbard. In his book Prophets on the Right: Profiles of Conservative Critics of American Globalism (1975), Radosh discusses the background and views of such Old Right figures as Oswald Garrison Villard (1872–1949), a journalist and editor; John Thomas Flynn (1882–1964), an economist, journalist, and a vocal opponent of President Franklin Roosevelt's New Deal; Charles A. Beard (1874–1948), a prominent historian; Lawrence Dennis (1893–1977), a journalist; and Robert A. Taft (1889–1953), who served as a Republican senator from Ohio and sought his party's presidential nomination in 1948 and 1952. In the years leading up to the United States's entry in World War II and during the Cold War, these men championed isolationism and warned of the dangers of interventionism, which they believed would lead to the suppression of civil liberties in the name of national security, the erosion of constitutional limits on the Executive Branch's abilities to make war, and the government's preoccupation with foreign policy at the expense of pressing domestic needs. They feared that the United States, which was founded on the principles of liberty and the respect for rights, was turning into a militaristic empire. The isolationists' views became increasingly unpopular during World War II, as Americans came to accept globalism, an activist foreign policy, and armed intervention as means to fight totalitarianism. Radosh, however, noted that many of the same criticisms of American foreign policy voiced by the Left, especially during the Vietnam War, had already been made decades earlier by the Old Right and still had relevance. In his review for Library Journal (February 1, 1975), Charles DeBenedetti expressed mixed feelings about the book. "Radosh's treatment, although skillful, is episodic in coverage and sermonizing in tone," DeBenedetti observed. "His sketches are true and fair; but they are just that—sketches or profiles. A comprehensive intellectual portrait of these critical figures remains to be written." However, writing for *Business Week* (April 21, 1975), William Wolman was more impressed with *Prophets on the Right*, noting that it "brilliantly documented" Taft's thinking. Wolman concluded, "The work of Radosh . . . is therefore well worth the time and careful attention of the broad center of the U. S. body politic that is disturbed by the current state of U. S. foreign policy and is casting about for constructive alternatives."

In 1973 Radosh visited Cuba with a group of American leftists. Radosh and the New Left backed the Cuban dictator Fidel Castro, who, in 1959, successfully waged a socialist revolution against a corrupt and brutal regime. As Radosh explained to Stephen Goode for *Insight on the News* (August 19, 2002, on-line), "We nothing short of extolled Cuba and Castro. Not only had Cuba broken out of the hated American sphere, it was our model. Different. A vibrant, fresh, humanist revolution." Radosh, however, became disillusioned with Castro after touring the country. Instead of finding a "workers's paradise," Radosh was shocked when he saw the economic misery caused by Castro's policies and numerous violations of human rights, including the imprisonment of homosexuals and the frequent use of lobotomies on mental patients. When he returned to the United States, Radosh published an article about his visit for *Liberation*, a left-wing publication. "My intention was to argue that the Cuban revolution could be strengthened by abandoning its repressive practices," he told Goode. "Almost all the reaction to the article [from the left] was hostile." In 1976 Radosh co-edited *The New Cuba: Paradoxes and Potentials*, which included his *Liberation* article and essays critical of Castro's regime written by various members of the New Left, including Frances Fitzgerald, Maurice Halperin, and Martin Duberman. Radosh's criticisms of Castro represented his first major break with the Left, but although he eventually turned against Communism, he still identified himself as a leftist. He then joined the Democratic Socialists of America, which was headed by the well-known political activist Michael Harrington.

During the mid-1970s the Rosenberg case resurfaced as the subject of intense debate among ideological partisans. Leftists continued to insist that Julius and Ethel Rosenberg were innocent of espionage charges and the victims of a political lynching during the McCarthy era. By contrast, the Right maintained that the Rosenbergs were guilty, and that the death sentence was justified by the severity of their crimes. The Rosenbergs' children, Robert and Michael Meeropol, who were given up for adoption after their parents' execution, published a book, *We Are Your Sons: The Legacy of Julius and Ethel Rosenberg* (1974). The Meeropols began a campaign to exonerate their parents and set up an advocacy group on their behalf, the National Committee to Re-Open the Rosenberg Case. The brothers also filed a lawsuit under the Freedom of Information Act (FOIA) to force the FBI to release documents related to the case. Many of the Rosenbergs' defenders expressed hope that evidence in the FBI documents would finally clear the couple and settle the controversy after two decades. Radosh, who still believed the Rosenbergs were innocent, joined the committee.

The Meeropols' lawsuit succeeded, and by 1978, the FBI had released about 200,000 pages of documents. As a leftist historian, Radosh thought he was the ideal person to study the new material and write a book vindicating the Rosenbergs. Radosh, however, decided to first write an article before publishing a book and recruited Sol Stern, a left-wing journalist and a classmate from the University of Iowa, to assist him. Radosh and Stern examined the FBI documents at the law office of Marshall Perlin, who represented the Meeropols, in New York City. After spending about one week studying the documents, Radosh began having second thoughts about the Rosenbergs' innocence. When Radosh and Stern began raising questions about information in the documents, Perlin threw them out of the office. The writers then traveled to Washington, D.C., at personal expense, resuming their research at FBI headquarters.

Radosh and Stern published their findings in an article for the *New Republic* (June 23, 1979), writing, "The full picture, as it turns out, confounds all the partisan versions to date." The writers concluded that Julius Rosenberg was guilty after all, but that Ethel Rosenberg was, at worst, only an accessory to her husband's crimes. The article received substantial attention in the media and outraged many of the Rosenbergs' staunchest defenders, including the Meeropols. Stern eventually decided against expanding the *New Republic* article into a book, and, in 1981, Radosh turned to Joyce Milton, a journalist and historian, to help him write it. (Stern, however, agreed to help Radosh and Milton with their research.) In 1983 Radosh and Milton published *The Rosenberg File: A Search for Truth*. Drawing on the FBI documents, interviews with the leading figures in the case, trial transcripts, and other unpublished sources, Radosh and Milton wrote that Julius Rosenberg, an electrical engineer who worked for the U.S. Army Signal Corps as a civilian employee during World War II, headed a spy ring—which included Ethel's brother, David Greenglass—that provided atomic secrets to the Soviet Union. However, Klaus Fuchs, the German-born physicist who worked on the atomic bomb at Los Alamos, New Mexico, had already given Soviets the information that allowed them to develop the atomic bomb. The Soviets used Julius Rosenberg's information to confirm the data supplied by Fuchs. In 1950 Fuchs, a British citizen, confessed and served nine years in prison. The book asserted that Ethel Rosenberg probably knew of her husband's activities, but found little evidence that directly implicated her in espionage. The authors, however, faulted the federal government's prosecution of the case and the trial. They wrote that Emmanuel Bloch, the lawyer who defended the Rosenbergs, made many mistakes that helped the prosecution. Radosh and Milton also cited FBI documents that revealed illegal *ex parte* communication between Irving Kaufman, the presiding judge, and the prosecution during the trial. Radosh and Milton wrote that the federal government's decision to seek the death penalty against the Rosenbergs was legally unjust. Julius Rosenberg had spied for the Soviet Union during World War II, when it was still an ally of the United States. Such a crime, in their opinion, did not merit the death penalty. The government, however, had sought the death penalty in order to frighten Julius Rosenberg into revealing information about other Soviet espionage activity in the United States and deter other Communists from spying for the Soviet Union. The government indicted Ethel Rosenberg on the same charges and sought the death penalty for her as well in order to pressure Julius into confessing. On the day of the execution, a team of FBI agents waited at Sing Sing Prison with a 13-page list of questions in case Julius decided to talk. (Only one of the questions, in fact, concerned Ethel.) The Rosenbergs, however, refused to talk and maintained their innocence as they went to their deaths. Radosh and Milton observed that the execution of the Rosenbergs, besides being legally unjust, also turned them into Communist martyrs and served the ends of Soviet propaganda.

The Rosenberg File became a best-seller and received mostly favorable notices in mainstream publications. In his review for the *Washington Post* (September 4, 1983), the historian Alan Brinkley described the book as a "sensitive, absorbing, and exhaustively researched study" that proved its case. "Rather than use the Rosenbergs to settle old ideological scores, [Radosh and Milton] have risen above the passions surrounding this case and produced a book of remarkable balance and restraint," Brinkley wrote. In the *New York Review of Books* (October 27, 1983), Murray Kempton wrote, "Radosh and Milton have been scrupulous in their research, persuasive in their deductions, and generally fair-minded in their exposition. Few of their readers can retain much doubt that Julius Rosenberg was a conscientious Soviet espionage agent and that his wife at the very least knew and approved of his vocational commitment, which was not, to be sure, a transgression that would excuse her dreadful punishment."

Radosh and Milton, however, failed to persuade many of the Rosenbergs' defenders on the left. Robert and Michael Meeropol, Marshall Perlin, and Walter and Miriam Schneir, the authors of the book, *Invitation to Inquest* (1965), which asserted that the government framed the Rosenbergs, accused Radosh and Milton of distorting documents, misquoting subjects, and even fabricating evidence; the two authors strongly denied such allegations. On October 20, 1983 the *New Republic* and *The Nation* co-sponsored a debate on the Rosenberg case at Town Hall in New York City with Radosh, Milton, and Stern on one side and the Schneirs and Perlin on the other. Both sides spent the evening trading charges and counter-charges. During one exchange, Radosh accused Perlin of engaging in left-wing McCarthyism. Many aging veterans of the Old Left packed Town Hall and frequently booed and shouted allegations whenever Radosh, Milton, or Stern spoke.

Radosh found himself essentially excommunicated from the Left for the heresy of writing that Julius Rosenberg was guilty. Both his *New Republic* article and *The Rosenberg File* offended many of the movement's die-hards, who considered the Rosenbergs' supposed innocence an article of faith. Several of Radosh's longtime friends and colleagues distanced themselves from him, and some even attacked him publicly. In *Commies*, Radosh wrote that several leftists, including Michael Harrington, privately admitted to him that they actually believed that the Rosenbergs were guilty, but continued to publicly insist that the couple were framed because it served political ends. "The stakes were high," Radosh elaborated in *Commies*. "For if the Rosenbergs were innocent, the Old Left was correct: America had been on the edge of fascism, and it was the United States, not the Soviet Union, that threatened the peace and sought to repress those who believed in freedom and democracy." Radosh, however, believed that a political cause could not be sustained by a lie. The experience of writing about the Rosenberg case and the hostile reaction he received from his leftist colleagues led Radosh to question his beliefs and eventually move to the right. In an interview with *World Authors, 1995–2000*, Radosh said, "Politically, I classify myself today as an independent moderate who leans to the conservative side on most key issues. I'm a registered Democrat, but one who often dissents from most Democratic Party policies and who voted for George W. Bush in the [2000] election."

In 1997 Radosh and Milton published an updated version of *The Rosenberg File*, which incorporated additional material that had become available since the original publication of the book. Among the evidence that supported the authors' conclusions were the "Venona" intercepts. In 1943 the U.S. Army Signal Security Agency began a top-secret project, codenamed "Venona," that involved the interception and decoding of thousands of double-encrypted messages sent and received between the Soviet Union and its diplomatic missions in the United States. In 1995 the National Security Agency (NSA) declassified the Venona intercepts, which revealed extensive Soviet espionage in the United States, especially by the American Communist Party. A number of intercepts made clear references to Julius Rosenberg, who had the codenames "ANTENNA" and "LIBERAL," and identified his wife, sister-in-law, and a college friend by name.

In 1996 Radosh published *Divided They Fell: The Demise of the Democratic Party, 1964–1996*. In it Radosh asserts that radical activists displaced the liberal New Deal coalition for control of the

Democratic Party during its national conventions in 1964 and 1968. The activists then pushed the Democratic Party to the far left on many issues, which, in turn, alienated millions of voters who made up the party's traditional base. According to Radosh, this contributed to the Democratic Party's defeat in five presidential elections—in 1968, 1972, 1980, 1984, and 1988—and its loss of both houses of Congress in the 1994 mid-term elections. In the *New York Times Book Review* (August 25, 1996), Hanna Rosin wrote, "While the minutiae in *Divided They Fell* can be riveting, there is something fundamentally unsatisfying in Mr. Radosh's account. He piles up the details without really deepening his explanation."

In 1996 Radosh also published, with Harvey Klehr, *The Amerasia Spy Case: Prelude to McCarthyism*. In this book Radosh and Klehr discuss the 1945 arrest and subsequent espionage trial of six individuals associated with *Amerasia*, a small pro-Communist journal that, although its circulation never topped 2,000, was read by almost everyone who specialized in the field of Far East politics. Philip Jaffe, the publisher and editor of *Amerasia*, received classified documents about China from several sources in the federal government. One of Jaffe's main sources was John Stewart Service, who worked with the State Department and leaked the documents with the hopes that they would discredit American support for Chiang Kai-Shek in the Chinese Civil War. Unbeknownst to Service, Jaffe was a Communist sympathizer who was eager to provide the documents to the Soviet Union. Jaffe never got the chance to carry out the espionage, however. Radosh and Klehr wrote that Thomas Corcoran, a prominent Democratic Party lawyer and lobbyist known as "Tommy the Cork," and U.S. Attorney General Tom Clark colluded to protect Service, a highly respected official, and minimize the damage caused by the leaks. Although the "*Amerasia* six" were indicted on minor charges, only Jaffe and Emmanuel Larsen, a civilian employee of the Navy Department, were convicted and paid modest fines. In 1950, however, the *Amerasia* controversy resurfaced when Senator Joseph McCarthy of Wisconsin alleged that the State Department was riddled with Communists. According to Radosh and Klehr, the fact that the *Amerasia* six had escaped serious punishment gave McCarthy's exaggerated charges serious credibility with many people. "Klehr and Radosh sift through an enormous amount of material here," John Corry wrote in the *American Spectator* (June 1996). "Political figures scarcely remembered now turn up frequently, and [the] chronology is often confusing. But the research is impeccable and the judgments are judicious."

In 2001 Radosh, Mary R. Habeck, and Grigory Sevostianov co-edited the book, *Spain Betrayed: The Soviet Union in the Spanish Civil War*, an annotated collection of documents culled from the Soviet archives and published as part of Yale University Press's *Annals of Communism* series. The Spanish Civil War began in July 1936 when a group of army generals led by Francisco Franco sought to overthrow the left-wing Republican government, which had been elected several months earlier. For the next three years, Franco's Nationalist forces battled the Loyalists, a coalition of left-wing factions that supported the government. Both Germany, under Adolf Hitler, and Italy, under Benito Mussolini, supplied arms to Franco. The Soviet Union, under Stalin, backed the Spanish Republic and the Loyalists, who were joined by thousands of volunteers from many countries, including the United States. In March 1939 the Nationalists defeated the Loyalists, and Franco established a dictatorship that ruled Spain until his death in 1975. The 81 documents in the book shed light on Stalin's true motivations for intervening in the Spanish Civil War and detailed the extent of the Soviet Union's assistance to the Republic and the Loyalist cause. Although for propaganda purposes, the Soviets claimed they were trying to save the Republic, in fact, Stalin wanted to strengthen Communism in Spain with the hope of eventually creating a satellite dictatorship that he would control from Moscow. Stalin disguised his intentions in order to entice Great Britain and France to intervene on the side of the Loyalists. (Both nations declared their neutrality.) Stalin actually undermined the Loyalists by bankrupting the Republican government by selling it arms at inflated prices. "The editors of this volume deserve the highest commendation for presenting an absolutely unique trove of original documentation as illuminates Soviet policy and internal republic politics as no other previous work has done," Stanley G. Payne observed in his review for the *Los Angeles Times* (July 15, 2001). "All students of Soviet policy, the Spanish war and European international relations, as well as all informed readers in these fields, will be indebted to them for an unprecedented collection of material that marks something of a watershed in the history of the period."

In 2001 Radosh also published his memoirs, *Commies: A Journey Through the Old Left, the New Left, and the Leftover Left*. The author writes about his Communist upbringing and his role in helping to found the New Left, and he offers his recollections about some of the most prominent figures of the movement, including the folksinger Pete Seeger and the activists Abbie Hoffman and Tom Hayden. Radosh also discusses writing about the Rosenberg case and explains why he gradually abandoned the left to "come home," meaning that he finally embraced the United States and its democratic institutions. "As a case study, [*Commies*] is invaluable: an exemplary text as notable for what it skirts over as it is for what it says," Jesse Walker wrote for *Reason* (December 2001). "*Commies* is crammed not with pedantic footnotes but with gossip, much of it gratuitous and most of it highly entertaining." Walker noted that "Radosh's portrait of a life as a young Red is engagingly written, filled with vivid characters (such as his mother's cousin

Jacob Abrams, a Bolshevik-hating anarchist exiled to Mexico City) and enjoyably odd details (such as the teacher who tried to relate everything he taught to dialectical materialism—including geology.)" Walker, however, had some criticisms of the book; he faulted Radosh, for example, for overlooking his associations during the late 1960s and 1970s with Old Right figures and libertarians such as Murray Rothbard.

Radosh frequently contributes articles to the *New Republic*, *Commentary*, *First Things*, and the on-line publication *Front Page Magazine*. Radosh told *World Authors* that his next book will be an "interpretative history of McCarthyism in the United States." Radosh currently serves as a senior fellow at the Hudson Institute, in Washington, D.C., and a senior research associate at the Center for Communitarian Policy Studies at George Washington University, also in Washington, D.C. (The John M. Olin Foundation's efforts in 1996 to fund a professorship for Radosh at George Washington University were successfully blocked by members of the history department.)

Ronald Radosh and his wife, Allis, live in Brookeville, Maryland. Radosh has three children, including two from his first marriage.

—D. C.

SUGGESTED READING: *America* p533 May 16, 1970; *American Spectator* (on-line) June 1996; *Business Week* p10 Apr. 21, 1975; *Insight on the News* (on-line) Aug. 19, 2002; *Journal of American History* p478 Sep. 1970; *Library Journal* p300 Feb. 1, 1975; *New Republic* p13+ June 23, 1979, with photos; *New York Review of Books* (on-line) Oct. 27, 1983; *New York Times* I p25+ Oct. 22, 1983, with photos; *New York Times Book Review* p12 Aug. 25, 1996; *Reason* p77+ Dec. 2001; *Washington Post Book World* p1+ Sep. 4, 1983

SELECTED BOOKS: *American Labor and United States Foreign Policy*, 1969; *Prophets on the Right: Profiles of Conservative Critics of American Globalism*, 1975; *The Rosenberg File: The Search for the Truth*, 1983 (with Joyce Milton); *The Amerasia Spy Case: Prelude to McCarthyism*, 1996 (with Harvey Klehr); *Divided They Fell: The Demise of the Democratic Party, 1964–1996*, 1996; *Commies: A Journey Through the Old Left, the New Left, and the Leftover Left*, 2001; as ed. *Teach-ins: USA*, 1967 (with Louis Menashe); *Debs*, 1971; *A New History of Leviathan: Essays on the Rise of the American Corporate State*, 1972 (with Murray Rothbard); *The New Cuba: Paradoxes and Potentials*, 1976; *El Salvador*, 1981 (with Marvin E. Gettleman, et al); *Spain Betrayed: The Soviet Union in the Spanish Civil War*, 2001 (with Mary R. Habeck and Grigory Sevostianov)

Rayner, Richard

Dec. 1955– Author; journalist

The English-born Richard Rayner is a journalist and the author of several books, including the novels *The Cloud Sketcher* (20000 and *Murder Book* (1997), and the memoir *The Blue Suit* (1995). His works have been enthusiastically adopted by the film industry. His first book, *Los Angeles Without a Map* (1988), was made into a 1999 movie directed by Mika Kaurismaeki. John Malkovich, the highly regarded actor and director, purchased the rights to *Murder Book* to direct himself, and *The Cloud Sketcher* screenplay is in development. Rayner, who moved to Los Angeles, California, in the early 1990s, writes frequently for the *New York Times*, the *New Yorker*, *Granta*, *Harper's Bazaar*, and other publications.

Richard Rayner was born in December 1955 near Bradford, England. In his 1995 memoir, *The Blue Suit*, he describes his roguish father, a car salesman who once sold £100,000 worth of cars and—instead of reimbursing the manufacturer—kept the money, faked his own death, and disappeared abroad. Rayner was 11 at the time. His father resurfaced years later, when Rayner was in college, to attend his wife's funeral. "Obviously he was a mythic figure for me," Rayner told Penelope Rowlands in an interview for *Publishers Weekly* (March 5, 2001).

Rayner attended Cambridge University, in England, where he studied philosophy and law. He dabbled in acting and entertained the idea of going into the theater, but changed his mind when he encountered the young actress, Emma Thompson, who was "so much more talented than I would ever be," as he told Rowlands. He graduated in 1977 and moved to London, where he worked briefly at a law firm before pursuing journalism. He got a job at *Time Out* magazine, which he described to Rowlands as "a sex and drugs and rock 'n' roll kind of place." He eventually became an editor there. "One was able to invent spurious reasons to do a story. . . . I kept finding reasons to come to L.A." His experiences in Los Angeles provided him with the material for his first novel, *Los Angeles Without a Map*. The book is about a young man, half British and half American, who meets a woman at a bar in Britain, falls in love, and follows her to Los Angeles. While there, he convinces his beloved (whom he discovers is a Playboy Bunny) to marry him, a decision with disastrous consequences. The novel combines a satiric take on 1980s L.A. with a thoughtful portrayal of the fleeting nature of love and the pain of loss. Rayner had arranged for the book to be published by a British company, but pulled out just before the book went to print. Bill

Jerry Bauer/Courtesy of Doubleday Publicity
Richard Rayner

Buford, a Cambridge friend and a founder of the literary journal *Granta*, had made him a proposition: Rayner would work as an assistant editor at *Granta*, while Buford edited his book. After this final revision, the book— according to Rayner—was much improved, and was printed, in the U.S., in 1988.

In 1991 Rayner moved to Los Angeles, where he found work as a freelance writer, contributing articles to the *New Yorker* and other publications. His next novel, *The Elephant* (1992), is a twisted morality tale loosely based on his own relationship with his father. Headingley Hamer narrates a series of raucous incidents that revolve around his depraved father, Jack, an incurable liar, drunk, and womanizer. The book was not well received. Anthony Quinn, in an appraisal for the *London Review of Books* (June 27, 1991), wrote that "Rayner works hard to orchestrate a galloping comedy of sexual hysteria, but can only manage a rather smutty slapstick. Detectable here is the influence of Martin Amis, whose gleeful nastiness in the bedroom has become quite a touchstone for many youngish male novelists. . . . Fatally, however, Rayner's performance as erotic farceur just isn't all that funny." Rayner himself was not very pleased with the effort, describing the novel to Rowlands as being "autobiographical and kind of undisciplined."

Rayner again took up the subject of paternal influence in *The Blue Suit*, a work that combines the stuff of memoir with the structure of fiction. Embarrassed by his con-artist father, a young Richard begins telling lies to his friends to hide his past. His search for a new identity takes root in a particular obsession—looting books. As a schoolboy he steals his first book, *Dracula*, and at Cambridge he steals compulsively, sometimes twice a day. He takes an eclectic range of works: valuable first editions; used paperbacks; novels by Anthony Burgess, Nabokov, and Bellow; the collected poems of A. E. Housman; and an edition of Byron's letters—nearly 12,000 in all. His penchant for looting spills over into other avenues of criminal behavior, as he forges stolen checks and burgles houses. He uses his stolen wealth on shopping trips in London, where he wears his "blue suit," a uniform with big lapels and a cardboard feel that, he imagines, lends him an aura of invulnerability.

"I spent my youth desperately afraid of someone finding out about my family," Rayner explained to Julia Llewellyn Smith in an interview for the *Times* (July 12, 1995). "I was so embarrassed with my own self. . . . I was scrambling round for any kind of identity that I invented this weird criminal career for myself. I lived in a state of terror, but I was very calmly able to do these reckless things. . . . Obviously, morally I can't defend myself. I'm not asking people to say it's all all right," he said. "I have made myself a hostage to fortune. I think it's actually a very moral book about an immoral period in my life. It's a story about someone learning what it means to be responsible."

Ben Macintyre, in a review for the *New York Times* (October 22, 1995), wrote that Rayner "tells his tale with a matter-of-factness that makes compelling if sometimes chilling reading. Quite how much of the forger is reflected in his writing remains a disquieting question. . . . Richard Rayner is a deft and dexterous writer, with the wit and self-irony to pull off what might otherwise be a hackneyed story of moral regeneration." Responding to critics who questioned the veracity of his account, Rayner told Smith: "People are always saying that some of the anecdotes are too far-fetched to have really happened but the ones they quote are almost invariably the truth. My experiences are too bizarre to invent. But the book is very structured and its aim was to be as compelling as possible."

For his next novel, *Murder Book*, Rayner drew upon his experiences shadowing the Los Angeles Police Department (LAPD), first in 1992 while covering the Los Angeles riots for *Granta*, and then in 1996 while writing a cover story on the LAPD for the *New York Times Magazine*. Billy McGrath, the narrator and protagonist of the novel, is a former philosophy student who has become a homicide detective for the LAPD. (He calls the binders of files on unsolved homicides that accumulate in his office "murder books.") Billy has fallen on hard times: he is divorced from his wife, whom he still loves, and struggles to be a good father to his young daughter. His desperation to make amends for past sins sets the stage for a profound moral dilemma. A middle-aged woman is found murdered, and the dead woman's son turns out to be Ricky Lee Richards, a powerful gangster and drug dealer. Richards, seeking vigilante justice, offers Billy $500,000 for the name of the killer. Though he at first ignores the offer, Billy is tempted by the money, which could help his ex-wife and daughter, and perhaps atone for his mistakes. He is further spurred on by a gnawing cynicism about the legal system and eventually sets in motion a scheme to seek his own justice.

Sybil S. Steinberg, writing for *Publishers Weekly* (September 1, 1997), called *Murder Book* "a taut, intricately plotted thriller" and noted that, "while Rayner's prose is occasionally too hard-boiled, as if it's parodying pulp detective novels, these missteps are rare. Mostly the novel has just the right punch, and its portraits of the contemporary American city gone bad are oddly moving." With *Murder Book* Rayner began to give more thought to structuring his plots. "Up until *Murder Book*, all I was trying to do was write an entertaining page and then write an entertaining page after that," he told Rowlands. He came to realize "that these things work better if you have a plan."

Rayner's planning is evident in *The Cloud Sketcher*, an epic story of love and ambition set in the early part of the 20th century. Esko Vaananen, a young boy with a scarred face and troubled relationship with his father, comes of age in Finland, fights in the Finnish Civil War of 1918, and eventually travels to America to pursue his dream of being an architect. From his remote and primitive Finnish village, Esko first learns of the technological advancements of the age—particularly the invention of the elevator. Struggling to decipher "the meaning of the elevator," he experiences a vision of a beautiful skyscraper—"*pilvenpiirtaja*" in Finnish, which means "cloud sketcher"—and from that moment determines to build such a marvel. He takes part in the Civil War out of love for Katerina Malysheva, the daughter of a Russian aristocrat whom he considers to be his muse. Years later, when Esko discovers some photographs taken by Katerina in an American magazine, *Vanity Fair*, he travels to New York City and discovers the pulsing excitement of Jazz Age New York, where skyscrapers are on the rise.

Meghan O'Rourke, in a review of *The Cloud Sketcher* for the *Los Angeles Times* (March 11, 2001) wrote that "Rayner has a strong sense for the textures of time and place—the pale, melancholic light of the Finnish landscape and the heated, highly sexual energy of New York during the 1920s—and the novel's greatest strength is its intensely filmic descriptions of the rhythms of pounding steel girders together high in the sky or the pleasurable claustrophobia of a reckless, drunken night in a Harlem club." Jabari Asim, in a review for the *Washington Post* (March 6, 2001), noted that "Rayner has written a completely engaging read, an impressive meditation on longing and obsession that's also a searching reflection on the act of creation itself."

Rayner did extensive research for the novel. "I read books, spoke to many architects and professors of architecture, spent days on end walking around buildings—churches and skyscrapers especially," he said in an interview posted on the HarperCollins Web site. "While I was doing this something rather wonderful happened. It's the book's gift to me, I guess. I began to experience architecture in a different way. That's to say, I realized the extent to which designed space can have an effect on you—for good or ill. When you walk inside a great building your spirit lifts. It's an actual physical experience. Some buildings kiss you, others comfort you, some put strength in your stride and make you walk with extra snap and confidence. Some buildings—like The Chrysler Building, or Frank Lloyd Wright's Guggenheim, or Lars Sonck's cathedral in Tampere in Finland—just make you gasp with joy and sheer amazement at the idea that someone, another human being, thought of and caused to be made this extraordinary, beautiful, breathtaking space. I became preoccupied with this and one of the things I tried hard to do in *The Cloud Sketcher* (I don't know whether I succeeded) was to describe the experience of architecture in this emotional way, and to consider what it might be like to be a man—my hero, Esko Vaananen—whose life's dream is to sculpt joy out of stone and air." Rayner attributes the book's Finnish setting to his Finnish wife, Paivi, whom he met in her homeland in 1990, while on a writing assignment. The film rights for *The Cloud Sketcher* were sold to the English director Alan Parker, who is developing the screenplay.

In his most recent work, *Drake's Fortune: The Fabulous True Story of the World's Greatest Confidence Artist* (2002), Rayner presents the life of the real-life swindler Oscar Hartzell, who between the years of 1914 and 1933 conned 100,000 Midwesterners out of millions of dollars. Hartzell was in his late 30s when he stumbled upon a scheme involving the allegedly misappropriated fortune of Sir Frances Drake. He began seeking donations for a legal fund that would return the mythical estate to its rightful heirs; in exchange, all investors would be guaranteed "shares" of the fortune, which was said to be valued at more than $1 billion. Although Hartzell had not invented the fraud, he used it to swindle millions from unsuspecting contributors. For a time he took the money abroad, living lavishly among London's aristocracy. Scotland Yard eventually built a strong enough case to deport him back to the U.S. to stand trial. Hartzell was imprisoned for his crimes and eventually died in a mental hospital. Rayner's biography was widely praised for its wealth of original research and its lively depiction of one of America's most notorious con artists. As one critic noted for *Publishers Weekly*, as quoted on *Amazon.com*, "Rayner's account of Hartzell's life and times is brisk and breezy, a terrifically entertaining read, and the author's obvious fascination with his subject is infectious." He continued, "But this is more than just a gripping tale: Rayner also laces his narrative with savvy commentary including insights into the psyches of swindler and victim alike that helps explain why cons like Hartzell occupy such a place in American history."

Rayner lives in Los Angeles, California, with Paivi and their two young children, Harry and Charlie.

—A. I. C.

SUGGESTED READING: London Review of Books p18 June 27, 1991; Los Angeles Times BR p2 Mar. 11, 2001; The Nation p712 Dec. 4, 1995; New York Times C p32 Oct. 27, 1995; Publishers Weekly p94 Sep. 1, 1997, p58+ Mar. 5, 2001; (London) Times p1 July 12, 1995; USA Today (on-line) Feb. 22, 2001; Washington Post B p2 Oct. 4, 1995, C p2 Mar. 6, 2001

SELECTED BOOKS: Los Angeles Without a Map, 1988; The Elephant, 1992; The Blue Suit, 1995; Murder Book, 1997; Cloud Sketcher, 2000; Drake's Fortune: The Fabulous True Story of the World's Greatest Confidence Artist, 2002

Graham Clark/Courtesy of HarperCollins

Ridley, Matt

(?)– Science writer; journalist

Matt Ridley, an acclaimed science writer, is the author of *Genome: The Autobiography of a Species in 23 Chapters* (2000). Following in the wake of successful efforts to sequence the entire human genome by the government-funded Human Genome Project and the private-sector organization Celera Genomics, Ridley wrote *Genome* to show the ways in which genes are connected to disease, intelligence, and human personality. The book was a popular success, and critics praised Ridley for his enthusiasm about the subject, his familiarity with the field, his avoidance of technical jargon, and his storytelling ability. Ridley is also the author of *The Red Queen: Sex and the Evolution of Human Nature* (1994), a work describing the link between natural selection and human behavior, and *The Origins of Virtue: Human Instincts and the Evolution of Cooperation* (1996), a book on evolutionary ethics. Ridley is a former science editor and journalist for the *Economist*.

Matt Ridley did not plan on becoming a writer. In an interview with Frederick Kaufman for *Publishers Weekly* (March 6, 2000), he explained: "I started out wanting to be a naturalist. My obsession in my youth was birdwatching. I collected things, I spent a lot of time outdoors. I only vaguely realized that science was a little more than natural history, but by then I was hooked." Ridley studied the works of Gerald Durrell, Richard Dawkins, and Stephen Jay Gould, and earned a Ph.D., in zoology, from Oxford University, in Oxford, England. He soon realized, however, that the actual practice of science was not something that interested him. "I didn't have sufficient patience for detail," Ridley recalled to Kaufman. "I liked big pictures rather than small details, and unlike my colleagues I enjoyed the process of writing up my thesis. I actually liked the writing, so I thought maybe journalism was the thing for me. I thought journalism would enable me to be a mile wide and an inch deep."

Ridley began submitting unsolicited manuscripts to numerous publications, and before long *New Scientist* featured one of his pieces for its cover story. Ridley told Kaufman: "Then I heard that the *Economist* science editor had died, and I thought maybe they were looking for new people on their science side, so I rang them up, and because I had a sheaf of clippings they gave me a three-month trial, at the end of which they offered me a job." Ridley worked as a journalist and science editor at the *Economist* for nine years. For a time he served as the magazine's Washington bureau chief and covered the 1988 presidential race. (He wrote a book on the election, *Warts and All: The Men Who Would Be Bush* [1989], which did not sell well.)

Ridley found that he enjoyed the process of writing a book, however, and in a few years completed a second book, *The Red Queen: Sex and the Evolution of Human Nature*. In it he discusses the theory that sex has evolved as a means of outwitting parasites—a theory some biologists see as a viable answer as to why sexual reproduction exists for some species when others are able to survive without it. As Ridley outlines in the book, living creatures in most environments are under continuous assault from microscopic parasites and viruses. Sex between organisms evolved as a means of swapping genetic material, which allowed the organisms to stay one step ahead of the parasites and accordingly increase the species' chances for survival. Since the parasites continue to adapt themselves to the new genetic combinations, the process is never-ending. This idea, credited to Oxford University's William Hamilton, is known as the "Red Queen" theory, after the character in Lewis Carroll's *Through the Looking Glass* who must keep running as fast as possible just to stay in the same place. Using this theory as his point of departure and drawing examples of mating behavior from the animal kingdom, Ridley makes some controversial arguments: for example, he posits that females have encouraged such masculine traits as aggression, promiscuity, and risk-taking by choosing males with these characteristics as mates. The book was a popular success and garnered mostly positive reviews. An anonymous critic for *Kirkus Reviews*, quoted on *Amazon.com*, wrote that the book was "extensively researched, clearly written: one of the best introductions to its fascinating and controversial subject." Peter Tallack, in a review for the *Economist* (November 20, 1993), cited some negative aspects, however: "Many of the evolutionary explanations in this book—seductive, imaginative and thought-provoking though they are—remain 'Just So' stories, dancing on the shores of speculation. [Ridley] pays scant regard, for instance, to the unpredictable contingencies of history, to the accidental by-products, relics and blind alleys of human evolution that have given rise to such superfluous features as the appendix and the male nipple." He admitted, though, that "Mr. Ridley explains the ins and outs of a complex and often controversial subject clearly, accurately, and entertainingly."

Ridley's next book, *The Origins of Virtue: Human Instincts and the Evolution of Cooperation*, is a continuation of Ridley's interest in applying the findings of biological science to questions of human motivation and behavior. In *The Origins of Virtue* he argues that many social traits considered to be virtuous are actually the result of natural selection. The book is Ridley's attempt to answer the apparent contradiction that natural selection, guided as it is by "selfish" genes seeking only to reproduce themselves, could result in virtuous behavior. According to Ridley, genes for such traits as cooperation are carried on to succeeding generations because cooperative behavior often results in better chances for survival. Ridley introduces an example known as "the prisoner's dilemma" to demonstrate this point: Two prisoners are caught by the police, and the state needs a confession to prove its case. If both prisoners deny the crime, both can go free. If interrogated separately, the prisoners are more likely to confess, not knowing what the other prisoner will do. When the scenario is programmed into a computer and played out repeatedly, however, the computer-generated prisoners learn over time that it's best to keep quiet. According to Ripley, this and other examples serve to show that where cooperation is mutually beneficial, it will be selected. From here Ripley develops his argument that self-interested cooperation can be seen as forming the basis of such human institutions as trade relationships, the division of labor, and property rights. Michael J. Behe, writing for the conservative publication *National Review* (June 2, 1997), noted that Ridley "defends economic and political ideas with which many readers of *National Review* will concur. But he does so from within the murky confines of Darwinism." He continued, "To defend free trade, private property, and limited government one need not invoke a dubious biological theory." An anonymous reviewer for the *Economist* (December 7, 1996) remarked that "Ripley is easily one of the best science writers around," but that compared to *The Red Queen*, "*The Origins of Virtue* comes as a disappointment: overambitious in scope, frustratingly muddled in argument and showing tell-tale signs of haste."

Ridley's next project was researching the unprecedented discoveries being made in the field of gene sequencing and the race to find and map the complete sequence of human genes. Ridley secured his first six-figure advance for *Genome: The Autobiography of a Species in 23 Chapters*, his best-selling book to date. He had to work fast to keep up with the pace of research; on June 26, 2000, President Bill Clinton announced the successful sequencing of the human genetic code. Scientists had succeeded in reading 3.2 billion DNA base pairs, years ahead of the original forecast made by the Human Genome Project.

Dean H. Hamer, in a review of the book for *Scientific American* (April 2000), wrote that "Ridley's excitement about the science has the benefit that the book is very much up-to-date, with many of the references from just the past year. And even the most speculative of his ideas is made palatable by the consistently graceful language and imaginative use of metaphors." He concluded, "*Genome* provides a delightful introduction to all who wish to follow the career of this rising star."

In *Genome*, Ridley explores how genetic sequencing reveals the genetic underpinnings of memory, intelligence, sex, personality, and language. He describes the genetic sequence as a sort of book, 800 times longer than the Bible, and extending back in time over three-billion years, tracing the historical forces that shaped our species. Extending this metaphor, Ridley explains that the words of the genetic book are called "codons," each codon a combination of three out of the four DNA bases (adenine, thymine, cytosine, and guanine). The 64 possible combinations are what make up the 20 amino acids, which in turn are the elements that comprise the proteins of the human body.

Genome is divided into 23 chapters to mirror the 23 chromosomes found in human DNA. In each chapter Ridley chooses one gene from each of the 23 chromosomes and uses it to tell a story about how the gene is related to human behavior. In chapter four, for example, he discusses the gene responsible for Huntington's chorea, a disorder involving the degeneration of nerve cells in the cerebrum resulting in abnormal body movements and dementia. The gene contains a codon, CAG (cytosine, adenine, and guanine), which is repeated as few as six and as many as 100 times. When the

CAG codon is repeated less than 35 times, there is no threat of disease, but if the repetition is higher, the chances increase that the disease will manifest itself. The benefit of such information, according to Ridley, is that in the future medical practitioners will be able to correct such disorders at the genetic level, before they can become a threat. Other ailments Ridley foresees as amenable to genetic engineering include heart disease, cancer, arthritis, and diabetes.

Not only will genetic research allow humans to combat disease, but it will make it possible to enhance personality traits as well. Ridley discusses research, for example, that shows that children with high IQ's are twice as likely as the general population to have a slightly different version of the IGF2R gene, which scientists believe is related to how bodies use glucose to produce energy. Based on findings like this, it is possible that parents will soon be able to modify certain genes in their children, thus enhancing their intelligence. In *Genome*, Ridley discusses the fact that such discoveries bring with them a host of moral questions about how humans ought to exercise these newfound capabilities. Ridley likes to emphasize the distinction between genetic engineering, used to correct disease, and cosmetic engineering, used to enhance personality traits (like athletic ability, for example). He unquestionably supports the former, but the latter, he acknowledges, is a difficult and divisive subject. In some sense, he prefers to sidestep the question. In an article he authored for *National Review* (July 31, 2000), titled "The New Eugenics," Ridley noted that, "it is fashionable to answer that we should not [pursue genetic enhancement], that we probably nonetheless will, and that that would be a disaster; I am more sanguine. Genetically modified people will not pose a great threat to society, even if we choose to create them: but we will, on the whole, not choose to create them, so there is little to worry about on this score." Ridley believes, for example, that parents will be less likely to genetically engineer their children than is commonly supposed: "I simply cannot think of a single feature of my own children that I would have liked to fix in advance. People do not want particular types of children; they just want their own children, and they want them to be a bit like themselves. When faced with a mediocre hand at poker, you change some of the cards and start again. But when faced with perhaps 40,000 human genes, any of which you could change for what may or may not be a slightly better version, which would you change?" Should cosmetic genetic engineering become acceptable, however, Ridley maintains that this will not be so terrible a fate. In response to the objection that genetic engineering will drive out diversity as people converge on an "ideal," he writes that "far from threatening genetic diversity, genetic engineering may actually increase it. . . . Musical people might seek out musical genes for their children; athletes might seek athletic genes; etc. It is very unlikely that everybody would choose the same priority."

Ridley maintains that he is not a genetic determinist. Although he reports that, in the case of intelligence for example, most studies find a substantial hereditary factor, he also says that distinguishing environmental from genetic influences on intelligence is virtually impossible. "You inherit not your IQ but your ability to develop a high IQ under certain environmental circumstances," Ridley writes in *Genome*, as quoted by Ronald Bailey in *Reason* (August/September 2000). Michael Shermer, in *American Scientist* (January/February 2001), noted that "in most cases Ridley does an admirable job of clarifying the enormous complexities involved in gene-environment interactions, demonstrating in numerous cases that it is next to impossible to say that any complex human trait (such as intelligence or athletic ability) is, say, 60 percent genetically determined and 40 percent environmentally shaped." Shermer also noted, however, that despite Ridley's caveats, readers are likely to take away from the book an inflated view of the role of genetics in determining behavior.

Ripley broadens his discussion of gene modification in *Genome* with a look at the ugly history of eugenics, documenting not only the well-known views propagated in Nazi Germany, but those espoused by such prominent figures as H. G. Wells, John Maynard Keynes, and George Bernard Shaw. One of Ridley's main arguments is that eugenics is a danger of politics, not of technological advancement. In his article, "The New Eugenics," he tries to separate eugenics from the morally offensive political ends in which it has become implicated in the 20th century: "The eugenic movement began with the best of intentions. Many of its most strident advocates were socialists, who saw eugenics as enlightened state planning of reproduction. But what it actually achieved, when translated into policies, was a human-rights catastrophe: the rejection of many immigrants, the sterilization of many people whose only crime was to have below-average intelligence, and eventually, in Germany, the murder of millions of people." As Ridley sees it, genetic research has made it possible for a new eugenics. This new eugenics is acceptable because, "whereas eugenics, conceived in the early part of the 20th century, was a public project, modern genetic screening is a private matter." He continued, "Modern eugenics is about individuals applying private criteria to improve their own offspring by screening their genes. The benefits are individual, and any drawbacks are social—exactly the opposite of the old eugenics."

In his writings and interviews, Ridley remains enthusiastic about the future of genetic research, while acknowledging the possible negative consequences. In a recent interview posted on the BBC News Web site, Ridley stated that "what I'm most looking forward to I think is understanding the entire human genome. I think that's a fantastic intellectual advance on the part of our species really." He admitted, though, "What I most fear I think about the future is that we haven't really done anything to improve human competence and human nature. The technology gets better and better but people don't get better and better and the potential for individuals to wreak havoc on the fellow members of the human race is still as great as ever."

Ridley recently helped establish the International Centre for Life, a visitors' center and research facility in the northeast of England. As chairman of the project, Ridley worked to find ways to tell the history of the gene and the brain in a manner that people without a science background would be able to understand. The experience of working with local politicians and businessmen on the project occupied most of his time, as Ridley told Frederick Kaufman: "These kinds of things are a bit of a string of crises. So I have no time to be writing a book." Ridley told Kaufman that he hopes to return to writing soon; this time, however, "I'd like to write a book in less of a hurry than I've done the previous books. Particularly *Genome*. Once I started I knew I had to finish within a year—because otherwise I'd have to keep going back and starting again, the subject is moving so fast. The kind of book I'd like to write would be a book that would take me five or six years to finish."

Ridley's most recent work is *Nature via Nurture: Genes, Experience, and What Makes Us Human*, published in May 2003. He currently lives in England with his wife, Anya Hurlbert, a professor of neuroscience, and their two children. He is a journalist for the *Daily Telegraph* and a contributor to numerous publications, including the *Wall Street Journal*, *National Review*, *Natural History*, and *Time*.

—A. I. C.

SUGGESTED READING: *American Scientist* p74+ Jan./Feb. 2001; *Economist* p110 Nov. 20, 1993; *National Review* p52+ June 2, 1997, p34+ July 31, 2000; *Publishers Weekly* p76+ Mar. 6, 2000; *Reason* p58+ Aug./Sep. 2000; *Sciences* p47+ July/Aug. 2000; *Scientific American* p114+ Apr. 2000; *Wall Street Journal* A p17 Mar. 26, 1997

SELECTED BOOKS: *The Red Queen: Sex and the Evolution of Human Nature*, 1994; *The Origins of Virtue: Human Instincts and the Evolution of Cooperation*, 1996; *Genome: The Autobiography of a Species in 23 Chapters*, 2000

Rivera, José

1955– Playwright

José Rivera, the Puerto Rican–born playwright, has achieved international recognition for his contributions to contemporary theater. Bruce Weber, in an article for the *New York Times* (April 12, 2001), remarked that "José Rivera writes with half his mind on credible reality and the other half in fantasyland. His characters tend to live in a world where magical and concrete forces coexist, where life's anchoring burdens do battle with uncommonly potent wishes and dreams." Rivera's plays have been translated into seven languages and performed at theaters across the United States, as well as in Mexico, Puerto Rico, Peru, Scotland, Greece, Sweden, Norway, England, and France. He received an Obie award for *Marisol*, in 1993, and one for *References to Salvador Dali Make Me Hot*, in 2001. His other plays include *The House of Ramón Iglesia*,*The Promise*, *Each Day Dies with Sleep*, *Cloud Tectonics*, *Giants Have Us In Their Books*, *Sueño*, *The Street of the Sun*, *Sonnets For an Old Century*, and *Maricela de la Luz Lights the World*. Rivera co-created and produced the critically acclaimed NBC series *Eerie, Indiana*, and his other television credits include episodes of *Goosebumps* and *Family Matters*. His movie credits include *The Jungle Book: Mowgli's Story* and the 3-D IMAX film *Riding the Comet*.

José Rivera was born in 1955 in Arecibo, Puerto Rico. His family moved to Long Island, New York, when he was four. He was inspired by his teachers in the New York public schools, and became the

Jeff Geissler/AP Photo

first in his family to go to college. "I had several male teachers," Rivera told Sandra Dillard-Rosen for the *Denver Post* (April 20, 1995). "That . . . was a revelation. The male teachers pushed me, and admired my writing." As a young man he lived in the Bronx and got a job as a copywriter at a publishing company, a position he held for four years. "I was the only Puerto Rican there," Rivera told Dillard-Rosen. "The only Puerto Ricans most of them were familiar with were doormen and delivery guys. I had to sort of challenge them about what a Puerto Rican was. They had very stereotypical ideas." In his spare time Rivera wrote plays, and in the spring of 1983, his first professional production, *The House of Ramón Iglesia*, premiered at the Ensemble Studio Theatre, a nonprofit group in New York City that develops new works. He quit his job that year to pursue a career as a playwright. In an article he wrote for *Parabasis* (Spring 1998), Rivera recalled the difficulties of making a living in theater. "I have survived on the strength of my family, on luck, love, persistence, friendships, and an obsessive desire to survive," he wrote. *The House of Ramón Iglesia* was a notable success, and in 1986 it was broadcast on the public-television series *American Playhouse*.

In two of his subsequent plays, *The Promise* and *Each Day Dies With Sleep*, Rivera used the techniques of magical realism to explore aspects of the Puerto Rican experience that he felt were being neglected by contemporary Latino drama. (For a time Rivera had studied under the Nobel Prize–winning writer Gabriel García Márquez, who is known for his use of magic realism.) "These plays were a response on my part to the prevailing tendency in Latino drama at the time I wrote them towards gritty realism and urban drug culture," Rivera wrote in a 1995 article for the Non-Traditional Casting Project, as reprinted on the group's Web site. "Instead, I wanted to incorporate more of the life I knew. I wanted to discuss Latino culture in a small town, semi-rural environment—with an emphasis on family, sexuality, spirituality, and the occult." *Each Day Dies with Sleep* premiered in 1989. "Here is a production to restore our faith in live theater, and a play to restore our interest in new theater," Alastair Macaulay wrote for the London *Financial Times*, as quoted on the Broadway Play Publishing Web site. "Its real subject is the primitive human struggle between animal instincts and civilized order. The language—poetic, intense, heightened, rude, stunted, funny, by turns—is always vivid." He continued, "[The play's] conception of the human condition as a psychic battleground—lively, funny, erotic, tragic—has a rare force."

Rivera's next play, *Marisol*, premiered in 1992 at the Humana Festival at the Actors Theatre of Louisville. The play's protagonist, Marisol Perez, is a young textbook editor who lives in the New York City borough of the Bronx and works in Manhattan. One day on the subway, a crazed homeless person threatens to bludgeon Marisol with a golf club. The next day, when she reads in the paper that someone with her name has been killed, Marisol wonders whether she is in fact alive or dead, awake or dreaming. As the play progresses, the division between reality and dream rapidly dissolves. Marisol meets her guardian angel, who informs her that God has become senile and is dying and that the angels are staging a rebellion. Marisol then journeys through a surreal cityscape that's been strangely distorted by the sedition in heaven: a pregnant man gives birth to a dead baby; a woman is brutally beaten for exceeding her credit-card limit; a burn victim appears, in search of his lost skin.

In *Marisol* the surreal encounters and apocalyptic visions function not as a prediction of a likely future, but as a commentary on the gruesome aspects of contemporary urban society. Following a well-received opening, the play moved to New York, where it was produced off-Broadway at the Joseph Papp Public Theater, in 1993. The successful production earned Rivera an Obie award for outstanding play of that year. Dan Hulbert, writing for *The Atlanta Journal-Constitution* (September 18, 1998) called *Marisol* a "funny, disturbing fever dream of a play" and praised Rivera for his "redeeming talent for language and an instinct for theatrical surprise." *Marisol* has sometimes been compared with Tony Kushner's *Angels in America*, which was also produced in New York in 1993, features a visiting angel, and conveys a similar millennial apprehension. William Tiplett, in a review of the Trumpet Vine Theater Company production for the *Washington Post* (April 12, 2000), wrote that "Rivera seems to have all of Kushner's passion but little of his narrative skill. . . . Overall the fragmented, episodic story, meant to evoke 'magical realism,' doesn't cohere. Events seem to come out of nowhere. A variety of creepy characters appear, then disappear. Unlike Kushner, Rivera develops no relationships that will show the bruising and bloodying effects of the corrupt world he envisions." In general, however, reviews were positive, and the play enjoyed numerous productions throughout the 1990s.

Giants Have Us In Their Books: Six Children's Plays for Adults premiered in 1994 at San Francisco's Magic Theater. The idea for the work originated with Rivera's four-year-old daughter, who speculated that if humans have giants in their fairytales, then the giants must have humans in theirs. Robert Huwitt, in a review for the *San Francisco Examiner*, as quoted on the Broadway Play Publishing Web site, wrote that the six one-act plays "have all the beautiful simplicity of fairy tales. . . . Rivera's prose has become more concentrated and spare, more pregnant with metaphor and poetry. The profuse and sometimes self-consciously fantastical stew of magic realism—which . . . Rivera insists is just another form of everyday reality—has been condensed so that each image carries greater weight. The six short fables in *Giants* add up to two hours of compelling, entertaining and provocative theater." In March 2001 the International Arts Relations (INTAR) Hispanic American Arts Center in New York City included *Giants* in its 35th-anniversary celebration.

Rivera's next work, *Sueño*, is an adaptation of the Spanish playwright Calderon de la Barca's 17th-century classic, *La Vida Es Sueño* (*Life Is a Dream*). Rivera's version, which premiered in 1995 at the Hartford Stage, in Connecticut, focuses on Prince Segismundo, son of Basilio, the king of

Spain. The king, in response to a prophecy that his newborn son will grow up to be a despot, has him imprisoned in a dungeon. Two decades later, Basilio relents and offers his son a chance at the throne. There is a catch, however: if Segismundo fails and the omens about his future bode true, then he will be returned to the dungeon and made to believe that his life as a ruler was only a dream. Segismundo's predicament thus provides the occasion for a meditation on the nature of reality and the forces of fate. Rivera altered some aspects of Calderon's original—the scene of the play, for example, has shifted from Poland in the Middle Ages to Spain in the 17th century. Most significantly, Rivera rewrote much of the dialogue to bring out the contemporary relevance of the play's themes. Ed Morales, writing in *American Theatre* (May/June 1998), noted that, "from Segismundo's opening soliloquies, where he proclaims himself a 'storm of chemical responses pretending to have a soul,' Rivera has reclaimed Calderon's florid use of metaphor and made it his own, spiced with science, sarcasm and sweetness." Rivera explained to Morales, "I wanted to find the language Calderon would have used if he was a 42-year-old playwright living in California." In bringing Calderon's play into modernity, Rivera also does away with some of its Christian underpinnings. "In the original, Segismundo gets attached to the idea that if everything is a dream, the dreamer must be God," Rivera told Morales. "What my version is trying to say is that the idea of God is unreliable."

References to Salvador Dali Make Me Hot premiered in January 2000 at California's South Coast Repertory Theater. The drama centers around Gabriela—a lonely Army wife stuck in a military town in the California desert—and her husband, Benito, who has just returned from the Persian Gulf War after a year's absence. Gabriela, frustrated by the limitations of her life, has been educating herself. Benito, a poorly educated Puerto Rican, has little patience with his wife's ambitions—especially when they cause her to neglect her domestic responsibilities. The human drama takes place within a surreal world of erotic fantasy: a house cat is seduced by a local coyote, and a lewd moon lusts after Gabriela. Rivera's play has political resonance as well; the marital disputes are accompanied by confrontations on such issues as government funding and the educational system.

A New York production of *Salvador Dali* opened at the Joseph Papp Public Theater in April 2001, starring Rosie Perez, the popular Hispanic actress who has appeared in such films as *Do the Right Thing* (1989) and *White Men Can't Jump* (1992). Bruce Weber noted that the production "contains a piquing nest of ideas. If its conscious juxtaposition of the literal and the surreal is more jarring than it means to be, under Jo Bonney's direction the play reaches an affecting emotional climax and it is intellectually provoking enough to linger." Randy Gener was positive in his review for *Broadway Online*: "Rivera's most lyrical creation since *Marisol*, *Salvador Dali* takes the form of a nightmare. . . . The language-driven play unravels the subconscious workings of a marriage that has reached a state of entropy." Some reviewers were more critical. Steven Winn, in an appraisal for the *San Francisco Chronicle* (November 22, 2000), remarked that the "overtly poetic scenes are self-conscious and overwritten. Where one image or metaphor might do, Rivera piles on a half-dozen to ever-decreasing effect." He concluded, "The desert rhapsodies and domestic turmoil don't merge in *Salvador Dali*. Rivera's overly decorated dramatic canvas never comes into focus." Rivera joined a small group of avant-garde luminaries, including Maria Irene Fornes, Eduardo Machado, and Mac Wellman, to offer writing classes for the 2001–2002 season at the Pataphysics Workshop for Playwrights at the Flea Theater in New York City. (The name derives from the French writer Alfred Jarry's definition of Pataphysics as the science of exceptions to general rules) According to the group's Web site, Rivera's course offered "discussion, exercises, and laughing at the whole deranged process of American playmaking."

Rivera has received support from the Kennedy Center Fund for New American Plays, the National Arts Club, the National Endowment for the Arts, the Rockefeller Foundation, the New York Foundation for the Arts, the Fulbright Commission, the Whiting Foundation, and the Berilla Kerr Foundation. He has served as a writer-in-residence at the Royal Court Theatre, in London.

In addition to his work for the stage, Rivera has written for television and film. In 1991 he collaborated with Karl Schaefer to create the television series *Eerie, Indiana*, which premiered on NBC on September 15 of that year. Rivera co-produced the show and wrote several of the episodes. A science-fiction drama following the otherworldly adventures of a 13-year-old boy, the show was inventive and humorous and managed to attract a small—but intensely loyal—group of fans. Ratings remained low, and the show was taken off the air after only seven months. Following the popular success of the TV series *X-Files*, the 19-episode series was re-aired in 1994.

—A. I. C.

SUGGESTED READING: *American Theatre* p42+ May/June 1998; *Atlanta Journal-Constitution* Q p6 Sep. 18, 1998; *Christian Science Monitor* Apr. 2, 1992; *Denver Post* E p8 Apr. 20, 1995; *Houston Chronicle* p1 Mar. 2, 1996; *Los Angeles Times* p1 Mar. 28, 1992; *New Republic* p29 July 19, 1993; *New York Times* C p11 Feb. 22, 1998, E p30 Mar. 3, 2000, E p5 Apr. 12, 2001; *Parabasis* Spring 1998; *San Francisco Chronicle* E p1 Nov. 22, 2000; *Village Voice* p90+ May 25, 1993, p97 June 8, 1993, p71 Mar. 14, 2000, p64 Apr. 3, 2001, p77 Apr. 24, 2001; *Washington Post* C p8 Jan. 17, 1995, C p8 Apr. 12, 2000, C p5 July 18, 2000

SELECTED PLAYS: *The House of Ramón Iglesia: A Drama In Two Acts*, 1983; *Promise*, 1988; *Marisol and Other Plays*, 1997; *Sueño: A Play In Three Acts*, 1999; *References to Salvador Dali Make Me Hot*, 2000

Lucy Bekeet/Courtesy of Random House

Roiphe, Katie

1968– Nonfiction writer; essayist

The American social critic Katie Roiphe has examined American attitudes toward sexuality, particularly among college students, in her widely discussed books: *The Morning After: Sex, Fear, and Feminism on Campus* (1993), in which she took to task militant feminist attitudes that she felt left women in a position of Victorian naïvete, ripe for sexual exploitation by men; and *Last Night in Paradise: Sex and Morals at the Century's End* (1997), in which she examined the influence of AIDS on this new puritanism. "I don't feel like I have the answers—I have the questions," Roiphe told the *Michigan Daily Online* (March 3, 1997). She recently brought themes of sexuality and feminism to her first novel, *Still She Haunts Me* (2001), a fictional account of the real-life relationship between Charles Dodgson—better known as Lewis Carroll—and his child-muse Alice Liddell.

The daughter of the novelist Anne Roiphe and Herman Roiphe, a psychoanalyst, Katie Roiphe was born in 1968 in New York City. She was one of the five daughters in her household, including her two stepsisters and her half-sister. Her mother, a progressive feminist, did not rear her daughters according to the strictures that had been placed on her own behavior when she was young. "I was always taught to be strong and assertive and to say what I thought," Roiphe told Paula Span in an interview for the *Washington Post* (October 22, 1993). Roiphe received her early education at the Brearley School, in New York. She did her undergraduate work at Harvard University and was a doctoral candidate in English literature at Princeton University when she entered the feminist dialogue with *The Morning After: Sex, Fear, and Feminism on Campus*. The book, which deals with date rape, caused a sensation, undermining as it did the militant feminists' claim that a "rape crisis" existed on the nation's college campuses. Roiphe described in an article for the *New York Times Magazine* (June 13, 1993) her impetus for writing the book: "One in four college women has been the victim of rape or attempted rape. One in four. I remember standing outside the dining hall in college, looking at a purple poster with this statistic written in bold letters. It didn't seem right." She went on to state that she would surely know if one-quarter of her friends had been raped, and she concluded that "the so-called rape epidemic on campuses is more a way of interpreting, a way of seeing, than a physical phenomenon. It is more about a change in sexual politics than a change in sexual behavior."

Roiphe went on to argue that, despite what the one-in-four statistic suggests, women today are not as naive as women of the 18th century, as depicted in Samuel Richardson's *Clarissa*, whose eponymous heroine fell prey to a bad man. She observed that the myth of innocence might be just that—a myth—"convenient, appealing, politically effective." Her argument went on to accuse the definers of date rape of creating a climate in which "everything that is unpleasant and disturbing about relations between the sexes" becomes a case of rape. Thus, she observed, "I wonder how many people there are, male or female, who haven't been date-raped at one point or another." She concluded with an attack on those who would warn women against men's sexual wiles and give all women victim status: "Rape-crisis feminists threaten the progress that's been made. They are chasing the same stereotypes our mothers spent so much energy escaping."

Roiphe's frankness in *The Morning After* drew the fire of committed feminists. In an interview with Roiphe and her mother, conducted by Barbara Presley Noble for the *New York Times* (November 10, 1993), Roiphe maintained that a "vital political movement" would survive criticism from within. "You should be able to say: 'I am a feminist. I do think that we need to modify the way we're talking about rape, the images we're projecting.' Feminism should be large enough to encompass . . . maverick positions."

Particularly outraged by Roiphe's views was Mary P. Koss, a social scientist at the University of Arizona, whose data Roiphe used—or, as Koss put it in a letter to the *New York Times Magazine* (August 15, 1993), "misstate[d] and dismisse[d]." Koss insisted that her definition of rape was a legal one and that although "rape prevalence numbers vary depending on the methodology used, all published studies describe a magnitude of rape that commands social concern." The philosopher Jean Bethke Elshtain, in an on-line review of *The Morning After* in *First Things* (April 1994), defended Roiphe, maintaining that numbers of forcible rapes had not increased and suggesting that Roiphe's insistence on "spheres of co-responsibility" was courageous, since "the dominant narrative, now a standard genre, holds that women are once more sexual innocents, men once more sexual brutes."

Many mainstream-media reviewers of *The Morning After*, such as Cathy Young—writing in the *Washington Post Book World* (September 19, 1993)—remained noncommittal with regard to Roiphe's arguments, while generally praising her writing. "Having grown up believing in feminism as a celebration of female autonomy and strength," Young wrote, "Roiphe is appalled by the assumptions of passivity and frailty implicit in the notion of rape by 'verbal coercion,' by the paternalism of attempts to protect women not just from sexual blackmail but from sexual innuendo. . . . The answer, she insists, does not lie . . . in 'chasing the same stereotypes our mothers spent so much energy running away from,' but in embracing the risks and burdens of freedom and adulthood."

In *Commentary* (September 1993), the conservative journal issued by the American Jewish Committee, Carol Iannone not only supported Roiphe's conclusions but expressed her opinion that Roiphe had not gone far enough. "In her fresh-faced, earnest way, Roiphe underestimates the rising feminist tyranny her book amply documents," she wrote, concluding, however, that Roiphe "is perfectly right to emphasize the need for individual responsibility; but one nevertheless understands that women want also to feel a sense of cultural support."

Last Night in Paradise: Sex and Morals at the Century's End (1997) is Roiphe's examination of how the AIDS crisis has affected sexual mores. In it, she lamented what she saw as the use of the epidemic to impose a new puritanism on society. "Roiphe dissects our obsession with . . . safety, our craving for rules, and our 'perverse nostalgia' for simpler times, asserting finally that sex, like everything else, is dangerous, complicated and confusing," Donna Seaman wrote in *Booklist* (March 15, 1997). Other reviewers were far less sympathetic toward Roiphe's discussion of the disease. Emily Gordon observed in the *Nation* (May 5, 1997) that Roiphe "conspicuously skirts the facts of AIDS . . . preferring instead to mark the cultural sign-posts and social trends it has produced." In the book, Gordon declared, "Roiphe manages to do just what she claims the 'date-rape feminists' and safer-sex missionaries do: create new myths instead of confronting reality."

Jean Bethke Elshtain, writing in the *Times Literary Supplement* (June 6, 1997), found contradictory attitudes in *Last Night in Paradise*. She cited Roiphe's description of her oldest sister's unrestrained sex life and drug use, which culminated in her being diagnosed with the HIV virus: "Roiphe describes her sister's appearance as 'upsetting' and her demeanor as strange and remote . . . but she cannot help romanticizing Emily's rebellion. . . . Why this need on Roiphe's part (and that of most of the book-writing class of Americans) to believe that those who experiment on the farthest edges of human possibility see more, know more, live fuller (if shorter) lives? . . . Her memoir is at odds with itself." Elshtain concluded, however, that "Roiphe does find 'true rebels' in the end, not in the sexually promiscuous, but in those young people 'resisting the pressure to be carefree and defying the seductive authority of their peers.'"

Roiphe's real crusade has not been against feminism, nor has she attempted to condone the behavior of rapists. What she has tried to express in her writings is the voice of reason: "The problem is not rage, but rage that is unexamined and uncontrolled," she wrote in an op-ed piece in the *New York Times* (November 29, 1993). "Unexamined anger misleads and divides us; it makes it impossible to talk and listen, to think in nuances, with clarity."

Most recently Roiphe expanded into the genre of fiction with her novel *Still She Haunts Me* (2001), an imagined account of the unusual friendship between the Oxford mathematician and photographer Charles Dodgson, more widely known by the pen name Lewis Carroll, and the young girl for whom he composed *Alice in Wonderland*, Alice Liddell. The novel opens with Alice's mother informing Dodgson, "It is no longer desirable for you to spend time with our family," as quoted by Stella Clarke for the *Australian* (December 22, 2001). In the book Roiphe explores the seven-year relationship that commenced when Alice was just four years old and Dodgson was in his early 20s. As she attempts to uncover the true nature of the friendship—whether it involved sexual overtones or was instead driven by Dodgson's attraction to the purity of childhood—Roiphe presents a complex exploration of Dodgson, relying on real letters, fictional diaries, and her own speculation to characterize the elusive figure.

Overall, the critical response to Roiphe's interpretation was decidedly mixed. While some critics praised her efforts to shed light on a curious piece of literary history, others were disappointed in the results. Some reviews criticized Roiphe's invented diary entries as incongruous and somewhat inconsistent with the real-life Dodgson's published works, and found fault in her tendency to match imagined scenes with their counterparts in *Alice in Wonderland*. Nevertheless, other critics applauded the piece as a powerful commentary on the Victorian era. While Clarke called the book "an intriguing first novel" and "enchanting," Jeanne

Schinto for the *Women's Review of Books* (October 2001) opined, "Fiction fans . . . may be just as disappointed as I was that Roiphe has squandered a stellar idea. . . . If Roiphe had been up to the task, we might have gone with her on a truly imaginative journey into the mind of a muse-haunted artist. As it stands, we've been shown the rabbit-hole, but not taken down it."

Roiphe resides in New York City.

—S. Y.

SUGGESTED READING: *Booklist* p1208 Mar. 15, 1997; *First Things* p43+ Apr. 1994; *Nation* p31 May 5, 1997; *New Yorker* p220 Oct. 4, 1993; *New York Times* C p1 Nov. 10, 1993, A p17 Nov. 29, 1993; *New York Times Magazine* p26 June 13, 1993, p6 Aug. 15, 1993; *Times Literary Supplement* p26 Nov. 11, 1994, p26 June 6, 1997; *Washington Post* C p1 Oct. 22, 1993; *Washington Post Book World* p3 Sep. 19, 1993

SELECTED BOOKS: nonfiction—*The Morning After: Sex, Fear, and Feminism on Campus*, 1993; *Last Night in Paradise: Sex and Morals at Century's End*, 1997; fiction—*Still She Haunts Me*, 2001

Courtesy of Harcourt Trade Publicity

Rosenblatt, Roger

Sep. 13, 1940– Nonfiction writer

Roger Rosenblatt has built a solid reputation over the last 30 years for his acclaimed writing and striking social commentaries. In addition to contributing essays to such national publications as *Time*, *Life*, *New Republic*, *U.S. News & World Report*, and the *New York Times Magazine*, Rosenblatt has written nine nonfiction books dealing with such diverse topics as the African-American literary tradition (*Black Fiction*, 1974), the realities of war (*The Children of War*, 1983, and *Witness: The World Since Hiroshima*, 1985), and abortion (*Life Itself: Abortion in the American Mind*, 1992). He has also produced a memoir on his years of teaching at Harvard, *Coming Apart: A Memoir of the Harvard Wars of 1969* (1997), and the patriotic reader, *Where We Stand: 30 Reasons for Loving Our Country* (2002). In addition, Rosenblatt has become a well-known media personality through his regular appearances on the PBS news program *The NewsHour With Jim Lehrer* (formerly known as *The MacNeil/Lehrer NewsHour*). He has held several high-level publishing positions, including a stint in the late 1980s as the editor of *U.S. News & World Report*. In 1991 Rosenblatt added the title of playwright to his resume, when his monologue *Free Speech in America* ran at New York City's American Place Theater; in 1992 *And*, his first full-length play, opened in New York and Los Angeles, and his second monologue, *Bibliomania*, enjoyed a short run in 1993. Rosenblatt has been recognized with several prestigious prizes, including two George Polk Awards, a George Foster Peabody Award, and an Emmy Award.

Roger Rosenblatt was born in New York City, on September 13, 1940 to Milton B. Rosenblatt, a physician, and Mollie Spruch Rosenblatt, an English teacher. He grew up in the borough of Manhattan, near Gramercy Park. As Rosenblatt recalled in an essay for *Modern Maturity* (September–October 1994), he loved to explore the city as a child, particularly the ethnic areas from which both of his parents hailed, about 10 blocks south of his own neighborhood. "Whenever I got the chance," he wrote, "I headed downtown to walk among the tenements and suck in the smells of the terrible boiled chicken, the pickle barrels, the hoots and bellows on the streets, the soda spraying the stoops, the old cronies planted in their folding chairs on the sidewalk, sweating in formal dresses, suits and vests, and yammering in Yiddish, Italian, Irish, Slovak. The past, the wonderful infinite past. Even then, I sensed that something of value lay back there, down there."

After reportedly neglecting his studies in high school, Rosenblatt improved his academic performance at New York University, and in 1962 he earned his B.A., with honors. He obtained a scholarship to pursue postgraduate study at Harvard University, in Cambridge, Massachusetts, where he earned his master's degree in 1963. Rosenblatt then remained at Harvard to pursue a Ph.D.; from 1965 to 1966 he studied in Dublin, Ireland, on a

Fulbright Scholarship, and in 1968 he completed his doctorate in English and American literature.

In 1963 Rosenblatt had married Virginia Jones, a teacher, and by the late 1960s, they were expecting their first child. In 1968—to support his growing family and his burgeoning writing career—Rosenblatt accepted a position in Harvard University's English department, where he proved a popular professor. Then in his late 20s, Rosenblatt was just a few years older than many of his students, some of whom included former Vice President Al Gore, the actor Tommy Lee Jones, the writer and comedian Al Franken, and the playwright Christopher Durang. In addition, Rosenblatt was greatly admired by the administration. At the age of 29, he was appointed master of Dunster House—becoming the youngest professor to ever hold the distinction—and was reportedly on a short list of candidates for the Harvard presidency. On April 9, 1969, a group of students protesting the Vietnam War took over University Hall. After a violent conflict between protesters and police, in which the police used tear gas and truncheons to quell the occupiers, the campus erupted into chaos. Students went on strike, and many faculty members were conflicted over whether to support the student body or the administration. Rosenblatt was appointed to the Committee of Fifteen, a faculty group that was designated to investigate the event and compile recommendations for Harvard's future. While students initially supported his appointment, many felt betrayed when the young professor began advocating harsh punishments for the student protesters. "I was the traitor," Rosenblatt told Erica-Lynn Gambino for the New York Times (April 6, 1997), "From that point on, my star really began to fall." Ultimately, the experience soured Rosenblatt on university life, particularly in the atmosphere of distrust that soon enveloped Harvard. As his disillusionment grew, he decided to leave academia, and in 1973 he departed Harvard. He accepted a position at the National Endowment for the Humanities (NEH), in Washington, D.C., where he served as the director of education until 1975.

In 1974 Rosenblatt published his first book, a work of literary criticism entitled Black Fiction. After noticing a shortage of critical works on African-American literature, he set out to provide a thorough academic critique of such writers as Richard Wright, James Baldwin, and Ralph Ellison, among others. Rosenblatt theorized that black fiction is characterized by a cyclical pattern, reflecting major events in African-American history. A. R. Shucard, writing for Library Journal (February 15, 1975), declared the book "a rare kind of critical work: it provides such keen and comprehensive insight that it is a landmark by which future studies should orient themselves and a standard against which future works should be measured." Barbara Smith, writing for the New Republic (January 4–11, 1975), affirmed, "This is an admirably perceptive work."

In 1975 Rosenblatt left his post at the NEH to become the literary editor of the New Republic; he also wrote a regular column for the magazine entitled "The Back of the Book." Three years later he left the New Republic to become an editorial writer and author of a weekly column for the Washington Post. (He served as a member of the Post's editorial board from 1976 to 1979.) In 1980 he changed positions again, this time becoming a senior writer for Time, where he remained until 1988, when he departed for U.S. News & World Report. There, Rosenblatt began as a senior writer and quickly rose to the position of editor; yet, after little more than a year, he resigned, attributing the decision to his taxing weekly commute between New York City (where his family had recently settled) and the magazine's headquarters in Washington, D.C. He served as a columnist and editor-at-large for Life magazine from 1989 to 1992 and, beginning in 1999, as editor-at-large for Time. Throughout the 1990s Rosenblatt's work appeared in numerous national publications, including the New York Times Magazine, Modern Maturity, Vanity Fair, Men's Journal, and the Atlantic. In 1983 he began making regular television appearances as an essayist and commentator on the PBS news program, The MacNeil/Lehrer NewsHour (subsequently named The NewsHour With Jim Lehrer)—a role he continues to perform.

While establishing himself as an acclaimed—and highly sought-after—journalist, essayist, and social commentator, Rosenblatt has also published many celebrated works of nonfiction. His 1983 book, The Children of War, expands on a 1982 cover story he wrote for Time; it chronicles the trials of children in various war-torn regions of the world, including Northern Ireland, Israel, Palestine, Lebanon, Thailand (where many people had fled to escape the violence in Cambodia), and Hong Kong. Rosenblatt traveled some 25,000 miles conducting interviews for the book, spending approximately one week in each country. The resulting work presents three common themes that Rosenblatt observed in the children he met—regardless of their differences in culture, race, geography, or religion. According to Rosenblatt's account, these children demonstrated a distinct seriousness, a firm belief in God, and little concern with revenge. Critics generally praised the journalist's sensitive presentation of the material, particularly his insight and dedication to providing the details of his subjects' lives, although because of the short time he spent in each area, some lamented his approach as that of a "typical American tourist," as Jack Riemer wrote for America (October 29, 1983). The Children of War garnered the Robert F. Kennedy Book Award, the Polk Award in journalism, and a nomination for the National Book Critics Circle Award.

Rosenblatt's next book, Witness: The World Since Hiroshima (1985), was essentially a reprint of a cover story he had written for Time the previous year. The book served to commemorate the

40th anniversary of the U.S. dropping of the atomic bomb on Hiroshima, Japan, during World War II. In it Rosenblatt examines the event from the perspectives of three people: a Japanese survivor who was 13 years old during the bombing, an American physicist who assisted on the project that developed the atomic bomb, and former President Richard Nixon. Robert Shaplen, writing for the *New York Times* (August 4, 1985), called the work, "a slim, provocative book that demonstrates boldness and bravado, originality and audacity, grace and gusto of style. It leaves one somewhat breathless in the final reach and flight of its conclusions." In a critique for *People* (October 14, 1985), Ralph Novak praised Rosenblatt's journalistic skills, declaring him "a superb interviewer, with a perceptive ear and an open mind."

The impetus for Rosenblatt's next book, *Life Itself: Abortion in the American Mind* (1992), was a monumental 1989 U. S. Supreme Court decision in the case of Webster v. Reproductive Health Services, which resulted in a 5-4 ruling to uphold state restrictions on abortion that had previously been deemed unconstitutional. Many abortion-rights advocates feared the Webster decision would set a precedent for the Supreme Court to further restrict, or even overturn, Roe v. Wade (the 1973 ruling that had legalized abortion). As the nation began focusing again on abortion, Rosenblatt decided the moment was opportune for exploring the topic further. He told Charles Truehart for the *Washington Post* (August 16, 1989) that the Webster decision marked the beginning of "the first period in all history in which all elements of this issue will be discussed." In a *Publishers Weekly* article (January 22, 1992), Rosenblatt observed that Americans had historically been able to resolve conflicts by what he called "our normal, sloppy, democratic way." Yet, he found the abortion issue to be an anomaly. "We talk about [most issues]," he wrote, "[and] work out laws and learn to live—uncomfortably—with them. The question 'Why have we *not* been able to live uncomfortably with abortion?' became the engine that propelled my book. It didn't take a long time to write it, but it took a long time to work out *before* I began writing. I had no flash of inspiration, but a continuous brooding." Rosenblatt begins the book by exploring the nation's ambivalence on the topic: He recalls a 1990 poll in which 77 percent of those surveyed found abortion to be a type of murder; nevertheless, 73 percent wanted it to remain legal. The book is divided into four sections; in them Rosenblatt assesses the current political debate on abortion, takes a historical perspective, explores why the issue has proven to be so divisive for Americans, and offers a possible solution. In his conclusion he argues for a policy that he calls "permit but discourage," whereby abortion would be kept legal but made increasingly unnecessary through sex education. As Rosenblatt explained in the *Publishers Weekly* article, "If that formula can be wholeheartedly absorbed into American thinking, we will be able to live—uncomfortably—with this deservedly troubling issue. . . . We *have* to talk about the problem, and if my book does any good at all, it will get people do to just that."

Like the abortion issue that it covered, *Life Itself* received a mixed response from critics. While Abigail Trafford for the *Washington Post* (March 26, 1992) praised Rosenblatt's style, calling it "rich and reasoned" as "he presents his insights with the impartial smoothness of a marriage counselor," she concluded that he is "not an impartial mediator." "He is asking the anti-abortion side to learn to live with abortion," Trafford observed. "Rosenblatt is very up front in saying that his 'stand on abortion is conventionally pro-choice.'" Writing for the *New York Times* (March 12, 1992), Christopher Lehmann-Haupt called the work a "thoughtful, healing" book and praised Rosenblatt's sensible approach. "Reason and humanity pervade Mr. Rosenblatt's entire argument, which might easily have come out dry and abstract but which instead reads comfortably," he noted. In contrast, Katha Pollitt for the *Nation* (May 25, 1992) criticized what she considered the oversimplified resolutions that Rosenblatt suggests. "[This book] asks the wrong questions, gives the wrong answers and offers a false solution," she opined. "Some of [the] material is interesting and worth pointing out. . . . But much of the historical material has a canned feel, like the research file for a *Time–Life* 'think piece.'" Despite the mixed reviews, *Life Itself* was awarded the 1993 Frederic G. Melcher Book Award from the Unitarian Universalist Association.

Rosenblatt's next book, *The Man in the Water: Essays and Stories* (1994), collects many of his previously published articles and showcases his diverse interests and distinct style. With pieces spanning the preceding two decades, the book includes scholarly essays, celebrity profiles, humorous pieces on family life and aging, and more serious reflections on his father's death and the devastations of war. Gilbert Taylor observed for *Booklist* (January 1, 1994), "Rosenblatt hones in on the human enigma, the quality of mysteriousness that exists in everyone. That's his trademark, and expressing it with a cerebral penchant for literary allusion—reflecting, still, his 1960s days as a Harvard English professor—adds relish to his substantial, quizzical human interest sketches."

In *Coming Apart: A Memoir of the Harvard Wars of 1969* (1997), Rosenblatt presents an account of the student takeover of University Hall that he witnessed at Harvard in 1969. Recounting his unique position as a young professor appointed to the Committee of Fifteen, he reveals how the war protests and the ensuing chaos ultimately affected his own life. While some critics questioned the significance of revisiting the experience nearly 30 years after the fact, many found the book to be an interesting slice of history. Bill Ott noted for *Booklist* (February 15, 1997), "As a reassessment of the sociopolitical forces on campus in the late sixties, the memoir tells us little we haven't heard before, but as an ironic psychodrama of how the period affected the life of one relatively uncommitted faculty member, it carves out a special niche for itself." Writing for the *New York Times* (April 10, 1997), Christopher Lehmann-Haupt praised Rosenblatt's impulse to approach the piece as a memoir. "By dramatizing a time of ideological crisis and knitting into it his own conflicted inner development," he said, "Mr. Rosenblatt has revealed new subtleties about all of our pasts."

Rosenblatt was the editor of *Consuming Desires: Consumption, Culture, and the Pursuit of Happiness* (1999), a collection of 13 essays exploring the connections between consumption and culture. In his introduction to the book, he argues that Americans often consume in order to fill spiritual or emotional voids in their lives; throughout the essays that follow, such writers as Alex Kotlowitz, Molly Haskell, David Orr, Andre Schiffrin, and Jane Smiley expand on these themes of materialism and popular culture. As a piece of cultural criticism, the book was widely praised for its insightful commentaries. Vanessa Bush, writing for *Booklist* (June 1–15, 1999), called *Consuming Desires* "a thoughtful exploration of what we buy and why." Peter Heinegg, in a review for *America* (November 20, 1999), affirmed: "Despite some inevitable unevenness, this is a pertinent survey of a life-and-death problem, op-ed writing at close to its quotable, discussible best."

While recovering from a back operation, Rosenblatt wrote his next book, *Rules for Aging: Resist Normal Impulses, Live Longer, Attain Perfection* (2000), a slim volume containing witty advice and providing a humorous guide to life. In a critique for *People* (December 11, 2000), a reviewer wrote, "Through bitingly cynical, [Rosenblatt's] advice on everything from party etiquette to office politics is also delightfully smart and to the point." His most recent book, *Where We Stand: 30 Reasons for Loving Our Country*, was released in 2002. This book, written in what Rosenblatt described as "an extension of feeling stemming from September 11," as quoted by Michael Lind for the *New York Times* (July 7, 2002), includes several essays and vignettes exploring the author's patriotic view of the U.S. In 2003 Rosenblatt published *Anything Can Happen: Notes on My Inadequate Life and Yours*, which an *Amazon.com* reviewer described as a collection of "cautionary notes and hilarious stories" that "pack the Rosenblatt punch."

In 1996 Rosenblatt joined the faculty of Long Island University's Southampton College, becoming the Parsons Family University Professor in Writing. In hiring Rosenblatt, the liberal-arts college—then known for its reputable program in marine and environmental science—was hoping to invigorate its English department. "Roger Rosenblatt's appointment is the first step in turning the English Program at Southampton College into a nationally recognized center for students of writing," David Steinberg, the university's president, announced at a press conference, as quoted on the school's Web site. Rosenblatt said of his goals for the new position, also as quoted on the Web site, "The marine biologists have the natural resource of Long Island's waters. Southampton College can use the human resources of our area's authors to build a nationally distinguished specialty in writing. I want to be the catalyst that makes such a program possible." In 1998 the college expanded the writing program to offer an MFA degree in English and writing, which Rosenblatt helped design.

Rosenblatt has been recognized with honorary doctoral degrees from the University of Maryland; Claremont Graduate School, in California; the University of Utah; Pace University, in New York; and Brigham Young University, in Utah. He currently resides in Quogue, New York, a picturesque town in the Hamptons, with his wife of nearly 40 years. They have three adult children: Carl Becker, Amy Elizabeth, and John Milton.

In a 1996 lecture at Southampton College, Rosenblatt addressed the question of "Why write?" As quoted by Erica-Lynn Gambino for the *Southampton Press* (October 17, 1996), he said in part, "The reason to write is to stay afloat, to tell others to stay afloat . . . and to tell them how. . . . Because for all the monsters, there will be a gleam, a spark, a light, and we will tell that story too." Rosenblatt concluded, "Why write? To make a connection with life."

—K. D.

SUGGESTED READING: *Modern Maturity* p38 Sep.–Oct. 1994; *New York Times* VII p1 Aug. 28, 1983, VII p3 Aug. 4, 1985, XIII p8 Apr. 6, 1987, C p22 Mar. 12, 1992, with photo, C p22 Mar. 9, 1994; *Publishers Weekly* p15 Jan. 22, 1992, with photo; *Washington Post* D p3 Mar. 26, 1992

SELECTED BOOKS: nonfiction—*Black Fiction*, 1974; *The Children of War*, 1983; *Witness: The World Since Hiroshima*, 1985; *Life Itself: Abortion in the American Mind*, 1992; *The Man in the Water: Essays and Stories*, 1994; *Coming Apart: A Memoir of the Harvard Wars of 1969*, 1997; *Rules for Aging: Resist Normal Impulses, Live Longer, Attain Perfection*, 2000; *Where We Stand: 30 Reasons for Loving Our Country*, 2002; as editor—*Consuming Desires: Consumption, Culture, and the Pursuit of Happiness*, 1999

Catherine Temerson/Courtesy of W. W. Norton & Company

Rosenfield, Israel

July 11, 1939– Nonfiction writer

Trained as a physician and political scientist, Israel Rosenfield has spent more than 30 years thinking and writing about human consciousness. In his first book, *Freud: Character and Consciousness* (1970), Rosenfield takes on the founder of psychoanalysis, arguing that Freud's theory of hidden motivations and neuroses is inadequate to explain the complexities of social behavior. In his next book, *DNA for Beginners* (1983), co-authored by Edward Ziff and Borin van Loon, Rosenfield narrates the history of genetics and the discovery of the building blocks of life in an unusual, comic-book format. In his celebrated work, *The Invention of Memory: A New View of the Brain* (1988), Rosenfield boldly suggests that memory is not a static function, localized in the brain, but is in fact a dynamic one. He followed this work with *The Strange, Familiar, and Forgotten: An Anatomy of Consciousness* (1992), in which he asserts that consciousness is the major function of the human brain. In his most recent work, Rosenfield returns once again to the subject of Freud, this time using fiction to explore the man and his legacy. The premise of the novel, *Freud's Megalomania* (2000), is the discovery of what is purported to be the psychiatrist's last work, a manuscript entitled "Megalomania" that sends shock waves through the psychiatric community because, in it, Freud totally rejects psychoanalytic theory.

Israel Rosenfield was born on July 11, 1939 in New York City, the son of high-school teachers Jacob Rosenfield and the former Mamie Keselenko. He was educated at New York University, where he received his bachelor's degree in 1958 and his M.D. in 1962. From there he continued his education at Princeton University, where he earned a master of arts degree in 1964 and a doctorate in 1966 (in either political science or history). That year Rosenfield began his teaching career at the City University of New York's Queens College campus as an assistant professor of political science. In 1975 he was made an associate professor. He left Queens College in 1985 to become a professor of history at John Jay College of Criminal Justice in Manhattan, where he continues to teach. (From 1966 to 1969 he also served as a visiting lecturer at Princeton University.)

Rosenfield's first book, *Freud: Character and Consciousness* (1970), is a critical analysis of the psychiatrist's theory of the unconscious. Rosenfield argues that both the theoretical and therapeutic bases of psychoanalysis are unsound, therefore casting doubt on the proposition that social behavior is grounded in hidden or repressed motivations. Although by the early 1970s Freudian psychoanalysis had fallen out of favor among many therapists, Rosenfield approaches his subject from the perspective of a political scientist, warning against the use of psychoanalysis to discern the motivations of political leaders. The book received mixed reviews. While a *Library Journal* (January 1, 1971) reviewer recommended it for "collections embracing everything written about Freud," a reviewer for *Choice* (March 1971) argued that "the aim of the book is not realized fully. The logical arguments . . . appear sound; but the reasons given for supposing that character has other roots are not compelling. Too often they consist simply in replacing analytic speculations with those of the political scientist."

Rosenfield's next book, *DNA For Beginners* (1983), co-authored by Edward Ziff and Borin van Loon, was a departure from his earlier academic writing. It takes the form of a comic book and gives a short history of DNA, from the early work done by Thomas Hunt Morgan and his students in the 1900s, to Watson and Crick's mapping out of the DNA structure, to recent debates over the role of genetic engineering in society. "I found the book to be thoroughly enjoyable and quite informative, . . . and I recommend it to the serious high-school or college student," Allen A. Badgett wrote in *Science Books and Films* (September/October 1984). Harold M. Schmeck, in the *New York Times Book Review* (March 11, 1984) agreed: "The humor is sharp, the cartoons imaginative, often outrageous—a sort of Monty Python treatment of molecular biology. The text, some of it in comic-strip balloons, is wry, terse and easy to understand. And it conveys a remarkable amount of information."

In 1988, with the publication of *The Invention of Memory: A New View of the Brain*, Rosenfield returned to more conventional academic study. He challenges "localization theory," which holds that memories are stored in specific areas of the brain, like documents in a computer's hard drive. He argues instead that memories are not fixed, but rather are manipulated to fit present conditions. To support his claim, he invokes David Marr's work in artificial intelligence, and Marcel Proust's fiction, among other examples. Although he disagreed with Rosenfield's theories, James W. Lance in the *New York Times Book Review* (May 22, 1988) conceded: "*The Invention of Memory* will stimulate interest in one of the most intriguing aspects of brain function." In a review for *Psychology Today* (May 1988), Anne H. Rosenfeld agreed, stating that "*The Invention of Memory* may inspire your brain . . . to form a whole new set of surprising connections." In *Science Books and Films* (November/December 1988), Max Fink wrote: "I highly recommend it to interested general adult readers as well as to professional psychologists and neuroscientists seeking a popular, simplified, and easily read guide to modern ideas of memory."

Four years later Rosenfield published a new work on the human mind, *The Strange, Familiar, and Forgotten: An Anatomy of Consciousness* (1992). Citing case studies of neurological impairment (a woman who must touch herself to be sure she exists; a 48-year-old man who can remember the first 30 years of his life but has no recollection of what happened yesterday), Rosenfield attempts to understand the normal functioning of the human mind. He suggests that consciousness is rooted in time and place, and that, furthermore, consciousness is the preeminent function of the human brain. Calling this work "a series of remarkable essays," Carol R. Glatt in her review for *Library Journal* (April 15, 1992) added: "His approach is challenging, controversial, and stimulating." In the *Student Library Journal* (February 1993) Nancy K. Craig remarked: "Students of psychology will appreciate the variety of primary source information included, as well as the concise discussion of the history of thought and theory on this topic." However, Michael R. Trimble, reviewing *The Strange, Familiar, and Forgotten* for the medical journal *Lancet* (April 3, 1993), concluded: "My main criticism of this book is that it is too loose and too poorly referenced to satisfy the scientific inquirer, and is dangerous for the uninitiated, pretending authority. . . . It lacks a depth of inquiry and left me reformulating one of the most famous statements on consciousness ever—namely Descartes' 'I think, therefore I am,' or, as this book suggests, 'I think, therefore I am. . . I think.'"

Eight years later Rosenfield reemerged with a new approach to his long study of the human mind. His first novel, *Freud's Megalomania* (2000), centers on the (fictional) discovery of a new Freud manuscript entitled "Megalomania." In it the eminent psychoanalyst reveals that he was a victim of his own self-delusions. He attempts through this paper to show that human behavior is not driven by subliminal urges but is really a result of our capacity to con ourselves into believing whatever we may want. In the *New York Times Book Review* (July 9, 2000), Adam Phillips remarked: "What is most striking about this fictional last work of Freud's . . . is that it is overtly autobiographical. It shows Freud making theory out of the most immediate life circumstances. And the novel is particularly poignant in its evocation, without cynicism, of Freud's ambition, and of the devastating impact of World War I on Freud's every impression. *Freud's Megalomania* is, in short, a triumph of that false-memory syndrome called contemporary fiction." A Kirkus reviewer, as quoted on *Amazon.com*, echoed this praise, calling the novel a "brilliant, learned, ambitious, and wildly thought-provoking masterpiece of fictional revisionism."

Israel Rosenfield married the translator, writer, and literary manager of a theater, Catherine Temerson, on April 11, 1970. He contributes to a number of periodicals, most notably the *New York Review of Books*.

—C. M.

SUGGESTED READING: *Choice* p144 Mar. 1971; *Lancet* p881 Apr. 3, 1993; *Library Journal* p88 Jan. 1, 1971, p112 Apr. 15, 1992; *New York Times Book Review* p18 Mar. 11, 1984, p37 May 22, 1988, p12 July 9, 2000; *Psychology Today* p68 May 1988; *Science Books and Films* p19 Sep./Oct. 1984, p77 Nov./Dec. 1988; *Science News* p47 July 17, 1993; *Student Library Journal* p130 Feb. 1993

SELECTED BOOKS: nonfiction—*Freud: Character and Consciousness*, 1970; *The Invention of Memory: A New View of the Brain*, 1988; *The Strange, Familiar, and Forgotten*, 1992; *DNA for Beginners*, 1983 (with Edward Ziff and Borin van Loon); fiction—*Freud's Meglomania*, 2000

Roth, Philip

Mar. 19, 1933– Novelist; short-story writer

Philip Roth first achieved prominence in 1959 with the publication of *Goodbye, Columbus, and Five Short Stories*, for which he won the National Book Award. Delineating the conflict between traditional and contemporary morals as manifested in a young, Jewish American man's search for identity, the title novella revived an enduring controversy (which had begun two years earlier with Roth's first *New Yorker* story) over whether his satirical treatment of Jewish themes constituted anti-Semitism. That controversy reached a fever pitch with his novel *Portnoy's Complaint*, which created a sensation in 1969 because of its explicit recounting of a young lawyer's sexual autobiography, consisting largely of compulsive attempts to free himself from the strict confines of his Jewish upbringing through incessant masturbation and sexual conquest. Since then, Roth's output has ranged from wild comedy and political satire to examinations of his role as a writer and son and metafictional ex-

Nancy Crampton/Courtesy of Vintage Anchor Publicity
Philip Roth

plorations of the relationship between art and life, fiction and reality, imagination and fact; or, as he has put it, the "relationship between the written and the unwritten world." In an interview with Mervyn Rothstein for the New York Times (August 1, 1985), Roth identified his primary theme as "the tension between license and restraint, . . . a struggle between the hunger for personal liberty and the forces of inhibition."

In their late 50s and 60s, some novelists begin to rest on their laurels, but Philip Roth instead produced some of his best work. Starting with Patrimony, in 1991, Roth has strung together seven superbly inventive books in a row, including Operation Shylock: A Confession (1993) and Sabbath's Theater (1995), which won the National Book Award for fiction. Roth's sociological and historical trilogy of modern American life began in 1997 with American Pastoral, which covered the Vietnam era; continued in 1998 with I Married a Communist, a look at the Red Scare of the 1950s; and concluded in 2000 with The Human Stain, a critique of America's obsession with moralizing, sex, and political correctness. For American Pastoral he earned the Pulitzer Prize in 1998. His most recent novel is The Dying Animal (2001).

Philip Milton Roth was born on March 19, 1933 to Herman Roth, the American-born son of Jewish immigrants from Galicia, Spain, and Bess (Finkel) Roth in Newark, New Jersey, where he and his older brother, Sandy, grew up. His father, whose shoe store had gone bankrupt during the Depression, was an insurance salesman who worked his way up into the echelons of management despite the openly anti-Semitic sentiments of his superiors. Like his father, Philip Roth faced similar prejudices that marred his otherwise "intensely secure and protected" childhood. His summer vacations at Bradley Beach on the New Jersey shore were sometimes spoiled by gangs of toughs who attacked Jews, and, even at the almost entirely Jewish Weequahic High School, he was subjected to violence inflicted by toughs from neighboring, non-Jewish schools. At the age of 12, he had decided that when he grew up he would "oppose the injustices wreaked by the violent and the privileged by becoming a lawyer for the underdog," a goal toward which he continued to work even after graduating from high school in 1950. His other passion during his youth was baseball, which, he has written, offered him "membership in a great secular nationalistic church from which nobody had ever seemed to suggest that Jews should be excluded."

From 1950 to 1951 Roth attended the Newark extension of Rutgers University before transferring to Bucknell University, in Lewisburg, Pennsylvania, to escape the "provincialism" of Newark and discover "the rest of America." But he discovered instead that Bucknell's "respectable Christian atmosphere [was] hardly less constraining than [his] own particular Jewish upbringing." A big man on campus nonetheless, he edited the literary magazine, appeared in student plays, and became a member of Phi Beta Kappa. After graduating magna cum laude with a B.A. degree in English in 1954, he obtained an M.A. degree in English from the University of Chicago the following year. Roth then moved to Washington, D.C., where he served briefly in the United States Army before he was discharged because of a back injury. Returning to the University of Chicago in 1956, he began teaching a full schedule of freshman composition while working toward a doctorate (a goal that he abandoned in the first quarter). During Roth's two years as an English instructor at the University of Chicago, he continued to write short fiction, which he had begun doing at least as early as 1955. Among those who read his work at that time was Saul Bellow, who has recalled that Roth's stories "showed a wonderful wit and great pace." Roth has said that he did not take his writing seriously at first because "everybody studying English wrote stories."

But Roth's stories, the first of which to see publication was "The Day It Snowed," which appeared in the Chicago Review in 1955, often proved to be of award-winning caliber, and it was not long before he was writing and teaching fulltime. After serving for a brief period as a reviewer of television and film for the liberal weekly journal of opinion the New Republic, Roth published Goodbye, Columbus in 1959. In the title novella the conflicting values of the impoverished, urban Neil Klugman and the affluent Brenda Patimkin, a Jewish-American "princess" whose suburban, upper-middle-class lifestyle is satirized mercilessly, doom the couple's relationship. In the opinion of most critics, the book showed great promise and signaled the arrival of an important new writer. "A brilliant new talent . . . ," Arnold Dolin wrote in the *Saturday Review* (May 16, 1959), "Philip Roth has looked penetratingly into the heart of the American Jew who faces the loss of his identity. The conflict involved in this choice between two worlds provides the focal point of drama for a memorable collection of short stories."

The earlier publication of one of the stories in *Goodbye, Columbus*, "Defender of the Faith," in the *New Yorker* in April 1957, had set off a barrage of charges that Roth's attitude toward his Jewish subjects was anti-Semitic, a controversy that was revived by Roth's unflattering portrayal of the consumerist lifestyle of the Patimkins, which prompted one rabbi to accuse him of presenting "a distorted image of the basic values of Orthodox Judaism." Nevertheless, the majority of critics were impressed by *Goodbye, Columbus*, which brought Roth a National Book Award, an award from the National Institute of Arts and Letters, a Daroff Award from the Jewish Book Council of America, and a Guggenheim fellowship that enabled him to travel to Rome. In 1960 he began a two-year stint as a visiting lecturer at the University of Iowa Writers' Workshop, followed by two years as a writer in residence at Princeton University.

Roth's next two books are now generally considered minor works. *Letting Go* (1962), his first full-length novel, concerns the ethical dilemmas of a young Jewish academic at the University of Chicago. Despite the "sharply observant" qualities of Roth's prose that were unfailingly mentioned by reviewers, *Letting Go* was invariably faulted for its sprawling length and its diffusiveness. *When She Was Good* (1967), which Roth once referred to simply as his "book with no Jews," is also his only novel to feature a female protagonist. Critics were sharply divided over its merits. Josh Greenfeld, writing in *Book Week* (June 4, 1967), ranked it "among the few novels written about America since World War II that may still be worth reading 25 years from now," but a reviewer for *Time* (June 9, 1967) found *When She Was Good's* heroine "theatrically unsatisfying and an ear-jarring bore." Saul Maloff's view, as expressed in *Newsweek* (June 12, 1967), occupied a middle ground: "With unerring fidelity, [Roth] records the flat surface of provincial American life, the look and feel and sound of it—and then penetrates it to the cesspool of its invisible dynamisms. Beneath the good, and impelling it, he says, lies the horrid."

The period between 1962 and 1967, during which Roth lived in New York City and underwent psychoanalysis, marked the longest hiatus in his productivity that he has ever experienced. He has characterized that period as one of "literary uncertainty," adding, "I didn't know what the hell to do. What do I write about? Do I pursue these Jewish subjects any further or get rid of them? . . . It was a period of debilitating disorder in my young life." In an interview with Hermione Lee for the *Paris Review* (Summer 1983–Winter 1984), he revealed how his disastrous marriage in 1959 to the former Margaret Martinson Williams (from whom he was legally separated in 1963 and who died in an automobile accident in 1968) had exhausted his emotional and financial resources. "I needed [analysis]," he said, "primarily to prevent me from going out and committing murder because of the alimony and court costs incurred for having served two years in a childless marriage. The image that teased me during those years was of a train that had been shunted onto the wrong track. In my early twenties I had been zipping right along there, you know—on schedule, express stops only, final destination clearly in mind; and then suddenly I was on the wrong track, speeding off into the wilds. I'd ask myself, 'How the hell do you get this thing back on the right track?' Well, you can't. I've continued to be surprised, over the years, whenever I discover myself, late at night, pulling into the wrong station."

Roth rehabilitated his career in the late 1960s, when he began teaching literature at the University of Pennsylvania, where he was on the faculty for about 11 years. In 1969 the release of the movie *Goodbye, Columbus*, starring Ali MacGraw and Richard Benjamin, coincided with the publication of *Portnoy's Complaint*, which sold 393,000 copies in hardcover, making its author financially secure. Roth became an instant celebrity—not only because of the grossness of his humor, which offended some (the book was banned in Australia) and delighted others, but also because the intimate nature of Portnoy's confessional monologue to his psychoanalyst led to considerable prurient speculation about Roth's own personal life. The inordinate amount of attention with which he was bombarded induced him to move out of New York City to the Yaddo Writers Colony in Saratoga Springs, in upstate New York.

More charitable and less voyeuristic in their assessment of *Portnoy's Complaint* than the gossipmongers on the television talk-show circuit, the literary critics were by and large wildly enthusiastic. Granville Hicks called *Portnoy's Complaint* "something very much like a masterpiece" in the *Saturday Review* (February 22, 1969), and John Greenfeld, writing in the *New York Times Book Review* (February 23, 1969), termed it a "deliciously funny book, absurd and exuberant, wild and uproarious." Those who were offended by the book included not only anti-obscenity crusaders of the Anthony Comstock breed, but also some members of the Jewish community, who felt that the novel was tinged with anti-Semitism. "The charges were several," Roth recalled in an interview with Curt Suplee for the *Washington Post* (October 30, 1983), "and in defense of my accusers, it was only the lunatic fringe who said I was anti-Semitic. The stronger case was that I was lending fuel to the fires of anti-Semites. . . . I don't think it's a matter of a right position or a wrong position. It's two right positions colliding."

Ironically, his critics may have unwittingly played a part in the genesis of *Portnoy's Complaint*, as Roth explained in his book *Reading My-*

self and Others (1975), by prompting him to set himself the goal "of becoming the writer some Jewish critics had been telling [him he] was all along: irresponsible, conscienceless, unserious." Both the reactions of Jews who resent his satire and those offended by his obscenity, wrote Raymond A. Sokolov for *Newsweek* (February 24, 1969), "will miss the essential literary achievement of this very important book. . . . He is not really prodding Jews but the myth about them in a 100 recent novels . . . in order to probe at all of our half-stifled conflicts over an emerging, 'freer' new morality." The brouhaha over *Portnoy's Complaint* did not impede Roth's election to the National Institute of Arts and Letters, in 1970.

In the early 1970s Roth completed three entirely different satirical novels that received mixed reviews and are generally perceived as being less impressive than his other books. *Our Gang* (1971), featuring a president of the United States named Tricky E. Dixon, was described by Dwight MacDonald in the *New York Times Book Review* (November 7, 1971) as "farfetched, unfair, tasteless, disturbing, logical, coarse, and very funny. . . . In short, a masterpiece." Explaining his chosen target, Roth said, "One ought to recognize that the present political chaos is connected with the decay of language, and that one can probably bring about some improvement by starting at the verbal end."

In *The Breast* (1972), Professor David Kepesh becomes transformed into a six-foot-tall mammary gland, a metamorphosis that he heroically survives by attempting to reconcile his intellectual and sexual natures. Although he does not succeed completely, his efforts bring him invaluable insights into how to cope with a self-image at war with his impulses. Roth once referred to Kepesh as the "first heroic character" he has been able to portray because he goes further than other Rothian protagonists in passing through "the barrier that forms one boundary of the individual's identity and experience: that barrier of personal inhibition, ethical restraint, and plain old conformism and fear, beyond which lies the moral and psychological unknown." (Kepesh reappears, as a professor who moves from the alternate gratification of his mental and physical selves to the achievement of a more integrated way of being, in *The Professor of Desire* [1977].) "*The Breast* heaves with weighty theme- ideas," Bruce Allen quipped in a review for *Library Journal* (October 1, 1972), "but it yields nothing fresh, lacking any consistent interplay between the serious and the grotesque."

After writing the ironically titled *The Great American Novel* (1973), a baseball satire that one critic dismissed as "a great American bore that's impossible not to put down shortly after you pick it up," Roth produced what many consider his finest novel: *My Life as a Man* (1974). Its multilayered story centers on the novelist Peter Tarnopol's attempts to solve his dilemmas by writing "Useful Fictions" about one Nathan Zuckerman, a young Jewish writer whose life resembles his own. Writing in *Newsweek* (June 3, 1974), Peter S. Prescott judged *My Life as a Man* to be "Roth's best novel. It is also his most complex and most ambitious."

Once introduced, Nathan Zuckerman was to return time and again to Roth's fiction. In *The Ghost Writer* (1979), a young Zuckerman visits the home of his literary mentor, where he meets a mysterious guest named Amy Belette whom he sees as Anne Frank resurrected. According to Jonathan Penner's review for the *Washington Post* (September 2, 1979), *The Ghost Writer* "provides further evidence that [Roth] can do practically anything with fiction. His narrative power . . . is superb." *Zuckerman Unbound* (1981) follows Zuckerman as he achieves notoriety with his scandalous novel "Carnovsky" and becomes the prisoner of his own reputation, which destroys his love life and his relations with his family. In *The Anatomy Lesson* (1983), Zuckerman, now racked by inexplicable neck and shoulder pain and grieving for the loss of his mother and the devolution of his hometown, Newark, into a slum, decides to abandon writing and become a doctor. Reviewing it in the *New Yorker* (November 7, 1983), John Updike discovered that "materials one might have thought exhausted by Roth's previous novelistic explorations, inflammations one might have thought long soothed, burn hotter than ever; the central howl unrolls with a mediated savagery both fascinating and repellent, self-indulgent yet somehow sterling, adamant, pure, in the style of high modernism, that bewitchment to all the art-stricken young of the 1950s."

The three novels were published in one volume in 1985 entitled *Zuckerman Bound: A Trilogy and an Epilogue*. Although the epilogue, *The Prague Orgy*, which was considered by many critics to be the best section of the volume, seemed to mark the end of the Zuckerman cycle, Roth brought his hero back once more in *The Counterlife* (1986), which won the National Book Critics Circle Award. Many reviewers of the experimental *The Counterlife*, in which nonlinear narrative tends to subvert the logical sequence of events, felt that Roth's talent had reached a new peak of expression. William H. Gass declared the novel "a triumph" in his article for the *New York Times Book Review* (January 4, 1987) and concluded that it "constitutes a fulfillment of tendencies, a successful integration of themes, and the final working through of obsessions that have previously troubled if not marred his work." Among the dissenters was Christopher Lehmann-Haupt, who wrote in the *New York Times* (December 29, 1986) that "we become so aware of the narrative's duplicity that all that is left to us is the burden of the author's self-consciousness as an artist and a Jew. It's like being trapped between two funhouse mirrors that reflect each other's distortions unto a point that vanishes into absurdity."

During his interview with Curt Suplee for the *Washington Post*, Roth defined the Zuckerman novels as " hypothetical autobiographies. It's very complicated. I have no great brief to make for my life as lived. In fact, it's basically sitting in a chair writing books. It's not very eventful. I don't know what I am—I'm a person who writes. But what excites my verbal life is imagining what I *might* be, what might befall someone like myself; imagining what kind of person I would be if I *were* a person. I'm really quite content to be what I am. I never entertained the idea of being a doctor in my life, but writing this book I had to. I don't have to do these things—I have people do them for me."

After writing so many "hypothetical autobiographies," Roth finally felt impelled to begin what turned out to be a genuine one, which he called *The Facts: A Novelist's Autobiography* (1988). A memoir of his first 36 years, *The Facts* began as a therapeutic exercise to help him recover from the deep depression he had fallen into after minor knee surgery in 1987. Because of the interaction of two drugs he was taking as a result of the surgery, he suffered for three months from hallucinations, panic attacks, suicidal thoughts, and other debilitating symptoms. "I thought, something is happening to me; I've got to fight my way out of it," he recalled in an interview with Stephen Schiff for *Vanity Fair* (April 1990). "And I would try to write down who I was, to remember who I was." Appraising *The Facts* for *USA Today* (September 2, 1988), William H. Pritchard demurred that "novelists, even when they try to play it straight and pass along naked truths about themselves, clothe those truths in sentences that construct an imagined self instead of handing it over unaltered." In reply to such comments, Roth told Mervyn Rothstein, "I called the book *The Facts*, not 'The Dirt.' I didn't write 'The Dirt.' That's another book."

In 1990 and 1991 Roth published two books that could not be more dissimilar in tone, style, and subject. *Deception* is the notebook of a 50-year-old married novelist provocatively named Philip, who records the dialogue between himself and his younger, married lover in an adulterous affair. The novelist Fay Weldon commented that *Deception* "reads like a brilliant radio play for a minority audience" in her article for the *New York Times Book Review* (March 11, 1990), while Peter S. Prescott wrote in *Newsweek* (March 26, 1990) that Roth was merely "revving his motor again, his gearshift still stuck in neutral."

In contrast, *Patrimony: A True Story*, which deals with the life and death of Herman Roth, who died at 86 from a brain tumor in October 1989, was unanimously admired for its "deeply resonant" portrayal of the author's father. "In celebrating his father," R. Z. Sheppard wrote in *Time* (January 21, 1991), "and by implication the source of his own character, Roth has not strayed from the long path he has cut for himself: to dramatize the adventure of assimilation in all its anxiety, humor, and fertile illusions. As a writer and a son, he has now dotted the i's and crossed the t's." In 1991 Roth received the National Arts Club's Medal of Honor for Literature for the body of his work.

In *Operation Shylock* (1993), Roth writes about having been a spy for the Israelis, encountering his double in Israel, and suffering prolonged depression while taking the sleeping pill Halcion. (Roth's publisher and reviewers called it a work of fiction, but Roth himself insisted that the story was true, despite many critics questioning the likelihood of Roth's having been recruited by the Mossad.) When the "real" Roth confronts his double, the two begin arguing fiercely about everything from the Holocaust to the slippery slope of politics in the Middle East. The novel received mixed reviews. Paul Gray, in *Time* (March 8, 1993), cheered: "Roth has not riffed with quite this comic abandon since *Portnoy's Complaint*. And the social and historical range of *Operation Shylock* is broader than anything the author has attempted before." In his review for *Newsweek* (March 8, 1993), Malcolm Jones was of a completely different opinion, writing: "If [Roth] intended to replicate the ironic contradictions in the Mideast, he succeeded all too well, exhausting our patience in the bargain. Our lasting impression is of a prodigally gifted writer searching for evermore complicated and arcane ways to keep himself amused."

For his next novel, *Sabbath's Theater* (1995), Roth returned to his study of sexuality, this time through the misadventures of Mickey Sabbath, a once-notorious New York street performer, now cheating on his second wife, Roseanna, with a Croatian immigrant named Drenka. When Drenka dies of ovarian cancer, the embittered Sabbath looks back on their relationship in order to better understand his own wild life. Calling the book "distasteful and disingenuous," Michiko Kakutani wrote in her *New York Times* (August 22, 1995) review: "Because Mr. Roth never offers much insight into Sabbath's heart, because he suggests that Sabbath is virtually incapable of sincerity, that even his post-Drenka breakdown may be an act of manipulation . . . the reader is hard pressed to tolerate, much less sympathize with, Sabbath." On the other hand, William H. Pritchard, in a review for the *New York Times Book Review* (September 10, 1995), found the book to be Roth's "richest, most rewarding novel." *Sabbath's Theater* went on to win the National Book Award for fiction, which carried a $10,000 stipend.

In 1997 Roth published *American Pastoral*, the first book in a trilogy of postwar American life, set primarily in the Vietnam era. Though narrated by Nathan Zuckerman, the story he relates is about the rise and fall of Seymour Irving Levov, known as "the Swede" for his Aryan good looks. Though Jewish, the Swede is not as alienated as many of Roth's other Jewish characters; in fact, because of his good looks, he becomes first a commanding athlete and later a successful husband and father—someone truly living the dream of the 1950s by assimilating completely into American life. His daughter, however, shows him the flip side of his American dream as a revolutionary in the 1960s, destroying his illusion of ordinariness forever.

American Pastoral received stellar reviews and earned Roth the Pulitzer Prize. In *America* (August 30–September 6, 1997), Sylvia Barack Fishman proclaimed: "Philip Roth . . . has written a powerful, painful and deeply moving masterpiece that will surprise many readers familiar with his 22 earlier books." "*American Pastoral*," noted Mayer Schiller in the *National Review* (June 16, 1997), "has everything one could want in a novel. Its rapid-fire insights into the human condition tumble down upon each other. Yet, they are delivered with just the right degree of irony, ambiguity, and humble humor."

I Married a Communist (1998), the second volume in Roth's trilogy, did not fair as favorably with the critics. Again told by Zuckerman, as well as his 90-year-old high-school teacher, Murray Ringold, it relates the story of Murray's brother Ira—a radio star known as Iron Rinn—who converts to communism during World War II and is later vilified for his beliefs. Betrayed by his wife, Eve, who writes a tell-all memoir about her life with him, Iron Rinn is devastated by the same anti-communist forces that brought down so many Americans in the 1950s. In the *New York Times* (October 8, 1998), Michiko Kakutani called the book "a wildly uneven novel that feels both unfinished and overstuffed, a novel that veers unsteadily between sincerity and slapstick, heartfelt melancholy and cavalier manipulation." Calling the book "a gripping novel" in the *New York Times Book Review* (October 11, 1998), Robert Kelly cheered: "This powerful novel leaves me haunted by the isolation in which each character, not just Ira, stands in history. The book's final page tells of the stars, whose brilliance is matched only by their apartness. A classic image fit to close this new novel by one of the real ones."

The Human Stain (2000) is the final installment of the trilogy. A portrait of contemporary American angst, set against the backdrop of the Monica Lewinsky scandal, in 1998, the novel looks at the decline of common sense and civility with regard to sex and privacy in the United States. Told once again by Nathan Zuckerman, the book relates the life of Coleman Silk, a black professor who has been passing for white for decades. Lorrie Moore, in the *New York Times Book Review* (May 7, 2000), called it "an astonishing, uneven and often very beautiful book." In *Time* (May 8, 2000), R. Z. Sheppard proclaimed: "At 67, Roth has not lost one ampere of his power to rile and surprise. . . . Most novelists wouldn't or couldn't handle the variety of elements that Roth does here. Few have his radical imagination and technical mastery. Fewer still have his daring."

With *The Dying Animal* (2001), Roth revived David Kepesh, who was last seen in the 1977 book *The Professor of Desire*. Though now an old man, Kepesh continues to have relationships with young students, particularly one beautiful Cuban American pupil named Consuela Castillo. The book received mediocre reviews. As Keith Gessen wrote in the *Nation* (June 11, 2001): "It seems obvious that at this point Roth can do little with sex that he hasn't done already (though he tries in *The Dying Animal*, he tries). This continued fixation is fictionally fallow. . . . Since sex is, in this view, overdetermined, it's like writing about gravity."

In 1990 Roth married the distinguished British actress Claire Bloom, with whom he had lived since 1976, after encountering her on a Manhattan street corner. (The couple had first met in 1965 at a party, when they were both otherwise attached.) They separated after four years of marriage. In 1996 Bloom published her autobiography, *Leaving a Doll's House*, in which her turbulent 18-year relationship with Roth is the centerpiece. (Eve, the traitorous wife in *I Married a Communist*, was generally thought by critics to be based on Bloom.) Since 1973 Roth has lived on his 200-year-old, 40-acre farm in northwestern Connecticut. "I don't lead a sociable life," Roth has said. "The concentration of writing requires silence," he told Michiko Kakutani in 1981. "For me, large blocks of silence. It's like hearing a faint Morse code—a faint signal is being given, and I need quiet to pick it up. Besides, what do I need the city for? A little bit goes a long way. One week in New York will take care of me for a year."

—C. M.

SUGGESTED READING: *America* p23+ Aug. 30–Sep. 6, 1997; *Commonweal* p22+ Jan. 15, 1999; *Nation* p53+ June 12, 2000; *National Review* p53+ June 16, 1997; *New Republic* p70+ Apr. 17–24, 2000; *New York Newsday* p14+ Nov. 27, 1983, II p4+ Jan 7, 1987; *New York Times* C p17+ Sep. 6, 1988, C p17 Aug. 22, 1995, C p29 Nov. 17, 1995, E p1 Oct. 6, 1998, IV p2 Oct. 11, 1998; *New York Times Book Review* p1+ Oct. 18, 1987, p7 Sep. 10, 1995, p7 Oct. 13, 1996, p6 Oct. 11, 1998, p7+ May 7, 2000; *New Yorker* p109 Mar. 15, 1993; *Newsweek* p55 Mar. 8, 1993, p70 May 15, 2000; *People* p97+ Dec. 19, 1983, p99+ Apr. 8 1991; *Publishers Weekly* p68+ Aug. 26, 1988; *Threepenny Review* p18+ Fall 2000; *Time* p68 Mar. 8, 1993, p88 May 8, 2000; *Washington Post* p1+ Jan. 12, 1987; Contemporary Literary Criticism Yearbook (1999); *Dictionary of Literary Biography Yearbook 1982* (1983); Jones, Judith Paterson, and Guinevera A. Nance. *Philip Roth* (1981); Kakutani, Michiko. *The Poet at the Piano* (1989); McDaniel, John N. *The Fiction of Philip Roth* (1974); Plimpton, George, ed. *Writers at Work* (1986); Rodgers, Bernard F. *Philip Roth* (1978);*World Authors 1950–1970* (1975)

SELECTED BOOKS: *Goodbye, Columbus and Five Short Stories*, 1959; *Letting Go*, 1962; *Portnoy's Complaint*, 1969; *The Breast*, 1972; *The Great American Novel*, 1973; *My Life as a Man*, 1974; *The Professor of Desire*, 1977; *Zuckerman Unbound*, 1981; *Zuckerman Bound*, 1985; *Patrimony: A True Story*, 1991; *Operation Shylock*, 1993; *Sabbath's Theater*, 1995; *American Pastoral*, 1997; *I Married a*

Communist, 1998; *The Human Stain*, 2000; *The Dying Animal*, 2001

Leslie Rule/Courtesy of Ann Rule

Rule, Ann

Oct. 22, 1935– True-crime writer

Sometimes called the "queen of true-crime writers," Ann Rule is the author of numerous books, most of which were best-sellers. The most popular of her works include *The Stranger Beside Me*, *A Rage to Kill: And Other True Cases*, *Bitter Harvest*, and two—*Small Sacrifices* and *Dead by Sunset*—that were made into television miniseries. In a review of *Dead by Sunset*, Walter Walker wrote for the *New York Times* (October 22, 1995) that Rule "brings to her work the passion, the prodigious research and the narrative skill to create suspense from a situation in which the outcome is a matter of fact, known to many readers before they open the book." Regarded as an expert on serial killers, Rule has testified at congressional hearings and lectured before behavioral scientists receiving instruction at the Federal Bureau of Investigation's training academy. She served as a member of the United States Justice Department task force that instituted the FBI's Violent Crime Apprehension Program (VI-CAP), which uses a computerized system to help the police discover patterns in what may appear to be unconnected crimes. In an interview with Cheryl Bartky for *Writer's Digest* (December 1992), Rule said, "I think I have a God-given instinct for people—for knowing what makes them tick and for making them come alive on the page."

Rule was born Ann Stackhouse on October 22, 1935 in Lowell, Michigan, to Chester Stackhouse and Sophie Hansen Stackhouse. Both of her parents worked at schools—her father as a football, basketball, and track coach, and her mother as a teacher for the mentally disabled. Her father changed jobs several times, forcing the family to move periodically; during her childhood they lived in Pennsylvania, Oregon, California, and New York. For 11 summers from the time she was seven, Rule stayed in Stanton, Michigan, with her maternal grandparents—who, like others among her relatives, held jobs in law enforcement. Her grandfather, Chris Hansen, was Stanton's sheriff; he and his wife lived in part of the same building that housed the town jail. In an interview with Montgomery Brower for *People* (September 14, 1987), Rule recalled that watching her grandfather in the process of solving crimes fascinated her. Her grandmother cooked meals for the prisoners, and young Ann would help by passing trays of food to them. The inmates almost always treated her well, and she often wondered what they had done to land them behind bars. "I grew up wanting to know: Why do nice, little kids grow up to be criminals?" she recalled to Angie Cannon for *womenconnect.com* (May 5, 2000). By the age of eight, she knew that she wanted to be a police officer.

Rule still harbored that ambition when she enrolled at the University of Washington. Knowing that she would get good grades in writing courses, she majored in English and took classes in psychology, criminology, and penology as well. After graduating she joined Seattle's police force, where she soon learned that her male co-workers did not regard female officers as equally qualified to do the job. Speaking of herself and her female colleagues, Rule told Marie Arana for the *Washington Post* (October 17, 1999), "We were glorified caseworkers. We didn't wear uniforms. . . . If things got dangerous, we were told to call for male back-up." Nevertheless, she told Angie Cannon, "I loved that job"—"the excitement of it, . . . never knowing what was going to happen," and "being able to help people." But after a little over a year at the job, she was forced to leave, because, although she got high marks on all her written and performance tests, her extreme nearsightedness prevented her from passing the eye examination. Rule later worked as a caseworker for the Washington State Department of Public Assistance.

By the 1960s she had married Bill Rule, a high-school English teacher and former classmate of hers, with whom she had four children. After her husband took a break from his job to further his education, she began writing to support her family. By 1969 she had become a full-time writer as well as a homemaker. Having chosen to focus on real crimes, she increased her expertise by talking with officers in the homicide and arson divisions of her local police department. She gradually widened her contacts to law-enforcement personnel throughout the Northwest and slowly gained their trust. (Later, when they learned that she had become her children's sole source of support, they helped her by giving her information that they might otherwise have withheld from her.) Her work appeared in newspapers and national magazines, among them *Cosmopolitan*, *Redbook*, and *Ladies Home Journal*. She has cited the acclaimed investigative reporter and true-crime writer Thomas Thompson, whose books include *Blood and Money* and *Serpentine*, and Truman Capote, the celebrated author of *In Cold Blood*, as influential in her development as a writer.

In the early 1970s Rule volunteered during the late shift at a Seattle crisis center, answering a telephone hotline whose callers included people who felt suicidal. There she befriended one of her coworkers, a good-looking, charming 24-year-old law student named Ted Bundy, who loved gourmet food and the music of Mozart. Bundy reminded her of her younger brother, Don, who had committed suicide, and she trusted him enough to confide in him. She revealed to him that she had decided to end her marriage but that she felt guilty about doing so, because her husband had been diagnosed with a potentially fatal form of skin cancer. "On the surface at least, it seemed that I had more problems than Ted did," Rule told Deb Price for the *Detroit News* (May 6, 1996, on-line). "He was one of those rare people who listen with full attention, who evince a genuine caring by their very stance. You could tell him things you might never tell anyone else." Rule divorced her husband in 1972, and from then on she raised her children alone. (Her ex-husband died when the children were between the ages of eight and 15.) To make ends meet, she shopped at a Goodwill store and sewed clothing for her children herself. She also took night classes, in such subjects as crime-scene investigation and photography; police administration; and arrest, search and seizure, first at Highline Community College, in Des Moines, Washington, and then at the University of Washington, where she eventually received an M.A. degree in criminal psychology. For 13 years she wrote two 10,000-word pieces each week for *True Detective*, which paid her $250 per article. At the insistence of the magazine's editors, who "thought nobody would want to read a crime story written by a female," as she told Robert Lindsey for the *New York Times* (February 21, 1984), she used the pseudonym Andy Stack.

In May 1975 Rule signed a contract to write a book about a series of unsolved murders in the Seattle area. The next year Ted Bundy was linked to those murders and others, after one of his former fiancées told Utah police about the bag filled with women's clothing, plaster of Paris, and instruments of torture she had seen in his room; he was subsequently arrested on charges of killing more than 30 women in five states. Bundy, who had graduated from college with honors in psychology, was serving as a mental-health counselor and as the assistant director of the Seattle Crime Prevention Advisory Commission; he had also written a popular pamphlet on rape prevention. In addition, he had been so successful in local Republican politics that some expected him to run for the governorship of Washington State someday. Expert at masking his true personality, he had manipulated many women—including Rule—into trusting him, often tricking them by wearing a fake cast on his arm and asking for their help.

For a long time Rule could not believe that the man who had always walked her to her car at 2:00 a.m. on her crisis-center nights was capable of the savage crimes he was accused of committing. She had found him to be "young, idealistic, clean, sure, and empathetic," she told Peter Gorner for the *Chicago Tribune* (September 17, 1980). "He seemed to ask nothing but friendship." Rule's perception of him changed when Bundy was tried for beating a woman to death in a Florida State University sorority house. During the trial, which ended in 1979, prosecutors displayed photographic proof that the teeth marks found on the buttocks of the dead woman exactly matched the configurations of Bundy's teeth. "Every single one of his teeth, every little broken spot, the shape, size, everything fit perfectly," Rule recalled to Deb Price. "There was no explaining that away. It made me physically ill. I had to run down the hall and throw up."

The Stranger Beside Me (1980), which she completed after 90 days of nearly nonstop writing, chronicles Rule's friendship with Bundy as well as his trials for murder. A best-seller, the book describes the physical resemblance between each of Bundy's victims and the first of his fiancées, who had rejected him and caused him to feel humiliated. "He got her back . . . ," Rule told Deb Price. "He was in effect killing her [when he killed other women], and each time he killed her image, he felt worse instead of better. . . . He just became more and more addicted to getting rid of this empty place inside him." In the *New York Times Book Review* (August 24, 1980), Thomas Thompson described *The Stranger Beside Me* as "dramatic and occasionally as chilling as a bedroom window shattering at midnight"; in the *Saturday Review* (August 1980), Arthur Spiegelman characterized the book as "serious, balanced, and absorbing."

Rule's next book, a novel called *Possession* (1983), apparently attracted little notice. She also published three true-crime books under her pseudonym, Andy Stack: *Lust Killer* (1983), *Want-Ad Killer* (1983), and *The I-Five Killer* (1984), all of which are about serial killers and have since been reissued. Her real name appears on the cover of the highly successful *Small Sacrifices: A True Story of Passion and Murder* (1987). That book focuses on Diane Downs, who was found guilty of shooting each of her three children—killing one and seriously injuring the others. Downs had claimed that the perpetrator was a "bushy-haired stranger," but according to the prosecutors, she had been driven to murder by her fear of losing her married lover, who did not want children. The television adaptation of *Small Sacrifices*, written by Joyce Eliason and directed by David Greene, starred Farrah Fawcett and Ryan O'Neal. The miniseries won a 1989 George Foster Peabody Award, which recognizes outstanding achievement in radio and television.

In 1989 Simon & Schuster paid Rule $3.2 million for her next two books. The first, *If You Really Loved Me: A True Story of Desire and Murder* (1991), describes how David Brown, a millionaire computer expert, murdered his fifth wife, so that he could collect more than $800,000 in insurance and marry his teenage sister-in-law; he pinned the blame on his 14-year-old daughter from an earlier marriage, who spent several years in a juvenile-detention facility before Brown's guilt was discovered. *If You Really Loved Me* was followed by *Everything She Ever Wanted: A True Story of Obsessive Love, Murder, and Betrayal* (1992), about Patricia Allanson, a sociopath who attempted to poison her husband's grandparents and later trapped her spouse into unwittingly killing his mother and father, while she maintained the façade of a "modern-day southern belle." Other books by Rule include *Dead by Sunset: Perfect Husband, Perfect Killer?* (1995), about Brad Cunningham, who for seven years escaped prosecution for the murder of his fourth wife; *Bitter Harvest: A Woman's Fury, a Mother's Sacrifice* (1998), about a Kansas physician who tried to poison her husband and set a fire that claimed the lives of two of her children; and *And Never Let Her Go: Thomas Capano, the Deadly Seducer* (1999), about a successful lawyer who was sentenced to death for the murder of his former lover Anne Marie Fahey, a secretary to the governor of Delaware.

In 1999 Rule published *The End of the Dream: The Golden Boy Who Never Grew Up and Other True Cases*, a book depicting, among other tales, the lives of four young men in Washington State who become embroiled in million-dollar bank robberies and drug dealing. Her second book of that year, *A Rage To Kill*, looked at the vicious murder spree of Silas Cool, who caused a bus to crash off the Aurora Bridge in Seattle and into an apartment building. Ten of her shorter pieces, written over the last 25 years, were collected in *Empty Promises* (2001).

Rule's second book of 2001, *Every Breath You Take*, had an unusual origin: it was written at the request of the murder victim. Sheila Bellush married and endured years of abuse at the hands of Allen Blackthorne, a rich swindler, even after giving birth to their two daughters. When she finally divorced him, Blackthorne remained obsessed with his ex-wife and vowed that she would be punished for leaving him. Bellush asked her sister to contact Rule in case she was killed, so that her story could be told. In a review for *Booklist*, as quoted on *Amazon.com*, Brad Hooper proclaimed: "Rule excels at painting psychologically perceptive portraits of all the characters in this stranger-than-fiction but nevertheless real-life drama."

Before deciding on the subject of a book, Rule considers as many as 500 possible cases, many of which are suggested by readers—including, in some instances, the relatives of crime victims. "When I get over three dozen messages, e-mail, letters, or phone calls [about a single case], I pay attention," she told Angie Cannon. "My readers know what I'm looking for." She has no interest in writing about high-profile cases, such as the O. J. Simpson trial. Her research includes reading newspaper accounts, interviewing both the lead detective and the prosecutor, and visiting the scene of the crime. She also attends the trial, where she makes contact with witnesses. She does not approach the accused until he or she is found guilty, because, as she told Angie Cannon, "I don't want to mess up the prosecutor's case." She explained to Cannon, "A lot of [criminals] are anxious to talk to me after they've been convicted. . . . Most of the people I write about are antisocial personalities, and they are so convinced that they're smarter than anyone else that all they have to do is just explain to a reporter or a jury what really happened." She has learned to be a good listener and to hide her feelings and opinions when interviewing a subject.

To discover as much as possible about the roots of a killer's behavior, Rule thoroughly investigates each suspect's childhood and family history. Although it is, in her words, "almost impossible" to feel sorry for the vicious criminals she meets, she told Cannon that she does "feel empathy and sympathy for the children that they were." Rule also tries to portray the victims accurately, although she sometimes omits personal details or changes people's names at the request of their families. Her books often detail the strenuous efforts of particular law enforcement officials or prosecutors who were determined to solve a case or put a murderer behind bars. "When you are dealing with the blackest side of the human soul," Rule told Cheryl Bartky, "you have to have someone who has performed heroically to balance that out." She tries to keep gore and sensationalism out of her books. "I try to be as sensitive as I can," she explained to Bartky, "and I try to think, 'Now if someone was writing about my family, . . . what would I want the writer to say?' I try to stick within those guidelines."

After writing several books about serial killers, Rule began to document the circumstances surrounding acts of violence perpetrated by women, whose motives, she realized, often differ from those of their male counterparts. "Women kill for two reasons, broadly defined: for love—and you've got to include jealousy, revenge, sex—or for money," Rule told Angie Cannon. "Women also tend to kill people they know, people who trust them, people they are very close to—their children, mother, their series of husbands. Women are willing to delay gratification for a long time. They plan their murders very, very carefully and coldly." Although the motives of sociopaths may differ, Rule learned that such people have certain characteristics in common. "These are people who have no conscience, no empathy," she told Deb Price. "They can lie with the clearest eyes and the nicest smiles. These people wear a mask that is so perfect. Where unless they choose to lift just a little piece of it, we never know that there's a monster behind."

Rule told Cannon that being a true-crime writer requires courage. "The hardest thing for me to do is to approach people who have been through so much stress and tragedy and then have the temerity to ask them to talk to me . . . ," she said. "Every time I'm amazed that people will talk to me. You have to have a compassionate heart." For many years Rule felt guilty about benefitting from the misfortunes of others, but over time she began to realize that her books had helped many people, and in some cases may have saved lives. Many of her readers are women, and some have thanked her for helping them to avoid potentially violent relationships. "I want to warn readers of the dangers—the ruses, devices, and techniques that sociopaths use to ensnare people," she told Cheryl Bartky. Rule regards her contributions to the development of the FBI's Violent Crime Apprehension Program (VI-CAP), in the early 1980s, as one "vindication for profiting from other people's tragedies," as she told Robert Lindsey.

Rule has received the Washington State Governor's Award and two Anthony Awards (named in honor of the mystery writer Anthony Boucher and bestowed at the annual World Mystery Convention), and she is a two-time nominee for the Mystery Writers of America's Edgar Award. She assists with programs that aid the victims of violent crimes and their families and also helps support groups for women and children who have been abused. She has often done book signings jointly with her best friend, the suspense writer Donna Anders, author of *Flower Man* and *Dead Silence*. A resident of Washington State, Rule lives with her two dogs and five cats. She enjoys gardening and collecting such objects as antique bottles, cobalt-blue glass, police memorabilia, wind chimes, and teddy bears. Rule's daughter Leslie has written two mysteries, *Whispers from the Grave* and *Kill Me Again*, both of which deal with supernatural phenomena. Her other daughter, Laura, works with the elderly and with children of battered women. Her son Mike serves as her office manager and conducts interviews for the Blind Radio Network; her son Andy works in the field of consumer research. According to her official Web page, she has a third son, Bruce Sherles, whose job is in the cookie industry. Rule also has three grandchildren.

—*C. L.*

SUGGESTED READING: *Chicago Tribune* I p15 Sep. 17, 1980; *Detroit News* (on-line) May 6, 1996, with photo; *New York Times* B p9 Feb. 21, 1984, with photo, VII p38 Oct. 22, 1995; *Washington Post* X p8 Oct. 17, 1999; *Writer's Digest* p27+ Dec., 1992, with photos

SELECTED BOOKS: *The Stranger Beside Me*, 1980; *Possession: A Novel*, 1983; *Small Sacrifices: A True Story of Passion and Murder*, 1987; *If You Really Loved Me*, 1991; *Everything She Ever Wanted*, 1992; *Dead By Sunset*, 1995; *Bitter Harvest*, 1997; *And Never Let Her Go: Thomas Capano: The Deadly Seducer*, 1999; *End of the Dream*, 1999; *Rage to Kill*, 1999, *Empty Promises*, 2001; *Every Breath You Take*, 2001; *Last Dance, Last Chance*, 2002

Courtesy of Crown Publicity

Rushkoff, Douglas

Feb 18, 1961– Nonfiction writer; novelist, editor

After the publication of *Cyberia: Life in the Trenches of Hyperspace* (1994), which extolled the virtues of the wireless world, Douglas Rushkoff was seen as a spokesman for the Internet generation. He soon found himself in demand as a media consultant to companies interested in selling products to young people who, it was thought, had become immune to traditional marketing techniques. In his subsequent books, *Media Virus!*, *Children of Chaos*, and *Coercion*, Rushkoff studied the confluence of youth culture, technology, and media. A *New Perspectives Quarterly* report described Rushkoff as "the brilliant heir to [Marshall] McLuhan," the late communications and media theorist whose ideas have been widely applied to the Internet; but Rushkoff has also been decried as a "sellout" for his consultation work. Both characterizations surprise Rushkoff, who never intended to set himself up as a "cyberpundit," an expert on the emerging Internet community and culture. "I [need] to show people how false all this cyberpunditry really is; that 'cyberpundit' is an oxymoron to the core," he told Michael Rust in an interview with the *Washington Times* (August 4, 1997). "All I've been trying to communicate is that we live in a culture where the tools of social programming are obsolete. And that kids were the first [to become] immune [to] so-called target media." His most recent book is *Nothing Sacred* (2003), a reflection on modern Judaism.

Douglas Rushkoff was born on February 18, 1961 in New York City and grew up in Larchmont and Scarsdale, suburbs of New York. His parents, Marvin and Sheila Rushkoff, were, respectively, a hospital administrator and a psychiatric social worker. He attended Princeton University, in Princeton, New Jersey, where he studied English and graduated magna cum laude in 1983. He then studied at the California Institute of the Arts, in Los Angeles, and earned an MFA in 1986. During the time he lived on the West Coast he considered a career in film, and received a director's fellowship from the American Film Institute, in 1988. Film, however, did not hold his interest for long.

In the late 1980s, at a time when the Internet was not widely known or available, Rushkoff began writing about computers and virtual reality for *Exposure*, a Los Angeles magazine. In 1991 he accepted a job as a senior editor with *Fame*, a monthly magazine based in New York. He had already shipped his belongings there when he learned that the magazine had folded, and so decided to move anyway. On the flight from Los Angeles to New York he sketched out an idea for a book, which was published in 1994 as *Cyberia: Life in the Trenches of Hyperspace*.

Rushkoff had already published, with Patrick Wells, *Free Rides: How to Get High without Drugs* (1991), an exploration of meditation and other ancient and modern mind-altering practices. (It was later reprinted under the title *Stoned Free: How to Get High without Drugs*, in 1995.) He struck a popular chord with *Cyberia*, a study of the then-emerging Internet culture. Rushkoff had noticed that many of his old friends, who had experimented with psychedelic drugs in their college years, had subsequently moved into the computer industry in the San Francisco Bay Area and gotten into large dance parties, known as raves, and formed a community centered around hallucinogens and the Internet. In *Cyberia*, he focuses on the mind-altering potential of the new information revolution and predicts a transformation of American culture, in which citizens use the power of the Internet to make more informed, independent decisions in their lives. A *Kirkus* reviewer, as quoted in *Contemporary Authors* (1998), characterized the book as a "provocative, wide-ranging survey of the current state of the interface between the longings of youth and the wild potentials of computer technology."

In his next work, *Media Virus!* (1994), Rushkoff introduces the concept of the "datasphere," the contemporary media culture that continually bombards us with images, advertisements, and information. Rushkoff argues that the datasphere is susceptible to viruses—whether through the "hijacking" of media by special interest groups (animal rights activists, religious conservatives) or by more "organic," spontaneous events, including the live broadcast of O. J. Simpson fleeing police in a Ford Bronco truck or the widespread dissemination of the amateur videotape of Los Angeles cops beating Rodney King. The book received mainly positive reviews. "[Despite an] irritating tendency to lump too many people into a vaguely defined Gen X category, *Media Virus!* obviously contains many ideas well worth considering," Aaron Cohen wrote for *Booklist* (October 1, 1994). Writing for *Library Journal* (October 15, 1994), Judy Solberg noted that "While [Rushkoff's] excessive use of viral-related concepts gets tiresome, the thesis that the popular media manipulate American culture is provocative and well argued."

The predictions in *Cyberia* and *Media Virus!* about the ongoing human-communications revolution peaked the interest of advertising executives, and Rushkoff became a much-sought-after new-media expert. In an interview with John Brockman for *Harper's Magazine* (January 2000), Rushkoff described his disillusionment after attending the American Association of Advertising Agencies conference. "They wanted me to talk to them about media viruses and youth culture. I was thrilled. I prepared a talk in which I claimed that advertising was over, that their tyranny over young people had come to an end, that they should give up their coercive ways," he told Brockman. "When I arrived, there were signs and handouts that read 'How to use Media Viruses to Capture New Audiences' and that sort of thing.... My books were primers, required texts for young executives on how to take advantage of new media to do the same old thing they were doing before." Realizing that he was "just as caught up in it as everyone else," Rushkoff began to work as a highly paid consultant to groups interested in marketing their products to Internet-savvy consumers. Trip Gabriel noted in the *New York Times* (November 25, 1996) that, "For eyebrow-raising fees of up to $7,500 an hour, Mr. Rushkoff has explained to the chief executive of a broadcast television network the meaning of 'whatever,' that shrug of generational indifference in the lyrics of Kurt Cobain." Gabriel's article generated a great deal of negativity towards Rushkoff, who was widely accused of hawking his generation's interests to marketing executives for cash. "The figures bandied about—that I make $7,500 an hour or that I got $500,000 for selling my book to a movie studio—are just plainly not true," Rushkoff noted in an interview with Rebecca Eisenberg for the *San Francisco Examiner* (June 22, 1997). "When I'm attacked by the right, it's because there are people who think that media literacy is dangerous. I can respect that. They are attacking my ideas. When the so-called left attacks me, it's not about ideas. They say, 'This guy is making a lot of money, so he's a sellout.'"

In 1994 Rushkoff developed, with Andrew Mayer and Jason Shankel, the "Cyber Tarot" software, an electronic tarot-card game. He also edited the *Gen X Reader*, an anthology of stories, screenplays, interviews, essays, and other entries by and about that generation's luminaries, including the screenwriter and director Richard Linklater, the cartoonist Matt Groening, and the fiction writer Walter Kirn. In 1995 he published *Children of Chaos: Surviving the End of the World As We Know It* in London; a year later it was published in the U.S. as *Playing the Future: How Kids' Culture Can Teach Us How to Thrive in an Age of Chaos*. In this work Rushkoff argues that young people, whom he calls "screenagers," adapt to evolving technologies more easily than adults, in part because their games, hobbies, and interests allow them to cope in a world bordering on the chaotic. The book received mixed reviews. In the *New York Times* (July 9, 1996) Michiko Kakutani proclaimed: "Mr. Rushkoff has taken a pedantic and heavy-handed approach to a potentially intriguing subject. The resulting book is decidedly less readable than its precursor, *Media Virus!* . . . and, as it turns out, considerably more dubious." Stuart Price in the *Daily Telegraph* (April 29, 1997) offered only praise: "Douglas Rushkoff is a class writer, and this is a class book. Just getting someone to think through some ideas and come to well-founded conclusions is a start; but this writer goes further, with an attractive, often humorous style and compelling insights into why those who have grown up with a background of computer technology—or 'screenagers'—are so baffling."

Rushkoff next published a novel, *Ecstasy Club* (1997), which focuses on the lives of alienated youths who follow a cult leader named Duncan. Duncan believes that the way to raise humanity to a higher level is by throwing ecstasy-taking raves in abandoned factories and warehouses in Oakland. Many critics agreed with Randall Lyman, who wrote in the *Bay Guardian* (May 28, 1997): "*Ecstacy Club* is a solid first novel but not a great one. Rushkoff's got the basic novelistic moves down, but he's not adroit yet. . . . Too often [it] makes me feel like I were still reading Rushkoff's other books, as if he hadn't broken free of their stylistic momentum."

In 1999 Rushkoff returned to nonfiction with *Coercion: Why We Listen to What "They" Say*. He argues that marketing people have become increasingly skilled at getting people to buy things that they do not need, and that corporations use ever-shadier techniques to increase their sales. Such techniques, Rushkoff noted to Brockman, become much more insidious when automated through on-line marketing tools. "An e-commerce site watches and records each user's interactions with it. What screens did the user look at and in what order? Where did he click? Where did he buy?" Rushkoff said. "And the computer can then dynamically reconfigure itself to make a Web site that identifies and then paces each individual exactly. Meanwhile the user thinks he's in control."

David Pitt noted in *Booklist* (August 1999) that, in *Coercion*, Rushkoff "reveals all the tricks we use on one another—and reminds us that, no matter how clever we think we are, we're always, inevitably, being manipulated." He concluded that it was "an essential book for anyone interested in the power of media and the mechanics of deception." In *Reason* (April 2000) Timothy Virkkala found Rushkoff's argument uneven and in some cases manipulative: "Like any good salesman, he tells a good story, and his wares do not wholly lack merit. But he's twisting words and arguments in untrustworthy ways."

In 2001 Rushkoff published one of the first "open source" novels, *Exit Strategy*, which was published in the same year in Great Britain under the title *Bull*. Rushkoff introduces Jamie Cohen, a young computer hacker who is betrayed by his friends and winds up becoming the right-hand man to venture capitalists in New York. This story was published in both print and electronic form, and readers were encouraged to modify and annotate the text in any ways they chose. One hundred of their comments were incorporated into the second U.S. printing of the book.

In April 2003 Rushkoff published *Nothing Sacred: The Truth About Judaism*, a detailed reflection on the meaning of Jewish culture and religion in the modern world.

Douglas Rushkoff writes monthly columns on cyberculture that are internationally distributed through the *New York Times* Syndicate and contributes commentaries to National Public Radio (NPR). He is a professor of media studies at New York University, a board member of the Media Ecology Association, and an adviser to the United Nations Commission on World Culture. His writing has been published in such periodicals as *Time*, *Esquire*, the (London) *Guardian*, *Paper*, *Gentleman's Quarterly*, and the *Silicon Alley Reporter*.
—C. M.

SUGGESTED READING: *Bay Guardian* (on-line) May 28, 1997; *Booklist* p216 Oct. 1, 1994, p2000 Aug. 1999; *Christian Science Monitor* p20 Aug. 5, 1999; *Daily Telegraph* (on-line) Apr. 29, 1997; Douglas Rushkoff Web site; *Forward* (on-line), Apr. 20, 2001; *Harper's Magazine* p23+ Jan. 2000; *Library Journal* p76 Oct. 15, 1994; *New York Times* C p16 July 9, 1996, D p1 Nov. 25, 1996; *Policy Studies Journal* p893+ 1999; *Reason* p70+ Apr. 2000; *San Francisco Examiner* D p5 June 22, 1997; *Washington Times* p 22 August 4, 1997

SELECTED BOOKS: nonfiction—*Free Rides*, 1991; *Cyberia*, 1994; *Media Virus!*, 1994; *Coercion*, 1999; *Nothing Sacred*, 2003; fiction—*Ecstasy Club*, 1997; *Exit Strategy*, 2001; as editor—*Gen X Reader*, 1994

J.D. Sloan/Courtesy of Knopf Publicity

Russo, Richard

July 15, 1949– Novelist; short-story writer

Richard Russo's comic portrayals of small-town American life have earned him comparison to Sinclair Lewis and Sherwood Anderson. The majority of his novels examine the lives of blue-collar characters after the local industries have closed down, men and women who get by on luck and tenacity. His first two books, *Mohawk* (1986) and *The Risk Pool* (1988), revolve around the struggles of the inhabitants of the fictional town of Mohawk; since the demise of the local leather-tannery there, troubles have increased with the unemployment rate. In one of his most commercially successful novels to date, *Nobody's Fool* (1993), readers are treated to the misadventures of Sully, a 60-year-old man whose badly injured knee is a harbinger of an impending streak of bad luck. Russo, a teacher for many years, shifted gears with *Straight Man* (1997), his humorous look at academia in a small Pennsylvania college town. Nevertheless, he returned to form with *Empire Falls* (2001), a sprawling multi-generational book about a collapsing New England mill town, for which he won the 2002 Pulitzer Prize for fiction.

Richard Russo was born in Johnstown, New York, on July 15, 1949, the son of James W. Russo and Jean Findlay (LeVarn) Russo, and grew up in Gloversville, New York. In 1967 he began his undergraduate work at the University of Arizona, in Tucson. "I went about as far away as I could get," Russo told Lewis Burke Frumkes in the *Writer* (December 2000). "After one semester I became an English major, and I really fell in love all over again with books, particularly with literature."

After receiving his undergraduate and master's degrees, Russo stayed on at the university to work on his doctorate in English literature, but was disappointed by the fact that, as a Ph.D. student, he spent considerably more time reading academic work about literature than actual literature. As he explained to Frumkes: "As I got closer to a degree and a career as a scholar, I slowly realized that this was not something I really wanted to do. When I passed my preliminaries and started work on my dissertation, things went along pretty well. I had published one article from my dissertation and had another one accepted. Everybody was encouraging me. I only had to write three more chapters to finish up the degree."

As Russo was coming to the end of his doctoral work, he realized that he didn't want to remain in academia for the rest of his life, although his entire education had been focused on that goal. As a graduate teaching assistant sharing an office with 23 other graduate assistants, he reevaluated his chosen path. As he told an interviewer for Nashville Public Radio, as transcribed on the Davis-Kidd Booksellers Web site: "It wasn't so much that I wanted to write books, but I loved literature. Reading books about books wasn't nearly as much fun as reading books. I also discovered that the only people having fun were the creative writers. So, while in school working toward finishing my Ph.D., I wandered across the aisle where people seemed to be having fun and took a course in creative writing."

For a year Russo worked on ridding himself of the bad writing habits he had formed while writing academic papers, and after a while he managed to write several solid 15-page stories. He earned his Ph.D. in 1980 and an MFA in 1981, and for the next five years, he taught literature at various colleges while working on his first novel, *Mohawk*, which would be published, in 1986, as part of the Vintage Contemporaries paperback series.

In Mohawk, a small upstate New York town on the decline, things have been falling apart for years: unemployment has been on the rise as leather-tanning factories close and chemicals are dumped into the local water supply. The book's dozen or so main characters have been hit hard by the times: Dan Wood has been confined to a wheelchair since the car accident that paralyzed him; Anne has been in love with Dan for years even though he married her cousin; Dallas Younger hit his peak as a high-school football star and has been drifting ever since. In the *New York Times* (October 15, 1986), Michiko Kakutani complained that the novel "has a tendency to swerve towards contrived melodrama," but believed that overall it "remains an immensely readable and sympathetic novel, a novel that attests to its author's considerable ambition and talent."

Russo returned to Mohawk for his second novel, *The Risk Pool* (1988), which is narrated by a character named Ned Hall. The novel details Ned's relationship with his father, Sam, who had fought in

World War II and returned from the service as a drifter, moving from pool hall to bar without ever thinking about the wife and child he had abandoned. After Ned's mother, Jenny, has a mental breakdown, Ned goes to live with his father in a loft above Mohawk's lone department store. In the *Chicago Tribune* (October 30, 1988), Hilma Wolitzer wrote that Russo "brilliantly evokes the economic and emotional depression of a failing town, a place where even the weather is debilitating and the inhabitants seem to struggle merely to stay in place." Walter Clemons, in *Newsweek* (December 26, 1988), noted: "In the gruff scenes between father and son, Russo risks sentimental overkill and narrowly avoids it. The result is very touching." Reviewing the novel for the *New York Times Book Review* (December 18, 1988), Jack Sullivan declared: "This is a superbly original, maliciously funny book, peopled by characters that most of us would back away from plenty fast if they ever lurched toward our barstool. It is Mr. Russo's brilliant, deadpan writing that gives their wasted lives and miserable little town such haunting power and insidious charm."

Russo's third novel, *Nobody's Fool* (1993), was also one of his most popular, thanks in part to his remarkable portrayal of Sully, a 60-year-old laborer who fears that his bum knee is just the start of a bad-luck streak. In quick succession he discovers that his landlady's son wants him evicted, his ex-wife is on the verge of a nervous breakdown, his estranged son has come for a visit, and his girlfriend blames him for her daughter's broken jaw. However, Sully's biggest problem might be trying to rid himself of memories of his own abusive father—which he attempts to do by taking the old man's house apart a piece at a time. Charles Michaud in *Library Journal* (April 15, 1993) remarked: "Russo knows the small towns of upstate New York and the people who inhabit them; he writes with humor and compassion. A delight." *Nobody's Fool* was made into a film starring Paul Newman by the director Robert Benton. Russo acted as a script consultant on the film and later co-wrote another movie with Benton, *Twilight* (1997), which starred Paul Newman, Gene Hackman, and James Garner.

Straight Man, Russo's send-up of academia and middle age, was published in 1997. In it the 50-year-old protagonist, Hank Deveraux, Jr., is named the interim chairman of the English department at a small-town Pennsylvania college, primarily because his colleagues hope he will maintain the status quo. Few realize the lengths to which Hank is willing to go to pull himself—and his backbiting petty colleagues in the English department—out of their stagnancy. In the course of a week, he threatens to kill a goose in retaliation for a cut in funds to the English department, has his nose bashed by a feminist poet colleague, and finds out his secretary is a better fiction writer than he is. In his interview for Nashville Public Radio, Russo said: "I think that this is a novel about being nearer than you want to be to the end of something. This is a story about what happens when we begin to suspect that all those important decisions that get made in the human lifetime have already been made and you're playing out the string." Joanne Wilkinson cheered in *Booklist* (May 15, 1997): "Russo has lost none of his gifts for fashioning wry comedy, endearing characters, and an artful blend of high jinks and heartache. . . . [He] proves himself a master of bighearted, old-fashioned storytelling." Scott Bradfield disagreed, however, noting for the *Times Literary Supplement* (July 25, 1997): "*Straight Man* is a funny novel; but somewhere around the middle pages, the thin plot starts to unravel, and scenes grow overly long and diffuse. Russo sets up some intriguing premises, . . . but he never tries to resolve any of them." The movie rights for *Straight Man* have reportedly been purchased by a major motion-picture studio.

In 2001 Russo published *Empire Falls*, another study of small-town America blighted by the loss of jobs and business. A generation earlier, Empire Falls, Maine, was a bustling textile and timber town; today it is filled with empty warehouses and factories and boarded-up stores. The once powerful Whiting Enterprises has one living heir, Francine Whiting, who enjoys pointing out the faults of the main character, Miles Roby, a generally nice guy who runs the local diner and may own it one day if Mrs. Whiting is inclined to turn it over to him. Russo introduces a host of secondary characters from every social circle—each dealing with the effects the town's slow demise has had on themselves and their family and friends. Writing for the *Washington Post* (May 27, 2001), Dan Cryer remarked: "Richard Russo layers these tangled relationships into a richly satisfying portrait of a man within a defining community. The author seems determined to subordinate style to honest and compassionate storytelling. That *Empire Falls* resonates so deeply is a measure of its unexpected truths." Janet Maslin in the *New York Times* (May 10, 2001) wrote: "Mr. Russo . . . has turned Empire Falls into a setting for a rich, humorous, elegantly constructed novel rooted in the bedrock traditions of American fiction." *Empire Falls* earned Russo the 2002 Pulitzer Prize for fiction.

In 2002 Russo published his first book of short fiction, *The Whore's Child: And Other Stories*, a seven-story collection that was widely praised for its wisdom, authenticity, and humor. The title story features the memorable Sister Ursula, who after enrolling in a college writing course begins composing her life story, recounting how she grew up in the convent as the abandoned daughter of a prostitute. Many of the stories tackle themes of complex parent-child or marital relationships, including "Joy Ride," in which a mother takes her 12-year-old son on a cross-country trek in search of freedom from her dull husband, and "The Mysteries of Linwood Hart," in which an astute 10-year-old boy ponders the behavior of his domineering mother. Still other stories depict characters engaged in serious self-reflection, such as "Monhegan Light," in which a troubled photographer finds love for his dead wife after discovering how hard she protected him from her long-term infidelity. Overall, *The Whore's Child* generated significant critical praise. In a review posted on *Amazon.com*, Ross Doll noted, "Russo, like Flannery O'Connor, has a gift for conveying the absurdity and severity of everyday life with brutal honesty, humor, and compassion." Meanwhile, another reviewer for *Publishers Weekly*, as quoted on *Amazon.com*, affirmed, "Russo's rueful understanding of the twisted skein of human relationships is sharp as ever, and the dialogue throughout is barbed, pointed and wryly humorous. The collection is a winner."

Richard Russo is married to Barbara Marie Russo. They have two daughters, Emily and Kate. Russo has contributed short stories to such periodicals as the *Prairie Schooner*, the *Mid-American Review*, the *Sonora Review*, the *New Yorker*, and *Harper's Magazine*. —C. M.

SUGGESTED READING: *Booklist* p1541 May 15, 1997; Davis-Kidd Booksellers Web site; *Harper's Magazine* p60+ February 1998; *Library Journal* p128 Apr. 15, 1993; *New Republic* p7 Mar. 30, 1998; *New Yorker* p74+ Dec. 23–30, 1996; *New York Times* E p22 Mar. 6, 1998, May 10, 2001; *New York Times Book Review* p14 Dec. 18, 1988, p13 June 20, 1993; *Newsweek* p67 Dec. 26, 1988; *Time* p78 July 14, 1997; *Times Literary Supplement* p634 June 9, 1989, p23 July 25, 1997; *Washington Post* T p7 May 27, 2001; *Washington Post Book World* p3 July 20, 1997; *Writer* p19+ Dec. 2000

SELECTED BOOKS: *Mohawk*, 1986; *The Risk Pool*, 1988; *Nobody's Fool*, 1993; *Straight Man*, 1997; *Empire Falls*, 2001; *The Whore's Child: And Other Stories*, 2002

Cheung Ching Ming/Courtesy of Oxford University Press

Santoro, Gene

Oct. 31, 1950– Music critic; biographer

Gene Santoro is a music critic whose columns, essays, and books explore wide swaths of musical styles and histories. He has written about legendary jazz greats and little-known world musicians and has a particular eye for musical cross-pollination—the development of new styles and hybrids from the fusion of existing musical traditions. He is a music columnist for *The Nation*, and has been a contributor to a number of periodicals, most notably, the New York *Daily News*, *New York Times*, *New York Post*, *New Yorker*, *Village Voice*, *Rolling Stone*, *Spin*, *Entertainment Weekly*, and *Down Beat*. In addition to publishing two collections of essays, *Dancing in Your Head* (1994) and *Stir It Up* (1997), he has written *Myself When I Am Real* (2000), which is considered one of the definitive biographies of the frequently misunderstood jazz legend Charles Mingus.

Born in the New York City borough of Brooklyn, on October 31, 1950, Eugene Santoro developed an interest in music at an early age. As he recalled in an e-mail interview with *World Authors*: "I don't remember not being interested in music. I started music lessons in 3rd grade. I'd always learned to sing songs from radio and TV, and made up my own. My parents were neither musicians nor music 'enthusiasts.' When she was young, my mother was a jitterbugger; as a kid I listened a lot to her handfuls of swing 78s. My father listened to opera on the radio, and Italian singers from Mario Lanza to Jerry Vale, and, when he was older, muzak."

Though Santoro has experimented with other instruments, including the mandolin and the keyboard, his true love has always been the guitar. At 12, he joined his first garage band and played at local parties and school dances. By the time he entered Regis High School, in Manhattan, he was working with more serious bands, including several that made demos for record producers and provided back-up music for singers. "I started writing about music in high school, the same time I was playing it," he told *World Authors*. "I was on the high school paper, and also spent some time trawling around clubs in Manhattan, even though I was underage (I drank a lot of overpriced cokes) with friends who wanted to check out our new heroes. So in little spots like the Scene, Café Au Go Go, Café Wha?, the Night Owl, Cheetah, and the Village Vanguard, I saw a lot of stuff, from the Blues

Project to John Coltrane. It was a wild time, and I got to write about some of what I saw—like the night Buddy Guy played at the Scene, and Jimi Hendrix showed up to jam."

After high school Santoro studied at the City University of New York, primarily at Queens College, where he won writing awards. His studies were interrupted, in 1971, when he was drafted during the Vietnam War. After getting out of the army, in late 1972, he worked as an electronics technician and also started a rock band. Unfortunately, his group did little more than play as the house band for restaurants and at weddings and bar mitzvahs. He did have some success as a musician, however, co-writing soundtracks for short films on the PBS show *Great American Dream Machine*. By 1974 he had realized that he wasn't suited for a musician's life, and so returned to college. He attended graduate school, at Stanford University, on a fellowship, and earned his doctoral degree in comparative literature and languages. He then won a Fulbright Scholarship to study classical, medieval, and renaissance culture in Italy for one year.

During that year in Italy, Santoro realized that he didn't want to be an academic. He returned to New York in the hopes of launching a writing career. "Not surprisingly, since I had zero contacts, I wasn't very successful," he told *World Authors*. "I did have a few poems published, and a couple of short stories, for which I was paid mostly in copies of the magazines and books they were published in. I got freelance editorial work at a major publisher, then became an editor at a small house in 1980. Three years later, having learned how to make a book from start to finish (I'd written and/or ghosted several books on topics from business travel to literary tourism to jazz, and overseen dozens from commissioning to publication), I co-wrote one under my own name, on the guitar. That launched me out of editing and into writing."

Over the next year, Santoro began to find work through query letters and contacts but discovered that his best stories were the ones on musicians. "Musicians liked talking to me—I understood their language," he remarked to *World Authors*. "And, as some of them told me once my stories started to appear, 'You get it right.' At first, I didn't know what they meant, then they'd explain that they too often found what they'd said or done misquoted or decontextualized. So my accuracy and empathy helped me land some big-name features and interviews, like Keith Richards and Jeff Beck, for the niche-market magazines—*Guitar World* and *Guitar Player*, *Downbeat*, *Pulse*—I'd begun writing for, and made me a valued contributor."

Santoro hoped to write more broadly about the cultural history of jazz, rock, pop, and soul. "After a couple of years," he went on to note, "I became *The Nation*'s music columnist, where I had the space and freedom to explore my evolving sense of the relationships defining art, history, culture, and society. Soon my byline appeared in a wide field of publications, each with its own editorial rules and slants and space allotments. What I did mutated, grew, encompassed new possibilities. I moved from oral history to more critical cultural analysis—something I had, in essence, been trained to do from high school on. You could say that I'm never just writing about music; I use music as a way to write about the world."

In 1994 Santoro published *Dancing in Your Head*, an essay collection about an eclectic group of musicians, including country music's k. d. lang, "free jazz" musicians Ornette Coleman and Sun Ra, rock's Neil Young, and the controversial rap group Public Enemy. Though it covers a broad range of contemporary music, the collection never seems sprawling or unfocused. Santoro supports avant-garde musicians, while criticizing major record labels for dominating music distribution. He diverges with many contemporary music critics who deride the marketing and consumption of Woodstock-era music as driven by nostalgia, rather than true appreciation for the era's bands. "This usually disposable music can and does find lasting meaning in people's lives," Santoro argues, as Aaron Cohen quoted him in *Booklist* (February 1, 1994). "If it didn't we'd need a radically new definition of culture." About the collection as a whole, Cohen remarked: "Santoro's recommendations make *Dancing in the Dark* a worthy guide for libraries expanding their sound recording collections."

Three years later Santoro published another essay collection, *Stir It Up*, this time aiming his critical eye at the evolution of musical styles. He argues that, as the world becomes smaller through better communication, musicians take the best of the world's music, blend it with their own styles, and produce something totally new. He also shows how lyrics have helped to develop new musical forms, from Bob Marley's political reggae to Bruce Springsteen's working-class rock anthems. As a reviewer noted for *Amazon.com*: "As always, Santoro is wonderfully attentive to the qualities of each artist, from Ornette Coleman to Elvis Costello, from P. J. Harvey to Manu Dibango. The heart of this book, though, is the cross-pollination of cultures. Nobody is better at describing those genres—like Tex-Mex or South African mbaqanga—in which (musical) worlds collide."

In 2000 Santoro published *Myself When I Am Real*, a critically acclaimed biography of the jazz bassist Charles Mingus, who died at age 56, in 1979. Santoro dismantles the "angry man of jazz" myth that has surrounded Mingus—and which Mingus himself helped to perpetuate in his autobiography—and seeks to reexamine his genius through interviews with his fellow musicians, family members, and former wives. Like many of the musicians who have fascinated Santoro, Mingus combined a variety of styles in his music, from gospel to classical, bebop to South American and Indian music. The biography displays Mingus's open-mindedness toward all forms of music while showing how difficult and narrow-minded he could be in his personal life, and yet it is by no means an armchair psychoanalysis of the jazz legend. As a critic in *The Nation* (October 4, 2000) noted: "Eschewing psychobiography, Santoro attempts to illustrate the postwar ferment of American culture by charting his subject within it—race, unsurprisingly, is a major leitmotif—often with anecdotes that cut against received wisdom. When Mingus first heard Dizzy Gillespie and 'Bird' Parker's bebop, who now would believe he wasn't turned on but instead found it 'chaotic and unlovely'?" In the *Philadelphia Inquirer* (August 30, 2000) Tom Moon noted: "By chronicling Mingus' milieu in such exhaustive detail, Santoro brings his readers into the mind of this conflicted genius. From there, it becomes easy to appreciate the ways Mingus cajoled and coaxed his music—charged with lusty emotion and righteous passion, taunting brass and rumbling rhythms—out of thin air, under often adverse conditions, on a nightly basis."

When asked by *World Authors* about his current projects, Santoro responded: "Right now, I'm gathering a collection of essays (some, which have been previously published, will be altered and expanded; some are being written from scratch) that is more overtly focused than my earlier ones. At least some of it will be autobiographical. It's grouped around figures from the 1950s (Max Roach, Lenny Bruce, Sonny Rollins) and the 1960s (Bob Dylan, John Coltrane, the Grateful Dead, Buffalo Springfield, Richard Pryor, Tom Wilson), and some of their cultural descendants (Tom Waits, Emmylou Harris, Cassandra Wilson), and tries to raise issues and pursue ideas about how postwar American pop culture has worked. For instance, one thesis of this book is that postwar countercultures, which I call the postwar American renaissance, represented significant feedback loops between genuine popular culture and the increasingly corporate nature of the entertainment industry. Another is that these countercultures disseminated what you could call jazz culture—everything from the value of improvisation to the civil rights movement—into the broad popular mainstream of American life, in ways that parallel the Swing Era."

In addition to writing the liner notes for at least a dozen albums, Santoro has contributed to the *Encyclopedia Britannica* and the *Encyclopedia of New York City*. He sits on the advisory board of the *New Grove Dictionary of Jazz*.

—C. M.

SUGGESTED READING: *Amazon.com*; *Library Journal* p98 July 2000; *The Nation* (on-line); *The Nation* p40 Oct. 7, 2000; *Philadelphia Inquirer* Aug. 30, 2000

SELECTED BOOKS: *Dancing in Your Head*, 1994; *Stir It Up*, 1997; *Myself When I Am Real*, 2000

Saunders, George

Dec. 2, 1958– Short-story writer

The short-story writer George Saunders discovered his writer's voice when he stopped trying to write in the realist tradition of Hemingway and started to have some fun. As he told Toby Lester in an interview for the *Atlantic Monthly* (May 17, 2000, online), "I started saying, 'Okay, I can't write a straight sentence. I can't describe nature. I don't really care what happens when a divorcing couple sits down in a café. I just don't care.'" With this admission, Saunders came to rely on his own strengths, including an ear for dialogue and a mordant sense of humor, and began writing finely tuned, startlingly original stories. Saunders's fiction takes place in surreal but recognizable landscapes of a near-future America—littered with discount mega-marts, artificial turf, and bombed-out strip malls—and light years away from waving fields of grain. Toiling in menial jobs and attending self-help seminars, his characters struggle for recognition, comfort, and for some version—however degraded—of the American dream. When Saunders published his first collection, *CivilWarLand in Bad Decline* (1996), which included short stories and a novella, the *New York Times* hailed "the debut of an exciting new voice in fiction" and the *New Yorker* named him one of the "20 Best American Fiction Writers Under 40," both as quoted on *Amazon.com*. The collection became a finalist for that year's PEN/Hemingway Award. The equally warm reception that met Saunders's second collection of stories, *Pastoralia* (2000), confirmed that Saunders has indeed hit his stride.

For *World Authors 1995–2000*, George Saunders writes, "I was born in Amarillo, Texas, in 1958, the first child of George R. Saunders and Joan (Clarke) Saunders. I have two younger sisters, Nancy and Jane, both of whom are funny and live in New Orleans. I was raised on the South Side of Chicago, attending St. Damian's, a local Catholic grade school, and then Oak Forest High School, the public high school. My father worked for Peterson Coal and Oil, a company that supplied heating products to apartment buildings, and would come home with hilarious and scary stories of the Chicago of that time (early- to mid-1960s). One of these, for example, involved a man who shot his own German Shepherd on the Dan Ryan Expressway, after the dog bit him on the neck. My father encouraged me to read Mike Royko, Machiavelli, Upton Sinclair, and Michael Harrington, and was a wonderful and charismatic storyteller, who underscored the power and value of humor by laughing himself into tears every Sunday night during *Monty Python's Flying Circus*. My mother stayed home with us, manifesting a humor and kindness and compassion that seemed to me embodiments of the more abstract Catholic versions of these virtues we were taught by the nuns. From her side of the family came a type of West Texas humor that used invented voices and long, exaggerated scenarios to induce a pathos/hilarity reaction that often lasted for entire afternoons.

"In my senior year of high school I met Joe Lindbloom, a geology teacher, and Sheri Williams, an English teacher, who influenced me tremendously and were responsible for my going to college. Prior to this, my career plan had consisted of: Join a Rock Band. They even went so far as to call admissions officers on my behalf, a necessary step given the condition of my grade point average. As if by miracle, I was accepted into the Colorado School of Mines, 'The World's Foremost College of Mineral Engineering.' This was not perhaps the obvious path for a kid who had flunked both Chemistry and Algebra II, but having read (possibly mis-read) Ayn Rand, I was convinced that the only worthy work was Technological Work, preferably done in spite of the efforts of a bunch of simpering leeches who were trying to live off one's labors, work done by someone with a short, harsh, Anglo-Saxon name, and so during this period I briefly considered changing mine to Dirk Frank.

"I attended Mines from 1977 to 1981. In what little spare time I had, I would sneak to the upper level of the library, where the fiction was kept. These rarely left their shelves, since everyone was busy studying Differential Equations. Because it was so rarely visited, this level had a musty smell I associated with the 1930s, with Hemingway and Thomas Wolfe, and, looking out at the lights of the town, I would imagine that I was Hemingway, and was about to ship out to, say, Spain, and then, three or four hours later, as the library was closing, I would remember that I myself had a Differential Equations test the next day, and would sprint home and study until the wee hours, cursing Hemingway.

"I graduated from Mines in 1981, barely, with a degree in Geophysical Engineering. Luckily an oil boom was in effect, and in light of the lower standards in effect at such a time, I obtained a job in Sumatra, Indonesia, as a field geophysicist. I worked in a jungle camp about 40 miles from the town of Pekanbaru, and started writing stories that were a painful combination of Hemingway, Kahlil Gibran, Thomas Wolfe, Joseph Conrad, and my actual life, in which, typically, a stoic young man who has just arrived in Asia witnesses something brutal and then recoils in silent horror, while mouthing dialogue which sounds something like Somerset Maugham on Qualludes.

"After two years of this, under the influence of a killer stomach virus, I quit this job and returned to the U.S. Between 1983 and 1986, reading Jack Kerouac, I traveled around the U.S. and held various jobs, including slaughterhouse laborer, roofer, convenience store clerk, and bar-band guitarist, and started to write stories that were a painful combination of Jack Kerouac, Kahlil Gibran, Thomas Wolfe, and my actual life, in which, typically, a stoic young man, just back from Asia, witnesses something brutal in a slaughterhouse and recoils in horror, while mouthing dialogue that sounds something like Steve Allen imitating Jack Kerouac.

"In 1986, after a catastrophic year in Los Angeles, I moved back in abject defeat to Amarillo, Texas, where my parents were living, took a job as a groundsman at an apartment complex, and wrote a new set of stories, three of which were published in small journals. Soon afterwards I was accepted into Syracuse University's Creative Writing Program, where I studied with Tobias Wolff and Douglas Unger and met my soon-to-be wife, Paula, a former ballet dancer who was also a student in that program. For once, I did something intelligent: I proposed three weeks after we met. We were married in May of 1987. Our first daughter, Caitlin, was born the following year, and I took a job at the Sterling-Winthrop Research Group, as a technical writer, summarizing animal test reports for the FDA. This was a sobering time, during which I would write about tortured monkeys for eight hours, walk out to my car past a suite of beagles hanging in slings awaiting the next day's round of tests, then go home and write late into the night. Unfortunately, my new responsibilities had somehow plunged me back into my faux Hemingway phase, although I had made some progress and was now writing stories in which, typically, a stoic young man, who had just fathered his first child, witnesses something brutal and recoils in horror, and, after considering returning to Asia, returns silently home and changes a diaper, while mouthing dialogue that sounds like Raymond Carver, if Raymond Carver was trying very hard to sound like Kahlil Gibran on Qualludes.

"In 1989 I took a job as a technical writer for Radian Corporation, an environmental engineering company in Rochester, New York. In 1990 our second daughter, Alena, was born. Shortly afterwards, during a torturous conference call, I, in a sort of heady despair, wrote a little book of Seussian poems that though not at all original (they were Seussian, after all) were at least sort of funny. People seemed to enjoy them, which was not true of the faux Hemingway/Kerouac/Wolfe stories, which were typically named something like O Autumn in the Field Not Far From the Mad Town.

"In this new mode, over the next five years or so, stealing time from my employer or on the bus on the way home, I wrote my first book, *CivilWarLand in Bad Decline*, which was published in 1996. All of the above-listed experiences combined to produce my main theme, if writing as silly-assed as mine can be said to have a Main Theme, which is: Capitalism, though not necessarily avoidable, is necessarily brutal. It takes our grace and our peace of mind, it affects our ability to respond to the people we care about; in short, it is not to be trusted.

"In 1997 I was able, with great joy, to quit my tech writing job and start teaching in the Syracuse University Creative Writing Program. My second collection of stories, *Pastoralia*, was published in 2000, as was an illustrated fable called *The Very Persistent Gappers of Frip*, illustrated by Lane Smith."

The six stories and one novella in *CivilWarLand in Bad Decline* are all first-person narratives. Often, the characters are grotesques, such as a misshapen girl named Boneless, a 400-pound businessman, and a black boy with skin so fragile that it tears when touched. Writing for *Choice* (July/August 1996), R. B. Shuman admired how Saunders is able to present such characters "in their full humanity, never sentimentalizing, ever withholding judgment." The title story is set in a historical theme park called CivilWarLand, in which a "verisimilitude inspector" toils to reconstruct mid-19th century America. Into this world intrudes the actual past, in the forms of the ghosts of the McKinnon family, Civil War–era farmers who met their bloody demise in one of the park's fields. The ghosts of the Vietnam War also appear, in the form of a park employee who, after his coworkers discover that he participated in a massacre during the Vietnam War, is given the job of inflicting revenge on the teenagers who have been vandalizing the park. In "The Bounty," the novella that ends the collection, environmental poisoning in a post-apocalyptic America has spawned a class of malformed, the "Flaweds," who work in menial jobs for the remaining "Normals." Although his job at a theme park called BountyLand ensures that the narrator, a "Flawed," gets three meals and a dose of cocaine each day, he leaves the security of his post to search for his sister, who has a tail.

Many critics have remarked on the originality of Saunders's vision, calling the stories in *CivilWarLand* "unforgettable," "inventive," and "exuberantly weird." Writing for the *New York Times Book Review* (February 4, 1986, on-line), Jay McInerney praised Saunders's idiosyncratic voice, his "ear for the offbeat cadences of the contemporary idiom, not least the language of businessmen." "Respect," McInerney quoted one of Saunders's corporate types as saying, "That's the quality I hope to imbibe to you during the confab that is to follow this present preface I'm extolling." Although he cautioned that "a style as singular as this . . . can seem mannered in a book length dose," McInerney found that he was often surprised by the directions the stories take: "Quite unexpectedly, between guffaws, you find yourself moved. Mr. Saunders is one of those rare writers who can effortlessly blend satire and sentiment."

Thomas Pynchon, as quoted by Toby Lester, called Saunders "astoundingly tuned" to American society. As part of an issue titled "The Future of American Fiction," the *New Yorker* (June 21–28, 1999) published the short story *I Can Speak!*, Saunders's parody of Americans' self-involvement and obsession with consumption. The story takes the form of a letter written to an unsatisfied customer of the "I Can Speak1900," a mask-like machine that is placed over the face of a real baby to simulate speech. The letter writer, a Product Service Representative for KidLuv, Inc., claims that his own child has become a much greater asset since they began using the "I Can Speak": "Now when childless friends are over, what we have found, my wife, Ann, and I, is that it's great to have your kid say something witty and self-possessed years before he or she would actually in reality be able to say something witty or self-possessed. . . . Here I must admit that we have several times seen a sort of softening in the eyes of resolute childless friends, as if they, too, would suddenly like to have a baby."

The hapless heroes of Saunders's second collection of stories, *Pastoralia*, endure hardscrabble lives in places where the economy has yet to "trickle down." In the title story, a woman named Janet and a male narrator worry about losing their jobs portraying Neanderthal cave dwellers in a historical theme park, a favorite Saunders setting. The pair live like zoo animals; forbidden from speaking English or walking upright, they spend their days making crude gestures, capturing and eating bugs, and scratching out pictographs in the dirt. Apart from a goat that is pushed through a slot each morning, a hidden fax machine provides their only connection to the outside world. Run by an invisible bureaucracy, the theme park world becomes a nightmarish microcosm of the more-familiar corporate one. For example, a bonus gift of a rabbit arrives one day along with a letter informing all employees of imminent "Staff Remixing," a euphemism for downsizing. When Janet begins to flout more and more of the company rules by smoking, talking instead of grunting, and harassing a visitor, the narrator is forced to decide between his loyalty to Janet and his own self-preservation.

In "Sea Oak," the poverty of the characters' existence comes across in the dialogue, which they do not so much speak as spew out. The protagonist works as a male stripper in an aviation-themed club called "Joysticks," and lives in an apartment complex with a crack house in the laundry room along with his unemployed sister and their female cousin, the women's babies, and a sweet old maid of an aunt. The story turns gothic when the aunt dies and then returns from the grave as a raging Fury, suddenly bitter that her own life was so lacking and goading her nieces and nephew to make something of themselves.

Writing for the *New York Times Book Review* (May 28, 2000, on-line), Lynne Tillman drew a link between Saunders's loser-characters and the legacy left by America's Protestant settlers: "The Puritans proved their worth in the New World by achieving worldly success that, they hoped, demonstrated God's love. . . . Anxiety and guilt drove the Puritans, and those were their psychological gifts to America's future." Tillman continued, "Saunders showcases Americans' fears, shames, and need to be accepted—all resonant reminders of this country's neurotic origins . . . his frantic characters . . . anxiously await punishment for nonexistent crimes and imperfections, suffering for the strange sin of wanting to be happy. His losers are threatened with losing even more—jobs, sexual attractiveness, their illusions, just about everything." In *Time* (May 22, 2000, on-line), Paul Gray wrote "these losers are too self-aware to pity, and the world they perceive is unsettlingly familiar." Most critics have agreed that Saunders's humor and generosity balance the bleak scenarios in his stories; as Tillman wrote, "Saunders can be brutally funny, and the better his stories are, the more melancholy, somber and subtle they are, too."

—M. A. H.

SUGGESTED READING: *Atlantic Monthly* (on-line) May 17, 2000; *Library Journal* p147 Jan. 1996; *New York Times Book Review* (on-line) Feb. 4, 1996, May 28, 2000; *Time* (on-line) May 22, 2000

SELECTED BOOKS: short-story collections—*CivilWarLand in Bad Decline*, 1996; *Pastoralia*, 2000; juvenile—*The Very Persistent Gappers of Frip*, 2000

Courtesy of Princeton University Press

Scarry, Elaine

June 30, 1946– Essayist; critic

In *The Body in Pain: The Making and Unmaking of the World* (1985), Elaine Scarry, a critic and literature professor in the U.S., created a cultural stir with her insights into human creativity and destructiveness. In her subsequent books—*Resisting Representation* (1994), *On Beauty and Being Just* (1999), and *Dreaming by the Book* (1999)—Scarry continued to explore aesthetics, religion, and literature from a unique perspective. Her books have been praised for their suggestive and sweeping claims, but many critics have faulted her lack of rigorous argument. Her most recent book, *Who Defended the Country?* (2003), looks at what defenses could have been made to prevent the terrorist attacks of September 11, 2001.

Scarry was born on June 30, 1946 in Summit, New Jersey. She graduated from Chatham College, in Pittsburgh, Pennsylvania, in 1968, and completed her Ph.D. at the University of Connecticut, in Storrs, in 1974. She joined the English Department of the University of Pennsylvania, in Philadelphia, where she won the Ira Abrams Award. She later became the Walter M. Cabot Professor of Aesthetics and the General Theory of Value at Harvard University, in Cambridge, Massachusetts.

Scarry's 1985 philosophical treatise, *The Body in Pain: The Making and Unmaking of the World*, was applauded by many for its revelations on the sources of human creativity and destructiveness. According to Susan Rubin Suleiman's review in the *New York Times Book Review* (January 5, 1986), Scarry argued that "the human body is the focus and central support for both making and unmaking. . . . It is the state of bodily pain or deprivation that impels the imagination to 'produce' objects that might relieve that pain, either in fact (hunger causes me to imagine, and then to seek, food) or merely by acting as a symbolic substitute for pain's attributes (when I say that my headache feels 'as if' a nail were being drive into my temple, I momentarily relieve the pain by imagining and verbally objectifying the hammer and the nail)." Suleiman pointed out that the "negative consequence of a dissociation between body and voice is one of . . . Scarry's recurring themes" and concluded that among "her most powerful and paradoxical insights is that 'to be intensely embodied . . . is the equivalent of being unrepresented and is almost always the condition of those without power.'"

Many reviewers found Scarry's argument extraordinarily difficult and complicated but rewarding. In "its breadth and humaneness of vision, in the density and richness of its prose, above all in the compelling nature of its argument, this is indeed an extraordinary book," Suleiman announced. A reviewer for *Choice* (January 1986) called the book "fascinating" as it "weaves through semantics, philosophy, psychology, sociology, art, and history. . . . Scarry succeeds in presenting provocative insights on the human condition and contemporary society." For a *Library Journal* (September 1, 1985) reviewer, Scarry "persuasively explores the fact that the human experience of bodily pain is inexpressible in words. . . . She also develops a link between the potency of human language and creativity in the spheres of religious, political, and esthetic endeavor." In a more negative review, Peter Singer wrote in the *New York Review of Books* (February 27, 1986) that "the book is cavalier in its disregard for the hard work of providing either factual evidence or serious philosophical argument for what it says."

In 1994 the Oxford University Press published *Resisting Representation*, a collection of Scarry's essays. The collection deals with how experience is represented in language and considers such authors as Thomas Hardy, Samuel Beckett, William Makepeace Thackeray, and Boethius. In a description of the book that appears on the Oxford University Press Web site, the publisher wrote, "We often assume that all areas of experience are equally available for representation. On the contrary, these essays present discussions of experiences and concepts that challenge, defeat, or block representation. Physical pain, physical labor, the hidden reflexes of cognition and its judgments about the coherence or incoherence of the world are all phenomena that test the resources of language." The publisher added that Scarry demonstrated in her essays how linguistic "resistance is at last overcome, thus suggesting a domain of plenitude and inclusion."

In 1998 Scarry published an article in the *New York Review of Books* (April 9, 1998) entitled "The Fall of TWA 800: The Possibility of Electromagnetic Interference." The article addressed the cause of the 1996 crash of TWA flight 800 into the ocean off New York—an unusual topic for a literary critic. Scarry noted that the crash investigators had searched for evidence of mechanical trouble, a bomb detonation, a missile impact, and even a meteorite collision. What the investigators overlooked, according to Scarry, was electromagnetic interference (EMI). A small amount of such interference emanates from computers, headsets, telephones, and other electronic devices; because EMI can disrupt operation of the plane during takeoff and landing, airlines typically ask passengers to turn off such devices during these times. As Scarry pointed out in the *New York Review of Books*, EMI "from military equipment can be thousands, even millions, of times as great, and can have much more serious consequences for airborne planes. Because 10 military planes and ships were in the vicinity of TWA 800 that night, we need to ask the airmen and sailors on the planes and ships to describe with precision the pieces of equipment that were in use." Scarry's speculation was often dismissed because she is not a professional accident investigator. However, reaction to her conjecture was not completely unfavorable. On the *Infowar.Com* Web site, John Young posted an article (April 2, 1998) that called Scarry's explanation "thoroughly researched . . . and highly informative about EMI hazards."

In her next book, *On Beauty and Being Just* (1999), based on her 1998 Tanner lectures at Yale University, Scarry asserted that beauty has become stigmatized by academic critics who see the search for beauty as a frivolous distraction from the search for social justice. Scarry believed the opposite: beauty arouses in the beholder a longing for truth and justice. For her the attraction of the symmetry and proportions of beautiful people and objects is like the attractive symmetry of notions like fairness, equality, and justice. Scarry has often found evidence of the power of beauty in her life. She told David Bowman in an interview for *Salon* (November 9, 1999, on-line): "During the past 13 years I've been working on a big project about nuclear weapons and the fact that the current military arrangements we have are not compatible with democracy. The more I work on that, the more it happens that I need to read poems. And work my garden. Beauty restores your trust in the world."

Stuart Hampshire wrote in the *New York Review of Books* (November 18, 1999) that "Scarry persuades me that there is an analogy between the recognition of beauty and the recognition of just or fair social arrangements, and that the analogy proceeds through the pleasure we find in just balances and in the equitable fitting together of disparate elements." He added that in "a light and allusive and gentle and unpolemical style . . . [Scarry] insinuates that we might learn to look and to listen better and to attend more closely to shapes and forms in art and nature, and to protect any beautiful things that we haphazardly encounter as we stumble along under the growing weight of the dull and indifferent things." Other critics, however, found the book impenetrable. Daniel Kunitz, the reviewer for the *New Leader* (November 29, 1999), complained about Scarry's misguided logic and her "jargon laden" language. "One of Scarry's most aggravating tactics is her insistence on politicizing her subject even while supposedly defending it from 'political critiques,'" he wrote. He added that while "she desperately wants to show that beauty leads to social equality," he found that the "notion is contradicted by the example of numerous 17th-century absolutist princes who sponsored some of the world's most astonishingly beautiful art and architecture, but who had little use for the idea of equality. . . . Scarry fails to acknowledge that contemplating beauty is as likely to direct one's thoughts to hierarchies of value as it is to promote social equality."

In 1999 Scarry also published *Dreaming by the Book*, which analyzes how authors engage the imaginations of their readers. For Scarry authors "instruct" readers in how to "see," thereby producing a collaboration that provides for "vivacity." She enumerates five techniques that authors use to produce their effects: radiant ignition, rarity, dyadic addition and subtraction, stretching, and floral supposition. In a positive review of the book, Kenneth Baker wrote in the *San Francisco Chronicle* (November 28, 1999), "Through diverse literary examples, introspection, and recent findings in cognitive psychology, Scarry deploys a truly revealing phenomenology of imagination. . . . For all its eccentricity . . . *Dreaming by the Book* will affect how one reads fiction and poetry as few critical works have done before." A reviewer for *Publishers Weekly* (August 2, 1999) agreed that "Scarry is an original, interdisciplinary thinker. She writes like someone enraptured by both the natural world—especially flowers—and by language." This reviewer concluded, however, that "Scarry appears lost in her own lush imaginative world." In a more scathing assessment in the *New York Times Book Review* (November 28, 1999), Wendy Lesser dismissed *Dreaming by the Book*: "Scarry's work trumps all parodic efforts. . . . If reading novels were as difficult and convoluted as Scarry makes out, why in the world would any of us do it for pleasure?" She concluded that Scarry, like "many literary critics who stumble in through the back door of philosophy . . . lacks that basic philosophical implement, a logical mind."

Scarry's next book, *Who Defended the Country?* (2003), uses phone records, official reports, accounts of the actions of passengers on two of the hijacked planes, and government responses, to reconstruct the terrorist attacks of September 11, 2001. She pointedly asks if anything could have been done to better defend the United States homeland. The only successful defense, she points out, was not a government response, but instead involved the passengers of Flight 93 who fought back against their hijackers and crashed their plane into a field in Pennsylvania. Nine prominent thinkers—among them Richard Falk, Ellen Willis, Admiral Eugene Carroll, and Antonia Chayes—respond to her arguments.

—S. Y.

SUGGESTED READING: *American Prospect* p61+ Dec. 20, 1999; *Choice* p751 Jan. 1986; *Flying 125* p111+ Oct. 1998; *Library Journal* p202 Sep. 1, 1985, p84 Sep. 15, 1999; *New Leader* p17+ Nov. 29, 1999; *New York Review of Books* p59+ Apr. 9, 1998, p42+ Nov. 18, 1999; *New York Times Book Review* p20 Jan. 5, 1986, Nov. 28, 1999; *Publishers Weekly* p60+ Aug. 2, 1999; *San Francisco Chronicle* p4 Nov. 28, 1999; *Village Voice* p140 Sep. 21, 1999

SELECTED BOOKS: nonfiction—*The Body in Pain: The Making and Unmaking of the World*, 1985; *Resisting Representation*, 1994; *On Beauty and Being Just*, 1999; *Dreaming by the Book*, 1999; *Who Defended the Country?*, 2003; as editor—*Literature and the Body: Essays on Populations and Persons*, 1988; *Fins-de-Siècle: English Poetry in 1590, 1690, 1790, 1890, 1990*, 1995

Schneider, Bart

July 23, 1951– Novelist; editor

Bart Schneider has written two well-received novels and is the founding editor of the critical publication the *Ruminator Review*, which was originally named the *Hungry Mind Review*. His first novel, *Blue Bossa* (1998), is the story of a jazz musician struggling to make a comeback in 1970s San Francisco. The work was a finalist for the *Los Angeles Times* Book Award for first fiction, as well as a *San Francisco Chronicle* best-seller. Schneider's next novel, *Secret Love* (2001), deals with issues of race and sexuality and is set against the tumultuous backdrop of the 1960s civil rights movement. Schneider also edited *Race: An Anthology in the First Person* (1997), a compilation of essays by an impressive array of well-known writers and lecturers.

Bart Schneider was born on July 23, 1951 in San Francisco, California, to David Schneider, a violinist with the San Francisco Symphony, and Geraldine (Schwartz) Schneider. He attended Saint Mary's College of California, in Moraga, where he received his B.A. in English in 1973. He earned his M.A. in creative writing from San Francisco State University in 1975. During the 1970s he published short stories in small journals and wrote plays that were produced by theaters in Los Angeles and in the San Francisco Bay Area. He moved to Minnesota, in 1983, to participate in a play-development program, but found the experience unrewarding.

In 1986 Schneider founded the *Hungry Mind Review*, a quarterly periodical that contains commentaries on fiction, poetry, drama, and nonfiction. Millicent Lenz, writing in the *School Library Journal*, as quoted in *Contemporary Authors* (2000), noted that the *Review* attracted "those iconoclastic, free-thinking persons who frequent independent bookstores." The publication has since been renamed the *Ruminator Review* and is published by Macalester College, a private liberal-arts college in St. Paul, Minnesota. A recent issue included essays by Wole Soyinka and Arundhati Roy, as well as an interview with the poet W. S. Merwin.

In May 1994 Schneider published a questionnaire about race-related issues in the *Hungry Mind Review*, generating considerable interest and drawing nearly 1,000 reader responses. He assembled these, along with book excerpts and previously published essays, in *Race: An Anthology in the First Person*. The book includes contributions from many distinguished writers and activists, including Richard Rodriguez, who writes about the difficulty of teaching in the multicultural classroom; Henry Louis Gates Jr., who analyzes the O. J. Simp-

Bart Schneider
Kathy Sawyer/Courtesy of Bart Schneider

son trial; and Peggy McIntosh, who examines white privilege. "These are eloquent reminiscences, angry screeds, even a terse, meaty history of race in the U.S. from the ACLU's Ira Glasser," Mary Carroll wrote in an assessment for *Booklist* (November 1, 1996). "A solid collection, calculated to convince nonparticipants that we all need to think and talk about this endlessly troubling issue."

Schneider, an avid amateur sax player, published *Blue Bossa* in 1998. It is the fictional story of Ronnie Reboulet, a once-celebrated jazz trumpeter and singer who in his glory days played with such greats as Charlie Parker. In the late 1960s he had the looks of a movie star and a sea of admirers, but he lost it all to a destructive heroin habit. At the outset of the novel, Ronnie hasn't played his horn in over five years. With the help and patience of his steadfast companion, Betty, he has weaned himself off heroin, but given up his music in the process. "It was in Florida that he made the point of banishing music," Schneider writes, as quoted by Peter Kurth for *Salon.com* (March 6, 1998). "He cast it out, isolated it like a disease from the rest of his one-foot-before-the-other life. He slipped it into an unlined case, the strongbox for all things gathered that would not of themselves dissolve. He tried to reenter the world with the peculiar posture of the tone-deaf. He felt confident that he could join the tribe of shambling gracelessness without incident." Having relocated to San Francisco, Ronnie is working at a dead-end job and is no longer the attractive man he once was; his face is prematurely aged and he's long since lost his teeth. Unexpectedly, he receives a visit from his estranged 20-year-old daughter, Rae, whom he had abandoned six years earlier. She has a small child of her own now and aspires to a career as a jazz singer. Rae and Betty become friends, and together they encourage Ronnie to take up the trumpet again. He makes an inspiring comeback, but along the way he succumbs to his old habits of drug addiction and detachment, inflicting pain and hardship on those close to him.

Critics welcomed *Blue Bossa* as an impressive first novel. Beth E. Anderson, writing for *Library Journal* (January 1998), referred to the inventive structure of the novel as a series of episodic, interconnected scenes, when she noted that Schneider "pulls the reader into the rhythm of this tale with vignettes of lovely artistry that weave back and forth throughout Ronnie's life." She continued, "The standard formula of drugs plus musical wizardry equals heartbreak does not necessarily apply to this poignant tale of good-hearted people working hard to carve a life, hopefully with each other." Many critics praised Schneider for his ability to write about music—a skill which, they acknowledge, is difficult to perform well. "To the task of describing music, Schneider brings a jazz fan's ardor and a poet's precision," Louis Bayard wrote for the *Washington Post* (April 12, 1998). David Thomson, writing for the *Los Angeles Times* (June 14, 1998), quoted Schneider as he evokes a salient moment of trumpet playing during Ronnie's comeback: "Ronnie walks tentatively through the theme. The trumpet is a thin man strolling up a trail with a trusty stick. He stumbles here, goes up the wrong fork there, and has to back his way down. No fancy stops yet, no switchbacks. Just a walking man telling a warm story with enough quick, pop laughs to punctuate the tale so that any dumb fool, wondering if he's pissed away his life, feels he has a compatriot on the stage, walking a deceptively simple trumpet line up the trail."

Blue Bossa is loosely based on the life of the jazz musician Chet Baker (1929–1988), who was the embodiment of hip culture in the 1950s and also struggled throughout his life with heroin addiction. Some critics contended that Schneider's attitude lapsed into reverence and that as a result the book was too sympathetic to its destructive protagonist. "*Blue Bossa* is honest about the craziness of music makers," Bayard wrote, "but you may end up feeling that Ronnie Reboulet has gotten off easy, that his ultimate transcendence is achieved at other people's expense and his detachment from his own behavior excused as an artist's last refuge. Ronnie leaves a lot of wounded souls in his wake and never really gets around to apologizing, but hey, he's more talented than the rest of us."

Schneider's next novel, *Secret Love*, was also set in San Francisco, this time in the turbulent 1960s. Jake Roseman is a political activist and a confident lawyer who juggles a steady stream of attention-getting civil rights cases. He has considerably more trouble with his personal life, however, as he raises his two children and comes to terms with his wife's recent suicide. At a political demonstration he meets Nisa Bohem, a young black actress and activist. A passionate romance ensues, and the two struggle with the obstacles that complicate the bi-racial affair—including Jake's bigoted father. The novel simultaneously chronicles a similarly vexed homosexual love story, between Simon Sims, a young black man whose interest in the Nation of Islam pits him against his Baptist minister father, and Peter Boswell, a white actor and a friend of Nisa's. The novel explores the damage that prejudice and social taboos can inflict on individual lives and relationships.

Most critics offered mixed reviews. "The novel offers a relaxed, friendly read, with a great feel for its time and place and some moving and dramatic moments," Jeff Zaleski wrote in *Publishers Weekly* (February 26, 2001). "But the lead characters, despite nice establishing touches and some well-turned speeches on themes of the era, never seem very convincing, and the lack of narrative drive and tension in the book make reading it ultimately a pallid experience." "Although the book's scenes are well-crafted, *Secret Love* suffers from Schneider's heavy plotting," John Freeman opined for the *Denver Post* (May 6, 2001). "The sit-ins, Joan Baez-led marches and firehose-wielding police officers that punctuate this novel feel like window dressing. *Secret Love . . .* mimics the flattened quality of television broadcasts from this period, rather than conjuring its own particular imagery, texture and shades of feeling." Although Gary Kamiya, writing in the *New York Times Book Review* (April 15, 2001), agreed that "history is essentially a stage set for Schneider," he nonetheless concluded that "he's a savvy and empathetic writer, and his real passion is for his characters, who refuse to become historical tintypes." Kamiya concluded that the novel is "flawed but irresistible."

Schneider is the literary director of the Loft Literary Center. Located in Minneapolis, Minnesota, the Loft is one of the nation's largest literary institutions, offering a variety of programs, readings, lecture series, and writing workshops. Schneider lives in St. Paul, Minnesota, with his wife, Patricia Kirkpatrick, whom he married in 1983. They have two children, Simone and Anton.

—A. I. C.

SUGGESTED READING: *Booklist* p463 Nov. 1, 1996, p986 Feb. 15, 1998; *Denver Post* I p2 May 6, 2001; *Library Journal* p145 Jan. 1998; *Los Angeles Times* p14 June 14, 1998; *New York Times Book Review* p15 Apr. 15, 2001; *Publishers Weekly* p38 Jan. 12, 1998, p58 Feb. 26, 2001; *Salon.com* Mar. 6, 1998; *Washington Post* p4 Apr. 12, 1998

SELECTED BOOKS: nonfiction—*Race: An Anthology in the First Person*, 1997; fiction—*Blue Bossa*, 1998; *Secret Love*, 2001

Schulman, Helen

Apr. 30, 1961– Novelist, short-story writer, editor, journalist

Helen Schulman is something of a literary chameleon—sometime serious novelist, sometime short-story writer, sometime comic novelist, sometime journalist, sometime screenwriter. *Not a Free Show* (1988), her first collection of stories, explores the relationships of young alienated urbanites; her second book, *Out of Time* (1991), is a linked series of tales about the death of a young man, told from the perspective of various narrators. Since that time she has co-edited (with Jill Bialosky) a collection on parenting, *Wanting a Child* (1998), and has written two novels: *The Revisionist* (1998), about a Jewish doctor and a Holocaust denier, and *p.s.* (2001), about a middle-aged woman's affair with a youthful version of her high-school love.

Helen Schulman was born in New York City, on April 30, 1961. Her father, David, was a doctor; her mother, Gloria, a social worker. In *Interview* (May 2001), she described to Karen Karbo how her interest in writing developed: "In high school I wasn't outwardly intellectual, nor was anybody around me. I wrote in secret, and I was a big reader. I went to Cornell . . . and suddenly everything I did in secret was applauded and encouraged. I came back to New York a semester early, my father had been ill. I needed a couple of credits to graduate so I ended up in Gordon Lish's workshop at Columbia. He was important for me as a teacher. He saw writing as this noble effort and truly as an art form. He taught me to read word-for-word, when before I had only read for plot and meaning."

After receiving her bachelor's degree, in 1983, from Cornell University, in Ithaca, New York, Schulman began regularly writing stories. In order to support herself while she honed her craft, she took a number of odd jobs—as a reader of book and movie scripts and as an assistant to a neurologist—and soon saved up enough money to go to Columbia University, where she received her MFA, in 1986. Two years later she published *Not a Free Show* with Knopf.

Most of the 16 stories comprising *Not a Free Show* revolve around people who have not dedicated themselves to either relationships or careers; they tend to drift from lover to lover and job to job. Like the characters in the works of Jay McInerney and Bret Easton Ellis, they tend to be abusers of drugs or alcohol and are disenchanted with the world without knowing what to do about it. The collection received mixed reviews. In the *Los Angeles Times Book Review* (May 15, 1988), Susan Heeger called the stories "a literature of opulence" filled with "imagistic language, full-spectrum emotion, large themes." Michiko Kakutani noted

Marion Ettlinger/Courtesy of Bloomsbury USA
Helen Schulman

in the *New York Times* (May 7, 1988), however, that "some of the slighter stories in this volume feel like creative-writing-class exercises in getting overheard dialogue down on paper. Yet in such larger, more commodious tales as 'James Dean's Widow,' the author uses her considerable powers of language and observation to delve beneath the surface of her characters' lives, carefully showing us how they have managed to misplace their innocence."

In 1991 Schulman published *Out of Time*, another work of fiction, but in 1998 she shifted gears and edited, with her friend Jill Bialosky, *Wanting a Child*. Although they had originally envisioned the book as a series of nonfiction essays, so many writers backed out of the project because of the personal, painful nature of the assignment, that Schulman and Bialosky were forced to fill in the gaps with fiction. The topics covered in the book include adoption, infertility, miscarriage, and childbirth. In addition to helping edit the volume, Schulman also contributed an essay regarding her own problems with infertility and three miscarriages. *Wanting a Child* received high praise in the press. In the *Women's Review of Books* (September 1998), Karen Propp wrote that the collection "contains the best writing I have seen on infertility, treatment by reproductive technology, and adoption. . . . The writers articulate their experiences across a wide and unusual range of family-building situations . . . emotion runs high, prose runs fast and tight." Writing for *Booklist* (April 15, 1998), Kathryn Carpenter proclaimed: "The loss, grief, and yearning felt by couples wanting a child yet, through miscarriage or infertility, unable to have one are hauntingly evoked. . . . The courage and determination the contributors reveal will inspire others."

Schulman's novel *The Revisionist* was published in 1998. Its somewhat comic story centers on David Hershleder, a middle-aged neurologist whose life is falling apart: His wife has left him, his work borders on the negligent, and he still mourns his mother, who died two decades earlier. After coming across a newspaper article about Jacques LeClerc, a one-time Holocaust denier who has publicly reversed his position, Hershleder becomes fascinated by the man's story, in part because his mother barely escaped Germany before the war. Hershleder feels a connection to LeClerc and seeks him out in order to better understand himself, his mother, and the Holocaust. Calling Schulman "an exceptionally daring writer" in the *New York Times Book Review* (November 1, 1998), Brian Morton cheered: "It's an original, bold and often moving book about a man so estranged from his feelings that he has to travel halfway around the world and look into the eyes of madness in order to gain some new perspective on his life." Daphne Merkin in the *New Yorker* (October 1998) felt that Schulman "has taken a somewhat tired subject, the sort of material that was fresh when Saul Bellow happened upon it—i.e., the occupational hazards of being brainy, horny, and Jewish—and given it an original, glistening spin."

In 2001 Schulman published *p.s.*, a comic novel about Louise Harrington, a 38-year-old who dreams of her high-school love, Scott Feinstadt, a painter and printmaker who died in a car crash on his way to art school. When Feinstadt appears in her life again, he is not a middle-aged man or a ghost, but is somehow just four years older than when she last saw him. After entering into an affair with the new Scott, Louise is able to feel the emotions she felt at 17, with all the confidence and experience of an older woman. Though Bliss Broyard called the novel a "fresh and funny love story" in the *New York Times Book Review* (May 20, 2001), she had some minor complaints: "[The book] does suffer from a slightly dashed-off quality— characters' responses don't always ring true; there are some suspiciously convenient plot turns and an occasional over-the-top, couldn't-resist passage that strains an already implausible story—but if fine-tuning these moments would mean hindering the elements that propel this novel, I say, don't change a thing."

In addition to writing fiction, Helen Schulman is a screenwriter—she has been the recipient of a Sundance fellowship—and a journalist, whose work has appeared in *Time*, *Vanity Fair*, *Vogue*, and the *Paris Review*, among other publications. She lives in New York City with her husband and two children.

—*C. M.*

SUGGESTED READING: *Booklist* p1402 Apr. 15, 1998, p1969 Aug. 1998; *Interview* p70+ May 2001; *Library Journal* p138 June 1, 1998; *Los Angeles Times Book Review*, May 15, 1988; *New*

York Times p14 May 7, 1988; New York Times Book Review p20 May 10, 1998, p26 Nov. 1, 1998, p13 May 20, 2001; New Yorker p105 Oct. 5, 1998; Women's Review of Books p10 Sep. 1998

SELECTED BOOKS: *Not a Free Show*, 1988; *Out of Time*, 1991; *The Revisionist*, 1998; *P.S.*, 2001; as editor—*Wanting a Child* (with Jill Bialosky), 1998

Aleksandra Crapanzano/Courtesy of Vintage Anchor Publicity

Schwartz, John Burnham

May 8, 1965– Novelist

John Burnham Schwartz's first novel, *Bicycle Days* (1989), was published when he was just 24 years old. But unlike many authors who are published that early and never live up to expectations, Schwartz has produced two highly regarded follow-up novels, *Reservation Road* (1998), which looks at the lives of two families after a tragedy, and *Claire Marvel* (2002), a love story between graduate students at Harvard. His sparse and delicate writing style has earned him praise in a wide range of periodicals, including *Library Journal*, *Entertainment Weekly*, *Time*, the *New York Times*, and the *Washington Post*.

John Burnham Schwartz was born on May 8, 1965. His father was an entertainment lawyer; his mother worked in children's book publishing. His parents had an apartment in Manhattan and a vacation home in East Haddam, Connecticut, where they entertained many famous authors and actors. Schwartz attended Choate, a prestigious boarding school in Connecticut, and while he was there, his parents divorced. In an essay for *Vogue* (January 1999) Schwartz wrote of the experience: "A dispersal was taking place in our family, an emigration that felt final to me and that I did not understand."

Though Schwartz sometimes dreamed of becoming an author and wrote an occasional poem or short story throughout his youth, when he went on to Harvard University, in Cambridge, Massachusetts, he embarked on a course of East Asian studies and planned on going into banking. The summer after his junior year, Schwartz traveled to Tokyo, Japan, where he worked in public relations at a computer company and lived with a Japanese family who did not speak English. When he returned to Harvard, he wrote of his experiences in his senior thesis and secured a job as a banker at First Boston a few days before his graduation. The thesis, however, had generated some interest among family friends who had seen it, including the noted author David Halberstam, who encouraged Schwartz to submit it to Amanda "Binky" Urban, a highly regarded literary agent. Urban was impressed and suggested that Schwartz turn the thesis into a novel.

Schwartz deferred his bank job for a year in order to write his novel. He went to a family home in Nantucket, a small island off the coast of Cape Cod, to write. Halberstam, who was also there that summer, called the young author every morning to see that he developed a steady work routine. Urban sold the completed book to Ileene Smith, an editor at Summit Books (and another family friend), who offered Schwartz a $25,000 advance. "I turned down the bank forever," he told Kelli Pryor, in an interview for *New York* (April 24, 1989). "I realized that I'd been on a track all my life, from Choate to Harvard, and whole parts of my life had gotten submerged. Writing the book is the most interesting thing I've done in terms of discovering myself and my life. I realized I felt very strongly about family and memory and the journeys one makes in various ways, both actually and imaginatively."

Bicycle Days, as the book was titled, was published on Schwartz's 24th birthday, and it reflected his deep disappointment with his time in Japan. The main character, Alec, is a young American working in that country. He tries to maneuver in Japanese society—awkwardly speaking Japanese at business meetings and interacting with the Japanese family in whose home he is boarding—but he finds few connections. He is shocked by Japanese prejudices against blacks, Koreans, and Americans—but is particularly horrified by their attitudes towards women, as exemplified by Kiyoko, a 33-year-old, who he is informed is "old Christmas cake," a derogatory reference to her still-unmarried status.

Schwartz's debut received mixed reviews. Peggy Payne, in the *New York Times Book Review* (July 9, 1989) wrote: "John Burnham Schwartz is a writer of significant potential who has made a tentative, faltering beginning in this novel. . . . Although *Bicycle Days* does not work as a fully satisfying narrative, many passages linger in the mind of the reader and yield continuing pleasure." The longtime *New York Times* (May 9, 1989) critic Michiko Kakutani had a similar assessment: "It's a familiar enough story, of course—the classic tale of a young man's coming of age, but as handled by Mr. Schwartz, it has freshness and energy, and it announces the debut of a bright new voice in fiction."

Schwartz's second novel, *Reservation Road*, was published in 1998. Equal parts thriller and family drama, the novel tells the story of two families linked by a tragedy. Ethan Lerner watches as his eldest son is killed by a hit-and-run driver, Dwight Arno, a local lawyer and himself the father of a small child. Schwartz, who had only written before from the point of view of a young man, now put himself in the place of someone older. "In that sense, *Reservation Road*, despite its painful subject, felt like a kind of liberation to me," he wrote in an essay posted on the Random House Web site. "The novel began with the simple but tragic idea of a father who had lost a son. Perhaps this was my way of reversing the order I'd felt myself chained to as a writer: to take away the son at the very start of the novel, leaving the father behind to live out the story and its consequences." Ethan becomes obsessed with hunting down and finding his son's killer, while Dwight struggles with his guilt. Tom De Haven, writing for *Entertainment Weekly* (September 11, 1998), cheered: "This is one of those rare—very rare—novels that you don't so much read as inhabit and that makes everyday life seem altogether mysterious and fragile, and infinitely perilous." In *Library Journal* (August 1998), Starr E. Smith wrote "this is a forceful psychological novel in which nobody wins—except readers appreciating Schwartz's well-wrought prose."

In 2002 Schwartz published *Claire Marvel*, a novel that, as an old-fashioned love story, surprised many reviewers used to high-concept modern novels from young authors. The book's protagonist, Julian Rose, meets Claire Marvel during a rainstorm near Harvard's Fogg Art Museum in May 1985. Julian, a graduate student at the university, is immediately taken with Claire, who is depicted as a spontaneous free spirit. The novel chronicles their love affair through the next 15 years, through several breakups and reconciliations. *Claire Marvel* received varying reviews. Daniel Mendelsohn, in *New York* (March 11, 2002), found little to like about it, remarking: "The problem here is that every relationship in *Claire Marvel*—between Julian and his parents, between Julian and the Machiavellian thesis advisor, between Julian and a troubled student at the prep school where he ends up teaching—turns out to be more textured, more authentic, than the one the book's supposed to be about." Mendelsohn continued, "It would be hard to find a recent novel that offers more overwrought verbiage. Claire's yellow umbrella is a 'thin sunlike carapace,' the lovers' arms are 'silent benedictions,' red wax is like 'an old prostitute's lipsticked mouth,' and winter daylight 'is as scarce as wartime rations. This is deeply, deeply phony writing. I doubt Schwartz, who's in his thirties, has ever laid eyes—or anything else for that matter—on an old prostitute's lipsticked mouth, let alone on a wartime ration." On the other hand, Valerie Sayers had somewhat more positive things to say in the *New York Times Book Review* (March 17, 2002). She praised how Schwartz writes "spare, elegant prose with old-fashioned inversions ('Too soon it ended') that seem to come from another era. His plot can be pretty sappy, but that's a sizable hazard of the genre. And while *Clare Marvel* has all the elements of a paperback romance—hesitant lovers, disease, separation, despair, reunion, death—it aims for the operatic tone of high art. . . . Its subject is not just romance but Grand Passion."

Journalists frequently make much of Schwartz's youthful good looks, and he has been profiled in such teen magazines as *Seventeen* and *YM*. He admitted to Paula Span for the *Washington Post* (May 23, 1989), "These days the way it works is, how old you are, what you look like, your background—they're all part of it."

—C. M.

SUGGESTED READING: *Entertainment Weekly* p125+ Sep. 11, 1998; *New York* p32 Apr. 24, 1989, p74+ Mar. 11, 2002; *New York Times* C p18 May 9, 1989; *New York Times Book Review* p11 July 9, 1989, p19 Mar. 17, 2002; Random House Web site; *Time* p85 Sep. 28, 1998; *Vogue* p73+ January 1999; *Washington Post* A p1 May 23, 1989

SELECTED BOOKS: *Bicycle Days*, 1989; *Reservation Road*, 1998; *Clare Marvel*, 2002

Sebald, Winfried Georg

(1944–2001) Novelist; poet; critic

The German-born novelist Winfried Georg Sebald, best known to English readers as W. G. Sebald, made a career as a professor of literature before he began writing his imaginative works, published in English as *The Emigrants* (1996), *The Rings of Saturn: An English Pilgrimage* (1998), and *Vertigo* (1999). These volumes broke new ground in experimental fiction, containing a hard-to-disentangle mélange of fact and fancy, illustrated with old snapshots, timetables, tickets, postcards, and other realistic artifacts. They are narrated by a man who may or may not be Sebald himself, and over them hangs a sense of loss and melancholy, although Sebald often interjects a note of drollery. "Against the violent legacies of nations and the relentless self-approbation of the living, he refers us to the silent community, the perfect deprivation of the dead. This is a very ancient idea," Edwin Frank wrote in the *Boston Review* (on-line). "Sebald's books are

Isolde Ohlbaum/Courtesy of Random House
Winfried Georg Sebald

resolutely plotless," James Atlas wrote in the *Paris Review* (Summer 1999). "Their narrative line follows the contours of the unconscious. His method is to build up a collage of apparently random details—stray bits of personal history, historical events, anecdotes, passages from other books—and fuse them into a story; Sebald, borrowing the term from Claude Levi-Strauss, calls it bricolage." His posthumous works in English translation include two novels, *Austerlitz* (2001) and *After Nature* (2002), as well as a collection of essays, *On the Natural History of Destruction* (2003).

Winfried Georg Sebald was born in 1944 in Wertach im Allgaeu, in the Bavarian Alps in southern Germany, while Hitler was in power. Sebald described his parents to David Streitfeld for an interview in the *Washington Post Book World* (November 9, 1997) as members of the "German petit bourgeoisie, largely identical with the class which was primarily responsible for setting up the fascist regime." His father had joined the army in 1939 and re-entered the service after the war, having served for a time as a clerical worker. "He retired early, as one does in that profession," Sebald told James Atlas during an interview for the *Paris Review* article, "and has done nothing for the last forty years but read the newspaper and comment on the headlines," having "very pronounced opinions about the issues of the day." Sebald's parents, he has told various interlocutors, were to have differing opinions about his writing career. His mother worried about what people would think when, in 1990, he published a novel about a man returning to his hometown, which was the same as his mother's and near where she still lived. "For weeks," he told Streitfeld, "she was in a state over this. . . . It was only when the book received public acclaim . . . that she began to see that perhaps this wasn't a bad thing after all." His father "took a certain interest when there was public attention," he told Atlas. "[T]hen he seemed to be jolly pleased about it."

Sebald studied German language and literature at Freiburg University, where he met the woman who was to become his wife. He told Atlas that all of his teachers "had gotten their jobs during the Brownshirt years and were therefore compromised"; Sebald felt that they were engaged in a "conspiracy of silence surrounding the Nazi era," and he found that "things were kept under wraps in the classroom as much as they had been at home." Such circumstances led him to complete his education in Switzerland, and in 1966 he went to Manchester, England, where he taught at the University of Manchester. In 1970 he began teaching at the University of East Anglia, in Norwich, where he became a professor of European literature. Sebald has been a permanent resident of England since 1970, and although he returns frequently to Germany, he told Atlas that to him Germany "feels like a cold country." He refused a post at the University of Hamburg because he did not want to "be drawn into the German culture industry." He served as director of the British Centre for Literary Translation from 1989 to 1994.

Sebald's first books were critical studies of Carl Sternheim and Alfred Doeblin, published in German in 1969 and 1980, respectively. Continuing to write in German, Sebald entered the realm of imaginative literature when he was 45 years old. His books were published in English as *The Emigrants*, *The Rings of Saturn: An English Pilgrimage*, and *Vertigo*. (The German edition of *Vertigo* appeared before that of *The Emigrants*.)

The Emigrants, translated by Michael Hulse, which was published in German in 1992 as *Die Ausgewanderten* (Those Who Went Off), is the story of the search for the pasts of four men who are connected, however tenuously, to the narrator. The lives of these four men are documented with journal excerpts and photographs. One of the men is an elderly English doctor, Henry Selwyn, who rents rooms to the narrator and his companion; another, Paul Bereyter, is the narrator's primary-school teacher, a man with a Jewish grandfather who has been forbidden for that reason to teach but later returns to his profession; the third is great uncle Ambros Adelwarth, the German-born butler of a Jewish family on Long Island; and last is Max Ferber, a German-Jewish painter in Manchester, England, whose parents have perished in the Holocaust and who gives the narrator his mother's letters and diaries—her memories of a sunny childhood. Richard Eder, in the *Los Angeles Times* (October 27, 1996), observed that "the Sebald-narrator has, like a tomb excavator, been taken over by the dead men's ghosts." The "faces that peer from the class pictures, excursions, holidays and eavesdropped intimacies bear two opposite messages: 'I am' and 'I no longer am.'" Each of the stories concerns a man who "displays a vital energy and earns some kind of success in the first years," Eder wrote. The shadow or foreshadowing of the Holocaust hangs over them, however, and at the end, "there is a break or an undermining: a nervous collapse or slow extinguishment."

Many English-language reviewers hailed Sebald as the creator of a new genre, "a striking mixture of fact, alleged fact, and fantasy, punctuated by often hazy, artless snapshots," as Philip Brady wrote in the *Times Literary Supplement* (July 12, 1996). James Atlas asked whether Sebald's work amounted to "[h]istory or a Borgesian fabrication built upon fact?"

The question of whether *The Emigrants* belongs to the genre of Holocaust literature has also preoccupied critics. For Gabrielle Annan, writing in the *New York Review of Books* (September 25, 1997), "it is really more general than that: it is about time, distance, absence, isolation, loneliness, depression, withdrawal, nostalgia, memory, and oblivion." Only one of the stories, "'Max Ferber,' is certainly a Holocaust story, although the Holocaust is barely alluded to and not mentioned in the other stories at all. Sebald's affection and pity for Jews is part of a general sorrow for the dead."

For Cynthia Ozick, whose critical piece appeared in the *New Republic* (December 16, 1996), Sebald's year of birth, 1944, froze him in the time of Germany's shame. She suspected that it was "not the democratic Germany of the economic miracle from which Sebald emigrated in 1970; it may have been, after all, the horribly frozen year of his birth that he meant to leave behind." She had an ambivalent reaction to the beauty of Sebald's language, "because sublime grieving is a category of yearning, fit for that which is irretrievable. But 1944 is always, always retrievable." In *The Emigrants*, Ozick maintained, "Sebald is haunted by Jewish ghosts—Europe's phantoms: the absent Jews, the deported, the gassed, the suffering, the hidden, the fled. . . . The Jews for whom he searches are either stricken escapees or smoke. Like all ghosts, they need to be conjured."

Annan pointed out the leitmotifs that tie the parts of *The Emigrants* together and make it thematically unified. In the first story, "Dr. Henry Selwyn," years after Selwyn has committed suicide, the narrator learns of a corpse retrieved from a Swiss glacier. It proves to be the body of Selwyn's lost love, who disappeared in 1914. "And so they are ever returning to us, the dead," the narrator remarks. Then, in "Paul Bereyter," the narrator observes, upon seeing Bereyter's photo album after his suicide: "Looking at the pictures in it, it truly seemed to me, and still does, as if the dead were coming back, or as if we were on the point of joining them." In that story also occurs another of Sebald's leitmotifs: Bereyter, serving in the German army in World War II, has written under a photo of himself, "about 2,000 km away—but from where?" Later, in "Ambros Adelwarth," the narrator's uncle Kasimir, the nephew of Adelwarth and also an immigrant in the United States, stands on a beach in New Jersey and muses, "I often come out here, . . . it makes me feel that I am a long way away, though I never quite know from where." Almost all reviewers pointed out the influence on the book of Vladimir Nabokov, who appears as a character. *The Emigrants* was awarded the Berlin Literature Prize.

Die Ringe des Saturn: Eine Englische Wallfahrt, published in 1995, was translated by Michael Hulse as *The Rings of Saturn: An English Pilgrimage* (1998). Like *The Emigrants*, *The Rings of Saturn* is narrated by a man called Sebald. The story, in this case, is that of his peregrinations through Suffolk—and through his own mind, as he muses on the past and the present—ending in his collapse into immobility in a hospital. *The Rings of Saturn* contains Sebald's thoughts on such topics as herring fishing; he also reflects on the lives of Edward Fitzgerald, the translator of the Rubaiyat of Omar Khayyam; Algernon Charles Swinburne, the Victorian poet; Chateaubriand; and Joseph Conrad. Still, the "true subject of *The Rings of Saturn* is death," James Wood commented in the *Guardian* (May 30, 1998). "He is especially attracted to the elegiac, to all that is dwindling and passing."

Blake Morrison, who reviewed *The Rings of Saturn* for the *New Statesman* (June 5, 1998), wrote that "the stories Sebald tells, whether about herrings or hangings, skulls or silkworms, are rarely less than fascinating. And even his absent-mindedness (there's a good deal of nodding off and dreaming) seems a part of the story: the story of a man with a curious mind and a long memory who can find no peace even in peaceful Suffolk."

"*The Rings of Saturn*—fragments of what were once moon—is a book of what dies," Richard Eder wrote in the *Los Angeles Times* (June 28, 1998). "As he plods along, transience on the ground, the narrator describes airy circles of transience in his mind and memory: an apparently random inventory of what he has encountered and read." Eder concluded that "*Rings* is an extension, an expansion of *The Emigrants*. . . . In the former the fact of the Holocaust provided a mighty current on which Sebald sailed his flotilla of stories, connections and disassociations each variously ramshackle, graceful, tragic and fearsomely armed." He found *The Rings of Saturn* lacking, however, in "the thunderous current; it eddies and scatters. . . . It may be a while before the reader realizes that for Sebald the Holocaust set in motion a shock wave for all, not just part, of mankind. It has leached away the illusion of life and permanence that allows humanity to take pleasure in its endeavors even if theoretically aware of their mortality." The purpose of Sebald's work becomes, accordingly, to demonstrate that neither the landscape around him nor "the narrator's lifetime store of art, language and remembrance can escape the blight." *The Rings of Saturn* was named a *New York Times* Notable Book of the Year in 1998 and won the 1998 *Los Angeles Times* Book Prize.

Sebald's 1990 novel *Schwindelgefühle*, his first venture into the experimental technique he was to apply successfully in *The Emigrants* and *The Rings of Saturn*, was translated into English by Michael Hulse and published in 1999 as *Vertigo*. That work, like *The Rings of Saturn*, deals with journeying and pilgrimage, but the journeys are undertaken by Stendhal (under his real name, Marie-Henri Beyle) and Franz Kafka in Italy and by Sebald himself in Vienna, Venice, and the Bavarian Alps, where he grew up. Like *The Emigrants*, *Vertigo* is divided into four sections, each involving travel across the Alps between Italy and northern Europe. Their titles are "Beyle, or Love Is a Madness Most Discreet," "All'Estero (Going Abroad)," "Dr. K. Takes the Waters at Riva," and "Il Ritorno in Patria (The Return to the Fatherland)." In "Beyle," Sebald tells the story of Beyle's love affairs, culminating with a romance between Beyle and Madame Gherhardi, the love of his life. In "All'Estero," the narrator describes his own depression (though not the reasons for it), which leads him to travel from England to Vienna to Venice. In Venice, seeing the Doge's Palace, he thinks of Casanova, who was imprisoned there and escaped on October 31, the "very day upon which our author finds himself in Venice," as Tim Parks noted in the *New York Review of Books* (June 15, 2000). "Dr. K. Takes the Waters at Riva" deals with a trip that Kafka, ill with tuberculosis, made to Italy. Anthony Lane, in his *New Yorker* (May 29, 2000) review, praised "Sebald's powers of précis as well as his tiny editorial twists": Although Sebald had borrowed heavily from Kafka's letters in writing this section, he wrote in *Vertigo* that "Kafka, when staying at the Hotel Sandwirth, in Venice, 'exchanged not a word with a living soul excepting the hotel staff.'" What Kafka actually wrote was that he spoke with almost no one during his stay. Lane pointed out that Sebald "has subtly deepened the pit of his subject's solitude—made it, dare one say, more Kafkaesque."

The theme of *Vertigo*, according to Benjamin Kunkel, the reviewer for the *Village Voice* (June 6, 2000), "is memory, but in Sebald memory does not so much restore the past as take the true measure of bottomless loss. Memory occasions vertigo—a sense of all that has vanished from under our feet— because it reminds us of the missing as well as the found." Although the Holocaust is not mentioned in *Vertigo*, according to Kunkel, "it casts its shadow across all of Sebald's pages." Nevertheless, even with "all its dark contents and burden of undeclared grief, *Vertigo* is dizzyingly light and transparent," Kunkel wrote. "As with its over- or underexposed snapshots, shading into a blankness white or black, we see through the book to the void from which it has rescued a few persons and things, and so it is its own double— itself and not itself, memory and oblivion, here and gone."

The novelist Anita Brookner, reviewing *Vertigo* in the *Spectator* (December 25, 1999), found that reading it was a disturbing experience. "A curious life of wandering," she wrote, "in itself a sign of fearlessness, and of taking notes in obscure rooms watched over by taciturn landladies, lays a hold on the reader's imagination, as if he too might be tempted to embark on such a life. This would be extremely dangerous. . . . Nothing like *Vertigo* is likely to be encountered in the course of one's regular reading. One emerges from it shaken, seduced, and deeply impressed. For this is freedom of a sort, and also the price that must be paid if such freedom, such extreme non- attachment, is sought by those unfitted to withstand the terrors which must be their accompaniment."

Although none of Sebald's critical studies has been translated into English, his 1998 volume *Logis in einem Landhaus: Uber Gottfried Keller, Johann Peter Hebel, Robert Walser und Andere* (Lodging in a Thatched Cottage: On Gottfried Keller, Johann Peter Hebel, Robert Walser and Others) has been reviewed in English. In the *Times Literary Supplement* (October 2, 1998), Michael Butler found in the collection of writings on Swiss or German writers a convergence of the literary and scholarly sides of Sebald. He saw in *Logis in einem Landhaus* "an exploration of spiritual affinities that indicate some of the sources of [Sebald's] own inspiration as a creator of fiction." The unifying theme behind these essays is that the writers discussed are "eccentric figures, men who were either in conflict with their environment . . . or lived their imaginative lives at a tangent to social reality." The last essay in the book deals with a painter, Jan Peter Tripp. "Like the writers Sebald discusses so illuminatingly," Butler wrote, "the painter poses frames of apparent order which reveal on closer gaze interstices of doubt." Robert Schwarz, writing in *World Literature Today* (Summer 1999), agreed, finding *Logis in einem Landhaus* "such a treasure" because of Sebald's "singular way . . . of commenting on the subtlest aspects of the lives and cultural contributions of the six geniuses he discusses." In addition, Schwarz concluded, Sebald does not "stress the droll or eccentric at the expense of the main thrust: literature, art, and philosophy."

Reviewing *Vertigo* in the *New York Times* (May 22, 2000), Richard Eder summed up Sebald's imaginative preoccupations as having to do with the effect of time: "The present that he explores is invaded, governed, sullied and eroded by the past. . . . Sebald has created a common market or free trade zone between memory and the senses. . . . There are no boundary markers or customs posts. . . . Time is not what we employ to measure the distance we have come or plan to go. It is a mechanism set off in the past and advancing balefully upon us. . . . It will not simply limit our future—the classical notion—it undoes our present. We resort to futile devices against it."

In 2001 Anthea Bell's translation of Sebald's novel *Austerlitz* was published. The novel begins in the late 1960s when the narrator encounters an unusual architecture student named Austerlitz in the waiting room of the Antwerp rail station. Over the next few years the narrator encounters Austerlitz in a number of places, until finally, Austerlitz reveals his life story, including his quest to discover his origins in Europe during World War II. The novel met with great praise, including that of Regina Marler, who wrote for *Amazon.com*, "If the mark of a great novel is that it creates its own world, drawing in the reader with its distinctive rhythms and reverberations, then W.G. Sebald's *Austerlitz* may be the first great novel of the new century. . . . Slow and meditative, relying on the cumulative effect of its sedate, musical prose and its dark subject matter (illuminated here and there with hope), Sebald's novel doesn't overturn the conventions of fiction, but transcends them. It is a love story to history and vanished beauty. Don't let the slow beginning turn you away. *Austerlitz* takes its time getting off the ground, but is well worth seeing in flight."

In 2002 *Nature* was published in an English translation by Michael Hamburger. In this book, three men—including two historical figures and the author himself—question the place of humanity in the natural world. Another of his recently translated and published works is *On the Natural History of Destruction* (2003), a collection of four essays on the impact of the Allied bombardment of Germany during World War II. In a review for *Booklist*, as quoted on Amazon.com, Brendan Driscoll wrote, "Sebald approaches his subject with sensitivity, yet avoids neither descriptions of horrible carnage nor criticism of writers too preoccupied with absolving themselves of blame to faithfully portray a destroyed Germany."

W. G. Sebald was killed in an automobile accident in Norfolk, England, on December 14, 2001.
—S. Y.

SUGGESTED READING: *Commentary* (on-line) June 1997; (London) *Guardian* p8 May 30, 1998, X p3 Dec. 18, 1999; *Los Angeles Times* p2 Oct. 27, 1996, p2 June 28, 1998; *New Republic* p33+ Dec. 16, 1996; *New Statesman* p45+ June 5, 1998; *New York Review of Books* p29+ Sep. 25, 1997, p44+ Dec. 3, 1998, p52+ June 15, 2000; *New York Times* (on-line) May 22, 2000; *New York Times Book Review* (on-line) Mar. 30, 1997; *New Yorker* p128+ May 29, 2000 with photo; *Paris Review* p278+ Summer 1999, with photos; *Review of Contemporary Literature* p173+ Spring 1997; *Spectator* p65+ Dec. 25, 1999; *Times Literary Supplement* (on-line) July 12, 1996, Nov. 29, 1996, Oct. 2, 1998, Nov. 12, 1999; *Village Voice* p125 June 6, 2000; *Washington Post Book World* p15 Nov. 9, 1997; *World Literature Today* p521 Summer 1999

SELECTED BOOKS IN ENGLISH TRANSLATION: *The Emigrants*, 1996; *The Rings of Saturn: An English Pilgrimage*, 1998; *Vertigo*, 1999; *Austerlitz*, 2001

Self, Will

1961– Novelist; short-story writer; journalist

Early in his career, the novelist and short-story writer Will Self was something of an enigma. Some postulated that he didn't exist, theorizing that his name was actually a pseudonym for the popular British writer Martin Amis. Others believed that his name was the clever invention of some unknown writer, because it seemed a tailor-made postmodern moniker. Following the publication of his successful first short-story collection, *The Quantity Theory of Insanity* (1991), it became clear that Self was a real person bearing the name given to him at birth, and his words, rather than his identity, became the subject of speculation. Critics have varied widely on how to read Self: his bizarre and often violent sexual imagery has provoked both disgust and intrigue. He has been compared to a range of writers, from William Burroughs, to Jonathan Swift, to Franz Kafka, to Nicholson Baker. His surreal narratives, often lacking traditional plots and characterizations, throw many readers off balance. However, most critics have agreed that Self possesses an exceedingly sharp wit and a gift for the incisive use of language (with which he employs a vast and often esoteric vocabulary). Another matter on which critics concur is that Self is a satirist. Beginning with his debut collection and continuing through his latest novel, *How the Dead Live* (2000), Self has used his barbed tongue to expose that which he deemed corrupt, laughable, or misguided in society. It was this talent that led Martin Amis to vote *The Quantity Theory of Insanity* Amis's book of the year for 1991 and to call Self "a very cruel writer—thrillingly heartless, terrifyingly brainy," as quoted by Zoë Heller in *Vanity Fair* (June 1993). Self's most recent novel is *Dorian: An Imitation* (2002).

Will Self was born in London, England, in 1961. His father was a professor of public administration, and his mother, Elaine, worked at a publishing house. In his interview with Heller Self characterized his family as "the standard, available-from-Woolworth's unhappy family." His parents often quarreled, so much so that when Elaine became pregnant with Will, she considered having an abortion rather than raising another child with her husband. However, a psychotherapist convinced her otherwise. As a writer whose work is fueled by raw images that take shape in his imagination, Self traces that proclivity back to his childhood. "I was forced back on my own resources, particularly my imagination," he told Chris Wright for the *Boston Phoenix* (March 14, 1996, on-line).

Don McCullin/Courtesy of Grove Atlantic Publicity
Will Self

Self began smoking marijuana at age 12, and later he experimented with LSD, cocaine, amphetamines and, at age 17, heroin. In addition to being a seasoned drug-user, by the time he entered college he also had a complicated psychiatric history: he'd been diagnosed as depressive, hypermanic, and manic-depressive. Then, at the age of 19, he was diagnosed as borderline schizophrenic. Years later, Self's view that human personality is oversimplified by most psychologists became a recurring theme in his fiction.

Self's father spent long hours writing in their house, and Self wanted to be a writer as well. Experimenting with vast quantities of drugs was part of his romantic conception of being a great author. "I always wanted be in print, to write," Self told Heller, "and part of the justification for the drugs was that this is what real writers do—you know, they leaped into their capsules and blasted off. But, of course, what the drugs were really doing was blanketing a lot of painful feelings I couldn't or wouldn't face."

In spite of his drug usage, Self was accepted into Oxford University in 1979 and maintained good grades for most of his stay there. However, around the time of his final examinations, Self was caught using drugs, and he ended up with a third-class degree, second to last on the British scale of degree rankings. (Later, he returned to Oxford and earned an M.A., with honors, in 1992.) Upon leaving Oxford in the early 1980s, Self took a series of menial jobs and fell further into drug addiction. He did clerical work, ran an adventure playground, and worked as a general laborer, all the while producing few finished pieces of writing. At the age of 25, Self checked into a drug rehabilitation center to rid himself of his heroin habit. In 1990 he married Kate Chancellor and had two children with her.

In 1991 Self was managing a trade-magazine publishing company. His real ambition, however, was to get his fiction published, which he did with *The Quantity Theory of Insanity* (1991), a collection of short stories that addressed topics such as mental health, death, and academia. In "The North London Book of the Dead," the narrator meets his recently deceased mother on the streets of London and goes with her to her new home. The house is just like her old one, except the people in the photos she has framed are unfamiliar to the narrator. He barrages her with questions about death, until she dispels his misconceptions with an impatient statement: "Look," she says, "there aren't any 'people in charge' of death. When you die you move to another part of London, that's all there is to it. Period," as quoted by Carol Anshaw in *Chicago Tribune* (March 5, 1995). In "Ward 9" an art therapist named Misha gets a job at a mental institution and quickly loses his mind, finally ending up as a patient himself. The title story is about a psychology graduate student who comes up with brilliant theories such as, "People who are severely mentally ill when they are left unconstrained tend to behave fairly badly. On reflection I suppose that is why they are diagnosed as being mentally ill in the first place," as quoted by Anshaw. The student's crowning glory is his quantity theory of insanity, which states that there are a finite number of sane people in the world and that if a group of insane people is cured, an equal number of previously sane people will lose their minds to maintain the equilibrium.

As David Bowman noted in the *New York Times Book Review* (February 26, 1995), "You either love Will Self or you hate him. . . . You find his writing wonderfully outrageous or merely adolescent." Bowman tended toward the latter group. He felt that although Self was a clever wordsmith, he was short on passion and heart. "Mr. Self's vocabulary is a vibrant one for sure," Bowman wrote, "composed of 'etiolated blues' and 'tonsured idiots' and men sitting 'vertiginously'—but there's little love in evidence." Bowman's reservations notwithstanding, the predominant critical opinion was that Self's debut was a smashing success. Vince Passaro, reviewing Self's collection in New York *Newsday* (February 15, 1995), wrote, "He is terrifically imaginative, probing and funny, and for certain of us, his unreality moves in and begins to overtake the ostensibly real with a remarkable power that only very fine artists can wield." Following the publication of *The Quantity Theory of Insanity*, Self was short-listed for the John Llewellyn Rhys Prize in 1991. In 1993 he won the Geoffrey Faber Memorial Prize. Although he had yet to write a novel, he was named one of the "Best Young British Novelists" in the literary magazine *Granta*, by a panel that included the writer Salman Rushdie. Self's book was published in the United States in 1995.

After *The Quantity Theory of Insanity* was published, Self's rise to fame was almost immediate. He enjoyed the endorsement of Martin Amis, who wrote a laudatory blurb for the book's back cover. Self's willingness to divulge his drug habits and odd personal traits also helped turn him into a sort of black-sheep celebrity in Great Britain. Though some have contended that Self's public persona is a carefully crafted form of self-promotion, he maintains that his bad boy image was initially an accident. In one of his first national newspaper interviews, he rather offhandedly described his drug use, and the journalist printed it all. "So having been outed in that way," Self explained to Chris Heath for *Details* (March 1995), "like some pederast bishop, I then thought: 'If you've got it, baby, flaunt it.' I had to make a virtue out of a necessity."

For those awaiting further controversy following *The Quantity Theory of Insanity* and Self's subsequent interviews, his dual novellas *Cock & Bull* (1992)—published in a single volume—did not disappoint. The first story, *Cock*, depicts a woman who grows a penis; the second, *Bull*, tells of a man who develops a vagina behind his left knee. In *Cock* a woman named Carol loses patience with her meek, alcoholic husband and looks elsewhere for sexual gratification. Soon she sprouts a penis, and, consequent with this, she develops a new love of driving, begins gazing at pin-up pictures, and starts bossing her husband around. In *Bull* an ex-rugby player turned sports journalist begins to grow weary of the macho perspective pervading his profession. When he discovers a vagina behind his knee, he goes to the doctor for treatment. The doctor gradually seduces him, and they engage in a bizarre form of sex, while John finds himself becoming more sensitive and "womanly."

Self told Heller that he wrote the book to express his "anger at the way gender-based sexuality is so predetermined, the way we fit into our sex roles as surely as if we had cut them off the back of a cereal packet and pasted them onto ourselves." The critic Michiko Kakutani, however, thought *Cock & Bull* paid lip service to just the opposite view. In the *New York Times Book Review* (May 31, 1993) she criticized Self's "misogynistic and ridiculously sophomoric vision," continuing, "Although Mr. Self writes under the guise of sending up sexual politics and gender wars, his stories end up buttressing the oldest, most sexist views of men and women." Carol Anshaw, in her review for the *Village Voice Literary Supplement* (June 8, 1993), was not offended by the book, although she felt the tone of Self's writing had definite limitations. "Self expresses a blackly humorous, mildly disgusted view of humanity; gender is significant only in being a dirty joke on all of us. Hermaphrodism, in *Cock & Bull*, merely offers new venues for one or another penis," she wrote. "Self never has to give reverence to this cynicism; the world of farce requires only outrageous or comic consequences." In a more whole-heartedly positive review, Jean-Christophe Castelli opined in *Esquire* (May 1993) that *Cock & Bull* was "the way sexual satire ought to be: a Swiftian kick in the who-knows-what."

Self's next book was *My Idea of Fun: A Cautionary Tale* (1993), his first full-length novel. It is narrated by Ian Wharton, a young man who has an eidetic memory: he can remember and manipulate all the images he's ever seen in his life. Ian is raised in Saltdean, England, by his father, a non-entity, and his mother, who treats him with a discomfiting, barely repressed sexuality. No one seems to recognize Ian's gifts until his mother's friend, Mr. Broadhurst (also known as Samuel Northcliff and the Fat Controller), comes to town and offers to take Ian under his wing. Mr. Broadhurst is a ruthless business tycoon with a harsh, barking voice, who commits murders without batting an eye. He teaches Ian to use his gifts and also threatens that if Ian has sex, he will instantly lose his memorial abilities. After Ian goes to college, Mr. Broadhurst disappears, and Ian finds a new mentor, the psychiatrist Dr. Gyggle. Dr. Gyggle instructs Ian to view his gifts as a delusion, and he convinces him that his attachment to Broadhurst was fueled by the need for a father figure. Ian goes on to graduate and succeed fabulously in business—until the Fat Controller returns and Ian must confront him as an adult.

Michiko Kakutani, the same critic who so disliked *Cock & Bull*, found much to celebrate in Self's new novel. In the *New York Times* (June 3, 1994), she wrote, "*My Idea of Fun* is a genuinely ambitious and accomplished novel, a novel that reads like an original and often willfully perverse Cuisinart mix of William Burroughs, William Gaddis, Thomas Pynchon, and Lewis Carroll." Many critics agreed with Kakutani, and *My Idea of Fun* became Self's most acclaimed book to date. In a dissenting view, Dwight Garner wrote in the *Village Voice* (May 10 1994) that Self had produced little more than surface linguistic pyrotechnics: "This werewolf is too enamored of his own artful huffing and puffing to blow any houses down." Furthermore, as other critics had noted about his fiction in general, Garner said that Self's characters were "emotional children, virtual cartoons." Self himself has agreed that his strengths as a writer do not lie in plot and characterization. In an interview with Robert Clarke for *Spike Magazine* (on-line), he said, "I think the real problem with my books is the lack of structure. I have great difficulty with plot and I have never got on with character, and have always found them very artificial, and essentially romantic in that way, but I have largely written about ideas, and I view descriptive prose, the metaphorical aspects of the work as part and parcel of the ideas."

The idea behind Self's next short-story collection, *Grey Area* (1994), is, according to Giles Foden in his review for the *Spectator* (November 19, 1994), "Political, philosophical, and social indeterminancy" and a "sense of things being neither one nor other." In "A Short History of the English Novel," a book editor named Gerard suddenly finds that the wait staff in the restaurants he frequents consist of aspiring authors angry at him and all those who reject their books. In "Between the Conceits" the narrator postulates that there are only eight people in London who matter and, at one point, says to the story's readers, "Whereas I am fortunately one of them—you are emphatically not." In "Inclusion," a new drug makes concepts blur together in the minds of its users and, ultimately, causes users' minds to meld with those of people nearby. Foden argued that Self's writing was at risk of being eclipsed by his public persona, commenting that *Grey Area*, "as knowingly unsure of itself as its title suggests, points both ways. That is, either to [Self's] consumption, [Truman] Capote-like, by his own image and reputation, or to true success as a writer." Other critics commended the collection. In *People* (June 3, 1996) Paula Chin wrote, "Self's tales are all nightmares. But rarely are bad dreams this wickedly entertaining." The *New York Times* named *Grey Area* one of its Books of the Year for 1996.

In 1995 Self published a collection of his journalistic writing entitled *Junk Mail*. Many of the pieces focused on drugs and British counterculture. Self, somewhat surprisingly, had spent a stint as a food critic for the *Observer*, writing reviews that incorporated his idiosyncratic and sometimes fantastical commentaries. In a review published on August 18, 1996, for example, he wrote about drinking a French wine in a restaurant. His companion, he explained, "thoughtfully ordered a bottle of Chorey-Les-Beaunes 1993 (Lite) to dilute my mood. This was fine, although a fly had insinuated itself into the bottle and rapidly adapted to its new environment by growing a minuscule tweed suit and joining the Garrick Club." In part because of his self-acknowledged drug-use, Self's career as a journalist had been riddled with controversy, which culminated in a national scandal in 1997. Self moved on to the role of television critic for the *Observer* and was later asked to write a political column for the newspaper. After writing one column, Self admitted to having snorted heroin on former British Prime Minister John Major's election campaign jet. After initially denying the allegations, Self said in an interview with the *Independent* (April 13, 1997), "So I was smacked out on the Prime Minister's jet, big deal." To officials at the *Observer*, it was a big deal, and Self was fired from the newspaper amidst a storm of publicity. As he told Ann Henchman for *Publisher's Weekly* (September 8, 1997) not long after the incident, "It's been pretty bad. Enormous public humiliation, your face smeared over every paper, paparazzi at my door. We had to virtually go on the run and live out of my car for a week."

In 1996 Self published the novella *Sweet Smell of Psychosis*, which included illustrations by Martin Rowson. In the story, the young Richard Hermes leaves his girlfriend and his pleasant suburban life and makes his way to London, where he hopes to make it big in a media position. He ends up meeting the center of London's media scene, a man named Bell, and falls in love with one of Bell's acquaintances, a sexy, jaded woman named Ursula Bently. Richard becomes obsessed with Ursula, and when the two become romantically involved, it plunges him further into the decay of London's fashionable media crowd. The book elicited a lukewarm review in *Publisher's Weekly* (July 19, 1999) by Sybil S. Steinberg, who wrote, "This short book, while capped off with a somewhat stunted punchline-like ending, will nevertheless provide readers with a mini-overdose of Self's signature detached licentiousness."

In 1997 Self remarried, to Deborah Orr, editor of the *Guardian Weekend Magazine*. He had left his first wife in 1993, when his son, Alexis, and daughter, Madeleine, were two years old and six months old, respectively. Also in 1997 he published a novel entitled *Great Apes*. Its main character, a painter by the name of Simon Dykes, wakes up after a night of debauchery to discover that his girlfriend has turned into a chimpanzee. So, it seems, has he, but Simon refuses to believe it. As a result, he is institutionalized and put under the care of Dr. Zack Busner (who bears resemblance to the well-known psychiatrist and author Oliver Sacks). In the outside world Simon sees chimpanzees walking the streets, communicating in a strange sign language, and copulating compulsively. Greeting cards and commercials feature humans dressed in ape clothing and humorously aping apes. Nevertheless, Simon continues to resist the idea that he is an ape himself. Gradually, Dr. Busner helps him accept his fate, and Simon is able to resume his life as before, the only difference being that now he is a chimpanzee.

"What should have been the literary equivalent of a parlor trick turns out to be an utterly absorbing and affecting work of fiction," Gary Krist wrote in the *New York Times* (September 21, 1997, on-line). However, many other critics seemed to think that *Great Apes* was in fact little more than a literary parlor trick. In *Library Journal* (October 1, 1997) Barbara Hoffert wrote, "Self is too busy with badboy language and obsessive sex to get at deeper issues." Michiko Kakutani wrote in the *New York Times* (September 12, 1997, on-line), "It is a slender idea for a satire, inflated into a fat, puffy novel, a 'Twilight Zone' episode blown into a full-length feature."

Self published another volume of short stories, *Tough, Tough Toys for Tough, Tough Boys*, in 1998. In "Flytopia" a man makes a pact with the bugs infesting his house. "The Rock of Crack as Big as the Ritz" tells the story of Danny, who discovers a vein of crack cocaine beneath his home. "A Story for Europe" finds a British toddler speaking his first words in German business jargon, a comment on the new unified Europe. In "Caring, Sharing" Americans engage in sex with "emotos," which are manifestations of their own selves programmed to constantly sing the praises of their originals. Depending on the reviewer, *Tough, Tough Toys for*

Tough, Tough Boys was judged as either more of the usual from Self or some of his best fiction in years. Michiko Kakutani, who seemed to swing back and forth between loving and hating Self's work, was much enamored of this collection. In the *New York Times* (May 21, 1999) she wrote of Self, "His tendency displayed in previous books to force his tales into predictable shapes with obvious, italicized morals, has given way in these pages to masterfully shaped narratives that are both complex and unexpected, just as his earlier, adolescent preoccupation with sex has evolved into a more deeply felt interest in the mysteries of identity and emotional (dis)connection."

Though Self had been "cured" of his heroin addiction at the age of 25, he had continued to use drugs and alcohol liberally throughout the rest of the 1980s and 90s. In his interview with Zoë Heller in 1993 he had explained that drugs were still an important part of his life. "I don't feel like I've just closed the door on my past," he said. "I feel a sense of doubleness. I still take occasional excursions into my old world, and I live, I suppose, with a kind of Janus face." Self's pattern was often to binge while in London and then take trips out to the country to sober up and get some writing done. However, his drug use was beginning to spiral out of control once again in 1997 when he lost his column at the *Observer*. In a deliberate attempt to regain power over his habit, he agreed to deliver his next novel, *How the Dead Live*, in 1998, hoping that the tough deadline would force him to clean up. In an interview with Lynn Barber for the *Guardian* (June 11, 2000, on-line), Self called *How the Dead Live* "the book that saved me." Before writing it he went cold turkey on all drugs and alcohol. As he told Barber, "I do think I have a responsibility to point out, very clearly, that I don't think that my talents or my success as a writer have anything to do with my drug use or drinking. On the contrary, I've always had to fight against them in order to get any serious literary work done."

In *How the Dead Live* (2000) Self works with the same premise that he used in the short story "The North London Book of the Dead" from *The Quantity Theory of Insanity*: life after death differs little from life before death. The story is narrated by Lily Bloom, a 65-year-old Jewish-American cancer victim who greatly resembles Self's own mother, as he told Barber during their interview. Lily, who is already deceased when the novel begins, has two living children, Charlotte and the heroin addict Natasha—both of whom Lily constantly criticizes and worries about, even in death. Two deceased children accompany her in the afterlife; Lithy is the cadaver of an aborted fetus, and Rude Boy is her bratty nine-year-old, who was killed in a car accident. Lily's guide through the world of the dead is an Aborigine named Phar Lap Dixon. First Lily must wait in line at the Deatheaucracy Office to be assigned a living space. Much to her chagrin, she also must attend Personally Dead (PD) meetings, a sort of support group for dead people, which bore her inordinately. Lily is unhappy as a dead woman, and she unleashes her bitterness on all that surrounds her while reminiscing about life as a young woman. Finally, in the year 2000, she gets her wish of being reborn as her daughter's daughter. However, the next cycle of life proves no more fulfilling than her previous one.

Reviews of the novel generally praised Self for his ambition. In the *Guardian* (June 17, 2000, on-line), Elaine Showalter applauded the novel's "lavishness of feeling and characterization," and concluded, "What begins as a satiric novel of ideas ends as a surprisingly moving elegy." However, although Self was congratulated for his novel's scope, many critics found the grumpy voice of Lily Bloom tedious and ultimately unrewarding. "Four-hundred pages is too long," a reviewer for the *Economist* (July 15, 2000, on-line) complained. "Bile, spleen, choler and gall don't have that many tunes." In the *Observer* (June 18, 2000, on-line) Adam Mars-Jones wrote that Lily's ranting was "a dutiful nihilism which over hundreds of pages becomes mysteriously vanilla for lack of anything to contrast with it." He concluded, "A book about death needs a pulse as much as any other, perhaps more than most."

Self lives with his wife and their two-year-old son, Ivan, in the Stockwell section of London. As he told Barber, he plans to explore new directions in his future novels: "Bigger canvas, longer time span, more characters and more gearing into the world. In my 20s and 30s, I had that kind of fashionable deconstructionist view that it was meaningless to write about what characters thought because it was such an artificial construct—and I think in my case it was also a reflection of my own immaturity. But the interesting thing about middle age is that you begin to see how people change over time, and how they change in relation to social change, and you begin to get an inkling of why the 19th-century novelists were so preoccupied by this phenomenon. It requires a big canvas and a lot of space and a lot of oomph to bring it off. I'm really interested in doing it."

In 2002 Self published *Dorian: An Imitation*, a retelling of *The Picture of Dorian Gray* by Oscar Wilde, set in this version in the late-20th-century homosexual community. In Self's work, Dorian is a narcissistic "seducer par excellence," of both men and women. In 1981 a young video artist named Baz films Dorian for a video installation. As in the original by Wilde, Dorian continues his decadent behavior but maintains his youth while the video ages. In a critique quoted on *Amazon.com*, a reviewer for *Publishers Weekly* noted: "The prose is laced with epigrammatic, lightly amusing pseudo-Wildean wit . . . but its wordplay and evocation of debauchery also owe something to Evelyn Waugh and Martin Amis (channeling Hunter Thompson and Irvine Welsh). Self's mannered prose can grow tedious, and there's hardly a sympathetic character to be found, but the writer has undertaken—and largely succeeded in pulling off—a daring act of literary homage."   —P. G. H.

SUGGESTED READING: *Details* p126+ Mar. 1995, with photo; *Esquire* p39 May 1993; *Guardian* (on-line) June 11, 2000; *New York Times* (on-line) Sep. 12, 1997, Sep. 21, 1997; *New York Times Book Review* p20 May 31, 1993, p11 Feb. 26, 1995; *Publisher's Weekly* p52+ July 19, 1999, with photo; *Vanity Fair* p125+ June 1993, with photo; *Village Voice* p25+ June 8, 1993, p5+ May 10, 1994; *Washington Post Book World* p3 Apr. 3, 1994

SELECTED BOOKS: essays—*Junk Mail*, 1995; Novels—*My Idea of Fun: A Cautionary Tale*, 1993; *Great Apes*, 1997; *How the Dead Live*, 2000; *Dorian: An Imitation*, 2002; novellas—*Cock & Bull*, 1992; *Sweet Smell of Psychosis*, 1996; short-story collections—*The Quantity Theory of Insanity*, 1991; *Grey Area*, 1994; *Tough, Tough Toys for Tough, Tough Boys*, 1998

Star Black/Courtesy of Graywolf Press

Seshadri, Vijay

Feb. 13, 1954– Poet; essayist; critic

The poet Vijay Seshadri writes of human displacement in his collection *Wild Kingdom* (1996). Set variously in both urban and rural milieus, many of the poems' protagonists—be they Jamaicans in the Bronx, in the poem "Made in the Tropics," or a truck driver lost in the woods after his vehicle crashes, in "Lifeline,"—find themselves out of context. Born in India and raised in Canada and the American Midwest, Seshadri has had his poetry published in many prestigious literary journals, including the *Threepenny Review*, the *New Yorker*, and the *Nation*. *Wild Kingdom* has been called "among the broadest, most intelligent new poetry of this decade," by a reviewer for *Publishers Weekly* (February 26, 1996).

Vijay Seshadri was born in Bangalore, India, on February 13, 1954. His father, K. S., was a research chemist and professor, and his mother, Champaka, was a homemaker. In an essay entitled "My Pirate Boyhood"—in reference to his affection for the Pittsburgh Pirates baseball team—that was published in the *Threepenny Review* (Spring 1998), Seshadri noted that his family left India because the work his father wanted to do would have required them to move to northern India, an area with a culture far removed from that of Bangalore, in southern India. According to Seshadri, his father's logic in moving to North America was that "if he had to go north he might as well go all the way," as Seshadri wrote in the essay. He added, "I happen to know for a fact that my parents' desire to see me have a great academic career in science was crucial to their setting out on their long journey to another civilization, but I've never challenged this explanation my father gives for his motives."

Seshadri and his mother lived in India until 1959, when he was five years old. At that point his father returned from the United States, where he had just earned a doctoral degree in physical chemistry, and moved his wife and son to Ottawa, in Alberta, Canada, where he had received a postdoctoral fellowship with the Canadian Research Council. Seshadri believes that, despite their outward optimism, the move must have been difficult for his parents. In the *Threepenny Review*, he described the Bangalore they left behind as "a gracious garden city, one of Asia's most beautiful. My parents were born into a community with deep roots in that region. They had only just stepped out of the old Indian world, the world that antedates the arrival of the British, and even of Islam, to the Subcontinent."

In late 1960 or early 1961, Seshadri's mother gave birth to his sister in Ottawa. Seshadri went to Sunday Bible school and played ice hockey with his new friends and neighbors, and, through a French-Canadian family who lived next door, he attended Catholic Mass and learned about baseball. Though he didn't much care for Mass, and he never took to ice hockey, he did fall in love with baseball—in particular the Pittsburgh Pirates, the favorite team of his next-door neighbors—during the 1960 World Series.

In August 1961 K. S. Seshadri was offered a position in Ohio State's chemistry department, and moved his family to Columbus, Ohio. Seshadri recounted in his autobiographical essay in the *Threepenny Review*, "When asked where I come from these days by people who expect to hear the name of a place in India, I say I come from Ohio and go on to describe my classic Ohio boyhood—tree-fort building, crawdad-hunting, fishing for bluegills with dough balls—and the streams and woods and railroad tracks near where we lived. Actually, my Ohio boyhood was classic only in its overall unhappiness." While living in Canada, Seshadri had skipped two grades, an occurrence that forced him to play with children who were older, bigger, and more athletic than he was. There was also the additional problem of his ethnicity. As he noted in the *Threepenny Review*, "Small, brown, bespectacled, alien, and saddled with a name that others thought was unpronounceable, I was an easy target for the casual cruelties of childhood." (At the time there were few South Asians living in the United States and even fewer living in the Midwest.) Seshadri, as he wrote in the essay, "didn't respond well to the social pressures" he encountered at that age. He began to develop a destructive side, first playing with matches and later with firecrackers at construction sites near the family's home. At age 10 he convinced his mother to buy him a BB gun, which his father quickly made her take back. "I mourned that gun for years," Seshadri recalled in the *Threepenny Review*, "and it was a long time before I recognized how shocking it must have been for my father, who grew up in an intellectual climate imbued by the presence of Gandhi, to come home and see his son cradling a not-lethal but nevertheless dangerous replica of a Winchester repeating rifle."

Seshadri's fondness for the Pittsburgh Pirates continued to grow after the family's move to Columbus, aided in part by the city's Triple-A baseball team, the Jets, which at that time was part of the Pirates farm system. In 1967 Seshadri's father accepted a position in Pittsburgh, and that summer, as the family prepared for the move, an elated Seshadri developed a "passionate identification" with the Pirates' star rightfielder, Roberto Clemente, as Seshadri wrote in the *Threepenny Review*. Over the next few seasons, he closely followed Clemente's life and performance on the field, as well as the Pirates' games, which he mostly watched on television or listened to on the radio. Clemente's career was fraught with problems, including an arthritic back and continual squabbles with fellow players, managers, and the press. He was outspoken about racism in baseball at a time when there were very few Hispanics and blacks playing in the major league. During Seshadri's adolescence and into his college years, he identified strongly with Clemente. "Moody, sensitive, forbidding, his coal-black, faintly Aztec features usually scowling, he walked the earth feeling aggrieved and misunderstood," Seshadri wrote in the *Threepenny Review*. He continued, "It took quite a while for me to recognize how perfect [Clemente] had been for my peculiar, Indian adolescent romance of hero-worship—complex, human, uncomfortable in the world he lived in but nevertheless astonishing and unequaled—and how much I had got from him."

When in 1972 Clemente died in a plane crash while shuttling supplies to earthquake victims in Nicaragua, Seshadri was a junior at Oberlin College, in Oberlin, Ohio, and had developed other interests, including becoming involved in the counterculture movement. Seshadri received his bachelor's degree from Oberlin in 1974 and later worked in the fishing and logging industries in Oregon for five years. He also lived on New York City's Upper West Side, where he was a student in Columbia University's doctoral program in Middle Eastern Languages and Literature. While he did not complete his doctorate, he did receive a master's degree in fine arts from Columbia in 1985. Around this time he also began submitting his writing to periodicals. His essays, reviews, and poems have been published in, among others, the *Nation*, the *New Yorker*, the *Paris Review*, *Boulevard*, the *Threepenny Review*, *Verse*, and *Shenandoah*, as well as in the anthologies *Under 35: The New Generation of American Poets* and *The Best American Poetry: 1997*.

In 1993 Seshadri became an editor for the *New Yorker*, and two years later he was appointed an adjunct professor at the New School for Social Research. A collection of his poetry, *Wild Kingdom*, was published in 1996 by Graywolf Press. As a critic for *Midwest Book Review* wrote, as quoted on Amazon.com, "Seshadri's poetry addresses some of the central motifs of American literature: the tensions between human history and wilderness and our relationships to both, and the complicated racial dramas underlying our collective experiences." The poems often touch on the theme of human isolation. In "Too Deep to Clear Them Away" the narrator, bothered by a continually ringing phone, remarks: "No, I don't want to go to a movie./I want to sit on my stump and read,/and plot, and imagine things. How,/for example, as night comes on and, grown/tired of the tunes from the buildings,/one lone window washer hangs his harness on the moon." Many of Seshadri's narrators are also full of anxieties in social situations, discomfort that seems to be fueled by the sense that they don't belong. In the first stanza of "Alien Nation," another poem from the collection, the narrator confides, "I think I'm around the wrong people today./Though I know their cousins (who say I'm nice),/veiling their faces they tiptoe away/some impassive, some afraid,/and others grumbling that they'd sooner fillet me than talk to me twice."

Wild Kingdom received mostly favorable notices, many of which applauded Seshadri's range, both in the tone of his writing and in the forms his poems take. A reviewer for *Publishers Weekly* (February 26, 1996) proclaimed, "In portrayals that fluidly embrace abstraction and detail, Seshadri practices a formal precision that is as easy with sonnets as with free verse," and went on to praise the poet's "compassionate, perceptive spirit." A critic for the *Virginia Quarterly Review* (Autumn 1996) wrote that although some of the lines "fade out and lack assurance," the book was "subtle and wry . . . a pleasing first collection." One negative review came from Rochelle Ratner, who remarked in *Library Journal* (March 1, 1996) that "Seshadri has been published in all the top places (the *Na-*

tion, the *New Yorker*, the *Paris Review*, et al.), yet his first collection has little to recommend it. . . . Hampered by clashing cultures, we don't quite know how to read [his poems]. Too many poems seem hollow exercises, often with strict, predictable rhyme schemes." Mary Park, describing the poems in a review for *Amazon.com* (on-line), wrote that "Seshadri is a poet of street scenes and seascapes, twisted alder stumps and spawning salmon, as well as drive-by shootings and thumping reggae bass." She continued, "[His] voice is elegant, energetic, and startlingly original."

Vijay Seshadri lives in Brooklyn, New York, with his wife and son. He has received grants from the New York Foundation for the Arts and the National Endowment for the Arts. He continues to work as an editor for the *New Yorker* and also teaches poetry at Sarah Lawrence College.

—C. M.

SUGGESTED READING: *Library Journal* p81 Mar. 1, 1996; *Publishers Weekly* p102 Feb. 26, 1996; *Southwest Review* p272+ Spring/Summer 1995; *Threepenny Review* Spring 1998; *TriQuarterly* p213+ Fall 1999; *Virginia Quarterly Review* p137 Autumn 1996; *Contemporary Authors*, vol. 156, 1997

SELECTED BOOKS: *Wild Kingdom*, 1996

Rembert Block/Courtesy of HarperCollins

Shakar, Alex

1968– Novelist; short-story writer

Alex Shakar has spent much of the last decade pursuing higher education: After graduating from Yale University in 1990 with a B.A. in literature, he became a Michener Fellow at the University of Texas at Austin, where he earned an M.A. in writing. Currently a doctoral candidate in English and creative writing at the University of Illinois, in Chicago, Shakar, according to Peter Wolfe for the *St. Louis Post–Dispatch* (October 14, 2001), "has both the vision and the rhetorical might to school most of the professors paid to school him and his fellow students in the same lore." From the publication of his award-winning debut collection of short stories, entitled *City in Love: The New York Metamorphoses* (1996), Shakar has distinguished himself as what Brian Lennon for *American Book Review* (as quoted on Shakar's *City in Love* Web site) called "an author unafraid to take risks." In his first novel, *The Savage Girl* (2001), Shakar again demonstrated his bold literary sensibilities, tackling themes of marketing and popular culture in a fantastical—yet recognizable—urban setting. The resulting work has been widely celebrated by critics, with Jeff Giles for the *New York Times* (October 7, 2001) calling it "a wild, ambitious, at times crazily overwrought dystopian novel so stuffed with satire, pathos, villainy, earnestness, doomsaying and marketing seminars that it's like a suitcase that won't shut unless you sit on it." Of the book's innovative author, Giles added: "It's exciting to meet a new novelist who's not afraid of heights."

Alex Shakar was born in 1968 in the New York City borough of Brooklyn. His father was the actor Martin Shakar, perhaps best known for his film role as John Travolta's brother, the priest, in *Saturday Night Fever* (1977). By witnessing the effects of his father's turbulent career, Shakar told Irene Lacher for the *Los Angeles Times* (December 14, 2001) that he learned early on the pitfalls of popular culture. "I think I had a different view of pop culture. I also had a kind of love-hate relationship with it," he explained. "When that movie came out in the '70s, I was in elementary school, and my dad was the local hero. But I also got to see how he had to struggle. Every so often I'd turn on the TV and see my dad getting strangled and being some insane killer. It's been very hard for him to be a serious artist and to be in this world of pop culture, where you're having to do these really cheesy or sometimes insulting roles." After spending his early childhood in Cobble Hill, a neighborhood in Brooklyn, Shakar attended Manhattan's Stuyvesant High School, widely considered one of the most prestigious public high schools in the city.

While pursuing postgraduate work in creative writing at the University of Texas at Austin and later in Chicago at the University of Illinois, Shakar began incorporating a strong literary bent into his work. His first collection of short stories, *City in*

Love: The New York Metamorphoses, published in 1996, is a series of seven stories set in 20th-century New York City but based on the mythological tales of the Roman poet Ovid's book *Metamorphoses*. Shakar told a reviewer for the on-line literary magazine the *Richmond Review*, "I was exploring a sense that modern urban society is in many ways better grasped by the ancient vision of the Metamorphoses—a universe in constant flux, the always-changing-always-the-same quality of things—than it is by more modern teleologies." He continued, "The latter demonizes chaos, whereas Ovid's mythological system embraces it and shows it to be part of the greater order."

Throughout these stories, Shakar drapes modern culture in the garbs of myth, parable, and legend. For example, in "On Morpheus, Relating to Orpheus," Shakar depicts Morpheus, known in Greek mythology as the god of dreams, as an underemployed actor struggling for survival in New York City, a place that Shakar describes as "a massive by-product of untold thousands of impossible dreams," as quoted by Brian Lennon. In "Waxman's Sun," he evokes the legend of Icarus, who in Greek mythology flew too close to the sun on a pair of wax wings; here, Shakar tells the story of Danny Waxman, who descends into the labyrinth tunnels of the city's subway system in search of his lost father. In "Maximum Carnage," Shakar describes fifth-grade girls in the New York City borough of Queens battling "sentors," which are half-man/half-motorcycle creatures inspired by Ovid's centaurs, beings that were, similarly, part-human/part-horse. Joseph Allen O'Rear for *The Review of Contemporary Fiction* (Spring 1997) observed, "All of the characters in the collection are recognizably human, yet striving to be more than human."

City in Love: The New York Metamorphoses was generally praised by critics for its ambition and originality. Noting Shakar's "often profound literary inventions," O'Rear acknowledged, "These stories are technically innovative in the best way; that is, Shakar's structural 'experimentation' is always at the service of, indeed, dictated by the thematics of his story at hand." Yet, many critics thought the collection as a whole was not an unqualified success. One reviewer for *Publishers Weekly* wrote, "Shakar is really good when he's on. Which is, admittedly, a cagey way of saying that he's not when he's not." Nevertheless, Lennon, who also described a few of the stories as "thin," concluded: "Over all, Shakar's debut work is characterized by elegance and creative honesty, and in a quadrant (if inclined to such things, you might label this book 'experimental') known best for smirking cleverness, he lends dignity to the notion of literary alchemy." The collection earned Shakar a 1996 National Fiction Competition prize, and it was named an Independent Presses Editors' pick of the year.

In 2001 Shakar published his first novel, *The Savage Girl*, which rose from an idea he had conceived 10 years earlier, after reading a 1991 article on trend spotters in *Spy* magazine. (Trend spotters are the marketing consultants who observe popular culture in order to predict lucrative consumer trends.) After conducting extensive research on such topics as marketing and advertising practices and terminology and behavioral psychology, Shakar set out to write an enlightened novel about popular culture and consumer marketing. "I thought that [trend spotters] would be the perfect people," he told Ron Hogan for *Beatrice.com*, "through which to look at whether our increasing tendency to express ourselves through our purchases gives us power or leeches our power away." In exploring this topic, Shakar told Dylan Foley for the *Denver Post* (November 11, 2001), he had to challenge his own preconceptions about consumer culture. "It was my struggle in writing the novel," he said. "Half the time, you see the ugliness of consumerism, then you look at the same thing in a different way, and see that consumerism is liberating and dynamic. Is it something that imprisons us and stifles our imagination, or is it something that gives us more creativity?"

The novel takes place in the fictional Middle City, an urban metropolis built on the side of a volcano—a backdrop that Jeff Zalenski for *Publishers Weekly* (August 20, 2001) called "a comic-book setting" that is "both familiar and fantastic." At the novel's center is Ursula Van Urden, a failed artist who arrives in Middle City to aid her sister, Ivy, a schizophrenic fashion model who has been institutionalized after attempting to commit suicide. While in Middle City, Ursula convinces Ivy's estranged boyfriend, Chas, who is president and founder of the trend-spotting firm Tomorrow, Ltd., to give her a job. In this capacity, Ursula confronts the exploitative world of consumer marketing and, in an attempt to revolt against its standard manipulation, proposes a public-relations campaign for "the savage girl," a waif she has observed in one of Middle City's parks killing her own food and constructing her own clothing out of natural materials. To Ursula's horror, the campaign is successful, and Chas begins marketing her sister, Ivy, as a "savage girl," to advertise a new product called "diet water."

In the novel, which Mark Rozzo for the *Los Angeles Times* (October 7, 2001) called "a frighteningly-smart take on an advertising-drenched society," Shakar also introduced several original marketing concepts, which he discovered and coined while researching marketing culture. For example, while training Ursula to become a trend spotter, Chas explains the idea of "paradessence"—or paradoxical essence—which is the notion that every product can promise to satisfy two paradoxical desires at the same time. "For example," Shakar told Lacher, "the paradessence of coffee is stimulation and relaxation, and every commercial or ad will promise you both of these things at the same time. When I came up with that idea, I was seeing it everywhere." Second, Shakar described a world steeped in what he calls "post-irony." He explained to

Lacher, "The trend spotters in the book are saying the culture is supersaturated with irony, and something's got to change, and they're predicting this new state of mind that they call post-irony. Post-irony is not knowing whether anyone's being ironic or earnest at any given moment, and moreover, the distinction ceases to matter." In an interview for the *Richmond Review*, Shakar added, "The question of whether post-irony is a good thing or a bad thing—whether it's the next phase in the evolution of modern consciousness or a virulent new kind of Orwellian doublethink—is an issue that divides [the characters]."

Shakar's ambition was noted by many literary critics, some of whom compared *The Savage Girl*'s themes to those set forth in *Purgatorio*, by the Italian writer Dante Alighieri (1265–1321). Reviewers regarded the novel as a revealing and freshly original critique of what Janet Maslin for the *New York Times* (September 20, 2001) called "fashion and consumerism gone mad." Maslin concluded, "*The Savage Girl* winds up as a sharply observant relic of the recent past. And the keenness of Mr. Shakar's satirical vision also carries it into the future. The age of cynicism and anomie that is captured here may have ended in a flash, but its hallmarks are revealing all the same. And Mr. Shakar preserves them here with a scathing intelligence that transcends the trendiness of any particular moment."

Shakar recently revealed one of his artistic intentions for the *Richmond Review* writer. "Good art at its best can lift us up outside the ideologies we inhabit and give us a bird's eye view of them," he said, "allowing us to see how they have shaped us, informed us and limited us. I'd argue this is something only good art can do. . . . A work of art, by connecting with us aesthetically and emotionally, can really hit us where we live and show us on every level of consciousness what's at stake in our own day-to-day."

Shakar currently resides in Chicago.

—K. D.

SUGGESTED READING: *Beatrice.com* 2001; *Los Angeles Times* Dec. 14, 2001; *New York Times* E p8 Sep. 20, 2001; *New York Times Book Review* p8 Oct. 7, 2001; *Review of Contemporary Fiction* p180 Spring 1997; *Richmond Review* (on-line) 2001; *Washington Post* C p9 Oct. 8, 2001

SELECTED BOOKS: *City in Love: The New York Metamorphoses*, 1996; *The Savage Girl*, 2001

Shapiro, Alan

Feb. 18, 1952– Poet; essayist; memoirist

The American poet, critic, and memoirist Alan Shapiro has made his life's work the examination of the human condition and spiritual striving. In his first book of poems, *After the Digging* (1981), he drew on history, portraying the eras of the Irish potato famine and the Salem witch trials. In later volumes of poetry, *The Courtesy* (1983) and *Happy Hour* (1987), he turned to his own life for themes, while continuing to demonstrate his ability to enter the minds of even Old Testament–era characters. He seemed to have reached a poetic pinnacle with the critically acclaimed *Covenant* (1991) and *Mixed Company* (1996). The death of his sister and the declining years of his parents drew responses from Shapiro that ranged from *The Last Happy Occasion* (1996), a series of autobiographical and critical essays, to *Vigil* (1997), an account in prose and elegiac poems of his sister's last weeks in a hospice. Critics found illuminating his discussions of the "New Formalism" in *In Praise of the Impure: Poetry and the Ethical Imagination: Essays, 1980–1991* (1993). In *The Dead Alive and Busy* (2000), a poetry collection, Shapiro gave Kate Daniels, writing in the *Southern Review* (Winter 2000), "hope for the future of our besieged American language" with poems "full of lovely human voices that call us to drown in them." In 2002 he published *Song and Dance*, another collection of poetry.

The son of Marilyn Katz and Harold Shapiro, Alan Shapiro was born February 18, 1952 in Boston, Massachusetts. His father was a salesman and his mother a secretary. Shapiro graduated from Brandeis University in Waltham, Massachusetts, in 1974.

Inspired by the work of the Nobel Prize–winning Irish poet Seamus Heaney, Shapiro left the United States, making his way to Ireland by way of Wales—a trip he described in *The Last Happy Occasion*. Shapiro remained in Ireland for some time, studying in Dublin and writing poetry, before heading to Stanford University, in California, where he had been awarded a Stegner Fellowship in Poetry. (He was soon joined there by his girlfriend from Ireland, Carol Ann, whom he married and later divorced.) At Stanford he came under the influence of Yvor Winters, a noted poet and critic. "Winters had died in 1968, six years before I came to Stanford," Shapiro wrote in *The Last Happy Occasion*. "But he was still very much a living presence to me and the other students in the writing program. . . . Early in his career, Winters had abandoned many of the modernist techniques and assumptions that had governed the work of his contemporaries and that still governed to some extent much of the work of mine. His poetry and criticism (*In Defense of Reason* especially) were our sacred texts, our Torah and Talmud. . . . [W]e believed that Winters's definitions and prescriptions were true not only for the poetry he wrote and admired, but for any poetry at all that aspired to be deathless and universal." Winters had decried the poetry of such troubled spirits as Hart Crane, Sylvia Plath, and John Berryman. "Like Crane, Plath, and Berryman, we too had the courage of our convictions," Shapiro declared, "but our convictions were life-enhancing, not life-threatening. For us, the act of writing and reading had all the urgency of a morality play in which the self heroically confronts the brute facts of irrational nature and, in the confrontation, renews, strengthens, and extends the fragile boundary of human consciousness." Shapiro remained at Stanford until 1979, when he went to teach at Northwestern University, in Evanston, Illinois, becoming a professor of English and editor of the Phoenix Poets series published by the University of Chicago Press.

In 1981 Shapiro published *After the Digging*, his first poetry collection. For a first book of poetry it is unusual, in that it draws on history rather than personal experience. The volume contains two suites of poems, the first a sequence on the Irish potato famine of the mid-19th century, the second a series on demonic possession in late-17th-century New England. In powerful dramatic narratives, Shapiro envisioned the atmosphere of those desperate times; the poems evoke the ills of our own times as well. In "Ploughing," his subject, Goodman Upton of Salem, thinks about the stricken and hysterical girls who were believed to be possessed, their writhings and shrieks attributed to the malignity of those accused of witchcraft:

> *Who have the girls*
> *cried out upon today?*
>
> His plough strikes rock, jolting away the reins and his hands burning,
> and stumbling to his knees as if he heard deep in the hedges
> the spade-foot frogs begin
> to sound too much like
> drumming in his ears,
> he tries with all his might to say the Lord's Prayer
> but, having learned that everywhere is listens as he recalls,
> *Let him that thinketh*
> *he standeth safe take heed now, lest he fall.*

Critics were struck by a young poet's having summoned so powerfully voices from the past and having attempted so successfully to infuse them with a modern sensibility. *After the Digging* was reissued in 1998 with a new afterword by Shapiro.

His 1983 volume, *The Courtesy*, was thought by many reviewers to be his first, because its themes were autobiographical. The poet J. D. McClatchy, writing about *The Courtesy* in the *New York Times Book Review* (July 26, 1987), declared himself "dismayed by all [Shapiro] had forsworn to write his plain, agreeable poems with their suburban settings and tactful epiphanies. Everywhere was intelligence, but no fizz, no fire." In the same review, however, discussing Shapiro's 1987 collection, *Happy Hour*, McClatchy found that those poems, in contrast, "use their calm surfaces to restrain a new, more difficult and unshapely material." He judged that Shapiro had deliberately narrowed his range and "cultivated a new generosity of detail and insight," particularly in the "longer narratives . . . of considerable power. . . . His character studies like 'Extra' or 'Astronomy Lesson' or the title poem recall the plangent bitterness in similar poems by Randall Jarrell or Anthony Hecht." McClatchy singled out for praise "Neighbors," which he termed "a chilling poem . . . about a young couple whose downstairs neighbor, a crone who blasts old love songs, becomes a crazed menace—an eerie counterpart to their own relationship." Shapiro is "a shrewd and sympathetic moralist," McClatchy concluded. "He never trivializes his subjects with high-minded flourishes or stylistic gimmicks."

Shapiro's 1991 poetry collection, *Covenant*, was highly praised, particularly by other poets. Robert Pinsky, twice poet laureate of the United States, declared in the *Yale Review* (April 1992) that Shapiro had achieved the pinnacle of poetic success, "bringing all the eloquence of poetry to the experience and language of the author's contemporary America." Pinsky quoted C. K. Williams, another poet, who had remarked that *Covenant* "brings the fugitive emotions" and "blunderings" of life into "contact with that which, for good and ill, links us to the mythic and historic." He stated his agreement with Williams "that the book is a marvelous work . . . which grows richer and richer on every reading."

In 1993 Shapiro published his first essay collection, *In Praise of the Impure: Poetry and the Ethical Imagination: Essays, 1980–1991*. When Shapiro was at Stanford, he got from Winters not only "a heady sense of mastery over everything we didn't know," as he wrote in *The Last Happy Occasion*, but a method of channeling the anarchically irrational self by means of the "New Formalism." A few years later, Shapiro recalled, "I began to feel constrained by the Wintersian injunction to 'write little, do it well.' To chisel every word of every poem as if in stone became, for me at least, a recipe for writer's block. . . . If not for Winters himself, then for many of his ardent followers, writing as if Ben Jonson were looking over their shoulder placed too great a burden on each and every line they wrote. Meter for them, moreover, seemed more a cage than a technique of discovery. And whereas Winters did in fact have a lion inside him that required caging, the poems by his epigones were lion cages holding pussycats."

Such is the background to Shapiro's analysis of his contemporaries' use of classical formalist techniques. He argued in *In Praise of the Impure* that form is only a tool and that when it is made the driving force of a poem, replacing meaning, it produces what Shapiro termed the "mechanical reaction." On the other hand, meter and rhyme can be used as an architect uses beams and girders—to support and delimit a poetic space or statement.

Shapiro's 1996 volume of poetry, *Mixed Company*, won the *Los Angeles Times* Book Prize for Poetry in 1997. Most critics argued that the collection was "without question his most satisfying performance," as James Longenbach wrote in the *Yale Review* (October 1996). Longenbach felt that for "Shapiro, the barriers of gender, age, class and race are nearly insurmountable. But what distinguishes *Mixed Company* is Shapiro's willingness to think hard—and then harder still—about his culture's inability to forge a true community. There is not," he concluded, "a single moment of nihilism in this dark, unflinching book."

Calvin Bedient, writing in the *Southern Review* (Winter 1997), also called *Mixed Company* Shapiro's "best book." He found the poetry at "once puritanical and urbane, stringent and compassionate" and termed "Shapiro's imagination . . . almost unremittingly 'ethical.'" In "The Basement," Shapiro evoked the play space he shared with his friend Gary when they were children watched over by Gary's nanny, Helen. Helen, a refugee, "the only German Jew I knew," treats Gary with excessive indulgence, trying to give him everything he wants and spoiling him in the process:

Did Helen mourn the trouble he got into? Or had she by the time we knew her had her fill of mourning, her heart by then concerned with other things, things he unwittingly provided, Gary never more enslaved than in the license she made him think was his? Could he have been her plaything too, as much as she was his, her puppet of a secret brooding on what couldn't be forgotten, all of her life from the war on (and she was just a girl then) a mere reprise, a deafening echo chamber?

Shapiro is careful to attribute Helen's "aura of dread and urgency" and her intense concentration on the children's toy trains to her childhood spent under the eye of the Nazis. When he speaks of her to his mother, Helen "rises from the dead through small talk to become/ my personal link to what I can't imagine."

Bedient noted a somewhat didactic quality in Shapiro's "articulate elegance, the 'prose' music of his syntax." He observed that "the harmony of Shapiro's language, its manifest love of illustrating a complex poise, makes it the most tactful of teachers." He concluded, however, that "the quality of the lines remains, throughout, that of a lights-on ethical analysis, even as manner closes seamlessly with matter."

Also in 1996 Shapiro published *The Last Happy Occasion*, a memoir in six parts. In it, he intertwined personal memories with illuminating poems. "*The Last Happy Occasion* is a model of a certain kind of confessional literature," Jonathan Kirsch wrote in the *Los Angeles Times Book Review* (November 6, 1996). "At moments, Shapiro allows his prose to take flight and soar into poetry— an appropriate self-indulgence, since he . . . seems to turn to poetry as the touchstone of reality in his own life. . . . Shapiro concedes that *The Last Happy Occasion* started out as 'a personal testimony to the power of poetry to alter how we live,' but ended up as something much less celebratory. Poetry, for instance, does not soften the sting of his sister's final illness; even though she asked him to write a poem for her as she lay dying, he came to realize that 'she was beyond the reach of anybody's love or kindness, of poetry, of conversation, of relatedness of any kind.'"

In one essay, about Shapiro's new neighbor who allowed his dog to attack Shapiro's dog, at a time when his wife was about to give birth to their first child—Shapiro took a more positive view of poetry's ability to affect people's lives. Not only poetry, but all literature, has the power to dull the sting of events and clarify their essential character: "Freed from the tyranny of sheer event, from the pressure of immediate feeling and the unconscious and semiconscious history that feeling bears, the contemplative field I enter when I write about this man now, and that you enter when you read about him, affords us both a latitude of response and attention not available in the experience itself. This contemplative field enables us to cultivate what [the critic] Wayne Booth calls an upward hypocrisy. . . . It enables us to enter into the inner world of people we might shun or dismiss in the normal course of our nonreading lives. This is the value of imaginative contemplation (literary or otherwise), and its limitation. . . . I'd like to think that the imaginative work of writing this, of telling and retelling this story over the years, will bring me sooner to a more inclusive, more flexible grasp of the experience."

For Jean Hanff Korelitz, who reviewed *The Last Happy Occasion* for the *Washington Post Book World* (October 13, 1996), Shapiro emerges as "serious, insightful and honest about his shortcomings." Korelitz observed, however, that Shapiro's transformation by poetry does not quite come through to the reader; "his homages to specific works by [Thom] Gunn and [Philip] Larkin, and more general praise of Heaney, Winters and others, do not quite present, let alone clarify, this sense of utter alteration." *The Last Happy Occasion* was nominated for a National Book Critics Circle Award in 1997.

Vigil, Shapiro's 1997 memoir about the last days of his sister Beth, who died of breast cancer, was a product not so much of "imaginative contemplation" as an attempt to make his "grief all the more palpable and recognizable," as Kathrine Varnes put it in *Parnassus: Poetry in Review* (1999). Shapiro's sister had been a left-wing activist, married to an African-American man and estranged from her parents. Her entry into a hospice to die, however, reunited her with her family, who kept a vigil around her bedside for an extended period of time. Varnes lauded the way in which Shapiro's "sinuous sentences stretch into all the possibilities of feeling." The reunion, Shapiro wrote, gave the family a paradoxical sense of joy: "Joy in the self-forgetfulness that came with tending Beth, with grieving for her, and in caring so tenderly for each other as we grieved; joy in the dissolution of the opaque privacies of daily life, in the heightened clarity of purpose and desire, in the transparency of understanding we all felt for the first time as a family; joy in other words, in an intimacy whose very rarity added sadness to the joy."

Critics generally showed enthusiasm for *Vigil*. The *Library Journal* (August 1997) reviewer noted that the book's disturbing subject was "handled with an unreserved elegance and an emotional honesty," observing that "The Afterwards," a series of poems that Shapiro included in the volume, "demonstrate how creativity can provide healing." Jeanne Braham, in an article entitled "The Power of Witness" in the *Georgia Review* (Spring 1998), found the "stories . . . inscribed with the effort to transform witness into insight: illness generates pain, pain converts to loss, and grief comes round to comprehension by listening to its own testimony."

In the 2000 poetry volume *The Dead Alive and Busy*, Shapiro confessed that death has had a kind of triumph in his life. "Something got loose/hunting the vision of itself," he acknowledged in the opening line of "Scarecrow." "What has got loose," Michael Hainey wrote in the *New York Times Book Review* (April 9, 2000), "is the dead—in all their guises and disguises. Shapiro, like a kind medium, offers these loose souls his hand so that he might know them and, in the process, give those of us on this side of the great divide a new way of seeing. His unblinking gaze yields unforgettable images."

In 2002 Shapiro continued his reflections on death in *Song and Dance*, a new collection of poems about his brother David, a Broadway stage actor who succumbed to brain cancer. In this book the poet recounts their relationship, including childhood memories of lip-synching Ethel Merman records for their parents, up until his brother's diagnosis and death. Ray Olson, in a review for *Booklist* as quoted on *Amazon.com*, wrote, "This book of poems in which not a word seems mischosen is one of the finest examples of the new secular poetry of illness and death that would assuage grief when the consolations of religion seem hollow." In 2003 Shapiro, who has translated other classic works, published a translation of *The Oresteia* by Aeschylus.

Shapiro lives with his second wife and two children in North Carolina, where he teaches at the University of North Carolina in Chapel Hill.

—S. Y.

SUGGESTED READING: *Boston Review* (on-line) 1998; *Commonweal* p26+ Feb. 26, 1993; *Georgia Review* p168+ Spring 1998; *Library Journal* p89 Aug. 1997; *Los Angeles Times Book Review* p6 Nov. 6, 1996; *New York Times Book Review* p9 July 26, 1987, Apr. 9, 2000; *Parnassus: Poetry in Review* p317+ 1999; *Poetry* p232 July 1992; *Southern Review* p136+ Winter 1997, p165+ Winter 2000; *Washington Post Book World* p7 Oct. 13, 1996; *Yale Review* p236+ Apr. 1992, p158+ Oct. 1996

SELECTED BOOKS: poetry—*After the Digging*, 1981; *The Courtesy*, 1983; *Happy Hour*, 1987; *Covenant*, 1991; *Mixed Company*, 1996; *The Dead Alive and Busy*, 2000; *Song and Dance*, 2002; nonfiction—*In Praise of the Impure: Poetry and the Ethical Imagination, Essays 1980–1991*, 1993; *The Last Happy Occasion*, 1996; *Vigil*, 1997; as translator—*The Orestia*, 2003

Jerry Bauer/Courtesy of Hyperion Press

Sharp, Paula

Nov. 12, 1957– Novelist; short-story writer; lawyer

The American writer Paula Sharp has used her childhood, her life in disparate places in the United States, and her later experiences as a public defender in her novels *The Woman Who Was Not All There* (1988), *Lost in Jersey City* (1993), *Crows Over a Wheatfield* (1996), and *I Loved You All* (2000), and in her short stories, collected in a volume entitled *The Imposter: Stories About Netta and Stanley* (1991). Sharp, who in her writing has dealt with such issues as the inability of family law to protect women and children from abusive husbands and fathers, and the havoc wrought by anti-abortion activists, has received accolades from reviewers who have praised her realism and attention to detail. One such critic is Megan Harlan, who, writing in *Publishers Weekly* (August 19, 1996), noted that Sharp is able to alternate "palpable suspense with thoughtful, multifaceted consideration of . . . heated issues."

Paula Sharp was born November 12, 1957 in San Diego, California. Her father, Rodman Alton Sharp, was a physicist, and her mother, Rosemary Cochran Sharp, became an archeologist. After her parents divorced, Sharp lived with her mother, younger brother, and older sister in various parts of the country. Some of the places, including Chapel Hill, North Carolina, and New Orleans, Louisiana, were later used as settings for Sharp's novels. "My mother is a Southerner by blood," Sharp told Megan Harlan. "I love that, in the South, people have such a high tolerance for eccentricity." Sharp attended high school in Ripon, Wisconsin, where her mother became a professor at a small college.

Paula Sharp attended Dartmouth College, in Hanover, New Hampshire, where she majored in comparative literature and was honored as a superior student. She received her bachelor's degree from that school in 1979. Her first job was teaching at an inner-city Catholic elementary school in Jersey City, New Jersey, while translating the works of Latin American writers who had been censored in their own countries. She went on to study at Columbia University Law School in New York City, graduating in 1985. While there, her translation of Antonio Sharmeta's novel, *The Insurrection*, was published, in 1984.

Since then, Sharp has had a distinguished career in the law, acting as a public defender and working for the Legal Aid Society in New York City. In an on-line interview with *George Jr.* (January 1997), however, Sharp declared, "I am a writer first. I wrote and translated fiction for years before I became a lawyer, and I continued to do so all through law school and afterwards. I also believed . . . that almost everything I was exposed to in the criminal-justice world would have to make me a better writer. You spend a lot more time as a criminal lawyer trying to puzzle people together, making sense of their motives and figuring out how the circumstances of their lives led them down the wrong roads." Sharp took a year off from the Legal Aid Society to live in Brazil, where her sister was doing anthropology field work. There she completed her first novel, *The Woman Who Was Not All There*, which was published in 1988. In it, the title character is a woman in a small southern town. After her husband deserts her, she must raise her four children on her own with her earnings as a nurse. By the end of the novel, she emerges as a more full human being from the rigid routine in which she has encased herself. Carolyn See, in the *Los Angeles Times* (October 31, 1988), praised the novel for its humor and for its "heartbreaking" qualities. Other reviewers liked the moral courage shown by the main character in taking control of her own life. The novel went on to win the QPB (Quality Paperback Book Club) New Voice Award.

Sharp's next book was *The Imposter: Stories About Netta and Stanley* (1991), which won a BANTA Award. Netta and Stanley are distant cousins, members of a clan of good-for-nothings. Their forbears, the Beaulieus, have drifted from Louisiana to Wisconsin over various routes, and Netta and Stanley meet up in Ripon. The first section of the book consists of three stories about Netta, and the second section is five stories about Stanley. Their lives are intertwined in the first story, "Joyriding," in which they take a lawyer on a ride in a stolen limousine. "The introduction is a flash-forward, as it turns out, a momentary cross section of the lives of the adult Stanley and Netta," Jack Butler wrote in the *New York Times Book Review* (September 15, 1991). Readers mainly experience Netta and Stanley as rebellious adolescents, trying with no success to escape their dreadful upbringings. "These stories," Butler noted, "range from the mid-1960s to the early 1970s, but they are strangely reminiscent of the Depression era: circumstances are bleak everywhere, and everywhere circumstances triumph over character." Butler also felt that the stories are mainly "examinations of a dysfunctional society" rather than portraits of two human beings. "The author does a remarkable job of describing real places. . . . But finally it is the author's portrayal of Ripon that comes to represent all the places in this book—a muddy and barren town, ruled by gossip and meanness. And it is this town that emerges as the main character." He concluded that "these stories are wonderfully observant, full of sharp detail and good prose."

In *Lost in Jersey City* (1992), another female character, Ida Terhune, migrates from Louisiana, this time to Jersey City. When Ida decides to leave her second husband, she gets into her large car and drives north with her children—Skeet, a nine-year-old boy, and his younger sister, Sherry—to live with a friend in her Jersey City apartment owned by a notorious slumlord. The first part of the book consists of the family's on-the-road story, but those adventures are only a prelude to what happens to the beehive-haired, polyester-clad Ida when she accidentally kills the landlord's son with her car.

The reviewer for *Publishers Weekly* (August 16, 1993) found that Sharp had concentrated on the comic value of "culture shock" to the detriment of character. "Thus, though the book has many humorous passages, much of its hilarity feels forced." Walter Satterthwait, however, writing in the *New York Times Book Review* (November 7, 1993), maintained exactly the opposite—that making Ida Terhune "so colorless as to be nearly invisible" was a risk that had paid off for Sharp. "If Ida sometimes tries our patience, the rest of this novel does not. Ms. Sharp, unlike Ida, has a fine, freewheeling sense of humor, and she provides her story with a terrific troop of characters, all vibrant and quirky: brash Betty Trombley, the towering, irreverent, quick-thinking, fast-talking reformed tomboy; Mike Ribeiro, the slovenly yet dashing, cynical yet romantic criminal lawyer; Angel Rodriguez, the proprietor of a pest-removal service whose jacket pockets sport, with a slight nod to Luis Buñuel, the words 'Exterminator Angel.'" *Lost in Jersey City* was a *New York Times* Notable Book of the Year in 1993.

Although Sharp used humor in *Crows Over a Wheatfield* (1996), "it is . . . a more complex and powerful book than Sharp's previous efforts," according to Megan Harlan. In the tradition of Charles Dickens's *Bleak House*, which helped inspire reform in 19th-century British laws of equity, *Crows* is designed to call attention to abuses in the American legal system. The narrator, Melanie, has grown up as the daughter of a criminal defense attorney who gets the guilty off in court and then comes home and attacks his own family. Melanie has responded by becoming an attorney and then a judge. Although she keeps herself insulated from real feeling as a result of her unhappy childhood, she is successful in her career. Her brother, Matt, fares less well. After their father forces him to help win an acquittal for a murderer of children, Matt suffers a schizophrenic break and winds up in a halfway house run by a minister who helps Central American refugees as well as the mentally disturbed. When Melanie arrives in Wisconsin to visit her brother and stepmother, whom her father has also oppressed, she becomes friendly with the minister's daughter, Mildred. Mildred's husband has been away doing research in Brazil, but when he returns, he shows his true colors as an abuser of their toddler child and something of a maniac. Melanie tries to get her friend disentangled from this marriage, but the judge awards custody of the child to his father. Mildred is forced underground, fleeing with her child and later becoming the founder of a service that helps other women escape from abusive husbands.

"The court scenes in this novel bristle with the interaction of the participants' personalities," the *Publishers Weekly* (June 10, 1996), reviewer wrote; "they are riveting. From start to finish, this is an emotionally involving story whose powerful message is commensurate with the social problem it illustrates with gripping accuracy." Other reviewers praised Sharp's artistry in making "this story as lush in detail (the frigid small-town Wisconsin setting bursts with all shades of Midwestern eccentricity) as it is grand in scale, with meditations on insanity and plain old evil swirled into the mix."

The novelist Jane Smiley, who reviewed *Crows Over a Wheatfield* for the *New York Times Book Review* (August 18, 1996), found herself feeling somewhat exploited by Sharp's appeal to readers to indict the legal system for its handling of child custody and spouse abuse cases. For Smiley, the most enjoyable parts of the novel were "the peripheral bits," which demonstrate that Sharp "is clearly a writer of significant talents. She brings precision and lyricism to her descriptions of northern Wisconsin, evoking quite neatly both the darkness of the winter and the brightness of the summer. . . . This beautiful sense of place, though, is crying out to be in another novel, one in which it is more than scenery." Smiley concluded that Sharp is to be commended for asking serious questions about "issues that many Americans deal with only reluctantly. That the novelist cannot resolve them is a testament to their importance and their mind-numbing difficulty."

Michael Harris, in his review for the *Los Angeles Times* (August 5, 1996), concurred that although the scenes involving Mildred and her family courtroom trials are emotionally exciting and involving, the novel weakens when Melanie's questions about the practice of law take over. At these moments, Harris contends, Sharp allows her readers to question the issues, "not what the author of a protest novel wants to happen." "The law may be a mess," Harris stated, "but what do we put in its place? Can society rely for justice on clandestine networks of anarchistic computer hackers and keepers of safe houses just because—unlike other 'outlaws,' such as the anti-abortion militants and 'freemen' types who lurk at the edges of the story—these are supposed to be the good guys?" He concluded that Sharp's statement of the problem— "There's a whole nation of women out there . . . who live in terror, trapped and dependent, with . . . children, and the law won't free them"—was, in his words, "ringing but not sufficient."

Sharp turned to another "women's issue" in her novel *I Loved You All* (2000), which takes on the "pro-life" movement. The novel has three principal characters: Marguerite Daigle, a Cajun merry widow living in upstate New York who drinks; Mahalia, her teenage daughter; and Isobel, the babysitter for Marguerite's younger daughter, Penny, a rebellious eight-year-old who narrates the story in retrospect. When Marguerite is sent by her brother to a rehab center for alcoholics, Isobel enlists Mahalia and Penny in her crusade to end abortion. The varied characters they encounter "seem ready to get up and step off the page," according to Craig Seligman, writing in the *New York Times Book Review* (August 27, 2000), who added: "Sharp has the born novelist's gift of breathing life into her characters." Although he noted that the ending had some weaknesses, Seligman nonetheless stated that Sharp has produced a "novel . . . strangely gentle and funny for a book about the escalating defiance of anti-abortion fanatics in the late 1970s."

Cheryl L. Conway, in a review for *Library Journal* (July 2000), agreed, terming *I Loved You All* "well worth reading." Sharp "intertwines the themes of family love, alcoholism, abortion, betrayal, and the power of a fanatically held belief," Conway wrote. A *Publishers Weekly* (June 26, 2000) reviewer praised Sharp's "carnival of characters," and noted that the "narrative moves swiftly from conflict to conflict, buoyed by Sharp's perfect timing and occasionally ecstatic prose that renders water moccasins as 'black ink dropped in water' and a truck headlight as 'a tilted goblet of gold liquid.'"

Sharp, a resident of a "working-class Westchester, N.Y., town," according to Megan Harlan, lives with her young son. As she told Harlan, she attributes her "love of people who are quirky and eccentric and sort of on a lunatic fringe" to her own upbringing, in which her family was regarded as eccentric by their strait-laced neighbors. "Of course, there are certain prices you pay if you don't fit in. But if you live in a conservative sort of place, you have such freedom," she added to Harlan. "You're kind of beyond the pale anyway, so you live by your own rules."

—S. Y.

SUGGESTED READING: *Entertainment Weekly* p57 Aug. 16, 1996; *George Jr.* (on-line) Jan. 1997; *Library Journal* p142 July 2000; *Los Angeles Times* (on-line) Oct. 31, 1988, p6 Aug. 5, 1996; *New York Times Book Review* p22 Sep. 15, 1991, p18 Nov. 7, 1993, p13 Aug. 18, 1996, p10 Aug. 27, 2000; *Publishers Weekly* p88 Aug. 16, 1993, p85 June 10, 1996, p41+ Aug. 19, 1996

SELECTED BOOKS: novels—*The Woman Who Was Not All There*, 1988; *Lost in Jersey City*, 1993; *Crows Over a Wheatfield*, 1996; *I Loved You All*, 2000; short-story collections—*The Imposter: Stories about Netta and Stanley*, 1991

Brigitte Lacombe/Courtesy of Knopf Publishing

Shepard, Sam

Nov. 5, 1943– Playwright; actor

Sam Shepard is a genuine American original, an unconventional playwright who has insisted that the theater accept him on his own terms. Since composing his first play, *Cowboys*, in 1964, Shepard has produced more than 40 works for the theater, many of which illustrate the uniquely independent vision and daring imagination that have made him a cult figure in American Off-Off-Broadway theater. The macabre landscape of a Shepard play is often a nightmarish America where myth collides with reality. As the critic Mel Gussow once observed, "Mr. Shepard is a playwright of the American frontier, but his plays generally take place in confined, even claustrophobic rooms. These plays . . . form an abundant body of work, one of the most sizable and tantalizing in the American theater." Another critic, Jack Kroll for *Newsweek* (October 30, 1978), said of Shepard's contribution: "Since his first play . . . he has almost certainly written and had produced more plays than any other American playwright—none of them on Broadway. In some crazy way, Sam Shepard seems almost to have *become* the alternative American theater." Despite his indifference to commercial Broadway theater, Shepard is widely considered one of the most important playwrights of his generation: Throughout the 1970s and '80s he was said to be one of the most produced American playwrights, second only to Tennessee Williams. He has garnered 10 Obie (Off-Broadway) Awards, as well as the 1979 Pulitzer Prize for drama for *Buried Child*—his second in a trilogy of critically acclaimed plays exploring the disintegration of the American family—and the 1986 New York Drama Critics' Circle Award for *A Lie of the Mind*. Although his once prolific output began to diminish in the 1980s (he produced only four new plays in the 1990s), Shepard has remained dedicated to creative pursuits. He has appeared in more than 30 films, often receiving serious acclaim for his acting, including an Oscar nomination for his portrayal of Chuck Yeager in *The Right Stuff* (1983).

In 1980 Sam Shepard submitted the following personal statement to *World Authors*: "I was born in the heart of the Cornbelt, Fort Sheridan, Illinois, in an Army hospital. This happened on November 5, 1943. My father was the son of a dairy farmer in Crystal Lake and was in the Air Force somewhere across the sea at the time of my birth. I never saw my father until I was five. My mother was a strong woman. She carted me from state to state in an old Plymouth. By the time I was six I had lived or spent time in: Illinois, Wisconsin, Florida, North and South Dakota, Iowa, Washington, Indiana, Idaho, Michigan, the Marianas Islands, and finally California, where I stayed more or less until the age of eighteen.

"After spending some time living with my aunt we moved to a small avocado ranch in Duarte, California, at the foot of the San Gabriel Mountains. It was in this place that I first began to smell the real adventure of my life. To the north of us were lush thoroughbred farms. Rolling green pastures, rainbird sprinklers, pick-up trucks and horse trailers. To the south, lined up along the highway, were staunch lower-middle-class tracts. To the east was a trailer camp for transient workers. Further south was a steaming, deep-country hovel of shacks and stucco boxes full of blacks and Mexicans only. (I still have nightmares of walking down the narrow dirt street that led into this section that all whites referred to as 'Rock Town'). To the west was 'civilization': Santa Anita Race Track, Arcadia, Pasadena and L.A., 'the home of the Angels.' Duarte was an absolute cross-section of everything American. This never struck me until later of course, when I hit the 'Big Apple.'

"My father was prone to violent bouts with various types of alcohol and his own bitter disappointment with his life. This culminated for me on a night when he decided to rip the front door off the house since my mother had locked him out, threatening to call the police. My sisters and I lived in a separate section of the house. The next morning I left home in my '51 Chevy with all my gear stuffed in cardboard boxes. For a while I lived at the Y.M.C.A., then got a job as an actor with the Bishop's Company out of Burbank. They gave me twenty bucks and a one-way ticket to Bethlehem, Pennsylvania, where I joined the troop.

"That was one of the most exciting times of my life. Suddenly I was on my own. The company was endowed with a brand new red bus which I volunteered to drive. We never spent more than one or two nights in the same place and our stages were always the altars of churches. We were all housed by different families in the parish of each town. We crisscrossed New England, up into Maine and Vermont. The country amazed me, having come from a place that was brown and hot and covered with Taco stands. Finally we hit New York City and I couldn't believe it. I'd always thought of the 'big city' as Pasadena and the Rose Parade. I was mesmerized by this place.

"Through a series of coincidences I made contact with an old high school friend of mine who had also come to New York. His name was Charles Mingus Jr. and it wasn't until New York that I found out who his father was. We lived together in a railroad flat on Avenue C and Tenth Street. His influence on me was very strong in those days. He was a painter and surrounded himself with his art. Night after night we'd get in free to the Five Spot on St. Mark's Place, since his father played there often. It was hearing that music and seeing Charlie's paintings all over the walls that gradually moved me from acting into playwrighting. I wanted to write something for the theater that might have the same kind of vibrant, pulsing life that I was feeling all around me. I arrived at the right time. 'Off-off-Broadway' was just being spawned and places were hungry for scripts. Ralph Cook, the head waiter at the Village Gate, where I was working as a busboy, was starting something called Theater Genesis at St. Mark's Church in the Bowery. He read a script of mine called *Cowboys* and decided to put it on. From then on I've been writing plays."

The son of Samuel Shepard Rogers, a teacher and farmer, and the former Jane Elaine Schook, Samuel Shepard Rogers Jr. was known by his family as "Steve." He attended Duarte High School, where he took little interest in his classes. Instead, he had strong passions for music and animals, playing drums in a garage band and participating in his local 4-H Club. He did have one academic interest, however—reading the contemporary poetry and fiction of such writers as Jack Kerouac, Lawrence Ferlinghetti, and Gregory Corso, who were then emerging on the literary scene. These "beat" writers emphasized a musical approach to their craft, often employing a technique known as jazz sketching, which aimed to create the equivalent of jazz riffs through language. Inspired by this progressive form, Shepard began composing poetry. A friend introduced him to the work of another unique modernist, the playwright Samuel Beckett, who had written *Waiting for Godot* (1949). Although Shepard's experience in theater had been thus far limited to a brief spell of acting with a local group, he found Beckett's language fascinating and was inspired to write a play of his own. His first work featured a young rape victim, whose father is unsympathetic after the attack. After completing high school, in 1961, Shepard attended Mount San Antonio Junior College, in Walnut, California, but dropped out after three semesters. He planned to take a job managing a sheep ranch, but instead joined a repertory theater that was then touring churches throughout the U.S. When he reached New York City, in 1963, he decided to stay and soon after changed his name from Steve Rogers (which happened to be the real name of the comic-book character Captain America) to Sam Shepard, "because it was shorter," as he told Robert Coe for the *New York Times* (November 23, 1980).

While working as a busboy at the Village Gate, a Greenwich Village cabaret, he met Ralph Cook, the founder of Theater Genesis, who was then a headwaiter. Shepard shared much of his beat-inspired poetry with Cook, who promptly encouraged him to write for the Off-Off-Broadway theater, a growing force in New York City theater. Off Off Broadway was considered an alternative outlet for many noncommercial, avant-garde companies, and was then located largely in storefronts, lofts, church basements, and other makeshift sites in Manhattan's East Village.

Following Ralph Cook's suggestion, Shepard began turning out one-act plays at a furious pace. Most of his early works were impressionistic mood pieces expressing an often-dark awakening to the social forces of modern times. The first plays to be produced were *Cowboys* and the *Rock Garden*, both one-act pieces directed by Cook in a Theater Genesis production at St. Mark's Church-in-the-Bowery, in October 1964. Both of these works dealt with themes from Shepard's own life. For example, *Cowboys*—which Coe called a "rowdy Beckettian western"— was based largely on Shepard's adventures with his friend Mingus and his rural life in Duarte. *Rock Garden*, as Shepard described to Coe, was "about leaving my mom and dad." (The last scene of *Rock Garden* was later incorporated into the multi-authored "erotic" Broadway musical *Oh! Calcutta!*) While many criticized Shepard's first efforts as merely poor emulations of Beckett, one reviewer, Michael Smith, writing for the *Village*

Voice, heaped significant acclaim on the 20-year-old playwright. That notable review, along with Shepard's prolific output of writing, soon helped establish him as an important theatrical voice for Off-Off-Broadway theater; it also gave him the encouragement to stay in New York, rather than to return to California. Of this intense period, during which he often composed plays in one sitting, Shepard described to David Ansen for *Newsweek* (November 17, 1980): "There was so much to write, I felt I couldn't spend time rewriting; I had to move on to the next thing. It was a furious kind of writing. Obsessive. I identified a lot with jazz at the time—there was no reason why writing shouldn't be exactly like a jazz improvisation. I figured to go and change it was like being untrue to the impulses that were making it happen."

Later in the 1964–65 Off-Off-Broadway season, the Café La Mama Experimental Theater Club staged Shepard's *Up to Thursday*, *Dog*, and *Rocking Chair*. In retrospect, Shepard described *Up to Thursday*, to Don Shirley for the *Washington Post* (January 14, 1979), as "a bad exercise in absurdity, I guess. This kid is sleeping in an American flag, he's only wearing a jockstrap or something, and there're four people on stage who keeping shifting their legs." He summarized *Dog* as being "about a black guy—which I later found out it was uncool for a white to write about." Of *Rocking Chair*, he told Shirley, "I don't even remember [it], except it was about somebody in a rocking chair." An important milestone in Shepard's career was the decision of Richard Barr, Clinton Wilder, and Edward Albee to include *Up to Thursday* in their New Playwrights series at the Off-Broadway Cherry Lane Theater, in February 1965.

Three plays by Shepard produced in the 1965–66 season, *Chicago*, *Icarus's Mother*, and *Red Cross*, won the young playwright his first Obie Awards (*Village Voice* citations for Off- and Off-Off-Broadway excellence), and *Chicago* was included in *Six From La Mama*, a program of one-act plays presented at the Martinique Theater, in April 1966. *Chicago*, in which a young man stands in a bathtub delivering a monologue about the life swirling about him, typified the angry-young-man theatrical pieces Shepard was creating at the beginning of his career.

A 1967 Rockefeller Foundation grant and a 1968 Guggenheim grant gave Shepard the freedom to write full time. (He also reportedly spent part of the money on a Dodge Charger and a classic Stratocaster guitar.) In the mid-1960s he became the drummer for a rock band known as the Holy Modal Rounders, which he described to Coe as an "amphetamine band." Touring with the Rounders Shepard was drawn into a world of drugs and alcohol. (He escaped the Vietnam draft in 1965 by pretending to be a heroin addict.)

In 1967, while in Mexico and under the influence of both amphetamines and dysentery, Shepard composed his first full-length play, *La Turista*. One week into the play's rehearsals in New York, Shepard made his first-ever revisions—combining the final two acts into a single act. The play premiered at the American Place Theater, then based in St. Clement's Church, in March 1967. On that occasion, Shepard exercised the option of not formally inviting critics, explaining that he did not see "why everything [has] to be evaluated in terms of success or failure." Nevertheless, theater critics hailed the piece, with one reviewer, Elizabeth Hardwick, writing for the *New York Review of Books*, as quoted by Coe, calling Shepard "one of the three or four most gifted playwrights alive." *La Turista* earned Shepard his fourth Obie Award.

Forensic and the Navigators and *Melodrama Play*—two one-act pieces—earned Shepard another Obie at the end of the 1967–68 season. Paired with John Guare's *Muzeeka*, a revival of Shepard's *Red Cross* played to a mixed reception at New York City's Provincetown Playhouse, in the spring of 1968. Among the positive reviews was that of Clive Barnes in the *New York Times* (May 28, 1968). After describing Shepard's work as an attempt to sever "an umbilical connection with the past," Barnes wrote: "As a result, a play like *Red Cross*, set presumably in some casualty station of the mind, is mysterious simply because it does not play the nice game of drama according to our rules. Two people are arguing in adjacent beds, and we ask, 'who are they?' They tell us what they are doing and how they are feeling, but never for a moment who they are. It is like meeting someone at a party whom you can't quite place. The results that Mr. Shepard gets are very, very funny. But much more than funny, they are stealthily disturbing."

London audiences became acquainted with Shepard's work through Off- and Off-Off-Shaftesbury Avenue productions of *Melodrama Play*, *Chicago*, and *La Turista* in the late 1960s. In a dispatch to the *New York Times* (April 13, 1969), Charles Marowitz reported that those London critics who were "not wholly dismissive" of *La Turista* agreed on one main point—"the play is baffling." Marowitz went on to observe: "Shepard is not so much obscure as he is disjointed. His is a quirky, fey, mildly Saroyanesque turn of mind which trusts its changes of direction as totally as the traveler trusts the instincts of the burro carrying him through the foothills of a foreign countryside. . . . If one hadn't seen *Chicago* and read other Shepard plays, *La Turista* would be a perfect case of the emperor's new clothes. But there is a consistency in Shepard and a richness of texture which encourages one to suspend judgment. He is a writer with a cool, idiosyncratic style and one waits to see what he will ultimately deliver."

In 1970 Michelangelo Antonioni hired Shepard to help write the screenplay for *Zabriskie Point* (1970), a strident polemic about the radicalization of a flower child. While the prospect of writing for film was enticing, the experience proved an unhappy one for Shepard, because Antonioni, in an effort to make a political statement about contemporary youth, wanted to include a lot of Marxist jargon and Black Panther speeches, and Shepard was not interested in writing in that style.

The influence of Shepard's cinematic stint was evident, however, in both the form and the content of *Operation Sidewinder*, a three-act play that was given its premiere by the Repertory Company of Lincoln Center, at the Vivian Beaumont Theater, in March 1970. Set in the Hopi Indian country of the American Southwest and featuring a secret Air Force computer project—a giant mechanical rattlesnake that runs amok—*Operation Sidewinder* delineates the dehumanization of the American spirit in 12 grotesquely satirical scenes, ending with an atomic holocaust. In the Lincoln Center production the scenes were divided by rock music interludes provided by the Holy Modal Rounders. The play was a critical disaster, with most reviewers—even those ordinarily sympathetic to the playwright—deeming it the most outrageous work of Shepard's career. Jack Kroll wrote for *Newsweek* (March 23, 1970), "[Shepard's] plays are rituals of confrontation . . . often ricocheting like esthetic shrapnel into the spectators to sting them with signs of the perversity that has taken hold in their lives. As in contemporary life itself, in a good Shepard play you can't tell where the horror ends and the joke begins. . . . But in *Operation Sidewinder* the energy has congealed in a half-slick pop machine with the feel of celluloid and the clackey sound of doctrinaire contemporaneity." In retrospect, Shepard himself admitted that the play deserved to fail because he was mistaken in trying to apply film technique to the stage. "That single frame editing kind of thing doesn't work on stage," he said in a *Guardian* interview. "It was very static."

A considerably warmer reception greeted *The Unseen Hand*, a science-fiction western in which an interplanetary fugitive raises three outlaws from the dead, when it premiered at the Astor Place Theater the following month. Marilyn Stasio, writing for *Cue* (April 11, 1970), was effusive: "Shepard is an awesomely talented writer with a freedom fixation. . . . Once you accept the basic 'flight patterns,' his outlandishly funny but dead-earnest plays seem perfectly logical within their own zany, surrealistic terms of reality." Reviewing a London production of *The Unseen Hand* for the *New Republic* (April 21, 1973), Robert Brustein wrote of Shepard: "He continues to confront American popular culture with a kind of manic exuberance—not exalting its every wart and pimple, like Andy Warhol, but nevertheless considerably turned on, like many of his generation, even by its more brutalized expressions. In a degenerate time, this may be a strategy for survival, and it certainly sparks the energy of *The Unseen Hand*."

Around that time Shepard wrote *Holy Ghostly*, a one-act play first produced in New York, in 1970; *Shaved Splits*, first produced Off Broadway at La Mama Experimental Theater Club, in July 1970; and *Mad Dog Blues*, a one-act produced at St. Mark's Church-in-the-Bowery, in March 1971. He also collaborated with the rock musician Patti Smith on the rock opera *Cowboy Mouth*—a stream-of-consciousness piece depicting a world of drugs and music—which premiered in Edinburgh, Scotland, in April 1971, and appeared at the American Place Theater later that month.

Somewhat disenchanted with Off-Broadway theater, in 1971 Shepard moved his young family—which included the actress O-Lan Johnson Dark, whom he had married in 1969, and their son, Jesse Mojo, born in 1970—to Hempstead, England, where he planned to become more involved with rock music. The increasing pressures of writing plays and his growing involvement in New York's drug scene were taking their toll on his career. As he recalled to Coe, "It was incredible luck to be around when something like Off Off Broadway was getting off the ground. But the 1960s were kinda awful. I don't even want to think about it." While in England, he grew immensely as a playwright and, as he told Coe, learned two fundamentals of theater: the importance of revision for quality theater and the value of his American identity.

One of his own favorites among his plays, *The Tooth of Crime*—a two-act musical fantasy about an Arizona outlaw-rock star whose turf, both in music and along the freeways, is taken over by a young gypsy upstart—had its premiere in London in 1972, and its first American production the following year. It became one of his most critically admired works. Theater reviewers on both sides of the Atlantic praised his near-perfect use of metaphor and language. As T. E. Kalem noted in *Time* (November 27, 1972), in order to glean what *The Tooth of Crime* is about, the playgoer must understand Shepard's continuing theme: "Fast cars, mechanical gadgetry, chrome, and plastic values form a symbolic veneer under which, he seems to be saying, older American ideals are shriveling." In 1973 Shepard received his sixth Obie Award, for *The Tooth of Crime*.

Other critics have described Shepard's major themes in terms of the degradation or displacement of the artist (seen as the natural hero) in our culture and of the corruption of innocence—a message certainly evident in *Geography of a Horse Dreamer*, a two-act mystery about a young cowboy who loses his ability to pick horse-race winners through his dreams when a group of gangsters try to exploit his powers. The premiere of *Geography of a Horse Dreamer* was directed by Shepard at the Royal Court's Theater Upstairs, in London, in February 1974, and the first American production was directed by David Schwelzer at the Yale Repertory Theater the following month. Reviewing a revival of the play, Edith Oliver of the *New Yorker* (December 22, 1975) called it "one more work of Sam Shepard's incomparable imagination."

Throughout 1973 and 1974 Shepard also produced *Blue Bitch*, which premiered at the Off-Off-Broadway Theater Genesis, in 1973; *Nightwalk* (with Megan Terry and Jean-Claude van Itallie), which first appeared Off Off Broadway at St. Clement's Church, in September 1973; and *Little Ocean*, which first appeared at London's Hampstead Theatre Club, in 1974. As Shepard told Stewart McBride for the *Christian Science Monitor* (December 26, 1980), his London plays marked a notable change in his approach to writing. "I used not to care about character," Shepard explained. "I would write these five-minute speeches, arias, and they were simply boring. Character has become much more important to me. I learned that from [the British director] Peter Brook. A playwright has to understand what an actor goes through. I've seen Beckett made to look like Abbott and Costello. I don't see how a playwright can grow if he doesn't get involved in the production of his work."

After returning to the United States, in late 1974, Shepard settled in California and became the playwright-in-residence at the Magic Theater in San Francisco. When Bob Dylan and his band toured the country with their Rolling Thunder Revue, in 1975, Shepard, at Dylan's request, went along as scriptwriter for a projected film of the tour. The film never materialized, but the tour was wittily chronicled by Shepard in words and pictures in *Rolling Thunder Logbook* (1977).

In April 1975 *Action*, first staged in London the year before, opened at the American Place Theater, on a bill with *Killer's Head* in its world premiere. *Killer's Head* is a brief, jarring exploration of a man's mind in the moment before his execution, as his thoughts turn, from habit, to plans he will never live to complete. *Action*, which won a 1975 Obie, is a study in inertia, or inaction, set in a dimension where there is neither sound nor time—a cold space where four humanoids are celebrating (or uncelebrating) Christmas. "His language reminds us of Pinter," Clarke Taylor observed in *After Dark* (June 1975), "his landscape of Beckett."

The stifling of creative freedom is again suggested in the musical play *Suicide in B-Flat*, first mounted at the Yale Repertory Theater, in 1976. In this "mysterious overture," police investigate the apparent suicide of Niles, a jazz musician who is "playing dead" just as he once "played alive," and who at one point says, "We've all lost our calling." In 1976 the Magic Theater staged the premiere of Shepard's *Angel City*, his first clearly autobiographical play, a scathing satire on the temptations that Hollywood sets before young writers.

More theatrically conventional than his previous work is Shepard's bitter three-act tragicomedy, *Curse of the Starving Class*, in which a self-destructive society is reflected in the dissolution of a Southern California farm family. The play marked a significant departure for Shepard; it was his first attempt to explore themes similar to those of his contemporaries, Arthur Miller and Eugene O'Neill—in particular, the disintegration of the American family. "I felt [the topic] was exploited in the past," Shepard told Coe, "by writers who didn't have anything else to write about. But then I felt that, rather than try to avoid it, I might as well try to meet it head on. The other thing is, my family is so idiosyncratic it verges on the bizarre." Set on a small avocado farm, *Curse of the Starving Class* presents a cruel, alcoholic father, a whiny mother, and two children who are stunned to learn that their parents have each been secretly developing plans to sell the farm and escape. Ultimately, it descends into gross vulgarity—a feature that stirred controversy at the play's 1977 London opening and its 1978 American premiere in New York City. Nevertheless, the piece was generally recognized as a major step forward in Shepard's career. In *Cue* (March 18, 1978) Marilyn Stasio advised her readers that "you must go with all your wits about you" to appreciate how Shepard opens the play "sneakily, under the false pretense of being a half-satiric, half-serious domestic drama" and then "rips away the dramatic trappings to reveal the inner darkness. It's a hellish place; violent, brutish, and ugly. Like Walt Whitman gone berserk, Shepard sings America in flames. . . . These people are real and poignant and dammed." *Curse of the Starving Class* brought Shepard his seventh Obie, for best play/best new American play.

Shepard's *Buried Child*—a tragicomedy about a decayed rural American family that harbors guilty secrets of incest and infanticide—opened Off Off Broadway, at the Theatre for the New City, in October 1978. Even more lucid and accessible than *Curse of the Starving Class*, *Buried Child* became Shepard's first real success in terms of box-office receipts and the endorsement of the critical establishment. Among the rave reviews was John Simon's in *New York* (November 27, 1978): "This tale of a silent-American farm family that seems to go crazier by the minute—but with a craziness containing both sardonic bite and the gift of holy terror—bears some resemblance to Pinter's *Homecoming*, which, in my estimate, it surpasses. Here, as in other Shepard works, the effect is rather as if Pieter Bruegel and Hieronymous Bosch had set about improving a Grant Wood canvas, until rustic creepiness grew into manic vitality and visionary madness." On April 16, 1979 *Buried Child* won the Pulitzer Prize for drama; that year it also won an Obie.

Shepard returned to acting as an affluent farm owner duped into a tragic marriage with a migrant worker in the film director Terrence Malick's *Days of Heaven* (1978). Critics generally agreed that Shepard was excellent in portraying the ill-fated farmer with, as one critic called it, "laid-back grit." "The real surprise of the film," Annette Insdorf wrote in *Take One* (November 1978), "is playwright Sam Shepard, who creates in his first screen role the most sympathetic, believable, and sustained character."

Despite this foray into film, Shepard soon returned to theater with *Seduced*, a play about a paranoid recluse modeled after Howard Hughes, which was first staged at the American Place Theater, on February 1, 1979. That year he also composed *Tongues* and *Savage/Love*, which were both produced at California's Eureka Theater Festival and later premiered Off Off Broadway in November 1979.

Throughout the 1980s Shepard became better known as an actor than as a playwright, especially after receiving an Academy Award nomination for his portrayal of the pioneering test pilot Chuck Yeager in *The Right Stuff* (1983). He also could be seen in such popular movies as *Resurrection* (1980), *Paris, Texas* (1984), *Crimes of the Heart* (1986), *Baby Boom* (1987), and *Steel Magnolias* (1989). After starring with Jessica Lange in the 1982 film *Frances*, the playwright and the film actress became a couple, and have remained long-term partners ever since. (Shepard divorced his first wife, O-Lan, in 1984.) Shepard made his directorial debut in 1988's *Far North*, a film which featured Lange.

As a result of his film work, Shepard produced only a handful plays throughout the entire decade: *True West* (1981); *Fool For Love* (1983), for which he won the 1984 Obie Award and which was later adapted into a 1985 film; the two one-acts, *The Sad Lament of Pecos Bill on the Eve of Killing His Wife* (1983) and *Superstitions* (1983); *A Lie of the Mind* (1987), for which he won the 1987 New York Drama Critics' Circle Award; and *Hawk Moon* (1989), which was first produced in London. Though Shepard was not as prolific, his plays were generally admired by critics. His most notable play of that decade, *True West*, completed a trilogy of plays about the American family. It recounts the story of two brothers—Austin, a screenwriter, and Lee, a petty thief and drifter who envies his brother's success—as they reunite in their mother's Los Angeles home to face unresolved demons regarding their father. Throughout, the characters voice radically different visions of the "true West." Of the impulse behind the play's realism, Shepard told Coe: "I wanted to write a play about double nature, one that wouldn't be symbolic or metaphorical or any of that stuff. I just wanted to give a taste of what it feels like to be two-sided." *True West* premiered at the Off-Broadway Public Theater and has since enjoyed several Off-Broadway revivals. Stewart McBride, like most critics, found much to praise about the play, noting, "This is [Shepard's] first true comedy and has the trademarks of a great dramatic work: realism, well-crafted character, and economy of language. Shepard has edited out any heavy-handed metaphysical symbolism which invaded some of his earlier writing, thus making *True West* an intriguing play open to broad interpretation." From his own perspective, Shepard called *True West* "the first one of my plays I've been able to sit through night after night and not have my stomach ball up in knots of embarrassment." He told McBride, "I worked longer on this than any other play and rewrote it 13 times. *True West* is the first play I've truly felt hooked up to."

In 1991 Shepard made something of a return to his theatrical roots with his production of *State of Shock*, an absurdist work dealing with war and death which stylistically resembled many of his earlier pieces. Written and produced during the Gulf War, the play takes place during a dinner party, to which a character called the Colonel has invited Stubbs, a disabled veteran, in an attempt to better understand his own son's death—which he believes was caused by the same shell that crippled his dinner guest. For *Simpatico*, his Off-Broadway show that opened in November 1994, Shepard employed a more realistic style, similar to that in which he had written *True West*. It concerned a bribery scheme cooked up by two friends, Vinnie and Carter, who 15 years earlier had used Vinnie's former wife, Rosie, to blackmail a horse-racing official. For the 1996 Olympic Arts Festival in Atlanta, Georgia, Shepard co-authored the one-act play *When the World Was Green* with Joseph Chaikin. Two years later he produced *Eyes for Consuela*, based on a story by Octavio Paz. (The play, about a bandit who asks for his victims' eyes, was unusual for Shepard because it was based on someone else's material.) In 2000 his next play, *The Late Henry Moss*, debuted at San Francisco's Magic Theater, where so many of his plays from the 1970s premiered. The piece concerns two sons, Ray and Earl, who return home to bury their father and, in the process, confront painful truths about him and their past. Ray wants to better understand the brutal man his father had become, while Earl continues trying to hide the truth from everyone, including himself. The play received mixed reviews. While believing there to be great moments in it, Hal Gelb, writing for *The Nation* (December 25, 2000), opined, "With great disappointment I report that Shepard hasn't returned to his former powers with this play. . . . There's not a whole lot to the characters, and their relationship lacks the continuously rich evolution of *True West*."

In addition to his work as a playwright and actor, Shepard has published three short-story collections: *Hawk Moon* (1973), *Motel Chronicles* (1982), and *Cruising Paradise* (1996). Throughout the last decade, he has also added a number of notable film credits to his name, including parts in *The Pelican Brief* (1993), *Safe Passage* (1994), *Snow Falling on Cedars* (1999), *All the Pretty Horses* (2000), *The Pledge* (2001), *Swordfish* (2001), and *Black Hawk Down* (2001). In 1997 he participated in a television special profiling his theater career, entitled *Great Performances Sam Shepard: Stalking Himself*.

Never a fan of the spotlight, Sam Shepard currently resides on a 400-acre ranch in Minnesota with long-term companion, Jessica Lange. In addition to his son, Jesse, from his first marriage, he has two children with Lange: Hannah Jane and Samuel Walker. He is said to be an avid horseman, golfer, and polo player. Of his seemingly endless creative drive, Shepard told McBride, "I'm driven by a deep dissatisfaction. What you accomplish in your work always falls short of the possibilities you know are sneaking around. The work never gets easier. It gets harder and more provocative. And as it gets harder you are continually reminded there is more to accomplish. It's like digging for gold. And when you find the vein, you know there's a lot more where that came from."

—K. D.

SUGGESTED READING: *Christian Science Monitor* B p2 Dec. 26, 1980, with photo; *Internet Movie Database* (on-line); *Guardian* p8 Feb. 20 1974; *Maclean's* p74 Oct. 2, 2000, with photo; *The Nation* p34+ Dec. 25, 2000; *New Republic* p31+ Nov. 12, 2001; *New York* p46+ Feb. 9, 1998, with photo; *New York Times* VI p56+ Nov. 23, 1980, with photo; *Newsweek* p106 Oct. 30, 1978, p117 Nov. 17, 1980; *Washington Post* p1+ Jan. 14, 1979, with photo

SELECTED WORKS: plays—*Cowboys*, 1964; *Up to Thursday*, 1965; *Red Cross*, 1966; *The Unseen Hand*, 1969; *The Tooth of Crime*, 1972; *Geography of a Horse Dreamer*, 1974; *Buried Child*, 1978; *Curse of the Starving Class*, 1978; *True West*, 1981; *Eyes for Consuela*, 1999; *The Late Henry Moss*, 2001; short-story collections—*Hawk Moon*, 1973; *Motel Chronicles*, 1982; *Cruising Paradise*, 1996; films as actor—*The Right Stuff*, 1983; *Steel Magnolias*, 1989; *Snow Falling on Cedars*, 1999; *Swordfish*, 2001; *Black Hawk Down*, 2001

Frederick Slaski/Courtesy of W. W. Norton & Company

Sherwood, Frances

June 4, 1940– Novelist; short-story writer

"I write fiction because I am interested in secrets of the human heart," Frances Sherwood told an interviewer for the *Writer* (April 1997). "Fiction is an attempt, through words, at a discovery of those mysteries. Nonfiction spells out the obvious. I suppose that poetry is even more elusive than fiction, but less expansive. I need more situation, more character, more words to encircle the truth, to approach it. I want to understand. In fiction, good fiction, I don't think we are talking about meaning, addressing 'The Why.' It is insider knowledge, the information of a confidant. Whenever I write I think of it as a journey, and not into the heart of darkness, but into something like the sacred heart, that is, illumination." A professor of creative writing and journalism at Indiana University, Sherwood has won acclaim for the short-story collection *Everything You've Heard Is True* (1989) and the novels *Vindication* (1993), *Green* (1995), and *The Book of Splendor* (2002).

The eldest of four children, Frances Sherwood was born in Washington, D.C., on June 4, 1940. Her father, William Sherwood, was a biochemist, lawyer, and linguist; her mother, Barbara, was a homemaker. She grew up in Brazil, California, and New York. In 1957 her father committed suicide rather than testify before Senator Joseph McCarthy's House Committee on Un-American Activities. In an interview with Joseph Olshan for *People* (June 28, 1993), the author reflected on her father's death: "Imagine that happening after growing up in an atmosphere of open discussion, after being ostracized as the village atheists, something that we were all really proud of."

After her father's death, Sherwood left the family home in Monterey, California, to study at Howard University, in Washington, D.C., a venerable black institution where she was the only white student at the time. "I was a radical at a black college that I must say was rather bourgeois," she told Olshan, explaining why she left Howard after two years of study. She then completed her undergraduate degree at New York City's Brooklyn College in 1967, and did a year of graduate work at New York University in 1968. In 1975 she earned her master of arts degree from Johns Hopkins University, in Baltimore.

While pursuing her degrees, Sherwood married twice, the first time only briefly. She has three interracial children, now grown: twin sons, Lark and Leander, and a daughter, Ceres Madoo. Initially, Sherwood supported her children by working a variety of odd jobs—waitress, house cleaner, census clerk, nursery-school teacher. She also wrote, and her short stories began to be published in such periodicals as the *Greensboro Review*, the *Sonora Review*, *Playgirl*, the *Seattle Review*, the *Kansas Quarterly*, the *California Quarterly*, *Sequoia*, and the *Cream City Review*.

Sherwood has also had several academic positions, including teaching fellowships at Johns Hopkins Writing Seminars (1973–1974) and California's Stanford University (1976). She became a full-time creative writing and journalism instructor at Indiana University, in South Bend, in 1986; in 1994 she became a full professor.

In 1989 Sherwood published a collection of short stories, *Everything You've Heard is True*. The stories were wide-ranging in their subject matter and ambitious in their scope. One of the stories, "History," was a 1989 O. Henry Award winner. (Another story, entitled "Demiurges," won her a second O. Henry Award, in 1992.) "History" follows an interracial couple who married before the civil rights movement. Although they had coped well with the attendant social pressures before, in the midst of that turbulent period, they find themselves redefining their relationship. In "Arrowhead," a story that Perry Glasser, writing for the *Chicago Tribune* (July 2, 1989), calls "a bizarre little gem," Sherwood adopts a male perspective. The story concerns an unusual relationship between a man and a woman who still lives with her ex-husband. Critics generally praised the collection. "A few of these stories are written in a thick, lilting Caribbean rhythm that makes them tough going," Glasser opined. "But most of the stories in *Everything You've Heard is True* are drawn with great authority and grace."

After receiving a 1990 National Endowment for the Arts fellowship, Sherwood began work on her first novel, *Vindication*. The book is a fictionalized account of the life of Mary Wollstonecraft, an 18th-century feminist who challenged her era's attitudes towards women. Wollstonecraft was the author of *The Vindication of the Rights of Women* (1792), now considered a seminal feminist treatise. While Sherwood was faithful to some of the details of Wollstonecraft's life, she diverged from fact often. (In one notable example, she confines her character to Bedlam, a notorious asylum, after a nervous breakdown.) Like many historical novels that deviate from the facts, *Vindication* received mixed reviews. Margaret Forster, writing for the *New York Times Book Review* (July 11, 1993), complained, "The reader familiar with Wollstonecraft is likely to be appalled [with the deviations]; the reader who is not, and who many never take trouble to find out, will have absorbed an interpretation of her that is utterly disloyal to her memory." A reviewer for *Publishers Weekly* (March 1, 1993), however, called it "an arresting and convincing portrayal."

The protagonist of the 1995 novel *Green* is another progressive young woman—this time a California teen of the 1950s. Zoe McLaren lives in a Mormon household with her mother, who drinks too much, and her father, who wakes her in the middle of the night to force her to scrub the floors. Zoe falls in love with an American Indian named Grey Cloud, who eventually leaves her, with a child, for another woman. She finds work—as a garment worker and an exotic dancer, among other positions—and in the process grows into a mature, self-realized woman. Like its predecessor, *Green* received mixed reviews. Penelope Mesic, writing for the *Chicago Tribune* (August 20, 1995), lamented, "At moments we seem to stand at the brink of valuable knowledge, seeing not the tangle of events but the way events are given shape by our hidden needs. Too often, though, those moments pass, leaving us with a young woman whom we are reluctant to pity and can't quite love." Claire Messud wrote for the *New York Times Book Review* (August 20, 1995), "Thematically as well as narratively, *Green* treads ground familiar to Ms. Sherwood's readers, but it remains—in spite of its length—a thinner, less realized novel that its predecessor, one striving for, rather than achieving, a satisfying form."

With *The Book of Splendor* (2002), Sherwood returned to the historical novel, this time setting her tale in 1601 Prague, during the reign of Emperor Rudolph II. The emperor asks two eminent alchemists, John Dee and Edward Kelley, to develop an eternal-life elixir for him, and as a secondary measure he orders Rabbi Loew, a legendary cleric, to prepare an immortality spell. This plot line is paralleled by the story of Rochel, a poor Jewish girl trapped in a loveless marriage to an older man. When Rabbi Loew uses mud to fashion a golem (a figure from Jewish folklore, traditionally meant to do household chores or protect the community), Rochel falls in love with the creature, who is named Yossel. The novel received generally favorable reviews, with some reservations. In the *Boston Globe* (July 14, 2002), Barbara Fisher expressed mixed feelings: "Both the imperial plot and the ghetto saga move along nicely, cleverly combining real characters and historical events with fictional people, myth, and fantasy. Yet the stories feel insufficiently motivated; and thus the history feels untrue." Richard Eder, in the *New York Times* (July 5, 2002), called Sherwood "the rare writer whose work goes far beyond what we think of as historical novels. Instead of history's retrospective certainty—this is how it was—Ms. Sherwood projects her readers, as if by time machine, back to a place where everything is still to be discovered. We do not feel that her characters are keeping appointments. Rather than moving confidently backward out of the clarity of Now, we move uncertainly forward from a foggy Then. We are only truly in the past when we feel lost in it."

—*C. M.*

SUGGESTED READING: *Antioch Review* p20+ Winter 1996; *Boston Globe* C p3 July 14, 2002; *Chicago Tribune* C p3 July 2, 1989, XIV p3+ Aug. 20, 1995; *Financial Times* II p11 June 26, 1993; *New York Observer* p15 May 10, 1993; *New York Times* E p40 July 5, 2002; *New York Times Book Review* p21 July 11, 1993, p7 Aug. 20, 1995; *People* p26+ June 28, 1993

SELECTED BOOKS: *Everything You've Heard is True*, 1989; *Vindication*, 1993; *Green*, 1995; *The Book of Splendor*, 2002

Shore, Jane

Mar. 10, 1947– Poet

Jane Shore is "one of the most accessible poets writing today," according to Judy Clarence for *Library Journal* (September 15, 1996), and Charles Guenther for the *St. Louis Post-Dispatch* counted her as "one of the finer craftsmen of free and semi-formal verse," as quoted on the Carnegie Mellon University Press Web site. Known for her distinct conversational style and rich autobiographical themes, which have invited comparisons to the legendary poets Robert Lowell and Elizabeth Bishop, Shore has produced work that is both critically admired and widely read. Her first two collections—*Eye Level* (1977) and *The Minute Hand* (1986)—garnered major literary prizes, and her third volume, *Music Minus One* (1996), sold more than 8,000 copies, an impressive sales record for a book of poems.

Born on March 10, 1947, Jane Shore grew up in North Bergen, New Jersey, in an apartment above Corduroy Village, the women's clothing store that her parents, George and Essie Shore, owned. Shore's father had been a big-band musician, but had abandoned his musical ambitions after returning from service in World War II. The elder of two daughters, Shore was surrounded by music, storytelling, and family warmth. She told Bonni Goldberg for the *Baltimore Jewish Times* (February 28, 1997), "My favorite stories as a child were fairy tales. Also, my father played in the big bands in the 1930s and 1940s, and I grew up in a house full of music, played the piano and sang songs. I heard my father's records by Gershwin, Porter and Berlin." North Bergen was a short commute to New York City, and in her teens Shore began exploring the artistic and literary communities then thriving in city neighborhoods such as Greenwich Village. In 1965 she entered Vermont's Goddard College, a small liberal-arts school known for its free-spirited and self-expressive student body. In a profile of the poet for *Ploughshares* (Winter 1997–1998), Lorrie Goldensohn, whose husband taught at Goddard during those years, remembered Shore as a college freshman. According to Goldensohn, Shore arrived at the school already determined to make poetry her life's work. "There was a sharp playfulness to her early poems," Goldensohn recalled, "a sense of lives and styles being tried out and examined for soundness, utility. Jane was checking out the tradition in the classroom, and all the while reading and memorizing contemporary poetry in great gulps elsewhere. In addition to the Yeats and Eliot we were feeding her, she'd bring us her latest acquisition, Adrienne Rich's *Snapshots of a Daughter-in-Law*, or Donald Finkel's *A Joyful Noise*, or *Somewhere Among Us a Stone is Taking Notes*, a new chapbook by Charles Simic that she'd found at Grolier's in Cambridge, testing these things on us, forcing us to open our own eyes, think about our allegiances, and, always, working fiercely at her own poems." While at Goddard, Shore attended workshops with such notable peers as Norman Dubie, Roger Weingarten, and David Mamet—who all went on to become accomplished poets and authors—in what she told Paula Routly for *Book* (September–October 2000, on-line) was "a funny confluence of people wanting to be creative all at once." She actively cultivated a community of writers with whom she could discuss poetry and openly share her work. As Goldensohn observed, "It was always clear to Jane that poetry, written in solitude, is still an act of live community making, community in the widest sense."

After graduating from Goddard, in 1969, with a B.A. in English, Shore enrolled in the prestigious Iowa Writers' Workshop at the University of Iowa. That year she published her first book of poems, a short chapbook entitled *Lying Down in the Olive Press*. (The book's title and the persona Shore invokes in several poems allude to the Greek poet Archilochus resting in an olive grove.) In his introduction to the chapbook, the poet George Starbuck (as quoted by Goldensohn) notes, "Jane Shore knows us, gets us, talks of us or hears us talk of ourselves, with a faultless, unsettling, illuminating interest."

Shore earned her M.F.A. degree from Iowa in 1971 and that year won a Radcliffe Institute Fellowship; she served as a poetry fellow at the institute, in Cambridge, Massachusetts, from 1971 to 1973. In 1973 she received a Briggs Copeland Lectureship at Harvard University, which allowed her to teach alongside Elizabeth Bishop and Robert Lowell, both of whom she greatly admired. She garnered additional literary prizes around this time, including the Bess Hokin Prize from *Poetry* magazine, in 1973, and two Borestone Mountain poetry awards, in 1973 and 1975. The following year she won a grant from the Massachusetts Endowment for the Arts and Humanities.

Shore published her first full-length volume of poetry, *Eye Level*, in 1977. Often originating with particular objects, characters, or experiences, the poems typically develop into more complex observations on such themes as love, survival, and understanding. As Margaret Gibson noted in her review for *Library Journal* (December 15, 1977), "This book offers a humane and intelligent exploration of worlds we encounter in objects, in other people, in ourselves. Shore begins within the innocent eye's exploration, often enchanted, often terrified, into lit interiors of advent calendar, glass paper-weight; moves through the minds of biblical women; and finally to woman's solitary self-recognition." Other critics found that the varied perspectives—with poems, for example, being narrated by Lot's wife, an astronaut, or a Haitian maid—allowed Shore to capture introspection with "a curiously effective objective quality . . . without lapsing into the sentimental," as Catherine O'Neill wrote for the New Republic (December 10, 1977). Gibson concluded: "The power of the eye to see, the mind to discern and know—these are themes Shore develops in language so deft, images so etched in light that one is constantly amazed and renewed." Some reviewers, however, found the poet's language and approach to be too simplistic. For example, Charles Moleworth, in the New York Times (May 21, 1978), opined, "Many of these poems might read well in magazines, because they're diverting and make few emotional or intellectual demands on the reader. But gathered in a book, they lose rather than add force." Despite these occasional detractors, Shore won the coveted 1977 Juniper Prize from the University of Massachusetts Press for the volume. That year she also received a Robert Frost fellowship to attend the Bread Loaf Writers Conference, which is held annually at Middlebury College, in Vermont.

In 1978 Shore acquired a grant from the National Endowment for the Arts. By 1981 she was working as an English professor at Tufts University, in Massachusetts. As Shore recalled to Chris Bohjalian for the Boston Globe (August 30, 1998), she was happy living in Boston at that time and was determined to dedicate her life to writing poetry—a calling that she considered incompatible with having a family. "I'd see that accomplished female poets like Sylvia Plath and Anne Sexton were miserable," she said, "and it appeared to me that you either chose art or you chose life. You couldn't have both." Then, on Thanksgiving Day 1981, Shore was invited to dinner at the home of the poet Philip Levine, where she met Howard Norman, a translator of Cree and Inuit folktales who had lived and traveled for extended periods in northern Canada and Greenland. Norman was a voracious reader with aspirations to write his own fiction. The two began a deep friendship and often discussed books and writing. "Here was somebody who spoke my language," Shore told Bohjalian, recalling her initial reaction to Norman. "[I thought] maybe you don't have to be lonely to be a poet." With her encouragement, Norman began writing his first novel, The Northern Lights, which was published in 1987 and nominated for the National Book Award. (Norman has gone on to publish four more critically acclaimed and commercially successful novels.) Norman's input also began influencing Shore's approach to writing poetry; at his suggestion she began looking toward her personal experiences and her childhood for poetic material. She recalled to Bohjalian, "We hadn't known each other long. . . . He was riffling through some of my poems, and we were talking about my life. Suddenly, he put the poems down and said, 'You have fantastic material to write about. All those dresses on iron shoulders in your parents' store? Right downstairs from where you were sleeping as a girl? That's great stuff, and you own it.'" Shortly after that, Shore composed a poem entitled "Dresses," which is included in her second collection, The Minute Hand (1986). Shore and Norman married in 1984.

In The Minute Hand, Shore again uses objects—a planter's clock, a home movie, a glass slipper that encases a Cinderella watch—as the starting points for explorations of relationships and her own life. As Linda Gregerson wrote for Poetry (February 1988), "Jane Shore's poems are memorabilia: they cultivate the leisure and faceted pleasure of retrospection; they favor the miniature and the artifactual; they are tender toward kitsch." Reviews of the book were largely positive and often acknowledged the poet's skill in capturing small details and in traveling what Fred Muratori, in Library Journal (April 15, 1987), called "the Wordsworthian path of personal memory." He concluded, "These graceful poems stay well within the realm of the conceivable, and for all their artistry rarely deviate from the now familiar mean of quiet introspection cast in mythic shades." The Minute Hand won the 1986 Lamont Poetry Prize from the Academy of American Poets.

Shore embarked on an even more personal narrative journey in her third volume of poems, Music Minus One (1996), a collection that many reviewers categorized as a poetic memoir. A series of autobiographical poems, the book follows Shore from her 1950s childhood through adolescence to adulthood, when she becomes a mother and faces the loss of both her parents. In Goldensohn's profile Shore described the process of compiling the book, which, she said, took approximately nine years. "There was a template in my head for this book," she explained. "I'd write an early childhood poem and there'd be another poem that would balance it, or fill in about a later part of my life. It was an arc, and there were points along this arc that needed to be told." Some of the book's most memorable poems include vivid childhood memories, often narrated from the child's point of view; for example, in "Holiday Season," the young Jewish narrator accidentally sings the refrain "Christ the Savior is born" during a Christmas concert at school. (Many of the poems involve Jewish themes, reflecting the poet's traditional Jewish upbringing and deepening association with her religion.) Meanwhile, other poems reveal more painful experiences from Shore's adult life. In the final poem, "The Visible Woman"—what Gardner McFall, in the New York Times Book Review (February 23, 1997), called "possibly its most moving"—Shore juxtaposes her mother's slow demise from a terminal illness with imagery pertaining to the construction of a Visible Woman model with her young daughter.

The critical response to Music Minus One was strongly favorable. A Publishers Weekly (July 22, 1996) reviewer called the collection "a virtuoso performance," and McFall affirmed, "This impressive sequence imparts a sense of deepening consciousness, of shifts in perspective over time. . . . These 31 poems all work together . . . forming a seamless arc of personal history, both artful and accessible." Many reviewers found that Shore's poems read more like prose than verse, but they acknowledged her natural gift for storytelling and her ear for the poetic sounds of language. In her *Library Journal* review, Clarence wrote, "At times, the 'prosy' nature of [Shore's] stories leads the reader to wonder why she's arranged her works into verses—prose poems may have been more suitable. But then a flash of pure poetry emerges—'At low tide, the today bore's puddle-raked mud flats / looked like a bolt of brown corduroy / running down the coast'—and her prosier moments are forgiven." In a critique for the *Kenyon Review* (Summer–Fall 1998), Rachel Hadas observed the influence of Elizabeth Bishop—to whom Shore had dedicated the poem "The Wrong End of the Telescope"—particularly in the meticulous attention to detail. While Hadas noted limitations in Shore's conversational style, she concluded, "Our attention isn't grabbed, it is reeled in. Shore's poetry . . . modestly reminds me how very much I have forgotten, omitted, just lost. And something like the miracle [the poet John] Koethe ascribes to books takes place: her memories become my memories, help me recover what I've misplaced—and after that her words are still there on the page." *Music Minus One* was a finalist for the 1996 National Book Critics Circle Award for poetry.

In her most recent book, *Happy Family* (1999), Shore again uses descriptive storytelling, this time in a series of poems focused on domestic themes. The title refers to a meal often served in Chinese restaurants—a "marriage of meat and fish, crab and chicken," as Shore describes in the title poem, as quoted by a reviewer for *Publishers Weekly* (August 30, 1999). The allusion also refers to the famous quotation that opens Leo Tolstoy's classic novel, *Anna Karenina*: "Happy families are all alike; every unhappy family is unhappy in its own way." Throughout *Happy Family*, Shore recounts scenes from her childhood; in "The Best-Dressed Girl in School," for example, she illustrates life at her parents' dress shop, and in "Mrs. Hitler" the young Shore invents a game about Auschwitz after hearing the name whispered in relatives' conversations. Several poems take on more painful and complex personal themes, particularly those regarding her mother's death and her own experiences growing older. In the two-part poem "Next Day"—alluding to Randall Jarrell's poem of the same name—Shore presents contrasting narratives from her older and younger selves, confronting the divided notion of herself as both artist and "the trapped housewife in the supermarket / I dreaded that I would one day be," as quoted by Bruce Murphy in *Poetry* (January 1, 2001). Overall, this collection received mixed reviews, with many critics characterizing Shore's language as too simple and conversational. Doris Lynch, in *Library Journal* (July 1999), observed, "Shore's poems have a directness and emotional intensity that will draw the reader in, but at times they are too rooted in everyday language—one longs for more lyricism." The *Publishers Weekly* reviewer opined, "Once such self-knowledge and frankness (especially in sexual matters) inspired readers. But Shore's own generation of poets has made the life passages she describes a regular and plentifully covered field of American poetry; her honesty no longer seems enough."

Jane Shore has taught at numerous colleges and universities across the country, including Princeton University, in New Jersey; Sarah Lawrence College, in Bronxville, New York; and the University of Hawaii. She is currently a tenured professor of English at the George Washington University, in Washington, D.C. With Howard Norman, she resides for part of the year in the nation's capital and the remainder of the year at the couple's 150-year-old farmhouse in Vermont. Shore and Norman have one daughter, Emma.

—K. D.

SUGGESTED READING: *Baltimore Jewish Times* p91 Feb. 28, 1997; *Boston Globe* Magazine Section p15+, Aug. 30, 1998, with photo; *Kenyon Review* p157 Summer–Fall 1998; *Ploughshares* p209+ Winter 1997–1998, with photo; *Publishers Weekly* p237 July 22, 1996, p79 Aug. 30, 1999

SELECTED BOOKS: *Lying Down in the Olive Press*, 1969; *Eye Level*, 1977; *The Minute Hand*, 1986; *Music Minus One*, 1996; *Happy Family*, 1999

Shreve, Anita

1946– Novelist

Like most aspiring fiction writers, Anita Shreve started her writing career by contributing short stories to small literary publications that "paid" writers with free copies of the issues in which their work appeared. Despite winning an O. Henry Award, in 1975, Shreve convinced herself she'd have a more lucrative career in journalism. She worked for several nationally known publications, and during the 1980s she wrote or co-wrote several nonfiction works, including a series on child rearing, written with Dr. Lawrence Balter, and a primer on health care for working women, written with Patricia Lone. Since the publication of her first novel, *Eden Close*, in 1989, she has published eight novels: *Strange Fits of Passion* (1991), *Where or When* (1993), *Resistance* (1995), *The Weight of Water* (1996), *The Pilot's Wife* (1998), *Fortune's Rocks* (1999), *The Last Time They Met* (2001), and *Sea Glass* (2002). *The Weight of Water* has been made into a feature film, and production has started on a movie version of *Resistance*, starring Bill Paxton and Julia Ormond; several of her other novels have also been optioned to be made into films. Popular notice of her work has extended to literary circles; *The Pilot's Wife* became a selection of Oprah Winfrey's book club, in 1998, and *Fortune's Rocks* was a main Book-of-the-Month Club selection when it was released in 1999.

SHREVE

Anita Shreve was raised in Dedham, Massachusetts, where she had been born in 1946. A high-school assignment opened the world of literature for her, as she would later recount in an essay for the *Boston Globe* (November 2, 1997): "I recall vividly my first reading of *Ethan Frome* on a wintry Sunday afternoon when I was 16, and the way the bleak, wet snow outside my windows seemed to echo perfectly the deeply interior mood of the novel. . . . I was of course thrilled that the work was so short. What I couldn't foresee then was that in the space of a few mesmerizing hours, most of my ideas about the purposes of storytelling and literature would be formed. A framed novel, *Ethan Frome* is a hard, sharp diamond of a book. That it is short is not beside the point. It is the point."

Shreve did her undergraduate work at Tufts University, in Boston, Massachusetts, earning a degree in English in 1968. She taught high school for a while after graduation and started to contribute short stories to small publications. In 1975 one of her first published stories, "Past the Island, Drifting," won an O. Henry Award, a major critical coup. She soon abandoned her teaching career and spent three years in the African nation of Kenya, where her husband was a graduate student. Beginning a career as a journalist, she wrote articles for American magazines such as *Newsweek*, *Quest*, and *US*. (Some sources say she contributed articles from Kenya, others say she started after her return to the U.S.) She became a deputy editor of *Viva* magazine, then embarked on a freelance-writing career in 1986. Her article about working mothers, which appeared in the *New York Times Magazine*, won a Page One Award from the New York Newspaper Guild. For her earliest books Shreve similarly highlighted issues of feminism, motherhood, and children's health. She co-wrote three books with Lawrence Balter—*Dr. Balter's Child Sense: Understanding and Handling the Common Problems of Infancy and Early Childhood* (1985), *Dr. Balter's Baby Sense* (1985), and *Who's in Control? Dr. Balter's Guide to Discipline Without Combat* (1988)—and a book with Patricia Lone, titled *Working Woman: A Guide to Fitness and Health* (1987). Shreve expanded her Page One Award–winning article for her first solo book, *Remaking Motherhood: How Working Mothers Are Shaping Our Children's Future* (1987), published by Viking, which also published her *Women Together, Women Alone: The Legacy of the Consciousness-Raising Movement* (1989).

For *Women Together, Women Alone*, Shreve conducted 65 interviews with women in their 30s, 40s, and 50s, all of whom were part of the early 1970s consciousness-raising movement (CR), a tool of feminist solidarity that urged women to discuss their feelings of powerlessness and encouraged them to find sisterhood and strength in numbers and in the depth of their mutual discussions. While Shreve's book recorded many examples of women whose lives were enhanced by that movement, her interviews also documented a fair amount of disillusion over the failure of CR to translate into meaningful change in women's lives.

By the late 1980s Shreve had begun to suspect that strict journalism was not the most effective way to convey the truths she wanted to tell, so she turned to fiction. During a vacation in New Hampshire, she chanced to read Alice McDermott's novel *That Night*. "I was taken with it. I loved the book and was inspired," she later recalled to Shelley West for the Amherst Student (September 30, 1998). She subsequently spent two years working on her first novel, *Eden Close*, published in 1989 by Harcourt Brace. In the book Andrew and Eden, a pair of childhood friends, are reunited in their 30s, when Andrew returns home for his mother's funeral. The novel gave Shreve confidence in her creative-writing ability and convinced her that she could succeed as a fiction writer.

Like *Eden Close*, Shreve's next novel, *Strange Fits of Passion*, deals with the psychological scars of crime, alcoholism, and domestic violence. It is set in the early 1970s, when many women were beginning to redefine their traditional roles as wives and mothers; the novel was sparked in part by some of the harrowing tales of wife-beating Shreve had heard while researching *Women Together, Women Alone*. The novel is structured around a series of interviews given by Maureen English, a battered spouse serving time in prison for murdering Harrold, her abusive husband, and then fleeing to establish a new life with a Maine lobster man.

Where or When, Shreve's third novel and the last to be published by Harcourt Brace, analyzes the mid-life crises of two characters who, 30 years earlier, had fallen in love at a summer camp as teenagers. Describing the novel as a "finely wrought book" in her evaluation for the *New York Times Book Review* (June 6, 1993), author Susan Isaacs wrote, "Ms. Shreve is too wise a writer to offer easy answers. Instead, she allows her characters to reveal their hearts and minds in their letters, through Sian's evocation of their love and through an intimate present-tense account of Charles's infatuation." Isaacs concluded, "*Where or When* is more than just an exquisitely written novel. It is also a gripping yarn."

With the publication of *Resistance*, in 1995, Shreve began an association with the publisher Little, Brown, which also issued the three novels that followed: *The Weight of Water* (1996), *The Pilot's Wife* (1998), and *Fortune's Rocks* (1999). As a setting for *Resistance*, Shreve abandoned her familiar New England coast for the Belgian village of Delahaut during the Nazi occupation in the 1940s. The novel narrates the story of Claire Daussois, the wife of a member of the Belgian resistance movement, who falls in love with Ted Brice, a wounded American pilot she shelters in their attic. By negotiating the always shifting quicksands of loyalties and trustworthiness during wartime, Shreve painted a picture of "how perfectly ordinary people, people who might not have amounted to much, people one hadn't even noticed or liked, had been transformed by the war," as her character Claire says. "It was as though the years since 1940, in all their misery, had drawn forth character—water from the earth where none had seemed to be before." Rebecca Radner, reviewing *Resistance* for the *San Francisco Chronicle* (July 2, 1995), wrote that "Shreve is an intelligent, powerful writer; the center of her story is the different ways people react to the terrors of war and the resulting changes in their character."

It took Shreve a quarter century to write *The Weight of Water* (1996), the "breakout" book that brought her work to the attention of a larger segment of the public. The narrative follows magazine photographer Jean as she visits Smuttynose Island, off the coast of Maine, to research a century-old ax-murder in which two women, both Norwegian immigrants, had been slain. Shreve herself learned about the crimes in 1973, while on a sailing vacation with her family on the Isles of Shoals, along the coast between New Hampshire and Maine. She first attempted to fictionalize the murder case in 1975, with the publication in the *Cimarron Review* of the short story "Silence at Smuttynose." Twenty years later, with four novels in print, she reread the story and decided to revisit the situation in a longer work of fiction. Although she has said that "the heart of the book has almost nothing to do with the facts," she read court transcripts and other historical records to ensure as much accuracy as possible.

For *The Weight of Water*, Shreve won a L. L. Winship/PEN New England Award and became a finalist for the Orange Prize, awarded in Great Britain. London critic Anita Brookner, writing for the *Spectator* (July 19, 1997), concluded that Shreve's novel "is a subversive narrative, as it is meant to be. Quite rightly we are spared the author's own reflections; indeed the author is notably absent, leaving poor glum Jean to do the work, or rather not do it. . . . *The Weight of Water* is a novel of the pioneer or North American school. Plainly told, it is a tease of the first order." John Taylor, reviewing the novel for the *Antioch Review* (Spring 1998), wrote that the "gale-torn" setting reminded him of the "claustrophobic ambience" of Goethe's *Elective Affinities* and concluded that the parallel tales—both of the ax murders and Jean's efforts to unravel them—"follow the relentless course of a Greek tragedy, with unsuspected character flaws, missteps that lead to mortal plot changes, and a violent storm-battered climax." *The Weight of Water* was made into a movie, released in 2000, starring Sean Penn and Elizabeth Hurley.

Shreve confessed on the Time Warner Bookmark Web site that her next novel, *The Pilot's Wife*, grew from a chance snippet of conversation she had overheard at a party, when a commercial airline pilot had told the guests that, after a plane crash, "the union always gets to the house of the pilot's wife first [because] it's the union representative's job to keep the wife from talking to the press." Shreve began to imagine what life would be like for that woman, especially if blame for the crash was attributed to her late husband, and to posit what the widow would do if confronted with signs of her late husband's infidelity. Shreve began working on the novel in spring 1996, but she put it aside for a while after the crash of TWA Flight 800 that summer brought up coincidences between her fiction and the real-life event. In an open letter to her readers posted on Time Warner Bookmark, Shreve wrote, "I took up the work again when I begin to convince myself that the novel really wasn't about the crash per se, but rather about secrets and betrayals and survival. Despite the darkness, much was learned. Perhaps because of the darkness."

By September 1998 it was reported that *The Pilot's Wife* had sold 1.8 million copies and that CBS was planning to turn it into a made-for-TV movie. In her review for *Publishers Weekly* (March 16, 1998), Sybil S. Steinberg described *The Pilot's Wife* as "a streamlined variation on Saint-Exupery's *Vol de Nuit* [*Night Mail*] told from the wife's point of view [which] explores in calm, clear prose a man's self-destructive desire for a world beyond the quotidian." Although Steinberg cautioned that "the climax, less dramatic than meditative, may strike some readers as too muted," she quickly asserted that "understatement is one of this novel's strengths. What haunts us is the way Jack's secret life gradually weakens its hold on Kathryn's imagination and ours. Like the plane in Saint-Exupery's tale, the soul of this pilot seems to have ended by running on empty."

Shreve's seventh novel, *Fortune's Rocks*, was designated as a main Book-of-the-Month Club selection when it was published in 1999. Set in 1899 on the New Hampshire coastline, its landscape and time frame evoke the settings of *The Weight of Water*. *Fortune's Rocks* deals, however, not with an unsolved murder but with the coming-of-age of Olympia Biddeford, the precocious 15-year-old daughter of a family of Boston Brahmins who becomes involved in a torrid summer romance with a physician 26 years her senior, a family friend named Dr. John Haskell. As a byproduct of her liaison with the socially conscious medical man, Olympia is also introduced to the plight of oppressed immigrant millworkers, giving her a rare window into a class far removed from her own family's pretensions. In his review for the *Christian Science Monitor* (December 2, 1999), Ron Charles called *Fortune's Rocks* "a morality tale that reads like something Edith Wharton would have written if she'd been a friend of Gloria Steinem instead of Henry James." Charles saw a "new feminist movement afoot" in the nearly simultaneous publication of Shreve's novel and Sena Jeter Naslund's *Ahab's Wife*. Both books, he argued, present heroines who "confront 19th-century challenges with a mixture of moxy and 20th-century liberalism." In a laudatory review for *Publishers Weekly* (October 4, 1999), Sybil S. Steinberg complimented the historical atmosphere of the book, praising it as "scandalous love story told with dignity and integrity, and a finely etched portrait of American society at the turn of the last century, a narrative that accurately reflects vanished manners and mores, while reconfirming the universality of human emotions." Steinberg declared that "while Shreve's books always show evidence of meticulous research, her hand has never been so sure as it is here" and predicted the book would "take off like a rocket." As for the themes, Christopher Lehmann-Haupt, in a *New York Times* (December 9, 1999) review, argued that novels like Judith Rossner's *Emmeline* and John Fowles's *The French Lieutenant's Woman* had covered some of the same territory, but he conceded that the "conventional power" of *Fortune's Rocks* brought pleasure by evoking "those elemental emotions that are reborn in every new reader and that remain like bedrock in the most sophisticated of readers. Some stories never grow tiresome, and in *Fortune's Rocks*, Ms. Shreve has captured one of them and kept it alive and pacing in its cage."

In *The Last Time They Met* (2001), Shreve recounts a life-long romance between two poets whose destinies are complexly intertwined. When the book opens, Thomas Janes and Linda Fallon, both middle aged, cross paths at a literary festival where they will be giving readings of their work. Linda has made a minor reputation for herself, and Thomas—the same Thomas from *The Weight of Water*—has become a famous poet. Linda is widowed; Thomas is divorced; Linda's son is gay and an alcoholic; Thomas is still grieved by the loss of his daughter. The two share memories of the times they once spent together, and their lingering regrets, and some unspecified tragedy in the past that unites them. They find their love for each other is still strong, even though they have only been together two other times in the last 35 years. From here the novel moves backwards in time: the next section finds Thomas and Linda in their mid-20s and living in Africa, married to other people but sharing an illicit love. In the third and final section, Thomas and Linda are 17 and falling in love. With each step backwards in time more questions are answered about the nature of their relationship, until the final tragedy is revealed.

"The latest work by this versatile novelist may be her most mature to date, as she demonstrates new subtleties in the unfolding of a complex plot," an anonymous reviewer wrote for *Publisher's Weekly*, as quoted on *Amazon.com*. "Shreve's compassionate view of human frailties—a recurring theme in much of her work—is at its most affecting here, as she meticulously interweaves past and present with total credibility." Shelby Hearon, writing for the *Chicago Tribune* (June 17, 2001), called the novel "a flat-out, can't-put-it-down page-turner. . . . *The Last Time They Met* is a riveting story that teases and confounds as it moves back in time from the end to the start of a love affair."

Sea Glass (2002) takes place in the late 1920s in New Hampshire, where newlyweds Sexton and Honora Beecher move into a large beach-side house (which also appeared in Shreve's earlier novels *The Pilot's Wife* and *Fortune's Rocks*). The marital bliss of their first few months together is suddenly uprooted following the stock market crash of 1929, when Sexton loses his job and is forced to work at a local mill where conditions are miserable and the mill hands are on the verge of a strike. Honora is at the center of the novel, although numerous other lives become entwined with hers. The narrative introduces the characters one by one, showing how they meet and come to know each other, all the while charting the progress of the workers' push to start a union, and the wayward passion of Honora for a millworker named McDermott. "The plot moves forward via kaleidoscopic vignettes from each character's point of view, building emotional tension until the violent, rather melodramatic climax when the mill owners's minions confront the strikers," a critic wrote for *Publishers Weekly*, as quoted on *Amazon.com*. "Shreve is skilled at interpolating historical background, and her descriptions of the different social strata—the millworkers, the lower-middle-class Sextons, the idle rich—enhance a touching story about the loyalty and betrayal, responsibility and dishonor." Reviews of the novel were positive, and after a week in stores it reached number seven on the *Publishers Weekly* best-selling fiction list.

Reviewers of Shreve's novels often caution against viewing Shreve as a mere "genre" writer. In a biographical profile that appeared in the *Boston Globe* (September 20, 1998), B. J. Roche remarked that Shreve's "themes of love, passion, and betrayal have often pigeonholed her in the 'chick book' category," but he hastened to add that she was beginning to receive prestigious literary awards and that several of her novels had been optioned to be made into films at one time or another. Shreve defended her choice of themes to Roche, declaring that "love is a very devalued subject to be writing about these days. That strikes me as sad. It's hard for me to imagine what is more serious to write about: how it affects people right down to their soul, how it affects their families, how it affects their future. It's the one thing that is guaranteed to happen to an ordinary person. That and death."

In the past Shreve has served as a visiting lecturer at Amherst College, in Massachusetts, an experience that she treasures for the opportunity it afforded her to connect with other people. "Writing is a solitary, and often lonely, pursuit. Teaching is not," she told Shelley West. "I remember when I was a journalist that particular feeling of energy when dealing with editors and copyeditors and from interviewing other people. Teaching at Amherst has some of that same energy." As a teacher, she explained, "I am from the carpenter school of writing. I am not so interested in the writer artist as the writer who can make a good chair," but then she added that "there is nothing I am teaching my students that they could not learn from reading the right things."

Shreve revealed her own short list of favorite authors in the essay she had written for the *Boston Globe*; the list includes *Lies of Silence* by Brian Moore, *Cal* by Bernard McLaverty, *That Night* by Alice McDermott, and *Ethan Frome* by Edith Wharton. "Each work on this idiosyncratic list illuminates with economical grace the consequences of an extraordinary event in an ordinary life," she explained. "Each tells its catastrophic story in a decidedly uncatastrophic manner. And each contains, within the elegant restraint of its language, a breathtakingly strong tale. Most important, each novel is remarkably short." To Shreve, brevity is admirable.

Shreve, who has been divorced twice, is married to John Osborn. They have five children between them. She met John at a summer camp in the 1960s, when they were both teenagers. He initiated correspondence with her after seeing her photograph in a newspaper book review. (Shreve wrote about a similar scenario in her 1993 novel, *Where or When*.) Some of Shreve's life experiences have found reflection in her fiction, as is evidenced by the unflinching examination of the failings of human relationships in her books. As she told B. J. Roche for his *Boston Globe* profile, "I don't not believe in marriage, and I don't not believe that wonderful companionships and partnerships can result. I've just had a lot of experiences with the realities of marriage that nobody tells you about, that nobody anticipates, and nobody expects. And the way passionate love wanes, and nobody prepares you for that, either."

—E. M.

SUGGESTED READING: *Booklist* p1276 Mar. 15, 1993; *Chicago Tribune* C p2 June 17, 2001; *Cosmopolitan* p32 June 1993; *Library Journal* p166 Aug. 1989, p156+ Aug. 1994; *Mother Jones* p47+ Oct. 1989; *New Woman* p26 Aug. 1993, with photo; *New Yorker* p101 July 5, 1993; *New York Times Book Review* p10 Aug. 13, 1989, p6 Sep. 3, 1989, p50 June 6, 1993, p21 July 3, 1994, p20 Nov. 13, 1994; *People Weekly* p41 June 14, 1993, with photo; *Publishers Weekly* p68 Mar. 22, 1993, p34+ June 6, 1994; *Times Literary Supplement* p23 Jan. 17, 1992; *Vogue* p85 July 1993, with photo

SELECTED BOOKS: fiction—*Eden Close*, 1989; *Strange Fits of Passion*, 1991; *Where or When*, 1993; *Resistance*, 1995; *The Weight of Water*, 1996; *The Pilot's Wife*, 1998; *Fortune's Rocks*, 1999, *The Last Time They Met*, 2001; *Sea Glass*, 2002; nonfiction—*Dr. Balter's Child Sense: Understanding and Handling the Common Problems of Infancy and Early Childhood* (with Lawrence Balter), 1985; *Dr. Balter's Baby Sense* (with Lawrence Balter), 1985; *Working Woman: A Guide to Fitness and Health* (with Patricia Lone), 1986; *Remaking Motherhood: How Working Mothers Are Shaping Our Children's Future*, 1987; *Who's In Control?* (with Lawrence Balter), 1988; *Women Together, Women Alone: The Legacy of the Consciousness-Raising Movement*, 1989

Silber, Joan

June 14, 1945– Novelist and short-story writer

Joan Silber has impressed many critics by creating memorable tales in which everyday characters face difficult or unusual circumstances. In her first novel, *Household Words* (1980), a woman struggles to cope with the unexpected death of her husband. Silber's second novel, *In the City* (1987), follows the adventures of a 19-year-old girl from New Jersey who moves to Greenwich Village in New York City during the 1920s. In her most acclaimed book to date, *Lucky Us* (2001), Silber portrays a couple whose marriage plans are disrupted when one of them is diagnosed with AIDS. Silber's prize-winning short-story collection, *In My Other Life* (2000), features characters who reflect on their lives and the mistakes they have made.

Joan Silber writes for *World Authors: 1995–2000*: "I grew up in Millburn, New Jersey, a small suburban town. I was born in 1945, and my childhood took place in that routinized pleasantness the fifties are famous for, though my home life had different textures. My father, who'd been a dentist, died when I was five. My mother, who never quite recovered from this loss, went back to teaching school. Our house was full of books that had been my father's, and I worked my way through the Best Known Works of Chekhov, de Maupassant, Ibsen, and Wilde (I could quote Wilde quite obnoxiously when I was ten); Thomas Wolfe had been my father's teacher at NYU, and we had a complete set of his novels too. I wrote poems and stories as soon as I could, though I planned for a career as a movie star. By the time I was a teenager, I was serious about poetry. For my high school term paper, I chose the topic, 'Why Did Rimbaud Stop Writing at Age Nineteen?'

"I went to Sarah Lawrence College, where I studied writing with Jane Cooper and Grace Paley. I moved to New York right after graduation, and I had the idea that I wanted to be a writer but not much of a clue as to what this writing would be, and I worked for several years as a waitress in a bar. This was a good job—the bar was a packed and frenetic place, an art-world hangout, stylish in a low-rent downtown way, and really very educating.

"In the mid-seventies, after I'd published a few stories in magazines, an agent wrote to ask if I had a novel. I didn't, but this question came not long after my mother had died, after decades of chronic illness, and her life—its expectations and sadness

Shari Caroline Diamond/Courtesy of Algonquin Books
Joan Silber

and what they might mean—was much on my mind. When I first began *Household Words*, I planned to alternate viewpoints between a mother and two daughters, but once I began in the mother's perspective, I stayed there. I already *knew* what the daughters would think, but the stretch of taking on the mother's role required a different empathy. I had often been embattled with my actual mother, but in fiction I could be more generous than in my own real life, where I'd had myself to watch out for. The decision to tell a family story from a viewpoint so clearly not my own is still something I'm glad about. The book won a PEN/Hemingway Award.

"The next novel, *In the City*, was set in New York in the 1920s, an era, it seemed to me, when social change was so fast that people (especially young women) couldn't rely on old certainties and were testing glamorous and airy new ones. I could see I was always going to want to write about the point at which the rug is pulled out from under a character. Working with both historical and contemporary material made it clear that each era has its own assumptions, its truisms about how life works, and they're never enough (events always outwit them). This is also what has kept me writing closely detailed realistic fiction, since I'm interested in the surprise of the particular.

"In these years I had grants from the Guggenheim Foundation, the NEA, and the New York Foundation on the Arts. After getting stuck on a novel I couldn't get off the ground, I turned to writing stories. The first one, begun at a time when I was feeling defeated in my work, was about a longstanding friendship between an ex-junkie and a woman who's adopted a baby with her female lover. My agent said she would send it to the *New Yorker* except for its content, which meant automatic rejection; after some pleading, she did send it, and, to my own surprise, it was accepted.

"This began several long and happy years working on stories, and most of these were about friendship, which I believe is often as complicated as romantic love. I had more or less skipped the usual apprenticeship as a story writer before becoming a novelist, because I thought (erroneously) that stories often made too much of a single moment or scene, whereas I had my eye on accumulated changes over time. Alice Munro, with her great leaps and switchbacks over years, showed me the span stories could contain. Since I was using characters with rocky pasts—drugs and other adventures in poor planning—I was glad for the chance to get then-and-now into a story and to parse out which casual decisions were crucial. The stories were collected as *In My Other Life*.

"*Lucky Us*, the most recent novel, is about a couple—an older man with a brief prison stint in his youth and a young woman who learns, as they're about to marry, that she's HIV-positive. Clearly I was thinking here too about the weight of the past—the book was originally titled, 'How Did It Happen?' Illness had always been part of my sense of what's possible and had entered my fiction before. In 1996, shortly after I began *Lucky Us*, I started volunteering as a Buddy for Gay Men's Health Crisis; both the book and the buddying came out of a late-dawning sense of the epidemic. (I am still a Buddy, and it's actually a great thing to do.) The male character also owes something to my being on the PEN Prison Writing Committee, whose members read manuscripts by inmates.

"Since the mid-eighties I have been teaching at Sarah Lawrence College and have taught off and on in the Warren Wilson College MFA Program. Right now I've just finished a cycle of stories, 'Ideas of Heaven.' They're about sex and religion, two impulses that sometimes fight over the same ground—forms of devotion and forms of consolation. They're linked a little oddly in that a minor element in one becomes major in the next. My interest in Buddhism finds its way in. I've loved working on them; two of them have historical settings—one is told by a Renaissance poet and one by a missionary wife in China in the late 1800s. I'm just beginning to think about a new writing project that will deal with the idea of travel."

Joan Silber was born on June 14, 1945 in Millburn, New Jersey. Silber graduated in 1967 from Sarah Lawrence College, in Bronxville, New York, with a B.A. That same year she began working as a copy editor for the publishing company Holt, Rinehart & Winston in New York City. In 1968 she worked briefly as a reporter for the *New York Free Press*. She then left the publishing industry for several years, working as a waitress, sales clerk, and daycare teacher.

Silber returned to publishing in 1975, serving as the editor of the fan magazines *Movie Stars* and *Movie Life* and writing book reviews. After she worked for a time as a legal assistant for the firm Warners & Gillers, Silber resumed her education, enrolling as a graduate student at New York University. She received her M.A. in 1979.

Silber earned acclaim for her first novel, *Household Words* (1980). The book is set in New Jersey during the 1940s and 1950s; its protagonist is Rhoda Taber, a happily married French teacher. Her life is disrupted when her husband, Leonard, a caring pharmacist, dies. The death of Rhoda's mother adds to her pain. Rhoda struggles to cope with her feelings of grief, loss, and anger while maintaining relationships with her two daughters and friends. "Though Miss Silber writes about the ordinary, her writing is extraordinary," Susan Isaacs wrote for the *New York Times Book Review* (February 3, 1980). "She never blathers on about the nobility of the human spirit; she simply has her character demonstrate it." Isaacs concluded that the novel "is about ordinary life. There is no zippy dialogue, no literary razzle-dazzle. People live, die, raise children, put on girdles and teach school. But the details add up to a novel full of dignity and humanity. Joan Silber is a gifted writer." In her review for the *Washington Post* (January 31, 1980), Linda B. Osborne observed that Rhoda's "voice is authentic and peppered with wise-cracks, yet she has dignity because Silber treats her with dignity." Osborne described *Household Words* as "a deeply moving account of a widow's ability to cope with loss and pain," concluding that the novel "is an optimistic book" that "concentrates not on sorrow, but on the life-affirming capacity to take on loss and still continue with sense and self-respect." *Household Words* won the 1981 PEN/Hemingway Award for best first novel and an honorable mention in a competition for new writers sponsored by the Great Lakes Colleges Association.

After a brief stint as a legal proofreader for the Women's Action Alliance, Silber began teaching at her alma mater, Sarah Lawrence College, in 1985. Her next novel, *In the City*, was published in 1987. It takes place during the 1920s, and its main character is Pauline Samuels, a 19-year-old girl from Newark, New Jersey. Pauline, who is the daughter of Russian Jewish immigrants, leaves her home and finds herself swept up in the bohemian atmosphere of Manhattan's Greenwich Village neighborhood. She finds a room in a boarding house, a job as a file clerk, and love with a failed writer. In an interview with Laurel Graeber for the *New York Times Book Review* (March 29, 1987), Silber said that she had originally set *In the City* during the 1960s, the time of her own coming-of-age. "Then I felt it was reducing itself too easily to too many familiar ideas," Silber explained. "To transfer it to the 1920s was a way of saying that I wanted it to be about youth, not just a particular time frame." Although the author shared a number of similarities with Pauline, such as having Jewish parents who immigrated from Russia, growing up in New Jersey, and leaving home for New York City, Silber assured Graeber that the events in the book were not based on her own experiences. "The incidents are made up," she said. "But I identified with that sense of starting out at a certain age—thinking that you know what's going on and slowly realizing you don't."

"Ms. Silber is at her best in her deft, elegant, wryly economical dissections of Pauline's elastic nature, and in the humor and authenticity with which she portrays the curiosity and self-protective detachment many young girls experience with sex," Joyce Johnson wrote for the *New York Times Book Review* (March 29, 1987). "Yet, at least for this reader, Pauline's very coolness works somewhat against this novel; one misses the energy that comes from intensities of feeling." Still, Johnson noted that Silber had written more than a period piece, opining that the work "has some of the immediacy of a novel actually written in the 1920s. The characters are not overly self-conscious of the features of their period as they are in much popular historical fiction; by what they take for granted, by what they fail to observe, they are made to seem more real."

In a review for the *Christian Science Monitor* (April 10, 1987), Merle Rubin praised the novel. "From the arch witticisms of high school humor to the sardonically undercutting rumblings of Pauline's suspicious immigrant parents, to the self-conscious sophistication of the literary and artistic types she meets in the Village, every intonation of voice and dialogue is utterly convincing," Rubin asserted. "*In the City* looks back on an earlier time—adolescence—and an earlier era—the 1920s—with affection and compassion, but without the least hint of condescension, capturing the feel of its time and place with the immediacy of felt experience and the wisdom of experienced feelings."

Silber next published a collection of short stories, *In My Other Life*. Writing for *Publishers Weekly* (March 20, 2000), Sybil S. Steinberg observed that in the book's 12 stories Silber "imagines households of mostly decent, though emotionally scarred, women and men trying to cope with kids, difficult exes or grown siblings. Some of these reflective characters can hardly believe they've outlived their perilous youth." Among the stories that Steinberg thought noteworthy were "Bobby Jackson," about a man who looks back at his life as a bartender and drug addict; "Lake Natasink," about a gay couple who move with their adopted baby to a farm in upstate New York; and "What Lasts," a look at a pair of high-strung newlyweds. Steinberg opined that this last "contains some of the book's most striking, skeptical writing, exemplary of the keen, expressive sense of the improbable, of dumb luck and ill luck, and of unlikely recovery that makes Silber's stories so warmly convincing."

In her review for *Newsday* (July 27, 2000), Georgia Jones-Davis wrote that the characters in the book look back "at who they were in the blossoming and dumbness of their youth. That we should start out as very different people from who we end up becomes a thematic given in Silber's universe. The ones who fail to evolve prove hopelessly immature or forever unfulfilled." Although Jones-Davis did find fault with the book, arguing that all of the stories were told from the same point of view and that "Lake Natasink" resembled a sketch rather than a completed story, she was impressed with many of the tales and concluded that "Joan Silber's former junkies, waitresses, bartenders, rock-star groupies and drug dealers are an oddly appealing lot." *In My Other Life* was honored with the Pushcart Prize in 2000. (One story, "Ordinary," was a finalist in the Nelson Algren Short Story Competition when it was originally published in 1994, in the *New Yorker*.)

In 2001 Silber returned with her third novel, *Lucky Us*, a tragic love story. Set in New York City, it chronicles the lives of Elisa, an artist, and Gabe, an ex-drug dealer, who tell their stories separately in alternating chapters. Silber explained to Chuck Leddy in an interview for *Bookreporter.com* (October 19, 2001) that she had both characters tell their stories because "I wanted the couple's conflicts to be seen fairly, and, in fiction as in life, one lover's version can too easily be a self-righteous plaint or a recitation of longing; I wanted the wider view. And then I came to like the occasional irony of one knowing things the other didn't." The couple's wedding plans are disrupted when Elisa is diagnosed with AIDS. Although Gabe remains steadfast, encouraging her to take her vitamins and reading everything he can find about the disease, Elisa rekindles a romantic relationship with Jason, her abusive ex-boyfriend who also has AIDS.

Silber drew from her own experiences in writing the book. She told Leddy, "As a kid, I grew up with an ill parent, and illness has always loomed large in my imagination; it's entered my fiction in previous books." A short time after she started the book, Silber volunteered as a "buddy" with the Gay Men's Health Crisis in New York City, spending one day a week with an AIDS patient. "Both the book and the buddying came out of a late-dawning sense of the epidemic's shadow over the time I was living in," she said.

Lucky Us received enthusiastic reviews from most critics. "The title [of the book], like the tone of the writing, is flip and wry, promising nothing more significant than a frothy comedy of manners," Dana Kennedy wrote in the *New York Times Book Review* (October 28, 2001). "What a pleasure, then, to discover how moving such a seemingly ordinary story can be." Kennedy observed that Silber's style is "direct and immediate . . . such that you never catch her self-consciously writing." The reviewer concluded that "while things do go from bad to worse, Silber manages both to satisfy the reader's hopes and to avoid soppy melodrama. The result is an unexpectedly powerful book." In her review for the *Chicago Tribune* (October 21, 2001), Laura Demanski wrote, "Silber ultimately believes in consequences and coping more than luck. The casually luminous wit that sparkles from every page of *Lucky Us* is underwritten by this wisdom, making for a novel that is not just effortlessly readable, but unexpectedly stirring."

Joan Silber's short stories have been published in such magazines as the *New Yorker* and *Paris Review*. She has earned a Guggenheim Foundation fellowship (1984–1985) and in 1986 she was awarded grants from both the New York Foundation for the Arts and the National Endowment for the Arts. Silber's next book, tentatively entitled "Ideas of Heaven," will be a collection of linked short stories that focus, as she told Chuck Leddy, on "forms of devotion and forms of consolation." The author lives in New York City.

—D. C.

SUGGESTED READING: *Bookreporter.com* Oct. 19, 2001; *Chicago Tribune* 14 p3 Oct. 21, 2001; *Christian Science Monitor* p24 Apr. 10, 1987; *New York Times Book Review* Feb. 3, 1980, p8 Mar. 29, 1987, p7 Oct. 28, 2001; *Newsday* B p12 July 27, 2000; *Publishers Weekly* p71 Mar. 20, 2000; *Washington Post* B p17 Jan. 31, 1980

SELECTED BOOKS: novels—*Household Words*, 1980; *In the City*, 1987; *Lucky Us*, 2001; short-story collection—*In My Other Life*, 2000

Sleigh, Tom

1953–Poet; writer; translator; educator

With just five volumes of poetry to his name, Tom Sleigh has already elicited comparisons to some of the most renowned poets. Liz Rosenberg, writing for the *New York Times* (June 30, 1991), noted, "[He] is nearly as prodigal with his gifts as Yeats," and his poetry has also frequently been compared to that of Wallace Stevens. Since the publication of his first collection, Sleigh has received consistent critical acclaim. His work, widely considered to be more accessible than that of many of his peers, explores the common threads of human existence—love, sickness, spirituality, and mortality—with an originality and a freshness that puts him, in the estimation of many critics, at the front ranks of modern American poets. In addition to being a poet, he is also a highly respected translator of ancient Greek texts, most notably Euripides' *Herakles*, published in 2000.

Tom Sleigh was born in 1953 in Mount Pleasant, Texas. He attended the California Institute of the Arts, in Valencia, and in 1977 he earned a master's degree from Johns Hopkins University, in Baltimore, Maryland. In 1983 he published his first collection of poetry, *After One*, which received highly laudatory press. Michael Hennessy wrote for *Li-*

Tom Sleigh
Courtesy of the University of Chicago Press

brary Journal (December 1, 1983): "Sleigh's romantic wonderment is made credible by a lurking sense of 'something monstrous' breaking through placid surfaces, and by the recognition of individual human suffering. Sleigh's deft handling of various rhythmic and stanzic patterns and his use of rhyme (especially slant rhyme) give his work a controlled, deliberate quality that is one of its most impressive features." Robert Pack, critiquing the volume for the New York Times Book Review (May 20, 1984), wrote, "Mr. Sleigh's poetry engages the self just as it engages the physical world that is there to be marveled at, enjoyed and lost. In language that is rhythmic, spare and lucid, he rewards his readers with poems genuinely designed with what Frost called 'a good look and a good listen.'"

After a number of his poems appeared in Ploughshares, the Boston Review, and Poetry, Sleigh published Waking, his next collection, in 1990. Critics again heaped praise on his work. Liz Rosenberg wrote, "Tom Sleigh's second book of poems, Waking, is so fine one can hardly do justice to it in a review." Citing the lines "The dull 'tick tock' of a manhole cover which the sleepless / Taxis rock back and forth," Rosenberg asserted that Sleigh "has the precision of a diamond cutter." She continued, "Nothing is lost on Mr. Sleigh—nothing felt, thought or imagined." She acknowledged that the collection was not perfect: "Mr. Sleigh is not at ease with dialogue; all his characters speak high rhetoric. The last section of the book . . . is weak, sentimental," but she concluded, "This is looking for faults where there are few." In a review for the Times Literary Supplement (May 31, 1991), Glyn Maxwell singled out one poem: "With many interested parties hailing the New Formalism, the death of Free Verse, . . . it is good to see Tom Sleigh's fine 'free' poem of mortality, 'Ending,' which serves to remind the average poet that shaping the space, the whiteness, the silence, is half the struggle." Maxwell was particularly impressed with the lines "The hypodermic plunged in my arm / And I shivered and repeated / With the insistence of a prayer / 'My temperature is a 104, 104, 104 . . .' / was this / What it meant to die?" The volume was named a Notable Book of the Year by the New York Times.

In his third collection, The Chain (1996), Sleigh reflects on past events, including the death of his father, and focuses on the nature of remembrance itself. In one wholly positive review, Elizabeth Millard wrote for Booklist (March 15, 1996), "Combining sophisticated language and often painful memory, Sleigh makes his mark as an original, unpredictable poet." Graham Christian, however, writing for Library Journal (March 1, 1996), expressed disappointment that "so many of Sleigh's poems are digressive, meandering narratives . . . that could have benefitted from revision and reduction." Andrew Frisardi noted in a review for Poetry (May 1997), "One difficulty of writing about childhood trauma these days is that some of our notions of it, deriving originally from psychoanalytic culture, have been hackneyed by talk show hosts, journalists, and even by poets. . . . Sleigh magnificently overcomes this handicap by treating the subject with considerable originality and dramatic flair." He opined, however, that while some of the pieces are "Sleigh's finest poetry to date," others are "weakened by slack, prosy language and insufficiently dramatized confessional detail."

The Dreamhouse (1999), Sleigh's fourth volume, is a collection of pieces about death and dissolution written in both rhyme and free verse. David Kirby wrote for the New York Times Book Review (April 23, 2000), "[These poems] are brightly lighted and accelerating . . . as though someone were flinging them into a cleansing fire." Rochelle Ratner, writing for Library Journal (October 15, 1999), noted, "Sleigh's powers of observation top any this reviewer has read." Bill Christophersen, in an assessment for Poetry (December 2000), also found much to praise: "Sleigh broods over traffic accidents, train wrecks, demons, ghosts, mass graves, an open sarcophagus, a hallucinating derelict, a razor-toting evangelist, the Civil War dead, and Holocaust survivors. . . . Sensationalistic? Very. Nonetheless, when Sleigh deals with personal and historical nightmares, he does so artfully." The Dreamhouse was a finalist for the 1999 Los Angeles Times Book Prize in poetry. Sleigh's latest work, Far Side of the Earth, was published in 2003.

Since 1986 Tom Sleigh has been a professor of English and creative writing at Dartmouth College, in New Hampshire. He has been a visiting professor at Johns Hopkins University. He is an advisory editor for the Agni Review, a Boston University publication, and a contributing editor for the Boston Review. Sleigh has received numerous honors for his work, including an Individual Writer's Award from the Lila Wallace–*Reader's Digest* Fund, the Shelley Memorial Award from the Poetry Society of America, and grants from the National Endowment for the Arts, the Ingram Merill Foundation, the Guggenheim Foundation, and the Fine Arts Work Center in Provincetown, Massachusetts. He lives in Cambridge, Massachusetts.

—C. M.

SUGGESTED READING: Academy of American Poets Web site; *Library of Congress* Web site; *Booklist* p1236 Mar. 15, 1996; *Library Journal* p 2253 Dec. 1, 1983, p82 Mar. 1, 1996, p73 Oct. 15, 1999; *New York Times Book Review* p37 May 20, 1984, p26 June 30, 1991, p18 Apr. 23, 2000; *Poetry* p104 May 1997, p217+ Dec. 2000; *Times Literary Supplement* p11 May 31, 1991

SELECTED BOOKS: *After One*, 1983; *Waking*, 1990; *The Chain*, 1996; *The Dreamhouse*, 1999; *Far Side of the Earth*, 2003; as translator—*Herakles*, 2000

Ben Murray/Retna/Camera Press

Smith, Zadie

Oct. 27, 1975– Novelist; essayist

The young British writer Zadie Smith took readers and the literary establishment by surprise with her first novel, *White Teeth* (2000), portraying the private hopes and fears of Londoners, native and immigrant. In colloquial dialogue, with humor and wit to spare, she displayed a profound understanding of the aspirations driving her characters, as each one struggles with the baggage of his or her cultural origins. Her most recent novel is *The Autograph Man* (2002).

Zadie Smith was born in England on October 27, 1975. Her mother had immigrated to England from Jamaica, settling in London to work as a model and later becoming a child psychoanalyst. Her father, who is British, worked as a photographer. Smith and her two younger brothers were raised in Willesden Green, a working-class suburb in northwest London, where much of her novel is set. When Smith was a child, she has recounted, the family spent holidays in the English town of Devon, where, "if you're black . . . everyone turns and looks at you. So my instinct . . . was always to over-compensate by trying to behave three times as well as every other child in the shop. . . . I think that instinct has spilled over into my writing . . . which is not something I like very much or want to continue," she told Maria Russo in an interview for *Salon* (April 28, 2000, on-line).

Smith's parents divorced when she was 12 years old, perhaps contributing to what she described to Nadya Labi for *Time* (May 8, 2000) as a "pathologically angst ridden" adolescence. For solace she turned to writing poetry and short stories as well as tap dancing, which she studied for 10 years and dreamt of pursuing as a career. She gave up that ambition after she "got too fat," as she told Nadya Labi. Similarly, she entertained hopes of being a jazz singer, but she "wasn't as good as Aretha [Franklin]."

Smith has said that she was a badly behaved teenager when she attended the local, state-run schools, but this did not prevent her from earning admittance to one of the oldest and most prestigious colleges in Britain—Cambridge University. She majored in English at the university's King's College, nicknamed "The People's Republic of King's" for the left-wing political views associated with it. While Smith discovered that there was only one other black girl at King's College, she did not feel alienated there, since she was able to find "kindred spirits," as she told Sam Wallace for *The Age* (February 5, 2000, on-line). During her years of study, she consciously pursued the prestigious Rylands Prize, awarded by King's College for student fiction and poetry. In her senior year she won the award with a collection of stories.

In 1996 Smith published the story "The Newspaper Man" in *May Anthologies*, a well-regarded annual collection of short stories and poetry by Cambridge and Oxford University students. The story brought her to the attention of the publishing house HarperCollins. It has been reported that Smith offered to write a novel for an advance of $5,000 from the publisher; a friend of hers then intervened and persuaded her to get a literary agent. As a result, Smith spent evenings in the college computer room during the exam-preparation period, writing an 80-page sample chapter to show to agents. The high-profile Andrew Wylie literary agency, whose clients include the novelist Salman Rushdie, signed her on. When the agency auctioned her novel to London publishers, a bidding war began. Smith, then only 21 years old, signed a two-book contract with Penguin Books for a figure said to be in the vicinity of $390,000.

The high level of excitement stirred by *White Teeth*, whose action begins in 1970s Britain, was partly a result of its appeal to a wide range of readers, regardless of age, gender, or politics. Two of the main characters in the sprawling novel are middle-aged men—Samad, a Bengali Muslim, and Archie, a white Englishman—navigating their wartime memories and their marriages to much younger women. The men find themselves bewildered by, and unable to conform to, late-20th-century conventions. Other prominent characters include Samad's twin sons and Archie's biracial daughter, all seeking to define themselves amid the expectations of others. In the novel Smith "exposes the hilarity of the rules we live by," as Nadya Labi put it in *Time* (May 8, 2000), her characters spending their lives in "a negotiation in disappointment." Salman Rushdie called *White Teeth* "an astonishingly assured début," according to the Random House Web site.

White Teeth became a tremendous success, climbing high on the best-seller lists and resulting in a steady flow of glowing reviews for the young writer. Jabari Asim, a senior editor of the *Washington Post Book World* (October 8, 2002), called it a "triumphant debut. . . . [Smith] displayed an admirable gift for tackling serious questions about identity and culture without being preachy or giving over huge stretches of the story to leaden, essayistic passages. In the end, she seemed to be suggesting that we humans are more alike than we are different—and we're all crazy." Daniel Zalewski, writing in the *New York Times* (October 6, 2002), opined, "Reading [Smith's] gloriously undisciplined first novel . . . was like going to a rip-roaring party where you met so many great people it didn't matter that at 4 a.m. the beer suddenly ran out—and some drunk knocked over the stereo. Before crashing to earth with its abrupt, tie-everything-together-in-knots ending, Smith's comic novel . . . soared higher than any other fiction debut had in years."

In addition to earning Smith the Whitbread First Novel Award, the James Tait Black Memorial Prize for fiction, and the Commonwealth Writers First Book Prize, *White Teeth* turned her into a literary celebrity—something that she continues to strongly resist. "I really don't think anyone should write a first novel at my age," Smith confessed to Kevin Jackson in an interview for the *New Yorker* (October 18–25, 1999). "The question is," she said to Sam Wallace, "do you want a writer to carry on writing? If you give them a huge amount of money, that's going to help them in that they're going to have food and heating, but if you turn them into celebrities then you're killing them." In that regard, Smith said she looks up to J. M. Coetzee, the South African writer who is the first novelist to win the prestigious Booker Prize twice and who declined to attend the award ceremony on the second occasion. Smith called this refusal to be drawn into celebrity culture "basic writer survival technique," according to Wallace.

Other novelists whom Smith has singled out as influences are E. M. Forster, John Updike, and Thomas Pynchon. Speaking of recent works by writers of the African diaspora, Smith told Labi, "A lot of black writing is this love-in, and I definitely don't write love-ins." In writing *White Teeth*, Smith sought to defy people's expectations of the subject matter she would tackle, given what Labi called her "personal demographics." "What did people think I was going to write?" Smith asked Labi. "Some kind of searing slave drama or single-girl-in-London tale?" Smith did not entirely avoid drawing from her own experiences, since the background of her character Irie—the daughter of an English man and a Jamaican woman—is similar in many ways to her own. At the same time, the novel's subject matter extends far beyond the autobiographical; her characters include Bengali Muslims, Jews, Jamaicans, teens, and octogenarians. Thanks to her remarkable ear for dialect, those characters' speaking styles emerge as distinct without lapsing into caricature.

All of the hype that Smith received—and its effects on a person and what it says about a society—became the grist for her second novel, *The Autograph Man*. The story's protagonist, Alex-Li Tandem, is a half-Chinese, half-Jewish inhabitant of London who makes a living buying and selling celebrity autographs. In comparison to the profuse, wandering style of *White Teeth*, her second novel was slimmer and more focused. It begins with a scene from Alex's childhood, a time when his father, Li-Jin, took him and his friends Adam, a black Jew, and Rubinfine to see a wrestling match. There, two important things happen—Alex meets Joseph Klein, a boy whose love for autographs leaves a lasting impression on Alex; and Alex's father dies. Back in the present day, Alex is a young man in his mid-20s with a slacker attitude who spends his time taking drugs, mistreating his girlfriend, and hunting down rare autographs. On the 15th anniversary of his father's death, Alex's more religious friends Adam and Joseph urge him to say Kaddish—a Jewish prayer for the dead—for his deceased father. Alex drops everything, however, when a signed photo of Kitty Alexander arrives in the mail. Kitty is a retired 1950s movie star who has bewitched Alex since his youth, and he takes off on a quest—of both commercial and spiritual dimensions—to New York City to meet the reclusive actress.

In the face of high expectations, *The Autograph Man* drew mixed reviews from critics. "Smith's eagerly awaited second novel begins with a bang, but rapidly loses momentum, slipping from tragicomedy to overdetermined farce," an anonymous critic wrote for *Publishers Weekly*, as quoted on *Amazon.com*. "Smith's pen portraits of the shabby, yobbish autograph trading circle are intermittently funny, but her prose is so busy being clever that the laughter never builds. This is disappointing but, even with its faults, the novel points to a literary talent of a high order." Other critics, however, found much to praise. "*The Autograph Man* is, if anything, more knowing and assured than Smith's first work," Sean Rocha remarked in *Library Journal*, as quoted on *Amazon.com*. "If Jewish mysticism and the collectibles market don't entice you, not to worry: the novel's real pleasure lies in the masterfully crafted characters and the small insights that capture something so true of the world that they make the reader sit up in startled recognition."

In an interview with Sarah Lyall for the *New York Times* (December 17, 2002), Smith confessed that—although she did not particularly mind the uneven critical response—she tended to become unhealthily obsessed with the negative reviews. "Everything in the culture is so hysterical," she explained to Lyall. "Everything is fantastic, or it's the worst thing; you should either be given a Nobel Prize or shot at dawn." In the same interview, Smith allowed that she did not think *The Autograph Man* was a great novel, in part because of the trickiness of the theme. "The actual subject of fame is so fatuous. I thought I'd try to deal with it instead of pretending it didn't exist, but maybe it can't be touched without an equal amount of fatuousness coming into the writing." The self-criticism was not new for Smith, who is often her own harshest critic. Earlier, she publicly derided her first novel as "the literary equivalent of a hyperactive, ginger-haired tap-dancing 10-year-old." She qualified the comment in the interview with Lyall: "If I ever criticize *White Teeth*, it's not because I don't think it's an enjoyable book. But sometimes things can be almost too enjoyable. Sometimes they can be morally light about the way life proceeds."

The suitability of the novel as a place for moral enquiry is the focus of a book of essays on which Smith is currently working, while on a writing fellowship at Harvard University, in Cambridge, Massachusetts. She has previously served as a writer-in-residence at the Institute of Contemporary Arts, in London, and her fiction has been published in the *New Yorker*. Smith, whom Sam Wallace described as being "tall with high cheekbones and long curly hair," has an apartment in London, five minutes away from her mother and two brothers, who still reside in Willesden Green.

Although recently some critics of *The Autograph Man* have accused Smith's writing of being derivative, she remains unconcerned—and even positive—about her future. "I'm influenced by everything I read, shamelessly," she told Lyall. "In a review someone said, 'Oh, she sounds very much like [Martin] Amis.' I was flattered by that. I love Amis. Thank you very much. I think if I carry on plagiarizing for 15 years, it will settle like silt, and I'll write something really great."

—V. K., A. I. C.

SUGGESTED READING: *The Age* (on line), Feb. 5, 2000, with photo; *New Yorker* p182 Oct. 18–25, 1999, with photo; *New York Times* VII p13 Oct. 6, 2002, E p1 Dec. 17, 2002; *Salon* (on-line), Apr. 28, 2000; *Time* p94 May 8, 2000, with photo; *Washington Post* C p1 Oct. 8, 2002

SELECTED BOOKS: *White Teeth*, 2000; *The Autograph Man*, 2002

Courtesy of HarperCollins Childrens Books

Snicket, Lemony

1970 (?)– Novelist; children's writer

As the author of *A Series of Unfortunate Events*, a best-selling collection of books, Lemony Snicket, whose real name is Daniel Handler, has created tales that mine the rich English tradition of satire and avoid the overly sentimental tone of much of American children's literature. Written in a droll style and narrated by Mr. Snicket himself, the books—with their tongue-in-cheek humor and over-the-top misadventures—have proven irresistible to children and adults alike. Snicket first warns readers that they will not find any happy endings in his stories of the three Baudelaire siblings and then relates their misery in spades—within the first chapter of the initial book in the series, their parents are killed and their house is burned to the ground. Thus far, Handler has written nine of the quasi-Victorian volumes; he expects to write 13 in all. In addition to *A Series of Unfortunate Events*, he has written two adult novels under his own name: *The Basic Eight* (1999) and *Watch Your Mouth* (2000).

Daniel Handler was born in around 1970 and grew up in San Francisco, California, in an upper-middle-class neighborhood. His mother was a college dean and his father an accountant. As a child he preferred reading quietly in corners to playing sports, but his interest in books never fell to such favorite children's authors as Laura Ingalls Wilder, who wrote the *Little House on the Prairie* books, or J. R. R. Tolkien, the mastermind of the *Lord of the Rings* trilogy. He had little interest in books with either happy endings or magical elements. "I was never much of a fan of books in which people were casting spells," he told Daphne Merkin for the *New York Times Magazine* (April 29, 2001), "and where you had to gather the three powerful rings to fell the dragon." Instead, he preferred reading dark books by such authors as Edward Gorey, Roald Dahl, and Zilpha Keatley Snyder.

After graduating from Wesleyan College, in Middletown, Connecticut, Handler lived in New York City for five years, before returning to his native San Francisco, in 2000. His first book was aimed at adults. *The Basic Eight* (1999), according to Merkin, "is told in pitch-perfect teenagerese and demonstrates an unerring comprehension of the murderous maneuvers of high-school cliques." His second adult book was titled *Watch Your Mouth* (2000). Billed as an "incest comedy," it received less-than-stellar reviews, including one from Rebecca Sturm-Kelm in *Library Journal* (June 1, 2000), who called it "ambitious but flawed." However, the strength of these works, in which Handler seemed to inhabit the lives of his teenage characters, led many editors to suggest that he write a children's novel. Up until that time he had never considered doing so, but he was eventually convinced by Susan Rich, an editor at HarperCollins, to try it. As Rich told Sally Lodge for *Publishers Weekly* (May 29, 2000), "I greatly admired his writing for adults and decided to try to lure him over to our side—the children's side. I knew we shared a similar sensibility about children's books, which I'd define as a resistance to fall into the overly trodden paths of traditional stories, and a resistance to anything that is too sweet or patronizing or moralistic."

Handler had been writing a mock-gothic adult novel, and after his discussions with Rich, he began to rework it for a young audience. Although he secretly felt that his ideas were too gruesome for children's literature, his editor and the staff at HarperCollins were encouraging, and Handler began to hope that the book might find an audience. "I thought maybe they'd [publish] two of them, and they'd have a tiny, tiny cult audience," he told Merkin. In order to separate these books from his adult work, he took on the pen name Lemony Snicket, which had been part of a joke between Handler and his friends; the group occasionally wrote letters to newspapers and reserved tables in restaurants under the fictitious name.

The first of Lemony Snicket's *A Series of Unfortunate Events* books, *The Bad Beginning*, was published in 1999. Though Handler, as Snicket, warns the reader: "If you are interested in stories with happy endings, you would be better off reading some other book," such a caveat only serves as an invitation to witness the miserable lives of Violet, Klaus, and Sunny Baudelaire unfold. Orphaned within the first few pages of the book, they are sent to live with their evil relative, Count Olaf, who schemes to get their fortune. There they are forced to clean his crumbling house, sleep in a single lumpy bed, eat oatmeal, wear itchy clothing, and do endless chores—including chopping wood for a fireplace that Olaf doesn't have.

The Bad Beginning was lauded in the press. In the *School Library Journal* (November 1999), Linda Binder wrote: "While the misfortunes hover on the edge of being ridiculous, Snicket's energetic blend of humor, dramatic irony, and literary flair makes it all perfectly believable. The writing, peppered with fairly sophisticated vocabulary and phrases, may seem daunting, but the inclusion of Snicket's perceptive definitions of difficult words makes these books challenging to older readers and excellent for reading aloud." Writing for *CNN.com* (December 27, 1999), Nancy Matson proclaimed: "This is a tale aptly told, never faltering from its humorous tone, and able to maintain a number of running jokes which enrich the story." This first book in the series was quickly followed by *The Reptile Room* (1999), in which, according to the official Lemony Snicket Web site, "the three siblings endure a car accident, a terrible odor, a deadly serpent, a long knife, a large brass reading lamp, and the reappearance of a person they'd hoped never to see again."

Three more sequels followed in 2000: *The Wide Window*, *The Miserable Mill*, and *The Austere Academy*. In each of these, as in their two predecessors, the Baudelaire children are subjected to a variety of horrible situations, including more encounters with Count Olaf. In *The Wide Window*, Olaf pursues them to the house of their Aunt Josephine, whom he shoves into the leech-infested waters surrounding her house. Handler's sardonic style is in full force here, but it had begun to grate on the nerves of some critics. As Marlene Gawron wrote in the *School Library Journal* (January 2000): "The narrator is humorous but intrusive, explaining words and providing many obvious clues that surface later. Aunt Josephine's constant correction of vocabulary and grammar, while at first humorous, becomes annoying. The book is really not bad; it just tries too hard and there are so many similar books that are much better."

Some found Snicket's style just as amusing by the time he wrote *The Austere Academy*. In the *New York Times Book Review*, Gregory Maguire (October 15, 2000) remarked: "Formulaic? Self-consciously, generously, joyously so. The fun derives from watching the formula work. . . . [Handler] has taken a small handful of storytelling tricks

... and he has made them convulse in convincing sequence, so that despite the contrivance there is something vivid and even urgent about these tales."

In 2001 Handler, as Snicket, published three more volumes about the Baudelaire children's misadventures: *The Ersatz Elevator, The Vile Village,* and *The Hostile Hospital.* In them, the siblings face even more twisted perils—secret passageways and darkened staircases, a creepy village populated by an angry mob, and a hospital where unnecessary surgery is performed. In the ninth and most recent volume in the series, *The Carnivorous Carnival* (2002), the Baudelaire siblings are hiding out at the Caligari Carnival, disguising themselves as carnival freaks in order to investigate the mysterious Madame Lulu. "Children faithful to the series won't be surprised when the book does NOT end happily; nor will they find it unusual that Snicket continues to entertain with witty asides and a satirical point of view," Susan Dove Lempke wrote for *Booklist,* as quoted on *Amazon.com.* "The overall story moves along nicely toward the conclusion of the planned 13-volume series; at the same time, the author successfully uses this book as a platform to communicate a good deal about individuals who belittle others and what it feels like to be on the end of the horrible barbs."

To satiate his fans' curiosity about the mysterious Snicket, who as the narrator of the *Unfortunate Events* series often appears to have some shadowy connection to the Baudelaire orphans, in 2002 Handler published *Lemony Snicket: The Unauthorized Autobiography.* The contents of the book—an odd assortment of documents such as letters, newspaper articles, and transcripts of meetings and conversations—playfully added to the series's lingering puzzles, however, rather than dispelling them. "[The book] is bizarre, abstruse, and truly entertaining," Emilie Coulter wrote in a review for *Amazon.com.* "Virtually every detail of the volume has Snicket's indelible mark, from the book jacket (reversible to help readers disguise this 'extremely dangerous' and 'objectionable' autobiography) to the copyright page text to the intentionally blurry and bewildering black-and-white photographs appearing throughout."

While not rivaling the astronomical sales of the Harry Potter series by J. K. Rowling, the series has grown in popularity since its initial volume's release, with each successive volume generating a larger first printing than the last. (Many critics have noted that the illustrations of Klaus bear an uncanny resemblance to those of Harry Potter; Handler explained to Daphne Merkin, "All bookish white boys with glasses look alike.") Cleverly packaged to resemble Victorian-era dime-store novels, the books feature patterned endpapers, a personalized bookplate, and sturdy bindings. The series has found admirers both young and old and seems likely to complete its expected 13-volume run. Nickelodeon has purchased the film and television rights and is currently developing a series based on the books. In addition, foreign rights to the books have been sold in Italy, Germany, Denmark, and Norway.

At his bookstore readings, Handler is part comic writer and part actor. He bursts into the room announcing that Mr. Snicket has taken ill from a bug bite under his arm and has sent him in his stead. He then passes around a bug so that the children can study it, warning them to never raise their hands in class because bugs like to bite people under the arm. "We get the occasional super-gullible bookstore clerk employee who comes over and says, 'I'm so sad Lemony Snicket wasn't able to be here,'" Handler told Merkin, "but for the most part people over 10—and under 10, really—figure it out."

Handler is currently working on the rest of the series chronicling the adventures of the Baudelaire siblings; he is also writing a collection of stories and a third adult novel. He is collaborating on a musical with his friend Stephen Merritt, of the rock group Magnetic Fields. Handler maintains a strict routine, getting up at seven to drive his wife, Lisa Brown, a designer and illustrator, to work, before returning home to write on a laptop computer from nine to four. "I do a draft, print it out and then ink things in," he told Daphne Merkin. "And then, I watch junky movies. That's my uncool life."

—C. M.

SUGGESTED READING: *CNN.com* Dec. 27, 1999; *Horn Book* p239+ Mar./Apr. 2001; Lemony Snicket Web site; *Library Journal* p196 June 1, 2000; *Maclean's* p84+ Dec. 18, 2000; *New York Times Book Review* p23 Aug. 20, 2000, p30 Oct. 15, 2000; *New York Times Magazine,* p62+ Apr. 29, 2001; *Publishers Weekly* p42+ May 29, 2000; *School Library Journal* p165+ Nov. 1999, p136 Jan. 2000; *Time for Kids* p7 Apr. 27, 2001

SELECTED BOOKS: as Lemony Snicket—*The Bad Beginning,* 1999; *The Reptile Room,* 1999; *The Wide Window,* 2000; *The Miserable Mill,* 2000; *The Austere Academy,* 2000; *The Ersatz Elevator,* 2001; *The Vile Village,* 2001; *The Hostile Hospital,* 2001; *The Carnivorous Carnival,* 2002; *Lemony Snicket: The Unauthorized Autobiography,* 2002; as Daniel Handler—*The Basic Eight,* 1999; *Watch Your Mouth,* 2000

Courtesy of Simon & Schuster

Solomon, Andrew

Oct. 30, 1963– Novelist; nonfiction writer

Andrew Solomon delves deeply into his topics, unearthing vast amounts of information for his books and magazine pieces, and including personal reflections and revelations, as well. For his first book, *The Irony Tower* (1991), Solomon immersed himself in the lives of avant-garde Soviet artists to gain an understanding of how their lives had changed under Mikhail Gorbachev's policy of *glasnost* (openness), in the mid- 1980s. His most recent book, *The Noonday Demon: An Atlas of Depression* (2001), provides a comprehensive overview of the mental illness and, in addition, chronicles Solomon's personal battle with depression. *A Stone Boat* (1994), his first work of fiction, also drew largely on his own life.

Andrew Solomon was born on October 30, 1963 in New York City, the son of Carolyn (Bower) Solomon and Howard Solomon, the president of Forest Laboratories, a $12- billion research firm that develops medicines. "I'm very proud of my father," Solomon told William Hamilton for the *New York Times* (May, 17, 2001, on-line). "He's an entirely self-made man. He grew up waiting on milk lines in the Bronx. His great love was always music, and he got a job when he was 13 selling librettos at the old Met because he loved opera. Now, he's chairman of the City Ballet and on the board of the opera." Solomon received his bachelor's degree, from Yale University, in 1985. He then attended Jesus College at Cambridge University, in England, and received a second bachelor's degree, in 1987, and a master's degree, in 1992.

In his first book, *The Irony Tower*, Solomon covers the history of avant-garde Soviet art, and details the artists' frequent clashes with government officials, who found their works to be obscene or antiauthoritarian. He traveled to the Soviet Union to study how the lives of artists there had changed since Gorbachev took power and granted them more freedom of expression than in any other period in the Communist state's history. He found that the Soviet art movement had split into two factions after the easing of restrictions; one group was comprised of those artists who sought the recognition long denied them and whose work sold well in Western auctions, and the others, who preferred to stay doggedly noncommercial.

The Irony Tower received mixed reviews. In the *New York Times Book Review* (July 28, 1991), Harlow Robinson called it a "timely, perceptive and highly entertaining combination of art criticism, social analysis and personal revelation," and later in the review noted: "Occasional lapses into condescension and pompous critical jargon notwithstanding, Mr. Solomon knows how to tell a good story. . . . What makes *The Irony Tower* special is not just its wealth of new and fascinating material, or even the lively intelligence of the analysis. It is Mr. Solomon's deep compassion for these artists." On the other hand, Amy Lewontin complained in her review for *Library Journal* (June 15, 1991): "While he writes extremely well about art and its relation to Soviet society, Solomon is not an accomplished storyteller, and the reader is left swimming alone with a string of names, unable to fully distinguish one artist from another either through their work or their personalities. This could have been a fascinating book, yet one never gets a clear sense of what effects glasnost or capitalist society have had on the Soviet art world or the individual artists."

In 1994 Solomon published his first novel, *A Stone Boat*. In it, Harry, a young bisexual pianist, deals with conflicting emotions when he discovers that his mother is dying from cancer. While he loves her for nurturing his musical talent, he is angered by her assertion that her cancer has been caused by the stress of having a bisexual son. (Solomon himself is bisexual, and his own mother committed suicide, after being diagnosed with ovarian cancer in 1989.) "*A Stone Boat* is a shimmering remembrance of things past and a meditation on love and death," Alison Carb Sussman wrote for the *New York Times Book Review* (November 13, 1994). "Mr. Solomon's novel could use less rumination and more dialogue, as well as fuller coverage of the motivations of minor characters; nevertheless, it evokes with sensitivity and compassion the severing of a deeply rooted, complex relationship."

Solomon returned to nonfiction for his next book, *The Noonday Demon: An Atlas of Depression*, in which he not only chronicles his own struggle with depression after the death of his mother, but the history of depression in societies around the world, as well as the various methods used to study and treat it. Critics reacted favorably to Solomon's frank discussions of his bisexuality, thoughts of suicide, and therapy, and were also greatly impressed with the research he had done for *The Noontime Demon.* "God knows Solomon's done his homework, and then some," David Gates wrote for *Newsweek* (June 11, 2001). "He's traveled to Greenland, Thailand and Africa to check out indigenous styles of depression, visited mental hospitals, talked to the obligatory experts with the obligatory conflicting points of view, poked around in history and done extensive interviews with real people . . . who tell stories both more awful and more uplifting than his own." In the *New York Times Book Review* (June 24, 2001), the novelist Joyce Carol Oates remarked: "*The Noonday Demon* is a considerable accomplishment. It is likely to provoke discussion and controversy, and its generous assortment of voices, from the pathological to the philosophical, makes for rich, variegated reading."

Solomon takes five medications daily, and his depression is currently under control. He credits his father, who nursed him during the worst periods of his illness, with "[giving] me life not once, but twice," as he told William Hamilton. He is a frequent contributor to *Artform*, *HG*, the *New York Times Magazine*, and the *New Yorker*. He has a brother, David, and lives alone in a five-story brownstone in Lower Manhattan that was once the home of the poet Emma Lazarus. Solomon told Hamilton that his house and its decor were reflections of himself: "Bigger than life, enthusiastic, imaginative, and a lot of fun."

—C. M.

SUGGESTED READING: *Interview* p48+ June 2001; *Library Journal* p74 June 15, 1991; *New York Times* (on- line) May 17, 2001; *New York Times Book Review* p5 July 28, 1991, p58 Nov. 13, 1994, p9+ June 24, 2001; *Newsweek* p56 June 11, 2001

SELECTED BOOKS: nonfiction—*The Irony Tower* (1991); *Noonday Demon: An Atlas of Depression* (2001); fiction—*The Stone Boat* (1994)

Staples, Brent

Sep. 13, 1951– Journalist; memoirist; editor

The African-American journalist and memoirist Brent Staples entered the literary consciousness of the English-speaking world when he published *Parallel Time: Growing Up in Black and White* (1994). The autobiography describes in poetic language Staples's childhood and young manhood, focusing on his growing detachment from his family members, who were drawn into a world of drug using and dealing, early childbearing, and early death. Staples, by contrast, went on to graduate school and eventually to a position on the editorial board of the *New York Times*, where the commentaries carrying his byline often address the topic of race.

Brent Staples was born on September 13, 1951 in Chester, Pennsylvania, one of the nine surviving children of Geneva Brown Staples and Melvin Staples and the oldest of their five sons. The family was poor; although Melvin Staples made "a handsome living" as a truck driver for the Blue Line Transfer Co., "much of what he earned he drank up," as Brent Staples wrote in *Parallel Time*. "My mother lacked the skill to stretch what was left." Staples's mother was charitable to an extreme, often taking in young people who had been abandoned by their families, sometimes after they had become pregnant. The family moved frequently, usually due to imminent—or actual—eviction. At one point Staples's mother and father split up; they later reconciled, only to separate again. The family lived for a time in Roanoke, Virginia, close to the parents' hometown.

The *New York Times*/Courtesy of Brent Staples

Staples was permanently marked by those moves. "As a child I was never where I was," he wrote in *Parallel Time*. "Part of me raced ahead looking for a foothold in the future. Part of me was somewhere behind rushing to catch up." (As an adult, he wrote, he lived for stretches of five years and longer in apartments that he could not bring himself to furnish: "Grown and out on my own, I was phobically wary of possessions, of anything that would trouble me when it was time to go.") One of Staples's greatest fears as a child was of losing his memories, of having no grasp on "moments I'd lived."

In high school Staples took what he described as a secretarial course of study. He also appeared in a production of Lorraine Hansberry's play *Raisin in the Sun*, emulating one of his heroes, Sidney Poitier. To try out for the play, he made up a monologue "on the spot," adopting the character of a man working in a bottling factory: "Cap on bottle. Cap on bottle. Cap on bottle," he repeated. "The monologue sprang from a primal source. The man watching the bottles go by was me. This was my failure dream, the ritual of meaningless acts that was out there, waiting to claim me." Staples exhibited political consciousness during this period, allying himself to the goals of the Black Panther Party.

Despite his family's poverty and his pessimism about his future, Staples was able to attend college with the help of a remedial-training and financial-aid program called Project Prepare, through which he participated in a kind of academic boot camp with 23 other young black men. He graduated cum laude from Penn Morton College (now Widener University), in Chester, in 1973, with a B.A. degree in behavioral science, after making the dean's list numerous times. From there he pursued graduate studies at the University of Chicago through a Danforth Fellowship, one of the nation's most prestigious academic awards.

Staples's success in his studies was coupled with an acute awareness of racism, both institutionalized and casual. One instance he wrote about involved a University of Chicago psychology professor, whom Staples approached in the hope of enrolling in her class. Disregarding, or unaware of, the fact that Staples as an undergraduate had fallen six one-hundredths of a percentage point short of graduating magna cum laude, she accepted him with the air of one making a benevolent gesture, based on the need for racial reparations. In another example in *Parallel Time*, Staples recalled learning that Robert Maynard Hutchins, developer of the "great books" program at the university, was implicated in efforts to clear people of color out of the neighborhood surrounding the campus. After Hutchins's death, these efforts continued, one result being that Staples saw his friends lose their basketball court. "A neighborhood that had once played host to [the jazz musicians] Charlie Parker, Miles Davis, and Earl (Fatha) Hines was devoid of music. By the time I arrived in Hyde Park, not a single jazz club remained. The ghetto had been beaten back, but sterility was the cost," he wrote.

Staples also noticed that his physical presence made many white strangers visibly uncomfortable. Whereas initially he tried to ease their fear—for example, by smiling at them on the street—he eventually came to resent their reactions to him. He directed his anger into a game that he called "Scatter the Pigeons." A fairly large man, he would walk toward couples, who, showing fear, would draw together; he would then position himself so that they had to separate to pass him. He would also approach white strangers and greet them loudly, delighting in their fear. Staples achieved a degree of notoriety after he wrote about how he had stalked the Nobel Prize–winning novelist Saul Bellow. While he admired the work of Bellow, who taught at the University of Chicago, Staples was disturbed by the way characters in the writer's novels viewed black men. "These passages made me angry," Staples wrote. "It was the same anger I felt when white people cowered as I passed them on the street." (Staples also revealed that he followed the novelist for other reasons: "I wanted something from him. The longing was deep. . . . I wanted to steal the essence of him, to absorb it right into my bones." He added, describing his beginnings as an essayist, that he sometimes stole from the works of Bellow, who was "the writer I knew best. I mimicked his phrasing and his body-snatching eye.")

After Staples received his Ph.D. in psychology, in 1982, having written a dissertation on the mathematics of decision making, he taught at the college level. Although he "had dreamed of becoming an Ivy League professor," no Ivy League college recruited him. He wrote that he "woke up from [his] Ivy League dream at Roosevelt University," where he came to see himself as merely one of an army of adjunct professors who had little chance of obtaining tenure-track positions and were forced to move from college to college. ("Adjuncts didn't get fired; they escaped," he wrote.)

Meanwhile, he wrote constantly, chronicling the happenings around him. He soon went into journalism, joining the staff of the *Chicago Sun-Times* as a reporter, in 1983. He remained in that post for two years, also contributing to the *Chicago Reader* and writing about jazz for *Down Beat* and *Jazz Hot–Paris*. In 1985 he began his association with the *New York Times*, serving as an editor of the paper's *Book Review* and then as assistant metropolitan editor before joining the editorial board, in 1990. In that post he continues to write about politics and culture, focusing often on race.

Meanwhile, the 1984 shooting death of Staples's younger brother Blake, a drug dealer, was a signal event in Staples's life. Both the first and last chapters of *Parallel Time* are accounts of Blake's murder, the path that led to it, and Brent Staples's attempts to remove his brother from that path. "Certain trains you can see coming," Staples told Mary Ann French, who interviewed him for the *Washington Post* (March 17, 1994). "There are some people who are standing right on the tracks. And no matter what you tell them, you find them back there on those tracks in the morning." A passage from *Parallel Time* discusses his absence from his brother's funeral: "I'd done my mourning in advance. But this was self-deception on a monstrous scale. The rituals of grief and burial bear the dead away. Cheat those rituals and you risk keeping the dead with you in forms that you mightn't like. Choose carefully the funerals you miss."

Parallel Time was praised by numerous reviewers and won the Anisfield-Wolf Book Award, which is given by the Cleveland Foundation to recognize works that address issues of racism and celebrate human diversity. In the *New York Times* (March 24, 1994), Michael Eric Dyson praised Staples's "resolutely distinct voice as he negotiates the treacherous shoals of racial identity in American culture. . . . *Parallel Time* reminds us that the best personal writing is born of the courage to confront oneself." Paul Galloway noted in the *Chicago Tribune* (March 7, 1994), "Staples writes with humor and insight about the warmth and the tyranny of family and the wondrous and frightening expedition through childhood, his serendipitous decision to attend college, and then gain a graduate fellowship at one of the nation's most prestigious universities." In a conversation with Galloway, Staples said that *Parallel Time* "is a literary work. Being black enriches my experience; it doesn't define me." David Nicholson, writing for *American Visions* (May 1994), agreed that it was "a book by a black man that does not focus on race. It is almost misleading to call *Parallel Time* a black book. The truth is that it is an *American* story, a celebration of one of the many strands of the American experience."

Placing Staples in a category with the Italian novelist, poet, memoirist, and Holocaust survivor Primo Levi, Verlyn Klinkenborg wrote for the *New York Times Book Review* (February 20, 1994) that for such writers "the sadness of memory comes from recognizing yet again what they have never really forgotten: how powerless they are to help others escape what they escaped." Staples has pointed out that his own "escape" owed much to affirmative action, which he continues to champion. Alluding to himself in an editorial for the *New York Times* (March 5, 1995), Staples wrote, "This black boy who was 'not college material' went on to earn a Ph.D. at the University of Chicago. . . . There are thousands of stories like this one. But in the Reaganaut 80's, many African-Americans who could tell those stories became converts to the gospel of Horatio Alger, suddenly claiming that success had been earned through hard work and rectitude alone. . . . The convert's role I will never play. . . . When I was 17, the society spotted me a few points on the S.A.T.'s and changed my life. I became a writer—and a middle-class taxpayer—as many other black men went on to prisons, cemeteries, and homeless shelters. Sounds like a smart investment to me. The country would be wise to keep making it."

Staples received an honorary doctorate in humane letters from Mount St. Mary College, in Newburgh, New York, in 2000. The school cited him for taking on, in his editorials, "some of today's hottest, often controversial, subjects, including racial profiling, the erosion of values and the literacy gap," and "for shining light in dark spaces." On September 16, 2000 Staples married Julie Williams Johnson, a former journalist who is currently a senior managing director at the public-relations firm Hill & Knowlton. In a *New York Times* (March 12, 2000) editorial titled "How a Black Man's Wallet Becomes a Gun" (which concerned the death of an unarmed West African immigrant at the hands of New York City police in 1999), Staples revealed that his then-fiancée has a teenage son.

—S. Y.

SUGGESTED READING: *American Visions* p28+ May 1994, with photo; *Chicago Tribune* XIV p3 Feb. 13, 1999, V p1 Mar. 7, 1994; *New York Times* C p15 Mar. 21, 1994, IV p14 Mar. 5, 1995, ST p12 Sep. 17, 2000, with photo; *New York Times Book Review* p1+ Feb. 20, 1994, with photo; *Times Literary Supplement* p14 June 10, 1994; *Washington Post* D p1 Mar. 17, 1994

SELECTED BOOKS: *Parallel Time: Growing Up in Black and White*, 1994

Stepto, Robert B.

Oct. 28, 1945– Critic; memoirist

A critic and scholar who specializes in the literature of the African diaspora in the United States, Robert Burns Stepto has for most of his career been affiliated with what is now called the Department of African and African-American Studies at Yale University, where he is also professor or English and American Studies. During the 1970s, as chair of a key Modern Language Association commission, he organized important scholarly conferences with the aim of more effectively including African-American literature in the nation's university curricula. His first book was *From Behind the Veil: A Study of Afro-American Narrative* (1979). He co-edited several other important critical and pedagogical studies, including (with Dexter Fisher) *Afro-American Literature: The Reconstruction of Instruction* (1979) and (with Michael S. Harper) *Chant of Saints: A Gathering of Afro-American Literature, Art, and Scholarship* (1979). He has also edited scholarly monographs on Sterling Brown and Jay Wright. Stepto's memoir, *Blue as the Lake: A Personal Geography*, was published in 1998; its nine essays of migration and memory mapped a nostalgic portrait of 20th-century life as lived by a relatively privileged strata of African-Americans.

Robert Burns Stepto was born in Chicago, Illinois, on October 28, 1945, the son of Robert Charles Stepto, a physician and professor of medicine, and Ann Burns Stepto, a teacher. He received his bachelor's degree in English from Trinity College, in Hartford, Connecticut, in 1966 and his master's and Ph.D. degrees in the same discipline from Stanford University, in 1968 and 1974. Stepto's first faculty appointment was as assistant professor of English at Williams College from 1971 to

1974, after which he joined the Yale University faculty as assistant professor of English (1971–79) and became affiliated with Yale University's Department of Afro-American Studies as director of undergraduate studies (1974–77). He also served as its director of graduate studies (1978–81, 1985–89, Spring 1994).

Stepto's first book, *From Behind the Veil: A Study of Afro-American Narrative*, was published in 1979 and reissued in 1991, around the time that he began to attract notice as a literary critic and chronicler of the African-American literary tradition. In 1977, as chair of the Modern Language Association's Commission on the Literatures and Languages of America, Stepto had directed at Yale a two-week seminar, "Afro-American Literature," which was funded by the National Endowment for the Humanities. The meeting, whose staff included the 31-year-old Stepto and a 27-year-old Henry Louis Gates Jr., among other junior scholars, invited participants to "reconstruct the instruction" of such literature. Thirteen papers from the seminar were published as *Afro-American Literature: The Reconstruction of Instruction*, co-edited by Stepto and Dexter Fisher; in it, the editors claimed that the seminar was "one of the first efforts of its kind in the Afro-American field to pursue aggressively such issues as folklore as process, intertextuality, black speech as poetic diction, and the distinction between literary history and literary chronology." Stepto contributed two of his own essays to this collection: "Teaching Afro-American Literature: Survey or Tradition: The Reconstruction of Tradition" and "Narration, Authentication, and Authorial Control in Frederick Douglass' Narrative of 1845." In the former paper, which introduced the collection, Stepto argued that, by and large, Afro-American literature is disserved "primarily because of the antiquated ways in which it is taught and discussed in critical writing." He criticized what he called the "all-purpose Black Studies essay," which leads students to feel that "an essay containing an occult potpourri of references to Frederick Douglass, Frantz Fanon, and Richard Wright is acceptable in any Afro-American studies course taught by any teacher regardless of the discipline in which the course is situated." Contrarily, Stepto raised the "simple, haunting fact that Afro-American history and social science are being taught while Afro-American language, literacy, and literature are not" and concluded, "Our mission as teachers is clear: Afro-American literature must be taught, and taught as a literature. Only then will our students learn of a culture's quest for literacy and in turn gain the literacy with which to sustain the tradition."

The year 1979 also saw the publication of *Chant of Saints: A Gathering of Afro-American Literature, Arts, and Scholarship*, an anthology of essays, interviews, and fiction that Stepto co-edited with Michael S. Harper. Original interviews, as with Ralph Ellison, Toni Morrison, and Gayl Jones, were "prepared expressly" for the book, Stepto wrote in a preface that explored the nature of the anthology and of the "Afro-American canon." Stepto himself conducted the interviews with Ellison and Morrison. He continued: "*Chant* is a gathering that has grown from a few poems and essays in hand in 1975 to the kind of rich tapestry that appears to embrace and define a literal and figurative world." He cautioned, however, that "*Chant* expresses the Afro-American canon in only a rough (but diamond rough!) way, primarily because the editors' energies were directed to another concern . . . we were far more greatly motivated by the goal of selecting first-rate expressions of varying genres and disciplines that speak to one another, and thereby suggest an artistic continuum, than by the tempting but ultimately secondary (or tertiary) concern of announcing who and what is in and out of some small circle. . . . In sum, we want *Chant of Saints* to be *read*; at its best, it is an epic and familial poem—and, for those who need it, it is a place to begin."

Stepto contributed two of his own essays to *Chant*: one on Richard Wright and the Afro-American literary tradition, and a second, entitled "After Modernism, After Hibernation: Michael Harper, Robert Hayden and Jay Wright." In the former essay, Stepto addressed the dilemma of how to place Wright within the "Afro-American canon" partly because of a "growing concern over how often 'canon,' 'survey,' and 'tradition' have been casually treated as synonymous terms and unthinkingly interchanged." Stepto expounded on the ways in which Wright's "ambivalent attitude toward his race and its rituals" made him a problematic figure in the continuum of African-American literary accomplishment. In "After Modernism, After Hibernation," Stepto examined the meaning of Ralph Ellison's definition of "hibernation" in his novel *Invisible Man* as "a covert preparation for a more overt action" and discussed poems by Harper, Hayden, and Wright "as responses to the prefiguring call of Mr. Ellison's novel and hence, in light of my definition, as post-modernist expressions." Stepto co-edited, with John M. Reilly, *Afro-American Literature: The Reconstruction of a Literary History* (1981) and edited two monographs on African-American writers of the 20th century: Sterling Brown (1901–1989) and Jay Wright (1935–). He also edited *Selected Poems of Jay Wright* (1987), to which he contributed the introduction.

Published in 1998 by Beacon Press, *Blue as the Lake: A Personal Geography* is Stepto's personal memoir, divided into three sections with three essays apiece, several of which had earlier appeared in the pages of *Callaloo*, an African-American literary journal. The first section, "Paths of One's Invention," describes the three anchorages of Stepto's boyhood: Idlewild, Michigan, the idyllic retreat where the Stepto family summered in the 1940s and 1950s; Washington Park, the thriving black neighborhood on the South Side of Chicago, where young Stepto lived with his extended, multigenerational family; and Woodlawn, another Chicago neighborhood, to which the Steptos migrated in the early 1950s. In "Woodlawn," the author reflected on the disappearance of community over the past generation, as when he wrote: "Driving around Woodlawn as I have recently, I am moved—stricken, actually—by how the neighborhood has been wasted, as if by war or disease." To the author, his boyhood neighborhood was "neither upscale nor (yet) downtrodden; it was simply full of people, black and white, bustling about, making a living, putting food on the table, seeking simple pleasures, finding respite from the summer heat in cool movie houses, restoring themselves after a trudge in the winter snow with a cup of coffee and maybe some lunch-counter banter. In short, there was activity, and while not all of the activity was wholesome or edifying . . . it mostly seemed to be about living, not dying—about getting on, not simply getting over." In "Migrations," the second part of the book, Stepto cast a fond glance at some of his immediate ancestors—including the celebrated jazz saxophonist Coleman Hawkins, a cousin of his mother's father—who, in the years around World War I, migrated from the South through Baltimore or Missouri. The final section, "Blue as the Lake," a reference to Lake Michigan, brought Stepto's meditations into the present, as he looked back on his roots of half a century. In "Hyde Park," the middle essay in this section, Stepto recounted an awkward visit with his elderly father, still living in Chicago.

In "Vineyard," the essay that followed and that concluded *Blue as the Lake*, Stepto mused, sometimes disdainfully, on the commercial culture that had invaded Martha's Vineyard in the 1990s, when it became the haven of many successful African-Americans. He wrote: "The Vineyard is my Idlewild, or rather I am in the process of seeking on the Vineyard the sense of well-being I believe Grandpa Burns found in Idlewild. . . . above all for me, the Vineyard is where my boyhood and adulthood collide and converge. It is where my inherited woodland, freshwater Midwest self and my invented shoreline, saltwater New England self look at each other—and embrace." Stepto wrote that his idyllic dreams for "the Vineyard" were often mediated, by "the charged sense of race that arrives with the droves of people vacationing in August, and that is in its way another kind of late summer humidity. Indeed, in August particularly, the business of vacation has become the business of race, and that is surely the biggest change on the island since my youth." Seeking a personalized image to represent his own stance, he rejects standardized posters and vulgar T-shirts in favor of the one he considers his "race shirt": one from the Penn Center on St. Helena, one of the South Carolina Sea Islands, the site of one of the first schools for former slaves. The shirt depicts woven seagrass baskets that demonstrate the ancestral heritage of St. Helena's settlers from Sierra Leone. "I like this tee-shirt," Stepto wrote. "It is my race shirt. It is an island shirt, it is a New World shirt. Its baskets, so beautifully woven, have room in them for me and mine."

Reviewing *Blue as the Lake* for *Publishers Weekly* (July 27, 1998), Deb Chapman declared: "Only the final essay, with its cranky observations about black youth culture and the marketing of black images on Martha's Vineyard, falls short of the elegance of the other pieces. Overall, though, these evocative meditations on home and family are thoughtful and moving." And Laurel Green, writing in the *New York Times Book Review* (October 11, 1998), found the "graceful family memoir" most engaging for "Stepto's recollections of his kin—a great-great-great grandmother who could describe in detail the building of the Smithsonian, the jazz saxophonist Coleman Hawkins, his great-granduncle Will, who one night lit his pipe, buttoned his coat and walked deep into the Missouri River to drown." These images, Green wrote, "meld beautifully with his generous evocations of time and place."

Stepto and Michele Leiss, now a college professor, were married in 1967. They have two children, Gabriel Burns and Rafael Hawkins Stepto.

—E. M.

SUGGESTED READING: *African American Review* p473+ Fall 1994; *American Literature* p673+ Dec. 1987; *Booklist* p1958 Aug. 1998; *Callaloo* p801+ Fall 1990, p907+ Fall 1991, p20+ Winter 1991, p94+ Winter 1996, p36+ Winter 1997, p940+ Fall 1998; *Condé Nast Traveler* p106 Sep. 1998; *Jet* p18 May 9, 1994; *New England Review* p94+ Winter 1995; *New York Times Magazine* p10 Apr. 4, 1993; *New York Times Book Review* p21 Oct. 11, 1998; *Publishers Weekly* p61 July 27, 1998; *Who's Who Among African Americans, 1998–99*

SELECTED BOOKS: nonfiction—*From Behind the Veil: A Study of Afro-American Narrative*, 1979; *The Selected Poems of Jay Wright*, 1987; *Blue as the Lake: A Personal Geography*, 1998; as co-editor—*Chant of Saints: A Gathering of Afro-American Literature, Art and Scholarship* (with M. S. Harper), 1979; *Afro-American Literature: The Reconstruction of Instruction* (with D. Fisher), 1979; *Afro-American Literature: The Reconstruction of a Literary History* (with J. M. Reilly), 1981; *The Collected Papers of Sterling Brown, Volume I* (with R. O'Meally), 1981; *The Harper American Literature* (with D. McQuade et al.), 1993

Jerry Bauer/Courtesy of Houghton Mifflin

Stevenson, Jane

Feb. 12, 1959– Novelist

Jane Stevenson has received praise from critics for her well-plotted stories, which tend to feature characters notable for their erudition and wit. Her first published fiction, *Several Deceptions* (1999), is a collection of four novellas. Marcel Theroux, writing for the *New York Times Book Review* (September 23, 2001), found it to be a "sly and sophisticated" work that "roamed confidently among unusual locations and difficult ideas." *London Bridges* (2000), set in contemporary London, is a self-conscious reworking of classic English detective fiction. Stevenson's next two novels, *Astraea* (2001; published in the U.S. in 2002 as *The Winter Queen*) and *The Pretender* (2002), are part of a projected trilogy which begins in 17th-century Holland story with an unlikely love affair between two exiles—an African prince and the Queen of Bohemia. She is also an editor of several scholarly texts.

Jane Barbara Stevenson writes the following autobiographical statement for *World Authors 1995–2000*: " I am a novelist who is also an academic—not that uncommon; think of A.S. Byatt, David Lodge, Umberto Eco, even J.R.R. Tolkien. I don't see these practices as antithetic, perhaps because I am a historian rather than a critic. My academic work, which has ranged from a study of St. Theodore of Tarsus and his school at Canterbury in the seventh century to a collection of early modern women's poetry, has always been very much focussed on people: how a particular milieu makes some patterns of thought likely, but others impossible, how actions follow from events. The art which goes into understanding the constraints which governed the life of a soap-boiler's daughter who was writing Latin verse in seventeenth-century Rome (a true story) is closely allied to the art of the novelist. All fiction has to be researched, not just historical novels, since it is necessary to understand the circumstances of character's lives in order to carry conviction. Groping for an understanding of human action and motivation is the business of my life, though some of the people I write about are imaginary and others are real.

"I was born in London in 1959, my parents' first child. My father, John Lynn Stevenson, was Scotto-Irish, my mother, Winifred Temple, was from Berwick on Tweed. Both were working-class high achievers, the first members of their respective families to go to University. My mother stayed in academia at first, while my father went into the Foreign Office and became a Chinese specialist. I don't think they quite realised at the time that it would be impossible for them both to pursue their careers because of the travelling. When I was three months old, they were sent to Beijing. Although Chinese was my first language, I have forgotten it entirely. The only thing I can remember is that when we came back, England seemed very peculiar indeed, and although there are many places I am now profoundly attached to, including London, the experience perhaps left me less inclined to put down roots than most.

"A couple of years later, we went to Bonn, but the life of a diplo-brat abruptly took a different turning when my father's health collapsed. The childhood I remember was dominated by his illness, and came to an end when he died, when I was twelve and my brother was ten. We were back in London by then, and my mother picked up what teaching she could in London's extra-mural and part-time sectors. I got on with my life as best I could, and tried to look after them both. Having been catapulted into a precocious maturity, I was no kind of a teenage rebel. Behaving obnoxiously demands an underlying security I no longer had, since I could see only too clearly how fragile the structure of our life was. Also, I had a great deal of sympathy for my mother, who had so clearly been given a rotten deal.

"My school was Haberdashers' Aske's, where I had followed parental tradition by winning a scholarship. I was neither popular nor despised: I wrote poetry and stories, studied Latin and Greek, and made no attempt to conform. I had a group of friends, all made in the art room—I draw quite well—and continued obstinately to go around with them despite the school's considerable pressure to keep me in an 'academic' environment with other Oxbridge-bound types. I was not a troublemaker, but I would not say I participated fully in the life of the school (as report cards used to say).

"I went to Cambridge to read Anglo-Saxon, Norse and Celtic, and discovered like-minded people, and began to enjoy myself as part of a community. I made an eclectic variety of friends, not all of them students, drank too much, slept around, and worked hard. I discovered research and how much I enjoyed it, and kept on writing stories. After ten years of Cambridge, I got a job teaching history at Sheffield University, and a year or so later, married Peter Davidson who was then teaching in St Andrews: we had been friends for six years. He is also an academic (now Regius Chalmers Professor of English at Aberdeen) and a published poet, and we have had no children, not by choice. In our early years, we commuted between England and Scotland, and then, when he was offered a job at Leiden, between England and the Netherlands. We did not manage to get ourselves to the same place until 1995, when we both taught at Warwick. We lived in a piece of a mansion ruined by Cromwell and reconstructed as a farmhouse in the seventeenth century, in what must have been one of the last real villages in middle England, with a succession of permanent house guests. The terms of life at home, which were socially and domestically archaic, made an extraordinary contrast with 'cutting edge' Warwick, which I enjoyed very much. It was during my time at Warwick, following pressure from my friend and colleague the poet David Morley that I finally made time to work seriously on my fiction, and became a published novelist.

"My first publication was four novellas on the common theme of deceit and self deception, which makes reference to two strong influences: Angela Carter's *Several Perceptions*, Umberto Eco's *The Island of the Day Before*. My second book, *London Bridges*, is a homage to the pre-war detective story. My parents had a large collection, and I delighted in them when I was a child. The book examines the themes and conventions of the 'thriller' in modern London: though it is playful, it has a small point to make, that the 'thriller' depends on a degree of cultural consensus which has ceased to exist.

"In 2000, the University of Aberdeen made us an extremely generous offer which brought us North, and I published my second novel, *Astraea*. This is altogether more serious in intention, the first volume of a trilogy concerned with questions of justice. In it, two remarkable people in the grip of the ideologies peculiar to their own time and place (mid-seventeenth century) set a course of action in motion which assumes that the world will continue to be governed by the sorts of consideration relevant to them. As the second and third books will show, since the working-out of their intended intervention in history is affected by variables they would have been unable to imagine, the results are either tragic or comic. The second volume, *The Pretender*, is just about to be published at the time of [this] writing.

"Work aside, my great pleasures are reading, working on the garden, cooking, enjoying the company of animals, and travel. Our new home in Scotland is near, but not in, a small town, and is surrounded by the derelict remains of a sizeable Victorian garden. The pleasures of middle age include the blue slopes of Bennachie on the horizon, learning about trees, and recreating Burnside into what it was intended to be. We travel extensively in Scotland and England, and visit Europe several times a year. We have kept up contacts with the Netherlands, and also spend a lot of time in Italy."

The four novellas that comprise *Several Deceptions* explore several ways in which deceit and self-illusion can undermine a person's sense of identity. In "The Island of the Day Before Yesterday" (a title derived from Umberto Eco's 1995 work), Professor Simone Strachey, an Italian semiotician, has undertaken the task of organizing the estate of his late father, a novelist. In London, the pretentious, name-dropping Strachey hires a secretary, "Dreary Dora," as he thinks of her, to help him catalog his father's papers for the *Times*. Strachey conceives a plan to deceive the newspaper by passing Dora off as a member of his father's literary scene and as his own ex-wife, but the hoax soon turns against him. In "Law and Order" identical twins, Hendrik and Florian, fall under the influence of their law professor Balder van Aldegonde, whose views on crime and responsibility verge on the nihilistic. Hendrik manages to extricate himself but cannot convince his brother to do the same. "The Colonel and Judy O'Grady," narrated by a graduate student, tells the story of Judy O'Grady, a woman who left Ireland as a teenager in the 1960s to become a Buddhist nun. At a Tibetan monastery, O'Grady—who has changed her name to Ananda—meets a retired British officer named James Hatherton, an experience that leads to a crisis of identity. In "Crossing the Water," the narrator, a disaffected artist named Oliver, is staying with a group of pretentious art historians on a lake trip in East Anglia. The inebriated Oliver indulges in vitriolic denouncements of his fellow guests, but his own scheming threatens to undo him.

Several Deceptions received predominantly enthusiastic responses. "Most of the book's characters are highbrow Europeans," Sybil S. Steinberg noted in a review for *Publishers Weekly* (August 14, 2000), "and their diction may be off putting to some readers. But Stevenson realizes the hilarious parodic effect of their ultra-proper intonations, especially when she places them in deliciously vulnerable situations." Hal Jensen, in a review for the *Times Literary Supplement* (April 30, 1999), described the book as "a very enjoyable display of deadly wit given with a relaxed literary confidence. . . . Here is a gossipy, smart, critical, intellectual, high-spirited and literate voice." Paul Baumann, in an appraisal for the *New York Times Book Review* (November 5, 2000), wrote that "Stevenson's novellas are strongly plotted, particularly in their expert thematic dovetailing. When her narrators are bombastic, they are usually winningly bombastic." Baumann added, "As a manipulator of actors, she is always in control; perhaps too much so. Despite disparate settings and narrative personas, a single voice—erudite, fastidious, self-aware—emerges. This doesn't fatally compromise the distinctiveness of each individual work, but it does leave the suspicion that Stevenson's carefully constructed denouements are closer to artifice than to fully imagined lives."

Stevenson's first novel was *London Bridges*. At the center of this tale's numerous plot lines is the character of Mr. Eugenides, an elderly Greek banker living a secluded life in London. Eugenides is the only surviving trustee of a church in Southwark that was destroyed during World War II—an estate that may contain considerable treasure. Edward, a crooked lawyer eager to get his hands on the riches, conspires with an unscrupulous Greek lawyer to bring about Eugenides' demise. Meanwhile, Sebastian, a young gay classicist, befriends Eugenides, believing the older man to be in possession of an ancient homoerotic poem that may help rekindle Sebastian's stagnant academic career. Other colorful London characters are drawn into the action: Dilep, a young Indian lawyer who practices with Edward; Jeanene, a student of Sebastian's who becomes Dilep's lover; and Alicia, an environmental crusader who wants to turn the site of the demolished church into a community garden.

London Bridges was widely reviewed, and critical reactions tended to be favorable. Jeff Zaleski for *Publishers Weekly* (August 13, 2001) described the novel as "an unusual mixture of genres: part thriller, part social comedy and part, as the cunningly punning title suggests, a study of how a variety of different people make unexpected connections in a great city." "It is rather overstuffed," Zaleski added, "but written with such tenderness, wit and brio, and deep affection for London and its people, that it is irresistible." Kathy Weissman for *Bookreporter.com* offered the following caveats: "The opening chapter is chronologically confusing rather than properly mysterious; the dialogue is rife with slang, shorthand, and arcane references (V&A, poofter, Past and Present) that may bewilder an American reader. But what will certainly grab anybody are the people—reading *London Bridges* is a bit like crashing a party and finding oneself in the company of fascinating strangers who soon become intimates." Although Marcel Berlins wrote for the London *Times* (June 24, 2000) that "the dialogue is mannered, the characters not quite believable and Stevenson passes on too much of her research," he concluded that "there is something about *London Bridges* which marks Stevenson out as a genuine and original talent."

Astraea (published in the U. S. by Houghton Mifflin under the title of *The Winter Queen*) is a work of historical fiction set in the Netherlands in the 1640s. Pelagius van Overmeer is an African prince who was born in the Yoruba kingdom of Oyo and subsequently sold into slavery in Asia. After having gained his freedom, Pelagius travels to Holland, where he hopes to train as a Protestant minister and eventually return to his homeland as a missionary. While there, his benefactor dies and he must resort to using his skills for shamanic prophecy to earn an income—a vocation that brings him to the attention of the exiled Queen Elizabeth of Bohemia, daughter of James I. The two begin a secretive affair that culminates in the birth of a son, Balthazar. The romance is set against the backdrop of political turmoil and the events leading up to the 1642 outbreak of civil war in England.

Astraea, the first book in a projected trilogy covering the 17th to the 21st centuries, received largely positive reviews. Patricia Duncker for the *New Statesman* (April 16, 2001) described *Astraea* as an "absorbing and intelligent tale of 17th-century passion and politics. . . . Stevenson's descriptive writing owes much to Dutch painting. Here are the still, scrubbed domestic interiors, kitchen objects, ornaments and carpets, plain and decorated, polished and cherished, as well as vivid action scenes, the stag-hunting sequence, the levees, the mechanics of the printing industry and the exotic skills and laces of aristocratic costume." Duncker added that the character of Pelagius "is sympathetic and convincing. Stevenson gives him a complex subjectivity. . . . His negotiation of 17th-century racism, astonishingly like the modern variety, is well imagined and portrayed." Emma Rea for the London *Times* (February 23, 2002) noted that "The workings of [Pelagius'] conscience are intricately drawn as he examines his Christian beliefs and carefully treads the thin line between doing God's will and simple self-delusion. . . . [The] journey [of Pelagius and Elizabeth] from cautious friendship to a rich love is utterly absorbing." "*Astraea*," she continued, "delivers superb entertainment." Michael Caines for the *Times Literary Supplement* (April 6, 2001) called the work "remarkable," adding that "Stevenson's calm prose [is] the perfect vehicle for the slow unfolding of extraordinary events. . . . [As] the first in a projected trilogy . . . *Astraea* certainly holds out the promise of a momentous history."

In the second book of the trilogy, *The Pretender*, Balthazar, the only son of Pelagius and Elizabeth, has come of age, and his parents are both now dead. Brought up in secrecy in Holland by his father, he met his mother only once. Denied of his identity and his royal lineage, he becomes a medical doctor and moves to London, where he meets a woman named Aphra Behn, an English spy (and later a famous playwright). Eventually he decides to make a new life for himself in Barbados, a colonial island in the West Indies, all the while trying to come to terms with his unusual upbringing, his conflicted past, and the difficulties of being a mulatto (of mixed racial descent) in Restoration England. "[Stevenson] has an absolute grasp of the language, literature and social formation of her period," Kathryn Hughes wrote in a review for the Web site of the London *Telegraph* (April 14, 2002). "It is perhaps because her knowledge is so securely held that she doesn't feel the need to wedge chunks of 'research' into her narrative. Instead she manages to pull of a near-perfect synthesis of setting and story. If a piece of information needs to be given to the reader—the cut of a sleeve, the smell of syphilitic gums, the economy of sugar-rich Barbados—it is delivered, expertly wrapped and precisely placed, in a way that makes it feel both necessary and natural." (*The Pretender* is scheduled to be published by Houghton Mifflin Co. in late 2003 as "The Shadow King.")

In 2000 Stevenson joined the English department at the University of Aberdeen, in Scotland. She is currently working on a study of women who wrote poetry in Latin, "Poetissae: Women and the Language of Authority," and a number of smaller projects concerned with elite women and culture in early modern Europe. She lives in Aberdeenshire with her husband, Peter Davidson, a professor of English.

—A. I. C.

SUGGESTED READING: *New Statesman* p58 Apr. 16, 2001; *New York Times Book Review* p31 Nov. 5, 2000, p7 Sep. 23, 2001; *Publishers Weekly* p330 Aug. 14, 2000, p286 Aug. 13, 2001; (London) *Times* p17 June 24, 2000, p14 Feb. 23, 2002; *Times Literary Supplement* p24 Apr. 30, 1999, Apr. 6, 2001

SELECTED BOOKS: *Several Deceptions*, 1999; *London Bridges*, 2000; *Astraea*, 2001 (*The Winter Queen*, 2002); *The Pretender*, 2002

Stewart, Susan

Mar. 15, 1952– Poet; critic

Susan Stewart, best known as a poet, has also produced four volumes of philosophical criticism that stem from her studies in folklore. Her first book in the field, *Nonsense: Aspects of Intertextuality in Folklore and Literature* (1979), was followed by *On Longing: Narratives of the Miniature, the Gigantic, the Souvenir, the Collection* (1984), *Crimes of Writing: Problems in the Containment of Representation* (1991), and *Poetry and the Fate of the Senses* (2001). Her volumes of poetry, *Yellow Stars and Ice* (1981), *The Hive: Poems* (1987), and *The Forest* (1995), have won almost universal critical acclaim. The essayist and critic Elaine Scarry declared, as quoted by *The Record* (February 5, 1998, on-line), a publication of Washington University in St. Louis, "Stewart renews and reinvigorates our relation to literature by continually setting in front of us startling categories. . . . Stewart is an original and deep thinker. . . . Her books are a model of intellectual life at its best."

Susan Stewart was born March 15, 1952 in York, Pennsylvania. She grew up in a family obsessed by its past. She wrote in the *Kenyon Review* (Winter 1997) of her "ruined family," explaining, "We had been ruined by history, by fate, by bad judgment and bad weather—a family with a fall. And when you are part of a family with a fall you know who fought in the French and Indian War, and who fought in the wars after that, and who started a school, and who converted the Persians, and who could hear a piece of music once and commit it instantly to memory—for these are the great dead of which you are merely a shadow." Whether or not those words refer to Stewart's own family, they express an emotional quality grounded in nostalgia—that has found its way into both her poetry and her philosophical works.

Stewart did her undergraduate work at Dickinson College, in Carlisle, Pennsylvania, earning her B.A. in 1973. She went on to obtain a master's degree in poetry from Johns Hopkins University, in Baltimore, Maryland, in 1975, and a Ph.D. in folklore and folk life from the University of Pennsylvania, in Philadelphia, in 1978.

Her first book was *Nonsense: Aspects of Intertextuality in Folklore and Literature*, published in 1979. The book is in large part a deconstruction of modernism. In children's literature, folk tales, and the works of such writers as James Joyce, Jorge Luis Borges, Alain de Robbe-Grillet, and Samuel Beckett, what may seem incomprehensible or "nonsense" is a method of "disorganizing the old order and . . . experimenting with new forms of order," Stewart wrote. She examined the way in which both traditional and folkloric material and the works of modern writers employ "reversals and inversions" and "play with infinity," "the uses of simultaneity," and "arrangement and rearrangement within a chosen field" to create new kinds of organization of discourse.

"Experience, common sense, and logic," Walter Blair wrote in *Modern Philology* (May 1981), "have led society to develop certain 'notions of process, development, hierarchy, and production.'" Stewart's observations, Blair noted, had led her to the notion "that nonsense playfully disrupts these notions. Her book explores the ways nonsensical creations do this." Blair concluded that Stewart's "learning and . . . wide- ranging research, making possible citations from folklore, fiction, literary criticism, philosophical works, anthropological treatises, linguistic studies, and other sources, are impressive," but he objected to her "highly abstract phrasings and convoluted sentences."

Stewart's first book of poetry, *Yellow Stars and Ice*, came out in 1981. The poems in the volume assert "the altruism of the poet listening to nature," according to Helen McNeil, the reviewer for the *Times Literary Supplement* (January 29, 1982), and celebrate "the 'true miracle' of natural processes." McNeil concluded that "the finest pieces, 'The Doves Are Swallowing Hard,' 'The Exact Middle of the Night' and 'Four Questions Regarding the Dreams of Animals,'" take "specific instances of nature imagery and move from observation to dream and back again; the effect is of mesmeric serenity."

Stewart continued alternating nonfiction with poetry. Her 1984 book, *On Longing: Narratives of the Miniature, the Gigantic, the Souvenir, the Collection*, is an exploration of the impulses to keep and collect objects, especially small ones, as an expression of mastery over nature and a physical embodiment of memory and experience. Although some reviewers found Stewart's language too dense and difficult, Dan Rose, the reviewer for *Language in Society* (June 1986), deemed Stewart the "leading figure in forming the new folklore," a folklore that has "broken with the sciences and joined the humanities." For Jerry Cullum, writing in *Art Papers* (February 1997), Stewart in *On Longing* displayed similarities to the surrealists through her unusual juxtapositions, though she has never acknowledged their influence on her work. Cullum also saw Stewart as having "identified precisely the reason why nostalgia . . . is the most politically and psychologically subversive emotion we have, ... Longing for the not-yet that is at the same time a never-was, nostalgia has the potential to produce visions of alternative futures," which may be "fulfilled in material invention."

In Stewart's 1987 collection of poems, *The Hive*, she continued her imaginative explorations of eternity, time, and loss, using images of nature and of the objects that surround people. *The Hive* won a Georgia Press Second Book Award in 1987. Stewart examined in her 1991 volume, *Crimes of Writing: Problems in the Containment of Representation*, the "underbelly" of literature, dealing with forgery, pornography, plagiarism, and graffiti. Critical opinion turned against *Crimes of Writing*. Wendy Steiner expressed her disappointment in the *Times Literary Supplement* (March 13, 1992): "Susan Stewart's earlier books on nonsense and on nostalgia showed such striking originality and sensitivity that we have come to expect only the best from her. Yet here we have . . . language so opaque as to mask any hint of argumentative rigour." Steiner did find "clarity and argumentative force" in Stewart's discussion of the Meese Commission Report on pornography, as when Stewart pointed out that that document "draws attention away from the material existence of rape, murder, assault . . . by displacing their import, and their remedy, to the domain of this 'underground' form of representation." Steiner added that Stewart "raises a host of interesting topics" when she "is presenting information," praising Stewart's suggestions of contradictions in the concept of "intellectual property" and her description of "the nostalgia of 'distressed genres': the literary fable, ballad, epic, fairy-tale and proverb beloved by eighteenth- and nineteenth-century revivalists and forgers." Steiner concluded that it might be that "the greatest crime of writing . . . for Stewart . . . is her own need to write in a climate so unconducive to the written word that she must reduce her significance to the moment of utterance and her audience to the alterity of herself."

In 1995 Stewart was appointed senior scholar at the Getty Center for the History of Art and the Humanities; received a Pew Fellowship in the Arts; and saw the publication of her most widely praised book of poetry, *The Forest*, which is divided into two parts: "Phantom" and "Cinder." "Narratives, often rooted in history and reminiscent of fairy tales, are told by unnamed speakers and peopled by figures that can't be pinned down," the *Publishers Weekly* (June 26, 1995) reviewer wrote of *The Forest*, concluding that the volume "is a rare phenomenon in recent poetry: poems which require several readings, and promise to be equally intriguing each time." Katherine Swiggart agreed in the *Electronic Poetry Review* (1996, on-line), terming the volume "mesmerizing." She observed that the "perpetual desire of these poems seems to be to restore and redefine the past through the language that both represents and distorts it. . . . It is, more than anything, the sense of inevitable loss which provides the occasion for these poems; they enact and continue to reenact an insoluble conflict between the idea that in language there is no difference among past, present, literature and life, and the disturbing losses resulting from too fervent a belief in that fact. The result is a postmodern lyricism as daring and frightening as it is consoling." In "The Forest," Stewart wrote:

> You should lie down now and remember the
> forest, for it is disappearing no, the truth is
> it is gone now and so what details you can
> bring back might have a kind of life.

"Her forest is one of fragmented memories, and the theme of remembering and forgetting that pervades the pages of this book is what effectively binds it together," Jean Hopkinson wrote in the *Alembic*, an on-line journal of the Providence College English department.

In 1997 Susan Stewart was the recipient of a MacArthur fellowship, commonly known as the "genius" grant. She had become a professor at the University of Pennsylvania in Philadelphia, after teaching at Temple University, in the same city, from 1978 until 1996.

In 1999 the question "How does poetry help us to live our lives?" was posed to Stewart, Robert Hass, Yusef Komunyakaa, W. S. Merwin, Joyce Carol Oates, and Gerald Stern by the editors of the *American Poetry Review*. Stewart's answer, published in that journal in October 1999, contained not only her philosophical remark that poetry "makes . . . experiences both particular and knowable," but also her thoughts on *poesis*: "Poetry also presents specific qualities of form. Foremost is the turn or volta that is synonymous with verse. Poetry emerges out of rhythms that are carried forward through the body by generation after generation; it is organized by what is unconscious to the reason and at the same time it struggles into the light of what can be said and known. The Greek word *poesis* conveys two kinds of creation: the inspired creation that resembles a god-like power and the difficult material struggle with making that is human labor." In 2001 Steward published *Poetry and the Fate of the Senses*, a large work drawing on examples of poetry ranging from the ancient Greeks to the postmoderns in an attempt to explore the relationship between the senses and poetic forms.

"Any work, including the work of art, is subject to contingency," Stewart wrote in *Representations 62*, an on-line publication of the University of California, Berkeley. One of the contingent factors for a creator is an audience, and Stewart, in an article entitled "Two Madmen," which appeared in the *American Poetry Review* (August 1999), described her problematic relationship with two audiences for her readings that included two "madmen": "Is it inevitable that stepping into the public world is stepping into the non-reciprocity of our relation with the mad? . . . The poet makes her bid for attention, but she may be, beyond her knowledge, in an auction of nightmares." Stewart, the recipient of a Guggenheim Fellowship and several grants from the National Foundation for the Arts, has transformed some of her own nightmares of loss and contingency into poetry that many critics have termed beautiful. —S. Y.

SUGGESTED READING: *Alembic* (on-line) 1996; *American Poetry Review* p8+ Aug. 1999, p21+ Oct. 1999; *Art Papers* p6+ Feb. 1997; *Boston Book Review* (on-line) 1998; *Kenyon Review* p145+ Win. 1999; *Library Journal* p404 Feb. 1, 1980, p1226 June 1, 1981; *Modern Philology* p463+ May 1981; *Publishers Weekly* p101+ June 26, 1995; *Raritan* p77+ Fall 1999; *Times Literary Supplement* p113 Jan. 29, 1982, p26 Mar. 13, 1992; *Washington Post Book World* p2 Dec. 17, 1995

SELECTED BOOKS: poetry—*Yellow Stars and Ice*, 1981; *The Hive: Poems*, 1987; *The Forest*, 1995; nonfiction—*Nonsense: Aspects of Intertextuality in Folklore and Literature*, 1979; *On Longing: Narratives of the Miniature, the Gigantic, the Souvenir, the Collection*, 1984; *Crimes of Writing: Problems in the Containment of Representation*, 1991; *Poetry and the Fate of the Senses*, 2001

Stollman, Aryeh Lev

Aug. 26, 1954– Novelist; short-story writer; neuroradiologist

Aryeh Lev's Stollman's fiction examines the borders we place around ourselves as human beings. To Stollman, these borders are not merely geographic or nationalistic; they are religious, political, and sexual, as well. Stollman has resided on either side of several such divides: as a child who lived in Canada but studied in the United States, as a practicing doctor who also writes fiction, as the son of a rabbinical scholar whose religious beliefs are challenged by the legacy of the Holocaust, and as a Jew in a predominantly Christian society.

Aryeh Lev Stollman writes for *World Authors 1995–2000*: "I was conceived in the border-city of Windsor, Ontario but taken across the Detroit River to be born [on August 26, 1954] in Michigan where my father had grown up in a large, close-knit family. This was only the beginning of my involvement and fascination with borders and human definitions of self. My father had come from Russia to the United States as an infant. After his ordination at the Rabbi Isaac Elchanan Seminary of Yeshiva University in New York City, he became the rabbi of an orthodox Jewish congregation in Windsor bringing my Brooklyn born mother with him for what they thought was a temporary career move. One day soon, they told themselves, they would move back to a big city in the United States or, even better, they would settle in Israel. Instead, they remained in Windsor for forty years before retiring to Jerusalem.

Steven Spewock/Courtesy of Riverhead Books

"As there was no Jewish day school in Windsor, a small group of boys and girls including my siblings traveled every day by bus across the international border to a yeshiva in Detroit. Overall my childhood was happy but I didn't quite fit in with many of the children in Windsor, even in my father's congregation, since I attended school in Detroit and my family was more religious than most. I was not quite at home with my American schoolmates what with going home every evening to Canada.

"Aside from pursuing his rabbinical duties, my father obtained his Ph.D. in English literature from Wayne State University in Detroit. His doctorate was entitled *Milton and Judaism* and was an exploration of Milton's profound knowledge and manipulation of Hebrew texts. Later my father would become the Chairman of the English Department at the University of Windsor. Our house was filled with books, including classic Jewish texts—the Talmud, Zohar, Bible studies—as well as English and American novels and plays. There was also a variety of scientific books. I remember in particular the *Life Magazine* science series my parents ordered for us children with titles such as *The Cell* and *Matter and Energy*. On Sabbath afternoons I would take one book or another out of my parents' library and read for hours, mostly in English but also in Hebrew. I thought I wanted to be either a writer or a scientist. I knew that to be a scientist you had to attend university but had no idea how to become a writer. Although my father was a scholar of literature there was never any discussion of the actual creative side of that endeavor.

"I attended Yeshiva University in New York City as a pre-medicine major, following in the footsteps of my older brother whom I have always admired. The competition at that time for medical school was fierce and grades were a seeming matter of life and death. I received almost straight A's with the exception of two or three courses among them English composition for which I received a B+. I then went to the Albert Einstein College of Medicine in the Bronx. In June 1980, on the day I graduated medical school, I bought a typewriter. I thought, Now I will figure out how to be a writer as well as a doctor. That took some time as I did six years of post-graduate residency and fellowship to become a neuroradiologist.

"In 1986, after finishing my training, I took a half-time position at the Mount Sinai Hospital and Medical Center in New York City. On my days off I began writing short stories, eventually submitting them on my own to various journals. After about four years I had my first story, 'The King of Sura and the Queen of Pumbedita,' accepted by Alistair MacLeod, the distinguished Canadian author, for the *University of Windsor Review*. Later I published in places like *Story*, *American Short Fiction*, *The Yale Review*, and *Southwest Review*.

"In 1995 I had a dream about a little boy being brought by several women to a tiny creature who lay upon a grand, sumptuously covered bed. The next day I began to write my first novel, *The Far Euphrates*, and the dream creature became Mademoiselle Dee Dee, the gypsy prophetess in Grosse Pointe, Michigan to whom the young Alexander in the novel is brought from Windsor by his worried mother. *The Far Euphrates* deals with, among other things, that which constitutes 'home,' exploring not only geographical place but also our physical selves and the inner psychological spaces in which we humans might try to find ourselves at home.

"My second novel, *The Illuminated Soul*, comes back to the theme of home but expands it to include not only the exile from home, but the exile from one's culture and the attempts and costs of trying to preserve that culture. Eva Laquedem Higashi, one of the central characters is someone in permanent exile, for me a female version of the Wandering Jew but removed from the anti-Semitic overtones of that Christian story with its notions of punishment. Eva is beautiful, broadly and deeply educated, multilingual, and in the possession of a magnificent illuminated manuscript, the *Augsburg Miscellany*, which she saves at great risk to her own life when she escapes her native Prague. I have always been fascinated with the way culture is preserved, kept alive, and transformed—and how at times it becomes an artifact, not unlike a laboratory specimen. And then there is always the question, Who is the legitimate carrier of any given culture? Although Eva's father is Jewish, her mother's origins are obscure in the novel, and so Eva, the woman bearing and preserving great culture is of uncertain designation at least according to orthodox definition of who is a Jew, which derives from the status of the mother.

"I have always been fascinated and troubled by the ways we define ourselves, which by their very nature are simultaneous acts of inclusion and exclusion: New World versus Old, American versus Canadian or European, Jew versus non-Jew, straight versus gay.

"In my writing, I am continually trying to understand what might constitute one's place in this world. And even if I do not have the answers it is in this ongoing attempt that I feel most at home."

Aryeh Lev Stollman's first novel, *The Far Euphrates*, was published in 1997. A coming-of-age story set in the author's hometown, Windsor, Ontario, it describes the lonely life of Alexander, the son of Holocaust survivors. His father, who is a rabbi, and his apprehensive mother try to keep young Alexander from all harm. They withhold from him the knowledge that his mother has a brother in an insane asylum and that the next-door neighbors, also survivors, were forced subjects of Dr. Josef Mengele's perverted medical experiments in Auschwitz. Alexander eventually discovers these things and becomes obsessed with the horror of the Holocaust.

The book received mostly favorable criticism. Molly Abramowitz wrote for *Library Journal* (September 1, 1997), "Alexander's small world is delightfully peopled by uncommon folk, and philosophical questions about the post-Holocaust world are probed through many of the boy's adventures." Margot Livesey, in the *New York Times Book Review* (September 21, 1997), heaped even more praise on the novel, noting that it "is remarkable both for Stollman's eloquently understated prose and for the ease with which he constructs his artful plot." She continued, "Most novels would be content to show how our lives are shaped by history, but this one seems to be after something even larger. At the heart of *The Far Euphrates* lie the vexed questions raised by the Holocaust and its legacy: how we must try to solve for ourselves the riddle of God's existence and cultivate a sense of mercy in an unforgiving age." The book won a 1998 Lambda Literary Award for best gay men's fiction; it also received a 1997 Wilbur Award from the Religion Communicators Council.

The Illuminated Soul (2002), Stollman's second novel, covers similar ground. As a young boy in Windsor, Ontario, the book's narrator, Joseph, meets a beautiful young woman named Eva when she rents a room in his mother's house a few years after World War II. A biologist and a scholar of Jewish studies, Eva traveled the world after her native Prague was overrun by the Nazis during the war. With her she carries two manuscripts: her father's discourse on clouds, titled *Enoch Laquedem*, and a 15th-century illuminated manuscript called the *Augsburg Miscellany*. Both books—and Eva herself—have a tremendous impact on the narrator, who grows up to become a scientist and author. Judith Bolton-Fasman wrote for the *Boston Globe* (April 28, 2002), "Aryeh Lev Stollman has forged a uniquely Jewish perspective on the classic mind-body problem. [This] is an admirable novel of ideas that grapples with the links between memory and the physiology of the brain as well as between information and imagination." She concluded, "*The Illuminated Soul* is a profound novel that sheds light on holy patterns and their endless confusions. But it is also a sturdy narrative that supports a strong and varied cast of characters while contemplating the place of sentience within the brain's function, and staking out that elusive stretch of middle ground between faith and science." Neil Freudenberger, writing for the *New York Times Book Review* (April 28, 2002), was less laudatory. He noted, "Eva doesn't escape her place in the allegorical pattern Stollman has created—a soul from the Old World, coming to help Jews in the new one—long enough to become a real person, and her story is never allowed to bear its own interesting fruit."

The Dialogues of Time and Entropy (2003) is a collection of several of Stollman's works of short fiction that previously appeared in literary magazines. The settings include Israel, Canada, and the U.S., and writers and scientists tend to figure prominently in the stories. In the title piece two physicists journey to Israel, talking all the while about time and entropy and find themselves caught up in the volatile political situation of the Middle East. An anonymous reviewer for *Publishers Weekly*, as quoted on Amazon.com, praised the "probing, intellectually acute story collection. . . . Stollman's moral intensity occasionally shades into grandiose sentiment ('she needs desperately to weep—for all of the children in everlasting time, compelled like their mother to wander forever in a wandering world'), but for the most part the stories offer lively conversations and likeably self-effacing characters who find themselves in an ethical or spiritual pickle."

Stollman continues to work as a neuroradiologist at the Mount Sinai Medical Center, in New York City. He has contributed short stories to a number of literary periodicals, including *Story*, the *Yale Review*, *American Short Fiction*, and the *Forward*.
—C. M.

SUGGESTED READING: Aryeh Lev Stollman's Official Web site; *Boston Globe* E p5 Apr. 28, 2002; *Library Journal* p221 Sep. 1, 1997; *New York Times Book Review* p11 Sep. 21, 1997, p15 Apr. 28, 2002

SELECTED BOOKS: *The Far Euphrates*, 1997; *The Illuminated Soul*, 2002; *The Dialogues of Time and Entropy*, 2003

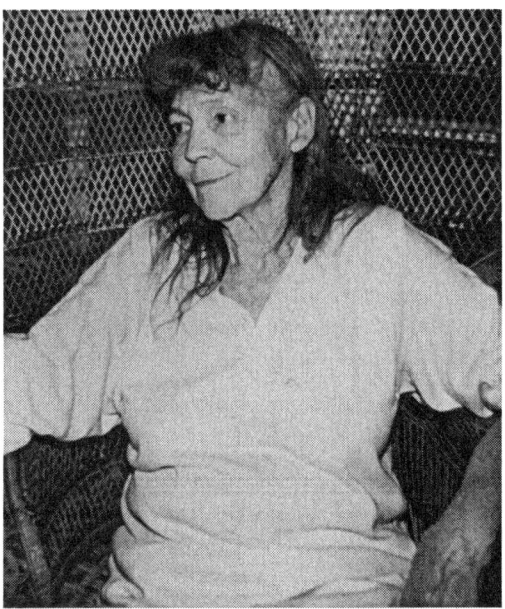

David Carlson/Courtesy of Copper Canyon Press

Stone, Ruth

June 8, 1915– Poet

Ruth Stone is among the foremost American poets of the postwar era. Her clean, fierce, and often hilarious poetry is difficult to define. As lyrical as the work of Alfred Lord Tennyson in its meter and rhyme, it is at the same time permeated with the mundane details of life. It also, however, discusses grander issues—the meaning of family, the beauty of nature, the definitions of femininity, and human struggles against loss. Her first collection, *In an Iridescent Time* (1959), was an ode to young family life, and her next, *Topography and Other Poems* (1971), looked at the passing of her husband with an unblinking eye. Some of her most notable collections over the years include *Cheap: New Poems and Ballads* (1973), *Second Hand Coat: Poems New and Selected* (1986), and *Simplicity* (1995). In 1999 her collection *Ordinary Words* won the National Book Critics Circle Award, and, along with the prize, brought its author some long overdue recognition.

Ruth Stone was born Ruth Perkins in Roanoke, Virginia, on June 8, 1915, the daughter of Roger McDowell Perkins, a musician, and the former Ruth Ferguson. Her father's family was of English descent and were members of high society in Indianapolis, Indiana: Ruth's paternal grandfather was a senator and her grandmother hosted formal tea parties. As a child Ruth was surrounded by talented relatives—teachers, poets, painters, and lawyers. An innate sense of humor was characteristic of the entire family, and Stone has recalled how her aunts and uncles thrilled their guests at dinner parties with one hilarious story after another. At the age of three she began reading books in her maternal grandparents' extensive library. By first grade she had moved from her home in Roanoke to that of her paternal grandparents, in Indianapolis. There, guided by her Aunt Harriet, she began writing and drawing, exercises that her mother also fully supported. Poetry was one of her mother's great loves, and she would often read to her daughter from the works of Alfred Lord Tennyson.

In addition to her early love of language, Stone developed a keen sense of rhythm from her father, who was a drummer. He would practice his instrument or play classical records during the evenings he spent at home. He would also frequently come through the door loaded down with boxes of chocolate, ready to read aloud to his family, sometimes from the Bible, other times from more humorous sources, such as the writings of Bill Nye.

The environment in which she spent her childhood fostered in Stone a lively intelligence and curiosity. Frequently intrigued by scientific phenomena, she would bring encyclopedias to bed with her to learn all she could about a particular subject. She took this curiosity with her to the University of Illinois, and later to Harvard University, in Cambridge, Massachusetts, where she received her bachelor's degree. Around the same time, she married the noted poet and novelist Walter B. Stone. While her husband was teaching at Vassar College, in Poughkeepsie, New York, Stone worked on the poems that would be collected in her first book, *In an Iridescent Time*, which was published in 1959; at the same time she raised three daughters—Marcia, born in 1942, Phoebe, born in 1949, and Abigail, born in 1953.

By 1955 Stone was beginning to receive accolades for her writing; in that year she won the Bess Hokin Prize for Poetry and the Kenyon Review Poetry Fellowship, and she recorded her poetry for the U.S. Library of Congress. Throughout the latter half of the 1950s she published poems in such literary journals as the *Kenyon Review*, the *Partisan Review*, *Poetry*, and the *New Yorker*. When *In an Iridescent Time* was published, Stone was hailed as a powerful new voice in American poetry. Though the subjects of many of her poems are tales of everyday family life, they are charged with "iridescent" feelings about the energy of youth. As P. S. Hurd noted in the *Christian Science Monitor* (March 3, 1960), "Ruth Stone . . . not only writes fresh and original and compelling poetry but lives and breathes in it." Kimon Friar, writing for the *Saturday Review* (February 6, 1960), commented, "With . . . Ruth Stone, we enter into an iridescent world of larks, brake, and crabgrass. . . . Although oftentimes her subject matter is grisly, not a line is in bad taste, for she treats her material with a brilliant lyricism, and carves it with such finesse that every gargoyle becomes a creation of love."

During the 1960s Stone taught English at a number of colleges, starting with Wellesley College in 1965, and Brandeis University in 1965 and 1966. In 1969 she and her family moved to Madison, Wisconsin, where she taught in the University of Wisconsin's English department.

The vitality of young family life in Stone's first collection gave way to a study of grief in her next, *Topography and Other Poems* (1971), which was written following the death of her husband. As she mourned, she began composing poems about her late husband and her attempts to come to terms with her sorrow. The poems collected in *Topography* reflect a change in her writing; these poems, while still lyrical, are looser, both in terms of form and meter. The poet's sense of loss permeates them, and many seem to suggest that life was now spoiled for her. A striking example of this sentiment is contained in her poem "The Excuse," as quoted in the *Dictionary of Literary Biography* (1991): "It is so difficult to look at the deprived, or smell their decay, / But now I am among them. I too, am a leper, a warning." As with her first collection, Stone received laudatory reviews for *Topography*. "To describe Ruth Stone's verse as unequivocally feminine and intellectually restrained," P. H. Marvin wrote in *Library Journal* (September 1, 1971), "is to miss the essential sanity and control which informs, and forms, her poems. . . . These poems reveal a generous and acute mind, not so much given to metaphor as to description and gentle fantasy." A critic for the *Christian Science Monitor* (May 6, 1971), agreed with this sentiment, adding, "With admirable restraint, [Stone] has allowed her gifts to mature slowly, deepening and strengthening her powers before new publication."

After spending two years as a member of the English department at the University of Illinois at Urbana-Champaign, Stone published another book of poetry, *Unknown Messages* (1973), and began her tenure as a visiting professor at Indiana University, at Bloomington, for the academic year 1973 to 1974. In 1975 Stone was appointed creative writing chair at Center College in Danville, Kentucky, the same year she published another collection of poems, *Cheap: New Poems and Ballads*. Some of the 71 poems in this collection first appeared in such literary journals as the *Boston Arts Review*, the *California Quarterly*, the *Iowa Review*, and the *Modine Gunch Anthology*; almost all were written during the migratory period in which the poet moved from university to university. In this volume, Stone migrates away from the grief-stricken poetry of *Topography* and toward a clear-eyed vision of what she has lived through and witnessed, arriving at amusing, sometimes terrifying revelations. A critic for the *Virginia Quarterly Review* (Spring 1976) proclaimed that Stone "has enormous humor and insight and so gracefully chooses the exact word. . . . She writes of bitter womanly experiences, observes nature with a sharp and balanced eye, and rollicks through some funny ballads." A reviewer for *Choice* (March 1976) noted that "The poems . . . explore with a mixture of gravity and wit women's experience in the roles of daughter, lover, wife, mother, artist."

In 1976 Stone returned to Brandeis University as a Hurst Visiting Professor, and in 1978 she became a lecturer at the University of California, Davis. Stone did not publish a new collection until the late 1980s, and when she began publishing her work again she did so with a vengeance: *American Milk* (1986), *Second Hand Coat: Poems New and Selected* (1987), *The Solution* (1989), and *Who is the Widow's Muse?* (1991), came out during a six-year period. In 1995 she published *Simplicity*, one of her most celebrated volumes to date. The collection reflects the persistent themes of her writing: nature, separation, everyday life, and loss. In one poem she writes of her dead husband, as quoted by Liz Rosenberg in the *Boston Globe* (December 24, 1995) and posted on the *Paris Press* Web site: "Memory becomes the exercise against loss. / Later, when we were naked on the bed, / and that tremble of heat lightening along the muscles, / you began the slow measures of 'Dover Beach' / in the only voice—the only voice— / 'Ah, love, let us be true to one another.'" Rosenberg proclaimed: "There is . . . great beauty in this collection, and a brilliance of imagery that comes from seeing the world freshly and clearly. . . . Above all, Stone's poetry speaks about and on behalf of love, which marries particles, photons, neutrons, the smallest particles alive, moving and connected." As many other fans and critics had done for years, Elana Frankel, in a review for *Small Press* (Fall 1995), asked, "What is most curious to me is why Stone, who has published nine previous collections of poetry and won numerous awards, is not better known. We all should be so fierce when we are eighty."

Simplicity did garner Stone a share of long overdue acclaim: the book was a finalist for the Academy of American Poets Lenore Marshall Prize, the Poet's Prize, and the Boston Review Award for Poetry. In 1996 one of the poems in this collection, "The News," won the Pushcart Prize. That same year *The House is Made of Poetry: The Art of Ruth Stone*, edited by Wendy Barker and Sandra M. Gilbert, was published. This volume, a collection of 17 essays by such noted figures as Sharon Olds, Willis Barnstone, and Diana Wakoski, includes discussions of Stone's life and the evolution of her work, critical readings of her poems, and recollections of the poet by those who have known her over the years.

In her 85th year, Stone published *Ordinary Words* (1999), a new collection that won the 1999 National Book Critics Award. Like much of her other poetry, *Ordinary Words* focuses on humanity and the natural world, displaying the poet's characteristic wit as well as her sober commentary. As a critic for *Publishers Weekly* (July 26, 1999), observed: "Stone often writes as aging observer, commenting wryly on a boring, line-up-at-the-counter existence; she laments the past's inability to break its frame—or her own inability to keep her late middle-aged daughters ('in over their hips') from falling into it. But Stone's other characters, with a contagious hope, look out with 'worn eyes / and see the bright new Pleiades.' The ordinary, for Stone, turns out to be more than enough."

The poems that comprise Stone's most recent publication, *In the Next Galaxy* (2002), cover subjects ranging from astronomy to fractals to the fatigue of aging. A reviewer for *Publishers Weekly*, as quoted on *Amazon.com*, remarked: "Stone veers easily between compressed stories of her Virginia upbringing and her own life, on the one hand, and scenic Americana on the other, finding material in 'New York mountain weather,' roaming cats, [and] 'the railroad's edge of metal trash.' A third sort of Stone poem begins and ends in abstraction, finding spare lines for dejection or reflection, or asking simply, 'how can I live like this?'" A reviewer for *Library Journal*, as quoted on *Amazon.com*, noted: "Stone writes conversationally, with lyricism, honesty, wit, and plenty of focus on the passage of time. . . . Her uses of subtle and occasional rhyme, off-rhyme, and inner rhyme are delicate and always appropriate."

In addition to her recent accolades, Ruth Stone has also received a Radcliffe Institute fellowship from Harvard University (1963–65); the 1963 Robert Frost fellowship for the Breadloaf Writers' Conference; the 1964 Shelley Memorial Award from the Poetry Society of America; a Kenyon Review fellowship, in 1965; and a grant from the Academy of Arts and Letters, in 1970. She has also received two Guggenheim fellowships, one for 1971–72, the other for 1975–76. As of 1996 she was living in Vermont, where she had resided for many years.

—*C. M.*

SUGGESTED READING: *Boston Globe* (on-line) Dec. 24, 1995; *Choice* Mar. 1976; *Christian Science Monitor* p7 Mar. 3, 1960, B p7 May 6, 1971; *Kenyon Review* p179+ Summer/Fall 1999; *Kirkus Reviews* p720 Sep. 15, 1959; *Library Journal* p3778 Dec. 1, 1959, p2650 Sep. 1, 1971, p1829 Oct. 1, 1975; *Massachusetts Review* p491 Winter 1996–1997, p455+ Winter 1997–1998, p682+ Winter 1999–2000; *New York Herald*

Tribune p3 Dec. 13, 1959; *New York Times Book Review* p6 Dec. 27, 1959; *New Yorker* p238 Nov. 28, 1959; *Paris Press* (on-line); *Publishers Weekly* p86 July 26, 1999; *Saturday Review* p21 Feb. 6, 1960; *Small Press* p88 Fall 1995; *Virginia Quarterly Review* p48 Spring 1976; *Women's Review of Books* p11 Dec. 1995; *Contemporary Authors New Revision Series*, vol. 2, 1981; *Dictionary of Literary Biography*, vol. 105, 1991

SELECTED BOOKS: *In An Iridescent Time*, 1959; *Topography and Other Poems*, 1971; *Unknown Messages*, 1973; *Cheap: New Poems and Ballads*, 1975; *American Milk*, 1986; *Second Hand Coat: Poems New and Selected*, 1987; *The Solution*, 1989; *Who is the Widow's Muse?*, 1991; *Simplicity*, 1995; *Ordinary Words*, 1999; *In the Next Galaxy*, 2002

Eamonn McCabe/Retna/Camera Press

Stoppard, Tom

July 3, 1937– Playwright

Tom Stoppard is widely considered to be one of the leading English-language playwrights of his time. The author of such Tony Award–winning works as *Rosencrantz and Guildenstern Are Dead* (1967), *Travesties* (1974), and *The Real Thing* (1982), Stoppard has forged a distinct brand of modern theater characterized by scintillating comedic wordplay, complex plot structures, and the witty exposition of erudite themes. Since *Rosencrantz and Guildenstern Are Dead* stunned audiences and critics alike when it premiered at London's Old Vic Theatre—marking the beginning of his long professional career—Stoppard has written more than 20 plays, including such acclaimed works as *Jumpers* (1972), *Every Good Boy Deserves Favor* (1977), *Arcadia* (1993), and *The Invention of Love* (1997). He has produced close to a dozen adaptations and translations of works by such writers as Anton Chekhov, Federico García Lorca, and Vaclav Hável, as well as written numerous television and radio plays. Also to his credit are the screenplays for such films as *Brazil* (1985), co-written with Terry Gilliam and Charles McKeown, and the Academy Award–winning *Shakespeare in Love* (1998), co-written with Marc Norman. "The tone, style, and subject matter of Stoppard's theatrical vision is striking," John Fleming wrote in *Stoppard's Theatre: Finding Order Amid Chaos*, as quoted by Carlin Romano for the *Philadelphia Inquirer* (May 12, 2002). "In an environment where socially and politically committed drama has long been valued, Stoppard's cerebral wit, philosophical and scientific inquiry, right-leaning political convictions, and theatrical showmanship set him apart from most of his contemporaries." "Stoppard has proven himself a wizard of language, a fountain of scholarship and a master of theatrical legerdemain," Richard Christiansen noted for the *Chicago Tribune* (July 14, 1993). "At the same time, along with the glitter of his intellectual juggling act, his best work also has contained a deeply humanistic spirit, lamenting the frail, ephemeral nature of man's existence yet reveling in the unquenchable force of life and love on the way to the grave."

Tom Stoppard was born Thomas Straussler in Zlín, Czechoslovakia (now the Czech Republic), on July 3, 1937, the second son of Eugene and Martha Straussler. Eugene Straussler was a company doctor for the Bata shoe-manufacturing company. In 1939 Dr. Straussler and his family—which was Jewish, a fact Stoppard did not find out until years later—moved to Singapore, thereby escaping the Nazi invasion of Czechoslovakia. When the Japanese invaded Singapore in 1942, Mrs. Straussler and her two sons were evacuated to India by the retreating British; Dr. Straussler remained behind and was killed. Mrs. Straussler then married Kenneth Stoppard, an officer with the British Army stationed in India, and Tom and his brother assumed that surname.

In 1946 the family moved to England, eventually settling in Bristol. Tom Stoppard was sent to a Nottinghamshire prep school and then to a public school at Pocklington in Yorkshire, which left him "thoroughly bored by the idea of anything intellectual," as he has told interviewers. His ambition then was to be a war correspondent, and at the age of 17 he joined the staff of Bristol's *Western Daily Press* as a general reporter. He has said that he "got a bigger thrill from seeing my first by-line . . . than I did from having my first play on at the National."

After four years with the *Press*, in 1958 Stoppard moved to the *Bristol Evening World* as a feature writer and drama critic. By that time John Osborne and the English Stage Company had arrived on the scene and "everybody of my age who wanted to write, wanted to write plays . . . and it struck me that I was never going to start writing unless I did something active about it." Feeling there was no more time to be lost, he turned freelance in 1960 and wrote his first plays—a one-act piece, called *The Gamblers*, and *A Walk on the Water*. Stoppard then moved to London, where he worked as a theater critic for *Scene* magazine. Under various pseudonyms, Stoppard reviewed 132 shows in the seven months that *Scene* was in operation. The *nom de plume* he preferred was "William Boot"—a reference to the innocent journalist in Evelyn Waugh's novel *Scoop*.

The Gamblers was staged once, in 1965, by Bristol University students and subsequently forgotten. *A Walk on the Water* was produced on British television in November 1963. A domestic drama about the family of an unsuccessful inventor, the play received little notice at the time. It was subsequently revised as a two-act stage play, *Enter a Free Man*. Meanwhile, Stoppard completed a number of radio plays, including *The Dissolution of Dominic Boot* (1964), *M Is for Moon Among Other Things* (1964), *If You're Glad I'll be Frank* (1966), and *Albert's Bridge* (1967), and several teleplays, among them *A Separate Peace* (1966), *Teeth* (1967), *Another Moon Called Earth* (1967), and *Neutral Ground* (1968). In addition to the plays he wrote during that early, prolific period, Stoppard wrote a number of short stories, often inspired by his favorite short-story writers: Damon Runyon, Ernest Hemingway, and Nathanael West. Some of his short stories were published in *Introduction 2: Stories by New Writers* (1964). Stoppard won the John Whiting Award from the Arts Council of Great Britain in 1967.

Earlier, in 1964, Stoppard went to Berlin on a Ford Foundation grant. For five months he lived and worked with a group of 20 other writers who had received similar grants. During his stay in Berlin he wrote a one-act burlesque in verse entitled *Rosencrantz and Guildenstern*, which bore little resemblance to his later hit *Rosencrantz and Guildenstern Are Dead*. In an interview with Dan Sullivan for a *New York Times* (August 29, 1967) profile, Stoppard admitted that initially he saw the situation of Rosencrantz and Guildenstern in terms of a farce. "Then," he went on to explain, "something alerted me to the serious reverberations of the characters. Rosencrantz and Guildenstern, the most expendable people of all time. Their very facelessness makes them dramatic; the fact that they die without ever really understanding why they lived makes them somehow cosmic."

In Shakespeare's *Hamlet*, Rosencrantz and Guildenstern are the pawns of King Claudius, who charges them with the task of diverting Hamlet from avenging the murder of his father. At the end of the play, they are sent as messengers to the king of England, carrying with them the instructions for their own executions. Stoppard used 250 lines from *Hamlet* to provide the framework for *Rosencrantz and Guildenstern Are Dead*, which focuses on the lives of the two courtiers; instead of developing their personalities, however, he leaves Rosencrantz and Guildenstern as vaguely drawn as they were in the original play. They are shown as adjuncts without individual identity who are swept along by events and personalities that they cannot comprehend. In their confusion about the meaning of their lives and their identities, they even mix up their own names. When they discover that they carry their own death warrants, they resolve to deliver them, hoping that the successful completion of their mission will give meaning to their existence.

Some critics viewed Stoppard's play as an existential work and compared it to Samuel Beckett's *Waiting for Godot*. Stoppard, however, has said, "I didn't know what the word 'existential' meant until it was applied to Rosencrantz." Moreover, Stoppard explained to Tom Prideaux in an interview for *Look* (February 9, 1968), "My play was not written as a response to anything about alienation in our times. One writes about human beings under stress—whether it is about losing one's trousers or being nailed to the cross."

Rosencrantz And Guildenstern Are Dead was first performed by Oxford University students at the Edinburgh Fringe Festival in 1966. The rave reviews of that production prompted the National Theatre's Kenneth Tynan, Sir Laurence Olivier, and the director Derek Goldby to stage the play in London, where it opened at the Old Vic Theatre in April 1967 (making Stoppard, at age 29, the youngest playwright ever to have a play staged by the National Theatre). Ronald Bryden, in a review for the London *Observer*, praised the "erudite comedy" as "the most brilliant debut by a young playwright since John Arden's." When the play opened in New York City, on October 16, 1967, it was an immediate critical and commercial success. A reviewer for *Time* (October 27, 1967) commented that *Rosencrantz and Guildenstern Are Dead* was "one of those rare plays able to open worlds of art, life, and death. . . . Broadway may not see a more auspicious playwriting debut this season." The *London Evening Standard* named Stoppard the most promising playwright of 1968. He also received the Antoinette Perry (Tony) Award and the New York Drama Critics Circle Award for the best play of 1968.

When Tom Stoppard's novel, *Lord Malquist and Mr. Moon*, was published in England in 1966, it received little attention from critics and was virtually ignored by British readers. (It sold almost as many copies in Venezuela as in England.) Although it was not a best-seller, the American edition, published by Knopf in 1968, was favorably reviewed. Commenting on the novel for the *Washington Post* (April 16, 1968), Geoffrey Wolff found it to be "a remarkable entertainment, remarkably funny." Thomas Roger, writing for the *New Republic* (June 15, 1968), compared the young writer to such established talents as Kingsley Amis, Evelyn

Waugh, and P. G. Wodehouse. Roger opined, "Farce, intellectual fantasy, and moments of genuine feeling succeed one another without apparent incongruity. Parody, as Stoppard uses it, is a way of looking with exuberant high spirits at a potentially dismaying reality."

Stoppard's winning streak in the theater continued with the London production of *The Real Inspector Hound*, a one-act comedy, in 1968. In the play two fiercely competitive drama critics attend the opening performance of a new play, a parody of an Agatha Christie murder mystery. Birdboot, the senior critic, is a philanderer who lusts after the actresses on stage. He is accompanied by Moon, an ambitious second-string critic, who fantasizes about the murder of Higgs, his immediate superior. Unwittingly, both men are inextricably drawn into the action of the stage thriller. Stoppard drew on his own experiences as a drama critic to create the stereotyped characters who muddle their way through a devilishly complicated play. When the play opened on Broadway, on April 23, 1972, the veteran critic Clive Barnes, in his *New York Times* (April 24, 1972) review, applauded the "extravagantly funny and inordinately clever" comedy. He noted that the "portraits of [the] two critics are moderately slanderous and highly amusing. . . . [Stoppard] is perhaps here at his best when he has his critical victims ponder out loud what they are going to write, for here his parodies are delicious and deadly." *After Magritte*, a diverting 40-minute play first produced in London in 1970, toured as a companion piece to *The Real Inspector Hound* in the United States.

Jumpers, Stoddard's second full-length play, premiered at the Old Vic in London early in 1972, with Michael Hordern and Diana Rigg in the leading roles. It received considerable critical attention. *Jumpers* is an absurdist play that evolved from Stoppard's fascination with the idea of men landing on the moon. In an interview with Kathleen Halton for *Vogue* (October 15, 1967), he said, "You can't just land on the moon. It's much more than a location, it's a whole heritage of associations, poetic and religious. There are probably quite a few people around who'll go mad when the first man starts chumping around this symbol in size-ten boots." Working from that premise, he set *Jumpers* in a future time when the earthly system of moral order has begun to disintegrate, perhaps as a direct consequence of a British moon landing. After discovering that there is not enough fuel for both men to make the return trip, one astronaut assaults the other and blasts off for Earth on his own.

For the principal characters in the play, that event signals the beginning of a pervasive spiritual and ethical decline. George Moore, an addlepated philosophy professor, inadvertently kills his two pets, a tortoise and a hare, while attempting to illustrate a lecture on moral standards. His wife, Dotty, a retired chanteuse, goes mad when she can no longer remember the lyrics to the songs that comprised her repertoire, and she begins a love affair with Sir Archibald Jumpers, the head of the philosophy department. Sir Archibald manages a team of philosopher-gymnasts, including a professor of logic who is shot dead while forming part of a human pyramid in the first scene of the play. The ensuing murder investigation develops along the farcical lines of *Inspector Hound*, while George remains obsessed with his agonizing quest for a moral absolute. "I don't claim to know that God exists," George announces at one point. "I only claim that he does without my knowing it."

Jumpers opened in the United States at the John F. Kennedy Center for the Performing Arts, in Washington, D.C., on February 18, 1974, starring Brian Bedford as George and Jill Clayburgh as Dotty. Critical reception was mixed. Although most critics praised the play, several found fault with the casting and production. Stoppard, who customarily attends the rehearsals of all his plays, made additional script changes and staging suggestions before the New York opening of the play, at the Billy Rose Theater, on April 22, 1974. Reviewing the play for the *New York Times* (April 23, 1974), Clive Barnes noted that Stoppard "plays with ideas like a juggler, and the ideas he is playing with are sharp, clear, and dazzling." Adopting the "jumpers" metaphor, he added, "Mr. Stoppard sees the theatre as a kind of trampoline for the intellect, a sauna bath for the mind. It is all very refreshing." Other critics were less impressed. Clifford A. Ridley, for one, commenting on *Jumpers* for the *National Observer* (March 9, 1974), complained about the play's "length," its "incessant circularity," and its theatrical construction: "The play doesn't build to a conclusion; it sort of aimlessly shoots off half-baked hypotheses like an orbiting planet divesting itself of moons."

A compulsive worker, Stoppard next adapted Federico García Lorca's *The House of Bernarda Alba* for the Greenwich (England) Theatre Company and completed a screenplay for Paramount Pictures based on Bertolt Brecht's drama *Galileo*. For a change of pace, he directed a British production of Garson Kanin's farcical *Born Yesterday*. Meanwhile, he continued to write plays for radio and television. "I would like ultimately before being carried out feet first to have done a bit of absolutely everything," he told Janet Watts in an interview for the *Guardian Weekly* (April 7, 1973). "I find it very hard to turn down offers to write an underwater ballet for dolphins or a play for a motorcyclist on the wall of death."

Travesties, Stoppard's next play, takes as its starting point the historical fact that the writer James Joyce, the communist revolutionary Vladimir Lenin, and the Dadaist poet Tristan Tzara were all living in Zurich during World War I. The protagonist of the play is a minor British official named Henry Carr, who meets the others during a production of Oscar Wilde's play *The Important of Being Earnest*. Carr, whose aging memory is beginning to falter, relates the interactions between the historical luminaries as they discuss the relationship of art and politics.

Travesties, which was first produced on London's West End in 1974 and on Broadway shortly thereafter, met with mostly positive reviews and is now considered one of Stoppard's most important works. Richard L. Coe, writing for the *Washington Post* (January 9, 1977), called it "a brilliant, pell-mell performance of words, ideas, allusions, mental gymnastics, music-hall nonsense and paradox. It is an absolute, glorious delight." Jack Kroll praised Stoppard in *Newsweek* (November 10, 1975) for creating "a theatrical master stroke, a marvelous comic character, a stunning tour de force of language and a crunchingly witty play that attacks his audience with a thousand laughs and nine hundred thoughts." Stoppard won a 1976 Tony for *Travesties*.

In 1977 Stoppard wrote two plays, *Every Good Boy Deserves Favour* (also known in the press as *EGBDF*) and *Professional Foul* (for television)—that evinced a heightened political sensitivity, surprising critics who had previously accused him of political evasiveness. *EGBDF* was a combination of theater and musical performance, which Stoppard created in cooperation with André Previn, then the conductor of the London Symphony Orchestra. The action takes place in a Soviet insane asylum, where two characters named Ivanov are sharing a cell. One of the men is deranged, believing himself to be the conductor (and triangle player) of a symphony orchestra—Previn's orchestra supplied the music that he hears in his head. His companion is sane, but has been placed in the mental ward for insisting publicly that sane people are put in Soviet insane asylums.

The play was widely performed in theaters throughout Europe and was generally well received, although critics tended to view it as something of a curiosity. "The short script," Mel Gussow, a respected reviewer, wrote in a representative assessment, "is filled with the author's usual felicitous turns of phrase, his deviously manipulative conceits, his lunatic lexicon of puns, literary allusions and rodomontade wordplays. Furthermore, a man with an orchestra in his head is a spectacular notion, and Mr. Stoppard improvises deliriously on the theme." Gussow noted, however, that he found the work to be "less a play than a playful puzzle." Other critics felt uneasy about the combination of frivolity and the weighty presentation of political oppression. Tim Taylor, writing for the *Washington Post* (September 1, 1978), noted that the speaking parts of the political prisoner are "written like a 'statement' on human rights. No matter how important the issue, we can demand of Stoppard some kind of dramatic embodiment of his ideas and not just the simple listing of Russian atrocities from a Kennedy Center soapbox."

Professional Foul was first seen on British television in September 1977 and in the United States the following year. Inspired by a 1976 trip Stoppard made to Russia and the imprisonment of the dissident Czech dramatist (and future president) Václav Havel in January 1977, the play is about a Cambridge University professor of ethics who goes to Prague to participate in an academic convention and is dramatically exposed to the realities of political oppression.

Stoppard's stage play *Night and Day* (1978) is set in an imaginary African country where three British journalists go to cover a civil war. The plot focuses partly on the professional rivalry between Wagner, an old pro, and Milne, an ambitious freelancer who has scooped an interview with the rebel leader. Wagner, a union militant, despises Milne as a "scab" who has defied a journalists' strike, and their conflict gains another dimension from the fact that they both want the same woman. The influential critic Irving Wardle observed that, unlike Evelyn Waugh in *Scoop*, "Stoppard writes as a man who still cherishes some ideals about journalism and even finds it glamorous, and therein lies both the strength and the weakness of the play. . . . Stoppard has always excelled in inventing theatrical forms for whatever he wants to talk about; but even for him, it is a signal triumph to have related . . . [an African war and the wars of Fleet Street] within the discipline of a nuts-and-bolts naturalistic play."

Stoppard surprised critics again with his play *The Real Thing*, which overcame one of the other accusations frequently leveled at him: that his plays, while intellectually captivating, were coldly unemotional. The action begins with a man accusing his wife of having an affair. It soon becomes clear that this is in fact the scene of a play, written by a successful dramatist named Henry who has earned a reputation for his sophisticated, detached representations of marital infidelity. Henry, as it turns out, is having an affair with his actress, Annie, and the two soon divorce their spouses and are married. Their own marriage begins to show strains before long, however. Meanwhile, Annie champions the cause of a political activist named Brodie, who has been jailed for defacing a monument. Brodie has concocted a poorly written political drama, which Annie asks Henry to rewrite. Henry resists, calling Brodie a "pacifist hooligan" and "a lout with language," but out of love for Annie undertakes the task. When Henry discovers that Annie is having an affair with a younger actor he is crushed—words fail the witty playwright, and all he can do is rock back and forth and mutter, "Oh, please, please, please, don't."

The Real Thing was produced on the West End in 1982 and premiered in New York City in 1984. David Richards wrote for the *Washington Post* (January 12, 1984), "*The Real Thing* is every bit as clever as *Travesties* or *Jumpers*, and it is studded with Stoppard quips. . . . But it also recognizes the impotence of the intellect when confronted with the ambiguities of love." Writing for the *Christian Science Monitor* (August 17, 1984), John Beaufort described the play as a "cerebral comedy with a heart. . . . The question Mr. Stoppard poses—and hintingly answers—is whether there is enough real love and understanding in the Henry-Annie relationship to overcome their differences on a variety of matters, from music and language to activist politics." Benedict Nightingale, writing for the *New York Times* (January 14, 1984), praised *The Real Thing* as a "remarkably complete and satisfying play: clever, amusing and everything we knew Mr. Stoppard was; as well as moving, painful and several things we never dreamed he could be." In addition to the 1984 Tony Award, Stoppard received a 1984 New York Drama Critics Circle Award and the 1982 London *Evening Standard* Drama Award for *The Real Thing*.

Stoppard spent the next few years working on various projects. He wrote *Squaring the Circle* (1984), a television drama-documentary about the Polish solidarity movement. He wrote *Rough Crossing* (1984), an adaptation of a work by Ferenc Molnar, and *Dalliance* (1986), adapted from Arthur Schnitzler's *Liebelei*. He joined Terry Gilliam and Charles McKeown to write the screenplay for the film *Brazil* (1985), a futuristic satire that received the Los Angeles Critics Circle Award for best original screenplay. He also wrote the screenplay for *Empire of the Sun* (1987), adapted from the novel by J. G. Ballard, and translated Václav Havel's *Largo Desolato* (1987).

Stoppard's next original play, *Hapgood* (1988), about a woman of the same name running a British intelligence network, was a heady combination of espionage intrigue and quantum physics. The result baffled audiences and critics alike, and ran for only six months at the Aldwych Theatre in London, where it premiered. "There's a fine line between tantalizing and frustrating an audience, and Tom Stoppard has crossed it with a vengeance," Tim Gray wrote for *Daily Variety*, as quoted by Janice Arkatov in the *Los Angeles Times* (May 28, 1989). "Ostensibly a philosophic/comic spy thriller, [the play is an] impenetrable, nearly three-hour talk fest." Irving Waddle, writing for the London *Times* (March 9, 1988), felt that the play lacked the "intellectual passion" of such earlier works as *Jumpers* and *Travesties*. "Rather," he wrote, "it comes over as a bright idea, which has laboriously to be hammered into shape, and which generates precious little in the way of dramatic action."

The 1993 National Theatre production of *Arcadia* put Stoppard once again at the forefront of English theater. The play presents two sets of characters that inhabit Sidley Park, an elegant country estate in Derbyshire, England, almost two centuries apart. In 1809 Thomasina, the 13-year-old daughter of Lady Croom, takes math lessons from her amusingly lecherous tutor, Septimus Hodge. "What is carnal embrace?" she innocently asks him in the play's opening line—setting the mood for the amorous atmosphere that develops, most notably around the (offstage) presence of the lascivious poet Lord Byron, a houseguest and acquaintance of Septimus's. Meanwhile, in the present day, a bumptious literary academic named Bernard has come to the house in hopes of discovering Byron's connection to a death that took place at the Croom residence in 1809. Bernard, who has no scruples about distorting history as long as he is able to get a popular book out of doing so, finds himself at odds with current lady of the house, the standoffish Hannah. Also an academic, Hannah is investigating the same period for a book on the history of gardening. As their research progresses, their focus falls upon the identity of a mysterious hermit who occupied the grounds at the time—and it begins to appear that the precocious Thomasina may have presciently hit upon the foundations of the new math.

Charles Spencer, writing for the London *Daily Telegraph* (April 15, 1993), heralded *Arcadia* as "a terrific return to form. The gags—and there are plenty of them—have all their old exuberance and elegance, but this is also a play that makes you think, and think hard. . . . It is amazing just how much Stoppard packs into this brilliantly plotted piece." "The intellectual substructure," Christopher Rawson wrote for the *Pittsburgh Post-Gazette* (November 21, 1993), "is as dense as ever, involving Fermat's Last Theorem, Newtonian physics, the third law of thermodynamics, chaos theory, the history of artistic styles in landscape and poetry, the real mystery of Byron's life, academic skulduggery, [and] the permutations of sex and English class attitudes. . . . But it is all kept in service to intriguing parallel stories of love, ambition and intellectual pursuit." "Once you weed through *Arcadia*'s exhilarating thicket of science and horticulture," Jan Stuart noted for *Newsday* (June 20, 1993), "you are left with a high-toned roll in the hay. . . . Stoppard's wildly abundant *Arcadia* indulges more notions than we should reasonably be asked to examine, but the fount of thinking is displaced in the final analysis by an unexpectedly touching swirl of feeling."

The Invention of Love, which premiered at London's National Theatre in 1997, is a memory play about A. E. Housman, the British poet and Latin scholar best known for his 1896 book of poems, *A Shropshire Lad*. The play begins with a dream in which the 77-year-old Housman is reflecting on his life as he is being ferried across the river Styx to Hades. Housman, who was a homosexual, recalls with sorrow his youthful love for Moses Jackson, a classmate at Oxford and the school track star. As Housman's longing for Jackson went unrequited, he turned his passion into poetry and devoted the remainder of his days to his classical studies. Housman's repressed sadness, as he tries to sort out the contradictions of his stifled life, is contrasted with the flamboyant attitude of his contemporary Oscar Wilde, who is frequently mentioned but doesn't appear on stage until late in the play. Although Wilde was imprisoned for his homosexuality and met with a dismal end, he lived his life according to an ethos of freedom and self-fulfillment, and he rebukes Housman for his incorrigible sullenness: "Better a fallen rocket than never a burst of light," he says, as quoted by Vincent Canby in the *New York Times* (December 14, 1997). "Dante reserved a place in his *Inferno* for those who willfully live in sadness."

Reviews of the play were positive. "The art of the play lies in the way one idea bleeds into another," Michael Billington wrote for the *Guardian* (November 5, 1998). "Stoppard is also concerned with the notion expressed in his punning title. Does love really exist before its literary invention? And is love itself capable of endless inventiveness?" Vincent Canby found *The Invention of Love* to be "so beautifully constructed that the playwright seems to be discovering his play only one jump ahead of the audience. It has that sense of surprise and wonder." Alistair Macaulay wrote for the London *Financial Times* (October 2, 1997) that the play contained "some of the finest, most passionate, and most disarmingly brilliant dramatic writing that [Stoppard] has given us." Although Macaulay noted that "at times . . . Stoppard is so concerned with being clever that he becomes merely callow," he concluded that "an immediate review can only scratch the surface of this most elaborately polished work of art."

Stoppard is perhaps best known to the general public for his next effort; in 1998 he co-wrote, with Marc Norman, the screenplay for *Shakespeare in Love*. The film envisions the young William as a not-yet-famous playwright, struggling to overcome a bad case of writer's block with a new script, *Romeo and Ethel, the Pirate's Daughter*. Will (played by Joseph Fiennes) soon falls in love with Viola De Lesseps (Gwyneth Paltrow)—an aspiring actress who must disguise herself as a man in order to perform, as women in Elizabethan England weren't permitted to act. Their passionate romance provides the inspiration for Will to complete the play, with Viola cast as the newly written character of Juliet. Jay Carr, writing for the *Boston Globe* (December 25, 1980), called it "the year's most exhilarating surprise. . . . Hurtling through a believable yeasty London with confidence and panache, *Shakespeare in Love* lives by the word. . . . It's a bawdy, exuberant, nimble-witted, impassioned lark." The idea for the script was Norman's, with Stoppard called in later to complete the work. As the film's director, John Madden, explained to Paula Span for the *Washington Post* (December 26, 1998), Stoppard was "literally the only person you could think of who could dare to put words in Shakespeare's mouth and get away with it." The New York Film Critics Circle voted it the year's best screenplay. At the 1999 Academy Award the movie received 13 nominations, of which it won seven, with Stoppard and Norman sharing an Oscar for best original screenplay.

The Coast of Utopia, Stoppard's long-awaited epic set in 19th-century Russia, premiered at the National Theatre in 2002. In what is actually a trio of sequential but self-contained three-hour plays—*Voyage*, *Shipwreck*, and *Salvage*—Utopia focuses on a group of intellectuals living under the repressive regime of Tsar Nicholas I. The main characters include the anarchist Michael Bakunin, the writer Ivan Turgenev, and the first self-proclaimed socialist Alexander Herzen—men for whom the word "intelligentsia" was coined. Spanning 30 years, the drama follows its protagonists as they struggle under oppression, forge varying strains of revolutionary thought and utopian idealism, and navigate the treacherous waters of life and love. Performed before London audiences in 12-hour Saturday marathons, with lunch and dinner breaks, the production received strong reviews and had its run extended until late 2002. The plays are scheduled for publication in individual volumes in mid-2003, but because of the size and complexity of staging such a work—it involves no less than 30 actors wearing 271 costumes—there are likely to be few performances in the United States. The Lincoln Center Theater plans to stage a production in spring 2005.

Stoppard, a fellow of the Royal Society of Literature, was made a Commander of the Order of the British Empire in 1978. He has two sons by his 1965 marriage to Jose Ingle, which ended in divorce, and two sons by his 1972 marriage to Miriam Moore-Robinson, a physician, author, and popular TV personality. That marriage ended in separation in 1990. Stoppard also had a relationship with the actress Felicity Kendall (who played leading roles in both *The Real Thing* and *Hapgood*). Now single, he lives in the Chelsea neighborhood of London, England—"with a lot of mess and books," as he told Robin Pogrebin for the *New York Times* (March 18, 2001).

—K. D.

SUGGESTED READING: *Boston Globe* C p1 Dec. 25, 1980; *Christian Science Monitor* p23 Aug. 17, 1984; *Daily Telegraph* p17 Apr. 15, 1993; Guardian p12 Nov. 5, 1998; Los Angeles Times p58 May 28, 1989; *New York Times* II p5 Jan. 14, 1984, II p4 Dec. 14, 1997, II p7 Mar. 18, 2001; *New Yorker* May 4, 1968; Dec. 19, 1977; Newsday p20 June 20, 1993; *Newsweek* p66 Nov. 10, 1975; Philadelphia Inquirer H p1 May 12, 2002; Pittsburgh Post-Gazette E p1 Nov. 21, 1993; (London) *Sunday Times Magazine* June 9, 1974;*Time* May 6, 1974, Nov. 10, 1975; (London) *Times* Nov. 11, 1972, Nov. 10, 1978, Mar. 9, 1988; *Times Literary Supplement* July 12, 1974; *Washington Post* M p1 Jan. 9, 1977, p13 Sep. 1, 1978, C p1 Jan. 12, 1984, C p1 Dec. 26, 1998

SELECTED WORKS: plays—*Rosencrantz and Guildenstern Are Dead*, 1967; *Enter a Free Man*, 1968; *The Real Inspector Hound*, 1968; *Jumpers*, 1972; *Travesties*, 1974; *Every Good Boy Deserves Favour*, 1977; *Night and Day*, 1978; *The Real Thing*, 1982; *Hapgood*, 1988; *Arcadia*, 1993; *Invention of Love*, 1997; screenplays—*Brazil*, 1985 (with Terry Gilliam and Charles McKeown); *Empire of the Sun*, 1987; *Billy Bathgate*, 1991; *Shakespeare in Love*, 1998 (with Marc Norman); novel—*Lord Malquist and Mr. Moon*, 1966

Straight, Susan

Oct. 19, 1960– Novelist; short-story writer

Susan Straight is the author of several novels and short stories that explore the world of working-class African-American men, women, and children. Yet as a white woman writing about the experiences of blacks, especially black males, Straight has been the subject of heated dispute. While some have praised her for bridging the racial gap, others have accused her of cultural appropriation. "Few authors in America manage (with the sort of easy confidence that makes the writing of fiction seem effortless) to do anything more difficult or (given the currently intense suspicion of anyone daring to write across the lines of race, gender, class) more nervy and brave," Francine Prose wrote of Straight for the *Washington Post* (July 21, 1996). Straight's published works, which include *Aquaboogie: A Novel in Stories* (1990), *I Been In Sorrow's Kitchen and Licked Out All the Pots: A Novel* (1992), *Getting Place* (1996), and *Highwire Moon: A Novel* (2001), have drawn praise from critics, in particular for their evocation of different forms of African-American speech. Donna Seaman in a review of *Blacker Than a Thousand Midnights* (1994) for *Booklist* (June 1– 15, 1994) wrote that "Straight has a great ear for the music of conversation, and her prose is potent, dignified, and lyrical, elevating the challenges of existence to a level of universal significance. And she writes under the banner of hope."

Susan Straight was born on October 19, 1960 in Riverside, California, which has been described by journalists as a tough, racially mixed town. Her mother was a Swiss immigrant and her stepfather was from Prince Edward Island in northeastern Canada. (Straight does not discuss her biological father with the press.) "The neighborhood [in Riverside] I came from, everyone was Air Force," she recalled to Michael Coffey for *Publishers Weekly* (July 4, 1994). "There were people that were half-German and half-black, half-Filipino and half-white. So we had friends who were half-half-half-half." When Straight was in the eighth grade, she met her future husband, Dwayne Sims, who is black.

After high school Straight attended Riverside Community College, where a professor encouraged her to write. She earned a scholarship to attend the University of Southern California, in Los Angeles, where she studied journalism and worked as a sportswriter for the *Daily Trojan*, a student newspaper. In a creative-writing class she worked on her fiction. At first, "I tried to write like everybody else," she recalled to Lynell George for the *Los Angeles Times* (December 1, 1994), but soon she began writing about the life she knew growing up in Riverside's diverse community. She received her B.A. in journalism in 1981. She applied for an MFA program at University of Massachusetts at Amherst and was accepted. After moving there with Sims, she sought out Jay Neugeboren, a white professor who had written *Big Man* (1966), a critically acclaimed novel about a black basketball player, and asked him to him read one of her stories. "And [Neugeboren] wrote on the bottom, 'This is wonderful, stop by and see me,'" she told Michael Coffey. "And it was like, if he'd laughed at me right then I'd've gone home. It woulda been over, I wouldn't even a stayed." Another important influence for Straight was James Baldwin, also a professor at the university and the author of the well-known work *Notes of a Native Son* (1963).

Straight completed her MFA in 1984. She and Sims, now married, returned to Riverside, where Straight began teaching English as a Second Language in programs for gang members, dropouts, and refugees. She continued writing and eventually *TriQuarterly*, a Northwestern University literary magazine, bought some of her stories. "Once I got that little bit of encouragement, it was just like everything changed for me," Straight told Michael Coffey. "My family used to say, Well what are you staying up all night typing for, I mean c'mon. Now I had a reason to do it, I'd say, Look, I sold this story, I made some money. I could show that check."

In 1990 Straight submitted a collection of her stories, *Aquaboogie*, for the Milkweed National Fiction Prize. She won the award, which confers $3000 and publication. *Aquaboogie: A Novel in Stories* is composed of several tales, most of which take place in a town about an hour outside of Los Angeles, California, called Rio Seco—a fictionalized version of Riverside. The stories sometimes overlap, with major characters from one story making appearances in another. In the title story, a young black artist named Nacho King has moved from California to Massachusetts. He works as a janitor to pay for an art class, but soon the racism becomes too hard to tolerate and he returns home, where his father reminds him of their limited horizons. "We don't take art classes and travel across the country. We just work," Straight writes in the voice of the father, as quoted by Margaret Camp for the *Washington Post* (March 3, 1991). In "Safe Hooptie," Darnell and his girlfriend, Brenda, are stuck in the house playing cards because police are trolling the area for a murder suspect. Darnell has learned that in a place where being black automatically makes you a suspect, it is best to stay out of sight.

"The great strength of *Aquaboogie*," Judith Freeman wrote for the *Los Angeles Times* (November 18, 1990), "is the way this 'novel-in-stories' brings to life the rich and vibrant life of an all-black-community. . . . A world of pain and love and longing is contained in these stories." "[Straight] has listened very carefully to the talking around her," Freeman added, "and by making a book that can be read by all, black and white, she has bridged worlds for us, bringing us the news, which has a quiet, very triumphant undertone, no matter how harsh the overlaying reality." Margaret Camp wrote that "Rio Seco seems surprisingly real—full of believable characters and events, created by a woman supremely sure of her environment. . . . She is keenly aware of people's habits, thoughts, speech patterns, indeed almost everything about them." *Publishers Weekly* named *Aquaboogie* as one of the best books of 1990.

Straight's first novel, *I Been in Sorrow's Kitchen and Licked out All the Pots*, follows the life of strong-willed Marietta Cook from her childhood in Pine Gardens, South Carolina, where the inhabitants speak Gullah (an African-influenced English dialect), into her middle-age. When Marietta is a teen, her mother dies and she is forced to fend for herself. She heads to the larger city of Charleston and finds work at a fish market, where she falls for a fellow employee named Sinbad. Their brief affair leaves Marietta, only 16, abandoned and the mother of twins. She returns to her hometown to raise the boys, Calvin and Nathaniel, before moving back to Charleston. Her children learn to play football, a skill that opens doors for them: they get into a college in California and eventually are recruited by the professional football team the Los Angeles Rams. Marietta follows them out to California, sampling the fruits of their success and moving into a luxury condo in Los Angeles. The lifestyle is not to her liking, however, so she settles in the outlaying town of Rio Seco (where several characters from *Aquaboogie* reappear).

Reviews of the novel were largely positive, although Straight's extensive use of Gullah dialect proved a point of contention among critics. Patricia Spears Jones, in an appraisal for the *Chicago Tribune* (June 21, 1992) found that "the cleverly honed language spoken by the men and women of *Aquaboogie*" had here been replaced "by language that is somewhat unintelligible and often dull." Leon Rooke for the *New York Times Book Review* (August 16, 1992), however, described the language as "wonderful talk . . . a patois that flows in delicious abundance through this yeasty, lavishly detailed . . . novel." "Her prose is lively and eloquent," Rooke continued, "most powerful when Ms. Straight is inside her remarkable character's head. For the most part . . . *I've Been in Sorrow's Kitchen and Licked Out All the Pots* is admirably constructed, and the author's vision sure." Henry Louis Gates, Jr., the chair of the Afro-American Studies Department at Harvard University, noted several flaws in the work; he wrote for the *Washington Post* (August 9, 1992) that the book was dangerously close to being "*The Beverly Hillbillies* in blackface." He continued, "Straight is a major talent, a first-rate writer who's written a decidedly second-rate novel. This is a book I read with growing irritation, but with steady admiration for her sentence-by-sentence craftsmanship, her ability to capture complex settings and situations."

In her second novel, *Blacker Than a Thousand Midnights*, Straight looks at a couple of years in the life of Darnell Tucker (a character that first appeared in *Aquaboogie*). A young black man, Darnell has been working as a seasonal firefighter in the mountains outside Rio Seco. He loves his job and would like to become permanent, but cutbacks in the Department of Forestry—and possible racism among his supervisors—deprive him of the opportunity. When the season ends Darnell returns to Rio Seco and to his girlfriend, Brenda, who is pregnant. The two marry and Brenda gives birth to a girl, Charolette. Desperate to do right by Brenda, Darnell takes whatever jobs he's able to get, including hauling trash for his father and working part time as a security guard. Often unemployed, however, he feels guilty that his wife has to support him and their daughter. He still dreams about being a firefighter, an internal conflict that is only exacerbated by friends who taunt him for choosing to be tied down to family life and for not doing drugs. "When I went on the [tour] for Darnell's book," Straight told Lynell George, "at black bookstores people said they were tired of reading about pathologies. They were tired of everything having to be so violent, so criminal to be a black story. They said what they like about Darnell was that is was about what they called a 'normal brother.' The guys who are going to work, and coming home and doing an ordinary thing."

"Darnell's painstaking struggle to do the ordinary things becomes extraordinary in Ms. Straight's gifted hands," Rosemary L. Bray wrote in an assessment of the novel for the *New York Times Book Review* (December 11, 1994). David Nicholson commented for the *Washington Post* (June 7, 1994) that the work evinced "an understanding of the irony and playfulness of black language, an understanding of the deepness of family ties and heritage." "The novel could have benefitted from a sympathetic editor," he added. "It's a little too long, it meanders, and it's hard to keep track of the large cast of characters. In the end, however, this is a triumph, a portrait of a young black man trying to find his way that ends not with prison, drug dealing or death, but with small moments of affirmation and the acceptance of responsibility that are a tribute to his will and his intelligence."

Straight's third novel, *Getting Place*, is a lengthy murder mystery that chronicles the lives of five generations of the African-American Thompson family. Hosea Thompson, the 76-year-old patriarch of the family, lives in Treetown, a poor black section of Rio Seco. Hosea grew up in Tulsa, Oklahoma, where he witnessed the infamous race riots of 1921—when white deputies and the Oklahoma National Guard set fire to an all-black neighborhood—and the memories of the event still haunt him. Hosea moved to Rio Seco in 1950, built a house, started a towing company, and with his wife, Alma, had five sons and a daughter (Demetrious, Octavious, Julius, Marcus, Finis, and Sofelia). Marcus, the main character in the story, is now a substitute-teacher who lives in a better part of town; his family members deride him for having white friends and for not working with his hands. His brother Finis's mind has been permanently damaged from smoking a "super cool"—a cigarette soaked in PCP. Sofelia, the daughter, was raped when she was 12 and in her desperation fled to Los Angeles, where she gave birth to a son, Mortice. The novel opens with the bodies of two young white women found in a burning car on Hosea's property. Hosea and his family become the prime suspects in the crime, and to help get his family off the hook, Marcus undertakes an investigation of his own. More murders follow, and soon Finis disappears. Sofelia meanwhile returns to Rio Seco, hoping to save her son from the ravages of gang violence—only to find Rio Seco just as afflicted.

"In this long, ambitious work," Francine Prose wrote for the *Washington Post* (July 21, 1996), "Straight combines her skill at accurately rending the complex nuances of character and community with the narrative momentum of a conventional novel of suspense. It is, as they say, a page-turner: a thriller with the sustained depth of a serious multigenerational family novel." Molly E. Rauch in a review for the *Nation* (July 15/22, 1996) found the work "extraordinarily detailed in its depiction of place and dialect. But the most compelling element in this ambitious novel is Marcus Thompson. . . . He's working against the clock, because he's trying to check the seemingly inevitable corruption of justice: black flesh for white flesh." "The underlying point of Ms. Straight's intricately plotted, exciting, infuriating novel is the degree of efficiency and energy lost to society when people like the Thompsons are mistrusted by the police and abused by the law," Phoebe-Lou Adams wrote in an assessment for *Atlantic Monthly* (September 1996). "It is a painful story, violent, ultimately sinister, and most expertly written."

In Straight's next novel, *Highwire Moon*, Serafina Mendez is a young Mixtec Indian girl who immigrates illegally to California from her home in the poor southern Mexican state of Oaxaca. She is 15 years old and alone when she becomes romantically involved with Larry Foley, a man who rescues her from the Immigration and Naturalization Service (INS). She gives birth to a daughter, Elvia. Three years later, Serafina leaves Larry and takes Elvia with her. In a moment of confusion, Serafina is picked up by the INS and deported to Mexico. Elvia grows up in Rio Seco in the care of a foster mother, believing all the while that her mother abandoned her. When, at age 15, Elvia becomes pregnant, she goes in search of Serafina.

"There's much to admire in Straight's heart-rending, take-no-prisoners fourth novel," Jeff Zaleski wrote for *Publishers Weekly* (July 30, 2001). "Straight portrays this world in imagery that can be quite poetic." Although Zaleski expressed minor grievances with the work, he concluded that, "As a novelist, Straight is unswervingly focused on the intersections of love, race, class and violence; despite its flaws, this is an engrossing demonstration of her dedication to that vision." "An intense, gripping, and beautifully wrought novel," Alix Madrigal opined for the *San Francisco Chronicle* (August 26, 2001). Suzanne Ruta for the *New York Times Book Review* (August 26, 2001) remarked that "Straight writes with great empathy about working-class men. . . . [Larry] is the most complex and convincing character in the novel." "*Highwire Moon* is an eye-opener. . . , a road map to the real California," she continued. "Straight's Rio Seco is a microcosm of the suspicious, segregated America, a place where racism often boils down to fear, ignorance and willful obliviousness." *Highwire Moon* was a finalist for the 2001 National Book Award.

Straight is a professor of creative writing at the University of California at Riverside, a position she has held since 1988. She has published short fiction and articles in such periodicals as *TriQuarterly*, *Ploughshares*, *Harper's*, *New York Times Magazine*, *Los Angeles Times Magazine*, and *Ontario Review*. She has also written a children's book, *Bear E. Bear* (1995). Straight is the recipient of a Guggenheim fellowship and a Lannan Foundation grant. She is divorced and the mother of three daughters—Gaila, Delphine, and Rosette.

—A. I. C.

SUGGESTED READING: *Atlantic Monthly* p112 Sep. 1996; *Booklist* p1774 June 1–15, 1994; *Chicago Tribune* p7 June 21, 1992; *Library Journal* p122 Apr. 15, 1992; *Los Angeles Times* p3 Nov. 18, 1990, p1 Dec. 1, 1994; *Nation* p42 July 15/22, 1996; *New York Times Book Review* p15 Aug. 16, 1992, p27 Dec. 11, 1994, p16 Aug. 26, 2001; *Publishers Weekly* p41 July 4, 1994, p60 July 30, 2001; *San Francisco Chronicle* p78 Aug. 26, 2001; *Washington Post Book World* p9 Mar. 3, 1991, p4 Aug. 9, 1992, p3 July 21, 1996

SELECTED BOOKS: *Aquaboogie: A Novel in Stories*, 1990; *I Been In Sorrow's Kitchen and Licked Out All the Pots: A Novel*, 1992; *Blacker Than a Thousand Midnights*, 1994; *Getting Place*, 1996; *Highwire Moon: A Novel*, 2001

Szirtes, George

Nov. 29, 1948– Poet; translator

The Hungarian-born poet, translator, and university professor George Szirtes has lived in England since he fled Budapest with his family during the uprising of 1956, when he was eight years old. He is now coordinator of creative writing at Norwich School of Art and Design and the author of more than a dozen collections of his own poetry, as well as many translations of contemporary Hungarian poets. With George Gomori, he edited *The Colonnade of Teeth: Modern Hungarian Poetry*, an anthology published in 1996. Several of Szirtes's collections from the 1990s, *Bridge Passages* (1991), *Blind Field* (1994), *Selected Poems 1976–1996* (1996), and *Portrait of My Father in an English Landscape* (1998), were published as part of the Oxford Poets series by Oxford University Press, which has stated of its author: "He wields English

Clarissa Upchurch/Courtesy of Bloodaxe Books
George Szirtes

with the particular skill, strangeness, and originality of one who mediates between the tone of his forebears and the voice he has acquired since childhood." Szirtes has regularly contributed reviews to publications such as the *Times Literary Supplement*, which has also published a number of his poems over the years.

George Szirtes was born in Budapest, Hungary, on November 29, 1948, during a period of postwar turmoil just months before a Communist-led government assumed power there. His father, Laszlo, was an engineer, and his mother, Magdalena Nussbacher Szirtes, was a photographer who had been imprisoned in a Nazi concentration camp during World War II. The family fled Hungary after the abortive uprising in 1956 and settled in England, where young George pursued studies in fine arts and painting. He studied at the Harrow School of Art for two years before receiving his bachelor's degree from Leeds College of Art, in 1972; he then continued his studies at the University of London. For several years during the 1970s, Szirtes taught creative writing at various schools, and from 1981 to 1987 he served as director of art at St. Christopher School in Letchworth. Since 1991 he has been senior lecturer in poetry at Norwich School of Art and Design.

The first collection of Szirtes's poetry, *Poems*, was published in 1972. Other collections published during that decade included *The Iron Clouds* (1975), *Visitors* (1976), and *An Illustrated Alphabet* (1978). He also engaged in collaborative works with other writers, such as *A Mandeville Troika* (1977), with Neil Powell and Peter Scupham, and *Poetry Introduction 4*, with five other writers. Szirtes's 1979 collection, *The Slant Door*, was the co-recipient of the Geoffrey Faber memorial prize from the Faber & Faber Arts Council in 1980.

In 1984 Szirtes revisited Hungary for the first time since he had fled there as a boy, and his next several collections of poetry, including *Short Wave* (1984), *The Photographer in Winter* (1986), *Metro* (1988), and *Bridge Passages* (1991), dealt with the reconciliation of his familial heritage and childhood memory with his adult identity as an English writer. *A Photographer in Winter* was written as a tribute to his mother. Metaphors inspired by camera work are found here and in other collections, notably *Blind Field*, whose title itself is a term used in photography; in an article for *Poetry Review*, Szirtes had earlier described his fascination with the "caught and frozen moment." In describing this book, his publisher, Oxford University Press, stated that "photographic themes supply the starting point for a number of poems of almost surrealistic dislocation. These give way at the end to a group of more warmly affectionate, personal poems." At the heart of the book is a long poem, "Transylvania," which finds the poet in his mother's former home in Romania.

Szirtes is also highly regarded as a translator from the Hungarian. He edited Ottó Orbán's *The Blood Song of the Walsungs* (1993) and Freda Downie's *Collected Poems* (1995) for Bloodaxe Books. His translation, for Oxford University Press, of Zsuzsa Rakovszky's selected poems, *New Life*, won the European Poetry Translation Prize in 1995. In the following year Bloodaxe Books published *The Colonnade of Teeth: Modern Hungarian Poetry*, an anthology Szirtes had edited with George Gomori. The book draws its title from a poem by Sándor Weöres (1913–89), widely regarded as Hungary's greatest late-20th-century poet. Works by 34 other Hungarian poets of the century are found in the volume, which includes five poems by Gomori but none, strangely, by Szirtes himself. In their joint introduction to the book, Szirtes and Gomori argue, "This anthology is not primarily about national obsessions—it simply presents what the editors consider to be, if not unarguably the best, then at least the best translated poetry written by Hungarian poets born in the specified period." Szirtes and his co-editor note that postmodernism had not yet affected Hungarian poetry "in any significant way" by the time the collection was published, and suggest that Hungary's unique political situation may have been at least partly responsible for this, as when they write: "The two most interesting poets of the post-1968 period, György Petri and Zsuzsa Rakovszky, achieved their present status by resisting the conformism-within-diversity imposed by the Kádár regime. Where Petri took to *samizdat* and direct political comment, Rakovszky's poetry established a persona that appeared introspective but in fact registered the realities of Hungarian society on its highly sensitive pulse." Rather than attempting to be all-inclusive in editing *The Colonnade of Teeth*, Szirtes and Gomori "regard the final result as the sum and overlap of our individual enthusiasms."

Szirtes's keen awareness of the Hungarian political culture is reflected in the introductions to several of his translated works. In 1991 New Directions in the United States published his translation of the novel *Anna Édes* (1926) by Dezsö Kosztolányi (1885–1936), who had founded the influential literary journal *Nyugat* (variously translated as *West* or *Occidental*) around the time of the First World War (modern Hungarian poets, noted Szirtes, are still classified as belonging to the first, second, or third *Nyugat* generation); Kosztolányi's works had fallen out of favor during the Communist period, when social realism dominated Hungarian literature. In his introduction to his translation, Szirtes wrote: "After the Communist takeover in 1949, so called 'art-for-art's-sake' aestheticism met with official disapproval and despite the social conscience so clearly evident in his work he was thought to be unsound. The wheel has turned again since then: few people would now query the classic status that is usually accorded him." Describing Kosztolányi as one of the major contributors to the "remarkable firework display of early and mid-century Hungarian literature that was characterized by the *Nyugat* movement," Szirtes added, "His was an ill-fated generation but a remarkably lively and intelligent one."

Szirtes received the European Poetry Translation Prize in 1995 for his English rendering of Zsuzsa Rakovszky's collection, *New Life*. In his essay "Translating Zsuzsa Rakovszky," published in the *Hungarian Quarterly* (Summer 1998), Szirtes offered a self-conscious evaluation of his own literary style and of his attitude toward the process of translation, which he called "a kind of love affair with the complementary Other whose shadow you have decided temporarily to become." Szirtes stated that he had initiated the project, that of translating Rakovszky's work, instead of waiting to be commissioned, and that he discovered in her work another affirmation of the overriding importance of form: "I bought or got hold of her books and began working things out for myself. I could see that the early poems owed something to Plath but that they had a political content beyond the personal. The poems were not always easy and at some points I felt they were very difficult indeed, but what was clear was that they did manage to synthesize both personal and public experience at a potent level, that the form provided a kind of intellectual discipline, and that—most importantly—there was something in the sensibility I recognized." In the same essay, he recounted that he had been sent "an interesting anthology" of American verse titled *Rebel Angels* from a group that calls itself the "New Formalists, most of whom are not ironic or postmodern in technique. They sent it to me because my own verse is often highly formal with ornate rhyme schemes and, less often, strict metrical patterns. The reasons for this are complex, possibly even unconscious." But, he added, "If I had to sum up my conscious attitude to form it would be to regard it as counterpoint. . . . Preferences and practices aside, it seems to me obvious that the poet's choice of form is an integral part of the poem as phenomenon. To translate a strictly formal poet into free verse seems a slightly incomplete enterprise—not because the result is in itself bad poetry . . . but because it is missing something worth having. It is also to regard form as decoration rather than structure, and I know, as a formal poet, that form is at least as structural as counterpoint in music."

Discussing his own experience, in the same essay, "with all my 40 years of English domicile," Szirtes frankly acknowledged his weaknesses: "Naturally, like any translator, I am highly fallible, fully aware that my bad work is very bad indeed, willing and able to defend the defensible but not unto the last ditch which would, I am convinced, be a foolish and vainglorious gesture. . . . Reading is, or should be, a matter of excitement. A bad translation of a good poem is a bad poem. An overweening and arrogant translation of a good poem into a different good poem is not a translation."

In 1998 Oxford University Press published Szirtes's *Portrait of My Father in an English Landscape*, a 63-page collection of poetry rendered predominantly in the sonnet form. It was originally titled *Hungarian Sonnet for an Irish Singer* after its 210-line poem of the same title, consisting of a sequence of 15 sonnets. The 12th sonnet in this poem expresses most directly Szirtes's quest for identity, as when he wrote:

> "This tiny world, part Hungary, part England, is the macaronic my parents speak— my dad especially. There is no bland unbroken stream. The words seem to leak In drips, wearing away all sensible matter, making minute impressions, exhausting them. I see this and am lost in multi-coloured chatter. . .

The concluding lines to the 15th sonnet in "Hungarian Sonnet for an Irish Singer" evoke once again Szirtes's dual identity as Hungarian and English: "Hungary, England are verbal shadowlands / of spotless glass where all may sit and preen, / blank languages whose words refuse to mean."

Reviewing the collection for *New Statesman* (April 24, 1998), Michael Glover wrote that the author "continues to be strikingly un-English—and yet he writes with brilliant precision in his adopted tongue. The effect is to give his imagery a delicious unpredictability. Szirtes was trained as a painter, and some of the best poems in this collection are to do with the particular moods and scenes evoked by colours: lemon yellow or, best of all, chalk white in the poem entitled 'Chalk White: Moon in the Pool'." Stephen Knight, In his review for the *Times Literary Supplement* (August 28, 1998), elaborated on this painterly interpretation: "As he must by now be tired of hearing, his training as a painter is again evident in the wealth of references to the visual arts, with nods to Hopper and Duchamp as well as to filmmakers John Frankenheimer—*The Manchurian Candidate* supplies Szirtes with one of his poem's titles—and Busby Berkeley. What is scarcely ever noticed, however, is that this training has not resulted in a no-ideas-but-in-things school of poetry; a typical Szirtes piece tends not to be worked around a single, defining image, but is rather an accumulation of details that tellingly incorporates a degree of verbal play." Knight compared Szirtes's work to that of the German-born Michael Hoffman, "another poet-exile writing in his second language," by citing lines from Szirtes's poem "The First, Second, Third and Fourth Circles":

> the cool air shuffles through a park
> with cedars, a cog-wheeled railway,
> a deserted tram stop, some concrete
> tables for ping-pong or for chess, and
> benches where migrant workers from
>   Romania
> sleep to shave in the morning by a
>   working fountain . . .

To Knight, Szirtes is "a poet neither fully English nor Hungarian . . . a condition explored at greater length in the three autobiographical sonnet-sequences that close *Portrait of My Father in an English Landscape.* Though eclectic in its choice of technique, the book is dominated by the sonnet, a quintessentially compact form that has always suited Szirtes's discursive purpose, deployed, in the title poem, to remember his father, 'the figure I feel I have to build / into and out of language.'"

Szirtes's literary credos are also revealed in his essays about the work of other Hungarian authors. In "Budapest Diaries," from *Hungarian Quarterly* (Summer 1997), Szirtes reviewed books by three Hungarian women who, like himself, returned to their homeland in the 1980s or 1990s after years of exile abroad: Magda Denes, Susan Rubin Suleiman, and Susan Varga. To Szirtes, their stories are woven from memories that are "of loss, deprivation and danger." His comment on Denes's memoir, *Castles Burning,* shed particular light on his own stance toward literature: "Denes writes with the intensity of an artist: her scenes are directly and immediately present. There is no postmodern hedging or decentering here. We follow the characters through their travails in war-time Budapest and we care deeply about them."

In the last few years Szirtes has published several books, including a new translation of a prominent Hungarian author, a book on art, and two collections of his own poetry. In 1999 he published a translation of *The Melancholy of Resistance,* by László Krasznahorkai. In *Exercise of Power: The Art of Ana Maria Pacheco* (2001), he traces the career of the Brazilian-born sculptor, painter, and printmaker who in 1999 was in residency at the National Gallery in London. *The Budapest File* (2000) contains a collection of poems on Hungarian themes gathered from Szirtes's earlier volumes, exploring universal issues of loss, danger, and exile. *An English Apocalypse* (2001) includes a selection of earlier poems as well as new work. Szirtes is currently at work on a translation of "The Night of Akhenaton: Selected Poems of Ágnes Names Nagy."

Szirtes lives in Norfolk and is married to the artist Clarissa Upchurch. Their two grown children live and work in London.

— E. M.

SUGGESTED READING: *Georgia Review* p368+ Summer 1999; *Hungarian Quarterly* (on-line) Spring 1995, Summer 1997, Summer 1998; *Library Journal* p103+ Jan. 1998; *New Statesman* p56 Apr. 24, 1998; *Times Literary Supplement* p28 Feb. 2, 1996, p26 June 7, 1996, p23 Apr. 18, 1997, p28 Oct. 24, 1997, p4 Oct. 31, 1997, p31 Aug. 28, 1998

SELECTED BOOKS: poetry—*Poems,* 1972; *The Iron Clouds,* 1975; *Visitors,* 1976; *A Mandeville Troika* (with N. Powell and P. Scupham), 1977; *An Illustrated Alphabet,* 1978; *Poetry Introduction 4* (with C. Clothier, A. Cluysenaar, A. Elliott, A. Hollinghurst, C. Raine), 1978; *At the Sink,* 1978; *Silver Age,* 1978; *The Slant Door,* 1979; *Sermon on a Ship,* 1980; *Homage to Cheval,* 1981; *November and May,* 1981; *The Kissing Place,* 1982; *Short Wave,* 1984; *The Photographer in Winter,* 1986; *Metro,* 1988; *Bridge Passages,* 1991; *Blind Field,* 1994; *Selected Poems, 1976–1996,* 1996; *Portrait of My Father in an English Landscape,* 1998; *The Budapest File,* 2000; *An English Apocalypse,* 2001; as translator—*The Tragedy of Man* (by I. Madach), 1988; *Through the Smoke: Selected Poems* (by I. Vas), 1989; *Anna Édes* (by D. Kosztoloányi), 1991; *The Melancholy of Resistance* (by L. Krasznahorkai), 1999

Tasker, Peter

1956 (?)– Novelist; nonfiction writer; financial analyst

Peter Tasker is a British expatriate who has been living in Tokyo, Japan, for more than 20 years. Tasker is a celebrity in his adopted country, enjoying a reputation as one of the country's most talented financial analysts. He has also earned critical acclaim as a writer, having published an analysis of Japanese society, *The Japanese: A Major Look at Modern Japan,* and three detective novels, *Silent Thunder, Buddha Kiss,* and *Samurai Boogie.* The hero of these novels, Kazuo Mori, is a Japanese version of the hard-boiled detective made famous by such American authors as Raymond Chandler, Dashiell Hammett, and Mickey Spillane. In each of his three adventures, Mori investigates a case and finds himself fighting for his life against a host of enemies, including a sinister right-wing group, a dangerous cult, vicious gangsters, and corrupt pol-

Courtesy of Kodansha International Ltd.
Peter Tasker

iticians and businesspeople. In an interview with Stephen Mansfield for *Japan Inc* (August 2001, online), Tasker said that his novels "reflect my perceptions, though not necessarily my personal experiences. Most of the characters are blends of people I've met, so my experience is there in an altered form."

Peter Tasker was born in the United Kingdom in about 1956 and graduated from Oxford University. He became a permanent resident of Japan in 1981. In an interview with Patrick J. Killen for *Tokyo Business Today* (July 1995), Tasker explained that his move to Japan "was like most things, it was an accident. I was planning to be a lawyer, working and studying at the same time. And I decided to take a year off, and that year turned out to be 14." Tasker spent two years working for the Japanese firm Suntory Ltd. In 1986 he joined the Tokyo branch of the investment bank Kleinwort Benson (later renamed Dresdner Kleinwort Benson), eventually becoming its head of Japanese research and investment strategy. During the 1990s Tasker emerged as one of Japan's most respected and sought-after financial experts. From 1992 to 1997, he was voted the number-one financial analyst and strategist in Japan in an annual survey of the nation's fund managers. In 1998 he co-founded Arcus Investment, a fund management company.

In his first book, *The Japanese: A Major Look at Modern Japan* (1988), Tasker focused on the influence on Japanese society of the media, political and economic groups, technology, and the nation's industrial and financial center. Tasker drew on his observations and experiences as a foreigner working in Japan's fast-paced financial sector. "In a crisp style peppered with pungent phrases, Tasker skillfully probes Japanese society, politics, and the economy," Steven I. Levine wrote for *Library Journal* (June 1, 1988). "Well-grounded in history and rich in revealing anecdotes, his book provides shrewd insights into the often contradictory essences of contemporary Japan. Well-balanced and fair-minded, the work avoids gross generalizations or sensationalism." In the *Times Literary Supplement* (April 29–May 5, 1988), W. G. Beasley observed that the book "lives up to its title: this is the work of an author who knows the place, the people, the society, the language." Beasley praised Tasker for writing "a highly readable and often witty discussion of all the themes that are debated about Japan today."

In 1992 Tasker published his first novel, *Silent Thunder*, in which Kazuo Mori attempts to thwart a conspiracy by far-right groups in the United States and Japan to seize control of Japan's financial markets. The novel received mixed reviews. "[Tasker] has produced an unbelievable tale of the seamy side of modern Japan, full of its corrupt lines between politicians, bureaucrats and gangsters and littered with dead bodies," Kevin Rafferty wrote for the London *Financial Times* (September 18, 1993). "Its sleazy hero is a character you can warm to. He has a sharp eye for the Japanese underworld." In the *New York Times Book Review* (November 15, 1992), Newgate Callendar praised the novel, describing Mori as a throwback to Raymond Chandler's Sam Spade and other literary private detectives. "Mori beats up people, gets beaten up himself and always manages to squeeze out of life-threatening situations," Callendar wrote. "Mr. Tasker provides some extra dividends, including a close look at the Japanese character and great flashes of humor, like the introduction of a father and two sons who want to be gangsters and hit men, a trade at which they are spectacularly inept. The premise of *Silent Thunder* may not be believable, but it's all great fun."

In 1997 Tasker brought Mori back for a sequel, *Buddha Kiss*. Mori investigates the death of an old friend's daughter and comes to the aid of Richard Mitchell, an aspiring stock analyst from England. Mori soon finds himself battling a drug-dealing, doomsday cult with ties to Japan's financial community. Buddha Kiss is the name of the highly addictive drug that the cult manufactures. In his review for *Business Week* (September 15, 1997), William Glasgall noted similarities between Peace Technology, the cult in the novel, and the Aum Shinrikyio, the real-life cult that released sarin gas in the Tokyo subway system in 1995, killing 12 people. (The novel was published in Japan before the incident.) "Indeed, with today's newspapers full of headlines about white-shoe Japanese bankers consorting with yakuza blackmailers," Glasgall observed, referring to the Japanese mafia, "it is Tasker's insider's perspective on the scandal-ridden Japanese market that gives *Buddha Kiss* its keen sense of immediacy." Glasgall described the novel as "a good read in its own right—and a perfect companion to the current headlines out of Tokyo." Reviewing the novel for *Publishers Weekly* (August 4, 1997), Sybil S. Steinberg noted that Tasker "provides well-observed details and cross-cultural references that make this tale a feast as full of confounding surprises as the sushi dinner depicted here, with a final course of poisonous blowfish. The emphasis on the detective work of Mori and Mitchell allows Tasker to develop a sense of the dramatic and divisive forces now erupting in tradition-loving Japanese society. This rich atmosphere and social acuity raises his second novel well above the standard in the genre."

Mori returned for his third adventure in Tasker's *Samurai Boogie* (1999). Tasker set *Samurai Boogie* during the mid-1990s, at the height of the Japanese recession that destroyed the country's global image as an invincible economic power and undermined the confidence of its people. Mori's former mistress asks him to investigate the murder of a bureaucrat in the health ministry. As Mori pursues the case, he unearths a nest of political and corporate corruption and becomes a target of a powerful gangster. In his review for the London *Times* (September 25, 1999), Peter Ingham wrote that the novel had "all the makings of an original thriller—tough, sexy, and fast-paced." Ingham concluded that "for its vigorous pace, the stark authenticity of its setting and its exhilarating immediacy, *Samurai Boogie* is outstanding." Writing in the Tokyo *Daily Yomiuri* (February 6, 2000), Paul Migliorato expressed mixed feelings about the narrative: "Some of it works, at least in the gruff, knowing tradition of Raymond Chandler and Dashiell Hammett: 'Some women are like songs. You think you've forgotten the tune and the words, but it's all there in the back of your head.' Some of it is cause to cringe: 'Shinjuku is as dank and steamy as a sumo wrestler's armpit.'" Migliorato, however, concluded that the novel is "brisk, edgy, suspenseful, and picaresque" and observed that Tasker "writes with an understanding of Japan that makes this tale . . . both plausible and convincing."

Peter Tasker has written several nonfiction books about Japan in the Japanese language. He is also a prolific journalist, having written a column for *Newsweek Japan* since 1991 and published articles on Japan and finance for the *New Statesman*, the London *Independent*, and the *Far Eastern Economic Review*, among other publications. Tasker's next novel, *Dragon Dance*, about a reporter who investigates a Japanese ultranationalist, was published in 2003.

—D. C.

SUGGESTED READING: *Business Week* p18 Sep. 15, 1997; (Tokyo) *Daily Yomiuri* p15 Feb. 6, 2000; London *Euromoney* p6 May 1993; *Financial Times* Observer p15 Sep. 14, 1992, p18 Sep. 18, 1993; *Guardian* p18 Aug. 15, 1996; *Japan Inc* (on-line) Aug. 2001, *Japanese Review Net* (on-line) Nov. 17, 2002; *Library Journal* p130 June 1, 1988; *New York Times Book Review* p21 Nov. 15, 1992; *Publishers Weekly* p64 Aug. 4, 1997; London *Times* p22 Sep. 25, 1999; *Times Literary Supplement* p479 Apr. 29, 1988; *Tokyo Business Today* p24 July 1995, with photo

SELECTED BOOKS: nonfiction—*The Japanese: A Major Look at Modern Japan*, 1988; fiction—*Silent Thunder*, 1992; *Buddha Kiss*, 1997; *Samurai Boogie*, 1999; *Dragon Dance*, 2003

Courtesy of Harcourt Trade Publishing

Theroux, Marcel

1968– Novelist

The novelist Marcel Theroux belongs to an unofficial club whose members include Benjamin Cheever, the son of John Cheever; Molly Jong-Fast, the daughter of Erica Jong and Jonathan Fast; Martin Amis, the son of Kingsley Amis; and James Reston Jr., the son of James Reston Sr. Having had parents who were respected and famous writers, they all hope to find success on their own merit and to establish separate literary voices and identities. Theroux is the son of Paul Theroux, the successful American-born fiction and travel writer. Although his two novels, *A Stranger in the Earth* (1999) and *The Confessions of Mycroft Holmes: A Paper Chase* (2001), which both follow the experiences of characters in new and unfamiliar surroundings, have been greeted with mixed responses, many critics have said that Marcel Theroux shows great potential as a writer and eagerly await his future books. "For a long time I didn't know what to do because I was frightened of failure," Theroux said to Catherine Wilson, a writer for London's *Daily Telegraph* (January 17, 1998), explaining why he had previously avoided writing. "The thought of my father reading it was crippling, but then I decided that I had to try."

In the mid-1960s Paul Theroux was living in Kampala, Uganda, where he taught English at Makerere University. While there Theroux fell in love with and eventually married Anne Castle, a British woman. Marcel Theroux was born in Kampala in 1968. That year they left Uganda to escape the nation's increasing political turmoil. The family moved to Singapore, where Paul Theroux got a job teaching 17th-century English literature at the University of Singapore. In 1970 Anne gave birth to her second son, Louis, and the next year, the Theroux family settled in London.

To collect research for his books, Paul Theroux traveled extensively and was often away from home for long periods of time. In an article published in the *World Reporter* (May 23, 1999), Marcel Theroux recalled, "Dad being off in exotic places annoyed me a little. It made London seem a bit unglamourous. We didn't feel neglected, because when he was around, he was tremendous fun." Like most children, Marcel often squabbled with his younger brother, Louis. "I used to be the sergeant major and he was my private, and I would march him around and make him do stuff," Marcel wrote in the *World Reporter*. Despite their sibling rivalry, Marcel and Louis enjoyed a close relationship growing up.

Marcel Theroux studied English at the University of Cambridge, in England, graduating with a bachelor of arts degree, in 1989. He later enrolled at Yale University, in New Haven, Connecticut to pursue a master's degree in international relations. "For some reason I got it in my head that I really need[ed] to learn about the real world, and it was a reaction to having studied English," he explained to Katy Emck, a contributor to *Newsday* (August 15, 1999). "I had an idea that I wanted to be a diplomat, but I went off the idea, partly because I don't know which country I'd be a diplomat for." (Theroux has a dual citizenship for the United States and the United Kingdom.) Theroux earned his master's degree, from Yale, in 1991.

Theroux worked briefly for the *Christian Science Monitor* in Boston, Massachusetts. He then returned to London, working for BBC television as a producer, host, and cameraman, among other positions. In 1998 Theroux published his first novel, *A Stranger in the Earth*, in Britain. (The American edition appeared a year later.) Like many children who follow famous parents into their profession, Marcel Theroux had to escape the immense shadow of his father. The younger Theroux told Emck that while "working at the *Christian Science Monitor*, an Englishwoman there said, 'Son of Paul Theroux, that must be a heavy cross to bear.' It really struck me, because I thought, 'Hard act to follow I can understand, but heavy cross to bear'!" Theroux admitted to Brendan Lemon, a writer for *Interview* (August 1999) that when "I started writing fiction, I stopped reading my dad's books. Though I admire his work enormously, I didn't want to be accused of sounding like him."

In *A Stranger in the Earth*, Horace Littlefair, a young resident of the rural British town of Great Much, accepts an offer from his great-uncle to write for the newspaper he owns in suburban London. Horace, who has never visited London before and is completely ignorant of big-city life, finds himself thrust into a new and even hostile environment. Theroux explained to Wilson that he "wanted to write a novel that was unhip about the unfashionable south London I remembered as a child, where I grew up, about contemporary life in as unknowing a way as possible." In his review for the *Boston Globe* (August 24, 1999), Robert Taylor observed that Theroux "has two significant strengths—an ironic narrative voice and the capacity to create convincingly styled comic characters." However, the reviewer wrote that "the tone of the story sputters between caricature's impish outrages and a kind of documentary texture." Although he described the novel as "uneven," Taylor concluded that it showed "spirited comic potential." By contrast, Ron Charles enthusiastically praised the book in his review for the *Christian Science Monitor* (July 15, 1999). "To straightforward Horace, the machinations of this modern world seem endlessly absurd," Charles noted. "Seeing a TV set for the first time, he notices that 'reporters look as though they'd been abducted from respectable jobs and forced to participate in the making of the newscast.'" Charles enjoyed the book's satire, writing that Theroux is a suitable heir to the author Evelyn Waugh. "The acerbic wit [Theroux] fires at politics and journalism is tempered by a tender compassion for his central characters," Charles wrote. "That breadth keeps the novel from developing the steely surface that renders some satire tedious. This is a smart debut from a writer who's no stranger to comedy."

Theroux followed up *A Stranger in the Earth* with a second novel, *The Confessions of Mycroft Holmes: A Paper Chase* (2001), which combined comedy and mystery. The plot concerns Damien March, a BBC television journalist who inherits a house on an island near Cape Cod from his late uncle, Patrick, a writer. Estranged from his family and not dating anyone, Damien, who was born in the United States, feels like he doesn't belong anywhere. He decides to leave England to live in his new house. As a condition of inheritance, Damien must agree not to dispose of the vast amounts of junk his uncle left in the house. One day, while sorting through the stuff, Damien discovers a manuscript Patrick wrote entitled *The Confessions of Mycroft Holmes*. (Mycroft Holmes is Sherlock Holmes' older and smarter brother; the character occasionally plays a minor role in the novels and stories of Sir Arthur Conan Doyle.) Reading the manuscript, Damien notes many similarities between Mycroft's actions and Patrick's actual life. Damien becomes alarmed when Mycroft does something horrible and investigates whether Patrick, in fact, committed the same act. In his review for the *Hartford Courant* (March 18, 2001), Ashley

Warlick believed that "because Damien is telling us this story, we expect him to be telling us the all of it, but his decisions seem to be made out of thin air. No sooner has he moved to Patrick's house than it seems he decides to leave it, without anything happening to motivate the change." Warlick asserted that Theroux "is a writer testing his wings, trying something different, and it's an interesting thing to watch, even when it's not a pure success." In the *New York Times Book Review* (March 25, 2001), John Lanchester was impressed with Damien as the novel's narrator, writing that "Theroux extracts full value from his rootless, skeptical, sharp-eyed perspective." Lanchester added that "there is in the end something very satisfying about the momentum of the novel. The story moves forward with a pleasant, unthrillerish pressure."

Marcel Theroux is the co-author, with Ted LeValliant, of the juvenile book, *What's the Verdict?: You're the Judge in 90 Tricky Courtroom Quizzes* (1991). Theroux also writes for the *Guardian*, the *New York Times Book Review*, and *Travel & Leisure*. He lives in the Notting Hill section of London.

—D. C.

SUGGESTED READING: *Boston Globe* C p3 Aug. 24, 1999; *Christian Science Monitor* p21 July 15, 1999, with photo; *Daily Telegraph* (on-line) Jan. 17, 1998; *Hartford Courant* G p3 Mar. 18, 2001; *Interview* p58 Aug. 1999, with photo; *New York Times Book Review* p7 Mar. 25, 2001, with illustration; *Newsday* B p11 Aug. 15, 1999, with photo; *World Reporter* p70 May 23, 1999; *World Authors 1970–1975*, 1975

SELECTED BOOKS: *A Stranger in the Earth*, 1998; *The Confessions of Mycroft Holmes: A Paper Chase*, 2001; juvenile literature—*What's the Verdict?: You're the Judge in 90 Tricky Courtroom Quizzes* (with Ted LeValliant), 1991

Courtesy of Simon & Schuster

Thompson, Jean

1950– Short-story writer; novelist

"If you are a writer, you make use of what comes your way. Your job is to process experience, as opposed to the journalist who goes out to research a story," author Jean Thompson explained to Susan Tekulve, a writer for *Web del sol* Editor's Picks (Summer 2000, on-line). Thompson continued, "I think a writer's job is to say here is the world that I filter through my instrument of writing and try to order and make sense of it in an aesthetic way." Jean Thompson's portraits of isolated and troubled Americans in her short stories and novels have earned her critical acclaim. After publishing two short-story collections and two novels in five years during the 1980s, Thompson at first encountered difficulty in finding a publisher for her third book of short stories. Harcourt Brace published that book, *Who Do You Love*, in 1999, and it was a finalist for the National Book Award that year.

Jean Thompson submitted the following statement to *World Authors 1995–2000*: "I was born in Chicago in 1950 and grew up there and in Louisville and Memphis, the eldest of four children. My mother taught me how to read before I entered school, and I hit the ground running. I read kids' books and adult classics, including much that was way over my head. (No child of twelve really needs to be reading Chekhov.) But it gave me a sense of the enterprise of literature, its breadth and its possibilities.

"Although I wrote in hit-or-miss fashion from an early age, I did not presume to think of myself as a writer until my twenties, and then only with trepidation. It seemed then, and still does, the most uncertain of careers, fitfully rewarded if at all, dependent not only on whatever you can wrestle out of your own talent, but on the vagaries of publishing and not least of all luck. Writers and readers find each other across a chasm bridged by threads. I have been fortunate in that from the beginning my writing received enough recognition, even on a small scale, to keep me moving forward. At some point writers realize they are in it for the long haul, in spite of the occupational hazards of discouragement and self-doubt.

"I gravitated toward prose rather than poetry because narrative is my way of organizing experience, as I suppose musicians and mathematicians and visual artists use their chosen forms to impose a structure on the random world. In narrative there is a beginning point that announces a life, a situation. There is conflict (as there is in life, although seldom can we take a step back from ourselves and see it as clearly), action that works out all the possibilities once character and conflict are set in motion, and an ending, a sense of finality or conclusion that must satisfy without seeming contrived.

"I've written both short fiction and novels. Short stories to me are like solving a puzzle. All the apparatus of narrative has to fit inside a more or less finite frame. (I love Alice Munro's stories, which are so often open-ended and mysterious and which punch holes in the frame.) A novel, by contrast, is like discovering a planet, where nothing can be taken for granted. Everything must be newly named, colonized, and constructed.

"I'm a hopeless realist, endlessly fascinated by the world we live in. At the time I was first starting out, there was among writers of serious fiction a sense that realism was a somewhat quaint, fusty, outmoded enterprise. 'You can't write stories like that any more,' I remember being told. In 1961 Philip Roth had declared that imaginative writing simply couldn't keep up with the absurd realities of American life. Just as cameras had trumped realistic painters, the daily newspaper or newscast served up better stories than writers could invent. There was a vogue for the experimental, which all too often was only an imitation of the truly experimental, a kind of hipster pose or collection of mannerisms. I still dislike writing that is stilted, disjointed, and self-conscious, artiness for artiness' sake.

"I know only one way to write, and that is by beginning with what disturbs or intrigues me. This is the seed you plant and hope takes root as a story. I often write about people who are isolated, vulnerable, or in distress, not because I'm fixated in despair, but to see how they, and we, endure what life keeps dishing out. I'm interested in the story, and the self, beneath the mundane surface. I hope that readers will find lives that they recognize and understand, even if the circumstances are far different than their own.

"Language is as important as event in my fiction. I aim for language that is evocative without being decorative, and flexible enough to render action as well as the intricacies of consciousness. I often write in a third person voice that is very close to the point of view character, a technique that best allows me to inhabit someone else's world and still maintain some authorial distance.

"People are always curious about how writing is accomplished. Is there some secret or trick to it, some recognizable way of proceeding? In spite of all the instruction manuals and how-to advice out there, the only universal imperative is putting in the hours. Writing is a discipline as well as an art. And discipline has its own reward, even in a world geared to immediate gratification. A lifetime of trying to write one's best becomes a way of trying to be one's best."

Thompson received her degree in English from the University of Illinois in 1971 and her master of fine arts degree from Bowling Green State University, in Ohio, in 1973. She recalled to Tekulve that her first serious attempt to write was at age 20 when, as a student at the University of Illinois, she enrolled in a writing workshop. "My teacher was Mark Costello, and I was such a little hot shot that I think I wrote the story before class started and turned it in the first day," Thompson said to Tekulve. "That tells you something, I guess. Then Mark came into class the next day and said, 'Oh, I read your story and I liked it.' And he said it in front of everyone. Wasn't that wonderful? So I was hooked at that point."

In 1980 Thompson published her first book, *The Gasoline Wars*, a collection of short stories. The title derives from the fact that several of the stories take place in cars. In his review for the *Washington Post Book World* (March 30, 1980), Terence Winch wrote, "Her stories, set in several different regions of the U.S., are often brilliant exposés of the paradoxical way love and hate combine in human relationships. Her characteristic emphasis is on couples and the effect someone or something else has on their relationships." Winch praised Thompson's stories as "intelligent, honest, and technically impressive," adding that her "work includes a hard-won faith in the ability of people (and literature too) to transcend evil." In the *New York Times* (July 27, 1980), reviewer David Evanier wrote, "Internal confusions beset Miss Thompson when she tries to deal with love entanglements. In all the more subjective stories, which are muddled in tone and point of view, she impedes the force of the narrative." However, in stories such as "The People of Color," "Birds in the Air," "Dry Spring," and "Applause, Applause," Evanier observed that "immediacy, real characters and spare language replace romantic Indians, religious fanatics and other staples of the safe short story." Despite his criticisms of some of her stories, Evanier concluded that "Miss Thompson is a real writer to watch."

Thompson followed *The Gasoline Wars* with her first novel, *My Wisdom* (1982). Through the eyes of the novel's protagonist, Mary Ann Edwards, Thompson gives readers a view of life during the turbulent decade of the 1960s. Mary Ann abandons college and heads west to San Francisco. During her journey, she gets married and settles down in Colorado. After her marriage collapses, Mary Ann proceeds to San Francisco where she experiments with drugs and becomes involved with radical politics. In her review for the *Village Voice* (January 25, 1983), Cheri Fein criticized the novel for failing to explain why "Mary Ann's character vacillates with every change of events. . . . One day she's a confused 20 year old lurching toward California living, then she is suddenly intent on cooking breakfast, cleaning house, clipping recipes, and being otherwise unexceptional." In the

Los Angeles Times (November 25, 1982), Caroline Thompson expressed a favorable view of the novel. "Mary Ann's story with all its ramblings and anecdotes and aura of indecisiveness sings solid and true probably because [Jean] Thompson writes so beautifully," she declared. "Her prose is seductive and elegant, her ear and eye unfailingly right." Caroline Thompson described *My Wisdom* as "an accomplishment hard to believe. The book is brave and [Jean] Thompson writes as well as anyone. She's the real thing."

In 1984 Thompson published her second short-story collection, *Little Face and Other Stories*. In the *Library Journal* (October 1, 1984), Janet Boyarin Blundell wrote that Thompson's short stories "are connected by a common theme: unusual relationships and the havoc they may wreak." In her review, Blundell described the title story, in which a girl's affair with a graduate student leaves her sadder but wiser; "Having Words," in which a marriage between a writer and an anti-intellectual comes to a tragic demise; and "Foreigners," about an eye-opening encounter between a young writer working in a bookstore and an Iranian student. "The voices we hear are sometimes middle-aged, wry, and intelligent, sometimes young and poignant: behind them is the powerful yet subtle voice of a sensitive writer," Blundell stated. Tekulve asked Thompson how she keeps from falling into the same despair that afflicts many of her characters. "Fiction is a way of working through what is difficult, or oppressive, or challenging about life, at least for me," Thompson replied. "And then I feel better once I've written it. There's something therapeutic about it."

Another novel, *The Woman Driver*, was published in 1985. The book's title refers to Flora, its main character, who, as Gerald Nemenic wrote in the *Chicago Tribune* (July 21, 1985), "comes fully alive only under the influence of her automobile." Nemenic described the novel's opening scene, in which Flora crashes her car while driving in the country, the most likely cause being her anguish over the disintegration of her marriage. "Upside down in the tangled steel," Nemenic wrote, "Flora vaguely realizes that the visible world has a fresher meaning for her now—viewed from so odd an angle—than it does when she is upright." Flora embarks on an affair with Mike, a married man. Mike is also having an affair with Suzanne, Flora's best friend. "Yet," Nemenic commented, "through all this contrivance Thompson keeps her eye on target: members of an apparently burned-out generation of the 1960s and '70s who have fallen into the same kind of passionless, cliche-ridden existence—in another guise—that they have so blithely condemned in their forbears." Nemenic observed that the novel contains "characters notable for their drabness and plots that spin in tedious circles." By contrast, in the *Los Angeles Times Book Review* (August 18, 1985), Roberta Smoodin wrote that the novel "is an immensely likable book, not because one becomes attached to any of the characters. It is the narrator whose tart wit, incisive observations and clarity of observation charms one. The narrator is firmly in touch with the reality of her created world and gives the reader a strong, powerful picture of this world with every word." Smoodin also praised Thompson as a "charming and witty writer, and because of her qualities, this book deserves to be read."

After the publication of *The Woman Driver*, Thompson spent the next 14 years writing short stories. Many of these were published in such journals and magazines as the *New Yorker* and *Ontario Review*, and two were anthologized, respectively, in *Best American Short Fiction* and *The Pushcart Prizes*, an annual collection of short fiction and poetry published by small presses. However, Thompson was initially unsuccessful in finding a publisher to market another collection of her stories. In an interview with *World Authors* on August 11, 2000, Thompson explained, "Publishers have traditionally been reluctant to bring out short-story collections, which has always seemed like a self-fulfilling prophecy to me—if you don't publish, promote, or distribute them, of course they won't sell. The novel is still the more glamorous genre, a trial to those of us who love the short form."

In 1999 Thompson published the collection *Who Do You Love*, her first book in more than a decade. In the *Women's Review of Books* (November 1999), Valerie Miner wrote that characters in these stories "ponder their solitude, asking themselves who they love and if they are loved in return. Thompson writes in a range of voices, often about working-class and middle-class mid-westerners, charting their frustrating desire for communion in a morally, economically, and socially disconnected world." In "The Lost Child," for example, which Miner described as one of the most successful stories in the collection, an ex-convict, driven by her fervid desire to be a mother, abducts a young boy. "Mercy" tells the story of Quinn, a divorced police-officer, and Bonnie, a single parent, who are brought together by the death of Bonnie's teenage son in a drunk-driving accident. Fate, a theme that appears in many of the stories, according to Miner, is most prominent in "Rich Man's House," in which a woman's life is dramatically changed after her mysterious, wealthy neighbor asks her to feed his cat while he's away. Miner added that Thompson "is an acute observer of people and place, and her lilting, original language suits these tales of wayward, cockeyed, star-crossed and sometimes—at least temporarily—successful relationships." In *Newsweek* (June 14, 1999), Jeff Giles wrote, "Thompson is fascinated by the sudden and unlikely communion of people. Her characters vary—there are junkies, cops, women who've lost men to drugs, religion and everything else—but she never condescends to them, no matter how hungry their hearts are, no matter how many screws they have loose. The best stories here are so sympathetic and true that they glow a little." Giles concluded by writing that Thompson's "fiction may never make her rich, but *Who Do You Love* is still a gold mine." *Who Do You Love* was a finalist for the National Book Award for fiction in 1999.

In 2002 Thompson returned with her third novel, *Wide Blue Yonder*. Set in the town of Springfield, Illinois, where President Abraham Lincoln is buried, the novel's protagonist is Josie Sloan, a 17-year-old girl. During the summer before her senior year of high school, Josie works at the local Taco Bell fast-food restaurant, where she eventually begins an affair with a customer, Mitchell Crook, a 25-year-old police officer. Josie conceals the relationship from her divorced mother, Elaine, who runs a small shop and takes care of Harvey, her ex-husband's elderly uncle. Nearly blinded by cataracts, Harvey lives in squalor and self-neglect and spends his time watching the Weather Channel. As the characters go about their lives, Rolando Gottschalk, a violent criminal from Los Angeles, makes his way to Springfield. "Thompson tells her story by alternating among the points of view of [Josie, Elaine, Harvey, and Rolando], a virtuoso performance in which she makes these disparate internal lives believable to the point of being inhabitable," the novelist Carol Anshaw wrote in the *Chicago Tribune* (January 20, 2002). "The reader experiences what it must be like to be 17 and bored, 45 and lonely, old and addlepated, criminally insane." Although slightly critical of the novel's plot, Anshaw was impressed with Thompson's characters, who are abundantly described to the smallest detail. "Thompson sketches people and the way their hearts beat and sympathies shift, the way they fumble around trying to find a direction that looks like forward," the reviewer observed. "She also captures the very particular place and time in which these characters live. And in the process, she creates a Springfield that is much more than just a place only good for being a state capital."

Jean Thompson has also been awarded fellowships from the Guggenheim Foundation and the National Endowment for the Arts. She teaches creative writing and rhetoric at the University of Illinois in Urbana, where she also lives. In her spare time, she teaches English to Spanish-speaking immigrants. "I would say that what any writer needs is a curiosity about other people and some degree of empathy so that you have some motivation for attempting to get inside somebody else's skin," Thompson said to Tekulve.

— D. C.

SUGGESTED READING: *Chicago Tribune* XIV p33 July 21, 1985, with photo, Books p1 Jan. 20, 2002; *Web del sol* Editor's Picks (on-line) Summer 2000; *Library Journal* Oct. 1, 1984; *Los Angeles Times* V p27 Nov. 25, 1982; *Los Angeles Times Book Review* p14 Aug. 18, 1985; *New York Times Book Review* p18 July 27, 1980; *Village Voice* p43 Jan. 25, 1983; *Washington Post Book World* p14 Mar. 30, 1980; *Women's Review of Books* p15 Nov. 1999

SELECTED BOOKS: short-story collections—*The Gasoline Wars*, 1980; *Little Face and Other Stories*, 1984; *Who Do You Love?*, 1999; novels—*My Wisdom*, 1982; *The Woman Driver*, 1985; *Wide Blue Yonder*, 2002

Thomson, Rupert

1955– Novelist

The British novelist Rupert Thomson has viewed his past, beginning with his almost Dickensian childhood, through a strange kind of looking glass to produce books that turn real experience into sometimes horrifying flights of the imagination. His novels have varied settings, including London, the American West Coast, 19th-century Mexico, and Europe, all given a fantastical gloss that turns them into a kind of dream—or nightmare—world. He has received critical acclaim on both sides of the Atlantic. "In all of Thomson's books, there is a thriller element, a search, a conspiracy, a chase. Otherwise, the characters might become becalmed in the intervals between memories and perceptions. Events remind the characters of previous events, lush worlds, full of transformation," as David Flusfeder wrote in the *Guardian* (March 14, 1998).

Rupert Thomson was born in Eastbourne, England, in 1955. He had a difficult childhood owing to family illnesses. His father had developed pneumonia while he was in the navy; the treatment he underwent required removal of ribs and major portions of his lungs. After 10 years in the hospital, he married a nurse who had taken care of him. The couple had three sons, the eldest of whom—Rupert—was eight when his mother died suddenly. Rupert had to assume responsibility for massaging his father's horribly damaged back, and he had to take care of his younger brothers as well. When Rupert was 15 his father married the family's 21-year-old Swiss au pair, with whom he had two daughters. Thomson and his brothers were sent to Christ's Hospital, a boarding school known for its high academic standards but peculiar methods of discipline.

At the age of 16, according to a thumbnail biography of him on a Borzoi Books Web page, Thomson won a scholarship to Cambridge University, where he studied political thought and medieval history. (According to another source, he concentrated in English.) Immediately after his graduation he traveled to New York and then Hollywood. He later taught English in Athens, Greece. In about 1978 he returned to Great Britain, where for the next five years or so he worked as an advertising copywriter. After leaving his last copywriting job, he moved to Tuscany, Italy, and wrote *Dreams of Leaving*, his first novel. Before its publication, in 1987, he supported himself by working as a bartender, a salesperson in a bookstore, a farmhand, and a caretaker. Since then, the on-line Borzoi biography reported, he has spent time in Los Angeles, Rome, Belfast, and other cities; he now makes his home in London.

Moses Highness, the main character in *Dreams of Leaving*, also lives in London, where he spends his time drinking in nightclubs and using drugs at parties. Like his biblical namesake, Moses was put in a basket when he was a small child and placed on a river—in his case, to enable him to escape New Egypt, a mysterious village that no one is allowed to leave and whose inhabitants are in a state of despair. Moses eventually returns to the village and finds his sad but resourceful father sickly and his mother dead. The village chief of police, Peach, plots against Moses, the only person who has ever escaped.

Reviewers generally praised *Dreams of Leaving*. Bruce Allen, in the *New York Times Book Review* (October 6, 1991), termed it an "irreverently comic first novel" in which "oddball metaphors and surrealist fantasy . . . depict an innocent youngster's escape from provincial complacency and his amazed introduction to wicked, swinging London." There was some divergence in critical opinion about whether Thomson had done a better job in rendering the strange village or swinging London. For Linda Barrett Osborne, writing in the *New York Times Book Review* (August 21, 1988), Thomson's novel "moves effortlessly from one setting to the other. His London is an atmospheric blend of humor, sleaze, and innocence, his fantasy village always true to human nature and complete to the last plausible, wonderfully surrealistic detail." By contrast, Andrew Hislop, the *Times Literary Supplement* (July 17, 1987) reviewer, found that although "Thomson in town often writes well, at times very well," the scenes in New Egypt left one "wondering whether Thomson, like Highness, in this village found himself approaching the limits of his imagination." In the *Guardian* (March 14, 1998), David Flusfeder wrote that he thought the "village scenes . . . funny and quite terrifying." For him, the "more 'realistic' London scenes don't work quite so well."

For *The Five Gates of Hell* (1991), his second novel, Thomson again drew on his memories of an often motherless family and an atmosphere heavy with illness. In this book the strange town submerged in an aura of death and dying is Moon Beach, located in an unidentified country with aspects of the southwestern United States and Mexico. The town is "a place where people went to die . . . pretending to be a beach resort." Two boys, Nathan and Jed, grow up there as "rootless young souls misshapen by family trauma and uncertain sexuality," according to Bruce Allen, writing in the *New York Times Book Review* (October 6, 1991).

Nathan becomes a rescuer of others, while Jed emerges as a blackmailer. Moon Beach's economy is dominated by funeral parlors, the most important of which, the Paradise Corp., is headed by Neville Creed. As a Moon Beach cab driver remarks, "The funeral parlours, that's a business, they got to expand, but people're living longer than before, advances in medicine, right? So there's all this advertising to get people to move here. . . . You know why? They've got to feed the funeral parlours, that's why. You listen to those buildings sometime. You can almost hear them chewing, man." Nathan and Jed are eventually dragged into Creed's machinations. "In the end Creed gets what he deserves," James W. Hall wrote in his review for the *Washington Post* (September 23, 1991). "The reader does as well. . . . And the language is honed and purified as the pace quickens. But *The Five Gates of Hell* is not a conventional thriller; . . . rather, it is a pastiche of the lurid and the literary, the page burner and the leisurely, the taut and the poetic . . . beautifully written, achingly vivid, and constantly teetering on the edge of disaster."

Air & Fire (1993) is also set in the suffocating atmosphere of a small town, this one in late-19th-century Baja California, where a French engineer, who has a dream of building a prefabricated metal church designed by Alexandre-Gustave Eiffel, has brought his bored wife, Suzanne. While Valence, the engineer, is absorbed in his work, his wife gets involved with other inhabitants of the town: Pharoah Wilson, an American who is on a search for a golden treasure, and Montoya, an army captain. Terming *Air & Fire* an "exquisite tale" that celebrates "dignity in the face of disillusion," Barbara Hoffert, the reviewer for *Library Journal* (November 15, 1993), also found a larger political implication in the novel. "Suzanne's growing alienation from those around her is paralleled by native resistance to outside domination, directed as much at the Mexican government as the Europeans." Dinitia Smith, assessing the novel for *New York Newsday* (January 30, 1994), likewise discerned a version "of the New World myth," in which "a slightly crazed white man ventures into uncivilized territory, carrying with him a vision of rationality, and tries to impose it on the indigenous population—only to be defeated by the 'primitive.'" "The plot . . . is less important than the haunting atmosphere that . . . Thomson skillfully describes: heat and dust and apathy and a sense of uselessness that pervades nearly everything," David Murray wrote for the *New York Times Book Review* (March 13, 1994).

With his fourth novel, *The Insult* (1996), Thomson hit best-sellerdom. David Flusfeder accounted for this when he called the novel "a book of a significantly higher order of ambition and subtlety" than Thomson's previous books. *The Insult* takes place in a vaguely middle-European locale, resembling Czechoslovakia, where Martin Blom, the protagonist and main narrator, is shot in the head by unknown assailants. He wakes up in a hospital, blind; a titanium plate is inserted to repair the damage to his skull. Martin discovers that he is not blind in darkness, and using his night vision, he finds files that lead him to believe that he is the victim of an experiment by the neurosurgeon who has treated him. (Among other oddities, the plate in his head seems to receive television broadcasts.) He leaves his old life and moves into a cheap hotel, where he encounters various strange characters and has a torrid interlude with a lovely woman, Nina. After she disappears, he goes off to find her; in the course of his search, he encounters an old woman, Edith, whose story of incest, rape, murder, and mental aberration accounts for a large portion of the novel. Edith turns out to be Nina's grandmother.

"Edith's monstrous story, written with an occasional touch of ghastly beauty, is so coldly grotesque as to seem hallucinatory. Yet, its detail is repellently real," Richard Eder wrote in his review for *New York Newsday* (August 15, 1996). Still, Eder felt that the "contrast with the abstract torment of Blom in the first part is too violent and arbitrary." "Apart from the story's mysteries," he continued, "there is the mystery of the story's deeper meaning. . . . Blom is all spooky quandary, but as his literal and metaphysical ordeal takes him among bewilderment, paranoia, and anger, he is very little else; not so much an unknown person as a virtual person." In Thomson's native England, however, critical reactions to *The Insult* tended toward lavish praise. In the *Guardian*, Flusfeder termed the novel "weird and terrifying and comic" and the grandmother's narrative "gruesome and touching"; her story, he declared, pulled "the strands of plot" together. "It's a risky tactic, introducing a second narrative voice so far into a book, but it works: this author is in utter control of his material." *The Insult* was shortlisted for the *Guardian* fiction prize.

In *Soft!* (1998) Thomson made use of his experiences in the world of advertising. Judging from the book, his impressions of that business and the impact it has had on the modern world were not favorable. *Soft!* is about the launching of a new soft drink. Jimmy, an American marketing executive, is sent to London to get the drink off the ground, no matter what the human cost. Arriving in London at the same time is a small-time criminal, Dodds Barker, who wants to improve his life but comes under the dark shadow of a man who forces him to accept a contract on the life of a young waitress, Glade Spencer. The stories of these three people eventually converge; it turns out that a sleep experiment in which Glade participates is part of a plot to implant the desire for the new soft drink into the minds of the public. When a reporter gets wind of the story, Glade must be stopped from talking to him.

Carolyn See, who reviewed *Soft!* for the *Washington Post* (September 18, 1998), detected a political subtext in the novel: "Money is behind every facet of this venture, of course. Jimmy wants more and more of it, and that is all that the author is able to do with his character. . . . On the other hand, Glade and Barker are beautifully drawn, sorrowful originals, both isolated beyond understanding. . . . The author knows that when a whole economy fails, millions of individual families fail along with it. The England he envisions is tapped out, raped, broke, bankrupt, flat. All of his characters, Barker and his mother, Glade and her father, even the repellent Jimmy, exist in a swirling vacuum. . . . The only possessions that . . . Glade and Barker get to have are the tawdry products that corporate interests cram down their throats."

In the opinion of the *Spectator* (June 6, 1998) critic, Michael Glover, Thomson was successful in building the novel's climax. At first, "we find ourselves in the company of a whole battalion of potentially mean and violent disaffected types who are not so much living their lives as washing around in the world like soapsuds in the sink. The language is laid down like bricks in a wall, solid, unadorned, utilitarian. It tastes as savoury as metal on the tongue. . . . But then the atmosphere begins to change. The plot gets burnished—and so does the language." Michiko Kakutani, the *New York Times* (November 10, 1998) reviewer, who had disparaged *The Insult* as "a shaggy dog story," lauded *Soft!* as "a fast-paced, almost cinematic narrative that holds the reader's attention with a combination of zany comedy, sardonic social satire, and old-fashioned psychological insight."

In *The Book of Revelation* (1999), Thomson created a fictional world that belongs in the realm of dream literature. A ballet dancer is drugged and kidnapped by three women and is forced to act out their erotic fantasies; years later, after his release, he travels the world and then returns to try to determine the identity of his captors. His attempt ends in failure, Nicholas Blincoe reported in the *Guardian* (September 18, 1999), because the women "left him no clues to their identity, only a fiction of female desire." Blincoe judged the novel "cool, stylish, and . . . in total sympathy with the intelligence of its audience. . . . *The Book of Revelation* is unbelievable. It takes place in a world overstuffed with fictional motifs where all the laws of reality are suspended, and the new law aims only at suspense. Yet it works because it generates real emotion out of this suspense." The *Publishers Weekly* (November 29, 1999) reviewer wrote that the action is "conveyed in Thomson's usual fluent and riveting style" but faulted the author for the ending of *The Book of Revelation*, deeming it anticlimactic. "Despite this narrative's glittering surface . . . it is not one of his sharper efforts," the reviewer concluded. To Henry Hitchings, writing for the *New Statesman* (September 27, 1999), the subject matter of *The Book of Revelation* seemed "gratuitously lurid," but, as he wrote, "Thomson is able to make it all work . . . because his writing is so nuanced and so evocative." Anthony Bourdain, in an assessment for the *New York Times Book Review* (March 12, 2000), praised Thomson as a "hugely talented writer" whose "sentences are as clean, cool and unsparing as a surgeon's blade."

In an interview for the *Guardian* (March 5, 1998), Thomson, having been asked what book he most wished he had written, cited *The Master and Margarita*, by Mikhail Bulgakov. What he considered "most extraordinary about *The Master and Margarita* is its scale, its daring, its sheer imaginative reach. Part satire, part love story, part mystical experience, it refuses to be pigeonholed. It's a book that makes other books look safe." Thomson has attempted, in all his novels, to meet those criteria, and for the most part, critical opinion has deemed him successful.

—S. Y.

SUGGESTED READING: *Guardian* p4 Nov. 21, 1996, p10 Sep. 18, 1999; *Library Journal* p148 Aug. 1991, p101 Nov. 15, 1993; *Los Angeles Times* p5 Aug. 22, 1996; *New York Newsday* p38 Jan. 30, 1994, B p6 Aug. 15, 1996; *New York Times Book Review* p20 Aug. 21, 1988, Oct. 6, 1991, Mar. 13, 1994; *Publishers Weekly* p47 July 6, 1998, p50 Nov. 29, 1999; *Spectator* p35 June 6, 1998; *Times Literary Supplement* p766 July. 17, 1987, p11 Mar. 15, 1991; *Washington Post* C p3 Sep. 23, 1991, C p2 Sep. 18, 1998

SELECTED BOOKS: *Dreams of Leaving*, 1987; *The Five Gates of Hell*, 1991; *Air and Fire*, 1993; *The Insult*, 1996; *Soft!*, 1998; *The Book of Revelation*, 1999

Thon, Melanie Rae

Aug. 23, 1957– Novelist; short-story writer

The novelist and short-story writer Melanie Rae Thon has received wide acclaim for her poignant depictions of the struggles of marginalized characters, many of them from small western towns like the one in which she grew up. Whether her character is white or Native American, poor or rich, male or female, a convict or a priest, Thon immerses herself entirely in that character, seeking to elicit compassion in her readers. "This," Thon wrote in the *Washington Post* (December 17, 2000), "is what we all need: long days of mercy in our own lives, hope and freedom from pain, so that we have space in our hearts and minds to imagine another person's anguish." Anguish is pervasive in Thon's work, and she has a remarkable ability to put her characters' inner turmoil, which might otherwise resist the strictures of language, into words. Thon, according to Claire Messud, who reviewed her novel *Iona Moon* (1993) for the *Times Literary supplement* (July 23, 1993), possesses a "rare and not inconsiderable talent for conveying the ineffable." This same penchant of Thon's has led some to criticize her for being too vague or too concerned with the affectations of literary style. Named among the "Best Young American Novelists" by *Granta* magazine in 1996, Thon is the author of five works of fiction. In a statement for World Authors *1995–2000* Melanie Rae Thon writes: "My sensibilities have been carved by glaciers, shaped by the jagged mountain peaks and deep, cold lakes of Northwestern Montana. Miners, soldiers, cowboys, widows—my father's ancestors were among the first white settlers in this territory. I was born in Kalispell, August 23, 1957, a fifth-generation Montanan.

"Though I belong to this land, I can make no claims on it: archeological evidence indicates that native peoples inhabited the region more than 14,000 years ago. My people were conquerors at their worst and displacers at their most benign.

"In a region with only six humans (and 896 catchable-size trout) per square mile, you cannot hide yourself from history. Most of Montana is still open and unpopulated enough to see how ice and wind, rain and rivers, volcanic eruptions and the earth's great underground movements continue to make and unmake landscape.

"It is no wonder I love doing research! I've climbed the Black Hills and the Absaroka Mountains, wandered alone through the Badlands in December. I toured Montana State Prison, where I encountered boys as vulnerable and violent as the children in my stories, and where I saw inmates—kidnappers, killers, rapists—planting columbines and poppies. I've witnessed an autopsy, been charged by a buffalo bull, chased by mountain goats, and besieged by swallows. One cold March day in Indianapolis, I learned to shoot a Taurus 85 revolver and a 9 mm pistol.

"Research is food for the imagination. I cannot survive without it. Whatever my characters remember or experience, I too must understand. But for every hour spent catching lizards whose tails regenerate or seeking buffalo that once traveled in herds twenty-five miles wide and fifty miles long, for every night spent walking the streets of Boston's Combat Zone, I may spend ten hours—or a hundred—in secluded contemplation. I need to learn and then forget, to recover memories and images in the voices of particular people, to describe the killing of a weasel as the potato farmer who wields the shovel sees it, to live through the blizzard as if I have been thrown away by my mother, as if I were a child again, already a criminal, forever homeless.

"The brilliant Russian psychologist L. S. Vygotsky believed that dialogue launches language, but that we come to know ourselves and our world through 'inner speech,' a private language almost without words, a ceaseless stream of images and associations that approaches pure meaning. It is through this inner speech that a child discovers and creates her own identity and vision of the world.

"Though I know it is impossible to capture inner speech through written words, I am always working in this direction, trying to evoke a web of connected images unique to each person.

"Sensory impressions come to me long before I can speak in sentences. When I first began working on the novel *Sweet Hearts*, a friend told me about a man whose hand was so badly burned that the doctors sewed it inside his chest, hoping his own body might heal him. I didn't understand what the image meant, but I realized I had to keep moving toward it, that this was the fire guiding my journey. Five years later, I finally began to see: we do not heal ourselves by severing our damaged limbs or by turning our hurt and troubled children into exiles and outcasts. We heal ourselves by taking the wounded inside, bringing them as close to our hearts as we can bear to hold them.

"But I confess: I am as terrified as anyone! Most of us long to believe in our own 'goodness,' and one of the ways we do this is to imagine all 'evil' lurks outside us— in the woods, in wolves or serpents, in other people's children. During the fall of 1998, I lived in an isolated cabin at the edge of Flathead Lake. One morning, hours before daybreak, I heard someone knocking hard on my window. I looked out but met only my own reflection. The visitor rattled the doors, front and back, then banged again at the glass.

"When I turned off the lights, I saw the long nose and furred back of an auburn bear. The huckleberry crop had been unusually sparse that year. Now, facing winter without enough fat to keep them alive through months of hibernation, the bears in Montana had become desperate.

"I had plenty to eat, a refrigerator stocked with soup and fish and vegetables. We could have shared. We might have eaten together. But I am no saint. I am not one of those monks in the desert who befriends beasts and tames their wild spirits. I had enough food but not enough faith to feed us. And I saw that the bear had come to teach me about Flint Zimmer, the boy in my novel, about his hunger and my fear, about my willingness to let 'dangerous' children starve in body and in spirit, about my need to make Flint an exile so that I might live with the illusion of safety. I saw the limits of my compassion and the failure of my courage.

"Like everyone in Flint's family, I refused to love him. I needed to meet the bear in order to understand my people. It is always my wish that the work will change me, that I will become braver in how I choose to live, more curious, less quick to judge, more observant, less fearful. "Michelangelo said: 'Miserable mortals! Open your eyes!' The act of writing helps me do this. My wise friend Mark Robbins once asked: 'Isn't that what prayer is, the dedicated concentration of your being on that which will help you become the person you know you should be?' If I were truly kind, already merciful, perhaps I could give up writing; but for now, writing is an act of faith, the practice that wakes me—not an end in itself, but a part of the journey."

Melanie Rae Thon is the daughter of Raymond Albert, an architect, and Lois Ann (Lockwood), a homemaker. Thon was not a particularly avid reader as a child, preferring to play in the vast Montana outdoors. By the time she was in college at the University of Michigan, in Ann Arbor, she began to think of reading—and writing—as a way to enhance and enliven her experience of the world. "For me, writing is the greatest discovery," she told Leslie Haynsworth for *Publisher's Weekly* (January 29, 2001). "So much of writing is a sense of excitement and curiosity and finding out something I didn't know before." Before she had even done much writing, Thon began to refer to herself as a writer among her fellow students. "I told people, 'I am a writer,'" she recalled to Haynsworth, "which was ridiculous, since I didn't have the first clue what that would mean in my life." Partly to validate her claims, Thon pursued writing as an undergraduate and received much encouragement, particularly from her teacher George Garrett.

Thon graduated with a B.A. in English, in 1980, and was accepted into the graduate creative-writing program at Boston University, in Massachusetts. After receiving her MFA, in 1982, Thon remained in the Boston area and worked as an adjunct professor, while supplementing her meager income by waiting on tables. From 1987 to 1990 she was a literature instructor at the University of Massachusetts, in Boston. She also held teaching positions during this time at Harvard University, in Cambridge, and at Wheelock College and Emerson College, in Boston. To make time for her writing, Thon woke as early as four in the morning. She often produced hundreds of pages of exploratory material before deciding what her characters would do next, a habit she still practices. "We make a covenant with the people we invent," Thon wrote in the *Washington Post*, "to serve and love them as honestly as possible, to bear witness to their lives without sentimentality or prejudice."

Thon's writing often concerns the nature of religious faith, usually from an untraditional, loosely Christian perspective. "I'm struggling to understand the Christian belief that Jesus died for our sins, giving us access to forgiveness," Thon told Haynsworth. "I imagine Jesus dying again and again; his spirit returns, and through the suffering of others, some people are inspired to live better lives." The pursuit of faith, Thon believes, is particularly difficult in modern times. "We're so alienated in the modern world," she told Haynsworth, "where faith and experience aren't shared. It often takes a catastrophe to make people reach across those barriers of religious and cultural difference."

While Thon continued to teach, in the mid-1980s she began writing her first novel, *Meteors in August*. It was repeatedly rejected for publication; then she sent the manuscript to her former teacher George Garrett, who returned it with a 40-page letter offering useful revision advice. The novel, finally published in 1990, tells the coming-of-age story of Lizzie Macon, who lives with her parents and older sister in the small town of Willis, Montana, during the late 1960s and early '70s. Willis offers few options to its inhabitants; the men generally work for the lumber company, and the women raise children and usually get involved with the local Lutheran church. Abutting Willis is a Native American reservation, which is viewed with displeasure by many of the townspeople, including Lizzie's father. When Lizzie's older sister, Nina, gets impregnated by a part–Native American man named Billy Elk, she is forced out of the house by her father. Now lonelier than ever, Lizzie looks for salvation through communion with God, though she avoids the services of the Lutheran church. She instead befriends Freda Graves, a fundamentalist who holds services in her living room. Lizzie's unique faith is continually challenged as she meets new hardships in Willis. *Meteors in August* was viewed by many critics as a flawed, but promising, debut. In the *New York Times* (October 21, 1990, on-line) Ralph Sassone wrote, "Thon is a talented writer whose prose features some lyrical passages and moments of undeniable power. She is adept at evoking the kind of rugged place where American Gothic citizens, fresh from running a man out of town, change from their bloodstained clothing to attend Sunday services. . . . On the whole, though, Lizzie's internal journey is obscured by the many melodramatic episodes that crowd the novel. . . . Lizzie is an appealing narrator, but the thinness of those who surround her often makes *Meteors in August* seem too schematic to be a thoroughly convincing work about guilt, growth and personal redemption."

In 1991 Thon's first collection of short stories, *Girls in the Grass*, was published. Many of the stories are about the nature of faith in God and the possibility of redemption, and many deal with the trials of growing up. In the title story a group of girls explore sexuality by playing truth or dare out in a field. In "Chances of Survival" a boy, who has recently moved from Idaho to Arizona, starts obsessively wearing a robe, which somehow reminds him of Jesus and will, he hopes, protect his family from misfortune. In "Repentance," Margaret, a young girl who is supposed to be caring for her grandmother, is distracted from her duties by her friend Delena, with whom she indulges in sexual play.

The 11 stories in *Girls in the Grass* conjure a unique world, an interpretation of which Carolyn See offered in the *Los Angeles Times* (July 8, 1991). See wrote, "The world according to Melanie Rae Thon: Pregnant women whose bodies swell and swell until their very mouths become little holes and their eyes shrink to tiny slits. Old people who get soft and drooly. Boys whose hair is cut so close you can see the configurations of their scalps. Ears so big and strange they seem to live lives of their own. Feet, long, well-shaped, but not stuck on good and proper to the human beings they support. A general sense of spiritual, emotional, sexual dislocation. A God who keeps watching, while people on the margins of things get saved or un-saved. (Or, maybe God isn't watching.) A string of young girls who would far rather be boys. A string of young women who learn, over and over, that their sexuality means degradation and shame: To be female is to be taunted, humiliated, shunned." See called some of the stories in the collection "literary to a fault" and found others guilty of a "dry, laconic style." However, other critics, including Beverly Langer, writing for the *San Francisco Chronicle* (July 7, 1991), applauded *Girls in the Grass*. "[Thon's] understanding of what truly matters—love, mothers, children, God and family—is so deep and so certain," Langer wrote, "that one is tempted to fall in love with her characters, and join them in that quest for a state of grace, however fleeting it is and however we define it."

Thon became a professor of writing and literature at Syracuse University, in 1993, the year she published her second novel, *Iona Moon*. Excerpts of the novel had appeared in various journals previous to its publication, and the novel's structure in many ways resembled a series of short stories bound by shared characters. The book's central character is Iona Moon, who lives with her parents and older brothers in White Falls, Idaho, a stifling place—especially for Iona and her family, who are very poor. *Iona Moon* is unrelenting in its rendering of hardship. Julia Cameron, in a review for the *Los Angeles Times* (July 25, 1993), summed up much of the novel's action: "Iona is molested by her brothers. Her friend Sharla is impregnated by her father. Their friends the Frye boys both come to bad ends: Everett returns from Vietnam with post-traumatic stress and kills himself by blowing his head off. His brother Matt also sustains a blow to the head. It renders him the village idiot in a village full of idiots. . . . Iona's mother dies a lingering death from cancer. We count her bedsores along with Iona. Then, Iona's brother gets Jeweldeen, Sharla's sister, pregnant. Jay Tyler, the town heartthrob and diving champion, has a philandering father, a drunken mother and impregnates Muriel Arnouz, himself. Then he breaks both his legs for good measure." After her mother's death, Iona goes to Seattle, Washington, where she gets a job in a convenience store, is groped by her boss, and returns home after being fired for shoplifting. Back home, Iona is forced to piece together the shards of her life and find some order into which she can fit herself and her neighbors.

As usual, Thon's novel provoked wide-ranging responses among critics. Cameron found the accumulation of tragic detail in *Iona Moon* stultifying. "Thon's compulsive specificity in rendering the negativity of [her characters'] lives," she wrote, "creates a skewed universe in which events, large or small, are accorded equal weight. Reading *Iona Moon* is like trying to sort through a family attic. If you sort long enough, through enough stuff, you stop caring or knowing what's valuable and what's just plain stuff." Conversely, Joan Mooney, who reviewed the novel for the *New York Times* (November 21, 1993, on- line), wrote, "Ms. Thon powerfully conveys the intense sufferings of adolescence, of the loneliness of small-town life." In her interview with Haynsworth, Thon explained, "I'm not trying to represent characters' external voices so much as I'm trying to understand the most intimate associations these people have, through memory, desire and sensation."

This intention was particularly evident in *First, Body*, a short-story collection published in 1997. The backgrounds of the characters in the collection vary widely—there is a morgue worker, a teenage crack-cocaine user, an alcoholic Vietnam veteran, and a mugging victim, among others—yet she offers an equally deep, compassionate portrait of each. The title story depicts a Vietnam vet who is now working in an emergency room and trying to understand the violence he experienced at war. In another story a drug dealer's girlfriend purposely gets him addicted to his own heroin. In "Nobody's Daughters" a young black woman breaks into people's houses, slips into their clothes, and thus slips into their lives for a few moments of escape. Many of the characters in the collection have so few options that they feel confined even in their own bodies.

Some critics found Thon's total immersion in her characters overbearing. "Writing like this makes for passionate admirers and grudging resisters," Rand Richards Cooper wrote of *First, Body* in the *New York Times* (February 16, 1997, on-line). "I resisted. Earnestness, intensity, unremitting interiority—the very combination of qualities that thrills one sensibility leaves another feeling trapped and badgered. Throughout *First, Body* I found myself longing for a little distance, a little room to breathe. Refusal to grant it constitutes not merely a basic aspect of Ms. Thon's style, but perhaps an act of solidarity with her walking wounded in the tight places they inhabit. If they don't get any respite, why should we?" Christopher Tilghman, who reviewed the collection for *Ploughshares* (Spring 1997), asserted that reading it was "simply to encounter genius. . . . The stories in *First, Body* are testimonies; the whole truth of the piece is in every line, which means that linear plot and character development are beside the point. Yet each one of them has a power that holds a reader transfixed. This collection feels like a book of photographs, and one reads knowing that every new page will contain unforgettable—perhaps horrible—images." "*First, Body*," Tilghman concluded, "leaves me completely in awe."

Thon's next novel, *Sweet Hearts* (2000), was based partly on a young convict of her acquaintance. Flint Zimmer, as she named her protagonist, is a descendant of the Metis, a Canadian ethnic group originated from European fur traders and Native Americans. The book is narrated by Marie, a deaf, Metis woman who lives with and takes care of her aging father. The story centers around Marie's nephew Flint, a 16-year-old who was conceived in a rape and whose mother, Frances, consequently wants little to do with him. In and out of trouble since he was a child, Flint has spent most of his life in juvenile detention and prison. After he escapes from prison, he returns to Frances's house, where she lives with her new husband and a daughter, Cecile. Cecile is Flint's half-sister and his only friend. When Frances and her husband insist that Flint move on, he obliges, taking with him Cecile, the family car, and a gun. Together they perpetrate a series of violent crimes, though it is unclear whether Cecile is another of Flint's victims, his accomplice, or his lover. When Flint finally encounters a woman capable of showing him mercy, he reacts in the only way he knows: with violence. Thon skillfully incorporates into the novel the wretched history of Flint's Metis family, a clan that has never been wanted by either whites or Native Americans. Thus Flint's story is placed within a broader perspective, and the question of his guilt seems more complicated the closer it is examined.

While Chris Bohjalian, who reviewed *Sweet Hearts* for the *Washington Post Book Review* (February 18, 2001), granted that Thon is "an immensely gifted prose stylist and storyteller," he also felt that Thon did not entirely achieve her goals for the novel. "She suggests," Bohjalian wrote, "that [Flint's and Cecile's] behavior results inevitably from two apparently disparate factors: the U.S. government's 19th-century war on Native Americans, and the frightening conditions inside modern correctional facilities. This is a pretty tall order . . . and the end result is decidedly mixed." In the *New York Times* (March 11, 2001, on-line) Maile Meloy suggested that the scope of the novel broadens the reader's compassion for Flint and the other characters. "Although *Sweet Hearts* mourns equally for Flint's forbears, for his victims and for Flint himself, it doesn't give any of them up for lost," Meloy wrote. "In this novel, as in the most bracing of her short stories, Thon gives voice to the inarticulate, making vivid the yearning of those left out in the cold."

After leaving her post at Syracuse University, Thon taught literature and writing at Ohio State University, in Columbus, for four years. She currently teaches in the English department at the University of Utah, in Salt Lake City, and is glad to have returned to an area that more closely resembles her childhood home in the West. "I had wonderful students and colleagues at Ohio State, but I felt as if I'd had one of my arms or legs amputated," Thon told Haynsworth. In the West, she said, "you have a sense of sharing responsibility for every living thing on the planet. It's easier to have that sensibility when you can get away from people, and where you know you can't dominate the landscape; you have to cooperate with it to survive."

In addition to the *Granta* award, Thon's honors and awards include the Hopwood Award from the University of Michigan, in 1980; the A. B. Guthrie, Jr. Award, in 1987; a Whiting Writer's Award; fellowships from the New York Foundation for the

Arts, the National Endowment for the Arts, and the Ohio Arts Council; inclusion in the *Best American Short Stories* anthology for 1998; and the *Five Points* Paul Bowles Prize for Fiction.
—P. G. H.

SUGGESTED READING: *Los Angeles Times* p2 Sep. 17, 1990, p2 July 8, 1991, p9 July 25, 1993; *New York Times* (on-line) Oct. 21, 1990, July 14, 1991, Feb. 16, 1997, Mar. 11, 2001; *Ploughshares* p208+ Spring 1997; *Publishers Weekly* p60+ Jan. 29, 2001; *San Francisco Chronicle* p6 July 7, 1991; *Washington Post* p8 Dec. 17, 2000; *Washington Post Book Review* p5 Feb. 18, 2001

SELECTED BOOKS: *Meteors in August*, 1990; *Girls in the Grass*, 1991; *Iona Moon*, 1993; *First, Body*, 1997; *Sweet Hearts*, 2000

Sophie Bassouls/Corbis SYGMA

Thorpe, Adam

May 12, 1956– Novelist; short-story writer; poet

Although he was born in France and returned to live there in later life, the poet, novelist, and short-story writer Adam Thorpe maintains a quintessentially English view of life, according to many reviewers. His first novel, *Ulverton* (1992), covers 300 years of English history from the perspectives of the inhabitants of a fictional town. His subsequent novels, *Still* (1995) and *Pieces of Light* (1998), feature characters and settings that reflect the realities of the British Empire as it declined. *Shifts* (2000), a book of short stories, portrays workers rarely seen in the contemporary world, such as blacksmiths.

Thorpe's poetry has been widely praised. *Mornings in the Baltic* (1988), *Meeting Montaigne* (1990), and *From the Neanderthal* (1999) have a largely elegiac tone. "The question of extinction hangs like a cloud of . . . unmentionable, poisonous substance over the entire collection," John Greening, the *Times Literary Supplement* (July 23, 1999) reviewer, wrote of *From the Neanderthal*. He went on to praise the work's "feeling of genuine experience."

Adam Thorpe was born on May 12, 1956 in Paris, France, to Sheila Greenlees and Bernard Naylor Thorpe. He was educated in England, attending Magdalen College of Oxford University from 1976 to 1979. In 1980 he started his career as an actor and mime, becoming one of the founders of the Equinox Theatre; he then taught mime in secondary schools in London, until 1987, before serving as a lecturer in English at the Polytechnic of Central London. Thorpe later married and returned to live in France with his wife and children.

His first two books were volumes of poetry: *Mornings in the Baltic*, which appeared in 1988, and *Meeting Montaigne*, published two years later. They were generally well received. But it was with his third book, *Ulverton*, published in 1992, that he made his literary mark. Containing a number of linked stories, all set in the fictional village of the title, the book chronicles lives lived in one place over a period of three centuries. The first story is set in 1650, when a soldier returns from war to learn that his wife has been unfaithful. Other voices in the book emerge from letters—in the 18th-century epistolary style—from a young woman who is carrying on a doomed love affair; a nearly illiterate mother sending messages to her imprisoned son; and a lawyer writing to his sweetheart, interspersing his letters with the statements of farmers and landlords after the riots of the 1830s that led to the Chartist uprising. The sections are narrated by a disparate collection of protagonists: young, old, and middle-aged women, workers, soldiers, civil servants, the sane and the insane.

For Malcolm Bosse, the *New York Times Book Review* (January 17, 1993) critic, *Ulverton* was "an impressive example of the flawed but exuberant first novel of exceptional promise." Bosse described the "pleasures" he found in Thorpe's writing: "He has an interesting way of embedding a revelation quite harmlessly in the middle of a paragraph, allowing the truth to emerge slowly out of a welter of facts. He knows the value of money and throughout the novel vividly shows its impact on people who live in a world where pence and pounds count. Technically, he has mastered a number of styles. . . . Moreover, he has a poet's deftness with imagery." John Bilston, who reviewed *Ulverton* for the *Times Literary Supplement* (May 8, 1992), approved of its "pleasing textural variety compounded of straightforward storytelling, tap-room reminiscence, letters, diary entries, a sermon, some ruminative captions for a set of nineteenth-century photographic plates, a garrulous bucolic monologue and a television documentary. . . . Thorpe manages to establish an agreeably oblique narrative interconnection between his dozen chapters."

Thorpe's 1995 novel, *Still*, did not win him the critical eclat that came with *Ulverton*. *Still* is narrated in the voice of one character, Rick Thornby, an English film director and critic teaching film studies in Houston. The novel consists of his memories and the story of his latest film. Reviewers, such as Laurence O'Toole in *New Statesman & Society* (April 21, 1995), described the cineaste-protagonist as a bore. His delvings into the past produce "a quivering, teeming mess of mordant recall and bad feelings," according to O'Toole. "Excavating the memory can be a dangerous game . . . inducing vertigo, disorientation and mental disintegration. That, ultimately, defines *Still*: a wordy, elaborate exposition of the art of falling apart."

Pieces of Light, Thorpe's 1998 novel, restored his reputation: "Thorpe approaches the achievements of postimperial British writers like Paul Scott and J. G. Ballard," according to the *Publishers Weekly* (November 1, 1999) reviewer. Set partly in Africa, partly back in the fictional town of Ulverton, *Pieces of Light* is a story whose narrator looks back, first during a mental breakdown and later during the confusion of his old age. Hugh Arkwright, an English boy born in equatorial Africa, where his father is an administrator of the British colonial regime, spends his childhood in "a world teeming with menacing spirits, secret rituals, good luck fetishes and portentous scars," and Thorpe "hits upon a rich natural synergy between the child's imagination and the pagan magic of native Africa," as Ra Page put it in the *New Statesman* (October 2, 1998). Hugh is wrested from his African idyll at the age of seven and sent to school in England. During holidays he is placed under the care of his uncle, who, having seen the horrors of World War I, has escaped into mysticism and leads a group of followers in an apocalyptic pagan cult. Hugh's fate is to remain with his uncle, as he is told that his mother has disappeared in the African jungle, leaving him to an unhappy adolescence. When World War II begins, he becomes an anti-aircraft gunner; later, he loses his sweetheart to his uncle and makes a career of directing Shakespeare's plays, then retires to Ulverton. Nicholas Wroe, the reviewer for the *Guardian* (August 15, 1998), deemed Thorpe successful in creating a "psychological adventure story." Thorpe, he wrote, "subtly takes on the two huge public and historical themes of colonialism and war alongside his affecting and sometimes unbearably poignant human story. . . . Thorpe has cast his eye wide as well as deep, and again proved himself astute and inventive as well as a skilled writer."

The *Publishers Weekly* (November 1, 1999) reviewer agreed, concluding that "Thorpe's intensely evocative prose, and his poetic imagination, create a mesmerizing narrative." David Crane, writing in the *Spectator* (August 29, 1998), compared Thorpe to Charles Dickens in his "delicate awareness of a boy's fears and anxieties" and in his "sure feel for the ways in which the irrational guilts of childhood linger despotically on to sour and darken adult life." Overall, however, Crane felt that "the central problem with Thorpe's novel is that he never finds any convincing way of linking the mysteries of Hugh's early years and the revelations of adult life, the magic of Africa where anything seems possible and an England where everything seems contrived."

Thorpe returned to poetry for his next volume, *From the Neanderthal*, published in 1999. Many of the entries in this short volume deal with limits and crossing borders. They "patrol frontiers and thresholds in time, scanning the past through powerful lenses, sharing irrational fears, keeping their distance from real danger," John Greening wrote in the *Times Literary Supplement* (July 23, 1999). Greening celebrated Thorpe's "returns to the popular English sources, to . . . those royal meeting-places of myth and history: the stone at the heart of the forest, the figure on the seas's edge."

Shifts, Thorpe's 2000 collection of short stories, takes its title from the workplace. All of the protagonists are workers or their family members. The occupations are mainly traditional ones: stoneworking, blacksmithing, lumbering, and collecting trash. (A woman who sells luxurious swimming pools has the most modern occupation.) Robert Potts remarked in the *Guardian* (January 8, 2000) that "most of the tales are told from a position of grief, or sometimes guilt." An example of the latter is "Glass," set in 1936, in which a French glazier tells his wife that they will have a paid holiday for the first time in their lives. She replies, "It isn't right, paying us to do nothing, Jean-Luc." The glazier secretly agrees: "To be paid to take a break! It went against the grain." While idling in a tent by a river on the vacation they finally decide to take, the glazier cannot avoid memories of the only work-related thing he has ever done wrong: dropping a piece of stained glass from the Amiens cathedral window, which workers were trying to preserve from the shelling in World War I. He is overwhelmed by guilt, which he has managed to hold at bay while working. Although they get paid vacations in the future, he and his wife do not leave their home: "Too much to do. It's not right doing nothing, letting it all go, staring into the sky like that."

Alex Clark, the reviewer for the *Times Literary Supplement* (January 7, 2000), describing the stories in *Shifts* as having "an archaeological tone," felt that in spite of "flashes of brilliance," Thorpe had not quite made his point. "Possibly, the theme of work, so iconic and all-consuming, has been made to work too hard, eclipsing the real subject of the book, which revolves around the individual desire to make sense of bewildering, painful experience." In 2001, Thorpe published *Nineteen Twenty-One*. Set during the drought summer of 1921, the book examines a young author striving to write the first great novel of the War.   —S. Y.

SUGGESTED READING: *Guardian* p10 Aug. 15, 1998, p9 Jan. 8, 2000; *New Statesman* p49+ Oct. 2, 1998; *New Statesman & Society* p36 Apr. 21, 1995; *New York Times Book Review* p12 Jan. 17, 1993; *Publishers Weekly* p73 Nov. 1, 1999; *Spectator* p27 Aug. 29, 1998; *Times Literary Supplement* p20 May 8, 1992, p27 Apr. 21, 1995, p27 July 23, 1999, p19 Jan. 7, 2000

SELECTED BOOKS: poetry—*Mornings in the Baltic*, 1988; *Meeting Montaigne*, 1990; *From the Neanderthal*, 1999; novels—*Ulverton*, 1992; *Still*, 1995; *Pieces of Light*, 1998; *Nineteen Twenty-One*, 2001; short-story collections—*Shifts*, 2000

Adam Nadel/AP Photo

Thubron, Colin

June 14, 1939– Novelist; travel writer

Colin Thubron, the British novelist and travel writer, recently published *In Siberia* (1999), the third in a series of Russian travelogues that includes the acclaimed *Among the Russians* (1983) and *The Lost Heart of Asia* (1994). Like these earlier works, *In Siberia* has been praised for providing a moving and insightful account of the Russian people and culture, and for its lyrical descriptions of landscapes and cities. Thubron rose to prominence in the late 1970s, along with his fellow travel writers Paul Theroux, Bruce Chatwin, and Jonathan Raban, at a time when the publishing industry began to realize "that travel writing could also be literature," as Thubron explained to Nicholas Wroe for the *Guardian* (September 23, 2000). Thubron has received less American recognition than some of his peers, "yet in his native England," Gayle Feldman noted in *Publishers Weekly* (February 28, 2000), "the long, lanky man with the boyish shock of hair . . . is recognized as one of the best literary traveling companions a reader can find." Thubron has also written six novels, including *A Cruel Madness* (1984), *Falling* (1989), and *Turning Back the Sun* (1991). His fictional works, it has been pointed out, are not what one might expect from a travel writer. "They are often set in enclosed places. I've used a mental hospital, a prison and inside someone's amnesiac head," he told Wroe. "They are anti-travel books, if you like, but they give their voice to something in me that a travel book can't. In travel writing your principal fascination is with something outside yourself. With fiction you can much more give voice to your personal life, however heavily disguised, and to all sorts of inner feelings and compulsions."

In a statement for World Authors 1995–2000, Colin Thubron writes: "I'm often asked what prompted my becoming a travel-writer—was it a fascination with writing or with the foreign? And I guess that most travel-writers fall into either the category of writers who travel, or of travellers who write. I'm aware, a bit uncomfortably, that I belong with the writers who travel. As a child I loved words. My parents may have had a hand in this—my mother's family was that of Dryden, the line of the first English Poet Laureate—and my childish attempts at verse were shamelessly applauded.

"My father worked in the USA and Canada when I was a boy, and my early journeys across the Atlantic aged 9–12 (holidays in America, school in England) gave me a premature excitement with travel. This has never left me, although I am obsessed by my destinations (heavily researched beforehand) rather than motivated by the sheer pleasure of being on the move.

"My earlier books—on the Middle East—were the result of a romantic fascination with a part of the world that mystified me, and all my subsequent journeys have been acts of discovery for myself as well as (I hope) for the reader. Asia has been my lasting obsession. This began with a love of ancient cultures—their history and architecture as well as their present state—and as a younger man I travelled through almost every Asian country in a kind of strenuous euphoria. I went with the high-coloured notions about them, but gradually became obsessed by the reality beneath.

"During the past twenty years I have concentrated on austere regions: the ex-USSR and China after the Cultural Revolution. Yet the same forces were, I think, at work in me: the desire to unravel lands I did not understand. But there was an added element, here, of wishing to humanize the countries that my generation was brought up to fear (the 'Russian Bear', the 'Yellow Peril'). I seem to need this kind of challenge, in which every encounter has the frisson of hard-won experience.

"Nevertheless, the true motive for writing has not been the creation of works of healing. That may be a justification, but the actual impulse is more self-indulgent. To me, a journey through a country I'm going to write about has always been far more intense than merely travelling. Normally I'm not especially observant, but when I'm travelling in order to write I become violently curious and sensitized.

"Yet the main challenge has been to communicate with the ordinary inhabitants of these countries (I dislike pre-set interviews), to give voice to people I have met by chance along the way. So much of my research is concentrated on learning the language (Russian, Mandarin)—however inadequately.

"At the same time I am aware that the voice most surely given is my own. On the whole (I'm told) my presence in the books is a reticent one: but travel-books, essentially, are one culture looking at another—and my own judgements, feelings (and sometimes prejudices) must be implicit everywhere.

"As a teenager I wanted to write novels, and there's a sense in which my love of travelling postponed this for a while. In some ways travel-writing came to me more naturally. I didn't find my voice so easily as a novelist. And most of the novels are violently different from the travel books. In fact several of them take place in states of grimly restricted movement: a mental hospital *(A Cruel Madness)*, a prison *(Falling)*, an amnesiac's head *(Distance)*.

"I'm still unsure where these novels come from. The preponderant feelings in them—although not the stories—are autobiographical (and scarcely original): complexities of love, loss of religious faith, conflicts of values. Nothing in my background—a privileged English one, with happy, compatible parents—offers much clue to fiction that has been described as tense and anguished. (Nor am I particularly anxious in ordinary life.) It seems that the writing of novels releases an angst which is otherwise dormant.

"My novels and travel-books tend to alternate. The novels feed something subjective; the travel books indulge a curiosity with the world. I like this pendulum, and would probably tire if either genre consumed me wholly.

"Sometimes I think writing is a kind of disease. I have many (too many) interests, but despite the intense difficulty of writing it gives me a unique pleasure when I sense it going well. Then I feel that this is the point of me."

Colin Gerald Dryden Thubron was born on June 14, 1939 in London, England. His father, Gerald Ernest Thubron, was a military attaché, posted to Canada and then America in the late 1940s. The young Thubron, who lived at boarding school in England, traveled alone across the Atlantic to visit his parents on holidays, something that instilled in him "an early physical love of movement and pleasure and excitement in travel," he recalled to Feldman. Thubron is a distant relative of the 17th-century poet John Dryden, through his mother, Evelyn. He confided to Feldman that "the love of writing came even before the love of travel. As a child, being descended from England's first poet laureate was a very grand thing. It was important to me that writing was something respectable and splendid." As a teen, he explained, "I imagined being a writer meant being a novelist." Now, having written both novels and travel books, he finds himself in possession of "two different identities, coming from two different parts of myself."

Thubron was educated at Eton College, a prestigious boy's school in England that fostered in him a great deal of self-confidence—an attitude that served him well in his future career, although not an inheritance he was entirely proud of. "The Englishness Eton represents is something I disliked," he admitted to Feldman. "In the late '50s Eton promulgated a cult of your own personality above everything, the cult of an effortlessly superior 'casual man' who was taught not to care too much because caring was bad form. Yet I was obsessively caring and still am. My characters are obsessive in the novels. On the other hand, I benefitted from the independence that Eton inculcated. It is that sense of entitlement that enables English travel writers to go with a surety that things will be all right and a confidence in their own perceptions."

After his schooling, in 1959, Thubron joined the editorial staff at the publishing company Hutchinson & Co., in London. Beginning in 1963, he worked as a freelance filmmaker, scripting and filming documentaries in Turkey, Morocco, and Japan for the British Broadcasting Corporation (BBC). After working for the Macmillan Co. in New York City from 1965 through 1966, he published his first travel book, *Mirror to Damascus*, in 1967. "I had been fascinated by the inland cities of Syria for years," Thubron told Wroe. "I suppose I chose Damascus as a subject partly because it had been so little written about. But it was a work of love, really. I had no idea whether anyone would publish it." This was followed by another travel book, *Jerusalem*, published in 1969. In the mid-1970s Thubron worked as a writer for hire, completing four books: *Journey into Cyprus* (1975), *Istanbul* (1978), *The Venetians* (1980), and *The Ancient Mariners* (1981), all assignments from the Time-Life Company. During this time he also penned his first novel, *The God in the Mountain* (1977). He published a second novel, *Emperor*, a year later.

"With the early books," Thubron told Feldman, "I suppose it was a young man's romantic curiosity about Arab urban life, the lure of a civilization not hopelessly out of reach of Western civilization." His perspective shifted when, in 1978, he had a car crash and suffered a fractured spine. "During the months of enforced leisure, I dreamt grandiose travel dreams. I wanted to approach the lands I had always been taught to fear." One of those lands was

Russia, or the former Soviet Union, a long-time Cold War enemy of the West.

In 1981 Thubron set out for the Soviet Union, which was then in the final years of Leonid Brezhnev's rule. In a sedan he traveled 10,000 miles across the Asian continent, from the northern Baltic republics to Georgia and Armenia in the south. From his experiences he composed *Among the Russians*, published in the U.S. as *Where Nights Are Longest: Travels by Car through Western Russia* (1984). Thubron impressed critics by weaving what were, for the most part, commonplace events and encounters into an insightful tapestry of Russian culture. S. Frederick Starr, writing for the *New York Times Book Review* (July 15, 1984), noted that "Mr. Thubron met no underground artists, regales us with no tales of heroic dissidents. His adventures are no more dramatic than being picked up by a teenage girl in Novgorod, boozing with a morose student at a rural eatery and visiting a friend's former fiancée in Moscow. And yet the results are glorious. A subtle and humane writer, Mr. Thubron is able to capture the fleeting words and gestures that define a culture. . . . The appeal of Mr. Thubron's account is deepened by his keen self-awareness, which pervades his narrative like an inner dialogue." Many critics praised Thubron for his captivating descriptions. "Thubron has an exceptional gift," Rosemary Dinnage wrote in the *New York Review of Books* (June 13, 1985), "for recreating cityscapes and buildings, and the book scintillates with architectural set pieces." Olgo Semenova, writing for the *New Statesman* (October 21, 1983), noted that Thubron "conveys the feel of places and their past with wonderful intensity, the golden domes of medieval Moscow, the desolate plains of Belorussia, the 'cold luminous skies' of Leningrad and the 'dynamic disorder' of Georgia. At the same time, he portrays the ugliness and emptiness of modern Russian life, with its tawdry tower blocks, interminable queues and tension, radiating outwards from the Kremlin." Thubron came close to losing all of his research when his notebooks were nearly confiscated, an experience he recalls as one of the worst in his many travels. "I thought I was going to lose my first book, [*Among the Russians*]," Thubron told a interviewer for *Geographical* (October 1999). "I was followed for several weeks, throughout southern Russia, by the KGB. At the border I was stripped and body searched, the panels were taken out of my car and the film was taken from my camera. The worst moment came when I was taken into the bowels of an office. They took my notes for the book and with granite faces made me read out parts, which I invented. I thought I was going to lose three years' work. All my memories were there."

Thubron's next journey took him to another "forbidden" land—China. After studying enough Mandarin to enable him to communicate, he spent many months exploring the region, visiting popular tourist destinations as well as less-frequented sites, including the grave of the Tang poet Li Bai, the old political pilgrimage sites of Shaoshan and Yunnan, and the desert province of Quinghai, the site of labor camps. Thubron chronicled his observations in *Behind the Wall: A Journey Through China* (1987), a work that was enthusiastically received by critics, winning both the Hawthornden Prize, from England's Hawthornden Trust, and the Thomas Cook Travel Award from the travel-book publisher. "By turns witty, melancholic, lyrical and cynical, *Behind the Wall* is an off-the-beaten-track account of China's beaten track, " Judith Shapiro wrote for the *New York Times Book Review* (November 27, 1988). "Although most of the places Colin Thubron visited over the course of his yearlong travels can be found on standard tourist itineraries, his literary gift is so formidable that some scenes are more compelling through his eyes than they are in reality. Even the most conventional and oft-depicted sites—the Great Wall, the Forbidden City, the Ming Tombs—are so vividly observed that those who have already visited may wish to return, book in hand." Jonathan Mirsky, in a review for the *Times Literary Supplement* (September 11–17, 1987), wrote that "Thubron . . . is a wonderfully perceptive writer. From the ordeal of a journey by local bus in freezing weather through China's far west—a region of gulags vaster than Siberia—to reach the country's largest lake, Kokor Nor, he gives us a mere six paragraphs, each a masterpiece of description." Thubron was especially affected by the history of cruelty in China, particularly during the Cultural Revolution (1966–1976). "Once authority had sanctioned violence, no monitor inside . . . had called a halt," Thubron writes, as quoted by Mirsky. "Such a pattern, I realized, ran back in China's history: a recurring cycle of constraint broken by ungovernable savagery. A student admitted that he had tormented his teachers because it was ordered. 'We didn't know—we didn't ask—why this or that man was bad. People hit him, so you hit him. It was simple. It wasn't even personal.'"

Thubron's third novel, *A Cruel Madness*, was published in 1984, and was better received that his first two attempts at fiction. The narrator, Daniel, is a volunteer worker at a Welsh mental hospital. One day he glimpses Sophia, a woman with whom he once had a disastrous love affair; she has become a patient at the hospital. Daniel is overwhelmed, recalling his passion for her and his desolation at the affair's bitter dissolution. However, as the story progresses, it becomes clear that the truth might not be quite as Daniel describes it. "Thubron stirs the muddy waters of passion to the point where reality and delusion are but different sides of the same occurrence, where reason and paranoia coexist," Sharon Dirlam wrote for the *Los Angeles Times* (October 6, 1985). "This isn't just another novel about madness and despair. It is a gripping tale of passion, however misspent, and the failure of an entire set of characters to come to grips with life seems not as distant from 'normal' as one might think, but simply a look deeper into the mind than most of us dare to probe." Some critics found fault with the narrative structure. Stephen Koch, in a review for *Washington Post Book World*, as quoted in *Contemporary Authors* (2001), expressed his distaste for "the absurdly simple device of omitting major pieces of information from an otherwise perfectly ordinary story. . . . I for one find it a cheap trick, an effort to make a story more portentous, merely because it is more perplexing." Koch nonetheless found the book to be an "an intriguing and sometimes rather moving novel about insanity and love, illusion and reality." Thubron won the PEN Silver Pen Award for this novel in 1985.

In *Falling* (1989), Thubron's next novel, the protagonist, Mark Swabey, narrates most of the book from prison. He is in some way implicated in the death of Clara, a circus acrobat with whom he fell in love; only later does the reader learn the exact reasons for his imprisonment. According to Michael Dibdin in a review for the London *Observer* (September 10, 1989), "this narrative bait is of secondary importance in a book which attempts—and largely achieves—an ambitious synthesis of realistic surface and symbolic depth." Clara, an aerial artist whose occupation demands an unwavering faith in her body, is a figure of self-reliance and self-mastery; she stands in stark contrast to Katherine, the woman with whom Mark is involved when he meets Clara. Katherine, a stained-glass artist, looks outside herself for reassurance, both to Mark and to her personal religion. Katherine struggles to understand the presence of evil in the world—a conflict represented by her failure to complete a stained-glass representation of the fall of Lucifer that she has been hired by a church to make. George Stade, writing in the *New York Times Book Review* (February 3, 1991), described *Falling* as an "anti-theodicy as well as a love story and symbolist novella, a humanistic revision of the fall. . . . Thubron's sentences are remarkable for being at once rapid and weighty, like bright stones that skip across a stream until they sink into turbulent depths." Dibdin, in his review, remarked that "the interpolated chapters narrated by other characters in the story are perhaps a mistake," but concluded that "this is the merest wobble on the high wire, a momentary failure of nerve that cannot diminish the effect of this extraordinary performance."

Thubron explored issues of colonialism and racism with his fifth novel, *Turning Back the Sun* (1991). Dr. Rayner, a young physician, has been exiled to a frontier town in an unnamed country that resembles Australia in the 1930s. Rayner grew up in the capital city by the distant coast, now 1,000 miles away, and he yearns for the life he could have had there, working as a doctor and living an easy and comfortable existence. He failed to perform well on his medical exams, however, and the government sent him to the isolated town in the outback where he now resides. Although he feels like an outsider among the townspeople, he also feels a certain sympathy for the Aborigines who live outside of town, partially because of their outsider status, but also because, in their myths about a paradise at the beginning of time, he finds a parallel to his own nostalgia for the past. He begins to find companionship with Zoë, a local striptease dancer and political radical who, like Rayner, is a pariah. The plot revolves around the strained relationship between the white townspeople and the black Aborigines, a situation that is exacerbated by a murder and the onset of a mysterious disease that, although mostly benign, gives white townspeople a rash that turns their skin a dark brown.

The work received mixed reviews. Christopher Walker, writing for the London *Observer* (September 8, 1991), attested that "schematic heavy-handedness is the novel's downfall. The themes are too crudely worked out and in the novel's many disparate elements never convincingly coherent. In the end, too much is resting on Rayner as a symbolic figure for us to care about him or to suggest that any truths he reveals extend beyond the formal arrangement of the narrative." Other critics were more sympathetic. "Though the framework is heavy, Thubron's writing has remarkable vigor and fluency," a reviewer noted for *Publishers Weekly* (April 27, 1992). "[Thubron] shows sharp psychological insight and creates considerable pathos. . . . It's by no means a casual read, but an ultimately rewarding one."

In 1992 the nations of Central Asia that were once a part of the Soviet Union—Kazakhstan, Tajikistan, Turkmenistan, Kirghizstan and Uzbekistan—were experiencing their first year of independence, and Thubron seized the moment to visit the beleaguered people of the region. Covering some 6,000 miles by bus, car, and train, he encountered a panoply of forlorn individuals beset by poverty and hopelessness, and recorded his melancholy observations in *The Lost Heart of Asia* (1994). Thubron sought primarily to discern signs of a national identity, and in particular whether or not the region would succumb to an Islamic fundamentalism like that of the nearby Middle East. From the testimonials he received over many vodka-drinking sessions, however, he found little in the way of an emerging national identity. Most of those he met fulminated against the Soviet Union and cheered its demise; a few hoped for its return. There were some who were stirred by feelings of nationalism—such as Uzbeks that dreamed of a pan-Turkic federation—yet many were too aware of their multi-racial history to find any real significance in nationalist ideals.

The book was well received, and as with his earlier travel writings, critics lauded Thubron for his beautifully descriptive passages. Luree Miller, in a review for the *Washington Post* (November 20, 1994), quoted Thubron depicting Islamic architecture in a harem courtyard: "A rank of wooden columns tapered like inverted tulips . . . scooped deep, shadowed bays from the walls. Every surface was worked into flowers, tendrils, inscriptions. It was as if for centuries, all over the courtyard, a legion of insects had been burrowing nervously across wood and marble, gnawing out, with minute, fastidious appetites, all the intricacy for which the patience of man was too short." Tina Rosenberg, in a review for *New York Newsday* (November 27, 1994) averred that "reading Thubron is the next best thing to being there, and in the case of most of the places he visits . . . better. His description is as rich with color and detail as the ochre, carnelian and peacock carpets in the mosques. He makes history burn with life." A.C. Grayling and Michael Thompson-Noel noted in the *Financial Times* (October 15, 1994) that "Thubron is happiest when he is saddest, picking his solitary way among poignant ruins and meditating on the fate of civilizations." Some critics interpreted this as a disregard for the land's people and history: "Given his weak, yet highly confident, hold on Central Asian history, Thubron at times goes so far as to deny Central Asians as having been part of history at all," Scott Malcolmson remarked in the *Times Literary Supplement* (September 30, 1994). "He is not interested in his characters but in the aesthetic possibilities of their ruination."

Thubron returned to Asia again for his third book about the region, this time exploring the desolate arctic regions of northern Russia. With *In Siberia* (1999), Thubron was largely concerned with the question of faith, and its disappearance from the Russian culture. "I was trying to find a core to Siberia, where there seemed none," he writes, as quoted by Adam Goodheart for the *Washington Post* (April 9, 2000). "Or at least for a moment," he continues, "to witness its passage through the wreckage of Communism—to glimpse that old, unappeasable desire to believe, as it fractured into confused channels, flowed under other names. Because I could not imagine a Russia without a faith." On his journey Thubron visited some of the notorious gulag prison camps in the area, including such places as Omsk—where Dostoevsky was imprisoned for four years—and Serpentinka, where in 1938 alone nearly 26,000 prisoners perished. Thubron "longed to find the Russians outraged at such places, but people seemed in some ghastly way to be accepting," he writes, as quoted by Gayle Feldman. "It was like the weather, it was how things were. The persecuted and persecutors were indistinguishable in so many ways. There was no sense of memory being a path to rectitude. The gulag is simply being allowed to rot."

"Through language that is alternately exuberant, poetic, and mournful, Thubron evokes the natural beauty of Siberia as well as its despoliation," Frank Caso wrote in a review for *Booklist* (January 1–15, 2000). "Equally powerful is his ability to capture on paper the personalities of the many people whom he meets during his sojourn." Ben Downing, writing for the *New Criterion* (June 2000), remarked that "*In Siberia* is distinguished as well by its author's nearly masochistic travel habits. Thubron would, on a whim, peel off into the middle of nowhere and sometimes get seriously stuck there . . . but his misery is our gain. His bulletins from these hyperborean hamlets strike just the right tonal balance between disgust at the old system and solicitude for those who groan beneath its rubble. And his prose is a precision instrument, able to conjure up, with a few brisk yet nuanced strokes, the whole atmosphere and sadness of a place."

As for the future of Siberia, Thubron told Feldman that "whatever happens, it will be very slow. I had hoped that the further I got from the bureaucratic center, the more communities would have held together. But the further I went the worse it became: without centralized control, everything was falling to bits. Russia can't get much worse. The people will dig in, wait, be patient—what the Russians are very good at doing."

Thubron lives in London, England, and is working on his next novel. He has become accustomed to alternating between genres, as he told Nicholas Wroe: "When I finish a travel book I want to write some fiction. Equally, after writing a novel I want to go out, meet a billion Chinese people or something like that."

—A. I. C.

SUGGESTED READING: *Booklist* p871 Jan. 1–15, 2000; *Financial Times* p15 Oct. 15, 1994; *Geographical* p98 Oct. 1999; *Guardian* p11 Sep. 23, 2000; *Los Angeles Times* p22 Oct. 6, 1985; *New Criterion* p82+ June 2000; *New York Newsday* p35 Nov. 27, 1994; *New York Review of Books* p29 June 13, 1985; *New Statesman* p23 Oct. 21, 1983; *New York Times Book Review* p24 July 15, 1984, p10 Nov. 27, 1988, p9 Feb. 3, 1991; (London) *Observer* p7 Sep. 10, 1989, p57 Sep. 8, 1991; *Publishers Weekly* p248 Apr. 27, 1992, p54+ Feb. 28, 2000; *Times Literary Supplement* p973 Sep. 11–17, 1987, p26 Sep. 30, 1994; *Washington Post* p5 Nov. 20, 1994, p5 Apr. 9, 2000

SELECTED BOOKS: novels—*Cruel Madness*, 1984; *Falling*, 1989; *Turning Back the Sun*, 1991; travel books—*Mirror to Damascus*, 1967; *Among the Russians*, 1983; *Behind the Wall: A Journey Through China*, 1987; *The Lost Heart of Asia*, 1994; *In Siberia*, 1999

Townsend, Sue

Apr. 2, 1946– Novelist; playwright

Sue Townsend's *The Secret Diary of Adrian Mole, Aged 13¾*, along with its sequels, were among the best-selling books in England during the 1980s. In Adrian Mole, a loveable loser, the British saw a reflection of their own travails, and the series inspired a spate of merchandise, including lunch boxes, T-shirts, and computer games. In the series Townsend, an avowed socialist, provides a gentle satire of English society and skewers the politics of the Thatcher era using the form of fictional diary

Sue Townsend

Townsend had enjoyed writing while in school, and continued to do so in between raising her children and performing odd jobs. Her first play, *Womberang*, takes place in a gynecologist's waiting room and features a heroine who rallies her fellow patients to defy the doctor's authority and stand up for themselves. It opened at the Leicester Haymarket Theatre in 1979 and later moved to the West End, the London equivalent of Broadway. After that success she continued as a playwright, producing *The Ghost of Daniel Lambert* and *Dayroom* in 1981, *Captain Christmas and the Evil Adults* in 1982, and *The Great Celestial Cow* in 1984, as well as several others.

In 1982 Townsend's first novel, *The Secret Diary of Adrian Mole, Aged $13\frac{3}{4}$*, was released by Methuen Publishing Ltd. in England. Adrian Mole, the book's young protagonist, is pretentious, sanctimonious, and insensitive—yet he manages to be oddly endearing instead of insufferable. Critics have posited that the universality of Adrian's adolescent problems—acne, schoolyard bullies, and his parent's inexplicable behavior, among them—ensure his appeal. Townsend herself told an interviewer for *Contemporary Authors* (1989), "Adolescence is such a strong experience, and the emotions bound up in it are so common to all of us, that everybody recognizes those feelings. And I think to a certain extent everybody sees himself [like Adrian] as this brave little soldier plodding through life misunderstood by the rest of the world." The teenaged Adrian has often been compared to Huck Finn and Holden Caulfield, and Norma Klein, writing for the *New York Times Book Review* (May 25, 1986), found him "part Woody Allen, part a kindred spirit to the heroes of Philip Roth's early novellas." The book, despite its emphasis on Adrian's dating woes and intellectual naivete, is more than simply a coming-of-age tale. Townsend also cleverly satirizes life for the British working-class during Margaret Thatcher's tenure as prime minister. For example, when the hot-lunch program at Adrian's school is eliminated, he theorizes that it is Thatcher's attempt to keep England's young too hungry and weak to demonstrate when they get older.

In 1984 Townsend wrote a second book, *The Growing Pains of Adrian Mole*, which details Adrian's life at ages 15 and 16. It was as popular as the first, and together the two volumes quickly sold more than five million copies in England alone. (They still sell steadily after more than 15 years.) Some critics wondered if the novels, with their distinctively British references and slang terms, could succeed in America, and when the pair was published by Grove in 1986 as a one-volume compilation called *The Adrian Mole Diaries*, it included a glossary of phrases apt to be unfamiliar to readers in the United States. (It was explained, for example, that when Adrian complains about his "spots," he is referring to his pimples.) The volume won Townsend an American following that, while smaller than its English counterpart, was no less enthusiastic, and she followed up with several

entries written by a self-absorbed adolescent boy. Although arguably best known for the Adrian Mole books, Townsend has written other comic novels, such as *Rebuilding Coventry: A Tale of Two Cities* (1990), in which a middle-aged housewife goes on the lam after killing her brutish neighbor, and *The Queen and I* (1993), in which the monarchy is overthrown and the royal family reduced to living on the dole in a housing project. Those who knew Townsend only as a comic writer, however, were surprised by *Ghost Children* (1998), which depicts a sordid world of isolation and despair in a manner that "builds slow momentum through stark prose, taut storytelling and relentless probing of each perspective to its darkest recesses," according to a reviewer for *Publishers Weekly* (March 23, 1998). Townsend has also written several plays, including stage adaptions of *The Diary of Adrian Mole, Aged $13\frac{3}{4}$* and *The Queen and I*, and in fact, started her writing career as a dramatist.

Townsend was born into a working-class family on April 2, 1946 in Leicester, England. She attended South Wigston Girls High School, but dropped out two weeks before her 15th birthday. (After the success of the first Adrian Mole book Leicester University awarded her an honorary master's degree.) Always an avid reader, she continued the habit after leaving school, and was particularly fond of Fyodor Dostoevski and John Updike. She married at an early age and had three children, but her husband soon abandoned the family. Townsend was then forced to work at a variety of unskilled jobs, including selling hot dogs and pumping gas, in order to earn a living. She worked as a waitress for a time, as well, and one of her duties was to strain the mouse droppings out of the restaurant's cream pitchers.

more installments chronicling Adrian's life. The latest, *Adrian Mole: The Cappuccino Years*, was published in the U.S. in 2000 and revisits the diarist as a 30-year-old divorced father of two. The series has currently been published in more than 20 languages, gaining Townsend a worldwide readership, and numerous Adrian Mole–related sites have appeared on the World Wide Web. Besides Townsend's stage version, the books were also adapted for a short-lived series on Thames Television and a multi-episode program on the British Broadcasting Corporation (BBC) Radio 4 channel.

Rebuilding Coventry: A Tale of Two Cities (1990), while still a comic novel, marked a departure from the Mole series for Townsend. Coventry Dakin, the book's eponymous protagonist, escapes from her dull suburban life and whining family when she picks up an action doll, bashes in the head of a neighbor who is strangling his wife, and flees to London, where she temporarily winds up as a bag lady, prostitute, and maid. Bill Kent wrote for the *New York Times Book Review* (April 22, 1990, on-line) that the book is "more a series of hilarious comic moments than a cohesive novel," but he praised "Ms. Townsend's crisp, clever prose and her unabashed glee at wringing from her wacky characters the essence of their vileness."

Townsend is no admirer of the royal family. At a debate in London, she was quoted by John Darnton for the *New York Times* (May 23, 1993) as calling the monarchy "the apex of our terrible class system which strangles people." She said, "When I was a child in school, I used to sit at my desk learning my [multiplication] tables and the Queen's portrait looked down on me and I believed in her. She was an icon. I also believed in fairies and Santa Claus and God. And one by one, I've stopped." In her satiric novel, *The Queen and I* (1993), Townsend imagines that a general election has resulted in the overthrow of the monarchy and the establishment of a republic. The royal family is unceremoniously ousted from the palace and sent to live in a public housing project. The individual royals behave very much according to the public's preconceptions of them: the Queen is resourceful and able to manage, but her husband, Prince Philip, degenerates into a bedridden madman, and her sister, Princess Margaret, becomes a chain-smoking harridan. Prince Charles is delighted with the possibilities for organic gardening in the housing project—and with a social worker's promise that the national health plan will pay to fix his protruding ears. Princess Anne rolls up her sleeves and learns plumbing. Princess Di, alive and well at the time of the writing, becomes a local good-time party girl, and her children run wild with the local kids. The Queen Mother, who in reality is regarded in Great Britain "like God, Jesus and Mother Teresa rolled into one," as Townsend told Suzanne Cassidy for the *New York Times* (December 25, 1993, on-line), weakens and dies in the novel. That particular scene occasioned a few angry letters from staunch royalists, but for the most part, the British reading public was unoffended by Townsend's mockery of the monarchy, and the book remained on the *Sunday Times* of London's best-seller list for months. It was adapted as a BBC radio series and a West End play and also enjoyed some success in other countries. When the novel was published in America, it was called "sui generis" and "great fun" by Michael Elliott for the *New York Times* (September 12, 1993), and it was named one of the notable books of 1993 in the *New York Times Book Review*.

With *Ghost Children*, her 1998 novel, Townsend departed from her comedic mode. Scott Alarik, writing for the *Boston Globe* (July 20, 1998), warned readers, "You might be browsing for a bouncy beach book and find *Ghost Children* by Sue Townsend. 'Ah,' you think, 'that witty Brit who wrote the eccentric Adrian Mole books and savaged the royal family in *The Queen and I*. Just the ticket.' Think again." Although the novel contains occasional touches of humor, its major themes are abortion, child abuse, and drug addiction. The main character, Christopher, is a lonely misfit, obsessed by feelings of loss for his old lover, Angela, and the child she aborted 17 years before. Angela, now grossly overweight and married to a tyrannical shopkeeper, has also been haunted by memories of the unborn child and agrees to rekindle the relationship. Crackle, another central character, is a devil-worshiping drug addict who, along with his companion, Tamara, abuses their infant daughter badly enough to land her in the hospital. Alarik wrote, "Nearly all the characters defy affection and yet somehow draw our sympathy, a credit to Townsend's wonderful ability to steer us into their interior lives and back out again." Jonathan Yardley wrote for the *Washington Post* (April 29, 1998), "This is an intense story, told in a most intense way," and concluded, "At times Townsend cannot disguise her disdain for the filthy, sordid lives that Crackle and Tamara live, but she finds a degree of humanity in them all the same. It is . . . her deep feeling for all her characters that is this novel's greatest strength." Townsend's latest novel is *Number Ten* (2002), a more typically comic romp featuring the adventures of a prime minister and his bodyguard.

Townsend contributed to a BBC-TV series called *Revolting Women* in 1981 and collaborated on a comedic radio series called *The Refuge* in 1987. She was a regular columnist for *Women's Realm* magazine in the mid-1980s and has contributed to numerous periodicals, including *New Statesman*, the London *Times*, and *Marxism Today*. Townsend eventually remarried and had a fourth child. She enjoys canoeing, gardening, and reading. Despite the success of her work, she prefers to live modestly, citing her main extravagances as traveling and purchasing a house with enough bedrooms for all of her children.

—S. Y.

SUGGESTED READING: *Atlantic* p78 July 1986; *Guardian* p70+ Apr. 22, 2000; *New York Times* I p9 May 23, 1993, VII p13 Sep. 12, 1993; *New York Times Book Review* p9 May 25, 1986, p24 Apr. 22, 1990, p16 Feb. 26, 1995; *Newsweek* p76 May 5, 1986; *Publishers Weekly* p77+ Mar. 23, 1998, p69 June 5, 2000; *Times Literary Supplement* p21 Oct. 29, 1999; *Washington Post* D p2 Apr. 29, 1998; *Washington Post Book World* p2 Aug. 29, 1993

SELECTED BOOKS: novels—*The Adrian Mole Diaries* (contains *The Secret Diary of Adrian Mole, Aged 13¾* and *The Growing Pains of Adrian Mole*), 1986; *Mr. Bevan's Dream*, 1989; *Rebuilding Coventry: A Tale of Two Cities*, 1990; *Adrian Mole from Minor to Major: Mole Diaries–The First Ten Years* (contains *The Secret Diary, The Growing Pains, True Confessions, Adrian Mole and the Small Amphibians*), 1991; *Adrian Mole: The Wilderness Years*, 1993; *The Queen and I*, 1993; *Adrian Mole: The Lost Years*, 1994; *Ghost Children*, 1998; *Adrian Mole: The Cappuccino Years*, 2000; *Number Ten*, 2002; plays—*Bazaar and Rummage; Groping for Words; Womberang*, 1984; *The Great Celestial Cow*, 1984; *The Secret Diary of Adrian Mole Aged 13 3/4: The Play*, 1985; *The Queen and I: A Play*, 1996

Kate Simon/Courtesy of David Trinidad

Trinidad, David

1953– Poet

The poet David Trinidad once watched and made plot synopses of 102 episodes of *The Patty Duke Show*, and then wrote about his favorites in a poem entitled "The Ten Best Episodes of The Patty Duke Show." In the poem "Living Doll" (1988), Trinidad assumes the persona of Barbie, recounting in detail the ensemble she wore on a special occasion: "formal, floor-length gown with flowing train . . . pearl necklace and drop earrings, pink dancing pumps with silver glitter, white elbow gloves and fur stole," as quoted by Barbara Raskin in the *Washington Post* (April 26, 1993). Much of Trinidad's work is driven by his obsessive fascination with popular culture, particularly with the toys, songs, television shows, comic books, and movies of his 1960s youth. "They were an amazing escape," Trinidad told Richard Marranca and Vasiliki Koros in an interview for the *Literary Review* (Winter 1999). "It makes sense that I'd try to capture, in my work, how important that stuff was (and still is) to me. . . . I suppose there is still, in some quarters, this attitude that poetry has to be above all that, that it has to be this serious, highbrow thing, that the rest is passing garbage and won't last. But it doesn't feel like that for me." By embracing popular culture in his poetry, Trinidad is also expressing parts of his self. "There's something about the things I'm attracted to that reflects the fact that I'm a gay male, or a particular kind of gay male. Certain icons give me permission to express that sensibility," Trinidad told Marranca and Koros. Using popular culture's artifacts as both points of reference and focal points of emotion, the poems chronicle nostalgia, longing, and desire.

In an autobiographical statement for *World Authors 1995–2000*, David Trinidad writes in the third person: "David Trinidad was born in Los Angeles in 1953 and raised in the San Fernando Valley. He received his B.A. in English from California State University, Northridge, where he studied poetry with Ann Stanford. From 1981 to 1984, he was the editor and publisher of Sherwood Press, established in memory of the poet Rachel Sherwood, which published titles by such poets as Dennis Cooper, Amy Gerstler, Tim Dlugos, and Alice Notley. Trinidad's first book of poems, *Pavane*, was published in 1981. It was followed by *Monday, Monday* in 1985, *Living Doll* in 1986, and *November*, published by Hanuman Books in 1987. In the early eighties, he was associated with the writers who frequented Beyond Baroque Literary/Arts Center in Venice, California. This group included Dennis Cooper, Amy Gerstler, Benjamin Weissman, Jack Skelley, and Bob Flanagan.

"In 1988, Trinidad moved to New York City. That year another Hanuman Book, *Three Stories*, was published. He received an M.F.A. in Poetry from Brooklyn College two years later. While at Brooklyn College, he studied with Joan Larkin and Allen Ginsberg. *A Taste of Honey*, Trinidad's collaboration with Bob Flanagan, appeared in 1990. It was followed by *Hand Over Heart: Poems 1981–1988* (Amethyst Press, 1991).

"His most recent books are *Answer Song* (High Risk Books, 1994), *Essay with Movable Parts* (Thorngate Road, 1998), and *Plasticville* (Turtle Point Press, 2000). About *Plasticville*, *Publisher's Weekly* wrote, 'Only via Trinidad will Chatty Cathy enter a villanelle, or Garbo's troll collection find itself unveiled in terza rima. . . . Trinidad's high/low playfulness thoroughly displays a smart, sharp art of arrangement. . . . The book masterfully renders the obsessive aspects of popular culture—collectibility, relentless camp, larger-than-life power dynamics—and the odd way they reflect the poignant complexities of making choices. . . . This is Trinidad's finest work to date, and readers will do well to take refuge in its shiny, humane splendors.'

"Trinidad has received grants from the Fund for Poetry and the New York Foundation for the Arts. In 1996, he edited *Powerless*, the selected poems of Tim Dlugos. He continues to live in New York City. He currently teaches poetry at Rutgers University [in New Brunswick, New Jersey], where he directs the Writers at Rutgers series, and is a member of the core faculty in the M.F.A. writing program at the New School. In the fall of 2000, he will be teaching at Princeton University."

The collection *Hand Over Heart: Poems 1981–1988* (1991) garnered mixed responses from critics. A reviewer for *Publishers Weekly* (April 12, 1991) deemed Trinidad more of a "diarist" than a poet, citing *November*, which records in journal-like entries one month in the life of the author. But David Yezzi, writing for *Parnassus* (1993), referred to Trinidad's "colloquial patter" and commented that "the poems work through accretion, building a kind of novelistic continuity from the various incidents and anecdotes that make up the poet's life." Yezzi continued, "[Trinidad's] feel for how two details or incidents—receiving bad news and a popular song lyric, for example—play off one another displays them to greatest advantage." Yezzi found the poems in the collection "tempestuous, groping, and romantic," characterizing them as "artifacts of a much sought after human contact."

Although they were written during the 1980s, Yezzi saw the poems in *Hand Over Heart* as anthems of the 1970s—the era of lava lamps, beanbags, and a newly liberated gay culture. In this context, Yezzi finds it appropriate that the AIDS epidemic, which rose to a crisis point during the 1980s, is only referred to by the poet obliquely. The *Publishers Weekly* reviewer, however, found fault with Trinidad for failing to discuss AIDS in his poetry, claiming that "Trinidad seems to have cruised through the '80s without giving the virus and its assault on the gay community a second thought."

In *Answer Song* (1994) Trinidad continued to interweave meditations on love and sex into the detritus of popular culture, including advertising jingles and television theme music. "The Ten Best Episodes of The Patty Duke Show" appears in this collection, along with poems featuring children's breakfast cereals from the 1970s and early 1980s. A reviewer for *Publishers Weekly* (September 26, 1994) was intrigued by Trinidad's juxtapositions of the "emotionality of human relationships with the infectious dissonance of pop culture," but ultimately found the collection lacking. "*Answer Song* may leave readers feeling like they have just eaten an entire box of Trix—satisfied and sugar-fed, yet nervous," he wrote.

Trinidad's most recent collection, *Plasticville* (2000), has been hailed by critics as his most sophisticated work to date. A reviewer for *BOMB* magazine, as quoted on the *Amazon.com* Web site, called *Plasticville* "part diary, part TV Guide, part history of the world according to B-movie epics, part excursion into the attic of one's formative years (and thus the idiosyncrasy of sexual identity)." In the *Lambda Book Report* (April 2000), Jim Cory connects Trinidad's use of "non-serious" material in "rigorous forms" to the New York School of poetry (others poets usually mentioned in this group are Frank O' Hara, Gary Soto, and James Schuyler). Cory cites as examples of this tendency the poems "Accessories," in which Barbie wardrobes are listed in tercets (units of three lines of verse); "Fortunes," a list of fortune cookie messages in rhymed couplets; and "Chatty Cathy Villanelle," five tercets and a quatrain (four lines of verse) consisting of the babble of a talking doll. Trinidad's acts of appropriation and regrouping—of the fortune cookie messages, for example—reach a highpoint, Cory writes, in the 116-line poem "Evening Twilight," in which every line is borrowed from a different poet, and the arrangement unfolds alphabetically, from Matthew Arnold to James Wright. Cory suggests that Trinidad's precise calibration of rhythm and control of form are ways of replacing the obsessions of childhood, such as dolls and toys, with the obsessions of a poet: "measuring, cutting, and pasting imagery and information into language contraptions with all the smooth, seductive sleekness of the promises pop culture makes," he writes.

Trinidad's work has appeared in such magazines as *Harper's*, the *Paris Review*, and *New American Writing*, and is included in *Postmodern American Writing: A Norton Anthology* and *Up Late: American Poetry Since 1970*. Trinidad, who typically writes at his kitchen table, told Richard Marranca and Vasiliki Koros, "I do think the process of writing poetry is kind of magical. I learn from writing the poems. Afterwards it's 'Wow, look what I said . . . look what I did.' It can be embarrassing, too. I have to learn to live with what I've revealed about myself."

—M. A. H.

SUGGESTED READING: *Lambda Book Report* p15 Apr. 2000; *Library Journal* p168 Feb. 15, 2000; *Literary Review* p323+ Winter 1999; *Parnassus* p460+ 1993; *Publishers Weekly* p52 Apr. 12, 1991, p58 Sep. 26, 1994, p70 Feb. 7, 2000

SELECTED BOOKS: *Hand Over Heart: Poems 1981–1988*, 1991; *Answer Song*, 1994; *Plasticville*, 2000

Elizabeth A. Lustig/Courtesy of Algonquin Books

Trotter, William

July 15, 1943– Novelist; historian

William R. Trotter first gained wide recognition with his nonfiction Civil War trilogy, *Silk Flags and Cold Steel: The Piedmont* (1988), *Bushwhackers!: The Mountains* (1989), and *Ironclads and Columbiads: The Coast* (1989). His subsequent works include *A Frozen Hell: The Russo-Finnish Winter War of 1939–40* (1991); *Priest of Music: The Life of Dimitri Mitropoulos* (1995), a biography of the respected composer and conductor; and *The Sands of Pride* (2002), an historical novel about the Civil War. An editor and computer-gaming expert, Trotter writes the "Desktop General" column for *PC Gamer* magazine and has published strategy guides for such computer games as Close Combat and Ascendancy. He contributes articles and stories to a diverse assortment of publications, including *Deathrealm*, a small-press horror magazine; *Eldritch Tales*, a science-fiction periodical; and *St. Andrews Review* and *Red Clay Reader*, both Southern literary journals.

William R. Trotter Jr. was born on July 15, 1943 in Charlotte, North Carolina, the son of William R. Trotter Sr. and Anne Pease Trotter. He studied at Davidson College, in North Carolina, and received a B.A. in European history in 1966. In 1974, while working as a writer and director for World Film Productions, in Greensboro, North Carolina, Trotter published his first book, an instructional volume called *Word Processing*. Over the next decade he held various jobs, including stints as a bookseller and as the head buyer in the classical section of a record store. He worked as a freelance writer and editor for a time, and in 1988 he joined Signal Research Corp. as a senior writer. That year he published *Deadly Kin: A True Story of Mass Family Murder*, which he co-authored with Robert W. Newsom III, one of the survivors of the incident recounted in the book.

Trotter's Civil War trilogy began as an article for a magazine. As the wealth of resource material became apparent to him, he expanded the project into a book—and then into a trilogy. *Silk Flags and Cold Steel*, the first volume, focuses on the events in the Piedmont region of North Carolina during the early 1860s. In addition to describing the political climate, Trotter discusses the Salisbury prison; the Union general William Sherman's march through the Carolinas; and the confrontations at Bentonville, Raleigh, and Greensboro. The sequel, *Bushwhackers!*, examines the fighting that occurred in the Tar Heel Mountains of North Carolina, home to both pro-Union and pro-Confederate factions. The ferocity of loyalties led to bloody internecine skirmishes, and Trotter recounts hundreds of incidents—alternately violent, humorous, heroic, and shameful—that typified the time. (The author Charles Frazier has acknowledged that *Bushwhackers!* was one of the main sources for his best-selling 1997 book, *Cold Mountain*.) In *Ironclads and Columbiads*, Trotter describes the important sea battles off the coast of North Carolina, a location of strategic import to the Confederacy. Michael Rogers, in a review of the trilogy for *Library Journal* (April 15, 1991), wrote, "The facts are presented with clarity for the general reader, but the text contains enough detail to keep Civil War buffs happy."

Trotter's next book, *A Frozen Hell*, describes the attempt of the outnumbered Finnish army to defend itself from the onslaught of Russian forces during the winter war of 1939–1940. Although the conflict was overshadowed by World War II and is now largely forgotten, it was widely covered in the international media at the time. In 1939 the USSR demanded that Finland cede portions of the 90-mile-long Karelian Isthmus, the only substantial land bridge between the Scandinavian peninsula and Russia, for strategic reasons in case of an attack from Nazi Germany. When the Finns refused, the Soviets attacked, expecting an immediate victory against the sparsely inhabited nation. The Finns, crippled by their smaller numbers and severe lack of modern weaponry, nevertheless executed a strategic guerrilla campaign marked by heroism and ingenuity—an effort that earned them many admirers in the Western world. The Soviets ultimately won, but the Finns managed to prolong what might have been a quick conquest into a fierce battle lasting more than three months.

"This history is a well-balanced blend of narrative and analysis," Dennis E. Showalter wrote for *Library Journal* (July 1991). "Trotter's overt sympathy for the justice of Finland's cause does not blind him to the justified fear of Nazi Germany that led Russia to demand a buffer zone in front of Leningrad. Similarly, Trotter's admiration for the Finnish army's fighting power does not prevent him from presenting its limitations as well as achievements." John Eisenhower noted in a more mixed critique for the *New York Times Book Review* (July 7, 1991), "The author is at his best when dealing with political matters. Describing the strategies of military campaigns, he throws in far too much detail." Eisenhower opined, however, "This defect is more than offset by vivid pictures and intriguing trivia. . . . The greatest value of *A Frozen Hell* is the perspective it affords. We will not often find a book written with such authority as this one by Mr. Trotter." Trotter won the 1992 Finlandia Foundation Arts and Letters prize for *A Frozen Hell*.

Winter Fire (1993), Trotter's first novel, is also set in Finland, although he now focuses on World War II. Erich Ziegler, a conductor and German intelligence officer, is on a secret mission when he meets the composer Jean Sibelius. The two form a friendship, and Ziegler learns that Sibelius's highly anticipated eighth symphony may be complete. Ziegler is abruptly dispatched to the Russian front, but he resolves to be the first to present the symphony to the world. "Trotter uses a blend of mysticism, music, greed, and ambition to craft a wonderful story," Karen Stewart wrote for *Library Journal* (January 1993). "[He] contrasts the brutality of war with the humanity of music. He vividly depicts the Finnish countryside, the extreme cold of Lapland, and the horrors of the Russian front. Yet he remains focused on his story and does not allow the inhumanity to take over."

Trotter pursued his interest in music with his next book, *Priest of Music: The Life of Dimitri Mitropoulos*. During his lifetime, Mitropoulos (1896-1960) was widely considered to be one of the most important conductors of the era. As a youth in his native Greece, he was drawn toward the priesthood, but his love for music exerted a greater pull. His work was frequently praised for its "religious" zeal. After gaining international recognition in Europe, he embarked on an American career that culminated in a decade-long tenure as the director of the New York Philharmonic. Mitropoulos's musical interpretations were frequently controversial and eventually a cabal of music critics led by the *New York Times* forced him out of the high-profile directorship. After leaving the New York Philharmonic, Mitropoulos joined the Metropolitan Opera and continued to conduct in the final years before his death, but his story is punctuated with various other misfortunes. For example, Leonard Bernstein, a fellow conductor whom Mitropoulos financially supported for a time, later turned against him and thwarted his attempt to become the director of the Boston Symphony.

Trotter wrote about Mitropoulos using approximately 150 interviews that were conducted by the musicologist Oliver Daniel; Daniel had planned to write the biography but died before he could do so. Bill Zakariasen, writing for *Opera News* (February 3, 1996), called the book "extraordinary" and an "engrossing tome," adding, "Mitropoulos' blessed spirit has been done justice by Trotter's book." Richard Dyer, in the *Boston Globe* (December 19, 1995), however, complained that Trotter was frequently sloppy with his facts, citing an example in which Dyer himself had been misidentified. Dyer conceded that "the biography remains valuable for the information it brings together—some of it, in fact, could not be assembled today because the sources have died," but, he continued, "it's hard to read the book without feeling an additional sense of loss—no one else is going to undertake this task, so it ought to have been done better."

In *The Sands of Pride*, a lengthy volume of historical fiction, Trotter again takes up the battles and political intrigues of the Civil War. As in his earlier nonfiction trilogy, the focus is on North Carolina. The novel features an extensive cast of characters, several drawn from actual historical figures, including: William B. Cushing, the daring Union naval commander; Major General Ambrose Burnside; Major General Ben Butler; Jefferson Davis, the president of the Confederacy; and Zebulon Vance, the future governor of North Carolina. The novel opens on December 31, 1860, just months before North Carolina agreed to secede from the Union, on May 20, 1861. The hub of the action is the lively coastal city of Wilmington, North Carolina, which served as a vital port for the South during the war. As other coastal areas fell to Union forces, Wilmington, protected by Fort Fisher, was one of the last viable ports in the South.

Trotter "throws everything into his literary plot," Ben Steelman wrote for the *Wilmington Star-News* (May 12, 2002). While Steelman praised Trotter for committing very few historical mistakes, he noted that the novel "may be overstuffed with history, with page after page of background, and elaborate tactical analyses poorly disguised as dialogue." Mark Johnson wrote for the *San Jose Mercury News* (May 5, 2002), "The author's love of the history [of the Civil War] for its own sake shines through on every page." Although Johnson faulted the book for its depiction of slavery as a "beneficent institution," he added, "If this is a theme that Trotter intends to develop in a sequel, I will happily withdraw my objection. In other ways, he has offered much to enjoy and much to think about." Jeff Zaleski, writing for *Publishers Weekly* (April 22, 2002), predicted a sequel, noting that the book ends in July 1863, "portending the fall of Fort Fisher some two years later." Zaleski concluded, "This masterful epic offers insight into the perfidious political agendas and personal greed underlying the bumbling and horrors suffered by both sides during the war."

Trotter, who is an avid record collector, lives with his wife in Greensboro, North Carolina. He has three children.

—A. I. C.

SUGGESTED READING: *Boston Globe* p67 Dec. 19, 1995; *Library Journal* p130 Apr. 15, 1991, p112 July 1991, p167 Jan. 1993; *New York Times Book Review* p11 July 7, 1991; *Opera News* p47 Feb. 3, 1996; *Publishers Weekly* p50 Apr. 22, 2002; *San Jose Mercury News* May 5, 2002; *Washington Times* B p6 Nov. 3, 1991; *Wilmington Star-News* D p8 May 12, 2002

SELECTED BOOKS: *Silk Flags and Cold Steel: The Piedmont* 1988; *Bushwhackers!: The Mountains*, 1989; *Ironclads and Columbiads: The Coast*, 1989; *A Frozen Hell: The Russo-Finnish Winter War of 1939–40*, 1991; *Winter Fire*, 1993; *Priest of Music: The Life of Dimitri Mitropoulos*, 1995; *The Sands of Pride*, 2002

Calvin Ferguson/Courtesy of Simon & Schuster

Tyree, Omar

1968(?)– Novelist

Omar Tyree's success as a published author mirrors the successes of many of his characters. After graduating from Howard University, Tyree self-published and promoted his first three novels, *Colored, On White Campus* (1992), *Flyy Girl* (1993), and *Capital City: The Chronicles of a D.C. Underworld* (1994). His books proved to be so popular that by July 1993, he had become a full-time, self-employed author; two years later he signed a two-book deal with Simon & Schuster. As part of that deal, *Flyy Girl* was republished in 1996 in a hardcover edition. Since then he has published several more novels: *A Do Right Man* (1997), *Single Mom* (1998), *Sweet St. Louis* (1999), *For the Love of Money* (2000), *Just Say No!* (2001), and *Leslie* (2002), each adding to his already considerable commercial success. His portraits of young, upwardly mobile African-Americans have earned him a solid fan base.

In an autobiographical statement written in the third person for *World Authors 1995–2000*, Tyree discussed his life and work: "Omar Tyree is an author, publisher, lecturer and performance poet who completed his undergraduate studies at Howard University in Washington, D.C., with honors in print journalism. He was born and raised in Philadelphia, Pennsylvania, where he graduated from the city's most prestigious Central High School in 1987. He is presently thirty-one years old and lives in Charlotte, North Carolina, with his wife, Karintha, and two sons Ameer and Canoy.

"After high school graduation, Tyree became one of thirty fortunate minority students to enroll at the University of Pittsburgh under a challenge grant scholarship program. He was later awarded the sum of $3,400 toward his school tuition after being recognized by the Phi Eta Sigma Freshman Honor Society for academic excellence in math and science studies.

"While attending the U. of Pitt. and studying to become a pharmacist, Tyree scored at the highest level of reading comprehension and discovered an uncanny ability to write. He penned a journal, 'The Diary of a Freshman,' which was published in the minority counseling news pamphlet. He then became one of few freshman allowed to enroll in a creative writing course during his first year of schooling after receiving an A grade mark in highest level of freshman English.

"In 1989, Tyree transferred to Howard University and began a new career interest in writing. In his senior year of 1991, he became the first student in Howard University history to have a featured column, 'Food For Thought,' published in *The Hilltop*, the school's award-winning newspaper.

"Following the completion of undergraduate studies in December of 1991, he was hired as a reporter and an assistant editor at *The Capital Spotlight* weekly newspaper in Washington, D.C., where he also sold advertising. He later served as the chief reporter for *News Dimensions* weekly newspaper while freelancing for the *Washington View Magazine*.

"Tyree made his next move writing and publishing books. After having first-hand experience with print shops and typesetting at newspaper plants, he organized MARS Productions, a sole-proprietorship, to publish his first novel, *Colored, On White Campus*. The small-scale book was published in October of 1992, with financial help from friends and family, who offered him personal loans. *Colored, On White Campus* sold well enough to produce funds to publish his second effort, *FLYY-GIRL*, in April of 1993. By July of 1993, Omar Tyree was self-employed.

"Tyree was the youngest participant on a BET (Black Entertainment Television) talk show pilot entitled, 'For Black Men Only,' which successfully aired in the fall of 1992. The show shared candid views of African-American men on stereotypes, lifestyles, social/economic politics, public issues and their effects on them. Hosted by *Washington Post* columnist and BET news commentator Courtland Milloy, the program's taped shows aired continuously throughout the summer of 1993 with positive national response.

"In the summer of 1993, Tyree was published in the Sunday 'Outlook' section at the nation's number two newspaper, the *Washington Post* ('Meet The New Invisible Man,' 7/18/93). At twenty-four-years of age, he again made history as one of the youngest African-American male journalists to be published in the *Post's* commentary page with his views on the lack of attention positive young black men (YBM's) receive in the American media. The story became syndicated and printed by newspapers nationally and internationally. The British Broadcast Channel (BBC) then sought out an interview for a network special on young black men and stereotypes in the United States.

"*Capital City: The Chronicles of a D.C. Underworld* was released in April of 1994, becoming Tyree's third successfully published book. In January of 1995, he republished *Colored, On White Campus* as *BattleZone: The Struggle to Survive the American Institution* with a new cover design. He was also published in a Beacon Press release entitled *Testimony: Young African-Americans on Self-Discovery and Black Identity* in February of 1995. Soon after, he was invited for a television interview with host Julian Bond on America's Black Forum to discuss present issues facing blacks and education on predominantly white campuses at the advent of director John Singleton's film, *Higher Learning*.

"Most recently, Tyree was honored with an entrepreneurial spirit and leadership plaque by the Multicultural Youth Incorporation (MCY Inc.) in Washington, D.C. His three published books, *FLYY-GIRL, Capital City* and *BattleZone* have all been picked up by book distributors in New York, New Jersey, Atlanta, Virginia, Baltimore and Chicago. Sales escalated to more than 25,000 copies, and are still selling through Tyree's persistence in marketing.

"In August of 1995, author Omar Tyree was picked up on a two-book contract deal, which included the republication of *FLYY-GIRL* in hardback form, by the major publishing house of Simon & Schuster.

"Tyree has now published a total of seven novels including *For The Love of Money, Sweet St. Louis, Single Mom, A Do Right Man, Flyy Girl, Capital City*, and *BattleZone*, and is continuously participating in national lecturing events to disseminate information to the African-American community and expand his popularity among readers. He continues to lecture to organizations, at colleges, high schools and community events on a variety of subjects. He recently finished his latest novel entitled *Just Say No!* about the indulgences of the America youth and the music industry to be published by Simon & Schuster on August 7, 2001.

"Last but not least, author Omar Tyree has begun pitching film ideas to Hollywood agents and producers, starting with his most successful novel, *FLYY GIRL*."

Tyree's first novel to be widely reviewed was the 1996 hardcover re-issue of *Flyy Girl*, which had received high praise from people who had read it as a self-published work. Many of those readers were moved by the experiences of Tracy Ellison, the teenager at the center of this morality tale, who uses sex to get the things she wants but then learns the unfortunate consequences of such actions. Critics, however, were not as kind to *Flyy Girl*. As one of them noted for *Kirkus Reviews* (August 1, 1996), "Tyree's shapeless docudrama seems written for an audience he intends to shock—why else would he pause so often (and so awkwardly) to translate slang terms that any watcher of Moesha would know? But for all its immoral behavior, it's a cautionary tale of the most heavy-handed sort: virtue rewarded; vice punished."

Tyree's next novel, *A Do Right Man* (1997), fared better with critics. The novel is about Bobby Dallas, a rising star in the radio industry, who tries in vain to keep up with women who are too fast for him. Motivated by the problems that result, Dallas begins to search for a soul mate; he eventually learns how to be monogamous and also responsible with regard to family obligations. Lillian Lewis, in her review for *Booklist* (November 1, 1997), noted, "Tyree presents refreshing insight into the world of an aspiring African American male and his relationships. . . . [He] shares the black male struggle, experience, and feeling with insight and humor. A great coming of age story for young African American males." In *Library Journal* (November 15, 1997), Shirley Gibson Coleman was less complimentary, writing that the "book has its problems," but also noting that the "author has done an impressive amount of research into the world of radio and gives an honest if tiring interpretation of a black man struggling to do right, while getting it all wrong."

In 1998 Tyree published *Single Mom*, which was considered a departure from the author's formula involving entangling sexual situations. As the title suggests, this novel is about the life of a single working mother, Denise Stewart, who has two teenage boys from two different fathers. The novel shows how her strength and determination to raise good sons aid her in making the men in her life better people. Though each of her sons' fathers is aware of his offspring, he has opted to have little to do with his son. Later, each attempts to reenter his child's life, at around the time Denise begins dating a truck driver who is developing a relationship with both boys. Lillian Lewis praised *Single Mom* in her *Booklist* (October 1, 1998) review: "Tyree's stories have become increasingly complex and thought-provoking. . . . This novel's warm and fuzzy ending will make you feel hopeful that the struggles people encounter as parents, partners, and friends can be less burdensome when people face issues rather than run from them."

In 1999 Tyree published *Sweet St. Louis*, about the differences between the behavior of black men and women in relationships and how they finally find true love. The story focuses on the love affair between womanizer Anthony Poole and Sharron Francis, who might help him to change his ways. In the course of the novel, the two grow by challenging and provoking each other. The novel received mostly mixed reviews. Regina Marler, in an undated on-line assessment for *Amazon.com*, complained, "Tyree sometimes generalizes too much about the sexes. He also relies on overly long, relaxed dialogue that can sometimes read like the transcript of an excruciating blind date. But Ant and Sharron are depicted as ordinary, multidimensional people who are full of contradictions." In a *Booklist* (September 15, 1999) review of *Sweet St. Louis*, by contrast, Lillian Lewis called Tyree a "masterful . . . storyteller."

In *For the Love of Money* (2000), the sequel to *Flyy Girl*, the story follows Tracy Ellison as she succeeds by sheer determination. "Tyree may turn off some readers with Tracy's clichéd poetry and occasional references to himself and his success throughout the narrative," an anonymous critic wrote for *Publishers Weekly* (July 3, 2000). "Although the prose (rife with self-important italicized words to make obvious points) is often clunky and the dialogue flat, Tracy's adventures provide cool commentary on ambition, love, friendship and the price of fame."

Tyree's next book, *Just Say No!* (2001), is about two lifelong friends, Darin Harmon and John Williams, who achieve fame and celebrity through John's ascending musical career, but soon find themselves struggling to overcome the usual pitfalls of sex and drugs. "If there's one thing that novelist Omar Tyree has, it's his finger on the pulse of the urban community," Kelley L. Carter wrote in the *Chicago Tribune* (August 15, 2001). "He's managed to get right in there with some of the issues that are facing young black people, toss his spin on them, and churn out some fairly decent literature. The plot, most times, isn't overwhelming, nor is the narrative style that he uses. But Tyree has carved a nice niche for himself. . . . Tyree demonstrates growth in this novel, finding clever ways to tell the story of growing up and learning to deal with the things around you."

Leslie (2002) is the story of a beautiful and mysterious New Orleans college student, Leslie Beaudet, who begins to dabble in Voodoo, the superstitious practice that developed in New Orleans through the slave trade and derives from the religious Vaudou culture of Haiti. "Tyree takes the easy way out in his latest effort, subjugating the more promising elements of his story line about an intelligent, exotic Haitian co-ed to a series of lurid subplots involving voodoo, drugs and murder," a critic wrote for *Publishers Weekly*, as quoted on *Amazon.com*. "This could have been a fascinating novel if there were more meaningful interactions between Leslie and those around her." Other reviewers were more positive. Lillian Lewis, in a review for *Booklist*, as quoted on *Amazon.com*, remarked,"Tyree has woven complex characters that overcome seemingly hopeless circumstances."

In 2001 Tyree received the National Association for the Advancement of Colored People (NAACP) Image Award for the best work of fiction. His next novel, "Diary of a Groupie," was published in June 2003.

—C. M.

SUGGESTED READING: *Booklist* (on-line) Oct. 1, 1998, Sep. 15, 1999; *Chicago Tribune* C p9 Aug. 15, 2001; *Kirkus Reviews* (on-line) Aug. 1, 1996; *Booklist* p456 Nov. 1, 1997; *Library Journal* p78 Nov. 15, 1997; *Publishers Weekly* p45 July 3, 2000

SELECTED BOOKS: *Colored, On White Campus*, 1992 (re-published as *BattleZone: the Struggle to Survive the American Institution*, 1995); *Flyy Girl*, 1993, 1996; *Capital City: The Chronicles of a D.C. Underworld*, 1994; *A Do Right Man*, 1997; *Single Mom*, 1998; *Sweet St. Louis*, 1999; *For the Love of Money*, 2000; *Just Say No!*, 2001; *Leslie*, 2002

Vance, Jack

Aug. 28, 1916– Novelist; short-story writer

While not a brand name in the genre of science fiction like H. G. Wells, Ray Bradbury, or Arthur C. Clarke, Jack Vance is considered by his many fans to be the premiere science-fiction writer of the 20th century. Since the mid-1940s his work has chronicled humanity's distant future and has suggested that people possess a certain energy that draws them toward exploration, adventures, or mysteries. Though Vance's more than 60 novels and many short stories are hard to define—falling somewhere between science fiction and escapist fantasy—all of his work is both entertaining and insightful. He is a reader's writer who shuns the cult of celebrity that exists around so many successful authors. "A reader is not supposed to be aware that someone's written the story," Vance remarked in an interview with Ralph B. Sipper, published in the *Los Angeles Times* (August 5, 1979) and archived on the Jack Vance Information Page Web site. "He's supposed to be completely immersed, submerged in the environment."

John Holbrook Vance was born on August 28, 1916 in San Francisco, California, the son of Charles Albert Vance and the former Edith Hoefler. Vance was raised on his father's ranch in the San Joaquin Valley. As a boy he loved to read adventure stories, including those of Jules Verne, Edgar Rice Burroughs, and Robert Chambers. He attended high school in Los Angeles and then enrolled at the University of California at Berkeley, receiving a B.A. in journalism in 1942 after changing his major from physics. During World War II he served as a merchant marine; using the astronomy skills he had gained at age 12, when he had constructed a star chart, he studied the night skies over the Atlantic and the Pacific. At sea he also began to compose short stories, and by the time he came home he was determined to become a writer.

Like many of the science-fiction writers of the day, including Isaac Asimov and Ray Bradbury, Vance's efforts first found publication in pulp magazines. His first story, "The World-Thinker," was published in *Thrilling Wonder Stories* in the summer of 1945. Many of his early stories feature Detective Magnus Ridolph and are a cross between science-fiction space adventures and true-crime tales. (A collection of these stories was first released in book form as *The Many Worlds of Magnus Ridolph* in 1966.)

Vance spent a few years learning his craft. "I'm not one of these chaps who has an instant success," he told Charles Platt in his book *Dream Makers, Volume II: The Uncommon Men and Women Who Write Science Fiction* (1983), as quoted in *Contemporary Authors* (1986). "There was a long period in which I wrote a lot of junk, as an apprentice, learning my trade. I found out I was no good at gadget stories, or at least they were very boring to me, and I found out that I didn't enjoy writing whimsy, and I finally blundered into this thing which I keep doing, which is essentially a history of the human future."

Vance's first major work, *The Dying Earth* (1950), is a collection of six interconnecting stories, which take place in a common setting with many recurring characters. Set in the distant future, in a time when the sun has grown large and fills the sky, humans live in a world of ruined cities and gigantic forests. Their society is a mix of high technology and magic and yet, as in the present era, people continue to battle for knowledge or power: a magician torments a man to gain the secret of intelligent life he has created; a witch exchanges a man's face with a demon's. The heroes overcome their troubles through courage, loyalty, and love, thereby lifting curses, or overthrowing some oppressor—common themes throughout Vance's work. Other books in *The Dying Earth* series include *The Eyes of the Overworld* (1966), *Cugel's Saga* (1983), and *Rhialto the Marvellous* (1984).

After *The Dying Earth*, Vance's best-known work of the 1950s is *Big Planet* (1957), an adventure novel in which a group of marooned Earthmen must journey 40,000 miles across an enormous planet in order to reach safety at the Earth Enclave. Along the way they face castoffs from human civilization—among the most ungovernable people in the galaxy—living in kingdoms, small fiefdoms, and expansive wildernesses. In a series of episodes, the Earthmen escape from bandits and other hostile factions and encounter strange, idiosyncratic societies.

Many of Vance's short stories from this period were collected in *Slaves of the Klau* (1958), *The Houses of Iszm* (1964), *Son of the Tree* (1964), *The World Between and Other Stories* (1965), and *Eight Fantasms and Magics* (1969). In one unusual, fairy-tale-like story, "The Moon Moth" (1961), a young man finds himself on the planet Sirene, where the inhabitants communicate by wearing elaborate masks and speaking only when accompanied by musical instruments. As a stranger to this planet he is only able to communicate with basic instruments, but he must quickly find an assassin hiding behind Sirenese customs and masks.

The mid-1950s through the 1960s proved to be an incredibly fruitful period for Vance, in which he wrote such major works as *To Live Forever* (1956), *The Languages of Pao* (1958), *The Blue World* (1966), and the first three *Demon Princes* novels: *The Star King* (1964), *The Killing Machine* (1964), and *The Palace of Love* (1967).

To Live Forever imagines a world in which everyone petitions to join the exclusive ranks of the Amaranth Society, a group granted immortality for their achievements. One man—a former immortal—questions the value of this endless, placid existence. In *The Languages of Pao*, a peaceful race must learn self-defense or risk domination by others. The "Demon Princes" series, which would later include *The Face* (1979) and *The Book of Dreams* (1981), follows the adventures of Kirth Gersen, who must track down the five criminals, or "demon princes," who destroyed his home and family. A combination of the mystery and thriller genres set in a futuristic universe, the novels are also morality tales about the abuse of power and the meaning of good and evil.

Though not part of a series, *Emphyrio* (1969) is considered one of Vance's most significant novels. It follows the coming-of-age of Ghyl Tarvoke, a woodcarver's son who will someday become the liberator of his people. He adopts the traits of the legendary hero Emphyrio, who died while striving for justice. The book has been praised for resisting melodrama while exploring freedom and the responsibility of leadership.

Vance began his *Planet of Adventure* cycle in 1968, with the publication of *City of the Chasch*; *Servants of the Wankh* (1969), *The Dirdir* (1969), and *The Pnume* (1970) soon followed. In the cycle an intergalactic scout named Adam Reith crashes on the planet of Tschai. In his attempts to find a way off the planet, he encounters a variety of alien species and human civilizations. In the "Durdane" trilogy, composed of *The Anome* (1973), *The Brave Free Men* (1973), and *The Asutra* (1974), the main character sets out to right the wrongs of his society, including overthrowing Anome, the Faceless Man, and defying the attempts of two alien civilizations to exploit the humans of this planet. Vance also published the *Alastor* series (1973–1978), the *Lyonesse* series (1983–1985), and the *Cadwal Chronicles* (1987–1992).

In the 1980s Vance published *Galactic Effectuator* (1980), *The Dark Ocean* (1985), *Strange Notions* (1985), and *The Complete Magnus Ridolph* (1984). In addition to these works, he has also published novels under the pseudonyms Peter Held and Alan Wade. Though much of his work remains out of print, the Vance Integral Edition project (VIE), an Internet-based effort run by volunteers, is planning to publish Vance's complete works in 60 volumes, beginning in 2002. These hardcover volumes will be published in chronological order and sell for about a $1,000 per set.

Legally blind and infirm, Jack Vance continued to write and appear at occasional science-fiction conventions well into his 80s. His work has spawned a role-playing game, as well as numerous fan Web sites. He has received several awards for his work, including the Edgar Allen Poe Award from the Mystery Writers of America (1961), the Hugo Award from the World Science Fiction Convention (1964 and 1967), the Nebula Award from the Science Fiction Writers of America (1966), the Jupiter Award for best novelette (1975), and the World Fantasy Lifetime Achievement Award (1984). He lives with his wife, the former Norma Ingold, in Oakland, California. The Vances married in 1946 and have one son, John Holbrook Vance II.
—C. M.

SUGGESTED READING: *Booklist* p226 Sep. 15, 1996; Infinity Plus Web site; *New York Times Book Review* p24 Nov. 3, 1996; *Utopia Studies* p186 1997; *Contemporary Literary Criticism* Vol. 35 1985; *Dictionary of Literary Biography* Vol. 8 1981; Platt, Charles. *Dream Makers, Volume II: The Uncommon Men and Women Who Write Science Fiction*, 1983

SELECTED BOOKS: *The Dying Earth*, 1950; *To Live Forever*, 1956; *Big Planet*, 1957; *The Languages of Pao*, 1958; *The Star King*, 1964; *The Killing Machine*, 1964; *The Palace of Love*, 1967; *Emphyrio*, 1969; *The Worlds of Jack Vance*, 1973; *The Best of Jack Vance*, 1976; *Galactic Effectuator*, 1980; *The Dark Ocean*, 1985; *Strange Notions*, 1985; *The Complete Magnus Ridolph*, 1984; *Night Lamp*, 1996

Vasilenko, Svetlana

(VASSI-len-KO, TSVET-lana)

Jan. 24, 1956– Short-story writer; novelist

In the last decade, Svetlana Vasilenko has emerged as one of Russia's leading women writers. In her profile of Vasilenko for the *Dictionary of Russian Women Writers* (1994), Elena Trofimova writes, "In her prose Vasilenko tells of the normal life of so-called plain Soviet people . . . which, in fact, is monstrously abnormal. In the author's own words, her prose is about 'a society where everything is allowed. Everything, that is, which is forbidden by Christian precepts.'" On the surface, Vasilenko's fiction seems bleak. Her characters often face unspeakable horrors such as rape, domestic abuse, neglect, radiation, and the threat of nuclear extinction. Out of this misery, however, Vasilenko believes that redemption, salvation and intellectual insight can be found. In 1999 Vasilenko was introduced to English-speaking audiences when Northwestern University Press published a collection of her work, *Shamara and Other Stories*.

Svetlana Vasilenko was born on January 24, 1956 in Kapustin Iar, the Soviet Union's equivalent of Cape Canaveral. Security in Kapustin Iar was extremely strict, and the area was also contaminated with radiation. Svetlana's father, V. G. Morev, worked as a rocket specialist and her mother, Mariia Vasilenko, was a construction technician. As a child, Svetlana witnessed the launch of cosmonaut Yuri Gagarin, the first man in space, in 1961. She was acutely aware of the ominous presence of nuclear weapons in her hometown. In her editorial introduction to *Shamara and Other Stories*, Professor Helena Goscilo of the University of Pittsburgh wrote that "Vasilenko contends [that Kapustin Iar] endeavored to instill a love of death in its residents." In the *Moscow Times* (July 29, 2000), Oliver Ready recounted a conversation Vaslienko purportedly had with her father. "Critic Pavel Basinsky claimed (in comments translated in the journal *Glas*) Vasilenko once asked her father: 'What did you all do, what did you all think about sitting facing all those buttons, facing the end of the world?' He thought for a moment and said: 'We played cards.'" Goscilo notes that Svetlana "enjoyed emotional closeness with her mother," while her father was often absent. Svetlana later adopted her mother's last name after her father abandoned the family.

As a child, Vasilenko showed immediate promise as a writer. In 1966, at the age of 10, she published a poem in the Soviet newspaper, *Komsomolka*. Over 1,000 readers sent letters, enthusiastically praising Vasilenko's work. Goscilo observes that this overwhelming praise ignited in Vasilenko a desire to become a writer.

Vasilenko's attempts to publish in the 1970s were unsuccessful. She found employment at a synthetic-fibers plant and later worked as a mail carrier and fruit hauler. In 1978 Vasilenko enrolled in the Gorky Literary Institute in Moscow and studied under Grigorii Baklanov, the veteran Soviet author. Goscilo quotes Vasilenko as saying that her years at the Institute were "the happiest period" of her life.

In 1982 Vasilenko earned critical acclaim in the Soviet Union when she published her first short story, "Going After Goat Antelopes." The story's narrator, a waitress, meets a soldier at a restaurant. The couple are attracted to each other, and she accepts his invitation to leave with him. They drive off together in his jeep to hunt for "goat antelopes," a rare animal hybrid. The narrator gives the reader the impression that the encounter ends tragically, but she admits that her account contains unspecified lies. According to Goscilo, Soviet literary critics hailed "Going After Goat Antelopes" as "the best story of the year."

Vasilenko graduated from the Gorky Literary Institute in 1983. Although "Going After Goat Antelopes" established her as a fresh talent, Vasilenko didn't publish another short story until 1989. Although perestroika was sweeping the Soviet Union in the late 1980s, Vasilenko and other female writers still encountered discrimination in literary circles. Trofimova quoted Vasilenko as saying that Soviet journals refused to publish her work due to what they deemed its "superfluous naturalism and an emphasis on the lack of spirituality in the lives of the Soviet people." Goscilo writes that Vasilenko and other women formed an informal writers' group, "The New Amazons," who were able to publish anthologies of their work. The first, *Ne pomniashchaia zla* (She Who Bears No Grudge) appeared in the Soviet Union in 1990, and *Novye Amazonki* (The New Amazons) was published there in 1991.

Vasilenko joined the Writers' Union in 1989 and the PEN Club in 1990. She later became the first secretary of the Union of Russian Writers, based in Moscow, and Goscilo cited Vasilenko's ascendence to a leadership role as evidence of a growing cultural acceptance of women writers following the breakup of the Soviet Union, which occurred in 1991. In 1989 Vasilenko completed a course of study in film directing and started work with Andrei Konchalovsky on a joint project, a film version of the fable *Tristan and Isolde* (1990). Goscilo compared one of Vasilenko's signature narrative techniques to "cinematic montage": "Abrupt, unexplained interpolations of strikingly visual scenes (often signaled by use of the present tense) reinforce a narrative rhythm that inscribes the relentless forces buffeting beings whose behavior seems equally disjointed and irrational." In 1990 Vasilenko published *Shamara*, which Goscilo referred to as a "video novella." Set in a labor camp contaminated by radiation, the story borrows from Vasilenko's childhood in Kapustin Iar. A representative passage reflects Vasilenko's sensibility: A woman knocks on the door of a cottage. She informs the man behind the door that she will die without him. The man comes out, hands the woman a rope with a noose and asks, "Anything else?" The novella also illustrates the importance of the female body in Vasilenko's fiction. In her book *Dehexing Sex: Russian Womanhood During and After Glasnost* (1996), Goscilo writes that the female body in Vasilenko's fiction "functions, in fact, as the field through which passes every conceivable experience, open to endless signification. A source of joy and suffering, the corporeal self is both metaphor and material entity, subject and object, depending upon the specifics of the give moment." The title character, Shamara, is physically abused by her husband and her co-workers and nearly killed on two occasions. However, Shamara, as Goscilo adds, also "articulates her sexual desire for a man, enjoys a drinking spree, and takes sensual delight in her own and others' physical appearance."

Throughout the 1990s, Vasilenko published numerous short stories and a short novel, *Little Fool*, which, according to several sources, was nominated for the Russian Booker Prize for fiction in 1998. The journal *Novyi mir* (New World), in which *Little Fool* initially appeared, named the novel its best publication of 1998. In the novel, the world is saved from nuclear war by an unlikely heroine: a deaf-mute child named Ganna who witnesses an apparition of the Virgin Mary and herself becomes a saint, rising into the air and giving birth to a new sun.

In 1999 six of Svetlana Vasilenko's best stories were published in English in the anthology, *Shamara and Other Stories*. In her review for *Publishers Weekly* (February 21, 2000), Sybil S. Steinberg wrote, "Though Vasilenko sometimes makes narrative jumps that are difficult to follow, she brings intelligence and soulfulness to these telling, moving stories." Steinberg stated that Vasilenko's longer works such as "Going After Goat Antelopes," *Shamara*, and *Little Fool* "critique Russian culture as they passionately examine the human psyche." In the *Moscow Times* (July 29, 2000), Oliver Ready observed, "The characters of *Shamara and Other Stories* seem to face apocalypse on a daily basis, whether it comes in the shape of an atomic bomb, a horrible disease or a despotic orphanage director. . . . Behind every story lurks the urgent question: How can a world bent on mutilation and wanton cruelty ever be saved? The answer also seems to lie between the lines: by a miracle as great as the surrounding evil." Ready criticized Vasilenko's use of "restrictive gender roles." In her fiction, men are identified with "unthinking destruction and the callous abuse of authority, women with unpredictability and heightened sensitivity." Although Ready describes Vasilenko's writing as "stark and abrupt," he concludes that she is "an adventurous and challenging writer."

Svetlana Vasilenko is married, and she and her husband live in Moscow. In addition to writing, Vasilenko is pursuing a career as a film director.
—D. C.

SUGGESTED READING: *Moscow Times* (on-line) July 29, 2000; *Publishers Weekly* p66 Feb. 21, 2000; Goscilo, Helena. *Dehexing Sex: Russian Womanhood During and After Glasnost*, 1996; Trofimova, Elena. *Dictionary of Russian Women Writers*, 1994

SELECTED BOOKS IN ENGLISH TRANSLATION: *Shamara and Other Stories*, 1999

Courtesy of Plume Publicity

Véa, Alfredo

1952(?)– Novelist; lawyer

"I have spent a great deal of my life inside the United States but far outside of America," the novelist Alfredo Véa has written on his Web site. He spent his childhood working among migrant farm workers, as society seemed to pass him by on the freeways next to the fields. He witnessed the Vietnam War firsthand, questioning the violence and machismo of his fellow soldiers. Overcoming his lack of formal education, he became an attorney, defending farm laborers and other people he felt were oppressed and victimized. These experiences formed the basis of his three novels, *La Maravilla* (1992), *The Silver Cloud Café* (1996), and *Gods Go Begging* (1999), all three of which employ magical realism in their depictions of rural and urban life in California. "All three books . . . celebrate the forgotten [and] illuminate the unseen. . . . They are from the 'underside' of our society, not written from the mainstream point of view," he told Randall Holdridge for *Tuscon Weekly* (September 12, 1999, on-line).

Born in the Arizona desert to a 13-year-old mother of Mexican origin, Véa is unsure of his date of birth; he believes it was sometime in the early 1950s. His father deserted him soon after his birth, and he and his mother lived just outside of Phoenix, in a community of squatters called Buckeye Road, where migrant laborers of all ethnic stripes huddled in hovels made of flimsy tar-paper or brittle adobe. Véa's mother took care of him for six years before she left to work as a migrant laborer in California's Central Valley fields. Left in the care of his maternal grandparents, Manuel Carvajal and Josephina Castillo de Carvajal, Véa absorbed a lot from them. From his grandmother he learned to appreciate such black singers and musicians as Sarah Vaughan, Dinah Washington, Duke Ellington, Count Basie, and Louis Armstrong. His grandfather introduced him to many different languages. Exiled from his Yaqui tribe because he had married a woman of Spanish origins, Manuel was fluent in English, Spanish, Yaqui, and other languages he picked up from the immigrants with whom he worked on the railroads; he could even sing songs in Gaelic. Although both of Véa's grandparents were Catholic, they imparted to Véa a strong sense of magic, mysticism, and spirituality, stemming from their gypsy and Native American roots. When Véa was nine, he even experimented with peyote tea, a mind-altering substance.

When he was 10 years old, Véa joined his mother to work as a seasonal laborer and to take care of his four younger half-siblings (a girl and three boys). Traveling up and down the Pacific Coast— he picked vegetables in California's Imperial Valley and packed salmon in Washington—he befriended Mexican, Filipino, and French-Canadian workers, who became his "tios" (uncles). They taught him everything from self-defense to reading and writing; they even bought him a 10-volume encyclopedia so that he could exercise his brain and escape the drudgery of farm labor. "I read about the Depression, the New Deal, Lewis and Clarke," he recalled on his Web site. "But I never found myself or my tios on those pages. When I looked up from my reading I saw children in rags, slave wages, and the hardest work on earth. America was out there somewhere. I wondered if she would ever have a place for me."

Before high school, Véa sporadically attended school and met pessimistic teachers who told him that he would never make it to college. At Livermore High School, however, he befriended Jack Beery, a teacher who taught Véa a great deal about academics and life; Véa later dedicated his first book to Beery, who died in 1992. Overcoming his poor educational background, Véa made it to the University of California at Berkeley, but had to take a leave of absence in 1967 because he lacked the money to continue his education. He resumed farm labor, then was drafted into the army in 1967. He tried to avoid participation in the Vietnam War by claiming to be a conscientious objector, but his petition was denied because he did not have a religious basis for his objection to war. Véa had been interested in electronics, so he became a radio telephone operator and was sent to Vietnam just days before the North Vietnamese launched the Tet Offensive. "There I was in a bare quonset, surrounded by bachelor men who were working like slaves under horrid conditions for little or no pay," he wrote on his Web site. "It was just like being back in the Imperial Valley." Profoundly marked by his wartime experiences, Véa lost his belief in white authority figures.

After Véa completed his two-year tour, he held various jobs, including driving a truck and operating a forklift. Beginning in 1970, he lived for a year in France (he had studied French in high school) and earned a living by working as a janitor. He soon became fluent in the language and read and studied in his spare time. He returned to the University of California at Berkeley in 1971 and graduated in 1975 with a bachelor's degree in English and physics. During this time, he supported himself by working in construction jobs and repairing carnival rides. He then entered the university's law school and earned his law degree in 1978.

Shunning a lucrative career as a corporate lawyer, Véa used his legal expertise for the benefit of underserved Mexican- Americans and other immigrant workers. He joined the United Farm Workers, led by Cesar Chavez, and worked for the Centro Legal de La Raza (Legal Center of the People) until 1980. He then became a public defender in San Francisco and remained in that position until 1986, when he opened his own legal practice.

Working as a specialist in capital punishment cases, Véa encountered much racism. "I began to write *La Maravilla* in 1989, when I was defending a Mexican-American boy against the charge of murder," Véa recalled on his Web site. "The judge and the jury in this small San Joaquin Valley town were so incredibly racist and abusive toward my client and myself. . . . The boy was convicted, but his sentence has since been reversed, specifically because of the judge's abuse of power." During the trial, Véa decided to rent a trailer and begin writing a novel expressing his love for his culture and people. "I began to write about ancestry, about archetypes that were not European, about forms that persist," he was quoted as saying by Roberto Cantú for a profile in the *Dictionary of Literary Biography* (1999). "I began with the most remarkable image in my possession: the image of my grandmother, in a mourning dress, playing her upright piano in front of her cardboard music."

Véa's first novel, *La Maravilla* (The Marvel), was published three years later. Borrowing heavily from incidents from Véa's life, *La Maravilla* describes the childhood of Beto, who is abandoned by his mother and raised by his grandparents. The clash between the Catholic grandmother, Josephina, who practices magical healing arts, and the grandfather, Manuel, whose spirit can fly with the aid of peyote, supplies much of the book's tension. Other characters, from various ethnicities and with many eccentricities, provide Beto with unusual growing-up experiences, often described in magical-realistic terms. The enormous prostitute Vernetta, for instance, begins to lose weight when she discovers her long-lost son; as she shrinks, baubles lost among the folds of her flesh pop out, visible reminders of the useless trinkets given to her by numerous suitors.

"Essentially the story of Beto's struggle for his own identity amid the poverty and passion of Buckeye . . . *La Maravilla* tries for much more," Sam Harrison wrote in a review for the *Washington Post* (April 27, 1993). "Véa at times seems to be a bit too conscious of his sociological/anthropological/historical platform, and forgets to let his marvelous characters tell their story. . . . Véa writes a prose that is intricate, controlled and frequently quite beautiful, but it tends to lose power and sputter. . . . One of the elements he tries to work into the narrative is the Yaqui nonlinear concept of time, which is that all events and time exist simultaneously." Harrison concluded that the story of the "loving struggle between Josephina and Manuel" results in "a love story that transcends . . . time itself. . . . Sometimes brilliant, sometimes frustrating, always rich and extravagant, *La Maravilla* almost does it all." Robert Cantú wrote, "*La Maravilla* endorses diversity in cultural expressiveness, encourages reflection on man's cognitive limits . . . and exhorts the reader to accept the multiform—the apparently disconnected—as a substantial representation of the protean qualities of the world."

Véa used his experiences as a migrant laborer and as a defense attorney to write his second novel, *The Silver Cloud Café* (1996). The protagonist, Zeferino del Campo, becomes the defense attorney for an accused murderer, Teodoro Cabiri, a diminutive, hunchbacked immigrant farmworker from the Philippines. As Zeferino investigates the case, he is forced to confront an old memory of the violent death of a landowner. *The Silver Cloud Café* received a warm critical reception. In a review for *Publishers Weekly* (August 5, 1996), Sybil Steinberg wrote that the "kaleidoscopic narrative renders a colorful panorama of cultures depicted through a motley cast of characters. A gay Filipino, a Mexican stripper, a black former prizefighter, a mad Bulgarian cab driver, an assassin, transvestites, migrant workers and the San Francisco police collide with angels, saints, martyrs, even Cesar Chavez and the ghost of a Greek poet. . . . Though the narrative is disjointed at times and Véa occasionally succumbs to heavy moralizing against American jingoism and free-market worship, his instinct for storytelling keeps us immersed in this zesty, poetic celebration of America's immigrant cultures."

In Véa's most recent novel, *Gods Go Begging* (1999), two females—one African-American, the other Vietnamese—have been shot, and a young African-American called Biscuit Boy stands accused. Defense attorney Jesse Pasadoble, who is plagued by memories of the Vietnam War, takes up Biscuit Boy's defense and discovers that he knew the two women's husbands, who served on opposite sides of the war in Vietnam and were supposedly killed in action. Véa intended the novel to be an examination of war. "I wrote what I so longed to read about [the Vietnam War], but could never find on the bookshelves," he told Randall Holdridge for the *Tucson Weekly* (September 13, 1999, on-line). "I attempted to answer for myself why so many boys were willing to go; why so many were surprised by the horror of it; why so many have returned home to find that 'home' is no longer. For 28 years I have lived with nightmares and anxieties. In *Gods Go Begging* I set out to explore the nature of war and why I was curious enough to seek it out." The book is also about how to escape the condition of war. "*Gods Go Begging* is at its base a book about communication," Véa explained to Holdridge. "The battle in Vietnam is set on a hill that is a cryptographic relay station. The North Vietnamese attempt to break the codes. The two women who begin and end the story attempt to break the code of their husbands' infatuation with violence. The Biscuit Boy character is saved by teaching him language. The entire Army experience, replete with sexual metaphor and symbol, operates only to deprive young men of the ability to speak to their own souls and to the souls of others. In this book, it is communication that changes the world."

Michael Harris observed for the *Los Angeles Times* (September 30, 1999) that Véa's "rendering of the Vietnam War and its aftermath—from the viewpoint of black and Chicano grunts—is thoroughly original. The magic doesn't disturb the realism; it enhances it, like the refrain to a song." James Lough, the reviewer for the *Denver Post* (October 31, 1999), noted that "Véa displays . . . a broad inside knowledge of, and sympathy for, San Francisco's variety of ethnic subcultures: Latino, African-American, Vietnamese, Sephardic, even Creole." In a review for *Publishers Weekly* (July 26, 1999), Sybil Steinberg called *Gods Go Begging* "a gritty, dark, and tightly wrapped tale of mystery, desire, hopelessness and death." Steinberg added, "Jesse's anguish actually heightens his awareness and allows him to finally unravel a Gordian knot of bizarre relationships, which not only brings justice for the victims, but a measure of peace to his own soul as well. Véa composes his plot with great skill, leaving the reader strongly convinced of his story's credibility."

Some of the writers Véa has acknowledged as influences include Herman Melville, William Faulkner, Octavio Paz, the Yaqui poet Refugio Zavala, Fyodor Dostoyevsky, Dylan Thomas, Theodore Roethke, and Gabriel García Márquez. In an interview with David Uhler for the San Antonio *Express News* (November 2, 1999, on-line), Véa stated, "I think it's time for Chicano writers to read Nabokov and Joseph Conrad and Dostoyevsky and start comparing their writing with those people, rather than just being this small enclave where everything seems to be OK because it's politically correct." In his interview with Randall Holdridge, Véa stated, "I don't like the idea of being characterized as a Chicano author. I would rather be characterized as an author who is Chicano. . . . Evolved cultural thinking never asks if James Joyce represents all the Irish people. In many of the universities where my books are read and where I have spoken it is the Chicano students who often question the necessity of reading the works of other races. Slowly this insipid posture is changing. Until it changes completely there will never be a Chicano intelligentsia."

Véa's first marriage ended in divorce. His second wife is Carole Conn. For his fourth novel, he plans to deal with the Mexican-American War. "It's about a couple of Mexican guys in the 1800s who are writing an opera about the Alamo," Véa told David Uhler. "This story is really, really out there."

—S. Y.

SUGGESTED READING: *Denver Post* I p5 Oct. 31, 1999; *Kirkus Reviews* Jan. 1, 1993, Aug. 15, 1996; *Los Angeles Times* p6 Sep. 30, 1996, p4 Sep. 30, 1999; *Publishers Weekly* p32 Aug. 5, 1996, p63 July 26, 1999; *Washington Post* B p2 Apr. 27, 1993; *Dictionary of Literary Biography, Volume 209: Chicano Writers*, 1999

SELECTED BOOKS: *La Maravilla*, 1992; *The Silver Cloud Café*, 1996; *Gods Go Begging*, 1999

Vonnegut, Kurt

(VON-nuh-guht)

Nov. 11, 1922– Novelist; short-story writer; essayist

Throughout his long career as a writer, Kurt Vonnegut has been pessimistic about the future of the human race, using elements of science fiction, satire, and dark humor to warn his readers about the dangers of rampant technological progress, environmental pollution, and war. Sometimes misinterpreted as straight science fiction, Vonnegut's

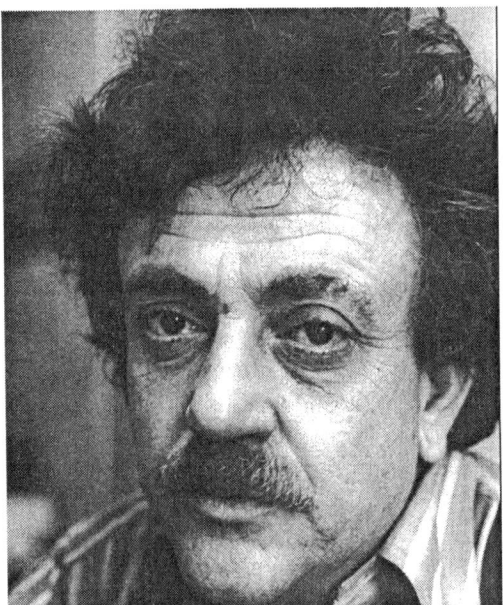

Kurt Vonnegut
Alan Weller/Retna/Camera Press

early novels were known only to a relatively small reading public until 1963, when *Cat's Cradle* earned him the admiration of his fellow writers and brought him wider popularity. *Slaughterhouse-Five* (1969), his classic antiwar novel about the 1945 Allied firebombing of Dresden, Germany, which he survived as a prisoner of war, made him a guru of the counterculture during the early 1970s. In 1997 Vonnegut published *Timequake*, which he announced would be his final novel; two years later he released *Bagombo Snuff Box*, a volume of previously uncollected short fiction from the 1950s. Vonnegut, also a prolific graphic artist, currently devotes much of his time to that pursuit.

Bridging the gap between popular fiction and serious literature, Vonnegut's novels employ simple, highly accessible language and a dazzling variety of innovative narrative techniques; they often supplant traditional linear structure with a cyclical style. Joseph Coates, in a review of the 1991 essay collection *Fates Worse Than Death* for the *Chicago Tribune* (September 1, 1991), neatly summed up the author's impact on American literature: "Vonnegut's work is whatever is the opposite of escapism—clear-eyed realism, perhaps, or the kind of total sanity often mistaken for madness. . . . I am convinced once again that America has had no writer so cheerfully, entertainingly, and less hectoringly sane—and hence truly subversive—since Mark Twain."

Kurt Vonnegut Jr. was born on November 11, 1922 in Indianapolis, Indiana, to Kurt Vonnegut Sr., a successful architect who built the family home on North Illinois Street, and Edith Sophia (Lieber) Vonnegut, the daughter of a prosperous brewer. Fourth-generation German-Americans, Kurt Vonnegut Jr, his older brother, Bernard (who became a physicist), and his older sister, Alice, were raised without any knowledge of the German language—despite their parents' fluency—because of the widespread anti-German sentiment in the United States that followed World War I. Referring to his parents, Vonnegut once remarked, "They volunteered to make me ignorant and rootless as proof of their patriotism."

In 1940, after graduating from Shortridge High School, in Indianapolis, Vonnegut entered Cornell University, in Ithaca, New York, to study biochemistry. Although he had wanted to become a journalist, he studied biology and chemistry at the behest of his father, who insisted that he learn something deemed practical. "Cornell was a boozy dream," Vonnegut has remembered, "partly because of booze itself, and partly because I was enrolled exclusively in courses I had no talent for." He became a columnist and editor of the *Cornell Daily Sun*, taking solace in the work to which he felt most suited.

About a year after the Japanese attacked Pearl Harbor, on December 7, 1941, Vonnegut enlisted in the armed services. "I was flunking everything by the middle of my junior year," he has said. "I was delighted to join the army and go to war." Trained as a mechanical engineer at the Carnegie Institute of Technology (now part of Carnegie Mellon University), in Pittsburgh, and then at the University of Tennessee, he was thoroughly acquainted with the 240-millimeter howitzer, then the largest mobile field weapon in use. With typical sarcasm, he has referred to it as the ultimate terror weapon—"of the Franco-Prussian War."

On Mother's Day 1944 Vonnegut obtained special leave from his duties as an infantry battalion scout. He arrived home to learn that on the previous night his mother had committed suicide by overdosing on sleeping pills. She had become increasingly prone to depression after she realized that writing fiction for magazines—a venture she had taken on after the loss of the family fortune during the Great Depression—would never be as lucrative as she had hoped. "She was a good writer, it turned out," Vonnegut explained in a self-edited compilation of four interviews for the *Paris Review* in 1977 (published in *Writers at Work* in 1984), "but she had no talent for the vulgarity the slick magazines required. Fortunately, I was loaded with vulgarity, so, when I grew up, I was able to make her dream come true. Writing for *Collier's* and the *Saturday Evening Post* and *Cosmopolitan* and *Ladies' Home Journal* and so on was as easy as falling off a log for me. I only wish she'd lived to see it."

Vonnegut was sent overseas three months after his mother's funeral. In December 1944 he was captured by German troops in the Ardennes during the Battle of the Bulge, in which there were some 77,000 Allied casualties. He spent the rest of the war as a prisoner quartered in a slaughterhouse in the city of Dresden, working in a factory that produced vitamin-enriched malt syrup for pregnant women. On the night of February 13, 1945, three consecutive British and American bombing raids annihilated Dresden in a firestorm that killed about 135,000 people in two hours.

In a firestorm, temperatures reach between 1,000 and 2,000 degrees Fahrenheit, which causes spontaneous combustion of all organic material. Those residents of Dresden who escaped that fate were probably asphyxiated in their basement shelters, because firestorms tend to consume all available oxygen in strong updrafts that approximate tornadoes. Vonnegut and the other prisoners with whom he was confined survived the firestorm only because they were kept in a huge, cold meat locker three stories beneath the slaughterhouse, which itself was located in wide-open stockyards. When they ventured out, nothing remained of the city or its population.

Vonnegut described the nightmarish aftermath of the bombing of Dresden, which had harbored no military industries or installations, in his *Paris Review* interviews: "Every day we walked into the city and dug into basements and shelters to get the corpses out, as a sanitary measure. . . . One hundred thirty thousand corpses were hidden underground. It was a terribly elaborate Easter-egg hunt. . . . We would bust into the shelter, gather up valuables from people's laps without attempting identification, and turn the valuables over to guards. Then soldiers would come in with a flame thrower and stand in the door and cremate the people inside." He continued, "It was a fancy thing to see, a startling thing. It was a moment of truth, too, because American civilians and ground troops didn't know American bombers were engaged in saturation bombing. It was kept a secret until very close to the end of the war." Although Vonnegut has dealt with Dresden in several of his novels, most notably in *Slaughterhouse-Five*, he was quoted in the *Dictionary of Literary Biography* (1983) as saying, "The importance of Dresden in my life has been considerably exaggerated . . . and I don't think people's lives are changed by short-term events like that. Dresden was astonishing, but experiences can be astonishing without changing you."

Liberated and repatriated in April 1945 after the occupation of Dresden by Soviet troops, Vonnegut went to work as a police reporter for the Chicago News Bureau while studying anthropology at the University of Chicago from 1945 to 1947. Although his master's thesis was unanimously rejected, he was granted an M.A. degree by the university in 1971 (when his reputation was approaching its zenith) on the basis of the anthropological elements of his fourth novel, *Cat's Cradle*. "[Studying anthropology] confirmed my atheism," Vonnegut once said, "which was the faith of my fathers anyway. Religions were exhibited and studied as the Rube Goldberg inventions I'd always thought they were."

From 1947 to 1950 Vonnegut worked as a publicist for the research laboratories of General Electric in Schenectady, New York, supplementing his income by publishing short stories, the first of which appeared in the February 11, 1950 issue of *Collier's*. Since he was soon earning more money through his fiction than he was making at General Electric, he quit his public-relations job in order to write fulltime. (He had also come to see public-relations work as hypocritical.) Moving to Cape Cod (first to Provincetown and later to West Barnstable), he had published more than 50 short stories by 1966.

Vonnegut's first novel, a pessimistic account of a totalitarian future in which technology reigns supreme, was published as *Player Piano* by Scribners in 1952 and as *Utopia 14* by Bantam Books in 1954. Although Vonnegut acknowledged that he had been influenced by Aldous Huxley's 1932 classic *Brave New World*, he drew directly on his experiences at General Electric for his story of clashing value systems: ruthless technocracy pitted against the individual's potential for taking independent action. Although *Player Piano* attracted scant critical attention, it sounded the ironical and compassionate tone that is apparent in much of his later work. Vonnegut spent the rest of the decade writing short stories in addition to holding down a succession of other jobs. He taught English at Hopefield High School on Cape Cod, worked at an advertising agency, and opened the first Saab auto dealership in the United States.

Since, by the late 1950s, the market for short stories had begun to shrink, Vonnegut concentrated on writing his second novel, *The Sirens of Titan* (1959), in which he weighed the possibility that humanity's destiny was already irretrievably beyond our control. A parody of science fiction, a description of the mythic journey of a modern-day hero, and a tongue-in-cheek exploration of a meaningless universe, *The Sirens of Titan* proved its author to be "a first-rate novelist," according to Robert Group, who wrote for the *Dictionary of Literary Biography* (1981), "He gives a perspective both sobering and entertaining, makes the reader wince and worry, and extracts a complex reaction."

In his next novel, *Mother Night* (1962), Vonnegut dealt with the ambiguities of guilt and complicity during World War II. Narrated in the first person, the novel recounts the experiences of an American dramatist living in Germany who broadcasts anti-Semitic propaganda for the Nazis that happens to contain coded messages for the Allies. After the war the former double agent changes his identity and settles in the United States, but he is eventually caught by the Israelis and tried as a war criminal.

Reviewing the reissued novel for the *New Republic* (April 26, 1969), Michael Crichton wrote, "*Mother Night* . . . begins by giving it to the Nazis . . . [but] finally manages to reduce any social or political affiliation to complete absurdity. . . . It is an astonishing book, very gentle and funny and quiet and totally destructive. Nobody escapes without being shown, in a polite way, what an ass he is. . . . The left-wing political activists, who generally count Vonnegut among their number, all have somehow never found time to read this particular book."

Cat's Cradle (1963), Vonnegut's fourth novel, which brought him to wide public attention, is still regarded as one of his best works. Taking its title from the children's string game originally played by Eskimos in a fruitless attempt to snare the sun, the novel illuminates the futility of certain human inventions, whether scientific or religious. The protagonist, who is researching a book about people's activities on the day of the atomic explosion in Hiroshima, travels to a Caribbean island, where he converts to Bokononism—a religion of "harmless untruths"—and, eventually, witnesses the destruction of the earth by Ice-9, a deadly substance, invented by Vonnegut's fictional protagonist, that freezes everything with which it comes into contact. *Cat's Cradle* was acclaimed by Nelson Algren, Conrad Aiken, Marc Connelly, Jules Feiffer, Graham Greene, and Terry Southern, among other notable fellow writers.

In *God Bless You, Mr. Rosewater: or Pearls before Swine* (1965), Vonnegut introduces his alter ego, the aging science-fiction writer Kilgore Trout, who also appears in the later novels in which the author satirizes his own profession. Although he has often disavowed the label of science fiction as a description of his own work, Vonnegut has his title character, the philanthropic millionaire Eliot Rosewater, interrupt a meeting of science-fiction writers with a torrent of affectionate praise: "I love you sons of bitches. You're all I read anymore. . . . You're the only ones with guts enough to *really* care about the future, who *really* notice what machines do to us, what wars do to us, what cities do to us, what big, simple ideas do to us, what tremendous misunderstandings, mistakes, accidents, and catastrophes do to us." The first of Vonnegut's books to be widely reviewed, *God Bless You, Mr. Rosewater* was, in the opinion of John R. May, writing in *Twentieth-Century Literature* (January 1972), "Kurt Vonnegut's finest novel to date. . . . We may not be able, Vonnegut is saying, to undo the harm that has been done, but we certainly love, simply because they are people, those who have been made useless by our past stupidity and greed, our previous crimes against our brothers." Rosewater's motto, accordingly, is "Goddamn it, you've got to be kind."

After completing a two-year residency at the University of Iowa Writers' Workshop, Vonnegut spent most of 1967 in Dresden on a Guggenheim fellowship, gathering material for his sixth and ultimately most influential novel, *Slaughterhouse-Five* (1969). Its protagonist, Billy Pilgrim, undergoes an ordeal in Dresden that parallels Vonnegut's experience there during World War II. He copes with his trauma by traveling to the planet Tralfamadore, whose inhabitants see all time—past, present, and future—as existing simultaneously. "I felt," Vonnegut told David Standish for a *Playboy* (July 1973) interview, "after I finished *Slaughterhouse-Five* that I didn't have to write at all anymore if I didn't want to. It was the end of some sort of career. . . . I suppose that flowers, when they're through blooming, have some sort of awareness of some purpose having been served."

Because it was published at the height of the Vietnam War, *Slaughterhouse-Five* created much controversy, and, though it quickly became required reading on some college campuses, it was contraband on others. (The book was excluded from several school and public libraries on the grounds of obscenity.) Suddenly much in demand as a campus speaker, Vonnegut was invited in 1970 to teach creative writing at Harvard University, in Cambridge, Massachusetts, and was awarded a National Institute of Arts and Letters grant that year. The release of *Slaughterhouse-Five* in 1972 as a feature film directed by George Roy Hill catapulted Vonnegut to a level of fame rivaled by few contemporary American authors. "I drool and cackle every time I watch that film," he wrote in 1972, "because it is so harmonious with what I felt when I wrote the book."

To pull himself out of the depression he suffered after the publication of *Slaughterhouse-Five*, Vonnegut wrote *Breakfast of Champions: or Goodbye Blue Monday!* (1973). Extravagantly illustrated with Vonnegut's doodles or felt-tip calligraphs, the book represents his attempt to come to terms with his despair over what he considered to be an ever-widening cultural vacuum in the United States. Despite its tremendous commercial success—the book sold more than a quarter of a million hardcover copies in less than a year—*Breakfast of Champions* met with unenthusiastic reviews, for the most part. The same apathy greeted his next novel, *Slapstick, or Lonesome No More* (1976), which was written as a tribute to his sister, Alice, who called her impending death of cancer at the age of 41 "slapstick."

Commenting on *Slapstick*'s critical reception in his *Paris Review* interview compilation, Vonnegut acknowledged that "*Slapstick* may be a very bad book. I am perfectly willing to believe that. Everybody else writes lousy books, so why shouldn't I? What was unusual about the reviews was that they wanted people to admit now that I had never been any good. . . . The hidden complaint was that I was barbarous, that I wrote without having made a systematic study of great literature, that I was no gentleman, since I had done hack writing so cheerfully for vulgar magazines—that I had not paid my academic dues."

Jailbird (1979), Vonnegut's longest and perhaps most ambitious book, is also his most overtly political—a bitter indictment of the American political system, which he characterizes as a xenophobic plutocracy rife with injustice, corruption, and greed. The novel juxtaposes the Sermon on the Mount and its plea for compassion and mercifulness with a recounting of Watergate, McCarthyism, the trials of Sacco and Vanzetti, and the history of the American labor movement. According to David A. Myers, writing for the *International Fiction Review* (Summer 1980), *Jailbird* "begins uncannily to resemble the parable in Bertolt Brecht's *The Good Woman of Setzuan*. In both works the capitalist economy is held by the author to make the practice of Christian altruism impossible, and in both works the Gods are revealed to be impotent anachronisms, leaving the only solution to be found in this world in the evolution of a new community founded on socialist ideals. But whereas Brecht's plays are resolutely optimistic, Vonnegut's novels waver irresolutely between the black humor of despair and a wistful hope beyond hopelessness."

By the time Vonnegut's next novel, *Deadeye Dick* (1982), was published, reviewers like Bruce Allen, appraising it for the *Christian Science Monitor* (December 3, 1982), seemed to be growing impatient with his "overload of sentimentalism" coupled with a plea for the underdog that pervades much of his work. "Vonnegut has taken us down this road too many times already," Allen observed, adding, however, "Fortunately the novel's preachy sentimentalism seldom interferes with its bizarre logic." But in the opinion of Cline Doucet, writing for the Toronto *Globe and Mail* (October 23, 1982), "the humor that relieved Vonnegut's pessimistic view of the human race has thinned into evanescence."

In *Galápagos* (1985), a Darwinian comic tale that takes place over the course of a million years and features Leon Trotsky Trout, Kilgore's son, as its narrator, Vonnegut tried "to show how random natural selection really is," he has said, "not [being] dependent on talent or fitness to survive." According to Thomas M. Disch, writing for the London *Times Literary Supplement* (November 8, 1985), the author's "targets are not the foibles of social behavior but . . . targets as broad as the pax Americana: war, genocide, economic imperialism. . . . The difficulty of aiming at such broad targets is not in scoring bulls-eyes but in avoiding preaching-to-the-converted complacency . . . and this Vonnegut achieves by irony."

Reviews of *Bluebeard* (1987), which deals with the life of an Armenian-American veteran of World War II who becomes a minor member of the abstract expressionist movement, were lukewarm. "Although not among his best novels," A. J. Wright conceded in the *Library Journal* (January 1988), "*Bluebeard* is a good one and features liberal doses of his off-balance humor." Writing for the *New Statesman* (April 29, 1988), Richard Deveson praised the author's inventiveness but added,"It's almost as if that inventiveness is the problem he's really writing about. His own brilliant draughtsmanship allows him to be fantastical at the drop of his funny hat and yet this book . . . ultimately lacks soul."

In *Hocus Pocus* (1990), Vonnegut casts a Vietnam veteran named Eugene Debs Hartke (after the well-known labor organizer) as yet another of his witnesses to the decay of the United States. In the book, which opens in 2001, racism has become so thoroughly entrenched that prisons are segregated, ignorance and illiteracy are rampant, cities are abandoned because of radioactive waste in their drinking water, and crime has become more prevalent than ever. "*Hocus Pocus*," John Leonard wrote for*The Nation* (October 15, 1990), "seems to me to be Vonnegut's best novel in years—funny and prophetic, yes, and fabulous, too, as cunning as Aesop and as gloomy as Grimm; but also rich and referential; a meditation on American history and American literature; an elegy; a keening."

Timequake, published in 1999, is purported to be Vonnegut's "final" novel. Kilgore Trout, Vonnegut's alter ego (who supposedly died in an earlier novel), appears as well. In the year 2001 time lurches back to 1991. The world's population is now forced to relive the last decade all over again—with no chance of altering those events. As a result, everyone loses their sense of free will, leading to major problems when the rerun decade ends, because people have forgotten how to think and act for themselves. The book received mixed reviews. M. John Harrison remarked for the *Times Literary Supplement* (September 26, 1997): "Some of this book is funny, some of it is touching, and a very little of it both. For the most part, it is as irritating as it is clever; and in the end, despite [Vonnegut's] efforts, it appeals, like even his best work, less to the human being in us than the adolescent."

In addition to his novels, Vonnegut has published three collections of short stories: *Canary in a Cathouse* (1961), *Welcome to the Monkey House* (1968), and *Bagombo Snuff Box* (1999). He wrote the text for *Sun Moon Star* (1980), a children's Christmas story illustrated by Ivan Chermayeff, and he has published five collections of essays: *Wampeters, Foma, and Granfalloons: Opinions* (1974); *Palm Sunday* (1981); *Nothing Is Lost Save Honor* (1984); *Fates Worse Than Death: An Autobiographical Collage of the 1980s* (1991); and *God Bless You, Dr. Kervorkian* (1999). His work has often been adapted for stage, screen, and television.

From 1945 until 1979 Vonnegut was married to Jane Marie Cox, whom he met in kindergarten. They have three children: Mark, Edith, and Nanette, born in 1947, 1949, and 1954, respectively. In 1958 he adopted his sister Alice's three children after her death, which came just a day after her husband, John Adams, was killed in a train crash. In June 1991 it was reported that Vonnegut was divorcing his second wife, the photographer Jill Krementz, whom he married on November 24, 1979, but the petition was later withdrawn. They have one child together, Lily.

In 1984 Vonnegut tried to commit suicide by overdosing on pills and alcohol, an event he recorded in *Fates Worse Than Death*: "I went briefly [crazy] in the 1980s in an effort to get out of life entirely, and wound up playing Eightball in a locked ward for thirty days instead." He discussed his suicidal feelings publicly during an interview with David Streitfeld for the *Washington Post* (August 29, 1991), saying that he was simply "pissed off. . . . If I do myself in sometime, and I might, it will be because of my mother's example. If I get really pissed off, screw it all. . . . [Suicide is] on my mind all the time. But I tried as hard as I could to kill myself, without any luck. So my feeling is, the hell with it." In January 2000 Vonnegut was hospitalized for smoke inhalation when fire broke out in his home; he has completely recovered and has recently taught advanced writing at Smith College, in Northampton, Massachusetts. In November 2000 he was named the state author of New York, a position he will hold until 2003.

—C. M.

SUGGESTED READING:*Booklist* p1849 Aug. 1997; *Christian Science Monitor* p13 Oct. 30, 1995; *Entertainment Weekly* p72 Sep. 26, 1997, p16 Feb. 11, 2000; *London Review of Books* p26 Dec. 11, 1997; *Publishers Weekly* p20+ Apr. 21 1969; *Times Literary Supplement* p22 Sep. 26, 1997; Allen, William Rodney, ed. *Conversations with Kurt Vonnegut*, 1988; Bellamy, Joe David, and John Casey. *The New Fiction: Interviews with Innovative American Writers*, 1974; Platt, Charles. *Dream Makers: Science Fiction and Fantasy Writers at Work*, 1987; Plimpton, George, ed. *Writers at Work: The Paris Review Interviews, Sixth Series*, 1984; Shenker, Israel. *Words and Their Masters*, 1974

SELECTED BOOKS: fiction—*Player Piano*, 1952; *The Sirens of Titan*, 1959; *Mother Night*, 1961; *Canary in a Cathouse*, 1961; *Cat's Cradle*, 1963; *God Bless You, Mr. Rosewater*, 1965; *Welcome to the Monkey House*, 1968; *Slaughterhouse-Five*, 1969; *Breakfast of Champions*, 1973; *Slapstick*, 1976; *Jailbird*, 1979; *Deadeye Dick*, 1982; *Galápagos*, 1985; *Bluebeard*, 1987; *Hocus Pocus*, 1990; *Timequake*, 1997; *Bagombo Snuff Box*, 1999; nonfiction—*Wampeters, Foma, and Granfalloons: Opinions*, 1974; *Palm Sunday*, 1981, *Nothing is Lost Save Honor*, 1984; *Fates Worse Than Death*, 1991, *God Bless You, Dr. Kervorkian*, 1999

Walker, Alice

Feb. 9, 1944– Novelist; poet; essayist; social activist

Alice Walker is not only an essayist, poet, and award-winning novelist and short-story writer, but also an ardent social activist. Walker's ability to create mythical tales and to evoke life in the rural South, along with her passionate intensity for social concerns—as demonstrated in such books as *Revolutionary Petunias*, a collection of poems, and her Pulitzer Prize–winning novel *The Color Purple*—have prompted many critics to rank her among the best of contemporary American writers. Walker's writings often address the dual horrors of racism and sexism that black women frequently face. Chris Wyatt observed for *Women's Studies* (December 2000), "Alice Walker's work continues to be some of the most widely read and most often taught texts authored by African-American women."

In an autobiographical statement previously published in *World Authors, 1975–1980*, Alice Walker writes: "At the time I was born my family already consisted of nine people: my five brothers and two sisters, and my mother and father. The house in which I was born was small, of unpainted wood, and stood beside a dirt road that wandered through the backwoods of Putnam County, Georgia. It is still a beautiful setting, though the house has long since disappeared; there are pecan and walnut trees lining the main road, and around where our house stood, oaks. My mother was at that house and at all the others we lived in a con-

Jakub Mosur/Corbis SYGMA

summate gardener, and if flowers turn up in almost everything I write, it is because I have a hard time imagining worlds in which they don't exist in profusion.

"I have at least two first memories: in one, my grandmother Nettie (after whom I named a childless African missionary in my book, *The Color Purple*) who was the mother of my mother and her eleven sisters and brothers, is standing over a wood stove cooking an enormous dinner (I realize it must have been enormous in retrospect; her family was huge) with a harassed, if stoic, look on her face. She is very dark brown, heavy (her spirit as heavy as her large body) and I can't imagine her laughing, or even smiling. In the second memory, my father is approaching the front porch of our house, on which I am standing, waiting in delight and anticipation for him to begin dancing for me, which I know he often does, laughing with his face and his eyes. I know when he finishes dancing he will pick me up for a kiss and a hug. My grandmother died when I was two; my father stopped picking me up, I'm sure, around the same time.

"I cherish these memories, and they stick with me. Perhaps it is from the harassed, trapped look on my grandmother's face that I received an interest in the oppression of women; perhaps it is from my father's playfulness and delight in me that I received faith in the possibility of companionableness with men. For certainly in everything I've written there is concern for women's freedom and the need to envision man as something other than master or marriage partner. My sister tells me I used to address Space when I was very small and continued to do so well into my teens. I would stand, with a very attentive expression—always out of doors—and listen to 'something' only I could hear. I would then reply in words only 'something' understood. I'm convinced that this is the beginning of myself as writer.

"I wrote my first book of poems while a student at Sarah Lawrence, which I attended on scholarship, as I had attended Spelman College before it, and also my first published short story (under the double lucky auspices of Muriel Rukeyser, my poetry teacher, and Langston Hughes). Since then I have written many poems and stories and novels, and no longer write—as I used to say—to survive, but because when I am writing I am so deeply happy. I imagine I feel as many pregnant women say they feel (and as I never felt while pregnant myself) totally attentive to an inner reality, an inner compulsion, an inner conversation, to which I know I will respond in a way that will reveal me even more to myself, while at the same time connecting me to other people.

"As I look at what I have written, it seems plain to me that writing, for me, has simply been about filling the space I always felt around me, peopling it with—instead of spirits—real listeners who understand because I have told them, through my work, how it is. Realizing this makes me long to reassure the little girl who addressed Space. Look, I want to tell her, the people you listened to and spoke to long ago have come. And it was your faith that they were there, in space, that brought them! And I see that that is perhaps what writing is. Sending out a voice—sometimes feeble, sometimes confused, sometimes strong and confident—but always just a human voice that has listened to the world and seeks to answer it, to say to it, You see, because we both listen and respond to each other, neither of us is alone."

Alice Malsenior Walker was born on February 9, 1944 in Eatonton, Georgia, the youngest of the eight children of Willie Lee and Millie Tallulah (Grant) Walker. Her father, who was, in her words, "wonderful at math [but] a terrible farmer," earned only $300 a year from sharecropping and dairy farming, while her mother, who helped him in the fields, supplemented the family income by working as a maid. Her parents were also storytellers, and at the age of eight Alice began to record those stories and some poems of her own in a notebook.

In 1952 Walker was accidentally wounded in the eye by a shot from a BB gun fired by one of her brothers. Because they had no access to a car, the Walkers were unable to take their daughter to a hospital for immediate treatment, and when they finally brought her to a doctor a week later, she was permanently blind in that eye. A disfiguring layer of scar tissue formed over it, rendering the previously outgoing child self-conscious and painfully shy. Stared at and sometimes taunted, she felt like an outcast and turned for solace to reading and to poetry writing. Although when she was 14 the scar tissue was removed—and she subsequently became valedictorian and was voted most-popular girl, as well as queen of her senior class—she came to realize that her traumatic injury had some value: it allowed her to begin "really to see people and things, really to notice relationships and to learn to be patient enough to care about how they turned out," as she has said. Because of the accident, she became eligible for and won a scholarship for handicapped students to attend Spelman College, a black women's college in Atlanta, beginning in 1961. Her neighbors raised the $75 for her bus fare to the state capital.

Already powerfully moved by what she had learned of the civil rights movement on television, at Spelman Walker came under the influence of the radical historians Staughton Lynd and Howard Zinn and soon became involved in civil rights demonstrations in downtown Atlanta. Zinn's dismissal during her sophomore year and Spelman's restrictive rules in general led her to accept a scholarship offer from Sarah Lawrence, the exclusive, but progressive, women's college in Bronxville, New York.

In the summer of 1964, Walker traveled around Africa in search of a "spiritual home," as Gloria Steinem phrased it in an interview with her for *Ms.* (June, 1982). When she returned to Sarah Lawrence in the fall, she was pregnant and for a time she contemplated suicide. Then she decided to have an abortion. Almost all of the poems in *Once*, her first volume of poetry, were written in the week immediately after the abortion. Barely pausing to eat or sleep, she wrote poems about Africa, suicide, love, and civil rights activism and slipped batches of them as they were completed under the door of her teacher, Muriel Rukeyser, the well-known poet. Impressed by her poems, Rukeyser showed them to her agent, who in turn gave them to Hiram

Haydn, an editor at Harcourt Brace Jovanovich. Although Haydn quickly accepted the poems, *Once* was not published by the company until 1968. Writing for *Poetry* (February 1971), Lisel Mueller, an acclaimed poet herself, lavished praise on *Once*, complimenting the "sensitive, spirited, and intelligent" young author on her spare but insightful poetry. "Feeling is channeled into a style that is direct and sharp, honest speech pared down to essentials. Her poems are like pencil sketches which are all graven outline: no shaded areas, no embellishments. Wit and tenderness combine into humanity."

After receiving her B.A. degree from Sarah Lawrence, in 1965, Walker canvassed voters in Liberty County, Georgia; later worked in New York City's Welfare Department (a job she detested); and wrote at night. When she won her first writing fellowship, in 1966, she initially planned to use it to move to Senegal, West Africa. Instead she spent the summer in Mississippi to be in the thick of the civil rights movement, helping people who had been taken off the welfare rolls or thrown off their farms for registering to vote. While there she met Melvyn Rosenman Leventhal, a young Jewish civil rights lawyer. She and Leventhal lived together contentedly for a year in New York City and were married on March 17, 1967. As Walker explained to Gloria Steinem during the *Ms.* interview, "We could challenge the laws against intermarriage at the same time. . . . Love, politics, work—it was a mighty coming together."

While they were living in New York City in a studio apartment overlooking Washington Square Park, Walker's first published essay, "The Civil Rights Movement: What Good Was It?," an impassioned declaration of her commitment to the cause, appeared in the *American Scholar* (August 1967) and won the $300 first prize in its annual essay contest. "To Hell With Dying," her best-known and first-published short story celebrating the love and loyalty of a young girl for a dying old man, also appeared that year. (In 1988 Walker adapted the story into an illustrated children's book of the same name.)

In September 1967 Leventhal and Walker moved to Mississippi, becoming the first legally married interracial couple in Jackson. There Leventhal sued racist real-estate dealers and fought to desegregate the state's schools, while Walker served briefly as a black-history consultant to Friends of the Children of Mississippi (a Head Start program) and as a writer-in-residence at Jackson State College (1968–69) and at Tougaloo (Mississippi) College (1970–71).

During their seven-year residence in Jackson, Walker's literary career advanced considerably. Her first novel, *The Third Life of Grange Copeland*, which she wrote during a 1967 fellowship at the MacDowell Colony in New Hampshire, was published in 1970. Beginning in the 1920s, the novel tells the story of Grange Copeland, a black tenant farmer in the South who deserts his wife and his son, Brownfield, for the promise of the North—a life that, in time, he finds even more degrading. Years later he returns to the South a mellower and wiser man, only to discover Brownfield repeating his own mistakes by viciously abusing his wife and his daughter, Ruth. When Brownfield goes to prison for murdering his wife, Grange takes custody of Ruth. Through his granddaughter, he is given a chance to rectify the errors he made in raising his own child, and their mutual love gives him his "third life." But when the angry and violent Brownfield tries to reclaim Ruth after his release from prison, the conflict between father and son results in the death of both men. "I was curious to know," Walker has said in a 1970 interview, discussing her intent for the novel, "why people in families, specifically black families, are often cruel to each other, and how much of this cruelty is caused by outside forces. . . . In the black family, love, cohesion, support, and concern are crucial since a racist society constantly acts to destroy the black individual, the black family unit, the black child. In America black people have only themselves and each other."

The critical response to *The Third Life of Grange Copeland* was mixed. Many reviewers applauded Walker's skill in developing characters, but found fault with her analysis of them. In an appraisal for the *Saturday Review* (August 22, 1970), Josephine Hendin observed that Walker "never probes the impact of poverty on Brownfield's inner life, or the psychic starvation that makes him so unable to love. . . . [She] disappoints by explaining Grange's conversion in political clichés [and her] solution ignores the depth and force of the loveless agony she describes."

To be close to her lecturing commitments in literature at both Wellesley College and the Boston campus of the University of Massachusetts, in 1972 Alice Walker moved to Massachusetts, where she spent a year and a half. Her enforced separation from her husband, who had to remain in Jackson to continue his work, and the death of her father, made 1973 a traumatic year for the author. That year also saw, however, the publication of three more of her books. *Revolutionary Petunias and Other Poems*, like *Once*, earned high marks from the critics. Writing in *Parnassus: Poetry in Review* (Spring–Summer 1976), Darwin Turner had high praise for its use of "plain, unaffected diction" and its revelations of "human behavior and emotion." A reviewer for *Choice* (September 1973) noted that Walker's "poetry is strongly narrative and compelling. One reads in order to follow the narrative thread, and the thread never gets gnarled or monotonous." *Revolutionary Petunias* was nominated for a National Book Award and won the Lillian Smith Award of the Southern Regional Council.

Walker's *In Love and Trouble: Stories of Black Women* (1973), her first collection of short fiction, also captured a prestigious prize: the Richard and Hinda Rosenthal Award from the American Institute of Arts and Letters. Most of the 13 stories, each of which has a black woman as its protagonist, had already been published, but assembling them in a single volume underlined the intensity of Walker's concern for the lives of black women, especially those who are poor, uneducated, and Southern. The author's skill at "getting inside the minds of the confused, the ignorant, [and] the inward-turning character" was singled out for special praise by J. H. Bryant in his review for *The Nation* (November 12, 1973). Writing in the *New York Times Book Review* (March 17, 1974), Mel Watkins was equally enthusiastic: "These stories are perceptive miniatures, snapshots, that capture their subjects at crucial and revealing moments. In this collection, Miss Walker is moving without being maudlin, ironic without being [gimmicky]." Written for children, *Langston Hughes: American Poet*, her biography of the "poet laureate of the Negro race," as he has been called, was also published in 1973.

In 1974 Melvyn Leventhal and Alice Walker moved back to New York City. There she accepted a position as a contributing editor for *Ms.*; completed work on her second novel, *Meridian* (1976); and published her third book of poems, *Goodnight, Willie Lee, I'll See You in the Morning* (1979). Walker has described these poems as a "by-product of the struggle to be, finally, an adult—grown up, *responsible* in the world—to put large areas of the past to rest." The book is divided into sections: "Confession" contains poems of love, and of the near-impossibility of finding a love that is mutually satisfying, enriching, and respectful; "On Stripping Bark from Myself" has poems of personal struggle and of black feminist history; in "Early Losses: A Requiem" there are poems of political involvement and African stories; "Facing the Way" consists of reflections on a revolutionary decade and its aftermath; and "Forgiveness" has four short poems reflecting that theme. In 1979 Walker also managed to find time to edit an anthology of the work of Zora Neale Hurston, the Harlem Renaissance writer and folklorist, entitled *I Love Myself When I'm Laughing . . . and Then Again When I Am Looking Mean and Impressive*.

Meridian, often praised as one of the finest novels to come out of the civil rights movement, is concerned with the explosive tensions and permanent impact of that movement on the lives of three young people—a black woman, Meridian Hill, whose refusal to say she will kill, as well as die, for the Revolution causes her to be thrown out of a radical political cell in New York; Truman Held, a black male activist and sometime lover of Meridian's who becomes an artist as the movement fades; and their friend Lynne Rabinowitz, a Jewish civil rights worker whom Held eventually marries. Recommending *Meridian* in *Newsweek* (May 31, 1976), Margo Jefferson wrote that Walker is "both ruthless and tender. Her eye for hypocrisy is painfully sharp, . . . [and] her eye for eccentricities and subtleties of character is equally astute." In *Commonweal* (April 29, 1977) Gordon Burnside criticized Walker's characterization of Meridian Hill because in her total selflessness and dedication to the cause of civil rights she becomes a "disappearing central character." Although Burnside considered *Meridian* "a failure as a novel," he valued it as "an extremely interesting historical document" that transports its readers to "the Movement's very heart."

Walker's second collection of short fiction, *You Can't Keep a Good Woman Down* (1981), deals with characters from a wider social spectrum than those that had figured in *In Love and Trouble*. In her evaluation for the *New York Times Book Review* (May 21, 1981), Katha Pollitt made a charge often leveled against Walker's work: she found the stories to be "too partisan." "The black woman," she observed, "is *always* the most sympathetic character." But Walker makes no attempt to hide her "womanist" (a term she coined for "black feminist or feminist of color") bias. As she explained to Barbara A. Bannon in an interview for *Publishers Weekly* (August 31, 1970): "The black woman is one of America's greatest heroes. . . . She has been oppressed beyond recognition. Her men have actually encouraged this oppression and insisted on it."

In *The Color Purple*, her third novel and perhaps most critically acclaimed to date, Walker again focused on the cruel domination of black men over black women, this time using an epistolary technique. *The Color Purple* spans about 30 years in the life of Celie, a Southern black woman. When she was a teenager her stepfather beat and raped her repeatedly, gave away the two children she bore him, and forced her into a loveless marriage with a widower who also beat her. Through her relationship with other women—mainly with Shug Avery, a dazzlingly vital blues singer who moves in with Celie and her husband as his mistress but also becomes Celie's lover—she transcends her degrading circumstances and is transformed and redeemed. The letters throughout *The Color Purple*—which are first addressed to God, whom Celie feels is the only one she can turn to, and later to her long-lost and dearest sister Nettie, who has become a missionary in Africa—are couched in a language that Walker calls "black folk English," which resembles dialect (a term she rejects as condescending) but is far easier to read and more musical.

Reviewers praised *The Color Purple*, and Peter S. Prescott pronounced it in *Newsweek* (June 21, 1982) to be "an American novel of permanent importance." Even those critics troubled by its feminist slant or weaknesses in plot and structure congratulated Walker on her eloquent use of black folk English. Robert Towers, writing for the *New York Review of Books* (August 12, 1982), admired "the conversion, in Celie's letters, of a subliterate dialect into a medium of remarkable expressiveness, color, and poignancy. . . . N[o] other novelist . . . has so successfully tapped the poetic resources of the idiom." *The Color Purple* was nominated for the National Book Critics Circle award, won both an American Book Award and the Pulitzer Prize for fiction, and remained on the *New York Times* list of best-sellers for more than 25 weeks. Warner Brothers bought the movie rights for $350,000. The film, directed by Steven Spielberg and starring Whoopi Goldberg, Danny Glover and Oprah Winfrey, became one of the highest-grossing films of 1985 and was nominated for 11 Academy Awards. In Walker's 1996 book, *The Same River Twice; Honoring the Difficult: A Meditation of Life, Spirit, Art, and the Making of the Film "The Color Purple," Ten Years Later*, she recounts the experience of making the film at a time when her mother was dying, she was ending a long-term relationship, and was herself ill with Lyme disease.

In 1983, Walker published *In Search of Our Mothers' Gardens: Womanist Prose*, a collection of her essays written between 1966 and 1982. Some of the pieces deal with politics or literature, but almost all contain biographical material, including an account of her depression and abortion during her senior year in college. Although she considered deleting some material, she decided against it. "It's my life, and I really respect it. If there are flaws, that's the way it was," she has said. The collection earned Walker a 1984 Best Books for Young Adults citation from the American Library Association. That year she also published her fourth collection of poetry, *Horses Make a Landscape More Beautiful*. In 1991, Walker published *Her Blue Body Everything We Know: Earthling Poems, 1965–1990 Complete*, a collection of all her poetry to date, including 16 new poems.

Walker amassed more of her nonfiction writings in *Living by the Word: Selected Writings, 1973–1987* (1988), including several essays, public addresses, letters, and journal entries. Writing for *Library Journal* (May 1, 1988), Mollie Brodsky declared the work "an important book" and described, "Entertaining and often stirring, [this book] ranges widely, moving from observations made on trips to China, Bali, and Jamaica to Walker's views on her connection with San Francisco's lesbian and gay communities." Noel Perrin, writing for the *New York Times* (June 5, 1988), found the book's spiritual journey to be even more captivating than the geographical ones chronicled. He observed, "It leads Ms. Walker through a path distinctly her own."

Walker's fourth novel, *The Temple of My Familiar* (1989), offers a mythical retelling of history, particularly as it pertains to the heritage of African-American women. The plot revolves around Suwelo, a black professor of American history, who travels to Baltimore to attend his uncle's funeral and to sell the home there that he has inherited; meanwhile, his wife, Fanny—the granddaughter of Miss Celie from *The Color Purple*—has discovered feminism and decided that she wants a divorce. When Suwelo meets Mr. Hall and Miss Lissie, two of his uncle's friends, the characters begin a regular dialogue in which Miss Lissie recalls her past lives since the beginning of time. Overall, the book received largely mixed reviews. Doris Davenport, writing for the *Women's Review of Books* (September 1989), like many feminists found the novel to be "one of the most important books of the late eighties: because of Walker's 'messages,' her possibility of 'saving' a large number of us—or of enabling us to see and save ourselves, through an Afracentric vision." Other critics faulted Walker's unflattering portrayal of men, particularly white men, throughout her revisionist take on world history. One such critic, Paul Gray for *Time* (May 1, 1989) noted, "Walker's relentless adherence to her own sociopolitical agenda makes for frequently striking propaganda. But affecting fiction demands something more: characters and events in conflict, thoughts striking sparks through the friction of opposing beliefs."

Walker again mixed fiction with politics in *Possessing the Secret of Joy* (1992), a novel in which she made a profound statement about the subject of female genital mutilation—a procedure still practiced by many African tribal cultures whereby parts of the women's reproductive system are removed. Here, Walker resurrected Tashi, a member of the Olinka tribe who appeared in both *The Color Purple* and *The Temple of My Familiar*. When Tashi is about to marry and move to North America, she decides to undergo the ritual of female circumcision in order to preserve the heritage of her tribe. "We had been stripped of everything but our black skins. Here and there a defiant cheek bore the mark of our withered tribe. These marks gave me courage. I wanted such a mark for myself," she explained, as quoted by Mel Watkins for the *New York Times* (July 24, 1992). As Tashi confronts the physical and emotional pain of the experience, struggling to understand why her people continue this tradition, she suffers a breakdown, spiraling into madness and eventually emerging defiant and strengthened, and possessing her own secret of joy. Throughout the novel Walker introduces narratives from various other characters, including Tashi's husband, sister-in-law, son, psychiatrist, and the female tribal circumciser who performed her ceremony.

While many critics acknowledged the difficulty in writing an effective political novel, most agreed that, in this work, Walker succeeded in her task. Janette Turner for the *New York Times* (June 28, 1992) observed, "The people in Ms. Walker's book are archetypes rather than characters as we have come to expect them in the 20th-century novel. . . . When the novel is operating genuinely on this archetypal level, it has mythic strength." Meanwhile, Laura Shapiro for *Newsweek* (June 8, 1992) declared, "[Walker] has pulled off an amazing feat here: she's written a powerful novel about brutal misogyny, and she's made it both horrifying and readable, angry and warm-hearted, political and human. . . . we have true rarity: a novel that's strengthened, not strangled, by its political mission." Walker also participated with the filmmaker Pratibha Parmar in making a documentary about female genital mutilation; in 1993, the two women co-wrote a book entitled *Warrior Marks: Female Genital Mutilation and the Sexual Blinding of Women*.

Walker published additional nonfiction collections throughout the 1990s, including *Alice Walker Banned* (1996)—an account of the events that led the California Board of Education to ban several of her stories, *Anything We Love Can Be Saved: A Writer's Activism* (1997), a collection of personal and political essays, and *Dreads: Sacred Rites of the Natural Hair Revolution* (1999).

In *By the Light of My Father's Smile* (1998)—her sixth novel—Walker again focuses on society's attitudes toward female sexuality. The novel examines the troubled relationship between a father, Senor Robinson—who narrates the book's opening chapter as a spirit in the afterlife—and his two daughters, Susannah and Magdalena. Throughout the novel Robinson reconciles his past behavior, specifically as it related to his treatment of his daughters during adolescence; ultimately, he learns to accept his daughters as sexual creatures. While the book contained important themes about sexuality, adolescence, and the nature of father-daughter relationships, most critics found the work somewhat disappointing. "[Despite its] strong and poetic beginning," Ellen Flexman wrote for *Library Journal* (August 1998), "the book is more like a Walker essay than a novel, as the characters expound upon a wide range of topics, from the influence of the Ice Age on the European psyche to the legacy of the Vietnam War. Sadly, they lack the humanity that made Walker's earlier novels so moving and inspiring." Similarly, Gayle Pemberton, writing for the *Women's Review of Books* (December 1998), observed, "[This] is neither Walker's strongest novel nor her weakest. It is a brave attempt to transverse the difficult ground, to celebrate eros shorn of vulgarity, shame or loathing, to light—paraphrasing the novel's final words—the darkness around it."

In 2000 Walker published a different type of novel, which many reviewers categorized as a "fictionalized autobiography."*The Way Forward Is With a Broken Heart* contains 14 short stories (including an epilogue); the work reminisces about Walker's experiences as a black woman living through the civil rights era and its aftermath. The first and longest story, "To My Young Husband," offers an account of the speaker's mourning following the breakup of her interracial marriage; though Walker fictionalizes aspects of the story by, for example, changing the characters' names, she is clearly reflecting on her own feelings about her 1976 divorce from Leventhal. Writing for *Ms.* (October–November 2000), Samiya A. Bashir opined, "I felt like a voyeur witnessing the intimate details of a daily life dissolving." Merle Rubin, writing for the *Christian Science Monitor* (November 9, 2000), called this story "in many ways the best. It recaptures the exhilaration, enthusiasm, and happiness of the young couple, . . . and tries, in a generous spirit, to analyze what went wrong." Critics praised the subsequent stories for their complexity and honesty, while Eleanor J. Bader for *Library Journal* (September 1, 2000) summarized the collection: "Brave and passionate, audacious and wise, this is Walker at her best."

Throughout her 35-year career, Walker has received numerous honors, including a grant from the National Endowment for the Arts (1969), a Radcliffe Institute Fellowship (1971–73), an honorary doctorate from the University of Massachusetts (1983), the O. Henry Award (1986), the Langston Hughes Award from the City College of New York (1989), the Nora Astorga Leadership Award (1989), the Fred Cody Award for lifetime achievement from the Bay Area Book Reviewers Association (1990), the Freedom to Write Award from PEN West (1990), the California Governor's Arts Award (1994), and the Literary Ambassador Award from the University of Oklahoma Center for Poets and Writers (1998). She has been a lecturer and a reader at numerous universities and literary conferences and serves as a member of the board of trustees at Sarah Lawrence College.

Walker has lived in northern California since 1978. She currently has a home in Berkeley, near her daughter, Rebecca Walker, who recently authored her own memoirs entitled *Black, White, and Jewish: Autobiography of a Shifting Self* (2001). Alice Walker also maintains a country home in the hills of Mendocino, where she gardens and writes. In an interview with Mel Gussow for the *New York Times* (December 26, 2000), she confessed that she is contemplating what her next "internal imperative" may inspire. "I'm not sure I want to keep writing," she explained. "I feel like this is the end of a 30-year cycle, and it's really a good time for me to think about what I want to do for another 30 years." Nevertheless, Walker told Gussow, she will continue to approach her craft as a spiritual exercise. "I've been given something really precious. And I have to wait until I know it is the time to use it," she said, adding, "There's an ecstatic side to writing. It's like jazz. It just has a life." In 2003 Walker published *Absolute Trust In the Goodness of the Earth: New Poems*.

—C. M.

SUGGESTED READING: *African American Review* p715+ Winter 1999; *Essence* p58 July 1992; *Ms.* p35+ June 1982; *New York Times* VII p7 Apr. 30, 1989, C p20 July 24, 1992, E p8 Oct. 7, 1998, E p1 Dec. 26, 2000; *New York Times* (on-line) June 5, 1988; *New York Times Magazine* p24 Jan. 8, 1984; *Time* p69 May 1, 1989; *Washington Post* G p1+ Aug. 8, 1976, E p1+ Oct. 15, 1982, X p1 July 5, 1992; *World Literature Today* p335 Spring 2001

SELECTED BOOKS: novels—*The Third Life of Grange Copeland*, 1970; *Meridian*, 1976; *The Color Purple*, 1982; *The Temple of My Familiar*, 1989; *Possessing the Secret of Joy*, 1992; *By the Light of My Father's Smile*, 1998; *The Way*

Forward Is With a Broken Heart, 2000; short-story collections—*In Love and Trouble*, 1973; *You Can't Keep a Good Woman Down*, 1981; poetry—*Once*, 1968; *Revolutionary Petunias*, 1973; *Good Night, Willie Lee, I'll See You in the Morning*, 1979; *Horses Make a Landscape Look More Beautiful*, 1984; *Her Blue Body Everything We Know: Earthling Poems, 1965–1990 Complete*, 1991; *Absolute Trust In the Goodness of the Earth: New Poems*, 2003; children's literature—*Langston Hughes: American Poet*, 1973; *To Hell with Dying*, 1988; *Finding the Green Stone*, 1991; nonfiction—*In Search of Our Mother's Gardens: Womanist Prose*, 1983; *Living By the Word: Selected Writings, 1973–1987*, 1988; *Warrior Marks: Female Genital Mutilation and the Sexual Blinding of Women* (with Pratibha Parmar), 1993; *Alice Walker Banned*, 1996; *Anything We Love Can Be Saved: A Writer's Activism*, 1997; *Dreads: Sacred Rites of the Natural Hair Revolution*, 1999; as editor—*I Love Myself When I'm Laughing . . . and Then Again When I Am Looking Mean and Impressive: A Zora Neale Hurston Reader*, 1979

Walker, Ted

Nov. 28, 1934– Poet; short-story writer; memoirist

"No poet writing in England today has a closer, more recondite knowledge of the secret life in the non- human universe than Ted Walker. . . . Walker has been contriving quiet, hair-raising (and musically precise) metaphors from his great gift for relating our inattentive senses to the cryptic features of animals, fish, birds—flowers even—in which, if we paused to look (with *his* patience and his occult powers) we would see ourselves, or the wreck of ourselves, writ plain." Such were the words of Vernon Young in *The Hudson Review* (Winter 1975), as quoted in *Contemporary Literary Criticism, Vol. 13* (1980), when Ted Walker had published one pamphlet and four volumes of poetry. In his first published pamphlet of poems, *Those Other Growths* (1964), Walker had emerged fully formed, writing closely observed nature poems in strict meter and rhyme and drawing poignant metaphors between humans and the rest of the natural world. He became known for his vivid, realistic imagery, described through exacting word choices, and more specifically, for his intimate sketches of England's Sussex seascapes. Through the 1980s and most of the 90s, Walker turned away from poetry in favor of autobiography and fiction. Then, in 1999, he brought out a long-awaited new volume of poetry called *Mangoes on the Moon*, which set the stage for new directions in Walker's poetry and recalled the artistry that had made him one of England's best nature poets.

In an autobiographical statement submitted to *World Authors 1995–2000*, Ted Walker writes, "I was born in the nondescript southern English seaside village of Lancing, within a stone's throw of high tide. My working-class parents had gone south from Birmingham in the midlands in search of work; my father was a carpenter, my mother a grocer's daughter. I started primary school at the beginning of World War II, the Battle of Britain was soon to take place in the skies above. Lessons were sometimes taken in the air raid shelters. The shoreline adjacent to my home was laid with mines which, with the puny tank- traps set up in our garden, prevented me from seeing the English Channel again until 1945. When the sappers removed the mines, I rediscovered the playground of my early infancy. Later, when I began writing poetry, the beach, the sand and shingle and the breakwaters provided the backdrop for my work. Here, I staked out my poetic territory.

"Despite his poverty, my father sent me at the age of nine for private French lessons—by the Berlitz Direct Method. I therefore had a head start when I went to High School; and to my early proficiency in languages I think I owe much of my career as a writer and teacher. At Cambridge University, which I went up to in 1953, I wasted my time academically but took every advantage of the opportunities offered to read only what I wanted and needed to read and to discover, in my loneliness, that I was an artist rather than a scholar.

"After graduation (I took a poor degree) I married my first love, Lorna, whom I had met seven years before when I was fourteen. We had four children—two boys and two girls—in quick succession. We were chronically short of money. I taught in various Secondary Schools, gaining rapid promotions until I became Head of a major Languages Department in a huge Comprehensive School. I enjoyed these jobs well enough, but what I wanted was to be a published poet. It took a long time for me to discover my 'true voice of feeling.' Indeed, I was 28 before I began to have poems accepted by the important magazines, journals and newspapers. And then, events accelerated when the *New Yorker* took a poem called 'Breakwaters.' In all, I was to publish almost thirty poems and the same number of short stories in that once great magazine.

"I brought out five collections of poetry with Jonathan Cape, beginning with *Fox on a Barn Door* in 1965. There followed *The Solitaries* (1967), *The Night Bathers* (1970) and *Gloves to the Hangman* (1973). Then, after *Burning the Ivy* (1978) the well of lyrical poems went dry. My *Selected Poems* (1987) from Secker & Warburg contained nothing new.

"Well, lyrical poetry is—and always was— essentially a young man's trade. I taught myself new skills: those of the short story, children's verse and light verse, TV and Radio drama (both comic and serious) and a miscellany of other types of writing from autobiography and travel writing, to essays and reviews to journalism and even football commentating and reporting. Always, though, I was on the *qui vive* for the return of the gift of poetry. I did hundreds of poetry readings up and down the country, was poet-in-residence on dozens of writers' courses and I broadcast regularly on the BBC. I enjoyed the freelance life; but when the well of short stories also went dry—and the Inland Revenue demanded a high percentage of my previous year's income—I had to return for a while to schoolmastering.

"Early in the 1970s I was fortunate enough to secure the temporary, part-time post of Poet-in-Residence and teacher of Spanish and Creative Writing at the newly-opened British Campus of an American liberal arts college, a short drive from my home in Sussex. Here I was given almost total freedom to teach whatever courses I chose to. From being temporary and part-time lecturer, I became, over the next 21 years, assistant, then associate, then full professor. When I took early retirement in 1992, the institution (New England College, whose base is in New Hampshire) created me Professor Emeritus.

"When I was an undergraduate at Cambridge, I sat at the feet of Robert Graves when he delivered the Clarke Lectures. He told us that a poet should *never, never, never* take a job as a teacher. "Sweep the roads first," he said. I know now that I was perhaps foolish to disregard that advice if I had expectations of becoming a poet of the first rank. If you're any good as a teacher, all your powers of inventiveness and creativity go into your classes not your real work. (Either that, or you woefully neglect your students: and that simply won't do.) Also—as Cyril Connolly argued so cogently in *Enemies of Promise*—the domestic life gets in the way too, with its not unreasonable demands upon the poet's time and freedom. However: the fact remains that I have had an extremely happy and fulfilled life both as a family man and an admittedly second-rate poet and writer. Happiness (though this sounds, I know, insufferably smug) ought to be enough.

"My wife Lorna died in 1987 of a long and painful illness, and I was inconsolable. I wrote about this and our time together in *The Last of England* (Cape, 1992) which had some success and which—more importantly—seemed to be of help to others similarly bereaved. I was unbelievably lucky to be able to re-marry quite soon: to Audrey, herself recently widowed. I have had two hugely successful marriages; few people have one. Smugness again!

"After retiring for good from the classroom, to my great delight I found poetry returning. Australia kick- started me again with its startlingly different flora, fauna and topography. After two visits, I wrote enough new poems for a new book, *Mangoes on the Moon*, which came out from London Magazine Editions in 1999. Much had changed, during the long gap since *Burning the Ivy*, both in my choice of subject-matter and my method of writing. Now I was writing more about people and family relationships, in a manner closer now to Larkin than to Hughes. Shortly I expect to bring out a second book of short stories, again from London Magazine Editions.

"I have always chosen to plough my own lonely furrow. I have never belonged to any literary school or group. Now that I am an old man, I hope for (perhaps) more poems of a philosophical nature. I have retired to Spain, to a beautiful valley full of oranges and lemons and almonds and olives and vines. I am surrounded by poems which maybe I don't need to write."

Ted Walker was born on November 28, 1934 in Lancing, England, the son of Edward Joseph Walker, a carpenter, and Winifred Schofield Walker. Walker's father encouraged his early interest in reading and always set aside money to buy books for his son, even during financial difficulties in the thirties. One of the books in his father's collection that influenced Walker was *The Natural History of the World in Pictures*. Illustrations of such animals as the tree-climbing crab and the warthog captured Walker's imagination, and nature would later become a central theme in all of his poetry. Walker spent much time exploring the beaches of the Sussex coast, where he encountered more animals, including eels, sticklebacks, and waterfowl. He attended primary school in the town of Shoreham-by-Sea. When he won admission to Steyning Grammar School, Walker's satisfaction was mixed with disappointment, because it seemed that this prestigious school would set him on a path that diverged from the tradesman's life of his father. This would prove true; Walker soon took an interest in the poetry of T.S. Eliot and then went on to study modern and medieval languages at St. John's College at Cambridge University, graduating with honors in 1956. (Later, in 1977, he received his M.A. from St. John's College.) After he graduated from St. John's, on August 11, 1956, Walker married Lorna Ruth Benfell, whom he had fallen in love with and proposed to when he was 15 years old. They eventually had four children together: Edward, Susan, Margaret, and William.

In 1956 Walker was appointed assistant master of the North Paddington School, in London. He became the head of the French department at Southall Technical Grammar school, in 1958. In 1963 he joined the Modern Languages Department at the Bognor Regis School. Meanwhile, he had also been reading and writing poetry. Among his favorite poets were Samuel Taylor Coleridge, Robert Frost, W. H. Auden, and Arthur Rimbaud, but, according to Walker, his greatest influence was F. L. Lucas's *The Decline and Fall of the Romantic Ideal*. Walker told Julia Gitzen for *The Dictionary of Literary Biography, Vol. 40* (1985) that the book taught him to "blend elements of the *classical* (as far as disciplined form is concerned) with my incurable *romanticism* of outlook, with the *realism* which springs from close observation of the world." This combination of the classical, romantic, and realistic would form the basis of much of Walker's poetry. However, he didn't formulate this until he moved back to the Sussex coast and rediscovered his childhood stomping grounds. "Having found my true voice, almost by accident," Walker told Gitzen, "—experimenting with new meters and stanza forms—and then finding my subjects as though mint- new, I was able to begin."

In 1964 Walker published a pamphlet of seven poems titled *Those Other Growths*. In 1965 he published a larger collection of poems, *Fox on a Barn Door*, which included those that had appeared in *Those Other Growths*. Many of the poems in *Fox on a Barn Door* focus on the animals, flora, and fauna of the Sussex coast. Porpoises, carp, eels, and other marine animals populate the pages of the collection, and many of the poems focus on the animal aspects of human beings. "In Walker's vison," wrote Laurence Lieberman in the *Yale Review* (Winter 1968), as quoted in *Contemporary Literary Criticism, Vol. 13*, "our suppressed animal impulses nearly always manifest themselves in our daily lives as mildly persistent fears, incipient edginess, emerging at odd moments from no detectable source." Walker uses traditional forms and strictly metered rhyme schemes in most of the poems. They are also characterized by sharply realized descriptive passages, as well as an underlying somberness. Philip Legler, in *Poetry* (March 1967), as quoted in *The Dictionary of Literary Biography, Vol. 40*, described Walker's early thematic concerns as "fear and loss which looks for the beauty that remains among the ruins of lost faith, lost innocence, and lost animal strength." *Fox on a Barn Door* drew many favorable reviews and established Walker as one of England's best nature poets. While Lieberman wrote that in some of Walker's poems "too many words with puzzling overtones, or connotations, pile up too fast," he added that in the best poems "meanings subtly add up to a forceful statement, inseparable from the persons or events which call them forth."

Walker's next collection of poetry was titled *The Solitaries* (1967). As the title suggests, Walker focused on solitude, and many of the people and animals in these poems are alone. The imagery of subdued light, both at dawn and dusk, suffuses many of the poems, heightening the sense of loneliness, while the vastness of the ocean provides another image of solitude. Solitude, for Walker, also carries positive connotations. It allows for meditation and provides a setting in which people can conquer their fears. Lieberman found *The Solitaries* an advancement of Walker's vision from his previous volume. "In *The Solitaries*," he wrote, "several poems deepen the vision, exploring psychic states in which the solitary human—or animal—soul, pushed or driven to harrowing extremity, finds a haunting beauty in the mere act of survival against powerful odds."

In his next volume of poetry, *The Night Bathers* (1970), Walker included some translations of other poets with his own work. He translated poems by Federico García Lorca and Pablo Neruda from the Spanish; Paul Verlaine and Charles Leconte de Lisle from French; Eugenio Montale from Italian; and Friedrich Hölderlin and Rainer Maria Rilke from German. *The Night Bathers* also marked a departure from Walker's previous work in that, in addition to writing about nature, he tackled the subject of family relations, often from an autobiographical standpoint. The title poem, for example, is about his visiting Wales after having a disagreement with his son. In the *Times Literary Supplement* (June 18, 1970), as quoted in *Contemporary Literary Criticism, Vol. 13*, Lieberman wrote that some of Walker's translations seemed a bit stilted and his own poetry was, at times, predictable, but he commended Walker's decision to break new ground with his autobiographical poems. "He seems," wrote Lieberman, "to be looking for a way out of the nature poetry he does to perfection and that comes to him with an ease which his artist's instinct is already teaching him to distrust."

In 1971 Walker became a professor of creative writing at the British campus of New England College, in Arundel, England, while continuing to write. In *Gloves to the Hangman* (1973), his fifth volume of poetry, Walker wrote more nature poetry—focusing on the changing seasons—but broke his own mold with two offbeat poems: "Letter to Marcel Proust," which follows a loose meter and has a humorous bent, and "Pig pig," which is narrated by a 14th-century hangman. Lieberman, reviewing the volume for the *Times Literary Supplement* (June 8, 1973), as quoted in *Contemporary Literary Criticism, Vol. 13*, called "Pig pig " a "poem of powerful narrative momentum, skillful characterization and truly hideous, though in no way gratuitous, violence. In seeking and exposing the roots of cruelty, Mr. Walker's savage drama is an exorcism, and his finest achievement." Lieberman also praised the volume in general, writing that Walker "united the compulsions of the natural world with the complexity of human energies. An elegant and sophisticated poet, despite the butch persona sometimes on view, he has consistently shown a rare delicacy in making the image that both precisely represents his natural subject and embodies psychological correspondences."

Many of the poems in Walker's next volume, *Burning the Ivy* (1978), are set in his Sussex residence with its well-tended gardens. "The *point* of my garden is that I foster my sanity there," he told Julian Gitzen. "In a sense, the walled garden became a kind of extended metaphor of life itself, of temporary endeavour and small achievement. Unhappinesses crept over my wall from the outside, however I tried to hack them back; within the boundaries, small joys would briefly flourish." As usual for Walker, *Burning the Ivy* captured the small joys of a close association with nature. It also contained meditations on the sometimes arduous art of writing itself. In one poem, for example, Walker writes, "I dread my craft, crabbed / words obdurate as sodden / bark." With this consideration of the writer's craft came experimentation with several forms new to Walker; he tried his hand at free verse and experimented with several convoluted rhyme schemes. Despite the formal experimentation, Craig Raine felt that *Burning the Ivy* was covering familiar ground. "Reading Ted Walker's well-made collection, *Burning the Ivy*," Raine wrote for *New Statesman* (December 22, 1978), as quoted in *Contemporary Literary Criticism, Vol. 13*, "I was reminded of the joke about the man who invented television—in 1975. It worked but it wasn't sufficiently original." Alan Brownjohn, in *Encounter* (March 1979), as quoted in *Contemporary Literary Criticism, Vol. 13*, found the volume admirable, but somewhat lackluster. "Carefully crafted notations of domestic existence, of change, and mortality come forward, and most of them. . . are honorably done, but solid instead of exciting."

After *Burning the Ivy* Walker took a long hiatus from writing poetry. In 1980 he published a children's book, *The Lion's Cavalcade*, and in 1982 he wrote an autobiography titled *The High Path*, which told of his early life. In 1985 Walker published his first collection of short stories, *You've Never Heard Me Sing*, which investigated, among other things, domestic relationships, especially those between fathers and sons. In the *Guardian* (December 19, 1985), Norman Shrapnel wrote favorably of Walker's first foray into fiction: "It's a satisfying harvest, fusing imagination and memory, those fecund wrestlers, into an issue more fruitful and certainly more lively than such bleak old records often manage to scratch out."

In 1987 a collection of Walker's old poetry, *Hands at a Live Fire*, was published, along with a travel memoir, *In Spain*. In 1992, the year he became professor emeritus at New England College, he wrote another autobiographical book, *The Last of England*, which recounts the death of his first wife, Lorna Benfell. Lorna had died of cancer, in 1987, and Walker had suffered with her through many ordeals, including surgical facial reconstruction. Alan Ross, in the *Times Literary Supplement* (April 24, 1992), wrote, "*The Last of England* is not a depressing book despite everything. Flooded by love, and written with unembarrassing reverence, it has a dignity and grace that make what might have been intolerable, tolerable."

It had been nearly 20 years since Walker had published any new poetry when *Mangoes on the Moon* was published, in 1999. The epigraph to his new volume of poetry was a quote of Philip Larkin's about encountering writer's block: "expressing sentiments in short lines having similar sounds at their ends seems as remote as mangoes on the moon." The volume contained some nature poems and some poems about Lorna's death. It also concentrated on his travels through Australia. Australia's people and social customs fascinated Walker, as evidenced in such poems as "Sunday Raffle in the Returned Servicemen's League." Alan Brownjohn, in the *Times Literary Supplement* (February 4, 2000), was impressed by Walker's return to poetry. He called *Mangoes on the Moon* "a group of poems unlike any he has previously written, the work of someone astonished by the Australian landscape and writing with relish and directness about its people," and concluded, "Ted Walker's rediscovery of inspiration will be welcome if he continues to write as well as this."

Walker continues to write and live in Spain. His awards include the Eric Gregory Award, 1964; the Cholmondeley Award, 1966; the Alice Hunt Bartless Award, 1967; an award from the Arts Council of Great Britain, 1969; the Campion Prize, 1974; and an honorary degree in literature from the University of Southampton, in Highfield, Great Britain, in 1995. Walker married Audrey Joan Hicks on July 8, 1988.

—P. G. H.

SUGGESTED READING: *Guardian* Dec. 19, 1985; *Times Literary Supplement* p12 Apr. 24, 1992, p23 Feb. 4, 2000; Bryfonski, Dedria ed. *Contemporary Literary Criticism, Vol. 13*, 1980; Sherry, Vincent B. Jr. ed. *Dictionary of Literary Biography, Vol. 40*, 1985

SELECTED BOOKS: *Those Other Growths*, 1964; *Fox On a Barn Door*, 1965; *Solitaries*, 1967; *Night Bathers*, 1970; *Gloves to the Hangman*, 1973; *Burning the Ivy*, 1978; *High Path*, 1982; *You've Never Heard Me Sing*, 1985; *Hands at a Live Fire*, 1987; *In Spain*, 1987; *The Last of England*, 1992; *Mangoes on the Moon*, 1999

Warner, Alan

1965 (?)– Novelist

In the 1990s the media began reporting a "Scottish Renaissance" in literature, fueled by the success of such writers as Irvine Welsh of *Trainspotting* (1993) fame and James Kelman, who won the Booker Prize for *How Late It Was, How Late* (1994). Over the course of the decade, Scottish authors had begun writing about the lives of ordinary Scots, with a special focus on the fringes of their society—drug addicts, eccentrics, and alcoholics. A *New York Times Magazine* article celebrating the movement referred to it as "a new beer-soaked, drug-filled, profanity-laced, violently funny literature," as quoted by Melissa Denes for the *Guardian* (May 25, 2002, on-line). Alan Warner, whose characters populate the underbelly of Scotland and use the language of the streets to express themselves, is often mentioned as a major participant in this renaissance. (Ironically, Warner was ejected from the *New York Times Magazine* photo shoot at one point, for being too drunk.) "The thing that's happened in Scotland is, the gulf between writers and readers has gotten smaller," he told Larry Weissman for an interview posted on the Random House Web site. "Writers feel divorced from the whole literary world and have more in common with the people who actually read the books than they used to. In the past there was this sort of ivory tower thing, but now some sort of democratization of lit-

Alan Warner

erature is going on, whereby it's becoming more open as an art form."

Alan Warner was born in about 1965 in Argyll, Scotland, and grew up in Oban, a town on the western coast of the country. His parents owned no books, and his friends tended to look down on anyone who seemed too interested in reading. "Where I came from is a small, backwards town," he told Weissman. "The whole culture was pretty repressive; guys who read books were looked upon as effeminate, so reading instantly became kind of an underground act. There was a reaction against the culture I was in, which was small town, philistine, patriarchal, sexist, violent." Despite this, Warner does not describe his childhood in purely negative terms. He lived with his parents in a 40-room hotel on a hillside near the port. "It was this incredible thing, like a palace," he told Melissa Denes. "It would close for winter and I'd get to know every room, the difference between every door handle— it was a real world of the imagination. I'd have my pal over and we'd play secret agents, me starting at the top, him at the bottom, and we'd hunt each other down."

In his teens Warner began arguing with his father, an ex-military man and heavy drinker. "He was a self-made man, and I was this hopeless case, a breakaway at 16," he described to Denes. He found some solace in writing stories. "I think writing for me is an extension of play," he noted to Weissman. "Like when you're a kid you play and you have this incredibly active imaginative life and then suddenly, society demands that we stop and that we start thinking about getting a job and stuff. I always found it difficult to keep the imagination down. All I want in life is to be involved in some creative process."

Warner moved to London to study at Ealing College and then continued his education at Glasgow University, where he wrote a thesis on Joseph Conrad and suicide. After completing his education, however, he began to drift from one dead-end job to the next, working variously as a bartender, bouncer, jazz guitarist, and eventually a train driver. "It was a good life, but hard work and long hours," he told Weissman of his time on the trains. "Weekends were just mad with drinking and drugs and dances." While on a holiday in Spain, however, Warner had an epiphany and realized that he needed to devote himself fully to writing.

He started submitting poetry and short stories to magazines. After reading Duncan McLean's short-story collection *Bucket of Tongues* and Jeff Torrington's *Swing Hammer Swing!*, he realized that there was a marketplace for contemporary, realistic Scottish fiction. His days of hard partying had provided him with plenty of material. He completed work on a novel but didn't think it was publishable, so he left it in a box in his bedroom for 18 months. Finally, he decided to write a letter to Duncan McLean, who subsequently asked to see part of it. McLean was impressed and called his agent, who found a publisher for the book, which was titled *Morvern Callar*, within a week. Warner received a modest advance of £3,000.

Morvern Callar was published in 1995. The title character is a disaffected young woman in northern Scotland who hates her low-level supermarket job and spends her free time at raves—all-night dance parties featuring techno music and often fueled by mood-altering drugs. When Morvern discovers her boyfriend's body the morning after he commits suicide, she is indifferent to his death and opens the Christmas presents he has bought her. One of them, a Walkman, provides a soundtrack for the rest of the novel, as Morvern (whose full name in Scottish means literally "quieter silence") tells the reader what song she's listening to at every moment—including the moment she hacks up her boyfriend's body and disposes of it. She then escapes with the money she inherits from him to the Mediterranean club scene. In *Library Journal* (February 1, 1997), Doris Lynch called the book a "compelling first novel [that] introduces a fresh, lyrical voice." She continued, "Warner has an eye for the shocking detail: ciggies fizzed out in blood; cookie-baking with a corpse nearby. Occasionally, the story stretches the believable, but Morvern and the supporting cast are compelling enough characters for the reader to accept a few inconsistencies. This novel may very well trigger a young, cult following." Jennifer Kornreich, writing for the *New York Times Book Review* (May 18, 1997), however, complained: "While Morvern's opacity is obviously meant to convey hip disaffection, the novel's matter-of-fact amorality quickly grows tiresome. Mr. Warner's true forte is his deadpan rendering of the idiosyncratic trappings of Morvern's morbid world. Unfortunately, these appalling but convincing details never add up to anything in particular;

ultimately, understanding their significance is as impossible for us as it is for Morvern herself." The book has been made into a film, released in late 2002, starring the actress Samantha Morton.

In *These Demented Lands* (1997), Warner continues the story of Morvern Callar, who has traveled across Europe for the last several years, bounding from one club scene to another. The reader is reintroduced to her on a skerry in the North Atlantic. There she meets a host of eccentric characters, including John Brotherhood, a manipulative hotelier and gun runner, and someone she refers to as the Aircrash Investigator, who is at Brotherhood's hotel piecing together an accident involving small planes that took place a decade previously. In *Booklist* (March 15, 1998), Joanne Wilkinson cheered, "Warner's novel, with its powerfully realized setting, evokes *The Road Warrior* with an alternative-rock soundtrack. Although those unfamiliar with the first novel might feel a bit lost, Warner's inventive prose and intriguing characters (especially the unpredictable Morvern) are the hooks here and ample evidence of the author's large talent." However, writing for the *Times Literary Supplement* (April 4, 1997), Liam McIlvanney offered a more mixed assessment of the novel: "There is little in the way of coherent narration or convincing characterization. Instead, we can admire Warner's prodigious powers of invention, his marvellously dynamic prose and, above all, his brilliant visual imagination." McIlvanney continued, "Its conspicuous virtues notwithstanding, there are aspects of this novel which weaken its impact. Too many of the characters are too similar, and Warner's deployment of religious symbolism is heavy-handed. It is perhaps best to see [this] as a greatly ambitious novel which finally fails to fulfil its promise. If a failure, however, it still outdoes most other writers' successes."

In his third novel, *The Sopranos* (1998), Warner examines the world of teenage Catholic-school girls. The members of Our Lady of Perpetual Succour School for Girls Choir are preparing for a national singing competition to be held in "the big, big city." Released from the confines of the school, they revolt against all of the conventions put upon them by their teachers. Writing for the *New Statesman* (August 7, 1998), Keith Martin observed that the girls "delight in disobeying authority; they smoke and drink; dance and have sex. The result is very funny. But these lives are not entirely empty. Warner's girls are not caricatures; they know about trust, loyalty and friendship." Dan Gunn was less enthusiastic in his review for the *Times Literary Supplement* (August 14, 1998): "Warner has a fine ear, and this may be partly what gets him into trouble with *The Sopranos*. . . . Wedding his narrative so slavishly to his adolescents means that when he does step back, he cannot make up his mind as to what sort of grown-up voice to adopt." Still, most reviewers were impressed by Warner's ability to write believable female characters, and Melissa Denes opined, "His familiarity with female behavior and private ritual is frankly spooky. He seems to have been places boys aren't invited—locked toilet cubicles, single-sex classrooms, teenage bedrooms. He gets the dialogue just right."

In 2002 Warner published *The Man Who Walks*, a mock epic featuring a protagonist known as "the Nephew," who is searching for his uncle, an eccentric drunkard who has stolen the World Cup kitty from his local pub. Katie Owen, in the *New Statesman* (April 29, 2002), proclaimed, "Alan Warner is arguably the most mature and original of [the modern Scottish fiction writers]. *The Man Who Walks* bears this out. . . . [The novel] confirms this Scot as one of the most unusual and provocative writers working on this side of the Atlantic." Paul Quinn, writing for the *Times Literary Supplement* (June 14, 2002), was more restrained in his praise: "Although the broad comedy and media parodies often work well, the attempts at Swiftian satire are not always successful."

Alan Warner lives in Dublin with his wife, Hollie, who is half-Irish and half-Spanish. He is currently at work on two novels; one about a Spanish businessman with HIV, the other about an Englishman, a Scotsman, and an Irishman who go to Spain to build swimming pools.

—*C. M.*

SUGGESTED READING: *Guardian* (on-line) May 25, 2002; *Spike Magazine* (on-line); *Booklist* p1203 Mar. 15, 1998; *Library Journal* (on-line) p23 Nov. 2, 1995; *New Statesman* p48 Aug. 7, 1998, p51 Apr. 21, 2002; *New York Times Book Review* p21 May 18, 1997; Random House Web site; *Times Literary Supplement* p23 Apr. 4, 1997, p8 Aug. 14, 1998, p22 June 14, 2002; *TriQuarterly* p48+ Fall 1999

SELECTED BOOKS: *Morvern Callar*, 1995; *These Demented Lands*, 1997; *The Sopranos*, 1998; *The Man Who Walks*, 2002

Waters, Sarah

1966– Novelist

The Welsh-born novelist Sarah Waters has built a solid reputation for her powerful historical fiction. Yet, as Marianne Brace for the London *Independent* (January 19, 2002) observed upon meeting Waters, "With her black T-shirt and jeans, she's a historical author in name only, and one with a contemporary agenda." Waters' published works to date, *Tipping the Velvet* (1999), *Affinity* (2000), and *Fingersmith* (2002), have all been set in Victorian-era Britain and depict classic gothic themes—with one significant twist: Her protagonists are often budding lesbians, forced to confront their sexuality within the restricted environments of 19th-century England. Waters, who studied the Victorian era in depth for her Ph.D. thesis on lesbian and gay historical fiction, has acknowledged her debt

Bernd Ott/Courtesy of Riverhead Books/The Putnam Publishing Group

Sarah Waters

to such Victorian writers as Charles Dickens, Wilkie Collins, and Joseph Sheridan LeFanu. Building upon their example, Waters told Brace, she set out to write complex literary novels that would expand the genre of lesbian literature. Her results have been widely celebrated as both effective Victorian-type novels and groundbreaking modern works. Brace noted, "[Waters's] books bulge with period detail and have gripping, carefully constructed plots. There's plenty of danger, mystery, hysteria, and corruption. Yet she also puts what's only ever hinted at in Victorian novels—drug addiction, sexuality, pornography—right up front."

Born in 1966, Sarah Waters was raised in Neyland, Pembrokeshire, on the southwestern coast of Wales—an environment far removed, both geographically and culturally, from the mainstream of British life. In an interview for the Melbourne *Sunday Age* (June 17, 2001), Waters described her hometown: "It was a place of contradictions," she recalled, "it was held in a mid-20th century time-warp. It's given me a taste for small-town life, families, the slightly claustrophobic. I remember all the women looking old." Many critics have suggested that the sense of isolation and marginalization that Neyland engendered contributed to Waters's gothic sensibilities as a writer. As a young child, Waters and her father shared a passion for storytelling and by the time she reached her teens, she was an insatiable reader. After attending Milford Haven Grammar School in Wales, she enrolled at the University of Kent to study English Literature. She obtained a B.A. degree and immediately pursued postgraduate study at Lancaster University, where she earned an M.A. degree. After working briefly as a bookseller and a librarian, Waters entered a doctoral program at London's Queen Mary and Westfield College, studying lesbian and gay literature dating from the 19th century to the present.

While finishing her Ph.D. thesis, Waters began to consider writing her own novel depicting homosexual relationships as they may have existed in the Victorian era. "I really got into the issue of what lesbians and gay men can do with history," she told the *Sunday Age* reporter, "whether you can reclaim it, recover it or invent it. I was finishing the thesis and I really began to think, there's a novel somewhere in here." Since Waters found Victorian literature largely lacking in complex homosexual themes—despite historical evidence suggesting that lesbian and gay communities were emerging at that time—she set out to "recover" this period for homosexual literature. "I touched on it when I was doing the thesis," she explained to Ron Hogan in an interview for *BookSense.com*, "looking at gay men's writing from the period—there's quite a lot of it, and it was very identifiable, you know [Irish writer Oscar] Wilde and the people around Wilde, and so on. It's a hinge time between earlier nineteenth century stuff . . . and the modernist stuff, as well as a time when we began to get a recognizably modern gay subculture. I thought about what there might be around for women, lesbians of the period, and so the music hall, male impersonation . . . I got into what that might mean for women viewers and for the women doing it. I have read a lot, and do still read a lot, of Victorian fiction because it's a way of really getting into the period—simply immersing yourself in it. I found it came quite naturally in a way to write in a Victorian style."

After completing her Ph.D. and obtaining a teaching position at the Open University, an unusual institution catering to students of all ages and abilities, Waters spent 18 months composing *Tipping the Velvet* (1999), a novel that begins in 1880s England and chronicles the adventures of a picaresque heroine, Nan King, as she confronts new aspects of her sexuality. (A picaresque is a type of fiction that presents a loosely connected series of episodic adventures, often featuring an appealingly roguish main character.) As the book opens, Nan is an innocent young girl raised in her family's oyster parlor on the southeast coast of England. Passionate about music-hall entertainment, Nan visits a nearby variety show where she becomes infatuated with Miss Kitty Butler—a "masher," or singing and dancing male impersonator—and returns night after night to watch Kitty perform. The two girls gradually develop a friendship, and Miss Kitty invites Nan to join the troupe as a hairdresser when the act moves to London. Later, as the relationship becomes sexual, Nan takes her own role in the provocative, cross-dressing show. Kitty, who expresses disdain for "toms," or openly lesbian girls, refuses to make their affair public and eventually marries her manager, causing the jealous and heartbroken Nan to flee. In the four sections that follow, Nan survives by working as a "renter," or male street prostitute, and later as the "kept woman" of a cruel and perverse widow. Eventually, she finds true love and takes up the cause of Britain's labor movement. Harriet Malinowitz observed for the *Women's Review of Books* (February 2000), "Nancy's evolution from sexual and theatrical ingenue to savvy professional is sumptuously described; the smells, textures, songs, swaggers and vernaculars of the England she inhabits are breathlessly and wittily detailed."

Overall, critics declared *Tipping the Velvet* a significant literary success, crediting Waters with providing an authentic example of how a 19th-century, lesbian picaresque might have looked. Miranda Seymour, writing for the *New York Times* (June 13, 1999, on-line), called the work a "buoyant and accomplished first novel," adding, "If lesbian fiction is to reach a wider readership—as much, though far from all, of it deserves to do—Waters is just the person to carry the banner." While some critics, including Seymour, considered certain portions of the book too political, they more often celebrated the author's tremendous storytelling gifts. Malinowitz observed, "*Tipping the Velvet* has already become something of a word-of-mouth sensation, and unsurprisingly so: besides its literary smarts, its rich cultural detail, its exceptional eroticism, its intense articulation of sensory experience, its insouciant depiction of life in drag and its brilliant showcasing of modes of performance, it has the terrific ability to reduce the reader to a weeping mess." *Tipping the Velvet* earned the Lambda Literary Award for fiction and was named a *New York Times* Notable Book and one of *Library Journal*'s Best Books of 1999; it is currently being adapted by the screenwriter Andrew Davies for one of Britain's largest television networks, the BBC2.

Waters' second book, *Affinity* (2000), is a psychological thriller set in 1870s London. While Waters called *Tipping the Velvet* "kind of a romp," she told Hogan she wanted this novel to explore something "a bit grimmer and a bit darker." As she explained to Brace, "I wanted to look at a whole range of lesbian identities and think about a world in which there was constraint." Told through a series of alternating journal entries, *Affinity* explores the relationship between two women: Margaret Prior, an upper-class, unmarried Victorian woman recovering from a suicide attempt, and Selina Dawes, a spiritual medium imprisoned in London's Millbank Prison for a mysterious death following one of her seances. As part of Prior's recuperation, she begins charity work as a "lady visitor" at the prison, meeting regularly with inmates to help improve their spiritual lives. There, she encounters Dawes and develops an intense affinity for her; as the women fall in love, Prior becomes increasingly certain of the medium's innocence. Waters keeps her readers in suspense as she juxtaposes the characters' narratives and gradually reveals several chilling plot twists. Sarah Van Arsdale observed for the *Lambda Book Report* (July–August 2000), "It is Waters' careful weaving of Dawes' story that gives the book its layered effect, as the reader sees the two protagonists' stories dovetail seamlessly as the book progresses."

In developing the novel, Waters has said she was interested in illustrating women's prisons as they existed in Victorian London, but also in exploring how the spiritualism of the day affected women's lives. "The more I researched and the further I got imaginatively into those worlds," she told Van Arsdale, "I realized that of course there were lots of overlaps—overlaps between, for example, the treatment of prisoners and the treatment of women mediums; a fetishisation of restraint and observation and darkness and silence—and that most importantly for me, these things were completely pertinent to our sense of the place of women in general, and lesbians in particular, in Victorian society."

Critics again applauded Waters's ability to evoke the Victorian era. "Waters creates a world so believable and richly detailed that readers will gladly follow her down the winding pathways into the dark catacombs of a women's prison in 1870s London. And those readers will soon be rewarded," Van Arsdale noted. Devon Thomas for *Library Journal* (May 15, 2000) affirmed, "Full of vivid descriptions of the sights, sounds, and smells of the labyrinthine prison and stultifying drawing rooms of Chelsea, *Affinity* is a dark, elegant, and subtle Gothic novel—a mix of Charlotte Perkins Gilman's *The Yellow Wallpaper* with a bit of Edgar Allen Poe." Mel Steel wrote for the London *Independent* (May 2, 1999), "[Waters'] skill is in taking the conventions and cliches of several genres at once—lady's journal, ghost story, mystery, romance—and drawing them together in an irresistible narrative, building the momentum of unraveling repression to a fevered—albeit ladylike—climax." He concluded, "She's a strong and original voice and consummate storyteller, and she obviously has a lot more up her writing sleeve." *Affinity* earned Waters the Somerset Maugham Prize, the *Sunday Times* Young Writer of the Year Award, the Ferro-Grumley Award for lesbian fiction, and an American Library Association Award.

In 2002 Waters published *Fingersmith*, another tale of psychological suspense and sexual obsession. (The title refers to a Victorian slang word for pickpocket.) Set in 1860s Britain, the novel is composed of two narratives, the first by Sue Trinder, an orphan raised in a London slum by a mercenary character named Mrs. Sucksby, and the second by Maud Lilly, another orphan, raised by her uncle at Briar, her family's country estate. When Richard Rivers, a con man, appears at Sue's door with a plan to seduce Maud into marriage, secure her inheritance, and then commit her to a madhouse, Sue agrees to assist him—for a cut of his proceeds—by becoming Maud's lady's maid. However, as Sue attaches herself to her young mistress, the two girls grow unexpectedly close and become sexually involved. This plot twist is the first of several, as Waters reveals that Maud is not the only character being deceived. Tom Gilling observed for the *New York Times* (February 24, 2002), "Waters spins an absorbing tale that withholds as much as it discloses. The revelation that ends Part 1 and sets up what follows is brilliantly handled; we can almost feel Waters smiling at her own cunning, though there is nothing precious or self-regarding about the way she carries it off on the page. This author finesses her readers as expertly as her villains finesse one another."

Most critics praised *Fingersmith* for its effectiveness as a Victorian-era thriller and the homage it paid to its predecessors. Patricia Duncker wrote for the *New Statesman* (March 4, 2002), "Waters unveils enough secrets, reversals and revelations to keep the most demanding fans of Victorian fiction happy and enthralled, bowing to the great novels of Wilkie Collins and Charles Dickens in ways that are both fanciful and intelligent." Also commenting on Waters' influences, Karla Jay for *The Gay & Lesbian Review Worldwide* (May 2002) noted, "With a wink to Dickens, Waters actually owes more to the works of the Brontë sisters and to the female Gothic in general, for the dark houses, ominous male figures, and interior settings." Waters' told Peter Terzian for *Newsday* (March 10, 2002), "I was interested in taking on those great melodramatic novels of the 1860s, those 'novels of sensation' by people like Wilkie Collins and [Joseph] Sheridan LeFanu and Mrs. Broughton, in which there's actually a lot of transgressive stuff going on around women's sexuality. I didn't have to do much to the genre to make it into a lesbian story that hopefully appeals to a modern readership."

Fingersmith also addresses the theme of Victorian-era pornography: Through the character of Maud's uncle, who forces his niece to spend her days cataloguing pornographic literature, Waters reveals the extent to which the genre proliferated in Victorian Britain. Waters explained to Brace, "I'm not trying to celebrate pornography, but I find it endlessly fascinating the way it both confounds our sense of what the Victorians are like and so obviously sits alongside what we know about the exploitation of the period."

Some critics found the overlapping narratives of the book to be somewhat repetitive, and Gilling observed, "It's only in the last 50 pages that Waters's touch lets her down. Herding her characters into a room is a rather contrived way of delivering their comeuppance; it robs a pulsating story of the narrative climax it promised, though the novel's emotional complexity is deepened." Nevertheless, most reviewers overwhelmingly applauded Waters's creation, with a critic for *Kirkus Reviews* (December 15, 2001) opining, "Nobody writing today surpasses the precocious Waters's virtuosic handling of narrative complexity and thickly textured period detail. This is a marvelous novel." Writing for the London *Sunday Times* (February 10, 2002), Joan Smith concluded, "It is a rare pleasure to discover a writer as startlingly assured and original as Waters's third novel proves her to be." In 2002, *Fingersmith* was shortlisted for Great Britain's prestigious Orange Prize for women's fiction.

Waters is currently at work on her fourth novel, a piece of historical fiction set in the years following World War II. Of her decision to move her setting outside the Victorian era, she recently told Peter Terzian, "Something about that clipped '40s style [of speaking] really appeals to me—buttoned-up, but sort of seething. I was surprised at how passionate and bitter a lot of the fiction of the period is—Graham Greene and even George Orwell."

Waters plans to continue expanding the genre of lesbian literature by exploring new themes, including the depiction of long-term lesbian relationships, which are often left out of traditional modern lesbian fiction. In the meantime, her historical approach to fiction helps expand the gay literary canon. "I'm not drawn to writing a novel with a contemporary setting: there are loads of people doing that, with lots of interesting things to say," she told Sarah Van Arsdale, "but so far, I've felt that— on however modest a scale—I have had things to say about history—about lesbian history in particular—about what it consists of, why we are drawn to it, how we might imagine and capture it. The nineteenth century in particular appeals to me because it's a time in which you can clearly see lesbian things going on, and sometimes they take a recognizably modern form . . . and sometimes they seem utterly strange."

Sarah Waters currently resides in London.

—K. D.

SUGGESTED READING: *BookSense.com*; *Gay & Lesbian Review Worldwide* p39+ May 2002; (London) *Independent* p11 May 2, 1999, p10 Jan. 19, 2002; *Lambda Book Report* p6 July–Aug. 2000; *New York Times* (on-line) June 13, 1999, July 23, 2000, Feb. 24, 2002; (London) *Times* Feb. 10, 2002; *Women's Review of Books* p11 Feb. 2000

SELECTED BOOKS: *Tipping the Velvet*, 1999; *Affinity*, 2000; *Fingersmith*, 2002

Weigel, George

Apr. 17, 1951– Theologian; nonfiction writer; biographer; journalist

The author and theologian George Weigel has devoted his career to studying the relationship between the Roman Catholic faith and the modern world. Joining such other influential Catholic neoconservatives as Michael Novak and the Rev. Richard John Neuhaus, Weigel offers traditional Catholic perspectives on foreign policy and political, moral, and religious controversies. Weigel's early books, which include *Peace and Freedom: Christian Faith, Democracy, and The Problem of War* (1983), *Tranquillitas Ordinis: The Present Failure*

John Earle/Courtesy of HarperCollins

George Weigel

and Future Promise of American Catholic Thought on War and Peace (1987), American Interests, American Purpose: Moral Reasoning and U. S. Foreign Policy (1989), and Idealism Without Illusions: U. S. Foreign Policy in the 1990s (1994), explore the disagreement among many Catholics on such difficult policy issues as nuclear disarmament, nuclear deterrence, superpower rivalry, state conflict, human rights, and the morality of war. Weigel analyzes Pope John Paul II's influence on the Catholic Church and the larger world in such works as A Century of Catholic Social Thought: Essays on Rerum Novarum and Nine Other Key Documents (1991), The Final Revolution: The Resistance Church and the Collapse of Communism (1992), A New Worldly Order: John Paul II and Human Freedom (1992), and Soul of the World: Notes on the Future of Public Catholicism (1996). In 1999 Weigel published what many critics consider his best book to date, Witness to Hope: The Biography of John Paul II. Although many books and articles about the pontiff have been published throughout his reign, Weigel enjoyed unprecedented personal contact with the pope, his friends, and many Vatican officials. With the pope's approval, the Vatican allowed Weigel to see personal papers, correspondence, and other documents. The result was a massive biography that detailed Pope John Paul II's life, thoughts, achievements, and setbacks, as well as his influence on the modern world and the pivotal role he played in the downfall of communism in Europe. Weigel's most recent books are The Truth of Catholicism: Ten Controversies Explored (2001) and The Courage to be Catholic: Crisis, Reform, and the Future of the Church (2002), which addressed the sexual abuse scandals that rocked the Catholic Church in the United States in 2002.

George Weigel submitted his official biography to World Authors 1995–2000: "George Weigel, a Senior Fellow of the Ethics and Public Policy Center, is a Roman Catholic theologian and one of America's leading commentators on issues of religion and public life.

"A native of Baltimore, he was educated at St. Mary's Seminary College in his native city, and at the University of St. Michael's College in Toronto. In 1975 Weigel moved to Seattle where he was Assistant Professor of Theology and Assistant (later Acting) Dean of Studies at the St. Thomas Seminary School of Theology in Kenmore. In 1977 Weigel became Scholar-in-Residence at the World Without War Council of Greater Seattle, a position he held until 1984. In 1984–85 Weigel was a fellow of the Woodrow Wilson International Center for Scholars in Washington, D.C. There, he wrote Tranquillitas Ordinis: The Present Failure and Future Promise of American Catholic Thought on War and Peace (Oxford University Press, 1987).

"Weigel is the author or editor of fourteen other books, including Catholicism and the Renewal of American Democracy (Paulist, 1989), The Final Revolution: The Resistance Church and the Collapse of Communism (Oxford, 1992), and Soul of the World: Notes on the Future of Public Catholicism (Eerdmans, 1994), The Truth of Catholicism: Ten Controversies Explored (HarperCollins, 2001), and The Courage to be Catholic: Crisis, Reform, and the Future of the Church (Basic Books, 2002). In addition to his books, Weigel has contributed essays, op-ed columns, and reviews to the major opinion journals and newspapers in the United States, and has appeared on numerous network television, cable television, and radio discussion programs. His weekly column, The Catholic Difference, is syndicated to several dozen newspapers around the United States. Both his scholarly work and his journalism have been translated into a variety of western languages.

"From 1986 until 1989, Weigel served as founding president of the James Madison Foundation. From 1989 through June 1996, Weigel was president of the Ethics and Public Policy Center, where he led a wide-ranging, ecumenical and interreligious program of research and publication on foreign and domestic policy issues. From June 1996, in his present role as a Senior Fellow of the Center, Weigel prepared a major study of the life, thought, and action of Pope John Paul II. Witness to Hope: The Biography of Pope John Paul II was published to international acclaim in the Fall of 1999, in English, French, Italian, and Spanish editions. Polish and Portuguese editions were published in the first half of 2000 and Czech, Slovak, Slovenian, Romanian, Ukrainian, and Russian editions are being prepared. Mr. Weigel is currently working on a documentary film based on the book.

"Weigel, who has been awarded four honorary doctorates and the papal cross, Pro Ecclesia et Pontifice, serves on the boards of directors of several organizations dedicated to human rights and the cause of religious freedom. He is also a member of the editorial boards of *First Things* and *Orbis*.

"George Weigel and his wife, Joan, live in North Bethesda, Maryland with their three children."

George Weigel was born on April 17, 1951. His father, George, worked as an insurance executive, and his mother, Betsy, was a homemaker. Weigel briefly considered the priesthood, graduating magna cum laude from St. Mary's Seminary and University, in Baltimore, in 1973. He received his master's degree from St. Michael's College, in Toronto, in 1975, graduating summa cum laude.

In his first book, *The Peace Bishops and the Arms Race: Can Religious Leadership Help in Preventing War* (1982), Weigel critiqued the public statements issued in 1981 by four American Catholic archbishops, Raymond G. Hunthausen of Seattle, Washington; John R. Quinn of San Francisco; Walter Sullivan of Richmond, Virginia; and Michael H. Kenny of Juneau, Alaska, condemning war and nuclear weapons as immoral. At the time, Ronald Reagan had been elected president, and his opposition to nuclear disarmament and his speeches attacking the Soviet Union alarmed many Americans who feared a nuclear war between the superpowers. Weigel argued that the four bishops had ignored traditional Roman Catholic teachings on just wars and had championed the same mistakes of disarmament and appeasement that were made by European governments during the 1930s that, although well intentioned, failed to stop Nazi aggression. "Our desperate need, as a Church and a country, is for a third voice," Weigel wrote in the book's conclusion, "a voice that faces our responsibilities; that does not weaken this political community; that gathers it for the job of changing our adversaries; and that in doing so points a way out of the twin dead-ends of accommodation and Armageddon."

In his book, *Tranquillitas Ordinis: The Present Failure and Future Promise of American Catholic Thought on War and Peace* (1987), Weigel faults many American Catholics for abandoning traditional Catholic perspectives on war and peace and adopting pacifist stances. He traces the change back to the conclusion of the Second Vatican Council (1962–1965) and growing opposition to the Vietnam War. Such pacifism, he argued, abetted the Soviet Union's agenda and communist expansion in Central America. In order to pursue a foreign-policy agenda that facilitated both peace and freedom, Weigel called for American Catholics to reclaim the tradition of a "tranquillitas ordinis," a Latin phrase used by St. Augustine to define the just peace of a properly ordered political community. "Mr. Weigel's argument rests on two theses—the Catholic tradition includes a theology of peace (tranquillitas ordinis), and from the early 19th century until Vatican II the American Catholic hierarchy supported and indeed developed this classic heritage of thought," Jay P. Dolan wrote in the *New York Times Book Review* (April 26, 1987). "The first thesis is doubtful and the second is simply not true." Dolan asserted that "Catholics never developed a theology of peace beyond the pacifist tradition, a tradition that Mr. Weigel never seriously considers" and that Weigel "fashions a theory of peace that has little if any relationship to the meaning of the traditional just-war theory." Dolan concluded that Weigel's theory of peace, which makes room for "the long-term goal of nuclear disarmament and support for deterrence in the interim, a strategic defense system, a strong anti-Communist stance, intervention by force if necessary in Nicaragua" reads more like a conservative political agenda than like Catholic teachings. In his review for the *Wall Street Journal* (August 10, 1987), William McGurn praised the book, writing, "Echoing [the Jesuit theologian] Karl Rahner's grumble that moral principles do not deliver policy prescriptions like 'freshly baked breakfast rolls,' Mr. Weigel argues that they do something far more fundamental: They provide a framework for intelligent discussion between fallible men and women grappling as best they can with greater goods and lesser evils. The author's achievement is that he manages to reconstruct this promising framework from its present tatters."

In 1989 Weigel published two books, *American Interests, American Purpose: Moral Reasoning and U. S. Foreign Policy* and *Catholicism and the Renewal of American Democracy*. Reviewing the first book for *Perspectives on Political Science* (Winter 1990), Hal Nieburg hailed it as "a terse and robust contribution to the debate over moral reasoning and foreign policy. It provides a useful resource for the ongoing discussion of public policy, keeping in full view the often obscured, but always ineluctable moral dimension." In his review for *Commonweal* (May 19, 1989), Dennis P. McCann had mixed feelings about the second book. While praising the author's discussion of abortion and "his occasionally brilliant applications of his framework to a variety of social issues," McCann observed that Weigel's "descriptions of the current predicament of American Catholicism are often so outrageously distorted and viscerally provocative as to make it almost impossible to keep one's mind firmly fixed upon the contribution he seems capable of making."

In 1991 Weigel and James Turner Johnson wrote essays for and co-edited *Just War and the Gulf War*. In his essay, Johnson argues that Gulf War, the 1991 effort by the United States and other nations to liberate Kuwait from Iraqi occupation by military force, met the conditions of Catholic just-war theory, which states that a nation can wage war only as a last resort, for the right intention, by competent authority and must abstain from deliberately harming innocent civilians. Weigel's article criticizes some leaders from the Protestant and Catholic Churches for failing to use just-war criteria to judge the morality of the conflict. The book also features the text of several speeches by religious leaders who opposed the war. In his review for *America* (April 24, 1993), Stephen J. Pope observed that "At times Weigel's critical observations have a point, as exemplified in his skepticism about certain pacifists who explicitly draw a 'moral equivalence' between Saddam Hussein and the coalition forces." However, the reviewer criticized Weigel's "consistently tendentious and highly polemical mode of argumentation. The desire to understand seems to have been eclipsed by the desire to comfort one's allies and ridicule one's opponents."

In 1991 Weigel and the Rev. John P. Langan, S.J. co-edited *The American Search for Peace: Moral Reasoning, Religious Hope, and National Security*, a collection of essays delivered at a seminar in 1987–1988, co-sponsored by the James Madison Foundation and the Woodstock Theological Center. "This is a scholarly analysis of the just-war tradition, national security, pacifism, intervention, and more from some of the heavy hitters in political ethical philosophy," James W. Gustafson wrote in *Ethics* (April 1993). "Well reasoned, cogent, often compelling, the essays reflect the complexity of ethical reasoning and range from Machiavelli to the Catholic bishops, to the National Association of Evangelicals, synthesizing secular and religious, ancient and recent, theoretical and practical."

In *The Final Revolution: The Resistance Church and the Collapse of Communism* (1992), Weigel writes that the Christian churches played a key role in the demise of communism in Eastern Europe in 1989. He credited Pope John Paul II's support for the Solidarity movement, headed by Lech Walesa, in his native Poland, for giving millions of people hope and the courage to resist communism. In turn, this set the stage for the first free elections in Poland in 1989. According to Weigel, the Polish people's election of Solidarity candidates to the parliament created a domino effect that toppled many of the other Communist governments in Eastern Europe the same year. In his review for *Commonweal* (April 9, 1993), Michael Lavelle noted that "Weigel's book, well-written and well argued, presents an accurate and moving picture of the church behind the Iron Curtain from 1948–89."

In 1994 Weigel explored the role of the United States in the post–Cold War world in his book, *Idealism Without Illusions: U. S. Foreign Policy in the 1990s*. Drawing from the policies that led to victory during the Cold War, Weigel argues that the United States must remain active in world affairs, by taking the lead against terrorism, ethnic cleansing, and "rogue" states such as Iraq and by supporting arms control, human rights, and democracy. He theorizes that inaction or renewed isolationism would have serious consequences for the United States and the rest of the world in the future. "Weigel's eminently readable book jogs our memory, our conscience, and our courage to act in uncertain circumstances," Sven F. Kraemer observed in *First Things* (January 1995, on-line). "It breaks through the idealist/realist impasse in its idealistic insistence on the moral foundations of policy and in its determination accurately to reflect reality. Weigel rediscovers historical truths, avoids the temptations of messianism and cynicism, and critically surveys global developments and foreign policy options as America redefines her national purpose abroad."

In 1992 Weigel and the Rev. Richard John Neuhaus co-edited the book, *Being Christian Today: An American Conversation*, a collection of papers on Christian social thought that were delivered at a neoconservative conference, in 1991. In his review for the *Catholic World* (March 1995), Lawrence S. Cunningham was impressed by several of the papers in the book, including Mark Noll's discussion of Evangelical Christian social ethics, an exploration of natural law within the framework of the Protestant Reformation by Carl Braaten, and an essay by Jean Elshtain that calls for shifting the discussion of abortion away from "individual rights to the arena of the commonweal." The reviewer, however, faulted the editors for failing to include Christian writers with different opinions and perspectives. Cunningham concluded that although the "essays are studded with valuable insights," the contributors to the book are simply "preaching to the choir."

In 1993 Weigel and Robert Royal co-edited a collection of essays for the book, *Building the Free Society: Democracy, Capitalism, and Catholic Social Teaching*. Such contributors as William Murphy, Thomas C. Kohler, and James Finn discussed various papal documents, including Pope Leo XIII's encyclical on labor, *Rerum Novarum* (1891), and Pope John Paul II's encyclical on the free market, *Centesimus Annus* (1991), which form the foundation of modern-day Catholic social thought. "This work is recommended for anyone interested in Catholic social teaching," Richard C. Bayer wrote in the *Journal of Church and State* (Winter 1995). "It is recommended not only because the essays are interesting and well written, but also because they present an important and underrepresented viewpoint in contemporary interpretations of Catholic social teaching."

In 1996 Weigel published a collection of his articles and lectures in *Soul of the World: Notes on the Future of Public Catholicism*. The author discusses Pope John Paul II's influence on Catholic social teaching and the relationship between the Catholic Church and democratic society. According to Weigel, the pope embraces religious pluralism, which benefits both the Church and the State. The Catholic Church cautions against totalitarianism by constantly reminding people that the world was divinely created and that the State is not God. In his review for the *Journal of Church and State* (Summer 1997), R. Bruce Douglass asserted that the book was "gracefully written, and develops a complex argument in such a way that it is easily accessible." However, Douglass objected to the book's polemical style, concluding that Weigel's "failure to even admit the existence of principled reasons why so many well-informed people cling to the beliefs and practices he dislikes makes it impossible for me to take what he has to say seriously as anything more than a sermon for the faithful." In the *Review of Politics* (Spring 1997), R. Scott Appelby wrote that "*Soul of the World* is a clear, engaging, and closely reasoned argument about the significance of 'public Catholicism'; it presents a single, if not singular, point of view without pretending to provide an inclusive, detailed account of various positions on the question at hand." Appelby observed that "despite a few obligatory swipes at old foes (radical feminists, 'tenured radicals' of the academy, and liberation theologians), a kinder, gentler George Weigel is on display, to good effect, in these pages."

In 1999 Weigel received substantial acclaim for his book, *Witness to Hope: The Biography of Pope John Paul II*. During a trip to Rome, in 1995, Weigel discussed writing a biography of the pontiff with Dr. Joaquin Navarro-Valls, the official Vatican press director. In December 1995 Weigel had dinner with the pope, who encouraged him to go forward with the project. In an interview with Sally McDonald, the religion reporter for the *Seattle Times* (November 8, 1999), Weigel quoted John Paul II as saying that many biographers had tried "to understand me from the outside. But I can only be understood from the inside." The pope agreed to Weigel's conditions that the author have unlimited access to him, his top advisors and friends, and classified documents, as well as complete editorial independence. "I told him I needed to do this without any supervision, any oversight, anybody exercising any form of editorial review or control," Weigel recalled to Paul Waters for the Montreal *Gazette* (December 4, 1999). "To which he said: 'Of course. That's the way it has to be, and that's the way it should be.'" Weigel interviewed John Paul II 10 times and spoke to many top officials at the Vatican. He also spoke to the pope's old friends, such as Jerzy Kluger, a boyhood friend in Poland, and saw the pope's private letters to such world leaders as Leonid Brezhnev and Mikhail Gorbachev of the Soviet Union, and Deng Xiaoping of China. After completing his research, which totaled 2,000 pages of transcribed interviews and nearly 10,000 pages of documents, Weigel went to a small Catholic parish outside of Charleston, South Carolina, to write the book. In an interview with Waters, Weigel said that he brought "16 linear feet of files and two magnums of Kentucky's finest product" with him to the parish.

In an interview with Cathy Lynn Grossman for *USA Today* (April 12, 2001), Weigel described Pope John Paul II as "a singular figure of our times because not only has he lived through so much of the horror of the 20th century, but he came out on the far side not a cynic but a man who believes the 21st century can be a springtime of the human soul." The man who became Pope John Paul II, in 1978, had been born Karol Wojtyla in Wadowice, a small Polish town, in 1920. During the Nazi occupation of Poland in World War II, when three million Polish Jews and three million Polish Catholics were killed, Weigel reports that Wojtyla studied for the priesthood in an underground seminary. Wojtyla became the Archbishop of Krakow, in 1964, and was elevated to cardinal by Pope Paul VI in 1967. In a surprise move, the College of Cardinals elected Wojtyla to the papacy in 1978, making him the Catholic Church's first non- Italian pope in 455 years. Unlike his predecessors, John Paul II traveled extensively, bringing his message to many nations. The pope frequently condemned totalitarianism and championed freedom and human rights. His first visit as pope to his homeland in 1979 inspired millions of Poles and provided a strong moral challenge to the authority of the Communist government. Weigel uncovered a letter in the Vatican archives written in French that the pope sent to Soviet President Leonid Brezhnev in 1980. The pontiff warned Brezhnev against invading Poland, which had declared martial-law to suppress the Solidarity movement, writing that such an action would be comparable to Germany's invasion of the country in 1939. John Paul II survived two assassination attempts in 1981 and 1982; the first one seriously wounding him. As pope, he encountered opposition from a significant number of Catholics by reaffirming the Church's teachings against contraception, divorce, abortion, and homosexuality, and keeping the ban on married and female priests. Weigel rejects branding the pope and his message with contemporary political labels such as "liberal" or "conservative." In an interview with Michael Rust for *Insight on the News* (November 15, 1999, on-line), Weigel said that in the book he argues that "John Paul can only be understood as a Christian radical, a profoundly convinced Christian disciple whose thoughts, decisions and actions all reflect his intense faith and his conviction that faith is not one option in a supermarket of spiritualities but the great truth of the world and of history." Weigel concluded that Pope John Paul II, the longest reigning pontiff of the 20th century, shaped nearly every aspect of the Catholic Church by naming over 100 cardinals and issuing many encyclicals, addresses, and statements on a whole range of topics. Many reviewers praised *Witness to Hope* as a remarkable achievement and asserted that it was superior to several of the other biographies of the pope. "As it stands, this book is a major contribution, invaluable for putting John Paul II's achievements into proper perspective," Avery Cardinal Dulles, S.J. asserted in *First Things* (November 1999). "Not content with vague generalities, Weigel spares no pains to furnish exact personal names, dates, places, and figures. His interest never seems to flag, whether he is writing about theological debates, political events, literature, or even medical data. He has been tireless in gathering information about the Philippines, Central America, Poland, France, Germany, and practically every corner of the globe." Dulles concluded that Weigel "has written a memorable biography of an extraordinary leader." In his review for *Commentary* (December 1999), Paul Johnson also lauded the book, writing, "In the providential destruction of the evil empire of Communism—with his native Poland being the first, pivotal stone to fall—John Paul played a leading role. George Weigel examines that role minutely in this huge authoritative tome, revealing much that is new about the history of Eastern Europe in our time." Johnson was impressed by Weigel's detailed account of how the pope improved relations with the Jews by condemning anti-Semitism as a sin and establishing diplomatic relations between the Holy See and Israel, in 1993.

Weigel's next book, *The Truth of Catholicism: Ten Controversies Explored*, appeared in 2001. In it he author discussed such topics as Jesus Christ, the meaning of freedom, the use and misuse of sex, the role of women in the Catholic Church, democracy, and the relationship of the Church with other faiths. "The chapters are short, the pace swift, and the territory covered daunting," Paul Baumann wrote in his review for the *Chicago Tribune* (November 18, 2001). "Weigel is quite good on democracy, Judaism, the church's dogmatic claims and missionary imperatives, less convincing on the redemptive meaning of suffering, and fairly tendentious about a host of other things."

In 2002 Weigel adapted ideas he had developed in his syndicated columns into the book *The Courage to be Catholic: Crisis, Reform, and the Future of the Church*. In the volume Weigel addressed the problem of sexual abuse by priests, which made national headlines early in the year. Citing church documents that were previously sealed, the *Boston Globe* published numerous stories revealing that the Archdiocese of Boston had covered up the abuse of children by several priests for decades. The archdiocese shuffled abusive priests to different parishes and quietly settled lawsuits with victims on the condition of anonymity. The revelations outraged many people, including Catholics who demanded accountability from their bishops for the scandal. In December 2002, Bernard Cardinal Law, the archbishop of Boston, who was accused of covering up for many abusive priests, resigned. Throughout the year, allegations of abuse also surfaced in many other dioceses, sparking calls from both conservative and liberal Catholics for reform. Weigel blamed many of the nation's Catholic bishops for the scandal; according to the author, these bishops refused to address ongoing problems in their dioceses, including sexual abuse and dissent from the Church's teachings on sexual morality. In his review for the *Wall Street Journal* (December 3, 2002), George Sim Johnston praised *The Courage to be Catholic* as a "clearheaded and elegant guide to the scandals," adding that it "is finally a hopeful and constructive book. Mr. Weigel knows his church history, and for two millennia there has been a pattern of decay, crisis, and renewal."

Since 2001, George Weigel, in his published articles, speeches, and interviews with the media, has frequently offered his thoughts on the application of the Church's "just war theory" in regard to the war against terrorism in Afghanistan and the possibility of conflict with Iraq and North Korea.
—*D. C.*

SUGGESTED READING: *America* p26 Apr. 24, 1993; *Catholic Historical Review* p635+ July 1994; *Catholic World* p88 Mar. 1995; *Chicago Tribune* Books p3 Nov. 18, 2001; *Commentary* p69+ Dec. 1999; *Commonweal* p312+ May 19, 1989, p39 Apr. 9, 1993; *Ethics* p626 Apr. 1993; *First Things* p64+ Jan. 1995, p49+ Nov. 1999; Montreal *Gazette* J p4+ Dec. 4, 1999, with photos; *Insight on the News* (on-line) Nov. 15, 1999; *Journal of Church and State* p164+ Winter 1995, p581+ Summer 1997; *New York Times Book Review* p30 Apr. 26, 1987; *Perspectives on Political Science* p4+ Winter 1990; *Review of Politics* p377+ Spring 1997; *Seattle Times* C p1+ Nov. 8, 1999; *USA Today* D p6 Apr. 12, 2001, with photo; *Wall Street Journal* (on-line) Aug. 10. 1987; D p4 Dec. 3, 2002

SELECTED BOOKS: *The Peace Bishops and the Arms Race: Can Religious leadership Help in Preventing War?*, 1982; *Peace and Freedom: Christian Faith, Democracy, and the Problem of War*, 1983; *Washington's Window on the World: A Guide to World Affairs Organizations and Institutions in Washington State*, 1983; *Tranquillitas Ordinis: The Present Failure and Future Promise of American Catholic Thought on War and Peace*, 1987; *American Interests, American Purpose: Moral Reasoning and U.S. Foreign Policy*, 1989; *Catholicism and the Renewal of American Democracy*, 1989; *Freedom and Its Discontents: Catholicism Confronts Modernity*, 1991; *The Final Revolution: The Resistance Church and the Collapse of Communism*, 1992; *Idealism Without Illusions*, 1994; *Soul on the World: Notes on the Future of Public Catholicism*, 1996; *Witness to Hope: The Biography of Pope John Paul II*, 1999; *Truth of Catholicism: Ten Controversies Explored*, 2001; *The Courage to be Catholic: Crisis, Reform, and the Future of the Church*, 2002; as editor—*American Search for Peace: Moral Reasoning, Religious Hope, and National Security* (with John P. Langan), 1991 ; *A Century of Catholic Social Thought: Essays on Rerum Novarum and Nine Other Key Documents* (with Robert Royal), 1991; *Just War and the Gulf War* (with James Turner Johnson), 1991; *Being Christian Today: An American Conversation* (with Richard John Neuhaus), 1992; *New Worldly Order: John Paul II and Human Freedom*, 1992; *Building the Free Society: Democracy, Capitalism, and Catholic Social Teaching* (with Robert Royal), 1993

Courtesy of Mac Wellman

Wellman, Mac

Mar. 7, 1945– Playwright; poet; novelist

Mac Wellman, the American playwright, poet, and novelist, has been described as a "linguistic exorcist," and his eccentric dialogue and manic wordplay have raised comparisons to James Joyce and Lewis Carroll. In the *New York Times* (January, 12, 1990), as quoted in *Contemporary Literary Criticism* (Vol. 65), Mel Gussow described Wellman's play, *Terminal Hip* (1990), as "a crazy quilt of slang and circumlocutions, double negatives and oxymorons," a statement that might describe much of Wellman's work. Other critics have placed Wellman in the company of the Language Poets, writers such as Gertrude Stein, Louis Zukofsky, Clark Coolidge, and John Ashbery who experiment with language's shapes and sounds. While some critics have found Wellman's writing too insular and his focus on language irrelevant to the larger world, in an article for *Theater* (Summer–Fall, 1990), as quoted in *Contemporary Literary Criticism* (Vol. 65), the playwright Eric Overmyer argued that Wellman's plays "are political in every line. Because at bedrock they are about language, and because of their formal strategies, they are simultaneous, multifaceted critiques of American politics, culture, jargon (and the modern degradation of language in the political, economic, and cultural realms), and American theater itself."

Wellman is a prominent figure in New York City's avant-garde theater community. In 1990 he received an Obie Award for three plays he published that year: *Terminal Hip*, a monologue subtitled "A Spiritual History of America Through the Medium of Bad Language"; *Bad Penny*, a work created and performed in New York City's Central Park that required actors to shout lines across a lake; and *Crowbar*, another site-specific piece, performed in Broadway's New Victory Theater, which dramatized the history of the century-old building. Wellman was awarded a second Obie, in 1991, for *Sincerity Forever*, a play that filters contemporary American society through the lens of two teenage girls in the Deep South. In 1997 he received a Lila Wallace-Reader's Digest Writer's Award. His plays have been published in four collections: *Bad Infinity: Eight Plays* (1994); *The Land Beyond the Forest: Dracula and Swoop* (1995); *Two Plays: A Murder of Crows and The Hyacinth Macaw* (1994); and *Cellophane: Plays* (2001). He has also published two novels, *Annie Salem: An American Tale* (1996) and *The Fortuneteller; A Jest* (1991), and four collections of poetry.

Mac Wellman, born John McDowell Wellman, submits the following autobiographical statement to *World Authors 1995–2000*: "I was born in Cleveland, Ohio, in 1945, a great year for red wines and human freedom. My family had been in the foundry business for several generations, and even today one of my dearest possessions is the leather bound book of my great- grandfather's numerous patents, beautiful drawings of heavy industrial machinery of all sorts. There were many inventors in the family and S. T. Wellman was only the most gifted. In many ways I think of myself as a rigorous and methodical inventor as a writer, even though in many ways my work is neither very methodical or machine-like. A parallel theme in the family has been the lure of the arts; my grandmother was a gifted composer who left among other works an opera on the subject of Noah & the Flood, and a song I remember loving (called Charley-Horse); one of my aunts spent time in Paris as a painter before returning to Cleveland to work as industrial editor for the Cleveland *Press*.

"I came of age in the difficult transition time between the Fifties and Sixties, and have vivid memories of Washington D.C. just before the Kennedy Assassination, at that time still almost a sleepy southern military town. I studied international relations at a diplomatic school there, the School of International Service at American University and was determined to enter the foreign service, or find a job in the general field of foreign affairs. A junior year abroad to the University of Bristol in England gave me the opportunity to hitch-hike my way all over Europe, and in the process I made the acquaintance of the Dutch Theater director, Anne Marie Prins, who hooked me on experimental, a thing I had not imagined could exist given my previous experience with theater in the states. At the time I was writing mainly poetry (which I still do), and initially at least had no idea how to proceed as a writer of plays.

"Progress was slow, and I spent ten years at least exploring what turned out to be mostly blind alleys. And reading, reading, reading. I don't think I wrote a poem I could stand till I was thirty, and I was in my mid thirties before I wrote a play,

Harm's Way, that I can stand to look at now. It was till I was past forty that I had a production of a play, (Anne Bogart's direction of *Cleveland* at BACA Downtown in Brooklyn in 1986) that I had a really good physical production of a theatre piece.

"I think because of my unusual introduction to theater, I have always been an outsider in this country, which is probably all for the best. My best work is about the slippage between propositions, the way people talk about their lives, and the actual physical realities themselves. Sentimental melodrama, that is most mainstream theater, tries to reconcile these, and heal the rift between; I do just the opposite. As I write, I have just finished the proofs for a second major collection of my plays, entitled *Cellophane*; it is striking to me how consistent this theme is, although the plays are ostensibly quite different: *Cellophane* is a pure language piece, a kind of homage to the general looniness of the American language as she has been spoken in what Greil Marcus has aptly called, 'The old, weird America'; *Cleveland* is a sprained sci-fi soap opera; *Hypatia*, a dense Steinian extrapolation based on real historical sources. A lot of what I write is what Eric McLuhan (Marshall's son) has called Mennippian satire—the kind of work designed to give the audience pause to think about his or her own assumptions. I am obsessed by the tendentious facticity of the print and television media, and am always trying to find my own slant to counter what I regard as the perniciousness of the corporate picture of the world, whether considered in specific instances, or in general.

"My work tends to be produced at very small theaters, because the big ones do exactly what the better class of cultural mandarins dictate. I spend a great deal of time and energy devoted to encouraging and helping, in whatever ways, the most talented of my younger colleagues on the art. I like teaching, and have learned a great deal from my students. My best plays to date are *The Lesser Magoo*, which was premiered in Los Angeles to very mixed notices, and received very little attention here in New York; and a new version of *Antigone*, which I have written for a dance theater company. I still write poetry and have a couple of books of prose on the shelf; but my life in the theater is simply too engrossing for me to have much time to get these around."

Responses to Wellman's work have been mixed. His references are often obscure, his characters speak in unusual ways, and his plots are at times barely discernable. It is just these attributes, however, that some critics celebrate, finding that Wellman's work offers a bold alternative to the social and psychological realism found in much contemporary American theater. According to Kirk Wood Bromley, in an article for *Theater Mania.com* (May 11, 2000), Wellman's business card reads "Mac Wellman/Damnable Scribbler," a handle Bromley found appropriate: "Perverse, elusive, and frantically neologic, Wellman's texts are damnable because daring, scribble because sincere, and good because inventive." Bromley quoted Wellman's *Hypatia or The Divine Algebra* (2000) to demonstrate his unconventional style:

Narrator #2:
A machine is revealed
Cries of
Hypatia:
Why why why why why.
Narrator #2:
No one has heard her
Cry
An infinite decimal an
Hypatia:
0

Hypatia is based on the story of a pagan philosopher and mathematician who was murdered by Christian monks in the fifth century. In Wellman's play, Hypatia travels through time delivering gifts: the zero to the eighth-century inventor of algebra, the first machine to the Emperor of Byzantium. But, as with many of Wellman's plays, this plot is not the focal point. In his review for the *New York Times* (May 22, 2000), Bruce Weber noted that "Mr. Wellman has never been a linear storyteller, and his interest in language has always had as much to do with exploiting the properties of its fundamental units—letters, syllables, words—as it has with using them to express meaning in its conventional sense. It's the kind of writing that, when it works, creates an enigmatic music of its own, the soundtrack for a theatrical tableau." Weber, however, was critical of the apparent obfuscation in Wellman's writing: "One hesitates to dismiss what one has tried and failed to apprehend. But though there is obviously a theatrical code at work here—the word cipher is bandied about like a shuttlecock—its adamant opacity comes across as smug. You don't feel beguiled by its presumed complexity; you feel taunted by it."

"It's not that I'm trying to make my stuff willfully obscure," Wellman told a *Los Angeles Times* interviewer, in 1997, as quoted by Richard Dodds in *BroadwayOnline.com* (October 11, 2000). "The world most of the time seems a very strange and complicated place to me, and I want to make plays that in some sense are as complicated and as strange as the world we live in." Wellman described to Bromley how his unique style developed: "I was very frustrated just with writing, so I got a legal pad and I decided to write one page of bad writing every day, and I did for two and a half years . . . ungrammatical, vague, disordered, everything. . . . I thought I'd explore the downside . . . and what I found in doing this is that there were all these interesting rhythms . . . very expressive, very speakable . . . full of ideas, and I found actually that this mysterious kind of narrative would emerge from it. It was not disordered at all. In fact, it was quite the opposite."

In his review of *Crowbar* for the *New Republic* (March 26, 1990), Robert Brustein expressed admiration for Wellman's linguistic virtuosity, but concluded "In view of all that's happening in the world these days . . . *Crowbar* seems peculiarly theater-enclosed. For all its technical ambitiousness, it's another melancholy sign of how little American art seems to matter in the universe at large." Others, however, describe Wellman's work as inherently political. Eric Overmyer argued: "Wellman's plays are not direct, they are oblique. Ironic. They have multiple, even contradictory meanings. They are dense texts. Their narratives are rebukes to more ordinary ways of thinking about and writing for the theater. . . . Wellman's subject is often simply language itself, its 'thingness,' its palpable existence, its matter, its uses and perversions. Therefore, by extension, his subject is also, inevitably, American culture and politics."

Two of Wellman's most overtly political plays are *Sincerity Forever* (1990), about art, politics, and the corruption of American values, and *7 BlowJobs* (1991), a satire set in the Washington, D.C. office of a fictitious Senator Bob, who is baffled by the arrival to his office of a package containing seven sexually explicit photographs. Wellman dedicated both plays to the conservative Republican senator, Jesse Helms, and to other political figures who, in the early 1990s, worked to scale back government support for the National Endowment for the Arts (NEA) in the wake of controversies over art and public funding.

Most of Wellman's plays are not so firmly grounded in real-world events. His dramatic universe is peopled by aliens, vampires, girl Huns, mystic fur-balls, and remarkably prescient teenage girls. In *FNU LNU* (1996), pronounced "fuh-NOO luh-NOO" and standing for the common designation in morgues of unidentified corpses as "First Name Unknown, Last Name Unknown," Wellman introduces Deezo, a man who may or may not be dead, guided by a trio of seductive women who periodically break into nonsense songs: "Why the Y in Ybor? Why the B in Bbor?" The play is set in Ybor City, which is now a part of Tampa, Florida, but at the turn of the last century was known as the "Cigar Capital of the World" because of the many Cubans, Sicilians, and other new immigrants who hand-rolled cigars in the many cigars factories there. Ybor City became a center for cultural intermingling and political activism; Cuban independence leader José Martí delivered a speech there and, nearly 100 years later, Fidel Castro paid a visit. (In Wellman's vision, the city is haunted by Castro's levitating beard.) "It's the kind of place," noted Peter Marks in the *New York Times* (October 17, 1996), in his review of a SoHo Repertory Theater production, "where history and legend mingle easily and where a playwright invigorated by myth and mystery might find inspiration." Marks, who noted that *FNU LNU*'s haunting, child-like songs echoed in his mind days later, concluded that Wellman's play is "seriously weird and weirdly addicting."

In such plays as *A Murder of Crows* (1994) and *Hyacinth Macaw* (1994), Wellman explores the moral and social terrain of Middle America. In the latter play, set in the small midwestern town of Gradual, a family slowly falls apart, an event precipitated by the arrival of a stranger, William Hard, who brings a letter full of secrets. Hard replaces the father, the mother is taken away, and the teenage daughter, Susannah, is left alone to make sense of what has happened. Susannah reappears in *The Lesser Magoo* (1997) as a power-hungry corporate woman who has left her youthful questioning far behind. In his review of a 78th Street Theatre Lab production in the *Village Voice* (April 28– May 4, 1999), Charles McNulty noted that the play constantly shifts genres—starting as an office drama, becoming a political monologue, and lapsing into an old-fashioned musical, featuring the classic song "Paper Moon," from the musical *The Great Magoo* (1932). *The Lesser Magoo*, McNulty wrote, continues Wellman's "exploration of the way in which contemporary society subverts not only our children but the very possibility of innocence. . . . Wellman's description of the rabid greed and self-interest that are transforming contemporary society into a shameful creature may seem bleak. But somehow the capacity for deep feeling in his play survives—even if, in the case of Susannah, it's merely a case of forlorn hope."

Wellman's plays have primarily been produced in smaller, New York–based theaters, although there have been productions in other cities as well. In 1997 he was honored with "The Mac Wellman Festival," a six-month tribute to his work. The festival showcased more than 20 of his plays, with productions staged in four cities, including New York. Stephen Nunns, in a profile of Wellman for the *Village Voice* (February 3, 1998), noted: "Wellman has attracted a whole new generation of directors, playwrights, actors, and theatergoers. Indeed, a number of younger playwrights—Ruth Margaff and Eric Ehn, for example—look on him as a kind of mentor." Nunns quoted the festival's director, Tim Farrell, as saying: "Young Downtown experimental theater artists who are working on readings of Mac's plays for the festival are suddenly realizing that they've been influenced by him."

Wellman has published four collections of poems, *Satires* (1985), *A Shelf in Woop's Clothing* (1990), *In Praise of Secrecy* (1997), and *Miniature* (2002), and two novels. In her *New York Times Book Review* (May 12, 1996) assessment of Wellman's second novel, *Annie Salem: An American Tale* (1996), which is posted on the Sun & Moon Press Web site, Susan Osborn noted that, "While much of his verbal playfulness seems, at first, just plain silly (in part because the author not only sustains it but shamelessly builds on it), the plot rises into true hilarity in the final pages." In an unsigned appraisal for *Kirkus Reviews*, also as posted on the Sun & Moon Press Web site, a reviewer concluded: "Part trenchant social commentary, part love story, part inscrutable sci-fi yarn, the novel reads a little like *Goodbye, Columbus* as rewritten by Kurt Vonnegut and Sherwood Anderson. . . . A wacky blend of fantasy, whimsy, and satire from an author who clearly knows what he's doing, even if almost no one else will."

Wellman has received fellowships from many institutions, including the NEA, the New York Foundation for the Arts, and the Guggenheim Foundation. In addition to his two Obie Awards, he has received an Outer Circle Critics Award, in 1990; an American Theater Critics Association Award, in 1992; and has been invited to be a resident artist at the MacDowell Colony and the American Conservatory Theatre, in San Franscisco, California. He is a founding member of the Bat Theater Company, based in New York City.

Mac Wellman resides in the New York City borough of Brooklyn. He is the Donald I. Fine Professor of Playwriting at Brooklyn College. —A. I. C.

SUGGESTED READING: *New Republic* p28+ Mar. 26, 1990; *New York Times* C p12 Jan. 21, 1997, E p3 Oct. 17, 1997, B p16 Feb. 6, 1999, E p3 May 22, 2000, E p35 Dec. 29, 2000; *Village Voice* p43+ Feb. 3, 1998; *Contemporary Literary Criticism*, Vol. 65

SELECTED BOOKS: play collections—*Bad Infinity: Eight Plays*, 1994;*Two Plays: A Murder of Crows and The Hyacinth Macaw*, 1994; *The Land Beyond the Forest: Dracula and Swoop*, 1995; *Cellophane: Plays*, 2001; novels—*Annie Salem: An American Tale*, 1996; poetry—*Satires*, 1985, *A Shelf in Woop's Clothing*, 1990; *In Praise of Secrecy*, 1997; *Miniature*, 2002

Wheatcroft, Geoffrey

Dec. 23, 1945– Nonfiction writer; journalist

Geoffrey Wheatcroft is a noted British journalist who has written two works on important historical events. His first book, *The Randlords* (1985), examines the ruthless exploitation of native workers in the 19th-century South African gold and diamond mines by a handful of European robber barons. His second, *The Controversy of Zion* (1996), presents a detailed history of Zionism and discusses how the movement to give the Jewish people a homeland has evolved since the late 19th century.

Geoffrey Wheatcroft was born on December 23, 1945 in London, England, the son of Stephen Wheatcroft, an economist, and the former Joyce Reed, a social worker. He grew up in a liberal upper-middle-class household in Hampstead, outside London. He received his education at New College, part of Oxford University, graduating with a master's degree with second class honors in 1968.

During the early part of his career, Wheatcroft worked in various publishing houses. From 1968 to 1970 he served as a production assistant and publicity manager at Hamish Hamilton Ltd. In 1971 he joined the staff at another publishing house, Michael Joseph Ltd., as an editor. He then worked from 1974 to 1975 as an editor at Cassel and Company before moving to newspaper publishing as an assistant editor at the *Spectator*. In 1977 he became the newspaper's literary editor, a position he held until 1981 when he became a freelance journalist.

The Randlords was published in 1985 in Great Britain and in 1986 in the United States, while Wheatcroft was working as an editor for the *Evening Standard*. (The book's title probably refers both to Witwatersrand, an area near Johannesburg with rich deposits of gold ore, and the South-African monetary unit known as a rand.) The volume looks at the brutal history of the South African diamond and gold fields of the 19th century. Wheatcroft explains how small miners were driven out by robber barons—or Randlords—and examines how race relations worsened after the mine owners began to oppress black workers. Maidel Cason, writing for *Library Journal* (Mar. 1, 1986), proclaimed *The Randlords* "a fascinating description of ingenuity, hard work, and greed. The book also illuminates the political and racial picture of South Africa and shows how the antagonism between the Boer farmers and the Uitlanders [foreigners] who had come to mine gold led to increasingly violent confrontations and eventually to the Anglo-Boer War." She concluded, "Though not easy reading, this will appeal to informed laypersons." David Welsh opined for the *Times Literary Supplement* (October 25, 1985), "[Wheatcroft writes] with freshness and verve. . . . The technology of mining and the financial legerdemain that underpinned it are complex subjects, which Wheatcroft handles with skill."

In 1996 Wheatcroft published *The Controversy of Zion: Jewish Nationalism, the Jewish State, and the Unresolved Jewish Dilemma*. In it he details the history of the Zionist movement, created in 1896 by Theodore Herzl, a Viennese journalist who believed that problems of anti-Semitism could be resolved if the Jewish people had a homeland of their own. Wheatcroft tracks the evolution of Zionism in the 20th century, showing how it has been influenced by such events as the Holocaust, the establishment of Israel in 1948, and the 1995 assassination of Israeli Prime Minister Yitzhak Rabin. Wheatcroft explained the impetus behind the book to Katie Bacon for *Atlantic Monthly* (February 1, 2000, on-line): "I just became deeply interested in the story of Zionism and its effect on the Jewish people, and there wasn't a book that seemed to say what I wanted to read." He continued, "I'm not Jewish, but my parents had a lot of Jewish friends and colleagues. And I lived through some of the period I'm writing about. I can remember when—in the fifties and sixties—Israel was still a popular cause among liberals. That has ceased to be the case in the past thirty years, and I wanted to try to explain why." Wheatcroft told Bacon, "I've been touched by the generosity of Jewish scholars who might possibly have resented an outsider's stepping in on their subject. Several have said that I've brought a fresh eye to the story precisely because I'm outside the loop and therefore am not committed in the way that someone who is Jewish inevitably would be."

The Controversy of Zion received generally favorable reviews. George Cohen, writing for *Booklist* (September 1, 1996), remarked: "Wheatcroft has written an absorbing and well-balanced book, bound to attract its share of—as the title suggests—controversy." A reviewer for the *Economist* (September 14, 1996) agreed with that assessment, noting: "A well-informed layman, Geoffrey Wheatcroft guides the reader gently through the thickets of Zionist history and thought without exhausting him with inaccessible detail." "There are books aplenty about Israel," Serge Schmemann noted for the *New York Times Book Review* (October 13, 1996). "Mr. Wheatcroft offers something else, and if approached for what it is, an essay on the genesis of Zionism and its consequences for Jews around the world, with no pretensions to a comprehensive history or a revolutionary thesis, *The Controversy of Zion* is a very readable and useful guide."

Geoffrey Wheatcroft is a frequent contributor to such periodicals as the *New York Times*, *Harper's*, the *Spectator*, and *New Republic*.

—C. M.

SUGGESTED READING: *Atlantic Monthly* (online) Feb. 1, 2000; *Booklist* p43 Sep. 1, 1996; *Economist* p77 Sep. 14, 1996; *Library Journal* p96 Mar. 1, 1986; *New Statesman* p47 July 19, 1996; *New York Times* D p12 Dec. 8, 1997, A p19 Oct. 12, 1998, A p25 Apr. 14, 1999, A p17 Sep. 6, 1999; *New York Times Book Review* p6 Mar. 30, 1986, p8 Oct. 13, 1996; *Times Literary Supplement* p1200 Oct. 25, 1985, p9 Aug. 23, 1986

SELECTED BOOKS: *The Randlords*, 1985; *The Controversy of Zion*, 1996

Wheeler, Kate

July 27, 1955– Novelist; short-story writer; travel writer

Fiction and travel writer Kate Wheeler keeps several packed suitcases in her apartment at all times, in case the impulse to take a journey should suddenly grab her. Wheeler, who moved an average of once per year for the first 17 years of her life, travels often, and this has played a defining role in her life and work. Indeed journeys, be they spiritual or physical, are a central theme in nearly all of Wheeler's writing. As a regular contributor to the *New York Times*' "Sophisticated Traveler" section, *Outside*, and other travel publications, Wheeler is an expert at depicting exotic locales. In her short-story collection *Not Where I Started From* (1993), her characters' outward journeys mirror their inner quests for enlightenment. In her most recent work and first novel, *When Mountains Walked* (2000), Wheeler tells the stories of a grandmother and granddaughter who, although separated by many years and many miles, are both living out similar lives searching for themselves in foreign locales.

Kate Wheeler was born in Tulsa, Oklahoma, on July 27, 1955. Her father, Charles Bowen Wheeler, was an oil prospector who moved all over the globe in search of oil with his wife and their children. Growing up, Wheeler lived in various countries in South America, and, as she told John Freeman for the *Boston Phoenix* (March 30, 2000), she became aware early on of the conflicts that result from living abroad at a young age. "My first word as a baby was in Spanish," Wheeler said. "But because I had all the sensory inputs of a Spanish person and all the cultural inputs of an American person, my identity always seemed to be an artifice that never quite fit."

At the age of 17, Wheeler returned to the United States to attend Rice University, in Houston, Texas, where she majored in English and fine arts. After graduating, Wheeler took a job as a reporter for the *Miami Herald*, partly because she wanted to live in the closest approximation of a Spanish-speaking city the United States had to offer. Gradually, however, Wheeler tired of writing small-time news stories and longed to have more room for embellishment in her writing. "I wanted more scope to blur the facts, so as to make the truth truer," Wheeler wrote in a brief autobiography for her publisher, Houghton Mifflin. It was with this impulse that she enrolled in the writing workshop at Stanford University, in Stanford, California, where she studied under John L'Heureux. Her second short story was eventually published in the *Threepenny Review* and included in the O'Henry Awards collection in 1982. Another short story she wrote in the workshop was selected for the Pushcart Prize. L'Heureux was impressed with Wheeler, as a writer and a person. As quoted by Freeman, L'Heureux said of Wheeler, "In person, [she] was quiet, charming, utterly unassuming, and at least as interested in dogs and people as she was in becoming a writer. Getting to know her, though, you saw that beneath her delicacy and gentleness was a spine of steel."

When her mother was diagnosed with breast cancer, Wheeler went to live with her parents. A year later, Wheeler was given a residency at the Fine Arts Work Center in Provincetown, Massachusetts, and her mother died while she was away. To help herself deal with her grief, Wheeler used her inheritance to attend a series of meditation retreats. Wheeler had begun reading books on yoga and Eastern religion in eighth grade; in 1988 she was ordained as a Buddhist nun, in Burma. Wheeler has said the retreats were also an excuse to indulge her wanderlust. In *Outside* (January 2000), Wheeler wrote, "I lust to touch what's real. Dirt paths trailing off to nowhere. The full moon over a black sea, the grief-stricken stillness of Sundays in the Andes, and the limb-tearing exuberance of the water games on Hindu Holi. I even confess a fondness for cringing street dogs, lurching buses, and ill-lit restaurants where it seems an evil dimension is trying to reach the surface. Anything that makes me say, 'So this is how it is!'" Motivated by this ethos and her spiritual interests, over the next couple years Wheeler traveled in Burma, Thailand, India, Germany, and England.

Following this period, Wheeler settled in Cambridge, Massachusetts, in order to "pick up the thread of writing," as she wrote in her autobiography for Houghton Mifflin. She began submitting short stories to various magazines, but for the most part, it was a discouraging process. She wrote in her autobiography, "Publications [of my writing] were few and rewards were low, so I decided to return to a life of meditation practice and perhaps become a teacher, or at least try to figure out what to do next." Wheeler told Richard B. Woodward in an interview for *Mirabella*, "It's so hard to write. I'd like to escape and be something else, but I don't think I can." After a month-long retreat, Wheeler returned home to find that while away, she had won a literary prize, and her answering machine was full of messages from literary agents and publishers.

This encouragement helped Wheeler finish 10 short stories, which were published by Houghton Mifflin as *Not Where I Started From* (1993). Many of the characters in the collection are American women whose spiritual journeys take them abroad. In "Ringworm," a woman forced out of a Burmese monastery for political reasons discovers that her profoundest spiritual connection has been with a cat. Other stories expose the hypocrisy of some spiritual seekers. In "Snow Leopard, Night Bird," a spiritual guru's sexual escapades are brought to light. "Under the Roof" tells the story of a young American monk living in Bangkok, Thailand, espousing asceticism and poverty; it turns out that a girlfriend in Vermont is mailing him monthly checks. Two stories, "Urbino" and "Improving My Average," are about an American girl growing up in South America. Indeed many of the stories in the collection borrow closely from Wheeler's own experiences, which is partly why they were deemed successful. In *Kirkus Reviews* (June 1, 1993), the collection was praised for its "unrestrained shapeliness born of intimate knowledge." In the *New York Times* (September 1, 1993), Janette Turner Hospital wrote that Wheeler's prose sometimes sounded too much like fashionable writing coming out of graduate writing programs, but also added, "Although each story stands alone, and there are no recurring characters, there is nevertheless a sort of progressive narrative thread that gives the collection heft and substance and renders it something more than disparate anecdotes, something closer to an episodic novel." Perhaps with this in mind, on the strength of *Not Where I Started From*, Wheeler was named by *Granta* as one of the 20 best novelists under 40, without having written a novel. The collection was also a finalist for the 1994 PEN/Faulkner Award, and it earned Wheeler a second O'Henry award.

Based on the critical success of *Not Where I Started From*, Wheeler got work as a travel writer and, while on assignment, she had her share of adventures. In *Outside* (January 2000) Wheeler wrote, "I've swum with piranhas in the Parana River, gotten fogbound in trackless valleys and stuck halfway up rock faces, touched dead people's bones, slept in a hut in Peru's Cordillera Central where a terrorist was thought to be hiding, [and] nearly drowned in a river in the Rockies." However, some of Wheeler's "intense, sometimes even shattering" experiences on these trips, as she wrote in her brief autobiography, wouldn't fit into the travel article format, and these began to wend their way into her novel-in-progress.

In 1993 Wheeler was thinking a lot about her parents and grandparents, and these ideas became the seed of *When Mountains Walked* (2000). Through alternating chapters, the novel depicts the separate but intertwined stories of a grandmother, Althea Barnes, and her granddaughter, Maggie Goodwin. In the 1940s, Althea travels with her seismologist husband from South America to India. She falls in love with the country, and with a Hindu priest. Unlike Maggie later in life, she decides to stay with her domineering husband, and on visits with her grandparents, Maggie hears her grandmother's stories. Years later, Maggie and her husband travel from New England to set up a medical clinic in Peru, where a government-backed mine is causing health problems for the villagers. Gradually, and with her grandmother's stories stirring in the back of her mind, Maggie begins to feel stifled by her marriage and starts a love affair with a former member of a militant terrorist group. As all that is familiar to Maggie is stripped away, she begins to discover that her own will had been buried beneath the surface of her everyday life.

Wheeler's intimate knowledge of South America allows her to create detailed descriptions that may surprise the reader. An example is her description of the cane liquor that is so destructive to the native Peruvians: "The resulting brew combined the oiliness of kerosene, the smell of an electrical fire, and pubic funk." The *Wall Street Journal* remarked on Wheeler's "lyrical use of language," adding, "She has a gift for tangible, descriptive writing." Susan Bolotin, writing for the *New York Times Book Review* (February 20, 2000), praised the novel but was surprised that Wheeler seemed unaware that she was rehashing themes that had been around since at least the 1960s. "The concerns of the book—finding one's self, knowing one's self, making sense of one's past, figuring out how to be a woman in relation to a man—are approached with such youthful directness and so little cynicism," Bolotin wrote. A reviewer in *Publisher's Weekly* (December 13, 1999) did not find Wheeler's themes as familiar as Bolotin had. "Ably articulating the themes of a woman's role as wife and mother in a patriarchal society, and the political realities that occur when relentless economic depravation victimizes people in third world cultures, she has written a psychologically lucid and emotionally resonant novel." *When Mountains Walked* went into a second printing before it became available in stores.

Wheeler is the editor of *In This Very Life: The Liberation Teachings of the Buddha* (1992) and the translator of *Borrowed Time/Lo Esperady Lo Vidido* (1987) by Enrique Márquez. She continues to do other work besides writing, such as teaching meditation practice at retreats. She currently lives in Somerville, Massachusetts, with her fiancé, David Guss, an anthropologist and an ordained Buddhist lama. The two of them travel in South America for half of every year, and for several years spent their summers in La Paz, Bolivia. Several grants, including one from the National Endowment for the Arts in 1994, a Guggenheim Fellowship in 1998–99, and a Somerville Arts Council Grant in 1999, have helped them finance their trips. In her autobiography for Houghton Mifflin, Wheeler writes, "In La Paz, David is working on a book about the festivals and I'm a member of a devil dance group, which I've persuaded him to join, even though it means an ordeal of five hours of dancing in a heavy mask and costume. I'm currently writing an article about La Paz, and wondering whether my suspicions about the topic of my next book are correct."

—P. G. H

SUGGESTED READING: *Boston Phoenix* (on-line) March 30, 2000; *New York Times Book Review* p11 Sep. 12, 1993; *New York Times Book Review* (on-line) Feb. 20, 2000; *Outside* (on-line) Jan. 2000; *People* p25 Sep. 27, 1993

SELECTED BOOKS: novels—*When Mountains Walked*, 2000; short-story collections—*Not Where I Started From*, 1993; as editor—*In This Very Life: The Liberation Teachings of the Buddha*, 1992; as translator—*Borrowed Time/Lo Esperady Lo Vidido*, 1987

Whitehead, Colson

1969– Novelist

After the publication of his first novel, *The Intuitionist* (1999), Colson Whitehead was heralded as the most exciting African-American voice of his generation and drew comparisons to such celebrated authors as Ralph Ellison. The story of a black elevator inspector turned sleuth, *The Intuitionist* received so much critical acclaim that it left many pundits wondering if Whitehead could possibly top his debut. Yet he did just that with *John Henry Days* (2001), an encyclopedic look at the modern era through the eyes of a young freelance journalist who finds himself on the same ill-fated course as the mythic railroad laborer John Henry, who died trying to outperform a steam engine in the Industrial Age.

Colson Whitehead was born in 1969 in New York City. As a child and teenager he was obsessed with pop culture—everything from television sit-coms to action movies to Marvel Comics. He also had an early interest in writing and attended Harvard University, in Cambridge, Massachusetts, with the intention of enrolling in creative-writing classes. Because he was not accepted into the writing seminars he wanted to take, he studied English and comparative literature instead, earning a degree in those subjects, in 1991. Shortly after his graduation Whitehead secured a job with the literary supplement of the *Village Voice*, as an editorial assistant. At the time he wanted to become a pop-culture critic and quickly found himself writing

Natasha Stovall/Courtesy of Doubleday

music, television, and book reviews. He was eventually promoted to the position of TV editor, and he wrote a regular column that gave him some sense of satisfaction. "All my wasted time as a child and teenager [was] now actually income-generating and [paid] my rent," he remarked to

Kevin Larimer for *Poets and Writers* magazine (July/August 2001).

During his time at the *Village Voice*, Whitehead wrote his first novel. "It was a kind of pop-culture-heavy book about a child-genius cherub, Michael Jackson-Gary Coleman type," Whitehead told Logan Hill for *New York* (May 7, 2001). "He's not a midget, but he gets plugged into all sorts of stereotypical black roles until he becomes a sort of super-bad-ass Shaft character." The book was turned down by almost 25 publishing houses. Six months later his agent dropped him. In an interview with the author Walter Mosley for *Book* (May/June 2001), Whitehead reflected on the loss of his agent. "It was [depressing], because you have all these rejection letters and the person who you thought was your one ally is like, 'So where do we send these manuscripts? Put them in the garbage? You want them back?' I think being dumped by the agent was actually beneficial because it was like, no one gives a crap, no one cares. I had to keep doing it, though no one cared except me."

One night in 1996, while watching a television segment on defective escalators, Whitehead stumbled on the inspiration for his next book. He changed the focus from escalators to elevators and wrote a detective novel, a genre that had recently begun to fascinate him. The result was *The Intuitionist*.

In the novel, Lila Mae Watson, one of the few black elevator inspectors in an unnamed city, has become the scapegoat in a political tug-of-war between two main factions in the Department of Elevator Inspectors: the Empiricists and the Intuitionists. (An Empiricist solves elevator problems through an exhaustive understanding of mechanical details; an Intuitionist, such as Lila Mae, solves problems through instinct and meditation.) After the crash of an elevator she has inspected, the Empiricists, who control the department, try to use the accident to stop the spread of their rivals. In order to save herself, as well as the Intuitionists, from being run out of the department, Lila Mae must find the missing blueprints for the "black box," a cutting-edge elevator design.

"In *The Intuitionist*," Brian Gilmore wrote for the *Washington Post* (June 21, 1999), "Whitehead somehow accomplishes two completely unrelated things: He educates the reader in some of the specifics of elevator technology and carves out an exclusive space for himself in America's literary canon." Writing for *Booklist* (December 1998), Donna Seaman cheered: "The story is mesmerizing, but it is Whitehead's shrewd and sardonic humor and agile explications of the insidiousness of racism and the eternal conflict between the material and the spiritual that make this such a trenchant and accomplished novel." In *Time* (January 25, 1999), Walter Kirn commented: "The invention of rich, new literary metaphors is difficult enough. When the subject is race in America, however, it's almost impossible. In his first novel, Whitehead has solved the problem, coming up with the freshest racial allegory since Ralph Ellison's *Invisible Man* and Toni Morrison's *The Bluest Eye*." *The Intuitionist* won the Quality Paperback Book Club's New Voices Award, in 1999, and a Whiting Writer's Award, in 2000.

For his next novel, *John Henry Days*, Whitehead used the legend of the folk hero John Henry—who died beating a steam engine in a race to cut a tunnel through a mountain—to reflect on the modern American obsession with popular culture. John Henry's legend is compared to the life of J. Sutter, a black freelance journalist trying to beat the record for most consecutive days covering staged events—including the unveiling of a commemorative stamp in John Henry's honor—on someone else's bill.

Most reviewers had only mild criticisms of the novel. In *Time* (May 21, 2001), Paul Gray noted: "*John Henry Days* is a narrative tour de force that astonishes on almost every page, but it generates more glitter and brilliance than warmth." In *Newsweek* (May 21, 2001), Malcolm Jones remarked on how Whitehead "extends his narrative every which way with little vignettes that use the John Henry legend as a jumping off point—a touchstone—to explore how pop culture subverts and destroys legitimate myths. . . . The amazing thing is, he nearly pulls it off. There's no way he could, of course. But if this novel is a mess, it's a grand mess, one of those stories where the getting there is all the fun." Though noting that *John Henry Days* has "encyclopedic aspirations," and includes many sections that have little direct impact on the central story, Jonathan Franzen, in the *New York Times Book Review* (May 13, 2001), nevertheless praised the work: "Again and again, you hit passages of wry and largehearted descriptive prose that are the clearest measure of Whitehead's achievement and promise as a writer."

Colson Whitehead is married to Natasha Stovall, a photographer he met while working at the *Village Voice*. He lives in the New York City borough of Brooklyn and is currently at work on a novel about Band-Aids.

—*C. M.*

SUGGESTED READING: *Book* p44+ May/June 2001; *Booklist* p651 Dec. 1, 1998; *New York* p38+ May 7, 2001; *New York Times Book Review* p8+ May 13, 2001; *Newsweek* p59 May 21, 2001; *Poets and Writers* p20+ July/Aug. 2001; *Time* p78 Jan. 25, 1999, p91 May 21, 2001; *Washington Post* C p3 June 21, 1999

SELECTED BOOKS: *The Intuitionist*, 1999; *John Henry Days*, 2001

Wiley, Ralph

Apr. 12, 1952– Essayist; journalist

In the hands of the American writer Ralph Wiley, the venerable essay becomes a tool of both pleasure and provocation. Whether he is writing about sports, celebrities, culture, or current events, Wiley deploys edgy humor and trenchant wit to elicit meaning beyond the headlines. Equal parts memoir, satire, and social commentary, his essays frequently invoke the meaning of race in America—be it Clarence Thomas's controversial appointment to the Supreme Court, Richard Pryor's comic genius, or the furor over teaching Mark Twain's purportedly racist novel *Huckleberry Finn* in public schools. The titles of his essays—for example "Do All Black People Know Each Other?," and "Why Black People Don't Buy Books"—are often hooks designed to snare a reader's attention. "I deal with irony and sarcasm," Wiley has told V. R. Peterson for *Essence* (November 1993). "That's my way of performing as a writer."

Ralph Wiley was born on April 12, 1952 in Memphis, Tennessee. His father, Ralph Heygood Wiley, had served in the Korean War and then worked as a night watchman. His mother, Dorothy Brown, taught English literature and humanities at S. A. Owen College, and instilled in her son a love of books and writing. "Until I was 18, I never slept where I couldn't reach my hand from my bed to a bookcase," Wiley told Peterson. Though he was offered a scholarship to Brown University, an Ivy League school, Wiley chose to attend Knoxville College, in Tennessee. While at college, Wiley became interested in writing and began working as a copywriter for the *Knoxville Keyana-Spectrum*. After graduating in 1975, he became a beat writer and later a columnist for the *Oakland Tribune*, in California. In 1982, he joined the staff of *Sports Illustrated* as a feature writer. Then, after many years as a journalist, Wiley embarked on a freelance writing career. Many of the observations in his first book, *Serenity: A Boxing Memoir* (1989), were gleaned during his days as a sports reporter. He has since written three collections of essays, *Why Black People Tend to Shout* (1991), *What Black People Should Do Now* (1993), and *Dark Witness* (1996).

In *Serenity: A Boxing Memoir* (1989), Wiley pooled his journalistic skills and personal sympathies to meditate on the boxing life. "What would you think if you couldn't get out of bed because of a traumatized liver?," Wiley writes, as quoted by Ray Murphy in the *Boston Globe* (June 26, 1989). "Can you imagine getting your jaw broken and not going to the hospital but fighting for ten more rounds? . . . Can you imagine thousands of your fellow humans screaming for your blood? . . . the look on your mother's face while all this is happening?" Wiley, who had both a grandfather and an uncle who were prizefighters, describes his own street-fighting days as a youth, his process of getting to know fighters as a young reporter, learning the strange art of taking notes during a fight, and the addiction of watching the sport. He also profiles boxers who have defined the game over the last several decades: Muhammad Ali (who Wiley once glimpsed sitting alone in an airport, looking "serene"), Joe Lewis, Sugar Ray Leonard, Larry Holmes, and Mike Tyson.

In the *New York Times* (July 13, 1989), Christopher Lehmann-Haupt pointed out that *Serenity* goes beyond the typical sports fan's memoir by providing a thoughtful look at the ugly realities and strange beauties of the fighting life. Wiley writes about the unseen battles that take place between a boxer's mind and body, and describes the stages on which fighters are made or broken, whether they be the streets, the boxing schools—Detroit's Kronk Boxing Club, Wiley says, is a place for "boys beyond boyhood, boys whose faces and hearts had been turned to stone and then only grew harder in the ring," as quoted by Lehmann-Haupt—or arenas in the Mecca of the fighting world—Las Vegas. "For fighters, or gamblers, or those related to them," Wiley writes, as quoted by Lehmann-Haupt, "Vegas was the most exciting trip to hell imaginable."

In a laudatory review in the *Los Angeles Times* (June 25, 1989), Sonja Bolle found that Wiley's book gives "poetic depth to the word that is so often applied to the ring warriors: grace." Lehmann-Haupt wrote that the book is at heart a story "about growing up in a world where you had to defend yourself physically." It is in such a world that fighters live and sometimes even thrive, Wiley says, finding a degree of "serenity" unknown to most of us.

In an interview with Delia O' Hara for the *Chicago Sun-Times* (June 28, 1992), Wiley described the impetus behind his next book, *Why Black People Tend to Shout: Cold Facts and Wry Views from a Black Man's World* (1991). Wiley recalled watching a segment of the news program *Nightline* about the drug war in Washington, D.C., in which the anchor, Ted Koppel, interviewed a black woman who had lost her son to drug-related violence. The woman made an appeal for real change in her community, challenging Koppel to "Tell me I'm worth it," as Wiley told O'Hara. Wiley, who had been working on some essays about race in America, realized that this woman was his audience, and she needed to hear from him. "I thought to myself, she doesn't know she's worth it. And Ted Koppel can't tell her," Wiley told O'Hara.

The 33 essays in *Why Black People Tend to Shout* range widely over America's social and cultural landscape, offering pungent, disturbing, and achingly funny answers to the question posed by the book's title. In one essay Wiley offers a solution to the persistent problem of racial stereotypes. Black people, he suggests, should wear buttons that read "I'M NOT . . ." and then fill in the blank. People at risk of being stopped by the police might wear "I'M NOT CARRYING NARCOTICS" buttons, for instance, and black actors could wear buttons that read "I'M NOT EDDIE MURPHY," as quoted by Clarissa N. West in *English Journal* (January 1996). In other essays, Wiley profiles figures such as the ex-Klansman and Louisiana politician David Duke, pop star Michael Jackson, and the novelist Alice Walker, and details accomplishments of black inventors and "cultural icons" who, Wiley says, have not been given their proper place in history.

Wiley's writing operates on many levels, mixing a colloquial voice and deadpan humor with anger and pathos. "Its not easy to express how it feels to be a black man in the 1990s," Alex Raskin observed in the *Atlanta Journal and Constitution* (April 14, 1991). He continued, "Ralph Wiley is one of the few who have been able to find just the right tone." Delia O' Hara noted that the book was published a year before one of the most racially polarizing events of the 1990s: the "Not Guilty" verdict in 1992 for the police officers who were caught on video tape beating a black man, Rodney King, and the riots in Los Angeles that followed the controversial courtroom decision. Although Wiley's book was written before the verdict, it includes a prescient chapter called "When Black People Lose Hope," in which a black man opens fire in an airplane after his boss squelches his hopes for advancement.

Wiley's next book, *What Black People Should Do Now: Dispatches from Near the Vanguard* (1993), drew mixed responses from reviewers. The essays in it are divided into five broadly titled sections—on media, personalities, perceptions, travel, and life—in which Wiley comments on cultural identity, history, and race. Some of the essays address hot-button issues and events of the 1990s, including the AIDS crisis; the tension and slow-simmering rage in Los Angeles surrounding the racially divisive trials of Rodney King and O. J. Simpson; and the Mike Tyson rape case. In his somewhat sympathetic portrait of Tyson, Wiley provoked the ire of feminists with his assertion that "women prove nothing by receiving [legal] judgments at the expense of black men while white men do the same as they've always done. If Mike Tyson cannot force himself on you, but William Kennedy Smith or a platoon of soccer players can, where's the progress really," he argued, as quoted by Lynell George in the *Los Angeles Times* (November 11, 1993). When asked by George about drawing heated responses from readers, Wiley responded that he views his role as that of "artist as agitator": "The very act of thinking is weighing options and disagreeing with yourself," he told George. "I'm trying to get you to think through your feelings."

Some critics voiced ambivalence about Wiley's provocations, best captured in James Conaway's observation in the *Washington Post* (December 23, 1993) that the essays are variously "engaging and exasperating." In *Black Enterprise* (March 1994), Frederick D. Robinson expressed appreciation for much of Wiley's humor, and described as "penetrating" Wiley's personal reminiscences of working with Spike Lee on a book about the making of Lee's film *Malcolm X* (1992). And yet Robinson balked at what he described as Wiley's "tenuous claims" about AIDS, including his assertion that the virus was meant to kill undesirables, including black men, drug users, and gays. "He is a veteran journalist and should know better," Robinson commented. Jill Nelson, writing in the *San Francisco Chronicle* (December 8, 1993), felt the book did not live up to the promise made in its title. "One finishes *What Black People Should Do Now* not only without a clue as to what black people should do, but with scarcely a hint as to what they should think about doing," she asserted, describing the essays as "half-baked, frivolous, or plain silly."

Other reviewers were more accepting of the book's hodgepodge of controversial ideas and polemics. A critic for *Kirkus Reviews* (August 15, 1993), as quoted on *Amazon.com*, praised Wiley for "always jabbing, testing, looking for the edge." While this reviewer noted that this tendency sometimes leads Wiley astray, as in his attacks on Arthur Schlesinger, Allan Bloom, and Saul Bellow, it also makes for some penetrating insights and a book that, taken as a whole, is a "rude, rousing defense and celebration of African-American culture." Veronica Chambers, in the *Los Angeles Times* (December 7, 1993), expressed relief that Wiley doesn't attempt to name "solutions" to the problems of race, but instead offers his personal experiences and observations as one man's perspective on race. "It's refreshing to realize that one can be a 'race man' (one who works for the uplifting of his race) and still be able to crack jokes," she wrote. In Chambers's opinion, Wiley's writing is strong and assured because he knows what he wants to say, and whom he wants as his listeners: "The book is called *What Black People Should Do Now* because Wiley assumes he is addressing a literate, intelligent, African American readership," she asserted. Wiley himself takes up this subject in his essay "Why Black People Don't Buy Books," in which he sets out to disprove the widespread view in the predominantly white publishing world that black people don't read.

Dark Witness: When Black People Should be Sacrificed (Again) (1996) is Wiley's third collection of essays. It includes "A Profuse Apology," written in the satiric tradition epitomized by Jonathan Swift's "A Modest Proposal." In this essay, Wiley apologizes for "all the incompetence, criminality, shiftlessness, and stupidity of the African American, the sum of which has held America down mightily," as quoted by Dean Wakefield in the *San Francisco Chronicle* (August 6, 1996). "I apologize for their failure to agree to my own proposal that they throw themselves off the nearest rooftops to save us the trouble of thinking up less obvious methods of disposal." As Wakefield noted, Wiley uses humor in this essay to respond to Charles Murray and Richard Herrnstein's *The Bell Curve* (1996), which purported to show scientific evidence that the common denominator of the underclass is low intelligence, and that this, rather than racial prejudice or class disadvantage, accounts for their position in society. Wiley skewers what he considers to be Murray and Herrnstein's unscientific methods, and exposes the flaws in their argument by taking it to its illogical and harrowing conclusions.

In examining what comprises blackness in America, Wiley recounts a visit with the scholar Cornel West, and cites the jazz musician Wynton Marsalis, who has observed that "United States Negro culture . . . includes all Americans," as quoted by a critic for *Kirkus Reviews* (April 1, 1996) and cited on *Amazon.com*. The Kirkus reviewer praised the essay "One Day, When I Was on Exhibit"—prompted by Wiley's visit to the Whitney Museum of American Art's "Black Male" exhibit—calling it "a long, sinuous, and altogether elegant essay . . . which effortlessly glides from professional basketball to the woes of former NAACP president Benjamin Chavis to the question of self-governance for Washington, D.C., and scores big points at every turn." However Dean Wakefield, along with other reviewers, found that Wiley "lurches from one subject to another without giving the reader the appropriate context." In *Quarterly Black Review of Books* (September 1996), Terri James argued that Wiley's rambling style is ultimately rewarding: "Reading *Dark Witness* is an experience much like finding yourself seated next to a chatty traveler on a long train trip. . . . Like many talkative travelers, Wiley occasionally goes off on long tangents, but in midst of wisecracks and Twain-like yarns, Wiley discusses substantial issues that have received little exposure," James wrote, as quoted on *Powells.com*.

Wiley has co-authored two books with Spike Lee, *Best Seat in the House: A Basketball Memoir* (1997), and *By Any Means Necessary: The Trials and Tribulations of the Making of Malcolm X*, (1992), and has written a book with the baseball player Eric Davis, *Born to Play* (1999). *Best Seat in the House*, a memoir of Spike Lee's lifelong love-affair with the New York Knicks basketball team, was called by John D. Thomas in the *Atlanta Journal and Constitution* (June 8, 1997) "one of the most honest, opinionated, and enjoyable sports books to come out in years, maybe ever." Wiley also contributed to Dexter Scott King's *Growing Up King: An Intimate Memoir* (2003), an account of what it was like to grow up as the youngest son of civil rights leader Martin Luther King, Jr.

Wiley is married to Holly Anne Cypress and has a son, Colen Cypress Wiley. When asked by Lynell George what African-Americans stand to gain at this point in history, Wiley turned to literature. "It's like what Dickens said: We're walking the line between tragedy and greatness. I smell a renaissance and I smell something burning. That's the challenge. You've got to make it go one way or another," he told George. "That's the beauty of being alive at this time."

—M. A. H.

SUGGESTED READING: *Atlanta Journal and Constitution* p10 Apr. 14, 1991; *Black Enterprise* p93 Mar. 1994; *Chicago Sun-Times* p38 June 28, 1992; *Essence* p62 Nov. 1993; *Los Angeles Times* p6 June 25, 1989; *Los Angeles Times* p1 Nov. 11, 1993, p3 Dec. 7, 1993; *New York Times* p21 July 13, 1989; *San Francisco Chronicle* E p5 Dec. 8, 1993, E p5 Aug. 6, 1996; *Washington Post* C p2 Dec. 23, 1993

SELECTED BOOKS: essays—*Why Black People Tend to Shout: Cold Facts and Wry Views from a Black Man's World*, 1991; *What Black People Should Do Now: Dispatches from Near the Vanguard*, 1993; *Dark Witness: When Black People Should be Sacrificed (Again)*, 1996; memoir—*Serenity: A Boxing Memoir*, 1989; as co-author—*By Any Means Necessary: The Trials and Tribulations of the Making of Malcolm X* (with Spike Lee), 1992; *Best Seat in the House: A Basketball Memoir* (with Spike Lee), 1997; *Born to Play* (with Eric Davis), 1999

Willis, Elizabeth

1961– Poet

Elizabeth Willis's poems have been likened to jigsaw puzzles, which "seem to leave out more than they leave in," as one reviewer wrote for the Georgetown University English Department Web site. Willis has gained notice as the author of *The Human Abstract*, a collection selected as one of the five winners in the 1994 National Poetry Series Competition. In addition to her work as a poet, she teaches at Wesleyan University, in Middletown, Connecticut.

Elizabeth Willis was born in 1961 in Awali, Bahrain, an independent sultanate in the Persian Gulf; she was raised in Eau Claire, Wisconsin. She received her bachelor's degree at the University of Wisconsin, in Eau Claire, graduating summa cum laude in 1983 with a major in English and a minor in Spanish. She then studied 19th- and 20th-century literature at the State University of New York (SUNY) at Buffalo and received a master's degree, with distinction, in 1986. In 1994 she earned a doctoral degree in the school's Program in Poetics.

In 1991 Willis published *A/O*, her first poetry chapbook, and in 1993 followed it with *A Maiden*. That same year she published *Second Law*, a book-length poem that the poet and critic Susan Howe, as quoted on the Duration Press Web site called "terse, precise, ecstatic and luminous." Willis's work was anthologized in *The Gertrude Stein Awards in Innovative North American Poetry (1993-1994)*, edited by Douglas Messerli.

In 1995 Willis published *The Human Abstract*, which had been one of the five winners of the National Poetry Series Competition a year earlier. Frank Allen, in *Library Journal* (May 1, 1995), called *The Human Abstract* "exhilarating but abstruse." He concluded, "Only the most dedicated poetry enthusiast will volunteer to accompany Willis on her journey to inaccessible, rarified meaning." A reviewer for *Publishers Weekly* (April 24, 1995) felt, however, that the "the poems' many seemingly unconnected references . . . leave readers at risk of being lost in a swirl of enjoyable sounds." Citing Willis's lines "no crisis/but of the iris in/containing light," the reviewer noted that "unexpected juxtapositions suggest strange relationships that often accrue in some lovely images, the best drawing on sound for further effect."

In addition to her work at Wesleyan University, Elizabeth Willis has taught at Cabrillo College, in Santa Cruz, California, and at Mills College, in Oakland, California.

—C. M.

SUGGESTED READING: Duration Press Web site; Georgetown University English Department Web site; *Library Journal* p101 May 1, 1995; Mills College Web site; *Publishers Weekly* p66 April 24, 1995; *Subtext Reading Series* (on-line)

SELECTED BOOKS: *A/O*, 1991; *A Maiden*, 1993; *Second Law*, 1993; *The Human Abstract*, 1995

Miriam Berkley/Courtesy of Harcourt Trade

Winegardner, Mark

Nov. 24, 1961– Novelist; nonfiction writer

Mark Winegardner emerged from his home state of Ohio, and from a childhood spent wandering the byways of America in his family's RV, with a fondness for Americana—particularly baseball—that he has expressed in several fiction and nonfiction books. *Elvis Presley Boulevard: From Sea to Shining Sea, Almost* (1988), an account of the author's cross-country journey with a friend, *Prophet of the Sandlots: Journeys with a Major League Scout* (1990), and *The 26th Man: One Minor Leaguer's Pursuit of a Dream* (1991) were followed by *The Veracruz Blues* (1996) and *Crooked River Burning* (2001), novels featuring many true stories and real-life characters. Winegardner has been deemed by critics to have fulfilled the promise found in his first book by the novelist Carolyn See, who in the *Los Angeles Times* (February 15, 1988, on-line) expressed her hope that he would continue to write.

Mark Winegardner was born November 24, 1961 in Bryan, Ohio, to Beverly and Gary Winegardner. His parents owned a business that involved recreational vehicles; every year, Winegardner and his sister were taken in a different model on a trip to a scenic point in the American countryside.

Winegardner was educated at Miami University, in Oxford, Ohio, where he received his B.A. degree in 1983, and at George Mason University, in Fairfax, Virginia, earning an M.F.A. degree there four years later. He taught creative writing around the Washington, D.C., area before becoming a professor of creative writing at Florida State University in Tallahassee.

Meanwhile, in 1983, when he was engaged to be married, Winegardner fondly recalling the family vacations of his childhood decided to take one last, carefree trip before settling down. He persuaded his friend Bob to join him on an odyssey that carried them, in Bob's 15-year-old car, from Bryan to Los Angeles, with stops in New Orleans; Elvis Presley's home, Graceland; Chicago; Colorado; Arizona; and Nevada.

Winegardner based his 1988 book, *Elvis Presley Boulevard: From Sea to Shining Sea, Almost*, on his experiences during that journey. Caroline See wrote about the book, "[I]f it's 'adulthood' these boys fear in all its most negative ramifications the rest of adult America reassures them greatly. Out there in the Boonies, Americans have created a strange, electrical, cultural inner life, and guess what? It's based on Elvis Presley. . . . Winegardner doesn't make a big deal out of any of this. He draw no profound conclusions. He knows enough simply to pray, 'Give us each day our daily Elvis,' and he knows enough simply to write down what it means to be recording the last days of his certified youth."

Winegardner's 1990 book, *Prophet of the Sandlots: Journeys with a Major League Scout*, follows the last season in the career of Tony Lucadello, who signed 49 big-leaguers during a 50-year career with the Chicago Cubs and the Philadelphia Phillies. The title refers to Lucadello's gift for spotting talent in immature baseball players. As Winegardner drove around the Midwest with Lucadello, scouting college and high-school sandlots, Lucadello told him some of the tricks of the trade, which included applying onion juice to his own eyes, in order to induce the tears that led one player to sign a contract for $96,000 less than other teams had offered. Lucadello loved baseball and nurtured its fledgling players until his team, the Philadelphia Phillies, rejected his methods of finding and training gifted athletes; he committed suicide after more than a half-century devoted to the game.

"Winegardner's engaging portrait of a scout's life is at its best when he simply allows Lucadello to talk," Diane Cole wrote in the *New York Times Book Review* (April 1, 1990). His "voice is so distinctive that the author's travelogue and personal asides cannot help suffering by comparison." She concluded that Winegardner's "assessment of the Phillies' decision to cut the team's and Lucadello's already tight player development budget a few months before the scout's death in May 1989 is sadly on the mark: 'Good plan, fellows. Enjoy your stay in the cellar.'"

Library Journal (January 1990) reviewer, Martin J. Hudacs, also had a favorable assessment of *Prophet of the Sandlots*: "Winegardner is reminiscent of David Halberstam in his research and reporting style, as he faithfully chronicles the events and emotions of the Lucadello scouting trips. The behind-the-scenes insight into baseball scouting alone is worthy reading, but the book's ending is more dramatic than any fictional account." Sara Paretsky in *USA Today* (July 6, 1990) named *Prophet of the Sandlots* "the best baseball book of the season" and praised Winegardner's "spare, unadorned style."

In 1991 Winegardner helped Steve Fireovid to tell his story in *The 26th Man: One Minor Leaguer's Pursuit of a Dream*. Written in diary form, the book recounted what Fireovid expected to be his last season as a minor-league baseball player. At the age of 33, he was disappointed when his younger teammates were tapped by the Montreal Expos. Though the Expos offered Fireovid the chance to serve as a minor-league pitching coach, he was unwilling to relinquish his dream of playing in the big leagues. "Fireovid engages in a good deal of philosophical musings on the dichotomy between his passion for the game, and his aversion to its unfairness. This is not the usual list of I-could-have-been-a-contender complaints," John V. Turner wrote in *Library Journal* (June 15, 1991). Walter Shapiro, the *Time* (June 17, 1991) critic, deemed *The 26th Man* a "poignant journal" and perhaps "the best recent glimpse of baseball's inner life."

Winegardner based his first novel, *The Veracruz Blues*, on the true story of an episode that took place in 1946, when Jorge Pasquel and his brothers, Mexican businessmen, offered lucrative contracts to American Major League Baseball players and Cuban players. Already playing in the Mexican league were African-Americans of great talent, who were barred from the major leagues because of racism. "Pasquel's dream was to upgrade the Mexican League to major league status," Roberto Gonzalez Echevarria wrote in the *New York Times Book Review* (April 7, 1996). "Pasquel improved the quality of the Mexican game by developing a truly democratic, multiethnic league in which ability and the open market determined a player's worth."

Winegardner's story, filled with real and fictional characters, deals with the failure of Pasquel's dream once his plan came to the attention of Happy Chandler, the baseball commissioner, and the other powers behind Major League Baseball in the U.S. The story is told by fictional baseball journalist Frank Bullinger, who writes it in 1994, as he looks back on the *temporada de oro*—the season of gold. Bullinger "sounds like Damon Runyon or Ring Lardner at their bourbon-soaked best," the *Publishers Weekly* (November 6, 1995) reviewer wrote. "Whether Pasquel was '(a) Mephistopheles, (b) Gatsby, (c) Barnum, (d) an egomaniacal war profiteer,' or a few other possibilities, including 'philandering murderer' and 'civil rights pioneer,' Bullinger leaves to the reader." Bullinger himself, as he tries to write the Great American Novel, is trapped in disintegrating relationships with his wife and two mistresses. "*The Veracruz Blues* is, in the modernist tradition, the story of the writing of the novel Bullinger never quite completed," according to Echevarria. Winegardner, Echevarria felt, had produced "the best baseball novel I have read . . . a book that delves deep into national myth making by looking at it from the outside, as only literature can do. Two American dreams collide in *The Veracruz Blues*: the game of baseball and the yearning to write the Great American Novel."

The Veracruz Blues "pokes holds in the pieties about breaking the color barrier in the major leagues," Echevarria wrote. "Racial integration in baseball has become a story about sacrifice and sublime courage that preserves the integrity of the American national game. But consider for a moment the following heresies: Branch Rickey was a pompous, money-grubbing hypocrite who cloaked himself in the mantle of a savior by signing one black baseball player . . . when there were dozens ready for the majors. . . . With unbearable condescension, organized baseball passed off this revolting tokenism as a crusade for equality. . . . Could such notions be thought, much less articulated, in 1946, during the frenzy of postwar jingoism?" Echevarria concluded that Winegardner, in doing the job in 1996, had produced "a moving and significant story." The novel was judged one of the year's most notable by the *New York Times*. The *Christian Science Monitor* (March 15, 1996) reviewer, Larry Eldridge, on the other hand, felt that the book's mixture of fact and fiction "leaves the reader confused and unsatisfied."

In *Crooked River Burning*, Winegardner's 2001 novel, the eponymous river is the Cuyahoga, which runs through Cleveland, Ohio, and which—because of pollution—has actually caught fire on several occasions. The novel covers a 20-year period starting in the late 1940s; like *The Veracruz Blues*, it involves real as well as fictional events and people. Two characters meet and fall in love in 1952: David Zielinsky, who was raised by his aunt and uncle, a detective who once worked for Eliot Ness; and Anne O'Connor, the daughter of the former mayor. While their love is not to be consummated, their meetings and partings give the novel its structure. David becomes a politician, and Anne a television journalist; they are both witnesses to the decline of the city of Cleveland.

"Cleveland may be on the decline in this urban portrait," the *Publishers Weekly* (November 20, 2000) reviewer wrote, "but Winegardner infuses his tale with an exhilarating energy" and "takes on the American metropolis, making Cleveland his own in plain, straightforward prose." In the *New York Times Book Review* (January 21, 2001), Peter Khoury agreed that as "we follow the adventures of David and Anne, we learn about a gritty, rich and misjudged city." Khoury enjoyed Winegardner's portraits of real people, finding those of "the legendary disc jockey Alan Freed and of Dorothy Fuldheim, a television commentator who worked into her 90s . . . classics." Khoury judged *Crooked River Burning* to be "bulky, yet brilliant."

That's True of Everybody (2002) is a collection of 13 stories, mostly about loss and emptiness, relayed in a lyrical, down-to-earth tone. In one story, the proprietor of a bowling alley becomes obsessed with a missing female employee, while at home he tries to cope with a daughter who insists on doing paintings of phalluses. In a section called "Tales of Academic Lunacy: 1991–2000," three stories satirize the oddities of life in a small college; one tale concerns a visiting poet who seduces students but is granted tenure and a pay raise. "Winegardner's ordinary midwestern characters often find themselves on extraordinary quests, and the results are uniformly riveting and revealing," James Klise noted in *Booklist*, as quoted on *Amazon.com*.

Winegardner is the Janet Burroway Professor of English and director of the creative writing program at Florida State University, in Tallahassee. He teaches fiction and nonfiction workshops, as well as American literature and the short story. Winegardner is the recipient of grants, fellowships, and residencies from the Ohio Arts Council, the Lilly Endowment, the Ragdale Foundation, the Sewanee Writers Conference, and the Corporation of Yaddo. He is also a national board member of the Associated Writing Programs. His work has appeared in such magazines as *Doubletake*, *Gentlemen's Quarterly*, *Men's Journal*, *New York Times Magazine*, *Oxford American*, *Playboy*, *Ploughshares*, *Story Quarterly*, *TriQuarterly*, and *Witness*.

Winegardner was recently selected by Random House and the literary executors of Mario Puzo to write a continuation of Puzo's legendary *Godfather* series, which chronicles the life of the Corleone organized-crime family. Tentatively titled "The Godfather Returns," the book is scheduled for publication sometime in 2004.

—S. Y.

SUGGESTED READING: *Christian Science Monitor* p11 Mar. 15, 1996; *Library Journal* p116 Jan. 1990, p82 June 15, 1991; *Los Angeles Times* p4 Feb. 15, 1988; *New Yorker* Apr. 11, 1988; *New York Times Book Review* p18 Apr. 1, 1990, p14 Apr. 7, 1996, p18 Jan. 21, 2001; *Ploughshares* p188+ Fall 2000; *Publishers Weekly* p81 Nov. 6, 1995, p45 Nov. 20, 2000; *Time* p72 June 17, 1991; *USA Today* D p4 July 6, 1990

SELECTED BOOKS: nonfiction—*Elvis Presley Boulevard: From Sea to Shining Sea, Almost*, 1988; *Prophet of the Sandlots: Journeys with a Major League Scout*, 1990; fiction—*The Veracruz Blues*, 1996; *Crooked River Burning*, 2001; *That's True of Everybody*, 2002

Wolfe, Tom

1930– Journalist; essayist; novelist

Instantly recognizable in his trademark white suit, Tom Wolfe is one of the best-known men of letters in the United States. He began his writing career as a reporter for newspapers in Springfield, Massachusetts; Washington, D.C.; and New York City. During the 1960s Wolfe and other journalists began experimenting with a new style of nonfiction writing that employed the creative techniques commonly associated with fiction. New Journalism, as the revolutionary style became known, influenced many writers and proved popular with audiences. Although he generally rejected the values of the counter-culture, Wolfe began covering the movement for magazines such as *New York* and *Esquire* at a time when virtually every facet of American society, from fashion to morals, was undergoing dramatic change. Wolfe reached a wider audience by publishing many of his essays in books such as *The Kandy-Kolored Tangerine-Flake Streamline Baby* (1965) and *The Pump House Gang* (1968), both of which received many favorable reviews. His humorous account of a party in 1970 thrown by the conductor Leonard Bernstein at his Park Avenue duplex to raise money for the Black Panther Party established his reputation as an iconoclast and biting social critic. That essay, which also brought him severe criticism in some circles, was republished in *Radical Chic and Mau-Mauing the Flak Catchers* (1970). Wolfe has published controversial broadsides against modern art, in *The Painted Word* (1975), and against modern architec-

Tom Wolfe
Jacques Lowe/Courtesy of Farrar, Straus and Giroux

ture, in *From Bauhaus to Our House* (1981). In 1979 he published one of his most acclaimed nonfiction books, *The Right Stuff*, which related the early history of the U.S. space program, focusing on the test pilots and the first seven astronauts of Project Mercury. The book earned several notable literary prizes.

Wolfe, who spent much of his journalistic career attacking what he considered the poor state of the American novel, published his first, *The Bonfire of the Vanities*, in 1987. It offered a look at how ambition drives people in different professions, from frenzied bond traders on Wall Street to New York City politicians. In addition to receiving many enthusiastic reviews, the novel eventually sold millions of copies. Wolfe's second novel, *A Man in Full* (1998), was a best-seller, but it divided the critics. In 2000 Wolfe's *Hooking Up*, a collection of essays and one novella, was published to critical acclaim.

Tom Wolfe submitted the following statement for *World Authors 1995–2000*: "I was born in Richmond, Virginia, in 1930, and named for my father, Thomas Kennerly Wolfe. By the time I was aware of work, jobs, and so forth, he was editor of one of the agricultural magazines of the day, the *Southern Planter*. By profession, he was not a journalist, however, but an agronomist who had made a name for himself during the golden era of American agricultural science, the 1920s, when agronomists at experimental stations across the country increased American crop yields per acre by astounding multiples (wheat: ten-fold). The agronomist part, however, was lost upon his three-year-old son. As far as I was concerned, my father was a man who sat at his desk writing with a pencil on a yellow legal pad. Two weeks later his not terribly legible handwriting would reappear as smartly turned out regiments of black type on graphically beautiful pages for thousands of people to read. To me that was magic, and my father was a writer.

"Meantime, my mother, Helen Hughes Wolfe, an adept in Georgian garden design, had introduced me to art. My first published art work (appearing in an afternoon daily, the *Richmond News Leader*) was a painting in a children's art show of a battleship firing artillery at night. The newspaper's art critic compared me to Matisse, although mainly, I realized much later, because the two artists shared a tendency to use hot-pastel colors to compensate for underdeveloped drawing skills. This was my first exposure to that most cutting of literary devices, irony. Fortunately, being seven years old, I didn't get it. I was going to be an artist *and* a writer.

"Simultaneously, it so happened, I fell victim to an endemic American male disease, athlonomania, a morbid obsession with sports stardom. My particular strain: baseball. I pitched for my high school, St. Christopher's, for my college, Washington and Lee, and for two seasons in the old amateur Sertoma League, hatchery of a number of major leaguers, including my rival Mel Roach. Both of us were waiting to be discovered by professional scouts. In no time, Mel was playing second base for the Milwaukee Braves. In my case, the very same scouts successfully contained their excitement. I later went through the box scores in the *Richmond Times-Dispatch* and discovered that Mel had hit .438 against me. Thereafter I claimed, bitterly, that I was the man who had sent Mel Roach to 'the Bigs.'

"That left writing and art.

"I was at least sensible enough to realize that if I was to become a writer—at the time a Writer of Novels—I would need gainful employment prior to lighting up the sky. So I headed off to Yale's graduate program in American Studies in order to qualify as a teacher at the college level. This was a fabulous program in many ways, but my greatest single discovery was sociology, which I soon came to regard as the queen of all disciplines (including biology). Lately the queen, debilitated by a weakness for fashionable intellectual trends, has been dethroned and exiled to Blue Johnnies Island. But I digress. . . .

"I completed work for my doctorate late in the summer of 1956 (the degree was awarded in 1957), too late to get a job teaching in the academic year that would begin in three weeks. Luckily I found work as a reporter for the *Springfield* (Mass.) *Union*. I would return to academia in the fullness of time. . . Instead, I wound up working for newspapers for the next decade and would have done so longer, had not two New York newspapers, the *Herald Tribune* and its still-born successor, the *World Journal Tribune*, sunk beneath me within eight months in 1966 and 1967. I felt like a Jonah.

"At the *Herald Tribune* I had been a general assignment reporter for the city desk, but during a long Newspaper Guild strike in the winter of 1962 I kept afloat by writing magazine articles for *Esquire*. After the strike ended, in the spring, I began writing articles for the *Trib*'s new Sunday supplement, *New York Magazine*, as well as *Esquire*, all the while still working as a reporter. Looking back on it, I blink in disbelief at the number of magazine pieces, many of them long, I turned out over the next twenty-one months. In 1965 I put together a collection of them as my first book, *The Kandy-Kolored Tangerine-Flake Streamline Baby*, and illustrated it with drawings I had done for newspapers over the preceding seven years.

"This, my long-postponed art career, had finally tracked me down in 1958. One day the *Springfield Union* city desk sends me to the courthouse to cover the most sensational murder trial in Springfield in years. I walk in, and I can't believe what I'm looking at. Right out in the middle of the courtroom is a cage-like coop containing the two defendants, whose lawyers have wrestled them into starched white shirts and felony-blue suits and ties. The coop is flanked by uniformed court officers carrying .45-calibre revolvers. Forty-fives are big guns. I couldn't take my eyes off this spectacle, the cop-heavy felony coop, which was apparently unique to Massachusetts. It *demanded* to be recorded, but cameras were not allowed. So I did a drawing of the entire courtroom with the coop as the focal point, in addition to a long story, both against a deadline less than three hours away. I went on to illustrate my own stories under daily deadline pressure for the *Washington Post* and the *Herald Tribune*. Frankly, it's a maddening business. The neuroscientists know what they're talking about when they say the brain has two hemispheres, one logical and the other intuitive, that have never been properly introduced. While you're doing a courtroom drawing, you can't absorb the testimony—not any of it. If you pay attention to the testimony, you can forget about drawing. It was a relief to do the mere illustrated features I undertook later on for newspapers, magazines, and my own books, including drawings with extended captions for *Harper's Magazine* every month for four years (1977–1981), culminating in a book of drawings, *In Our Time*, in 1980.

"But above all there was the experiment in what would by and by be labeled (not by me) 'the New Journalism,' which by my definition (there were others) meant writing non-fiction, from newspaper stories to books, using basic reporting to gather the material but techniques ordinarily associated with fiction, such as scene-by-scene construction, to narrate it. I plunged into this movement—a movement was what the experiment quickly became—with abandon, along with such dazzling practitioners as Gay Talese and Jimmy Breslin. If this new approach to non-fiction is not regarded by historians in 2025 as the most important American literary phenomenon of the second half of the 20th century, I (up on a cloud or elsewhere) will be very surprised. I soon lost interest in the old Writer's El Dorado, the Novel. In non-fiction I could combine two loves: reporting and the sociological concepts American Studies had introduced me to, especially status theory as first developed by the German sociologist Max Weber. One result was *The Right Stuff* (1979), a story of the first seven American astronauts, in Project Mercury [the U.S.'s first manned space-flight program]. Whatever popularity or praise the book enjoyed was due in no small part to its sociological approach. It was not about space or astronauts per se but the secret, and, in fact, taboo status competition among American military pilots who lived by what I called—the taboo kept them from giving it a name— 'the code of the Right Stuff.' Whatever uproar two books I wrote about Modern art (*The Painted Word*, 1975) and Modern architecture (*From Bauhaus to Our House*, 1981) managed to set off was thanks to the fact that they were not critiques—I have never burdened a reader with an aesthetic pronouncement of my own—but sociological accounts of the 'charming aristocracies' that have been dictating taste to obedient multitudes ever since the late 1940s.

"Borrowing a term Truman Capote had coined after writing a superb piece of New Journalism, *In Cold Blood*, I rather grandly began to think of *The Right Stuff* as a non-fiction novel. In the early 1980s I was set to write another one, this one about New York City high and low. I did months of reporting but at the last minute started wondering what would happen if I used the same material in that by now retrograde and dying form, the capital-N Novel. The experiment was entitled *The Bonfire of the Vanities*. Granted, there is more than one good way to write a novel. I could scarcely admire Eugene Zamyatin's science fiction masterpiece, *We*, or George Orwell's out-and-out knock-off of it, *1984*, more extravagantly. Both were, at bottom, political. Orwell once said he never wrote a decent line that didn't have a political purpose. I would turn that around. I can't think of anything that reduces prose to rubbish faster than a political purpose. In my opinion, a writer should have enough pride to write with an egotistical form of objectivity. The goal of exploring the lurid carnival of contemporary life and bringing it alive on the page brilliantly enough to light up the sky should be more important than any political purpose. Putting literary talent at the service of a cause is P.R.

"I have been rash enough to write three essays since 1973 arguing that the future of the American novel, if it is to have any at all, will be in the form of hyper-realistic fiction based upon intensive reporting, 'naturalism,' to use Zola's term. For my pains, I have received little other than averted eyes and charges of self-promotion. But como Fidel lo ha dijo, history will absolve me."

Tom Wolfe attended college not far from his home town, at Washington and Lee University, in Lexington, Virginia, from which he graduated cum laude in 1951. He then enrolled at Yale University, in New Haven, Connecticut, earning his doctorate in American studies in 1957. After completing his studies, he turned to writing, eventually joining the *Washington Post* as a reporter and Latin American correspondent. In 1961 Wolfe received the Washington Newspaper Guild's awards for foreign-news reporting and humor.

In 1965 Wolfe published a collection of his magazine pieces in his first book, *The Kandy-Kolored Tangerine-Flake Streamline Baby*, which also included a number of his drawings. The pieces address such topics as stock-car racing, status seeking, bouffant hairdos, the city of Las Vegas, contemporary art, rock concerts, and the Twist (the dance popularized by the rock star Chubby Checker). The title piece discusses the cars designed and built by teenagers in California. In the *Saturday Review* (July 31, 1965) Emile Capouya expressed mixed feelings about the book. Although impressed with Wolfe's "industrious researches, his eye for the characteristic triviality, and his very lively style," Capouya asserted that the pieces in the book were exclamatory and too long and that the drawings were mean-spirted. "One wants to say to Mr. Wolfe," Capouya wrote, "you're so clever, you can talk so well, tell us something interesting." In contrast, a reviewer for *Newsweek* (June 28, 1965) wrote, "[Wolfe] is full of raw talent, and it is that which has touched so many nerves and created such anger and delight. . . . Partly, Wolfe belongs to the old noble breed of poet-journalists like Ben Hecht, and partly he belongs to a new breed of supereducated hip sensibilities like Jonathan Miller and Terry Southern, who see the complete human comedy in everything from a hair-do to a holocaust." The reviewer concluded that Wolfe's debut would be "a sharp pleasure to reread years from now, when it will bring back, like a falcon in the sky of memory, a whole world that is currently jetting and jazzing its way somewhere or other. By that time, Wolfe may have buffeted himself through the journalism barrier and produced the work of art that is obviously jouncing around in those kaleidoscopic cells of his."

In 1968 Wolfe published two books, *The Electric Kool-Aid Acid Test* and *The Pump House Gang*. The first book examines the psychedelic movement via Ken Kesey—the author of the acclaimed novel *One Flew Over the Cuckoo's Nest* (1964)—and his band of "Merry Pranksters," who travel across the country in their psychedelic bus. The product of a comfortable, middle-class upbringing, Kesey began experimenting with hallucinogenic drugs in the 1960s and became a hippie icon. In the *National Review* (August 27, 1968) Lawrence Dietz called *The Electric Kool-Aid Acid Test* the "best work Wolfe has done, and certainly the most profound and insightful book that has been written about the psychedelic life." Dietz added that "Wolfe has brought to his reportage a sense of historical perspective, and more important, a willingness to let accuracy take the place of the hysterical imprecations that have passed for reportage in most magazine articles and books on the subject." In a review for *The Nation* (September 23, 1968), Joel Lieber maintained that the book was about 100 pages too long and fell short of capturing Kesey. However, he concluded that Wolfe has "come as close as seems possible with words, at re-creating the entire mental atmosphere of a scene in which one's understanding is based on feeling rather than verbalization. His book . . . is nonfiction told as experimental fiction; it is a genuine feat and a landmark in reporting style."

The Pump House Gang is a collection of revised articles that Wolfe had previously published in magazines and newspapers. In it he provides a look at how contemporary society was changing during the 1960s and examines such groups as social climbers in New York City, society girls in London, motorcyclists, pop-art collectors, and a band of elite surfers in California who called themselves the Pump House Gang. In the *New York Times Book Review* (August 18, 1968), C. D. B. Bryan observed that Wolfe "manages somehow to imbue [his subjects] all with a semblance of life, no matter how depressing they may seem," but he concluded that it was little more than a remake of *The Kandy-Kolored Tangerine-Flake Streamline Baby*. In his review for *Newsweek* (August 26, 1968), Jack Kroll wrote, "Wolfe is one of the few writers of any sort who have truly caught the seeping miasma of modern madness that is drifting over the modern world. But he does this not in the cold, bright, heartless fake way of most absurdity-mongering journalists, but by seizing in a brilliant ritual of language the dissonances and occlusions that rack the protoplasms and the polity of mid-century America. . . . He creates the most vivid, most pertinent possible dimension of his subject."

Wolfe's next book, *Radical Chic and Mau-Mauing the Flak Catchers* (1970), was a republication of two of his essays. In "Radical Chic," which was originally published in *New York* magazine in June 1970, Wolfe scrutinized the late-1960s trend of wealthy elites courting and seeking to identify themselves with political radicals. Wolfe attended a party thrown by the conductor Leonard Bernstein and his wife at their duplex on Park Avenue in New York City to raise money for the legal defense of the Black Panthers (an African-American militant organization), several of whom faced criminal charges for allegedly planning a series of terrorist bombings in the city. Wolfe offered his amusing observations of the event as well as a number of barbs directed against the Bernsteins and their wealthy guests. The publication of the essay in *New York* generated substantial controversy. When asked by a reporter if Wolfe's account of the party was accurate, a minister of the Black Panther Party's shadow government replied, "You mean that dirty, blatant, lying, racist dog who wrote that fascist disgusting thing in *New York* magazine?" as quoted by Timothy Foote in *Time* (December 21, 1970). In *Commentary* (March 1971) Joseph Epstein wrote, "Wolfe has his own theory about the [Bernsteins' party]. He sees it as a classic instance of *nostalgie de la boue*, the 19th-century European upperclass phenomenon of imitating, whoring after, and generally romanticizing the primitive lower classes. There is something to this, though one suspects that the correspondences between the Bernsteins' set and 19th-century aristocratic circles probably ought best not be pressed too firmly." Epstein observed that Wolfe was probably the journalist best suited to cover the party because he "has always been marvelously attuned to all the nuttiness of the small gradations of status that play so large a role on these fringes" and "is invariably able to convey a vivid sense of what it is about these things that exhilarate those who go in for them—what it is, in short, that turns people on."

In "Mau-Mauing the Flak Catchers," Wolfe detailed the confrontation between white liberal bureaucrats who were in charge of administering a government anti-poverty program in California's Bay Area and several groups of racial-minority militants. Peter Michelson, reviewing the book for the *New Republic* (December 19, 1970), preferred "Mau-Mauing the Flak Catchers" to "Radical Chic," which he dismissed as a "vacuous parody." By contrast, "Mau-Mauing the Flak Catchers," Michelson wrote, contains "genuine humor" and "not only exposes and spanks social absurdities but also suggests ethical alternatives to bureaucratic paralysis."

In 1973 Wolfe and E. W. Johnson co-edited *The New Journalism: With an Anthology*, in the first part of which Wolfe contributed an essay explaining the New Journalism style. The second part of the book included excerpts from pieces written in the New Journalism style by such writers as Norman Mailer and Gay Talese. "Wolfe's boundless enthusiasm for the new style is contagious, although some may question his assertion that it has dethroned the novel as the reigning literary genre," Barbara Zelenko wrote for the *Library Journal* (May 1, 1973). "Taken together, these selections (dealing with politics, war, show business, the youth revolution, and other topics) comprise a fascinating panorama of recent American life. A lively textbook for would-be-writers."

In 1975 Wolfe published *The Painted Word*, an adaptation of an essay published in *Harper's Magazine* (April 1975) in which he offered a social history of modern art. According to Wolfe, modern art began as a revolution against literary content in art, but eventually adopted the same literary and academic content it once opposed. Wolfe faults contemporary modern art for capitulating to the theories of such powerful art critics as Clement Greenberg, Harold Rosenberg, and Leo Steinberg, who, Wolfe argues, stifle creativity by setting and enforcing standards for artists to follow. *The Painted Word* outraged many in the art community and sharply divided reviewers. "Nothing can escape the precise prose of the author," John Harvath wrote for the *Library Journal* (June 1, 1975), "and this brilliant essay cuts the world of 20th-Century art to the quick." In *Newsweek* (June 9, 1975) Douglas Davis took issue with Wolfe's arguments. "In brief, [Wolfe argues that] the critics have put modern art over on us," Davis wrote. "But theory has been part of the success of any art as far back as we can go—Victorian, neoclassical, Renaissance, medieval and even Greco-Roman art were surrounded by written analyses and statements, some of them still surviving. Michelangelo, Leonardo, and Delacroix were prodigious talkers and writers. So was Picasso." Davis refuted Wolfe's claim that modern art is unpopular with many ordinary people, pointing out that "museum attendance, print buying, and cheap reproduction sales have soared," and he attributed the flaws in *The Painted Word* to Wolfe's apparent failure "to get away from the typewriter and out into the thick of his subject. Imagine Wolfe dining with Greenberg, drinking with Rosenberg, going to an opening with Steinberg—and reporting it all. Then we would have the tang of reality, the feel of what it is like to be *inside* Cultureburg [Wolfe's pejorative term for the elite art world], instead of outside peering in, through the lens of theory."

In *Mauve Gloves & Madmen, Clutter & Vine, and Other Stories, Sketches, and Essays* (1976), a collection of his pieces and drawings, Wolfe offered his thoughts on such topics as minicomputers, pornography, hailing a taxicab in New York City, and summer fashions in Martha's Vineyard in Massachusetts. "Perhaps the chief delight of this collection is watching [Wolfe's] style shift with his varying subjects," Jack Beatty wrote in his review for *The Nation* (March 5, 1977). "To re-create the look and feel of a jet taking off from an aircraft carrier Wolfe unleashes a forty-five line sentence that puts you as close to the horror, noise and confusion of the real thing as you are ever likely to get." Beatty concluded that the pieces in the book "offer a lively picture of the surface of our society; one wishes life were this interesting. But they tell us little of what lies beneath the surface." Reviewing the collection for *America* (February 4, 1977), the Reverend Gerard Reedy wrote, "In his energetic accumulation of detail and in his clever way of isolating cultural metonyms, Wolfe is a marvel, a phenomenon for any writer to admire. Although Wolfe is anti-fad and anti-elite throughout, the exact moral or philosophical position from which he satirizes his subjects is not always clear." Reedy described Wolfe as "an old-fashioned moralist who, at the same time, knows intimately the way we live now."

In one of his best-known nonfiction books, *The Right Stuff* (1979), Wolfe wrote about the origins of the U.S. space-exploration program. He focuses on such test pilots as Chuck Yeager, who flew experimental aircraft during the 1950s, paving the way for manned spacecraft. "I was interested in who do you get to sit on top of those enormous rockets, on top of really enormous amounts of liquid oxygen," he told Adrianne Blue for the *Washington Post* (September 9, 1979). Wolfe found that there was nothing special in the backgrounds of the seven astronauts who participated in Project Mercury except that most of them had been test pilots. "So there you go," Wolfe elaborated to Blue. "The way to approach it was to find out what test pilots are like—and this led to the whole theory of 'the right stuff.'" Wolfe conducted extensive research for the book, interviewing many pilots and astronauts. In his review for the *Washington Post* (September 9, 1979), Michael Collins, one of the astronauts of the Apollo 11 mission that landed on the moon in 1969, lauded the book. "Wolfe's profile of Yeager and his description of the Air Force Flight Test Center at Edwards Air Force Base are absolutely first class," Collins observed. "I've flown with Yeager, and I lived at Edwards for four years, and, improbable as some of Tom's tales seem, I know he's telling it like it was." Collins added that another "superlative part of the book deals with the diversity of the astronaut group, as opposed to the homogenized mush of personality stereotypes that *Life* magazine and others pushed in the Mercury days." Although critical of the author's accounts of the space flights, Collins concluded that "*The Right Stuff* is not vintage, psychedelic Tom Wolfe, but if you . . . have ever been curious about what the space program was really all about in those halcyon [President John F.] Kennedy and Mercury years, then this is your book." *The Right Stuff* was a national best-seller and earned the American Book Award for nonfiction, the National Institute of Arts and Letters Harold Vursell Award for prose style, and the Columbia Journalism Award. In 1983 *The Right Stuff* was adapted into a popular and critically acclaimed film with Ed Harris, Scott Glenn, Dennis Quaid, and Sam Shepard.

In 1980 Wolfe published *In Our Time*, a collection of drawings that had appeared in *Harper's Magazine* as well as captions and several short articles. "The scratchy black-and-white ink drawings, populated by the inhabitants of Wolfe's Me Generation—from alcoholic . . . executives to fat Hollywood moguls—strain toward [Honoré Daumier's] social consciousness without that great artist's skill or compassion," Kay Larson asserted in the *Saturday Review* (October 1980). "Each picture is accompanied by a lengthy Wolfean exegesis, usually far funnier than the drawing it accompanies. The drawings, unfortunately, stand or fall with the prose, and the prose can flame as brightly (and die as quickly) as lighter fluid." In his review for *Quill & Quire* (April 1981), Paul Stuewe described *In Our Time* as a "mere chip from the Wolfe-ian lode, but solid gold all the same. Several short essays act as scintillating appetizers to a tasty main course of drawings, and together they add up to a most satisfying repast."

In Wolfe's next book, *From Bauhaus to Our House* (1981), an adaptation of an essay that he published in *Harper's Magazine*, the author turned his attention to modern architecture. According to Wolfe, the post–World War I Bauhaus school of design in Germany greatly influenced contemporary architectural styles in the United States, resulting in the design of new buildings and homes that ignored aesthetics and did not reflect the spirit of the nation. "As in *The Painted Word*, Wolfe's explanation is that modernism has been a conspiracy," Benjamin Forgey wrote for the *Washington Post* (November 15, 1981). "In place of the New York critics who foisted abstract art upon us, we have the European giants of architecture (Walter Gropius, Mies van der Rohe of the Barcelona chair and other icons, and Le Corbusier) and their abject American followers. In Wolfe's view the motivation was pretty much the same, too. They were all playing the hypocritical bohemian game of spitting on the bourgeois." Although Forgey acknowledged the truth of some of Wolfe's points, he observed that the author's "own outlook is quite rigid. He obviously has no interest, none at all, in the internal [aesthetics] of architecture, in that sense of serious play that can result in surprising, beautiful, and efficacious new forms. Nor does he demonstrate much interest, other than as a way of putting it down, in the social, cultural, political, economic, demographic or technological conditions that gave rise to the modernist movement." Conversely, in the *Library Journal* (November 1, 1981) Edward Nilsson wrote, "Wolfe has done it again. This historical vignette on the ideas behind modern architecture is always entertaining and often brilliant. . . . The architect and student will be thoroughly delighted with the biographical sketches of Le Corbusier, Gropius, et al., although the serious historian might object to some of the author's metaphors and characterizations (e.g., 'hog stomping Baroque exuberance of American civilization')."

Wolfe next assembled a collection of his best work from the 1960s and 1970s in *The Purple Decades* (1982). "*The Purple Decades* is . . . Wolfe's greatest hits as ordained by the master himself," Jonathan Yardley observed in the *Washington Post* (November 7, 1982). "What *The Purple Decades* tells us, then, is that Wolfe sees himself as a chronicler of three broad subjects: the vulgarity, pretension and cynicism of life during the period that he has penetratingly characterized as 'the Me Decade;' the con game played on the public by the high priests and priestesses of modern art and architecture; the daring deeds of those few remaining souls—stock-car drivers, combat pilots, test pilots, astronauts—who undertake acts of individual courage during an age of collective timidity. His marks in the first category are startlingly high, but rather lower in the second and third; and too often his feats of social observation are gravely diminished by his showy, self-declarative prose." In his review for the *Christian Science Monitor* (February 2, 1983), Bruce Allen wrote, "Although Tom

Wolfe's surrealistic buoyancy occasionally masks conservative postures (see his funny diatribes against modern art and architecture), and his satirical cartoons are derivative, he emerges as a brilliant reporter, whose prose comes through as the honest and appropriate expression of his impish sensibility."

In 1981 Wolfe began writing a novel about life in New York City, where he lived. "It struck me that nobody any longer seemed to be writing novels of the city, in the sense that Balzac wrote novels of Paris and Dickens and Thackeray wrote novels of London," he told Mervyn Rothstein for the *New York Times* (October 13, 1987). Although he recognized that writing fiction is different than writing nonfiction, Wolfe believed that good reporting is necessary to both. After struggling with the project and writing very little, Wolfe approached *Rolling Stone* magazine about publishing the novel in serial form, a practice that had served Charles Dickens, Honoré de Balzac, and Emilé Zola well. "I knew this would force it out of me," he told Rothstein. "I knew from my newspaper days that I could make a deadline. Even if it wasn't very good, I could make a deadline." *Rolling Stone* accepted Wolfe's proposal, and *The Bonfire of the Vanities* appeared in issues of the magazine from 1984 to 1985. Wolfe subsequently revised the novel and expanded it to more than 600 pages for its publication in book form in 1987. Whereas in the serialized version, the protagonist, Sherman McCoy, was a writer, in the book version Wolfe turned Sherman into a bond salesman who has everything and considers himself a "master of the universe." Sherman owns a Mercedes and lives in a 14-room duplex on Park Avenue with his wife, Judy, and their young daughter, Campbell. Sherman's life begins to unravel when his wife discovers that he is unfaithful to her and when he is accused of running down an African-American teenager with his car in a crime-ridden neighborhood in the South Bronx. Although his mistress, Maria, actually hit the teenager, Sherman is eventually arrested for the crime, which sparks a media frenzy. A whole host of characters—including the mayor of New York City, the Bronx County district attorney, a local prosecutor, a trial lawyer, a British tabloid journalist, and a demagogic African-American minister—are eager to exploit the case, and possibly send an innocent man to prison, in order to advance their own individual ambitions. The title of Wolfe's novel was based on the exploits of the 15th-century Italian priest Girolamo Savonarola, who encouraged people to burn items he considered sinful. "In the real 'bonfire of the vanities,'" Wolfe explained to Rothstein, "Savonarola sent his 'Red Guard' units into people's homes to drag out their vanities—which were anything from false eyelashes to paintings with nudes in them, including Botticellis. This bonfire is more the fire created by vain people themselves, under the pressure of the city of New York. It may happen in other places, but it certainly happens here. People are always writing about the energy of New York. What they really mean is the status ambitions of people of New York. That's the motor in this town. That's what makes it exciting—and it's also what makes it awful many times." *The Bonfire of the Vanities* was a huge success. In addition to receiving many enthusiastic reviews, the novel spent two months at the top of the *New York Times* best-seller list and remained on the list for more than a year. "The fun of the book, and much of its energy, comes from watching Mr. Wolfe eviscerate one pathetic character after another," the novelist Frank Conroy wrote for the *New York Times Book Review* (November 1, 1987). "And he is good at it, really brilliant sometimes." Conroy, however, noted that "the fun can turn sour. Malice is a powerful spice. Too much can ruin the stew, and Mr. Wolfe comes close." In his review for *Time* (November 9, 1987), R. Z. Sheppard also hailed the novel. "Wolfe is a master of social satire," Sheppard wrote. "*Bonfire* is merciless and unrelenting in its depiction of New York as a city driven by ethnic and racial hostility, political ambition and status." The reviewer observed that the novel's controversial content is "embedded in convincing contexts and experienced through the eyes, ears, and nerve endings of the characters. This technique is what makes Wolfe's journalism so vital and gives him authority as a novelist. This, and his ability to handle an imaginative and intricate plot that welds his descriptions of dinner parties, restaurant games, Wall Street trading and courthouse chaos into more than a tour de force." In 1990 the director Brian De Palma adapted *The Bonfire of the Vanities* into a film that failed with both critics and audiences.

Wolfe spent much of the 1990s writing his second novel, *A Man in Full*, which was published in 1998. Setting the novel in the multiracial city of Atlanta, Georgia, Wolfe expanded on the themes he explored in *The Bonfire of the Vanities*. The title's "man in full" is Charlie Croker, a bigoted old Southerner and former star football player at Georgia Tech who frequently boasts about his physical and sexual prowess. Despite being a wealthy real-estate developer and the head of a national conglomerate, Charlie spends much of his time hunting quail on his 29,000-acre estate. Charlie is a poor businessman, and his conglomerate has accumulated billions in debt. Under pressure from creditors, he lays off workers at one his subsidiaries, Croker Global Foods in California's Bay Area. Among the displaced workers is an idealistic young man named Conrad Hensley, who ends up in prison. After reading the work of the ancient Roman philosopher Epictetus in prison, Conrad becomes a Stoic, basing his life on virtue, logic, and nature. An earthquake allows Conrad to escape (which he attributes to divine intervention), and he flees to Atlanta, where he eventually finds employment with Croker and converts him to Stoicism. Meanwhile, racial tensions are threatening to tear Atlanta apart over the upcoming trial of Fareek "the Cannon" Fanon, a star African-American football player with Georgia Tech, who is accused of date raping a white girl from one of the city's most prominent families. Eager to avoid race riots and not alienate both the African-American and white communities, Wesley Dobbs Jordan, the city's African-American mayor, reaches out to Croker for help, offering to get the creditors off Croker's back if he agrees to speak out on Fanon's behalf and plead for calm. Because the alleged victim is the daughter of his best friend, the offer presents a dilemma for Croker. The other major character in the novel is Roger White II (known as "Roger Too White"), an African-American lawyer from a privileged background who represents Fanon. In the *Atlanta Journal and Constitution* (November 5, 1998), John Huey described *A Man in Full* as a "big, rich book, chock-full of wonderful descriptive writing, clever social commentary, and comprehensive, sophisticated reporting." Huey, however, asserted that Wolfe had misrepresented the state of race relations in modern-day Atlanta. "For one thing, the white racism in contemporary Atlanta is so much more subtle and sophisticated than what we see in Charlie Croker, who is such a Hollywood-style cliché that it's hard to believe someone as sophisticated as the great Tom Wolfe could have wrote him," Huey wrote. "Beyond that, there's Wolfe's primary plot premise—that an alleged date rape of a white society girl by a black football player would endanger the public peace. Give me a break! This is a city that has endured, among other things, the missing and murdered children crisis, [and] bombings at the Olympics and abortion clinics." In the *New Yorker* (November 9, 1998) the writer John Updike also expressed disappointment with the novel. "[Wolfe] concocts a good, if sometimes laborious read, which becomes perfunctory and implausible only toward the end," Updike observed. "The laboriousness derives, in part, from the worked-up quality of many scenes, masterpieces of creative journalism but a little thick for floating suspense and characters with free will." Updike concluded that *A Man in Full* "amounts to entertainment, not literature, even literature in a modest aspirant form. Like a movie desperate to recoup its bankers' investment, the novel tries too hard to please us." Despite the mixed reviews, the book was a best-seller. A testament to Tom Wolfe's reputation, *A Man in Full* was nominated for the National Book Award before its publication.

In 2000 Wolfe published *Hooking Up*, a collection that included several nonfiction essays and the novella "Ambush at Fort Bragg." The essays present Wolfe's thoughts on such topics as left-wing college professors, dating on college campuses, the sculptor Frederick Hart, and the Vietnam Veterans Memorial in Washington, D.C. In "My Three Stooges" Wolfe answers the authors John Updike, Norman Mailer, and John Irving, who had all criticized *A Man in Full*. (The article set off a storm of well-publicized disputes between Wolfe and the three authors.) *Hooking Up* also includes Wolfe's famous broadside against the *New Yorker*, which he published in 1965, and his profile of Bob Noyce, the co-founder of the Intel Corporation, which first appeared in 1983. The novella, which had appeared in two parts in *Rolling Stone*, follows a television news magazine that tries to obtain evidence against three soldiers who are suspected of murdering a gay comrade. "Wolfe may have made millions off his fiction, but at heart he is and always will be a terrific reporter," Malcolm Jones wrote for *Newsweek* (November 13, 2000). "*Hooking Up* provides a great introduction to Wolfe the nonfiction stylist: the peerless portraitist (Robert Noyce, Frederick Hart), the contrarian social critic ('In the Land of the Rococo Marxists') and the literary bomb thrower ('My Three Stooges'). Yes, there is a piece of fiction here ('Ambush at Fort Bragg,' a self-contained novella cut from *A Man in Full*). But the strongest entries are factual pieces on everything from teen sex to sociology. The book's title is a sexual metaphor, but in Wolfe's hands, it means making connections among the culture's disparate corners. And nobody hooks up better than he does."

Tom Wolfe's many awards and honors include the Society of Magazine Writers award for excellence (1970), the John Dos Passos Award (1984), the Gari Melchers Medal (1986), the Washington Irving Medal for literary excellence from the Nicholas Society (1986), and honorary degrees from many colleges.

Wolfe was forced to take a break from writing in 1996, after having quintuple-bypass heart surgery. He and his wife, Sheila, have two children, Alexandra and Thomas, and make their home in New York City.

—D. C.

SUGGESTED READING: *America* p113 Feb. 5, 1977; *Atlanta Journal and Constitution* D p1+ Nov. 5, 1998; *Christian Science Monitor* p15 Feb. 2, 1983; *Commentary* p98+ Mar. 1971; *Library Journal* p1479 May 1, 1973, p1114 June 1, 1975; *Nation* p232 Sep. 23, 1968, p278 Mar. 5, 1977; *National Review* p865 Aug. 27, 1968; *New Republic* p17 Dec. 19, 1970; *New York Times* C p13+ Oct. 13, 1987, with photo; *New Yorker* p99+ Nov. 9, 1998; *Newsweek* p90 June 28, 1965, p88 June 9, 1975, with photo, p84 Nov. 13, 2000; *Quill & Quire* p39 Apr. 1981; *Saturday Review* p23 July 31, 1965, p90 Oct. 1980; *Time* p72+ Dec. 21, 1970, p101+ Nov. 9, 1987; Tom Wolfe Official Web site; *Washington Post* p9 Sep. 9, 1979, with photo; *Washington Post Book World* p1+ Sep. 9, 1979, p10 Nov. 15, 1981, p23+ Nov. 7, 1982; Shomette, Doug ed. *The Critical Response to Tom Wolfe*, 1982; Scura, Dorothy ed. *Conversations with Tom Wolfe*, 1990; McKeen, William. *Tom Wolfe*, 1995; Ragen, Brian Abel. *Tom Wolfe: A Critical Companion*, 2002

SELECTED BOOKS: as editor—*The New Journalism* (with E. W. Johnson), 1973; nonfiction—*The Kandy-Kolored Tangerine-Flake Streamline Baby*, 1965; *The Electric Kool-Aid Acid Test*, 1968; *The Pump House Gang*, 1968; *Radical Chic and Mau-Mauing the Flak Catchers*, 1970; *The Painted Word*, 1975; *Mauve Gloves & Madmen, Clutter & Wine, and Other Short Stories*, 1976; *The Right Stuff, 1979*; 1979; *In Our Time*, 1980; *From Bauhaus to Our House*, 1981; *The Purple Decades: A Reader*, 1982; *Hooking Up*, 2000; novels—*The Bonfire of the Vanities*, 1987; *A Man in Full*, 1998

Katie Estill/Courtesy of Penguin Putnam, Inc.

Woodrell, Daniel

Mar. 4, 1953– Novelist

Daniel Woodrell has won critical acclaim for his novels, which are set in fictional towns in the Louisiana bayou and the Ozark region in Missouri. The inhabitants of such places—blue-collar workers, hillbillies, wanderers, and criminals—are witty, passionate, and eloquent; what one critic has called "back-country Shakespeares." Woodrell sends the police detective Rene Shade to battle corruption and racism in *Under the Bright Lights* (1986) and gangsters in *Muscle for the Wing* (1988). Shade is on hand to help his father and half-sister when they are pursued by a ruthless gambler in *The Ones You Do* (1992). A writer goes home to the Ozarks and gets caught in the middle of a blood feud between two families in *Give Us a Kiss* (1996). A lonely man is recruited by two opportunistic teenagers into an unsavory scheme in *Tomato Red* (1998). In a heart-wrenching story, *The Death of Sweet Mister* (2001), Woodrell presents a 13-year-old boy who is trapped in a life of crime by an abusive father-figure and neglectful mother. Such characters reflect their environment, which is often rough, chaotic, and dangerous. Reviewers have lauded Woodrell for skillfully using language to bring the bayou country and the Ozark region to life and for creating memorable dialogue that gives his characters authenticity. "I don't really consider myself a crime writer in the narrow sense," Woodrell said to Liz Rowlinson, a contributor to *The Richmond Review* (on-line). "I *do* often love the sort of people and situations novels that get called crime novels deal with. . . . Most of the work I am going toward will be very much to the periphery of crime writing, and possibly out of its bounds."

Daniel Woodrell was born on March 4, 1953 in Springfield, Missouri. His father, Robert Lee, worked in sales, and his mother, Jeanneanne Monique (Daily), was a nurse. He and his two brothers grew up in the town of St. Charles, near the banks of the Missouri River. "My mom taught us to read before we started school," he told Richard H. Weiss, a reporter for the *St. Louis Post-Dispatch* (April 19, 1992). "Twain was the first real writer I read."

When he was 15 Woodrell and his family moved to Overland Park, Kansas. He began writing short stories and writing for newspapers when he was in high school. He dropped out of high school, at age 17, to enlist in the marines, serving two years as a sharpshooter on a military base on the Pacific island of Guam. Woodrell recalled to Weiss that after leaving the military he did "the normal early '70s stuff hitchhiking around the country. I went to school once in a while on the GI bill and once in a while I didn't. When I was 23 I ended up at the University of Kansas and got serious about trying to write. It was a long time before anyone got serious about what I was trying to write."

Woodrell attended Johnson County Community College, in Overland Park, from 1972 to 1976 and also Fort Hays Kansas State College (later renamed Fort Hays State University), in Hays, Kansas, from 1972 to 1974, never receiving a degree from either institution. In 1976 he enrolled at the University of Kansas, in Lawrence. He earned two Edna Osborne Whitcomb awards for creative writing, in 1976 and 1979, and the Edgar Wolfe Award for fiction, in 1981. He graduated, in 1980, with a bachelor of general studies (B.S.G.) degree. In 1983 he received a master of fine arts degree from the University of Iowa, and was then awarded a James A. Michener fellowship to attend the prestigious Iowa Writers' Workshop, from 1984 to 1985. Woodrell found that he did not always fit in with the other writers in the workshop. "I'm from a regular, blue-collar background, and there were lots of people from the elite segments of society there," he told Michael Carlson, a writer for the London *Daily Telegraph* (October 29, 1999). "I was even asked to leave, because they said I wasn't fit to put in front of a classroom. I refused to go. They've got a point of view, and I've got one." For one of the classes, Woodrell wrote part of his Civil War novel, *Woe to Live On*, which was published in 1988. The class, he elaborated to Carlson, "was incensed because my characters, fighting for the Confederacy, didn't apologise for slavery with a modern sensibility!"

In 1986 Woodrell published his first novel, *Under the Bright Lights*. Woodrell created the fictional town of St. Bruno, inspired in part by his childhood memories of St. Charles. St. Bruno is located in Louisiana's bayou country and is divided into three sections: Frogtown, the original French settlement, now home to cajuns; Pan Fry, where the town's African-American population lives; and Hawthorne Hills, home to the city's elite. The novel's protagonist is Rene Shade, a Cajun police detective. Shade and his partner are assigned to investigate the murder of an African-American mayoral candidate. Racial tensions threaten to tear the town apart, and Shade finds racism and corruption nearly everywhere in St. Bruno as he pursues the case. "Although perhaps too gamy for some and somewhat overwritten, the story is gripping," Sybil S. Steinberg wrote in *Publishers Weekly* (June 20, 1986). "Dialogue that is pithy and full of vitality personalizes the characters in St. Bruno, Louisiana."

Woodrell's second novel, *Woe to Live On* (1987), is set during the start of the Civil War, in 1861. It depicts the lawlessness and guerilla warfare that raged along the border of Kansas and Missouri, far from the heat of the action on the battlefields of Gettysburg or Antietam. The story is narrated by Jake Roedel, a teenager who heads the "Kansas Irregulars," a roving band of robbers and murderers. Fueled by a lethal combination of youthful idealism, Southern pride, and whiskey, the Irregulars make raids and attacks on suspected Yankee sympathizers, and finally lead a doomed attack on the town of Lawrence, Kansas. For Donald McCaig, in the *Washington Post* (June 21, 1987), the tight focus on this narrative led to problems. "We aren't told much about Jake Roedel's past or that of his companions. . . . Without our knowing him better (his past, his beliefs), Jake Roedel isn't very appealing," McCaig argued. "His character change, brought on by an overload of grimness, isn't convincing." He praised the book's language as "sharp and convincing," writing that the "speech rhythms, locutions and slang ring true." The director Ang Lee secured the rights to *Woe to Live On* and adapted it into the film *Ride With the Devil* (1999). Although it received a number of favorable reviews, the film failed at the box office because it was screened in only a handful of theaters. (*Woe to Live On* was republished in 1999 as *Ride With the Devil*.)

Woodrell's hero, Rene Shade, returned in *Muscle for the Wing* (1988). Shade battles a group of vicious ex-convicts and Dixie gangsters who plan to take over St. Bruno by violently displacing Auguste Beaurain, the town's long-established boss. In the *Washington Post* (November 29, 1988) Robert Campbell praised the book's "off-the-wall characters, quirky and bizarre, yet as authentic as any I've ever met in a novel about a milieu I don't know." Describing the novel as "the perfect or nearly perfect mystery," Campbell noted that Woodrell's language set the novel apart. He cited a description of the town: "From the winging city pigeon's vantage point the neighborhoods of St. Bruno looked like a fist clutching at the lifeline that was the big greasy river."

In 1992 Woodrell published his third novel set in St. Bruno, *The Ones You Do*. John X. Shade, the father of the police detective Rene Shade, the hero in two of Woodrell's previous novels, is left by his younger wife, who hopes to become a singer and takes with her the $47,000 that was locked in his safe. The money, however, wasn't his. It was owed to Lunch Pumphrey, a murderous gambler with jailhouse tattoos—one reads "Cubs Win!"—and a strict habit of smoking only seven cigarettes a day. When Pumphrey comes to collect the money, John knocks him out with a whiskey bottle and leaves town, taking his 10-year-old daughter, Etta, with him. They seek shelter in John's hometown, St. Bruno, and meet up with his ex-wife and three grown sons. Pumphrey follows Shade to St. Bruno, determined to exact revenge. In the *Los Angeles Times* (July 19, 1992) Fred Schruers lauded *The Ones You Do*, noting that Woodrell has a gift for balancing violence and savagery with wit. "That gift frees him to treat us to the irresistible dialogue his characters pour forth; they're virtually all backcountry (or trailer- park or slum) Shakespeares," he observed. Schruers added that some readers might find the conclusion "a bit murky, but Woodrell makes us read it almost prayerfully as he clues us in—a tribute to how much we care for the book's broken-down hero." In the *Washington Post* (April 1, 1992) Carl Hiaasen described the novel as "great fun," writing that "the dialogue is dazzling. . . . And the characters are slippery and warped just as they are in true life, if you're hanging out at the right joints. Woodrell's white-trash philosophers might see things in a peculiar way, but they see clearly."

Woodrell's next novel, *Give Us a Kiss: A Country Noir* (1996), revolves around Doyle Redmond, a college-educated writer who goes home to the backwoods town of West Table, in the Ozark region of Missouri, to see his family. Doyle meets up with his older brother, Smoke, a fugitive from justice; Big Annie, Smoke's hippie girlfriend; and Niagra, Big Annie's seductive, 19-year-old daughter. When Doyle agrees to help this group harvest their marijuana patch—rationalizing that the experience will make good fodder for a novel—he becomes enmeshed in a feud with their sworn enemies, the Dollys, who are planning to steal the crop. In the *New York Times Book Review* (March 10, 1996, on-line) Robert Houston described this world as "the pre-Wal-Mart mountain South, where people are still connected to the land in old ways, where blood feuds still exist, where toughness and meanness and stubbornness are virtues and survival tactics." Noting that Woodrell "creates that vanishing South with an accuracy and understanding beyond any genre writer's capability," Houston concluded that the book was a "good read, with salty dialogue, tough-guy prose, quick- sketched characters and sharp, terse imagery."

Woodrell's sixth novel, *Tomato Red* (1998), also takes place in West Table, Missouri. The book's narrator, Sammy Barlach, works in the town's dog-food factory. One night, after burglarizing a mansion, Barlach encounters two teenagers, Jamalee and Jason Merridew, who have also broken into the house. Jamalee, who has dyed, "tomato red" hair, wants to escape the dreary life of West Table. Her hopes depend on her brother, an extremely attractive 17-year-old, who is more interested in other boys than in the wealthy women who pursue him. Jamalee recruits Barlach, who longs for companionship, to help facilitate her schemes. In his review for the London *Times* (March 27, 1999) Steve Jelbert wrote that Woodrell's "ability to draw characters is indisputable and his dialogue is rich, brutal and often hilarious." Jelbert added that Sammy "is a wonderful fall guy" and concluded that *Tomato Red* is "highly stylised and very funny." In *Newsday* (August 9, 1998) Sonja Bolle had mixed feelings about the novel. She noted that the language was not up to Woodrell's usual standard, writing, "He's one of those storytellers you lean into, so mesmerized by his cadences that even when he's telling you ugly things you want to hear more." However, she asserted that *Tomato Red* is not as good as his previous novels, dismissing it as "a shaggy-dog story." Woodrell has sold the film rights to *Tomato Red.*

Woodrell tapped into his childhood memories for his novel, *The Death of Sweet Mister* (2001). Set in the Ozarks during the late 1960s, the story centers on a 13-year-old boy, nicknamed "Shug," who is forced into a life of crime by Red, his mother's abusive husband. Shug and his alcoholic mother, Glenda, serve as caretakers for the local cemetery. Although Glenda loves her son, she cannot help him escape from Red. In an interview with Robert W. Butler, a reporter for the *Kansas City Star* (June 10, 2001), Woodrell recalled that, growing up in St. Charles, he had a friend who was in similar circumstances to Shug. "We hung out together, but I was never allowed in his house, and never really understood why," Woodrell told Butler. "But one day he did invite me to his home, and we walked in on what I now realize was some sort of criminal enterprise. His father was there with another guy, surrounded by stacks of what was certainly stolen merchandise. The father got mad, exploded, punched my friend, and I ran away. It took me awhile to figure out what I'd seen." After his family moved to Overland Park, Woodrell lost track of his friend. Since several of his childhood friends landed in prison, Woodrell told Butler that "it would have taken real good luck for him not to have a rap sheet by now."

In her review for the *Boston Globe* (May 18, 2001), Amy Graves wrote, "This novel . . . has many familiar emotional threads and an almost predictable plot, yet it's still compelling. What makes it hum is that Woodrell's descriptions—of a long walk wandering in the dark, Shug's ornery uncle's arrival home from Vietnam, or even just a hot summer day—seem real and alive and linger long after reading." Graves was also moved by Shug, writing that his miserable "upbringing is just as hard to forget as it is to forgive." Reviewing the novel for the *Washington Post* (May 27, 2001), Lawrence Block argued that "it is the voice of Shug that makes this book such a joy to read. . . . My guess is that Woodrell found Shug somewhere within his own imagination, let him talk and let what he heard inform his narrative."

Daniel Woodrell's first marriage ended in divorce, in 1980. He is currently married to Katherine Estill, a writer. The couple lives in West Plains, Missouri.

—D. C.

SUGGESTED READING: *Boston Globe* D p10 May 18, 2001; London *Daily Telegraph* p24 Oct. 29, 1999; *Kansas City Star* Arts p17 June 10, 2001; *Los Angeles Times* Book Review p2 July 19, 1992; *New York Times Book Review* (on-line) Mar. 10, 1996; *Newsday* B p12 Aug. 9. 1998; *Publishers Weekly* p93 June 20, 1986; *Richmond Review* (on-line); *St. Louis Post-Dispatch* C p3 Apr. 19, 1992; (London) *Times* (on-line) Mar. 27, 1999; *Washington Post* p9 June 21, 1987, p9 Nov. 20, 1988, p3 Apr. 1, 1992, p6 May 27, 2001

SELECTED BOOKS: *Under the Bright Lights*, 1986; *Woe to Live On*, 1987 (republished as *Ride with the Devil*, 1999); *Muscle for the Wing*, 1988; *The Ones You Do*, 1992; *Give Us a Kiss: A Country Noir*, 1996; *Tomato Red*, 1998; *The Death of Sweet Mister*, 2001

Wright, C. D.

Jan. 6, 1949– Poet

C. D. Wright has been influenced throughout her career by memories of a childhood spent in the Ozark mountains of Arkansas, recollections that lend a spirit of simplicity and artisanal craft to her major poetry collections: *Translation of the Gospel Back Into Tongues* (1983), *Further Adventures With You* (1986), *String Light*, (1991), *Just Whistle* (1993), *Tremble* (1996), and *Deepstep Come Shining* (1998). The recipient of many honors, including a 1999 Lannan Literary Award, Wright has made her living by teaching at Brown University, where she is a distinguished professor.

C. D. Wright was born on January 6, 1949 in Mountain Home, Arkansas, in the Ozark mountains. Her mother, Alyce E. Wright, was a court reporter, and her father, Ernie E. Wright, a judge. She

Forrest Gander/Courtesy of Copper Canyon Press

C. D. Wright

chose to use the initials C. D. instead of her given name—Carolyn—so that she would not be confused with another poet of a very similar name, who began her writing career at about the same time.

Wright was educated at Memphis State University, where she received a bachelor's degree in French in 1971, and at the University of Arkansas in Fayetteville, where she earned a master of fine arts degree in 1976. She later moved to San Francisco, becoming director of the writing workshops at the Intersection Center for the Arts and lecturing at San Francisco State University. In 1983, the year she married Forrest Gander, a fellow poet, she became an English professor at Brown University, in Providence, Rhode Island. Wright and Gander named their son Brecht, as a tribute to Bertolt Brecht, the German poet and playwright.

Wright's first three poetry collections were chapbooks. *Alla Breve Loving* was issued in 1976 by Mill Mountain Press; the next two, *Room Rented By a Single Woman* (1977) and *Terrorism* (1979), were brought out by Lost Roads, under the editorial direction of Frank Stanford. Stanford had become her mentor while she was at the University of Arkansas, and after his suicide, at the age of 29, Wright and Stanford's widow took over the directorship of Lost Roads. Wright and Gander, her husband, have continued its management. In an essay entitled "The Choice for Poetry," published in the *Writer* (May 1993), Wright wrote of her commitment to poetry while acknowledging that poets "remain hopelessly unprofessional. . . . Income must be derived elsewhere. The poet whose work had the most influence on my young life, the late Frank Stanford, earned his living as a land surveyor."

Wright's first full-length collection of poems, *Translations of the Gospel Back Into Tongues* (1983), embodies in its title her enduring themes. Her Ozark background comes through in her sometimes irreverent—though formal—appropriation of biblical speech. "Disenchanted views of deprivation and the inertia or violence it engenders are joined to an awareness of the ordinary that survives amid extremes," Robert Shaw observed in the *New York Times Book Review* (September 4, 1983). He singled out for particular praise "Obedience of the Corpse" for its "casual, relentless clarity. . . . A midwife is laying out the body of a woman who died giving birth: 'She smells apples,/Wonders where she keeps them in the house./Nothing is under the sink/But a broken sack of potatoes/Growing eyes in the dark.'"

Wright published an essay in the *Southern Review* (Autumn 1994), "Provisional Remarks on Being/A Poet/Of Arkansas," in which she used the words *poetry* and *Arkansas* as verbs: "I poetry. I write it, study it, read it, edit it, publish it, teach it. . . . Sometimes I weary of it. I could not live without it. Not in this world. Not in my lifetime. I also Arkansas. Sometimes these verbs coalesce. Sometimes they trot off in opposite directions." She explained that, for her, conscious "southern identity is a bromidal fallacy," adding that if "I have any particular affinity for poetry associated with the South, it is with idiom. I credit hill people and African Americans for keeping the language distinct." She quoted the jazz great Miles Davis as saying, "Those dark Arkansas roads, that is the sound I am after," and she concluded, "He had his own sound. He recommended we get ours."

Wright's collection *Further Adventures With You* was published in 1986, followed by *String Light* (1991), *Just Whistle* (1993), *Tremble* (1996), and *Deepstep Come Shining* (1998). In a discussion of Wright's poetry in the larger context of "the private lyric poem," Jenny Goodman observed in *Melus* (Summer 1994) that Wright's "forms have become more and more experimental," while her voice "has become more and more personal; that is, the distance between speaker and poet in her poems has narrowed."

In "Like Someone Driving to Texas by Herself," a poem from the collection *Tremble*, Wright seems to compare her life and career to a drive to Texas: "in the trunk unpowered steering the arduous turning/around/and skies amassing at the border/words appeared/by which she wanted to live not singularly but/companionate/in a wandering and guilty life everyone makes/orthographic errors."

For Wright, poetry serves not as an escape, but rather as a vehicle for human connection. In "On the Beach," from *Tremble*, the poet is visited by her father, "clutching a poke of tomatoes": "Courage and sex" He said/setting his poke down/at last "Caroline,/is all love is" finally with a faint sound/as a loneliness sewn by hand the wing/sheared away finally the loneliness sheared/away as a wing sewn by hand."

In 2002 Wright published *Steal Away: Selected and New Poems*, which includes samples of her work from over a 20-year period. The poems chronicle her journey from a poor, Southern childhood to an esteemed New England professorship. "Wright's skeptical, smoky, and ambushing poems are oddly ventriloquial, especially when she writes of the body as though it were severed from the soul and the self," Donna Seaman remarked in *Booklist*, as quoted on *Amazon.com*. "New works accompany selections from nine previous, mostly out of print collections, and all are electrifying in their clear-eyed reports on desire, determination, and survival. For all the darkness she plumbs, Wright reminds readers, 'The world spins / nightly toward its brightness and we are on it.'"

Among Wright's honors have been a Lila Wallace–Reader's Digest Writers' Award, National Endowment for the Arts fellowships in 1981 and 1988, the Witter Bynner Prize for Poetry from the American Academy and Institute of Arts and Letters in 1986, a Guggenheim fellowship in 1987, a Whiting Writers Award in 1989, and the Rhode Island Governor's Award. In 1999 she received a Lannan Literary Award.

Wright observed of the poet's dilemma in the *Writer* (May 1993): "You will not find our books except in the independently owned and operated literary stores of our most cerebral cities and headier colleges. This is not our choice, to be removed from the larger public sphere; it is our loss. To resolve to be a poet in the face of this predetermined dilemma leaves you free to sing as you will, with the lungs God gave you—even if no one but God might hear. It leaves you that naked and obligated to sing your best."

—S. Y.

SUGGESTED READING: *Melus* p35+ Summer 1994; *New York Times Book Review* p8 Sep. 4, 1983; *Southern Review* p809+ Autumn 1994; *Writer* p19+ May 1993

SELECTED BOOKS: poetry—*Alla Breve Loving*, 1976; *Room Rented by a Single Woman*, 1977; *Terrorism*, 1979; *Translations of the Gospel Back Into Tongues*, 1983; *Further Adventures With You*, 1986; *String Light*, 1991; *Just Whistle: A Valentine*, 1993; *Deepstep Come Shining*, 1998; *Steal Away: Selected and New Poems*, 2002; nonfiction—*The Lost Roads Project: A Walk-in Book of Arkansas* (with D. Luster), 1994

Wright, Jay

May 25, 1935– Poet

Jay Wright is an award-winning poet who, in his 10 volumes of poetry, has steadfastly explored the nature of African-American identity, drawing on African and Native North and South American cosmologies to light his path. A learned scholar, Wright has brought his extensive knowledge of the world's cultures, both ancient and contemporary, to bear upon his work, leading some to criticize his poetry for being overly intellectual and inaccessible. However, Wright has enjoyed a fond reception by many critics, who have commended him for his ambition, insight, and musical verse. In the *Atlantic Monthly* (November 2000), Peter Davison characterized Wright's work following the publication of a comprehensive collection of his poetry entitled *Transfigurations* (2000): "It turns out that Jay Wright . . . has been writing impassioned and lucid poetry for more than 30 years. Adept at narrative, at visionary celebration, at the imagery and symbolism of half a dozen cultures from Europe, Africa, Latin America, and the United States, [his] poems range in multiple voices through history and over several continents, dwelling on a sense of place and striving toward cultural self-definition."

Jay Wright was born on May 25, 1935 in Albuquerque, New Mexico, where he was exposed to the mix of Native American, Mexican, and American cultures that characterizes the Southwest. Wright's teenage years were spent in San Pedro, California. After high school he briefly played

Don Usner/Courtesy of Louisiana State University Press

minor league baseball before enrolling at the University of New Mexico, in Albuquerque, to study chemistry. After less than a term, he left school to join the U.S. Army, serving three years in the Medical Corps. Upon his discharge, Wright enrolled at the University of California at Berkeley, where he received his bachelor of arts degree in 1961. Wright won a Rockefeller Brothers theological fellowship and studied for a semester at the Union Theological Seminary in New York City. He went on to earn his master of arts degree in comparative literature from Rutgers University, in New Brunswick, New Jersey, in 1967.

Wright published his first collection of poetry in 1967, a short pamphlet entitled *Death as History*. Around this time he was awarded a Woodrow Wilson National Endowment for the Arts Poets-in-Concert fellowship. In 1971 about half of the poems in *Death as History* were re-published in revised form together with new poetry in *The Homecoming Singer*. David Kalstone, in the *New York Times Book Review* (July 30, 1972), noted that the poems in *The Homecoming Singer* often return to the theme of being a stranger in one's own society, and even a stranger to one's self. "Jay Wright is black," wrote Kalstone, "and his book is partly informed by a young black's sense of exclusion. He stands apart from the white society of his childhood—the railroad men and hunters and redneck homeowners of the Southwest, the Slavic fishermen of Southern California—but he also, as a child, stood apart from the mysteries of his own blackness." In "The Hunting Trip Cook" the poem's young narrator feels a mixture of pride and embarrassment when his father, who serves as camp cook for a group of white doctors, comes home from a hunting trip with meat to feed his family. In "Wednesday Night Prayer Meeting," the narrator senses that the Christian religion leaves the black congregation vaguely unfulfilled; some part of them must reject the alien teachings of Jesus. "They have taken his strangeness/and given it back, the way a lover/will return the rings and letters/of a lover that hurts him," Wright wrote, as quoted by Kalstone. Wright himself said of *The Homecoming Singer* that the poems reflect an urge to transcend the limitations of his own experience. "I discovered the pattern of that book," he said, as quoted in *Melus* (Fall 1998), "almost a posteriori. I had, as I looked at it, the record of my developing African-American life in the United States, but I also saw that I had the beginning of forms to express lives that transcend that particular life." *The Homecoming Singer* was praised by critics. Kalstone wrote, "Most first books of poems are scatterings, a necessary shedding of skin. Not Jay Wright's. . . . It is a tense and memorable collection." In *Poetry* (April 1988), Robert B. Shaw said that the volume contained "one of the more eloquent evocations of an American muse that I have read," as quoted in *Contemporary Authors* (2000).

From 1968 to 1971 Wright lived in Mexico, after which he resided in Scotland for two years. In 1974 he won an Ingram Merrill Foundation award and a Guggenheim fellowship. During those years he published his poetry in various journals, and in 1976 he published both *Dimensions of History* and *Soothsayers and Omens*. The later volume, which consists of four sections, begins with an exploration of Wright's New Mexican roots and incorporates images and ideas from Native American cosmology. By the fourth section, Wright's focus has shifted toward the cosmologies of traditional African societies, particularly that of the Dogon, an ethnic group from Mali, in western Africa. The spiritual beliefs of the Dogon are more abstract than those of many other peoples: they consist partly of a central creation myth, in addition to a method for classifying objects and a code of spiritual principles.

In *Melus* (Fall 1998) Isidore Okpewho postulated that African cosmology is more integral to Wright's identity, as reflected in *Soothsayers and Omens*, than is Native American cosmology: "In the early poems of the first section, so frequent is the poet's recourse to images of dreams and strained memory, so shaky the spiritual epiphanies that greet the postulant's quest, it is clear he is left with somewhat circumscribed feelings. . . . By the time we get to the third and fourth 'Sources,' we realize the [N]ative American symbols are gradually yielding to those of native African theology and environment. . . . The poet is slowly discovering that his purposes have not yet been served by the right spiritual forces, and gains increasing clarity and confidence in the memory of a distant ancestry." *Soothsayers and Omens* met with complimentary reviews. In *Library Journal* (May 1, 1987) E. Ethelbert Miller wrote, "Wright's explorations into African philosophy and the poems that result must be considered bridges healing the wounds that exist within the souls of black Americans," as quoted in *Contemporary Authors* (2000). The eminent literary critic Harold Bloom proclaimed the volume "the year's best book of poems from a small press," in the *New Republic* (November 20, 1976), also quoted in *Contemporary Authors* (2000).

Wright continued to develop the theme of African cosmology in *The Double Invention of Komo* (1980), for which he studied the works of various anthropologists. As he wrote in the notes to the volume, as quoted in *Melus* (Fall 1998), "My major texts have been those assembled by the group of French anthropologists, associated with Marcel Griaule, on an expedition to Dakar and Djibouti beginning in 1929 and subsequent expeditions to Mali, Chad, and Cameroon. . . . The study of Dogon and Bambara cosmology has led me to search and to explore other African religions and cosmologies." The Komo is one of the six male societies of the Bambara, another ethnic group from Mali, who have their own cosmology that is related to, yet also differentiated from, that of the Dogon. The Komo is the custodian of tradition and community life for the Bambara, including rituals of initiation. In some sense, *The Double Invention of Komo* is an initiation for the poet and his readers into the ways of the Bambara and the Dogon. Furthermore, it represents Wright's attempt to transform his identity through an imaginative identification with these African peoples. In one poem, as quoted in *Contemporary Poets* (1996), Wright writes, "I am about to be born./I forget where I come from/and where I'm going./I cannot distinguish/right from left, front from rear./Show me the way of my race/and of my fathers . . . You take me to kneel, forehead to earth, before Komo./You present me to sacred things./I am reborn into a new life./My eyes open to Komo."

In *Contemporary Poets* Paul Christensen concluded, "In the end [*The Double Invention of Komo*] seems to prove the reverse of its intention—that one cannot easily leap from one's own culture to grasp the reality of another's. [It] is stuck in its own metaphysical and linguistic provinciality, with much intelligent laboring exerted for a noble but unreached goal." However, many critics considered the volume to be Wright's most ambitious and difficult to date, as well as the most rewarding. "Unlike most modern poetry," a reviewer for *Choice* (October 1980) observed, "it is not an artifact, but a dynamic rite, enigmatic and alien, and without precedent in mainstream English poetry. It mixes/blends incantation, gnomic utterance, and folkloric perception in piercingly concrete terms and all in a sinewy language. . . . Probably not since Pound's Pisan cantos has there been, in itself, so pregnant a book, one so tough, or one so tantalizing." In the *Times Literary Supplement* (January 30, 1981) John Hollander called the volume "the considerable achievement of a major imagination engaged in the continuing struggle of poetry to free itself from its imprisonment in the comfortable halfway house of Good Writing," and called Wright "the most imaginatively serious and ambitious black American poet I know of."

In 1984 Wright published *Explications/Interpretations*, which contained poems he had written prior to those in *The Double Invention of Komo*, when he was living in Scotland in the early 1970s. In *Explications/Interpretations*, Wright, whose father was part-Celtic, introduces figures from Scottish history and also begins his investigations into the Dogon cosmology. Okpewho postulated that the volume represented Wright's attempt to reject his Western-based identity and embrace his African heritage. "It is clear," Okpewho wrote, "from his interlocutions with these Scottish figures, that he is determined to dissociate himself from their positions and so exorcize that strain in his personality that is decidedly at odds with his quest for a guiding African sensibility."

In 1986 Wright was awarded a MacArthur "genius" grant. The following year the *Selected Poems of Jay Wright* was published, which brought together many of the "strongest poems of one of America's strongest poets," as R. G. O'Meally wrote in *Choice* (April 1988). In *Library Journal* (July 1987) Jack Shreve said of the collection, "Wright has said that the aim of his poetry is to discover the weave of things already woven: but the expanse of his weave is far greater than most poets lay claim to, embracing the polyglot history and myth of white, black, and Indian in this hemisphere."

In 1988 Wright published *Elaine's Book*, a poetry collection he dedicated to his wife's sister for her birthday. The volume represents a further expansion of Wright's cultural vision. It contains poems, such as "Zapata and the Egungun Mask," that examine events from an African perspective, much as in his earlier works. It also contains poems that embrace a broader cultural spectrum, such as "The Power of Reeds," in which Wright celebrates old civilizations from Africa, Europe, Babylonia, and ancient America on equal terms. According to Okpewho, Wright also seems to have modified his view of women, who, according to the critic, were conspicuously overlooked in much of his earlier work. "In *Elaine's Book* our poet reflects with mature tenderness and understanding on females in his family (especially his wife)," Okpewho noted, "as well as on female figures of a symbolic or spiritual order." In the *Virginia Quarterly Review* (Summer 1989) a critic wrote, "Wright's language . . . is sinuous, beautiful. This is a book worth puzzling over for along time," as quoted in *Contemporary Authors* (2000).

Returning to the region of his upbringing, Wright focused on the cultural history of Mexico and New Mexico in his next collection of poems, *Boleros* (1991). As Christensen described *Boleros*, "The plot of the book is a travel memoir of the poet and his wife moving from one world (Scotland, New England) to the other (Mexico), from Protestant rationality to the depths of the Mayan and Aztec worlds with their layering of Spanish Catholicism and other New World elements." In many of the poems, Wright includes idiomatic phrases in Spanish. The book received mixed reviews. Rochelle Ratner, writing in *Library Journal* (May 15, 1991), commented that while "moments of lyric beauty are scattered throughout," the book as a whole was disjointed and disappointing. In *Choice* (March 1992) M. Waters wrote, "At their best, these poems are unlike any being written in America today as they attempt to articulate 'traces of desire.' At their worst, they allow Wright's fondness for 'new words' to put off the reader. . . . Luckily, the better poems constitute the majority as they explore 'love and naming,' and reward the patient reader with line after line of resplendent and evocative language."

In 1996 Wright was awarded the 62nd Fellowship of the Academy of American Poets for "distinguished poetic achievement," a prize worth $20,000. In 1999 he was asked to serve on the board of chancellors of the Academy of American Poets, but turned down the offer so that he could continue to devote his time to his upcoming work, *Transfigurations: Collected Poems* (2000). The volume, which is more than 700 pages long, contains poems from all of his previous collections in addition to poems he had written since the publication of *Boleros*. Though Wright has enjoyed the acclaim of a small group of critics for many years, *Transfigurations* has helped bring him a wider readership. Jeff Zaleski, in *Publisher's Weekly* (September 18,

2000), wrote, "Particularly in its movement between Africa and the Americas, Wright's poetry continually insists upon the notion of a diasporic history, but it refuses to allow its characters and speakers [to] be completely determined by it, making this book a true life lesson."

Shortly after the publication of *Transfigurations*, Wright was awarded the Lannan Literary Award for poetry. Wright has been a poet-in-residence at several universities, including Alabama's Talledega College; Tougaloo College, in Mississippi; Texas Southern University, in Houston; and Scotland's University of Dundee. He has contributed to such journals as *Black World*, *Callaloo*, the *Nation*, and the *Journal of Negro Poetry*. His work is anthologized in various collections, and his plays have been performed by various theater groups. He currently lives in Vermont.
—P. G. H.

SUGGESTED READING: *Choice* p252 Oct. 1980, p1249 Apr. 1988, p1082 Mar. 1992; *Library Journal* p86 May 15, 1991; *Melus* p51+ Fall 1993, p187+ Fall 1998; *New York Times Book Review* p4 July 30, 1972, with photo; *Poetry* p45 Apr. 1988; *Publishers Weekly* p105 Sep. 18, 2000; *Times Literary Supplement* p115 Jan. 30, 1981; Riggs, Thomas ed. *Contemporary Poets*, 1996; *Contemporary Authors* vol. 82, 2000

SELECTED BOOKS: *Death as History*, 1967; *Homecoming Singer*, 1971; *Dimensions of History*, 1976; *Soothsayers and Omens*, 1976; *Double Invention of Komo*, 1980; *Explications/Interpretations*, 1984; *Elaine's Book*, 1988; *Selected Poems of Jay Wright*, 1987; *Boleros*, 1991; *Transfigurations: Collected Poems*, 2000

Courtesy of Harcourt Publishing

Yoshimura, Akira

(YO-SHEE-MER-AH)

1927– Novelist; short-story writer; nonfiction writer

In his native Japan, Akira Yoshimura has been a prominent author of fiction and nonfiction for nearly five decades. Having published more than 50 books, he is credited with popularizing the genre of "technohistory"—nonfiction that relates the history of a technological achievement—and at least 20 of his novels have been best-sellers in Japan. His fiction is characterized by a spare, concentrated style and somewhat removed perspective, from which he addresses such weighty themes as death and free will. Despite his success, his work was little known outside Japan until several recent English translations of his books appeared in the United States, where they have been reviewed favorably by many critics.

Akira Yoshimura was born in 1927 in Tokyo, Japan. He began writing while attending Gakushuin University, in Tokyo, and his first book was published in Japan in 1955. The first of Yoshimura's books to be translated into English was *Build the Musashi!: The Birth and Death of the World's Greatest Battleship*, in 1991. The Musashi was a celebrated Japanese battleship built in 1937. The largest ship ever constructed, it weighed 72,800 tons and was armed with 18.1–inch guns. Toward the end of World War II, the new dominance of air-based warfare reached a symbolic climax when U.S. airplanes sank the Musashi in October 1944. The English translation went out of print and was re-issued in 1999 as *Battleship Musashi: The Making and Sinking of the World's Biggest Battleship*.

In 1996 Yoshimura's book *Zero Fighter* was translated into English. This nonfiction work is a technohistory of a World War II Japanese fighter plane, the Mitsubishi A6M Type 0 Carrier Fighter, known as the "Zero." The exceptional Zero gave Japan a distinct air advantage in its war against China and later, before the United States developed a comparable aircraft in 1943, in the early part of World War II. Yoshimura recounts, among other stories, the odd collision of the modern and the primitive in Mitsubishi's manufacturing procedures: because of Japan's lack of good roads, the company was forced to disassemble regularly all the airplanes built at the factory so that they could be transported in pieces via oxcart over the approximately 30-mile stretch of rough road that led from the factory to the Kagamigahara airfield. Yoshimura also points out that the U.S. military ignored the early warnings of an American pilot who encountered the Zero while flying for China in its war against Japan. In Japan the book was a best-seller, but in the U.S. it drew some unenthusiastic responses from critics, who found the book to be marred by a nationalistic agenda. For example, in *Air Power History* (Summer 1999), Scott A. Willey accused Yoshimura of criticizing sanctions placed against Japan preceding World War II by the U.S., the U.K., and Holland, without mentioning that the sanctions were levied to discourage human rights offenses being made by Japan against China. Willey wrote of *Zero Fighter*, "It well describes both the development of the Japanese aircraft industry and the process by which this particular aircraft was developed and fielded. . . . The book fails, however, in operational history. With no reference notes or bibliography, one cannot tell where 'facts' come from." Nevertheless, critics commended Yoshimura's involving narrative and fresh insights. A reviewer for *Publishers Weekly* (March 4, 1996) wrote "there is much here that is poignant," and praised *Zero Fighter* as a "knowledgeable history."

Though Yoshimura had written 20 novels in Japanese, the first to be translated into English was *Shipwrecks*, in 1996. In an isolated fishing village in medieval Japan, inhabitants barely eke out an existence by gathering what they can from the sea. Many of the village's men are forced to work as indentured servants outside of the village, including the father of the main character, the nine-year-old boy Isaku. In his father's absence, Isaku must support his mother and younger brother by himself. After he is ordered by the village chief to help boil sea water to make salt, Isaku discovers a dark secret of the island: the giant fires lit under the cauldrons at night are meant to lure ships to shore in the hope that they will be dashed against the rocks. When a ship founders on the rocks, the villagers row out to it, slay the survivors, take the goods, break down the ship for firewood, and hide the evidence. The shipwrecks, called *O-fune-sama*, are prayed for by the villagers, for whom the ships' cargos provide temporary relief from their terrible poverty. Their prayers appear to be answered one day when a ship washes ashore, but the ill-supplied crew is dead and clad in mysterious red garments. After the scant supplies are distributed throughout the village, a tragedy unfolds that leaves no one untouched. The novel explores the grim paradox of living off of the deaths of others, and Yoshimura's unadorned style suits the somber mood of the book. In his review in the *New York Times* (September 22, 1996), Randall Short wrote, "It's not inconceivable that, in the context of his larger body of work, the book might take on a more compelling heft. But at this point, its interest seems more ethnographic than literary." Other reviewers found the book powerful. In *World Literature Today* (Winter 1997), Yoshiko Yokochi Samuel commented, "Written in a style characterized by detachment and indifference, with the theme of death interwoven with another theme of the boy's developing sexuality, this narrative forces the reader to peer into the terrifying depth of the human instinct for survival." Richard Bernstein, in the *New York Times* (July 24, 1996), wrote of the novel, "One reads it with sadness and appreciation and a great deal of tenderness for one Isaku, who never lived and yet reminds us of our common past."

In 1999 another of Yoshimura's novels was translated into English and titled *On Parole*. The book opens with the release from prison of Shiro Kikutani, on parole after being incarcerated for 16 years. His parole officer finds work for him at a chicken farm, and Kikutani, after many years of blocking out his dark past, finds solace in the routine of work. Gradually, the reader learns that Kikutani's was a crime of passion. After discovering his wife with a lover, he killed them both and then burned down the lover's house, inadvertently killing an old woman who lived there as well. Kikutani makes some attempts to atone for his past, visiting, for instance, the cemetery where the woman who died in the fire is buried. However, despite his efforts, he cannot summon much remorse. He is more at ease absorbing himself in the numbing details of everyday life, which Yoshimura recounts in every particular. Eventually, Kikutani marries again; when his wife encourages him to perform a ritual expression of sorrow in the hope that he will be released from parole, it seems she may drive him to revisit his crimes in more ways than one. Emily Gordon, in *Salon* (March 9, 2000, on-line), found the character of Kikutani "soullessly flat" and "the essence of a cold fish." "Still," she wrote, "as a portrait of a killer that avoids the familiar psycho terrain, the novel has an austere remoteness that is admirable in its craft." Reviewer Michael Pye was more enthusiastic in his praise. In the *New York Times* (February 13, 2000, on-line) he wrote, "Yoshimura's exactness is also a passionately concentrated way of investigating the question of what it means to be free—and that breeds tension and finally horror."

The English translation of *On Parole* came on the heals of a Japanese film, *The Eel* (1997), that was based on the novel. The movie followed the general structure of *On Parole*, though it differed from the novel somewhat: The main character's name is Yamashita, and, while in jail, he engages in conversation only with an eel. After his release, he opens a barber shop rather than working in a chicken hatchery. Directed by Shohei Imamura, the film won the Palme d'Or at the 1997 Cannes Film Festival.

A translation of his third novel, which Yoshimura orginally published in 1978, appeared in 2001 as *One Man's Justice*. Set in post–World War II Japan, the novel explores moral questions through the eyes of Takuya, a former officer in the Japanese army who is on the run. The U.S. occupying forces are looking for war criminals, and Takuya is wanted for decapitating a captured

American pilot. Takuya believes he did his duty by executing the pilot, who participated in the bombing of Japanese cities and towns and killed many innocent civilians. "A deft, accurate writer, Yoshimura captures a man in limbo with unnerving insight and definition," Terry Hong wrote in a review for the *Christian Science Monitor* (August 23, 2001). "He's unflinching in his descriptions of brutality, and neither side is spared: the Japanese with their medical experiments on U.S. prisoners, the victorious U.S. and their senselessly violent postwar treatment of the occupied inhabitants. Yoshimura daringly explores the way honor, duty, and justice are tested when manmade death and destruction reign."

Akira Yoshimura lives in Tokyo and continues to write.

—P. G. H.

SUGGESTED READING: *Library Journal* p110 May 1, 1996; *Publishers Weekly* p48 Mar. 4, 1996, p52 Apr. 29, 1996; *New York Times* (on-line) July 24, 1996, Feb. 13, 2000; *Salon* (on-line) Mar. 9, 2000; *World Literature Today* p230 Winter 1997

SELECTED BOOKS IN ENGLISH TRANSLATION: fiction—*Shipwrecks*, 1996; *On Parole*, 1999; *One Man's Justice*, 2001; nonfiction—*Zero Fighter*, 1996; *Battleship Musashi: The Making and Sinking of the World's Biggest Battleship*, 1999

Zelitch, Simone

Dec. 15, 1962– Novelist

Simone Zelitch writes, she says, in order to be read. "Wanting to be read is not the same thing as wanting to be famous," she told John Coyne in an interview for *Peace Corps Writers* (on-line). "It may not even be the same thing as wanting to be published. I get real pleasure out of holding an audience, making them care about people or circumstances I invent, and making them anxious to find out what happens next." To judge by the reception of her books, which are imaginative recreations of historical and biblical events, Zelitch excels at doing just that. Her first novel, *The Confession of Jack Straw* (1991), won the prestigious Hopwood Award for major fiction, and her second novel, *Louisa* (2000), won the National Foundation for Jewish Culture's Samuel L. Goldberg and Sons Award for emerging Jewish writers. She also won a fellowship from the Pennsylvania Council for the Arts. Her most recent novel, *Moses in Sinai*, was published in 2001.

In a 2001 statement for *World Authors 1995–2000*, Simone Zelitch writes: "I was born in Northeast Philadelphia, a sprawling, deliberately anonymous not-quite-suburban neighborhood. I hated it there. Even the trees seemed inorganic. My sisters and brothers were much older than I was and did exciting, early 70's sorts of things, like running away from home and living on a commune. As a teenager, I saw myself as born ten years too late. I wore a lot of hand-me-down peasant blouses, identified as an anarchist, and observed the comings and goings of my classmates [with] a detachment which was half shyness and half snobbery. I used to think I wanted to be a psychiatrist. I would have been a bad one. I was far more interested in conflict than in resolution and had a disquieting habit of confusing people with characters.

"On the other hand, I also confused characters with people. I read everything I could get my hands on, but had a preference for what is usually called Science Fiction, although science played little part in Vonnegut, Burgess and Orwell. I loved the way that my own alienation was reflected in their work and shaped the structure of the world that they imagined. My greatest stroke of luck was the discovery of Ursula LeGuin. Her elegance, ambition, and insistence that fiction was fiction, that Tolkien should be put on the shelf next to Tolstoy, confirmed my belief that good writing has no boundaries, that I could write anything I wanted any way I wanted, so long as I wrote well.

"Another major influence was the Jewish form called Midrash, a tradition of elaborating on biblical narrative, often taking up the stories of nonentities, such as the Pharaoh's cook or Moses' mother. This form, taken up most directly in my forthcoming novel, *Moses in Sinai*, has had an impact on all of my fiction. I have a tendency to fixate on minor figures and to try to tell a story from the point of view of a marginal character. I steal most of my stories from familiar sources, but I try to tell them in unfamiliar ways. Like Midrash, the aim is to both clarify and confound, to force a reader to acknowledge that a situation is less simple than it appears.

"When I began to write novels, I was immediately drawn to historical or mythological subjects. I discovered, long after the fact, that my years of observation and my own emotional life, my friendships, betrayals, frustrations and anxieties, were all played out in stories about medieval peasants, Hungarian chain-smokers, or biblical rebels. Many of my characters are, like me, observers, and their conflicts are brought to the surface when history overtakes them. Like my early models, my books are, essentially, speculative. How do flawed, cranky, unheroic people respond to extraordinary circumstances? To what extent are those circumstances metaphors for their own troubled lives, or their lives metaphors for history? Where does one end, and the other begin?

"As my own life took me from Southern Illinois to a stint in the Peace Corps in Hungary, to Philadelphia, where I teach at a community college and live with my husband and stepdaughter, I have come to realize that present circumstances are extraordinary indeed. Yet I suspect that I am still best served by projecting what I have learned into somebody else's story. I like being on the outside, looking in. It keeps me honest, and it sets me free."

Zelitch attended Wesleyan University, in Connecticut, and then earned her M.F.A. in creative writing from the University of Michigan, in 1986. She taught writing at Southern Illinois University before joining the Peace Corps in 1991. She resides in a century-old house in Mt. Airy, near Philadelphia, and teaches at the Community College of Philadelphia, where she co- directs the college's Poets and Writer's Series.

The Confession of Jack Straw, written while Zelitch was a student at Wesleyan, set the pattern for all of her novels: it falls into the genre of historical fiction, is rich in incident, texture, and detail, and is driven by finely drawn characters. It is set near the end of the 14th century, the era of the devastating "Black Death" plague and the bloody and drawn-out conflict between France and England known as the Hundred Years' War. The "Jack Straw" of the title was a pivotal figure in the English Peasant Revolt of 1381. This uprising was sparked by the imposition of a new tax on peasants, who had little use for the monarchy's expensive war, and were already feeling disenfranchised under their landowning masters. One peasant—Jack Straw—joined the radical clergyman John Ball and the warrior Wat Tyler in leading a group of about 100,000 supporters through the countryside, freeing prisoners, killing lawyers, and creating havoc along the way. The group then headed to London, where they burned the Savoy Palace and murdered the Archbishop of Canterbury. Eventually, the rebels were met in an open field by 14-year-old King Richard II, who calmed them by promising reforms, and the group dispersed. After the danger had passed, however, the king's advisors forced him to revoke his promises and hanged all the rebel leaders, including Jack Straw.

In Zelitch's hands, this story takes the form of Jack Straw's confession, before his execution. He describes life in his small village leading up to the revolt, and his feelings during the uprising and after the king's betrayal. Critics appreciated the fact that Zelitch moves beyond conventional depictions of life in the Middle Ages. The science-fiction writer Ursula Le Guin observed (as quoted on Amazon.com) that, "In most novels about the Middle Ages, the deck is all face cards. Jack Straw is rare and admirable in its uncompromising, unpatronizing identification with a peasant—an intelligent, vulnerable man caught up in the dream of equality that flared into the Peasant Revolt." A Kirkus reviewer noted that "The Middle Ages are rendered not on silver platters or thrones but on the dusty roads and straw beds of peasants who are given center stage here, not limited to comic relief." Jack Straw is driven by what the reviewer Graham Purchase, in Rebel Worker Magazine (June 15, 1996, on-line), termed "a blend of liberation theology and revolutionary socialism."

Zelitch's second published novel was Louisa. It opens in 1949 in the port city of Haifa, in the newly created country of Israel. A recent immigrant to Israel, Nora Gratz narrates the story of her life as a Jew in Hungary, from the time of the empire of Franz Josef, through WWII and the Holocaust. Zelitch began the novel as an writer's exercise, following the example of Chekhov, who was supposed to have picked up an ashtray and decided: "Today I will write a story called 'The Ashtray,'" as Zelitch quoted in an essay for Peace Corps Writers. Thinking about Chekhov's ashtray led her to the novel's opening line: "I smoked my first cigarette when I was six years old. . . now where the hell can I get a cigarette?" Nora, the speaker, evolves as a somewhat prickly, but always entertaining character. She has what Zelitch described to Terry Matthews, in an interview for BookBrowser.com (October 2000), as a "Hungarian sensibility": "ironical, humorous, tough, and very conscious of the past." Zelitch's experiences in Hungary, where she taught English at the University of Veszprem and lived in a small village, shaped her novel's explorations of identity and place. "I spent a lot of time on trains, staring into space, and being stared at by Hungarians. I'd never felt more vulnerable, or more American," she told Coyne. "I think my experience of displacement had an enormous impact on the way I wrote about Louisa's central characters, who are all, essentially, displaced."

The title character of the book is a young, blond, lieder-singing German, the daughter of a bureaucrat in the Third Reich. Passionate, romantic, and naive, Louisa falls in love with Nora's son, Gabor, a struggling composer and music teacher, whose indifference to her only spurs her affection. When Gabor is killed by Nazi thugs, Nora and Louisa are thrown together and—despite their many differences—come to depend on each other for survival, forming wary, but resilient, bonds. After narrowly making it through the war alive—thanks to Louisa's protection—and after losing her parents, son, and husband, Nora emigrates to Israel to seek out her male cousin, Bela, who years earlier had moved to what was then British Palestine. Bela and Nora were childhood friends, and have maintained a passionate, somewhat flirtatious correspondence through their marriages and separate adult lives. When Nora decides to move to Israel, Louisa insists on coming along.

Why would this young German want to cut off ties to her family and country and move to Israel, where her appearance and accent will mark her as an outsider at best, and an enemy at worst? To create her story, Zelitch reworked the Old Testament parable of Ruth and Naomi. In the Book of Ruth, Naomi is an Israelite woman who escapes famine by taking her two sons to the land of Moab, where her sons marry Moabite women, from a tribe that has been cursed by God. When the plague arrives, both sons are struck down, and their wives left widowed. Naomi decides to return to the Israelis in Canaan, and Ruth, one of her daughters-in-law, insists on joining her, saying: "Whither thou goest, I shall go. Your nation shall be my nation, and your God my God." Louisa echoes these words, bluntly telling her mother-in-law: "I want to be where you are." Eventually, Louisa learns Hebrew, converts to Judaism, and becomes a symbol of the human capacity for survival and transformation. In the *Boston Review* (on-line), Leora Bersohn described *Louisa* as less about mourning and loss than about "what happens after tragedy, about unexpected finales." The novel is evidence, Bersohn maintained, "that sometimes life's post-scripts make the best reading."

Many critics noted Zelitch's skillful handling of the complex narrative, with its epic reach and constant fluctuations. "While often poignant, the storytelling avoids melodrama, self-righteousness and graphic horror—all the pitfalls of Holocaust fiction," David Sacks wrote for the *New York Times* (November 19, 2000, on-line). "Instead, suspense, surprising revelations and dry humor enliven the mix." Maralyn Lois Polak described the novel, in her review for the *Philadelphia Inquirer* (October 8, 2000, on-line), as "a lush, lavish, atmospheric literary symphony, building up to a stirring dramatic crescendo of action and revelation in the last third."

Louisa earned widespread critical attention. A *Boston Globe* reviewer, as quoted on BookBrowser.com, called *Loiusa* "A grand, brave, openhearted novel that is not afraid of its own ambitions," and Sacks wrote that the novel invites comparison to Isaac Bashevis Singer's *The Family Moskat* or William Styron's *Sophie's Choice*, and "remarkably . . . holds its own, thanks to a satisfying plot, vivid characters, a tart narrative voice and a bold conceit."

Zelitch's novel *Moses in Sinai* was published in late 2001. In the book the character of Moses is subjected to one horror after another throughout his long life: abandoned by his father Amram, he is taken into the house of Bityah, his adoptive mother, who convinces him to suck on a hot coal, leaving him scarred and with a permanent stutter. Even after he rises up to lead the Hebrew people out of Egypt, he is filled with doubt about his abilities and often questions God. The book received mixed notices. In a review for *Booklist*, quoted on Amazon.com, Michelle Kaske observed, "Occasionally one glimpses Zelitch's imaginative and romantic style, but the story line dominates the novel, which is unfortunate. In *Louisa* (2000), Zelitch more impressively showed her talent for combining harsh and earthy subject matter with graceful and picturesque prose."

The protagonist of Simone Zelitch's next book will reportedly be an American girl in Jerusalem.
—M. A. H.

SUGGESTED READING: BookBrowser.com; BookReporter.com; *Boston Review* (on-line); *New York Times* (on-line) Nov. 19, 2000; *Peace Corps Writers* (on-line); *Philadelphia Inquirer* (on-line) Oct. 8, 2000

SELECTED BOOKS: *The Confession of Jack Straw*, 1991; *Louisa*, 2000; *Moses in Sinai*, 2001

Courtesy of HarperCollins

Zimmer, Carl

July 13, 1966– Science writer; journalist

Carl Zimmer is a science journalist who has written accessible books on very complicated subjects. In *At the Water's Edge: Macroevolution and the Transformation of Life* (1998), he outlines the peculiar quirks of evolution that allowed some organisms, including whales, to adapt to life on land and then return to the seas. His next book, *Parasite Rex: Inside the Bizarre World of Nature's Most Dangerous Creatures* (2000), is a study of the effects of parasites on the plants and animals that host them. In 2001 Zimmer published *Evolution: The Triumph of an Idea*, which is the richly illustrated companion volume to a PBS television series of the same name.

Carl Zimmer was born on July 13, 1966, the son of Richard, a lawyer, and the former Marty Goodspeed. He received a bachelor's degree from Yale University, in New Haven, Connecticut, in 1987. From 1993 to 1999 he served as a science journalist and senior editor at *Discover*. After writing about evolution in the magazine, he expanded on this work in book form. *At the Water's Edge* (1998) was the result. In an interview with Amazon.com, as quoted in *Contemporary Authors* (1999), he remarked that such a work was the natural extension of his interests. "I've been writing since I was a kid, but writing about science became my passion when I started working at *Discover* magazine," he noted. "Sometimes a subject needs more space than a magazine can allow, and that's when I turn to writing books."

At the Water's Edge is a study of Charles Darwin's theory of macroevolution, an explanation of how entire species change over generations in an attempt to better adapt to their environments. In the first section of the book, Zimmer looks at how several early types of fish shifted from living in water to living on land. In the second half he details how certain mammals, including whales and dolphins, returned to the water after spending a significant number of generations as land-based animals. His study focuses on the major evolutionary transitions involving vertebrates that took place "at the water's edge," a barrier that has caused remarkable evolutionary changes. In the *Atlantic Monthly* (May 1998), Phoebe-Lou Adams cited a passage from the book: "There is always a little sadness mixed into great discoveries because they take away some of the confusion that brightens life." She concluded: "Mr. Zimmer avoids confusion but leaves life among the fossils agreeably bright." Reviewing *At the Water's Edge* for *Booklist* (March 1, 1998), Bryce Christensen wrote: "Tracing the ancestry of early land animals back to fish and of whales back to later land animals has long required strong faith in Darwinian doctrine, largely unsupported by biological or fossil evidence. The recent discovery of that long-sought evidence—paleontological, genetic, and anatomical—makes a fascinating story which Zimmer unfolds as a tale of high-stakes scientific sleuthing. Thanks to marvelously lucid writing, readers can decipher clues . . . right alongside some of the world's greatest researchers, starting with Darwin himself." Christensen concluded, "While steering clear of technical minutiae, Zimmer allows readers to wrestle with theoretical problems that have long attracted strong minds (and combative personalities) to evolutionary biology." In 1999 *At the Water's Edge* was published in paperback with a new subtitle, *Fish With Fingers, Whales With Legs, and How Life Came Ashore But Then Went Back to the Sea.*

In 2000 Zimmer published *Parasite Rex*, a study of parasites (including worms, viruses, and bacteria) that argues that these complex creatures have a vast influence on their host organisms, even regulating their sex drives. Zimmer does not argue that all parasites should be eliminated; in fact he suggests that if we destroy a large number of these creatures, the body's immune system, in the absence of such foreign antigens, may begin to attack itself. A reviewer for *Scientific American* (September 2000) remarked: "Zimmer presents a vivid portrayal of how parasites evolved, how resilient and adaptable they are, the effects they have on their hosts and the strategies the hosts have developed to combat them." Citing the example of the candiru, a thin fish found in Latin America that lodges itself in the urethras of unsuspecting swimmers, Susan Adams wrote for *Forbes* (September 18, 2000), "Some of the organisms in this book are truly hideous to contemplate." She concludes, however, that "Zimmer is such an accomplished, vivid writer that he is able to weave these revolting beasts into an engrossing story that you will read to the last page." Calling Zimmer "as fine a science essayist as we have," Kevin Padian wrote for the *New York Times Book Review* (October 22, 2000): "The importance of [his] book lies not only in its accessible presentation of the new science of evolutionary parasitology but in its thoughtful treatment of the global strategies and policies that scientists, health workers and governments will have to consider in order to manage parasites in the future."

In 2001 Zimmer published *Evolution: The Triumph of an Idea*, with an introduction by Stephen Jay Gould, a noted biologist. It was written as a companion to the seven- part PBS television series of the same name, which aired in September 2001. A review printed on *Scientific American.com* contained praise for the book: "Don't be misled by the polished prose, the gorgeous illustrations, the elegant design or the book's status as a 'companion volume': Zimmer neglects neither underlying biological concepts nor current controversies. His coverage is as thorough as it is graceful. This is as fine a book as one will find on the subject."

Since 1999 Carl Zimmer has been a freelance journalist, writing frequently for *National Geographic*, *Audubon*, and *Science*. He contributes a regular column on evolution to *Natural History*. He is a member of the National Association of Science Writers and has won several prizes for his scientific journalism, including the American Institute of Biological Sciences Media Award, the Pan-American Health Organization Award for Excellence in International Health Reporting, and the Everett Clark Award. He currently resides in the New York City borough of Brooklyn and is working on a book about neurology.

—C. M.

SUGGESTED READING: *Atlantic Monthly* p130 May 1998; *Booklist* p1078 Mar. 1, 1998; *Discover* p84+ Apr. 1998; *Forbes* p274+ Sep. 18, 2000; *Library Journal* p108 Feb. 1, 1998; *Natural History* p44+ Sep. 2000; *New York Times Book Review* p 22 May 3, 1998, p18+ Oct. 22, 2000

SELECTED BOOKS: *At the Water's Edge*, 1998; *Parasite Rex*, 2000; *Evolution: The Triumph of an Idea*, 2001

Courtesy of University of MN Press

Zimmer, Paul

Sep. 18, 1934– Poet; memorist; publisher

Paul Zimmer is both poet and publisher: Since the appearance of his first chapbook, in 1961, he has written hundreds of poems for literary journals that have been collected into a dozen books. Also since the 1960s, he has worked in scholarly publishing and is now director of the University of Iowa Press, where he established the Iowa Poetry Prize. His collections include *The Zimmer Poems* (1976), *With Wanda: Town and Country Poems* (1980), *Family Reunion: Selected and New Poems* (1983), *The Grêat Bird of Love* (1989), *Big Blue Train* (1993), and his retrospective *Crossing to Sunlight: Selected Poems* (1996), which contains several earlier pieces, as well as 21 new works. A wry and self-deprecating tone marks Zimmer's poems, which are often written as autobiographical narratives—starring "Zimmer," the poet's stand-in—or parodies of familiar works. In 2002 Zimmer published his memoirs, *After the Fire: A Writer Finds His Place.*

For *World Authors 1995–2000*, Paul Zimmer writes: "I was born in Canton, Ohio in 1934. Not a particularly successful young person, from the beginning I cherished the resonance and bearing of words. When I was in the army, bored by the mentality and soporific routine, I decided I wanted to be a writer and then, more particuarly, a poet. Very quickly I learned the value of practice and patience.

"There were some highly intimidating poets prominent in the fifties, and it seemed almost presumptuous to want to be a poet, but I desired nothing else. In those days there were no poetry workshops (at least available to me), so I worked for many years on my own, suffering my wife and friends to be my audience, and trying my work with the editors of literary journals and magazines. An artist friend and I enthusiastically produced a privately published chapbook in 1961. I blithely sent off a dozen copies to well known poets whose addresses I found in *Who's Who in America*. There were no responses or acknowledgments. Finally in the mid-sixties I had some poems accepted by publications and this spurred me to to form a full book manuscript.

"In 1967, after much tribulation and rejection, to my everlasting astonishment and joy, David Way accepted my first book for publication by his small New York firm, October House. Since then eight full books of my poems have been published by various publishers, including *Crossing to Sunlight: Selected Poems*, by the University of Georgia Press in 1996, and five chapbooks.

"I am very pleased to say that my work goes on and my interest and desire to make poems remains undiminished. For forty years I worked full time in the book business as a retailer, and then as university press publisher, until my retirement in 1998. I had to find the odd hours to work at poetry—usually my lunch breaks or early in the morning before heading off to my job. Now I have the great luxury of unencumbered hours to work at the craft. This does not necessarily increase my productivity, but it affords me time for more careful reflection and consideration. As I have matured, so has my work, and I am discovering new possibilities because of this new time for rumination. I will not claim wisdom, but I do feel a deeper, more reflective quality in my work that pleases me and spurs me on.

"Poetry remains the center of my life. In fact, for the first time, I can say I am a fulltime poet, and I rejoice in this development. It also pleases me that I now have the time to work at some considered prose, which enhances and extends my activity as a poet.

"It seems to me implicit in the act of writing that one wishes to share something if they write it down. Thus I want my poems to be about *something*. I take great pleasure in the sound of language and the discoveries I make as I chew my cud, connecting words and ideas, but I don't want my poems to rely on this process, to be simply flashy litanies of my intellect. I want my stuff to have an individual, vigorous poetic voice, and to present story and resonance. I try not to forget that our heritage from the first primitive poets is narrative, memory, invocation, recitation of triumph and failure, and a feeling of vulnerability and humanness. It seems to me that endeavoring to reflect these qualities in my poetry is the best thing I can do. It is work that I love and hope to continue until all my lights go out."

Paul Zimmer was born on September 18, 1934, the son of Jerome F. Zimmer, a shoe salesman, and Louise (Surmount) Zimmer, and received his early education in Catholic schools in his Ohio hometown. The slow-paced Midwestern cadences of his youth, during the late Depression and World War II years, are chronicled in his essay "The Catcher," published in the *Gettysburg Review* (Summer 1999). "In the early autumn of 1945, a great inquietude lifted from the world," he recalled. "The War had ended that summer, and adults seemed happier and more relaxed; even the life of an eleven-year-old boy was less restricted." Recalling his boyhood dream of wanting to be a catcher for the Cleveland Indians, he wrote, "I liked the idea of playing baseball and looking like a crusader." Although Zimmer stopped playing team baseball when he was 19, he added that "I have been a catcher all my life. Warehouse manager, technical writer, soldier, bookstore buyer, editor, publisher, husband, father, gardener, poet—I have borne the catcher's attitude to all these tasks. I have given signals, received pitches, watched the field, kept my eye on the ball, avoided most cheap shots, backed up bases, stayed busy, chattered encouragement, made decisions." He attended Kent State University intermittently during the 1950s, but did not receive his bachelor of arts degree until 1968. Earlier, while serving in the United States Army for a year in the mid-1950s, Zimmer experienced an epiphany that had a profound impact on his life and career as a poet. During a time when Cold War tensions had created a sense of national anxiety over atomic weapons, it was Private Zimmer's fate to witness several atomic-bomb tests in the Nevada desert. He described the experience in his essay "The Blind World, Atomic Battlefields" published in *The Georgia Review* (Winter 1998). In his account, he recalled how he and his colleagues had been "terrified speechless" as a result of the experience, but noted that "it was in this violent place that I discovered I wanted to be a poet." His army days were also mentioned in "The Catcher," in which Zimmer recounted how, during this trying period, "I had a visitation from some benevolent god—I discovered that I liked to read books. I became obsessed with novels and popular history until one day on barracks duty I found an anthology of modern poetry under someone's bunk. I read and read, not fully understanding. But I was tremendously excited by the words, the language and allusions, the accounts of triumph and failure, the masks and the reality. That is the only book I ever pilfered. I claimed it as my own and read it all the time." Zimmer soon began writing his own poetry--"now I realize that it was the only activity for me that could have replaced catching. The pictures of Birdie Tebbetts, Sherm Lollar, and Jim Hegan came down from my wall, and Robert Frost, Dylan Thomas, and Walt Whitman went up. Catching had taught me how to approach poetry: patience, diligence, doggedness, alertness, and practice, practice, practice."

In California during the 1960s, Zimmer managed bookstores for Macy's Department Store, in San Francisco, and the University of California at Los Angeles (UCLA) before returning east, in 1967, to serve as assistant director of the University of Pittsburgh Press, where he edited the "Pitt Poetry" series. He held this post until 1978, when he became director of the University of Georgia Press, in Athens. In 1984 he assumed the directorship of the University of Iowa Press, in Iowa City. In 1990 he turned down a $12,000 grant from the National Endowment for the Arts because he objected to the requirement that he pledge not to use the funds for "obscene" work.

Since 1960, when he published *A Seed on the Wind*, Zimmer has seen a dozen of his poetry collections come to print. During that time he won two National Endowment for the Arts Fellowships (in 1974–75 and 1982–83), the 1975 Helen Bullis Memorial Award for the journal *Poetry Northwest*, three Pushcart Prizes (in 1977, 1981, and 1991), an Amerian Academy and Institute of Arts and Letters Award in Literature in 1985, and a National Poetry Series Selection in 1988.

Published in 1976 by Dryad Press, *The Zimmer Poems* includes lyrics about adolescent crises of faith ("Father Animus and Zimmer," "The Day Zimmer Lost Religion"), about the stirrings of sexuality ("One for the Ladies at the Troy Laundry Who Cooled Themselves for Zimmer") and parodies of evergreen poetry classics ("A Zimmershire Lad"). "The Day Zimmer Lost Religion" describes a crisis familiar to many Catholic grade-school boys as they grow old and bold enough to question the omnipotence of God. "A Zimmershire Lad," one of the parodies in this collection, ends with the tongue-in-cheek warning: "Oh lads, ere your flesh decay, / And your sight grows dimmer, / Beware the ale foam in your way / Or you will end like Zimmer."

With Wanda, Town and Country Poems (1980) used a passage from Joseph Conrad's novel *Nostromo* to introduce the "Wanda" that plays muse to Zimmer's imagination: "She had come into the world like a thing unknown. She had come upon him unawares. She was a danger—a frightful danger." Again Zimmer peppered his text with parodies ("Robyn Hode and Maid Wanda") and allusions to other notable poets, but also included lyrics that suggest his earlier adolescent stirrings have been replaced by equally incomprehensible adult ones, as in "Zimmer's Last Gig":

Years ago I wanted to Take Wanda to Birdland, Certain that the music Would make her desire me. . . But Wanda was no quail. Bud could have passed Out over the keys, Bird could have shot Up right on the stand, Wanda would have missed The legends. The band Could have riffed All night right by Her ear, she never Would have bounced.

Zimmer's 1983 collection, *Family Reunion: Selected and New Poems*, was published by the University of Pittsburgh Press. It received more critical attention than his earlier collections, which had appeared in small-press editions. Reviewing the work for *Poetry* (July 1984), Peter Stitt called it "a book that grows in power as it is being read. The protagonist is a very attractive character—humane, humanly vulnerable, sensitive, as tough as he has to be, with a good eye for the funny and the grotesque." Joseph A. Lipari, reviewing the collection for *Library Journal* (August 1983), found the poems "heartbreaking and hilarious," leavened equally by "wit and sadness."

The publication of *Big Blue Train* by the University of Arkansas Press in 1994 elicited more praise for Zimmer. The voice for the poems in this collection is that of a maturer figure, as in "The Persistence of Fatherhood," which evokes a bittersweet mood as the poet is summoned from raking autumn leaves to accept what he momentarily believes was a telephone call from his father, who had been dead for five years. After the shock of realizing his mistake, Zimmer wrote:

Then last night this dream:
Suddenly leaves were children's clothing,
Blue jeans, caps, and flannel shirts.
I raked them up, bent over by sadness,
Fatherhood all used up and gone,
Playthings and storytimes gone,
I swept and piled, doing my duties,
Only this caretaking left to do.

Other poems in this collection resonate with the memories of loss and the unfulfilled expectations of youth, as when Zimmer reminisces about baseball games ("Raw and Absolute," "The Light," "Remembering Power Hitters"), sitting in on jazz jam sessions in New York in the 1950s ("But Bird," "Romance"), or contemplating news from London of an old friend's death ("A Rant Against Losses"). *Big Blue Train* was pronounced "a book filled with genuine emotion and consistently moving poems" by an anonymous reviewer in the *Virginia Quarterly Review* (Spring 1994), who added that "the humor here is more muted [than in his earlier work]. Zimmer is working in a serious vein. Loss permeates the book."

In 1996 the University of Georgia Press published *Crossing to Sunlight: Selected Poems*, a collection of 100 poems, of which 21 were new and the remainder reprinted from earlier volumes. An unsigned review in *Publishers Weekly* (June 3, 1996) acknowledged Zimmer's "talent for gentle humor, thoughtful observation and melancholy reminiscence. A representative Zimmer poem concerns a moment of metaphoric insight recalled at leisure and presented in accessible, yet cultured language." In the final poem in this collection, "In Apple Country," one of the 21 new poems, the poet contemplates "consummation of dusts, caverns of blossoms / Endless circles forming and expanding" via the metaphor of ripening and harvesting apples.

Zimmer's next book, the memoir *After the Fire: A Writer Finds His Place*, appeared in 2002. In it he recalls his experiences during the 1950s as a young soldier stationed in Nevada, where atomic bombs were tested, and reflects on his passions for jazz music, baseball, and poetry, which have given him tremendous pleasure over the years. Zimmer also offers his thoughts on living on an isolated farm in southwestern Wisconsin with his wife, Suzanne, whom he married in 1959. "Paul Zimmer, an award-winning poet, has a sharp eye, a love for the land and people of southwestern Wisconsin, and considerable talent as a writer," a critic for the *Virginia Quarterly Review* (Autumn 2002) observed. "This book is part notebook, part memoir, part philosophy, part therapy as the author works through his pain at being forced into retirement. Even so, it succeeds as one man's effort to make sense of his life, taking stock of where he is, where he's been and where he's going."

Paul and Suzanne Zimmer have two grown children, Erik Jerome and Justine Mary. The couple divide their time between their home in rural Wisconsin and southern France.

—E. M.

SUGGESTED READING: *Chronicle of Higher Education* A p3 Oct. 10, 1990; *Georgia Review* p736+ Winter 1990, p331+ Summer 1997, p286+ Summer 1998, p617+ Winter 1998; *Gettysburg Review* p325+ Summer 1997, p273+ Summer 1999; *Iowa Review* p82+ Spring 1999; *Library Review* p1487 August 1983; *Poetry* p231 July 1984; *Publishers Weekly* p227 Feb. 24, 1989, p73 June 3, 1996; *Virginia Quarterly Review* pSS64+ Spring 1994, p123+ Autumn 2002

SELECTED BOOKS: *A Seed on the Wind*, 1960; *The Ribs of Death*, 1967; *The Republic of Many Voices*, 1969; *The Zimmer Poems*, 1976; *With Wanda: Town and Country Poems*, 1980; *The Ancient Wars*, 1981; *Earthbound Zimmer*, 1983; *Family Reunion: Selected and New Poems*, 1983; *The American Zimmer*, 1984; *The Great Bird of Love*, 1989; *Big Blue Train*, 1993; *Crossing to Sunlight: Selected Poems*, 1996; nonfiction—*After the Fire: A Writer Finds His Place*, 2002

OHIO UNIVERSITY LIBRARY
Please return this book as ... as you have ... must